SIXTH EDITION

Nonprofit Corporations, Organizations, & Associations

HOWARD L. OLECK

MARTHA E. STEWART

PRENTICE HALL
Englewood Cliffs, New Jersey 07632

Prentice-Hall International (UK) Limited, *London*
Prentice-Hall of Australia Pty. Limited, *Sydney*
Prentice-Hall Canada, Inc., *Toronto*
Prentice-Hall Hispanoamericana, S.A., *Mexico*
Prentice-Hall of India Private Limited, *New Delhi*
Prentice-Hall of Japan, Inc., *Tokyo*
Simon & Schuster Asia Pte. Ltd., *Singapore*
Editora Prentice-Hall do Brasil, Ltda., *Rio de Janeiro*

© 1994 *by*
PRENTICE HALL
Englewood Cliffs, NJ

10 9 8 7 6 5 4 3 2 1

Library of Congress Cataloging-in-Publication Data

Oleck, Howard Leoner
    Nonprofit corporations, organizations, and associations / Howard
L. Oleck and Martha E. Stewart.—6th ed.
       p.   cm.
    Includes bibliographies and index.
    ISBN 0-13-121310-5
    1. Nonprofit organizations—Law and legislation—United States.
2. Unincorporated societies—United States.   I. Stewart, Martha E.
II. Title.
KF1388.O44 1994
346.73′064—dc20
[347.30664]   93–47544
                                        CIP

ISBN 0-13-121310-5

PRENTICE HALL
Career and Personal Development
Englewood Cliffs, NJ 07632
Simon & Schuster, A Paramount Communications Company

Printed in the United States of America

This book is dedicated to all the people whose lives and deeds exemplify the altruism, charity and volunteer work that is the essence of the noblest part of any country or culture—its non-profit organizations.

"Though I speak with the tongues of men and angels, and have not *charity*, I am become as sounding brass, or a tinkling cymbal."

1 Corinthians, XIII, 1

Voluntary associations are the key devices by which Americans obtain the benefits of the *dangerous freedom* of their *Constitution*, today as in the *Mayflower Compact* days of 1620. Their clubs and societies are what make the individual loneliness of freedom endurable and the individual anonymity of government tolerable; what make their lives something finer than the soulless pursuit of wealth/power. ["Congress shall make no law ... abridging the right of the people peaceably to assemble ..." *Amendment I, U.S. Constitution.*] ["... A dangerous freedom ... the principle of association ... is applied to a great multitude of objects ... in America. ..." Alexis de Tocqueville, *Democracy in America* (1831).] [Bradford Smith, *A Dangerous Freedom* (1952).]

ABOUT THE AUTHORS

HOWARD L. OLECK, the leading authority on nonprofit organization law and management since his treatise on the subject appeared in 1956, is Distinguished Professor of Law (and Dean) Emeritus of Cleveland State University College of Law and Professor of Law Emeritus of Stetson University College of Law, and also has been law professor at Wake Forest University and New York Law Schools. An active member of the New York, Ohio, and Federal Bars for 56 years, he has served as Special Master of Federal Courts on complex corporate cases, Consultant for Congressional Committees, several state legislatures, foreign nations, and many organizations worldwide, and as Counsel and Organizer and Officer of many kinds of nonprofit organizations. He is the author of many books and articles, including *Modern Corporation Law* (6 volumes) and (with Green) *Parliamentary Law and Practice for Nonprofit Organizations* (Amer. Bar Assn.-Amer. Law Inst.), has been listed in *Who's Who in America* since 1950, and is now semiretired and resides in St. Petersburg, Florida.

MARTHA E. STEWART is an attorney specializing in nonprofit organizations cases. As colleague, researcher, teaching fellow, editor, co-counsel, and co-author, she has worked with Professor Oleck for six years at Stetson University College of Law on Nonprofit Organizations Law and Practice courses, seminars, cases, and problems, and on Advanced Torts Law seminars, following 16 years of service in biologic scientific environmental research worldwide. She has been chief researcher and now co-author of the annual supplements to the Fifth Edition of this book for several years, and will be the chief researcher-writer of future supplements and editions. She practices and resides in St. Petersburg, Florida.

PREFACE
TO THE SIXTH EDITION

Nonprofit organizations long have been an important part of the lives of millions of people worldwide, but in 1994 it may well be true that they now are the *most* important factors in the lives of *most* Americans. Churches, schools, clubs, trade and professional societies, political and civic associations, sports, cultural, social, public service, residential and many other kinds of nonprofit organizations now number in the millions, and their membership in the multimillions. Tax-exempt organization practices applicable to NPO now are very voluminous and detailed.

Today, in addition, many NPOs carry on active "for profit" activities, and many business organizations conduct important nonprofit activities. These mixtures of profit and nonprofit organizations and operations now are so widespread as to be routine in both kinds of organizations.

This is a one-volume *desk book*, especially for officers and members of NPOs, and for others, as a detailed survey resource; a working guide for almost every aspect of NPO law and practice. It is a compendium of the research and analysis work of many contributors as well as of the co-authors. The name of each contributor, and acknowledgment of his/her help, appear at the beginning points where his or her contribution is set forth.

This Sixth Edition will be kept current by annual supplements keyed to each chapter and subject, as the volume of modern court, legislative, administrative agency, and evolving management practice now mandates.

Howard L. Oleck
Martha E. Stewart

v

CONTENTS

Chapter 5. Unincorporated Associations   **143**

Chapter 6. Forms for Unincorporated Associations   **170**

HOW THIS NEW EDITION
WILL HELP YOU

This completely revised and updated Sixth Edition provides an indispensable guide to all the recent developments in the nonprofit field. Executives of nonprofit organizations and their legal counsel will have a "one volume library" that

- covers all the relevant aspects of the impact of the Tax Reform Acts to date on nonprofit organizations;
- includes new forms and other government documentation necessary for nonprofit status application and reporting;
- points out the important details of application of the Revised American Bar Association Model Nonprofit Corporation Act, and new state statutes;
- contains new sections and whole new chapters on such important subjects as:
  —religious organizations
  —mixtures of profit and nonprofit activities
  —NPO ethics
  —charitable subscriptions
  —fund raising
- incorporates chapters contributed by leading specialists on
  —federal and state tax exemptions
  —tax deductions
  —accounting
  —condominiums and cooperatives
  —trade associations
  —lobbying
  —affiliations
  —antitrust
  —management techniques
  —accreditation

—international organizations

—parliamentary law, and

• has major revisions of chapters on international organizations and the effects of the Bankruptcy Act.

Organized for easy reference, this Sixth Edition provides the same high quality for its users as the first edition when it was published in 1956. Since then, it has been hailed as the recognized authority on nonprofit law and practice.

1

NATURE OF NONPROFIT ORGANIZATIONS

[*Acknowledgments*: Research assistance for this chapter was contributed by Keith R. Anderson, Patricia A. Baldwin, Robert E. Griffin, and Laura M. Watson.]

§1. IMPORTANCE OF NONPROFIT (VOLUNTARY) ORGANIZATIONS

Nonprofit Organizations now (in 1994) are second to no other kind of organizations in their importance in American (and increasingly in all modern/industrial) society. For many Americans they often are more essential to a decent life in a decent society than are business organizations; for the carrying on of much production and services and sources of paid employment often can be done by NPOs as well as (or better than) profit-businesses. In short, NPOs probably are the most important organizations in many aspects of human society today. NPOs now can (and do) provide the socio-economic legal vehicles for both capitalist-oriented and socialist-oriented management of human states or nations, in addition to being the main quality-of-life vehicles for most people. Just to list some of the main types of NPOs is enough to demonstrate their actual primacy in modern society; (just try to imagine modern society *without*): (NPO) churches, public schools, public charities, public clinics/hospitals, political organizations, sports/health/recreation clubs and leagues, savings & loan associations, legal aid societies, volunteer services organizations, orphanages, condominium/residents associations, labor unions, professional associations, research institutes, arts and sciences societies, museums, environmental protection societies, and many governmental (NPO) agencies, etc.

Nonprofit associations benefit society through educating their members, setting professional standards, developing and disseminating information,

1

informing the public, ensuring representation for private interests, exercising and supporting political choice, and stimulating and organizing volunteer efforts, while enriching the lives of their members.

A study of 5,500 national associations conducted by the Hudson Institute on behalf of the American Society of Association Executives and released in 1990 found that seven out of ten Americans belong to one association, while four out of ten belong to more than four associations. Associations spent $8.5 billion in 1989 on courses to educate their members and the public about technical and scientific matters and business practices. Educational courses are offered to the public by 90 percent of the associations surveyed. Associations spent $14.5 billion on industry standard-setting activities. Nearly one fourth of the professional societies set professional standards. Half of the standard-setting societies set and enforce product standards. Associations used the skills of their members, for the common good, to donate 100 million hours of community service in 1989. Only one third of the associations surveyed use money to promote political activity; those associations devote only an average of 5 percent of their expenditures to politics.[1]

On the other hand—high salaries to charity executives were attacked in 1993 by Rep. J. J. Pickle (D., Tex.) of the House Ways and Means oversight committee and IRS Commissioner M. M. Richardson, both promising to reduce the six-figure salaries and lush "perks" given to many executives of the top 2000 (of the total 1.2 million) tax-exempt NPOs. [*Washington Post* article, June 15, 1993.] And religious freedom does not protect a private religious college from liability for defaming a plaintiff by saying that he lived with "a well-known homosexual." [*Nazeri v. Missouri Valley College,* 75201, MO Supr. Ct., Aug. 17, 1993.]

In response to successive rounds of state budget cuts in 1991 and 1992, a decade of steep cuts in federal social programs, and a lengthy recession, nonprofits have become important in the struggle to fill gaps in social services. Welfare benefits were cut or frozen in 1991 by 41 states. States also cut general cash-assistance funds. Twelve states cut special needs or emergency cash-assistance funds. The cuts were worst in Michigan, Massachusetts, California, Maryland, Ohio, Illinois, Maine, and the District of Columbia.

As a result of government social services cuts, nonprofits have noticed a sharp increase in people who are sicker and seeking health care, because lost welfare means lost health insurance. Those seeking aid from the Salvation Army increased by 14 percent in 1991. Catholic Charities of Chicago reports that requests for assistance have increased by 10 to 15 percent each year since 1991. Catholic Charities USA says that those requesting food, clothing, and shelter (emergency aid) rose to 67 percent in 1991. In 1981, only 23 percent of charity clients needed emergency services. Walter Ousley, division manager for community development services for Catholic Charities in Chicago, says that he believes the situation will get even worse, as the government reduces social services funding further. Nonprofits are becoming the most important "social safety net" of the future.[2]

"Americans of all ages, all stations in life, and all types of disposition are forever forming associations . . . religious, moral, serious, futile, very general and very limited, immensely large and very minute . . . Americans combine great individualism with an attitude towards community action that knows no counterpart in the world."[3] "Associations are formed for purposes of trade, and for political, literary and religious interests."[4] The Pilgrims' *Mayflower Compact* of 1620 was a *contract* "to combine ourselves together into a civil body politic." Today, too, membership in a nonprofit organization is basically *contractual* in nature.[5]

At the same time, Americans conduct studies and seminars on such pragmatic aspects of *voluntarism* as "The nonprofit as entrepreneur: development options for . . . tax-exempt entities."[6] Overlapping (mixtures) of profit-seeking and not-for-profit enterprise is viewed as both natural and desirable. This dichotomy—altruistic voluntarism plus opportunistic profit-seeking—runs through all the history of nonprofit enterprise and community service of the American "nation of joiners."[7] Thus, in 1807 in Boston, a number of inventors joined together "to patronize themselves by associating to exchange mutual aids," and by the 1820s such formal associations of like-minded persons were being established at the rate of 85 a year in Massachusetts alone.[8] In the latter part of the nineteenth century many mutual-interest groups of this kind were formed—farmers' granges, trade and occupational associations, and labor unions. Then in the early twentieth century many more social service and welfare groups were added. In the final decades of the twentieth century great numbers of charitable and other foundations were established, plus enough political-action groups (PACs) to raise serious fears of domination of the American democracy by special interest societies and powers.[9]

Some students of American history think that individual freedom in a democracy causes many people to feel a sense of personal isolation that is counterbalanced by "belonging" in nonprofit organizations. Such associations define some people as "in," and some as "out," seeming to believe that life requires organization to deal with a hostile world if people are to survive.[10]

NPO Education

Far more Americans now participate in the activities of nonprofit organizations than in those of profit-seeking organizations. About half of the organizations and enterprises in the United States are now nonprofit in nature. Yet this vast area for potential legal practice was almost ignored until recently by lawyers and law professors; an astonishing fact, considering the fact that lawyers have the largest voluntary professional organization in the world—The American Bar Association, numbering close to 370,000 members in 1993.[11] It was not until 1979, for example, that the Association of American Law Schools, Business Organizations Section, first made *nonprofits* the subject of one of its annual meetings.[12] In the late 1980s the subject of nonprofit organizations law was still offered as an elective in only about twenty law schools.[13] But many undergraduate and business colleges have offered courses on such organizations.[14]

College instructors generally, other than law school professors, have long recognized the importance of these social phenomena, at least as sociology and
management factors in American society. Law professors today still seem to
fear the subject. Corporation law casebooks almost never mention it, probably
because of the intimidating range of kinds of law applicable to legal governance of nonprofits—from "corporations," "partnerships" and "agency" to
"trusts," "administrative," "wills," "international," "constitutional," "insolvency,"
"parliamentary," and complex portions of state and federal "tax law." The final
turnoff to many lawyers has been the superficial impression that "there's no
money in it" because of the term *nonprofit*—as wrong-headed a conclusion as
can be imagined, because nonprofits actually are involved with enormous
wealth.

Management of NPOs had become such big business in 1993 that more
than 32 American colleges and universities were offering graduate degrees in
that subject, not to mention undergraduate-degree programs and courses and
seminars and conferences in the hundreds.[15]

An example of *Master's Degree* programs today (at Case Western Reserve
University's "Mandel Center for NPOs") listed (in 1990) a 45-credit-hour program of 17 months full-time or 24 months part-time, with classes available on
weekends, evenings, and five-day intensive residency periods for working students; admission criteria include a bachelor's degree, GMAT scores, potential
for leadership, and experience with NPOs. The Curriculum includes NPO
Introduction, Ethics/Leadership, Quantitative Methods, Economics, Accounting, Management (Financial, Marketing, Systems, Human Resources), Law,
Practicums on various aspects, Electives, Special Lectures, and Special Computer Workshops, and so on. Tuition was $500/hr. or $6,000/semester in 1990.[16]

A fund-raising school operates at the Center on Philanthropy of Indiana
University. Courses offered in 1992 were: 101 Principles, Techniques of Fund
Raising, 103 Planned Giving: Getting the Proper Start, 105 Fund Raising with
Limited Budgets, 201 Leadership Development for Fund Raising, and 203
Interpersonal Skills for Fund Raising. For information on current courses, con-
tact The Fund Raising School, 550 West North Street Suite 301 Indianapolis,
Indiana 46202-3162, 800/962-6692.

The Support Center of Washington offers Management Workshops for
Nonprofits. The Center offers public training programs, contract training and
consulting programs, as well as a business volunteer program. Courses offered
cover the subjects of Organizational Development, People Development,
Fundraising, Financial Management, and Marketing. Contact The Support
Center of Washington, 2001 O Street, N.W., Washington, D.C. 20036, (202)
833-0300, (202) 223-8048.

Charitable Contributions Data

The impact of nonprofit organizations on the American economy and
social structure, and on the world, is evident in even a casual sampling of the

numbers and variety of such organizations and their wealth and influence. Leaf through the yellow pages of a telephone directory, especially in a big city, and you will be astonished by the number and variety of nonprofits listed as having an office and a telephone, under such headings as associations, chambers of commerce, charities, churches, clubs, condominiums, foundations, fraternal orders, golf courses, hospitals, labor unions, libraries, museums, religious organizations, research institutes, schools and colleges, social service organizations, societies, trade associations, and others. If one then includes governmental agencies, and considers that most of the smaller voluntary organizations—PTAs, local sports and hobby groups, cultural, ethnic, veteran, retiree, patriotic, occupational, regional, and other social groups—are unincorporated and maintain no office or telephone listing, the impact of nonprofits becomes impressive indeed.

One bright constant in American society, moreover, always has been a degree of voluntarism and charity that is unique in the world. In 1985, for example, latest available national statistics on *charitable* contributions (*not* for *all* nonprofit organizations' fundings) showed that 54.5 million of the 96.3 million couples and individuals who filed tax returns the year before claimed a deduction for charitable giving; the total deductions being $38 billion.[17] In 1980 corporate contributions were $2.7 billion.[18] In 1981 the nation's 300,000 charitable institutions received $53.6 billion (up from $47.7 billion in 1980), with contributions to religious institutions being $24.8 billion (46.3 percent of all giving in the United States).[19] It was $37.7 billion in 1985.[20] In 1983 Americans donated $64.93 billion to the 300,000 charitable organizations[21] (an 8.1 percent increase). In 1985 a survey reported that 89 percent of Americans said they had a *duty* to contribute to charity.[22] In 1983 a survey of 503 major U.S. companies showed $1.4 billion in gifts to charities, or 46 percent (almost half) of the estimated $3 billion given by all U.S. corporations that year (much for community improvement purposes—14.8 percent, and 28.75 percent for health and human services, and 11.4 percent to culture and arts, with 6.1 percent for mainly foreign people-aid programs), while 11 percent were in noncash form (products, etc.), and $553 million of it came from company foundations.[23] In 1983 Florida residents' gifts to charities (by three-fourths of the state's households) averaged $564 each, while half of those polled reported doing an average of 7.5 hours of volunteer work per month.[24] In 1985 it was estimated that Americans would contribute $65 billion to charity.[25] They actually gave $79.84 billion.[26]

Giving USA, 1991 Edition, AAFRC Trust for Philanthropy, New York, the American yearbook on philanthropy, reported that total giving in 1990 was about $122.6 billion (up about 5.8% from 1989, but really under 1% in inflated dollars). Individual giving was about $101.8 billion (up 5.2%). Religion got about $65.8 billion in gifts (up about 5.2%). Health groups got $9.9 billion (a 5% drop). The arts got $7.9 billion (up less than 1/2%). Schools, libraries and other educational and research institutions got about $12.4 billion (up 13.3%). Society-community groups got $4.9 billion (up 2.8%). Environmental groups got $2.3 billion (up 30%). International services groups got about 2.2% (up 30%). Corporate philanthropy rose 5.4% to $5.9 billion. Foundation grants rose 8.1% to $7.1 billion. Bequests rose 11.8% to about $7.8 billion.[27]

Private gifts to U.S. *colleges* totaled $9.8 billion in 1990, up 10% from the prior year, according to a 1991 survey.[28]

Gifts to *nonprofit hospitals* in 1990 were $3 billion, while about $377 million was spent on fundraising, according to a 350 member survey by the Association for Healthcare Philanthropy of 1370 NPO hospitals queried out of the about 3500 NPO hospitals in the United States Corporate gifts to member hospitals rose 11% to $278 million, while cash gifts from foundations dropped 10% to $328 million and individual gifts fell 1% to $1.07 billion.[29]

Giving USA, 1992 Edition, AAFRC Trust for Philanthropy, of New York City, the American yearbook on philanthropy, reported that total giving to nonprofit organizations in 1991 was estimated to be nearly $125 billion. This was a 1.4 percent increase over the 1990 total estimate, which may mean only the effect of the annual inflation rate. The American rate of giving has remained about 2 percent of the gross domestic product for over three decades as compared to other uses of its money. Percentage division of the $125 billion was about 53 percent to religion, 11 percent to education, nearly 9 percent to human services, 8 percent to health, over 7 percent to arts, 4 percent to public/society uses, 2 percent international, and 2 percent environment.[30]

In 1991, individuals gave 82.7 percent of the total charitable contributions. Foundations and bequests gave 6.2 percent each. Corporations contributed the least, at 4.9 percent.[31]

The greatest percentage increase in giving in 1991 was in the area of international affairs, with an 11.2 percent increase over 1990 and a total revenue figure of $2.59 billion. The second largest increase in giving was in the area of arts and culture, which showed a 6.58 percent increase over 1990, and $8.81 billion in revenues. Wildlife causes also showed an increase in giving of 5.75 percent, reflecting revenues of $2.54 billion.

The largest decreases in giving in 1991 were experienced by the human services area (−14.28%), health (−6.66%), and public society benefit (−4.39%).

According to a survey of 563 institutions, *anonymous* giving in 1991 accounted for less than one percent of contributions, for a full two-thirds of the organizations.[32]

The *size* of these organizations' impact on American society is suggested by the *dollar volume* of just *one* (of many) kinds of NPO—the *charity contributions.* In 1993 charity contributions were reported by the American Association of Fund Raising Counsel's Trust for Philanthropy to have been $124.3 billion in donations for the year before, despite a prolonged economic depression. This was (as usual) 2 percent of personal income for the year. Individuals gave nearly $110 billion, foundations $3.3 billion, and corporations $6 billion.[33]

Giving to *religious* institutions in 1992 increased by 5 percent (+1.2 percent in inflated 1992 dollars) and accounted for $56.7 billion and 45.6 percent of all contributions. Contributions to *education* increased by 4.2 percent (+.24 percent in 1992 dollars) but were a distant second at $14.02 billion and 11.3 percent of all contributions. In response to natural disasters, donations to *human services* organizations increased 4 percent (+.02 percent in 1992 dollars) equaling $11.57 billion and 9.3 percent of contributions, reversing a dramatic decline in 1991 of 6 percent. *Health* organizations received a 6 percent increase in donations (+1.7 percent in 1992 dollars) amounting to $10.24 billion and 8.2 percent of contributions. The *arts, culture, and humanities* garnered an increase in donations of 6 percent (+1.8 percent in 1992 dollars) totaling $9.32 billion and 7.5 percent of contributions. *Environment/wildlife* causes continued to increase their contributions, up 6.5 percent (+2.4 percent in 1992 dollars) at $3.12 billion and 2.5 percent of contributions. Donations to *public/society benefit* associations were up 2.4 percent, (actually −1.5 percent in 1992 dollars) at $5.05 billion and 4.1 percent of all contributions. Reflecting concerns about the ability of *international* organizations to function effectively, those organizations showed a sharp decrease in donations, down 2.1 percent (−5.9 percent in 1992 dollars) to 1.4 percent of all contributions. Undesignated contributions equaled 10 percent of all funds donated.[34]

From the English *corpora corporata* of the 18th century[35] to the Abolitionist groups of the early 1800s to the environmental protection groups of today, the impact of volunteer groups has been profound. It is not an overstatement to say that today the nonprofit organizations of the United States are the finest flowering of the idea of a free society and, in the long view of history, perhaps its most important feature.

§2. NUMBERS AND WEALTH OF NONPROFITS

[See the preceding section.]

Religious organizations consistently continue to be the most important kind of nonprofit groups in the U.S.A. and also the type that draws the most contributions (about half of all contributions to tax-exempt NPOs every year). But shifts of interest have been marked in other kinds of organizations in recent years. *Environmental* organizations increased extraordinarily in 1989–90. *Greenpeace U.S.A.* had 1.9 million members by the first of 1990, for example, while several other conservation organizations had well over a half million members each.[36]

Membership in *environmental groups* increased even more dramatically in 1990–92. Greenpeace U.S.A. had 2 million members by 1992; Sierra Club had 650,000; Nature Conservancy had 588,000; Wilderness Society had 377,000; and National Wildlife Federation had 6,200,000 members.[37]

In 1990 the biggest-income charities in the USA were Catholic Charities USA ($1,538 million), Lutheran Social Ministry Organizations (1,486 M), American Red Cross (1,465 M), YMCA (1,438 M), Salvation Army (1,215 M), UNICEF (821 M), etc.[38]

The "biggest" American Charities reported their income for 1991 about as follows: (1) Catholic Church $1.8 billion; (2) Lutheran Social Ministry Organization $1.6 billion; (3) YMCA of USA $1.5 billion; (4) American Red Cross $1.4 billion; (5) Salvation Army $1.3 billion.[39]

Over half a million organizations are now listed in the IRS cumulative list of organizations that are tax-exempt, to which contributions may be deductible. A recent study at the Yale University Institution for Social and Policy Studies (program on nonprofit organizations) gives an illuminating approach to the size and weight of American nonprofit organizations:[40] It began with a comparison of only certain *philanthropic* sectors of American nonprofits with the *budgets* of foreign nations. The budgets of U.S. philanthropic organizations exceeded the budgets of all nations of the world except the United States, France, West Germany, the United Kingdom, Japan, probably China and the U.S.S.R. The annual expenditures have been over $130 billion in recent years. The share of Gross National Product (GNP) originating in the nonprofit sector has been growing in recent years, while the share originated by business firms has declined. Nonprofits are a "growth" field. Philanthropic organizations in the United States in the 1980s have employed at least 5.6 million people annually as full-time employees, exceeding such leading industries as automobile manufacturing and construction. By 1975 the assets of the nonprofit sector exceeded $200 billion, and inflation and more contributions have swollen that number today. The study, *Philanthropic Organizations*, includes charitable, educational, health, scientific, religious and other groups to which contributions are tax-deductible under the Internal Revenue Code.[41]

Recent 1991 figures from the *Statistical Abstract of the United States* show counts of 358,194 churches, with 156,336,384 members.[42] A national survey of religious organizations made by the Washington-based Independent Sector in 1987 involved questionnaires sent to a national sample of 1,003 congregations, with 717 completed surveys. The aggregate revenues of an estimated 258,000 religious congregations in the U.S. total $48.4 billion, of which 81 percent comes from individual donors. Operating expenditures were 72 percent or $34.2 billion while 14 percent, or $6.8 billion, was spent on capital outlays, savings, and individuals. Another 14 percent, or 6.8 billion, was donated to other organizations and individuals.

Fifteen million people worked for religious organizations each month in 1991. Of that, 549,000 (4 percent) were clergy, of which 402,000 (73 percent) were paid and 147,000 or 27 percent were volunteers. Of the million paid employees, 28 percent (313,000) were full-time, 44 percent, or 488,000, were part time, and 27 percent (304,000) were "nominally" paid. The value of volunteer time donated to congregations was $19.2 billion in 1991.

Of the 258,000 congregations with telephones, 52,000 had fewer than 10 members, 134,000 had 100 to 399 members, and 72,000 had membership of more than 400.[43]

Major national nonprofit organizations with large memberships totaled about 23,000 in 1992. In addition, there are 11,000 international nonprofit membership organizations.[44] The *Statistical Abstract of the United States* indicates that in 1990 there were 3,918 trade, business, and commercial groups; 940 agriculture associations; 792 legal, governmental, public administration, and military groups; 1,417 scientific, engineering, and technical associations; 1,291 educational associations; 1,886 cultural organizations; 1,705 social welfare groups; 2,227 health and medical associations; 2,249 public affairs groups; 573 fraternal, foreign interest, nationality and ethnic groups; 1,172 religious groups; 462 veteran, hereditary, and patriotic societies; 1,475 hobby and avocational groups; 840 athletic groups; 253 labor unions; 168 Chambers of Commerce; 340 Greek and non-Greek letter societies; and 581 fan clubs.[45]

A four-year study by the Nonprofit Coordinating Committee of New York found that there are 19,500 nonprofits operating in New York alone. That number is more than twice the number estimated before the study. The average salary of nonprofit executive directors in New York is less than $30,000. Less than 4 percent of the nonprofits pay their executives more than $150,000. New York's nonprofits employ 450,000 people or 12.5 percent of the city's work force.[46]

The voluntary sector continues to expand internationally. For example, England is wrestling with the formation of a Charities Act in response to 1990 statistics indicating 170,000 existing charities, which represents a growth rate of almost 25 percent in 10 years.[47]

The giant of American (and probably of world) private charities is the Howard Hughes Medical Institute,[48] a Delaware corporation with a nine-member board of trustees, with executive offices in Bethesda, Maryland, and administrative offices in Coconut Grove, Florida.

The top ten in public support amounts in 1993 were [according to J. McIlquham article in 7 *Nonprofit Times* (12)23 (Dec. 1993)]:

Salvation Army	$905,195,971
United Jewish Appeal	407,440,087
Second Harvest	407,155,237
American Red Cross	394,732,700
American Cancer Society	354,663,271
Catholic Charities	305,741,095
Catholic Relief Services	235,561,000
American Heart Association	235,369,000
UNICEF	231,000,000
YMCA of the USA	219,743,090

Growth of nonprofits continues. By 1900, for example, over 5 million members belonged to over 70,000 fraternal lodges.[49] By 1992 the American Legion had 3 million members.[50] The American Automobile Association had 13.6 million members in 1972, 25.1 million by 1985, and 28+ million by 1992.[51] The Order of the Eastern Star, the women's branch of the Masonic Order, had 1.7 million members in 1992.[52] Also in 1992, a typical college fraternity (*Phi*

Delta Theta) had about 180,000 members; a typical law school fraternity (*Phi Alpha Delta*) about 130,000 members; and a typical engineering fraternity (*Tau Beta Phi*) about 270,000 members, while in 1988 private colleges enrolled 2,887,000 students and public institutions enrolled 10,156,000 students.[53] The numbers of members in labor unions has decreased. The 1992 data indicates that Teamsters number 1,600,000; automobile workers number 1,000,000; carpenters number 595,000; and machinists 826,000. Earlier 1983 figures for labor union members were: Teamsters, 2 million; automobile, 1.15 million; carpenters, 800,000; and machinists, 943,280.[54]

Economic interdependence of philanthropies and the rest of the economy obviously is great today. Business sells at least seven dollars in goods and services to these organizations for every dollar it returns to them by buying their services or by making donations.[55] The philanthropic payroll was $75 billion per year by 1980, exceeding the growth rate of business and government in the preceding 20 years; and philanthropic organizations bought $43 billion per year from business that year.[56] Remembering that the Rudney study considered only some (not all) kinds of nonprofits, the actual size of the overall economic interdependence obviously is enormous, especially in view of the inflation of the past decade and the push by the Reagan and Bush administrations for more private and less governmental support of nonprofits since 1980.

§3. DEFINITIONS OF "NONPROFIT"

A *nonprofit organization* is defined by the American Bar Association, in the 1964 revision of the American Law Institute *Model Nonprofit Corporation Act*,[57] as a corporation "no part of the income or profit of which is distributed to its members, directors or officers." Many state corporation law statutes have adopted this definition.[58] Some term such organizations "non-stock corporations," to convey the idea that no distributions or dividends are made to shareholders (*i.e.*, members). Presence or absence of *equity shares* is the single clear feature distinguishing a business corporation from a not-for-profit corporation."[59] The ABA 1986 revision of the Model Act, in its *Definition* [Subchapter 1.40] does not define "Nonprofit" at all.

All nonprofit corporations share three general *characteristics*:[60] (1) they are specifically designated as "nonprofit" when organized; (2) profits or assets may not be divided among corporate members, officers or directors in the manner of corporate share dividends; and (3) they may lawfully pursue only such purposes as are permitted for such organizations by statutes. They are divided into three nonprofit *categories*: (1) *public benefit* (such as museums, schools, and hospitals); (2) *mutual benefit* (such as cooperatives, trade or professional associations, and clubs); and (3) *private benefit* (such as tax-exemption-benefit-seeking organizations as low-cost housing developments, etc.).[61] The proposed (1987) ABA Model Act defined public and mutual benefit.[62]

Limitation, or more accurately, elimination of participatory proprietary

interests in assets is the key idea. Thus, the 1986 Illinois statute draft[63] effectively eliminated any real "member derivative rights" (*i.e.*, "standing" to sue on
behalf of the corporation) even in noncharitable nonprofit organizations, let
alone in charitable ones, unless the organization's rules or a particular contract
specifically grants such rights.[64]

Governmental corporations, although they are nonprofits, of course, must be
treated as *sui generis* in many respects. Primarily, the privileged status of "government" often applies to them. For example, the laws that apply to other nonprofits may not apply to them; *e.g.*, a state's Fair Information Practices Act did
not apply to a municipally operated nursing home, which was treated as a city
or town bureau for liability purposes,[65] but its employees could be held liable.[66]

More elaborate statutory definitions, such as those of New York, define a
not-for-profit organization as "one exclusively for a purpose or purposes, not
for pecuniary profit or financial gain, and no part of the assets, income, or
profits of which is distributable to, or enures to the benefit of its members,
directors, or officers, except to the extent permitted under this statute."[67]

Nonprofit or Not-for-Profit

Some people see a subtle distinction between not-for-profit and nonprofit, in that the first term is more accurate because nonprofits may seek profit as
long as that profit is employed only to fulfill the organization's major (nonprofit) purpose.[68] Some states' statutes now allow nonprofit corporations to
engage freely in largely business operations as long as they conduct them for
ultimately nonprofit objectives.[64] The American Bar Association's Model Nonprofit Corporations Act, and many state statutes, permit nonprofit corporations
to be formed for any lawful purpose, including, but not confined to, some purposes stated in those statutes.[70] California and Canadian movements in this
same direction have been evident in recent years, following New York's radi-
cally new statute of 1970 and Pennsylvania's emulation of such mixture of business and altruistic purposes soon after.[71]

There is no real difference between the two terms. A general law dictionary
definition says that a *profit* corporation is "a business corporation, organized with
a view toward realizing gains to be distributed among its members."[72] Black's
Law Dictionary defines nonprofit by adopting the 1964 Model Act definition.[73]

The words *nonprofit* and *charitable* seem to mean much the same thing to
most people. But they often are distinctly different in nonprofit organization
law. In common use, the word nonprofit is defined in a standard dictionary as
an adjective, meaning "not intending or intended to earn a profit [as, a nonprofit corporation]."[74] Charitable is defined as "of or for charity . . . Syn. see
Philanthropic . . ."; while the word charity is described in one definition as "a
welfare institution, organization, or fund. . . ."[75] Philanthropic is defined as an
adjective, meaning:

> [O]f, showing or constituting philanthropy; charitable; benevolent;
> humane. . . . Syn.—Philanthropic implies interest in the general human

welfare, esp. as shown in large-scale gifts to charities, the endowment of
institutions for human advancement, etc. . . . charitable implies the giving
of money or other help to those in need; altruistic implies putting the welfare of others before one's own interests and therefore stresses freedom
from selfishness.[76]

A nonprofit corporation is not necessarily a charitable corporation; but a
charitable corporation necessarily is a nonprofit corporation. Nonprofit is a
general term, while charitable is a specific one.

The Texas statute states that:

"Nonprofit Corporation" is the equivalent of "not-for-profit corporation"
and means a corporation no part of the income of which is distributable to
its members, directors, or officers.[77]

Right after adoption of the radical New York Statute in 1970, a Practicing Law Institute seminar suggested the idea that *nonprofit* and *not-for-profit* have
different meanings.[78] But this mystical semantic distinction evaporates on close
inspection.[79]

Thus, the Alaska[80] statutes speak of "not-for-profit." Arkansas' statute says
that nonprofit is, in effect, a synonym for not-for-profit.[81] California[82] has spoken only of "nonprofit." Both Colorado[83] and Alabama[84] had a "Corporations Not
for Profit" Act, but now have entitled their statues "Nonprofit Corporations."[85]

Connecticut has a "Non-Stock Corporation Act."[86] Delaware's statute
speaks of corporations, generally, for "any lawful business or purpose," and
mixes its few nonprofit provisions right in among its general business corporation provisions.[87] And Florida's statute says "Corporations may be organized
and incorporated under this act for any one or more lawful purposes, not for
pecuniary profit."[88] There is no need to labor the point. There is no real distinction between the terms nonprofit and not-for-profit.

§4. CHARITY—ORGANIZATION STANDARDS

[ACCREDITATION]

National Charities Information Bureau of New York City issued new standards as
to what constitutes a charity organization in 1988, eliminating any direct statement as to how much should be spent on fund raising, but requiring that at
least 60 percent of annual expenses be related to its charity programs. Also, its
(nonbinding) rules require boards of directors to spell out "conflicts of interests" policies. In brief, the standards require:

1. An independent, volunteer board, with a minimum of five members and at
   least two (in person) meetings a year, with no fees paid for merely being
   a member, no more than one paid staff member who does not chair the
   board nor serve as treasurer, and no material conflicts of interests.
2. Formally stated purpose(s).
3. Programs consistent with those purposes.

4. Information accurately describing its activities for fund raising and public information.

5. The board is accountable for financial and other activities, and their descriptions to outsiders.

6. Reasonable use of funds; at lest 60 percent to its stated purposes, in reasonable annual programs.

7. Annual reports, documented, available on request, listing activities, board members, and audited financial statements (or at least summary).

There are many more detailed NCIB standards for interpretations and applications.

Philanthropic Advisory Service of the Council of Better Business Bureaus requires that fundraising costs not exceed 35 percent of related contributions, and administrative costs not exceed 50 percent, with at least 50 percent spent on programs.[89]

Charitable organizations that meet standards appropriate for contributions from the public are listed (hundreds of them) in guides issued by such offices as the following:

National Charities Information Bureau, 19 Union Square West, New York, NY 10003.

Philanthropic Advisory Service, Council of Better Business Bureaus, Inc., 1515 Wilson Blvd., Arlington, VA 22209.

Salary Disclosure Requirements/Standards

Disclosure of executives' salaries and administrative costs is beginning to be strictly required in some states (e.g., California, effective January 1993, for charities raising over 50% of their annual income and over $1 million annually from California donors the prior year and that allot over 25% of income to such expenses).[90]

The IRS has revised Form 990 to include additional reporting on fundraising costs, levels of compensation, and lobbying expenditures, three topics that are receiving attention in the press.[91]

Tax Exemption Privilege [See "tax," "licenses," etc.]

In a *NonProfit Times*/Barna Research nationwide survey, 1009 people were asked whether nonprofit organizations should be exempt from property taxes. Of those polled, 54 percent were in favor of the exemption, 29 percent were against, and 17 percent had no opinion.[92]

Nonprofit businesses actually make billions of dollars. At the same time, the government loses more than $36 billion in potential taxes per year through nonprofit tax-exemptions. Tax exemptions for nonprofits amount to $18 billion for individual income tax deductions; $16 billion for tax obligations that would have been collected from hospitals, universities, and foundations, had they not been nonprofit; and $2.5 billion in tax-exempt bonds and postage discounts.

Some criticize tax exemption for nonprofits, noting that (1) hospitals don't have to pay taxes in return for free care for the poor, and are still exempt even though there is now less charity care; (2) colleges are exempt while stockpiling millions each year from investment and research, while tuition climbs; (3) nonprofit executive salaries skyrocket, some approaching $350,000 to $400,000 a year, plus bonus, luxury car, country-club membership, interest-free house loans, and domestic help provided; (4) nonprofits receive cheap loans through tax-exempt bonds designed to allow taxpayers to underwrite the loans to meet society's needs. Need to fuel construction booms? (5) foundations, tax-exempt due to the grants they give, now earn more money than they give away.

Perhaps nonprofits need to realize that "the reason we exist is not to be 'nonprofit,' but rather to profit our communities and society in ways that families, governments, and corporations cannot. We might, in other words, discover the soul of a sector that has been lost by many contemporary nonprofits, blinded as they are by their quest to be both 'businesslike' and 'tax free.' "[93]

Many NPOs are set up by persons interested mainly in the *tax exemption* they may obtain for their operations, as any worldly wise person knows. There are persons who actually urge extension of "charity" tax exempt status to politicians' campaign fund organizations; this, despite the long established policy of not giving tax exemption to political candidacy for public office. [See Chapters 9, 11, 39.][94]

A 1989 study by the *Center for Responsive Politics* suggested that more and more nonprofit organizations are being formed to further the political careers of politicians. A 1987 study had found about 30 tax-exempt organizations (charities and foundations) were affiliated with federal office-holders or seekers, such as Gary Hart, Bruce Babbitt, Senators Jesse Helms (R.-N.C.), William Bradley (D.-N.J.), and Robert Dole (R.-Kan.). The 1989 study said that many donors to such NPOs contribute in order to support certain congress members (citing some names).

Florida Senator Connie Mack and Tampa Electric Co. Chairman H. L. Culbreath were said (by the article) to have set up a Tampa nonprofit research group (Horizon Institute for Policy Research, Inc.), to be financed by contributions by businesses and foundations, to conduct conferences on foreign policy, economics, housing, and so on, beginning with one in Miami on January 29, 1990 featuring former U.N. Ambassador Jeane Kirkpatrick, with Mack serving as unpaid, honorary chairman of the new organization.[95]

Criteria for Nonprofit Status

In determining the profit or nonprofit status of an organization the following criteria are the ones usually examined by public authorities.[96]

Detailed fiscal and other records of the organization's assets and operations, especially of the immediately preceding fiscal year, showing:

a. reasonableness of salaries, fees, gifts, transfers, or payments to any person or group directly or indirectly controlled by or controlling the organization;

b. similar reasonableness as to any loans or liens or guaranties or the like made for services tendered;

c. similar reasonableness of any contracts or sales or purchases or management arrangement or change of interest in property of the organization;

d. similar reasonableness as to any salaries, services, supplies, payment, encumbrances, etc.;

and as to all such things the organization must affirmatively prove that no part of any such asset or interest "will inure to the benefit of its members, directors, or officers or any person or firm operating for profit or for a nonexempt tax purpose."[97]

Similar criteria are examined in determining when a *portion* of an organization's property is entitled to tax-exemption.[98] These criteria include the nature and extent of the exempt activity and its relative size and scope as compared with all the activities of the organization, or to others at lower-than-otherwise charges or costs; but with special leeway allowed for some profit (income) producing support activities such as bingo games,[99] or qualified profit-sharing plans.[100]

Special (similar) criteria are involved in the cases of nonprofit hospitals, nursing homes, homes for special services,[101] homes for the aged,[102] educational institutions' fraternities, sororities and expositions,[103] labor unions,[104] governmental units,[105] and some nonprofit public utilities.[106] The categories vary from state to state.

Purposes of the organization are key elements in its evaluation for nonprofit status. For example, the new, proposed Illinois Not-for-Profit Corporation Act of 1985[107] listed 29 specific purposes proper for such organizations:[108] (1) charitable; (2) benevolent; (3) eleemosynary; (4) educational; (5) civic; (6) patriotic; (7) political; (8) religious; (9) social; (10) literary; (11) athletic; (12) scientific; (13) research; (14) agricultural; (15) horticultural; (16) soil improvement; (17) crop improvement; (18) livestock or poultry improvement; (19) professional, commercial, industrial or trade association; (20) promoting the development, establishment or expansion of industries; (21) electriciation cooperatives; (22) telephone cooperatives; (23) water supply cooperatives; (24) property ownership cooperatives; (25) property operation condominiums; (26) consumer cooperatives; (27) community mental health patient services boards; (28) consumer credit counseling boards; (29) ride-sharing cooperatives. These are not all the possible purposes, of course. To them may be added such more specific purposes as environmental protection organizations, community development corporations, human rights groups, alumni associations, credit unions, and many others that merit the respect (and privilege) of nonprofit status.

[See, §11 *Kinds of Nonprofit Organization Structures.*]

A *nonprofit* organization is one that is not used for personal financial

enrichment of any of its members or managers, and no portion of the money
or property of which is permitted to inure to the benefit of any private individual, except as a proper grant according to its state-approved purpose, or as
salaries paid for employee-type services rendered to the organization.[109]

Financial gain accruing to the organization from its own operation, however, does not make it a *profit* or *business* organization if such gain is devoted
to its maintenance or improvement. *Profit* means gain from a transaction or
operation. More precisely, it means the excess of income over expenditure in
an enterprise, during a given period.[111] In a corporation, the classic test of
whether or not it is nonprofit is whether or not dividends or other pecuniary
"divvy-up" benefits are paid to its members. But that test is not conclusive.[112] A
nonprofit corporation operating social and recreation clubs, issuing corporate
stock (not membership cards) is subject to execution and sheriff's sale of the
stock.[113] But a social club may lease its land for construction of a condominium and not lose its status.[114]

Altruistic Motives Earn Nonprofit Privileges

Motive is the acid test of the right to nonprofit status, in most cases. When
altruistic, ethical, moral, or social motives are the clearly dominant ones in an
enterprise, that enterprise is nonprofit. Obviously, it is difficult to test for human
motives in an enterprise. Abuse of nonprofit status, however, often is best tested by testing the motives of the organizers or officers of nonprofit organizations. The status in our society of nonprofit enterprises and organizations very
definitely is a privileged one. In recognition of services rendered to us without
profit, our communities reciprocate by granting various benefits to them.

To distinguish between *taxable* and *nontaxable* revenue in nonprofits, the
basic rule is that:

> If the for-profit activity produces 'related' business income that furthers the
> tax-exempt purpose of the organization, then the IRS can't touch it. If, on
> the other hand, the activity is 'unrelated,' then the IRS should get its
> share.[115]

Application of this principle, however, is not simple. Accountants and tax specialists are unsure about what should be taxed and not taxed.[116]

Problems often arise as a result of novel fund-raising methods. For example, Chicago's Lincoln Park Zoo Shop raised a problem for the IRS. This shop
takes in about $10,000 a week, selling souvenirs and elegant gifts. The IRS had
to determine which business activities are related to the Zoo's main reason for
existence and which are not.[117] The IRS decision exempts items that try to
teach something about animals, but holds other items taxable.[118] If the item is
in the shape of an animal it qualifies for tax-exemption, because it helps children to learn to identify physical characteristics of different kinds of animals.[119]
But jewelry with pictures of animals does not qualify; nor do T-shirts, caps or
pendants bearing such pictures.[120] These distinctions are not very convincing.

§5. ETHICS IN NONPROFIT ORGANIZATIONS

[Patrick Real contributed most of the following section.]

Before the ethical standards of nonprofit organizations (nonprofits) can be discussed, they must be defined. Webster defines ethics as the system of morals of a particular person, religion, group, etc.[121] Webster further defines morals as teaching, or in accordance with principles of right and wrong.[122] Thus, the ethical standards to be imposed upon nonprofits will be nothing more than someone's definition of right and wrong. However, there are many different opinions of what is right and what is wrong. The law of ethics governing nonprofits is going through some profound changes.[123] To understand where the law might be headed one must understand how nonprofit law evolved in the United States.

Prior to the nineteenth century, nonprofits consisted mainly of religious, educational and other charitable organizations. Most of these organizations were not incorporated, with many operating as charitable trusts.[124] As a result, trust law played an important role in governing nonprofits. As charitable entities, most nonprofits were supported by donations and were seen as providing a public benefit to society. Consequently, nonprofits gained the reputation of being the "good samaritans" of society.

Because nonprofits were seen as the "good samaritan," the government was reluctant to sternly regulate them. Furthermore, the government's best interests were served by promoting such charitable activities, since they relieved the government from having to provide similar services. In fact, the government subsidized such activities by granting tax exemptions to nonprofits.[125] Moreover, the U.S. Constitution prohibited government-sponsored religion while guaranteeing individual religious freedom.[126] Therefore, regulation of religious nonprofits bore the added risk of violating the First Amendment. Consequently, a great deal of deference and favoritism were afforded nonprofits. For example, the doctrine of "charitable immunity" exempted nonprofits from tort liability.[127] During the period 1850–1950, nonprofits were exempted from sales, income, and property taxes.[128] They were also exempted from laws involving involuntary bankruptcy, collective bargaining, securities registration, Social Security, unemployment insurance, the minimum wage, and unfair trade practices.[129] Furthermore, nonprofits were given advantageous treatment under the copyright and antitrust laws.[130]

During the nineteenth century, the number of nonprofits grew dramatically. Eventually, these organizations became more sophisticated and began to incorporate. Thus, much of the nonprofit law was a derivative of general corporate law. However, general corporate law proved inadequate since it ignored the difference between nonprofits and for-profit corporations. For example, a nonprofit has no shareholders to whom the director could be held accountable. To respond to these differences, nonprofit law became a mix of corporate and trust law, with corporate law being applied to the internal workings of nonprofits, while trust law governed the fiduciary duties of the officers and directors.[131]

Although the states are limited in their regulatory roles, there are private organizations, such as the Philanthropic Advisory Services (PAS), that set up voluntary standards for charitable solicitations.[132] One of the standards, set by PAS, is that at least 50 percent of contributions must be spent directly on the programs described in the solicitation.[133] However, compliance with these standards is voluntary. As a result, PAS's only means of enforcement is to publish the names of charities that don't comply with the standards. If the contributing public is unaware of the service, then the standards will not be effective in discouraging unscrupulous fund raising.

The law governing nonprofits, although more formalized, is still an ad hoc system borrowing from different parts of the law. Different states, such as California and New York, have attempted to promulgate a more uniform nonprofit law.[134] Later the American Bar Association drafted the Revised Model Nonprofit Corporation Act (RMNCA).[135] However, the one common flaw among all these acts is their continued deference to religion.[136] If religious organizations are already assumed to act with a higher ethical standard, then ethical regulation would affect only those violating the standards. Hence, there is no reason to avoid equal standards for religious nonprofits. Yet, the taboo surrounding the separation of church and state has continued to impede effective government regulation of religious nonprofits.

The problem with nonprofit law is the attempt to deal with both commercial and noncommercial nonprofits under one body of law. There needs to be a completely separate body of law for commercial nonprofits and another for noncommercial nonprofits. Although the California code and the RMNCA classify nonprofits into three categories, the acts still attempt to deal with nonprofits as one entity comprised of subdivisions. However, since commercial nonprofits operate more like corporations, general nonprofit law is not effective. Commercial nonprofits compete directly with for-profit corporations while unfairly benefiting from tax exemptions. Therefore, commercial nonprofit law should be handled under corporate law, while nonprofits with more philanthropic purposes should have a separate body of law.

Legislatures must face up to the fact that religious and "good samaritan" charities are as fallible as any other business.

[Too high, self-serving "overhead", salaries, etc., of charities are being attacked by attorneys-general, despite Supreme Court decisions barring interference by government authorities. Use of fraud and deception statutes and use of the media to broadcast warnings are major devices to get around the Supreme Court view. *See:* Bush, article, *Non Profit Times*, p.1 (Nov. 1993).]

A good current summary of the matter of *Ethics* in USA organizations is that of the INDEPENDENT SECTOR, a major national forum to encourage voluntarism and NPO initiative [1828 "L" St., N.W., Washington, D.C. 20036; Tel. # (202) 223-8100]. Some extracts are the following [from *Leadership IS*; Vol. 1, No. 1, p. 4 (Summer 1991), a new I.S. newsletter]:

"... While all are under scrutiny, violations of legal as well as commonly held ethical standards in voluntary and philanthropic organizations are particularly troublesome because of the special trust the public has vested in the sector.

"... INDEPENDENT SECTOR asked a broadly representative group to provide guidance on what these institutions and their leaders should stand for ....

"The final statement of the committee, published as a booklet entitled *Obedience to the Unenforceable* includes recommendations that all organizations in the sector:

- Adopt an organizational credo.
- Conduct an ethics review every year. The committee believes this is as important as an annual fiscal audit, and refers to the ethics review as an "ethics audit" or "self-evaluation."

"Larger organizations should expand to:

- Develop a supportive set of codes or standards.
- Involve all of their constituencies in the process.
- Infuse the process and the documents into the culture of the total organization.

"The committee recommends that trustees be involved in and ultimately responsible for examinations of ethical behavior. ...

"The report was approved in principle by the INDEPENDENT SECTOR Board of Directors on September 12, 1990."

ETHICAL GUIDELINES are easy to demand, but hard to construct. But it can be done. Thus, colleges today usually forbid romantic relationships between teachers and students. Experience taught the wisdom of this "ethics rule."[137]

Ethics Bibliography (Sample books, and materials)

[See the main bibliography herein, at Section 16]

Berman, *Law and Revolution* (1983).

The Better Board's Role, board evaluation, American Society of Association Executives, 1575 Eye Street, NW, Washington, DC 20005, 202/626-2708, the annual supplement, *Leadership* is available for $4.50.

Board Member, Handling An Ineffective Chair, NCNB, 2000 L Street, NW, Suite 411, Washington, DC 20036-4907, 202/452-6262, membership is $48/yr. for individuals and begins at $195 for organizations.

Bottom-Up Evaluation, National Academy of Public Administration, 1120 G Street, NW, Suite 850, Washington, DC 20005, 202/347-3190.

Bradley, *Church-State Relations Today* (1987).

Brockett, *Ethical Issues in Adult Education* (1988).

Corey, S. & C., *Issues and Ethics in the Helping Professions* (1984).

Effective Nonprofit Board Leadership, training video tape, ARDI, 1805 South Bellaire Street, Suite 219, Denver, CO 80222, 303/691-6076, $149.95.

Eliade (Ed.), *Encyclopedia of Religion* (1987).

"Ethical Dimensions of Nonprofit Administration," Customer Service, Jossey Bass Publishers, 350 Sansome Street, San Francisco, CA 94104; Foundation News is available for one year (6 issues) for $29.50.

Ethical Dos and Don'ts; "Sticky Issues" and Calvin & Hobbes JEJI, 310 Washington Blvd., #104, Marina del Rey, CA 90292, 310/306-1868, basic membership is $35.

Evaluation for Foundations, Jossey Bass Publishers, Inc., 350 Sansome Street, San Francisco, CA 94104, 415/433-1767; $39.95 + $3 shipping.

Garnett, *Ethics* (1960).

Greenawalt, *Religious Convictions and Political Choice* (1988).

Insights on Global Ethics, monthly newsletter. $35 membership, Public Service Fellows Programs, Tufts University, Medford, MA 02155, 617/627-3453.

Leadership IS:, Independent Sector, 1828 L Street, NW, Washington, DC 20036, 202/223-8100.

Monitoring and Supporting Your Executive Director, Marline Cararillo, Neighborhood Reinvestment Corporation, 1325 G Street, NW, Suite 800, Washington DC 20005, 202/376-3216.

Morals and Ethics in the Education of a Trustee: Chester I. Barnard at the Rockefeller Foundation, Fred W. Beuttler, University of Chicago, Department of History, 1126 East 59th St., Chicago, IL 60637.

Mothershead, *Ethics* (1955).

Noonan, *The Believer and the Powers That Are* (1987).

Perry, *Morality, Politics and Law* (1988).

The Program Evaluation Standards, Dr. James R. Sanders, Western Michigan University, College of Education, The Evaluation Center, Kalamazoo, MI 49008-5178, 616/387-5895.

Save the Children's Ethics Code, Terrence Meersman, Executive Vice President, Save the Children, 54 Wilton Road, Westport, CT 06880, 203/221-4123.

Self-Assessment Tool, for small/mid-sized organizations. The Drucker Foundation, 666 Fifth Avenue, 10th Floor, New York, NY 10103, 212/399-1710.

Tushnet, *Red, White and Blue* (1988).

Welch, *Law and Morality* (1987).

Independent Sectors' *Obedience to the Unenforceable* (1990), of course, is recommended.

Two opposing views of modern statutory trends in nonprofit organizations law are placed in contrast in a 1989 Symposium issue of the *Northern Kentucky Law Review* [Vol. 16, No. 2, at pp. 225 and 251].

The first is the writer's (Oleck) view that the 1987 Revision of the *Model Nonprofit Corporation Act* by the Business Law Section of the American Bar Association is not only unwise but is almost an invitation to unethical abuses. [Oleck, *Mixtures of Profit and Nonprofit Corporation Purposes and Operations*, 16 No. Ky. L. Rev. (2) 225 (1989).] The second is approval by a writer (Moody) of the revision's proposal to abolish the ancient principle that a director of a charitable or religious or educational corporation is a fiduciary (trustee) of its assets, who ought not to seek to use the organization for his/her personal enrichment. [Moody, *The Who, What and How of the Revised Model Nonprofit Corporation Act*, 16 No. Ky. L. Rev. (2) 251 (1989).]

§6. POTENTIAL ABUSE OF NONPROFIT STATUS

As in all human activities, a number of people (estimated at about 5 percent) always seem willing to evade or violate the rules or laws of decent society in order to obtain personal power or wealth. They view nonprofit status (especially charitable status) as ideal camouflage for self-enrichment. No national law requires charities to account to donors; many states require annual reports but few check them for accuracy; accounting standards for nonprofits are not yet well established; requirements of uses of certain percentages of income for proper programs are easily evaded by treating as "program" or "education" the advertising solicitations for more contributions. There are other devices for abuse of alleged status as well.[138]

[Most of the following material in this section was contributed by Patrick Real.]

By 1950, a large number of commercial nonprofit organizations sold personal services and derived their income from those sales. These organizations basically operated as for-profit, yet benefited from their nonprofit status. Consequently, this raised new ethical questions about the equity of such tactics, which seemed devoid of any philanthropic purposes. This advent of commercial nonprofits seemed to tarnish the good-samaritan image of the entire nonprofit sector. In turn, the government was more willing to scrutinize the operations of nonprofits. Evidence of this is the "unrelated business income tax" (UBIT) passed in 1950.[139] UBIT allows the government to tax the noncharitable activity of any nonprofit.[140] Eventually, the government went as far as to revoke the tax exempt status of certain commercial nonprofits.[141]

Recently, the government has even started to more zealously peruse the operations of this country's most prestigious educational institutions. In *The United States v. Brown University*, the government alleged that Massachusetts Institute of Technology (MIT) and other universities formed the Ivy League Overlap Group (ILOG), which conspired to restrain trade in violation of the

Sherman Act, 15 U.S.C. § 1 (1990). The government claimed that MIT and the others had collectively determined the amount of financial assistance to be awarded students. MIT contended that its activities were neither trade nor commerce and, therefore, did not violate the Sherman Act. MIT also argued that its activities were a charitable component of higher education and that Congress did not intend to subject charitable functions of nonprofits to the Sherman Act. The court discussed the historical reluctance of Congress to exercise control in educational matters, but noted that this did not immunize a nonprofit from antitrust laws. The court held that MIT's activities were commercial and that the ILOG's purpose was to eliminate economic competition. Thus, MIT and the other Ivy League schools were banned from similar activity.[142] But in 1993 this view was changed.

Another example of the judiciary's refusal to exempt nonprofits from the law is the abrogation by most jurisdictions of the "charitable immunity" doctrine.[143] However, the legislatures responded by passing laws that limited the liability of nonprofits. For example, in the late 1950s, after the court had abrogated "charitable immunity," New Jersey passed the Charitable Immunity Act, which limited the liability of a nonprofit hospital to $10,000.[144] Needless to say, this kind of protectionism meant great injustice to someone who had been injured by the negligence of a nonprofit hospital.

Many states have recognized the injustice caused by limiting nonprofit liability and have raised the liability limits.[145] In 1991, even New Jersey, one of the last states to do so, finally amended its Charitable Immunity Act so as to increase nonprofit hospital liability from $10,000 to $250,000.[146] However, many wanted the courts to make nonprofits accountable for their past negligence by applying the amendment retroactively. Not willing to go that far, the New Jersey Supreme Court held that there was neither legislative intent nor any reasonable expectation on the part of the parties that would warrant applying the amendment retroactively. Thus, the amendment would apply only to injuries occurring after July 31, 1991.[147]

The courts have also attacked limited liability statutes on the basis of equal protection. In *Hanvey v. Oconee Memorial Hosp*,[148] the South Carolina Supreme Court held that the South Carolina statute § 44–7–50 (1976), was a violation of equal protection. The statute limited a nonprofit hospital's maximum liability to $100,000, while the maximum liability for all other nonprofits was $200,000.[149] The court found this classification to be unconstitutional because there was no rational basis for differentiating between a nonprofit hospital and other nonprofits. So, there appears to be a trend toward making nonprofits more accountable for their negligent actions by increasing their liability exposure.

The doctrine of preemption has also been used to attack the limits imposed by state liability statutes. In *Power v. Arlington Hosp.*, [150] the court held that Virginia's law,[151] which limited the tort liability of charitable hospitals to their maximum insurance coverage, could not limit the amount recoverable under a federal "patient dumping" action.

Recently, even the most traditional charities have been held accountable for negligence and fraud. In *Roe v. Catholic Charities of the Dioceses*,[152] despite long-standing precedent otherwise, the court held that it would recognize an action for fraud based on an adoption agency's intentional misrepresentation of a child's health and psychological background. The court also recognized an action for social worker malpractice, which allowed for an action grounded in negligence. These types of cases may mark the end of the carte blanche protectionism afforded church-run charities.

Many times religious organizations seek to promote their views through involvement in politics. However, the Internal Revenue Service has banned tax-exempt organizations from participating in political campaigns on behalf of specific candidates. As a result of such violations, religious organizations, such as Jerry Falwell's Old-Time Gospel Hour, have lost their tax-exempt status.[153]

Despite the government's increasing willingness to scrutinize nonprofits, including traditional charities, not all protectionism is gone. In the 1960s, charity fund-raising came under heavy state regulation.[154] However, during the 1980s the United States Supreme Court, in several decisions, held that these regulations were unconstitutional under the First Amendment.[155] As a result of these decisions, states can neither mandate what percentage of donations must go to the recipient nor set limits on the amount spent on fund raising.[156] Also, the court in *Riley v. National Federation of the Blind*,[157] struck down a state statute requiring the disclosure of fund-raising costs at the time of solicitation. This battle between the legislature and judiciary has resulted in regulation that goes too far in protecting charities while prohibiting donors from requiring fund-raising information.[158]

Even the fine-sounding aspects of nonprofit activity often are not as noble as they claim to be. For example, the nonprofit annual conventions of over 26 million Americans involve expenditures of over $15 billion per year, and in fact often serve mainly as excuses for vacations, and partying and tax-evasion, under the pretense that they are serious conferences.[159] The horror story of 900 murder-suicide victims of Jimmy Jones' Peoples' Temple in 1978 in Guyana is an example of how far some operators of "nonprofit" organizations will go in abusing their status.[160] Similarly, the nation stood in horror as David Koresh orchestrated the destruction of his cult of Branch Davidians in Waco, Texas, in 1993, when federal troops ended a hostage standoff there. The standoff began with an attack on federal troops by the cult members as the troops executed a warrant to search for suspected federal weapons violations by the members of the cult.

Hancock and Chafetz's cynical but well-researched book, *The Compleat Swindler*, p. 225) says: "Promotion of some national charity or church or community welfare project . . . forms the base on which this country's most extraordinary rackets build monolithic ("nonprofit" and tax-free) empires." They estimate that every year over $11 billion is taken from Americans' pockets by "charity" swindlers, America's "fourth largest industry." Paul Blanshard, the noted columnist, urged taxation of churches,[161] citing C. Stanley Lowell, whose book, *The Church-State Fraud*, said that "the simple tax-exemption for a modest house of worship has burgeoned into virtual establishment of religion. The favorable tax position of the churches is an irresistible stimulant to their wealth. Tax-exemption enables churches to expand their domain with scarcely theoretical limitations." Wholesale sales of mail-order "ordaining" certificates for ministers of various "churches" are recurring rackets, as are "degree-mill colleges," with plenty of takers responding to advertised offers.[162]

Sales of souvenir buttons to aid the victims of the Mount Saint Helens volcanic eruption in 1984 turned out to be a racket, in which the con men escaped with the take.[163]

"Missing children's" fund-raising groups have multiplied in recent years. There are half a dozen in the Tampa Bay area alone, for example.

How to Avoid Fakes

1. Never send cash.
2. Ask to see the charity's financial statement, which should be prepared annually by an independent auditor.
3. Find out whether at least half of the money raised goes to the cause itself rather than for fund-raising and administrative costs.
4. Make sure the solicitor has proper identification, and inquire about whether he works for the charity or for a fund-raising firm that is paid a percentage of the proceeds.
5. Be cautious about responding to strongly emotional appeals.
6. If you have unanswered questions about a telephone or door-to-door solicitation, get it in writing and then check with your local Better Business Bureau.

Philanthropic Advisory Service (PAS) and the *National Information Bureau* (NIB) monitor nonprofit organizations, and report on the charities that do and don't meet their requirements. These reports can be obtained by the public for a nominal fee. Monitoring by PAS and NIB has curbed some, but not all, of the abuses by fraudulent "charitable" organizations.

The PAS revised booklet, *Standards for Charitable Solicitations*, makes the standards easier for people to use when checking out charities. You can get a free copy of a tip sheet on evaluating charities in general and reports on up to three charities you name, by sending a stamped self-addressed, business-size envelope to PAS, Council of Better Business Bureaus, 1515 Wilson Blvd., Arlington, VA 22209. For a copy of its current list rating about 400 charities, send a check for one dollar.

The NIB will send you a free copy of its *Wise Giving Guide* and reports on up to three charities if you send a postcard request to the NIB at 419 Park

Avenue South, New York, N.Y. 10016. You will also receive material urging you to become an NIB contributor: a donation entitles you to request additional reports on specific charities.

Council of Better Business Bureaus (CBBB) will send three short reports to people who send specific queries, one dollar and a postpaid return envelope (self-addressed) to 1150 Seventeenth St., N.W., Washington, D.C. 20036.

Though fraudulent practices continue, "there are probably fewer scams today because the public has become more educated about what to look for. They're much more sophisticated than they were even ten years ago,"[165] contends John J. Schwartz, president of the *American Association of Fund-Raising Counsel.*

Independent Sector—an association of major nonprofit associations—will provide much information about management of organizations. Address either 1828 L Street N.W., Washington, D.C. 20036, or its National Center for Non-profit Boards, at 2000 L Street, NW, Suite 411, Washington, DC 20036-4907, 202/452-6262.

§7. PRIVILEGES OF NONPROFIT STATUS

Tax Exemption Privilege

Chief among the privileges flowing from nonprofit (and especially from *charitable*) status is freedom from most of the burdens of federal income taxation. The same is true with state exemption of charitable operations from real property and other state taxes, and other such benefits granted to nonprofit organizations.[166] Tax-exemption today is so rampant that it threatens the viability of many communities and is totally opposed by some people.[167]

Those who oppose tax exemption for nonprofits point out that nonprofits actually earn billions of dollars every year. Nonprofit hospitals are giving less charity care, even though their tax exemption was given in return for free care for the poor. Colleges and universities earn millions from investments and research while tuition climbs out of reach for most Americans. The IRS cannot adequately police nonprofit businesses because of dwindling staff and money. Audits of nonprofit businesses would take years, so they operate unfettered and unchecked. Nonprofit executive salaries rapidly approach $350,000 to $400,000 plus bonus and expensive perks. Nonprofit organizations are conducting a huge building boom that rests on the backs of the taxpayers, who underwrite tax-exempt bonds. Foundations, exempt from taxation because of the grants they give, now make more money than they give away. Conservatives believe that no corporation, profit or nonprofit, should be taxed. Liberals believe that the U.S. government should join the rest of the world and impose a value-added tax, as floated by the Clinton administration, mentioned in *Business Week's* April 1993 issue, and supported by business executives. Radicals think that high salaries should be taxed at high rates, perhaps the 71 percent that followed World Wars I and II. Perhaps a combination of the positions voiced here would continue the nonprofit tax exemption, eliminate the nonprofit war with small business, and reduce nonprofit executive salaries.[168]

> Exemption from certain special imposts or customs duties (such as those on art imports for use by educational or charitable organizations[169] is found in the Internal Revenue Code and other provisions.

Postage Privilege

Another privilege is the right to special low postage rates for mailing by nonprofit organizations. However, faced with a projected $490 million shortfall in 1994, the U.S. Postal Service has proposed phasing out the nonprofit preferred rates completely by October 1995. The cost increase, averaging 35 to 40 percent, could jump to 57 percent for third-class carrier-delivered mail. Nonprofits are scrambling for Congressional action to bring back $540 million—the amount that's needed in President Clinton's 1994 budget to avert a rate increase. Most nonprofits will have to experience deep program and service reductions to ameliorate the impact of a major postal-rate shock. Most will have to decrease mailings, which will hurt income in the future.[170]

The Alliance of Nonprofit Mailers recently voiced support for postal rate decreases for nonprofits that use recycled paper. Executive Director Neal Denton wants the proposal to pass as an important social mission for nonprofits. However, the proposal is opposed by the Direct Marketing Association and the Postal Service.[171]

For some nonprofit organizations, the current (1993) postal rate privilege saves millions of dollars. Some well known magazines are products of nonprofit corporations, and these corporations especially benefit from this privilege; *National Geographic, Consumer Reports,* and the *Smithsonian,* for example.[172]

> Depending on weight, distance and percentage of advertising pages, a half-pound magazine that would cost 14 cents to mail at regular second-class rates would go nonprofit for perhaps 7 cents. For a 500,000 circulation monthly, that's worth $420,000 a year. More important, when a nonprofit company uses third-class circulars to drum up new subscribers, it pays 3.5 cents postage per piece, against 8.4 cents for commercial competitors. Figure on a 1 percent response rate, considered good for a cold-prospect mailing, and that seemingly trivial spread translates into a $4.90 saving per subscriber. On top of that, the reader can usually call his subscription a tax-deductible 'donation.'[173]

Reginald Brick, Jr., publisher of The Times, Inc.,'s new scientific magazine *Discover,* said, "If I had my druthers, I would rather not compete with a nonprofit organization."[174]

By 1980, nonprofit postal permits were costing taxpayers 522 million dollars a year. It was Congress that made the appropriation to the postal service for the revenue it lost.[175] In recent years, the postal service has started charging nonprofit agencies higher fees. The cost of mailing an appeal, for instance, was raised from 3.5 cents to 4.9 cents at the end of 1982.[176] Nonprofit organizations probably will be required to do even more in the future.

Another major advantage of lower postage rates is derived when a nonprofit corporation increases its use of direct-mail fund-raising. At least 100 million letters asking for donations are mailed each year. And although fewer than 3 out of 100 people will respond, tens of millions of dollars will be raised in this manner.[177]

Labor & Unemployment Compensation Privilege

Exemption from labor union collective-bargaining rules is part of the privilege package in many states under the protection of the National Labor Relations Act.[178] In some jurisdictions, nonprofit organizations are exempt from statutory requirements of contribution to state or other unemployment compensation funds.[179] It was only in 1970, for example, that the American Association of University Professors obtained passage of unemployment coverage in the Employment Security Amendments of 1970.[180]

Exempting hospital-based extended-care units from state (Illinois) Nursing Home Care Reform Act provisions is not a violation of the "equal protection" constitutional clause.[181]

In some jurisdictions, nonprofit organizations are exempt from the statutory requirements of state or other unemployment-compensation funds. Still argued, however, is whether or not nonprofit institutions and their employees should have to pay social security taxes.[182] About 80 percent of the nonprofit corporations have elected coverage. But this decision is optional, and recently several institutions have revoked their original options. The National Commission on Social Security Reform proposed new standards that require mandatory coverage by nonprofit institutions.[183]

But the problems involved are, first, the problem of enforcement, and secondly, the question of principle. First, it is difficult to enforce this rule on small nonprofit organizations with few employees. Second, determining the type of taxes that a nonprofit organization should pay is a policy consideration involving questions about whether or not the tax would impose so heavy a burden on tax-exempt organizations that it would discourage private support.[185] Tax exemptions to nonprofit organizations tell the public that these organizations are important; and thus the public is encouraged to support such groups.[186] Conversely, if the government does not seem to think these programs are important enough to support, then neither will the public. "The power to tax is the power to destroy."[187] Taxation of nonprofit organizations might devastate them. The government's continued support in the form of tax breaks encourages public giving. Another question is whether the money to be raised by the tax would be better spent directly on the programs of the tax-exempt organizations or on the purposes for which the tax is imposed. This is a difficult value judgment.

Immunity from Tort Liability

Immunity of charitable organizations from tort liability for damages for negligence or other harms caused by their agents or employees still continues in a few states, with varying degrees of completeness in some, and abolition of all immunity in others.[188]

Statutes limiting the tort liability of charitable organizations are not unconstitutional even if very low ($20,000). Damage caps are an expression of a legitimate state interest in preserving the resources of the organization and do not violate "equal protection."[189]

Charitable immunity for negligent injuries is being restored in many jurisdictions in order to protect volunteer activity. Since 1986 nearly half of the states have enacted volunteer-immunity laws.[190]

Solicitation Privilege

[See the chapter on Fund Raising.]

A privilege to solicit donations, gifts, bequests, and contributions is a major feature of nonprofit organizations.[191] To some extent, the very filing of articles of incorporation by the Secretary of State is an approval of this privilege,[192] and some states (*e.g.*, California, Florida, Illinois, Ohio, and Massachusetts) have special requirements about filing reports with various offices including the office of the attorney general.[193] But local controls in cities and towns vary considerably.[194] State attempts to control fund raising abuses are valid if they require registration, financial disclosure reports, and modest fees to finance administration of regulations. However, if broadly worded, such statutes may be violations of First Amendment free speech.[195]

Direct mail "magnates" fees often are based on the size of the mailings; the more they mail the more they make.[196]

Not all the money sent in response to these direct-mail pleas for aid goes directly to the cause. In the initial stages, the money contributed often is reinvested in further mailings.[197] In effect, "The big and expensive job of finding kindred spirits who will become reliable contributors is paid for by the kindred spirits themselves."[198]

New Nonprofit Corporation Statutes

The newest NPC statute is Florida's completely revised Act; and it is perhaps the most modern and complete NPC statute ever enacted. Signed into law on June 25, 1990, Florida's new *Not-for-Profit Corporation Act* is a total re-writing of Florida Statutes Chapter 617; effective July 1, 1991. See:

> Florida Session Laws, 1990 Regular Session, Chapter 90-179, Committee Substitute for Senate Bill No. 1460. Numbered sections Fl. St. 617.01011-617.2101 (Sess. L. §§1-130) cover NPCs, while the rest of the lengthy bill (Sess. L. §§131-190) provides detailed revisions and "bridging" sections tying it to the Business Corp. Act (§§607. _____) and other statutes related to NPCs.

See: Florida Bar 1990 CLE Program of Business Law Section: "Florida's New

Not for Profit Corporation Act." Address 650 Apalachee Pkwy., Tallahassee, FL 32399-230. Course Materials $15; Videotapes plus Course Materials $160; Audiocassettes $55; all + tax.

Favored Status

One major advantage that flows from nonprofit, and especially from charitable, status, of course, is the high social regard that it receives from most people. Many special kinds of ordinances and statutes, governmental agencies, and private organizations provide that special preference shall be given in various matters to organizations of charitable nature. One example is the price support given by the U.S. Commodity Credit Corporation of the Department of Agriculture, to cooperative marketing associations.[199] Tax-exemption of "the land of the priests" traces back to biblical times in ancient Egypt: *Genesis 47:26.*

§8. ACCREDITATION

See, Section 5, and in the INDEX see Licensing, Incorporation, Tax Exemption, etc. Note that accreditation and other agency/authority office addresses and telephone numbers may change often.

Records relating to the performance of a medical or quality assurance review function are exempt from disclosure, even where the records are those of a private accreditation organization prepared at the request of a hospital.[200]

§9. STATUTORY DEFINITIONS

Every state's corporation statutes contains some definitions of important terms used in nonprofit organization activities.[201] Some of these statutes attempt to define the word *nonprofit.* For example, the Ohio statute states:

> (C) "Nonprofit corporation" means a corporation which is not formed for the pecuniary gain or profit of, and whose net earnings or any part thereof is not distributable to, its members, trustees, officers, or other private persons; provided, however, that the payment of reasonable compensation for services rendered and the distribution of assets on dissolution . . . shall not be deemed pecuniary gain or profit or distribution of earnings. In a corporation all of whose members are nonprofit corporations, distribution to members does not deprive it of the status of a nonprofit corporation.
>
> (D) "Charitable corporation" means a corporation organized and operated exclusively for religious, charitable, scientific, testing for public safety, literary, or educational purposes, exclusively for the prevention of cruelty to children or animals, or exclusively for a home for the aged. . . .[202]

Most notable in this statutory provision is the distinction, by definition, between a corporation that is organized and operated merely not for profit, such as a private golf club, and a truly *charitable* corporation, such as an orphan asylum maintained by contributions from private citizens.

The North Carolina statute wisely emphasizes *intention* in its definition:

> "Nonprofit corporations" means a corporation intended to have no income or intended to have income none of which is distributable to its members, directors, or officers, and includes all marketing associations without capital stock. . . .[203]

More typical of the definitions found in most statutes, and not very clear, are the older provisions, such as those in the Kentucky statutes. They say simply that a nonprofit corporation is one that is incorporated "for the purposes of carrying out any lawful purpose or objective not involving pecuniary gain or profit to its members or associates."[204]

A modern definition is that of the New York Not-for-Profit Corporation Law, which became effective in 1970. It provides:

> "Corporation" or "domestic corporation" means a corporation (1) formed under this chapter, or existing on its effective date and therefore formed under any other general statute or by any special act of this state, exclusively for a purpose or purposes, not for pecuniary profit or financial gain, for which a corporation may be formed under this chapter, and (2) no part of the assets, income, or profit of which is distributable to, or enures to the benefits of, its members, directors, or officers except to the extent permitted under this statute.[205]

But this New York statute definition must be read along with two other sections of that statute in order to determine its meaning. Under the statute's rule of *application* of the provisions,[206] this statute does not apply to corporations which are subject to the state's education laws, such as colleges. This law further introduced the concept of four *different purpose* categories of nonprofit corporations, as follows:[207]

> Type A-A not-for-profit corporation of this type may be formed for any lawful non-business purpose or purposes including, but not limited to, any one or more of the following non-pecuniary purposes: civic, patriotic, political, social, fraternal, athletic, agricultural, horticultural, animal husbandry, and for a professional, commercial, industrial, trade, or service association. Type B-A not-for-profit corporation of this type may be formed for any one or more of the following non-business purposes: charitable, educational, scientific, literary, cultural, or for the prevention of cruelty to children or animals.
>
> Type C-A not-for-profit corporation of this type may be formed under this chapter when such formation is authorized by any other corporate law of this state for any business or non-business, or pecuniary or non-pecuniary purpose or purposes specified by such other law, whether such purpose or purposes are also within types A,B,C above or otherwise.

The statute further qualifies these distinctions:

> If a corporation is formed for purposes which are within both type A and type B above, it shall be considered a type B corporation. If a corporation has among its purposes any purpose which is within type C, such corporation shall be considered a type C corporation.[208]

Another type of statutory definition is the indirect kind, provide by such statutes as the Internal Revenue Code provisions. This, the term *private foundation* was described (rather than defined), in the Tax Reform Act of 1969, to exclude "public safety" organizations, as well as the so-called "30-percent organizations" which are exempt from income tax, under Internal Revenue Code Section 501 (c)(3),[209] because they are "publicly supported" and qualify for charitable contribution deductions, in that at least one-third of their (or their parent organization's) income comes from public support, and less than one third from investment income.[210]

§10. SELF-DESIGNATION AS TEST OF STATUS

Self-designating or self-describing statements do not suffice to obtain nonprofit status and its benefits. The fact that a corporation or association styles itself as a nonprofit organization does not make it one. For example, in an Ohio case,[211] a corporation had stated in its charter that its purpose was to "promote the social welfare of the community," while in fact it was organized as a real estate, home-building, "development" operation. The court said that such self-designation was not conclusive when the purpose to act as a real estate tract-development operation was apparent.

The real tests of nonprofit qualification are in the corporation's activities and methods, in the use or non-use of dividend-bearing capital stock, and especially in whether income is distributed as dividends or profits among the organizers or operators.[212] In this connection, such antiquated concepts as those of the statutes which in Delaware still permit use of stock (as equivalent to certificates of membership) in nonprofit organizations, are anachronisms that encourage misconceptions about the proper nature of such organizations.[213]

Nonetheless, self-designation is one of the test elements in determining nonprofit status. For example, in a suit against the University of Georgia Athletic Association, Inc., injunction was sought against that association's operation of a laundry business on the university campus, for cleaning athletic uniforms and equipment. It was objected that the association used state trucks and equipment in a private commercial enterprise.[214] The Georgia court ruled that the association was a nonprofit organization, and denied the injunction. It rested its decision largely on a provision in the association's charter that the "object of said corporation is not pecuniary gain by its members but is to promote the physical and moral welfare of the student body." That statement apparently was true.

Self-designation in its charter as nonprofit is *required* of an organization by statute in some states, and is required by administrative custom in others. Thus, California's statute in 1977 required that the articles of incorporation set forth "[t]he specific and primary purposes for which it is formed."[215] Obviously, the nonprofit nature of the corporation must be indicated by the nature of these purposes. The same is true where statutory provisions are less precise, as in the present Kentucky,[216] Ohio,[217] and Florida statutes,[218] which respectively require merely a statement of "[t]he purpose or purposes for which it is formed." New Jersey and North Carolina require only a statement of "[t]he purpose for which it is formed."[219]

In 1985, Illinois still lumped profit and nonprofit corporations in the same chapter of its statutes,[220] and did not place in the nonprofit section the usual outline of contents of articles of incorporation. Instead, the provision as to the purposes of nonprofit corporations implied that the statement of purposes must indicate their nonprofit nature.[221] But by 1986, Illinois' General Not-For-Profit Corporation Act was passed (805 ILCS 105). Missouri's statute does not provide any requirements for a form of incorporation in its nonprofit organization statute, but permits use of articles of agreement, which are recorded in the county and then filed with the secretary of state.[222] Such articles, too, would necessarily declare nonprofit purposes.

In practice, *all states require* that an organization clearly indicate in its articles of incorporation that its purpose or purposes are nonprofit. For income-tax-exemption purposes, it is desirable that the articles clearly state charitable rather than merely nonprofit purposes, if such be the case. Otherwise, difficulties with the Internal Revenue Service are to be expected when tax-exempt status is sought.

§11. KINDS OF NONPROFIT ORGANIZATIONS' STRUCTURES

Purposes of an organization largely determine the choice of ideal form for the organization. [See in §4, the listing of purposes as criteria for obtaining nonprofit status.] The Illinois statute's list is fairly typical of current kinds, types, or forms of nonprofit corporations. Another example is the North Carolina statute, which covers the broad range of kinds in its Chapter 55A, but then adds a number of special provisions for some other, special kinds of organizations: agricultural societies and fairs,[223] marketing associations[224] which are distinguished from cooperative associations,[225] religious societies[226] including corporation sole[227] but excluding educational-denominational institutions,[228] nonprofit hospital and/or medical and/or dental service plans exempted from state insurance laws,[229] (HMOs) health maintenance organizations,[230] credit unions,[231] fraternal orders,[232] cemetery associations,[233] the state crop improvement association,[234] the state fireman's association,[235] the Roanoke Island Historical Association[236] and other outdoor historical-drama presentation societies.[237]

Main Kinds of Organization Structures

Unique, odd, or rare *titles* of *kinds* of organizations, such as Michigan's old "trustee corporations," are not discussed here; which means only that control is vested in a self-perpetuating board of trustees or directors.[238]

Individual Enterprise of course is the most basic form of any kind of enterprise, and very often is used for nonprofit purposes.

Individual charitable *contributions* and public-benefit work are allowed, within certain statutory limits, as tax deductions. But, in general, deductions are allowed only for *gifts* to a formally organized *entity* such as a corporation, association, or trust. Even a contribution to an informal group devoted to aiding servicemen has been disallowed.[239] Besides tax relief, there is little legislative support for individual philanthropic activity. The little legislation on individual charities aims primarily to keep swindlers from posing as philanthropists. Licensing of solicitation of contributions and of persons who solicit contributions is the principal check on such abuse of nonprofit status.[240]

Partnership for nonprofit purposes is actually a contradiction in terms, but the expression does occasionally appear. This is because an ordinary business partnership is, by statutory definition, an association of two or more persons to carry on, as co-owners, a business *for profit*.[241] If the profit element is eliminated, we are left with an organization of two or more co-owners to carry on certain activities. That peculiar body is usually termed an *association*.

The *unincorporated association* was once the principal form of organization for nonprofit purposes. *Association* is a vague term for a group of people who have joined in a common purpose.[242] Sometimes the word *society* is used in the same sense, but this word is confusing because of its frequent use in other contexts. Many other terms are also used to convey the idea of a group or association (*e.g., fraternal order, club, brotherhood, union*, etc.). Ordinarily, an association is not incorporated. If it is, it is more accurately called a corporation, whether its purposes be profit or nonprofit.

Unincorporated, an association is a body of people united in purpose and acting together, usually with a formal charter. Yet, it usually employs the methods and forms used by corporations, and is often treated by tax and governmental authorities as a quasi-corporation.[243] This is especially likely if its organization and operation are governed by a written agreement among the members (*i.e.,* articles of association). The unincorporated association has many disadvantages and few advantages. Fundamentally, it is not, as the corporation is, a legal entity separate from the people who control it. Yet, often, if it suits governmental purposes, it is treated as if it were. Also, the laws governing such groups are few, vague and inadequate to spell out a system of organization and operation.

The *corporation* is now by far the best and most popular form of organization for most group enterprises. It combines several advantages: freedom from personal liability, continuity of existence, flexibility—and great range and scope because of joinder of resources and efforts. Detailed and plentiful legislative, administrative, and executive studies, during the past century, have produced a wealth of plans for effective organization and operation, especially as far as business organizations are concerned.

A corporation may be considered an artificial person. More precisely, it is a legal entity, organized to meet legal requirements, consisting of a number of individuals but considered by the law as an aggregate body distinct from its component members, having a specific name or title and specific powers granted by the law, and having continuous existence though its membership changes.[244]

The *condominium* is now such an important form of cooperative ownership and management of jointly owned real property, and so thoroughly governed by special statutes, that it is treated separately herein, in a special chapter. It is a system of separate ownership of individual units in a multiple-unit building or parcel of land, with each unit-owner having a right in common to use the common areas or elements.[245]

The *foundation* is a relatively modern form, providing endowment of a nonprofit enterprise and the setting up of a corporation or an association to carry out the originator's plans.[246] Michigan's *trustee corporations*, formed to execute specific written grants, are very similar to the ordinary incorporation foundation; and the special wording[247] governing it seems to be a redundancy.

Some foundations are set up in *charitable trust* form. That is, the grantor of the foundation endowment, by a *deed of trust*,[248] conveys money or property to a named trustee or trustees, to be disbursed as directed in that document. This differs from a private trust in that the beneficiaries are not named individuals, but are unnamed members of a specified group or class of people or of the public generally.[249] The grantor usually directs that a charitable corporation be formed to serve as the corporate trustee; the corporation itself being governed by a board of its trustees, who are usually persons named by the grantor. Or, the grantor directs the named trustees to organize a *charitable corporation*[250] which becomes the corporate trustee. Occasionally, the unincorporated group of trustees is given the option of incorporating or not incorporating, as they see fit.

The document of incorporation or endowment—for instance, of a scholarship fund—is the *foundation*. The grantor (an individual or an organization), who usually specifies the purposes for which the fund or the property is to be used, is the *founder*. The organization that is set up is the *trustee*. In popular usage, foundation may mean the entire enterprise, or, more often, *the organization* that administers the fund itself.[251] Now and then, a few other forms of organization or management are used for nonprofit purposes, including such varied devices as *individual trusteeship, committee control, governmental supervision,* and *bank or insurance company management.* Combinations of forms, at different stages of operation, are also used. Thus, corporate form may be converted into unincorporated trust form for winding up a foundation, while a bank is designated to handle final distributions.[252]

The *corporation sole* is a special type, originally only religious in purpose, being an incorporated church (one-man) bishopric, in effect. But some modern statutes allow its use for scientific organizations, or even for "any lawful purpose."[253]

For practical purposes, the modern *one-man corporation* (one incorporator is all that is required), which is now permitted by statutes in many states, is the equivalent of the corporation sole.

Combinations of various profit with nonprofit aspects, structures, and systems of organization, such as those permitted under the New York and Pennsylvania statutes, are mentioned in the preceding sections. Combinations in the nature of *affiliations*, or *parent and subsidiary entities*, require separate and detailed treatment.

POINTS TO REMEMBER

- Nonprofit form for carrying on enterprises is highly flexible and useful.
- Use nonprofit form as even more useful than business form in appropriate activities.
- Use both nonprofit and profit form, each for appropriate purposes, even in a single enterprise.
- Make sure that local state statutes permit use of both business and nonprofit form in one enterprise, if you plan to combine them.
- Do not use nonprofit form for what is really a profitmaking purpose. This is illegal as well as immoral.
- If anyone is to gain more than salary for services as an employee, the organization is not nonprofit.
- Assert nonprofit status in the charter and elsewhere if the organization is nonprofit in purpose.
- Calculate tax-exemption as a valuable feature of an altruistic organization.
- Choose the form of organization carefully.
- Corporate form usually is most desirable. When in doubt, incorporate.
- Use unincorporated form only when that is clearly desirable for specific reasons.
- Expect increasing governmental supervision in the future.
- Do not rely on amateur leadership for complex enterprises that require professional skill and knowledge, especially in technical operations.

NOTES TO CHAPTER 1

1. Burek (Editor), *Encyclopedia of Associations: 1993*, (27th edition.) Detroit, Michigan 1992.

2. Castelli, J., 7 *NonProfit Times* (2) 1, 57 (February 1993).

3. Alexis de Tocqueville, *Democracy in America* (1831), J.P. Mayer and M. Lerner, eds., 485 (1966). Tufts University Center for Public Service, Medford, MA 02155, in 1988 had its Sociology Department develop course materials for a class "America's Voluntary Spirit." ESLM Quarterly, p. 3 (*Independent Sector* newsletter, Washington, D.C. 20036; Feb. 1988).

4. Alexis de Tocqueville, *Journey to America*, 212 (Notebook, 1831), J.P. Mayer, ed. (1966). Religious organizations are the largest; e.g., 1.07 billion Christians and 600 million Muslims in 1983; about 783 million Catholics, according to the Vatican. *Guinness Book of World Records*, 284 (1985).

5. See, Village Square Shopping Center Assn. v. Nelson, 522 So. 2d 163 (La. App., 4 Cir., 1988). Implied agreements apply even in unincorporated associations. Seaview Assn. of Fire Island v. Williams, 69 N.Y. 2d 987, 510 N.E. 2d 793 (1987); *Smith v. Ohio State University*, 557 N.E. 2d 857 (Ohio Ct. Clm. 1990); *Douglas Manor Assn., Inc. v. Popovich*, 562 N.Y.S. 2d 170 (App. Div., 1990); *Brenner v. Powers*, 584 N.E. 2d 569 (Ind. App. 3 Dist. 1992). See, D.B. Robertson (ed.), **Voluntary Associations** (1966, John Knox Press, Richmond, VA.)

6. Institute for Professional and Executive Development, Inc., Washington, D.C.; two-day workshop program in 1985 on how to "develop, finance and manage . . . profitable projects to supplement . . . physical and capital assets . . . of the nonprofit." See S. Rose-Ackerman, ed., *Economics of Nonprofit Institutions, Yale Studies on NPOs* (New York: Oxford University Press, 1986); cf. R.W. Hamilton, *Corporations* (casebook), 3rd ed., 1986 and 1987 Teacher's Manual typically does not mention nonprofit corporations; *See Also* the *Symposium* on various aspects of this subject in 16 *No Ky. L. Rev.* (2) 225-396 (publ. Apr. 1989).

7. A. Schlesinger, "Biography of a Nation of Joiners," 50 *Amer. Hist. Rev.* 1 (1944); Henn and Alexander, *Laws of Corporations* §1, 3rd ed. (1983); cf., Hamilton casebook above, n.6.

   As to *Mixtures of profit and nonprofit corporate purposes and operations*, see Oleck *article* (pp. 1–57) in Seminar Course Materials book NONPROFIT CORPORATIONS, Chase College of Law, Northern Kentucky Univ. (Feb. 1988); *See Also* the *Symposium* on various aspects of this subject in 16 *No Ky. L. Rev.* (2) 225-396 (publ. Apr. 1989); L. Blumenthal (report), 2 *NonProfit Times* (2) 15 (May 1988); (Study) *NCI Research* at Institute for Urban Economic "Development Studies, 1800 Sherman Ave., Evanston, IL 60201 (1988); Note, *Harvard Forms Profit Making Company . . . , 1 Ethics: Easier Said Than Done*, 19 (Marina del Rey, CA, 1989); 6 *NonProfit Times*, (8) 26 (August 1992).

8. Bailyn, Davis, et al., *The Great Republic*, 401 (1977).

9. L. Hollman and M. Travis, "Curbs Are Sought on the Power of PAC's," *St. Petersburg Times* (Fla.), preview of 1985 Florida Legislature, p. 31 (April 1985); and G.H. Malandra, *Lobbying by Non-Profit Organizations* (Natl. Fed. of State Humanity Councils, 1985). In the 1984 election of Congress alone, PAC's gave $112.6 million in campaign donations, mostly to conservative candidates. AP Dispatch, May 18, 1985. *See also, PAC for Equality v. Dept. of State*, 542 So. 2d 459 (Fla. 2d D.C.A., 1989).

10. L.M. Friedman, *History of American Law*, 297 (1973). This is not new: "The spirit of association . . . of America . . . where absolutely democratic laws and habits hinder the accumulation of wealth in the hands of a few individuals, has already succeeded in carrying out undertakings and accomplishing works which the most absolute kings and the most opulent aristocracies would certainly not have been able to undertake and finish in the same time." Alexis de Tocqueville, *Journey to America* 252 (notebook E, 1831), J.P. Mayer, ed. (1959).

11. Telephone inquiry figure from staff member of the A.B.A. membership office in Chicago in June 1993.

12. Professor Oleck presented the theme paper (overview) for discussion by a panel of experts in Chicago.

13. *E.g.*, Arizona State Univ., Cleveland State Univ., Duke Univ., Northern Kentucky Univ., Stetson Univ., Wake Forest Univ., Univ. of California (Los Angeles), Univ. of Pennsylvania, Univ. of South Carolina, Univ. of Texas, Yale Univ.

14. *E.g.*, Antioch College, Eckerd College, Long Island Univ., Stetson Univ., Univ. of South Florida, Wake Forest Univ., and many others; under titles of business law, economics, political science, sociology, etc.; *See also infra*, article at note 15.

15. N.B. Wish, *Colleges Offering More Nonprofit Graduate Programs*, 7 *NonProfit Times* (6) 22 (June 1993).

16. CWRU circular (1990); address—2035 Abingdon Rd., Cleveland, Ohio 44106; Tel. 216/368-2275.

17. *Internal Revenue Service Report*; Associated Press (Washington, D.C.) May 8, 1985.

18. *Conference Board Report* (business research group) New York: *St. Petersburg Times* (Fla.), p. 11A (June 20, 1982).

19. Amer. Assn. of Fund-Raising Counsels report; (*Giving USA*); *St. Petersburg* (Fla.) *Times*, p. 7A (June 22, 1982).

20. *Giving U.S.A.* (Assn. of Fund Raising Councils, 1986).

21. Amer. Assn. of Fund Raising Counsels report; *St. Petersburg Times* (Fla.) (July 2, 1984).

22. Yankelovich, Skally & White survey for Rockefeller Bros. Fund (reported March 1986). It said that 72 percent of all money donated went to religious organizations.

23. *Conference Board Report* (N.Y.); *Miami Review*, p. 9 (November 7, 1984).

24. Univ. of Florida survey; *Miami Review*, p. 3 (November 6, 1984).

25. W. Briston, ed. of "Charitable Giving Techniques Newsletter," article in *Pinellas County Review* (Fla.) p. 9 (April 19, 1985).

26. *Giving USA* (Amer. Assn. of Fund Raising Councils, 1986).

27. L. Sterne (article), 5 *NonProfit Times* (3) 1 (June 1991). For copies of the report address: American Association of Fund Raising Council (AAFRC) Trust at 25 West 43rd St., New York, New York 10036; phone (212) 354-5799 ($45/copy prepaid).

28. *St. Petersburg (FL) Times*, p. 14A (May 3, 1991).

29. 5 *NonProfit Times* (2) 1 (May 1991).

30. L. Keenan (article), 6 *NonProfit Times* (7) 1 (July 1992). American Association of Fund Raising Counsel (AAFRC) Trust at 25 West 43rd ST., New York City 10036; phone (212) 354-5799.

31. 6 *NonProfit Times* (8) 1 (August 1992).

32. 6 *NonProfit Times* (6) 7 (June 1992) (citing the Survey on Anonymous Giving, Eleanor T. Cicerchi, Marymount College, Tarrytown, NY).

33. Associated Press Report (N.Y. City) May 27, 1993.

34. McIlquham, article, 7 *NonProfit Times*, (6) 1,27 (June 1993).

35. Blackstone's *Commentaries of the Laws of England*, Book 1, c.8 (Chase, 4th ed., 1938).

36. D. Sterne (article), 4 *Non-Profit Times* (1) 1 (Apr. 1990). [See also §10 Statistics, below.]

37. *Encyclopedia of Associations* (27th edition.) Gale Research, Inc., Detroit, MI 1992.

38. 5 *Non-Profit Times* (8) (Nov. 1991); Blackband Micro Systems data.

39. C. Swan (tabulation), 6 *NonProfit Times* (11) 14 (Nov. 1992).

40. Conducted by Gabriel Rudney, a U.S. Treasury official who had been the research director of the Filer Commission on private philanthropy, while a visiting fellow at the Yale program. See its *Research Reports*, beginning with No. 1 (September 1981) et seq.

41. *Ibid.*

42. 1992 Yearbook of American and Canadian Churches.

43. McIlquham, J., 7 *NonProfit Times* (6) 26 (June 1993). Burek (Editor), *Encyclopedia of Associations: 1993*, (27th edition.) Detroit, MI, 1992: Irvin (Editor), *Encyclopedia of Associations: International Organizations: 1992*, (26th edition.) 1991.

45. U.S. Bureau of the Census, *Statistical Abstract of the United States: 1991* (111th edition.) Washington, DC, 1991.

46. Mason, M., (article) 6 *NonProfit Times*, (8) 4 (August 1992). Copies of the study are available for $25 from the Nonprofit Coordinating Committee of New York, 121 Avenue of the Americas, New York, NY 10013.

47. S.F. Cohen, (article), *6 NonProfit Times* (3) 1 (March 1992).

48. N. Henderson, article, *Washington Post* (synd.); and UPI and AP wire services (June 5, 1985).

49. A. Schlesinger, "Biography of a Nation of Joiners," *50 Am. Hist. Rev.* 1, 19 (1944).

50. *Encyclopedia of Associations* (27th ed., 1992).

51. *Ibid.*

52. *Id.*

53. *Id., Statistical Abstract of the U.S.* (111th ed., 1991).

54. 1984 World Almanac; *Statical Abstract of the U.S.*, (111th ed., 1991).

55. G. Rudney, "Budget of Philanthropic Organizations," in 1 *Research Reports* 3 (Yale Inst. for Soc. and Policy Studies, Sept. 1981).

56. *Ibid.*

57. §2(c), in the 1964 revision.

58. *E.g.*, Ala. Code tit. 10-3A-2(9); N.M. Stat. §53-8-2(C); W.Va. Code §31–1–144; N.Y. Not-for-Profit Corp. L. §102(5).

59. J.K. Notz, Jr., Subcommittee Chairman of Illinois Not-for-Profit Act Revision Subcommittee Report to Secretary of State of Illinois (February 21, 1985) on Draft of 1985 Il1. NFPCA (February 20, 1985 version).

60. B.B. Harvey, Jr., "The Public-Spirited Defendant and Others; Liability of Directors and Officers of Not-for-Profit Corporations," 17 J. Marshall L. Rev. (3) 665-741 (1984).

61. *Ibid.*

62. Exposure Draft (1986) §1.40.

63. IL. Gen. Assembly S.B. 1320 (1985–6; eff. Jan. 1, 1986) "General Not-for-Profit Act," ch. 32, rep. pars. 163-a-163a 100 §107.80 (*See now* 805 ILCS 105/107.80).

64. *Ibid.*, §107.80.

65. Spring v. Geriatric Authority of Holoke, 475 N.E.2d 727 (Mass., 1985); Mass. G.L.A. c. 66A, §1; St. 1971, c. 554, §8(b) as amended.

66. *Ibid.*; c. 258, §1 *et seq.*

67. N.Y. Not-for-Profit Corp. L §102 (a)(5)(10) (McKinney, 1970).

68. J. Weeks, "The Not-for-Profit Business Corporation," 19 *Clev. St. L. Rev.* 303 (1970); P. Cumming, *Proposals for a New Not-for-Profit Corporations Law for Canada* (1974).

69. N.Y. Not-for-Profit Corp. L §508.

70. Model Act §4 (1964 rev.); Ala. Stat. §10-3A-4; Tex. Rev. Civ. Stat. Ann. art. 1396-2.01; Vt. Stat. Ann. tit. 11 §2351.

71. *See* N.Y. and Pa. statutes, above, n. 69, Cumming article above, n. 68; and California Assembly Bill No. 2180 (Knox) of 1978 in which definition is made by a series of references from one section to another that end in no definition at all.

72. *Ballentine's Law Dictionary*, 3rd ed., 1005 (1969).

73. *Black's Law Dictionary*, 5th ed., 953 (1979).

74. *Webster's New World Dictionary*, 2d ed., 968 (1970).

75. *Id.* at 240.

76. *Id.* at 1068.

77. Tex. Civ. Stat. tit. 32, ch. 9, art 1396-1.02(A)(3).

78. Practising Law Institute, New York Not-for-Profit Corporations, a circular announcing course. Speakers for the course, offered in the summer of 1970, included the author, as well as Robert S. Lesher, Esq. of Buffalo, New York; Professor James K. Weeks and Assistant Professor Jon Bischel of Syracuse University law School, and Julius Greenfield, Chief of the Bureau of Charitable Foundations, Office of the N.Y. Attorney General. Lesher and Greenfield had participated in the drafting of the new statute.

79. Practising Law Institute, *supra.*

80. Ala. Stat. tit. 10, §§10.20.005 *et seq.*

81. Ark. Stat. Ann. §4-28-202.

82. Calif. Corp. Code §§5,000-10,846.

83. Colo. Rev. Stat. ch. 31, art. 19 §1.

84. Code of Ala. tit. 10 ch. 10, §204 (b).

85. Colo. Rev. Stat. tit 7, art. 20; Ala. Code §10-3A-3.

86. Conn. Gen. Stat. Ann. ch. 600 §33-419.

87. Del. Code Ann. tit. 8, ch. 1., §§101 *et seq.*

88. Fla. Stat. §617.2001 (1992).

89. 2 *NonProfit Times* (article) (4) 1 (July 1988).

90. B.H. Bush, Regulation Watch, 6 *Nonprofit Times* (12) 6 (Dec. 1992).

91. 7 *NonProfit Times* (6) 20 (June 1993).

92. 6 *NonProfit Times* (5) 1 (May, 1992).

93. Van Til, J., (article) 7 *NonProfit Times* (6) 14 (June 1993).

94. See, L.B. Chisolm, *Politics and Charity: A Proposal for Peaceful Coexistence*, 58 *Geo. Wash. L. Rev.* (2) 308-367 (1990); a very heavily footnoted article.

95. D. Dahl (article), Washington Notebook, *St. Petersburg Times*, 10A (Dec. 10, 1989).

96. Fla. Stat. §196.195. Considerations for tax-exempt status involve additional criteria; treated in separate chapters herein. *See*, for example: G.C. Walker, *North Carolina Business Practice Handbook*, rev. (1985) c. 6.

97. Fla. Stat. §196.195(3).

98. Fla. Stat. §196.196. For charitable, religious, scientific or literary purposes.

99. *Ibid.*

100. (IRS) G.C.M. 38283 (Nov. 17, 1984).

101. Fla. Stat. §196.197.

102. Fla. Stat. §196.1975.

103. Fla. Stat. §196.198.

104. Fla. Stat. §196.1985.

105. Fla. Stat. §196.199.

106. Fla. Stat. §196.2001.

107. Ill. SB 1320 (84 Genl. Assembly 1985–86) new ch. 32, rep. pars, 163a-163a 100, eff. 1986 (ILCS §805/105/103.05 also lists low income utility services).

108. *Ibid.*; ILCS §805/105/103.05.

109. See *In re* Troy, 300 N.E.2d 159, 183 (Mass. S.J., 1973); Hoffman v. Lehnhauser, 48 Ill. 2d 323, 269 N.E.2d 465 (1971); Baltimore Country Club, Inc. v. Comptroller, 321 A.2d 308 (Md. 1974); First National Bk. v. State Property Tax App. Bd., 60 Ill. App. 3rd 810, 377 N.E.2d 339 (1978); Leader v. Cullerton, 62 Ill. 2d 453, 343 N.E.2d 897 (1976); Rochester Liederkranz, Inc. v. U.S., 456 F.2d 152 (2d Cir. 1972).

110. Grodjeski v. Jersey City Medical Center, 135 N.J. Super. 393, 343 A.2d 489 (Super. Ct., ch. D 1975). See generally Note, *Preventing the Operation of Untaxed Business by Tax-Exempt Organizations*, 32 U. Chi. L. Rev. 581 (1965).

111. *In re* Letts' Estate, 200 Calif. App. 2d 708, 713, 19 Calif. Rptr. 502, 505 (2d Dist. 1962); Burnacaszel v. Spivey, 11 N.C. App. 269, 181 S.E.2d 151 (1971).

112. Ky. Rev. Stat., c. 273 §161(3); Gen. Stat. No. Car. §55A-2(8); People ex rel. County Collector v. Hopedale Medical Foundation, 46 Ill. 2d 450, 264 N.E.2d 4 (1970).

113. Icardi v. National Equipment Rental, Inc., 378 S. 2d 113 (Fla. DCA 1980).

114. Reynolds v. Surf Club, 473 S.2d 1327 (FL 3rd DCA, 1985).

115. Rudolph, B., "The Less Said the Better [tax-exempt status]," 129 *Forbes* 72 (April 26, 1982).

116. *Id.* But advertising revenue from a professional journal is taxable. U.S. v. Amer. College of Physicians; U.S. Supr.Ct. #84-1737 (Apr. 1986).

117. "When Should the Profits of Nonprofits Be Taxed?" *Business Week*, 191 (December 5, 1983).

118. *Id.*

119. *Id.*

120. *Id.*

121. *Webster's New World Dictionary*, (3rd. Edition, 1990).

122. *Id.*

123. Hereinafter referred to as nonprofits.

124. Hansmann, *The Evolving Law of Nonprofit Organizations: Do Current Trends Make Good Policy?*, 39 *Case W. Res.* 807 (1989).

125. Bittker & Rahdert, *The Exemption of Nonprofit Organizations from Federal Income Taxation*, 85 *Yale L.J.* 299 (1976).

126. U.S. Const. Amend. 1.

127. W. Prosser & W. Keeton, *Prosser and Keeton on the Law of Torts* 1069 (5th ed. 1984).

128. *Supra* at note 124.

129. *Id.*

130. *Id.*

131. Fishman, *The Development of Nonprofit Corporation Law and an Agenda for Reform*, 34 *Emory L.J.* 617 (1989).

132. Revised Standards for Charitable Solicitations, Philanthropic Advisory Service, Council of Better Business Bureaus, Inc. (1982).

133. *Id.*

134. See, *CAL. CORP. CODE* @ 841, 5000-10 (West 1990& Supp. 1992); *N.Y. NOT-FOR-PROFIT CORP. LAW* @ 201 (McKinney 1970 & Supp. 1992).

135. *Revised Model Nonprofit Corp. Act* (1987).

136. Hansmann, *Supra* note 124, at 819.

137. See: Boulmetis & Russo (article), *Community Education Journal*, p. 15 (Winter 1991).

138. Quinn, J.B., "Caveat Donor," *Newsweek* 65 (December 18, 1978).

139. *Revenue Act of 1950*, ch. 994, @ 301, 64 Stat. 906, 947–53.

140. *Id.*

141. For example, the *Tax Reform Act of 1986* revoked the tax exemption for life and health insurance companies operating as commercial nonprofit organizations; *Tax Reform Act of 1986*, Pub. L. No. 99-514, @ 1012, 1986 *U.S. CODE CONG. & ADMIN. NEWS* (100 Stat.) 2390 (codified at I.R.C. @ 501(m)M (1986).

142. *The United States v. Brown University*, 805 F. Supp. 288 (U.S. Dist. 1992).

143. W. Prosser & W. Keeton, *Prosser and Keeton on the Law of Torts* 1070 (5th ed. 1984), (noting that almost all jurisdictions have abandoned complete charitable immunity).

144. *N.J.S.A.* 2A:533A-7 (1992).

145. See S.C. Code @ 44-7-50 (1977); also Va. Code @ 8.01-38 (1992).

146. See *N.J.S.A.* 2A:53A-8 (1991).

147. *Schiavo v. John F. Kennedy Hosp.*, 1993 Lexis 50 (N.J. 1993).

148. *Hanvey v. Oconee Memorial Hosp.*, 416 S.E. 2d 623 (S.C. 1992).

149. *See S.C. Code* @ 33-55-210 (1991).

150. *Power v. Arlington Hosp.*, 800 F. Supp. 1384 (U.S. Dist. 1992).

151. *Va. Code.* @ 8.01-38 (1991).

152. *Roe v. Catholic Charities of the Dioceses*, 588 N.E. 2d 354 (Ill. App. 5th 1992).

153. *St. Petersburg Times*, Apr. 10, 1993, pg. 1E.

154. Espinoza, *Straining the Quality of Mercy: Abandoning the Quest for Informed Charitable Giving.*, 64 *S. Cal L. Rev.* 605, 667 (1991).

155. See *Village of Schaumburg v. Citizens for a Better Environment*, 444 U.S. 620 (U.S. 1980); *State v. Joseph H. Munson Co.*, 467 U.S. 947 (U.S. 1984); *Riley v. National Fed'n of the Blind*, 487 U.S. 781 (U.S. 1988).

156. Mann, *The Constitutionality of Regulating Charitable Solicitation: State Regulations and Enforcement after Riley, in Nonprofit Organizations 1990: Current Issues and Developments* 419, 421–423 (Daniel L. Kurtz & Jonathan A. Small eds., 1990).

157. Riley v. National Fed'n of the Blind, 487 U.S. 781 (U.S. 1988).

158. Espinoza, *Supra* note 154, at 607.

159. "The Convening of America," *Time* 54-63 (December 18, 1978).

160. *New York Times*, 1 (issues of November 26–December 4, 1978). Describe how the remnant of the congregation in San Francisco applied for court order of dissolution and use of the assets "to recompense the families of the victims"; also, *St. Petersburg Times* (Fla.), 3N (December 6, 1978).

161. *St. Petersburg Times* (Fla.), (December 4, 1978).

162. New York refused tax-exemption application of a California-based church, for example, in the State Board of Equalization Case; *New York Times*, p. 85 (March 9, 1979).

163. Kittle, R.A., "Do You Know Where Your Charity Dollars Go?," 89 *U.S. News & World Report* 61 (July 7, 1984).

164. Huntley, H., (article), *St. Petersburg Times* (Fla.), 1B (September 9, 1984).

165. "How to Check Out Charities Before You Give" 36 *Changing Times* 33 (October 1982).

166. *See* Kittle article, above, n. 163.

167. People *ex rel.* County Collector v. Hopedale Medical Foundation, 46 Ill. 2d 430, 264 N.E.2d 4 (1970); State Bd. of Tax Comm'n. v. Fort Wayne Sport Club, Inc., 258 N.E.2d 874 (Ind. App. 1970); *In re* application of Dana W. Morey Foundation, 21 Ohio App. 2d 230, 256 N.E.2d 232 (1970); see Surrey, *Tax Incentives as a Device for Implementing Government Policy: A Comparison with Direct Government Expenditures*, 83 Harv. L. Rev. 705 (1970); Ohio Children's Soc., Inc. v. Porterfield, 26 Ohio St. 2d 30, 268 N.E.2d 585 (1971); Small v. Pangle, 60 Ill. 2d 517, 328 N.E.2d 285 (1975); *In re* Estate of Casner, 325 N.E.2d 487 (Ind. App. 1975); Transue and Williams, *etc.* v. Lindley, 54 Ohio St.2d 351, 376 N.E.2d 134 (1978); Tacoma Goodwill Ind. R. Ctr. Inc. v. County of Pierce, 10 Wash. App. 197, 518 P.2d 196 (1973).

168. Van Til, J., (article) 7 *NonProfit Times* (6) 14 (June 1993).

169. 26 U.S.C. §3301 (1978); *see* 4 *Academe* 1 (1970).

170. Seglem, L., 7 *NonProfit Times* (5) (May 1993).

171. 7 *NonProfit Times*, (6) 1 (June 1993).

172. 7 C.F.R. §1425.13.

173. Baldwin, W., "Those Nonprofit Profits" [magazine's postal subsidies], 126 *Forbes*, 98 (September 1, 1980).

174. *Id.*

175. *Id.*

176. *Id.*

177. Kelly, O., "Nonprofit Groups: Are They Worth Their Tax Breaks?," 94 *U.S. News and World Report,* 40 (January 31, 1983).

178. See M. Larson and C. Lowell, "Praise the Lord for Tax Exemption," 159-65 (1969) for a full-scale attack on church tax-exemptions. In Ohio, for example, by 1971, $4.7 billion of assessed value of land in the state was tax-exempt, *i.e.,* 17 percent of the area of the state, 69 percent of this land being located in cities. *Cleveland Press,* Oct. 4, 1971, at 6, col. 10; see Bromberg, "The Charitable Hospital;" 20 Catholic U.L. Rev. 237 (1970).

179. 29 U.S.C. §152 (2) N.L.R.B. v. Yeshiva Univ., 582 F.2d 686 (2d Cir. 1978); cf., Coyne v. Stack, 404 N.Y.S.2d 908 (App. Div. 1978); *Billington, Hospital, Unions and Strikes,* 18 Clev.-Mar. L. Rev. 70, 75-76 (1969) where the author lists states that had statutes varying or changing the rule—including Colorado, Connecticut, Massachusetts, Michigan, Minnesota, Montana, New Jersey, New York, Utah, Vermont, and Wisconsin. But see, Univ. of Missouri v. Dalton, 456 F.Supp. 985 (D.C. Mo. 1978).

180. Ducks, Unlimited, Inc. v. Grabjec, 272 N.E.2d 657 (Ill. App. 1971); Gulf Oil Corp. v. Koysdan, 44 Ohio St. 2d 208, 339 N.E.2d 820 (1975).

181. *Illinois Health Care Assn. v. Ill. Dept. of Public Health,* 879 F. 2d 282 (7th Cr., Ill., 1989).

182. "Dear Friend, Send Money," [mail-order fraud], 36 *Changing Times,* 55 (August 1982).

183. "Taxing Tax-Exempt Organizations," 148 *America,* 82 (Feb. 5, 1983).

184. *Id.*

185. *Id.*

186. *Id.*

187. McCullouch v. Maryland, 17 U.S. 316 (1819).

188. Moral Re-Armament, Inc. v. United States, 317 F.Supp. 261 (Cust. Ct. 1970); Acme Marble and Granite Co. v. U.S., 324 F.Supp. 503 (Cust. Ct. 1971).

189. *American Red Cross Blood Service, S.C. Region,* 377 S.E. 2d 323 (S.C., 1989); *English v. New England Medical Center,* 541 N.E. 2d 329 (Mass. S. J., 1989); *English v. New England Medical Center,* 541 N.E. 2d 329 (Mass. S.J., 1989).

190. L.G. Markoff (article), 11 *National L.J.* (2) 1 (Sept. 1988).

191. *See,* Oleck, H., Tort Law Practice Manual, 197 (1982); Prosser and Keeton, *Torts,* 5th ed., 1069 (1984).

192. N.Y. Not-for-Profit Corp. Law §§202, 513, Ohio Rev. Code §1702.121, People v. Caldwell, 290 N.E.2d 279 (Ill. App. 1972).

193. M. Fremont-Smith, *Philanthropy and the Business Corporation* (1972).

194. See, *e.g.,* Fla. St. §447.06. Div. of Labor of Dept. of Commerce (annual) for labor unions.

195. *See* Harris, Holley & McC. Article in 24 *U. of San Fran. L. Rev.* 571-652 (1990).

196. "Dear Friend, Send Money," [mail order fraud], 36 *Changing Times,* 55 (August 1982).

197. *Id.*

198. *Id.*

199. M. Fremont-Smith, *supra* note 193, at Appendix A, Table 2, 479-90. Pinellas County (Fla.) charges $10 for a one year solicitor's permit. Pinellas County (Fla.) Review, p. 21 (Apr. 10, 1987).

200. *Zion v. New York Hosp.,* 590 N.Y.S. 2d 188 (N.Y.A.D. 1 Dept., 1992).

201. *See,* Fla. Stat. §§618.01; N.Y. Not-for-Profit Corp. L. §102; N.C. Gen. Stat. §55 A-2; Ohio Rev. Code §1702.01, Tex. Civ. Stat. tit. 32, c. 9, art. 1396-1.02; Ill. Comp. Stat. Ann. 805/105/101.80.

202. Ohio Rev. Code §1702.01 (C),(D).

203. Gen. Stat. N.C. §55A-2(8).

204. Ky., Rev. Stat. §273.167; Wis. Stat. Ann. §181.03.

205. N.Y. Not-for-Profit Corp. Law §102(a)(5).

206. N.Y. Not-for-Profit Corp. Law §103(a).

207. N.Y. Not-for-Profit Corp. Law §201(b).

208. N.Y. Not-for-Profit Corp. Law §201(c).

209. 26 U.S.C. §4942.

210. Int. Rev. Code of 1954, §501(c)(3); *and see,* Cleveland Foundation, *Challenge and Response,* 3 (1970).

211. State *ex rel.* Russell v. Sweeney, 153 Ohio St. 66, 91 N.E.2d 13 (1950); cited in Foreman v. Community Services, Inc., 500 F.2d 1246 (2d Cir. 1974).

212. Cummins-Collins Foundation, 15 T.C. 613, 622 (1950); Cleveland Chiropractic College, §62-001, Prentice-Hall Memo T.C. (1962); P. Verrucoli, *Non-Profit Organizations (A Comparative Approach),* c.1 (Milan, Italy: Giuffre 1985).

213. Or *see,* Mich. Stat. Ann., §§450.2302, 450.2303.

214. Westbrook v. University of Georgia Athletic Association, 206 Ga. 667, 58 S.E.2d 428 (1950).

215. Calif. Corp. Code §9300 (repealed).

216. Ky. Rev. Stat. §273.247(b).

217. Ohio Rev. Code Ann. tit. 17, §1702.04(A)(3).

218. Fla. Stat. §617.0202 (1991).

219. N.J. Stat. Ann. tit. 15A:2-8 Gen. Stat. No. Car. §55A-7.

220. Ill. Ann. Stat. ch. 32 §§163a *et seq.*

221. Ill. Ann. Stat. ch. 32 §§163a *et seq. See,* Baker v. Loe's Park S. and L. Asso., 61 Ill. 2d 119, 333 N.E.2d 1 (1975).

222. Ann. Mo. Stat. ch. 352, §352.060. *See,* Jackson County v. State Tax Commission, 521 S.W.2d 383 (Mo. 1975).

223. N.C. Gen. Stat. §106-505 *et seq.*

224. *Id.* §§54-129 to 166.

225. *Id.* §§54-111 to 128.

226. *Id.,* ch. 61.

227. *Id.,* §61-5.

228. *Thomas v. Harris,* 140 N.C. 498, 53 S.E. 341 (1906).

229. N.C. Gen. Stat. §57-1; ch. 57B.

230. *Id.* §57-1.1 to 57-18; ch. 57B.

231. *Id.* §§54 B-1 to 262.

232. *Id.* §§54B-263 to 315.

233. *Id.* §§65-16 to 17.1; 65-47.

234. *Id.* §106-273.

235. *Id.* §§118-1 to 17.

236. *Id.* §§143-199 to 203.

237. *Id.* §143-204.8.

238. Mich. Comp. L. §§450.117 *et passim. See,* Welleby Condominium Assn. One, Inc. v. W. Lyon Co., 522 So. 2d 35 (Fla. App. 4th Dist., 1987).

239. Tripp v. Commissioner, 9 CCH Tax Ct. Mem. 622 (1950).

240. *E.g.*, National Foundation v. Forth Worth, 415 F.2d 41, 43 n.1 (5th Cir. 1969). *See* McGeorge, *Control of Charity Solicitations*, 14 Clev.-Mar. L. Rev. 265 (1965), cited in Williams v. Westinghouse Elec. Corp. 488 F.2d 1353 (2d Cir. 1973).

241. *See* generally Uniform Partnership Act §6; Crane and Bromberg, *Partnership* (1968).

242. *Black's Law Dictionary*, 5th ed., 111 (1979). Treated as a corporation if it resembles one, under IRC §7701(a)(3).

243. IRC §7701(a)(3); Rabkin and Johnson, *Federal Income, Gift and Estate Taxation* §§2.10-2.12 (1978).

244. *See*, Louis K. Liggett Co. v. Lee 288 U.S. 517 (1932) (Brandeis J., dissenting); Trustees of Dartmouth College v. Woodward, 17 U.S. (4 Wheat.) 518, 636 (1819); H. Oleck, (Vol. 1) *Modern Corporation Law* §§2,3 (1978 Supp.); Fla. Stat. c. 718.

245. *Black's Law Dictionary*, 5th ed., 267 (1979); Calif. Civil Code §783.

246. See, IRC §509(a) for definition of a "private foundation" for tax purposes.

247. Mich. Comp. L. §§450.148 *et seq.*

248. It is called "essentially a security" in *Black's Law Dictionary*, 5th ed., 373 (1979). *See also* "charitable trust," *Ibid.* p. 1353.

249. See, Brown v. Buyer's Corp., 35 Ohio St.2d 191, 299 N.E.2d 279 (1973); Estate of Southwick v. First Natl. Bk., 515 P.2d 486 (Colo. App. 1973); Saffron v. Dept. of the Navy, 561 F.2d 938 (D.C. Cir. 1977); Ohio Rev. Code §109.23.

250. See, *Chiechi and Gustafson, Private Foundations*, Secs. 4940 and 4944 (1983); *Corporate Foundation Profiles*, 3rd ed., (New York: Foundation Center; 1983); D.R. Gray, *Nonprivate Foundations: A Tax Guide* (1978); R. Bogert, *Law of Trusts* (current ed.).

251. *Ibid.*

252. L. Hanna, Jr., *Final Fund* (1963), is an example.

253. Ariz. Rev. St. §§10-421, 427; Calif. Corp. Code §§10,000,-15; Nev. Rev. St. §§84.010,-.080; Ore. Rev. St. §61.055 and §61.125 that the number of directors of nonprofit corporations *other than sole* may not be less than three; Rev. Code Wash. Ann. c. 24.12.
    The Arizona statute permits corporations sole for scientific as well as religious purposes. Iowa repealed its provision in L. 1977, c. 28 (eff. January 1, 1978). Oregon's modification of the ABA Model Act, permits one-man directorates only for religious purposes. District Col. Code §29-902 does not specify any minimum number of directors for a religious society. Similarly, Ky. Rev. Stat., ch. 273 makes no mention of the number of directors required for religious, charitable, or educational organizations. Code S.C. §33-31-140 renumbering §12-762, is unique insofar as it mentions and recognizes corporations sole, but makes no provision for their incorporation.
    Many other statutes, while not expressly authorizing the formation of corporations sole, give validity to the acts and conveyances of land by a bishop and his successors in office. Typical of such statutes are N.C. Gen. Stat. §61-5; Ohio Rev. Code Ann. §1715.17, Okla. Ann. tit. 18, §563.

2

STATISTICS AND BIBLIOGRAPHY

§12. GENERAL STATISTICS

The numbers of nonprofit organizations in the United States, and their wealth and numbers of members, are touched on in Chapter 1, Section 1 (latter part) and Section 2 (Numbers and Wealth) in some detail. See also the chapters relevant to the statistical information you need.

Biggest Charities (See §1)

The Washington D.C. based American Society of Association Executives (ASAE), ranks the top 100 largest associations in the nation each year. Their study indicates that more than 260 million members belonged to the top 100 associations in 1992. The top 100 associations employ 233,700 people and spend more than $12.68 billion annually. Ranked by membership, the top ten associations are: American Association of Retired Persons, American Automobile Association, YMCA-USA, National Geographic Society, Internat'l Assn. for Medical Assistance to Travelers, National Forensic Language, National Wildlife Federation, National PTA, Council of Industrial Defense, Fndn. for the Support of Internat'l Medical Training, and the Boy Scouts of America.[1]

State Associations of Associations

Twenty-two statewide NPO associations, with combined 5850 agencies, of which over 34 are themselves associations, in early 1991 were leading a new evolution of policy advocacy and combined action (e.g., purchasing, lobbying, and so on) that indicates that soon every state will have such an association center.[2]

There are an estimated 20,000 nonprofit organizations that are enrolling in state-wide nonprofit associations. Twenty to thirty states have some form of state-wide organization in development.[3]

§13. INADEQUACY OF STATISTICS

Typical of the difficulty in obtaining *reliable* data about nonprofit organizations is the history of foundations, in particular the most frequently studied types. Even the subpoena power of Congress has been ineffective in obtaining reliable data.[4] (See Section 11).

In the 1930s, there were about 240 foundations in this country (six in Ohio, 58 in New York, etc.).[5] Later, the Foundations Directory reported that there were 6,803 nonprofit foundations in 1966 (463 in Ohio, 1,822 in New York) as of 1965 figures.[6] It also said there were 18,000 foundations in all, but that 10,000 were "very small" (*i.e.,* assets of less than $200,000, or making grants of less than $10,000 per year). By 1968, the IRS Official List of tax-free foundations *registered* with it, numbered 30,262.[7] This latter listing showed 1,493 registered in Ohio, while the Foundation Directory reported 463 (a disparity of 1,030). The Patman Committee study in 1960 had estimated that there then were already about 50,000 foundations.

Assets of several foundations then were Ford (3.6 billion dollars),[8] Carnegie ($320 million),[9] Rockefeller ($854 million).[10] In 1969, the Internal Revenue Service reported 30,000 foundations filing reports.[11] There then probably were double that number, in fact, acting as foundations, without bothering to report to anyone. Prior to the Tax Reform Act of 1969,[12] an organization was tax-exempt if it met the requirements of the Internal Revenue Code, even if it had not obtained a letter of exemption from the IRS.

The *Foundation Directory* of 1967 said foundations then owned $19.6 billion in assets.[13] But in early 1969, the New York attorney-general's investigation in New York alone, found an "alarming rate" of cases of foundation funds diverted to personal uses, and one-third of the 13,500 foundations that had registered there at that time owned $25 billion in the state of New York alone.[14] This investigation reported that in New York alone the number of foundations then was increasing by about 100 a month, and that abuses by many foundations had become serious. It was then that Congress enacted the Tax Reform Act, and in 1970 more thorough supervision of foundations began, with a resulting sharp decline in the number of abuses.

The 1978 *Foundation Directory*[15] said that there were then about 26,000 foundations, of which 23,000 were "quite small," but with about 300 of them holding assets of over $10 million each. This directory contains data on about 3,000 foundations—those that are fairly large and make sizable grants per year.

The foregoing statistics about one type of NPO indicate how fragmentary and sketchy is the published information available about nonprofit organizations.

For listing national associations alone, the directory published by the U.S. Department of Commerce in 1949 required 634 pages.[16] In 1973 the *National Trade and Professional Associations Directory* covered 4,700 national associations.[17] Today's multivolume *Encyclopedia of Associations* consists of over 1,000 pages.[18]

The *Cumulative List* of the Internal Revenue Service, published periodically to show organizations in which gifts get tax exemption, is a large, small-print book.

Published collections of data or information about nonprofit organizations continue to be fragmentary and sketchy.[19]

See the Bibliography in Section 16 in this chapter. See also such publications as the current issues of the *Statistical Abstract of the United States*, the *World Almanac*, such state annual Statistical Abstracts as that of Florida, *National Trade and Professional Associations of the United States*, the *Yearbook of American Churches*, etc. *See also* the Ethics Bibliography in Section 5 of Chapter 1 and the Fundraising Bibliography in the chapter on fundraising.

§14. GOVERNMENTAL SUPERVISION

[See Sections 12 and 13.]

Many states have enacted registry-board of commission laws governing nonprofit organizations, but few have adequately staffed or funded them. The New Hampshire legislature began a *register* of *charitable trusts* in 1943, and then other states followed, with powers in the director to supervise them. By 1992 charitable solicitation laws had been enacted by 37 states.[20] But supervision by attorneys general remains cursory or non-existent in most states.[21] According to the Ohio attorney general not long ago, many states require annual reports by foundations and charitable trusts, but few have staffs adequate for effective regulation.[22] State secretary of state (corporation division) supervision continues to be almost pathetically scanty.[23] A survey by Richard A. Manger[24] revealed the following illuminating data: Massachusetts had a public charities division of the attorney general's office, with a staff of 14, supervising some 11,000 charities with assets in the hundreds of millions of dollars; the staff included four attorneys. Ohio had 23 people in its Charitable Foundations Section, handling 3,000 charitable trusts then with aggregate assets of over $2 billion; the staff included nine attorneys, four accountants, and three investigators—an astonishingly large staff compared to most states.[25] New York and California have fair-sized staffs.

Washington's staff was more typical. Its Division of Charitable Trusts had three part-time staff people, including two attorneys, to supervise about 600 trusts, with assets of about $600 million.[26] At least ten states mixed supervision of nonprofit and profit corporations in one batch under the new staff, while seven had separate staffs.[27] Delaware started a nonprofit staff only in 1976, consisting of two volunteer workers, and one paid attorney and secretary.[28]

Massachusetts and Washington define annual reports of charitable organizations as public documents, open for public inspection.[29] Texas says that such information is not published nor made available.

It was only relatively recently that the Internal Revenue Service set up a separate division to supervise nonprofit (tax-exempt) organizations. And note that most of the supervision referred to above applies almost exclusively to charitable trusts, not to nonprofit organizations generally.

Governmental Revenues vs. Tax-Exemption

[*See* the chapters on tax-exemption.]

The impact of nonprofits, in the matter of tax-exemption, is now known to be very great. In some big cities, tax exemption of property now removes from 15 to over 50 percent of the revenue from property tax rolls. By 1978 over 55 percent of all land in Washington, D.C. was exempt from real estate taxes, or $181 million per year in lost revenues; but only $19 million applied to *private* tax-exempt land.[30] The result is highlighted in a report[31] of a futile plea by Mayor Koch of New York City. In a letter addressed to 2,300 hospitals, universities, and certain other tax-exempt real estate, he implored them to make "voluntary payments" *in lieu* of property taxes that they are exempt from paying. These properties were worth about $2 billion and would yield at least $180 million a year in tax revenues if they were taxable. No letters were sent to churches or certain other highly privileged types of nonprofit institutions. The problem of the cost to the city of providing services to tax-exempt organizations was diffidently mentioned, but not pressed.

Another aspect of tax-exemption is the Connecticut program. It was begun in 1978 to give cities 25 percent of the sums they would have collected if the state had not granted tax-exemption to nonprofits in those cities. This was the result of a statute enacted in Connecticut, to compensate cities for the burden placed on them by state grants of tax exemptions to nonprofit organizations.[32] New Jersey did likewise in 1978. A study[33] in the Lowell (Mass.) *Sun*, by Lee Mitgang, Associated Press Urban Affairs expert, in January 1978, cited some startling figures about tax-exemption: $15 billion a year in extra property taxes ($300 a family) to make up the exempt loss. By 1980 one third of America's real estate was tax-exempt; about $800 billion according to the Advisory Commission on Inter-Governmental Relations. Fifty states exempt such property, 39 exempt college dormitories, 34 exempt YMCA's and YMHA's, 31 exempt veterans' organizations, 24 exempt fraternal orders, 10 exempt labor and professional organizations—to name just a few examples—with the exempt list growing faster than property value. Denver, Milwaukee, and Pittsburgh get "service payments" from tax-exempt organizations. Harvard, Northwestern, the University of Michigan, and some churches, make voluntary payments to local governments. Attempts by communities (*e.g.*, New York City) to remedy their tax losses are often beaten down by the courts while legislatures find it politically easier to grant new exemptions than to reduce or abolish old ones.

Proposals to limit, or even abolish, some kinds of tax-exemption, have begun to be pressed in recent years. Columnist Paul Blanshard, in his December 4, 1978 article in the *St. Petersburg Times*, pointed out that in Pinellas County, Florida (St. Petersburg, Largo, Clearwater, Tarpon Springs) $116 million of 1,465 separate parcels of *religious* property *alone* was tax exempt. This exemption traces back to *Genesis 47:26* and *Ezra 7:24* granting *Old Testament* exemption to Jewish "ministers of the House of God." Presidents Madison, Grant and Garfield dared, in vain, to oppose this traditional privilege, but today every state allows it, 32 by constitutional provisions. However, the federal constitution nowhere directs it. Martin A. Larson, in his 1965 book, *Church Wealth and Business Income*, estimated that by 1960 religious tax-exemption was costing each American family about $32 a year. This contrasts strangely with the Supreme Court decision of Torasco v. Watkins (1961) that outlawed "requirements which aid all religions as against unbelievers." Blanshard, doubting that anything less that a constitutional amendment could deal with so established a privilege, urged churches to contribute voluntarily to local property taxes—perhaps $200 a year—one-tenth of what ordinary tax rates would require from taxable property for a $100,000 church.

Across the nation, nonprofit groups are becoming increasingly popular targets for taxes. Cities, counties, and states are seeking new sources of funds to offset the cost of government services and to launch new programs in tough economic times.

A recent example of community attempts to revoke the tax exempt nature of nonprofits can be seen in Erie County, Pennsylvania. In that county, 600 nonprofits lost their tax exempt status in 1991. Many nonprofit hospitals in Erie County, Pennsylvania, can expect to lose their tax exempt status if they do not meet the state's test as a "purely public charity." In Erie County, nuns have been forced to take out an advertisement asking readers to write their legislators to demand a law saying that religious orders won't be taxed. Pennsylvania's property tax statute exempts only religious places regularly used for worship services. The nuns realize that the state property taxes on their motherhouse, where nuns are taught and where they reside, could approach $100,000 per year. Property taxes on their soup kitchen could reach $3,000. Nonreligious nonprofits have also been targeted in Pennsylvania. The Erie Art Museum may have to pay a $6,000 property tax bill.

In Minnesota, a 2 percent tax was imposed on 149 hospitals, 55 percent of which are nonprofit, in order to get funding for the state's health insurance program. In Berkeley, California, local government officials started to enforce an ordinance that requires all 800 nonprofit groups in the city to pay a business license fee, regardless of the size or religious affiliation of the nonprofit. Yale University, in New Haven, Connecticut, was forced to pay taxes on such noneducational property as its golf course to defray costs of fire protection and other city service programs. Yale now contributes almost $2 million in taxes to city revenues. Some experts indicate that nonprofits can and should pay for city services that are provided to them. Others cite the fact that national programs have been pushed to the state and local level and that the cities must logically look to any new base of taxpayers to fund more programs with increased expenditures.

Registration fees for nonprofit fundraisers have been used as a "tax" in many states. For example, in Massachusetts, registration for nonprofit firms

rose from $25 to a maximum of $250 in 1992. The cost of registering professional fundraisers in New York and Tennessee went from $100 to $800 in New
York and $1,000 in Tennessee. The states usually contend that fees are often
raised to offset increased reporting requirements. There were, in 1992, 37
states that required some form of reports and registration by nonprofits. However, such "fees" are believed by some to be simple "taxes" for services.[34]

§15. HISTORY OF NONPROFIT ORGANIZATIONS: SUMMARY

[Melissa Mince wrote the draft study from which this section was
abridged.]

(See Chapter 1.)

The primitive clan and village temple may have been the first nonprofit organizations.[35] The *Code of Hammurabi* (about 1850 B.C.) clearly referred to such
organizations in requiring that the first fruits of all crops or productions go to
the priests for support of the temple and the poor.[36] The *Old Testament*
required tax exemption of the priests and temples, in *Genesis 47:26*, and *Ezra
7:24*. The church became the first center of charity and welfare and remained
that way for thousands of years. In the eleventh century, two religious military
organizations were founded to escort pilgrims to Jerusalem and to protect
them from the Muslims. The *Knights Templar* was begun by eight or nine
French knights who vowed to devote their lives to that purpose.[37] They founded a religious community that amassed great wealth throughout Europe. King
Philip IV (the Fair) of France suppressed the order in 1312.[38]

The second such organization, the *Hospitallers* was founded by the merchants of Amalfi, Italy, to provide hospitals for the pilgrims.[39] After the crusaders conquered Jerusalem in 1099, more hostels were begun in Italian cities
along the route to the Holy Land. Many knights wounded in battle left part of
their estates to the hospital in gratitude for the care and nursing they had
received. Other crusaders stayed with the hospital and helped tend the sick,
and at the same time waged war on the Muslims. For centuries, the Hospitallers gained and lost power and territories, especially in the island of Malta
where they attained formidable strength and maintained an advanced hospital
until almost 1800 A.D. The order still continues its humanitarian projects in
many parts of the world.[40]

As Church power declined, society provided for the less fortunate, largely through unincorporated nonprofit organizations, such as trade unions.

A group of Philadelphia shoemakers organized the first union in 1792.[41]
In 1794 the shoemakers reorganized and called themselves the Federal Society
of Cordwainers,[42] until the group disbanded in 1806.[43] In the following decades,
many small local unions were formed. Uriah S. Stephens founded the nationwide Noble Order of the Knights of Labor in 1869.[44] Originally, it was a secret
society designed to shield its members from the wrath of employers. Membership in the Knights rapidly increased to a high of 702,000 in 1886. In Decem-

ber of that year, the once powerful Knights were supplanted by the American Federal of Labor (AFL).[45] Samuel Gompers, one of the founders and the first president, pushed for collective bargaining, the end of racial discrimination among affiliates, union dues, strike benefits, the end of racial discrimination among affiliates, union dues, strike benefits, and one union per trade.[46] In 1935 John L. Lewis, founder of the United Mine Workers, encouraged eight AFL unions to establish industrial unions. The AFL would not accept these unskilled members into their ranks, so Lewis set up the Committee for Industrial Organization. (The name was later changed to Congress of Industrial Organizations (CIO).)[47] Both unions merged under the leadership of George Meany and Walter Reuther in 1955.[48] Membership was at an all-time high of 15 million in 1955. Since then, membership has been steadily declining. The National Association of Manufacturers conducts seminars to help companies prevent their employees from unionizing, and the U.S. Chamber of Commerce supplies booklets with tips for defeating union organization drives.[49]

While most nonprofit organizations actively support idealistic and altruistic goals, there is a dark side to NPOs—the "hate" organizations. Probably the most infamous one of all is the Ku Klux Klan. What began as a harmless diversion for six bored young Confederate veterans quickly snowballed into a national nightmare.[50] On Christmas Even, 1865, Richard R. Reed, John B. Kennedy, and four of their friends decided to start a secret social club.[51] They devised ridiculous-sounding names for all of the offices.[52] The president would be the Grand Cyclops, the vice-president the Grand Magi, the Grand Scribe would be the secretary, and the Grand Turk would greet all new members, or Ghouls as they were called. The name of the organization is derived from the Greek word "kuklos" (circle or cycle are both derived from that root).[53] The Klan members donned bed sheets and rode galloping horses through their sleepy little hometown of Pulaski, Tennessee. That prank created such a stir that the Klansmen decided to adopt the sheets as their official dress.[54] To add to their fun, they embellished the outfits with pointed hats and grotesque masks. New members were welcomed to the club with elaborate initiation ceremonies, replete with hazing and ridiculous oaths. By early 1866 some members had discovered that the midnight rides were reminiscent of pre-war slave patrols and had a terrifying effect on local blacks, especially those who were exercising their new-found freedom.[55] With their anonymity protected by hoods, and their persons protected by hidden weapons and numbers, the night riders paid late night visits on certain people, to threaten them. Soon the threats turned into actual violence and the Ku Klux Klan was no longer a social joke, but something deadly serious, attempting to reinstate slavery.[56]

The Klan's reign of terror has gained and lost strength several times since its humble beginnings. It was at its peak during the years just after World War I.[57] Membership then declined sharply, only to rise again during the civil rights unrest of the 1960s.[58] Today the Klan often uses as its uniform, instead of white sheets and pointed caps, camouflage fatigue clothes and automatic weapons. Its members find appropriate fellowship with Neo-Nazis, who also enjoy threatening and attacking defenseless people.[59] Such sadistically evil terrorist perversions of the concept of nonprofit organization are protected by the Constitutional guarantees of free speech and assembly. But in 1987 a North Carolina Klan was found liable for $7 million in civil damages for its acts.

The original "disaster relief" fund-raiser was the International Red Cross, which had its beginnings in 1859, and was officially established in 1864. Another, less successful, international nonprofit organization, formed shortly after World War I, was the League of Nations. It was a failure. The United Nations was formed during World War II, but members' self-interest now seems to be rendering it, too, a failure.

Some disaster-relief groups have met with success. American and British rock and pop music groups have banded together to raise money for the victims of famine in Africa. "Live Aid," the transcontinental rock concert that was telecast live on July 13, 1985, reached about 80 percent of the world's 600 million television sets.[60] Viewers pledged $65 million and in 1985 over $60 million was collected.[61] One million tons of food was distributed in Ethiopia that year.[62]

The success of "Live Aid" inspired the 1985 "Farm Aid" concert.[63] Its organizers hoped to raise more than the $8 to $10 million in pledges to save America's farmers. The bulk of "Live Aid's" money, about $40 million, came from worldwide donations.[64] Americans contributed only $9 million out of their own pockets.[65] Great Britain raised more than $15 million—and that country has only one-fourth the number of people in the United States. That disparity is explained by the fact that only a few charities are allowed to solicit funds in Great Britain, while literally thousands of American organizations plead daily for funds, and Americans contribute billions of dollars each year.[66]

These are impressive developments arising from the seed of the Pilgrims' *Mayflower Compact* agreement "to combine ourselves together into a civil body political."[67] By 1985 charitable contributions by U.S. business corporations *alone* was estimated at $4.4 billion per year.[68]

In 1992, charitable contributions were reported by the American Association of Fund Raising Counsel's Trust for Philanthropy to be $124.3 billion. Individuals gave $110 billion, foundations $3.3 billion, and corporations gave $6 billion.[69]

§16. BIBLIOGRAPHY OF NONPROFIT ORGANIZATIONS

[Roman Yoder, Assistant Librarian of the Stetson University College of Law, prepared the following "Selected Bibliography" of Nonprofit Organizations. Rebecca Forman assisted.]

Accounting & Financial Reporting: A Guide for United Ways & NP Human Service Orgns. (Rev. ed., 1990; 286 pp., $37.50; United Way, Sales office; Alexandria, VA, 1990.) *Accounting principles and reporting practices for certain nonprofit organizations.* New York: American Institute of Certified Public Accountants, 1979.

The 1991–92 Administrative Compensation Survey, higher education institutions, College and University Personnel Association, 1223 20th Street, NW, Suite 503, Washington, DC 20036 (202-429-0311).

Anosike, Benji O. *How to form your own profit/non-profit corporation without a lawyer.* New York: Do-It-Yourself Legal Publishers, 1981.

Anthony, Robert Newton, *Management Control in Nonprofit Organizations,* 4th ed.—Homewood, Ill.: R.D. Irwin, 1988.

Ashton, D., *Complete Guide to Planned Giving: Everything You Need to Know to Compete Successfully for Major Gifts.* Cambridge, MA, JLA Publications, 1988.

The 1992 Association Benefits Survey, Greater Washington Society of Association Executives, 1426 21st Street, NW, Suite 200, Washington, DC 20036-5901 (202-429-9370).

Association Management, (monthly magazine), American Society of Association Executives, 1575 Eye St., NW, Washington, DC 20005.

Association taxation. Washington, D.C.: Tax Policy Center, Chamber of Commerce of the United States. Monthly newsletter.

Bachmann, *Nonprofit Litigation;* J. Wiley & sons, Inc., N.Y.C.; 1992, 425 pp. $95.

Barocci, Thomas A. *Non-profit hospitals: their structure, human resources, and economic importance.* Boston, Mass.: Auburn House Pub. Co., 1981.

Barrett, Agnes P. *Cases and Materials on Not-for-Profit Corporations.* rev. ed. Indianapolis, Ind.: The author, 1979.

Becker, Sarah and Glenn, Donna. *Off Your Duffs and Up the Assets: Common Sense for Nonprofit Managers.* Rockville Center, N.Y.: Farnsworth Pub. Co., 1985.

Beckwith, Edward J. *Estate and Gift Tax Charitable Deductions.* Washington, D.C.: Tax Management, Inc., 1984. (Tax management portfolio)

Bennett and DiLorenzo, "Are Nonprofits Wolves in Sheep's Clothing?" *Business & Society Review* 40–44, Fall 1988.

Bergan, H., *Where the Money Is: A Fund Raiser's Guide to the Rich,* Second Edition, 272 pages, ($29.95 plus $2 shipping) BioGuide Press, P.O. Box 1602-N, Alexandria, VA 22303.

Blazek, *Tax and Financial Planning for Tax-Exempt Organizations: Forms, Checklists, Procedures* (1990).

Blodgett, Merry Selk. *Bookkeeping for Nonprofits.* 1st ed. San Francisco, Calif.: Public Management Institute, 1979.

Bowett, D.W. *The Law of International Institutions.* 4th ed. London: Stevens, 1982.

Boyer, R.E. *Cases on Condominiums, Coops., and Cluster Developments.* Clearwater, Fl. D.&S. Publ. 1986.

Bremner, R.H., *American Philanthropy* (history). University of Chicago Press, (1987 revision).

Bromberg, Robert S. *Tax-exempt Organizations.* Englewood Cliffs, N.J.: Prentice-Hall, Inc., 1970-[current].

Bryan, E. Lewis. *A Financial Reporting Model for Not for Profit Associations.* Ann Arbor, Mich.: UMI Research Press, 1981. Revision of thesis (Ph.D.), George Washington University, 1980.

Bryce, H., *Financial & Strategic Management for Nonprofit Organizations 2nd*, (Prentice Hall, Englewood Cliffs, N.J., 1992), (201) 767-5937.

Bryson, John M., *Strategic Planning for Public and Nonprofit Organizations: A Guide to Strengthening and Sustaining Organizational Achievement.*—San Francisco: Jossey-Bass, 1988.

Budgeting for Nonprofits. 2nd ed. San Francisco: Public Management Institute, 1980.

Burchfield, Beth Anne. *Tax-exempt Organizations: Profit from Nonprofit.* Thesis (M.S.), University of Virginia, 1981.

Building Bridges to the Twenty-First Century: Compassion and Excellence in Nonprofit Organizations, (changes, opportunities, and challenges), Center for Nonprofit Excellence, 3003 East Third Avenue, Suite 105, Denver, CO 80206, $10, (303-399-3253).

Cassiday, B. *The Complete Condominium*, guide. New York. Dodd, Mead. 1979.

Catalog of Federal Domestic Assistance, ($45), Superintendent of Documents, U.S. Government Printing Office, Washington, DC 20402.

Charitable Gift Planning News. Little Brown & Co., Law Div., 34 Beacon St., Boston, MA 02108, ($120/yr.) Monthly Newsletter-4 page. Tax law.

Chiechi and Gustafson. *Private Foundations, Section 4940 and Section 4944.* Washington, D.C.: Tax Management, Inc., 1983. (Tax management portfolio)

Christian Ministries Salary Survey, 1992–1993, 12th Edition, Christian Ministries Management ASsociation, P.O. box 4638, Diamond Bar, CA 91765 (714-861-8861).

Chronicle of Philanthropy (newspaper). ($60 per year) P.O. Box 1989, Marion, OH 43306.

1992 Church Funding Resource Guide, Ninth Edition, Women's Technical Assistance Project, 733 15th St. NW, Suite 510, Washington, D.C. 20005; $55, prepaid.

Church/State Symposium, 22 Cumberland L. Rev. 471–680 (1991–2).

Clark and Erickson. *Taxation of Cooperatives.* Washington, D.C.: Tax Management, 1984. (Tax management portfolio)

Clarkson and Martin. *The Economics of Nonproprietary Organizations.* Greenwich, Conn.: JAI Press, 1980. Proceedings of a conference held at the Law and Economics Center, University of Miami, April 28–May 1, 1977, sponsored by the Liberty Fund.

Clifford, Marcia L., *Nonprofit Organizations: Forms for Creation Operation and Dissolution*, Callaghan, Wilmette, IL., c1987.

Clotfelter, Charles T. *Federal Tax Policy and Charitable Giving.* Chicago: University of Chicago Press, 1985.

Cohen and Loeb. *Duties and responsibilities of outside directors.* New York: Practising Law Institute, 1978.

Commission on Foundations and Private Philanthropy. *Foundations, Private Giving, and Public Policy: Report and Recommendations.* Chicago: University of Chicago Press, 1971.

Compensation in Nonprofit Organizations, 5th Edition, Abbott, Langer & Associates Inc., 548 First Street, Crete, IL 60417 (708-672-4200).

The 1992 Compensation Survey Report of Management Positions in Not-For Profit Organizations, Towers Perrin, 1001 19th Street North, Suite 1500, Rosslyn, VA 22209 (202-466-4440).

Computer Resource Guide for Nonprofits. 3rd ed. San Francisco, Calif.: Public Management Institute, 1985. vol. 1. Software directory. vol. 2. Funding source directory.

Computer Software for Nonprofits (information on):

Technology Resource Consortium, Marshall Mayer, Chair, Desktop Assistance, 23 South last Chance Gulch, Helena, MT 59601, 406/442-3101.

Support Center, 2001 O St., NW, Washington, D.C. 20036, 202/462-2000.

Computer Use in Social Services, Dick Schoech, Ph.D., Associate Professor, Graduate School of Social Work, University of Texas at Arlington, UTA Box 19129, Arlington, TX 76019-0129.

Communal Computing, P.O. Box 6599, Silver Spring, MD 20916, 301/589-9062 (voice and fax).

COMSEARCH *printouts.* New York: The Foundation Center, 1960-[current]. Contains a complete list of grants to nonprofit organizations of $5,000 or more recorded in the Foundation Grants Index Data Bank by year . . . available in either paper or microfiche.

Connors and Callaghan. *Financial Management for Nonprofit Organizations.* New York: American Management Association, 1982.

Connors, Tracy Daniel. *The Nonprofit Organization Handbook.* New York: McGraw-Hill, 1980.

Corporate Foundation Profiles. 3rd ed. New York: Foundation Center, 1983.

Corporate Giving Directory, 1992, ($327), The Taft Group, 835 Penobscot Building, Detroit, MI 48226, (800) 877-8238.

Corporate Philanthropy Report (Newsletter). 2727 Fairview Ave. East, Suite D, Seattle, WA 98102-3199; Tel. (206) 329-0422 or FAX (206) 325-1382.

Currents, (monthly magazine), (colleges and universities), ($85 per year for non-members) Case Publication Ordering Department, 2700 Prosperity Ave., Fairfax, VA 22031. (703) 204-0411.

Dermer, Joseph, ed. *Where America's Large Foundations Make Their Grants.* New York: Public Service Materials Center, 1983.

Description of S. 1564 (Governmental Lease Financing Reform Act of 1983, Relating to Tax Treatment of Property Leased to Tax-Exempt Entities), Scheduled for a Hearing Before the Committee on Finance on July 19, 1983. Washington, D.C.: U.S. Government Printing Office, 1983.

Desiderio and Taylor. *Planning Tax-exempt Organizations.* Colorado Springs, Colo.: Shepard's/McGraw-Hill, 1983.

Developments in the Law-Nonprofit Corporations, 105 Harv. L. Rev. 1578–1699 (1992).

Dillon, Clarence Douglas. *Tax Impacts on Philanthropy.* Princeton, N.J.: Tax Institute of America, 1972.

Directory of Associations in Canada. 6th ed. Toronto: Micromedia, Ltd., 1985–[current].

Directory of British Associations and Associations in Ireland. Beckenham, Kent: CBD Research Ltd., 1974–[current].

Directory of Corporate Affiliations. Skokie, Ill.: National Register Pub. Co., 1973–[current].

The Directory of Corporate and Foundation Givers, ($195) The Taft Group, 835 Penobscot Building, Detroit, MI 48226, (800) 877-8238.

Directory of Building and Equipment Grants (Second Edition, $49.50); Research Grant Guides, Dept. 18 P.O. Box 1214, Loxahatchee, FL 33470.

Directory of Computer and High Technology Grants (first Edition, $44.50); Research Grant Guides, Dept. 18 P.O. Box 1214, Loxahatchee, FL 33470

Directory of European Associations. 3rd ed. Detroit, Mich.: Gale Research, 1981–[current].

Directory of Financial Aids for Minorities, 1991–1993, $47.50 plus $4 shipping and handling prepaid), 600 pages, TGC/Reference Service Press, 1100 Industrial Road, Suite #9, San Carlos, CA 94070.

Directory of Financial Aids for Women 1991–2 (TGC/Reference Service Press, San Carlos, CA 94070) (468 pp., $45 plus $3 shipping).

Directory of Grant-making Trusts. Tonbridge, England: Charities Aid Foundation, 1975. Covers Great Britain, 4th compilation.

Directory of International Corporate Giving in America, Taft Group, Washington, DC 20016 (1988), 249 pp. $160.

Directory of Japanese Giving, ($190), The Taft Group, 1-800-877-8238.

Directory of New and Emerging Foundations, New York, NY 10003, Foundation Center, 1988, $75 + 2.

Dove, Kent E., *Conducting a Successful Capital Campaign: A Comprehensive Fundraising Guide for Nonprofit Organizations*—San Francisco: Jossey-Bass, 1988.

Do You Comply With Fundraising Law? Chicago Area Technical Assistance Providers (CATAP), (Illinois law), ($10) CATAP, P.O. Box 4852, Chicago, IL, 60680-4852.

D&O Yes or No?: Directors and Officers Insurance for the Volunteer Board, National Center for Community Risk Management & Insurance, 1828 L St., NW, Suite 505, Washington, D.C. 20036; telephone: 202-785-3891.

Duca, Diane J., *Nonprofit Boards: A Practical Guide to Roles, Responsibilities, and Performance*—Phoenix, AZ.: Oryx Press, 1986.

Eckstein, R.M., *Handicapped Funding Directory*; Research Grant Guides, Dept. 18 P.O. Box 1214, Loxahatchee, FL 33470. Now *"Directory of Grants for Orgns. Serving People with Disabilities"* (8th ed., 1993).

Economics of Nonprofit Institutions: Studies in Structure and Policy, The–New York: Oxford University Press, 1986.

Elliott, Homer L. *Charitable Contributions—General Rules.* Washington, D.C.: Tax Management, Inc., 1981. (Tax management portfolio)

Encyclopedia of Associations: A Guide to National and International Organizations. Detroit: Gale Research, 1988; 27th ed. 1992.

Energize, Inc., 5450 Wissahickon Ave., Philadelphia, PA 19144, 1-800-395-9800, catalog of many titles including: Ellis and Noyes, *By the People, A History of Americas as Volunteers*, ($24.95) 1990 revision, 432 pp.; Ellis, *From the Top Down, The Executive Role in Volunteer Program Success* ($18.75), 1986, 185 pp.; Schindler-Rainman and Lippett, *The Volunteer Community*, second edition, ($17.50), 1984, 176 pp.; Scheier, *Staff Volunteer Relations Collection*, ($15.00), 1988, 80 pp.; Brudney, *Fostering Volunteer Programs in the Public Sector*, $28.95), 1990, 243 pp.; Ellis, *Volunteer Centers: Gearing Up for the 1990s*, United Way of America, ($20.00), 1989, 92 pp.; Ellis and Noyes, *Proof Positive, Developing Significant Volunteer Recordkeeping Systems*, revised 1990, ($12.75), 60 pp.; Dalsimer, *Self-Help Accounting, A Guide for the Volunteer Treasurer*, ($18.75), 1989, 104 pp.; *Volunteer Information Management Software*, ($25.00); Ellis and Noyes, *No Excuses: The Team Approach to Volunteer Man-*

agement, ($10.25), 1981, 64 pp.; Ellis, Weisbord and Noyes, *Children as Volunteers*, revised 1991, ($14.75), 68 pp.; Mizenko and Smith, *The Significance of Volunteering*, 1991, ($125.00) 50 pp., 20 slides; *Vytal Manual: Volunteer Youth Training and Leadership*, ($35.00), Fall 1990, 189 pp.; Ellis, *Colleagues: The Volunteer/Employee Relationship*, 45 minutes, *Together, Volunteer-To-Volunteer Relationships*, 38 minutes, tape and trainer's guide, ($395 or $699 for both); *The Church Puzzle Game*, 1989, how your congregation works, ($9.50), 40 pp.; Scheier, *Meanwhile . . . Back at the Neighborhood*, community organizing, 1984 ($5.00), 62 pp.; Morris, *Volunteer Ministries, New Strategies for Today's Church*, 1990, ($12.95), 162 pp.; Schindler-Rainman and Lippitt, *Building the Collaborative Community*, 1980, ($17.50), 164 pp.

Espy, Siri N., *Handbook of Strategic Planning for Nonprofit Organizations*—New York: Praeger, 1986.

Exempt Organizations Reports. Chicago: Commerce Clearing House, 1981–[current]. Previously called Private Foundation Reports; bi-weekly, loose-leaf.

The Exempt Organization Tax Review, (monthly, $499 per year), Tax Analysts, 6830 North Fairfax Drive, Arlington, VA 22213.

Exempt Organizations: Tax Strategies and Legal Problems. New York: Practising Law Institute, 1982.

The Federal Assistance Program Retrieval System (FAPRS), computerized guide to federal grants, Federal Domestic Assistance Catalog Staff, General Services Administration, 300 7th St., SW, Washington, DC 20407, or, (202 708-5126.

Federal Educational and Scholarship Funding Guide, P.O. Box 1291, West Warwick, RI Grayco Publishing, 1989.

Federal Grants and Contracts Weekly, ($349 per year), Capitol Publications, Inc., 1101 King Street, PO Box 1453, Alexandria, VA 22313.

Federal Register, (weekdays, $350 per year), (federal funding), Superintendent of Documents, New Orders, PO Box 371954, Pittsburgh, PA 15250.

J. Fergus, Associates Must Weigh Future Goals (in studying facts prior to reaching a board decision), *12 Natl. L.J.* (38) 22 (May 28, 1990).

Feuer and Johnston. *Personal Liabilities of Corporate Officers and Directors.* 2nd ed. Englewood Cliffs, N.J.: Prentice-Hall, 1974.

Financial Accounting Standards Board. *Deferral of the Effective Date of Recognition of Depreciation by Not-for-Profit Organization: An Amendment of FASB Statement No. 93*—Norwalk, Conn.: The Board, 1988.

Firstenberg, P.B. *Managing for Profit in the N-P World.* New York: Foundation Center, 1986.

Fisch, Freed, and Schachter. *Charities and charitable foundations.* Pomona, N.Y.: Lond Publications, 1974.

Fisher, John. *How to Manage a Nonprofit Organization.* American ed. Toronto, Ont.: Management and Fund Raising Centre, Publishing Division, 1978. Also published under title: *Money Isn't Everything.*

Fitch Institutional Report. New York: Fitch Investors Service, 1979–[current]. Each issue also has a distinctive title, e.g., "Hospital and other nonprofit institutional ratings." Includes hospital, nursing, and retirement center bond ratings.

Flanagan, J., *Successful Fundraising*, (1991, $19.95), contemporary Books, 180 N. Michigan Ave., Chicago, IL 60601.

Flanagan, Joan. *The Successful Volunteer Organization: Getting Started and Getting Results in Nonprofit, Charitable, Grass Roots, and Community Groups.* Chicago: Contemporary Books, 1981.

Fletcher and Jones. *Cyclopedia of the Law of Private Corporations.* rev. and permanent ed. Chicago: Callaghan, 1931–[current]. Later volumes have title: *Fletcher cyclopedia of the Law of Private Corporations.* Kept current with pocket parts and replacement volumes.

Forrester, *Tips for Auditing Nonprofit Organizations.* 165 J. of Accountancy 56(8), May 1988.

Foundation Center, *The Literature of the NP Sector: A Bibliography with Abstracts* (Foundation Center, N.Y.C., 1989, $50).

Foundation Center Publications (Many). Catalog on request. Includes two libraries (New York, NY and Washington, DC) and two field offices (San Francisco, CA and Cleveland, OH), Publishes *The Foundation directory, N.Y. State Foundations, Foundation Grants,* (various), *The Nonprofit Entrepreneur, Philanthropy in Action, National Data Book of Foundations, Foundation Grants Index, Grant Guides* (various), *Foundation Fundamentals, The Foundation Center's User-Friendly Guide, The National Directory of Corporate Giving, Corporate Foundation Profiles* and others. The Foundation Center, 79 Fifth Avenue, New York, NY 10003, (800) 424-9836.

Foundation Center Source Book Profiles. New York: Foundation Center, 1982–[current]. Quarterly.

Foundation Directory, 1992 Edition, $150 soft cover, The Foundation Center, 79 Fifth Avenue, New York, NY 10003, (800) 424-9836.

The Foundation Grant's Index: A Cumulative Listing of Foundation Grants. 13th ed. New York: Foundation Center, 1984.

Foundation News, (bimonthly magazine), ($29.50 per year), Council on Foundations, 1828 L Street, NW, Washington, DC 20036.

The Foundation Reporter, 1992, Comprehensive Profiles and Giving Analysis of American's Major Private Foundations, ($327), The Taft Group, 835 Penobscot Building, Detroit, MI 48226, (800) 877-8238.

The 1992 Foundation Salary Update, Publications Department, Council on Foundations, 1928 L Street, NW, Washington, DC 20036 (202-466-6512).

Fox and Rudnick. *Private Foundations—Excess Business Holdings.* Washington, D.C.: Tax Management, 1978–[current]. (Tax management portfolio)

Fram, E.H., and Pearse, R.F., *The High Performance Nonprofit,* (management) Family Service America, 11700 West Lake Park Drive, Milwaukee, WI 53224 (414-359-1040).

Fryer and Haglund. "New California Nonprofit Corporation Law: A Unique Approach." In *Pepperdine Law Review,* vol. 7, 1979, pgs. 1–40.

Fund Raising Management, (monthly magazine), ($50 per year), Hoke Communications Inc., 224 Seventh Street, Garden City, NY 11530.

*Future of the Nonprofit Sector, The/*eds. Virginia A. Hodgkinson, Richard W. Lyman—San Francisco: Jossey-Bass, 1989.

Gaby and Gaby. *Nonprofit Organization Handbook: A Guide to Fund Raising, Grants, Lobbying, Membership Building, Publicity, and Public Relations.* Englewood Cliffs, N.J.: Prentice-Hall, 1979.

Gaedeke, Ralph M. *Marketing in Private and Public Nonprofit Organizations: Perspectives and Illustrations.* Santa Monica, Calif.: Goodyear Pub. Co., 1977.

Gaffney, Edward McGlynn, *Ascending Liability in Nonprofit Organizations,* Macon, GA: Mercer. 1984.

Gaffney and Sorensen. *Ascending Liability in Religious and Other Nonprofit Organizations.* Macon, Ga.: Center for Constitutional Studies and Mercer University Press, 1984.

Galaskiewicz, Joseph. *Social Organization of an Urban Grants Economy: A Study of Business Philanthropy and Nonprofit Organizations.* Orlando, Fla.: Academic Press, 1985.

Galloway, Joseph M. *The Unrelated Business Income Tax.* New York: Wiley, 1982.

Gassler, Robert Scott. *The Economics of Nonprofit Enterprise: A Study in Applied Economic Theory.* Lanham, Md.: University Press of America, 1986.

Gelatt, James P., *Managing Nonprofit Organizations in the 21st Century,* Oryx Press, 4041 N. Central, Phoenix AZ 85012-3397. 208 pages, paper, $29.96.

Getting Funded: A Complete Guide to Proposal Writing, (1988, $19.95), Continuing Education Publications, PO Box 1394, Portland, OR 97207.

Getting Organized—Mt. Kisco, N.Y.: M. Bell, 1989. (FPS) (discussed especially taxation and nonprofits in the U.S. and New York).

Gift Givers Guide (Fla. Dept. of Agric. and Consumer Services, Dec. 1993) lists 1954 charities registered, showing amounts spent on overhead, on programs, etc.

1992–1993 Grant Guide, The Foundation Center, 79 Fifth Ave., New York, NY 10003-3076 (800-424-9836) $60 prepaid.

Grantsmanship Center. *Whole Nonprofit Catalog.* Biennial. Los Angeles 90014.

Green, *Corporate Philanthropy and the Business Benefit,* 20 Golden Gate U.L. Rev. 239 (1990).

Greer, Thomas L. *Exempt Organizations: Exemption Requirements.* Washington, D.C.: Tax Management, 1984. (Tax management portfolio)

Greer, Thomas L. *Private Foundations—Definition and Classification.* Washington, D.C.: Tax Management, 1982. (Tax management portfolio)

Giving USA. New York: American Association of Fund-Raising Counsel, 1956–[current]. A compilation of facts and trends on American philanthropy.

Godfrey, Howard. *Handbook on Tax-Exempt Organizations.* Englewood Cliffs, N.J.: Prentice-Hall, 1983.

Gray, David Ross. *Nonprivate Foundations: A Tax Guide for Charitable Organizations.* Colorado Springs, Colo.: Shepard's, Inc., of Colorado Springs, 1978.

Gross, W. & L. *Financial & Accounting Guide for N.P.O.s* (4th ed., 1991). Accounting procedures.

Groves and Osteen. *Charitable Contributions by Corporations.* Washington, D.C.: Tax Management, Inc., 1983 (Tax management portfolio)

Guide to Government Resources for Economic Development. Washington, D.C.: Northeast-Midwest Institute, 1983–[current]. A handbook for nonprofit agencies and municipalities.

Haller, Leon. *Financial Resource Management for Nonprofit Organizations.* Englewood Cliffs, N.J.: Prentice-Hall, 1982.

Hamlin, Petkun, and Bednarz. *Charitable Income Trusts.* Washington, D.C.: Tax Management, Inc., 1982. (Tax management portfolio)

Hansmann, *Condominium and Cooperative Housing*, 20 J. Legal Stud. 25–71 (1991).

Hansmann, Henry. *Nonprofit Enterprise in the Performing Arts.* New Haven, Conn.: Institution for Social and Policy Studies, Yale University, 1980.

Hansmann, Henry. "Reforming Non-profit Corporation Law." In *University of Pennsylvania Law Review.* v. 129, pg. 497 +.

Hansmann, Henry. *The Role of Non-profit Enterprise.* New Haven, Conn.: Institution for Social and Policy Studies, Yale University, [1980?]. Reprinted from: *Yale Law Journal.* v. 89, no. 5, April 1980.

Hardy, James M. *Corporate Planning for Nonprofit Organizations.* New York: Association Press, 1972.

Harmon & Weiss. *Tax Monthly for Exempt Organizations.* Wash., D.C. (newsletter). 1988
_____.

Harris, Holley & McCaffrey, *Fundraising into the 1990s: State Regulation of Charitable Solicitation After Riley*, N.Y.U. Program on Philanthropy and the Law, paper re-done in 24 U. of San Fran. L. Rev. 571–652 (1990).

Harris, Susan R. "The Dangers of Incorporating Nonprofit Corporations." In *Colorado Lawyer*, v. 13, May 1984, pgs. 765–771. Incorporating procedures, especially drafting of articles and bylaws.

Hartwell and Bromberg, *Private Foundations—Special Rules (Sec. 508).* Washington, D.C.: Tax Management, 1981. (Tax management portfolio)

Hartwell, Sugarman, and Bromberg. *Private Foundations—Termination.* Washington, D.C.: Tax Management, 1979 (Tax management portfolio)

Hauser, *Social Fraternities at Public Institutions of Higher Education*, 19 J.L. & Educ. 433–466 (1990).

Hay, Leon Edwards, *Essentials of Accounting for Government and Not-for-Profit Organizations*—Homewood, Ill.: Irwin, 1987.

Health Care Industry (Taxes; Nonprofit Corporations). Chicago, IL, Commerce Clearing House, 1988.

Henke, Emerson O. *Accounting for Nonprofit Organizations.* 4th ed. Boston, Mass.: Kent Pub. Co., 1986.

Henke, Emerson O. *Introduction to Nonprofit Organization Accounting.* Belmont, Calif.: Wadsworth Pub. Co., 1980.

Henn and Boyd, "Statutory Trends in the Law of Nonprofit Organizations: California Here We Come~!" In *Cornell Law Review*, v. 66, 1981, pg. 1103 +.

Hennessey, Paul. *Managing Nonprofit Agencies for Results: A Systems Approach to Long-range Planning.* San Francisco: Public Management Institute, 1978.

Holeman, Jack R. *Condominium Management.* Englewood Cliffs, N.J.: Prentice-Hall, 1980.

Hone, Michael C., ed. *Advising California Nonprofit Corporations.* 3rd ed. Berkeley, Calif.: California Continuing Education of the Bar, 1984.

Hopkins, Bruce R. *Charitable Giving and Tax-exempt Organizations: The Impact of the 1981 Tax Act.* New York: Wiley, 1982.

Hopkins, *Charity, Advocacy and the Law,* Wiley, Colorado Savings, CO, 1992; $85.

Hopkins, *Law of Fund-Raising* (Wiley, Colorado Springs, CO 1990) $95, plus annual suppl.

Hopkins, Bruce R. (ed.). *The Law of Tax-Exempt Organizations.* 4th ed. New York: Wiley, 1983.

Hopkins, Bruce R. (ed.). *Nonprofit Counsel* (monthly newsletter). New York. John Wiley & Sons, 1988 _____.

Hopkins, Bruce R., *Starting and Managing a Nonprofit Organization: A Legal Guide,* New York: Wiley, 1989.

Horowitz, Harvey. *Non-profit Cultural Organizations.* New York: Practising Law Institute, 1979.

Hospital Liability: Law and Practice, PLI; New York, 5th ed., 1987.

C.O. Houle, *Governing Boards: Their Nature and Nurture* (Natl. Center for NP Boards; Wash., D.C., 1989; $19.95).

Howe, *Board Member's Guide to Fund Raising* (1991, Jossey-Bass).

How to Apply for and Retain Status for Your Organization. rev. February 1980 ed. Washington, D.C.: Treasury Department, Internal Revenue Service, U.S. Government Printing Office, 1980–[current].

How to Form a Nonprofit Corporation, Berkeley, CA: Nolo Press, 1990.

Hummel, Joan M. *Starting and Running a Nonprofit Organization.* Minneapolis, Minn.: University of Minnesota Press, 1980.

Hunter, Richard J. *Not for Profit Business: Reading, Legal Documents and Commentary.* South Bend, Ind.: Icarus, 1980.

Huntsinger, J., *Making Direct Response Fund Raising Pay Off,* Bonus Books, 160 East Illinois St., Chicago, IL 60611; 225 pages, ($49.95).

Hutton and Schwarz. *Exempt Organizations: Tax Strategies and Legal Problems.* New York: Practising Law Institute, 1982.

Hyatt, W.S., *Condominium and Houseowner Association Practice: Community Association Law.* Philadelphia, PA, ALI-ABA, 2nd ed., 1988.

Inc., (monthly magazine), (financing), Inc. Magazine, P.O. Box 54129, Boulder, CO 80322.

An Independent Sector Resource of Education and Training Opportunities and Other Services. Washington, D.C.: Independent Sector, 1985–[current].

Independent Sector and the Tax Laws, 64 S. Cal. L. Rev. 461–509 (1991).

Insurance Basics for Nonprofits, booklet, Nonprofits' Mutual Risk Retention Group 1-800-533-3097 or the Granite State Association of Nonprofits, 125 Airport Road, Concord, NH 03301; telephone 603-225-4346.

I.R.S. Cumulative List of Organizations: lists 501(c)(3) [tax exempt] organizations (about

400,000 in January 1994); less than the actual number. It was 2060 pages long in Jan. 1994.

Jackson, James K. *Charitable Contributions—Percentage Limitations.* Washington, D.C.: Tax Management, Inc., 1981. (Tax management portfolio)

Japanese Corporate Connection: A Guide for Fundraisers, ($90), The Taft Group, 1-800-877-8238.

John B. Stetson University, College of Law. *Nonprofit Corporations in Florida.* Tallahassee, Fla.: Florida Bar, Continuing Legal Education, 1981. Based on a seminar conducted at Stetson University college of Law, August–December 1979, conducted by Howard Oleck.

Johnson, James Leonard. *Profits, Power and Piety.* Irvine, Calif.: Harvest House, 1980. Previously published as *The Nine to Five Complex.* Zondervan, 1972.

Johnston, Joseph F. *Protecting the Corporate Officer and Director from Liability* (a series). New York: Practising Law Institute, 1947–1979.

Josling and Alexander. *The Law of Clubs: With a Note on Unincorporated Associations.* 4th ed. London: Oyez, 1981.

Keating and Keating. *Not-for-Profit.* Glen Ridge, N.J.: T. Horton, 1980.

Kibbe, B., and Setterberg, F., *Succeeding with Consultants: Self Assessment for the Changing Nonprofit,* Foundation Center, 79 fifth Ave., New York, NY 10003-3076. ($19.95, plus $4.50 shipping).

Kielbowicz and Lawson, *Reduced-Rate Postage for Nonprofit Organizations . . .* 11 Harv. J. of Law & Publ. Policy, 347–406, Spring, 1988.

Kirgis, Frederick L. *International Organizations in Their Legal Setting: Documents, Comments, and Questions.* St. Paul, Minn.: West Pub. Co., 1977.

Knittle, Fred D. *How to Obtain Foundation Grants.* Los Angeles: R.L. Houts Associates, 1972.

Kotler, Ferrell, and Lamb. *Cases and Readings for Marketing for Nonprofit Organizations.* Englewood Cliffs, N.J.: Prentice-Hall, 1983.

Kotler, Philip. *Marketing for Nonprofit Organizations.* 2nd ed. Englewood Cliffs, N.J.: Prentice-Hall, 1982.

Kurtz and Green, *Liabilities and Duties of Nonprofit Directors and Officers.* 16 N.Y.U. Conf. on Tax Planning for Charity. Section II-1 (17), Ann. 1988.

Landy, L., *Something Ventured, Something Gained: A Business Development Guide for NPOs.* In vinyl binder. Trenton, NJ 08608, Center for Nonprofit Corporations, 1987, $19.95.

Lane, Marc J. *Legal Handbook for Nonprofit Organizations.* New York: AMACOM, 1980.

Lashbrooke, E.C. *Tax-Exempt Organizations.* Westport, Conn.: Quorum Books, 1985.

Lee, James C. *Do or Die: Survival for Nonprofits.* Washington, D.C.: Taft Products, 1974.

Lewis, William, *Profitable Careers in Nonprofit—*New York: Wiley, 1987.

Literature of the Nonprofit Sector: A Bibliography with Abstracts, The / Foundation Center staff and Margaret Derrickson—[Foundation Center], 1989.

Lobbying and Political Activity for Nonprofits: What You Can (and Can't) Do Under Federal Law. Washington, D.C.: Children's Defense Fund, 1983.

Lobbying by Non-Profit Organizations: A Summary of Regulations. Minneapolis, Minn.: National Federation of State Humanities councils, rev. 1985.

Long, David F. *How to Organize and Raise Funds for Small Nonprofit Organizations.* South Plainfield, N.J.: Groupwork Today, 1979.

R. Lord, *Nonprofit Problem Solver: A Management Guide,* Praeger Press; Westport, CT, 1989; $35.95; 159 pp.

Lovelock & Weinberg, *Public and Nonprofit Marketing* (Scientific Press, Redwood City, CA, 94063; $37.50; 2d ed., 1989).

LRC Newsbrief, (monthly), (Lutheran, Presbyterian, Methodist), LRC, 5 Thomas Circle, NW, Washington, DC 20005.

Lunin, Joseph, *New Jersey Nonprofit Corporation Act Forms.* Newark, NJ: New Jersey Institute for Continuing Legal Education, 1983.

Lynn and Thompson. *Introduction to Fund Accounting.* Reston, VA.: Reston Pub. Co., 1974.

Mackie, Sam A., *How to Form a Nonprofit Corporation in Florida*—Clearwater, FL: Sphinx Pub. FL, 1988.

Maddalena, Lucille A. *A Communications Manual for Nonprofit Organizations.* New York: AMACOM, 1981.

R. Magat (ed.), *Philanthropic giving: Studies in Varieties and Goals* (Oxford U. Press; N.Y., N.Y., $49.95; 1990).

Management Circulars: A-21, A-87, A-88, A-102, A-110, A-122, and A-128, Rules that all agencies should follow in administering federal grants, (Free), Publications Office, Executive Office of the President, Room 2200, Washington, DC 20503.

Mancuso and Warner. *The California Non-profit Corporation Handbook.* 2nd ed. Berkeley Calif.: Nolo Press, 1980.

Mann and McCoy. *Management Remuneration: SEC and Tax Aspects of Corporate Prerequisites.* New York: Practising Law Institute, 1978.

Marketing Workbook for Nonprofit Organizations and Strategic Planning for Nonprofit Organizations, Amherst H. Wilder Foundation, 919 Lafond Ave., St. Paul, MN 55104, ($25.00 plus shipping and handling).

McAdam, T.W., *Doing Well by Doing Good* (guide to careers in NPOs). New York, Penguin Books, 1986.

McConkey, Dale. D. *MBO for Nonprofit Organizations.* New York: AMACOM, 1975.

McGovern, A., and S., *The Revised Lobbying Regulations—A Difficult Balance.* 41 Tax Notes 1425, Dec. 26, 1988.

McKee, *The Amended Open Meetings Law: New Requirements for Publicly Funded Corporations. . . ,* 25 Ga. State Bar J. 78(6), Nov. 1988.

McLaughlin, Curtis P. *The Management of Nonprofit Organizations.* New York: Wiley, 1986. Wiley series in management.

Metzger, Vaccaro, and Richards. *Successful Meetings.* 1st ed. San Francisco, Calif.: Public Management Institute, 1980.

Meyer, Mary Keysor. *Meyer's Directory of Genealogical Societies in the U.S.A. and Canada.* Pasadena, Md.: M.K. Meyer, 1982–[current].

Miller, Joel E. *Cooperative and Condominium Apartments.* Washington, D.C.: Tax Management, Inc., 1984. (Tax management portfolio)

Model Non-profit corporation Act. rev., exposure draft. Philadelphia, Pa.: Joint committee on Continuing Legal Education of the American Law Institute and the American Bar Association, 1986. American Bar Association, Committee on Corporate Laws.

Montana, Patrick J. *Marketing in Nonprofit Organizations.* New York: AMACOM, 1978.

Monthly Portfolio. Ambler, Pa.: Fund-Raising Institute, 1983–[current]. Monthly. Also called FRI monthly portfolio, FRI newsletter.

Moody, L., *Who, What, and How of Revised Model N.P.C. Act.* 16 No. Ky. L. Rev. 251, 1989.

Moore, Harry E. *Financing the Nonprofit Organization for Recreation and Leisure Services.* South Plainfield, N.J.: Groupwork Today, 1981.

Nagel, *The Use of For-Profit Subsidiaries by Nonprofit Corporations.* 17 Colo. Lawyer 1293 (4), July 1988.

National Center for Nonprofit Boards, many publications for nonprofit boards, for catalog, National Center for Nonprofit boards, Suite 411, 2000 L Street, NW, Washington, DC 20077-6333, 202/452-6262.

National Date Book. 5th ed. New York: foundation Center, 1981–[current].

National Trade and Professional Associations of the United States. Washington, D.C.: Columbia Books, 1985.

New York Not-for-Profit Corporations. New York: Practising Law Institute, 1970.

Nicholas, Ted. *How to Form Your Own Non-profit corporation Without a Lawyer for Under $75.* Wilmington, Del.: Enterprise, 1980.

Nicholas, Ted. *Non-profit Tax-Exempt Corporations: The Alternative Tax Shelter: All You Need to Know About SEtting Up and Maintaining a Non-profit corporation without a Lawyer.* 3rd ed. (rev.) Wilmington, Del.: Enterprise Pub., 1983.

Nichols, J., *Targeted Fund Raising: Defining and Refining Your Development Strategy,* Precept Press, 160 East Illinois St., Chicago, IL 60611, 210 pages ($39.95).

Nicholson, Miklos S. *Duties and Liabilities of Corporate Officers and Directors.* Englewood Cliffs, N.J.: Prentice-Hall, 1972.

Nielsen, Waldemar A. *The Endangered Sector.* New York: Columbia University Press, 1979.

Nonprofit Almanac 1992–1993: *Dimensions of the Independent Sector.* For copies address: Independent Sector, 1828 L St., N.W., Suite 1200, Washington, D.C. 20036 ($49.95 + $3.50 shipping and handling prepaid).

Nonprofit Corporations in Florida. Tallahassee, Fla.: The Florida Bar, Continuing Legal Education, 1981. Based on a seminar conducted at John B. Stetson University College of Law August–December 1979, conducted by Howard Oleck.

The Nonprofit Counsel, (monthly, $96 per year), John Wiley and sons, Inc., 605 Third Avenue, New York, NY 10158.

Nonprofit Management & Leadership (quarterly journal) management studies by academics. Jossey-Bass, Inc., San Francisco, CA 94104. $45/yr. for individuals, began 1991.

The Nonprofit Management Handbook: Operating Policies and Procedures, John Wiley & Sons, $95, 800-CALL-WILEY.

Non-profit Organizations: Current Issues and Developments. New York: Practising Law Institute, 1984, 1986.

Nonprofit Organizations: Forms of Creation, Operation and Dissolution/Clifford, Marcia L., et al.—Wilmette, IL: Callaghan, 1987.

Nonprofit Organizations Seminar, 1983 at Stetson College of Law. St. Petersburg, Fla.: Pinellas County Review, 1983. Seminar conducted by Howard Oleck.

Nonprofit Organizations. Symposium. 21 U. of San Francisco L. Rev. 585 (1987).

The Nonprofit Sector Series, includes *Governing, Leading, and Managing Nonprofit Organizations, Designing and Conducting Survey Research, The Nonprofit Sector in the Global Community, Government and The Third Sector* and *Strategic Planning for Fund Raising,* Jossey Bass publishers at 415-433-1767 or fax 415-433-0499.

Nonprofit Sector: A Research Handbook, The—New Haven, Conn.: Yale University Press, 1987.

NonProfit Tax Letter, Prentice Hall, Englewood Cliffs, N.J. 07632-9940, biweekly; $9.95/mo. plus shipping.

The NonProfit Times, (monthly), (Free or $39 per year), The NonProfit Times, 190 Tamarack circle, Skillman, NJ 08558.

B. O'Connell, *Volunteers in Action*; Foundation Center, N.Y.C. (1990). $19.95 + $2.00 shipping.

Not-for-Profit Organizations: The Challenge of governance in an Era of Retrenchment, April 9–10, 1992 Santa Monica, CA: ALI-ABA course of study materials, 4025 Chestnut St., Philadelphia, PA 19104, 1992.

Notre Dame Studies in the Management of Not-for-Profit Institutions. Notre Dame, Ind.: University of Notre Dame Press, No. 1, 1978-

O'Connell, B. *Philanthropy in Action.* Wash., D.C., Independent Sector. 1987.

Odendahl, *Charity Begins at Home: Generosity and Self-Interest Among the Philanthropic Elite* (1990).

Oleck, Howard L. *ALI-ABA Course of Study: Officers' Powers and Duties in Nonprofit Organizations: Study Materials.* Philadelphia, PA.: American Law Institute-American Bar Association Committee on Continuing Professional Education, 1975.

Oleck, Howard L. *ALI-ABA Course of Study–Legal Problems in the Management of Non-profit Corporations, November 8 and 9, 1974: Study Materials.* Philadelphia, PA.: American Law Institute-American Bar Association Committee on Continuing Professional Education, 1974.

H. Oleck, *The Church and the Law* (monograph, 39 pp.), for Stetson Univ. Conference (May 1990), c/o Continuing Educ. Dept. DeLand, FL.

Oleck, Howard L. *Management's Liabilities in Nonprofit Organizations.* St. Petersburg, Fla.: Stetson University, College of Law, 1979. Course materials for a seminar held at the Bayside-Concourse Hotel, St. Petersburg, Fla., Friday–Saturday, March 30–31, 1979.

Oleck, H., *Mixtures of Profit and Nonprofit Corporate Purposes and Operations.* 16 No. Ky. L. Rev. 225–250, 1989.

Oleck, Howard L. *Modern Corporation Law.* Indianapolis: Bobbs-Merrill, 1958–1960, with 1978 cumulative supplement. See Index Volume, vol. 6, for various aspects.

Oleck, H., *Nonprofit Corporations, Organizations and Associations.* (6th ed., 1994) [This treatise, with annual supplements]. Englewood Cliffs, NJ, Prentice Hall, 1994.

Oleck, H., *Nonprofit Corporations, Organizations and Associations.* (5th ed., 1988) (and annual supplements). Englewood Cliffs, NJ: Prentice Hall, 1988.

Oleck, Howard L. *Nonprofit Organizations' Problems—1980.* St. Petersburg, Fla.: John B. Stetson University, College of Law, 1980.

Oleck, Howard L. *Nonprofit Corporations, Organizations, and Associations.* 4th ed. Englewood Cliffs, N.J.: Prentice-Hall, 1980.

Oleck, Howard L. *Parliamentary Law for Nonprofit Organizations.* Philadelphia, PA.: American Law Institute-American Bar Association Committee on Continuing Professional Education, 1979. Based on work presented at a seminar held in 1977 at Wake Forest University.

Oleck H. and Green, C., *Parliamentary Law & Practice for Nonprofit Organizations*, 2nd ed., Philadelphia, PA: American Law Inst.-Amer. Bar Assn. Comm. on Continuing Professional Education, 1991.

Oleck, Howard L. *Religious Nonprofit Organizations' Legal Problems 1981: Course Materials for Registrants at Seminar, March 13–14, 1981.* St. Petersburg, Fla.: Stetson University, College of Law, 1981.

Oleck, Howard L. *Religious Nonprofit Organizations' Legal problems in 1982.* St. Petersburg, Fla.: Stetson University, College of Law, 1982.

Oleck, Howard, and Clark, Millard W. *Trends in Nonprofit Organizations Law: A Wake Forest University Law Seminar.* Philadelphia PA.: American Law Institute-American Bar Association Committee on Continuing Professional Education. 1977. Held at the University's School of Law, 1976. "1979 Supplement" by Millard W. Clark, Jr. covers revisions provided by Tax Reform Act of 1976 and the Revenue Act of 1978.

M. O'Neill, *The Third America: The Emergence of the Nonprofit Sector in the U.S.*; Jossey-Bass, Inc., San Francisco, CA (1990). $22.95.

Orlans and Derthick. *Nonprofit Organizations: A Government Management tool.* New York: Praeger, 1980. Papers from a conference sponsored by the National Academy of Public Administration.

Orlikoff, J.E., *Malpractice Prevention and Liability Control for Hospitals.* Chicago, IL, American Hospital Publishers, 2nd ed., 1988.

O'Rourke, H., *Standards for Charitable Solicitations*, (Free), Philanthropic Advisory Service, Council of Better Business Bureaus, Inc., 4200 Wilson Blvd, Suite 800, Arlington, VA 22203, (703) 276-0100.

Ott, J. Steven, *The Facts on File Dictionary of Nonprofit Organization Management*—New York, N.Y.: Facts on File, 1986.

Packel, Israel. *Law of the Organization and Operation of Cooperatives: The Organization and Operation of Cooperatives; Including Consumer, Marketing, Purchasing and Trade Associations, Labor Unions and Condominiums.* 4th ed. Philadelphia, PA.: Joint Committee on Continuing Legal Education of the American Law Institute and the American Bar association, 1970.

J. Panas, *Official Fundraising Almanac* (Pluribus Press, Chicago: $39.95; 400 pp.; 1990).

Personnel Matters in the Nonprofit Organization by Earl W. Antes and Jerry Cronin—Englewood Cliffs, N.J.: Prentice-Hall, 1987.

Petkun, Hamlin, and Downing. *Charitable Remainder Trusts and Pooled Income Funds.* Washington, D.C.: Tax Management, Inc., 1982 (Tax management portfolio)

Phelan, Marilyn E. *Nonprofit Enterprises: Law and Taxation.* Wilmette, Ill., 1985.

Phelan, Marilyn E., *Nonprofit Enterprises: Law and Taxation*, Callaghan, Wilmette, IL, 1985.

Phelan, Marilyn E., *Representing the Nonprofit Organization*—Wilmette, IL: Callaghan, 1987.

PLAN letter—Planning for Legislation and Administration for Non-profits. Garden City, N.Y.: Hoke Communications Inc., (196?)–[current].

Powell, Walter W., ed. *The Nonprofit Sector: A Research Handbook.* New Haven, Conn.: Yale University Press, 1987. Projected publication: April 1987.

Prentice Hall *NonProfit Tax Letter.* Bi-weekly. Prentice Hall, Englewood Cliffs, NJ, since 1991; $9.95/mo., plus shipping.

Program Planning & Proposal Writing, ($3 for introductory version). Grantsmanship Center Publications, PO Box 17220, Los Angeles, CA 9017.

Pugh, Joanne. *Managing Staff for Results.* San Francisco, Calif.: Public Management Institute, 1980.

Pugh, Joanne. *Nonprofit Management Skills for Women Managers.* 1st ed. San Francisco, Calif.: Public Management Institute, 1980.

Rados, David L. *Marketing for Non-Profit Organizations.* Boston: Auburn House Pub. Co., 1981.

Ramanathan and Hegstad. *Readings in Management Control in Nonprofit Organizations.* New York: Wiley, 1982.

Ramanathan, Kavasseri V. *Management Control in Nonprofit Organizations: Text and Cases.* New York: Wiley, 1982.

Reiss, A. H., *Arts Management: A Guide to Finding Funds and Winning Audiences*, (sourcebook for art administrators), Taft, 800-877-TAFT.

Research Grant Guides (Co.), publishes various directories of "Handicapped Funding," "Building & Equipment," "computer Grants," etc. P.O. Box 1214, Loxahatchee, FL 33470.

Retirement and Deferred Compensation Plans for Employees of Tax Exempt and Governmental Employers: ALI-ABA of Study Materials—Philadelphia, PA: American Law Institute-American Bar Association Committee on Continuing Professional Education, 1988.

Retirement Plans for employees of Tax Exempt Organizations and Governments: ALI-ABA Course of Study Materials—Philadelphia, PA: American Law Institute-American Bar Association Committee on Continuing Professional Education, 1987.

1986 Revised Model Nonprofit Corporation Act: exposure draft/Committee on Nonprofit Corporations, Section of Corporation, Banking and Business Law, American Bar Association, Chicago IL 1986.

Revised Model Nonprofit Corporation Act: Official Text with Official Comments and Statutory Cross-References—Clifton, N.J.: Prentice-Hall, *Law & Business*, 1988.

Robertson, D. B. (ed.), *Voluntary Associations*, John Knox Press, Richmond, VA, 1966.

Robinson, Skip. *Charitable Employee Benefit Design*. San Francisco, CA: San Francisco Study Center, 1985.

Rose-Ackerman, Susan, ed. *The Nonprofit Sector: Economic Theory and Public Policy*. New York: Oxford University Press, 1986.

Rose-Ackerman, S., (ed.), *Economics of Nonprofit Institutions*. New York, Oxford Univ. Press, 1988.

Rules on Corporate Charity Modified. 166 J. of Accountancy 15 (1), Dec. 1988.

Salem, Mahmoud. *Organizational Survival in the Performing Arts: The Making of the Seattle Opera*. New York: Praeger Publishers, 1976.

Sanders, Michael I. *Private Foundations—Taxable Expenditures (Sec. 4945)*. Washington, D.C.: Tax Management, 1984 (Tax management portfolio)

Schindler-Rainman and Lippitt. *The Volunteer Community: Creative Use of Human Resources*. 2nd ed. La Jolla, Calif.: University Associates, 1977.

The 1992 Survey of Nonprofit Organizations' Compensation & Benefits, New York City, Ernst & Young, 787 Seventh Avenue, New York, NY 10019 (212-773-5202).

Scialabba, K. and S., *Mail-Order Ministries Under the Section 170 Charitable Contribution Deduction*: . . . , 11 Campbell L. Rev. (1) 1 1988.

Scott, Austin Wakeman. *The Law of Trusts*. 4th ed. Boston: Little, Brown, 1987.

Shafritz and Ott. *The Facts on File Dictionary of Nonprofit Organization Management*. New York: Facts on File, 1986.

Simpson, Steven D. *Exempt Organizations: Public Charities*. Washington, D.C.: Tax Management, 1984. (Tax management portfolio)

Singer, Barbara, *Nonprofit Organizations: Operations Handbook for Directors and Administrators*—Wilmette, IL: Callaghan, 1987.

Skloot, E., *The Nonprofit Entrepreneur: Creating Ventures to Earn Income*. New York, Foundation Center, 1988.

Smith, G. Stevenson. *Accounting for Librarians and Other Not-for-Profit Managers*. Chicago: American Library Association, 1983.

Statham and Buek. *Associations and the Tax Laws*. Washington, D.C.: Chamber of Commerce of the U.S., 1978.

Statistical Abstract of the United States. Washington, D.C.: U.S. Dept. of Commerce, Bureau of the Census, current.

Steinberg, *Religious Exemptions as Affirmative Action*, 40 Emory L. J. 77–139 (1991).

Symposium: Nonprofit Organizations. 16 No. Ky. L. Rev. (2) 225–408, 1989.

Symposium: Nonprofit Organizations. 24 U. San Fran L. Rev., 571 (1990).

Taft Directory of Nonprofit Organizations: Profiles of America's Major Charitable Institutions. Washington, DC 20016, Taft Group, Public Service Materials Center, New, 1989, 535 pp., $97.

Tax-Exempt Organizations. Englewood Cliffs, N.J.: Prentice-Hall, 1981–[current]. Loose-leaf service.

Tax Monthly for Associations. Washington, D.C.: Martineau Corp., (1977?)–[current].

Tax shelters: analyses. Chicago: Commerce Clearing House, 1976. (Or see most recent edition.)

Taxwise Giving, (monthly, $155 per year), Taxwise Giving, 13 Arcadia Road, Old Greenwich, CT 06870.

Topinka, et al. *A Guide to the California Nonprofit Public Benefit Corporation Law.* 1st ed. San Francisco, Calif.: The Management Center, 1981.

Tremper, Charles R., *Reconsidering Legal Liability and Insurance for Nonprofit Organizations*—Lincoln, NE: Law College Education Services, Inc., 1989.

Treusch, P.E., *Tax-Exempt Charitable Organizations.* Philadelphia, PA, ALI-ABA, 3rd ed., 1988.

Treusch and Sugarman. *Tax-Exempt Charitable Organizations.* 2nd ed. Philadelphia: American Law Institute-American Bar Association Committee on Continuing Professional Education, 1983.

Troyer, S., & M., *Final Lobbying Regulations Provide Workable Guidances,* 74 J. Taxation 124 (1991).

United States Government Manual, ($23), Superintendent of Documents, U.S. Government Printing Office, Washington, DC 20402.

Unterman, Israel. *Strategic Management of Not-for-Profit Organizations: From Survival to Success.* New York: Praeger, 1984.

The USA Salary & Benefits Report, Association for Healthcare Philanthropy Foundation, 313 Park Avenue, Suite 400, Falls Church, VA 22046 (703-532-6243).

Vargo and Dierks. *Readings and Cases in Governmental and Nonprofit Accounting.* Houston, Tex.: Dame Publications, 1982.

Verrucoli, P. *Non-Profit Organizations (A Comparative Approach).* Milan, Italy: Giuffre, 1985.

Volunteer Action Leadership. Quarterly. Arlington, Va. Volunteer-Natl. Center. 1987–8.

The 1992 Wage and Benefit Survey for Northern California Nonprofit Organizations, Management Center, 944 Market Street, Suite 700, San Francisco, CA 94102 (416-362-9735).

Walton and Egan, *Not-for-Profit Reorganizations Under the New Illinois Law.* 77 Ill. Bar J. 14 (9), Sept. 1988.

Warwick, M., *You Don't Always Get What You Ask For: Using Direct Mail Test to Raise More Money for Your Organization,* Strathmoor Press, 2550 Ninth St., Suite 1040 Berkeley, CA 94710 ($19.95 plus $2.50 shipping).

Webster, George D. *The Law of Associations: An Operating Manual for Executives and Counsel.* New York: M. Bender, 1975.

Webster, George D. *Trade and Professional Assns.–Taxation.* Wash., D.C., Tax Management, 1986.

Weisbrod, Burton Allen. *The Voluntary Nonprofit Sector: An Economic Analysis.* Lexington, Mass.: Lexington Books, 1977.

Weithorn, Stanley S. *The New York Not-for-Profit corporation: Its Creation, Maintenance, and Termination.* New York: Practising Law Institute, 1975.

Weithorn, Stanley S. *Tax Planning for the Charitable Sector.* New York: New York Law Journal, 1980.

Weithorn, Stanley S. *Tax Techniques for Foundations and Other Exempt Organizations.* New York: M. Bender, 1964–[current].

Wellford, W. H., and Gallagher, J. G., *Unfair Competition: The Challenge to Tax Exemption.* Washington, DC 20004, National Assembly; 273 pp., 1988, $23.45.

Whole Nonprofit Catalog: Sources and Resources for Managers and Staff of NPOs, Los Angeles, CA Grantsmanship Center, 1988 issue.

Wilson, Jane L. *New Information Technologies for the Nonprofit Sector: Report of a Joint Conference of the Foundation Center and the Aspen Institute held at Wye Plantation, Queenstown, Maryland, November 16–17, 1981.* New York: The Foundation Center, Aspen Institute for Humanistic Studies, 1982.

Winslow, Peter M. *Exempt Organizations–Declaratory Judgments.* Washington, D.C.: Tax Management, Inc., 1985. (Tax management portfolio)

Wise Giving Guide, current issues, issued intermittently, by National Charities Information Bureau, Inc., 19 Union Sq. W., N.Y. City 10003-3395.
    To check on local or state charities call your county Charitable Solicitations Officer; or, in Florida call the C.S. Section of the Dept. of Agriculture and Consumer Services (800) 435-7352, for the 1994 *Gift Givers Guide.*

Witte, Tax Exemptions of Church Property, 64 S. Cal. L. Rev. 363–418 (1991).

Yearbook of American and Canadian Churches. Nashville, Tenn.: Abingdon Press, 1973–[current].

Yearbook of California Charitable Organizations (1989, directory of NPOs with revenues over $25,000 or assets over $250,000; data). Also, *Yearbook of N.Y. State Charitable Orgns.* both from Independent Sector, Washington, D.C. Series to be expanded.

Yale Studies on NPOs. New York: Oxford University Press, 1987. A series of books.

Zaltman, Gerald. *Management Principles for Nonprofit Agencies and Organizations.* New York: AMACOM, 1979.

POINTS TO REMEMBER

- Statistics on NPOs are fragmentary and incomplete in all states.
- Quote and use statistics with caution; always emphasize their incompleteness and uncertainty.
- ask your local and national association's office to help you; and be amazed by how much help you can get by just asking (and credit to the source should be given).
- Expect little help from public officials, and much "double talk," about their statistics.
- Use current statistical abstracts; the numbers change often.

- Expect little governmental supervision, except where governmental revenues are concerned.

- Tax exemption is not hard to obtain, in most cases, if the formalities are followed.

- Much published guidance material (books, articles, etc.) is now available for NPOs.

- Ask your (local) (or national) association's office to help you; and be amazed by how much help you can get by just *asking* (and creditting your source).

NOTES TO CHAPTER 2

1. McIlquham, (article) 6 *NonProfit Times* (8) 4 (August 1992).

2. Stanton article, 14 *Whole Nonprofit Catalog* p. 4 (Grantsmanship Center, Spring 1991). See, for example, Calif. Assn. of Nonprofits, P.O. Box 1478; Santa Cruz, CA 95601-1478; Phone # (408) 458-1955 (1900 NPOs). *National Council of Non-profit Ass'ns* also formed in 1989.

3. Mcilquham, (article), 6 *NonProfit Times* (8) 1 (August 1992).

4. In 1959–60 Professor Oleck was consultant to the Congressional (Patman) Committee study of foundations, in Washington, D.C. and in Cleveland (where tabulations were begun). The Mills Committee study in 1969 led to the Tax Reform Act of 1970, which began to check abuse of foundation tax-exemption privileges.

5. *Foundation Directory*, 1st ed. (Russell Sage Foundation, 1939), and p. 13 in 2nd ed. (1964).

6. *Foundation directory*, 3rd ed. (Russell Sage Foundation, 1967).

7. *New York Times*, 28 (January 6, 1969).

8. *New York Times Encyclopedic Almanac 1971*, at 298. but in 1975–76, in the stock market drop of that time, the Ford investment securities portfolio was said to have dwindled to $2.6 billion, at lest for a while, because of that depression.

9. *Id.*

10. *Id.*

11. *Id.*

12. 26 U.S.C. §4940 (1970).

13. *Foundation Directory*, 3rd ed. (Russell Sage Foundation, 1967).

14. Clines, "Abuses Alleged in Charity Funds," *New York Times*, p. 1 (January 18, 1969).

15. *Foundation Directory*, 6th ed. (Russell Sage Foundation, 1978). And see: Oleck, "Nonprofit Types, Uses, and Abuses 1970," 19 *Clev. St. L. Rev.* 207, 225 (1970); W. Weaver, *U.S. Foundations*, 14–16 (1967). But about 5,000 foundations control all but a fraction of the total of foundation assets. F. E. Heimann, *The future of Foundations*, 20 (1973).

16. C. Judkins, *National Associations of the United States* (1949).

17. Columbia Books, Inc., Washington, D.C. publishers.

18. Gale Research Co., *Encyclopedia of Associations* (curr. ed.)

19. Yale Studies on Nonprofit Organizations began publishing studies on specific types (e.g., the Arts, Private Education, Economics) in separate books in 1986 (Oxford Univ. Press, NY).

20. See, Gray, State Attorney General-Guardian of Public Charities???, 14 Clev. Mar. L. Rev. 236 (1965). See Oleck, *Trends in Nonprofit corporation Law in 1976* 10 Akron L. Rev. 71 (1976); Oleck (Chm.) *Trends in Nonprofit Organization Law* (1977); Amer. Law Inst.-Amer.

Bar Assn. Committee on Continuing Legal Education; with 1978–79 supp; Bush, B. H., (article) *7 NonProfit Times* (5) 14 (May 1993); Stepneski, R., (article) *7 NonProfit Times* (3) 1 (March 1993).

21. Friedman, *State Administration of Charities*, 19 Clev. St. L. Rev. 273 (1970).

22. Letter to Richard Manger, April 9, 1976, cited in Manger (contributed chapter 5) of Oleck (Chm.), *Trends in Nonprofit Organizations Law* (1977).

23. The writer adds, parenthetically, that too much government is bad but too little is worse.

24. *See* n. 22.

25. In 1960 only on assistant attorney general and one clerk supervised 1,130 registered trusts, with assets of over $250 million.

26. Manger, above, n. 22, at p. 53. Letter from Office of atty. gen. of Washington, State (April 9, 1976).

27. *Id.*

28. *Id.* Letter from Delaware Dept. of Justice (April 6, 1976).

29. *Id.* Letter from dept. of attorney general of Massachusetts (April 5, 1976); and above n. 26.

30. Letter to Carl Nelson (the survey conductor in the writers' Stetson University seminar in November 1978), and no answer in 1985 survey.

31. *New York Times*, p. 1 (July 21, 1978). It produced no cash. *New York Times*, p. 1 (August 4, 1978).

32. *New York Times*, p. A7 (May 29, 1978).

33. *Tax Monthly for Associations*, 5 (March 1979).

34. Stepneski, R., *7 NonProfit Times* (3) 1 (March 1993).

35. See, C. Svoboda, (article), *Pinellas County* (Fla.) *Review*, 9 (February 10, 1984). Priests in ancient Ur collected the taxes. W. Keller, *The Bible as History*, 18 (1956).

36. *Ibid.*; and 11 *Encyc. Britannica* 624 (1985 issue).

37. *Id.*

38. *Id.*

39. *Id.*

40. *Id.*; and 6 *Encyclopedia Britannica* 78 (1985 issue).

41. P. Taft, *Organized Labor in American History* 5 (1964).

42. *Ibid.*; and Vol. 6, 13, 16 *Encyclopedia Britannica, et passim.*

43. *Id.*

44. *Id.*

45. *Id.*

46. *Id.*

47. *Id.*

48. *Id.*

49. Bernstein, *Union Busting*, 14 U.S. D.L. Rev. 9 (1980).

50. Turner, "From Social Club Beginnings," 8 *The Ku Klux Klan* (1982).

51. *Ibid.*

52. *Id.*

53. *Id.*

54. *Id.*

55. Turner, "Klan Nightriding: Shades of Slave Patrols," 10 *The Ku Klux Klan* (1982).

56. Turner, "Origins of the KKK," 9 *The Ku Klux Klan* (1982).

57. 5 *Encyclopedia Britannica* 935 (1985 issue) estimated its membership then at 4 to 5 million.

58. *Ibid.*

59. Turner, The "Klan Today," 48 *The Ku Klux Klan* (1982).

60. *Newsweek* 52 (July 15, 1985).

61. *St. Petersburg Times*, ID (October 23, 1985).

62. *Ibid.*, p. 11A.

63. Cooks, "Songs from the Highground," *Time* 78 (October 7, 1985).

64. *St. Petersburg Times*, 2D (October 23, 1985).

65. *Ibid.*

66. *Id.*

67. J. Whitaker, *St. Petersburg Times* (Fla.), p. 2 (November 23, 1985).

68. Conference Board annual survey (November 9, 1986), reported in *United Press International-al* wire news item (November 9, 1986).

69. Associated Press Report (New York City) May 27, 1993.

3

MIXTURE OF PROFIT AND NONPROFIT ACTIVITIES

[Laura M. Watson, Robert Landt, and Robert E. Griffin contributed to the research in this chapter. Discussions of the latter parts of the sections on statutes of N.Y., Tex., Cal., Mich. were drafted by Gloria Smith.]

§17. MIXTURE OF PROFIT AND NONPROFIT PURPOSES

Obtaining, or *making* money with which to carry out a nonprofit organization's *purpose* is a constant concern of most such organizations. A church bingo-games program, for example, is a business operation used for fundraising. The endowment of a community-welfare foundation by a business corporation often is a public relations project, aimed at increasing the "parent" corporation's business profits. Many other examples can also be added.

Nonprofit corporations today routinely employ many *development options* or business-type devices for supporting their ultimate nonprofit purposes. These may involve such diverse projects as housing, publishing, real estate, communications, financial underwriting, and manufacturing operations; which in turn may employ sale-leasebacks, tax-exempt (or, floating) bond issues, equity syndications, joint-venture building (*e.g.,* housing) developments, telephonic and cable TV systems, and many other devices.[1]

Some say that *most* of the revenues of many nonprofit organizations come from business-type sales income, producing substantial net profits.[2] It is the reinvestment of the business income, in achieving the nonprofit purpose, and its nondistribution of profits, that gives the nonprofit its special character.[3] Often a "commercial" nonprofit will compete directly with business corporations in providing goods and services.[4] Moreover, the dwindling of governmental support of income to most commercial nonprofits in recent years has forced them to turn more and more to money-raising operations.[5] Religious (church) corporations pose special constitutional problems; the courts do not have juris-diction when matters of religious doctrine are involved to a major extent.[6]

The launching of a business (profit) operation may be decided upon and executed by the board of directors of the nonprofit—even against the votes of some members where the asset employed is owned by the corporation as an entity, and the operation has the vote of the "proprietor members." An exam-ple would be a social club that owns land and leases it for construction of a condominium on it.[7] Another such example is the contracting of control of a parcel of college land by Eckerd College of Florida to Centerbanc Corporation for construction and operation of "lifecare" condominiums on the campus in 1985; and a municipal "authority" corporation that operated a nursing home was held to possess governmental immunity when sued for negligence and invasion of privacy and infliction of emotional distress.[8]

The quest for profit is the chief motivating force in our society, especial-ly in commerce and industry. Our economic system has grown and developed considerably from the initial search for pecuniary profit. Our social system, too, is strongly affected by the human impulse to obtain prestige and advantages over other people. But profit seeking has never been the only determinant of the development of Western society. Parallel to the profit motive in the devel-opment of our civilization, down through the ages, has been another great ten-dency which is exactly the opposite of the desire for personal gain. This ten-dency is a compound of many motives, all of which can be called nonprofit. These motives include the nobler human impulses: religious and moral con-cepts and principles, tenderness toward children, resentment of injustice and oppression, the desire to help the needy. Use of profit-seeking devices in order to accomplish nonprofit purposes is not inconsistent.

It is clear that a mixture of profit-seeking activities into or with ultimate nonprofit purposes is not only an acceptable, but usually necessary part of many nonprofit organizations' operations. But see: R. Nader, *Masks of Deception: Corporate Front Groups in America* (1991), S. Holton article, *Orlando (FL.) Sentinel*, pp. 1 and 16 (Sept. 4, 1993).

[Ann E. Snow contributed most of the rest of this section.]

Of course, the basic restraint on any ongoing nonprofit organization is that profits or assets are not to be distributed to individual shareholders, mem-bers, directors, or officers.[9] To direct the contributions away from the ultimate purpose for which they were intended constitutes a betrayal of the donor's trust in the organization. A prime illustration of donors' intolerance of such betrayal is the reduced contributions to local United Way chapters in response to revelations of extravagant personal gains distributed to United Way of Amer-ica directors.[10]

It appears, however, that most states are tolerant of the mixing of profit and nonprofit agendas. There is an absence of prohibitive state legislation. In light of that absence, the regulation of mixtures of profit and nonprofit operations has been delegated to the tax authorities in a particular jurisdiction.[11] Such regulation generally takes the form of sales and use tax exemption, real property tax exemption, and unrelated business income taxation (UBIT).[12]

Because there is no uniform system of law, an organization intending to synthesize profit and nonprofit activities must consult the relevant case law and statutes of that jurisdiction. Litigation of profit/nonprofit mixtures is most prevalent in the nonprofit sectors involving educational, religious, or health care organizations.

Education

The Internal Revenue Service issued an advance announcement in late December of 1992, which set forth the proposed examination guidelines for agents to use during examinations of tax-exempt college and university financial operations.[13] The proposed instructions focus on contributions and detecting profits made through unrelated business income. Examples include: the use of real property, including rental of facilities; the use of tax-exempt bonds; the sources of athletic department income; the contractual relationships of joint ventures formed to conduct research; and the source of bookstore revenues.[14] The detailed IRS checklist indicates that the IRS is aware of the increasingly complex ways that exempt organizations—in this case, educational organizations—now operate.

In the proposed guidelines, the IRS notes that real property owned by universities is exempt from taxation under many state and local statutes if used "exclusively" for "educational" purposes.[15] A review of current case law shows that these terms are defined differently from jurisdiction to jurisdiction.

In Illinois, for example, a nonprofit university foundation held title to 74 acres of partially developed land, which it leased to the university. The university in turn used the property primarily for rental of a conference center located on the property to for-profit groups unrelated to the university. The appellate court denied the request for property tax exemption, stating that the use of the land was not shown to be for educational purposes but rather with a view to profit.[16]

In Ohio, a private nonprofit corporation that served as the major fundraising arm of a public university was considered a "public office" and the list of donors to that foundation was deemed a public record and therefore subject to disclosure upon request.[17]

Pennsylvania's state constitution provides for tax exemption to institutions of "purely public charity."[18] The state Supreme Court established a definitive test to determine when an entity qualifies as pure charity. The test requires an entity to possess all of the following five characteristics:

1) Advances a charitable purpose;
2) Donates or renders gratuitously a substantial portion of its services;
3) Benefits a substantial and indefinite class of persons who are legitimate subjects of charity;

4) Relieves the government of some of its burden; and

5) Operates entirely free from private profit motive.[19]

This standard was applied to nonprofit corporations owning land on which they operated summer camps for children to study the Judaic religion. The county tax board deemed the land taxable, with the exception of buildings where primary religious services were conducted and a surrounding five-acre buffer. The nonprofit camps appealed, claiming they provided religious education, drug awareness programs, and other social and recreational activities. The court held, however, that the camp corporations (which charged $2,800.00 per eight-week session) failed to prove that there was a governmental burden to provide such activities over the summer, hence there was no relief of a governmental burden as required by the fourth requirement necessary to qualify as a purely public charity.[20]

Joint ventures mixing profit and nonprofit operations and purposes are increasingly common. Harvard University has announced a new plan for a "limited partnership" to raise outsiders' money to commercialize its medical research, whereby Harvard will get 10 percent of the company profits. Most research universities use *licensing* offices which patent and market professors' work through existing companies, and then divide royalties with the employees. Now Harvard *itself* will raise the money and form the *business* company. This plan may raise ethical conflicts. In licensing activities in 1988, Stanford University earned $9.1 million fees, and M.I.T. made about $3 million. The temptations for abuse are obvious in either technique.[21]

Health Care

The health care industry is a target of reform by the White House and a critical eye is focused on nonprofit hospitals subsidized by taxpayers. In March of 1993, Congress heard testimony scrutinizing the funding and expenditures of nonprofit hospitals across the country.[22] Watchdogs claim that hospitals are abusing the public trust by turning their back on indigent patients, while at the same time investing in diverse businesses such as landscaping, collection agencies, hunting lodges, and four-star restaurants. For example, the Texas attorney general's office has alleged that Methodist Hospital of Houston, one of the nation's largest nonprofit hospitals, spends only $5 million a year on the average to pay for indigent care, compared to the $40 million in subsidies the hospital receives from tax-exempt benefits.[23]

Traditionally, the public policy has been to encourage the establishment of hospitals. To do so, they have long been accorded an unusual consideration, unlike most exempt institutions, in that they are permitted to charge patients reasonable fees and still be regarded as charitable. Today, some argue that not all hospitals provide a sufficient community benefit to justify the loss of government revenue caused by their tax exemption.[24]

Contrary to that opinion, a gift shop in a nonprofit hospital in Oregon was granted property tax exemption. The tax court there, viewed the "emotional medicine" provided by the shop as being reasonably necessary for the welfare of the patients.

A charitable health care provider's fitness center in Missouri was ruled exempt from sales and use taxation because its primary purpose was education. Despite charging a flat monthly fee and conducting retail sales of apparel, juices, and food items, the center operated below cost and incurred operating losses.[25] The court noted that the purpose of an organization takes precedence over any purported competition when determining if the activity satisfies exemption requirements.[26]

McDonalds (profit) restaurants in NPO hospitals by 1988 numbered eight such restaurants opened and five more in process. Some hospital spokespeople favor this mixture, while the Public Citizen Health Research Group (Washington, DC) attacks it as medical madness in dietetics. Burger King and Wendy's also have opened restaurants in hospitals.[27]

The fact that a foundation's primary source of funding is not public or private charity does not require a conclusion that it is not a charitable enterprise. In Illinois, a physicians' group formed in affiliation with a hospital sought and received property tax exemption. The foundation employed physicians who received below-market income and were not allowed to maintain private practices. These physicians spent 52 percent of their time in educational, research, and administrative activities. The patients treated were not denied treatment due to the inability to pay. All of this, the court held, indicated that the property was used for the primary benefit of the public.[28]

The owner of property is the only lawfully authorized entity entitled to apply for property tax exemption, and to qualify, that owner must be an exempt entity, according to Florida statutory law. The fact that the property is leased to an exempt entity and used for an exempt purpose is irrelevant.[29]

Hospital-Physician Joint Ventures

[This subsection was contributed by David C. Bearden.]

As late as 1978, the position of the IRS was any investment by an NPO that shared profits or was in partnership with private investors removed a nonprofit organization's tax-exempt status. GCM 37259 (Sept. 19, 1977); GCM 36293 (May 30, 1975). But changes in political attitudes and rising costs opened a window that gave an NPO flexibility to joint venture.

In 1984, the IRS issued a favorable unpublished ruling to a nonprofit hospital regarding the sale of its "net revenue stream" of certain profitable operations, in this particular case four of its outpatient departments (surgery, imaging, ophthalmology, and nuclear medicine). The hospital sold the operations to a new corporation that formed four limited partnerships with the stock owned 50 percent by the hospital and 50 percent by a broad cross-section of its medical staff. The outpatient departments remained under the hospital license, and their services continued to be billed under the hospital provider number. This series of transactions were considered consistent with the hospital's tax exempt purpose.

Another favorable ruling was issued regarding a hospital subsidiary that issued limited partnership interests in the "net revenue stream" of the outpatient surgery center and gastroenterology laboratory (Ltr. Rul. 8820093). The limited partnership interests were purchased by members of the hospital's medical staff, and the units continued to operate as departments of the hospital under its license and billed for its services under the hospital provider number.

Other more specific memoranda were issued dealing with the types and structures of hospital-physician joint ventures. The chief council's office issued some clear lines concerning these joint ventures, particularly if the "net revenue stream" flows from the hospital to the physician (GCM 39862; November 22, 1991). The GCM discussed a community-benefit standard, expanded the list concerning types of joint ventures, reconsidered and recommended revocation of the three favorable rulings discussed previously, recommended the notifying of key IRS district offices to be alert for potential abuse and to have the district take affirmative steps to identify and evaluate hospital-physician joint ventures. It was estimated by the General Accounting Office that State and Federal Taxing Authorities forego approximately $8 billion dollars per year by granting tax exemptions to NPO hospitals (62-APR PABAQ 74). The IRS wants to be sure this tax exempt status is not being used to improperly benefit certain individuals.

All these clarifications create a need for hospitals to carefully scrutinize their own policies regarding their financial structure. To do this, it is necessary to understand what the IRS will and will not allow.

Since 1979, any arrangement between the NPO and one or more for-profit entities requires a careful scrutiny of the circumstances due to the potential conflicts that may arise (GCM 37852; Feb. 9, 1979). The IRS applies a three-prong test to determine if the NPO is jeopardizing their tax exemption (C693 ALI-ABA 101).

The first prong is whether the partnership is serving its charitable purpose. The IRS will not sanction a tax exempt status for a partnership whose purpose is not substantially related to an organizations tax exempt status (GCM 39444; Nov. 13, 1985). Through a series of letters issued since 1979, the IRS has provided a list of substantially related activities for hospital-physician joint ventures. These partnerships with for-profit purposes include:

1. Medical office buildings. Ltr. 89040039;
2. C.T. Scanners. Ltr. 8917055;
3. Diagnostic imaging centers. GCM 39732 (May 19, 1988);
4. Lithotripsy services. Ltr. 9109066;
5. Cardiac diagnostic center. Ltr. 8909036;

6. Ambulatory surgical centers. GCM 39732 (May 19, 1988);

7. Cancer center. Ltr. 8925052;

8. Alcoholism/substance abuse treatment center. Ltr. 8521055;

9. Women's health center. Ltr. 8727080;

10. Physical therapy center. GCM 39732 (May 19, 1988);

11. Rehabilitation center. Ltr. 9035072;

12. Psychiatric hospital center. Ltr. 8912041;

13. Acute behavioral medicine specialty hospital. Ltr. 8903060;

14. Chemical dependency. Ltr. 8903060;

15. Home health care services. Ltr. 8945063;

16. Nursing home. Ltr. 9014050;

17. Hospital laboratory. Ltr. 8921091;

18. Health maintenance organization. Ltr. 8723065;

19. Hospital equipment. Ltr. 8936073;

20. Pharmaceutical production facility. GCM 37852 (Feb. 9, 1979);

21. Blood fractionation facility. Ltr. 7921018;

22. Office buildings in which operations conducted. Ltr. 8344110.

The second prong attempts to scrutinize the facts surrounding the affiliation (GCM 39546; Aug. 15, 1986). The concerns run to the conflict between a general partner's duty to maximize profits and pursuing the NPO's tax exempt goals. The fact that a general partner assumes the liabilities of the limited partner is also in conflict with the purposes of an NPO.

The third prong deals with whether the affiliation impermissibly benefits the private parties. The benefits received from the NPO must be incidental to the public purposes served. Incidental was defined in GCM 39598 (May 19, 1988) as requiring both a qualitative and quantitative threshold be met. Qualitative analysis determining whether the benefit to the public could be accomplished only by involving a private entity. Quantitative analysis that the private entity benefit must not be substantial after considering the overall benefit to the NPO's public purpose. Insiders will be held to a higher standard and the IRS expects the joint venture to be completed using an arm's-length standard.

The IRS drew a clear line on certain transactions in GCM 39862 (Nov. 11, 1991). The GCM divided its analysis into three basic components: private inurement, private benefit, and the antikickback statute for Medicare and Medicaid.

Their focus on private inurement is in the area of whether the hospital-physician joint venture furthers the hospital's purpose. If only a restructuring of the cash flow occurs without an expansion of their purpose, an improvement in treatment, or a reduction in costs, no charitable purpose is being served. In effect, what you have is a disguised equity interest.

The GCM went on to explain a private benefit will result to the physician if a "substantial share on the profits of the hospital" or "an extremely profitable investment" is arranged. Improving financial health by better utilization of a hospital's facilities bears only a tenuous relationship to the hospitals charitable purposes. The GCM also observes improving the competitive position, though referrals or eliminating competition is not the same as benefiting its community.

What the GCM does do is suggest types of joint ventures that may further a hospitals charitable purpose. These include a joint venture that:

1. results in a new health care provider, service, or resource being made available to the community;
2. raises capital for a bona fide purchase or purpose;
3. owns or leases a facility/service and operates it as a separate provider;
4. involves substantial risk;
5. involves the pooling of expertise;
6. measurably improves the quality of service or costs to the patients.

Suggested types of joint ventures that are clearly suspect include a joint venture that:

1. involves the restructuring of existing capacity to maintain and enhance use;
2. upon analysis, appears to be little more than a shell and does not involve meaningful risk sharing between the hospital and their physician partners.

Because some of the earlier rulings are narrowed in GCM 39862, the chief council created an amnesty period for hospitals to change existing agreements in Announcement 92-70 1992-19 I.R.B. This period was to last until September 1, 1992. When the deadline passed only twelve hospitals had notified the IRS that they were rescinding joint venture/partnership agreements with physicians. Although the number coming forward seems low, the IRS believes that most hospitals terminated their agreements privately (11 TMWR 1316; Sept. 28, 1992).

What is clear is that there are still many permissible joint ventures. The IRS is working on an issue paper continuing the work of GCM 39862 regarding a tax exempt hospital entering into a joint venture with a related health care organization to share its revenue stream (12 TMWR 477; Apr. 5, 1993).

Physician recruiting is also a focus of examination (11 TMWR 244; Sept. 24, 1992). Recruitment and retention must be justified in terms of their net benefit to the services provided the community and not just depending on improved efficiency as their rationale (76 JTRAX 164; March, 1992). Where Medicare or Medicaid are involved, the Social Security Act prohibits renumeration in exchange for referrals (42 U.S.C.A. s 1320a-7b(b). As of September 1992, the inspector general of the Department of Health and Human Services had about 230 active investigations of joint ventures under way. The inspector general has civil authority to exclude violators from the federal Medicaid program. Such a finding could also result in an NPO losing its tax exemption (11 TMWR 1316; Sept. 28, 1992).

The Chief Council also is paying close attention to joint ventures whose purpose may be to benefit physicians for referrals (10 TMWR 1485; Dec. 9, 1991). Specifically, the service will focus its analysis around how the arrangement benefits the community and not the hospital. Examination guidelines for hospitals were published in Announcement 92-83 1992-22 I.R.B. 59. Joint ventures are covered in Sec. 333.4.

The IRS has provided some clear guidelines for a hospital to analyze a joint venture opportunity. While recognizing that changes in the way government pays for medical services, competition, burgeoning medical costs, and the need to better serve the community, the IRS is still allowing only a narrow scope of investment possibilities. The line between allowable and disallowed joint ventures for tax exempt status is becoming more defined and clear.

The IRS announced that it would audit many hospitals and colleges in September of 1992, paying special attention to for-profit subsidiaries, joint ventures, partnerships, exempt bonds, fund raising efforts, employee wages, treatment of UBIT, credit cards issued to alumni, sales of alumni mailing lists, commercial use of property financed by tax-exempt bonds, educational travel programs, and corporate-sponsored events. The increased scrutiny reflects the complex ways that exempt hospitals and colleges have tried to mix profit and nonprofit operations.[30]

Financial

When a debtor filed for bankruptcy, she sought dischargeability of her Law Access Loan program ("LAL") loan obligation which was obtained from, serviced by, and insured by for-profit entities. The loan insurer claimed that the loan was nondischargeable because LAL is substantially funded by a nonprofit corporation. The court held that although the LAL umbrella serves as a conduit to both profit and nonprofit funded loans, the debtor's particular loan was entirely funded by for-profit entities, and therefore, was dischargeable. To hold otherwise would enable a for-profit organization to "boot strap" onto nonprofit programs and attain nondischargeability.[31]

Mixtures of Individual Interests

Sacramento housing advocates fear that for-profit companies that own low-income complexes are selling these properties to nonprofit organizations while retaining lucrative management and consulting contract ties with the new owners. Critics claim the nonprofit purchasers are used as fronts for for-profit entities thereby obstructing HUD's goal of independent ownership and control of low-income housing by community based nonprofit groups.[32]

Traditional Nonprofit-Profit Mixtures

Museums have traditionally sold souvenirs to supplement funding for operational costs. The revenue from such sales are subject to UBIT[33] if they are not directly related to the tax exempt organization's purpose. The primary aim of UBIT is to eliminate unfair competition, whereby the tax-free status of organizations enables them to use their profits tax free to expand operations, while competitors have only the revenue remaining *after* taxes to invest.[34]

Spokespersons for commercial tour operators and travel agencies have been asking the IRS to apply the UBIT standard to museums and other nonprofit organizations that have been offering low-cost tour programs labeled as educational. The IRS recently responded by conducting an audit of three National Trust tours to see if they were so weakly linked to the organization's purpose as to justify taxation as unrelated business income.[35]

The Public Broadcasting System (PBS) is being criticized by independent producers and distributors who claim the not-for-profit company has a mini-monopoly over video sales. PBS offers videos at retail prices through an "800" number while the program airs. The for-profit distributors who hold the rights to the videos are precluded from offering the same videos on the air unless they offer the tapes at a nominal price, which PBS has set at $10 a cassette. Distributors protest that they cannot afford to drop prices that low, whereas PBS can because they purchase the videos at discounts of 45 to 65 percent. PBS maintains that the UBIT test allows the profit venture because the revenues are used in a manner consistent with the organization's purpose.

Nontraditional

Center for Independent Living, a nonprofit Virginia organization, is seeking $21.5 million in bonds to buy a Niagara Falls water park that is already in receivership. Local legislators and citizens criticize the proposal asking, "What business is it of a nonprofit organization [to] be running something that traditionally is a for-profit venture?"[36]

New Trends

Whether it be a purely commercial marketing maneuver or purely philanthropic (or a combination of the two), the hottest nonprofit/profit mixture trend involves commercial entities taking on nonprofit activities as part of their commercial efforts. For example, the sales of new "environmentally correct" foods produced by commercial corporations such as R. W. Knudsen Co. result in a percentage of profits being directed to nonprofit organizations.[37]

The co-founder of Ben & Jerry's Ice Cream, Ben Cohen, reported that his for-profit enterprise recently opened a shop in Harlem that is 75 percent owned by a nonprofit organization there. Their goal in doing this is "So the profits go back toward helping improve the quality of life ... [t]he aim is to help people who have traditionally been cut out of the capitalistic equity track to get some business ownership.[38]

Examples of Money-Making Devices

A Washington, D.C. public broadcasting service (PBS) TV station produced TV commercials and rented out space in its quarters.

A nonprofit hospital sold music records produced by volunteers.

A health organization sold computerized financial programs to its members, based on a charter provision for providing financial assistance to members.

A children's aid organization sold items from a Christmas catalog.

An organization that helps disabled persons to acquire new skills for making a living won a state highway department contract for picking up litter.

Colleges often lease out facilities for conferences and meetings.

Some research groups have rented out time (use) of their computers.

A museum sells display space to manufacturers of baby foods and toys for exhibits at an annual "parenting fair," and also produced books for corporate sponsors.

See the *Symposium* on various aspects of this subject in *16 No. Ky. L. Rev.* (2) 225–396 (publ. Apr. 1989).

Growing dominance of "commercial" nonprofit organizations (e.g., mixing much profit with their nonprofit operations) may involve two-thirds of American NPOs by the year 2000, and may lead to loss of tax exemption by all but a few organizations, said Prof. Henry Hansmann of Yale Law School at a 1988 conference in San Francisco, referring especially to organizations relying mainly on fees, such as NPO hospitals, HMOs, medical laboratories, nursing homes, day care centers, fitness centers, and health and life insurance organizations. Of the 6000 hospitals in the United States, 70 percent are nonprofit organizations; but Brian O'Connell, president of *Independent Sector* (650 big NPOs coalition) is more optimistic that the NPOs will bridle their profit-seeking operations.[40]

In many areas, it is unsettled whether a nonprofit corporation should or may own a for-profit subsidiary which will be funded by revenues of the nonprofit corporation. In Maryland, a case was recently reversed and remanded back to an insurance commissioner with the suggestion that he rule on whether Blue Cross, a nonprofit health service plan, may or should own a for-profit subsidiary. [See ch., Affiliations.][41]

[Research for the following five items was contributed by Mark A. Catchur.]

The Woman's Club of Morristown, a nonprofit organization, owns a building that has been certified as an historic landmark. When the Club leased a portion of the building to commercial tenants, the city challenged the Club's tax exempt status. The court held that there is a rational and reasonable difference between a for profit corporation and a nonprofit organization that needs rental income to preserve its property. Thus, the tax exemption was preserved.[42]

The American Society for Metals International, a nonprofit corporation, used its facilities for lectures, courses, and presentations of scientific papers at a discount for members. Revenue and profits were generated. The court held that the Society did not use its property as a charitable institution or public institution of learning. The tax exemption was denied.[43]

An organization whose bylaws restricted membership to companies who own large scale computer equipment, manufactured by IBM, sought a tax refund as a business league under section 501(c)(6), which requires activities to be directed to the improvement of business conditions of one or more lines of business. The court held that the organization served primarily the interests of IBM and accordingly denied their business league status under section 501(c)(6).[44]

A nonprofit organization can be a limited partner in a partnership formed for the purpose of developing real estate, a for profit venture.[45]

A church that purchased an inner city apartment building, in order to offer affordable housing to the poor and jobs for church members, received more than expected for the bargain. The building's maintenance problems and destructive tenants, who had to be evicted, placed a drain on the church's meager finances to the point of threatening its existence.[46]
[See § 425 (Mergers) outline of "Corporate Takeover" litigation; "Corporation raiders" case; *Poynter Institute* as an NPO with security holder demands; 1991 Cum. Supp.]

The Poynter Institute in St. Petersburg, Florida, dedicated to teaching and improving journalism, settled a minority (1990) shareholder claim in its "holding company" control of the city's newspaper by buying back the claimant's stock and making the NPO-Profit Corporation mixture into a more complete control-of-stock arrangement.[47]

A for-profit nursing home for congregate care was so valuable for housing community senior citizens, so good for the "general welfare," so helpful to the community, and so little burden on traffic, that it was entitled to a use variance for construction of the housing unit.[48]

Debt-Programs Mixtures

Interaction and interdependence of profit and nonprofit corporate purposes and operations is increasing most rapidly in health, defense, housing and community development financing, and other debt-programs. As yet, however, the problems and pitfalls in these areas have received insufficient attention and analyses.[48] However, a nonprofit borrower/sponsor that secures a loan from HUD, under the Housing Act of 1959, for the development of housing for the elderly and handicapped may not earn profits to the benefit of any member, founder, contributor or individual. For example, the same identity can not borrow from HUD and then receive profits as a contractor on the project.[50]

§18. STATUTES AUTHORIZING MIXTURE OF PURPOSES

New York's Not-for-Profit Corporation Law (NY-NPCL) enacted in 1970, was the first modern statute that frankly departed from the stern old rule of absolute separation of nonprofit from profit purposes.[51] Of course, the old rule in practice had been largely ignored for a long time. The New York statute divides nonprofits into four categories, each subject to some different rules. *Commercial* nonprofits are designated as "Type C" corporations, but these still are not allowed to distribute profits to members or officers. However, upon *dissolution* and payment of creditors and judicial approval, members of Type C corporations may participate in distribution of the dissolved corporation's assets.

The most drastic "new" statute, the California Nonprofit Corporation Law of 1980, which was the model for the American Bar Association's 1986 Revised Model Nonprofit Corporation Act proposals, also permits distribution of assets to members, upon dissolution of a nonprofit.[52] But California permits *commercial* nonprofits to incorporate under the same category as social clubs.[53] Commercial nonprofits are categorized as "Mutual Benefit Nonprofits."[54] Some persons argue that the no-distribution-of dividends rule is enough to prevent abuse of nonprofit status.[55] But the more general view has long been that profit-seeking adversely affects the quality of services performed by nonprofit organizations.[56] Often, *too easy* freedom of gain in nonprofits encourages abuse of the nonprofit status.[57]

"Business corporation" is a term so widely understood that statutes usually do not trouble to define it, even in statutes titled by that name.[58] The Internal Revenue Service defines the term by listing its characteristics.[59] The 1964 revision of the American Law Institute–American Bar Association Model Nonprofit Corporation Act[60] defined nonprofit corporation as "a corporation no part of the income of which is distributable to its members, directors or officers"—which does not suggest any prohibition of any *commercial* or *profit-making activities*, as long as the profits are not so distributed. The ABA 1987 Revised Model Nonprofit Corporation Act did not define "nonprofit" at all.

New York's corporation statute system in recent years has set forth statutory provisions for public corporations; special rules for certain nonstock corporations—fraternal orders, religious corporations, and education corporations; special rules for certain stock corporations subject to insurance, cooperative and education laws; a four-types nonprofit corporations law; and a business corporations law.[61] California's corporation code provides a general corporations law; a nonprofit corporations law; a special part for such special categories as cooperatives and professional corporations; a part for nonprofit public-benefit corporations; one for mutual-benefit types; and one for nonprofit religious corporations.[62] The 1986 Revision of the Model Nonprofit Corporation Act (§3.01) allows all kinds of activities in both "public benefit" and "mutual benefit" organizations [§2.02(a)(2)].

Subventions

New York's statute provides in detail for an investment-in-nonprofits device, whereby an investor can finance a nonprofit's project such as a housing development, and get income while the corporation uses his capital, and then get his capital back when it has served its purpose. These are called *subvention certificates*, and resemble a special-stock issue of a business corporation; *e.g.*, like a limited certificate of stock.[63]

Ultimate Test: Whether or not income (profit) producing activities are proper (*e.g.*, tax-exempt) is tested by whether or not the profit is "achieved incidentally to accomplishment of the dominantly charitable objective"; and it must not be "a primary goal of the project," but "must be dedicated unconditionally to the charitable activity."[64]

§19. COLLISIONS OF PURPOSES

There is inherent difficulty in mixing profit and nonprofit purposes, of course; the boundary between the two types usually is indistinct. The result—charitable tax-exemption, or denial of exemption—usually is critical to the organization.[65]

"Limited dividends" corporations, for example, often involve strongly proprietary feelings of the people involved.[66] Charitable trust concepts now seem to be under erosive attack. New York's statute says that trustees of Type B (charitable, educational, religious, cultural, and prevention of cruelty) corporations shall be deemed to be owners in effect, rather than trustees, of property received by the corporation.[67] Thus, the trustees may be deemed not accountable to donors, though the purpose attributed to the new rule may be to allow trustees more freedom in treating income as not part of the principal *corpus* of the trust.[68]

Social welfare primacy tendencies seem to collide with this provision. Thus, derivative actions by members are now allowed.[68] Ordinary persons (citizens) in taxpayer's actions are held to have standing to sue to enforce charitable trusts.[70]

The judiciary's concern for the preservation of the public interest is increasingly apparent. Interposition of interested parties, through use of *ami-cus curiae* briefs, is common.[71] Members' inherent rights to belong to associations are strongly favored where the right to earn a living is involved.[72] The *cy pres* rule still applies to preserve the rights of those intended to be benefited from grantors.[73] Minority rights are favored on one hand, and overruled for "social architect purposes" on the other) as where a church turned over its assets to a "black caucus of members" group, despite objections from some members).[74]

One problem which inevitably plagues courts and legislators is that the tendency of some human beings to pretend to charitable purposes while seeking only (or primarily) personal advantage is still as strong as ever.[75] This tendency seems to be universal.[76] And debate on how to establish reliable criteria for the conduct of nonprofit (and other) organization officers and directors goes on and on.[77]

The American Bar Association 1987 Revised Model Nonprofit Corporation Act was drafted with committee *intention* to abolish the trust nature of grants establishing even charitable trusts; so said the committee chairperson of 1986.[78] But the California court, in the celebrated *Buck Trust* case said the outcome of the case will provide a reminder that *fiduciary responsibility* and loyalty to a permanent trust will remain the law.[79]

The American Bar Associations' committees on drafting nonprofit corporation law have consisted almost entirely of business corporation lawyers—mainly of management counsel. Yet some of them occasionally have displayed a sense of uneasiness about their own work as to the Model Nonprofit Corporations Act. Several years ago, for instance, the author was asked to serve as a consultant to the A.B.A. special committee for revision of this act, because of the committee's dissatisfaction with their own product. Eagerly, he went to Washington for a meeting at which he entreated the members to consider a totally different approach. They listened politely, and then resumed their business-corporation-concept-oriented discussion.

The author's view was, and is, this: That lawyers who think in terms of *profit-oriented* organization law are basically not the right people to decide what concepts and principles should undergird nonprofit organization law. The nonprofit organization basically is (or ought to be) an altruistic, voluntaristic undertaking, in which the satisfactions sought are those derived from aid to charity, service to others, compassion, religious exaltation, fellowship, beauty, and other moral compensations. This does not mean that it is wrong for a member to have a proprietary interest that the law will protect.[80] But stock issued (besides a membership) is open to execution and sheriff's sale.[81]

A proper committee to draft nonprofit organizations law should consist of philosophers, anthropologists, biologists, statisticians and demographers, theologians, sociologists, economists, psychologists, and the like, plus a few lawyers to crystallize the principles enunciated by the committee into workable rules of law.

The essence of nonprofit organization law principles should be analogized out of the guiding principles of religious and fraternal, and community-service and charitable, and mutual aid groups such as have illuminated civilization for many centuries. The fact that the concept of the Bronze Age temple or agricultural commune also often turned into the idea of a pirate crew should not make us conclude that we must make the pirate crew the model for our laws.

These high-sounding, admittedly almost-sanctimonious-sounding, views are diametrically opposed to the views of many people that nonprofits really are only just another form of cooperation for pecuniary profit. Advocates of that view are not necessarily crass opportunists. Many aspects of nonprofit operation may, do, and should involve profit seeking as an instrumentality of altruism.

In recent state changes in nonprofit corporation statutes toleration of the mixing of profit and nonprofit purposes and motives is apparent. For example, in Florida's amendments to its nonprofits statutes,[82] very easy merger of a business corporation into a nonprofit is authorized; scholarship and other funds are administered by Department of Insurance (*e.g.*, business) procedures; and business-style qualification of foreign corporations is adopted. In addition, the Florida punitive provisions for abuse by nonprofit status for the purpose of self-enrichment (like many state statutes) remain chiefly in the category of misdemeanors rather than (white collar) felonies, though deliberate falsification of records now will be treated as perjury. Also nonprofit agricultural cooperative marketing associations are authorized to convert easily into profit corporation form. The net effect is to create a strong impression that the difference between profit and nonprofit purposes is of diminishing consequence in Florida corporation law, and in the law of a growing number of states.

Mingling of legalized taxable and tax-exempt operations now is becoming a noticeably strong tendency in American society.[83]

Nonprofits now often are referred to as "tax-exempt organizations," as though their tax-exemptions were their chief characteristics. If that *is so*, about any particular organization, that organization is a burden imposed on the society, not a benefit to it. Tax evasion is not a legitimate basis for forming or continuing a nonprofit organization. Happily, nonprofit organizations would continue to be numerous in a free society, and very valuable to that society, even if tax-exemption were to be utterly abolished.

§20. STATUTORY CLASSIFICATIONS

The typical "trunk system" of corporate legislation beings with a general business corporation chapter, and then follows with a general nonprofit corporation chapter; thereafter providing a whole series of chapters for various specific kinds of organizations. Ohio's statutory system is a good example.[84]

OHIO CORPORATIONS

Chapter

1701	General Corporation Law
1702	Nonprofit Corporation Law
1703	Foreign Corporations
1707	Securities
1711	Agricultural Corporations; Amusement Rides
1713	Educational Corporations
1715	Religious and Benevolent Organizations
1716	Charitable Organizations
1717	Humane Societies
1719	Charitable Trusts
1721	Cemetery Associations
1723	Appropriation of Property by Certain Corporations
1724	Community Improvement Corporations
1725	Trade Associations
1726	Development Corporations
1727	Farm Laborers' Associations
1728	Community Redevelopment Corporations
1729	Cooperatives
1733	Credit Unions
1735	Title Guarantee and Trust Companies
1737	Medical Care Corporations
1738	Health Care Corporations
1740	Dental Care Corporations
1741	Bridge Companies
1742	Health Maintenance Organizations
1743	Miscellaneous Provisions and Types of Companies
1745	Unincorporated Associations
1747	Real Estate Investment Trusts
1761	Credit Union Shareowners' Guaranty Association

Kentucky's statute, with 1984 amendments, is a reasonable short guide. Its Chapter 272, for agricultural and livestock *cooperatives*, is *business*like. Its Chapter 273, for *religious, charitable,* and *educational* societies (not labor unions nor insurance nor banking), also includes community service and institutional fund managing groups.

Maine's statute, like many state nonprofit corporation acts, specifically avoids presentation in one chapter of all the specialized statutes that may relate to this subject.[85]

Nevada's statute typifies the structure of most of the modern nonprofit codes or statute systems of most states.[86]

    c. 81. Nonprofit and Cooperative Corporations and Associations
       82. Specific Fraternal Orders, Churches, and Other Organizations
       83. Cemetery Associations
       84. Corporations Sole

85. Hospitals and Charitable Asylums
86. Religious, Charitable, Literary, and Scientific Associations

Delaware's statute makes almost no provisions for nonprofit corporations.[87]

Statutory Permissiveness

The 1987 *American Bar Association's Model Nonprofit Corporations Act Revision* is extraordinarily permissive. It is criticized severely by this author in his article on "Mixtures of Profit and Nonprofit Corporate Purposes and Operations" in the Seminar Coursebook, *Non-Profit Organizations*, Northern Kentucky Univ., Chase College of Law, 1988. This proposed revision suggests division into Mutual Benefit, Public Benefit, and Religious Categories of NPO's. Tennessee and Mississippi quickly adopted it.

Statutes granting great leeway in mixing profit and nonprofit operations are being made ever more permissive. Florida's statutes are typical of this trend. They especially provide, for example, for nonprofit cooperative corporations as marketing organizations for agricultural products, aquatic products, confections, oils or juices products, and to dissolve and reform easily, and to own and manage stock in corporations in these lines of business. Also, the indemnity and liability powers of officers and agents of nonprofit organizations are made substantially as permissive as those of business corporations.[88]

The Internal Revenue Code as Corporate Regulatory Law

NOTE: [The balance of this Supplement Section contains reproduced extracts from the author's article (dated 1988, but published in 1989) in 16 *No. Ky. L. Rev.* 225–250.]

Tax law, especially income tax law, is fundamentally a body of rules meant to enable government to obtain funds needed for diverse governmental and administrative purposes. It is not the proper vehicle for selecting and establishing public morality-policy. Yet American tax law—especially federal income tax law—is the main body of legislation that in practice chooses and establishes the law of nonprofit tax-exempt privilege, and determines what mixtures of profit and nonprofit purposes and operations are valid.[89]

In fact, many lawyers think of "nonprofit organizations" as important only insofar as they are *tax-exempt* organizations.[90] They speak of tax-exempt organizations (i.e., those granted tax exemption by the IRS) as though any other kind of nonprofit organization is not worth mentioning.

Tax law continues to be the main avenue both for favoring and regulating mixtures of profit and nonprofit operations. However, decisions in various jurisdictions have been inconsistent. Two recent decisions suffice to outline the present uncertain state of the law. For example, Illinois recently held that *incidental* acts of charity by a fraternal lodge were not enough to justify property tax exemption, where the main purpose of the lodge was to provide a building for social use by its members. The court held that use of the property must be "exclusively" for charitable purposes.[91] In a Florida case, however, it was held that a tax exemption will apply to nonreligious use of property by a tax-exempt church (as a parking lot) where the religious use is the "predominant" use or the "most significant activity" on land which may support multiple activities.[92]

Many state corporation law statutes now contain at least one specific section that refers to the Internal Revenue Code's rules as the definition of "prohibited transactions" for nonprofit organizations.[93] The 1987 Revised Model Nonprofit Corporation Act also refers to I.R.C. §501(c)(3) as the test standard for distributions of assets of both tax-exempt and non tax-exempt nonprofit corporations upon dissolution.[94]

In practical effect, therefore, the IRS is the chief architect of public policy as to legal status of nonprofit organizations' mixed profit and non-profit purposes and operations. The key idea in state law seems to be that property of a tax-exempt organization satisfies the "exclusive use" requirements for tax-exemption if it is primarily used for the exempted purpose, even though it is used for a secondary or incidental purpose.[95]

Many states[96] gear their income tax structures to "taxable income" as defined under the federal Internal Revenue Code.[97] I.R.C. section 501(c) lists twenty-three types of associations, corporations, and trusts that can qualify for federal tax exemption, plus subdivision (c)(24) trusts under ERISA section 4049, and section 501(c)25 real estate title holders or distributors to nonprofit organizations.[98] The major exempt-purpose classifications under section 501(c)(3) are religious, scientific, charitable, and educational; but Congress has added such new purposes as prevention of cruelty to children and fostering of international athletic competitions.[99] The service itself has added exemptions such as that for aid to distressed persons.[100] There are now many more such exemptions.[101]

The gearing of state tax rules to federal tax law means that by engaging in "prohibited transactions," as defined in the federal statute, some trusts, pensions, or other such plans will lose their tax-exempt status if they lend funds without adequate security, pay unreasonably high salaries, give preferences, pay unduly high prices, sell at unduly low prices, or otherwise cause substantial diversion of assets.[102] Self-dealing, as defined in I.R.C. section 4941(d), will have the same result in private foundations.[103] There are many other federal tax law rules which influence the operation of nonprofits.[104]

State Tax Exemptions

The tax structures of various jurisdictions also affect what mixtures of profit/nonprofit organizations and activities will be granted tax-exempt status. State taxation includes incorporation fees, annual franchise taxes, income taxes (not in all states), property taxes, death and gift taxes, and more. Charitable organizations are granted exemption from many state taxes. To a lesser extent, "merely nonprofit" (other than charitable, religious, and the like) organizations that are somewhat public in nature are similarly excepted.[105] This applies to franchise taxes,[106] income taxes,[107] sales and use taxes[108] and especially to property taxes of charitable and similar organizations.[109] Only the property used for "charitable" purposes is exempt, however.[110] The requirement that such use be exclusive is satisfied if that use is the primary one, even if it also is used for other purposes.[111]

The inconsistency between state schemes is illustrated by the following examples. In some states, property held by an exempt organization under a lease, even though used to produce income (e.g., a college dormitory) is not entitled to the exemption because it is not owned.[112] In other states the lessor of property can get the tax exemption by renting the property to such a non-profit organization as a church.[113] There is need for legislative clarification of public policy of such mixtures of profit and nonprofit purposes and operations.

§21. NEW YORK'S STATUTES

New York's Not-for-Profit Corporation Law[114] divides nonprofit corporations into four types (*A, B, C,* and *D*) as described below (at note 118). The *general* statute is more typical of the concepts in most American corporation laws, recognizing three main clauses of corporations:

1. *Public corporations.* These include municipal, district, and public-benefit corporations: the organs or agencies of government for administrative purposes. In some cases, the statutes which create them grant limited legislative powers.

2. *Stock corporations.* These are the ordinary business (profit-seeking) corporations. The newer statutes put cooperative corporations in this group, because cooperatives may be run for profit, but nonprofit cooperatives are provided for by the laws of some states, such as New York; and other profit operations now can be added in some stated situations.[115]

3. *Nonstock corporations.* These are the ordinary social, charitable, fraternal, and other nonprofit corporations. Ordinarily, they issue "certificates of membership" instead of certificates of stock. It should be noted that sometimes a certificate of membership in a nonprofit corporation is called a "certificate of stock." This is not necessarily fatal to the corporation's nonprofit status, if no distribution of dividends to such "stockholders" is contemplated. But the use of this term shows a misconception about the real nature of nonprofit corporations, as the new New York statute does with its "business corporations not for profit."

   A fourth general classification is added to the foregoing by special statutes in New York (the General Associations Law) and Ohio (Unincorporated Associations Law).[117]

4. *Unincorporated associations.* These include every unincorporated company, enterprise, or "joint stock association," especially those having written articles of association and shares of stock. Here, "shares of stock" may be read also as "certificates of membership." A joint stock association is not the same thing as a business trust, but is characterized by written *articles of association* providing for:

a. Continuity of existence even on the death of a shareholder.

b. Transferability of shares.

c. Management by three or more directors.

New York's Not-for-Profit Corporation Law[118] (the N-PCL) classifies nonprofit organizations into four types—A, B, C, D.[119] Type A is the typical nonbusiness membership type. Type B covers charities, educational, scientific, literary, cultural or prevention of cruelty to children or animals. Type C is for mixed nonprofit/profit corporations, covering organizations which carry out business activities for profit, but in which the principal purpose is other than to make money. This approves, in effect, the view that nonprofits may be simply another means for taking profit; a most doubtful policy.[120] Type D is basically a permission to form a nonprofit under this chapter when authorized under some other law of the state.

Among other provisions in the New York N-PCL are requirements of annual reports, and continuous supervision of nonprofits by the attorney general.[121] Also, judicial and administrative approvals are required except for mutual benefit corporations.[122]

Another important concept introduced by the New York N-PCL is that of "subventions," a form of debt financing.[123] The subvention, similar to a capital contribution, does not create a debt of the corporation, but is an obligation, allowing investors to have their contributions returnable to them, upon accomplishment of the purpose. It can be described as a long-term goal, guaranteed by stock for each unit of loan, with the subventioner getting his money back at the end of a stated time.[124] The subventions "shall consist of money or other property, tangible or intangible, actually received by the corporation or expended for its benefit . . ."[125] A board resolution, the means of accepting subventions, can make provisions for setting a "fixed or contingent periodic payment from corporate assets" to be a percentage of the subvention's original value and not to exceed "2/3 of the maximum interest rate authorized."[126] The resolution may provide for redemption (whole or partial) and subventioners may have the right to require redemption after a stated period.[127] The subvention is a unique method of flexible financing but could lead to abuses.

Some new membership legislation is found in Article 6 of the N-PCL, and states that the certificate of incorporation or bylaws may provide for one or more classes of members, and no members are required in Type B (charitable) corporations.[128] Voting changes fix the quorum requirement at "a majority of the total number of votes entitled to be case thereat"[129] and in very large membership corporations it reduced the minimum quorum requirement formerly stated by the membership corporation law.[130] Another feature is that "no derivative action can be brought unless the plaintiffs in such action consist of at least five percent of any class of members."[131] Also, the complaint must state the plaintiff's prior efforts to obtain initiation of action by the board, or if no effort is made, the reasons for not doing so. The five percent rule has met with disapproval by many who feel that it is too great a burden for a member's derivative action.

Article 7 of the N-PCL deals with directors and officers, and incorporates business-type rules for a strong board of directors, but allowing this standard to be changed by stipulation in the articles of incorporation[132] and granting safeguards against abuse of authority in nonmember corporations. As for the directors' duties and liabilities, the N-PCL utilizes the "prudent person" standard.[133]

Overall, the New York N-PCL system clearly delineates areas of previous uncertainty, including memberships and director's duties and liabilities. However, the strong economic overtones concerning subventions, relaxed and flexible authorization of mergers, consolidations, and reduction of judicial supervision, make this statute radical, appearing to show little concern for the voluntaristic and altruistic nature of the true nonprofit organization.

§22. TEXAS CODE

Texas, adopting the ABA Model Corporation Act in 1961, and amending it in 1977, provided a clear statute while retaining the essence of nonprofit.[134] The Act excludes from its scope cooperatives, group health services, rural credit unions, or fraternal organizations, which are incorporated under Articles 1399-1407; brand or insurance companies; and organizations for water or sewer services.[135]

Other distinctions include flexible rules for amendment of the articles, allowing for approval by two-thirds of all votes which members present (in person or by proxy) are able to cast; and if there are no voting members, amendment can be achieved by majority votes of the directors.[136]

Concerning the structure of nonprofit corporations, the Texas statute allows for one or more classes of members, or for organizations with no members.[137] If there are members, the articles or bylaws must set forth the classes, manner of appointment, qualifications, and rights of members. Membership meetings are handled in the same way as are shareholder meetings under the Business Corporation Act, with the exception that church notice may be announced orally at services prior to the meeting; if the corporation has over 1,000 members, notice by publication in a newspaper of general circulation is sufficient (if stated in the bylaws). The bylaws may eliminate altogether the requirement or notice.[138] A quorum consists of members holding one-tenth of all votes to be cast.[139]

Just as in a business corporation, the board of directors is to manage the corporation, except that a church may be managed by its members or may limit the directors' authority. And in nonprofits directors may vote by proxy.[140] The board must have at least three directors.[141]

The Act requires reports to be made every four years,[142] and annual financial reports must be filed. Financial records should be kept at the principal or registered office for three years.[143]

This Act is extensive and clearly drafted, but is not as flexible or as lenient as its California and New York counterparts. Texas upholds the traditional nonprofit concept, and does not condone dominance of economic motivation such as has become the recent trend in some states.

§23. CALIFORNIA'S STATUTE

In 1980 California seemed to follow in New York's footsteps when it adopted a new Nonprofit Corporations Law (NCL)[144] as a separate statute within the Corporations Code. California's system classifies nonprofits into three main categories: mutual benefit,[145] public benefit[146] and religious[147]—with specific provisions that deal with each type.

The California NCL states the standard of care applicable to directors to be that of the "prudent director."[148] Other provisions include authorization for committees, to which the board can delegate powers,[149] that self-dealing by officers is allowable (the only restriction is that it be "reasonable"),[150] and the startling provision allowing up to 49 percent of the directors to have personal interests in the "nonprofit" business they manage.[151] This provision would almost seem to guarantee corruption and abuse by directors.

The California statute, however, recognizes an inherent need to monitor the activities of nonprofits, and provides for increased governmental supervision. It differentiates according to the three types listed above, and subjects public benefit corporations to scrutiny by the attorney general at all times.[152] By contrast, mutual benefit corporations are deemed to require less supervision, with the attorney general exercising powers only with respect to assets held in charitable trusts, and involuntary dissolutions.

Other rules include elimination of annual and third-year meeting requirements,[153] allowance of special meetings called by not less than five percent of the members,[154] and prohibition of adjournment of meetings for over 45 days.[155] As for members derivative actions, the California NCL authorizes actions to be brought by members or public benefit[156] and mutual benefit corporations,[157] but still necessitates a demand requirement and the same "contemporaneous membership" rule found in the General Corporation Law. This is a more realistic approach than New York's five-percent rule that discourages even meritorious actions.

§24. MICHIGAN'S STATUTE

In 1983, Michigan joined the group of states that have enacted statutory formulations intended to liberalize government of nonprofit corporations. The laws in Michigan had been virtually unchanged for fifty years, and the New Nonprofit Corporations Act,[158] otherwise known as "Act 162," was said to be created to "simplify, clarify and modernize the law governing nonprofit corporations and provide a general corporate form for conduct of lawful nonprofit activities. . . ."[159] The basic restraint on nonprofits, that they may not have the ultimate purpose of making money, was retained in Act 162, which states that a nonprofit corporation may not "pay dividends or distribute any part of its assets, income or profit to its shareholders, members, directors, or officers. . . ."[160] There are the usual exceptions to this, such as reasonable compensation for services rendered to the corporation, and distribution of assets to shareholders or members (in dissolution).

Two basic forms of nonprofits allowable under Michigan law—stock and nonstock membership—continue to be permitted by Act 162, with certain discrepancies having been eliminated.[161] For instance, under Act 162, membership in a membership corporation and shares of a stock nonprofit corporation are not transferable except if the articles or bylaws provide otherwise; but the General Corporation Act only applied this restriction to stock nonprofit corporations. The form—stock, nonstock membership, or nonstock directorship— must be chosen when the corporation is organized.[162] "Stock corporations" are those organizations in which members (or investors) as in New York's statute, have property rights or economic interests. Nonstock membership is appropriate for those organizations in which members (or investors) as in New York's statute, have property rights or economic interests. Nonstock membership is appropriate for those organizations in which the members have an active role in the association's affairs, and usually are typified by the rule of one member-one-vote, democracy.[163] Act 162 has sought more flexible procedures for both types, allowing to stock corporations more leeway in regard to allocation of control with respect to property interests, and allowing to membership corporations more relaxed procedures regarding relations between members and other organizations. Also, the Act states that shareholders in a stock corporation are allowed votes equal to the number of shares held, unless the articles or bylaws provide for a one shareholder-one vote basis.[164] The use of the term "stock" nonprofit corporation is disturbing to people in most states. New York's "subventions" at least sound different.

A major change concerning nonstock corporations is the directorship of organization. This is a form of self-government by the board of directors, as a single entity. This allows the directors alone to approve the amendment of articles of incorporation, mergers and dissolutions, whereas previously shareholder or membership approval was required. The directorship may have members as long as they have no votes.[165] The directors may be removed only for cause, and the articles of incorporation must specify their term and manner of appointment. This directorship form is basically intended for organizations in which a relatively small group of individuals participates, or where there is need for a specialized board of directors. For example: hospitals, symphonies, or joint ventures are appropriate types for use of Michigan's directorship form.[166]

Act 162 directly addresses the issue of fiduciary duties of directors, and makes the "prudent person"[167] standard of the Business Corporation Act applicable, not subjecting directors to a higher trust standard, as had been suggested. The duties of directors are clearly delineated, and the principles of business corporate law pertaining to conflicts of interest, dissents from improper actions of the board, and so forth, are now expressly applied to nonprofit directors.

Michigan's Act 162 is an organized and practical statute, while maintaining a clear distinction of the nonprofits from other corporations. In this respect the state did not follow the economic dominance trend of New York, Pennsylvania and California. However, the "directorship form" is a dramatic change from prior law and may lead to abuse by a too powerful board of directors.

It is ironic that in 1985 Delaware, the leading "permissiveness" state in corporation law, abandoned the "prudent person" (presumption of innocence-"business judgment" rule) standard as to directors, and adopted a higher standard of due negligence and care required of directors and officers.[168]

POINTS TO REMEMBER

- Profit-making projects and activities may be used to achieve ultimately nonprofit purposes.
- Profit-seeking activities that aim at profit as the ultimate purpose are improper and illegal.
- Some states are more tolerant of profit-seeking in nonprofit organizations that are other states' authorities; notably California and New York.
- Federal tax law tests of tax-exempt status are the chief criteria of what is or is not proper profit-versus-nonprofit purposes and activities.
- Some state tax statutes are quite detailed in setting forth criteria for tax exemption; notably, Florida.
- If in doubt, remember that the ultimate purpose of a nonprofit organization must be charity, education, research, or other altruistic—voluntaristic purpose, not personal profit.
- Mix profit-seeking with nonprofit status only with caution, and with the best nonprofit interests of the community as the ultimate test of propriety.

NOTES TO CHAPTER 3

1. *See*, Oleck, *Mixtures of Profit and Nonprofit Corporate Purposes and Operations*, in Seminar Course book: *Non-Profit Organizations*, pp. 1–59, No. Ky. Univ., Chase College of Law (Feb. 1988); and **rule** No. Ky. L. Rev.—(late 1988); and also notes on a two-day seminar "The

Nonprofit as Entrepreneur: Development Operations for Universities, Hospitals, Governmental Bodies and Other Tax-Exempt Entities" of Institute for Professional and Executive Development, Inc., 2300 M Street NW; Washington, D.C. 20037 (1985), covering these subjects. *See* generally, P. Verrucoli, *Non-Profit Organizations* (A Comparative Approach), c. 1 (Milan, Italy: Giuffre 1985); Firstenberg, *Managing for Profit in a N-P World* (New York: Foundation Center, 1986).

2. Hansmann, *Rationale for Exempting Nonprofit Organizations from Corporate Income Taxation*, 91 Yale L. J. 54, 56, 59 (1981).

3. Hansmann, *Reforming Nonprofit Corporation Law*, 129 U. Pa. L. Rev. 497, 556 (1981). *See, above*, Verrucoli, n.1.

4. *Ibid.*, at 586. *See,* Hotel Dieu v. S. Williams, 410 S.2d 1111 (La. 1982); S.S. Bd. of S. Baptist Convention v. Mitchell, 658 S.W.2d 1, 5 (Mo. 1983).

5. Stern, *Conversion of Operating Charitable Enterprises from Nonprofit to For-Profit Status*, 16 J. Bev. Hills B.A. 85, 94 (1982); and see, "How Reaganomics Cuts Philanthropy," 100 *Newsweek* Mag. 42 (September 13, 1982).

6. Archdiocese of Miami v. Sama, 519 So. 2d 28 (Fla. App. 3rd Dist., 1987).

7. Reynolds v. Surf Club, 473 S. 2d 1327 (Fla. 3rd D.C. App., 1985).

8. Spring v. Geriatric Authority of Holyoke, 475 N.E.2d 727 (Mass., 1985).

9. *See* Tex. Rev. Civ. Stat. Ann. art 1396-1.02(A)(3) (Vernon 1993); Tex. Tax Code Ann. § 11.18(e) (Vernon 1993); Ga. Code Ann. §§ 14-3-140(21), 14-3-1301 (1992).

10. Marshall, *United Way Tries to Portray United Front, Los Angeles Times*, April 13, 1993, at 5. (Former UW president forced to resign after press reports made public his spending on chauffeured limos, Concord flights to Europe, a $463,000 pay package, and allegations he and his aides created several for-profit spinoff business that they used to purchase property for their personal enjoyment. Local chapters respond to public outrage by declaring their independence from the UW of American operation.)

11. E.g., 26 USCA § 501(c)(3). (Tax code definition of tax-exempt charity; referred to by many states in their nonprofit statutes.)

12. I.R.C. §§ 512(a), 513(a) (1985).

13. Rev. Ann. 93-2, 1993-2 I.R.B. 39, *Proposed Examination Guidelines Regarding Colleges and Universities*, issued December 22, 1992. (Published to invite feedback from educational organizations before final framework announced.)

14. Retail sales revenue is exempt when it results from sales related to the educational purposes of the college or university, which includes texts and items required for courses as well as "materials that further the unstructured intellectual life of the campus community." *Id.* at § 354(4).

15. Rev. Ann. 93-2, 1993-2 I.R.B. 39 at §342.32(3). It goes on to say that "university-owned real property may be nonexempt if used for noneducational purposes, such as faculty residences or operating a trade or business," an example of which would be a retail store.

16. *Northern Illinois University Foundation v. Sweet*, 603 N.E.2d 84 (Ill. App. 2d 1992).

17. *State ex. rel. Toledo Blade v. Univ. of Toledo Foundation*, 602 N.E.2d 159 (Ohio 1992).

18. Pa. Const. article 8, § 2(a)(v). "The General Assembly may by law exempt from taxation: . . . Institutions of purely public charity . . ."

19. *Hospital Utilization Project (HUP) v. Commonwealth*, 507 PA. 1, 21-22, 487 A.2d 1306, 1317 (1985).

20. *Associated YM-YWHA v. County of Wayne*, 613 A.2d 125 (Pa. Commw. Ct. 1992).

21. Note, *Harvard Forms Profit Making Company . . .*, 1 Ethics: Easier Said Than Done, 19 (Marina del Rey, CA, 1989).

22. Day, *Panel Told of Hospital Spending Abuses, The Washington Post*, April 1, 1993, at B12.

23. *Id.*

24. *Mercy Medical Center v. Dept. of Revenue*, 12 Or. Tax 305 (1992); *See* Simpson, *How Good a Samaritan? Federal Income Tax Exemption for Charitable Hospitals Reconsidered*, 14 U. Puget Sound L. Rev. 633 (1991).

25. *See also Rideout Hospital Foundation v. County of Yuba*, 8 Cal. App. 4th 214, 10 Cal. Rptr. 2d 141 (Cal. Ct. App. 3d 1992) (no set amount of earned revenue that automatically disqualifies a nonprofit hospital from property exemption; consideration is directed at how the revenue is spent).

26. *Director of Revenue v. St. John's Regional Health Center*, 779 S.W.2d 588 (Missouri 1989).

27. *Associated Press* (Report) (July 14, 1988).

28. *Lutheran General Health Care System v. Dept. of Revenue*, 231 Ill. App. 3d 652, 595 N.E.2d 1214 (Ill. App. 1st 1992).[15]

29. *Mastroianni v. Memorial Medical Center*, 606 So.2d 759 (Fla. 1st DCA 1992); *See also Lincoln Street, Inc. v. Town of Springfield*, 615 A.2d 1028 (Vt. 1992) (property owned by private individuals and leased to nonprofit organization for public or charitable use is not exempt; need concurrence of ownership and use by a nonprofit entity to qualify.)

30. 6 *Nonprofit Times*, (8) 26 (August, 1992).

31. *In re Pilcher v. Hemar Service Corp.*, 139 Bankr. 948 (D. Ariz. 1992).

32. Vellinga, *Keeping Capital's Housing Affordable, Sacramento Bee*, March 15, 1993, at C1.

33. I.R.C. §§ 512(a), 513(a) (1985). H.R. Rep. No. 2319, 81st Cong. 2d Sess. (June 1950), 1950-2 C.B. 380, 409; S. Rep. No. 2375, 81st Cong. 2d Sess. (Aug. 22, 1950) 1950-2 C.B. 483, 504.

34. *Id.*

35. Nichols, *Home Video, The New York Times*, January 14, 1993, at C-20; *See also* Maler, *MPR Hopes Idea Climbs Profit Chart: Mailorder CD Sales Revive Debate on Nonprofit Status*, Minneapolis-St. Paul City Business, January 8, 1993, at 1.

36. Robinson, *Doubt Swirls Around Proposal for Nonprofit to Buy Water Park, Business First of Buffalo*, November 30, 1992, at 10.

37. Crichton, *"Eco-Foods," Dallas Morning News*, January 20, 1993, at 1F.

38. Lenson, *Ben & Jerry's Trades on the "Spiritual" Side of the Boomers, The Boomer Report*, January 15, 1993, at 6; *See also* Mehegan, 5, *For Charity Businesses Springing Up*, 7 *Nonprofit Times* (4) 2 (April 1993).

39. James R. Hopkins, a specialist in representing nonprofit groups, provided these examples in an article.

40. L. Blumenthal (report) 2 *NonProfit Times* (2) 15 (May 1988).

41. *Lubman v. Insurance Com'r of State*, 585 A.2d 269 (Md. App. 1991).

42. *Town of Morristown v. Woman's Club of Morristown*, 592 A.2d 216 (N.J. 1991).

43. *American Soc. for Metals v. Limbach*, 569 N.E. 2d 1065 (Ohio 1991).

44. *Guide Intern. Corp. v. United States*, 948 F.2d 360 (7th Cir. (Ill.), 1991).

45. *Macklowe v. 42nd Street Development Corp.*, 566 N.Y.S. 2d 606 (N.Y.A.D. 1 Dept. 1991).

46. Kotlowitz, "Being a Landlord Is a Mixed Blessing for Chicago Church," *Wall Street Journal*, April 2, 1992, at 1, col. 5.

47. S. Koff, article, *St. Petersburg Times*, P. 1B (Dec. 19, 1990); and May 1991 news items.

48. *Jayber v. Municipal Council of Tp. of W. Orange*, 569 A. 2d 304 (N.J. Super., App. D., 1990).

49. (Study) *NCI Research* at Institute for Urban Economic Development Studies, 1800 Sherman Ave., Evanston, IL 60201 (1988).

50. *Homewood Corp. v. Kemp*, 786 F. Supp. 1315 (S.D. Ohio 1992).

51. Henn and Boyd, *Statutory Trends in the Law of Nonprofit Organizations: California Here We Come!*, 66 Cornell L. Rev. 1103, 1114 (1981).

52. Cal. Corp. Code §7111.

53.   *See*, Hansmann *supra* n. 3, at 585.

54.   Cal. Corp. Code §5059.

55.   Hansmann, supra n. 3, at 557.

56.   Marjorie Webster Jr. College v. Middle States Assn., 432 F.2d 650 (D.C. Cir., 1969), at 657; cert. den. 400 U.S. 965 (1970).

57.   *See*, Oleck, *Proprietary Mentality and the New Nonprofit Corporation Laws*, 20 Clev. St. L. Rev. 145 (1971).

58.   *E.g.*, ALI-ABA Model Bus. Corp. Act §2; N.Y. Bus. Corp. L. §102.

59.   Treas. Reg. §301.7701-2.

60.   §2(a),(b),(c). Adopted in many state statutes: Ala. Code tit. 10 §3A-2; N.M. St. Ann. §53-8-2.

61.   *See*, Henn and Alexander, *Laws of Corporations*, 44 (3rd ed., 1983).

62.   *See*, Dessant, *California Corporation Manual*, (curr. supp. ed.).

63.   N.Y. Not-for-Profit Corp. Law, §505.

64.   S.S. Bd. of S. Baptist Convention v. Mitchell, 658 S.W.2d 1, 5 (Mo., en banc, 1983); *cf.*, Hotel Dieu v. Williams, 410 S.2d 1111 (La. 1982).

65.   See the cases in n. 64, above. Jerry Rubin's Yippie "Social Education Foundation" did not qualify, as his wife was sole trustee and the foundation was used to further his private purposes. New York *Times*, December 15, 1970, at 65, cols. 2-3. *See* Ohio Children's Soc., Inc. v. Porterfield, 26 Ohio St. 2d 30, 268 N.E.2d 585 (1971). For a definition of charity, see People ex. rel. Redfern v. Hopewell Farms, 291 N.E.2d 288 (Ill. App. 1972), questioned in 367 N.E.2d 1023.

66.   *See* Oleck, *Proprietary Mentality and the New Non-Profit Corporation Laws*, 20 Clev. St. L. Rev. 145 (1971) with reference to the New York and New Jersey Statutes.

67.   N.Y. Not-for-Profit Corp. Law §513.

68.   N.Y. Not-for-Profit Corp. Law §103(a).

69.   Atwell v. Bide-a-Wee Home Ass'n., 59 Miscs. 2d 299, 321, 323 N.Y.S. 2d 40, 41 (Sup. Ct., N.Y. Cty 1969).

70.   *See* Gordon v. Baltimore, 258 Md. 682, 267 A.2d 98 (1970) cited in Langeweld v. L.R.Z.H. Corp., 130 N.J. Super. 486, 327 A.2d 683 (Super. Ct. Ch. Div. 1974); Lefkowitz v. Cornell Univ., 62 Misc. 2d 95, 308 N.Y.S. 2d 85 (Sup. Ct., Erie Cty 1970), 316 N.Y.S. 2d 264 (App. Div. 1970). As to *taxpayers' actions see*: Article, 13 Wake Forest L. Rev. 397-444 (1977) These also may be called "Citizen's Actions" or "Mandamus," etc.

71.   *E.g.*, Matthews v. Ingleside Hosp., Inc., 49 Ohio Op. 2d 382, 254 N.E.2d 923 (C.P., Cuyahoga Cty 1969).

72.   Pinsker v. Pacific Coast Soc'y of Orthodontists, 1 Cal. 3d 160, 81 Cal. Rptr. 623, 460 P.2d 495 (1969) (professional society); Grempler v. Multiple Listing Bureau, 258 Md. 419, 266 A.2d 1 (1970) (trade association), cited in Pomanowski v. Monmouth Bd., 152 N.J. Super. 100, 377 A.2d 791 (Super Ct., Ch. Div. 1977).

73.   Bell v. Carthage College, 103 Ill. App. 2d 289, 243 N.E.2d 23 (1968), cited in In re Estate of Fuller, 10 Ill. App. 3d 460, 294 N.E.2d 313 (1973).

74.   *See* Atwell v. Bid-a-Wee Home Ass'n, *supra* note 69.

75.   Mack v. Huston, 51 Ohio Op. 2d 407, 256 N.E.2d 271 (C.P., Cuyahoga Cty 1970).

76.   Prof. Oleck received a letter from an English law professor then visiting at the University of Lima, Peru. Referring to his article, *supra* note 66, the correspondent commented as follows on his cynical conclusion that at least half of all American nonprofit organizations are used for personal profit:

> I was particularly interested in your article in the January 1971 issue. I am not competent to comment in depth, on its content, but would second most whole-heartedly your conclusion at page 165, which tallies with my own experience. I was for many years with the Department of Inland Revenue. Had it not been for

the accruing tax advantages, the English Charitable Trust, would, like the Deed of Covenant, have died out long ago. In many cases, self-interest shows through to such an extent as to obscure entirely any incidental motive of a charitable nature behind the setting up of the foundation. I humbly join you in your cynicism.

77. W.F. Jarvis, *The Nonprofit Director's Fiduciary Duty: Toward a New Theory of the Nonprofit Sector*, 77 N.W. Univ. L. Rev. 34 (1982).

78. L. Moody, *The Who, What and How of the Revised Model Nonprofit Corporation Act*, p. 5, in Course Book of Seminar on *Non-Profit Organizations*; No. Ky. Univ., Chase College of Law, (Feb. 1988).

79. Malone, McE. & C., *The Buck Trust Trial*, 21 *W. San Fran. L. Rev.* (4) 585, a 639 (1987); In re Estate of Buck, #23259 (Jan. 23, 1986) Cal. Super. Ct., Marin County; in Symposium on NPO's, 21 *U. San Fran. L. Rev.* (4) 585–762 (1987).

80. Surf Club v. Long, 325 S. 2d 66 (Fla. DCA 1975).

81. Incardi v. National Equipment Rental, Inc. 378 S. 2d 113 (Fla. DCA 1980).

82. Fla. Stat. §§ 618.221, 617.1101, 617.1805.

83. *See*, for example, O'Malley article on Walt Disney World, in *New Times* magazine 40-49 (October 16, 1978), and the New York and Pennsylvania statutes, capped by the California statute that took effect in 1980. Or, the report of the granting of nonprofit status to *Ms. Magazine* in 1980; *Los Angeles Times* report in *St. Petersburg* (Fla.) *Times*, p. 4D (January 30, 1980).

84. Ohio Rev. Code, tit. 17; with ch. 1702 as the nonprofit organizations chapter, and then many specific chapters as shown above.

85. Me. Nonprofit Corp. Act, tit. 13-B.

86. Nev. Rev. Code, cc.81-86.

87. Del. Code, tit. 8, §§101-398.

88. See *Fla. Stat.* §§617.0830 et seq. (eff. July 1, 1991).

89. I.R.C. §501(c)(3) and 26 C.F.R. §1.501(c)(3)-1 specify the organizational and operational tests for determining the tax exempt status of a nonprofit organization.

90. *See* DESIDERIO & TAYLOR, PLANNING TAX-EXEMPT ORGANIZATIONS (1983); GREER, EXEMPT ORGANIZATIONS: EXEMPTION REQUIREMENTS (1984); GODFREY, HANDBOOK ON TAX-EXEMPT ORGANIZATIONS (1983); HOPKINS, LAW OF TAX EXEMPT ORGANIZATIONS (4th ed. 1983); LASHBROOKE, TAX EXEMPT ORGANIZATIONS (1985); NICHOLAS, NONPROFIT TAX-EXEMPT ORGANIZATIONS (rev. ed., 1983); Tax-Exempt Org. (P-H, current issue); Treusch & Sugarman, Tax-Exempt Organizations (ALI-ABA, 1983).

91. Morton Temple Ass'n v. Dep't of Revenue, 158 Ill. App. 3d 794, 511 N.E.2d 892 (1987). *See also*, Lutheran Child & Family Serv. v. Dep't of Revenue, 7 Ill. App. 3d 420, 513 N.E.2d 587 (1987) (building used for residence).

92. Grady v. Hausman, 509 So. 2d 1316 (Fla. Dist. Ct. App. 1987).

93. For example, the Florida statute says "as used in this section, section references, unless otherwise indicated, shall refer to the Internal Revenue Code of 1954, Title 26 of the United States Code, as in effect on December 16, 1971, including corresponding provisions of any subsequent federal tax laws." FLA. STAT. ANN. §617.105 (West 1988). Other states which refer to the Code include Alabama, Alaska, Arkansas, California, Kentucky, Louisiana, Minnesota, New Mexico, North Carolina, Ohio, Oklahoma, Rhode Island, Tennessee and Texas.

94. REVISED MODEL NONPROFIT CORPORATION ACT §14.06(a)(6) (1987).

95. Benedictine Sisters of the Sacred Heart v. Dep't of Revenue, 155 Ill. App. 3d 325, 508 N.E.2d 470 (1987); *See also* Le Sea Broadcasting Corp. v. State Bd. of Tax Comm'rs, 525 N.E.2d 637 (Ind. Tax Ct. 1988); Community Christian Church, Inc. v. State Bd. of Tax Comm'rs, 523 N.E.2d 462 (Ind. 1988); Baptist Health Care Corp. v. Okmulgee County Bd. of Equalization, 750 P.2d 127 (Okla. 1988); Illinois Conference of the United Church of Christ v. Ill. Dep't of Revenue, 165 Ill. App. 3d 200, 518 N.E.2d 755 (1988).

96. ARIZ. REV. STAT. ANN. §43-308 (1980); CAL. REV. & TAX CODE §17071 (West 1988); COLO. REV. STAT. §39-22-104 (1987); DEL. CODE ANN. tit. 30 §1105 (1985); D.C. CODE ANN. §47-1803.2 (1988); GA. CODE ANN. §48-7-27 (1988); HAW. REV. STAT. §235-1 (1987); IDAHO CODE §63-3002 (1987); IND. CODE ANN. §6-3-1-3.5 (West 1988); IOWA CODE ANN. §422-7 (West 1988); KAN. STAT. ANN. §79-32, 117 (1987); KY. REV. STAT. ANN. §141.010 (Michie/Bobbs-Merrill 1988); ME. REV. STAT. ANN. tit. 36, §5102 (1987); MD. ANN. CODE art. 81, §280 (1987); MASS. ANN. LAWS ch. 62, §2 (Law. Co-op. 1988); MICH. COMP. LAWS ANN. §206.12 (West 1988); MINN. STAT. ANN. §290.01 (West 1988); MONT. CODE ANN. §15-30-111 (1987); NEB. REV. STAT. §77-2715 (1986); N.D. CENT. CODE §57-38-01 (1987); OHIO REV. CODE ANN. §5747.01 (Anderson 1987); OKLA. STAT. ANN. tit. 68, §2353 (West 1988); OR. REV. STAT. §316.013 (1987); I.R. GEN. LAWS §44-30-2 (1980); S.C. CODE ANN. §12-7-1510 (Law Co-op 1987); UTAH CODE ANN. §59-10-11 (1987); VT. STAT. ANN. tit. 32, §5811 (1988); VA. CODE ANN. §58.1-322 (1988); W. VA. CODE §11-21-12 (1988).

97. I.R.C. §63 (1988).

98. *See* I.R.S. Notice 87-18, I.R.B. 1984, 29 instructions.

99. 1976 Pub. L. No. 94-455 §§1307(d)(1)(a), 1313(a); and I.R.C. §501(j) (1988); Pub. L. No. 97-248 §286(a).

100. Rev. Rul. 69-174, 1969-1 CB 149.

101. *See* Gershon, *Tax-Exempt Entities; Achieving and Maintaining Special Status Under the Watchful Eye of the Internal Revenue Service,* 16 CUMB. L. REV. 301 (1985–86).

102. I.R.C. §503(b) (1988).

103. I.R.C. §4941(a) (Supp. 1986). A tax is imposed on self-dealing transactions. *See id.* at §§507(d), 4946(a)(1)–(2) & 4942.

104. B. HOPKINS, THE LAW OF TAX EXEMPT ORGANIZATIONS 855–860 (5th ed. 1987). *See generally* I.R.C. §§6033, 6034, 6051(g)(2) (Supp. 1986) (annual information for returns); I.R.C. §6050 (charitable transfers); I.R.C. §6056 (annual private foundation reports); I.R.C. 6072(e) (filing time); I.R.C. §7701 (a)(3) (definition of nonprofit corporation for tax law purposes); I.R.C. §7701 (classification as a nonprofit corporation); I.R.C. §4946 (A)(1)(B), (b)(1) (regulation of managers on nonprofits).

105. *See* Hospital Utilization Project v. Pennsylvania, 507 Pa. 1, 487 A.2d 1306 (1985).

106. See, e.g., OHIO REV. CODE ANN. § 5733.01 (Baldwin 1988).

107. See, e.g., 72 PA. CONS. STAT. §7401 (1988).

108. See, e.g., N.Y. TAX LAW §§1105, 1116 (McKinney 1987).

109. See, e.g., OHIO REV. CODE ANN. §5739.02 (Baldwin 1988).

110. See, e.g., FLA. STAT. ANN. ch. 196 (West Supp. 1988).

111. See, e.g., Benedictine Sisters of the Sacred Heart v. Dep't of Revenue, 155 Ill. App. 3d 325, 508 N.E.2d 470 (1987).

112. See, e.g., Wheaton College v. Dep't of Revenue, 115 Ill. App. 3d 945, 508 N.E.2d 1136 (1987).

113. See, e.g., Skycrest Baptist Church case (Fla. 2d Dist., June 19, 1987). But the county property appraiser was appealing the case, lest it "open the floodgates" of tax exemption of profit organizations and owners.

114. N.Y. Laws 1969, c. 1066; ch. 35 of N.Y. Consol. Laws. It is less specific than Ohio's chapters.

115. N.Y. Coop. Corp. L.

116. C.29 of N.Y. Consol. L.

117. Ohio Rev. Code, c. 1745.

118. *N.Y. Not-for-Profit Corp. Law* §§101-1515. Henn and Boyd, *Statutory Trends in the Law of Nonprofit Organizations: California, Here We Come,* 66 Cornell L. Rev. 1103 (1981).

119. N.Y. N-PCL at §201(b).

120. Oleck, *Proprietary Non-Profit Corporations,* 20 Clev. St. L. Rev. 145 (1971).

121. N.Y. N-PCL at §720.

122. *Id.* at §404(a).

123. Joint Legislative Committee to Study Revision of Corporation Laws, Explanatory Memoranda on Not-for-Profit Corporation Law XV (McKinney) in N.Y. N-PCL.

124. Henn and Boyd, *supra* n. 118, at 1120.

125. N-PCL, §504(b).

126. *Id.* at §504(d).

127. *Id.* at §504(e) and (f).

128. *Id.* at §601.

129. *Id.* at §608.

130. *N.Y. Memb. Corp. Law §20 (repealed 1971). It required a quorum of one-third of membership. The N-PCL reduces this to "the members entitled to cast one hundred votes or one-tenth of the total number of votes entitled to be cost, whichever is lesser." N-PCL, §608(a).*

131. N-PCL, §623.

132. Id. at §701(b).

133. *Id.* at §717(a).

134. Vernon's Rev. Civ. Stat. of Tex., Anno., c. 9, tit. 32, at. 1396.

135. *Id.* §2.01.

136. *Id.* §4.02.

137. *Id.* §2.08(A) and (B).

138. *Id.* at §2.11.

139. *Id.* at §2.12(A). In §2.12(B), applicable to churches states that "members present at a meeting, notice for which shall have been duly given, shall constitute a quorum."

140. *Id.* §2.17(D).

141. *Id.* §2.15.

142. *Id.* §9.01.

143. *Id.* at 2.23(A). The periodic report sets forth (1) the name and state of incorporation, (2) address of registered office and name of registered agent, and address of principal office of foreign corporation, and (31) names and addresses of directors and officers.

144. Cal. Corp. Code §§5000-10,846.

145. *Id.* §5059.

146. *Id.* §5060.

147. *Id.* §5061.

148. *Id.* §5230.

149. *Id.* §5212.

150. *Id.* §5233.

151. *Id.* §5227. This states that 49 percent or less of board may be interested persons and defines "interested persons" to "include directors compensated by the corporation for full or part-time services rendered during the previous twelve months, and their relatives." The ABA 1987 Revised Model Nonprofit Corporation Act adopted this extraordinary legislation of conflicts of interests.

152. *Id.* §5250.

153. *Id.* §5510(b).

154. *Id.* §5510(e).

155. *Id.* §5511(d).

156. *Id.* §5710.

157. *Id.* §7710.

158. Mich. Comp. Laws Act §450.2101 *et. seq.*; 1982 P.A. 162.

159. *Id.* §103(a) and (b).

160. *Id.* §301(3).

161. Darlow, *Michigan Nonprofit Corporations*, 62 Mich. B.J. 530 (1983).

162. Act 162, §§202, 302.

163. Darlow, *supra* note 161 at 533.

164. Act 162, §303(3).

165. *Id.* §305(1).

166. Darlow, *supra* n. 161, at 533.

167. Act 162, §541. This provides for duties discharged "in good faith and with that degree of diligence, care and skill which an ordinarily prudent person would exercise under similar circumstances in a like position."

168. Smith v. Van Gorkom, 488 A.2d 858 (Del. 1985); *cf.*, Henn and Alexander, *Laws of Corporations*, 3rd ed., §242 (1983) as to "business judgment" rule.

4

SPECIAL-TYPE
ORGANIZATIONS

§25. CLASSIFICATIONS, GENERALLY

Classification of a nonprofit organization has directly important results. This is generally true in that the classification indicates the nature of an organization and the treatment of it by public authorities.

Once a given organization has been classified under its state's statutory system, it almost automatically becomes subject to specific statutes in the main nonprofit chapter or chapters, and also to related statutes which usually are either suggested or specified in the main statute. Thus the *classification of an organization often determines how it must be operated, or dissolved, what supervision it may expect from the public authorities, and so forth.*

For example, considering only some of the special types of corporations, other than business (stock) corporations, the following governing statutes are found to apply:

Agricultural and horticultural corporation (such as cooperatives or county-fair organizations) must be formed under specific agricultural corporations statutes in some states,[1] and under the general nonprofit statutes in others.[2]

Clubs must be formed under general nonprofit statues if they are to be incorporated.[3] Business organizations using the word "club" (*e.g.,* Silver Slipper Supper Club) must be organized under business corporation statutes.

Churches involve much constitutional law privilege, and must be formed under religious or church corporation statutes.[4]

Educational organizations may be formed under the educational corporations statutes if they are to be nonprofit,[5] and under the business corporation statutes otherwise.[6] In either case, the statutes usually require compliance with the education laws as to academic standards, facilities, instruction, reports, and the like. Classification may result in supervision by the State Board of Regents, for colleges, for example.

Condominiums and *other cooperatives* may be formed under either nonprofit or business cooperative statutes, depending on which type is desired, in many states.[7]

Farmers' associations may be formed as cooperatives, as stated above about agricultural and horticultural corporations,[8] or under farm laborers' statutes in some states, depending on their composition and purposes.

Fraternal benefit societies and mutual indemnity organizations are subject to state insurance statutes in most states, and also to benevolent society statutes, both types of statutes being applicable to their organization.

Credit unions (special quasi-nonprofit organizations) must be formed under credit union statutes in some states, and under banking laws in the absence of special statutes.[9]

Medical indemnity plan groups (such as the Blue Cross) are formed under the insurance statutes in many states, and under special medical care or hospital service statutes in some states.[10]

Savings and loan associations must be formed under banking laws, which often have special savings and loan provisions.

Municipal corporations must be formed under village, town, or city corporation statutes (whichever is appropriate), depending primarily on population. *District corporations,* such as school, road, or water districts, also must be organized under special statutes in most states.

Urban development corporations now have various statutes to help them.[11]

Foundations must be organized under charitable corporations statutes in most states, if they are to be incorporated, or under charitable trust law if not to be incorporated. Some states also have *charitable trust* corporation statutes.[12]

Trade Associations must be organized under special trade association statutes in some states,[13] and under the general nonprofit statutes in others. There is little point in attempting to itemize every conceivable type of organization and every applicable statute. The foregoing examples should indicate the nature of modern legislation on this subject.

Use Key Words: Language itself is the main classification key, of course. If an organization is to be called *Whist Club of Chicago,* it sounds like, and prima facie is, a social club. If it is called *Ridgeville P.T.A.,* it presumably is a para educational organization. And if it is to be named *Diabetes Sufferers Relief Foundation,* it patently seems to be a charitable organization. The applicable statutes that govern then should not be hard to decide in such cases.

Purpose as the Ultimate Test

If a name is noncommittal sounding, the purpose of the organization as stated in its articles of incorporation, bylaws, or constitution, probably is determinative; especially if the actual operation of the organization is already sufficient to indicate its real purpose.

Purpose will override the seeming import of a name or descriptive term, of course, in determining the proper classification of an organization.

For example, in one case in Texas, a nonprofit country club's officers filed a "statement" required by statute, in connection with a requirement of the state's Business Corporation Act, that a statement be filed regarding an annual report for franchise tax purposes. The filing of the form seemed to indicate that this was a profit type corporation by its own admission. But the filing was held to be not sufficient to determine the corporation's status. It was a nonprofit country club in actual purpose (and operation), and the underlying purpose was not changed by the mere filing of a form that seemed to be required by law.[14]

§26. NONPROFIT ORGANIZATIONS AS "PUBLIC"

Public Purpose

A nonprofit organization will be subject to Open Public Meetings Acts and Open Records Acts if the court deems the organization to be a "public body," a "public agency," or a "public office." Open Public Meeting Acts apply to all matters of substantial importance to the general public in the state. The quasi-judicial exception to the Act applies only where (1) the court could have been charged with making the agency decision (2) the action is one historically performed by courts (3) the action involves application of the law to past or present facts to determine or enforce liability or (4) the action resembles the ordinary business of courts rather than that of legislators or administrators.[15]

For example, a nonprofit corporation that leases property in excess of $1,500,00 to the Pennsylvania Commonwealth is deemed to be an agency for purposes of the Pennsylvania Sunshine Act and Right to Know Law. Such statutes are constitutional and are rationally related to the state's need to monitor the soundness of the corporation's business to assure rental space for government operations.[16]

The Washington state Open Public Meeting Acts (OPMA) do not apply to public agencies of the State of Washington when decision-making authority is placed in an individual director, and not in a multimember body. The Acts also do not apply if the agency is not a "governing body."[17]

A state *Public Records Act* allows inspection of private NPC records when the nonprofit is organized to foster a *public* (university) *interests* and collaborates in performance of the university's functions; it too is a "public body" then.[18]

A private nonprofit foundation is a "public office," for purposes of public records disclosure requirements if it acts as a major gift-receiving and soliciting arm of a public university that receives support from public taxation. Such a foundation can be compelled to disclose the names of donors.[19] A state university foundation is a "public agency" for the purposes of an Open Records Act.[20]

Advocacy Societies [*See: Lobbying*]

Many nonprofit organizations are started in order to advocate a political opinion or agenda, or to protect the rights of a particular class of people. For example, nonprofit corporations can be formed to advocate and protect the rights of the mentally ill pursuant to 42 U.S.C. § 10801, *et seq.* One such society, the Advocacy Center for People With Disabilities, was not required to exhaust all of its administrative remedies prior to bringing a civil rights action because the hearing officer lacked jurisdiction to hear the society's constitutional claims and therefore could not grant appropriate remedies.[21] Another court, considering a handicap advocacy case, held that under the Handicapped Access Law, an enforcing agency may grant zoning exceptions in cases of practical difficulty, where it is clearly evident that equivalent facilitation and protection of the physically handicapped remain intact. Exceptions for floors or spaces containing mechanical equipment and for alteration of historic buildings are invalid.[22]

Many pro-choice (abortion) advocacy groups have organized to challenge state and federal laws restricting the government funding of abortions. A Michigan court has ruled that its state statute, that prohibits the public funding of abortions unless the abortion is necessary to save the mother's life, is constitutional under equal protection analysis.[23]

Organizations are often formed by communities when they are faced with governmental action of which they disapprove. For example, a coalition of parents of school children was recently told by the court that a writ of certiorari, rather than a declaratory judgment action, is the proper procedure for a nonprofit coalition of parents to challenge a school board's decision to realign the attendance areas for school children.[24]

As refugees continue to flee to the United States, advocacy groups representing their interests are becoming more common. The Haitian Refugee Center, in Florida, challenged former President Bush's executive order allowing interdiction of refugees and their subsequent forced repatriation back to Haiti. However, the court held that Haitian refugees have no right to judicial review, under the Administrative Procedure Act, of their repatriation back to Haiti if they are interdicted on the high seas and have never presented themselves at a U.S. border. Further, a refugee center has no first Amendment right of access to the aliens. An executive order to interdict the aliens gives them no private right of action for improper return.[25] The President upheld this view in 1993.

Legal Aid Societies

Legal aid societies are being formed in increasing numbers to represent the rights of those unable to afford counsel. When a legal aid society challenged the constitutionality of a magnetometer center for weapons for people trying to enter family court, the court held that such a search is reasonable under the Fourth Amendment.[26]

A legal aid attorney, who was employed by a nonprofit corporation that was funded by the city and county at public expense, is the equivalent of appointed counsel. The defendant has no right to substitute appointed counsel on the day of trial after asserting that certain motions were not filed.[27]

Volunteer Fire Department

Volunteer fire departments, organized by the communities they serve, are frequently faced with financial and liability issues. A volunteer fire department's assets and obligations are those of a *Charitable Trust*, and subject to rules as to use of assets, cy pres doctrine applicability, etc. District residents may sue to prevent sale of its assets that would deprive them of fire protection.[28]

Adoption Organizations

Adoption organizations are facing increased litigation over the rights of their clients, adoptive parents and adopted children. A foster parent has no constitutionally protected liberty interest in a foster child, despite their long-term relationship and assurances of adoption by the state, where the natural parents never fully lost their paternal rights.[29]

Savings and Loan Associations

A state-charted subsidiary service corporation of a federal savings association is subject to state regulation (as well as federal) insofar as the state regulation does not conflict with the federal.[30] The FSLIC does not have exclusive powers of adjudication over creditors of insolvent savings and loan associations. If its administrative procedures are inadequate (e.g., as to foreclosure of a mechanic's lien), a claimant is not obliged to exhaust those procedures before bringing action in the state courts.[31]

Environmental Societies

Environmental societies usually form in order to pool the resources of individuals to enable them to challenge governmental and private action that threatens environmental concerns. Environmental groups often face the obstacle of obtaining standing to sue. Citizen suits, however, are authorized by some environmental statutes. A Massachusetts environmental society brought a citizen's suit against their town, alleging that the town discharged pollutants from its water treatment facility in violation of the federal Clean Water Act. The Clean Water Act bars citizen suits where "comparable action" has been initiated by the state. The court found that an administrative order issued by the state was "diligent prosecution" by the state. Thus, the citizen's suit was barred.[32]

Environmental organizations frequently bring suit to demand environmental impact reports or to challenge governmental permitting decisions. A decision by the Secretary of Commerce to set limits on pollock fishing in the Gulf of Alaska, without requiring an environmental impact statement, is not arbitrary and capricious if the agency took a hard look at the environmental consequences, the court carefully reviewed the record for the agency's reasoned evaluation of relevant factors, and the agency's inquiry into the facts is searching and careful.[33]

A trial court may set aside approval of a development project, pending preparation of an additional environmental impact report, if a proposed site-specific project might cause significant adverse effects on the environment that were not examined in a prior more general environmental impact report.[34]

When a nonprofit defense fund sued to prevent construction and operation of geothermal wells in Hawaii, the court held that the Department of Health (DOH) had violated the requirements of the Hawaii Administrative Procedure Act when it imposed special conditions, limiting the emission of sulfide into the air, as a condition of the permit. The emission limits were ambient air quality standards that could be adopted only after proper notice and hearing rules. Thus, the DOH had to refuse issuance of the permit.[35]

A nonprofit environmental group brought action to force a National Pollutant Discharge Elimination System (NPDES) permittee to pay penalties for violation of its discharge permit limitations. Violation of the monthly limitations is a daily violation for each day of the month, for purposes of a penalty calculation.[36]

Environmental societies recently challenged the United States Forest Service to stop the motorized portaging of canoes between lakes in Minnesota. Such portaging is now allowed only where no "feasible" means of transportation exists. Three person carry teams are "feasible."[37]

Credit Unions

[James D. Wood and Michael E. Ciochina contributed the material in the following subsection.]

A credit union is not a private corporation for profit but is a cooperative nonprofit association, organized under special statutory provisions for the purposes of encouraging thrift among its members, creating sources of credit at fair and reasonable rates of interest, and providing an opportunity for its members to use and control their resources on a democratic basis in order to improve their economic and social condition.[38]

In the early thirties the overall purchasing power of working-class Americans was reducing at an astounding rate. Much of this may have been attributable to the stock market crash. However, many believed our purchasing power was diminishing because the majority of working Americans could not obtain credit at reasonable rates. In the midst of the Great Depression most working Americans did not have the necessary security to obtain loans from the banks so they had to turn to loan sharks who usually charged usurious interest rates.

Congress saw the solution to this problem in a system of federal credit unions that would provide credit at reasonable rates and thus would help spur economic recovery. Therefore, in 1934 Congress passed the Federal Credit Union Association (FCUA) to help the working class obtain credit. S. Rep. No. 555, 73d Cong., 2d Sess. 3 (1934). The supervision and chartering control was given to the Board of the National Credit Union Administration (NCUA), a three-member panel appointed by the President upon the advice and consent of the Senate. 12 U.S.C. §§ 1752a, 1754, 1756. The NCUA promulgates the rules and regulations that govern credit unions.

For example, credit union loans to members were limited, to prevent risky business investments and loans, by amendment of the rules by the National Credit Union Administration (NCUA) Board, effective Jan. 1, 1992, by FR48421 (No. 186) in 1991, to provide guidance to credit union officials.[39]

The National Credit Union Administration began (with the Dec. 31, 1990 reporting cycle) releasing nonrestricted credit union data to the U.S. Department of Commerce, National Technical Information Service (NTIS). Now, under the Freedom of Information Act, the NTIS may give information to those requesting it, about financial, historical and statistical data and lists of credit unions and other matters concerning credit unions.[40]

Contrary to the desires of the credit union industry the NCUA voted on March 25, 1993, to issue for comment a proposed regulation that would require an annual opinion audit by a certified public accountant for all of its federally insured institutions with more than $50 million in assets.

Currently, only the credit unions that are experiencing financial difficulties or those with serious record-keeping problems are required to obtain a certified public accountant opinion audit.

Under the FDICIA, banks and thrifts with more than $150 million in assets will be required to obtain an annual opinion audit. This law will apply to approximately 2,300 banks and 850 thrifts.

For credit unions, this annual requirement would apply to approximately 29 percent of all federally insured credit unions, which would affect about 3,680 credit unions. The NCUA is recommending that the smaller credit unions also obtain an annual CPA audit.[41]

The Federal Financial Institutions Examination Council consists of representatives of the Federal Reserve Board, the Federal Deposit Insurance Corp., the National Credit Union Administration, the Office of the Comptroller of the Currency, and the Office of Thrift supervision. The council's main goals was to draft uniform examination standards for all give of the Federal Financial Institutions. Needless to say, the council has failed to live up to its expectations.

William M. Isaac, the FDIC chairman from 1981 to 1985, said that the overall objective of the council was just not practical. He said that each of the five agencies has its own agenda, and they are all coming from a different direction.

In 1992, the NCUA became so frustrated with the council that it decided not to follow the council's slow pace and drafted its own statement on how financial institutions should treat securities for accounting purposes. The NCUA had its statement on securities in place even before the council issued a statement describing the issues to be considered.[42]

Unlike banks, credit unions do not receive "deposits" creating a debtor/credit relationship. Instead credit union "shares" are part of the capital stock of the credit union. The shares become liens against any outstanding loans.[43]

A credit union's equitable security interest in a joint passbook savings account by making a loan to one of the joint owners of the account is not wiped out by the death of the joint owner who borrowed the loan.[44]

Credit unions (CU) rates and services drew customers to them (and away from commercial banks) in 1991, because they offered to members better deals than banks and savings and loan organizations. Thus a CD one year rate at a CU was 6.54 percent, at a bank was 6.12 percent and at a S.& L. was 6.41 percent, while the new car loan rate was 10.15 percent against 11.8 percent and 11.94 present. The nonprofit (tax exempt) nature of the CUs is the chief advantage, plus volunteer staff and often free buildings.[45]

In 1992, credit unions were growing at double-digit rates and usually offered higher savings rates, lower loan rates, and the lowest service fees, while offering expanded services such as checking accounts, ATM privileges and home mortgages. This, while Florida Savings & Loans were having many losses and failures, for example; and most CUs in that state have obtained federal insurance though some remain privately indexed. Nationwide there were 12,763 CUs. Tampa-based Suncoast Schools Federal Credit Union, for example, had 129,000 customers/members and $769 million in assets.[46]

The banking industry, citing unfair competition, has repeatedly challenged the expansion of credit unions as well as the tax exemption privilege afforded to credit unions. The FCUA has a requirement that membership in federal credit unions be limited to "groups having a common bond of occupation or association." 12 U.S.C. § 1759. In 1991, when the NCUA allowed AT&T Family Federal Credit Union to expand its field of membership, the First National Bank and Trust Company and many other banks challenged the ruling by the NCUA. The banks stated that allowing AT&T Family Federal Credit Union to expand its membership base violates the "common bond of occupation or association" requirement set out in 12. U.S.C. § 1759. The banks also stated that it would be an unfair advantage to the credit union if they were allowed to expand without meeting the requirement set out in 12 U.S.C § 1759. However, on the ninth day of August, 1991, the United States District Court, District of Columbia, held that the banks could not challenge the NCUA's ruling because they lacked "prudential standing."[47]

In the appeal the banks realleged that when the NCUA approved the amendments, it acted arbitrarily and capriciously and violated the statutory requirement under the Federal Credit Union Act, 12 U.S.C. § 1751; the common bond of occupation or association requirement. The appeal was argued in front of the United States Court of Appeals, District of Columbia Circuit, on November 16, 1992, and on April 2, 1993, the court found that even though the appellants were not the intended beneficiaries of the FCUA, they are suitable challengers because the statute arguably prohibits the unfair competition of which the banks complained.[48]

In 1992, credit union officials were stunned by a Bush Administration budget proposal that would repeal their institutions' coveted tax-exempt status. The proposal would have applied to credit unions with more than $50 million in assets. However, the credit union industry's lobbyists prevailed over the bank sponsored proposal.[49]

Because credit unions enjoy nonprofit status, student loans made by them are not dischargeable in bankruptcy.[50]

Credit unions with assets in the $15-million to $50-million range have had Electronic Funds Transfer (EFT) services for quite some time. However, the smaller credit unions with assets in the $5-million to $7-million range didn't even know how to spell debit card according to James Stewart, Dallas-based Affiliated Computer Systems Inc. (ACS) vice president.

ACS has developed a turnkey program for credit unions with less than $10 million in assets. However, ACS is not the only one who has been working on minimizing the cost of EFT systems. The Credit Union National Association has been developing a national EFT network in hopes that it will lower the costs of exchanging EFT transactions between regions.

Florida-based Credit Union 24 stated that because the network will allow them to contract for services as a group they should have greater bargaining power with third-party processors. David Pace, vice president of Credit Union 24, said that the network will be able to offer a service that the third-party processors can't; interstate ATM deposits. He also noted that credit unions will like the fact that the 45-cent interchange fees will go back to the credit union system rather than to their competitors.[51]

Political Purpose

Nonprofit groups that wish to influence legislation are forming in increasing numbers. These groups can often control legislation through petitions and initiatives.

When a nonprofit organization, seeking enactment of a "toxic chemical right to know" law, filed petitions with the Secretary of State, the petitions were challenged in order to compel the Secretary to reject them. The court held that the Secretary has no clear duty to ascertain whether the petitions are properly verified. The Secretary can certify the petitions to the General Assembly as soon as it convenes.[52]

A nonprofit citizens group tried to force a city council to place on the ballot an initiative to repeal nondiscrimination ordinances against homosexuals and HIV victims, and to require future similar ordinances to be submitted to voters. The court held that the initiative was unconstitutionally vague in its prohibition of future ordinance promotion and was an invalid attempt to amend the city's charter by deleting substantial city council powers.[53]

A nonprofit organization, that collects 12,500 signatures on a petition, in support of a proposed county charter amendment, cannot unilaterally decide not to file the petition. When the petition is complete the circulators must fulfill their promise, file the petition, and submit the amendment to the voters.[54]

A group of nonprofit organizations failed to prevent a Governor from placing an initiative, for budget and welfare reform, on the ballot. The initiative was held to be valid because it did not violate the single subject rule, was not overly broad, and the individual provisions were "reasonably germane" to the initiative's stated purpose.

Protection of Agricultural Producers

In our global economy, associations of agricultural producers are facing increasing problems in the areas of international trade. Regulations are multiplying and often conflict. For example, one association found that a regulation, providing that foreign poultry be subject to inspection standards "at least equal to" those imposed on American poultry, violates a statutes that requires foreign poultry inspection to be "the same as" the American standard.[56]

The Agricultural Fair Practices Act protects individual producers from interference by processors and protects the producers from coercion by associations of producers. A Michigan nonprofit cooperative agricultural association brought action to enjoin a milk broker from interfering with milk marketing agreements between the cooperative and its members. The court held that even if standing was conferred by the Agricultural Fair Practices Act, the cooperative's motion for preliminary injunction was rightly denied because the cooperative would not suffer "irreparable harm" as required under federal law.[57]

§27. SPECIAL CLASSIFICATION CHOICE

When organizing a nonprofit corporation or association it is not enough to decide merely to form a public benefit rather than a mutual benefit organization. The organizers must select a specific type of organization category, and then employ the statutes and other rules applicable to *that type* of organization. For example, a mutual benefit *residence* project should look to the law of *condominiums*, or of *redevelopment corporations*, depending on whether they plan a single-center project or an urban-area project. Thus, too, a religious group may be concerned about organizing a specific denomination church; this would lead to very specific statutes in some states whose statutes provide express guidance for Baptists, Methodists, Catholics, et cetera. Contrariwise, a "church" or a "school" may be intended for very different purposes. For example, in 1970, atheist Madelyn Murray O'Haire, well-known for her opposition to all religion, said in Austin, Texas, that she and her husband, Richard, had organized the "Poor Richard's . . . Church" for tax evasion purposes.

Among the special types covered by various state systems, for example, are cemetery corporations,[58] fire associations,[59] organizations for prevention of cruelty,[60] Christian associations,[61] soldiers' monument corporations,[62] professional societies (*e.g.*, medical),[63] alumni associations,[64] historical societies,[65] agricultural and horticultural societies,[66] boards of trade and chambers of commerce,[67] and others.

Ohio's provisions include all these, and more (see the list in Section 20). In addition, it contains such highly specialized enactments as those for corporations organized to maintain lodge hall or chapel or scientific buildings,[68] to care for dead bodies,[69] aged or indigent women,[70] deaf and dumb persons,[71] battlefield and memorial sites,[72] historic sites,[73] or museums or parks.[74] Ohio's statutes also now contain the Uniform Management of Institutional Funds law.

California since 1980 has three major categories under which nonprofit corporations may be organized: mutual benefit corporations,[75] public benefit corporations,[76] and religious corporations.[77] All nonprofit corporations are subject to the control of one of these statutes.[78] In addition to these large categories, California has specific statutes, as do most other states, which regulate special organizations and corporations. Several states, Delaware chief among them, have not yet succeeded in organizing their law of nonprofit corporations and associations in a system which can be easily recognized or researched. California has statutes concerning nonprofit corporations in such various volumes as their Finance Code, Corporations Code, Business and Professions Code, Revenue and Taxation Code, Government Code, and the Pregnancy Freedom of Choice Act of the Welfare and Institutions Code, to name only a few. A person interested in researching nonprofit corporations law often finds his or her way tediously and painstakingly through such legislative quagmires as exist in many states.

Persons interested in special types of nonprofit corporations are encouraged to research state law as it relates to nonprofit corporations generally first, and then proceed to research state law using the generic names of activities which the organization will be engaged in (*e.g.*, "agricultural shows," "cemetery associations"). Particular attention should, of course, be paid to licensing and registration requirements. These precautionary steps need to be taken for every state the proposed nonprofit organization may be operating in.

Texas, for example, has special sections dealing with eye banks, business development corporations, cooperatives, health organizations, and legal service nonprofit corporations.[79]

Florida's statutes include fraternal benefit societies, warranty associations (auto, home, and service), professional service plans (optometry and pharmaceutical), health care (hospital, medical, health maintenance), legal expense insurance (service corporations), automobile clubs, credit unions, etc.[80] Missouri's statutes are quite technical.[81]

The following sections highlight some general areas dealing with special nonprofit organization law.

[Rashmika A. Mehta drafted some of the material on Agricultural, Fraternal, Cemetery, Community, and Religious organizations. Jerry Oliver checked many citations.]

§28. AGRICULTURAL ORGANIZATIONS

Most states have fairly detailed provisions for county agricultural societies. Ohio's statute, for example, is quite lengthy, and shows a large number of case decisions interpreting the various sections of this chapter.[82]

State and county support of agricultural organizations, such as reimbursement for junior club work,[83] or provision of county fair land and buildings,[84] or financial grants for agricultural fairs,[85] are not uncommon.[86] The purpose of these organizations is to encourage the advancement of agricultural interests by promoting educational programs, to provide needed information to farmers, and to organize county fairs to promote agricultural activities.[87]

The number of persons or groups required to form an agricultural society varies; Florida requires three,[88] whereas Ohio requires five.[89] Where an agricultural society has been properly formed, and its purpose is to benefit the interests of agriculture and livestock raising, a member will not be held personally liable for any claims against the society.[90]

In some jurisdictions, the courts view such societies as agents working for the state, for the purpose of promoting and developing agriculture.[91] The Tennessee Supreme Court held that even though the agricultural association was receiving state appropriation of nearly ten thousand dollars per year, the organization still qualified as a private corporation.[92] Where the state has not imposed any of its agents upon the board of directors the corporation is free to act as any private corporation and to direct its own affairs.[93] Agricultural societies are liable in tort for injuries sustained by a guest on a fairground operated by the society.[94]

Public fairs are often associated with agricultural associations. These fairs educate the public about agricultural technology.[95]

Unlike the public benefit aspect of agricultural societies, agricultural marketing-cooperative associations serve primarily to benefit their members. These associations are formed for the purpose of "economically, effectively and equitably distributing and marketing" agricultural products.[96] The Florida Supreme Court said that the purpose of these associations is (1) to promote, foster and encourage the intelligent and orderly marketing of agricultural products through cooperation; (2) to eliminate speculation and waste in such marketing; (3) to distribute agricultural products between producer and consumer as efficiently and directly as possible; and (4) to stabilize the marketing of agricultural products.[97] Agricultural marketing associations provide certain benefits to the members individually at a lower cost than the individual could obtain them without the association's aid.[98]

A unique feature of Florida's statutory treatment of these organizations is that members have the right to receive an 8 percent dividend on common and preferred stock.[99] One may question the nonprofit status of an association that distributes dividends to its members. Such associations are not nonprofit in the traditional sense; rather they are quasi-business.[100] The statute does note, however, that an agricultural association incorporated under Florida Statutes Chapter 618 is nonprofit because profit is distributed to the members as *producers* of agricultural products and not to the members as members of an agricultural association.[101]

§29. ANIMAL WELFARE SOCIETIES

There have been increases in the numbers and members of animal welfare societies. These societies work toward humane treatment of animals through litigation for animal rights and legislation against cruelty. An example of such legislation is the New York Agriculture and Markets Law § 374(1) which allows any agent or officer of the American Society for the Prevention of Cruelty to Animals to humanely destroy any animal found so maimed, diseased, disabled, or infirm as to be unfit for any useful purpose. The animal may be destroyed on recommendation of a veterinarian, or two reputable citizens, or upon consent of the owner. A court order is needed for entry onto the premises where the animal is kept.[102]

Animal welfare societies also operate shelters for lost and abused animals throughout the United States. Animal rights activists expressed outrage at a United States Supreme Court decision stating that a city's prohibition of ritual animal sacrifice violates the free exercise rights of a church practicing the Santeria religion.[103]

§30. HEALTH CARE ORGANIZATIONS

Health care organizations must deal with complex governmental regulations in order to receive Medicaid payments. Recently, the Department of Social Services used a random sample audit to determine that a nonprofit health care provider had received Medicaid overpayments which would have to be reimbursed. The court held that the random sample audit was arbitrary and capricious where the health care provider had adequate records for the audit period, even though the records were voluminous.[104]

Health care organizations must also face contract issues in dealing with their clients' coverage. For example, a nonprofit group health care contractor's exclusion of coverage, to the extent that benefits were available under any automobile, medical, medical "no-fault," or uninsured or underinsured motorist coverage, was found to be valid even though full compensation had not been received by the victim for his injuries.[105]

Many states have enacted special statutes for health care organizations. For example, Ohio has chapters for medical care corporations,[106] hospital service associations,[107] health care corporations generally,[108] and dental care corporations.[109]

California has a general statute, applicable to nonprofit corporations, which deals with health care organizations,[110] and also special statutes for home health service, and for community clinics and free clinics.[111] These organizations usually are under the supervision of the state commissioner of insurance.

In many states such organizations are governed simply by the general nonprofit, and insurance, statutes.

Typical of such organizations are the well-known Blue Cross, Blue Shield, and other like groups.

"Asylums,'" Care of Residents

Liability for patient care is always a serious concern for health care organizations. A nonprofit corporation, that is a court appointed guardian of an incompetent individual in a persistent vegetative state, may refuse life sustaining medical treatment on the patient's behalf without obtaining prior authority of the court. The decision may be reviewed by the court at the instance of the parties in interest.[112]

A "reasonable" standard of care applies to nursing, mental health, drug treatment, and like institutions; thus, an aide need not constantly accompany ambulatory patients.[113]

Knowing abuse or neglect of residents may be criminal for such organizations; often by statute.[114]

California has particularly protective statues as to the rights of patients; such as the right to challenge treatment methods (even for minors).[115]

Government Status

A community hospital association is not an "institution of the state or a political subdivision," for purposes of open-meetings law, even though it provided services as required by its contract with the hospital district authority, when its board of trustees were elected by private individuals acting as a private nonprofit organization and operations were not under the district's control.[116]

Local Government Financial Support

Some statutes allow payment by the county to nonprofit hospitals for expenses incurred in treating "indigent" patients.[117]

In Washington, the county is responsible for a jail inmate's medical costs at a nonprofit hospital. However, the Department of Social and Health Services must reimburse the county if the indigent jail inmate is eligible for DSHS's public assistance medical program.[118]

Health Maintenance Organizations (HMOs)

HMOs offer low-cost premiums, little paperwork, and lists of participating physicians. Critics of HMOs point out that few physicians participate and that there are long waits for an appointment. Some say that patients get patronizing treatment at HMOs.

Most HMOs have to deal with all the federal regulations and rules involved in the receipt of Medicare payments. A nonprofit Health Maintenance Organization is entitled to reasonable notice and an opportunity for a hearing prior to denial, termination, or suspension of its ability to participate as a vendor, by contract with the state, to Medicare recipients.[119]

§31. BENEVOLENT AND FRATERNAL ORDERS, AND HEALTH, DEATH, AND BURIAL SOCIETIES

These usually are intended, among other things, to provide benefits in the event of members' illness, death, and burial.[120] If they have insurance features, they must conform with state insurance law.[121] Special statutes for their organization and management are found in many states.[122] Often they are classified under the general nonprofit statutes rather than under the public-benefit enactments.

Among such organizations are the Masons, Oddfellows, American Legion, Amvets, Knights of Pythias, Elks, and many other well-known groups. For a directory of the major national organizations, *see Encyclopedia of Associations* (Detroit, Michigan, Gale Research Co.). In these organizations, usually the provision of social, financial and moral support only extends to the *members* of the organization. Usually these organizations have been denied *charitable* status because they do not work for the *public* good, although they are nonprofit.[123]

Membership is based upon contract. Consideration for the contractual relationship consists of dues or fees paid on a periodic basis.[124] Florida Statutes §732.291, for example, requires that the society issues to each member a certificate setting the amount of benefits contained therein. The contract upon which the relationship is founded, and in which the member's rights are defined, must consist also of the certificate, riders, the articles of incorporation, and the member's application.[125] Membership in a fraternal organization constitutes an acceptance by the individual of the regulations and provisions in the bylaws.[126]

The general rule in many jurisdictions is that the contract shall be construed according to the laws of insurance.[127] The contract may include death benefits, endowment benefits, annuity benefits, and hospital or medical benefits due to illness, bodily infirmity or accident.[128] The corporations often are organized under the insurance laws.[129] Many states, however, provide exemptions from the Insurance Code as to certain types of *fraternal* associations.[130] Examples of these societies include domestic fraternal benefits societies that provide no more than $400 in death benefits or $350 for disability, to any person in any year, and associations whose members are engaged in crafts or hazardous occupations, and grand or subordinate lodges for societies which provide benefits solely through local lodges.

§32. CEMETERY ASSOCIATIONS

Cemetery associations may be for profit[131] or not-for-profit.[132] These organizations maintain and care for the cemetery and surrounding grounds; inter, entomb, or inurn human remains; sell the rights to an appropriate repository; and most importantly, acquire real estate in order to fulfill the purposes.[133] A nonprofit cemetery corporation has nonprofit membership, and its property is devoted to public use.[134] A cemetery association in Florida is subject to the approval of the Florida state department of finance.[135] Ohio mandates that a cemetery corporation may hold up to 640 acres of tax-exempt land, provided that it is held exclusively for cemetery or burial purposes.[136] Other jurisdictions allow various degrees of flexibility, and state that such corporations may acquire and hold only as much land as may be necessary for proper use as a cemetery.[137]

A membership corporation that operates a columbarium is classified as a cemetery corporation.[138] Cemetery associations have the legal right to draft and enforce rules regulating the association and the cemetery.[139] The rules must be reasonable, enacted in good faith,and apply equally to all persons.[140] Cemetery associations may not discriminate between lot owners by imposing special demands upon one member that should properly be borne by all.[141]

Cemetery associations may also be *charitable*. In determining charitable status one must look to the *public* nature of the services performed.[142] Cemetery associations have been denied charitable status where they did not provide free burial space for the indigent.[143] Most states have covered such organizations with specific statutory treatment.[144]

New York has a statute requiring that benevolent societies first offer cemetery plots for sale at the original purchase price plus four percent interest before offering the plots on the open market. The court found the statute addressed a strong public concern and was a valid exercise of police power that did not effect an unconstitutional taking without just compensation.[145]

Under New York's not-for-profit corporation law, formal notice and summons requirements do not apply to an application for disinterment. A homicide defendant is not entitled to exhume a body without proof to call into question the findings and conclusions of a medical examiner. The applicant must show good and substantial reasons to support removal.[146]

§33. RESIDENTS ASSOCIATIONS

[See Condominiums and Cooperatives]

Residents Associations frequently must litigate to enforce or set aside restrictive covenants in their communities. The fundamental rule in construing restrictive covenants is the intention of the parties. Intention is reflected by the entire instrument of the covenant, including the surrounding circumstances and objects which the covenant is designed to accomplish. Where property is part of a subdivision, new owners are limited to the use to which the tract had already been placed, even if is never depicted as part of the subdivision on any recorded map and no filed document specifically includes the tract as subject to the subdivision's restrictive covenants. Any additions have to be built, operated, and maintained in such a manner as not to constitute a nuisance.[147]

When developers amend restrictive covenants, contrary to the wishes of a homeowner's association, the test of enforceability of those amendments is one of reasonableness. Amendments cannot destroy the general plan of the development. If the developer does not reserve the power to amend, amendments can be validly enacted by the approval of two thirds of the lot owners. An amendment to a restrictive covenant, which imposes mandatory membership in a homeowner's association is invalid if it significantly restricts a lot owner's use of his or her property.[148]

If language in a restrictive covenant is ambiguous about how a covenant can be amended, the court will construe the language in line with the maxim favoring free and unobstructed use of real property.[149] For example, the term, "commercial vehicle," is not ambiguous in restrictive covenants. Covenants prohibiting the parking of commercial vehicles in subdivisions will be upheld if each property owner had adequate notice of the restrictions and purchases his property knowing of, accepting, and relying upon them. The courts will not invalidate restrictions unless they are clearly ambiguous, wholly arbitrary, unreasonable in application, or violative of public policy or a fundamental constitutional right.[150]

A nonbusiness (golf club land) group of homeowners had bought lots under a "restrictive covenant" not to have businesses there. Defendant (plot owner) built a house and used it as a licensed home for aged persons, living on the income of that use. Held: that is a "business" even though licensed, and violates the covenant. Injunction was granted, to stop such use.[151]

A senior citizen's association, representing residents of age restricted housing, sued to challenge an amendment to the Fair Housing Act which prohibits discrimination on the basis of familial status in the sale or rental of units. The court held that the amendment is constitutional.[152] A residential subdivision can bar children under 16 years of age by satisfying the "policies and procedures" requirement for the "55 or older" exemption to the Fair Housing Amendments Act. A bylaw limiting occupancy of housing units so that at least 80% of the units would be required to contain at least one person over 55 years satisfies that policy.[153]

The owners of a home in a subdivision waive the right to erect a 35 foot flag pole on their roof if they agree to abide by restrictive covenants designed to protect existing and future property owners in the subdivision.[154]

Resident Associations violate the Fair Housing Act if they interfere with the sale of a neighbor's home, to the operator of a group home for the mentally retarded, by filing state court action to enforce a restrictive covenant.[155]

A residents' association, is relieved of its contractual obligation to provide residents with an easement if the residents breach the easement agreement.[156]

[The rest of this subsection was contributed by Robert D. Wooten].

Homeowners and homeowners associations brought a civil rights action against a developer and the county challenging the construction of a stadium in a predominately black neighborhood. The court held that the association had standing to seek injunctive relief, but had no standing to seek monetary damages. The association's allegations were insufficient to state a takings claim or a racial discrimination claim against the county.[157]

[See the chapter on Condominiums and Cooperatives.]

§34. COMMUNITY IMPROVEMENT CORPORATIONS (DEVELOPMENT CORPORATIONS)

Community improvement corporations are organized and operated for the purposes of relieving and reducing unemployment, aiding the economic and social prosperity of a community, and the like. They seek to improve the economic, commercial and civic life and development of the community.[158] They are governed by special statues, and their powers are limited to the specific provisions of the statute under which they were created. In order to accomplish this stated purpose, these powers usually include: the power to acquire machinery and equipment for specific projects,[159] the power to obtain real estate for the purpose of constructing industrial plants,[160] the power to have capital stock and issue capital shares as stated in the articles of incorporation,[161] and the power to foster the expansion of industrial plants.[162] A county or municipality may designate such a corporation as its agent for the industrial, commercial and research development of an area.[163]

State Support for public-welfare organizations is illustrated by state grants to "nonprofit institutions only" for students' fees,[164] and loans to nonprofit corporations organized for encouragement of new small businesses.[165]

Deterioration of the American countryside and of downtown areas of many American cities since World War II has elicited much action aimed at remedying this and allied problems. One method is legal encouragement of *community improvement* and *development* corporations.

In Ohio[166] and California, for example, statutes adopted since 1961 provide for community improvement corporations and development corporations.[167]

These organizations have borrowing, lending,and finance powers considerably broader than those permitted to other nonprofit organizations. They also may employ business corporation techniques such as stock (shares).[168] Thus, members may have voting power based not only on the number of share held but also on the amount of money contributed to the corporate loan fund.[169]

A nonprofit corporation, that purchases property for the purpose of renovation, is required, under federal law, to reimburse a displaced tenant for moving expenses.[170]

§35. LABOR UNIONS

[See the Index.]

Labor unions often are unicorporated associations. Special aspects of their organization, status, and operation are touched on a various points in this work (see the index).

They usually are exempt from antimonopoly laws.[171] It is estimated that over 20 million people belong to American labor unions; that they have about 70,000 local organizations and about 200 national organizations. See data in Chapters 1 and 2. Labor law is too specialized to be treated here. In Florida, for example, "right to work" law weakens labor unions powers.[172]

Federal preemption labor law (Labor-Management Reporting and Disclosure Act) does not apply to such state court tort actions as a former union business representative's suit against a union for breach of the covenant of good faith and fair dealing or negligent infliction of mental suffering, and violates the covenant. Injunction was granted, to stop such use.[173]

A police officer's association affiliated with the labor law council of a state fraternal order of police is not *per se* in a conflict-of-interests position thereby, in dealing with the State Labor Relations Board. A village's refusal to deal with (bargain with) the association was an unfair labor practice.[174]

A union's failure to disclose four employees who were its long-term organizers in the area, in its application for registration as a certified collective bargaining agent for a particular unit of employees, was a substantial deficiency; but that may be cured if that is timely done.[175]

Under the *Railway Labor Act* a labor union's right to "self-help" is not barred by changes of circumstances or the passing of time.[176]

Nurses in private hospitals now may organize (or join) *labor unions* in *individual* bargaining units in *privately* owned hospitals. Until May 1991 they had to join other groups of employees, including maintenance workers, to form a union. A Supreme Court decision (in an NLRB vs. Hospital industry case) unanimously upheld the new (1989) NLRB rules allowing separate nurses' organization, as already was allowed in public hospitals. Now many big labor unions are attempting to organize (white collar) nurses unions as a positive off-set to their reputation of being basically blue-collar organizations.[177]

See also: *Directory of National and International Labor Unions in the United States, Including State Labor Organizations* (Wash., D. C.: Dept. of Labor, Bureau of Labor Statistics, Gov't. Printing Office) annual.

§36. RELIGIOUS ORGANIZATIONS

[See the Index, and the separate chapter on this topic.]

§37. EDUCATIONAL CORPORATIONS

Educational corporations may be either business (profit) or nonprofit organizations. If nonprofit in purpose, they must, in most states, incorporate under special statutes.[178]

Supervision of these organizations, by a state department of education (or commission), is the rule in all states. And this supervision is so detailed that many states provide their own books of regulations for the purpose.[179] Supervision of schools above the grade-school level is usually entrusted to a commission or to a board of regents (or supervisors).[180]

Trustees usually manage such organizations, and have rather broad powers.[181] Special, complicated tax exemptions apply to many of their activities. And many detailed local laws and rules apply to them.[182]

Accrediting authorities. Schools usually must be accredited by certain authoritative agencies or organizations in order for their students' diplomas to be recognized. Likewise, colleges must obtain accreditation from regional agencies.

For example, a school in Ohio should seek approval from the North Central Association of Colleges and Secondary Schools, and other accrediting agencies. In other states, equivalent agencies and approvals apply.

Special types of schools often must obtain other, additional (or prerequisite) accreditation. Thus, a law school in Ohio must be approved by (1) the secretary of state, for incorporation; (2) the Ohio Supreme Court, for enabling graduates to take the bar examinations; (3) the League of Ohio Law Schools, for approval of standards of legal education; (4) the American Bar Association, for basic qualification nationally; (5) the coordinating authority of the Ohio Board of Regents; and (6) the Association of American Law Schools for the highest accreditation.

A large body of special law applies to educational organizations.[183] For example, colleges must reveal crime rates on campus each year; must reveal graduation rates of athletes by sport, sex and race; and must provide their rules and policies as to such matters, for students.[184]

For directories, see: *Education Directory* (various sections, including one on educational associations) (annual bulletin; Wash., D. C.: U. S. Department of Education).

There also are a number of directories of schools, libraries, and colleges, which are available in practically any library. See, for example *American Educational Directories,* published regularly by B. Klein & Co., New York, N. Y. 10011; or, *Yearbook of Higher Education,* published by Academic Media, 32 Lincoln Ave., Orange, N. J. 07050; or *Standard Education Almanac* published by the same company.

§38. COOPERATIVES

[See the chapter on Condominiums and Cooperatives.]
Cooperative organizations are those for mutual help and service among and to their members.[185] They are a rapidly evolving form of organization,and express legislation for them (especially for agricultural organizations) is found in many states. Food producers and marketers and consumers are especially favored in this respect.[186]

These organizations may be run for profit, as well as not for profit.[187] Both individuals and organizations may be members.[188] Their powers, liabilities, and methods of formation and management often are set forth in detail in local statutes.[189]

For directories see:

Annual Surveys of Consumer Organizations (Wash., D. C.: U. S. Dept. of Labor).

Annual Surveys of Farmers Cooperatives (Wash., D. C.: Farmer Cooperative Service).

[*See also* the Bibliography in Chapter 2.]

§39. MUTUAL ASSOCIATIONS

Mutual-insurance, banking, credit-union, credit-bureau, and other such organizations are governed by highly complex local statutes and regulations. These are a mixture of local insurance or banking law with corporation and administrative law.[190] They often also involve, in part, benevolent and fraternal organization law.[191]

These organizations are more important than this brief section may suggest. Credit unions, for example, had outstanding loans of over *$10 billion by 1978.* But such organizations are so specialized that they cannot be discussed in detail in a work such as this.

Mutual insurance organizations are being formed in increasing numbers by statute and by the insurance industry. These organizations are usually started in order to provide a mutual fund to carry out the obligations of insolvent insurers. Such funds may provide a mechanism for the payment of claims asserted by policyholders against insolvent insurers.[192] A liability action, for unfair methods of competition and unfair or deceptive acts or practices, cannot be maintained against a statutorily mandated, nonprofit unincorporated association of insurers, organized to settle unpaid claims against insolvent insurers. Such associations do not engage in a "trade" or "commerce" and their activities are not performed within a "business context" as required by statute.[193] Also, a nonprofit statutorily created association of Nevada insurers, organized to assume the obligations of Nevada insurance companies that become insolvent, does not owe a duty of good faith and fair dealing to the insured of the insolvent insurer. Such a duty can only arise out of contract. Bad faith damages and attorney fees cannot be awarded where there is a statutory issue of first impression.[194] In addition, an unincorporated association of insurers, or insurance guarantee association, is not an "insurer" for purposes of a statute imposing liability for bad faith failure to settle claims.[195]

Employers who participate in the Florida Nonprofit Multiple-Employer Welfare Arrangement Act, to provide collective health insurance benefits for their employees, may be assessed for shortfalls in funds if their (MEWA) collapses and becomes insolvent.[196]

An automobile accident victim does not have to exhaust his remedies against his uninsured motorist carrier, prior to seeking recovery from the nonprofit Illinois Insurance Guaranty Fund, upon insolvency of the tortfeasor's liability insurer.[197]

§40. MUNICIPAL CORPORATIONS

Municipal corporations are governmental organizations, such as cities, towns, villages, and school or water districts. They often are called *public corporations.*[198] They are subject in all the states to highly specialized and detailed statutes and laws.[199] In fact they are so specialized that they properly are classified as a separate type of organization, distinct from all other kinds of nonprofit groups.

§41. DEFENSE PRODUCTION POOLS

A relatively recent innovation was the defense production pool, an association of defense-equipment manufacturers and processors. Such pools usually are nonprofit (for the association) but may be for profit, too. They usually are incorporated, but may be unincorporated. They are similar to the *Webb Associations* in export, which are exempted from the antitrust laws (by the Webb-Pomerene Act) to encourage small exporters. One hears little about them nowadays.

For information about such organizations see: *Small Business Production*

Pools for Defense (Wash., D. C.: Small Defense Plants Admin., Office of Information, free). Small Business Administration, Washington, D. C. 20416, and local branch offices.

§42. TRADE ASSOCIATIONS

[See the Index, and the separate chapter on this topic.]
One of the greatest single groups is that described as *trade associations*. These include local and area boards of trade and chambers of commerce, and local and area associations of business organizations. They must operate within the antimonopoly laws (Sherman Act, Clayton Act, Federal Trade Commission Act, Robinson-Patman Act, McGuire Act, and similar state laws).[200]

Exchange and compilation of information is one of their chief purposes. This is legal so long as it does not include exchange of customer, current-contract-and-work, price, and other such information, aimed at monopolistic practices.[201] Most of the general discussion of nonprofit organizations, throughout this work, applies to trade associations as well as to other nonprofit groups.

§43. FASHIONABLE SPECIAL TYPE CORPORATIONS

A few illustrations should suffice to indicate the kind of highly special types of nonprofit organization form that should be considered. The popularity of some types varies with the business climate, the kind of government administration in power at a given time, and other variables. Anyone contemplating the organizing of a nonprofit organization ought to investigate the state of the law and of administrative agency and public attitudes towards the special varieties fashionable at the time.

Urban Renewal Corporations

Under the Federal Housing Act, nonprofit organizations built and operated low-rent housing projects, with urban renewal land almost *given* to them, and 100 percent of the capital loaned by the government at low mortgage rates (while the prime business interest rate zoomed upward). Then federal rent supplements are available, etc. State Local Development Corporation statutes also help to provide state money for such projects.[202]

Bootstrapping

A discussion of special nonprofit organizations must include the now moot subject of bootstrapping. This was an arrangement for installment purchase of a business, without investment, by a nonprofit organization (often specially organized for this purpose), using as payment the income of the business itself. It was sanctified as lawful, by the United States Supreme Court, in the case of *Clay Brown v. Commissioner*[203] despite the protests of the IRS. The Tax Reform Act of 1969 began the end of this device by imposing a tax on such "unrelated business income."[204]

Nonprofit Organizations for Housing the Elderly

Congress in 1956, passed a law to provide public housing for elderly people. Then more laws encouraged nonprofit building organizations to do this, with F. H. A.-insured loans at very low interest rates and covering most costs.[205]

By 1965 a $100 million retirement city of 5,000 units (for example) was in business in San Diego, with a church on the highest hill. The University of Arizona set up a separate nonprofit corporation for F. H. A. funding of Tucson Green Valley ($100 million).

The retirement-building industry is big business today. Practically all states have such housing. Political fireworks occur when a large number of minorities escape from the city ghetto to the suburban green belt, where many residents want no poor old people's housing project planted in their midst. This happens in many cities.

Fringe income sources of housing for the elderly include 24-hour medical service and other services and facilities, while the age limit for "the elderly" fell to 52 at Leisure World, 50 at Sun City, and 45 at New Horizons in Santa Barbara, all in California. Twenty percent of our population was said to be so housed, by 1980. Cemetery annexes (also nonprofit), undertaking services, etc., are growing too, and the possibilities, income, troubles, etc., are very involved.[206] Church-related housing is particularly popular.[207]

Senator John Williams of Delaware once said, "These so-called nonprofit homes for the elderly are being constructed under the guise that they are being sponsored by nonprofit organizations." When, as sometimes happens, the cream of free money support is skimmed off to contractors, etc.; bankruptcy is no real worry, as the F. H. A. then has to take over. "The Government furnishes all the money, takes all the risk, and the promoter gets a sure profit," the Senator added, in the *Congressional Record*[208] (titled "Irresponsible Use of F. H. A. Insurance").

Meanwhile, the numbers of "senior citizens" grow, and so do the opportunities for organizers and operators of nonprofit organizations.

Group Law Practice "Feeder Organizations"

Group law practice (*e.g.,* counsel for all the members of a nonprofit organization) was made O.K., under the famous *Button,*[209] *Brotherhood of Railroad Trainmen,*[210] and *United Mine Workers*[211] cases. Labor unions are only one type of "feeder organization." Fraternal order, trade associations and other types of nonprofit organizations can be (and are being) used.[212] This should be distinguished from "feeder organizations" aimed at supporting tax-exempt organizations. Under the Tax Reform Act of 1969, such operation often will not be penalized by taxation as unrelated business income.[213] But see, below, the chap-

ter on tax exemption, as to current rulings; and do not merely rely on these
older citations.

§44. PROPRIETARY MENTALITY

Organizers officers, or employees, who think that they "own the company" are
found in many organizations. Sometimes they are correct—where, for example, the officer is the controlling stock-holder in a business corporation. But
the same human phenomenon is seen, all too often, in nonprofit organizations. And there, that kind of proprietary mentality is quite improper—even if
the organization was founded and funded entirely by "the owner." This is
because a nonprofit organization is, by definition, one that nobody owns, in
that nobody is supposed to get from it any personal profit (in the pecuniary
sense) such as owners get from their property.[214]

Control agreements are permitted by the new New York statute,[215] and the
California statute,[216] but such control is meant for protection of investors' rights
in New York's nonprofit-plus-business corporations. Control in the proprietary
sense of one-man ownership is not what the New York statute intends, although
it may be acceptable under the California statute.[217]

The proprietary mentality is most thoroughly improper and unhealthy in
nonprofit organizations that have fallen under the domination of *one* or a *very
few* domineering officers or employees or members. It is all too common in
such organizations, though seldom openly criticized, usually because of fear of
defamation suits or of reprisals, by the dominating person or persons, against
critics. Such danger of reprisal is a very effective silencer. The ones in the best
position to know of improper domination usually are the employees of the
organization and they usually cannot afford to risk their jobs by openly stating
unpleasant facts about their "employers." Third persons who are aware of
improper "ownership attitudes" in various organizations seldom are able or
willing to *prove* such unedifying attitudes. The "owners" hold the aces in the
game, under our system of defamation tort law and of scant or nonexistent
supervision or inspection by public officers and agencies.[218]

This last, parenthetically, is the key element in abuse of nonprofit status.
Privilege without scrutiny is fatally tempting to most people.

The history of abuse of the benefits of charitable status is long and disheartening. Today, as in centuries past, the "trustees" (in the generic sense of
that term) usually can and do make the organization pay the expenses of
defending their abuses, while the one who questions the abuses usually pays
out of his own pocket for his concern about propriety and morality.[219] The
history of occasional (and futile) public investigations of abuses of charitable
status is long and depressing to everyone except the persons who abuse that
status.[220]

Even in the time of Queen Elizabeth I, of England, the prevalence of abuse of trust in charitable activities was common enough to require legislative action. The preamble to The Statute of Elizabeth I, in 1601, said:

> Whereas lands tenements rentes annuities, profittes hereditamentes, goods chattels money and stockes of money, have been heretofore given . . . , some for the reliefe of aged impotent and poore people, some for he mainte- nance of sick and maymed souldiers and marriners, schooles of learninge, free schooles and schollers (etc.) . . . which lands tenements (etc.) never- theless have not byn imployed accordinge to the charitable intente of the givers and founders thereof, by reason of fraudes breaches of truste and negligence in those that should pay deliver and imploy the same . . . [221]

The Charities Act of 1960 in England repealed that preamble, but did not change human nature and the tendency of many people to treat trust proper- ty as their own.

Professor H. H. A. Cooper, an English law professor, wrote to me regard- ing a worried analysis of mine in 20 Cleve. St. L. Rev. 145 (1971):

> I was particularly interested in your article in the January, 1971 issue. I am not competent to comment, in depth, on its content; but would second most wholeheartedly your conclusion at page 165, which tallies with my own experience. I was for many years with the Department of Inland Revenue. Had it not been for the accruing tax advantages, the English Charitable Trust would, like the Deed of Covenant, have died out long ago. In many cases, self-interest shows through to such an extent as to obscure entirely any incidental motive of a charitable nature behind the setting up of the foundation. I humbly join you in your cynicism.

§45. DIRECTORY INFORMATION

[See also the *Bibliography* in Chapter 2]

Some of the principal sources of directory and statistical information about American organization (aside from the federal statistical guides found in most good libraries) are the following

Encyclopedia of Associations. (Detroit, Mich.: Gale Research Co.).

Foundation Directory. (Foundation Center; N. Y. City).

Directory of National Trade and Professional Associations of the United States. Annual. (Columbia Books, Washington, D. C. 20005).

Cumulative List published by the Treasury Department periodically, carries the names of all organizations approved as recipients of tax-deductible contributions. It is a large, closely printed book; titled *Organizations Described in Section 170(c) of the I. R. C. of 1954 [I. R. S. Publ. No. 78, reissued biennially, with bimonthly supplements].*

Annual Register of Grant Support. (Academic Media Co., Orange, N. J.

07050) gives worldwide information about programs, sponsors, how to apply, etc.

Directory of Consumer Protection and Environmental Agencies. (Academic Media Co., see directly above); compiled by California Center for Public Affairs, an affiliate of Claremont College.

These are a very few organizations that publish specialized studies and guides about nonprofit organizations. *"Independent Sector"* a consortium of major nonprofit organizations (1828 L Street, N. W.; Washington, D. C. 20036), for example, publishes *Resource Directory of Education and Training Opportunities and Other Services.* Other (private) organizations that make studies of the operations of nonprofits include; *Yale University Institute for Social and Policy Studies* (P. O. Box 154, Yale Station, New Haven, CT. 06520), and *National Information Bureau, Inc.* of New York City and *Council of Better Business Bureaus, Inc.* of Washington, D. C. N. I. B. will send a *free* list, plus three specific reports to persons who write to them at 419 Park Avenue South, New York, N. Y. 10016. CBBB will send three very short reports, on specific charities to persons who send to them $1 and a business-size, self-addressed, stamped envelope to 1150 Seventeenth Street, N. W., Washington, D. C. 20036.

The *Council of Better Business Bureaus* publishes an "Annual Charity Index" (by its *Philanthropic Advisory Service)* setting standards for charitable organizations, giving data on 200 of the most-asked-about charities; plus a bimonthly list of its approved charities. 2nd Annual "Index" (1990) costs $9.95 plus $1.00 postage. Address PAS/CBBB, Washington, D. C. 20042–0024.

Principal classifications. Categories or classes typical of nonprofit organizations which are of major importance are as follows:

INDUSTRY ORGANIZATIONS

Metal Products Associations

Food and Tobacco Associations

Textile, Apparel, and Leather Associations

Lumber, Furniture, and Paper Associations

Transportation and Other Public Utility Associations

Chemical and Rubber Associations

Stone, Clay, and Glass Associations

Printing and Publishing Associations

Finance and Real Estate Associations

Advertising and Allied Associations

Insurance Associations

Petroleum, Coal, and Gas Associations

Hotel, Hospital, and Allied Associations

Amusement and Allied Associations

General Associations

MISCELLANEOUS ORGANIZATIONS

Agricultural Associations

Better Business Bureaus

Commodity and Stock Exchanges

Cultural Organizations

Ethnic Associations

Foreign Chambers of Commerce

Fraternal Organizations

Hispanic Organizations

International Associations

Labor Unions

Management Associations

Negro Associations

Professional Associations

Religious Associations and Bodies

School and College Associations

Manufacturers' Associations

Multiple Associations' Offices

Organization in the Educational, Scientific, Social Welfare, and Other Fields

Wholesales and Retail Associations

Sport and Recreation Activities

State Organizations and City Chambers of Commerce

Veterans', Military, and Allied Associations

Women's Organizations

OTHER TYPES OF ORGANIZATIONS

Advertising Clubs

Civic Associations

Conventions

Cooperative Associations

Credit Associations

Educational Associations

Employers' Associations

Engineering Associations

Federations

Foreign Associations

Government Officials' Associations

Hobbies

Institutes

Law Associations

Lobbies

Medical Associations

Peace Associations

Research Associations

Residential Organizations Associations

Salesmen's Associations

Secretaries' and Executive Associations

Small Business Associations

Social Welfare Associations

Trade Directories

Traffic, Rate, and Tariff Bureaus

FUNCTIONAL AND SPECIAL INDUSTRY GROUPINGS

Construction Industry Associations

Foreign Trade Associations

Foundations

Machinery Associations

§46. CONFLICT OF GENERAL AND SPECIAL ORGANIZATION STATUTES

Not only in special types of nonprofit organizations, but in all types, conflicts often are found between provisions of the general nonprofit statute and of special statutes, in the same state.

For example, the educational corporations law will speak of management by the trustees, but there may be no "members" of the corporation. In the general statute, however, basic control is vested in the members; apparently assuming that there are members.

Such conflicts are resolved by applying the principle that a specific provision overrides a general provision, in case of conflict, where both statute provisions deal with the same subject and question. This is a basic principle of construction in conflicts of law.[222]

Modern corporation statutes often make specific provision for this problem. Usually they state the rule thus: Where a general provision conflicts with a specific provision, within the various corporation laws of the state, the specific or particular provision shall govern, unless they are cumulative in effect, in which case both apply.[223]

POINTS TO REMEMBER

- Consider alternatives available before choosing the *kind* (category) of organization to adopt.

- Consider the statute and other advantages of your home state first, but also heed those of other states.

- Study directories and other data sources in your field of interest before choosing a category.

- Current "fashion" as to popular kinds of organization should be examined.

- Popularity of a particular kind of form suggests that it has been found to have advantages.

- Consult specialist (such as the secretary of state, corporation division, assistant-in-charge in your state) as to which kinds are popular.

- Use the New York or California types (business and nonprofit combined) with caution.

- Expect IRS scrutiny of mixtures-of-purposes types.

- Clear with the IRS, in advance, if you can.

- Avoid "proprietary mentality" in nonprofit organization work.

- Control agreements must be limited to "investment purpose" under New York type statutes.

- Consult the "approving" or "parental" offices that may have regulatory or consultative reference to your organization.

- Get as much information as you can before incorporating, rather than rely on later research alone.

NOTES TO CHAPTER 4

1. Fla. St., c. 618; Agricultural Cooperative Marketing Associations; c. 616 public fairs and expositions; Ill. Comp. Stat. Ann. § 805/315/8.

2. Ohio Rev. Code, c. 1711; N.Y. N-P-C L. § 1409.

3. Ohio Rev. Code, tit. 17, c. 1702; Ann L. Mass. c. 180, § I *et seq.*

4. Ohio Rev. Code, c. 1715; N.Y. Relig. Corp. L., c. 51 of NY Consol. L.; Nev. Rev. Code, c. 82. As to courts refusal of jurisdiction in church matters, *see*, Archdiocese of Miami v. Sama, 519 So. 2d 28 (Fla. 3rd Dist. Ct. App., 1987).

5. Ohio Rev. Code, c. 1713; Smith-Hurd Ill. Ann. Stat. c. 144 § 13; Fla. St. c. 623.

6. Ohio Rev. Code, c. 1701; Gen. St. N.C., c. 55-A-1 to 55 A-89.1.

7. Condominiums: *see*, Fla. St. c. 718; and as to Cooperatives *see* Fla. St. cc. 619 nonprofit, and c. 719 generally. *See also*: Ohio Rev. Code c. 1729; Ky. Rev. St. tit. xxiii, c. 272.

8. *See*, n. 1.

9. Ohio Rev. Code c. 1733.

10. *Id.* (Ohio); Mich. Comp. L. Ann. §§550.1101 *et seq.*

11. Ohio Rev. Code cc. 1724, 1726, 1728; N.Y. State Urban Devel. Act, L. 1978 c. 174 § 1, c. 24 subc. 1, Unconsol. L. of NY (with cum. supp.).

12. *See* in the index "foundations." For a definition of a charitable trust see Ohio Rev. Code § 109.23. For a more detailed set of definitions (and rules) *see* Fla. St. c. 737 part V).

13. Ohio Rev. Code c. 1725.

14. Argue v. Goldcrest Country Club, 461 S.W.2d 248 (Tex. Civ. App. 1970); cf. Vernon's Ann. Tex. Civ. St. art. 1396-5.09, subd. a(1); V.A.T.S. Bus. Corp. Act., arts. 1.02, subd. a(3) 2.24, 9.14, subd. F, 5.10; V.A.T.S. Tex. Gen. art. 12.08.

15. *Protect the Peninsula's Future v. Clallam County*, 833 P.2d 406 (Wash. App. Div. 2, 1992).

16. *Harristown Development Corp. v. Com. Dept. of General Services*, 614 A.2d 1128 (Pa., 1992).

17. *Salmon For All v. Department of Fisheries*, 821 P.2d 1211 (Wash. 1992). *See also Humphrey v. Posluszny*, 562 N.Y.S.2d 598 (S. Ct., Erie County, 1990).

18. *Guste v. Nicholls College Foundation*, 564 So. 2d 682 (La. 1990).

19. *State ex. rel. Toledo Blade Co. v. Univ. of Toledo Found.*, 602 N.E.2d 1159 (Ohio, 1992).

20. *Frankfort Pub. Co., Inc. v. Kentucky State University Foundation, Inc.*, 834 S.W.2d 681 (Ky., 1992).

21. *Gonzales v. Martinez*, 756 F. Supp. 1533 (S.D. Fla. 1991).

22. *D.I.A.L., Inc. v. New Jersey Dept. of Community Affairs*, 603 A.2d 967 (N.J. Super. A.D. 1992).

23. *Doe v. Department of Social Services*, 487 N.W.2d 166 (Mich., 1992).

24. *Neighborhood School Coalition v. Independent School Dist. No. 279*, 484 N.W.2d 440 (Minn. App. 1992).

25. *Haitian Refugee Center, Inc. v. Baker*, 953 F.2d 1498 (11th Cir. (Fla.), 1992).

26. *Guste v. Nicholls College Foundation*, 564 So.2d 682 (La. 1990).

27. *People v. Turner*, 9 Cal. Rptr. 2d 388 (Cal. App. 1 Dist. 1992).

28. *Riverton Fire Prot. Dist. v. Riverton Volunteer Fire Dept.*, 566 N.E.2d 1015 (Ill. App., 1991).

29. *Procopio v. Johnson*, 785 F. Supp. 1317 (N.D. Ill. 1992). Cf., *Kingsley* case (divorce from parent), *St. Petersburg (FL) Times*, p. 1 (Sept. 26, 1992).

30. *Spitz v. Goldome Realty Credit Corp.*, 569 N.E.2d 43 (Ill. App. 1991); Home Owners Loan Act § 1 *et seq.*, 12 U.S.C.A. § 1461 *et seq.*

31. *ABC Plumbing and Heating Co., Inc. V. Vernon Savings and Loan Association*, 257 Cal. Rptr. 139 (App., 4th Dist., 1989).

32. *North and South Rivers Watershed Ass'n, Inc. v. Town of Scituate*, 755 F. Supp. 4844 (D. Mass. 1991).

33. *Greenpeace Action v. Franklin*, 982 F.2d 1342 (9th Cir. (Wash.), 1992).

34. *Sierra Club v. County of Sonoma (Syar Industries, Inc.)*, 8 Cal. Rptr. 2d 473 (Cal. App. 1 Dist. 1992).

35. *Aluli v. Lewin*, 828 P.2d 802 (Hawaii 1992).

36. *Atlantic States Legal Foundation, Inc. v. Universal Tool & Stamping Co., Inc.*, 786 F. Supp. 743 (N.D. Ind. 1992).

37. *Friends of the Boundary Waters Wilderness v. Robertson*, 978 F.2d 1484 (8th Cir. (Minn.), 1992).

38. *Oiciyapi Federal Credit Union v. National Credit Union Admin.*, 936 F.2d 1007 (8th Cir. 1991).

39. See, 56 FR56000 (No. 211) (eff. Dec. 2, 1991).

40. See, 55 FR5109 (No. 244) (1990).

41. *The Thrift Accountant*, The American Banker-Bond Buyer a division of Thompson Publishing, Apr. 5, 1993.

42. *The Thrift Accountant*, The American Banker-Bond Buyer a division of Thompson Publishing, Mar. 29, 1993.

43. *First Nat. Bank and Trust Co. v. National Credit Union Admin.*, 772 F. Supp. 609 (D.D.C. 1991).

44. *Hefferman v. Wollaston Credit Union*, 567 N.E.2d 933 (Mass. App. 1991).

45. V. Marino (article), *Associated Press* (May 20, 1991).

46. R. Trigaux article, *St. Petersburg Times* business section, p. 10 (Dec. 21, 1992).

47. *First Nat. Bank and Trust Co. v. National Credit Union Admin.*, 772 F. Supp. 609 (D.D.C. 1991).

48. 1993 WL 92494 (D.C. Cir), 61 *USLW* 2597.

49. Atkinson, *Industry Gears Up for Tax Fight*, The American Banker, Feb. 4, 1992.

50. *BNA's Banking Report*, The Bureau of National Affairs, Inc., Mar. 1, 1993; Bankruptcy Code Section 523(a)(8).

51. *Bank Network News*, Predicasts, a Division of Ziff Communications Co. Faulkner & Gray, Inc., Apr. 12, 1992.

52. *State, ex rel. Hodges v. Taft*, 591 N.W.2d 1186 (Ohio 1992).

53. *Citizens for Responsible Behavior v. Superior Court (Riverside City Council)*, 2 Cal. Rptr. 648 (Cal. App. 4 Dist. 1991).

54. *Ficker v. Denny*, 606 A.2d 1060 (Md. 1992).

55. *League of Women Voters v. Eu (Wilson)*, 9 Cal. Rptr. 2d 416 (Cal. App. 3 Dist., 1992).

56. *Mississippi Poultry Ass'n, Inc. v. Madigan*, 790 F. Supp. 1283 (D. Miss., 1992).

57. *Southern Milk Sales, Inc. v. Martin*, 924 F.2d 98 (6th cir. 1991); Fed. Rules Civ. Proc. Rule 65, 28 U.S.C.A.

58. N.Y. Not-for-Profit Corp. L. § 1401.

59. *Ibid.* § 1402.

60. *Ibid.* § 1403.

61. *Ibid.* § 1404.

62. *Ibid.* § 1405.

63. *Ibid.* § 1406.

64. *Ibid.* § 1407.

65. *Ibid.* § 1408.

66. *Ibid.* § 1409.

67. *Ibid.* § 1410.

68. Ohio Rev. Code § 1743.01.

69. *Ibid.* § 1743.03.

70. *Ibid.* § 1743.04.

71. *Ibid.* § 1743.05.

72. *Ibid.* § 1743.06.

73. *Ibid.* § 1743.07.

74. *Ibid.* § 1743.10.

75. CA. Nonprofit Corp. L. § 7110 *et seq.*

76. *Ibid.* § 5001 *et seq.*

77. *Ibid.* § 9110 *et seq.*

78. *Ibid.* § 9912(a).

79. Tex. Nonprofit Corp. Act, Art. 1396, *et seq.*

80. FL. Stat. cc. 632, 634, 637, 641, 642, 649, 657.

81. *See,* Hubbard, article, 39 J. Mo. Bar 209 (1983).

82. *See,* Ohio Rev. Code Anno. tit. 17. c. 1711.

83. *Ibid.* § 1711.03.

84. *Ibid.* § 1711.15.

85. *Ibid.* § 1711.22.

86. FL. Stat. §604.09; Ohio Rev. Code. Ann. § 1711.01; NY Not-for-Profit Corp. Law § 1409; Ill. Ann. Stat. ch. 805 § 105.

87. NY Not-for-Profit Corp. Law & 1409(a); Carswell v. State, 118 FL. 72, 159 So. 15 (1935).

88. FL. Stat. §604.10.

89. Ohio Rev. Code. Ann. § 1729.05.

90. Roper v. Ulster County Agricultural Soc., 139 A.D. 97, 120N.Y.S. 644 (1909).

91. Berman v. Minnesota Agricultural Soc., 93 Minn. 732   100 N.W. 732 (1904).

92. Tri-State v. Rowton, 140 Tenn. 204 (1918).

93. *Id.*

94. Platt v. Erie County Agricultural Soc., 164 A.D. 99, 149 N.Y.S. 520, (1914); Roper v. Ulster County Agricultural Soc., 136 A.D. 97 120 N.Y.S. 644 (1909).

95. Carswell v. State, 118 Fla. 72, 159 So. 15, 17 (1935).

96. Lee v. Clearwater Grower's Ass'n., 93 Fla. 214 111 So. 723 (1927).

97. *Id.,* at 723.

98. California Employment Commission v. Butte County Rice Growers Ass'n. 154 P.2d 892 (Cal., 1944).

99. Fla. St. §618.15(3).

100. Stetson University College of Law, *Nonprofit Corporations in Florida,* Tallahassee: Florida Bar, Continuing Legal Education, 61 (1981).

101. Fla. Stat. §618.01.

102. *Hampton Animal Shelter, Inc. v. A.S.P.C.A.P., 564 N.Y.S.2d 461 (A.D. 2 Dept. 1991).*

103. Church of the LuKumi, Babalu Aye v. Hialeah, 91-948.

104. *Mercy Hospital of Watertown v. New York State Dept. of Social Services,* 565 N.Y.S.2d 285 (A.D. 3 Dept. 1991).

105. *Brown v. Snohomish County Physicians Corp., 822 P.2d 336 (Wash. App. 1992).*

106. *Ohio Rev. Code c. 1737.*

107. *Ibid.* c. 1739.

108. *Ibid.* c. 1738.

109. *Ibid.* c. 1740; *and see,* Calif. Health and Safety Code, §33000 *et seq.*

110. Calif. Corp. Code §§10810 *et seq.*

111. *Ibid.* §§10820, 10830, 10840; and Calif. Ins. Code §§10123.10, 10176, 11512.20; Calif. Health & Safety Code §§1246 *et seq.*

112. *Matter of Guardianship of L.WP>, 482 N.W. 60 (Wis. 1992).*

113. Kildron v. Shady Oaks Nursing Home, 549 S.2d 395 (La. App., 1989); *c.f., Stropes v. Heritage House Children's Center, 546 N.E.2d 244 (Ind., 1989).*

114. *State v. Dale,* 775 S.W.2d 126 (Mo. 1989).

115. Note, 14 Amer. Acad. Psych. & Law (3) Newsletter (1989).

116. *Prescott Newspapers, Inc. v. Yavapai Community Hosp. Assn., 785 P.2d 1221 (Ariz. App. 1990);* cf: Guste v. Nicholls College Foundation, 546 So. 2d 682 (La. 1990).

117. *Washoe Medical Center, Inc. v. Churchill County,* 836 P.2d 624 (Nev. 1992).

118. *Our Lady of Lourdes Hosp. v. Franklin County,* 842 P.2d 956 (Wash., 1993).

119. *MEDICARE HMO v. Bradley,* 788 F. Supp. 1460 (N.D. Ill. 1992).

120. N.Y. Not-for-Profit Corp. L. § 103; Ohio Rev. Code, c. 1715, esp. Secs. 1715.42, 1715.43; *and see,* tendency to facilitate transfers of benefits today, in view of such authorities as North Carolina Mutual Burial Ass'n. Commission: Gen. Stat. N.C. §58-224.2; Adair v. Orrell's Mutual Burial Assn., 199 S.E.2d 129 (N.C. App. 1973), cf., Kenton v. Campbell Benevolent Burial Ass'n. 244 Ky. 260, 50 S.W.2d 554 (1932) based on a narrower statute.

121. N.Y. Insur. L. § 466; Ohio Rev. Code, cc. 1737, 1738, 1739, 1740.

122. See N.Y. Benev. Ord. L. §2(44), 3-a, 9, 11.

123. Georgia Congress of Parents and Teachers, Inc. v. Boynton, 239 Ga. 472, 238 S.E.2d 113 (1977); Camp v. Fulton County Medical Society, 219 Ga. 602, 135 S.E.2d 277 (1964).

124. State v. Shain, 342 Mo. 199, 114 S.W.2d 965 (1938).

125. Durkin v. Brotherhood of Locomotive F. & E., 170 Md. 562, 185 A. 322 (Md. App. 1936).

126. Crossen v. Duffy, 90 Ohio App. 252, 103 N.E.2d 769 (1951).

127. Brotherhood's Relief and Compensation Fund v. Cagnina, 155 So. 2d 820, 824 (Fla. D.C.A., 1963).

128. Fla. Stat. § 632.231(1).

129. Fla. Stat. §632.051 (1983); Brotherhood's Relief and Compensation Fund case, above, n. 127 at 823.

130. Fla. Stat. §632.051.

131. Fla. Stat. §559.35.

132. Fla. Stat. §617.0301.

133. Sunset Memorial Gardens v. Idaho State Tax Commission, 80 Id. 206, 327 P.2d 766 (1958).

134. State *ex rel.* Stephan v. Lane, 228 Kan. 379, 614 P.2d 987 (1980).

135. Fla. Stat. §§559.30-559.48.

136. Ohio Rev. Code. Ann. §1721.01.

137. Mich. Comp. Laws Ann. §456.2; Ill. Ann. Stat. ch. 805 § 125/5.

138. U.S. Columbarium Co. v. Tax Commission of City of New York, 19 Misc. 2d 256, 187 N.Y.S.2d 602 (1959); N.Y. N-PCL § 1401.

139. Lehman v. Evergreen Cemetery Association, 5 Wis. 2d 213, 92 N.W.2d 756 (1958).

140. *Ibid.,* at 758.

141. Jewish Center of Mt. Vernon, Inc., v. Mt. Eden Cemetery Association, Inc., 15 A.D.2d 94, 222 N.Y.S.2d 644 (1961).

142. Estate of Edwards, 88 Cal. App. 3d 383, 151 Cal. Rptr. 770 (1979).

143. *Id.* at 151 Cal. Rptr. 776; Child v. United States, 540 F.2d 579, 583-584, (2d Cir. 1976).

144. Ind. Code §23-14-1-1; Ohio Rev. Code. Ann. § 1721.

145. *Warchauer Sick Support Soc. v. State of N.YP>*, 754 F. Supp. 305 (E.D.N.Y. 1991).

146. In re Elman, 578 N.Y.S. 2d 95 (Supp. 1991); *People v. Radtke*, 578 N.Y.S. 2d 827 (Supp. 1991); *Isola v. Siani*, 577 N.Y.S. 2d 487 (A.D. 2 Dept. 1991).

147. *Teays Farms Owners Ass'n, Inc. v. Cottrill*, 425 S.E.2d 231 (W.Va, 1992).

148. *Holiday Pines Property Owners Ass'n, Inc. v. Wetherington*, 596 So. 2d 84 (Fla. 4th DCA 1992). *See also Zito v. Gerken*, 587 N.E. 2d 1048 (Ill. App. 1 Dist. 1992); *Settlers Village Community Imp. Ass'n, Inc. v. Settlers Village 5.6, Ltd.*, 828 S.W. 2d 182 *(Tex. App.-Houston [14th Dist.] 1992);* Shipyard Property Owners' Ass'n v. Mangiaracina, 414 S.E.2d 795 (S.C. App. 1992).

149. *City of Gulfport v. Wilson*, 603 So.2d 295 (Miss., 1992).

150. *Cottrell v. Miskove*, 605 So.2d 572 (Fla. App. 2 Dist., 1992).

151. *Hagemann v. Worth*, 782 P.2d 1072 (Wash. App., 1989).

152. *Senior Civil Liberties Ass'n, Inc. v. Kemp*, 965 F.2d 1030 (11th Cir. (Fla.), 1992).

153. *Massaro v. Mainlands Section 1 and 2 Civic Ass'n., Inc.*, 796 F. Supp. 1499 (S.D. Fla., 1992).

154. Stone Hill Community Ass'n v. Norpel, 492 N.W.2d 409 (Iowa, 1992).

155. *U.S. V. Scott*, 788 F. Supp. 1555 (D. Kan. 1992).

156. *Snow Lake Shores Property Owners Corp. v. Smith*, 610 So. 2d 357 (Miss., 1992).

157. *Lake Lucerne Civic Association, Inc. v. Dolphin Stadium Corp.*, 801 F. Supp. 684 (S.D. Fla. 1992).

158. *Ohio Rev. Code. Ann. §1724.01; N.Y. Not-for-Profit Corp. Law §14011 (a); Mich. Comp. Laws Ann. §125.1602; Ky. Rev. Stat. §273.410; Martin v. North Carolina Housing Corp.*, 175 S.E.2d 665 (N.C. 1970).

159. *Mich. Comp. Laws Ann. §125.1607(b).*

160. *Ohio Rev. Code. Ann. §1724.02(1); N.Y. Not-for-Profit Corp. Law §1411(c).*

161. *Ill. Ann. Stat. ch. 805 §125/15.*

162. *N.Y. Not-for-Profit Corp. Law §1411(c).*

163. *Burton v. Greater Portsmouth Growth Corporation*, 7 Ohio St. 2d 34, 218 N.E.2d 446 (1966).

164. *Talley v. So. Car. Higher Ed. T.G. Comm.*, 347 S.E.2d 99 (S.C. 1986).

165. *Utah Technology Fin. Corp. v. Wilkinson*, 723 P.2d 406 (Utah 1986).

166. *Ohio Rev. Code, c. 1724.*

167. *Ibid.* c. 1726.

168. *Ibid.* §§ 1726.02, 1726.05. These presumably were the inspiration for the New York N-P-C Act of 1970.

169. *Ibid.* § 1726.07.

170. *Boylston Development Group, Inc. v. 22 Boylston Street CorpP>*, 591 N.E. 2d 157 (Mass. 1992).

171. *Clayton Act, 15 U.S.C.A.; N.Y. Gen. Bus. L. §340;* and see, Anti-Trust Laws, with Amendments (U.S. Govt. Printing Office, current edition) pamphlet.

172. Fla. Const. Art 1 §6; Stat. §§447.01 *et seq.*

173. *Hagemann v. Worth*, 782 P.2d 1072 (Wash. App. 1989). [See Condominiums and Cooperatives: Chap. 36.]

174. *Oak Park v. Illinois State Labor Rel. BdP>*, 522 N.E.2d 161 (IL App. 1988).

175. *Sanitation Employees Association, Inc. v. Metropolitan Dade County Water and Sewer Authority*, 526 So. 2d 128 (FL 3d DCA 1988).

176. *Pan American World Airways, Inc. v. International Brotherhood of Teamsters, CP. W. & H. of Amer.*, 894 F.2d 36 (2d Cir., N.Y., 1990).

177. *D. L. Amos (article)*, St. Petersburg Times "Business" Section, p. 7 (June 3, 1991).

178. N.Y. Not-for-Profit Corp. L. §103; N.Y. Educ. L. §216; Ohio Rev. Code, c. 1713.

179. E.g., *Procedure with Respect to Incorporation by the Regents* (Albany, N.Y.: Univ. of State of N.Y., Pamphlet #9, with forms).

180. Am. Jur., Schools, §§29-37; 55 Am. Jur., *Universities and Colleges* §§12-24 (curr. ed.).

181. N.Y. Educ. L. §226; Ohio Rev. Code c. 1713.

182. *See*, the New York system, detailed discussion, in Oleck, *New York Corporations*, c. 96 (New York: Robert Slater Corp., 1959 Supp.).

183. *See*, Blackwell, *College Law Manual*, a looseleaf service for college and university administrators and their attorneys, Santa Monica, Calif. (curr. ed.).

184. Public L. 101-542 (1990).

185. Ohio Rev. Code, c. 1729; Fla. St., cc. 618, 619, 718, 719.

186. Ohio Rev. Code. §1729.02; Fla. St. cc. 618, 619, 718, 719.

187. Ohio Rev. Code, §1729.03; Fla. St. cc. 618, 619, 718, 719; Calif. Food and Agric. Code §§54000 *et seq.*

188. Ohio Rev. Code §1729.01(C); Fla. St., cc. 618, 619, 718, 719.

189. *See* N.Y. Not-for-Profit Corp. L. §103; N.Y. Educ. L. §216; Fla. Stat. §617.01; N.Y. Relig. Corp. Law §2a,b; Fla. Stat. §617.2005.

190. *See*, Fla. St. cc. 641, 628, *et passim*, for example, or Ohio Rev. Code c. 1733 credit unions; Fla. St., c. 657 credit unions.

191. Fla. St., cc. 627, 632.

192. *Washington Physicians Service v. Marquardt*, (Wash. App. Div. 1, 1992).

193. *Barnett v. Massachusetts Insurers Insolvency Fund*, 592 N.E. 2d 1317 (Mass. 1992).

194. *Nevada Ins. Guar. Ass'n v. Sierra Auto Center*, 844 P.2d 126 (Nev., 1992).

195. *T&N Plc v. Pennsylvania Ins. Guar. Ass'n*, 800 F. Supp. 1259 (E.D. Pa., 1992).

196. *In re International Forum of Florida Health Ben. Trust*, 607 So. 2d 432 (Fla. App. 1 Dist., 1992).

197. *Urban v. Loham*, 592 N.W. 2d 292 (Ill. App. 1 Dist. 1992).

198. In N.Y. statutes, for example.

199. *E.g., see, Fla. St., cc. 165, 170, 171, 180, 215, 286, 380,* et passim.

200. *See*, Glazer and Sills, *The Government of Associations* (1966); Packel, *Organization and Operation of Cooperatives* (A.L.I. 1970).

201. Sugar Institute v. U.S., 297 U.S. 553, 56 S. Ct. 629 (1936); *See* Goldfarb, et. ux., v. Virginia State Bar, *et al.* 421 U.S. 781 (1975), wherein a bar association was held not to engage in trade or commerce, but, by publishing a minimum fee schedule, had violated sec. 1 of the Sherman Act. As to anti-trust laws, and corporations, *see* 4 Oleck, *Modern Corporation Law*, c. 74 (1978 supp.). *See also*, Bradley, *The Role of Trade Associations and Professional Business Societies in America* (Penna. State Univ. Press, University Park, Pa., 1965); Webster, *Associations and the IRS.* (Chamber of Commerce of the U.S., Washington, D.C., 1966).

202. *E.g., Fla. St., c. 163; Ohio Rev. Code, cc. 1724, 1726, 1728.*

203. *380 U.S. 563 (1965).*

204. *57 CCH Standard Fed. Tax Reports (3) Explanation, etc. (Dec. 30, 1969), Par. 1241 §511 of the I.R.C. now imposes a tax on such "unrelated business income."*

205. *Federal Housing Admin. Office of Public Info.: "Mortgage Insurance on Housing for the Elderly," F.H.A. Consumer Bulletin #247 (revised).* See also, §167(K) of the I.R.C. which provides certain tax incentives to encourage rehabilitation expenditures on low-income rental housing.

206. Simon, *The New Years*, c. 5 (Knopf, N.Y., 1968).

207. Scholler, *Churches Enter the Housing Business*, 80 Christian Century (#42) (Oct. 10, 1966). In St. Petersburg, Florida, in 1988 many such buildings (mainly high-rise) were being operated by religious denominations.

208. Of June 21, 1966. This was still substantially true in 1993.

209. N.A.A.C.P. v. Button, 371 U.S. 415 (1963).

210. Brotherhood of Railroad Trainmen v. Virginia Bar Assn., 377 U.S. 1 (1964).

211. United Mine Workers of Amer., Distr. 12 v. Illinois State Bar Assn., 389 U.S. 217 (1967).

212. See, *Symposium on Group Law Practice*, 18 Clev.-Mar. L. Rev. (1)1-52 (1969).

213. Act, Sec. 121(b)(7), amending I.R. Code Sec. 502.

214. See definitions herein, and in Oleck, *Nonprofit Types, Uses, and Abuses*; 1970, 19 Clev. St. L. Rev. 207, at 211 (1970). Control of business organizations by majority stock vote, or by cumulative voting is approved by statute in most states; see, *e.g., Ohio Rev. Code Sec. 1701.55.*

215. *N.Y. Not-for Profit Corp. L. §§601* et seq.

216. Calif. Nonprofit Corp. L., art. 3 (esp. §5334).

217. *Ibid.*

218. *See,* Gray, *State Attorney General, Guardian of Public Charities???*, 14 Cleve.-Mar. L. Rev. 236 (1965); Bogert, *State Supervision of Charities*, 52 Mich. L. Rev. 639 (1954). Ownership by management, in most nonprofit organizations, is a flat contradiction of the *pro bono publico* idea that is the essence of (proper) group activity not-for-profit. And *see,* Oleck, (chm.), *Trends in Nonprofit Organizations Law*, c. 6 (Maraghy) (1977).

219. *See,* Lord Eldon's opinion in Corporation of Ludlow v. Greenhouse (1827), 1 Bli. N.S.P.C., 17, 48; *and see* Jones, *History of the Law of Charity*, 1532-1827, at p. 161 (Cambridge Univ. Press. 1969); Chester New, *The Life of Henry Brougham* 217, 218, 223, 224 (Oxford Univ. Press, 1961). The public is concerned especially when tax or other benefits are enjoyed by people who abuse tax-free status. *See,* DiMarco and Kane, *Privileges and Immunities of Nonprofit Organizations*, 19 Clev. St. L. Rev. 264 (1970).

220. *E.g., Jones* op. cit. supra, n. 214 at 167; *and see,* for example, *The Commission of 1818* (in England) described therein, and the next one in the 1840s, *etc,* down to the Mills Committee and the resulting (U.S.) Tax Reform Act of 1969 described in the Symposium in 19 Clev. St. L. Rev. (No. 2) 207-322 (May 1970).

221. As to the history of the Act, subsequently, see generally, Jordan, *Philanthropy in England 1480-1660* (1959) and Marshall, *The Charities Act, 1960* (1961) 24 M.L.R. 44, 445-446.

222. *See,* 2 Beale, *Conflict of Laws*, §179.2 *et passim* (1935).

223. *See,* Oleck, *Modern Corporation Law*, §6 (1978 supp.), citing: Mont. Rev. Code §15-1201, N.Y. Gen. Corp. L. §6, Nev. Gen. Corp. L. §1, Ohio Rev. Code §1701.98, 1702,58 (B).

5

UNINCORPORATED ASSOCIATIONS

[Acknowledgment to Dee Mateer and Phillip Zies for research in updating this chapter.]

§47. VOLUNTARY ASSOCIATIONS, IN GENERAL

Humans tend to form groups for cooperative purposes; this tendency seems to be instinctive. Many anthropologists, sociologists, and political philosophers speak of humans as a "social animal" who normally hunts and lives in groups or "packs."[1] Some speak of these tendencies as "shared commitment"' *contractual* in nature—for the achievement of shared ends or purposes, which in turn involves a need for express or *implied* agreement, and for rules to hold the group together (*e.g.*, its "legal principles").[2] Organization of groups usually is informal, loose, and "unincorporated" at first, and then increasingly formal, tight, and corporate as the society becomes more sophisticated.

Western civilization has been (and is) characterized by voluntary associations of people, from the earliest warrior bands and "churches" to towns, and universities, and guilds, etc.[3] Corporations, as vehicles for such associations, did not exist until relatively recently, and associations were (and very many still are) unincorporated.[4] Unincorporated associations as a form of organization have been losing ground to the corporation, but are far from obsolete.[5]

§48. NONPROFIT ASSOCIATIONS, IN GENERAL

[See Sections 443, 444 as to "legal entity."]

Statutory provisions for unincorporated associations are fragmentary and inadequate in almost all of the states. In most cases, they consist of short sections scattered through the state's code. Thus, there usually is a provision for agricultural associations in one place, one for firemen's associations in another, one for fraternal associations in still another part of the state's code, and so on.

Incomplete and sketchy provisions of this kind are found in the statutes of such states as California, Delaware, Florida, Illinois, New York, and Ohio. In some states, there are hardly any provisions for unincorporated associations.

New Jersey's statute for *Unincorporated Organizations*[6] is an example of a relatively integrated provision. It consists of a few short sections, and deals with lawsuits involving such organizations. Its primary purpose is to allow lawsuits to be brought by or against an unincorporated association in its recognized name, if it has one. It allows service of legal process on the president or other officer, agent, or person in charge of its business, and execution of judgement against its assets. But it also allows suit and judgement against any members who are personally liable, if the organization does not satisfy a judgment against it, or even without suit against the association as an organization.[7]

The New Jersey statute, at its end, expressly exempts from its application, in regard to lawsuits of equitable nature, charitable and fraternal organizations.[8] This is not explained.

The New Jersey statutes also contain a small volume, in the set, dealing with various *special types* of organizations and certain of their problems.[9] This, however, mixes corporate and unincorporated matters in confusing style.

California's bulky statutes contain bits and pieces about unincorporated associations, scattered through volumes, and chapters, and sections dealing with corporations, probate, finance, military matters, etc.[10]

New York's short statute on unincorporated associations, like New Jersey's, consists mainly of a few provisions concerning lawsuit procedures by or against associations, service of process, and the like.[11]

Statutes of most states, such as they are, usually are much like those of California, New Jersey, or New York.[12]

It is easy to see, from the examples of these statutes, how undesirable the unincorporated form of organization usually is to its members. Use of this form of organization today usually results from sheer ignorance of the possible degree of personal liability of its members.

Either natural persons or corporations may be members of unincorporated associations.[13] The most familiar type of association of corporations is the trade association.

Modern associations usually are organized on roughly the following basis:

1. Articles of Association. This is an agreement (contract) among the original members, to which new members also agree. It sets up the general plan of organization, the purpose to be accomplished, and the method of operation.

    In a few states, where statutes exist as to this matter, they direct merely that articles of association shall provide:

    a. That the death or departure of a member shall not work a dissolution of the association.

     b. That the board of directors or trustees shall consist of (3), (5) members who shall have the sole management of association affairs.

     c. Any other management of association affairs not inconsistent with law.[14]

2. Constitution. This is the basic internal law of the organization, equivalent to a national or a state constitution. Sometimes it is implicit in the articles of association.

3. Bylaws. This is the detailed set of internal laws covering internal procedures and regulations. It is equivalent to the specific statutes of a state, as contrasted with the general provisions of a constitution. Sometimes the bylaws are in the constitution or even in the articles of association.

4. Management is carried on by an elected board of directors or trustees, who often are also the officers of the association.

5. Membership is evidenced by certificates of membership (or membership cards), which sometimes are transferable.

6. Continuity of existence in the event of the death, resignation, or expulsion of any member usually is provided by the articles of association.

7. Property-holding power is vested in the board of directors or trustees.

8. Income tax exemption applies to the organization if its activities as a whole are not for the profit of its members.[15]

    Because a nonprofit association is neither a partnership nor a corporation, it has a very indefinite character. Except insofar as statutes in a few states provided, it was not viewed as a legal entity in the past, and still is not in some respects, while it *is* in others. It suffers constant difficulties in acquiring, holding, and passing title to property, in making contracts, and in bringing or defending legal actions.

    In recent years, governmental authorities have applied regulatory administration to many unincorporated as well as incorporated group activities. As a result, few advantages remain to the modern association. It is a desirable form of organization only for very special purposes.

§49. ASSOCIATION TAXED LIKE CORPORATION

If a not-for-profit association qualifies as a tax-exempt organization it will, for the most part, avoid the problems of taxation. [See the Chapters on Tax Exemption]. However, many not-for-profit entities must pay federal, state and local taxes.[16]

    For purposes of the federal income tax, any entity, whether or not it is incorporated under state law, will be taxed as a corporation if:

1. It has a continuity of life beyond the natural lives of its members.

2. It has centralized management.

3. Its shareholders have limited liability.

4. Its shares are freely alienable.[17]

If an organization has only three of the four aforementioned attributes, it will still be taxed as an association.[18]

§50. WHAT ORGANIZATIONS SHOULD USE ASSOCIATION FORM?

Small local organizations, such as the following types, are the kinds of organizations that best can use unincorporated association form:

1. *Local clubs.* Social and sport groups of a local or neighborhood character often find the formalities of incorporation undesirable But it should be understood by them that informal oral agreements of association are full of uncertainties. Formal articles of association (*e.g.,* a constitution and bylaws) are the minimum provisions to avoid both misunderstanding and possible full personal liability.

2. *Local societies.* Musical, literary, or religious societies may take the unincorporated association form, subject to the dangers pointed out in item 1, above.

3. *Fraternal benefit societies.* These must use written articles of association. Their activities that have the character of insurance or indemnity are strictly subject to regulation by state insurance and public welfare statutes and authorities.

4. *Political clubs and committees.* These should use written articles of association. They are subject in all states to special statutes. They are usually required to have the approval of county or state party headquarters if their activities or names are party-organizational. *Propaganda organizations* may *have to* employ unincorporated form as in the case of the organization to favor liberal homosexual laws, which was, for a time, refused a chapter of incorporation because its purpose was (as yet) illegal, although the refusal finally was reversed in 1973.[19]

5. *Labor unions.* This is by far the most important group of unincorporated associations. Labor unions, particularly, often find it preferable not to incorporate.[20]

    The vagueness of organizational liability is here an advantage. Activities of these associations sometimes fall in a liability twilight zone, and the association form further obscures both personal liability and that of the group. Such legislation as the Taft-Hartley Act (Labor Management Act of 1947) failed to clarify this uncertainty. The effect of viewing associations as *entities* is discussed below and in the section on Lawsuits by or

Against an Association. *Requiring* incorporation would make the lines of liability very clear. There was an abortive attempt of this kind in 1944 in Colorado (*American Federation of Labor v. Reilly*),[21] but it failed to have effect.

At common law, a labor union did not have an existence separate from its members.[22] As a result, union liability in such situations as picket line assaults was often based on the theory of conspiracy.[23] Today, however, courts rarely apply this theory, for most jurisdictions statutorily permit unions to be sued as unincorporated associations.[24] And although the courts are hardly consistent in their treatment of union liability, courts oftentimes apply the usual principles of agency law in determining union liability in the event of unfair labor practices.[25] The implication of such application is treated in more detail below.

6.   *Charitable trusts (unincorporated foundations).* This type of nonprofit organization is not treated as a legal entity, but rather, involves the legal and equitable rights and duties among the trust properties, the trustees, and the beneficiaries.[26] Legal title to the trust properties is in the trustees, who manage trust affairs.[27] These charitable trusts have become numerous in recent years. They are predominantly controlled by traditional trust law, although there is an increasing body of statutory law which is replacing many of the traditional aspects.[28]

According to the Patman Committee investigation report in 1962,[29] wherein the author served as Consultant to the Congressional Committee, foundations (incorporated and unincorporated) increased to 45,124 tax-exempt foundations in 1960 as against 12,295 in 1952.[30] Congressman Patman charged that many foundations were used as tax-free cloaks for private business operation.[31] Others, including the author, had pointed out such abuses earlier.[32] For such a purpose, the unincorporated charitable trust form has some advantages over incorporation.[33]

It is doubtful that the "self-dealing" prohibitions of the Tax Reform Acts of 1969, 1984 and 1986 will completely cure this. Such a unit often is set up with endowment consisting of stock of business corporations controlled by the founder.

Six types of trusts generally are regarded as charitable: relief of poverty, aid to education, aid to religion, health promotion, community benefit, and aid to government.

Mere benevolence, such as a trust for division of a fund among a group of school children, is not an "educational purpose," as the children might use the money for other than educational purposes. Thus it is not a charitable trust.[34] If the trustee had been directed to buy books for the children, on the other hand, that would have been a charitable trust.

A trust for the benefit of a small group such as relatives (or employees) of the settlor, even for an educational purpose, in some states is not a valid *charitable* trust because it lacks the required true trust concept of public spirit.[35]

Likewise, the American and Canadian Internal Revenue Services may refuse tax exemptions for a trust that benefits only employees of the settlor.

Cy pres doctrine: usually the trust will not fail even if that particular purpose becomes impossible to achieve. The court will order use of the fund for a similar charitable purpose. This is on the theory that the settlor would have wanted his intention carried out "as nearly as possible," if his main motive was charitable.[36]

If the purpose of the settlor is very specific, and is not fundamentally an expression of a general charitable intent, failure of that purpose means failure of that trust. In such case the *cy pres* doctrine ordinarily will not be applied.[37]

§51. ASSOCIATION PROPERTY

Only a human being, or a group of humans recognized as a legal entity, can hold title to property, unless specific statutes provide otherwise. Early common law established that rule, and it still applies. When title to property is conveyed to a group having an artificial name, the conveyance to that name is meaningless unless the group is a legal entity (such as a corporation) except as special statutes may validate such a transfer.

Therefore, when property is conveyed to an informally associated group, the courts ordinarily view the conveyance as a transfer to the individual persons who comprise the group.[38] What this means is that each person has become a part-owner. Title can now be conveyed only with his consent, and subject to the legal rights of his family, heirs, and creditors.[39] A clumsier method of holding title to property is hard to imagine.

The following recent case illustrates the problems often encountered in unincorporated associations concerning the ownership of property. A nonprofit unincorporated association, named the Bass Anglers Sportsman Society, had filed suit against BASS, Inc. and its founder, Ray W. Scott Jr., alleging that Scott owed the members of the unincorporated association $75 million allegedly looted from the nonprofit association. The complaint stated that Scott, after forming the nonprofit Sportsman Society, started a new profit corporation, BASS, Inc., some 18 months after the nonprofit association was formed, using a name that was deceptively similar to the nonprofit association's name. The profit society is alleged to have converted assets (BASS Master Magazine) and revenues of the unincorporated nonprofit society to the profit corporation without a vote from the members or notification to the member/subscribers. The suit seeks ouster of the BASS, Inc. leadership and formation of a trust for the property as well as punitive damages.[40]

A partial cure for this impossible situation is the designation, by the association members, of trustees to take hold and convey title on their behalf.[41] But this solution is made undesirable by another rule of law—the *rule against perpetuities.* This rule forbids title to be tied up: (*e.g.,* in trust) by the wishes of the transferor for a period longer than that measured by *"lives in being plus 21 years."* (i.e., the lifetime of the longer-lived of two designated persons).[42]

This rule makes an exception for charitable trusts—an exception that may not apply if the association is merely "nonprofit" and not actually "charitable" in purpose. Thus, trusts for fraternal associations have been held to be invalid under this rule,[43] and in other cases have been held to be valid.[44]

Solution of this puzzle was provided for in some states by statutes affecting specially designated types of religious societies and other highly charitable associations. These statutes permitted taking title in the group name.[45] All the states make a general provision to this effect for profit-making associations (partnerships).[46] A similar general provision for nonprofit associations would simplify the problem. As it is, many associations prefer to incorporate simply to gain this advantage. In New York, for example, incorporation is encouraged by a statute that permits an incorporated association to take title to association property merely by incorporating.[47]

Tax Exemption: Insofar as property is used within the state for the truly charitable purposes of an association, it is free in most states from property taxes, inheritance, and gift taxes.[48] Tax exemption is a subject that requires separate treatment, and it cannot be treated here.[49]

Such property as association records is subject to ordinary governmental regulation and supervision, including investigation. But the Constitutional guaranties against unreasonable searches and seizures, which apply to natural persons, do not protect association property. The unincorporated association is not a "person" in this sense.[50]

Such property as an automobile must be registered in the name of an individual, not of the association. This, again, is because the association is not a legal "person" for this purpose, unless a specific statute so provides.[51]

Such property as a name or its goodwill usually is protected by general statutes against unfair appropriation by third persons.[52]

§52. LAWSUITS BY OR AGAINST AN ASSOCIATION

[See below, the chapter on *Lawsuits and Litigation*.]
At common law, not being a legal entity, an association can sue or be sued only in a representative capacity.[53] That is, a trustee or director must act on behalf of the association. He personally is named as a party, though only in a representative sense.

But by 1922 the United States Supreme Court had ruled that, even in the absence of statutes, an unincorporated association (there, a labor union) could be sued as an entity, in its own name, for its agents' torts.[54] This rule was codified in the Federal Rules of Civil Procedure.[55] It later was restated, as to labor unions, by the Labor Management Relations Act, to make damages payable only by the association, not against a member.[56] But then the State of Oregon first reaffirmed the common law rule as its rule and then made it not the rule for unions.[57] And in 1960 a federal court upheld a suit against a trustee of a union welfare fund which, under Pennsylvania law, could be sued as a "foreign corporation or similar entity."[58]

Then, in 1962 in the case of *Marshall v. ILWU*, the Supreme Court ruled that a member could sue an unincorporated association (labor union) as an entity, for torts committed by members.[59] And in 1965 Ohio adopted the "legal entity" view of nonprofit organizations.[60] The difficulties of the old view of unincorporated associations have about worn out the patience of the courts.[61] In 1972, for example, Illinois ruled that unincorporated associations may be treated as corporations for lawsuit purposes.[62]

Today, many states specifically authorize legal action to be brought in the association name, or against the association itself.[63] Statutes permitting legal action are now found in several states, including Florida, Illinois, California, Virginia and New York; often referring to Condominium Associations.

In addition to statutory change, procedural rules[64] and judicial decisions authorize an incorporated association to sue and be sued in the association name or the names of specific officers. The law favors this view.[65]

New York and Ohio permit action naming either the association or its representatives,[66] but Florida (until recently)[67] did not allow suits against associations as such.

The recent state rule of Indiana allowing suit in its common name against an unincorporated association does not change the substantive rule that the association is not liable for torts of members against other members.[68]

Louisiana holds that an unincorporated association may be an "entity" like a corporation, separate from its members and shielded from personal liability for torts if the tort was within the organization purpose; *e.g.*, nature of acts of members of a hunting club.[69]

An unincorporated association (of business companies forming a franchisees *advertising pool*) proving partial performance by some members, followed by failure to continue to contribute by some, shows a breach of contract situation. An association suit and judgment *in the association name* is error, but the award may be amended and remanded so as to allow *paying members* to collect the damages from those who did not pay. Otherwise, the defendants would be unjustly enriched.[70]

An unincorporated association cannot be a party to a lawsuit in Massachusetts; but individuals may have "standing."[71] Massachusetts does not permit suit against a "representative" of an unincorporated association.[72]

The local courts usually assume jurisdiction over unincorporated associations whenever a branch of the association (such as a union local) carries on activities within the state. In New Jersey, New York, Pennsylvania, and many other states, the tests of "doing business" that apply to any foreign (out-of-state) corporation are applied also to foreign associations. The presence and representative activity of local agents is the basic test of local court jurisdiction over foreign organizations.[73]

The law favors the right of unincorporated associations to sue or be sued in the organization name, rather than as partnerships, for procedural-reasoning convenience, in uncertain cases.[74] However, partnership law is still applied to unincorporated associations in some cases. For example, in *partnership* litigation under 28 U.S. Code § 1654 the "firm" cannot appear *pro se* by a partner. This is the same as when a *layperson* represents others having an interest in a corporation or partnership (or an *unincorporated association*). An attorney should be retained.[75]

§53. ASSOCIATION AGENTS' AND MEMBERS' POWERS AND LIABILITIES

[G. Phillip Zies contributed research for some of the cases in this section.]

As in a multimember partnership, each member of an unincorporated association is liable for the acts of the others done in the course and scope of the association's business.[76] However, an unincorporated association has no legal entity or existence apart from its members.[77] In legal effect, each member becomes both a principal and an agent as to all other members for the actions of the group itself; accordingly, as a principal he has no cause of action against a co-principal (the group) for the wrongful conduct of their common agent.[78] Typically, the cases have involved fraternal organizations or beneficial associations.[79] For example, in an unincorporated (college fraternity) association tort injury of a member by a member is part of the joint enterprise and is imputed to all; e.g., in a hazing injury (the imputed negligence doctrine).[80]

Similarly, a *member* of a Fraternal Order of Police (unincorporated association) who fell from a scaffold while helping in renovation of the clubhouse, may *not* sue the association for negligence of its members in erecting the scaffolding, which is a joint enterprise in which the tort of one is attributed to all (e.g., as though suing herself) in Indiana.[81]

The general rule as to associations was arrived at by applying to other forms of voluntary unincorporated associations the rules of law developed in the field of business partnerships. Under traditional legal concepts the partnership is regarded as an aggregate of individuals, with each partner acting as agent for all other partners in the transaction of partnership business, and the agents of the partnership acting as agents for all of the partners. When these concepts are transferred bodily to other forms of voluntary associations, such as fraternal organizations, clubs, and labor unions, which act normally through elected officers and in which the individual members have little or no authority in the day-to-day operations of the association's affairs, reality is apt to be sacrificed to theoretical formalism. The courts, in recognition of this fact, have from case to case gradually evolved new theories in approaching the problems of such associations, and there is now a respectable body of judicial decision, especially in the field of labor-union law, which recognizes the existence of unincorporated labor unions as separate entities for a variety of purposes, and which recognizes as well that the individual members of such unions are not in any true sense principals of the officers of the union or of its agents and employees, so as to be bound personally by their acts under the strict application of the doctrine of "respondeat superior."[82]

Like a corporation, which is an artificial entity, an association can act only through agents or representatives. The amount of authority delegated to an agent must be determined by the executive board or the trustees, pursuant to the powers granted by the members.

The agent can bind the association only to the extent to which he is authorized to act.[83] But the general rules of principal and agent (agency law) also apply. The apparent (seeming) authority of an agent may bar the association from later denying that he actually had such authority. But if an agent clearly exceeds his authority, the members are not liable, if they have not negligently or fraudulently permitted third persons to be misled. Persons dealing with an agent have a duty to make reasonable inquiry, and to demand reasonable proof of the actual scope of his authority.[84]

The acts of the association's agents may either be authorized in advance or ratified or adopted afterwards. In both cases, the members of the association assume liability.[85]

Members of an unincorporated civic association are not bound by an association contract as to land use when they indicate dissent by letters or resignation from the group, where their *property rights* are affected by the contract.[86]

An uncertain implied authority inheres in some types of agency. Thus, an agent who is authorized to buy something for a certain price has implied power either to pay cash or to give association notes or other paper in payment, unless the authorization is specific on these points. In certain types of associations, such as social clubs, it is generally held that an agent can bind only the funds of the association, such as dues and contributions. The personal liability of members of such associations cannot be involved by the agent, at least in routine matters. This is because it is generally understood that most such associations are very limited in their purposes and operations.[87]

But if the facts and circumstances give to the agent the apparent power to commit the members personally, they may actually be bound by his actions. For example, if a club's agent leases a clubhouse in the name of the club, some cases have held that this binds the members. Ordinarily, of course, club members expect and consent to no such extent of liability. But if the lessor has reasonable causes to believe they did so consent, he may enforce his rights against them personally as well as against the association.[88]

Similarly, a nonprofit unincorporated political committee is liable to a printer for printing orders, under the doctrine of apparent authority, if the political committee fostered a reasonable belief that campaign workers were authorized to place printing orders for campaign materials in reasonable amounts, and where the committee did not communicate to the printer that only particular persons could place orders. The candidate is also jointly and severally liable for the debts, if the candidate's unawareness of the transaction is a result of her failure to repudiate the unauthorized transactions upon receipt of invoices from the printer. The candidate is also liable if the committee had no personality separate from the candidate under a theory similar to "piercing the corporate veil."[89] In a contrasting decision, a New York court held that as long as the members and officers of a voluntary unincorporated nonprofit campaign committee don't intend to be personally liable for the debts of the committee, they will not be held liable. The candidate is not liable for the debts if he never agreed to assume the debts of his campaign committee.[90]

In most cases, the liability of members of an association is determined by the general principles of agency law. Little significant legislation exists on this precise point (except for labor unions, which are treated in the next section). In one case a member of a trade association was held to be not liable for the salary of the editor of the association's journal, because the member was inactive.[91] But in another (old) case, the members of a college alumni group were held liable for the costs of a yearbook because they had chosen one member to publish it.[92] Acceptance of the benefits of an unincorporated association (e.g., a home owners association) may imply contract-type duty to pay a share of its expenses.[93]

In most associations, the directors also are the officers of the association, and thus are its principal agents. A large association may also have many employees, some of whom may have the status of agents.

An association is liable, as a principal, for the negligence or other wrongful acts of an agent, when these acts are committed by him during, and within the scope of, his authorized duties. What is and what is not "in the course and scope of his employment" is a question of fact in each case.[94]

Members' Lawsuits Against Their Association (for Torts): Most states do not allow a member to sue his or her unincorporated association for tort (*e.g.*, negligent) injury to him or her, but some states do.[95] See Chapter 44.

In Indiana, members of fraternal organization (unincorporated association) are not personally liable for its bar sale or serving of alcoholic drinks to a nonmember who is injured, if they are not officers or board members and are not specifically involved in the sale.[96]

In New York, statutes authorizing actions against individual members of unincorporated associations do not create new substantive rights or liabilities. An unincorporated association has no existence independent of its members. All liability for the tortious conduct of agents or employees of unincorporated associations is that of each member individually. Members must have authorized or ratified the tortious conduct to be liable.[97]

In Texas, a member of an unincorporated association is not precluded from bringing a negligence action against the association solely because he/she is a member of the association. Satisfaction of a judgment against the association may be obtained by reaching any assets of an unincorporated charitable association, held either by the association or in trust by a member of the association.[98] Similarly, the South Carolina Supreme Court said, "We hold that . . . an unincorporated association, regardless of its underlying purpose, is amenable to suit by its members for tortious acts."[99]

In New Jersey, when a plaintiff was injured after he fell down an elevator shaft in a lodge building, a New Jersey court held that the imputed negligence doctrine was an anachronism that resulted in injustice and no longer advanced public policy.[100]

§54. SPECIAL RULES FOR LABOR UNIONS

Agents of a labor union may bind the union only on the express authorization of the members.[101] In fact, courts have held that the employer acts at his peril if he acts merely on the implied or apparent authority of union representatives.[102] However, many state courts have applied the theory of "implied consent" to hold both the international and local unions liable for picket line assaults. In addition, under this theory, the courts may imply authorization or ratification from union silence or omissions concerning acts of violence.[103]

This is unlike the general law of agency, and clearly tends to contribute to the corruption of the labor movement. A partial remedy for this difficulty was attempted by the 1947 Federal Act in making consent or ratification not controlling.[104]

Distinctly the leading case on modern views of the labor union as an association (*e.g.*, an *entity* rather than a loose partnership) is the 1962 *Marshall* case, which has been cited several times hereinabove. Even before that, the federal courts had said that an unincorporated labor union could be sued as an entity in federal courts. The Supreme Court also said:[105]

> Structurally and functionally, a labor union is an institution which involves more than the private or personal interests of its members. It represents organized, institutional activity as contrasted with wholly individual activity. This difference is as well-defined as that existing between individual members of the union. The union's existence in fact, and for some purposes in law, is as perceptual as that of any corporation, not being dependent upon the life of any member . . . 'The actions of one individual member no more bind the union than they bind another individual member unless there is proof that the union authorized or ratified the acts in question. At the same time, the members are not subject to either criminal or civil liability for the acts of the union or its officers as such *unless it is shown that they personally authorized or participated in the particular acts . . .*'[106]

The labor union then was labeled "a separate legal entity," similar to a corporation; and described as *sui generis* and no longer comparable to voluntary fraternal orders or partnerships.[107] The conclusion in the *Marshall* case was that an injured member could sue the union for damages and not be defeated by the old concept that he was suing his "partners" and thus himself.

Contracts. A representative cannot bind the union as an entity in some states. He can bind only the current membership, which changes constantly.[108] In Massachusetts (according to some decisions) and New York, on the other hand, the union is viewed as a legal entity for this purpose.[109] In either case, the membership and the agents change quite often, creating a very foggy agency situation, though *procedural* statutes usually permit suits.

In a state such as Mississippi, the union's contract is a "third-party beneficiary contract." The union members are the beneficiaries. The beneficiaries can enforce the agreement against the parties, but the parties rarely have any enforcement powers other than those specifically stated in the contract.[110] Usually such contracts are strictly enforced by the courts against the individual employee.

Union arbitration agreements have been held to bind nonunion employees. An association of nonunion public school teachers sought to set aside arbitration awards upholding the deduction of union service fees from teachers' pay. The court required nonunion members of the bargaining unit to pay their fair share of the costs for collective bargaining, contract administration and grievance adjustment to the exclusive bargaining representative.[111]

A more logical view is that of the federal courts, adopted by such states as Missouri and Nebraska, that a labor contract is a direct contract between each employee and the employer.[112] In this view, the union representatives are merely agents for the individual employees. Only under this theory can an employer logically obtain specific performance of the contract. Otherwise, an employee always can defy his own union, if necessary. All the union can do to force him to honor his agreement is to expel him. If he is not afraid to seek other kinds of work, this threat is futile.[113]

If the union representatives act intentionally, in causing harm to members, the union clearly is liable.[114] The same is true where a special duty of representation is owed to the particular member.[115] Such a duty often is a question of discretion on the part of union officers; and the courts prefer not to interfere unless abuse of a fiduciary duty is shown.[116] And if business judgment is involved, the discretionary aspect usually bars court interference.[117] In Massachusetts, an employee is entitled to relief for the union's breach of duty of fair representation where his or her grievance was not clearly frivolous.[118]

All in all, the state of union responsibility vis-à-vis members is still unclear. For example, it was held that a union did not violate N.L.R.B. rules by fining strike-breaker members; the contract theory being viewed as governing the case.[119]

Recently a longshoreman's union local sought to compel pretrial disclosure of the names of Union members who told government officials that the union had attempted to extort money and property from them. The government could not use the informer's privilege to shield the member's identity because their testimony was the sole evidence of the members' state of mind.[120]

Whether or not one agrees with the precise provisions of such statutes as the Taft-Hartley Act, or the Norris-LaGuardia Anti-Injunction Act, it is clear that carefully drawn, specific legislation still is necessary. The modern labor union is only partly a nonprofit organization in the sense of an eleemosynary or charitable association. To lump it indiscriminately with such organizations is simply unrealistic. It is "big business" in itself (more aptly, "big labor"). Its social importance demands special treatment and special legislation.

§55. EXEMPTION OF ASSOCIATIONS FROM COLLECTIVE BARGAINING

The exemption of some nonprofit organizations, such as hospitals, from the duty to engage in collective bargaining with labor unions has led to some difficulties.[121]

The Taft-Hartley Act of 1947 was intended to impose a duty on employers to collectively bargain with their employees.[123] Since the American national policy was to encourage workers to organize in order to achieve better working conditions, this imposed duty was a means to reach the objective of better conditions.[123] Thus, the duty of the employers to bargain was purely statutory.[124]

However, the exemption of some nonprofit organizations, such as hospitals, from the definition of "employer" enabled such organizations to avoid the duty of collective bargaining,[125] in addition to causing some other difficulties. But, in 1951, a Utah decision reopened the matter and gave the states the power to control the question, with the result that the Utah hospital employees could utilize collective bargaining.[127]

In 1974, however, the definition of "employer" was amended so as to no longer exempt hospitals from its coverage.[128] Nevertheless, subsequent case law remained inconsistent in its treatment of hospitals; some courts held that they were now political subdivisions while others deemed them to be employers.[129] Suffice it to say that state law will probably still be determinative of whether hospitals are employers, and whether they have an affirmative duty to collectively bargain.

Of course, the rising costs of hospital care have been attributed in large part to costs of workers' services, which is quite unfair.[130] If anything, it is the physicians and the drug and supply people who, between them, have been drawing great wealth from their hospital connections. New York settled the debate, there, in 1967, by statute amendment granting bargaining rights to employees of charitable hospitals.[131] This would be the simplest and most reasonable way for all states to end the exploitation of hospital service workers.

§56. ORGANIZING THE ASSOCIATION

In practice many unincorporated associations just "sort of grow" into going organizations, out of informal (often social) meetings of their members. This is very human but not very wise.

The members ought to meet more or less formally, and discuss purposes, plans, and proposals. Then the persons concerned should reduce their agreement to written form.

The agreement is the *Articles of Association,* or sometimes, the *Constitution,* or the *Charter.* These may contain rules for internal management procedures, or the body of internal rules may be stated in a separate document; in either case, the rules are the *Bylaws.*

Forms of articles, constitutions, and bylaws should be understood to be merely guides. The provisions of the articles for each association must be tailored to its purposes, personnel, funds, facilities, and the agreed plan of operation. When the articles are duly signed and adopted, the association comes into existence.

In some states, articles of association must be filed with the secretary-of-state and with the clerk of the county in which the association's principal office is located. In a few states, a certificate stating the name of the organization, its office, and its officers is required instead. Use of an assumed (group) name also may require filing, in the nature of licensing, with penalties for failure to file.[132]

§57. MANAGING THE ASSOCIATION

Internal management of an unincorporated association must be carried on as provided by the articles of association. In most states where statutes cover the subject, the management must be in the hands of a board of directors or trustees, consisting of at least three (or five) persons.[133]

The rights of members of the association (other than mere social relations) often are viewed as property rights. Interference with such rights mainly is treated much as is any improper interference with any property rights, by the issuance of injunctions or damage awards by the courts.[134] (See the next section, below.)

The courts ordinarily will not interfere with the purely internal affairs of an association, except to prevent fraud or to protect property and civil rights.[135] If, for example, a member is expelled, he must exhaust all the remedies provided by the association's rules before the courts will aid him, unless these remedies obviously are futile.[136] And then the courts will move only if he can show some illegality in the action against him. If he can show unfair or improper treatment, the courts can and will grant damages or even order his reinstatement.[137] When membership is valuable or necessary to him, or is tinged with public stature or purpose as in a professional or trade association, the courts will scrutinize an exclusion or expulsion with particular care.[138]

Membership in a private association, society, or club, or (to some extent) in a labor union, is open only to those the members choose to admit. And membership is not transferable unless the association's rule so provides. This right of choosing associates is called *delectus personae.* But restrictions must be reasonable.[139]

The managers of an association (the directors or trustees) are fiduciaries. They stand to the members almost in the position of full trustees. But among members there is no such fiduciary relationship except in special circumstances.[140]

Submission to the constitution and direction of apparent body or authority often is found in such subsidiaries as fraternal lodges, unions, and religious associations.

The *cy pres* rule of the law of trusts applies to nonprofit organizations. A trust fund always must be devoted as nearly as (cy pres) is possible to the trust purpose specified by the founder. If, for example, property is given to a religious association to benefit that association's faith, it may not be used for a different faith. If the association dissolves, the courts will order the property used for other, *closely similar* purposes, unless specific provision for such an eventuality was made by the founder.[141]

§58. EXCLUSION AND EXPULSION OF MEMBERS

[See index and text on *Freedom to Associate*.]

Denial of membership to would-be members, and expulsion of existing members, are basically civil rights (constitutional law) problems.[142] These matters are only incidentally questions of nonprofit association law, and the principles applicable are generally the same for unincorporated as for incorporated organizations. These often are problems of racial or religious discrimination and of the privilege to exercise the ordinary rights of citizenship, such as the right to vote, free speech, freedom of petition, right to resort to the courts, equal protection of laws in many respects, employment right, etc.

Basically, a private organization may limit its membership (exercise *delectus personae* choice of the person),[143] unless the organization is affected by a strong *public interest*.[144] A "strong public interest" may be said to be present, for example, in the constituency of a professional society or a trade association.[145] The exceptions and limitations are affected by such questions as when the 14th and 15th Amendments to the Constitution involve "state action" as against private action. Thus leases of public premises to organizations, and economic aid, and public licensing may inject "state action."[146]

The Civil Rights Act of 1964[147] particularly applies to clubs and organizations according to one view, and particularly does not apply according to another view.[148] Private school discrimination or segregation based on race is illegal,[149] and so is social fraternity or sorority discrimination, especially at public (state) institutions,[150] welfare organizations,[151] or a political "club" that is used as a mere device for exclusion.[152] But in June 1972 the United States Supreme Court held that a private club may exclude blacks from its restaurant, on the theory that the granting of a liquor license is not such "state action" as violates the constitution, and in August 1972 the Pennsylvania Supreme Court held otherwise.[153]

Where exclusion or expulsion involves the right to earn a living or other economic interests, today such action usually is viewed as improper. This is by case law decisions in some respects,[154] and more effectively by statutes forbidding racial discrimination by labor unions.[155] So, too, the right to belong to a professional society is upheld when it affects the right to practice one's profession and earn a living.[156] However, a medical clinic that expelled a member physician by following its procedural rules, for misconduct, is not to be dissolved on the basis of his claim of interference with his prospective economic advantages.[157]

§59. AMENDMENTS OF ARTICLES, CONSTITUTION, OR BYLAWS

[See chapter on amendments.]

Articles of association always should set forth precise procedures, including the number of votes necessary, for the amendment of the articles, the constitution, or the bylaws of the association. Or each document may contain provisions for its own amendment. Changes must, of course, be consistent with the law. The requirement of a two-thirds vote is customary.

Notice provisions are important. At least 10 days' notice of a meeting should be required, and *notice* should be defined to include purpose as well as time and place.

The statutory provisions, in the various states, for amendments of corporate articles and bylaws are good guides for similar action in unincorporated associations.[158]

§60. FOREIGN ASSOCIATIONS

[See the chapter on *Foreign Organizations.*]

If an association wishes to carry on activities in a state other than where its home office is located, it is a *foreign* organization in that other state.[159] Operation in another state usually involves filing in the other state and *qualifying* for license to do business there.[160]

Most state statutes provide that a foreign association must register if it undertakes more than occasional, isolated transactions, unless its activities can be classified as "interstate commerce."[161] Interstate commerce is exempt from state regulation.

Registration usually consists of the filing of a certificate with the secretary of state, designating him as the agent for the service of legal process against the association. This certificate usually must be signed by the president, vice president, or secretary, and the signature must be notarized. The certificate usually must set forth:

1. The names and places of residence of its officers and trustees.
2. Its principal place of operation.
3. The address of its office within the state.

Failure to file usually is punished by denying the association the right to use the local courts to enforce its contracts in the state.[162]

§61. DISSOLUTION

[See chapters on Dissolution.]
Statutory procedures for dissolution of corporations are good guides for dissolution formalities of unincorporated associations.[163]

Rules as to property disposal and other matters should be outlined, in case of dissolution of the organization, ideally in its articles of association. The procedure usually is to dissolve upon at least a two-thirds vote, or by consent of all the members. Some articles provide that no dissolution may be voted so long as seven members vote to continue. The other members then have little choice except to resign, unless fraud can be shown.

§62. "MIXED" UNINCORPORATED-CORPORATE ORGANIZATIONS

Cooperatives, and to some extent *professional "corporations"* and *trusts*, incorporated or unincorporated, present a special problem that resembles the reverse of the liability-fixing question discussed in the earlier parts of this paper.

A *trust*, for example, can be liable *as an entity* for wrongs done by its employees. But beneficiaries and/or trustees may be *personally liable* for wrongs done *by the trust*; and such liability depends mainly on the extent of *control* of (or, *right* to control) the trust organization. This is only obliquely a matter of the law of unincorporated nonprofit associations. In effect, a *corporate* organization (and of course, an *unincorporated* one) can involve personal liability that closely resembles that of a partnership.[164]

Professional corporations (or *associations*) of physicians or lawyers, are corporations almost solely for tax and pension purposes. For most other purposes they are treated as partnerships (*e.g.*, for ethics or personal liability purposes).[165]

Real estate cooperatives and condominiums can involve substantial risks of personal liability for members, which is proportionate to the amount of *control* of (or, *right* to control) common areas, whether the formal organization is based on corporate, trust, association, or individual-title-plus-cross-easement (or undivided interest in common areas). *Farm cooperatives* usually involve little personal liability for members, under most state statutory systems.[166]

POINTS TO REMEMBERS

- Always use articles of association. Do not rely on oral agreements.
- Tailor your articles to your purposes and plans.
- Use corporate form, if possible. It is better for all but a few kinds of organizations.
- Check your state laws to see whether or not the association as such can take title to property. If it cannot, appoint trustees to hold title for the association.
- Obey licensing and registration laws.
- Check your state laws as to whether the association can sue or be sued in its own name. If it cannot, designate an officer for this purpose and protect him with a bond.
- Remember that bankruptcy and insolvency laws make special provisions for nonprofit organizations.
- Remember that the law of "principal and agent" governs acts of association representatives; and beware of "implied" or "apparent" authority. Acceptance of benefits may imply agreement to contribute to association expenses and rules.
- Labor unions are subject to special laws. These laws change often. Check the latest statutes before you act.
- Provide carefully for internal management, meetings, members' rights, admission, and expulsion.
- Provide exact procedures for amendment of the charter, constitution, and bylaws.
- Register as a foreign association if you carry on any real activity in another state.
- Provide exact procedures for dissolution vote sand for distribution of property after payment of debts.
- Consider the use of unincorporated association form for effectuating the winding up process in dissolving a nonprofit organization.
- Consider the use of combinations of incorporated and unincorporated operation.

NOTES TO CHAPTER 5

1. L.L. Fuller, "Two Principles of Human Association," in *Voluntary Associations,* Pennock and Chapman, eds., (1969).

2. Contractual-type agreements may be implied as well as express. Seaview Assn. of Fire Island v. Williams, 69 N.Y. 2d 987, 510 N.E. 2d 793 (1987). Fuller suggests a series of eight "laws" governing the interrelations of the two aspects ("principles") of human "association." And see, S. Dickerson and M. Chapman, *Contract Law, Due Process, and the NCAA,* 5

J. Coll. and U.L. 107-21 (1978–9); T.D. Conners (ed.), The Nonprofit Organization Handbook, 1–4 (1978); 4 FL. Juris. 2d 110 (curr. ed.).

3. J.W. Chapman, "Voluntary Association and the Political Theory of Pluralism," in Voluntary Associations 87 (Pennock and Chapman, eds., 1969).

4. See generally, McNeill, The Rise of the West: A History of the Human Community (1963); Trevor-Roper, The Rise of Christian Europe (1965).

5. See, 1 Oleck, Modern Corporation Law, chs. 1, 2, 4 (1978 supp.); H. Ross, Florida Corporations, 23–25 (1984).

6. N.J. Stat. Anno., tit. 2A, c. 64, §64-1 to 64-6.

7. Id.

8. Id., §64-6.

9. N.J. Stat. Anno., tits. 15–16, Corps. & Ass'ns. Not-for-Profit.

10. See, Ann. Calif. Code, Gen. Index (West).

11. N.Y. Gen. Ass'ns., and N.Y. Consol. Laws., ch. 29. See, e.g., Lloyd v. Sloan, 259 App. Div. 615, 19 N.Y.S.2d 842 (1940) (judgment only to be satisfied out of the association's property).

12. N.C. Stat., §1, A-1, Rule 4(j)(8) (service of process).

13. N.J. Stat. Anno., tits. 15–16, Corps. & Ass'ns. Not-for-Profit, §64-9.

14. Id.

15. See generally, IRC §501(c).

16. E.g., Curran v. Mount Diablo Council of the Boy Scouts of America, 147 Cal. App. 3d 712, 195 Cal. Rptr. 325 (1983).

17. Internal Revenue Reg. §§301.7701-2, 301.7701-3.

18. Morrissey v. U.S., 296 U.S. 344 (1935), see also, Larson v. Cir, 66 TC 159 (Acq.) (1976).

19. Gay Activists Alliance v. Lomenzo, 320 N.Y.S.2d 994 (N.Y. Sup. Ct. 1971), revd. 38 A.D.2d 981, 329 N.Y.S.2d 181, affd. 331 N.Y.2d 965, 293 N.E.2d 255 (1973); and see Application of Thom, 33 N.Y.2d 609, 301 N.E.2d 542 (1973).

20. But this strategy now is not as effective as it used to be.

21. American Fed'n. of Labor v. Reilly, 113 Colo. 90, 155 P.2d 145, 160 A.L.R. 873 (1944).

22. Walker v. Locomotive Engineers, 186 Ga. 811, 199 S.E. 146 (1930); St. Paul Xypothetae v. St. Paul Bookbinders Union, 94 Minn. 351, 102 N.W. 725 (1905). See generally, Witmer, Trade Union Liability: The Problem of the Unincorporated Corporation, 51 Yale L.J. 49 (1941).

23. Wallick v. International Union of Elec. R. & M.W., 90 Ohio L. Abs. 584 (C.P. 1962); Koehring Co. v. National Automatic Tool Co., 257 F. Supp. 282 (N.D. Ind. 1966). See also, Burdick, The Tort Conspiracy as a Crime, and Conspiracy as a Tort, 7 Colum. L. Rev. 229 (1907); Hall v. Walters, 226 S.C. 430, 85 S.E.2d 729 (1955) (conspiracy theory in a picket line assault), cert. denied, 349 U.S. 953 (1955).

24. Sturges, Unincorporated Associations as Parties to Actions, 33 Yale L.J. 383 (1933); Myers, State Damage Suit by an Employer Against a Labor Union for Inquiries Incurred Through Violence During a Strike, 34 Tenn. L. Rev. 609, 622 (1967).

25. See R. Gorman, Labor Law, 216 (1976).

26. See Restatement (Second) of Torts §348 (1959). See also G.G. Bogert and G.T. Bogert, Law of Trusts, §1 (2d ed., 1964).

27. Henn and Pfeifer, Nonprofit Groups: Factors Influencing Choice of Form, Wake Forest L. Rev. 181, 197 (1975).

28. Id. at 199 n. 86. And see, Mohonk Trust v. Board of Assessors, 47 N.Y. 2d 476, 392 N.E. 2d 876 (1979).

29. House, U.S. Congress-Select Committee on Small Business. Tax-Exempt Foundations and Charitable Trusts: Their Impact on OUr Economy; chairman's report (1962).

30. Ibid.

31. Id. See, Krasnowiecki and Brodsky, Comment on the Patman Report, 112 U. Pa. L. Rev. 190 (1963); Good Will Home Ass'n. v. Erwin, 266 A.2d 218 (Me. Sup. Jud. Ct. 1970).

32. Oleck, Foundations Used as Business Devices, 9 Cleve-Mar. L. Rev. 339 (1960). Of course other types of organizations may also cloak business purposes behind a mantle of charity or education, etc., such as the "boys home" that ran a school that charged a tuition fee of $2,800. Good Will Home Ass'n. v. Erwin, 266 A.2d 218 (Me. Sup. Jud. Ct. 1970); this "purpose" being held to be ultra vires.

33. Id. See, Wallace, How to Save Money by Giving it Away, 47 Marquette L. Rev. 1 (1963); Comment, Charitable Trusts and Inducements to Violate the Law, 20 Wash. and Lee L. Rev. 85 (1963); Lusk, The Uncertain Future of Charitable Trusts, 15 Ala. L. Rev. 390 (1963).

34. Shenandoah Valley Nat'l. Bank. v. Taylor, 192 Va. 135, 63 S.E. 2d 786 (1951).

35. In re Compton (1945), Ch. 1923. Not valid for employees: Pennsylvania Bar Ass'n. Endowment v. Robbins, 10 Pa. D. & C. 2d 637 (C.P. Dauph. 1955); Valid: In re Barbieri 8 Misc. 2d 753, 167 N.Y.S. 2d 962 (1957); Boxer v. Boston Symphony, 339 Mass. 369, 159 N.E. 2d 336 (1959). The trustee, even if corporate, is not really the owner. Lefkowitz v. Cornell Univ., 62 Misc. 2d 95, 308 N.Y.S. 2d 85 (1970). Policy, rather than "magic words" is the test. Trustees of Dartmouth College v. City of Quincy, 258 N.E. 2d 745 (Mass. Sup. Jud. Ct. 1970).

36. Thatcher v. St. Louis, 335 Mo. 1130, 76 S.W. 2d 677 (1934); In re Byrd's Will, 62 Misc. 2d 232, 308 N.Y.S. 2d 97, 101 (1970); Haywood House v. Trustees of Donations and Bequests, 27 Conn. Sup. 176, 233 A.2d 5 (1967); and see, Brookes, "Foundations and Their Tax Problems," 41 Taxes 742 (1963). See also, Henn and Pfeifer, supra note 27, at 199 nn. 84 and 85.

37. Industrial Nat'l. Bank v. Drysdale, 83 R.I. 172, 114 A.2d 191 (1955); Industrial National Bank v. Drysdale, 83 R.I. 172, 114 A.2d 191 (1955); Industrial National Bank of R.I. v. Guiteras, 267 A.2d 706, 711 (R.I. Sup. Ct. 1970). But, the Doctrine of Approximation may apply. Daggert v. Children's Center, 28 Conn. Super. 468, 266 A.2d 72 (1970).

38. Normandy Consol. School Dist. v. Haral, 315 Mo. 602, 286 S.W. 86 (1926); Carpenters and Joiners Local 1846 v. Stephens Broadcasting Co., 214 La. 928, 39 So. 2d 422 (1949).

39. Apolostic Holiness Union v. Knudson, 21 Idaho 589, 123 P. 473 (1912); Adams v. Bethany Church, 361 S.2d 510 (Ala. 1978). Many states have statutes defining "corporations" as including associations for jurisdictional, tax, and other purposes, but these statutes apply primarily to business organizations. See, U.M.W. v. Coronado Coal Co., 259 U.S. 344, 27 A.L.R. 762 (1922) unincorporated union held liable, in union name, to treble damages under Sherman Anti-Trust Act, 15 U.S.C.A. §§1–7, 15 note (1963) and Stevens, Corporations §7 (2d ed. 1949); Bankers Trust Co. v. Knec, 222 Iowa 988, 263 N.W. 549 (1935). Corporations can be members of associations: 4 Oleck, Modern Corporation Law §1795 (Supp. 1978).

40. Cox, (article) 14 Nat. L.J. (30) 8 (March 30. 1992).

41. Venus Lodge No. 62, F.A.&M. v. Acme Benevolent Ass'n., Inc., 231 N.C. 522; 58 S.E. 2d 109, 15 A.L.R. 2d 1446, 1451 (1950).

42. See, Black's Law Dictionary, 4th ed., 1299, 1498 (1951).

43. In re Rathbone, 170 Misc. 1030, 11 N.Y.S. 2d 506 (1939) (fraternal order).

44. Bancroft v. Cook, 264 Mass. 343, 162 N.E. 691 (1928) (college fraternity). Trusts to a church for masses are usually upheld. O'Brien, Seventy Years of Bequests for Masses in New York Courts, 23 Fordham L. Rev. 147 (1954); Curran, Trusts for Masses, 7 Notre Dame Law 42 (1931). See also, Scott, Trusts, 3rd ed., 298 (1940) (cases).

45. See, Brown v. Father Divine, 163 Misc. 796, 298 N.Y.S. 642 (1937). See, e.g., N.J. Stat Anno. 15: 14-7 (repealed 1983) for a case dealing with the construction and application

of this statute, see, First Methodist Church in the City of New Brunswick, 141 N.J. Eq. 92, 56 A.2d 120 (1947). Florida statute 692.101 vests title to property of an unincorporated church in the trustees.

46. Uniform Partnership Act §§8(3), 8(4), 10(2).

47. N.Y. Not-for-Profit Corp. L. §§402, 403, 1405.

48. MacGregor v. Commissioner, 327 Mass. 484, 99 N.E. 2d 468 (1950 inheritance and gift taxes). See, e.g., N.J. Stat. Anno. 54:4-3.6.

49. See, e.g.: Nonprofit organization's apartment house gets no property tax-exemption where tenants pay rent. Friendship Manor Corp. v. Tax Comm'n., 487 P.2d 1272 (Utah 1971); Leased-out parts of a building of a charity organization may get no tax exemption. Milton Hospital and Convalescent Home v. Board of Assessors, 271 N.E. 2d 745 (MA. S. Ct. 1971); No state tax-exemption for fraternal order. In re Estate of Allen, 94 Cal. Rptr. 648 (App. 1971); Nor for sports club. State Bd. of Tax Comm'rs. v. Fort Wayne Sport Club, Inc., 258 N.E. 2d 874 (Ind. App. 1970); Not for veteran's association. In re Application of Am. Legion, 20 Ohio St. 2d 121, 254 N.E.2d 21 (1969). Nor for an old people's "home" that charged ample fees: ($9,000 to $25,000). Willow v. Munson, 43 Ill. 2d 203, 251 N.E.2d 249 (1969). Nor for a university restaurant. Ohio Northern Univ. v. Tax Comm'rs. 21 Ohio App.2d 133 255 N.E. 2d 297 (1970). As to charitable operation as the test of tax exemption right (as against social and other functions), see, Sahara Grotto & Styx, Inc. v. State Bd. of Tax Comm'rs. 261 N.E. 2d 873 (Ind. App. 1970); In re application of Dana W. Morey Foundation, 21 Ohio App. 2d 230, 256 N.E. 2d 232 (1970). The following articles may prove helpful: Note, Tax-Exempt Status of Public Interest Law Firms, 45 S. Cal. L. Rev. 228 (1972); Graves, When Will Political Activities of Unions and Associations Cost Them Their Exemption? J. Taxation 254 (1971); Fleming, Charitable Trusts Under the Tax Reform Act, 48 Taxes 757 (1970).

50. United States v. White, 322 U.S. 694 (1944); see also, Bellis v. United States, 417 U.S. 85, 87 (1974); United States v. Beattie, 522 F.2d 267, 270 (2d Cir. 1975).

51. Hanley v. American Ry Express Co., 244 Mass. 248, 138 N.E. 323 (1923).

52. Ancient Egyptian Arabic Order of Nobles of the Mustic Shrine v. Michaux, 279 U.S. 737 (1929); see also, Missouri Federation of the Blind v. National Federation of the Blind of Missouri, Inc., 505 S.W. 2d 1, 10 (Mo. 1973).

53. See Sturges, Unincorporated Associations as Parties to Actions, 33 Yale L.J. 383 (1924).

54. U.M.W. v.Coronado Coal Co., 259 U.S. 344 (1922).

55. Fed. R. Civ. P. 17(b).

56. 29 U.S.C. §185(b).

57. Benz v. Companio Naviera Hidalgo, S.A., 233 F.2d 62, 68 (9th Cir. 1956), aff'd. 353 U.S. 138 (1957); Note, 43 A.B.A.J. 638 (1957), but, said that labor unions will be viewed as entities for everything in Bronwer v. Sanders, 244 Ore. 302, 417 P.2d 1009, 1012 (1966).

58. Parlovscak v. Lewis, 274 F.2d 523 (3d Cir. 1960).

59. Marshall v. ILWU Local 6, Dist. 1, 57 Cal. 2d 781, 22 Cal. Rptr. 211, 371 P.2d 987 (1962); Note, 50 Calif. L. Rev. 909 (1962); Note, 1963 Duke L.J., 197. This decision was limited to labor unions by the court. See also, Daniels v. Sanitarium Ass'n., Inc., 30 Cal. Rptr. 838, 381 P.2d 652 (1963), Note, 10 Wayne L. Rev. 444 (1964).

60. Miazga v. International Union of Oper. Engrs., 2 Ohio St. 2d 49, 205 N.E. 2d 884 (1965); of United Bhd. of Carpenters & Joiners of Amer. v. Humphreys, 230 Va. 781, 127 S.E. 2d 98 (1962), cert. denied 371 U.S. 962 (1963); and see, United Steelworkers of Amer. v. R.H. Bouligny, Inc., 382 U.S. 145 (1965).

61. Kingsley v. Amalgamated Meat Cutters, Local 530, 323 Ill. App. 353, 55 N.E.2d 554 (1944); Curtis v. Albion-Brown's Post 590 Am. Legion, 74 Ill. App. 2d 144, 219 N.E. 2d 386, 389 (1966). See, note, Hazards of Enforcing claims Against Unincorporated Associations in Florida, 17 U. Fla. L. Rev. 211 (1964).

62. Boozer v. U.A.W. Local 457, 279 N.E. 2d 423 (Ill. app. 1972).

63. E.g., Fla. Stat. §718.111(1); Ill. Ann. Stat. Ch. 765, 605/18.3; Stockton, Civil Procedure—Acquiring Diversity Jurisdiction Over an Unincorp. Assn., 60 N.C.L. Rev. 194 (1981).

64. E.g., Johnson v. Chilcott, 599 F. Supp 224 (D. Colo. 1984); Heifetz v. Rockaway Point Volunteer Fire Department, 126 N.Y.S. 2d 604 (1983).

65. Rivard v. Chicago Firefighters Union, 494 N.E. 2d 756 (Ill. App. 1986).

66. Tanner v. Columbus Lodge No. 11, Loyal Order of Moose, 337 N.E. 2d 625 (Ohio 1975); Heifetz v. Rockaway Point (Note 64 supra.).

67. Johnston v. Albritton, 101 Fla. 1285, 134 So. 563 (1931). Cf., Fl. St. §718.111(2), as to condominium associations.

68. Calvary Baptist Church of Marion, Inc. v. Joseph, 522 N.E.2d 371 (IN 1988), overruling O'Bryant case: 376 N.E.2d 251.

69. Ermert v. Hartford Insur. Co., 559 So. 2d 467 (La. 1990), revg. 531 So. 2d 506 (La. App. 1988); Dartez v. Western World Insur. Co., 569 So. 2d 1089 (La. App. 1990).

70. Parton v. West Palm Beach AAMCO Dealers Advertising Pool, 539 So. 2d 1184 (FL 4th DCA, 1989).

71. Harvard Square Defense Fund, Inc. v. Planning Board, 540 N.E.2d 182 (MA App. 1989).

72. Northbrook Excess of Surplus Ins. Co. v. Medical Malpractice Joint Underwriting Assn., 128 F.R.D. 10 (D.C., Mass. 1989).

73. See, Quinn v. Pershing, 367 Pa. 426, 80 A.2d 712 (1951); and 29 U.S.C. §185(c) (labor unions).

74. Rivard v. Chicago Firefighters Union, 494 N.E. 2d 756 (Ill. App. 1986).

75. Eagle Associates v. Bank of Montreal; U.S. 2d Cir., N.Y.; Feb. 11, 1991.

76. Annot., 14 A.L.R. 2d 473; and see generally, Crane and Bromberg, Partnership, §24 (1968); Crane, Liability of Unincorporated Association for Tortious Injury, 16 Vand. L. Rev. 319 (1963); Conard, Knauss and Siegel, Enterprise Organization (cases) (4th ed. 1972).

77. *Ibid.*

78. Marshall v. I.L.W.U., 57 Cal. Rptr. 211, 371 P.2d 978 (1962). See generally, Henn and Pfeifer, supra, note 27, at 195–96.

79. Carr v. Northern Pac. Beneficial Ass'n., 128 Wash. 40, 221 P. 979 (1924) (negligent selection of physicians and negligent hospital care furnished); Koogler v. Koogler, 127 Ohio St. 57, 186 N.E. 725 (1933) (negligent maintenance of fire escape); Roschmann v. Sanborn, 315 Pa. 188, 172 A. 657 (1934) (negligent operation of a bus); DeVillars v. Hessler, 363 Pa. 498, 70 A.2d 333, 14 A.L.R. 2d 470 (1950) (negligent operation of a steam table); Mastrini v. Nuova Loggia Monte Grappa, 1 Pa. D. & C. 2d 245 (1954) (negligent maintenance of lodge floor); Duplis v. Rutland Aerie No. 1001, Fraternal Order of Eagles, 118 Vt. 438, 111 A.2d 727 (1955) (negligent maintenance of stairway).

80. Foster v. Purdue Univ. Chapter. the Beta Mu . . ., 567 N.E.2d 865 (Ind. App. 1991).

81. Maroney v. Fraternal Order of Police Lodge #71, 546 N.E.2d 99 (Ind. App. 1989).

82. Marshall v. I.L.G.W.U., 57 Cal. Rptr. 211, 371 P.2d 987 (1962). E.g., 14 A.L.R. 2d 473 (recovery by member from unincorporated association for injuries inflicted by tort of fellow member). See also, Comment, Tort Liability of Labor Unions for Picket Line Assaults, U. Mich. L.J. Ref. 517, 525–28 (1977).

83. Humphrys v. Republican Cent. Campaign Comm., 320 Pa. 353, 182 A. 366 (1936); International Union of Operating Engineers, Local 675 v. Lassiter, 295 S.2d 634 (1974); United Board of Carpenters v. Humphreys, 203 VA. 781, 127 S.E. 2d 98 (1962).

84. See, Haldeman v. Addison, 221 Iowa 218, 265 N.W. 358 (1936). See generally, W. Seavey, Agency §22 (1964).

85. See, Empire City Job Print v. Harbord, 244 App. Div. 6, 277 N.Y.S. 795 (1935); Lester v. International Brotherhood of Boilermakers, 113 Ga. App. 396, 148 S.E. 2d 195 (1966);

Roddy v. Independent Oil and Chemical Workers Union, 181 So. 2d 285 (La. 1965). See also, Seavy, supra note 84, at §§33, 37, 39.

86. Will v. View Place Civic Assn., 580 N.E. 2d 87 (Ohio Com. Pl. 1989, reported 1991).

87. See generally, Crane & Bromberg, supra note 76.

88. See, Korstad v. Williams, 80 Wash. 452, 141 P. 881 (1914).

89. Progress Printing Corp. v. Jane Byrne Political Committee, 601 N.E. 2d 1055 (Ill. App. 1 Dist., 1992).

90. Xerox Corp. v. Rinfret, 589 N.Y.S. 2d 723 (N.Y. City Civ. Ct., 1992).

91. Stone v. Guth, 232 Mo. App. 217, 102 S.W. 2d 738 (1937).

92. Wilcox v. Arnold, 162 Mass. 577, 39 N.E. 414 (1895).

93. Seaview Assn. of Fire Island v. Williams, 69 N.Y. 2d 987, 510 N.E. 2d 793 (1987).

94. See generally, Crane and Bromberg, supra, note 76; Oleck, Tort Law Practice Manual, c. 21 (1982); note, Liability of Members and Officers of Non-Profit Associations for Contracts and Torts, 42 Calif. L. Rev. 812 (1954); and, Note, Enforcing a Contractual Claim Against an Unincorporated Association in Wisconsin, 1960 WI. L. Rev. 444.

95. 7 C.J.S. Associations §51; DeVillars case, 70A. 2d 333 (Pa. 1950); Joseph v. Calvary Baptist Church, 500 N.E. 2d 250 (Ind., App. 1986).

96. Hatton v. Fraternal Order of Eagles, 551 N.E.2d 479 (Ind. App. 1990).

97. Jund v. Town of Hempstead, 941 F.2d 1271 (2nd Cir. N.Y.), 1991). See also Hutchins v. Grace Tabernacle United Pentecostal Church, 1991 WL 11337 (Tex. App. 1991) See also Guyton v. Howard, 525 So.2d.948 (FL 1st Dist. Ct. App., 1988) (Shriner's Lodge).

98. Cox v. Thee Evergreen Church, 836 S.W. 2d 167 (Tex., 1992).

99. Crocker v. Barr, 409 S.E. 2d 368 (S.C. 1991).

100. Buteas v. Raritan Lodge No. 61 F. & A.M., 591 A.2d 623 (N.J. Super. A.D. 1991).

101. State v. Kansas City Firefighters Local 42, 672 S.W. 2d 99 (Mo., 1984).

102. Coats v. Construction and Gen'l. Laborers Local 185, 15 Cal. App. 3d 908, 93 Cal. Rptr. 639 (1971); McDaniel v. Textile Workers, 36 Tenn. App. 236, 254 S.W.2d 1 (1962); Hall v. Walters, 226 S.C. 430, 85 S.E. 2d 729 (1955), cert. denied, 349 U.S. 953 (1955).

103. Coats v. Construction and Gen'l. Laborers Local 185, 15 Cal. App. 3d 908, 93 Cal. Rptr. 639 (1971). See Comment, Tort Liability of Labor Unions for Picket Line Assaults, 10 U. Mich. J.L. Ref. 517, 523–25 (1977); Maggio, Inc. v. United Farm Workers of America, AFL-CIO, 278 Cal. Rptr. 250 (Cal. App. 4 Dist. 1991).

104. See, Humphrys v. Republican Cent. Campaign Comm., 320 Pa. 353, 181 A. 366 (1936). And for a case on difficulty of proof of deliberate wrongs, see Hill v. Eagle Glass and Mfg. Co., 219 F. 719 (4th Cir. 1915).

105. 57 Cal. 2d 781, 22 Cal. Rptr. 211, 371 P.2d 987 (1962), and see, supra notes 76–82.

106. UMW v. Coronado Coal Co., 259 U.S. 344 (1922).

107. Id., citing Chavez v. Sargent, 52 Cal. 2d 162, 193, 339 P.2d 801, 820 (1959). See also, Tanner v. Loyal Order of Moose, 44 Ohio St. 2d 49, 337 N.E. 2d 625 (1975) (conferred upon unincorporated association a legal identity separate from that of its individual members for all purposes of the law). For an excellent discussion of this case, see, note, Unincorporated Associations, 9 Akron Law Rev. 602 (1976). See also, 92 A.L.R. 2d 499.

108. Wilson v. Airline Coal Co., 215 Iowa 855, 246 N.W. 753 (1933).

109. Donovan v. Travers, 285 Mass. 167, 188 N.E. 705 (1934); Ribner v. Rasco, Butter and Egg Co., 135 Misc. 616, 238 N.Y.S. 132 (1929). But see, supra note 92, contra. Tanner v. Loyal Order of Moose, 44 Ohio St. 49, 337 N.E. 2d 625 (1975) (action against an unincorporated association would not be affected by a change in officers or membership).

110. McCoy v. St. Joseph B. Ry., 229 Mo. App. 506, 77 S.W. 2d 175 (1934); Yazoo and M.V.R.R.

v. Sideboard, 161 Miss. 4, 133 S. 699 (1931); Burns v. Washington Savings, 251 Miss. 789, 171 So. 2d 322, 325 (1965).

111. Kilpatrick v. Connecticut Education Ass'n, Inc., 584 A.2d 479 (Conn. App. 1991).

112. McCoy v. St. Joseph B. Ry 77 SW 2d 175 (Mo., 1934); Hantschler v. Missouri P.R.R. 126 Nebr. 4933, 253 N.W. 694 (1934), See 429 F.2d 249 (8th Cir. 1970).

113. Associated Master Plumbers v. Warnock & Zahrndt, Inc., 236 A.D. 882, 260 N.Y.S. 573 (1932).

114. Svete, Disposition of Local's Funds Upon Disaffiliation, 12 Clev.-Mar. L. Rev. 539 (1963).

115. See, N.Y. Labor L. Art. 20, §715 Hebrew Home and Hosp. for Chronic Sick, Inc. v. Davis, 38 Misc. 2d 173, 235, N.Y.S. 2d 318 (1962).

116. See, Billington, Hospitals, Unions, and Strikes, 18 Clev-Mar. L. Rev. 70 (1969).

117. 29 U.S.C. §141 et. seq.

118. Pattison v. Labor Relations Com'n, 565 N.E. 2d 801 (Mass. App.Ct. 1991).

119. Id. §152(2). See, Peters v. Poor Sisters, 267 N.E. 2d 558 (Ind. App. 1971).

120. United States v. Local 1804-1, International Longshoreman's Ass'n, AFL-CIO, 753 F. Supp., 1158 (S.D.N.Y. 1990).

121. See, Billington, Hospitals, Unions and Strikes, 18 Clev.-Mar. L. Rev. 70 (1969); LaVerne, Toward Equal Protection for the Non-Profit Employee, 5 Suffolk L. Rev. 365 (1971).

122. See 29 U.S.C. 141 et seq.

123. See, 29 U.S.C. §152 et passim.

124. See, NLRB v. Jones and Laughlin Steel Corp., 301 U.S. 1, 45 (1937).

125. 29 U.S.C. § 152(2). See, e.g., Building Service and Maintenance Union Local No. 47 v. St. Luke's Hospital, 11 Ohio Misc. 218, 227 N.E. 2d 265 (1967); Pennsylvania Labor Relations Board v. Mid-Valley Hospital Ass'n, 385 Pa. 344, 124 A. 2d 108 (1956).

126. See, 18 U.S.C. §3692 (1964) and 29 U.S.C. §§101–115 (1964) (dealing with injunctions). See also, Billington, Hospitals, Unions and Strikes, 18 Clev.-Mar. L. Rev. 70 (1969); LaVerne, Toward Equal Protection for the Non-Profit Employee, 5 Suffolk L. Rev. 365 (1971).

127. Utah Labor Relations Board v. Utah Valley Hosp., 120 Utah 463, 235 P. 2d 520 (1951).

128. 29 U.S.C. §152(2) (as amended).

129. Highview, Inc., 223 N.L.R.B. No. 80 (1976) (not a function of local government). but cf., Camden-Clark Memorial Hospital, 221 N.L.R.B. No. 160 (1975) (hospital was a political sub-division).

130. See, G. Kirstein, Why Hospitals Exploit Labor, 189 The Nation 3 (July 4, 1959); D. Kockery and G. Strauss, The Non-Profit Hospital and the Union, 9 Buff. L. Rev. 255 (1960); E. Weissman, Non-Profit Hospitals and Labor Unions, 8 Clev.-Mar. L. Rev. 482 (1959).

131. N.Y. Labor L., Art. 30 §§700–717.

132. N.Y. Gen. Bus. L. §130.

133. N.Y. Gen. Ass'n L., Book 18A, Art. 1. See also, Marvin v. Manash, 175 Or. 311, 153 P. 2d 251 (1944).

134. See Elfer v. Marine Engr. Ben. Ass'n. 179 La. 383, 154 So. 32 (1934); Green v. Obergfell, 121 F. 2d 46 (1941); Leo v. Local Union No. 162, 174 P. 2d 523 (Wash. 1946); Jones v. Hansen, 57 So. 2d 224 (La. 1952).

135. See, as to civil rights: Quimby v. School Dist. No. 21 of Pinal County, 10 Ariz. App. 69, 455 P. 2d 1019, 1022 (1969) (dicta that discrimination in a voluntary non-profit association, as to membership, will be subject to a judicial review in order to safeguard constitutional rights). As to labor unions, see, Krause v. Sander, 66 Misc. 601, 122 N.Y.S. 54 (1910) (union member expelled). And see (inherent right, not merely property right, of political association member who was expelled, and question to share of value of clubhouse

use), Berrien v. Pollitzer, 83 U.S. App. D.C. 23, 165 F. 2d 21 (1947). Jackson v. American Yorkshire Club, 340 F. Supp. 628 (N.D. Iowa 1971); Crandall v. North Dakota High School Activities Ass'n., 261 N.W. 2d (N.D. 1978).

136. Jennings v. Jennings, 56 Ohio L. Abs. 258, 91 N.E. 2d 899 (1949); Hurwitz v. Directors Guild of America Inc., 364 F. 2d 67, 72 (2d Cir. 1966) (union member could not be expelled for failure to take a loyalty oath; the property basis was rejected and the proceeding was based on tort). See generally, 33 A.L.R. 3d 1309. See also, Pinsker v. Pacific Coast Society of Orthodontists, 526 P. 2d 253 (Cal. 1974); Mercury Motor Express v. Brinke, 475 F. 2d 1086, 1091 (5th Cir. 1973); Rosenberg v. Amer. Bowl. Cong., 589 F. Supp. 547 (M.D. Fla., 1984).

137. Hurwitz v. Directors Guild of America, Inc., 364 F. 2d 67, 72 (2d Cir. 1966); Van Deale v. Vinci, 282 N.E. 2d 728 (Ill. 1972); McCune v. Wilson, 237 S. 2d 169, 173 (Fla. 1970).

138. Pinsker v. Pacific Coast Soc. of Orthodontists, 81 Cal. Rptr. 623, 460 P. 2d 495 (1969) and see, supra note 130, Van Daele v. Vinci, 282 N.E. 2d 728 (Ill. 1972) (association of grocers); Commonwealth v. Beiler, 168 Pa. Super. 469, 79 A. 2d 134 (1951) (religious association); courts seldom will interfere in doctrinal disputes; Dragelvich v. Rajsich, 263 N.E. 2d 778 (Ohio App. 1970); Serbian Orthodox Church v. Keleman, 21 Ohio St. 2d 154 (1970).

139. See, Johnston v. Winn, 105 S.W. 2d 398, 400 (Tex. Civ. App. 1937) (definition of delectus personae). See also, Page v. Egmonds, 187 U.S. 596 (1903) (transfer of stock exchange membership). But, concerning unions, see Ryan v. Simmons, 18 N.Y.L.W. 2305 (Sup. Ct. 1950) (restriction to family members is illegal), and Penna. Lab. Rel. Act. §3(f), 43 Penna. Stat. §211.3(f) (restrictions of race or religion are illegal). Marjorie Webster Jr. College, Inc. v. Middle States Ass'n. of Colleges and Secondary Schools, Inc., 432 F. 2d 650 (D.C. Cir.) cert denied, 91 S. Ct. 367 (1970); Booster Lodge No. 405 v. N.L.R.B., 412 U.S. 84 (1973); Hawkins v. North Carolina Dental Society 230 F. Supp. 805 (D.C.N.C.) rev. 355 F. 2d 718 (4th Cir. 1966).

140. Boston B.B. Club v. Brooklyn B.B. Club, 37 Misc. 521, 75 N.Y.S. 1076 (1902).

141. Note, Cy Pres Doctrine and Anonymous Donors, 6 Stan. L. Rev. 729–734 (1954); Sheridan, The Cy Pres Doctrine, 32 Can. B.R. 599–623 (1954); Note, Cy Pres Doctrine, 5 Baylor L. Rev. 205–210 (1953); See, Bell v. Carthage College, 243 N.E. 2d 23 (Ill. App. 1968) (applies to college that moves to another state); but cf., City of Paterson v. Paterson Gen. Hosp., 250 A. 2d 427 (Super. Ct. 1969), aff'd 251 A. 2d 131 (N.J. 1969) (taxpayer cannot stop relocation of a hospital).

142. Pasley, Exclusion and Expulsion from Non-Profit Organizations—The Civil Rights Aspect, 14 Clev.-Mar. L. Rev. 203 (1965); Chafee, The Internal Affairs of Associations Not-for-Profit, 43 Harv. L. Rev. 993 (1930); Holland, Clubs and the Race Relations Act of 1968, 122 New L.J. 258 (1972); Holden, Judicial Control of Voluntary Associations, 4 N.Z.U.L. Rev. 343 (1971); Note, Discrimination in Private Social Clubs, 1970 Duke L.J. 1181.

143. Supra, note 135.

144. Madden v. Queens County Jockey Club, Inc., 296 NY 249, 72 N.E. 2d 697 (1947); Cline v. Insurance Exch. of Texas, 140 Tex. 175, 166 S.W. 2d 677 (1943); Pinsker v. Pacific Coast Soc. of Orthodontists, 81 Cal. Rptr. 623, 460 P. 2d 495 (1969); McCune v. Wilson, 237 S. 2d 169, 173 (Fla. 1970); Van Daele v. Vinci, 282 N.E. 2d 728 (Ill. 1972); McCreery Angus Farms v. American Angus Ass'n. 379 F. Supp. 1008, aff'd. 506 F. 2d 1404 (7 Cir. 1974).

145. Pinsker v. Pacific Coast Soc. of Orthodontists, 81 Cal. Rptr. 623, 460 P. 2d 495 (1969); Marjorie Webster Jr. College, Inc. v. Middle States Ass'n. of Colleges and Secondary Schools, Inc., 432 F. 2d 650, cert denied, 91 S. Ct. 367 (1970).

146. Grempler v. Multiple Listing Bureau, 266 A. 2d 1 (Md. App. 1970); Van Daele v. Vinci, 282 N.E. 2d 728 (Ill. 1972). See generally, 72 A.L.R. 3d 412. See also, Gashgai v. Maine Medical Ass'n., 350 A. 2d 571 (Maine 1976); Rosee v. Board of Trade of City of Chicago, 356 N.E. 2d 1012 (Ill. App. 1976); Board of Regents of University of Oklahoma v. NCAA, 561 P. 2d 499 (Okla. 1977).

147. Civil Rights Cases, 109 U.S. 3 (1883); Comment, A Statement Against State Action, 37 S. Cal. L. Rev. 463 (1964).

148. Refer to discussion and cases in Pasley article supra, note 142 at 206–212. See also, United States v. Guest, 183 U.S. 745 (1965) (the state's involvement need be neither exclusive nor direct in order to create rights under the Equal Protection Clause).

149. Pub. L. 88-352, 78 Stat. 243, esp. §201(e) of the Act.

150. Castle Hill Beach Club, Inc. v. Arbury, 2 N.Y. 2d 596, 142 N.E. 2d 186 (1957) (does apply); Tillman v. Wheaton-Haven Recreation Ass'n., Inc., 451 F. 2d 1211 (D.C. Md. 1972) (does not apply).

151. Brown v. Board of Education, 347 U.S. 483 (1954). See also, Evans v. Buchannan, 379 F. Supp. 1218 (D. Del. 1974); Judith AMC Jeep, Inc. v. NLRB, 562 F. 2d 1081 (8th Cir. 1977); Vaughns v. Board of Education of Prince George's County, 355 F. Supp. 1034 (D. Maryland 1972). And see, statutes such as N.Y. Exec. L. §296(4).

152. Comment, 8 U.C.L.A. L. Rev. 168 (1961).

153. Statom v. Board Comm'rs. of Prince George's County, 233 Md. 57, 195 A. 2d 41 (1963); Shapiro v. Thompson, 394 U.S. 618. See also, 28 U.S.C. §2282; 62 P.S. Pa. §432(6).

154. Pasley, supra, note 142, at 225.

155. Moose Lodge No. 107 v. Irvis, 40 U.S.L.W. 4715,-U.S.-.92 S. Ct. 1965 (1972). A Moose Lodge must serve blacks if it allows any nonmembers to use its facilities. Matter of Moose Lodge 107 of Harrisburg, Penna., Supr. Ct. unanimous opinion, reported in N.Y. Times, p. 40 (Aug. 2, 1972).

156. Pasley, supra, note 142 at 227, citing cases; and cases cited supra notes 144–146.

157. Willcutts v. Galesburg Clinic Assn., 560 N.E.2d 1 (Ill. App. 1990).

158. Civil Rights Act of 1964, Pub. L. 88-352, 78 Stat. 241 (Title 7); see Note, 78 Harv. L. Rev. 684 (1965); N.Y. Civil Rights Law §43.

159. Falcone v. Middlesex County Med. Soc., 34 N.J. 582, 170 A. 2d 791 (1961); Annot. 89 A.L.R. 2d 964 (1963); Pima County Medical Society v. Felland, 565 P. 2d 188 (Ariz. App. 1977); Walsky v. Pascack Valley Hospital, 367 A. 2d 1204 (N.J. 1976); Marlboro v. Association of Independent Colleges and Schools, 416 F. Supp. 958 (D. Mass. 1976).

160. E.g., N.Y. Not-for-Profit Corp. L., Art. 8, §§801 et seq.; Ohio Rev. Code §1702.38.

161. See, Black's Law Dictionary, 775 (4th ed. 1951).

162. See, for rules and fees in all states and Canadian provinces, statutes regarding filing as a foreign corporation, 1 H. Oleck, Modern Corporation Law, §§107-166 (1978 Supp.). See, esp., N.Y. Not-for-Profit Corp. L., Art. 13 §§1301 et seq. Ohio Rev. Code §§1703.01 et seq. and, Taylor v. State, 29 Wash. 2d 638, 188 P. 2d (1971).

163. Id.

164. N.Y. Not-for-Profit Corp. L., Art. 13, esp. §1313 Ohio Rev. Code §1703.02; but see, Selama-Dindings Plantations v. Durham, 216 F. Supp. 104 (S.D. Ohio 1963) (as to members' right to sue; Local Trademarks, Inc. v. Derror Motor Sales, 120 Ohio App. 103, 201 N.E. 2d 222 (1963) (as to what is interstate commerce).

165. See, for samples for forms from various states, 5 H. Oleck, Modern Corporation Law; Forms 1079, 1080, 1085–1095, et passim (1978 Supp.); and esp. Ohio Rev. Code §§1702.47–1702.52; and see, in regard to dissolution: In re Cleveland Savings Soc., 90 Ohio Abs. 3, 183, N.E. 2d 234 (1962); In re Springfield Savings Soc., 12 Ohio Misc. 51, 230 N.E. 2d 139 (1965); N.Y. Not-for-Profit Corp. L., Arts. 10, 11.

166. E. Roy, Collective Bargaining in Agriculture (1970). See Fla. Stat. 618.15; Ohio Rev. Stat. § 1729.10.

6

FORMS FOR UNINCORPORATED ASSOCIATIONS

§63. SCHEMATIC FORM FOR ARTICLES OF ASSOCIATION

Agreement among the organizers (members) of an unincorporated association is the keynote in drafting forms for such an organization. This means that the necessary articles, bylaws and other instruments should be expressions of the wishes of the members, rather than pre-existing formulae which are reworded to cover the wishes of the members.

Many people are overwhelmed by legal forms. They think, erroneously, that they must copy forms, and that they are free only to insert names and other data in prescribed forms. This error is particularly troublesome in unincorporated associations. Such organizations, in fact, are the ones least obliged to follow prescribed forms in drafting their governing documents.

Forms provided herein (or in any book of forms) should be used as guides rather than considered mandatory. There are exceptions, in some jurisdictions, where *official forms* are provided by public authorities for some purposes. Such official forms usually pertain to corporate matters and are found in a few states, or to tax reports and returns of the federal government.

Many forms useful for unincorporated associations are like those used by incorporated associations. Consult the Index for those forms and for forms and clauses on specific subjects.

Form No. 1 is a skeleton suitable generally for any unincorporated association. It illustrates the construction of a complete but simple set of articles. All the elements are set forth in their usual order.

Exact wording is not given in every section of the form. The wording of certain sections must represent the agreement of the organizers—not merely a prescription.

Note that the essentials of articles of association are these:

1. Name
2. Purposes (Nonprofit)

3. Office

4. Duration

5. Powers

6. Membership

7. Dues

8. Directors (Trustees)

9. Officers

10. Committees

11. Meetings

12. Expulsion and Resignation

13. Amendments

14. Dissolution

15. Acceptance of Articles

16. Signatures

FORM NO. 1
Articles of Association
of Unincorporated Association
(Schematic)

[*Note.* Articles of association need follow no particular form. They simply state an agreed plan for organization and operation. The form given here is intended only as a suggestion. For specific matters, such as officers or meetings, many clauses in the forms for *corporate* organization may be used as models. It should be remembered, however, that certain corporate provisions, such as those for quorums and powers, are determined by statute.]

Article I

Name and Purposes

§1. We, the undersigned, desiring to form a nonprofit association for the (popularization of the sport of . . . . . . ; or, improvement of the breed of . . . . . . ; or, other purpose), do hereby constitute ourselves a voluntary nonprofit association under the name of . . . . . . Association.

§2. Our principal purpose(s) are (specify purposes, such as):

To acquire grounds as facilities for the playing of the sport of . . . . . . by members of this Association and by their guests; and to popularize the game of . . . . . . by the holding of championship contests and the offering of voluntary instruction and assistance to prospective followers of the game; all without pecuniary profit to any officer, director, or member.

Article II

Office and Duration

§1. The principal office of this Association shall be located in the City of . . . . . . , State of . . . . . .

§2. The duration of this Association shall be . . . . . . years.

§3. The death, removal, or resignation of any member of this Association shall not result in the dissolution of this Association.

Article III

General Powers

§1. This Association shall have the power to own, accept, acquire, mortgage, and dispose of real and personal property, and to obtain, invest, and retain funds, in advancing the purposes stated in Article I, above. [See other forms in this book for clauses vesting this power in the governing board.]

    [*Note*: This power is ineffective where statutes forbid certain gifts of property to unincorporated associations. It may be necessary to incorporate to accept such a gift.]

§2. This Association shall have the power to do any lawful acts or things reasonably necessary or desirable for carrying out the Association's purposes, and for protecting the lawful rights and interests of its members in connection therewith.

Article IV

Membership and Dues

§1. There shall be (only one) (two) class(es) of membership, namely (for example):

    a. Life Members [e.g., who contribute $100].

    b. Regular Members [e.g., who pay annual dues].

§2. Application for membership shall be (specify; for example:) written, on Association forms, personally signed, and submitted to the Membership Committee.

§3. All membership applications shall contain a statement that the applicant agrees to abide by the Articles of Association (or Constitution), and the Bylaws (if any) as presently or hereafter duly adopted.

§4. (Specify method of acceptance or of election to membership.)

§5. (Specify any particular agreements or obligations which application for membership shall include.)

§6. (Specify method and form of enrollment, initiation, or the like.)

§7. The annual dues of each member shall be . . . . . . dollars, payable each year, on or before . . . . . .

Article V

Directors (or Trustees)

§1. The management and government of the affairs of this Association shall be vested in a Board of Directors (or Trustees) which shall consist of . . . . . . members.

§2. (Specify their qualifications, terms of office, quorum, and other such general rules.)

§3. (Specify rules, notices, and procedures for their meetings.)

§4. (Specify the method of their election and of filling vacancies by directors.)

§5. (Specify what reports shall be made to the members, when, and in what detail. At least one annual meeting of all members, and a report thereat, should be required.)

§6. Power to enter into contracts on behalf of the Association shall be vested in the President, who must be a member of the Board of Directors. But all such contracts shall be subject to ratification or disapproval by the said Board. (Or specify other rules for contracts.)

§7. All Directors shall serve without salary for their services as Directors, but they may receive reasonable compensation for special work or services rendered in other capacities at the request of the Board of Directors.

§8. (Specify methods for filling vacancies by members.)

§9. (Specify methods of removal, for what causes, and by what procedures.)

§10. (Specify other powers, such as procedure to hear complaints and to expel, suspend, or reinstate members; and special powers.)

Article VI

Officers

§1. The Officers of this association shall be: (specify titles, such as: President, Vice-President, Secretary, and Treasurer).

§2. The Officers of this Association shall be selected (or, elected) by the Board of Directors, who also shall fix their salaries and who may remove them from office at the Directors' pleasure [or provide for removal by the members, and procedures].

§3. Legal counsel shall be selected by the Board of Directors [or, by the President] on terms to be fixed by the Board.

§4. (Specify details for appointments, compensation, vacancies, removals, and chain of authority.)

§5. The President, who must be a member of the Board of Directors, shall (specify his powers and duties).

§6. The Vice-President (specify his powers and duties).

§7. The Secretary (specify his powers and duties).

§8. The Treasurer (specify his powers and duties).

§9. The Association's Counsel (specify his powers and duties).

Article VII

Committees

§1. (Specify committee selection, quorum, control, meetings, and reports. State which shall be standing committees. Specify a power to create special committees when necessary. Next, set forth for each committee, separately, its name, membership, powers, and duties, thus:)

§2. The Membership Committee . . . . . .

§3. The Executive Committee, exercising powers of the Board of Directors, under Board direction, when the board is not in session, ...

§4. The Budget Committee . . . . . .

§5. The Grievance Committee . . . . . .

§6. (Other committees) . . . . . .

Article VIII

Meetings of the Membership

§1. An annual meeting of the members of the Association shall be held in the month of . . . . . . , at a place in the City of . . . . . . , State of . . . . . . , to be designated by the Board of Directors [or, in a place to be designated by the Board].

§2. At the annual meeting a report of the past year's activities and of projects for the future shall be made by the Board and by such others as the Board may invite to report. A financial report shall be made by the Treasurer.

§3. (Specify other regular matters on the agenda.)

§4. (Specify methods of sending notice.)

§5. (Specify procedures for election of directors.)

§6.   Parliamentary procedure shall be that stated in Oleck & Green, *Parliamentary Law and Practice for Nonprofit Organizations,* 2d ed., Philadelphia, PA: ALI-ABA, 1991.

Article IX

Expulsions and Resignations

§1.   (Specify grounds and methods of expulsion, including notices, hearings, appeals.)

§2.   (Specify procedures for resignations.)

Article X

Amendments

§1.   (Specify methods and procedures for amending these Articles or the Bylaws.)

Article XI

Dissolution

§1.   (Specify procedures for dissolution.)

§2.   (Specify methods of distribution of assets.)

Article XII

Approval of Articles

§1.   These Articles shall become binding and effective when they are duly accepted and signed by (specify the number of the organizers whose signatures shall constitute approval. At least two-thirds of the organizers should sign, if possible, in order to avoid later recriminations).

Signatures	*Dates*
....	....
....	....
....	....
....	....
....	....
....	....

[*Note:* Notarization of each signature may be attached below the group of signatures but is not required in most states.]

§64. DETAILED FORMS FOR ARTICLES (CONSTITUTIONS AND BYLAWS)

Detailed articles of association usually contain statements suitable for the particular organization and for no other. Certain phrases may seem florid and declamatory. Such statements, however, are important in expressing the character of the organization.

The articles also serve special purposes such as setting forth suitable parliamentary procedure. In Forms No. 2 and 3, which are based on labor union constitutions and bylaws, many clauses amount only to statements of the ordinary rules of good manners and courtesy.

Both local (subsidiary) and general (parent) forms are given below. Their relationships and references to each other should be noted. Labor unions, for example, have three levels of organization:

1. National (*e.g.*, AFL-CIO)
2. Industry or area (*e.g.*, "international" union)
3. Local

These same local-to-parent relationships exist in religious, political, trade, and other associations.

FORM NO. 2
Constitution and Bylaws
of Labor Union Local

Preamble

As almost every improvement in the condition of the working people was accomplished by the efforts of Organized Labor and as the welfare of the members of a craft can best be protected and advanced by their organized Local No. . . . . of the . . . . . . Employees' International Union, *affiliated with the* . . . . . . , *and adopted the following Constitution:*

Article I

Name of Organization

This organization shall be known as the . . . . . . Employees' International Union, Local No. . . . . . .

Article II

Jurisdiction

This Local Union shall be composed of . . . . . . and . . . . . . , whose work shall be confined solely to all types of . . . . . . excepting . . . . . . , ... , or . . . . . . ;

but all workers employed as . . . . . . and . . . . . . , by contracting companies shall be eligible for membership in this Union.

The jurisdiction of this Local shall embrace . . . . . . and vicinity.

Article III

Opening of Meeting

President: "By the authority vested in this Union by the Charter in our midst, and the formal consent of our members, we are pledged to the emancipation of our class from poverty, ignorance, and selfishness. This can best be accomplished by organization, education, and fraternity. Organization is necessary for the sake of education; education is necessary to organization; and fraternity is the cause and effect of unity. In union there is strength, so while we cannot hope to be successful when working individually, by combining our efforts the most skillful and beneficent results may be attained."

"I now declare this meeting open for the transaction of such business as may legally come before it."

The President will then conduct the meeting according to the laws governing the Union.

Article IV

Order of Business

1. Salute the American flag.

2. Roll call of officers.

3. Reading of minutes of previous meeting.

4. Initiation of candidates.

5. Reading of communications.

6. Reports of delegates, committees, and shop stewards.

7. Reports of auditors (semi-annually).

8. Unfinished business.

9. New business.

10. Nomination of officers.

11. Election of officers.

12. Installation of officers.

13. Adjournment.

Article V

Installation of Officers

"I, ..., do hereby sincerely pledge my honor to perform the duties of my office as prescribed by the laws of this Union, and to bear true allegiance to the ...... Employees' International Union, Local No. ...... I will deliver to my successor in office all books, papers, and other property of this Union that may be in my possession at the close of my official term. I will also deliver all property of the ...... Employees' International Union, Local No. ......, to the President of the same upon demand. All of this I solemnly promise with the full knowledge that to violate this pledge is to stamp me as a person devoid of principle and destitute of honor."

President: "You will now proceed to your respective stations, and perform the duties devolving upon you."

The outgoing President next surrenders the chair to his successor.

Article VI

Initiation of Members

When there is but one candidate, use the singular. When the candidate is a woman or a girl, use the term "sister."

"I, ..., pledge my honor to faithfully observe the Constitution and bylaws of this Union and of the ...... Employees' International Union of America, and will never consent to subordinate its interests to those of any private organization of which I may now or hereafter be a member.

"I promise never to discriminate against a fellow worker on account of creed, color, or nationality, nor will I knowingly wrong a brother or sister or see him or her wronged if it is in my power to prevent it.

"I agree to educate myself and fellow workers in the history of the Labor Movement and to defend to the best of my ability the trades-union principle, which guards its autonomy, and which recognizes that Capital is the product of past Labor and that wages can never be regarded as the full equivalent for Labor performed.

"I further promise, whenever and wherever possible, to purchase only Union-made goods and to influence others to do the same."

President: "You are now members of the ...... and I give you my right hand in full acknowledgment thereof."

Article VII

Rules of Common Procedure

§1. On motion, the regular order of business may at any time be suspended by a two-thirds vote of the meeting to dispose of anything urgent.

§2. All motions (if requested by the chair) or resignations must be submitted in writing.

§3. Any conversation, by whispering or otherwise, that is calculated to disturb a member while speaking or to hinder the transaction of business shall be deemed a violation of order.

§4. Sectarian discussion shall not be permitted in the meetings under any circumstances.

Motions

§5. A motion to be entertained by the presiding officer must be seconded, and the mover as well as seconder must rise and be recognized by the chair.

§6. Any member having made a motion can withdraw it by consent of his second, but a motion once debated cannot be withdrawn except by a majority vote.

§7. A motion to amend an amendment shall be in order, but no motion to amend an amendment to an amendment shall be permitted.

Debate

§8. A motion shall not be subject to debate until it has been stated by the chair.

§9. When a member wishes to speak, he shall rise and respectfully address the chair, and, if recognized by the chair, he shall be entitled to proceed.

§10. If two or more members rise to speak at the same time, the chair shall decide which is entitled to the floor.

§11. Any member speaking shall confine himself to the question under debate and avoid all personal, indecorous, or sarcastic language.

§12. No member shall interrupt another while speaking, except to a point of order, and he shall definitely state the point, and the chair shall decide the same without debate.

§13. If a member, while speaking, be called to order, he shall take his seat until the point of order is decided, when, if it is decided that he is in order, he may proceed.

§14. If any member feels himself personally aggrieved by a decision of the chair he may appeal to the body from the decision.

§15. When an appeal is made from the decision of the chair, the Vice-President shall then act as chairman: said appeal shall then be stated by the chairman to the meeting in these words: "Shall the decision of the chair be sustained as the decision of this Union?" The members shall then have the right to state the grounds of appeal, and the chair shall give reasons for his decision. Thereupon the members shall proceed to vote on the appeal without further debate, and it shall require a majority vote to sustain such an appeal.

§16. No member shall speak more than once on the same subject until all have spoken, nor more than twice without unanimous consent, nor more than five minutes at any one time without consent of a two-thirds vote of all members present.

§17. The presiding officer shall not speak on any subject, unless he retires from the chair, except on points of order, and in case of a tie shall cast the deciding vote.

Article VIII

Privileged Questions

§1. When a question is before the meeting, no motion shall be in order, except:

a. To adjourn.

b. To table.

c. For the previous question.

d. To postpone to a given time.

e. To refer or commit.

f. To amend.

These motions shall have precedence in the order herein arranged. The first three of these motions are not debatable.

§2. If a question has been amended, the question on the amendment shall be put first. If more than one amendment has been offered, the question shall be put as follows:

a. Amendment to the amendment.

b. Amendment.

c. Original proposition.

§3. When a question is postponed indefinitely, it shall not come up again except by a two-thirds vote.

§4. A motion to adjourn shall always be in order, except:

a. When a member has the floor.

b. When members are voting.

§5. Before putting a question to vote, the presiding officer shall ask, "Are you ready for the question?" Then it shall be open for debate. If no member rises to speak, the presiding officer shall then put

the question in this form: "All in favor of this motion say 'aye' ";
and, after the affirmative vote is expressed: "Those of the contrary
opinion, say 'no.' " After the vote is taken, he shall announce the
result in this manner: "It is carried (or lost) and so ordered."

§6. Before the presiding officer declares the vote on a question, any
member may ask for a division of the house; then the chair is duty
bound to comply with the request, and a standing vote shall be
taken, and the Secretary shall count the same.

§7. When a question has been decided it can be reconsidered only by
a two-thirds vote of those present.

§8. A motion to reconsider must be made and seconded by two members who voted with the majority.

§9. A member being ordered to take his seat three times by the chair
without heeding shall be debarred from participating in further
business at that session.

§10. All questions, unless otherwise provided, shall be decided as a
majority vote may direct.

Article IX

Nominations and Election of Officers

§1. Election of officers shall be by secret paper ballot or by voting
machine. Determination of which of these methods shall be used
at any particular election of officers shall be made at the general
membership meeting wherein said officers are nominated.

§2. No person shall be eligible for nomination or election as an officer,
member of the Executive Board, or Auditor in Local . . . . . ., unless
he has been a member in good standing in Local . . . . . . and in
the . . . . . . Employees' International Union for three (3) continuous
years immediately prior to his nomination and election.

§3. Nominations of officers of this Local shall be made once every
three (3) years at the first regular general membership meeting in
April in the year wherein the election shall take place, as hereinafter set forth. Elections of officers of this Local shall be held
once every three (3) years on a day decided by the general membership at the meeting wherein officers are nominated.

§4. Officers shall be installed at the first regular general membership
meeting following their election.

§5. In the event any office becomes vacant, the President shall appoint
a member qualified pursuant to §2 of this Article to fill such vacancy.
Said officer shall act until the vacancy has been filled by a person

duly elected to such office at a special election which shall take
place on a date determined by the Executive Board of this Local.

Article X

Officers

§1.   Officers of this Local Union shall consist of the President, Vice-
       President, Secretary-Treasurer, Recording Secretary, seven (7)
       members elected to the Executive Board, at least two of whom
       shall be employed by . . . . . . contractors, and three (3) members
       elected to the Board of Auditors. The President, Vice-President,
       Secretary-Treasurer, Recording Secretary, and seven members
       elected to the Executive Board shall constitute the Executive
       Board of Local . . . . . . The terms of office of the officers of this
       Local Union shall begin immediately following their election, and
       they shall continue to hold office for a period of three (3) years
       thereafter, or until their successors are duly elected.

Article XI

Duties of the President

He shall preside at all Union meetings, including general membership meetings and Executive Board meetings, and shall generally perform the duties
appertaining to the office of President and Chairman of the Executive Board.

The President shall act as Business Manager of Local . . . . . . and as such
shall have full authority and supervision over any and all organizers, delegates,
and business representatives of the Local. He shall appoint from time to time
such delegates, organizers, and business representatives for the Local as may in
his opinion be to the best interests of this Local. All such appointments must
be ratified by a majority of the Executive Board.

The President shall familiarize himself with the facts and conditions existing in the operation of non-union . . . . . . and shall use his best judgment to
bring about their unionization.

The President shall appoint all committees and shall cast the deciding
vote on all questions where there is equal division. The President shall decide
all questions relating to the Local's contractual relationship with others, after
consultation with the Executive Board, and shall interpret points of law and
order when called upon to do so, after hearing the interested parties. The President's decisions are reversed by the Executive Board, the general membership,
or other bodies of appeal within the International Union as prescribed by the
Constitution and Bylaws of the . . . . . . Employees' International Union.

The President shall have the power to suspend or remove any officer or employee of this Local Union for neglect of duty or malfeasance in office. In the case of defalcation or misappropriation of funds, he shall proceed legally to protect the Union on the bonds.

The President, after consultation with the Executive Board, shall be a member, ex-officio, of all committees. He shall have power to retain counsel on any and all matters pertaining to the business of the Local Union, subject to the approval of the Executive Board. He shall countersign all checks, bills, notes, and vouchers issued by the Secretary-Treasurer in behalf of the Local Union.

The President, after consultation with the Executive Board, shall appoint all delegates to labor bodies with which this Local Union is affiliated. He shall call such special meetings of shop stewards or shop meetings as he deems them necessary. He shall from time to time appoint such Sergeants-at-Arms as he deems necessary.

And he shall have such further powers and duties as may be granted to him in other Articles and Sections of this Constitution and these Bylaws.

Article XII

Duties of the Vice-President

In case of the death, resignation, or disability of the President, the Vice-President shall assume all the responsibility of the President until his successor shall have been elected; which elections shall be held within sixty (60) days after such death, resignation, or prolonged period of complete and continued disability.

Article XIII

Duties of the Secretary-Treasurer

The Secretary-Treasurer shall receive all moneys paid into the Union and immediately make record of the same in books kept by him for that purpose. He shall keep a correct account of the financial standing of all members with their full names and residence, as well as their places of employment. He shall keep a record of any and all moneys paid out by the organization.

The Secretary-Treasurer shall make an itemized statement on the first meeting of each quarter, to the body, of all moneys received and paid out by him.

He shall file a bond with the Board of Auditors of the Union as security for the funds of the Union in such amount as shall be fixed by the Executive Board. Any expense in securing of the bond shall be borne by the Union.

The Secretary-Treasurer shall be a member of the Executive Board. He shall have charge of the seal and affix the same on all legal orders, and conduct all official correspondence and perform such other duties as the Union or the Executive Board may direct.

Article XIV

Duties of the Recording Secretary

The Recording Secretary shall keep the correct minutes of each meeting of the body and of the Executive Board, and shall read and preserve all documents and correspondence. Under instruction of the President and the Secretary-Treasurer, he shall issue all summonses for meetings, special meetings, and meetings of the Executive Board.

Article XV

Duties of the Sergeant-at-Arms

The Sergeant-at-Arms shall have charge of the Inner Door and shall not admit any member who is more than thirty (30) days in arrears, unless authorized to do so by the chair, and shall not allow any member under the influence of liquor or drugs to enter the hall.

Article XVI

Duties of the Board of Auditors

The Board of Auditors shall consist of three (3) qualified members who shall be elected by the membership and whose duty it shall be to examine into and report the entire assets and property owned by the Union at least once every three (3) months.

The Chairman of the Board of Auditors shall be empowered, whenever requested by the President or Executive Board, to call for a meeting of the Auditors and examine any matters of finance brought to their attention that may affect the Union.

Article XVII

Duties of the Executive Board

§1. The Executive Board shall have power to transact all business between meetings, subject to approval of members. Any business which they transact must get the approval of the members at the next regular meeting before becoming final.

§2. They shall act as a trial board and shall be unbiased and impartial in all trials.

§3. The Executive Board shall hold meetings the first Thursday of each month at 2 p.m. The minutes of such meetings are to be read at the next regular membership meeting of the Local Union.

§4.   Should any officer of this Local Union fail to attend three consecutive Executive Board meetings, except for sickness, absence on business
for the Union, or for other just cause, his office shall be declared
vacant by the President, subject to the approval of the Executive Board.

Article XVIII

Shop Stewards

§1.   Shop stewards shall be elected by a majority vote of the members
employed in their respective places. One so elected shall remain shop
steward during the term of the agreement. He shall examine the
dues books of each member once a month. He shall see that all members pay their dues and in the event of laxity in payments of the members, he shall report the same to officers of the Union immediately.

§2.   When a member has a complaint, he must report to the steward,
whose duty it is to take the matter to the employer, hear both sides
of the case, and if the employer is right, tell the member so; if the
member is not satisfied, the steward must send him or her to the
officials of the Local. If an employer refuses to comply with his
decision, the steward must at once notify the officers of the Union.

§3.   In order to remove a steward from office, charges must be preferred
against him in writing, and said charges must be proven. Charges
may be for violation of his obligation or for some act in connection
with the organization which would unfit him as a steward. Shop stewards
are prohibited from calling strikes without the consent of the Union.

Article XIX

Committees

All committees shall function immediately upon being assigned to their
duties, and the said committees shall perform the duties assigned them
within the time specified, and they shall report their results to the Union
in writing.

Article XX

Salaries

§1.   Salaries for officers and all employees of the Union shall be fixed
by the President, subject to the approval of the Executive Board.

§2.   Officers who are not on a salary basis shall be compensated by payment of at least five dollars ($5.00) for each Executive Board meet-

ing, regular membership meeting, or shop meeting which they attend. The unsalaried officers shall, in addition, be compensated ...... per week as and for expenses, which sum shall be paid to them by the Union annually in the month of December of each year.

Article XXI

Application for Membership

§1. Any person who desires to become a member of the Local must fill out the regular application blank and sign his name in full.

§2. Any such applicant may be accepted for initiation by the Union after payment of the initiation fee.

§3. Any such accepted applicant failing to present himself for initiation on the date designated by the Union after paying his initiation fee may be stopped from work until initiated.

§4. All newly initiated members, after payment of initiation fees and dues, shall receive a dues book, which shall remain the property of the Union and which shall be surrendered to the Union, for cause, at any time upon request in writing by the President.

Article XXII

Dues and Assessments

§1. The membership dues of this Union shall be determined from time to time by the membership at regular meetings; but in no event shall said dues be less than ...... per month.

§2. The Union may make such assessments upon its members as the interest of the Union shall demand. All assessments and fines shall be charged as dues and must be paid in fifteen (15) days after the levy of said fine or assessment; but the Union may further extend the time if it considers this advisable.

Article XXIII

Delinquencies

§1. Any member failing to pay the dues and assessments of the Local Union on or before the last day of the month in which the same are due shall stand automatically suspended as a member of the Local Union and from all rights and privileges of such membership. A suspended member must pay the Local Union all back dues and assessments before being readmitted to membership.

§2.   Members to be in good standing must have their dues paid on or before the end of the first month of their dues period, as fixed and determined by the membership.

Article XXIV

Quorum

Fifty (50) members in good standing shall constitute a quorum for the carrying on of a general membership meeting. Seven (7) members in good standing shall constitute a quorum for the carrying on of a shop meeting. Seven (7) members of the Executive Board in good standing shall constitute a quorum for the carrying on of a meeting of the Executive Board. Two-thirds of the members in good standing of any such committee shall constitute a quorum for the carrying on of a meeting of such committee.

Article XXV

Property Rights

Membership in this organization shall not vest any member with any right, title, or interest in or to the funds, property, or other assets of the Local Union, now owned and possessed, or that may hereafter be acquired, and each member hereby expressly waives any right, title, or interest in or to the property of this Local Union, including the funds of this Local Union.

The title to all property, funds, and other assets of this Local Union shall at all times be vested in the Executive Board of this Local Union in trust for the joint use of the membership of this Local Union, but no member shall have any severable proprietary right, title, or interest therein.

Article XXVI

Contracts and Agreements

Any and all contracts and agreements for and on behalf of Local . . . . . . and its members shall be signed by the President, with the approval of the Executive Board. The President shall be and is the only person vested with such authority.

Article XXVII

Dissolution

This Local Union cannot dissolve if there are seven (7) dissenting members.

Article XXVIII

Charges

§1. Charges and the basis for charges shall be governed by the provisions of the Constitution and Bylaws of the International Union.

§2. Every member or officer of the Local Union against whom charges have been preferred and disciplinary action taken as a result thereof shall be obliged to exhaust all remedies provided for in this Constitution and the Constitution and Bylaws of the International Union before resorting to any court or other tribunal.

Article XXIX

Per Capita Tax

This local Union shall pay per capita tax to the International Union for any person from whom the Local Union receives revenue, whether called dues or otherwise.

Article XXX

Records

All records pertaining to initiation fees, readmission fees, and other revenue of the Local Union must be kept for a period of seven (7) years.

Article XXXI

Definitions

Wherever the words "he," "him," "his," or "himself" are used in this Constitution and these Bylaws, they shall include in their meaning "she," "her," "hers," or "herself."

Article XXXII

Rules and Regulations*

§1. No member shall make any individual agreement with his employers.

§2. Members in arrears of payment of their dues, fines, or assessments may be removed from their employment.

---

*Equivalent to Bylaws.

§3.   Members may be fined, suspended, or expelled for failing to obey orders issued by the Executive Board.

§4.   Any member who shall resign or be suspended or expelled from the Union shall not be entitled to be refunded any moneys he paid as dues, fines, or assessments.

§5.   Any member appearing at a Union meeting or a shop meeting in an intoxicated condition shall be put on probation for a period of time by the presiding officer of such meeting, and if a member under probation appears at a Union or shop meeting in an intoxicated condition, the presiding officer of such meeting may, without debate, prohibit such member from attending all Union meetings during the remainder of the probationary period.

§6.   Every member shall be an American citizen, or such member who is not shall agree to become a citizen of the United States as soon as he or she is eligible for citizenship.

§7.   No member or officer of the Communist or of any Fascist or Nazi or other subversive organization, nor any person who subscribes to their doctrines, shall be allowed to hold membership or office or be admitted to membership in the Local Union. It is not necessary that the individual charged with membership in the Communist Party or any Fascist or Nazi or other subversive organization admit his membership in said party or organization. If the Local Executive Board, by majority vote, shall find from the evidence presented that the individual is a member of the Communist Party or of any Fascist or Nazi or other subversive organization, or subscribes to their doctrines, the Local Executive Board shall expel such individual after he has obtained a proper trial.

§8.   No member shall be expelled from this Union without a fair trial before the Executive Board.

Article XXXIII

Transfer Card

Any member may transfer from one local union to another within this international, subject to approval of the local to which application is made for entrance.

Article XXXIV

Honorable Withdrawal Card

Any member in good standing for the current month may obtain an honorable withdrawal card from this Local Union by making proper application to the officers of this Union. The withdrawal card entitles him to readmission. However, should the member be found working in a non-union ...... without permission of this Union, the card will be immediately revoked and the matter brought before the Executive Board.

Article XXXV

Regular Meetings

Regular meetings shall convene on the last Sunday in every month and shall be called to order promptly at 2:30 p.m., except that when a holiday falls on the last Sunday of the month, other arrangements will be made by proper notifications.

Article XXXVI

No amendments to or alterations of this Constitution and these Bylaws shall be made unless the same be drafted in proper form. They shall include all sections of Articles amended or repealed, which shall be placed in blackface brackets. Amendments to existing laws and also new laws shall be printed in blackface type. All propositions as provided above shall be submitted to the next regular meeting of the Executive Board for its consideration and recommendations, and thereafter shall be presented and read to a meeting of the entire Union, with a second reading at the second regular meeting of the entire Union.

Article XXXVII

Approval by International

§1. This Constitution and its Bylaws and each section and provision hereof are subject to the approval of the ...... Employees' International Union. It shall become effective only upon approval by the International Union.

§2. The ultimate places of determination of all interpretations of this Constitution and Bylaws shall be as provided for in the International Constitution and Bylaws.

§3. In the event any grievance, charge, or situation arises which is not provided for herein, the matter shall be determined by the General President and the Executive Board of the ...... Employees' International Union in the first instance, and, in the second and third instances, by the ...... Employees' International Union General Executive Board and the International Convention.

FORM NO. 3
Form for Association of Churches

FLORIDA DISTRICT
UNITARIAN UNIVERSALIST ASSOCIATION
CONSTITUTION AND BY-LAWS
(April 1984—Revision)

Article I—Name

The name of this organization is the *Florida District of the Unitarian Universalist Association.*

Article II—Purpose

The purpose of this organization shall be:

a. To cultivate cooperative relationships among the societies in the Florida Dɪ. ·ict and their constituents.

b. To promote the religious life of the societies.

c. To assist the societies in carrying on active and effective programs within their respective communities.

d. To support the Unitarian Universalist Association and to assist in formulating and implementing its policies and programs.

Article III—Membership and Representation

Section 1.   Membership shall be comprised of societies within the Florida District which are members of the Unitarian Universalist Association and which indicate their wishes to assume the privileges and responsibilities of membership in this District.

Section 2.   Each member society in good standing shall be entitled to three (3) voting delegates and any member society with membership of more than fifty (50) persons shall be entitled to one additional delegate for each additional 100 members, or fraction thereof, to a maximum of eight. Each minister professionally serving a society shall be entitled, if he or she so chooses, to be one of the voting delegates for that society.

Section 3.   In order to maintain good standing, a society must have made its contributions to the UUA Annual Program Fund and to the Florida District for the current fiscal year. Only delegates from societies which are in good standing shall have the right to participate in meetings of this District.

Article IV—Officers and Directors

Section 1. The Board of Directors shall consist of the officers of the District and the directors representing the clusters.

Section 2. The officers of the District shall be a President, a Vice President, a Secretary, each of whom shall be elected for one term of two years, and a Treasurer, who may be elected for two successive terms of two years each. After the end of the stated terms, at least one year out of office must elapse before a member may serve in the same office again. No more than two members from the same society may serve at the same time as officers of the district. All officers shall serve as voting members of the Board.

Section 3. All elections shall be held at the Annual Meeting each year. The President and Vice President shall be elected in odd numbered years and the Secretary and Treasurer shall be elected in even numbered years. All newly elected officers shall assume office at the close of the Annual Meeting at which elected.

Section 4. Any Director representing a Cluster shall be elected according to the procedures of his or her Cluster. If a Cluster fails to conduct an election, the District Board may appoint a representative from one of the Societies within that Cluster to serve as Director for one term or the remainder of an unexpired term or until the Cluster elects its representative. The regular terms of Directors shall be for two years. There shall be one Director from each Cluster which is made up of five or fewer societies, and two Directors from each Cluster with six or more societies. Each Director shall assume office at the District Board meeting which follows his or her election. Certification of election shall be provided in writing to the Board of Directors by the Cluster.

Section 5. One Director, 18 years old or less, shall be elected by the delegates at the Annual Meeting for a term of one year and shall represent Florida Young Religious Unitarian Universalists.

Section 6. The Nominating Committee shall nominate the officers and youth representative, all of whom shall be active members of affiliated societies.

Section 7. Meetings of the Officers and Directors shall be held not less than twice a year. Special meetings may be called by the President or upon the request of three members of the Board. Notices shall be sent to members at least ten (10) days before the time of the meeting. A quorum shall consist of fifty percent (50%) plus one of the current Board membership. A report of the actions of the Board shall be submitted to all member societies and to the District Annual Meeting.

Section 8.   The general direction of the affairs of this organization and the general authority necessary for exercising such direction, together with authority to adopt all measures necessary for promoting the interests of this organization, shall be vested in the Board of Directors, subject to annual review by the delegates of the member societies.

Section 9.   It shall be the duty of the Board of Directors:

    a. To authorize the disbursement procedures to be followed by the Treasurer.

    b. To appoint each year a Committee on Credentials.

    c. To submit to the Annual Meeting recommendations concerning policies and programs for the following fiscal year. These recommendations shall be included in the Call and Notice for the Annual Meeting.

    d. To fill a vacancy in any office (except that of President) until the next annual meeting when an unexpired term can be filled by election.

Section 10.   Notwithstanding the specific duties of the Board, the primary function of the Board is the making of policy and plans. The Board is hereby empowered to determine its own procedures in order to expedite routine business so that proper attention can be given to policy and planning.

Article V—District Meetings

Section 1.   The Annual Meeting of this organization shall be held at least fifty (50) days before the date of the UUA General Assembly at a place within the Florida District to be specifically selected by the Board of Directors.

Section 2.   Special meetings of the District may be called by the Board of Directors and shall be called at the written request of five (5) or more member societies. At any such meeting, consideration may be given only to business for which the meeting has been called as stated in the notice of the meeting.

Section 3.   The Secretary shall provide notice of any meeting of delegates by depositing the same in the United States mail, regular first-class postage prepaid, not less than twenty-one (21) days before the date of the meeting, with a separate copy of the notice to be addressed to the minister, Chairman of the Board or President, and the Secretary or Clerk of each member society.

Section 4.   At all meetings of the District, those entitled to vote shall be the officers and directors of this organization and the delegates from each society in good standing.

Section 5.   At meetings of the District, a quorum shall require at least thirty (30) delegates representing at least ten (10) separate member societies. In determining a quorum, officers and directors of the District shall be counted as delegates and as representing the society of which the officer or director is a member.

Section 6.   At the discretion of the chair, the privilege of the floor shall be extended to those in attendance who are not voting delegates.

Section 7.   Action taken at the Annual Meeting of the District shall constitute the final authority in all policy matters and shall constitute general direction to the Board on budgetary matters. A majority vote of those present and voting shall decide all substantive questions presented at meetings of the District, except as otherwise provided herein.

Article VI—Clusters

The boundaries of each Cluster and the member societies within each Cluster shall be determined by the District Board. A request for realignment of Clusters may be made by the Board of Directors of the Cluster or by any Society which is involved. All societies involved in proposed changes as well as the Clusters shall be notified in writing at least sixty (60) days in advance of any meeting of the Board of the District at which the matter may be presented for vote.

Article VII—Duties of Officers

Section 1.   The President shall:

    a. Exercise general supervision over the activities and programs of the District.

    b. Preside at all meetings of the District and of the Board of Directors.

    c. In consultation with the Board, appoint all committee chairs not otherwise chosen.

Section 2.   The Vice President shall:

    a. In the absence or disability of the President to serve, be vested with the powers of the President and perform those duties.

    b. Perform such other duties as the President and the Board may assign.

Section 3.   The Secretary shall:

    a. Keep minutes of all meetings of the District and of the Board of Directors, and send copies of minutes to the appropriate member groups and individuals.

    b. Provide all required notices of the meetings of this organization.

Section 4.   The Treasurer shall:

    a. Receive all moneys collected under the authority of the District and give receipts therefore.

    b. Pay all debts, including the travel expenses of Officers and Directors in accordance with procedures authorized by the Board of Directors.

    c. Keep accounts of all financial transactions, which accounts shall be annually examined and certified by an auditor selected by the Board of Directors. The report of the auditor shall be presented at the Annual Meeting.

Article VIII—Committees and Appointments

Section 1.   The Board of Directors shall recommend to the President the appointment of committee chairs for such periods as they may deem appropriate and shall specify the duties of each committee at the time of appointment.

Section 2.   Each committee shall make a written report to the Board of Directors for inclusion in the Annual Report to Delegates.

Section 3.   The Nominating Committee shall consist of three persons who shall serve for three years each. One member shall be elected by the delegates each year at the Annual Meeting and may not serve for a second consecutive term. The Committee shall present at least one nomination for each office to be filled. No person shall be nominated by the Committee nor from the floor at the Annual Meeting without the nominee's consent. It is recommended that the report of the Committee include biographical material for each nominee. The report shall be submitted to the Board of Directors at least sixty (60) days before the Annual Meeting and copies shall be included in the Notice of the Annual Meeting. The Committee shall also nominate one person to serve on the Nominating Committee during the next year, two persons to serve on the Board of the Southeast Unitarian Universalist Summer Institute (SUUSI) and one person to serve on the Board of the Southeast Unitarian Universalist Winter Institute (SWIM).

Section 4.   There shall be a committee on Credentials composed of at least three (3) members, to be appointed by the Board of Directors before the Annual Meeting. It shall be responsible for determining the credentials for voting members and the supervision of elections and balloting procedures at the Annual and Special Meetings of the District and shall make such reports to each meeting as the delegates or the Secretary shall direct. In order to be recognized as a voting delegate, a representative must be certified as a delegate by his or her society. The certification should be in writing over the signature of an officer of the society. However, the committee on credentials shall have the authority to use other reasonable criteria in determining credentials.

Section 5.   There shall be a Youth Council which shall be appointed by the District Board. One (1) youth member (age 12–22) shall be nominated by and from each local youth group in the District. The remaining members shall be appointed as follows:

   a. Additional youth members, if necessary to maintain a minimum of two (2) representatives from each of the following age groups: Jr. High (12–14); Sr. High (14–19); and post-high (19–22).

   b. Sufficient adult members to maintain a three-to-one (3:1) youth-to-adult ratio.

   c. The purpose of the youth council shall be to promote and coordinate youth programming (for ages 12–22) throughout the District.

Section 6.   Subject to the By-Laws of the Southeast Unitarian Universalist Summer Institute, two (2) representatives shall be nominated to its Board by the Florida District at its Annual Meeting for three (3) year terms. Vacancies occurring between Annual Meetings may be filled by the District Board.

Section 7.   Subject to the By-Laws of the Southeast Unitarian Universalist Winter Institute (SWIM), one representative shall be elected to its Board at the Annual Meeting of the Florida District for a two (2) year term to serve not more than two consecutive terms. Vacancies occurring between Annual Meetings may be filled by the District Board.

Article IX—Administration

A District office with a mailing address shall be maintained at the direction of the Board. To staff this office, the Board may employ an Executive Secretary to serve at the discretion of the Board and to be supervised by the President.

Article X—General Provisions

Section 1.   The fiscal year of this organization shall be from July 1 through June 30.

Section 2.   The business of each District Meeting shall be conducted in accordance with these By-Laws and Oleck & Green, *Parliamentary Law and Practice for Nonprofit Organizations* (Amer. Law Inst.-Amer. Bar Assn.; 2d ed. 1991).

Section 3.   The annual budget of this organization shall be supported by its member societies, together with such funds as may be secured from other sources. The "fair share" of member societies shall be determined at the Annual Meeting preceding the fiscal year in which it is to be collected.

Section 4.   The Florida District of the UUA shall be incorporated under the laws of the State of Florida.

Section 5.   Any notice required by these By-Laws shall be deemed sufficiently given if a Waiver of Notice is subsequently signed by a majority of the members of the group entitled to the notice.

Article XI—Nomination and Election of UUA Trustee from Midsouth and Florida Districts

The trustee representing the Florida and Mid-South Districts shall be elected in accordance with the By-Laws of the Unitarian Universalist Association. Future amendments to the UUA By-Laws shall take precedence over the provisions of this Article. For the purpose of this Article, active member societies shall be those qualified to send delegates to the General Assembly in the year of the election.

Section 1.   Two hundred and fifty days before the General Assembly in the year in which the two districts are entitled to elect a UUA Trustee, or in the event of a vacancy in the office, the district boards shall each appoint one person to an Election Committee, shall designate a mailing address for the Committee, and shall cause notice of the appointment of this Committee to be mailed to all active member societies in both districts, together with a request for nominations. The Election Committee shall carry out the requirements of this By-Law in such a manner that the election will be completed forty-five days before the General Assembly.

Section 2.   Each active member society in either district may nominate one (1) and no more than one candidate for the post of UUA Trustee. Such nominations shall be certified by the clerk or secretary of the society and sent to the Election Committee so that it is received no less than one hundred and twenty-five days before the General Assembly. No one shall be nominated without his or her consent.

Section 3.   The Election Committee shall receive the nominations, confirm the qualifications of the nominees, prepare ballots, and mail one ballot to each of the active member societies in the districts at least one hundred and ten days before the General Assembly. If more than two candidates are nominated, the ballots shall be prepared and the election conducted in the same manner as the provision for the election of President in the UUA By-Laws, Article V, Section 9, Paragraph 3.

Section 4.   Each society shall vote on the nominees at a local meeting of the congregation, and shall cast the number of votes equal to the number of delegates to which it would be entitled at the General Assembly based on the number of members given on the UUA Membership Certification Form. Ministerial and accredited DRE General Assembly delegates can be counted in the vote total when permitted by UUA By-Laws. The total number of votes allowed the society shall be distributed among the nominees as the society shall determine, with fractions of a vote permitted. The vote shall be recorded on the ballot, certified by an officer of the society, and returned to the Election Committee so that it is received no later than fifty-five days before the General Assembly.

Section 5.   The Election Committee shall meet and count the votes no later than forty-five days before the General Assembly. The two members of the Committee shall appoint a third person to observe the tabulation and recording of the vote. A letter signed by the two Committee members shall be sent the Secretary of the UUA giving the name and address of the newly elected Trustee.

Article XII—Resolutions

No resolution shall be presented for adoption at any meeting of the District unless it shall have been furnished in writing to each member or member societies at least twenty-one (21) days before such meeting. Provided, however, this rule may be waived by the favorable vote of three-fourths (3/4) of the delegates present at any meeting of the membership.

Article XIII—Amendments

These By-Laws may be amended by the favorable vote of three-fourths (3/4) of the delegates present and voting at any Annual or Special Meeting, provided a copy of the proposed amendment shall be mailed to the member societies with the call of such meeting. Further amendments to the By-Laws and to any related provision of the By-Laws may be acted upon at such meeting.

Article XIV—Dissolution

In the event of dissolution of this organization, all of its assets shall be vested in the UUA.

POINTS TO REMEMBER

- Tailor your articles to your purposes and plans.
- Use corporate form, if possible. It is better for all but a few kinds of organizations.
- Check your state laws to see whether or not the association as such can take title to property. If it cannot, appoint trustees to hold title for the association.
- Obey licensing and registration laws.

- Check your state laws as to whether the association can sue or be sued in its own name. If it cannot, designate an officer for this purpose and protect him with a bond.

- Remember that bankruptcy and insolvency laws make special provisions for nonprofit organizations.

- Remember that the law of "principal and agent" governs acts of association representatives; and beware of "implied" or "apparent" authority.

- Labor unions are subject to special laws. And these laws change often. Check the latest statues before you act.

- Provide carefully for internal management, meetings, members' rights, admission, and expulsion.

- Provide exact procedures for amendment of the charter, constitution, and bylaws.

- Register as a foreign association if you carry on any real activity in another state.

- Provide exact procedures for dissolution votes and for distribution of property after payment of debts.

- Consider the use of unincorporated association form for effectuating the winding up process in dissolving a nonprofit organization.

- Consider the use of combinations of incorporated and unincorporated operation.

7

FOUNDATIONS
(CHARITABLE TRUSTS)

[Christopher E. Dougherty, of Jacksonville, North Carolina, contributed the first five sections of this chapter]

§65. FOUNDATIONS DEFINED

A *foundation* is a "permanent fund established and maintained by contributions for charitable, education, religious or other benevolent purpose."[1] The organization (or, institution) that administers such a fund also is referred to as *the foundation*. It is a kind of *charitable trust*, of which the grant or "endowment" is the *corpus* (body) and the (settlor) endower (grantor) is the founder, and the beneficiaries (unlike a "private" trust) are an uncertain group, such as a class of people (*e.g.*, "children"; or "Baptists") or the public generally.[2] Trust law terminology, such as "cestui qui trust" to mean "beneficiary" and other legalese now usually is not often employed in discussion of the modern foundation. The word foundation has a generic rather than a precise meaning. These may be private and also state-founded types of such "trusts."[3]

The Internal Revenue Code reflects the problems associated with its definition, as it defines a private foundation by exception.[4] F. Emerson Andrews, a former director of the Foundation Center, of New York City, defined the foundation as:

> "a non-governmental, non-profit organization having a principal fund of its own, managed by its own trustees or directors, and established to maintain or aid social, educational, charitable, religious or other activities serving the common welfare."[5]

One cynical view of foundations is embodied in the statement that foundations are "a pile of money totally beyond the reach of the tax collector—and of anyone else we don't like."[6]

In either case, we usually distinguish foundations from other charitable organizations. Foundations generally received their assets from a single donor, or small group. Also, the basic *function* of foundations usually is to make grants and distribute money rather than to provide services to others.[7]

Charitable Gift Funds

Charitable Gift Funds, run by Investment Companies, get immediate tax breaks for investments—grants of $10,000 or more, for small businesses and individuals, by combining such philanthropic "charitable" accounts; like a grouping of private foundations in which the founder(s) "recommend" how and when the money shall be disbursed. An example is Boston-based Fidelity Investment's Charitable Gift Fund.[8]

There is also a foundation fund bill on Capitol Hill that would allow foundations to pool their assets in a tax-free "mutual fund." The cooperative fund would be managed by professional money managers, who would make all of the investment decisions on behalf of the foundations. However, the bill was blocked as an amendment to President Clinton's omnibus bill. It may be attached by a "technical corrections package" to another major tax measure, or to the Senate version of Clinton's tax bill. The bill was previously attached to two major tax bills vetoed by President Bush.[9]

Functions of Foundations

The function of a particular foundation usually varies with the size of the foundation and the wishes of the donor.[10] While the $2.4 million headquarters of the Ford Foundation houses a "foundation," so too does a desk drawer in which sits a small family foundation in the form of a document stating a charitable trust.[11] The wishes of the donor determine the function of the foundation, since a foundation is created as a vehicle to accomplish the objectives of its founder.[12] Traditionally, the general function of foundations has been to set up experimental models and demonstrations for solving long-range problems. The Reagan Administration pushed foundations to alter this traditional role and function. President Reagan encouraged the private sector to concentrate on the role of providing for *immediate social needs,* which previously had been accomplished through tax-supported government programs.

Foundations have begun to fill the void left by the curtailment of social programs which have lost public funding, a trend which disturbed such leaders as Dr. David Rogers, the Chairman of the Council on Foundations.[13] Dr. Rogers and others insisted that foundations should be one step ahead of society, not behind it. They should be examining the root causes of societal problems, so that serious need does not arise, rather than merely try to respond to health, shelter, and food needs after those needs have arisen.[14]

§66. CLASSES OF FOUNDATIONS

Foundations are generally classified according to their sources of funds, and thus fall into three general categories: (1) *private* foundations; (2) *company*-sponsored foundations; and (3) *community* foundations. Private foundations are the independent grant-makers, which are generally family backed. These foundations receive special IRS attention. Company-sponsored foundations are, as their name suggests, set up with the corporate officers or directors serving as the trustees of the foundation. Community foundations make grants to a specific geographical area, and therefore usually draw their trustees from the community which the foundation serves. A fourth category of foundations, unrelated to the source of funds, is the *exempt operating foundation*. This category of foundation is afforded more lenient tax treatment, pursuant to the Deficit Reduction Act of 1984. Generally, an exempt operating foundation is a private organization which has substantial public involvement.[15] There are also other classifications of foundations, relevant, chiefly for tax considerations, such as private operating foundations, non-private foundations, and non-private foundations *per se*. These last types are too specialized to warrant treatment here since they are largely governed by tax law. See IRS Pub. 578 ("Tax Information for Private Foundations and Foundation Managers") and IRM 7752 ("Private Foundations Handbook").

Corporation or Charitable Trust

Foundations are set up in two main types of structures—the non-profit corporation, and the charitable trust. The nonprofit corporation is generally the preferred form, since it is more flexible than the charitable trust. The purposes of a nonprofit corporation are more expansive than those of a charitable trust, and the fiduciary obligations imposed on the officers and directors are purported to be less stringent than those imposed on trustees of a charitable trust.[16] Like a nonprofit corporation, the charitable trust does afford limited liability and centralized management, and it may be established for an unlimited period of time. Despite these similarities, the charitable trust form is hampered by the inflexible requirement that it only serve a charitable purpose and must conform to the stringent fiduciary obligations (which can arise *constructively*, or by *implication*) imposed on a trustee.[17] Whether these fiduciary obligations are in fact more onerous to trustees *vis-à-vis* officers of a nonprofit charitable corporation is debatable. Without directly comparing the fiduciary obligations imposed on an officer of a nonprofit corporation to those imposed on a trustee of a charitable trust, the Supreme Judicial Court of Massachusetts has declared that the powers given to officers of nonprofit charitable corporations are to be more narrowly construed than the powers given to officers of a business corporation. This heightened scrutiny is the result of the high degree of accountability owed to the individual donors and to the community when these officers are entrusted with money earmarked for charitable purposes.[18] Some courts also object to the broad statement that trustees are hampered by stringent fiduciary obligations. The Florida 1st District Court of Appeal has decided that a trustee of a charitable trust has wide discretion in the exercise of his powers.[19] The trustee is not disqualified to act as such merely because he is also an officer or director of a corporation, the stock of which constituted the primary asset of the foundation. The same court characterized this dual representation as merely being a "potential" conflict of interest, and the court would not interfere with the trustee's exercise of his duties until shown a clear abuse of his discretion.[20] [See section 78.]

§67. STATE SUPERVISION OF FOUNDATIONS

Since a foundation formed as a charitable trust is not a statutory organization, no filing with a state agency is required as a predicate to its existence, as is required for a nonprofit corporation. Though this may afford a limited degree of privacy to the donor, it creates problems of enforcement when trustees abuse their discretion in administering the funds of the foundation. While private trusts may be enforced by their beneficiaries, charitable trusts ordinarily should be enforced by the attorney general, since charitable trusts have no individual beneficiaries *per se*.[21] The attorney general is called the *parens patriae* of charitable trusts.[22] Because charitable trusts are designed to benefit the community as a whole, and not identifiable individuals, attorneys general have a duty to protect, supervise, and enforce charitable trusts,[23] and to see to it that the funds are distributed to their intended charitable uses.[24] How effectively abuses are ferreted out, in fact, by attorneys general is impossible to ascertain. Most experts believe that most attorneys general need a lot of pressure and help in order to get them properly to enforce charitable trusts.[25] The Uniform Supervision of Trustees Charitable Purposes Act thus far has not cured the problem.[26]

An independent foundation to raise money for religious organizations is not a religious organization, and thus is not exempt from the requirement that it register with the state *before* beginning solicitations.[27]

§68. COMMON LAW BASES OF FOUNDATIONS

Cy Pres Doctrine

The most illuminating common law doctrine important to charitable trusts (foundations) is the *cy pres* doctrine. The *cy pres* doctrine is an equitable rule which courts use in order to prevent destruction of a charitable trust by death or other interfering event. When a charitable purpose is evidenced by a settlor of a charitable trust, the courts will adopt a substitute plan of administration for such a trust, as similar as possible to the original plan, when that original plan is no longer able to function.[28] The *cy pres* doctrine simply says that if the stated purpose of the settlor becomes impossible to achieve or continue, some similar purpose (dedication) of the funds should be made, "as nearly as possible" (*cy pres*) to what the settlor *intended* the fund to help achieve.[29] Thus the Buck Foundation (San Francisco Foundation) set up as a community foundation for Marin County poor, was taken over by Shell Oil Co., becoming the then wealthiest foundation in the nation.[30] As Marin County is the third wealthiest county in California, the evaluation of who was "needy" 'in that county perhaps hinged on whether or not one owned a hot tub or swimming pool.[31]

Succumbing to pressure from nonprofit corporations outside the delineated five counties, the trustees of the San Francisco Foundation petitioned for expansion of the geographical boundaries of the foundation, pursuant to the *cy pres* doctrine. The counties which were the recipients of the trust income opposed the application of *cy pres*, arguing that Mrs. Buck would have wanted Marin and the four other counties to reap the windfall of increased income. They opposed the attempt to loosen Mrs. Buck's spectral grasp of the trust, contending that "if the San Francisco Foundation is permitted to continue as a trustee, the beneficiaries of the Buck Trust will suffer irreparable loss and injury because the San Francisco Foundation has spurned Mrs. Buck's charitable intent in order to indulge its compulsion to embark on vainglorious philanthropic adventures."[32] Marin County sought removal of the foundation's trustees, and a prohibition on the foundation's use of trust funds in its attempt to modify the trust, whether or not the change in dedication of the trust fund to "as near as possible" to Mrs. Buck's purpose was the test of *cy pres*. The Supreme Court of California first determined that the foundation's motion for a transfer to a neutral county was best resolved by assigning a disinterested judge, from a neutral county, to hear the case.[33]

[The court ruled that the *cy pres* doctrine allows modification of a charitable trust only if impossibility or illegality or permanent impracticability are the bases for change. Estate of Beryl H. Buck, deceased, #23259 Marin Co. Super. Ct. (Aug. 15, 1986). See, Symposium on NPO's, 21 U. San Fran. L. Rev. 585-762 (1987).]

A "vested" remainderman of a charitable trust has an absolute right to a periodic accounting of the trust, even without alleging any abuse of the trust.[34]

Charity Is a Favorite of the Law

Since charitable trusts are created for charitable purposes, they generally are designed to benefit a community or group as a whole. This contrasts with the objective of a private trust, which is to benefit identifiable individuals. The "dedication" to a "public purpose" explains why charitable trusts are viewed with special favor by the law.[35] When the beneficiaries of a private trust cannot be determined, or if they are incapable of talking, the trust will fail and the fund revert to the settlor.[36] But a charitable trust will be upheld as long as the intent to benefit a charitable purpose is evident. A charitable trust will not fail even if the specific beneficiaries are uncertain or indefinite. It is sufficient for the trust simply to identify the beneficiary with reasonable certainty.[37] When a charitable trust describes a purpose of substantial public interest, the trust will remain viable for as long as it is able to serve some kind of community benefit, although it may have become impossible to achieve the benefit which had been the object of the trust for years.[38]

§69. INTERNAL REVENUE SERVICE SUPERVISION

[See Chapter 9.]

Many of the foundations in existence today were created purely as devices to avoid taxation. Prior to 1969, foundations could accumulate huge amounts of wealth, generate immense business income, and generally receive favorable tax treatment, even if only a small portion of their money actually went for charitable purposes.[39]

Congress enacted strict anti-abuse laws in 1969 in order to combat the use of foundations as tax-avoidance devices. The most stringent provisions of the Internal Revenue Code then (until 1984) limited deductions of gifts of cash and ordinary income property to private non-operating foundations to 20 percent of the donor's adjusted gross income.[40] Additionally, Congress levied an excise tax of 2 percent of the private foundation's net investment income.[41] This excise tax was imposed, ostensibly, to pay for the added administration incidental to auditing these foundations. Congress also imposed a strict payout rule, mandating that non-operating foundations must make distributions to charitable objects in an amount equal to at least 5 percent of the foundation's net assets.[42]

These rules were designed to prevent abuses and may have intimidated the smaller family-backed or community foundations, and stopped some from taking risks and supporting the causes which the larger foundations forget. At least that was the view of President Reagan's Task Force on Private Sector Initiatives, whose kindness to private foundations led to an easing of some of those tough 1969 restrictions.[43]

In 1984, Congress passed the Deficit Reduction Act. Due to the Reagan administration's view of private foundations as the "venture capitalists of philanthropy,"[44] and the administration's aim to limit federal spending on social programs, Congress eased some of the 1969 anti-abuse provisions, in order to encourage smaller foundations to fill the void left by the governmental cutbacks.

In particular, the 1984 Act increased the deduction limitation from 20 percent to 30 percent of adjusted gross income for contributions of cash and ordinary income to non-operating foundations.[45] The 20 percent limitation remained for contributions in the form of capital gain property.[46]

The 1984 Act also created a new class of foundations, termed "exempt operating foundations." An exempt operating foundation is any private oper-

ating foundation which (1) has been publicly supported for 10 years or qualified as an operating foundation on January 1, 1983; and (2) is governed by
individuals who are broadly representative of the general public and at least 75
percent of whom are not disqualified individuals, and (3) if no officer of the
foundation is a "disqualified individual."[47] If a foundation qualifies as an
exempt operating foundation, it will be exempt from the 2 percent excise tax
on net investment income.[48]

Pre-1984 law treated private foundation grants to non-charitable organizations as taxable expenditures, thus subject to a 10 percent excise tax on that
expenditure.[49] A foundation could avoid the excise tax if it demonstrated that
it could exercise expenditure responsibility over the grant.[50] If a foundation
made a grant to a private charity, the grant was not subject to the 10 percent
excise tax. The 1984 Act placed exempt operating foundations on the level of
public charities, so that foundations now may make grants to exempt operating foundations without fear of the 10 percent excise tax.[51]

Another change in the strict 1969 laws is a reduction of the 2 percent
excise tax on net investment income of a private foundation to 1 percent.[52] To
reap the benefits of this change, a foundation is required to make a certain
percentage of distributions for charitable purposes ("qualifying distributions")
in the taxable year.[53]

It is doubtful that the 1984 changes to the IRC will bring the motives of
all potential foundation donors full circle back to "altruistic." On the other
hand, the changes[54] should encourage the founding of new foundations, which
declined dramatically after the 1969 crackdown.[55]

§70. CONGRESSIONAL INVESTIGATIONS OF FOUNDATIONS

In the 1950's, foundations were accused of widespread abuse of their (chiefly
tax-exemption) privileges.[56] Several Congressional committees looked into the
problem, which culminated in the formation of the Patman Committee.
Howard L. Oleck was a consultant to this committee in 1961–62. He and a staff
of over 30 lawyer-accountants studied the files of some 540 major foundations.
After several months of work, he found himself in disagreement with Congressman Wright Patman's liaison representative concerning procedures and
policies; so he resigned, accepting no fee for the work. He returned the voluminous files to Washington for completion of the study and the writing of the
reports by Representative Patman and his committee. These reports were published in 1962, 1963 and 1964; and hearings were held and more reports issued
almost yearly until 1969.[57]

The Patman Reports pointed out serious abuses and defects in the law,
and demanded legislative action.

They found that the 1960 reports of the 546 foundations studied had
revealed untaxed receipts of over $1.4 billion against $556 million in 1951.

One hundred and eleven of these foundations each owned 10 percent or more of at least one class of stock of 263 different corporations (including many large business corporations) on December 31, 1960.[58]

For example, they stated that one personal foundation grew from 2,000 shares of one common stock ($320,000 value) in 1926, to assets of $76 million in 1960, including 227,012 shares of the same common stock valued at $9.2 million. They valued a 1963 contribution of the same stock, by the founder, at $143 million. In 1962 the taxable dividends to the founder, on these shares, amounted to almost $5.5 million.[59]

The Report accused Treasury Department officials of "deliberate obstructionist tactics," and of the placing of ten foundation executives on the Treasury's Advisory Committee on Foundations. That committee was to make recommendations for tightening supervision of tax-exempt foundations.[60]

Congressman Patman expressed deep concern because "of the ever-increasing erosion of our tax base."[61] But it was not until 1969 that the Mills Committee finally obtained Congressional action to reform the federal tax law that had invited abuses. That reform began its effects in 1970.[62]

The changes made by the Tax Reform Act, and those of the 1984 Reagan-Administration period tax law changes, are sketched in the preceding sections of this chapter.

§71. FOUNDATIONS' PROBLEMS

[William L. Bondurant, Executive Director of the Mary Reynolds Babcock Foundation (Winston-Salem, N.C.) contributed material from which this section was abridged].

[Foundations' problems now are] more managerial than tax-related. These problems are more important because they get at what the foundations were created to do, and given tax exemption to do, in the first place.

Basically these problems deal with the efficient foundation management: selection of personnel (board and staff); managing the foundation's endowment, selecting program interests and the most talented grantees within those interests, monitoring the grants made; understanding the important needs of society and the likelihood that foundation grants may have an appreciable impact on those needs; a sense of trusteeship in the use of private money committed to the public good and a corresponding willingness to be open and "public" about what the foundation does and why. [Since the Tax Reform Act] the first problem is increasing costs and decreasing resources. For private foundations the Tax Reform Act increased operating expenses because of the excise tax, the cost of increased public accountability, and greater legal and auditing work, including the additional work needed to exercise "expenditure responsibility" over grants made to other private or private-operating foundations. All of this reduces the funds available for granting. At the same time, the

Tax Reform Act reduced the incentive for contributions to the endowments of private foundations through the (lower) percent of income limitation on gifts to private foundations as opposed to allowable gifts to other charities. This, of course, has a chilling effect on foundation creation and enlargement.

The "expenditure responsibility" requirement placed on private foundation grants to other private operating foundations has turned out in practice not to be as onerous as had been feared. In fact much of the information requested under expenditure responsibility should be requested from a grantee in an ordinary situation, just as a matter of thorough pre-grant investigation and post-grant monitoring.

Additional problems faced by private foundations include board underestimation of the value of using professional staff. A number of foundations have no professional staff, and as a result, miss countless opportunities to enlarge their effectiveness. Another problem area is that of establishing priorities of foundation interests and selecting the best programs within those fields after careful, onsite investigation. The next problem which foundations generally run into is taking insufficient time to monitor the grants made in past years to see whether the funds were spent for the purposes granted or whether better grants could have been made in the first place.

One of the greatest problems facing foundations today, not unique to foundations, is that of the *information reporting explosion*.[63] Foundation staffs tend to be generalists, and they are constantly faced with the difficulty of acquiring in-depth information about a variety of human endeavors. As a result, many wheels have been reinvented with the aid of foundation grants.

Another problem of foundations is their tendency to provide "seed" or startup funding for a program without carefully investigating its potential for securing long-term funding after the foundation has moved on. The first cousin of that problem is the temptation to grant funds to programs which look terribly important but they are in fact fads, and which in time will burn out with or without the foundation's help.

Finally, foundations, whose total capital assets are far less than HEW's annual budget, must make their grants in constant awareness of the presence of the federal government in the grant-making business. Considerable private-public granting cooperation is possible, but unwary smaller foundation grants can be simply swamped by larger federal funding. The loss is a real one, because the foundation has an opportunity to pinpoint its limited dollars into selected growth areas that larger tax dollars simply cannot go into; the relatively scarce foundation dollars should not be used to relieve the government of its responsibilities with tax dollars.

§72. STATE REGULATION OF CHARITABLE TRUSTS

State laws as to regulation of charitable trusts are generally brief and vague. The Ohio Statute, adopted in 1955, is typical. It permits incorporation of charitable trusts by filing of articles, to which must be attached the will or deed of trust establishing the foundation.[63] It requires adoption of a code of bylaws,[64] names the usual officers, permits acceptance of subsequent gifts, and makes some perfunctory provisions about educational foundations and their members, officers' titles, bylaw adoption, and place of meetings.[68] The IRS Tax Requirement Rules are adopted.

It provides for increases in the number of members or directors, filling of vacancies, and inclusion of public officials in the managing board when the will or deed of trust establishing the trust so provides.[69]

It permits the local prosecuting attorney to examine the foundation records, and to bring court action to enforce administration in accordance with the founding instrument's provisions. It also requires filing of an annual finance report with the county probate judge. It also permits court action by the attorney general to enforce gifts made in the document that establishes the trust.[70]

Elsewhere in Ohio statutes enacted in 1953, charitable trust is defined, and the attorney general is directed to enforce such trusts on his own initiative, or when directed by the Supreme Court, governor, or assembly. He is also to be a party to any enforcement proceedings. All charitable trusts must register with him, and report biennially; or more often if required. Violations theoretically involve severe criminal penalties.[71]

It would seem, from these statutes, that supervision by public officials is provided for. This would seem to be adequate provision to prevent abuse. Enforcement is another matter.

In fact, national surveys have shown that supervision by state officials has long been inadequate.[72]

Even where reports are required to be filed, as in Ohio, such reports usually are simply filed and forgotten, if they are filed at all. Nor can the attorney general in some states be compelled to enforce the duties of a charitable trustee.[73]

In New York, an independent foundation to raise money for religious organizations must register with the state *before* beginning solicitations. Such a foundation is *not* a "religious organization, exempt from registration."[74]

Foundations Are Prima Facie Valid

Unless clearly unlawful, (*e.g.*, with a stated purpose that is patently contrary to public policy) a foundation will usually be held to be valid under these arguments.[75] It is axiomatic that charities are favorites of the law, and courts will try to support a doubtful instrument in order to sustain a charitable gift.[76] Valid portions will be sustained, while invalid portions are severed.[77] Or equity courts will reform a deed of trust in order to carry out the intent of the settlor when he has made a mistake.[78] Or they will freely allow him to amend the instrument.[79]

In addition it is argued that no member of the public nor relative of the settlor has standing to attack the trust.[80] Even claims of legal heirs of the settlor are given little consideration when they attack it. It is usually reasoned that abuses are correctable only at the instance of the attorney general,[81] although some cases hold otherwise.

Not only events contemporaneous with the establishment of the foundation, but also subsequent events will be considered in seeking to uphold the grant.[82] General expressions of charitable intent often will prevail.[83]

In the interpretation of any trust, charitable or otherwise, the polestar is the intent of the settlor as defined by the language he used.[84]

Usually the instrument involved is long and complex and must be considered in its entirety. There are many cases which have held that instruments are to be construed liberally in order to sustain a charitable gift.

Truly charitable trusts enjoy a special status in our society, justified because they perform valuable services for the community, and thereby decrease the general tax burden. The case of *Bennet Estate*[85] emphasized this very point thus.[86]

> . . . charitable trusts perform some public functions which a governmental body should perform . . . deducting money from the charitable trust for tax purposes, which would then be applied to the same or some other charitable use, would only result in a waste of funds because the process of collecting taxes is costly . . .

§73. TESTS OF FOUNDATION VALIDITY

Certainly, deliberate abuse of legal classification should be held to a minimum.[87] "Classification . . . as 'charitable' rather than as 'for profit' depends on the actual nature of its activities rather than on its name, purpose clause, or other formal indicia of character."[88]

Motive as the test. When ethical, moral or social motives are the dominant ones in an enterprise, that enterprise is nonprofit. If an enterprise is to be viewed as nonprofit, it is not enough that it merely subordinate the profit motive. It must entirely eliminate profit-making from its basic purposes, although it is not necessary that profit be eliminated from all the activities of an organization.[89] The fact that a corporation or association styles itself as a nonprofit organization does not make it one. Some tax experts have utterly confused the very real distinction between charity or public-benefit purposes and merely not-for-profit purposes (not to mention business purposes).[90] Naturally, such a confusion of terms and purposes is highly desirable for tax avoidance, but it is also highly unethical.

Improper and Proper Purpose Provision

In the sense of legal or formal organization of a nonprofit group, the word *purpose* has a special meaning, identical to the meaning of that word in corporation law.[91] Statutes in almost all states require that nonprofit corporations or associations state in their articles a definite purpose or purposes.[92]

A "trust instrument" includes any form of grant or device for charitable or public purposes.[93]

Purpose clauses are supposed to tell the public authorities, the member, the officers and trustees or directors, creditors, and other persons, precisely what the organization is authorized to do and what it is not authorized to do.[94] The typical "business foundation's" deed of trust, or purpose clause, often states or implies a variety of objectives and purposes.

The statement must be definite and exact.[95] Application for a nonprofit charter may be refused if purposes stated are so unrelated as to fall within different clauses of the statute.[96] A charter may be not granted for purposes which are distinct and unrelated to each other *inter sese.*[97]

Fraudulent statement of purpose, or the misleading of supervisory authorities is a serious crime in many states.[98] In a number of states special approvals by supervisory authorities must be obtained for many "public welfare" activities. Thus, hospital-type aid must be approved by the department of health in Pennsylvania, and by the state board of social welfare in New York; hospital-expense aid must be approved by those agencies and also by the commissioner of insurance in both states.[99] Public assistance and funds must be supervised by state authorities.[100] Many of the purposes stated in the usual "business foundation" instrument are "public welfare" in nature and must be approved and supervised by various public authorities. No incorporation ordinarily is permitted, for example, for an organization which will merely duplicate the work already being done by another nonprofit organization.[101]

The requirement of nonprofit purpose approval by supervisory authorities is illustrated by the requirement of basic approval, besides that of the secretary of state, by the Court of Common Pleas of the County where the registered office is to be located.[102] So, too, approval of education organizations is vested in the State Board of Private Licensed Schools.[103]

Nonprofit organizations for the benefit of employees of a certain company or companies only (besides being not tax exempt) must obtain special approval of the proper state supervisory authority (*e.g.*, Board of Standards and Appeals).[104]

Actual purpose (motive), rather than the purpose stated, is the real test of legality.[105] And the state may challenge any corporation or foundation for grasping more powers than it is authorized to use.[106]

See, also, in the Index, "annulment" or "forfeiture" of charter.

Challenge of a Charitable Trust

Where heirs at law challenged a settlor's gift to a charitable trust, on the ground that it contained an unenforceable racial-restriction provision, they must prove that they were so clearly the real objects of the testator's (settlor's) affections that he would not have wanted the trust to survive without the racial-restriction provision. Prima facie a racial (or religious) restriction clause is against public policy and the charitable trust should be enforced without the restriction.[107]

A grant of property to a town, to hold "in trust" as a library, does not create a charitable trust when the grant states that the grant will terminate and title will revert to the grantor or his heirs if the property ceases being used as a library.[108]

Under Arkansas' law and in other states, a charitable trust is exempt from the rule against perpetuities. If the trust instrument refers to or limits the trust to a general charitable purpose, such as the relief of poverty, the trust sufficiently indicates a class of intended beneficiaries.[109]

A pension fund is not a charitable trust but is in fact a contractual obligation. Thus, the cy pres doctrine is inapplicable to pension funds.[110]

§74. QUO WARRANTO PROCEEDINGS (CORRECTION OF ABUSES)

Statutes in practically every state give to the state's attorney general the power, and duty, to challenge misuse of corporate or other organization authority. *Quo warranto* proceedings may and should be brought by the attorney general to vacate, revoke, or annul the charter of a corporation or other organization guilty of improper conduct, or neglect or failure to use its powers, or use of unauthorized powers. Such action may be based on the attorney general's" own information and volition, or on the complaint of a private person.[111] Thus the New York general corporation law[112] says: "The attorney general may maintain an action upon his own information or upon the complaint of a private person."

The detailed provisions of Ohio statutes governing charitable trusts[113] and attorney general enforcement rules[114] are set forth above.[115]

State administrative officers or agencies, other than the attorney general, also may initiate proceedings based on improper conduct or abuse of the real functions of public welfare type organizations.[116]

Courts themselves, of their own motions (*sua sponte*), may act summarily when perversion or willful disregard of corporate propriety occurs.[117]

Affected individuals, as well as the attorney general, have the right to attack abuse of the privileges involved in charitable trust status. Courts of Equity have inherent power to correct improper results of the use of rules of law.[118]

As early as 1907, courts recognized the true facts when a partnership used a corporation as a mere instrument, and the courts disregarded the seeming form and attached the consequences of the "corporate" acts to the partnership.[119] "Where several corporations became in effect a single enterprise and merged their operations (*i.e.*, as in so many foundations), their several entities were disregarded.[120] . . . The cycle is completed by reference to classic cases in which the fiction of corporate organization has been disregarded, but without recreating or recognizing any other entity . . . In fact, the courts have repeat-

edly examined the underlying enterprise to find what its real purport was. . . .
The nature of the enterprise determines the result, negativing the corporate
personality or any other form of organization of that enterprise . . ."[121]

In other words, the courts and their agencies (such as attorneys general)
now can treat enterprises as what they are, not as what they say they are. It is
most disheartening, in this day and age, that any attorney general should revert
to the blindly formalistic doctrines of the past century—stubbornly saying, in
effect, that the label or form adopted by an enterprise is the final determinant
of what the enterprise really is. Today, "in effect the courts look through the
paper delineation to the actual enterprise; and then determine whether it is
criminal, illegal, contrary to public policy, or otherwise bad (as the circumstances may be) for individuals to conduct that enterprise by any kind of organization."[122]

§75. FORMS FOR FOUNDATIONS

FORM NO. 4
Articles of Incorporation of a Private Foundations

Articles of Incorporation
of _____ Foundation

THIS CERTIFIES that the undersigned is more than 18 years of age and does
hereby organize a corporation under the Nonprofit Corporation Act of the
State of North Carolina (Chapter 55A of the General Statutes) and to that end,
does hereby set forth:

I.

The name of the corporation is _____ FOUNDATION.

II.

The period of duration of the corporation shall be perpetual.

III.

The purposes for which the corporation is organized are:

> To operate exclusively for charitable, educational, religious, and scientific
> purposes as referred to in Sections 501 (c) (3) and 170 (c) (2) of the Inter-
> nal Revenue Code of 1954 (or the corresponding provisions of any future

United States Internal Revenue Law), herein generally called "exempt purposes," including, but not restricted to, the following more specific purposes but only to the extent that they are within the scope of such exempt purposes.

1. To construct, preserve, maintain, and operate a facility to be operated in ...... County, North Carolina, as a center for the encouragement and advancement of the Arts and literature and education with respect thereto.
2. To operate the above-described facility as a place for work and companionship and temporary abode of artists and writers in order to encourage and promote their development and, through their works, to encourage and promote public appreciation of the Arts and literature generally.
3. To encourage and advance the Arts through the public display of fine paintings, sculpture, and other art objects.
4. To provide public enlightenment and education in matters important to the Arts in all of their manifestations.

IV.

The corporation shall have no members.

V.

The method of election of directors shall be set forth in the bylaws of the corporation.

VI.

The address of the initial registered office of the corporation is ...., North Carolina, and the name of the initial registered agent of the corporation at such address is ....

VII.

The number of persons constituting the initial board of directors of the corporation shall be three, and the persons who are to serve as the initial board of directors, together with their addresses, are as follows:

VIII.

The name and address of the incorporator is as follows:

IX.

1. The corporation shall distribute its income for each taxable year at such time and in such manner as may be required so as not to become subject to the tax on undistributed income imposed by §4942 of the Internal Revenue Code of 1954, or to corresponding provisions of any subsequent federal tax laws.
2. The corporation shall not engage in any act of self-dealing as defined in §4941(d) of the Internal Revenue Code of 1954, or corresponding provisions of any subsequent federal tax laws.
3. The corporation shall not retain any excess business holdings as defined in §4943(c) of the Internal Revenue Code of 1954, or corresponding provisions of any subsequent federal tax laws.
4. The corporation shall not make any investments in such manner as to subject it to tax under §4944 of the Internal Revenue Code of 1954, or corresponding provisions of any subsequent federal tax laws.
5. The corporation shall not make any taxable expenditures as defined in §4945 (d) of the Internal Revenue Code of 1954, or corresponding provisions of any subsequent federal tax laws.

X.

No part of the net earnings of the corporation shall inure to the benefit of or be distributable to any member, director, or officer of the corporation, or any other private person, except that the corporation shall be authorized and empowered to pay reasonable compensation for services rendered and to make payments and distributions in furtherance of its purposes as set forth in these Articles of Incorporation. No substantial part of the activities of the corporation shall be the carrying on of propaganda or otherwise attempting to influence legislation, and the corporation shall not participate in or intervene in (including the publishing or distribution of statements) any political campaign on behalf of any candidate for public office. Notwithstanding any other provision of these Articles of Incorporation, the corporation shall not carry on any other activities not permitted to be carried on by a corporation organized and operated exclusively for example purposes within the meaning of the Internal Revenue Code.

XI.

In the event of termination, dissolution, or winding up of the corporation in any manner or for any reason whatsoever, the directors shall, after paying or making provision for the payment of all of the liabilities of the corporation, dispose of all of the remaining assets of the corporation to an entity or organization which is then an exempt organization described in Sections 501 (c)(3) and 170 (c)(2) of the Internal Revenue Code of 1954 or corresponding provisions of any prior or future law, or to more than one such exempt entity or organization or to the State of North Carolina or any governmental subdivision thereof exclusively for public purposes all as shall be determined by the board of directors of the corporation or, in default of any such determination, to the State of North Carolina exclusively for public purposes.

IN WITNESS WHEREOF, the incorporator has hereunto set . . . . . . hand and seal this . . . . . day of . . . . . , 19 . . .

. . . . (SEAL)

FORM NO. 5
Charitable Trust Instrument of a Community Foundation

PINELLAS COUNTY COMMUNITY FOUNDATION

Table of Contents

PINELLAS COUNTY COMMUNITY FOUNDATION

January 1, 19XX

Each bank or trust company which causes this instrument or a duplicate of it to be executed on its behalf declares and agrees that all gifts accepted and received by it in trust under this Instrument shall be held and administered by it as Trustee, upon the following trusts and terms:

Article 1

Purpose and Definitions

Sec. (1). The purpose of Pinellas County Community Foundation is to receive and accept property to be administered under this Instrument exclusively for charitable purposes primarily in and for the benefit of the community of Pinellas County, Florida, and the vicinity thereof, including, for such purposes,

a. The administration of funds given in trust for charitable purposes,

b. The making of distributions for such purposes in accordance with the terms of gifts, bequests, or devises to the Foundation not inconsistent with the purposes of this Instrument or in accordance with determinations by the Board of Governors pursuant to this instrument,

c. The making of distributions to qualified charitable organizations, and

d. Providing for distributions from time to time from property held under this Instrument in such manner that charitable purposes will be effectively served notwithstanding changed conditions that may have arisen or will arise in the charitable needs of the area to be served by the Foundation from the time of the original receipt of property by the Foundation from a donor.

Sec. (2). No part of the net earnings of the Foundation shall inure to the benefit of, or be distributable to, any Foundation Trustee, or to any officer, director or employee thereof, except that the Foundation shall be authorized and empowered to pay reasonable compensation for services rendered and to make payments and distributions in furtherance of the purposes set forth in Section (1) of Article I hereof. No substantial part of the activities of the Foundation shall be the carrying on of propaganda, or otherwise attempting, to influence legislation. The Foundation shall not participate in, or intervene in (including the publishing or distributing of statements) any political campaign on behalf of any candidate for public office.

Notwithstanding any other provision of this Instrument, the Foundation shall not carry on any activities not permitted to be carried on:

a. By an organization exempt from Federal income tax under Section 501(c)(3) of the Internal Revenue Code of 1954 (or the corresponding provision then in effect of any future United States Internal Revenue law) or

b. By an organization, contributions to which are deductible under Section 170(c)(2) of the Internal Revenue Code of 1954 (or the corresponding provision then in effect of any future United States Internal Revenue law).

Sec. (3). In this Instrument:

a. "Pinellas County Community Foundation" and "the Foundation" mean the organization established and funds held from time to time under this Instrument as from time to time amended.

b. "Board of Governors" and "the Board" mean the Board of Governors of the Foundation from time to time in office pursuant to the terms of this Instrument.

c. "Trustee" means, and applies separately to, each bank and trust company which causes this Instrument, or a duplicate to it, to be executed on its behalf, and accepts and receives a gift to or for the use of the Foundation, and without necessity for Board approval, each such bank and trust company under any alter extensions or amendments of its charter, and any corporation with which it may merge or consolidate or which is organized as its successor and takes over its business.

d. "Charitable purposes" means those purposes which are included in both:

  i. purposes for which under the law of the State of Florida property may be held in trust free from the rule against perpetuities; and

  ii. charitable purposes under Section 501 (c)(3) of the United States Internal Revenue Code of 1954 (or the corresponding provision then in effect of any future United States Internal Revenue law).

e. "Qualified charitable organization" and "qualified charitable organizations" mean an organization or organizations for charitable purposes and qualified as exempt from Federal income tax under Section 501 (c)(3) of the Internal Revenue Code of 1954 (or the corresponding provision then in effect of any future Federal income tax law).

f. "Donor" means the maker of any gift to or for use of the Foundation, whether an individual, corporation, partnership, trust or other person or organization.

g. "Fund" means property from time to time held in trust hereunder regardless of the nature of the property or its investment.

h. "Gift" applies whether of money or other property of any kind, real, personal or mixed, or any interest in property, and whether made by delivery, grant, conveyance, payment, devise, bequest or any other method of transfer.

i. "Pinellas County community" means the area of Pinellas County, Florida, and such surrounding areas as the Board may from time to time determine.

Article II

Donors' Gifts and Directions

Sec. (1). Donors may make gifts to or for the use of the Foundation by naming or otherwise identifying the Foundation, whether or not a trustee is designated. A donor may designate one or more of the Trustees to hold and administer the gift, and if more than one, the portions of the gift to be held and administered by each. In case of failure of a donor to designate a Trustee or Trustees of such portions, or failure of a designated Trustee to accept a gift, the Board may in each case so far as necessary designate one or more of the Trustees to hold and administer the gift, and if more than one, the portions to be held and administered by each.

Sec. (2). Each donor by making a gift to or for the use of the Foundation accepts and agrees to all the terms of this Instrument, and provides that the fund so created shall be subject to the provisions for presumption of donors' intent, for variance from donors' direction and for amendments and termination, and to all other terms of this Instrument as from time to time amended.

Sec. (3). If a gift is made to a Foundation Trustee or other trustee in trust to make income or other payments for a period, of a life or lives or other period, to any individuals or for non-charitable purposes, followed by payments to or for the use of the Foundation, or in trust to make income or other payments to or for the use of the foundation, followed by payments to any individuals or for non-charitable purposes, only the payments to or for the use of the Foundation shall be regarded as Foundation funds subject to this Instrument and only when the Foundation becomes entitled to their use, but a Trustee or the Board may take such actions as it from time to time deems necessary to protect the Foundation's rights to receive such payments.

Sec. (4). Any donor may, with respect to a gift made by such donor to or for the use of the Foundation, give directions at the time of the gift as to the geographical limits for use of the gift, including use in or for areas within or outside the Pinellas County community. Any donor may also, with respect to any gift of Five Thousand Dollars ($5,000.00) or more, give directions as to: (a) field of charitable purposes or particular charitable organizations or purposes to be supported, (b) manner of distribution including amounts, times, and conditions of payments and whether from principal or income, (c) a name as a memorial or otherwise for a fund given, or addition to a fund previously held, or anonymity for the gift, and (d) reasonable limits on or additions to investment or administrative powers of a Trustee.

Sec. (5). All such directions by donors shall be followed except as provided in Sections (7) and (8) of this Article II.

Sec. (6). No gift shall be required to be separately invested or held unless the donor so directs, or it is necessary in order to follow any other direction by the donor as to purpose, investment or administration, or in order to prevent tax disqualification, or is required by law. Directions for naming a fund as a memorial or otherwise may be satisfied by keeping under such name accounts reflecting appropriately the interest of such fund in each common investment.

Sec. (7). Each fund of the Foundation shall be presumed to be intended (a) to be used only for charitable purposes, (b) to be productive of a reasonable return of net income which (except during the period referred to in Section (3) of this Article II) is to be distributed at least annually or if accumulated is to be accumulated only in a reasonable amount and for a reasonable period for a charitable purpose or purposes, and (c) to be used only for such of those purposes and in such manner as not to disqualify the gift from deduction as a charitable contribution, gift or bequest in computing any Federal income, gift or estate tax of the donor or his estate and not to disqualify the Foundation from exemption from Federal income tax as a qualified charitable organization; and shall not be otherwise applied. If a direction by the donor, however expressed, would, if followed, result in use contrary to the intent so presumed, or if the Trustee or the Board is advised by counsel that there is a substantial risk of such result, the direction shall not be followed, but shall be varied by the Board so far as necessary to avoid such result, except that if the donor has clearly stated that compliance with the direction is a condition of such gift, then the gift shall not be accepted in case of such advice unless an appropriate judicial or administrative body first determine that the condition and direction need not be followed. Reasonable charges and expenses of counsel for such advice and proceedings shall be proper expenses of administration.

Sec. (8). Whenever the Board of Governors decides that conditions or circumstances are such or have so changed since a direction by the donor as to purpose, or as to manner of distribution or use, that literal compliance with the direction is unnecessary, undesirable, impractical or impossible, or the direction is not consistent with the Foundation primarily serving effectively the charitable needs of the Pinellas County community, it may, by affirmative vote of at least 2/3 of its members communicated to the Trustee holding the fund, order such variance from the direction and such application of the whole or any part of the principal or income of the fund to other charitable purposes, as in its judgment will then more effectively serve such needs. Whenever the Trustee decides that a donor's direction as to investment or administration has because of changed circumstances or conditions or experience proved impractical or unreasonably onerous, and impedes effectual serving of such needs, the Trustee may order variance from such direction to such extent as in its judgment is necessary.

Article III

Trustees' Powers and Duties

Sec. (1). Gifts to or for the use of the Foundation shall upon acceptance and receipt vest in the Trustee designated by the donor or by the Board, subject to the terms of this Instrument and to directions given or varied pursuant to Article II. Whenever any Trustee is succeeded by another corporation through merger or consolidation or by a corporation organized as its successor taking over its business, the Foundation funds then held by it shall thereupon vest likewise in the succeeding corporation. Any Trustee may at any time resign as Trustee of any or all funds it holds, by designating with approval of the Board another consenting Trustee and transferring the funds to such Trustee, and the funds shall thereupon vest likewise in such Trustee, and the transferring Trustee shall thereupon be discharged from obligation for further administration thereof.

Sec. (2). No Trustee shall be responsible for the validity of any gift received. Any Trustee may decline to accept any gift, but in such case shall promptly notify the Secretary of the Foundation so that another Trustee may be designated if possible. If a donor's direction would, if followed, result in use contrary to the intent presumed by Section (7) of Article II, or if a Trustee is advised by counsel that there is substantial risk of such result, the Trustee may notify the Secretary of the Foundation and decline to accept the gift until a determination is obtained as provided in said Section (7) or the direction is varied as provided in Article II. Each Trustee upon acceptance and receipt of any gift to or for the use of the Foundation shall furnish the Secretary of the Foundation with a statement of the property given and its value or estimated value and a copy of any directions given by the donor, and in case or receipt of property in a trust under which the Foundation has, or may have, a contingent or vested interest although not then accepted as a Foundation fund, a like statement and a copy of the instrument creating the trust.

Sec. (3). Solely for the purpose of carrying out the charitable purposes of the Foundation, each Trustee shall have, in addition to Trustee's powers under the law of the State of Florida and other powers granted by this Instrument or by donor's directions, but subject to limitations expressly provided by donor's directions and the provisions of Section (7) of Article II hereof or other provisions of this Instrument, the following discretionary powers with respect to each fund held by it:

a. to retain property in the form and condition in which it is received, to invest and reinvest from time to time in any securities, obligations or other property of any kind it may deem advisable, including any common trust fund maintained by it;

b. to sell, lease for any period, convey, transfer, exchange, deliver and dispose of all or any part of the assets of any fund, and make contracts concerning any such assets, all at such prices, for such terms as to credit and otherwise and whether by public auction or private negotiation, as it deems best;

c. to vote or refrain from voting any corporate or other securities; to give proxies; to exercise or sell subscription rights and pay security assessments; to consent to extension or renewal or refunding of obligations and liens or security therefor; to hold property in its name or the name of a nominee without disclosing the interest of the Foundation except in its accounting; to participate in reorganizations, members, consolidations, foreclosures and liquidations, and to join with other security holders in delegating authority to, depositing securities with, and acting through, committees, depositories, voting trustees and the like, and receive and hold securities or property thereby received; and to settle, compromise, contest, prosecute or abandon claims in favor of or against any trust assets, all as it deems best;

d. to allocate receipts and disbursements to principal or income in accordance with reasonable accounting principles;

e. to execute and deliver receipts, bills of sale, conveyances, assignments, transfers, powers of attorney, contracts, releases, deeds of trust, mortgages and other instruments incident to any transaction; and

f. to employ attorneys and agents and special assistance as needed, and retain and pay reasonable compensation for services and expenses thereof, and to retain and receive for its services as Trustee such compensation as is fair, reasonable and customary at the time, and as may be established from time to time by advance written agreements with the Board, and to charge all such amounts in equitable proportions to the funds held by it.

Sec. (4). No one dealing with any Trustee need inquire concerning the validity of anything the Trustee purports to do, nor see to the application of anything paid or transferred to or upon order of a Trustee, and anyone dealing with any Trustee with respect to any asset of any fund may rely without inquiry upon the authority of the Trustee in any action it purports to take, and upon a certificate by any executive officer of the Trustee with respect to any fact pertinent to any fund or funds, asset or administration.

Sec. (5). Each Trustee shall quarterly certify to the Secretary of the Foundation a statement showing the receipts and disbursements of income and principal for the preceding quarter for each fund by it, and the amount, if any, of income available for distribution at the end of the quarter and after the end of each fiscal year shall similarly certify an inventory of the capital assets of each fund at the year end with book values and its estimates of market values.

Sec. (6). Each Trustee shall be subject to audits and inspection as provided in Article VII, and shall retain for such audits and for a reasonable time thereafter invoices, receipts and other original records of transactions, and directions from the Board for distribution, disbursements and accumulations.

Sec. (7). Each Trustee shall serve in a fiduciary capacity and shall refrain from exercising any powers in such manner as to disqualify the Foundation from Federal income tax exemption as a qualified charitable organization or any gift from deduction as a charitable contribution, gift or bequest in computing Federal income, gift or estate tax of the donor of his estate.

Sec. (8). No Trustee shall be liable for acts, neglects or defaults of any other Trustee or of any employee, agent or representative selected with reasonable care, nor for anything it may do or refrain from doing in good faith, including the following if done in good faith: errors in judgment, acts done or committed on advice of counsel, or any mistakes of fact or law.

Article IV

Board of Governors' Organization and Administration

Sec. (1). The Board of Governors of the Foundation shall consist of United States Citizens who reside in or near Pinellas County, Florida. No person who is a salaried officer or employee of any Trustee or who is holding a salaried public office shall be a member of said Board. Each Board member is to be selected for knowledge of the educational, cultural, civic, moral, public and other charitable needs of the Pinellas County community and shall serve without compensation except for reasonable expenses incurred for the Foundation. Members appointed by the holder of any office or an officer or board member of any other organization are to act in their own right and not as representative of any interest or group.

Sec. (2). Nine regular members of the Board shall be appointed and elected as follows:

a. One appointed by the President or governing body of the Pinellas County Medical Society, or its successor organization.

b. One appointed by the Presidents or governing bodies of the Bar Associations of Pinellas County, acting jointly.

c. One appointed by the President or governing body of the United Fund of Pinellas County, or its successor organization.

d. One appointed by the Chairman of the County Commission of Pinellas County.

e. One appointed by the Chairman of the Pinellas County Board of Public Instruction.

f. One appointed by the Senior Circuit Judge of Pinellas County.

g. One appointed by the Presidents or governing body or bodies of the various chapters of the League of Women voters in Pinellas County, acting jointly.

h. Two appointed by majority vote of the Trustees' Committee (as described in Article V).

Sec. (3). The regular members initially appointed or elected shall serve from appointment or election for the following terms: Three for five years, three for three years and three for one year, respectively, in the order above listed, and until the first Board meeting of the fiscal year following. Thereafter the terms of all regular members shall be five years. Each regular member shall further continue in office until his successor is appointed or elected.

Sec. (4). If, in the judgment of the regular members, the purposes of the Foundation at any time would be furthered by obtaining the services of any person or persons as additional Board members, the Board may, by vote of at least five regular members, elect not more than two additional members who shall thereupon become members, with the same powers as the other Board members, and shall serve for the term of office, not exceeding five years, specified at time of election. Upon expiration of the term of any additional member it shall be optional with the regular members whether to elect a successor.

Sec. (5). Members who by change of citizenship, residence, office or employment cease to be qualified shall automatically cease to be members. Failure without excuse acceptable to the Board to attend three consecutive regular meetings of the Board shall operate as a resignation. Vacancies by death, resignation, refusal to serve or otherwise shall be filled for the unexpired term in the same manner as the original appointment or election. If those entitled to fill any vacancy by appointment fail to do so within sixty days after request by the Board, the Board may fill the vacancy.

Sec. (6). In the event that an office or an organization having appointing authority shall cease to exist, then the Trustees' Committee shall designate the holder of another office or another organization to exercise the appointing authority.

Sec. (7). The Board shall first organize as soon as convenient and shall thereafter meet annually in January and whenever called by the Chairman, or Vice Chairman, or any three members, by at least three days advance notice to all members. It may adopt and from time to time amend bylaws and rules and procedures not inconsistent with this Instrument and provide for methods of voting and action between meetings, and appoint and delegate duties to committees. A majority of the Board shall constitute a quorum and a majority of those present may act, except when larger vote is expressly required. At the first meeting and each annual meeting and whenever a vacancy exists the Board shall elect a Chairman and a Vice Chairman from among its members, and a Secretary of the Foundation who may, or may not, be a member of the Board or an employee of the Foundation and shall be subject to removal at any time. The Secretary shall perform such duties as the Board may determine and shall keep a complete record of the proceedings of the Board, and inform each Trustee of each change in membership and officers. Any action or direction of the Board may be relied upon by any Trustee or others concerned if in writing signed by the Chairman or other person duly authorized by the Board.

Sec. (8). The Board may, from time to time, appoint, as Advisors, persons whose advice, assistance and support may be deemed helpful in determining policies and formulating programs for carrying out the Foundation's purposes.

Sec. (9). The Board is authorized to employ such persons, including an executive officer, attorneys, agents, and assistants, as in its opinion are needed for the administration of the Foundation and to pay reasonable compensation for services and expenses thereof.

Sec. (10). The Board shall take all appropriate actions to make the Foundation known to the people of the Pinellas County community and in that connection seek gifts to the Foundation from a wide segment of the population of the Pinellas County community.

Sec. (11). Each member of the Board shall serve in a fiduciary capacity, and shall refrain from exercising any powers in such manner as to disqualify the Foundation from Federal income tax exemption as a qualified charitable organization or any gift from deduction as a charitable contribution, gift or bequest in computing Federal income, gift or estate tax of the donor of his estate.

Sec. (12). Neither the Board nor any of its members individually, shall be liable for acts, neglects or defaults of an employee, agent or representative selected with reasonable care, nor for anything it may do or refrain from doing in good faith, including the following if done in good faith: errors in judgment, acts done or committed on advice of counsel, or any mistakes of fact or law.

Sec. (13). No member of the Board shall serve more than two consecutive terms.

Article V

The Trustees' Committee

Sec. (1). The President for the time being or each of the Trustees, or such other officer of a Trustee as its governing body shall appoint, together shall constitute the Trustees' Committee. The Trustees' Committee shall

a. Exercise the authority granted the Trustees' Committee under Article IV to select certain members of the Board and to designate an office or organization to exercise appointing authority (under the circumstances described in Section (6) of said Article IV) and

b. Perform such other acts as may aid in completion of the organization of the Foundation and its continued operation, and as may accomplish appropriate cooperation among the Trustees.

Sec. (2). The Trustees' Committee may prescribe such rules for its procedure as it may deem expedient. Action at a meeting shall be taken only if authorized by a majority of the votes of all members of the Trustees' Committee; action may be taken without a meeting only if authorized by a written instrument subscribed by all of the members of such Committee. The members of the Trustees' Committee shall receive no compensation for their services. Neither the Trustees' Committee nor any of its members individually, shall be liable for acts, neglects or defaults of any employee, agent or representative selected with reasonable care, nor for anything the Committee or any member may do or refrain from doing in good faith, including the following if done in good faith: errors in judgment, acts done or committed on advice of counsel, or any mistakes of fact or law. The Trustees shall not be liable for the acts of the Trustees' Committee or of any member thereof as such.

Article VI

Distributions and Disbursements

Sec. (1). The Board shall from time to time but not less frequently than yearly (a) determine all distributions to be made from net income and principal of each fund pursuant to provisions of this Instrument and donors' directions from time to time applicable, and make, or authorize and direct the respective Trustees to make, payments to organizations or persons to whom payments are to be made, in such amount and at such times and with such accompanying restrictions, if any, it deems necessary to assure use for the charitable purposes and in the manner intended, and (b) determine all disbursements to be made for administrative expenses incurred by the Board and direct the respective Trustees as to payment thereof and funds to be charged.

Sec. (2). All determinations shall be by affirmative vote of a majority of the Board, unless otherwise expressly provided herein or by direction of the donor as a condition of the gift (which is nevertheless subject to variance as provided in Article II).

Sec. (3). Determinations may be made to distribute capital from funds given without directions as to principal or income as well as pursuant to directions expressly permitting use of principal, but the Board shall inform the Trustee holding the funds as far in advance as the Board deems practicable so as to permit the Trustee to adjust its investment policies accordingly, and may, upon advice from the Trustees as to how the desired distribution and any necessary liquidation of investments can most economically be accomplished, adjust its directions for distribution so far as it deems practible accordingly.

Sec. (4). The Board shall gather and analyze facts and conduct investigation and research as from time to time is necessary in order to determine the most effective agencies and means for meeting the needs of the Pinellas County community through distribution of funds given for charitable purposes, and may direct disbursements for such fact gathering and analysis, investigation and research from funds given for such purposes or from funds given without direction as to purpose. Disbursements for other proper administrative expenses incurred by the Board, including salaries for such professional and other assistance as it from time to time deems necessary, shall be directed paid so far as possible, first from any funds directed by the donor for such purpose, and any balance out of the Foundation funds.

Sec. (5). The Board may, in furtherance of the Foundation's charitable purposes, when needs therefor have been determined, and with appropriate provisions to assure use solely for such purposes, direct distributions to such persons, organizations, governments or governmental agencies as in the opinion of the Board can best carry out such purposes or help create new qualified charitable organizations to carry out such purposes.

Sec. (6). Each Trustee shall make or withhold such distributions and disbursements as the Board may direct, and shall be fully protected in acting on any written direction signed by the Chairman or other person duly authorized by the Board and shall not be responsible for any act or omission by the Board.

Article VII

Audits and Reports

Sec. (1). The accounts of each Trustee for each fund shall, without revealing the identity of any donor who directed anonymity at the time of gift, be audited in accordance with accepted auditing practices by an independent auditor appointed or approved by the Board, at such times as the Board may determine but at least annually.

Sec. (2). An independent auditor appointed or approved by the Board shall at such time as the Board may determine but at least annually, prepare for the Foundation as a whole a consolidated financial statement, including a statement of combined capital assets, and liabilities, and a statement of income, expenses, and distributions, and a list of projects and/or organizations to or for which funds were used or distributed for charitable purposes, and such other additional reports or information as may be ordered from time to time by the Board. The auditor shall also prepare such financial data as may be necessary for returns or reports required by state or federal government to be filed by the Foundation. The auditor's charges and expenses shall be proper expenses of administration.

Sec. (3). Copies of all audits, statements, lists, reports and data delivered by the auditor to the Board shall be made available or furnished to each Trustee. The Board shall at least annually make such distribution of a written report of its financial condition, activities and distributions to representative persons and organizations in the Pinellas County community (including to at least one daily newspaper generally circulated in Pinellas County and to the chief executive officer of at least one radio station, television station or other news distribution organization in Pinellas County) as will, in the opinion of the Board, reasonably inform the interested public of the operations of the Foundation.

Article VIII

Amendments and Termination

Sec. (1). The Board by affirmative vote of all its members, approved by all Trustees then acting may, subject to the limitations of Section (2) of this Article VIII,

a. amend this Instrument in order to maintain Federal income tax exemption for the Foundation as a qualified charitable organization and deductibility of gifts to the Foundation for Federal income, gift and estate tax purposes for donors and their estates, and in such other respects, consistent with the purposes of the Foundation, as the Board may from time to time find necessary;

b. direct transfer of all Foundation funds to a new corporation organized for exclusively charitable purposes and with provisions consistent with those of this Instrument, including the employment of any of the Trustees of fiscal agent; and

c. terminate this Foundation and its Board, in which case each Trustee shall continue to hold the Foundation funds then held by it, but with all powers to determine variances, distributions and disbursements granted to the Board by this Instrument.

Sec. (2). In the event of a termination of the Foundation for any reason, or in the event of termination of any fund, either by the Foundation or a Trustee (other than as provided in Section (1) of Article III or upon complete distribution of a fund for charitable purposes in accordance with its provisions), the property then held shall (after payment of, or provision for, all liabilities) be disposed of exclusively for charitable purposes in such manner, or to such qualified charitable organization or organizations as the Board (or the Trustee, if the Board has been terminated) shall select. Any property not so disposed of shall be disposed of by the court which has general jurisdiction for the county in which the principal office of the Foundation shall then be located, exclusively for such charitable purposes or to such qualified charitable organization or organizations as said court shall select.

Sec. (3). A court determination that any provision of this Instrument is invalid shall not affect the validity of the remaining provisions.

IN WITNESS WHEREOF each of the banks and trust companies whose name is subscribed hereto has pursuant to resolution of its Board of Directions, caused this Instrument to be signed, sealed with its corporate seal, and delivered on its behalf.

Article IX

Any other provisions of this instrument notwithstanding, the trustees shall distribute its income for each taxable year at such time and in such manner as not to become subject to the tax on undistributed income imposed by section 4942 of the Internal Revenue Code of 1954, or corresponding provisions of any subsequent Federal tax laws.

Any other provisions of this instrument notwithstanding, the trustees shall not engage in any act of self-dealing as defined in section 4941(d) of the Internal Revenue Code of 1954, or corresponding provisions of any subsequent Federal tax laws; nor retain any excess business holdings as defined in section 4943(c) of the Internal Revenue Code of 1954, or corresponding provisions of any subsequent Federal tax laws; nor make any investments in such manner as to incur tax liability under section 4944 of the Internal Revenue Code of 1954, or corresponding provisions of any subsequent Federal tax laws; nor make any taxable expenditures as defined in section 4945(d) of the Internal Revenue Code of 1954, or corresponding provisions of any subsequent Federal tax laws.

FORM NO. 6

TRUST AGREEMENT
CREATING
FOUNDATION

THIS AGREEMENT, creating the_____
FOUNDATION, is made at _____ , Florida, this 26th day of
August, 19 ____ , between _____ , of _____ ,
Florida, as the Settlor and _____ , _____ and
_____ , as the Trustees.

The Settlor hereby transfers the property listed on Schedule A attached hereto to the Trustees, and the Trustees hereby acknowledge receipt thereof and agree to hold such property and all investments and reinvestments thereof irrevocably in trust as the "trust estate," upon the following terms and conditions:

Article I

The name of the Trust shall be the _____ FOUNDATION.

Article II

The Trust is created exclusively for charitable, religious, scientific, literary or educational purposes, including for such purposes, the making of distributions to organizations that qualify as exempt organizations under Section 501(c)(3) of the Internal Revenue Code of 1986 (or the corresponding provision of any future United States Internal Revenue law).

Article III

The Trustees may receive and accept property, whether real, personal, or mixed, by way of gift, bequest, or devise, from any person, firm, trust, or corporation, to be held, administered, and disposed of in accordance with and pursuant to the provisions of this Trust Agreement, but no gift, bequest or devise of any such property shall be received and accepted if it is conditioned or limited in such manner (a) as to require the disposition of the income or its principal to any person or organization other than a "charitable organization" or for other than "charitable purposes" within the meaning of such terms as defined in paragraphs (h) and (i) of Article VI of this Trust Agreement, or (b) as shall in the opinion of the Trustees, jeopardize the federal income tax exemption of this Trust pursuant to Section 501(c)(3) of the Internal Revenue Code of 1986 (or the corresponding provision of any future United States Internal Revenue law).

Article IV

a. The principal and income of all property received and accepted by the Trustees to be administered under this Trust Agreement shall be held in trust by them, and the Trustees may make payments or distributions from income or principal, or both, to or for the benefit of such one or more organizations that qualify as exempt organizations under Section 501(c)(3) of the Internal Revenue Code of 1986 (or the corresponding provision of any future United States Internal Revenue law), as the Trustees shall from time to time determine; and the Trustees may make payments or distributions from income or principal, or both, directly from the charitable purposes of this Trust, as defined in paragraph (i) of Article VI, as the Trustees shall from time to time determine.

b. Income or principal derived from contributions by corporations shall be distributed by the Trustees for use solely within the United States or its possessions.

c. No part of the net earnings of this Trust shall inure or be payable to or for the benefit of any private individual, and no substantial part of the activities of this Trust shall be the carrying on of propaganda, or otherwise attempting to influence legislation.

d. No part of the activities of this Trust shall be the participation in, or intervention in (including the publishing or distributing of statements), any political campaign on behalf of any candidate for public office.

e. The Trustees shall distribute the income of this Trust for each tax year at such time and in such manner as not to become subject to the tax on undistributed income imposed by Section 4942 of the Internal Revenue Code of 1986 (or the corresponding provision of any future United States Internal Revenue law). Further, the Trustees shall not engage in any act of self-dealing as defined in Section 4941(d) of the Internal Revenue Code of 1986 (or the corresponding provision of any future United States Internal Revenue law), nor retain any excess business holding as defined in Section 4943(c) of the Internal Revenue Code of 1986 (or the corresponding provision of any future United States Internal Revenue law), nor make any investments in such manner as to incur tax liability under Section 4944 of the Internal Revenue Code of 1986 (or the corresponding provision of any future United States Internal Revenue law), nor make any taxable expenditures as defined in Section 4945(d) of the Internal Revenue Code of 1986 (or the corresponding provision of any future United States Internal Revenue law).

Article V

This Trust Agreement may be amended at any time or times by written instrument or instruments signed and acknowledged by the Trustees, provided that no amendment shall authorize the Trustees to conduct the affairs of this Trust in any manner or for any purpose contrary to the provisions of Section 501(c)(3) of the Internal Revenue Code of 1986 (or the corresponding provision of any future United States Internal Revenue law). An amendment of the provisions of this Article V (or any amendments to it) shall be valid only if and to the extent that such amendment further restricts the Trustees' amending power. All instruments amending this Declaration of Trust shall be noted upon or kept attached to the executed original of this Trust Agreement held by the Trustees.

Article VI

a. Any Trustee under this Trust Agreement may, by written instrument, signed and acknowledged, resign his office. The number of Trustees shall be at all times not less than (3), and whenever for any reason the number is reduced below three (3), there shall be, and at any other time there may be, appointed one or more additional Trustees. Appointments shall be made by the Trustee or Trustees for the time in office by instruments signed and acknowledged.

b. Upon any change in any trusteeship hereunder, the continuing Trustee or the next successor Trustee or Trustees, as the case may be, shall have all of the powers, authorities, rights, discretion, immunities, estates, titles, duties and obligations of the original Trustees, without the necessity of any conveyance or the taking of any action whatsoever.

c. None of the Trustees shall be required to furnish any bond of surety. None of them shall be responsible or liable for the acts of omissions of any other of the Trustees or of any predecessor or of a custodian, agent, depositary or counsel selected with reasonable care.

d. The Trustee or Trustees from time to time in office, shall have full authority to act even though one or more vacancies may exist. A Trustee may, by appropriate written instrument, delegate all or any part of his powers to another or others of the Trustees for such periods and subject to such conditions as such delegating Trustee may determine.

e. The Trustees serving under this Trust Agreement are authorized to pay to themselves amounts for reasonable expenses incurred and reasonable compensation for services in the administration of this Trust, but in no event shall any Trustee who has made a contribution to this Trust ever receive any compensation thereafter.

f. The Trust shall continue forever unless the Trustees terminate it and distribute all of the principal and income, which action may be taken by the Trustees in their discretion at any time; provided, however, that if and to the extent that state law prohibits perpetual duration, this Trust shall not extend beyond the maximum period permitted under applicable state law. On termination, the trust fund as then constituted shall be distributed to or for the use of such charitable organizations in such amounts and for such charitable purposes as the Trustees shall then select and determine.

g. The Trustees are authorized to form and organize a not-for-profit corporation limited to the uses and purposes provided for in this Trust Agreement, such corporation to be organized under the laws of any state or under the laws of the United States as may be determined by the Trustees. Such corporation when organized shall have power to administer and control the affairs and property and to carry out the uses, objects, and purposes of this Trust. Upon the creation and organization of such corporation, the Trustees are authorized and empowered to convey, transfer, and deliver to such corporation all the property and assets to which this Trust may be or become entitled. The articles, bylaws, and other provisions for the organization and management of such corporation and its affairs and property shall be such as the Trustees shall determine, consistent with the provisions of this paragraph.

h. In this Trust Agreement and in any amendments to it, references to "charitable organizations" or "charitable organization" mean corporations, trusts, funds, foundations, or community chests created or organized in the United States or in any of its possessions, whether under the Laws of the United States, any state or territory, the District of Columbia, or any possession of the United States, organized and operated exclusively for charitable purposes, no part of the net earnings of which inures or is payable to or for the benefit of any private shareholder or individual, and no substantial part of the activities of which is carrying on propaganda, or otherwise attempting to influence legislation, and which do not participate in or intervene in (including the publishing or distributing of statements), any political campaign on behalf of any candidate for public office. It is intended that the organization described in this paragraph (h) shall be entitled to exemption from federal income tax under Section 501(c)(3) of the Internal Revenue Code of 1986 (or the corresponding provision of any future United States Internal Revenue law).

i. In this Trust Agreement and in any amendments to it, the term "charitable purposes" shall be limited to and shall include only charitable, religious, scientific, literary, or educational purposes within the meaning of those terms as used in Section 501(c)(3) of the Internal Revenue Code of 1986 (or the corresponding provision of any future United States Internal Revenue law), but only such purposes as also constitute charitable purposes under the law of trusts of the State of Florida.

Article VII

The Trustees shall have, in addition to all powers granted by law, and subject to paragraph (e) of Article IV hereof, the following powers with respect to this Trust, exercisable in the Trustees' discretion:

a. To invest and reinvest the principal and income of the Trust in such properties, real, personal, or mixed, and in such manner as they shall deem proper, and from time to time change investments, as they shall deem advisable; to invest in or retain any stocks, shares, bonds, notes, obligations, or personal or real property (including without limitation any interests in or obligations of any corporation, partnership, association, business trust, investment trust, common trust fund, or investment company) although some or all of the property so acquired or retained is of a kind or size which but for this express authority would not be considered proper and although all of the trust funds are invested in the securities of one company. No principal or income, however, shall be loaned, directly or indirectly, to any Trustee or to anyone else, corporate or otherwise, who has at any time made a contribution to this Trust, not to anyone except on the basis of an adequate interest charge and with adequate security.

b. To sell, lease, or exchange any personal, mixed, or real property, at public auction or by private contract, for such consideration and on such terms as to credit or otherwise, and to make such contracts and enter into such undertakings relating to the trust property, as the Trustees consider advisable, whether or not such leases or contracts may extend beyond the duration of this Trust.

c. To borrow money for such periods, at such rates of interest, and upon such terms as the Trustees consider advisable, and as security loans to mortgage or pledge any real or personal property with or without power of sale; to acquire or hold any real or personal property, subject to any mortgage or pledge on or of property acquired or held by this Trust.

d. To execute and deliver deeds, assignments, transfers, mortgages, pledges, leases, covenants, contracts, promissory notes, releases, and other instruments, sealed or unsealed, incident to any transaction in which the Trustees engage.

e. To vote, to give proxies, to participate in the reorganization, merger or consolidation of any concern, or in the sale, lease, disposition, or distribution of its assets; to join with other security holders in acting through a committee, depositary, voting trustees, or otherwise, and in this connection to delegate authority to such committee, depositary, or trustees and to deposit securities with them or transfer securities to them, to pay assessments levied on securities or to exercise subscription rights in respect of securities.

f. To employ a bank or trust company as custodian of any funds or securities and to delegate to it such powers as the Trustees deem appropriate; to hold trust property without indication of fiduciary capacity but only in the name of a registered nominee, provided the trust property is at all times identified as such on the books of this Trust; to keep any or all of the trust property or funds in any place or places in the United States of America; to employ clerks, accountants investment counsel, agents, attorneys and any special services, and to pay the reasonable compensation and expenses of all such services in addition to the compensation of the Trustees.

Article VIII

The Trustees' powers are exercisable solely in the fiduciary capacity consistent with and in furtherance of the charitable purposes of this Trust as specified in paragraph (i) of Article VI and not otherwise.

Article IX

The term "Trustees" as used in this instrument shall include the original Trustees and any successor or continuing Trustee or Trustees at the time acting. Where appropriate, with reference to the Trustees, the use of the masculine shall include the feminine and the neuter, and the plural shall include the singular, and vice versa.

Article X

Any person may rely on a copy, certified by a notary public, of the executed original of this Trust Agreement held by the Trustees, and of any of the notations on it and writings attached to it, as fully as he might rely on the original documents themselves. Any such person may rely fully on any statements of fact certified by anyone who appears from such original documents or from such certified copy to be a Trustee under this Trust Agreement. No one dealing with the Trustees need inquire concerning the validity of anything the Trustees purport to do. No one dealing with the Trustees need see to the application of anything paid or transferred to or upon the order of the Trustees of this Trust.

Article XI

The validity, effect and construction of this Trust shall be determined in accordance with the laws of Florida. The original situs and original place of administration of the trust estate shall also be Florida, but the situs and place of administration of the trust estate may, however, be transferred at any time or from time to time to such place or places as the Trustees deem to be for the best interest of the trust estate. In so doing, the Trustees may resign and appoint a substitute Trustee, but may remove each substitute Trustee and appoint another, including any one or more of the appointing Trustees, at will. Each substitute Trustee so appointed may delegate any and all of such substitute Trustee's powers, discretionary or ministerial, to the appointing trustees.

IN WITNESS WHEREOF, the Settlor and the original Trustees have executed this Trust Agreement on the day and year first above written.

_____   _____
Settlor   Trustee

_____   _____
                                     Trustee

                                     _____
                                     Trustee

SCHEDULE A

to

THE _____ **FOUNDATION**

TRUST AGREEMENT

Identified:

_____   _____

Settlor   Trustee

_____   _____

                                                     Trustee

                                                     _____

                                                     Trustee

FORM NO. 7

Grant-Seeking Project Proposal to Foundation(s) [Based on a Medical Health Care Community Center Project Proposal]

[*Cover Page* should show (1) Name of the Project or its Sponsor(s); (2) Names and Titles (*e.g.*, such as professional, academic, or other degrees); (3) Address; (4) Telephone Number(s).]

[Each Foundation may have its *own* Forms for Application for Grant. Ask, and You Shall Receive.]

Background:

Over the last _____ years, hundreds of thousands of _____ have migrated to _____ towns and cities along the border, attracted by plentiful, low-paying jobs in the maguila plants. The infrastructures of these communities—housing, sanitation, water, schools, health, transportation—have been overwhelmed by the increased population. _____ , _____ for example, has grown from a sleepy town of 50,000 long-time residents to 250,000 during this period.

The vast majority of migrants, 70 percent of whom are estimated to be women, live in squatters' communities—urban shantytowns without electricity, gas, water, sanitation—known as "colonias." The thousands of families that live in the colonias are generally supported by poorly educated single working

moms who lack the support of the traditional family structure so important in
_____ The average salary is _____ minimum
wage, approximately $3 a day.

As more jobs are created along the border, migration from the rural
south to the border is expected to continue. This rural migration is likely to
increase during this period of high unemployment and economic crisis in
_____.

There is a tremendous need to improve primary health care in these
colonias. Residents say they have received little outside help. While there are
_____ and multinational organizations working in northern rural areas,
none as far as we know have specifically targeted the new urban shantytowns.

Goals:

To develop a grassroots, community-based primary health care program
to improve the general health of colonia residents, especially women and children under five year. Our programs will be based on UNICEF child survival
model (GOBI-IAM-EFF)—growth monitoring, ORT, breastfeeding, immuniza-
tions, nutrition, family spacing and sanitation (safe water).

To implement the primary health care program by providing training for
health care workers (_____) within the colonias. To develop a clinical component to address specific health needs and issues of residents.

To interface with the University of _____ medical school,
_____medical community and private agencies to provide
resources and referrals for the colonia residents.

Executive Summary:

_____ is a bilingual, bicultural three-phase COMMUNITY-
BASED PRIMARY HEALTH CARE PROGRAM of the residents of the colonias
in the city of _____ , _____ . The ideas
behind _____ come from the residents of colonia communities
themselves and were communicated to us through _____ ,
_____ resident _____ , who has been work-
ing on a volunteer and professional basis with colonia communities for the last
ten years.

The project's goal is to "empower" colonia residents to help themselves on
a long-term basis. The project will train people respected in their communities—"_____"—as primary health care workers so that they
can train others. The word _____ denotes a special bonding between women—that of co-mother or godmother. What each group of
_____ is trained for, i.e., family spacing, depends on community
needs.

Supported by grant monies, _____ stresses the involvement of health professionals and resources from both sides of the border. Our advisory board is made up of a wide range of professionals in _____ and _____ who contribute both their experience and expertise. _____ is a collaboration with the University of _____ Department of Family and Community Medicine.

_____ will be working in two colonias. One is _____ , a colonia with a large migrant population of about 1,000 households. Less than three years old, _____ is located around the city's red light district (prostitution is legal in _____). The other, _____ is an older colonia with 2,000 households built around the _____, _____ garbage dump. Unlike other squatter communities, these two very different colonias are not involved in _____ party politics. _____ is purely interested in working with residents on needed health issues and services.

The tools and educational programs developed in _____ will be transferable to other _____ squatter communities along the _____ mile border.

Project Plan:

Phase I: Community
Organization/Needs Assessment

October 1, _____ to March 1, 19____

Stage 1: To encourage community participation and awareness we will hold community meetings in _____ and _____ . The community development meetings will concentrate on basic health issues such as family spacing, nutrition, oral rehydration, water quality, infectious diseases, and sanitation.

Stage 2: Based on community input, priorities will be set for a community development needs assessment survey for the two colonias. We feel a survey is an important first step since there has been so little documentation of health needs in the colonias that can be shown to government and private agencies. It also facilitates the involvement of residents.

Individuals will be chosen from among those actively involved in the community development phase to be our "_____ ." Usually women will be selected because they are the natural _____ of the communities; perhaps midwives or other women to whom people already turn to for advice. (We're not trying to exclude men, if there is a man who fits these criteria he would naturally be included.)

Project members, _____, and other volunteer consultants will write a _____ language survey to cover a wide range of topics including basic socio-economic information, nutrition, prenatal care, family spacing, where people go for health care, how health care is paid for, attitudes toward health care, sanitation/waste disposal, water (a major problem in colonias), dental care, immunization, schools and day-care for children, family history, etc. We estimate it will take about six weeks to hold the formal community meetings and develop the survey in a concise, user-friendly form.

Stage 3: The project staff and other volunteer consultants will develop a training program for the _____ on how to conduct the house to house survey. The survey will give the _____ the opportunity to get to know their community and at the same time, inform people about the program. We plan to reach 10 percent of households in each colonia using a random sample approach to every third household. Survey training will take no more than two weeks. The _____ will help decide how best to disperse the survey throughout the colonias. (Squatter's makeshift dwellings have been built without any plan, streets, or even public services.)

Stage 4: _____ who participate will receive an incentive payment per survey and will be expected to product 30 surveys over a one month period. The project director will provide guidance and support as well as enter the data into a computer for analysis.

Through the community development phase residents will be aware of the survey and why it is a necessary step. In addition, we plan to offer donated incentives (food, clothes, blankets) for households that participate in the survey.

Stage 5: The data will be analyzed by the project director and a statistician from the university. A report based on the findings will be written in _____ and English. The finished product will also include reports from _____ and the communities as a whole. The data will be used to develop the primary health care training modules of Phase II.

Phase II: Primary Health Care Training

Phase II depends on the findings of Phase I. The community will decide—based on the needs assessment—what the highest health care priorities are for the colonias. We will prvide primary health care training modules for _____ based on the expressed needs. (The number of _____ actively involved is likely to be expanded at this point, depending on the needs of the community.) The training modules will cover areas from family spacing to sanitation. The _____ will also be trained to teach or refer others how to take advantage of existing resources.

Stage 1: Meet with the community and _____ to report the findings of the needs assessment survey and prioritize the needs to establish training modules topics.

Stage 2: Develop an overall training program for the topics including information, skills, materials, and resources to address each training module.

Stage 3: Organize committees based on _____ interests and skills to decide on approaches, methods and strategies for each training module.

Stage 4: Develop an evaluation tool for each module. _____ will use this after their presentations so that the residents can evaluate the usefulness, relevance and quality of presentation. The evaluation will be used to improve subsequent training programs.

Phase III: Clinical Medical Component/Referral

Phase III is the development of a primary health care clinic that networks with the trained _____ , augmented by _____ and interfacing with local _____ agencies and health care workers.

Stage 1: _____—Commitment to Underserved Populations—a University of _____ College of Medicine Department of Family and Community Medicine faculty-student program—is a very important long-term component of _____ . _____ students will offer a clinic providing primary care based on the community assessment. Fourth-year medical students and family practice residents (MDs) will organize this aspect of the program with faculty guidance and support. _____ students, residents and faculty will be offering their services on a volunteer basis.

The students will work with _____ , _____ health care specialists in preceptorships supervised by University of _____ College of Medicine's Department of Family and _____ Community Medicine faculty. This relationship with _____ is especially important since there are no full-fledged medical schools in the state of _____ and the University of _____ is the closest medical training center to _____ , _____ .

Stage 2: Development of a referral network among all available health resources.

Stage 3: The total program will be evaluated to see if the desired outcome has been achieved; e.g., decreased incidence of diarrhea or decreased unplanned pregnancies.

Phases I, II and III will be implemented within the first year and will continue for a minimum of three years.

Phase IV: Future Development

Develop liaisons and funding sources with agencies who are committed to serving underserved populations.

Stage 1: Grant development

Stage 2: Bring _____ to other needy communities along the border

Who's Who

_____: Project Director

_____ is a bilingual _____,
_____ resident who was director of the city of
_____, _____ (Department of Family Services)
between 19 _____–_____ . She has worked on issues regarding the
colonias for the last 10 years. The mother of eight children, she has a BA and
MA in rural and social anthropology. She has taught in programs of the Universidad de _____ , Universidad Pedagogica del _____
and the University of _____ .

_____: Program Director/consultant

_____ writes on international affairs, medical issues and other
topics for national and international publications including the *New York Times*,
the *Christian Science Monitor, Ms.*, and *Life*. She is a contributing editor to *American Medical News*, the weekly magazine of the American Medical Association.
She was Research Associate of an international food aid study in Kenya and
Egypt, funded by the Rockefeller Foundation and U.S.A.I.D. She earned her
BA and MA in International Affairs specializing in development at the University of _____ . She later was a political science fellow
at _____ University in _____ .

_____: Principal Investigator/consultant

_____ is coordinator of the International Health Program at
University of _____ College of Medicine and coordinator of
the College of Medicine's AIDS Educational Project. She has developed health
education and training programs worldwide. A consultant to primary health
care projects targeted at underserved populations, she received her Masters in
Health Education from the University of _____ .
_____: student liaison:

   Faculty: _____ Md, _____ MD (volunteer)

FORM NO. 8
Annual Report of a Community Foundation

THE BOARD OF GOVERNORS

Nine members, serving five-year terms, and appointed by various public officials and organizations.

MR. LARRY K. MEYER, *Chairman*
Attorney at Law
By the Bar Association of Pinellas County

REV. C. CURTIS HESS, *Vice Chairman*
Central Christian Church, St. Petersburg
By the Senior Circuit Judge
of Pinellas County

MRS. CONSTANCE MARQUARDT, *Secretary*
By the League of Women Voters

RAYMOND H. CENTER, M.D.
By the Pinellas County Medical Societies

MR. EDWARD R. TURVILLE
Attorney at Law
By the Chairman of the County Commission of Pinellas Co.

MR. STEPHEN R. MILLER
Certified Public Accountant
By the United Way of Pinellas, Inc.

MR. J. FRED CAMPBELL, JR.
Certified Public Accountant
By the Trustees Committee

MRS. SANDRA M. CASSIDY
President, Pro-Guard Services
By the Trustees Committee

MR. GLENN KRANZOW
Supervisor of Pinellas County
Schools Social Work Service
By the Chairman of the County Board of Public Instruction

STAFF: MR. THOMAS R. BRUCKMAN
Executive Director

THE PINELLAS COUNTY COMMUNITY FOUNDATION

A charitable foundation established by Trust Agreement dated January 1, 1969, and recorded in Official Records 3588, Page 20, public records of Pinellas County.

1253 Park Street
Clearwater, Florida 33516
Phone: 443-3281

1984
ANNUAL REPORT

FUNDS OF THE FOUNDATION	Market Value December 31, 1984
First National Bank of Clearwater, Trustee	$ 480,044.56

Funds for the discretionary use of the Foundation, provided by various persons but largely by the will of Mary K. Haworth. Includes donations from Sarah Louise Halmi, friends of Ralph Richards in his memory, Frances R. Breeden in memory of her father Ralph Richards, Caroline G. Larkin, Marjorie B. Vary, Marjorie D. Bowen, Paul Stiegelmaier, Edith K. Archer and the law firm of Richards, Nodine, Gilkey, Fite, Meyer & Thompson, P.A.

First National Bank of Clearwater, Trustee	10,125.47

Fund provided by U.S. Home in memory of Maurice Condon. Income to go to the scholarship fund of the University of South Florida.

First National Bank of Clearwater, Trustee	5,061.29

Fund provided by Mr. and Mrs. David G. Perkins, Jr. in memory of Edward H. Heidt, Jr. to provide an annual scholarship of $500 for ten years, to a student at St. Petersburg Junior College; thereafter the income becomes unrestricted.

First National Bank of Clearwater, Trustee 50,778.10
Funds provided by the will of Mrs. Donald Roebling
with income to go to Boy Scouts Council and Florida Sheriff's Youth Fund.

Landmark Union Trust Bank of St. Petersburg, NA,
Trustee 713,547.30
Fund provided by the will of Marjorie B. Vary with income
to go to the Museum of Fine Arts, St. Petersburg.

Landmark Union Trust Bank of St. Petersburg, NA,
Trustee 1,108,542.15
Fund provided by the will of Agnes M. Reuter, income to
go to St. Anthony's Hospital, St. Petersburg.

Florida National Bank of Florida, Trustee 69,859.05
Funds for the discretionary use of the Foundation provided by the will of Florence Stillwell.

First National Bank of Florida, Trustee 70,701.96
Fund provided by the will of Selma A. Fields in memory of
her deceased son, Michael Fields. The income goes to
Morton F. Plant Hospital, Clearwater, for the benefit of
leukemia patients.

Total funds .... $ 2,508,659.88

INCOME DISTRIBUTIONS IN 1984

Restricted Income:

Boy Scouts of America, Area Council 3,084.27
Florida Sheriff's Youth Fund 3,084.27
Morton Plant Hospital Leukemia Fund 21,087.76
St. Anthony's Hospital 92,547.44
St. Petersburg Jr. College Scholarship 301.92
St. Petersburg Museum of Fine Arts 56,192.38
Univ. of South Florida Scholarship Fund 1,105.06

Unrestricted Income, Discretionary:

Abilities Inc. Rehabilitation Center   1,000
Big Brothers/Big Sisters of Pinellas   2,000
Boley Manor   1,500

Boy Scouts of America, Area Council	1,000
Channel Markers For the Blind	1,500
Child Development Center, Peace Memorial	2,000
Clearwater Free Clinic	2,000
Clearwater Neighborhood Housing Services	2,000
College Fund of Pinellas	2,000
Community Services Foundation	2,500
FACE Learning Center	1,000
Family Service Centers of Pinellas	2,500
Friends of Happy Workers	2,000
Friends of Ridgecrest	2,000
Girls Clubs of Pinellas	2,500
Hospice Care Inc.	1,500
Junior Achievement of Pinellas	1,000
PARC Housing (Retarded)	2,000
Prevention of Child Abuse, Exchange Club	2,500
St. Petersburg Emergency Shelter	2,000
St. Petersburg Free Clinic, Food Bank	1,500
St. Petersburg YWCA, Womens Resource	1,000
Spouse Abuse Center, Religious Comm.	2,000
Star Foundation	2,000
Suncoast Guardianship, Lutheran Min.	1,000
Upper Pinellas Assoc. For Retarded Cit.	1,000

TOTAL INCOME DISBURSED in 1984 .... $222,393.10

Restricted income is generally distributed in the year that it is earned in accordance with the directions of the donors. Unrestricted, discretionary income is distributed after the close of the year in which it is earned faster the recipients are selected by the Board of Governors and the size of the grants determined.

HOW GIFTS CAN BE MADE

All banks in Pinellas County with trust powers, listed as follows, serve as Trustees of the Foundation. Consult the bank of your choice, your attorney, or your accountant as to how best to serve your interests and the needs of the community.

PIONEER SAVINGS BANK
RUTLAND BANK
SOUTHEAST BANK, NA
SUN BANK/SUNCOAST

WHAT IT IS AND HOW IT WORKS

A community foundation is a community trust to which anyone can make contributions to be used for charitable purposes. Every large city in the United States has a community foundation, and there are now well over 200 of them in operation.

In 1969, a group of Pinellas County citizens decided to form a community foundation. The trust agreement creating the Foundation was dated January 1, 1969, and every bank in Pinellas County having a trust department signed the trust agreement agreeing to serve as a trustee. Therefore, persons wishing to make a contribution to the Foundation, either during their lifetimes or by will, can if they wish designate the particular bank which is to serve as trustee for the Foundation. If a gift is made merely to the Foundation, then the Board of Governors will decide which bank is to hold it as trustee.

Any person contributing $5,000 or more may specify the purpose for which the gift is to be used. The Foundation has received funds restricted in this manner and earmarked for the benefit of leukemia patients at Morton Plant Hospital, the general use of St. Anthony's Hospital, the scholarship fund of the University of South Florida, the area council of the Boy Scouts, the Florida Sheriff's Youth Fund and the St. Petersburg Museum of Fine Arts. The funds may only be used for charitable purposes and persons not wishing to specify a particular charity will find this Foundation useful in helping Pinellas County in those areas that the Board finds to be worthy of support. The needs in a community change and unrestricted gifts enable a board composed of interested citizens to channel the funds where they are needed most at any given time.

The Pinellas County Community Foundation has been approved by the Internal Revenue Service so that all gifts to the Foundation are tax deductible.

The organizers of this Foundation thought it would be especially appropriate in a community like Pinellas County have so many retired persons. Some of these persons wish to help, by living gifts or by Wills, the general interests of charities in this area. The existence of the Pinellas County Community Foundation makes it unnecessary to set up a private trust for such purposes, as the Foundation is an ideal instrument for handling and distributing funds for these purposes.

The governing body of the Foundation is the Board of Governors. It consists of nine members, seven of whom are appointed by public officials, and the other two are appointed by the Trustees Committee. Members of the Board cannot serve more than two consecutive five-year terms.

The Board determines grant making policies and authorizes all disbursements in the manner the donor has directed. The Board disburses available funds in the way it believes will best meet the needs of the community where unrestricted gifts exist.

If the original purpose of a restricted or designated gift has been impractical or impossible to accomplish, the Board may direct the use of these funds for such other purposes as it deems most appropriate at the time.

Gifts to the Foundation are managed by the trustee bank selected by the donor. Each gift is ordinarily managed as a separate fund bearing the name of the donor or any other name he or she may select. Unrestricted gifts are consolidated and invested as a single fund.

While each trustee invests independently, the policy of all trustee banks is to develop the highest level of income consistent with safety.

While the trust agreement authorizes disbursement of principal as well as income, it is the policy of the Board to distribute income only. Distribution of principal would be made only in the case of an extreme emergency.

The principal founder of this Foundation, Mr. Ralph Richards, passed away in 1980. He had devoted more than 11 years to the development of what is today a very significant community foundation. This Annual Report is dedicated to the memory of Ralph Richards, he gave much to the improvement of our community.

POINTS TO REMEMBER

- True charities are the favorites of the law.
- False self-seeking or tax evasion, under the guise of charity, is illegal as well as immoral
- Make the endowment document specific. Pick one or two purposes (*e.g.*, educational, scientific); do not try to cover all kinds of charity.
- Incorporate the foundation at once. Specify the IRS forbidden transactions.
- Pick trustees who will serve, and who know something of the field of service chosen.
- Make trustees' terms of office specific; avoid lifetime trusteeships and the proprietary mentality.
- Do not make the board of trustees a family group.
- Make the duration of the foundation specific (*e.g.*, 25 years maximum), except where the nature of the purpose is a continuing one (such as maintenance of a research center).
- Pick a trained, objective chief executive (such as a law professor); not a man whose chief qualification is charm or obsequiousness.
- Apply promptly for tax-exemption.

- Keep accurate, detailed records; and make full and correct reports to public authorities.

NOTES TO CHAPTER 7

1. *Black's Law Dictionary*, 591 (5th ed., 1979); *Ballentine's Law Dictionary*, 494 (3rd ed., 1969).

2. *Ibid.* pp. 1353 (Black), 194 (Ballentine); 15 Am. Jur. 2d *Char.* §5.

3. *See* Jaar v. University of Miami, 474 S.2d 239 (Fla. App., 1985).

4. IRC §509. See IRC § 507 for termination of private foundation status.

5. F. Emerson Andrews, *Philanthropic Foundations*, 11 (N.Y., Russell Sage Foundation, 1956).

6. Goulden, *The Money Givers*, 8 (N.Y., Random House, 1971).

7. G. Peterson, *Foundations, Private Giving and Public Policy (Report of the Commission on Foundations and Private Philanthropy)* (Chicago, Univ. of Chicago Press, 1970).

8. H. Huntley article, *St. Petersburg Times*, p. 24A (Nov 27/92).

9. Mehegan, S., (article) 7 *NonProfit Times* 6 (10) (June 1993).

10. B. Whitaker, *The Philanthropoids: Foundations and Society*, 135 (N.Y. William Morrow and Co., 1974).

11. Goulden, *The Money Givers*, p. 8 (*supra* n.6).

12. Arthur Anderson and Co., *Tax Economics of Charitable Giving* (8th ed., 1982).

13. "How Big Foundations Spend Their Millions", *U.S. News and World Report* (Sept. 19, 1983).

14. *Id. See also* Castelli, J., 7 *Nonprofit Times* (2) 1, 57 (February 1993).

15. IRC §4940(d)(2) as amended by 1984 Act §302(a). Such exempt operating foundations are exempt from the 2 percent excise tax on net investment income of a private foundation.

16. R. Desiderio, and S. Taylor, *Planning Tax-Exempt Organizations*, 2, 3; Colo. Springs, McGraw-Hill, 1984).

17. *Id.* But a charitable trust can arise by *implication*; e.g., in a release deed. Hillman v. Roman Catholic Bishop of Fall River, 24 Mass. App. 241, 508 N.E. 2d 118 (1987).

    Or by *constructive trust*. American Diabetes Assn. v. Diabetes Soc., 509 N.E. 2d 84 (Ohio App. 1986).

18. Boston Athletic Association v. International Marathons Inc., 457 N.E.2d 58, 64 (Mass. 1984).

19. Mills v. Ball, 344 So. 2d 635 (Fla. 1st DCA 1977).

20. State of Delaware v. J.C. Belin, 456 So. 2d 1237, 1241 (Fla. 1st DCA 1984).

21. P. Haskell, *Preface to the Law of Trusts*, 76 (1975). *But see*, the sections below.

22. Takabuki v. Ching, 695 P.2d 319 (Hawaii 1985). *See*, note 6.

23. People ex rel. Hartigan v. National Anti-Drug, 464 N.E.2d 690, 695 (Ill. App. 1 Dist. 1984).

24. People v. George F. Harding Museum, 374 N.E.2d 756 (Ill. 1978).

25. Illinois has a Charitable Trust Act, to guide the Attorney General in enforcing charitable trusts. The Act requires trustees to make the attorney general aware of their existence. See 760 ICCS 55/1-55/19. Other states which have adopted this Uniform Supervision of Trustees for Charitable Purposes Act are California (West's Ann. Cal. Gov. Code, §12580-12599.5); Michigan (M.C.L.A. §14.251-14.266); and Oregon (ORS 128.610 to 128.990). See also Connecticut General Statutes §3-125, and Lieberman v. Rodgers, 481 A.2d 1295 (Conn. Super. 1984), when an Attorney General was given broad power to enforce charitable trusts by invalidation, administration, termination, or enforcement of the trust terms.

26. *Ibid.*

27. *Abrams v. N.Y. Foundation For Homeless*, 562 N.Y.S.2d 3225 (S. Ct., N.Y. County, 1990).

28. Restatement (2d) of Trusts §399. [*Equitable deviation* doctrine differs from *cy pres* in dealing only with *administrative* provisions of a trust, not the trust *purpose. See, Matter of Estate of Offerman*, 505 N.E.2d 413 (Ill. App. 1987).]

29. *Black's Law Dictionary*, 349 (5th ed., 1979).

30. P. Allen, "Mrs. Buck's Millions", 4 *Calif. Lawyer* (Oct. 1984). Shell purchased the Beldridge Oil Co. for $3.5 billion, which allowed the foundation's coffers to swell to $360 million.

31. *Id.*

32. San Francisco Foundation v. The Superior Court of Marin County, 690 P.2d 1 (Cal. 1984).

33. *Id.*

34. *Shriner's Hospital for Crippled Children v. Smith*, 385 S.E.2d 617 (Va. 1989).

35. *Succession of Mizell*, 468 So. 2d 1371, 1376 (La. App. 1st Cir. 1985).

36. D.R. Lowell and J.G. Grimsley, *Florida Law of Trusts*, §19-1 (Norcross, Ga., Harrison Co., 3rd ed., 1984).

37. Valley Forge Historical Society v. Washington Memorial Chapel, 479 A.2d 1011 (Pa. Super. 1984).

38. Kohn v. Pearson, 670 S.W.2d 795, 796 (Ark. 1984).

39. University Hill Foundation v. Commissioner of Internal Revenue, 51 T.C. 548 (1966).

40. IRC §170(6)(1)(B). This section is referred to in its form prior to the Deficit Reduction Act of 1984, which amended this section.

41. IRC §4940(a).

42. IRC §4942.

43. "Shoring Up Foundations", *Forbes* (Mag.) (July 18, 1983).

44. *Id.*

45. IRC §170(b)(1)(B) as amended by DRA 1984 §301(a).

46. IRC §170(b)(1)(D) as amended by DRA 1984 §301(c).

47. IRC §4940(d)(2). See IRC §4940(d)(3)(B) for definition of disqualified individuals.

48. IRC §4940(d)(1).

49. IRC §4945(a)(1).

50. IRC §4945(d)(4)(A). This provision applies to grants to exempt operating foundations made after December 31, 1984.

51. IRC §4945(d)(4) as amended by DRA 1984 (§302(b).

52. IRC §4940(e) as amended by DRA 1984 §303 and TC 1986 §1832.

53. *Ibid.* n.50, 51.

54. *Ibid.*

55. "How Big Foundations Spend Their Millions," *U.S. News and World Report* (Sept. 19, 1983). 759 foundations with assets over $10 million started up in the 1960s. In the 1970s, this number dropped to 255.

56. Oleck, *Foundations Used as Business Devices*, 9 Clev. St. L. Rev. 339 (1960); Comment, *Charitable Trusts and Inducements to Violate the Law*, 20 W. & L. L. Rev. 85 (1963).

57. *See*, for example, U.S. Congress, House, Reports to Subcommittee No. 1, Select Committee on Small Business; Tax-Exempt Foundations and Charitable Trusts: Their Impact on Our Economy (Washington: U.S. Govt. Printing Office, 1962, 1963, 1964); Subcommittee Chairman's Report No. 1 (1962), No. 2 (1963), No. 3 (1964), No. 4 (1966), No. 5 (1967), No. 6 (1968), No. 7 (1969). *See*, Riecker, *Foundations and the Patman Committee Report*, 63 Mich. L. Rev. 95 (1964).

58. *Ibid.*, Report No. 3, at II.

59. *Ibid.*, at IV.

60. *Ibid.*

61. *Ibid.*, at 1; *and see*, Peril, *Tax-Exempt Targets: The Patman Report and Private Charitable Foundations*, 42 Taxes 69 (1964); Pamphlet, *Charitable Dispositions*, 14 V. L. Weekly, Dicta. Comp. 1 (1963).

62. *See*, Weithorn, *Tax Planning for Foundations, Tax Exempt Status and Charitable Contributions* (1976).

63. *See* (Book) *Public Information Reporting by Tax-Exempt Private Foundations Need More Attention by IRS.* U.S. Genl. Acctg. Office GGD-83-58 (Sept. 26, 1983).

64. Ohio Rev. Code §1719.01.

65. *Ibid.* §1719.02.

66. *Id.* §1719.03.

67. *Id.* §1719.04.

68. *Id.* §1710.06–1719.11.

69. *Id.* §1719.13, 1719.14.

70. *Id.* §1719.05, 1719.12. But trustees' failure to file annual reports as required was not reason enough for their removal. Attorney general v. Olson, 191 N.E.2d 132 (Mass. Supr. Jud. 1963).

71. Ohio Rev. Code §109.23-109.99; and see, Ohio att'y gen. Info. Sheet No. 2, Form CT-4 (Mar. 30, 1960); Klapp and Wertz, *The Ohio Charitable Trusts Act*, 18 Ohio St. L.J. 181 (1957); Bailey v. McElroy, 89 Ohio L.A. 289, 186 N.E.2d 213 (1961) (att'y genl. is not necessary party in a will construction); but he is if the will affects a charitable trust therein; Blair v. Bouton, 15 Ohio Op. 2d 474; and see, Spang v. Cleveland Trust Co., 1 Ohio Op.2d 288, 134 N.E.2d 586 (1956), 176 N.E.2d 280 (1956).

72. Karst, *The Efficiency of the Charitable Dollar: An Unfulfilled State Responsibility*, 73 Harv. L. Rev. 433–483 (1960); Gray, *State Attorney-General, Guardian of Public Charities???*, 14 Clev.-Mar. L. REv. 236 (1965).

73. Ames v. Attorney General, 332 Mass. 246, 124 N.E.2d 511 (1955).

74. *Abrams v. N.Y. Foundation For Homeless*, 562 N.Y.S. 2d 325 (S. Ct., N.Y. County, 1990).

75. *In re* Scholler's Estate, 169 A.2d 554 (Pa., 1961); Est. of McFetridge, 372 A.2d 823 (Pa., 1977); based on the attorney general's brief in the Scholler case.

76. Funk's Estate, 353 Pa. 321 45 A.2d 67 (1946); *In re* Little's Estate, 404 Pa. 247, 168 A.2d 738 (1961).

77. Restatement of Trusts, §3398(2); Manners v. Philadelphia Library Co., 93 Pa. 165, 174; 39 Am. R. 741 (1881); *In re* Coxen, 1948 Ch. 747 (Engl.).

78. Spiegel Estate v. Commissioner, 335 U.S. 701 69 S. Ct. 301, 93 L. Ed. 330 (1949); Miller v. National Bank, 38 N.W.2d 863 (Mich. 1949); Flagg v. Flagg, 80 D. and C. 544 (1952); Yohe v. Yohe, 353 A.2d 417 (Pa. 1976); Com. v. Gibson, 375 A.2d 132 (Pa. 1977).

79. Restatement of Trusts, §367, Comment(c); Par. 333, Comment(e).

80. Weigand v. The Barnes Foundation, 374 Pa. 149, 97 A.2d 81 (1953).

81. *See*, Scott, *Trusts*, §391, p. 2761 (2d ed. 1956); Tudor, *Charitable Trusts* 341 (5th ed. 1929); *and see*, Murphey v. Dalton, 314 S.W.2d 726 (Mo. 1958); Gredig v. Sterling, 47 F.2d 832 (5th Cir. 1931), cert. den. 284 U.S. 629; Stoner Mfg. Corp. v. Y.M.C.A., 13 Ill.2d 162, 148 N.E.2d 441 (1958); Greene v. Art Institute of Chicago, 16 Ill. App. 2d 84, 147 N.E.2d 415 (1958); *In re* Vassar's Estate, 27 N.E. 394 (N.Y.); Trustees of Alexander Linn Hospital Assn. v. Richman, 46 N.J. Supr., 594, 135 A.2d 221; Anno., 124 A.L.R. 1237 (1957). *But see*, State *ex rel.* Tennessee Children's Home Soc. v. Hollinsworth, 193 Tenn. 491, 246 S.W.2d 345 (1952), that district atty's. have the powers; and Hedin v. Westdala Luth. Church, 59 Idaho 241, 81 P.2d 741, 745 (1958) that an interested party has the power. *And see*, Estate of Tomlinson, 359 N.E.2d 109 (Ill. 1976).

82. Scholler case, above, n. 75.

83. *Ibid.*

84. Britt Estate, 369 Pa. 450, 87 A.2d 243 (1952); Hill v. Lewis, 318 A.2d 850 (Md. App. 1974).

85. 18 D. and C. 2d 595 (O.C. Luz, Pa., 1959).

86. *Id.* at 609. But there must be an actual, and direct, benefit to the public, to justify classification as a charity with all the privileges of that status. Mass. Medical Society v. Assessors
of Boston, 164 N.E.2d 325 (Mass. 1960).

87. Lightfoot v. Poindexter, 199 S.W. 1152 (Tex. Civ. App. 1918). See, J. Riley, *Tax-Exempt
Foundations: What Is Legal?*, 9 Natl. L.J. (24)1 (Feb. 23, 1987) (political activities).

88. Oleck, *Modern Corporation Law*, 15 (1978 Supp.); cf. Gilbert v. McLeod Infirmary, 219 S.C.
174, 64 S.E.2d 524 (1951); Leeds v. Harrison, 7 N.J. Super., 558, 72 A.2d 371 (1950);
Kubick v. American Composers Alliance, Inc., 54 N.Y.S.2d 764 (1945); *In re* Estate of Bailey, 19 Cal. App. 2d 135, 65 P.2d 102 (1937); Federal Chem. Co. v. Paddock, 264 Ky. 338,
94 S.W.2d 645 (1936). For the broader view of what is "private charity" *see*, Karst, *The Efficiency of the Charitable Dollar: An Unfulfilled State Responsibility*, 73 Harv. L. Rev. 433, n.2
(1960).

89. *See*, Penna. Stat. Ann., tit. 15, §7002 (repealed). *See now* 15 Pa. C.S.A. §5545.

90. *See*, Massachusetts Medical Society v. Assessors of Boston, 164 N.E.2d 325 (Mass. 1960),
that merely indirect benefits to the public from a medical society do not suffice to warrant recognition as "charity" and tax exemption.

91. *See*, 6 Fletcher, *Cyc. Law of Private Corporations*, §2475 (perm. ed.); Oleck, *N.Y. Corporations*,
Chap. 17 (1954, with 1961 Cum. Supp.).

92. Del. Code Anno. tit. 8; N.Y. Not-for-Profit Corp. L., Art. II. *And see*, as to "trust funds":
Calif. Corp. Code, Div. 8, §10250 *et seq.* (1980).

93. Calif. Corp. Code, Div. 8, §§10250 *et seq.* (1980); Pa. Stat. § 7213.

94. Oleck, *Modern Corporation Law*, 864 (1978 Supp.).

95. *In re* Application for Jocard Club, 85 D. and C. 89 (Pa.); Citizens League of Wheatfield
Tp., 65 D. and C. 70 (Pa.); *cf.*: Tinnin v. First Bank of Miss., 502 S.2d 659 (Miss. 1987).

96. Pa. Stat. §§2851-201. Charter Application, 21 Dis. 1135, 8 Sch. 179 (Pa.). *See* Pa. C.S.A.
§5301.

97. *In re* Charter of Evangelical Lutheran Church, 4 Del. 154 (1892).

98. N.Y. Penal Law, §§660, 661 (ten-year prison term).

99. N.Y. Not-for-Profit Corp. L. §404(c); 40 Pa. C.S.A. 6101–6301, 6302, 6306, 6321.

100. *In re* Gold Star Parents Association, 67 N.Y.S.2d 73 (1946).

101. *In re* Gold Star Parents Association, above, n. 100; *In re* Boy Explorers of America, 67
N.Y.S.2d 108 (1946); *In re* Victory Committee of Greenpoint, 59 N.Y.S.2d 546 (1945); *In
re* Certificate of Incorporation of Humanity Club, 155 N.Y.S.2d 210 (1956).

102. See 15 Pa. C.S.A. §5309.

103. 24 P.S. 6501–6518.

104. Wilson v. Picard, 173 Misc. 788, 20 N.Y.S.2d 119 (1932).

105. Vanderbilt v. Commissioner, 93 F.2d 360 (1st Cir. 1937); Cummins-Collins Foundation, 15
T.C. 613, 622 (1950); Trinity Operating Co. v. Corsi, 269 A.D. 716, 53 N.Y.S.2d 744 (1945);
Kubik v. American Composers Alliance, Inc., 54 N.Y.S.2d 764 (1945). *See*, as to valid pur-
pose in what might seem to be self-dealing: IRS Ltr. 8533059 (Noted) in 8 Natl. L.J.(7)3
(Oct. 28, 1985).

106. Syracuse Savings Bank v. Yorkshire Insurance Co., 301 N.Y. 403; 94 N.E.2d 73 (1950);
Note, Distinction Between Powers and Objects in Articles of Incorporation, 46 Harv. L.
Rev. 1337 (1933).

107. *Tinnin v. First United Bank of Mississippi*, 570 So. 2d 1193 (Miss., 1990).

108. *Walton v. City of Red Bluff*, 3 Cal. Rptr. 2d 275 (Cal. Ap. 3 Dist. 1991).

109. *Lancaster v. Merchants Nat. Bank of Fort Smith, Ark.*, 961 F.2d 713 (8th Cir. (Ark.), 1992). *See also In re Estate of Breeden*, 256 Cal. Rptr. 813 (App. 4th Dist., 1989).

110. *Fireman's Annuity and Ben. Fund of Chicago v. Municipal Employees', Officers', and Officials' Annuity and Ben. Fund of Chicago*, 579 N.E. 2d 1003 (Ill. App. 1 Dist. 1991).

111. Ohio Rev. Code §1713.31 (on written application by five citizens, verified by the oath of one, and stating specific charges. Applies to educational corporations); N.Y. Genl. Corp. L. §83 (any person); *D.C. Code Encyclopedia* §16-3502; Calif. Ann. Civ. Proc. Code §803; *and see* Com. ex. rel. Truscott v. Yiddisher Kultur Farband, 382 Pa. 553, 116 A.2d 555 (1955); Southerland *ex rel.* Snider v. Decimo Club, Inc., 16 Del. Ch. 183, 142 A. 786 (1928); People v. Stilwell, 157 A.D. 839, 142 N.Y.S. 881, affg. 78 Misc. 96, 138 N.Y.S. 693 (1912) (misuse of powers); Nicolai v. Maryland Agric. and Mech. Assn., 96 Md. 323, 53 A. 965 (9103) (misuse of powers); State v. Dyer, 200 S.W.2d 813 (Tex. 1947) (misuse of powers); Bennett v. American-Canadian Ambulance Corps, 179 Misc. 21, 37 N.Y.S.2d 470 (1942) (misuse of profit); Ames v. Kansas, 111 U.S. 499, 4 S. Tc. 437, 28 L. Ed. 482 (1884); Aitken v. Stewart, 129 Calif. App. 38 18 P.2d 988 (1933); Syracuse Savings Bank v. Yorkshire Ins. Co., 301 N.Y. 403, 94 N.E.2d 73 (1950); Red Ball Motor Freight Co., Inc. v. Southern Pacific Trans. Co., 231 S.W.2d 462 (Tex. 1950); 35 Words and Phrases, *Quo Warranto* (1978 Cum. Supp. Ed.).

112. N.Y. Genl. Corp. L. §83.

113. *Supra* at n. 111 (Ohio Rev. Code §109.23–109.99).

114. *Ibid.*

115. *Supra,* at n. 111 *et seq.*

116. N.Y. Genl. Corp. L. §130; Walker Memorial Baptist Church v. Saunders, 173 Misc. 455; 17 N.Y.S.2d 843, affd. without op. 259 A.D. 1010, 21 N.Y.S.2d 512 (1940), revd. on other gds. 285 N.Y.S. 462, 35 N.E.2d 42, rehear. den. 286 N.Y. 607, 35 N.E.2d 944 (1941).

117. People v. Volunteer Rescue Army, Inc., 262 A.D. 237, 28 N.Y.S.2d 994, affd. without op. 39 N.Y.S.2d 1022 (1943); Com. *ex rel.* Truscott v. Yiddisher Kultur Faband, 382 Pa. 553, 116 A.2d 555 (1955); Morrison v. Philadelphia College of Law, Inc., 57 Dauph. 265 (Pa.); Kardo Co. v. Adams, 231 F. 950 (6th Cir. 1916); 19 C.J.S., Corporations, §1651.

118. Oleck, *Historical Nature of Equity Jurisprudence,* 20 Fordham L. Rev. 23 (1951). But see, In re Scholler's Estate, 403 Penna. 97, 169 A.2d 554 (1961).

119. *In re* Rieger, 157 F.609 (S.D., Ohio 1907).

120. Sampsell v. Imperial Paper Co., 313 U.S. 215 (1941).

121. Berle, *Enterprise-Entity Theory,* 47 Columbia L. Rev. 343 (1947), citing among many cases, United States v. Lehigh Valley Ry., 220 U.S. 257 (1911); Chicago, etc. Ry. v. Minneapolis Civic Assn., 247 U.S. 490 (1918); United States v. Reading Co., 253 U.S. 26 (1920); Brundred v. Rice, 49 Ohio St. 640, 32 N.E. 169 (1892); Northern Securities Co. v. U.S., 193 U.S. 197 (1904). Corrigan v. West Shore Center, 31 Ohio St. 2d 192, 287 N.E.2d 803 (1972) (dissolution of nonprofit corporation where actual activities bore no relation to its stated purpose).

122. Berle, n. 121.

8

CHARITABLE
SUBSCRIPTIONS

[See *Tax Exemption* as to deductions by Contributors]

[Suzanne L. Underberg and Prof. I. Richard Gershon assisted in updating this material]

§76. SOLICITATION OF CONTRIBUTIONS

[See also, in the Index, *Fundraising.*]

One important aspect of charitable organizations is their ability to solicit contributions. Such contributions are often essential to the existence of the organization.

In order to determine whether an entity is nonprofit, or charitable, or neither—and thus entitled or not entitled to favorite-of-the-law-treatment—it is necessary to turn to the statutory provisions of the various states.

Florida's statutes, for example, contain a variety of provisions for this matter, in separate chapters on tax-exemption (§196.012), solicitation of contributions (§496.404), and charitable trusts (§737.501). It defines "charitable organization" in the first above-listed provision (§496.404), as does Pennsylvania's law.[1] Florida's statutory analysis of the criteria for determining profit or nonprofit status is particular helpful (Fl.St.§196.195):

196.195 *Criteria for determining profit or nonprofit status of applicant—*

1. Applicants requesting exemption shall supply such fiscal and other records showing in reasonable detail the financial condition, record of operation, and exempt and nonexempt uses of the property, where appropriate, for the immediately preceding fiscal year as are requested by the property appraiser or the property appraiser adjustment board.

2. In determining whether an applicant for a religious, literary, scientific, or charitable exemption under this chapter is a nonprofit or profit-making venture or whether the property is used for a profit-making purpose, the following criteria shall be applied:

   a. The reasonableness of any advances or payment directly or indirectly by way of salary, fee, loan, gift, bonus, gratuity, drawing account, commission, or otherwise (except for reimbursements of advances for reasonable out-of-pocket expenses incurred on behalf of the applicant) to any person, company, or other entity directly or indirectly controlled by the applicant or any other officer, director, trustee member, or stockholder of the applicant;

   b. The reasonableness of any guaranty of a loan to, or an obligation of, any officer, director, trustee, member, or stockholder of the applicant of any entity directly or indirectly controlled by such person, or which pays any compensation to its officer, directors, trustees, members, or stockholders for services rendered to or on behalf of the applicant;

   c. The reasonableness of any contractual arrangement by the applicant or any officer, director, trustee, member, or stockholder of the applicant regarding the rendition of services, the provision of goods or supplies, the management of the applicant, the construction or renovation of the property of the applicant, the procurement of the real, personal, or intangible property of the applicant, or other similar financial interest in the affairs of the applicant;

   d. The reasonableness of payments made for salaries for the operation of the applicant or for services, supplies and materials used by the applicant, reserves for repair, replacement, and depreciation of the property of the applicant, payment of mortgages, liens, and encumbrances upon the property of the applicant, or other purposes;

   e. The reasonableness of charges made by the applicant for any services rendered by it in relation to the value of those services . . .

3. Each applicant must affirmatively show that no part of the subject property, or the proceeds of the sale, lease, or other disposition thereof, will inure to the benefit of its members, directors, or officers or any person or firm operating for profit or for a nonexempt purpose.

4. No application for exemption may be granted for religious, literary, scientific, or charitable use of property until the applicant has been found by the property appraiser or, upon appeal, by the property appraisal adjustment board to be nonprofit as defined in this section.

196.196 *Criteria for determining that portion of charitable, religious, scientific, or literary property entitled to tax exempt status.-*

1. In the determination of whether an applicant is actually using all or a portion of its property predominantly for a charitable, religious, scientific, or literary purpose, the following criteria shall be applied:
   a. The nature and extent of the charitable, religious, scientific, or literary activity of the applicant, a comparison of such activities with all other activities of the organization, and the utilization of the property for charitable, religious, scientific, or literary activities as compared with other uses.
   b. The extent to which the property has been made available to groups who perform exempt purposes, at a charge that is equal to less than the cost of providing facilities for their use, or the extent to which services are provided to persons at a charge that is equal to or less than the cost of providing such services. Such rental or service shall be considered as part of the exempt purposes of the applicant.

2. Only those portions of property used predominantly for charitable, religious, scientific, or literary purposes shall be exempt. In no event shall an incidental use of property either qualify such property for an exemption or impair the exemption of an otherwise exempt property.

3. Except as otherwise provided herein, property claimed as exempt for literary, scientific, or charitable purposes which is used for profit-making purposes shall be subject to ad valorem taxation. Use of property for functions not requiring a business or occupational license conducted by the organization at its primary residence the revenue of which is used wholly for exempt purposes shall not be considered profit making. In this connection the playing of bingo on such property shall not be considered as using such property in such a manner as would impair its exempt status.

The Florida statues then add provisions for hospitals, nursing homes, etc. *"Charitable Purpose"* is defined in Section 196.012(b) as "a function or service which is of such a community service that its discontinuance could legally result in the allocation of public funds for the continuance of the function of service."

See (cases on solicitation, *e.g.*, in public malls or airports) City of Watseka v. Illinois Public Action Council, 55 LW 2083, 3492, 3607; and N.J. Citizen Action v. Edison Township, 55 LW 2093, 3571; also TC. (1986) §1601(a) permitting distribution of articles worth up to $5 in connection with solicitation of charitable contributions.

State Regulation

Registration of solicitors of contributions to charitable organizations is the chief method of state regulation of their actions; also requirements that they disclose, in writing, that a financial statement and other information are available on request. Professional fund raiser disclosures are required to be ample in most states; less for volunteer fundraisers.[2] [See, below, Ch. 43 §440]

Local licensing of solicitors now is required in many places. Thus a *permit* (on payment of $10 fee per year) is required by the Pinellas County Charitable Solicitations Board (Clearwater, Florida).

Most state codes require professional (or paid) solicitors to disclose their professional status or explain their relation to the charities for which they solicit contributions.[3] However, regulation must not invade the constitutional freedom of organizations or solicitors.[4]

Florida's 1989 attempt to *reduce* registration was an acknowledged failure, abandoned in 1991. Currently, in Florida, all nonexempt charitable organizations, professional solicitors, and their sponsors must register with the Department of Agriculture and Consumer Affairs. Professional solicitors must post a $50,000 bond. Nonexempt organizations must provide a financial report or budget within 14 days of any request for such information.[5]

Increasingly strict disclosure requirement laws were enacted in Ohio and Pennsylvania, with tougher penalties, by 1991, broadening a tendency begun in Illinois and Virginia to reduce the number of exempt (including religious) organizations. Every solicitation receipt or pledge now must contain a mandatory statement (such as Pennsylvania's):

> "A copy of the official registration and financial information may be obtained from the Pennsylvania Department of State by calling toll-free, within Pennsylvania, (800) 732-0099. Registration does not imply endorsement."

Pennsylvania's statute lists 15 prohibited acts, and denominational groups (not church institutions) that raise money from the public are not exempt. Florida took steps in 1991 to repeal its 1989 statute that had eliminated registration requirements.[6]

Fund Raisers' Registration Costs increased to $20,000 bonds for solicitors in Massachusetts and $50,000 in Florida for 1992. Registration fees are $800 in New York and $1,000 in Tennessee (1992).[7]

§77. DEFINITIONS OF CHARITABLE STATUS

[As to Internal Revenue Code definitions, see the next Chapter. As to Criteria (statutory), see the preceding section.]

State law definitions of terms such as "charitable organization" or "charitable purpose" often depend upon court decisions.[8] However, there have been many statutory attempts to define these somewhat vague terms. Virginia, for example, uses the following definitions.[9]

> *Charitable Organization.* Any person which is or holds itself out to be organized or operated for any charitable purpose, or any person which solicits or obtains contributions solicited from the public. This definition shall not

be deemed to include any church or convention or association of churches, primarily operated for nonsecular purposes and no part of the net
income of which inures to the direct benefit of any individual; nor shall it
include any political party, or campaign committee.

Charitable Purpose. Any charitable, benevolent, humane philanthropic, patriotic or eleemosynary purpose and the purposes of influencing legislation or
influencing the actions of any public official or instigating, prosecuting, or
intervening in litigation.

Notice that Virginia considers *lobbying* a charitable purpose, while the
Internal Revenue Code clearly does *not*.[10]

It is also important to note that the statutory definitions of charitable
organizations are narrower than those of not-for-profit organizations in general.

When these definitions are compared with the definitions of *non-profit* in
the same statute (see the general discussion herein Chapters 1, 2), difficulties
multiply.

Differences in meaning have real importance when the same word is used
with respect to truly *charitable* organizations *and* organizations which are *merely
nonprofit* in nature.

For example, the word *contribution* is defined in the Ohio statute as meaning "the promise or grant of any money or property of any kind or value."[11]

But a contribution to a charitable organization (*e.g.*, an orphan asylum)
is not legally the same thing as one to a merely nonprofit organization (*e.g.*, a
private golf club). The contract implications, tax implications, and other legal
aspects differ in the two cases.

This is why precision in definition is important. Confusion of charitable
and merely nonprofit aspects of such a thing as a gift or *contribution* usually is
desired by hypocrites, such as those who seek tax benefits for gifts given to personally controlled pseudo-charities.

"*Charitable subscription*" conveys the idea of a promise to make a gift, not
a return for consideration.[12] It is gratuitous in nature. Nevertheless, the general American rule is that a charitable subscription is a binding contract or offer
to contract.[13]

Subscription (literally, *writing under*) is the act of signing one's name on a
written document or instrument—usually at the bottom of the paper. The signature to what is stated represents an agreement, an authentication, or an
adoption.[14]

A *subscription* may also be a written contract whereby the singer (*subscriber*) agrees: to contribute a sum of money or something else of value, to take
and pay for stock, or to take and pay for something that is yet to be issued,
such as a book or play.[15]

In this chapter, a *subscription* is *a promise to contribute*.[16]

To *contribute* means to give something, together with other givers, in furtherance or aid of a common purpose.[17] The gift or assistance itself is the *contribution*. *Contribution* has certain other technical legal meanings (in the sense

of reimbursement outlays, among co-debtors),[18] with which we need not concern ourselves here.

Charitable means *liberal to those in need.* It is equivalent to *benevolent,*[19] *beneficient,*[20] or *eleemosynary.*[21] *Eleemosynary* itself means *pertaining to the distribution of alms or bounty.*[22] Thus, an *eleemosynary corporation* is a corporation organized for the accomplishment of charitable or benevolent purposes.[23]

A *charitable corporation* purposes more specifically to aid those who need aid.[24] Yet both charitable and eleemosynary corporations, in a more general sense, promote the welfare of a group, a class, a community, or all of mankind.[25]

A *charitable organization* is one that is dedicated to actual charitable purposes, rather than to merely nonprofit purposes.[26] Unfortunately, the term is also used as a synonym for simply *nonprofit.*[27] It would be much better to distinguish clearly between mere *nonprofit* and truly *charitable* organizations. The distinction between a nonprofit social club or trade union and a hospital or orphan asylum should not be permitted to become blurred.

A *charitable institution* is one devoted to performing a public service,[28] or one supported at least in part by public aid,[29] or one that administers a charity.[30] Thus a *charitable hospital* is one that is operated not for profit,[31] or that is operated for the giving of free hospital services.[32] But for tax purposes, the giving of free services to those unable to pay makes a hospital charitable, though it charges persons who are able to pay.[33] In another view, even the mere devotion of income from patients to charitable facilities makes the hospital charitable.[34] A *charitable school,* similarly, may be merely one operated not for profit,[35] or one partly supported by public contributions,[36] or one wholly supported by charitable contributions.[37] (Concerning freedom of charitable organizations from liability for negligence or other wrongs by their agents, see Chapter 17.)

A *charitable society* is an organization (*e.g.,* a school) that would be classified as charitable under the above definitions.[38]

Charity is a word of many meanings. It may mean merely good intention and benevolence of attitude.[39] It may mean an organization that is dedicated to public service or use,[40] or to some particular aspect of public or group welfare[41] (especially to religious, educational, or benevolent purposes[42]) or to scientific research that will be of public benefit, or to any activity or thing or group that aids or improves mankind or some considerable group of persons[43] (or even animals—as in the case of a society for the prevention of cruelty to animals[44]).

One important characteristic of a true charity is that the specific persons who are to receive its benefits are not certain, though the class or group that is to be aided is certain.[45] Thus *charity* may imply almost anything from actual almsgiving,[46] to merely nonprofit objects.[47]

Dues, fines and assessments of members become organization property unless contrary provisions are made in the organizations' fundamental documents.[48]

So loose a term as *charity* is readily subject to abuse or misunderstanding. It seldom should be used without qualification or explanation.

Pure charity is entirely gratuitous aid, with no return or benefit to the giver.[49] *Public charity* confers benefits on a number of persons, indefinite or comprising a class, among the general public.[50] So far as tax exemption goes, incidental aid (and saving) to the state is one of the primary bases for classification as pure charity.[51]

A *foreign charity* is organized or supported in a state other than that in which the contributors or the benefactor reside.[52]

§78. CHARITABLE TRUSTS IN GENERAL

(See the preceding chapter on foundations.)

For the making of substantial gifts or contributions dedicated to public welfare, the *foundation* or *charitable trust* is a major legal vehicle. In recent years foundations have become so important that a chapter has been added to this work, dealing solely with them.

The importance of foundation grants is illustrated by a study conducted by the New York-based Foundation Center in 1991. The study analyzed 58,000 recent grants and shows that there is an upswing in large grants: 145 grants of $2.5 million or more reported in 1991, up 71 percent in two years. The largest recipients were health associations, followed by children's groups. Education received a quarter of the grant dollars in 1991. Higher education received just under 16 percent of all grant dollars. Overall grants to science dropped slightly in 1991. Foundations have nearly tripled their investments in Eastern Europe since 1990. Foundation support for the arts, particularly in the area of arts programming, increased rapidly in the last decade. Support for the arts increased from 1983 to 1989 by 18 percent a year, rising from $653 million to $1.2 billion.[53]

The subject of charitable trusts (foundations) in respect to their establishments as "unincorporated associations," is touched on in Chapter 5. Most foundations today are incorporated.

Discussion in this section is intended only to indicate the utility of charitable trusts as an important technique for charitable contribution.

A *charitable trust* of property or funds is one for the benefit of the public or of some class or group of the public.[54] Its creation amounts to the appointment of some person, persons, or group, as trustees to hold the trust fund or property and to apply or manage it for a charitable purpose.[55] In the absence of a reserved power, neither the donor nor the donee can alter or terminate a charitable trust.[56]

The chief characteristics of a charitable trust are: (1) *designation* of a trustee or trustee group (2) to *hold* certain property (3) and *apply* it or its income (4) to a *specific* charitable purpose (5) for *unidentified beneficiaries* (6) who are of a *specified class or group* of the public.[57] Thus, a church is a charitable trust.[58]

The chief difference between an ordinary *trust* and a *charitable trust* is that in a charitable trust the beneficiaries are unspecified,[59] while in an ordinary trust the beneficiary [*cestui(s) qui* trust] are specified.[60]

So far as nonprofit organizations are concerned, trusts are chiefly important in the endowment of foundations and in support of public-benefit work. For unincorporated associations, use of the trust device is necessitated by the vague structure of the multi-partner equity. (See Chapter 5.)

Trust situations also involve the *cy pres* doctrine. (See the Index.) Trust instruments, such as a trust deed or foundation instrument, must be construed as nearly as possible (*cy pres*) to carry out the donor's purpose. If, for example, the organization is dissolved, the trust fund must be devoted to closely approximate purposes—when the original gift instrument failed to specify other alternatives, or failed to make them clear.[61]

A trust is an "association" for real property tax law exemption and other purposes.[62]

There is a vast literature on the trusts, both in their purely private and in their charitable aspects. The multi-volume *Bogert on Trusts*[63] should be consulted. The *Restatement of the Law of Trusts* issued by the American Law Institute is another important authority.[64] The special trust law applicable to *foundations* is often treated as a separate branch of the law of trusts.

There also is a large literature on charities, especially heavy in articles and notes in legal journals and periodicals. [See the Bibliography in Chap. 2, Section 16.] A sample bibliography of literature on charities is included in the footnotes to this section.[65] Charitable contributions by corporations, tax exemption, and immunity for liability are treated elsewhere in this book.

Some states have adopted Uniform Supervision of Trustees for Charitable Purposes Acts[66] with extensive rules.[67] Many states have adopted the Uniform Management of Institutional Funds Act with similar rules.[68]

§79. SUBSCRIPTIONS AND CONTRIBUTIONS TO CHARITIES

[See the preceding chapter.]

A principal problem in subscriptions to charities is that of whether or not a promise to contribute results in an enforceable contract. The laws of various states differ on this point.

In terms of ordinary contract law, there is no technically valid contract. Every contract must contain a promise or a *consideration* on each side.[69] It is hard to see how a mere promise to *accept* a benefit can be adequate consideration for a promise to *give* that benefit.[70]

But this logic is countered, in many states, by the reasoning of *promissory estoppel.* This holds that one who makes a promise is estopped to deny it later if the promisee has already acted in reasonable reliance on that promise.[71]

Challenges to gifts to charities may be based on *mortmain* statutes in some states.[72]

But "charitable trusts" are favorites of the law, and courts tend to uphold them.[73] Thus, "public policy" is enough to make a *charitable contribution* pledge enforceable by the courts in some states.[74]

England and a few of the United States hold to the logic that a promise to contribute to charity is not binding because there is no valid exchange of consideration.[75]

In most of the United States, the public desire to aid charities has resulted in action to hold promisors to their promises. This action is justified by a variety of reasons, none of them legally logical.[76]

The prevailing American rule can be stated thus:

A subscription (promise to contribute) to a charity is an *offer* to enter into a binding contract. It becomes *binding* when it is *accepted* (1) by *beginning or doing the work* for which it was promised, or (2) by *incurring liability* in respect to such work *in reliance* on the good faith of the promisor.[77]

An offer is revocable until it is accepted. Either the promisor's actual revocation or his death or insanity may end the offer.[78]

Mutual reliance (merely theoretical) among promisors is sometimes said to be the consideration that makes the promise binding.[79]

Statutes in some states (*e.g.*, Georgia) specifically state that a promise by one party is good consideration for a promise by the other.[80] Even without statutes, many cases hold that the promise of each subscriber is supported by the promises of the others.[81]

A few cases have held that the fact that the subscription in question induced others to subscribe constitutes sufficient consideration.[82] Some cases rest on the view that public policy requires that charitable subscriptions be deemed to be binding.[83]

Some cases have held that charitable subscriptions are not binding contracts.[84] Others have held that a request by the contributor, that the promisee obtain other subscribers, is sufficient consideration.[85] Or, the doing of the act, towards which the contribution was made, is sufficient.[86] Or, the grantees promise to apply the contribution properly and in accordance with the contributor's wishes, is sufficient consideration.[87]

In most states charitable contributions are held to be binding contracts, on the theory of promissory estoppel.[88]

In cases involving the ongoing administration of a charitable corporation, "standing" is restricted to the Attorney-General. The policy behind that rule is to prevent vexatious litigation and suits by irresponsible parties who have not conducted proper investigations and have no tangible stake in the matter.[89] The *Attorney-General*, as representative of the people, has sufficient interest to check up on reasonableness of fees given by a charitable trust, as the state is the ultimate *cestui qui trust* of any charitable bequest; and he/she may require that a judicial hearing be conducted if he/she challenges executor or attorney fees.[90]

Bequests to charities may be overturned by survivors' (mortmain) actions if the will was executed less than six months before the relative's (grantor's) death, in Georgia, Idaho, and Mississippi. In 1990 the Florida Supreme Court ruled that the law allowing this is "feudal" and violates the state and federal constitutions (5 to 2 decision).[91]

[Daniel M. Young contribued the rest of this section.]

When the words describing a charity fail to enumerate an existing, functioning, legal charity, then the court will "as near as possible" attempt to replicate the testator's intent by allowing the bequest to be bestowed on a charity of similar character. This is the doctrine of cy pres.[92]

The *Cy pres* doctrine applies to grant of land for public usage, and the *municipality* becomes the trustee for benefit of the public when it accepts dedication of the land; and if literal performance of a general charitable purpose is impossible or impractical, the *cy pres* doctrine decision as to the land's use is decided by a court, not by the municipality.[93] Similarly, when a volunteer fire service, operating from a charitable trust, tried to liquidate its fire fighting assets so that it no longer would provide fire protection, the court held that the service could not change its charitable activity while the original intent of fire fighting remained "possible, practical, and legal." Otherwise, the donor's intent would be thwarted.[94] *Cy pres* always looks to the intent of the donor.

The intent of the donors was paramount when about 742 people contributed to a memorial fund for an eight-year-old girl who had been murdered. $10,000 remained after payment of her funeral expenses. The court queried some contributions and decided that help to the child's family also had been intended by some contributors; two of whom received refunds, while half of the balance was ordered to go to the parent and the rest to charity.[95]

In North Carolina, a specific institution was named by a decedent in his charitable devise. The purpose of his devise was "aiding the sick, injured and suffering humanity." The court held that there was *specific charitable intent*, on the part of the testator, when he named a *specific institution*. Therefore the cy pres doctrine would not apply to transfer the gift to a similar institution.[96]

Solicitation of Contributions

[See the preceding chapter.]

Whether or not an organization is charitable, and thus able to solicit funds from generous contributors, is a determination that will be made by each individual state.[97] However, the average person who is approached by someone claiming to represent a worthy charity is generally not privy to any state action concerning the authenticity of the purported charitable organization or its authority to solicit contributions. It is this fact which has given rise to many confidence scams in which illegal organizations prey upon the philanthropic nature of people in general in order to garner personal gain.

The National Catholic Development Conference has published a new brochure entitled *Giving Is an Act of Faith*. The brochure suggests points for donors to consider before they decide to contribute to a charitable organization: (1) The appeal letter should state the soliciting organization's full name and address, be in good taste, present the needs of the organization factually, and fully describe the purpose for which the contribution will be used. (2) Premiums or gifts, sent with the appeal, do not obligate you to give. Such gifts do not have to be returned if you do not give. (3) Expect a prompt thank-you or acknowledgment if you give. (4) Write to ask that your name be removed from the mailing lists of organizations whose mail you don't want to receive. (5) Write, before you give, to the organization if you have questions about programs, finances, or beneficiaries, or if you want your gift to be applied to a specific program.[98]

Many states have acted to protect the public from fraudulent charities by adopting legal criteria for charitable solicitations. [See the next sections.] Solicitation of Charitable Contributions Acts are meant to protect the public.[99]

§80. REGISTRATION OF CHARITIES

One protective measure adopted by the various states involves the registration of charities.

As to *local licensing* of solicitors, see the beginning portion of Section 76 above.

Rhode Island's statute, which is typical of modern registration statutes, provides as follows:

5-53-2. Registration of charitable organizations.—(a) No charitable organization, except those granted exemption in §5-53-1, which intends to solicit contributions from persons within the state of Rhode Island, or have funds solicited on its behalf by a professional fund-raising counsel, professional solicitor or other charitable organizations shall solicit contributions unless it shall, prior to any solicitation, file a registration statement with the department upon prescribed forms. In addition, in order to obtain a renewal of registration, such charitable organizations shall file the statements required by this chapter within 90 days subsequent to the end of its fiscal year. It shall be the duty of the president, chairman or principal officer of such charitable organization to file the statements required under this chapter. Such statements shall be sworn to and shall contain the following information:

1. The name of the organization and the purpose for which it was organized.

2. The principal address of the organization and the address of any offices in this state. If the organization does not maintain an office, the name and address of the person having custody of its financial records.

3. The names and addresses of any chapters, branches or affiliates in this state.

4. The place where and the date when the organization was legally established, the form of its organization, and a reference to any determination of its tax exempt status under the internal revenue code.

5. The names and addresses of the officers, directors, trustees and the principal salaried executive staff officer.

6. A copy of the annual financial statement of he organization audited by an independent certified public accountant for the organizations' immediately preceding fiscal year, or a copy of a financial statement audited by an independent certified public accountant covering, in a consolidated report, complete information as to all the preceding year's fund-raising activities of the charitable organization, showing kind and amount of funds raised, costs and expenses incidental thereto, and allocation or disbursements of funds raised, and if the organization employs a professional solicitor the report shall indicate how and from whom each contribution obtained by said professional solicitor was received and how the contribution was used.

   Organizations having annual gross budges of $100,000 or less shall be considered to have met the financial requirements of this section by providing the following financial statements for the immediately preceding fiscal year prepared by an independent public or certified public accountant.
   1. Statement of Revenues, Expenses, and Changes in Fund Balances
   2. Balance Sheet
      At the discretion of the director, audited annual financial statements of organizations with budgets of $100,000 or less may be required.

7. A description of the method or methods of solicitations including whether the organization intend to solicit contributions from the public directly or have such done on its behalf by others.

8. Information as to whether the organization is authorized by any other governmental authority to solicit contributions and whether it is or has ever been enjoined by any court from soliciting contributions.

9. The general purpose or purposes for which the contributions to be solicited shall be used.

10. The name or names under which it intends to solicit contributions.

11. The names of the individuals or officers of the organization who will have final responsibility for the custody of the contributions.

12. The names of the individuals or officers of the organization responsible for the final distribution of the contributions. The director of business regulation or his designee shall examine each initial application of charitable organizations for the right to solicit funds and each renewal application of charitable organizations for the right to solicit funds and if found to be in conformity with the requirements of this chapter and all relevant rules and regulations it shall be approved for registration.

13. A listing of the names, addresses, and the compensation of all individuals, directors, officers, agents, servants and/or employees of the organization who receive an annual compensation, commission or

other remuneration in excess of $12,500. Each chapter, branch, affiliate or member agency of a federated fund-raising agency may report the information required by this subsection to its parent organization and such parent organization shall furnish such information as to its Rhode Island chapters, branches, affiliates or member agencies in consolidated form to the department, or each chapter, branch, affiliate or member agency of a federated fund-raising agency may report the information required by this subsection separately to the department.

Most registration statutes require the application of the organization to be signed by an authorized officer and an independent certified public accountant, and verified under oath.[100]

§81. EXEMPTIONS FROM REGISTRATION REQUIREMENTS

Most states allow certain organizations to be exempt from registration statutes. The most common of these exempt organizations are churches[101] and educational institutions.[102] However, an independent foundation to raise money for religious organizations is not a religious organization and thus is not exempt from the requirement that it register with the state *before* solicitation.[103]

Other organizations which can be exempt from the registration requirements are charitable hospitals, public libraries,[104] and organizations which will solicit only relatively small amounts during a given calendar year[105] especially where members' dues are the primary support solicited.[106]

§82. DENIAL OF APPLICATION TO SOLICIT

A state will deny an organization's application for authority to solicit charitable contributions for a number of reasons. The most common grounds for denying such an application are:

1. false statements in the application.[107]
2. that the applicant is or has engaged in a fraudulent transaction or enterprise.[108]
3. that the applicant's solicitation would be a fraud on the public.[109]
4. that the organization's actual or expected expenses for items like salaries to professional solicitors would be too high compared with the funds remaining after such salary expenditures,[110,111] A less-than 25 percent fee to solicitors and/or expenses of fund-raising now seems to be the validity test,[112], unless a higher rate is reasonable.[113]
5. that the activities to be financed will be incompatible with the health, safety or welfare of the state's citizens.[114]

§83. IDENTIFICATION BADGES OF SOLICITORS (PERMITS)

As a further protection, some jurisdictions now require those soliciting funds to display or wear a badge identifying the charity they work for, and stating that such charities are authorized to make solicitations.[115] For example, Pinellas County, Florida, charges $10 for a permit for a solicitor for charitable contributions, valid for one year. [Pinellas County Charitable Solicitations Officer, 400 S. Fort Harrison Ave., Clearwater, FL. 33516.]

§84. CONTRIBUTIONS BY CORPORATIONS AND ASSOCIATIONS

In practically all the states, the authority of a corporation (including business corporations) to contribute to charities or public welfare organizations or programs now is well settled. In the past this was considered to be "waste" of corporate funds. But today, argument that corporations should *not* so contribute often evokes resentful criticism—as evasion of a public organization![116] Canada's top corporations are said to contribute less than 1 percent of their pre-tax profits to charity, and to do it mainly in obsolete ways.[117]

In both England and America corporate contributions are valid, especially where they benefit the purposes or business of the corporation.[118] But this does not authorize political contributions.[119]

Many state statutes authorize corporate contributions, for example, for "the betterment of the social and economic conditions in any community or communities in which such corporation is operating." "Foreign" corporations may also contribute[120] (See the sections below.)

The Internal Revenue Code grants deductions to corporations and unincorporated associations for their charitable contributions.[121] So, too, expenditures incurred in rendering services to a charitable organization are deductible as contributions.[122]

The contribution must be made to a corporation, trust, or other formal organization.[123] It must be made to an organization created or organized in American territory or under American law.[124] Special rules apply to gifts to unincorporated associations (must be used in the United States or its possessions, for exempt purposes), and for Canadian organizations.[125] Contributions to American political subdivisions or states, or agencies serving them, are deductible.[126] But political activity may result in loss of tax-exempt status of the corporation.[127]

1990s Trends in Corporate Giving

The 1990s recession decreased corporate giving. Most corporate foundations are "pass through" organizations. Cash contributions are dependent on corporate profits. In order to continue giving, some corporations have cut back on staff. In most organizations the emphasis is on strategic giving, designed to mesh with community needs while serving corporate interests with an eye toward maximum impact.[122]

Corporate and foundation giving to nonprofit hospitals dropped in 1991 about 20 percent according to a 1992 membership survey conducted by the Association for Healthcare Philanthropy. Total cash giving fro all sources decreased about 5.5 percent in 1991.[129]

The faltering 1991 economy meant less giving. However, the economy has also caused an increase in charitable trusts. The benefits of a charitable rust are that the donors can gift their favorite charity, avoid capital gains liability on appreciated assets, get a sizable tax deduction, and receive a steady stream of income for life, or postpone payments until retirement.[130]

In response to *A Nation at Risk* and other reports in the 1980s, documenting the sad state of the American public educational system, corporations have increased contributions in the 1990s to restructure the educational system. In the community, corporations increasingly support affordable housing units, jobs created, and early childhood initiatives. In the area of health care, corporations seem to be promoting wellness and cost containment. The general trend in the 90s is for corporate giving to expand into areas of civic and social responsibility in order to face the increasing competition of the global economy. There is increased giving, in response to the perceived ineffectiveness of government, to tackle the tough management problems involved in governmental charitable programs. There is a trend away from corporate giving to large nonprofit organizations in response to revelations at the United Way of America.[131]

Corporate donations, by socially responsible product manufacturers, often help both the manufacturer and the charities. For example *Newman's Own*, owned by Paul Newman, donates 100 percent of its profits to charitable and educational causes.[132]

Socially responsible money-market concepts were becoming more and more popular and beneficial for corporations in 1993. For example, "Working Assets" combines business and fundraising for socially committed nonprofits. The Working Assets group donated 1 percent of its customers' phone charges to 36 nonprofit organizations working with the environment, peace, human rights, and economic justice. Buying phone service in bulk rates from commercial carriers, Working Assets has 150,000 telephone customers across the U.S. and raised $100,000 for nonprofits in 1992. The company also markets a VISA card that takes five cents from each credit card bill to donate to nonprofits chosen by its subscribers each year.[133]

Corporate donations of inventory skyrocketed in 1992. The National Association for the Exchange of Industrial Resources, an Illinois-based nonprofit, solicits donations of inventory and then redistributes products to 7,000 nonprofits and schools nationally. Donations as of May 1993 are $30 million ahead of donations in 1992. Donated items include office supplies, computer accessories, clothing, toys, games, paper good, arts, and maintenance supplies. Members average $7,000 in new products per year.[134]

Hartford, Connecticut-based Northeast Utilities donated its license to emit pollutants to the American Lung Association in 1993. The 1990 clean Air

Act allows companies to buy and sell pollution rights from one another, supervised by the Environmental Protection Agency (EPA), which administers the act. The donation will be placed in a "repository" of ALA's Connecticut chapter and marketed to the public for donations. Donors who contribute a certain amount to the Connecticut chapter of ALA will receive a certificate stating that a ton of the pollutant has been retired in their names[135]

Drawing the line between corporate donor recognition and advertising on behalf of a corporation can be a problem. If a nonprofit organization actively promotes a sponsor or its product line, payments by the sponsor may be considered to be advertising revenue and taxable unrelated business income. Simple recognition of donors, however, is not considered to be advertising for the corporation.[136]

Worldwide "corporate citizenship," including NPO and philanthropic activities, are covered by the *Corporate Philanthropy Report* newsletter (and CPR also conducts conferences on various aspects). Address: 2727 Fairview Ave. East; Suite D, Seattle, WA 98102-3199; Tel.: (206) 329-0422 or FAX (206) 325-1382.

Grant Proposals

Grant Proposal Writing "workshop" (training) programs are held in various cities, throughout the year, by *The Grantsmanship Center.* Inquire by phone to # (213)-482-9860 or toll-free (800) 421-9512, or to P.O. Box 17220, Los Angeles, CA 90099-4522.

Gender-Sensitive Giving

Women and girls are specifically targeted by only 4.1 percent of all foundation giving, even though they represent 52 percent of the population, according to the *Foundation Grants Index,* for 1990. Though women and children make up the majority of the nation's poor, only 8.6 percent of the funding for employment programs, 7.5 percent of adult continuing education programs, and 3.2 percent of food and nutrition programs are targeted at women and girls.[137]

However, the National Network of Women's Funds (NNWF) released a report on the women's funding movement during 1991 that indicates that grants/allocations, endowment sizes, donations, and sources of contributions show increased funding. The survey of 34 women's funds showed total grants/allocations of $5.5 million in 1991, an increase of 1.2 percent from 1990. The 20 funds reporting in '90 and '91 indicated that grants/allocations showed a 39 percent increase, or almost $1.3 million. By comparison, the 1985 survey of 10 funds reported $1.2 million in grants/allocations. Therefore, since 1985, there has been a 358 percent increase in funds monitored by NNWF.[138]

International Giving

Giving by Americans to international causes has increased in response to the growing knowledge that problems in the rest of the world impact on Americans. The environment, peace, drugs, migration, and education are problems that must be solved on a global basis. Environmental, conservation, and wildlife issues are the causes that garner the most contributions. For example, The World Wildlife Fund has grown from 58,000 members to over one million donors. Grants and contributions to the American Council for Voluntary International Action (InterAction), an association of 136 international organizations, including The World Wildlife Fund, total $2.1 billion. InterAction plans to unify private independent organizations to participate in foreign government aid programs. Currently, aid to foreign governments is 80 percent government supplied. InterAction wants to see at least half of all aid to foreign governments handled by private or unilateral agencies. Such Nongovernment Organizations (NGOs) will attempt to manage and control funds more efficiently.[139]

Japanese Contributions

Japanese corporate contributions to American nonprofit organizations remained the same in 1991 as in 1990 at about $300 million. Japanese corporate foundations operating in the United States rose in number from three to twenty-five between 1984 and 1991. In general, it serves the interests of Japanese companies to develop programs for community giving and volunteering. Benefits result from the good will generated with state and local government officials. Favorable tax status may benefit Japanese subsidiaries filing returns in the United States. More than $100 million was donated to American colleges and universities by the Japanese in the 1990s. Such donations may benefit the Japanese "corporate recruitment strategy" and their interest in educating the next generation of American employees and consumers.[140]

Political Purpose Gifts

Contributions or spending of money by corporations, both *profit and nonprofit*, on behalf of *political purposes*, may be *limited* by state or federal statutes, and that does not violate constitutional rights of free speech. This is in addition to the governmental right to restrict direct contributions of money to or for political *candidates*. Michigan's (and 20 other states') statutes making it a crime for a corporation to spend money to promote political candidacies are valid. The limitation of use of corporate wealth to influence the political process is necessary in order to prevent corruption of the political process.[141]

Philanthropy in the Former Soviet Union

Goodwill Industries reports that the concept of philanthropy needs revival in the former Soviet Union, even though Soviet philanthropy has deep roots in the church. Goodwill is working with the Association for Charity and Culture in the former Soviet Union to instill the twin concepts of giving and private enterprise by importing used clothes to a thrift shop and using the funds obtained by selling the clothes to buy property for an orphanage.[142]

POINTS TO REMEMBER

- Consult state and local statutes and ordinances as to profit or nonprofit status.
- Look for state "criteria" provisions (such as those of Florida).
- Look to the IRS criteria for guidelines.
- Look at your state's "charitable trusts" law.
- Make your subscription forms "mutual-consideration" agreements.
- Register with state and local authorities.
- Follow registration requirements precisely.
- Register your solicitation agents, and have them wear identification badges.
- National Charities Information Bureau and other organizations provide guidance information for contributors. Address 1841 Broadway, N.Y. City, N. Y. 10023.

NOTES TO CHAPTER 8

1. Packel v. Frantz Advertising, Inc., 353 A.2d 492 (Pa. Cv. Ct. 1976). Pennsylvania generally defined contribution as any promise or grant of money or property. 10 Pa. Cons. Stat. §162.3.

2. See, *Telco Communications v. Barry*, 731 F. Supp. 670 (D.C., N.J. 1990); *Telco Communications v. Carbaugh*, 885 F.2d 1235 (4th Cir. 1989); *Famine Relief Fund v. West Virginia*, 905 F.2d 747 (4th Cir. 1990).

3. See, Harris, Holley & McC. article in 24 *U. of San Fran. L. Rev.* 571 at 640-1 (1990); *Telco Communications v. Carbaugh*, 885 F.2d 1235 (4th Cir., 1989).

4. *U.S. v. Kokinda*, 110 S. Ct. 3115 (1990); See Carbaugh case, above.

5. *St. Petersburg (FL) Times*, p. 8S (June 29, 1992).

6. B.H. Bush (article), 4 *NonProfit Times* (12)1 (Mar. 1991).

7. B.H. Bush, Regulation Watch, 5 *NonProfit Times* (8) 6 (Nov. 1991.

8. *See e.g.*, Application of Green, 167 N.Y.S.2d 607, (1957); Joseph H. Munson Co. v. Secretary of State, 294 Md. 160, 448 A.2d (1982), *cert.* granted, 459 U.S. 1102, aff'd, 104 S. Ct. 2839 (1984).

9. Code of Vvirginia §§57-48.

10. IRC §501(c)(3). Many states also deny charitable status to organizations seeking to influence legislation. *E.g.* Businesses and Professions Code of Rhode Island §5-53-1(b).

11. Ohio Rev. Code §1716.01(B); Fla. St. §496.404(5).

12. L. Williston on *Contracts*, §166 (3d ed. 1597); American Univ. v. Todd, 39 Del. 449, 1A 2d 595 (1938).

13. *Ibid; In re* Lord's Will, 175 Misc. 921, 25 N.Y.S.2d 747 (1941); Furm an Univ. v. Waller, 124 S.C. 68, 117 S.E. 356, 33 A.L.R. 615 (1923). In England a charitible subscription is not binding: *Re* Hudson 56 L.J. Ch. 811; Dalhousie College v. Boutiler, [1934] S.C.R. (Canada) 642, [1934] 3 Dom L. Rev. 593; 95 A.L.R. 1298, 1305; *but cf.*, Reinhart v. Burger, 43 Ont. L.R. 120.

14. *Black's Law Dictionary,* 1596 (4th ed., 1951); *and see,* Anno., 50 Am.Jur. 777. *See* Little Switzerland Brew. Co. v. Oxley, 197 S.E.2d 301 (W. Va. 1973).

15. Davis v. Rolley, 124 Kans. 132; 257 P. 746 (1927).

16. Jefferson County Farm Bureau v. Sherman, 208 Iowa 614; 226 N.W. 182, 185 (1929).

17. Park v. Missionary Society, 62 Vt. 19; 20 A. 107 (1890); Christman v. Reichholdt, 150 S.W.2d 527, 532 (No. App. 1941); Dartmouth College v. Woodward, 4 Wheat. (U.S.) 518 (1819).

18. Saint Lewis v. Morrison, 50 F. Supp. 570, 572 (D.C. Ky. 1943).

19. *In re* Carlson's Estate, 88 Cal. Rptr. 229, 9 C.A.3d 479 (1970).

20. Stockton Civic Theatre v. Board of Supv'rs of San Joaquin County, 56 Cal. Rptr. 658, 423 P.2d 810 (1967).

21. State *ex rel.* Brennan v. Bowman, 503 P.2d 454 (Nev. 1972).

22. *In re* Bailey's Estate, 19 Calif. App.2d 135; 65 P.2d 102 (1937).

23. Society for Propagation of Gospel v. New Haven, 8 Wheat. (U.S.) 465; 5 L. Ed. 662 (1823).

24. Lynch v. Spilman, 62 Cal. Rptr. 12, 431 P.2d 636 (1967).

25. *In re* Dol's Estate, 182 Calif. 159, 187 P. 428, 1886 Calif. 64, 198 P. 1039 (1921).

26. Manassas Lodge No. 1380, Loyal Order of Moose, Inc. v. Prince William County, 237 S.E.2d 102 (Va. 1977).

27. Stearns v. Association of the Bar of City of N.Y., 154 Misc. 71, 276 N.Y.S. 390 (1934).

28. Methodist Old Peoples Home V. Korzen, 39 Ill.2d 149, 233 N.E.2d 537 (1968).

29. City of Vicksburg v. Vicksburg Sanitarium, 117 Miss. 709; 78 S. 702 (1918).

30. Saint Albans Hospital v. Town of Enosburg, 96 Vt. 389; 120 A. 97 (1923).

31. *In re* Farmers Union Hospital Assn., 190 Okla. 661; 126 P.2d 244 (1942).

32. White v. Charity Hospital of Louisiana in New Orleans, 239 So.2d 385 (La. 1970).

33. Commissioner v. Battle Creek, 126 F.2d 405 (5th Cir. 1942).

34. Benton County v. Allen, 170 Ore. 481; 133 P.2d 991 (1943).

35. College Preparatory School for Girls v. Evatt, 144 Ohio St. 408; 59 N.E.2d 142 (1945); Southern Methodist Univ. v. Clayton, 142 Tex. 179; 176 S.W.2d 749 (1943).

36. New York Univ. v. Taylor, 251 A.D. 444; 296 N.Y.S. 848 (1937).

37. Bodenheimer v. Confederate Memorial Assn., 5 F. Supp. 526 (D.C. Va. 1933).

38. *In re* Cooper's Estate, 229 Iowa 921; 295 N.W. 448, 454 (1940).

39. *In re* Gatlin's Estate, 94 Cal. Rptr. 295, 16 C.A.3d 644 (1971).

40. Central Board on Care of Jewish Aged, Inc. v. Henson, 120 Ga. App. 627, 171 S.E.2d 747 (1969).

41. People *ex rel.* Redfern v. Hopewell Farms, 9 Ill. App.3d 16, 291 N.E.2d 288 (1972).

42. *In re* Jordan's Estate, 329 Penna. 427; 197 A. 150 (1938).

43. *In re* Kidd's Estate, 467 P.2d 770 (Ariz. App. 1970); Lefkowitz v. Cornell University, 308 N.Y.S.2d 85 (Sup. Ct. 1970).

44. Waddell v. Y.W.C.A., 133 Ohio St. 601, 15 N.E.2d 140 (1938). *E.g.,* Society for Animal Rights, Inc., with offices in Clark's Summit, Pa. 18411 (formerly in New York City).

45. Goode's Administrator v. Goode, 238 Ky. 620, 38 S.W.2d 691, 694 (1931).

46. *In re Rathbone's Estate,* 170 Misc. 1030; 11 N.Y.S. 2d 506 (1939).

47. Stearns case, n. 27, above.

48. Solomon v. Edgewater Yacht Club, Inc., 519 N.E. 2d 429 (Ohio Mun. Ct. 1987).

49. *In re* Lenox's Estate, 9 N.Y.S. 895 (1890).

50. Continental Ill. Natl. Bk. and Tr. Co. v. Harris 359 Ill. 86; 194 N.E. 250 (1935).

51. City of Houston v. Scottish Rite Benev. Assn., 111 Tex. 191, 230 S.W. 978 (1921).

52. Taylor's Exec. v. Trustees of Bryn Mawr College, 34 N.J. Eq. 101 (1881).

53. 7 *NonProfit Times*, (2) 4 (February 1993); 7 *NonProfit Times* (5) 1 (May 1993).

54. Delaware Trust Co. v. Fitzmaurice, 31 A.2d 383, 388 (Del. Ch. 1943). *See* the definition in Treas. Dept. *Report on Private Foundations*, p. 1 (U.S. Govt. Printing Office 1965).

55. *In re* White's Estate, 340 Penna. 92; 16 A.2d 394 (1940).

56. Grand Lodge of Ind. Order of Odd Fellows v. Gunnoe, 177 S.E.2d 150 (W. Va. 1970), citing W. Va. Code (1931) c. 35, Art. 2, §4 (35-2-4).

57. Woodcock v. Wachovia Bk. and Tr. Co., 214 N.C. 224, 199 S.E. 20 (1938).

58. Burgie v. Muench, 65 Ohio App. 176; 29 N.E.2d 439 (1940).

59. Bauer v. Myers, 244 F. 902, 911 (8th Cir. 1917); *In re* Hall's Estate, 193 S.2d 587 (Miss. 1967).

60. King v. Richardson, 136 F.2d 849, 856 (4th Cir. 1943).

61. *See,* Crane v. Morristown School Foundation, 120 N.J. Eq. 583; 187 A. 632, 635 (1936); Doyle v. Whalen, 87 Me. 414; 32 A. 1022; 31 L.R.A. 118 (1895), Tincher v. Arnold, 147 F. 665 (7th Cir. 1906); Good Samaritan Hospital and Medical Center v. U.S. Natl. Bk., 425 P.2d 541 (Ore. 1967); Howood House, Inc. v. Trustees of Donations and Bequests for Church Purposes, Inc., 233 A.2d 5 (Conn. 1969); Trammel v. Elliott, 199 S.E.2d 194 (Ga. 1973); *Restatement of Trusts*, 2d §399, p. 297. *See,* as to *Equitable Deviation* doctrine comparison, Burr v. Brooks, 393 N.E.2d 1091 (Ill. App. 1979).

62. Mohawk Trust v. Board of Assessors, 47 N.Y.2d 476, 392 N.E.2d 876 (1979).

63. Bogert, *Law of Trusts and Trustees* (curr. ed.) multi-volume set.

64. *Restatement* (Second), Trusts (St. Paul, Minn.: American Law Inst., 1959), 2 volumes.

65. *See* n. 63 and 64, above. *See also books*:
     Cary, William L., *The Law and the Lore of Endowment Funds; Report to the Ford Foundation* (New York, Ford Foundation 1967).
     Commerce Clearing House, *The Tax Exempt Organization: A Practical Guide* (New York 1967).
     Report on *Relations Between Foundations and Education and Between Foundations and Government* (1954).
     Report No. 3: *Economics and the Public Interest* (1954).
     Report No. 4: *Summary of Activities of Foundations* (1954).
     U.S. Congress, House, Reports to Subcommittee No. 1, Select Committee on Small Business; *Tax-Exempt Foundations and Charitable Trusts: Their Impact on Our Economy* (Washington, U.S. Govt. Printing Office 1962, 1963, 1964).
     Subcommittee *Chairman's Report No. 1* (1962).
     Subcommittee *Chairman's Report No. 2* (1963).
     Subcommittee *Chairman's Report No. 3* (1964).
     Walton and Lewis (eds.), *Foundation Directory,* current Edition (New York, Russell Sage Foundation).
     Note, *Wills-Charities-Validity of a Bequest of a Labor Union Fund as a Charitable Trust,* 23 Fordham L. Rev. 220 (1954).
     Wentworth, *Accumulation Trusts,* 117 Trusts and Est. 621 (1978).
     Williamson, *Cases and Materials on Trusts* (So. Tex. Coll. of Law, 1977).

66. *E.g.* 760 ILCS 55/1-55/19; M.C.L.A. §§14.251-14.266; ORS 128.610-128.750; West's Ann. Cal. Gov. Code §§12580-12599.

67. *E.g.,* Cal. Civ. Code §2290.4; Ill Rev. Stat. C. 55 §§1-19; Ohio Rev. Code §1715.54.

68. *Ibid.*

69. I. Williston on *Contracts,* §116 (3d ed. 1957). *See,* Jordan v. Mount Sinai Hospital, 276 S.2d 102 (Fla. App. 1973).

70. American Univ. v. Todd, 9 Del. 449, 1 A.2d 595 (1938); Wesleyan Univ. v. Hubbard, 20 S.E.2d 677 (W. Va. 1942).

71. Floyd v. Christian Church Widows and Orphans Home, 296 Ky. 196; 176 S.W.2d 125 (1943).

72. See *Shriners Hospitals v. Zrillic,* 563 So.2d 64 (Fla. 1990); See, Ga. code § 53-2-10 (1990).

73. *Application of Troy Savings Bank,* 549 N.Y.S.2d 910 (Sup. Ct. 1989).

74. See, *Jewish Federation of Central N.J. v. Baroness,* 560 A.2d 1353 (N.J. 1989). Cf., *Congregation Kadimah v. DeLeo,* 540 N.E.2d 691 (Mass. 1989).

75. Dalhousie College v. Boutilier, 3 Dom. L. Rev. 593; noted, 13 Can B. Rev. 108 (1935); *and see,* above, n. 13.

76. 1. Williston, *Contracts* above, n. 69.

77. More Game Birds in America, Inc. v. Boettger, 125 N.J. J. 97; 14 A.2d 778 (1940); *In re* Lord's Will, 175 Misc. 921; 25 N.Y.S.2d 747 (1941); Long v. Board of Chosen Freehold- ers, 16 N.J. Super. 448; 84 A.2d 765 (1951); Missouri Wesleyan College v. Schulte, 346 Mo. 628; 142 S.W.2d 644 (1940); Rouff v. Washington and Lee Univ., 48 S.W.2d 483 (Tex. Civ. App. 1932); noted, 39 W. Va. L. Rev. 159 (1933).

    And See:
    Billig, *The Problem of Consideration in Charitable Subscriptions,* 12 Cornell L. Rev. 467 (1927).
    Gregory, *Contracts-Enforceability of Charitable Subscriptions in Kentucky,* 42 Ky. L. J. 487 (1954).
    Murtagh, *Charitable Subscriptions in Illinois,* U. Chicago L. Rev. 430 (1937).
    O'Brien, *Seventy Years of Bequests for Masses in New York Courts,* 23 Fordham L. Rev. 147 (1954); Brennan, *Bequests for Religious Services,* 17 Clev.-Mar. L. Rev. 388 (1968).
    And See: Restatement Contracts §§45, 90.

78. Davis v. Campbell, 93 Iowa 524; 61 N.W. 1053 (1895); *In re* Taylor's Estate, 251 N.Y. 257; 167 N.E. 434 (1929).

79. University of So. Calif. v. Bryson, 103 Calif. App. 39; 283 P. 949 (1929); De Pauw Univ v. Ankeny 97 Wash. 451; 166 P. 1148 (1917).

80. Ga. Code Ann. §13-3-44; Miller v. Oglethorpe Univ., 24 Ga. App. 388, 100 S.E. 78 (1919).

81. Home Missions and Church Ext. v. Manley, 129 Calif. App. 541, 19 P.2d 21 (1933); First Church v. Pungs, 126 Mich. 670, 86 N.W. 235 (1902); *Re* Stack's Est., 164 Minn. 57, 204 N.W. 546 (1925); Edinboro Academy v. Robinson, 37 Pa. 210 (1860).

82. Irwin v. Lombard Univ., 56 Ohio St. 9, 46 N.E. 63 (1897); *Re* Converse's Est., 240 Pa. 458, 87 A. 849 (1913).

83. More Game Birds, above, n. 77.

84. Floyd v. Christian Church Widows and Orphans Home, 296 Ky. 196, 176 S.W.2d 125 (1943); Albert Lea College v. Brown, 88 Minn. 524, 93 N.W. 672; 60 L.R.A. 870 (1903); *Re* Tummond's Est., 160 Misc. 137, 290 N.Y.S. 40 (1936).

85. Washington Hts. M.E. Church v. Comfort, 128 Misc. 236, 246 N.Y.S. 450 (1930).

86. Rague v. N.Y. Evening Post Publ., 164 A.D. 126 149 N.Y.S. 668 (1914).

87. Allegheny College v. National Chautauqua County Bk., 246 N.Y. 369, 159 N.E. 173, 57 A.L.R. 980 (1927).

88. *Restatement, Contracts* §90; Small v. Paulson, 187 Ore. 76; 209 P.2d 779 (1949); Hunter v. Sparling, 87 Calif. App.2d 711; 197 P.2d 807 (1948); Clement v. Clement, 230 N.C. 636; 55 S.E.2d 459 (1949); Lake Bluff Orphanage v. Magill's Exec., 305 Ky. 391; 204 S.W.2d 224 (1947).

89. Matter of De Long, 565 N.Y.S. 2d 569 (A.D. 3 Dept. 1991).

90. *Matter of Estate of Laas,* 525 N.E.2d 1089 (IL App. 1988).

91. L. Zrillic (Motion), in *Estate of L. Romans,* Fla. S. Ct. (May 31, 1990); report in *St. Petersburg*

Times, p. 4B (June 1, 1990); see Shriners Hospitals v. Zrillic, 563 So. 2d 64 (Fla. 1990) (A Lineal Descendant of a testator may challenge a bequest to a charity if he/she is eligible to receive an interest in the devise (if it is to be overruled); under the *Mortmain* statute. But the *Mortmain* statute violates equal-protection rights by failing to prevent undue influence by charities and not reaching others who may act equally improperly, and by overriding clearly intended bequests by testators who were not improperly influenced.)

92. *Cowden v. Sovran Bank/Central South*; 816 S.W. 2d 741 (Tenn. 1991).

93. *Matter of Village of Mount Prospect*, 522 N.E.2d 122 (IL App. 1988); Restatement (2d) of Trusts §399 Comment b, at 297.

94. *Riverton Area Fire Protection. Dist. v. Riverton Volunteer Fire Dept.*, 566 N.E. 2d 1015 (Ill. App. 4 Dist. 1991).

95. See, *Estate of Crenshaw*, 806 P.2d 1014 (Kans. 1991).

96. *Trustees of L.C. Wagner Trust v. Barium Springs Home for Children, Inc.*, 401 S.E. 2d 807 (N.C. App. 1991).

97. *E.g.*, No. Car. Gen. Stat. §131C-4; Fla. Stat ch. 496.

98. 7 *NonProfit Times*, (2) 28 (February 1993); For a copy of the brochure, write: NCDA, 86 Front Street, Hempstead, NY 11550 (516-481-6000).

99. *E.g.*, Fla. Stat. §496.404; 10 Pa. Cons. Stat. §162.3; CA. Bus. & Prof. Code §17510 et seq.; Ohio Rev. Code § 1716.03.

100. *E.g.*, 225ILCS460/1 et. seq.

101. *E.g.*, 225ILCS460/4(a).

102. *Id.*

103. *Abrams v. N.Y. Foundation For Homeless*, 562 N.Y.S.2d 325 (S. Ct., N.Y. County, 1990).

104. Penna. Stat. §162.6.

105. *Ibid.*, §162.6(8).

106. Fla. Stat. §496.406; Heritage Village Church and Missionary Fellowship, 263 S.E.2d 726 (NC 1980).

107. R.I. Code §5-53-2(e)(1).

108. *Ibid.*, 5-53-2(e)(2).

109. *Ibid.*, 5-53-2(e)(3).

110. *Ibid.*, 5-53-2(e)(4).

111. Holloway v. Brown, 403 N.E.2d 191 (Ohio 1980); Village of Schaumberg v. Citizens for a Better Environment, 100 S.Ct. 826 (1980).

112. Streich v. Pa. Comm. on Charitable Orgns., 579 F. Supp. 172 (Pa. D.C. 1984).

113. R.I. Code §5-53-4.

114. MA. Code Ann. §68-19.

115. *See* literature listed in note 65, above. *And see:*
      Note, *Corporate Donations to Religious and Educational Bodies*, 37 Notre Dame Law 206 (1961).
      Note, *Corporate Power to Make Charitable Contributions Further Liberalized*, 6 Utah L. Rev. 270 (1958).
      Prunty, *Love and the Business Corporation*, 46 Va. L. Rev. 391 (1960).

116. N. Hartley, Memo from Turner (Group), 1 *The Philanthropist* (2) 45 (1973). But see, article, *Charities left in the dust by Reagonomics*, in St. Petersburg (Fl.) *Times*, p. 2 Community Section (July 27, 1987).

117. *See*, note, 34 Harv. L. Rev. 555 (1921) about English cases. *And see*, Corning Glass Works v. Lucas, 37 F.2d 798 (D.C., App. 1929); Amer. Rolling Mill v. Commissioner 41 F.2d 314 (6th Cir. 1930); 1. Williston, *Contracts*, §116 (3d ed. 1957); and Oleck, *New York Corpora-*

tions, §54 (New York, Robert Slater Co. 1961 rev.).

118. N.Y. Penal L. §671; Tenn. Code Ann. §48-13-102(14), I.R.C. §170(c).

119. Ohio Rev. Code §1701.13, 1702.12; N.Y. Not-For-Profit Corp. L. §202.

120. *Ibid.*

121. I.R.C. §170(b)(2). *See,* 4 Rabkin and Johnson, *Federal Income, Gift and Estate Taxation,* §59.04(7)(curr. ed.).

122. Reg. §1.170-2(a)(2); *see,* Henry Cartan, 30 T.C. 308 (1958).

123. Carolyn Trippe, T.C. Memo., C.C.H. 17,775, P-H §50,176; Eppa Hunton, 1 T.C. 821 (1943); Riker v. Commissioner, 244 F.2d 220 (1957); *cert. den.* 355 U.S. 839 (1957).

124. I.R.C. §§170(c)(2), 882(c)(3).

125. *See,* Rabkin and Johnson, above, n. 221, at §59.04(2).

126. *Ibid.* §59.04(2).

127. *See,* J. Riley, *Tax-Exempt Foundations: What Is Legal?,* 9 Natl. L.J. (24) 1 (Feb. 23, 1987).

128. Fisch, (article) 6 *Nonprofit Times* (6) 1 (June 1992).

129. 6 *NonProfit Times* (7) 28 (July 1992). The Report on Giving is available through AHP for $25 for members, $50 for nonmembers. HP, 313 Park Avenue, Suite 400, Falls Church, VA 22046.

130. Huckins, (article) 6 *NonProfit Times* (8) 6 (August, 1992).

131. Ostergard, (article) 6 *NonProfit Times* (7) 34 (July 1992).

132. L. Keenan, (article), 6 *NonProfit Times* (3)3 (March 1992).

133. 7 *NonProfit Times* (2) 15 (February 1993).

134. 7 *NonProfit Times* (5) 1 (May 1993).

135. Mehegan, S., (article) 7 *NonProfit Times,* (5) 4 (May 1993).

136. J. Fisch (article), 6 *NonProfit Times* (3) (March 1992).

137. Fisch, J. (article) 6 *NonProfit Times* (6) 1 (June 1992), (citing *Getting It Done: From commitment to Action on Funding for Women and girls,* Women and Foundations/Corporate Philanthropy).

138. Fasanella, D., (article) 7 *NonProfit Times* (2) 45 (Feb. 1993).

139. Cohen, S.F., (article) 6 *NonProfit Times* (9) 1 (Sept. 1992).

140. Grunberg, Greg, *Land of the Rising Funds,* (article), The Grantsmanship Center Whole Nonprofit Catalog, Summer 1992. *See also Japanese Corporate Connection: A Guide for Fundraisers,* ($90); *Directory of Japanese Giving,* ($190); *Inside Japanese Support* ($195), The Taft Group, 1-800-877-8238.

141. *Austin v. Michigan Chamber of Commerce,* U.S. Supreme Court; March 27, 1990; 6 to 3 decision (Scalia, Kennedy, and O'Connor dissenting).

142. Cohen, S.F., (article) 6 *NonProfit Times* (9) 1 (Sept. 1992).

* * *

See such publications (current) as:

Gift Givers Guide, by Florida Dept. of Agriculture & Consumer Services, published December 1993, lists 1954 charities registered, to show amounts (%) each one spent on administration and program services, as a guide to contributors to charities. Thus, the American Association of State Troopers was reported to have spent $2.6 million in its fiscal year, 44% to administrative costs, 43% to fund raising, and 13% to program services.

See: A. Yoemans report, Associated Press, *St. Petersburg (FL) Times,* p. 4B (Dec. 21, 1993).

9

TAX EXEMPTION (FEDERAL)

[The first version of this chapter originally was contributed in 1988 by Prof. I. Richard Gershon of Stetson University College of Law] [Pre-published in 16 Cumberland L. Rev. 301-327 (1987).] [See, generally: IRM 7751 (Exempt Organizations Handbook)] Most material added by Oleck and Stewart or others after 1988 is identified at the starting points of each item.]

85. TAX EXEMPTION, IN GENERAL

[See also Chapter 11]

Generally speaking, all corporations,[1] trusts,[2] and associations[3] are subject to federal, state and local taxation. This includes nonprofit organizations unless they qualify for tax-exempt status. In order for a nonprofit corporation, association or trust to become a tax-exempt entity for *federal* income tax purposes, it must meet specific requirements of the Internal Revenue Code,[4] the treasury regulations thereunder,[5] and the Internal Revenue Service.[6] While many states[7] gear their income tax structures to "taxable income" as defined under the federal Internal Revenue Code,[8] which effectively grants a state income tax exemption to all federally-exempt organizations, an organizer must also consider the possibility of other important state tax exemptions, such as exemptions from property,[9] sales and use,[10] and occupational licensing[11] taxes.

Another important consideration is whether or not an entity, which is qualified as tax-exempt, will be a qualified donee of charitable contributions. If an entity is a qualified donee, contributors can often deduct their donations from their income,[12] estate,[13] gift,[14] or generation-skipping transfer[15] taxes.

This chapter deals with the tax-exempt status of organizations under the federal law, the various types of exempt organizations, the procedures for obtaining and maintaining exempt status, and the possible penalties for failure to comply with stated requirements. Such penalties can include special excise taxes levied only against tax-exempt entities[16] and even revocation of exempt status.[17]

Succeeding chapters will deal with the requirements for achieving exempt status under state laws; and see also the preceding chapter as to the deductibility of charitable contributions to qualified donees.

NPO Tax Exemption Support

A survey of Minnesota peoples' views on tax exemption of NPOs, by Minnesota Center for Survey Research, showed about 41 percent "strongly" and 38 percent "generally" favor such exemption (e.g., almost 80 percent). Minnesota Council of NPOs helped in the survey, and said that three bills to reduce the exemption had been proposed in the legislature in the past three years.[18]

The *Congressional Research Service*, in the Library of Congress, prepared CRS *Reports for Congress*, and makes these reports available and also has its specialists and analysts available for personal consultations for committee members. Copies of the reports can be obtained.

Charitable donations for $250 or more now (1994) are deductible by the contributor only if the donor gets and keeps written substantiation (receipt) from the charity, under the 1993 tax bill.

[See, *Non-Profit Tax Letter*, Prentice Hall, Englewood Cliffs, NJ 07632–9940, bi-weekly; $9.95/mo. plus shipping.]

§86. TYPES OF EXEMPT ORGANIZATIONS

Internal Revenue Code §501 states that all organizations described in §501(c), or (d), or §401(a) are exempt from federal income taxation. Generally, organizations described in §501(c) and (d) are organizations which perform some type of societal, as opposed to private, good. While the specific organizations described in those sections are tremendously diverse in nature, they all have as a common component the requirement that no part of their net earnings can "inure to the benefit of any private shareholder or individual."[19]

Organizations described under §401(a) are essentially employee benefit trusts, which provide tax incentives to employers and employees who make contributions for employee retirement (apparently as a supplement, or even a replacement for social security). While employee benefit trusts clearly inure to the benefit of private individuals, they are similar to organizations under §501(c) and (d) in that they are subject to procedural and operational requirements.

[In 1987 the Commissioner of the IRS appointed an Exempt Organizations Advisory group to advise him on various tax-exempt organization issues, such as lobbying excesses, unrelated business income law as to churches, etc.

§87. 501(C) ORGANIZATIONS

IRC §501(c) lists 23 types of associations, corporations and trusts which can qualify for federal tax exemption [plus (c)(24) trusts under ERISA §4049, and

501(c) 25 real estate title holders or distributors to nonprofit organizations. See IRS notice 87-18, IRB 1984-4, 29 instructions.]

1. Instrumentalities of the United States

All corporations created or organized by Act of Congress are exempt from federal income taxation, as long as the exemption is provided for in the Internal Revenue Code,[20] even though a non-revenue related Act might state otherwise.[21] Some examples of such Congressionally exempted corporations are:

Central Liquidity Facility[22]

Farmer's Home Corporation

Federal Credit Unions

Federal Deposit Insurance Corporation

Federal Reserve Banks

National Mortgage Associations

2. Corporations Organized to Hold Title to Property for Exempt Organizations

The code specifically exempts any corporation operated for the purpose of "holding title to property, collecting the income therefrom, and turning over the entire amount thereof, less expenses, to an organization which itself is exempt.[23] Such a corporation will lose its exempt status if it retains or accumulates income from property,[24] or has any business powers other than the right to hold title and collect income. Expenses of 501(c)(2) organizations include ordinary and necessary business expenses,[25] as well as a reasonable reserve for expenses and depreciation.[26]

It should be noted that a corporation under §501(c)(2) can hold title for more than one exempt organization (which can be called parent organizations). If, however, any parent organization has its exempt status revoked, the title-holding organization will also have its exempt status revoked.[27]

Employees' Taxes

Basic employee benefits such as sick leave, vacation time, disability or death benefits, and severance pay are taxable when received, not when they accrue, under IRS §457.[28]

An insurance-benefits trust, providing coverage for employees of two religious schools (tax exempt) association, is not itself tax exempt; it is an unrelated (nonreligious) operation.[29]

Costs of sponsoring free-enterprise (employee training) seminars are not deductible expenses under I.R.C. §162, as they are too tremendously related to improving specific job skills to be proper under §162.[30]

[Nonprofits (with the exception of certain religious charities) are required to pay Social Security taxes on employees earning more than $100 a year. An organization need report only the names and amounts disbursed to the five highest-paid consultants who earned $30,000 or more from the non-profit in one year.[31]]

§88. 501(c)(3) ORGANIZATIONS

Probably the most important category of tax-exempt organizations is found at §501(c)(3) of the Internal Revenue Code. §501(c)(3) deals with organizations which are *"organized and operated exclusively for religious, charitable, scientific, testing for public safety, literary, or educational purposes, and to foster national or international amateur sports competition or for the prevention of cruelty to children or animals".*[32] The general requirements for all 501(c)(3) organizations are that no personal benefit (profit in the nature of a dividend) may inure to private individuals, members or officers, and that they must not engage in prohibited lobbying activities (discussed *infra*).

[The presence of any substantial nonexempt purpose will destroy an organization's exemption, regardless of the number and importance of truly exempt purposes.[33]]

Organized and Operated Test

The statutory language set forth specifically requires that organizations exempt under §501(c)(3) be organized and operated exclusively for permitted purposes. The regulations state that an entity is not exclusively organized for exempt purposes unless the articles of organization (corporate charter, trust instrument, or any instrument by which the organization is formed) expressly:

a. Limit the purposes of the organization to one or more exempt purposes; *and*

b. Do not expressly empower the corporation, trust, foundation or association to engage in activities which themselves are not in furtherance of one or more exempt purposes, unless the non-exempt activities are insubstantial.[34] Thus, even if an organization's actual operation falls within the limits of exempt purposes, it will not be granted exemption unless its powers are limited to exempt purposes.[35]

On the other hand, the mere limitation of statement of purpose and enumeration of powers in the organization's creating document is not enough to give rise to exemption unless the entity actually acts in accordance with that purpose. Organizations have been denied exempt status when their operations benefitted private interests such as the creator of the organization or his family.[36]

The broadness of §501(c)(3), as well as the constitutional aspects of its exemption of religious organizations, leads to continuing litigation by taxpayers and the IRS alike, concerning the exempt status of organizations purportedly satisfying the requirements of §501(c)(3).

§89. RELIGIOUS PURPOSES

[See the chapter on Religious Organizations]

"The power to tax, is the power to destroy,"[37] as any taxpaying person will surely attest. The exemption of religious organizations by §501(c)(3) reflects Congress' concern that taxation of churches and other religious entities could have substantial adverse effects on the freedom of religion guaranteed by the Constitution.[38] The exemption created for churches in §501(c)(3) has, interestingly enough, been challenged as an unconstitutional establishment of religion,[39] since churches are given preferential tax treatment. However, courts have continued to uphold the constitutionality of tax exemptions for religions.

While the constitutionality of §501(c)(3) seems well settled, its very provisions present the IRS with the problem of determining whether an organization engages in religious activity. This, as a matter of practicality, requires the government to decide whether or not the organization deals with a *bona fide* religion.[40] The government has been faced with many taxpayers who see §501(c)(3) as an excellent opportunity for avoiding taxation.[41]

For example, a church (Zion Coptic Church) that claimed that smoking of marijuana by its members was a religious sacrament lost its claim for constitutional protection and lost its tax exemption when the IRS investigation found that it was formed as a device for large-scale commercial drug smuggling. This decision was upheld by the Tax Court, and damages for carrying on a "frivolous" defense were assessed (over $1 million in taxes and penalties).[42]

The government must tread lightly in its denial of 501(c)(3) religious status; thus no definition of religion is given by 501(c)(3) or its regulations, in order to afford a high degree of flexibility and discretion to the IRS in its decisions to grant or deny exempt status. The closest thing to a definition of religion can be found in the regulations under §511, which deal with unrelated taxable business income (discussed *infra*). Those regulations provide:

> What constitutes conduct of religious worship or the ministration of sacredotal functions depends on the interests and practices of a particular religious body constituting a church.[43]

It must be reiterated that, even if an organization qualifies as religious under 501(c)(3), it will not be exempt if any of its benefits inure to private individuals, or if it engages in prohibited lobbying activities. (See *infra*).

[For example, Reverend Jerry Falwell's Old Time Gospel Hour was fined $50,000 and had its tax-exempt status revoked for 1986 and 1987 after it used personnel and assets to raise funds for a political action committee backing congressional candidates. The IRS agreed to reinstate the group's exemption for 1988 in exchange for an agreement by the organization to make changes to ensure that it will not participate in future political campaigns.[44]]

Payments to Church of Scientology for "auditing" *instruction*, provided for in its religious tenets, until 1993 were held not qualified for deduction as contributions to religious organizations.

Church housing and automobile use provided for its minister (apartment located on church property), and also for its custodian and caretaker, which would have cost as much if paid as salary by the church, do not justify IRS revocation of its tax exemption when all other aspects of operation were the usual free church services and the church received over half its contributions from members and trustees and its main expenditures were mortgage and utility payments and repairs.[46] [IRC §501(c)(3).]

Persons claiming to be ministers, who deduct (as charitable contributions) amounts paid to that church but used to meet their personal expenses (a "mail-order church"), are subject to "substantial understatement penalty" under I.R.C. 6661; the use of the church as a tax shelter is penalized.[47]

A nonprofit organization that operated restaurants and food stores, in accordance with the doctrines of the Seventh Day Adventist Church, was denied a federal tax-exemption because it was not operating exclusively for exempt purposes. The court found no unconstitutional discrimination against a "less orthodox" religion.[48]

[Mia Wood contributed the rest of this subsection.]

The Church Audit Procedures Act (CAPA) allows IRS to demand documents only "to extent necessary" to determine tax liability or tax-exempt status. The IRS must show actual necessity for documents it seeks, not merely an allegation of relevance. The court held, however, that under the CAPA, a document may be used to shift the burden to the taxpayer to show otherwise.[49]

IRS did not act in bad faith by conducting an investigation of a church under CAPA, despite the church's allegation of nationwide offensive against its organizations and individuals. Thus, the IRS was entitled to enforcement of summons against the church with respect to documents that could logically be expected to give IRS overview of flow of money into and out of the organization to shed light on possible commercial purposes.[50]

Scientologists believe in reaching spiritual awareness with the help of an auditor who receives a mandatory "fixed donation" for the sessions of counseling. Following several unfavorable rulings by the IRS, church officers carried out a number of obstructionist actions designed to thwart further financial audits and investigations. Upon the revocation of its tax exempt status, the church claimed that the IRS was motivated by hostility to Scientology.[51]

In October 1993 the Scientology Church was ruled to be a valid tax-exempt church by I.R.S. "determination letters."

The Scientology group earlier had been said to have had a "commercial character," and "scripturally based hostility to taxation;" also that the organization seeking exemption had an "enormous potential for both accumulating wealth and bestowing shelter from taxation."[52]

[See Chap. 36; Religious Organizations]

Unrelated business income is taxable only if it comes from an activity, in churches and other religious organizations, that is regular, not merely occasional. That includes such income as that from rental of church property (such as automobiles or computers), and debt-financed investment income. But, income volunteer services, bingo weekly games, or sales of contributed goods, or from services for members only or for employees or students is not taxable income.[53]

Supporters of "pro-choice" abortion-rights view do not have "standing" to bring lawsuits challenging the *tax exemption* of the (anti-abortion-view) Catholic church.[54]

Religious Charities Disclosure of Finances

IRS requirement of disclosure of their finances on form 990 tax reports by religious charities does not apply to churches, synagogues or their auxiliaries. But inquiries to private watchdog organizations may obtain voluntary reports that some churches do provide to them. Some such groups are: National Charities Information Bureau (N.Y. City); Evangelical Council for Financial Accountability (Washington, D.C.); Council of Jewish Federations (N.Y. City); Philanthropic Advisory Service (Arlington, VA); or state groups such as Charities Review Council of Minnesota or Better Business Bureaus.[55]

§90. CHARITABLE PURPOSES

The regulations under §501(c)(3) define "charitable" in its generally accepted legal sense. There is no attempt to limit the term to the list of exempt purposes enumerated in the code. Specifically, "charitable' includes: relief of the poor, distressed, or the underprivileged; advancement of religion, education, or science; erection or maintenance of public buildings, monuments or works, lessening of the burdens of government, and promotion of social welfare. The fact that an organization structured and operated for the relief of indigent persons might receive contributions from such persons will not necessarily cause a revocation of exempt status.[56]

Thus, an agency which provided for the adoption of orphan children by parents in the United States,[57] an organization which provided skills training for Native Americans[58] and a nonprofit corporation organized to tend to the nonmedical needs of patients in a hospital (which was a proprietary entity),[59] were all allowed exempt status as charitable organizations.

On the other hand, a corporation formed to pay legal fees of its teacher-members,[60] a scholarship fund for the "Miss Georgia Pageant,"[61] and an organization formed to protect a community's aesthetic beauty for the benefit of its residents[62] were denied "charitable" status on the basis that their benefits were private, as opposed to public in nature. These organizations were not found to be organized and operated exclusively for charitable purposes.

It should be noted that many organizations which do not qualify as 501(c)(3) charitable organizations, can qualify as §501(c)(4) social welfare organizations.[63] The difference being that 501(c)(4) organizations are not qualified donees, and therefore contributions to them are not deductible by the donor.[64]

Food stands and a gift shop on the property of a charitable organization did not affect the tax exempt status where they were adjunct to the operation and enjoyment of concerts held on the property. The primary use of the property was charitable.[65]

Hospitals

Since a 1969 IRS ruling, *hospitals* have been held to fulfill a *charitable purpose* by providing a community service, such as I.R.C. § 501(c)(3) calls tax exempt. In 1991 Rep. Brian Donnelly (D-Mass.) introduced HR 1374 which would require three tests of charity status: An emergency room open to needy patients, a Medicaid provider agreement, and proof that it did not systematically refuse service to Medicaid patients.[66]

About 43 percent of nonprofit hospitals give charitable care that amounts to less than the amounts of their tax-exemption, a General Accounting Office report said in 1990. A House Committee proposal of legislation to require nonprofit hospitals to provide a minimum stated amount of charitable services was being studied in 1990. States' efforts to remove tax exemption from such hospitals is increasing.[67]

In May 1992 the IRS published new guidelines for its field examiners for auditing tax-exempt hospitals. The guidelines require that an exempt hospital provide an emergency room that is open to all, regardless of ability to pay, except where the state determines that such an emergency room would duplicate care, or where a hospital specializes in care that is unlikely to involve emergencies. Closer scrutiny of doctors regarding private inurement includes analysis of compensation, physician recruitment and retention arrangements, and business relationships between doctors and hospitals. Joint ventures and partnerships must serve the hospital's exempt purposes. Financial analysis of records will be extensive. Unrelated business income will be evaluated for laboratory testing, pharmacy sales, parking facilities, medical research, laundry services, and leasing of medical buildings.[68]

[Mia Wood contributed the rest of this subsection.]

The determination as to whether a health maintenance organization (HMO) qualifies for tax exempt status as a corporation organized and operated exclusively for an exempt purpose must be based upon totality of circumstances, with an eye toward discerning whether the HMO in question benefits the community, as well as its subscribers. In deciding whether an organization qualifies for tax exempt status, the issue is not whether it primarily benefits the community. Although the HMO had implemented or planned to implement a subsidized dues program to permit a small number of people who could not otherwise subscribe for its services to become members, it did not provide any health care services or the like. As this HMO provided no significant benefits to anyone other than its subscribers, the HMO did not qualify for a tax exempt status.[69]

The "integral part doctrine" is a means by which an organization can qualify for tax exempt status vicariously through related organizations. They must, however, be engaged in activities that would be exempt if related organizations engaged in them, and those activities must be in furtherance of the exempt purposes of the related organizations.[70]

The theory under which an "integral part" of a larger entity is entitled to share in a larger entity's tax-exempt status does not apply to the determination of "political subdivision" status. This would bypass the sovereign power requirement.[71]

§91. SCIENTIFIC PURPOSES

A scientific organization must serve a public interest, rather than a private one, if it is to attain exemption under §501(c)(3).[72] Thus, allowable scientific activity does not include research incident to commercial activities, such as testing of construction materials.[73] Scientific activities will be regarded as serving the public interest if the results of such activities are made available to the public on a nondiscriminatory basis;[74] if the research is carried on by or for federal or state governments, or agencies or instrumentalities thereof;[75] or if the research is directed towards benefiting the public, such as research carried on to find a cure for cancer.[76]

On the other hand, a scientific organization does not operate in the public interest if it performs research only for persons who are not exempt from taxation under §501(c)(3) and who are the creators (directly or indirectly) of the corporation,[77] it retains substantial benefits from the control of patents, copyrights or formulate which are products of its research.[78]

[The 1987 Federal Tax Act requires fund raising solicitations by a noncharitable tax-exempt organization to place a conspicuous statement, on its solicitations, that gifts to it are not deductible as charitable contributions. *I.R.S Notice 835*, eff. Feb. 1988].

§92. EDUCATIONAL PURPOSES

The regulations broadly define education to include the instruction of private individuals as well as the public in general.[79] While it is obvious that colleges, universities, and professional schools with regular faculties, course offerings, and student bodies qualify as educational organizations,[80] it might be surprising to note that museums, zoos, planetariums,[81] and organizations presenting public discussion groups[82] can qualify as tax-exempt educational organizations as well.

While the regulations allow such educational organizations to present opinions or to advocate a particular point of view, they expressly deny exemption to groups who have as their principal purpose the presentation of unsupported propaganda.[83] Furthermore, the government has taken a strong position in requiring that educational organizations will be denied tax-exempt status if they practice improper discrimination in either their hiring or their admission policies.[84] Thus, a private secondary school which admits only whites will be denied tax exemption, even though it technically qualifies as an educational institution under §501(c)(3).

The government's position disfavoring discrimination has clashed with questions of religious freedom in connection with religious schools.[85] In 1975, the government issued Revenue Ruling 75-231[86] which clearly states that a church-run school will lose its exempt status if the school engages in a policy of racial or ethnic discrimination. However, the IRS has a great deal of discretion in determining whether or not the school practices involve a "substantial" degree of discrimination.[87]

[The rest of this section was contributed by Mia Wood.]

Education is defined in Treasury Regulation §1.501(c)(3) as "the instruction or training of the individual for the purpose of improving or developing his capability and the instruction of the public on subjects useful and beneficial to the community."

> An educational organization may advocate a particular position as long as it "presents a sufficiently full and fair exposition of the pertinent facts." An organization, however, is not considered educational "if its principal function is the mere presentation of unsupported opinion."[88]

§93. OTHER EXEMPT PURPOSES UNDER §501(c)(3)

While the major classifications for exemption under §501(c)(3) are religious, scientific, charitable and educational, Congress has, from time to time, made additions to the list of permitted purposes. For example, the list now includes the prevention of cruelty to children, and the fostering of national and international athletic competition.[89] In fact, it would not be at all surprising to see further additions to the list in the future, such as societies for the protection of natural resources, or organizations providing care for battered or deserted spouses,[90] because §501(c)(3) was designed to take into account the changing needs of society. Whether Congress chooses to update the section or not, it is clear that all organizations which are structured and operated to benefit the public, and which do not provide a benefit to any private individual or shareholder, will qualify under one of the more general classifications, such as charitable or educational.

[For a discussion of private foundations that are involved with 501(c)(3) permitted purposes, see Chapter 7.]

§94. SOCIAL WELFARE ORGANIZATIONS

Closely related to charitable organizations under §501(c)(3) are social welfare organizations which are exempt from taxation under §501(c)(4) of the Code. These organizations include civil leagues established "for the purpose of bringing about civic betterments and social improvements,"[91] and local employee associations, whose membership is limited to the employees of a designated employer, from a particular municipality.[92] The net earnings from such organizations must be devoted exclusively to charitable, educational, or recreational purposes.[93]

The primary distinction between 501(c)(3) organizations, and social welfare organizations, is that social welfare groups can be "action" organizations, which engage in attempts to influence legislation. A 501(c)(3) organization would be disqualified if it participated in any lobbying effort. However, a 501(c)(4) organization, like its cousin under 501(c)(3), would lose its exempt status if it became involved in any direct or indirect political campaign involving a candidate for public office. Thus, an anti-abortion organization which engaged in an effort to educate the public on abortion, while actively seeking legislative changes which would curtail abortions, would qualify as a social welfare organization, even though it could not qualify as a 501(c)(3) public education organization.[94] On the other hand, if such an anti-abortion group expressed its opposition to a congressional candidate who espoused personal choice in abortion decisions, it would lose its tax-exempt status.

Another major difference between 501(c)(3) and 501(c)(4) organizations is that 501(c)(4) organizations are generally not qualified donees of charitable contributions, which means that donors to such organizations usually do not receive the benefits of being able to deduct their contributions when calculating their federal tax liabilities for the year.[95]

Finally, §501(c)(4) organizations, unlike organizations under §501(c)(3), can provide incidental social benefits for the pleasure or recreation of their members. If such benefits become substantial, however, the organization must be classified as a social club, rather than a social welfare organization.

§95. OTHER ORGANIZATIONS EXEMPT UNDER §501(c)

Some other organizations which derive their tax-exempt status from §501(c) are: business leagues,[96] such as the Clearwater (Florida) (city) Chamber of Commerce, or the National Football League;[97] social or pleasure clubs, such as country clubs;[98] fraternal beneficiary societies, orders, or associations which operate under the lodge system; and which provide for the payment of sick, life, accident or other benefits to their members;[99] domestic fraternal societies, orders, or associations which devote their net earnings to religious, scientific, educational, literary, and fraternal purposes;[100] voluntary employees' beneficiary associations (VEBAs), which are for the payment of life, sick and accident benefits to their employee members;[101] local teachers' retirement funds;[102] and nonprofit cemetery companies.[103]

New section 501(c)(25) of the *Internal Revenue Code of 1986* allows as many as 35 unrelated and tax-exempt organizations to pool their resources in order to invest in real property. The corporation investing these pooled resources will be tax-exempt, provided that it only has one class of stock. In essence, §501(c)(25) allows for tax-exempt organizations to create their own exempt corporation under rules interestingly similar to the subchapter S rules (IRC §§1361–1378).

§96. EXEMPT STATUS DERIVED OUTSIDE OF §S501(c)

Because §501(c) is such a massive document in terms of mere words, as well as content, it is hard to imagine that any other sections provide for tax-exemption. However, such sections do exist. For example, §501(d) awards an exemption to religious and apostolic orders. this exemption is allowed even though such orders engage in a business for the common benefit of their members. It is clear that Congress enacted §501(d) in order to avoid the constitutional problems that might arise from the taxation of religious orders. However, the individual members of the order are taxed on their proportionate share of the income derived by the order's business. Thus, the tax consequences of exempting religious and apostolic associations are very similar to those which arise in the taxation of partners and partnerships,[104] or S corporations and their shareholders.[105] That is, the religious order is merely a conduit of income to its members.

Homeowner's associations, of management character, (like condo) are another type of tax-exempt entity which fall outside the scope of §501(c).[106] These associations are exempt as long as they derive at least 60 percent of their income from dues, fees or, assessments of member owners,[107] at least 90 percent of their expenditures are for the acquisition, maintenance, construction, management, or care of association property.[108] and the organization elects to have the exemption apply by filing a Form 1120-H with its return for the tax year for which the election will apply.[109] Any taxable income[110] derived by the association from sources other than fees, dues, or assessments of owner members will be taxed at a rate of 30 -percent.[111]

Thus, there are a wide variety of organizations which can qualify for tax-exemption under the Internal Revenue Code. Once a planner has determined that his particular organization is of a type which can have the benefits of tax exemption, he must take the proper procedural steps in order to secure those benefits.

§97. PROCEDURES FOR OBTAINING TAX-EXEMPTION

In order for a corporation, association, foundation, or trust to obtain tax-exempt status, it must first meet the statutory requirements discussed in preceding sections. The taxpayer has the burden of showing that it falls within the statutory parameters of the exemption it is claiming.[112] While the IRS resolves any doubts against the taxpayer, some courts have been more liberal in their construction of requirements for exemption.[113] However, even the strictest compliance with the provisions of the Internal Revenue Code will not give rise to exemption unless certain administrative formalities are observed.[114] Furthermore, the government will not be bound by the fact that other similar organization have been granted exemption on prior occasions.[115] Thus, all procedural steps are essential and the organizer should not take short-cuts.

Applications:

All organizations seeking a ruling or determination of exempt status must file a written application with the director for the district where the organization's principal office or place of business is located.[116] Generally, such applications must be filed on official forms, but even where no official forms exist an application must be filed. The organization must attach to its application a conformed copy of its articles of incorporation, declaration of trust, or other creating document, set forth the permitted powers or activities of the organization, its bylaws or other regulations, and its latest financial statement. Such application must contain a written declaration that it is made under penalty of perjury.[117] It should be emphasized that any power granted to the organization which is not permitted as part of the basis for exemption will give rise to automatic disapproval of the application.[118]

[Recently, a tax court ruled that Section 501(c)(4), (5), and (6) organizations are no longer required to file an application with the IRS as a *precondition* of claiming tax exempt status. Thus, noncharitable organizations may be able to save staff time, legal fees, and a $375 filing fee. However, most organizations will want to file in order to obtain the benefits of recognition or to prove their status. Organizations under 501(c)(4), (5), and (6) may be able to avoid penalties and interest for failure to file as taxable corporations through the use of this new court decision.[119]]

Application Forms:

Usually, an organization must file an official application form, similar to a tax return, when it is seeking to establish its exemption. However, there are some organizations for which no official form exists. These organizations are: Instrumentalities of the United States, created by Acts of Congress,[120] Black Lung Benefit Trusts,[121] Teachers' Retirement Fund Associations,[122] and religious and apostolic orders.[123] Other applicants will use Form 1023, Form 1024, or Form 1028 depending upon their bases of exemption.

Form 1023 should be filed by organizations claiming exemption under §501(c)(3) (as charitable, religious, scientific, or educational organizations), §501(d) (as cooperative hospital service associations), or §501(f) (as cooperative service organizations of operating educational corporations).

Form 1024 should be filed by civil leagues,[124] social clubs,[125] cemetery companies.[126] VEBAs,[127] fraternal societies,[128] and agricultural organizations.[129]

Finally, an applicant should file Form 1028 if it is a farmer's cooperative association under §521(a) of the Internal Revenue Code.

Withdrawal of Application

An organization may withdraw its application for exemption at any time prior to the issuance of a determination letter or ruling. However, the IRS is entitled to use any information obtained in such application during subsequent audits of the corporation's tax returns.[130]

Other Forms Required

In addition to the proper application for exemption, an organization is required to file the following information:

(a) An Application for an Employer Identification Number: Form SS-4

While 501(c)(3) organizations,[131] any tax-exempt organizations which pay renumeration to an employee of less than $100 per year,[132] and state instrumentalities,[133] are exempt from withholding under FICA, all other exempt organizations withhold income taxes from employee salaries.[134] Thus, the government requires organizations applying for exempt status to obtain an employer identification number by filing a Form SS-4.

(b) Power of Attorney

If an organization will be represented by an attorney or an agent, whether in person or by letter, it must file in duplicate a power of attorney.[135] The power of attorney must authorize the agent or attorney to represent the organization before the Internal Revenue Service. The organization may use Form 2848 or 2848-D to make such authorization.

"Private Inurement" of NPO Assets

[Margaret A. Fonvielle contributed some of the following material in this subsection.]

If distribution of a church's assets goes to a private individual (here, the founder), as other than *reasonable* amount for salary, such "private inurement" violates the rule that "no part" of net earnings shall be so granted, and causes loss of tax exemption. Cumulative effect of the founder's use of the church to promote his book-royalty income, plus much "debt repayments" of not-bona-fide "debts,' shows improper "inurement."[136,137]

Leasing property, such as antique automobiles, to a nonprofit foundation is considered a fraudulent conveyance when made to evade payment of taxes by the donor if the donee organization is just an "alter ego" that may be ignored by the courts.[138]

Inurement will be found when a nonprofit organization makes an interest free loan to a corporation, formed by a member of the NPO, without any written security or evidence of indebtedness. Reasonableness of the transaction will be measured by the degree of control retained by the individuals who appear to benefit personally, and evidence of the appropriateness of expenses.[139]

The United States may levy against the property of a nonprofit charitable corporation to satisfy an individual taxpayer's tax liability where the charitable corporation is the alter ego of the taxpayer and the conveyance of the property to the charity was fraudulent as to the United States.[140]

Criminal penalties arise when "corporate shells" and tax exempt religious organizations are used to receive benefits for payments fraudulently represented to be contributions. For example, an attorney was recently found guilty of conspiracy to defraud the U.S. and the IRS when he provided the tax identification number of a tax-exempt religious corporation's account to the IRS, making it appear that the tax settlement funds would go to a tax-exempt religious corporation, when the lawyer, his partner, and the partner's client intended to divide among themselves the settlement proceeds.[141]

[The following case was contributed by Mia Wood.]

A Michigan Education Trust (MET) was established by state statute to help parents finance their children's college education. The Trust's purpose of providing the tuition guaranteeing service was a substantial private purpose that destroyed the Trust's exemption. Thus, MET was found not to qualify for income tax exemption as a charitable or educational organization or as a nonprofit social welfare organization.[142]

§98. SPECIAL RULES FOR §501(c)(3) ORGANIZATIONS

Most charitable, religious, scientific and educational organizations exempt under §501(c)(3) must file a Form 1023 with their District Director in order to obtain tax-exempt status. Such status will apply only for the period beginning with the filing of the application, unless the form 1023 is filed within fifteen (15) months from the end of the month in which the organization was created.[143]

Therefore, timely filing can be crucial if the organization desires to have its exemption be retroactively applied to the day it was organized. Failure to file within the required fifteen-month period would mean that any contributions made to the charity, prior to the date it filed its application for exemption, would be nondeductible.[144]

Along with its application, an organization claiming exemption under §501(c)(3) must show that its creating document (a) permits it to exercise only those powers which will further its exempt purpose, and (b) contains an adequate provision for distribution of its assets upon dissolution. Such distribution must be solely for an exempt purpose.[145]

Some §501(c)(3) organizations, however, are automatically exempt, and need not file an application Form 1023. These organizations are churches, church auxiliaries, conventions or associations of churches, and organizations having annual gross receipts of less than $5000, which are not private foundations.

Officers' Tax Liability

Officers can be personally liable for not paying over employee withholding taxes and FICA taxes.[146] I.R.C. attempts to hold unpaid volunteers (officers and directors) of NPOs personally liable for employee withholding, and FICA taxes not paid by organization administrators are based on I.R.C. §6672, which allows "responsible persons" to be held liable. If they use these funds to pay other debts the IRS goes after their personal assets. By mid-1987 the IRS had assessed $5.6 billion against such individuals. Discouragement of volunteerism is a serious problem, especially since the volunteer bears the burden of proof; and proof of IRS error still leaves no attorney fee for the successful volunteer, under I.R.C. §7430, unless he can prove lack of substantial IRS justification. See, *Holley v. U.S.*, 89-1 U.S.T.C. §9196. (E.D. WI, 1989) holding for the volunteers; and *Simpson v. U.S.*, 88-2 U.S.T.C. §9474 (E.D., N.Y., 1987) holding for the volunteers in a case of $989,671 taxes of a nonprofit hospital.[147]

§99. DETERMINATION LETTER OR RULINGS

After an organization files all necessary documents with the key director for its district, a determination letter or ruling will be issued.[148] Except as discussed in §96–98, *supra*, a letter or ruling recognizing exemption is effective from the date the organization was formed. The IRS can, however, specify a later date for the recognition of exemption, if it requires the organization to make alterations in its operations.[149]

It is possible for an organization to be given an advance ruling on its exempt status; that is, the government can issue a ruling before the organization begins operation. In order to obtain an advance ruling an organization must show its expected activities, sources of income, and principal expenditures.[150] Even if the organization provides the appropriate information, the IRS can require that the organization present a record of actual operations before it issues a ruling.[151]

Not all applications for exemption are granted. When an organization receives an adverse letter or ruling it has the right to have the matter considered by an Appeals Office. An organization seeking to protest an adverse determination must file a statement with the key district director establishing its desire to have an Appeals Office conference; this statement must be filed no later than 30 days after the receipt of the adverse determination. If the key district director maintains his or her ruling, the case will be sent to the chief of the proper appeals office.[152]

If a determination was issued after 1975, and the IRS denied exemption, or no determination was issued within 270 days of a request for a determination, the taxpayer can seek a declaratory judgment in the district court for the District of Columbia, or the U.S. Tax Court.[153]

Tax Secrecy at Hearings

Federal income tax return statutory *secrecy* applies to administrative nonadversarial proceedings (local rent review board) as well as to court proceedings; no duty to reveal.[154]

§100. MAINTAINING EXEMPT STATUS

All exempt organizations, except for Instrumentalities of the United States created by Acts of Congress,[155] are required to file yearly tax returns. The form filed by most organizations is Form 990. However, private foundations are required to file the special Form 990-PF, while Black Lung Trusts must file a 990-BL. Finally, because §501(d) religious and apostolic associations are treated like partnerships, they must file a Form 1065 partnership tax return, instead of a Form 990.[156]

In order to maintain exempt status, an organization must continue to operate exclusively for exempt purposes.[157] Failure to do so an cause the imposition of excise taxes or even the revocation of exemption. Examples of activities which will give rise to punitive action by the IRS are: prohibited transactions, [158] certain lobbying activities,[159] conducting an unrelated trade or business,[160] engaging in discriminatory practices,[161] and violating the private foundation provisions.[162] These improper activities, and the penalties imposed upon organizations involved in them, are discussed next.

[In 1988 the IRS announced plans to study 5000 of the 1987 nonprofit tax returns, to obtain information about commercial activities of tax exempt organizations, and to complete the study by 1990. See, Oleck, *Mixtures of Profit and Nonprofit Corporate Purposes and Operations*, in Seminar Course Book; Northern Kentucky Univ., Chase College of Law (Feb. 1988) pp. 1–59; also— *No. Ky. L. Rev.*—(late 1988)].

IRC §6104 now requires organizations exempt under §501(c) and (d) to make a copy of their application for exemption and all annual information returns available for public inspection during normal business hours at the organization's principal office. Each return must be kept open to the public for a three year period.

IRC §6652(c)(1)(C) assesses a penalty of $10 per each day that the organization fails to comply with the public inspection requirement. While failure to supply annual information returns carries a $5000 maximum penalty, there is no cap on the failure to supply the organization's original application for exemption. IRC §6652(c)(1)(1).

§101. LOSS OF TAX EXEMPTION (PROHIBITED TRANSACTIONS)

If certain government or church pension and profit sharing or stock bonus plans,[163] or trusts forming part of a supplemental unemployment plan under §501(c)(17),[164] or trusts created before June 25, 1959 which provide pension benefits funded only by employee contributions,[165] engage in "prohibited transaction," they will lose their exempt status.[166]

The organization will be engaged in a prohibited activity if it:[167]

1. lends its income or corpus without adequate security, to;

2. pays unreasonably high compensation, to:

3. makes its services preferentially available, to;

4. purchases securities or property at an unreasonably excessive price, from;

5. sells securities or properties at an unreasonably reduced price, to; or

6. engages in any other transaction which results in a substantial diversion of its income or corpus, to;

its creator, or a person who made substantial contributions to the organization.

It is important to note that any demand loan which remains outstanding after 1955 without adequate security or interest will be a prohibited transaction.[168]

Feeder Organizations:

Corporations or other organizations which are operated for the primary purpose of carrying on a trade or business, but which are required to pay over their profits to one or more exempt entities, are called feeder organizations.[169] Feeder organizations are fully subject to tax as corporations,[170] trusts,[171] or individuals.[172] Tax exempt *status* is determined by *use of the property* in question rather than ownership of the property. In Montana, a cattle company used cattle as a capital investment to produce funds which in turn were donated to member evangelical organizations to provide services to the needy. The cattle of this *feeder organization* were found to be taxable.[173]

[Mia Wood contributed the rest of this subsection.]

Such difficulties associated with nonprofit organizations occur outside the United States, as well. A 1993 Canadian newspaper reported problems during the campaign for the October 26 referendum on the Charlottetown constitutional accord.

The three main political parties joined forces to create a national "Yes" committee. Shortly after the "Yes" committee was incorporated, it received advice that it could qualify for a refund on the GST it paid out on goods and services if it sold memberships as a nonprofit organization. Following this advice, the committee sold about 70 $10 memberships, and after submitting its GST returns, the committee received three refund cheques totalling about $527,000. Experts are saying that it is "absolutely unconscionable" that Canadian taxpayers, who voted against the three main political parties in last October's constitutional vote, are now forced to subsidize them, and that if this tactic had been tried by another group or business, they would have found themselves in the courts on fraud or tax evasion charges.[174]

Action and Propaganda Organizations:

[See *"Lobbying"* in the Index]

§501(c)(3) specifically provides that a religious, scientific, charitable or educational organization will lose its exempt status if it engages in attempting to influence legislation as a substantial part of its activities. Organizations which become too entangled in the legislative process are called action[175] or propaganda[176] organizations. The determination of whether or not the lobbying activities of the organization are substantial will be made in light of all of the organization's activities, its governing instruments, and the pertinent facts and circumstances.[177]

An organization which fails to qualify for §501(c)(3) status, because it is an action organization, may still qualify under §501(c)(4) as a social welfare organization.[178] On the other hand, a §501(c)(3) organization which *lost* its exempt status, because of its lobbying activities, cannot become a §501(c)(4) organization.[179]

While §501(c)(3) organizations have always been prohibited from lobbying, Congress clarified this prohibition in the Omnibus Budget Reconciliation Act of 1987 (OBRA).

First, Act §10711 states that the organization's exempt status can be revoked if the organization engages in campaigning for, or against, a political candidate. Secondly, §10711 provides that a 501(c)(3) which loses its exempt status because it engages in prohibited political activities *cannot* retain exempt status under §501(c)(4).

OBRA also added taxes for 501(c)(3)s making political contributions. IRC §4955. The taxes start at 10 percent of the expenditure on the organization. There is an additional tax of 2.5 percent of the expenditure on any manager authorizing a political expenditure, up to $5000 maximum.

IRC §4955(d) increases the number of prohibited political expenditures by adding: any expenses which have the primary effect of promoting public recognition of a candidate including voter registration; advertising for a candidate; travel expenses for a candidate; honoraria paid for speech by a candidate.

Finally, IRC §7409 now authorizes the Internal Revenue Service to seek injunctive relief against 501(c)(3) organizations if they are about to engage in making flagrant political expenditures. A court can grant such a injunction to prevent a public charity from using its assets to fund a political campaign. In conjunction with §7409, §6852 grants the IRS the power to assess immediately any taxes owed because of prohibited political expenditures by exempt organizations.

Funds caused by a political organization to promote ballot measures are exempt expenditures that are not taxable if their referenda expenditures are part of a campaign strategy to influence the elections of state and local officials and where the referenda on the ballot had a substantial influence on elections.[180]

The *Omnibus Reconciliation Act of August 1993* eliminated the tax deduction for lobbying expenses except for local and county lobbying by chambers of commerce and the like.

A presidential candidate was excluded from a Democratic party presidential debate cosponsored by a nonpartisan voter education group. She had "competitive advocate standing" to challenge the tax exempt status of the group for violation of statutory nonelectioneering prohibitions. The injury was that voters had received a message from this nonpartisan, federally tax-exempt group that her candidacy did not warrant serious attention. Further, the group was using funds it raised through its tax exempt status to obtain television exposure for her competitors. Finally, harm flowed from the federal government's allegedly partisan restriction of her opportunities to communicate her political ideas to the voting public at large.

The candidate also had a cause of action under the First Amendment. The federal government, in allowing the group to act in a partisan manner while benefiting from tax exempt status, removed the vital element of governmental neutrality from primary process, which encroached upon her first Amendment rights.[181]

When the Inaugural Committee sponsored a ball, a fundraising reception, a parade, and the swearing-in ceremony, it claimed that it had lessened the burdens of the government, an exempt purpose under the IRC. For an activity to be identified as a governmental burden, there must be an objective manifestation by the government that confirms the activity is part of its obligation. The IRS determined that while there was some evidence that the state considered the inauguration part of its burden, the activities of the organization did not actually relieve the government's burden. The state was merely required to perform a swearing-in ceremony and had budgeted only a small fraction of what the organization spent for the occasion. Thus, the IRS found that the organization did not qualify for exempt status.[182]

NPOs as Political Investment

[David E. Bricker did research for the first part of this subsection.]

Public concern about the potential for abuse of the tax law privileges of politicians' NPOs has increased in recent years.[183] Use of tax-exempt organizations as instrumentalities created by politicians became noticeably greater in the 1980s. Financial disclosure forms of Congress members in 1988 showed 51 Senators and 146 House Members to be founders, officers, or directors of tax-exempt organizations.[184]

Political-career NPOs usually are organized as *educational* charities under IRC §501(c)(3), and are supposed to do no partisan political acts and limited lobbying.[185] Federal Election Commission rules allow committees to serve for political activity, but require revelation of some sources of funds and limit use of corporate sources.[186] The IRS uses a "facts and circumstances" (common sense) test of compliance.[187]

In late 1989 Congress approved a potentially great loophole in their pay raise ethics package: It thenceforth would be lawful for an "interest group" to donate money to a Congress members' favorite charity if that NPO was tax-exempt.[188]

§102. PRIVATE FOUNDATIONS' TAXES

[See Chapter 7.]

Private foundations are, as a general rule, exempt from taxation. There are, however, several exceptions to that general rule in the form of "excise" taxes. A private foundation is a §501(c)(3) organization which is not a public charity qualifying for the maximum deduction for charitable contributions,[189] and is not broadly public supported. An organization receives broad public support if it receives more than two-thirds of its annual income from its members and the public and less than one-third from investment income. In addition, exempt organizations which are engaged in public testing, or which support public charities are not private foundations.[190] Absent notice to the contrary, the government will presume that all §501(c)(3) organizations are private foundations.[191] This is a rebuttable presumption, however.[192]

Private foundations are subject to a tax equal to two (2) percent of their net "investment income."[193] Net investment income includes rents, royalties, interest, dividends, and capital gain net income.[194] [See Chapter 7.]

Persons or entities in close proximity to private foundations will be taxed on any act of "self-dealing" with those organizations.[195] An act of self-dealing occurs when a disqualified person engages in selling, leasing, borrowing, or performing services for compensation, with the private foundation.[196] A disqualified person is one who is a substantial contributor to the foundation, a foundation manager, or a corporation,[197] partnership, or trust, which is related to a substantial contributor or manager.[198]

The Code defines a substantial contributor as either the creator of a charitable trust, or one who contributed more than $5000 in all years if his total contributions are more than 2 percent of the total contributions received by the foundation in all years through the end of the taxable year in which the contribution was received.[199] That is, the question of whether or not a contributor is a substantial contributor must be determined in relation to contributions to the foundation as a whole.

The tax imposed on self-dealing transactions can take two forms. First, there is an *initial* tax of 5 percent of the amount involved in the self-dealing transaction. This tax must be paid by the disqualified person.[200] There is also a tax on a foundation manager who knowingly participates in a self-dealing transaction. This tax is 2 1/2 percent of the amount involved.[201]

Second, there are *additional* taxes which may be assessed. If an initial tax is imposed, but the act of self-dealing continues, a disqualified person will be required to pay 200 percent of the amount,[202] and a foundation manager who refuses to correct the act will be liable for 50 percent of the amount[203] as an excise tax. The additional tax imposed on the manager will not exceed $5,000.[204]

A private foundation is required to distribute its income on an annual basis. Failure to do so will cause the foundation to pay a tax of 15 percent of its "undistributed income."[205] For years beginning after 1984, the distributable income of the foundation is its minimum investment return,[206] plus net short-term capital gains,[207] minus the private foundation taxes paid by the organization.[208]

In addition to the 15 percent tax on undistributed income, the government will impose a 100 percent tax if the foundation does not distribute within 90 days after they received a notice of deficiencies for failure to distribute.[209]

Private foundations are discouraged from maintaining too great an ownership interest in corporations and partnerships engaged in an active trade or business. As usual, the government's method of discouraging such "excess business holdings" is to impose a tax equal to 5 percent of the amount of the excess.[210] The tax will be imposed on the last day of the foundation's tax year, but will be determined as of the day on which the excess business holdings were at their greatest.[211]

Excess business holdings are defined as any ownership of a corporation's voting stock in excess of 20 percent of the outstanding shares,[212] or the excess over 35 percent if the control of the corporation is shown to be in the hands of a third party.[213]

A foundation which held stock ownership prior to May 26, 1969, may retain such ownership to the extent of 50 percent of the voting stock of the corporation.[214]

An additional tax of 200 percent of the excess holdings will be applied if the foundation fails to dispose of its excess holdings within 90 days of receiving a deficiency notice based on those holdings.[215]

Investments made by a private foundation, which might jeopardize the completion of the foundation's exempt purpose, are subject to a 5 percent tax payable by the foundation.[216] Another 5 percent tax (not to exceed $5,000) will be imposed on a foundation manager who knowingly participates in such "speculative investments."[217]

As with other private foundation taxes, a failure to remove the investments from jeopardy within 90 days of the assessment of the initial tax will give rise to an additional tax; this tax is 25 percent on the foundation.[218] and 5 percent on the manager (not to exceed $10,000),[219] of the speculative investments.[220]

Taxable expenditures of a private foundation include amounts paid for "lobbying, electioneering, and other prohibited transactions" such as grants to individuals which are awarded on a discriminatory basis.[221] Such expenditures subject the foundation to a 10 percent initial tax[222] and the manager to a two and one-half percent tax if he knowingly participates.[223] If the expenditures continue for a period of more than 90 days after mailing of deficiency notice, the foundation will be subject to an additional tax of 100 percent,[224] while the manager will be taxed to the extent of 50 percent[225] (of a maximum $10,000).[226]

A private foundation may terminate its status voluntarily by notification of the IRS[227] or it may be terminated involuntarily by IRS action.[228]. The "termination of a private foundation" will give rise to a tax equal to the lesser of the foundation net assets,[229] or the tax benefit received by substantial contributors through charitable deductions, including interest on such benefits.[230]

However, this tax can be avoided if the assets are distributed to a charitable organization which has been in existence for five consecutive years,[231] or if state officials notify the IRS that the assets will be preserved for charitable use through a court order.[232]

Sales of abusive tax shelters are calculated as a percentage of gross income, for statutory penalties computation, not based on the number of such sales. The penalty is $1,000 or 10 percent of the gross income to be derived from such activity, under the federal statute, as a minimum deterrent, rather than as a flat fee for each such sale.[233]

§103. "UNRELATED BUSINESS" TAXABLE INCOME [UBIT]

The government grants tax-exemptions under the expectation that organizations will not engage in business unrelated to their purpose as exempt entities. Thus, all organizations exempt under §501(c) are subject to tax on income generated by their involvement in regularly carrying on a trade or business unrelated to their exempt purpose.[234]

Some examples of "unrelated trade or business" activities are:

The auctioning of prize-winning animals by an agricultural organization,[235]

The sale of computer time to the public by a university,[236]

and pet grooming services provided by a society for the prevention of cruelty to animals.[237]

If the IRS determines that an organization regularly engages in an unrelated trade or business, the taxable income from that trade or business will be subject to either the corporate[238] or trust[239] tax rates depending upon the nature of the organization. In essence the tax imposition works as a limited denial of tax-exemption, which causes the unrelated business to be taxed as any other business.

It must be stressed that an organization which operates an unrelated business could be in danger of losing its exempt status if the IRS determines that it is no longer operated exclusively for exempt purposes.[240]

[Tax information that is given during an enforcement proceeding can be disclosed if it tends to show that the IRS had reasons to suspect that organization's services were being utilized for business purposes inconsistent with tax exempt status. Disclosure of information will be permitted if it relates directly to the transactional relationship between exempt organization and taxpayer. The IRS, however, must satisfy an objective standard of "good faith." If it does, IRS will not be held liable for disclosure.[241]]

Income from "affinity" *credit cards* issued by nonprofit organizations is taxable unrelated business income. Banks are given permission by NPOs to use their names to sell credit cards, in exchange for a percentage of the fees and charges.[242]

Income from a special endowment used for publishing a quarterly, by a college fraternity, but not set up as a special set-aside fund, and not exclusively nonprofit in publishing, is not tax-exempt income under I.R.C. §512(a)(3)(B).[243]

[The IRS has conducted examinations and hearings on its guidelines for auditing colleges and universities in a number of ares, including unrelated business income tax. Examiners will look into such areas as athletic departments that derive income from sporting events, including that income often earned through the rental of facilities or the provision of goods and services to nonuniversity groups. Examiners will also scrutinize research funded by private firms or the government and review minutes of governing board and fundraising committee meetings to determine if any contributions are contingent upon conditions that suggest private benefit.[244]

In a recent UBIT case, the plaintiff, a charitable trust and a qualified tax exempt organization, was held not to have been evading taxation assessed on rent from a farm the plaintiff owns as an unrelated business income tax. The rent, in the form of 50 percent of the farm's production under a crop-share lease, was nontaxable as a fixed percentage of receipts or sales. It also was not taxable as an amount dependent on the income or profits of the lessee.[245]

The interest from "debt-financed property," such as certificates of deposit bought with borrowed funds, is subject to UBIT. An organization that buys high-yielding CDs with borrowed money to increase its interest earnings must pay unrelated business income tax on the interest. "Debt-financed income property" is defined as property acquired by incurring debt, retained to produce income, and unrelated to the organizations' exempt purposes.[246]

Nonprofit organizations have been trying to evade taxation by obtaining legislative protection from the IRS's effort to enforce the UBIT on income from corporations sponsoring athletic and other events.[247]]

Advertising income from sports programs is tax-free (not UBIT) (unrelated business taxable income) only if it is occasional and not regularly and/or continually earned/ e.g., a Final Four NCAA basketball tournament.[248]

"Dues" paid by nonmembers of a tax-exempt labor union for some federal employees' health insurance coverage offered by the union (regular insurance payments plus a $35 annual fee, called "dues") are *Unrelated Business Income* in a trade or business, not truly "membership" dues ($32.50 of it being net income) and taxable.[249]

Joint Ventures with Profit Organizations now are allowed (tax exempt by IRS) if the "general partner" NPO serves a charitable purpose, and presents assurances that the NPO will not be prevented from so doing by the for-profit investors.[250]

Income received by a tax-exempt organization for the use of its logo is a royalty payment and is not subject to the unrelated business income tax (UBIT). Income that is received from another noncharitable organization for the names and addresses of donors is taxable.[251]

When exempt organizations contract out for the publication of magazines and the sale of advertising, the IRS may determine that the advertising income is subject to unrelated business income tax. This may be true even if the nonprofit has a minimal role in the sale of advertising. The income does not fall within the "royalties" exception to UBIT taxation even if it is called "royalties" in a contract.[252]

All of the tax aspects of unrelated business income are too complex to warrant more detailed discussion here. Thus the 1986 Tax Code §1605(a) amended Code §277(b)(4) to allow "news" organizations to qualify for exemption; and there were other changes. [See §100]

§104. THE IRS "HIT LIST"

The director of the IRS Exempt Organization Technical Division told a NPO tax seminar at NYU in 1991 that prime targets for IRS audits in 1992 were hospitals and educational multi-unit groups, tax exempt bond issues, political activities, gambling-fund raising, and private school discriminations.[253]

In 1992 the IRS began to focus on nonprofits in the areas of physician-hospital joint venture, fund raising, compensation, unrelated business income tax, employee-independent contractor classifications, lobbying, and corporate sponsorships. In particular, the IRS will concentrate on Form 990 reporting which requires disclosure of all compensation to officers and other high paid employees, even where the income is not taxable. The service also monitors political activity; nonprofits cannot support political activities that sponsor one candidate over another.[254]

The Internal Revenue Service is increasing enforcement of tax regulations concerning student scholarships given by colleges. A scholarship given to a U.S. student is not taxable if used to pay for tuition, fees, books, and equipment. Funds that go toward nonacademic expenses are taxable, including those spent for room, board, and traveling expenses. Colleges are required to withhold tax from grants given to international students if the funds are to be used for nonacademic purposes.[255]

The IRS believes that exempt organizations are trying to avoid covering employees in their employee health and benefit plans by classifying "employees" as "independent contractors." Employers, thus, do not have to withhold income taxes or Social Security taxes or pay the employer's share of the worker's Social Security taxes. Control is the major issue in the determination of whether a worker is an employee or independent contractor. If an exempt organization controls a worker's hours, what he/she does, and demands performance in the organization's office, the worker is probably an employee. If a worker performs specific assignments, at his/her own convenience, for a fixed fee, he/she is probably an independent contractor.[256]

§105. FUTURE OF TAX EXEMPTIONS

Tax-exempt organizations are a major factor in present society. However, such entities maintain exemption purely through the grace of Congress.[257] Congress is definitely aware that exempt organizations engage in various commercially motivated activities.[258] Thus, there is no guarantee that the next great tax reform act will include any provision for tax exemption.

Yet, it seems unlikely that Congress would ever totally dismantle tax-exempt organizations, for it is their exempt status which serves, in no small measure, as their motivation for providing charitable, educational, agricultural, and social welfare services, *etc.* In fact, these organizations perform functions which would fall squarely on the government if private volunteers were not willing to devote their time and energies to them. Thus, if the exempt organizations ceased to exist, the government would have to spend more tax dollars in order to fill the void left in society by their absence.

[The 1986 reduction of the top tax-deductible contributions rate from 50 percent to 28 percent is estimated to cost charitable or educational or other tax-exempt organizations about $13 billion a year]. [*Independent Sector* estimate (AP report) Aug. 21, 1986.]

POINTS TO REMEMBER:

- Retain a tax law expert as a regular consultant; use his/her services even if you are knowledgable about tax law.
- Decide whether or not your organization can qualify as a tax-exempt organization.
- Make sure that the organization is not empowered to perform any activity beyond the scope of its exempt activities.
- Make sure that you file the appropriate form required.
- Remember to include a power of attorney in your application.

- Do not allow the organization to involve itself in any disqualifying activities.

- Be particularly cautious with profit-seeking "unrelated business", and "lobbying," activities.

NOTES TO CHAPTER 9

1. IRC §11; Florida Statutes Annotated (West's) [hereinafter F.S.A.] F.S.A. §220.03(aa).

2. IRC §641. F.S.A. §220.11, 199.185, 220.03(1)(aa).

3. Reg. §301.7701-2.

4. The Code provides specific categories of exempt organizations, most of which are found under IRC §501.

5. *E.g.*, §1.501(a)-1.

6. The Internal Revenue Service has issued detailed revenue rulings and procedures which must be met before exemption is granted, even though all statutory requirements for exemption have been satisfied.

7. *E.g.*, Idaho Code §63-3022 (1985) which specificlaly refer to the Internal Revenue Code definition of taxable income, in defining income for state law purposes; Fla. Stt. 220.13(2)(h).

8. IRC §63 defines taxable income as adjusted gross income minus itemized deductions. Since exempt organizations to not have "taxable" income, at least to the extent of their exemptions, they cannot have taxable income under stte law either, if the stte law derives its definition from the Internal Revenue Code.

    [But income from group insurance offered to the organizations' members is "unrelated business income." United States v. american Bar endowment, 106 S. Ct. 2426 (1986)].

9. F.S.A. §§196.195; 196.011.

10. F.S.A. §212.08.

11. F.S.A. §205.192.

12. IRC §170.

13. IRC §§2001, 2055, 2106(a)(2).

14. IRC §§2501, 2522(a) and (b).

15. IRC §§2601, 2602(c)(2).

16. See IRC §§4911 and 4940-4948 which impose excise taxes on public charities which engage in prohibited transactions, and private foundtions under a variety of circumstances.

17. IRC §§(a)(1)(A), (B) and (C) which provide for loss of exemption of supplemental unemployment benefit trusts, certain funded trusts created before 6/25/59 and certain employee benefit plans maintained by governments and churches when those means engage in prohibited transactions.

18. 3 *NonProfit Times* (12) 4 (News Briefs) (Mar. 1990). *Cf.*, S.P. Cole, *Volunteerism Can Be Taxing*, 12 Natl. L.J. (10) 13 (Nov. 13, 1989).

19. IRC §§501(c)(3), (c)(6), (c)(7), (c)(9), (c)(11)(A), and (c)(13).

20. IRC §501(c)(1).

21. IRC §501(c)(1)(A)(ii); (c)(1)(B).

22. IRC §501(c)(1)(1).

23. IRC §501(c)(2).

24. Regs. §1.501(c)(2) - 1(b).

25. IRC §162.

26. Rev. Rul. 66-102, 1966-1 CB 133.

27. Rev. Rul. 68-371, 1968-2 CB 204.

28. I.R.S. Notice 88-68; summarized in Harmon and Weiss, *Tax Monthly* for Exempt Organizations, p. 1 (July 1988) (Wash., DC.).

29 *American Association of Christian Schools voluntary Beneficiary Welfare Plan rust by January v. U.S.*, 850 F.2d 1510 (11th cir., AL 1988).

30. *Love Box Co., Inc. v. Commissioner of I.R.; Tax Ct.* §85-1804, 3-2 (9th Cir., July 1988).

31. 7 *NonProfit Times* (4) 29, 33 (April 1993).

32. Emphasis supplied.

33. *Michigan v. U.S.*, 802 F.Supp. 120 (July 1992).

34. Regs. §1.501()(3)-1(b)(1)(i)(a). The determination of whether or not granted powers permit the corporation to engage in substantial non-exempt activities is a question of fact. However, such determination will be constructed in a manner which is least favorable to the taxpayer, thus presenting it with the burden of showing that it has no power to act in a manner which involves substantial nonexempt activity. See *e.g.*, Lewis v. U.S., 189 F. Supp. 950.

35. Regs. 1.501(c)(3)-1(b)(1)(ii).

36. Regs. 1.501(c)(3)-1(c); *See also,* General Conference of the Free Church of America, 71 TC 920 (1979), and U.S. v. Dale, 756 F.2d 1076 (5th Cir., 1985).

37. Or more exactly, "an unlimited power to tax involves, necessarily, a power to destry," McCulloch v. Maryland, 117 U.S. 316 (1819).

38. U.S. Const. amend. I.

39. The Supreme Court said in Walz v. Tax Commissioner of the City of New York that "granting tax-exemptions to churches necessarily operates to afford an indirect economic benefit and also gives rise to some, but yet a lesser, involvement in taxing them. In analyzing either alternative, the questions are whether the involvement is excessive, and whether it is a continuing surveillance leading to an impermissible degree of entanglement." 297 U.S. 664, (1970), at 674–75.

40. *E.g.*, Stephenson v. Commissioner, 748 F.2d 331 (6th Cir., 1984) which involved a "church" which had no congregation, no regular worship services, no liturgy or creed. The Sixth Circuit held that such an entity was not operated exclusively for religious purposes.
    [The better view is that "Tax-free status bears burden of proof" that the organization's tax eemption is valid. "Religious organizations, by state law, are subsidized by all property taxpayrs. At the least, they must show, financially, why they qualify." Editorial, *St. Petersburg (Fl.) times*, p. 2 D (Aug. 23, 1987).]

41. *E.g.*, Levy Family Tribe Foundation, Inc., 69 TC 615 (1978).

42. *Olsen v. Drug Enforcement Admin.*, 878 F.2d 1458 (D.C. App. 1989); *aff'd*, Ethiopian Zion Coptic Church, _____. TC _____ (1990); (Report 3 *NonProfit Times* (11) 35 (Feb. 1990). For details see Harmon, Curran & T, *Tax Monthly.*

43. Reg. §1.511-2(a)(3)(ii).

44. Harmon, G., (article) 7 *NonProfit Times* (6) 20 (June 1993).

45. *Neher v. C.I.R.*, 852 F.2d 848 (6th Cir., 1988) and *foley v. C.I.R.*, 844 F.2d 94 (2d civ. 1988), both reversed by U.S. Supreme Court (5 to 2) June 5, 1989; Reported in *St. Petersburg* (FL) *Times*, p. 1 (June 6, 1989).

46. *Truth Tabernacle Church, Inc. v. Commissioner*, TM Document #22350-87; Harmon, C & T., *Tax Monthly*, p. 8 (Nov. 1989).

47. I.R.S. Rev. Rul. 89-74, clarifying (same rule) of *Tweeddale* case, 92 T.C. 31 (1989).

48. *Living Faith, Inc. v. C.I.R.*, 950 F.2d 365 (7th Cir. 1991).

49. *U.S. v. Church of Scientology Western United Sttes*, 973 F.2d 715 (August 1992).

50. *Tougher Standard for Church Documents, Nonprofit Times*, April 1993.

51. *Constitutional Issues in Revoking Religious Tax exemptions: Church of Scientology of California v Commissioner*, XXXVII U.Fla.L. Rev.

52. *Church of Spiritual Technology v U.S.*, 26 Cl.Ct. 713, June 1992.

53. *IRS Publication 598* is "Tax on Unrelated Business Income of Exempt Organizations.' Or clal your state-located IRS "Forms Only' toll-free phone number, *such as Florida 1-800-424-3676 in Jacksonville.*

54. *In re U.S. Catholic Conference*, 885 F.2d 1020 (2d Cir., N.Y., 1989).

55. J.B. Quinn article, *Newsweek* magazine, p. 50 (Dec. 28, 1992).

56. Reg. §1.50(c)-1(d)(2).

57. Rev. Rul. 80-200, 1980-2 CB 173.

58. Rev. Rul. 77-272, 1977-2 CB 191.

59. Rev. Rul. 68-73, 1968-1 CB 251.

60. Retired Teachers Legal Defense Fund, Inc., 78 TC 280 (1981).

61. Miss Georgia Scholarship Fund, Inc. 72 TC 267 (1979).

62. Rev. Rul. 67-6, 1967-1 CB 135.

63. Taxation With Representation of Washington v. Regan, 459 U.S. 819 (1983).

64. IRC §170(b)(1)(C).

65. *Highland Women's Club v. Dep't opf revenue*, 564 N.E. 2d 890 (Ill. App. 2 Dist. 1990).

66. N. Lipschitz, Tax Briefs, 13 *Natl. L. J.* (31) 4 (4/8/91).

67. L. Blumenthal article, 4 *NonProfit Times* (5) (Aug. 1990).

68. Harmon, G. and Ladd, J., (article) 6 *NonProfit Times* (6) 28 (June 1992).

69. *Geisinger Health Plan v. Commisioner of Internal Revenue*, 61 U.S.L.W. 2512 (3rd Cir. 1993).

70. *Id.*

71. *Texas Learning Technology Group v. Commissioner of Internal Revenue*, 958 F.2d 122 (U.S. 5th C.Ct Appeals April 1992)

72. Reg. 1.501(c)(3)-1(d)(5)(i).

73. Reg. 1.501(c)(3)-1(d)(5)(ii).

74. Reg. 1.501(c)(3)-1(d)(5)(iii)(a).

75. Reg. 1.501(c)(3)-1(d)(5)(iii)(b).

76. Reg. 1.501(c)(3)-1(d)(5)(iii)(c).

77. Reg. 1.501(c)(3)-1(d)(5)(iv)(a).

78. Reg. 1.501(c)(3)-1(d)(5)(iv)(b).

79. Regs. 1.501(c)(3)-1(d)(3)(a) and (b).

80. Reg. §1.501(c)(3)-1(d)(3)(ii) Example 1.

81. Reg. §1.501(c)(3)-1(d)(3)(ii) Example 4.

82. Reg. §1.501(c)(3)-2(d)(3)(ii) Example 2.

83. Reg. §1.501(c)(3)-1(d)(3)(ii).

84. In Rev. Rul. 71-447, 1971-2 CB 230 the government's position was that a charitable trust must not violate public policy, and that racial discrimination was clearly in violation of well-established federal public policy. Thus, even though there was no reference to discrimi-

nation in §501(c)(3), the government would deny tax-exemption to any §501(c)(3) charitabl or educational institution practicing a substantial amount of discrimination.

The government requires an educational institution exempt under §501(c)(3) to keep records of its non-discriminatory policy, which must appear in all school advertising. Further, the school must operate all programs, including scholarship programs in a non-discriminatory manner. Ann. 76-143, 1976-47 IRB 19.

85. Bob Jones University had a policy of racial segregation based on religious practices. The school admitted members of all races, but enforced rules which prohibited interracial dating on or off campus. The Supreme Court held that the IRS's revocation of Bob Jones' exempt status was valid, and not violative of religious protections under the First Amendment. Bob Jones University v. U.S., 461 U.S. 574 (1983).

86. 1975-1 CB 158.

87. Furthermore, a recent Supreme Court decison disallowed an injunction against the IRS's granting of exempt status to racially discriminatory schools. The rationale for the court's decision was that the parents seeking the injunction had based their claim on their position as taxpayers, rather than on any direct harm to their children. Thus, the parents did not have standing. The Court did not decide whether or not the injunction would have been granted, had the children actually been denied the benefits of the schools after applying for admission. Allen v. Wright, U.S., 104 S. Ct. 3315 (1984). Petition for rehearing denied in 105 S. Ct. 51 (1984).

88. *Developments in the Law, Nonprofit Corporations—Tax Exemption*, 105 Harv. L. Rev. 1612, 1613 (May 1992).

89. Added in 1976 by Pub. L. 94-455 §§1307(d)(1)(A), 1313(a). In 1982, Congress also added IRC §501(j), which allows already exempt amateur sports organizations to involve the provision of athletic facilities and equipment and to be regional or local in nature. This was designed, in part, to help in the U.S. Olympic effort. Pub. L. 97-248, §286(a).

90. Similar organizations which provide aid to distressed persons have already been granted exemption. Rev. Rul. 69-174, 1969-1 CB 149.

91. Reg. §1.501(c)(4)-1(a)(2)(i).

92. Reg. §1.501(c)(4)-(1)(b).

93. Reg. §1.501(c)(4)-1(a)(2)(i), which provides that the term "charitable' will have the same definition as it had in Reg. §1.501(c)(3)-1(d)(2).

94. Rev. Rul. 76-81, 1976-1 CB 156. *See*, Abortion Rights Mobilization Inc. v. Regan, 603 F. Supp. 970 (D.C., N.Y. 1985).

95. IRC §170(b)(1)(C); for a discussion of charitable contributions, see Chapter 8, above.

96. IRC §501(c)(6).

97. Regs. §1.501(c)(6)-1; Rev. Rul. 65-164, 1965-1 CB 238.

98. IRC §501(c)(7).

99. IRC §501(c)(8).

100. IRC §501(c)(10).

101. IRC §501(c)(9).

102. IRC §501(c)(11).

103. IRC §501(c)(13).

104. IRC §701–761.

105. IRC §§1361–1379.

106. IRC §528. *See* IRS Publ. 588, and Reg. §1.528-4.

107. IRC §528(c)(1)(B).

108. IRC §528(c)(1)(C).

109. IRC §528(c)(1)(E); Reg. §1.528-8(a).

110. "Taxable income" is defined by IRC §528(d) to be the excess of the gross income of the organization over its expenses, except that no deduction for either net-operating loss unders §172 shall be allowed. For the purpose of §528 there is a specific deduction of $100, and gross income will not include the exempt function income of the organization.

111. IRC §528(b).

112. *E.g.*, American Bar Endowment v. U.S., 761 F.2d 1573 (Fed. cir., 1985).

113. *E.g.*, Dillingham Transportation Building, Ltd. v. U.S., 146 F. supp. 953 (1957).

114. IRC §6033(a); Reg. §1.501(a)-1(d).

115. Minnesota Kingsmen Chess Association, Inc., TC Memo 1983-495.

116. Reg. §1.501(a)-1(a)(2).

117. Reg. §1.501(a)-1(a)(3)(i).

118. *E.g.*, Stephenson v. Commissioners, 748 F.2d 331 (6th Cir., 1984).

119. 7 *NonProfit Times* (3) 37 (March 1993).

120. IRC §501(c)(1).

121. IRC §501(c)(21).

122. IRC §501(c)(11).

123. IRC §501(d).

124. IRC §501(c)(4).

125. IRC §501(c)(7).

126. IRC §501(c)(13).

127. IRC §501(c)(9).

128. IRC §§501(c)(8) and (10).

129. IRC §501(c)(5).

130. IRS Pub. No. 557 ('80 ed.), p. 4.

131. IRC §3121(b)(8)(B), repealed by P.L. 98-21 (4/20/83), but ministers are still exempt if they elect to be included for related activities.

132. IRC §3121(a)(16).

133. IRC §3121(b)(7).

134. IRc §3121.

135. IRS Pub. No. 577 ('80 ed.), p. 2.

136. *Church of Scientology of Calif. v. Commr. of I.R.*, 108 S. Ct. 1752 (1989) denying cert. on 823 F.2d 1310 (9th Cir. 1988); see 92 ALR Fed. 255; and *see, Tweedale*, 92 T.C. 31 (1989) "mail-order" church and I.R.C. 6661 penalty for "substantial understatement" and Rev. Rul 89-74.

137. *Church of Scientology of Calif v. Commissioner*, 108 S. Ct. 1752 (1989), denying cert. on 823 F.2d 1310 (9th Cir., 1988); and see 92 ALR Fed. 255.

138. *Towe Antique Ford Foundation v. I.R.S.*, 791 F. Supp. 1450 (D. Mont. 1992).

139. *Orange County Agr. Soc., Inc. v. C.I.R.*, 893 F.2d 529 (2d Cir. 1990).

140. *Towe Antique Ford foundation v. I.R.S., Dept. of Treasury, U.S.*, 791 F. Supp. 1450 (D. Mont., 1992).

141. *United Sttes v. Sprecher*, 783 F. Supp. 133 (S.D.N.Y. 1992).

142. *Michigan v. U.S.*, 802 F.Supp. 120 (July 1992).

143. Reg. §1.508-1(a)(2)(i).

144. IRC §508(d)(2).

145. IRS Pub. No. 557 ('80 ed.), p. 16; Treas. Rel. TIR-359 1/18/62; Ann. 62-19, 1962-8 IRB
      20.

146. *Carter v. U.S.*, 717 F. Supp. 188 (D.C., N.Y., 1989); but *c.f.*, *contra: United States v. burger*,
      717 F. Supp 245 (D.C., N.Y., 1989) (that a director is not a "responsible person" in just
      such a failure to pay over unpaid withholding taxes); See, *Cole* (article), *12 Natl. L.J.* (10)
      13 (Nov. 13, 1989).

147. S.P. Cole, *Volunteerism Can Be Taxing* 12 *Natl L. J.* (10) 13 (Nov. 13, 1989).

148. Rev. Proc. 80-25, 1980–1 CB 667.

149. Proc. rules §601.201(n)(3)(i).

150. IRS Pub. No. 557 ('80 ed.), p. 5.

151. Rev. Proc. 80-25, 1980–1 CB 667.

152. *Id.*

153. IRC §7428.

154. *King v. Mobile Home Rent Review Board of County*, 265 Cal. Rptr. 624 (2d Dist. App., 1989).

155. IRC §501(c)(1).

156. IRC §6033(a).

157. Reg. §1.501(c)(3)-1(c).

158. IRC §503(b).

159. IRC §501(c)(3).

160. IRC §512.

161. *E.g.*, Bob Jones University v. U.S., note 85, *supra.*

162. IRC §509.

163. IRC §§503(a)(1)(B); 401(a) and 4975(g)(2) or (3).

164. IRC §503(a)(a)(A).

165. IRC §§503(a)(1)(C) and 501(c)(18).

166. IRC §§503(a)(1) and (2).

167. IRC §503(b).

168. IRC §503(d)(2); The government was allowed to apply the excise tax provision of IRC
      §4975 (tax on prohibited transactions) to a prohibited loan that was outstanding even
      though the loan was made before §4975 was enacted by Pub. L. 93-406, sec. 2003, 88 Stat.
      829, 971, in 1974. The Tax Cout held that §4975 is not an *ex post facto* law. Hockaden and
      Associates, Inc. v. Commissioner, 84 TC 13 (1985).

169. IRC §502.

170. IRC §11.

171. IRC §1(e).

172. IRC §1.

173. *Steer, Inc. v. Dept. of Revenue*, 803 P.2d 601 (Mont. 1990).

174. *The Vancouver Sun, Pacific Press Lmd.*, March 19 1993 Pg. A9,

175. Reg. §1.501(c)(3)-1(c)(3)(ii).

176. Reg. §1.501(c)(3)-1(d)(3)(i).

177. Reg. §1.501(c)(3)-1(c)(3).

178. Reg. §1.501(c)(3)-1(d)(3)(N).

179. IRC §504(a).

180. 7 *NonProfit Times* (3) 37 (March, 1993).

181. *Fulani v. Brady*, 809 F.Supp. 1112 (Jan. 6, 1993).

182. *IRS Rains on Inaugural Committee's Parade, Nonprofit Times*, April 1993.

183. *Role of Politicians in Public Charities*, Vol. 2, p. 23, Center for Responsive Politics (1987).

184. Cohen & Matlock, "All-Purpose Loophole," *Natl. Journal*, p. 2981 (Dec. 9, 1989).

185. *New Trends in Voter Registration Groups*, Vol. 1, p. 26, Center for Responsive Politics (1989); 26 C.F.R. 1.501(c) (3)-(d) (1) (ii) (1987).

186. 2 U.S.C. §§441b(a),(e); 11 C.F.R. 100.7; Rev. Rul. 67-71, 1967-1 C.B. 125.

187. Treas. Reg. 1.170A-9(e) (3).

188. Cohen & Matlock, *supra*, note 184, p. 2983.

189. IRC §509(a).

190. Which is currently 50 percent of the taxpayer's contribution base nder IRC §170(b)(1)(A).

191. IRC §508(b).

192. Rev. Rul. 73-504, 1973-2 CB 190 1/2.

193. IRC §4940(a). Only 1 prcent if adequate distributions are made. See Prentice-Hall Tax Service, Par. 34,936.

194. IRC §§4940(c)(1) and (2).

195. IRC §4941(a).

196. IRC §4941(d).

197. Using the attribution rules under IRC §267.

198. IRC §4946(a).

199. IRC §507(d).

200. IRC §4946(a)(1).

201. IRC §4946(a)(2).

202. IRC §4946(b)(1).

203. IRC §4946(b)(2).

204. IRC §4946(c)(2).

205. IRC §4942(a).

206. IRC §4942(d)(1).

207. IRC §4942(f)(2)(B).

208. IRC §4942(d)(2).

209. IRC §4942(b).

210. IRC §4943(a)(1).

211. IRC §4943(a)(2).

212. IRC §4943(c)(2)(A).

213. IRC §4943(c)(2)(B).

214. IRC §4943(c)(4)(A).

215. IRC §4943(b) and (d)(3).

216. IRc §4944(a)(1).

217. IRC §4944(a)(2) and (d)(2).

218. IRC §4944(b)(1).

219. IRC §§4944(b)(2) and (d)(2).

220. Reg. §53.4944-1(a)(2) defines a jeopardizing investment as one in which the managers

have failed to exercise ordinary care and prudence under the facts and circumstances pre-
vaiing at the time of investment. Factors to be considered are the risks involved and the
long-and-short-term needs of the foundation.

221. IRC §4945(d).

222. IRC §4945(a)(1).

223. IRC §4945(b)(1) and (i)(2).

224. IRC §4945(b)(1) and (i)(2).

225. IRC §4945(b)(2).

226. IRC §4945(c)(2).

227. IRC §507(a)(1).

228. IRC §507(a)(2).

229. IRC §507(c)(1).

230. IRC §507(c)(2).

231. IRC §507(g)(1).

232. IRC §507(g)(2).

233. *Bond v. U.S.*; 9th Cir., CA; Apr. 13, 1989.

234. IRC §511.

235. Ltr. Rul. 78421023.

236. Ltr. Rul. 7902019.

237. The pets were not unwanted, and were not victims of the cruelty which the organization
     sought to prevent. Rev. Rul. 73-587, 1973-2 CB 192.

238. IRC §11, 511(a)(1).

239. IRC §1(e), 511(b).

240. Reg. §1.501(c)(3)-1(c)(1).

241. *Lebaron v. U.S.*, 794 F.Supp. 947 (Jan. 1992).

242. IRS Ruling (Jan. 1989); Report in, Grantsmanship Center, *Whole Nonprofit Catalog #9*, p. 4
     (Spring 1989).

243. *Phi Delta Theta Fraternity v. C.I.R.* (6th Cir., Oct. 24, 1989).

244. *Service Issues University Audit Guidelines, Nonprofit Times*, April 1993.

245. *Harlan E. Moore Charitable Trust v. U.S.*, 71 A.F.T.R. 2d 93–932, 93-1, USTC P 50,090 (Jan
     1993).

246. 7 *NonProfit Times* (6) 20 (June 1992) (citing *Kern County Electrical Pension Fund v. Commis-
     sioner.*

247. *IRS Official Warns Nonprofits*, Janne Gallagher, *Nonprofit Times* (April, 1993).

248. *National Collegiate Athletic Assn. v. Commissioner*, #89-9005 (U.S. 10th Cir.); in N.L. Tax
     Briefs, 13 *Natl. L. J.* (5)5 (Oct. 8, 1990).

249. *American Postal Workers Union v. U.S.*; U.S.D.C. Cir. Ct. App. #88-01091, reported in 13 *Natl.
     L. J.* (27)5 (Mar. 11, 1991).

250. 1 *NonProfit Tax Letter* (10), (Nov. 18, 1991) giving illustrations. Prentice Hall Co.

251. 6 *NonProfit Times* (8) 26 (August, 1992).

252. 6 *NonProfit Times* (5) 29 (May 1992).

253. 1 *NonProfit Tax Letter* (9) 1 (Nov. 4, 1991), Prentice Hall Co.

254. 1 *NonProfit Times* (8) 20 (August, 1992).

255. *See* 6 *NonProfit Times* (7) 26 (July 1992).

256. 6 *NonProfit Times* (5) 4 (May 1992); *Exempts, A newsletter for the non-for-profit service organiza-tion*, quartelry, Grant Thornton's National Exempt Organizations Committee, 312-856-0001.

257. IRC §501; although it could be argued that churches are constitutionally protected from taxation.

258. *E.g.*, IRC §511.

10

FORMS FOR TAX EXEMPTION (FEDERAL)

IRS Publication 557, *Tax-Exempt Status for Your Organization*, is highly recommended. These and other forms and publications that may be necessary can be obtained from the IRS by writing to:

Form Distribution Center
P.O. Box 9903
Bloomington, IL 61799
[If you are in Alabama, Arkansas, Louisiana, Mississippi or Tennessee.]

Form Distribution Center
P.O. Box 25866
Richmond, VA 23289
[If you are in Florida, Georgia, North Carolina or South Carolina.]
    To order IRS Tax Forms/Publications by telephone, call: 1-800-829-3676.
    To ask IRS tax questions, dial: 1-800-829-1040.

FORM No. 9

[IRS Form 990 and Schedule A]

§106. IRS FORM 990; RETURN FOR EXEMPT ORGANIZATIONS.

[Instructions for use with this form are available from the IRS.]

Form **990**	**Return of Organization Exempt From Income Tax** Under section 501(c) of the Internal Revenue Code (except black lung benefit trust or private foundation) or section 4947(a)(1) charitable trust	OMB No. 1545-0047 **1992**

Department of the Treasury
Internal Revenue Service   **Note:** *The organization may have to use a copy of this return to satisfy state reporting requirements.*   This Form is Open to Public Inspection

A For the calendar year 1992, or fiscal year beginning _____ , 1992, and ending _____ , 19 ____

Please use IRS label or print or type. See Specific Instructions.	**B** Name of organization		**C** Employer identification number
	Number and street (or P.O. box if mail is not delivered to street address)	Room/suite	**D** State registration number
	City, town, or post office, state, and ZIP code		**E** If address changed, check box . . . ▶ ☐

F Check type of organization—Exempt under section ▶ ☐ 501(c)( ) (insert number),
OR ▶ ☐ section 4947(a)(1) charitable trust   **G** If exemption application pending, check box . ▶ ☐

H(a) Is this a group return filed for affiliates? . . . . ☐ Yes ☐ No   **I** If either box in H is checked "Yes," enter four-digit group exemption number (GEN) ▶

(b) If "Yes," enter the number of affiliates for which this return is filed:. . ▶ _____

(c) Is this a separate return filed by an organization covered by a group ruling? ☐ Yes ☐ No   **J** Accounting method: ☐ Cash ☐ Accrual   ☐ Other (specify) ▶

K   Check here ▶ ☐ if the organization's gross receipts are normally not more than $25,000. The organization need not file a return with the IRS; but if it received a Form 990 Package in the mail, it should file a return without financial data. **Some states require a complete return.**

Note: *Form 990EZ may be used by organizations with gross receipts less than $100,000 and total assets less than $250,000 at end of year.*

Part I   **Statement of Revenue, Expenses, and Changes in Net Assets or Fund Balances**

Revenue	**1**	Contributions, gifts, grants, and similar amounts received:		
	a	Direct public support	1a	
	b	Indirect public support	1b	
	c	Government grants	1c	
	d	**Total** (add lines 1a through 1c) (attach schedule—see instructions)	1d	
	2	Program service revenue (from Part VII, line 93)	2	
	3	Membership dues and assessments (see instructions)	3	
	4	Interest on savings and temporary cash investments	4	
	5	Dividends and interest from securities	5	
	6a	Gross rents	6a	
	b	Less: rental expenses	6b	
	c	Net rental income or (loss)	6c	
	7	Other investment income (describe ▶)	7	
	8a	Gross amount from sale of assets other than inventory	(A) Securities / 8a	(B) Other	
	b	Less: cost or other basis and sales expenses	8b		
	c	Gain or (loss) (attach schedule) . . .	8c		
	d	Net gain or (loss) (combine line 8c, columns (A) and (B))	8d	
	9	Special fundraising events and activities (attach schedule—see instructions):		
	a	Gross revenue (not including $_____ of contributions reported on line 1a)	9a	
	b	Less: direct expenses	9b	
	c	Net income . . . . ·.	9c	
	10a	Gross sales less returns and allowances	10a	
	b	Less: cost of goods sold	10b	
	c	Gross profit or (loss) (attach schedule)	10c	
	11	Other revenue (from Part VII, line 103)	11	
	12	**Total revenue** (add lines 1d, 2, 3, 4, 5, 6c, 7, 8d, 9c, 10c, and 11)	12	
Expenses	**13**	Program services (from line 44, column (B)) (see instructions)	13	
	14	Management and general (from line 44, column (C)) (see instructions)	14	
	15	Fundraising (from line 44, column (D)) (see instructions)	15	
	16	Payments to affiliates (attach schedule—see instructions)	16	
	17	**Total expenses** (add lines 16 and 44, column (A))	17	
Net Assets	**18**	Excess or (deficit) for the year (subtract line 17 from line 12)	18	
	19	Net assets or fund balances at beginning of year (from line 74, column (A)) . . .	19	
	20	Other changes in net assets or fund balances (attach explanation)	20	
	21	Net assets or fund balances at end of year (combine lines 18, 19, and 20)	21	

For Paperwork Reduction Act Notice, see page 1 of the separate instructions.   Cat. No. 11282Y   Form **990** (1992)

Part II | **Statement of Functional Expenses** — All organizations must complete column (A). Columns (B), (C), and (D) are required for section 501(c)(3) and (4) organizations and 4947(a)(1) charitable trusts but optional for others. (See instructions.)

Do not include amounts reported on line 6b, 8b, 9b, 10b, or 16 of Part I.		**(A)** Total	**(B)** Program services	**(C)** Management and general	**(D)** Fundraising
22	Grants and allocations (attach schedule) . .	22				
23	Specific assistance to individuals (attach schedule)	23				
24	Benefits paid to or for members (attach schedule)	24				
25	Compensation of officers, directors, etc. . .	25				
26	Other salaries and wages	26				
27	Pension plan contributions	27				
28	Other employee benefits	28				
29	Payroll taxes	29				
30	Professional fundraising fees	30				
31	Accounting fees	31				
32	Legal fees	32				
33	Supplies.	33				
34	Telephone	34				
35	Postage and shipping	35				
36	Occupancy.	36				
37	Equipment rental and maintenance . . .	37				
38	Printing and publications	38				
39	Travel.	39				
40	Conferences, conventions, and meetings .	40				
41	Interest	41				
42	Depreciation, depletion, etc. (attach schedule) .	42				
43	Other expenses (itemize): **a**	43a				
b	....	43b				
c	....	43c				
d	....	43d				
e	....	43e				
f	....	43f				
44	**Total functional expenses** (add lines 22 through 43) *Organizations completing columns (B)-(D), carry these totals to lines 13-15* .	44				

Reporting of Joint Costs.—Did you report in column (B) (Program services) any joint costs from a combined educational campaign and fundraising solicitation? . . . . ▶ ☐ Yes ☐ No

If "Yes," enter **(i)** the aggregate amount of these joint costs $_____ ; **(ii)** the amount allocated to program services $_____ ;
(iii) the amount allocated to management and general $_____ ; and **(iv)** the amount allocated to fundraising $_____ .

Part III | **Statement of Program Service Accomplishments** (See instructions.)

Describe what was achieved in carrying out the organization's exempt purposes. Fully describe the services provided; the number of persons benefited; or other relevant information for each program title. Section 501(c)(3) and (4) organizations and section 4947(a)(1) charitable trusts must also enter the amount of grants and allocations to others.

Expenses
(Required for 501(c)(3) and (4) organizations and 4947(a)(1) trusts; optional for others.)

a ....
....
....
(Grants and allocations $ _____)

b ....
....
....
(Grants and allocations $ _____)

c ....
....
....
(Grants and allocations $ _____)

d ....
....
....
(Grants and allocations $ _____)

e Other program services (attach schedule) . . . (Grants and allocations $ _____)

f **Total** (add lines **a** through **e**) (should equal line 44, column (B)) . . . . ▶

Part IV   **Balance Sheets**

Note: *Where required, attached schedules and amounts within the description column should be for end-of-year amounts only.*	**(A)** Beginning of year	**(B)** End of year
Assets		
45 Cash—non-interest-bearing	45	
46 Savings and temporary cash investments	46	
47a Accounts receivable **47a**		
b Less: allowance for doubtful accounts . . . **47b**	47c	
48a Pledges receivable **48a**		
b Less: allowance for doubtful accounts . . . **48b**	48c	
49 Grants receivable	49	
50 Receivables due from officers, directors, trustees, and key employees (attach schedule)	50	
51a Other notes and loans receivable (attach schedule) **51a**		
b Less: allowance for doubtful accounts . . . **51b**	51c	
52 Inventories for sale or use	52	
53 Prepaid expenses and deferred charges	53	
54 Investments—securities (attach schedule)	54	
55a Investments—land, buildings, and equipment: basis **55a**		
b Less: accumulated depreciation (attach schedule) **55b**	55c	
56 Investments—other (attach schedule)	56	
57a Land, buildings, and equipment: basis . . . **57a**		
b Less: accumulated depreciation (attach schedule) **57b**	57c	
58 Other assets (describe ▶ _____)	58	
59 **Total assets** (add lines 45 through 58) (must equal line 75)	59	
Liabilities		
60 Accounts payable and accrued expenses	60	
61 Grants payable	61	
62 Support and revenue designated for future periods (attach schedule) . .	62	
63 Loans from officers, directors, trustees, and key employees (attach schedule).	63	
64 Mortgages and other notes payable (attach schedule)	64	
65 Other liabilities (describe ▶ _____)	65	
66 **Total liabilities** (add lines 60 through 65)	66	
Fund Balances or Net Assets		
Organizations that use fund accounting, check here ▶ ☐ and complete lines 67 through 70 and lines 74 and 75 (see instructions).		
67a Current unrestricted fund	67a	
b Current restricted fund	67b	
68 Land, buildings, and equipment fund	68	
69 Endowment fund	69	
70 Other funds (describe ▶ _____)	70	
Organizations that do not use fund accounting, check here ▶ ☐ and complete lines 71 through 75 (see instructions).		
71 Capital stock or trust principal	71	
72 Paid-in or capital surplus	72	
73 Retained earnings or accumulated income	73	
74 Total fund balances or net assets (add lines 67a through 70 OR lines 71 through 73: column (A) must equal line 19 and column (B) must equal line 21)	74	
75 **Total liabilities and fund balances/net assets** (add lines 66 and 74) . .	75	

Form 990 is available for public inspection and, for some people, serves as the primary or sole source of information about a particular organization. How the public perceives an organization in such cases may be determined by the information presented on its return. Therefore, please make sure the return is complete and accurate and fully describes the organization's programs and accomplishments.

Form 990 (1992)   Page **4**

| **Part V** | **List of Officers, Directors, Trustees, and Key Employees** (List each one even if not compensated. See instructions.) |

(A) Name and address	(B) Title and average hours per week devoted to position	(C) Compensation (if not paid, enter -0-)	(D) Contributions to employee benefit plans	(E) Expense account and other allowances
....				
....				
....				
....				

Did any officer, director, trustee, or key employee receive aggregate compensation of more than $100,000 from your organization and all related organizations, of which more than $10,000 was provided by the related organizations? ▶ ☐ Yes ☐ No
If "Yes," attach schedule (see instructions).

| **Part VI** | **Other Information** |

Note: *Section 501(c)(3) organizations and section 4947(a)(1) trusts must also complete and attach Schedule A (Form 990).*

			Yes	No
76	Did the organization engage in any activity not previously reported to the Internal Revenue Service? . .	76		
	If "Yes," attach a detailed description of each activity.			
77	Were any changes made in the organizing or governing documents, but not reported to the IRS? . . .	77		
	If "Yes," attach a conformed copy of the changes.			
78a	Did the organization have unrelated business gross income of $1,000 or more during the year covered by this return?	78a		
b	If "Yes," has it filed a tax return on **Form 990-T**, Exempt Organization Business Income Tax Return, for this year?	78b		
c	At any time during the year, did the organization own a 50% or greater interest in a taxable corporation or partnership?	78c		
	If "Yes," complete Part IX.			
79	Was there a liquidation, dissolution, termination, or substantial contraction during the year? (See instructions.)	79		
	If "Yes," attach a statement as described in the instructions.			
80a	Is the organization related (other than by association with a statewide or nationwide organization) through common membership, governing bodies, trustees, officers, etc., to any other exempt or non-exempt organization? (See instructions.)	80a		
b	If "Yes," enter the name of the organization ▶ .... and check whether it is ☐ exempt **OR** ☐ nonexempt.			
81a	Enter amount of political expenditures, direct or indirect, as described in the instructions . .	81a		
b	Did the organization file **Form 1120-POL**, U.S. Income Tax Return for Certain Political Organizations, for this year?	81b		
82a	Did the organization receive donated services or the use of materials, equipment, or facilities at no charge or at substantially less than fair rental value?	82a		
b	If "Yes," you may indicate the value of these items here. Do not include this amount as revenue in Part I or as an expense in Part II. See instructions for reporting in Part III .	82b			
83a	Did anyone request to see either the organization's annual return or exemption application (or both)? . .	83a		
b	If "Yes," did the organization comply as described in the instructions? (See General Instruction L.) . . .	83b		
84a	Did the organization solicit any contributions or gifts that were not tax deductible?	84a		
b	If "Yes," did the organization include with every solicitation an express statement that such contributions or gifts were not tax deductible? (See General Instruction M.)	84b		
85a	*Section 501(c)(5) or (6) organizations.*—Did the organization spend any amounts in attempts to influence public opinion about legislative matters or referendums? (See instructions and Regulations section 1.162-20(c).) . .	85a		
b	If "Yes," enter the total amount spent for this purpose	85b			
86	*Section 501(c)(7) organizations.*—Enter:			
a	Initiation fees and capital contributions included on line 12	86a			
b	Gross receipts, included on line 12, for public use of club facilities (see instructions)	86b			
c	Does the club's governing instrument or any written policy statement provide for discrimination against any person because of race, color, or religion? (If "Yes," attach statement. See instructions.)	86c		
87	*Section 501(c)(12) organizations.*—Enter amount of:			
a	Gross income received from members or shareholders	87a			
b	Gross income received from other sources. (Do not net amounts due or paid to other sources against amounts due or received from them.)	87b			
88	*Public interest law firms.*—Attach information described in the instructions.			
89	List the states with which a copy of this return is filed ▶			
90	During this tax year did the organization maintain any part of its accounting / tax records on a computerized system?	90		
91	The books are in care of ▶ ....Telephone no. ▶ (........) .... Located at ▶ .... ZIP code ▶			
92	*Section 4947(a)(1) charitable trusts filing Form 990 in lieu of* **Form 1041**, *U.S. Fiduciary Income Tax Return,* should check here ▶ ☐ and enter the amount of tax-exempt interest received or accrued during the tax year . . ▶	92			

Form 990 (1992)   Page **5**

Part VII   Analysis of Income-Producing Activities

Enter gross amounts unless otherwise indicated.	Unrelated business income		Excluded by section 512, 513, or 514		(e) Related or exempt function income (See instructions.)
	(a) Business code	**(b)** Amount	**(c)** Exclusion code	**(d)** Amount	
93 Program service revenue:					
(a) _____					
(b) _____					
(c) _____					
(d) _____					
(e) _____					
(f) _____					
(g) Fees from government agencies					
94 Membership dues and assessments					
95 Interest on savings and temporary cash investments .					
96 Dividends and interest from securities . . .					
97 Net rental income or (loss) from real estate:					
(a) debt-financed property					
(b) not debt-financed property					
98 Net rental income or (loss) from personal property .					
99 Other investment income					
100 Gain or (loss) from sales of assets other than inventory					
101 Net income from special fundraising events . .					
102 Gross profit or (loss) from sales of inventory .					
103 Other revenue: (a)_____					
(b) _____					
(c) _____					
(d) _____					
(e) _____					
104 Subtotal (add columns (b), (d), and (e)) . . .					

105 TOTAL (add line 104, columns (b), (d), and (e)) . . . . ▶ _____

Note: *(Line 105 plus line 1d, Part I, should equal the amount on line 12, Part I.)*

Part VIII   Relationship of Activities to the Accomplishment of Exempt Purposes

Line No. ▼	Explain how each activity for which income is reported in column (e) of Part VII contributed importantly to the accomplishment of the organization's exempt purposes (other than by providing funds for such purposes). (See instructions.)

Part IX   Information Regarding Taxable Subsidiaries (Complete this Part if the "Yes" box on 78c is checked.)

Name, address, and employer identification number of corporation or partnership	Percentage of ownership interest	Nature of business activities	Total income	End-of-year assets

Please Sign Here

Under penalties of perjury, I declare that I have examined this return, including accompanying schedules and statements, and to the best of my knowledge and belief, it is true, correct, and complete. Declaration of preparer (other than officer) is based on all information of which preparer has any knowledge.

▶ _____   _____   ▶ _____
    Signature of officer   Date   Title

Paid Preparer's Use Only

Preparer's signature ▶	Date	Check if self-employed ▶ ☐
Firm's name (or yours if self-employed) and address ▶	ZIP code	

IRS Form 990 Schedule A

[Instructions for use with this form are available from the IRS.]

SCHEDULE A (Form 990) Department of the Treasury Internal Revenue Service	**Organization Exempt Under Section 501(c)(3)** (Except Private Foundation), 501(e), 501(f), 501(k), or Section 4947(a)(1) Charitable Trust Supplementary Information ▶ **Attach to Form 990 (or Form 990EZ).**	OMB No. 1545-0047 19**92**

Name	Employer identification number

Part I — Compensation of the Five Highest Paid Employees Other Than Officers, Directors, and Trustees
(See specific instructions.) (List each one. If there are none, enter "None.")

(a) Name and address of employees paid more than $30,000	(b) Title and average hours per week devoted to position	(c) Compensation	(d) Contributions to employee benefit plans	(e) Expense account and other allowances

Total number of other employees paid over $30,000 . . . . ▶

Part II — Compensation of the Five Highest Paid Persons for Professional Services
(See specific instructions.) (List each one. If there are none, enter "None.")

(a) Name and address of persons paid more than $30,000	(b) Type of service	(c) Compensation

Total number of others receiving over $30,000 for professional services . . . . ▶

Part III — Statements About Activities

		Yes	No
1	During the year, has the organization attempted to influence national, state, or local legislation, including any attempt to influence public opinion on a legislative matter or referendum? **1**		
	If "Yes," enter the total expenses paid or incurred in connection with the lobbying activities. $ _____ Organizations that made an election under section 501(h) by filing Form 5768 must complete Part VI-A. Other organizations checking "Yes," must complete Part VI-B AND attach a statement giving a detailed description of the lobbying activities.		
2	During the year, has the organization, either directly or indirectly, engaged in any of the following acts with any of its trustees, directors, principal officers, or creators, or with any taxable organization or corporation with which any such person is affiliated as an officer, director, trustee, majority owner, or principal beneficiary:		
a	Sale, exchange, or leasing of property? **2a**		
b	Lending of money or other extension of credit? **2b**		
c	Furnishing of goods, services, or facilities? **2c**		
d	Payment of compensation (or payment or reimbursement of expenses if more than $1,000)? **2d**		
e	Transfer of any part of its income or assets? **2e**		
	If the answer to any question is "Yes," attach a detailed statement explaining the transactions.		
3	Does the organization make grants for scholarships, fellowships, student loans, etc.? **3**		
4	Attach a statement explaining how the organization determines that individuals or organizations receiving grants or loans from it in furtherance of its charitable programs qualify to receive payments. (See specific instructions.)		

For Paperwork Reduction Act Notice, see page 1 of the Instructions to Form 990 (or Form 990EZ).   Cat. No. 11285F   **Schedule A (Form 990) 1992**

Schedule A (Form 990) 1992   Page **2**

Part IV   **Reason for Non-Private Foundation Status** (See instructions for definitions.)

The organization is not a private foundation because it is (please check only **ONE** applicable box):

5   ☐   A church, convention of churches, or association of churches. Section 170(b)(1)(A)(i).

6   ☐   A school. Section 170(b)(1)(A)(ii). (Also complete Part V, page 3.)

7   ☐   A hospital or a cooperative hospital service organization. Section 170(b)(1)(A)(iii).

8   ☐   A Federal, state, or local government or governmental unit. Section 170(b)(1)(A)(v).

9   ☐   A medical research organization operated in conjunction with a hospital. Section 170(b)(1)(A)(iii). **Enter name, city, and state of**
         hospital ▶ ....

10   ☐   An organization operated for the benefit of a college or university owned or operated by a governmental unit. Section 170(b)(1)(A)(iv).
         (Also complete Support Schedule.)

11a ☐   An organization that normally receives a substantial part of its support from a governmental unit or from the general public.
         Section 170(b)(1)(A)(vi). (Also complete Support Schedule.)

11b ☐   A community trust. Section 170(b)(1)(A)(vi). (Also complete Support Schedule.)

12   ☐   An organization that normally receives: **(a)** no more than ⅓ of its support from gross investment income and unrelated business
         taxable income (less section 511 tax) from businesses acquired by the organization after June 30, 1975, and **(b)** more than ⅓ of
         its support from contributions, membership fees, and gross receipts from activities related to its charitable, etc., functions—subject
         to certain exceptions. See section 509(a)(2). (Also complete Support Schedule.)

13   ☐   An organization that is not controlled by any disqualified persons (other than foundation managers) and supports organizations
         described in: **(1)** boxes 5 through 12 above; or **(2)** section 501(c)(4), (5), or (6), if they meet the test of section 509(a)(2). (See
         section 509(a)(3).)

Provide the following information about the supported organizations. (See instructions for Part IV, box 13.)

(a) Name(s) of supported organization(s)	**(b)** Box number from above

14   ☐   An organization organized and operated to test for public safety. Section 509(a)(4). (See specific instructions.)

Support Schedule (Complete only if you checked box 10, 11, or 12 above.) *Use cash method of accounting.*

Calendar year (or fiscal year beginning in) . ▶	**(a)** 1991	**(b)** 1990	**(c)** 1989	**(d)** 1988	**(e)** Total
15 Gifts, grants, and contributions received. (Do not include unusual grants. See line 28.). .					
16 Membership fees received					
17 Gross receipts from admissions, merchandise sold or services performed, or furnishing of facilities in any activity that is not a business unrelated to the organization's charitable, etc., purpose.					
18 Gross income from interest, dividends, amounts received from payments on securities loans (section 512(a)(5)), rents, royalties, and unrelated business taxable income (less section 511 taxes) from businesses acquired by the organization after June 30, 1975. . . .					
19 Net income from unrelated business activities not included in line 18					
20 Tax revenues levied for the organization's benefit and either paid to it or expended on its behalf .					
21 The value of services or facilities furnished to the organization by a governmental unit without charge. Do not include the value of services or facilities generally furnished to the public without charge . .					
22 Other income. Attach schedule. Do not include gain or (loss) from sale of capital assets. . .					
23 Total of lines 15 through 22.					
24 Line 23 minus line 17.					
25 Enter 1% of line 23					/////////
26 Organizations described in box 10 or 11:					
a Enter 2% of amount in column (e), line 24					
b Attach a list (not open to public inspection) showing the name of and amount contributed by each person (other than a governmental unit or publicly supported organization) whose total gifts for 1988 through 1991 exceeded the amount shown in line 26a. Enter the sum of all excess amounts here . . . . ▶					

(Continued on page 3)

| **Part IV** | **Support Schedule** (continued) (Complete only if you checked box 10, 11, or 12 on page 2.) |

27 Organizations described in box 12, page 2:

a Attach a list for amounts shown on lines 15, 16, and 17, showing the name of, and total amounts received in each year from, each "disqualified person," and enter the sum of such amounts for each year:

(1991) .... (1990) .... (1989) .... (1988) ....

b Attach a list showing, for 1988 through 1991, the name of, and amount included in line 17 for, each person (other than a "disqualified person") from whom the organization received more during that year than the larger of: **(1)** the amount on line 25 for the year; or **(2)** $5,000. Include organizations described in boxes 5 through 11 as well as individuals. Enter the sum of these excess amounts for each year:

(1991) .... (1990) .... (1989) .... (1988) ....

28 For an organization described in box 10, 11, or 12, page 2, that received any unusual grants during 1988 through 1991, attach a list (not open to public inspection) for each year showing the name of the contributor, the date and amount of the grant, and a brief description of the nature of the grant. Do not include these grants in line 15. (See specific instructions.)

| **Part V** | **Private School Questionnaire** |
| | **(To be completed ONLY by schools that checked box 6 in Part IV)** |

		Yes	No
29	Does the organization have a racially nondiscriminatory policy toward students by statement in its charter, bylaws, other governing instrument, or in a resolution of its governing body? **29**		
30	Does the organization include a statement of its racially nondiscriminatory policy toward students in all its brochures, catalogues, and other written communications with the public dealing with student admissions, programs, and scholarships? **30**		
31	Has the organization publicized its racially nondiscriminatory policy through newspaper or broadcast media during the period of solicitation for students, or during the registration period if it has no solicitation program, in a way that makes the policy known to all parts of the general community it serves?. **31**		
	If "Yes," please describe; if "No," please explain. (If you need more space, attach a separate statement.)		

32	Does the organization maintain the following:		
a	Records indicating the racial composition of the student body, faculty, and administrative staff? **32a**		
b	Records documenting that scholarships and other financial assistance are awarded on a racially nondiscriminatory basis? **32b**		
c	Copies of all catalogues, brochures, announcements, and other written communications to the public dealing with student admissions, programs, and scholarships? **32c**		
d	Copies of all material used by the organization or on its behalf to solicit contributions? **32d**		
	If you answered "No" to any of the above, please explain. (If you need more space, attach a separate statement.)		

33	Does the organization discriminate by race in any way with respect to:		
a	Students' rights or privileges? **33a**		
b	Admissions policies? **33b**		
c	Employment of faculty or administrative staff? **33c**		
d	Scholarships or other financial assistance? (See instructions.). **33d**		
e	Educational policies? **33e**		
f	Use of facilities? **33f**		
g	Athletic programs? **33g**		
h	Other extracurricular activities? **33h**		
	If you answered "Yes" to any of the above, please explain. (If you need more space, attach a separate statement.)		

34a	Does the organization receive any financial aid or assistance from a governmental agency? **34a**		
b	Has the organization's right to such aid ever been revoked or suspended? **34b**		
	If you answered "Yes" to either 34a or b, please explain using an attached statement.		
35	Does the organization certify that it has complied with the applicable requirements of sections 4.01 through 4.05 of Rev. Proc. 75-50, 1975-2 C.B. 587, covering racial nondiscrimination? If "No," attach an explanation. (See instructions for Part V.) **35**		

Schedule A (Form 990) 1992   Page **4**

Part VI-A   **Lobbying Expenditures by Electing Public Charities** (see instructions)
                (To be completed **ONLY** by an eligible organization that filed Form 5768)

Check here ▶   **a** ☐ If the organization belongs to an affiliated group (see instructions).
Check here ▶   **b** ☐ If you checked **a** and "limited control" provisions apply (see instructions).

Limits on Lobbying Expenditures ("Expenditures" means amounts paid or incurred)		**(a)** Affiliated group totals	**(b)** To be completed for ALL electing organizations
36	Total lobbying expenditures to influence public opinion (grassroots lobbying) **36**		
37	Total lobbying expenditures to influence a legislative body (direct lobbying) **37**		
38	Total lobbying expenditures (add lines 36 and 37) **38**		
39	Other exempt purpose expenditures (see Part VI-A instructions) **39**		
40	Total exempt purpose expenditures (add lines 38 and 39) (see instructions) **40**		
41	Lobbying nontaxable amount. Enter the amount from the following table—		

If the amount on line 40 is—	**The lobbying nontaxable amount is—**
Not over $500,000	20% of the amount on line 40 . . . . .
Over $500,000 but not over $1,000,000.	$100,000 plus 15% of the excess over $500,000
Over $1,000,000 but not over $1,500,000	$175,000 plus 10% of the excess over $1,000,000
Over $1,500,000 but not over $17,000,000	$225,000 plus 5% of the excess over $1,500,000
Over $17,000,000	$1,000,000. . . . .

41

42	Grassroots nontaxable amount (enter 25% of line 41) **42**		
43	Subtract line 42 from line 36. Enter -0- if line 42 is more than line 36 . . . . . **43**		
44	Subtract line 41 from line 38. Enter -0- if line 41 is more than line 38 . . . . . . **44**		

Caution: *File Form 4720 if there is an amount on either line 43 or line 44.*

4-Year Averaging Period Under Section 501(h)

(Some organizations that made a section 501(h) election do not have to complete all of the five columns below.
See the instructions for lines 45–50 for details.)

Calendar year (or fiscal year beginning in) ▶	**Lobbying Expenditures During 4-Year Averaging Period**				
	(a) 1992	**(b)** 1991	**(c)** 1990	**(d)** 1989	**(e)** Total
45 Lobbying nontaxable amount (see instructions)					
46 Lobbying ceiling amount (150% of line 45(e))					
47 Total lobbying expenditures (see instructions)					
48 Grassroots nontaxable amount (see instructions)					
49 Grassroots ceiling amount (150% of line 48(e))					
50 Grassroots lobbying expenditures (see instructions)					

Part VI-B   **Lobbying Activity by Nonelecting Public Charities**
                (For reporting by organizations that did not complete Part VI-A.)

During the year, did the organization attempt to influence national, state or local legislation, including any attempt to influence public opinion on a legislative matter or referendum, through the use of:	Yes	No	Amount
a Volunteers			
b Paid staff or management (include compensation in expenses reported on lines c through h) . . .			
c Media advertisements			
d Mailings to members, legislators, or the public			
e Publications or published or broadcast statements			
f Grants to other organizations for lobbying purposes			
g Direct contact with legislators, their staffs, government officials, or a legislative body			
h Rallies, demonstrations, seminars, conventions, speeches, lectures, or any other means			
i Total lobbying expenditures (add lines c through h)			

If "Yes" to any of the above, also attach a statement giving a detailed description of the lobbying activities.

Schedule A (Form 990) 1992   Page **5**

Part VII	**Information Regarding Transfers To and Transactions and Relationships With Noncharitable Exempt Organizations**

51 Did the reporting organization directly or indirectly engage in any of the following with any other organization described in section 501(c) of the Code (other than section 501(c)(3) organizations) or in section 527, relating to political organizations?

				Yes	No
a	Transfers from the reporting organization to a noncharitable exempt organization of:				
	(i) Cash		**51a(i)**		
	(ii) Other assets		**a(ii)**		
b	Other Transactions:				
	(i) Sales of assets to a noncharitable exempt organization		**b(i)**		
	(ii) Purchases of assets from a noncharitable exempt organization		**b(ii)**		
	(iii) Rental of facilities or equipment		**b(iii)**		
	(iv) Reimbursement arrangements		**b(iv)**		
	(v) Loans or loan guarantees		**b(v)**		
	(vi) Performance of services or membership or fundraising solicitations		**b(vi)**		
c	Sharing of facilities, equipment, mailing lists or other assets, or paid employees		**c**		

d If the answer to any of the above is "Yes," complete the following schedule. The "Amount involved" column below should always indicate the fair market value of the goods, other assets, or services given by the reporting organization. If the organization received less than fair market value in any transaction or sharing arrangement, indicate in column (d) the value of the goods, other assets, or services received.

(a) Line no.	(b) Amount involved	(c) Name of noncharitable exempt organization	(d) Description of transfers, transactions, and sharing arrangements

52a Is the organization directly or indirectly affiliated with, or related to, one or more tax-exempt organizations described in section 501(c) of the Code (other than section 501(c)(3)) or in section 527? . . . . ☐ **Yes** ☐ **No**

b If "Yes," complete the following schedule.

(a) Name of organization	(b) Type of organization	(c) Description of relationship

§107. IRS FORM 990-T; TAXABLE BUSINESS INCOME OF EXEMPT ORGANIZATIONS.

[Instructions for use with this form are available from the IRS.]

Form **990-T**	**Exempt Organization Business Income Tax Return**	OMB No. 1545-0687
	For calendar year 1992 or other tax year beginning ...., 1992, and ending ...., 19	**1992**
Department of the Treasury Internal Revenue Service	Instructions are separate. See page 1 for Paperwork Reductions Act Notice.	

A ☐ Check box if address changed	**Please Print or Type**	Name of organization	C **Employer identification number** (Employees' trust, see instructions for Block C)
B Exempt under section ☐ 501(c)( ) or ☐ 408(e)		Number, street, and room or suite no. (If a P.O. box, see page 3 of instructions.)	
		City or town, state, and ZIP code	D **Unrelated business activity codes** (See instructions for Block D)

E   Check type of organization . . . . ▶ ☐ Corporation   ☐ Trust   ☐ Section 401(a) trust   ☐ Section 408(a) trust

F   Group exemption number (see instructions for Block F) ▶

G   Describe the organization's primary unrelated business activity. (see instructions for Block G)

H   During the tax year, was the corporation a subsidiary in an affiliated group or a parent-subsidiary controlled group? . . ▶ ☐ Yes ☐ No
If "Yes," enter the name and identifying number of the parent corporation. (see instructions for Block H) ▶

Part I **Unrelated Trade or Business Income**		(A) Income	(B) Expenses	(C) Net
1a	Gross receipts or sales _____			
b	Less returns and allowances _____ c Balance ▶ 1c			
2	Cost of goods sold (Schedule A, line 7) 2			
3	Gross profit (subtract line 2 from line 1c) 3			
4a	Capital gain net income (attach Schedule D) 4a			
b	Net gain (loss) (Form 4797, Part II, line 20) (attach Form 4797) 4b			
c	Capital loss deduction for trusts 4c			
5	Income (loss) from partnerships (attach statement) . . . 5			
6	Rent income (Schedule C) 6			
7	Unrelated debt-financed income (Schedule E). 7			
8	Interest, annuities, royalties, and rents from controlled organizations (Schedule F) 8			
9	Investment income of a section 501(c)(7), (9), (17), or (20) organization (Schedule G) 9			
10	Exploited exempt activity income (Schedule I). 10			
11	Advertising income (Schedule J) 11			
12	Other income (see instructions for line 12—attach schedule) . 12			
13	TOTAL (add lines 3 through 12) 13			

Part II **Deductions Not Taken Elsewhere** (See instructions for limitations on deductions.) (Except for contributions, deductions must be directly connected with the unrelated business income.)		
14	Compensation of officers, directors, and trustees (Schedule K)	14	
15	Salaries and wages	15	
16	Repairs.	16	
17	Bad debts.	17	
18	Interest (attach schedule).	18	
19	Taxes	19	
20	Charitable contributions (see instructions for limitation rules)	20	
21	Depreciation (attach Form 4562) 21		
22	Less depreciation claimed on Schedule A and elsewhere on return . 22a	22b	
23	Depletion	23	
24	Contributions to deferred compensation plans	24	
25	Employee benefit programs	25	
26	Excess exempt expenses (Schedule I)	26	
27	Excess readership costs (Schedule J)	27	
28	Other deductions (attach schedule)	28	
29	TOTAL DEDUCTIONS (add lines 14 through 28)	29	
30	Unrelated business taxable income before net operating loss deduction (subtract line 29 from line 13).	30	
31	Net operating loss deduction	31	
32	Unrelated business taxable income before specific deduction (subtract line 31 from line 30) . .	32	
33	Specific deduction	33	
34	Unrelated business taxable income (subtract line 33 from line 32). If line 33 is greater than line 32, enter the smaller of zero or line 32	34	

Cat. No. 11291J   Form **990-T** (1992)

Form 990-T (1992)　　　　　　　　　　　　　　　　　　　　　　　　　　　　　　Page **2**

Part III　　Tax Computation

35	Amount from line 34 (unrelated business taxable income)	**35**	
36	**Organizations Taxable as Corporations** (see instructions for tax computation) Controlled group members (sections 1561 and 1563)—Check here ☐ and:		
a	Enter your share of the $50,000 and $25,000 taxable income bracket amounts (in that order): *(i)* |$ |_____| |_____| *(ii)* |$ |_____| |_____|		
b	Enter your share of the additional 5% tax (not to exceed $11,750) \|$ |_____|		
c	Income tax on the amount on line 35	**36c**	
37	**Trusts Taxable at Trust Rates** (see instructions for tax computation) Income tax on the amount on line 35 from: ☐ Tax rate schedule or ☐ Schedule D (Form 1041)	**37**	

Part IV　　Tax and Payments

38a	Foreign tax credit (corporations attach Form 1118; trusts attach Form 1116) .	**38a**		
b	Other credits (see instructions)	**38b**		
c	General business credit—Check if from: ☐ Form 3800 or ☐ Form (specify) ▶...................................	**38c**		
d	Credit for prior year minimum tax (attach Form 8801 or 8827) . . .	**38d**		
39	Total (add lines 38a through 38d)		**39**	
40	Subtract line 39 from line 36c or line 37.		**40**	
41	Recapture taxes. Check if from: ☐ Form 4255 ☐ Form 8611		**41**	
42a	Alternative minimum tax .... **b** Environmental tax		**42c**	
43	**Total tax** (add lines 40, 41, and 42c).		**43**	
44	**Payments: a** 1991 overpayment credited to 1992	**44a**		
b	1992 estimated tax payments	**44b**		
c	Tax deposited with Form 7004 or Form 2758	**44c**		
d	Foreign organizations—Tax paid or withheld at source (see instructions) . .	**44d**		
e	Other credits and payments (see instructions).	**44e**		
45	Total credits and payments (add lines 44a through 44e)		**45**	
46	Estimated tax penalty (see the instructions on page 2). Check ▶ ☐ if Form 2220 is attached .		**46**	
47	**Tax due** —If line 45 is less than the total of lines 43 and 46, enter amount owed . . . . . ▶		**47**	
48	**Overpayment** —If line 45 is larger than the total of lines 43 and 46, enter amount overpaid . . ▶		**48**	
49	Enter the amount on line 48 you want: **Credited to 1993 estimated tax** ▶ 　　**Refunded** ▶		**49**	

Part V　　Statements Regarding Certain Activities and Other Information (See instructions on page 8.)

		Yes	No
1	At any time during the 1992 calendar year, did the organization have an interest in or a signature or other authority over a financial account in a foreign country (such as a bank account, securities account, or other financial account)? If "Yes," the organization may have to file Form TD F 90-22.1. If "Yes," enter the name of the foreign country here ▶		
2	Was the organization the grantor of, or transferor to, a foreign trust that existed during the current tax year, whether or not the organization had any beneficial interest in it? . . . . If " Yes," the organization may have to file Forms 3520, 3520-A, or 926.		
3	Enter the amount of tax-exempt interest received or accrued during the tax year ▶ $		

SCHEDULE A—COST OF GOODS SOLD (See instructions on page 8.)

Method of inventory valuation (specify) ▶

1	Inventory at beginning of year	**1**		6	Inventory at end of year. . . .	**6**		
2	Purchases.	**2**		7	Cost of goods sold. Subtract line 6 from line 5. (Enter here and on line 2, Part I.)	**7**		
3	Cost of labor	**3**						
4a	Additional section 263A costs (attach schedule)	**4a**		8	Do the rules of section 263A (with respect to property produced or acquired for resale) apply to the organization?		Yes	No
b	Other costs (attach schedule)	**4b**						
5	TOTAL—Add lines 1 through 4b	**5**						

The books are in care of ▶　　　　　　　　　　　　　　Telephone number ▶ (　　　)

Please Sign Here	▶			
	Signature of officer or fiduciary	Date	Title	

Paid Preparer's Use Only	Preparer's signature ▶	Date	Check if self-employed ▶ ☐	Preparer's social security number
	Firm's name (or yours, if self-employed) and address ▶		E.I. No. ▶ ZIP code ▶	

Form 990-T (1992)   Page **3**

SCHEDULE C—RENT INCOME (FROM REAL PROPERTY AND PERSONAL PROPERTY LEASED WITH REAL PROPERTY)
(See instructions on page 8.)

1 Description of property

(1)

(2)

(3)

(4)

2 Rent received or accrued		**3** Deductions directly connected with the income in columns 2a and 2b (attach schedule)
a From personal property (if the percentage of rent for personal property is more than 10% but not more than 50%)	**b** From real and personal property (if the percentage of rent for personal property exceeds 50% or if the rent is based on profit or income)	
(1)		
(2)		
(3)		
(4)		
Total	Total	

Total Income (Add totals of columns 2a and 2b. Enter here and on line 6, column (A), Part I, page 1.) ▶

Total deductions. Enter here and on line 6, column (B), Part I, page 1. ▶

SCHEDULE E—UNRELATED DEBT-FINANCED INCOME (See instructions on page 9.)

1 Description of debt-financed property	**2** Gross income from or allocable to debt-financed property	**3** Deductions directly connected with or allocable to debt-financed property	
		(a) Straight line depreciation (attach schedule)	**(b)** Other deductions (attach schedule)
(1)			
(2)			
(3)			
(4)			

4 Amount of average acquisition debt on or allocable to debt-financed property (attach schedule)	**5** Average adjusted basis of or allocable to debt-financed property (attach schedule)	**6** Column 4 divided by column 5	**7** Gross income reportable (column 2 × column 6)	**8** Allocable deductions (column 6 × total of columns 3(a) and 3(b))
(1)		%		
(2)		%		
(3)		%		
(4)		%		
			Enter here and on line 7, column (A), Part I, page 1.	Enter here and on line 7, column (B), Part I, page 1.

Totals . . . . ▶

Total dividends-received deductions included in column 8 . . . . ▶

SCHEDULE F—INTEREST, ANNUITIES, ROYALTIES, AND RENTS FROM CONTROLLED ORGANIZATIONS
(See instructions on page 9.)

1 Name and address of controlled organization(s)	**2** Gross income from controlled organization(s)	**3** Deductions of controlling organization directly connected with column 2 income (attach schedule)	**4** Exempt controlled organizations		
			(a) Unrelated business taxable income	**(b)** Taxable income computed as though not exempt under sec. 501(a), or the amount in col. (a), whichever is larger	**(c)** column (a) divided by column (b)
(1)					%
(2)					%
(3)					%
(4)					%

5 Nonexempt controlled organizations			**6** Gross income reportable (column 2 × column 4(c) or column 5(c))	**7** Allowable deductions (column 3 × column 4(c) or column 5(c))
(a) Excess taxable income	**(b)** Taxable income, or amount in column (a), whichever is larger	**(c)** Column (a) divided by Column (b)		
(1)		%		
(2)		%		
(3)		%		
(4)		%		
			Enter here and on line 8, column (A), Part I, page 1.	Enter here and on line 8, column (B), Part I, page 1.

Totals. . . . . ▶

SCHEDULE G—INVESTMENT INCOME OF A SECTION 501(c)(7), (9), (17), OR (20) ORGANIZATION
(See instructions on page 10.)

1 Description of income	2 Amount of income	3 Deductions directly connected (attach schedule)	4 Set-asides (attach schedule)	5 Total deductions and set-asides (col. 3 plus col. 4)
(1)				
(2)				
(3)				
(4)				
Totals .... ▶	Enter here and on line 9, column (A), Part I, page 1.			Enter here and on line 9, column (B), Part I, page 1.

SCHEDULE I—EXPLOITED EXEMPT ACTIVITY INCOME, OTHER THAN ADVERTISING INCOME
(See instructions on page 10.)

1 Description of exploited activity	2 Gross unrelated business income from trade or business	3 Expenses directly connected with production of unrelated business income	4 Net income (loss) from unrelated trade or business (column 2 minus column 3). If a gain, compute cols. 5 through 7.	5 Gross income from activity that is not unrelated business income	6 Expenses attributable to column 5	7 Excess exempt expenses (column 6 minus column 5, but not more than column 4).
(1)						
(2)						
(3)						
(4)						
Column totals .... ▶	Enter here and on line 10, col. (A), Part I, page 1.	Enter here and on line 10, col. (B), Part I, page 1.				Enter here and on line 26, Part II, page 1.

SCHEDULE J—ADVERTISING INCOME (See instructions on page 10.)

Part I Income From Periodicals Reported on a Separate Basis (For each periodical listed in Part I, be sure to fill in columns 2 through 7 on a line-by-line basis.)

1 Name of periodical	2 Gross advertising income (Enter the total of this column on line 11, col. (A), Part I, page 1)	3 Direct advertising costs (Enter the total of this column on line 11, col. (B), Part I, page 1)	4 Advertising gain or (loss) (col. 2 minus col. 3). If a gain, compute cols. 5 through 7.	5 Circulation income	6 Readership costs	7 Excess readership costs (column 6 minus column 5, but not more than column 4). Enter the total of this column on line 27, Part II, page 1.
(1)						
(2)						
(3)						
(4)						

Part II Income From Periodicals Reported on a Consolidated Basis (If you listed periodicals in Part I above, use a separate Schedule J to report income from periodicals on a consolidated basis in Part II and see the instructions.)

(1)						
(2)						
(3)						
(4)						
Column totals .... ▶	Enter here and on line 11, col. (A), Part I, page 1.	Enter here and on line 11, col. (B), Part I, page 1.				Enter here and on line 27, Part II, page 1.

SCHEDULE K—COMPENSATION OF OFFICERS, DIRECTORS, AND TRUSTEES (See instructions on page 10.)

1 Name	2 Title	3 Percent of time devoted to business	4 Compensation attributable to unrelated business
		%	
		%	
		%	
		%	
Total (enter here and on line 14, Part II, page 1) . . . . ▶			

§108. IRS FORM 2758; APPLICATION FOR EXTENSION OF TIME TO FILE FORM 990.

Form 2758
(Rev. August 1992)
Department of the Treasury
Internal Revenue Service

**Application for Extension of Time To File
Certain Excise, Income, Information, and Other Returns**

▶ File a separate application for each return.

OMB No. 1545-0148
Expires 5-31-95

Please type or print. File the **original and one copy** by the due date for filing your return. (See instructions on back.)

Name	Employer identification number
Number and street, (or P.O. box no. if mail is not delivered to street address.)	Apt. or suite no.
City, town or post office, state, and ZIP code. (For a foreign address, see instructions.)	

Note: Taxpayers who file a corporation income tax return, including Forms 990-C, 990-T, and 1120S, must use **Form 7004** to request an extension of time to file.
Partnerships, REMICs, and trusts (except those filing Form 990-T) must use **Form 8736** to request an extension of time to file.

1   An extension of time until ...., 19 ...., is requested to file (check only one):

☐ Form 706GS(D)   ☐ Form 990-PF   ☐ Form 1041-A   ☐ Form 3520-A   ☐ Form 8612
☐ Form 706GS(T)   ☐ Form 990-T (401(a) or 408(a) trust)   ☐ Form 1042   ☐ Form 4720   ☐ Form 8613
☐ Form 990 or 990EZ   ☐ Form 990-T (trust other than above)   ☐ Form 1042S   ☐ Form 5227   ☐ Form 8725
☐ Form 990-BL   ☐ Form 1041 (estate) (see instructions)   ☐ Form 1120-ND (4951 taxes)   ☐ Form 6069   ☐ Form 8804

If the organization does not have an office or place of business in the United States, check this box. . . . . . ▶ ☐

2a   For calendar year 19 ....., or other tax year beginning .... and ending ....
b   If this tax year is for less than 12 months, check reason: ☐ Initial return ☐ Final return ☐ Change in accounting period
3   Has an extension of time to file been previously granted for this tax year? . . . . ☐ Yes ☐ No
4   State in detail why you need the extension. ....

5a   If this form is for Form 706GS(D), 706GS(T), 990-BL, 990-PF, 990-T, 1041 (estate), 1042, 1120-ND, 4720, 6069, 8612, 8613, 8725, or 8804, enter the tentative tax, less any nonrefundable credits. (See instructions.) $ _____
b   If this form is for Form 990-PF, 990-T, 1041 (estate), 1042, or 8804, enter any refundable credits and estimated tax payments made. Include any prior year overpayment allowed as a credit . . . . . $ _____
c   **Balance due** (subtract line 5b from line 5a). Include your payment with this form, or deposit with FTD coupon if required. (See instructions.) . . . . $ _____

Signature and Verification

Under penalties of perjury, I declare that I have examined this form, including accompanying schedules and statements, and to the best of my knowledge and belief, it is true, correct, and complete; and that I am authorized to prepare this form.

Signature ▶   Title ▶   Date ▶

FILE ORIGINAL AND ONE COPY. The IRS will show below whether or not your application is approved and will return the copy.

Notice to Applicant—To Be Completed by the IRS

☐ We **HAVE** approved your application. Please attach this form to your return.
☐ We **HAVE NOT** approved your application. However, we have granted a 10-day grace period from the later of the date shown below or the due date of your return (including any prior extensions). This grace period is considered to be a valid extension of time for elections otherwise required to be made on a timely return. Please attach this form to your return.
☐ We **HAVE NOT** approved your application. After considering the reasons stated in item 4, we cannot grant your request for an extension of time to file. We are not granting the 10-day grace period.
☐ We cannot consider your application because it was filed after the due date of the return for which an extension was requested.
☐ Other: ....

Director   By: _____   Date

If you want a copy of this form to be returned to an address other than that shown above, please enter the address to which the copy should be sent.

Please Type or Print

Name	
Number and street, (or P.O. box no. if mail is not delivered to street address.)	Apt. or suite no.
City, town or post office, state, and ZIP code. (For a foreign address, see instructions.)	

For Paperwork Reduction Act Notice, see back of form.   Cat. No. 11976B   Form **2758** (Rev. 8-92)

General Instructions

(Section references are to the Internal Revenue Code unless otherwise noted.)

Paperwork Reduction Act Notice.—We ask for the information on this form to carry out the Internal Revenue laws of the United States. You are required to give us the information. We need it to ensure that you are complying with these laws and to allow us to figure and collect the right amount of tax.

The time needed to complete and file this form will vary depending on individual circumstances. The estimated average time is:

Recordkeeping.	3 hr., 35 min.
Learning about the law or the form	6 min.
Preparing and sending the form to the IRS	10 min.

If you have comments concerning the accuracy of these time estimates or suggestions for making this form more simple, we would be happy to hear from you. You can write to both the **Internal Revenue Service,** Washington, DC 20224, Attention: IRS Reports Clearance Officer, T:FP; and the **Office of Management and Budget,** Paperwork Reduction Project (1545-0148), Washington, DC 20503. **DO NOT** send the tax form to either of these offices. Instead, see **Where To File** below.

Purpose of Form.—Use Form 2758 to request an extension of time to file any of the returns listed under line 1, page 1.

Note: *An extension of time granted by filing Form 2758 will apply only to the specific return checked on line 1. It does not extend the time for filing any related returns. For example, an extension of time for filing an estate's income tax return will not apply to the individual income tax returns of the beneficiaries.*

When To File.—File Form 2758 by the regular due date (or the extended due date if a previous extension was granted) of the return for which an extension is needed. However, to avoid a possible late filing penalty in case your request for an extension is not granted, you should file Form 2758 early enough to allow the IRS to consider your application and reply before the return's regular or extended due date.

No Blanket Requests.—File a separate Form 2758 for each return for which you are requesting an extension of time to file. Blanket requests for extensions will not be granted.

Note: *Black lung benefit trusts, their trustees, and any disqualified persons filing Form 990-BL must each file separate applications. Also, trustees and disqualified persons filing Form 1120-ND to report section 4951 taxes must each file separate applications.*

Exempt Organization Group Returns.—A central organization may request an extension of time to file a group return. Attach a schedule to Form 2758 showing the name and employer identification number of the local organizations that will be included in the group return.

Reasons for Extension.—The IRS will grant a reasonable extension of time for filing a return. You must file an application on time and show reasonable cause why the return cannot be filed by the due date. Generally, we will consider the application based on your efforts to fulfill the filing requirements, rather than on the convenience of your tax return preparer. However, if your tax return preparer is not able to complete the return by the due date for reasons beyond his or her control or, in spite of reasonable efforts, you are not able to get professional help in time to file, the IRS will generally grant the extension.

Caution: *If an extension is granted and the IRS later determines that the statements made on this form are false and misleading, the extension is null and void. You will be subject to the late filing penalty explained below.*

Extension Period.—Generally, we will not grant an extension of time for more than 90 days unless sufficient need for an extended period is clearly shown. In no event will we grant an extension of more than 6 months to an applicant living in the United States.

Where To File.—File the **original and one copy** of this form with the Internal Revenue Service Center serving the taxpayer's address. If you are requesting an extension for Form 1042 or 1042S and **do not** file Form 1042S on magnetic tape, or if you do not have a principal office or place of business in the United States, file this form with the Internal Revenue Service Center, Philadelphia, PA 19255.

If you are filing Form 1042S on magnetic tape, file this form with the Martinsburg Computing Center, P.O. Box 1359, Martinsburg, WV 25401.

File Form 2758 for Forms 990-BL and 6069 with the Internal Revenue Service Center, Cincinnati, OH 45999.

Filing Your Tax Return.—You may file your tax return any time before the extension of time is up.

Interest.—Interest is charged on any tax not paid by the regular due date of the return from the due date until the tax is paid. It will be charged even if you have been granted an extension or show reasonable cause for not paying on time.

Late Payment Penalty.—Generally, a penalty of ½ of 1% of any tax not paid by the due date is charged for each month or part of a month that the tax remains unpaid. The penalty cannot exceed 25% of the amount due. The penalty will not be charged if you can show reasonable cause for not paying on time.

Late Filing Penalty.—A penalty is charged if the return is filed after the due date (including extensions) unless you can show reasonable cause for filing late. The penalty is 5% of the tax not paid by the regular due date (even if an extension of time to pay has been granted) for each month or part of a month that the return is late, up to a maximum of 25% of the unpaid tax. For an income tax return more than 60 days late, the minimum penalty is $100 or the balance of the tax due on the return, whichever is smaller.

Different late filing penalties apply to information returns. See the specific form instructions for details.

Specific Instructions

Address.—If your address is outside the United States, or its possessions or territories, enter the information on the line for "City, town or post office, state, and ZIP code" in the following order: city, province or state, postal code, and the name of the country. Do not abbreviate the country name.

Note: *If your mailing address has changed since you filed your last return, use* **Form 8822,** *Change of Address, to notify the IRS of the change. (A new address shown on Form 2758 will not update your record.) To order Form 8822, call 1-800-TAX-FORM (1-800-829-3676).*

Line 1.—Check the box for the form for which you are requesting an extension. You must file a separate Form 2758 for each return. Check only one box. Use Form 2758 for **estates** that file Form 1041, U.S. Fiduciary Income Tax Return. **Trusts** that file Form 1041 must use Form 8736 to apply for an extension.

Line 4.—Clearly describe the reasons causing delay in your filing the return. We cannot approve applications that give incomplete reasons, such as "illness" or "practitioner too busy," without adequate explanations. If a request for an extension is made for no important reason but only to gain time, we will deny both the extension request and the 10-day grace period.

Line 5a.—See the specific form and form instructions to estimate the amount of the tentative tax, reduced by any nonrefundable credits.

Line 5c. Balance Due.—Form 2758 does not extend the time to pay tax. To avoid interest and penalties, send the full balance due with Form 2758.

Note: *If you are requesting an extension of time to file Form 990-T, do not send a payment with Form 2758. Instead, deposit the payment with* **Form 8109,** *Federal Tax Deposit Coupon. If you are requesting an extension of time to file Form 990-PF or 1042, see the deposit rules in the instructions for Form 990-PF or 1042 to determine whether payment must be made with a coupon or may be made with Form 2758.*

Signature.—The person who signs this form may be:

- A distributee, or an authorized representative of a distributee, filing Form 706GS(D).
- A trustee filing Form 706GS(T).
- A fiduciary, trustee, or an officer representing the fiduciary or trustee of an exempt trust filing Form 990, 990EZ, 990-BL, 990-PF, or 990-T.
- A principal officer of a corporate organization filing Form 990, 990EZ, 990-PF, 4720, 6069, 8612, or 8613.
- A foundation manager, trustee, or disqualified person filing Form 990-BL, 1120-ND, or 4720 for their own liability.
- A fiduciary, trustee, executor, administrator, or an officer representing the fiduciary or trustee filing Form 1041, 1041-A, 4720, or 5227.
- A withholding agent filing Form 1042 or 1042S.
- A grantor or transferor filing Form 3520-A.
- An individual filing Form 6069.
- A person authorized to sign Form 8725 for greenmail recipients.
- A general partner of a partnership filing Form 8804.
- An attorney or certified public accountant qualified to practice before the IRS.
- A person enrolled to practice before the IRS.
- A person holding a power of attorney.

§109. IRS FORMS FOR APPLICATION FOR RECOGNITION OF EXEMPTION.

FORM NO. 10 [IRS Form 2670: Exemption Certificate]

Form **2670** (Rev. November 1984) Department of the Treasury Internal Revenue Service	**Credit or Refund—Exemption Certificate For Use By A Nonprofit Educational Organization**

This certificate is for sales to a nonprofit educational organization to support: (1) a claim for credit or refund to the person who paid the manufacturers excise tax on the sale of articles under Chapter 32 of the Internal Revenue Code, or (2) the exemption of sales from the special fuels excise tax under Chapter 31 of the Code.

I certify that the articles specified in the accompanying order or the attached statement are being or were purchased from

-- by the organization named below for its exclusive use:

(Name and address of seller)

(a) ---

(Name and address of tax-exempt nonprofit educational organization described in section 501(c)(3) of the Code)

(b) ---

(Name and address of school operated as an activity of a church, parish, or other exempt organization described in section 501(c)(3) of the Code)

I further certify that all of the requirements explained on the back of this certificate have been met to permit: (1) credit or refund of the tax paid under Chapter 32 of the Code, or (2) exemption from the tax imposed by Chapter 31 of the Code.

If any article referred to in this certificate is used for other than the exempt purpose, I will report this fact to the manufacturer, importer, or retailer of the article.

---   -------------------------------------   ---------------------

(Signature)   (Title)   (Date)

Form **2670** (Rev. 11-84)

Instructions

(Section references are to the Internal Revenue Code.)

Section 6416 provides that a person who paid the manufacturers excise tax on an article may claim a credit or refund of this tax if the article was sold to a nonprofit educational organization for its exclusive use.

Section 4041 provides that a person who sells liquid fuel (diesel fuel and special motor fuels such as benzol, benzene, liquefied petroleum gas, etc.) to a nonprofit educational organization for its exclusive use may claim exemption from the special fuels excise tax.

The nonprofit educational organization must fill out this form and give it to the seller in order for the seller to claim a credit or refund of the manufacturers excise tax or an exemption from the special fuels excise tax.

A "nonprofit educational organization" is one that is exempt from income tax under section 501(a) and that meets the following tests:

(1) Its main function is formal education.

(2) It has a regular faculty and curriculum.

(3) It has a regularly enrolled body of students who attend the place where the instruction normally occurs.

A nonprofit educational organization also includes a school operated by a church or other organization described in section 501(c)(3) that meets the above tests.

The organization (other than a church, parish, or other religious body) operating a school must have a valid determination letter or ruling from IRS that states it is exempt from income tax under section 501(c)(3).

When tax-free sales of liquid fuel are regularly made to a nonprofit educational organization, this form can be used to cover all orders for a specified period of up to 12 calendar quarters.

Do not use this form to make tax-free sales to a nonprofit educational organization of articles subject to the manufacturers excise tax under Chapter 32 of the Code. Make such sales according to the registration requirements of section 4222(a) and applicable regulations.

The penalty for the fraudulent use of this certificate is a fine of not more than $10,000 or imprisonment for not more than 5 years or both, plus costs of prosecution.

☆ U.S. Government Printing Office: 1984—461-495/10086

FORM NO. 11 [IRS Form 5578: Statement of Nondiscrimination]

| Form **5578**
(Rev. February 1993)
Department of the Treasury
Internal Revenue Service | **Annual Certification of Racial Nondiscrimination
for a Private School Exempt From Federal Income Tax**
(For use by organizations that do not file Form 990 or Form 990-EZ) | OMB No. 1545 0213
Expires 1-31-96
**For IRS
use ONLY** ▶ |

For the period beginning _____ , 19____ and ending _____ , 19____

1a	Name of organization that operates, supervises, and/or controls school(s)	**1b** Employer identification number
	Address (number and street or P.O. box no. if mail is not delivered to street address) — Room/suite	
	City or town, state, and ZIP code	

2a	Name of central organization holding group exemption letter covering the school(s). (If same as 1a above, write "Same" and complete 2c.) If the organization in 1a above holds an individual exemption letter, write "Not Applicable."	**2b** Employer identification number
	Address (number and street or P.O. box no. if mail is not delivered to street address) — Room/suite	**2c** Group exemption number (see instructions under **Definitions**)
	City or town, state, and ZIP code	

3a	Name of school (if more than one school, write "See Attached," and attach list of the names, addresses, ZIP codes, and employer identification numbers of the schools). If same as 1a above, write "Same."	**3b** Employer identification number, if any
	Address (number and street or P.O. box no. if mail is not delivered to street address) — Room/suite	
	City or town, state, and ZIP code	

Under penalties of perjury, I hereby certify that I am authorized to take official action on behalf of the above school(s) and that to the best of my knowledge and belief the school(s) has (have) satisfied the applicable requirements of section 4.01 through 4.05 of Revenue Procedure 75-50 for the period covered by this certification.

_____ (Signature)   _____ (Title or authority of signer)   _____ (Date)

Instructions

This form is open to public inspection.

Paperwork Reduction Act Notice.—We ask for the information on this form to carry out the Internal Revenue laws of the United States. You are required to give us the information. We need it to ensure that you are complying with these laws.

The time needed to complete and file this form will vary depending on individual circumstances. The estimated average time is 4 hours and 45 minutes. If you have comments concerning the accuracy of this time estimate or suggestions for making this form more simple, we would be happy to hear from you. You can write to both the **Internal Revenue Service,** Washington, DC 20224, Attention: IRS Reports Clearance Officer, T:FP; and the **Office of Management and Budget,** Paperwork Reduction Project (1545-0213), Washington, DC 20503. **DO NOT** send the form to either of these offices. Instead, see **Where To File** below.

Purpose of Form

Form 5578 may be used by organizations that operate tax-exempt private schools to provide the Internal Revenue Service with the annual certification of racial nondiscrimination required by Rev. Proc. 75-50, 1975-2 C.B. 587.

Who Must File

Every organization that claims exemption from Federal income tax under section 501(c)(3) of the Internal Revenue Code and that operates, supervises, or controls a private school or schools must file a certification of racial nondiscrimination. If an organization is required to file **Form 990,** Return of Organization Exempt From Income Tax, or **Form 990-EZ,** Short Form Return of Organization Exempt From Income

Tax, either as a separate return or as part of a group return, the certification must be made on **Schedule A (Form 990),** Organization Exempt Under Section 501(c)(3), rather than on this form.

An authorized official of a central organization may file one form to certify for the school activities of subordinate organizations that would otherwise be required to file on an individual basis, but only if the central organization has enough control over the schools listed on the form to ensure that the schools maintain a racially nondiscriminatory policy as to students.

Definitions

A **racially nondiscriminatory policy as to students** means that the school admits the students of any race to all the rights, privileges, programs, and activities generally accorded or made available to students at that school and that the school does not discriminate on the basis of race in the administration of its educational policies, admissions policies, scholarship and loan programs, and other school-administered programs.

The IRS considers discrimination on the basis of race to include discrimination on the basis of color or national or ethnic origin.

A **school** is an educational organization that normally maintains a regular faculty and curriculum and normally has a regularly enrolled body of pupils or students in attendance at the place where its educational activities are regularly carried on. The term includes primary, secondary, preparatory, or high schools and colleges and universities, whether operated as a separate legal entity or as an activity of a church or other organization described in Code section 501(c)(3). The term also includes preschools and any other organization that is a school as defined in Code section 170(b)(1)(A)(ii).

A **central organization** is an organization that has one or more subordinates under its general supervision or control. A subordinate is a chapter, local, post, or other unit of a central organization. A central organization may also be a subordinate, as in the case of a state organization that has subordinate units and is itself affiliated with a national organization.

The **group exemption number (GEN)** is a 4-digit number issued to a central organization by the IRS. It identifies a central organization that has received a ruling from the IRS recognizing on a group basis the exemption from Federal income tax of the central organization and its covered subordinates.

When To File

Under Rev. Proc. 75-50, a certification of racial nondiscrimination must be filed annually by the 15th day of the 5th month following the end of the organization's calendar year or fiscal period.

Where To File

If the principal office of the organization is located in	Use the following Internal Revenue Service Center address
Alabama, Arkansas, Florida, Georgia, Louisiana, Mississippi, North Carolina, South Carolina, or Tennessee	Atlanta, GA 39901
Arizona, Colorado, Kansas, New Mexico, Oklahoma, Texas, Utah, or Wyoming	Austin, TX 73301
Indiana, Kentucky, Michigan, Ohio, or West Virginia	Cincinnati, OH 45999
Alaska, California, Hawaii, Idaho, Nevada, Oregon, or Washington	Fresno, CA 93888

Cat. No. 42658A   Form **5578** (Rev. 2-93)

Connecticut, Maine, Massachusetts, New Hampshire, New York, Rhode Island, or Vermont	Holtsville, NY 00501
Illinois, Iowa, Minnesota, Missouri, Montana, Nebraska, North Dakota, South Dakota, or Wisconsin	Kansas City, MO 64999
Delaware, Maryland, New Jersey, Pennsylvania, Virginia, District of Columbia, any U.S. possession, or foreign country	Philadelphia, PA 19255

Certification Requirement

Section 4.06 of Rev. Proc. 75-50 requires an individual authorized to take official action on behalf of a school that claims to be racially nondiscriminatory as to students to certify annually, under penalties of perjury, that to the best of his or her knowledge and belief the school has satisfied the applicable requirements of sections 4.01 through 4.05 of the Revenue Procedure, reproduced below:

Rev. Proc. 75-50

4.01 Organizational Requirements. A school must include a statement in its charter, bylaws, or other governing instrument, or in a resolution of its governing body, that it has a racially nondiscriminatory policy as to students and therefore does not discriminate against applicants and students on the basis of race, color, and national or ethnic origin.

4.02 Statement of Policy. Every school must include a statement of its racially nondiscriminatory policy as to students in all its brochures and catalogues dealing with student admissions, programs, and scholarships. A statement substantially similar to the Notice described in subsection (a) of section *4.03, infra,* will be acceptable for this purpose. Further, every school must include a reference to its racially nondiscriminatory policy in other written advertising that it uses as a means of informing prospective students of its programs. The following reference will be acceptable:

The (name) school admits students of any race, color, and national or ethnic origin.

4.03 Publicity. The school must make its racially nondiscriminatory policy known to all segments of the general community served by the school.

1. The school must use one of the following 2 methods to satisfy this requirement:

(a) The school may publish a notice of its racially nondiscriminatory policy in a newspaper of general circulation that serves all racial segments of the community. This publication must be repeated at least once annually during the period of the school's solicitation for students or, in the absence of a solicitation program, during the school's registration period. Where more than one community is served by a school, the school may publish its notice in those newspapers that are reasonably likely to be read by all racial segments of the communities that it serves. The notice must appear in a section of the newspaper likely to be read by prospective students and their families and it must occupy at least 3 column inches. It must be captioned in at least 12 point bold face type as a notice of nondiscriminatory policy as to students, and its text must be printed in at least 8 point type. The following notice will be acceptable:

Notice Of Nondiscriminatory Policy As To Students

The (name) school admits students of any race, color, national and ethnic origin to all the rights, privileges, programs, and activities generally accorded or made available to students at the school. It does not discriminate on the basis of race, color, national and ethnic origin in administration of its educational policies, admissions policies, scholarship and loan programs, and athletic and other school-administered programs.

(b) The school may use the broadcast media to publicize its racially nondiscriminatory policy if this use makes such nondiscriminatory policy known to all segments of the general community the school serves. If this method is chosen, the school must provide documentation that the means by which this policy was communicated to all segments of the general community was reasonably expected to be effective. In this case, appropriate documentation would include copies of the tapes or script used and records showing that there was an adequate number of announcements, that they were made during hours when the announcements were likely to be communicated to all segments of the general community, that they were of sufficient duration to convey the message clearly, and that they were broadcast on radio or television stations likely to be listened to by substantial numbers of members of all racial segments of the general community. Announcements must be made during the period of the school's solicitation for students or, in the absence of a solicitation program, during the school's registration period.

Communication of a racially nondiscriminatory policy as to students by a school to leaders of racial groups as the sole means of publicity generally will not be considered effective to make the policy known to all segments of the community.

2. The requirements of subsection 1 of this section will not apply when one of the following paragraphs applies:

(a) If for the preceding 3 years the enrollment of a parochial or other church-related school consists of students at least 75% of whom are members of the sponsoring religious denomination or unit, the school may make known its racially nondiscriminatory policy in whatever newspapers or circulars the religious denomination or unit utilizes in the communities from which the students are drawn. These newspapers and circulars may be those distributed by a particular religious denomination or unit or by an association that represents a number of religious organizations of the same denomination. If, however, the school advertises in newspapers of general circulation in the community or communities from which its students are drawn and paragraphs (b) and (c) of this subsection are not applicable to it, then it must comply with paragraph (a) of subsection 1 of this section.

(b) If a school customarily draws a substantial percentage of its students nationwide or world-wide or from a large geographic section or sections of the United States and follows a racially nondiscriminatory policy as to students, the publicity requirement may be satisfied by complying with section *4.02, supra.* Such a school may demonstrate that it follows a racially nondiscriminatory policy within the meaning of the preceding sentence either by showing that it currently enrolls students of racial minority groups in meaningful numbers or, when minority students are not enrolled in meaningful numbers, that its promotional activities and recruiting efforts in each geographic area were reasonably designed to inform students of all racial segments in the general communities within the area of the availability of the school. The question whether a school satisfies the preceding sentence will be determined on the basis of the facts and circumstances of each case.

(c) If a school customarily draws its students from local communities and follows a racially nondiscriminatory policy as to students, the publicity requirement may be satisfied by complying with section *4.02, supra.* Such a school may demonstrate that it follows a racially nondiscriminatory policy within the meaning of the preceding sentence by showing that it currently enrolls students of racial minority groups in meaningful numbers. The question whether a school satisfies the preceding sentence will be determined on the basis of the facts and circumstances of each case. One of the facts and circumstances that the Service will consider is whether the school's promotional activities and recruiting efforts in each area were reasonably designed to inform students of all racial segments in the general communities within the area of the availability of the school. The Service recognizes that the failure by a school drawing its students from local communities to enroll racial minority group students may not necessarily indicate the absence of a racially nondiscriminatory policy as to students when there are relatively few or no such students in these communities. Actual enrollment is, however, a meaningful indication of a racially nondiscriminatory policy in a community in which a public school or schools became subject to a desegregation order of a federal court or otherwise expressly became obligated to implement a desegregation plan under the terms of any written contract or other commitment to which any Federal agency was a party.

The Service encourages schools to satisfy the publicity requirement by the methods described in subsection 1 of this section, regardless of whether a school considers itself within subsection 2, because it believes these methods to be the most effective to make known a school's racially nondiscriminatory policy. In this regard it is each school's responsibility to determine whether paragraph (a), (b), or (c) of subsection 2 applies to it. On audit, a school must be prepared to demonstrate that the failure to publish its racially nondiscriminatory policy in accordance with subsection 1 of this section was justified by the application to it of paragraph (a), (b), or (c) of subsection 2. Further, a school must be prepared to demonstrate that it has publicly disavowed or repudiated any statements purported to have been made on its behalf (after November 6, 1975) that are contrary to its publicity of a racially nondiscriminatory policy as to students, to the extent that the school or its principal official were aware of such statements.

4.04 Facilities and Programs. A school must be able to show that all of its programs and facilities are operated in a racially nondiscriminatory manner.

4.05 Scholarship and Loan Programs. As a general rule, all scholarship or other comparable benefits procurable for use at any given school must be offered on a racially nondiscriminatory basis. Their availability on this basis must be known throughout the general community being served by the school and should be referred to in the publicity required by this section in order for that school to be considered racially nondiscriminatory as to students. . . . [S]cholarships and loans that are made pursuant to financial assistance programs favoring members of one or more racial minority groups that are designed to promote a school's racially nondiscriminatory policy will not adversely affect the school's exempt status. Financial assistance programs favoring members of one or more racial groups that do not significantly derogate from the school's racially nondiscriminatory policy similarly will not adversely affect the school's exempt status.

FORM NO. 12 [IRS Form 1023]

**Department of the Treasury
Internal Revenue Service**

Instructions for Form 1023
(Revised September 1990)
Application for Recognition of Exemption Under Section 501(c)(3) of the Internal Revenue Code

(Section references are to the Internal Revenue Code unless otherwise noted.)

Retain a copy of the completed Form 1023 in the organization's permanent records. See **General Instruction G** regarding public inspection of approved applications.

General Information

Paperwork Reduction Act Notice.—We ask for the information on this form to carry out the Internal Revenue laws of the United States. If you want to be recognized as tax exempt by IRS, you are required to give us this information. We need it to determine whether you meet the legal requirements for tax-exempt status.

The time needed to complete and file these forms will vary depending on individual circumstances. The estimated average times are:

Form	Recordkeeping	Learning about the law or the form	Preparing, and sending the form to IRS
1023 Parts I to IV	54 hrs., 17 min.	4 hrs., 53 min.	9 hrs., 34 min.
1023 Sch. A	7 hrs., 10 min.	-0- min.	7 min.
1023 Sch. B	4 hrs., 47 min.	30 min.	36 min.
1023 Sch. C	5 hrs., 1 min.	35 min.	43 min.
1023 Sch. D	4 hrs., 4 min.	42 min.	47 min.
1023 Sch. E	9 hrs., 20 min.	1 hr., 5 min.	1 hr., 17 min.
1023 Sch. F	2 hrs., 38 min.	2 hrs., 53 min.	3 hrs., 3 min.
1023 Sch. G	2 hrs., 38 min.	0 min.	21 min.
1023 Sch. H	1 hr., 55 min.	42 min.	46 min.
1023 Sch. I	3 hrs., 35 min.	-0- min.	4 min.
872-C	1 hr., 12 min.	24 min.	26 min.

If you have comments concerning the accuracy of these time estimates or suggestions for making these forms more simple, we would be happy to hear from you. You can write to both the **Internal Revenue Service,** Washington, DC 20224, Attention: IRS Reports Clearance Officer, T:FP; and the **Office of Management and Budget,** Paperwork Reduction Project (1545-0056), Washington, DC 20503. DO NOT send the tax form to either of these offices. Instead, see the instructions below for information on where to file.

General Instructions

User Fee.—The Revenue Act of 1987 requires payment of a user fee with determination letter requests submitted to the Internal Revenue Service. **Form 8718,** User Fee for Exempt Organization Determination Letter Request, must be submitted with this application along with the appropriate fee as stated on Form 8718. Form 8718 may be obtained through your local IRS office or by calling the telephone number given below for obtaining forms and publications.

Helpful Information.—For additional information see **Publication 557,** Tax-Exempt Status for Your Organization; **Publication 578,** Tax Information for Private Foundations and Foundation Managers; and **Publication 598,** Tax on Unrelated Business Income of Exempt Organizations. You may also call **1-800-554-4477 (after October 1, 1990, call 1-800-829-4477);** ask for **Topics #109** and **#110** (a push-button telephone is required). For additional forms and publications, call **1-800-424-3676 (after October 1, 1990, call 1-800-829-3676).**

A. Purpose of Form

1. Completed Form 1023 required for section 501(c)(3) exemption.—Unless it meets either of the exceptions in item 2

below, or notifies the IRS that it is applying for recognition of section 501(c)(3) exempt status, no organization formed after October 9, 1969, will be considered tax exempt under section 501(c)(3).

An organization "notifies" IRS by filing a completed Form 1023. Form 1023 also solicits the information that IRS needs to determine if the organization is a private foundation.

2. Organizations that are not required to file Form 1023.—The following organizations will be considered tax exempt under section 501(c)(3) even if they do not file Form 1023: **(a)** Churches, their integrated auxiliaries, and conventions or associations of churches, or **(b)** Any organization which is not a private foundation (as defined in section 509(a)) and the gross receipts of which in each taxable year are normally not more than $5,000.

Even if these organizations are not required to file Form 1023 to be tax exempt, they may wish to file Form 1023 and receive a determination letter of IRS recognition of their section 501(c)(3) status in order to obtain certain incidental benefits such as: public recognition of their tax-exempt status; exemption from certain state taxes; advance assurance to donors of deductibility of contributions; exemption from certain Federal excise taxes; non-profit mailing privileges, etc.

3. Other organizations.—In applying for a determination letter, cooperative service organizations, described in section 501(e) and (f), and child care organizations, described in section 501(k), use Form 1023 and are treated as section 501(c)(3) organizations.

4. Group exemption letter.—Note: *Generally, Form 1023 is NOT used to apply for a group exemption letter. For information on how to apply for a group exemption letter, see Publication 557.*

B. What To File

1. All organizations—Pages 1 through 9, Form 1023 and additional schedules, if applicable
2. Churches—Schedule A
3. Schools—Schedule B
4. Hospitals or Medical Research—Schedule C
5. Supporting Organizations (509(a)(3))—Schedule D
6. Private Operating Foundations—Schedule E
7. Home for the Aged or Handicapped—Schedule F
8. Child Care—Schedule G
9. Scholarship Benefits or Student Aid—Schedule H
10. If your organization has taken over or will take over a "for profit" institution—Schedule I.

Attachments.—Every attachment should state that it relates to Form 1023 and identify the applicable part and line item number. The attachments should also show the organization's name, address, and employer identification number and be on 8½" × 11" paper.

In addition to the required documents and statements, you should file any additional information citing court decisions, rulings, opinions, etc., that will expedite processing of the application. Generally, attachments in the form of tape recordings are not acceptable unless accompanied by a transcript.

C. When To File

An organization formed after October 9, 1969, must file Form 1023 to be recognized as an organization described in section 501(c)(3). Generally, if an organization files its application within 15 months after the end of the month in which it was formed, and if IRS approves the application, the effective date of the organization's section 501(c)(3) status will be the date it was organized.

Generally, if an organization does not file its application (Form 1023) within 15 months after the end of the month in which it was formed, it will not qualify for exempt status during the period before the date of its application.

D. Where To File

File the completed application, and all information required, with the key district office for your principal place of business or office as listed below. As soon as possible after the complete application is received, you will be advised of IRS's determination and of the annual returns (if any) that the organization will be required to file.

When the principal place of business or office of the organization is in one of the districts or locations shown below ▼	Send your application to the key district listed below ▼
Anchorage, Boise, Honolulu, Laguna Niguel, Las Vegas, Los Angeles, Portland, San Jose, Seattle	Internal Revenue Service EO Application Receiving Room 5127, P.O. Box 486 Los Angeles, CA 90053-0486
Sacramento, San Francisco	Internal Revenue Service EO Application Receiving Stop SF 4446 P.O. Box 36001 San Francisco, CA 94102
Atlanta, Birmingham, Columbia, Ft. Lauderdale, Greensboro, Jackson, Jacksonville, Little Rock, Nashville, New Orleans	Internal Revenue Service EP/EO Division P.O. Box 941 Atlanta, GA 30370
Aberdeen, Chicago, Des Moines, Fargo, Helena, Milwaukee, Omaha, St. Louis, St. Paul, Springfield	Internal Revenue Service EP/EO Division 230 S. Dearborn DPN 20-5 Chicago, IL 60604
Baltimore, District of Columbia, Newark, Philadelphia, Pittsburgh, Richmond, Wilmington, any U.S. possession (except Virgin Islands) or foreign country	Internal Revenue Service EP/EO Division P.O. Box 17010 Baltimore, MD 21203
U.S. Virgin Islands	Virgin Islands Bureau of Internal Revenue Lockharts Garden No. 1A Charlotte Amalie, St. Thomas, VI 00802
Albany, Augusta, Boston, Brooklyn, Buffalo, Burlington, Hartford, Manhattan, Portsmouth, Providence	Internal Revenue Service EP/EO Division P.O. Box 1680, GPO Brooklyn, NY 11202
Cincinnati, Cleveland, Detroit, Indianapolis, Louisville, Parkersburg	Internal Revenue Service EP/EO Division P.O. Box 3159 Cincinnati, OH 45201
Albuquerque, Austin, Cheyenne, Dallas, Denver, Houston, Oklahoma City, Phoenix, Salt Lake City, Wichita	Internal Revenue Service EP/EO Division Mail Code 4950 DAL 1100 Commerce Street Dallas, TX 75242

E. Signature Requirements

An officer, a trustee who is authorized to sign, or another person authorized by a power of attorney must sign this application. Send the power of attorney with the application when you file it. **Form 2848,** Power of Attorney and Declaration of Representative, or **Form 8821,** Tax Information Authorization, may be used for this purpose.

F. Deductibility of Contributions

Deductions for charitable contributions are not allowed for any gifts or bequests made to organizations that do not qualify under section 501(c)(3). The effective date of an organization's section 501(c)(3) status determines the date that contributions to it are deductible by donors. (See General Instructions, **When To File.**)

G. Public Inspection of Form 1023

IRS Responsibilities.—If the application is approved, it and any supporting documents will be open to public inspection, as required by section 6104, in any key district office and in the Internal Revenue Service's National Office. In addition, any letter or other document issued by the IRS with regard to the application will be open to public inspection. However, information relating to a trade secret, patent, style of work or apparatus which, if released, would adversely affect the organization, or any other information which would adversely affect the national defense, will not be made available for public inspection. You must identify this information by clearly marking it "NOT SUBJECT TO PUBLIC INSPECTION" and attach a statement explaining why the organization asks that the information be withheld. If the Internal Revenue Service agrees, the information will be withheld.

Organization's Responsibilities.—The organization must make available for public inspection a copy of its approved application and supporting documents, along with any document or letter issued by the IRS. These must be available during regular business hours at the organization's principal office and at each of its regional or district offices having at least 3 paid employees. See Notice 88-120, 1988-2 C.B. 454. If any person under a duty to

comply with the inspection provisions fails to comply with these requirements, a penalty of $10 a day will be imposed for each day the failure continues.

H. Appeal Procedures

Your application will be considered by the key district office, which will either:

(1) issue a favorable determination letter;

(2) issue a proposed adverse determination letter denying the exempt status you requested; or

(3) refer the case to the National Office.

If you receive a proposed adverse determination, you will be advised of your appeal rights at that time.

I. Language and Currency Requirements

Form 1023 and attachments must be prepared in English. If the organizational document or bylaws are in any other language, an English translation must be furnished. If the organization produces or distributes foreign language publications that are submitted with the application, you may be asked to provide English translations for one or more of them during the processing of your application.

Report all financial information in U.S. dollars (state conversion rate used). Combine amounts from within and outside the United States and report the total for each item on the financial statements.

For example:

Gross Investment Income	
From U.S. sources	$4,000
From Non-U.S. sources	1,000
Amount to report on income statement	$5,000

J. Annual Information Return

If the annual information return for tax-exempt organizations becomes due while your application for recognition of exempt status is pending with IRS (including any appeal of a proposed adverse determination), you should file **Form 990,** Return of Organization Exempt From Income Tax (or **Form 990EZ,** Short Form Return of Organization Exempt From Income Tax) and **Schedule A (Form 990),** Organization Exempt Under Section 501(c)(3), or **Form 990-PF,** Return of Private Foundation, if a private foundation, and indicate that an application is pending.

K. Special Rule for Canadian Colleges and Universities

A Canadian college or university that has received a **Form T2051,** Notification of Registration, from Revenue Canada (Department of National Revenue, Taxation) and whose registration has not been revoked, does not have to complete all parts of Form 1023 that would otherwise be applicable. Such an organization must complete only Part I of Form 1023 and Schedule B (Schools, Colleges, and Universities). The organization must also attach a copy of its **Form T2050,** Application for Registration, together with all the required attachments that it submitted to Revenue Canada. If any attachments were prepared in French, an English translation must be furnished.

Other Canadian organizations seeking a determination of section 501(c)(3) status must complete Form 1023 in the same manner as U.S. organizations.

Specific Instructions

The following instructions are keyed to the line items on the application form:

Part I.—Identification of Applicant

Line 1. Full Name and Address of Organization.—Enter the organization's name exactly as it appears in its creating document including amendments. If the organization will be operating under another name, show the other name in parentheses.

Line 2. Employer Identification Number.—All organizations must have an EIN. Enter the 9-digit EIN assigned to the organization by the IRS. If the organization does **not** have an employer identification number, enter "none" and attach a completed **Form SS-4,** Application for Employer Identification Number, to the application. If the organization has previously applied for a number, attach a statement giving the date of the application and the office where it was filed.

Line 3. Person to Contact.—Enter the name and telephone number of the person to be contacted during business hours if more information is needed. The contact person should be familiar with the organization's activities, preferably an officer, director, or authorized representative.

Line 4. Month the Annual Accounting Period Ends.—Enter the month the organization's annual accounting period ends. The accounting period is usually the 12-month period that is the organization's tax year. The organization's first tax year depends on the accounting period you choose (it could be less than 12 months).

Line 5. Date Formed.—Enter the date the organization became a legal entity. For corporations, this would be the date that the articles of incorporation were approved by the appropriate State official. For unincorporated organizations, it would be the date its constitution or articles of association was adopted.

Line 6. Activity Codes.—Select up to three of the code numbers listed on the back cover that best describe or most accurately identify the organization's purposes, activities, or type of organization. Enter the codes in the order of importance.

Line 7.—Indicate if the organization is one of the following:

> 501(e) Cooperative hospital service organization;
>
> 501(f) Cooperative service organization of operating educational organization;
>
> 501(k) Organization providing child care.

If none of the above applies, make no entry on line 7.

Line 8.—Indicate if the organization has ever filed a Form 1023 or **Form 1024**, Application for Recognition of Exemption Under Section 501(a) or for Determination Under Section 120, with the Internal Revenue Service.

Line 9.—Indicate if the organization has ever filed Federal income tax returns as a taxable organization or filed returns as an exempt organization (e.g., Form 990, 990EZ, 990-PF, or **990-T**, Exempt Organization Business Income Tax Return).

Line 10. Type of Organization and Organizational Documents.—Submit a conformed copy of the organizing instrument. A "conformed" copy is one that agrees with the original and all amendments to it. The conformed copy may be a photocopy of the original signed and dated organizing document OR it may be a copy of the organizing document that is not signed but is accompanied by a written declaration signed by an authorized individual stating that the copy is a complete and accurate copy of the original signed and dated document.

In the case of a corporation, a copy of the certificate of incorporation, approved and dated by an appropriate State official, is sufficient by itself. If an unsigned copy of the articles of incorporation is submitted, it must be accompanied by the written declaration discussed above. Signed or unsigned copies of the articles of incorporation must be accompanied by a declaration stating that the original copy of the articles was filed with, and approved by, the State. The date filed must be specified.

In the case of an unincorporated association, the conformed copy of the constitution, articles of association, or other organizing document must indicate in the document itself, or in a written declaration, that the organization was formed by the adoption of the document by two or more persons.

In the case of a trust, a copy of the signed and dated trust instrument must be furnished.

If your organizing instrument does not contain a proper dissolution clause, and if State law does not provide for distribution of assets for one or more exempt (section 501(c)(3)) purposes upon dissolution, the organization will not qualify for exempt status. If you rely on State law, please cite the law and briefly state its provisions on an attachment. Your organizing instrument must also specify your organizational purposes and the purposes specified must be limited to one or more of those set out in section 501(c)(3).

If the organization does not have an organizing instrument, it will not qualify for exempt status. The bylaws of an organization alone are not an organizing instrument. They are merely the internal rules and regulations of the organization.

See Publication 557 for detailed instructions and for sample organizing instruments that satisfy the requirements of section 501(c)(3) and the related regulations.

Page 3

Part II.—Activities and Operational Information

Line 1.—It is important that you report all activities carried on by the organization to enable the IRS to make a proper determination of the organization's exempt status.

Line 2.—If it is anticipated that the organization's principal sources of support will increase or decrease substantially in relation to the organization's total support, attach a statement describing anticipated changes and explaining the basis for the expectation.

Line 3.—For purposes of this question, "fundraising activity" includes the solicitation of contributions and both functionally related activities and unrelated business activities. Include a description of the nature and magnitude of the activities.

Line 4a.—Furnish the mailing addresses of the organization's principal officers, directors, or trustees. Do not give the address of the organization.

Line 4b.—The annual compensation includes salary, bonus, and any other form of payment to the individual for services while employed by the organization.

Line 4c.—Public officials include anyone holding an elected position or anyone appointed to a position by an elected official.

Line 4d.—For purposes of this application, a "disqualified person" is any person who, if the applicant organization were a private foundation, is:

(1) a "substantial contributor" to the foundation (defined below);

(2) a foundation manager;

(3) an owner of more than 20% of the total combined voting power of a corporation that is a substantial contributor to the foundation;

(4) a "member of the family" of any person described in (1), (2), or (3) above;

(5) a corporation, partnership, or trust in which persons described in (1), (2), (3), or (4) above, hold more than 35% of the combined voting power, the profits interest, or the beneficial interests; and

(6) any other private foundation that is effectively controlled by the same persons who control the first-mentioned private foundation or any other private foundation substantially all of whose contributions were made by the same contributors.

A substantial contributor is any person who gave a total of more than $5,000 to the organization, and those contributions are more than 2% of all the contributions and bequests received by the organization from the date it was created up to the end of the year the contributions by the substantial contributor were received. A creator of a trust is treated as a substantial contributor regardless of the amount contributed by that person or others.

See Publication 578 for more information on "disqualified persons."

Line 5.—If your organization controls or is controlled by another exempt organization or a taxable organization, answer "Yes." Examples of special relationships would be: common officers and the sharing of office space or employees.

Line 6.—If the organization conducts any financial transactions (either receiving funds or paying out funds), or non-financial activities with an exempt organization (other than 501(c)(3) organizations), or with a political organization, answer "Yes," and explain.

Line 7.—If the organization must report its income and expense activity to any other organization (tax-exempt or taxable entity), answer "Yes."

Line 8.—Examples of assets used to perform an exempt function are: land, building, equipment, and publications. Do not include cash or property producing investment income. If you have no assets used in performing the organization's exempt function, answer "N/A."

Line 9a.—Answer "Yes," if the organization is managed by another exempt organization, a taxable organization, or an individual.

Line 9b.—If the organization leases property from anyone or leases any of its property to anyone, answer "Yes."

Line 10.—A membership organization for purposes of this question refers to an organization that is composed of individuals or organizations who:

(1) share in the common goal for which the organization was created;

(2) actively participate in achieving the organization's purposes; and

(3) pay dues.

Line 11.—Examples of benefits, products, and services would be: meals to homeless people, home for the aged, museum open to the public, and a symphony orchestra giving public performances.

Line 12.—An organization is attempting to influence legislation if it contacts or urges the public to contact members of a legislative body, or if it advocates the adoption or rejection of legislation.

If you answer "Yes," you may want to file **Form 5768,** Election/Revocation of Election by an Eligible Section 501(c)(3) Organization to Make Expenditures to Influence Legislation.

Line 13.—An organization is intervening in a political campaign if it promotes or opposes the candidacy or prospective candidacy of an individual for public office.

Part III.—Technical Requirements

Line 1.—If you check "Yes," proceed to question 7. If you check "No," proceed to question 2.

Line 2.—If you fit one of the exceptions, do not answer questions 3 through 6. Proceed to question 7.

Line 3.—Relief from the 15-month filing requirement may be granted under certain circumstances. (See the instructions for Line 4 below.)

Line 4.—The reasons for late filing should be specific to your particular organization and situation. Revenue Procedure 79-63, 1979-2 C.B. 578 lists the factors that will be taken into consideration by the Service in determining whether good cause exists for granting an extension of time to file the application. (Also see Publication 557.) To address these factors, your response on line 4 should provide the following information:

(1) Whether or not you consulted an attorney or accountant knowledgeable in tax matters or communicated with a responsible Internal Revenue Service employee (before or after the organization was created) to ascertain the organization's Federal filing requirements and, if so, the names and occupations or titles of the persons contacted, the approximate dates, and the substance of the information obtained;

(2) How and when you learned about the 15-month deadline for filing Form 1023;

(3) Whether any significant intervening circumstances beyond your control prevented you from submitting the application timely or within a reasonable period of time after you learned of the requirement to file the application within the 15-month period; and

(4) Any other information that you believe may establish good cause for not filing timely or otherwise justify granting the relief sought.

Line 5.—If you answer "No," you may receive an adverse letter limiting the effective date of your exempt status, if:

(1) You are not filing this application within 15 months from the end of the month you were formed;

(2) You do not satisfy any of the exceptions listed in Line 2 of Part III; or

(3) You do not wish to request relief in Line 3, Part III.

Line 6.—The organization may still be able to qualify for exemption under section 501(c)(4) for the period preceding the effective date of its exemption as a section 501(c)(3) organization. If the organization is qualified under section 501(c)(4) and page 1 of Form 1024 is filed as directed, the organization will not be liable for income tax returns as a taxable entity. Contributions to section 501(c)(4) organizations are generally not deductible by donors as charitable contributions.

Line 7.—Private foundations are subject to various requirements, restrictions, and excise taxes under Chapter 42 of the Internal Revenue Code that do not apply to public charities. Also, contributions to private foundations may receive less favorable treatment than contributions to public charities. (See Publication 578.) Therefore, it is usually to an organization's advantage to show that it qualifies as a public charity rather than as a private foundation if its activities or sources of support permit it to do so. Unless an organization meets one of the exceptions below, it is a private foundation. In general, an organization is **not** a private foundation if it is:

(1) a church, school, hospital, or governmental unit;

(2) a medical research organization operated in conjunction with a hospital;

(3) an organization operated for the benefit of a college or university that is owned or operated by a governmental unit;

(4) an organization that normally receives a substantial part of its support in the form of contributions from a governmental unit or from the general public as provided in section 170(b)(1)(A)(vi);

(5) an organization that normally receives not more than one-third of its support from gross investment income and more than one-third of its support from contributions, membership fees, and gross receipts related to its exempt functions (subject to certain exceptions) as provided in section 509(a)(2);

(6) an organization operated solely for the benefit of, and in connection with, one or more organizations described above (or for the benefit of one or more of the organizations described in section 501(c)(4), (5), or (6) of the Code and also described in (5) above), but not controlled by disqualified persons other than foundation managers, as provided in section 509(a)(3); or

(7) an organization organized and operated to test for public safety as provided in section 509(a)(4).

Line 8.—Basis for Private Operating Foundation status: (Complete this question **only** if you answered "Yes" to question 7.)

A "private operating foundation" is a private foundation that spends substantially all of its adjusted net income or its minimum investment return, whichever is less, directly for the active conduct of the activities constituting the purpose or function for which it is organized and operated. The foundation must satisfy the income test and one of the three supplemental tests: **(1)** the assets test; **(2)** the endowment test; or **(3)** the support test. (For additional information, see Publication 578.)

Line 9.—Basis for Non-Private Foundation status: Check the box that shows why you are not a private foundation.

Box (a). A church or convention or association of churches.

Box (b). A school.—See the definition in the instructions for Schedule B.

Box (c). A hospital or medical research organization.—See the instructions for Schedule C.

Box (d). A governmental unit.—This category includes a State, a possession of the United States, or a political subdivision of any of the foregoing, or the United States, or the District of Columbia.

Box (e). Organizations operated in connection with or solely for organizations described in (a) through (d) or (g), (h), and (i).—The organization must be organized and operated for the benefit of, to perform the functions of, or to carry out the purposes of one or more specified organizations described in section 509(a)(1) or (2). It must be operated, supervised, or controlled by or in connection with one or more of the organizations described in the instructions for boxes **(a)** through **(d)** or **(g), (h),** and **(i).** It must not be controlled directly or indirectly by disqualified persons (other than foundation managers or organizations described in section 509(a)(1) or (2)). To show whether the organization satisfies these tests, complete Schedule D.

Box (f). An organization testing for public safety.—An organization in this category is one that tests products to determine their acceptability for use by the general public. It does not include any organization testing for the benefit of a manufacturer as an operation or control in the manufacture of its product.

Box (g). Organization for the benefit of a college or university owned and operated by a governmental unit.—The organization must be organized and operated exclusively for the benefit of a college or university that is an educational organization within the meaning of section 170(b)(1)(A)(ii) and is an agency or instrumentality of a State or political subdivision of a State; is owned or operated by a State or political subdivision of a State; or is owned or operated by an agency or instrumentality of one or more States or political subdivisions. The organization must also normally receive a substantial part of its support from the United States or any State or political subdivision of a State, or from direct or indirect contributions from the general public or from a combination of these sources. An organization described in section 170(b)(1)(A)(iv) will be subject to the same publicly supported rules that are applicable to 170(b)(1)(A)(vi) organizations described in box (h) below.

Box (h). Organization receiving support from a governmental unit or from the general public.—The organization must receive a substantial part of its support from the United States or any State or political subdivision, or from direct or indirect contributions from the general public or from a combination of these sources. The organization may satisfy the support requirement in either of two ways. It will be treated as publicly supported if the support it normally receives from the above-described governmental units and the general public equals at least one-third of its total support. It will also be treated as publicly supported if the support it normally receives from governmental or public sources equals at least 10% of total support and the organization is set up to attract new and additional public or governmental support on a continuous basis. If the organization's governmental and public support is at least 10%, but not over one-third of its total support, questions 1 through 13 of Part II will apply to determine both the organization's claim of exemption and whether it is publicly supported. Preparers should exercise care to assure that those questions are answered in detail.

Box (i). Organization described in section 509(a)(2).—The organization must satisfy the support test under section 509(a)(2)(A) and the gross investment income test under section 509(a)(2)(B). To satisfy the support test, the organization must normally receive more than one-third of its support from: **(a)** gifts, grants, contributions, or membership fees, and **(b)** gross receipts from admissions, sales of merchandise, performance of services, or furnishing of facilities, in an activity which is not an unrelated trade or business (subject to certain limitations discussed below). This one-third of support must be from organizations described in section 509(a)(1), governmental sources, or persons other than disqualified persons. In computing gross receipts from admissions, sales of merchandise, performance of services, or furnishing of facilities in an activity that is not an unrelated trade or business, the gross receipts from any one person or from any bureau or similar agency of a governmental unit are includible only to the extent they do not exceed the greater of $5,000 or 1% of the organization's total support. To satisfy the gross investment income test, the organization must not receive more than one-third of its support from gross investment income.

Box (j).—If you believe the organization meets the public support test of section 170(b)(1)(A)(vi) or 509(a)(2) but are uncertain as to which public support test it satisfies, check box (j). By checking this box, you are claiming that the organization is not a private foundation and are agreeing to let the IRS compute the public support of your organization and determine the correct foundation status.

Line 10.—To receive a definitive (final) ruling under sections 170(b)(1)(A)(vi) and 509(a)(1) or under section 509(a)(2), an organization must have completed a tax year consisting of at least 8 months. Organizations that checked box (h), (i), or (j) on line 9 that do not satisfy the 8-month requirement must request an advance ruling covering its first 5 tax years instead of a definitive ruling.

An organization that satisfies the 8-month requirement has two options:

(1) It may request a definitive ruling. In this event, the organization's qualification under sections 170(b)(1)(A)(vi) and 509(a)(1) or under section 509(a)(2) will be based on the support that the organization has received to date; or

(2) It may request an advance ruling. If the Internal Revenue Service issues the advance ruling, the organization's public support computation will be based on the support it receives during its first 5 tax years. An organization should consider this option if it has not received significant public support during its first tax year or during its first and second tax years, but it reasonably expects to receive such support by the end of its fifth tax year. An organization that receives an advance ruling is treated, during the 5-year advance ruling period, as a public charity (rather than a private foundation) for certain purposes, including those relating to the deductibility of contributions by the general public.

Line 11.—For definition of an unusual grant, see instructions for Part IV-A, line 12.

Page 5

Line 12.—Answer this question only if you checked box (g) or (h) in question 9.

Line 13.—Answer this question only if you checked box (i) in question 9 and are requesting a definitive ruling in question 10.

Line 14.—Answer "Yes" or "No" on each line. If "Yes," you must complete the appropriate Schedule. Each Schedule is included in this application package with accompanying instructions. For a brief definition of each type of organization, see the appropriate Schedule.

Part IV.—Financial Data

The Statement of Revenue and Expenses must be completed **for the current year and each of the 3 years immediately before it** *(or the years the organization has existed, if less than 4). Any applicant that has existed for less than 1 year must give financial data for the current year and proposed budgets for the following 2 years.* We may request financial data for more than 4 years if necessary. All financial information for the current year must cover the period ending within 60 days of the date of application. Prepare the balance sheet as of the last day of the current year period covered by the Statement of Revenue and Expenses. Prepare the statements using the method of accounting the organization uses in keeping its books and records. If the organization uses a method other than the cash receipts and disbursements method, attach a statement explaining the method used.

A. Revenue and Expenses

Line 1.—Do not include amounts received from the general public or a governmental unit for the exercise or performance of the organization's exempt functions. However, payments made by a governmental unit to enable the organization to provide a service to the general public should be included. Also, do not include unusual grants. (For an explanation of unusual grants, see instructions for line 12 below.)

Line 2.—Include amounts received from members for the basic purpose of providing support to the organization. Do not include payments to purchase admissions, merchandise, services, or use of facilities.

Line 3.—Include on this line the income received from dividends, interest, payments received on securities loans, rents, and royalties.

Line 4.—Enter the organization's net income from any activities that are regularly carried on and not related to the organization's exempt purposes. Examples of such income include fees from the commercial testing of products; income from renting office equipment or other personal property; and income from the sale of advertising in an exempt organization periodical. See Publication 598 for information about unrelated business income and activities.

Line 5.—Enter the amount collected by the local tax authority from the general public that has been allocated for your organization.

Line 6.—To report the value of services and/or facilities furnished by a governmental unit, use the fair market value at the time the service/facility was furnished to your organization. Do not include any other donated services or facilities in Part IV.

Line 7.—Enter the total income from all sources that is not reported on lines 1 through 6, or lines 9, 11, and 12. Attach a schedule that lists each type of revenue source and the amount derived from each.

Line 9.—Include income generated by the organization's exempt function activities (charitable, educational, etc.) and by its nontaxable fundraising events (excluding any contributions received). Examples of such income include the income derived by a symphony orchestra from the sale of tickets to its performances; and raffles, bingo, or other fundraising-event income that would not be taxable as unrelated business income because the income-producing activities were not regularly carried on or because they were conducted with substantially all (at least 85%) volunteer labor.

Line 11.—Attach a schedule that shows a description of each asset, the name of the person to whom sold, and the amount received. In the case of publicly traded securities sold through a broker, the name of the purchaser is not required.

Line 12.—Unusual grants generally consist of substantial contributions and bequests from disinterested persons that:

(1) are attracted by reason of the publicly supported nature of the organization;

(2) are unusual and unexpected as to the amount; and

(3) would, by reason of their size, adversely affect the status of the organization as normally meeting the support test of section 170(b)(1)(A)(vi) or section 509(a)(2), as the case may be.

If the organization is awarded an unusual grant and the terms of the granting instrument provide that the organization will receive the funds over a period of years, the amount received by the organization each year under the grant may be excluded. See the regulations under sections 170 and 509.

Line 14.—Fundraising expenses represent the total expenses incurred in soliciting contributions, gifts, grants, etc.

Line 15.—Attach a schedule showing the name of the recipient, a brief description of the purposes or conditions of payment, and the amount paid. The following example shows the format and amount of detail required for this schedule:

Recipient	Purpose	Amount
Museum of Natural History	General operating budget	$9,000
State University	Books for needy students	4,500
Richard Roe	Educational scholarship	2,200

Line 16.—Attach a schedule showing the name of each recipient, a brief description of the purposes or condition of payment, and amount paid. Do not include any amounts that are on line 15. The schedule should be similar to the schedule shown in the line 15 instructions above.

Line 17.—Attach a schedule that shows the name of the person compensated; the office or position; the average amount of time devoted to business per week, month, etc.; and the amount of annual compensation. The following example shows the format and amount of detail required:

Name	Position	Time devoted	Annual salary
Philip Poe	President and general manager	16 hrs. per wk.	$7,500

Line 18.—Enter the total of employees' salaries not reported on line 17.

Line 19.—Enter the total interest expense for the year, excluding mortgage interest treated as occupancy expense on line 20.

Line 20.—Enter the amount paid for the use of office space or other facilities, heat, light, power, and other utilities, outside janitorial services, mortgage interest, real estate taxes, and similar expenses.

Line 21.—If your organization records depreciation, depletion, and similar expenses, enter the total.

Line 22.—Attach a schedule listing the type and amount of each **significant** expense for which a separate line is not provided. Report other miscellaneous expenses as a single total if not substantial in amount.

B. Balance Sheet

Line 1.—Enter the total cash in checking and savings accounts, temporary cash investments (money market funds, CDs, treasury bills or other obligations that mature in less than 1 year), change funds, and petty cash funds.

Line 2.—Enter the total accounts receivable that arose from the sale of goods and/or performance of services.

Line 3.—Enter the amount of materials, goods, and supplies purchased or manufactured by the organization and held to be sold or used in some future period.

Line 4.—Attach a schedule that shows the name of the borrower, a brief description of the obligation, the rate of return on the principal indebtedness, the due date, and the amount due. The following example shows the format and amount of detail required:

Name of borrower	Description of obligation	Rate of return	Due date	Amount
Hope Soap Corporation	Debenture bond (no senior issue outstanding)	10%	Jan. 1999	$ 7,500
Big Spool Company	Collateral note secured by company's fleet of 20 delivery trucks	12%	Jan. 1998	62,000

Line 5.—Attach a schedule listing the organization's corporate stock holdings. For stock of closely held corporations, the statement should show the name of the corporation, a brief summary of the corporation's capital structure, the number of shares held and their value as carried on the organization's books. If such valuation does not reflect current fair market value, also include fair market value. For stock traded on an organized exchange or in substantial quantities over the counter, the statement should show the name of the corporation, a description of the stock and the principal exchange on which it is traded, the number of shares held, and their value as carried on the organization's books. The following example shows the format and the amount of detail required:

Name of corporation	Capital structure (or exchange on which traded)	Shares	Book amount	Fair market value
Little Spool Corporation	100 shares nonvoting preferred issued and outstanding, no par value; 50 shares common issued and outstanding, no par value.			
	Preferred shares:	50	$20,000	$24,000
	Common shares:	10	25,000	30,000
Flintlock Corporation	Class A common N.Y.S.E.	20	3,000	3,500

Line 6.—Report each loan separately, even if more than one loan was made to the same person. Attach a schedule that shows the borrower's name, purpose of loan, repayment terms, interest rate, and original amount of loan.

Line 7.—Enter the book value of securities held of the U.S., State, or municipal government. Also enter the book value of buildings and equipment held for investment purposes. Attach a schedule identifying and reporting the book value of each.

Line 8.—Enter the book value of buildings and equipment **not** held for investment. This would include plant and equipment used by the organization in conducting its exempt activities. Attach a schedule listing these assets held at the end of the current tax-year period and the cost or other basis.

Line 9.—Enter the book value of land **not** held for investment.

Line 10.—Enter the book value of each category of assets not reported on lines 1 through 9. Attach a schedule listing each.

Line 12.—Enter the total of accounts payable to suppliers and others, such as: salaries payable, accrued payroll taxes, and interest payable.

Line 13.—Enter the unpaid portion of grants and contributions that the organization has made a commitment to pay other organizations or individuals.

Line 14.—Enter the total of mortgages and other notes payable at the end of the current tax-year period. Attach a schedule that shows each item separately and the lender's name, purpose of loan, repayment terms, interest rate, and original amount.

Line 15.—Enter the amount of each liability not reported on lines 12 through 14. Attach a separate schedule.

Line 17.—Under fund accounting, an organization segregates its funds, liabilities, and net assets into separate funds according to restrictions on the use of certain assets. Each fund is like a separate entity in that it has a self-balancing set of accounts showing assets, liabilities, equity (fund balance), income, and expenses. If the organization does not use fund accounting, report only the "net assets" account balances, such as: capital stock, paid-in capital, and retained earnings or accumulated income.

Form **1023** (Rev. September 1990) Department of the Treasury Internal Revenue Service	**Application for Recognition of Exemption** **Under Section 501(c)(3) of the Internal Revenue Code**	OMB No. 1545-0056 If exempt status is approved, this application will be open for public inspection.

Read the instructions for each Part carefully.
A User Fee must be attached to this application.

If the required information and appropriate documents are not submitted along with Form 8718 (with payment of the appropriate user fee), the application may be returned to you.

Part I   **Identification of Applicant**

1a Full name of organization (as shown in organizing document)	2 Employer identification number (If none, see instructions.)
1b c/o Name (if applicable)	3 Name and telephone number of person to be contacted if additional information is needed
1c Address (number, street, and room or suite no.)	
1d City or town, state, and ZIP code	( )
	4 Month the annual accounting period ends

5 Date incorporated or formed	6 Activity codes (See instructions.)	7 Check here if applying under section: a ☐ 501(e) b ☐ 501(f) c ☐ 501(k)

8 Did the organization previously apply for recognition of exemption under this Code section or under any other
section of the Code? . . . . ☐ **Yes**   ☐ **No**
If "Yes," attach an explanation.

9 Has the organization filed Federal income tax returns or exempt organization information returns? . . . . . ☐ **Yes**   ☐ **No**
If "Yes," state the form numbers, years filed, and Internal Revenue office where filed.

10 Check the box for your type of organization. BE SURE TO ATTACH A COMPLETE COPY OF THE CORRESPONDING DOCUMENTS TO
THE APPLICATION BEFORE MAILING.

a ☐ Corporation— Attach a copy of your Articles of Incorporation, (including amendments and restatements) showing approval by
the appropriate State official; also include a copy of your bylaws.

b ☐ Trust—   Attach a copy of your Trust Indenture or Agreement, including all appropriate signatures and dates.

c ☐ Association— Attach a copy of your Articles of Association, Constitution, or other creating document, with a declaration (see
instructions) or other evidence the organization was formed by adoption of the document by more than one
person; also include a copy of your bylaws.

If you are a corporation or an unincorporated association that has not yet adopted bylaws, check here . . . . ► ☐

I declare under the penalties of perjury that I am authorized to sign this application on behalf of the above organization and that I have examined this application, including the accompanying schedules and attachments, and to the best of my knowledge it is true, correct, and complete.

Please
Sign ►
Here   ------------------------------------   ------------------------------------   ------------------
(Signature)   (Title or authority of signer)   (Date)

For Paperwork Reduction Act Notice, see page 1 of the instructions.

Complete the Procedural Checklist (page 7 of the instructions) prior to filing.

Part II	**Activities and Operational Information**

1   Provide a detailed narrative description of all the activities of the organization—past, present, and planned. **Do not merely refer to or repeat the language in your organizational document.** Describe each activity separately in the order of importance. Each description should include, as a minimum, the following: **(a)** a detailed description of the activity including its purpose; **(b)** when the activity was or will be initiated; and **(c)** where and by whom the activity will be conducted.

2   What are or will be the organization's sources of financial support? List in order of size.

3   Describe the organization's fundraising program, both actual and planned, and explain to what extent it has been put into effect. Include details of fundraising activities such as selective mailings, formation of fundraising committees, use of volunteers or professional fundraisers, etc. Attach representative copies of solicitations for financial support.

Part II **Activities and Operational Information** *(Continued)*

4 Give the following information about the organization's governing body:

a Names, addresses, and titles of officers, directors, trustees, etc.	**b** Annual Compensation

c Do any of the above persons serve as members of the governing body by reason of being public officials or being appointed by public officials?. . . . . ☐ **Yes**   ☐ **No**
If "Yes," name those persons and explain the basis of their selection or appointment.

d Are any members of the organization's governing body "disqualified persons" with respect to the organization (other than by reason of being a member of the governing body) or do any of the members have either a business or family relationship with "disqualified persons"? (See the specific instructions for line 4d.) . . . . ☐ **Yes**   ☐ **No**
If "Yes," explain.

5 Does the organization control or is it controlled by any other organization? . . . . ☐ **Yes**   ☐ **No**
Is the organization the outgrowth of (or successor to) another organization, or does it have a special relationship with another organization by reason of interlocking directorates or other factors? . . . . ☐ **Yes**   ☐ **No**
If either of these questions is answered "Yes," explain.

6 Does or will the organization directly or indirectly engage in any of the following transactions with any political organization or other exempt organization (other than 501(c)(3) organizations): **(a)** grants; **(b)** purchases or sales of assets; **(c)** rental of facilities or equipment; **(d)** loans or loan guarantees; **(e)** reimbursement arrangements; **(f)** performance of services, membership, or fundraising solicitations; or **(g)** sharing of facilities, equipment, mailing lists or other assets, or paid employees?. . . . . ☐ **Yes**   ☐ **No**
If "Yes," explain fully and identify the other organizations involved.

7 Is the organization financially accountable to any other organization? . . . . ☐ **Yes**   ☐ **No**
If "Yes," explain and identify the other organization. Include details concerning accountability or attach copies of reports if any have been submitted.

Part II   **Activities and Operational Information** *(Continued)*

8   What assets does the organization have that are used in the performance of its exempt function? (Do not include property producing
investment income.) If any assets are not fully operational, explain their status, what additional steps remain to be completed, and
when such final steps will be taken. If "None," indicate "N/A."

9a Will any of the organization's facilities or operations be managed by another organization or individual under a
contractual agreement? . . . . □ **Yes**   □ **No**

  b Is the organization a party to any leases? . . . . □ **Yes**   □ **No**

     If either of these questions is answered "Yes," attach a copy of the contracts and explain the relationship
between the applicant and the other parties.

10 Is the organization a membership organization? . . . . □ **Yes**   □ **No**

     If "Yes," complete the following:

  a Describe the organization's membership requirements, and attach a schedule of membership fees and dues.

  b Describe your present and proposed efforts to attract members, and attach a copy of any descriptive literature
or promotional material used for this purpose.

  c What benefits do (or will) your members receive in exchange for their payment of dues?

11a If the organization provides benefits, services or products, are the recipients required, or will they be
required, to pay for them? . . . . □ **N/A**   □ **Yes**   □ **No**

     If "Yes," explain how the charges are determined, and attach a copy of your current fee schedule.

  b Does or will the organization limit its benefits, services or products to specific individuals or classes
of individuals? . . . . □ **N/A**   □ **Yes**   □ **No**

     If "Yes," explain how the recipients or beneficiaries are or will be selected.

12 Does or will the organization attempt to influence legislation? . . . . □ **Yes**   □ **No**

     If "Yes," explain. Also, give an estimate of the percentage of the organization's time and funds which it devotes
or plans to devote to this activity.

13 Does or will the organization intervene in any way in political campaigns, including the publication or distribution
of statements? . . . . □ **Yes**   □ **No**

     If "Yes," explain fully.

Form 1023 (Rev. 9-90)   Page **5**

Part III   Technical Requirements

1   Are you filing Form 1023 within 15 months from the end of the month in which you were created or formed?   ☐ **Yes**   ☐ **No**
      If you answer "Yes," do not answer questions 2 through 6.

2   If one of the exceptions to the 15-month filing requirement shown below applies, check the appropriate box and proceed to
      question 7.
      Exceptions—You are not required to file an exemption application within 15 months if the organization:

      ☐ **(a)** Is a church, interchurch organization, local unit of a church, a convention or association of churches, or an integrated
             auxiliary of a church;

      ☐ **(b)** Is not a private foundation and normally has gross receipts of not more than $5,000 in each tax year; or,

      ☐ **(c)** Is a subordinate organization covered by a group exemption letter, but only if the parent or supervisory organization timely
             submitted a notice covering the subordinate.

3   If you do not meet any of the exceptions in question 2, do you wish to request relief from the 15-month filing
      requirement? .   .   .   . ☐ **Yes**   ☐ **No**

4   If you answer "Yes" to question 3, please give your reasons for not filing this application within 15 months from the end of the month
      in which your organization was created or formed. **(See the Instructions before completing this Item.)**

5   If you answer "No" to both questions 1 and 3 and do not meet any of the exceptions in question 2, your
      qualification as a section 501(c)(3) organization can be recognized only from the date this application is filed
      with your key District Director. Therefore, do you want us to consider your application as a request for
      recognition of exemption as a section 501(c)(3) organization from the date the application is received and not
      retroactively to the date you were formed? .   .   .   . ☐ **Yes**   ☐ **No**

6   If you answer "Yes" to question 5 above and wish to request recognition of section 501(c)(4) status for the **period beginning with the**
      date you were formed and ending with the date your Form 1023 application was received (the effective date of your section
      501(c)(3) status), check here ▶ ☐ and attach a completed page 1 of Form 1024 to this application.

Form 1023 (Rev. 9-90)   Page **6**

Part III **Technical Requirements** *(Continued)*

7 Is the organization a private foundation?
☐ **Yes**   (Answer question 8.)
☐ **No**   (Answer question 9 and proceed as instructed.)

8 If you answer "Yes" to question 7, do you claim to be a private operating foundation?
☐ **Yes**   (Complete Schedule E)
☐ **No**

After answering this question, go to Part IV.

9 If you answer "No" to question 7, indicate the public charity classification you are requesting by checking the box below that most appropriately applies:

THE ORGANIZATION IS NOT A PRIVATE FOUNDATION BECAUSE IT QUALIFIES:

(a)	☐	As a church or a convention or association of churches (CHURCHES MUST COMPLETE SCHEDULE A).	Sections 509(a)(1) and 170(b)(1)(A)(i)
(b)	☐	As a school (MUST COMPLETE SCHEDULE B).	Sections 509(a)(1) and 170(b)(1)(A)(ii)
(c)	☐	As a hospital or a cooperative hospital service organization, or a medical research organization operated in conjunction with a hospital (MUST COMPLETE SCHEDULE C).	Sections 509(a)(1) and 170(b)(1)(A)(iii)
(d)	☐	As a governmental unit described in section 170(c)(1).	Sections 509(a)(1) and 170(b)(1)(A)(v)
(e)	☐	As being operated solely for the benefit of, or in connection with, one or more of the organizations described in (a) through (d), (g), (h), or (i) (MUST COMPLETE SCHEDULE D).	Section 509(a)(3)
(f)	☐	As being organized and operated exclusively for testing for public safety.	Section 509(a)(4)
(g)	☐	As being operated for the benefit of a college or university that is owned or operated by a governmental unit.	Sections 509(a)(1) and 170(b)(1)(A)(iv)
(h)	☐	As receiving a substantial part of its support in the form of contributions from publicly supported organizations, from a governmental unit, or from the general public.	Sections 509(a)(1) and 170(b)(1)(A)(vi)
(i)	☐	As normally receiving not more than one-third of its support from gross investment income and more than one-third of its support from contributions, membership fees, and gross receipts from activities related to its exempt functions (subject to certain exceptions).	Section 509(a)(2)
(j)	☐	We are a publicly supported organization but are not sure whether we meet the public support test of block (h) or block (i). We would like the Internal Revenue Service to decide the proper classification.	Sections 509(a)(1) and 170(b)(1)(A)(vi) or Section 509(a)(2)

**If you checked one of the boxes (a) through (f) in question 9, go to question 14.
If you checked box (g) in question 9, go to questions 11 and 12.
If you checked box (h), (i), or (j), go to question 10.**

Part III **Technical Requirements** *(Continued)*

10 If you checked box (h), (i), or (j) in question 9, have you completed a tax year of at least 8 months?
☐ Yes—Indicate whether you are requesting:
☐ A definitive ruling (Answer questions 11 through 14.)
☐ An advance ruling (Answer questions 11 and 14 and attach 2 Forms 872-C completed and signed.)
☐ No—**You must request an advance ruling by completing and signing 2 Forms 872-C and attaching them to your application.**

11 If the organization received any unusual grants during any of the tax years shown in Part IV-A, attach a list for each year showing the name of the contributor; the date and the amount of the grant; and a brief description of the nature of the grant.

12 If you are requesting a definitive ruling under section 170(b)(1)(A)(iv) or (vi), check here ▶ ☐ and:

a Enter 2% of line 8, column (e) of Part IV-A _____

b Attach a list showing the name and amount contributed by each person (other than a governmental unit or "publicly supported" organization) whose total gifts, grants, contributions, etc., were more than the amount you entered on line **12a** above.

13 If you are requesting a definitive ruling under section 509(a)(2), check here ▶ ☐ and:

a For each of the years included on lines 1, 2, and 9 of Part IV-A, attach a list showing the name of and amount received from each "disqualified person."

b For each of the years included on line 9 of Part IV-A, attach a list showing the name of and amount received from each payer (other than a "disqualified person") whose payments to the organization were more than $5,000. For this purpose, "payer" includes, but is not limited to, any organization described in sections 170(b)(1)(A)(i) through (vi) and any governmental agency or bureau.

14 Indicate if your organization is one of the following. If so, complete the required schedule. (Submit only those schedules that apply to your organization. **Do not submit blank schedules.**)

	Yes	No	If "Yes," complete Schedule:
Is the organization a church?			A
Is the organization, or any part of it, a school?			B
Is the organization, or any part of it, a hospital or medical research organization?			C
Is the organization a section 509(a)(3) supporting organization?			D
Is the organization an operating foundation?			E
Is the organization, or any part of it, a home for the aged or handicapped?			F
Is the organization, or any part of it, a child care organization?			G
Does the organization provide or administer any scholarship benefits, student aid, etc.?			H
Has the organization taken over, or will it take over, the facilities of a "for profit" institution?			I

Form 1023 (Rev. 9-90)   Page **8**

Part IV	**Financial Data**

Complete the financial statements for the current year and for each of the 3 years immediately before it. If in existence less than 4 years, complete the statements for each year in existence. **If in existence less than 1 year, also provide proposed budgets for the 2 years following the current year.**

A.—Statement of Revenue and Expenses

		Current tax year	3 prior tax years or proposed budget for 2 years			
		(a) From_____ to	**(b)** 19	**(c)** 19	**(d)** 19	**(e) TOTAL**
Revenue	1 Gifts, grants, and contributions received (not including unusual grants—see instructions) . .					
	2 Membership fees received . .					
	3 Gross investment income (see instructions for definition) . .					
	4 Net income from organization's unrelated business activities not included on line 3					
	5 Tax revenues levied for and either paid to or spent on behalf of the organization					
	6 Value of services or facilities furnished by a governmental unit to the organization without charge (not including the value of services or facilities generally furnished the public without charge)					
	7 Other income (not including gain or loss from sale of capital assets) (attach schedule) . .					
	8 **Total** (add lines 1 through 7) .					
	9 Gross receipts from admissions, sales of merchandise or services, or furnishing of facilities in any activity that is not an unrelated business within the meaning of section 513					
	10 **Total** (add lines 8 and 9) . . .					
	11 Gain or loss from sale of capital assets (attach schedule)					
	12 Unusual grants					
	13 **Total** revenue (add lines 10 through 12)					
Expenses	14 Fundraising expenses					
	15 Contributions, gifts, grants, and similar amounts paid (attach schedule) . .					
	16 Disbursements to or for benefit of members (attach schedule) .					
	17 Compensation of officers, directors, and trustees (attach schedule).					
	18 Other salaries and wages . . .					
	19 Interest					
	20 Occupancy (rent, utilities, etc.) .					
	21 Depreciation and depletion . .					
	22 Other (attach schedule) . . .					
	23 **Total** expenses (add lines 14 through 22)					
	24 Excess of revenue over expenses (line 13 minus line 23).					

Form 1023 (Rev. 9-90)   Page 9

Part IV   **Financial Data** *(Continued)*

B.—Balance Sheet (at the end of the period shown)	Current tax year Date ....

Assets

1	Cash	**1**
2	Accounts receivable, net	**2**
3	Inventories	**3**
4	Bonds and notes receivable (attach schedule)	**4**
5	Corporate stocks (attach schedule)	**5**
6	Mortgage loans (attach schedule)	**6**
7	Other investments (attach schedule)	**7**
8	Depreciable and depletable assets (attach schedule)	**8**
9	Land	**9**
10	Other assets (attach schedule)	**10**
11	**Total assets** (add lines 1 through 10)	**11**

Liabilities

12	Accounts payable	**12**
13	Contributions, gifts, grants, etc., payable	**13**
14	Mortgages and notes payable (attach schedule)	**14**
15	Other liabilities (attach schedule)	**15**
16	**Total liabilities** (add lines 12 through 15)	**16**

Fund Balances or Net Assets

17	Total fund balances or net assets	**17**
18	**Total liabilities and fund balances or net assets** (add line 16 and line 17)	**18**

If there has been any substantial change in any aspect of your financial activities since the end of the period shown above, check the box and attach a detailed explanation . . . . ▶ ☐

Form **872-C**	**Consent Fixing Period of Limitation Upon Assessment of Tax Under Section 4940 of the Internal Revenue Code**	OMB No. 1545-0056
(Revised 9-90) Department of the Treasury Internal Revenue Service	(See instructions on reverse side.)	To be used with Form 1023. Submit in duplicate.

Under section 6501(c)(4) of the Internal Revenue Code, and as part of a request filed with Form 1023 that the organization named below be treated as a publicly supported organization under section 170(b)(1)(A)(vi) or section 509(a)(2) during an advance ruling period,

----
(Exact legal name of organization as shown in organizing document)

(Number, street, city or town, state, and ZIP code)

} and the

District Director of Internal Revenue, or Assistant Commissioner (Employee Plans and Exempt Organizations)

Consent and agree that the period for assessing tax (imposed under section 4940 of the Code) for any of the 5 tax years in the advance ruling period will extend 8 years, 4 months, and 15 days beyond the end of the first tax year.

However, if a notice of deficiency in tax for any of these years is sent to the organization before the period expires, the time for making an assessment will be further extended by the number of days the assessment is prohibited, plus 60 days.

Ending date of first tax year --------------------------------------
                                         (Month, day, and year)

Name of organization (as shown in organizing document)	Date

Officer or trustee having authority to sign

Signature ▶

For IRS use only

District Director or Assistant Commissioner (Employee Plans and Exempt Organizations)	Date

By ▶

For Paperwork Reduction Act Notice, see page 1 of the Form 1023 Instructions.

329-124 O - 92 - 3

You must complete this form and attach it to your application if you checked box (h), (i), or (j) of Part III, question 9, and you have not completed a tax year of at least 8 months.

> For example: If you incorporated May 15 and your year ends December 31, you have completed a tax year of only 7½ months. Therefore, Form 872-C must be completed.

(a) Enter the name of the organization. This must be entered exactly as it is written in the organizing document. Do not use abbreviations unless the organizing document does.

(b) Enter the current address.

(c) Enter ending date of first tax year.

> For example:

>> (a) If you were formed on June 15 and you have chosen December 31, as your year end, enter December 31, 19 ....

>> (b) If you were formed June 15 and have chosen June 30 as your year end, enter June 30, 19......... . In this example your first tax year consists of only 15 days.

(d) The form must be signed by an authorized officer or trustee, generally the President or Treasurer.

(e) Enter the date that the form was signed.

DO NOT MAKE ANY OTHER ENTRIES.

Schedule A.—Churches

1   Provide a brief history of the development of the organization, including the reasons for its
    formation.

2   Does the organization have a written creed or statement of faith? . . . . . . ☐ **Yes**   ☐ **No**
    If "Yes," attach a copy.

3   Does the organization require prospective members to renounce other
    religious beliefs or their membership in other churches or religious orders to
    become members? . . . . ☐ **Yes**   ☐ **No**

4   Does the organization have a formal code of doctrine and discipline for its
    members? . . . . ☐ **Yes**   ☐ **No**
    If "Yes," describe.

5   Describe your form of worship and attach a schedule of your worship services.

6   Are your services open to the public? . . . . ☐ **Yes**   ☐ **No**
    If "Yes," describe how you publicize your services and explain your criteria for admittance.

7   Explain how you attract new members.

8   **(a)** How many active members are currently enrolled in your church?

    (b) What is the average attendance at your worship services?

9   In addition to your worship services, what other religious services (such as baptisms, weddings,
    funerals, etc.) do you conduct?

Schedule A.—Churches *(Continued)*

10 Does the organization have a school for the religious instruction of the young? . ☐ **Yes** ☐ **No**

11 Were your current deacons, minister, and pastor formally ordained after a prescribed course of study? . . . . ☐ **Yes** ☐ **No**

12 Describe your religious hierarchy or ecclesiastical government.

13 Does your organization have an established place of worship? . . . . ☐ **Yes** ☐ **No**

If "Yes," provide the name and address of the owner or lessor of the property and the address and a description of the facility.

If you have no regular place of worship, state where your services are held and how the site is selected.

14 Does (or will) the organization license or otherwise ordain ministers (or their equivalent) or issue church charters? . . . . ☐ **Yes** ☐ **No**

If "Yes," describe in detail the requirements and qualifications needed to be so licensed, ordained, or chartered.

15 Did the organization pay a fee for a church charter? . . . . ☐ **Yes** ☐ **No**

If "Yes," state the name and address of the organization to which the fee was paid, attach a copy of the charter, and describe the circumstances surrounding the chartering.

16 Show how many hours a week your minister/pastor and officers each devote to church work and the amount of compensation paid each of them. If your minister or pastor is otherwise employed, indicate by whom employed, the nature of the employment, and the hours devoted to that employment.

Form 1023 (Rev. 9-90)   Page **13**

Schedule A.—Churches *(Continued)*

17 Will any funds or property of your organization be used by any officer, director, employee, minister, or pastor for his or her personal needs or convenience? . . . . ☐ **Yes**   ☐ **No**

If "Yes," describe the nature and circumstances of such use.

18 List any officers, directors, or trustees related by blood or marriage.

19 Give the name of anyone who has assigned income to you or made substantial contributions of money or other property. Specify the amounts involved.

Instructions

Although a church, its integrated auxiliaries, or a convention or association of churches is not required to file Form 1023 to be exempt from Federal income tax or to receive tax deductible contributions, such an organization may find it advantageous to obtain recognition of exemption. In this event, you should submit information showing that your organization is a church, synagogue, association or convention of churches, religious order or religious organization that is an integral part of a church, and that it is carrying out the functions of a church.

In determining whether an admittedly religious organization is also a church, the Internal Revenue Service does not accept any and every assertion that such an organization is a church. Because beliefs and practices vary so widely, there is no single definition of the word "church" for tax purposes. The Internal Revenue Service considers the facts and circumstances of each organization applying for church status.

The Internal Revenue Service maintains two basic guidelines in determining that an organization meets the religious purposes test:

(a) that the particular religious beliefs of the organization are truly and sincerely held, and

(b) that the practices and rituals associated with the organization's religious beliefs or creed are not illegal or contrary to clearly defined public policy.

In order for the Internal Revenue Service to properly evaluate your organization's activities and religious purposes, it is important that all questions in this Schedule are answered accurately.

The information submitted with this Schedule will be a determining factor in granting the "church" status requested by your organization. In completing the Schedule, the following points should be considered:

(a) The organization's activities in furtherance of its beliefs must be exclusively religious,

(b) An organization will not qualify for exemption if it has a substantial nonexempt purpose of serving the private interests of its founder or the founder's family.

Schedule B.—Schools, Colleges, and Universities

1 Does, or will, the organization normally have: **(a)** a regularly scheduled curriculum, **(b)** a regular faculty of qualified teachers, **(c)** a regularly enrolled body of students, and **(d)** facilities where its educational activities are regularly carried on? . . . . ☐ **Yes** ☐ **No**

If "No," do not complete the rest of this Schedule.

2 Is the organization an instrumentality of a State or political subdivision of a State? . . . . ☐ **Yes** ☐ **No**

If "Yes," document this in Part II and do not complete items 3 through 10 of this Schedule. (See instructions for Schedule B.)

3 Does or will the organization (or any department or division within it) discriminate in any way on the basis of race with respect to:

a Admissions? . . . . ☐ **Yes** ☐ **No**

b Use of facilities or exercise of student privileges? . . . . ☐ **Yes** ☐ **No**

c Faculty or administrative staff? . . . . ☐ **Yes** ☐ **No**

d Scholarship or loan programs? . . . . ☐ **Yes** ☐ **No**

If "Yes" for any of the above, explain.

4 Does the organization include a statement in its charter, bylaws, or other governing instrument, or in a resolution of its governing body, that it has a racially nondiscriminatory policy as to students? . . . . . . ☐ **Yes** ☐ **No**

Attach whatever corporate resolutions or other official statements the organization has made on this subject.

5a Has the organization made its racially nondiscriminatory policies known in a manner that brings the policies to the attention of all segments of the general community that it serves? . . . . ☐ **Yes** ☐ **No**

If "Yes," describe how these policies have been publicized and how often relevant notices or announcements have been made. If no newspaper or broadcast media notices have been used, explain.

b If applicable, attach clippings of any relevant newspaper notices or advertising, or copies of tapes or scripts used for media broadcasts. Also attach copies of brochures and catalogues dealing with student admissions, programs, and scholarships, as well as representative copies of all written advertising used as a means of informing prospective students of your programs.

6 Attach a numerical schedule showing the racial composition, as of the current academic year, and projected as far as may be feasible for the next academic year, of: **(a)** the student body, and **(b)** the faculty and administrative staff.

7 Attach a list showing the amount of any scholarship and loan funds awarded to students enrolled and the racial composition of the students who have received the awards.

8a Attach a list of the organization's incorporators, founders, board members, and donors of land or buildings, whether individuals or organizations.

b State whether any of the organizations listed in **8a** have as an objective the maintenance of segregated public or private school education, and, if so, whether any of the individuals listed in **8a** are officers or active members of such organizations.

9a Indicate the public school district and county in which the organization is located.

b Was the organization formed or substantially expanded at the time of public school desegregation in the above district or county? . . . . ☐ **Yes** ☐ **No**

10 Has the organization ever been determined by a State or Federal administrative agency or judicial body to be racially discriminatory? . . . . ☐ **Yes** ☐ **No**

If "Yes," attach a detailed explanation identifying the parties to the suit, the forum in which the case was heard, the cause of action, the holding in the case, and the citations (if any) for the case. Also describe in detail what changes (c) your operation, if any, have occurred since then.

For more information, see back of Schedule B.

Instructions

A "school" is an organization that has the primary function of presenting formal instruction, normally maintains a regular faculty and curriculum, normally has a regularly enrolled body of students, and has a place where its educational activities are carried on. The term generally corresponds to the definition of an "educational organization" in section 170(b)(1)(A)(ii). Thus, the term includes primary, secondary, preparatory and high schools, and colleges and universities. The term does not include organizations engaged in both educational and non-educational activities unless the latter are merely incidental to the educational activities. A school for handicapped children would be included within the term, but an organization merely providing handicapped children with custodial care would not.

For purposes of this Schedule, "Sunday schools" that are conducted by a church would not be included in the term "schools," but separately organized schools (such as parochial schools, universities, and similar institutions) would be included in the term.

A private school that otherwise meets the requirements of section 501(c)(3) as an educational institution will not qualify for exemption under section 501(a) unless it has a racially nondiscriminatory policy as to students. This policy means that the school admits students of any race to all the rights, privileges, programs, and activities generally accorded or made available to students at that school, and that the school does not discriminate on the basis of race in the administration of its educational policies, admissions policies, scholarship and loan programs, and athletic, or other school-administered programs. The Internal Revenue Service considers discrimination on the basis of race to include discrimination on the basis of color and national or ethnic origin. A policy of a school that favors racial minority groups in admissions, facilities, programs, and financial assistance will not constitute discrimination on the basis of race when the purpose and effect is to promote the establishment and maintenance of that school's racially nondiscriminatory policy as to students. See Rev. Proc. 75-50, 1975-2 C.B. 587, for guidelines and recordkeeping requirements for determining whether private schools that are applying for recognition of exemption have racially nondiscriminatory policies as to students.

Line 2.—An instrumentality of a State or political subdivision of a State may qualify under section 501(c)(3) if it is organized as a separate entity from the governmental unit that created it and if it otherwise meets the organizational and operational tests of section 501(c)(3). (See Rev. Rul. 60-384, 1960-2 C.B. 172.) Any such organization that is a school is not a private school and, therefore, is not subject to the provisions of Rev. Proc. 75-50.

Schools that incorrectly answer "Yes" to line 2 will be contacted to furnish the information called for by lines 3 through 10 in order to establish that they meet the requirements for exemption. To prevent delay in the processing of your application, be sure to answer line 2 correctly and complete lines 3 through 10 if applicable.

Schedule C.—Hospitals and Medical Research Organizations

☐ Check here if you are claiming to be a hospital; complete the questions in Section I of this Schedule; and write "N/A" in Section II.

☐ Check here if you are claiming to be a medical research organization operated in conjunction with a hospital; complete the questions in Section II of this Schedule; and write "N/A" in Section I.

Section I   Hospitals

1a How many doctors are on the hospital's courtesy staff? . . . . _____

b Are all the doctors in the community eligible for staff privileges? . . . . ☐ **Yes**   ☐ **No**
If "No," give the reasons why and explain how the courtesy staff is selected.

2a Does the hospital maintain a full-time emergency room? . . . . ☐ **Yes**   ☐ **No**

b What is the hospital's policy on administering emergency services to persons without apparent means to pay?

c Does the hospital have any arrangements with police, fire, and voluntary ambulance services for the delivery or admission of emergency cases? . . . . ☐ **Yes**   ☐ **No**
Explain.

3a Does or will the hospital require a deposit from persons covered by Medicare or Medicaid in its admission practices? . . . . ☐ **Yes**   ☐ **No**
If "Yes," explain.

b Does the same deposit requirement apply to all other patients? . . . . ☐ **Yes**   ☐ **No**
If "No," explain.

4 Does or will the hospital provide for a portion of its services and facilities to be used for charity patients? . . . . ☐ **Yes**   ☐ **No**
Explain your policy regarding charity cases. Include data on the hospital's past experience in admitting charity patients and arrangements it may have with municipal or government agencies for absorbing the cost of such care.

5 Does or will the hospital carry on a formal program of medical training and research? . . . . ☐ **Yes**   ☐ **No**
If "Yes," describe.

6 Does the hospital provide office space to physicians carrying on a medical practice? . . . . ☐ **Yes**   ☐ **No**
If "Yes," attach a list setting forth the name of each physician, the amount of space provided, the annual rent, the expiration date of the current lease and whether the terms of the lease represent fair market value.

Section II   Medical Research Organizations

1 Name the hospitals with which you have a relationship and describe the relationship.

2 Attach a schedule describing your present and proposed (indicate which) medical research activities; show the nature of the activities, and the amount of money that has been or will be spent in carrying them out. (Making grants to other organizations is not direct conduct of medical research.)

3 Attach a statement of assets showing the fair market value of your assets and the portion of the assets directly devoted to medical research.

For more information, see back of Schedule C.

Additional Information

Hospitals.—To be entitled to status as a "hospital," an organization must have, as its principal purpose or function, the providing of medical or hospital care or medical education or research. "Medical care" includes the treatment of any physical or mental disability or condition, the cost of which may be taken as a deduction under section 213, whether the treatment is performed on an inpatient or outpatient basis. Thus, a rehabilitation institution, outpatient clinic, or community mental health or drug treatment center may be a hospital if its principal function is providing the above described services. On the other hand, a convalescent home or a home for children or the aged would not be a hospital. Similarly, an institution whose principal purpose or function is to train handicapped individuals to pursue some vocation would not be a hospital. Moreover, a medical education or medical research institution is not a hospital, unless it is also actively engaged in providing medical or hospital care to patients on its premises or in its facilities on an inpatient or outpatient basis.

Cooperative Hospital Service Organizations.—Cooperative hospital service organizations (section 501(e)) should not complete Schedule C.

Medical Research Organizations.—To qualify as a medical research organization, the principal function of the organization must be the direct, continuous and active conduct of medical research in conjunction with a hospital that is described in section 501(c)(3), a Federal hospital, or an instrumentality of a governmental unit referred to in section 170(c)(1). For purposes of section 170(b)(1)(A)(iii) only, the organization must be set up to use the funds it receives in the active conduct of medical research by January 1 of the fifth calendar year after receipt. The arrangement it has with donors to assure use of the funds within the five-year period must be legally enforceable. As used here, "medical research" means investigations, experiments and studies to discover, develop, or verify knowledge relating to the causes, diagnosis, treatment, prevention, or control of the physical or mental diseases and impairments of man. For further information, see Regulations section 1.170A-9(c)(2).

Schedule D.—Section 509(a)(3) Supporting Organization

1a Organizations supported by the applicant organization: Name and address of supported organization	b Has the supported organization received a ruling or determination letter that it is not a private foundation by reason of section 509(a)(1) or (2)?	
---	☐ Yes	☐ No
---	☐ Yes	☐ No
---	☐ Yes	☐ No
---	☐ Yes	☐ No
---	☐ Yes	☐ No

c If "No" for any of the organizations listed in 1a, explain.

2 Does the organization you support have tax-exempt status under section 501(c)(4), 501(c)(5), or 501(c)(6)? ☐ Yes ☐ No
If "Yes," attach: **(a)** a copy of its ruling or determination letter, and **(b)** an analysis of its revenue for the current year and the preceding three years. (Provide the financial data using the formats in Part IV-A (lines 1–13) and Part III (questions 11, 12, and 13).)

3 Does your governing document indicate that the majority of your governing board is elected or appointed by the supported organizations? . . . . ☐ Yes ☐ No
If "Yes," skip to question 9.
If "No," you must answer questions 4 through 9.

4 Does your governing document indicate the common supervision or control that you and the supported organizations share? . . . . ☐ Yes ☐ No
If "Yes," give the article and paragraph numbers. If "No," explain.

5 To what extent do the supported organizations have a significant voice in your investment policies, in the making and timing of grants, and in otherwise directing the use of your income or assets?

6 Does the mentioning of the supported organizations in your governing instrument make you a trust that the supported organizations can enforce under state law and compel to make an accounting? . . . . ☐ Yes ☐ No
If "Yes," explain.

7a What percentage of your income do you pay to each supported organization?

b What is the total annual income of each supported organization?

c How much do you contribute annually to each supported organization?

For more information, see back of Schedule D.

Schedule D.—Section 509(a)(3) Supporting Organization *(Continued)*

8   To what extent do you conduct activities that would otherwise be carried on by the supported organizations? Explain why these activities would otherwise be carried on by the supported organizations.

9   Is the applicant organization controlled directly or indirectly by one or more "disqualified persons" (other than one who is a disqualified person solely because he or she is a manager) or by an organization which is not described in section 509(a)(1) or (2)? . . . . ☐ **Yes**   ☐ **No**

If "Yes," explain.

Instructions

For an explanation of the types of organizations defined in section 509(a)(3) as being excluded from the definition of a private foundation, see Publication 557, Chapter 3.

Line 1.—List each organization that is supported by your organization and indicate in item 1b if the supported organization has received a letter recognizing exempt status as a section 501(c)(3) public charity as defined in section 509(a)(1) or 509(a)(2).

If you answer "No" in 1b to any of the listed organizations, please explain in 1c.

Line 3.—Your governing document may be articles of incorporation, articles of association, constitution, trust indenture, or trust agreement.

Line 9.—For a definition of a "disqualified person," see specific instructions for Part II, line 4d, on page 3 of the application's instructions.

Schedule E.—Private Operating Foundation

Income Test		Most recent tax year
1a Adjusted net income, as defined in Regulations section 53.4942(a)-2(d)	1a	
b Minimum investment return, as defined in Regulations section 53.4942(a)-2(c)	1b	
2 Qualifying distributions:		
a Amounts (including administrative expenses) paid directly for the active conduct of the activities for which organized and operated under section 501(c)(3) (attach schedule)	2a	
b Amounts paid to acquire assets to be used (or held for use) directly in carrying out purposes described in section 170(c)(1) or 170(c)(2)(B) (attach schedule)	2b	
c Amounts set aside for specific projects that are for purposes described in section 170(c)(1) or 170(c)(2)(B) (attach schedule)	2c	
d Total qualifying distributions (add lines 2a, b, and c)	2d	
3 Percentages:		
a Percentage of qualifying distributions to adjusted net income (divide line 2d by line 1a)	3a	%
b Percentage of qualifying distributions to minimum investment return (divide line 2d by line 1b) . . . . . (Percentage must be at least 85% for 3a or 3b)	3b	%

Assets Test		
4 Value of organization's assets used in activities that directly carry out the exempt purposes. Do not include assets held merely for investment or production of income (attach schedule)	4	
5 Value of any stock of a corporation that is controlled by applicant organization and carries out its exempt purposes (attach statement describing corporation)	5	
6 Value of all qualifying assets (add lines 4 and 5)	6	
7 Value of applicant organization's total assets	7	
8 Percentage of qualifying assets to total assets (divide line 6 by line 7—percentage must exceed 65%) . . .	8	%

Endowment Test		
9 Value of assets not used (or held for use) directly in carrying out exempt purposes:		
a Monthly average of investment securities at fair market value	9a	
b Monthly average of cash balances	9b	
c Fair market value of all other investment property (attach schedule)	9c	
d Total (add lines 9a, b, and c)	9d	
10 Acquisition indebtedness related to line 9 items (attach schedule)	10	
11 Balance (subtract line 10 from line 9d)	11	
12 Multiply line 11 by 3⅓% (⅔ of the percentage for the minimum investment return computation under section 4942(e)). Line 2d above must equal or exceed the result of this computation	12	

Support Test		
13 Applicant organization's support as defined in section 509(d)	13	
14 Gross investment income as defined in section 509(e)	14	
15 Support for purposes of section 4942(j)(3)(B)(iii) (subtract line 14 from line 13)	15	
16 Support received from the general public, 5 or more exempt organizations, or a combination of these sources (attach schedule)	16	
17 For persons (other than exempt organizations) contributing more than 1% of line 15, enter the total amounts that are more than 1% of line 15	17	
18 Subtract line 17 from line 16	18	
19 Percentage of total support (divide line 18 by line 15—must be at least 85%)	19	%
20 Does line 16 include support from an exempt organization that is more than 25% of the amount of line 15? . .	☐ Yes	☐ No

21 Newly created organizations with less than one year's experience: Attach a statement explaining how the organization is planning to satisfy the requirements of section 4942(j)(3) for the income test and one of the supplemental tests during its first year's operation. Include a description of plans and arrangements, press clippings, public announcements, solicitations for funds, etc.

22 Does the amount entered on line 2a include any grants that you made? . . . . ☐ Yes ☐ No
If "Yes," attach a statement explaining how those grants satisfy the criteria for "significant involvement" grants described in section 53.4942(b)-1(b)(2) of the regulations.

For more information, see back of Schedule E.

Instructions

If the organization claims to be an operating foundation described in section 4942(j)(3) and—

   (a) bases its claim to private operating foundation status on normal and regular operations over a period of years; or

   (b) is newly created, set up as a private operating foundation, and has at least one year's experience;

provide the information under the income test and under one of the three supplemental tests (assets, endowment, or support). If the organization does not have at least one year's experience, provide the information called for on line 21. If the organization's private operating foundation status depends on its normal and regular operations as described in (a) above, attach a schedule similar to the one shown on the front of this schedule showing the data in tabular form for the three years preceding the most recent tax year. (See Regulations section 53.4942(b)-1 for additional information before completing the "Income Test" section of this schedule.) Organizations claiming section 4942(j)(5) status must satisfy the income test and the endowment test.

A "private operating foundation" described in section 4942(j)(3) is a private foundation that spends substantially all of the lesser of its adjusted net income (as defined below) or its minimum investment return directly for the active conduct of the activities constituting the purpose or function for which it is organized and operated. The foundation must satisfy the income test under section 4942(j)(3)(A), as modified by Regulations section 53.4942(b)-1, and one of the following three supplemental tests: **(1)** the assets test under section 4942(j)(3)(B)(i); **(2)** the endowment test under section 4942(j)(3)(B)(ii); or **(3)** the support test under section 4942(j)(3)(B)(iii).

Certain long-term care facilities described in section 4942(j)(5) are treated as private operating foundations for purposes of section 4942 only.

"Adjusted net income" is the excess of gross income for the tax year over the sum of deductions determined with the modifications described below. Items of gross income from any unrelated trade or business and the deductions directly connected with the unrelated trade or business will be taken into account in computing the organization's adjusted net income:

Income modifications (adjustments to gross income).—

(1) Section 103 (relating to interest on certain governmental obligations) does not apply. Thus, interest that otherwise would have been excluded should be included in gross income.

(2) Except as provided in (3) below, capital gains and losses are taken into account only to the extent of the net short-term gain. Long-term gains and losses will be disregarded.

(3) The gross amount received from the sale or disposition of certain property should be included in gross income to the extent that the acquisition of the property constituted a qualifying distribution under section 4942(g)(1)(B).

(4) Repayments of prior qualifying distributions (as defined in section 4942(g)(1)(A)) will constitute items of gross income.

(5) Any amount set aside under section 4942(g)(2) that is "not necessary for the purposes for which it was set aside" will constitute an item of gross income.

Deduction modifications (adjustments to deductions).—

(1) Expenses for the general operation of the organization according to its charitable purposes (as contrasted with expenses for the production or collection of income and management, conservation, or maintenance of income producing property) should not be taken as deductions. If only a portion of the property is used for production of income subject to section 4942 and the remainder is used for general charitable purposes, the expenses connected with that property should be divided according to those purposes and only expenses related to the income producing portion will be allowed as a deduction.

(2) Charitable contributions, deductible under section 170 or 642(c), should not be taken into account as deductions for adjusted net income.

(3) The net operating loss deduction prescribed under section 172 should not be taken into account as a deduction for adjusted net income.

(4) The special deductions for corporations (such as the dividends-received deduction) allowed under sections 241 through 250 should not be taken into account as deductions for adjusted net income.

(5) Depreciation and depletion should be determined in the same manner as under section 4940(c)(3)(B).

Section 265 (relating to the expenses and interest connected with tax-exempt interest) should not be taken into account.

You may find it easier to figure adjusted net income by completing Column (c), Part 1, Form 990-PF, according to the instructions for that form.

An organization that has been held to be a private operating foundation will continue to be such an organization only if it meets the income test and either the assets, endowment, or support test in later years. See Regulations section 53.4942(b) for additional information. No additional request for ruling will be necessary or appropriate for an organization to maintain its status as a private operating foundation. However, data related to the above tests must be submitted with the organization's annual information return, Form 990-PF.

Schedule F.—Homes for the Aged or Handicapped

1 What are the requirements for admission to residency? Explain fully and attach promotional literature and application forms.

2 Does or will the home charge an entrance or founder's fee? . . . . ☐ Yes   ☐ No
If "Yes," explain and specify the amount charged.

3 What periodic fees or maintenance charges are or will be required of its residents?

4a What established policy does the home have concerning residents who become unable to pay their regular charges?

b What arrangements does the home have or will it make with local and Federal welfare units, sponsoring organizations, or others to absorb all or part of the cost of maintaining those residents?

5 What arrangements does or will the home have to provide for the health needs of its residents?

6 In what way are the home's residential facilities designed to meet some combination of the physical, emotional, recreational, social, religious, and similar needs of the aged or handicapped?

7 Provide a description of the home's facilities and specify both the residential capacity of the home and the current number of residents.

8 Attach a sample copy of the contract or agreement the organization makes with or requires of its residents.

For more information, see back of Schedule F.

Instructions

Line 1.— Provide the criteria for admission to the home and submit brochures, pamphlets, or other printed material used to inform the public about the home's admissions policy.

Line 2.— Indicate whether the fee charged is an entrance fee or a monthly charge, etc. Also, if the fee is an entrance fee, is it payable in a lump sum or on an installment basis? If there is no fee, indicate "N/A."

Line 4.— Indicate the organization's policy regarding residents who are unable to pay. Also, indicate whether the organization is subsidized for all or part of the cost of maintaining those residents who are unable to pay.

Line 5.— Indicate whether the organization provides health care to the residents, either directly or indirectly, through some continuing arrangement with other organizations, facilities, or health personnel. If no health care is provided, indicate "N/A."

Form 1023 (Rev. 9-90)   Page **25**

Schedule G.—Child Care Organizations

1 Is the organization's primary activity the providing of care for children away
from their homes? . . . . □ **Yes**   □ **No**

2 How many children is the organization authorized to care for by the State (or local governmental
unit), and what was the average attendance during the past 6 months, or the number of months the
organization has been in existence if less than 6 months?

3 How many children are currently cared for by the organization?

4 Is substantially all (at least 85%) of the care provided for the purpose of
enabling parents to be gainfully employed or to seek employment? . . . . . . □ **Yes**   □ **No**

5 Are the services provided available to the general public? . . . . □ **Yes**   □ **No**
If "No," explain.

6 Indicate the category, or categories, of parents whose children are eligible for your child-care
services (check as many as apply):

□   low income parents

□   any working parents (or parents looking for work)

□   anyone with the ability to pay

□   other (explain)

Instructions

Line 5.— If your services are not available to the general public, indicate the particular group or groups
that may utilize your services.

REMINDER—If this organization claims to operate a school, then it must also fill out Schedule B.

Form 1023 (Rev. 9-90)   Page **27**

Schedule H.—Organizations Providing Scholarship Benefits, Student Aid, Etc., to Individuals

1a Describe the nature and the amount of the scholarship benefit, student aid, etc., including the terms and conditions governing its use, whether a gift or a loan, and how the availability of the scholarship is publicized. If the organization has established or will establish several categories of scholarship benefits, identify each kind of benefit and explain how the organization determines the recipients for each category. Attach a sample copy of any application the organization requires individuals to complete to be considered for scholarship grants, loans, or similar benefits. (Private foundations that make grants for travel, study, or other similar purposes are required to obtain advance approval of scholarship procedures. See Regulations sections 53.4945-4(c) and (d).)

b If you want this application considered as a request for approval of grant procedures in the event we determine that you are a private foundation, check here . . . . ▶ ☐

c If you checked the box in 1b above, indicate the sections for which you wish to be considered.

☐ 4945(g)(1)   ☐ 4945(g)(2)   ☐ 4945(g)(3)

2 What limitations or restrictions are there on the class of individuals who are eligible recipients? Specifically explain whether there are, or will be, any restrictions or limitations in the selection procedures based upon race or the employment status of the prospective recipient or any relative of the prospective recipient. Also indicate the approximate number of eligible individuals.

3 Indicate the number of grants you anticipate making annually . . . . ▶

4 If you base your selections in any way on the employment status of the applicant or any relative of the applicant, indicate whether there is or has been any direct or indirect relationship between the members of the selection committee and the employer. Also indicate whether relatives of the members of the selection committee are possible recipients or have been recipients.

5 Describe any procedures you have for supervising grants (such as obtaining reports or transcripts) that you award, and any procedures you have for taking action if the terms of the grant are violated.

For more information, see back of Schedule H.

Additional Information

Private foundations that make grants to individuals for travel, study, or other similar purposes are required to obtain advance approval of their grant procedures from the Internal Revenue Service. Such grants that are awarded under selection procedures that have not been approved by the Internal Revenue Service are subject to a 10% excise tax under section 4945. (See Regulations sections 53.4945-4(c) and (d).)

If you are requesting advance approval of your grant procedures, the following sections apply to line 1c:

4945(g)(1)— The grant constitutes a scholarship or fellowship grant that meets the provisions of section 117(a) prior to its amendment by the Tax Reform Act of 1986 and is to be used for study at an educational organization (school) described in section 170(b)(1)(A)(ii).

4945(g)(2)— The grant constitutes a prize or award that is subject to the provisions of section 74(b), if the recipient of such a prize or award is selected from the general public.

4945(g)(3)— The purpose of the grant is to achieve a specific objective, produce a report or other similar product, or improve or enhance a literary, artistic, musical, scientific, teaching, or other similar capacity, skill, or talent of the grantee.

Form 1023 (Rev. 9-90)   Page **29**

Schedule I.—Successors to "For Profit" Institutions

1   What was the name of the predecessor organization and the nature of its activities?

2   Who were the owners or principal stockholders of the predecessor organization? (If more space is needed, attach schedule.)

Name and address	Share or interest

3   Describe the business or family relationship between the owners or principal stockholders and principal employees of the predecessor organization and the officers, directors, and principal employees of the applicant organization.

4a Attach a copy of the agreement of sale or other contract that sets forth the terms and conditions of sale of the predecessor organization or of its assets to the applicant organization.

  b Attach an appraisal by an independent qualified expert showing the fair market value at the time of sale of the facilities or property interest sold.

5   Has any property or equipment formerly used by the predecessor organization been rented to the applicant organization or will any such property be rented? . . . . ☐ **Yes**   ☐ **No**
If "Yes," explain and attach copies of all leases and contracts.

6   Is the organization leasing or will it lease or otherwise make available any space or equipment to the owners, principal stockholders, or principal employees of the predecessor organization? . . . . ☐ **Yes**   ☐ **No**
If "Yes," explain and attach a list of these tenants and a copy of the lease for each such tenant.

7   Were any new operating policies initiated as a result of the transfer of assets from a profit-making organization to a nonprofit organization?. . . . . ☐ **Yes**   ☐ **No**
If "Yes," explain.

Additional Information

A "for profit" institution for purposes of this Schedule includes any organization in which a person may have a proprietary or partnership interest, hold corporate stock, or otherwise exercise an ownership interest. The institution need not have operated for the purpose of making a profit.

Activity Code Numbers of Exempt Organizations (select up to three codes which best describe or most accurately identify your purposes, activities, operations or type of organization and enter in block 6, page 1, of the application. Enter first the code which most accurately identifies you.)

Code

Religious Activities

001 Church, synagogue, etc.
002 Association or convention of churches
003 Religious order
004 Church auxiliary
005 Mission
006 Missionary activities
007 Evangelism
008 Religious publishing activities
---- Bookstore (use 918)
---- Genealogical activities (use 094)
029 Other religious activities

Schools, Colleges and Related Activities

030 School, college, trade school, etc.
031 Special school for the blind, handicapped, etc.
032 Nursery school
---- Day care center (use 574)
033 Faculty group
034 Alumni association or group
035 Parent or parent-teachers association
036 Fraternity or sorority
---- Key club (use 323)
037 Other student society or group
038 School or college athletic association
039 Scholarships for children of employees
040 Scholarships (other)
041 Student loans
042 Student housing activities
043 Other student aid
044 Student exchange with foreign country
045 Student operated business
---- Financial support of schools, colleges, etc. (use 602)
---- Achievement prizes or awards (use 914)
---- Student bookstore (use 918)
---- Student travel (use 299)
---- Scientific research (see Scientific Research Activities)
046 Private school
059 Other school related activities

Cultural, Historical or Other Educational Activities

060 Musuem, zoo, planetarium, etc.
061 Library
062 Historical site, records or reenactment
063 Monument
064 Commemorative event (centennial, festival, pageant, etc.)
065 Fair
088 Community theatrical group
089 Singing society or group
090 Cultural performances
091 Art exhibit
092 Literary activities
093 Cultural exchanges with foreign country
094 Genealogical activities
---- Achievement prizes or awards (use 914)
---- Gifts or grants to individuals (use 561)
---- Financial support of cultural organizations (use 602)
119 Other cultural or historical activities

Other Instruction and Training Activities

120 Publishing activities
121 Radio or television broadcasting
122 Producing films
123 Discussion groups, forums, panels, lectures, etc.
124 Study and research (non-scientific)
125 Giving information or opinion (see also Advocacy)
126 Apprentice training
---- Travel tours (use 299)
149 Other instruction and training

Health Services and Related Activities

150 Hospital
151 Hospital auxiliary
152 Nursing or convalescent home
153 Care and housing for the aged (see also 382)
154 Health clinic
155 Rural medical facility
156 Blood bank
157 Cooperative hospital service organization
158 Rescue and emergency service
159 Nurses register or bureau
160 Aid to the handicapped (see also 031)
161 Scientific research (diseases)
162 Other medical research
163 Health insurance (medical, dental, optical, etc.)
164 Prepared group health plan
165 Community health planning
166 Mental health care
167 Group medical practice association
168 In-faculty group practice association
169 Hospital pharmacy, parking facility, food services, etc.
179 Other health services

Scientific Research Activities

180 Contract or sponsored scientific research for industry

Code

181 Scientific research for government
---- Scientific research (diseases) (use 161)
199 Other scientific research activities

Business and Professional Organizations

200 Business promotion (chamber of commerce, business league, etc.)
201 Real estate association
202 Board of trade
203 Regulating business
204 Promotion of fair business practices
205 Professional association
206 Professional association auxiliary
207 Industry trade shows
208 Convention displays
---- Testing products for public safety (use 905)
209 Research, development and testing
210 Professional athletic league
---- Attracting new industry (use 403)
---- Publishing activities (use 120)
---- Insurance or other benefits for members (see Employee or Membership Benefit Organizations)
211 Underwriting municipal insurance
212 Assigned risk insurance activities
213 Tourist bureau
229 Other business or professional group

Farming and Related Activities

230 Farming
231 Farm bureau
232 Agricultural group
233 Horticultural group
234 Farmers cooperative marketing or purchasing
235 Financing crop operations
---- FFA, FHA, 4-H club, etc. (use 322)
---- Fair (use 065)
236 Dairy herd improvement association
237 Breeders association
249 Other farming and related activities

Mutual Organizations

250 Mutual ditch, irrigation, telephone, electric company or like organization
251 Credit union
252 Reserve funds or insurance for domestic building and loan association, cooperative bank, or mutual savings bank
253 Mutual insurance company
254 Corporation organized under an Act of Congress (see also 904)
---- Farmers cooperative marketing or purchasing (use 234)
---- Cooperative hospital service organization (use 157)
259 Other mutual organization

Employee or Membership Benefit Organizations

260 Fraternal beneficiary society, order, or association
261 Improvement of conditions of workers
262 Association of municipal employees
263 Association of employees
264 Employee or member welfare association
265 Sick, accident, death, or similar benefits
266 Strike benefits
267 Unemployment benefits
268 Pension or retirement benefits
269 Vacation benefits
279 Other services or benefits to members or employees

Sports, Athletic, Recreational and Social Activities

280 Country club
281 Hobby club
282 Dinner club
283 Variety club
284 Dog club
285 Women's club
---- Garden club (use 356)
286 Hunting or fishing club
287 Swimming or tennis club
288 Other sports club
---- Boys Club, Little League, etc. (use 321)
296 Community center
297 Community recreational facilities (park, playground, etc.)
298 Training in sports
299 Travel tours
300 Amateur athletic association
---- School or college athletic association (use 038)
301 Fundraising athletic or sports event
317 Other sports or athletic activities
318 Other recreational activities
319 Other social activities

Youth Activities

320 Boy Scouts, Girl Scouts, etc.
321 Boys Club, Little League, etc.

Code

322 FFA, FHA, 4-H club, etc.
323 Key club
324 YMCA, YWCA, YMHA, etc.
325 Camp
326 Care and housing of children (orphanage, etc.)
327 Prevention of cruelty to children
328 Combat juvenile delinquency
349 Other youth organization or activities

Conservation, Environmental and Beautification Activities

350 Preservation of natural resources (conservation)
351 Combating or preventing pollution (air, water, etc.)
352 Land acquisition for preservation
353 Soil or water conservation
354 Preservation of scenic beauty
---- Litigation (see Litigation and Legal Aid Activities)
---- Combat community deterioration (use 402)
355 Wildlife sanctuary or refuge
356 Garden club
379 Other conservation, environmental or beautification activities

Housing Activities

380 Low-income housing
381 Low and moderate income housing
382 Housing for the aged (see also 153)
---- Nursing or convalescent home (use 152)
---- Student housing (use 042)
---- Orphanage (use 326)
398 Instruction and guidance on housing
399 Other housing activities

Inner City or Community Activities

400 Area development, redevelopment or renewal
---- Housing (see Housing Activities)
401 Homeowners association
402 Other activity aimed at combating community deterioration
403 Attracting new industry or retaining industry in an area
404 Community promotion
---- Community recreational facility (use 297)
---- Community center (use 296)
405 Loans or grants for minority businesses
---- Job training, counseling, or assistance (use 566)
---- Day care center (use 574)
---- Referral service (social agencies) (use 569)
---- Legal aid to indigents (use 462)
406 Crime prevention
407 Voluntary firemen's organization or auxiliary
---- Rescue squad (use 158)
408 Community service organization
429 Other inner city or community benefit activities

Civil Rights Activities

430 Defense of human and civil rights
431 Elimination of prejudice and discrimination (race, religion, sex, national origin, etc.)
432 Lessen neighborhood tensions
449 Other civil rights activities

Litigation and Legal Aid Activities

460 Public interest litigation activities
461 Other litigation or support of litigation
462 Legal aid to indigents
463 Providing bail
465 Plan under IRC section 120

Legislative and Political Activities

480 Propose, support, or oppose legislation
481 Voter information on issues or candidates
482 Voter education (mechanics of registering, voting, etc.)
483 Support, oppose, or rate political candidates
484 Provide facilities or services for political campaign activities
509 Other legislative and political activities

Advocacy

Attempt to influence public opinion concerning:
510 Firearms control
511 Selective Service System
512 National defense policy
513 Weapons systems
514 Government spending
515 Taxes or tax exemption
516 Separation of church and state
517 Government aid to parochial schools
518 U.S. foreign policy
519 U.S. military involvement

Code

520 Pacifism and peace
521 Economic-political system of U.S.
522 Anti-communism
523 Right to work
524 Zoning or rezoning
525 Location of highway or transportation system
526 Rights of criminal defendants
527 Capital punishment
528 Stricter law enforcement
529 Ecology or conservation
530 Protection of consumer interests
531 Medical care service
532 Welfare system
533 Urban renewal
534 Busing students to achieve racial balance
535 Racial integration
536 Use of intoxicating bevarage
537 Use of drugs or narcotics
538 Use of tobacco
539 Prohibition of erotica
540 Sex education in public schools
541 Population control
542 Birth control methods
543 Legalized abortion
559 Other matters

Other Activities Directed to Individuals

560 Supplying money, goods or services to the poor
561 Gifts or grants to individuals (other than scholarships)
---- Scholarships for children of employees (use 039)
---- Scholarships (other) (use 040)
---- Student loans (use 041)
562 Other loans to individuals
563 Marriage counseling
564 Family planning
565 Credit counseling and assistance
566 Job training, counseling, or assistance
567 Draft counseling
568 Vocational counseling
569 Referral service (social agencies)
572 Rehabilitating convicts or ex-convicts
573 Rehabilitating alcoholics, drug abusers, compulsive gamblers, etc.
574 Day care center
575 Services for the aged (see also 153 and 382)
---- Training of or aid to the handicapped (see 031 and 160)

Activities Directed to Other Organizations

600 Community Chest, United Way, etc.
601 Booster club
602 Gifts, grants, or loans to other organizations
603 Non-financial services or facilities to other organizations

Other Purposes and Activities

900 Cemetery or burial activities
901 Perpetual care fund (cemetery, columbarium, etc.)
902 Emergency or disaster aid fund
903 Community trust or component
904 Government instrumentality or agency (see also 254)
905 Testing products for public safety
906 Consumer interest group
907 Veterans activities
908 Patriotic activities
909 4947(a)(1) trust
910 Domestic organization with activities outside U.S.
911 Foreign organization
912 Title holding corporation
913 Prevention of cruelty to animals
914 Achievement prizes or awards
915 Erection or maintenance of public building or works
916 Cafeteria, restaurant, snack bar, food services, etc.
917 Thrift shop, retail outlet, etc.
918 Book, gift or supply store
919 Advertising
920 Association of employees
921 Loans or credit reporting
922 Endowment fund or financial services
923 Indians (tribes, cultures, etc.)
924 Traffic or tariff bureau
925 Section 501(c)(1) with 50% deductibility
926 Government instrumentality other than section 501(c)
927 Fundraising
928 4947(a)(2) trust
930 Prepaid legal services plan exempt under IRC section 501(c)(20)
931 Withdrawal liability payment fund
990 Section 501(k) child care organization

FORM NO. 13 [IRS Form 1024]

Note: *Retain a copy of the completed Form 1024 in the organization's permanent records.*

General Information

(Section references are to the Internal Revenue Code unless otherwise noted.)

Paperwork Reduction Act Notice.—We ask for this information to carry out the Internal Revenue laws of the United States. We need it to determine whether you meet the legal requirements for tax-exempt status. If you want to be recognized as tax-exempt by IRS, you are required to give us this information.

The time needed to complete and file this form will vary depending on individual circumstances. The estimated average times are:

Form	Recordkeeping	Learning about the law or the form	Preparing and sending the form to IRS
1024	52 hrs., 51 min.	2 hrs., 45 min.	4 hrs., 56 min.
1024, Sch. A	58 min.	18 min.	19 min.
1024, Sch. B	1 hr., 40 min.	18 min.	20 min.
1024, Sch. C	58 min.	12 min.	13 min.
1024, Sch. D	4 hrs., 4 min.	18 min.	22 min.
1024, Sch. E	1 hr., 4 min.	18 min.	20 min.
1024, Sch. F	2 hrs., 9 min.	6 min.	8 min.
1024, Sch. G	1 hr., 55 min.	6 min.	8 min.
1024, Sch. H	1 hr., 40 min.	6 min.	8 min.
1024, Sch. I	5 hrs., 30 min.	30 min.	37 min.
1024, Sch. J	2 hrs., 23 min.	6 min.	8 min.
1024, Sch. K	3 hrs., 21 min.	6 min.	10 min.
1024, Sch. L	3 hrs., 7 min.	24 min.	28 min.
1024, Sch. M	1 hr., 20 min.	12 min.	13 min.

If you have comments concerning the accuracy of these time estimates or suggestions for making this form more simple, we would be happy to hear from you. You can write to the **Internal Revenue Service,** Washington, DC 20224, Attention: IRS Reports Clearance Officer, T:FP; or the **Office of Management and Budget,** Paperwork Reduction Project, (1545-0057), Washington, DC 20503.

General Instructions

User Fee.—The Revenue Act of 1987 requires payment of a user fee with determination letter requests submitted to the Internal Revenue Service. **Form 8718,** User Fee for Exempt Organization Determination Letter Request, must be submitted with this application along with the appropriate fee as stated on Form 8718. Form 8718 may be obtained through your local IRS office or by calling the telephone number given below for obtaining forms and publications.

Helpful Information.—For additional information, see **Publication 557,** Tax-Exempt Status for Your Organization. You may also call **1-800-554-4477** (or the IRS Tele-Tax number for your area; ask for Topic #109 and #110 (push button telephone is required). For additional forms and publications call **1-800-424-3676 (1-800-424-FORM).**

A. Purpose of Form.—Form 1024 is used by most types of organizations to apply for recognition of exemption under section 501(a) and by all applicants for a determination of plan qualification under section 120.

Even if these organizations are not required to file Form 1024 to be tax-exempt, they may wish to file Form 1024 and receive a determination letter of IRS recognition of their section 501(c) status in order to obtain certain incidental benefits such as: public recognition of their tax-exempt status; exemption from certain state taxes; advance assurance to donors of deductibility of contributions (in certain cases); non-profit mailing privileges, etc.

Note: *Generally, Form 1024 is NOT used to apply for a group exemption letter. For information on how to apply for a group exemption letter, see Publication 557.*

B. What To File.—

(1) Section 501 applicants.—Most organizations applying for exemption under section 501(a) must complete Parts I through III. However, see Special Rules for Certain Canadian Organizations. In addition, each organization must complete the Schedule indicated on page 1 of the application for the section of the Code under which it seeks recognition of exemption. (For example, an organization seeking recognition under section 501(c)(19) must complete Parts I through III and Schedule K.)

(2) Section 120 applicants.—

Applicants seeking a determination of plan qualification under section 120 must complete Part I, and Schedule L.

Do not submit any blank schedules that do not apply to your type of organization.

Attachments.—Every attachment should state that it relates to Form 1024 and identify the applicable part and line item number. The attachments should also show the organization's name, address, and employer identification number, and preferably be on size 8½" × 11" paper.

In addition to the required documents and statements, you may include any additional information citing court decisions, rulings, opinions, etc., that will help to speed the application's processing. Generally, attachments in the form of tape recordings are not acceptable unless accompanied by a transcript.

C. Where To File.—File the completed application, and all information required, with the key district office for your principal place of business or office as listed below. As soon as possible after the complete application is received, you will be advised of the Internal Revenue

Service's determination and of the annual returns which the organization will be required to file.

When the principal place of business or office of the organization is in one of the districts or locations shown ▼	Send your application to the key district listed below ▼
Anchorage, Boise, Honolulu, Laguna Niguel, Las Vegas, Los Angeles, Portland, San Jose, Seattle	Internal Revenue Service EO Application Receiving Room 5127, P.O. Box 486 Los Angeles, CA 90053-0486
Sacramento, San Francisco	Internal Revenue Service EO Application Receiving Stop SF 4446 P.O. Box 36001 San Francisco, CA 94102
Atlanta, Birmingham, Columbia, Ft. Lauderdale, Greensboro, Jackson, Jacksonville, Little Rock, Nashville, New Orleans	Internal Revenue Service EP/EO Division P.O. Box 941 Atlanta, GA 30370
Chicago, Aberdeen, Des Moines, Fargo, Helena, Milwaukee, Omaha, St. Louis, St. Paul, Springfield	Internal Revenue Service EP/EO Division 230 S. Dearborn DPN 20-5 Chicago, IL 60604
Baltimore, District of Columbia, Newark, Philadelphia, Pittsburgh, Richmond, Wilmington, any U.S. possession (except Virgin Islands) or foreign country	Internal Revenue Service EP/EO Division P.O. Box 17010 Baltimore, MD 21203
U.S. Virgin Islands	Virgin Islands Bureau of Internal Revenue Lockerts Garden No. 1A Charlotte Amalie, St. Thomas, VI 00802
Albany, Augusta, Boston, Brooklyn, Buffalo, Burlington, Hartford, Manhattan, Portsmouth, Providence	Internal Revenue Service EP/EO Division P.O. Box 1680, GPO Brooklyn, NY 11202
Cincinnati, Cleveland, Detroit, Indianapolis, Louisville, Parkersburg	Internal Revenue Service EP/EO Division P.O. Box 3159 Cincinnati, OH 45201
Albuquerque, Austin, Cheyenne, Dallas, Denver, Houston, Oklahoma City, Phoenix, Salt Lake City, Wichita	Internal Revenue Service EP/EO Division Mail Code 4950 DAL 1100 Commerce Street Dallas, TX 75242

D. Signature Requirements.—An officer who is authorized to sign or another person authorized by a power of attorney must sign this application. Send the power of attorney with the application when you file it. **Form 2848,** Power of Attorney and Declaration of Representative, or **Form 2848-D,** Tax Information Authorization and Declaration of Representative, may be used for this purpose.

E. Public Inspection of Form 1024.

IRS Responsibilities.—The application, if approved, and any supporting papers will be open to public inspection, as required by section 6104, in any IRS district office and in the Internal Revenue Service's National Office. In addition, any letter or other document issued by the IRS with regard to the application, will be open to public inspection at the time and in the manner prescibed by the regulations. However, information relating to a trade secret, patent, style of work, or apparatus, which if released would adversely affect the organization; or any other information, which if released would adversely affect the national defense, will not be made available for public inspection. You must identify this information by clearly marking it, "NOT SUBJECT TO PUBLIC INSPECTION," and attach a statement explaining why the organization asks that the information be withheld. If the Internal Revenue Service agrees, the information will be withheld.

Organization's Responsibilities.—An organization that submits an application to the Internal Revenue Service, and has it approved, must make a copy of the application and supporting documents, as well as any letter issued by the Internal Revenue Service, available for public inspection. The application and related documents must be made available for inspection during regular business hours at the organization's principal office and at each of its regional or district offices having at least 3 employees.

F. Appeal Procedures.—Your application will be considered by the key district office, which will either:

(1) issue a favorable determination letter;

(2) issue a proposed adverse determination letter denying the exempt status you requested; or

(3) refer the case to the National Office.

If you receive a proposed adverse determination, you will be advised of your appeal rights at that time.

G. Language and Currency Requirements.—Form 1024 and attachments must be prepared using the English language. If the organizational document or bylaws are in any other language, an English translation must be furnished. (See conformed copy requirements in the Specific Instructions for Part I.) If the organization produces or distributes foreign language publications that are submitted with the application, you may be asked to provide English translations for one or more of them during the processing of your application.

Report all financial information in U.S. dollars (state conversion rate used). Combine amounts from within and outside the United States and report the total for each item on the financial statements.

For example:

Gross Investment Income
From U.S. sources	$4,000
From non-U.S. sources	1,000
(Amount to report on income statement)	$5,000

H. Annual Information Return.—If the filing date for the annual information return for tax-exempt organizations falls due while your application for recognition of exempt status is pending with the IRS (including any appeal of a proposed adverse determination), you should file a **Form 990,** Return of Organization Exempt From Income Tax (or **Form 990EZ,** Short Form Return of Organization Exempt From Income Tax), and indicate that an application is pending. Applicants under sections 501(c)(5), (9), (17), and (20) should see the Form 990 (or Form 990EZ) instructions for special provisions regarding substitutions for certain parts of that form. Section 120 plans should see **Form 5500,** Annual Return/Report of Employee Benefit Plan, and instructions.

I. Special Rule for Certain Canadian Organizations.—A religious, scientific, literary, educational, or charitable organization formed in Canada that has received a **Form T2051,** Notification of Registration, from Revenue Canada

(Department of National Revenue, Taxation) and whose registration has not been revoked may apply for recognition of exemption as a social welfare organization under section 501(c)(4) without completing all parts of Form 1024 that would otherwise be required. Such an organization that desires recognition of exemption under section 501(c)(3) must complete **Form 1023,** Application for Recognition of Exemption Under Section 501(c)(3) of the Internal Revenue Code. Exemption under section 501(c)(3) is needed to establish eligibility to receive contributions that are deductible by U.S. residents to the extent provided by the U.S.-Canada tax treaty.

A registered Canadian religious, scientific, etc., organization seeking exemption under section 501(c)(4) must complete only Part I and the signature portion of Form 1024. To indicate that this special rule applies, the organization should write, "Registered Canadian Organization," across the top of page 1 of Form 1024. The organization must also attach a copy of its current Form T2051 and a copy of Application for Registration, **Form T2050,** together with all required attachments that it submitted to Revenue Canada. If any of the attachments to Form T2050 were prepared in the French language, an English language translation must be furnished with Form 1024. In the case of organizing documents and bylaws, see the conformed copy requirements in the Specific Instructions for Part I.

Specific Instructions

The following instructions are keyed to the line items on the application form:

Part I.—Identification of Applicant

Line 1. Full name and address of organization.—Enter the organization's name exactly as it appears in its creating documents, including amendments. If the organization will be operating under another name, show the other name in parenthesis.

Line 2. Employer Identification Number (EIN).—All organizations must have an EIN. Enter the 9-digit EIN assigned to the organization by the IRS. If the organization does **not** have an employer identification number, enter "none" and attach a completed **Form SS-4,** Application for Employer Identification Number, to the application. If the organization has previously applied for a number, attach a statement giving the date of the application and the office where it was filed.

Line 3. Person to Contact.—Enter the name and telephone number of the person to be contacted during business hours if more information is needed. The contact person should be familiar with the organization's activities—preferably an officer, director, or authorized representative.

Line 4. Month the Annual Accounting Period Ends.—Enter the month the organization's annual accounting period ends. The organization's accounting period is usually the 12-month period which is the organization's taxable year. The organization's first taxable year depends on the accounting period you choose (it could possibly be less than 12 months).

Line 5. Date Formed.—Enter the date the organization became a legal entity. For corporations this would be the date that the articles of incorporation were approved by the appropriate state official. For unincorporated organizations, it would be the date its constitution or articles of association was adopted.

Line 6. Activity Codes.—Select up to three of the code numbers listed on the back cover that best describe or most accurately identify the organization's purposes, activities, or type of organization. Enter the codes in the order of their importance.

Line 7.—Indicate if the organization has ever filed Form 1023, Form 1024, or other exemption application with the Internal Revenue Service.

Line 8.—Indicate if the organization has ever filed Federal income tax returns as a taxable organization or filed forms as an exempt organization (e.g. Forms 990, 990EZ, 990-PF, and **990-T,** Exempt Organization Business Income Tax Return).

Line 9. Type of Organization and Organizational Documents.—Submit a conformed copy of the organizing instrument. A "conformed" copy is one that agrees with the original and all amendments to it. The conformed copy may be a photocopy of the original signed and dated organizing document OR it may be a copy of the organizing document that is not signed but is accompanied by a written declaration signed by an authorized individual stating that the copy is a complete and accurate copy of the original signed and dated document.

In the case of a corporation, a copy of the certificate of incorporation, approved and dated by an appropriate State official, is sufficient by itself. If an unsigned copy of the articles of incorporation is submitted, it must be accompanied by the written declaration discussed above. Signed or unsigned copies of the articles of incorporation must be accompanied by a declaration stating that the original copy of the articles was filed with and approved by the State. The date filed must be specified.

In the case of an unincorporated association, the conformed copy of the constitution, articles of association, or other organizing document must indicate in the document itself, or in a written declaration, that the organization was formed by the adoption of the document by two or more persons.

In the case of a trust, a copy of the signed and dated trust instrument must be furnished.

If the organization does not have an organizing instrument, it will not qualify for exempt status. The bylaws of an organization alone are not an organizing instrument. They are merely the internal rules and regulations of the organization.

Part II.—Activities and Operational Information

Line 1.—It is important that you report all activities carried on by the organization to enable the Internal Revenue Service to make a proper determination of the organization's exempt status. It is also important that you provide detailed information about the nature and purpose of each of your activities. You will be contacted for such information if it is not furnished.

Line 2.—If it is anticipated that the organization's principal sources of support will increase or decrease substantially in relation to the organization's total support, attach a statement describing anticipated changes and explaining the basis for the expectation.

Line 3a.—Furnish the mailing address of the organization's principal officers, directors, or trustees. Do not give the address of the organization.

Line 3b.—The annual compensation would include salary, bonus, and any other form of payment to the individual for services performed for the organization.

Line 4.—If your organization's activities were formerly performed under another name or if your organization was a part of another organization (tax-exempt or non-exempt), furnish the requested information. Otherwise indicate "N/A."

Line 5.—Indicate your current or planned connection with any tax-exempt or non-exempt organization.

Line 6.—If your organization has issued stock as a means of indicating ownership by its members or others, furnish the requested information. Otherwise, indicate "N/A."

Line 7.—If your organization is a membership organization, furnish the requested information. Otherwise, indicate "N/A."

Line 8.—If your organization should cease operations as a tax-exempt organization, explain to whom its assets will be distributed.

Line 9.—Indicate if the organization distributes, or plans to distribute, any of its property or funds (such as a distribution of profits) to its shareholders or members.

Line 10.—Indicate if the organization performs any services for any other organization or individual for which it is paid a fee.

Line 11.—Do not include the normal salary of officers or employees.

Line 12.—Answer "Yes," if the organization either provides insurance through a third party or provides the insurance itself.

Line 13.—Examples of public regulatory bodies are: HUD, HHS, Public Utilities Commission, Housing Commission, and a state Insurance Commission.

Line 14.—Provide the specified information about leased property whether it is used for exempt functions or for other purposes.

Line 15.—Provide the specified information about political expenditures whether they were made to support or to oppose particular candidates.

Line 16.—This includes any printed material that may be used to publicize the organization's activities, or as an informational item to members or potential members.

Part III —Financial Data

The Statement of Revenue and Expenses must be completed for the current year and each of the 3 years immediately before it (or the years the organization has existed, if less than 4). **Any applicant that has existed for less than 1 year should give financial data for the current year and proposed budgets**

for the following 2 years. Any applicant that has been in existence more than one year but seeks recognition of exemption only for the current year and future years (rather than from the date of its formation), should give financial data for the current year and proposed budgets for the following 2 years. We may request financial data for more than 4 years if necessary. All financial information for the current year must cover the period ending within 60 days of the date of application. Prepare the balance sheet as of the last day of the current-year period covered by the Statement of Revenue and Expenses .

Prepare the statements using the method of accounting the organization uses in keeping its books and records. If the organization uses a method other than the cash receipts and disbursements method, attach a statement explaining the method used.

A. Revenue and Expenses

Line 1.—Include amounts received from the members that represent the annual dues and any special assessments or initiation fees.

Line 2.— Do not include amounts received from the general public or a governmental unit for the exercise or performance of the organization's exempt function.

Line 3.—Examples of such income would be: the income derived by a social club from the sale of food or beverage to its members; the sale of burial lots by a cemetery association; and fees charged by a social welfare organization or trade association for an educational seminar it conducted.

Line 4.—Enter the organization's gross income from activities that are regularly carried on and not related to the organization's exempt purposes.

Examples of such income would include: fees from the commercial testing of products; income from renting office equipment or other personal property; and income from the sale of advertising in an exempt organization periodical. See **Publication 598,** Tax on Unrelated Business Income of Exempt Organizations, for information about unrelated business income and activities.

Line 5.—Attach a schedule showing the description of each asset, the name of the person to whom sold, and the amount received. In the case of publicly traded securities sold through a broker, the name of the purchaser is not required.

Line 6.—Include on this line the income received from dividends, interest, payments received on securities loans (as defined in section 512(a)(5)), rents, and royalties.

Line 7.—Enter the total income from all sources that is not reported on lines 1 to 6. Include, for example, income from special events such as raffles and dances that is not taxable as unrelated business income. Attach a schedule that lists each type of revenue source and the amount derived from each.

Line 9.—Enter the expenses directly related to the income sources reported on line 3 of this part.

Line 10.—Enter the expenses directly related to the income sources reported on line 4 of this part.

Line 11.—Attach a schedule showing the name of the recipient, a brief description of

the purposes or conditions of payment, and the amount paid.

Line 12.—Attach a schedule showing the total amount paid for each benefit category, such as disability, death, sickness, hospitalization, unemployment compensation, or strike benefits.

Lines 13-18.—Use lines 13 through 18 to report expenses that are not directly related to the expense categories listed on lines 9 and 10. For example, salaries attributable to the organization's exempt purpose activities should be included with any other expenses reportable on line 9 rather than being reported separately on line 14. Salaries reportable on line 14 would include, for example, those attributable to special events; to the solicitation of contributions; and to the overall management and operation of the organization.

Line 13.—Attach a schedule that shows the name of the person compensated; the office or position; the average amount of time devoted to business per week, month, etc.; and the amount of annual compensation.

Line 14.—Enter the total of employees' salaries not reported on line 13.

Line 15.—Enter the total interest expense for the year, excluding mortgage interest treated as occupancy expense on line 16.

Line 16.—Enter the amount paid for the use of office space or other facilities, heat, light, power, and other utilities, outside janitorial services, mortgage interest, real estate taxes, and similar expenses.

Line 17.—If your organization records depreciation, depletion, and similar expenses, enter the total.

Line 18.—Indicate the type and amount of each **significant** expense for which a separate line is not provided. Report other miscellaneous expenses as a single total.

B. Balance Sheet

Line 1.—Enter the total interest and non-interest bearing cash in checking accounts, savings and temporary cash investments (money market funds, CD's, treasury bills or other obligations that mature in less than 1 year), change funds, and petty cash funds.

Line 2.—Enter the total accounts receivable that arose from the sale of goods and/or performance of services.

Line 3.—Enter the amount of materials, goods, and supplies purchased or manufactured by the organization and held to be sold or used in some future period.

Line 4.—Attach a schedule that shows the name of the borrower, a brief description of the obligation, the rate of return on the principal indebtedness, the due date, and the amount due.

Line 5.—Attach a schedule listing the organization's corporate stock. For stock of closely held corporations, the schedule should show: the same name of the corporation; a brief summary of the corporation's capital structure; the number of shares held; and their value as carried on the organization's books. If such valuation does not reflect current fair market value, also include fair market value. For stock traded on an organized exchange or in substantial quantities over the counter, the schedule should show: the name of the corporation; a description of the stock and the principal exchange on which it is traded; the number of shares held; and their value as carried on the organization's books.

Line 6.—Attach a **schedule** that shows the borrower's name, **purpose of loan,** repayment terms, interest rate, and original amount **of loan. Report each loan** separately, even if more than one loan was made to the same person.

Line 7.—Enter the book value of securities held of the U.S., state, or municipal governments. Also enter the book value of buildings and equipment held for investment purposes. Attach a schedule identifying each.

Line 8.—Enter the book value of buildings and equipment not held for investment. This would include plant and equipment used by the organization in conducting its exempt activities. Attach a schedule listing these assets held at the end of the current tax-year period and the cost or other basis.

Line 9.—Enter the book value of land not held for investment.

Line 10.—Enter the book value of each category of assets not reported on lines 1 through 9. Attach a schedule listing each.

Line 12.—Enter the total of accounts payable to suppliers and others, such as: salaries payable, accrued payroll taxes, and interest payable.

Line 13.—Enter the unpaid portion of grants and contributions that the organization has made a commitment to pay other organizations or individuals.

Line 14.—Enter the total of mortgages and other notes payable at the end of year. Attach a schedule that shows each item separately and the lender's name, purpose of loan, repayment terms, interest rate, and original amount.

Line 15.—Enter the amount of each liability not reported on lines 12 through 14. Attach a separate schedule.

Line 17.—Under fund accounting, an organization segregates its assets, liabilities, and net assets into separate funds according to restrictions on the use of certain assets. Each fund is like a separate entity in that it has a self-balancing set of accounts showing assets, liabilities, equity (fund balance), income, and expenses. If the organization uses fund accounting, report the total of all fund balances on line 17. If the organization does not use fund accounting, report only the "net assets" account balances, such as: capital stock, paid-in capital, and retained earnings or accumulated income.

Procedural Checklist
Make sure your application is complete.

If you do not complete all applicable parts of the application or do not provide all required attachments, we may return the incomplete application to you for resubmission with the missing information or attachments. This will delay the processing of your application and may delay the effective date of your exempt status. You may also incur additional user fees.

Have you . . .

_____ Attached **Form 8718** (User Fee for Exempt Organization Determination Letter Request) along with the appropriate fee?

_____ Located the correct **key district office** for the mailing of your application? (See "Where To File" on page 1 under General Instructions.) Do **not** file the application with your local Internal Revenue Service Center.

_____ Completed Parts I through III and any other schedules that apply to the organization?

_____ Shown your **employer identification number**?
a. If your organization has one, write it in the space provided.
b. If you are a newly formed organization and do not have an employer identification number, attach a completed Form SS-4 if you have not already applied for one.

_____ Described your organization's **specific activities** as directed in Part II, question 1 of the application?

_____ Included a **conformed copy** of the complete organizing instrument? (Part I, question 9)

_____ Had the application signed by one of the following:
a. an officer, or trustee, who is authorized to sign (e.g., President or Treasurer); **or**
b. a person authorized by a power of attorney (submit Form 2848, Form 2848-D, or other power of attorney)?

_____ Enclosed **financial statements** (Part III)?
a. Current year (must include period up to within 60 days of the date the application is filed) and 3 preceding years.
b. Detailed breakdown of revenue and expenses (no lump sums).
c. If the organization has been in existence less than one year, you must also submit proposed budgets for 2 years showing the amounts and types of receipts and expenditures anticipated.

Note: *During the technical review of a completed application by the Employee Plans/Exempt Organizations Division in the key district or by Exempt Organizations Technical Division in the National Office, it may be necessary to contact you for more specific or additional information.*

Do not send this checklist with your application.

Form **1024** (Rev. December 1989) Department of the Treasury Internal Revenue Service	**Application for Recognition of Exemption** **Under Section 501(a)** **or for Determination Under Section 120**	OMB No. 1545-0057 If exempt status is approved, this application will be open for public inspection

Read the instructions for each Part carefully.
A User Fee must be attached to this application.
If the required information and appropriate documents are not submitted along with Form 8718 (with payment of the appropriate user fee), the application may be returned to you.
Complete the Procedural Checklist on page 4 of the instructions.

Part I.—Identification of Applicant (Must be completed by all applicants; also complete appropriate Schedule.)

Check the appropriate box below to indicate the section under which you are applying:

a ☐ Section 501(c)(2)—Title holding corporations (Schedule A, page 6)

b ☐ Section 501(c)(4)—Civic leagues, social welfare organizations (including certain war veterans' organizations), or local associations of employees (Schedule B, page 7)

c ☐ Section 501(c)(5)—Labor, agricultural, or horticultural organizations (Schedule C, page 8)

d ☐ Section 501(c)(6)—Business leagues, chambers of commerce, etc. (Schedule C, page 8)

e ☐ Section 501(c)(7)—Social clubs (Schedule D, page 9)

f ☐ Section 501(c)(8)—Fraternal beneficiary societies, etc., providing life, sick, accident, or other benefits to members (Schedule E, **page 11**)

g ☐ Section 501(c)(9)—Voluntary employees' beneficiary associations (Schedule F, page 12)

h ☐ Section 501(c)(10)—Domestic fraternal societies, orders, etc., not providing life, sick, accident or other benefits (Schedule E, **page 11**)

i ☐ Section 501(c)(12)—Benevolent life insurance associations, mutual ditch or irrigation companies, mutual or cooperative telephone companies, or like organizations (Schedule G, page 13)

j ☐ Section 501(c)(13)—Cemeteries, crematoria, and like corporations (Schedule H, page 14)

k ☐ Section 501(c)(15)—Mutual insurance companies or associations, other than life or marine (Schedule I, page 15)

l ☐ Section 501(c)(17)—Trusts providing for the payment of supplemental unemployment compensation benefits (Schedule J, page 16)

m ☐ Section 501(c)(19)—A post, organization, auxiliary unit, etc., of past or present members of the Armed Forces of the United States (Schedule K, page 17)

n ☐ Section 501(c)(20)—Trust/organization for prepaid group legal services (Parts I, II, and Schedule M, page 21)

o ☐ Section 501(c)(25)—Title holding corporations or trusts (Schedule A, page 6)

p ☐ Section 120—Qualified group legal services plans (Parts I, II, and Schedule L, page 19)

1a Full name of organization (as shown in organizing document)	**2** Employer identification number (**if none, see Specific Instructions**)

1b c/o Name (if applicable)

1c Address (number and street)

1d City or town, county, state, and ZIP code	**3** Name and telephone number (including area code) of person to be contacted during business hours if more information is needed ( )

4 Month the annual accounting period ends	**5** Date incorporated or formed	**6** Activity codes (see back cover)

7 Did the organization apply for recognition of exemption under this Code section or under any other section of the Code? ☐ **Yes** ☐ **No**
If "Yes," attach an explanation.

8 Has the organization filed Federal income tax returns or exempt organization information returns? . . . . ☐ **Yes** ☐ **No**
If "Yes," state the form number(s), years filed, and Internal Revenue office where filed.

9 Check the box for your type of organization. BE SURE TO ATTACH A COMPLETE COPY OF THE CORRESPONDING DOCUMENTS TO THE APPLICATION BEFORE MAILING.

a ☐ Corporation—Attach a copy of your Articles of Incorporation, (including amendments and restatements) showing approval by the appropriate state official; also attach a copy of your bylaws.

b ☐ Trust—Attach a copy of your Trust Indenture or Agreement, including all appropriate signatures and dates.

c ☐ Association—Attach a copy of your Articles of Association, Constitution, or other creating document, with a declaration (see instructions) or other evidence that the organization was formed by adoption of the document by more than one person. Include also a copy of your bylaws.

If you are a corporation or an unincorporated association that has not yet adopted bylaws, check here ▶ ☐

PLEASE
SIGN
HERE ▶

I declare under the penalties of perjury that I am authorized to sign this application on behalf of the above organization, and that I have examined this application, including the accompanying schedules and attachments, and to the best of my knowledge it is true, correct, and complete.

---   ---   ------------------------------
(Signature)   (Title or authority of signer)   (Date)

Part II.—Activities and Operational Information (Must be completed by all applicants)

1 Provide a detailed narrative description of all the activities of the organization—past, present, and planned. Do not merely refer to or repeat the language in your organizational document. Describe each activity separately in the order of importance. Each description should include, as a minimum, the following: (a) a detailed description of the activity including its purpose; (b) when the activity was or will be initiated; and (c) where and by whom the activity will be conducted.

2 List the organization's present and future sources of financial support, beginning with the largest source first.

Form 1024 (Rev. 12-89)   Page **3**

Part II.—Activities and Operational Information (continued) **(Must be completed by all applicants)**

3   The membership of the organization's governing body is:

a Names, addresses, and titles of officers, directors, trustees, etc.	**b** Annual compensation

4   If you are the outgrowth or continuation of any form of predecessor(s), state the name of each predecessor, the period during which it was in existence, and the reasons for its termination. Submit copies of all papers by which any transfer of assets was effected.

5   If you are now, or plan to be connected in any way with any other organization, describe the organization and explain the relationship (such as: financial support on a continuing basis; shared facilities or employees; same officers, directors, or trustees).

6   If you have capital stock issued and outstanding, state: (1) class or classes of the stock; (2) number and par value of the shares; (3) consideration for which they were issued; and (4) whether any dividends have been paid or whether your creating instrument authorizes dividend payments on any class of capital stock.

7   State the qualifications necessary for membership in the organization; the classes of membership (with the number of members in each class); and the voting rights and privileges received. If any group or class of persons is required to join, describe the requirement and explain the relationship between those members and members who join voluntarily. Submit copies of any membership solicitation material. Attach sample copies of all types of membership certificates issued.

8   Explain how your assets will be distributed on dissolution.

Part II.—Activities and Operational Information (continued) **(Must be completed by all applicants)**

9 Have you made or do you plan to make any distribution of your property or surplus funds to shareholders or members?　☐ **Yes**　☐ **No**
If "Yes," state the full details, including: (1) amounts or value; (2) source of funds or property distributed or to be distributed· and (3) basis of, and authority for, distribution or planned distribution.

10 Does, or will, any part of your receipts represent payments for services performed or to be performed? . . ☐ **Yes**　☐ **No**
If "Yes," state in detail the amount received and the character of the services performed or to be performed

11 Have you made, or do you plan to make, any payments to members or shareholders for services performed or to be performed? . . . . ☐ **Yes**　☐ **No**
If "Yes," state in detail the amount paid, the character of the services, and to whom the payments have been, or will be made.

12 Do you have any arrangement to provide insurance for members, their dependents, or others (including provisions for the payment of sick or death benefits, pensions or annuities)? . . . . ☐ **Yes**　☐ **No**
If "Yes," describe and explain the arrangement's eligibility rules and attach a sample copy of each plan document and each type of policy issued.

13 Are you under the supervisory jurisdiction of any public regulatory body, such as a social welfare agency, etc.? . . ☐ **Yes**　☐ **No**
If "Yes," submit copies of all administrative opinions or court decisions regarding this supervision as well as copies of applications or requests for the opinions or decisions.

14 Do you now lease or do you plan to lease any property? . . . . ☐ **Yes**　☐ **No**
If "Yes," explain in detail. Include the amount of rent, a description of the property, and any relationship between your organization and the other party. Also, attach a copy of any rental or lease agreement.

15 Have you spent or do you plan to spend any money attempting to influence the selection, nomination, election or appointment of any person to any Federal, state, or local public office or to an office in a political organization? . . . . ☐ **Yes**　☐ **No**
If "Yes," explain in detail and list the amounts spent or to be spent in each case.

16 Do you publish pamphlets, brochures, newsletters, journals, or similar printed material? . . . . ☐ **Yes**　☐ **No**
If "Yes," attach a recent copy of each.

Form 1024 (Rev. 12-89)   Page **5**

Part III.—Financial Data (Must be completed by all applicants)

Complete the financial statements for the current year and for each of the 3 years immediately before it. If in existence less than 4 years, complete the statements for each year in existence. ***If in existence less than 1 year, also provide proposed budgets for the 2 years following the current year.***

A—Statement of Revenue and Expenses

Revenue	(a) Current Tax Year From _____ To _____	3 Prior Tax Years or Proposed Budget for 2 Years			(e) Total
		(b) 19 ____	(c) 19 ____	(d) 19 ____	
1 Gross dues and assessments of members . . .					
2 Gross contributions, gifts, etc.					
3 Gross amounts derived from activities related to the organization's exempt purpose (attach schedule) .					
4 Gross amounts from unrelated business activities (attach schedule)					
5 Gain from sale of assets, excluding inventory items (attach schedule)					
6 Investment income (see instructions)					
7 Other revenue (attach schedule)					
8 Total revenue (add lines 1 through 7)					
Expenses					
9 Expenses attributable to activities related to the organization's exempt purposes					
10 Expenses attributable to unrelated business activities					
11 Contributions, gifts, grants, and similar amounts paid (attach schedule)					
12 Disbursements to or for the benefit of members (attach schedule)					
13 Compensation of officers, directors, and trustees (attach schedule)					
14 Other salaries and wages					
15 Interest					
16 Occupancy					
17 Depreciation and depletion					
18 Other expenses (attach schedule)					
19 Total expenses					
20 Excess of revenue over expenses (line 8 minus line 19)					

B—Balance Sheet (at the end of the period shown)

Assets		Current Tax Year as of _____
1 Cash	1	
2 Accounts receivable, net	2	
3 Inventories	3	
4 Bonds and notes receivable (attach schedule)	4	
5 Corporate stocks	5	
6 Mortgage loans (attach schedule)	6	
7 Other investments (attach schedule)	7	
8 Depreciable and depletable assets (attach schedule)	8	
9 Land	9	
10 Other assets (attach schedule)	10	
11 **Total assets**	11	
Liabilities		
12 Accounts payable	12	
13 Contributions, gifts, grants, etc., payable	13	
14 Mortgages and notes payable (attach schedule)	14	
15 Other liabilities (attach schedule)	15	
16 **Total liabilities**	16	
Fund Balances or Net Assets		
17 Total fund balances or net assets	17	
18 **Total liabilities and fund balances or net assets** (add line 16 and line 17)	18	

If there has been any substantial change in any aspect of your financial activities since the end of the period shown above, check the box and attach a detailed explanation . . . . ▶ ☐

| **Schedule A** | **Organizations described in section 501(c)(2) or 501(c)(25) (Title holding corporations or trusts)** |

1 State the complete name, address and employer identification number of each organization for which title to property is held and the number and class(es) of shares of your stock held by each organization.

2 State whether the annual excess of revenue over expenses is or will be turned over to the organization for which title to property is held and, if not, the purpose for which the excess (income) is or will be held.

3a In the case of a corporation described in section 501(c)(2), state the purpose(s) of each organization for which title to property is held (as shown in its governing instrument) and the Code section(s) under which each is classified as exempt from income tax.

3b In the case of a corporation or trust described in section 501(c)(25), state the basis whereby each shareholder is described in section 501(c)(25)(C).

INSTRUCTIONS

Line 1.—Provide the requested information on each organization for which your organization holds title to property. Also indicate the number and type(s) of shares of your organization's stock that are held by each.

Line 2.—For purposes of this question, "excess of revenue over expenses" is all of the organization's income for a particular tax year less operating expenses.

Line 3a.—Give the exempt purpose of each organization which is the basis for its exempt status and the Internal Revenue Code section that describes the organization (as shown in its IRS determination letter).

Line 3b.—Indicate if the shareholder is one of the following:

(1) a qualified pension, profit-sharing, or stock bonus plan that meets the requirements of the Code;

(2) a government plan;

(3) an organization described in section 501(c)(3); or

(4) an organization described in section 501(c)(25).

Form 1024 (Rev. 12-89)   Page **7**

Schedule B	**Organizations described in section 501(c)(4) (Civic leagues, social welfare organizations (including posts, councils, etc., of veterans' organizations not qualifying or applying for exemption under section 501(c)(19)) or local associations of employees.)**

1   Has the Internal Revenue Service previously issued a ruling or determination letter recognizing you
    (or any predecessor organization listed in item 4 of Part II) to be exempt under section 501(c)(3)
    and later revoked that recognition of exemption on the basis that you (or your predecessor) were
    carrying on propaganda or otherwise attempting to influence legislation or on the basis that you
    engaged in political activity? . . . . □ **Yes** □ **No**

    If "Yes," indicate the earliest tax year for which recognition of exemption under section 501(c)(3)
    was revoked and the IRS district office that issued the revocation.

2   Do you perform or plan to perform (for members, shareholders, or others) services, such as
    maintaining the common areas of a condominium; buying food or other items on a cooperative
    basis; or providing recreational facilities or transportation services, job placement, or other similar
    undertakings? . . . . □ **Yes** □ **No**

    If "Yes," explain the activities in detail, including income realized and expenses incurred. Also,
    explain in detail the nature of the benefits to the general public from these activities. (If the answer
    to this question is explained in Part II (pages 2, 3, and 4), enter the page and item number here.)

3   If you are claiming exemption as a homeowners' association, is access to any property or facilities
    you own or maintain restricted in any way?. □ **Yes** □ **No**

    If "Yes," explain.

4   If you are claiming exemption as a local association of employees, state the name and address of each employer whose
    employees are eligible for membership in the association. If employees of more than one plant or office of the same
    employer are eligible for membership, give the address of each plant or office.

Form 1024 (Rev. 12-89)   Page **8**

Schedule C	Organizations described in section 501(c)(5) (Labor, agricultural, including fishermen's organizations, or horticultural organizations) or section 501(c)(6) (business leagues, chambers of commerce, etc.)

1 Describe any services you perform for members or others. (If the description of the services is contained in Part II, enter the page and item number here.)

2 Fishermen's organizations only.—What kinds of aquatic resources (not including mineral) are cultivated or harvested by those eligible for membership in your organization?

3 Labor organizations only.—Are you organized under the terms of a collective bargaining agreement? . . . . . ☐ **Yes** ☐ **No**

If "Yes," attach a copy of the latest agreement

Form 1024 (Rev. 12-89)   Page **9**

| **Schedule D** | **Organizations described in section 501(c)(7) (Social clubs)** |

1   Have you entered or do you plan to enter into any contract or agreement for the management or operation of
your property and/or activities, such as restaurants, pro shops, lodges, etc.? . . . . ☐ **Yes** ☐ **No**

If "Yes," attach a copy of the contract or agreement. If one has not yet been drawn up, please explain your plans.

2   Do you seek or plan to seek public patronage of your facilities or activities by advertisement or otherwise? . . . . ☐ **Yes** ☐ **No**

If "Yes," attach sample copies of the advertisements or other requests.

If you plan to seek public patronage, please explain your plans.

3a Are nonmembers, other than guests of members, permitted or will they be permitted to use the club facilities
or participate in or attend any functions or activities conducted by the organization? . . . . ☐ **Yes** ☐ **No**

If "Yes," describe the functions or activities in which there has been or will be nonmember participation or
admittance. (Submit a copy of your house rules, if any.)

b   State the amount of nonmember income included in Part III, lines 3 and 4, column (a) . . . .

c   Enter the percent of gross receipts from nonmembers for the use of club facilities . . . .   %

d   Enter the percent of gross receipts received from investment income and nonmember use of the club's
facilities . . . .   %

4a Does your charter, bylaws, other governing instrument, or any written policy statement of your organization
contain any provision which provides for discrimination against any person on the basis of race, color, or
religion? . . . . ☐ **Yes** ☐ **No**

b   If "Yes," state whether or not its provision will be kept.

c   If you have such a provision which will be repealed, deleted, or otherwise stricken from your requirements,
state when this will be done . . . . _____

d   If you formerly had such a requirement and it no longer applies, give the date it ceased to apply . . . . _____

e   If the organization restricts its membership to members of a particular religion, check here and attach the
explanation specified in the instructions . . . . ☐

See reverse side for instructions

Instructions

Line 1.——Answer "Yes," if any of the organization's property or activities will be managed by another organization or company.

Lines 3b, c, and d.——Enter the figures for the current year. On an attached schedule, furnish the same information for each of the prior tax years for which you completed Part III of the application.

Line 4e.——If the organization restricts its membership to members of a particular religion, the organization must be:

(1) an auxiliary of a fraternal beneficiary society that:

    (a) is described in section 501(c)(8) and exempt from tax under section 501(a), and

(b) limits its membership to members of a particular religion; or

(2) a club which, in good faith, limits its membership to the members of a particular religion in order to further the teachings or principles of that religion and not to exclude individuals of a particular race or color.

If you checked 4e, your explanation must show how you meet one of these two requirements.

Form 1024 (Rev. 12-89)   Page 11

Schedule E   Organizations described in section 501(c)(8) or 501(c)(10) (Fraternal societies, orders, or associations)

1   Are you a college fraternity or sorority, or chapter of a college fraternity or sorority? . . . . ☐ Yes   ☐ No

If "Yes," read the instructions for Line 1 before completing this schedule.

2   Does or will your organization operate under the lodge system? . . . . ☐ Yes   ☐ No

If "No," does or will it operate for the exclusive benefit of the members of an organization operating under the lodge system? . . . . ☐ Yes   ☐ No

3   Are you a subordinate or local lodge, etc.? . . . . ☐ Yes   ☐ No

If "Yes," attach a certificate signed by the secretary of the parent organization, under the seal of the organization, certifying that the subordinate lodge is a duly constituted body operating under the jurisdiction of the parent body.

4   Are you a parent or grand lodge? . . . . ☐ Yes   ☐ No

If "Yes," attach a schedule for each subordinate lodge in active operation showing: (a) its name and address; (b) the number of members in it; and (c) how often it holds periodic meetings.

Instructions

Line 1.—To the extent that they qualify for exemption from Federal income tax, college fraternities and sororities generally qualify as organizations described in section 501(c)(7). Therefore, if you are a college fraternity or sorority, please refer to the discussion of section 501(c)(7) organizations in Publication 557. If section 501(c)(7) appears to apply to you, complete Schedule D instead of this schedule.

Line 2.—Operating under the lodge system means carrying on activities under a form of organization that is comprised of local branches, chartered by a parent organization, largely self-governing, and called lodges, chapters, or the like.

Forms for Tax Exemption (Federal) 381

Form 1024 (Rev. 12-89)   **Page 12**

| **Schedule F** | Organizations described in section 501(c)(9) (Voluntary employees' beneficiary associations) |

1 Describe the benefits available to members. Include copies of any plan documents that describe such benefits and the terms and conditions of eligibility for each benefit.

2 Are any employees or classes of employees entitled to benefits to which other employees or classes of employees are not entitled? . . . . ☐ **Yes** ☐ **No**

If "Yes," explain.

3 Give the following information as of the first day of the first plan year for which you are filing this application and enter that date here . . . . _____

a Total number of persons covered by the plan who are highly compensated individuals (See instructions.) . . . _____
b Number of other employees covered by the plan . . . . _____
c Number of employees not covered by the plan . . . . _____
d Total number employed* . . . . _____

* Should equal the total of **a, b,** and **c**—if not, explain any difference. Describe the eligibility requirements that prevent those employees not covered by the plan from participating.

4 State the number of persons, if any, other than employees and their dependents (for example, the proprietor of a business whose employees are members of the association) who are entitled to receive benefits . . . . . ▶ |_____|

Instructions

Line 3a.—The definition of "highly compensated individual" varies depending on the tax year. For tax years beginning after December 31, 1984, and beginning before January 1, 1988, it is defined as any individual who is:

(a) one of the five highest paid officers of the employer;

(b) a shareholder who owns more than 10% of the value of the stock of the employer; or

(c) among the 10% of the highest paid employees of the employer.

For tax years beginning after December 31, 1987, "highly compensated individuals" are employees who at any time during the year (or preceding year):

(a) owned a 5% or larger interest in the employer;

(b) had compensation from the employer in excess of $81,720;*

(c) were in the top 20% of employees in compensation and had compensation in excess of $54,480;* or

(d) were officers of the employer and received compensation in excess of $45,000.*

*At some point in the future, these figures may change because of an inflation factor built into the Internal Revenue Code.

Form 1024 (Rev. 12-89)   Page **13**

| **Schedule G** | **Organizations described in section 501(c)(12) (Benevolent life insurance associations, mutual ditch or irrigation companies, mutual or cooperative telephone companies, or like organizations)** |

1 Attach a schedule in columnar form for each tax year for which you are claiming exempt status.
On each schedule:

a Show the total gross income received from members or shareholders.

b List, by source, the total amounts of gross income received from other sources.

2 If you are claiming exemption as a local benevolent insurance association, state:

a The counties from which members are accepted or will be accepted.

b Whether stipulated premiums are or will be charged in advance, or whether losses are or will be paid solely through assessments.

3 If you are claiming exemption as a "like organization," explain how you are similar to a mutual ditch or irrigation company, or a mutual or cooperative telephone company.

4 Are the rights and interests of members in your annual savings determined in proportion to their business with you? ☐ **Yes** ☐ **No**

If "Yes," do you keep the records necessary to determine at any time each member's rights and interests in such savings, including assets acquired with the savings? . . . . ☐ **Yes** ☐ **No**

5 If you are a mutual or cooperative telephone company and have contracts with other systems for long-distance telephone services, attach copies of the contracts.

Instructions

Mutual or cooperative electric or telephone companies should show income received from qualified pole rentals separately. Mutual or cooperative telephone companies should also show separately: the gross amount of income received from nonmember telephone companies for performing services that involve their members and the gross amount of income received from the sale of display advertising in a directory furnished to their members.

Do not net amounts due, or paid to, other sources against amounts due, or received from those sources.

Form 1024 (Rev. 12-89)   Page **14**

Schedule H   Organizations described in section 501(c)(13) (Cemeteries, crematoria, and like corporations)

1   Attach the following documents:

a   Complete copy of sales contracts or other documents, including any "debt" certificates, involved in acquiring cemetery or crematorium property.

b   Complete copy of any contract you have that designates an agent to sell your cemetery lots.

c   A copy of the appraisal (obtained from a disinterested and qualified party) of the cemetery property as of the date acquired.

2   Do you have, or do you plan to have, a perpetual care fund? . . . . ☐ **Yes** ☐ **No**
     If "Yes," attach a copy of the fund agreement and explain the nature of the fund (cash, securities, unsold land, etc.)

3   If you are claiming exemption as a perpetual care fund for an organization described in section 501(c)(13), has the cemetery organization, for which funds are held, established exemption under that section?. . . . . . ☐ **Yes** ☐ **No**
     If "No," explain.

Form 1024 (Rev. 12-89)   Page **15**

| Schedule I | Organizations described in section 501(c)(15) (Small insurance companies or associations) |

Note: *Section 501(c)(15) was amended in 1986 to provide new requirements for qualifying under that section. Therefore, complete lines 2 through 5 below only for years beginning after December 31, 1986, for which the organization claims to qualify under section 501(c)(15).*

1   Is the organization a member of a controlled group of corporations as defined in section 831(b)(2)(B)(ii)?
    (Disregard section 1563(b)(2)(B) in determining whether the organization is a member of a controlled group.)   . . ☐ **Yes**   ☐ **No**
    If "Yes," include on lines 2 through 5 the total amount received by the organization and all other members of
    the controlled group.
    If "No," include on lines 2 through 5 only the amounts that relate to the applicant organization.

	(a) Current Year	3 Prior Tax Years		
	From _____ To _____	(b) 19	(c) 19	(d) 19 ....
2 Direct written premiums				
3 Reinsurance assumed				
4 Reinsurance ceded				
5 Net written premiums (line 2; plus line 3; minus line 4) . . .				

6   If you entered an amount on line 3 or line 4, attach a copy of the
    reinsurance agreements you have entered into.

Instructions

Line 1.—Answer "Yes," if the organization would be considered a member of a controlled group of corporations if it were not exempt from tax under section 501(a). In applying section 1563(a), use a "more than 50% " stock ownership test to determine whether the applicant or any other corporation is a member of a controlled group.

Line 2.—In addition to other direct written premiums, include on line 2 the full amount of any prepaid or advance premium in the year the prepayment is received. For example, if a $5,000 premium for a 3-year policy was received in the current year, include the full $5,000 amount in the Current Year column.

Form 1024 (Rev. 12-89)   Page **16**

| Schedule J | Organizations described in section 501(c)(17) (Trusts providing for the payment of supplemental unemployment compensation benefits) |

1   If benefits are provided for individual proprietors, partners, or self-employed persons under the plan, explain in detail.

2   If the plan provides other benefits in addition to the supplemental unemployment compensation benefits, explain in detail and state whether the other benefits are subordinate to the unemployment benefits.

3   Give the following information as of the first day of the first plan year for which you are filing this application and enter that date here . . . . _____

a   Total number of employees covered by the plan who are shareholders, officers, self-employed persons, or highly compensated (see instructions for line 3a of Schedule F) . . . . _____

b   Number of other employees covered by the plan . . . . _____

c   Number of employees not covered by the plan . . . . _____

d   Total number employed* . . . . _____

*Should equal the total of **a, b,** and **c**—if not, explain the difference. Describe the eligibility requirements that prevent those employees not covered by the plan from participating.

4   At any time after December 31, 1959, did the trust engage in any of the transactions listed below with any of the following: the creator of the trust or a contributor to the trust; a brother or sister (whole or half blood), a spouse, an ancestor, or a lineal descendant of such a creator or contributor; or a corporation controlled directly or indirectly by such a creator or contributor?

Note: *If you know that you will be, or are considering being, a party to any of the transactions (or activities) listed below, check the "Planned" box. Give a detailed explanation of any "Yes" or "Planned" answer in the space below.*

a   Borrow any part of your income or corpus? . . . . ☐ **Yes** ☐ **No** ☐ **Planned**

b   Receive any compensation for personal services? . . . . ☐ **Yes** ☐ **No** ☐ **Planned**

c   Obtain any part of your services? . . . . ☐ **Yes** ☐ **No** ☐ **Planned**

d   Purchase any securities or other properties from you? . . . . ☐ **Yes** ☐ **No** ☐ **Planned**

e   Sell any securities or other property to you? . . . . ☐ **Yes** ☐ **No** ☐ **Planned**

f   Receive any of your income or corpus in any other transaction? . . . . ☐ **Yes** ☐ **No** ☐ **Planned**

5   Attach a copy of the Supplemental Unemployment Benefit Plan and related agreements.

Schedule K   **Organizations described in section 501(c)(19)—A post or organization of past or present members of the Armed Forces of the United States, auxiliary units or societies for such a post or organization, and trusts or foundations formed for the benefit of such posts or organizations.**

1   *To be completed by a post or organization of past or present members of the Armed Forces of the United States.*

a   Total membership of your post or organization . . . .

b   Number of your members who are present or former members of the U.S. Armed Forces . . . .

c   Number of members who are cadets (include students in college or university ROTC programs or at armed services academies only), or spouses, widows, or widowers, of cadets or past or present members of the U.S. Armed Forces

d   Do you have a membership category other than the ones set out above? . . . . ☐ **Yes** ☐ **No**

  If "Yes," please explain in full. Enter number of members in this category . . . . _____

e   If you wish to apply for a determination that contributions to you are deductible by donors, enter the number of your members from line 1b who are war veterans, as defined below . . . . _____

  A war veteran is a person who served in the Armed Forces of the United States during the following periods of war: April 21, 1898, through July 4, 1902; April 6, 1917, through November 11, 1918; December 7, 1941, through December 31, 1946; June 27, 1950, through January 31, 1955; and August 5, 1964, through May 7, 1975.

2   *To be completed by an auxiliary unit or society of a post or organization of past or present members of the Armed Forces of the United States.*

a   Are you affiliated with and organized according to the bylaws and regulations formulated by such an exempt post or organization? . . . . ☐ **Yes** ☐ **No**

  If "Yes," submit a copy of such bylaws or regulations.

b   How many members do you have? . . . .

c   How many are past or present members of the Armed Forces of the United States themselves, their spouses, or persons related to them within two degrees of blood relationship? (Grandparents, brothers, sisters, and grandchildren are the most distant relationships allowable.) . . . .

d   Are all of the members themselves members of a post or organization, past or present members of the Armed Forces of the United States, or spouses of members of such a post or organization, or are related to members of such a post or organization within two degrees of blood relationship? . . . . ☐ **Yes** ☐ **No**

3   *To be completed by a trust or foundation organized for the benefit of an exempt post or organization of past or present members of the Armed Forces of the United States.*

a   Will the corpus or income be used solely for the funding of such an exempt organization (including necessary related expenses)? . . . . ☐ **Yes** ☐ **No**

  If "No," please explain.

b   If the trust or foundation is formed for charitable purposes, does the organizational document contain a proper dissolution provision as described in section 1.501(c)(3)-1(b)(4) of the Income Tax Regulations? . . . . ☐ **Yes** ☐ **No**

Schedule L Qualified Group Legal Services Plans (Section 120)

1a Name of plan ▶ _____

 b Plan number (See instructions.) . . . . ▸ _____

 c Date the plan year ends . . . . ▶ _____

2 A qualification determination or ruling is requested for:

 a ☐ Initial qualification—date the plan was adopted . . . . _____

 b ☐ Amendment—date adopted . . . . _____

If you check "a," submit a copy of the documents establishing the plan, including a copy of the plan and any related trust instrument. If the plan was subject to collective bargaining, include a copy of the collective bargaining agreement pertaining to it. If you check "b," submit a copy of the amendment.

3 Describe the legal services covered by the plan, if they are not described in the plan or collective bargaining agreement.

4 Give the following information as of the first day of the first plan year for which you are filing this application and enter that date here . . . . _____

 a Total number of employees covered by the plan who are shareholders, officers, self-employed persons, or highly compensated (see instructions for line 3a of Schedule F) . . . . _____

 b Number of other employees covered by the plan . . . . _____

 c Number of employees not covered by the plan . . . . _____

 d Total number employed* . . . . _____

*Should equal the total of **a, b,** and **c**—if not, explain the difference. Describe the eligibility requirements that prevent those employees not covered by the plan from participating.

5 If all eligible employees are NOT entitled to the same benefits, explain the differences.

6 Manner of funding the plan (Check the appropriate box(es).)

 a ☐ Payments to insurance companies

 b ☐ Payments to organizations described in section 501(c)(20)

 c ☐ Payments to organizations described in section 501(c), which are to pay or credit your payments to other organizations described in section 501(c)(20)

 d ☐ Prepayments to providers of legal services

See reverse side for instructions.

Instructions

If you are filing separate applications under sections 120 and 501(c)(20) at the same time, please indicate this in each application.

Applicants for plan approval under section 120 should read all instructions for Schedules L and M before filling in the application because the same rules do not apply in every situation. Unless you are aware of all the exceptions, you may spend time giving unnecessary information or omit some necessary information. Either could delay getting the plan approved.

(a) In general, all applicants under section 120 should complete Part I and Schedule L. When completing Schedule L, each applicant should supply information regarding its own employees only, not all employees covered by the plan.

(b) Usually, when two or more employers contribute to the same plan, only one applicant must submit a completed application as indicated in (a). Any other or subsequent applicant under the same plan only has to supply enough information to identify the employer and the plan, plus information on Schedule L relating to its own employees.

(c) Except as noted in (d), if an application is filed for a plan to which more than one employer contributes, and the plan is maintained pursuant to a collective bargaining agreement, then only one application, as outlined in (a), is required.

(d) When more than one employer contributes to a plan pursuant to a collective bargaining agreement, and all the employers are corporations that are members of a controlled group, the filing requirements in (b) apply.

(e) If an employer has employees covered by multiple collective bargaining agreements, and one or more of such agreements includes a group legal services plan, which excludes employees under any of the other agreements from participating, then explain such arrangements. The explanation should include a list of the agreements; show the employees included; and explain why.

Line 1a.——Enter the name you chose for your plan.

Line 1b.——Enter the plan number. You must assign a 3-digit number to each adopted plan to identify it. All plan number sequences begin at "501." If you have more than one plan, number them 501, 502, etc. Once you have assigned a plan number, it cannot be changed or used for another plan.

Form 1024 (Rev. 12-89)   Page **21**

Schedule M	Trust or organization set up under section 501(c)(20)

1a Was this trust or organization created or organized in the United States? . . . . ☐ Yes ☐ No
b If "Yes," was it created or organized to form part of a group legal services plan or plans qualified under section 120? ☐ Yes ☐ No
  If "Yes," enter name of plan: _____
c Has the plan (or plans) qualified under section 120? . . . . ☐ Yes ☐ No
  If "Yes," submit a copy of the ruling or determination letter(s). If "No," attach an explanation.

2 If the trust or organization provides legal services or indemnification against the cost of legal services unassociated with a qualified group legal services plan, describe the nature and extent of these services.

Attach copies of all plan documents.

Instructions

Complete this schedule if you are applying for exempt status as a trust or other organization organized as part of one or more qualified group legal services plans under section 120. An exemption under 501(c)(20) cannot be recognized unless you are part of a section 120 plan.

If you are filing separate applications under section 120 and 501(c)(20) at the same time, please indicate this in each application.

Line 1c.—If you answered "No" to 1c, but have requested a determination letter, please attach an explanation giving the plan name; the IRS office to which the request was submitted; and the date submitted. All other "No" answers for Schedule M also must be explained.

Activity Code Numbers of Exempt Organizations (select up to three codes which best describe or most accurately identify your purposes, activities, operations or type of organization and enter in block 6, page 1, of the application. Enter first the code which most accurately identifies you.)

Code

Religious Activities

001 Church, synagogue, etc.
002 Association or convention of churches
003 Religious order
004 Church auxiliary
005 Mission
006 Missionary activities
007 Evangelism
008 Religious publishing activities
---- Bookstore (use 918)
---- Genealogical activities (use 094)
029 Other religious activities

Schools, Colleges and Related Activities

030 School, college, trade school, etc.
031 Special school for the blind, handicapped, etc.
032 Nursery school
---- Day care center (use 574)
033 Faculty group
034 Alumni association or group
035 Parent or parent-teachers association
036 Fraternity or sorority
---- Key club (use 323)
037 Other student society or group
038 School or college athletic association
039 Scholarships for children of employees
040 Scholarships (other)
041 Student loans
042 Student housing activities
043 Other student aid
044 Student exchange with foreign country
045 Student operated business
---- Financial support of schools, colleges, etc. (use 602)
---- Achievement prizes or awards (use 914)
---- Student bookstore (use 918)
---- Student travel (use 299)
---- Scientific research (see Scientific Research Activities)
046 Private school
059 Other school related activities

Cultural, Historical or Other Educational Activities

060 Musuem, zoo, planetarium, etc.
061 Library
062 Historical site, records or reenactment
063 Monument
064 Commemorative event (centennial, festival, pageant, etc.)
065 Fair
088 Community theatrical group
089 Singing society or group
090 Cultural performances
091 Art exhibit
092 Literary activities
093 Cultural exchanges with foreign country
094 Genealogical activities
---- Achievement prizes or awards (use 914)
---- Gifts or grants to individuals (use 561)
---- Financial support of cultural organizations (use 602)
119 Other cultural or historical activities

Other Instruction and Training Activities

120 Publishing activities
121 Radio or television broadcasting
122 Producing films
123 Discussion groups, forums, panels, lectures, etc.
124 Study and research (non-scientific)
125 Giving information or opinion (see also Advocacy)
126 Apprentice training
---- Travel tours (use 299)
149 Other instruction and training

Health Services and Related Activities

150 Hospital
151 Hospital auxiliary
152 Nursing or convalescent home
153 Care and housing for the aged (see also 382)
154 Health clinic
155 Rural medical facility
156 Blood bank
157 Cooperative hospital service organization
158 Rescue and emergency service
159 Nurses register or bureau
160 Aid to the handicapped (see also 031)
161 Scientific research (diseases)
162 Other medical research
163 Health insurance (medical, dental, optical, etc.)
164 Prepared group health plan
165 Community health planning
166 Mental health care
167 Group medical practice association
168 In-faculty group practice association
169 Hospital pharmacy, parking facility, food services, etc.
179 Other health services

Scientific Research Activities

180 Contract or sponsored scientific research for industry

Code

181 Scientific research for government
---- Scientific research (diseases) (use 161)
199 Other scientific research activities

Business and Professional Organizations

200 Business promotion (chamber of commerce, business league, etc.)
201 Real estate association
202 Board of trade
203 Regulating business
204 Better Business Bureau
205 Professional association
206 Professional association auxiliary
207 Industry trade shows
208 Convention displays
---- Testing products for public safety (use 905)
209 Research, development and testing
210 Professional athletic league
---- Attracting new industry (use 403)
---- Publishing activities (use 120)
---- Insurance or other benefits for members (see Employee or Membership Benefit Organizations)
211 Underwriting municipal insurance
212 Assigned risk insurance activities
213 Tourist bureau
229 Other business or professional group

Farming and Related Activities

230 Farming
231 Farm bureau
232 Agricultural group
233 Horticultural group
234 Farmers cooperative marketing or purchasing
235 Financing crop operations
---- FFA, FHA, 4-H club, etc. (use 322)
---- Fair (use 065)
236 Dairy herd improvement association
237 Breeders association
249 Other farming and related activities

Mutual Organizations

250 Mutual ditch, irrigation, telephone, electric company or like organization
251 Credit union
252 Reserve funds or insurance for domestic building and loan association, cooperative bank, or mutual savings bank
253 Mutual insurance company
254 Corporation organized under an Act of Congress (see also 904)
---- Farmers cooperative marketing or purchasing (use 234)
---- Cooperative hospital service organization (use 157)
259 Other mutual organization

Employee or Membership Benefit Organizations

260 Fraternal beneficiary society, order, or association
261 Improvement of conditions of workers
262 Association of municipal employees
263 Association of employees
264 Employee or member welfare association
265 Sick, accident, death, or similar benefits
266 Strike benefits
267 Unemployment benefits
268 Pension or retirement benefits
269 Vacation benefits
279 Other services or benefits to members or employees

Sports, Athletic, Recreational and Social Activities

280 Country club
281 Hobby club
282 Dinner club
283 Variety club
284 Dog club
285 Women's club
---- Garden club (use 356)
286 Hunting or fishing club
287 Swimming or tennis club
288 Other sports club
---- Boys Club, Little League, etc. (use 321)
296 Community center
297 Community recreational facilities (park, playground, etc.)
298 Training in sports
299 Travel tours
300 Amateur athletic association
---- School or college athletic association (use 038)
301 Fundraising athletic or sports event
317 Other sports or athletic activities
318 Other recreational activities
319 Other social activities

Youth Activities

320 Boy Scouts, Girl Scouts, etc.
321 Boys Club, Little League, etc.

Code

322 FFA, FHA, 4-H club, etc.
323 Key club
324 YMCA, YWCA, YMHA, etc.
325 Camp
326 Care and housing of children (orphanage, etc.)
327 Prevention of cruelty to children
328 Combat juvenile delinquency
349 Other youth organization or activities

Conservation, Environmental and Beautification Activities

350 Preservation of natural resources (conservation)
351 Combating or preventing pollution (air, water, etc.)
352 Land acquisition for preservation
353 Soil or water conservation
354 Preservation of scenic beauty
---- Litigation (see Litigation and Legal Aid Activities)
---- Combat community deterioration (use 402)
355 Wildlife sanctuary or refuge
356 Garden club
379 Other conservation, environmental or beautification activities

Housing Activities

380 Low-income housing
381 Low and moderate income housing
382 Housing for the aged (see also 153)
---- Nursing or convalescent home (use 152)
---- Student housing (use 042)
---- Orphanage (use 326)
398 Instruction and guidance on housing
399 Other housing activities

Inner City or Community Activities

400 Area development, redevelopment or renewal
---- Housing (see Housing Activities)
401 Homeowners association
402 Other activity aimed at combating community deterioration
403 Attracting new industry or retaining industry in an area
404 Community promotion
---- Community recreational facility (use 297)
---- Community center (use 296)
405 Loans or grants for minority businesses
---- Job training, counseling, or assistance (use 566)
---- Day care center (use 574)
---- Referral service (social agencies) (use 569)
---- Legal aid to indigents (use 462)
406 Crime prevention
407 Voluntary firemen's organization or auxiliary
---- Rescue squad (use 158)
408 Community service organization
429 Other inner city or community benefit activities

Civil Rights Activities

430 Defense of human and civil rights
431 Elimination of prejudice and discrimination (race, religion, sex, national origin, etc.)
432 Lessen neighborhood tensions
449 Other civil rights activities

Litigation and Legal Aid Activities

460 Public interest litigation activities
461 Other litigation or support of litigation
462 Legal aid to indigents
463 Providing bail
465 Plan under IRC section 120

Legislative and Political Activities

480 Propose, support, or oppose legislation
481 Voter information on issues or candidates
482 Voter education (mechanics of registering, voting, etc.)
483 Support, oppose, or rate political candidates
484 Provide facilities or services for political campaign activities
509 Other legislative and political activities

Advocacy

Attempt to influence public opinion concerning:
510 Firearms control
511 Selective Service System
512 National defense policy
513 Weapons systems
514 Government spending
515 Taxes or tax exemption
516 Separation of church and state
517 Government aid to parochial schools
518 U.S. foreign policy
519 U.S. military involvement

Code

520 Pacifism and peace
521 Economic-political system of U.S.
522 Anti-communism
523 Right to work
524 Zoning or rezoning
525 Location of highway or transportation system
526 Rights of criminal defendants
527 Capital punishment
528 Stricter law enforcement
529 Ecology or conservation
530 Protection of consumer interests
531 Medical care service
532 Welfare system
533 Urban renewal
534 Busing students to achieve racial balance
535 Racial integration
536 Use of intoxicating beverage
537 Use of drugs or narcotics
538 Use of tobacco
539 Prohibition of erotica
540 Sex education in public schools
541 Population control
542 Birth control methods
543 Legalized abortion
559 Other matters

Other Activities Directed to Individuals

560 Supplying money, goods or services to the poor
561 Gifts or grants to individuals (other than scholarships)
---- Scholarships for children of employees (use 039)
---- Scholarships (other) (use 040)
---- Student loans (use 041)
562 Other loans to individuals
563 Marriage counseling
564 Family planning
565 Credit counseling and assistance
566 Job training, counseling, or assistance
567 Draft counseling
568 Vocational counseling
569 Referral service (social agencies)
572 Rehabilitating convicts or ex-convicts
573 Rehabilitating alcoholics, drug abusers, compulsive gamblers, etc.
574 Day care center
575 Services for the aged (see also 153 and 382)
---- Training of or aid to the handicapped (see 031 and 160)

Activities Directed to Other Organizations

600 Community Chest, United Way, etc.
601 Booster club
602 Gifts, grants, or loans to other organizations
603 Non-financial services or facilities to other organizations

Other Purposes and Activities

900 Cemetery or burial activities
901 Perpetual care fund (cemetery, columbarium, etc.)
902 Emergency or disaster aid fund
903 Community trust or component
904 Government instrumentality or agency (see also 254)
905 Testing products for public safety
906 Consumer interest group
907 Veterans activities
908 Patriotic activities
909 4947(a)(1) trust
910 Domestic organization with activities outside U.S.
911 Foreign organization
912 Title holding corporation
913 Prevention of cruelty to animals
914 Achievement prizes or awards
915 Erection or maintenance of public building or works
916 Cafeteria, restaurant, snack bar, food services, etc.
917 Thrift shop, retail outlet, etc.
918 Book, gift or supply store
919 Advertising
920 Association of employees
921 Loans or credit reporting
922 Endowment fund or financial services
923 Indians (tribes, cultures, etc.)
924 Traffic or tariff bureau
925 Section 501(c)(1) with 50% deductibility
926 Government instrumentality other than section 501(c)
927 Fundraising
928 4947(a)(2) trust
930 Prepaid legal services plan exempt under IRC section 501(c)(20)
931 Withdrawal liability payment fund
990 Section 501(k) child care organization

U.S. GOVERNMENT PRINTING OFFICE : 1992 O - 317-147

FORM NO. 14 [IRS Form 1028]

[Instructions for use with this form are available from the IRS.]

Form **1028** (Rev. April 1991) Department of the Treasury Internal Revenue Service	**Application for Recognition of Exemption** Under Section 521 of the Internal Revenue Code For the use of farmers', fruit growers', or like associations applying for recognition of exemption as cooperatives. ▶ See separate Instructions.	OMB No. 1545-0058 Expires 3-31-94

If Your Organization Does Not Have an Organizing Document, Do Not File This Application. Every organization must furnish all the information specified in the Instructions. An attachment may be used if more space is needed for any item. If the required information and appropriate documents are not submitted along with Form 8718 (with payment of the appropriate user fee), the application may be returned to you.

Part I Identification (see instructions.)

1a Full name of organization	b Employer identification number (see instructions.)

2a Number, street, and room or suite no. (or P.O. box number if mail is not delivered to street address)

b City or town, county, state, and ZIP code

3 Name and telephone number (including area code) of person to be contacted during business hours	4 Date incorporated or formed
( )	5 Month the annual accounting period ends

6a Has the organization filed Federal income tax returns? . . . . ☐ Yes ☐ No

b If "**Yes**," state the form numbers, years filed, and Internal Revenue office where filed ▶ ....
....

Part II Type of Entity and Organizational Documents (see Instructions.)

Check the applicable entity box below and attach a conformed copy of the organizing and operational documents listed.
☐ Corporation—Articles of Incorporation, bylaws
☐ Other—Constitution or Articles of Association, bylaws

Part III Activities and Operational Information (see instructions.)

1 State the number of shares of each class of capital stock currently outstanding, if any, the value of the consideration for which issued, and the rate of dividend paid:

		Shares	Amount	Rate of Dividend
a Preferred stock (voting)	1a			
b Preferred stock (nonvoting)	1b			
c Common stock (voting)	1c			
d Common stock (nonvoting)	1d			

2 Number of shares of capital stock (other than nonvoting preferred) owned by:

a Producers	2a	
b Nonproducers	2b	
c Current and active producers	2c	
d Total number of shares—Add lines 2a and 2b	2d	
e Percentage owned by current and active producers—Divide line 2c by line 2d	2e	%

3 What provision is made for retiring the voting stock held by a nonproducer?

4 Describe who is accorded voting rights in the cooperative and how many votes one person may have. If a person may be entitled to more than one vote, describe in detail how voting rights are acquired.

5 Legal rate of interest in the state where the association is located . . . . ▶

Please Sign Here ▶	Under penalties of perjury, I declare that I am authorized to sign this application on behalf of the above organization; and I have examined this application, including the accompanying statements, and to the best of my knowledge and belief it is true, correct, and complete. (See General Instruction "C.")
	.... (Signature) .... (Title or authority of signer) .... (Date)

For Paperwork Reduction Act Notice, see page 1 of the separate Instructions   Form **1028** (Rev. 4-91)

Form 1028 (Rev. 4-91)   Page **2**

Part III **Activities and Operational Information** *(Continued)*

6   If the association issues any nonvoting preferred stock, explain whether the owners, upon dissolution or liquidation, may participate
in the profits of the association beyond fixed dividends.

7a Does state law require the accumulation and maintenance of reserves? . . . .   ☐Yes ☐No
   b If **"Yes,"** state the names and purposes of the reserves and enter the amount of each: Amount

....
....

8a Does the association maintain or plan to maintain any reserve or reserves other than those required by state law?☐Yes ☐No
   b If **"Yes,"** state the names and purposes of the reserves and enter the amount of each: Amount

....
....

9   Does the association deal or plan to deal with both members and nonmembers? . . . .   ☐Yes ☐No
10a Does the association pay or plan to pay patronage dividends? . . . .   ☐Yes ☐No
   b If **"Yes,"** are they paid or will they be paid to all patrons, both member and nonmember, on the same basis? .   ☐Yes ☐No

11a Is the allocation of patronage dividends based on an obligation in existence before the cooperative received
the amounts allocated? . . . .   ☐Yes ☐No
   b If **"Yes,"** is this obligation in:
      ☐ Organizing document (specify) ▶ ....
      ☐ Bylaws

12 Explain below all of the activities in which the association is or will be engaged.

13 Explain below how distribution is or will be made of the proceeds of products marketed for members and nonmembers. Also, if
the organization operates on a basis of allocated units (i.e., functional, departmental, etc.), explain how losses are or will be treated.

14 Explain below how the association charges for supplies and equipment bought for members and nonmembers.

Form 1028 (Rev. 4-91)   Page **3**

Part III **Activities and Operational Information** *(Continued)*

15 Explain the requirements for membership in the association.

16 Federated cooperatives only:

a Are all of the association's member cooperatives exempt under section 521? . . . . ☐ **Yes** ☐ **No**

b If **"No"** to 16a, do the nonexempt member cooperatives have the same annual accounting period as the association's? . . . . ☐ **Yes** ☐ **No**

c If **"No"** to 16b, check the method below that the association used, or will use, to provide a common or comparable unit of time for analyzing and evaluating its operations and those of its members.

Note: *Methods listed below do not apply to the filing of returns or the manner in which operating results are reported by a federated cooperative and its members.*

(i) ☐ Method 1—The association uses the operations of members for those months that correspond to the months that make up its tax year.

(ii) ☐ Method 2—The association uses the tax years of members that end within its tax year.

(iii) ☐ Method other than 1 or 2 above (explain) ▶ ....
....

17 Value of agricultural products marketed or handled for: (see instructions.)	**Current tax year**	**3 prior tax years**		
	(a) From .... to	**(b)** 19	**(c)** 19	**(d)** 19 .....
•a Members—				
(i) Actually produced by members				
(ii) Not actually produced by members but marketed by them through the association				
b Nonmembers—				
(i) Actually produced by nonmembers				
(ii) Not actually produced by nonmembers but marketed by them through the association .				
c Nonproducers (purchased from nonproducers for marketing by the association).				
18 Value of supplies and equipment purchased for or sold to: (See instructions.)				
•a Members who were producers				
b Nonmembers who were producers				
c Members and nonmembers who were not producers				
19 Amount of business done with the United States Government or any of its agencies				

20 Does the association plan to do business with the United States Government or any of its agencies in the future? ☐ **Yes** ☐ **No**

21a Were all of the net earnings (after payment of dividends, if any, on capital stock) for the years shown on lines 17–19 distributed as patronage dividends? (See instructions.) . . . . ☐ **Yes** ☐ **No**

b If **"No,"** were undistributed net earnings apportioned on the records to all patrons on a patronage basis? . . . ☐ **Yes** ☐ **No**

22a Has the organization operated in a manner consistent with the information given since the date formed? . . . ☐ **Yes** ☐ **No**

b If **"No,"** state the changes that have occurred and dates of the changes.
....
....
....

---

* If it is necessary to own one or more shares of stock in order to become a member, include on lines 17a and 18a only the amount of business transacted with persons actually owning the required number of shares.

Forms for Tax Exemption (Federal)

Form 1028 (Rev. 4-91)

Page **4**

Part IV **Financial Data (see instructions.)**

Complete a statement for the current year and for each of the three immediately preceding years that the organization was in existence.

Statement of Receipts and Expenditures, for period ending ...., 19 ......

(If you prepare a statement of receipts and expenditures that is more descriptive and detailed than the statement below, you may submit that statement instead of this one.)

Receipts	1	Gross dues and assessments from members		1	
	2	Gross dues and assessments from affiliated organizations		2	
	3a	Gross amount derived from activities related to organization's exempt purpose (attach schedule)	3a		
	b	Less cost of goods sold	3b ( )	3c	
	4a	Gross amount from other business activities (attach schedule)	4a		
	b	Less cost of goods sold	4b ( )	4c	
	5a	Gross amount received from sale of assets, excluding inventory items (attach schedule)	5a		
	b	Less cost or other basis and sales expense of assets sold (attach schedule)	5b ( )	5c	
	6	Interest, dividends, rents and royalties		6	
	7	Other receipts (attach schedule)		7	
	8	**Total receipts**—Add lines 1 through 7 in far right column		8	
Expenditures	9	Compensation of officers, directors, and trustees (attach schedule)		9	
	10	Other salaries and wages		10	
	11	Interest		11	
	12	Rent		12	
	13	Depreciation and depletion		13	
	14	Dues and assessments to affiliated organizations		14	
	15	Other expenditures (see instructions—attach schedule)		15	
	16	Patronage dividends (see instructions—attach schedule)		16	
	17	**Total expenditures**—Add lines 9 through 16		17	
	18	Excess of receipts over expenditures (line 8 less line 17)		18	

Balance Sheets

Enter dates ▶

				Beginning date	Ending date
Assets	19	Cash	19		
	20	Trade notes and accounts receivable (less allowance for bad debts)	20		
	21	Inventories	21		
	22	Investments (attach schedule)	22		
	23	Other current assets (attach schedule)	23		
	24	Depreciable and depletable assets (less accumulated depreciation/depletion)	24		
	25	Land (net of any amortization)	25		
	26	Other assets (attach schedule)	26		
	27	**Total assets**	27		
Liabilities and Capital	28	Accounts payable	28		
	29	Mortgages, notes, bonds payable in less than one year	29		
	30	Other current liabilities (attach schedule)	30		
	31	Mortgages, notes, bonds payable in one year or more	31		
	32	Other liabilities (attach schedule)	32		
	33	Patronage dividends allocated in noncash form, other than capital stock and interest-bearing obligations	33		
	34	Per-unit retains allocated in noncash form	34		

	Capital stock (enter numbers at end of year):	Number of shareholders	Number of shares			
			Issued for money	Issued as patronage benefits		
35						
a	Voting preferred stock	35a				
b	Nonvoting preferred stock	35b				
c	Voting common stock	35c				
d	Nonvoting common stock	35d				

36	Paid-in or capital surplus	36		
37	Retained earnings (attach schedule)	37		
38	Less cost of treasury stock	38 ( )	( )	
39	**Total liabilities and capital**	39		

11

TAX DEDUCTIONS FOR CHARITABLE CONTRIBUTIONS

[*Note:* This is *outline only*. Consult Tax Counsel]

[The first writing of this chapter was contributed in 1988 by Prof. I. Richard Gershon of Stetson University College of Law. Material by Oleck and Stewart was added thereafter. Individual contributor's names appear at the beginning of each such contribution.]

§110. FEDERAL CHARITABLE DEDUCTIONS, GENERALLY

[See Chapter 9]

Gifts[1] of property are expressly excluded from the gross income of the donee by the Internal Revenue Code.[2] The gift exclusion applies to all donees, whether they are tax-exempt or not. However, the donor of a gift generally derives no income tax benefit from this generosity,[3] and, in fact, might actually be required to pay a gift tax on the transfer of his wealth.[4] Thus, the tax system often serves as a disincentive for gift giving. [The 1987 federal tax law revision lowered individual tax rates from a top of 38.5 percent to either 28 or 33 percent, thus making donations by wealthy persons less advantageous tax-wise. See Section 113.]

Congress has recognized[5] that certain gifts foster such important societal good, that a person making such a gift should be given a tax incentive in the form of income,[6] gift[7] and estate[8] tax deductions.

Contribution Benefits

In the 1993 tax bill, charitable donations of *$250 or more* are *deductible only* if the donor obtains a written receipt from the charity stating that there was no consideration given for the contribution. Also, contributors of highly appreciated property never have to pay tax on the appreciation and get a tax deduction for the full market value of the property. See, G.K. Yin, article, *St. Petersburg (FL) Times*, p. 11A (Dec. 30, 1993); *Religious News Service Note, St. Petersburg (FL) Times*, p. 3E (Jan. 15, 1994).

Contribution of motion picture rights to the Library of Congress is not deductible where the taxpayer got the *benefit* of having the nitrate-based film converted to safety film and kept commercial rights in the film.[10]

A contributor, who gave to a nonprofit conservancy organization, had donative intent at the time of the conveyance of a scenic easement and was entitled to a charitable contribution. The contributor's inquiry about tax matters did not negate his primary gift motive. An expectation of substantial benefit from a quid pro quo contribution would defeat deductibility.[11]

Contribution to a NPC without investigating the circuitous arrangement whereby the NPC would enable the contributor to get a tenfold charitable deduction is not conclusively deductible.[12]

A donor who receives a *benefit* from the charity in return for the contribution is a *contracting party* rather than a donor, and may not lawfully deduct that contribution from adjusted gross income.[13]

Charitable Gift Funds, run by *Investment Companies*, get immediate tax breaks for investments—grants of $10,000 or more, for small businesses and individuals, by combining such philanthropic "charitable accounts;" like a grouping of private foundations in which the founder(s) "recommend" how and when the money shall be disbursed. An example is Boston-based Fidelity Investment's Charitable Gift Fund.[14]

A gift cannot be properly characterized as charitable if it is so structured as to advance a significant private interest of a financial or pecuniary nature. However, there is often a fine line between charity and self-interest. The largest gift ever received by a state school, $100 million, may not have been totally altruistic. The donor stood to save $31 million in taxes. Further, the gift provided for a full college scholarship for eligible children of his 4,200 employees worldwide as an incentive to keep employees with the company. The gift would have also brought an engineering school within 25 miles of the donor's headquarters, thereby providing the donor with a source of trained labor. The scholarship was not available to the children of union members, arguably punishing union members, a private benefit to the donor, which runs counter to public policy. After adverse publicity, the donor made union members' children eligible for the scholarship.[15]

IRS "Checks" on Non-Cash Contributions

The IRS now (since Feb. 1990) makes available to interested NPOs and others the "check sheet" list of questions/criteria used by its tax auditors in testing the propriety of tax exemptions claimed by NPOs for contributions to them of non-cash gifts/donations. The check sheet is titled "Exempt Organizations Charitable Solicitations Compliance Improvement Program Study Checksheet—

Phase II," and can be obtained from any of the IRS seven regional offices.[16]

Most gifts of property of over $5000 value, to charities, must be appraised, and summaries filed. Gifts of money must be noted in records, at least such as a cancelled check or receipt from the charity (donee), or a letter from it. Otherwise, some "reliable written record" must be kept by the donor; or diary entries, or emblem-award, or the like. Similar, but more complete, record of property donations of under $5000 value also must be kept by the donor, for each gift.[17]

IRS Regulations for donors (to charitable organizations) of gifts of *property* worth over $5000: The donor must submit a "Qualified Appraisal" (on Form No. 8283) by a "qualified appraiser," with his or her tax return, and must supply copies to the NPO and its partners or deduction-claiming shareholders. The appraisal must be dated within 60 days before the gift (90 days after if honest mistake and IRS demand). There are additional rules for small-item packages. "Charitable deduction property" is anything other than money or some types of securities traded on securities markets.[18]

The most probative evidence of fair market value is the price of similar items, that are sold in arms length transactions, within a short time of the date of contribution. Taxpayers who are misinformed about the value of a donation must bear the burden of the increase in taxes due.[19] For example, the price paid for videotapes of a ballet, by the contributor of them, is the measure of his validity claimed charitable contribution deduction.[20]

Contributions are deductible from gross income when paid within the taxable year and are valued at the fair market value at the time of contribution. Gifts given over a period of years may be considered by the IRS to be one gift and valued at the time of the first gift.[21]

Prompted by a $5 billion gap between what charities say they get and what donors are deducting, charities should inform donors of the fair market value of contributions. The law now denies deductions for contributions of $250 or more without a written acknowledgment from the charity.[22]

§111. QUALIFIED DONEES

In order for a donor to receive an income tax-deduction in recognition of his generosity, he must first make sure that he has chosen a proper donee for his contributions. Section 170(a) of the Internal Revenue Code states that "there shall be allowed as a deduction any charitable contribution . . . which is made within the taxable year." Section 170(c) defines charitable contribution to mean "a contribution or gift to or for the use of:"

1. a state or possession of the United States, or a political subdivision thereof, but only if the contribution or gift is made for exclusively public purposes.[23]
2. an organization exempt from taxation under Section 501(c)(3).[24] [See Chapter 9 on Federal Tax-Exemptions.]
3. a post or organization of war veterans, including any auxiliary unit there-

of, which is a domestic organization, but only if no part of the net earnings of such an organization inures to the benefit of any private shareholder or beneficiary.[25]

4. a domestic fraternal society or order, operating under the lodge system,[26] but only if the organization uses the contribution exclusively for
   religious, charitable, scientific, or literary purposes, or for the prevention
   of cruelty to animals.[27] It is important to note that only individuals (as
   opposed to corporations or trusts) can make deductible gifts to a fraternal society.[28]

5. a cemetery company owned and operated exclusively for the benefit of its
   members.[29]

§112. LIST OF QUALIFIED ORGANIZATIONS; IRS PUBLICATION 78

A complete list of organizations qualified to receive charitable contributions
can be obtained from the Superintendent of Documents, US Government
Printing Office, Washington, DC. This list, which is known as IRS Publication
Number 78 (IRS Pub. No. 78),[30] is issued annually in a bound volume. The government also issues quarterly cumulative supplements to this document. Any
deletions or changes concerning an organization's status are announced weekly in the Internal Revenue Bulletin (IRB).[31]

Taxpayers are entitled to rely on determinations of deductibility as set
forth in IRS Pub. No. 78 to the extent that they did not know of revocation or
impending revocation, of an organization's exempt status.[32] Thus, a gift will
usually be deductible as long as it was made on or before the date of an IRS
proclamation of non-deductibility in the Internal Revenue Bulletin.[33]

§113. INCOME-TAX DEDUCTIONS FOR CHARITABLE CONTRIBUTIONS BY INDIVIDUALS

An individual taxpayer who makes contributions to an organization described
in Section 170(c) of the Internal Revenue Code[34] will be entitled to deduct his
contribution from his adjusted gross income[35] in calculating his taxable
income,[36] if he complies with the requirements of Section 170.

The income tax-deduction is limited to 50 percent of the taxpayer's gift
base[37] for contributions made to public charities[38] and to some operating private foundations[39] during the tax year. Deductible contributions to other private foundations[40] do not qualify for the 50 percent maximum, and are limited to the lesser of 30 percent of the taxpayer's contribution base,[41] or 50
percent of the contribution base minus the amount already given to charities

qualifying for the 50 percent maximum.[42] Thus, in no year can a taxpayer's charitable deductions exceed 50 percent of his contribution base.

[See Section 110 above]

Religious Contributions

[See Chapter 36]

[In 1993 the I.R.S. sent 30 "determination letters" finding the Scientology Church to be entitled to classification as (and tax privileges of) a church.]

[Margaret A. Fonvielle contributed this subsection.]

A minister leased, to the Universal Life Church for one dollar per year, an apartment building that was purported to generate rental income for the church. The income was attributed to the minister because he collected the rents and deposited them in an account under his control. Continuous dominion over the property and all of the income produced was found to be a substantial benefit to the donor.[44]

The trustee of a temple held other positions including choir director, youth director, and Sunday school teacher. The trustee's cash contributions to the temple were disallowed because he did not prove that the transfer of money was devoid of any anticipated benefit, when the money was used to run his household.[45]

Contribution of a support expenses for sons serving as church missionaries is not a deductible item when the *control* of the funds is not in the church.[46]

Contribution Tax: In late 1992 churches in Berkeley, California were ordered to pay taxes on *contributions* (60¢ per $1000 received) and also to *register* like other nonprofit organizations. City finance director Sonali Bose reported that only half of the 600 NPOs in that city had registered yet. The tax is based on the unanimous ruling of the U.S. Supreme Court in 1990 (*Jimmy Swaggart Ministries v. Calif. Board of Equalization*, 110 S. Ct. 688 (1990)) upholding the California sales tax on religious organizations as well as other NPOs. The trend seems to be to require churches to pay such taxes as other NPOs are required to do, said Joe Conn, a spokesman for Americans United for Separation of Church and State, based in Silver Spring, Maryland.[47]

§114. CARRYOVERS OF EXCESS CONTRIBUTIONS

If an individual taxpayer makes contributions in excess of 50 percent of contribution base for a given tax year, he may carry forward the excess contributions for five years.[48] The contributions carried over are treated as if they were made after all other contributions in the succeeding year, and are subject to the same limitations as contributions actually made in that succeeding tax year.[49]

§115. CONTRIBUTIONS OF APPRECIATED PROPERTY

(See Table I at the end of this section).

[*Note:* Tax Code of 1986, §301 limited deductions for contributions of appreciated tangible property not related to the exempt purpose of a public charity, or any appreciated property to a private non-operating foundation, to the taxpayer's basis in the property. Note also the changes in corporate (business) donations, stock, etc., in Code §§ 170(e)(5), (e)(3), and 3304(f). [See IRS Publication 561 as to valuation problems. 1993 Tax law liberalized this; see page 395.]

The entire Internal Revenue Code is based upon a system of cash equivalence.[50] The same theory holds true in dealing with contributions to charities. For example, a taxpayer who gives $50 in cash to a charity has been subject to tax to the full extent of that $50.[51] On the other hand, a taxpayer who contributes a painting for which he paid $2, but which has a fair market value[52] of $50 at the time of the contribution, has been subject to tax on only the $2 he paid for the painting.[53] If the taxpayer was allowed a full and unconditional deduction of $50 upon the contribution of either the cash or the appreciated property, he would be foolish not to make his contribution using the painting, since this would confer a double tax benefit, by giving him a deduction for a donation of unrealized appreciation.[54]

Congress has recognized the possibility that the use of appreciated property can be abused by taxpayers in seeking an inordinate, and unintended, tax benefit. Thus, Congress enacted Section 170(e) of the Internal Revenue Code, which requires the taxpayer to reduce the amount of the contribution, taken into account in calculating the charitable deduction, when certain types of appreciated property are involved.

Section 170(e) states that in calculating the amount of a gift of property,[55] the fair market value must be reduced by the amount which would have been an ordinary income[56] gain had the property been sold or exchanged.[57]

Furthermore, if the taxpayer contributes tangible personal property to a charity, and the property is unrelated in purpose or use to the charity's exempt function, the amount of the contribution taken into account for purposes of the charitable deduction must be reduced by 40 percent of what would have been long-term capital gain[58] had the taxpayer sold or exchanged the property. Thus, for example, if a taxpayer, who was not an art dealer,[59] contributed a sculpture to a church, and the fair market value of the sculpture, for which the donor paid $2000 in 1984, was $3000 in 1986 when he made the gift, his charitable contribution would be $2600.[60]

Another situation which calls for a reduction of a fair market value in calculating a charitable contribution occurs when a taxpayer contributes appreciated property to a private foundation described in Section 170(b)(1)(B).[61] The fair market value of appreciated property to such a charity, must be reduced by 40 percent of what would have been long-term capital gain had the taxpayer sold or exchanged the property.[62]

All other gifts of appreciated property will be considered contributions of the fair market value of the asset at the time of the gift. However, a gift which is not reduced by the provisions of Section 170(e) will be subject to a special deduction limitation instead. Such gifts will be deductible only to the extent of the lesser of 30 percent of the taxpayer's contribution base,[63] or the excess of thirty-percent of the contribution base over the other deductible contributions made during the tax year.[64]

Even though Section 170(e) does not require a taxpayer to reduce certain gifts of appreciated property in calculating his charitable contributions, the code does provide for an election.[65] The election allows a taxpayer to reduce the amount of his contribution, as though Section 170(e) required such a reduction. After a taxpayer has reduced the amount of gift by 40 percent of what would have been long-term capital gain, he will be entitled to deduct his gift to the extent of 50 percent of his contribution base, rather than being forced to use the lower 30 percent limitation imposed upon non-reduced capital gain contributions.[66]

ILLUSTRATIVE TABLE

[Prof. Richard Gershon contributed the following Table (pages 402-403) and the update note about the deduction]:

Note in Table I, how the election to reduce a contribution of long-term capital gain property can increase a current year's deduction. However, also note that the increase in a current deduction must be weighed against the fact that contributions in excess of the allowable yearly percentage can be carried over for five years.[67] Thus, when a taxpayer elects to reduce contribution, he loses any chance to carry over his contribution to the extent of the reduction.

The following table assumes that a taxpayer with a contribution base of $100,000 is considering making only one contribution to charity in the current year. Notice how his income tax deduction will be affected by the type of property he chooses to give, and by the type of charity he chooses to benefit.[68]

The deduction for capital gains previously found in §1202 of the Internal Revenue Code of 1954, was repealed by the Tax Reform Act of 1986. Consequently, §170(b)(1)(C)(iii) was amended, and now requires an electing tax payer to reduce his contribution by the entire amount which would have been long-term capital gain, rather than only 40 percent of the amount which would have been capital gain. As a result, unless the property's fair market value is quite close to its basis, the election will not be of benefit to most taxpayers.

The contribution under #5 of Table I should now read only $25,000, rather than $55,000, if the election under §170(b)(1)(c)(iii) is made.

TABLE 1 [under 1988 rules]
Computation of Income Tax Charitable Contribution, Deduction, and Carryover (Individual w/$100,000 contribution base as defined by §170(b)(1)(F))

Gift	Contribution (§170(e))	Type of Charity (§§170(b)(1)(A), (B))	% of Contribution Base Deduction Limitation	Deduction (§170(a))	Carryover (§170(d))
1. $75,000 cash	$75,000	Public (§170(b)(1)(A))	50%	$50,000	$25,000
2. $75,000 cash	$75,000	Private (§170(b)(1)(B))	30%	$30,000	$45,000
3. INVENTORY, or other ordinary income property. Cost: $20,000 Fair Market Value: $75,000 FMV	$20,000 (which = cost under §170(e)(1)(A))	Public (§170(b)(1)(A))	50%	$20,000	0
4. INVENTORY, or other ordinary income property. Cost: $20,000 FMV	$20,000 (which = cost under §170(e)(1)(A))	Private (§170(B)(1)(B))	30%	$20,000	0
5. LONG-TERM CAPITAL GAIN PROPERTY (a) Land, Cost: $25,000 FMV: $75,000 No	$75,000 (which = FMV under §170(e)(1))	Public	30%	$30,000	$45,000[A]

§170(b)(1)(c)(iii) Election; (b) Land, Cost: $25,000 FMV: $75,000 Taxpayer makes the §170(b)(1)(c)(iii) election to reduce his contribution	Public	50%	$25,000 (FMV – long term capital gain sold) or $75,000 – $50,000)	$25,000	$0
(c) Land to Private Foundation Cost: $25,000 FMV: $75,000	Private	20%	$55,000 (automatic reduction under §170(d)(i)(B)(ii)	$20,000	$35,000
(d) Diamond Necklace given to a law school (unrelated to the charitable purpose of the school Cost: $25,000 FMV: $75,000	Public	50%	$55,000 (FMV – 40% of what would have been long-term capital gain) [This reduction is automatic— §170(e)(1)(B)(i)	$50,000	$5,000

Notes:
  *Gain is calculated by subtracting cost from fair market value. Thus, in this example gain would be $75,000 – $25,000 = $50,000. (I.R.C. §1001(a)&(b).)

(A) Note how the taxpayer here only gets a $30,000 current deduction, but is entitled to carryover $45,000 as a contribution of capital gain property. Thus, potentially the taxpayer could take deductions for the full $75,000 contribution, even though he only gets a $30,000 deduction in the current year.

§116. INCOME TAX CHARITABLE DEDUCTION FOR NON-ITEMIZERS

In order for an individual taxpayer to make use of the income tax deduction (discussed in §§ 1-6) until 1986 he must have had itemized deductions in excess of his "zero bracket" amount.[69] Thus, a large segment of generous taxpayers are precluded from taking the charitable deduction under Section 170(a), because they do not have sufficient itemized deductions.[70]

In 1981, Congress, recognizing that there should be some provision allowing non-itemizing taxpayers a charitable deduction, enacted Section 170(i).[71] Section 170(i) allowed a non-itemizing taxpayer a maximum deduction of $25 in 1982 and 1983.[72] The amount increased to $75 in 1984,[73] and to 50 percent of the taxpayer's contributions[74] in 1985. For 1986, the deduction was scheduled to increase to 100 percent of the taxpayer's contributions.[75] Unfortunately, Section 170(i) self-destructed on December 31, 1986[76] as Congress did not renew it.[77]

Additional help in calculating the income-tax charitable deduction for individuals can be obtained from Internal Revenue Publications 527[78] and 561.[79] Taxpayers should order those publications from the IRS Forms Distribution Center.

§117. INCOME TAX CHARITABLE DEDUCTION FOR ITEMIZERS

Through his 1993 budget proposal, President Clinton attempted to make the 3 percent floor on itemized deductions a permanent part of the tax code. Under the 1992 formula a single filer, making just over $208,000 annually, cannot itemize the first $3,000 of his/her charitable contributions. Some 300 non-profits opposed the measure, citing that it discourages initiating a donation and that the floor will inevitably creep up. The *Independent Sector* drafted a letter to both houses, urging reconsideration of the 3 percent floor, which is to expire in 1995 if Clinton's proposal failed.[80]

§118. INCOME TAX DEDUCTION FOR CONTRIBUTIONS BY CORPORATIONS AND ASSOCIATIONS[81]

Contributions by corporations are valid under both English and American law, where such contributions benefit the purposes or business of the corporation.[82] However, such contributions are not authorized where they constitute political contributions.[83]

Generally, state statutes authorize corporate contributions for such things as "the betterment of the social and economic conditions in any community or communities in which such corporation is operating.[84]

A corporation making contributions to charitable organizations will be entitled to deduct such contributions only to the extent that they do not exceed 10 percent of the corporation's taxable income.[85] Computed without taking into account: the corporation's charitable deductions for the year,[86] the special deductions for the year,[87] the special deductions allowed to corporations under Part VIII of the Internal Revenue Code (except for Section 248),[88] net operating loss carrybacks,[89] or capital loss carrybacks.[90]

The 10 percent limitation imposed upon corporations is a flat percentage which applies notwithstanding the classification of the donee. That is, the corporation's deductions are not increased when gifts are made to public charities as opposed to private charities.[91]

§119. CARRYOVER OF EXCESS CONTRIBUTIONS BY CORPORATIONS

If a corporation's contributions for a given tax year exceed 10 percent of its taxable income, it can carry its excess contribution forward for a period of up to five years.[92] In each succeeding year, contributions carried over will be taken into account only after taking into account the current year's contributions.[93] Carryover contributions from the immediate preceding year are always used before any carryover contributions, if any of the 10 percent limitation remains.[94]

§120. CONTRIBUTIONS OF APPRECIATED PROPERTY BY CORPORATIONS

Corporate gifts are subject to the same reductions[95] as gifts made by individual taxpayers. Please refer to §7 for the rules relating to such contributions.

Deduction for Exempt Organizations Subject to Tax on Unrelated Business Income.

Section 511 imposes upon certain exempt organizations a tax on unrelated taxable business income.[96] A trade or business is generally "unrelated" if its conduct is not substantially related to the exempt function of the organization.[97]

The tax levied by Section 511, can be offset, to some extent, by the deduction for charitable contributions.[98] Such deduction may not exceed 10 percent of the unrelated business taxable income.[99] It must be noted that an exempt organization can only take a charitable deduction for gifts to another exempt organization.[100] Therefore (at least as of 1987) a church with unrelated business income cannot receive a charitable deduction if it gives 10 percent of that income to itself, or one of its auxiliaries.[101] On the other hand, the church could give up to 10 percent of its unrelated business income to any art museum, which would then qualify it for the deduction.[102]

Contribution of options to buy business corporation (or foundation) stock would cause violation (as self-dealing) of IRC §4941; but sale of the stock to unrelated other tax-exempt organizations by the grantee is legally valid as to the difference (when the options are exercised) between the fair market value of the shares and the exercise price.[103]

§121. ESTATE, GIFT AND GENERATION-SKIPPING TRANSFER TAX CHARITABLE DEDUCTIONS

Because estate,[104] gift[105] and generation-skipping transfer[106] taxes are not imposed upon corporations, it is logical that the charitable deductions allowed[107] in computing wealth-transfer tax liability are only allowed to individuals and their estates.[108]

Unlike the income tax charitable deduction,[109] charitable deductions from wealth transfer taxes can be taken to reduce the taxpayer's tax liability without limit.[110] Also, unlike the income-tax deduction, there is no reduction in the amount of a taxpayer's contribution where appreciated property is involved.[111] Therefore, a taxpayer who gives a $75,000 painting to a church is entitled to a $75,000 gift tax deduction, even if he only paid $25,000 for the painting.[112]

In order for a contribution to be deductible for the purposes of wealth transfer taxation a bequest, legacy, devise or transfer must be made:

1. to or for the use of the United States, any political subdivision thereof, or the District of Columbia, for exclusively public purposes;[113]

2. to or for the use of any corporation organized and operated exclusively for religious, charitable, scientific, literary, or educational purposes, including the encouragement of art, or to foster national or international amateur sports competition (but only if no part of its activities involve the provision of athletic facilities or equipment), and the prevention of cruelty to children or animals, no part of the net earnings of which inures to the benefit of any private stockholder or individual, which is not disqualified for tax-exemption under Section 501(c)(3) by reason of attempting to influence legislation.[114]

3. to a trustee or trustees, or a fraternal society, order, or association operating under the lodge system, but only if such contributions or gifts are to be used by such trustee or trustees, or by such fraternal society, order or association, exclusively for religious, charitable, scientific, literary, or educational purposes, or for the prevention of cruelty to children or animals.[115]

4. to or for the use of any veterans' organizations incorporated by an Act of Congress, or of its departments or local chapters or posts, no part of the net earnings of which inures to the benefit of any private shareholder or individual.[116]

§122. GIFTS AND BEQUESTS OF REMAINDER INTERESTS

(Transfers), Generally

Transfers to charitable organizations can take many forms. The most common transfers involve outright gifts, and deferred giving through the use of charitable remainder annuity trusts, unitrusts and pooled income funds. Such transfers apply to the estate, gift, generation-skipping and income tax deductions.

Estate planning when the donor wishes to keep a life estate for his/her self and spouse, and the remainder to a charity, should consider many alternatives available: *viz.*: Marital deduction Q-TIP Trust, Qualified Charitable Remainder Trust, Pooled Income Fund or Remainder Interest in a Residence or Farm, or Charitable Gift Annuity; all of which turn on such factors as need for income or for corpus, business interests affected, private foundation rules, family transfers possibilities, etc.[117]

In computing the taxable estate under a will's split-interest gift to a charitable group, no deduction is allowed under I.R.C. § 2055(a) for a remainder interest unless the gift is through a pooled income fund, charitable remainder trust, or unitrust. I.R.C. § 2055(e).

Under a pooled-income fund gift to a school, when the heirs challenged the gift of the remainder to it after their life interest in the net income, a cash settlement of $250,000 to the school resulted in only a $14,746 allowance by the IRS, the actuarial value of the remainder interest. To deduct 250,000 the school would have to show a present right to that sum at some point under a valid will or state law. Here the gift came from the heirs, not the decedent.[118]

§123. OUTRIGHT GIFTS

An outright gift is the simplest type of transfer, because it requires only that the taxpayer relinquish control[119] over the property or cash given to charity. A taxpayer is required to furnish the amount of each contribution, the name of the donee organization, and the date of payment of each contribution.[120]

If the taxpayer's gift consists of property (as opposed to cash) he must be able to ascertain the fair market value of the property. To that end, the taxpayer should always obtain a certified appraisal[121] of the property's value, when large gifts are involved. In any event, the taxpayer must provide detailed information concerning any deduction generated by property valued at more than $200.[122]

Over-valuation of an asset given to charity can subject the taxpayer to a penalty of not less than 10 percent nor more than 30 percent of the amount of the taxpayer's underpayment of the tax.[123] The penalty results whenever a taxpayer reports the value of an asset to be 150 percent of its correct valuation.[124] However, no penalty is assessed if the underpayment of the tax is less than $1000, or if the taxpayer held the property for more than five years.[125]

Finally, a taxpayer is not entitled to a deduction for any "gift" which arises from a bargained for exchange.[126] Therefore, outright gifts do not include donations to educational institutions in lieu of tuition,[127] amounts paid for church raffle tickets,[128] or amounts paid for tickets to a concert, the proceeds of which will benefit a charitable organization,[129] to the extent that the donor receives something of value in exchange for his payment.[130]

A chemical manufacturer, who pleaded guilty to 940 counts of unlawful chemical discharge, contributed $8 million to create a tax-exempt fund which was organized to alleviate the effects of the manufacturer's discharges. When the manufacturer tried to deduct the contribution as an ordinary and necessary business expense, the IRS disallowed it because a deduction for payment of a fine or penalty is prohibited. The tax court found that the manufacturer had made the contribution in a quid pro quo attempt to reduce a criminal fine.[131]

§124. TRANSFERS OF PARTIAL INTERESTS

Generally speaking, a taxpayer will not be entitled to a deduction for gifts of partial interests in property. The five exceptions to that general rule involve transfers of:

1. a remainder interest in a personal residence or farm,[132]
2. an undivided interest in a portion of the taxpayer's entire property interest,[133]
3. property to be used exclusively for conservation purposes,[134]
4. copyrighted works of art[135] and
5. property to charitable remainder annuity trusts, unitrusts and pooled income funds.[136]

The greatest benefit derived from using charitable remainder trusts, is that the donor can take the charitable deduction in the current year, even though the charity will not receive its interest until the death of a non-charitable income beneficiary. The taxpayer must use caution in choosing the trust best suited to his or her needs.

§125. CHARITABLE REMAINDER ANNUITY TRUST

Charitable remainder trusts allow taxpayers to take current charitable deductions, even though the actual gift to the charity is deferred. So it is not surprising that the Internal Revenue Code requires that the remainder interest (which will be distributed to a charitable organization) can be given an appropriate valuation.[137] Without such a provision, it would be possible for the noncharitable income beneficiary to receive most of the value of the trust over his lifetime, leaving very little of value to be distributed to the (remainder beneficiary) charity.[138]

The requirements for a charitable remainder annuity trust are:

1. There must be a trust, from which a fixed sum of at least 5 percent of the initial net fair market value is to be paid to at least one non-charitable beneficiary.[139] Such payments must occur at least once each year, and must continue for either the life of the beneficiaries, or for a term of years not in excess of 20 years.[140]

2. No other payments (except for the required fixed sum discussed in (1) above) may be made to or for the use of any non-charitable beneficiary.[141]

3. Upon the termination of the payments to non-charitable beneficiaries, because of their deaths, or because of the expiration of the specified term, the remainder of the trust must either be distributed to, or for the use of, a charitable organization, or must be retained by the trust for such use.[142]

Note that the charitable remainder annuity trust provides the non-charitable income beneficiary with a fixed sum each year. Such a trust is, therefore, good advice for providing needed income for a family member of the creator of the trust.[143] However, because the sum is fixed at the beginning, an annuity trust cannot compensate for inflation, and no additions may be made to the trust.

The charitable deduction for property transferred into an annuity trust is the present value of the property transferred minus the present value of the fixed annuity. Present values are based upon a 10 percent discount rate as determined by the estate tax mortality tables.[144] As long as the fixed annuity is between 5 and 10 percent of the value of the property transferred, the chargeable remainder annuity trust will generate a higher valued remainder, and, thus, a higher valued deduction than will a charitable remainder unitrust.

Trust-for-Retirement Plans

Charitable gifts now are being used, more often than in the past, in *trusts*, as a *retirement* plan tactic. They are an attractive alternative to retirement savings plans such as Keogh and Individual Retirement Accounts. An individual charitable trust is the main choice when the gift is over $50,000; it being too expensive in legal and administrative costs for smaller amounts. For the smaller amounts a gift annuity paying a fixed return, or a pooled trust fund, gives many of the benefits of a trust. Also helpful are charitable lead trusts, giving trust income to charity for less than ten years before reverting to the donor, or insurance policies naming a charity as owner and beneficiary while allowing the donor to deduct the premiums on new policies.[145]

§126. CHARITABLE REMAINDER UNITRUST

In order for a trust to qualify as a charitable remainder unitrust it must:

1. distribute a fixed percentage of the trust assets, valued annually, to a non-charitable beneficiary who is living at the time of the creation of the trust. Such a fixed percentage cannot be less than 5 percent.[146]
2. make the distributions (discussed in (1) to the noncharitable beneficiary (or beneficiaries) each year for the life of such beneficiaries) or for a term not in excess of 20 years.[147] No other distributions may be made to a non-charitable beneficiary.
3. distribute the remainder interest to or for the use of a charitable beneficiary, or return the remainder in the trust for use by the charity, upon the termination of the required distributions to non-charitable beneficiaries.[148]

Unitrusts afford greater flexibility than annuity trusts, in that they are valued annually, as opposed to only one such annual valuation. This allows the grantor to add more property to the trust, and provides for adjustment in the annual distribution which will take into account inflation during the past year.[149]

Unfortunately, such annual valuation can also be a disadvantage, because it involves the expense and effort of having the assets appraised annually. One solution might be to fund the unitrust with assets which have easily ascertainable values. (Such as securities sold on the New York Stock Exchange).

§127. POOLED INCOME FUNDS

Pooled income funds involve transfers of money or property to a trust funded by several donors. The transferor must retain an income interest for life, or must create an income interest for the life of at least one beneficiary.[150]

The trust itself must be maintained by the charitable organization[151] which is to receive the remainder interest.[152] The assets of the trust must not be invested in tax-exempt securities.[153] Each income beneficiary will receive a portion of the trust's earnings for the year.[154]

Unlike charitable remainder annuity trust or charitable remainder uni-trusts, pooled income funds are fully taxable under the general rules of trust taxation found in Subchapter J of the Internal Revenue Code.[155]

Pooled income funds can be very advantageous to smaller contributors because they can combine with other small contributors to achieve diversification of investment unattainable by one small investor by himself. The cost of utilizing a pooled income fund is generally quite reasonable.

The trust must be maintained by the donee/charity, and neither donors nor income beneficiaries may serve as trustees. Although the transferred property is commingled with property from other donors, the fund may not com-mingle the assets with any other assets. The governing instrument of a pooled fund must also prohibit investing in or accepting donations of depreciable or depletable property or require a depreciation or depletion reserve in line with accepted accounting principles.[156]

§128. STATE LAW PROVISIONS

Generally, state laws allow charitable deductions similar to those utilized in reducing federal tax liability. California, for example, exempts from the provision of its inheritance tax any property transferred to:

a. the United States,
b. California,
c. a California Public corporation (such as a city),
d. a society, corporation, institution or association exempt from tax.[157]

§129. TAX COUNSEL

This chapter deals with basic provisions of a complex area of the tax law. It is designed to acquaint persons who work with nonprofit corporations with some of the tax savings available to possible contributors to such organizations. This chapter is not designed to take the place of tax counsel in structuring charitable gifts. "Use tax counsel."

POINTS TO REMEMBER

- Check Publication Number 78 to see if an organization is a qualified donee.
- Determine whether a charity qualifies as a 50 percent charity as opposed to a 30 percent charity.

- Check to see if a reduction of the contributed amount is necessary where gifts of appreciated property are used.
- Remember the estate, gift and generation-skipping deductions, as well as the income tax deduction.
- Remember that deferred gifts are not deductible unless they are made to a proper charitable remainder trust.
- Remember to check for state tax charitable deductions.
- If you have any doubts, see tax counsel.

NOTES TO CHAPTER 11

1. A gift is a transfer of property that arises out of "disinterested generosity." To the extent that there is a bargained for exchange in money or money's worth, the taxpayer has not made a gift. *Commission v. Duberstein*, 363 U.S. 278 (1960).

2. *IRC* §102. In 1962, rich ($1 million/year) Americans gave $1 of every $5 they earned; but in 1985 it was $1 of every $15, with "yuppies" giving little and the poor and middle class giving much. D. Johnston (article), *N.Y. Times*, p. 10A (March 24, 1985). [In 1988 this tendency was even more marked. *Los Angeles Times* article, and reprint in *St. Petersburg Times*, p. 10 E (Dec. 21, 1987). *And see*, L. Blumenthal article in 1 *Nonprofit Times* (11) 1 (Feb. 1988).]

3. Even gifts of property to employees cannot be deducted as ordinary and necessary business expenses to the extent they exceed $25 per donee. *IRC* §274(b)(1).

4. *IRC* §2501.

5. Congress enacted the first charitable deduction in 1917, as an incentive for taxpayers to give to charity. War Revenue Act of 1917, ch. 63, tit. xii, §1201(2), 40 Stat. 300. The deduction was created because of the fear that taxpayers were using the money they would have given to charity to pay their income taxes, which were constitutionally imposed for the first time by the Revenue Act of 1913, ch. 16, 38 Stat. 114.

6. *IRC* §170(a).

7. *IRC* §2522.

8. *IRC* §2055.

9. A complete discussion of qualified tax-exempt entities occurs in Chapter 9, above.

10. *Trans America Corp. v. U.S.*, 902 F.2d 1540 (2d Cir., 1990).

11. *Alfred Cooper v. United States*, 779 F. Supp. 833 (E.D.N.C. 1991).

12. *Allen v. C.I.R.*, 925 F.2d 348 (9th Cir., 1991).

13. *Hernandez v. Commissioner*, 109 S. Ct. 2136, 2143 (1989); I.R.C. § 170 (spiritual "counselling," similar to psychology counselling, goods and services by Church of Scientology).

14. H. Huntley article, *St. Petersburg Times*, p. 24A (Nov. 27/92.)

15. *Sua Sponte*, Marcia Chambers, 15 *Nat'l. L.J.* (24) (Feb. 15, 1993).

16. G. Harman & S. Pfau Article, 3 *NonProfit Times* (12) 30 (March 1990).

17. *I.R.S. Regs., T.D. 8199* (1988).

18. The *Nonprofit Counsel*, p. 1 (July 1988; Newsletter; John Wiley & Sons, Inc.; New York).

19. *Taylor v. United States*, 782 F. Supp. 1207 (S.D. Ohio, 1991).

20. *Saltzman v. U.S.*, 750 F. Supp. 61 (D.C., N.Y., 1990).

21. *The Hearst Corp. v. U.S.*, 704-89T (Cl. Ct., 1993).

22. Bush, (article) 6 *NonProfit Times* (8) 5 (August, 1992); and see p. 395 above.

23. *IRC* §170(c)(1).

24. *IRC* §170(c)(2).

25. *IRC* §170(c)(3).

26. *IRC* §170(c)(4).

27. None of the favored activities can involve lobbying on behalf of a candidate, or to influence legislation.

28. *IRC* §170(c)(4).

29. *IRC* §170(c)(5).

30. Rev. Nov. 1985.

31. The number of organizations listed in Publication No. 78 are too numerous to count. However, exclusive of states and cities, which are exempt, but not listed, there are many pages in the publication, with literally hundreds of organizations on each page.

32. *See* n. 30, above.

33. *Ibid.*

34. Note that these rules apply only to individuals and not to corporate taxpayers under *IRC* §170(b)(11).

35. *IRC* §62 defines adjusted gross income to be income minus specific deductions. Generally speaking, adjusted gross income is the amount of net income the taxpayer made after comparing his gross income with the expenses involved in generating that income.

36. *IRC* §63(b) defines taxable income as adjusted gross income minus the sum of the deduction for personal exemption under *IRC* §151 and the excess itemized deductions. Excess itemized deductions, until 1986, were the extent to which a taxpayer's itemized deductions exceed his "zero bracket" amount. *IRC* §63(c); TC 1986 reinstituted the standard deduction.

37. *IRC* §170(b)(1)(F) defines contribution base as adjusted gross income computed without regard to any net operating loss carryback to the taxable year under *IRC* §172. For all practical purposes, therefore, contribution base equals adjusted gross income as defined in *IRC* §62. (See note 36, *supra*.)

38. *IRC* §170(b)(1)(A). Such public charities include churches, universities which maintain regular faculties and student enrollment, states, cities, and the federal government, to name but a few.

39. *IRC* §§170(b)(1)(A)(vii), 170(b)(1)(E). Private foundations can only qualify under stated conditions.

40. *IRC* §170(b)(1)(B).

41. *IRC* §170(b)(B)(i).

42. *IRC* §170(b)(1)(B)(ii). More simply stated, if a taxpayer has already made contributions totalling 50 percent of his contribution base to §170(b)(1)(A) charities, he cannot deduct any of his contributions to §170(b)(1)(B) charities. That is, the 30 percent limitation under §170(b)(1)(B) is the maximum for contributions to such charities. HOWEVER, IN NO EVENT CAN THE TAXPAYER TAKE DEDUCTIONS FOR ANY CONTRIBUTIONS IN EXCESS OF 50 PERCENT OF HIS CONTRIBUTION BASE. §170(B)(1)(B) tells the taxpayer to deduct the lesser of 30 percent of his contribution base or whatever is left of the absolute maximum limit, which is 50 percent of his contribution base.

43. *St. Petersburg, (FL) Times* (Oct. 1993).

44. *Burke v. C.I.R.*, 929 F.2d 110 (2d Cir. 1991). *See also Macklem v. United States*, 757 F. Supp. 6 (D. Conn. 1991).

45. *Williamson v. C.I.R.*, T.C. Memo 1991-420; 1991 Tax Ct. Memo LEXIS 469.

46. *Davis v. U.S.*, 110 S. Ct. 2014 (1990).

47. Note, *St. Petersburg (FL) Times*, Religion Section, p. 3E (Aug. 15, 1992).

48. *IRC* §170(d)(1)(A).

49. For example, if a taxpayer had carry-over contributions for each of the past five years, he would first compare his current contributions to the 50 percent limit. If the current year's contributions were less than 50 percent of the taxpayer's contribution base, he would be entitled to apply the carry-over from the most recent year in determining his deduction. The taxpayer would continue to do this until he had either taken into account contributions to the extent of 50 percent of his contribution base, or had used up all of his carry-over contributions from the five previous years. *IRC* §170(d)(1)(A)(i), (ii).

50. For example, the concept of basis in *IRC* §§1011, 1012, 1013, 1014, 1015, 1016, 1017 and 1041 is simply a way of determining how much after-tax income the taxpayer has invested in property. *IRC* §1001 defines gain as the difference between what a taxpayer receives ("Amount Realized") and his adjusted basis. Gain is, therefore, defined in terms of cash. If taxpayers dealt solely in cash, and not property, the Internal Revenue Code would be only a few pages long. However, the practical realities are that taxpayers deal in property which must be taxed like cash.

51. In reality, taxpayers can only spend after-tax income, because any tax owed on income belongs to the government. Thus, a taxpayer who spends $50 does so only after that money has been subject to tax. This is true even if the taxpayer received the money as a gift, because, while gifts are not taxed to a donee under *IRC* §102, the gift has been subject to tax in that the government could tax it, but has decided not to under §102. The same can be said for any excluded income.

52. Fair market value is defined as the price a willing buyer would pay a willing seller, if neither the buyer nor the seller is under any compulsion, duress or distress, and where both have a reasonable knowledge of the facts surrounding the transaction. Andrews v. Commissioner, 135 F.2d 314 (2nd Cir. 1983), *cert. den.* 320 U.S. 748.

It should be noted that willing buyers might be willing to pay various prices, but as long as the sale is made to any willing buyer, and the other requirements for fair market value are met, the government will accept the sales price as fair market value. *IRC* §1001(b), 1010(a) and 1015(a). It should be noted that transactions between family members will be more closely scrutinized than transactions involving unrelated parties.

53. From the time the taxpayer purchased the painting, until the time of his contribution he had no gain realized under *IRC* §1001(a). The government has deemed that it would be inappropriate, as well as impractical, to tax an asset every time it appreciated in value. Instead, §§1001(a) and 61(a)(3) require realization of gain only upon an appropriate disposition of the property. Thus, the taxpayer would have a $48 gain realized if he had sold his painting for $50.

54. If the taxpayer sold the asset for $50 he would be subject to tax on the difference between his cost and the cash he received (*IRC* §§61(a)(12); 1001(a)). He could then contribute the cash to charity. If, on the other hand, he could get a $50 deduction by giving the property itself to charity, without incurring a tax on the gain, he would clearly be better off by making an asset contribution rather than a cash contribution.

55. *IRC* §170(e)(1).

56. IRC §64 defines ordinary income as income which arises from a transaction which does *not* involve the sale or exchange of a long-term capital asset (IRC §1221) or a track or business asset (IRC §1231). Thus, sales of inventory, for example, generate ordinary income (IRC §1221(1)). Ordinary income assets are not entitled to the sixty-percent deduction for net capital gains (IRC §1201). The reduction required by §170(e)(1)(A) also applies to sales of short-term (held less than six months) capital assets and trade or business property.

57. *See* above, n. 56.

58. IRC §170(e)(1)(B). The rationale behind this is really quite logical, because a taxpayer selling an asset which generates long-term capital gain will be entitled to a deduction of sixty percent (60%) of the gain. Thus, the taxpayer will only be taxed on forty-percent (40%) of his gain. When a taxpayer contributes tangible personal property unrelated in service or use to a charity, and that property would have generated a long-term capital gain if sold, then the taxpayer is only escaping tax on the asset to the extent of forty percent (40%) of what would have been gain had he sold it. Therefore, §170(e)(1)(B) requires a reduction of the contribution by forty percent of what would have been gain had the property been sold; that is, the reduction is equal to the portion which would have been subject to tax if the asset was sold.

The government's concern here is that the charity will sell the asset for cash, but not be taxed on the sale since it would be tax-exempt (IRC §501(c)(3)). Similarly, contributions of services are not deductible. Reg. §1.170A-1(g).

59. If the taxpayer was a dealer, the sculpture would be inventory, and thus an ordinary income asset subject to a reduction under §170(e)(1)(A).

60. IRC §179(e)(1)(B) mandates a reduction of forty percent of what would have been gain had the property been sold. Gain is calculated by subtracting the taxpayer's cost from the fair-market-value of the asset. Here, there would be a gain of $1000. ($3000 is the fair market value—$2000 the cost).

Forty percent of the gain is, therefore, $400, leaving a contribution of $2600 ($3000 fair market value—$400 reduction). IRC §1001(a)).

61. See, IRC §509.

62. IRC §170(e)(1)(B). Reg. §1.70A-1(c)(2) defines fair-market-value as "the price at which property would change hands between a willing buyer and a willing seller, neither being under any compulsion to buy or sell and both having a reasonable knowledge of the relevant facts."

63. IRC §170(b)(1)(C)(i).

64. IRC §170(b)(1)(A).

65. IRC §170(b)(1)(C)(iii).

66. This is because the taxpayer's election to reduce his contribution allows him to treat his gift as a gift of cash, rather than a gift of capital-gain property. The reduction limit applied to a contribution of cash, or property to which §170(e) applies, is 50 percent, when the gift is made to a public charity.

67. IRC §170(b)(1)(C)(ii); IRC §170(d).

68. This is because the carryover applies only to the excess contributions actually taken into account after reduction. Reg. §1.170A-4(d) example (4)(c).

69. IRC §63(C). IRC §63(D) until 1986 defined "zero bracket" amount as the maximum amount of taxable income on which no tax is imposed by IRC §1. This amount was $3400 for married couples filing jointly and $2300 a single taxpayer. IRC §1(a)(c).

70. In other words, a single taxpayer would need to have $2300 of itemized deductions (which also include interest, taxes, medical expenses, etc.) before he could deduct any of his charitable contributions under §170(a).

71. Sec. 121(a) of P.L. 97-34 (1981).

72. In 1982 and 1983 a taxpayer was allowed under §170(i)(2) to take a maximum deduction of 25 percent of his contributions without itemizing. Unfortunately, under §170(i)(3), the maximum contribution taken into account in 1982 and 1983 was $100.

73. In 1984, 25 percent of a taxpayer's contributions were deductible without itemizing, but those contributions could not exceed $300. IRC §§170(i)(2), (3).

74. For 1985 and 1986, there is no maximum allowable contribution under §170(i)(3).

75. For 1986, there is neither a percentage limit under §170(i)(2), nor a contribution limit under §170(i)(3).

76. IRC §170(i)(4).

77. There has been considerable discussion concerning possible tax reform. One area which seems specifically targeted for an early demise is the charitable deduction for non-itemizing taxpayers.

78. Rev. Nov. 1984.

79. Rev. Nov. 1984.

80. Mehegan, S., (article) 7 *NonProfit Times* (6) 10, 11 (June 1993).

81. Associations are taxed like corporations if they exhibit most of the following attributes:

    1. Centralized Management

    2. Perpetual existence

    3. Limited liability

    4. Alienability of ownership

    Reg. §301.7701-2(g).

82. *See* generally, Prunty, "Love and the Business Corporation," 46 Va. L. Rev. 467 (1960).

83. Regs. §1.170A-1(h)(5).

84. IRC §170(b)(1).

85. IRC §170(b)(2).

86. IRC §170(b)(2)(A).

87. IRC §170(b)(2)(B).

88. IRC §170(b)(2)(B).

89. IRC §170(b)(2)(C).

90. IRC §170(b)(2)(D).

91. Compare their treatment with the treatment given to individuals under §§170(b)(1)(A) and (B); for individuals, the percentage limit is higher when contributions are made to public charities.

92. IRC §170(d)(2)(A).

93. IRC §170(d).

94. Thus, for example, a carryover from 1985 would be used before one from 1984, when a corporation calculates its deductible contributions for any year after 1985.

95. IRC §170(e).

96. IRC §511(a)(1).

97. IRC §512(a).

98. IRC §512(b)(10).

99. Reg. §1.512(b)-1(g).

100. Reg. §1.512(b)-1(g)(3).

101. Regs. §1.512(b)-1(g)(2); Crosby Valve & Gage Co. v. Commissioner, 380 F.2d 146 (1st Cir. 1967), cert. denied, 389 U.S. 976 (1967).

102. Regs. §1.512(b)-1(g).

103. *IRS Letter 8825069* (July 1988).

104. IRC §2001.

105. IRC §2501.

106. IRC §2601.

107. IRC §§2055, 2522.

108. This is also logical in light of the fact that corporations can have a perpetual existence, while people cannot.

109. IRC §§170(b)(1)(A), (B).

110. IRC §2055.

111. Compare this result with IRC §170(e), which requires a reduction.

112. This is because the wealth transfer taxes concern the value of an asset transferred, while income taxes concern gain which accrues.

113. IRC §170(c)(1).

114. IRC §170(c)(2).

115. IRC §170(c)(3).

116. IRC §170(c)(4).

117. *Planners Forum* (article), 6 *Charitable Gift Planning News* (7)3 (July 1988).

118. *Terre Haute First Natl. Bank v. U.S.*, TH83-31-C (S.D. Ind., 1991); N. Lipschitz (note), 13 *Natl. L. J.* (38)5 (May 27, 1991).

119. Regs. §25.2501-1.

120. Regs. §1.170A-1(a)(2).

121. Appraiser's fees are deductible under IRC §213(3). Failure to have property properly valued can lead to penalties under IRC §6659; such penalty payments are not deductible.

122. Regs. §1.170A-1(a)(2).

123. IRC §6659.

124. IRC §6659(b).

125. IRC §6659(d).

126. IRC §170(c).

127. Rev. Rul. 83-104, 1983-2 CB. 46.

128. Rev. Rul. 67-246, 1967-2 CB. 104.

129. Rev. Rul. 67-246, example 1.

130. For example, the taxpayer will be entitled to a $90 deduction when he pays $100 for a charity ball, if the ball itself would normally cost $10.

131. *Allied-Signal Inc. v. Commissioner of Finance*, 588 N.E. 2d 731 (N.Y. 1991).

132. IRC §170(f)(3)(B)(i).

133. IRC §170(f)(3)(B)(ii).

134. IRC §170(f)(3)(B)(iii).

135. IRC §170(f)(3)(B)(iv).

136. IRC §170(f)(3)(B).

137. IRC §664(d)(1); Regs. §1.664-2(a).

138. Thus, the IRS issued Revenue Ruling 72-395, 1972-2 C.B. 340, modified by Rev. Rul. 80-123, 1980-1 C.B. 205, clarified by Rev. Rul. 82-165, 1982-2 C.B. 117, which contains mandatory provisions for charitable remainder trusts.

139. IRC §664(d)(1).

140. IRC §664(d)(1)(A).

141. IRC §664(d)(1)(B).

142. IRC §664(d)(1)(C).

143. Because there is a reliable rate of income, but see note 37.

144. IRC §664(d)(2).

145. H. Huntley, *When it's better to give than to pay taxes, St. Petersburg* (FL) *Times* (Dec. 4, 1988).

146. IRC §664(d)(2)(A).

147. IRC §§664(d)(2)(B), (C).

148. This provides a greater benefit to the income beneficiary of the trust.

149. IRC §642(c)(5)(A); Regs. §1.642(c)-5(b).

150. IRC §642(c)(5)(B).

151. IRC §642(c)(5)(C).

152. IRC §642(c)(5)(D).

153. IRC §§642(c)(5)(E), (F).

154. IRC §641, *et seq.*

155. *Ibid.*

156. 7 *NonProfit Times* (2) 47 (Feb., 1993).

157. *See* Chapter 12.

12

STATE TAX EXEMPTIONS

[The 1988 first writing of this chapter was contributed by Prof. I. Richard Gershon of Stetson University College of Law. Material by Oleck and Stewart and others was added since then. Names of contributors are set forth at the beginning of each such contribution.]

§130. STATE TAXATION, IN GENERAL

In order to cover fully all aspects of state taxation, and the exemptions relating to such taxes, one would need to write substantially more than one chapter in one book. Therefore, the purpose of this chapter is simply to acquaint the reader with a few of the more common[1] state taxes, and then to discuss which types of organizations can be exempt from the application of those taxes. In-depth research into this area would require reference to a currently supplemented looseleaf service, such as Prentice Hall's *State and Local Taxes* (also known as the *All States Reporter*).

[Corporations created by Congress, such as federal credit unions, may be given tax immunity by Congress. Barksdale Federal Credit Union v. Louisiana Tax Comm. 506 So. 2d 895 (La. App., 1st Cir., 1987).]

"Fee" or "Tax"?!

A nonstock association of home builders challenged a fee imposed by the city upon those adding or expanding connections to the city's water system. The Supreme Court of Virginia found that the fee was a *proprietary fee* rather than a *tax* or an *impact fee* requiring specific legislative authority. Those who were paying the fee were receiving a present, particular benefit of access to the water system. Access would not have been possible without the fee and the proposed project. Therefore the fee was validated.[2]

A church, which owns and operates a school, can be required to pay a life hazard use registration *fee* under a Uniform Fire Safety Act without excessive entanglement of church and state. A *fee is not a tax* as long as the fee is reasonably related to the cost of government regulation or the services rendered by the government are reasonably related to development.[3]

§131. SOME COMMON STATE TAXES

Incorporation fees.[4] These are also called "initial" or "organization fees" and are imposed before a corporation may begin to operate within a state. When such a tax is imposed upon a foreign corporation (*i.e.*, one incorporated in another state), it is called a "qualification fee," an "entrance fee," or a "license fee."

The amount of such fees in business corporations is often determined by the par value of authorized stock or of issued and outstanding stock.[5] Others measure the tax by the number of shares authorized, regardless of par value.[6] Certain allocation formulas are used, so that only "intrastate" business of foreign corporations is taxed.[7]

Since the tax is based upon the value or number of capital shares, any subsequent increase in capital is also taxed, usually at the same rates as at the time of organization.

It is important to distinguish these taxes or fees from the filing fees which must be paid for filing the certificate of incorporation with the secretary of state, and, if necessary, the county clerk. This latter fee is usually a fixed sum, not varying with the value or number of shares of the corporation.[8]

Franchise taxes.[9] These are annual taxes for the privilege of doing business within a state, whether or not such privilege is exercised. While the most frequently used basis for this tax is capital stock outstanding, such items as property, surplus, gross receipts, or income may be factors. Frequently alternative computations using several bases may be used, with the highest result being the tax due.[10]

Even if "income" is one of the bases or the only base upon which a franchise tax is computed, such a tax is still not an "income tax." In theory, a franchise tax is an "indirect" tax or an "excise" tax which is imposed upon the privilege of doing business in the state; the mere fact that the amount of tax is measured by the amount of income does not mean that the income itself is being taxed. A true "income tax" (discussed later) is a "direct" tax imposed directly upon the realization or enjoyment of income. This distinction may be important because of certain Constitutional requirements. For example, interest on federal bonds may not be subjected to a state income tax, but such federal interest may be in the base of a franchise tax.

Some states impose both an income tax and a franchise tax on corporations[11] Usually, however, where income is a major factor in computing the franchise tax, an income tax is not imposed on the same income.[12]

Income taxes.[13] In general, these are similar to the federal income tax. They are imposed upon the taxable entity at the time it realizes income. While franchise taxes are much more common than income taxes for corporations, income taxes are more common for unincorporated associations[14] and individuals.

Contribution Tax: In late 1992 churches in Berkeley, California were ordered to pay taxes on *contributions* (60¢ per $1000 received) and also to *register* like other nonprofit organizations. City finance director Sonali Bose reported that only half of the 600 NPOs in that city had registered yet. The tax is based on the unanimous ruling of the U.S. Supreme Court in 1990 (*Jimmy Swaggart Ministries v. Calif. Board of Equalization*, 110 S. Ct. 688 (1990)) upholding the California sales tax on religious organizations as well as other NPOs. The trend seems to be to require churches to pay such taxes as other NPOs are required to do, said Joe Conn, a spokesman for Americans United for Separation of Church and State, based in Silver Spring, Maryland.

Sales and use taxes.[15] In general, sales taxes are excises imposed upon sales (broadly defined) made to ultimate consumers (*i.e.*, not meant for resale) and are imposed at the time of transfer.[16] Use taxes are "compensating" in that they equalize users within the state who have bought goods within the taxing jurisdiction (and hence paid the sales tax), with those who have bought goods outside the taxing jurisdiction (and have not paid the sales tax). Thus the use tax is imposed upon beneficial enjoyment of goods which were not subject to sales tax because they were bought outside the state or city imposing the sales tax.[17]

Property taxes.[18] In general, these taxes are imposed upon property (broadly defined) within the state, owned by the taxpayer on a given date (usually called "tax day" or "assessment day"). The property subject to tax usually includes realty, tangible personal property, and intangible personal property.[19] The tax is a specified percentage of the assessed value of the property. Often such a different type of property is subject to a different rate of tax.

Leased property used by the lessee church for school purposes was held to be tax exempt in Florida. Skycrest Baptist Church (Clearwater) v. _____, Fla. 2d Dist. Ct. App. (June 1987). But Illinois refused tax exemption to a building leased by a College (lessee) for use as a residence for students. Wheaton College v. Dept. of Revenue, 508 N.E. 2d 1136 (Ill. App. 2d Dist., 1987).]

Death and gift taxes.[20] Almost all states impose a tax upon transfers at death.[21] If the tax is imposed upon the decedent's estate, it is called an "estate"; if it is imposed upon the beneficiaries, it is called an "inheritance tax." Since the beneficiaries may well be liable for an estate tax if the estate does not pay the tax (under some form of transferee liability), the practical effect of the two taxes is often the same.

A few states impose a tax upon gifts.[22] Again, although the tax is imposed upon the donor, the donee may be liable for any tax not paid by the donor.

§132. STATE EXEMPTIONS, IN GENERAL

[Sheila M. Bond, James F. Haggerty, and Nicola Jaye Trevethan contributed illustrative cases in this section.]

In general, charitable organizations[23] are granted exemption from many state taxes. However, merely nonprofit organizations are usually taxable to a greater degree.[24]

Any exemption depends on the given statute, and even within one state each type of tax may have a different test for exemption. Thus, an organization which might be exempt as charitable for purposes of one tax might not be exempt for purposes of some other tax, even if both taxes are levied by the same state. Logically, the test should be based on the actual operations of the organization. However, some states look only to the articles, and if any purpose stated is not charitable, the organization is not deemed "charitable."[25] Thus, either an "organization" test or an "operations" test (or both) may apply.

The following discussion of the types of taxes just mentioned is by no means exhaustive, but is intended to be merely illustrative:

Initial taxes.[26] In general, nonprofit organizations do not issue capital stock (*i.e.*, stock upon which dividends may be paid). Hence, they would not be liable for organization taxes.

In New York, for example, the organization tax is imposed upon "... every stock corporation ... and every corporation formed under the business corporation law. . . . "[27] And a not-for-profit corporation may not have any stock or shares.[28] Therefore, the organization tax does not apply to nonprofit corporations.

However, the fee required for filing the articles of incorporation in New York does apply to a not-for-profit corporation.[29]

Some states, which in effect combine the filing fee with the organization tax based on capital stock,[30] provide for a filing fee for a corporation which "shall not be authorized to issue any shares of capital stock. . . . "[31] The result is much the same as if the two taxes were separately stated.

Franchise taxes.[32] Exemption of charitable corporations from franchise taxes is almost universal, and exemption of at least some "merely nonprofit" corporations is not unusual. The given state's statute will, of course determine the scope of any exemption. For example, in Ohio nonprofit cooperative agricultural or marketing associations are subject to the franchise tax, but other nonprofit organizations are exempt.[33]

Income taxes.[34] States which impose corporate income taxes usually exempt certain nonprofit corporations (if not all) from the tax.[35]

Similarly, unincorporated associations are often exempted from income tax, if they are nonprofit. For example, New York, which imposes an income tax on "unincorporated businesses," says:

A trust or other unincorporated organization which by reason of its purposes or activities is exempt from federal income tax shall not be deemed
an unincorporated business (regardless of whether subject to federal
income tax on unrelated business-taxable income).[36]

Almost identical language exempts nonprofit unincorporated organizations for the personal income tax.[37]

Most states which impose an income tax on individuals permit them a
deduction for their contributions to a charity, often in terms quite similar to
the rule for federal income tax.[38] For example, an income tax deduction may
not be allowed until payment (or setting aside) is actually made even for an
accrual-method taxpayer.[39]

Sales and use taxes.[40] In general, sales to (or for the use of) charitable organizations have been not subject to any sales (or use) tax.[41]

Sales by charitable organizations to noncharitable entities or to individuals are usually subject to the sales tax if they are "engaged in business"; if the
sales are so few that the charity is not "engaged in business," they may be
exempt.[42] In some instances, sales by charities are exempt so long as profit does
not inure to the benefit of private individuals.[43]

Illustrative Sales and Use Tax Cases:

Tips left by customers at private club's restaurant (open to the public) are
not *mandatory* because placed on the bill, and are subject to *sales tax*, because
they go to food service personnel and not the club. *Summit Club, Inc., v. Indiana Dept. of State Revenue,* 528 N.E.2d 129 (IN Tax 1988).

A business need not have presence in the state for the state to force an
out-of-state company to collect use taxes that in-state customers owe on purchases. however, the out-of-state company must have a "substantial nexus" with
the taxing state, as required by the commerce clause. *Quill Corp. v. North Dakota,* 112 S. Ct. 1904 (U.S.N.D., 1992).

Service, use, transportation, and taxes are applicable to funds from private sources, used for patient care, even though patients also received payments from State Department of Public Aid. *Wentworth Nursing Center v. Director of Dept. of Revenue,* 544 N.E. 2d 971 (Ill. App. 1989).

An Arizona rule, that exempts purchases made by licensed nursing care
and residential care institutions from use tax, requires that those institutions
be licensed. Neither a Department of Insurance permit nor a Department of
Revenue letter, indicating approval of an application for use tax exemption,
are sufficient absent licensure. *People of Faith, Inc. v. Arizona Dept. of Revenue,* 829
P.2d 330 (Ariz. App. 1992).

A nonprofit laundry owned by hospitals must pay sales tax even with no
profit on its transactions. *Associated Hospital Services, Inc. v. State Dept. of R&T,*
588 So. 2d 356 (La. 1991).

Sales Tax (6% in Florida) now applies to all *publications* except newspapers (i.e., to the part of association dues that goes to such publications); except for NPOs that don't publish estimates on that percentage of the dues, (?!?). News Item, *Non Profit Times*, p. 6 (Oct. 1993).

In Wyoming, a contractor who purchases materials and resells them to a tax-exempt institution is not required to pay sales or use tax when another contractor installs those materials. However, where the purchasing contractor installs the materials, the purchasing contractor is considered to be the user or consumer of the materials, and owes sales or use taxes on the amount it paid for the materials. *Memorial Hosp. of Laramie County v. Dep't of Revenue and Taxation, State of Wyoming*, 805 P.2d 276 (Wyo. 1991).

A country club, in Idaho, has to pay sales tax on initiation fees, membership dues, assessments and unused dining minimums. *Crane Creek Country Club v. idaho State Tax Com'n*, 841 P.2d 410 (Idaho, 1992).

Property taxes.[44] In general, charitable organizations are exempt from real property taxes, so long as the property so exempted is used for charitable purposes.[45] This exemption is strictly construed,[46] as long as such construction does not defeat the purpose of the exemption statute.[47] If less than all of the property owned by a charitable organization is used for charitable purposes, only that portion used for the charitable purpose is exempt.[48]

Charities are also usually exempted from any property taxes on personal property.[49]

Even if a charity is exempted from real estate taxes, it will usually be liable for local assessments for improvements benefitting the real property (*e.g.*, water districts, garbage disposal districts, fire districts, or sewer districts).[50]

The test of "charitability" must be met on the "tax day" or "assessment day."[51] And the exemption applies even if the property is owned by a foreign organization on that day,[52] or if the property is being made ready for charitable use rather than being actually used for charity on that day.[53]

Illustrative Property Tax Cases:

Alabama

The "exclusive use" test is applied to determine whether the property at issue for religious worship, schools, or charity is exempt. Who owns the property at issue is unimportant; how the property is used is determinative.

The property must be "exclusively" used for religious, worship, schooling, or charity, in the sense that the property must be used solely, only or wholly for a religious, educational, or charitable purpose. No partial [property tax] exemption is available in Alabama. *Most Worshipful Grand Lodge of the Free and Accepted Masons of the State of Alabama v. Norred*, 603 So. 2d 996 (Ala. 1992).

The ownership of the property is important when the religious, educational, or charitable organization using the property does not own the property, in Alabama. *Crim v. Phipps*, 601 So. 2d 474 (Ala. 1992).

Arizona

A statute stating that classification of a NPO by the state Board of Tax Appeals shall not be conclusive in subsequent years does not limit or abrogate the doctrine of collateral estoppel (e.g., by arbitrary discrimination) if that is proved. *Hibbs v. Calcot, Ltd.*, 801 P.2d 445 (Ariz. App. 1990).

California

Amendment of a lease of tax-exempt real property, to extend the term of possession, is not a "change of ownership" that (under the state Revenue and Taxation Code) will permit a reassessment of the property for tax purposes. *Wrather Port Properties, Ltd. v. County of Los Angeles*, 257 Cal. Rptr. 266 (App. 2d Dist. 1989).

A "public schools" property tax exemption does not apply to a privately held leasehold interest in real property, owned by a state university and improved with homes, which are owned and occupied by university employees, who hold the leases. *Connolly, v. County of Orange*, 824 P.2d 663 (Cal. 1992).

In California, a nonprofit hospital earning over ten percent in surplus revenue, must prove that it is not organized for profit in order to qualify for a "welfare" property tax exemption. *Rideout Hosp. Foundation Inc. v. County of Yuba*, 10 Cal. Rptr. 2d 141 (Cal. App. 3 Dist., 1992).

The court will consider the community benefit offered by the entire complex of activities, offered at a facility being used for "charitable purposes," rather than determining whether each of the activities would qualify for property tax exemption. *Clubs of California For Fair Competition v. Kroger (Young Men's Christian Ass'n of Oakland)*, 9 CA1. Rptr. 2d 247 (Cal. App. 1 Dist., 1992).

Colorado

When a nonprofit golf club challenged the tax appraiser's valuation of the club's property, the court held that the assessor's failure to consider and fully document the market approach to property valuation was harmless, if the trial court subsequently gave "appropriate consideration" to comparable sales of golf courses in a de novo review of the assessor's decision. *Cherry Hills Country Club v. Board of County Com'rs of County of Arapahoe*, 832 P.2d 1105 (Colo. App., 1992).

A fraternal organization was denied property tax exemption under a statute that provided exemption only where the property was owned and used "exclusively" for strict charitable purposes and not for private gain or corporate profit. The court found the association provided a very small amount of its net income for charitable causes, but primarily dedicated the net income toward the bylaws' stated purpose of promoting Slavic culture, providing and contracting with its members for insurance, and carrying on business activities, which would be for the benefit of the members upon dissolution. *Western Slavonic Association v. Property Tax Administrator*, 835 P.2d 621 (Colo. Ct. App. 1992).

Connecticut

While a lease of property by a charitable corporation does not disqualify the nonprofit organization's exemption, the lessee may not claim the exemption in the place of the lessor. *Whole Life, Inc. v. Board of Tax Review of Hebron*, 1992 WL 360649 (Conn. 1992).

Florida

If property is owned by a for-profit entity, improvements made on that property by a tax-exempt organization (port authority) leasing the property are not exempt from ad valorem property taxes, even if the improvements are used exclusively for the operation of the tax exempt organization. *Ocean Highway and Port Authority v. Page*, 609 So. 2d 84 (Fla. App. 1 Dist., 1992).

A *lawsuit challenging* a tax assessment as void is barred by a 60-day limitation, because legislative intent was that this is a "jurisdictional statute of nonclaim," not merely a *statute of limitations*, which latter a tax assessor may be estopped from claiming. *Markham v. Neptune Hollywood Beach Club*, 527 So. 2d 814 (FL 1988); FL St. §194.171(2).

On-campus *faculty housing* at a church-related school is "used exclusively for educational purposes," under Florida law requirement for tax exemption, where such presence of faculty is needed for accreditation as a boarding school and for dealing with student emotional needs, and also for classes taught in these homes. *Saint Andrews School of Boca Raton, Inc. v. Walker*, 540 So. 2d (FL 4th DCA 1989).

The fact that a NPO's source of support was federal loans and grants does not destroy its right to ad valorem tax exemption when it serves exclusively to provide low income housing for indigent farm workers. *Public Housing Assistance, Inc. v. Havill*, 571 So. 2d 45 (Fla. App., 1990); Fl. St. § 196.192(2).

Georgia

A property qualifies as an institution of "purely public charity," within the meaning of the property tax exemption, if the owner is an institution devoted entirely to charitable pursuits for the benefit of the public, and the use of the property is exclusively devoted to those charitable pursuits. *York Rite Bodies of Freemasonry of Savannah v. Board of Equalization of Chatham County*, 408 S.E. 2d 699 (Ga. 1991).

Idaho

In Idaho, a county board of equalization granted a property tax exemption to the skilled nursing portion of a care facility for the elderly provided by a religious organization, but denied the tax exemption to the individual living units and common areas where the elderly lived. *The burden is on the taxpayer to clearly establish the right to the exemption, with no room for doubt.* The independent living portion did not qualify as a "hospital" even though claimed as a part of the "continuum" of services included in the nursing home. *Appeal of Evangelical Lutheran Good Samaritan Society (Good Samaritan Village) v. Board of Equalization of Latah County*, 804 P.2d 299 (Idaho 1990); I.C. §63-105C. *See also Village North, Inc. v. State Tax Comm. of Mo.*, 799 S.W.2d 197 (Mo. App. 1990); c.f., *Better Living Services, Inc. v. County*, Miss. Supr. Ct. #90-CA-0509 (Oct. 16, 1991).

In Idaho, a nonprofit labor council is entitled to a property tax exemption if it is a "fraternal organization, established to achieve some worthy objective of its members, or men and women generally, without regard to profit." Portions of the property of such organizations, leased to members, are exempt. However, portions of a building leased for a "commercial purpose" are not exempt, to the extent that that portion exceeds 3 percent of the total value of the building. *Boise Center Trades & Labor Council, Inc. v. Board of Ada County Com'rs*, 831 P.2d 535 (Idaho 1992).

Illinois

Church land (park) next to caretaker's residence, used for meditation, but also for grazing of horses, is tax exempt. *Illinois Conference of U.C. of C.V. Illinois Dept. of Revenue*, 518 N.E. 2d 755 (Ill. App. 3d Dist., 1988).

Convent caretaker's residence property is not tax exempt. *Benedictine Sisters v. Dept. of Revenue*, 508 N.E. 2d 470 (Ill. App. 2d Dist., 1977).

Church housing also used by non-member visiting missionary persons is tax exempt. *Evangelical Alliance v. Dept. of Revenue*, 517 N.E. 2d 1178 (Ill. App. 2d Dist., 1987).

Land planned to be used for care-center and parking by hospital (non-profit), but not yet built on, is entitled to tax exemption in year of purchase. *Weslin Properties v. Dept. of Revenue*, 510 N.E. 2d 564 (Ill. App. 2d Dist., 1987).

Taxable status of property is determined by its use, not by its ownership. *Faith Christian Fellowship of Chicago, Illinois, Inc. v. Dept. of Revenue*, 589 N.E.2d 796 (Ill. App. Ct. 1992).

Even the United States has to obey Illinois law if it sought property tax exemption; must follow state exemption procedures. *U.S. v. Hynes*, 771 F. Supp. 928 (D.C., Ill., 1991).

Property owned by a university foundation and leased to a state university is not entitled to a property tax exemption as property of the state or as property primarily for "educational use" if also rented to for-profit groups, in

Illinois. *Northern Illinois University Foundation v. Sweet*, 603 N.E. 2d 84 (Ill. App. 2 Dist., 1992).

A leased residential retirement facility is "owned" by its for-profit lessor, for purposes of a property tax exemption, if the sale/lease agreement reserves in the lessor the right to convey title when and if it chooses. *Henderson County Retirement Center, Inc. v. Department of Revenue*, 604 N.E. 2d 1003 (Ill. App. 3 Dist., 1992).

When the licensee operator of restaurant in a community college does not own, but *leases* space and furniture therein, it is taxable when the agreement seems to speak of a long term and no college control of the area. *Stevens v. Rosewell*, 523 N.E.2d 1098 (IL App. 1988).

The Illinois statute specifically relating to the exemption of parking lots used by churches, school districts, nonprofit hospitals, or religious or charitable institutions requires not only that the property be used by the tax exempt entity, but that it be owned by the entity in order to qualify for tax exemption. *Faith Christian Fellowship of Chicago, Illinois v. Dept. of Revenue*, 589 N.E. 2d 796 (Ill. App. Ct. 1992).

A child care center, serving professional employees of a charitable hospital, is entitled to a property tax exemption because it is "reasonably necessary" to accomplish efficient administration of the hospital. The center alleviated difficulties encountered in hiring and retaining professionals with young children. *Memorial Child Care v. Department of Revenue*, 604 N.E. 2d 530 (Ill. App. 4 Dist., 1992).

In Illinois, property that is purchased or otherwise transferred from an exempt use to a nonexempt use is subject to property taxation from the date of purchase or conveyance. *American Medical Ass'n v. Rosewell*, 606 N.E. 2d 68 (Ill. App. 1 Dist., 1992).

The Yale Club of Chicago (YCC) is a nonprofit organization whose primary goal is to promote the welfare of Yale University. The organization's foundation does not dispense its benefits to an indefinite number of people but reserves the benefits exclusively for Yale alumni and students. Thus, the YCC serves no exempt "charitable purpose." *Yale Club of Chicago v. Department of Revenue*, 574 N.E. 2d 31 (Ill. App. I Dist. 1991).

To create an open campus-like setting, a hospital acquired parcels of property and razed abandoned structures. Such open parcels need not be absolutely indispensable to the hospital's main charitable purpose for proper exemption. *Norwegian American Hosp., Inc. v. Department of Revenue*, 569 N.E. 2d 83 (Ill. App. 1 Dist. 1991).

A statute that covers *valuation* of "open space land," when applied to a golf course must assess it as open space land, not on the basis of its value as a golf course. Proper *valuation* process is a *question of law*. *Lake County Board of Review v. Property Tax Appeal Board*, 548 N.E. 2d 1129 (Ill. App. 1989).

No tax exemption applies to the manager's residence of a girl scout campsite of 120 acres and several buildings, because the site manager was not absolutely needed to reside there and could live elsewhere, and statutes granting exemption must be construed strictly in favor of taxation. *Girl Scouts of DePage County C., Inc. v. Dept. of Revenue*, 545 N.E. 2d 784 (Ill. App. 1989).

A private foundation operating a number of one city's softball *playing fields* for use by various persons and organizations, which otherwise would have to be provided at taxpayer's expense, thus benefiting an *indefinite number* of people by using funds derived from private and public charitable sources, is exempt from property taxation of those fields, even though it charged *user fees* to outside groups. *Decatur Sports Foundation v. Dept. of Revenue*, 532 N.E.2d 576 (IL App., 4th Dist., 1988).

A private institution for services mainly to chest-disease physicians, not for indefinite number of persons or educational, religious, etc. purposes, and deriving most income from members, is not tax exempt. *American College of Chest Physicians v. Illinois Dept. of Revenue*, 559 N.E.2d 774 (Ill. App. 1990).

Property tax exemption does not apply to five *residences* on 200 acres of charitable *trust land* made available as *public park* if the operator cannot prove that those *employee residences* were necessary for performance of the charitable purposes and functions. Employee maintenance duties are not per se enough to require residence on the property. Tax exemptions must be strictly construed. *Cantigny Trust v. Dept. of Revenue*, 526 N.E.2d 518 (IL App. 1988).

Thrift Store operated by charitable organization as a source of money for its rehabilitation programs is taxable property (unrelated business) even though it also provided charitable *incidental* services. The *primary use* of the property, rather than use of income or incidental uses, determines qualification for tax exemption. *Salvation Army v. Department of Revenue*, 524 N.E.2d 628 (IL App. 1988).

The primary source of funding for a medical foundation need not be a public or private charity for the foundation to be exempt from real estate taxes. *Lutheran General Health Care System v. Department of Revenue*, 595 N.E. 2d 1214 (Ill. App. 1 Dist., 1992).

To qualify for a state property tax exemption, property owned by a nonprofit lessor must be used exclusively for charitable purposes. The entire space leased for operation of a pharmacy, by a nonprofit hospital, is taxable if the lessor fails to allocate space between the exempt purpose of serving the corporation's own charitable hospital, and the nonexempt purpose of serving an outside firm at a marked up price. *Evangelical Hospitals Corp. v. Department of Revenue*, 584 N.E. 2d 1004 (Ill. App. 1 Dist. 1991).

A charitable organization which operated hospitals and a physicians' group constituting a medical foundation affiliated with the hospital, is entitled to a property tax exemption because its clinic was used for the benefit of the public, the doctors received below market income, and were not allowed to develop and maintain prior practices. The foundation was exempt from property taxes even though it had capital, capital stock and shareholders, because the stock conferred only the right to vote on administrative issues, but conveyed no ownership interest in the corporation, no dividends were paid, and the stock did not appreciate in value. The possibility of future compensation for directors implied no profit to directors. The medical clinic was exempt because it dispensed care to all who needed and applied for it and gain or profit was not provided in a private sense to any person connected with the charitable institution. *Lutheran General Health Care System v. Department of Revenue*, 595 N.W. 2d 1214 (Ill App. 1 Dist., 1992).

Indiana

A port authority lost it property tax exemption for property used "exclusively for the public" when it leased the property, for 70 years, to a private for-profit developer. *Klein-Albrandt v. Lamb*, 597 N.E. 2d 1310 (Ind. App. 5 Dist, 1992).

Medical office buildings owned by a nonprofit hospital, that were occupied and used by doctors and dentists on staff for the conduct of their private medical practices, are not entitled to a tax exemption because they are not reasonably necessary to hospital operation. *St. Mary's Medical Center of Evansville, Inc. v. State Bd. of Tax Com'rs*, 571 N.E. 2d 1247 (Ind. 1991).

A *state's constitution* that gives permission to the state legislature to grant property tax exemption to educational organizations (e.g., the state university's fund-raising foundation) is valid, and does not violate *federal constitutional* law. Tax exemption was validly provided as to the foundation's partial ownership of an apartment building partially used for educational purposes. *Indiana University Foundation v. State Board of Tax Commrs.*, 527 N.E. 2d 1166 (IN Tax. 1988).

Iowa

In Iowa, charitable property "under construction" is exempt from property taxes, even though the property is unoccupied during renovations. *Des Moines Coalition for the Homeless v. Des Moines City Bd. of Review*, 493 N.W. 2d 860 (Iowa, 1992).

A nursing home owned by a nonprofit entity is not entitled to a property tax exemption where it is managed by a for-profit entity in order to generate profits, especially where the owner's payment to the manager is not a necessary and reasonable cost of doing business but is an attempt to shift profits to the manager. *Care Initiatives v. Board of Review of Wapello County*, 488 N.W. 2d 460 (Iowa App., 1992).

A taxpayer may challenge the granting of tax exemption to a NPC owner-operator of a community for the elderly, because of the pecuniary effect on him. *Richards v. Department*, #92/89-988; Iowa Supr. Ct. (Apr. 18, 1990).

In Iowa, for property to be exempt from taxation, three conditions must be satisfied: (1) the property must be used by a charitable institution; (2) the property must be used solely for the appropriate objects of the institution; and (3) the property must not be used with a view to pecuniary gain. *Care Initiatives v. Board of Review of Wapello County*, 488 N.W.2d 460 (Iowa Ct. App. 1992).

Kansas

In Kansas, "special care housing" is exempt from ad valorem property tax liability. Such housing includes organizations whose total operating costs exceed "charges to the residents" as a group, including room, board and other fees. Tax deductible contributions to elderly housing are not to be considered in figuring the amount of "charges to residents." *Application of Presbyterian Manor, Inc.*, 830 P.2d 60 (Kan. App. 1992).

Minnesota

A lodging (*housing*) *facility* owned and operated by a public hospital on *land adjacent* to it, for pre-admission patients, out-patients, and persons attending medical seminars at the hospital, is exempt from real property taxes. *Abbott v. Northwestern Hospital, Inc.*, 389 N.W.2d 916 (MN 1988).

Mississippi

Proprietary-Function Operation by an NPC loses tax exemption if it is in competition with for-profit enterprise and its property and revenues are primarily invested in business for profit, such as operating an apartment complex for the elderly; that is not "charitable". *Better Living Services, Inc. v. County*, 90-CA-0509; Miss. Supr. Ct. (Oct. 16, 1991).

Missouri

A charity that leases out part of its real property (while it itself also occupies a part), with no intention of making a profit, leasing only to other charitable organizations, does not lose any of the property's tax exemption. *United Cerebral Palsy Assn. v. Ross*, #7201, MO Sup. Ct. (June 19, 1990).

Nebraska

The Nebraska State Bar Association asserted that its property, a law center, was tax-exempt because it was used for educational and charitable purposes. Strictly construing the exemption, the court held that the property was not charitable because it did not confer any social or physical benefit on the general public. *Nebraska State Bar Foundation v. Lancaster County Board of Equalization*, 465 N.W. 2d 111 (Neb. 1991).

New Jersey

A building owned by a nonprofit corporation and used both as a nursing care facility and a residential unit was not entitled to a "hospital purposes" exception from property taxation since it was not organized exclusively for hospital purposes. *Woodstown Borough v. Friends Home at Woodstown*, 12 N.J. Tax 197 (1992).

Tax exemption of property as historically unique is a valid public purpose basis for the privilege. *Town of Morristown v. Women's Club*, 592 A. 2d 216 (N.J. 1991).

New York

In New York, while exemption statutes are to be strictly construed against the taxpayer, the interpretation of those statutes should not be so narrow and literal as to defeat their settled purpose, that of encouraging, fostering, and protecting religious and educational institutions.

The test of entitlement to the tax exemption under the "exclusive use" test is whether the particular use is "reasonably incidental to the primary or major purpose of the facility." Whether the property is used exclusively for the statutory purposes depends upon whether its primary use is in the furtherance of the permitted purpose.

In the Matter of Yeshivath Shaerith Hapletah v. Assessor of the Town of Fallsburg, 590 N.E.2d 1182 (N.Y. App. Div. 1992).

If a property exemption statute does not require a nonprofit to file any prescribed application form, in order to gain the exemption, an administrative agency cannot require that such a form be completed and filed. An administrative board cannot promulgate regulations not existing under a statute, but can only promulgate rules to implement the law as it exists. *Emunim v. Town of Fallsburg*, 577 N.E. 2d 34 (N.Y. 1991) (corporation organized for religious purposes).

North Carolina

If the land of a a nonprofit corporation and charitable trust is not marketable for purposes of determining the property's true value for tax purposes, cannot be sold without approval by the court, and cannot be developed, there is substantial evidence for the Property Tax Commission's valuation of the property as timber land, rather than residential and recreational property. *Appeal of Perry-Griffin Foundation*, 424 S.E. 2d 212 (N.C. App., 1993).

Ohio

Realty held by a charitable institution under a lease renewable in 20-year segments is not property "belonging to" it, and is not tax exempt for the title owner. *Evans Investment Co. v. Limbach*, 554 N.E.2d 941 (Ohio App. 1988, reported July 1990).

A nonprofit corporation's use of real property, to conduct conferences and exhibitions, resulted in "profit." Thus, the corporation was disqualified from receiving a property tax exemption. Benefits cannot be reserved only for members. *American Soc. For Metals v. Limbach*, 569 N.E. 2d 1065 (Ohio 1991). *See also Du Page Art League v. Dept. of Revenue*, 532 N.E.2d 1116 (IL App. 1988).

Oregon

The receipt of payments from the state, to perform indigent defense, does not disqualify a public defender service from seeking a charitable exemption. If the taxpayer has no expectation of remuneration from the recipient of its services, the exemption is proper. *Southwestern Oregon Public Defender Services, Inc. v. Department of Revenue*, 817 P.2d 1292, (Or. 1991).

Pennsylvania

The designation of a university as a Pennsylvania Commonwealth Agency, exempt from property taxes, may be revoked if circumstances existing at the time of the designation have changed. *Pennsylvania State University v. County of Centre*, 615 A.2d 303 (Pa., 1992).

The law of Pennsylvania provides that an entity is qualified as a purely public charity if it possesses all of the following characteristics adopted in *Hospital Utilization Project v. Commonwealth of Pa.*, 487 A.2d 1306 (Pa. 1985), identified as the "H.U.P. test": (1) it advances a charitable purpose; (2) it donates or renders gratuitously a substantial portion of its services; (3) it benefits a substantial and indefinite number of persons who are legitimate subjects of charity; (4) it relieves the government of some of its burden; and (5) it operates entirely free from private profit motive. *Associated YM-YWHA of Greater New York v. County of Wayne*, 613 A.2d 125 (Pa. Commw. 1992), *Allentown Hospital-Lehigh Valley Hosp. Center v. Board of Assessment Appeals*, 611 A.2d 793 (Pa. Commw. 1992), *In Re Appeal of Capital Extended Care*, 609 A.2d 896 (Pa. Commw. 1992), and *St. Margaret Seneca Place v. Board of Property Assessment*, 604 A.2d 1119 (Pa. Commw. 1992).

A personal care home for the elderly is only a "purely public charity" for purposes of a property tax exemption if it can prove that it donates or renders a substantial portion of its services gratuitously. It must actually provide services to someone who cannot afford to pay. *Appeal of Capital Extended Care*, 609 A.2d 896 (Pa. Cmwlth., 1992).

A county redevelopment authority is not a "nonprofit industrial development agency" so as to be exempt from realty transfer taxes in Pennsylvania. *Eastern Inv. Co. v. Com., Bd. of Finance and Revenue*, 614 A.2d 223 (Pa., 1992).

A nonprofit hospital was denied a "purely public charity" state property tax-exemption because it aggressively pursued every avenue to collect from patients, who did not pay. The court noted that the hospital did not operate entirely free from a private profit motive, even though it offered emergency health care to the poor as a condition of its licensure. *School Dist. of City of Erie v. Hamot Medical Center of City of Erie*, 602 A.2d 407 (Pa. Cmwlth. 1992).

Texas

A water supply corporation is not a "purely public charity" where it is not organized to provide charitable services to the community as a whole, but is organized solely for the purpose of selling water to those within the boundaries of a district who can afford to pay the costs assessed. *North Alamo Water Supply Corporation v. Willacy County Appraisal Dist.*, 804 S.W. 2d 894 (Tex. 1991).

A building, owned by a nonprofit college, is not exempt from property tax if it is primarily used as a private residence for the college president and is not used in educational functions. *Bexar Appraisal Dist. v. Incarnate Word College*, 824 S.W. 2d 295 (Tex. App.-San Antonio 1992).

State improvements to a prison unit are equitable state public property, used for a public purpose. Such property is exempt from county ad valorem taxation, even though the legal title is held by a private trustee. *Texas Dept. of Corrections v. Anderson County Appraisal Dist.*, 834 S.W. 2d 130 (Tex. App.-Tyler, 1992).

Exemption from *ad valorem* property taxes may be had only when the claimant clearly demonstrates satisfaction of both the statutory and the constitutional rules that apply; but "*exclusive use*" issue is a question of facts similar to question of "*primary*" use. *Dallas County Appraisal Dist. v. Institute for Aerobics Research*, 766 S.W.2d 318 (TX App., Dallas 1989).

Vermont

Property owned by private individuals, but leased to a private nonprofit state corporation for charitable use, is not exempt from property taxes in Vermont. *Lincoln Street, Inc. v. Town of Springfield*, 615 A.2d 1028 (Vt., 1992).

Washington State

A portion of a nonprofit college's property that serves as a buffer between the college and a highway is exempt from property tax. Such property is reasonable necessary and principally designed to further the educational purposes of the college. *St. Martin's College v. Department of Revenue*, 841 P.2d 473 (Wash., 1992).

Washington, D.C.

A property exemption statute, that requires that a charity impact principally in a specific district, does not apply to a building owned by a nonprofit corporation representing the interests of black physicians nationwide. *National Medical Ass'n. Inc. v. District of Columbia*, 611 A. 2d 53 (D.C. App., 1992).

Wisconsin

An off-campus summer camp, where a university conducted mandatory physical education curriculum, is "grounds" of the university and exempt from property taxation, even though the off-campus property was leased to the alumni association as a family campground. *Trustees of Indian University v. Town of Rhine*, 488 N.W. 2d 128 (Wis. App., 1992).

If the educational function of an organization in Wisconsin is merely incidental to the nonexempt activities or if the facts as a whole show that the educational function is incidental to activities that serve the personal interests of the organization's directors or members, an exemption will not be granted. *Trustees of Indiana University v. Town of Rhine*, 488 N.W.2d 128 (Wis. Ct. App. 1992).

The Wisconsin statute that exempts real property from taxes contains no provision that a religious, educational, or benevolent association must be domiciled or incorporated in the state in order that property located in the state, which is owned and used exclusively by the organization, be exempt from taxation. If the legislature intended to require churches and religious associations to incorporate to gain tax exempt status, it would have so specifically provided. Incorporation is therefore not a prerequisite to tax exempt status. *Waushara County v. Graf*, 480 N.W.2d 16 (Wis. 1992).]

* * *

Death and gift taxes:[54] Transfers to charity are usually not subject to state inheritance or estate or gift taxes.

General observations: As stated previously, no general rule can be stated regarding exemptions from state and local taxation of nonprofit organizations. In general, charitable organizations receive total or partial tax exemptions with respect to most state and local taxes. "Merely nonprofit" organizations receive a much more limited degree of exemption. However, as the above brief survey shows, one must look to the particular statute to determine the exact nature of any exemption.

License taxes: Group Health Association, Inc., a nonprofit health maintenance organization did not qualify for an exemption from the Fairfax County Business, Professional and Occupational License Tax where the statute providing for the exemption extended to "nonprofit organizations operating a community center . . . and facilities for the welfare of the residents of the area." The court found it was a membership organization that provided services only to its members. *Board of Supervisors of Fairfax County v. Group Health Association, Inc.*, 414 S.E.2d 602 (Va. 1992).

Realty transfer tax exemption: The Revenue Authority of Berks Co. was held not to be a "nonprofit industrial development agency" within the meaning of a statute making transfers to industrial development agencies tax exempt. In exempting transfers to nonprofit industrial development agencies from the realty tax transfer, the legislature did not extend the exemption to redevelopment authorities. Therefore, Eastern Investment Co.'s transfer of property to the Authority was not tax exempt. *Eastern Investment Co. v. Commonwealth of Pa., 614 A.2d 223* (Pa. 1992).

§133. STATE TAX EXEMPTION STATUTES

Statutes on the exemption of nonprofit organizations from income, property and sales and use taxes are too varied and subject to changes to be detailed here. Reference should be made to the specific state and statute, *and its latest supplements*, in each case.

Some state statutes group all tax exemptions under the same title, while in other states the exemptions are spread throughout the various state laws. It is also interesting to note that some of the exemptions are constitutional in nature; that is, the legislature is constitutionally prohibited in those states from taxing certain organizations.

§134. SAMPLE STATUTES—NORTH CAROLINA REAL AND PERSONAL PROPERTY EXEMPTION

The North Carolina statutes §105-278.5 and §105-278.6 provide a clear example of a modern state exemption for charitable, religious and educational institutions. Those sections state:

> §105.278.5. Real and personal property of religious educational assemblies used for religious and educational purposes.
>
> a. Buildings, the land they actually occupy, and additional adjacent land reasonably necessary for the convenient use of any such building or for the religious educational programs of the owner, shall be exempted from taxation if:
>   1. Owned by a religious educational assembly, retreat, or similar organization;
>   2. No officer, shareholder, member or employee of the owner, or any other person is entitled to receive pecuniary profit from the owner's operations except reasonable compensation for services; and
>   3. Of a kind commonly employed in those activities naturally and properly incident to the operation of a religious educational assembly such as the owner; and
>   4. Wholly and exclusively used for
>   a. Religious worship or
>   b. Purposes of instruction in religious education.
>
> b. Notwithstanding the exclusive-use requirement of subsection (a), above, if part of a property that otherwise meets the subsection's

requirements is used for a purpose that would require exemption if the entire property were so used, the valuation of the part so used shall be exempted from taxation.

c. The fact that a building or facility is incidentally available to and patronized by the general public, so long as there is no material amount of business or patronage with the general public, shall not defeat the exemption granted by this section.

d. Personal property owned by a religious educational assembly, retreat, or similar organization shall be exempted from taxation if it is exclusively maintained and used in connection with real property granted exemption under the provisions of subsection (a) or (b), above.

§105-278.6. Real and personal property used for charitable purposes

a. Real and personal property owned by:
   1. A Young Men's Christian Association or similar organization;
   2. A home for the aged, sick, or infirm;
   3. An orphanage or similar home;
   4. A Society for the Prevention of Cruelty to Animals:
   5. A reformatory or correctional institution; or
   6. A monastery, convent, or nunnery;
   7. A nonprofit, life-saving first aid, or rescue squad organization;
   8. A nonprofit organization providing housing for individuals or families with low or moderate incomes shall be exempted from taxation if: (i) As to real property, it is actually and exclusively occupied and used, and as to personal property; it is entirely and completely used, by the owner for charitable purposes; and (ii) the owner is not organized or operated for profit.

b. A charitable purpose within the meaning of this section is one that has humane and philanthropic objectives; it is an activity that benefits humanity or a significant rather than limited segment of the community without expectation of pecuniary profit or reward. The humane treatment of animals is also a charitable purpose.

c. The fact that a building or facility is incidentally available to and patronized by the general public, so long as there is no material amount of business or patronage with the general public, shall not defeat the exemption granted by this section.

d. Notwithstanding the exclusive-use requirements of this section, if part of a property that otherwise meets the section's requirements is used for a purpose that would require exemption under subsection (a) above, if the entire property were so used, the valuation of the part so used shall be exempted from taxation.

Notice that the North Carolina Statutes treat religious, educational, and charitable institutions differently from other nonprofit organizations. You must be certain that your particular organization meets the requirements of your state's statutes, before you can expect the benefits of the tax exemption.

§135. SAMPLE STATUTE: SALES TAX EXEMPTION IN FLORIDA

The following transactions are exempt from sales taxes in Florida:

a. Sales or leases directly to churches or sales or leases of tangible personal property by churches.

b. Sales or leases to nonprofit religious, nonprofit charitable, nonprofit scientific, or nonprofit educational institutions when used in carry on their customary nonprofit religious, nonprofit charitable, nonprofit scientific, or nonprofit educational activities, including church cemeteries.

c. Sales or leases to state headquarters of qualified veterans' organizations and the state headquarters of their auxiliaries when used in carrying on their customary veteran's organization activities. If a qualified veteran's organization or its auxiliary does not maintain a permanent state headquarters, then transactions involving sales or leases to such organization and used to maintain the office of the highest ranking state official are exempt from the tax imposed by this part.

This is a common practice in state exemption statutes, it utilizes the federal government's determination as to the exempt organization and operation of a particular entity. [For a complete discussion of the federal tax exemptions, please see Chapter 10.]

§136. LEADING CASES ON STATE TAX EXEMPTIONS

While the vast majority of state tax considerations are covered by statute,[55] there have been some cases in the area of state tax exemptions which are indeed noteworthy.[56] Two of the pivotal cases dealing specifically with property tax exemptions, but applicable to all state tax exemptions, were *Whyy, Inc. v. Glassboro*[57] and *Walz v. Tax Commissioner.*[58]

In *Whyy,* the United States Supreme Court discussed the validity of a New Jersey Statute[59] which denied tax exemption to an educational organization, solely because the organization was a foreign corporation. The Supreme Court held that a state statute which limits an exemption to a domestic corporation violates the equal protection clause[60] of the United States Constitution. Thus, state tax exemptions, when granted to nonprofit and/or charitable domestic organizations must be granted to foreign corporations, which are qualified to do business within the state.

In the *Walz* decision, the court discussed the validity of state-tax-exemptions for church property. Mr. Walz, who was an owner of taxable property in New York, challenged the right of the state to exempt churches from the same type of taxation. Walz argued that a state tax exemption for churches amounted to establishment of religion in violation of the U.S. Constitution. The Supreme Court did not agree with Walz's argument, stating that:

FORM NO. 15
Application for Certificate of Tax Exemption (Florida)

DR-5
N. 08/87

STATE OF FLORIDA
SALES AND USE TAX
APPLICATION FOR CONSUMER CERTIFICATE OF EXEMPTION

DO NOT WRITE IN THIS SPACE
Cert. #
Issue Date   Expires

Organization Name	Current Sales Tax Exemption Number (If Renewal)
Street Address	Business Phone: ( ) - Home Phone: ( ) -
City: State: Zip:	County:
Mailing Name (If different than above)	Organization Incorporated: ☐ Yes ☐ No Date of Incorporation:
Mailing Address (If different than above)	FEDERAL EMPLOYER ID. NO. SOCIAL SECURITY NUMBER
City: State: Zip:	☐☐-☐☐☐☐☐☐☐ ☐☐☐-☐☐-☐☐☐☐

Does organization receive income from the sale or lease of tangible personal property, ☐ YES (_____)
the lease of real property or the sale of taxable services?   ☐ NO   Enter sales tax registration #

Federal Income Tax Exemption: ☐ YES: If "yes", attach current copy of federal exemption letter.
☐ NO

Type of Organization: (check only one)
☐ Federal Agency   ☐ State Agency   ☐ County Agency
☐ Federal Credit Union   ☐ City Agency   ☐ Religious   ☐ Charitable
☐ State Credit Union   ☐ Veterans   ☐ Educational   ☐ Other _____
☐ Scientific   ☐ Youth Organization   ☐ Home for the Aged, Nursing Home or Hospice

Copies of the following documents must be attached to support your claim for exemption:

A   A detailed statement fully describing your organizational activities

B   If incorporated, a copy of your articles of incorporation, or if not incorporated, a copy of other organizing documents

C   A copy of constitution and bylaws or a similar code of regulations and amendments

D   Statement of income and expenses for the preceding fiscal year categorizing funding and expenses as well as a Statement of Assets and Liabilities for the same accounting period

E   A statement which explains the manner in which your assets will be distributed upon dissolution or termination of your organization

ALL DOCUMENTS SUBMITTED WILL BE RETAINED AS PART OF YOUR APPLICATION

CERTIFICATION

I hereby attest to my knowledge as an officer of the above named entity that a Consumer Certificate of Exemption is to be extended in lieu of Sales and Use Tax only on the purchase or lease of items directly used or consumed in carrying on the customary nonprofit activities of the nonprofit entity granted such exemption certification. The sale of services to or by the above named entity will be subject to the provisions of Rule 12A-46, Florida Administrative Code.

Additionally, I certify that the above information entered on this application, including attached statements, has been examined by me and is to the best of my knowledge and belief, correct and complete.

Signature Of Officer: Title: Date:

MAIL TO:	INFORMATION
Florida Department of Revenue Application Acceptance Section Carlton Building Tallahassee, FL 32399-0100	This application is to be used by organizations applying for an exemption from Florida Sales and Use Tax and must be renewed every five (5) years. Failure to furnish all required data will delay the processing of your application.

If an organization sells or leases tangible personal property, charges taxable admissions, is the lessor of transient accommodations, real property or docking spaces, or sells taxable services, such organization must register as a dealer pursuant to Part I of Chapter 212, Florida Statutes, and collect and remit sales tax on such transactions to this Department. Churches are exempt from this requirement except when they are acting as the lessor of real property. |
| **NO FEE REQUIRED** | SEE LAW ON REVERSE SIDE |

FLORIDA STATUTES
SECTION 212.08(7)

The provisions of this section authorizing exemptions from sales and use tax shall be strictly defined, limited, and applied in each category as follows:

a.   "Religious institutions" means churches, synagogues, and established physical places for worship at which nonprofit religious services and activities are regularly conducted and carried on. The term "religious institutions" includes nonprofit corporations the sole purpose of which is to provide free transportation services to church members, their families, and other church attendees. The term "religious institutions" also includes state, district, or other governing or administrative offices the function of which is to assist or regulate the customary activities of religious organizations or members.

b.   "Charitable institutions" means only nonprofit corporations qualified as nonprofit pursuant to s.501(c)(3), United States Internal Revenue Code, 1954, as amended and other nonprofit entities, the sole or primary function of which is to provide, or to raise funds for organizations which provide, one or more of the following services if a reasonable percentage of such service is provided free of charge, or at a substantially reduced cost, to persons, animals, or organizations that are unable to pay for such service:

(I)   Medical aid for the relief of disease, injury or disability;

(II)   Regular provision of physical necessities such as food, clothing, or shelter;

(III)   Services for the prevention of, or rehabilitation of persons from, alcoholism or drug abuse; the prevention of suicide; or the alleviation of mental, physical, or sensory health problems;

(IV)   Social welfare services including adoption placement, child care, community care for the elderly, and other social welfare services which clearly and substantially benefit a client population which is disadvantaged or suffers a hardship;

(V)   Medical research for the relief of disease, injury, or disability;

(VI)   Legal services; or

(VII)   Food, shelter, or medical care for animals or adoption services, cruelty investigations, or education programs concerning animals;

and the term includes groups providing volunteer manpower to organizations designated as charitable institutions hereunder.

c.   "Scientific organizations" means scientific organization which hold current exemptions from federal income tax under s. 501(c)(3) of the Internal Revenue Code and also means organizations the purpose of which is to protect air and water quality or the purpose of which is to protect wildlife and which hold current exemptions from the federal income tax under s. 501(c)(3) of the Internal Revenue Code..

d.   "Educational institutions" means state tax-supported or parochial, church and nonprofit private schools, colleges, or universities which conduct regular classes and courses of study required for accreditation by, or membership in, the Southern Association of Colleges and Schools, the Department of Education, the Florida Council of Independent Schools, of the Florida Association of Christian Colleges and Schools, Inc., or which conduct regular classes and courses of study accepted for continuing education credit by the American Medical Association or the American Dental Association. Nonprofit libraries, art galleries, and museums open to the public are defined as educational institutions and are eligible for exemption. The term "educational institutions" includes private nonprofit organizations the purpose of which is to raise funds for schools teaching grades kindergarten through high school, colleges, and universities. The term "educational institutions" includes any nonprofit newspaper of free or paid circulation primarily on university or college campuses which holds a current exemption from federal income tax under s. 501(c)(3) of the Internal Revenue Code,and any educational television or radio network or system established pursuant to s. 229.805 or s. 229.8051 and any nonprofit television or radio station which is a part of such network or system and which holds a current exemption from federal income tax under s. 501(c)(3) of the Internal Revenue Code. The term "educational institutions" also includes state, district, or other governing or administrative offices the function of which is to assist or regulate the customary activities of educational organizations or members.

e.   "Veterans organizations" means nationally chartered or recognized veterans' organizations, including, but not limited to, Florida Chapters of the Paralyzed Veterans of American, Catholic War Veterans of the U.S.A., and Jewish War Veterans of the U.S.A. and Disabled American Veterans, Department of Florida, Inc., which hold current exemptions from federal income tax under s. 501(c)(4) or s. 501(c)(19) of the Internal Revenue Code.

f.   Volunteer fire departments. - Also exempt are fire fighting and rescue service equipment and supplies purchased by volunteer fire departments, duly chartered under the Florida Statutes as corporations not for profit.

n.   Organizations providing special educational, cultural, recreational and social benefits to minors. There shall be exempt from the tax imposed by this part nonprofit organizations which are incorporated pursuant to chapter 617, or which hold a current exemption from federal corporate income tax pursuant to s. 501(c)(3) of the Internal Revenue Code the primary purpose of which is providing activities that contribute to the development of good character or good sportsmanship, or to the educational or cultural development, of minors. This exemption is extended only to that level of the organization that has a salaried executive officer or an elected nonsalaried executive officer.

q.   State Theater Program Facilities. - Nonprofit organizations incorporated in accordance with chapter 617 which have qualified under s. 501(c)(3) of the Internal Revenue Code of 1954, as amended, and which have been designated as State Theater Program facilities as provided in s. 265.287 are exempt from the tax imposed by this chapter.

r.   Florida Retired Educators Association and its local chapters.- Also exempt from payment of the tax imposed by this chapter are purchases of office supplies, equipment, and publications made by the Florida Retired Educators Association and its local chapters.

u.   Home for the aged, nursing home, or hospice. - Nonprofit corporations which hold current exemptions from federal corporate income tax pursuant to s. 501(c)(3), U.S. Internal Revenue Code, 1954, as amended, and which either qualify as homes for the aged pursuant to s. 196.1975(2), or are licensed as a nursing home or hospice under the provisions of Chapter 400, are exempt from the tax imposed by this chapter.

v.   Specified nonprofit corporations. - Also exempt are sales to nonprofit corporations which hold current exemptions from federal corporate income tax pursuant to s. 501(c)(3), U.S. Internal Revenue Code, 1954, as amended, and whose primary purpose is to raise money for military museums.

[g]ranting tax exemptions to churches necessarily operates to afford an indirect economic benefit and also gives rise to some, but yet a lesser, involvement than taxing them. In analyzing either alternative the questions are whether the involvement is excessive and whether it is a continuous one.[61]

Thus, exemptions for churches are not volative of the first amendment.

Church Tax-Exempt Purposes

[Sheila M. Bond contributed some of this subsection.]

[See above sections and Chapter 36.]
[See, Witte, *Tax Exemption of Church Property*, 64 So. Cal. L. Rev. 363-415 (1991).]

California, Virginia, and Indiana law say that *churches* or other religious organizations must pay *sales taxes* on sales of goods (including bibles and religious articles), and such tax is lawful; so ruled the U.S. Supreme Court (unanimously) in 1990. This decision does not violate the Constitution's First Amendment provision that "Congress shall make no *law respecting an establishment of religion*, or prohibiting the *free exercise* thereof. . . . " It involved a California tax on Louisiana evangelist Jimmy Swaggart's TV sales of bibles, pamphlets, and tapes. As long as such *tax does not endanger* the seller's ability to practice his (its) *religion* it is valid, said the court. The same rule probably applies to other taxes (e.g., property taxes), as long as the tax is *not so "onerous"* that it "might effectively choke off an adherent's religious practices," said the decision. Most states specifically *exempt* churches from "broadly based" taxes. But this decision makes it clear that there is no constitutional right to tax exemption for churches.[62]

Churches and other religious institutions and charitable corporations or societies enjoy no inherent right to exemption from taxation; all tax exemption statutes should be strictly and narrowly construed against the taxpayer, who must show a clear entitlement, and in favor of the state.[63]

In determining whether a taxpayer is a bona fide church or religious association entitled to property tax exemption, a court is to consider the sincerity of an organization's asserted beliefs in light of all evidence presented by the organization. The court should determine whether the beliefs asserted are held in good faith, or whether forms of religious organization are erected for sole purpose of cloaking secular enterprise with legal protections of religion. Here, taxpayer was not a bona fide "church" or "religious organization" entitled to property tax exemption, but rather a subterfuge designed to evade taxation.[64]

While it is not a prerequisite for an exemption, a showing that the petitioning organization is incorporated as a church or a religious association will lend credence to that organization's claim that it is a "bona fide" church or religious organization. Property satisfies requirements for tax exempt status if its "use" is for occasional secular purposes other than religious worship, it does not result in the loss of the exemption if the primary purpose of the property is for religious worship and all income from the other use is devoted exclusively to the maintenance and development of the property as a place of religious worship.[65]

Florida's statute that exempts church (parochial) facilities from the state's requirement of licenses for such facilities is not in violation of the "Establishment" clause of the U.S. Constitution (First Amendment).[66]

A North Carolina exemption of "Holy Bibles" from sales and use tax was held to be a violation of the First Amendment "free press" and "establishment" clause in 1990.[67]

Where a question of taxability arises under the W. Va. Code, and the question involves the constitutionality of a statute granting exemption from taxation, the matter must be heard de novo by the circuit court before the court of appeals will pass upon the constitutionality of the statute granting the exemption.[68]

In Pennsylvania, a religious summer camp is not a "purely public charity," exempt from property taxes, unless the camp can show that the government was obligated to provide the social, recreational, or educational activities, or food and medical services that the camp provides.[69]

A Clearwater, Florida city ordinance requiring churches to file financial disclosure forms was upheld against the Church of Scientology, the court saying that donations for "auditing" (psychoanalysis!?!) and training were not covered by the ordinance because such moneys are Unrelated Business Income and not religious activities and are Taxable under U.S. Supreme Court and other rulings. County officials continue to press claims for property taxes on the church's hotel headquarters and other property in Pinellas County, arguing that most of the church's income is UBIT-vulnerable and that Scientology's tax exemption should be ended.[70] [In 1993 the I.R.S. held this to be a valid, Tax exempt church. See page 395 (Chap. 11).]

The Roman Catholic Diocese (RCD) improperly tried to exclude two residential parcels of land, which were primarily benefiting four individuals who worked with the church. RCD's theory was that their residential lots and buildings were "parsonages," but the residences were not "parsonages," because that means more than merely being a residence owned by a religious organization in which an ordained member of that organization resides. A "parsonage," as employed in I.C. §63-105B, is a building that is owned by a religious organization. It should be occupied as a residence by a designated minister who ministers to a specific localized congregation that gathers to worship at frequent and regular intervals. Since the house was occupied by a semi-retired priest without a designated congregation, administrators, and traveling ministers, the residence does not qualify.[71]

Property belonging to a nonprofit religious organization and used to provide residential housing accommodations to its faculty, staff, students and their families is exempt from property taxes if "necessary and reasonably incidental" to the facility's primary religious purpose. Property tax exemption statutes should be construed so as not to defeat their settled purpose of encouraging, fostering, and protecting religious and educational institutions.[72]

Contribution tax: In late 1992 churches in Berkeley, California were ordered to pay taxes on *contributions* (60¢ per $1000 received) and also to *register* like other nonprofit organizations. City finance director Sonali Bose reported that only half of the 600 NPOs in that city had registered yet. The tax is based on the unanimous ruling of the U.S. Supreme Court in 1990 (*Jimmy Swaggart Ministries v. Calif. Board of Equalization*, 110 S. Ct. 688 (1990)) upholding the California sales tax on religious organizations as well as other NPOs. The trend seems to be to require churches to pay such taxes as other NPOs are required to do, said Joe Conn, a spokesman for Americans United for Separation of Church and State, based in Silver Spring, Maryland.[73]

§137. BURDEN OF PROOF CONCERNING EXEMPT STATUS

[Sheila M. Bond contributed some of the following section.]

The overwhelming majority of states place the burden of proving exempt status on the organization itself.[74] However, once an organization has been granted exempt status, the burden generally shifts to the government, or taxing entity, that seeks to revoke the exemption.[75]

Revocation of exempt status can occur whenever an organization's actions violate the statutory authority for exemption. Thus, for example, an organization practicing racial discrimination, can have its exemption revoked.[76] In fact, a state *must* revoke the exempt status of an organization if there is proof that the organization practiced discrimination.[77]

While a fraternal organization was entitled to the presumption that property it owned was used for charitable purposes, the presumption did not relieve the organization from the burden of showing irrevocable dedication of net income from the property to statutory uses and purposes that entitled it to the exemption. The burden of proof is on the petitioner to establish its right to exemption.[78]

The burden of proving tax exempt status is upon the taxpayer. Tax exemption statutes are matters of legislative grace, and they are to be strictly construed against the granting of the exemption.[79] Where there is any doubt, the doubt must be resolved against the one claiming the exemption.[80]

Exemption of a public transportation corporation from special fuel tax (for needed wreckers' and supervisors' vehicles' fuel) was held necessary for operation of the system, and tax-exempt. An *ambiguous statute exemption* provision usually is *strictly construed* against the party seeking exemption. But ultimately it is primarily a function of the court to determine what the legislative intent was.[81]

A property tax evaluation, assessed by a town, is presumed valid, unless it is so unreasonable, under the circumstances, that injustice results or there is unjust discrimination or the assessment is fraudulent, dishonest or illegal. The taxpayer must prove the valuation to the "manifestly wrong."[82]

In trial court, the taxpayer has the burden of proving state tax-exempt status, whether or not he prevailed in prior hearings before the board of assessment or appeals.[83]

A trial court can make a *de novo* review of decisions allowing a hospital tax-exempt status for property taxes if the record is incomplete. One example is where the hospital refused to turn over relevant documents in prior hearings before the board of assessment and board of appeals.[84]

POINTS TO REMEMBER

- Use *tax counsel*, for these complex and changeable law problems.

- Remember to determine which taxes apply to your organization under your state statutes.

- Remember to determine whether or not you can qualify for exemption from state-imposed taxes.

- Remember to check your exemption from each type of tax, since some states only exempt nonprofit organizations from specified types of taxes.

- Remember that the burden of proving exempt status falls on the taxpayer.

- Remember that the tax laws are subject to frequent change; be up to date.

- Remember to seek the advice of competent counsel when you are unsure of your position.

NOTES TO CHAPTER 12

1. The state taxes most often applied against corporations are income, sales and use, and property taxes. However, organizations should carefully check their state statutes, or, better still, seek the advice of competent counsel, to determine what other types of taxes might apply to their particular activities.

2. *Tidewater Ass'n of Homebuilders, Inc., v. City of Virginia Beach,* 400 S.E. 523 (Va. 1991).

3. *New Life Gospel Church v. State, Dept. of Community Affairs, Div. of Housing Bureau of Fire Safety,* 608 A.2d 397 (N.J. Super. A.D., 1992).

4. For a discussion of such taxes see, ¶90,500 ff. of Prentice-Hall *All States Unit of State and Local Taxes* (hereinafter *All States*).

5. *See eg.* 805 ILCS §§5/15.20 - 5/15.95.

6. *See eg.* 805 ILCS §5/15.20 (domestic corporations); 5/15.55 (foreign corporations).

7. 805 ILCS §§5/15.55, 5/15.60

8. See, *e.g.*, New York Executive Law, §96(9)(b); Fla. Stat. 607.0122; 805 ILCS §5/15.10.

9. These are discussed in Prentice-Hall *All States* ¶92,200 ff.

10. See, *e.g.*, New York Tax Law, §209; 805 ILCS §§5/15.35, 15.40, 15.45, 15.65, 15.70, 15.75.

11. See, *e.g.*, 72 Pa. Stat. §7401.

12. Generally states impose a franchise tax measured by corporate income.

13. Income taxes are discussed in Prentice-Hall *All States*, 91,100 ff.

14. The individuals and unincorporated organizations are not generally treated as separate entities for tax purposes.

15. Sales and use taxes are discussed in Prentice-Hall *All States* at ¶92,501 ff. See, *e.g.*, Fla. Stat. §212.05, 212.08, 212.02.

16. See, *e.g.*, Fla. Stat. §212.05 (1992).

17. Ohio, for example, imposes such a tax at §5709.01 of the Ohio Revised Code.

18. Property taxes are discussed in Prentice-Hall *All States* at ¶93,601 ff.

19. See, *e.g.*, Ohio Rev. Code, §5709.01.

20. See, Fla. Stat. §198.02 (1992).

21. *E.g.* New York Tax Law, §952.

22. *E.g.* Tenn. Code Ann., §67-8-100 through 67-8-117.

23. For a complete discussion of the distinction between "charitable" and "non-profit" corporations, please see Chapter 1, *supra*.

24. *Ibid.* See, *e.g.* Hospital Utilization Project v. Pennsylvania, 487 A.2d 1306 (Pa. 1985), which imposed further that the organization must prove to be a public, rather than private, organization.

25. This two-part test is to be fully consistent with the test applied by the Internal Revenue Service in granting federal tax exemption under section 501(c)(3) of the Internal Revenue Code of 1954. For a complete discussion of the federal exemption requirements, please see Chapter 10, *supra*.

26. See, Prentice-Hall *All States*, ¶90,500 ff.

27. New York Tax Law §180(1).

28. See, generally, the New York Not-for-Profit Corporation Law.

29. New York Exec., §96(9)(b).

30. *E.g.*, Ohio Rev. Code, §111.16(A)(2).

31. Ohio Rev. Code, §111.16(A)(1).

32. See, Prentice-Hall *All States*, ¶92,260.

33. Ohio Rev. Code, §5733.01.

34. See, Prentice-Hall *All States*, ¶91,192.

35. See, n.11, *supra*.

36. New York Gen. City Laws §103(g).

37. New York Tax Laws §601(g).

38. See, *e.g.*, Colorado Stat. §39-22-115.

39. Kings County Trust Co. v. Law, 234 N.Y. 610, 138 N.E. 466 (1922).

40. See Prentice-Hall *All States* §93,601.

41. See, *e.g.*, New York Tax Law §§1105, 1116.

42. See, *e.g.*, Fla. Stat. §212.04 to .08.

43. See, *e.g.*, Georgia Code Ann. §48-8-3.

44. See, Prentice-Hall *All States* ¶93,601.

45. See, Ohio Rev. Code §5739.02.

46. *E.g.*, Mechlin v. Comptroller, Md. App., 426 A.2d 1387 (1981).

47. *Ibid.*

48. See, *e.g.*, Fla. Stat. §196.192 (1992).

49. Fla. Stat. Ch. 196.

50. People ex rel. New York School for the Deaf v. Townsend, 298 N.Y. 645, 82 N.E.2d 37.

51. See, *e.g.*, *Appeal of Town of Seabrook*, 470 A.2d 855 (N.Y. 1983).

52. *E.g.*, Whyy, Inc. v. Glassboro, 393 U.S. 117 (1968).

53. Clarkson Memorial College v. Haggett, 300 N.Y. 595.

54. *E.g.* Ohio Rev. Code Ann. §5731.17.

55. *See* specific state statutes applicable.

56. It would be impossible to discuss the possible judicial determinations for every state, thus organizers should be aware of the caselaw in their particular jurisdiction.

57. 393 U.S. 117 (1968).

58. 297 U.S. 664 (1970).

59. The former New Jersey Stat. Ann. §54:4-36.

60. Fourteenth Amendment, U.S. Const.

61. 297 U.S. 664, at 674-75.

62. *Jimmy Swaggart Ministries v. Calif. Board of Equalization*, #88-1374; 110 S. Ct. 688 (1990), Supr. Ct., 12 *Natl. L. J.* (21) 37 (Jan. 29, 1990); c.f.: Religious property tax exemption may not be limited by *burdensome filing requirements* imposed by an administrative agency. *Emunion v. Town of Fallsburg*, 577 N.E. 2d 34 (N.Y. 1991).

63. *ADA County Assessor v. Roman Catholic Diocese of Boise*, 1993 WL 48922 (Idaho 1993).

64. *Waushara County v. Graf*, 480 N.W.2d 16 (Wis, Feb. 1992).

65. *First Baptist Church of San Antonio v. Bexar County Appraisal Review Board*, 833 S.W.2d 108 (Tex. 1992).

66. S.P. Cole, *Volunteerism Can Be Taxing*, 12 *Natl. L. J.* (10) 13 (Nov. 13, 1989).

67. *Finlator vs. Powers*, U.S. 4th Cir. Ct. App.; May 10, 1990.

68. *New Vrindaban Community, Inc. v. Rose*, 419 S.E.2d 478 (W. Va. 1992).

69. *Associated YM-YWHA of Greater New York/Camp Poyntelle v. County of Wayne*, 613 A.2d 125 (Pa. Cmwlth., 1992).

70. C. Krueger (article), *St. Petersburg (FL) Times*, p. 1 City Times Section (Feb. 9, 1991) [See §110 above].

71. *ADA County Assessor v. Roman Catholic Diocese of Boise*, 1993 WL 48922 (Idaho 1993).

72. *Hapletah v. Assessor of Town of Fallsburg*, 582 N.Y.S 2d 54 (Ct. App. 1992).

73. Note, *St. Petersburg (FL) Times*, Religion Section, p. 3E (Aug. 15, 1992).

74. *E.g.*, Southern Baptist Convention v. Mitchell, 658 S.W.2d 1 (Mo. banc 1983).

75. *E.g.*, Rockford Life Insurance Company v. Department of Revenue, 470 N.E.2d 596 (Ill. App., 2 Dist. 1984). *See also*, New York Botanical Garden v. Assessors, App. Div. 438 N.Y.S.2d 580 (1981).

76. *E.g.*, Palleon v. Musolf, 345 N.W.2d 73 (Wis. App. 1984).

77. *Id.* The Wisconsin Court of Appeals stated that the continued exemption of an organiza-

tion which was discriminatory would violate the Fourteenth Amendment to the U.S. Constitution.

78. *Western Slavonic Association v. Property Tax Administrator,* 835 P.2d 621 (Colo. Ct. App. 1992).

79. *Waushara County v. Graf,* 480 N.E.2d 16 (Wis. 1992).

80. *Board of Supervisors of Fairfax County v. Group Health Association, Inc.,* 414 S.E.2d 602 (Va. 1992).

81. *Indiana Dept. of Revenue v. Indianapolis Public Transp. Corp.,* 550 N.E.2d 1277 (Ind., 1990).

82. *Camps Newfound/Owatonna, Inc. v. Town of Harrison,* 604 A.2d 908 (Me. 1992).

83. *School Dist. of City of Erie v. Hamot Medical Center of City of Erie,* 602 A.2d 407 (Pa. Cmwlth. 1992).

84. *School Dist. of City of Erie v. Hamot Medical Center of City of Erie,* 602 A.2d 407 (Pa. Cmwlth. 1992).

13

LICENSES AND APPROVALS

§138. STATE CONTROL BY AMENDMENT OR REPEAL

All grants of corporation status (and resulting privileges) are subject to legislative amendment or repeal. This power of the state is implied generally, subject to reasonable due process and "grandfather" privilege continuation in proper cases. Statute statement of this limitation, in state grants of nonprofit status, is sometimes express. For example, the 1986 draft of the proposed American Bar Association's Revised Model Nonprofit Corporation Act says: "The (name of state legislature) has power to amend or repeal all or part of this Act at any time and all domestic and foreign corporations subject to this Act are governed by the amendment or repeal."[1] The "vested rights" argument of the old case of *Trustees of Dartmouth College v. Woodward*[2] may no longer be effective today, but such statutory expression removes the concern of legislators about that argument.[3]

Refusal of the secretary of state's office to file articles of incorporation or other documents may be appealed to the state court.[4] And specific grants (or limitations) of secretary of state supervision power (*e.g.*, control) now are increasing; for example, in South Carolina's statute *requiring* that officer to *investigate* the validity of an organization's claim for a charter or amendment, and to revoke the charter of an organization that is no longer qualified for the desired status.[5]

Constitutional law limitations on the powers of state officials (or even state legislatures) serve to keep state control within reasonable bounds. For example, though political activity may cause the IRS to deny tax exemption to most charitable organizations, a nonprofit *ideological* corporation may not be forbidden to publish promotional materials about candidates for federal public office.[6] In addition, a state statute may validly place family (personal) rights above those of an organization; as where a state statute[7] permits a devise to a charitable, benevolent, educational, literary, scientific, religious, or missionary organization to be set aside in its entirety if a lineal descendent or spouse of the grantor files written claim of his or her interest therein within four months after the date of issuance of letters thereon.[8]

§139. STATE LICENSING STATUTES

Today every state, and almost every municipality, has extensive legislation on the licensing of various kinds of activities and organizations. These statutes should, of course, be consulted in any specific case.

As an example of a state's provisions in respect to licensing, Florida's statute index requires three pages to list the various items covered by its enacted state laws. These provisions are very general in some matters and very specific in others. Thus, there are specific enactments concerning abortion clinics (§390.014), child care institutions (§409.175), child placement agencies (§63.202), educational cooperative scholarship plans (§617.62), fairs (§616.12), labor union business agents (§447.04), migrant labor camps (§381.432 *et passim*), military organizations (§870.06), optometric service plans (§637.131), pharmaceutical service plans (§637.291), rodeos, shows and vaudeville (§616.12), *etc.* In addition, whole blocks of provisions are stated (cross-referenced). These include adult congregate living facilities, agricultural products, alcoholic beverages, *etc.* And municipal ordinances today can be expected to be almost as detailed in large urban areas everywhere.

License-Statute Construction

Legislative authorities enact license statutes. However, it is often left to the courts to interpret the meaning of the statutes as well as their zone of application.

Statutes that impose penalties for failure to obtain licenses must be strictly construed, with doubts resolved in favor of the one against whom the license statute is sought to be enforced.[9]

The Illinois "Charitable Games Act" (Ill. Rev. Stat 1987), c. 120, par. 1121 et seq.) lists 14 games (roulette, blackjack, poker, and so on) to permit NPOs to use *gambling for fund raising*, while gambling is otherwise illegal. A civil penalty (fine) is applicable to violations for not obtaining a license. The statute is constitutional even though it does not define "charitable games," because the list is *clear and understandable*, and the statute's confinement to NPOs does not violate the Equal Protection (14th Amendment) clause because of the state's interest in helping charitable purposes. A restaurant that ran other games, in a fund-raising benefit for charity (Multiple Sclerosis Society), without a license, was fined.[10]

Nonprofit or charitable bingo operations must comply with the prerequisite conditions and strict regulations, for operating bingo games, under any statutory exemption provided for them under state gambling laws.[11]

The governor's power to appoint real estate agents to a state licensing commission may be statutorily limited to a list supplied by a private, nonprofit organization of real estate agents without violating the separation of powers in the state constitution.[12]

Statutes, enacted to invalidate subdivision restrictions on group homes for the developmentally disabled or mentally ill persons, cannot be applied retroactively.[13]

The state Department of Mental Health and a nonprofit residential home care provider were joint employers of the organization's direct-care workers, since the department's control over the NPO extended beyond mere licensing and included establishing minimum qualifications for employment and setting a maximum hourly rate for the direct-care workers.[14]

A *new statutory approach,* favoring the licensee/franchisee in business franchising agreements (e.g., giving the franchisee freedom to sell the franchise; limiting the franchisor's power to grant more than one license per geographic area; etc.) was enacted in Iowa in 1992. Florida and other states soon may enact similar laws.[15]

An administrative regulation that governs criteria for licensing new cemeteries, and that requires consideration of the needs of the community is not invalidated by a statute, governing the same subject, that required consideration of the adequacy of existing cemeteries within the county.[16]

A nonprofit corporation's preserve or park was not considered to be a "public playground," for purposes of denial of a nearby restaurant's liquor license, where there were no swings, ball playing was not permitted, and the park did not contain separate recreational facilities for children.[17]

See, Section 142 on specific licenses and permits.

§140. NATURE OF LICENSING LAW, IN GENERAL

Licensing law basically is governmental *administrative* law. For example, in Florida statutes the *Administrative Procedure Act* (Chapter 120) is the main set of rules as to government agency rulemaking and supervision of permission for the *privilege* of doing (or not doing) various things by various persons and organizations. It is a lengthy and detailed set of administrative rules. In fact, the granting of corporation status is, in itself, a kind of grant of a license (*i.e.,* to have corporate status, with the privileges that such status enjoys). So, too, the granting of tax exemption amounts to a kind of license. We mean, here, *license* in the same sense that it is "A permission, by a competent authority to do some act which without such authorization, would be illegal, or would be a trespass or tort."[18] Licensing is one method of protecting "legitimate state interests",[19] such as public interest in being protected from improper (false) charity-solicitations.[20]

In an administrative hearing about license revocation, due process requires definite charge, adequate notice, and a full and impartial hearing. The procedures must conform to fundamental principles of justice.[21]

As concerns governmental licensing of nonprofit organizations and operations, there has been complaint that governmental supervision is inadequate rather than too onerous.[22] This contrasts strangely with the widespread complaint that government in this era is becoming unbearably domineering in its control of even the details of business and private life. Constant increase of supervision of nonprofit organizations and operations is almost certain to continue in the years to come.

Licensing is one of the principal methods of modern governmental supervision. It also is an important source of revenue for the state and for local government divisions and departments. Fees for most licenses and permits must be paid by nonprofit organizations just as by businesses. Licensing statutes and regulations, besides serving as sources of government revenue, establish prerequisites to the doing of certain acts.[23] The "right" to do the act, when licensed by the state or city, sometimes is viewed by the licensee as property, but usually is not treated by the law as a property right.[24] Neither is it a contract with the granting authority,[25] nor a "vested interest."[26] Usually it is deemed to be a specially granted and limited privilege. Licensing statutes of all kinds ordinarily convey, explicitly or implicitly, the idea that the grant of the privilege to be "licensed" (permitted or authorized) to do something is a special but limited favor from the licensing authority; but the governmental authority may not lawfully interfere with constitutional rights, such as free speech or communication.[27] This is an aspect of the state's "police powers."

Punitive provisions almost always are found in these enactments. Failure to obey may result in fines or even imprisonment, particularly if deliberate evasion of the law is shown.[28] The state or municipality thereby makes certain that the specified activity will be carried on only by those who satisfy the requirements.

Although license requirements apply to all kinds of organizations and activities, a number of them apply primarily to nonprofit organizations. These are discussed in this chapter.

Many license statutes are highly technical, and difficult even for lawyers to interpret. It is not unusual, in some states, to find that the license laws are scattered through as many as 70 to 80 different sections and parts of the state's legal code.

Some attempts have been made, in recent years, to clarify the confused development of licensing laws. Adoption of Administrative Procedure Acts has been the chief technique employed for this purpose.[29]

As far back as 1940 in Ohio (using that state as an example of the nationwide problem), there were 187 different types of state licenses, administered by 47 different agencies, under 76 separate licensing acts.[30] Most of these acts had been adopted in the prior 25 years.

Ohio adopted an Administrative Procedure Act in 1943, and has improved it by amendments since then.[31] Like other such statutes, of which Florida's is a good example, in many states today, it provides for adoption of new regulations only after notice and hearing on the proposal, guarantee of a hearing in a refusal to issue or renew a license, safeguards such as notice and hearing rules, and uniform procedures for hearings.[32]

A chief test of the validity of a licensing authority's conduct in granting or denying a license often is whether or not that decision was arbitrary, capricious, or *discriminatory* enough to amount to denial of due process.[33] Another criterion is the *reasonableness* of a license grant or denial.[34]

Government supervision, for protection of the public interest in any activity, often is based on the nature of the impact of that kind of activity on the community. Building of a hospital will surely affect other hospitals and the nature of its setting in a residential neighborhood. Thus, an applicant for a license to operate a hospital must obtain a "Certificate of Need" from the State Department of Health and Rehabilitation, and must show "standing" if it challenges board approval of a competing applicant.[35]

Licensing Constitutionality

[Thomas Flanigon contributed some of the following subsection.]

A school district, that licenses temporarily available school facilities to others for expressive activities, is barred by the First Amendment from refusing to lease school facilities to a nonprofit religious organization for the purpose of giving a free Christmas community dinner.[36]

Statutory regulation of (proprietary) schools does not per se violate First Amendment or due process or equal protection constitutional rights; but such violation must be specifically proved.[37]

A city ordinance, regulating parades, that requires a nonprofit civil rights organization to pay a permit application fee and to prepay the cost for traffic control, is a constitutionally permissible regulation of expressive conduct. However, an ordinance, granting an administrative body or government official unfettered discretion to regulate the licensing of activities protected by the First Amendment, is unconstitutional.[38]

A community may not impose higher permit fees on groups that are controversial in order to afford greater police protection. A higher fee financially burdens free speech.[39]

An association of unlicensed persons brought suit to challenge the constitutionality of the State Board of Accountancy's regulation, prohibiting unlicensed persons from using the terms "accountant" or "accounting" in referring to their services. The court held that the terms could only be banned where used to potentially mislead the public about the licensee's or nonlicensee's status.[40]

A city ordinance that requires a potential solicitor for a charitable organization to submit to fingerprinting before being issued a permit, but which exempts from the fingerprinting requirement those organizations that have been headquartered in its city for three years, violates equal protection.[41] But, a municipal ordinance that requires charitable organizations to file registration statements is not an unconstitutional invasion of their freedoms.[42]

[Howard Goldstein contributed the rest of this subsection.]

Religious organization's **land-use plans** are good illustrations of the interplay of laws (e.g., constitutional privileges and other community residents concerns) in granting or withholding of licenses or other approvals. [See Chap. 36.]

Recent appellate decisions suggest three significant legal questions in land-use ordinance vs. church-conflict cases. First, the threshold question, is the use clothed in enough religious garb to invoke a review standard stricter than that applied to nonprivileged, nonreligious users? If so, the next question is whether the infringement on the religious use is intolerably burdensome? And the final inquiry is whether the local administrative agency abused its discretion?

When an organization of independent contractor-counselors claimed a statutory exemption from permit laws, so it could offer "pastoral counseling" from a rented office in a church, the Appellate Court of Massachusetts found the mere "layer of theological content" involved was not enough to offset facts that evinced a business use. The court looked at facts that: Fair market rent was paid, the center charged substantial overhead, counseling was open to the public, there was no proselytizing, and even professed atheists would be treated without mention of religion.[43]

Another case where the court questioned the "Religious-ness" of the use involved a church using its building solely for the purpose of manufacturing printed religious tracts, but without the required special use permit. The church claimed it did not need a special use permit, by virtue of a statutory exception to the requirement for "assemblies of religious, public worship." But, applying the plain-meaning-of-language rule to construe the exemption, the court found that the church's use of its building as a printing plant was not the kind of religious, public worship anticipated by the statute.[44]

If the use is religious but statutory exceptions do not apply, the aggrieved church may still have a cause of action based on the First Amendment's free exercise clause, incorporated by the Fourteenth Amendment. When the county requires "Industrial" zoning, yet there is only residential land and no vacant Industrial land, and the zoning board twice rejects the church's petitions to rezone because of public opposition even though the church offers to implement aesthetic and safety features, the county has directly affected the exercise of religion so severely that the court was obliged to order the county to rezone in accordance with the request.[45]

Denial of a church application to expand its parking facilities, under *zoning law,* by requiring it to establish (by clear and convincing evidence) its right to expand, is not a valid exception to *freedom of religion,* when granting of a *conditional* use permit would be prima facie valid on the facts of the case.[46]

Illustrative of the California view is a recent case where the court upheld the planning commission's finding that the proposed use of a residence as a place for home worship, would create noise, traffic, and affect the character of the neighborhood. Key to the decision was the church's claim that home worship was a fundamental tenet of the religion, but facts at trial showed the church repeatedly held services in a rented hotel room prior to its application for a special use permit. Finding the impact on religion minimal but the state interest substantial, the court upheld the refusal.[47]

Religious instruction is an aspect of some religions and therefore qualifies for some deference. But the municipality can reasonably cap the enrollment therein when the school is located in a residential area.[48]

Also protected to some extent is the church's ability to obtain the necessary zoning variance for worshipers' parking. Even if the parking lot was shown to hurt adjacent property values, one court declared that "First amendment freedoms rise above mere property values." That court then proceeded to reverse the zoning board's refusal, since 191 parking spaces for a church comprised of 2900 members was clearly inadequate and thus an infringement upon the free exercise rights of commuting church members who would either be unable to attend, or severely inconvenienced by remote parking.[49]

Basic real property law concepts continue to apply, however. In another parking case, a state court of last resort answered the narrow question, whether the zoning board could rezone a lot *across the street* from the church for parking? Held: The non-conforming accessory use was not permitted since the use would not occur on the subject lot.[50]

Well-meaning lawmakers can go too far protecting religion. A blanket exception permitting religious day care providers to operate without the permit required of others was found to violate the secular provider's right to equal protection under the law.[51]

Landmarks Preservation laws are another area of potential church-government conflict. In a recent second circuit case, a church and adjacent ancillary building were designated landmarks 23 years previous to the church's denied application for permission to construct an office tower on the ancillary building's midtown Manhattan lot. Even though it presented evidence that the inability to raze the old building impaired its ability to raise funds it would use to facilitate religious functions, the court held that since the Landmarks law was neutral, applying to churches and non-churches alike, it was immune from free-exercise clause attacked under the "Law of General Applicability" doctrine expressed in *Employment Division v. Smith*, 110 S. Ct. 1595 (1990) (State may penalize *bona-fide* religious use of narcotic), and *Jimmy Swaggart Ministries v. Bd. of Equalization*, 110 S. Ct. 688 (1990). (Free exercise rights not implicated by neutral regulations that reduce religious organization's income).[52]

If a nonprofit religious corporation owns residential property and uses its administrative offices there as a business operation, such use is a prior non-conforming use that can be conveyed to a subsequent purchaser.[53]

The land use regulatory agency fulfills a quasi-judicial role, obliging the body to act upon competent, substantial evidence, enter findings of fact, and render decisions in accordance with the essential requirements of law. Thus, the planning board's conclusory findings and denial of a special use permit improperly ignored the principle presuming that nearby religious use has a beneficial impact on the surrounding area, and was reversible *abuse of discretion*.[54]

In *Neddermeyer* the court itself directed the board to issue a permit. Predictably, then, when another town board voted down a special use permit but entered no findings of fact, the court found reversible error in the failure to enter findings and suggest reasonable mitigating measures.[55]

And in another case, the agency erred when it denied a permit to construct parking required by ordinance since it improperly considered preexisting traffic congestion, and failed to consider the fact that the particular religion involved would likely generate substantially fewer vehicles than others because the religion prohibits most driving to worship.[56]

When the agency errs, it may find itself as a defendant in a Federal civil rights action under 42 U.S.C. § 1983. On cross motions for summary judgment, the Board and Township were held liable for section 1983 damages since the court found the Board's stated reasons for withholding the permit—radio interference and safety concerns—were illegitimate by virtue of complete federal preemption of radio interference issues and exaggerated, unreasonable safety concerns about towers only 184 feet tall on 106 acres of land. Finding the Board's stated reasons invalid, it and the Township were held liable for monetary damages since the improper refusal to issue the permit deprived the church of its free-exercise rights, under color of an ordinance.[57]

In the majority of cases the court granted great deference to the purported religious use. The application by the Supreme Court of the "Law of General Applicability Doctrine" in *Smith* and *Swaggart* seems to suggest that state interference with religion can nearly always be justified, provided the law is rational, and the law applies to both religious and secular objects. Given the present court's conservative makeup, a general deference towards religion is probable.

§141. INFORMATION ABOUT LICENSES AND PERMITS

In every state, and in the federal government, there is a central license bureau, office, or department, usually in the capital city. Branch offices of the central authority usually are found in principal cities of the particular state.

Cities, towns, villages, and counties also have license departments or bureaus to administer local licensing enactments.

A direct source of information about licenses and permits is the nearest license bureau office. This is listed in the local telephone directory, under the name of the state, county, city, town, or village. Any clerk should be able to tell you who is in charge of a particular license authority, and where to find him.

Every state has an annual official directory of governmental offices and personnel, as does the federal government. The federal Congressional Directory is paralleled by state directories, such as the New York State *Red Book*. Official directories also are published annually by many cities. Typical of these is the *Little Green Book* of New York City. Lists of licensing offices and authorities are important parts of such official publications.[58]

Departmental supervision of licenses and permits is the usual rule. There-fore, an inquiry to the department probably in charge usually elicits the desired information. For example, an inquiry about school matters obviously should be addressed to the department of education, one about farm matters should be addressed to the department of agriculture and markets, and so on.

Privately published directories also are helpful. Many of them list license and other governmental offices, classifying types of activity.

Branch or subsidiary organizations usually must obtain charter authority from their parent organizations (*i.e.*, in the nature of licenses) for permission to use the parent's name as well as for other purposes. Such is the case, for example, when a local trade association is being organized and is to be affili-ated with a national trade organization. Specific permission (*i.e.*, license) to carry on certain activities must ordinarily be obtained from the parent organi-zation.

Directories of such organizations, unfortunately, are few and some are incomplete. There is a directory of *National Trade and Professional Associations of the United States* published by Columbia Books, Inc. of Washington, D.C.[59] There is a *Foundation Directory* published by the Russell Sage Foundation; it lists pri-marily the larger and older foundations.[60] *The Patman Study* back in 1962 stat-ed that there were 45,124 tax-exempt foundations in 1960.[61] The major direc-tory is the *Encyclopedia of Associations*, in three volumes, published by the Gale Research Co. of Detroit.

The simplest, practical way to get information about the home address and list of officers of a national organization is to telephone or write to the nearest branch office. The latter usually is listed in the local classified tele-phone directory, under the heading of *associations and lodges, associations-trade, clubs*, or the like.

§142. SPECIFIC LICENSES AND PERMITS

[Thomas Flanigon contributed some of the following section.]

[See the Section on State Licensing Statutes.]
The following list, although it is not intended to cover the whole field, gives an idea of the types of activity that must be licensed.

Admission tickets. The charge for admission to theaters or other public places is usually declared by statutes to be a matter of public interest, and subject to supervision by the appropriate local political subdivision of the state. Licensing is required particularly if admission tickets are to be sold by agents or brokers. Certain information must usually be printed on such tickets, concerning price, limitation of liability in case of accident, and other matters.[62]

Adoption agencies. Granting of permission to a foreign (other state) adoption agency to place children in Connecticut is not also granting permission for it to place Connecticut children.[63]

Alcoholic beverages or food. Sale or distribution of alcoholic beverages or food almost always requires licensing and payment of taxes. However, in some states, special freedom from taxation is occasionally granted: for example, when beer is sold to or by a voluntary, nonprofit association aiding the military forces.[64] Upon filing of an application, the director of the beverage administration may issue a permit authorizing a nonprofit civic organization to sell alcoholic beverages for consumption on the premises only.[65]

Blind persons. Many city ordinances authorize the mayor or some other public authority to issue licenses without charge to blind persons for the vending of goods or sale of newspapers at stated places.[66] Organizations for aid to the blind often are clearing agencies for this purpose.

Boxing or wrestling exhibitions. State and municipal boxing and wrestling commissions usually are empowered to license all exhibitions of boxing or wrestling. This applies to exhibitions staged boys' clubs and amateur athletic associations as well as by professional promoters. Provision of proper premises and of medical and other supervision is usually required.[67]

Building permits. Nonprofit organizations, as well as others, must almost always obtain building permits from local housing and building departments before undertaking construction or alternation of any building or structure.[68]

Charitable annuity societies or medical indemnity groups. State insurance statutes provide, in some detail, for the licensing of nonprofit organizations that wish to carry on annuity or other insurance activities. Many express requirements are projected by these statutes, especially concerning minimum reserve funds and the regular submission of financial statements.[69] A State Insurance Commissioner may require that a nonprofit association of retired persons obtain a license before distributing materials that offer or "solicit" insurance.[70]

Child-care organizations. Most states, and many municipalities, require the granting of a permit by a social welfare department to any organization that wishes to provide day-nursery or other child-care supervision for more than one or two children. There are strict prerequisites for the qualification of premises and personnel, as well as for compliance with health department rules and regulations.[71]

A school that offered programs for children less than three years old, attending without parents, is a *"day-care"* organization, and is subject to Child

Care Act requirements of licensing as such. State interest overrides (Montessori) school doctrines as to what is good education for young children.[72]

County zoning law applies to state-licensed child-care facilities.[73]

Refusal of a regular license to a *personal care (nursing home, or asylum)* corporation is proper when an inspector's report and other evidence show overcrowding that amounts to noncompliance with state Department of Public Welfare regulations. "Substantial" evidence must be shown, however.[74]

Child care centers that are part of churches or parochial schools in Florida are exempt, by state law, from state-licensing standards as to personnel, facilities, emergency medical care, disease control, nutrition, food preparation, record-keeping, and transportation, but are required to obey local health and safety standards and to screen employees.[75]

> *Cooperatives.* In most states, nonprofit cooperative organizations are tax-exempt. In lieu of all franchise, license, or corporation taxes, they usually are required to pay a small annual license fee.[76]
>
> *Dispensaries.* Operation of clinics or dispensaries falls within the general category of hospital operation. Licensing is required, usually with the approval of social welfare department and hospital-supervisory bureaus or commissions.[77]
>
> *Farmer's associations' licensing powers.* In some states, farmers' associations (e.g., county fair organizations) are specifically empowered by statutes, themselves to license exhibitors, peddlers, or vendors at their association exhibitions or fairs.[78]
>
> *Gaming.* By law, bingo is a charity game in Florida. All games must be conducted by bona fide members of the charitable organization sponsoring the bingo. All proceeds after expenses must go to the charitable sponsor. An estimated one billion dollars a year, wagered by Florida bingo players, is free from state gambling taxes.[79]

The Louisiana "Charitable Raffles, Bingo, and Keno Licensing Law" regulates charitable gaming by nonprofit organizations as well as the relationship between charitable organizations and various providers. This law, however, does not extend to regulating the relationship between two private non-charitable organizations. Thus, the Attorney General could not enforce a newly adopted rule limiting the rental rate charged by a commercial lessor of a bingo hall to the distributor of electronic bingo machines.[80]

A prosecutor's objection to granting of a *bingo license* must set forth specific grounds (e.g., common scheme or plan) of misconduct complained of (e.g., notice to applicant).[81]

The Indian Gaming Regulatory Act, 25 U.S.C. Section 2701 *et seq.* (1988) regulates gaming on Indian reservations. A governor may negotiate with the tribes, under the act, but may not bind the state without legislative approval or appropriate delegation of power.[82]

Health permits and licenses. Institutions, particularly hospitals or asylums, are subject to the supervision of boards of health, food inspection, and other health and sanitation authorities. Compliance with requirements must usually be shown by obtaining from the supervisors various permits and certificates.[83]

A Public Health Council may regulate the bathing beaches of a private nonprofit noncommercial homeowners' association and require that the beaches meet the State Sanitary Code.[84]

A nonprofit health maintenance organization, which failed to take any Medicaid patients and had no emergency room, was denied an exemption from a business, professional, and occupational license tax. The assistance of low-income families with health care needs, training programs, medical research, and shared medical rounds with pediatricians at a local hospital were not enough to show specific enhancement of the welfare of the residents of the county.[85]

Hospitals. Administrative due process requires an agency to be consistent when reviewing certificate of need (CON) applications among like petitioners or respondents. In accepting certificate of need applications for an open heart surgery program, needs must be fixed, as of the application filing date, by the Department of Health and Rehabilitative Services (HRS).[86]

The addition of an operating room, to an outpatient hospital facility, does not fall within the statutory definition of a project subject to significant change. Thus, the hospital is not required to obtain a certificate of need for the addition.[87]

A Florida nonprofit corporation, which constructs nursing home facilities, cannot be granted a certificate of need (CON) for additional beds for a licensed nursing home facility if another unrelated entity, as sublessee, is the actual licensed operator of the facility. Only the license holder can apply for the certificate of need.[88]

The equal protection clause of the New Hampshire state constitution is not violated by a state regulation, that requires a review board to apply travel access standards to a certificate of need application for the construction of a new hospital, but not for the expansion of an existing hospital.[89]

Boards of health and state departments of health sometimes use "batching cycles" in ruling on a grant of a Certificate of Need (CON) to an applicant. Then an applicant not in such a "batch," or without an established competitive treatment system, lacks "standing" to challenge another applicant.[90]

Laborers and employees. Provision of safe and sanitary working places and equipment for laborers and employees is required, both for nonprofit and business organizations alike. Licenses and permits attesting to the adequacy of facilities and the elimination of fire and machinery hazards, and the like, are required. Local boards of standards, labor departments, and other regulatory bodies supervise these matters in all the states, and on the municipal-government level.

Mailing privileges. Some nonprofit organizations are entitled to special low mailing rates. Inquire at your local post office. But note that the post office has cut down on the kinds of organizations entitled to "philanthropic organization rates." Humane organizations, for example, are being stripped of bulk-rate mail privileges. Title 39, Code of Federal Regulations, Section 134.5(b)(3) confines the lower rates to specified types of nonprofit organizations, while many types of organizations are expressly excluded from the rate privileges.

Maternity homes and hospitals. It is a misdeameanor, in most states, to operate a maternity home or a hospital without first obtaining a license from the appropriate department of health or hospital commission.[91]

Mental institutions. It is a misdeameanor, in most states, to operate a private institution for the care or treatment of persons with mental disorders or defects without first obtaining a license from the proper department of mental hygiene or hospital.[92]

Professional practice. Practice of the learned professions may not be carried on by organizations. Only licensed individuals may practice law, medicine, and the other such professions. The exceptions are administrative organizations. Their members, not they, practice the professions. But they must be licensed by the same authorities which license individuals to practice those professions.[93] Exceptions exist, if they may be called such, for charitable-service organizations such as legal aid societies, free medical clinics, and the like, although statutes require nonprofit optometric and pharmaceutical service corporations to be licensed.

Professional corporations or associations have been authorized by statutes in most states. The Ohio statute, for example,[94] refers to them as *professional associations*, and permits incorporation of legal, medical, and other professional partnerships.[95] This is typical of these new statutes. The purpose is to enable professional people to obtain the tax advantages open to business corporation officers and employees, such as pension and retirement-plan participation.[96] In other respects, the members of professional corporations organized under such statutes continue to be personally responsible to their clients, and subject to the usual rules as to professional ethics. In fact, the Ohio Supreme Court for a time held that lawyers may not utilize the statute, because only that court can license legal professional practice, and would not do so for corporations.[97]

Aside from the special tax-benefit purpose of such statutes, any unlicensed practice of the professions is illegal.[98] But practice of accounting as a business seems to be permissible in some states, and the same is true as to architecture in some states.[99]

In any event, the *professional associations* statutes refer to business, not non-profit, organization of professional firms.[100]

Professional Trade associations are often governed by administrative rules, especially those rules restricting the scope of licensure. If an administrative agency adopts a rule *de facto*, without promulgating the rule or formally adopting it as required by the Administrative Process Act, the rule is not subject to circuit court review under provisions in the Administrative Process Act. A *defacto rule* may be challenged in court only if there is unlawfulness of an agency case decision, concerning a named party, who is in violation of or in compliance with a licensing requirement.[101]

> *Delegation of licensing power.* Delegation of state licensing power to private organizations is unconstitutional. For example, a New Jersey statute governing medical service corporations required approval by the New Jersey Medical Society of the persons nominated as trustees, prior to their election. The court said that this requirement violated the state constitution, and "sets forth no standards or safeguards to protect against unfairness, arbitrariness, or favoritism, and is therefore void for lack of due process."[102]

> *Public welfare organizations and institutions.* Great latitude in establishing and enforcing license requirements for public welfare organizations usually is left to state social welfare boards or commissions. Such boards of commissions often have what amounts to limited legislative power. They always have considerable discretionary power in the administration of laws within their spheres of supervision.[103]

> *Schools.* Extensive licensing requirements apply to all educational organizations and to their personnel. Boards of education usually supervise on the state level, and sometimes also on the municipal level. In addition, college-level institutions sometimes are under state university supervision. Trade schools must, depending on the trades they tech, comply with other special requirements, such as those set by agriculture commissions or supervisors and by aviation and marine departments.[104]

"Standing" to Challenge Licensing Decisions

When nonprofit environmental organizations sue to set aside construction permits and easements for development, agency decisions are reviewed under the "arbitrary and capricious" standard of the Administrative Procedure Act. Thus, it is difficult to overthrow such decisions.[105]

An environmental nonprofit organization lacks standing to challenge the approval of an application to build residential units when the organization makes only generalized claims of harm, no different in kind or degree from the public at large.[106] However, Environmental associations have standing to challenge the delegation to one agency, as opposed to another, the right to issue permits if that delegation will lead to regulations with insufficient environmental safeguards.[107]

A nonprofit trade organization, consisting of more than 2000 representatives of the plastic industry, lacks standing to challenge a county law banning the use of certain plastics when it fails to demonstrate that its asserted interests are relevant to the organization's purposes.[108] But, Members of a nonprofit trade association may intervene in an action challenging National Discharge Elimination System (NPDES) permits where their permits are those challenged.[109]

Zoning

Residential Care Facilities

A statute that authorized placing (by developers) of group homes for mentally disabled persons in a residential single family subdivision is not valid use of police power of the state; it condemns (lowers value of) private homes without payment of compensation, because the group homes are multiinhabitant "commercial" buildings. [Presumably the placing of such a development by a nonprofit organization would not be "commercial," though it would lower property values.][110]

Prospective residents of a group home for recovering alcoholics and drug addicts can get a preliminary injunction to prevent a township from enforcing zoning ordinances that interfere with their occupancy of group homes, located in a single-family residential zone, if there is a likelihood that they will prevail in proving a violation of the Fair Housing Act based on the disparate-impact theory.[111]

A city violates the handicap provisions of the Fair Housing Act if it refuses to give zoning approval to homeowners, who seek to operate an adult foster care home for elderly disabled persons in single family residential areas, if the city could have reasonably accommodated the homeowners' proposal.[112]

Under the Fair Housing Act, a city may zone special safety standards for the protection of developmentally disabled persons different from those that apply to the general population for single-family home housing, as long as the protection is warranted by the unique and special needs of the disabled. However, an ordinance that is not individualized to particular kinds of disabilities and subjects disabled persons to standardless and unpredictable variance process violates the act.[113]

A statute directing that a state license office shall not license the establishing of a new *residential-care building* if it will cause overconcentration does not apply to granting (or refusal) of a special-use permit by a city for that same construction.[114]

The definition of "family" in a zoning ordinance often determines whether a *nonprofit group home* violates a single-family zoning restriction. There was no violation found where a Pennsylvania ordinance merely required that individuals live together and maintain a common household. There was no requirement, in the ordinance, that the individuals be related.[115]

A zoning commission cannot require that a foundation get a special exception before it uses two-family residences for HIV-infected persons. An injunction can be had in order to stay enforcement of such a zoning regulation.[116]

A church may use a former church personnel residence as an office for administration of domestic violence, crime victims, and community residence programs without violating a single-family residence zoning restriction. Such a use is a "church-nonprofit" use permitted under the zoning ordinance. Owners of adjacent property may not intervene in the Article 78 proceeding brought by the church if the question is one of law.[117]

The issue of whether a nonprofit children's home is a "one-family dwelling" cannot be presented initially to a board of zoning adjustment or a circuit court. The home must request that an administrative officer decide that issue, and then appeal that decision if necessary. If the home does not qualify as a "one-family dwelling," it must prove an "unnecessary hardship" to justify a zoning variance.[118]

When a city council was sued by a nonprofit property owner, who had been denied his application for a conditional use permit to build a rest home on his property, the court found the denial to be arbitrary and capricious. The county does not have immunity of its agents in actions for compensatory damages under §1983.[119]

A Mayor's statement, that a conditional use permit, issued for a homeless shelter, was valid based on a "consensus" of the city council, is a "land use decision" and is appealable.[120]

Child Care Facilities

A state-licensed child care facility that is to be operated by a charitable corporation is not exempt from county zoning law and zoning supervision. The charity is not a governmental unit, and thus not immune from local zoning regulations.[121]

Educational Facilities

Educational facilities are often exempt from local zoning regulations. A group residence, for elderly and mentally ill individuals, was recently held to have an exempted "educational purpose," despite the fact that it was residential, served the elderly, and used nontraditional curriculum.[122]

A state statute permitting reasonable municipal zoning of buildings of religious and educational institutions, as to dimensions and parking, does not extend to state land and/or governmentally operated functions such as a state college.[123]

Zoning Changes

A city council must take a hard look at the relevant and important environmental impacts of proposed zoning amendments. Otherwise, their determinations and zoning ordinances will be properly annulled.[124]

A landowner, who tried to change the use of his property from a nonprofit private social club to a public restaurant, was denied an occupancy permit by a zoning board because the proposed use was not a continuation of the prior nonconforming social club. The landowner had no vested right to use the premises as a restaurant.[125]

§143. APPROVAL OF ORGANIZATIONS, IN GENERAL

Formal organizations, such as corporations or limited partnerships, must obtain some sort of governmental approval to become legal entities separate from their component members. For a corporation, this approval is the acceptance-for-filing of its certificate of incorporation. It is given by the secretary of state (or equivalent officer) of the particular state, and is evidenced by delivery to the corporation, by his department of a receipt or certificate indicating such filing and acceptance.[126] For a limited partnership, a certificate of the filing of partnership articles serves the same purpose, and is delivered by the county clerk, clerk of the court, or other appointed official.

Nonprofit associations and corporations are subject to much more specialized approval requirements. They must obtain the ultimate approval of the secretary of state for their certificates of incorporation, just as business corporations must. But this is not all.

A nonprofit organization rarely may commence lawful activity until it obtains certain specific approvals. Requirements for these approvals are statutory and vary from state to state. The principal types and categories of approvals and approving agencies are set forth in the sections that follow.

Tax exemption approval: See chapters on taxation. See pamphlet: "How to Apply for Recognition of Exemption of an Organization." [U.S. Treas. Dept., IRS Publication 557 current issue.]

§144. BASIC APPROVAL OF NONPROFIT ORGANIZATIONS

Ultimate approval of the formation of a nonprofit organization is the final filing of its charter or articles of association, as described in the foregoing section. But this document may not lawfully be filed unless it bears on its face, or annexed to it, the required certificate or certificates of preliminary approval.[127]

The fundamental preliminary approval, in some states, is that of a judge of the state's superior or supreme court. In some states it is that of the commissioner of institutions and agencies.[128]

Such approval *must* be annexed to the charter of a nonprofit organization. Other preliminary approvals may also be required.[129]

For an organization chartered by special act of a legislature, these approvals, are, of course, not necessary.

In practice, the charter is prepared, and to it is attached a blank form of approval (see Form below). It is submitted to a judge of the state's supreme or superior court. In the large cities, the courts have special divisions (or special "terms") for the submission of such charters. In most states mere filing of a copy in the local Recorder's Office is required (*e.g.*, in North Carolina).[130]

Submission must be in the county where the organization's home office will be.

The judge's clerk usually will suggest changes in the charter if he believes them advisable to make the charter acceptable to the judge. The clerk knows the particular judge's preference and prejudices. It is good policy to follow his suggestions.

FORM NO. 16
Approval by Judge

The foregoing (annexed) Certificate of Incorporation of the (name of organization) is hereby approved.

Dated: . . . . day of . . . . . . , 19 . .   . .

State of . . . .   Judge of the Supreme Court

County of . . . . Judicial District

In a few states, submission of the charter to a special investigating and supervisory agency (*e.g.*, The New Jersey Department of Institutions and Agencies) takes the place of submission to a judge. Submission for such approval follows the preliminary filing of the charter with the clerk of the county in which the home office of the organization is to be located.[131]

§145. SPECIAL APPROVALS

In most states there is no single general approving agency like the New Jersey Department of Institutions and Agencies. Approval by a judge is sometimes the preliminary general approval. But *additional* approvals by agencies often are required for certain organizations and activities.[132]

The typical breakdown of state approving agencies is shown in the list below. Titles vary from state to state. Equivalent local titles should be substituted. It should be noted that some state statutes designate private organizations as approving agencies. [See second section in this chapter.]

Abandoned children. Department of social welfare.

Asylums or homes. Department of social welfare.

Cemetery associations. Cemetery board of commission, the clerk of the county where the cemetery is to be situated, and the city, town, or village where any part of the cemetery may lie. All three approvals are required.

Child-care (placing or boarding out). Department of social welfare.

Churches, synagogues, and parishes. Official consent of the bishop of the diocese (or equivalent) is often required.

Clinics. Department of hospitals or department of social welfare.

College. Superintendent or commissioner of education and/or (in some states) state Regents or university. Also, for denominational institutions, denominational authorities.

County professional societies. State professional societies.

Cruelty prevention. State Society for Prevention of Cruelty to Children, or Prevention of Cruelty to Animals.

Delinquents. Department of social welfare.

Destitute persons. Department of social welfare.

Dispensaries. Department of hospitals or department of social welfare.

Educational purposes. Board or department of education, and/or of Regents. Also other appropriate authorities, such as the Civil Aeronautics Authority for air pilot schools.

Existing society, club, league, association. Parent organization's executive body, pursuant to its bylaws or charter.

Fire department. Fire commission of the fire district. The city, town, or village must also approve unless the fire commission is its agency.

Hospital expense groups. Superintendent of insurance and department of social welfare. Both must approve.

Hospitals. Department of hospitals or department of social welfare.

Labor organizations. Labor department or board of standards.

Legal aid society. State appellate court, Dept. of Legal Affairs, or Department of State.[133]

Libraries. Department of education.

Medical expense indemnity groups. Superintendent of insurance and department of social welfare. Both must approve.

Mental illness care. Commissioner of mental hygiene or (in some states) department of hospitals; and department of social welfare. Both approvals are required.

Military organization aid groups. Adjutant General.

Monuments and memorials. Public authorities of the city, town, or village, if public property is to be used.

Neglected children. Department of social welfare.

Political party organizations. Chairman of county committee of the particular political party. (If he unreasonably withholds his approval, the superior court may order it dispensed with).

Religious organizations. Diocesan, synod, bishopric, or like approval is required for official "branch" organization.

Schools. Superintendent or commissioner of education and/or (in some states) board of regents or state university.

Trade associations. Parent association's executive officers, pursuant to the parent constitution or bylaws. Such approval is not required for local or separate associations.

Workers' organizations. Labor department or board of standards.

YMCA or YWCA. State YMCA or YWCA executive committee.

How to Apply for Tax Exemption

[See Chapter 9, especially Section 97.]
[See Prentice Hall, *Tax-Exempt Organizations,* esp. Par. 7021 (current service).]
The Department of The Treasury prints a booklet entitled "How to Apply for Recognition of Exemption for an Organization." It can be obtained free of charge at any local IRS office or by writing to the Commissioner of Internal Revenue, Washington, D.C. 20224.

§146. AUTHORITY TO SOLICIT CONTRIBUTIONS

[See Chapter 8 and the chapter on Fund Raising.]
Solicitation of funds ordinarily may not be carried on without special authorization, which is implied by the state's acceptance of a character of a charitable organization. Tax exemption by the Internal Revenue Service, of course, also implies authorization to solicit contributions. Although many charters expressly permit the accepting of gifts to the corporation, they also should specifically authorize solicitation of contributions to the corporation.[134]

Statutory rules governing the solicitation of charitable funds have been enacted in a number of states. Florida's "Charitable Funds Act" provided a good example.[135] It even stated that more stringent local provisions were not to be overridden (preempted) by the state statute. But this statute was repealed,[136] effective July 1, 1982. Instead, specific empowering provisions for specific kinds of organizations were enacted; for example, revisions of rules for nursing homes, adult care centers, and hospices; all scheduled to expire on October 1, 1993.[137] Deregulation of solicitors in Florida failed miserably. In response, the legislature passed the new "Solicitation of Contributions Act," effective in 1991, and found in Chapter 496 of the Florida Statutes.

A statute governing solicitation of funds for charitable organizations is a valid exercise of state "police powers."[138]

Fund-Raising Costs: About 35 states have statutes requiring a stated proportion of money raised to go directly to charity (*e.g.*, staff salaries and solicitation expenses are *not* charity). But in 1980, in an 8-to-1 decision, the U.S. Supreme Court held such a village ordinance (requiring 75 percent to go to charity) to be unconstitutional interference with freedom of speech (too broad).[139] But *registration* requirements are upheld.

Municipal Ordinances: Jacksonville, Fla. Ordinance Ch. 404, requiring registration with the consumer affairs officer before soliciting contributions on selling articles (*i.e.*, a *Permit*) is constitutional.[140] Similar Los Angeles, Calif. ordinance is valid exercise of the "police power."[141]

Unincorporated associations have special difficulty in accepting property. This is because the unincorporated association may be deemed not an entity able to hold and pass title. Property then must be held by a trustee or trustees—a most convenient method.[142]

Unauthorized soliciting of alms falls into the category of begging. Begging in a public place is disorderly conduct.[143]

Authority for a nonprofit organization to solicit for its proper purposes usually is stated as a power in the certificate of incorporation. Approval of the charter by the proper authorities constitutes approval of this power. The final seal of approval is found in the acceptance and filing of the charter by the secretary of state, and in some places in local ordinances.[144]

A provision for soliciting contributions will lead to a charter's being closely scrutinized before it is approved. The practice sometimes is to require an affidavit as to the character and background of each of the incorporators. Many states investigate the incorporators. Some authorities are most reluctant to approve a charter containing such a power.

In some states, such as Ohio (but see the 1980 Supreme Court decision above at note[145]) there are specific statutory provisions as to solicitation of charitable contributions.[146] It is interesting to note that the Ohio statute as enacted only in 1955.[147] Such statutes usually apply only to solicitations of funds that may exceed a stated sum. (*e.g.*, $25,000 or $50,000 per year, or when solicitation expenses will be small); usually exempt certain types of organizations such as church, or degree-granting college, or other special institutions; usually require annual statements to be filed; usually require registration of professional fund raising solicitors; usually bar certain (*e.g.*, political) action; and usually exempt some types of organizations.[148]

Typically, such statutes are short and vague. The Ohio statute, for example, provides only nine sections, none lengthy: (1) definitions, (2) registrations of solicitors, (3) exemptions, (4) annual financial reports, (5) professional fund raisers, (6) contracts with fund raisers, (7) professional solicitors, (8) omitted, (9) penalties for violations.[149] The Massachusetts act is similar.[150] Case annotations to these statutes seem to be surprisingly sparse. Violations of the

statutes usually are punishable by up to $500 fine or six months imprison-
ment—hardly enough to scare off a bold racket operator.

Action by the state's attorney general, to protect the public against fraudulent solicitations or sales or contracts by nonprofit organizations (domestic or
foreign) also are provided for in some statutes, such as that of New York.[151]

Capital contributions in financing of nonprofit "business corporations"—
as in the New York statute's provisions—involve a special problem. This is the
question of honest valuation of such contributions of property or services. The
statute provides that, "In the absence of fraud in the transaction, the judgement of the board as to the value of the consideration received by the corporation[152] (for the capital certificate[153] given to it) shall be conclusive."[154]

Local statutes to control abuses of fund raising seem to be the main trend
in recent years, plus the rather doubtfully effective regulation by the Federal
Trade Commission, Post Office Department, and the like. Abuses have been a
problem for many years, and continue to be.[155]

Securities Issues: S.E.C. supervision generally applies to "securities issues,"
including those of nonprofit organizations. As to what is a *security*, works on
corporation law must be consulted. Exemptions from registration mainly are
certain ones granted by the Securities Acts to charitable and benevolent and
educational and the like organizations, "private offerings," and intrastate offerings. This subject is too complex for treatment here.[156] [See the chapter on
Finance Management.]

Prevention of Abuses and Swindles: See, in Chapters 1, 2, herein, a discussion of statistics on abuses, and citations of studies of them.

Fund-raising today is a business in itself. Individual experts and professional fund-raising advisory organizations are found in many large cities. They
are listed in local telephone directories under such classifications as "fund raising organizations" and "public relations consultants."

Payment of a high percentage of collections obtained to fund raising
experts or organizations should be avoided if possible. Such an arrangement
suggests abuse of privilege. It often is attacked as an abuse of public generosity, especially if the percentage retained by the professional fund raiser is very
high.

Most fund raising organizations require a minimum flat fee, plus a small
percentage of contributions obtained. If the percentage is reasonably low, such
an arrangement is proper and effective.

Experience has shown that least criticism and best results come from the
use of a trained, full-time, fund-raising expert as a member of the staff of the
charitable organization, on a regular salary basis.

Binding effect of promise to contribute: [See Chapters 8 and 11.]

Management Responsibility: It must be remembered, in analysis of "authority" of a nonprofit corporation (to solicit funds or to do other things), that
directors may be held personally liable for breach of fiduciary duties if they act
in bad faith.[157]

Tax "Substitutes." In some states (*e.g.*, North Carolina) instead of the complex problems of taxes and exemptions, small specific fees are charged by the state for such licensing as that for vehicles owned by orphanages or fire departments or associations and a church or Sunday school bus, or Red Cross disaster vehicles.[158]

POINTS TO REMEMBER

- Consider in advance the probable licenses that will be needed.

- Know that when a license is required, it is illegal to carry out the activity before a license is granted.

- Remember that fine or imprisonment may result from a violation of a licensing law.

- Get all possible license and permit information in advance.

- When in doubt, ask the local license office.

- Use directories and other such sources of information.

- Remember, the usual license requirements apply to nonprofit organizations as well as to business organizations—plus some special requirements.

- Find out what approvals are required for your type of organization. Do not be surprised to find that two or even three separate approvals are required.

- Avoid the use of political influence in getting approvals. Approvals granted "on the merits" will stand up later, if questioned.

- Draft your charter with blank forms, ready for signature by the required approving authorities.

- Do not include a power to solicit contributions, unless it is necessary.

- If power to solicit contribution, is included, expect very sharp scrutiny of your charter. Prepare for it: attach affidavits giving, in capsule form, the personal background of each incorporator.

NOTES TO CHAPTER 13

1. ABA Model Nonprofit Corp. Act, Revision Exposure Draft (Mar. 1986) §1.02.

2. 17 U.S. (4 Wheat) 518 (1819).

3. Official Comment to Model Act Revision §1.02, above n.l.

4. Model Act §1.26.

5. So. Car. Code, tit. 33 §31-60.

6. Federal Election Comm. v. Mass. Citizens for Life, Inc., 769 F.2d 13 (1st Cir., 1985). An agricultural society may not be required to file reports as a "charity," when organized for benefits to its members. Attorney General v. Brockton Agric. Society, 509 N.E. 2d 1198 (Mass. 19870; also Weymouth Agr. & I. Soc., p. 1193.

7. Fla. Stat. §733.212 (1992). *See also* Fla. Stat §732.5165.

8. Arthritis Foundation v. Beisse, 456 S.2d 954 (Fla. 4th D.C.App., 1984); Taylor v. Payne, 17 S.2d615 (Fla. 1944), app. dism. 65 S.Ct. 49; reh. den. 65 S.Ct. 113,89 L.Ed. 647 (1944).

9. Wilcox v. Safley, 766 S.W.2d 12 (AR 1989).

10. Earnhart v. Dir. of Ill. Dept. of Rev., 548 N.E. 2d 81 (Ill. App. 1989).

11. U.S. v. Hurst, 951 F.2d 1490 (6th Cir. 1991).

12. Kentucky Ass'n of Realtors, Inc. v. Musselman, 817 S.W. 2d 213 (Ky. 1991).

13. Clem v. Christole, Inc., 582 N.E. 2d 780 (Ind. 1991).

14. Michigan Council 25 American Federation of State, County and Mun. Employees (AFSCME) v. Louisiana Homes, Inc., 480 N.W. 2d 280 (Mich. App. 1991).

15. See: Joan Oleck, The Battle of Iowa, 91 RB (Restaurant Business magazine) 78 (Aug. 10, 1992); how Iowa adopted the most restrictive law on franchising (licensing), in a fast-food restaurants dispute. Address (for this, and for Franchising Report 1992) 355 Park Ave. So., New York, NY 10010.

16. Pershing Industries, Inc. v. Department of Banking and Finance, 591 So. 2d 991 (Fla. App. 1 Dist. 1991).

17. K & K Enterprises, Inc. v. Pennsylvania Liquor Control Bd., 602 A.2d 476 (Pa. Cmwlth. 1992).

18. Ballentine's Law Dictionary 736 (3d ed. 1969); Black's Law Dictionary 829 (5th ed. 1979); and see, as to the limitations of the "license" implied by the approval of articles of incorporation: H. Oleck, Remedies for Abuses of Corporate Status, 9 Wake Forest L. Rev. 463 (1973).

19. Ohio Academy of Chiropractic Physicians v. State Board, 508 N.E.2d 1013 (Ohio App. 1986).

20. Wickman v. Firestone, 500 So. 2d 740 (Fla. App. 4th Dist., 1987).

21. Cooper v. Illinois Dept. of Children and Family Services, 599 N.E. 2d 537 (Ill. App. 4 Dist., 1992).

22. H. Oleck, Trends in Nonprofit Corporation Law, 10 Akr. L. Rev. 71, at 79 (1976); Friedman, State Administration of Charities, 19 Clev. St. L. Rev. 273 (1970); Zeitzheim, Refusal of Charter of Nonprofit Corporation, 15 Clev.-Mar. L. Rev. 162 (1966); H. Oleck, Nature of Nonprofit Organizations in 1979, 10 Toledo L. Rev. 962 (1979).

23. State ex rel. Biscayne Kennel Club v. Stein, 130 Fla. 517, 178 S. 133, 135 (1938); Palm Springs Turf Club v. California Horse Racing Board, 155 Cal. App. 2d 242, 317 P.2d 713 (1957).

24. Garford Trucking v. Hoffman, 114 N.J.L. 522, 177 A. 882, 887 (1935). But see Jordan v. United Ins. Co. of Amer., 289 F.2d 778 (C.A.D.C. 1961). A license to occupy a city stall is property: In re Enrich, 101 F. 231 (D.C. Pa. 1900).

25. Rosenblatt v. California State Board of Pharmacy, 67 Cal. App. 2d 69, 158 P.2d 199, 203 (1945); State ex rel. 12501 Superior Corp. v. City of East Cleveland, 158 N.E.2d 565 (Ohio 1959).

26. Asbury Hospital v. Cass County, 22 No. Dak. 359, 7 N.W.2d 438, 452 (1943).

27. City of N.Y. v. American School Publications, 509 N.E. 2d 311 (N.Y. 1987), citing Metromedia, Inc. v. City of San Diego, 101 S. Ct. 2882, 2889, 69 L. Ed. 2d 800. And see below, N. 21 and 21a; and see State v. Kabayama, 94 N.J. Sup. 78, 226 A.2d 760, 763 (1967); and see above, H. Oleck, articles at n.18, 22.

28. E.g., see, Conard v. State, 2 Terry (Del.) 107, 16 A.2d 121, 125 (1940); Bogert, State Supervision of Charities, 52 Mich. L. Rev. 639 (1954); Elway, Michigan Licensing Boards, 41 U. Detroit L. J. 347 (1964); Gray, State Attorney General, Guardian of Public Charities, p.597, 14 Clev.-Mar. L. Rev. 236 (1965); Fla. Stat. 400.623 (adultfoster homes); Fla. Stat. 400.614 (nursing homes); Fla. Stat. 402.305, 402.319 (childcare facilities).

29. See, 5 U.S.C. §§551-701; and, Note, Procedural Safeguards for Licenses: Section 9(B) of the APA, 75 Harv. L. Rev. 383 (1961); D.A. Wallace, Occupational Licensing and Certification, Remedies for Denial, 14 Will. & Mary L. Rev. 46 (1972); W. Gellhorn, Abuses of Occupational Licensing, 44 Chi. L. Rev. 6 (1976).

30. Report of the Admin. Law Comm. to the Governor and General Assembly of Ohio, pp. 8–9 (Dec. 13, 1942).

31. Ohio Laws 358 (1943-4); Ohio Laws 578 (1945-6); etc.; Ohio Rev. Code §119.01 et seq.

32. See, Giles, Licensing, and Administrative Procedure Acts, 6 Clev.-Mar. L. Rev. 301 (1957); Note, a Survey of Principal Procedural Elements. . . , 22 Clev. St. L. Rev. 281 (1973). See, Fla. St., c. 120.

33. See, City of Tampa v. Islands Four, Inc., 364 S.2d 738 (Fla. App. 1978) (dance-hall license). A village ordinance requiring licenses for door-to-door solicitations by commercial organizations, but not by political or charitable or religious ones, violates the equal protection clause of the constitution. Chicago Tribune Co. v. Village of Downers Grove, 508 N.E. 2d 439 (Ill. App., 2d Dist., 1987).

34. Trustees of Boston Univ. v. Licensing Board of Boston, 510 N.E. 2d 283 (Mass. App. Ct. 1987). And see, above, n. 27.

35. First Hospital Corp. v. Dept. of H. & R.S., 566 So. 2d 917 (Fla. 1st DCA, 1990).

36. Grace Bible Fellowship, Inc. v. Maine School Administrative Dist. No. 5, 941 F.2d 45 (1st Cir. (Me.), 1991).

37. N.Y. State Assn. of Career Schools v. State Educ. Dept., 749 F. Supp. 1264 (D.C., N.Y., 1990).

38. Stonewall Union v. City of Columbus, 931 F.2d 1130 (6th Cir. (Ohio), 1991).

39. Forsyth County, Ga. v. Nationalist Movement, 112 S. Ct. 2395 (U.S. Ga., 1992).

40. Moore v. California State Bd. of Accountancy, 9 Cal. Rptr. 2d 358 (Cal., 1992).

41. Greenpeace, U.S.A. v. City of Glendale, 4 Cal. Rptr. 2d 672 Cal. App. 2 Dist. 1992).

42. Church of Scientology Flag Services Orgn., Inc. v. City of Clearwater, 756 F. Supp. 1498 (D.C. Fla., 1991).

43. Needham Pastoral Counseling Center, Inc. v. Board of Appeals of Needham, 29 Mass. App. Ct. 31, 557 N.E.2d 43 (1990).

44. Cochise County v. Broken Arrow Baptist Church, 161 Ariz. 406, 778 P.2d 1302 (Ariz. Ct. App. 1989).

45. Church of Jesus Christ of Latter-Day Saints v. Jefferson County, 741 F. Supp. 1522 (N.D. Ala. 1989).

46. Our Saviour's Evangelical Lutheran Church v. City of Naperville, 542 N.E. 2d 458 (Ill. App. 1989).

47. Christian Gospel Church, Inc. v. City of San Francisco, 896 F.2d 1221 (9th Cir. 1990).

48. Bethel Evangelical Lutheran Church v. Village of Morton, 201 Ill. App. 3d 858, 559 N.E.2d 533 (1990).

49. Our Savior's Evangelical Lutheran Church of Naperville v. City of Naperville, 186 Ill. App. 3d 988, 542 N.E.2d 1158 (1989).

50. Ex parte Fairhope Bd. of Adjustment and Appeals, 567 So. 2d 1353 (Ala. 1990).

51. Cohen v. City of Des Plaines, 742 F. Supp. 458 (N.D. Ill. 1990) (classification failed rational basis test).

52. Rector of Saint Bartholomew's Church v. City of New York, 914 F.2d 348 (2d Cir. 1990), cert. denied, Committee to Oppose Sale v. Rector, 111 S. Ct. 1103 (1991).

53. Vermont Baptist Corp. v. Burlington Zoning Bd., 613 A.2d 710 (Vt., 1992).

54. Neddermeyer v. Town of Ontario Planning Bd., 155 A.D.2d 908, 548 N.Y.S.2d 951 (N.Y. App. Div. 1989).

55. Harrison Orthodox Minyan, Inc. v. Town Bd. of Harrison, 159 A.D.2d 572, 552 N.Y.S.2d 434 (N.Y. App. Div. 1990).

56. Orthodox Minyan of Elkins Park v. Cheltenham Township Zoning Hearing Bd., 123 Pa. Commw. 29, 552 A.2d 772 (1989).

57. Burlington Assembly of God Church v. Zoning Bd. of Adjustment of Florence, 238 N.J. Super. 634, 570 A.2d 495 (1989).

58. For example: official U.S. Congressional Directory (printed annually) obtainable from Office of Congressional Directory, U.S. Capitol, Washington 25, D.C., or from Superintendent of Documents, U.S. Gov't. Printing Office, Washington 25, D.C.; official N.Y. Red Book (printed annually) (William Press, Inc., Albany, N.Y.).

59. There is also a U.S. Dept. of Commerce Directory of National Associations, but it is not brought up to date often enough. In 1913 the Department began to publish such directories, and the 1949 issue was only the 13th revision. Published by U.S. Govt. Printing Office, Washington 25, D.C.; $3.75 (buckram).

60. Published by the Foundation Center, New York, and Columbia University Press.

61. Tax-Exempt Foundations and Charitable Trusts: Their Impact on Our Economy (Chairman's Report to the Select Committee on Small Business, House of Representatives, 87th Congress), p. V (Dec. 31, 1962; U.S. Govt. Printing Office, Washington 25, D.C.).

62. N.J. St. Ann. §40:52-1; N.Y Genl. Bus. L. §§167–169(repealed 1983).

63. Easter House, Inc. v. Dept. of Children & Youth Services, 573 A.2d 304 (Ct. Sup. Ct., 1990).

64. See, Aurora Country Club v. Dept. of Revenue, 365 N.E.2d 224 (Ill. App. 1977); N.Y. Tax L., §424(1)f, and see, Collier v. State, 54 Ga. App. 346, 187 S.E. 843, 845 (1936). Sale of food or drink at social clubs is not exempt from retailers' occupation tax. Women's Athletic Club of Chicago v. Isaacs, 30 Ill.2d 207, 195 N.E.2d 647 (1964).

65. Fla. St. §561.422.

66. Fla. St. §413.051; N.Y. Genl. City L. §10; Ohio Rev. Code §3304.29.

67. See, McAdams, v. Windham, 208 Ala. 492, 94 S. 743 (1922); 47 A.L.R. 1092; N.Y. Unconsol. L.C. 7 §§5–8, 11, 15, 27 licenses, and see, N.Y. Penal L. §482 (1951) repealed by L. 1965 c. 1046 §2 (eff. 1967); and, Mich. Comp. L. Ann. §331.430 [see current supp. in each statute.]

68. N.Y. Vill. L. §7-734, 6.

69. E.g., N.Y. Ins. L., §§41(1), 45,466 (1 b,c,e).

70. National Federation of Retired Persons v. Insurance Com'r, 838 P.2d 680 (Wash., 1992).

71. E.g., N.Y. Soc. Services L. §390; N.Y. Soc. Welfare L. §390; Ohio Rev. Code, c. 5104.

72. People ex rel. Johnson v. Kulle, 557 N.E. 2d 488 (Ill. App. 1990).

73. Board of Child Care of Baltimore A.C. etc. v. Harker (MD app., July 28, 1989).

74. Holmes Constant Care Center v. Com., Dept. of Public Welfare, 555 A.2d 282 (PA Commwlth., 1989).

75. U.S. Dist. Ct. Jacksonville, FL, Judge John H. Moore II ruling (based on a 1987 Supreme Court decision) (May 24, 1989, reported in St. Petersburg (FL) Times (p. 2B) May 25, 1989. Cf. People ex rel. Johnson v. Kulle, 557 N.E. 2d 488 (Ill. App. 1990).

76. E.g., N.Y. Coop. Corp. L., §77; see Contra, Ill. Stat. ch. 805 §310/5.

77. See, Hospital Accreditation References (Amer. Hosp. Assn., current ed.); c.f., Group Health Insur. of N.J. v. Howell, 40 N.J. 436, 193 A.2d 103 (1963); Fla. St. ch. 395.

78. E.g., N.Y. Agric. & Mark. L., §290.

79. D. DeWitt and D. Olinger (article), St. Petersburg (FL) Times, p. A1 (April 12, 1992).

80. American Coin Machines, Inc. v. Atiyeh, 577 So. 2d 234 (La. App. 1 Cir., 1991).

81. In re Bingo License of New Day Tabernacle, 801 P.2d 742 (Okla. App. 1990).

82. State ex rel. Stephan v. Finney, 836 P.2d 1169 (Kan. 1992).

83. See, n. 71; N.Y. Publ. Health L., §§2570–2575 (childrens' institutions); and 504, 505a. (animals for scientific tests).

84. Rainbow Beach Ass'n Inc. v. New York State Dept. of Health, 590 N.Y.S. 2d 561 (N.Y.A.D. 3 Dept., 1992).

85. Board of Sup'rs of Fairfax County v. Group Health Ass'n, Inc., 114 S.E. 2d 602 (Va. 1992).

86. Central Florida Regional Hosp., Inc. v. Department of Health and Rehabilitative Services, 582 So. 2d 1193 (Fla. 5th DCA 1991).

87. Fairfax Surgical Center, Inc. v. State Health Com'r, 405 S.E. 2d 430 (Va. App., 1991).

88. Brookwood-Jackson County Convalescent Center v. Department of Health and Rehabilitative Services, 591 So. 2d 1085 (Fla. App. 1 Dist. 1992).

89. Appeal of Salem Regional Medical Center, 590 A.2d 602 (N.H. 1991).

90. First Hospital Corp. v. Dept. of Health & R. Services, 566 So. 2d 917 (Fla. 1st DCA, 1990); Charter Hospital v. Dept. of H. & R.S., 563 So. 2d 181 (Fla. 1st DCA, 1990).

91. E.g., Fla. Stat. ch. 383 (Maternity and Infancy Hygiene).

92. N.Y. Mental Hyg. L. §§9.01-9.17; Calif. Health and Safety Code §§1290; Fla. Stat. §394.875.

93. See, Anno. 91 A.L.R. 173; N.Y. Ed. L. §§7002, 7004; Rockett v. Texas State Board of Med. Examiners, 287, S.W.2d 190 (Tex. Civ. App. 1956) gives a comprehensive list of A.L.R. annotations and case citations on governance of licensing of professions and professional activities. See also, Law profession: Florida Bar v. Town, 174 S.2d 395 (Fla. 1965); Florida Bar v. Arango, 461 S.2d 932 (Fla. 1984); Smith v. Illinois Adjustment Finance Co., 326 Ill. App. 654, 63 N.E.2d 264 (1945); N.J. Stat. Anno. §2A: 170–178; Medicine (hospitals): Godfrey v. Medical Society, 177 A.D. 684, 164 N.Y.S. 846 (1917); and see, pamphlet, Incorporation, Taxation and Licensing of Hospitals in the U.S. (Amer. Hosp. Assoc., current ed.); Dentistry: Basford v. Department, 390 IU. 601, 62 N.E.2d 462 (1945); Pharmacy: Ohio atty. genl. Opinions (1937) No. 225; Podiatry: N.Y. Ed. L. §§7002, 7004; Optometry: State ex rel. Sisemore v. Standard Optical Co., 187 Ore. 452, 188, P.2d 309 (1947); Kelley v. Duling Enterprises, Inc., 172 N.W.2d 727 (So. Dak. 1969); but compare, Scadron's Sons, Inc. v. Susskind, 132 (N.Y.) Misc. 406, 229 N.Y.S. 209 (1928).

94. Ohio Rev. Code, c. 1785.

95. Associations should be viewed as corporations. O'Neill v. U.S., 14 (Ohio) Misc. 61, 281 F. Supp. 359 (1968) (e.g., for corporate income tax purposes).

96. Physicians may incorporate, to practice as a group. Cleveland Clinic v. Sombrio, 6 (Ohio) Misc. 48 (1966).

97. State ex rel. Green v. Brown, Secretary of State, 173 Ohio 114, 180 N.E.2d 157 (1962) 2 cases. See Jones, Should Lawyers Incorporate?, 11 Hastings L. J. 50 (1959); Wormser, A Plea for Professional Incorporation Laws, 46 A.B.A.J. 755 (1960); Dunkel, Professional Corporations, 22 Ohio St. L. J. 703 (1961); Vesely, The Ohio Professional Assn. Law, 13 W.R.U. Law Rev. 195 (1962); Stavole, Corporate Employee Tax Status for the Professional Man, 11 Clev.-Mar. L. Rev., 176 (1962). But see, 4 A.L.R.3d 383, Practice by Attorneys and Corporate Entities Under Professional Corporation Statutes.

98. See, N.Y. State Optometric Assn. v. Whelan, 389 N.Y.S.2d 161 (1976); and Rockett case, above n.93; and 91 A.L.R. 173, 102 A.L.R. 343.

99. See, as to accounting: Calif. Bus. and Prof. Code §§5033, 5034; Ga. Code Ann. 43-3-23; Ill. Rev. St. c. 225-450/17.1; Iowa Code §§116.2, 116.3; Mich. St. Ann. §339.705; Mo. Rev. St. §326.021; N.C. Gen. St. §93A-6; and see as to architecture; Ark. Stat. 17-14-301; Folsom v. Summer, Locateli & Co., 90 Ga. App. 696, 83 S.E.2d 855 (1954); 225 ILCS 305/11 et. seq.

100. E.g., see, Ohio Rev. Code c. 1785; O'Neill v. U.S., 14 Ohio Misc. 61,281 F.Supp. 359 (1968).

101. Virginia Bd. of Medicine v. Virginia Physical Therapy Ass'n, 413 S.E. 2d 59 (Va. App. 1991).

102. Group Health Insur. of N.J. v. Howell, 40 N.J. 436, 193 A.2d 103 (1963); and see, Kugler v. Yocum, 71 Calif. Rptr. 687 445 P.2d at 306 (Supr. Ct. 1968) and cases cited therein. On the question of self-regulation see, S. Wex, Natural Justice and Self-Regulating Associations, 18 McGill L.J. 262 (1972).

103. E.g., see, Butel, Law Making by Professional and Trade Associations, 34 Nebr. L. Rev. 431 (1955); and, N.Y. Soc. Services L. §§2(9), 20, 56.

104. See, for example, N.Y. Educ. L., §5001 et seq.; and typical provisions in (pamphlets): Association of American Law Schools Articles and Standards (adopted Dec. 30, 1962, as amended to date); and Standards of the American Bar Assn. for Law Schools (publ. 1957 and completely revised in 1973).

105. See e.g., Holy Cross Wilderness Fund v. Madigan, 960 F.2d 1515 (10th Cir. (Colo.), 1992).

106. Otsego 2000, Inc. v. Planning Bd. of the Town of Otsego, 575 N.Y.S. 2d 584 (N.Y.A.D. 3 Dept. 1991).

107. Friends of Crystal River v. U.S. E.P.A., 794 F. Supp. 674 (W.D. Mich., 1992).

108. Society of Plastics Indus., Inc. v. County of Suffolk, 573 N.E.2d 1034 (N.Y. 1991).

109. Dioxin/Organochlorine Center v. Washington State Dept. of Ecology, 837 P.2d 1007 (Wash., 1992).

110. Clem v. Christole, Inc., 548 N.E. 2d 1180 (Ind. App. 1990).

111. Oxford House, Inc. v. Township of Cherry Hill, 799 F. Supp. 450 (D.N.J., 1992).

112. U.S. v. City of Taylor, Mich., 798 F. Supp. 442 (E.D. Mich., 1992).

113. Marbrunak, Inc. v. City of Stow, Ohio, 974 F. 2d 43 (6th Cir. (Ohio), 1992).

114. Centinela Hospital Assn. v. City of Inglewood, 275 Calif. Rptr. 901 (App. 1990).

115. Human Services Consultants, Inc. v. Zoning Hearing Bd. of Butler Tp., 587 A.2d 40 (Pa. Cmwlth. 1991).

116. Steward B. McKinney Foundation, Inc. v. Town Plan and Zoning Com'n of Town of Fairfield, 790 F. Supp. 1197 (D. Conn., 1992).

117. Catholic Charities of Roman Catholic Diocese of Syracuse v. Zoning Bd. of Appeals of City of Norwich, 590 N.Y.S. 2d 918 (N.Y.A.D. 3 Dept., 1992).

118. Bedgood v. United Methodist Children's Home, 598 So. 2d 988 (Ala. Civ. App. 1992).

119. Lutheran Day Care v. Snohomish County, 829 P.2d 746 (Wash. 1992), overruling, Collins v. King Cy., 742 P.2d 185 (Wash. App. 1987).

120. Weeks v. City of Tillamook, 832 P.2d 1246 (Or. App., 1992).

121. Board of Child Care of Baltimore A.C., etc. v. Harker; Md. App., July 28, 1989.

122. Campbell v. City Council of Lynn, 586 N.E. 2d 1009 (Mass. App. Ct. 1992).

123. Inspector of Buildings of Salem v. Salem State College, 546 N.E. 2d 388 (Mass. App. Ct., 1989).

124. Save the Pine Bush Inc. v. Common Council of City of Albany, 591 N.Y.S. 2d 897 (N.Y.A.D. 3 Dept., 1992).

125. Limey v. Zoning Hearing Bd. of Port Vue Borough, 601 A.2d 433 (Pa. Cmwlth. 1991).

126. E.g., see, Fla. St. §617.0203 that endorsement of approval by the Department of State, with time and date, on the original articles, when payment of filing fee was also made, shall "constitute" the corporation.

127. N.Y. Not-for-Profit Corp. L. §404; and see, In re Boy Explorers of America, 67 N.Y.S.2d 108 (1946). Such approval is judicial rather than a ministerial act. In re Policyholders Information Office of N.Y., Inc. 23 (N.Y.) Misc.2d 1093, 206 N.Y.S.2d 897 (1960); Application of International Sports Foundation, Inc., 24 (N.Y.) Misc.2d 23, 203 N.Y.S.2d 399 (1960).

128. See above, n. 127, and N.J. Rev. Stat., tit. 15 (sections that deal with the Department of Institutions and Agencies). In New York it is a Justice of the Supreme Court who must approve in some cases. N.Y. Not-for-Profit Corp. L. §404.

129. Ibid.

130. The Office of the Secretary of State. Gen. Stat. No. Car. §55A-4.

131. N.J. Rev. Stat., tit. 15, cited above in n. 128, in the sections dealing with county clerks' functions.

132. N.Y. Not-for-Profit Corp. L. §404, specifies a number of such agencies for various specific kinds of organizations. And see, for example: (political approvals) In re Independent Republican Club, 58 N.Y.S.2d 162 (1945); (conflicting names) In re Gold Star Parents Assn., 67 N.Y.S.2d 73 (1946); (para-military organization) In re Long Beach Defense Guards, 100 (N.Y.) Misc. 584, 166 N.Y.S. 459 (1917); (medical work that requires approval by the commissioner of education) Association for Psychoanalysis v. Simon, 21 A.D.2d 209, 250 N.Y.S.2d 253 (1964).

133. Young Lords Party v. Supreme Court of N.Y. [U.S. Supreme Ct. Docket No. 73-623], reported in *N.Y. Times*, p. 14 (Dec. 11, 1973). In Florida, the Dept. of State has broad supervisory powers. See, Fla. Stat. §§617.01301.

134. State statutes often have not been explicit on this point, generally. See, typically, Ohio Rev. Code, §1702.12(c) that a nonprofit corporation may accept gifts unless its articles provide otherwise; and 1702.12(D) that it may give donations in furtherance of its purposes. And see, N.Y. Not-for-Profit Corp. L. §§1404(c), 1405(a), 1408(a) as to acceptance of gifts.

135. Fla. St. c. 496 (but see the next citation).

136. Repealed by s. 3, c. 76-178, as amended by s. 1, c. 77-457, effective July 1, 1982.

137. Fla. Sess. L., c. 83-181; Fla. St., c. 400.

138. Wickman v. Firestone, 500 S.2d 740 (Fl. 4th D CA, 1987); Fl. St. §496.01 et seq.

139. Citizens for a Better Environment v. Schaumburg, Ill., U.S. Supr. Ct., Feb. 20, 1980 (8 to 1 decision), on appeal from U.S. 7th Cir. And see, PLAN Newsletter (Sept. 27, 1979) p. 1 (Fund Raising Mgmt. Magazine).

140. League of Mercy Assn., Inc. v. Walt, 376 S.2d 892 (Fla. App. 1979).

141. Perlman v. Municipal Court for Los Angeles (Assoc. Justice L.T. Hanson Dec. 11, 1979).

142. Venus Lodge No. 62 v. Acme Benevolent Assn., 231 N.C. 522; 58 S.E.2d 109; 15 A.L.R.2d 1446, 1451 (1950); Hartman v. City of Pendelton, 96 Ore. 503; 186 P. 572; 8 A.L.R. 904 (1920) (acceptance of gift or bequest sustained); Grand Lodge of Independent Order of Odd Fellows of Pa. v. Baker, 192 Pa. Super. 14, 159 A.2d 552 (1960) (trust should have been judicially enforced).

143. N.Y. Penal L. §240.35. As to contributions generally, see: Fisch, E.L., American Acceptance of Charitable Trusts, 28 Notre Dame Law, 219-33 (1953); Marts, Philanthropy's Role in Civilization (Harper 1953); Note, Public Charity and Tax Exemptions, 36 Temple L.Q. 198 (1963). See above, the chapters on tax exemption.

144. City Code of St. Petersburg, Florida, §11-366, declares it to be unlawful for any person to solicit for charitable contributions unless such person is first registered by the Charitable Solicitations Board. See also: Maurice, Registration of Charities, 25 Convey, 263 (1961); D'Armours, State Supervision of Charities: Present Status, 4 N.H. B.J. 76 (1962); Neuhoff, How to Make Money by Giving It Away: Tax Consequences of Creating a Charitable Trust, 7 Prac. Law. 49 (1961), 23 U. Pitt. L. R. 105 (1961). See McGeorge, Control of Charity Solicitations, 14 Clev.-Mar. L. Rev. 265 (1965) citing typical city ordinances (of Shaker Heights, Ohio; Los Angeles, Calif.; etc.).

145. Ohio Rev. Code c. 1716. See, Gray, State Attorney General, Guardian of Public Charities, p.605, 14 Clev.-Mar. L. Rev. 236 (1965); and as to Florida's statute see, above, text at n. 137.

146. Ohio Rev. Code, c. 1716.

147. Ibid.

148. Id., see: 1956 Ohio Atty. Genl. Op. No. 6593, that YMCA is exempt.

149. Mass. Anno. Laws, c. 68 §§18 to 32.

150. N.Y. Not-for-Profit Corp. L. §112. See, for example, People v. Singer, 193 (N.Y.) Misc. 976, 85 N.Y.S.2d 727 (1949) improper fees of officers; People v. Abbott Maint. Corp., 11 A.D.2d 136, 201 N.Y.S.2d 895, affd. 9 N.Y.2d 810, 215 N.Y.S.2d 761, 175 N.E.2d 341 (1960) loss of corporate franchise; William G. Roe & Co. v. State, 43 (N.Y.) Misc.2d 417, 251 N.Y.S.2d 151 (1964) Atty. Genl. power to enjoin ultra vires activity of a corporation.

151. E.g., for membership, in a single class, or in different classes of membership in different amounts. N.Y. Not-for-Profit Corp. L. §502(b).

152. Ibid., §502(d).

153. Id., §502(b).

154. See, Bogert, Solicitation of Gifts for Charity, 5 Hastings L.J. 96 (1954); McGeorge, Control of Charity Solicitations, 14 Clev.-Mar. L. Rev. 265 (1965) citing city ordinances of Shaker Heights, Ohio; Los Angeles, Calif.; etc. And see citations in Chapter 1 herein, such as Hancock and Chafetz, The Compleat Swindler (1968); J.B. Quinn article, Newsweek magazine, p. 65 (Dec. 18, 1978); P. Blanshard article, St. Petersburg (Fla.) Times (Dec. 4, 1978).

155. See, L. Moody, Securities Issues of Nonprofit Organizations, in, Stetson Univ. Seminar Course Materials, Nonprofit Organizations' Problems 1980 (Stetson College of Law, Feb. 22, 23 1980); and generally, H. Oleck, Modern Corporation Law (1978) Supp. Ed.); Uniform Securities Act (now in most states); and see, Dunwoody Country Club of Atlanta, Inc. v. Fortson, 253 S.2d 700 (Ga. 1979) that redeemable membership certificates without interest or gain are not securities under the Georgia Securities Act.

156. Raven's Cove Townhomes, Inc. v. Knuppe Development Co., Inc., 171 Cal. Rptr. 334 (App., 1981); and see generally, N.C. Gen. Stat. §57B-7.

157. See e.g., Fla. Stat. 617.0830.

158. See your state's current statutes; N.C. Gen Stat. §20-84.

14

PROMOTERS AND ORGANIZERS

[Howard Weber assisted in the updating research for this chapter.]

§147. DEFINITIONS OF "PROMOTER" AND ORGANIZER

A *promoter*, in business corporation law is "a person who, acting alone or in conjunction with one or more other persons, directly or indirectly takes initiative in founding and organizing the business or enterprise of an issuer" of securities.[1] Such action is more a matter of business or enterprise than of law. The word has a derogatory connotation, in its common use, as a synonym for *sharp operator*, but in business and law it refers to people who perform a useful economic and social function.[2] A promoter of a corporation, for profit or not-for-profit, is the person who obtains for the new entity-to-be the legal rights, instrumentalities, capital, and original personnel to enable it to begin to conduct the business or enterprise.[3] The same is true of nonprofit (or profit) unincorporated associations.[4]

Organizers and promoters of nonprofit organizations usually are not corporation law experts. In most cases they are people with altruistic and voluntaristic purposes. Yet they, like business-corporation promoters and organizers, are charged with legal duties that are highly *fiduciary* in nature. They are legally bound to use good faith in their organization work. This duty relationship with the corporation continues until the promotional plan has been completed, even through the initial operation of the corporation, if that was included as part of the plan. This is because corporations can only be planned, organized, and set in motion by *promoters* who often continue to be the main motivating personnel after the corporation comes into legal being.[5]

The term *organizer* means any person who organizes any kind of a group or enterprise.[6] The term promoter, however, has a very specific meaning in the law of business associations and corporations.[7] It means anyone who takes part in the organization of a corporation. Such a person has a very specific status in corporation law and custom, and is subject to special rules.[8]

There is no basic difference between the rules and standards that apply to promoters of nonprofit corporations and those that apply to profit-purpose business corporations. Whether in a stock or nonstock corporation, a promoter owes to the corporate constituent, be he a shareholder or member, the same duties of good faith and fair dealing.[9] This is especially so in situations where either profit or nonprofit form might be employed to achieve the particular purpose.[10]

The need for special legislation to control promoters and prevent unfair dealing has been remarked upon often by the courts and legal writers.[11] The Florida legislature has responded by requiring the promoter of condominiums to adhere to stringent disclosure standards, imposing restrictions on management contracts, and encouraging early transfer of control of nonprofit condominium associations to the unit owners.[12] The Federal Securities Act and state "blue sky" laws also have some utility.[13]

Incorporators of a corporation may or may not also be the promoters. Technically, an *incorporator* is a person who signs the original articles of incorporation.[14] So, too, a promoter may or may not also be a member of the organization. A member means one having membership rights and privileges in an organization in accordance with its articles or bylaws.[15] No one can be a member until the organization has been brought into existence, but once it is in existence a promoter may be a member of it.

The promoter may be defined more precisely as a person who interests other persons in the organizing of a corporation to achieve a certain purpose or to carry on a certain enterprise, obtains their active assistance and membership in the projected organization, starts the actual mechanics of formation of the projected corporation, and sees to the completion of the mechanical process and the actual creation of a going corporation.[16]

A promoter is in a very real sense an agent who acts for the corporate entity by assisting at its birth. But in terms of law and logic, no one can be an agent for a nonexistent principal or employer.[17] Until the corporation comes into existence, it is not an entity. It cannot be bound by the acts of an agent, because it cannot have any agents until it is an entity.[18] This logical puzzle would make it impossible to form any corporation, unless some special solution were offered by the law. For this reason, a special solution is offered. The promoter of a corporation is given status as a special kind of agent, subject to special rules and possessing special rights.[19]

Unlike any ordinary agent, a promoter is legally viewed as a partner with his fellow promoters or organizers.[20] Like those of any agent, his acts or even contracts made on its behalf may be *adopted* or *ratified* by the corporation (principal) when it comes into existence. But if the corporation does not so ratify and adopt his acts, his fellow organizers are responsible for them, as partners.[21]

This is a rule of practical necessity. Without it no one ever would care to be a promoter, because his work always could be disowned by the corporation after it had benefited from his labors, and he would have no recourse and no assurance at all of being compensated. In practice, of course, the promoters usually become the original members of the corporation, and do (as a corporation) adopt the acts and contracts of the promoters. Thereby they transfer responsibility for such acts (and for compensation) to the corporation.

All the organizers of a corporation are promoters in this sense of partnership activity. They are partners in the "joint venture" of organizing the corporation. In addition, however, unlike ordinary partners or "joint ventures," they also have a special fiduciary duty of the highest good faith to each other *and* to the corporation which they are organizing.[22]

Promoters may not transfer *all* their transactions and obligations to the corporation, because this may unfairly burden the corporations's members. For example, if one promoter deals improperly with another promoter in the process of organizing, the injured promoter's remedy must be against the person who wronged him, not against the corporation.[23]

Likewise, the joint fiduciary duty of the promoters to the corporation theoretically forbids them from fastening their *personal control* onto the corporation by depriving the corporation's board of directors of effective control. In practice, the promoters usually become the directors of a nonprofit corporation, and thus this problem of separation of rights and powers becomes academic. Even voting agreements are provided for in the New York Not-for-Profit Corporation statute and other recently enacted statutes.[24] [See Section 152, on Control Agreements.]

§148. TWO METHODS OF INCORPORATION

The promotion and organization of a corporation usually follow a set pattern fixed by statutes. In all the states there exist general statutes which permit any reputable persons to form a corporation (profit or nonprofit) by following a prescribed procedure and by filing prescribed documents and certificates. This is by far the most commonplace method of incorporating.

In the past, however, this was not the way to form a corporation. Originally a corporation was created only by the granting of a special "charter" (document of authority) by the king. Later, the English parliament granted such special charters. In turn, the legislatures of the American colonies granted charters.

Today, state legislatures still can (and do) grant such special charters.[25] This is termed "incorporation by Special Act of the Legislature." It is becoming quite unusual because it is permitted by the law only when incorporation of a particular enterprise under the general incorporation statutes is impractical or undesirable in the view of the legislature.[26]

Promoters thus have two methods of incorporating their project: first, regular incorporation under the general statutes, and second, incorporation by the legislature through a special enactment.

The latter method involves special lobbying and other obvious difficulties. It now has become so unusual that we may confidently say that the first method is *the* method of incorporating.

§149. PHASES OF PROMOTION ACTIVITY

A promoter's processes of action in carrying on his or her promotion of a corporate venture are usually in three stages or phases: (1) conception (or discovery), (2) investigation, and (3) assembly.[27] Conception or discovery of the needs that exist, or the benefits to be obtained, is the first phase. Investigation of the scope and feasibility and those benefits and/or needs, and of the best way to attain or satisfy them, is the second phase. And the final phase is the procurement or furnishing (assembly) of the necessary capital and start-up personnel and legal machinery for beginning the enterprise.

The third phase (assembly) is the one in which the promoter usually acts as the risk-taking entrepreneur. It is then that he makes commitments for such items as attorney's services and other needed services, plus commitments of funds and/or property, for licenses, leases, employees, *etcetera*.[28]

It is at about this time or sometimes earlier that the legal problem of *promoter's contracts* becomes acute. Such a contract of a promoter with a third party is entered into for the benefit of a corporation that does not yet exist.[29] *See the next section.*

§150. PROMOTER'S CONTRACTS

(See the preceding section).

Four theories of law for dealing with promoters' contracts with other parties have been developed by various courts.[30] The primary doctrine, followed in all but a very few states, is that the corporation will not be liable for its promoters' contracts, when it comes into existence unless it expressly or impliedly adopts (*ratifies*) the contract in question.[31] Among the important factors in determining whether or not the promoter of the corporation is bound are: nature of the signature, statements of the parties in the agreement, time sequences, *etcetera*.[32]

One construction of a pre-incorporation agreement, which would relieve a promoter of all liability, is called the *revocable offer* theory; a sort of "gentlemen's agreement:"[33] The third party offer to the corporation to be formed will result in a contract only if the corporation is formed and accepts the offer before revocation. This construction applies when there is a clear intent of the parties that the agreement be such as this.

A second view of promoters' contracts is the *revocable offer* approach. These agreements take immediate effect, because the promoter promises, in consideration of the offer, to use his best efforts to procure the creation of the corporation and its acceptance of the offer. If the organization then is not formed, the promoter may be personally liable on his contract.[34] But in practice not many third parties make irrevocable offers in exchange for a promoter's own promise.

Another view of pre-incorporation agreements is that under which the promoter is primarily liable, but may become only secondarily liable on the contract. The corporation, when it is formed, may choose to receive the benefit of the promoter's contract, and thereby step into the position of primary liability. Such action of the corporation may be by express or implied *ratification* or *adoption*, or by the *third-party-beneficiary* theory, or by *novation* or *estoppel*.[35] However, even where ratification is found the promoter may still be held jointly liable on the contract.[36] If no theory of relief is found, the promoter is held primarily liable.[37]

The fourth theory of promoter liability applies when the corporation substitutes itself for the promoter. In this *novation* theory the promoter is divested of rights and relieved of all liabilities under the contract.[38] The promoter, however, has the burden of proving that he was not intended to be held liable on the contract.[39] The promoter is not personally liable if the third party knew of the non-existence of the corporation and agreed to look solely to the corporation.[40]

§151. PROMOTERS' DUTY AND CARE AND RIGHTS

Besides the standards applied to promoters' pre-incorporation agreements they may also infer liability based on duties to co-promoters, to the corporation, and to the shareholders or members of the corporation. While no specific statutory duties are set forth as to promoters, they have been held to have the same fiduciary status as do corporation directors.[41] Since nonprofit statutes generally provide the same duties for directors as do for-profit corporate statutes, the nonprofit promoter's performance usually will be evaluated by the same standards as those that apply in business corporations.[42]

A promoter is a fiduciary. His responsibility is similar to but not quite as stringent as that of a trustee. His fiduciary relationship extends to his fellow organizers, to the corporation as an entity, and to the membership of the corporation as an entity. It means that he is personally liable to each of these groups for any damages which they may suffer as a result of any material misrepresentation or concealment of facts by him. But once the organization has been incorporated, his liability ordinarily no longer extends to the members of it as individuals.

Avoidance of secret personal profit is the chief duty of a promoter.[43] The basic standard applied to promoters is like that of directors—ordinary prudence.[44] It applies in most kinds of nonprofit corporations.[45] Courts should, and usually do, take into account the fact that organizers of nonprofit corporations often are not experienced business people.[46]

If a promoter of a nonprofit association contracts on behalf of the association with himself, or with another for his personal benefit, he may be liable to the association for that amount by which he is unjustly enriched as a result of his contract.[47] This does not mean that he may not be duly paid for his services—but it indicates that with respect to personal profit, the law for nonprofit corporation transactions is strict.

One recent case illustrates the problems involved when the promoter of an unincorporated association allegedly benefited financially from the manipulation of organization property. A nonprofit unincorporated association, named the Bass Anglers Sportsman Society, filed suit against BASS, Inc. and its founder, Ray W. Scott Jr., alleging that Scott owed the members of the unincorporated association $75 million allegedly looted from the nonprofit association. The complaint stated that Scott, after forming the nonprofit Sportsman Society, started a new profit corporation, BASS, Inc., some 18 months after the nonprofit association was formed, using a name that was deceptively similar to the nonprofit association's name. The profit society was alleged to have converted assets (BASS Master Magazine) and revenues of the unincorporated nonprofit society to the profit corporation without a vote from the members or notification to the member/subscribers. The suit sought ouster of the BASS, Inc. leadership and formation of a trust for the property as well as punitive damages.[48]

Even in a business corporation matter, a promoter is forbidden to obtain secret profits.[49] For example, when 40 percent of the amount of contributions to a charitable corporation went to one of its promoters as payment of commissions for solicitation work, the certificate of incorporation of the organization was revoked by the state's attorney-general.[50] In another case, even a proposed sale of a nonprofit corporation's property to a business corporation, in exchange for shares of its stock which were to be given to the members (not only to the promoters), was enjoined.[51]

Open dealing with the corporation is not forbidden. For example, if the promoter openly offers property for sale to the corporation, and it openly and reasonably buys that property, his personal profit then is not a corporate matter.[52] But any such transaction is scrutinized sharply by the courts if anyone objects to it. All such transactions are best avoided entirely.

If one promoter injures another, this is a private matter between them. The injured promoter has no right to expect the corporation to make good his damages, unless it took part in the matter and gained improperly at his expense.[53]

As it is pointed out above, promoters are joint-venturers (i.e., partners) among themselves, with the usual rights and duties among themselves of such a special kind of partnership venture.[54]

Contracts to organize the corporation sometimes are made, particularly when professional corporation organizers and managers are employed. Such a contract is an express undertaking and usually makes provisions for rights and remedies in case of a breach by either party. The usual rules of contract law apply to such agreements.

If one promoter abandons the project, the others may go on with it, and he loses any rights for work already done by him.[55]

If promoters employ their own agents in the organizing of a corporation, the usual rules of principal and agent apply. The employer is responsible, in general, for all acts of his employee in the course of the employment.

Once the certificate of incorporation has been filed, the corporation comes into being. Thereupon the promoter's status as a promoter ceases. But if the filing is wholly defective or improper, no corporation may come into existence. In that event, the promoter's status as a promoter continues, and the joint status of all the promoters as partners continues.[56]

§152. CONTROL AGREEMENTS

Perpetuation of the organizer's control of the corporation often is desired and/or sought by the promoter or other organizers. Very typical is the drive of a "developer" of a condominium to keep the property and control, even after he "sells" them to unit-owners and the condo association, by such devices as long-term leases instead of sales, contracts for maintenance by him, or his corporation, division into recreational and residential units, one of which he retains and leases, retention by him of some of the units and their votes in the association, *etc.*

Agreements among the promoters to perpetuate their control over the corporation, as by electing certain promoters to certain positions, may be ignored or rejected by the corporation. Such agreements are not uncommon, nor are they necessarily immoral. Nevertheless, the corporation as such is in no way bound by them. Moreover, the law in most states requires that the control of a nonprofit corporation basically must reside with the corporation as an entity. This means in the board of directors or trustees, subject to their election by the general membership.[57]

New York's Not-for-Profit Corporation Law, in 1970, introduced an entirely new concept. It authorizes a contractual voting agreement (control agreement) among two or more members.[58] It is an adaptation of the New York Business Corporation Law,[59] and authorizes a vote-pooling arrangement. This would be particularly effective when coupled with the irrevocable proxy device also authorized by the corporation statute of New York,[60] and in effect eliminates the need for the voting trust in nonprofit corporations; for which reason the *latter* kind of vote-pooling device is not proper under the new law. California's statute that took effect in 1980, also includes very permissive control agreements.[61] The 1986 American Bar Association proposed Revised Model Nonprofit Corporations Act contains similar provisions. (See the Index).

As the parties who draft and file the articles of incorporation, promoters are in a position to grasp control of the operation. Along with the articles of incorporation, bylaws often are employed to establish this control in even greater detail. Articles of incorporation may provide for the same controls as do the bylaws; however, bylaws are more readily amended.[62] The articles of incorporation state the number of directors who will serve on the initial board, as well as their names and addresses.[63]

But the bylaws provide the real rulebook for operation of the corporation, and govern its internal affairs.[64] On the other hand, bylaws are required to be filed with the IRS before tax-exempt status will be granted.[65] At least partial control is available through the bylaws.

Promoters often set themselves up in the articles of incorporation as the initial directors. Bylaws then are set forth and formally adopted during the first meeting of the board.[66] Generally, state statutes provide that any provision not inconsistent with law may be provided in the bylaws.[67] Some areas where control may be set up within the bylaws are: membership, the board of directors, committees, and officers' selection processes and powers.

If a nonprofit corporation is to have a general membership, in addition to the board of directors or trustees, certain bylaw provisions are desirable.[68] Special qualifications for members and the manner of their admission may be stated; for example, qualifications for membership may be based on the amount of monetary support donated. *Classes* of membership, and corresponding voting privileges, may be provided for. This is sometimes a promotional device to encourage donations; or it attractively names each membership class. It often has a reverse effect on potentially large contributors who may not like the availability of membership to less wealthy persons. Length of membership, termination procedures and criteria, resignation rights, and transfers of membership are other matters covered in the bylaws. Of chief importance in this respect is the designation of just what the powers of the members are to be, and how they are to be exercised. Also, how many members will be enough to make a *quorum* for conduct of business, who may call a meeting, and what notice must be given to members, are factors that may have control effect. Cumulative voting and proxy voting are other such considerations.

Provision for domination of the board of directors is a key element of control. Other considerations in devising a system of control may involve the board's size (a small board suffers from deadlocks and lack of diverse experience, while a board that is large lacks speed of action and manageability); board member eligibility, tenure, replacement, removal, compensation rules and voting rules are useful; while staggering the terms of board members will defeat cumulative voting.

Major control devices in the law of corporations include *vote-pooling* agreements to assert a more powerful portion in a matter to be voted on; they are recognized by corporation law and may be oral as well as written.[69] *Voting trusts* differ from vote-pooling agreements in that they involve transfer of voting rights to voting trustees.[70] These voting trustees hold legal title to the shares and vote them pursuant to a written trust agreement. The agreement is usually kept by the corporation while voting trust certificates are issued; and they may be irrevocable.[71] Proxy grants are another useful control technique.

A *stockholder's agreement* is an agreement among the "owners" of the controlling number of shares of stock in a corporation, primarily intended to perpetuate their control of future corporate policy and management.[72] In a nonprofit corporation, such an agreement is rather futile, as well as incompatible with the democratic basis of a "membership corporation." Since each member ordinarily has only one vote, an agreement of this kind would have no real effectiveness unless it included a majority of the members. If the promoters made such an agreement to vote together, they would be outweighed by the majority as soon as a number of new members joined the organization.

In any event, even in a business corporation, and far more positively in a nonprofit corporation, unfair treatment of the minority members is not legally tolerated. More important the members may not, by private agreement, take control out of the hands of the board of directors or trustees. Nor may they prevent at least annual general elections, in which they each will have only have only one vote. An attempt to do any of these things in most states is simply illegal.[73]

In actual practice the organizers can (and do) fasten their control on the corporation by drafting bylaws to suit themselves and by occupying key offices. If the membership grows, they lose the power to control the voting. Then the bylaws may be amended by the general membership, in whom the ultimate control must lie, and new officers may be elected to take over management.

Even so, the inertia which is characteristic both of stockholders and of members of nonprofit corporations often permits the organizers to continue in office and in control, so long as abuse of such control does not become evident, or until a rival group obtains enough support to win control.[74]

New York's new, statutory *vote-pooling* authorization must be limited to the purposes and procedures envisaged in the "nonprofit for profit" types of organizations.[75] These are special-situation provisions, apparently intended for the protection of investors in these special projects. The California statute is an outright grant of power to control a nonprofit corporation *from outside.*[76]

The modern trend in legislative permissiveness is epitomized in the American Bar Association's draft 1986 revision of the Model Nonprofit Corporation Act: "Section 10.30—Approval by Third Persons." The articles may require an amendment to the articles or by-laws to be approved in writing by a specified person or persons other than the board.

§153. COMPENSATION OF PROMOTERS

In most cases, the work of the promoters of a nonprofit corporation is purely a labor of love. The promoters neither expect nor receive any pecuniary compensation for their own services.[77] But in many cases, the promoters do expect to receive, and do receive, payment for their services.

When the corporation has been organized, at the first meeting for the adoption of the bylaws a resolution usually is adopted for the repayment of the promoters. This often also includes payment for work done as well as for actual outlays of moneys. This resolution is equivalent to a contract to make such payment. (For the form of such a resolution, see the forms of bylaws in the chapters dealing with that subject.) But liability may be incurred without a resolution, by implied ratification.[78]

It hardly needs to be said that the valuation of pre-incorporation services must be fair and reasonable. Otherwise it will be viewed as a mere device to evade the laws forbidding personal profit in nonprofit corporations. Yet ordinarily the value of such services is not a fixed price. The services of one particular individual may be worth far more than those of another individual, depending on the surrounding circumstances.

§154. COMPENSATION OF THE ATTORNEY

When the services of an attorney are involved, a special consideration enters the compensation picture. The attorney not only serves, but he also disburses, and he may be one of the promoters as well.

The attorney's services are almost indispensable in preparing and filing the certificate of incorporation. They are almost essential in the drafting of the bylaws. These services involve various actual disbursements: of filing fees, of fees for corporate seals and "kits" (minute book, book of certificates, *etc.*), for stenographic and stationery services. By current standards of money-value, in most states these disbursements average at least $200. This reckoning excludes the value of the attorney's time.

Especially in the case of a nonprofit corporation, the attorney often becomes, at least to some extent, one of the organizers (promoters). He must discuss all the plans and ideas involved in order to be able to put them into operating form. The process leads naturally to his becoming a promoter.

Though he may volunteer his legal services, the attorney's out-of-pocket disbursements are usually returned by the corporation. If he arranges to be paid for his legal services, the corporation becomes liable when it adopts a resolution for compensation of promoters. If he is not duly paid, he is entitled to demand payment from the individuals who expressly or by implication retained him, unless he waives this right.

It is apparent that the attorney in an incorporation may legitimately serve both as an attorney and as a promoter.[79] The ethics and standards of attorneys are high—despite the recurrent popularity of abusing the legal profession.[80] The attorney leans over backward to avoid any suggestion that he is taking advantage of his special skill and knowledge. Common sense and courtesy require the nonattorney promoters to use equal consideration in deciding upon compensation for, and other participation by, the attorney. If this consideration is present, the corporation will avoid great trouble and expense in the long run, because its attorney will be a skillful, vigilant, and enthusiastic guardian of its rights and interests.

The attorney who incorporates the association is a logical candidate for retention as counsel to the corporation. Often this prospect of retainer makes it worthwhile for an attorney to carry through the incorporation at only a nominal charge for his services.

§155. PROFESSIONAL ORGANIZERS AND MANAGERS

The organization and management of nonprofit corporations and associations has become a new profession. In the large cities, there are organizations that specialize in association organization and management as a business.

In Chicago, New York City, and other metropolitan centers, there are various companies devoted to such work. They usually are listed in classified directories under the heading of "association management."

Individuals and firms in the "management consultant" business also offer such services. Some persons and firms in the "public relations" business also are skilled in such work. Attorneys who are experienced in this field, of course, often are management experts as well as legal experts.

Association management organizations are interested chiefly in trade associations, but are quite capable of handling almost any kind of association. In addition, a considerable number of individuals, often originally lawyers, make a profession of association organization and management.

The services of such experts save the organizers considerable work, time, and money invested in preparatory self-education. They also help eliminate some of the self-seeking and bickering among nonprofessional organizers that so often blight the birth of a new organization. Lack of mutual trust among the interested parties is partially assuaged when a disinterested specialist guides the enterprise, at least as respects its mechanical organization and operation.

The approach of a professional to the usual problems of association is illuminating. The following illustrative section, which is based on the problems of a *trade association*,[81] embodies suggestions by Mr. Stewart N. Clarkson, treasurer and general executive officer of Stewart N. Clarkson Associates, Inc., of New York City, trade-association management consultants. The substance of these suggestions appeared in the *American Trade Association Executives Journal*, and they are presented here with Mr. Clarkson's consent.

[See the chapter on Management.]

§156. HOW TO ORGANIZE A TRADE ASSOCIATION

The techniques that follow have been used primarily for the organization of relatively small groups of manufacturers who are individually in competition with each other and whose products are, in many instances, in competition with the products of one or more other industries. It will be found that some of the principles are basic of the organization of other types and sizes of associations.

Procedure. There are three stages in the organization of a trade association:

1. The first stage is to determine why there should be an association and who should be in it.

2. The second requirement is to bring about an agreement by a sufficient number of industry members to form an association for one or more specific purposes.

3. The final stage is to establish a firm foundation of sound policies and practices for the association's operation: bylaws, an outline of practical objectives, a budget, a basis for dues, a management operating plan. This third stage also involves the election of officers and committees and the election of a competent manager.

First stage. Initiative to organize those associations usually comes from members of the industry, from a trade-association management firm, or from a large association interested in establishing products or geographical divisions in its field. Occasionally the initiative is taken by a lawyer or by other professional individuals outside the industry or by a trade association executive.

Second stage. Associations that are successfully organized from within the industry often complete the first two stages without calling in qualified trade association counsel. But after they have decided that there should be an association, who should be in it, and what should be its functions, outside counsel is needed.

A meeting of prospective members will help—and may be essential—to crystallize the ideas of the membership.

Third stage. After the group decides what they want to do, they reach the final and very important stage: determining the best procedures to follow. This is the function of the organizing individual or committee. The life and efficacy of the association will depend largely on the experience and thoroughness that go into these recommendations.

At this point internally organized industry groups often call in a lawyer to do nothing more than write up the bylaws. The members would, however, sometimes be better advised to seek the counsel of a trade association executive or lawyer who is experienced in the organization of associations. If the group pays the trade association counsel a consultant fee, they then feel no obligation to engage him to serve the association after it is organized.

The incorporation of the association always should be carefully considered. Incorporation does give added protection to the members as well as a sense of permanence and ease in holding and transferring property. If this step is decided upon, a state should be selected that has a favorable law for the incorporation of nonprofit membership organizations.

Conclusion. These suggestions are based on experience in organizing some two dozen or more industry groups, each of which required individual treatment. The laying down of any rigid set of rules for the organization of a trade association is impractical, and all that has been attempted here is an outline of practices and policies that have been successfully tested in actual operation.

POINTS TO REMEMBER

- Distinguish between "organizing members" and "promoters."
- Use experienced promoters whenever possible.
- Legal counsel by specialists is essential every step of the way—especially in the process of incorporating.
- Corporations must ratify acts of promoters before these acts bind the corporations.
- Ratification can be expressed or implied.
- If you accept the benefits, you ratify the act.
- All the active organizers are promoters. They are subject to the law that applies to promoters.
- If incorporation fails to materialize, the promoters are "joint-venturers" (partners) personally liable for obligations.
- Seek a special charter from the legislature only if incorporation is impossible under the general law.
- Remember the fiduciary status of a promoter. Avoid all secret personal profit: it is illegal.
- Use a formal resolution, when adopting the bylaws, to ratify the promoters' acts, and another resolution to reimburse the promoters.
- Attorneys are also organizers (promoters) if they assist substantially in the nonlegal work of organizing.
- Avoid "control agreements." Put the control powers in the bylaws. Use *vote-pools* only in New York-type "investment" organizations (or California, cautiously).
- Use professional association experts, if possible, both for organizing and for later management.

NOTES TO CHAPTER 14

1. S.E.C. Rule 405, 17 C.F.R. 230.405; 18 Am. Jur. 2d, Corporations §106; 15 Am. Jur., Con. Apt. §21.

2. Hamilton, *Corporations* (casebook), 182 (3rd ed., 1986).

3. Henn and Alexander, *Laws of Corporations* (casebook) 237 (3rd ed., 1983).

4. *See* Chap. 5, herein above.

5. Hamilton book and Henn and Alexander book (above n. 2,3) both set forth detailed analyses of business corporation promoters. See also: Oleck, *Modern Corporation Law*, c.7 (1978 Supp. ed.).

6. See, *Black's Law Dictionary*, 991, 1093 (5th ed., 1979); *Ballentine's Law Dictionary*, 898, 1007

(3rd ed., 1969); *Webster's New World Dictionary*, 1033, 1166 (1962). The term "organizer" is usually employed in connection with labor unions; *e.g.*, "a union organizer."

7. Geving v. Fitzpatrick, 371 N.E.2d 1228 (III. App., 1978).

8. The main cases governing the legal status of promoters are: Old Dominion Copper Mining & Smelting Co. v. Lewisohn, 210 U.S. 206, 28 S. Ct. 634, 52 L. Ed. 1025 (1908); pre-incorporation compared with post-incorporation, in, Old Dominion copper Mining & Smelting Co. v. Bigelow, 203 Mass. 159, 89 N.E. 193 (1909), *affd.* 225 U.S. 111, 32 S. Ct. 641, 56 L. Ed. 1009 (1912); *and also* McCandless v. Furlaud, 296 U.S. 140, 56 S. Ct. 41, 80 L. Ed. 121 (1935), *affg.* 75 F.2d 977, rehearing denied 296 U.S. 644, 56 S. Ct. 304, 80 L. Ed. 473 (1935), *and see*, Blocke, *A Primer for Corporate Promoters*, 9 Prac. Law, 13 (1963); Guthmann & Dougall, *Corporate Financial Policy* 248 (4th ed. 1962). *And see*, Swafford v. Berry, 152 Colo. 493, 382 P.2d 999, 1001-2 (1963); Bowers v. Rio Grande Investment Co., 163 Colo. 433, 431 P.2d 478, 480 (1967).

9. Post v. United States, 407 F.2d 319, 328–330 (C.A. D.C. 1969); *cert. den.* 393 U.S. 1092 (1969) (criminal case, saying that this was a case of first impression).

10. Riviera Condominium Apts. v. Weinberger, 231 S.2d 850 (Fla. App. 1970); Fountainview Assn., Inc. v. Bell, 203 S.2d 657 (Fla. App. 1967).

11. *See*, Riviera Condominium case, *supra* n. 10; Anderson, *Legal Protection for Florida Condominium and Cooperative Buyers and Owners*, 27 Miami L. Rev. 451 (1973); Rosenstein, *Inadequacies of Current Condominium Legislation*, 47 Temple LQ 655 (1974); 73 A.L.R.3d 613.

12. Fla. St. §§718.503, 718.302, 718.301. See herein the chapter on Condominiums and Cooperatives.

13. Note, *Florida Condominiums Developer Abuses . . . , 35 Fla. L. Rev. 350 (1973)*; Note *Federal Securities Regulation of Condominiums: A Purchaser's Perspective*, 62 Georgetown L.J. 1403 (1974).

14. Ohio Rev. Code, §1702.01(G).

15. *Ibid.*, §1702.01(11). And a "voting member" means a member possessing voting rights, either generally or in respect of the particular question involved, as the case may be. *Id.*

16. *See* discussions, above n. 1–5; and *Directors and Officers' Encyclopedic Manual* 410–414 (N.Y., Prentice-Hall, Inc. 1955); Ehrlich, *Law of Promoters* (1916).

17. Henderson v. Plymouth Oil Co., 16 Del. Ch. 347, 141 A. 197, 212 (1928); Restatement, Agency, §102; Stanley J. How & Associates, Inc. v. Bass, 222 F. Supp. 936 (D.C. Iowa 1963).

18. *See*, Hamilton, *Law of Corporations*, c.5 (2d ed., 1987).

19. Old Dominion cases, above, n. 8; Arnold v. Searing, 78 N.J. Eq. 146, 157, 78 A. 762 (1910).

20. Granik v. Perry, 418 F.2d 832, 836 (5th Cir. 1969); MacMorris Sales Corp. v. Kozak, 69 Calif. Rptr. 719, 723 (Calif. App. 1968); Meinhard v. Salmon, 249 N.Y. 458, 462, 164 N.E.2d 545, 62 A.L.R. 1 (1928).

21. Chartrand v. Barney's Club, Inc., 380 F.2d 97 (9th Cir. 1967).

22. *See* above, n. 17; and, Park City Corp. v. Watchie, 249 Ore. 493, 439 P.2d 587, 591 (1968).

23. B. K. K. Co. v. Schultz, 7 Calif. App.2d 786, 86 Calif. Rptr. 760, 766 (1970); Morris v. Whittier Amusement Co., 123 Calif. App. 121, 10 P.2d 1017 (1932); Killeen v. Parent, 23 Wis.2d 244, 127 N.W.2d 244, 127 N.W.2d 38 (1964); *and see*, McCrea, *Disclosure of Promoters' Secret Profits*, 3 U.B.C.L. Rev. 183 (1968).

24. N.Y. N-P-C Law, §619.

25. *E.g.*, "by any special act of this state," in N.Y. N-P-C Law §102(a)(5) recognizes this fact, and, *Ibid.*, §104(c).

26. State v. Western Irrig. Canal Co., 40 Kan. 96, 19 P. 349 (1888); 1 Pollock and Maitland, *History of English Law* 669 (2d ed. 1911); Culp v. Trio TV Sales and Serv. 350 F.2d 1106, 1112 (Colo. 1958); Friedman, History of American Law 166 (1973).

27. Henn and Alexander, *Law of Corporations*, 237 (3rd ed., 1983).

28. See, Handley v. Ching, 627 P.2d 1132 (Hawaii App., 1981).

29. See, Stanley J. How & Assoc., Inc. v. Boss, 222 F. Supp. 936 (D.C. Iowa, 1963); Quaker Hill, Inc. v. Parr, 364 P.2d 1056 (Colo., 1961); McArthur v. Times Printing Co., 51 N.W. 216 (Minn., 1892).

30. Restatement, Agency 2d §326, Comment b.

31. Ibid., McArthur case, above n. 29; Hamilton, *Corporations*, 198 (3rd ed., 1986).

32. Henn and Alexander, *Law of Corporations*, 250 (3rd ed., 1983).

33. *Ibid.*, at 248.

34. *Ibid.* Southern Gulf Marine Co. v. Camcraft, Inc., 410 So. 2d 1181 (La. App., 1982).

35. A.A. Martin Transportation Co. v. Almonte, 468 A.2d 268 (R.I. 1983) (Ratification found through initiation of suit by the newly formed corporation to force the third party to perform on the promoter's agreement). *Speedee Oil Change No. 2, Inc. v. National Union Fire Insurance Company*, 444 So. 2d 1304 (La. App. 1984) (Third-party beneficiary theory used, finding the corporation liable where both the promoter and the third-party intended the corporation to benefit from the contract and the corporation accepted such benefit).

36. Ratner v. Central National Bank of Miami, 414 So. 2d 210 (Fla. 3rd DCA, 1982).

37. Quality Wood Chips, Inc. v. Adolphsen, 636 S.W.2d 94 (Mo. App. 1982).

38. Henn and Alexander, *supra* note 32, at 257.

39. Goodman v. Damon and Stafford Association, 653 P.2d 1371 (Wash. App. 1982).

40. *Id.* at 1372.

41. Christy v. Combran, 710 F.2d 669 (10th Cir. 1983).

42. Fla. Stat. §607.0830 as incorporated in Fla. Stat. §617.0830.

43. See, Gladstone v. Bennett, 38 Del. Ch. 391, 153 A.2d 577 (1959); Park City Corp. v. Watchie, 439 P.2d 587 (Ore. 1978); Whaler Motor Inn v. Parsons, 339 N.W.2d 197 (Mass. App. 1975).

44. Fla. Stat. §607.0830(1)(b); N.Y. N-P-C Law §717(a); Ga. Code §14-3-830(1)(B); Note, 19 Ga. St. B.J. 164 (1983).

45. Note, 66 Cornell L. Rev. 1103, 1122 (1981).

46. Unterman and Davis, *Strategic Management of Not-For-Profit Organizations*, 146 (1984).

47. Avila South Condominium Association v. Kappa Corporation, 347 So.2d 599 (Fla. 1976).

48. Cox, (article) 14 *Nat. L.J.* (30) 8 (March 30, 1992).

49. Rohrlich, *Organizing Corporate and Other Business Enterprises*, 53 (4th ed. 1967).

50. Bennett v. American-Canadian Ambulance Corps, 179 (N.Y.) Misc. 21, 37 N.Y.S. 2d 470 (1942).

51. Richter v. Sea Gate Assn., 207 A.D. 573, 202 N.Y.S. 68 (1923); and as to legal rights of third parties, Clark v. Daniels, 250 Mich. 22, 29, 229 N.W. 495 (1930).

52. Brooker v. Thompson Trust Co., 254 Mo. 125, 146, 162 S.W. 187 (1914). Sometimes a "Fair and reasonable compensation" is allowed even though improper profits must be returned: Mason v. Carruthers, 105 Me. 392, 74 A. 1030 (1909); Allenhurst Park Estates, Inc. v. Smith, 101 N.J. Eq. 581, 609, 138 A. 709 (1927).

53. Meinhard v. Salmon, 249 N.Y. 458, 464, 164 N.E. 545, 546, 62 A.L.R. 1, 4–5 (1928); Noted 29 Colum. L. Rev. 367 (1929), 13 Minn. L. Rev. 711 (1929).

54. *See*, Henn, *Law of Corporations*, §49 (2d ed. 1970).

55. Parks v. Gates, 84 A.D. 534, 82 N.Y.S. 1070 (1903). But his liability to third persons does not end, as to his past transactions. Noble v. McKinley, 72 N.Y.S.2d 515 (1947).

56. Bunzl & Ehrich, *Promoters' Contracts*, 111 S.W. L.J. 509 (1957); Lattin, *Corporations*, c.3 (1959).

57. See, generally, Oleck, *Proprietary Mentality and the New Nonprofit Corporation Laws*, 20 Clev. St. L. Rev. 145 (1971). Compare the 1980 California statute.

58. N.Y. N-P-C L. §619.

59. N.Y. Bus. Corp. L. §620(a).

60. N.Y. Bus. Corp. L. §619(f)(5).

61. Calif. Corps. Code, Div. 2 and 3, §5240(b)(3) in its draft included control by contracts with outsiders.

62. *See*, Fla. Stat. §617.1002, Calif. Code §5342.

63. *See*, Fla. Stat. §617.013(f).

64. J. Hummel, *Starting and Running a Nonprofit Organization*, 22 (1980).

65. *Ibid.*

66. *Ibid.* at 23.

67. *See*, Fla. Stat. §617.0206.

68. Hummel, above, n. 64, at pp. 23–24.

69. *See*, Fla. Stat. §607.0731, Del. Corp. Law §218; Calif. Code §5614 (voting agreements by members are limited).

70. *See*, Fla. Stat. §607.0730.

71. *Id.*

72. Oleck, *Modern Corporation Law*, c. 56 (1978 Supp.); Rohrlich, *Organizing Corporate and Other Business Enterprises*, §§3.02, 4.27 (rev. ed. 1953); Oleck, *New York Corporations*, cc. 6, 25 (New York: Robert Slater Co. 1959 Supp. ed.); Hornstein, *Stockholders' Agreements in the Closely Held Corporation*, 59 Yale L.J. 1040 (1950).

73. Potter v. Patee, 493 S.W.2d 58 (Mo. App. 1973) (attempt by some officers to hold a meeting at a place other than the specified place stated in the notice rendered the acts done at the meeting a nullity). *See also* Benintendi v. Kenton Hotel Co., 294 N.Y. 112; 60 N.E.2d 829 (1945); Long Park, Inc. v. Trenton-New Brunswick Theatres Co., 297 N.Y. 174; 77 N.E.2d 633 (1948); Glazer v. Glazer, 374 F.2d 390, 405–06 (5th Cir. 1967) noted 61 Harv. L. Rev. 1251 (1948); 43 Ill. L. Rev. 561 (1948), 47 Mich. L. Rev. 119 (1948). *See*, Fronklin v. Merrall Realty, Inc., 30 Misc.2d 288, 215 N.Y.S.2d 525 (1961) *affd.* 15 A.D.2d 919, 225 N.Y.S.2d 632 (1962). But "voting trusts" are permitted in business corporations. Gen. Stat. No. Car. §55–72. Also, stockholders' agreements. *Id.*, §55–73.

74. *See*, Anno., *Enforcement of Invalid Corporate Bylaw as Contract, 159 A.L.R. 290*; Dodd, *For Whom Are Corporate Managers Trustees?*, 45 Harv. L. Rev. 1145 (1932); First National Bk. v. Shanks, 34 Ohio Op. 359, 73 N.E.2d 93 (1945) Ward v. City Drug Co., 235 Ark. 767, 362 S.W.2d 27, 31-2 (1962); (invalid bylaw enforced as a contract). A promise to vote for a certain person is valid. Slonim v. Brodie, 109 N.Y.S.2d 440 (1951) *affd.* 281 A.D. 861, 119 N.Y.S.2d 916 (1953).

75. N.Y. N-P-C L. §619, *esp.* subd. (f)(5).

76. Calif. Corps. Code, Div. 2 and 3, §5240(b)(3) (1978 draft).

77. Ritchie v. McMullen, 79 F. 522 (6th Cir. 1897) (no compensation expected); Cuba Colony Co. v. Kirby, 149 Mich. 453; 112 N.W. 1133 (1907) (promoter represented that he expected no payment).

78. Bishop v. Parker, 103 Utah 145; 134 P.2d 180 (1943); Ramsay v. Brooke County Bldg, and Loan Assn., 102 W. Va. 119; 135 S.E. 249 (1926); 49 A.L.R. 668. No duty to pay, if no express or implied ratification: Garnder v. Equitable O.B. Corp., 273 F., 441 (2d Cir. 1921); Oleck, *Modern Corporation Law*, §41 (1978 Supp.); 17 A.L.R. 431; 123 A.L.R. 783; Johns, *Compensation of Promoters*, 20 Marquette L. Rev. 95 (1936). But acceptance of benefits, plus reasonable expectation of payment, results in a duty to pay: Brace v. Oil Fields Corp., 173 Ark. 1128; 293 S.W. 1041 (1927); Chartland v. Barney's Club, Inc., 380 F.2d 97 101–02 (9th Cir. 1967); and citations above. *And see*, Abrams v. Puziss, 235 Ore. 60, 383 P.2d 1012 (1963); Bailey v. Interstate Airmotive, 358 Mo. 1121, 219 S.W.2d 333 (1949); Coastal Pharmaceutical Co. v. Goldman, 213 Va. 831, 195 S.E.2d 848 (1973).

79. Attorney who receives benefits (business corporation) is a promoter, according to the

S.E.C. view; *Re* Continental Distributors of Importers Corp., 1 S.E.C. Rep. 54. Not so, according to the New York view: Tucillo v. Pittelli, 127 N.Y.S. 314 (1911).

80. *See*, Drinker, *Laymen on the Competency and Integrity of Lawyers*, 22 Tenn. L. Rev. 371 (1952).

81. *See*, Bradley, *Role of Trade Associations and Professional Business Societies in America* (Penna. State Univ. Press, University Park, Pa. 1965).

82. *Ibid.*

15

PURPOSES, AND PURPOSE CLAUSES

§157. ORGANIZATION PURPOSES, IN GENERAL

Nonprofit corporations usually state, in their articles of incorporation, the purposes for which they are formed; so do unincorporated associations in their organization documents. Statutes in most states expressly *require* such statements, as public notice of what this group is or means to be. For example, the Florida Not-for-Profit Corporation Statute[1] says that the articles of incorporation . . . . . . must set forth: . . . (c) The purpose or purposes for which the corporation is organized." Statutes in most other states contain similarly specific wording.[2] And unincorporated associations usually state their purposes with similar wording.[3] Even a corporation specially chartered by a legislature must have some such statement in its charter, lest its charter be found unconstitutional as a too-general grant of authority by the legislature.

But recent statute changes, such as those of New York and California, have loosened this express requirement. Instead they require only that the articles of incorporation state whether the corporation is to be a "charitable," "mutual benefit" or a "religious" organization;[4] in addition to "educational" and "cooperative" (or a few more specific ones) in some states.[5] The specific requirements of most state laws, as to such self-identification, now are attacked as too restrictive by some people.[6] Mingling of nonprofit and profit purposes also are enthusiastically approved by these persons, as long as the profits are not actually "divided up" among the operators and/or members as dividends. The American Bar Association's Model Nonprofit Corporation Act Revision, proposed in 1986, set forth an even looser view, saying that "The articles of incorporation *may* [emphasis supplied] [but are not required to] set forth (1) the purpose or purposes for which the corporation is organized. . . ."[7]

It is true, however, that the enormous multiplication of organizations in this century has resulted in a decline in the requirement of particularization of stated purposes. The public now expects business-type operations, for fund

raising, in even "charitable" organizations; and it also expects social-responsi-
bility-type operations (at least as public relations activities) in even strictly
"business" corporations.[8]

It is still the great majority rule that a specific purpose must be declared
in its articles of incorporation by a nonprofit corporation; including the new
revisions of state statutes, such Illinois' proposed total statute revision of 1985.[9]
This clearly is the sound view because the public and the organization's own
personnel ought to have clearly stated just what their organization is and does,
particularly if it is to receive such legal privileges as tax exemption.

Purpose, *in the language of corporation law, is a technical term.*

In the ordinary sense of the word, the *purpose* of a nonprofit corporation
is the object for which the corporation is formed; the aim, intention, or plan
which it is meant to effectuate. Such purpose, of course, must be of a charitable, educational, religious, social, or other nonprofit nature.

For example, a state bar association's proper (constitutional) purposes or
activities are valid if they meet the criteria of public interest, improvement of
justice and the courts, regulation of attorneys and their relation to client trust
accounts, and the education and ethics and competence of the legal profession.[10]

Common sense makes it obvious that every organization must have been
formed for some *purpose*, in the ordinary sense of the word. But in the sense
of legal or formal organization of a nonprofit group, the word *purpose* has a
special meaning, identical to the meaning of that word in corporation laws.[11]

In corporation law *purpose*, or more often, *purpose clause*, means the clause
in a corporation's charter which formally states the object or objects the corporation was organized to accomplish.[12] Thus, the word refers to the usually
short (one-paragraph) summary of the reason for the existence of the corporation. This is the *stated* reason, of course, as distinguished from the underlying (personal) reasons of its members for its existence. The underlying reason
in a business corporation usually is the desire for profit, and in a nonprofit corporation may be many moral objectives, or even (as in a trade association) also
the desire for profit.

§158. PURPOSES AND POWERS MUST BE DISTINGUISHED

It should be clear, from the foregoing section, that the *purpose clause* in a charter expresses the object of the corporation's existence and operation.

In contrast, the term *power*, or *power clauses*, means the abilities or capacities of the corporation to act as an entity.[13] The term is most important in corporation law, because a corporation is artificial. As such it does not have all the
capacities (rights) to act that a natural person has. It has only those capacities
(powers) that the law allows. These are the general powers granted by the law

to all corporations of its kind of class plus those granted by the approval of its specific charter.[14]

It follows, then, that ideally every conceivable power that a corporation might want should be stated in its charter to obtain governmental approval of them all at once. This is not practicable, of course, nor is it necessary. The law permits a corporation, in every state, to have and use all the powers reasonably necessary for the carrying out of its approved purposes, with certain specific exceptions. Thus, a general approval of its stated purposes amounts to implied approval of all reasonably necessary powers for the accomplishment of those purposes.[15] Statutes usually specifically except from this approval certain powers, such as the power to make profit in the case of a nonprofit corporation, or the power to carry on banking or insurance activities (for which special procedures and approvals are required).[16]

As a result of this distinction between *purposes* and *powers*, it is sufficient for most nonprofit corporations that their charters state only their purposes, in brief, general terms. Power clauses are useful, in a charter, only to clarify a few uncertain matters, such as the organization's power to mortgage property, to make loans to its members, or for its officers or members to receive salaries or do business with the corporation.

The corporation name or title itself often gives a general indication of the organization's purposes.

§159. EFFECT OF THE PURPOSE CLAUSES

Besides general explanation of the reason for the existence of the corporation, the purpose clauses in its charter have other important functions.

For a nonprofit organization, the very approval of incorporation depends largely on the purpose clause in its proposed charter. If the purpose is contrary to the public policy of the state (for example, a purpose to spread bigotry or race hatred or advocate statutes that would limit free speech and association), the charter cannot lawfully be approved.[17] Or if the purpose amounts to an evasion of other laws, approval cannot be granted.[18] Such is the case, for instance, when the purpose of the organization is to carry on profit-making activities under the guise of nonprofit form, or solely to evade the burden of taxes on private income.[19]

§160. DISCLAIMER OF IMPROPER PURPOSES

It is necessary, in preparing a certificate of incorporation or articles of association, to include a clause or phrase indicating the nonprofit intentions of the organization. Often this is done in a negative manner, by stating that the purpose of the organization is not to be for pecuniary benefit of the officers or members.[20] This is especially necessary for obtaining tax exemption. A typical clause is one such as the following:

FORM NO. 17

Disclaimer of Profit-Purpose

This corporation is not organized for the pecuniary profit of its directors, officers, or members; nor may it issue stock nor declare nor distribute dividends, and no part of its net income shall inure, directly or indirectly, to the benefit of any director, officer, or member; and any balance of money or assets remaining after the full payment of corporate obligations of all and any kinds shall be devoted solely to the charitable, educational, and benevolent purposes of the corporation.

FORM No. 18

Disclaimer of Political Purpose

No substantial part of the activities of the corporation shall be the carrying on of propaganda, or otherwise attempting to influence legislation, and the corporation shall not participate in, or intervene in (including the publishing or distribution of statements) any political campaign on behalf of or in opposition to any candidate for public office.

[Note: The right of *religious* organizations to do this is not clear at the time of this notation, in 1994.]

§161. CONTRADICTORY PURPOSES

[See Chapter 3, and Section 166]

Approval of incorporation usually will be refused if the purposes stated in a proposed charter are contradictory. For example, a stated purpose to aid and assist a given benevolent society, together with a stated purpose to own and manage property for that society, is contradictory. The corporation cannot consistently claim to be both a nonprofit and a profit organization at the same time, except under such special provisions as those of the California or New York system of statutes. Or, a purpose to practice law or medicine (which is unlawful for corporations, except where permitted by special statutes for limited purposes) is not consistent with a statement disclaiming such an intention.

A clear illustration of contradictory purposes is the statement of a truly nonprofit purpose, followed by the use of stock and the distribution of dividends by the corporation. In one case, a corporation had as its purpose the furnishing of bus transportation to its members on a nonprofit basis. This was nonprofit in fact, but the state law classified all bus companies as public utilities (*i.e.*, as business corporations). Accordingly, the stated purpose and the purpose declared by the law were contradictory, and the charter was refused approval.[21]

In recent years some special types of combined profit and nonprofit purposes have been encouraged by law, notably the building and operation of low rent housing developments. For this purpose "*limited profit housing companies*," organized under New York's *Private Housing Finance Law*, are good examples.[22]

Disclaimer clauses, discussed above, often declare that it is not the purpose of the corporation to engage in any activity forbidden to it. Then the self-serving disclaimer clause represents an attempt to clarify the real intentions of the interested persons. Whether or not such a disclaimer clause is effective depends ultimately on the actual nature of the corporate activities. This is so important that even one who participated in the improper activities is not barred from asserting their illegality.

As to combination of profit with nonprofit purposes, as permitted by the California and New York statutes for specific public-policy reasons, see Section 166 in this chapter, and Chapter 3.

§162. ILLEGAL PURPOSES

It is fundamental, in all states, that no organization, corporate or unincorporated, may carry on certain types of activities. These activities are such as depend on special, personal qualifications and relationships; for example, the practice of the learned professions.[23] Chief among these are the practice of law, medicine, and other such professions.[24] These all require a relationship of such special, personal trust and confidence that only duly licensed individuals may conduct them.

Corporations are generally forbidden to practice law and medicine, and also dentistry, podiatry, and optometry, and even engineering, architecture, and other professions in some states.[25] While a hospital, clinic, or legal aid society seems to be a contradiction under this general rule, there is no contradiction in fact. These organizations are chartered as *administrative* corporations or as "professional corporations" for tax benefit purposes only. They do not, and may not, practice medicine or law as artificial entities.[26] Such exceptions as the rendering of legal services by title companies, or of medical services by nurses employed by the Red Cross, are specially permitted by express legislation in the public interest.[27]

Parenthetically, it should be noted that many states now permit the incorporation of professional firms, such as partnerships of physicians or attorneys. This seems to be inconsistent with other statutes that forbid corporate practice of the learned professions. But there is no inconsistency in fact, because incorporation is permitted only for the purpose of allowing professional persons to obtain the tax law advantages available to corporations, as in pension and other compensation plans.[28] For all other purposes, corporate practice of the professions continues to be improper. Even if a charter erroneously should be accepted and filed by the state, later discovery of the contradictory purposes will result in cancellation proceedings. These proceedings are termed *quo warranto* (by what authority?) proceedings.[29]

In general, the test is whether or not licensing is required. If a license to practice is required, such a license ordinarily may be granted only to a qualified individual, not to a corporation. Then the corporation may not lawfully have as its purpose the practice of a profession for which such licensing is required.[30] But a corporation may be formed for the purpose of aiding a profession or the members of a profession, as in the case of aid to aged or needy members, or for popularization of public use of the services of that profession, or for intraprofession regulation, as in the case of a bar association or medical society.[31]

§163. FRAUD AND VAGUENESS

Purpose clauses give public notice of the nature of the organization for the information of those who deal with it. They also indicate to the corporation directors and officers the scope and range of their proper activities. And at the same time, they assure members that their membership will not involve them in remote and uncontemplated lines of activity and liability,[32] also, activities not in accord with the approved purpose warrant dissolution of the corporation.[33]

As our system of law presumes that a declared purpose is legitimate until proved otherwise, the approval of a stated purpose, by the fact of state approval of the charter, raises a strong presumption of legitimacy. This is not conclusive, however. If the facts of actual operation show the purposes to be illegal in effect or in underlying aim, the original presumption will be ineffective. Actual fraud, in such a case, is punishable under penal statutes. Vagueness may result in refusal of approval. And deceptiveness may result in withdrawal of approval after it has been granted.[34] Thus, an organization that seeks to carry on medical-insurance activities under the guise of a social or labor union purpose may be dissolved by the state.

Amendment or change of purposes, of course, is available at all times, if it will not work unjust effects or is not forbidden for certain specific purposes. In the case of a nonprofit corporation (as contrasted with the rule for business corporations), members usually have no "vested interest" in preserving the status quo. Therefore, changes in the organization's purposes may be made very freely, if the formalities are followed correctly.

§164. PUBLIC POLICY CONSIDERATIONS

Corporate purposes must not be contrary to public policy.

Duplication of purposes by several organizations is contrary to public policy. For example, a charter would be refused to an organization that wished to carry on exactly the same functions as the American Red Cross, the National Cerebral Palsy Association. The American Cancer Society, or the National Multiple Sclerosis Society.[35]

Racial and religious prejudice purposes are against public policy. In 1987 the Supreme Court ruled that defamation or discrimination based on *ethnic* group membership is actionable as a tort, as well as criminal in nature, *e.g.*, such as Jews or Arabs as ethnics. But religious or racially cultured purposes, aimed at mutual enjoyment or improvement, and not intended to promote bigotry or unhealthy exclusivism, are valid. This is a vague and uncertain borderline area of public policy and depends largely on the place and time.[36]

Mere unpopularity of the purpose generally does not make it contrary to public policy, nor bar its incorporation. For example, dislike of its purpose does not warrant rejection by the approving agency of the charter of a labor union, or of a society of friends of German or Chinese "culture"; nor generally justify rejection of an attempt to incorporate a "gay" (*e.g.*, homosexual) group.[37] The Supreme Court of Ohio, nevertheless, has held the rejection of the charter of a homosexual group valid, stating that "the promotion of homosexuality as a valid life style is contrary to the public policy of Ohio."[38]

Religious proselytization purposes are valid, but not if they aim solely at the conversion of the domestic members of another faith.[39]

Voluntary military societies of the nature of private armies now generally are illegal, but the purpose to aid and comfort the members of the official military services is valid.[40]

Preservation of national-origin group differences to prevent the working of the American "melting pot" is an improper purpose; but preservation of foreign-origin cultural qualities is a valid purpose.[41]

A corporate charter cannot be approved where the overthrow of the government is the declared object of the submitting organization.[42]

Anticommunist or antifascist purposes, and the like, are valid as long as they do not involve activities which themselves violate other principles of democratic fair play.[43]

Of course, evasion of the supposed nonprofit purpose of any organization is a fundamentally improper purpose, contrary to public policy as well as contrary to express statutory provisions.

§165. GOVERNMENTAL SCRUTINY OF PURPOSE CLAUSES

As is pointed out in some detail in Chapter 13, scrutiny of the purposes of nonprofit organizations is provided for in all states. The minimum scrutiny is that by the secretary-of-state at the time of filing of the organization documents. Many states have much more detailed administrative procedures in this respect.[44] Often approval by a judge and also various departmental approvals are required.[45] These are discussed in Chapter 13.

The administrative scrutiny is directed primarily to the purposes stated or implied, as well as to the persons concerned and the satisfaction of formal requirements.[46]

Since the revelations of abuses of the foundation form of nonprofit activities by the Patman Committee in 1962, and especially since enactment of the Tax Reform Act of 1969 and the creation of the Office of Exempt Organizations in 1974, more careful scrutiny of all nonprofit organizations by the Internal Revenue Service is to be expected. Indeed, warning of more careful scrutiny has been given by the IRS, applicable particularly to foundations but also to all organizations that have or seek tax-exempt status.

Political Activity: "Lobbying" by PACs (Political Action Committees), or "Grassrooting" purposes, may result in loss of tax exemption if extensive in nature.[47] See Form 18 above.

§166. COMBINATION (MIXTURE) OF PROFIT AND NONPROFIT PURPOSES

[See Chapter 3.] Mixtures of profit and nonprofit corporate purposes and operations now are the norm in American enterprise. This is treated in detail in Chapter 3.

New York's Not-for-Profit Corporation Law, which became effective in 1970, permits four types of corporations, including Type C and Type D corporations "for any lawful business purposes."[48] New Jersey's *Long Term Tax Exemption Law* is similar in concept, but limits profits to the percentage per annum arrived at by adding 1 1/4 percent to the annual interest rate of the project's mortgage or to the prevailing rate on mortgage financing for comparable projects.[49] California's permissive new statute is discussed in Chapter 3 and Section 157.

What is involved in this kind of "purpose" is actually a Not-for-Profit Business Corporation.

[The balance of this Section consists of extracts from an article by Prof. James W. Weeks of Syracuse University, titled "The Not-for-Profit Business Corporation," published in *19 Cleveland State Law Review* 303-315, and reproduced here with permission of that periodical.]

Although restrictions are placed upon the division or distribution of income, statutory recognition of profits opens the door to greater flexibility in operations by NPC's which hitherto had been denied or at least made hazardous by uncertainty of judicial construction. At least in New York it does remove some of the previous need for great ingenuity which was employed to create business facilities in spite of the lack of express statutory authorization. For example:

> Membership corporations desiring to provide housing facilities for the aged were apparently incapable of incorporating for that purpose under existing law if a profit element was involved in such operations. However, incorpo-

rating for purposes of rendering services to the aged was permissible, and if housing facilities are regarded as incidental to and an implied power resulting from the general purpose of the corporation to care for the aged, it was regarded as all right.

Final legislative recognition of the right to make "incidental profits" at least injects a note of honesty if nothing else. There need not be an equating of gains and losses throughout the year on all business activities. Surpluses engendered by the business operations of the NPC may be used to maintain or improve the business.[50]

[He then speaks of the *foundation* as a business instrumentality.]

The modern practitioner must undertake a degree of rethinking in the nonprofit area; no longer should the term conjure up only a mental picture of schools, hospitals, homes for the aged, fraternal organizations, churches, trade associations, agricultural organizations, and cemetery plots. Today one is required to think in addition to these of research and development companies, capital development corporations, residential and industrial, homeowner associations, and so forth. Several of these, particularly the development corporations, are multimillion dollar entities, no longer dependent upon private giving for their existence, but containing the potential of making large profits while conducting a necessary public function. Some are mixtures of the private and public sector, where the management skills of the private are blended with the power of the public to renovate central city areas, stop environmental pollution, and the like. . . .[51]

The NPC is really the logical development or extension of current societal demands. It permits the modern corporation to engage in socially useful enterprises without the previously required sacrifice of foregoing an economic advantage. This, of course, decreases the burden upon the government, which might or might not be in a position to adequately supply the need which the particular NPC desires to fill. Although not intended to supplant government, the NPC is a vehicle for "good works" constructed in such a fashion as to attract private capital by permitting some return thereon, rather than the traditional prohibition leveled against nonprofit organizations forbidding the distribution of income or earnings to members. The NPC is still restricted but can now attract considerably more private capital to carry out its corporate purposes.

To illustrate what I mean by those "activities," I cite from the Purposes section[52] of the NPCL re: Local Development Corporations—Type C.

Corporations may be incorporated or reincorporated under this section as nonprofit local development corporations operated for the exclusively charitable or public purposes of relieving and reducing unemployment, promoting and providing for additional and maximum employment, bettering and maintaining job opportunities, instructing or training individuals or improving or developing their capabilities for such jobs, carrying on scientific research for the purpose of aiding a community or geographical area by attracting new industry to the community or area or by encouraging the development of, or retention of, an industry in the community or area, and lessening the burdens of government and acting in the public interest.

In carrying out these purposes, the corporation is permitted considerable flexibility in financial matters and may issue notes and bonds and "other obligations" and dispose of its assets without leave of the court.

The NPC appears to be the answer to the problem of how to liberate private capital for devotion to charitable purposes rather than to channel such funds to the public coffers via taxation for later redistribution as public monies. . . .

§167. FORMS OF PURPOSE CLAUSES

See, in Section 160, Form No. 17, "Disclaimer of Profit-Purpose." [*Note*: Many of the following forms are reproduced here from the Prentice Hall *Encyclopedia of Incorporating Forms.*[53]]

In all cases, there should be some statement of the nonprofit purposes of the organization.

In all cases, an introductory phrase is used, such as:

"The purpose of this organization shall be:"

FORM NO. 19

Athletic Club

To provide, construct, develop, acquire, lease, own, operate, and maintain a club and facilities and equipment for the promotion of amateur baseball, basketball, football, boxing, wrestling, swimming, tennis, golf, and any and all kinds of athletic sports, for the benefit of the members and their guests.

To promote, arrange, and hold any and all kinds of amateur athletic contests, exhibitions, and competitions, and to contribute towards and provide for the awarding of prizes and trophies therein;

To raise funds by membership subscription or otherwise for the encouragement of amateur athletic sports, and to grant commensurate rights and privileges to members and subscribers;

To acquire, own, buy, sell, lease, mortgage, or otherwise manage and deal in and with real property suitable for the above-stated purposes.

FORM NO. 20

Archery Club

To promote and encourage public interest in archery and the use of bow and arrow and other nonchemical missile projectiles and firing devices;

To arrange annual or more frequent archery contests and the award of prizes to members and invited competitors;

To provide social and sporting recreation and entertainment for its members.

FORM NO. 21

Art Institute

To devise and perpetuate a code or ethics of practice of the fine arts and the teaching thereof, and also of applied and commercial arts, so that higher standards of achievement and instruction and criticism shall prevail;

To promote and encourage talent and ability through exhibitions, awards, scholarships, and sales of art works;

To establish and maintain schools and courses of study of the fine, applied, and commercial arts.

FORM NO. 22

Artists' League

To promote and encourage public interest in and support of art in general, and the work of the members of this league in particular;

To promote and facilitate social and professional relations and cooperation between and among the members of this league and the members of the allied arts of music, literature, sculpture, and the patrons of all the arts;

To create and maintain a library, recreation center, and center of professional activities relating especially to American painting and sculpture.

FORM NO. 23

Automobile Club

To establish, maintain, and conduct a club composed primarily of automobile owners;

To advocate the enactment of laws, ordinances, rules, and regulations relating to the use of motor vehicles, and the rights and privileges of the owners and users thereof;

To promote the construction and maintenance of improved highways;

To collect and disseminate touring and travel information;

To promote street and highway safety;

To endeavor to do all things necessary to promote the interests and welfare of the motor vehicle owner and driver;

To assist in the proper enforcement of all laws pertaining to automobiling;

To maintain a service organization furnishing to, or procuring for, members or patrons any and all services designated for the protection, comfort, or convenience of owners and operators of automobiles.

To edit, publish, and distribute to members and patrons, periodicals, tour books, maps, and other printed matter useful to motorists.

To provide for the relief of disabled or destitute members, or their families, and to maintain a fund for that purpose; to contract with its members to pay death benefits according to such rules or bylaws as may be adopted by the corporation from time to time, and to agree to pay the same to the families, heirs, blood relatives, affianced husbands or affianced wives, the legal representatives of its members, or to persons dependent upon its members, after their deaths.

To do all things necessary, suitable and/or proper for the accomplishment of the above purposes, and any one or more of them.

FORM NO. 24

Automobile Dealers' Association

To promote goodwill and cooperation among the automobile dealers of . . . . . . association;

To reform abuses and to encourage protective legislation for the benefit of the members;

To reduce unjust legislation and to distribute reliable information about the members and the trade generally.

FORM NO. 25

Boys' Camp

To acquire, organize, operate, and maintain without any charge (or, at a nominal charge) a summer camp for boys of . . . . . . (city) in . . . . . . (state) who because of family financial limitations cannot otherwise attend such camps, and to do any and all acts proper and suitable for this purpose;

To solicit contributions and donations from the public residents of . . . . . . (city) to pay the expenses of the operation of said camp.

FORM NO. 26

Building and Loan Association

To loan money to its members for the erection of dwellings and other buildings, for the improvement of real estate, or for other investments or purposes, and to take mortgages on real estate or pledges of stock of said corporation and to secure such loans, and to do the general business of a building and loan association as prescribed by the law of the State of . . . . . .

FORM NO. 27

Building of Public Project

To promote the building of a . . . . . . (insert project) at and . . . . . . Streets, County of . . . . . . , City of . . . . . . , State of . . . . . . , as contemplated in the act of the Legislature of the State of . . . . . . , providing for the location of such . . . . . in the City of . . . . . . ; to acquire by purchase, gift, donations, or devise, and to hold for the purposes hereinafter mentioned, real estate in or as additions to the City of . . . . . . , and to lay out and plat the same into streets, alleys, lots, and blocks, and to sell and dispose of the lots and blocks so surveyed, laid out, and platted, for the purpose of providing a fund for the construction of said building; to act as trustee for the donors of such fund, and for the State of . . . . . . ; and to do generally such other and further business, and have such other and further powers as are necessary or desirable to effectuate and carry out the above purposes.

FORM NO. 28

Club or Clubhouse

To own, operate, conduct, and maintain a membership club, clubhouses, clubrooms, recreation centers, and reception and assembly rooms, and other facilities for the purpose of providing for the members' entertainment, sport, recreation, and instruction of all kinds; to furnish, equip, decorate, and fit up such clubs and clubrooms; to promote social and friendly intercourse among the members of such club or clubs and their guests; and to provide and supply any and all appurtenances that may be necessary, useful, or convenient for the carrying on of sports, recreations, and diversions of all kinds and descriptions for the entertainment, welfare, and convenience of the members of such club or clubs and their guests and friends.

FORM NO. 29

Community Development

To publish authentic information regarding the resources, opportunities, and attractions of the (City, Town, or State) of . . . . . . ; to provide a service of advice, direction, and assistance to persons desiring to visit or settle within the boundaries of the (City, Town, or State) of . . . . . . ; to participate in activities for the development of the (City, Town, or State) of . . . . . . ; to cooperate with other communities by initiating or assisting similar activities in the interests of . . . . . . (insert locality); to do all acts and things necessary or convenient in furthering the purposes hereinabove set forth.

FORM NO. 30

Conservation

To conserve, preserve, and otherwise prevent the waste and depletion of petroleum rock or carbon oils, natural gas, or other volatile mineral substances by under-reaming and laterally drilling old, abandoned, or unused wells and other deposits, and to employ any and all other means and processes known, and which may become known to science, for accomplishing the conservation, preservation, restoration, and development of such old, abandoned, or unused wells and other deposits.

FORM NO. 31

Cooperative Apartment House [Condominium]

To acquire by purchase, or otherwise, hold, own, develop, improve, sell, convey, exchange, mortgage, lease, and otherwise deal or trade in, and dispose of real property and any estate, interest, or rights therein; to lend money on bonds secured by mortgage on real or personal property, or otherwise; to erect, construct, alter, manage, rent, and operate, for its own account or for others, and to maintain and improve houses and buildings and the several parts and apartments and other space of any building or buildings erected on any lands of the corporation, or upon any other lands, and to rebuild, alter, and improve existing houses and buildings thereon to the extent now or hereafter permitted by law.

It is not the purpose of this corporation to make profits, but rather to provide homes for its members by building, erecting, operating, and maintaining apartment houses or hotels and leasing to them, under leases now commonly known as proprietary (or, condominium) leases, rooms, suites and duplex apartments in buildings owned by the corporation, and to sell, rent, or lease to its members such space.

FORM NO. 32

Cooperative Apartment House[*]
([*]another form)

To acquire real estate in the City of . . . . . . , State of . . . . . . ; to hold mortgage, sell, or exchange the same; to erect a building or buildings thereon, and any replacements thereof and additions thereto; to manage, operate, and maintain such real estate, and to rent the several parts of and apartments and other space in any building or buildings erected or to be erected thereon; to do and transact all such business necessary, incidental to, or in any way connected with said purposes, or any of them.

It is not the purpose of this corporation to make profits, but rather to provide homes for its members by leasing to them, under leases now commonly known as proprietary (or, condominium) leases, apartments in a building owned by the corporation.

After the acquisition by this corporation of premises on the southwest corner of . . . . . . Street and . . . . . . Avenue, the City of . . . . . . , State of . . . . . . , now known as number . . . . . . Avenue and number . . . . . . Street, this corporation shall not acquire any other real estate nor shall it sell or exchange any real estate owned by it except when authorized so to do by the consent in writing, or by vote at a members' meeting duly called for such purpose, of two thirds of the members.

FORM NO. 33

Country Club

To organize and maintain a club for the promotion of the physical and social welfare of, and the social intercourse among, its members; to erect, maintain, purchase, rent, hire, lease, let or otherwise acquire or dispose of buildings or structures for said purposes; to acquire, sell, mortgage, lease, or otherwise acquire or dispose of real or personal property necessary or convenient to such purpose.

FORM NO. 34

Dog Protective Association

To promote public understanding, appreciation, and care of the dog, man's best friend;

To establish and maintain a home for the care and disposition of homeless dogs, and to assist in the restoration of lost dogs to their owners;

To encourage the improvement of the breed by shows and prizes;

To establish and maintain a system of ownership identification of dogs.

FORM NO. 35

Farmers' Association

To associate together for their mutual benefit the farmers, agriculturalists, and horticulturists of . . . . . . , for their mutual benefit as such, and to assist them in the promotion of the demand for the sale of . . . . . . and . . . . . . products, by promotional work;

To provide marketing and other information to members;

To represent them and their interests in common in state and federal agencies, the market, and before the public;

To perform and aid all functions in aid and furtherance of their legitimate interests as farmers, agriculturists, and horticulturists.

FORM NO. 36

Foundation

To support and assist, and to make grants and gifts in aid and support and assistance of (prevention of cruelty to children; or, the education of needy law students; or, etc.) And the entire income and principal of the endowment and assets of this corporation shall be held and distributed solely for such purposes, except for the modest amount needed for the expenses of administration of this corporation in order to effectuate the said purpose(s).

No part of its net earnings shall inure to the benefit of any individual except as a grant as above described; no substantial part of its activities shall be the carrying on of propaganda or otherwise attempting to influence legislation; and it shall not participate in nor intervene in (including the publishing or distributing of statements) any political campaign on behalf of any candidate for public office or referendum. If by reason of change in Section 501(c) of the United States Internal Revenue Code, or otherwise, the carrying out of any of the said purposes would cause the assets or income of this corporation to be subject to federal income tax, no further distributions shall be made for such nonexempt purpose or purposes.

FORM NO. 37

Gun Club

To promote public interest and skill in the use of small guns and firearms, hunting, fishing, trapping, and other lawful sports;

To aid in the conservation of game and wildlife;

To promote healthy social and athletic recreation for the members.

FORM NO. 38

Hospital

To acquire, buy, construct, establish and maintain, equip, and operate a public hospital in . . . . . .

FORM NO. 39

Medical Research

To engage in, carry on, and conduct research, experiments, investigations, analyses, and studies as to disease, deformities, functional disorders, afflictions, and other conditions, normal and abnormal, of any and all parts of the human body, and to foster and develop scientific methods for the diagnosis, prevention, treatment, alleviation, and cure thereof;

To establish, maintain, and operate laboratories, clinics, hospitals, plants, and any and all other establishments, for the purposes aforesaid.

FORM NO. 40

Propaganda (or, PACs)

To promote, foster, and encourage, by the preparation and distribution of literature, pamphlets, magazines, periodicals, tokens, and otherwise, the sentiment and belief that ...... (insert aim of organization); to create and maintain a compact, representative, and centralized agency for concerted action upon all matters affecting the welfare and betterment of the people of the United States; to mold public opinion, and to promote, foster, and encourage the interest of the people of the United States in good government; to compile, distribute, and disseminate information as to civic, state, and governmental matters;

To prepare, compile, select, distribute, and disseminate scientific data and information of all kinds which may be useful in furthering the purposes of this corporation;

To print, publish, distribute, and circulate among the people books, pamphlets, periodicals, papers, and magazines in connection with the activities of the corporation;

[*Note*: See statutory limitations on the right to carry on propaganda of certain kinds, especially *political*, in many states. Political activity also may cause loss of tax exemption.[54]] [See index herein: *Lobbying and Grassrooting*.]

FORM NO. 41

Purchasers' (Consumers') Protective Association

To aid and assist the manufacturers of nationally advertised products, by any and all proper and lawful means, in protecting themselves and the general purchasing public from the imitation of and the substitution of other products, merchandise, and commodities for the products, merchandise, and commodities of such manufacturers of nationally advertised products; to educate, encourage, and direct public opinion against the use of such imitations and against such substitution of products; to assist and collaborate with federal, state, and municipal authorities in prosecuting individuals, firms, partnerships, associations, corporations, and all others involved in any and all such imitations and substitutions which are unlawful; to investigate, compile, and procure data and information concerning the imitation of and the substitution of the other products, merchandise, and commodities for those produced and manufactured by the manufacturers of nationally advertised products, and in connection therewith to adopt, formulate, and carry out any and all protective measures possible and proper for the welfare and interests of the manufacturers of such nationally advertised products, merchandise, and commodities, and of the general purchasing public;

To prepare, compile, select, distribute, and disseminate scientific data and information of all kinds, which may be useful in furthering the purposes of this corporation;

To print, publish, distribute, and circulate books, pamphlets, periodicals, papers, and magazines in connection with the activities of the corporation.

FORM NO. 42

Savings and Loan Association

To transact the general business of a mutual savings and loan association; to receive money and accumulate funds to be loaned, and to loan the same to shareholders, stockholders, and others; to permit shareholders and investors to withdraw part or all of their payments, investments, or stock deposits, and to prescribe the terms and conditions of such withdrawal; to cancel shares of stock on which the payments have been withdrawn; to receive deposits of money and to execute certificates therefor; to borrow money for the purpose of making loans and of paying withdrawals at maturity; to encourage industry, frugality, home building, and saving among shareholders and members; to accumulate savings; to loan to its shareholders, members, and others the money so accumulated, with the profits and earnings thereon, and to repay to each his savings and profits whenever they have accumulated to the full par value of the shares, or at any time when he shall desire the same, or when the corporation shall desire to repay the same, as may be provided by the bylaws, and to do all other acts authorized by law.

FORM NO. 43

School

To establish and carry on a nonprofit school or college where students may obtain a sound classical, mathematical, technical, and general education; to provide for the delivery and holding of lectures, exhibitions, public meetings, classes, and conferences, calculated directly or indirectly to advance the cause of education, whether general, professional, or technical;

To give instruction in stenography, typewriting, bookkeeping, and other subjects which relate to the preparation for trained service in any and all branches of business and commerce;

To gather, receive, and disseminate such information as may seem helpful in the instruction of its students;

To provide helpful vocational advice and guidance; to maintain and operate a general free employment agency for placing or replacing in employment individuals who have taken courses at, or are graduates of, the school or schools conducted by this corporation;

To confer diplomas or other certificates of merit upon those who become proficient in one or more of the branches of instruction offered at the school or schools maintained by this corporation.

FORM NO. 44

Traffic Research

To give to members free advice and information concerning freight, passenger, and other kinds of traffic and transportation, on land, on sea, in air, or otherwise, as to rates, routes, methods, and means of shipping and transporting goods, wares, and merchandise, and on all or any matters pertaining thereto;

To analyze and give information as to the adjustment of rates, to handle rate adjustments, to gather and furnish statistics and data on the subject of freight and transportation rates, and to carry on research work in traffic rates and problems;

To print, publish, and sell books, newspapers, journals, magazines, periodicals, lists, pamphlets, and reports concerning matters relating to transportation and freight, and to set forth therein advice and information to members about all or any matters connected with or pertaining to the giving of service and advice on freight and transportation matters; and, in general, to render a complete and comprehensive service on all matters pertaining to and in any way connected with transportation and the handling of freight of all kinds and descriptions.

FORM NO. 45

Sports Club

To promote games, contests, physical exercise, sports, and athletics of every kind and description; to provide and maintain therefor buildings, grounds, and facilities, including clubhouses for the accommodation of its members; to elevate the standard of games, contests, athletics, and sports; to maintain a high plane of physical and moral excellence and to enlist the cooperation of all persons to that end; to hold contests and physical competitions and exhibitions of every kind; to give and grant to others, so far as empowered by law, the right and privilege to hold such contests, competitions, and exhibitions under its auspices or otherwise, in accordance with its prescribed rules and regulations and subject to such conditions as it may lawfully impose; to enact and establish rules and regulations governing such contests, competitions, and exhibitions, classifying those participating therein, determining and defining awards and prizes for winning contests, defining and awarding tokens and insignia of championships, and determining and defining breaches and infractions of its rules and regulations and imposing penalties therefor in accordance with law; to exercise disciplinary authority so far as is lawful over all persons engaged in such contests, competitions, and exhibitions to the end that games, contests, sports, and athletics of every kind may be subject to clean, manly, dignified competition, and that supremacy therein once attained by any individual shall be by him defended and kept in competition under penalty of forfeiture and permanent disqualification; to promote the physical and moral well-being of all athletes; to educate public opinion; and by all lawful means to elevate, improve, and promote games, contests, physical exercises, athletics, exhibitions, and all sports.

FORM NO. 46

Truck Owners' Association

To advance the mutual interests of members who own or operate trucks; to reform abuses, and to establish and maintain principles and standards of fair and equitable operation;

To protect members from irresponsible customers and from unfair attacks by other persons or groups;

To promote safety and compliance with the law;

To promote reasonable and fair insurance coverage, rates, and practices;

To eliminate unfair competition and unfair practices;

To do any and all proper things for the advancement of the legitimate interests of the members as truck owners or operators.

POINTS TO REMEMBER

- The "purpose clause" is all-important. Think it out before you decide on what purposes you will adopt.
- Word your purpose clause carefully. Make it broad, but don't bite off more than you can chew.

- Distinguish between "purposes" and "powers."

- Always use a specific "purpose clause" in your charter.

- Beware of contradictory purposes. [Study the statute, when using New York Type C or D purposes.]

- Use a "disclaimer clause" to show good intentions.

- Beware of illegal purposes. Look out for licensing requirements. They are danger signals.

- Remember that "public policy" is the final test. Ask yourself: "Is this good for the public?"

- Do not be afraid of unpopular purposes, if they are good for the public.

- Use forms of purpose clauses as a *guide*. Do not copy them word for word.

- *Your* purpose always is a little different. Write yours out yourself, after studying the model forms.

- Just say what you mean to do, in simple words, briefly. That is the ideal "purpose clause."

- Provide for alternative purposes only if that is essential. Keep purposes limited and practical.

- Do not make your purpose clause unnecessarily grandiose or sweeping; that may bring your tax-exempt status into question.

- Use "PACs" (Political Action Committees) for "Lobbying" or "Grassrooting" cautiously, lest you lose tax exemption.

NOTES TO CHAPTER 15

1. Fla. Stat. §617.0202; *Nonprofit Corporations in Florida* §3.1 (Florida Bar C.L.E., 1981; Oleck, Chairman of Seminar).

2. See, Del. Code tit. 8 §102(a)(3); Genl. St. No. Car. §55a-7(3); Ohio Rev. Code §1702.04(a)(3); Proposed Ill. Not-for-Profit Corp. Act (SB 1320) Art. 2 §102.05(a)(2) of 1985.

3. Note, *Judicial Protection of Membership in Private Associations*, 14 Wes. Res. L. Rev. 346 (1963); Note, *The Memorandum of Association: A Point on the Objects Clause*, 83 Sol. J. 330 (1939).

4. Calif. Corp. Code §§5035, 5059, 5060, 5111, *etc. See* Fryer and Haglund, *New California Nonprofit Corporation Law*, 7 Pepperdine L. Rev. (1) 1–40 (1979).

5. N.Y. Not-for-Profit Corp. L. §§101 *etc.*; Henn and Boyd, *Statutory Trends in the Law of Nonprofit Organizations: California Here We Come!*, 66 Cornell L. Rev. (6)1103 (1981).

6. See, Hansmann, *Reforming Nonprofit Corporation Law*, 129 U. of Penna. L. Rev. (3)497–623 (1981). But they are required by Ill. Not-for-Profit Corp. Act (Proposed), Art. 2 §102.05(a)(2) of 1985 (S.B. 1320); Illinois lists 30 purposes under which nonprofits may organize, 805 ILCS 105/103.05.

7. A.B.A. Model Nonprofit Corp. Act §2.02(b)(1): Exposure Draft (March 1986).

8. P. Verrucoli, *Non-Profit Organizations* (A Comparative Approach) 5 (Milan, Italy—Dott. A. Giuffre Editore; Cappalletti Studies in Comparative Law, 1985). In English.

9. §103.05 of that Act (SB 1320).

10. *Florida Bar re Schwarz*, 552 So. 2d 1094 (Fla. 1989).

11. *See*, 1, Oleck, *Modern Corporation Law*, §§596,603 (1978 Supp.); 6 Fletcher, *Cyc. of Law of Private Corporations*, §2475 (perm. ed.). The "charitable purposes" expressed in a trust become vested when the rights of present or future use or enjoyment become fixed and irrevocable. Brown v. Buyer's Corp., 35 Ohio St.2d 191, 299 N.E.2d 279 (1973), citing Ohio Rev. Code §109.23.

12. Good Will Home Assn. v. Erwin, 266 A.2d 218, 221 (Me. S.J. 1970); State *ex rel.* Russell v. Sweeney, 153 Ohio St. 66, 91 N.E.2d 13 (1950); Westbrook v. Univ. of Ga. Athletic Assn., Inc. 206 Ga. 667, 58 S.E.2d 428 (1950); (all, purposes clauses in nonprofit corporations); Henn, *Corporations*, 144 (2d ed. 1986, casebook); Hamilton, *Corporations* 164 (3rd ed. 1986, casebook).

13. *See*, 1 Oleck, *Modern Corporation Law*, c. 26 (1978 Supp.); Note, *Distinction Between Powers and Objects in Articles of Incorporation*, 46 Harv. L. Rev. 1337 (1933); Freligh v. Saugerties, 70 Hun. (N.Y.) 589, 24 N.Y.S. 182 (1893); Vanderbilt v. Commissioner, 93 F.2d 360 (C.C.A. 1 1937); Kubik v. American Composers Alliance, Inc., 54 N.Y.S.2d 764 (1945); *and see* State of Ohio *ex rel.* J. F. Russell, Jr., 153 Ohio St. 66 (1950); that a statement in the articles, characterizing purposes or powers as nonprofit, is not conclusive as to the nature of the corporation; *see also*, Celina and Mercer County Tel. Co. v. Union-Center Mutual Tel. Assn., 102 Ohio St. 487 (1921); American Jersey Cattle Club v. Glander, 152 Ohio St. 506 (1950).

14. Northwest Civic Assn. v. Sheldon, 317 Mich. 416; 27 N.W.2d 36 (1947); Luttenberger v. Restland Memorial Park Assn., 51 N.J. Super. 507, 144 A.2d 12 (1958).

15. *See* n. 13, above; Henn, *Corporations*, 144 (2d ed. 1986, casebook); Hamilton, *Corporations* 164 (3rd ed. 1986, casebook).

16. Statutes cited in n. 4, above.

17. *Re* We Americans, Inc., 166 Misc. 167; 2 N.Y.S.2d 235 (1938); *Re* Patriotic Citizenship Assn., 53 N.Y.S.2d 595 (1945); *Re* Voters Alliance for Americans of German Ancestry, 64 N.Y.S.2d 298 (1946); Matter of Certif. of Incorp. of Council for Small Businesses, 195 N.Y.S.2d 530 (1956) (purposes too vague); *and see*, Vance, *Freedom of Association in N.Y. State*, 46 Cornell L.Q. 290 (1961).

18. Bernstein v. Moses, 133 Misc. 513; 231 N.Y.S. 669 (1928); Castle Hill Beach Club v. Arbury, 142 N.Y.S.2d 432 (1955) (racial tolerance).

19. Profit purpose: People *ex rel* Davenport v. Rice, 68 Hun. (N.Y.) 24; 22 N.Y.S. 631 (1893); Meisel v. National Jewelers Board of Trade, 90 Misc. 19; 152 N.Y.S.913 (1915); Tax purpose: Columbia Univ. Club v. Higgins, 23 F. Supp. 572 (D.C.N.Y. 1938); *and see*, Oleck, *Foundations Used as Business Devices*, 9 Clev.-Mar. L. Rev. 339 (1960).

20. In many states such a statement in the charter is mandatory. *See* the statutes cited in n. 1–5, above. It is vital in respect to later application for income tax exemption.

21. Opinions N.Y. Atty.-Genl. (1942) p. 219; Bartlett v. Lily Dale Assembly, 139 Misc. 338; 249 N.Y.S. 482 (1931) (use of stock).

22. Mitchell-Lama Act. discussed in Fuller v. Urstadt, 28 N.Y.2d 315, 270 N.E.2d 321 (1971).

23. State Electro-Medical Inst. v. Nebraska, 74 Nebr. 40; 103 N.W. 1078 (1905); State *ex rel.* Sisemore v. Standard Optical Co., 182 Ore. 452; 188 P.2d 309 (1947); State *ex rel.* Harris v. Myers, 128 Ohio St. 366; 191 N.E. 99 (1934); Parker v. Panama City, 151 S.2d 469 (Fla. 1963).

24. State *ex rel.* Green v. Brown, 173 Ohio St. 114, 180 N.E.2d 157 (1962); Thompson Optical Inst. v. Thompson, 119 Ore. 252; 237 P. 965 (1925); Matter of Cooperative Law Co., 198 N.Y. 479; 92 N.E. 15, 32 L.R.A. (N.S.) 55 (1910).

25. Ohio Rev. Code §1701.03; Consol. Laws N.Y., Judiciary L. §495 prohibits practice of law by corporations; N.Y. Stock Corp. L. §7 (law); Matter of New York County Lawyers Assn. v. Bercu, 273 A.D. 524; 78 N.Y.S.2d 209; *affd.*, 299 N.Y. 728;87 N.E.2d 451 (1949) (accountancy and law); Smith v. Illinois Adj. Fin. Co., 326 Ill. App. 654; 63 N.E.2d 264 (1945); Land Title Abstract Co. v. Dworkin, 129 Ohio St. 23; 193 N.E. 650 (1934); Auerbach v.

Wood, 139 N.J. Eq. 599; 53 A.2d 800; *affd.*, 142 N.J.Eq. 484, 59 A.2d 863 (1948); Dworkin v. Apartment House Owners Assn., 28 Ohio N.P. (n.s.) 114, 117, *affd.*, 38 Ohio App. 265, 176 N.E. 577 (1931) (law practice).

But some states do permit corporate practice of some professions, such as optometry. *See*, Seadron's Sons, Inc. v. Susskind, 132 Misc. 406; 229 N.S. 209 (1928); Cleveland Clinic v. Somprio, 6 Misc. 48, 214 N.E.2d 740 (1966). Matter of Dr. Bloom, Inc. v. Cruise, 259 N.Y. 358; 182 N.E. 16; *appl. dism.*, 288 U.S. 588; 53 S. Ct. 320; 77 L. Ed. 408 (1932) (Dentistry).

26. Godfrey v. Medical Society, 177 A.D. 684; 164 N.Y.S. 846 (1917); *and see, Incorporation Taxation and Licensing of Hospitals in the United States* (Amer. Hosp. Assn. 1937). Ohio Rev. Code §1701.03 specifically exempts sanitariums. As to "professional corporations," *see* Genl. Stat. No. Car., Ch. 55B.

27. *See* Ohio Rev. Code §1785.01 *et seq.*; Mich. Comp. L. §450.221 *et seq.*; 15 P.S. §§ 9301 and 9303–9319. (all, authorizing professional associations and corporations); Smith, *Professional Corporations in Ohio*, 30 Ohio St. L. J. 439 (1969); Comment, *Professional Corporations and Associations*, 75 Harv. L. Rev. 776 (1962).

28. *See*, Empey v. U.S., 277 F. Supp. 851 (D. Colo. 1967) holding that a law firm is a "corporation" for tax purposes; O'Neill v. U.S., 410 F.2d 888 (6th Cir. 1969). For a typical statute *see*, Genl. Stat. No. Car. Ch. 55B (Professional Corporation Act).

29. Ames v. Kansas, 111 U.S. 449; 4 S. Ct. 437, 28 L. Ed. 482 (1884); State *ex rel.* Johnson v. Conservative Savings and Loan Assn., 143 Nbr. 805; 11 N.W.2d 89, 92 (1943); Wilder v. Brace, 218 F. Supp. 860 (D. Me. 1963); *see*, Ohio Rev. Code §§2733.02–2733.39; 735 ILCS 5/18-101 *et seq.*

30. Cases cited in n. 23–26 above.

31. *Re* Certificate of Incorporation of N.Y. County Lawyers Assn. Fund, 81 N.Y.S.2d 724 (1948); *In re* Society for Social Responsibility in Sciences, Inc., 23 D.&C.2d 538, 10 Bucks. 194 (Pa. 1960).

32. Kubik v. American Composers Alliance, Inc., 54 N.Y.S.2d 764 (1945).

33. State *ex rel.* Corrigan v. West Shore Center, 31 Ohio St.2d 192, 287 N.E.2d 803 (1972); a nonprofit employment placement service that engaged only in activities unrelated to any employment placement, dissolved by *quo warranto* proceedings.

34. *See*, N.Y. Educ. L. §§6509, 6511–6514; Ohio Rev. Code §1702.52(A)(1)(general).

35. *Re* Boy Explorers of America, Inc., 67 N.Y.S.2d 108 (1946); *Re* Gold Star Parents Assn., Inc., 67 N.Y.S.2d 73 (1946); *In re* Waldemar Cancer Research Assn., 130 N.Y.S.2d 426 (1954).

36. *Symposium on Group Defamation*, 13 Clev.-Mar. L. Rev. 1–117 (1964).

37. *Re* German and Austrian-Hungarian War Veterans, 13 N.Y.S.2d 207 (1939); Hagan v. Picard, 171 Misc. 475, 12 N.Y.S.2d 873, *affd.*, 288 A.D. 771, 14 N.Y.S.2d 706 (1939) (unpopular union); Application of Thom, 33 N.Y.2d 609, 301 N.E.2d (1973); Matter of Gay Activists Alliance, 31 N.Y.2d 965, 293 N.E.2d 255 (1973) (homosexuals).

38. State *ex rel.* Grant v. Brown, 39 Ohio St.2d 112, 313 N.E.2d 847 (1974), dismissed for lack of jurisdiction, 420 U.S. 916 (1975).

39. Matter of American Jewish Evangelization Society, 183 Misc. 634; 50 N.Y.S.2d 236 (1944).

40. Matter of Long Beach Defense Guards, Inc., 100 Misc. 584; 166 N.Y.S. 459 (1917) (private volunteer military unit); N.Y. Mil. L. §241; *Re* Victory Committee of Greenpoint, 59 N.Y.S.2d 546 (1945) (purposes approved, but incorporation denied because of unnecessary duplication of work of existing organizations).

41. *Re* Columbia Assn., 175 Misc. 876; 24 N.Y.S.2d 901 (1940) (denied); *Re* Mazzini Cultural Center, 185 Misc. 1031; 58 N.Y.S.2d 529 (1945) (purposes approved, but name rejected because of its political connotation).

42. Matter of Lithuanian Workers Society, 196 A.D. 262; 187 N.Y.S. 612 (1920). *And see*, Butel, *Law Making by Professional and Trade Assns.*, 34 Nebr. L. Rev. 431 (1955).

43. *Re* Patriotic Citizenship Assn., 53 N.Y.S.2d 595 (1945).

44.   *E.g.,* New Jersey.

45.   *E.g.,* New York.

46.   Association for the Preservation of Freedom of Choice v. Shapiro, 214 N.Y.S.2d 388, 9
      N.Y.2d 376, 174 N.E.2d 487 (1961); *In re* Fraternidad Hispana-Americana, 39 Misc.2d 106,
      240 N.Y.S.2d 110 (App. Div. 1963).

47.   *See,* Buck, *Grass Roots Lobbying of Nonprofit Organizations' Problems 1980,* 176 (1980); Associa-
      tion of the Bar of City of N.Y. v. Commissioner, 89 T.C.—(No. 42) (1987); Note, 53 U.
      Cinc. L. Rev. 277 (1984).

48.   Consol. L. of N.Y. c. 37.

49.   N.J. Stat. Anno., tit. 40A:20-1 *et seq.*

50.   Burton-Potter Post No. 185, American Legion v. Epstein, 219 N.Y.S.2d 244 (S. Ct. Suffolk
      County 1961).

51.   But this can be done by specific legislation too—such as N.Y. Private Housing Finance Law,
      limited profit corporations. *See,* Fuller v. Urstadt, 28 N.Y.2d 315, 270 N.E.2d 381 (1971);
      and Mitchell-Lama Act §§22,23.

52.   N.Y. Not-for-Profit Corp. L. §1411(a).

53.   Current edition.

54.   *But see* 1918 Ohio Atty. Genl. Op. 1480 (nonprofit corporation may be formed for the pur-
      pose of furthering a political candidacy); 1912 Ohio Atty. Genl. Op. 617 (company orga-
      nized solely to publish religious books, using profits only for relief of ministers, is a non-
      profit corporation); 1935 Ohio Atty. Genl. Op. 4216 (nonprofit corporation library run by
      library association is not a public library, and cannot participate in distribution of certain
      tax-obtained monies). As to tax exemption and political activity, *see* Note, *The Revenue Code
      and a Charity's Politics,* 73 Yale L.J. 661 (1964). *See,* Stafford, on PACs (Political Action Com-
      mittees), p. 1, *St. Petersburg (Fla.) Times* (Jan. 14, 1980). *And see* n. 47, above.

16

POWERS AND POWER CLAUSES

§168. WHAT ARE THE POWERS OF A CORPORATION OR ASSOCIATION?

The *powers* of a corporate organization are "The *right* or *capacity* to act or be acted upon in a particular manner or in respect to a particular subject; as the power to have a corporate seal, to sue and be sued, to make bylaws, to carry on a particular business or construct a given work;" an organization's *powers* are the rights-of-action or procedure which it may *lawfully* employ in order to attain its stated *purposes*.[1]

"The powers possessed by a corporation can be no broader than the purposes for which it is organized." See *Blue Cross & Blue Shield of Connecticut v. Mike*, 184 Conn. 352, 439 A.2d 1026 (1981). This is particularly the case where the corporation is organized for special, as opposed to, general purposes.[2]

In *legal* language, a *power* of a corporation or an association means a legal authority to do something, such as to borrow money or to carry on certain kinds of activities.[3]

Formerly, corporations were viewed as possessing only such powers as were specifically granted to them by the state. This grant of powers was found in the certificate of incorporation, as approved by the state, or in the special statute granting a charter to the corporation.[4]

Addition of powers is usually restricted. For example, restrictive covenants as to age of residents may *not be imposed* by a retirement community corporation on original takers of plotted lots (sold in a realty development by the developers) by the device of changing the recorded deed restrictions stated by the original developer. The corporation had the function of collecting maintenance fees and of maintenance, and the developer had had no authority to later assign such power to change deeds sold to the original purchasers; so the corporation also had no such power.[5]

Modern rule. Today, in all the states, a corporation is deemed to possess all the powers of a natural person except those powers which are specifically

519

forbidden to such corporations by the law. The old concept of a corporation as a bundle of only a few, specifically granted powers, has been replaced by the concept of a corporation as an artificial person, lacking only those powers which the law specifically denies to it.

Associations' powers. The powers of an unincorporated association in many respects are quite similar to this modern concept of a corporation. Most of the natural powers of the individual persons who are its members are available also to the association, except insofar as specifically limited by the law, or by the very nature of group action. These powers and limitations are discussed in Chapter 5.[6]

It should be remembered that an unincorporated association is viewed as a kind of partnership for many purposes. Unless authorized by local statute, for example, it may have difficulty in taking title to property or transferring title, in the association's name. Personal liability of members often is found for association debts.

The powers of an unincorporated association thus are not clear in certain respects. While its powers are generally similar to those of a corporation, as above stated, the possibility of differences in some matters continues to exist.

Such uncertainty is one of the chief reasons for avoidance of use of the unincorporated form of organization. Uncertainty as to powers, however, is of less importance than uncertainty as to liabilities. There is great uncertainty as to the limits of liability of an unincorporated association or of its members.

Statutory statements. Modern corporation statutes usually express in broad terms the basic powers (or authority) of corporations. In most states, the general corporation statutes specifically grant to each corporation organized in the state at least the following basic powers:[7]

1. To use a corporate name or title.
2. To have continuous existence as a legal entity, though the membership changes.
3. To have a corporate seal or symbol.
4. To have perpetual existence, or to exist for any desired number of years.
5. To acquire, own, deal with, and dispose of property, both real and personal.
6. To appoint and compensate necessary officers and agents, and to act through them.
7. To sue and be sued in the corporate name.
8. To make bylaws, not inconsistent with the law, for the internal regulation of the organization, and to establish procedures for carrying out its approval purposes.

    In addition, the statutes of most states now contain a general grant authority, which provides, in substance, that every corporation shall have the power:

9. To "do all things permitted by law and exercise all authority within the purposes stated in its articles or incidental to those purposes."[8] If a nonprofit corporation exceeds its proper powers, this may bring into effect the legal doctrine of *ultra vires*; see the discussion of this doctrine later in Chapter 17.

§169. STATUTE STATEMENT OF CORPORATE POWERS[9]

Detailed Powers Statute (Ohio Rev. Code Sec. 1702.12) Authority of Nonprofit Corporations

[Note: But see, below, Form No. 62]

(A) A corporation may sue and be sued.

(B) A corporation may adopt and alter a corporate seal and use it or a facsimile of it, but failure to affix the corporate seal shall not affect the validity of any instrument.

(C) Unless otherwise provided in the articles, a corporation may take property of any description, or any interest in property, by gift, devise, or bequest.

(D) Subject to limitations prescribed by law or in its articles, a corporation may make donations for the public welfare, for religious, charitable, scientific, literary, or educational purposes, or in furtherance of any of its purposes.

(E)(1) A corporation may indemnify or agree to indemnify any person who was or is a party, or is threatened to be made a party, to any threatened, pending, or completed civil, criminal, administrative, or investigative action, suit, or proceeding, other than an action by or in the right of the corporation, by reason of the fact that he is or was a trustee, officer, employee, or agent of or a volunteer of the corporation, or is or was serving at the request of the corporation as a trustee, director, officer, employee, or agent of or a volunteer of another domestic or foreign nonprofit corporation or corporation for profit, or a partnership, joint venture, trust, or other enterprise, against expenses, including attorney's fees, judgments, fines, and amounts paid in settlement actually and reasonably incurred by him in connection with such action, suit, or proceeding, if he acted in good faith and in a manner he reasonably believed to be in or not opposed to the best interests of the corporation, and, with respect to any criminal action or proceeding, if he had no reasonable cause to believe his conduct was unlawful. The termination of any action, suit, or proceeding by judgment, order, settlement, or conviction, or upon a plea of nolo contendere or its equivalent, shall not create, of itself, a presumption that the person did not act in good faith and in a manner he reasonably believed to be in or not opposed to the best interests of the corporation, and, with respect to any criminal action or proceeding, a presumption that the person had reasonable cause to believe that his conduct was unlawful.

(2) A corporation may indemnify or agree to indemnify any person who was or is a party, or is threatened to be made a party, to any threatened, pending, or completed action or suit by or in the right of the corporation to procure a judgment in its favor, by reason of the fact that he is or was a trustee, officer, employee, or agent of or a volunteer of the corporation, or is or was serving at the request of the corporation as a trustee, director, officer, employee, or agent of or a volunteer of another domestic or foreign nonprofit corporation or corporation for profit, or a partnership, joint venture, trust, or other enterprise against expenses, including attorney's fees, actually and reasonably incurred by him in connection with the defense or settlement of such action or suit, if he acted in good faith and in a manner he reasonably believed to be in or not opposed to the best interests of the corporation, except that no indemnification shall be made in respect of any of the following:

(a) Any claim, issue, or matter as to which such person is adjudged to be liable for negligence or misconduct in the performance of his duty to the corporation unless, and only to the extent that, the court of common pleas or the court in which the action or suit was brought determines, upon application, that, despite the adjudication of liability but in view of all the circumstances of the case, such person is fairly and reasonably entitled to indemnity for such expenses as the court of common pleas or such other court considers proper;

(b) Any action or suit in which liability is asserted against a trustee and that liability is asserted only pursuant to section 1702.55 of the Revised Code.

(3) To the extent that a trustee, director, officer, employee, agent, or volunteer has been successful on the merits or otherwise in defense of any action, suit, or proceeding referred to in division (E)(1) or (2) of this section, or in defense of any claim, issue, or matter in such an action, suit, or proceeding, he shall be indemnified against expenses, including attorney's fees, actually and reasonably incurred by him in connection with that action, suit, or proceeding.

(4) Unless ordered by a court and subject to division (E)(3) of this section, any indemnification under division (E)(1) or (2) of this section shall be made by the corporation only as authorized in the specific case, upon a determination that indemnification of the trustee, director, officer, employee, agent, or volunteer is proper in the circumstances because he has met the applicable standard of conduct set forth in division (E)(1) or (2) of this section. Such determination shall be made in any of the following manners:

(a) By a majority vote of a quorum consisting of trustees of the indemnifying corporation who were not and are not parties to or threatened with the action, suit, or proceeding referred to in division (E)(1) or (2) of this section;

(b) Whether or not a quorum as described in division (E)(4)(a) of this section is obtainable, and if a majority of a quorum of disinterested trustees so directs, in a written opinion by independent legal counsel other than an attorney, or a firm having associated with it an attorney, who has been retained by or who has performed services for the corporation or any person to be indemnified within the past five years;

(c) By the members;

(d) By the court of common pleas or the court in which the action, suit, or proceeding referred to in division (E)(1) or (2) of this section was brought.

If an action or suit by or in the right of the corporation is involved, any determination made by the disinterested trustees under division (E)(4)(a) of this section or by independent legal counsel under division (E)(4)(b) of this section shall be communicated promptly to the person who threatened or brought the action or suit under division (E)(2) of this section, and, within ten days after receipt of such notification, such person shall have the right to petition the court of common pleas or the court in which such action or suit was brought to review the reasonableness of such determination.

(5)(a)(i) Unless, at the time of a trustee's or volunteer's act or omission that is the subject of an action, suit, or proceeding referred to in division (E)(1) or (2) of this section, the articles or regulations of the corporation state, by specific reference to this division, that its provisions do not apply to the corporation, or unless the only liability asserted against a trustee in an action, suit, or proceeding referred to in division (E)(1) or (2) of this section is pursuant to section 1702.55 of the Revised Code, or unless division (E)(5)(a)(ii) of this section applies, the expenses incurred by the trustee or volunteer in defending the action, suit, or proceeding, including attorney's fees, shall be paid by the corporation. Upon the request of the trustee or volunteer and in accordance with division (E)(5)(b) of this section, those expenses shall be paid as they are incurred, in advance of the final disposition of the action, suit, or proceeding.

(ii) Notwithstanding division (E)(5)(a)(i) of this section, the expenses incurred by a trustee or volunteer in defending an action, suit, or proceeding referred to in division (E)(1) or (2) of this section, including attorney's fees, shall not be paid by the corporation upon the final disposition of the action, suit, or proceeding, or, if paid in advance of the final disposition of the action, suit, or proceeding, shall be repaid to the corporation by the trustee or volunteer, if it is proved, by clear and convincing evidence, in a court with jurisdiction that the act or omission of the trustee or volunteer was one undertaken with a deliberate intent to cause injury to the corporation or was one undertaken with a reckless disregard for the best interests of the corporation.

(b) Expenses, including attorney's fees, incurred by a trustee, director, officer, employee, agent, or volunteer in defending any action, suit, or proceeding referred to in division (E)(1) or (2) of this section may be paid by the corporation as they are incurred, in advance of the final disposition of the action, suit, or proceeding, as authorized by the trustees in the specific case, upon receipt of an undertaking by or on behalf of the trustee, director, officer, employee, agent, or volunteer to repay the amount if it ultimately is determined that he is not entitled to be indemnified by the corporation.

(6) The indemnification authorized by this section is not exclusive of, and shall be in addition to, any other rights granted to those seeking indemnification, pursuant to the articles, the regulations, any agreement, a vote of members or disinterested trustees, or otherwise, both as to action in their offi-

cial capacities and as to action in another capacity while holding their offices or positions, and shall continue as to a person who has ceased to be a trustee, director, officer, employee, agent, or volunteer and shall inure to the benefit of the heirs, executors, and administrators of such a person.

(7) A corporation may purchase and maintain insurance, or furnish similar protection, including, but not limited to, trust funds, letters of credit, or self-insurance, for or on behalf of any person who is or was a trustee, officer, employee, agent, or volunteer of the corporation, or is or was serving at the request of the corporation as a trustee, director, officer, employee, agent, or volunteer of another domestic or foreign nonprofit corporation or corporation for profit, or a partnership, joint venture, trust, or other enterprise, against any liability asserted against him and incurred by him in any such capacity, or arising out of his status as such, whether or not the corporation would have the power to indemnify him against that liability under this section. Insurance may be so purchased from or so maintained with a person in which the corporation has a financial interest.

(8) The authority of a corporation to indemnify persons pursuant to division (E)(1) or (2) of this section does not limit the payment of expenses as they are incurred, in advance of the final disposition of an action, suit, or proceeding, pursuant to division (E)(5) of this section or the payment of indemnification, insurance, or other protection that may be provided pursuant to division (E)(6) or (7) of this section. Divisions (E)(1) and (2) of this section do not create any obligation to repay or return payments made by a corporation pursuant to division (E)(5), (6), or (7) of this section.

(9) As used in division (E) of this section, "corporation" includes all constituent corporations in a consolidation or merger, and the new or surviving corporation, so that any person who is or was a trustee, officer, employee, agent, or volunteer of a constituent corporation or is or was serving at the request of a constituent corporation as a trustee, director, officer, employee, agent, or volunteer of another domestic or foreign nonprofit corporation or corporation for profit, or a partnership, joint venture, trust, or other enterprise, shall stand in the same position under this section with respect to the new or surviving corporation as he would if he had served the new or surviving corporation in the same capacity.

(F) In carrying out the purposes stated in its articles and subject to limitations prescribed by law or in its articles, a corporation may do the following:

(1) Purchase or otherwise acquire, lease as lessee, invest in, hold, use, lease as lessor, encumber, sell, exchange, transfer, and dispose of property of any description or any interest in property of any description;

(2) Make contracts;

(3) Form or acquire the control of other domestic or foreign nonprofit corporations or corporations for profit;

(4) Be a partner, member, associate, or participant in other enterprises or ventures, whether profit or nonprofit;

(5) Borrow money, and issue, sell, and pledge its notes, bonds, and other

evidences of indebtedness, and secure any of its obligations by mortgage, pledge, or deed of trust, of all or any of its property, and guarantee or secure obligations of any person;

(6) Become a member of another corporation;

(7) Conduct its affairs in this state and elsewhere;

(8) Resist a change or potential change in control of the corporation, if the trustees, by a majority vote of a quorum, determine that the change or potential change is opposed to or not in the best interests of the corporation, upon consideration of any of the matters set forth in division (E) of section 1702.30 of the Revised Code;

(9) Do all things permitted by law and exercise all authority within the purposes stated in its articles or incidental to those purposes.

(G) Irrespective of the purposes stated in its articles, but subject to limitations or prohibitions stated in its articles, a corporation, in addition to the authority conferred by division (F) of this section, may invest its funds not currently needed in carrying out its purposes in any shares or other securities of another nonprofit corporation or corporation for profit or another business or undertaking.

(H)(1) Notwithstanding any other provision of this section to the contrary, no corporation that is a "private foundation," as defined in section 509 of the Internal Revenue Code, shall do the following:

(a) Engage in any act of "self-dealing," as defined in section 4941 (d) of the Internal Revenue Code, that would give rise to any liability for any tax imposed by section 4941 of the Internal Revenue Code;

(b) Retain any "excess business holdings," as defined in section 4943 (c) of the Internal Revenue Code, that would give rise to any liability for any tax imposed by section 4943 of the Internal Revenue Code;

(c) Make any investment that would jeopardize the carrying out of any of its exempt purposes, within the meaning of section 4944 of the Internal Revenue Code, so as to give rise to any liability for any tax imposed by that section;

(d) Make any "taxable expenditures," as defined in section 4945 (d) of the Internal Revenue Code, that would give rise to any liability for any tax imposed by section 4945 of the Internal Revenue Code.

(2) Each corporation that is a "private foundation," as defined in section 509 of the Internal Revenue Code, shall, for the purposes specified in its articles, distribute at such time and in such manner, for each taxable year, amounts at least sufficient to avoid liability for any tax imposed by section 4942 of the Internal Revenue Code.

(3) Divisions (H)(1) and (2) of this section apply to all corporations described in them, whether or not contrary to the provisions of the articles or regulations of such a corporation, except that divisions (H)(1) and (2) of this section do not apply to a corporation in existence on September 17, 1971, to the extent that such corporation provides to the contrary by amendment to its articles adopted after that date.

(4) Violation of a provision of division (H)(1) or (2) of this section by a

corporation to which the provisions of those divisions are applicable is not cause for cancellation of its articles. No trustee or officer of a corporation to which the provisions of division (H)(1) or (2) of this section are applicable is personally liable for a violation of a prohibition or requirement of those provisions, unless he participated in such violation knowing that it was a violation, and no such trustee or officer is personally liable if such violation was not willful and was due to reasonable cause, except that this division does not exonerate a trustee or officer from any responsibility or liability to which he is subject under any other rule of law, whether or not duplicated in division (H)(1) or (2) of this section.

(5) Except as provided in division (H)(4) of this section, nothing in division (H) of this section impairs the rights and powers of the courts or the attorney general of this state with respect to any corporation.

(6) As used in division (H) of this section, "Internal Revenue Code" means the "Internal Revenue Code of 1986," 100 Stat. 2085, 26 U.S.C. 1, as amended.

(I)(1) No lack of, or limitation upon, the authority of a corporation shall be asserted in any action except as follows:

(a) By the state in an action by it against the corporation;

(b) By or on behalf of the corporation against a trustee, an officer, or a member as such;

(c) By a member as such or by or on behalf of the members against the corporation, a trustee, an officer, or a member as such.

(2) Division (I)(1) of this section shall apply to any action brought in this state upon any contract made in this state by a foreign corporation.

Ohio's 1988 revision of its NPC statute is a lengthy and detailed listing of proper and forbidden *powers* of a nonprofit corporation; probably the best statutory statement available on that subject.[10]

Compare the lengthy and detailed new Florida NPC statute that took effect in 1991.[11]

Limitation of powers: Note that many statutes today (see the Ohio statute above, the Florida statute, and the North Carolina statute, for example) *require* a statement (*e.g.*, in a foundation charter) forbidding self-dealing, and the like, as provided by the Internal Revenue Code since 1970.[12]

§170. CHARTER AS A SUMMARY OF THE ORGANIZATION'S POWERS

The breadth of nonprofit organization powers was shown in a Supreme Court decision that a fraternal organization may advise injured worker members to obtain legal counsel, and may recommend specific lawyers.[13] Such actions by other kinds of organizations (certainly by business organizations) would constitute unlawful solicitation of legal business and unauthorized practice of law.

A trade association was held to be privileged to interfere with third persons' business in order to protect its members' or public interests.[14]

In the modern view, a corporation possesses all those powers reasonably necessary for the accomplishment of its proper purposes.[15]

What those proper purposes are is stated in the charter of the corporation, as set forth in the foregoing chapter. When the state accepts the corporate charter for filing, it thereby approves the purposes stated in that charter.

Therefore, the corporation has all those powers reasonably necessary for the accomplishment of its stated purposes, except insofar as specific rules of law, or specific statutes, limit such implied powers.[16] (See, below Form 62, delineating the powers that must be specifically disclaimed under the Tax Law since 1970.)

Even the statutes which limit corporate powers in specific matters are often themselves avoidable. Many times they state, in effect, that no corporation shall posses a certain power (such as the power to mortgage its property) unless the charter (or bylaws) specifically claims this power for the corporation.[17] Then the corporation may acquire this otherwise forbidden power by merely claiming (stating) it in its charter or bylaws. This is why corporate charters (particularly of business corporations) often contain so many specific power clauses.

Nonprofit corporations need no power clauses. Actually, this elaborate listing of desired powers is quite unnecessary for nonprofit corporations. The absence of the profit motive, and the consequent absence of the need for careful protection of investors, has a clarifying effect. In the case of nonprofit corporations, the presumption or implication of powers is checked by few or no conflicting interests of shareholders or investors. As a result, nonprofit corporations have the implied power to do anything reasonably necessary to accomplish their purposes, except what specific statutes and public policy forbid.

A nonprofit corporation thus needs to state practically no particular powers in its charter. Its powers are implied by its stated purposes, and elaborated in its bylaws.

In addition, the statutes that set forth procedures for incorporation always state just what is to appear in the charter. In those statutes that deal with nonprofit corporations, the only requirement uniformly is for a purpose clause and a statement that the purpose is not for profit.

§171. ALL-POWERS CLAUSES

Although nonprofit corporations generally need no power clauses in their charters, they often include one such clause. This is the so-called *all-powers* clause. It is a catch-all affirmation that the corporation possesses all the implied powers reasonably needed to attain its objectives.

Forms Nos. 47 and 48 exemplify all-powers clauses.

FORM NO. 47

All-Powers Clause

[*Note.* This clause usually is placed immediately after the purpose clauses in the articles.]

The foregoing statement of corporate purposes shall be construed as a statement of both purposes and powers, and not as restricting or limiting in any way the general powers of this corporation, or their exercise and enjoyment, as they are expressly or impliedly granted by the laws of the State of
. . . . . .

FORM NO. 48

All-Powers Clause (another form)

[*Note.* See the note to Form 47.]

To do everything and anything reasonably and lawfully necessary, proper, suitable, or convenient for the achievement of the purposes above stated, or for any of them, or for the furtherance of the said purposes.

§172. WHERE ARE THE CORPORATION'S POWERS STATED?

An attempt to itemize all the powers possessed by a nonprofit corporation is quite impracticable. This is because the corporation possesses substantially all the powers of an individual, with certain specific limitations.

The general scope of these powers can be gathered from the following sources:

1. The charter of the corporation (especially its purpose clauses) and its bylaws.

2. The state's general corporation statute.

3. The state's nonprofit corporations statute (if any) [see above].

4. The statute governing the particular type of corporation, if there is such a statute (*e.g.*, Religious Corporations Law; Cooperative Corporations Law; Labor Law, for unions; General Association Law, for trade associations).

5. Special statutes applicable to special activities (*e.g.*, licensing statutes for fairs or assemblies).

6. Case law applicable to specific acts or transactions.

§173. HOW ARE THESE POWER-GRANTS INTERPRETED?

When a statement of a power is not absolutely clear and understandable in one of the sources listed in the foregoing section, certain tests or standards of interpretation must be applied. These are called *rules of construction*. When there is doubt as to the meaning of a word or phrase, these rules are employed to resolve the doubt.

    Rules of construction. The principal rules of construction are these:

1. Legislative intent must govern, if it can be ascertained.[18] It may be ascertained from:
   a. Statements in the statute section itself.
   b. Statements elsewhere in the statute.
   c. Statements in other statutes.
   d. Legislative documents reporting the debate during the enactment of the statute.
   e. Court decisions interpreting it.
   f. Authoritative interpretations by the attorney-general or other authorities.
   g. Law treaties, etc.
2. Public policy must govern in all cases.[19] It may be ascertained from:
   a. Statutory declarations, expressed or implied.
   b. Court decisions.
   c. Administrative agency decisions.
   d. Custom and usage.
   e. Law and social treaties.
3. Listing of many express purposes or powers implies exclusion of all purposes or powers not so listed, except those reasonably needed in order to carry out the listed purposes and powers.[20]
4. A general power, if followed and described by a particular explanation, is to be understood as so explained.[21] Thus, a power to distribute charity (general power), to members of a certain church (specific explanation), bars distributions to other faiths.
5. Customary powers of all corporations of the same particular type are useful as a general basis of interpretation, but are not conclusive.
6. Prior practices of the corporation in similar matters are useful as a last-resort basis of interpretation, but are not conclusive.[22]

Burden of proof. Anyone who asserts that a particular corporation lacks, or has exceeded, a particular power has the burden of proving his assertion. Only when the lack of the power, or the exceeding of it, is very obvious, does this burden shift to the corporation. Then it has the burden of proving that it does have the power, or that it has not exceeded the power.[23]

Ultra vires means "beyond the powers." When a corporation exceeds its lawful powers, it is said to have committed an *ultra vires* act.[24] The effect of such conduct is discussed in some detail in Chapter 17. In general, all acts of the corporation are prima facie presumed to be within its proper powers, unless these acts are obviously outside the scope of its proper powers.

§174. PARTICULAR POWERS

As Oleck has emphasized in his work on business corporations:[25] It may be said that *all* corporation law is nothing but a detailed analysis . . . of particular corporation powers.

Corporate powers are so many and varied that it is futile to attempt to list all of them. The illustrations of particular nonprofit corporation powers set forth below should suffice to indicate the nature of these powers and to suggest what provisions should be made for them in the charter or bylaws.

It usually is wiser to state in the charter only (1) the purpose clauses, and (2) an all-powers clause. Only when a special situation makes it advisable to emphasize, clarify, or limit a particular power from the outset, should particular powers be stated in the charter. Ordinarily, important powers should be described in the bylaws. It is best to leave out all but especially important powers and to rely upon general corporation law and statutes to specify the extent and limitations of most powers.

Borrowing power. When a nonprofit corporation may have to sell some property, or borrow money (*e.g.*, to build an orphanage or a clubhouse), and will have the security needed for this purpose (*e.g.*, land which it can mortgage or sell) it should include in its bylaws a power clause covering this possibility. This should be rather detailed, and should establish procedures, because statutes sometimes require approval by two-thirds of the members for such action.[26]

Contracts. Every corporation has the implied power to enter into contracts. A power clause indicates which officers shall exercise this power, and by what procedures. It belongs in the bylaws. The same is true of a power to indemnify the incorporators for their disbursements and expenses—which actually is a ratification of a contract.

Contributions. If a corporation intends to grant gifts or to make contributions to charities, it is well to specify this power in the charter, in general terms, and in the bylaws, in particular terms.

The law of almost every state now permits corporations to make charitable contributions in furtherance either of the corporate purposes or of the public welfare.[27] It may be desirable to *limit* this power, by a provision in the charter or in the bylaws.

Court proceedings. A corporation or association may appear in a legal proceeding in most states only by a duly admitted attorney.[28] No power clause is necessary to establish this rule.

Illegal activities. If any doubt about the legality of the corporation's activities in any field is suggested by its charter and proposed operations, it is well to clarify the matter with a negative power clause in the charter. For example, if clinic or dispensary activities are planned, care must be taken lest the corporation engage in the practice of medicine (which is illegal for corporations). A power clause forbidding such practice is desirable in such a case.

Loans and guarantees. If mutual or public assistance by way of low-cost loans is one of the purposes of the corporation, specific power clauses, as well as purpose clauses, should be included in both the charter and the bylaws.

In most nonprofit corporations such loans are forbidden to officers or members. They may be made to third parties only when the loans (or guarantees of loans) will further the corporation's legitimate purposes.[29] In nonprofit corporations, this seldom occurs; and when it does, local statutes usually govern the matter. Therefore, no power clause is ordinarily necessary or desirable.

Partnership ventures. Many states, by statute, now permit nonprofit corporations to become partners as long as the purpose of the partnership is incidental to the corporation's nonprofit purpose.[30] In some states, however, corporations may not become partners with other corporations or with individuals. It is argued that by that act the corporation would lose control of its operations, which must be vested in its own board of directors or trustees.[31]

But a corporation may enter into a single-transaction joint venture with temporary "partners." No special power clause is necessary for this purpose, as it includes no mutual agency power, and actually amounts to a single-transaction contract.[32]

Property holding. All corporations may acquire, hold, and dispose of property, both real and personal. This is a generally implied power for which no power clause ordinarily is necessary.

Several states limit some types of corporations in the amounts and kinds of property they may hold. Some states let them mortgage or sell property only with judicial consent and the consent of two-thirds of their members.[33] Often, therefore, power clauses regarding property appear in charters, although for most practical purposes they are unnecessary.

Some states limit the amount of property charities or religious organizations may hold.[34] These provisions are simply evaded by the formation of several corporations to hold any excess. These are *mortmain* (dead hand) laws, aimed at preventing excessive (and *perpetuity*) accumulation of property by religious and charitable organizations. But there is no limit on the duration of charitable trusts, in general. (See the chapter on *foundations.*)

Local statutes should be consulted if this embarrassment of riches, or of special kinds of property, should occur.

Unincorporated associations have very great difficulties in taking, holding, or transferring property. An unincorporated association often is not a legal entity: it must take title in the names of trustees. This problem is discussed in Chapter 5.

In a growing number of states statutes are being enacted to aid unincorporated associations in this respect. These statutes usually provide that, when a gift or bequest is made to such an association, and the association cannot accept it because of its vague title-holding powers (*e.g.*, a bequest specifically to "*X* Association" cannot legally be accepted by "Mr. *Y*, in trust for *X* Association"), the gift need not be lost. If the association incorporates within one year after the gift is made, these statutes permit the corporation (as an entity) then to accept the title.[35]

If such a situation arises, as it does surprisingly often, the association must adopt a resolution (equivalent to a power clause) to incorporate. In its certificate of incorporation, or its bylaws, no power clause is needed to enable it to accept the gift. Nevertheless, such a clause usually is included in the charter, as an explanation of why the association suddenly decided to incorporate, and as a clear expression of its readiness to accept the property.

Purposeless holding of property by a nonprofit corporation is illegal. And this illegality is not cured by a power clause. Property not devoted to the corporation purposes must be disposed of.[36] All property or funds held by nonprofit corporations must be devoted to the declared purpose of the organization.

Removal of officers. Removal of officers and agents always is a touchy subject. It is wise to include in the bylaws specific power clauses governing such removals.

These powers apply only to officers or agents of the corporation, as such. Thus, a minister of a church may not be an officer of the religious corporation, but is an agent of the parent religious society. He may be immune to a power clause. But a deacon, who is an agent of the corporation, can be removed pursuant to such a clause.

Whenever a removal is contemplated, it should be remembered that this *power* to remove is not the same thing as a *right* to remove. Thus, if a bylaw provides that officers may be removed at any time, with or without cause, even arbitrary removal gives the affected officer no legal redress. If the removal is not based on legal cause (right), it is effective as a practical power (*i.e.*, it can be done), but may give to the wrongly removed person a cause of action for breach of contract.

A removal power clause may bar such rights if it specifically so provides, and if the contract of employment reiterates the power to discharge the agent without cause.

Security holdings. In all states today, a corporation may own the stocks, bonds, notes, and other securities of other corporations, with certain limitations.[37] These limitations are intended to prevent monopoly and undue restraint of trade, such as can occur through the use of the "holding company" device.[38] They also serve to prevent the transfer of too much economic wealth to tax-free status, or to impractically managed ownership.[39]

No power clause is necessary to enable a corporation to own securities. The presence of such power clauses in many charters actually is only an echo of the former rule, now generally abandoned, under which corporations were not permitted to own the stock of other corporations.

Trust powers. Nonprofit corporations have the general power to serve as trustees of property and to accept property in trust for charitable or educational purposes. This is not generally true for business corporations.[40]

In foundations particularly, the *trust purpose* specified by the founder of the trust usually is the stated purpose in the charter of the corporation.[41]

No clause is necessary for trust powers, but explanatory clauses often appear. It is hard to classify these clauses, which often combine purpose and power provisions.

A nonprofit corporation needs no power clause to accept the benefits of a trust.[42] (See Chapter 7, as to Charitable Trusts).

§175. SPECIFIC POWER CLAUSE FORMS

Most of the following power clauses are based on forms provided by the Prentice-Hall *Encyclopedia of Incorporating Forms*. All-power clauses are given in the preceding Forms No. 47 and 48.

FORM NO. 49

Power to Hold Real Property

To purchase or otherwise acquire lands and interest in lands whether leasehold, in fee, or otherwise, situated within or without the State of . . . . . . , and to own, hold, improve by building or otherwise, and to deal in and with, or to lease out or otherwise use for corporate and income purposes, or to encumber, sell, and dispose of any such real estate or improvements, or any interest therein, or to lease the same either as landlord or tenant; and to purchase, construct, and otherwise acquire, and to own, maintain, and operate buildings of any character, for the corporate purposes.

FORM NO. 50

Power to Hold Real Property (Limited)

To acquire, own, lease, mortgage, convey, or assign in trust, occupy, use, develop, deal in or with, sell, or otherwise dispose of real estate for corporate purposes; but the aggregate amount of real estate which the corporation may hold at any one time is limited to . . . . . . (. . .) acres.

FORM NO. 51

Power to Have Buildings for Employees and Members

To buy, purchase, own, build, construct, hold, keep, control, maintain, operate, conduct, occupy, use, take by lease, or otherwise acquire, sell, assign, transfer, exchange, convey, let deal, or traffic in or with, lease, mortgage, pledge, or otherwise dispose of any and all kinds of houses, buildings, structures, places of worship, rest, or recreation for employees and members of the corporation; to do and transact all matters incident thereto or connected therewith; and to apply for, take, purchase, or otherwise acquire, own, hold, use, sell, assign, transfer, exchange, convey, mortgage, pledge, or otherwise dispose of any and all rights, permits, powers, privileges, franchises, licenses, and concessions necessary or in any manner requisite for the doing of anything mentioned in this paragraph.

FORM NO. 52

Power of Eminent Domain

To exercise the right of eminent domain to the extent and as the same may be conferred and bestowed by law.

FORM NO. 53

Power as to Patents and Copyrights

To apply for, obtain, purchase, lease, take licenses in respect of, or otherwise acquire, and to hold, own, use, operate, enjoy, turn to account, grant licenses in respect of, introduce, sell, assign, mortgage, pledge, or otherwise dispose of, for corporate purposes:

1. Any and all inventions, devices, and processes, and any improvements and modifications thereof.

2. Any and all letters patent of the United States or of any other country, state, or locality as aforesaid, and all rights connected therewith or appertaining thereunto.

3. Any and all copyrights granted by the United States or any other country, state, or locality as aforesaid.

4. [Any and all trade-marks, trade names, trade symbols, and other indications of origin and ownership granted by or recognized under the laws of the United States, or of any other country, state, or locality as aforesaid. (This is of limited use, as it may constitute business for profit.)]

FORM NO. 54

Power to Own Securities

To purchase, subscribe for, or in any manner acquire, to sell, transfer, mortgage, pledge, or in any manner dispose of, to hold as investment or otherwise, and to deal in and exercise all the rights of individual natural persons, for corporate purposes, with respect to:

1. Bonds, warrants, mortgages, debentures, notes, obligations, contracts and evidences of indebtedness of, and claims, demands, and choses in action against individuals, firms, associations, trusts, joint stock companies, private, public, or municipal corporations, the Government of the United States, or any state, district, territory, or colony thereof, and the governments, dominions, territories, and colonies of foreign countries.

2. Shares of stock or certificates and interests in corporations, firms, associations, trusts, partnerships, and joint stock companies.

FORM NO. 55

Power to Invest Funds

To invest and deal with the monies of the Corporation, for corporate purposes, in any manner, and to acquire by purchase, by the exchange of stock or other securities owned by the Corporation, by subscription, or otherwise, and to invest in, to hold for investment or for any other purpose, and to use, sell, pledge, or otherwise dispose of, any stocks, bonds, notes, debentures, and other securities and obligations of any government, state, municipality, corporation, association, or partnership, domestic or foreign, and, while owner of any such stocks, bonds, notes, debentures, or other securities or obligations, to exercise all the rights, powers, and privileges of ownership, including among other things the right to vote thereon for any and all purposes.

FORM NO. 56

Power to Contract

To enter into, make, perform, carry out, or cancel and rescind contracts of every kind for any lawful corporate purposes, with any persons, entity, syndicate, partnership, association, corporation, or governmental, municipal, or public authority, domestic or foreign.

FORM NO. 57

Power for Directors to Contract with the Corporation

[*Note*: This power is much better *omitted*. It is usually inconsistent with the proper attitude of a director of a nonprofit corporation towards his fiduciary position.]

To authorize and permit any or all of the directors (trustees) of the Corporation, notwithstanding their official relations to it, to enter into, negotiate, consummate, and perform any contract or agreement of any name or nature, consistent with fiduciary duties and with complete revelation of personal interest involved, between the Corporation and themselves, or any or all of the individuals from time to time constituting the board of directors of the Corporation, or any firm or corporation in which any such director may be interested, directly or indirectly, whether such individual or individuals, firm, or corporation thus contracting with the Corporation shall thereby derive personal or corporate profit or benefits, or otherwise; the intent hereof being to relieve each and every person who may be or become a director of the corporation from any disability that might otherwise exist to contract with the Corporation for the benefit of himself, or of the copartnership or corporation in which he may be in any wise interested, so long as the real relationships are open and clear.

FORM NO. 58

Power to Borrow

To borrow or raise money for corporate purposes to any amount permitted by the General Corporation Laws of the State of . . . . . . , by the sale or issue of bonds, notes, debentures, collateral trust certificates, or other obligations of any nature, or in any manner, and to secure the same by mortgage or other liens upon any and all of the property, real, personal, or in action, of every description whatsoever, or any portion thereof, of this Corporation, whether at the time owned or thereafter acquired.

FORM NO. 59

Power to Mortgage Property

To authorize and cause to be executed mortgages and liens, without limit as to amount, upon the real and personal property of the Corporation, for corporate purposes. [But see local statutes as to this power. They often require two-thirds vote-consent of the members for the making of a mortgage.]

FORM NO. 60

Power to Issue Bonds

To issue, sell, or dispose of the Corporation's bonds, debentures, notes, certificates of indebtedness, and other obligations, secured or unsecured, for corporate purposes, and however evidenced, upon any terms and in any lawful manner, and as security therefor, to mortgage, convey, or assign in trust, pledge, grant any charge, or impose any lien upon, all or any part of the real or personal property, including rights, or interests, of the Corporation, whether owned by it at the time or thereafter acquired.

FORM NO. 61

Power to Operate Outside the State

But if this Corporation shall undertake to do any of the things hereinabove set forth in any state other than the State of ......, in the District of Columbia, in any territory, colony, or dependency of the United States, or in any foreign country or in any colony or dependency thereof, then as to such jurisdictions and each of them this Corporation shall be deemed to have such powers only insofar as such jurisdictions respectively permit corporations such as this one within their several respective jurisdictions to be organized for or to execute such powers.

FORM NO. 62

Power Disclaimer: Powers Forbidden by I.R.S. [Prohibited Transactions]

[Use the following provision as your guide in drafting verbiage consistent with the Tax Reform Act of 1969 and many state's statutes, for your organization.]

The foregoing powers shall be limited as follows for any corporation organized under this chapter, which shall be classified as a "private foundation" as that term is defined by section 509 of the Internal Revenue Code of 1954 or corresponding provisions of any subsequent federal tax laws, unless any such corporation shall, by its articles of incorporation or amendment thereto, specifically state that it does not intend to be so limited:

(1) As used in this section, section references, unless otherwise indicated, shall refer to the Internal Revenue Code of 1954, Title 26 of the United States Code, as in effect on December 16, 19 [??] p.616, including corresponding provisions of any subsequent federal tax laws.

(2) No corporation, during the period it is a "private foundation" as defined in s. 509(a), shall:

(a) Engage in any act of "self-dealing," as defined in s. 4941(d), which would give rise to any liability for the tax imposed by s. 4941(a);

(b) Retain any "excess business holdings," as defined in s. 4943(c), which would give rise to any liability for the tax imposed by s. 4943(a);

(c) Make any investment which would jeopardize the carrying out of any of its exempt purposes, within the meaning of s. 4944, so as to give rise to any liability for the tax imposed by s. 4944(a); and

(d) Make any "taxable expenditures," as defined in s. 4945(d), which would give rise to any liability for the tax imposed by s. 4945(a).

(3) Each corporation, during the period it is a "private foundation" as defined in s. 509, shall distribute, for the purposes specified in its articles of organization, for each taxable year, amounts at least sufficient to avoid liability for the tax imposed by s. 4942(a).

(4) The provisions of subsections (2) and (3) shall not apply to any corporation to the extent that a court of competent jurisdiction shall determine that such application would be contrary to the terms of the articles of organization or other instrument governing such corporation or governing the administration of charitable funds held by it and that the same may not properly be changed to conform to such subsections.

(5) Nothing in this section shall impair the rights and powers of the courts or of the Department of Legal Affairs with respect to any corporation.

FORM NO. 63

Power to Pay Organizational Expenses

To pay out of the funds of the Corporation all costs and expenses of and incidental to the incorporation and organization of the Corporation.

FORM NO. 64

Disclaimer of Prohibited Powers

Nothing herein contained shall be deemed to authorize or permit the Corporation to carry on any activities, or to exercise any power, or to do any act which a corporation formed under the act herein referred to, or any amendment thereof or supplement thereto or substitute therefor, may not at the time lawfully carry on or do. [*Note:* Express prohibition of exercise of the "prohibited transactions" stated or implied in the Internal Revenue Code should be based on a reading of the latest revision or regulations thereof.]

POINTS TO REMEMBER

- Assume possession of all "reasonably necessary" powers, without trying to list them all.
- Your purpose clause is the real measure of your corporate powers.
- You have all lawful powers reasonably needed to carry out your approved purposes.
- Acceptance of your charter, by the state, amounts to grants of such "reasonably necessary" and logical powers.
- Consult the state corporation statutes as to what, if any, powers must be stated in order to be had. They are very few and highly specialized.
- Avoid stating powers in your charter, except for the all-powers clause. Always use an all-powers clause. Repeat it in the preamble to the bylaws.
- State only purposes, if possible. State powers in the charter only when it is essential that they be emphasized.

- Put your power clauses in your bylaws. Put them in the preamble or in the article relating to their subject matter.

- Examine the charter, statutes, and case decisions, in order to estimate the range of the corporation's powers.

- Interpret power clauses in the light of legislative intent, public policy, court decisions, administrative rulings, and general custom.

- Anyone who challenges the powers must ordinarily show why they are illegal.

- Use the forms of power clauses as guides. Do not simply copy them. Tailor your power clauses to suit your particular purposes and objects.

- Disclaim the "prohibited transactions" (*e.g.*, of self-dealing nature). Forbid them, in both articles of incorporation and bylaws. [See your state's statute as to terminology.]

NOTES TO CHAPTER 16

1. *Black's Law Dictionary*, 1053 (5th ed., 1979); Hamilton, *Corporations*, 164–5 (3rd ed., 1986); Revised Model Nonprofit Corp. Act. §3.02 (1986 Exposure Draft); Ill. Not-For-Profit Corp. Act §103.10 (Ill. S.B. 1320; 1985); Ill. General Not For Profit Corporation Act of 1986, 805 ILCS 105/101.01 *et. seq.* Fla. Stat. §617.0302. Williams v. United Most Worshipful St. John's Grand Lodge, 140 S.2d 206 (La. App. 1962) Cornell University v. Fiske, 136 U.S. 152, 10 S. Ct. 775, 34 L. Ed. 427 (1889); State v. Joe Must Go Club of Wisconsin, Inc., 270 Wis. 108, 70 N.W.2d 681 (1955); *In re* Morrison's Estate, 173 Misc. 503, 18 N.Y.S.2d 235, 241 (1939); 1 Oleck, *Modern Corporation Law*, §603 (1978 Supp.); Henn, *Corporations*, 144–6 (2d ed., 1986 casebook); 6 Fletcher, *Corporations*, §2485 (current ed.).

2. *Blue Cross v. Protective Life Ins. Co.*, 527 So. 2d 125 (AL Civ. App. 1987, publ. Aug. 1988); citing *Woodyard v. Arkansas Diversified Ins. Co.*, 594 S.W.2d 13 (AR 1980); *Blue Cross of S.W. Va. v. Commonwealth*, 338 S.E.2d 849 (VA 1986).

3. Ohio Rev. Code, §§1701.13, 1702.12; Vt. Genl. L. (1917) 4919, 4923; Vt. Stat. Ann. 11 §2352 Rev. Model Non Profit Corp. Act, §3.02; Clifford v. Helvering, 105 F.2d 586, 591 (8th Cir. 1939); Freligh v. Saugerties, 70 Hun. 589, 24 N.Y.S. 182 (1939); Genl. Stat. No. Car. §55A-15(b)(8).

4. Rev. Model Non-Profit Corp. Act, § Comment 3.02; 2 Oleck *Modern Corporation Law*, c. 38 (1978 Supp.); Stone, *Ultra Vires and Original Sin*, 14 Tulane L. Rev. 190 (1940); Ohio Rev. Code, §1702.12(H); Plairs, *Corporate Powers in Massachusetts*, 28 B.U.L. Rev. 301 (1948).

5. *Brookridge Community Property Owners, Inc. v. Brookridge, Inc.*, 573 So. 2d 972 (Fla. DCA, 1991); *White Egret Condominium, Inc. v. Franklin*, 379 So. 2d 346 (Fla. 1979).

6. *See also*, Smith, *Law of Associations* (1914); Witherspoon, *Legal Guideposts for Trade Associations*, 33 N.D.L. Rev. 202 (1957) as to corporate membership in an association.

7. *See*, n. 4, above; *also*, Wyo. Stats., §17-19-302 Wyo. Const., Art. X, §6. Many state statutes also contain scattered provisions as to various specific and optional powers; *see* 1 Oleck, *Modern Corporation Law*, §599(1978) for examples. Some statutes say almost nothing about specific powers, *e.g.*, Ariz., Iowa, Me., Miss., Okla., So. Car. business corporation statutes. *See also*, Aitken v. Stewart, 129 Calif. App. 38, 18 P.2d 988 (1933). Some statutes set out powers in detail; *e.g.*, Genl. Stat. No. Car. §55A-15, which also covers "foundations' powers."

8. Ohio Rev. Code, §1702.12(F)(9) Nev. Genl. Corp. L. §§78.070, 81.110; Genl. Stat. No. Car. §55A-15(b)(8); Fla. Stat. §617.0302(15).

9. Based on Model Non-Profit Corp. Act, §5. *See also*, Fenn College v. Nance, 4 Misc. (Ohio) 183, 210 N.E.2d 418 (1965).

10. Ohio Rev. Code Ann. §1702.12 (eff. 3/29/88).

11. Fla. St., ch. 617 (1992).

12. Genl. Stat. No. Car. §55A-15(c).

13. Brotherhood of Railroad Trainmen v. Virginia, 84 S. Ct. 1113 (1964).

14. Middlesex Concrete P.&E. Corp. v. Carteret Industrial Assn., 37 N.J. 507, 181 A.2d 774 (1962).

15. Park v. Alta Ditch and Canal Co., 458 P.2d 625 (Utah 1969); Ohio Rev. Code, §1702.12(F)(9); 1, Oleck, *Modern Corporation Law*, c.26 (1978 Supp.); Oleck, *New York Corporations*, §115 (1961 Supp. ed); Sutton's Hospital Case, 10 Coke 23A, 30b (Engl. 1613); Gause v. Commonwealth Trust Co., 196 N.Y. 134, 153; 89 N.E. 476; 24 L.R.A. (n.s.) 967 (1909); Northwest Civic Assn. v. Sheldon, 317 Mich. 416; 27 N.W.2d 36 (1947); South Carolina Elec. and Gas Co. v. So. Car. Publ. Serv. Authority, 215 S.C. 193; 54 S.E.2d 777 (1949).

16. *See*, n. 8–14, above.

17. *E.g.*, Power to convey realty to members for use as dwelling houses must be stated in the bylaws, and approved by a court. N.Y. Memb. Corp. L., §22 (now superseded by N.Y. N-P-C Act §509).

18. *See*, First Methodist Episc. Church of Chicago v. Dixon, 178 Ill. 260; 52 N.E. 887 (1899); State *ex rel.* Walker v. Payne, 129 Mo. 468; 31 S.W. 797; 33 L.R.A. 576 (1895).

19. Central Transportation Co. v. Pullman's Palace Car Co., 139 U.S. 24, 49; 11 S. Ct. 478; 35 L. Ed. 55 (1891); Lea County Elec. Coop., Inc. v. City of Plains, 373 S.W.2d 90 (Tex. 1963).

20. "Expressio unius est exclusio alterius"; State Bank of Blue Island v. Benzing, 383 Ill. 40; 48 N.E.2d 333 (1943); John B. Waldbillig, Inc. v. Gottfried, 21 A.D.2d 872, 251 N.Y.S.2d 991 (1964); Agassiz. Odessa Mut. Fire Ins. Co. v. Magnusson, 272 Minn. 156, 136 N.W.2d 861 (1965).

21. Prairie Slough Fishing and Hunting Club v. Kessler, 252 Mo. 424, 433; 159 S.W. 1080 (1913).

22. Nowell v. Equitable Trust Co., 249 Mass. 585; 144 N.E. 749 (1924).

23. *See*, n. 21, above. *See also*, Breckenridge Hotel Co. v. Radford Grocery Co., 33 S.W.2d 1074 (Tex. Civ. App.), *reh. den.*, 35 S.W.2d 464 (1931); Dyer v. Broadway Central Bank, 252 N.Y. 430; 169 N.E. 635 (1930).

24. State *ex rel.* Supreme Temple of Pythian Sisters v. Cook, 234 Mo. App. 898, 136 S.W.2d 142, 146 (1940); Wing Memorial Hospital Assn. v. Town of Randolph, 120 Vt. 277, 141 A.2d 645 (1958).

25. Oleck, *Modern Corporation Law* §603 (1978 supp.)

26. N.Y. N-P-C Law, §509. But in Ohio the trustees may mortgage property without consent of the members, unless the articles or regulations (bylaws) provide otherwise. Ohio Rev. Code, §1702.36.

27. *E.g.*, Ohio Rev. Code, §1702.12(D); Texas Acts 1917, c. 15, §§1, 3; N.Y. Bus. Corp. L., §202(a12); 26 U.S.C.A., §§170(a)(2), 170(b)(2) (Internal Revenue Code, allowing a deduction); *See also*, Cousens, *How Far Corporations May Contribute to Charity*, 35 Va. L. Rev. 401 (1949); Andrews, *Corporation Giving* (Russell Sage Foundation 1952); Rohr, *Corporate Philanthropy*, 33 Mich. S.B.J. 14–21 (1954); Thiele, *Corporation Giving*, 8 Rutgers L. Rev. 527–40 (1954); Wallace, *How to Save Money by Giving It Away*, 47 Marquette L. Rev. 1 (1963).

28. N.Y. Civ. Prac. Law and Rules, §321(a).

29. *See*, Nowell Case (guarantee), n. 22, above; Holmes, Booth and Haydens v. Willard, 125 N.Y. 75, 25 N.E. 1083; 11 L.R.A. 170 (1890) (loan to supplier upheld); Herbert v. Sullivan, 123 F.2d 477 (1st Cir. 1941) (ultra vires loan); Ohio Rev. Code, §1701.95(A)(3) (forbidden to officers, except in usual course of business). As to tax effects of loans to members (business corporations), *see*, 3 Oleck, *Modern Corporation Law*, §1379 (1978). Building and loan, and other such organizations, of course, do make loans to members, lawfully.

30. Ohio Rev. Code §1702.12(F)(4); Ga. Code §14-3-302(9).

31. People v. North River Sugar Ref. Co., 121 N.Y. 582, 625; 24 N.E. 834; 9 L.R.A. 33 (1890); Sherman & Ellis v. Indiana Mut. Cas. Co., 41 F2d 588 (7th Cir. 1930).

32. Bates v. Coronado Beach Co., 109 Calif. 160, 162, 41 P. 855 (1895); Sturm v. Ulrich, 10 F.2d 9 (8th Cir. 1925) (Mining partnership).

33. N.Y. N-P-C Law, §509. But trustees may do so without member's consent under Ohio Rev. Code, §1702.36.

34. N.Y. Relig. Corp. L., §14 (judicial investigation of amount held). As to mortmain statutes, *see*, Hart v. Gould, 119 Calif. App.2d 231, 259 P.2d 49, 51 (1953); Anno., 45 Am. Jur. 760, Religious Societies, §49. *See*, Ohio Rev. Code, §2107.06 as to requirement that a will giving a grant to a corporation or association in trust must be executed a year before the grant takes effect. As to perpetuities, *see* (400-year accumulation is unreasonable) *In re* James' Estate, 199 A.2d 275 (Pa. 1964); Ould v. Washington Hospital, 95 U.S. 303, 24 L. Ed. 450 (1877).

35. *See*, First Methodist Church v. Putnam, 189 Misc. 519; 72 N.Y.S.2d 70 (1947); and c. 5, above.

36. *See*, n. 34, above.

37. Rohrscheib v. Barton-Lexa Water Assn., 437 S.W.2d 230 (Ark. 1969); Robotham v. Prudential Ins. Co., 64 N.J. Eq. 673, 53 A. 842 (1903); Ohio Rev. Code, §1702.12(C); Del. Genl. Corp. L., §77; 8, §123.

38. Clayton Act, §7; 15 U.S.C.A., §18; Note, *Securities Regulations*, 51 Georgetown L. J. 855 (1963) (Charitable exemption of charitable corporation securities).

39. *See*, local state "lists of legal investments" issued periodically by state superintendents of banking or other officers; Tilt, *Legal Incidents to the Investment of Corporate Funds of Charitable Corporations of New York* (1952); Bogert, *Recent Developments Regarding the Law of Charitable Trusts*, 5 Hastings L. J. 95–102 (1954); Hanger, *Investments by Charitable Corporations*, 2 U. Queensland L. J. 145–9 (1953).

40. Trustees of Phillips Academy v. King, 12 Mass. 546 (1815); Conley v. Daughters of the Republic, 156 S.W. 197 (Tex. 1913). But a noncharitable corporation apparently has no such power, though it is nonprofit: Opinions N.Y. Atty.-Genl. (1936) 206.

41. *See*, Brown v. Buyer's Corp., 35 Ohio St.2d 191, 299 N.E.2d 279 (1973), citing Ohio Rev. Code, §109.23, as to vesting of trust purpose.

42. *See*, Bogert article, n. 39, above; Fisch, *American Acceptance of Charitable Trusts*, 28 Notre Dame Law 219–33 (1953); Gray, *Charitable Trusts*, 16 Modern L. Rev. 95–7 (1953); Scott, *Trusts for Charitable and Benevolent Purposes*, 58 Harv. L. Rev. 548–72 (1945); note, *Trusts— Gifts to Charitable Corporations—Nature of Interest Created—Duties of Trustee*, 26 So. Calif. L. Rev. 80–6 (1952); Comment, *Charitable Trusts and Inducements to Violate the Law*, 20 W. & L. L. Rev. 85 (1963); Lusk, *The Uncertain Future of Charitable Trusts*, 15 Ala. L. Rev. 390 (1963); Boylan, *Endowment Funds—Collision of Corporate and Trust Standards*, 18 Bus. Lawyer 807 (1963).

17

UNAUTHORIZED AND
IMPROPER ACTS

[Carol Ann Masio, George F. McLaughlin, and Francisco Garcia helped in updating this chapter.]

§176. ACTIONS BEYOND CORPORATE POWERS

[See Chapter 16 herein, on "Powers and Power Clauses."]
Actions by a corporation that are not within the kinds authorized by law are termed *ultra vires* actions; *ultra vires* means "beyond the powers" of the corporation.[1] This doctrine originated in the old view of the corporation as a legal entity that possessed only those limited powers granted to it by the state. Today, it still exists, but in most states it is a limited doctrine of law.[2] The concept is well illustrated by a case in which an English court issued an injunction to restrain the trustees of a "friendly society" (for mutual relief of members' sickness or old age) when they were exhausting the society's funds too freely.[3] And a dining club was held to have acted *ultra vires* when its articles of incorporation stated that it was to have the purpose of serving lunch to members and guests, but it refused to serve women or admit them to membership.[4]

Likewise, when a nonprofit corporation's stated purpose, in its articles of incorporation, was "to provide a home for the reception and support of needy boys," it had no legal power to run an expensive private school instead. The court noted that the charter of a corporation "is the index to the powers with which the corporation has been endowed," declared the operation of the school to be *ultra vires*, and ordered the corporation to conform its actions to its allotted powers.[5] Likewise, a corporation organized for religious purposes had no legal power to operate a general commercial printing and publishing business.[6] But in 1980, *Ms. Magazine*, published by a subsidiary corporation of Ms. Foundations for Women, was converted from a business to a tax-exempt (nonprofit) operation with IRS approval.[7]

The incidental carrying on of a profit-making business, with the profits devoted to the main (and proper) objectives of a nonprofit corporation, is lawful and proper.[8] Thus, the purchase and operation of a cemetery facility, in which plots were sold at a profit, was held to be a proper collateral activity of a corporation chartered as a religious congregation.[9]

A 1984 Massachusetts case illustrates the continuing importance of the *ultra vires* doctrine as a basis for regulating the authority of an officer of a nonprofit corporation. In *Boston Athletic Association v. International Marathons, Inc.*,[10] the president of the Boston Athletic Association (BAA) entered into a contract with International Marathons, Inc. (IMI) which gave IMI the exclusive right to be the promoter of the annual, prestigious road race, the Boston Marathon. The contract limited the amount of money the BAA would receive from commercial sponsors of the race to $400,000, and IMI would receive the excess profits. Before the signing of this contract, the BAA would promote the race by soliciting individual commercial sponsors, and the BAA would receive a percentage of the revenues which the sponsors earned from the race. The BAA, in turn, would use this income to carry out its corporate purpose, to support the marathon the following year. But when a court examined this arrangement, it found that the antithetical effect of the contract between BAA and IMI was that it "turns the solicitation of sponsors from a way to support the marathon to a way for IMI to make a profit."[11]

Although the board of governors of the BAA had authorized the president to execute a contract on behalf of the BAA for the perpetuation, sponsorship or underwriting of the marathon, the board never had specifically reviewed or approved the contract which was entered into. The BAA challenged the contract and the president's authority to bind the BAA.

The Supreme Judicial Court of Massachusetts held that the contract was void because the president was without power to bind the BAA without specific ratification by the BAA's board of governors.

An ultra vires corporation situation may be such as to bar corporate legal relief, and yet not be disabling for its members. For example, *members* of a church with a black congregation may sue under *civil rights* statutes for discriminatory repudiation of a contract for sale of a school building to the church corporation.[12]

An unmarried woman, member of the defendant church, had an affair with a man and was *publicly castigated* for that by the church minister, *after* she had withdrawn from the church. She sued the church for damages, for "tortious invasion of her rights." She won the case, because she impliedly consented to religious (church) *discipline while she was a member*, but not after she ceased to be a member. Her continued discipline was thus ultra vires.[13]

A realty subdivision owners' association's *articles* and *bylaws* are subsidiary to the *declaration of covenants* for the subdivision. Therefore it is *ultra vires* (beyond the powers) of the corporation to *sell* common areas where it was authorized in the declaration only to levy assessments, maintain the areas, and assign rights to dock areas in the subdivision.[14]

§177. MODERN LIMITATION OF ULTRA VIRES DOCTRINE

Today the *ultra vires* doctrine has been sharply limited by legislation in many states.[15] The modern rule is typified in the Florida statutory provision.[16] It permits questioning of the power of a nonprofit corporation only by:

A. (1) the state

    (2) the corporation itself, against a trustee, officer, or member as such, or

    (3) a member as such, or on behalf of the members, against a trustee, officer, or member as such; *but*

B. improper organization or lack of capacity to act or to convey property shall not be deemed *ultra vires* deficiencies.

Nevertheless, the doctrine of *ultra vires* continues to be followed according to the old common law rules in many states. It often is invoked by persons who contracted with the corporation and who seek to avoid the contract by arguing that the corporation had no authority to enter into such a contract. Sometimes the corporation uses the same argument, or a member invokes the doctrine.

While the modern view of corporate authority generally is that a corporation has substantially all the powers to achieve its purposes that a natural person has,[17] the limiting effect of the doctrine of *ultra vires* continues. This limiting effect is minimal in states that have adopted statutes on the subject,[18] and of various degrees of effect in other states.

The discussion that follows is based primarily on the law in states that do not have statutory limitations of the doctrine. It is probably true that the *ultra vires* concept has more application today to nonprofit corporations than to business corporations. This is because of the higher moral degree of fiduciary responsibility of officers of nonprofit organizations.

For example, if a corporation is duly chartered as a trade association, it has no power to contract for the building or establishment of an orphan asylum. If it does so, this action is *ultra vires*. Or, if a charitable corporation grants a gift to accomplish a purpose not included in its own charter, this grant is *ultra vires*.

An *ultra vires* act is beyond the limits of the powers stated in the corporation's charter or bylaws, or beyond the implied powers which are reasonably necessary for the carrying on of its stated purposes.[19]

The same principle applies to a contract made in excess of his powers by an agent of an unincorporated association.[20]

Effect of ultra vires action. An *ultra vires* action is merely unauthorized, not illegal.[21] It is *not* necessarily invalid. In most cases it is voidable; but it is not automatically void. This is the rule in most states. But in a few states, and in federal court cases, it is viewed as altogether void.[22]

Under either view, if the transaction is completely ended and finished, it is treated as a *fait accompli*, and is not disturbed unless it is fraudulent or directly harmful to some interested party.[23]

Unfinished transactions. If the transaction is not yet fully completed (executory contract) the courts will, on the application of any interested party, set it aside. The corporation itself, as an entity, usually is barred from applying for such a recission. This is because nobody should be permitted to use his own unauthorized act as a means for escaping the consequences of his own conduct. But members are free to raise the *ultra vires* objection to acts of the corporation officers or directors.[24]

Ultra vires as a defense. In most cases, *ultra vires* is said to be a legal defense against enforcement of an *ultra vires* contract. That is, any interested party (*e.g.*, the other contracting party, or a member of the corporation) may interpose the rule of *ultra vires* as a defense against an attempt to enforce such a contract. But one who has accepted the benefits of such an unauthorized act is said to be *estopped* from thereafter claiming that the act is *ultra vires*.[25]

Quo warranto proceedings. The state, too, may object to *ultra vires* actions. Such a proceeding by the state is called a *quo warranto* (by what authority) proceeding. It may lead to revocation of the corporate charter, unless the statute of limitations has run.[26]

Burden of proof. But anyone who asserts that an act is *ultra vires* has the burden of proof, except when the lack of authority is glaringly obvious.[27]

When members sue the corporation (foundation) directors for allegedly *unauthorized* (*Ultra Vires*—"Beyond the powers") corporation acts, they may do so today only insofar as specifically authorized by state *statutes*. Then they must allege *specific* demand on the directors to correct their acts, or why such request was futile. Ordinarily only the officers may sue for damages for harm to the corporation.[28]

The state is the proper party to challenge the *ultra vires* acts of a nonprofit corporation, in Indiana.[29]

Rules adopted by the board of a coop. apartment association must be reasonable and if they are not that then they are *ultra vires*.[30]

The doctrine of *ultra vires* is *not* a complete bar to corporate liability. Thus, a vendetta by police officers and their union against one police officer justified a damage award of $575,000.[31]

Dues of members required by an integrated (e.g., mandatory membership) bar association must be proportionately reduced for dissenters as to certain bar activities to which they object as outside core bar purposes. Not to reduce the amount is ultra vires.[32] An organization may also be liable for the "*misuse*" of members' dues.[33]

The U.S. Legal Services Corporation is not entitled to cut federal funds from an association that participated in a challenge to state abortion legislation. It exceeded its powers.[34]

§178. UNAUTHORIZED, IMPROPER, TORTIOUS, AND ILLEGAL ACTS MUST BE DISTINGUISHED

Corporate abuse of the privileges of corporate status has been a subject of much concern and discussion in recent years. For a summary and recommendations see, H. Oleck, *Remedies for Abuses of Corporate Status*, 9 Wake Forest Law Review 463.

An *illegal* act is contrary to a specific statute or law. The term means, primarily, acts that are criminal, but also includes acts clearly contrary to public policy or morals.[35]

A *tort* is an injury or harm to someone that is (usually) more than a breach of contract yet not a crime. Negligence, defamation, and trespasses of various kinds are typical torts.[36]

An *ultra vires* act is an *unauthorized* act; one that is beyond the powers granted to a corporation.[37]

An act may be *improper* because it is illegal, or because it is tortious, or because it is *ultra vires*.[38]

Effect of *classification*. The legal consequences of each type of improper action differ.

An illegal act is void; often it is also punishable as a crime or misdemeanor.

A tortious act results in liability for damages to the injured party, both on the part of the individual who commits it and on the part of the corporation he represents as agent.

An *ultra vires* act may be either void or voidable, as described in the preceding section. For example, deeds, conveying land, that are signed by "former officers" without authority are void ab initio, at the time the deeds are executed. The nonprofit association involved is entitled to have the land re conveyed to it in these circumstances.[39]

Members' duty to their organization, such as a condominium unit owner's duty to note and report dangerous conditions (e.g., unsafe elevator) is basically the same as anyone using the elevator; to look out for herself in a reasonable manner.[40]

Assumption of risk is not a good defense if a NPO member/beneficiary (student) is injured because of negligent supervision of sports/stunts at the school. *Nova University v. Katz*, 18 FLW-D1880 (FL. 4th DCA, 8/25/93; *Kirk v. Washington State*, 746 P.2d 285 (WA 1987).

Tort Immunity

A statute that exempted "health services corporations" from some kinds of patient-tort-liability is not an unconstitutional violation of equal protection and due process rights of nonprofit hospitals and HMOs, if there is a rational basis for legislature's different treatment and if remedies against the wrongdoing physician continue.[41]

Illinois amended its Voluntary Health Services Plans Act to remove the *statutory immunity* that was previously granted to nonprofit health care providers. However, the immunity still applies to cases pending on the effective date of the amendment.[42]

The state of Washington has a Blood Shield Statute that removes civil liability, except in the case of willful or negligent conduct, as a result of the handling of blood products and blood derivatives for the purpose of injecting or transfusing them into the human body. The Washington Supreme Court held that the statute applies to both for-profit and nonprofit corporations even though the statute does not apply to transactions where a donor is compensated.[43]

Immunity may be extended by the court through protection from punitive damages. For example, in Nevada, a court found that *corporation liability* for *punitive damages* should not be ordered unless the factual nature of its alleged malice or grossness of conduct was "brought home" to the corporation directly or vicariously. If no evidence of intent-type conduct is shown, mere disregard of appropriate safety precautions is not enough. Assault on the plaintiff in a casino parking lot, and robbery, is proper basis for $45,000 compensatory damages, but not for $1,000,000 punitive damages, absent conduct motivated by ill will and intent to injure.[44]

"Recreational use" statutes also provide immunity. A spectator, who was injured by a falling canopy at an outdoor community festival, sued the nonprofit festival committee that organized the festival. Even though there was a recreational use statute, which protected landowners and occupiers of land who opened their land to the public for "outdoor recreation" from liability, the court held that "outdoor recreation" does not include attending a weekend celebration or watching entertainment on an outdoor stage during a community festival.[45] Similarly, a homeowner's association is not immune from tort liability under a recreational use statute if the facility concerned is not available for public use and the access for the ultimate user is paid for by valuable consideration.[46]

However, "residential exceptions" to liability don't usually apply to nonprofits. Nonprofit organizations have a duty to nonbeneficiary pedestrians to maintain abutting sidewalks. A "residential exception" to a rule, making abutting landowners liable for injury to pedestrians caused by the poor condition of sidewalks, does not apply to nonprofit charitable and religious organizations.[47]

Immunity can also be granted by way of privileges. An association of horse racing companies has *qualified privilege* to distribute reports of alleged impropriety to the horse racing community, for *protection of its members.*[48] Similarly, a humane society has only qualified (not absolute) privilege to criticize medical research mistreatment of animals. It can be held liable for merely negligent defamation, and need not be shown to have had actual malice (as a "public" figure). Suit by animal dealers.[49]

§179. CHARITABLE IMMUNITY

[Michael J. Kapperman, Rebecca J. Casagrande, Susan A. Machata, and Allison E. Bradice did research for some of this section.]

Few states still follow the doctrine that *charitable* (not merely nonprofit) corporations are immune from liability for the torts committed by their agents in the course and scope of corporate activity.[50] The immunity applies only to charitable activities, not to such non-charitable functions as a church's bazaar sale.[51] The doctrine arose out of an 1846 English court decision[52] that was quickly repudiated in England[53] but was followed by American courts.

Today all but a very few American courts have discarded this immunity doctrine, mostly by case decisions,[54] but also by statute in some states.[55] New Jersey reestablished the immunity by statute.[56]

Charitable common-law-immunity still seems to be complete only in Arkansas[57] and Maine.[58] But even in those states statutes allow tort action against the insurer of the charity,[59] at least to the extent of insurance coverage.[60]

A few other states still allow immunity up to limits of insurance coverage; thus preserving the idea of a charitable corporation's *own* funds as a trust, immune from seizure.[61] Special legislation to deal with the so-called "insurance crisis" of the eighties sometimes made complex provisions as to hospital malpractice cases.[62] A few statutes have retained immunity of specified types of charitable corporations such as educational, religious or hospital organizations, but only as to suits by their beneficiaries.[63]

Liability to non-beneficiaries. Charitable immunity does not extend to non-beneficiaries of the charity, such as business visitors,[64] employees or officers of the charity,[65] or volunteer workers.[66]

Non-charitable organizations, such as a country club or swimming pool association, cannot claim charitable immunity.[67] For example, to benefit from the New Jersey Charitable Immunity Act, an organization must be devoted solely and exclusively to religious, charitable, educational, or hospital purposes. Thus, a fraternal benevolent society is not immune to a negligence suit brought by a bride who slipped and fell in a rented room of its fraternal hall.[68]

Limitation of liability to income derived from noncharitable sources is the rule in a few states.[69] Immunity usually applies only to "beneficiaries" of the charity and "charitable" operations.[70] And if the conduct is a departure (*abandonment*) of the charitable purpose (e.g., a cubmaster's sex with a 12-year-old scout) the organization is not liable.[71]

Sometimes charitable immunity is granted through a lower standard of care. For example, a parish home, owned by a religious corporation, is not a dwelling used for "commercial purposes" and is not required to provide scaffolding and the other safety features required by Labor Law during construction on the parish, in New York.[72]

An amendment to a charitable immunity act, which increased hospital liability from a maximum of $10,000 to $250,000, applies prospectively only to claims arising on or after the date the amendment became effective.[73]

A $5 million punitive damages award against a religious corporation for infliction of mental anguish on a former member was held to be excessive when that sum was one and a half times its total assets. This injury was not that outrageous. Reduced, on appeal, to $2 million.[74]

Charitable immunity for negligent injuries is being restored to nonprofit organizations, in a growing number of jurisdictions, in order to protect *volunteer* activity in charitable organizations, after a sharp drop in immunity-allowance beginning in the 1950s. By 1986, over two-thirds of the states had abolished charitable immunity. But in the 1980s the "insurance crisis" caused increases in liability insurance costs and then in cost of NPOs first for directors and officers, and not to protect *volunteers* from liability. Since 1986 nearly half the states have enacted volunteer-immunity laws. Illinois Congressman John E. Porter is pushing for federal adoption of such a law (Volunteer Protection Act; H.R. 911), which would cut Social Services grants to states that do not enact such statutes. Some NPOs are conducting special training for volunteer workers, on how to avoid liability; some are joining in *insurance pools.*[75]

The ABA 1987 revision of its *Model Nonprofit Corporation Act* especially favored directors and officers and agents immunity, particularly by corporate purchase of liability insurance.

NPC hospitals claimed to be unable to compete with for-profit hospitals without charitable immunity.[76] In response by 1989, over half of the state legislatures and courts had come to the rescue with immunity and/or damages-caps limitations, which have been widely upheld.[77] For example, the South Carolina Supreme Court held that *statutes limiting tort liability* of charitable organizations to actual damages not over $200,000 are valid expressions of legitimate state interest in preserving the resources of such organizations, and do not violate "equal protection" rights.[78]

In Massachusetts, statutory *limitation* of the amount of *damages* awarded for a charitable organization's torts (malpractice by hospital physicians, here), committed in carrying out its charitable purposes, is not unconstitutional, even if very low ($20,000).[79] A hospital giving negligent care to a patient is entitled to the statutory limitation (cap) on charities' damages liability, even though the patient paid $26 for emergency room care.[80]

In Missouri, statutory immunity for nonprofit corporation (health services corporation) torts (hospital negligence) serves a proper legislative purpose, and is not unconstitutional where the plaintiff's right to sue the physician for medical malpractice is not barred.[81]

New Jersey seems to be the leader, at present, in granting charitable immunity, but with a $10,000 "cap" in some cases.[82] But the New Jersey statute does not bar suits against the individual agent or servant of the NPO.[83] Yet, New Jersey has held a church immune for the sexual abuse of a boy by his boy scout camp instructor, leading to the boy's suicide, holding the church immune for mere "administrative" negligence.[84] And a "slip and fall" claim by a plaintiff on a sidewalk was dismissed by the New Jersey court on tenuous "charity" and "beneficiary" bases.[85]

Some "volunteer" protection statutes apply only to directors and officers.[86]

Limited *statutory immunity* has been extended to some nonprofit corporations. The parents of a severely retarded adult who choked to death sued a nonprofit organization that performed mental health intake and referral services for the county. The court noted that as a nonprofit health care provider, the organization was, by state statute, immune from simple negligence claims for anything done pursuant to the Pennsylvania Mental Health and Mental Retardation Act. The court also extended the immunity to persons employed under the Act.[87]

Virginia charitable institutions are immune from liability to their beneficiaries for negligent acts of servants and agents if due care has been exercised in the selection and retention of those servants and agents. However, the claim of an out-of-town invitee or stranger, having no beneficial relation to the charitable institution, is not barred by charitable immunity.[88]

Waiver/Immunity Clauses

In some states, a *club membership application* that agrees to *limit* club liability for inquiries is *assumption of risk* by the applicant.[89] However most states agree that such waivers of liability are against "public policy." For example, a nursing home must use reasonable care for the safety of its patients, but this does not require that an attendant follow each ambulatory patient; it is not liable for accident to a mentally handicapped patient who somehow escaped and was killed while crossing a street at night not at a crosswalk. But the home's *immunity*—from negligence—claims *clause* in its *contracts* is against *public policy* and is not admissible.[90] However, specific waiver protection is still required of beneficiaries by some charities, especially by hospitals.[91]

§180. GOVERNMENTAL IMMUNITY

Some nonprofit organizations are governmental agencies; *e.g.*, a housing development or management corporation, or an environmental research corporation set up by a state, federal, county or other governmental action. They are governmental agencies primarily, and nonprofit corporations only incidentally. Waivers of governmental immunity for torts of agents (and agencies) are now numerous, ranging from the Federal Tort Claims Act to municipal ordinances.

The federal government has waived immunity for torts of its agents or employees committed in the course and scope of their employment, in the Federal Tort Claims Act.[92] Some states have enacted statutes that waive the immunity of governmental authorities and corporations in the operation of state motor vehicles, and in such public places as schools, public buildings, or parks; these statutes may apply to municipal corporations and their agencies, county agencies, or the like.[93] Violations of civil rights have no immunity.[94]

For example, an organization that aided handicapped and black individuals in obtaining housing, sued a city and its officials, under the Fair Housing Act, for using police powers to exclude its clients from middle class white neighborhoods. Under the theory of respondeat superior and the Federal

Housing Act, the city is liable for illegal discriminatory acts of its employees even when the employees act against established municipal policy or custom, and despite directions by the city not to discriminate.[95]

Governmental, administrative, and proprietary functions. In most states the immunity of governmental agencies (including cities, towns, villages, and school or water districts) is now limited to torts committed in the course of performance of purely governmental functions. (Police work is governmental.) No immunity applies to merely administrative ("proprietary") operations. (Waterworks are proprietary.) For example, governments are shielded from tort liability under governmental immunity for the creation and operation of public parks and recreation programs. Such programs are legitimate and traditional functions of government, and are, thus, governmental and not proprietary in nature.[96] This is the rule for example, in Alabama, Florida, Georgia, New Mexico, Pennsylvania, Texas, and other states, while immunity has been abolished in Alaska, Arizona, Illinois, Minnesota, New York, and Wisconsin.[97] In Pennsylvania, a nonprofit volunteer fire company is entitled to absolute governmental immunity, as a local agency, regardless of whether it is engaged in fire fighting activities. However, the fire company must be one officially accorded the status of volunteer fire company by the political subdivision it serves.[98]

In a few states liability attaches to governmental acts of misfeasance, not to those of nonfeasance.[99]

In Hawaii, a nonprofit corporation has standing to bring a suit on behalf of its members if there are "generalized" injuries for which the relief granted would provide remedy to any individual member. State officials are not entitled to sovereign immunity when their acts are unconstitutional or violate state laws.[100]

In almost all states, with respect to most nonprofit organizations, the old immunity rules applied (or now apply) only, if at all, to "purely charitable" activities, and not to "administrative" activities. For example, in the case of a hospital, the wrongful acts of a physician in treating a patient were deemed "charitable," and the corporation immune. But the negligent acts of an orderly in cleaning, or of an elevator operator, were (and are) *administrative* and the corporation is not immune.[101]

Status of the employee (*e.g.*, a physician as a "professional" may determine whether he or she is an employee or an "independent contractor."[102]

Selection of employees. In all cases, failure to use due care in selecting competent and careful employees results in liability for injuries caused by such persons in the course of their employment.[103]

Punitive damages. In most states and in federal cases where corporate liability does exist, it may even include punitive damages, if the wrongful acts of the employee were willful or malicious and if they were approved or ratified by the corporation.[104]

A medical center, that is not controlled by or directly answerable to one or more public officials, public entities, or the public itself, is not a public entity for purposes of sovereign immunity. Joint ventures of public entities with private persons, firms, associations, or corporations do not convert the private entities into governmental bodies. The method by which the board of directors is elected determines whether a nonprofit will function as a public entity.[105]

A state university board of governors (curators) is a "public entity," entitled to governmental immunity from liability for torts, in absence of express statutory provision.[106]

Under Mississippi law the *university's* football team *instructors* (coach, trainer and team doctor) have qualified immunity in damage suit by estate of a player who died after a team practice session.[107]

Downstream landowners sued and alleged that a dam operator acted negligently when he released water from a reservoir and flooded the plaintiffs' property. The court held that the dam operator had a duty of reasonable and ordinary care. Governmental immunity could not shield the operator by way of summary judgment until there was a resolution of the existing genuine issues of material fact.[108]

A city's hospital and health corporations' phone operator's statement to a person calling for help for his wife, on a 911 phone call, that an ambulance was being sent, is evidence of a duty of the corporation to aid the person promptly.[109]

§181. TORT LIABILITY OF AGENTS AND OFFICERS

[See the preceding section, and Chapter 32.]

An agent ordinarily is personally liable for his own torts.[110] Enforcement of the additional liability of his principal (the corporation) usually is strongly sought, because the agent usually has little but his salary with which to pay damages.

Officers and directors are not personally liable for torts of other employees unless they participated in the wrongful acts.[111] (See chapters on directors' and officers' duties and liabilities.)

But if an officer or employee intentionally interferes with business or employee-relations to which the corporation is a party, he or she may be personally liable in tort, even if the corporation cannot be liable for interfering with its own contract relation.[112]

In Illinois board officers of an unincorporated condo unit owners association were held to be individually not exempt from liability for association negligence forced by the NPC Act where the organization was one not federally tax exempt, but the board members were viewed as fiduciaries of the unit owners so that breach of the duty was not a tort; but under the state's Condominium Act (which governs) they were protected from liability in a wrongful death action for drowning of a unit owner's child where they individually were not involved in the giving of a key to the child by a manager-agent.[113]

Florida's 1989 statute amendment permits courts to force disgorging of improperly obtained personal profits taken by directors or officers of NPOs; but the complaining member or other citizen must submit enough money to pay the costs of the legal proceedings.[114]

Member Liability

Shareholders or members, of either profit or nonprofit corporations, are not responsible for the debts of the corporation.[115] In order to "pierce the corporate veil" and hold individual members of a nonprofit corporation, who were not involved, responsible for an accidental shooting at a nonprofit hunt club, the injured party had to show one of two exceptional circumstances. Those two circumstances are that (1) the members acting through the corporation committed fraud or deceit on a third party, or (2) the members failed to conduct the business on a corporate footing by disregarding the corporate entity so that it became indistinguishable from the members.

Even if there is a duty on the part of a nonprofit hunt club to make and enforce safety rules, violation of that group duty is not enough to result in individual liability for corporation members.[116]

Members and officers of an unincorporated nonprofit reelection committee are personally liable for contractual obligations if they authorized the contract or subsequently ratified its terms.[117]

Organization Liability [See §178, above]

Utah's Dramshop Act gives a cause of action, against nonprofit or for-profit providers of intoxicants, to third parties who are injured by intoxicated persons. But, there is no action for the intoxicated person to sue a provider for his own injuries.[118]

A nonprofit committee and landowner, that held a fund raising event for local firemen, is not liable under the Dram Shop Act for injuries sustained by a motorist who was involved in an accident with a drunken motorist who had attended the fund raiser, unless the committee and landowner "sold" alcohol at the event. However, the nonprofit vendors that "sold" beer may be liable if they sold directly to the alleged tort-feasor.[119]

A fraternal organization is not liable for negligent supervision of its insurance agent where the agent induced others to invest in noninsurance related business schemes that benefited the agent. The organization has no duty to supervise the agent unless he was on its premises or using the chattel of the organization in his capacity as an insurance agent. The organization must have known or should have known that it should exercise control over the agent.[120]

An employment agency, that failed to discover a camp counselor's homosexual sexual orientation, owed no duty of care to a camper who was sexually assaulted by the counselor, after the agency placed the counselor, because the agency had no prior knowledge of deviance on the part of the counselor. The court would not presume that homosexuals are predisposed toward molestation.[121]

A student who slipped and fell while walking across a snow covered lawn sued Villanova University. A motion for nonsuit was granted because the doctrine of "hills and ridges," requiring that land owners remove accumulations of snow, did not apply to lawns. Further, the University breached no duty to provide a direct sidewalk where there was a properly maintained sidewalk indirectly connecting the points.[122]

A charitable organization is not liable for negligence of an amusement park's employees where the charity was promoting an event at the park for *fundraising purposes.* It had no duty of care as to the rides run by *park personnel.*[123]

A religious college is liable for defamation by its officers; implying that the plaintiff was homosexual. [Nazevi v. Missouri Valley College, 75201, Mo. Sup. Ct., Aug. 17, 1993.]

A nonprofit boarding school was held not to be liable for molestation of a student by a staff member because the misconduct was personal in nature and unrelated to employment. No negligence in hiring was found because a records check, indicating no criminal record or propensities, was conducted on the employee prior to hiring.[124]

A church member may not sue the church for negligence of another member in a roof repair project of members.[125]

A religious (church) conference is not liable for sexual assault by a pastor on a minor parishioner; his conduct was outside the scope of his employment, though he had sexually assaulted a child before.[126]

A church minister's alleged affair with the wife, while counseling a husband and wife, is not "religious" activity and not an "agent" act, and does not come under protection of the First Amendment free-exercise clause protections. Minister, but not the church, may be held liable in tort, as "intentional tort," not "malpractice."[127]

A *parent* may collect damages for infliction of mental suffering by a religious organization that enticed plaintiff's 15-year-old daughter to leave home, and concealed her whereabouts from them.[128]

Punitive damages have been awarded regularly against nonprofit as well as profit organizations.[129]

Ownership of only part of a subsidiary corporation may not be enough to make the "parent" liable for the torts of the subsidiary corporation if there is little domination and control.[130]

Nonprofit corporations, that serve as adoption agencies, may be liable for fraud, intentional misrepresentation or negligence for misrepresenting the health or psychological background of adopted children.[131]

Hospital and Blood Bank Liability

When a nonprofit hospital warrants that a parking lot is safe, through employment of a security service, the hospital is liable for injuries perpetrated by third parties and sustained by a hospital employee in that lot. This is true, especially where there is failure of the guard service to adequately patrol the area, despite warnings of an intruder's presence.[132]

A big hospital complex, with only one *security* guard, in a *high crime area,* was sued for negligence by the estate of a woman (a hospital driver) who was raped and murdered by a parolee after being abducted from the hospital parking ramp, which was frequented by drunks and weird persons. *Held:* that testimony as to *foreseeability*, in that the security was as good as that at similar institutions in similar communities, must be limited to evidence as to such facilities in the immediately nearby area.[133]

A NPO (hospital) has a duty to monitor its personnel, including independent contractors (physicians) who care for its patients, by using care in their selection and retention, independent of their (physician's) duty of care. Corporate negligence may be based on common law and/or statutes. "Proximate care" is the test.[134]

A nursing home is not strictly liable (as if it were an insurer) for the injury of a patient who fell while alone. It is required to use only "reasonable care" for even mentally confused patients (e.g., one with Alzheimer's disease).[135] Thus, a hospital employees' standard of care, in a negligence suit, is not higher than usual merely because of the elderly or sick nature of persons on the premises.[136]

A nonprofit hospital was recently held liable in the amount of $25,000 to a patient who was burned by a heating pad. On appeal, the court upheld the trial court's decision not to instruct the jury that a percentage of the fault belonged to the patient, because he had refused to allow a nurse to check his condition or the heating pad.[137]

The standard of care for a nonprofit blood bank is one of a professional, exercising reasonable care in a manner consistent with the knowledge and ability possessed by members of the profession in good standing. There is a rebuttable presumption that the standard adopted by members in good standing constitutes due care. However, the plaintiff may introduce evidence that the adopted school of practice is deficient by not incorporating readily available practices that provide increased protection. Compliance with the FDA recommendations is not conclusive proof that additional precautions are not required.[138]

The parents of a child infected with AIDS from a blood transfusion filed an action for negligent misrepresentation against the nonprofit blood bank that supplied the blood. The bank's receptionist had mistakenly stated that family blood donations could not be earmarked and directed for use in the child's operation. The Court of Appeals held that the trial court improperly excluded evidence that was offered to show that the rareness of the child's blood type was the cause of the infection, to the extent that the child could not have used the family's directed blood. A new trial on negligent misrepresentation was ordered. The blood bank was held not to be negligent for its failure to use tests that no other blood bank in the nation was using.[139]

Is an action against a nonprofit blood bank, for negligent collection and supply of human blood which causes the transmission of the HIV virus, a "malpractice" action, for purposes of a statute of limitation or repose? The question has been certified to the Georgia Supreme Court.[140]

Liability Releases

A dental patient brought a malpractice suit against the New York University Dental Center. The court found that an agreement signed by the patient under which the patient released the university, its doctors, and employees and students from all negligence liability was void and contrary to public policy.[141] [For form-signature law see: *Deboer v. Florida O.D. Assn.*, 18 FLW-D1805 (FL. 5th Cir., 8/13/93.]

Nuisance

The activities of the members of a radio-controlled model airplane club do not rise to the level of private noise nuisance where neighbors testified that they were not bothered by the airplanes or the noise.[142]

Defamation

Like any corporation, a nonprofit corporation may be guilty of libel or slander (civil or criminal) (See note 166).

Recent cases have held corporations to be "persons" for purposes of prosecuting a defamation action.[143] If the corporation has "assumed roles of special prominence in the affairs of society," or has "thrust itself to the forefront of particular public controversies in order to influence the resolution of the issues involved," it has become a "public person" under the test stated by the Supreme Court in *Gertz v. Robert Welch, Inc.*[144] As a public person, the corporation must show that the alleged defamatory statement about it was made "with knowledge that it was false or with reckless disregard of whether it was false or not" in order to recover damages.[145]

But the mere fact that a person was the *founder* of a nonprofit religious corporation did not make him a "public figure" for purposes of this rule of defamation law.[146]

Statements about the unsatisfactory results of a physician's approach to cancer treatment, made by the director of a nonprofit organization, which counseled patients about alternative treatments for cancer, are protected opinion, not actionable defamation. The four factors to be considered are (1) whether the language has precise meaning or is indefinite and ambiguous, (2) whether the language is capable of being objectively viewed as true or false, (3) consideration of the full context of the communication, (4) and consideration of the broader social context surrounding the communication, including applicable customs or conventions which alert the listener that he/she is hearing opinion and not fact.[147]

Statements made by individual animal rights advocates, about the alleged deplorable treatment of New York City carriage horses, are opinion and communications on a matter of public interest. Such statements are entitled to a qualified privilege against defamation under the First Amendment. However, when the ASPCA, a nonprofit corporation having the enforcement responsibilities of animal protection laws, distributes a flyer that repeats the advocate's statements and calls for restrictive legislation, the statements create an action for libel against the ASPCA.[148]

Association *Posting of Notice* of dismissal of its management (contractual) company on a bulletin board in an area open to others besides members is "publication" for a claim of libel by the company in a lawsuit for damages.[149]

A college is liable for defamation by its officers. See *Nazeri v. Missouri Valley College*, 75201, MO Supr. Ct., Aug. 17, 1993.

When a nonprofit corporation published the picture of a child and alleged that the child had been sold to neighborhood men to support a crack habit, a defamation action was brought on behalf of the child. By statute in New York, the use of names or pictures, for advertising purposes, is prohibited without authorization. Summary judgment for the nonprofit was reversed to determine whether the publication was an advertisement or whether the child was defamed.[150]

A published article, that merely investigates and questions claims made by a nonprofit project, that sent holiday care packages to the Persian Gulf during Operation Desert Shield, is not defamation, where the article did not intend or endorse a charge of profiteering or gouging. Stating that the organizer had benefited from the project is not defamatory.[151]

A nonprofit organization may be sued for slander and libel for damaging false statements contained in letters.[152]

When a newspaper erroneously reported that a contract between a nonprofit Private Industry Council and a youth training program had been subpoenaed by a federal grand jury and confiscated by the FBI, enrollment and funding of the training program dropped. The proper action against the newspaper is libel or slander and not contractual interference.[153]

A nonprofit art historical corporation, organized under French law, made disparaging statements about the genuineness of a painting and the quality of its restoration. The seller failed in his suit, on a claim of product disparagement, because he did not establish that the remarks had been transmitted to the potential buyers. To prevail in product disparagement cases, the plaintiff must show falsity of the statements, publication to a third person, malice, and special damages.[154]

§182. CRIMES COMMITTED BY CORPORATIONS

Corporations formerly were not viewed as convictable of the commission of a crime, because they are artificial, existing only in the contemplation of the law.[155]

Today they can be so convicted, because they are deemed to be groups of natural persons.[156] If their agents act criminally, the entire corporate group may be liable criminally. This is seldom based now on an attempt to impute the criminal intent of the agents to the corporation. It is based on practical public policy, which holds the corporation liable in order to force the corporation to control its agents.[157]

Criminal liability of the corporate entity is based on the conduct of its controlling officers or managers. This liability attaches if such officers authorize, acquiesce in, ratify, or knowingly accept the benefits of criminal acts of the corporation's agents.[158] (See notes 155, 156).

Nonfeasance (failure to perform duties imposed by the law) may be the basis of an indictment of the officers or agents of a corporation.[159] For example, failure to account for funds collected from the public may be a basis for such liability.[160] Most states require periodic reports of this kind from all nonprofit organizations. Failure to report often is made a statutory misdemeanor.[161]

Misfeasance (improper performance of duties imposed by the law) may be the basis of an indictment.[162] For example, fraudulent misuse of funds, false records or reports, or solicitation for purposes other than those authorized, is misfeasance; or improper loans to officers, trustees, or members.

A very common requirement is that nonprofit corporations maintain records in a prescribed manner. Failure to do so is a misdemeanor.[163]

Contributions to political parties often are forbidden to all corporations under penalty of criminal prosecution for disobedience of this statutory rule.[164]

Certain personal crimes of violence, such as rape or murder by its agents, obviously cannot be imputed to the corporation.[165] Likewise, a corporation cannot commit bigamy.

But today most crimes, including those such as libel or conspiracy, in which criminal intent (*mens rea*) is an essential element, can be imputed to a corporation.[166] There have even been cases of corporations being charged[167] or convicted of manslaughter (in California, New Hampshire and New Jersey).[168]

Even municipal corporations have been convicted of criminal conduct (maintenance of a criminal nuisance—a filthy sewage basin—in Maine and in New York.)[169]

A corporation officer's testimony may be impeached by evidence of criminal conviction of his corporation.[170]

Violation of law by church officials, for religious reasons, nevertheless is criminal conduct, not immune from prosecution. Clergy aid to persons illegally entering the U.S. (the "sanctuary" movement, for refugees from Central America) makes valid the government's use of tape recordings of clergy meetings, to convict them. "The *government's interest* in controlling immigration *outweighs* (the clergy's) purported religious interest."[171]

Insurance and Environmental Liability

A nonprofit Institute for Plant Research, affiliated with Cornell University, was required to contribute to the cleanup of a pesticide contaminated site pursuant to the Comprehensive Environmental Response, Compensation & Liability Act (CERCLA). The Institute sought summary judgment and a declaration that its insurer had breached its duty to defend. The court held that the existence of one policy covering some of the years during which the alleged contamination occurred would be sufficient if that policy clearly covered the property on which the damage occurred. Also the damage must have occurred while the premises were being used as envisioned in the policy (in this case as an "office and related purposes"). Issues of material fact precluded summary judgment.[172]

Penalties for Crimes

Plaintiffs are entitled to attorney fees for·litigation that results in a determination of a violation of the Voting Rights Act.[173]

Attorney's fees may be awarded by statute to the party that prevails on damage claims. A candidate seeking re-election as a state representative filed action alleging election *law violations* by a voters-league organization supporting his opponent. An injunction was issued. The Supreme Court of Texas held that a statutory award of $22,500 in attorney fees against the voters league was reasonable considering the time involved and the nature of services rendered.[174]

The U.S. Sentencing Commission in 1991 adopted guidelines to punish corporate crime, by fines taking (1) the bulk of financial profits of illegal conduct, or (2) of the amount of the victims' loss, or (3) on a table listing various grades of severity of offenses, whichever is the greatest amount.[175]

§183. OFFICERS' AND AGENTS' LIABILITY FOR CRIMES

The guilty officers and agents of the corporation, of course, are personally liable for their criminal acts. The imputation of their acts to the corporation does not exonerate them.[176]

Executive officers and directors have been held to be personally liable to criminal prosecution for the acts of subordinates, even without participating in those acts. If the corporation is generally engaged in illegal activities, this personal liability attaches, even though the executive officers do not personally direct or supervise the specific criminal acts of the subordinates.[177] See, below, the chapters on officers' and directors' duties and liabilities.

A corporation may be held criminally liable for homicide by a vehicle in Pennsylvania,[178] but not in Texas.[179] But in Oregon the word "person" does not include a corporation in the involuntary manslaughter statute.[180]

A physician who devised and implemented a scheme to receive public funds for nonexistent patient "home visits" was found to be personally liable for treble damages. He was personally enriched because he had de facto control, through his family, of two realty corporations that collected funds from the Medicaid fraud through inflated rents charged to the clinic for its buildings.[181]

A defendant, who started a local chapter of an international nonprofit basic trauma life support educational group, converted some of the fees charged to his personal use. However, the state charged him with conversion by a bailee, an improper charge that it could not prove.[182]

A clergyman giving counseling to a married woman member of the church violates the state (criminal law) statute about psychotherapists by having sex with the (woman) patient. The statute is constitutional exercise of state police power, is not too vague, protects victims with dependent personality disorders, and does not violate privacy.[183]

Punishment for Crimes

Crimes that are punishable by imprisonment obviously must be treated specially. A corporation cannot be imprisoned, as a practical matter, although its guilty members can be.

Fines are the usual criminal punishments for corporations.[184] Inasmuch as these fines may penalize innocent contributors and members, the tendency is to punish the guilty persons individually. The statutes specify their punishments, which may be imprisonment, or fines, or both.[185]

Revocation of the corporate charter, of course, is another method of punishment.[186]

§184. CIVIL RIGHTS LIABILITY

[See cases above in this chapter, and Chapter 36.]
42 U.S.C. 2000(e) (1970),[187] recognizes an individual's right to associate with whom he chooses, by granting to private clubs an exemption from compliance with the federal prohibition against discrimination in public facilities.[188] This exemption can be lost if membership is based in part on such nonpersonal grounds as closeness of residence to corporate facilities.[189] The Fourth Circuit has held that reliance on legal counsel's erroneous opinion that the corporation was entitled to the private club exemption does not prevent corporate directors from being personally liable for discriminatory membership policies.[190]

The Supreme Court defined the limits of public school officials' qualified civil rights immunity in 1975.[191] Since that time a number of suits have been brought against such officials under section 1983 of the Civil Rights Act.[192] If the "state action" required by that section can be found—possibly through government funding which gives the government a right of control[193]—there appears no reason why suits under section 1983 may not be brought against private school officials.

The impact of the *Bakke*[194] "reverse discrimination" suit was still uncertain almost a decade later. The following cases serve to illustrate commonly litigated civil rights issues.

Disability Advocates, Inc. (DIA) is a nonprofit advocacy corporation dedicated to providing legal representation and advocacy to persons diagnosed as mentally ill. When DIA sued to challenge the involuntary commitment of patients, the court held that the private hospital was a "state actor" for the purposes of a civil rights action because there was a close nexus between the state and the hospital's commitment activities. Also, the power to deprive a person of liberty is normally reserved to the states.[195]

If state officials place a minor in a nonprofit foster care and shelter facility, that they knew or suspected to be dangerous to minors, the officials incur liability if harm results. The standard of care for officials is whether they exhibited deliberate indifference, and not whether they failed to exercise professional judgment. Individual causes of action may exist under § 1983 for violation of a child's right, under the Adoption Assistance and Child Welfare Act, to care in a foster home that reasonably meets the standard of national organizations.[196]

A hospital's refusal to admit a patient because it had no bed available, where the hospital had no obligation to that person, does not suffice to constitute deprivation of the patient's federal *civil rights* (42 U.S.C. §1983).[197]

"*Compelling state interests*" in a matter involving church activity may *justify state imposition* of liability on the church and/or its officers; for example, "fraud" in recruiting members by "brainwashing," despite First Amendment (free exercise of religion) constitutional law. A California Supreme Court (6 to 1) order to try a claim by aggrieved church members was supported by U.S. Supreme Court refusal to hear the church's appeal from that decision.[198]

A church teaching that parents are ordered by God to educate their own children (at home), and not allow teaching by teachers who took courses based upon secular humanism, does not excuse violation of state "compulsory attendance" statute rules for all schools. Home "school" is not a "private school." The statute does not offend due process rules (14th Amend.). Requirement of "certificated" teachers does not violate First Amendment.[199]

§185. CONTEMPT OF COURT

A corporation may be guilty of contempt of court. Punishment usually is by the imposition of a fine.[200] Guilty officers and agents also may be liable.[201]

Imprisonment can be imposed as a civil contempt sanction if demonstrators refuse to obey an injunction. Antiabortion activists were jailed in Oregon when they interfered with the operation of a medical clinic despite an injunction against that behavior. The fact that the demonstrators could secure their release if they agreed to comply with the injunctive order was held not to improperly compel self incrimination or sworn statements against the demonstrators' conscience.[202]

The "choice of evils" defense does not apply to prevent the finding that abortion protesters are in contempt when they block access to abortion clinics in violation of a preliminary injunction. The choice of evils defense applies only if the defendant's conduct is "necessary" and not inconsistent with other provisions of law. Since abortion is legal in Oregon, the action of the protesters was inconsistent with other provisions of law.[203]

§186. JURY TRIAL

The right to trial by jury exists for corporate defendants as well as for individuals.[204]

§187. DOUBLE JEOPARDY

As a corporation has been held to be a "person" entitled to both equal protection and due process under the constitution,[205] the courts have found no reason why a corporation should not also be entitled to the constitutional guarantee against double jeopardy.[206]

§188. SELF-INCRIMINATION

The privilege of refusing to incriminate oneself, under the Fifth Amendment to the Constitution, does not apply to corporations. The initial theory for this was that the state withheld this right in exchange for the granting of the privilege of incorporation.[207] Now the corporate nature of the organization is held to be the determining factor.[208] Corporate records thus can be used against the corporation, although it is immune under the Fourth Amendment from "unreasonable search and seizure."[209]

Most states now have statutes which *compel* corporation officers and agents to testify in corporation-crime cases. But the privilege against self-incrimination is preserved to them by guarantees that no personal prosecution shall be brought against such officers or agents for personal crimes revealed while so testifying.[210]

The United States Supreme Court has held that the Fifth Amendment privilege against self-incrimination is protected even against *state* action, under the Fourteenth Amendment.[211]

§189. CONSTRUCTIVE TRUST REMEDY

A *constructive trust* may be imposed, by a court, on funds collected for charitable purposes but diverted to other purposes. This may be done in a suit by the attorney general, brought by him *sua sponte* or on the complaint of an interested person. The attorney general's power to protect public donations goes beyond mere enforcement of express charitable trusts.[212] This was the ruling of the Ohio Supreme Court in a case concerning proceeds of *bingo* operations and two persons' knowledge of falsity of entries made in the corporation's books.[213]

The courts' powers to employ specific (equity) remedies have long been well-established.[214]

§190. LOBBYING AND GRASSROOTING

[See Chapter 39, on Lobbying and Political Action.]

The Internal Revenue Service is often re-writing proposed regulations as to the elective rules about lobbying, under IRC §§ 501(h) and 4911. "Nonpartisan analysis, study, or research" is not lobbying under the elective rules. The newly created *IRS Commissioner's Exempt Organization Advisory Group* was helping in early 1988. But, considering that the 1950 proposed regulations of lobbying under the business expense deduction rules [IRC § 162(e)] and private foundation rules [IRC §4945] have *not yet* been finalized, we can only continue to watch the developments. See, for example, such newsletter services as the John Wiley and Sons (publishing company) monthly *Nonprofit Counsel.*

Before the 1976 Tax Reform Act, the Internal Revenue Code required tax-exempt organizations to make sure that "no substantial part of (its) activities is carrying on propaganda, or otherwise attempting to influence legislation." This vague rule was partly clarified in 1955 by the decision in *Seasongood v. Commissioner*[215] that held that devotion of less than five percent of corporate efforts to such attempts did not lose tax exemption. But the rule was so vague as to be unenforceable.

Since 1976 the tax law[216] allows a tax-exempt [IRC §501(c)(3)] (charitable) organizations to *elect* to follow a test of limitation of budget amounts, rather than the "substantial part" test. A special IRS *form* is provided for this election.[217] Such choice applies only to taxable years beginning January 1, 1977 and after. Some special types of organizations are ineligible to use this election provision: churches or church associations, private foundations, and organizations that support labor unions, trade associations, and certain social welfare organizations.

The statutory *nontaxable lobbying budget amounts*, per year, was set at 20 percent of the first $500,000, plus 15 percent of the second $500,000 plus 10 percent of the third $500,000, plus 5 percent of any additional expenditures; but in no case more than the *cap* sum of $1 million per year. As to *grassrooting* (influencing other people to write or phone, *etc.*) the nontaxable amount was set at 25 percent of the nontaxable lobbying sum.

Violation of these limits is punishable by an excise tax of 25 percent of the excess lobbying expenditures and loss of exempt status if the permitted amounts are exceeded by over 50 percent over a period of four years. State or federal statutes *may properly limit* political expenditures of funds by both NPOs and profit organizations, and this does not violate the First Amendment[218]. [See above, § 84.]

What constitutes *lobbying* is described in detail.[219] *Grassrooting* by tax-exempt trade and professional associations also is treated in detail by the Internal Revenue Code,[220] with political intervention allowed no deductions.[221] Since 1978 the Internal Revenue Service has issued Revenue Rulings on grassrooting expenses in attempts to influence legislation.[222] Lobbying now is being called a peril to a society when it employs "contributions" to legislators, or the like (*e.g.*, buying influence).[223]

IRS Tax Regulation §1.501(c)(3): Lobbying by Public Charities

—Sec. 501(h) sets optional rules for permissible lobbying by certain public charitable organizations, basically in terms of dollar limitations and election of coverage under various statutory choices offered. Thus the 25 percent excise tax on excess lobbying may apply, or loss of tax exempt status if lobbying exceeds 150 percent of the limitations. Form 5768 must be filed if limited lobbying is to be carried on. Churches or church associations are exempted, and may not elect to come under these rules. Especially forbidden is direct or indirect support of a candidate for election to public political office. An organizations that engages in such support is an "action" organization and usually is not tax exempt under Sec. 501(c)(3). But nonpartisan research and analysis is valid activity.[224]

POINTS TO REMEMBER

- Know what powers your corporation has.

- If in doubt, reason from the purposes stated in the charter. What powers are reasonably needed to carry out the purposes? These powers you have.

- If in doubt about a possibly *ultra vires* act—don't commit it.

- Do not rely on the immunity of nonprofit corporations from liability for torts. This immunity is disappearing rapidly.

- Use competent agents and employees as the best insurance against tort liability.

- And get insurance, too.

- Crimes of nonprofit corporation officers may be crimes of the whole corporation.

- Punishment is severe for guilty officers.

- Compulsory testimony statutes now exist in most states. The corporation cannot hide behind the Fifth Amendment, although individuals can.

- The problems of torts, crimes, and *ultra vires* are tough. Expert knowledge of tort law, criminal law, and corporation law is required for them.

- Be especially watchful against violations of civil rights by nonprofit organizations.

- Beware of "political" action that may cause loss of tax-exemptions; especially beware of supporting a candidate for political office.

NOTES TO CHAPTER 17

1. Henn and Alexander, *Laws of Corporations* § 184 (3rd ed., 1983); Hamilton, *Corporations*, 172 (3rd ed., 1986); 2 Oleck, *Modern Corporation Law*, c.38 (1978 supp.); Oleck, *Remedies for Abuses of Corporate Status*, 9 Wake For. L. Rev. 463, 476–481 (1973); Note, *Ultra Vires in Georgia*, 16 Mercer L. Rev. 320 (1964); and see for examples: State *ex rel.*, Supreme Temple of Pythian Sisters v. Cook 234 Mo. App. 898, 136 S.W.2d 142, 146 (1940); Wing Memorial Hospital Assn. v. Town of Randolph, 120 Vt. 277, 141 A.2d 645 (1958). This is one aspect of the view of corporations generally as "privileged classes." *See* Ewing, *The Corporation as Public Enemy No. 1, Saturday Review* (mag.) 12 (Jan. 21, 1978).

2. *Ibid.* See, Notes, 132 U. Pa. L. Rev. 901 (1984); 69 Va. L. Rev. 1303 (1983); 69 Va. L. Rev. 1153 (1983); 83 Columbia L. Rev. 1210 (1983).

3. Reeve v. Parkins [1820] 2 Jacob and Walker 390; *and see,* J. T. Pratt, *The Law Relating to Friendly Societies* (Garland Publ. N.Y. and London 1978) regarding Stat. 10 Geo. IV cap. 56 (1829); and Stats. 4 and 5 Will. IV cap. 40 (1834).

4. Cross v. Midtown Club, Inc., 365 A.2d 1227 (Conn. Sup., 1976); and see Note, *Corporate Standing to Allege Race Discrimination in Civil Rights Actions*, 69 Va. L. Rev. 1153 (1983).

5. Good Will Home Association v. Erwin, 266 A.2d 218 (Me. S.J.); app. den. 281 A.2d 453 (Me. 1971).

6. State *es rel.* v. Southern Publishing Assn., 169 Tenn. 257, 84 S.W.2d 580, 100 A.L.R. 576 (1935). Cf., Louisa T. York Orphan Asylum v. Erwin, 281 A.2d 453 (Me., 1971); City of Nashville v. Board of Equalization, 360 S.W.2d 458 (Tenn., 1962).

7. N. Yoshihara (*Los Angeles Times*, article), in *St. Petersburg (Fla.) Times*, p. 4D (Jan. 30, 1980).

8. *See,* Cedars of Lebanon Hospital v. County of Los Angeles, 35 Cal.2d 729, 745 (1950) (thrift shop in a hospital); Y.M.C.A. v. County of L.A., 35 Cal.2d 760, 772 (1950) (restaurant, barbershop, valet store, and gym store in a Y.M.C.A.)

9. People *ex rel.* Groman v. Sinai Temple, Calif. App.2d App. Dist., Div.4, Civ. No. 36407 (Oct. 18, 1971). *Quo warranto* action dismissed, citing Cal. Corp. Code, §9200 (1949); 33 Ops. Cal. Atty-Genl. 33, 35 (1959).

10. 467 N.E.2d 58 (Mass., 1984)

11. *Ibid.,* at 64.

12. *New Christian Valley M.B. Church v. Board of Educ.,* 704 F. Supp. 868 (D.C., IL, 1989).

13. *Guinn v. Church of Christ of Collinsville,* #62-154 (Ok.; Jan. 17, 1989).

14. *S. & T. Anchorage, Inc. v. Lewis,* 575 So. 2d 696 (Fla. 3rd DCA, 1991).

15. Tex. Rev. Civ. St. Ann., Art. 1396-203; Utah Code Ann., 16-6-23; N.C. Genl. Stat. Ann. § 55A-17; N.D. Sess. L. 1957, 10-24-06 Ohio Rev. Code, §1702.12(H); Va. Code 1950 §13. 1-828; Wis. Stat. §181.057; D.C. Code, §29-506.

16. Fla. St. § 617.0304; Ohio Rev. Code, §1702.12(H). *And see,* First United Presbyterian Church v. Young, 21 Ohio N.P.(n.s.) 569, 29 Ohio Dec. (N.P.) 477 (1919); Manufacturer's Fire Assn. v. Lynchburg Drug Mills, 8 Ohio C.C. 112, 4 Ohio C.D. 350 (1893).

17. *See,* above Chapter 16.

18. Such as those cited in n. 15.

19. *See,* n. 1; Northwest Civic Assn. v. Sheldon, 317 Mich. 416; 27 N.W.2d 36 (1947); South Carolina Elec. and Gas Co. v. So. Car. Public Service Authority, 215 S.C. 193; 54 S.E.2d 777 (1949).

20. Rianhard v. Hovey, 13 Ohio 300, 302 (1844); and *see* n. 10.

21. *In re* Grand Union Co., 219 F. 353; 363 (2d Cir. N.Y. 1915); Staacke v. Rutledge, 111 Tex. 489; 241 S.W. 994, 998 (1922); Healy v. Geilfuss, 37 Del. Ch. 502, 146 A.2d 5 (1958); St. Joseph Telephone & Tel. Co. v. Southeastern Tel. Co., 5 S. 55 (Fla., 1941).

22. *See,* 7 Fletcher, *Cycl. of Corporations,* §§3407-3409, 3411 (perm. ed); Henn, *Corporations,* 399 (2d ed. 1986 casebook).

23. City of Williston v. Ludowese, 53 N.D. 797; N.D. 208 N.W. 82 (1926); 19 C.J.S., *Corporations,* §975 p. 430; American Casualty Co., v. Dakota Tractor, 234 F. Supp. 606 (D.C., N.D., 1964).

24. Foote v. Community Hospital of Beloit, 405 P.2d 423 (Kan. 1965); Holt v. College of Osteopathic Phys. and Surg., 61 Cal.2d 750, 394 P.2d 932, 40 Cal. Rptr. 244 (1964); Shannons Co-Executor v. Marcum, 230 S.W.2d 457 (Ky. 1950); Fletcher, *op. cit. supra,* n. 22 at §3459.

25. Aitken v. Stewart, 129 Calif. App. 38; 18 P.2d 988 (1953); 7 Fletcher, *op.cit, supra,* §407-3409, 3411; Ross v. Realty Abstract Co., 141 A.2d 319 (N.J. 1958).

26. Ames v. Kansas, 111 U.S. 449, 4 S. Ct. 437; 28 L. Ed. 482 (1884); Syracuse Savings Bank v. Yorkshire Ins. Co., 301 N.Y. 403; 94 N.E.2d 73 (1950); Red Ball Motor Freight Co., Inc. v. Southern Pacific Trans. Co., 231 S.W.2d 462 (Tex. 1950); Cedars of Lebanon case, *supra,* n. 8. Ohio has a *quo warranto* authoirization statute: Ohio Rev. Code. §2733.02 (five years); and a limitation period of 20 years, Ohio Rev. Code, §2733.35; *see,* State *ex rel.* Mcelroy v. Trumbull Savings and Loan Co., 176 Ohio St. 85; 26 Ohio Op.2E 398 (1964).

27. Nowell v. Equitable Trust Co., 249 Mass. 585, 595; 144 N.E. 749 (1924); Moate v. H. L. Green Co., 95 Ga. 493, 98 S.E.2d 185 (1957).

28. *Jackson v. Stuhlfire,* 547 N.E. 2d 1146 (Mass. App., 1990).

29. *Brenner v. Powers, 584 N.E. 2d 569 (Ind. App. 3 Dist. 1992).*

30. Buddin v. Golden Boy Manor, Inc., 585 So. 2d 435 (Fla. 4th DCA, 1991).

31. *Hughes v. Patrolmen's Benevolent Association, 850 F.2d 876 (2d Cir., NY, 1988).*

32. *Schneider v. Colegio de Abogados de Puerto Rico,* U.S. 1st Cir. Ct. App., Puerto Rico (Oct. 24, 1990); *Florida Bar v. Frankel,* 581 So. 2nd 1301 (Fla. 1991), objectionable lobbying; *Keller v. State Bar,* 496 U.S. 1 (1993); see 16 Natl. L.D. (18)3 (Jan. 17, 1994).

33. See *Keller v. State Bar of Calif.*, 110 S.Ct. 2228 (1990); *Abood v. Detriot Board of Educ.*, c.38 §373 of this suppl.; *Florida Bar v. Frankel*, 581 So. 2d 1301 (Fla. 1991).

34. *National Center for Youth Law v. Legal Services Corp.*, 749 F. Supp. 1013 (D.C. Calif., 1990).

35. Protest of Downing, 164 Okla. 181; 23 P.2d 173 (1933).

36. Coleman v. California Yearly Meeting of Friends Church, 27 Calif. App.2d 579; 81 P.2d 469 (1938). *See*, K. Spero, *Hospital Liability: Vicarious and Direct Corporate Responsibility. . .* , 17 Trial 22-7 (1979).

37. *See* the preceding section.

38. *See*, Godbey v. Godbey, 70 Ohio App. 455; 44 N.E.2d 810, 813 (1942).

39. *Catawba County Horsemen's Ass'n, Inc. v. Deal*, 419 S.E. 2d 185 (N.C. App., 1992).

40. Coastal Towers Condo Apts. v. Trainor, 509 So. 2d 351 (Fla. App., 4th Dist., 1987).

41. *Harrell v. Total Health Care, Inc.*, 781 S.W. 2d 58 (Mo. 1989); And see, similar concept of "governmental immunity" of hospitals; *Armendarez v. Tarrant County Hosp. Dist.*, 781 S.W. 2d 301 (Tex. App. 1989).

42. *Jolly v. Michael Reese Health Plan Foundation*, 587 N.E. 2d 1063 (Ill. App. 1 Dist. 1992).

43. *Rogers v. Miles Laboratories, Inc.*, 802 P.2d 1346 (Wash. 1991).

44. *Craigo v. Circus-Circus Enterprises*, 786 P. 2d 22 (Nev. 1990).

45. *Matthews v. Elk Pioneer Days*, 824 P.2d 541 (Wash. App. 1992). *See also Cheneau v. Apostolic Outreach Center*, 529 So. 2d 149 (LA App. 1988); LA St. A-R.S. 9: 2791.

46. *Simchuk v. Angel Island Community Ass'n*, 833 P.2d 158 (Mont., 1992) (guest injured by falling basketball court light).

47. *Avallone v. Mortimer*, 599 A.2d 1304 (N.J. Super. A.D. 1991); *Brown v. St. Venantius School*, 544 A.2d 842 (1988). *See also Market Street Mission v. Bureau of R & B. H. Standards*, 541 A.2d 668 (NJ 1988).

48. *Catrone v. Throughbred Racing Associations of North America, Inc.*, 727 F. Supp. 744 (D.C., Mass., 1990).

49. *Buddin v. Golden Boy Manor, Inc.*, 585 So. 2d 435 (Fla. 4th DCA, 1991).

50. Prosser and Keeton, *Torts* §133 (5th ed., 1984); Oleck, *Tort Law Practice Manual* §132 (1982); Noel and Philips, *Cases on Torts* 170 (1980).

51. Williams v. First United Church of Christ, 318 N.E.2d 562 (Ohio App. 1974); Mason v. Southern New Engl. Conf. Assn., 696 F.2d 135 (1st Cir., 1982).

52. Feoffees of Heriot's Hospital v. Ross, (1846) 12 C. & F. 507, 8 Engl. Rep. 1508.

53. Mersey Docks Trustees v. Gibbs (1866), 11 H.L. Cas. 686, 11 Engl. Rep. 1500.

54. *E.g.*, Nicholson v. Good Samaritan Hospital, 199 S. 344 (Fla., 1940); Garlington v. Kingsley, 289 S.2d 88 (La., 1974); Annot., 25 A.L.R.2d 29; Restatement (2d) Torts, §895 E; Friend v. Cove Methodist Church, 396 P.2d 546 (Wash., 1964); Albritton v. Neighborhood Centers Assn., 466 N.E.2d 867 (Ohio, 1984); Community Blood Bank v. Russell, 196 S.2d 115 (Fla. 1967); Sibley v. Board of Supervisors, 446 S.2d 760 (La. App. 1983).

55. Gen. Stat. N.C., Art. 43B, §1-539.9 (now abolished in N.C. by Gen. Stat. N.C., §1-539.9); R.I. Gen. L. §9-1-26. Reestablished in New Jersey: See, Joralamo v. Fairleigh Dickinson Univ., 488 A.2d 1064 (N.J. Super., 1985).

56. N.J. Rev. Stat. §2A:53A-7. *See* n. 55.

57. Williams v. Jefferson Hospital Assn., 442 S.W.2d 243 (Ark., 1969); J.W. Resort, Inc. v. First Amer. Natl. Bk., 625 S.W.2d 557 (Ark. App. 1981).

58. Rhoda v. Aroostock Genl. Hospital, 226 A.2d 530 (Me. 1967). But it must be "majority charitable." Thompson v. Mercy Hospital, 483 A.2d 706 (Me. 1984).

59. Ark. Stat. §16-120.

60. Me. Rev. Stat., tit. 14, §158.

61. Morehouse College v. Russell, 135 S.E.2d 432 (Ga., 1964).

62. *E.g.*, see newspaper accounts in 1986–1988.

63. N.J. Stat., 2A:53 A-7.; Rabon v. Rowan Memorial Hospital, 152 S.E.2d 485 (N.C. 1967). Charitable hospital: Douglas v. Florence General Hospital, 259 S.E.2d 117 (S.C. 1979); but not for intentional torts: Terry v. Boy Scouts of Amer., 471 F. Supp. 28 (D.C., S.C. 1978).

64. Edwards v. Hollywood Canteen, 27 Cal.2d 807, 167 P.2d 729 (1946); Cohen v. General Hospital. Society, 113 Conn. 188, 154 A. 435 (1931); Blankenship v. Alter, 171 Ohio St. 65, 167 N.E.2d 922 (1960).

65. Stearns v. Schenectady Day Nursery, 262 A.D. 638, 31 N.Y.S.2d 277, *affd.* 288 N.Y. 574, 42 N.E.2d 24 (1942).

66. Roehl v. Whelpley, 290 N.Y. 852, 50 N.E.2d 241 (1943).

67. Langheim v. Denison F.D.S.P. Assn., 21 N.W.2d 295 (Iowa, 1946).

68. *Beicht v. American Polish Veterans, Inc.*, 611 A.2d 168 (N.J. Super. A.D., 1992).

69. *Ponder v. Fulton-DeKalb Hospital Authority*, 353 S.E.2d 515 (SC 1987).

70. *Gray v. St. Cecilia School*, 526 A.2d 265, 266 (NJ Sup., A.D., 1987).

71. *Dunn v. Garcia*, 768 P. 2d 419 (Or. App. 1989); *cf., Dunn v. Catholic Home Bureau*, 537 N.Y.S. 2d 742, 744 (Sup. Ct. 1989); and see as to what is "volunteer," E. A. Longfellow, *Volunteers and Liability*, 14 Curr. Munic. Problems 447 (1988).

72. *Pigott v. Church of the Holy Infancy*, 583 N.Y.S. 2d 534 (A.D. 3 Dept. 1992) (worker injured when he slipped off roof).

73. *Schiavo v. John F. Kennedy Hosp.*, 609 A.2d 781 (N.J. Super. A.D., 1992).

74. *Wollersheim v. Church of Scientology of Calif.*, 260 Calif. Rpts. 331 (App. Ct., 1989).

75. *Note*, 100 *Harv. L. Rev.* 1384 (1987); Trolin, *Legislatures Awaken to Nonprofits Hit by Liability Insur. Crisis*, 6 *Preventive L. Rpt.* 12 (June 1987); L.G. Markoff (article), 11 *National L.J.* (2) 1 (Sept. 19, 1988) citing *Big Brother/Big Sister of Metro Atlanta, Inc. v. Terrell*, 359 S.E.2d 241 (GA App. 1987); *Schultz v. Boy Scouts of Amer., Inc.*, 65 N.Y.2d (NY 1985) applying N.J. law; *Burke v. St. Raphael's Church* _____, (OH App., Cuy. Co., 1983). *Cf.*, Some states instead adopted *mandatory insurance* (to protect employees of ambulance services or the like), W. VA Code §16-4C-16. See also, Note, *The Quality of Mercy: "Charitable Torts"*..., 100 *Harv. L. Rev.* 1382 (1987).

76. Richards, *Businesslike NP Hospitals Losing Traditional Special Treatment*, 6 *Preventive L. Rpt.* 3 (June 1987).

77. See, *Boyd v. Bulala*, 877 F. 2d 1191 (4th Cir., VA, 1989); *English v. New England Medical Center*, 541 N.E. 2d 329 (MA. S.J., 1989); Wagner & Teiter, *Damages Caps in Medical Malpractice*, 1987 Detroit C. L. Rev. 1005; *Whalen v. U.S.*, 100 S. Ct. 1432 (1989). Longfellow, *Volunteers and Liability*, 14 Curr. Munic. Problems 447 (1988).

78. *American Red Cross Blood Service, S.C. Region*, 377 S.E. 2d 323 (S.C., 1989).

79. *English v. New England Medical Center*, 541 N.E. 2d 329 (Mass. S. J., 1989).

80. *Harlow v. Chin*, 545 N.E. 2d 602 (Mass. 1989).

81. *Harrell v. Total Health Care, Inc.*, 781 S.W. 2d 58 (Mo. 1989).

82. See, *Seiderman v. American Institute for Mental Studies*, 667 F. Supp. 154 (D.C., NJ 1987); and *Schultz v. Boy Scouts of Amer.*, 480 N.E.2d 679, 685 (NY 1985) based on NJ law. *N.J. Charit. Imm. Act*, §§16:1–48 to 53 of Rev. Stat.NJ Stat.

83. *NJ Stat. Ann. §2A:53A-7.*

84. Schultz v. Roman Cath. Archdiocese of Newark, 472 A.2d 531 (NJ 1984).

85. *Heffelfinger v. Town of Morristown*, 507 A.2d 761 (NJ Super. 1985).

86. Ariz. Rev. St. § 10-1017D; Fl. St. § 617.0834 (1992).

87. *Fialkowski v. Greenwich Home for Children, Inc.*, 921 F.2d 459 (3rd Cir. 1990).

88. *Straley v. Urbanna Chamber of Commerce*, 413 S.E. 2d 47 (Va. 1992) (out-of-town woman injured while watching a parade when hit in the eye by candy thrown by a clown.)

89. *Finkler v. Toledo Ski Club*, 577 N.E. 2d 1114 (Ohio App., 1989, publ. 1991).

90. *Fields v. Senior Citizens Center, Inc.*, 528 So. 2d 573 (LA App. 1988).

91. Richards and Tucker, *Nonprofit Organizations: Business Nonprofit Hospitals...*, 6 Preventive L.J. (2)3 (1987).

92. *See,* Prosser & Keeton, *Torts,* §131 (1984); Oleck, *Tort Law Practice Manual,* §§133–139 (1982).

93. Statutes are so varied and many that no list can be supplied here. *See* local enactments such as city ordinances, county enactments, school district enactments, *etc. See,* McQuillan on *Municipal Corporations* (curr. ed.).

94. Scherer v. Rhodes, and Krause v. Rhodes, 94 S. Ct. 1683 (1974). *And see,* Williams v. First United Church of Christ, 318 N.E.2d 562 (Ohio App., 1974).

95. *People Helpers, Inc. v. City of Richmond,* 789 F. Supp. 725 (E.D. Va. 1992).

96. *Hickman by Womble v. Fuqua,* 422 S.E. 2d 449 (N.C. App., 1992) (child killed by car near a public high school after tennis clinic).

97. *See,* Fairweather, *Test of Sovereign Immunity for Municipal Corporations,* 13 Clev.-Mar. L. Rev. 151 (1964); Alaska Comp. L. Ann., §9.65.070; 745 ILCS 10/1-101 *et seq.*; N.Y. Ct. Cl. Act. P. 8; Stone v. Ariz. Highway Comm., 93 Ariz. 384, 381 P.2d 107 (1963); Holytz v. City of Milwaukee, 17 Wis. 26, 115 N.W.2d 618 (1962); Fla. St., §768.28; Village of El Portal v. City of Miami Shores 362 S.2d 275 (Fla. 1978).

98. *Plavi v. Nemacolin Volunteer Fire Co.,* 618 A.2d 1054 (Pa. Cmwlth., 1992) (claim by parents of boy allegedly sexually abused in firehouse by suspected child molestor / employee). *Miller by Miller v. Elderton Dist. Volunteer Fire Co.,* 618 A.2d 1143 (Pa. Cmwlth., 1992) (negligence claim by person injured at carnival sponsored by fire company).

99. Rhodes v. Palo Alto, 100 Calif. App.2d 335; 223 P.2d 639 (1950); Stevenson v. Raleigh, 232 N.C. 42; 59 S.E.2d 195 (1950); City of Hazard v. Duff, 287 Ky. 427; 154 S.W.2d 28 (1941).

100. *Pele Defense Fund v. Paty,* 837 P.2d 1247 (Hawaii, 1992).

101. Reavey v. Guild of St. Agnes, 284 Mass. 300, 187 N.E. 557 (1933); Cadicamo v. Long Island College Hospital, 308 N.Y. 196, 124 N.E.2d 279 (1954).

102. Kelley v. Rossi, 481 N.E.2d 1340 (Mass. S. J., 1985).

103. *See,* Schultz v. Roman Catholic Archdiocese, 472 A.2d 531 (N.J., 1984); Rosane v. Senger, 112 Colo. 363; 149 P.2d 372 (1944); Howe v. Medical A.C. Hospital, 261 A.D. 1088; 26 N.Y.S.2d 957; *affd.,* 287 N.Y. 698; 39 N.E.2d 303 (1942). *See,* as to pleading of negligence: Oleck, *Negligence Forms of Pleading* (New York: Central Book Co. 1957 revision).

104. *See,* as to "punitive" damages, Brause v. Brause, 190 Iowa 329; 177 N.W. 65, 70 (1920); 25 C.J.S. *Damages. And see generally,* Oleck, 1 *Encyc. of Negligence,* §168 (1962); De Foe v. Potomac Elec. Power Co., 123 A.2d 920 (Mun. Ct. App., D.C. 1956); Note, 11 Stet. L. Rev. 570 (1981); Mercury Motors v. Smith, 393 S.2d 545 (Fla. 1981).

105. *Stacy v. Truman Medical Center,* 836 S.W. 2d 911 (Mo., 1992).

106. *Krasney v. Curators of University of Missouri,* 765 S.W.2d 646 (MO App. 1989).

107. *Sorey v. Kellett,* 849 F.2d 960 (5th Cir., MS, 1988).

108. *Burgess v. Salmon River Canal Co.,* 805 P.2d 1223 (Idaho 1991).

109. *Canty v. N.Y. City Health and Hospitals Corp.,* 550 N.Y.S. 2d 673 (App. Div., 1st Dept., 1990).

110. *See,* generally, Prosser & Keeton, and Oleck works on torts, n. 92.

111. *Id.,* Briggs v. Spaulding, 141 U.S. 132, 11 S. Ct. 924, 35 L. Ed. 662 (1891); Symposium on *Corporate Torts Problems,* 12 Clev.-Mar. L. Rev. 100 (1963).

112. Hickman v. Winston County Hosp. Bd., 508 So. 2d 237 (Ala. 1987).

113. *Robinson v. La Casa Grande Condo Assn.,* 562 N.E.2d 678 (Ill. App. 1990):

114. Fl. Stat § 617.09 (eff. June 1989), overriding *State of Florida v. Anclote Manor Hospital, Inc.* case. *See now* Fla. Stat: § 617.2003 (1992).

115. *Jones v. Briley,* 593 So. 2d 391 (La. App. 1 Cir. 1991).

116. *Id.*

117. *Victory Committee v. Genesis Convention Center, of City of Gary,* 587 N.E. 2d 361 (Ind. App. 3 Dist., 1992).

118. *Horton v. Royal Order of the Sun,* 821 P.2d 1167 (Utah 1991).

119. *Haskell v. Chautauqua County Fireman's Fraternity, Inc.,* 590 N.Y.S. 2d 637 (N.Y.A.D. 4 Dept., 1992).

120. *Degenhart v. Knights of Columbus,* 420 S.E. 2d 495 (S.C., 1992).

121. *Doe v. British Universities North American Club,* 788 F. Supp. 1286 (D. Conn. 1992).

122. *Gilligan v. Villanova University,* 584 A. 2d 1005 (Pa. Super. 1991).

123. *McGrath v. United Hospital,* 562 N.Y.S.2d 193 (App. Div. 1990).

124. *Doe v. Village of St. Joseph, Inc.,* 415 S.E. 2d 56 (Ga. App. 1992).

125. *Calvary Baptist Church of Marion, Indiana v. Joseph,* 522 N.E.2d 371 (IN 1988), overturning the prior state rule.

126. *Mt. Zion State Bank & Tr. v. Central Illinois Annual Conf. of United Methodist Church,* 556 N.E.2d 1270 (Ill. App. 1990).

127. *Strock v. Pressnell,* 527 N.E.2d 1235 (OH 1988). Mt. Zion State Bank & Tr. v. Central Illinois Annual Conf. of United Methodist Church, 556 N.E. 2d 1270 (Ill. App. 1990) sexual assault by a pastor is outside the employment.

128. *George v. International Society for Krishna Consciousness,* 262 Calif. Rptr. 217 (App. Ct. 1989).

129. *Pombriant v. Blue Cross/Blue Shield of Maine,* 562 A. 2d 656 (Me. 1989) for interference with contract. *Albright v. Longview Police Dept.,* 884 F. 2d 835 (5th Cir., 1989) for racial discrimination. *Wollersheim v. Church of Scientology,* 260 Calif. Rptr. 331 (App., 1989) for infliction of mental suffering. *Lloyd Lions Club v. Intntl. Assn. of Lions Clubs,* 724 P. 2d 887 (Or., 1986) for discrimination in public accommodations.

130. *Lener v. Club Med, Inc.,* 562 N.Y.S.2d 556 (App. Div. 1990).

131. *Roe v. Catholic Charities of Diocese of Springfield, Ill.,* 588 N.E. 2d 354, (Ill. App. 5 Dist. 1992).

132. *Hanewinckel v. St. Paul's Property & Liability Ins. Co.,* 611 So. 2d 174 (La. App. 5 Cir., 1992).

133. *Small v. McKennan Hospital,* 437 N.W.2d 194 (SD 1989).

134. *Insinga v. La. Bella,* 543 So. 2d 209 (Fla. 1990); Fl. St. § 768.60; *Darling v. Charleston Community Hospital,* 211 N.E.2d 253 (Ill. 1965), cert. den. 383 U.S. 946 (1966); 14 A.L.R. 3rd 860.

135. *Kildron v. Shady Oaks Nursing Home,* 549 S. 2d 395 (La. App. 1989).

136. *Stinson v. Cleveland Clinic Foundation,* 524 N.E.2d 898 (OH App. 1987; publ. 1988).

137. *Hackathorn v. Lester E. Cox Medical Center,* 824 S.W. 2d 472 (Mo. App. 1992).

138. *United Blood Services, a Div. of Blood Systems, Inc. v. Quintana,* 827 P.2d 509 (Colo. 1992).

139. *Osborn v. Irwin Memorial Blood Bank,* 7 Cal. Rptr. 2d 101 (Cal. App. 1 Dist. 1992).

140. *Bradway v. American Nat. Red Cross,* 965 F.2d 991 (11th Cir. (Ga.), 1992).

141. *Ash v. New York University Dental Center,* 564 N.Y.S. 2d 308 (A.D. 1 Dept. 1990).

142. *Kaiser v. Western R/C Flyers, Inc.,* 477 N.W. 2d 557 (Neb. 1991).

143. Reliance Insurance Co. v. Barron's, 442 F. Supp. 1341 (S.D. N.Y. 1977); Trans World Accounts, Inc. v. Associated Press, 814 (N.D. Cal. 1977).

144. 418 U.S. 323 (1974).

145. New York Times Co. v. Sullivan, 376 U.S. 254 (1964).

146. Davis v. Keystone Printing Service, Inc., 507 N.E. 2d 1358 (Ill. App., 2d Dist., 1987).

147. *Gonzalez v. Sackman,* 585 N.Y.S. 2d 435 (N.Y.A.D. 1 Dept., 1992).

148. *McGill v. Parker,* 582 N.Y.S. 2d 91 (A.D. 1 Dept. 1992).

149. *American Ideal Mgmt., Inc., v. Dale Village, Inc.*, 15 FLW 2357 (Fla. 4th DCA, Sept. 19, 1990).

150. *Smith v. Long Island Youth Guidance, Inc.*, 581 N.Y.S. 2d 401 (N.Y.A.D. 2 Dept., 1992).

151. *Chapin v. Greve*, 787 F. Supp. 557 (E.D. Va. 1992).

152. *See e.g. Muck v. Van Bibber*, 585 N. E. 2d 1147 (Ill. App. 4 Dist. 1992).

153. *Evans v. Philadelphia Newspapers, Inc.*, 601 A.2d 330 (Pa. Super. 1991).

154. *Kirby v. Wildenstein*, 784 F. Supp. 1112 (S.D.N.Y. 1992).

155. State v. Passaic County Agricultural Society, 54 N.J.L. 260, 23 A. 680 (1892); Anonymous, 12 Mod. 559, 88 Engl. Rep. 1518 (K.B. 1701) I.B.L. Comm. 476; Lee, *Corporate Criminal Liability*, 28 Columbia L. Rev. 1 (1928).

156. United States v. George F. Fish, Inc., 154 F.2d 798 (2d Cir. 1946); Miller, *Criminal Law* §45 (1934); Henn, *Corporations*, 354 (rev. ed. 1970); 3 Oleck, *Modern Corporation Law*, c. 66 (1978 supp.); and *see*, Chernside, Note, 80 A.L.R. 3rd 1220. (1977).

157. New York Central and H.R.R. Co. v. U.S., 212 U.S. 481; 29 S. Ct. 304; 53 L. Ed. 613 (1909); Edgerton, *Corporate Criminal Responsibility*, 36 Yale L. J. 827 (1927); and n. 156.

158. Perrymore v. State, 189 Ark. 519; 73 S.W.2d 470 (1943); *and see*, 3 Oleck, *Modern Corporation Law*, §§1681–1686 (1978 Supp.); U.S. v. Carter, 311 F.2d 934 (6th Cir. 1963).

159. *See*, n. 156, above; and, Southern Ry. Co. v. State, 125 Ga. 287; 54 S.E. 160 (1906).

160. N.Y. Penal L., §665(1) repealed; *see now*, §190.35.

161. N.Y. Penal L., §661 repealed; *see now*, §190.35.

162. People *ex rel.* Price v. Sheffield Farms Slawson-Decker Co., 225 N.Y. 25; 121 N.E. 474 (1918) (labor law violation); Ohio Rev. Code, §§1702.54, 1702.55.

163. N.Y. Penal L., §§20.20(2), 20.25.

164. N.Y. Penal L., §671 repealed; *see now* N. Y. Election L., §460.

165. Delaware Division Canal Co. v. Comm., 60 Penna. 367; 100 Am. Dec. 570; Rex v. Cory Bros. and Co., 1 K.B. 810 (1927).

166. Comment, *Increasing Community Control Over Corporate Crime*, 71 Yale L. J. 280 (1961); Hamilton, *Corporate Criminal Responsibility in Texas*, 47 Tex. L. Rev. 60 (1968).

167. Granite Construc. Co. v. Superior Ct., 197 Calif. Rptr. 3 (App., 1986).

168. Boston, C.&M. R.R. v. State, 32 N.H. 215; State v. Lehigh V. R.R., 90 N.J. L. 372; 103 A. 685; *contra*: Only a natural person can be guilty of this: Commissioner v. Ill. Central R.R., 152 Ky. 320; 153 S.W. 459.

    As to libel: State v. Atchison, 3 Lea (Tenn.) 729; 31 Am. Rep. 663.

    As to conspiracy: Joplin Mercantile Co. v. U.S., 213 F. 926 (C.C.A., Mo.); *cert. gtd.*, 235 U.S. 699; 35 S. Ct. 200; 59 L. Ed. 431; *affd.*, 236 U.S. 531; 35 S. Ct. 291; 59 L. Ed. 705 (1914).

169. State v. City of Portland, 74 Me. 268; 43 Am. Rep. 586; People v. Albany, 11 Wend. (N.Y.) 539, 27 Am. Dec. 95.

170. *CGM Contractors, Inc., v. Contractors Environmental Services, Inc.*, 383 S.E. 2d 861 (W. Va., 1989).

171. *United States v. Aguilar*, #86-1208; U.S. 9th Cir. Ct. App., San Francisco (Mar. 30, 1989). But, *cf., Contra*: Infiltration by agents wearing "body bugs" was held to violate the First Amendment, in *Presbyterian Church (USA) v. U.S.*, U.S. 9th Cir. Ct. App., Ariz. (Mar. 15, 1989).

172. *Boyce Thompson Institute for Plant Research, Inc. v. Insurance Co. of North America*, 751 F. Supp. 1137 (S.D.N.Y. 1990). *See also* Comprehensive Environmental Response, Compensation & Liability Act (CERCLA), 42 U.S.C. § 9601 et seq.

173. *Mississippi State Chapter Operation Push v. Mabus*, 788 F. Supp. 1406 (N.D. Miss 1992).

174. *St. Petersburg Times*, p. 21A (Apr. 27, 1991).

175. *Ragsdale v. Progressive Voters League*, 801 S.W. 2d 880 (Tex. 1990).

176. *See* cases cited in n. 157–169, *esp.* n. 158.

177. United States v. Dotterweich, 320 U.S. 277; 65 S. Ct. 134; 88 L. Ed. 48 (1943); N.Y. Penal L., §20.20; Storch, Note, Florida Bar C.L.E. (1981).

178. Commonwealth v. McIlwain School Bus Lines, Inc., 423 A.2d 413 (Pa. Super., 1980).

179. Vaughn & Sons, Inc. v. State, 649 S.W.2d 677 (Tex. App. 1983).

180. State v. Pacific Powder Co., 360 P.2d 530 (Or., 1961).

181. *People v. Brooklyn Psychosocial Rehabilitation Institute*, 585 N.Y.S. 2d 776 (N.Y.A.D. 2 Dept., 1992).

182. *Lahr v. State*, 840 P.2d 930 (Wyo., 1992).

183. *State v. Dutton*, 450 N.W. 2d 189 (Minn. App. 1990); Minn. Stat. §§ 609.344, subd. 1 (i); 609.345 subd. 1(i).

184. N.Y. Penal L., §§60.25, 80; Ohio Rev. Code, §1702.99.

185. State v. Truax, 130 Wash. 69; 226 P. 259; 33 A.L.R. 1206, 1211 (1924); United States v. Union Supply Co., 215 U.S. 50; 30 S. Ct. 15; 54 L. Ed. 87 (1918).

186. State *ex inf.* Hadley v. Delmar Jockey Club, 200 Mo. 34; 92 S.W. 185 (1905); States *ex rel.* Crabbe v. Thistle Down Jockey Club, 114 Ohio St. 582; 151 N.E. 709 (1926); Commonwealth v. Kentucky Jockey Club, 238 Ky. 739; 38 S.W.2d 987 (1931).

187. "The provisions of this subchapter shall not apply to a private club or other establishment not in fact open to the public. . . ."

188. 42 U.S.C. 2000a(a) (1970): "All persons shall be entitled to full and equal enjoyment of the goods, services, facilities, privileges, advantages, and accommodation, as defined in this section, without discrimination or segregation on the ground of race, color, religion, or national origin."

189. Tillman v. Wheaton-Haven Recreational Association, Inc., 410 U.S. 431 (1973).

190. Tillman v. Wheaton-Haven Recreational Association, Inc., 517 F.2d 1141 (4th Cir. 175), on remand from 410 U.S. 431 (1973).

    Other civil rights cases include Sullivan v. Little Huntington Park, Inc., 396 U.S. (1969); Watkins v. Mercy Medical Center, 364 F. Supp. 799 (D. Idaho 1973); Greco v. Orange Memorial Hospital Corporation, 513 F.2d 873 (5th Cir. 1975). See, U.S. v. Trustees of Fraternal Order of Eagles, 472 F. Supp. 1174 (D.C., Wis., 1980) as to what is a "private club" for §2000a(e).

191. Wood v. Stickland, 420 U.S. 308 (1975). In that case the Supreme Court held that a "school board member is not immune from liability for damages under §1983 if he knew or reasonably should have known that the action he took within this sphere of official responsibility would violate the constitutional rights of the student affected, or if he took the action with the malicious intention to cause a deprivation of constitutional rights or other injury to the student."

192. 42 U.S.C. §1983 (1970): Every citizen who, under color of any statute, ordinance, regulation, custom or usage, or any State or Territory, subjects, or causes to be subjected, any citizen of the United States or other person within the jurisdiction thereof to the deprivation of any rights, privileges, or immunities secured by the Constitution and laws, shall be liable to the party injured in an action at law, suit in equity, or other proper proceeding for redress.

    See, Endress v. Brookdale Community College, 144 N.J. Super. 109, 364 A.2d 1080 (1976); Jacobs v. College of William and Mary, 495 F. Supp. 183 (D.C., Va., 1980).

193. *See*, Pendrell v. Chatham College, 370 F. Supp. 494 (E.D.Pa. 1974).

194. Regents of University of California v. Bakke, 98 S. Ct. 2753 (1978).

195. *Rubenstein v. Benedictine Hosp.*, 790 F. Supp. 396 (N.D.N.Y. 1992).

196. *Yvonne L. By and Through Lewis v. New Mexico Dept. of Human Services*, 959 F.2d 883 (10th Cir. (N.M.), 1992).

197. *Ritter v. Wayne County General Hospital*, 436 N.W.2d 673 (MI App. 1988, publ. 1989).

198. *Molko v. Holy Spirit for the Unification of World Christianity*, 762 P. 2d 46 (Calif. 1988), app. dism. by U.S. Sup. Ct. (May 22, 1989).

199. *People v. DeJonge*, 449 N.W. 2d 899 (Mich. App. 1989) (publ. 1990).

200. Franklin Union No. 4 v. People, 200 Ill. 355, 370; 77 N.E. 176, 181, 185; L.R.A. (n.s.) 1001 (1906).

201. Auto Highball Co. v. Sibbett, 11 Ga. App. 618, 75 S.E. 914 (1912). But *contra*: dissent in, Geller v. Flamount Realty Corp., 260 N.Y. 346; 183 N.E. 520 (1932); State v. Unique Ideas, Inc., 376 N.E.2d 1301 (N.Y., 1978).

202. *Lovejoy Specialty Hosp. v. Advocates for Life, Inc.*, 802 P. 2d 684 (Ore. App. 1990).

203. *Downtown Women's Center, P.C. v. Advocates for Life, Inc.*, 826 P.2d 637 (Or. App. 1992).

204. *See*, N.Y. Bus. Corp. L., §1101 (formerly Genl. Corp. L., §94).

205. Wheeling Steel Corp. v. Glander, 337 U.S. 562 (1949).

206. United States v. Security National Bank, 546 F2d 492 (2d Cir. 1976); United States v. Armco Steel Corp., 252 F. Supp. 364 (S.D. Cal. 1966); United States v. Martin Linen Supply Co., 534 F.2d 585 (5th Cir. 1976), *affd.*...... U.S. ..... (1977); United States v. Southern Ry., 485 F.2d 309 (4th Cir. 1973); Fong Foo v. United States, 369 U.S. 141 (1962).

207. Wilson v. U.S., 221 U.S. 361 (1911).

208. United States v. White, 322 U.S. 694 (1944).

209. Hale v. Henkel, 201 U.S. 43, 26 S. Ct. 370.50 L. Ed. 652 (1906); 1 Oleck, *Modern Corporation Law*, §7 (1978 Supp.).

210. N.Y. Genl. Bus. L., §§345, 359, and other statutes as to real property, insurance debts, and other matters. *But see*, as to liabilities, also, Ohio Rev. Code, §1702.54 (false statements).

211. Malloy v. Hogan, 378 U.S. 1 (1964).

212. Brown v. Concerned Citizens for Sickle Cell Anemia, Inc., 56 Ohio St.2d 85, 382 N.E.2d 1155 (1978).

213. *Ibid.*

214. *See*, cases cited in Pratt, *The Law Relating to Friendly Societies* (Garland Publ., N.Y. and London 1978); and Restatement of Restitution 640, §160.

215. 227 F.2d 907 (6th Cir. 1955).

216. Tax Reform Act of 1976, §1307; The Conable-Muskie Act; Public Law 94-585 (Oct. 1976). J. Nix, Limitations on the Lobbying of Section 501(c)(3) Organizations, 81 W. Va. L. Rev. 407-26 (1979).

217. I.R.S. Form 5768.

218. *Austin v. Michigan Chamber of Commerce*, U.S. Supr. Ct. (Mar. 27, 1990); 6 to 3 decision.

219. *See*, Gaby and Gaby, *Nonprofit Organization Handbook: A Guide to Fund Raising, Grants, Lobbying, Membership Building, Publicity and Public Relations*, c. 6 (Prentice-Hall 1979); *and see*, Course Materials for Registrants, *Management's Liabilities in Nonprofit Organizations* (Stetson Univ. Seminar 1979) (Buek, *Legislative and Political Activities: Their Tax and Other Consequences*, pp. 129–138).

220. I.R.C., §162(e)(1).

221. *Ibid.*, §162(e)(2).

222. IRS Rev. Rulings 74–40, 78–111, 78–112, 78–113, 78–114, etc.

223. Powell, *Lobbyists Spending More on Lawmakers* (A. P. article), *St. Petersburg (Fla.) Times*, p. 11B (Jan. 27, 1980).

224. *See* current "services" such as Prentice-Hall, *Federal Taxes*, Par. 21,026.10 and 21,026.15.

18

CORPORATE NAME, SEAL, AND OFFICE

[Paul R. Wallace assisted in updating this and the next three chapters; and some extracts in this chapter were provided by Sheila M. Kahoe (of the New York Bar) article, Nonprofit Corporations' Names, 21 Clev. St. L. Rev. 114.]

§191. NEED FOR A CORPORATE NAME

Statutes generally require a corporate name to be stated in a corporation's articles of incorporation, and sometimes also require that the name indicate incorporated status by including the word "Incorporated" or "Inc."[1] But most nonprofit corporation statutes do not require nonprofit corporation names to indicate incorporated status. (See Section 201.)

Most states impose statutory restrictions on the selection of a name, with little or no distinction between the rules governing the business corporation and the nonprofit corporation. For example, in Ohio and Florida the two sections of the Code (profit, and nonprofit) relating to corporate names are virtually identical.[2]

These statutes serve to illustrate the policy reasons for a state's policing of the selection of a corporate name. Two important considerations are set forth in the statute: first, that the name selected shall not mislead the public, and second, that a name selected not be so similar to that of an existing corporation as to cause confusion.[3]

Certain exceptions to this last provision are noted. If the previously incorporated group files a written consent with the secretary of state, the name may be approved.[4] Also, when dealing with the merger or consolidation of two or more groups, the name of the surviving or new corporation may be the same as or similar to that of any constituent corporation.[5] A similar statutory exception is provided when a merger takes place between a domestic and foreign corporation.[6]

The state's authority to refuse authorization of a name extends to a foreign corporation (profit or nonprofit) wishing to do business in the state. This power is considered necessary to protect the public. It has been held that it is not an abuse of discretion to withhold authorization, even though the businesses of the two parties are so dissimilar that they could not be confused.[7]

Just how extensive the state's discretion is can be seen in the following example. A domestic corporation filed a written consent with the secretary of state, indicating its willingness to allow the use of a similar name by an incoming corporation. When the secretary refused to authorize the use of the selected name, a mandamus action was brought. The appellate court reversed a judgment issuing the writ, reasoning that the purpose of the statute was to protect the public as well as the domestic corporation. In this case, the court felt that because of the nature of the business, the public might be harmed by confusing the two corporations. So, despite the consent of the domestic corporation, the foreign corporation was not permitted to do business in the state under the selected name.[8]

Assumed Name. A corporation may use an assumed or fictitious name, just as an individual may, as long as the purpose is not to defraud.[9]

§192. DECEPTIVE NAMES

Choice of a name for a nonprofit organization is affected by legal restrictions similar to those governing choice or use of a business organization name. The basic principle is that the law will protect a prior user of a name against unauthorized use by another.[10]

Public policy in the United States and elsewhere is to prevent confusion and unfair use of organization names. Protection of the public as well as of the prior user of a name is the principal policy.[11] Statutory protection of organization names now is found in all American jurisdictions,[12] while common law protection also is available.[13]

Typically, state statutes forbid the secretary of state to file articles if the corporate name is likely to mislead the public or is not clearly distinguishable from the name of any other corporation (whether nonprofit or for profit), unless written consent of the other corporation is attached.[14]

When a corporation or association is dissolved, its name becomes available for adoption by others. This availability begins upon the filing of the certificate and completion of dissolution of the former user. But if confusion or deception may occur through the adoption of such name by another organization, its adoption will be refused; or it may itself indicate fraud if unwisely permitted as a result of mistaken acceptance for filing. But see, below, §200, n. 86.

Not all names are subject to protection. Words which indicate merely geographic locale, or type of organization, do not vest exclusively in a first user (*e.g.*, ... Association of Florida; or ... Educational Association).[15] A distinction is drawn between unique or identifying words and words that are merely descriptive. Of course, the general right to use geographic or descriptive words will not be allowed where there is intent to deceive,[16] or, sometimes, where deception actually occurs unintentionally.[17]

The courts have classified trade names as generic, descriptive, suggestive, or arbitrary, under federal common law, in order to determine the degree of protection to which the mark is entitled. Descriptive terms may be protected only if they acquire secondary meaning. Generic terms are generally not protected. Both suggestive and arbitrary terms qualify automatically for protection under the Lanham Trade-Mark Act.[18]

Ordinarily, it is not necessary that actual confusion of names, or deception, be shown. It is enough if use of a name is likely to cause confusion or deception in the minds of people of reasonable intelligence.[19] Innocent intention on the part of the second user of an existing name is not justification.[20] And actual competition between the organizations now is not deemed to be essential in order to enjoin use of a name by a new organization, if any confusion or deception at all may occur.[21]

Any person or organization injured by use of a deceptive name by another person or organization may enjoin such use, or at least obtain damages for his or its injuries.[22] For example, the *International Kennel Club* may enjoin marketing of defendant's toy dogs with the name "International Kennel Club" on them; it has "trademark" rights in the name.[23]

A certificate of incorporation bearing a deceptive name may not be accepted for filing by any public office. Even if it is filed, as a result of clerical mistake or other error, this does not authorize the free use of the deceptive name, nor prevent injunctive action or damage suits.[24]

The decision of a secretary of state or other administrative officer not to accept a name on these grounds is usually final. The courts will not overrule such administrative decisions unless they are clearly unreasonable or illegal, or unless a clear abuse of discretion can be proven.[25]

One court in viewing the policy reasons for protecting names has stated, "If there is no possibility that corporate names will tend to confuse the public or mislead them in any way, there is no reason for protection of that name."[26] However, it has also been held that it is not necessary to show actual confusion; if persons of ordinary intelligence would likely be confused, that is enough.[27]

This last interpretation is not the rule in every jurisdiction. The determination as to whether corporate names are confusing is a question of fact.[28] The theory is that a "greater similarity of names is allowed when the customers are capable of close discrimination."[29] This is a matter of Unfair Competition, primarily.[30]

This more sophisticated attitude, however, is not being accepted universally. Courts continue to apply the "likely to cause confusion test," giving less weight to evidence of lack of actual confusion.[31]

It is not necessary for the offended organization or person to be locally resident, incorporated, or licensed in order to obtain relief against unfair use of a name. For example, a nationally known corporation (such as the Red Cross, or the Knights of Pythias) may bring injunctive and damage suits anywhere, when improper use of a similar name is discovered.[32]

Under the common law, there are three basic theories for the protection of a name: unfair competition, libel, and invasion of privacy.[33] An example of damage to an organization through unfair competition would be the loss of contributions to one organization by people who contribute to another through confusion of names. The law is protecting both the public and the organization.[34] The theories of libel[35] and invasion of privacy[36] are relatively little used.

The *good will* of an organization will be protected, especially when the name is so similar to another as to induce membership in the latter or to cause in any way treatment of one as the other.[37] Careful consideration may be given the conduct of the newcomer. If this organization attempts to palm itself off as the earlier one or makes no conspicuous effort to disclaim identification with the former, use of a similar name will certainly be prohibited.[38]

The courts have been explicit in pointing out that the selection of a name is restricted to prevent fraud in dealing with the public.[39] They are no longer solely concerned with the same as a property right.[40] However, the protection will not be extended indefinitely. In Pilgrim Holiness Church v. First Pilgrim Holiness Church,[41] the plaintiff church sought to enjoin the defendant from using the words "Pilgrim Holiness" in its name. In this case, the plaintiff church had previously merged with another church and was known as the Wesleyan Church. Because a considerable amount of property was held in trust for the plaintiff, it was argued that the defendant should not be allowed to use the name, despite the fact that the plaintiff no longer used the name. The Court of Appeals of Illinois found that nothing in the record indicated that the plaintiff in any way retained the use of the name. This, concluded the court, was an effective abandonment of the name and thus the defendant could not be enjoined from using the designation "Pilgrim Holiness" as a part of its name.[42]

A further exception applies to the use of a generic or geographic terms if an intent to deceive can be shown.[43] In Lincoln Center for the Performing Arts, Inc. v. Lincoln Center Classics, Record Society, Inc.,[44] it was held that despite the argument that "Lincoln Center" is a geographical location, the name would be protected since the evidence showed that the name was adopted "with intent to acquire or obtain for personal or business purposes a benefit or advantage."[45]

Also, in Anti-Defamation League of B'nai B'rith v. National Mexican American Anti-Defamation Committee, the Court of Appeals for the District of Columbia held that a secondary meaning had attached to the phrase "anti-defamation league" which tied that concept to the plaintiff organization. Due to this secondary meaning a substantial likelihood of confusion would arise and therefore the name was protected.[46]

This idea of deliberate misrepresentation in the use of a generic term was explored in a New Jersey case. A man began operating an animal dealership under the name Humane Animal Shelter (Center) of New Jersey, Inc. Suit was brought by several local and national humane societies on the theory that the use of the word "humane" constituted a fraud upon the public at large since it deliberately misrepresented the true character and nature of the defendant's operation.[47] In this case, the court did not rely on the theory of unfair competition in fashioning its decision. Here it was dealing with a charitable (nonprofit) corporation seeking to enjoin the use of a generic term, claiming that the defendant's use of the term damaged the reputations of the several plaintiffs (and all others similarly situated). Note that the damage claimed was to reputation, although the court commented that there was also a possibility of financial harm to the plaintiffs by way of decreased membership and/or contributions.[48]

After exploring the meaning which the general public commonly places on the word "humane," the court found that the defendant's business did not conform to the concept of "humane" as understood by the public and upon which the public relies. The defendant was therefore found to be "through the use of the word humane in its title ... foisting a fraud upon the public."[49] An injunction was granted because the court felt that the public would ultimately be damaged because of the misrepresentation inherent in the use of a generic term which normally would not be restricted.[50]

An unincorporated association called the Bass Anglers Sportsman Society, filed suit against BASS, Inc. and its founder, Ray W. Scott Jr., alleging that Scott owes the members of the unincorporated association $75 million allegedly looted from the nonprofit association. The complaint stated that Scott, after forming the nonprofit Sportsman Society, started a new profit corporation, BASS, Inc., some 18 months after the nonprofit association was formed, using a name that was deceptively similar to the nonprofit association's name. The profit society was alleged to have converted assets (BASS Master Magazine) and revenues of the unincorporated nonprofit society to the profit corporation without a vote from the members or notification to the member/subscribers. The suit sought ouster of the BASS, Inc. leadership and formation of a trust for the property as well as punitive damages.[51]

Several states have provided for this type of situation by statute. New York and Massachusetts, for instance, impose criminal penalties for the fraudulent use of a name which so nearly resembles that of a benevolent charitable, humane, or fraternal organization as to deceive the public.[52]

§193. USE OF FAMILY NAME

Ordinarily one may use his own name for business purposes. However, in some cases the courts have been called upon to balance the natural right of one to use his own name against the right of an established corporation against unfair competition. The laws governing unfair competition usually involve the passing off of goods or services as the goods or services of another.[53] The courts have taken this idea and formulated some restrictions on the use of family names.

An individual may not use his own name with the fraudulent intent of passing his name off as that of another and thus taking advantage of another's good reputation.[54] In some cases that deal with this problem, the courts have extended this rule and presumed fraud even without evidence of an actual intent to deceive, when the effect of the use of the name has created confusion in the mind of the public and thus has been a cause of deception.[55] One Tennessee court has gone even further. They held that it is enough to show that the ordinary or unwary purchaser might be confused.[56]

In addition, if one has a name which has already been made famous by another family (*i.e.*, J. P. Morgan, Rockefeller, etc.) it may be *prima facie* deceptive to use that similar name because of the possibility of confusion.[57]

§194. "SECONDARY" MEANING OF A NAME

Whether the use of a name is proper may also depend on whether the prior use has acquired a secondary meaning because of long use or extensive publicity. For instance, permission to use the name "Bacardi" was refused since the name had been used so long and had become so closely identified with the product as to be almost synonymous.[58] Other examples of this sort of usage are readily available.

A name is entitled to the protection described above only when it has been so much used or advertised as to acquire a special, "secondary" meaning. This is largely a matter of time and expenditures used in publicizing the name. For example, the name "Masons" now means the "Free and Accepted Masons" to most people (*i.e.*, The Masonic Order, Freemasons, or Masonic Lodges), despite the fact that the word "mason" has a general reference to stoneworkers or bricklayers. No other group may use such a name.

Another example is the term "Platters." In Five Platters, Inc. v. Purdie, the court found that the phrase "Platters" had developed a secondary meaning and therefore its use could be enjoined nationwide.[59]

Generic and geographic names. Words of general, universal, or classificatory nature are *generic* terms. For example, the word "music" is generic, and so is "culture," or "charity," or "god."

No organization may now entirely preempt such words.[60] Thus, no corporation would be permitted to adopt the name "The Music Association." But use of such a term as part of a name is valid. Thus, "The Music Association of Des Moines, Ia." would be valid. And corporations that already have long-used generic names may continue to do so.[61]

The same is true of geographical words. For example, probably no new organization would be permitted to call itself "The Ohio Association," and certainly not "San Francisco, Inc." But "The Youth Club of New Orleans," and "The Chamber of Commerce of Wheeling, W. Va." are proper.

United Nations. The term "United Nations" has been placed under special limitations, by statutes. No use of that phrase as a name ordinarily is permitted, except with the specific approval of the Secretary-General of the United Nations (address him, by title, c/o United Nations Headquarters, New York, N.Y.).[62]

Existing organizations. Those organizations which had adopted the various forbidden types of names described above, before the law forbade this, may continue to use those names.

For example, those private organizations that had adopted the name "United Nations" ("U.N."), or "The New York Society," or "The Advertising Club," or "American Federation of Labor" may continue to use them.[63]

Well known names, such as Red Cross, Boy Scouts, *etc.,* also are not available.[64]

§195. VULGAR OR OFFENSIVE NAMES

Use of vulgar, or distasteful, or offensive names is generally not permitted. This is largely a matter of local taste and standards of propriety and decency.[65]

For example, such a name as "The Homosexual Club" until 1973 was viewed as offensive and not entitled to a corporate charter, while "The Anti-Catholic Association" still would be deemed offensive and against public policy.[66]

§196. RESTRICTED NAMES AND TERMS, AND OFFICIAL APPROVALS

In many states, statutes expressly forbid the free adoption of certain names or terms by any organizations. Often these terms may be used, however, with the consent of existing organizations which long have used them, or with the approval of certain governmental agencies. Local statutes should be consulted as to the specific names covered by these provisions in various states. (See also Chapter 13 on licensing and approvals.) Also consult private research organizations, such as TCT Service, Inc. of Englewood Cliffs, New Jersey (See Section 190).

Typical of restricted terms are the following:[67]

University or School may require Education Department consent.[68]

Social Welfare (or terms suggesting that idea) may be adopted only with the approval of state social welfare departments.

Labor Union (or terms suggesting that idea) may be adopted only with the approval of state labor departments or boards of standards; and often, also, of national parent-unions. Among restricted terms are *Labor, Union, Trades Council, Brotherhood of Labor, Industrial Union, Congress of Industrial Organizations,* and *American Federation of Labor.*[69]

Cooperative (or terms suggesting that idea) may be adopted only with the approval of state agricultural, housing, or other appropriate authorities.

Housing may require approval, as for a cooperative. Use of "governmental" terms (*State, National, City;* or *Chicago* or *Atlanta*) in conjunction with

Housing is forbidden if it creates an impression of official status or public character.

Banking, Insurance, or similar terms may be adopted only with the approval of state banking or insurance departments. Among the restricted words are *Bank, Finance, Savings, Insurance, Assurance, Annuity, Loan, Investment, Bond, Underwriter, Acceptance, Mortgage, Trust, Indemnity, Surety, Guarantee, Casualty, Fidelity, Title,* and *Endownment.* However, the use of the word "banknote" is not likewise precluded. Also, a corporation other than a moneyed corporation is prohibited from using the word "trustors" as part of its corporate name.[70]

Mason (or terms suggesting the F. & A. Masons), *Pythian* (or terms suggesting the Knights of Pythias), and *Columbian* (or terms suggesting the Knights of Columbus) are restricted.

Doctor and *Lawyer* are available only to professional societies.

Court is absolutely forbidden, if it suggests judicial status.

State and *Federal* (or other such items suggesting governmental status) are forbidden to all except public corporations.

Dentist, Podiatrist, Oculist, and names suggesting organizations of learned professionals are generally available only to professional societies.

Army and *Navy* (if official-sounding) must be cleared with the federal and state adjutant-generals.

§197. HOW TO CLEAR THE DESIRED NAME

Choice of an organization name is a matter of great importance and should be made only after careful research, inquiry, and study. It should indicate the nature of the organization in broad terms—but not in unrealistically broad terms.

First sift the general knowledge of the prospective organizers for names and types of names already in use.

Consult telephone and other classified directories, available in most libraries, for "Associations," "Clubs," "Unions," "Labor Unions," "Trade Associations," "Boards of Trade," "Schools," "Governmental," "Chambers of Commerce," and other appropriate listings.

The most complete reference work covering major organizations is the *Encyclopedia of Associations* published by the Gale Research Co., Book Tower, Detroit, Michigan 48226. This set is published in three volumes and includes: v. 1, National Organizations of the United States; v. 2, Geographic and Executive Index; and v. 3, New Associations and Projects (quarterly reports). This is an expensive set, and like the other directories mentioned, may be consulted at most public libraries.

Another important work is the *Foundations Directory.* Although the Foundation Center's files include many more foundations, only major ones meet the criteria for inclusion in the directory, available from Columbia University Press. Columbia University Press also publishes *The Foundation Grants Index*. This publication is a summary of grants given by larger American foundations. It is indexed in such a fashion as to allow the user to identify the larger foundations making grants in the various areas of concern. The amounts of the grants from each foundation are listed for the purpose of aiding in selection of an appropriate foundation from which to seek funds. Each foundation is categorized according to particular purposes which it seeks to further.

A directory that may be useful is *National Trade and Professional Associations of the United States*, containing data on national associations. This publication is revised regularly and is available from Columbia Books, Inc., Ste. 300, 917 15th St., N.W., Washington, D.C. 20005.

Private research companies may be of aid, such as TCT Service, Inc. of Englewood Cliffs, New Jersey.

There are many specialized directories available, an example of which is *Scientific, Technical, and Related Societies of the United States*, available from the Printing and Publishing Office, National Academy of Sciences, 2101 Constitution Avenue, Washington, D.C. 20418. Comparable directories in other fields may be found in public library collections.

State offices. Each state, in the corporation division of its department of state, maintains lists of names already in use. This information is available, free or at a nominal charge, to any inquirer. Similar county-wide listings are available in the offices of the county clerks. They include unincorporated assumed trade names.

Method of inquiry. A letter or telegram of inquiry should be addressed to the secretary of state. Four or five names should be submitted in the order of preference. Usually the department will indicate the first name on the list not already in use.

If a telegram is sent, the reply will be sent "collect," of course. The inquiry should indicate willingness to accept this charge.

If a more detailed search is desired, there are small fees, about 10 to 20 cents for each year's records so searched.

§198. RESERVATION OF A NAME

Many states now permit reservation of a corporate name by incorporators. In some states the reservation is for a 60-day period, often renewable in addition. In Florida a 120-day reservation is permitted, and the reservation may be renewed.[71] Moreover the reserved name may be transferred to any other corporation or person by filing a notice of transfer with the Department of State.[72] Most states expressly do permit such a reservation.[73] When a corporate name is to be *changed*, many states grant a 30- to 60-day reservation of the desired name while the certificate of amendment is being prepared and filed.[74] Usually a fee of $5 or $6 is charged.

Registration of a "trade name" is permitted in most states.

In an application for reservation, if the secretary of state finds the name is available, he will endorse the application. The applicant then has the exclusive rights to the use of the selected name reserved for the statute-indicated number of days. During this time the applicant may, if he chooses, transfer these rights by filing with the secretary a written notice of the transfer, including the name and address of the transferee.[75]

FORM NO. 65

Reservation of Name (Maine)

Filing Fee $ This Space for Use by
                                                        Secretary of State

For Use by the
Secretary of State
File No. _____
Fee Paid_____
C. B._____
Date _____

NONPROFIT CORPORATION

STATE OF MAINE

APPLICATION FOR RESERVATION
OF CORPORATE NAME

Pursuant to 13-B MRSA §302 the undersigned hereby applies to the Secretary of the State of Maine to reserve the following corporate name:

_____

for a period of one hundred twenty days from the date of filing this application. Name of applicant _____
State whether individual, foreign or domestic corporation _____
Address of applicant _____
                       (If a corporation, use address of principal or registered office)
                            indicating street, city, state and zip code)

Date:_____   _____ *
                                             (applicant)

                          By _____
                                          (signature)

Legibly print or type name   _____
and capacity of all signers   (type or print name and capacity)
13-B MRSA §104.
                          By _____
                                          (signature)

                                     _____
                                        (type or print name and capacity)

*If the applicant is an individual, it is to be signed by the applicant.
If the applicant is a corporation:
The name of the corporation should be typed and the document must be signed (1) by clerk or secretary or (2) by the president or a vice-president and by the secretary, or an assistant secretary or such other officer as the bylaws may designate as a 2nd certifying officer or (3) if there are no such officers, then by a majority of the directors or by such directors as may be designated by a majority of directors then in office or (4) if there are no such directors then by the members or such of them as may be designated by the members at a lawful meeting or (5) as otherwise permitted by law.

FORM NO. 66

Reservation of Name (Washington, D.C.)

APPLICATION FOR RESERVATION
OF
CORPORATION NAME
OF

_____

To: The Recorder of Deeds, D.C.
    Washington, D.C.

Pursuant to the provisions of the District of Columbia Nonprofit Corporation Act, the undersigned hereby applies for reservation of _____ (Note 1) for a period of sixty (60) days. If a foreign corporation, name of state where organized _____

Dated:_____   _____ (Note 2)
                                          Applicant

                    By _____

                    Its _____

                    Address _____

Notes: 1. Insert corporate name to be reserved.

        2. A corporate name may be reserved by any person or corporation domestic or foreign

Mail to: **Fees Due**
    OFFICE OF RECORDER OF DEEDS D.C.   Filing Fee $
    CORPORATION DIVISION   Indexing Fee
    SIXTH AND D STREETS, N/W   _____
    WASHINGTON, D.C. 20001   Total $

                                        MAKE CHECK PAYABLE TO
                                        RECORDER OF DEEDS, D.C.

FORM NO. 67

Transfer of Reserved Name
(Maine)

Filing Fee $

This Space for Use by
Secretary of State

For Use by the Secretary of State
File No. _____
Fee Paid_____
C. B. _____
Date _____

NONPROFIT CORPORATION

STATE OF MAINE

NOTICE OF TRANSFER OF
RESERVED CORPORATE NAME
of

_____

Pursuant to 13-B MRSA §302, you are hereby notified that the undersigned has transferred to_____
whose address is _____
the corporate name of_____
which was reserved in your office for the exclusive use of the undersigned on
_____ 19____, for a period of one hundred twenty days thereafter.

If transferor is a corporation, complete the following:

The principal or registered office of the undersigned corporation is currently located at _____
(street, city, state and zip code)

Dated:_____   _____ *
(applicant)

By _____
(signature)

Legibly print or type name
and capacity of all signers
13-B MRSA §104.

_____
(type or print name and capacity)

By _____
(signature)

_____
(type or print name and capacity)

*If name reserved by an individual, notice must be signed by such individual transferor.
If name reserved by a corporation:
The name of the corporation should be typed and the document must be signed (1) by clerk or secretary *or* (2) by the president or a vice-president and by the secretary, or an assistant secretary or such other officer as the bylaws may designate as a 2nd certifying officer *or* (3) if there are no such officers, then by a majority of the directors or by such directors as may be designated by a majority of directors then in office *or* (4) if there are no such directors then by the members or such of them as may be designated by the members at a lawful meeting.

FORM NO. MNPCA-1A

FORM NO. 68

Transfer of Reserved Name
(Washington, D.C.)

NOTICE OF TRANSFER
OF
RESERVED CORPORATE NAME
OF

_____

To: The Recorder of Deeds, D.C.
Washington, D.C.

Pursuant to the provisions of the District of Columbia Nonprofit Corporation Act, the undersigned hereby notified that the undersigned has transferred to _____ whose address is _____ the corporate name of _____, 19____, for a period of sixty (60) days thereafter.

Date: _____ (Note 1)

       By _____

       Its _____

       Address _____

Note   1. Signature of individual or name of corporation in whose name Certificate of Reservation was issued.
         The right to the exclusive use of a specified corporate name so reserved may be transferred to any other person or corporation. The transfer must be executed by the applicant for whom the name was reserved.

Mail to:	**Fees Due**	
OFFICE OF RECORDER OF DEEDS D.C.	Filing Fee	$
CORPORATION DIVISION	Indexing Fee	
SIXTH AND D STREETS, N/W		_____
WASHINGTON, D.C. 20001	Total	$

MAKE CHECK PAYABLE TO
RECORDER OF DEEDS, D.C.

FORM NO. 69

Renewal of Name Registration

Filing Fee $_____ per Month (See Sec. 1401)   This Space for Use by
(Renewal Fee $_____)   Secretary of State

For Use by the Secretary of State	NONPROFIT CORPORATION

For Use by the
Secretary of State

File No. _____

Fee Paid_____

C. B._____

Date _____

NONPROFIT CORPORATION

STATE OF MAINE

**APPLICATION FOR (RENEWAL OF)
REGISTRATION OF
CORPORATE NAME
OF**

_____
(a foreign corporation)

Pursuant to 13-B MRSA §303 the undersigned corporation, the principal or registered office of which is currently located at:_____

_____
(street, city state and zip code)

hereby applies for (renewal of) the registration of its corporate name to and including December 31, 19_____, and submits the following statement:

FIRST: The state or territory under the laws of which it is incorporated is

_____

_____

SECOND: The date of its incorporation is   _____

THIRD: It is actually engaged in the following corporate activities:

_____

FOURTH: This application is accompanied by a certificate executed by the official having custody of the records pertaining to corporations in the state or territory in which it is incorporated showing that the corporation is in good standing.

Date:_____   _____ *
                                              (applicant)

                                    By _____
                                              (signature)
Legibly print or type name
and capacity of all signers   _____
13-B MRSA §104.   (type or print name and capacity)

                                    By _____
                                              (signature)

                                     _____
                                       (type or print name and capacity)

The filing of this application does not authorize a corporation to engage in corporate activities in Maine.

*The name of the corporation should be typed and the document must be signed (1) by the clerk or secretary *or* (2) by the president or a vice-president and by the secretary or an assistant secretary, or such other officer as the bylaws may designate as a 2nd certifying officer *or* (3) if there are no such officers, then by a majority of the directors or by such directors as may be designated by a majority of directors then in office *or* (4) if there are no such directors, then by the members or such of them as may be designated by the members at a lawful meeting.

FORM NO. MNPCA-2

§199. CHANGE OF NAME

In all states, a corporation is free to change its name. It must comply with all the above-mentioned rules for selection and clearance of the new name. And it must file a formal certificate amending its charter in this respect.[76]

Provisions are set forth for any corporation or nonprofit corporation wishing to change its name[77] General corporation law recognizes no power in the corporation to change or alter its name except through the formal procedures set forth in the controlling statutes.[78]

There is some question as to the effect on the corporate existence in the event of an illegal or unauthorized name change or alteration. Some courts have held that the corporate identity is not destroyed, but rather becomes a partnership, with the officers and stockholders liable as partners.[79] The opposite conclusion has been reached in other jurisdictions, following the theory that abandonment of the name is equal to the abandonment of the corporation itself.[80]

An authorized change of name has the same effect as the name change of a natural person. It does not change the corporation's liabilities under the old name.[81] However, it allows the corporation to continue its operation under a new name.

§200. REMEDIES FOR INVASION OF RIGHTS IN A NAME

[See Sections 191–194.]

The general rule of law is that a corporation, whether profit or nonprofit, chooses its name at its own peril.[82] The grant of a charter or certificate of incorporation from the secretary of state carries with it no immunity for fraudulent or deceptive use of a corporate name.[83]

A corporation having prior rights to a name may ask for an injunction against the new corporation to prevent its use of the name.[84] This protective remedy is equally available to nonprofit corporations.[85]

The injunction, however, will issue only if the name is so similar as to cause confusion in the public mind. As discussed previously, the reason for the protection is twofold: first, to protect the public, and second, to protect the corporation from unfair competition.

Proprietary interest in a corporate name can arise from use of it, so that cancellation of its corporate status for failure to file a statement of continued existence [required by statute: Ohio R.C. § 1702, 59] does not end common law ownership interest in the name; but the injunction will be granted only if unfair competition by use of the name is shown—injury to the corporation or the public.[86] Because the relief is equitable in nature, the courts have been careful to scrutinize the likelihood that the public will be misled and the extent to which the complaining party is likely to be injured.[87]

A slightly different question of liability may arise in cases where the secretary of state's office accepts and files a name which in fact conflicts with a presently existing and previously certified corporation. In a New York case[88] an employee of the secretary of state accepted and filed a certificate for Baron Decorator's, Ltd. This corporation was later informed that a corporation named Baron Decorating Service, Inc. had been incorporated (in compliance with all statutory requirements) some 31 years earlier. The new corporation was then required to go through the statutory name change procedures. This corporation tried to bring an action in negligence against the employee and the state. The New York Court of Appeals found that the accepting or rejecting of a corporate name is a quasi-judicial act requiring the exercise of discretion, and thus the state was immune from suit despite the damage to the party forced to change its corporate name.[89]

The use of a corporate name has caused the courts some small problems in the past. With the rapid growth in the area of nonprofit corporation law,[90] the likelihood is that even more judicial interpretation of the use of corporate names will soon be required. Because of the unique function of the nonprofit corporation, the chances for abuse and misuse of names is great. It may be desirable to masquerade as a "charitable" organization. How simply this could be accomplished if one could freely select a name which implied "good deeds." Obviously the opportunity for misleading the public is present. "The danger is that nonprofit corporations, partly because of their charitable character, have a public image which can be usurped by being used as fronts for illicit interests."[91]

If the general public relies on a name which implies a charitable purpose, and then discovers that the name is deceptive, faith of the public in all charitable organizations is undermined.[92]

The name of a corporation, profit or nonprofit, gives the organization a legal identity. This identity should be maintained with the highest degree of integrity possible, and that integrity should begin with the corporate name.

§201. USE OF INC. OR CORP.

[See Section 191, first paragraph.]

Unlike business corporations, nonprofit corporations often need not add to their names explanatory terms such as *Incorporated (Inc.)*, *Corporations (Corp.)*, or *Limited (Ltd.)*.[93] An incorporated business in most states must use such a suffix or prefix.[94]

The same requirement applies in some states to ordinary (not "charitable") nonprofit corporations.[95] For example, if a social club is incorporated, its name usually must include the identifying *Inc.* (*e.g.*, Hazelton Social Club, Inc.). This is notice to persons (say, creditors) dealing with the corporation that it has limited liability. But the word *Club* may suffice for this purpose.[96]

But in most states, incorporated associations directly oriented to benefit the public are not required to add this explanatory tag. This usually holds for truly charitable, religious, benevolent, or professional societies, and for state-supervised educational corporations.[97]

§202. CORPORATE SEALS

A corporate seal is, in most uses these days, a secondary indication of corporate approval (*i.e.*, by the managers) of a corporate action or agreement. It is seldom equivalent to signature by a duly authorized officer. Usually the secretary keeps the corporate seal and affixes it to documents when directed by the directors or officers, as a token of corporation assent. But signature by a duly authorized officer usually is required to make that assent official.[98]

In virtually all states today, the old common law consideration of a seal as a binding evidence of assent (*e.g.*, proof of valid "consideration" in a contract) no longer is effective.[99] Today's seal is for most practical purposes merely a decoration.

Almost every corporation does officially adopt a seal bearing its name, home state, and year of incorporation. This may be impressed on paper documents by a "seal press." But it may also be a label, a wafer, or wax impression. Often a facsimile is engraved or printed on formal certificates.

Many states now permit but do not require corporations to have seals.[100] The bylaws often include adoption of a seal. Use of the letters "L.S." (*locus sigilli*) or of any mark or device will suffice if duly adopted. The seal of the officer who signs for the corporation may be adopted for the transaction as that of the corporation.[101]

If a seal is used on a document together with a signature of an officer, this raises a rebuttable presumption that the officer was duly authorized to sign. It is evidence of authority—not proof of it. The presumption can be rebutted by evidence to the contrary given by or for the corporation.[102]

Real property transfers by corporations in a few states must still bear the corporate seal. But a seal may be adopted for the particular occasion.[103]

Nonprofit organizations should adopt and use handsome seals and insignia. This is especially true for institutions such as schools, and for fraternal organizations. Such seals have value for group spirit and public relations purposes.

§203. THE CORPORATION'S OFFICE

A corporation resides in the county in which its charter states that its office is located.[104] Every certificate of incorporation must contain such a statement.[105] The fact that it has branch offices ordinarily does not make it a "resident" elsewhere.[106]

The *domicile* of a corporation is the state in which it was incorporated.[107] If a corporation is incorporated in two states, it has two domiciles. But for court jurisdiction under the federal "diversity of citizenship" rule, its first domicile now is not determinative.[108] For other jurisdiction purposes, domicile has the same effect as does that of a natural person. An unincorporated association has no domicile,[109] and no "citizenship."[110]

The *principal office* is wherever the chief affairs of the corporation are carried on. This is usually where its records are kept, its meetings are held, and its officers do their work.[111]

Every NPC in Florida must maintain at its registered office, information *readily available to the public,* such as the text of its charter and all amendments, its current address, federal identification number, officers' names and addresses, and registered agent name and address. Failure to do so may result in dissolution (automatic) by July 2, 1992 (with stated exceptions).[112]

It is important to remember that *official residence, domicile,* and *principal office* differ. A given statute often applies to one of these but not to the others.[113]

The original statement in a charter of the location of the corporate office usually need only include the city, town, or village—not the street address.[114] Thus no correction of the charter is necessary when the office is moved, unless it is moved to another town.

But in some states a street address must be specified: when the secretary of state is designated an agent on whom legal process against the corporation can be served. He then is able to mail any such process.

The state office of a corporation can be changed in most states by filing an amendment to the corporate charter setting forth city-to-city or town-to-town change, without street addresses.[115] Failure to file such an amendment may bring action by the state to annul the corporate charter and to punish guilty officers and directors, if the omission involves fraud or other wrongdoing.

The same is true of notice to the secretary of state, for mailing of process, whenever the street address is changed, in states where specific designation of the secretary of state as an agent for this purpose is required. [See also, the next Section.]

§204. AGENT-FOR-PROCESS

As mentioned in the foregoing section, most states require designation of an agent-for-service-of-process; if none is designated the secretary of state may be designated by the statutes.

Every corporation must designate a *resident agent*—a person or corporation to serve as such agent.[116] And the Department of State must be informed of changes of the corporation's office or agent.[117]

FORM NO. 70

Appointment of Agent
(Ohio)

Form C-103 Prescribed by Secretary of State Ted W. Brown

Original Appointment of Agent

The undersigned, being at least a majority of the incorporators of _____

_____

(Name of Corporation)

hereby appoint _____

(Name of Agent)

(a natural person resident in the country in which the corporation has its principal office) or (a corporation having a business address in the county in which the corporation has its principal office) (strike out phrase not applicable) upon whom (which) any process, notice or demand required or permitted by statute to be served upon the corporation may be served. His (Its) complete address is _____, _____

(Street or Avenue)   (City or Village)

_____County, Ohio, _____

(Zip Code)

_____

_____

_____

(Incorporators' names should be typed or printed beneath signatures)

(AGENT'S ADDRESS _____, Ohio

MUST BE ZIP CODED) _____, 19____

_____

(Name of Corporation)

Gentlemen: I hereby accept appointment as agent of your corporation upon whom process, tax notices or demands may be served.

_____

(Signature of Agent)

By _____

(Signature of Officer Signing and Title if Agent is a Corporation)

REMARKS: ALL ARTICLES OF INCORPORATION MUST BE ACCOMPANIED BY AN ORIGINAL APPOINTMENT OF AGENT. THERE IS NO FILING FEE FOR THIS APPOINTMENT.

FORM NO. 71

Agent's Consent
(Georgia)

CONSENT TO APPOINTMENT AS REGISTERED AGENT

TO: Ben W. Fortson Jr.
     Secretary of State
     Ex-Officio Corporation
     Commissioner
     State of Georgia

I(We) _____
                    (Type or print name of person(s))

do hereby consent to serve as registered agent for the corporation _____

_____
                    (Type or print name of corporation)

This _____ day of _____ 19_____.

                                    _____

                                    _____

Address of registered agent(s):
          (Type or print address)

          _____

          _____

          _____

          _____

FORM NO. 72

Office and Agent Statement of Unincorporated Association
(California)

STATEMENT BY UNINCORPORATED ASSOCIATION OF
ADDRESS OF PRINCIPAL OFFICE AND DESIGNATION
OF AGENT FOR THE SERVICE OF PROCESS
*(For filing with the Secretary of State of California
pursuant to Section 24003, Corporations Code.)*

(**OFFICE USE ONLY**)

_____an
unincorporated association makes the following statements:

(Use ONLY the following paragraph I if *no* agent is being designated for the
purpose of receiving process against the association.)

    I. The location and address of its principal office in the State of California
       is _____

                      (Number, Street, City and State; Do not Use Post Office Box)

(Use ONLY the following paragraph II if an agent is being designated for the
purpose of receiving process against the association. Fill in either subparagraph A or B, whichever is applicable, AND either subdivision (1) or (2) of
subparagraph C.)

  II. A. The address and location of its principal office in the State of Cali-
         fornia is _____

                      (Number, Street, City and State; Do not Use Post Office Box)

OR

    B. The association does not have an office in the State of California, but
       the address to which the Secretary of State shall send required
       notices is:

                      (Number, Street, City and State; Do not Use Post Office Box)

AND

C. (1) (*Use this subdivision if the process agent is a natural person.*)

_____a natural person residing in the State of California, whose complete [ ] business [ ] resident address is: _____

_____

is designated as its agent for the purpose of service of process.

NOTE: Either the business address or the residence address must be given. Indicate which by check mark in proper box.

(2) (*Use this subdivision if the process agent is a corporation. See Instruction No. 1.*) _____

_____, a corporation, organized and existing under the laws of _____ is designated as agent upon whom process directed to the undersigned unincorporated association may be served within the State of California, in the manner provided by law.

III. Has the association previously filed a statement: Yes [ ] No [ ]

If the answer is "Yes," then complete the following subparagraphs. The requested information will be shown on the copy of the statement which was returned to the association.

A. The file number of the last previously filed statement is_____

B. The date on which said statement was filed is _____

C. The name of the association as shown on such previous statement is _____

D. The address of the principal office (or the address to which notices are to be sent by the Secretary of State) as shown on such previous statement is _____

_____

_____
(Name of Unincorporated Association)

By _____
(Title)

_____
(Typed Name of Person Signing)

INSTRUCTIONS:

1. No domestic corporation may be designated as agent for service of process unless it has filed with the Secretary of State the certificate provided for by Section 1505, Corporations Code, and no foreign corporation may be designated unless it has qualified for the transaction of intrastate business in California and has filed with the Secretary of State of the State of California the certificate provided for by Section 1505, California Corporations Code. A domestic or foreign corporation must be currently authorized to engage in business in this State and be in good standing status on the records of the Secretary of State of the State of California, in order to file a certificate pursuant to this section.

2. After this statement has been filed the association may from time to time file a new statement superseding the last previously filed statement. If the new statement does not designate an agent for service of process, the filing of the new statement operates to revoke a process agent previously designated. A statement expires 5 years from December 31 following the date of filing with the Secretary of State, unless previously superseded by the filing of a new statement.

3. The fee for filing this statement or any new statement superseding it is $15.00.

THIS STATEMENT MUST BE SUBMITTED IN DUPLICATE ORIGINAL.

FORM NO. 73

Change of Office or Agent
(New Jersey)

CERTIFICATE OF CHANGE OF REGISTERED OFFICE
OR REGISTERED AGENT, OR BOTH

(For Use by Domestic or Foreign Corporations)

"Federal Employer Identification No."

To: The Secretary of State
    State of New Jersey

Pursuant to the provisions of Section 14A:4-3, Corporations, General, of the New Jersey Statutes, the undersigned corporation, organized under the laws of the State of _____,
submits the following certificate for the purpose of changing its registered office or its registered agent, or both, in the State of New Jersey:

FIRST: The name of the corporation is _____

_____

SECOND: The name of its new registered agent is _____

_____

THIRD: The address* of its new registered office is _____

_____
(*Include Zip Code)

FOURTH: The name of its former registered agent is _____

_____

FIFTH: The address* of its former registered office is _____

_____
(*Include Zip Code)

SIXTH: The corporation further states that the address of its new registered office and the address of its new registered agent are identical.

SEVENTH: The changes designated above were authorized by resolution duly adopted by its board of directors.

Dated this _____ day of _____, 19_____

_____
Corporation Name)

By_____ *

_____
Type or Print Name and Title)

(*May be executed by the chairman of the board, *or* the president *or* a vice-president of the corporation.)

FORM NO. 74

Resignation of Agent
(Washington, D.C.)

RESIGNATION OF REGISTERED AGENT
OF

_____

To: The Recorder of Deeds, D.C.
    Washington, D.C.

Pursuant to the provisions of the District of Columbia Nonprofit Corporation Act, the undersigned hereby resigns as registered agent of

_____

_____

effective as of the date of filing. The appointment of the undersigned shall terminate upon the expiration of 30 days after receipt of such notice by the Office of Recorder of Deeds, D.C., Corporation Division, or upon the appointment of a successor agent becoming effective, whichever occurs sooner.

Date _____

                              _____
                                   (Print name of agent)

                              _____
                                   (Signature of agent)

                              _____
                                   (Address of agent)

Domestic Corporation Execute in Triplicate
Foreign Corporation Execute in Duplicate

Mail to:

OFFICE OF RECORDER OF DEEDS, D.C.   **NO FEE REQUIRED**
CORPORATION DIVISION
SIXTH AND D STREETS, N.W.
WASHINGTON, D.C. 20001

POINTS TO REMEMBER

- Avoid use of deceptive names. If in doubt about a particular name, do not use it.
- Avoid use of names similar to those used by other organizations, especially those having purposes like yours.
- Beware of words or names having "secondary meaning."
- Avoid use of "suggestive" or offensive terms.
- Check your state statutes for restricted or forbidden names.
- If you use a restricted name, get approval from the statute-stated government authority.
- Get approval from your parent organization.
- Write to your state secretary to clear the desired name. Or wire, including "reply collect."
- Reserve a name, especially if you are changing your corporate name.
- Choose a new name with fresh caution.
- Use *Inc.* or *Corp.* when in doubt whether your corporation is required to do so.
- Adopt a seal; but use it merely for decorative purposes.
- Make your home town the corporation's office whenever possible.
- Do not put a street address in the charter. The city, town, or village name is enough.
- Put a street address in the "designation" of the secretary of state, for mailing legal process to you.
- Amend the town name in the charter if you move to another town.
- Amend the street address in the "designation" if you move to another address.
- Appoint an agent for service of notices and processes. Notify the Department of State when you change the agent or office address.

NOTES TO CHAPTER 18

1. Cal. Corp. Code §202(a); Colo. Corp. Code §7-3-106; Fla. Stat. §§617.0202, 617.0401; Rev. Mod. Nonprofit Corp. Act §2.02(a)(1) (1986) requires also a statement of public benefit or mutual benefit or religious status, and contains other elaborate rules in §4.01. *See,* Henn and Alexander, *Laws of Corporations,* 268–270 (3rd ed., 1983); Hamilton, *Corporations,* 160 (3rd ed., 1986); 1 Oleck, *Modern Corporation Law* c. 19 (1978 supp.) summarizes the statutes of all states.

2. Ohio Rev. Code §§1701.05, 1702.05; Fla. Stat. §§607.0401, 617.0401. As to other states see Henn and Alexander, supra, at p. 268.

3. *Id.,* §§1702.05 (A); Genl. Stat. No. Car., §55A-10; but Ohio Rev. Code, *Id.,* §1702 does provide for use of same name if there is filed in the office of the secretary of state the con-

sent of the other corporation in writing, evidenced by a resolution of the directors or trustees.

4. *Id.* (Ohio), §1702.05(A).

5. Ohio *Id.*, §1702.41(B)(2); Fla. §617.1101.

6. *Id.*, §1702.45; Fla. St., §617.1106–617.1107.

7. Jervis Corp. v. Secretary of State, 43 Misc.2d 185, 250 N.Y.S.2d 544 (Super. Ct. Nassau County 1964); 26 A.L.R.3d 1008, §5.

8. John Roberts Mfg. Co. v. University of Notre Dame Du Lac, 258 F.2d 256 (7th Cir. 1958); White Tower System v. White Castle System of Eating Houses Corp., 90 F.2d 67 (6th Cir. 1937), *cert. den.*, 58 S. Ct. 41, 302 U.S. 720, 82 L. Ed. 556 (1937); 1 Oleck, *Modern Corporation Law*, c. 19 (1978 Supp.); Diamond, *Unfair Competition in Use of Corporate Names*, 12 Clev.-Mar. L. Rev. 146 (1963); Annot., 37 A.L.R.3d 277; Covington Inn Corp. v. White Horse Tavern, Inc., 445 S.W.2d 138 (Fla. 1969) (unauthorized use constitutes common law tort of unfair competition).
    But *cf.*, Trans-Americas Airlines, Inc. v. Kenton, 491 A.2d 1139 (Del. 1985).

9. United States v. Dunn, 564 F.2d 348, 354, n. 12 (9th Cir. 1977); Rev. Model Bus. Corp. Act §§4.01(e), 15.06(a)(2); Rev. Mod. Nonprofit Corp. Act §4.01 Comment 2 (E of 1986).

10. Benevolent and Protective Order of Elks v. Improved Benevolent and Protective Order of Elks of the World, 205 N.Y. 459, 98 N.E. 756, L.R.A. 1915 B 1074; Parma Democratic Club v. Democratic Club of Parma, Inc., 29 Ohio L. Abs. 30 (1939); Investors Syndicate of America v. Hughes, 378 Ill. 413, 38 N.E.2d 754 (1941); Prince Hall Lodge v. Universal Lodge, 381 P.2d 130 (Wash. 1963). *And see*, Annot., 37 A.L.R.3d 277.

11. U.S.C., §§1051–1127; 18 U.S.C., §709; Ohio Rev. Code, §1702.05; Calif. Corp. L. §5122, 7121 Purdon's Penna. Statutes Annotated 15, §5303–5305; these are typical. For statutes of all states, *see*, 1 Oleck, above, n. 1. *And see*, Trimble, *Effect of Statutes on Similarity of Corporate Names*, 44 Ky. L J. 439 (1956). 18 U.S.C., §709; 15 U.S.C., §§1051–1127; N.Y. Bus. Corp. L. §§301, 302; N.Y. Not-For-Profit Corp. L. §§301, 302; Del. Code Ann. 8–312; Ann. L. Mass. 180:5, 7, 10, 11, 266:71A.

12. Meridian Yellow Cab Co. v. City Yellow Cabs, 206 Miss. 812, 41 S.2d 14 (1949); Annot., 66 A.L.R. 948 (1930); Callmann, *Unfair Competition and Trade Marks* (2d ed. 1950). *But see* (that statutes govern) Cleveland Opera Co. v. Cleveland Civic Opera Assn., 22 Ohio App. 400, 154 N.E. 352 (1926); Covington Inn Corp. v. White Horse Tavern, Inc., 445 S.W.2d 138 (Fla. 1969).

13. Ohio Rev. Code, §1702.05; *and see* above, n. 10. Also, Mayo Clinic v. Mayo Drug and Cosmetic, Inc. 113 N.W.2d 852 (Minn. 1962).

14. *Ibid.*

15. *See*, Burnside Veneer Corp. v. New Burnside Veneer Co., 247 S.W.2d 524 (Ky. 1952); Note, 30 Iowa L. Rev. 120 (1944).

16. Lincoln Center for Performing Arts, Inc. v. Lincoln Center Classics Record Society, Inc., 210 N.Y.S.2d 275 (1960).

17. Jackson v. Stephens, 391 S.W.2d 702 (Ky. 1965).

18. *Healing the Children, Inc. v. Heal the Children, Inc.*, 786 F. Supp. 1209 (W.D. Pa. 1992).

19. Yale University v. Benneson, 147 Conn. 254, 159 A.2d 169 (1960); General Finance Loan Co. v. General Loan Co., 163 F.2d 709 (8th Cir. 1947), *cert. den.* 68 S. Ct. 356, 332 U.S. 851, 92 L. Ed. 421 (1947); First Congressional District Democratic Party Organization v. First Congressional District Democratic Organization, Inc., 177 N.W.2d 224 (Mich. 1970).

20. National Circle, Daughters of Isabella v. National Order of Daughters of Isabella, 270 F. 723 (2d Cir. 1920), *cert. den.* 255 U.S. 571, 41 S. Ct. 376, 65 L. Ed. 791 (1920); Annot., 76 A.L.R.2d 1396.

21. Lawyers Title Insurance Co. v. Lawyers Title Insurance Corp., 109 F.2d 35, 71 App. D.C. 120 (D.C. Cir. 1939), *cert. den.* 309 U.S. 684, 60 S. Ct. 806, 84 L. Ed. 1028 (1940); Diamond, *op. cit.* above, n. 8, at 153.

22. Meridian Yellow Cab Co. v. City Yellow Cabs, 41 S.2d 14 (Miss. 1949); noted 21 Miss. L. J. 411 (1950); 18 U.S.C., §709; Del. Rev. Code 1915, §1919; McCollum, *Protection by Equity of Corporate Names Against Unfair Competition*, 6 Columbia L. Rev. 244 (1906); Note, *Protection of Corporate Name—Nature of Right Involved*, 20 Calif. L. Rev. 633 (1932). As to jurisdiction of U.S. courts when such use occurs in a foreign country, *see*, Wells Fargo and Co. v. Wells Fargo Express Co., 358 F. Supp. 1065 (D.C. Nev. 1973).

23. *International Kennel Club of Chicago, Inc. v. Mighty Star, Inc.*, 846 F.2d 1079 (7th Cir., 1988).

24. National Tool Salvage Co. v. National Tool Salvage Industries, Inc., 60 N.Y.S.2d 308 (1946).

25. Motor Club of America v. Curran, 193 Misc. 157, 83 N.Y.S.2d 733; *affd.*, 274 A.D. 1083, 85 N.Y.S.2d 552 (1949), *affd.* without opinion, 299 N.Y. 776, 87 N.E.2d 678 (1949); Motor Club of America v. Curran, 193 Misc. 157, 83 N.Y.S.2d 733, *affd.* 274 A.D. 1083, 83 N.Y.S.2d 553, *affd. without op.* 229 N.Y. 776, 87 N.E.2d 678 (1949).

26. Pilgrim Holiness Church v. First Pilgrim Holiness Church, 115 Ill. App.2d 448, 252 N.E.2d 1, 4 (1969).

27. First Congressional Dist. Democratic Party Org. v. First Congressional Dist. Democratic Org., Inc., 22 Mich. App. 386, 177 N.W.2d 224 (1970).

28. General Adjustment Bureau, Inc. v. General Ins. Adjustment Co., 381 F.2d 991, 992 (10th Cir. 1967); Beatrice Foods Co. v. Neosho Valley Coop. Creamery Assn., 297 F.2d 447 (D. Okla. 1961).

29. General Adjustment Bureau, Inc. v. General Adjustment Co., 381 F.2d 991, 992 (10th Cir. 1967). *See also* Lawyers' Title Ins. Co. v. Lawyer's Title Ins. Corp., 109 F.2d 35 (D.C. Cir. 1939). Here the court points out that the more sophisticated and discerning the customers likely to use the services of the organization, the less reason there is for protection.

30. *See*, McCarthy, *Trademarks and Unfair Competition*, Sec. 9.2 (2d ed., 1984).

31. First Congressional Dist. Democratic Party Organization v. First Congressional Dist. Democratic Organization, Inc., 22 Mich. App. 386, 177 N.W.2d 224 (1970). *See also* General Adjustment Bureau, Inc. v. Fuess, 192 F. Supp. 542 (S.D. Tex. 1961), relying on Abramson v. Coro, Inc., 240 F.2d 854 (5th Cir. 1957) and Pure Foods v. Minute Maid Corp., 214 F.2d 792 (5th Cir. 1954).

32. Sterling Products Corp. v. Sterling Products, Inc., 43 F. Supp. 548 (D.C. N.Y. 1942). *But contra*, for names not so well-known: Sweet Sixteen Co. v. Sweet "16" Shop, Inc., 15 F.2d 920 (8th Cir. 1926).

33. Annot., 37 A.L.R.3d 277.

34. *See* n. 21 above; Annot. 115 A.L.R. 1241; Note, *Right to Exclusive Use of Corporate Name*, 28 Calif. L. Rev. 766 (1940); Bear Mill Mfg. Co. v. F.T.C., 98 F.2d 67 (2d Cir. 1938); B.&P.O. of Elks, v. Improved B.&P.O. of Elks, 205 N.Y. 459 (1912); L.R.A. 1915B 1074; Wheeler Syndicate, Inc. v. Wheeler, 99 Misc. 289, 163 N.Y.S. 817 (1917); annot. 68 A.L.R.3d 1168.

35. *Supra*, n. 27.

36. Brandeis and Warren, *The Right to Privacy*, 4 Harv. L. Rev. 193 (1890); Kacedan, *The Right to Privacy*, 12 B.U.L.L. Rev. 353, 600 (1932); Weeks, *Comparative Law of Privacy*, 12 Clev.-Mar. L. Rev. 484 (1963); Serge Koussevitzkey v. Allen, Town and Health, Inc., 188 Misc. 479, 68 N.Y.S.2d 779 (1947); Simpson, *Equity*, 24 N.Y.U.L.Q. Rev. 1265, 1270 (1949). A corporate name is not protected by N.Y. Civil Rights L. §51: Jaccard v. R. H. Macy and Co., 176 Misc. 88, 26 N.Y.S.2d 829, *affd.*, 265 A.D. 15, 37 N.Y.S.2d 570 (1942).

37. Most Worshipful Hiram of Tyre v. Most Worshipful Sons of Light, 94 Cal. App.2d 25, 210 P.2d 34 (1949).

38. American Gold Star Mothers v. National Gold Star Mothers, 191 F.2d 488 (D.C. Cir. 1951).

39. Pilgrim Holiness Church v. First Pilgrim Holiness Church, 115 Ill. App.2d 448, 252 N.E.2d 1 (1969).

40. *Id.*

41. *Id.*

42. Id. at 7.

43. *Id.*

44. *25 Misc.2d 686, 210 N.Y.S.2d 275 (Sup. Ct. 1960).*

45. *Id.*, at 277, citing N.Y. Penal Law, §948.

46. Anti-Defamation League of B'Nai B'Rith v. National Mexican American Anti-Defamation Committee, 510 F.2d 1246 (C.A. D.C. 1975).

47. National Catholic Society of Animal Welfare, Inc. v. Grohsman, No. C-1842-70 (N.J. Super. April 6, 1971).

48. *Id.*, at 7–8.

49. *Id.*, at 7.

50. *Id.*

51. Cox, (article) 14 *Nat. L.J.*. (30) 8 (March 30, 1992).

52. Mass. Ann. Laws ch. 266, §71A; N.Y. Genl. Bus. Law, Art. 9B, §§134, 135. *See also* N.Y. Genl. Bus. Law Art. 26, §397.

53. Griesedieck Western Brewing v. Peoples Brewing Co., 56 F. Supp. 600 (D. Minn. 1944).

54. Annot., 44 A.L.R.2d 1159.

55. *Id.*

56. Neuhoff, Inc. v. Neuhoff Packing Co., 167 F.2d 459 (D. Tenn. 1948).

57. Al S. Holtz v. Holtz and Son, 105 N.Y.S.2d 454 (1951); Great A.&P. Tea Co. v. A.&P. Radio Stores, Inc., 20 F. Supp. 703, 706 (D.C. Pa. 1937); Charles S. Higgins Co. v. Higgins Soap Co., 144 N.Y. 462; 27 L.R.A. 42 (1895); Note, *Use of One's Own Name as Unfair Competition*, 26 Columbia L. Rev. 870 (1926).

58. Compania "Ron Barcardi" S.A. v. American Barcardi Rum Corp., 63 N.Y.S.2d 610 (Sup. Ct. 1934). *And see,* Annot., 37 A.L.R.3d 277 (1971); United States Jaycees v. San Francisco Jr. Cham. of Comm., 354 F. Supp. 76 (D.C. Cal. 1972).

59. The Five Platters, Inc. v. Purdie, 419 F. Supp. 372 (D.C., D. Md. 1976).

60. American Gold Star Mothers v. National Gold Star Mothers, 191 F.2d 488 (D.C. Cir. 1951); *and see,* Goodyear India Rubber Glove Mfg. Co. v. Goodyear Rubber Co., 128 U.S. 598 (1888); Saunders System Atlanta Co., Inc. v. Drive-It-Yourself Co., 158 Ga. 1, 123 S.E. 132 (1924); General Industries Co. v. 20 Wacker Drive Bldg. Corp., 156 F.2d 474 (7th Cir. 1946); Blackwell's Durham Tobacco Co. v. American Tobacco Co., 145 N.C. 367, 59 S.E. 123 (1927); Anti-Defamation League of B'Nai B'Rith v. National Mexican-American Anti-Defamation Committee, 510 F.2d 1246 (C.A., D.C. 1975).

61. Goodyear's India Rubber Glove Mfg. Co. v. Goodyear Rubber Co., 128 U.S. 598; 9 S. Ct. 166; 32 L. Ed. 535 (1888); *Note,* L.R.A. 1917C, 958; *In re* Church of God World Headquarters, Inc., 182 Misc. 851; 46 N.Y.S.2d 545 (1944).

62. *Restatement, Torts,* §§715–717, 727, 732; New York World's Fair, 1939 v. World's Fair News, 163 Misc. 661; 297 N.Y.S. 923; *affd.,* 256 A.D. 373; 10 N.Y.S.2d 56 (1939); N.Y. Gen. Bus. L. §141.

63. N.Y. Penal L., §946-a.

64. 18 U.S.C. §706; 36 U.S.C. §27. *See* n. 61 above; also, N.Y. Not-for-Profit Corp. L. §301(a)(8).

65. *Re* Jiggs Nut Club, Inc., 142 Misc. 309; 256 N.Y.S. 273 (1932); Gay Activists Alliance v. Lomenzo, 320 N.Y.S.2d 994 (1971), revd. 38 A.D.2d 981, 329 N.Y.S.2d 181, *affd.,* 31 N.Y.2d 965, 293 N.E.2d 255 (1973); Application of Thom, 33 N.Y.2d 609, 301 N.E.2d 542 (1973); Grant v. Brown, 313 N.E.2d 847 (Ohio 1974).

66. Thus, only labor unions may use the word "union." Tool Owners Union v. Roberts, 190 Misc. 577, 76 N.Y.S.2d 239 (1947); *and see* N.Y. Genl. Corp. L., §9; Ohio Rev. Code, §1702.05.

67. N.Y. Educ. L. §224.

68. N.Y. Bus. Corp. L. §301(a)(6).

69. 1959 Op. Atty.-Genl. 100 (N.Y.).

70. N.Y. Gen. Bus. L. §138.

71. Fla. St., §607.0402 is in the business corporation statute. See Model Bus. Corp. Act §9; Rev. Model Nonprofit Corp. Act §4.02 (1986 Exposure Draft); Fla. Stat. 617.0402 (nonprofit corporations).

72. *Ibid.*

73. *E.g.*, permitted by: Calif., Genl. Corp. L., §201; 805 ILCS 105/104.10; N.Y. N-P-C Law, §303; Ohio Rev. Code, §1701.05(C) (for business corporations); Ohio Rev. Code §1702.05(C) (for nonprofit corporations).

74. *See*, Ohio Rev. Code, §1701.05(C); N.Y. Not For Profit Corp. L. §303; N.Y. Bus. Corp. L., §303, 801(3); and statutes cited above in n. 73. As to procedural requirements, *see*, Sykes v. People, 132 Ill. 32, 23 N.E. 391 (1890). As to abandoned names, *see*, Cincinnati Realty Co. v. St. Nicholas Plaza, 28 Ohio N.P. (n.s.) 354 (1931). As to misleading names, *see*, 1947 Ohio Atty.-Genl. Op. 1759; Model Non-Profit Corp. Act, §4.01 (1986 Exposure Draft).

75. Ohio Rev. Code Ann., §1702.05(C) Fla St., §617.0402.

76. Ohio Rev. Code, §1702.38(B)(1); 1931 Ohio Atty.-Genl. Op. 3429; amendment intended only to make the name correspond with the recorded title to corporate property does not change the corporate structure or powers. East End Church of God v. Logan, 102 Ohio App. 552, 75 Ohio Abs. 29, 131 N.E.2d 439 (1956); *and see*, Sykes case, above, n. 74; N.Y. Bus. Corp. L., §303; N.Y. Educ. L., §219; N.Y. N–PCL §303.

77. *Id.*

78. Pilsen Brewing Co. v. Wallace, 291 Ill. 59, 125 N.E. 714 (1919).

79. *Id. See also*, Richard v. Minnesota Savings Bank, 75 Minn. 196, 77 N.W. 822 (1899); Robinson v. First National Bank, 98 Tex. 184, 82 S.W. 505 (1904).

80. Cincinnati Cooperage Co. v. Bate, 96 Ky. 356, 26 S.W. 538 (1894); Senn v. Levy, 111 Ky. 318, 63 S.W. 776 (1901); Stafford National Bank v. Palmer, 47 Conn. 443 (1880); Annot. 8 A.L.R. 583 (1920).

81. Michigan Ins. Bank v. Eldred, 143 U.S. 293 (1891).

82. American Order of Scottish Clans v. Merrill, 151 Mass. 558, 24 N.E. 918 (1890).

83. Staples Coal Co. v. City Fuel Co., 55 N.E.2d 934 (1940).

84. American Gold Star Mothers v. National Gold Star Mothers, 191 F.2d 488 (D.C. Cir. 1951); The Five Platters, Inc. v. Purdie, 419 F. Supp. 372 (D.C., D. Md. 1976).

85. Parma Democratic Club v. Democratic Club of Parma, Inc., 29 Ohio L. Abs. 30 (8th Dist. Ct. App. 1939).

86. Hinckley Chamber of Commerce v. Hinckley Chamber of Commerce, Inc., 27 Ohio App. 3rd 264, 501 N.E. 2d 47 (1985; reported 1987).

87. 18 Am. Jur.2d Corporation, §148; 18 C.J.S. Corporations, §173.

88. Gross v. State of N.Y., 33 App. Div.2d 868, 306 N.Y.S.2d 28 (1969).

89. *Id.*

90. Lesher, *The Non-Profit Corporation—A Neglected Stepchild Comes of Age*, 22 Bus. Law 951 (1967).

91. *Id.*, at 966.

92. This is not to suggest that this writer is equating charitable and nonprofit corporations but is merely using the charitable corporation as an example of this class.

93. N.Y. N-PCL §301,302. Nor need business corporations do so in Ohio; *see* Ohio Rev. Code, §§1701.05, 1702.05. *And see*, Model Nonprofit Corp. Act, §4.01 (1986 Draft).

94. Fla. St., §617.0202; Unif. Bus. Corp. Act., §4; *In re* American Cigar Lighter Co. 77 Misc. 643; 138 N.Y.S. 455 (1912).

95. Two opinions, N.Y. Atty.-Genl. (1913) 144.

96. *In re* Nyack Country Club, 166 N.Y.S. 611 (1917).

97. *Ibid.*

98. United Surety Co. v. Meenan, 211 N.Y. 39; 105 N.E. 106 (1914). As to what is a seal, *see,* Ann. Cas. 1912C, 42; N.Y. Genl. Construction L., §§44, 45, 44a.

99. *E.g.,* Ariz. Rev. Stat. Ann. §1-202; Minn. Stat. Ann. §302A.163; N.Y. Genl. Construction L., §44-a; Ohio Rev. Code, §5.11; Wyo. Stat. §34-2-126, *See,* 1 Williston, *Contracts,* 218 (rev. ed. with cum. Supp.). See, Henn & Alexander *Corporations,* 318 (3rd ed., 1983).

100. Valente v. International Milling Co., 119 A.D. 127; 103 N.Y.S. 966 (1907); Feder v. Forest Hill Apts., Inc., 100 N.J. Eq. 455; 136 A. 297 (1927); District of Columbia v. Camden Iron Works, 181 U.S. 453; 21 S. Ct. 680; 45 L. Ed. 948 (1900); Ohio Rev. Code, §1701.13(B).

101. N.Y. Genl. Construction L., §45.

102. United Surety Co. case, n. 98 above.

103. N.Y. Real Prop. L., §292-a.

104. Wienbroer v. U.S. Shipping Bd. Emergency Fleet Corp., 299 F. 972 (D.C., N.Y. 1924); Fla St., §617.0501 (1992).

105. *See* list of statutes in footnotes to c. 4.

106. Mason and H. Co. v. Sharon, 231 F. 861 (2d Cir. 1916), *cert. den.,* 241 U.S. 670; 36 S. Ct. 554; 60 L. Ed. 1230 (1916). But it does for railroads and airlines, pursuant to statutes, in most states.

107. *Restatement, Conflict of Laws,* §41, *esp.* comment (c).

108. *See,* Henn, *Corporations,* §81 (rev. ed. 1970); 28 U.S. C.A., §1391. See, as to *transnational* corporations: Henn, *Corporations* 28–31 (2d ed., 1986; casebook).

109. *Restatement, Conflict of Laws,* §41 comment (d); Puerto Rico v. Russell and Co., 288 U.S. 476, 482; 53 S. Ct. 447; 77 L. Ed. 903 (1933).

110. Thomas v. Board of Trustees of Ohio State University, 195 U.S. 207; 25 S. Ct. 24; 49 L. Ed. 160 (1904).

111. *Re* Lone Star Shipbuilding Co., 6 F.2d 192 (2d Cir. 1925).

112. Fl. St. § 617.1623 (eff. July 1, 1991), Fla. 1990 Sess. L., Chap. 90–179, § 109 (eff. July 1, 1990).

113. *See, generally,* Goodrich, *Conflict of Laws* (3d ed. 1949).

114. N.Y. N-P-C Law, §402(3).

115. *See,* Canal Bank and Trust Co. v. Greco, 177 La. 507; 148 S. 693 (1933); Estes v. Bank of Walnut Grove, 172 Miss. 499; 159 S. 104 (1935); N.Y. N-P-C Law, §801(6); Ohio Rev. Code, §1701.69(B)(2).

116. Fla. St., §617.0501.

117. Fla. Stat §617.0502.

19

INCORPORATION: ARTICLES AND PROCEDURES

§205. PREPARATION OF ARTICLES (CERTIFICATE) OF INCORPORATION

Incorporation documents are called by different names in different states. In most states the term *Articles of Incorporation* is used.[1] In some states the term is *Certificate of Incorporation*.[2] A few states utilize special kinds of documents, such as *Articles of Organizations* in Massachusetts, *Articles of Agreement* in New Hampshire, and *Charter of Incorporation* in Tennessee.[3]

The articles of incorporation should be prepared by the attorney for the organizers. He usually becomes the attorney for the corporation, at least at first. Use of the widely advertised "do it yourself" forms sold in some states is very unwise and likely to produce trouble for the corporation.

As with all kinds of forms, reference should be made to form books, but the draft of the form actually to be used should be adapted to the particular case under consideration. Never slavishly copy forms.

Preparation of the articles is a cooperative action. The organizers tell the attorney what they propose to do, who is going to sign the certificate, and so forth. He then drafts the set of articles, and submits it to the organizers for approval. When they have approved it, especially its purpose clause, he puts it into clean, final form, ready for their signatures.

Form. The form of the certificate is determined, in outline, by the provisions of the state's nonprofit corporations statute. As has been pointed out before, this form is not clearly defined in many states. Where no separate nonprofit corporations statute exists, the general corporation statute is followed.[4] In such cases, the certificate differs from the ordinary stock corporation certificate only insofar as the statute directs. Usually this means only that a statement of the nonprofit nature of the corporation must be included, and that provisions regarding capital stock and the division of dividends should be omitted. A few states now use, and provide, "official" forms.

Consents. In addition, a form for the consents of the affected governmental authorities sometimes must be annexed to the certificate, as described in Chapter 13, above. If more than one consent is required, a form must be added for each.

Affidavit of no previous application. In some states the attorney must add a personal affidavit that no previous application for this incorporation has been made; or, if one has been made, why it was not approved, and how the present application has corrected any deficiency in the rejected application.[5]

Language. Use of English in drafting the certificate is compulsory in all the states.[6]

In some states, the name of the organization need not be in English. But if a foreign language is used for the name, an affidavit explaining its meaning should accompany the certificate.[7] In either case, English letters or characters must be used.

The certificate must be worded in reasonably clear and understandable language.

Many useful hints for the preparation, filing, and maintenance of legal documents, such as certificates of incorporation, are given in such standard reference books as Prentice-Hall, Inc., *The Corporate Secretary's Handbook*[8] and Miller, *Manual and Guide for the Corporate Secretary.*[9]

Corporation Service Companies, in New York City and elsewhere, will prepare and file articles in Delaware, inexpensively and quickly.

§206. CONTENTS OF THE CERTIFICATE OF INCORPORATION

Although there is some variation in the form prescribed by states for the certificate of incorporation, this variation is surprisingly small. Usually the chief difference is in the minimum number of incorporators required. In many states one-man incorporation now is allowed.[10] In some states the minimum is three (3) incorporators (signers). In some states the minimum is seven (7). Other differences are in the titles of the approving agencies or in the procedures for filing the certificate.

In almost all the states, the essentials of a certificate (articles) of incorporation are the following:

1. Title (*e.g., Articles or Certificate of Incorporation*).
2. Name and number of the statute under which incorporation is sought.
3. Name of the corporation.
4. Purpose clause.
5. Statement of nonprofit nature of the corporation.

6. Statement barring "prohibited" (self-serving) transactions [necessary, in order to obtain tax exemption].

7. Locality where corporate activities are to be conducted.

8. City, town, or village (and county) where the principal corporation office is to be located.

9. Number of directors or trustees, or a stated maximum and minimum number (usually at least three).

10. Names and residence addresses of the persons who are to be the directors until the first annual meeting (same number as that stated in item 8).

11. Statement (in some states) that all the subscribers to the certificate are of legal age (over 21 in some states; over 18 in some, such as New York and North Carolina), that two-thirds of them are citizens of the United States, and that at least one of the directors named is a citizen of the United States and a resident of the states. [Incorporation by *one* incorporator now is allowed in New York, North Carolina, and some other states.[11]]

12. Statement that the corporation shall (or, shall not) have members; shall be public benefit (or, mutual benefit) in nature; and how its assets shall be distributed on dissolution; also, for religious corporations a statement of religious nature. [These requirements are stated to be "required" in the Revised Model Nonprofit Corporation Act (of the A.B.A.) (1986 Exposure Draft) §2.02, Official Comment.] While these are not yet widely required, they are very desirable.

13. Name and address of the designated Agent for Service of Process.

14. Signatures, addresses, and (in some states) acknowledgments (notary's statement that each signer swore or affirmed that he signed in the presence of the notary, and that the notary knew him to be the signer). [Usually at least five or seven signatures.]

15. Approval statement and signature from each governmental agency whose approval is required (if any are required). Detailed provisions are found in some states.[12]

16. Attorney's Statement of "no previous application" [in some states].

17. [In some states.] Designation of the secretary of state as the corporation's agent for the service of legal process against the corporation.

Note. Even under the newer statutes (*e.g.*, N.Y. N-P-C Law §402) most of these requirements are continued.

§207. EXECUTION OF THE CERTIFICATE (ARTICLES)

When the certificate is in final form, each incorporator must sign it. In some states the signing must be notarized; *e.g.*, signed before a notary. His signature must be acknowledged by him, to the notary.[13] The notary then fills in and signs the form of acknowledgment provided for each incorporator. One form of acknowledgment can be used for all the acknowledgments, or separate forms can be used.

In order to avoid all uncertainty, an outside notary should be used, even though one of the incorporators himself is a notary.

Acknowledgments may be taken by persons other than notaries, including judges, county clerks, mayors, military officers (for military personnel), and ambassadors; consuls, and local authorities in foreign nations. State statutes usually set forth detailed provisions as to who may take such acknowledgments.[14]

The notary must know the signer personally, or have reasonably good evidence of his identity.

Next, the attorney signs and has his own signature witnessed. This is not required in some states.

Then the certificate is submitted for approval by the appropriate governmental approving agencies (each in turn). If approval must be given by a judge, submission is made to the judge's clerk. If a commissioner must approve, a submission is made to the proper clerk in the commission office. In many cases, a special part (e.g., the "motions" part) of the court or commission is devoted to handling such applications.[15]

§208. FILING FEES

In Florida in 1985 the filing fee for articles of incorporation or any amendment thereto, or merger or other document for nonprofit corporations was $30 for filing and $5 in each case for a certified copy, and $15 for filing papers relating to dissolution or amendment or merger. [Fla. Stat. §617.015.] Filing fees change almost annually nowadays; invariably become higher.

Floridian nonprofits have experienced rapid increases in filing fees for corporations. In 1992, the filing fee for registration with the state was $61.25. In 1993, the fee was raised to $200. The 1992 summer tax bill raised the fee, which excludes some religious and educational organizations. Other nonprofits must pay the full $200 fee. The rate increase is expected to generate about $47 million in new revenues for Florida, which is in a financial crisis. Small neighborhood groups, with small budgets, are especially burdened. Senator Curt Kiser, R-Palm Harbor, intended to propose a bill during the Legislature's session in the fall of 1993 to return most small nonprofit groups to the old $61.25 fee.[16]

In some states a flat fee of $50 is charged, while in some the fee amounts to $11 ($5 to the county clerk, $5 to the secretary of state for filing, and $1 to him for recording).[17] In some the filing fee for a nonprofit corporation is $25, and $50 for a business corporation.[18]

In California the filing fee for a not-for-profit corporation in the 1980s was as low as $20.[19] It is currently (1994) $30.

The check for the filing fee ordinarily should be drawn to the order of the department of state. It must be certified, or a money order may be used, in some states.

No taxes apply to the organization of a nonprofit corporation, as they do to a business corporation, on which both state and federal organization taxes are imposed.

Under New York's statute, existing corporations had to file statements as to their proper classification by September 1, 1973 (filing fee was $10).[20]

§209. FILING THE CERTIFICATE (ARTICLES)

The fully executed articles are sent, together with all the annexed affidavits and approvals, and with the filing fee check attached, to the secretary of state, or to the equivalent designated office, such as the Recorder of Deeds in Washington, D.C. Ordinarily only one original need be sent. The attorney sends it with a brief covering letter. Some states require more than one copy.

In a few cases, it is good policy to send record copies to the interested approving agencies. Usually this is not required. In a few states (*e.g.*, New Jersey), a copy must be filed in the county clerk's office.

When the secretary of state (through the corporation division of his department) approves the certificate by signature or stamping and by indexing (numbering), the corporate existence begins.[21] In some states (*e.g.*, New Jersey) the secretary first asks a department of institutions and agencies for approval.

Notice of acceptance and filing usually is given in a receipt-acknowledgment-certificate mailed to the attorney. The receipt-certificate is the usual *prima facie* evidence of the incorporation. It should be fastened into the corporation's minute book together with a copy of the certificate of incorporation.

The secretary of state in some states has the original certificate photostated and sends a copy to the clerk of the county in which the corporation's office is located. He also usually sends about $5 out of the filing fee as the filing fee for the county clerk's filing.[22]

The county clerk puts his copy in the county office or county court files. This, or the copy in the secretary-of-state's office, is the *public record* of the incorporation which may be inspected by interested persons. Interested persons can obtain certified copies (usually photocopies) by applying to the county clerk's or secretary of state's office. The usual fee is about 50¢ per page.

Reincorporation Requirement

Older nonprofit organizations, in Florida, were incorporated by a judge's ruling. The state legislature recently required that all nonprofit organizations, incorporated before Sept. 1, 1959, reincorporate through the Secretary of State's office. Any organization that missed the deadline faced dissolution.[23]

§210. CORPORATION-SERVICE-COMPANIES

In some major cities there are businesses that serve as corporation agents for filing documents and other administrative work. Thus, the Prentice-Hall Corporation Service, or Corporation Trust Company, and others, maintain offices in state capitals for such work. In Wilmington, Delaware there are several such "services," because of that state's popularity with business corporation management people. These companies provide low service fees, almost instant reservation-of-name service, resident agent service (for process), etc.

Look in the yellow pages of your telephone directory for the names of corporation service companies.

You can incorporate in some states (*e.g.*, Delaware) without ever going there. But remember that other people know that fact too.

§211. FORMS OF CERTIFICATES FOR INCORPORATION

The following forms of documents and certificates (articles) for incorporation are generally suitable for use in any state. However, it must be remembered that there are some differences in statutory provisions. Local corporation statutes should be consulted before a certificate is drafted.[24] Some statutes provide official forms.

For purposes of comparison, several certificates are here provided.

A copy of a labor union constitution may be obtained by writing to the National Union of Hospital and Health Care Employees (AFL-C10), 330 West 42 Street, New York, N.Y. 10036. Call 1-800-223-1199.

FORM NO. 75

Inquiry as to Availability
of
Corporate Name [Letterhead]

Secretary of State   [Date]
  State of
Corporations Division
  [Address]

Dear Sir:

    Please inform me, by return mail in the enclosed prepaid self-addressed return envelope, of the availability of the following Nonprofit Corporation name(s), and oblige:

> Name 1, Inc.
> Name 2, Inc.
> Name 3, Inc.

    With thanks for your courtesy,

[Encl.]   Yours truly,
                                                        (Signature)

    [Note: Usually the answer will be *one* name (the first one available from the list given) for use by the inquirer.]

FORM NO. 76

Approval of Incorporation
by
Outside Authority

(Political Club)

_____(name)_____, duly elected Chairman of the _____
County Committee of the _____ Party of _____,
    hereby approve the incorporation of _____(name)_____ Corporation
    as a _____(describe)_____.

                          Date _____ 19_____
                          Address _____
                          Signature_____

FORM NO. 77

Notice of Application for Incorporation
(to Attorney General)

_____ Court

Address _____

In the Application
of the Not-for-Profit Corporation
named _____ _____
(name)
for approval and filing.

Please take notice that the attached Certificate of Incorporation will be
presented to Judge _____, at _____ Court, on
(name)   (name)
_____ at the chambers of the named judge,
(date)
at _____.
(address)

_____
(name)

_____
(name)
Attorney for Corp.

FORM NO. 78

Affidavit of No Previous Application

_____
(address)

(Title of Corporate
Application)

In the _____ Court, ___(attorney's name)___, being first duly
sworn, do make affidavit that he is the attorney for the incorporators of the
_____ Corporation signatory to the attached Certificate of Incor-
(name)
poration, and that no previous application for approval of this incorporation
has been made to any other Judge of the _____ Court.

_____
(Signature)

[Notary's Concurrence]

FORM NO. 79

Approval of Incorporation
by Judge

Date _____, 19_____.

_____ Court

_____(name)_____, Judge of _____ Court of ____(county)____, ____(state)____

____(district)_____, hereby approves the attached (or, foregoing) Certificate of Incorporation of the _____ Corporation.

_____ _____
(Signature)

FORM NO. 80

Certificate of Incorporation (New York)
(Schematic)

[*Note.* This form follows the provisions of the New York Statute, N.Y. N-P-C Law §401.]

Certificate of Incorporation
    of _____ Corporation
Under Section 402
    of the
New York Not-for-Profit Corporation Law   (county)   (state)
    1. The name of the corporation is_____.
It is a corporation as defined by the N.Y. statute.
    2. This corporation is not organized for pecuniary profit, and no part of its net earnings or income shall inure to the benefit of any officer or member or employee or persons. [Also, the I.R.S. "prohibited transactions" clause.]
    3. The purpose(s) of this corporation shall be ____(state them)____.
    4. This corporation shall be a (Type. . . .) corporation under Section 201 of the New York N-P-C Law.
    5. The principal office of the corporation shall be located in the (village, town, or city) of _____, State of New York.
    6. The activities of this corporation will be conducted principally in the territory comprised of _____
    7 The initial directors are to be
        (1) _____ ; _____
        (2) _____ ; _____
        (3) _____ ; _____
    8. The duration of this corporation shall be _____ years, (or _____ perpetual).
    9. The post office address to which notices may be sent by the Secretary-of-State will be _____.

The secretary of state is designated as an agent for service of legal process on the corporation.

10. The designated agent for service of process and notices for this corporation is _____(name)_____ of _____(address)_____

11. Approval of this Certificate of Incorporation by _____, as required by law, is attached herewith [attach consents or approvals as required by N.Y. N-P-C Law §404]; *or*, [if no approvals are required for this particular activity, simply say]: No approval of this certificate by any authority is required by law.

12. All of the subscribers to this certificate are of full legal age, and at least (2, 3) of them are citizens of the United States, and at least one of them is a resident of New York State, and at least one of the directors named is a citizen of the United States, and a resident of New York State.

In Witness Whereof, the undersigned incorporators have signed and acknowledged this certificate and file it in duplicate.

Date _____, 19_____.

(1) <u>Signature_____Address_____</u>

(2) <u>(name typed)_____(typed)_____</u>

(3) _____

[Acknowledgment]

FORM NO. 81

Certificate of Adaptation to Revised Statute

[*Note.* This is for *continuing* an existing corporation, under such enactments as the drastic revision of New York's statutes into new form. See, N.Y. N-P-C Law §113. *Add this certificate* to the preceding (old; existing) form (80).] [See footnote 19.]

Certificate of Type
of
Non-for-Profit Corporation

_____(name)_____ Corporation, a nonprofit corporation duly incorporated on _____(date)_____, in (New York) State under the said name by filing with the Secretary of State (or, Special Act, or etc.).

FORM NO. 82

Articles of Incorporation (Florida)
(Free Library)
Articles of Incorporation
of
_____, Inc.

The undersigned by these Articles associate themselves for the purpose of forming a corporation not for profit under Chapter 617, Florida Statutes, and certify as follows:

I.
Name

The name of the corporation, hereinafter called the "Corporation," shall be _____, Inc., and its principal place of business shall be in the City of _____, _____ County, Florida.

II.
Purpose

A. The purposes for which the Corporation is to be organized are exclusively for free library, educational, charitable, and scientific purposes within the meaning of Section 501(c)(3) of the Internal Revenue Code of 1986 and to that end to take and hold by bequest, devise, gift, grant, purchase, lease or otherwise, any property, real, personal, tangible or intangible, or any undivided interest therein, without limitation as to amount or value; to sell, convey, or otherwise dispose of any such property and to invest, reinvest, or deal with the principal or the income thereof in such manner as, in the judgment of the Directors, will best promote the purposes of the Corporation without limitation, except such limitations, if any, as may be contained in the instrument under which such property is received, this Certificate of Incorporation, the bylaws of the Corporation, or any laws applicable thereto. To enhance the cultural, educational and information environment of the community by providing library services, facilities, and collections beyond that provided for by the traditional tax base funding of the _____ Public Library.

- To provide access to library facilities throughout greater _____ _____ neighborhoods for all people.
- To provide and maintain special collections of rare books, art, collectibles, media, historic documents, equipment, etc. for people with special cultural, informational and educational needs.
- To provide library services to the deaf, blind, handicapped, and economically disadvantaged.

- To provide cultural enrichment to the community through special programs.

III.
Registered Agent

The registered office of the Corporation and its registered agent to accept service of process within the State is _____, located at _____, _____, _____ County, Florida 33516.

IV.
Limitations and Restrictions

A. No part of the net earnings of the Corporation shall inure to the benefit of any member, Director, officer of the Corporation, or any private individual (except that reasonable compensation may be paid for services rendered to or for the Corporation affecting one or more of its purposes), and no member, Director, officer of the Corporation, or any private individual shall be entitled to share in the distribution of any of the corporate assets on dissolution of the Corporation. No substantial part of the activities of the Corporation shall be the carrying on of propaganda, or otherwise attempting to influence legislation, and the Corporation shall not participate in or intervene in (including the publication or distribution of statements) any political campaign on behalf of any candidate for public office.

B. Notwithstanding any other provision of these Articles, the Corporation shall not conduct or carry on any activities not permitted to be conducted or carried on by an organization exempt from federal income tax under Section 501(c)(3) of the Internal Revenue Code and its Regulations as they now exist or as they may hereafter be amended, or by an organization, contributions to which are deductible under Section 170(c)(2) of such Code and Regulations as they now exist or as they may hereafter be amended.

C. Upon the dissolution of the Corporation or the winding up of its affairs, the assets of the Corporation remaining after payment of all costs and expenses of such dissolution shall be distributed exclusively to library, charitable, religious, scientific, literary, or educational organizations which would then qualify under the provisions of Section 501(c)(3) of the Internal Revenue Code and its Regulations as they now exist or as they may hereafter be amended, and none of the assets will be distributed to any member, officer or director of the Corporation or to any private individual.

V.
Term

This Corporation shall exist perpetually, unless terminated by due process of law.

VI.
Members

The members of the Corporation shall constitute all persons hereinafter named as subscribers and directors and such other persons as, from time to time hereafter, may become members, in the manner provided in the Bylaws of the Corporation or as may be elected by the members at each annual meeting.

VII.
Subscribers

The names and residences of the subscribers to these Articles of Incorporation are as follows:

_____   (Address) _____
                                      _____, Florida 33516

_____   (Address) _____
                                      _____, Florida 33546

_____   (Address) _____
                                      _____, Florida 33516

_____   (Address) _____
                                      _____, Florida 33516

VIII.
Directors

A. The affairs, property and business of the Corporation shall be managed and controlled by a Board of Directors consisting of the number of Directors determined by the Bylaws, but not less than three Directors, and in the absence of such determination, the Board shall consist of three Directors.

B. Directors of the Corporation shall, at the annual meeting, be elected and hold office in the manner determined by the Bylaws of the Corporation. Directors may be removed and vacancies on the Board of Directors shall be filled in the manner provided in the Bylaws.

C. The names and addresses of the members of the first Board of Directors who shall hold office until their successors are elected and have qualified, or until removed, are as follows:

_____   (Address) _____
                                      _____, Florida 33516

_____ (Address) _____
_____, Florida 33546

_____ (Address) _____
_____, Florida 33516

_____ (Address) _____
_____, Florida 33516

IX.
Board of Honorary Trustees

A Board of Honorary Trustees composed of not more than 100 prominent men and women may be selected in the manner and for such duties as shall be provided and set forth in the bylaws, provided, however, that said Board of Honorary Trustees shall constitute only an advisory board to consult and advise with said Board of Directors.

X.
Officers

A. The affairs of the Corporation shall be administered by the officers designated in the Bylaws of the Corporation.

B. The officers of the Corporation shall be the President, Vice President, Secretary, Treasurer (which may be combined with another office as allowed by law), and such other officers as may be provided in the Bylaws of the Corporation.

C. The officers shall be elected by the Board of Directors at its first meeting following the annual meeting of the members of the Corporation and shall serve at the pleasure of the Board of Directors.

D. The names of the officers who shall serve until their successors are elected by the Board of Directors are as follows:

_____ President
_____ Vice President
_____ Secretary/Treasurer

XI
Bylaws

The Board of Directors of this Corporation shall make, adopt, alter, amend and repeal such Bylaws of the Corporation for the conduct of the business of the Corporation and the carrying out of its purposes as such Directors may deem necessary from time to time. The Bylaws may be altered, amended or repealed at any meeting of members of the Corporation in the manner provided in the Bylaws.

XII.
Amendment

The Articles of Incorporation may be amended by a two-thirds vote of the membership of the Corporation at a regular meeting or at a duly called special meeting of the membership upon notice given, as provided by the Bylaws, of intention to submit such amendments to the membership of the Corporation.

XIII.
Defense and Indemnification of
Officers and Directors

The Corporation shall defend, indemnify and hold harmless, every registered agent, director or officer and his or her heirs, personal representatives and administrators against liability and against expenses reasonably incurred by him or her in connection with any action, suit or proceeding to which he or she may be made a party by reason of his or her having been a director or officer of this corporation, except in relation to matters as to which he or she shall be finally adjudged in such action, suit or proceeding to be liable for willful misconduct. The foregoing rights shall be exclusive of other rights to which he or she may be entitled.

IN WITNESS WHEREOF, the undersigned subscribers have executed these Articles of Incorporation this _____ day of _____, 19 _____.

STATE OF FLORIDA
COUNTY OF _____

BEFORE ME, a Notary Public authorized to take acknowledgments in the County and State aforesaid, personally appeared, and to me known to be the persons described in and who executed the foregoing Articles of Incorporation, and they acknowledged before me that they executed the same.

WITNESS my hand and official seal in the County and State last aforesaid, this _____ day of _____, A.D. 19 _____.

_____
Notary Public
My Commission Expires:

(*Notary Seal*)

CERTIFICATE DESIGNATING PLACE OF BUSINESS OR DOMICILE FOR THE SERVICE OF PROCESS WITHIN THIS STATE, NAMING AGENT UPON WHOM PROCESS MAY BE SERVED.

_____

In pursuance of Chapter 48.091, Florida Statutes, the following is submitted, in compliance with said Act:

First—That _____,
desiring to organize under the laws of the State of _____
with its principal office, as indicated in the articles of incorporation at City of _____, County of _____, State of _____ has
named _____
located at _____
        (street address and number of building; Post Office Box address not acceptable)
City of _____, County of _____, State of Florida, as its agent to accept service of process within this state.

–Acceptance by Agent–
ACKNOWLEDGMENT: (MUST BE SIGNED BY DESIGNATED AGENT)

Having been named to accept service of process for the above stated corporation, at place designated in this certificate, I hereby accept to act in this capacity, and agree to comply with the provision of said Act relative to keeping open said office.

_____
                                    Signature

FORM NO. 83

Certificate Certifying a Copy
of Articles of Incorporation (Florida)

[This usually is a decorative certificate, suitable for framing. *See eg.* Form No. 87.]

STATE OF FLORIDA
Department of State

I certify that the attached is a true and correct copy of the Articles of Incorporation of
_____, INCORPORATED
filed on March 11, 198X.
The Charter Number for this corporation is 751485.

Given under my hand and the
Great Seal of the State of Florida,
at Tallahassee, the Capital, this the
11th day of March, 198_____.

George Firestone
Secretary of State
CORP 104 Rev. 5-79

FORM NO. 84

Articles of Incorporation
(Oklahoma)

ARTICLES OF INCORPORATION

(CHARITABLE, BENEVOLENT, RELIGIOUS, EDUCATIONAL,
OR SCIENTIFIC PURPOSE)

STATE OF OKLAHOMA   )
) ss.   Fee: $25.00
COUNTY OF _____)

TO SECRETARY OF STATE OF THE STATE OF OKLAHOMA:
We, the undersigned trustees or directors

NAME	NO. & STREET	CITY & STATE
_____	_____	_____
_____	_____	_____
_____	_____	_____

being persons legally competent to enter into contracts, for the purpose
of forming a corporation under the laws of the State of Oklahoma (18
O.S. 1961 SECS. 541-594), do hereby adopt the following Articles of
Incorporation:

ARTICLE ONE
The name of this corporation is: _____
_____

ARTICLE TWO
The address of its registered office in the City State of Oklahoma is ___
_____ in the City of _____ County of
          (Street Address)
_____ and the name of its Registered Agent at such
address is _____
_____

ARTICLE THREE
The duration of the corporation is _____
_____

ARTICLE FOUR
The purpose or purposes for which the corporation is formed are:
A. ___(Specify the Category as either Religious, Charitable, Educational,
Benevolent, or Scientific _____;)

B.   (Set forth the Purpose or Purposes of the Particular Corporation):

_____

ARTICLE FIVE

A.   The corporation is not organized for pecuniary profit nor shall it have any power to issue certificates of stock or declare dividends, and no part of its net earnings shall inure to the benefit of any member, director, trustee, or individual. The balance, if any, of all money received by the corporation from its operations, after the payment in full of all debts and obligations of the corporation of whatsoever kind and nature, shall be used and distributed exclusively for carrying out only the purpose or purposes of the corporation particularly set forth in Article Four hereof.

B.   Upon the dissolution of the corporation, the board of trustees shall, after paying or making provision for the payment of all of the liabilities of the corporation, dispose of all of the assets of the corporation exclusively for the purposes of the corporation in such manner, or to such organization or organizations organized and operated exclusively for charitable, educational, religious, literary, or scientific purposes as shall at the time qualify as an exempt organization or organizations under Section 501(c)(3) of the Internal Revenue Code of 1986, or the corresponding provision of any future United States Internal Revenue Law, as the board of trustees shall determine. Any such assets not so disposed of shall be disposed of by the district court of the County in which the principal office of the corporation is then located, exclusively for such purposes or to such organization or organizations, as said court shall determine, which are organized and operated exclusively for such purposes.

ARTICLE SIX

The number of directors to be elected at the first meeting of the trustees is: _____.

(TRUSTEES SIGN BELOW)

_____

_____

_____

_____

_____

STATE OF OKLAHOMA   )
)   SS.
COUNTY OF _____   )

        Before me, _____ a Notary Public in and for said county and State, on this _____ day of _____, 19_____, personally appeared, _____

to me known to be the identical persons who executed the foregoing Articles of Incorporation and acknowledged to be that they executed the same as their free and voluntary act and deed for the uses and purposes therein set forth.

IN WITNESS WHEREOF, I have here unto set my hand and seal the day and year above written. _____
Notary Public

(SEAL)

My Commission expires _____

CERTIFICATE TO BE FILLED OUT
BY PRESIDING OFFICER

I hereby certify that the within named Directors or Trustees were duly elected at a meeting held for said purpose at _____ on the _____ day of _____, 19 _____.

_____
Presiding Officer

(SEAL)

My Commission expires _____

STATE OF OKLAHOMA   )
) SS.
COUNTY OF _____   )

_____, of lawful age, being first duly sworn, says; that he is the presiding officer above named, that he has read the foregoing certificate and knows the contents thereof, and that the facts set forth therein are true, as he verily believes.

_____
Presiding Officer

Subscribed and sworn to before me this _____ day of _____, 19 _____.

_____
Notary Public

(SEAL)

My Commission expires _____

FORM NO. 85

Articles of Incorporation
of a Foundation
(Washington State)

Articles of Incorporation
of
_____ University Foundation

The undersigned persons, acting as the incorporators of a corporation under the provisions of the Washington Non-Profit Corporations Act, adopt the following Articles of Incorporation.

Article I
Name

The name of this private, nonprofit corporation shall be THE _____ UNIVERSITY FOUNDATION (thereinafter called the "Foundation").

Article II.
Duration

The duration of the Foundation shall be perpetual. Upon dissolution, the Board of Trustees of the Foundation shall conclude its affairs, pay or make adequate provision for payment of all of its liabilities and obligations, and distribute the remaining assets to Washington State University. In the event _____ University is not then in existence, said assets shall be distributed to an organization or organizations organized and operated exclusively for charitable, educational or scientific purposes as shall at that time qualify as an exempt organization under Section 501(c)(3) of the Internal Revenue Code of 1986 and any amendments thereto, as the Board of Trustees shall determine.

Article III
Purpose

The purposes for which this Corporation is formed are as follows:

A.   This Corporation is organized and shall operate exclusively to receive, hold, invest, and administer funds and property and to make expenditures to or for the benefit of _____ University (an institution of higher education and an agency of the _____ of _____), thereby promoting, supporting, developing, and extending the educational undertakings of

_____ University; and, in furtherance thereof, in support and conduct any and all scientific, literary, charitable and educational activities permitted both to an organization exempt under Section 501(c)(3) of the Internal Revenue Code, or acts amendatory thereof or supplementary thereto, and by chapter 24.03 of the Revised Code of Washington, as now or hereafter amended.

B.   To that end, it shall be within the purpose of the Foundation to conduct such activities and to operate in such a manner as shall be designed or intended to facilitate or enhance the educational, cultural, living, and operational conditions at _____ University; to provide support for, maintaining, enlarging, and extending the curricula, services, faculty, staff, and the real or personal properties of _____ University; and, to provide financial or other assistance to the students, faculty, and staff of _____ University in their efforts to acquire new knowledge and to extend the educational services and endeavors of _____ University.

C.   The Foundation is intended to be an organization which is exempt from Federal income tax under Section 501(c)(3) of the Internal Revenue Code of 1986 and which is an organization described in Section 509(a)(3) of said Internal Revenue Code. Said foundation is organized exclusively for charitable, religious, educational, and scientific purposes, including, for such purposes, the making of distributions to organizations that qualify as exempt organizations under section 501(c)(3) of the Internal Revenue Code of 1986 (or the corresponding provision of any future United States Internal Revenue Law). All terms and provisions of these Articles and all operations of this Corporation shall be constructed, applied, and carried out in accordance with such intent.

Article IV
Powers

The Foundation shall have, in furtherance of its foregoing purposes, all of the powers and authority allowed to a nonprofit corporation under the laws of the State of Washington (Chapter 24.03 of the Revised Code of Washington, as now or hereafter amended), but specifically to include the power to:

A.   Design and implement such programs and procedures among all the _____ University constituents as to persuade continuous and special philanthropic support and benefactions in furtherance of the purpose of the Foundation and for the exclusive benefit of the University.

B.   Apply for, accept, hold, and administer the corpus and income of any donation, grant, devise, or bequest, or any part thereof, in such manner as may have been stipulated or provided in the instrument creating such donation, grant devise, or bequest.

C.   Accept, hold, administer, invest, and disburse such funds and properties of any lawful kind or character as from time to time may be given to it by persons, corporations, or governmental agencies absolutely or in trust, as the case may be; employ and retain proper employees, agents, experts, consultants, accountants, advisors, and investment counselors for the proper accepting, holding, administering, investing, and disbursing of proper funds and properties; and in general to do all things that may appear lawful and necessary and useful in accomplishing these purposes.

D.   Apply for and aid in the processing of applications for patents and copyrights; receive or purchase patents and copyrights, inventions, discoveries and processes; hold, manage, use, and develop the same; sell, license or otherwise dispose of the same; and collect royalties thereon.

E.   Sell, mortgage, pledge, lease, or exchange all or any part of the real or personal property or funds of the Foundation, unless otherwise specifically provided in its creating instrument, at such prices and upon such terms and conditions as it may deem best; and invest or reinvest its funds in any such lawful loans or securities or in any such real or personal property as it may deem suitable for the investment of trust funds, whether or not such investments are approved as investments for Trustees under the laws of the State of Washington.

F.   No part of the net earnings of the Foundation shall inure to the benefit of or be distributable to any person having a personal and private interest in the activities of the Foundation, but the Foundation shall be authorized and empowered to pay reasonable compensation for services rendered and to make payments and distributions in furtherance of the purposes set forth in Article IV hereof. No substantial part of the activities of the Foundation shall be the carrying on of propaganda or otherwise attempting to influence legislation, and the Foundation shall not participate in, or intervene in (including the publishing or distributing of statements), any political campaign on behalf of any candidate for public office.

G.   Notwithstanding any other provisions of these Articles of Incorporation to the contrary the Foundation shall not carry on any activities outside the scope of the purposes set forth in Article III and not permitted to be carried on:
    1. by an organization exempt from Federal income tax under Section 501(c)(3) of the Internal Revenue Code of 1986 and any amendments thereto; or
    2. by an organization, contributions to which are deductible under Section 170(c) (2) of the Internal Revenue Code of 1986 and any amendments thereto.

H..   In addition to devising, directing, and conducting the affairs of the Foundation, the Corporation and its Trustees also serve to advise and counsel the President of the University and the President of the Foundation on devising, directing, and conducting the _____ University development program.

Article V
Membership

The general members of the Foundation shall be the members of the Visiting Committee of _____ University who are from time to time appointed to the Visiting Committee by the President of the University. The term of a general member shall continue as long as such individual is a member of the Visiting Committee as specified in the Bylaws of the Foundation.

Other persons by virtue of their offices shall be general members of the Foundation as specified in the Bylaws. In addition, other persons, independently or by virtue of their offices, may be selected for *ex-officio* membership by a majority of general members. *Ex-officio* members shall be accorded full rights and privileges of Foundation membership, as specified in the Bylaws of the Foundation.

There shall be a category of general members without right to vote but with the privilege to attend all meetings of the general membership to be known as general member emeritus as specified in the Bylaws of the Foundation.

In addition, there shall be special members of the Foundation, named through resolution adopted by the Board of Trustees, who shall not be entitled to vote. The classification of special memberships and their rights and privileges shall be as specified in the Bylaws of the Foundation.

Article VI
Trustees

The initial board of directors shall consist of five Trustees, who shall manage the affairs of the Foundation according to provisions of the ByLaws. The names, offices, and addresses of the initial Board of Trustees shall be as follows:

Name	Office	Address
	Chairman of the Board	
	Recording Secretary	
	Treasurer	

Name	Office	Address
	Ex-Officio Trustee	
	Executive Secretary	

The term of the first Trustees shall be until the first annual meeting of the membership of the Foundation and until their successors are elected.

The appointment, qualifications, manner of election and removal, number, powers and duties, terms of office, time and place of meetings, and voting rights of the members of the Board of Trustees, including Trustees designated as emeriti and ex-officio, shall be as provided in the Bylaws of the Foundation.

The Trustees of the Foundation shall receive no compensation for their services as Trustees.

The Board of Trustees may delegate any or all of its authority and powers to any committee, as specified in the Bylaws, insofar as is allowed by law.

Article VII
Bylaws

The authority to make, alter, amend, or repeal the Bylaws of the Foundation is vested in the Trustees and general membership subject to right of the general membership to repeal or amend any alterations made by the Trustees. The Bylaws may contain any provision for the regulation and management of the affairs of the Foundation not inconsistent with law or these Articles of Incorporation.

Article VIII
Registered Office and Registered Agent

The registered office of the Foundation's registered agent, unless changed by resolution of the Board of Trustees, shall be:

> Office of University Development
> Administration Bldg.
> _____ University
> _____, WA

The name and address of the Foundation's registered agent, unless changed by resolution of the Board of Trustees, shall be:

> Office of University Development
> Administration Bldg.
> _____ University
> _____, WA

Article IX
Incorporators

The name and post office address of each of the incorporators are as follows:

Name   *Address*

IN WITNESS whereof the incorporators hereinabove named have hereunto put their hands in duplicate this _____ day of _____, 19 _____.

_____   _____
_____   _____
_____   _____
_____   _____

Signatures

FORM NO. 86

Articles of Incorporation
of a Local
Fund-Raising Foundation

[For assisting a nonprofit organization formed for training divorced or widowed women (and others) for self-supporting employment.]

Articles of Incorporation
of
Learning Center Foundation, Inc.

We the undersigned natural persons of the age of 18 years or more, acting as incorporators for the purpose of creating a Nonprofit Corporation under the laws of the State of Florida, as contained in Chapter 617 of the Florida Statutes, and the several amendments thereto, do hereby set forth:

1. The name of the Corporation is _____ LEARNING CENTER FOUNDATION, INC.
2. The period of duration of the Corporation shall be perpetual.
3. The purposes for which the Corporation is to be formed are exclusively charitable, to wit:

To accept, hold, invest, reinvest, and administer any gifts, bequests,

(a) devises, benefits of trusts (but not to act as trustee of any trust), and property of any sort, without limitation as to amount or value, and to use, disburse, or donate the income or principal thereof for exclusively charitable purposes.

(b) To give, convey, or assign any of its property outright, or upon lawful terms regarding the use thereof, to other organizations, provided that:

(1) such organizations engage in activities which allow the charitable, scientific and educational purposes of _____ LEARNING CENTER, INC., to be accomplished; (2) transfers of property to such organizations shall, to the extent then permitted under the

statutes of the United States Government, be exempt from gift, succession, inheritance, estate, or death taxes (by whatever name called) imposed by the United States Government; and (3) such organizations shall, to the extent then permitted under the statutes of the United States Government, be exempt from the income taxes imposed by the United States Government.

(c) To provide funds to or for the benefit of, to help conduct and support activities which benefit, to maintain, improve, expand, advance the services of, to enhance the quality of services of, to provide funds for the buildings, facilities, equipment and administration of, to sustain, to support, to perpetuate, and to accumulate funds in perpetuity for the support of _____ LEARNING CENTER, INC., so long as it remains a "qualified organization." An organization is a qualified organization for purposes of these Articles only if it is described in Section 501(c)(3) of the Internal Revenue Code of 1986, as amended.

(d) To be operated at all times solely in connection with _____ LEARNING CENTER, INC., provided, however, if _____ LEARNING CENTER, INC., ceases to be a qualified organization, the _____ LEARNING CENTER FOUNDATION, INC., shall not operate for the benefit of or in connection with said organization but shall be operated exclusively for the benefit of and solely in connection with one or more qualified organizations as shall be selected by the Board of Directors of _____ LEARNING CENTER FOUNDATION, INC.

(e) To the extent permitted by law, to exercise its rights, powers, and privileges, to hold meetings of its Board of Directors, to have one or more offices, and to keep the books of the Corporation, in any part of _____ County.

(f) Alone or in cooperation with other persons or organizations to do any and all lawful acts and things which may be necessary, useful, suitable, or proper for the furtherance, accomplishment, or attainment of any or all of the purposes or powers of the Corporation.

4. The Corporation will be a nonmembership corporation.

5. Directors of the Corporation shall be elected in the manner provided by the Bylaws.

6. The address of the initial registered office of the Corporation is as follows:

_____ Towers

12945 _____ Boulevard

_____, Florida 34648

The name of the initial registered agent of the Corporation at the above address is _____.

7. The number of trustees constituting the initial Board of Trustees shall be three (3), and the names and addresses of the persons who are to serve as directors until the first meeting of the Corporation or until their successors are elected and qualified are:

Name	Street Address	City or Town
(President)	417 _____ Drive	_____, Florida 34616
(Secretary)	19 _____ Island	_____, Florida 34630
(Treasurer)	211 _____ Lane	_____, Florida 34640

8. The names and addresses of all the incorporators are:

Name	Street Address	City or Town
(President)	417 _____ Drive	_____, Florida 34616
(Secretary)	19 _____ Island	_____, Florida 34630
(Treasurer)	211 _____ Lane	_____, Florida 34640

9. The Corporation shall have all the powers granted corporations under the laws of the State of Florida. However, notwithstanding anything herein to the contrary, the Corporation shall exercise only such powers as are in furtherance of the exempt purpose of organizations set forth in the subsection of Section 501(c) of the Internal Revenue Code of 1986 under which the Corporation chooses to qualify for exemption, as the same now exists, or as it may be amended.

10. In the event of the dissolution of the Corporation, no member shall be entitled to any distribution or division of its remaining property or its proceeds, and the balance of all money and other property received by the Corporation from any source, after the payment of all debts and obligations of the Corporation, shall be used or distributed exclusively for purposes within the intendment of Section 501(c) of the Internal Revenue Code as the same now exists or as it may be amended.

In witness whereof we have hereunto set our hand, March 16, 19_____.

_____
(President)

_____
(Secretary)

_____
(Treasurer)

STATE OF FLORIDA

ss.

COUNTY OF _____

Before me, the undersigned authority, personally appeared _____, to me well known to be the person described in and who executed the foregoing Articles of Incorporation, and who acknowledged before me that he executed the same for the uses and purposes therein expressed.

WITNESS my hand and official seal at _____, in the County and State last aforesaid, this 25th day day of May, 19_____.

_____

NOTARY PUBLIC
My Commission Expires:

Notary Public, State of Florida
My Commission Expires Sept. 2, 19_____
Bonded through Insurance, Inc.

FORM NO. 87

Certificate of
Secretary of State as to
Articles of Incorporation (Copy)

State of Florida

Department of State

I certify that the attached is a true and correct copy of the Articles of Incorporation of   **LEARNING CENTER FOUNDATION, INC.**, a corporation organized under the Laws of the State of Florida, filed on May 30, 1989, as shown by the records of this office.

The document number of this corporation is N32559.

Given under my hand and the
Great Seal of the State of Florida,
at Tallahassee, the Capital, this the

30th   day of   May, 19■■

CR2EO22 (6-88)

Secretary of State

FORM NO. 88

Articles of Incorporation of an Unincorporated Association
(North Carolina)
Articles of Incorporation of SCRIBES

[This was an incorporation done by Oleck, who was President of SCRIBES in 1972–73]

The undersigned, acting as the present President of SCRIBES, which hitherto has been an *unincorporated* association or society of members of the legal profession in good standing who have done significant legal writing or editing in published form, and acting with the consent of the officers and directors of that association, now wishing to incorporate the said unincorporated association, does hereby state:

One. The name of the society is SCRIBES.

Two. The duration of this corporation shall be perpetual.

Three. The purposes for which this society is formed are not-for-profit, fraternal, and educational, in that:

Its objects are: (1) to promote and foster a feeling of fraternity between those who write concerning the law, and particularly between those who are members of this organization; (2) to seek to create an interest in writing about the law, substantive or procedural, about its origin, history, and philosophy, and about those who make, define, interpret, and enforce it; (3) to endeavor to foster a clear, succinct, and forcible style in legal writing, whether the writing be in the format of book, brief, annotation, article, pleading, or legal instrument; (4) to lend assistance and encouragement to those who write and to those who want to write on legal subjects; (5) to broaden the objectives of the society by the encouragement of the interchange of information among the members through educational study courses, seminars, symposiums, lectures, workshops, and conferences; and (6) to convey to the public an adequate and correct knowledge of the role of the lawyer in the community, state, and nation, and to foster in the public mind a wholesome respect for the proper enforcement of the law and for the equal administration of justice.

These objects are the same ones declared in the Constitution of this society and elaborated in the said constitution and bylaws of the society.

Four. Regular membership in this society shall be based upon qualification, in that:

Any member of the legal profession in good standing who shall have written at least one book on a legal subject which has been published, or who has written three or more articles on legal subjects which have been published in magazines or journals, or who is or has been an editor of an established legal publication, shall be eligible to membership in SCRIBES upon nomination by an existing member. Thus eligible one may be elected to membership as provided by the Bylaws.

Honorary Membership in this society shall be based upon special qualification and election, in that:

Persons of distinction in the field of legal writing and members of the legal profession of another country may be elected to Honorary Membership in SCRIBES upon a majority vote of the Board of Directors in Annual or Special Meeting. Such Honorary Members shall have no right to vote, shall pay no dues, and shall have no interest in property of SCRIBES.

Five. The method of election of officers and directors shall be that stated in the constitution and bylaws; and the original officers and directors of this corporation, as of the time of the filing of these articles of incorporation are specifically those presently in office pursuant to election under the said constitution and bylaws for the current year.

Six. The assets of this corporation, present and future, are to be devoted to not-for-profit, educational, and fraternal encouragement and improvement of good legal writing and editing, and the said assets are to continue to be devoted to such purposes if and when this society should be dissolved.

Seven. The address and initial registered office of this society shall be at Wake Forest University School of Law, Winston-Salem, North Carolina 27109; and the name of its initial registered agent at such address shall be Dean ....

Eight. The names and address of the incorporators and initial officers and board of directors of this corporation, they being the present officers and directors of this society, are as follows:

[Names and addresses of incorporators]

President: ....   Treasurer: ....
          ....
          ....
          ....
Vice-Pres.: ....   Secretary: ....
          ....
          ....
          ....

Board of Directors

19XX-XX	19YY-YY	19ZZ-ZZ
....	....	....
....	....	....
....	....	....
....	....	....
....	....	....
....	....	....
	....	....
	....	....

[*Note*. Duration is perpetual unless a term is limited by the articles. Purposes clause now need state only that they shall be "those lawful under this chapter of" the N.C. statute.]

Ninth: The powers of this corporation shall be all those lawful, necessary, and proper, pursuant to the provisions of Chapter 55A (Non-profit Corporation Act) of the General Statutes of North Carolina.

IN WITNESS WHEREOF, we have made, subscribed, and acknowledged these Articles of Incorporation this day of March, 19XX.

_____
Howard L. Oleck
(President)

_____
James J. Brown
(Secretary)

State of North Carolina   )
) ss:
.... County   )

Personally appearing before me, a Notary Public in and for the State of North Carolina, Howard L. Oleck and James J. Brown, who are personally known to me to be the individuals who signed the foregoing Articles of Incorporation and acknowledge the same to be their act and deed.

Given under my hand and notarial seal this _____ day of _____, 19XX.

_____
Notary Public

FORM NO. 89

Certificate of Incorporation
(Ohio)

[*Note*. This form is based on that of a professional-trade association, local in scope, organized in Cleveland, Ohio, by Oleck as attorney.]

Articles of Incorporation
of
.... PHARMACEUTICAL ASSOCIATION, INC.
(a Corporation Not for Profit)

The undersigned, a majority of whom are citizens of the United States, desiring to form a corporation, not for profit, under Sections 1702.01 et seq., Revised Code of Ohio, do hereby certify:

FIRST.   The name of said corporation shall be .... Pharmaceuti-
                cal Association, Inc.
SECOND.   The place in Ohio where the principal office of the corporation
                is to be located is the City of Cleveland, Cuyahoga County.
THIRD.   The purpose of this organization shall be to unite the members
                of the profession of Pharmacy in the area in and about the City
                of Cleveland; to promote the ideals of Pharmacy among them
                and in relation to the public; to aid and encourage cooperation
                and improvement in the practice of Pharmacy; to provide media
                for such cooperation and improvement; and to do all lawful
                things consistent with the purpose of the organization and help-
                ful to it, its membership, and the profession, both as a separate
                organization and in cooperation with national, state, and other
                local organizations.
FOURTH.   The following persons shall serve said corporation as trustees
                until the first annual meeting.
                G . . . . H. B . . . . Avenue, Cleveland 13, Ohio;
                N . . . . C. F . . . . Road, Rocky River 16, Ohio; G
                . . . . E. H . . . . Ave., Lakewood 7, Ohio; J
                . . . . H. H . . . . Road, Shaker Heights 20,
                Ohio; D . . . . . . H. W . . . . Drive, Moreland
                Hills, Ohio.
FIFTH.   Pursuant to Ohio Revised Code Section 1702.08, the . . . .
                Pharmaceutical Association, Inc. (to wit, this corporation) shall
                succeed to and be vested with the rights, privileges, immunities,
                powers, franchises, authority, property, and obligations of the . .
                . . . . . Pharmaceutical Association (unincorporated) of Cleve-
                land, Ohio; the said unincorporated association having duly
                authorized such succession and vesting by proper vote at a meet-
                ing duly called on proper notice as provided by the said Section
                1702.08; and the members of the said unincorporated association
                shall be members of this corporation upon the filing of these
                articles of incorporation.
SIXTH.   This corporation shall engage in no activity which is prohibited
                by corporations exempt from Federal income taxes under the
                relevant subdivisions of Section 501(c) of the Internal Revenue
                Code. It shall not engage in propaganda or otherwise attempt to
                influence legislation as a substantial part of its activity.
SEVENTH.   No part of the income or assets of this corporation shall be dis-
                tributed, directly or indirectly, to members, except as reasonable
                compensation for services rendered.

_____

G . . . . H. B . . . .

N . . . . . . C. F . . . . . .
_____

G . . . . . . E. H . . . . . .
_____

J . . . . . . H. H . . . . . .
_____

D . . . . . . H. W . . . . . .
_____

ORIGINAL APPOINTMENT OF AGENT

The undersigned, being at least a majority of the incorporators of . . . . .
. . . . PHARMACEUTICAL ASSOCIATION, INC., hereby appoint HOWARD L.
OLECK, Attorney at Law, a natural person resident in . . . . . . County in
which the corporation has its principal office, upon whom any process, notice,
or demand required or permitted by statute to be served upon the corporation
may be served. His complete address is

. . . . . . Cleveland (Cuyahoga County), Ohio
. . . . . . PHARMACEUTICAL ASSOCIATION, INC.

G . . . . . . H. B. . . . .
_____

N . . . . . . C. F . . . . . .
_____

G . . . . . . E. H . . . . . .
_____

J . . . . . . H. H . . . . . .
_____

D . . . . . . H. W . . . . . .
_____

Cleveland, Ohio
. . . . 26, 19 . . .

. . . . . . PHARMACEUTICAL ASSOCIATION, INC.

Cleveland, Ohio

Gentlemen: I hereby accept appointment as agent of your corporation upon
whom process, tax notices, or demands may be served.

Howard L. Oleck
Attorney at Law
_____

FORM NO. 90

Original Appointment of Agent
Official Form (Ohio)

Form C-103 Presented by Secretary of State Ted W. Brown

Original Appointment Of Agent

The undersigned, being at least a majority of the incorporators of

_____
(Name of Corporation)

hereby appoint _____
(Name of Agent)

a natural person resident in the county in which the corporation has its principal office, a corporation having a business address in the county in which

_____
(Name of Corporation)

has its principal office (strike out phrase not applicable), upon whom (which) any process, notice or demand required or permitted by statute to be served upon the corporation may be served. His (Its) complete address is

_____ _____
(Street or Avenue)   (City or Village)

_____ County, Ohio, _____
(Zip Code)

_____
(Name of Corporation)

_____
_____
_____
_____
(Incorporators names should be typed or printed beneath signature)

_____, Ohio
_____, 19_____

_____
(Name of Corporation)

Gentlemen: I, It (strike out word not applicable) hereby accept(s) appointment as agent of your corporation upon whom process, tax notices or demands may be served.

_____
(Signature of Agent or Name of Corporation)

By _____
(Signature of Officer Signing and Title)

Remarks: All articles of incorporation must be accompanied by an original appointment of agent. There is no filing fee for this appointment.

FORM NO. 91

Certificate of Incorporation (Universal Form)
[club]

[*Note.* This is a generally usable form suitable for any nonprofit corporation when adjusted to local statutory requirements for number of directors and number of incorporators. It is based on the charter of a *local club*, for which no approvals from any governmental agencies usually are required.]

Certificate of Incorporation
of
The .... *Club, Inc.*

We, the undersigned, desiring to form a Membership Corporation pursuant to the (nonprofit) corporation Law of the State of ...., do hereby state:

One. The name of the proposed Corporation is the........... Club, Inc.

Two. The purposes for which said Corporation is formed are as follows:

   a. To encourage interest in ....

   b. To provide economical .... for its members, not for profit.

   c. To bring to more people the social benefits and pleasures of .... activity.

Three. The powers of the Corporation shall be as follows:

   a. To own and hold and/or lease, purchase, mortgage, sell or otherwise dispose of in its name personal property—namely, one or more .... or .... appurtenances—and to purchase in its name, lease, mortgage, sell, or otherwise divest itself of real property, or any interest therein for use in connection with its .... activities, all property both real and personal to be used or disposed of only in the interest of the Corporation and in furtherance of its objects; and the Corporation shall operate as a non-profit-making enterprise; to perform or contract for the performance by others of any work or service deemed necessary or desirable in carrying on or furthering the purposes of the Corporation, and in the upkeep, improvement, or preservation of the Corporation's property interests;

   b. To promulgate rules and regulations governing the rights and activities of its members in their use of the Corporation's facilities; and

   c. To carry on all other business not specifically herein above mentioned and not inconsistent with law in furtherance of the above-stated purposes of this Corporation.

   d. But not to engage in any activities forbidden by I.R.C. Section 501(c) for tax-exempt corporations.

   e. No income or assets of the corporation may be distributed, directly or indirectly, to members, except as reasonable compensation for services rendered.

[Duration statement is required in some states.]

Four. The operations of this Corporation are principally to be conducted in the Counties of .... and ...., State of ....

Five: The office of the Corporation is to be located in the Village of .... County of ...., State of ....

Six: The number of directors shall not be less than three nor more than seven.

Seven: The directors of this Corporation need not be members.

Eight: Any one or more of the directors may be removed either with or without cause at any time by a vote of *two-thirds* of the members of the Corporation at any special meeting called for that purpose.

Nine: The name and post-office addresses of the directors until the first annual meeting are as follows:

Name	*Address*			
1.	....	Road,	....	....
2.	....	Street,	....	....
3.	....	Avenue,	....	....
4.	....	Avenue,	....	....
5.	....	Street,	....	....

Ten: The time for holding the annual meeting of the Corporation shall be the first Monday in the month of May or, if such day shall be a holiday, the next day thereafter.

Eleven: The majority in person or by written proxy of all the members of this Corporation entitled to vote shall be necessary to constitute a quorum at every regular or special meeting of the members, except as to a special election as provided for in the .... Corporation Law.

Twelve: All of the subscribers of the certificate are of full age, at least two-thirds of them are citizens of the United States, and at least one of them is a resident of the State of ....; at least one of the persons named as a director is a citizen of the United States and a resident of the State of ....

In witness whereof, we have made, subscribed, and acknowledged the certificate, this .... day of ...., 19.....

....
.... Avenue, ..., ...

....
.... Street , ..., ...

....
.... Avenue, ..., ...

....
.... Avenue, ..., ...

....
.... Avenue, ..., ...

[Acknowledgments]

FORM NO. 92

Articles of Incorporation: Schematic
(Washington, D.C.)

ARTICLES OF INCORPORATION
OF

_____

To: The Recorder of Deeds, D.C.
    Washington, D.C.

We, the undersigned natural persons of the age of 21 years or more, acting as incorporators of a corporation, adopt the following Articles of Incorporation for such corporation pursuant to the District of Columbia Non-profit
Corporation Act:

FIRST: The name of the corporation is _____

SECOND: The period of duration is _____

THIRD: The purpose or purposes for which the corporation is organized

_____

FOURTH: A statement as to whether or not the corporation is to have
members _____

FIFTH: The corporation is to be divided into _____ classes of
members. The designation of each class of members, the qualifications and
rights of the members of each class and conferring, limiting, or denying the
right to vote are as follows: _____

SIXTH: A statement as to the manner in which directors shall be elected
or appointed, if the directors or any of them are not to be elected or appointed by one or more classes of members, or that the manner of such election or
appointment of such directors shall be provided in the bylaws _____

_____

SEVENTH: Provisions for the regulation of the internal affairs of the corporation, including provisions for distribution of assets on dissolution or final
liquidation _____

EIGHTH: The address, including street and number, of its initial registered office is _____,
and the name of its initial registered agent at such address is _____

_____

NINTH: The number of directors constituting the initial board of directors is _____ and the names and addresses, including street and number
of the persons who are to serve as the initial directors until the first annual
meeting or until their successors be elected and qualified are:

Name   *Address*

....
....
....

TENTH: The name and address, including street and number, of each incorporator is:

Name   *Address*

....
....
....
                                                      ....
                                                      ....
                                                      ....

                                                                  Incorporators

Date _____

)
)   SS

    I, _____, a Notary Public, hereby certify that on the _____ day of _____, 19_____, personally appeared before me _____ _____, and _____, who signed the foregoing document as incorporators, and that the statements therein contained are true.

(Notarial Seal)   _____

                                                    Notary Public

Mail to: **Fees Due**

OFFICE OF RECORDER OF DEEDS, D.C.   Filing Fee $
CORPORATION DIVISION   Indexing Fee
SIXTH AND D STREETS, N.W.   _____
WASHINGTON, D.C. 20001   Total $
                                       MAKE CHECK PAYABLE TO
                                       RECORDER OF DEEDS, D.C.

FORM NO. 93
Amended Articles of Incorporation (Church)
(Florida)

[Actually, a "Restatement" of the Articles.]

Amendment to Charter
of
Lutheran Church, Unaltered
Augsburg Confession, Of.....................,
Florida, Incorporated
(A Corporation Not for Profit)

Pursuant to the provisions of Section 617.02, Florida Statute, the under-signed nonprofit Corporation, whose original Charter was approved by the Circuit Court of the Judicial Circuit of Florida, in and for the County, on June 10, 19........., and which Charter was amended and reincorporated with the Secretary of State, of the State of Florida, on February 6, 19........., have agreed, adopted, and resolved that the Charter of this Corporation be amended to read, in its entirety, as follows [restated]:

Article I. Name

The name of this corporation shall be LUTHERAN CHURCH, UNALTERED AUGSBURG CONFESSION, OF FLORIDA, INCORPORATED

Article II. Purposes

The purpose of this body shall be that of a religious organization established and maintained, not for profit, but to disseminate the Gospel of Jesus Christ according to the confessional standard as set forth in the Declaration of Creed, as follows to-wit:

This congregation and all its members as individuals accept without reservation:

(A) The Scriptures of the Old and New Testaments as the written Word of God and the only rule and norm of faith and of practice.

(B) All symbolical Books of the Lutheran Church as a true and unadulterated statement and exposition of the Word of God. These Symbolical Books are:

The three Ecumenical Creeds: The Apostolic Creed, the Nicene Creed, and the Athanasian Creed.

The Unaltered Augsburg Confession.

The Smalcald Articles.

The Large Catechism of Luther.

The Small Catechism of Luther.

The Formula of Concord.

Article III. Term of Existence

This corporation is to exist perpetually.

Article IV. Qualification of Members

The membership of this corporation shall consist of all persons whose names appear in the membership rolls of this corporation on the date of this amendment and such persons as, from time to time hereafter, may be or become members, in the manner provided by the bylaws.

Article V. Subscribers

The subscribers to original Charter of this Corporation were:

Name   *Address*

Article VI. Officers

Section 1. The officers of this corporation shall be a Pastor(s), a President, a President-Elect, a Secretary, a Treasurer, and The Board of Elders. The officers shall be elected and have such duties, obligations, and authority as provided in the bylaws.

Section 2. The name of the persons who are to serve as officers of the corporation until the next election or appointment as provided in the bylaws are:

Office	*Name*
Pastor	
Pastor	
President	
President	
President-elect	
Secretary	
Treasurer	
Elder	
Elder	
Elder	
Elder	
Elder	
Elder	

Section 3. The officers shall be elected at a regular meeting of the Voters' Assembly as provided in the bylaws.

Article VII. Voters' Assembly

Section 1. The governing body of this corporation shall be the Voters' Assembly, who shall be members of this corporation and shall manage the spiritual and temporal affairs of the corporation in the manner provided in the bylaws.

Section 2. The Voters' Assembly shall consist of all persons whose names appear as voting members in the membership rolls of this corporation on the date of this amendment and such persons as, from time to time hereafter, may be or become voting members in the manner provided in the bylaws, provided, however, the number shall never be less than three members.

Article VIII. Bylaws

Section 1. The Voters' Assembly of this corporation may provide such bylaws for the conduct of its business and affairs and the carrying out of the purposes of this corporation as they may deem necessary from time to time.

Section 2. Upon proper notice the bylaws may be amended, altered, or rescinded by a majority vote of those members of the Voters' Assembly present and voting at any regular meeting or any special meeting called for that purpose.

Article IX. Nonprofit Tax-Exempt Status

Section 1. This corporation shall engage in no activity which is prohibited by corporations exempt from Federal income taxes under Section 501(c)(3) of the Internal Revenue Code. It shall not engage in propaganda or otherwise attempt to influence legislation as a substantial part of its activity.

Section 2. No person, firm, or corporation shall ever receive any dividends or profits from the undertaking of this corporation and upon dissolution of its assets remaining after payment of all costs and expenses of such dissolution shall be distributed to the District of the Lutheran Church—Missouri Synod, of which this corporation was a member at the time of such dissolution, provided said Synod has qualified for exempt under Section 501(c)(3) of the Internal Revenue Code, or if not, then to a District of the Lutheran Church—Missouri Synod that has qualified for exemption under Section 501(c)(3) of the Internal Revenue Code, or if none, then to such other organization of the Lutheran Church that has qualified for exemption under the said Internal Revenue Code, or if none, then to the State or Local government, or the Federal Government, for a public purpose, and none of the assets will be distributed to any member or officer of this corporation.

Section 3. No part of the net earnings of the corporation shall inure to the benefit of any individual or member, but the corporation may pay reasonable compensation for services rendered.

Article X. Principles

Section 1. This corporation shall confer the office of Pastor(s), and any teaching position within the corporation only upon those pastors, teachers, or candidates who unreservedly pledge their acceptance of and adherence to the Declaration of Creed as contained in this Charter and who are qualified for their work in the manner provided in the bylaws.

Section 2. Removal from office of a Pastor, teacher, or officer may be effected only by observance of right and Christian principles and procedures. Valid and urgent reasons for removal from office are persistent adherence to false doctrine, scandalous life, willful neglect of official duty, or evident and protracted inability to perform the functions of the office.

Section 3. It shall be the duty of every member to support all of the purposes, work, and programs of this corporation and the Synod to which it belongs according to their ability.

Section 4. Only such hymns, prayers, liturgies, books, and literature shall be used in public worship, religious instructions, and other official acts as conform to the confessional standard of Article II.

Article XI. Amendments

This Charter, with the exception of Article II which may not be revised or repealed, may be amended by an affirmative vote of two-thirds (2/3) of those members of the Voters' Assembly present at any regular meeting or any special meeting called for that purpose, provided any proposed change in this Charter shall have been presented and submitted in writing at a previous regular meeting of the Voters' Assembly.

Resolved, further, that the President and Secretary of this corporation be, and they are hereby authorized and directed to make, execute, and acknowledge a Certificate under the corporate seal of this corporation, embracing the foregoing Resolution, and to cause such Certificate to be filed and recorded in the office of the Secretary of State in the manner required by Florida Statutes.

The Amendment was adopted at a meeting of the Voters' Assembly held on the 2nd day of March, 19 . ., at which a quorum was present and the Amendment received at least two-thirds (2/3) of the votes of the members present at such meeting.

DATED at _____ Florida, this 2nd day of March, 19_____
                                   LUTHERAN CHURCH, UNALTERED
                                   AUGSBURG CONFESSION, OF _____
                                   FLORIDA, INCORPORATED.

(CORPORATE SEAL)

                              By: _____
                                             President

                                   _____
                                        Recording Secretary

FORM NO. 94

Certificate, Charter of Incorporation, and Acknowledgment
for Horticultural Society (APPLICATION)
(Tennessee)

Certificate

STATE OF TENNESSEE
DEPARTMENT OF STATE

I, E. . . .F. . . . , Secretary-of-State of the State of Tennessee, do hereby certify that the annexed Instrument with Certificate of Acknowledgment was filed in my office and recorded on the 15th day of September 19 . . in Corporation Record Book Miscellaneous A-32 page 92.

IN TESTIMONY WHEREOF, I have hereunto subscribed my Official Signature and by order of the Governor affixed the Great

(SEAL)

Seal of the State of Tennessee at the Department in the City of Nashville, this 15th day of September A.D. 19_____

/s/ _____ E.F . . . . . .
                    Secretary-of-State

Charter Application

STATE OF TENNESSEE
CHARTER OF INCORPORATION

BE IT KNOWN That S . . . . K. J . . . . . , H . . . . . M. H . . . . . R . . . . . N. C . . . . . M . . . . . S. C . . . . . ,and W. C. C . . . . . are hereby constituted a body politic and corporate, by the name and style of R . . . . . R . . . . . , for the general purpose of operating a modified arboretum, promoting the conservation of resources by demonstrating to the public the need for conserving animal life, forests, water, soil, a love of nature and its beauty, and acquainting the public with the history of the area in which R . . . . . R . . . . . is located, including also the support and encouragement of agriculture, horticulture, and the mechanic arts, as, agricultural, societies, or societies for the promotion of the mechanic arts, or other objects of like nature; all not-for-profit.

The general powers of said corporation shall be:

(1) To sue and be sued by the corporate name.

(2) To have and use a common seal, which it may alter at pleasure; if no common seal, then the signature of the name of the corporation, by any duly authorized officer, shall be legal and binding.

(3) To establish bylaws, and make all rules and regulations not inconsistent with the laws and Constitution deemed expedient for the management of corporate affairs not-for-profit.

(4) To appoint such subordinate officers and agents, in addition to a president and secretary, or treasurer, as the business of the corporation may require.

(5) To designate the name of the office and fix the compensation of the officer.

(6) To issue income bonds, constituting an obligation to pay interest and liquidate principle by setting aside net operating income, to be used in payment of property bought by it, making improvements, and for other purposes germane to the objects of its creation, but no obligation may be executed that would be a general indebtedness on which a lien or judgment might be obtained, except one for purchase money on land bought.

(7) To receive property, real, personal, or mixed, by purchase, gift, devise, or bequest, sell the same and apply the proceeds toward the promotion of the objects for which it is created, or hold any such property and apply the income and profits toward such objects; however, notwithstanding the powers herein given, it shall have no power to solicit gifts or money or property or to seek to raise funds from its members or the public.

(8) Unless otherwise specifically directed in the trust instrument by which any real or personal property, money, or other funds, are given, granted, conveyed, bequeathed, devised to, or otherwise vested in, the directors, the governing board, or the authorized finance committee thereof, when authorized by the corporation, shall have power to invest funds thus received or the proceeds of any property thus received, in such investments as in the honest exercise of their judgment they may, after investigation, determine to be safe and proper investments and to retain any investments heretofore so made.

(9) The general welfare of society, not individual profit, is the object for which this charter is granted, and the members are not stockholders in the legal sense of the term, and no dividends or profits shall be divided among the members; nor shall the IRC §501(c) rules be evaded.

(10) The said five (5) or more corporators shall, within a convenient time after the registration of this charter, elect from their number a president, secretary, and treasurer, or the last two (2) officers may be combined into one (1), said officers and the other corporators to constitute the first board of directors. They may also enlarge the board and the board may elect an advisory committee of such size and with such powers, privileges, and capacities as they may determine.

(11) The term of officers may be fixed by the bylaws, the said term not, however, to exceed three (3) years. All officers hold office until their successors are duly elected and qualified.

(12) At any time and for any period when the corporation does not have funds sufficient to carry on the objectives of the trust, it may (a) reduce the operation and employ a mere custodian who will be allowed to graze and farm the property, (b) rent to those who without hindering substantial development will be allowed to live on and utilize the property, (c) sell timber in sufficient amounts to maintain a custodian, or (d) adopt other expedients for mere

preservation or conservation that will make the property available later for the general objectives.

(13) To accept members, the incorporators or directors being such without the necessity of application, each incorporator or director to have the power of designating a successor and also naming two members, future members to be admitted upon such terms and conditions and with such privileges as may be fixed in the bylaws, etc., referred to in section (3) above, but in any event to be by fee and classified as in like organizations, life membership to pass one time by will of the deceased member.

(14) The members will meet periodically at such times as the directors fix, after five years of operation have enabled them to form an opinion as to the need, and in all elections each member to be entitled to one (1) vote either in person or by proxy, the result to be determined by a majority of the votes cast. Due notice of any election must be given by advertisement in a newspaper, personal notice to the members, or a day stated on the minutes of the board one (1) month preceding the election.

We, the undersigned, the incorporators above mentioned, hereby apply to the State of Tennessee for a charter of incorporation for the purposes declared in the foregoing instrument.

WITNESS our hands this, the 14th day of September 19...

/s/ S . . . . . K. J . . . . .
/s/ H . . . . . M. H . . . . .
/s/ R . . . . . N. C . . . . .
/s/ M . . . . . S. C . . . . .
/s/ W. C. C . . . . .

Subscribing witness:
/s/ M . . . . . S. C . . . . .

Acknowledgment

STATE OF TENNESSEE
COUNTY OF HAMILTON

Personally appeared before me F . . . . . M. .P . . . . . of said County, the within named M . . . . . S. C . . . . ., the subscribing witness and incorporator, with whom I am personally acquainted, and who acknowledged that she executed the within application for a Charter of Incorporation for the purposes therein contained and expressed; and the said M . . . . . . S. C . . . . ., subscribing witness to the signatures subscribed to the within application, being first duly sworn, deposed, and said that she is personally acquainted with the within named incorporators, S . . . . K. J . . . ., H . . . . M. H . . . ., R . . . . . N. C . . . . . and W. C. C . . . . . and they did in her presence acknowledge that they executed the within application for a Charter of Incorporation for the purposes therein contained and expressed.

WITNESS my hand and official seal at office in Chattanooga, Tennessee, this 14th day of September 19. . .

/s/ F . . . . . M . . P . . . . .
Notary Public

My commission expires:
October 10, 19. .

STATE OF TENNESSEE, HAMILTON COUNTY

The above instrument and certificates were filed September 18, 19. . at 3:05 p.m. entered in Note Book No. 48, Page 437 and recorded in Book 1239, Page 557.

Witness my hand at office in Chattanooga, Tennessee

/s/ D . . . . . P. B . . . . ., Register
/s/ R. H. T . . . . ., Dep. Register

[*Note*: Tenn. Acts 1986, c. 887 §17.05 affects corporations until Oct. 1, 1987.]

FORM NO. 95

Notice of Incorporation
(Georgia)

Publisher's Notice

Dear Sirs:

You are requested to publish, four times, a notice in the following form:

_____

_____

(Name of Corporation) has been duly incorporated on _____,
19_____ (Month, day, and year to be inserted by the Secretary of State) by the issuance of a certificate of incorporation by the Secretary of State, in accordance with the applicable provisions of the Georgia Nonprofit Corporation Code.
The initial registered office of the corporation is located at _____

_____

(address of registered office) and its initial registered (Agent) (Agents) at such address (Is) (Are) _____
_____ (Name or names of agent or agents).
Enclosed is a check, draft or money order in the amount of $60.00, in payment of the cost of publishing this notice.

Very truly yours,

(Name and address of incorporator or incorporators or his or their representatives)

POINTS TO REMEMBER

- First, be sure that the incorporators themselves may prepare and file the articles of incorporation in your state. In some states, this may be viewed as unauthorized practice of law.
- Best avoid all doubt and mistakes—retain an attorney to incorporate the organization.
- Find out what outside approvals are required; and get them.
- Clear the desired name; reserve the name.
- Look up in the state statute the required contents of a certificate of incorporation (in the state's nonprofit corporations law, if there is one; or else in the general corporation law).
- Follow the statutory requirements for the number of incorporators, number of directors, and governmental agency approvals required (if any).
- Agree on the wording of the purpose clause.
- Agree on the persons who are to be the first directors.
- Sign the final form of certificate.
- Get a notary public to witness the signatures, and to sign acknowledgments for each (if your state statute requires this).
- Submit the certificate to the interested state departments for any approvals required by law.
- Draw a certified check or money order to the order of the secretary of state (see the state statute for the fees).
- Send the certificate, the check, and a brief covering letter, by registered mail, to the secretary of state.
- Wait for the return of his receipt to you. The corporation should not take any corporate action until the receipt arrives.
- Fasten an exact copy of the certificate into the first pages of your minute book.
- Fasten the receipt into the next page of your minute book.
- Now your corporation officially exists (technically it existed from the day on which its certificate was filed).
- Publish notice of incorporation if your state statute so requires.

[*Note*. See an article arguing in favor of "close corporations" not-for-profit: J. J. Fishman, *Development of Nonprofit Corporation Law and an Agenda for Reform*, 34 Emory L.J. 617 (1985).]

NOTES TO CHAPTER 19

1. *E.g.*, in Florida, Illinois, Ohio, and Oklahoma.
2. *E.g.*, in New York and New Jersey.

3. For examples of both official and unofficial forms of many states, *see,* 5 Oleck, *Modern Corporation Law,* c. 91 (1978 Supp.). *See, In re* Articles of Incorporation of Defender Assn. of Philadelphia, 307 A.2d 906 (Pa. 1973); 6 Am. Jur. Legal Forms (2d) 74:54; 74:115; 224:29. *See,* Rev. Model Nonprofit Corp. Act §1.20 (1986 Exposure Draft).

4. *See* the list of statutes, above, in c. 4; and *see,* Henn and Alexander, *Corporations* §116 (3rd ed., 1983).

5. *E.g.,* New York.

6. *See,* N.Y. Bus. Corp. L., §104(a); Pa. C. St. §5306; N.Y. N-P-C Law §104, 403.

7. *Re* Daughters of Israel Orphan Aid Society, 125 Misc. 217; 210 N.Y.S. 541 (1921); Rev. Model Nonprofit Corp. Act §1.20(e). (1986 Exposure Draft).

8. (Prentice-Hall, Inc., Englewood Cliffs, N.J.)

9. (Prentice-Hall, Inc., Englewood Cliffs, N.J.)

10. Tenn. Code Ann. §48-52-101.

11. *Id., E.g.,* Genl. Stat. No. Car. §55A-6. as to age of 18 *see* N.Y. N-P-C. L. §401.

12. *E.g.,* Genl. Stat. No. Car., §55A-4 (1968).

13. Fla. St., §617.013(2)(repealed); as to what is "acknowledgment," *see,* Favello v. Bank of America Ntl. Tr. and Savings Assn., 24 Calif. App. 2d 342; 74 P.2d 1057 (1938); Jemison v. Howell, 230 Ala. 423; 161 S. 806 (1935); 99 A.L.R. 1511 (1935); Williford v. Davis, 106 Okla. 208; 232 P. 828, 831 (1924). Not required in Penna.: Pa. St., §7318. Acknowledgment is no longer *required* in Fla. Stat §§617.0202, 617.01201 (1992). *See also* Ann. Cal. Code §§5120, 5030; Cal. Civ. Code art. 3 ch. 4 §§1180 *et seq.*; 805 ILCS 105/101.10.

14. *E.g.,* in a Real Property Act, for realty matters; in a Sales Act (or Uniform Commercial Code), for sales, *etc.; and generally,* in Practice Acts.

15. *E.g.,* in New York City, it is the Supreme Court, Special Term, Part 1. As to other procedures, *see,* Calif. Corp. Code, §5008; Del. Genl. Corp. L., tit. 8, §102; Fla. St., §617.0203; 805 ILCS §§105/101.10, 105/102.10., N.J. Stat., §15A:1–7; N.Y. N-P-C Law, §404; Ohio Rev. Code, §1702.04; Pa. Stat. 15,§§5308, 5309.

16. *St. Petersburg Times,* p. S1 (June 2, 1993).

17. N.Y. Exec. L., §96(9b), N.J. Stat. Anno. tit. 22A:2-29.

18. Ohio Rev. Code, §111.16(A)(1).

19. Calif. Govt. Code, §12200.

20. N.Y. N-P-C Law, §113. Must state that it is "Type A," or "Type B," or *etc.,* or will be *deemed* "Type B."

21. Fla. St., §617.0203; Ohio Rev. Code, §1702.07. The endorsed articles are returned by the secretary of state, who keeps a photocopy, in Ohio. In New York, a different procedure is followed, and merely the receipt is returned. *See,* Opinions N.Y. atty. genl. (Nov. 14, 1941).

22. N.Y. N-P-C Law §104.

23. *St. Petersburg (FL) Times,* p. 8S (June 29, 1992).

24. For exhaustive text and forms for many states, *see,* Oleck, *Modern Corporation Law* (1978 Supp.), *esp.* vol. 5 for forms and vol. 1 for statutes.

20

ORGANIZATION MEETINGS

[See, as to meetings procedures: Oleck & Green, *Parliamentary Law & Practice for NPOs* (2d ed, 1991, Amer. Law Inst.-Amer. Bar Assn.)] [Debbie Lev assisted in updating this chapter.]

§212. ORGANIZATION MEETING REQUIREMENT

"In American law various forms of rules exist that are applicable to the organizational phases of the nonprofit corporation, but more with respect to the type of activity that is to be carried out than with respect to the formation of the group as a legal entity."[1] In other words, there is considerable variety, from state to state, as to the legal requirements in the organizing process.[2] The American Bar Association's 1986 Exposure Draft of the Revised Model Nonprofit Corporation Act, Section 1.20, Official Comment says that it "standardizes the filing requirements .... (in order) to simplify .... minimize the number of pieces of paper .... (and) eliminate all possible disputes ...." How successful that is is still uncertain.

In unincorporated associations, the general rule in most states is that contract law and procedures are all that are available as guides for their organization processes.[3]

State statutes have sometimes been vague as to the requirement of an organizational meeting to form a corporation. But now most states require an organizational meeting. For example Florida requires the initial directors to call an organizational meeting, with three days' notice, to elect directors and complete organization of the corporation.[4] In most statutes, the General Corporation Act (business corporations) does require such a meeting for all corporations.[5] It is usually express in requiring notice of the meeting.[6] Illinois, too, requires an organizational meeting for nonprofit corporations.[7]

As a practical matter, a meeting for completion of the organizing process is required, unless the corporation is really an organization set up by counsel and merely "signed" by the organizers.[8] It is good practice to deposit a set of the incorporation *minutes* and other documents with the attorney or other reliable person, for safekeeping in case of a fire or other disaster. In case a dispute arises, about what was done, this duplicate record may be very important.[9]

Minutes of the incorporation meeting may become important many years later.[10] See Chapter 21.

§213. WHAT IS THE ORGANIZATION MEETING?

Formal organization of a corporation is usually completed at a meeting of the incorporators, while in some cases a similar organization meeting of the directors named in the articles of incorporation is required. Many statutes require that an organization meeting be called by the initial board members, on at least three days' notice to members, after the issuance of a certificate of incorporation by the secretary of state.[11]

Meetings of the organizers of a corporation occur before the articles of incorporation are prepared. But none of these meetings is the *organization meeting*.

The organization meeting is the first general meeting of the corporation officers or members *after* the articles of incorporation have been filed. The corporation technically *comes into existence* when that filing occurs; but usually, as a practical matter, it cannot *operate* until an organization meeting is held.[12]

Purposes of the organization meeting. At the organization meeting, the following matters ordinarily must be accomplished:

1. Directors named in the charter must be confirmed in office, or else new ones must be elected.

2. Bylaws (or a constitution) must be adopted.

3. Officers must be elected (by the members generally, or, quite often, by the directors).

In addition, the meeting serves to make sure that the corporate organization is complete and is not merely *de facto*. (See Section 217, following). It usually also ends the personal liability of promoters thereafter.[13]

A directors' organization meeting often is the only real meeting.

When to hold the meeting. As a practical matter, the organization meeting should be held as soon as it conveniently can be arranged, after the filing of the articles of incorporation.

In a few states, the general corporation laws specify within what period the first meeting must be held.[14]

Do not postpone the meeting. If the first meeting is unduly postponed, a real danger arises. In many states a corporation is deemed to exist only *conditionally*, when its articles are filed, until it enters upon the activities for which it was chartered. If it fails to do so within a reasonable time (by holding its organization meeting, and thus commencing activities), its corporate existence fails.[15] Then its members may be held liable as *partners*, as in an unincorporated association.[16]

Many state statutes set definite periods for validation of corporate status by activity after incorporation. These periods range from six months to two years. Failure to comply may result in loss of corporation status or even in revocation of the charter by the state.[17]

§214. HOW THE MEETING IS CALLED (NOTICE)

By the attorney. Usually the attorney who incorporated the organization calls the organization meeting. When he has the receipt showing acceptance of the charter for filing by the department of state, he should notify the incorporators. At this time oral agreement is usually reached on a time and place for the organization meeting. An attorney may be disciplined for failure to act correctly in the organizing process.[18]

Theoretically, formal written notice should be sent to all the incorporators. In practice, however, the attorney almost always uses a *waiver of notice*. This waiver is included in the minutes of the first meeting and is signed by the incorporators.

Such a waiver is valid and effective. A waiver of notice may be signed either before or after an event, except in a few special matters when statutes forbid it.[19]

By an incorporator. Sometimes one of the incorporators calls the meeting. He does this after receiving notice from the attorney that the charter has been duly filed. (See also section 216, following.)

It is best for the incorporator to send formal written notice instead of relying on telephone or other oral arrangements. Written notice prevents later disputes.

Record of sending of notice. A copy of the notice should be retained by the sender, whether he is the attorney or one of the incorporators.

At the time of the meeting, this copy should be fastened into the minute book with an affidavit by the sender, testifying that he sent it, to whom, and when.

Period of notice. Ten days is the usual safe period of notice before a meeting. A shorter period—say, four or five days—may be used if no one will be seriously inconvenienced. The provisions in the bylaws as to the period of notice should be followed exactly.[20]

FORM NO. 96
Notice of Organization Meeting

............, Esq.
.... (address)

(To) ...., 19....
.... Street
.... (city), ... (state)

Dear Sir:

Please take notice that an organization meeting of the .... Assn., Inc., will be held at .... o'clock (a.m. or p.m.) at .... Street, ... (city), ... (state), in Room ....

At this meeting the agenda will include:

1. Acceptance of the Certificate of Incorporation, which was duly filed in the office of the Secretary of State of .... on ...., 19...

2. Election of Directors (Trustees).

3. Adoption of Bylaws.

4. [If officers are to be elected by the members directly, mention of that fact should be included.]

5. A meeting of those persons elected as directors will immediately follow the general meeting.

If you will not be able to attend, please communicate with the undersigned before ...., 19...

Yours truly,

....
Attorney for the incorporators ......

FORM NO. 97
Waiver of Notice of Organization Meeting

We, the undersigned, being the (incorporators) (directors) of .... *Association, Inc.,* do hereby severally waive notice of the time, place, and purpose of the (first) meeting of the (incorporators) (directors) of the said Corporation, and consent that the meeting be held at ....o'clock, a.m. (p.m.), on ...., 19......, in Room ...... at .... (street), ... (city), ... (state); and we do further consent to the transaction of any business required in order to complete the organization of the said (corporation) (board of directors of the said corporation), and to do any and all business that may properly come before the said meeting.

Dated: ...., 19...   ....
....
....
....
....

§215. WHERE TO HOLD THE MEETING

Organization meetings theoretically *must* be held within the state in which incorporation took place. The first meeting is, in effect, completion of the process of incorporation. Meetings may be held outside the state if articles or bylaws so provide.[21]

The corporation has no agents (officers or directors) until some are selected at the organization meeting, or pursuant thereto. This is why it theoretically cannot act outside the state for the first meeting. An as-yet-nonexistent principal cannot have any agents.[22]

This theoretical reason makes it wise to hold the first meeting within the state. But, if no one will be hurt thereby, the meeting may, as a matter of fact, be held elsewhere and its decisions ratified at a later meeting within the state.

Ordinarily, too, the city or town where the corporation's office is to be located is the logical place for the meeting.

§216. WHAT TO DO IF NO MEETING IS CALLED

If no organization meeting is called within a period set by local statute (usually within one year), or within a reasonable time, the corporation may not properly act as such.

The incorporators, if they incur obligations for the group, are then in the position of partners in an unincorporated association. And the state may revoke the charter. (See section 213, preceding.)

Although it often happens that the formalities of an organization meeting are not properly carried out, this omission is dangerous. Creditors (or the state) may then be able to refuse to acknowledge the corporate status (and rights) of the organization and may be able to fasten personal liability on the organizers themselves.[23]

Ordinarily, if no one is affected by the failure to complete these formalities, no one objects. The state becomes interested only when the required annual reports are not filed. But any interested person may call the omission to the attention of the state's attorney general. This may bring immediate *quo warranto* proceedings against the corporation.

Carryover of first directors' terms. If no organization meeting is held, the directors named in the certificate of incorporation continue in office until an election is duly held.[24] Or, at the organization meeting (as often happens), their tenure of office may be confirmed by election, until the next annual election.

Call of meeting by an organizer. In many states, the general corporation statutes expressly authorize any one of the incorporators to call a first meeting if none is called by the others within a reasonable time (usually, within one year after filing of the certificate.)[25]

Most such statutes provide that notice of such a meeting must be mailed to the last-known address of each incorporator at least two weeks before the meeting. In addition, the notice must be published in a newspaper in the home county of the corporation once a week for at least three successive weeks.[26]

These statutes usually provide also that court supervision or confirmation of such a meeting shall apply.[27]

The object of such statutes is to permit the member who calls such a meeting to free himself of responsibility for the acts of his fellow incorporators. These procedures also enable incorporators to bypass any deliberately dilatory blocking of action by those who normally should call the first meeting.

Local statutes should be consulted for the exact procedure to be followed in the particular state.

§217. DEFECTIVE INCORPORATION (DE FACTO, DE JURE, AND ESTOPPEL)

One of the prime purposes of the organization meeting is to examine the charter of the incorporation, and to make certain that all the required formalities have been satisfied.

If the corporation procedure was carried out improperly, or incompletely, the corporation is not a *de jure* corporation. That is, it is not a corporation as a matter of full, technical right.[28] This is not necessarily fatal, but it may be very serious.

If all the important requirements have been substantially met, the corporation is a corporation *de jure* (as a matter of law).[29]

De facto status. A corporation that has reasonably sought to fulfill the legal requirements for incorporation, but has omitted some minor requirement, is a *de facto* corporation. It is a corporation as a matter of fact, but not as a matter of law.[30] If it has *de facto* status, *only the state may object* to the technically defective incorporation and require that it be corrected under penalty of loss of the charter for failure to do so.[31]

Status as a *de facto* corporation exists if the defect in the incorporation is minor. For example, if *substantial compliance* with all major legal requirements has been made, but the signature of one incorporator is missing, or witnessed by an unqualified notary (in states where notarization of signatures is required), this is a minor defect. The corporation may even be viewed as *de jure*, when the defect is so trivial. It certainly is *de facto.*

Lack of even *de facto* status results if the defect is serious. Most serious, for example, would be a failure to file the certificate of incorporation.[32] Since it is generally agreed that one cannot even be said to colorably comply with applicable law until taking the basic step of filing the corporate articles,[33] such a lack means that there is no corporate status.

The "incorporators" then are, in contemplation of law, partners, and are fully liable as such to any affected persons.[34] In practice, most states limit such liability to managing members. In addition, of course, their use of a corporate name is improper, and may result in action by the state to stop such conduct (*quo warranto* proceedings).

Tests of *de facto* status. Some states have statutory tests of *de facto* status, and the others have established similar tests by case decisions. These tests are listed below. If all four of these tests are met, the organizers are entitled to (at least) *de facto* corporate status, and to personal immunity as corporation members.

1. *An incorporation statute must exist*, under which such a corporation *could* be formed.[35] This means either a nonprofit corporation act, or a general corporation act containing some provision whereby the formation of a nonprofit corporation under its provisions is permitted. If no such statute exists, no corporate status, not even *de facto*, is possible.

If the act did exist at the time of incorporation, and then was repealed or found to be unconstitutional, most states hold that *de facto* status results,[36] but a few states hold that not even *de facto* status can exist in such a case.[37]

2. *Reasonable attempt to comply* with the statute's requirements, in good faith, must have been made.[38] What is an adequate attempt depends on many factors, and is a question of fact in each case. (See also *Corporation by estoppel*, below.)

3. "*User*" of corporate powers, to some extent, must have occurred.[39] What is an adequate *user* of corporate powers to indicate an intention to act as a corporation is a question of fact. Certainly the holding of an organization meeting and the election of officers indicates such an intention.

4. *Unintentional omission* of some part of the incorporation requirements.[40] If the omission is not material, *de facto* status exists.

Corporation by estoppel. When a corporation has failed to achieve even *de facto* status, personal liability of the organizers results, subject to the general equitable principle of *estoppel.*

Estoppel means this: a person's own act or words may be such as to make it unfair for him later to argue that the truth is other than what those words or that act seemed to indicate.[41]

If the organizers acted as though they were a corporation, and other persons reasonably relied on their conduct, the organizers will not later be heard (they are estopped) to deny that they are a corporation, insofar as these third persons are concerned.[42]

If the "corporation" has assets, for example, the members who contracted with a third person may not later deny the corporate status in order to prevent the third party from reaching those assets.[43] Nor may they deny it in order to avoid liability under criminal statutes.[44]

Conversely, one who dealt with a defectively organized corporation as a corporation cannot later assert that it is not a corporation, in order to proceed against the members personally. Such an attack on the corporate status is called a *collateral attack*, and is not permitted, except when it is the only way to prevent injustice to the person who brings it.[45]

For example, if the members should seize the assets themselves, such a collateral attack presumably would be permitted, in order to prevent use of the corporate status as a device with which to cheat a creditor. Then the members would be estopped to deny the corporate status and the corporate title to the assets concerned.[46]

One class of creditors particularly is not permitted to bypass the *de facto* corporation in order to reach the members personally. This is the class of creditors whose claims are based on injuries that were caused by *negligence* or other *torts* of employees of the *de facto* corporation.[47]

§218. QUO WARRANTO PROCEEDINGS

The state's attorney general may bring *quo warranto* proceedings to revoke the charter of a corporation if it has been guilty of:[48]

1. Defective incorporation.
2. Failure to complete its organization.
3. Failure to use its powers.
4. Prolonged inactivity.
5. Use of unauthorized power.
6. Violation of a statute.

There often is a statute of limitations provided for each of these cases and for various violations of statutes. Statutes of limitations vary from state to state but usually set a period of about five years for improprieties other than penal violations.[49]

Any person may complain to the attorney general and thus instigate *quo warranto* proceedings. These proceedings must follow the pattern of procedure provided by the statutes of the particular state.[50]

In most states, the attorney general has a considerable degree of discretion in deciding whether or not to institute the proceedings.

§219. AGENDA FOR ORGANIZATION MEETINGS

Although no formal procedure is mandatory for organization meetings, the following sequence of business is that which is usually followed. It should be understood that these matters may be attended to in a different order, or that different titles may be used, and that other variations will be required in various different situations. Many matters listed in the agenda below may be postponed until later meetings.

It should be particularly noted that the order of business at any meeting of a nonprofit corporation differs somewhat from that of a business corporation. Although the meetings of both types of corporations are generally similar, these differences are of real importance. It is not safe practice to use general corporation rules and procedures unless they are modified to suit the special nature of a nonprofit corporation.

1. Incorporators assemble at the appointed time and place.

2. Attorney for incorporators (or the person who was the leader in the organizational stage) calls the meeting to order. (Roll call and collection of proxies sometimes are conducted at this point, and waivers of notice).

3. Brief welcoming and explanatory remarks by the person in charge of the meeting.

4. Election of a temporary chairman of the meeting.

5. Temporary chairman takes the gavel.

6. Election of a temporary secretary of the meeting.

7. Temporary secretary begins to take notes for minutes of the meeting (or use a tape recorder).

8. Chairman calls on the attorney to report on the incorporation of the organization.

9. Attorney briefly reviews the incorporation process, and delivers:

    a. A copy of the certificate (articles) of incorporation.

    b. The receipt showing its filing (which he sometimes retains in his files, but which ordinarily should be delivered to the corporation).

    c. The corporation's seal (if he obtained one with the corporation "kit").

    d. The book of membership certificates (if he obtained one).

    e. The minute book.

10. Secretary takes these, after they have been inspected by those present. Later, the permanent secretary will keep minutes in this minute book (or a better one) and will fasten the charter and receipt into its first pages. A resolution adopting the certificate and other documents sometimes is formally passed.

11. Directors (trustees) are elected, or the ones named in the charter are confirmed (elected) to serve until the next election. (Proxies often are introduced and accepted at this point when voting is held, where proxy voting is allowed.)[51]

12. Officers are elected. (But sometimes they are elected by the directors, if the bylaws so provide.)

    Appointment of a "parliamentarian" is made by the chairperson.

13. Permanent officers take their proper places, relieving the temporary chairman and secretary. The secretary takes custody of the corporation kit delivered by the attorney. (Usually the president is also one of the directors and presides also as chairman of the meeting.)

14. Officers and directors take oaths of office.

15. Bylaws are read and adopted; or a committee is appointed to draft bylaws.

(In practice, today, very often the bylaws contain all the first-year directors' and officers' names, which are filled in as they are elected. The adoption of the bylaws, thus naming first officers, is the equivalent of the "control agreements" in business corporations. Although self-perpetuation-in-control is theoretically improper, this method, plus lethargy of the members in voting, may serve to prolong control by the organizers for a long time.)

16. Bylaws (or the constitution, or both), if ready and if duly adopted by majority vote, should be in final form.

17. Waivers of notice of meeting may be signed (if no written notice was sent).

18. Initiation fees, and/or dues, are paid by all those present, and are collected by the treasurer.

19. The treasurer is required to be bonded. (Resolution to this effect is adopted. Other officers also may be required to be bonded, or this is done at the directors' meeting.)

20. Corporate seal is adopted.

21. Secretary is authorized to buy, and set up, books and records.

22. President and treasurer (or two other officers) are authorized to open a bank account in a named bank. (This is done by resolution, but the bank's own form of resolution will have to be obtained and executed. A copy of it later will be affixed in the minutes. Often this is done at the directors' meeting.)

23. President or other officers are directed to file any reports required by governmental agencies. (For example, in Mississippi, filing of lists of officers, location of office, et cetera, was required.)[52]

24. Application for tax exemption is directed to be filed. (Usually this is to be done by the president and the attorney. Often it is done later by an attorney selected by the directors.)

25. Agent for receipt of legal process against the corporation is designated (if state law so requires).

26. Treasurer is authorized to pay the expenses of organizing the corporation.

27. Fiscal period is adopted (this is optional).

28. Authorization to accept new members is given to the membership committee (when it is appointed).

29. Date and place for directors' organization meeting is established (if it is not immediately to follow this meeting, as it usually is). Often a date for the next general meeting also is established.

30. New business (special new matters, such as acceptance of a gift to the organization, plans for the future).

31. Adjournment.

32. Secretary types up the minutes and signs them, for reading, correction, and approval at the next meeting. [See the next chapter, for forms.]

Directors' (Trustees') Organization Meeting[53]

1. Directors (trustees) assemble at the appointed time and place.

2. Chairman of the board (who usually also is the president) presides.

3. Secretary of the board (who usually also is the general secretary) takes minutes.

4. Roll call. (Proxies may be received and noted at this point, or when voting is carried on, in states where directors may vote by proxy.)[54]

5. Waivers of notice of the meeting are signed (if no written notice was sent, and if not all the directors are present).

6. Minutes of the general organization meeting are read (or knowledge of their contents is admitted).

7. Bylaws are read (or knowledge of their contents is admitted).

8. Officers are elected (insofar as all officers were not filled by general election by the members, and insofar as the board may elect officers).

9. Elected officers take oaths (if they are present).

10. Compensation of officers (if any compensation is to be paid) is fixed.

11. Particular tasks are assigned to the officers (pursuant to the bylaws).

12. Committee appointments are made (if they are to be made by the entire board, or with its consent).

13. Membership certificate or card contents and forms are decided (or a committee is appointed to draft them).

14. Contracts or agreements essential for commencement of activities are accepted (or their negotiation is authorized; a committee or individual officer is designated to complete them). These may be for purchase of essential equipment, or the like. This must be done in compliance with the bylaws.

15. New business.

16. Date and place for next board meeting are established (if not established in the bylaws, or not subject to the sole discretion of the President-Chairman).

17. Adjournment.

18. Secretary of the board types up the minutes and signs them, for reading, correction, and approval at the next meeting. [See the next chapter, for forms.]

POINTS TO REMEMBER

- Call an organization meeting immediately on receipt of proof of filing of the charter.

- Send written notice to all the incorporators (usually, about 10 days' notice).

- Keep a copy. Affix an affidavit stating when you sent the notice and to whom.
- Do no "corporate acts" until *after* this meeting.
- If the one who should call the meting fails to do so, you can call it yourself by following the proper procedure.
- Do not unduly delay the organization meeting—the delay may cause loss of the charter.
- Hold the meeting at a central location and at an hour and place convenient for the majority of those who are to attend.
- Hold this meeting at a place within the state of incorporation.
- Be sure that the incorporation was correctly carried through.
- Beware of *de facto* status, and estoppel and *quo warranto* proceedings.
- Follow the organization-meeting agenda given here merely as a guide, not as a mandatory procedure.
- Be sure to include all the essentials, especially elections and adoption of bylaws.
- Try to complete all the organizational details at one meeting, but call additional meetings if necessary.
- Hold the board of directors meeting right after the general meeting. Schedule the general meeting early enough so that there will be time for the board meeting.
- Discuss controversial matters only after finishing the basic, required points. If the discussion becomes heated, call a recess for tempers to cool. Vote immediately after re-assembly.

NOTES TO CHAPTER 20

1. P. Verrucoli, *Non-Profit Organizations (A Comparative Approach)* 66 (Dott. A. Giuffre, S.P.A., Milan, Italy; 1985).
2. Expressly required in 1985 (Proposed) Illinois Not-for-Profit Corp. Act. §102.20 (S.B. 1320), for example. *See,* Henn and Alexander, *Laws of Corporations* §135 (3rd ed., 1983).
3. Florida Bar, *Nonprofit Corporations in Florida,* §2.7 (1981); 4 Fla. Jur. 2d, Associations and Clubs §2.
4. Fla. Stat., §617.0205.
5. *Ibid.,* §607.0205.
6. *Nonprofit Corporations in Florida* §4.7 (*supra,* n.3); *Florida Basic Corporate Practice* §2.29 (C.L.E. 1977); Fla. Stat. 617.0205.
7. 805 ILCS 102.20.
8. Matter of Rappaport, 487 N.Y.S.2d 376 (App. Div. 1985); N.Y. Bus. Corp. L. §404(b).
9. Gregory v. Gregory, 338 S.E.2d 7 (Ga. App. 1985).
10. Metal Tech. Corp. v. Metal Techniques Co., 703 P.2d 237 (Or. App. 1985).
11. *See* n. 2, 4, 5.
12. *See,* 1 Oleck, *Modern Corporation Law,* §§521-575 (1978 Supp.): *and see,* Fla. St., 607.0205 (1979) (business corporation); Genl. St. N.C., §55A-9 (1978) (nonprofit corporation);

Ohio Rev. Code, §1701.10 (1978) (business corporation), and §1702.08(A) (nonprofit corporation), and §1702.10 (adoption of bylaws, called regulations in Ohio); *and see*, Murdock v. Lamb, 92 Kans. 857; 142 P. 961 (1914). But legal existence may begin without completion of full organization. Hammond v. Williams, 215 N.C. 657; 3 S.E.2d 437 (1939). Glenn v. Wagner, 329 S.E.2d 326 (N.C. 1985); Matter of Rye Psychiatric Hospital v. Schoenholtz, 476 N.Y.S.2d 339 (App. Div. 1984).

The *members*, rather than the trustees of a nonprofit corporation usually are vested with the power to adopt the fundamental rules of the corporation. Veterans of World War I v. Levy, 70 Ohio L. Abs. 49, 118 N.E.2d 670 (1952). *See*, Ohio Jur.2d:13, Corporations, §§953–956. *See also* Potter v. Patee, 493 S.W.2d 58 (Mo. App. 1973) (members of a nonprofit organization have right to conduct a meeting when officers are absent; but see n. 43 below).

13. Almac, Inc. v. JRH Development, Inc., 391 N.W.2d 919 (Minn. App. 1986).

14. About 17 months, in New York. N.Y. Bus. Corp. L., §603. Two years, in Connecticut. Di Francesco v. Kennedy, 114 Conn. 681; 160 A. 72 (1932). *See also* N.Y. N-P-C Law §604.

15. People v. Stilwell, 78 Misc. 96; 138 N.Y.S. 693 (1912); Bonaparte v. Baltimore, H.&L.R. Co., 75 Md. 340; 23 A. 784 (1892).

16. Culkin v. Hillside Restaurant, 126 N.J. Eq. 97;8 A.2d 173 (1939); Geisenhoff v. Mabrey, 58 Calif. App.2d 481; 137 P.2d 36 (1943); Beck v. Stimmel, 39 Ohio App. 510; 177 N.E. 920 (1931).

17. *See* n. 10, above; *and see*, Wortney, *What Every Lawyer Should Know About Organizing a Not-for-Profit Corporation*, 43 Ill. B. J. 856 (1955).

18. People v. Fleming, 716 P.2d 1090 (Colo. 1986).

19. Prentice v. Knickerbocker Life Ins. Co., 77 N.Y. 483 (1879); *and see*, Sherrard State Bank v. Vernon, 243 Ill. App. 122 (1928); Frankel v. 477 Central Park West Corp., 176 Misc. 701;28 N.Y.S.2d 505 (1941); Guaranty Loan Co. v. Treadwell, 53 Calif. App. 538; 200 P. 653 (1921). And as to ratification by a later meeting, when no waiver was signed, *see*, Howard v. Tatum, 81 W. Va. 561, 94 S.E. 965 (1918).

20. *In re* Election of Directors of the FDR-Woodrow Wilson Democrats, 57 Misc.2d 743, 293 N.Y.S.2d 463 (1968).

21. Ohio Rev. Code, §1702.17(B). 18 Am. Jur.2d. *Corporations*, §602; Fla. Stat. 617.0205.

22. Bank of Augusta v. Earle, 13 Pet. (U.S.) 519; 10 L. Ed. 274 (1839); Michael Bros. v. Davidson and Coleman, 3 Ga. App. 752; 60 S.E. 362 (1908).

23. *See* n.14 above, and n.12.

24. N.Y. Bus. Corp. L. §703; Ohio Rev. Code, §1702.28(A); N.Y. N-P-C Law §703(c).

25. N.Y. Bus. Corp. L., §603; N.Y. N-P-C Law §604.

26. N.Y. N-P-C Law §605.

27. N.Y. N-P-C Law §618.

28. *See* 1 Oleck, *Modern Corporation Law*, c. 25 (1978 Supp.); Harris v. Ashdown Assn., 171 Ark. 399, 384 S.W. 755 (1926); Tulare Irrigation District v. Shepard, 185 U.S. 1;22 S. Ct. 531, 46 L. Ed. 773 (1901); Baltimore and P.R. Co. v. Fifth Baptist Church, 137 U.S. 568; 11 S. Ct. 185;34 L. Ed. 784 (1890).

29. Kosman v. Thompson, 204 Iowa 1254, 1260; 215 N.W. 261, 264 (1927).

30. Cases cited in n.19, above; *also*, Methodist Episcopal Union Church v. Pickett, 19 N.Y. 482 (1859); *In re* Johnson-Hart Co., 34 F.2d 183 (D.C. Minn.) (1929); Barber v. Irving, 226 Cal. App.2d 560, 38 Cal. Rptr. 143 (1964); *cf.*, Audubon Park Commission v. Board of Comrs., 153 S.2d 574 (La. App.), *cert. den.* 244 La. 1011, 156 S.2d 223 (1963); 18 C.J.S. Corporations, §§93, 99 (1939).

31. State v. U.S. Realty Improv. Co., 15 Del. Ch. 108; 132 A. 138 (1926); Atty.-Genl. v. Gay, 162 Mich. 612; 127 N.W. 814 (1910). *And see*, note, 7 A.L.R.2d 1407 (1949); Robertson v. Levy, 197A.2d 443 (App. D.C. 1964); Cardellino v. Comptroller, 511 A.2d 573 (Md. App. 1986).

32. Hughes Co. v. Farmers' Union Produce Co., 110 Nebr. 736; 194 N.W. 872 (1923); 37 A.L.R. 1314 (1925); Baker v. Bates Street Shirt Co., 6 F.2d 854 (C.C.A. Me. 1925).

33. Kiamesha Dev. Corp. v. Guild Properties, 4 N.Y.2d 378, 175 N.Y.S.2d 63, 151 N.E.2d 214 (N.Y. 1958); 2 Model Business Corp. Act, Chapt. 50, §4.

34. *See* n. 28, above. *But see,* Di Francesco v. Kennedy, 114 Conn. 681; 160 A. 72, 74 (1932); holding that nonfiling within two years results in *de facto* status. A typical *quo warranto* statute is N.Y. N-P-C Law §§112, 1101.

35. Imperial Bldg. Co. v. Chicago Open Board of Trade, 238 Ill. 100; 87 N.E. 167 (1908).

36. Gwynne V. Board of Education, 259 N.Y. 191, 198; 181 N.E. 353 (1932); Winget v. Quincy Bldg. and Homestead Assn., 128 Ill. 67; 21 N.E. 12 (1889). *See,* Fields, *The Status of a Private Corporation Organized Under an Unconstitutional Statute,* 17 Columbia L. Rev. 327 (1917).

37. Miller v. Davis, 136 Tex. 299; 150 S.W.2d 973 (1941); 136 A.L.R. 177 (1942); Brandenstein v. Hoke, 101 Calif. 131;35 P. 562 (1894).

38. *See* cases in n.28-30, above; also, Burstein v. Palermo, 104 N.J. L. 414; 140 A. 326 (1928).

39. Martin v. Deetz, 102 Calif. 55; 36 P. 368 (1894); Emery v. De Peyster, 77 A.D.65; 78 N.Y.S. 1056 (1902); Methodist Epis. Un. Church, n.30, above.

40. *See,* Kosman case, n.29, above.

41. Agoodash Achim of Ithaca v. Temple Beth-El, 147 Misc. 405; 263 N.Y.S. 81 (1933); Albemarle County v. Massey, 183 Va. 310; 32 S.E.2d 228, 230 (1944).

42. Rogers v. Toccoa Power Co., 161 Ga. 524; 131 S.E. 517, 521 (1926); 44 A.L.R. 534 (1926); Pearson Drainage District v. Erhardt, 201 S.W.2d 484, 491 (Mo. App. 1947).

43. *See* cases in n. 32 above; *and see,* Kinney v. Bank of Plymouth, 213 Iowa 267;236 N.W. 31 (1931). "Members" who have not paid in their contributions (dues), but put them in an escrow account, are not members for meeting-call statute purposes. American Hungarian Federation v. Nadas, 519 N.E.2d 677 (Ohio App. 1987).

44. Smith v. State, 28 Ind. 321 (1867); Mears v. State, 84 Ark. 136; 104 S.W. 1095 (1907).

45. For an excellent discussion of "collateral attack," *see,* Stevens, *Corporations,* §29 (2d ed. 1949); Henn and Alexander, *Corporations,* C.7 (3rd ed., 1983).

46. *See,* n. 45, above, citing many illustrations, mostly involving business corporations.

47. *See,* Trustees of East Norway Lake Church v. Froislie, 37 Minn. 447, 451; 35 N.W. 260, 262 (1887); Baltimore and P.R. Co. v. Fifth Baptist Church, 137 U.S. 568, 11 S. Ct. 185; 34 L. Ed. 784 (1890). *See, generally,* Frey, *Legal Analysis and the "De Facto" Doctrine,* 100 U. Pa. L. Rev. 1153-1180 (1952).

48. N.Y. N-P-C Law §112, 1101.

49. Ohio Rev. Code, §2733.35 (5 years for *quo warranto* actions); §2733.36 (one year for officer's misconduct); but note that failure to bring *quo warranto* action for 20 years bars the action. *And see,* as to officer's misconduct limitation periods, N.Y.C. P.L.R., §214(4); People v. Society of St. Joseph P.D.C., 177 Misc. 419, 30 N.Y.S.2d 551 (1941).

50. *See* n. 49, above.

51. Ohio Rev. Code, §1702.20 provides that no member who is a natural person may vote by proxy unless the articles or regulations (bylaws) provide otherwise. *See,* Oleck, *Proxy Voting Power in Nonprofit Organizations,* 14 Clev.-Mar. L. Rev. 273 (1965). Florida's law allows proxy voting unless the articles or bylaws provide otherwise. FL. St. §617.0721(2).

52. Miss. Bus Corp. Act, §150 (applies only to nonprofit and nonshare corporations). *See now* Miss. Code 1972 §§79-11-143 (1992).

53. Bostetter v. Freestate Land Corp., 426 A.2d 404 (Md. App. 1981).

54. *See* n. 51, above.

21

MINUTES OF MEETINGS

[See, as to Meetings procedures, Oleck & Green, *Parliamentary Law & Practice for NPOs* (2nd ed., 1991, Amer. Law Inst.-Amer. Bar Assn.)]

§220. WHAT ARE MINUTES?

Minutes are a record of the business transacted at a meeting of the members or directors of an association or corporation, in the form of written memoranda or notes, kept in a book (or file) that is called the *minute book*.[1] It is the official memory, recollection, and record of the organization.[2]

Minutes are a summary, not a *verbatim* record of everything that was said (ordinarily), and should be objective in nature, not an expression of the personal views of the corporation's secretary.[3]

The importance of minutes. The importance of such records is made clear in the typical statutory provision of Ohio regarding them:[4]

> 1702.15. Books, records of account, and minutes.
>
> Each corporation shall keep correct and complete books and records of account, together with minutes of the proceedings of its incorporators, members, trustees, and committees of the trustees or members. Subject to limitations prescribed in the articles or the regulations upon the right of members and charitable corporations to examine the books and records, all books and records of a corporation, including the membership book prescribed by section 1702.13 of the Revised Code may be examined by any member or trustee, or the agent or attorney of either, for any reasonable and proper purpose and at any reasonable time.

The main function of minutes is to serve as an accurate history of the life of the organization.[5] When no minutes are kept, parole (oral) evidence of what occurred at a meeting can and will be admitted in evidence in court proceedings.[6] In recent years there has been some dissatisfaction with the failure of some organizations to keep, and make available to properly interested authorities, thorough and accurate minutes and other records; notably dissatisfaction of the tax (exempt) authority with such records of private foundations.[7]

Limitations on Examination of Books and Records

Permissive power to prescribe limitations on members' rights to examine minutes and other books and records is stated in the foregoing statute from the Ohio law. Similar provisions are found in some other states, sometimes repeatedly. Thus, another section of the Ohio law[8] states that provisions may be included in the articles or rules that provide

> . . . in the case of charitable corporations, limitations upon or regulations governing their (members') rights to examine the books and records of the corporation.

This limitation on members (but not on trustees) is based on the view that members properly may be denied detailed reports on the amounts of individual contributions of individual members of a church, YMCA, or other such charitable organization. Also, some donors wish to have their names omitted from lists of contributors.[9]

[See Section 227, below, as to the legal *right* to inspect corporation minutes.]

§221. WHO KEEPS THE MINUTES?

Almost invariably, the organization's secretary has responsibility for making and maintaining the minutes.[10] In a few cases some other officer, such as a vice-president, or the treasurer, is charged with this duty.

The keeping of the minutes is so important that several excellent books have been written for the guidance of organization secretaries, principally in regard to this duty. [For example, Miller, *Manual and Guide for the Corporate Secretary* (Englewood Cliffs, N.J.: Prentice-Hall, Inc., 1969); and Doris and Friedman, *Encyclopedia of Corporate Meetings, Minutes, and Resolutions* (Englewood Cliffs, N.J.: Prentice-Hall, Inc., 1958).]

The secretary, in close cooperation with the president, takes notes at business meetings, prepares minutes from these notes, reads them to the assembly, and certifies them by his or her signature when the organization has approved them.[11]

Bylaws usually designate the secretary as the keeper of the organization's books and records. He should keep these books and records in a safe place, of course.

Often, today, the attorney for the organization also is its secretary.

§222. THE MINUTE BOOK

Minutes usually are kept in a bound or looseleaf book. A separate *minute book* sometimes is kept for the meetings of the general membership, and another for the meetings of the board of directors.[12]

Keep all minutes in one book. In nonprofit organizations, experience has shown that use of a single minute book is preferable. In this book (or set of books), all meetings of members and of directors are recorded in sequence, by dates.

The reason for use of a single, chronological minute book is this: in business corporations, meetings of the stockholders are relatively few and far between. Moreover, the members are interested almost exclusively in results, not in details of procedure. A single annual report by the board of directors, plus a single annual financial statement, often is the only (and sufficient) practical way to tell the shareholders about the corporation's affairs.

In a nonprofit organization, however, the members usually are interested in all the day-by-day activities of the organization. They feel a much more direct and proprietary interest, and view the directors as primarily their agents. Usually they are unimpressed by claims to lofty "managerial status."

It follows that the keeping of all minutes as a record of a single stream of activities is what the members desire. This maintains the direct knowledge and control by the members that is the basic principle of nonprofit organization operation.

Contents of the minute book. The minute book usually contains at least:

1. Title page.
2. Copy of the Certificate (Articles) of Incorporation (and any amendatory certificates) fastened to one of the first pages of the book. (Or the constitution, if it is an unincorporated association.) [Use certified copies, if possible.]
3. Original receipt from the secretary-of-state, showing the acceptance of the charter and its filing.
4. Bylaws (and any amendments thereto).
5. Minutes of the organization meeting of the members.
6. Minutes of the organization meeting of the directors (or, trustees, if it is an unincorporated association).
7. Minutes of subsequent meetings, by dates (with important documents annexed to each meeting record to which they pertain).

It is customary to begin the minutes of each meeting at the top of a new page.

Form minutes. Printed forms of minutes, prepared by legal stationery and office supply companies, can be used for some few, small business corporation meetings. They are unsatisfactory, impractical, and even dangerous for such use.

For nonprofit organizations, they are altogether useless and undesirable.

Physical details. Use of looseleaf books seems to be preferred by most secretaries. Some, however, prefer the bound blank-book type. At the end of every year, it is desirable to bind the year's record.

The elaborateness and quality of the book depend on taste and available funds. Good quality paper and binding obviously are desirable.

The handwritten meeting notes taken by the secretary should be carefully amplified into good English and neatly typed.

Pages should be numbered. An *index* by subject, date, and page is very desirable. It can be placed at the end of the minutes for a year when that volume is sent to be bound.

The book always should be treated as an entire unit. Pages should not be removed to be taken to a meeting or anywhere else. The entire book should be taken.

Corrections and verifications. Minutes of each meeting should end with the signature of the secretary. After they are read (and corrected, if necessary, in ink) at the next meeting, the corrections should be initialed in the margin by the secretary and also by the officer presiding at that meeting.[13] Any such correction ordinarily may be made only with the consent of those present at the meeting.[14] But the directors also may correct the minutes to indicate official actions not already stated therein.[15]

After the minutes have been approved in corrected form, the counter-signature of the presiding officer shall be added below that of the secretary, in verification of their correctness.[16]

Some organizations require that each page of the minutes must be initialed by the secretary and the presiding officer.

No changes or alterations properly may be made in the minutes after this verification. Even corrections of typographical or grammatical errors may then be made only with the approval of the members present at a meeting.[17]

If changes in decisions or records (actual changes) are to be made, they may be indicated in the minutes of subsequent meetings—not by rewriting history.

§223. CONTENTS OF MINUTES OF MEETING

The minutes of each meeting, after the organization meetings, should contain at least the following minimum details. Though most minute books omit some of these in practice, this is undesirable, and may lead to serious difficulties later.

1. Time (date and hour).
2. Place (address; and even the room number).
3. Statement that the meeting was duly called:
   a. By whom;
   b. By what kind of notice;
   c. (Attach a copy of the notice or attach a waiver of notice, duly signed.)
4. Presiding officer.
5. Secretary of the meeting.
6. Names of those present.

7. Quorum statistics (how many were present in person, and how many by proxy).

8. Reading, correction, and adoption of minutes of the previous meeting.

9. Record of what occurred at this meeting, including:

    a. Resolutions proposed;

    b. Resolutions adopted (names of proposers and seconders need not be stated, ordinarily, unless they so request);

    c. Record of those who voted for or against a proposal (if they wish to have this record);

    d. Reports of officers and committees.

10. Adjournment (time).

11. Signature of secretary.

12. Counter-signature of presiding officer (obtained at next meeting, when these minutes are adopted).

[Note: For a typical set of actual[18] minutes of a routine meeting, see Forms in Section 226.]

For a *parliamentary* approach, see *Oleck & Green, Parliamentary Law and Practice for Nonprofit Organizations* (ALI-ABA, 2d ed., 1991).

§224. BINDING EFFECT OF MINUTES

Minutes of a meeting are prima facie evidence of what occurred at that meeting.[19] They are effective (but not conclusive) evidence of what was there said and done. But this evidence can be rebutted by the testimony of those who were present at that meeting.[20] Whether or not such testimony is so strong as to outweigh the written record lies within the discretion of the jury, if the matter comes before a court.

In practice, it is very difficult to prove that the facts in issue were not as they were said to be in the duly adopted minutes. Original written records are *best evidence* (superior to *secondary evidence* by testimony of witnesses), under the legal rules of evidence.[21] They *are* the transaction, in this sense, rather than merely *evidence* (testimony) of it.

For example, one court recently held that a subdivision owner, who reserved the right to construct docks on common area parcels he retained, had superior dock rights to those of the individual lot owners. The minutes of an owners' association meeting, held in conjunction with the acceptance of the subdivision owners' deed to the common areas, were sufficient evidence of unanimous agreement by all the lot owners to recognize and accept the subdivision owner's dock rights.[22]

Unsigned minutes. Duly signed and countersigned minutes fall within the *best evidence* rule, as the embodiment of the actions they record.

When minutes have been made, but not yet countersigned, nor even signed by the secretary, they nevertheless are admissible as *evidence.*[23] This means that they then are equivalent to testimony. But they are not as effective as minutes which have been duly signed.

Minutes are evidence for either side. Minutes may be used as evidence for the organization.

They also may be used as evidence against the organization.[24]

In most states, when a party seeks to use the evidence contained in minutes, an application must be made to the court. This application asks that the court issue a *subpoena duces tecum* ("bring with you").[25] This order usually is directed to the organization's president or secretary.

Self-incrimination. The Fifth Amendment to the United States Constitution guarantees individuals against being compelled to testify against themselves. But this guarantee does not apply to such artificial persons as corporations.[26]

Refusal to produce minutes, an order of a court, may not be rested on the constitutional privilege against self-incrimination. This is true under both the federal and the various state constitutions.

Both the federal government and most of the states now also have enacted compulsory testimony statutes. These provide that an officer or agent of a corporation or association must testify about organization affairs, when ordered to do so by a duly constituted authority, even though he may tend to incriminate or degrade himself by so doing. He is guaranteed, however, against personal prosecution for criminal conduct he thereby may be forced to admit.[27]

§225. MUST MINUTES BE KEPT?

Statutes in some states specifically require that nonprofit corporations keep and maintain minutes of their proceedings and complete books and records of account. The Ohio and Florida rules set forth in Section 220 are illustrative. In fact, failure to keep such records by Ohio business corporations[28] is penalized.[29]

On the other hand, New York's general nonprofit corporations statutes made adoption of even a constitution or bylaws an optional matter, let alone the keeping of minutes.[30] Most states have few or no specific requirements as to the keeping of minutes, unlike the specific requirement spelled out in the Ohio and Florida statutes.[31]

It thus is true, in some states, that there is no express legal requirement that a nonprofit organization must keep minutes of its meetings.[32]

Failure to keep minutes does not invalidate organization acts or decisions, if they are otherwise valid. Nor does it provide a basis for denial of organization responsibility for such acts or decisions.[33]

When must records be kept? In certain specific matters, statutes in many states do require that some record be kept. Usually the minutes may serve as such record.

For example, by statute in some states, a sale, lease, or mortgage of substantial assets (especially real property) often may be made only with the consent of a majority of the members or directors.[34] The obtaining of these consents, usually at a duly called meeting, must be recorded.

Again, in respect to payment of compensation to officers or agents, or entry into a contract, if the charter or bylaws do not contain authority for this, the problem of records arises. If authority is not given by the members, and if authority is not recorded in the minutes, the payment or contracting may amount to violation of the law. At best, lack of minutes in such a case will make it very difficult to prove that authority was granted.

Keeping of records by nonprofit organizations as well as by businesses is expressly required for tax and regulatory purposes. Public welfare agencies must also keep records for some purposes. Often the minutes are the primary record on which required tax and other reports must be based.[35]

FORM NO. 98

Certificate of Custody of Minutes
(Maine)

Nonprofit Corporation

State of Maine

**Certificate of Person
Having Custody of the Minutes
of**

_____

This is to certify that I have in my custody the minutes of the corporation which properly reflect the action taken by the members of the corporation as set forth in the foregoing instrument(s) to which this Certificate is attached.

Dated _____   _____
                                          (signature)

                             _____
                                  (type or print name and capacity)

FORM NO. MNPCA-X

FORM NO. 99

Minutes of Organization Meeting of Incorporators

[*Note:* The descriptive headings of the various parts of the minutes, here shown, seldom are actually reproduced in the minutes.]

(Time and Place)

The first (organization) meeting of the incorporators of ....
Association, Inc. was held at .... o'clock p.m. on ....,
19......, a .... Street, ... (city), State of
....

(Persons Present)

Present in person were:

....
....
....

(Proxies Present)

Present by written proxy were:

....

Both proxies provided that Mr. .... was to have general
voting power at this meeting on behalf of the grantors of these proxies.

(Temporary Officers)

By unanimous vote, ... was elected to serve as temporary
chairman and .... was elected as temporary secretary of the
meeting.

(Waiver of Notice)

The temporary Secretary submitted a waiver of notice of this meeting,
which was duly signed by all those present. The written proxies of Messrs.
.... and .... were accepted by the temporary
chairman and were attached to the waiver.

The temporary chairman directed that the waiver and proxies be annexed
to these minutes.

(Atttorney's Report)

...................., Esq., the attorney for the incorporators, reported
on the pre-incorporation meetings of the organizers of this Corporation, and
presented a certified copy of the Certificate of Incorporation and the original
Receipt showing the acceptance and filing by the Secretary-of-State of the State
of ...., on ...., 19......

(Acceptance of Charter)

By unanimous vote of all the incorporators present, the Certificate of
Incorporation and the Receipt for Filing were accepted.

The temporary chairman directed that they annexed to these minutes.

(Delivery of Corporation Kit)

The attorney also delivered to the temporary chairman the following items of the Corporation outfit:

Seal of the Corporation (hand press seal).

Book of membership certificates.

Minute book.

Draft of Bylaws.

(Adoption of Bylaws)

The secretary read aloud the proposed Bylaws for the regulation and management of the affairs of the Corporation. Suggested changes were passed upon by voice vote of those present, as the various sections were read. The proposed Bylaws were unanimously accepted and adopted. [*Note:* signing of the Bylaws by those present is very desirable.]

The temporary chairman directed that the Bylaws be annexed to these minutes.

(Election of Directors or Trustees)

The Temporary Chairman then announced that nominations were in order for the election of Directors to replace those who had been named in the Certificate of Incorporation to serve until this meeting.

[*Note:* Election of directors for staggered periods of office should be provided in the Bylaws. This provides continuity of experienced directors in office.]

Election of a Director to serve for three (3) years was first conducted. Mr. .... was unanimously elected to this office.

Election of a Director to serve for two (2) years was next conducted. Mr. .... was unanimously elected to this office.

Election of a Director to serve for one (1) year was next conducted. Mr. .... was elected to this office by a majority vote.

(Oath of Directors)

Messrs. ...., ..., and .... accepted their elections as Directors and took oaths of office.

(Election of President)

Nominations for the office of President then were heard. Mr. .... was unanimously elected as President and took his oath of office.

[*Note:* Bylaws often provide that the President also shall serve as the Chairman of the Board of Directors.]

The President took over the chair of the meeting, after thanking Mr. .... (the temporary chairman) for this work.

(Election of Secretary)

Mr. .... then was unanimously elected as Secretary of the Corporation and took his oath of office. He took over the notes of the temporary secretary and continued to take the minutes of the meeting.

The President delivered into custody of the Secretary the Corporation's seal, membership certificate book, minute book, and Bylaws, pursuant to the provisions of the Bylaws.

(Election of Other Officers)

Elections of officers continued.

Mr. .... was unanimously elected to be the Vice-President of the Corporation, and Mr. .... was elected by majority vote to be the Treasurer of the Corporation; and both took their oaths of office.

(Payment of Dues)

The Treasurer then accepted the payment of the sum of $ .... as membership dues for the period .... 19...... to .... 19...... from all the members present.

(Payment of Organization Expenses) (Opening of bank Account)

[*Note*. These sometimes are resolved at the meeting of the incorporators. More often they are done at the first meeting of the Directors.]

(Delivery of Membership Certificates)

The President directed the Secretary to deliver to each member who had paid his dues a certificate (card) of membership, pursuant to the Bylaws. [*Note*. In practice, today, membership cards are often used rather than certificates. Delivery, of course, must await the printing of such cards.]

(Organization Meeting of Directors Directed)

The President suggested that the organization meeting of the Board of Directors be held immediately after the adjournment of this meeting. This suggestion was unanimously approved by the meeting.

(Meeting Date Selected)

The President requested suggestions from the floor for the next meeting date. After discussion, it was unanimously agreed that the next general meeting of the members be held on ...., 19......, at .... o'clock p.m. at .... Street, ... (city), State of ....

The President also directed the Secretary to send due notice of this meeting to all members, in accordance with the provisions of the Bylaws.

(Adjournment)

There being no other business before the meeting, the meeting was, upon motion duly made and carried, adjourned, at .... o'clock p.m.

Respectfully submitted,

....

Secretary ....

(Counter-Signature)

[*Note*: The minutes are counter-signed by the president or other officer designated in the Bylaws, after these minutes are duly read, corrected, and accepted, at the next meeting.]

Corrected; and approved on ...., 19......

....

President

(Appendices)

[Annexed to these minutes (usually before the first minutes in the minute book) are:

[1. Certificate of incorporation (certified copy).

[2. Receipt for filing of the certificate.

[3. By laws.

[Also, annexed to the *end* of these minutes are:

[4. Waiver of notice of the meeting.

[5. Proxies.]

FORM NO. 100

Waiver of Notice of Organization Meeting

We, the undersigned, being all the incorporators of .... Association, Inc., do hereby severally waive all notice of the time, place, and purposes of the first (organization) meeting of the incorporators of the said Corporation, and consent that this meeting be held at .... o'clock p.m. at .... Street, ... (city), State of ...., and consent to the transaction at this meeting of any and all business that may properly come before the meeting.

Dated: .... 19......   ....

....

....

....

....

....

FORM NO. 101

Proxy for Organization Meeting

[*Note.* A proxy may be revoked by the grantor at any time, in most states.]
To Whom It May Concern: *know that*

    I, ..., an incorporator of .... Association, Inc., hereby do make, constitute, and appoint ....
(name; usually another incorporator) my proxy and attorney-in-fact, to act and vote in my place and stead at the organization meeting of the said Corporation at .... Street, ... (city), State of ...., at .... o'clock p.m., or at any adjournment thereof, as fully as though I myself were there present and voting [or, state the express voting powers: *e.g.,* "to vote for .... for President"] in any and all matters that properly come before the said meeting; and expressly ratify and confirm all that the said .... may do in my name, place, and stead.

    In witness whereof I have hereunto set my signature this .... day of ...., 19......

....

Witness:

FORM NO. 102

Minutes of Organization Meeting of Directors

[*Note.* The descriptive headings of the various parts of the minutes, here shown, seldom are actually reproduced in the minutes.]

(Time and Place)

    The first (organization) meeting of the Board of Directors of .... Association, Inc., was held at .... o'clock p.m. on ...., 19...., at .... Strect, ... (city), State of ....

(Persons Present)

Present in person were: ....

....

....

....

[*Note.* Presence of directors or trustees by proxy is highly undesirable except in very special circumstances. In some states, they may not vote by proxy at all.]

These constituted a quorum (or, the full membership) of the Board.

(Presiding Officer)

Mr. ...., the President of the Corporation, presided as Chairman. Mr. ...., the Secretary of the Corporation, took minutes.

[*Note:* Usually the bylaws make the President and Secretary members of the Board. Or the persons holding those offices are selected by the Board to serve in the same capacities at Board meetings.]

(Waiver of Notice)

The Secretary presented and read a waiver of notice of the meeting, signed by all the Directors. The Chairman directed the Secretary to file this waiver. [Or it may be annexed to these minutes.]

(Approval of Minutes)

The minutes of the first (organization) meeting of the incorporators were read aloud by the Secretary, and were approved by the Board. [Of course, if this meeting immediately follows that of the incorporators, this is unnecessary.]

(Bonding of Officers)

The Board directed that the Treasurer give a surety bond to the Corporation in the sum of $ .... The Treasurer is to present the form of such a bond, from a first-class surety company having an office in .... (city), at the next meeting of the Board, for approval. The Corporation is to bear the cost of this bond.

[Bonding of other officers may be directed.]

(Retention of Attorney)

The Board directed the President to arrange and enter into a retainer agreement with ...., Esq., of .... (address), for the retention of the said Attorney as Counsel to the Corporation, on the following terms and conditions:

[State the desired terms.]

(Resident Agent)

It was resolved that .... (name), of .... Street, ... (city), State of ...., be appointed as the Agent for the service of legal process against the Corporation, and that the Attorney for the Corporation communicate this information to the Secretary-of-State of .... upon acceptance of this appointment by the said Agent. The Secretary was directed to notify the said Agent of his appointment, and to deliver to him a duly executed certificate of authorization to this effect.

(Opening of Bank Account)

The Board directed the Treasurer to open a bank account for the Corporation with the .... Bank, in the City of ...., which bank is to be authorized to recognize as signatory officers for the Corporation on checks and drafts against deposits, only the joint co-signatures of the President, Vice-President, and Treasurer, as long as there is a balance in favor of the Corporation.

(Payment of Organization Expenses)

The Board directed the Treasurer to pay all properly evidenced fees and expenses incident to and necessary for the organization of this Corporation.

(Preparation of Membership Certificates)

The Board directed the President to arrange for the printing and distribution to the members of the Corporation of membership certificates (cards) in a form to be approved by him in consultation with the members of the Board.

(Meeting Schedule)

It was resolved that, unless otherwise ordered for special meetings which may be called pursuant to the provisions of the Bylaws, the Board of Directors shall meet regularly at the Office of the Corporation in the City of ...., State of ...., on the (third) Friday of each month at .... o'clock p.m. The Secretary shall send notice of these meetings pursuant to the provisions of the Bylaws.

(Committee Appointments)

The Chairman (President) announced the appointment of the following members to committees:

Membership Committee:
................, Chairman
....
....

Finance Committee:
................, Chairman
....
....

Publications Committee:
................, Chairman
....
....

(Adoption of Seal)

[If the Bylaws do not contain an adoption of a seal, as they usually do, the Board may adopt one.]

(Acceptance of Gift)

It was resolved by the Board that the Corporation accept the offer of (describe the property offered), which was offered as a gift by Mr. .... The President was directed to arrange, together with the Corporation's Attorney, the completion of formalities of acceptance by the Corporation and the proper filing or recording of title in the corporate name.

The Secretary was directed to have prepared, and delivered to Mr. ...., a suitable written or engraved testimonial of the gratitude and thanks of the Corporation.

(Appointment of Inspectors of Election)

The Chairman, with the approval of all the members of the Board, appointed as Inspectors of Election for all Corporation elections until ...., 19......, Messrs. ...., and ...., who immediately took their oaths of office.

(Adjournment)

There being no other business before the meeting, the meeting adjourned at .... o'clock p.m.

Respecfully submitted,

....

Secretaty

(Counter-Signiture)

[*Note:* The minutes are countersigned at the next meeting by the chairman after they are duly read, corrected, and accepted.] Corrected; and approved on ...., 19......

....

Chairman

(Appendix)

[If the waiver of notice of the meeting is directed to be annexed to the minutes, this should be done. Ordinarily, board meetings direct that the waiver be filed.]

[Resolutions, contracts, fascimiles of the seal, and other important documents often are annexed to the minutes.]

§226. ROUTINE MEETING MINUTES

Once the organization has settled down to routine operation, most of the specifically important elements shown above in the first (organization) meeting minutes no longer need to be in the minutes.

Minutes of routine meetings should always show the giving of due notice; or else the holding of meetings must be established in schedule style by the bylaws. In addition, the presence of a quorum must be shown, if the meeting is to be legally proper and effective. Signature of the secretary always should appear at the end of the minutes. Counter-signature by another officer also is desirable, as is pointed out above.

Other than this, minutes of routine meetings need contain only a clear and concise narrative of what occurred at the meeting.

For a list of the elements of minutes of a routine meeting, see section 223.

Typical minutes of a meeting of an established nonprofit organization follow. They are from the minute book of a local civic organization.

FORM NO. 103

Minutes of Regular Meeting (Civic Association)

Meeting of .... 19......, of the general membership of the .... (civic) Association, held at ....

A quorum of over .... members being present, the Chairman (President) called the meeting to order at .... p.m.

1. The minutes of the previous meeting were read by the Secretary and accepted, and various items that had been left for action by the Association were reported upon.

2. Mr. .... mentioned that ....

3. A report was rendered by Mr. .... on the situation with respect to ....

4. A motion was made and duly carried out that the Association appropriate $ .... for the purpose of ....

5. It was reported in regard to ....

6. Traffic conditions on .... Road were discussed at some length. Mr. .... suggested that ....

7. Special questions raised by various members of the Association were the following:

  a. One member indicated that ....

  b. It was pointed out that ....

8. Mr. .... brought up for discussion the question of whether the Association should ....

9. Mr. .... mentioned that volunteers for civilian defense will be needed and asked any interested members to leave their names with the President and Secretary.

10. Mr. .... rendered his report as Treasurer. The report brought out that after dues of $............... collected in the last Association year and disbursements for various purposes of $ ...., the balance on August 31, 19..... was $ ....

11. In behalf of the Nominating Committee, Mr. .... proposed the following slate for election for the forthcoming Association year:

President:.......................
Vice-President:...................
Secretary:........................
Treasurer: ....
Directors:........................
....
....
....
....
....

There were no other nominations. The slate as submitted was thereupon unanimously elected.

12. The incoming president, Mr. ...., thereupon took the chair and had the pleasure of presenting to Mr. ...., on behalf of the Association, a handsome gavel in recognition of the valuable services that Mr. .... had rendered to the Association. As his first act of office, Mr. .... named the following committee chairmen:

Block Captain Appointments:............................
School Committees:.......................................
Ordinance and Zoning:...................................
Federation of Civic Associations of................., Inc.:
....

13. The meeting was closed and the members then partook of refreshments. There were about 60 members present by the time of closing.

Respectfully submitted,

....
Secretary

Approved,...................... 19....

....
President

FORM NO. 104

Meeting Agenda Notice
School

Interoffice Correspondence

.... UNIVERSITY

COLLEGE OF ....

To   The Faculty   February 5, 19. .

From   The Dean's Office

Faculty Agenda

1. Commence meeting.
2. Approve minutes.
3. Announcements.
4. Old Business.
5. Assistant Dean ....:   Curriculum Committee policy
                                   proposal on the requirement of
                                   written final examinations
6. Dean ....:   Appointments Committee report
7. Professor ....:   Appointment of faculty liaison
8. Assistant Dean ....:   Transient student status of ....
                                   and ....

9. New business.

FORM NO. 105

Minutes of School Faculty Meeting

.... University
College of ....

Faculty Meeting

Wednesday, January 17, 19. .

The faculty of .... University College of .... held its regular
meeting at 3:00 p.m., Wednesday,January 17, 19.., with Dean ....
presiding. Present were: Professors ...., ... (etc.).
Absent were: Professors .... and ....,

Professor .... began the meeting with a prayer.

The minutes of the faculty meeting of November 15, 19..., were approved as submitted.

Assistant Dean .... moved that the petition of Professor ...., with respect to a grade change for .... be added to the agenda. Motion was seconded and carried by the required 2/3 vote.

Dean .... announced that Assistant Dean ....would be taking a leave of absence for the academic year 19..., 19..., to do graduate work. It was further announced that effective starting with the Spring Semester 19..., Professor .... had been appointed Assistant Dean with the responsibility of assisting Assistant Dean .... with student matters, along with such further responsibilities as might be assigned to him.

Professor ...., as Chairman, gave a report by the Admissions Committee on Admissions for the Autumn Term, 19...

Assistant Dean .... moved that the petition of .... be added to the agenda. Motion was seconded and carried by the required 2/3 vote.

Professor .... presented his petition to change the grade for .... in .... for the Fall Semester, 19... from .... to .... Professor .... moved that the petition be granted. Motion was seconded and carried.

Professor ...., announced that the following students had been elected to the following positions on the ...., *Review.*

........................: Research Editor
........................: Activities and Notes Editor
........................: Activities and Notes Editor
........................: Activities and Notes Editor

Professor .... moved that the foregoing students be appointed to the said editorial positions. Motion was seconded and carried.

Professor .... presented the petition of ...., a copy of which is attached and made a part of these minutes, and outlined the procedure which the Grading Committee intended to follow in this matter. No objections were expressed by the faculty.

Assistant Dean .... presented the petition of ...., a copy of which is attached and made a part of these minutes, and moved to waive the three-hour .... requirement. Motion was seconded and carried.

Assistant Dean .... presented the petition of ...., a copy of which, together with the referral letter of the Chairman of the Faculty Committee on Readmissions, is attached and made a part of these minutes. Mr. .... appeared and spoke on behalf of his petition. Professor .... moved to deny the petition. Motion was seconded and carried.

Assistant Dean .... presented petition of .... , a copy of which is attached and made a part of these minutes, and moved that .... be granted transient student status for the Summer Session of 19... Motion was seconded and carried.

No new business was presented.

The meeting adjourned at 6:10 p.m.

Respectfully submitted,

[Signature]

Secretary to the Faculty

[Attachments]

§227. INSPECTION OF MINUTES AND RECORDS

Express statutory provision of the right of members to examine minutes and other books and records is found in many states.[36] Limitation of inspection rights, in charitable organizations, for the protection of donors and for other reasons, is provided for in some statutes.[37] See section 220 for extracts from such statutes, authorizing limitation rules.

At common law, the members have a general right to inspect books and records.[38] No mismanagement need be shown, according to most decisions.[39] Inspection ought to be made for proper purposes, of course, and some cases now tend to place the burden of proof on the corporation officers if improper purpose is alleged.[40] For example, in New York, a qualified member of a not-for-profit corporation may examine the corporation's books and records to obtain a list of the corporate members, absent established bad faith and improper purpose on the member's part.[41]

It has been held that a court does have the authority to order that members be permitted to examine books and records of accounts, and that members could bring suit for the appointment of an auditor to investigate a non-profit corporation's accounts without the society first being required to file formal charges of grievance concerning fiscal discrepancies with the society's grand master.[42] However, the court did say that the inspection should not interfere with the internal economy, policy, discipline, operation, or management of the society.[43]

Typical "improper purposes" would be the obtaining of "sucker lists" or an intention to find material to use for blackmail extraction.[44]

The member may be accompanied by his attorney and accountant, and may copy extracts from the record.[45] In general, the reduction of these rules to statute form should not be understood to mean impairment of inspection rights, unless the restriction is clearly intended.[46]

Other records, such as computer data, also may be inspected.[47] Membership lists may be inspected.[48]

Directors' rights of inspection are deemed absolute in some jurisdictions and qualified (by good faith) in others.[49] Even a former director has the right to inspect records covering his period of office, in order to protect his personal rights and responsibility interests, if there is some indication that he may be charged with improper conduct.[50] Directors' rights are based on their duties to keep themselves informed about the organization's affairs.[51]

Statute provisions concerning the right to inspect books and records of a corporation now are so common, and so specific as to various subjects and situations, that it is wise to consult specific statutes and case law in a dispute about such rights.[52] But these statutes generally do not nullify common law rights except as specifically so intended as to specific records and situations.[53] Time limits and other restrictions on the right to inspection are numerous.[54] Fines and penalties for refusal of the right also may apply,[55] especially where "securities" are involved.[56]

State inspection rights, of course, are almost absolute.[57]

Improper purpose may cause loss of the right of inspection.[58]

POINTS TO REMEMBER

- Keep minutes of all meetings.
- Keep them in clear, short form, properly verified.
- Keep them in a minute book (looseleaf or bound).
- Transcribe meeting notes as soon as possible after the meeting.
- The secretary should keep the minutes and *guard* them.
- Do not use printed-form minutes.
- Make changes or corrections only with approval of the members. Initial every change.
- Include the essential points each time.
- Remember the binding legal effect of the minutes. Be careful of what is said in them.
- But remember that minutes are prima facie evidence—not conclusive proof of what they state. They can be opposed by oral testimony.
- No privilege against self-incrimination applies to the minutes.
- Be particularly careful in writing up the organization meeting minutes.
- Fasten important documents (charter, waivers) into the minute book.
- Do not put every routine document into the minute book.
- Do not permit minutes of routine meetings to degenerate into fragmentary notes.

• Make sure that directors are given easy access to minutes and other books and records.

NOTES TO CHAPTER 21

1. *Black's Law Dictionary*, 900 (5th ed., 1979); Henn and Alexander, *Corporations* §199 (3rd ed., 1983); *Directors' and Officers' Encyclopedic Manual* 314 (Prentice-Hall, Inc. 1955); 18 Am. Jur.2d, *Corporations*, §1132; Chapin v. Cullis, 299 Mich. 101, 299 N.W. 824 (1941).

2. So important that even when the original is lost or destroyed (as by fire) a court may receive as evidence an abstract or sworn copy of it. Fla. St., §§92.25-92.28.

3. Oleck & Green, *Parliamentary Law & Practice for NPOs* §13 (2d ed., 1991; H.M. Robert, *Robert's Rules of Order* New Revised 389 (1981). *See* Forms in Oleck, *Modern Corporation Law*, Numbers 573-583 *et passim* (1978 supp.).

4. Ohio Rev. Code §1702.15; Fla. St. §§817.15, 817.16, 607.1601, 617.1601; Ohio Rev. Code Ann. §1702.

5. W.T. Carnes, *Effective Meetings for Busy People*, 92 (1980).

6. G.S. Hills, *Managing Corporate Meetings*, 656 (1977).

7. Comptroller General (GAO), *Public Information Reporting by Tax-Exempt Private Foundations Need More Attention by the IRS* (Sept. 23, 1983).

8. Ohio Rev. Code, §1702.11(A)(4).

9. Ohio Legislative Committee Comment 1955, following Ohio Rev. Code, §1702.11, in *1970 Ohio Corporation Laws Annotated*, issued by Ted W. Brown, Secretary of State.

10. Dendinger v. J. D. Kerr Gravel Co., 158 La. 324, 104 S. 60 (1925); Hornaday v. Goodman, 167 Ga. 555, 146 S.E. 173 (1928); Glencoe Board of Education v. Trustees of Schools 174 Ill. 510, 74 Ill. App. 401 (1898); Sturges, *Standard Code of Parliamentary Procedure*, 198 (2d ed. 1966); Mauritz v. Schwind, 101 S.W.2d 1085, 1090 (Tex. Civ. App. 1937).

11. *Ibid.*

12. *See,* Miller, *Manual and Guide for the Corporate Secretary* (Prentice-Hall, Inc., Englewood Cliffs, N.J.c. 1969); Doris and Friedman, *Encyclopedia of Corporate Meetings, Minutes and Resolutions* (Prentice-Hall, Inc., Englewood Cliffs, N.J. 1958).

13. *See* n. 10.

14. Those present may demand that the minute book be produced. State *ex. rel.* Dendinger v. J. D. Kerr Gravel Co., 158 La. 324, 104 S. 60 (1925).

15. Brown v. Ramsdell, 139 Misc. 360; 249 N.Y.S. 387 (1931). To show what actually was done. Caldwell v. Dean, 10 F.2d 299 (D.C. N.Y. 1926).

16. *But* the reading and tacit acceptance actually is sufficient acknowledgement of correctness. Hornaday v. Goodman, 167 Ga. 555; 146 S.E. 173 (1928). Signature by the secretary validates the minutes, even if the secretary actually did not read them out before signing. Teiser v. Swirsky, 137 Ore. 595; 2 P.2d 920; 4 P.2d 322 (1931).

17. *See* cases in n. 9-12.

18. For samples of many specific types of minutes of meetings (*e.g.,* of organization meeting, trustees' meeting, official forms provided in some states, *etc.*) *see,* 5 Oleck, *Modern Corporation Law*, Forms 579-583, 716, 1048 (1978 Supp.).

19. Stipe v. First National Bank of Portland, 301 P.2d 175 (Ore. 1956); *In re* Mandelbaum, 80 Misc. 475, 141 N.Y.S. 319 (1913), *affd.,* 159 A.D. 909, 144 N.Y.S. 1128 (1913).

20. Keogh v. St. Paul Milk Co., 205 Minn. 96; 285 N.W. 809 (1939).

21. *See* cases in n.16; Supreme Kingdom, Inc. v. Fourth Natl. Bk., 174 Ga. 779, 164 S.E. 204 (1932).

22. *Dowd v. Ahr*, 563 N.Y.S. 2d 917 (A.D. 3 Dept. 1990).

23. Woodhaven Bank v. Brooklyn Hills Impr. Co., 69 A.D. 489; 74 N.Y.S. 1023 (1902); 48 A.L.R.2d 1261, Gale-Hasslacher Corp. v. Carmen Contracting Corp., 219 N.Y.S.2d 212 (1961).

24. *See*, Annot., 19 A.L.R.3d 869 (1968); 15 A.L.R.2d 11 (1951); Ochs v. Washington Hts. Fed. S.&L. Assn., 17 N.Y.2d 82, 268 N.Y.S.2d 294, 215 N.E.2d 485 (1966); 5 Fletcher, *Private Corporations*, §§2213-2226.4 (curr. ed.).

25. *See, Ex parte* Harte, 240 Ala. 642; 220 S. 783, 785 (1941); General records are not privileged. *In re* Keough, 151 Ohio St. 307, 85 N.E.2d 550 (1949); Ohio Civil R. 45; Ohio Crim. R. 17.

26. Shapiro v. United States, 335 U.S. 1; 68 S. Ct. 1375; 92 L. Ed. 1787 (1948).

27. *E.g.*, Federal Compulsory Testimony Act, 49 U.S.C., §46; N.Y. Genl. Corp. L., §13 (Omitted in N.Y. Bus. Corp. L. and N.Y. N-P-C Law). *And see*, United States v. Monia, 317 U.S. 424; 63 S. Ct. 409, 87 L. Ed. 376 (1943), concerning the then Emergency Price Control Act of 1942 (Publ. L. 421, Jan. 30, 1942). Similar provisions are found in other statutes, such as, Social Security Act, 42 U.S. C.A., §405 (a, d-f); Labor Management Rel. Act. 29 U.S. C.A., §§156, 161, 177(c).

28. Ohio Rev. Code, §1701.37.

29. Ohio Rev. Code, §1701.94.

30. N.Y. Memb. Corp. L., §20 (now repealed).

31. Ohio Rev. Code, §1702.15; Fla. Stat. §617.1601.

32. Wright v. Phillips Fertilizer Co., 193 N.C. 305; 136 S.E. 716 (1927); Woodhaven Bank v. Brooklyn Hills Impr. Co., 69 A.D. 489; 74 N.Y.S. 1023 (1902).

33. Redstone v. Redstone Lumber and Supply Co., 101 Fla. 226; 133 S. 882 (1931); Sorge v. Sierra Auto Supply Co., 47 Nev. 217; 218 P. 735; 221 P. 521 (1924).

34. Fla. Stats. §617.1202. But no members consents needed under Ohio Rev. Code, §1702.36; and Fla. Stats. §617.1201 as to mortgages.

35. Int. Rev. Code, §§441, 446; *see* Mertens, *Law of Federal Income Taxation*, §47.44 (curr. supp. ed.), citing, as to information returns, Int. Rev. Code, §6033(a). *And see*, 220 at n.7, for the mid-1980's situation.

36. Ohio Rev. Code, §1702.15; Ga. Code, §§14-3-1602 through 14-3-1604; Or. Rev. Stats. §61.161; Fla. Stat. 617.1601.

37. *Ibid.*, §1702.11(A)(4); *and see* above, n.9.

38. *See*, Ochs v. Washington Hts. Fed. S.&L. Assn., 17 N.Y.2d 82, 268 N.Y.S.2d 294, 215 N.E.2d 485 (1966); Annot., 19 A.L.R.3d 869 (1968); Weisfeld v. Spartans Industries, Inc., 58 F.R.D. 570 (D.C. N.Y. 1972). *Also*, voting lists: Magill v. North Amer. Refr. Co., 36 Del. 185, 128 A.2d 233 (1956); 36 Del. 305, 129 A.2d 411 (1957); *see also*, Henn and Alexander, *Corporations*, 536-546 (3rd ed., 1983).

39. *See*, 5 Fletcher, *Private Corporations*, §§2222 *et seq.* (curr. rev.). But some cases say that reasonable grounds for suspecting mismanagement must be shown: Matter of Martin v. Columbia Pictures Corp., 307 N.Y. 922, 123 N.E.2d 572 (1954).

40. Hagy v. Premier Mfg. Corp., 404 Pa. 330, 172 A.2d 283 (1961); Smooth Ashlar Grand Lodge (compact) of F.&A.A. York Masons v. W. H. Odom, 136 Ga. App. 812, 222 S.E.2d 614 (1975).

41. *Gardega v. Washington St. Marine Officers Corp.*, 562 N.Y.S. 2d 688 (A.D. 1 Dept. 1990).

42. Smooth Ashlar Grand Lodge (compact) of F.&A.A. York Masons v. W. H. Odom, 136 Ga. App. 812, 222 S.E.2d 614 (1975).

43. *Ibid.*, p. 616.

44. Slay v. Polonia Publ. Co., 249 Mich. 609, 229 N.W. 434 (1930); Fletcher, above, n.39, at §2226; *See* Fla. Stat. 607.1602 (6).

45. Fletcher, above, n.39, at §§2233, 2241, Brandt v. New Orleans H., 193 S.2d 32 (La. App. 1966).

46. Weck v. District Court, 158 Colo. 521, 408 P.2d 987 (1965); Tucson Gas and Elec. Co. v. Schantz, 5 Ariz. App. 511, 428 P.2d 686 (1967); Model Bus. Corp. Act, §46; Schwartzman v. Schwartzman, 659 P.2d 888 (N.M. 1983); *cf.*, Caspary v. Louisiana Land & Exp. Co., 707 F.2d 785 (4th cir. 1983).

47. Freed, *Providing by Statute for Inspection of Corporate Computer and Other Records Not Legibly Visible* . . . , 23 Bus. Law 457 (1968).

48. Ochs v. Washington Heights Fed Sav. and Loan Assn., 17 N.Y.2d 82, 268 N.Y.S.2d 294, 215 N.E.2d 485 (1966).

49. Note, *Right of Directors to Inspect Corporate Books and Records*, 11 Villa. L. Rev. 578 (1966); Henn and Alexander, *Corporations*, §216 (3d ed. 1983); Cal. Corp. Code §1602.

50. Matter of Cohen v. C-C Clubs, Inc., 10 Misc.2d 57, 171 N.Y.S.2d 873 (1958).

51. *See*, 2 Oleck, *Modern Corporation Law*, cc. 41, 42 (1978 Supp.).

52. *See*, Henn and Alexander, *Corporations* (3d ed., 1983; §199 as to members' rights and §216 as to directors' rights.

53. *Ibid.; and see* 5 Fletcher, *Private Corporations* §§2222 *et passim* (curr. ed.).

54. *E.g.*, N.Y. CPLR §217 (within 4 months after refusal of demand). *See also* Fla. Stat. 607.1602.

55. Fritz v. Belcher Oil Co., 363 S.2d 155 (Fla. App. 1978).

56. *See*, Henn and Alexander, *Corporations* §297 (3rd ed., 1983); N.Y. Stock Exch., *Company Manual* §A4 (curr. ed.).

57. Okl. Const. Art. II §28.

58. Dusel v. Castellani, 350 N.Y.S.2d 258 (App., 1973): director may be personally liable for breach of fiduciary duty in exercising his absolute right to inspect. *Cf.*, Javits v. Investors League, 92 N.Y.S.2d 267 (1949).

22

BYLAWS

[Julian J. Izydore assisted in the researching to update this chapter.]

§228. BYLAWS ARE NECESSARY

Bylaws are the set of rules adopted by an organization for its internal management and government.[1] They constitute a code of internal laws, even if not in writing.[2] They are valid if they do not contradict the organization's charter but only add to it;[3] but void if they contradict it.[4] They are contractual in nature, binding the members[5] and the organization.[6]

Most state statutes *permit*, or suggest, use of *bylaws* by nonprofit organizations, rather than specifically *require* them. Ohio's statute says that nonprofits "may adopt" regulations (bylaws),[7] while New York's statutes "permit" them.[8] Florida's old NPC statute permitted (but did not require) adoption of bylaws, but the state ruled that a court has no power to *require a church* corporation "to pass or not pass bylaws." Most states permit or suggest adoption of bylaws; common sense says that they should be adopted in order to avoid disputes about procedures, if nothing else.[9] Florida's new (1991) statute impliedly requires bylaws, and places adoption powers in the directors unless the articles of incorporation state otherwise.[10]

Any set of internal rules, whether called *bylaws* or *regulations*[11] or by any other name, constitute bylaws.[12] They amount to a binding contract among the members, as to how internal management shall be carried on, insofar as they are not contrary to law or public policy.[13] They are secondary only to the charter of the organization (constitution of an unincorporated association) in force and binding effect, so far as the members are concerned.

Practical necessity. Lack of bylaws, or inadequate bylaws, are almost certain sources of friction and trouble in any organization. When differences of opinion arise, as to proper procedures or rights and powers of members or officers, well-drawn bylaws serve to resolve most differences.

Legal necessity. Some state statutes specifically require that bylaws be adopted, particularly by corporations.[14] In almost all states, there are statutory provisions that assume that bylaws will be adopted by corporations. For example, many statutes state that the procedure for amending the organization's charter may be that specified in the bylaws.[15] Commonly, statutes governing voting, elections, meetings and notices, and the like, refer to the procedures stated in the bylaws.[16]

It is well-settled that corporations and other organizations have an inherent power to adopt and amend bylaws.[17] Tax benefits of nonprofit status are difficult to obtain when an organization cannot show reasonably adequate provisions for internal management.[18]

Constitution, means any fundamental body of rules or principles of an organization (or state or nation), embodied in a written document, or implied in custom and practice.[19] Often the term is applied to an organization's charter; if the constitution and bylaws conflict, the constitution governs.[20] This is the same rule that applies to conflicts between articles of incorporation and bylaws; the articles govern.[21]

The term *constitution* is vague and general. It usually is applied to the basic governing document of an unincorporated association, but sometimes is used by corporations. Often it is used as a joint-term for the bylaws; *e.g.*, "Constitution and Bylaws of . . . . . . Association." Sometimes it is used to mean the articles of incorporation (or association) *plus* the *bylaws*; occasionally, to mean merely the bylaws.

Constitutional means conforming to the provisions of a constitution.[22]

Experienced lawyers, aware of the uncertain and varied meanings of the word, avoid using *constitution* in relation to nonprofit organizations. Instead, they use specific terms, such as articles of association, articles of incorporation, bylaws, regulations, and so forth.

Purposes of bylaws. In summary, bylaws:

1. Regulate the internal practices and procedures of the organization.

2. Define the relations, rights, and duties of the members amongst themselves and in relation to the organization.

3. Define the powers, duties, and limitations of trustees (directors), officers, and other agents.[23]

Adoption of bylaws may be proven by the records of the organization or minutes of meetings, even if the bylaws are not written out as a single body of rules.[24] Oral proof must suffice if there is no written record,[25] or proof by evidence of custom, usage, or acquiescence.[26]

Court Review. Courts may view internal procedural rules of associations, especially as to fairness;[27] and particularly if membership is an economic necessity.[28]

Courts are usually reluctant to interfere in internal matters, but will do so if justice requires it,[29] especially if economic necessity is involved, but seldom if anti-trust violations are alleged.[30] Arbitrary or discriminatory actions of an organization will invite court scrutiny,[31] or expulsion based on private disagreement.[32]

Fairness and reasonableness may be tested in terms of *balancing* of the equities.[33] Equal protection clause violations by members seldom are found to involve state action or property rights.[34] Violations of federal law or public policy will bring court scrutiny.[35] Generally, the courts are hesitant to compel admission to membership.[36] The internal remedies available in an organization must be exhausted before judicial review will be granted.[37]

§229. WHO ADOPTS THE BYLAWS?

The power to adopt or amend the bylaws of nonprofit corporations ought to be placed fundamentally in the general membership.[38] Trustees' or directors' powers, in this respect, basically ought to be limited to adoption of board bylaws, binding only for government of meetings of the board of trustees.[39] But the newer statutes, such as Florida's [see above, n.10] place the power basically in the directors unless the articles or bylaws provide otherwise. EMERGENCY BYLAWS are left to the discretion of the directors (e.g., as in wartime) by the new statutes such as Florida's [Fl. St.§617.0207].

The 1986 Exposure Draft of the Revised Model Nonprofit Corporation Act (ABA) Section 2.06 places the power to adopt bylaws in "The incorporators or board of directors." In the case of a foundation or one-man or other small-group organization, there is some sense in having directors so empowered. In a true membership organization it is a device (or invitation) for domination.[40]

Bylaws of limited application must not be inconsistent with the general bylaws.

At the organization meeting of a corporation or of an unincorporated association, the adoption of bylaws by the members almost always is one of the first matters attended to.

The statutes in most, but not all, states permit directors or trustees to amend the bylaws, or add to them, only insofar as the general membership grants the right in the original bylaws or in the charter.[41]

But the members may grant quite general powers to the directors to amend or add to the bylaws. This is perfectly legal (though often undesirable). It does not transfer the primary power from the members in regard to the bylaws. Such power given the directors or trustees remains secondary to that of the general membership, and may be withdrawn. It is well if the bylaws state an exact procedure for the purpose.

Many persons urge that absolutely no power to change the bylaws ever be delegated to the directors. But in routine procedural matters, granting such power to them is convenient.

In granting of power to anyone, it is wise to reflect on the cynical saying attributed to Lord Acton, that "all power corrupts, and absolute power corrupts absolutely."

§230. HOW BYLAWS ARE ADOPTED

Few state statutes specify procedure for adopting bylaws. Usually the members simply adopt by majority vote at the organization meeting.

The attorney for the incorporators usually drafts the original bylaws immediately after the filing of the charter. He follows the general directions of the incorporators. As the incorporators are usually the original members, the adoption of the bylaws at the organization meeting may be a mere formality. But sometimes a committee is appointed to draft the bylaws after incorporation.

In the organization of an association, the articles of association and bylaws often are all contained in one document—the *constitution*. Almost always a committee draws up this document, or separate bylaws, after the organization meeting. Then the bylaws are adopted by majority vote.

State statutes sometimes specify the percentage of votes required for adoption of a bylaw.[42] If adoption customarily is by voice vote or other special procedure, such custom may be required to be proved, if court proceedings are invoked.[43]

Waiver of the right to vote on a bylaw adoption may be spelled out by conduct of a member at the voting meeting.[44]

The charter or articles may require a greater-than-majority vote for adoption. A two-thirds or even a three-fifths vote-requirement is a prolific source of difficulty in reaching final agreement.[45]

Adoption usually takes the form of a resolution, but oral consents, or mere tacit consents implied by use of the drafted bylaws, may suffice.[46]

The aid of an experienced attorney is almost indispensable in drafting the bylaws.

§231. RESOLUTIONS ARE NOT BYLAWS

Bylaws should not be confused with *resolutions*. A resolution may be used to adopt the bylaws; but the bylaws are not resolutions.

A *resolution* is a formal expression, usually in writing, of a decision, opinion, or attitude of an organization, or of a group (such as the board of directors or a committee), adopted by vote in accordance with a regular procedure. Ordinarily the idea or viewpoint thus to be embodied is introduced by a motion at a meeting. A resolution is used for a *single decision* or act, or to express an official attitude towards a single matter.[47]

In contrast, a *bylaw* is a *permanent enactment* of a generally applicable, continuing rule, intended to serve as a governing regulation for all members concerned with its subject matter.[48]

An example of purpose of a resolution is the issuance of "subvention" paper (contractual debt acknowledgement) for financing purposes under the New York statutory authorization, which does not permit issuance of stock.[49]

Which should be used for what: When the purpose is *to establish a fixed policy*, a *bylaw* should be adopted. The same is true for giving notice of a permanent policy.

When the matter is *transient or temporary* (*e.g.*, to accept or reject a contract or gift, or to approve or disapprove a specific matter) a *resolution* should be used.

It is undesirable to lay down a more precise rule for choosing between a bylaw and a resolution. Each is an internal law when adopted. Often either may serve. But it is good policy not to clutter up the bylaws with many provisions that will have no particular utility later on.

In general, use of a resolution rather than a bylaw is appropriate in the following cases:

1. If a statute specifically requires a resolution.
2. If the matter is temporary or transient in nature.
3. If the matter is unlikely to arise again.
4. If the matter is of small importance.
5. If notice of a single matter needs to be given (*e.g.*, a requirement to file a certain report).
6. If an amendment to the charter or bylaws thereby is to be adopted.
7. If permanent record of a matter is to be made.
8. If a procedural change in management practice is not lasting enough to make desirable its recording in the bylaws.

Resolutions book. Many organizations keep a separate book of resolutions, carefully indexed, as a convenient permanent record. This saves considerable searching through the minutes, and also preserves the privacy of the minutes. When a stranger is to be shown a particular resolution, he need not be permitted to read the whole private history of the organization.

No particular form is required for a resolution, so long as its sense is clear. One simple form (fixing salaries) follows:

FORM NO. 106

Resolution on Salaries

Resolved, that the following shall be the salaries paid to the respective officers of the Association (Corporation) during the year of 19 . . for their services other than those rendered in their capacities as Directors:

President	$
Vice-President	$
Secretary	$
Treasurer	$

FORM NO. 107

Resolution Appointing Special Agents

UPON MOTION duly made, seconded, and passed, the Board of Directors of . . . . Heights Civic Club, Inc. on the day of . . . . , 19. . . hereby resolves:

RESOLUTION #4
     The following persons are approved and named officers of the ....
Heights Buying Club.
President   _____
Vice-President   _____
Secretary   _____
Treasurer   _____
Chairman of Packaging Committee   _____
Chairman of Ordering (Purchasing) Committee   _____
Chairman of Finance Committee (Financial Secretary)   _____

§232. BYLAWS AND CONTRACTS

The bylaws and articles of incorporation, of a nonprofit corporation, are a form of contract between the corporation and its members, and among members themselves. Applicable statutes are, by implication, included in the relationship between the members and the nonprofit corporation.[50] However, as a general rule the court will not interfere in the internal affairs of nonprofit corporations, absent fraud or bad faith. This is the *"business judgment rule."* Thus, it is within a homeowners association's discretion to approve the construction of a fence that is in violation of an association covenant.[51]

     NPC *hospital bylaws* are *not* part of an integrated *contract of employment* of an independent contractor radiologist (as to procedures for dismissal from staff privileges) where the contract *expressly stated* that termination of the contract would also terminate staff privileges.[52]

     When the directors of a nonprofit water system company adopted rate structures, in violation of a corporate by-law, which required consent of the Farmers Home Administration along with notice to the members of the amount of such charges and dates for payment, the rate structure was voided.[53]

     Though a shipper's association's bylaws did not say that it was an agent for its members, agency was found because the members had the ability to control operation of the association, and the association provided low shipping rates to its members.[54]

§233. AMENDMENT OF BYLAWS

The charter or articles may contain provisions regulating the manner of amendment of the bylaws. In most cases, the bylaws themselves provide for the method of their amendment. Sometimes alternate methods are set forth. In only a few cases do statutory provisions govern such amendments. Almost any reasonable rules may be adopted for this purpose. For example, the amendment of an association bylaw, requiring a two-thirds majority to amend bylaws, is not unreasonable or oppressive, especially where the membership votes to retain the amendment. A member has no contractual or property right to an associational bylaw, based upon his reliance on the bylaw.[55]

It is possible to amend a bylaw *de facto* without formal adoption of any changed provision. If, for example, a custom or practice contrary to a given bylaw is followed (and acquiesced in) for a considerable period, the customary practice may become the rule, though never written down.[56] A unanimous decision by the members (*e.g.*, a resolution) may have the same effect.[57]

Most bylaws provide fairly detailed procedures for their own amendment—usually, that certain notice of a proposed change must be sent, that the change must be voted upon at a formal meeting, and that a certain majority or plurality vote must be obtained to carry the proposal.

Consistent disregard or nonuse of a bylaw by the board of directors, with the acquiescence of the members, may have the same effect as outright repeal or amendment.[58]

Tests of validity of an amendment. Any amendment to the bylaws, adopted in accordance with the procedures prescribed by the charter, bylaws, or statutes, is valid and effective if it is:

1. Consistent with the general laws
2. Consistent with the charter
3. Consistent with the rest of the bylaws
4. Generally reasonable
5. Able to be obeyed
6. Not in violation of an established right
7. Not in violation of a contract

These latter tests, of course, refer to the validity of the amendment with respect to individuals. If the change violates someone's established rights, for example, it is invalid as far as he is concerned.[59] Such invalidity may suffice to invalidate the amendment entirely. Yet in some instances, it may be invalid to one person and bind others (*e.g.*, those who approved it in order to injure the one).[60]

Directors' power to amend bylaws usually requires state statute authorization of such grant of power.[61] Absence of a provision in the articles or bylaws may be interpreted to leave the power open.[62]

Amendments may not abrogate established rights.[63] Changes to require unanimity of vote, may override the usual statutory requirement of a simple majority vote.[64] Amendments must be prospective in effect, not retroactive.[65] Unless otherwise provided, the ones who adopted the bylaws have the power to amend them.[66]

§234. BINDING EFFECT OF BYLAWS ON MEMBERS AND OTHERS

The binding effect of bylaws among the members of an organization lies in the contract nature of the bylaws adoption.[67] Acceptance of the bylaws amounts to submission to internal laws. Those who, by joining, agree to the charter's provisions agree to abide by its other rules—its bylaws.[68] Those who adopt the bylaws, of course, expressly bind themselves thereby.

Third persons. Third persons who deal with the organization are not ordinarily bound by its bylaws.[69] If they expressly, or impliedly, agree to be bound by them, they are bound. This can happen if they know the bylaws, and act with such knowledge.[70]

Constructive notice, without actual knowledge, may be equivalent to knowledge. This applies to members, who should know their bylaws, and therefore are (by construction) deemed to have such knowledge.[71] Third persons are not ordinarily charged with such notice.[72] But in a few states, all corporations are required to post their bylaws conspicuously in their offices or places of activity. This may amount to constructive notice to third persons dealing with the corporation.[73]

Bylaws are internal documents. Ordinarily they need not be filed in any public office (except in the Internal Revenue Department, in an application for exemption from income taxation, where law requires privacy be protected). Thus they are *not public documents,* as court and other public records (such as a charter) usually are.[74]

Waiver of bylaws. Even on its members, or on informed third persons, an organization can waive the binding effect of its bylaws.[75] This can be done by resolution or by action contrary to the bylaws. These actions amount to adopting a different bylaw for the particular matter.

Bylaw adoption (and vote) may amount to abandonment of existing rights.[76] Rules of contract interpretation may be applied to bylaws,[77] and such rules may vary from state to state.[78]

Bylaws and Statutes

Court enforcement of a *condominium* rule barring display of flags except on stated occasions is "state action" and makes private conduct into constitutionally covered action.[79]

If the bylaws of a *member* club of the Professional Golf Association Tour contests allows use of certain kinds of clubs that are not in accordance with PGA bylaws, the golfer members and approved club manufacturer may enjoin the use of the only-local-club-rules type of golf clubs.[80]

A former occupant of a cooperative apartment complex brought suit to redeem shares of stock in the cooperative pursuant to a state statute applying to the redemption of real property. However, the rights, remedies and procedures for enforcing rights between the occupant and the cooperative association were spelled out in the occupancy agreement and association bylaws. The court held that the bylaws, and not the real property redemption statute, controlled the occupant's redemption rights, even though the controlling redemption period fell short of redemption rights the occupant would have had under the real property statute.[81]

A bylaw of a religious association that forbade election of delegates aged 66 years or more is a violation of a statute barring age (of 40 to 70) discrimination for "job openings."[82]

§235. RELATION BETWEEN CHARTER AND BYLAWS

Bylaws are the secondary law of the organization; the charter is its primary law. But ordinarily these supplement each other. Therefore, the bylaws must be interpreted in the light of the charter. Similarly, the charter sometimes can be interpreted by viewing the bylaws as an elaboration of its general terms. But if there is a conflict between the charter and the bylaws, the charter must govern.[83] *Charter* is a synonym for *articles of incorporation*, ordinarily.

Bylaws always must be consistent with the provisions of the charter; otherwise, they are of no effect.

The charter, being on file in a public office (*e.g.*, in the secretary-of-state's office and in the county clerk's office), is constructive notice, to third persons, of what it contains. This is not true of the bylaws. Only members and those third parties who have actual or constructive knowledge of their provisions ordinarily are charged with knowledge of them. (See the foregoing section.)

Bylaws need not be so-entitled in order to be such. Whatever they are called, if they have the nature of bylaws, that is what they are.[84]

Neither the charter nor the bylaws may override statutes or ordinances. But statutes, ordinances, and the duly issued regulations of governmental administrative agencies may override both the charter and the bylaws.[85] (And see notes 27 and 28.)

Either the charter or the bylaws may specify the quorum required for a general meeting, and make other such provisions. But today's charter ordinarily contains little more than a statement of the purpose of the organization. The bylaws therefore must do most of the providing for operation and management. They must be *reasonable*, and should at least provide for the election of directors and officers, and specify their powers and duties.[86]

Members of the organization have an inherent right to see and make extracts from the bylaws, at reasonable times (*i.e.*, during business hours[87]). Directors have not only an absolute right, but also a duty, to see the bylaws and familiarize themselves with their provisions.[88] The charter, being a public record, is available at the secretary of state's corporation division, or county clerk's office, for inspection by any person who cares to see it (the certified copy there on file); and anyone may obtain a certified copy by paying the fee charged by the county clerk (from 50 cents to one dollar per page of photostatic copy).

It has been held that the *ultra vires* doctrine does not apply to bylaws.[89] And some aspects (or kinds) of bylaws are covered by express state statutes. Today the *ultra vires* doctrine is limited by state statutes, in many states, so as to limit challenges to the corporation's power to act.[90]

§236. CONTENTS OF BYLAWS

Bylaws must not offend public policy,[91] and they may be governed by express statutes sometimes.[92]

It should be obvious that there is no fixed form for bylaws. They must be tailored to the purpose and special situation of each organization. Their content, length, and amount of detail are largely a matter of common sense. Like a lady's dress, they should be long enough to cover the subject and short enough to invite study.

Corporate and noncorporate bylaws. Differences in details are dictated by the unincorporated or incorporated status of the organization. If the organization is incorporated, many details are covered by the corporation laws of the state. It is generally true that the bylaws of a corporation need not be quite as detailed as those of an unincorporated association.

Yet it is wise to think of probable difficulties before they arise. It is good general policy to provide in advance in the bylaws for many possible eventualities. This includes both corporate and noncorporate bylaws.

Some bylaws drafted by attorneys name the attorney's office (or firm) as "Registered Agent" for the client organization. This means, in effect, that a change of agent will require formal revision (amendment) of this bylaw. This practice, in the opinion of many lawyers, is very questionable when the client (e.g., a condominium association for example) is officered by laypersons who do not understand what such a bylaw really involves.

Forms of bylaws for *unincorporated associations* are provided in Chapter 6.

Forms for *corporations* are provided in Chapter 23.

Contents of bylaws. Typical important provisions in the bylaws of any organization are these.[93]

1. Purposes stated in the charter should be restated in somewhat greater detail.

2. Qualifications for membership, methods of admission of members, rights and privileges.

3. Initiation or admission fees, dues, termination of membership for nonpayment or otherwise.

4. Rules for withdrawal, censure, suspension, and expulsion of members (including appeals).

5. Officers' titles, terms of office, times and manner of election or appointment, qualifications, powers, duties, and compensation (for each office, respectively).

6. Vacancies in offices or on the board of directors: when they shall be deemed to require action, and the method of filling such vacancies.

7. Voting by the members, including what number shall constitute a quorum. This may include cumulative voting, voting by bondholders on the

basis of the number of bonds held, and other such special provisions, in many states, but not in all. Voting procedures should be carefully detailed.

8. Meetings for elections and for other than election purposes, including notice, quorums, and agendas (general and special meetings).

9. Voting qualifications, individually or by groups; proxies, etc.

10. Director's (or trustees') qualifications.

11. Classification of directors (or trustees) into two, three, four, or five classes, each to hold office so that the terms of one class shall expire every year.

12. [Optional] Executive committee of the board of directors to exercise all (or certain) powers of the board between board meetings.

13. Directors' titles, terms of office, times and manner of election, meetings, powers, and duties.

14. Convention and assembly rules (if part of a larger organization).

15. Property holding transfer.

16. The seal: its adoption, custody, and method of use.

17. Bank depository, and which officers may act for the organization.

18. Bonding of the treasurer and other officers and agents.

19. Fiscal details: fiscal year, regular (at least annual) audits of books.

20. Principal office, and other offices.

21. Books, records, and reports.

22. Amendment methods and rules, for the charter as well as for the bylaws.

23. Principal committees.

24. Dissolution procedures.

25. Disposition of surplus assets on dissolution (following the *cy pres* doctrine, whereby trust funds go to a similar purpose).

POINTS TO REMEMBER

- Adopt a full set of bylaws soon after organization—but not hastily.
- Tailor your bylaws to your organization's purposes and capabilities and to hard facts. Suit them to your special situation and prospects.
- Do not simply copy another organization's bylaws.
- Do not let amateurs draft the bylaws. An attorney's aid is almost indispensable.
- Have only a charter and bylaws. Avoid use of a third "constitution." It usually causes confusion.
- Do not try to operate without bylaws.

- The members should control the adoption and amendment of the bylaws as to matters other than formalities.

- Give amendment powers to the directors only in minor matters, and with plenty of caution and safeguards.

- But do not shackle the directors and then expect good results.

- Resolutions are not bylaws.

- Use resolutions for temporary problems.

- Use bylaws for permanent or recurrent problems.

- Keep a resolutions book. Index it.

- Provide detailed rules for adoption of amendments.

- Avoid amendments when they are not really necessary. Too many amendments lead to confusion.

- Remember that outsiders are not bound by what is in the bylaws unless you can prove they had actual or constructive knowledge of their contents.

- Charter is primary; bylaws are explanatory and regulatory.

- Draft your bylaws with care, thoughtfully.

NOTES TO CHAPTER 22

1. Bosch v. Meeker Co-Op. Light and Power Assn., 253 Minn. 77, 91 N.W.2d 148 (1958); *In re* Flushing Hospital, 27 N.Y.S.2d 207 (1941), *affd.* 262 A.D. 749, 28 N.Y.S.2d 155 (1941), *affd.* with modifications, 288 N.Y. 125, 41 N.E.2d 917 (1942); Vernon Manor Co-Op. Apartments, Inc. v. Salatino, 15 Misc.2d 491, 178 N.Y.S.2d 895 (1958); Diskin v. City of Phila. Police Pension Fund Assn., 168 Pa. Super. 76, 76 A.2d 663, 665 (1950); Van Atten v. Modern Brotherhood of Amer., 131 Iowa 232, 108 N.W. 313 (1906); Griffith v. Klamath Water Assn., 68 Ore. 402, 137 P. 226 (1913); Coulee Constr. Co. v. Cay Constr. Co., 221 S.2d 792 (Fla. App. 1969); Elisian Guild, Inc. v. U.S., 412 F.2d 121 (C.A. Mass. 1969).

2. *Ibid.*, District Grand Lodge v. Cohn, 20 Ill. App. 335 (1886) (bylaws are binding even if not in writing). But the one who alleges existence of an unwritten or implied bylaw has the burden of proof: *see*, Hinckley v. Swaner, 13 Utah 2d 93, 368 P.2d 709, 3 A.L.R.3d 620 (1962); *c.f.*, Olincy v. Merle Norman Cosmetics, Inc., 200 Cal. App.2d 260, 19 Cal. Rptr. 387 (1962) (no implied rule amendment where no notice was given); Comment, *Informal By-Law Amendment by Inconsistent Employment Contracts*, 1961 Duke L. J. 619.

3. Kingston Dodge, Inc. v. Chrysler Corp., 449 F. Supp. 52 (D.C. Pa., 1978).

4. Missouri State Teachers Assn. v. St. Louis Suburban Teachers Assn., 622 S.W.2d 745 (Mo. App. 1981); *In re* Oceanside Properties, Inc., 14 B.R. 95 (Hawaii 1981).

5. Wells v. Mobile County Board of Realtors, 307 S.2d 140 (Ala. 1980); American Hungarian Federation v. Nadas, 519 N.E.2d 677 (Ohio App. 1987).

6. Kendler v. Rutledge, 396 N.E.2d 1309 (Ill. App. 1979).

7. Ohio Rev. Code, §1702.10 ("may adopt"). Bylaws are called "regulations" in the Ohio code, while board of directors' rules are called bylaws. Ohio Rev. Code, §1702.30.

8. N.Y. N-PCL §§602, 608(b).

9. *Matthews v. Adams*, 520 So. 2d 334 (Fla. DCA, 1988).

10. Fl. St. §617.0206; *Skane v. Star Valley Ranch Ass'n*, 826 P.2d 266 (Wyo. 1992).

11. *See* above, n. 7. "Regulations" usually are minor rules, secondary to the bylaws, and dealing with discretionary matters, able to be changed easily. *See* forms in other chapters. But, for a different meaning, *see*, Vernon Manor Coop. v. Salatino, 15 Misc. 2d 491, 178 N.Y.S.2d 895 (1958).

12. Thompson v. Wyandanch Club, 70 Misc. 299, 127 N.Y.S. 195 (1911).

13. STP Corp. v. U.S. Auto Club Inc., 286 F. Supp. 146 (D.C. Ind. 1968); Oklahoma Assn. of Insur. Agents v. Hudson, 385 P.2d 453 (Okl. 1963); Strong v. Minneapolis Auto. Trade Assn., 151 Minn. 406, 186 N.W. 800 (1922); Cratty v. Peoria Law Library, 219 Ill., 516, 76 N.E. 707 (1906); Anno. 159 A.L.R. 195; *In re* American Fibre Chair Seat Corp., 241 A.D. 352, 272 N.Y.S. 206 (1934), *affd.*, 265 N.Y. 416, 193 N.E. 253 (1934); Commonwealth v. Union League, 135 Pa. St. 301, 19 A. 1030, 8 L.R.A. 195 (1890); People's Home Savings Bank v. Sadler, 1 Cal. App. 189, 81 P. 1029 (1905); Notes, 45 Columbia L. Rev. 960 (1945); 19 St. John's L. Rev. 144 (1944); Leon v. Chrysler Motors Corp., 358 F. Supp. 877 (D.C. N.J. 1973).

14. *See*, Conn. Genl. St. §33-442; Idaho Code, §30-3-21; Mont. Rev. Code, §35-2-118 No. Dak. Century Code 10-24-12; So. Dak. Codified Laws 47-22-33; Ohio Rev. Code, §1729.11 (cooperatives).

15. *See*, Ohio Rev. Code, §1702.38(C).

16. Mich. Compiled Laws Annot. 450.122; Ohio Rev. Code, §§1701.39–1701.45; 1702.38(C); Fla. St., §617.0721.

17. Steen v. Modern Woodmen of America, 296 Ill. 104, 129 N.E. 546 (1920); Interstate B.&L. Assn. v. Wooten, 113 Ga. 247, 38 S.E. 738 (1901); Superior Bedding Co. v. Serta Associates, Inc., 353 F. Supp. 1143 (D.C. Ill. 1973).

18. Exemption based on articles and bylaws: I.R.C. Reg. 1.501(a)-1; 3 CCH Standard Fed. Tax Rpts. 3025.04; Lewis v. United States, 189 F. Supp. 950 (D.C. Wyo. 1961).

19. Fairhope Single Tax Corp. v. Melville, 193 Ala. 289, 69 S. 466, 470 (1915); Anno., 11 Am. Jur. 602.

20. Thompson v. Wyandanch Club, 70 Misc. 299, 127 N.Y.S. 195 (1911).

21. Christal v. Petry, 275 A.D. 550, 90 N.Y.S.2d 620 (1949), *affd.* 301 N.Y. 562, 93 N.E.2d 450 (1950); Bergman v. St. Paul Mut. Assn., 29 Minn. 275, 13 N.W. 120 (1882).

22. *Black's Law Dictionary*, 282 (5th ed. 1979); Ballentine, *Law Dictionary*, 253 (3d ed. 1969); *and see*, State v. Main, 69 Conn. 123, 37 A. 80, 36 L.R.A. 623 (1897); American Legion of Honor v. Perry, 140 Mass. 580, 5 N.E. 634 (1886); State v. Greenville, etc. Assn., 29 Ohio St. 92 (1876).

23. *See* cases above, n. 2, 21; and, State *ex rel.* Schwab v. Price, 121 Ohio 114, 167 N.E. 366 (1929).

24. *See*, as to writing not being mandatory, case above, n.3; and Commonwealth v. Woelper, 3 S.&R. (Pa.) 29, 8 Am. Dec. 628 (1819); Hagerman v. Ohio Bldg. etc. Assn., 25 Ohio St. 186 (1874).

25. Masonic etc. Benev. Assn. v. Severson, 71 Conn. 719, 43 A. 192 (1899); Espy v. American Legion of Honor, 7 Luz. Leg. Reg. (Pa.) 134.

26. 1 Oleck, *Modern Corporation Law*, 796 (1978 Supp.), citing cases.

27. Kendler v. Rutledge, 396 N.E.2d 1309 (Ill. App. 1979).

28. Treister v. American Academy of Orthopedic Surgeons, 396 N.E.2d 1225 (Ill. App. 1979).

29. Dietz v. American Dental Association, 479 F. Supp. 554 (D.C. Mich. 1979); Brennan v. Minneapolis Society for the Blind, Inc., 282 N.W.2d 515 (Minn. 1979); Spain v. Louisiana High School Athletic Association, 393 So.2d 226 (La. App. 1980).

30. Marresse v. American Academy of Orthopedic Surgeons, 692 F.2d 1083 (7th Cir. 1982) antitrust change; Koszela v. National Association of Stock Car Racing, 646 F.2d 749 (2d Cir. 1981) economic necessity.

31. Dietz case, n.29.

32. Steiner v. Saugatuck Harbor Yacht Club, Inc., 450 A.2d 369 (Conn. 1982).

33. California Dental Assoc. v. American Dental Assoc., 590 P.2d 401 (Cal. 1979); Coventry Square Condominium Association v. Halpern, 436 A.2d 580 (N.J. Super. 1981); Spain case, n.29.

34. Kite v. Marshall, 661 F.2d 1027 (5th Cir. 1981); Moran v. Vincent, 588 S.W.2d 867 (Tex. Civ. App. 1979); McDonald v. Lake Hauto Club, 428 A.2d 785 (Pa. Civ. 1980).

35. Pavey v. Univ. of Alaska, 490 F. Supp. 1011 (D.C., Alaska 1980); James v. Camden County Council, N.J. Civil Serv. Assoc., 457 A.2d 63 (N.J. Super. 1982); Booneville Properties, Inc. v. Simons, 677 P.2d 1111 (Utah 1984); Spain case, n.29.

36. Matthews v. Bay Head Improvement Association, 471 A.2d 355 (N.J. 1984).

37. Morgan v. New York Racing Association, 421 N.Y.S.2d 249 (App. Div. 1979); Travis v. Lost Tree Village Corp., 388 S.2d 319 (Fla. 4th D.C. App., 1980).

38. N.Y. N-PCL §§602, 701, 707; Ohio Rev. Code, §1702.10; Veterans of World War I v. Levy, 70 Ohio Abs. 49, 118 N.E. 2d 670 (1954); *Re* Buckley, 183 Misc. 189, 50 N.Y.S.2d 54 (1944); Arizona Southwest Bank v. Odum, 38 Ariz. 394, 300 P. 195 (1931); Bradley v. Cincinnati Camp Meeting Assn., 9 Ohio App. 321 (1918) (who may assess dues).

39. Ohio Rev. Code, §1702.30. The (old) Model Non-Profit Corp. Act, §12, places bylaw powers in the directors "unless otherwise provided in the articles of incorporation or the bylaws," which indicates a "proprietary" view of "management" powers. *See*, Oleck, *Proprietary Mentality and the New Nonprofit Corporation Laws*, 20 Clev. St. L. Rev. 145 (1971).

40. *See*, Hollins v. Edmonds, 616 S.W.2d 801 (Ky. App. 1981); Dimieri & Weiner, *Public Interest and Governing Boards of Nonprofit Health Care Institutions*, 34 Vand. L. Rev. 1029 (1981); Harris v. Board of Directors of Community Hospital of Evanston, 370 N.E.2d 1121 (Ill. 1977).

41. N.Y. N-PCL §§602, 701, 707; N.Y. N-P-C Law, §602; Rogers v. Hill, 289 U.S. 582; 53 S. Ct. 731 (1933) revg., 62 F.2d. 1079 (C.C.A.2d 1933); Templeman v. Grant, 75 Colo., 519; 227 P. 555 (1924). Or by general resolution: Hingston v. Montgomery, 121 Mo. App. 451; 97 S.W. 202 (1906).

42. N.H. Rev. Stat. §301-A:10 (consumer coop. assoc.) Casita De Costilian, Inc. v. Kanrath, 629 P.2d 562 (Ariz. 1981).

43. Hernandez v. Banco De Las Americas, 570 P.2d 494 (Ariz. 1977); O'Leary v. Board of Directors of Howard Young Medical Center, Inc., 278 N.W.2d 217 (Wis. 1979).

44. Rowland v. Rowland, 633 P.2d 599 (Ida. 1981).

45. *See*, Benintendi v. Kenton Hotel, Inc., 181 Misc. 897; 45 N.Y.S.2d 705 (1943), *affd.*, 50 N.Y.S.2d 843 (1944), modified, 294 N.Y. 112; 60 N.E.2d 829 (1945); noted, 45 Columbia L. Rev. 960 (1945); which led to revision of N.Y. Stock Corp. L., §9 in 1948 and 1949.

46. Bay City Lumber Co. v. Anderson, 8 Wash.2d 191; 111 P.2d 771 (1941); noted, 30 Calif. L. Rev. 195 (1942); Pomeroy v. Westaway, 70 N.Y.S.2d 449 (1947); *In re* Ivey v. Ellington, 42 A.2d 508 (Del. 1945).

47. Conley v. Texas Division of United Daughters of the Confederacy, 164 S.W. 24, 26 (Tex. Civ. App. 1913); *Ex parte* Hague, 104 N.J. Eq. 31; 144 A. 546, 559 (1929). *See* above, n.11.

48. *Ex parte* Hague, n.47; Brennan, n.29.

49. N.Y. N-P-C Law §§801, 504.

50. *Brenner v. Powers*, 584 N.E. 2d 569 (Ind. App. 3 Dist. 1992).

51. *Black v. Fox Hills North Community Ass'n, Inc.*, 599 A.2d 1228 (Md. App. 1992).

52. *Szczerbaniuk v. Memorial Hospital*, 536 N.E.2d 136 (IL App. 1989).

53. *Clardy v. Tri-Community Water System*, 591 So. 2d 65 (Ala. 1991).

54. *Central States Trucking Co. v. J.R. Simplot Co.*, 965 F.2d 431 (7th Cir. (N.Y.), 1992).

55. *Skane v. Star Valley Ranch Ass'n*, 826 P.2d 266 (Wyo. 1992).

56. Usage: Bay City Lumber Co. v. Anderson, 8 Wash.2d 191; 111 P.2d 771 (1941); noted, 30

Calif. L. Rev. 195 (1942); Elliot v. Lindquist, 94 Pittsb. L. J. 295 (1946, Ct. Com. Pl., Alleg. Co., Penna.); Osteopathic Hosp. Assn. of Del., 195 A.2d 759 (Del. 1963). Nonusage: Pomeroy v. Westaway, 70, N.Y.S.2d 449 (1947). Inconsistent action: Hill v. American Coop. Assn., 195 La. 590; 197 S. 241 (1940); noted, 3 La. L. Rev. 235 (1940). Unanimous consent: In re Ivey and Ellington, 42 A.2d 508 (Del. 1945).

57. In re Ivey and Ellington, n.56.

58. N.46.

59. Farrier v. Ritzville, 116 Wash. 522; 199 P. 984 (1921).

60. See, Bay City case, n.48; Hueftle v. Farmers Elevator, 145 Nebr. 424; 16 N.W.2d 855 (1944). McConnell v. Owyhee Ditch Co., 132 Ore. 128; 283 P. 755 (1930); Board of Managers of Genl. Apart. Corp. Condominium v. Gans, 72 Misc.2d 726, 340 N.Y.S.2d 826 (1972).

61. See, Cal. Corp. Code §§5610, 5813; Mass. Gen. L.C. 180 §3; N.Y. N-P-C L. §612; Ohio Rev. Code §1702.38(C)(E).

62. Harris case, above, n.40.

63. Petition of Board of Directors . . . , 472 A.2d 731 (Pa. Civ. 1984).

64. See, Weona Camp v. Gladis, 457 A.2d 153 (Pa. Civ. 1983).

65. Winston Towers Assn. v. Saverio, 360 S.2d 470 (Fla. 3rd DCA 1978).

66. Whitman v. N.H. Elec. Coop., 459 A.2d 224 (N.H. 1983).

67. Re American Fibre Chair Seat Corp., 241 A.D. 352; 272 N.Y.S. 206 (1934); affd., 265 N.Y. 416; 193 N.E. 253 (1934); noted, 34 Columbia L. Rev. 1361 (1934); and they ordinarily are not retroactive, Roblin v. Knights of the Maccabees, 269 Pa. 139, 112 A. 70 (1920); Petition case, above, n.63; Edison Club v. Harvey, 434 N.Y.S.2d 639 (1981); Gastonia Board of Realtors v. Harrison, 306 S.E.2d 809 (N.C. 1983); Delmakino Assoc. v. N.J. Engrg., 424 A.2d 847 (N.J. Super. 1980); Adams v. Amer. Quarterhorse Assn., 583 S.W.2d 828 (Tex. Civ. App. 1979).

68. Members and officers are charged with knowledge of the valid bylaws. Model Land and Irrig. Co. v. Madsen, 87 Colo. 166; 285 P. 1100 (1930); State v. Shaw, 103 Ohio 660; 134 N.E. 643 (1930); Jones v. Wallace, 616 P.2d 575 (Ore. App. 1980).

69. Green v. Ashland 63rd State Bank, 346 Ill. 174; 178 N.E. 468 (1931); Lutz v. Webster, 249 Penna. 226; 94 A. 834 (1915); Uline Loan Co. v. Standard Oil Co., 45 S.D. 81; 185 N.W. 1012; 27 A.L.R. 585 (1921).

70. Fleming v. Reinhardt, 153 Wash. 526; 280 P. 9 (1929) (course of dealings).

71. N.69, above; City of Chicago v. Severini, 344 N.E.2d 67 (Ill. App. 1980).

72. N.69, above; and, Ohio Rev. Code, §1702.11(F).

73. Department of Trade v. Bankers, etc., Co., 117 Nebr. 388; 220 N.W. 830 (1928); Iowa-Missouri Grain Co. v. Powers, 198 Iowa 208; 196 N.W. 979 (1924).

74. Charter is a public record. N. A. Berwin and Co., Inc. v. Hewitt Realty Co., 199 A.D. 453; 191 N.Y.S. 817 (1922); affd., 235 N.Y. 608; Browne v. Hare, 112 W. Va. 648; 166 S.E. 362 (1932). This rule is opposed by some authorities, who propose that such filing should not bind third persons. Unif. Business Corp. Act (proposed), §10.

75. Ledebuhr v. Wisconsin Trust Co., 112 Wis. 657; 88 N.W. 607 (1902); State ex rel. Liegley v. Potter, 42 Ohio App. 489; 182 N.E. 242 (1932) (waiver by acquiescence by the corporation). The members also may waive the bylaws. Grand Valley Irrig. Co. v. Fruita Improv. Co., 37 Colo. 483; 86 P. 324 (1906) (waiver of a required publication of notice). One who alleges a waiver or amendment by custom or usage has the burden of proving it. Belle Isle Corp. v. MacBean, 49 A.2d 5 (Del. 1946).

76. Ryan v. Baptiste, 565 S.W.2d 196 (Mo. App. 1978).

77. See, Figure Eight Beach Homeowner's Assn. v. Parker, 303 S.E.2d 336 (N.C. App. 1983); LeFeure v. Ostendorf, 275 N.W.2d 154 (Wis. 1979).

78. See, Storrs v. Lutheran Hospital & H. Assn., 609 P.2d 24 (Alaska 1980); Hibbert v. Holly-

wood Park, 457 A.2d 339 (Del. 1983); Natl. Bank v. Interbank Card Assn., 507 F. Supp. 1113 (D.C., N.Y. 1980).

79. *Gerber v. Longboat Harbor North Condo., Inc.*, 724 F. Supp. 884 (D.C. Fla., 1989).

80. *Gilder v. PGA Tour, Inc.*, 727 F. Supp. 1333 (D.C. Ariz., 1989).

81. *Mehralian v. Riverview Tower Homeowners Ass'n, Inc.*, 464 N.W. 2d 571 (Minn. App. 1990).

82. *Mizenko v. First Catholic Slovak Ladies Assn.*, 550 N.E.2d (Ohio App. 1989).

83. Thompson v. Wyandanch Club, 70 Misc. 299; 127 N.Y.S. 195 (1911); Christal v. Petry, 275 A.D. 550; 90 N.Y.S.2d 620 (1949); *affd.*, 301 N.Y. 562; Oceanside case, n.4.

84. Thompson v. Wyandanch Club, n.83.

85. Saint John of Vizzini Assn. v. Cavallo, 134 Misc. 152; 234 N.Y.S. 683 (1929); Veverka v. Suffolk County Patrolmen's Benev. Assn., 236 N.Y.S.2d 917 (1963).

86. As to reasonableness requirement, *see*, Selama-Dindings Plantations v. Durham, 216 F. Supp. 104 (D.C. Ohio 1963). Thus, a hospital bylaw that barred staff privileges to a licensed osteopath, by requiring membership in the county medical society which admitted only M.D.'s, was invalid. Greisman v. Newcomb Hospital, 40 N.J. 389, 192 A.2d 817 (1963); Hodges v. Arlington N. Center, 628 S.W.2d 537 (Tex. Civ. App. 1982); Belmar v. Cipolla, 475 A.2d 533 (N.J. 1984); Sarasota Co. Pub. Hosp. v. El Shahwg, 408 S.2d 646 (Fla. DCA 1981).

87. Ohio Rev. Code, §1702.15. "May be examined by any member or trustee or the agent or attorney of either, for any reasonable and proper purpose and at any reasonable time" (applied to "all books and records," including the membership book). But the bylaws may limit members' (not trustees') inspection rights. Ohio Rev. Code, §1702.11(A)(4). See, American Hungarian Federation v. Nadas, 519 N.E.2d 677 (Ohio App. 1987).

88. *Re* Coats, 75 A.D. 567, 78 N.Y.S. 429 (1902).

89. Greenbelt Homes, Inc. v. Nyman Realty, 426 A.2d 394 (Md. App. 1981).

90. *E.g.*, Conn. Gen. St. §33-459(a); FL St. §617.0304; Minn. St. §317.25, subd.1(2); and see, below, n.92.

91. *See*, Wells case, above, n.5 (mandatory arbitration may be invalid); and Casita case, n.42 (condominium rules in bylaws).

92. Dulaney Towers Maintenance Corp. v. O'Brien, 418 A.2d 1233 (Md. App. 1980); and *see* above, n.90.

93. Ohio Rev. Code, §1702.11 sets forth lengthy provisions suggesting what matters may (and should) be covered in the bylaws (called "regulations" in Ohio).

23

FORMS OF BYLAWS

§237. FORMS OF BYLAWS, IN GENERAL

[*See* the Index for examples of bylaws in chapters other than this one. *Resolutions* are not bylaws. *See* §231]

Bylaws should be tailored to the purposes and needs of the particular organization. No two organizations have exactly the same purposes and needs. Bylaws of another organization, therefore, should not be copied slavishly. If verbatim copying is done it is likely to cause difficulty some day for the copier organization.

Form books: It is an axiom, in drafting bylaws or other legal documents, that form books should be used only as general guides. They should not be copied slavishly.

Various form books are available that can be helpful to nonprofit organizations. Among them are:

Joint Committee on Continuing Legal Education of the American Law Institute with the American Bar Association, *Model Nonprofit Corporation Act*, With Official Forms (revised edition 1964) (27 general, outline forms); but *cf.* the 1986 Revised Act (Exposure Draft).

Oleck, *Modern Corporation Law*, Volume 5 and Supplemental Volume 5, Forms ([Michie—Bobbs-Merrill]) (1168 forms in main volume, hundreds of forms in the supplement).

Size of a set of bylaws: The range of size and completeness of bylaws is illustrated by the following examples:

A city trade association uses a 16-page pamphlet (3 by 6 inches) printed in large type.

A university faculty set of bylaws uses a 24-page pamphlet (7 by 8 inches).

A nationwide labor union uses a 96-page booklet (3 by 6 inches).

A school alumni association uses a four-page, legal cap size set of mimeographed, single-spaced, typed material.

One local church uses a ten-page, letter size set of photocopied, single-spaced, typed material; another local church uses a similar seven-page set of bylaws.

For its "Faculty Manual," stating all pertinent rules and regulations applicable to faculty members, a small college publishes a bound book (9 by 11 inches) of 87 pages.

A national fraternal order sets forth its "Constitution and Statutes" in a bound book (almost 7 inches by 5 inches) of 127 pages.

A college residential alumni club in one large city used a bound book (over 7 inches by 5 inches) including 42 pages of bylaws and rules.

A national professional association uses a bound book (3 1/2 by 6 inches) of 106 pages of formal bylaws and rules.

A local professional association in one county, on the other hand, finds that a small pamphlet (3 by 6 inches) of 12 pages is sufficient to set forth its bylaws.

A national religious auxiliary union uses for its bylaws a bound book in two languages (3 1/2 by 5 inches) of over 450 pages.

A national professional institute sets forth its bylaws and rules in a pamphlet (9 1/4 by 6 1/4 inches) of 15 double-column pages.

A corporation's credit union uses a bound booklet (3 by 5 inches) of 20 pages).

A company contributory retirement plan (a trust plan) is set forth in a bound pamphlet (8 1/2 by 5 1/2 inches) of 20 pages.

A small private foundation sets forth its bylaws in 13 typewritten pages, double-spaced.

A small national health association employs a simple mimeographed set of bylaws, on ordinary letterhead-size paper, of 23 pages.

A business executives' institute uses a bound booklet (7 by 4 1/2 inches) of 19 pages.

A company-employees' club in one large factory uses a mimeographed set of bylaws, on ordinary letterhead-size paper, of only seven pages.

A group-health-pian organization in one large city breaks it bylaws into several distinct sets of rules, some of which are not labelled "bylaws"; each set being applicable to one aspect of its operations.

The size and contents of labor union (unincorporated association) bylaws are illustrated by the forms in Chapter 6.

§238. SMALL, AND LOCAL, ORGANIZATIONS' FORMS OF BYLAWS

FORM NO. 108

Local Association's Bylaws

Bylaws
of

_____ **ASSOCIATION OF**

_____

Article I

Purpose and Name

The purpose, name, and qualifications for membership in the _____ _____ Association (herein referred to as "Association"), are set forth in the Articles of Incorporation approved by the voting membership on _____.

Article II

Management

Section 2.1 The management of this Association shall be vested in a Board of Directors of not less than eighteen nor more than twenty-two persons who are at least Eighteen years of age and who possess the qualifications for voting membership in the Association. In the event the President's tenure expires with his term of office, he shall become an ex-officio voting member for the period of One (1) year.

Section 2.2 The Board of Directors shall have and exercise all the powers necessary to control the work and policy of this Association. No contract, debt, or obligation shall be binding unless contracted under the authority of the Board of Directors.

Section 2.3 The Board of Directors shall have the power to fill, for the unexpired terms, all vacancies occurring in their number between annual elections. All such vacancies shall be filled by first recommending names to the Board Selection Committee, who shall act as a nominating committee, for screening and recommendation to the Board of Directors.

Section 2.4 The Board of Directors shall have the power to establish or disband departments, operations, or branches of the Association, or may establish policies of their government and appoint and remove Boards of Management for the same.

Section 2.5 The Board of Directors shall have the power to enter into cooperative relationships with other agencies or organizations when, in their judgment, such a relationship is desirable toward achieving the Association's objectives in the area concerned, in which case they shall have the power, on behalf of the Association, to execute Articles of Agreement setting forth the rules of the government of the cooperative operation—which Articles shall contain provisions for severing relationships any time when, in the judgment of the Board of Directors, it is in the best interests of the Association to do so.

Section 2.6 The Association, through its Board of Directors, may hold or dispose of such property, real or personal, as may be given, devised, or bequeathed to it or entrusted to its care and keeping, and may purchase, acquire, and dispose of such property as may be necessary to carry out the purposes of the Association.

Section 2.7 The Board of Directors shall have the control and management of the property of the Association, with power to borrow money for corporate purposes.

Section 2.8 The Board of Directors shall meet monthly at such time and place as they shall determine. One-third of the membership of the Board of Directors shall constitute a quorum. Any member who misses three consecutive meetings may be dropped as a Board Member, unless such absences are approved by the Board.

Section 2.9 Special Meetings of the Board of Directors may be called by the President, or may be called upon the written request of Five (5) Directors. The call for a Special Meeting shall specify the purpose of the meeting and shall give seven days' notice thereof to the remaining Members of the Board.

Section 2.10 The Board of Directors shall employ the General Executive Director, define his duties and fix his compensation. Also, the Board of Directors shall employ such special employees as they, from time to time, deem necessary.

Section 2.11 The Board of Directors may honor One or more of their members from time to time, for long and faithful service by electing him an Honorary Board Member for life. An Honorary Board Member may attend all meetings and participate in the discussion, but shall not vote or hold office.

Article III

Officers and Their Duties

Section 3.1 The Officers of this Association, as elected by the Board of Directors, shall be a President, a First Vice President, a Second Vice President, a Recording Secretary, and a Treasurer, each of whom shall hold office for one year or until his successor is elected and qualified.

Section 3.2 The President shall preside at all meetings of the Board of Directors and of the Association. With the Recording Secretary, he shall execute all legal papers, documents, and instruments ordered to be executed by the Board of Directors. The President shall appoint all committees and shall be a member *ex-officio* of all committees of the Association and shall perform such other duties as may, from time to time, be prescribed by the Board of Directors.

Section 3.3 The Vice Presidents, in order, shall act in the absence or disability of the President.

Section 3.4 The Recording Secretary shall, together with the President or a Vice President, execute such legal papers, documents, or instruments as authorized by the Board of Directors. The Recording Secretary shall keep the Minutes of all meetings of the Association and of the Board of Directors.

Section 3.5 The Treasurer shall have charge of the funds and securities of the Association, and shall cause them to be deposited in depositories approved by the Board of Directors. He shall see that accurate record is kept of the funds and shall make monthly reports to the Board of Directors. All checks upon bank accounts of the Association shall be signed as directed by Resolution of the Board of Directors. The Treasurer of the Board of Directors shall be the Treasurer of all of the Branches of the Association.

Section 3.6 All officers handling funds shall be bonded.

Article IV

Committees

Section 4.1 The Board of Directors, upon the recommendation of the General Executive Director, shall designate the various areas or departments into which the program and administrative work of the Association shall be divided; shall determine the division of responsibility and the relationship between such departments; and shall authorize the President to appoint necessary committees.

Section 4.2 Executive Committee: There shall be an Executive Committee consisting of the Officers of the Association, the Chairman of the Finance Committee, the Chairman of the Personnel Committee, the Chairman of the Membership Committee, the Chairman of the International Committee, the Chairman of the Physical Education Committee and the Chairman of the Community Program Committee. The Executive Committee shall act for the Board of Directors in the interim between Board meetings, but they shall not have the power to reconsider or reverse any action or policy of the Board. The President or any two members of the Executive Committee, may call meetings at any time, giving the purpose of the meeting and seven days' notice to the remaining members thereof; and three members shall constitute a quorum.

Section 4.3 The Board of Directors may determine the Standing Committees of this Association. Each Standing Committee of the Association and its Chairman shall be appointed annually by the President. All Standing Committees of the Association must be chaired by a member of the Board of Directors, but may have as a part of its membership, any current member of this Association. Only Members of the Board of Directors or other current members of the Association shall be eligible for membership on any Standing Committee. The President and the General Executive Director shall be *ex-officio* members of all Committees. A written charter of the responsibilities of each Committee shall be prepared by the Board of Directors and filed with the Minutes of the Board.

Section 4.4 Each Standing Committee shall keep the Minutes of its meetings and file the Minutes in the Association's office, and it shall submit to the Board of Directors a monthly report of work done. It shall not enter into any contract or incur any indebtedness or financial obligation of any kind, except under the authority of the Board of Directors. It shall have the power to appoint such sub-committees for carrying on the work under its direction as it may deem necessary.

Section 4.5 Subject to the approval of the Board of Directors, each Committee shall have the power to adopt such rules as may be necessary for the conduct of the work entrusted to it.

Section 4.6 The President shall have the authority to appoint such other Committees as shall be necessary for the conduct of the business of the Association.

Section 4.7 The Board of Directors shall prescribe the duties, powers, and functions of each Committee herein authorized.

Article V

Elections

Section 5.1 Terms of office of the Officers and Directors of this Association shall begin on January 1st and end on December 31st of each year.

Section 5.2 The annual election of Directors shall be held in December and there shall be chosen by ballot one-third of the legal number of Directors whose terms shall be for three years.

Section 5.3 The President shall appoint a Board Selection Committee of Five (5) members to screen candidates for the Board membership. At a regular meeting of the Board of Directors, not later than the regular October meeting, the Board Selection Committee shall recommend candidates for consideration. Names will not be placed on the ballot until screened and approved by the Board of Directors. Any member of the Association may recommend names to the Board Selection Committee. Such names shall be proposed in writing to the Committee at least one week prior to the report of the Committee to the Board of Directors. Any Director may nominate at the October meeting, the final nominees to be determined by the Directors.

Section 5.4 At least one month prior to the date of election, a sample ballot and a brief biographical sketch on each of the nominees shall be posted in the lobby of the downtown office of the Association, and notice of said posting shall be placed on each bulletin board in the Association. Members may obtain an official ballot from the front desk at the Association at any time during said period, the same to be returned to the ballot box which will be available in the lobby of the downtown office during said period until ten o'clock p.m. on election day. The Board Selection Committee shall have charge of the election, shall count the ballots on the day following the election, and shall certify the returns to the Board of Directors. The ballot box shall remain sealed until opened by the Board Selection Committee, and each ballot returned by mail shall remain sealed until opened by the Board Selection Committee.

Section 5.5 At the first regular meeting of the Board of Directors after the annual election of the Association, the Board shall elect by ballot from their own number, the Officers of this Association. They shall have the power to perform the duties incumbent upon the Officers of like name and in similar Associations, subject to these Bylaws and such regulations as may be provided.

Article VI

Staff

Section 6.1 The General Executive Director shall be employed by the Board of Directors after consultation with the Executive Officer of the Region Council with which the Association is affiliated. He shall be an *ex-officio* member of all Committees of the Board and of the Association; he shall be responsible for the employment of all other members of the Staff and Branch Directors, in accordance with the policies and procedures set forth by the Board of

Directors, and as specified in the Operations Policy and shall designate their duties and have general supervision of their work; he shall attend all meetings of the Board of Directors, except as provided by personnel policy; and he shall make monthly reports on the operation of the Association.

Section 6.2 All other employees of the Association shall be employed by the General Executive Director in consultation with the Personnel Committee and in accordance with Association personnel policies.

Article VII

Annual Meeting

There shall be an Annual Meeting of the Association, within ninety days after the close of the fiscal year or at such time as the Board of Directors may determine. The purpose of this meeting shall be to review the work of the Association, to develop fellowship among members, and to develop their united action in planning and carrying forward the program of the Association. No business of the Association will be conducted at the Annual Meeting, except as provided in the Articles of Incorporation.

Article VIII

Amendments

These Bylaws may be amended as provided in the Articles of Incorporation.

Article IX

Procedure

Unless provided otherwise in these Bylaws, procedure at all meetings shall be governed by Oleck's *Parliamentary Law for Nonprofit Organizations.*

These Bylaws were approved and adopted at the regular meeting of the Board of Directors in the month of _____, 19_____.

FORM NO. 109

Constitution of Music (Musicians') Association

[Based on an unincorporated (but tax-exemption-approved) association for encouragement of interest in jazz music]

CONSTITUTION
of
_____ JAZZ ASSOCIATION
(Officially Adopted After Second Reading August 30, 19___)

Article I

Name and Affiliation

Section 1. Name

This organization shall be known as _____ JAZZ ASSOCIATION. Initial Post Office address: _____ Street, _____, FL 33712. The official address may be changed from time to time as the members of the association may agree.

Section 2. Affiliation

_____ ASSOCIATION shall be affiliated with other organizations promoting the cause of jazz.

Article II

Objectives and Strategies

Section 1. Objectives

This Association is organized for educational, cultural and other non-profit purposes pursuant to Section 501(c)(3), Internal Revenue Code, with objectives generating interest in preserving, understanding and performing jazz music.

Section 2. Strategies

Objectives shall be accomplished by:

A. Encouraging active performance and creation of jazz music.

B. Assisting and guiding in the organization and development of jazz activities.

C. Encouraging the development by music educators of curricula that will explore jazz composition, jazz improvization.

D. Disseminating news about jazz and pertinent news about the music industry.

E. Participating in clinics, festivals and symposiums.

F. Organizing jazz concerts.

Article III

Membership

A. Professional Membership

Professional Membership shall be granted to any individual who is engaged in performing, teaching, supervision or administration of music within the State of Florida. Professional Membership provides the privileges of participation in all activities of the Association including the right to vote and hold office.

B. Associate Membership

Associate Membership shall be granted to any individual who is interested in the pursuit and advancement of the objectives and strategy as stated in Article II, Sections 1 and 2 of this Constitution. Other than for elections they may not vote or hold office, except that one Associate Member and one Alternate Associate Member shall be elected to the Board as otherwise provided for under Article VII hereof.

Article IV

Dues

Section 1. Professional Membership

Annual dues for Professional Members shall be $_____. (January 1 through December 31) Dues are payable to the Treasurer of the Association.

Section 2. Associate Membership

Annual fees shall be $_____. (January 1 through December 31) Dues are payable to the Treasurer of the Association.

Article V

Officers

Section 1. Elected

Elected Officers shall be President, Vice President, Secretary and Treasurer.

Section 2. Appointed

Appointed Officers shall be any other individual as may be provided for in the Bylaws of the Association.

Section 3. Term of Office

All officers will hold office for one year.

Section 4. Duties

A. It shall be the duty of the President to:
   1. Preside at all meetings.
   2. Enforce due observance of the Constitution and Bylaws.
   3. Call emergency meetings when necessary of the Executive Board.
   4. Appoint all committees for which no provisions have been made.
   5. Serve as member *ex-officio* of all committees.

6. Serve as Executive Officer and to act upon his best judgment in representing the Association in any matter upon which he has received no previous instruction from the Association or Executive Board.

7. Be responsible to the Executive Board at all times and must accept and carry out any instructions given him by the Board.

8. Co-sign with the treasurer, checks and financial transactions.

9. Prepare newsletters to be distributed by mail to all members.

B. It shall be the duty of the *Vice President* to:

1. Perform the duties of the President in the event of the absence of the President.

2. Serve as advisor to the President.

3. Assume other duties assigned to him by the President or the Executive Board.

4. Coordinate the work of all standing or special committees.

C. It shall be the duty of the *Secretary* to:

1. Keep an accurate record of all business transacted at all regular or special called meetings of the Executive Board and full association.

2. Present in writing the Minutes of previous meeting to members in session.

3. Present in writing records of all business transacted in the monthly newsletter.

D. It shall be the duty of the *Treasurer* to:

1. Collect all dues and funds of the Association.

2. Deposit all monies collected.

3. Pay all bills or demands against the Association when duly authorized by the Executive Board.

4. Keep accurate account of all receipts and disbursements in proper account books.

5. Make available all books and records for professional audit and inspection of the Executive Board fifteen days prior to his end of term.

6. Render an annual statement in writing to the full membership.

7. Co-sign with the President all checks.

Article VI

Nomination and Election of Officers

Nominations for the election of officers shall be made by a nominating committee appointed by the President no later than February 1st of each year. The Committee shall consist of the President and three members from the voting membership to submit nominations for each office no later than March 1st of each year. A brief biographical sketch of each nominee shall appear in the newsletter. These selections shall not prevent further nominations from the floor at the April meeting immediately prior to elections. Nominations from the floor shall be governed by *Oleck & Green Parliamentary Law and Practice for Nonprofit Organizations* (ALI-ABA 2d ed., 1991).

Article VII

Section 1. Members Executive Board

The Executive Board shall consist of the President, Vice President, Secretary, Treasurer, immediate Past President, one Professional Member and one Associate Member.

Section 2. Duties and Responsibilities

The Executive Board shall be responsible for the proper handling of all business and finance of the association as well as determining the activities of the Association. The Executive Board shall have the right to appoint an officer for an unfilled term of office for any position of the Association.

Section 3. Reporting

All business transacted by the Executive Board shall be reported to the entire Association membership through the newsletter.

Article VIII

Meetings

Section 1. Time and Places

A. *Executive Board*

The Executive Board shall meet at least once each quarter. These meetings are to be held in a centrally located place within the State agreeable to the majority of the Executive Board members. Special emergency meetings may be called if deemed necessary by the President or any four members of the Board. Meeting times and places will be published at least thirty days prior to the proposed meetings.

B. *General Membership*

The general membership business meeting shall be held at a time and place to be published in the newsletter.

Section 2. Procedures and Order of Business

All meetings of the Executive Board and General Membership shall be governed by Oleck & Green *Parliamentary Law and Practice for Nonprofit Organizations* in all cases which they are applicable and in which they are not inconsistent with the By-laws or the Special rules of the Association.

The Order of Business shall be:

1. Call to Order
2. Roll Call
3. Presentation of Minutes of last regular meeting and all special meetings held since then.
4. Treasurer's Report
5. Report of Standing Committees
6. Report of Special Committees
7. Unfinished Business
8. New Business
9. Adjournment

Article IX

Standing Committees

Section 1. Committee on University, 2nd College, Jazz Activities

The purpose of this committee is to keep abreast of the existing jazz activities on the campuses of Florida, exchange ideas, promote new and creative programs, and make complete reports to the entire Association membership via the newsletter and Association meetings.

Section 2. Committee on Senior High Jazz Activities (9–12)

The purpose of this committee is to keep abreast of the existing jazz activities in the High Schools of Florida, exchange ideas, promote new and creative programs and make complete reports to the entire Association membership.

Section 3. Committee on Middle School Activities

The purpose of this committee is to keep abreast of the existing jazz activities in the Middle Schools of Florida, exchange ideas, promote new and creative programs and make complete reports to the entire Association membership.

Section 4. Committee on Elementary School Activities (1–5)

The purpose of this committee is to keep abreast of the existing jazz activities in the Elementary Schools of Florida, exchange ideas, promote new and creative programs and make complete reports to the entire Association membership.

Section 5.

Each of these committees shall consist of at least six members. The Vice President of the Association shall serve as chairman for each committee. The President of the Association shall be an *ex-officio* member of each committee.

Section 6. Public Relations Committee

It shall be the duty of the Public Relations Committee to handle all matters of publicity concerning the activities of the Association.

Article X

Special Committees

The President shall be approved to appoint special committees to study and recommend to the Executive Board, action on any matters that arise concerning the Association.

Article XI

Amendments

Section 1.

The Constitution may be amended by a two-thirds vote of the total Professional Membership present at the annual meeting.

Section 2.

Any proposed amendment must first be presented in writing to the Executive Board at least three months before the annual meeting.

Section 3.

Any proposed amendment must be published in the newsletter not later than two months prior to the business meeting.

Section 4.

Proposed amendments will be presented to the membership at the next general business meeting of the organization.

Article XII

Quorum

Section 1.

A *quorum* for regular business meetings and for the annual meeting of the Association shall consist of a majority of the elected officers and board plus five Professional and/or Associate Members.

Section 2.

The President shall determine that a *quorum* is present before conducting official business of the Association.

Article XIII

Ratification

Section 1.

This Constitution may be ratified at the annual business meeting by a two-thirds vote of those Professional Members present providing that a *quorum* exists.

Section 2.

This Constitution shall be in effect immediately upon ratification.

Article XIV

Term

The term of this Association shall be perpetual.

Article XV

Distribution of Assets Upon Dissolution

It is intended that this Association shall operate as an organization not for profit under Section 501 of the Internal Revenue Code and that no part of the net earnings shall inure to the benefit of any provate share holder or individual. Should the Association be dissolved, all of the assets remaining after payment of all just debts, costs and expenses shall be distributed to similar organizations which have qualified for exemption under Section 501 of the Internal Revenue Code and none of the assets shall be distributed to any member, officer or trustee of this Association.

Article XVI

Powers

The Association shall have such additional powers as may be authorized or permitted by law, provided, however, no power shall be adopted or exercised which would disqualify the Association from the status as a tax exempt organization.

Article XVII

The Bylaws of this Association shall be those that may be adopted by a majority of the Executive Board at any regularly called meeting of the Board, provided, however, that any Bylaw in conflict with this Constitution shall have no validity or effect.

FORM NO. 110

Local Church Bylaws

BYLAWS

of the

_____ CHURCH OF _____ FLORIDA

(As adopted October 14, 1979 and as amended April 12, 1981,
February 12, 1984, May 19, 1985, May 31, 1987 and May 17, 1992.)

The purpose of this corporation shall be to maintain a church society where the individual may explore, develop and express a personal religious philosophy in an environment free of established or implied doctrines, tenets or beliefs and where the human causes and concerns for truth, equal rights, environment and community may be advocated and espoused. (Article II of the Articles of Incorporation, as amended October 14, 1979.)

ARTICLE 1–MEMBERSHIP

Section 1.–Qualification. Any person who has reached the age of fourteen years and is in sympathy with the purpose and methods of this Church may become a member by signing the Church Membership Book.

Section 2.–Vote. The right to vote at any meeting of the Church shall be reserved to those persons who have been members for a period of sixty days and the right to vote on any matter, question or proposal involving the creation or continuance of a financial obligation on behalf of the Church shall be further reserved to those voting members who are eighteen years of age or older.

Section 3.–Service. Eligibility to serve as an Officer, Trustee or as a Trustee for Endowments shall be reserved for voting members of the Church who are eighteen years of age or older.

Section 4.–Revocation. Membership may be revoked for just cause by action of the Board of Trustees. Notice of any proposed revocation shall be given by mail to the member no more than thirty and not less than seven days before the meeting of the Board of Trustees at which such action will be considered.

Section 5.–Review. The membership roll shall be reviewed annually by the Board of Trustees, or a designated committee, for the purpose of determining which members have not contributed, financially or through service, directly or indirectly, to the support of the Church. The absence of such support shall be considered sufficient reason for revocation of membership.

Section 6.–Honorary. The Board of Trustees shall be empowered to grant, at its discretion, Honorary Life Membership to any member who may have been deemed to have become permanently incapable of any such contribution due to disability or infirmity.

ARTICLE II–MEETINGS

Section 1.–Annual. The Annual Meeting of the Church shall be held within a month prior to April 30th, unless changed by action of the members, for the purpose of electing Officers, Trustees and Trustees for Endowments to hold office, commencing with the first day of the Fiscal Year, for the terms as provided elsewhere in these Bylaws, to adopt a budget for the current fiscal year, and to conduct such other business as may come before the meeting.

Section 2.–Special. Special meetings may be called by the President, or by four members of the Board of Trustees, or upon written request to the President subscribed to by at least twenty-five voting members of the Church.

Section 3.–Quorum. At all meetings of the Church, except as may be provided elsewhere in these Bylaws or in the Articles of Incorporation, it shall be necessary that at least twenty percent (20%) of the voting members of the Church shall be personally present to constitute a quorum.

Section 4.–Voting method. At all meetings of the Church the method of voting shall be by voice, except in the case of elections when there is more than one bona fide candidate for any one office, then the voting shall be by secret ballot. The presiding officer shall, at the request of a voting member, call for a show of hands or a division of the house. Proxy voting is permitted.

Section 5.–Votes required. Except as provided elsewhere in these Bylaws or the Articles of Incorporation, a majority of the votes cast at any meeting of the Church at which a quorum is present shall be sufficient to take or authorize action upon any matter, question or proposal which may properly come before the meeting.

Section 6.–Notice. Formal notice of the Annual Meeting and/or special meetings shall be given through the Church newsletter or Church bulk mail and/or first class mail to all Members no less than ten days before such meeting. Notice of any special meeting shall state the specific purpose of said meeting. Notice of all meetings of the Church shall be given from the pulpit when the Church is in session.

ARTICLE III—BOARD OF TRUSTEES

Section 1.–Composition. The Board of Trustees shall consist of nine voting members. Trustees shall serve for a term of three years on a staggered basis with three Trustees being elected each year at the Annual Meeting. The Minister and the D.R.E. shall be ex-officio members of the Board without a vote.

Section 2.–Election. The Board of Trustees shall, following the Annual Meeting, elect from their number a President and a Vice President to serve as Officers of the Church for the Administrative Year.

Section 3.–Regular meetings. Regular meetings of the Board of Trustees shall be held each month at a mutually agreed upon time and day. Except in the case of emergency, such meetings shall be announced to the members of the Church in the newsletter and/or from the pulpit.

Section 4.–Special meetings. Special meetings of the Board of Trustees may be held at such times as the Board may, from time to time, determine, or at the call of the President, or at the request of at least three Trustees made to the President.

Section 5.–Notice. Notice of all meetings of the Board of Trustees may be made by telephone, provided that no less than twenty-four hours notice is given. Meetings of the Board may be held without notice provided that all Trustees sign a Waiver of Notice prior to any such meeting.

Section 6.–Quorum. At all meetings of the Board of Trustees a majority of the members of the Board shall constitute a quorum. The consent of five Trustees shall be necessary to take or authorize action. However, during the months of June through September, three Trustees shall constitute a quorum solely for the purpose of ordering routine maintenance of Church property and filling any vacancy on a committee or of any non-elective office. The consent of three Trustees shall be required to take or authorize action at any such reduced quorum meetings.

Section 7.–Prohibitions. (A) Any Trustee whose period of service is two years or longer shall be ineligible for re-election during the following year. (B) A member of the Board of Trustees shall not concurrently serve as a Trustee for Endowments.

Section 8.–Responsibilities. The Board of Trustees shall be responsible for: (1) Managing and safekeeping of the assets of the Church; (2) Conducting the business of the Church; (3) Providing leadership in authorizing and directing activities which will provide operating funds; (4) Arranging for a review of the financial records of the Church following the close of the Fiscal Year; (5) Acting in accordance with the provisions of the Trust Agreement for Endowments, and (6) Creating and establishing committees as required or determined necessary or desirable.

Section 9.–Activity Report. The Board of Trustees shall provide the members of the Church with a written report at least one week prior to the Annual Meeting which shall account for the activities of the Board, all standing Committees, organizations and such other committees as requested by the Board to submit a report.

Section 10.–Financial Report. (A) The Board of Trustees shall make available to the members of the Church at least one week before the Annual Meeting a written report which shall include a financial statement for the Fiscal Year just ended and a proposed budget for the current Fiscal Year. (B) No expenditure, budgeted or unbudgeted, shall be allowed unless full funding is available.

Section 11.–Rentals. The Board of Trustees may permit the use of the Church property by such persons or organizations and upon such terms as it deems advisable.

Section 12.–Maintenance Reserve Fund. (A) The Board of trustees of the Church shall direct the Trustees for Endowments to set aside from the net income of the unrestricted properties of the Trust Fund for Endowments in a separate account to be identified as the "Maintenance Reserve Fund" amounts equal to 2% of the current replacement value of the property of the Church as determined each year in good faith by the Board of Trustees then in office. Such set asides shall be limited to replacements of funds appropriated from the Maintenance Reserve Fund when the account reaches $90,000 plus an annual increment of interest at the rate of the Consumer Price Index beginning in fiscal year 1988–89. (B) The Trustees for Endowments shall determine: (1) the depository for such funds and the signatories thereto and (2) if and when any or all of such funds shall be committed to other forms of liquid investment. (C) Cash provided from such investments whether from income or by conversion, shall be returned to this Maintenance Reserve Fund. (D) Withdrawals from said Maintenance Reserve Fund, other than for the purpose of investment, may be made only for the purpose of making *major repairs* and replacements of the property of the Church. Written guidelines for the use of this Maintenance Reserve Fund shall be established by the Board of Trustees of the Church and the Trustees for Endowments, and shall include estimates of the capital outlay needs in the foreseeable future and a routine procedure for determining the current replacement value each year. (E) The use of the remainder of the net income shall also be for the purpose of making major repairs and/or replacements to the property of the Church to the extent that the Maintenance Reserve Fund is insufficient, for the acquisition of real property, and for such religious purposes of the Church as may be determined in good faith by the Board of Trustees of the Church and the Trustees for Endowments. (F) If agreed upon by the Board of Trustees of the Church and by the Trustees for Endowments, the Board of Trustees of the Church shall direct the Trustees for Endowments to make a loan to the Church from the principal of the Trust Fund in such amount as may be amortized and repaid to the Trust Fund over a reasonable period of time. (G) In the ever the Trustees of the Church and the Trustees for Endowments are not in agreement the matter shall be submitted for decision by a two-thirds majority of the Church membership eligible to vote, by signed ballot.

ARTICLE IV—OFFICERS

Section 1.–Titles. (A) The Officers of the Church elected by the Board of Trustees shall be a President and a Vice President. (B) The Officers of the Church elected by the members of the Church shall be a Clerk, a Treasurer, an Assistant Treasurer, and a Financial Secretary. (C) All Officers shall serve for the Administrative Year.

Section 2.–President. The President shall: (1) Preside at all meetings of the Church and the Board of Trustees; (2) Make such appointments as directed, authorized or required, including appointing Trustees to serve as liaison representatives to Standing Committees who shall be responsible for reporting to the Board of the activities of their respective committees; (3) Execute all documents necessary to carry out the purpose and functions of the Church; (4) Be responsible for carrying out the directives and requirements of applicable law, these Bylaws and the Articles of Incorporation, and (5) Serve without a vote as an ex-officio member of all committees except the Nominating Committee.

Section 3.–Vice President. The Vice President shall: (1) Assist the President in the exercise of his or her duties; (2) In the absence or inability of the President, execute the duties of the President, and (3) In the absence or inability of the Treasurer or the Assistant Treasurer, have the authority to receive all monies on behalf of the Chruch.

Section 4.–Treasurer. The Treasurer shall: (1) Be responsible for the safekeeping of all funds and assets of the Church, except for those assets assigned to the trusteeship of the Endowment Trust; (2) Keep a full and accurate record of all receipts and disbursements in ledgers kept for such purposes which shall be the property of the Church; (3) Prepare written monthly and annual reports on the financial condition of the Church and make them available to the Board of Trustees and members of the Church; (4) File any and all tax and other financial reports as required by applicable law; (5) Deposit all monies, drafts and checks in the name or to the credit of the Church at such banks and/or depositories as the Board of Trustees shall designate, and (6) Disburse funds of the Church for all expenses authorized by the Board of Trustees or by action of the members of the Church.

Section 5.–Assistant Treasurer. The Assistant Treasurer shall: (1) Assist the Treasurer in the exercise of his or her duties, and (2) In the absence or inability of the Treasurer, execute the duties of the Treasurer.

Section 6.–Clerk. The Clerk shall: (1) Prepare detailed and accurate minutes of all business meetings of the Church and Board of Trustees; (2) Preserve all records, reports and official documents of the Church; (3) Prepare and file reports, other than financial, as required by applicable law; (4) Conduct official correspondence in the name of and for the Church; (5) Communicate to the members via official newsletter or such other publications as deemed appropriate, actions or concerns of the Board of Trustees, and (6) Be custodian of the corporate seal.

Section 7.–Financial Secretary. The Financial Secretary shall: (1) Keep an accurate record of all collections of financial support for the Church; (2) Transmit all such collections to the Treasurer, and (3) Prepare a written report for presentation to members of the Church at the Annual Meeting as to the total amount pledged and the amount collected, and make such additional reports as requested by the Board of Trustees.

ARTICLE V—TRUSTEES FOR ENDOWMENTS

Section 1.–Composition. The Trustees for Endowments shall consist of seven voting members of the Church. Trustees shall serve for a term of three years on a staggered basis with two Trustees being elected each year at the Annual Meeting. Trustees may be re-elected. A Trustee for Endowments shall not concurrently serve as a member of the Board of Trustees.

Section 2.–Trust Agreement. The Trustees for Endowments shall be bound and guided in their stewardship by the TRUST AGREEMENT FOR ENDOWMENTS dated January 25, 1962, as amended February 27, 1963, and recorded as Clerk's instruments numbered 916419-A and 44602-B, respectively, with the Office of Clerk of Circuit Court, Pinellas County, Florida, and any subsequent amendments made thereto and properly recorded with said office.

Section 3.–Officers. The Trustees for Endowments shall elect from their number at the beginning of the Administrative Year a Chairperson, a Vice Chairperson, a Treasurer, and a Recording Secretary to serve for one year.

Section 4.–Representative. The Trustees for Endowments shall elect from their number at the beginning of the Administrative Year a Representative to the Board of Trustees to act as a liaison to the Board. The Representative shall serve for one year.

Section 5.–Regular Meetings. Regular meetings of the Trustees for Endowments shall be held quarterly from September through May, inclusive. Such meetings must be announced to the members of the Church in the newsletter and/or from the pulpit.

Section 6.–Special Meetings. Special emergency meetings of the Trustees for Endowments may be held at the request of the Board of Trustees or the Trustees for Endowments. Notice of all special meetings of the Trustees for Endowments shall be extended to the President of the Church Board of Trustees. Such notice of special meetings may be made by telephone provided that no less than twenty-four hours notice is given.

Section 7.–Quorum. At all meetings of the Trustees for Endowments, majority of the members shall constitute a Quorum and the consent of four Trustees shall be necessary to take or authorize action.

Section 8.–Financial Report. (1) The Trustees for Endowments shall make available to the Board of Trustees on a quarterly basis, a written report which shall include a financial report which shall include a financial statement; (2) The Trustees for Endowments shall make available to the Church, at least one week before the Annual Meeting, a written report which shall include a financial statement.

ARTICLE VI—THE MINISTER

Section 1.–Duties. The Minister shall have a free pulpit and, in addition to ministerial duties and functions, shall: (1) Be an Administrative Officer of the Church in carrying out the directives and policies established by the Board of Trustees; (2) Provide general supervision to other paid church staff, and work with the DRE and others to create and implement activities and programs for the entire congregation; (3) Bring to the attention of the Board of Trustees any matter or thing which is considered to be in the general interest and concern of the Church, making any observations and/or recommendations thereon, and (4) Serve without a vote as an ex-officio member of the Board of Trustees and all other committees except the Nominating and Ministerial Search Committees.

Section 2.–Qualification. The Minister shall be fellowshipped by the Unitarian Universalist Association or in preparation for such fellowship.

Section 3.–Contract. The Minister after two annual contracts shall be considered to have indefinite tenure. The contract for service shall be reviewed at least biennially by the Board of Trustees. If the Trustees and the Minister are not able to agree on a contract for the ensuing two year period, then the matter shall be presented to the members at a meeting of the Church.

Section 4.–Selection. The Minister shall be chosen by the members of the Church upon the affirmative vote of at least two-thirds of the voting members present at a meeting of the Church. Following the selection of the Minister, the members shall approve a contract for service upon the affirmative vote of a majority of the eligible voting members present.

Section 5.–Search Committee. Upon notification of an immediate or future vacancy of the ministerial office, the Board of Trustees shall elect a Search Committee to seek out qualified candidates. The Search Committee shall consist of at least seven voting members of the Church and three alternates. The Committee shall be representative of the membership of the Church. The Committee shall elect from their number a Chairperson and a Recording Secretary.

Section 6.–Dismissal. The Minister may be dismissed and the contract terminated upon the affirmative vote of a majority of the voting members present at a meeting of the Church at which a quorum of fifty-one percent (51%) of the members shall be required. The vote shall be taken by secret ballot. Notice of any such dismissal shall be given in writing by the President to the Minister. A severance payment equal to two months salary shall be given upon dismissal.

ARTICLE VII—DIRECTOR OF RELIGIOUS EDUCATION

Section 1.–Duties. The Director of Religious Education (DRE) shall be responsible for the administration of the religious education department and shall work with the minister and others to create and implement activities and programs for the entire congregation.

Section 2.–Line of responsibility. The DRE serves under the general direction of the minister, but serves at the pleasure of the Board.

Section 3.–Contract. The DRE may be offered a contract for service by the Board on an annual basis.

Section 4.–Search Committee. Upon a decision by the Board and Minister to look for a DRE, the Board of Trustees shall select a Search Committee to seek out a qualified candidate. The Search Committee shall consist of at least seven members of the Church representative of the Church membership and shall select their own Chairman and Recording Secretary. The Minister shall serve without a vote as an ex-officio member of the committee.

ARTICLE VIII—GENERAL PROVISIONS

Section 1.–Fiscal Year. The Fiscal Year shall begin July 1 and end June 30.

Section 2.–Administrative Year. The Administrative Year shall coincide with the Fiscal Year.

Section 3.–Signature Authorization. All checks, notes, drafts, orders for payment of money and other evidences of indebtedness issued in the name of the Church shall be signed by either the President, the Treasurer or other authorized signatories.

Section 4.–Nominating Committee. The Nominating Committee shall consist of five voting members, including a Chairman appointed by the President and four other members elected by the Board of Trustees. The Committee shall provide a slate of candidates for election at the Annual Meeting, which slate shall be published in said meeting notice. The Committee shall obtain the consent of each candidate and shall construct a slate that will maintain a Board of Trustees representative of the Church membership. Additional candidates may be nominated in writing at least one week before the meeting by action of at least three Church members with consent of the proposed candidate. Such additional nominees shall be listed on the official ballot, together with those submitted by the Nominating Committee.

Section 5.–Vacancies. Any vacancy occurring among the elected Officers or Board of Trustees shall be filled by appointment by the President with the approval of the Board of Trustees until the next Annual Meeting.

Section 6.–Removal. Any elected Officer or Trustee may be removed from office for just cause upon the affirmative vote of two-thirds of the voting members present at any meeting of the Church. Notice of any proposed removal from office shall be given by mail to the Officer or Trustee involved no more than thirty and no less than seven days before the meeting at which such action will be considered. Any Officer or Trustee shall automatically be removed from office for three consecutive unauthorized absences from regular meetings of the Board of Trustees.

Section 7.–Bonding. All Officers and Trustees shall be bonded in an amount determined by the Board of Trustees.

ARTICLE IX—AMENDMENTS

These Bylaws may be amended upon the affirmative vote of two-thirds of the voting members present at any meeting of the Church, provided, however, that the notice of said meeting shall contain an advisory that an amendment or amendments shall be included in the order of business and, provided further, that a copy of the text of the proposed amendment or amendments shall be included with said notice.

ARTICLE X—PARLIAMENTARY AUTHORITY

Oleck & Green, *Parliamentary Law and Practice for NPOs* (2d ed., 1991) shall prevail on matters of parliamentary procedure to the extent that they are not inconsistent with these Bylaws, the Articles of Incorporation or applicable law.

ARTICLE XI—DISSOLUTION

In the event of the dissolution of the Church, the Board of Trustees shall, after paying or making provision for the payment of all the liabilities of the corporation, dispose of all of the assets of the corporation exclusively for the purposes of the corporation in such manner, or to such organization or organizations organized and operated exclusively for religious or like purposes, charitable, educational or scientific purposes as shall at the time qualify as an exempt organization or organizations under Section 501(c) (3) of the Internal Revenue Code as it exists at the time of dissolution.

FORM NO. 111

Bylaws of Society for Support of Public Libraries (Local)

Bylaws

_____

Article I

Name, Seal and Offices

Section 1. Name. The name of this Corporation is _____

_____

Section 2. Seal. The seal of the Corporation shall be circular in form and shall bear on its outer edge the words "_____, _____." The Board of Directors may change the form of the seal or the inscription thereon at pleasure.

Section 3. Offices. The principal office of the Corporation shall be in the County of _____, City of _____. The Corporation may also have offices at such other places as the Board of Directors may from time to time appoint or the purposes of the Corporation may require.

Article II

Activities

Section 1. Activities will be limited to those permitted under Section 501(c)(3) of the Internal Revenue Code.

Section 2. The public library system exists and is supported by citizens of the community to provide open access to collections and services which reflect the ideas and experiences of humanity.

Section 3. The public library alone, of all society's institutions, is dedicated to (1) the preservation of materials which typify and epitomize the quality of the past, and (2) the acquisition and presentation of contemporary materials and services which are for citizens' informational, cultural, and recreational reading, viewing, and listening.

Section 4. The philosophy of library service presumes a careful, caring and dynamic determination of community needs and individual concerns succeeded by responsive development of resources and services. Continuing community receptivity and support of such a philosophy is vital to survival and symbolizes the Foundation's commitment to the existence of an informed and educated public with a perspective for self-government and personal fulfillment.

Section 5. The purposes of the Foundation of _____, are:

1. to promote public support of the local public library system by establishing a framework for receipt and distribution of contributions in a variety of form;

2. to offer a project oriented, rather than a function oriented program of assistance to local public libraries;

3. to develop a year-round program for the development of public support to establish supplemental funding for the local public library system which can provide additional, special, and extraordinary funds in addition to those provided by the traditional tax-base funding;

4. to encourage public support of the local public libraries and their branches by providing special or additional goods and services not otherwise available through the traditional tax base funding program.

Article III

Members and Meetings of Members

Section 1. Membership. The members of the Corporation shall consist of the persons signing the Certificate of Incorporation and such other persons qualifying as hereinafter set forth. The Corporation shall have three classes of members:

A. Individual Members. Individual members of the Corporation shall consist of those natural persons whose annual dues are paid for the current year. Such dues shall be fixed from time to time by the Board of Directors and payable as provided in Section 2 hereof.

B. Corporate Members. Corporate members of the Corporation shall consist of firms, partnerships, associations, corporations, or other business entities whose dues are paid for the current year. Such dues shall be fixed from time to time by the Board of Directors and payable as provided in Section 2 hereof. Each corporate member shall designate one person to vote at meetings of members.

C. Honorary Members. Honorary membership may be conferred upon individuals who in the opinion of the Board of Directors have returned distinguished service to the greater _____ public library system. A candidate for honorary membership may be proposed by any member of the Board of Directors and shall be selected to such membership upon a three-fourths vote of all Directors at a regularly constituted meeting of the Board of Directors. Honorary Members shall be exempt from payment of any dues whatever and shall be entitled to all the privileges of regular members, except the right to vote or hold office.

Section 2. Members' Dues. Members' dues shall be fixed from time to time by the Board of Directors. The dues of all members of the Corporation shall be payable annually in advance upon the first day of January. If the dues of any member be unpaid for a period of sixty (60) days after the same become payable, the Treasurer of the Corporation shall mail a notice of delinquency. If the dues of any member be not paid within thirty (30) days after the mailing of such notice of delinquency, his membership shall automatically terminate on that date by reason of such nonpayment, but the Board of Directors may provide for subsequent reinstatement.

Section 3. Rights of Members. The right of a member to vote and all his right, title, and interest in or to the Corporation shall cease on the termination of his membership. No member shall be entitled to share in the distribution of the corporate assets upon the dissolution of the Corporation.

Section 4. Resignation of Members. Any member may resign from the Corporation by delivering a written resignation to the President or Secretary of the Corporation.

Section 5. Annual Meetings. The Annual meeting of the members of the Corporation shall be held during January of each year at the principal office of the Corporation or at such other place as the Board of Directors shall designate, for the purpose of electing Directors, and for the transaction of such other business as may properly come before the meeting.

Section 6. Notice of Annual Meetings. Notice of the time, place, and purpose or purposes of the annual meeting shall be served by publication in local newspapers of general circulation once each week for three consecutive weeks. Said notice shall commence not more than nine weeks nor less than seven (7) weeks before the meeting. For annual meetings at which an election of Directors will occur, the notice shall set forth the slate of Directors nominated by the Nominations Committee and the procedure for the nomination by members of additional individuals for the position of Director.

Section 7. Nomination of Directors. Any member may nominate individuals for the position of Director. Such nomination must be in writing, signed by the nominee authorizing that his name be placed on the ballot, and delivered to the Board of Directors not less than two weeks nor more than four weeks before such meeting. Any such additional nominees shall be included on the Ballot at an annual meeting at which an election of Directors will occur.

Section 8. Special Meetings. Special meetings of the members, other than those regulated by statute, may be called at any time by the President or Vice President or by two Directors and must be called by the President or Secretary on receipt of the written request of one-third of the members of the Corporation.

Section 9. Notice of Special Meetings. Notice of special meeting stating the time, place, and purpose or purposes thereof shall be served by publication in local newspapers of general circulation once each week for two consecutive weeks. Said notice shall commence not more than five weeks nor less than four weeks before such meeting.

Section 10. Quorum. At any meeting of members of the Corporation the presence of one-third of the membership or 50 members, whichever is less, shall be necessary to constitute a quorum for all purposes except as otherwise provided by law, and the act of a majority of the members present at any meeting at which there is a quorum shall be the act of the full membership except as may be otherwise specifically provided by statute or by these bylaws. In the absence of a quorum, or when a quorum is present, a meeting may be adjourned from time to time by vote of a majority of the members present in person or by proxy, without notice other than by announcement at the meeting and without further notice to any absent member. At any adjourned meeting at which a *quorum* shall be present, any business may be transacted which might have been transacted at the meeting as originally notified.

Section 11. Voting. At every meeting of members each member of the Corporation shall be entitled to one vote. Proxy votes shall be recognized. All elections shall be had and all questions decided by a majority vote of the members present in person or by proxy.

Section 12. Waiver of Notice. Whenever under the provisions of any law or under the provisions of the Certificate of Incorporation or Bylaws of this Corporation, the Corporation or the Board of Directors or any committee thereof is authorized to take any action after notice to the members of the Corporation or after the lapse of a prescribed period of time, such action may be taken without notice and without the lapse of any period of time, if at any time before or after such action be completed, such requirements be waived in writing by the person or persons entitled to such notice or entitled to participate in the action to be taken or by his attorney thereunto authorized.

Section 13. Removal of Members, Directors, or Officers, any member, Director, or Officer may be removed from membership or from office by the affirmative vote of two-thirds of the full membership, voting in person at any regular or special meeting called for that purpose, for conduct detrimental to the interests of the Corporation, for lack of sympathy with its objectives, or for refusal to render reasonable assistance in carrying out its purposes. Any such member, officer, or director proposed to be removed shall be entitled to at least five days' notice in writing by mail of the meeting at which such removal is to be voted upon and shall be entitled to appear before and be heard at such meeting.

Article IV

Board of Honorary Trustees

Section 1. A Board of Honorary Trustees composed of not more than 100 prominent men and women in the community shall be selected in the manner and for such duties as determined by the Board of Directors, provided, however, that said Board of Honorary Trustees shall constitute only an advisory board to consult and advise with the Board of Directors and shall have no authority to act on behalf of or as agent for or in any manner bind the Foundation's duly acting and appointed Board of Directors.

Article V

Directors

Section 1. Election of Directors and Term. At the annual meeting next held after the adoption of these Bylaws, there shall be an election by ballot of thirteen Directors of the Corporation, four of whom shall be elected for a term of one year, four for two years, and five for three years. At each annual meeting thereafter, a number of Directors equal to that of those whose terms have expired shall be elected for the term of three years. At the expiration of any term of three years, any Director may be reelected. The Directors shall be members of the Corporation and shall be chosen by ballot at the Annual Meeting by a majority of the votes of the members present at such meeting.

Section 2. Number. The number of Directors of the Corporation shall be thirteen, but such number may be increased or decreased by amendment to these Bylaws, in the manner set forth in Article XIV hereof. When the number of Directors is so decreased by amendment adopted by the Board of Directors, each Director in office shall serve until his term expires, or until his resignation or removal as herein provided.

Section 3. Resignation. Any Director may resign at any time by giving written notice of such resignation to the Board of Directors.

Section 4. Vacancies. Any vacancy in the Board of Directors occurring during the year, including a vacancy created by an increase in the number of Directors made by the Board of Directors, may be filled for the unexpired portion of the year by the Directors then serving, although less than a quorum, by affirmative vote of the majority thereof. Any Director so elected by the Board of Directors shall hold office until the next succeeding annual meeting of the members of the Corporation or until the election and qualification of his successor.

Section 5. Annual Meetings. Immediately after each annual election, the newly elected Directors may meet forthwith at the principal office of the Corporation for the purpose of organization, the election of officers, and the transaction of other business, and, if a quorum of the Directors be then present, no prior notice of such meeting shall be required to be given. The place and time of such first meeting may, however, be fixed by written consent of all the Directors.

Section 6. Special Meetings. Special meetings of the Board of Directors may be called by the President or Vice President and must be called by either of them on the written request of any member of the Board.

Section 7. Notice of Meetings. Notice of all Directors' meetings, except as herein otherwise provided, shall be given by mailing the same at least seven days before the meeting to the usual business or residence address of the Director, but such notice may be waived by any Director. Regular meetings of the Board of Directors may be held without notice at such time and place as shall be determined by the Board. Any business may be transacted at any Directors' meeting. At any meeting at which every Director shall be present, even though without any notice or waiver thereof, any business may be transacted.

Section 8. Chairman. At all meetings of the Board of Directors, the President or Vice President, or in their absence a chairman chosen by the Directors present, shall preside.

Section 9. Quorum. At all meetings of the Board of Directors, a majority of the Directors shall be necessary and sufficient to constitute a quorum for the transaction of business and the act of a majority of the Directors present at any meeting at which there is a quorum shall be the act of the Board of Directors, except as may be otherwise specifically provided by statute or by these Bylaws. If at any meeting there is less than a quorum present, a majority of those present may adjourn the meeting from time to time without further notice to any absent Director.

Article VI

Officers

Section 1. Number. The officers of the Corporation shall be the President, Vice President, Secretary, Treasurer, and such other officers with such powers and duties not inconsistent with these Bylaws as may be appointed and determined by the Board of Directors. Any two offices, except those of President and Vice President, may be held by the same person.

Section 2. Election, Term of Office, and Qualifications. The President shall be elected annually by the Board of Directors from among their number, and the other officers shall be elected annually by the Board of Directors from among such persons as the Board of Directors may see fit, at the first meeting of the Board of Directors after the annual meeting of members of the Corporation.

Section 3. Vacancies. In case any office of the Corporation becomes vacant by death, resignation, retirement, disqualification, or any other cause, the majority of the Directors then in office, although less than a quorum, may elect an officer to fill such vacancy, and the officer so elected shall hold office and serve until the first meeting of the Board of Directors after the annual meeting of members next succeeding and until the election and qualification of his successor.

Section 4. President. The President shall preside at all meetings of members and of the Board of Directors. He shall have and exercise general charge and supervision of the affairs of the Corporation and shall do and perform such other duties as may be assigned to him by the Board of Directors.

Section 5. Vice President. At the request of the President, or in the event of his absence or disability, the Vice President shall perform the duties and possess and exercise the powers of the President; and to the extent authorized by law the Vice President shall have such other powers as the Board of Directors may determine, and shall perform such other duties as may be assigned to him by the Board of Directors.

Section 6. Secretary. The Secretary shall have charge of such books, documents, and papers as the Board of Directors may determine and shall have the custody of the corporate seal. He shall attend and keep the minutes of all the meetings of the Board of Directors and members of the Corporation. He shall keep a record, containing the names, alphabetically arranged, of all persons who are members of the Corporation, showing their places of residence, and such book shall be open for inspection as prescribed by law. He may sign with the President or Vice President, in the name and on behalf of the Corporation, any contracts or agreements authorized by the Board of Directors, and when so authorized or ordered by the Board of Directors, he may affix the seal of the Corporation. He shall, in general, perform all the duties incident to the office of secretary, subject to the control of the Board of Directors, and shall do and perform such other duties as may be assigned to him by the Board of Directors.

Section 7. Treasurer. The Treasurer will initiate financial policies of the Corporation for review by the membership. He shall represent the Corporation in discussions of financial matters with outside agencies, as required, but with full knowledge and support of the officers. He also shall have the care and custody of any monies, funds and properties of the Corporation, and shall render an annual statement of the receipts and disbursements at each annual meeting of the members, and prepare reports for the Internal Revenue Service and any other governmental agencies. The Treasurer shall have the custody of all funds, property, and securities of the Corporation, subject to such regulations as may be imposed by the Board of Directors. He shall be required to give bond for the faithful performance of his duties, in such sum and with such sureties as the Board of Directors may require. When necessary or proper he may endorse on behalf of the Corporation for collection checks, notes, and other obligations, and shall deposit the same to the credit of the Corporation at such bank or banks or depositary as the Board of Directors may designate. He shall sign all receipts and vouchers and, together with such other officer or officers, if any, as shall be designated by the Board of Directors, he shall sign all checks of the Corporation and all bills of exchange and promissory notes issued by the Corporation, except in cases where the signing and execution thereof shall be expressly designated by the Board of Directors or by these Bylaws to some other officer or agent of the Corporation. He shall make such payments as may be necessary or proper to be made on behalf of the Corporation. He shall enter regularly on the books of the Corporation to be kept by him for the purpose full and accurate account of all moneys and obligations received and paid or incurred by him for or on account of the Corporation, and he shall exhibit such books at all reasonable times to any Director or member on application at the offices of the Corporation. He shall, in general, perform all the duties incident to the office of treasurer, subject to the control of the Board of Directors.

Section 8. Removal. Any officer may be removed from office by the affirmative vote of two-thirds of all the Directors at any regular or special meeting called for that purpose, for non-feasance, malfeasance, or misfeasance, for conduct detrimental to the interests of the Corporation, for lack of sympathy with its objects, or for refusal to render reasonable assistance in carrying out its purposes. Any officer proposed to be removed shall be entitled to at least five days' notice in writing by mail of the meeting of the Board of Directors at which such removal is to be voted upon and shall be entitled to appear before and be heard by the Board of Directors at such meeting.

Article VII

Committees

Section 1. Executive Committee. There shall be an Executive Committee, the size of which shall be determined by the Board of Directors, consisting of the Chairman of the Board, the principal officers of the Foundation, the most recent past president, and may include one or more members of the Board of Directors. The Executive Committee shall have the power to act for the Board of Directors between meetings of the Board of Directors and to perform such other duties as may be prescribed by the Bylaws or delegated to it by the Board of Directors from time to time. It shall be responsible to report to the Board of Directors at each regularly scheduled meeting concerning its activities.

Section 2. Standing Committees. The Foundation President shall appoint standing committees and designate chairperson for each such committee, and, except when otherwise specifically provided by the Bylaws, shall determine the membership. The standing committees shall be:

1. Membership
2. Resource Development
3. Nominating
4. Budget and Finance
5. Community Relations
6. Planning

The function of these standing committees is to plan and conduct broad base year around fund raising activities for the Foundation.

Section 3. Nominations Committee. Not less than three months before an annual meeting of members at which an election of Directors will take place, the Chairman shall appoint a Nominations Committee comprised of current Directors for the purpose of identifying qualified persons to serve as Directors of the Corporation. The Nominations Committee shall nominate a number of Directors equal to that of those whose terms have expired. The Committee shall provide a slate of nominees which shall be set forth in the notice of annual meetings of the members. Directors shall be elected as provided in Article V, Section 1.

Section 4. Other Committees. It is anticipated that from time to time *ad hoc* committees and possibly other standing committees will be appointed and approved by the Board of Directors or the members.

Article VIII

Executive Director

The Board of Directors may appoint or employ an Executive Director whose duties and functions shall be those prescribed by the Board of Directors, provided that any such delegation of authority to the Executive Director shall not operate to relieve the Board of Directors or any individual directors of any responsibility imposed upon it or him by law. The Board of Directors shall, from time to time, determine the compensation to be paid, if any, to the Executive Director. The Executive Director is authorized to employ, on the approval of the Executive Committee, a staff responsible to assist with the duties of the Executive Director. The Executive Director shall be bonded and shall be responsible for the bonding of other staff members in such manner under such conditions as the Board of Directors and the Executive Director may direct.

Article IX

Out-of-Pocket Expenses

Members, directors and officers are expected to contribute their services. It is not expected that they will bear out-of-pocket expenses directly related to meetings and projects.

Article X

Contracts

The Board of Directors, except as in these Bylaws otherwise provided, may authorize any officer or agent to enter into any contract or execute and deliver any instrument in the name of and on behalf of the Corporation, and such authority may be general or confined to a specific instance: and unless so authorized by the Board of Directors, no officer, agent, or employee shall have any power or authority to bind the Corporation by any contract or engagement, or to pledge its credit, or render it liable pecuniarily for any purpose or to any amount.

Article XI

Prohibition Against Sharing in Corporate Earnings

No member, Director, officer, or employee of or member of a committee of or person connected with the Corporation, or any other private individual shall receive at any time any of the net earnings or pecuniary profit from the operations of the Corporation, provided that this shall not prevent the payment to any such person of such reasonable compensation for services rendered to or for the Corporation in effecting any of its purposes as shall be fixed by the Board of Directors; and no such person or persons shall be entitled to share in the distribution of any of the corporate assets upon the dissolution of the Corporation. All members of the Corporation shall be deemed to have expressly consented and agreed that upon such dissolution or winding up of the affairs of the Corporation, whether voluntary or involuntary, the assets of the Corporation, after all debts have been satisfied, then remaining in the hands of the Board of Directors shall be distributed, transferred, conveyed, delivered, and paid over, in such amounts as the Board of Directors may determine or as may be determined by a court of competent jurisdiction upon application of the Board of Directors, exclusively to charitable, religious, scientific, testing for public safety, literary, or educational organizations which would then qualify under the provisions of Section 501(c)(3) of the Internal Revenue Code and its Regulations as they now exist or as they may hereafter be amended.

Article XII

Investments

The Corporation shall have the right to retain all or any part of any securities or property acquired by it in whatever manner, and to invest and reinvest any funds held by it, according to the judgment of the Board of Directors, without being restricted to the class of investments which a Director is or may hereafter be permitted by law to make or any similar restriction, provided, however, that no action shall be taken by or on behalf of the Corporation if such action is a prohibited transaction or would result in the denial of the tax exemption under Section 503 or Section 507 of the Internal Revenue Code and its Regulations as they now exist or as they may hereafter be amended.

Article XIII

Indemnification of Officers

The Foundation shall defend, indemnify, and hold harmless every registered agent, director, or officer, the Executive Director, his or her heirs, executors, administrators against liability and against expenses reasonably incurred in connection with any action, suit, or proceeding to which such individual or individuals shall be made a party by reason of being or having been a director, officer, or Executive Director of the Foundation, except with regard to such actions or matters that such individual shall be finally adjudicated in such action, suit, or proceedings to be liable for willful misconduct. The foregoing right shall be exclusive of any other rights to which such individual may be entitled.

Article XIV

Amendments

Section 1. By Directors. The Board of Directors shall have power to make, alter, amend, and repeal the Bylaws of the Corporation by affirmative vote of a majority of the Board, provided, however, that the action is proposed at a regular or special meeting of the Board and adopted at a subsequent regular meeting, except as otherwise provided by law. All Bylaws made by the Board of Directors may be altered, amended, or repealed by the members.

Section 2. By Members. The Bylaws may be altered, amended, or repealed at any meeting of members of the Corporation by a majority vote of all the members present in person, provided that at least seven days written notice is given to the intention to alter, amend, repeal or adopt new Bylaws at such meeting.

Article XV

Exempt Activities

Notwithstanding any other provision of these Bylaws, no member, Director, officer, employee, or representative of this Corporation shall take any action or carry on any activity by or on behalf of the Corporation not permitted to be taken or carried on by an organization exempt under Section 501(c)(3) of the Internal Revenue Code and its Regulations as they now exist or as they may hereafter be amended, or by an organization contributions to which are deductible under Section 170(c)(2) of such Code and Regulations as they now exist or as they may hereafter be amended.

The foregoing were adopted as the Bylaws for _____, _____, a corporation not for profit under the Laws of the State of _____, at the first meeting of the Board of Directors on _____, 19___

By _____

President

FORM NO. 112

Bylaws of

...... MOBILE HOME CLUB, INC.

AN ADULT PARK OWNED AND OPERATED BY

THE HOME OWNERS

Article I

Offices

The principal office of the corporation in the State of _____ shall be located at _____ Mobile Home Park, _____, _____

Article II

Shareholders

§1. Ownership of shares in _____ Mobile Home Club, Inc. is available to owners of mobile homes in _____ Mobile Home Park. Any buyers of a mobile home to be located in the park must buy the share of stock and the 99-year lease on the lot relating to the lot on which the mobile home is located or to be placed.

§2. The annual meeting of the shareholders shall be held in the Recreation Hall the fourth Tuesday of January each year to receive the reports of the outgoing Board of Directors, to install Directors and alternate Directors for the ensuing year and to transact such other business as may come before the meeting. The time and place of such meeting shall be posted on the bulletin board of the Recreation Hall 15 days prior to the meeting.

§3. A special meeting of the shareholders may be called at any time by the President, or in his absence by the Vice President, or the Secretary, or at the written request of any three Board members, upon 15 days notice, which notice shall be posted on the bulletin board of the Recreation Hall, stating the time, place, and purpose of such meeting.

§4. A quorum shall consist of a majority of the shareholders, in person or by proxy—each share being entitled to one vote. Unless otherwise stated in these bylaws the act of a majority of the shareholders present at a meeting in which a quorum is present shall be the act of this corporation.

§5. Informal action by shareholders. Any action required to be taken at a meeting of the shareholders, or any other action which may be taken at a meeting of the shareholders, may be taken without a meeting if a consent in writing, setting forth the action so taken, shall be signed by all of the shareholders entitled to vote with respect to the subject matter thereof.

Article III

Board of Directors

§1. All business of the corporation shall be managed by the Board of Directors.

§2. The Board of Directors shall consist of seven persons elected by the shareholders of the corporation. Of the seven directors, two may be designated by the previous owners to represent them until they control less than 23 shares. They shall then designate one representative to the Board until all but eight of their shares are sold.

§3. Two alternate Board members shall be elected by the shareholders to serve as voting members of the Board during the absence of any elected Board member. They are to serve the same term as a regular Board member and may attend all regular and special meetings of the Board of Directors.

§4. Any vacancy on the Board of Directors shall be filled for the unexpired term by one of the alternate Board members. Should no alternate Board member be available, the Board of Directors shall select a Board member and an alternative Board member to fill the unexpired term. A member of the Board of Directors who misses three consecutive regular meetings without being excused will be considered inactive and the Board will vest an alternate Director for that seat on the Board with full responsibility of directorship for the balance of the term. A Board member may resign at any time, said resignation to be in writing directed to the President.

§5. During December of each year a Nominations and Elections Committee shall prepare a slate of nominees and conduct an election by secret written ballot of all shareholders in good standing and post in the Recreation Hall the results 10 days before the annual meeting. Any shareholder desiring to have his/her name or the name of another shareholder placed on the slate of nominees must advise the chairman of the Nominations and Elections Committee before December 1st of each year that he desires his/her name or the name of another shareholder to be placed on the nominations slate, and the Nominations Committee must place the name submitted on the slate of nominees.

§6. A regular meeting of the Board of Directors shall be held on the third Thursday of each month at the time and place fixed by the Board.

§7. A special meeting of the Board of Directors may be called at any time by the President, or in his absence by the Vice President, or the Secretary, or at the written or oral request of any three members of the Board, upon five days notice, which notice shall state the time, place, and purpose of such meeting.

§8. A quorum shall consist of four Directors. The act of the majority of the Directors present at a meeting at which a quorum is present shall be the act of the Board of Directors.

§9. Any action required to be taken at a meeting of the Board of Directors, or any other action which may be taken at the meeting of the Board of Directors, may be taken without a meeting if a consent in writing, setting forth the action so taken, shall be signed by all of the Directors entitled to vote with respect to the subject matter thereof.

§10. Immediately following the Annual Meeting of the Corporation, the Board of Directors shall elect from its members a President, a Vice President, a Secretary, and a Treasurer. One person may be elected to hold the offices of Secretary and Treasurer. The Board may also elect or appoint such other officers, associates, or assistants as the Board shall deem necessary. Associates and assistants need not be members of the Board. Vacancies in offices may be filled by the Board at any meeting at which a quorum is present.

§11. All Officers and Directors shall be elected annually or re-elected annually.

§12. The Board may employ a Park Manager, if necessary, and fix the terms of his employment salary. It may remove the Park Manager whenever in its best judgment such action is in the best interests of the corporation.

Article IV

Officers and Committees

§1. *The President* is the chief executive officer of the corporation. He shall preside at all meetings of the shareholders and the Board of Directors. He shall appoint all standing and special committee chairmen. Unless otherwise directed by the Board, he shall represent the corporation and the Board of Directors at any meeting at which representation is requested or is considered advisable.

§2. *The Vice President* shall preside in the absence of the President and perform all the duties of the President in the event of his absence or disability.

§3. *The Secretary* shall keep or have under his supervision all records and proceedings of the corporation and the Board of Directors. He shall preside at any meeting in the absence of the President and Vice President. He shall maintain the record of shareholders and control transfers of stock as approved by the Board. He shall perform such other duties as the Board of Directors may designate.

§4. *The Treasurer* shall:

a. Receive and keep in safe custody all monies, funds, and property of the corporation; all monies of this corporation shall be deposited in a bank designated by the Board of Directors in the name of and to the credit of this corporation; all legal documents and papers of importance shall be kept in a safe deposit box in a bank designated by the Board of Directors.

b. Pay all proper bills and vouchers.

c. Establish and maintain the books of accounts of the corporation including rental records of tenants and shareholders.

d. Report in writing the state of accounts of the corporation at each regular meeting of the Board of Directors and to the Finance Committee whenever requested.

e. Produce a statement of the accounts of the corporation for the 12-month period ending December 31st each year to the Board of Directors prior to the annual meeting of the shareholders of the corporation.

f. Make the accounts and vouchers available to a Certified Public Accountant, named by the Board of Directors, for inspection and audit at any time.

g. Perform such other duties as the Board may designate.

All records, books, accounts, and vouchers shall be the property of this corporation and subject to the control of the Board of Directors.

§5. *The Finance Committee* shall consist of shareholders appointed by the Chairman. The Chairman shall be a member of the Board of Directors and in the absence of all the officers shall preside at Board meetings. It shall:

a. Audit and advise with the officers in connection with the budget and financial affairs of the corporation, and shall report to the Board at each regular meeting.

b. Prepare the annual budget of the corporation.

c. Recommend to the Board any changes to be made in monthly rates to tenants and shareholders.

d. Recommend to the Board any changes to be made in fees for services rendered to tenants and shareholders by the park.

e. Have prepared for filing with the proper governmental agencies all reports required of owners or operators of mobile home parks.

§6. *The Development Committee* shall consist of shareholders appointed by the Chairman. The Chairman shall be a member of the Board of Directors. It shall:

a. Be the duty of this committee to receive, review, and report to the Board of Directors any suggestions, comments or criticisms submitted by tenants or shareholders relative to the facilities or rules of the park.

b. Formulate, publish, and report to the Board of Directors the Rules and Regulations in effect in the park, and any changes thereto; and, upon approval of the Board, deliver a printed copy of such Rules, or changes, to the tenants and the shareholders.

c. Prepare a long-range plan for keeping the facilities of the park in first-class condition.

d. Prepare the annual budget for improvements to the park for review by the Board and the Committee on Finance for inclusion in the annual budget.

e. Establish coach standards for all units brought into the park.

f. Recommend to the Board of Directors admission of any person or persons desiring to reside in any mobile home in the park.

g. Carry out such other duties and assignments as the Board may designate.

§7. *The Building and Grounds Committee* shall consist of shareholders appointed by the Chairman. The Chairman shall be a member of the Board of Directors. It shall be the duty of this committee to:

a. Secure the necessary manpower, materials, and equipment to maintain all common property of the corporation.

b. Prepare an annual budget of expenses for review by the Board of Directors and the Committee on Finance.

c. Carry out such other duties and assignments as the Board may designate.

§8. *The Nominating Committee* shall consist of three shareholders, not more than one of whom may be a member of the existing Board of Directors. It shall be appointed by the President not later than November 1st of each year and shall submit its election report of Directors and alternate Directors to the annual meeting of the shareholders.

Article V

Rules and Regulations

The Rules and Regulations as adopted by the Board of Directors shall be in force and binding on tenants and shareholders until such time as amended by the Board of Directors.

Article VI

Legal Counsel

An attorney, designated by the Board of Directors, shall advise in all legal matters and shall render such legal services as may be requested by the Board of Directors.

Article VII

Seal

The Corporate Seal of the corporation shall bear the words: . . . . . . MOBILE HOME CLUB, INC., 19 . . .

Article VIII

Bonding

All officers, employees, and assistants authorized to handle money or funds, at the direction of the Board of Directors, shall be bonded in an amount deemed appropriate by the Board of Directors.

Article IX

Contracts, Loans, Checks, and Deposits.

§1. *Contracts:* The Board of Directors may authorize any officer or officers, agent or agents, to enter into any contract or execute and deliver any instruments in the name of and on behalf of the corporation, and such authority may be general or confined to specific instances.

§2. *Loans*: No loans shall be contracted on behalf of the corporation and no evidence of indebtedness shall be issued in its name unless authorized by a resolution of the Board of Directors. Such authority may be general or confined to specific instances.

§3. *Checks, Drafts, Etc.*: All checks, drafts, or other orders for the payment of money, notes, or other evidences of indebtedness issued in the name of the corporation shall be signed by such officer or officers, agent or agents of the corporation and in such manner as shall from time to time be determined by resolution of the Board of Directors.

§4. *Deposits*: All funds of the corporation not otherwise employed shall be deposited from time to time to the credit of the corporation in such banks, trust companies, or other depositories as the Board of Directors may select.

Article X

Certificates for Shares and Their Transfer

§1. Certificates representing shares of the corporation shall be in such form as shall be determined by the Board of Directors. Such certificates shall be signed by the President or a Vice President and by the Secretary or an assistant Secretary. All certificates surrendered to the Corporation for transfer shall be cancelled and no new certificate shall be issued until the former certificate shall have been surrendered and cancelled, except that in case of a lost, destroyed, or mutilated certificate a new one may be issued therefor upon such terms and indemnity to the corporation as the Board of Directors may prescribe. Certificates will be issued for one share and shall be numbered the same number as the lot number of the lot being leased, except for Lot 1A, which certificate shall be numbered 107. On resale of a certificate the new certificate shall bear the same number, but letters of the alphabet will be used to differentiate that it is not an original certificate.

§2. Subject to requirements in Article XI transfer of shares of the corporation shall be made only on the stock book of the corporation by the holder of record thereof or by his legal representative, who shall furnish proper evidence of authority to transfer, or by his attorney thereunto authorized by power of attorney duly executed and filed with the Secretary of the corporation, and on surrender for cancellation of the certificates for such share. The person in whose name shares stand on the books of the corporation shall be deemed by the corporation to be the owner thereof for all purposes. The corporation shall have a first and prior lien upon all the shares registered in the name of each shareholder for debts due the corporation by such shareholder, except to the extent the same may be subject to a prior pledge or mortgage to an institutional lender. Except as otherwise provided, the registration of a transfer of shares upon the books of the corporation shall operate as a waiver of the corporation's lien on the shares so transferred as to pre-existing obligations of the transferor.

Article XI

Leases and Their Assignment

§1. The form of the lease and all the provisions and conditions and terms of the lease are prescribed by these bylaws by incorporation of said lease as a part hereof, the same being attached hereto and made a part hereof.

§2. A shareholder-lessee shall not assign his lease nor transfer the demised premises, or any part thereof, nor the stock certificate appertaining thereto, except on the following terms and conditions:

A shareholder-lessee may assign the leasehold estate hereby created and the stock certificate appertaining thereto only with the previous consent of the Board of Directors of lessor, provided the assignee shall also simultaneously acquire shareholder-lessee's share of stock of the corporation as hereinbefore provided, and shall have in writing assumed all obligations of the shareholder-lessee to the corporation and shall have delivered to it a duplicate of such assignment and assumption duly executed by shareholder-lessee and the assignee in accordance with the provisions hereof. A shareholder-lessee so assigning shall be relieved from all liability thereafter accruing under said lease, or these bylaws.

The shareholder-lessee desiring to make such assignment shall make written application to the Board of Directors through the Development Committee, giving the name, address, and occupation or business of the party to whom he proposes to assign his lease, together with any other information required by the Board of Directors. The Board of Directors shall pass upon the application within 30 days from the date of its receipt, and the decision of the Board of Directors shall be final and conclusive. In exercising its authority, the Board of Directors shall take into consideration that it is to the best interests of this corporation to have compatible residents to maintain the harmonious relationship of all residents. No fee shall be charged in connection with a transfer or approval in excess of the expenditures reasonably required for credit report expense and legal expense, and this shall not exceed $50.

Article XII

Fiscal Year

The fiscal year of the corporation shall be determined by the Board of Directors.

Article XIII

Assessments

§1. Determination: The Board of Directors shall, from time to time, fix and determine the sum or sums necessary and adequate for the continued ownership, operation, and maintenance of the corporation property including its operating expenses, the payment for any items of betterment, and the establishment of appropriate reserve funds as the Board shall deem proper. That sum or sums shall include provisions for property taxes and assessments of the corporation, insurance premiums for fire, windstorm, and extended coverage insurance on the real property and improvements thereon, and such personal property as is part of the common elements, which may include a deductible provision, premiums for adequate public liability insurance as determined by the Board, legal and accounting fees, management fees, operating expenses of the property and this corporation, maintenance, repairs and replacements, charges for utilities and water used in common for the benefit of the corporation, cleaning, and janitor service of the common elements, lawn maintenance, any expenses and liabilities incurred by the corporation in connection with the indemnification of officers and directors provided for herein and in and about the enforcements of its rights or duties against the lessees or others, and the creation of reasonable contingency or reserve requirements.

Regular assessments shall be paid by each lessee-shareholder on a monthly basis, or such other basis as the Board may from time to time determine. The assessment fixed hereunder is based upon the projection and estimate of the Board of Directors and may be in excess of or less than the sums required to meet the cash requirements of the corporation, in which event the Board of Directors by the appropriate action may increase or diminish the amount of said assessment and make such adjustments respecting the reserves as in its discretion is proper, including the assessment of each lessee-shareholder of his proportionate share of any deficiency or the distribution to each lessee-shareholder of his proportionate share of any excess of sums paid beyond the requirements of the corporation or its reasonable reserves as fixed by the Board of Directors.

The aforedescribed assessment charges shall not include assessment or utilities separately charged and metered to each mobile home lot and consumed therein. Nor shall said assessments include any charges for alteration, repairs, painting, or maintenance within the interior or exterior of any mobile home, but only for such alteration, repairs, maintenance, *etc.*, to the common elements of the corporation, unless, as aforesaid, repairs or replacements which would ordinarily be the obligation of the lessee-shareholder must be made for the protection of the common elements of the corporation, and same have not been made by the lessee-shareholder of the mobile home lot concerned.

After the first estimated budget is established, the Board of Directors, on or before December 10th of each year, shall prepare an estimated budget to cover all operating expenses and otherwise for the ensuing calendar year; and shall post the same in the Recreation Hall and mail a copy of said estimated budget to each lessee-shareholder; and shall disclose the amount of assessment necessary for each lessee-shareholder to pay for each month during the ensuing calendar year. The budget and the assessment for each lessee-shareholder shall be used for the calendar year for which it is prepared, unless changed as hereinafter stated. The budget will be an agenda item at the annual meeting of the corporation and may be changed by a vote of a majority of the lessee-shareholders of the corporation (not merely a majority of the shareholders attending a meeting).

Special assessments, should they be required, shall be levied and paid in the same manner as heretofore provided for regular assessments. Special assessments can be of two kinds:

a. Those chargeable to all lessee-shareholders in the same proportions as regular assessments to meet shortages or emergencies.

b. Those assessed against one or more lessee-shareholders to accomplish repairs, maintenance, or utility services (including water and sewer hookup fees) for which he or they are responsible within their designated lot area.

Common expenses not hereinabove listed which are to be the subject of said assessment shall be defined from time to time by the Board of Directors, provided, however, that material alterations or substantial additions to the common elements may be authorized only upon a three-fourths (3/4) vote of the Board of Directors and shareholders.

§2. Liability, Lien and Priority, Interest, Collection: The holder of a lease, regardless of how acquired, including without limitation a purchaser at a judicial sale, shall be liable for all assessments coming due while he is the holder thereof. In a voluntary conveyance the grantee shall be jointly and severally liable with the grantor for all unpaid assessments against the latter for his share of the common expenses up to the time for such voluntary conveyance, without prejudice to the rights of the grantee to recover from the grantor the amounts paid by the grantee therefor.

The liability for assessments may not be avoided by waiver of the use or enjoyment of any common elements or by abandonment of the lease against which the assessments are made.

Assessments and installments thereon not paid when due shall bear interest from the date when due until paid at the rate of 10 percent per annum.

Lessor shall have a lien on each lease and attendant stock certificate for any unpaid assessments, and interest thereon, as well as a claim against the lessee. Said lien shall also secure reasonable attorney's fees incurred by lessor incident to the collection of such assessment or enforcement of such lien.

Article XIV

Mortgage of Corporate Assets

The corporation shall not mortgage the land or buildings thereon or any part thereof without the express approval of three-quarters (3/4) of the shareholders of the corporation.

Article XV

Dissolution

This corporation shall have a perpetual existence. In the event of dissolution of the corporation, it shall require the vote of 100 percent of the shareholders.

Article XVI

Amendments

The bylaws of the corporation may be altered, amended, or repealed at any regular or special meeting of the shareholders by a majority vote of all the shareholders of the corporation, not merely a majority of shareholders attending a meeting of shareholders.

[Reasonable regulations are binding. Wilshire Condominium Assn., Inc. v. Kohlbrand, 368 S.2nd 629 (Fla. App. 1979).]

Rules and Regulations of
_____ Mobile Home Club, Inc.
October, 19 ___

Address: _____
_____, State of _____

PREFACE: THE PURPOSE OF THESE RULES AND REGULATIONS IS PRIMARILY FOR THE PROTECTION OF YOUR INVEST-MENT IN, AND ENJOYMENT OF, YOUR HOME AND PARK FACILITIES. BY HAVING THESE CLEAR-CUT DEFINITIONS EVERYONE IS ASSURED OF EQUAL PROTECTION AND KNOWS HIS INDIVIDUAL POSITION, AS WELL AS HIS NEIGHBORS'. THIS ASSURES US OF A HIGH STANDARD OF QUALITY AS THE PARK REACHES ITS MAXIMUM DEVELOPMENT. YOUR OBSERVANCE OF THESE RULES AND REGULATIONS IS APPRECIATED AND EXPECTED BY ALL. THE BOARD OF DIRECTORS OF . . . . . MOBILE HOME CLUB, INC., WHICH IS REFERRED TO BELOW AS MANAGEMENT

GENERAL RULES:

1. Each mobile home which is placed on a mobile home site must first meet a set standard as to type, age, and quality.

2. Each mobile home is required to have management-approved awnings, porches, carports, and utility buildings and shall be enclosed around the base with management-approved materials in a neat and orderly manner.

3. Management reserves the right to establish building codes for any and all buildings and appurtenances placed on or within the boundaries of each mobile home site.

4. Management, or its designee, shall have the sole right to place, level, and

hook-up mobile homes on their sites; said mobile homes to be placed in accordance with the position initially designated by management.

5. Davits or any mooring device may be erected on waterfront lots only with the written consent of management in accordance with approved plans and specifications.

6. A mailbox showing name of occupant and/or a name sign will be permitted under common specifications set forth by management.

7. To plant any trees or shrubs, other than in raised planters, special permission must be obtained from management due to underground location of utilities and in order to protect the rights of neighbors. Also, specific care should be taken to avoid any obstacle in management's cutting of the lawn.

8. Under no circumstances will clotheslines be permitted outside the mobile home itself. Small clothes stands will be permitted within the utility or screened porch to facilitate the drying of bathing suits, beach towels, etc.

9. No signs of any kind (except as in #6) shall be displayed on anything within the park without permission from management. General notices and articles for sale may be posted on the clubhouse bulletin board, after management's approval.

10. No storage of any kind will be permitted under or around the mobile home except in an approved utility building.

11. Suitable areas will be designated and set aside by management for maintenance and repair of boats, automobiles, recreational vehicles, furniture, accessories, and equipment. Such is strictly prohibited in any other area, including the individual homesite and the public streets; washing and polishing exempted.

12. All personal cars, trucks, utility trailers, recreational vehicles, boat trailers, boats, etc., must be parked fully on the occupant's property in the carport and drive provided. No vehicles, or equipment, may be parked alongside or behind the mobile home without consent of management. No street parking will be permitted at any time except for approved deliveries, pickups, or short-time visitors, or loading and unloading of vehicles.

13. Management reserves the right to prohibit parking of trucks, utility trailers, vans, recreational vehicles, boat trailers, boats, *etc.*, in the parking places of the recreation areas. Management also has the right to prohibit the operation of motorbikes and motorcycles within the park.

14. Commercial and/or professional activities may not be carried on within a mobile home site, or within a mobile home, other than by the written consent of management.

15. Management reserves the right to enter upon all lots at all reasonable

times for the purpose of inspecting the use of said lot, and for the purpose of utility maintenance, lawn cutting and edging, and for the purpose of cleaning or trimming the premises as authorized herein.

16. Propane gas is piped individually to each lot by Northern Propane Gas; no other gas is to be used in the park as the distribution system is under contract.

17. For use in the event of emergencies the management shall be furnished with name of family member or friend to contact, including address and telephone number.

18. It is the responsibility of all homeowners to see that their guests comply with park rules, regulations, and customs.

19. Small house pets are permitted. Pets must be kept on a leash at all times whenever off the homesite. Pick up messes. Management reserves the right to screen pets as it does tenants (State Law).

20. Owner, or lessee, shall be held responsible for damage to property of others, including recreational facilities and equipment, caused by him, or guests, whether caused by negligence or deliberate act.

21. Each homeowner, or lessee, shall use his site and the improvements thereon in such a manner as to allow his neighbors to equally enjoy the use of their sites; so as to insure that everyone in the park may live in peace and tranquility. Radios, record players, televisions, voices, and other sounds should be kept at a moderate level observing an 11 p.m. until 9 a.m. quiet period.

22. Management, individually or in conjunction with the proper governmental authorities, specifically reserves the right to control all peddling, soliciting, selling, delivering, and vehicular traffic (also pedestrian traffic) and to establish speed limits within the boundaries of the park. Any of the aforementioned activities for commercial purposes are strictly prohibited, except upon the written consent of management.

23. Each occupant is entitled to the use of the common recreational facility; specific rules governing the use of each facility will be posted.

24. All garbage or trash must be stacked or wrapped and placed in an approved container, which must be kept closed and in good condition, with tight cover. Collection schedules and information as to the collection are available from management. Collection of garbage or trash and certain trimmings is provided by management each week.

25. Mowing and lawn-edging will be done by the park. Other than this, each occupant is responsible to keep the mobile home, setup, planters, plantings, sod, etc., neat and orderly at all times. For the protection of all, management reserves the right to have the work done, for which the owner will be billed.

26. Any irregularities affecting the park, or any mobile home property, shall

be reported immediately to management. Remember—YOU CAN CALL THE SHERIFF'S OFFICE AT ALL TIMES. PHONE . . . -. . . .

27. If you have any complaints or recommendations, please discuss them with management, who will be glad to furnish the facts and do everything possible to correct unfair situations.

28. Everyone is expected to abide by the above rules and regulations, and any others deemed necessary by management and posted on the clubhouse bulletin board. Management will allow reasonable time to correct any infraction. Any persistent breach may be deemed by management as sufficient grounds for eviction.

NOTE: The foregoing rules and regulations are, of course, subject to all federal, state, and local laws, rulings, and zoning restrictions.

MANAGEMENT RESERVES THE RIGHT TO CHANGE THE ABOVE RULES AND REGULATIONS AT ANY TIME, AND SUCH CHANGES WILL BE POSTED ON THE CLUBHOUSE BULLETIN BOARD.

[*Inspection of Membership List*: Right to "discovery" proceedings may be limited by the corporation in order to protect its members' rights. KQED, Inc. v. Hull, 185 Calif. Rptr. 630(1985), 37 A.L.R. 4th 1199, 1206.]

FORM NO. 113

Bylaws of Residential Social Club
[Based on bylaws of a community alumni clubhouse of alumni of a large university.]

. . . . . . Club
Bylaws

Article I

Officers and Their Duties

§1. The officers of the Club shall be a President, a Vice-President, a Secretary, a Treasurer, and such other officer or officers as may be appointed by the Council pursuant to the authority given to it in bylaw 8.

§2. The President, and in his absence the Vice-President, shall preside at the meetings of the Club and of the Council, and shall exercise the usual functions of a President.

§3. The Treasurer shall collect all revenues of the Club and shall pay all debts of the Club incurred by the Council or by its authority. He shall keep the Club's accounts. At the first regular meeting after the end of the fiscal year, or at any earlier special meeting, the Treasurer shall submit to the Council the annual balance sheet and profit-and-loss account. He shall also report at each regular meeting the financial condition of the Club at the close of the previous month. His accounts and reports shall be subject to such directions and to such audits as the Council may prescribe.

§4. The Secretary shall keep the records of the Club and of the Council and shall give notice of their meetings. He shall keep a roll of membership and inform the Treasurer of all changes therein. He shall have the custody of the seal of the Club. He shall file the records and documents of this office in the Clubhouse, subject to such regulations as may be prescribed by the Council.

§5. Each officer shall also perform such other duties as may be assigned by the Club or the Council.

Article II

The Council

§6. Twenty-one Directors, to be known collectively as the Council, shall control and manage the affairs, funds, property, and expenditures of the Club, shall carry out its corporate purposes, and shall execute its bylaws.

§7. The Council shall be divided into three classes of seven members each. The term of office of each class shall be three years, and until successors are elected. At each annual meeting seven directors shall be elected by the Club, by ballot, to succeed the class whose term then expires. Of such seven directors to be elected, no more than five may have served as directors at any time during the year prior to such annual meeting. The seven eligible candidates having the highest number of votes shall be elected, a tie to be decided by lot. The Council may fill vacancies occurring therein otherwise than by expiration of term.

§8. As soon as may be after each annual meeting, the Council shall elect from its own body the President and the Vice-President of the Club, and also from the resident membership the Secretary and Treasurer, who shall hold office until the next annual meeting, and until successors are elected. The Council may appoint, by resolution, at any time from the resident membership of the Club, such other officer or officers as may be deemed expedient, and any such officer shall perform the duties assigned by the Council, and hold office during the pleasure of the Council. The Council shall elect at least four of the Directors to constitute, with the President, an Executive Committee, which shall have general direction of the management and operation of the Club while the Council is not in session, subject to such rules and orders as may be prescribed by the Council.

§9. The Council shall submit at each annual meeting a general report of the affairs of the Club, which shall be distributed to members ten days before the meeting.

§10. The Council shall hold a regular meeting in each month except July and August. Special meetings shall be held when ordered by the President or by three Directors. A majority shall be a *quorum.*

§11. The Council shall make rules regulating the use of the house and property of the Club by members and guests, and for admitting guests, and may make rules not inconsistent with these bylaws for any other purpose, and may prescribe and enforce penalties for their breach.

§12. The Council may remit penalties at its discretion.

§13. Any member of the Council who shall be absent from three successive meetings without satisfactory explanation shall thereby cease to be a director.

Article III

Committees

§14. There shall be the following standing committees: Committee on Admissions, House Committee, Library and Arts Committee, Committee on the . . . . . . , Finance Committee, and Committee on Public and Labor Relations. Each of the foregoing, except the Committee on Admissions, shall be such number as the Council shall from time to time determine, and shall be appointed by the Council from its own members or from the Club at large; but at least the Chairman of each shall be a member or a former member of the Council. Each standing committee, subject to the direction and control of the Council, may make rules for its own government and to regulate the matters with which it is specially charged, and may prescribe and enforce penalties for their breach. The Council shall also constitute and appoint from the membership of the Club, a Club Activities Committee, a Committee on Athletics and Games, a Committee on Business Information, and such other committees as it may deem to be required. Neither the Clubhouse, nor the services of the employees shall be put to any extraordinary use by any officer, committee, member, or employee without first having obtained the approval of the House Committee, unless otherwise ordered by the Council.

§15. The Committee on Admissions shall be 15 in number, and shall be divided into three classes of five members each. The term of office of each class shall be three years and until successors are elected. At each annual meeting five members shall be elected by the Club, by ballot, to succeed to the class whose term then expires. The five candidates having the highest number of votes shall be elected, a tie to be decided by lot. The Committee may fill vacancies occurring therein otherwise than by expiration of term. The Committee shall not contain more than one member of any single business or profession. No member of the Council shall serve on this Committee.

§16. The Committee on Admissions shall consider and vote upon, separately, by ballot, all candidates for membership who have become eligible, as prescribed in bylaw 35. Five negative votes shall reject a candidate. The Secretary of the Committee shall promptly notify the Secretary and Treasurer of the Club of all elections to membership.

The Committee may meet at such times as it shall determine and shall meet at least once in every month, except July and August. A majority shall be a quorum. Its proceedings shall be secret and confidential. The names of the Committee shall remain posted in a conspicuous place in the house. No candidate for membership shall be proposed or seconded by a member of the Committee, or by an officer or Director of the Club. Any member of the Committee who shall be absent from three consecutive meetings without satisfactory explanation shall be deemed to have resigned.

§17. The House Committee, subject to the direction and control of the Council, shall have charge of the House, employ and discharge servants, provide furniture and supplies, regulate prices, and audit current bills. It shall consider complaints and suggestions of members, and report thereon to the Council.

§18. The Library and Arts Committee, subject to the direction and control of the Council, shall have charge of the Library and Reading Room, and of the books, papers, periodicals, and works of art belonging to the Club, and may ask for and receive gifts, purchase books, periodicals, and works of art for the Club, and audit the bills therefor.

§19. The Committee on ...... shall have the duty, subject to the direction and control of the Council, to see that the purposes of the Club in relation to the ......, as stated in its Certificate of Incorporation, are carried out.

§20. The Finance Committee, subject to the direction and control of the Council, shall have general supervision of the finances of the Club and shall determine all matters of financial policy.

§21. The Committee on Public and Labor Relations, subject to the direction and control of the Council, shall have charge of labor negotiations and any affairs affecting public relations.

§22. The Club Activities Committee, subject to the direction and control of the Council, shall have charge of special social meetings, or "Club Nights," and all entertainments in the Clubhouse.

§23. The Committee on Athletics and Games, subject to the direction and control of the Council, shall have charge of the departments devoted to athletics and games and of all exhibitions and competitions in connection therewith.

§24. The Committee on Business Information shall have the duty, subject to the direction and control of the Council, to aid communications between ...... men seeking employment and persons in need of service, and to give information, advice, and assistance in reference to business relations and opportunities.

§25. A vacancy in any of the standing committees, except the Committee on Admissions, may be filled by appointment by the President until the next meeting of the Council.

Article IV

Nominations

§26. Before each annual meeting, the Council shall appoint a committee of seven members who shall nominate candidates for the Council, for the Committee on Admissions, and for representatives of the ...... Board of .... The names of such candidates shall be posted in the House at least 15 days before the election. Any five members of the Club may nominate other candidates for all or any of such offices, but the names of all such candidates shall be posted in the house at least 15 days before the election. No person shall be elected whose name is not so posted, unless no nominations are made and posted by a Nominating Committee as hereinbefore provided, in which event resident members of the Club may be elected.

Article V

Club Meetings

§27. At the annual meeting, the order of business, after the reading of the minutes shall be:

a. The election of members of the Council and of members of the Committee on Admissions.

b. The report of the Council.

c. General business.

§28. The Council may at any time, and upon the written request of 25 resident members, call a special meeting of the Club. Such request, and the notice of every special meeting, shall state the object for which it is called, and no subject not stated in the notice thereof shall be acted on at a special meeting.

§29. The Club shall hold at least four special social meetings, or "Club Nights," in each year, upon dates to be fixed by the Council.

§30. Notice of the annual meeting and of a special meeting shall be posted in the Clubhouse and mailed to the resident members at least 10 days before such meeting, unless shorter notice be directed by the Council.

§31. Thirty resident members shall be a quorum at any meeting of the Club, and none but members shall be present at any business meeting.

Article VI

Qualifications and Classes of Membership

§32. Any person, not . . . . . . , is eligible who has attained the age of 21 years and who has (state qualifications).

§33. A member neither living nor having an office or place of business within 20 miles of the Clubhouse may be a nonresident member; all other members shall be resident members. No nonresident member shall vote or hold office in the Club.

§34. (Rules for assuming resident status). . .

§35. No person shall be considered for election to membership until he is proposed by a member and seconded by another member, in writing, with information on the kind of membership desired, the details of his qualifications for membership, (other data), his occupation, his residence, and business addresses; and until his name has been posted in a conspicuous place in the Clubhouse for at least two weeks.

§36. A candidate so qualified shall be referred to the Committee on Admissions, and if elected by such Committee, shall become a member upon payment of the entrance fee and proportionate semi-annual dues for the period from the first of the month in which he is elected to the end of the semi-annual dues period.

A nonresident member shall pay one half of the entrance fee required of a resident member, but upon becoming a resident members shall pay the balance of such entrance fee.

The election of any candidate shall be void if he fails to make such payment within 60 days after notice of his election is mailed, addressed to him at the place given as his residence by his proposer.

§37. Any member whose name has been upon the roll of the Club for 15 consecutive years shall be entitled to become a Life Member on the payment of $. . . . . . The number of Life Members of the Club shall not exceed 100. A Life Member shall have the rights and privileges and be subject to all the penalties of a resident member, but shall be exempt from payment of annual dues.

§38. The Council, by the affirmative vote of all of its members, cast in person or by signed letter at a regular meeting, may elect as an Honorary Member of the Club any distinguished man who is or has been . . . . . . (state qualifications). There shall be no more than ten Honorary Members at any time. Honorary Members shall have all the privileges of non-resident members and shall be exempt from the payment of entrance fees and annual dues.

The Council, by the affirmative vote of all of its members, cast in person or by signed letter, may elect as an Associate Member of the Club any person who . . . . (state qualifications). There shall be no more than 50 Associate Members at any time. Associate Members shall have all the privileges of non-resident members and shall be exempt from the payment of entrance fees and annual dues.

Article VII

Entrance Fees and Dues

§39. The entrance fee shall be . . . . . . dollars for a resident member and . . . . . . dollars for a nonresident member. The Council may cancel or commute such entrance fees for all those elected to membership during a period not to exceed six months in any fiscal year of the Club.

The annual dues shall be . . . . . . dollars for a resident member and . . . . . . for a nonresident member.

§40. The fiscal year of the Club shall begin on the first day of March. One-half the annual dues shall be payable in advance on that day and one-half in advance on September 1st. The status of a member on the first day of March and September shall determine whether he shall pay resident or nonresident dues for the fiscal half year then beginning.

§41. Notice of dues shall be sent by the Treasurer to every member in February and August of every year. The name of any member whose dues remain unpaid on the first day of the following April and October, respectively, shall be posted in the House, and a second notice shall be sent to him by the Treasurer, and if the dues remain unpaid upon the first day of the following May or November, respectively, he shall cease to be a member of the Club. He may be reinstated by the Council or the Executive Committee upon showing satisfactory excuse for his default, and paying a charge of . . . . . . dollars reinstatement fee, the dues for which he was in default at the time his membership ceased, and the proportion-semi-annual dues for the period from the first of the month in which he is reinstated to the end of the semi-annual dues period.

§42. Any member who is not indebted to the Club may, upon written application, be relieved by the Council or Executive Committee from payment of dues, wholly or partly, while temporarily in active military service.

§43. Upon election to membership, or reinstatement thereto (except where reinstatement falls under the provisions of bylaw 41), a candidate shall be charged $ . . . . . . reinstatement fee and proportionate semi-annual dues for the period from the first of the month in which he is elected or reinstated to the end of the semi-annual dues period.

Article VIII

Resignation and Expulsion

§44. A member may resign by writing to the Secretary, and his resignation shall not be effective until all indebtedness to the Club is discharged, including dues for the current half year; but deferred entrance fees may be waived by the Council.

The Council may reinstate any former member of the Club who resigned in good standing, and in such case may waive payment of entrance fees previously waived by it.

§45. Any member may be suspended or expelled for nonpayment of indebtedness to the Club (other than annual dues) by a vote of two-thirds of a quorum of the Council, or for any other cause by a vote of two-thirds of all the members of the Council; provided that notice in writing, stating the grounds of proposed suspensions or expulsion, shall have been delivered to him or mailed to his last address carried in the records of the Club, 15 days before. The Council, by similar vote, may rescind any such action and reinstate the member, upon or without conditions, at its discretion. The Council may vest in the House Committee, subject to such regulations as the Council may prescribe, and subject at all times to its control, the power to exclude for disorderly conduct any member from the Clubhouse until action by the Council thereon.

Article IX

Addresses

§46. Any member may enter in a book, to be kept at the House, a mail address to which all notices to be sent to him under the bylaws or rules shall be directed. In default of such entering, such notices may be served by mailing them addressed to him at the last address carried in the records of the Club.

Article X

Gambling

§47. No betting or playing of any game for stakes shall be allowed in the House.

Article XI

Amendment of Bylaws

§48. The bylaws may be amended at any regular or special meeting of the Club, at which not less than 50 members are present, by a vote in favor of the amendment of two-thirds of the members present; provided that notice of the proposed amendment is posted by the Secretary in the Clubhouse at least 20 days before such meeting and is mailed to each resident member ten days before such meeting. The Secretary shall so post and mail notice of a proposed amendment when requested to do so in writing by the Council, or by 25 resident members of the Club; but not otherwise.

FORM NO. 114

Bylaws of Civic Association
[Based on bylaws of a neighborhood civic association]

§1. *Name.* The name of this Association is . . . . . . Association, Inc., incorporated under the Membership Corporation Laws of the State of . . . . . . on February 23, 19 . . .

§2. *Objects.* The objects of this Association shall be to protect and promote the best interests of the residents of the area hereinafter set forth; to promote and strive for the improvement and betterment of all public facilities and services within said area; to promote and encourage a better community and civic spirit; and to foster good will and friendship between and among all the residents of said area; to cooperate with county, town, and village officials and with other civic and public organizations for the general welfare of the entire community of . . . . . .

§3. *Area.* The area to be covered and encompassed by the activities of this Association shall be bounded on the north by . . . . . . Road, on the east by . . . . . . Road, on the south by . . . . . . Road, and on the West by . . . . . . Road.

§4. *Membership.* Membership shall be of two classes A and B.

a. Property owners and any adult members of their immediate families in the area hereinabove set forth shall be eligible for class A membership in this Association.

b. Any person renting or leasing a residence or a part thereof in said area shall be eligible for class *B* membership in this Association upon application approved and accepted by the Board of Directors.

c. Every member shall be eligible to vote on all matters affecting this Association and shall be entitled to all membership privileges therein, except that any person holding class *B* membership shall not be eligible to hold any elective offices therein.

§5. *Dues.* The annual dues of each member of this Association shall be ...... dollars ($ ... 00) per annum, payable in advance. Any member who shall be in arrears in the payment of dues for a period of 30 days shall be ineligible to vote at any meeting until all such arrears have been fully paid.

§6. *Fiscal Year.* The fiscal year of this Association shall commence on the 1st day of October and end on the 30th day of September.

§7. *Meetings.*

a. An annual meeting for the election of Directors and officers of this Association shall be on the 3rd Tuesday in each May.

b. Regular meetings shall be held on the 3rd Tuesday in each November, January, and March.

c. Special meetings shall be called by the President whenever he shall deem the same necessary or whenever he shall be called upon to do so by two members of the Board of Directors.

Notices of all such meetings shall be in writing given (or mailed) to each member not less than five days nor more than ten days before the date set for any such meeting.

All notices of any special meeting shall state the purpose of the meeting.

A quorum of all meetings shall consist of at least 15 members in good standing. Voting thereat shall be by a majority vote cast in person or by proxy. Proxies shall be in writing subscribed by the member and shall be presented to the presiding official of the meeting to be qualified.

§8. *Directors.* The affairs and business of this Association shall be managed by a board of ten Directors, of which four members shall be the officers of the Association and the additional six members shall be those elected at the annual meeting by a plurality vote of the members present thereat. Such Directors shall serve for the ensuing year or until their successors have been elected and qualified.

Special or regular meetings of the Board of Directors shall be called by the President whenever he deems them necessary or whenever he is called upon to do so by two of the Directors.

§9. *Officers.* The officers of this Association shall be four in number: a President, a Vice President, a Secretary, and a Treasurer.

a. The President shall be the chief executive of the Association, charged with the duty of supervising all of its functions, subject to the orders of the Board of Directors. He shall be ex-officio a member of all committees.

b. In the President's absence or in the event of his inability to act, the Vice President shall perform the duties of the President. He shall also perform such other functions as the Board of Directors may from time to time assign.

c. The Secretary shall conduct the correspondence of the Association, issue notices of and keep minutes of all meetings of the Association, be custodian of the records, keep the roll of all members, and discharge such other duties as may be assigned to him by the Board of Directors or the President.

d. The Treasurer shall collect all membership dues and shall have the care and custody of all the funds and property of this Association, which shall be disbursed by him only upon the order of the Board of Directors or of the President. He shall submit a report for the preceding year at the annual meeting and shall render special reports whenever requested to do so by the Board of Directors. He shall deposit all funds in the name of the Association in such bank or banks as may be designated by the Board of Directors.

e. Should any vacancy occur by death, resignation, or otherwise, the same shall be filled without undue delay by the Board of Directors.

§10. *Committees.* Committees shall be designated and appointed by the President as may be required.

§11. *Seal.* The seal of the Association shall be circular and shall show around its circumference the words: .... Association, Inc., and at its center

$$\left(\begin{array}{c} \text{seal} \\ \text{impressed} \\ \text{here} \end{array} \right)$$ the words and figures: Corporate Seal, 19 ..., ..., in accordance with the impression made at the margin gin of this page.

§12. *Amendments.* The bylaws of this Association may be amended or revised by the Board of Directors by unanimous vote of all Directors, or by the affirmative vote (a majority, or two-thirds, or etc.) of the members present at the annual meeting or at any regular or special meeting, provided that the notice of any such meeting contains a summary of the proposed amendment or amendments.

(Dated) ......, 19 ..

FORM NO. 115

Condominium Bylaws: Leasing Clauses

Add to Chapter on The Association as a Section. A unit owner in this condominium association, once a year, may lease that owner's unit to a tenant who will occupy the unit subject to the bylaws and other rules of the association, subject also to the following provisions:

a. The consent of the board of director's president, in writing, must be obtained before the lease is granted, and that consent shall not be denied for reasons of racial or religious or other such civil rights discrimination; but the leasing of units basically is not favored in this condominium.

b. No more than a maximum of seven units in the condominium may be leased-out at any one time, and no further leasing shall be permitted when seven units have been leased, until one or more of those leases has ended; the unit owners agreeing that this is a unit-owner residential association in its essence and that such essence-quality should be maintained.

c. A lessor shall continue to be fully responsible to the association as a unit owner, and the lessee shall be responsible as a unit occupant.

d. Leases may be only for residential, not business, occupance, and shall be for a minimum of six months and a maximum of two years in duration, with renewal options subject to the limitations above stated (subd. b) as to total number of leases in effect at the time of renewal.

e. Leasehold law as to condominiums stated in Florida Statutes §718.401 shall apply to leases insofar as that statute is relevant, such as its provisions as to the lessor's obligations, reservation of possession or control of the leased property, conspicuousness of disclosure of reservations, subordination to mortgages or liens, escalation clauses, and so on.

§239. LARGE, AND WIDESPREAD, ORGANIZATIONS FORMS OF BYLAW

The size and scope of the bylaws of a large national organization are illustrated by the following table of contents of the constitution and bylaws of a large national fraternal order.

FORM NO. 116
Table of Contents of National Fraternal Order's Bylaws

CONSTITUTION
Article I
The Supreme Law
Article II
Departments of Government
Article III
Legislative Department
Article IV
Executive Department
Article V
National Foundation
Article VI
Judicial Department
Article VII
Subordinate Lodges
Article VIII
General Provisions
Article IX
Amendments

STATUTES

[In addition, this organization's book of bylaws contains an appendix setting forth the order's Certificate of Incorporation with amendments and a Form of Complaint for internal use. It also contains a detailed index of the contents of the book.]

FORM NO. 117

National Professional Association's Bylaws

Bylaws

Article 1

Title and Functions

§1. The name of this association shall be the American . . . . . . Association.

§2. The functions of the American . . . . . . Association shall include the following:

a. To define functions of . . . . . . and promote standards of professional . . . . . . practice.

b. To define qualifications for the practitioners of . . . . . . including those in the various . . . . . . specialties.

c. To promote legislation and to speak for . . . . . . in regard to legislative action concerning general . . . . . . and programs.

d. To survey periodically the . . . . . . resources of the nation.

e. To promote and protect the economic and general welfare of . . . . . .

f. To provide professional counselling service to individual . . . . . . and to their employers in regard to employment opportunities and available personnel.

g. To cooperate with the National League for . . . . . . in activities which concern both organizations.

h. To represent . . . . . . and serve as their national spokesman with allied professional and government groups and with the public.

i. To serve as the official representative of American . . . . . . in the International Council of . . . . . .

Article II

Constituent Associations

§1. State . . . . . . associations whose members now constitute the membership of the American . . . . . . Association shall be termed "constituent associations" of the American . . . . . . Association.

§2. State . . . . . . associations that hereafter may be organized may be recognized as constituent associations upon approval of their articles of incorporation (or constitution) and bylaws by a majority vote of the board of directors of this association. Not more than one association from any state may become a constituent association of the American . . . . . . Association.

§3. A state . . . . . . association which fails to comply with these bylaws or for other cause deemed sufficient may be disqualified as a constituent association of the American . . . . . . Association by unanimous vote of the board of directors, provided due notice has been given the state . . . . . . association at least three months before such vote is taken.

§4. A state . . . . . . association which has been disqualified may be reinstated by unanimous vote of the board of directors of the American . . . . . . Association.

§5. The term "state" in these bylaws . . . (defined).

Article III

Membership

§1. The membership of the association shall consist of the active and associate members of the constituent state . . . . . . associations and the individual active and associate members of this association as defined in §§2,3, and 4, which follow. All members shall be registered . . . . . . graduates of state accredited schools of . . . . . . offering programs of not less than . . . . . . years of instruction and . . . . . . practice in . . . . . . and in other community agencies. The preparation for women . . . . . . must include [standards].

§2. The active members of this association shall be the active members of the constituent state . . . . . . association and the individual active members of this association, and shall have all privileges of membership. Only active members shall have the privileges of voting and serving as delegates or alternates at conventions and special meetings of this association. Only active members shall be eligible to hold office and to serve as chairmen of standing committees of this association.

The term "active members" as used hereinafter in these bylaws shall include the active members of the constituent state . . . . . . associations and the individual active members of this association.

§3. The associate members of this association shall be the associate members of the constituent . . . . . . associations and the individual associate members of the association, provided that such membership shall not be denied to any eligible . . . . . . unless such . . . . . . anticipates employment for more than 30 days during the current calendar year. No member or applicant for membership shall be required to become an associate member if active membership is preferred.

The term "associate members" as used hereinafter in these bylaws shall include the associate members of the constituent state . . . . . . associations and the individual associate members of this association.

§4. (Special memberships) . . .

Application for individual membership in this association shall be made on a form provided by the association and shall be accompanied by dues for the current year.

§5. The presentation to this association of official lists of active and associate members in good standing in the constituent . . . . . . associations, together with the dues of such members, shall establish such members of state . . . . . . associations as active and associate members, respectively, of the American . . . . . . Association.

(Foreign members) . . .

§6. Active members of the American . . . . . . Association have representation through this association in the International Council of . . . . . .

§7. (Change of residence) . . .

§8. Honorary recognition (provisions) . . .

Article IV

Dues

§1. *a.* The annual dues received from the constituent state . . . . . . associations for active members of the American . . . . . . Association shall be . . . . . . dollars per capita.

The annual dues for individual active members of the American ......
Association shall be ...... dollars per capita payable in advance to the treasurer of the association.

b. The annual dues received from the constituent state ...... associations
for associate members of the American ...... Association shall be ...... dollars ...... per capita.

The annual dues for individual associate members of the American
...... Association shall be ...... dollars per capita payable in advance to the
treasurer of the association.

Dues for associate members who become active members during any fiscal year, and who have paid dues as associate members for the year, shall be
...... dollars in addition to the ...... dollars previously paid.

c. Dues for .... who graduate and are licensed to practice professional .... after July 1 of any year and are admitted to active membership in a constituent state ...... association or to individual active membership in the American ...... Association shall be ...... dollars for the same
year.

§2. Dues for the current calendar year shall be paid not later than March
15 by the constituent state ...... associations for the members of such associations, and shall be paid by January 1 by the individual members of this association.

§3. (Failure to pay dues) ...

§4. Individual members who have been dropped from membership for
nonpayment of dues may be reinstated upon payment of dues for the current
year.

§5. Dues received by state ...... associations after March 15 shall be paid
to this association monthly during the remainder of the year.

§6. All dues paid to this association by the state ...... association shall
be accompanied by a classified list of the members for whom dues are paid.

Article V

Officers

§1. The officers of this association shall be a president, a first vice president, a second vice president, a third vice president, a secretary, a treasurer,
and ten directors.

§2. The officers of the association shall perform the duties usually performed by such officers, together with such duties as shall be prescribed by the
bylaws of the association or by the board of directors.

§3. The terms of office of all officers elected at any biennial convention
shall commence at the adjournment of such convention.

§4. No officer shall be elected to the same office for more than two successive terms.

§5. No person shall be elected to serve as an officer or board member of
the American ...... Association who is at the same time an officer or board
member of the National League for ......

Article VI

Duties of Officers

§1. The president shall be chairman of the board of directors, of the advisory council, and of the executive committee, and an *ex-officio* member of all committees except the committee on nominations, and in the even years shall serve as chairman of the Coordinating Council of the American . . . . . . Association and the National League for . . . . . .

§2. In the absence of the president, the vice presidents, in the order of rank, shall assume the duties of the president. They shall also assume such other duties as are assigned to them by the board of directors. In the event of a vacancy occurring in the office of president, the first vice president shall serve as president until the adjournment of the next biennial convention or until her successor is elected.

In the event of a vacancy occurring in the office of first vice president, the second vice president shall serve as first vice president until the adjournment of the next biennial convention or until her successor is elected. In the event of a vacancy occurring in the office of second vice president, the third vice president shall serve as second vice president until the adjournment of the next biennial convention or until her successor is elected.

§3. The secretary shall keep the minutes of all meetings of the association, of the board of directors, and of the advisory council; preserve all papers, letters, and transactions of the association; and have custody of the corporate seal. She shall present to the board of directors all applications of state . . . . . . associations for recognition as constituent associations of this association with the report of the committee on constitutions and bylaws on the same. She shall deliver to her successor within one month after the biennial convention all association property in her possession. The executive secretary shall assume such duties in connection with the work of the secretary as shall be specified by the board of directors.

§4. The treasurer shall collect, receive, and have charge of all funds of the association; shall have deposited such funds in a bank designated by the board of directors; and shall provide for the expenditure of such funds. She shall report to the board of directors the financial standing of the association whenever requested to do so and make a full report to the association at each biennial convention. She shall give a bond, subject to the approval of the board of directors. Her accounts shall be audited annually by a nonmember certified public accountant approved by the board of directors. The executive secretary shall assume such duties in connection with the work of the treasurer as shall be specified by the board of directors.

The retiring treasurer shall within one month after the close of the biennial convention deliver to the treasurer all money, vouchers, books, and papers of the association in her custody, with a supplemental report covering all transactions from January 1 to the close of the biennial convention.

§5. All officers except the secretary and treasurer shall on expiration of their terms surrender all property in their possession belonging to their respective offices to the newly elected president.

§6. Any one of the officers of the association, except the president, the first vice-president, the second vice-president, and the third vice-president, is eligible for the position of executive secretary contingent upon her resignation from the board of directors.

Article VII

Board of directors

§1. There shall be a board of directors of the association. The board shall consist of the president, the first vice president, the second vice president, the third vice president, the secretary, the treasurer of the association, and ten directors who shall be elected as hereinafter provided, together with the chairmen of sections of the American . . . . . . Association.

§2. Regular meetings of the board of directors shall be held immediately preceding and immediately following each biennial convention of the association at the place where such biennial convention shall be held. Meetings of the board also shall be held at such times and places as may from time to time be determined by resolution of the board.

§3. Special meetings of the board of directors may be called by the president on five days' notice to each director either personally or by mail or telegraph and shall be called by the president in like manner or like notice on the written request of not less than three state . . . . . . associations or three members of the board. Special meetings shall be held at such time and place as may be specified in the notice thereof.

§4. In the intervals between meetings of the board of directors, the president of the association may refer and submit by mail or telegraph to the members of the board of directors definite questions relating to the affairs of the association which, in the opinion of the president, require immediate action on the part of the board of directors. The result of such a referendum, which requires a majority vote of the personnel of the board of directors, shall control the action of the association and of its board of directors, officers, sections, committees, agents and employees.

Article VIII

Duties of Board of Directors

§1. The board of directors shall:

a. Transact the general business of the association in the interim between biennial conventions.

b. Establish major administrative policies governing the affairs of the association and devise and mature means for the association's growth and development.

c. Provide for the maintenance of national headquarters and for making such office the center of activities of the association, including such work of the officers and committees as may be deemed expedient; provide for the proper care of materials, equipment, and funds of the association, for the payment of legitimate expenses and for the annual auditing of all books of account by a nonmember certified public accountant.

d. Assume responsibility with regard to constituent state . . . . . . associations as specified in Article II of these bylaws.

e. Act upon applications for individual membership in this association.

f. Appoint an executive secretary, define her duties, and fix her compensation.

g. Appoint standing committees and all committees not otherwise provided for.

h. Have power to fill any vacancies on the board of directors, except vacancies occurring in the office of the president, the first vice-president, or the second vice-president.

i. Decide upon the exact date and place for holding the biennial convention and provide for the payment for a place of meeting when necessary; decide upon the time and place for meetings of the advisory council; hold meetings of the board of directors as hereinbefore provided.

j. Verify referendum votes of the board of directors.

k. Provide for the establishment and dissolution of sections in accordance with these bylaws.

l. Represent the American . . . . . . Association in the association's capacity as a sole stockholder of the American Journal of . . . . . . Company, meeting in this capacity at the time and place specified in the bylaws of the American Journal of . . . . . . Company.

m. Represent the American . . . . . . Association in the association's capacity as sole stockholder of the American . . . . . . Association Professional Counseling and Placement Service, Inc., meeting in this capacity at the time and place specified in the bylaws of the American . . . . . . Association Professional Counseling and Placement Service, Inc.

n. Represent the American . . . . . . Association at meetings of the Coordinating Council of the American . . . . . . Association and the National League for . . . . . .

§2. There shall be an executive committee of the board of directors composed of the president, the three vice presidents, the secretary, and the treasurer of the association, meeting as a committee of the whole. This committee shall have all the powers of the board of directors to transact business of an emergency nature between board meetings. All transactions of this committee shall be reported in full at the next regularly scheduled meeting of the board of directors. [Note that in some states directors only may be members of the executive committee, and may not hold any salaried position.]

Article IX

Advisory Council

(Its composition and functions) . . .

Article X

Coordinating Council

(Its composition and functions) . . .

Article XI

Student Council

(Its composition and functions) . . .

Article XII

Standing Committees

§1. Standing committees, except the committee on nominations and the executive committee, may be composed of both active and associate members of the association and shall assume such duties as are specified in these bylaws and such other duties as may be assigned by the board of directors. Only active members shall be chairmen of standing committees.

§2. The following standing committees, with the exception of four members of the committee on nominations who shall be elected as hereinafter provided, shall be appointed at or immediately after each biennial convention to serve until the next biennial convention, and until their respective successors are appointed:

    a. Constitution and Bylaws.

    b. Nominations.

    c. Convention Program.

    d. Relief Fund.

    e. Finance.

    f. Promotion of . . . . . . Membership.

    g. Legislation.

    h. Credentials.

§3. The Committee on Constitutions and Bylaws shall consist of at least five members of the association. It shall be the duty of this committee to review the articles of incorporation (or constitutions) and bylaws of all state . . . . . . associations that apply for recognition as constituent associations of the American . . . . . . Association and to report its findings to the board of directors whose decision shall be final. [Add other functions.]

§4. The Committee on Nominations shall consist of seven active members of the association, including three members appointed by the board of directors and four members who shall be elected as hereinafter provided. This committee shall perform the duties described in article XIII of these bylaws.

§5. The Committee on Convention Program shall consist of three members of the association and the chairman of the program committee of each section. This committee shall be responsible for planning the program for conventions, subject to the approval of the board of directors.

§6. The Committee on Relief Fund shall consist of at least three members of the association, two of whom shall be the secretary and the treasurer of the association. The work of the committee shall be defined by the board of directors.

§7. The Committee on Finance shall consist of at least five members of the association, including the treasurer of the association who shall serve as chairman. This committee shall prepare an annual budget, advise on expenditure of funds, and report the same to the board of directors.

§8. The Committee on Promotion of American . . . . . . Association Membership shall be composed of members of the association chosen to represent various geographic sections of the country. This committee shall devise ways and means of cooperation with state . . . . . . associations in securing members and in methods of organization for making such membership effective. Such action shall be subject to the approval of the board of directors.

§9. The Committee on Legislation shall consist of at least three members of the association. The membership of this committee shall be representative of all major branches of . . . . . . and various geographic sections of the country. This committee shall assume such duties as shall be assigned to it by the board of directors.

§10. The Committee on Credentials shall consist of at least three members and shall consider all applications for individual membership in this association and shall present such applications with recommendation to the board of directors.

Article XIII

Nominations

§1. Immediately after each biennial convention, the Committee on Nominations shall request of each state the names of 10 outstanding . . . . . . qualified to serve the national organization and willing to serve if elected. From these lists from the several state associations, a composite list shall be compiled by January 1 of the year following the biennial convention. (State how nominations shall be made.)

Article XIV

Elections

§1. A president, a first vice president, a second vice president, a third vice president, a secretary, a treasurer, and four members of the committee on nominations shall be elected biennially to serve for two years or until their successors are elected; and five directors shall be elected biennially to serve for five years or until their successors are elected.

§2. Elections shall be carried out by delegates voting either in person or by proxy as hereinafter provided.

§3.*a.* Each section of a state ...... association shall be entitled to one delegate vote for every 200 active members or fraction thereof. (State method of computing the number of delegate votes.)

§4. (Selection of State Supervisors of Voting is optional) ...

§5. (Method of mailing votes) ...

§6. (Ballot and proxy rules) ...

§7. (Voting procedure) ...

§8. (Proxy procedure) ...

§9. (Proxy delivery) ...

§10. (Alternates) ...

§11. (Representation for individual active members) ...

§12. (Individual votes) ...

§13. (Ballots) ...

§14. A second ballot shall not be given or sent to any delegate for any reason.

§15. (Proxy for delegates) ...

§16. (Voting by delegate's proxy) ...

§17. On the first day of the convention, the president shall appoint tellers who shall act also as inspectors of election.

§18. A plurality vote shall constitute an election. The five nominees for directors and the four nominees for the committee on nominations who receive the highest number of votes shall be declared elected. In case of a tie, the choice shall be decided by lot.

§19. Polls shall be open for such a period of time as shall be specified in advance by the board of directors.

Article XV

Sections

§1. (Composition and functions) ...

§2. Functions of sections shall include the following (stated in detail).

Article XVI

Convention or Special Meeting

§1. The voting body of this association at each convention or special meeting shall consist of the regularly accredited delegates from each section of the state . . . . . . associations, three delegates-at-large from each state . . . . . . association, the delegates representing the individual active members of this association, and all officers and members of the board of directors of the American . . . . . . Association. Each delegate, officer, or board member shall be entitled to one vote on all matters coming before the convention or special meeting. If a delegate is represented by an alternate, the alternate shall have the same voting privileges as a delegate, except in the election of officers for the American . . . . . . Association, in which instance the regular delegate would vote by mail.

§2.*a*. Each section of a state . . . . . . association shall be entitled to one delegate for every 200 active members or fractional part thereof, such delegate or delegates to be elected in a manner to be determined by the section. For the purpose of computing the number of delegates to which any section shall be entitled at any convention or special meeting, the number of its active members shall be deemed to be the number of its active members in good standing as members of the American . . . . . . Association on December 31 of the year preceding a biennial convention or special meeting, as evidenced by dues paid to this association or postmarked by such time. Each section, through the state . . . . . . association of which it is a part, shall certify the names and addresses of the delegate or delegates and their respective alternates elected for such section.

b. Each state . . . . . . association shall be entitled to three delegates-at-large who shall be elected in the manner determined by the respective state . . . . . . associations.

§3. Individual active members shall be entitled to one delegate for each 50 individual active members in good standing in the American . . . . . . Association on December 31 of the year preceding a biennial convention or a special meeting, as evidenced by dues paid to this association or postmarked by such time. Individual active members shall be entitled to one delegate if total individual active membership is less than 50.

At least three months before the opening day of a biennial convention or six weeks before the date of a special meeting, a form shall be mailed to each individual active member with blank spaces equal to the number of delegates to which the individual active members are entitled and with blank spaces, twice the number of delegates, for the alternates. Not later than two months prior to the opening day of a biennianl convention or four weeks prior to the date of a special meeting, the individual active members shall return the forms to the American . . . . . . Association, with the names of the delegates and alternates for whom each individual active member wishes to vote. Individual active members shall vote for candidates without distinction between delegates and alternates;

and no individual active member may cast more than one vote for any one candidate. The forms shall be tabulated at the headquarters of the American ...... Association. Election of delegates and alternates shall be by plurality vote. Candidates equal to the number of delegates to which the individual active members are entitled, who receive the highest number of individual active member votes, shall be declared elected as individual active member delegates; and the remaining candidates in the order of the highest number of votes received shall be declared elected as alternates. In case of a tie, the choice shall be decided by lot.

§4.*a.* A delegate may be represented by an alternate who shall be elected in such manner as each section of the state......association naming such delegate shall determine, provided, however, that no delegate or alternate shall be permitted to cast more than one vote on any matter coming before a convention or special meeting.

b. An individual member delegate may be represented by an alternate as hereinbefore determined, provided, however, that no delegate or alternate shall be permitted to cast more than one vote on any matter coming before a convention or special meeting, and provided, further, that if more than one alternate shall attend as representative of the same individual member delegate, the alternate who received the highest number of votes shall be recognized.

c. Alternates representing delegates shall vote on all matters coming before a convention or special meeting, except that no alternate shall vote for officers of the American ...... Association.

§5. The delegates at any convention may adopt such rules of procedure for the transaction of business at their meetings as they may deem suitable.

§6. If a special meeting is held in the month of January or February for the purpose of computing the number of delegates to which any section of a state ...... association or individual active members shall be entitled, the number of active members shall be deemed to be the active members in good standing as active members of the American ...... Association on November 1 of the year preceding a special meeting, as evidenced by dues paid to this association or postmarked by such time.

Article XVII

Biennial Conventions

§1. This association shall hold conventions biennially in the even years. The time and place of biennial conventions shall be designated by the board of directors and announced by publication in the American Journal of ....

§2. Special meetings of this association may be called by the board of directors and shall be called by the president upon the written request of ten or more constituent state ...... associations. The time and place of any special meeting shall be designated by the board of directors of this association. Official notice of a special meeting shall be mailed to the president and secretary of each state ...... association and to the individual members of this association at least six weeks prior to the meeting. The time, place, and purpose of the meeting shall be stated in the official notice thereof.

§3. The order of business at each biennial convention shall be fixed at the beginning of the convention and shall include, among other things:

a. Address of the president.

b. Reports of board of directors.

c. Reports of officers.

d. Reports of standing committees.

e. Reports of special committees.

f. Reports of sections.

g. Election of officers and directors.

h. Miscellaneous business.

Article XVIII

Quorum

§1. Five officers of the American . . . . . . Association (including the president or a vice-president) and representatives of at least 15 constituent state . . . . . . associations shall constitute a quorum for the transaction of business at any meeting of the American . . . . . . Association.

§2. A majority of the board of directors, including the president or a vice president, shall constitute a quorum at any meeting of the board of directors.

§3. Members of the advisory council representing at least 15 constituent state . . . . . . associations, together with the president or a vice president of the American . . . . . . Association, shall constitute a quorum of the advisory council of the association.

§4. A majority of the members of any standing or special committee shall constitute a quorum.

Article XIX

Fiscal Year

The fiscal year of this association shall be the calendar year.

Article XX

Parliamentary Authority

The rules contained in Oleck & Green, *Parliamentary Law and Practice for Nonprofit Organizations* (2d ed., 1991) shall govern meetings of this association in all cases to which they are applicable and in which they are not inconsistent with these bylaws.

Article XXI

Duties of State . . . . . . Associations

It shall be the duty of each constituent state . . . . . . association:
a. To require . . .

Article XXII

American Journal of . . . (Rules for the Association's journal) . . . .

Article XXIII

Amendments

§1. These bylaws may be amended at any biennial convention by a (majority, two-thirds, etc.) vote of the accredited delegates present in person and voting. All proposed amendments shall be referred to the committee on constitutions and bylaws for study and recommendation. The committee shall see that all proposed amendments with the committee's recommendations shall be in the possession of the secretary at least two months before the date of the biennial convention and shall be appended to the call for the meeting.

§2. These bylaws may be amended at any biennial convention by a two-thirds vote without previous notice.

Form NO. 118

Bylaw Regulations for State Chapters of a National Organization

Regulations Pertaining to Chapters
of
_____ Institute, Inc.

Organization

   II. Directors and Officers
  III. Meetings
  IV. Dues and Finances
   V. Nominations
  VI. Committees
 VII. Rules of Procedure

Chapters of the . . . . . . Institute, Inc. (hereinafter referred to as the Institute) shall be governed by the following regulations which have been duly authorized at a meeting of the board of directors of the Institute pursuant to the provisions of article VIII of the bylaws of the Institute.

Article I

Organization of Chapters

§1. The board of directors of the Institute may authorize a chapter to be organized in any city upon receipt of a petition signed by ten or more persons who are members of the Institute in good standing or who are qualified for membership in accordance with article I of the bylaws and have submitted applications for membership. Chapters shall be designated in this manner: (name of city) Chapter of the . . . . . . Institute, Inc.

§2. Members of a chapter shall be members of the Institute and may vote for directors and officers of the Institute as set forth in the bylaws.

§3. Each chapter shall have a membership committee, which shall obtain from each applicant a signed application on a form prescribed by the Institute. After the board of directors of the chapter approve such application, it shall be forwarded to the Institute where admission to membership shall be by vote of the board of directors of the Institute.

§4. Resignation from membership in a chapter shall be presented to the board of directors of the chapter, but shall not relieve any member from liability for any dues accrued and unpaid at the time when such resignation is filed. Upon acceptance by the board of directors of the chapter, a copy of the resignation shall be forwarded to the secretary of the Institute for disposition, as set forth in §4 of article I of the bylaws.

§5. The bylaws of the Institute, unless excepted by these regulations, shall apply to all chapters of the Institute.

Article II

Directors and Officers

§1. Since §1 of article II of the bylaws vests control of the Institute and its affairs and property in the board of directors of the Institute, all property of the chapter becomes property of the Institute.

Except as otherwise required by the bylaws or these regulations, the entire management of the affairs of each chapter shall be vested in a board of directors, subject to the approval of the board of directors of the Institute.

The board of directors of each chapter shall consist of six members elected from and by the chapter in the same number of classes and for the same period as the directors of the Institute elected by the membership at large as set forth in §1 of article II of the bylaws. Officers of the chapter shall also be members of the board of directors.

A duplicate copy of the minutes of each meeting of the board of directors shall be mailed to the secretary of the Institute for submission to the board of directors of the Institute for approval.

§2. The officers of each chapter shall include at least a president, one or two vice-presidents, a secretary, and a treasurer, all of whom shall be members of the chapter.

§3. Chapters of the Institute shall elect their officers in the same manner and for the same period as provided in §3 of article II of the bylaws.

§4. All other provisions of the bylaws with respect to directors and officers of the Institute shall apply concerning directors and officers of the various chapters of the Institute.

Article III

Meetings

§1. The date of the annual meeting of members of chapters of the Institute at which members of the board of directors and officers shall be elected shall be at the discretion of the chapter.

§2. The president of each chapter shall present at the annual meeting of the chapter a report, verified by a majority of the board of directors, reflecting all operations of the chapter during the 12 months immediately preceding the month in which the annual meeting of the chapter is held. Such report shall be prepared in duplicate, the original filed with the records of the chapter and the duplicate submitted forthwith to the secretary of the Institute.

The board of directors shall appoint three members of the chapter, other than members of the board of directors, to act as auditors, who shall examine the annual report referred to in this section, and express their opinions thereon, furnishing copies of such opinion to the board of directors of the chapter. A copy shall be appended to the copy of the annual report filed with the secretary of the Institute.

§3. All other rules concerning chapter meetings shall be the same as those provided under article III of the bylaws.

Article IV

Dues and Finances

§1. The dues of all members of the chapters shall be payable to the Institute annually in advance upon the first day of January. If the dues of any member be unpaid for a period of 60 days after the same become payable, the treasurer of the Institute shall mail a notice of delinquency. If the dues of any member be not paid within 30 days after the mailing of such notice of delinquency, his membership shall automatically terminate on that date by reason of such nonpayment, but the board of directors of the Institute may provide for subsequent reinstatement.

§2. The Institute shall remit annually to the chapter an amount of $ . . . 00 from the dues paid by each member of the chapter and $ . . . 00 from each initiation fee paid by members of the chapter, as a working fund.

§3. The working fund of a chapter (described in §2 of this article) shall be deposited or kept with a bank or trust company doing business in the city in which the chapter is located. Such account shall be in the name: (name of city) Chapter of . . . . . . Institute, Inc.; and the officers of the chapter shall be authorized by the board of directors of the chapter to draw on such bank account. Duly authorized officers of the Institute shall also be authorized by the board of directors of the chapter to draw on such account.

Article V

Nominations

§1. All provisions with respect to nominations as set forth in article V of the bylaws are applicable to chapters of the Institute, except that the report of the nominating committee, as provided in §2 of article V of the bylaws, shall be filed with the secretary of the chapter not later than 60 days prior to the date of the annual meeting, and nominations made by members of the chapter, as provided in §3 of article V of the bylaws, shall be filed with the secretary of the chapter not later than 45 days prior to the date of the annual meeting.

Article VI

Committees

§1. Rules provided in article VI of the bylaws are applicable to chapters of the Institute.

Article VII

Rules of Procedure

The rules of procedure at meetings of chapters of the Institute shall be according to Oleck, *Parliamentary Law for Nonprofit Organizations*, so far as applicable and when not inconsistent with these regulations.

FORM NO. 119

Bylaws of Statewide Trade Association

Bylaws
of
_____**Packers**

Article I

Purposes—Powers

The purposes for which this association is formed and the powers which it may exercise are as set forth in the Articles of Incorporation of the association.

Article II

Membership

Members of this association shall be only persons, firms, partnerships, associations, corporations, or other business units engaged primarily in the packing, shipping, selling, and marketing in interstate and/or interstate and/or foreign commerce of fresh . . . . fruit in commercial quantities (other than express or gift fruit shippers) and who own and operate or have available to them facilities for packing fresh . . . . . . fruit handled by them and who have been approved and elected to membership by the Board of Directors of the association; provided, however, that any common marketing agency handling the sales of fresh . . . . . . fruit for the account of any of the members of this association who do not maintain their own sales force or organization shall be eligible for membership in this association. If any member fails to market any . . . . . . under its own labels during two consecutive seasons, it shall be placed on the inactive list until such time as it resumes marketing . . . . . . under its own labels. Inactive members have no vote and pay no assessment. Every member of this association must be and remain a duly licensed . . . . . . fruit dealer under and as required by the . . . . Code of 1949, as amended, the same being Chapter 601, ... Statutes.

Article III

Members—Annual Meeting

The annual meeting of the members of this association shall be held in May of each year commencing with the year 19 . . . The members themselves at any regular monthly meeting or special meeting called for the purpose, or the Board of Directors or the Executive Committee, shall determine and fix the date, time, and place of each such annual meeting. Written notice of the date, time, and place of holding each annual meeting shall be mailed to each member of the association at his or its last address as shown by the books and records of the association at least two weeks prior to such meeting.

The order of business at the annual meeting of the members of this association shall be as follows:

1. Roll call
2. Approval of the minutes of previous meeting
3. Reports of officers
4. Reports of committees
5. Unfinished business
6. New business
7. Miscellaneous
8. Certification, election, and seating of directors

Article IV

Members—Regular and Special Meetings

§1. A regular meeting of the members shall be held on the first Wednesday in each month at such time and place as the members shall fix from time to time, except that such regular monthly meeting may be dispensed with by the members for such months in each year as the members may determine. Notice of each such regular monthly meeting of the members is hereby dispensed with and the members at such meeting may transact any and all business coming before the meeting.

§2. Special meetings of the members may be called by the Board of Directors or the President at any time to be held at such time and place as it or he may designate for the purpose of transacting any particular business which requires the vote of the membership, and such action cannot be delayed until the next regular monthly meeting. Notice of any such special meeting may be served upon the members by mail at least 48 hours or by telegram at least 24 hours prior to the date fixed for such meeting.

§3. Ten percent of the members of the association entitled-to vote may at any time file with the directors or the President a petition demanding a special meeting and stating the specific business to be brought before the association at such special meeting. It shall thereupon become the duty of the Board of Directors or the President of the association, as the case may be, to call such special meeting within five days after the receipt of said petition and fix the date thereof at not more than ten days after the filing of said petition. Written notice of such special meeting, together with a statement of the purpose thereof, shall be mailed to each member entitled to vote at least three days prior to the meeting. No business shall be transacted at any such special meeting except such as may be comprehended in the statement of the purpose or purposes thereof as mailed to the members entitled to vote.

Article V

Members—Voting, Proxies, Quorum

At all annual, regular, and special meetings of the members, each member of the association shall be entitled-to one vote except as provided in Article XIV hereof. Members entitled to vote shall have the right to vote by written proxy at annual, regular, and special meetings, and members who are not individuals must be represented at all such meetings by a duly accredited representative appointed in writing. Members may also appoint in writing alternates or substitutes to represent them at any and all meetings. No paid employee of this association shall represent or act for any member at any meeting of the members. No member may appoint as proxy or representative, or alternate or substitute representative; any person whose position or function in the .... fruit industry is in any way or to any extent incompatible with the requirements for membership in the association, and the Board of Directors or the Executive Committee of the association shall be the judge of whether such incompatibility exists in any particular situation.

Cumulative voting shall not be permitted.

Fifty members or 30 percent of the members, whichever is less, present in person or by proxy, shall constitute a quorum at any annual, regular, or spe-

cial meeting but the members present at a duly organized meeting may continue to do business until adjournment notwithstanding the withdrawal of
enough members to leave less than a *quorum.* If a meeting cannot be organized
because a quorum was not attended, those present may adjourn the meeting
until such time and place as they may determine.

Adjournment or adjournments of any organized or unorganized annual,
regular, or special meeting of the members may be taken. Upon such adjournment, it shall not be necessary to give any notice of the adjourned meeting or
of the normal business to be transacted other than by announcement at the
meeting at which such adjournment is taken.

Article VI

Board of Directors—Officers

§1. The affairs of this association shall be managed by a Board of Directors of not less than three members and said Board shall consist of as many
members as there are members of this association. Each member shall be entitled at all times to have one director on the Board of Directors of this association.

§2. Each member of this association shall on or before the date of each
annual meeting of the members of this association certify in writing to this
association the name of a person to represent such member on the Board of
Directors of this Association for the ensuing year and until his successor shall
be chosen and seated and such certified representative of such member shall
be forthwith elected as a director and seated on the Board of Directors of this
association.

Each member of this association shall have the right at any time to
remove its representative on the Board and to certify another person to fill
such vacancy or any vacancy occasioned by the resignation or death or incapacity of its representative, and any such new representative shall be forthwith
elected as a director and seated on the Board at any regular or special meeting of the Board. Term of office of any such Director shall extend to the next
annual meeting of the members of this association and until his successor shall
be chosen and seated. In case of a vacancy, if any member shall fail for a period of 30 days to certify its representative, then such vacancy on the Board may
be filled by the Board by the action of the remaining directors until such member certifies its representative on the Board.

§3. Immediately after each election of directors at the annual meeting of
the members in May of each year, the newly elected directors shall be seated
and shall hold their annual meeting and organize by the election of a Chairman of the Board, a President (who may also hold the office of Chairman of
the Board if a majority of a quorum of the directors so determines) and one
or more vice presidents, and the members of the Executive Committee and
each of them at the time of filling said office to which he is elected, must be
a director of the association. The directors at said meeting shall also elect a

General Manager, a Secretary, and a Treasurer, who may or may not be directors and either one of which may at the time of holding such position, hold and exercise the functions of either one or more of such positions if otherwise qualified for the same. The directors may also at said meeting elect one or more assistants to the officers last above-mentioned and referred to.

§4. A special meeting of the Board of Directors shall be held whenever called by the Chairman of the Board or the Executive Committee or by request in writing by not less than 10 percent of all directors in office. Any and all business may be transacted at a special meeting. Each call for a special meeting shall be in writing signed by the person or persons making the same, addressed and delivered to the Secretary, and shall state the time and place of such meeting.

§5. Notice of each special meeting of the Board of Directors shall be mailed to each director at his last known address at least three days prior to the time of such meeting or may be telegraphed to each director at his last known place of address at least 24 hours prior to the time of such meeting.

§6. The directors present at any meeting shall constitute a quorum of the Board.

§7. The order of business at all meetings of the Board of Directors shall be determined by the Chairman of the Board, subject to revision, if any, by the directors present.

Article VII

Powers and Duties of Directors

§1. The directors shall have the power:

a. To conduct, manage, and control the affairs and business of this association; and to make rules and regulations for the guidance of the officers and the management of the affairs of the association;

b. To elect and/or appoint and remove at pleasure all officers, agents, and employees of the association, prescribe their duties, fix their compensation, and require from them, if advisable, security for faithful service;

c. To select or authorize the selection of one or more banks to act as depository of the funds of the association and to determine the manner of receiving, depositing, and distributing the funds of the association and the form of checks and the person or persons by whom same shall be signed with the power to change such banks, person, or persons signing such checks and the form thereof at will;

d. To incur such indebtedness as shall be deemed necessary and required to properly conduct the business of the association;

e. To determine and fix the amount to be assessed against and collected upon the fresh . . . . . . fruit handled by the members of this association for the purpose of paying all expenses of the association; provided, however, that during no . . . . . . fresh . . . . . . shipping or marketing season shall any such assessment exceed $.002 per packed box of 1-3/5 bushels of fresh . . . . . . fruit or the equivalent thereof in volume as evidenced by inspection certificates issued according to law. The Board of Directors shall have authority to adopt or promulgate rules or regulations governing the way and manner and the time within which all such assessment shall be paid and the books and records of each member of this association relating to the volume of fresh ...... fruit shipments shall be open to inspection during reasonable business hours by any authorized representative of this association. No member of this association shall pay annual assessments for defraying expenses of the association in an amount less than $100, regardless of the volume of fresh ...... fruit packed and handled by such member.

f. Assessments for capital purposes over and above the maximum rate of assessment of $.002 per box of 1-3/5 bushels of fresh ...... fruit or the equivalent thereof in volume hereinabove referred to, shall not be permitted except with the written approval and consent of at least 75 percent of the members of the association and such assessments levied and collected pursuant to such written approval and consent of not less than 75 percent of all members of the association shall be in the nature of loan capital evidenced and made repayable in the way and manner prescribed by the Board of Directors.

§2. It shall be the duty of the Board of Directors:

a. To keep a complete record of all its acts and of the proceedings of its meetings and to present a full statement at the annual meeting of the members showing in detail the condition of the affairs of the association;

b. To supervise all officers, agents, and employees and to see that their duties are properly performed, and also to see that all officers and employees who handle funds are adequately bonded;

c. To cause to be issued proper membership certificates;

d. To cause to be installed and/or maintained such a system of bookkeeping and auditing that each member may know and be advised fully from time to time concerning the receipts, disbursements, and operations of the association; and

e. To authorize the execution by this association of all contracts between it and its members and others.

Article VIII

Executive Committee

§1. The Board of Directors shall at its annual organization meeting immediately following adjournment of the annual meeting of the members, elect an Executive Committee from within the membership of the Board to serve during the pleasure of the Board. Such Executive Committee shall consist of not less than seven members, of whom the President shall be one and its Chairman. All vice presidents shall likewise be members of such Executive Committee.

§2. During the intervals between the meetings of the Board of Directors, the Executive Committee shall possess and may exercise all the powers and functions of the Board of Directors in the management and direction of the affairs of the Association in all cases in which specific directions shall not have been given by the Board of Directors.

§3. All actions by the Executive Committee shall be reported to the Board of Directors at its meeting next succeeding such action. Regular minutes of the proceedings of the Executive Committee shall be kept. Vacancies in the Executive Committee shall be filled by the Board of Directors. A majority of the members of the Executive Committee in office at the time shall be necessary to constitute a *quorum* and in every case an affirmative vote of a majority of the members of the Committee present at a meeting shall be necessary for the taking of any action.

§4. The Executive Committee shall fix and establish its own rules of procedure and shall meet as provided by such rules, and it shall also meet at the call of its Chairman or of any member of the Committee. Anything in the rules of procedure of the Executive Committee to the contrary notwithstanding, all acts at any meeting of said Executive Committee however called or held, shall be valid for all purposes if such meeting is held pursuant to a written waiver of notice and call signed by not less than three-fourths of the Committee in office at the time and made a part of the minutes of such meeting.

§5. The members of the Executive Committee shall receive no compensation for their services as such other than reimbursement for travelling at the mileage rate fixed by the Board of Directors to and from all meetings of the Executive Committee which they are required or requested to attend, together with a *per diem* not to exceed $15.

Article IX

Powers and Duties of Officers

§1. Chairman of the Board. The Chairman of the Board of Directors shall when present preside at all meetings of the Board and shall have such other powers and perform such other duties as may from time to time be prescribed by the Board of Directors.

§2. President. The President shall be the chief executive officer of the association and shall have full supervision and control over the association and the management of its affairs, subject to the control of the Board of Directors. He shall:

a. Preside over all meetings of the members of the association;

b. Call meetings of the members as provided by these bylaws;

c. Perform all acts and duties usually performed by an executive and presiding officer; and

d. Sign all membership certificates and such other papers of the association as may be authorized or directed to be signed by the Board of Directors; provided, however, that the Board of Directors may authorize any person to sign any or all contracts and other instruments in writing on behalf of the association. The President shall perform such other duties as may be prescribed by the Board of Directors.

§3. Vice Presidents. In case of the absence or disability of the President, the senior Vice President available shall perform the duties of the President required to be performed during such absence or disability.

§4. General Manager. Under the direction and subject to the control of the Board of Directors, the General Manager shall have general charge of and shall direct, supervise, and control all of the activities and business of the association. He shall, subject to the control of the Board, employ and discharge all employees, agents, and representatives of the association who are not employed by the Board of Directors itself or whose employment is not otherwise provided for. It shall be his duty to secure information from time to time as to crop and marketing conditions and when requested by them to furnish the same to the directors and members and to encourage production of the best quality of . . . . . . fruit handled by members of the association.

§5. Secretary. It shall be the duty of the Secretary to keep a record of the meetings of the Board of Directors and the members as well as of the Executive Committee in a well-bound book or books and to furnish copies thereof in the way and manner and to the extent prescribed by the Board of Directors. He shall keep a book of membership certificates. He shall make out and countersign the certificates of membership and make corresponding entries on the margin of the book of issuance. He shall have no power to issue a certificate of membership to any person, firm, partnership, association, corporation, or other business unit whomsoever until so ordered by the Board of Directors. He shall have the custody of the seal of the corporation and all books and records of the association. He shall issue notices of all meetings of the members, directors, and Executive Committee, as required by these bylaws or by the Board of Directors. He shall discharge such other duties pertaining to his office as Secretary or such as may from time to time be prescribed by the Board of Directors. The Secretary may be assisted in the exercise of his powers and the discharge of his duties by one or more assistant secretaries duly elected by the Board of Directors for that purpose.

§6. Treasurer. The Treasurer shall receive, have in charge, and be responsible for all money, bills, notes, bonds, and other property coming into his possession belonging to this association and shall do with the same as may be ordered by the Board of Directors. He shall keep such financial accounts and statements as may be required of him by the Board of Directors. On the expiration of his term of office, he shall turn over to his successor or to the Board of Directors all property, books, papers, money, and other property of the association in his hands. The Treasurer may be assisted in the exercise of his powers and the discharge of his duties by one or more assistant treasurers duly elected by the Board of Directors for that purpose.

Article X

Members—Withdrawal—Expulsion

§1. Any member of this association may withdraw from membership as of August 1 of any year hereafter by giving written notice of such withdrawal to the association during the month of April immediately preceding such August 1, but such withdrawal shall not affect his or its existing liabilities to the association.

§2. Any member of this association may be expelled from membership who shall violate any of the rules, regulations, orders, or bylaws of this association or who violates any contract made by or with this association or who does any act which tends to interfere with the accomplishment of the objects sought to be accomplished by this association. When any member of this association is charged with any act for which such member may be expelled, notice of the same shall be served on such member personally or by mail at his, her, or its last known address, and if, after due opportunity to be heard, the Board of Directors or the Executive Committee, as the case may be, by a majority vote of those present so decides, such member may be expelled and his, her, or its name dropped from the list of membership; provided, however, that any member so expelled may appeal such expulsion to the membership of the association, and the action of a majority of the members at any duly called and held meeting at which such appeal is considered, shall be final. Expulsion or death or dissolution of a member shall not affect his or its existing liabilities to the association.

Article XI

Dissolution

Upon the dissolution or winding up of this association in any manner after the payment of all outstanding indebtedness of the association, including unpaid loan capital however evidenced, any remaining assets shall be distributed among the then members on an equal basis, share and share alike.

Article XII

Fiscal Year

The fiscal year of this association shall commence on the *1st* day of *August* of each year.

Article XIII

Corporate Seal

The corporate seal of this association shall be in circular form in the center of which shall appear the year of incorporation and a design of . . . . . . fruit in conjunction with the words "Union Makes Strength" and around the outer edge of which shall appear the words". . . . . PACKERS" and "SEAL."

A facsimile of such corporate seal may, if the Board of Directors so directs, constitute the emblem or insignia for use by this association and by its members in connection with their business, subject to such rules and regulations governing the use of same as the Board of Directors may adopt or promulgate.

Article XIV

Miscellaneous Provisions

§1. All activities and functions of this association shall be in accordance with its Articles of Incorporation and these bylaws as well as all applicable laws and by and under such uniform rules, regulations, or orders as the Board of Directors or the members themselves may from time to time adopt or promulgate; provided, however, that in all cases where it is deemed wise, necessary, or expedient to determine the position and action of this association with respect to State or Federal legislation and/or rules and regulations thereunder affecting the fresh . . . . . . fruit industry of . . . . . . or the obtaining of appropriate rulings and/or interpretations with respect to any such law, rule, or regulation or any part or parts thereof, only the membership of this association shall have power to act in determining any such position and action by the affirmative vote of not less than 75 percent of the members present and voting at a meeting duly called and held for such purpose, and be it further provided that when the question regarding legislation and regulations or rules and interpretations thereunder pertains to a specific . . . . . . variety (for the purpose of these bylaws, all . . . . . . constitute one variety, all round . . . . . . constitute one variety, and all reticulata type . . . . . . constitute one variety), the voting shall be weighted by volume if such a vote is requested by a member present at the time of voting who ships the variety affected. Approval shall require, based on the record of the latest complete shipping season, the affirmative vote of at least 75 percent of the volume of the variety affected represented and voted at the meeting, with the further provision that the volume of the variety affected represented at the meeting shall equal at least 50 percent of the volume of the variety shipped by the members of this association during the latest complete shipping season.

§2. Whenever a controversy arises between two or more members of this association which involves a matter in which this association has an interest direct or indirect, the same shall be settled after full hearing by the Board of Directors of this association and its decision shall be final; and whenever such controversy involves the welfare of this association, an officer or director of this association may bring the same to the attention of the Board of Directors for action.

Article XV

Amendments

These bylaws may be altered or amended by a majority vote of the members of this association attending a duly called and held meeting of which notice of the proposed amended or amendment to bylaw or bylaws shall have been given.

FORM NO. 120

Bylaws of National Patriotic/Service Association

Bylaws

of the

Association of _____ **Officers, Inc.**

Article I

Purpose and Activities

A. The Corporation was founded on a belief that a responsive and efficient American _____ service is vital to the security of the nation. To that end the Corporation will promote public understanding of the role of American _____ by means of education and dissemination of factual material to all segments of the American public. To assist in this purpose, the Corporation will:

1. Conduct research on the function of _____ in the United States Government, historically, currently and prospectively. Provide the results to colleges, universities, secondary schools and other educational groups.

2. Provide lecture material and speakers from the membership of the Corporation at educational institutions for courses such as political science, government and history. Offer from the membership of the Corporation individuals for participation in seminars, panels, forums and discussion groups sponsored by educational institutions.

3. Provide speakers and writers from the membership of the Corporation for lectures and discussion groups, panels, and other forums conducted by the electronic media which involve the conduct of _____ as a function of the United States Government, with special interest in the public service radio and television stations.

4. Provide speakers to address civic, fraternal and social organizations which desire discussion of the _____ function of the United States Government.

5. Provide to the printed media factual information and material relative to _____ functions.

6. Provide assistance to Congressional Committees and individual Members of Congress on _____ matters.

Article II

Membership

A. Any adverse actions by the Board of Directors under paragraphs B or G of Article VI of the Articles of Incorporation shall be taken only after receipt of recommendations from the President.

B. Provision is made for industrial or other patrons whose status and donation shall be determined by the Chairman of the Board of Directors or his designee.

Article III

Chapters

A. Upon application, the Board of Directors may approve the establishment of local Chapters of the Association of _____ Officers, Inc. but in the form of unincorporated associations. Such Chapters shall be composed of at least five (5) members of any class and should be based on a commonality or compatibility of former association or geographical location.

B. Bylaws of such local Chapters, as approved by the Board of Directors, shall be in consonance with the Articles of Incorporation of this Corporation and these Bylaws with such additions as may be necessary for appropriate local administration. All classes of members are eligible to vote and hold office in local Chapters.

C. Upon application or on its own cognizance, the Board of Directors may reorganize or consolidate local Chapters in the interest of Corporate objectives or administration.

Article IV

Directors

A.1. The Board of Directors shall consist of not less than fifteen nor more than twenty members. Vacancies for membership on the Board of Directors will be filled by votes of Full Members voting in person or by proxy at the National Convention. The number of nominees receiving a plurality of votes cast for the number of vacancies will be elected.

A.2. Tie breaker procedures will be determined by the sitting Board of Directors. The Board will determine basic policies of the Corporation and review its activities. The Board will supervise and furnish guidance to the Executive Committee.

B. The Board of Directors shall elect its own Chairman and an Executive Committee composed of not more than five Directors to provide interim advice and assistance to the President. All actions and decisions of the Board shall be by a majority vote of the Directors present, or represented by proxy, at a duly scheduled meeting of the Board, except that any amendment to these Bylaws shall be by a two-thirds vote of the Directors present at a duly scheduled meeting of the Board, and subject to ratification by a majority of the members eligible to vote and present or represented by proxy at the next membership meeting.

C. The Board of Directors shall designate the term of office of each of the Directors pursuant to paragraph C of Article IX of the Articles of Incorporation giving due consideration to terms of office in predecessor organizations.

Article V

Officers

A. By the Directors the President, Vice President, Secretary and Treasurer shall be elected at the National Convention subsequent to the election of Directors by the members. Such officers shall act for the Corporation between meetings of the Board of Directors within their respective functions. Such officers shall hold office for a period of one year and, thereafter, until their successor may be elected. In the event of a death, removal, or resignation of any officer, the Chairman of the Board of Directors shall designate an interim replacement until the next meeting of the Board.

B. The *President* shall be the chief executive officer of the Corporation. He shall be *ex-officio*, a member of all committees and he shall perform the usual duties pertaining to the office.

C. The *Vice President* shall perform the duties and exercise the powers of the President during the absence or disability of the President. He shall perform other duties as directed by the President.

D. The *Secretary* shall act as Clerk of the Board of Directors and of the Executive Committee. The Secretary shall be responsible for the scheduling and preparation for meetings of the Board of Directors and shall record minutes of such meeting and such reports as directed by the Board. The Secretary shall keep the corporate minute book recording all actions of the Board of Directors and actions approved by the members. The Secretary shall give, or cause to be given, notice of all meetings of the Board of Directors, and Executive Committee, and the members. The Secretary shall perform such other duties as may be prescribed by the Board of Directors or by the President.

E. The *Treasurer* shall be responsible for a full and accurate account of all Corporation receipts and disbursements which will be kept in books belonging to the Corporation. All funds shall be kept in depositories as may be designated by the Board of Directors in separate accounts in the name of the Corporation. The Treasurer shall be responsible for disbursement of Corporation funds as may be directed by the Board of Directors, the President, or as delegated to any member of the Executive Committee by the Board. The Treasurer shall voucher each disbursement and shall render reports of all transactions to the President and Board of Directors, as required, including certifications by institutions in which Corporation funds are deposited. All instruments drawing on Corporation accounts will be signed by the Treasurer and countersigned by the President or the Vice President acting for him. All financial reports, tax returns, and other reports required under law to Federal, State or local government authority shall be prepared by the Treasurer.

Article VI

Meetings

A. In addition to any meeting of the Board of Directors called by the Chairman, a majority of the Directors may call a meeting. A quorum for any meeting of the Board shall be nine members present or represented by proxy at such meeting.

B. For any meeting of the members of the Corporation, the Secretary shall be responsible for providing not less than ten nor more than fifty (50) days notice of such meetings. A quorum shall be one hundred (100) full members of the Corporation eligible to vote present or represented by proxy in order to transact any business. The Chairman of the Board of Directors shall preside at any such meeting.

C. *Oleck & Green, Parliamentary Law and Practice for NPOs* (2d ed., 1991) shall govern the procedure and forms of business except where otherwise provided in the Articles of Incorporation and these Bylaws.

D. Procedures for representation by proxy for voting by Directors and by members at membership meetings shall be as established by the Executive Committee.

Article VII

National Conventions

A. The President shall appoint all committees necessary for the transaction of business at the National Convention and such committees shall make their reports to the Convention at a time to be determined by the Board of Directors.

B. Nominating Committees for the candidacy of members of the Board of Directors may be appointed by the Chairman of the Board or the President. Such nominations may be made from the floor of the Convention.

C. All elections at the National Convention shall be conducted and supervised by a committee of three members appointed by the President and approved by the Board of Directors.

D. Resolutions proposed for adoption and approval by the members at the National Convention must be in the hands of the President not less than thirty days prior to the National Convention at which any resolution shall be presented.

FORM NO. 121

Bylaws of Statewide Cultural-Support Foundation

BYLAWS

Article I

Name and Location

Section 1: Name. The name of this Corporation is The _____ Endowment for _____, Incorporated.

Section 2: Location. The principal office of the corporation is located at _____ of _____, in the city of _____, in the County of _____ and the State of _____. The corporation may have such other offices as the Board of Directors may authorize.

Article II

Purposes

The corporation shall be organized exclusively as a nonprofit, tax-exempt organization under Section 501(c)(3) of the U.S. Internal Revenue Code of 1954, as amended, and shall be operated exclusively for the following exempt purposes: 1) to support activities which foster public knowledge and appreciation of _____ and strengthen the bond between _____ and the people of Florida (the _____ shall be defined as those disciplines listed in 20 U.S.C. 952(a) which established the National Endowment for _____), and 2) to distribute grant money received by the corporation from the National Endowment for _____ and from the general public to nonprofit, non-political _____ groups who will conduct the activities listed above.

Article III

Membership

The corporation shall have no members other than the persons elected or appointed from time to time as members of the Board of Directors, who shall be considered to be the members of the corporation for the purposes of any statutory provision or rule of law relating to members of a non-stock, non-profit corporation.

The Board of Directors may provide for associates such as "_____ Associates." Such associates will have no authority to act for or incur any liability against the corporation, and will have no vote in corporate affairs.

Article IV

Board of Directors

Section 1: General Powers: The duly elected or appointed Board of Directors shall have control and policy management of the affairs, business, property, and funds of the corporation. The board may adopt such rules and regulations for the conduct of its meetings and the management of the corporation as the board may deem proper, not inconsistent with Federal and/or state law or these bylaws.

Section 2: Number, Qualification, and Tenure: The Board of Directors shall consist of eighteen residents, who shall be elected from time to time by the Board of Directors, and up to four residents who may be appointed by the Governor of the State of _____ in consultation with the Chairman and the Executive Director of _____. The elected members of the Board of Directors shall consist of persons interested in promoting and encouraging _____, and chosen for the purpose of assuring wide access to groups and individuals interested in the promotion and encouragement of _____. Approximately one-half will be professional _____, or academic administrators at institutions with a commitment to _____. The other one-half will be representatives of the public of _____.

The term of board members begins July 1st and extends four years, through June 30th of the fourth year. At least one year must elapse between terms. Approximately one fourth of the Directors' terms shall expire each year, assuring staggered classes of terms. Terms of Governor's appointees also will be four years, but not beyond the Governor's term of office.

Section 3: Nomination and Election: a) *Nomination process:* Nominations for membership shall be solicited from a wide cross-section of the _____ public and _____ representatives, in terms of race, religion, sex, ethnicity, occupation, institutional affiliation, level of educational achievement, and geographical distribution within the state. The nomination process will include: publication of membership vacancies to the general media and to _____ departments in colleges, universities, and junior colleges, and to various civic, business, labor, professional, educational, minority, women's and other organizations. b) *Selection process:* Nominations are to be solicited and proposed by an *ad hoc* committee derived from one member of each-standing committee (nominated by the chair of that committee) and one additional member appointed by the _____ chair. This committee shall prepare a list of candidates to fill board member vacancies created by term expirations, and shall mail this list to each incumbent board member at least seven days before the meeting at which new members are to be elected. Nominations will also be received from the floor, provided, however, that the consent of the nominee to his or her election has been obtained in advance and a resume of the nominee's background is made available to the Board of Directors at or before the meeting at which the election occurs. Appointments will be made by majority vote of the board.

Section 4: Vacancies: Vacancies due to resignation or removal of a member on the Board of Directors shall be filled at a regular meeting of the Board of Directors occuring within six months of the date of removal or resignation. A director elected to fill a vacancy shall be elected to serve for the unexpired portion of the departing member's term, and may be elected to an additional term consecutive to this service if the term of the previous member had one year or less to run.

Section 5: Attendance: Attendance at meetings of the Board of Directors is a responsibility of each member. A member of the board who fails to attend two meetings in any one membership year shall be given notice by the Executive Director that if the member concerned shall miss one more meeting within one year after the second absence, then that member will be deemed to have resigned from the board. Members of the Board of Directors must attend all scheduled activities of the board at any given meeting in order to receive credit for attendance at that meeting. The board may move, upon request from a member, to count that member as present at a particular meeting for which attendance is questionable. All members of the board, elected or appointed, must observe the attendance policies of the board. In the case of members appointed by the Governor, the Governor will be notified when an appointee has been placed on probation because of absence, and the Governor will be requested to make a new appointment to serve out the term of the member in question.

Article V

Meetings

Section 1: Regular Meetings: Meetings of the Board of Directors shall be held at such times and places as may be determined by the chair with the consent of the majority of the members of the board. Written notice of the time and location of such meetings shall be posted to the members at least one month in advance. There shall be at least four regular meetings per year.

Section 2: Special Meetings: A special meeting may be called at the discretion of the chair, or Executive Committee, or upon written request of three members of the Board of Directors, provided that notice of such meeting be mailed to each member at least seven days prior to the time of such meeting, or communicated by telephone at least 24 hours before such meeting. Such notice shall state the purpose for which the special meeting is called.

Section 3: Notice: Written notice stating the place, date and time of the meeting and, in case of a special meeting, the purpose or purposes for which the meeting is called and the name of the person or persons by whom or at whose direction the meeting is called shall, except in extraordinary situations, be given to each member of the Board of Directors not less than fifteen (15) days before the date of any annual, regular, or special meeting, either by personal delivery or by mail. If mailed, such notice shall be deemed to be delivered when deposited in the United States mails, properly addressed and with the postage thereon prepaid. Each member shall be responsible for keeping the Secretary informed as to such member's proper mailing address.

Section 4: Quorum: One half plus one of the members shall constitute a quorum for the transaction of business at any meeting of the Board of Directors, but if less than such quorum is present at a meeting, a majority of the members present may adjourn the meeting from time to time without further notice.

Section 5: Presumption of Assent: A member of the corporation who is present at a meeting of the Board of Directors at which action on any corporate matter is taken shall be presumed to have assented to such action unless he shall file his written dissent to such action with the Secretary of the meeting before the adjournment thereof.

Article VI

Officers and Committees

Section 1: Chair: The Chair shall be the chief executive officer of the board, having the authority to call meetings, to appoint committees, and generally to direct the activities of the board. The term of office of the Chair shall be one year, beginning July 1. The Chair may be eligible for election to a second term of one year.

Section 2: Vice Chair: The Vice Chair shall be the chief executive officer of the board after the Chair and shall assist the Chair in such ways as the latter may direct in the conduct of the affairs of the board. In the absence of the Chair, the Vice Chair shall conduct meetings and perform the other duties of the Chair. The term of office of the Vice Chair shall be one year, beginning July 1. The Vice Chair is eligible for the election to the Chair.

In the event that the office of Chair shall be vacated by resignation, incapacity, or death, the members of the board shall declare the office vacant, and the Vice Chair shall serve as Chair for the remainder of the term (*i.e.*, until the next July 1). In this case, this Chair may be reelected to one succeeding term.

Each officer shall continue to serve until a successor is duly elected and installed.

Section 3: Secretary: The Secretary shall: keep, or supervise the keeping of, the minutes of the meetings of the Board of Directors, and, to the extent ordered by the Board of Directors or the Chair, the minutes of committee meetings; cause notice to be given of all such meetings; have custody of the corporate seal and general charge of the records, documents, and papers of the corporation not pertaining to the performance of the duties vested in others; affix and attest the corporate seal to corporate papers; and perform such other duties as may be prescribed from time to time by the bylaws, the Board of Directors, or the Chair. In the absence of the Secretary, a Secretary *Pro Tem* may be appointed by the presiding officer at any meeting. The Executive Director is *ex-officio* Secretary of the board.

Section 4: Committees: The Chair and the Executive Director are *ex officio* members of all committees.

a) *Executive Committee:* There shall be an Executive Committee composed of the Chair, the Vice Chair, Secretary, and three other members elected by the board for a period of one year. The Executive Committee shall, in intervals between meetings of the Board of Directors, have general control of the affairs of the corporation, but nothing herein shall be construed to allow the Executive Committee to act to the exclusion of, or contrary to the expressed direction of the Board of Directors. The Chair of the Board of Directors shall be the Chair of the Executive Committee.

The two chief elected officers shall be elected by majority vote of the board. The three remaining elected members shall each be the elected Chair by one of the three standing committees, confirmed by vote of board.

b) *Major Administrative committees:* The structure of the administrative committee system shall be on two levels: the first level shall be three large standing committees: 1) Grants 2) Program Development 3) Operations, the second level will be the subcommittees, appointed by the Chair of each standing committee, on a semi-permanent and on an *ad hoc* basis. The standing committees shall be composed of members selected by the Chair. They shall serve one-year terms concurrent with that of the Chair.

c) *Reading Committees:* Reading committees shall be appointed by the Executive Director, who also appoints the chairs. Membership of reading committees is changed at each meeting.

Section 5: Removal of Officers: Officers may be removed if, upon repeated evaluation, their performance is found consistently poor. [Also, provisions for notice and a hearing should be included.]

Article VII

Staff

Section 1: Executive Director: The Board of Directors shall employ an Executive Director who shall be charged with the administrative and executive management of the affairs of the corporation, subject to review by the Board of Directors. In the event of a vacancy in the position of Executive Director, the Chair shall forthwith appoint an *ad hoc* search committee whose responsibility shall be to identify, investigate, and interview candidates for the position and make recommendations to the Board of Directors for filling the vacancy.

Section 2: Additional Personnel: From time to time, _____ may change its staff structure according to available administrative funds and needs.

Article VIII

Regranting

Section 1: Process: The regranting process shall begin with the receipt of proposals in the principal office. After the proposals are reviewed by the staff for technical eligibility, the eligible proposals will be distributed among reading committees which meet separately, recording their decisions for or against funding and delineating their reasons therefore. The board will then vote their acceptance of the reading committees' decisions. In the case of proposals for small amounts or proposals recommended for revision by the board, the board may delegate authority to make grants to the Executive Committee or to an *ad hoc* committee, subject to ratification by the board. The Executive Director will inform all proposal writers of the status of their proposals.

Article IX

Miscellaneous

Section 1: Ability to Amend: A majority of the Board of Directors may amend these bylaws by resolution at any meeting.

Section 2: Conflict of Interest: An _____ board member should not submit an application for _____ funds on behalf of himself or be the recipient of funds for himself through an institution or organization which employs him, or with which he is affiliated. An _____ board member should not be designated in an application as a principal investigator, nor as serving a similar role. An _____ board member may take part in projects undertaken with support from _____ but should not personally receive any remuneration out of _____ funds for his services to a project, except for travel and per diem. If an _____ Board member is a participant in any way, a proposal should clearly indicate the nature of his participation in the project. An _____ board member should not participate in any way in support of, or vote on, an application for _____ funds on behalf of an institution or organization which employs him or with which he is affiliated, or in support of an application for a project in which he will participate. All negotiations in support of such applications should be carried on by persons who are not _____ board members.

Section 3: Public Access Information: The _____ Endowment for _____ as a *quasi*-governmental organization, recognizes its responsibility to the people of _____ under the Sunshine Law and will adhere to the guidelines stated therein.

Meetings of the board are announced in an _____ newsletter. Board meetings are open to the public, except for deliberations of reading committees and the nominations subcommittee, but these committees report their conclusions to the board, and the reading committees provide written explanation of principal funding recommendations other than unconditional approval. This information, along with minutes of the meeting, is available for public scrutiny in the _____ central office.

Information about _____ and its program is published regularly in a newsletter, and will be available in various papers and brochures describing aspects of _____'s program. _____'s proposal to the National Endowment for _____ will be available for public scrutiny. _____ will issue a report to the people of the State following the completion of each grant period.

Section 4: Rules of Order: Unless otherwise specified in this document, Oleck & Green *Parliamentary Law and Practice for NPOs* (Amer. Law Inst.-Amer. Bar Assn., 2d ed., 1991) shall be this organization's Rules of Order.

24

MEETINGS AND CONVENTIONS OF MEMBERS

[See MEMBERS in the *Index*]
[See Chapter 30 as to Directors' Meetings]

§240. MEETINGS, IN GENERAL

[See, *Successful Meetings* (magazine) as to current hotel and other meetings facilities, supplies, services, etc., 355 Park Ave., So.; N.Y. City, N.Y. 10010; Tel. (212) 592-6403 (Editorial office).]

Members' relationships to the organization and each other are basically contractual.

While day-to-day management of the affairs of a nonprofit corporation basically is the province of the board of directors, the making of corporation policy (or changes of policy) and selection of the directors, is the province of the members of the organization. This is so because it is ordinarily impractical to have a mass meeting of members for dealing with the details of the organization's operation.[2] But meetings are usually essential for the exercise of their "ownership" rights by the members of an organization; *e.g.*, their mutual—contract—implied in becoming members.[3]

Meetings of the members, of the board of directors, of the various committees, and of other special groups of members are the very essence of nonprofit organization life. These meetings may range from a gathering of two or three persons to a general convention representing thousands of persons or many associated member organizations.

In the largest or in the smallest meeting, certain fundamental principles and procedures apply.

Bylaws govern meetings. Methods for holding and conducting meetings are almost always provided in the bylaws of the organization. In fact, the provision of rules for meetings probably is the most important function of the bylaws. If a meeting of the members can be properly called and held (with a minimum of dispute and confusion), those present can make all the other necessary provisions for the operation of the organization.

Statutory requirements. Organization meetings are specifically required by statutes in some states, as is discussed previously in Chapter 20. Statutes in many states specifically require that nonprofit corporations hold at least annual meetings.[4] The Ohio statute actually states the date on which it must be held if the bylaws do not set a different date.[5]

Some state laws, such as Florida's, have specific details as to meetings of members and assume that they will be held. The Georgia statute says that bylaws *may* specify the date of annual meetings.[6]

Corporation law statutes usually provide that a nonprofit corporation *may* adopt bylaws fixing the dates of certain kinds of meetings, such as an annual meeting for the election of officers and directors (trustees).[7] And they usually make provisions for election of trustees "at a meeting of members."[8]

Special types of organizations. Statutory rules governing some special types of organizations (*e.g.*, cooperatives) sometimes specifically require the holding of at least annual meetings.[9] This is particularly true as to organization meetings.[10]

Officers and trustees of special types of nonprofit organizations should take care to acquaint themselves with any special statutes applicable to their kind of organizations. It should not be assumed that compliance with general nonprofit organization laws always will satisfy statutory requirements.

Conventions. (See Sections 247, 248.) A *convention* is an assembly of delegates or representatives chosen by the members of an organization, or of delegates or members of subsidiary chapters or branches. It usually is called as an annual meeting for the election of officers or trustees of the parent (national or regional) organization, or for framing or revision of the parents' constitution or bylaws.[11] Often conventions are held periodically and include educational and social meetings as well as business meetings. [See Chapter 23.]

See "Members" in the Index.

Many special rules apply as to *Members' Rights and Duties.*

For example: Members' dues to a bar association may not be used to fund *political causes opposed by members,* but may be used only to regulate or improve the profession and its services.

Keller v. State Bar, 496 U.S., (1993); Crosetto v. State Bar of Wisconsin, 92-F.2d 3899 (7th Cir., Dec. 1993), 16 Natl. L.J.(18)3 (Jan. 17, 1994).

FORM NO. 121 A

Members' Rights and Duties in Residential Club
[*Agreement* applicable to NPOs and/or For-Profit "Clubs" for Retirees]

CLUB MEMBERSHIP AGREEMENT

THIS AGREEMENT is made this _____ day of _____, 19_____, by and between _____ **MANAGEMENT COMPANY, INC.**, a Florida Corporation (referred to as the "MANAGEMENT COMPANY"), whose address is 8333 Blvd., Florida 34642, and _____ (referred to as the "MEMBER" OF _____ "CLUB"),

whose address is _____. If
two persons are named as the MEMBER, the term MEMBER shall refer to both
persons separately and together as the context requires.

SECTION 1. STATEMENT OF INTENTION AND PURPOSES

The intent and purpose of the MANAGEMENT COMPANY shall be to
provide a congenial atmosphere for the MEMBER'S living pleasure, promote
the general physical and mental well being of the MEMBER and to provide a
place where the MEMBER and the MEMBER'S guests may dine in a congenial
atmosphere. The CLUB facilities shall be located in Commercial Condominium Unit A of Lake Seminole Square, a Condominium.

SECTION 2. GENERAL SERVICES TO MEMBERS

The MANAGEMENT COMPANY shall provide the MEMBER with the following services:

A. *Transportation.* The MANAGEMENT COMPANY will provide routine
transportation from _____, a Condominium, for medical, financial and
shopping services within a reasonable proximity of _____, a Condominium, in the discretion of the MANAGEMENT COMPANY, as well as for social
and leisure activities scheduled by the CLUB.

B. *Social and Leisure Activities.* Social and leisure activities will be planned
and coordinated with the MEMBER and other members by an Fitness and
Activities Director employed by the MANAGEMENT COMPANY.

C. *Food Service.* The MANAGEMENT COMPANY will provide, without
additional charge, one meal per day. This meal can be either lunch or dinner.
Additional meals are available for a separate charge. Guests of the MEMBER
will be permitted to use the dining room on a reservation basis. Charges for
additional or guest meals will be in addition to the MEMBER's Monthly Fee.
Therapeutic diets are available at an additional charge.

D. *Miscellaneous.* Since the CLUB facilities owned or operated by the
MANAGEMENT COMPANY are in close proximity to the residential units in
_____, a Condominium, the MANAGEMENT COMPANY shall also offer
to those MEMBERS who are owners of residential units in _____, a Condominium, the additional services included on Exhibit "B" and Exhibit "C" as
provided in the condominium documents.

SECTION 3. HEALTH SERVICES

A. *Health Facilities.* The MEMBER is entitled to priority admission to
either The Inn at _____, a licensed adult congregate living facility locat-

ed in Commercial Condominium Unit B of _____, a Condominium, The Inn at _____, a licensed adult congregate living facility located at _____, Seminole Nursing Pavilion, a licensed nursing facility located at _____ and _____ Nursing Center, a licensed nursing facility located nearby at _____. A discount is available for these four facilities. In the event that it is necessary for the Resident to stay at a facility other than The Inn at _____ or _____ Nursing Facilities as listed above, the rate charged to the Resident will not be greater than the applicable rate charged by the Inn at _____ or _____ Nursing Facilities with the applicable discount taken into consideration.

B. *Temporary Stay in Assisted Living and/or Skilled Nursing.* If the MEMBER needs the services of an assisted living facility and/or skilled nursing center and takes advantage of priority admission to either The Inn at _____ or _____ Nursing Facilities, the Monthly Fee will be suspended during the first 90 days of such care in any year, with a maximum of 360 days during the life of the MEMBER.

If two persons are named as the MEMBER, the monthly fee for single membership will be suspended and only the Monthly Fee for the second person will continue during the first 90 days of the stay of one of the persons named. If both persons require assisted living and/or skilled nursing at the same time and both persons take advantage of priority admission to either The Inn at _____ or _____ Nursing Facilities, the Monthly Fee for both persons will be suspended during the first 90 days of care.

C. *Non-Resident of _____—A Condominium/Permanent Stay in Assisted Living and/or Skilled Nursing.* If the MEMBER becomes a permanent resident of The Inn at _____ and/or _____ Nursing Facilities as determined by the sale of the MEMBER'S current home, or by 180 continuous days of care at either the assisted living facility and/or skilled nursing center subject to the terms of section 3 B., (whichever occurs first), then the Monthly Fee will be suspended and the MEMBER will receive a 15% discount on a semi-private room at either the assisted living facility and/or skilled nursing center.

If two persons are named as the MEMBER and one (1) person requires the services of assisted living and/or skilled nursing on a permanent basis, then the Monthly Fee will be reduced to single occupancy for the person not requiring assisted living and/or skilled nursing, and the person requiring the services of assisted living and/or skilled nursing on a permanent basis, will receive a 15% discount on a semi-private room. If both persons require assisted living and/or skilled nursing on a permanent basis, then the Monthly Fee for both persons will be suspended and each person named will receive a 15% discount on a semi-private room in either assisted living and/or skilled nursing facility.

D. *Resident of* _____—A *Condominium/Permanent Stay in Assisted Living and/or Skilled Nursing.*

1. If the MEMBER becomes a permanent resident of The Inn at
_____ and/or _____ Nursing Facilities as determined by the sale
of the balance of the MEMBER'S life estate, the Monthly Fee will be suspended and the MEMBER will receive a 15% discount on a semi-private
room at either the assisted living facility and/or skilled nursing facility.

2. If the MEMBER becomes a permanent resident of The Inn at
_____ and/or _____ Nursing
Facilities as determined by 180 continuous days of care at either the assisted living facility and/or skilled nursing center, then the MEMBER will
receive a 15% discount on a semi-private room at either the assisted living facility and/or skilled nursing center and the Monthly Fee will be suspended during the first 90 days of such care in any year, with a maximum
of 360 days during the life of the MEMBER.

If two persons are named as the MEMBER and one (1) person
requires the services of assisted living and/or skilled nursing on a permanent basis, then the Monthly Fee will be reduced to single occupancy
for the person not requiring assisted living and/or skilled nursing, and
the person requiring the services of assisted living and/or skilled nursing
on a permanent basis, will receive a 15% discount on a semi-private
room. If both persons require assisted living and/or skilled nursing on a
permanent basis, then the Monthly Fee for both persons will be suspended and each person named will receive a 15% discount on a semi-
private room in either assisted living and/or skilled nursing facility.

E. *Functional Impairment.* If the MEMBER becomes "functionally
impaired," as defined in Chapter 10A-4"Specialized Adult Services" of the regulations of the Florida Department of Health and Rehabilitative Services, then
the Monthly Fee will be suspended. In addition, in such event, if the MEMBER
owns a life estate in a residential unit in _____, A Condominium, the
MANAGEMENT COMPANY, as the MEMBER'S authorized agent, shall notify
_____ Group—_____, Inc., its successors or assigns (referred to as
the "Developer"), in writing, that the MEMBER desires to sell the life estate to
the Developer. The sale of the life estate to the Developer shall be upon those
terms set forth in the Purchase Agreement for the unit. The MEMBER hereby
appoints the MANAGEMENT COMPANY as his authorized agent for this purpose and the MANAGEMENT COMPANY hereby accepts said appointment.
This appointment may not be revoked for so long as this Agreement remains
in full force and effect.

SECTION 4. FEE REFUNDS, INCREASE AND EFFECTIVE DATES

A. *Club Fees.* There are no initial membership fees. The only fees charged
to the MEMBER shall be the Monthly *MANAGEMENT COMPANY* Fee set forth
on Exhibit "A" to this Agreement and the fees for additional services set forth

on Exhibit "B" and Exhibit "C".

B. *Monthly Fee Refunds.* The Monthly Fees shall be pro-rated based upon the date of termination and as provided in Chapter 2–18 "Contracts for Future Consumer Services" of the regulations of the Florida Department of Legal Affairs.

C. *Monthly MEMBER Fee Increase.* The Monthly Fee for Club Membership can only be increased once annually after sixty (60) days notice to the MEMBER. Any increase shall not be greater than the sum of:

> 1.   The percentage increase in the Consumer Price Index for all urban consumers (all items) for Class A areas of the South East Region, published by the Bureau of Labor Statistics, U.S. Department of Labor, Washington, D.C., or the successor of that Index, plus two (2) percentage points.

> 2.   The MEMBER'S proportionate share of any increase in direct MANAGEMENT COMPANY costs caused by any new governmental taxes, charges, assessments or levies.

D. *Future Repairs and Replacements.* The MANAGEMENT COMPANY shall be required to make all future repairs and replacements to the common elements of the condominium at its sole cost and expense without assessing the CLUB MEMBERS. The MANAGEMENT COMPANY shall be entitled to utilize all funds budgeted for such expenses prior to funding the expenses from its own account.

E. *Commencement.* Monthly Fees shall commence on the _____ day of _____, 19_____ as agreed.

SECTION 5. TERM OF AGREEMENT

A. *Original Term and Additional Terms.* This Agreement shall have an original term of thirty-six (36) months and shall be automatically renewable for additional twelve (12) month terms thereafter, unless otherwise terminated pursuant to Section 6 or upon the MEMBER providing written notice to the MANAGEMENT COMPANY at least thirty (30) days prior to MEMBER'S intention to cancel this Agreement.

B. *Subrogation.* The MANAGEMENT COMPANY has the right of subrogation with respect to any claim a MEMBER may have against a third party on account of injuries inflicted on the MEMBER by such third party, to the extent of all damages and expenses incurred by the MANAGEMENT COMPANY by reason of such injury.

C. *Liability for Losses.* The MANAGEMENT COMPANY shall not be responsible for any loss, damage, injury or expense incurred for services provided by persons other than employees of the facilities owned or operated by the MANAGEMENT COMPANY.

D. *Liability for Fees.* The MEMBER is liable for payment of all fees and charges incurred by the MEMBER. If the MANAGEMENT COMPANY has to institute legal procedures to recover these fees and charges, the MANAGEMENT COMPANY shall also be entitled to receive legal fees and costs incurred to effect this recovery.

SECTION 6. TERMINATION OF AGREEMENT

A. *Death.* This Agreement shall be terminated by the death of the MEMBER. If this Agreement applies to two (2) MEMBERS, it will remain in effect after the death of one of the MEMBERS, except the Monthly Fee shall be adjusted to single membership.

B. *Misstatement of Fact.* This Agreement may be terminated by the MANAGEMENT COMPANY upon ninety (90) days written notice to the MEMBER upon discovery of the misstatement of a material fact in the application for admission, physician's medical status report, or any information submitted by or on behalf of the MEMBER to induce the MANAGEMENT COMPANY to enter into this Agreement.

C. *Default in Payment.* This Agreement may be terminated by the MANAGEMENT COMPANY upon ninety (90) days written notice to the MEMBER if the MEMBER fails to pay the Monthly Fee. However, the MANAGEMENT COMPANY *will not* terminate this Agreement if the MEMBER is unable to pay the full Monthly Fee as a result of financial reverses, *unless* such reverses, in the judgment of the MANAGEMENT COMPANY, are the result of willful and unreasonable dissipation of the MEMBER'S assets by the MEMBER.

For the period that the MEMBER is unable to pay the full Monthly Fee as a result of financial reverses, under circumstances acceptable to the MANAGEMENT COMPANY, the amount of each Monthly Fee that the MEMBER is unable to pay shall be calculated and all of these amounts shall be totaled. The MEMBER or his estate shall pay this total to the MANAGEMENT COMPANY upon the earlier of one hundred and twenty (120) days of the death of the MEMBER, or at such time as the non-residential MEMBER sells his current home or, in the case of a MEMBER who owns a life estate in a residential unit in _____, A Condominium, at such time as the MEMBER sells the balance of the life estate.

SECTION 7. MEMBERS' PROPERTY

A. *Responsibility for Member's Property.* The MEMBER shall be responsible for all of his property located at the facilities owned or operated by the MANAGEMENT COMPANY. In the event of the MEMBER'S death, the MANAGEMENT COMPANY shall exercise care in maintaining the MEMBER'S personal property in the possession of the MANAGEMENT COMPANY until delivery can be made to those entitled to receive the property. If such property is not removed within thirty (30) days, the MANAGEMENT COMPANY may store it in a warehouse at the expense and risk of the MEMBER'S estate.

B. *Insurance.* MEMBER shall maintain a policy of insurance covering MEMBER'S personal property as may be contained at _____, excluding such items as the appliances and fixtures, which were provided by _____ Group—_____ ("Developer") and remain the property of the Developer upon termination of this Agreement. MEMBER shall also maintain a policy of public liability insurance for at least $100,000.00, naming the Developer, as the owner of the remainder interest and as an additional insured.

SECTION 8. BURIAL

MEMBER may furnish the MANAGEMENT COMPANY with instructions concerning burial arrangements. The MANAGEMENT COMPANY will cooperate, where possible, in implementing such arrangements. The MEMBER or his estate, is responsible for the cost of funeral and burial.

SECTION 9. LEGAL INCOMPETENCY

If a MEMBER is believed to be mentally incompetent or physically incapacitated, the MANAGEMENT COMPANY is authorized to take action to protect the MEMBER, which may include guardianship proceedings. In the event a relative is unable or unwilling to make application for adjudication of incompetency and appointment of a guardian, the MANAGEMENT COMPANY may initiate such proceedings at the expense of the MEMBER. The MANAGEMENT COMPANY shall not be appointed as conservator or guardian for a MEMBER.

SECTION 10. EMERGENCY INFORMATION

The MEMBER shall furnish to the MANAGEMENT COMPANY on the MANAGEMENT COMPANY'S request therefor, complete emergency information including medications being taken by MEMBER, and shall immediately notify the MANAGEMENT COMPANY of any changes.

SECTION 11. ASSISTANCE

The MANAGEMENT COMPANY will assist the MEMBER in applying for financial assistance from any Federal, State, or other program. MEMBER agrees to cooperate in applying for any programs for which the MEMBER or the MANAGEMENT COMPANY may be entitled.

SECTION 12. RULES AND REGULATIONS

The MANAGEMENT COMPANY shall adopt reasonable rules for orderly operation of the facilities owned or operated by the MANAGEMENT COMPA-

NY and for the health, safety and welfare of the MEMBERS. The MEMBER agrees to abide by such rules.

SECTION 13. ASSIGNMENT

This Agreement is binding upon the successors and assigns of the MANAGEMENT COMPANY and the representatives of the MEMBER, and is not assignable by the MEMBER.

THIS AGREEMENT IS FOR FUTURE CONSUMER SERVICES AND PUTS ALL ASSIGNEES OF THE MANAGEMENT COMPANY ON NOTICE OF THE CONSUMER'S RIGHT TO CANCEL UNDER FLORIDA'S FAIR TRADE PRACTICES RULE.

SECTION 14. AMENDMENT

This Agreement may be amended by the MANAGEMENT COMPANY upon receiving approval of a majority vote of the Residents Advisory Council of _____. Any such amendment shall become effective upon receiving said approval of the Residents Advisory Council. A MEMBER who notifies the MANAGEMENT COMPANY, in writing, of the MEMBER'S intention to cancel his/her Agreement must do so within 30 days of said approval.

SECTION 15. MEMBER'S RIGHTS AND ACKNOWLEDGMENTS

THE MEMBER, BY EXECUTING THIS AGREEMENT, ACKNOWLEDGES THAT THE MANAGEMENT COMPANY PRESENTED A PRINTED COPY OF THIS AGREEMENT TO THE MEMBER PRIOR TO THE TRANSFER OF ANY MONEY OR PROPERTY TO THE MANAGEMENT COMPANY.

CONSUMER'S RIGHT OF CANCELLATION

MEMBER MAY CANCEL THIS AGREEMENT WITHOUT ANY PENALTY OR OBLIGATION WITHIN SEVEN (7) DAYS FROM THE ABOVE DATE. IN THE EVENT OF SUCH CANCELLATION, ALL SUMS PAID BY MEMBER SHALL BE FULLY REFUNDED BY THE MANAGEMENT COMPANY.
MEMBER MAY ALSO CANCEL THIS AGREEMENT IF UPON A DOCTOR'S ORDER MEMBER CANNOT PHYSICALLY RECEIVE THE SERVICES OFFERED BY THE MANAGEMENT COMPANY, OR MEMBER MAY CANCEL THIS AGREEMENT IF THE SERVICES CEASE TO BE OFFERED AS STATED IN THE AGREEMENT. IF THE MEMBER CANCELS THIS AGREEMENT FOR EITHER OF THESE REASONS, MEMBER SHALL BE OBLIGATED TO PAY TO THE MANAGEMENT COMPANY ONLY THE AMOUNT THE MEMBER OWES THROUGH THE DATE OF CANCELLATION.

THE MEMBER MAY NOTIFY THE MANAGEMENT COMPANY OF THE MEMBER'S INTENT TO CANCEL BY NOTICE TO _____ MANAGEMENT COMPANY, INC., AT 8333 SEMINOLE BOULEVARD, SEMINOLE, FLORIDA 34642.

IN WITNESS WHEREOF, the MANAGEMENT COMPANY and the MEMBER have signed this agreement as of the day and year first written above.

_____ MANAGEMENT COMPANY, INC.

By: _____

_____, its _____

(CORPORATE SEAL)

_____   _____
Date Executed by Member   (MEMBER)

_____   _____
Date Executed by Member   (MEMBER)

FEES FOR SERVICES
EXHIBIT "A"

MONTHLY MANAGEMENT COMPANY FEE $ _____

EXHIBIT "B"

1. *Housekeeping and Laundry Services.* The MANAGEMENT COMPANY will perform in the MEMBER'S unit, on an "as needed" basis, strenuous housekeeping tasks such as heavy vacuuming, cleaning of carpets, scrubbing of bath tile, window washing, etc., as determined by the MANAGEMENT COMPANY. On a weekly basis, the MANAGEMENT COMPANY will vacuum, clean all vinyl floors, and clean bathrooms. The MEMBER agrees to otherwise maintain the unit in a clean, sanitary and orderly condition. The MANAGEMENT COMPANY will furnish the MEMBER with a change of towels and wash cloths on a weekly basis. The MANAGEMENT COMPANY will also change bed linens and make the MEMBER'S bed on a weekly basis. The MANAGEMENT COMPANY will provide service and maintenance at no charge to the MEMBER on the following items, if these

items are included in the original purchase price of the
MEMBER'S Unit, and replacements thereof, if the replacements are purchased from the MANAGEMENT COMPANY:
stoves, ovens, refrigerators, disposals, dishwashers, plumbing
and air-conditioning and heating equipment, carpet,
drapes, tile, wallpaper, linoleum, enclosures, verticals and
other upgrades.

2. *Twenty-Four Hour Emergency Call Systems.* The MANAGE-
MENT COMPANY shall monitor and respond to an emergency call and response system for the MEMBER.

3. *Real Property Taxes.* The MANAGEMENT COMPANY shall
pay all real property taxes assessed against the MEMBER'S
unit at _____, A Condominium, provided the MEM-
BER files for homestead exemption and any other available
exemption.

The services set forth on this Exhibit "B" shall be billed to
the MEMBER at a monthly cost of:

$ _____

EXHIBIT "C"

MONTHLY CONDOMINIUM FEE: $ _____

TOTAL MONTHLY SERVICE FEE $===============

GUARANTY OF PAYMENT

The undersigned hereby guarantees payment of the MEMBER'S Monthly Fee, plus any costs of collection.

_____   _____
Date Executed by Guarantor   (GUARANTOR)

§241. MEETINGS OF THE MEMBERS

Ordinarily, at least one *general meeting* must be held each year, for election of
trustees and consideration of reports.[12] Some state statutes specifically so
require.[13]

Some state statutes make such a meeting necessary by their provision that
at least one-fifth of the total number of the board of trustees be elected annually.[14]

Many organizations now use such a rotating system of board elections as
a matter of convenience. Election of one trustee each year, each trustee being

elected for a term of five years, for example, assures the organization of continued experience of most of the trustees at any given time.

These elections, however, may be conducted at special meetings as well as at general meetings if the requirements of due notice and quorum are met.

Other matters besides elections may be taken up at a general meeting. Reports on and discussion of the organization's plans and finances usually are important parts of such a meeting. Members of a corporation ordinarily can act only in this way, concurrently, at a meeting, except when statutes expressly permit consents in writing.[15]

Unqualified members (*e.g.*, who call a meeting although they have not paid their dues properly) cannot bind the organization by that meeting.[16]

Constitutional rights usually continue to apply to members; *e.g.*, union members have *standing* to challenge organization restriction of *freedom of speech*.[17]

If *extraordinary matters* (such as proposals to change election rules or to dissolve the organization) are to be considered, the general meeting may not properly pass on them, unless the notice of meeting stated that they would be brought up for decision.[18]

Statutes in many states provide that *even a single member can call a general meeting* for the required annual election, or for decision of an important matter, if the persons who should call it fail to do so.[19] This power usually passes to individual members about a month after the meeting should have been called.[20] Such power should be exercised only after a demand has been made on the officer who should call the meeting. If he still refuses or neglects to act, the individual member may act under the statutory authority.[21]

Presumably no demand for action need be made when it obviously would be futile—for example, when the officer who should call the meeting has committed an error or a crime for which the members, once assembled, would proceed to punish him. This is another reason for inclusion in the bylaws of alternative means of calling a meeting.

Special power usually is given by the statutes to individual members for the calling of the first (organization) meeting, if the organizers of a corporation fail to call it within one year after the filing of the certificate of incorporation.[22]

The first member to send proper notice of such a meeting is the one whose choice of time and place will govern. Whenever possible, he should specify the organization's usual meeting place. Statutes also provide that any number of members who attend shall constitute a quorum.[23]

Individual members are also given power by some statutes to call special meetings to deal with important matters, when the proper officers fail to do so.[24] The individual member who calls such a special meeting negligently or maliciously may be punished by the organization.

Bylaws often provide that general meetings shall be held at least semiannually, or quarterly, or even monthly. They usually also specify that the president (or some other officer) shall call meetings and designate their times and places. The secretary is generally charged with giving proper notice. Usually the Board of Directors is also given the power to call meetings, especially special meetings, by instructing some officer to send notice.[25]

Most state laws permit the meetings of nonprofit organizations to be held outside the state, as well as within it, if the bylaws so permit.[26]

Stated time and place must be strictly observed. If, for example, a meeting is held at a place other than the one announced, it is not valid insofar as it concerns members who were not properly notified. But any member who attends without objecting waives this defect in notice.[27]

At any time before a meeting adjourns, those present may reconsider a matter that already has been passed upon. They may change their general decision by another vote.[28] A decision made at a previous meeting also may be repealed or altered, if this will not injure rights that have legally accrued under the former decision.[29]

All business stated or reasonably implied in the notice may be attended to at a meeting. Matters not so stated or implied may not properly be brought before the meeting.[30]

For example, if the stated purpose of the meeting is to hire a new executive secretary, this reasonably implies that removal of the one currently employed is also to be decided. But if the purpose stated is the acceptance or rejection of an offered gift to the organization, it is not proper to hold an election, too (insofar as members who do not attend are concerned).

Special meetings. When some special matter must be attended to, at a time between regularly scheduled meetings, a special meeting may be called by the board, or by persons authorized by the bylaws or articles to do so; or by a demand filed by (a usually stated number of) members.[31] The urgency and reasonableness of the matter (and manner of calling of the meeting) will determine its validity.[32] Often the articles or bylaws provide for the calling of a special meeting by the president or secretary at the request of a stated number of members.[33]

Extraordinary meetings. When neglect of the members to attend meetings causes difficulties for the organization, it may be necessary to call an extraordinary meeting. New York's corporation law, until revised in 1963, actually had a specific statute covering this situation.[34] The sheer common sense of calling such a meeting makes the provision of a statute authorizing it seem unnecessary.

For example, an important matter may need to be decided and not enough members may respond to meeting notices, thus making it impossible to obtain the quorum required by the bylaws. Then, unless authority can be obtained to waive these bylaw requirements, or proxies obtained, the neglect by even a minority of the members may effectively stop all operations of the organization.

In such a situation, the officers may petition the state court for an order that will authorize them to call an extraordinary meeting. If the court agrees with the officers' assertion that this is necessary, it will order such notice sent. Under this court order, the members who attend constitute a quorum.[35]

Parliamentary procedure. Bylaws often specify that, where no rule is provided in the articles or bylaws, meetings shall follow the procedure recommended by a given authority, such as the old *Roberts,* the later *Sturgis,* and the (1991) modern Oleck works on parliamentary procedure.[36]

Sometimes more specialized procedural works are specified, such as *Mason's Manual of Legislative Procedure.*[37] Such a reference, good as it is for its purpose, is not intended for use by private nonprofit organizations.

Today, with the wealth of statutory materials available, reliance on such authorities as *Robert's Rules of Order*[38] is becoming less common. The well-known old authority, General Henry M. Robert, was a military man, not a lawyer. His *Rules* long have been widely used. Alice Sturgis, on the other hand, based her works on parliamentary procedure on modern corporation and other statutes and cases. (See, in the Index, "parliamentary procedure.")

The most authoritative set of *Rules of Order* for nonprofit organizations is Oleck & Green, *Parliamentary Law & Practice for Nonprofit Organizations* (2d ed., 1991) published by the highly authoritative American Law Institute-American Bar Association Joint Committee of C.L.E. (4025 Chestnut Street, Philadelphia, Penna. 19104—telephone number 215-387-3000). This handbook is based on modern statute and case law of all states. It is more likely to be upheld by the courts in legal disputes about procedure than is probable when more arbitrary sets of rules of order are cited. *See* Chapter 51 for a summary of the rules of order.

Doris and Friedman, *Encyclopedia of Corporate Meetings, Minutes, and Resolutions*[39] is a useful work on meetings and their procedures.

Sturgis, *Standard Code of Parliamentary Procedure*[40] is a general book based on corporation and association law.

This book itself (*Nonprofit Corporations, Organizations, and Associations*), of course, is general in nature. It is not limited to meetings and procedure at meetings. Yet, it is based almost entirely on modern statutory and case law.

Many courts have said, repeatedly, that they are bound by law, not by lay authorities on parliamentary procedure. They also have said that, in the absence of a provision in bylaws as to procedure on a particular question, the president (or chairman) should follow the ordinary usages of parliamentary procedure.[41]

In order to avoid doubt, it is best to provide in the bylaws that meetings shall follow the procedure recommended by . . . . . . (state the authority) . . . . . . when the bylaws are silent on a particular question of procedure.

§242. WHEN ARE MEETINGS OF THE MEMBERS NECESSARY?

In a few situations (usually specified by statutes), consent of the members may be had by obtaining a number of signatures on a document.

But a meeting must be held to obtain approvals by the directors or members for the following:

1. Acceptance of charter.[42]

2. Election of officers.[43]

3. Adoption of bylaws.[44]

4. Amendment or correction of charter or bylaws.[45]

5. Real property sales, mortgages, or leases.[46]

6. Guaranteeing the obligations of others.[47]

7. Substantial grants or donations of organization funds or property.[48]

8. Extension of life of a corporation (if its duration was stated in years, and is expiring).[49]

9. Voluntary bankruptcy or insolvency proceedings (but probably the directors may do this, if no real choice is available).[50]

10. Voluntary dissolution.[51]

11. Special situations for which the bylaws require meetings.

Failure to hold annual meetings and to properly adopt and amend bylaws, according to a nonprofit corporation's own articles of incorporation, is not sufficient disregard of corporate formality to make members, who are not involved in an accident, individually liable for an injury.[52]

§243. QUORUMS AT MEETINGS OF MEMBERS

A *quorum* is the number of members of an organization that a rule of public or private law (*e.g.*, bylaws) requires to be present before business done at a meeting can be valid and binding on the organization. In the absence of a private rule, a quorum usually is a majority of the members.[53]

Bylaws usually provide what percentage of the number of all the members shall constitute a quorum for meetings. Sometimes special quorums are provided for specific matters.

It is unwise to establish quorums in terms of numbers. Percentages are more practicable. For example, if membership should decrease, it might become impossible to muster enough members to meet a numerical quorum.

Presumptions of quorum. It is a general rule of parliamentary procedure that, when a meeting is held, a quorum is presumed to be present unless someone present questions the fact, or unless the lack of quorum is shown by the minutes or other records of the meeting.[54]

"... If a number of members leave a meeting, thereby breaking the quorum, their departure should not ordinarily be permitted to render the meeting invalid." This is especially true where the "*walkout*" is *intended* to break the required quorum; so too of refusal to attend, for such a purpose.[55]

[Special quorum rules apply to *extraordinary* meetings and to special meetings called by one member. These are discussed in Section 241.]

High-quorum rules. Bylaws or the charter may provide that a quorum shall be *greater* than the law requires for a certain kind of action, but provision of a number *smaller* than the law requires is invalid.

For example, statutes often require attendance by a majority, and also a two-thirds vote of all members, for the making of a mortgage. At least two-thirds of the members must therefore be present in person or by proxy. It is invalid, as well as unwise, to set the quorum at less than the percentage specified by the statute.[56]

You may include proxies in quorums. Many times a member attends a meeting representing other members, in that he holds their proxies for voting. It is important that the bylaws set precise quorum rules on this point.

Proxies may be counted toward a quorum at a meeting or a convention.[57] But then a single member, if he has enough proxies in his pocket, can constitute a quorum, and hold a one-person meeting.[58] This is hardly democratic practice. The law usually requires personal presence of at least *two* persons,[59] but the bylaws must establish further requirements, if there are to be any. (See, also, the chapter on *Proxies.*)

§244. NOTICE OF MEETINGS OF MEMBERS

For the mandatory meetings listed in Section 242, statutes generally require that a certain formal notice be given the members. If such notice is not given, the meeting is invalid—at least as it affects the members who were not properly notified.

How to give minimum formal notice. Proper notice includes at least the following formalities:[60]

1. Written or printed notice,
2. Signed by an officer,
3. Stating the time and the place,
4. Stating the purpose of the meeting,
5. Sent reasonably in advance,
6. By mail or personal delivery.

Bylaws' notice rules. Bylaws are in themselves notice of regular meetings provided therein.[61] Most bylaws also specify the notice that must be given for various meetings. For important meetings, they usually require written notice. Sometimes they set time limits, require use of registered mail, or set other exact rules. But ordinarily they specify only *written,* or *oral,* or *telephone* notice. Many and serious disputes result from such vague rules.

The more precisely the rules of notice are drawn at the beginning, the less trouble later.

Statutory notice rules. For meetings to transact certain business (*e.g.*, approving a mortgage of assets) statutes often specify that certain formal notice be given.[62]

Such statutes usually require the *minimum formal notice* outlined above. They also specify when the notice must be sent or delivered—usually "at least ten, but not more than 40 days before the date of the meeting."[63]

Publication of the notice, in local newspapers, is often allowed for special meetings of organizations having more than 500 members. Statutes ordinarily call for publication once each week for at least two or three weeks before the meeting.[64]

Mailing of notice must be to the latest address given by the member to the organization.[65]

FORM NO. 122
Notice of Meeting of Members

...... Association
...... (address)

...... , 19 ..

Mr. ......
...... (address)
Please take notice that

A (general) (special) meeting of the members of the .... Association will be held at (the clubhouse) (the office of the Association) at .... Street, ... (city), State of ...., on ...... (day of week), ..., 19 .., at .... o'clock (a.m.) (p.m.), in Room No. .... for the (election of directors) (decision on a proposal to sell the following Association property: ....) and for the transaction of such other business as may come before the meeting.

Voting will commence at ...... o'clock (a.m.) (p.m.).

If you will not be able to attend in person, you may execute a proxy to any other member of the Association, authorizing him to vote on your behalf, in accordance with the provisions of Article ......, Section ......, of the Association's Bylaws.

By order of the (President) (Board of Directors)

....
Secretary

FORM NO. 123
Notice of Annual Meeting of Members
Yacht Club Condominium Building-B, Inc.

TO ALL MEMBERS:

On March 1, 199_____, at 3:30 p.m. at the Clubhouse, the Annual Meeting of the Association will be held for the purpose of electing Directors and such other business as may lawfully be conducted.

A majority of members of the Association (a "quorum") must be present, in person or by proxy, at the meeting, in order for the business to be conducted, including election of Directors. It is therefore *VERY IMPORTANT* that you either *attend* or provide a *proxy*.

Please note the following information about *PROXIES*:

A *proxy* is for the purpose of appointing *another person* to vote on your ballot in the event that you might not be able to attend the meeting. It must be signed by all owners of the unit or the one among them that they designate on a voting certificate (see below). If you appoint a proxy and later decide you will be able to attend the meeting in person, you may *withdraw* your proxy when you register at the meeting.

Please note the following information about *VOTING CERTIFICATES*:

A *voting certificate* is for the purpose of establishing who is authorized to vote for a unit owned by *more than one person* (including husband and wife) *or a corporation*. A voting certificate is *not* needed if the unit is owned by only one person. A voting certificate must be signed by *all* of the owners of the unit or the appropriate corporate officer.

Again, please be sure to either attend the Annual Meeting or submit a proxy or voting certificate if your unit is owned by more than one person or a corporation. Thank you for your assistance in conducting the business of your Association.

DATED:_____, 199___.

BY ORDER OF THE BOARD OF
DIRECTORS

_____
Secretary

§245. ADJOURNED MEETINGS

Once a meeting has been duly called, on due notice and duly assembled, with a proper quorum, no repetition of written notice is legally necessary (unless the bylaws specifically require it) if the meeting is adjourned to another time.[66] The decision to reconvene at an agreed time and place is sufficient notice to those present. (But it is good practice for the secretary to send notice again, especially if the adjournment is a fairly long one.)

In effect, reassembly on the agreed date is a continuation of the same meeting.[67] The reassembled meeting may properly deal only with the matters stated in the original notice.[68]

Ordinarily, adjournment is final conclusion of a meeting unless those present adopt a formal or informal resolution to the contrary.

§246. WAIVER OF NOTICE OF MEETING

Statutes in all the states authorize *waiver of notice* of a meeting.[69] Before, during, or *even after* a meeting, those who did, or might have, attended, may formally waive the giving of notice to them.[70] They may do this by signing a formal waiver. Personal signature or the signature of an attorney-in-fact (duly authorized in writing) may be used.[71]

Waiver by conduct. The *conduct* of a member may imply waiver of notice. If a member receives no proper notice, but in fact attends the meeting and takes an active part, he thereby waives the defect in notice.[72] Only if lack of due notice makes it impossible for him to act as he desires (*e.g.*, to investigate the matter), and only if he registers his protest, will his participation not bar his disowning the decision of the meeting.[73]

FORM NO. 124

Waiver of Notice of Meeting

We, the undersigned, being all the (members) (Directors) of the . . . . . Association of (address), do hereby waive any and all notice as provided by the Statutes of . . . . . ., and/or by the Charter or Bylaws of the said Association, and do hereby consent to the holding of a (special) meeting of the (members) (Directors) of the said Association, to be held on the . . . . . day of . . . ., 19 . ., at . . . . o'clock (a.m.) (p.m.), or at an adjournment or adjournments thereof, at Room No. . . . . . ., at . . . . . . Street, ... (city), State of . . . . . ., for the following purposes: (state them), and for the transaction of such other business as may come before the meeting. [Add waiver of publication of notice, if that applies.]

(Signatures)

Dated . . . ., 19. . . . .
. . . . (city), State of. . . . .
                                                           . . . .
                                                           . . . .

§247. CONVENTIONS AND ASSEMBLIES

Nonprofit organizations often include a number of chapters, lodges, locals, or branches, under the auspices of a national or regional parent organization. Often the local branches are formed pursuant to the overall rules of the parent body.

Each branch or chapter is equivalent, in many respects, to an individual member of an organization. The members of the local chapter are usually members, *ipso facto*, of the parent organization.

General (annual) meetings of the parent body (*conventions* or *assemblies*) bring together *representatives* of its constituent organizations. Individual members of the various branches usually are welcome to attend, and many do. But conventions or assemblies fundamentally are meetings of representatives of constituent organizations. Especially in the larger organizations, each representative appears as bearer of the proxies of his chapter's members.[74]

Delegates. The representative is usually called a *delegate*. This title indicates his authority to speak and vote for his branch organization. He has been *delegated* the whole voting power of the local organization he represents.[75]

This power-of-attorney (proxy) may be *general* or it may be *limited* to certain specified acts. An *instructed delegate* is one who is empowered to act or vote only as he has been specifically directed.[76]

Bylaws usually provide in some detail for delegates' selection, qualifications, and powers, and for other particulars of their functions. The bylaws of the parent organization usually state that such delegates, when assembled as the bylaws provide, shall have and exercise all the powers, rights, and privileges of members of an organization in annual meeting. Restrictions on the powers of a delegate are not binding on the parent organization unless it is notified— for example, by stating the restrictions on the delegate's credentials.[77]

Examples of bylaws covering conventions. Bylaw articles and clauses covering conventions and assemblies appear in Chapters 22 and 23, *Forms*. See below, Section 248, as to *Convention Bureaus and Services*.

Pointers for Conventions

1. Pick the date carefully. Suit the date, the day of the week, and the hour to the tastes and habits of the people who will attend.

2. Pick the place carefully. Central location is only one factor. Consider the problems for transportation, parking, accommodations, food, entertainment, and expense.

3. Decide whether the convention will be social, strictly business, or a blend. Make arrangements accordingly. At least one luncheon or dinner meeting should be at the expense of the organization; but if too much money is spent on the delegates, some members will object.

4. Prepare an agenda and have it (and a general program) ready in advance. Be sure that notices, bulletins, and lists of speakers are clear,

plentiful, and readily available. If possible, send them in advance to all chapters or branches.

5. Set up a convention office as a central clearing-house for information, contacts, and assistance.

6. Keep meetings short and interesting. Vary the subject matter and speakers. Use seminars or committee meetings for special problems that are not interesting or suitable to the general assembly.

7. Get press coverage. Prepare press releases, ready to distribute. If possible, get photographers. TV coverage may be appropriate.

8. Use registration tables, badges, signs, page-boys, and other administrative helps, especially in the convention office and auditorium. Have sideroom committee sessions only while the main meeting is not in session.

9. Send "thank you" letters after the convention has been concluded.

10. Gather (and write down) comments and suggestions to guide future conventions. Do this during and immediately after the convention.

11. Remember that 1986 Tax Code §142(d) amended §170(k) to deny a charitable deduction to travel expenses involving a significant element of pleasure.

(See, Section 241, and Section 248.)

See: *Successful Meetings* Magazine note, above, at page 602.

§248. AGENDA FOR MEETINGS OF MEMBERS

Bylaws often establish the agenda (order of business) for certain kinds of meetings—especially for general, annual meetings. But a rigid formal agenda, not tailored to the purposes and problems of the particular meeting, is of doubtful value. Sometimes it is positively clumsy and undesirable. An agenda should be adopted in the bylaws only in very general terms, leaving plenty of room for adaptation to particular meetings and problems.

Agendas for *organization meetings* are set forth in Chapter 20.

An Agenda for a General Meeting

1. Members assemble at the appointed time and place.

2. Call to order by presiding officer.

3. Invocation by a minister, priest, or rabbi. (Ordinarily this applies only to convention meetings.)

4. Brief welcoming remarks by presiding officer.

5. Collection of delegates' credentials. (Ordinarily this applies only to convention meetings. Credentials may also be collected before the meeting assembles or at the door.)

6. Formal recognition of the due sending of notice, and of the presence of a quorum, are noted and recorded by the secretary.

7. List of those present is recorded. (This may be done later. At a convention, it may precede the meeting.)

8. Minutes of the previous meeting are read (or the reading is waived, by vote), corrected, and adopted.

9. Reports (especially financial reports) are delivered by various officers and by chairmen of important committees. Various pertinent recommendations are made. Discussion and voting may follow, or further committee studies may be ordered.

10. Inspectors of election, and tellers, are appointed and introduced.

11. Elections of officers and directors are conducted according to the procedure established by the bylaws. (Delegated votes and proxies may have been turned in earlier.)

12. Inspectors of election announce election results.

13. New officers and directors take their oaths.

14. Voting on important issues is conducted.

15. Old business that is still not concluded may be discussed at this point.

16. New business is introduced (followed by discussion and voting or by designation of committees to study various proposals).

17. Selection of next meeting date and place (if the bylaws do not determine these).

18. Recessional (closing prayer by minister, priest, or rabbi). This applies ordinarily only to convention meetings.

19. Adjournment.

20. (Optional). Social program(s).

Convention bureaus and services. (See Section 247.) Most major cities today have *convention bureaus,* maintained at public expense, to assist organizations in holding conventions in their cities. Indeed, there is much competition among cities to win conventions, which are valuable sources of local business.[78] Chambers of Commerce often offer services for convention planning. St. Petersburg, Florida, a very popular center for conventions, for example, has a special *Convention and Visitors Bureau* in its Chamber of Commerce, and so do nearby communities in its Tampa Bay and Gulf of Mexico beaches area. These organizations offer many services without charge. Use of such bureaus for information and assistance is very helpful in planning and holding a convention.

Convention services and supplies. In major cities, there are various companies that supply services and supplies for conventions. They can be found listed in telephone book yellow pages under the heading of "convention services and facilities."

Thus, for example, the list includes chair, table, china, and display rental companies, flower supplies, photographers, actors' and musicians' personnel agencies, caterers, reporters and stenographers, display and decoration designers and producers, hostesses, badge and banner companies, and many other kinds of services and supplies. [See SUCCESSFUL MEETINGS magazine.]

POINTS TO REMEMBER

- Provide in the bylaws for meetings and for their scheduling, calling, and procedures. Provide amply and in detail.
- Provide for all possible types of meetings.
- Provide alternatives, whenever possible, as to who may call meetings, when, and by what procedures.
- Local statutes provide that certain matters, such as amendments and mortgages, must be attended to only at meetings even if the bylaws do not so provide.
- Set quorum requirements with an eye to the probable attendance and with an eye to legal requirements.
- Use formal written notice for every important meeting. Check local statutes' requirements for formal notice on particular matters.
- Remember that the law may also require publication of notice.
- Adjourn meetings to another day only by formal resolution.
- Use formal waivers if you fail to send notice in advance, but do not depend on them as a regular substitute.
- Treat conventions and assemblies as general meetings of representatives—like a legislative session.
- Prepare for conventions in great detail. Suit the preparations to your organization's special character and situation.
- Prepare an agenda for every meeting, large or small.
- Appoint special committees to arrange and run conventions. Do not depend on amateurs, if you can get experienced people to do this.
- Make use of convention bureaus and services. Try to obtain the help of a "local arrangements" man or organization at the site selected for your convention.
- Be sure that your convention committee makes on-the-spot inspections and arrangements. Do not depend entirely on mail or telephone arrangements.
- Try to make the convention a "fun" gathering for members and their family members, as well as an efficient business meeting.
- But beware of tax law denial of charitable deduction of travel expenses if pleasure is a too significant element of the convention.

NOTES TO CHAPTER 24

1. *Jones v. Briley*, 593 So. 2d 391 (La. App., 1st Cir., 1991).

2. *See*, Henn and Alexander, *Corporations* §188 (3rd ed., 1983) that (p. 491): "Inherent, then, in the corporate setup is the idea that the shareholders (members) own the corporation, but the board of directors manages it."

3. See, Village Square Shopping Center Assn. v. Nelson, 522 So. 2d 163 (La. App. 1988); Revised Model Nonprofit Corp. Act, c.7 (ABA Exposure Draft, 1986). [Herein cited as RMN-PCA.]

4. RMN-PCA §7.01 (1986); Model Bus. Corp. Act §28; Cal. Corp. Code §600(b); N.Y. N-P-C Law, §603(a). Fla. Stat §617.070

5. Ohio Rev. Code, §1702.16.

6. Fl. St. §617.0701; Ga. Nonprofit Corp. Code, §14-3-206, 14-3-207.

7. N.Y. N-P-C Law, §603(b).

8. Ohio Rev. Code, §1702.26.

9. Ohio Rev. Code, §1729.12.

10. *E.g.*, of credit unions: Ohio Rev. Code, §1733.12.

11. *See, In re* Opinion of the Justices, 132 Me. 491, 167 A. 176, 179 (1933).

12. Ohio Rev. Code, §1702.16; and n.3.

13. *Ibid.*; see FL. St. §617.0701.

14. Permissive rather than mandatory in New York, where bylaws may provide for "two, three, four, or five classes" of directors. N.Y. N-P-C Law, §704.

15. RMN-PCA §7.04 (1986). Action without a meeting; Ohio Rev. Code, §1702.25; this must be recorded in writing and unless articles or regulations prohibit such; N.Y. N-P-C Law, §3614 (consent of all members). *And see*, Duke v. Markham, 105 N.C. 138; 10 S.E. 1003(1890); Stott v. Stott, 258 Mich. 547; 242 N.W. 747 (1932), Kappers v. Cast Stone Constr. Co., 184 Wis. 627; 200 N.W. 376 (1924). But even without a meeting, the corporation's acts may be binding, by estoppel. *See*, Kearneysville Creamery Co. v. American Creamery Co., 103 Va. 259; 137 S.E. 217; 51 A.L.R. 938 (1927); Sovereign Camp. W.O.W. v. Johnson, 64 S.W.2d 1084, 1087 (Tex. Civ. App. 1933).

16. American Hungarian Federation v. Nadas, 519 N.E. 2d 677 (Ohio App. 1987).

17. Nelson v. Intnati. Assn. of Bridge, Structural & Orn. Iron Workers, 680 F. Supp. 16 (D.D.C. 1988).

18. Klein v. Scranton Life Ins. Co., 139 Penna. Super. 369; 11 A.2d 770 (1940); Des Moines Life and Annuity Co. v. Midland Insur. Co., 6 F.2d 228 (D.C. Iowa 1925). But a notice in general terms, if it substantially states the purpose, is sufficient. *See*, Lawrence v. I.N. Parlier Estate, 15 Calif.2d 220, 100 P.2d 765 (1940).

19. RMN-PCA §7.03; 15 Penna. Stat., §5755 (after 6-month delay); 805 ILCS 105/107.03; N.Y. Genl. Corp. Law allows one-month delay: This applies to nonprofit corporations: *In re* Atwater, 85 N.Y.S.2d 738 (1948); Potter v. Patee, 493 S.W.2d 58 (Mo. App. 1973); N.Y. N-P-C Law §603.

20. *See* n. 18.

21. The statutes usually do not expressly state that a demand must be made, but common sense indicates this should be done.

22. *See* n. 19, and c.23 herein above.

23. N.Y. N-P-C Law, §604(b).

24. *See* n. 19, and *see*, Hamilton, *Corporations* (Black Letter Series) c. 7 (2d ed., 1986).

25. If the bylaws are silent, and if no express statute states who shall call meetings, the directors may call meetings. Walsh v. State *ex rel.* Cook, 199 Ala. 123; 74 S. 45 (1917); Ohio Rev. Code, §1702.17; FL. St. §617.0701.

26. N.Y. N-P-C Law, §603(a); Calif. Corp. Code, §5510; Ohio Rev. Code, §1702.17(B); Del. Code, tit. 8, §211; 805 ILCS 105/107.05; Minn. Stat., §317A.431; 15 Penna. Stat., §5755.

27. Caldwell v. Kingsberg, 451 S.W.2d 247 (Tex. 1970); State *ex rel.* Blackwood v. Brast, 98 W. Va. 596; 127 S.E. 507 (1925); Beggs. v. Myton Canal and Irrig. Co., 54 Utah 120 179 P. 984 (1919), Frankel v. 447 Central Park West Coop., 176 Misc. 701; 28 N.Y.S.2d 505 (1941). But if he attends merely in order to protest, this is not a waiver. People v. Matthiessen, 193 Ill. App. 328; *affd.*, 269 Ill. 499; 109 N.E. 1056 (1915); Ohio Rev. Code, §1702.19; N.Y. N-P-C Law, §606.

28. Cumberland Coal and Iron Co. v. Sherman, 20 Md. 117 (1863).

29. Sagness v. Farmers Coop. Creamery Co., 67 S.D. 379; 293 N.W. 365 (1940); Terry v. Eagle Lock Co., 47 Conn. 141; Naftalin v. La Salle Holding Co., 153 Minn. 482, 190 N.W. 887 (1922).

30. Rogers v. Hill, 289 U.S. 582, 53 S. Ct. 731, 77 L. Ed. 1385 (1933); Noted, 46 Harv. L. Rev. 854 (1933); 18 Minn. L. Rev. 192, 221 (1934).

31. RMN-PCA §7.02 (suggests at least 5 percent); or see Cal. Corp. Code §5510, Del. Corp. L. §211(d).

32. *See,* Aver v. Dressel, 118 N.E.2d 590 (N.Y. 1954); 48 ALR 2d 604; Darwin v. Belmont Ind., Inc., 199 N.W.2d 542 (Mich. 1972).

33. RMN-PCA §7.02; and Rev. Model Bus. Corp. Act §7.02.

34. This was former N.Y. Stock Corp. L., §52, and presumably the same concept would apply to nonprofit corporations. The N.Y. Bus. Corp. L. omitted this provision, possibly because it is mere common sense that hardly needs statutory authorization.

35. *Ibid.*

36. *See,* People v. American Institute of N.Y., 44 How. Pr. (N.Y.) 468; Marvin v. Manash, 175 Ore. 311, 153 P.2d 251 (1944); *In re* Election of Directors of Bushwick S.&L. Assn., 70 N.Y.S.2d 478 (1947).

37. McGraw-Hill Book Co., Inc. (1953).

38. Robert's *Rules of Order Revised* (1970 rev. ed.).

39. Three volume set (Prentice-Hall, Inc. 1958).

40. 2d ed., McGraw-Hill, New York, c. 1966.

41. Commissioner v. Vandergrift, 232 Penna. St. 53; 81 A. 153 (1911); Young v. Jebbett, 213 A.D. 774; 211 N.Y.S. 61 (1925); Alliance Coop. Ins. Co. v. Gasche, 93 Kans. 147; 142 P. 882 (1914); Landers v. Frank Street M.E. Church, 114 N.Y. 626; 21 N.E. 420 (1889).

42. *See* c. 23.

43. *See* c. 23.

44. *See* c. 18; N.Y. Bus. Corp. L., §601; *but cf.,* N.Y. N-P-C Law, §602 (bylaws adoptable by directors unless prohibited).

45. *E.g.,* N.Y. N-P-C Law, §801(1).

46. *E.g.,* Fla. Stat. §617.1202; N.Y. N-P-C Law §509 (2/3 vote of directors); Ohio Rev. Code, §1701.76 (sale of substantial assets); *but cf.,* Ohio Rev. Code, §1701.65, Fla. Stat. §617.1201(mortgages); N.Y. Bus. Corp. 1., §909(a).

47. N.Y. Bus. Corp. L., §§202(a)(7), 908. The analogy is even stronger in a nonprofit corporation; *cf.,* N.Y. N-P-C Law, §506(d).

48. *See,* Ohio Rev. Code, §1701.13(d), and old N.Y. Bus. Corp. L., §202(a)(12). The remark in n. 47, above, applies. Foundations, of course, are not necessarily so bound, due to their special nature.

49. N.Y. Genl. Corp. L., §45. N.Y. N-P-C Law §§801, 802, 803.

50. *See* Oleck, *Debtor-Creditor Law,* 221 (1959 Supp.). (Reprint ed. 1986).

51. Ohio Rev. Code, §1702.47(D). Fla. Stat. §617.1402.

52. *Jones v. Briley,* 593 So. 2d 391 (La. App. 1 Cir. 1991).

53. Application of McGovern, 180 Misc. 508; 44 N.Y.S.2d 132, 137 (1943), Mountain States Tel. and Tel. Co. v. People, 68 Colo. 487, 190 P. 513, 517 (1920). But the Ohio statute states that, in the absence of provision otherwise, a quorum shall be "the voting members present at any meeting of voting members." Ohio Rev. Code, §1702.22. *But see* Schroder v. Scotten, Dillon Co., 299 A.2d 431 (Del. Ch. 1972) (quorum obtained by trickery is invalid). RMN-PCA §7.22.

As to the more general view, *see also,* Hill v. Town, 172 Mich. 508, 138 N.W. 334; 42 L.R.A.

(n.s.) 799 (1912); State *ex rel.* Schwab v. Price, 121 Ohio St. 114; 167 N.E. 366, 63 A.L.R. 1100; Duffy v. Loft, Inc., 17 Del. Ch. 140; 151 A. 223 (1930); *affd.*, 17 Del. Ch. 376; 152 A. 849. N.Y. N-P-C Law, §608.

54. Coombs v. Harford, 99 Me. 426; 59 A. 529 (1904). Communist Party of the U.S. v. Commissioner, 332 F.2d 325 (D.C. Cir. 1964); Lewis v. Steinhart, 338 N.Y.S.2d 552 (N.Y. A.D. 1972).

55. Oleck & Green, *Parliamentary Law & Practice for Nonprofit Organizations*, (2nd ed., American Law Institute—American Bar Association, 1991), citing statutes and cases from various states; *California Corp. Code* §9211(a)(8); *N.Y. N-P-O Law* §708(d); *Matter of Gearing v. Kelly*, 182 N.E.2d 391 (NY 1962). [See §315.]

56. *E.g.*, Ohio Rev. Code, §1702.32. *See*, Benintendi v. Kenton Hotel, Inc., 294 N.Y. 112, 60 N.E.2d 829; 159 A.L.R. 280 (1945), which led to enactment in 1948 of N.Y. Stock Corp. L., §9(c) permitting a requirement of two-thirds or even of three-fifths but not of unanimous approval.

57. Ohio Rev. Code, §1702.21(A); Franklin Trust Co. v. Rutherford Elec. Co., 57 N.J. Eq. 42, 41 A. 488 (1898); 58 N.J. Eq. 584, 43A. 1098 (1899); N.Y. N-P-C Law, §608.

58. *See*, Morill v. Little Falls Mfg. Co., 53 Minn. 371, 55 N.W. 547 (1893).

59. Addi Laurenzano v. Einbender, 264 F. Supp. 356 (D.C. N.Y. 1966); Green v. Felton, 42 Ind. App. 675, 84 N.E. 166 (1908); Gilchrist v. Collopy, 119 Ky. 110, 82 S.W. 1018 (1904).

60. Boericke v. Weise, 68 Calif. App.2d 407; 156 P.2d 781 (1945) (time and place). No particular form is required unless bylaws or statutes specify. Citrus Growers Devel. Assn. v. Salt River Valley Water Users Assn., 34 Ariz. 105; 268 P. 773 (1928). *See*, Height v. Democratic Women's Luncheon Club of New Jersey, Inc., 131 N.J. Eq. 450, 25 A.2d 899 (1942) to the effect that members must be given notice of extraordinary proceedings or are not bound thereby; *also*, Strong v. Garvey Memorial Liberty Hall, 380 Pa. 236, 110 A.2d 244 (1955), notice must be sent to all members; State of Ohio v. Anti-Vivisection Society of Ohio, Inc., 185 N.E.2d 790 (Ohio App. 1962), where only a third of the members received notice, all action at meeting invalid; Stone v. Dean, 344 P.2d 649 (Okla. Sup. Ct. 1959), where merger attempt required more than regular notice of annual meeting; Estes v. Tompkins, 371 P.2d 86 (Okla. Sup. Ct. 1962).
    Purpose should be indicated. Rogers v. Hill, 60 F.2d 109 (2d Cir. 1932), *affd.*, 62 F.2d 1079 (1933); *cert. gtd.*, 289 U.S. 716; 53 S. Ct. 593; 77 L. Ed. 1469 (1933).

61. State v. Kreutzer, 100 Ohio St. 246; 126 N.E. 54 (1919). Unless statutes require certain specific notice; then the statute governs. Piedmont Press Assn. v. Record Publ. Co., 156 S. C. 43; 152 S.E. 721 (1930); *and see*, Oleck, *Proxy Voting Power in Nonprofit Organizations*, 14 Clev.-Mar. L. Rev. 273 (1965).

62. *See* the list in §242.

63. *See* the list in §242; N.Y. N-P-C Law, §605 (ten days, no more than 50).

64. *See*, N.Y. N-P-C Law, §605. *And see*, State *ex rel.* Webber v. Shaw, 103 Ohio 660; 134 N.E. 643 (1921). Affidavit of the publisher is proof of publication. Dolbear v. Wilkinson, 172 Calif. 366; 156 P. 488 (1916).

65. N.Y. N-P-C Law, §605; 15 Penna Stat., §5702.

66. Unless the bylaws require another notice. People *ex rel.* Loew v. Batchelor, 22 N.Y. 128 (1860); Morris Alpert and Sons, Inc. v. Kahler, 502 P.2d 98 (Colo. App. 1972); N.Y. N-P-C Law, §605(b); Ohio Rev. Code, §1702.18 (if time and place announced).

67. *See* n. 66.

68. Sagness v. Farmers Coop. Creamery Co., 67 S.D. 379; 293 N.W. 365 (1940); Naftalin v. La Salle Holding Co., 153 Minn. 482; 190 N.W. 887 (1922); N.Y. N-P-C Law, §605(b).

69. Ohio Rev. Code, §1702.19; People *ex rel.* Carus v. Matthiessen, 193 Ill. App. 328, *affd.*, 269 Ill. 499, 109 N.E. 1056 (1915). *See*, as to forms, 5 Oleck, *Modern Corporation Law* (1978 Supp.), forms 560, 561; N.Y. N-P-C Law, §606.

70. *Ibid.*

71. *See* n. 68; Opinion of Atty.-Genl., Mo. (1935) (waiver by proxy after the meeting is valid). Or, ratification: Howard v. Tatum, 81 W. Va. 561; 94 S.E. 965 (1918).

72. Frankel v. 447 Central Park West Corp., 176 Misc. 701; 28 N.Y.S.2d 505 (1941); Beggs v. Myton Canal and Irrig. Co., 54 Utah 120; 179 P. 984 (1919); N.Y. N-P-C Law, §606; Ohio Rev. Code, §1702.19; mere attendance without protest waives notice.

73. People *ex rel.* Carus, n. 69.

74. N.Y. N-P-C Law, §603(d).

75. *See* n. 74.

76. *See,* Duncan, *Trade Association Management,* c. 16 (rev. ed.: Natl. Inst. for Coml. and Trade Org. Executives, Chicago 1948); Bradley, *Role of Trade Associations and Professional Business Societies in America* (Penna. State Univ. Press, University Park, Pa. 1965).

77. *See,* Di Silvestro v. Sons of Italy Grand Lodge, 130 Misc. 494; 223 N.Y.S. 791 (1927); 129 Misc. 521; 222 N.Y.S. 203 (1927) (void bylaw provision as to *quorum* of delegates).

78. Write to local and state chambers of commerce for valuable information and assistance. Most of them have literature and brochures in stock, ready for immediate mailing to inquirers. Local tourist and convention bureaus will not only provide a wealth of information but often will perform other services such as seeing to the bulk of accommodations, and entertainment planning at no charge.

25

VOTING AND ELECTIONS

§249. VOTING PRINCIPLES, IN GENERAL

A few state statutes, such as Florida's 1992 revision, [§617.0721] say that "members are not entitled to vote except as conferred by the articles of incorporation or the bylaws." This is about as contrary to the idea of "voluntary organizations" as one can get.

"One man (or woman), one vote" is the essential principle of democracy, especially in nonprofit organizations. The American Bar Association's Model Nonprofit Corporation Act (1986 Revision Draft) says:[1] "Unless the articles or bylaws provide otherwise, each member is entitled to one vote on each matter voted on by the members."[2] But then the official comment adds that: "Corporations which wish to provide different voting rights may do so in their articles or bylaws. Different voting rights can be based upon the amount of dues paid or contributions made, the number of hours devoted to the corporation's activities, the net worth, sales volume, or number of outlets of a corporate member or innumerable other factors considered significant by the organization. These distinctions will be upheld by the courts unless they violate some federal or state law or are adopted in violation of some provision of the Model Act."[3]

Courts usually are hesitant to grant the extraordinary remedy of *Mandamus* to compel a nonprofit organization to do something (*e.g.*, hold an election) where its bylaws do not clearly require that.[4] But courts will compel or enjoin meetings and votes, by mandamus or injunction or other judicial remedies, in a proper case.[5] Exhaustion of internal remedies often must be proved before a court will accept such a case.[6]

A state has authority to prohibit the buying or selling of votes; but for "anything of value" is too vague to be constitutional as a standard or measure.[7]

§250. RIGHT TO VOTE

[This section consists of extracts from a Note by P.L. Nesbill in 16 Clev.-Mar. L. Rev. 384, used with permission.]

[As to voting control and power in business corporations, *see* 3 Oleck, *Modern Corporation Law*, cc. 57, 58 (1978 Suppl.).]

Statute provisions as to voting in nonprofit organizations are inadequate both in coverage and precision. There appears to be some divergence of views among the various courts as to the existence of a property right in voting aspects of nonprofit organizations. Since the right to earn a living has been deemed to be property within the concept of the Fifth Amendment to the Federal Constitution, *a fortiori* membership in a trade union, in the service of its interest, is a property right which the courts will protect.[8] The National Labor Relations Act recognizes that rights of members of unions are economic in nature, so as to constitute property rights.[9] It has been held that a member of a voluntary association, not a charity, has a property right in its assets.[10] An Ohio case even said that, "Inherent in memberships in churches, or any other nonprofit incorporated or unincorporated organizations and societies, is the right to a share of the organization's properties ... a property right does exist."[11] Yet, a member of a club organized as a corporation not for profit, whose membership is terminated, has no right or interest in the property of the corporation except such as is given him by the articles and regulations of the corporation.[12] In situations where life memberships are used, the member is a part owner of the property of the organization only during his lifetime.[13]

Some courts refuse to accept the property right theory. An Indiana court approached the right to vote in an election for officers of a voluntary association as a right stemming from membership, but treated it as a privilege extended by the organization's constitution to members in good standing.[14] The court proceeded to say, "Membership in an unincorporated association ... is a privilege and is neither a civil nor property right."[15] A like conclusion was reached by a New York court in response to a petition to set aside the election of directors of the New York State Council Knights of Columbus.[16] The court said that a member of a *charitable* corporation does not have a vested right to vote for its directors or trustees, as he has no interest in the property of the corporation.[17] The same conclusion was reached in an earlier New York decision which held that members of a charitable corporation, a hospital, did not have a vested right to vote for trustees, and that such a right was not constitutionally protected.[18]

In an attempt to resolve the problem, some courts have developed a contract theory which is used as a substitute for finding a property right. An early Massachusetts case held that "The bylaws constituted in effect a contract between the different members and the corporation."[19] This view also is followed in Alabama,[20] Illinois,[21] Kansas,[22] Louisiana,[23] Minnesota,[24] New York,[25] Ohio,[26] and Oklahoma.[27] (*Harington v. Sendall*, 1 Ch. 921, a 1903 decision, apparently maintains this same rule for England.) Members are presumed to be acquainted with the constitution, bylaws, and regulations.[28] One court pointed out that, "In churches, lodges, and all other like voluntary associations, each person, on becoming a member, either by express stipulation or by implication, agrees to abide by all rules and regulations adopted by the organization ..."[29]

A voluntary association may adopt bylaws and rules which will be controlling as to all questions of doctrine or internal policy,[30] provided such bylaws and rules are not immoral, unreasonable, contrary to public policy, nor in contravention of the law of the land.[31] The bylaws reflect a member's rights in the organization. In light of this, an appeal to a constitutional bill of rights (which is designed to protect the citizen against oppression by the *government*) is usually unsuccessful.[32] Since the constitution and bylaws of a voluntary association have no legal validity and effect except as contracts among members, they are binding only on members who are shown to have assented to them.[33]

Dissatisfied members of nonprofit organizations generally appeal to courts of equity. But the office and jurisdiction of a court of equity, unless enlarged by express statute, sometimes are said to be limited to the protection of rights of property.[34] As stated by an Ohio court ". . . courts of equity have no authority to interfere with the action of voluntary and unincorporated associations where no property right is involved."[35] Yet, the term "property right" is understood to include contract rights, and any civil right of a pecuniary nature, whether technically "property" or not.[36] In many cases, the slightest color of, or circumstances tending to suggest, a so-called "property right" is grounds for jurisdiction. This tendency indicates that the principle supposedly limiting the jurisdiction of equity to the protection and enforcement of property and contract rights lacks substantial basis. Some courts have said that equity will protect purely personal rights.[37] A federal court has clearly stated that:

> The doctrine that equity jurisdiction is limited to the protection of property rights conflicts with the familiar principle that equity may give preventive relief when the legal remedy of money damages, if available at all, is inadequate to redress a wrong. Obviously money has little in common with such personal rights or interests as reputation, domestic relations, or membership in nonprofit organizations.[38]

It then goes on to say that injunctions are much better suited to protect interests of personality than a speculative action for damages.[39] Ohio courts are in accord with the federal view, and have recognized that in a great number of cases the courts have issued injunctions to protect purely personal rights.[40]

Judicial interference in the internal affairs of a voluntary association is justified where there is a violation of contract obligations or an invasion of property rights.[41] Thus, courts will not hesitate to entertain jurisdiction and afford relief where property rights[42] or purely personal rights[43] are involved.

In *American Aberdeen-Angus Breeders' Association v. Fullerton*, the court held that a nonprofit corporation may make any reasonable regulation (*i.e.*, limiting voting rights) for election of directors by members or convention where no conflict with a state statute is present.[44] The same court in a later case reasoned that the State, through the legislature, retains the right to amend the statute, and the organization, pursuant to the statute, reserves the power to amend the

bylaws. It thus would follow that the right of members of a charitable corporation to vote is not constitutionally protected.[45] This rationale was followed by
New York in a case where the state legislature passed a statute amending the
charter of a charitable corporation so as to provide for the election of trustees
by trustees whose terms have not expired instead of by the members of the
organization.[46] The court stated that the right of members of a charitable corporation to vote for trustees is not a vested interest entitled to protection
under the Constitution. It further held that there was no denial of due process
of law by making the board of trustees self perpetuating and transferring the
right to vote from the members to the board itself. Prior to the *Mt. Sinai* decision the court had enlarged its holding to include membership in nonprofit
corporations, by finding that bylaw provisions creating a self-perpetuating
board of managers do not infringe on any property or other enforceable right
of members.[47]

    In the absence of rules to the contrary, an association acting through its
members may elect such officers as it chooses.[48] Regulation of the election is
by the articles of the association or the constitution and bylaws of the organization, or, if none exist, by the usage of the association and regulations adopted by it.[49] An Indiana court held that "The majority rule is final unless it violates property rights or liberties protected under the constitution and laws of
the state."[50] Elections must be held in accordance with the bylaws and constitution of the society.[51] If the action by a member is concerned solely with the question of proper title to an office in a club or other nonprofit organization, a
court of equity has no jurisdiction, the remedy of *quo warranto* being available.[52]

    It may thus be seen that the court will not interfere with the internal
affairs of a religious organization when no property rights are involved.[53] It has
been pointed out that courts will accept as conclusive the decision of an association tribunal except in cases involving a property right.[54] Lacking a method
for redress of grievances, a member of a nonprofit organization may turn to
the court of equity to enjoin any unlawful act by the organization towards one
of its members.[55] Minority stockholders in business corporations may bring an
action when the directors and majority have breached their fiduciary duties to
the minority.[56]

The *Ethical Practices Code* of the AFL-CIO states that:

> 1. Each member of a union should have the right to full and free partici-
> pation in union self-government. This should include the right (a) to vote
> periodically for his local and national officers, either directly by referendum
> vote or through delegate bodies, (b) to honest elections, (c) to stand for
> and hold office, subject only to fair qualification uniformly imposed, (d) to
> voice his views as to the method in which the union's affairs should be con-
> ducted.[57]

    It is evident that the right to vote in nonprofit organizations has been
judicially recognized but has received uneven protection.[58] As a general rule,
unless the right to vote is specifically restricted, every member of a nonprofit
organization is entitled to vote. The right to vote may be defined in the pro-

visions by which the organization is governed, and in that case the right to vote is restricted to those within the terms of the governing provision.[59] Illinois courts, for example, have held that an organization not for profit may adopt a constitution or bylaws by which the members can be deprived of the right to vote for the election of trustees.[60] As long as even one court will rule that the voting power is a basic contractual right which cannot be taken away without consent, some member will protest the deprivation or dilution of his voting power.

State statutes regulating voting rights of nonprofit organizations offer little help in assuring the right to vote. Most statutes permit articles or bylaws of the organization to limit or eliminate the members' voting rights.[61] The (old and the Revised) Model Nonprofit Corporations Act, showing the heavy influence of general business corporation law, distinctly fails to protect the individual member . . ."[62] [See §249, as to the Revised Act.]

§251. VOTING RULES, IN GENERAL

Parliamentary Law. Most questions and problems about voting and elections can be avoided by adopting, in advance, a set of guideline rules, such as those in: Oleck & Green, *Parliamentary Law & Practice for Nonprofit Organizations*, Amer. Law Inst.-A.B.A., (2d ed., 1991).

While provisions as to voting have been amplified in recent nonprofit corporation statutes, these provisions still are not very ample or specific.

Unincorporated association statutes are almost devoid of any rules as to voting. California's, New York's, and Ohio's unincorporated association statutes, for example, contain absolutely no provisions as to voting. The statement of voting rules for such associations is based largely on analogy with corporate voting and informal partnership voting, and on ordinary parliamentary procedure.

What is a vote? A *vote* as a noun, means the suffrage, voice, or choice of a person for or against a measure, or in the election of a person to office. It is not the same thing as a *ballot*, which is the instrument by which one expresses his choice.[63]

A *voter* is (1) a person who performs the act of voting, or (2) who has the qualifications entitling him to vote.[64]

Voting by ballot means the opposite of open, voice, or public voting. Secrecy is the essence of voting by ballot.[65]

Ohio's enactments, among the most complete nonprofit statutes in the nation, along with New York's provisions, illustrate the fragmentary nature of the voting legislation.

The main Ohio provision dealing with voting rights of members provides that:

> Except as otherwise provided in the articles or the regulations, each member, regardless of class, shall be entitled to one vote on each matter properly submitted to the members for their vote, consent, waiver, release, or

other action. The articles or the regulations may provide that voting at elections and votes on other matters may be conducted by mail. . . .[66]

It also contains a provision about proxy voting (see the next chapter), voting by corporate members,[67] special voting requirements for members or trustees (greater or less than majority votes),[68] and votes required for a rescission of a decision (must be the same as required for the original decision).[69] That is all.

New York's enactments say that the bylaws may make provisions as to qualifications of voters,[70] may allow bondholders to vote for directors in certain situations,[71] or may change the basic one-member, one-vote rule.[72] These statutes forbid sale of votes or proxies,[73] and require records and inspectors of election to be made available at vote meetings.[74]

Greater or less than majority vote rules. While majority vote usually is the basic system of decision of questions or of elections, that is not always true. Statutes in many states permit provision in the articles or bylaws for decision by greater than majority, or less than a majority vote.

For example, Ohio's statute permits provision for vote, on any action by the members or trustees, by "a greater proportion or number . . . than otherwise required."[75] California's 1980 statute allowed use of either a greater or less than majority vote.[76] California's current statute allows a "greater proportion" of votes to be mandated in the articles or bylaw.

Such special voting rules, of course, must be reasonable. Thus, the Michigan statute (referring to a quorum for directors' meetings) permits special rules to be set, but not less than one-third of the number of trustees.[77] The implication is that it would be improper to allow decision by less than one-third.

Special voting percentage rules normally should be provided only as to special matters, such as borrowing by the organization, sale of assets, change of purpose, dissolution, or the like.

In most (but not all) states, the right to vote ordinarily is deemed an inherent part of membership in a nonprofit organization.[78] Nonvoting membership, if used at all, is honorary rather than true membership. Restrictions on stock voting power, common in business corporations, and sometimes used by nonprofit organizations, are business-control devices.[79] *Voting control techniques,* such as stockholders' agreements, classification of shares, or voting trusts, are more characteristic of business than of nonprofit corporations.[80] Voting control of businesses by foundations is a special recent development.[81] New York's 1970 Not-For-Profit Corp. Law has extensive voting control rules. So does California's amended 1980 statute.[82]

Voting Agreements

The A.B.A. 1986 Revision of the Model Nonprofit Corporations Act [§7.30] specifically allows members to sign a *voting agreement,* valid for a period of up to ten years, and makes such agreement specifically enforceable; but in "public benefit corporations such agreements must have reasonable purposes not inconsistent with the corporation's public or charitable purposes." It will be interesting to see how many states adopt this proposal.

Who may vote. The records of the organization (*e.g.,* membership lists) usually determine who is entitled to vote.[83] Usually the right to vote is determined when the meeting is held in which the voting is to be done.[84] [See §255].

Labor union elections. The Labor-Management Reporting and Disclosure Act of 1959 (Title IV) made provisions for the election of union officers, aimed at safeguarding democratic processes. Much of what is said in this book applies to labor unions as well as other types of nonprofit organizations.

A pamphlet published by the United States Department of Labor, entitled "Requirements for Electing Union Officers," may be obtained from the Superintendent of Documents, Government Printing Office, Washington, D.C. 20402. It contains a simple explanation of the law in question and answer form. Order as L1.48:5/3.

§252. VOTING BY NONMEMBERS

Certain nonprofit statutes of New York State expressly refer to voting by persons or organizations other than members. They grant voting rights to holders of stock in cemetery corporations, which formerly could be organized on a stock basis there (the old cemetery corporations still exist).[85] Such corporations now must allow lot owners to vote, in person or by proxy, on the basis of one vote per lot owned.[86]

Voting by security holders. New York's statute[87] permits the bylaws to "authorize holders of bonds of the corporation to vote for directors, and (to) apportion the number of votes that may be cast with respect to the bonds on the basis of the amount of bonds held."

The purpose of such a law is to give to lenders and mortgagees some measure of control of the organization in case of default on the loan or mortgage. Without such a security arrangement available in case of need, lenders would refuse loans in many cases. New York's 1970 Statute has detailed rules as to this. So does California's 1980 Law.[88]

Many states have similar provisions for the protection of bondholders or other creditors—for example, Delaware, Minnesota, Ohio, and Virginia.[89] Case law to the same effect is found in Massachusetts.[90] In Illinois, on the other hand, the granting of voting power to bondholders was viewed as improper and unconstitutional,[91] until 1985, when a drastic revision of the Illinois Not-for-Profit Corporation Act[92] expanded the loan and other rules of the state. Today it is not unusual for statutes to allow the granting of voting power to creditors if and when that is necessary to induce them to make loans to nonprofit corporations. Thus, the bylaws may authorize the granting of some voting power to a creditor if and when the corporation defaults on a loan to it by that creditor.

§253. MULTIPLE VOTING POWER

Basically, in nonprofit organizations, the rule is one-vote-per-member, unless the articles or bylaws provide otherwise.[93] Some organizations do apportion voting power as to certain matters in terms of classification of members (*e.g.*, two votes for life membership holders, one for other members, in elections).

In one much-cited case, a charitable corporation employed shares of stock instead of membership certificates. An attempt to grant each member one vote for each share of stock he owned was held to be invalid and void.[94]

It seems to be public policy in most states to allow one vote per member in nonprofit corporations.[95] Business corporations commonly base shareholders' voting rights on the number of shares held, and also issue nonvoting preferred stock.[96]

Cumulative or multiple voting. In business corporations, a device for the protection of minority stockholders, called *cumulative voting*, is permitted by statute in some states, is mandatory in some, and is not provided for in others.[97] Florida's statute [§617.0721(4)] lets the articles or bylaws allow it.

This system gives to each "vote" (*i.e.*, share of stock) a number of votes equal to the number of officers to be chosen, at a given election. The shareholder (voter) may concentrate the whole number of his votes on one person, or distribute them as he wishes among several directorship candidates. For instance, if ten directors are to be elected, he may cast ten votes for one person, or five votes for each of two persons etc. Thus the minority shareholders, by concentrating their votes on one or two candidates friendly to them, can assure the election of these persons. This system is intended to secure some representation for the minority.[98]

The (old and new) Model Nonprofit Corporation Act, of the American Law Institute and the American Bar Association, contains a suggested provision for cumulative voting.[99] A few states, such as California, Florida, Indiana, and Pennsylvania, have adopted such a provision.[100]

Some states had rejected the idea, for nonprofit corporations.[101] The Ohio statute, for example, in the Committee Comment dealing with adoption of the Model Act provision, specifically excluded the cumulative voting part.[102] But *multiple voting* (*i.e.*, one vote for every $100 subscribed) was allowed in Tennessee, as long as each member had at least one vote.[103] In 1987 Tennessee adopted the ABA Revised Model Nonprofit Corporation Act of 1986.

Staggered elections and cumulative voting. Statutes based on the Model Acts (for business and nonprofit corporations) of the A.L.I.-A.B.A., above mentioned, follow the Model suggestions to have both cumulative voting and staggered elections (*i.e.*, rotating boards of directors).

Classification of directors, with differing terms of office, is meant to assure constant presence of experienced directors on the board.[104]

When both devices are included in a charter, the cumulative voting provision may be made meaningless by holding periodic elections at which only one or two directors are elected at a given election. Then the "bullet voting" of the minority will always be defeated by the majority, which also has the power to cumulate its votes.

It has been held that a provision to classify the board of directors is in conflict with a provision to vote cumulatively, and is unlawful, in Illinois and West Virginia; but in Pennsylvania, on the other hand, such provision has been held to be lawful.[105]

The prevailing view seems to be that use of such conflicting rules is improper, unless enough offices are to be filled, at any given election, to enable minority voters to utilize the cumulative voting right.[106]

Classification of members (and voting powers). Occasionally an organization will grant more than one vote to each member who belongs to a stated class of members (*e.g.*, members who are donors). Thus a grant of one vote for every $1,000 contributed was upheld by a California court in one case, though a grant of one vote per lot owned in a nonprofit cooperative subdivision was overruled by another California court. The new California statute permits classification and granting of different membership class voting powers, and all sorts of other unique arrangements.[107]

§254. VOTING BY PROXY, IN GENERAL

[See the next chapter, as to *Proxies.*]
A *proxy* is a person substituted or appointed by another to vote or act for him; or the instrument containing the appointment of such person.[108]

The power to vote by proxy, in nonprofit organizations, now is affirmed by statute in most states, although it did not exist at common law.[109]

While proxies are the chief device for self-perpetuation of management, and this tendency is aided by such legislation as that proposed by the Model Business Corporation Act,[110] they are widely used by business and nonprofit organizations.

Most nonprofit corporation laws now specifically allow proxy voting. Some statutes, such as that of Ohio, however, forbid proxy voting by members who are natural persons unless the articles or bylaws expressly provide otherwise.[111]

Directors probably should *not* vote by proxy, although most statutes are silent or not clear on this point. Thus the Model Nonprofit Corporations Act (1986 Proposal) §8.24 "Quorum and Voting" is pointedly silent on this, and so is §7.24 "Proxies." And the typical Ohio statute seems to disfavor (but tolerate) provisions for proxy voting, even by members who are natural persons, as noted above; yet the statute governing Executive Committee action permits decisions to be reached "by a writing or writings signed by all of its members." Executive Committee members must be trustees. It seems that court decisions view proxy voting by trustees as a delegation of their powers (and duties) to exercise their own discretion in management.[112] (*See* the next chapter.)

Most charters or bylaws expressly provide for voting by proxy.[113] But their

failure to do so does not abridge the right.[114] Even an express bylaw requirement that voting be done in person cannot destroy the right to vote by proxy—
certainly not where the right is expressly or impliedly recognized by some
statute of the state.[115]

A *proxy* is a person who is deputized by another to represent him and act
for him, especially in voting at a meeting.[116] He is given the authority of an
attorney-in-fact (a power of attorney) to vote on behalf of the person who has
the real power to vote. The term may also mean the written authorization
given to such a representative.[117]

A typical general statute governing the power to vote by proxy is that of
New York. It states that "Every member entitled to vote at a meeting of members or to express consent or dissent without a meeting may authorize another person or persons to act for him by proxy.[118]"

Proxies are discussed fully in the next chapter.

§255. VOTING LISTS

Statutes often require corporations to keep lists and records about their members (shareholders), available for inspection by persons entitled to see them,
at the corporation's main office or its "registrar's" office.[119] This is a common-
law right, insofar as nonprofit organizations are concerned.[120]

The ABA Model Non-Profit Corporations Act Revision of 1986 [§7.20]
specifically requires the corporation to prepare, and make available to members, a list of its members and their addresses, before a meeting. The members, or their agents or attorneys, are entitled, on written demand, to make
copies, at their own expense, at reasonable times. The list must be available at
the meeting. Refusal to allow the member to inspect the lists may result in a
court-ordered inspection, with the corporation ordered to pay the expenses.
But the action taken at the meeting is not invalid unless the written demand
was made in advance.

In Idaho, statutory penalties may be imposed on nonprofit corporations
for failing to allow a member to inspect its books and records.[121]

Elements of a member's (shareholder's) right of action for bad-faith
denial of the right to inspect (and copy from) corporate records are: (1) Proper written demand, (2) Bad-faith refusal, (3) Proof of cost (and expenses) of
a proceeding to enforce such right (including special damages). Burden of
proof is on the member.[122]

An unsuccessful candidate for director of a ranch association has no *pos-
sessory interest*, necessary to maintain an action for trespass to chattels, in *voting
records*, by way of an untimely request for recount or a resolution requiring candidates to sign releases indicating satisfaction with the vote's accuracy. Breach
of fiduciary duty is not indicated if association voting records are *lost by officers*,
absent proof of damages beyond nominal damages.[123]

§256. ELECTIONS AND ISSUES, IN GENERAL

Provision of rather detailed regulations for elections usually is made in the charter and bylaws. These may include rules for the election of delegates or representatives to assemblies or conventions.[124]

Directors, other than those named in a certificate of incorporation, must be elected by the members and other persons entitled to vote.[125]

Occasionally statutes provide express voting and election rules for certain kinds of organizations. The New York statute permits election of YMCA delegates on the basis of one delegate per ten members.[126] But such precise provisions are unusual.

The California statute, effective 1980, contains extraordinarily detailed provisions about voting and elections.[127]

Unless the charter, the bylaws, or statutes provide otherwise, a majority vote (out of the total number of votes cast) decides an issue or an election.[128] This is so even when the majority vote is not a numerical majority of the number of members, nor of the number of those present at the election meeting.[129] Any provision is strictly construed, and must be quite clear and specific, if it is to change this "rule of simple majority."[130]

Higher-than-majority voting may be required by the charter or bylaws— so long as they do not require unanimous votes, or votes so close to unanimity that they defeat the basic control by the members.[131] (*See* Sections 251, 252.)

Statutes require a two-thirds vote for certain specific issues. Thus, a two-thirds vote (of directors, in many cases) often is required for the making of a sale, mortgage, or lease of corporate assets.[132]

Statutes generally require annual election of directors by the members.[133] Even for an insolvent or dormant corporation, such elections may, and should, be conducted.[134] Nor may the directors or officers directly or indirectly take this power away from the members.[135]

Members may agree among themselves to vote for certain persons.[136] But, of course, they may not sell their votes.[137]

Nominations. Once nominations have been closed, no others may be made;[138] but *write-in* of names is not thereby always (in all states) barred. Such write-ins may lead to election.[139]

It is generally deemed unnecessary to second a nomination for the office of director. But seconds are required for most other purposes. Bylaws often make express provision for nominations. Specific provisions forestall disputes. [See, herein, the chapter on Parliamentary Law.]

§257. BALLOTING

Casting ballots is, after all, only a method of determining the will or opinion of the voting body. The exact method is secondary. The voting may be by written or printed ballot, by different colored balls or pellets, by voice or roll call, or by show of hands. It may be secret or open. It may be by signature on a document stating the proposition in issue. It may be by mail if bylaws so provide.

The terms *vote* and *ballot* are used interchangeably.[140] But, more precisely, a ballot is an instrument whereby a choice may be expressed, while a vote is the choice itself.[141]

Unless statutes specify a method of balloting for a particular issue or election, the bylaws may provide any reasonable method.

A member is entitled to cast one vote for each office that the election is to fill. The bylaws may not validly cut down this right.[142] Conversely, the casting of fractional votes is improper unless such a procedure is expressly permitted by the bylaws.[143]

Time allowed to complete the voting. Voting ordinarily is completed on one given day, at a given hour—but not necessarily so. Voting may extend over a period of days or even longer. For example, one director may be elected at a meeting, and another director at a subsequent meeting.[144]

Closing of the polls. The physical closing of the polls is not the completion of an election or vote. If additional votes then are accepted this does not invalidate the entire vote, provided that the result has not yet been announced.[145] Of course, the acceptance of late votes may be a source of dispute, and is best avoided. Exact rules are desirable.

Until the formal announcement of the result, a member may change his vote or even vote additional proxies in his possession, unless the bylaws forbid.[146]

True *closing of the polls* occurs when the officer in charge of the election announces the result.[147] Thereafter, no further votes or changes may validly be accepted.[148] But an announcement of the result by a member, or even by a teller who counts the votes, is not a formal closing of the polls.[149]

Rival voting or elections. If two factions conduct rival meetings and rival voting, the first one completed is *prima facie* valid. Of course, this holds only until the question is settled or adjudicated.[150] (*See also* Section 258.)

Challenged votes. If the validity of a proxy or the right of a member to vote is challenged, examination and cross-examination should be permitted, and proof should be taken. But this should be done before the actual voting time. Disruption of the voting by a surprise challenge should not be permitted.[151] Preferably, the bylaws should make provisions for *inspectors of election*, whose determinations are *prima facie* evidence of validity.[152] One to three persons usually serve as "inspectors of election" (also called "tellers" or "supervisors"). [See §§258, 259.]

Voting methods, and *motions,* and other aspects of the election process may involve detailed principles and rules of parliamentary procedure. *See,* Oleck, *Parliamentary Law for Nonprofit Organizations,* c. 8 and Chart of Procedures (pp. xii and xiii) (Amer. Law Inst.—Amer. Bar Assn., 1979); Oleck & Green, *Parliamentary Law & Practice for Nonprofit Organizations,* (2d ed., 1991; American Law Inst.—Amer. Bar Assn. Join Comm, American Law Institute, 4025 Chestnut St., Philadelphia, PA 19104. [*See also* the list in Chapter 51, herein.]

The organization's records should be at the voting place. They settle, for the time being, the right of a member to vote. The chairman or president may not decide who may and who may not vote unless the bylaws, the charter, or specific statutes permit him to do so.[153] The corporate books are the basic arbiters.[154]

Concerning challenge procedures, *see* the Index and Sections 250 and 251.

Strong measures, such as injunctions in disputed elections or votes, can be used but are not favored by the courts. This holds for court appointment of a special master to oversee a vote.[155]

FORM No. 125

Ballot for Election

. . . . . Association, Inc.,

Annual Election of Directors

The undersigned, being a member in good standing of the . . . . . Association, hereby votes for the following named persons to serve as Directors for the period . . . . . . , 19 . . , to . . . . . . , 19 . . .

. . . .
. . . .

.... (L.S.)

By .... (Proxy)

[*Note*: When a member himself votes, the last line is left blank. A proxy signs the member's name and also his own.]

FORM NO. 126

Ballot on Resolution

. . . . . . Association, Inc.

Special Meeting of Members   . . . . . . , 19 . .

On the following proposed Resolution:
[Set forth the resolution]
The undersigned votes

For the resolution.
                                   [Mark one]
Against the resolution.

.... (L.S.)

By .... (Proxy)

[See the Index as to *Resolutions* and *Bylaws*.]

§258. CHALLENGED ELECTIONS

[See §257, at n. 151, 152.]

When the entire result of an election is challenged, a serious problem exists. Such a challenge and dispute can easily be fatal to a nonprofit organization. Eligibility of voters, correctness of procedure, and interpretation of bylaws are closely interwoven in these cases.

Unless the charter or bylaws grant the power to his discretion, the chairman or president may not settle a disputed right to vote.[156]

If no bylaw or charter provision exists, the members may settle such a dispute by a vote on it, subject to court review.[157]

A disputed election usually is not void *per se.* Its propriety must be settled first. Usually a change in the result of an election caused by illegal votes is the basis for legal voiding of the election.[158]

Even when officers or directors are illegally elected, they are nevertheless *de facto* officers or directors, with such powers as the power to call a meeting required by the bylaws, until their election is duly set aside.[159]

Warning: Use of *summary* court proceedings (*e.g.,* injunction) to set aside an election is improper when fundamental issues of voting rights are the ultimate criteria. Such issues must be settled by *plenary* proceedings (*e.g.,* full hearings, on due notice).[160]

Even when two *rival elections* are held, a court may consider the votes at both in deciding the question involved.[161]

Trial of a candidate for election in a *labor union,* held just before the election and based on campaign statements, is *interference* with (reprisal against) union members.[162]

Statutory procedures. In some states, detailed statutory provisions cover challenged elections. Such statutes are most helpful. In New York, for example, they provide as follows:

1. Any aggrieved person may apply to a Special Term of the Supreme Court, on notice to other parties, for an *immediate* hearing of the question of a challenged election. The court then may confirm the election or order a new one.[163]

2. Correction of an error in an election—for example, by the inspectors of election—may be accomplished by more summary proceedings under another statute.[164] These proceedings, though summary in time, provide for plenary hearing.[165]

3. Even such organizations as federal saving and loan organizations are subject to these statutory procedures.[166]

4. A party who seeks to use these procedures may be *aggrieved* either in that he is adversely affected or in that the result of the election is improper or inequitable.[167] But mere *irregularity* does not void an election.[168]

5. If the applicable bylaws under which an election was held (*e.g.,* amend-

ments) were invalid, an election held under them is invalid and may be set aside.[169]

6.   If a particular practice in elections is customary in the organization, though contrary to the bylaws, it will be upheld by the court.[170] Similarly, acquiescent conduct bars later objection.[171] And delay beyond a reasonable time, in objecting, also bars later objection.[172]

7.   The court may not pass upon the validity of the qualifications of voters in advance, but must merely confirm an election or order a new one.[173]

8.   The forms used in these proceedings are the usual local legal forms of petitions in special proceedings.[174]

9.   Appeals are not permitted, under these statutes, as to the court's appointment of a referee to hear the dispute.[175]

§259. INSPECTORS OF ELECTION

[See §257, at n. 150, 151.]

Inspectors of election (or *supervisors*, or *judges of election*) should oversee the conduct of a vote, in an election or any other voting. Most states encourage this salutary method of forestalling disputes.

Inspectors are most important in business corporation voting[176] but not mandatory unless the bylaws so provide and a member demands enforcement of these bylaws.[177] The demand of a member for inspectors, even when not backed by bylaws, ordinarily must be honored.[178]

The president or chairman usually appoints the inspectors of election. But if a member so demands, they must be elected.[179] Two or more inspectors must be selected.[180] If none are appointed, or if those selected fail to appear, the members may elect new ones at the meeting.[181]

An inspector need not be a member; he may even be an officer or a candidate for office.[182] That a candidate for office should be an inspector of an election is, of course, undesirable. The same holds for an officer who has any conceivable interest in the voting.

When inspectors of election are not used, the presiding officer should at least appoint *tellers* to count the votes.

Inspectors ordinarily are required to take an oath of office, but their failure to do so does not invalidate the election.[183] However, if an inspector fails to take the oath, and this (or any act of his) is challenged at the time, he must take the oath; otherwise, all his acts are improper and invalid.[184]

Any fraudulent conduct by inspectors, or by officers in relation to such inspectors, results in liability for damages to persons affected.[185]

Inspectors' duties and powers. Inspectors of election are primarily administrative officers.[186] But they do have some discretion in running the election or vote.[187]

Fundamentally they must base their acceptance or rejection of ballots on the records of the organization.[188] But they, like others interested, may challenge any vote.[189] Their objections, like those of others, are subject to court review.[190]

The inspectors' administration of the voting should be practical and reasonable. For example, they may keep the polls open after the appointed closing time if this is necessary in order to permit fair casting of ballots.[191] Inspectors have a reasonably wide practical discretion in such administrative decisions.[192]

Once the inspectors have counted the ballots, they ordinarily may not again examine them in order to reject some, and thus change the result of the vote.[193]

Challenge procedure. When a voter's right to vote is challenged, the voter must in some states take an oath as to his right to vote. This oath ordinarily affirms primarily that the voter has not sold his vote.[194]

Procedures for handling challenges are quite completely left to the discretion of the inspectors of election in some states.[195]

POINTS TO REMEMBER

- Provide detailed voting rules in the bylaws. They prevent disputes and save much time.
- Prepare and distribute copies of voting rules.
- Do not rely on the statutes to provide detailed voting regulations.
- Remember that nonmembers, such as creditors, can be given voting rights. Give them sparingly.
- Proxy voting always is proper for members, if bylaws so provide.
- In special types of organizations, such as cooperatives, see your local statutes as to the right to vote by proxy.
- Do not try to bar rights to vote by proxy.
- Directors may not vote by proxy, in some states.
- Avoid higher-than-majority voting rules, except in special matters.
- Avoid use of multiple-voting power devices.
- Provide detailed rules for balloting.
- Use written ballots whenever convenient, or when the vote is important.
- Save the marked ballots for a reasonable time.
- Avoid disputes over elections. Like the plague, they destroy the organization.
- Use court action to enforce rights only when truly necessary.
- Make provisions for inspectors of election in the bylaws.
- Always select inspectors of election. Select them with care. Do not interfere with them, once they are selected, unless absolutely necessary.
- Consult texts on Parliamentary Law for Nonprofit Organizations.

NOTES TO CHAPTER 25

1. ABA Revised Model Nonprofit Corp. Act §7.21(a) [1986 Exposure Draft].

2. *Ibid.*, Comment; and *see* §6.10 as to permitted differences or classes authorized by the articles or bylaws.

3. *Ibid.*, Official Comment.

4. Lawnwood Medical Center v. Cassimally, 471 S.2d 1346 (Fla. 2d D.C. App., 1985); M. Lane, *Legal Handbook for Nonprofit Organizations*, 79 (1980).

5. *See*, Henn and Alexander, *Corporations*, 510 (3rd ed., 1983).

6. *Anno.*, 48 A.L.R.2d 615, 630.

7. *Commonwealth v. Foley*, 798 S.W. 2d 947 (Ky., 1990).

8. *See*, DeMille v. American Federation of Radio Artists, 31 Cal.2d 139, 187 P.2d 769, 175 A.L.R. 382, *cert den*, 333 U.S. 876 (1947), citing, Lo Bianco v. Cushing, 117 N.J. Eq. 593, 117 A. 102 (1935); Dusing v. Nuzzo, 29 N.Y.S.2d 882, *aff'd*. 31 N.Y.S.2d 849 (1941) and Cameron v. International Alliance, 118 N.J. Eq. 11,176 A. 692, 697, 700, 97 A.L.R. 594 (1935).

9. National Labor Relations Act, 29 U.S.C.A. Supp., §101 amending §§8a(3), (5), and 9 (3).

10. Bacon v. Paradise, 318 Mass. 649, 63 N.E.2d 571 (1945), citing, Balukonis v. Lithuanian Roman Catholic Benefit Society, 272 Mass. 366, 172 N.E. 505 (1930); Hamaty v. St. George Ladies Society, 280 Mass. 58, 181 N.E. 775 (1932).

11. Randolph v. First Baptist Church, 68 Ohio L. Abs. 100, 120 N.E.2d 485, 488 (1954).

12. Chestnut Beach Association v. May, 44 Ohio App. 217, 184 N.E. 856 (1933); DeBruyn v. Golden Age Club of Cheyenne, 399 P.2d 390 (Wyo. 1965).

13. Flaherty v. Manufacturers' Club of Philadelphia, 104 Pa. Super 546, 159 A. 209 (1932).

14. State *ex rel* Givens v. Superior Court of Marion County, 233 Ind. 235, 117 N.E.2d 553 (1954).

15. *Ibid.*, 117 N.E.2d at 555, citing, 7 C.J.S., *Associations*, §23, p. 56.

16. Petition of Sousa, 203 N.Y.S.2d 3 (Sup. Ct., 1960). *Also see* McClintock, *Equity*, 434 (2d ed. 1948).

17. *Ibid.*, 203 N.Y.S.2d at 5.

18. *In re* Mt. Sinai Hospital, 250 N.Y. 103, 164 N.E. 871 (1928); *see also* Westlake Hospital Association v. Blix, 13 Ill.2d 183, 148 N.E.2d 471, *app. dism.* 358 U.S. 43, 79 S. Ct. 44, 3 L. Ed.2d 43 (1958).

19. Boston Club v. Potter, 212 Mass. 23, 98 N.E. 614, 615 (1912), citing, Flint v. Pierce, 99 Mass. 68, 70, 96 Am. Dec. 691 (1868); Dolan v. Court Good Samaritan, 128 Mass. 437 (1880).

20. Waugaman v. Skyline Country Club, 277 Ala. 495, 172 So.2d 381 (1965).

21. Bostedo v. Board of Trade, 227 Ill. 90, 81 N.E. 42 (1907); Werner v. International Association of Machinists, 1 1 Ill. App.2d 258, 137 N.E.2d 100 (1956), *cert. den.* O'Brien v. Matual, 14 Ill. App.2d 173, 144 N.E.2d 446 (1957). The latter two cases both involve disputes in labor unions and point out how the rule in the leading case is applied.

22. Lake of the Forest Club v. Buttles, 142 Kan. 538, 51 P.2d 18 (1935).

23. Colonial Country Club v. Richmond, 19 La. App. 272, 140 So. 86, 87 (1932), citing the rule in 11 C.J. 924; Elfer v. Marine Engineers Beneficial Association No. 12, 179 La. 383, 154 So. 32 (1934), citing 5 C.J. *Associations*, §72, p. 1355.

24. Anderson v. Amidon, 114 Minn. 202, 130 N.Y. 1002 (1911); Rensch v. General Drivers, Helpers, and Truck Terminal Emp. Local 120, 268 Minn. 307, 129 N.W.2d 341 (1964), illustrating the result of a breach of the contract on the part of the union.

25. People v. New York Motor Boat Club, 70 Misc. 603, 129 N.Y.S. 365 (1911), showing that

a member following the method prescribed in the bylaws for resignation was acting in accordance with contract.

26. Leahigh v. Beyer, 67 Ohio L. Abs. 69, 116 N.E.2d 458 (1953), which holds that having established the contractual basis for membership in unions, internal remedies within the bylaws must be exhausted before resorting to the courts, and a bylaw denying the right to appeal is not unconstitutional.

27. Oklahoma Association of Insurance Agents v. Hudson, 385 P.2d 453 (Okla. 1963).

28. Colonial Country Club v. Richmond, *supra* n. 23.

29. Langer v. North Central Association of Colleges and Secondary Schools, 23 F. Supp. 694, 699 (D.C. Ill. 1936), *aff'd.*, 99 F.2d 697 (7th Cir. 1938).

30. Bostedo v. Board of Trade, *supra* n. 20; Ginossi v. Samatos, 3 Ill. App.2d 514, 123 N.E.2d 104 (1954); Campbell v. Brotherhood of Railroad Trainmen, 4 Ohio App.2d 81, 212 N.E.2d 650 (1965).

31. Greene v. Board of Trade, 174 Ill. 585, 51 N.E. 599 (1898).

32. *In re* Mt. Sinai Hospital, *supra* n. 12; Westlake Hospital Association v. Blix, *supra* n. 18.

33. Leahigh v. Beyer, *supra* n. 26, *obiter dictum.*

34. State *ex rel.* Moyer v. Baldwin, 77 Ohio St. 532, 546, 83 N.E. 907 (1908); Riggs v. Cincinnati Waiters Alliance Local, 5 Ohio N.P. 386, 8 Ohio Dec. N.P. 565 (1898); *See* Oleck, *Maxims of Equity Re-Appraised*, 6 Rutgers L. Rev. 528 (1952).

35. State *ex rel.* Ohio High School Athletic Assn. v. Judges of the Court of Common Pleas of Stark County, 173 Ohio St. 329, 181 N.E.2d 261 (1962), quoting from 5 Ohio Jur.2d 440, §7 and Boblitt v. Cleveland, Cincinnati, Chicago and St. Louis Ry. Co., 73 Ohio App. 339, 56 N.E.2d 348 (1943).

36. International News Service v. Associated Press, 248 U.S. 215, 236, 63 L. Ed. 211 (1918).

37. Randolph v. First Baptist Church, *supra* n. 11, 489 ff. has an excellent treatment of this point; Stark v. Hamilton, 149 Ga. 227, 99 S.E. 861 (1919), in this case the court granted a prohibitive injunction against a man who had induced a minor girl to abandon her parental home and live with him; *also see* 6 Am. Jur.2d, *Associations*, §40.

38. Berrien v. Pollitzer, 83 U.S. App. D.C. 23, 165 F.2d 21, 22 (1947) referring to Chafee, *Does Equity Follow the Law of Torts?* 75 U. of Pa. L. Rev. 1, 27, 35 (1926–27).

39. *Ibid.*, quoting from Chafee, *The Internal Affairs of Associations Not for Profit*, 43 Harv. L. Rev. 933, 938 (1929–30).

40. Snedaker v. King, 111 Ohio St. 225, 145 N.E. 15 (1924). *See* dissenting opinion of Marshall, C.J., at 245, for this analysis.

41. Green v. Obergfell, 73 U.S. App. D.C. 298, 121 F.2d 46, 138 A.L.R. 258, *cert den.* 314 U.S. 637 (1941); Werner v. International Association of Machinists, *supra* n. 20; Potter v. Patee, 493 S.W.2d 58 (Mo. App. 1973).

42. *Supra* n. 34.

43. *Supra* n. 37.

44. American Aberdeen-Angus Breeders' Association v. Fullerton, 325 Ill. 323, 329, 330, 156 N.E. 314 (1927); Mackey v. Moss, 278 Ala. 713, 175 So.2d 749 (1965).

45. Westlake Hospital Association v. Blix, *supra* n. 18.

46. *In re* Mt. Sinai Hospital, *supra* n. 18.

47. Bailey v. American Society for Prevention of Cruelty to Animals, 282 App. Div. 502, 125 N.Y.S.2d 18 (1953) *affd.* 307 N.Y. 679; Petition of Sousa, *supra* n. 16; Leahigh v. Beyer, *supra* n. 26.

48. Ostrom v. Greene, 161 N.Y. 353, 55 N.E. 919 (1900).

49. Grand Rapids Guard v. Bulkley, 97 Mich. 610, 57 N.W. 188 (1893); Strempel v. Rubing, 4

N.Y.S. 534 (1889); *In re* Osteopathic Hospital Ass'n. of Delaware, 41 Del. Ch. 369, 195 A.2d 759 (1963).

50. Standsberry v. McCarty, 238 Ind. 338, 149 N.E.2d 683, 686 (1958); State *ex rel.* Givens, *supra* n. 14; 45 Am. Jur., Religious Societies, §61.

51. Long v. Harvey, 177 Pa. 473, 35 A. 869 (1896).

52. Hornady v. Goodman, 167 Ga. 555, 146 S.E. 173 (1928). This rule was questioned in Cummings v. Robinson, 194 Ga. 336, 21 S.E.2d 627, 634 (1942) which points out that the decision that *quo warranto* was the more "speedy remedy," was not concurred in by all the justices and is not binding as precedent.

53. Gibson v. Singleton, 149 Ga. 502, 101 S.E. 178 (1919).

54. Note, *Protection of Membership in Voluntary Associations*, 37 Yale L.J. 368 (1927–28), citing State *ex rel.* Buckner v. Landwehr, 261 S.W. 699 (Mo. App. 1924) and others, Howard v. Betts, 190 Ga. 530, 9 S.E.2d 742 (1940) citing 5 C.J. 1357.

55. Engel v. Walsh, 258 Ill. 98, 101 N.E. 222 (1913), rehearing denied. This was a case in which the court held the labor union was acting lawfully and properly within its own rules in fining a member.

56. Kruger v. Gerth, 16 N.Y.2d 802, 210 N.E.2d 355 (1965).

57. Summers, *Judicial Regulation of Union Elections*, 70 Yale L.J. 1221, 1236 (1961), n. 87, citing the AFL-CIO Ethical Practices Code on Union Democratic Processes.

58. *Ibid.*, 1230 ff.

59. Randolph v. Mt. Zion Baptist Church of Newark, 139 N.J. Eq. 605, 53 A.2d 206 (1947).

60. People *el rel.* Hoyne v. Grant, 283 Ill. 391, 119 N.E. 344 (1918).

61. Illinois: "The right of the members, or any class or classes of members, to vote may be limited, enlarged, or denied to the extent specified in the articles of incorporation or the bylaws." Ill. Stats. 32, §163a 14.

    Ohio: "Except as otherwise provided in the articles or the regulations, each member, regardless of class, shall be entitled to one vote on each matter properly submitted to the members for their vote. . . . . . ." Ohio Rev. Code, §1702.20.

    California: "The authorized number and qualifications of members of the corporation, the different classes of membership, if any, the property, voting, and other rights and privileges of members . . . . . . shall be set forth either in the articles or in the bylaws, ..." 25 Cal. Code, §9301 [but see the revised California statute Cal. Corp. Code §§5610, 5510, 5132, 5151].

62. ALI-ABA Model Nonprofit Corporations Act, §15, Voting (1964 revision).

63. *See*, Jenkins v. State Board of Elections, 180 No. Car. 169, 104 S.E. 346, anno. 14 A.L.R. 1247 (1920).

64. Board of Education of Oklahoma City v. Woodworth, 89 Okla. 192, 214 P. 1077, 1079 (1923); State v. Williams 100 Fla. 996, 130 S. 428, 430 (1930).

65. Smith and Son v. MacAulay, 196 A. 281, 283 (Vt. 1938).

66. Ohio Rev. Code §1702.20.

67. *Ibid.*, §1702.21.

68. *Ibid.*, §1702.23.

69. *Ibid.*, §1702.24.

70. N.Y. Not-for-Profit Corp. L. §611.

71. *Ibid.*

72. *Ibid.*, §611(e); and N.Y. Genl. Corp. L. §20 (omitted in Bus. Corp. L. and N-P-C Law).

73. *Ibid.*, §609(a)(5).

74. *Ibid.*, §610.

75. Ohio Rev. Code §1702.23.

76. Calif. Nonprofit Corp. L. §§5034, 5510, 5132, 5151(e).

77. Comp. L. Mich. §450.124(d).

78. *Inherent right: See* State *ex rel.* Givens v. Superior Court, 223 Ind. 235, 117 N.E.2d 553 (1954); Drob v. National Memorial Park, Inc., 41 A.2d 589 (Del. 1945); State *ex rel,* Johnson v. Heap, 1 Wash.2d 316, 95 P.2d (1039) (1939); Reimer v. Smith, 105 Fla. 671, 142 S. 603 (1932). *Not inherent: See,* Westlake Hosp. Assoc. v. Blix 148 N.E.2d 471 (Ill. 1958). Voting rights may be changed if the articles so provide (there is no "property right" to vote in a charitable corporation). *In re* Sousa's Petition, 203 N.Y.S.2d 3 (1963) (specially chartered corp.).

79. *See,* for summaries of statutes of all states, 3 Oleck, *Modern Corporation Law,* c. 57 (1959).

80. *See,* 3 Oleck, *Modern Corporation Law,* c. 58 (1978 Supp.). Class votes given (1 per $1,000 contributed) are valid. Erickson v. Gospel Foundation of Cal., 275 P.2d 474 (Calif. Sup. 1954).

81. *See below,* the discussion of foundations; also, 3 Oleck, *Modern Corporation Law,* §1471 (1978 Supp.); Oleck, *Foundations Used as Business Devices,* 9 Clev.-Mar. L. Rev. 339 (1960).

82. Calif. Nonprofit Corp. L. §§5124 *et seq.* (1980).

83. State *ex rel.* Breger v. Rusche, 219 Ind. 559, 39 N.E.2d 433 (1942); N.Y. Not-for-Profit Corp. L. §611(b).

84. McLain v. Lanova Corp., 39 A.2d 209 (Del. 1944).

85. N.Y. Not-for-Profit Corp. L. §140(i).

86. *Ibid.*, §1401(i).

87. *Ibid.*, §506(c).

88. Calif. Nonprofit Corp. L. §§5000 *et seq.* (1980).

89. Del. Code Anno., tit. 8, §221; Minn. Stat. Anno. §302A.445; Ohio Rev. Code §1701.84; Va. Code §13.1-662. *See,* State *ex rel,* Devine v. Baxter, 78 Ohio L. Abs. 549, 153 N.E.2d 452 (1958), appeal dism. 168 Ohio St. 559, 156 N.E.2d 746 (1959).

90. New England Mutual Life Ins. Co. v. Phillips, 141 Mass. 536, 6 N.E. 534 (1886); *and see,* Fehr v. Hadden, 300 P.2d 533 (Colo. 1956) that members should not easily be deprived of their votes.

91. Durkee v. People *ex rel.* Arkren, 155 Ill. 354, 40 N.E. 626 (1895).

92. Ill. S.B. 1320 (1985 Subcommittee Proposed Act), esp. §§103.10, 106.10, 109.10(a)(1), *et passim. See now* 805 ILCS 105/107.40.

93. Ohio Rev. Code §1702.20.

94. Bartlett v. Lily Dale Assembly, 139 Misc. 338, 249 N.Y.S. 482 (1931).

95. *E.g.,* N.Y. Not-for-Profit Corp. L. §611(e).

96. *See, generally,* as to statutes of all states, 3 Oleck, *Modern Corporation Law,* c. 46, 57 (1978 Supp.).

97. *Ibid.*, c. 57.

98. *See,* Bridgers v. Staton, 150 N.C. 216, 63 S.E. 892 (1909); Attorney General v. McVichie, 138 Mich. 387, 101 N.W. 552 (1904). As to the mathematics of cumulative voting, *see* Cole, *Legal and Mathematical Aspect of Cumulative Voting,* 2 So. Car. L. Q. 225 (1950).

99. Model Nonprofit Corp. Act, §7.25 (1986 Rev. Proposal).

100. Calif. Nonprofit Corp. L. §5616 (1980); Fl. St. §617.0731(4); 15 Ann. Ind. Code §23-7-1.1-11 (directors); 15 Penna. Stat. §5758.

101. *See*, Westlake Hospital Assn. v. Blix, 13 Ill.2d 183, 148 N.E.2d 471 (1958); Saylor v. Gray, 41 Ariz. 558, 20 P.2d 441 (1933); but *cf.*, of N.Y. Not-for-Profit Corp. L. §617.

102. Ohio Rev. Code §1702.20 (official copy of Ohio Corp. L., Anno., 1960, by Ted W. Brown, Secy. of State).

103. Bedford County Hospital v. Bedford County, 42 Tenn. App. 569, 304 S.W.2d 697 (1957).

104. Model Nonprofit Corp. Act. §18; and §8.06 in the 1986 Revisions.

105. Wolfson v. Avery, 6 Ill.2d 78, 126 N.E.2d 701 (1955); State *ex rel.* Syphers v. McCune, 101 S.E.2d 834 (W. Va. 1957); Janney v. Philadelphia Transport Co., 387 Pa. 282, 128 A.2d 76 (1956).

106. Stilley, *Corporations—Election of Directors* . . . , 19 U. Pittsburgh L. Rev. 806–808 (1958).

107. Calif. Nonprofit Corp. L.§§5000 *et. seq.* (1980); Erickson v. Gospel Foundation of Calif., 275 P.2d 474 (Calif. Super. 1954); *but see* (not allowed) Green Gables Home Owners Assn. v. Sunlite Homes, 202 P.2d 143 (Calif. 1949).

108. Manson v. Curtis, 223 N.Y. 313, 119 N.E. 559, 561 (1918); Cliffs Corp. v. United States, 103 F.2d 77, 80 (6th Cir. 1939). *See*, 3 Oleck, *Modern Corporation Law*, c. 59 (1978 Supp.).

109. *E.g.*, N.Y. Not-for-Profit Corp. L §609, Fisher v. Bush, 35 Hun (N.Y.) 641, 644 (1885) (contract not to give a proxy held void). *See*, Oleck, *Proxy Voting Power in Nonprofit Organizations*, 14 Clev.-Mar. L. Rev. 273 (1965).

110. Harris, *The Model Business Corporation Act; An Invitation to Irresponsibility*, 50 Northwestern U. L. Rev. 1 (1955); Oleck, *Proxy Voting Power in Nonprofit Corporations*, 14 Clev.-Mar. L. Rev. 273 (1965).

111. Ohio Rev. Code §1702.20.

112. Craig Medicine Co. v. Merchants Bank, 59 Hun (N.Y.) 561; 14 N.Y.S. 16 (1891); Stevens v. Acadia Dairies, Inc., 15 Del. Ch. 248; 135 A. 846 (1927).

113. *See*, Commonwealth v. Detwiler, 131 Penna. 614; 18 A. 990; 7 L.R.A. 357 (1890).

114. Flynn v. Kendall, 195 Misc. 221; 88 N.Y.S.2d 299 (1950).

115. *See*, No. 48, above; People v. Younger, 238 Ill. App. 502 (1947).

116. Cliffs Corp. v. United States, 103 F.2d 77; 80 (6th Cir. 1939).

117. *See, Directors' and Officers' Encyc. Manual*, 415 (New York: Prentice-Hall, Inc. 1955).

118. N.Y. N-P-C Law §609.

119. *See*, Henn and Alexander, *Corporations*, 508, 536 (3rd ed., 1983); R. Stevenson, *Corporations and Information: Secrecy, Access, and Disclosure* (1980); Ochs v. Washington Hts. Fed. Sav. & L. Assn., 215 N.E.2d 485 (N.Y. 1966); 5 Fletcher, *Private Corporations* §2222–2224 (curr. ed.).

120. Ochs case, n. 119; and Henn & Alexander, n. 119 at 537; and citations there.

121. *Stueve v. Northern Lights, Inc.*, 838 P.2d 323 (Idaho App., 1992).

122. *Directional Wireline Services, Inc. v. Tillett*, 552 So. 2d 1201 (La. App. 1989).

123. *Skane v. Star Valley Ranch Ass'n*, 826 P.2d 266 (Wyo. 1992).

124. *E.g.*, N.Y. Not-for-Profit Corp. L. §603(d).

125. *Ibid.*, §703.

126. *Ibid.*, §1404(e)(2).

127. Calif. Nonprofit Corp. L. §§5000 *et seq.* (1980).

128. Stratford v. Mallory, 70 N.J. L. 294; 58 A. 347 (1904).

129. *See*, n. 56, above; State v. Chute, 34 Minn. 135; 24 N.W. 353 (1885); N.Y. Not-for-Profit Corp. L. §613(b) (majority of votes cast).

130. *See*, Standard Power and Light Corp. v. Invest. Associates, Inc., 51 A2d 572 (Del. 1947).

131. Benintendi v. Kenton Hotel, Inc., 294 N.Y. 112; 60 N.E.2d 829 (1945) (which case led to revision of old N.Y. Stock Corp. L. §9).

132. N.Y. Not-for-Profit Corp. L. §509.

133. *See*, Finkelstein, *The Conduct of Corporate Elections*, 17 St. John's L. Rev. 75 (1943); Arenow & Einhorn, *Proxy Contests for Corporate Control*, 40 (2d ed., 1968).

134. Beardsley v. Johnson, 121 N.Y. 224; 24 N.E. 380 (1890).

135. State v. Cronan, 23 Nev. 437; 49 P. 41 (1897). *See*, Henn & Alexander, *Corporations* §192 (3rd ed., 1983).

136. Benintendi case, n. 131, above; Rev. Model N-P-C Act §7.30 (1986 Draft).

137. Drob v. National Memorial Park, Inc., 41 A.2d 589 (Del. 1945); State *ex rel.* Johnson v. Heap, 1 Wash.2d 316; 95 P.2d 1039 (1939); 15 Penna. Stat. §5758(d).

138. *See*, Moon v. Moon Motor Car Co., 17 Del. Ch. 176; 151 A. 298 (1930). *And see*, State *ex rel.* Devine v. Baxter, 78 Ohio L. Abs. 549, 153 N.E.2d 452 (1958).

139. Commonwealth *ex rel*, Laughlin v. Green, 351 Penna 170; 40 A.2d 492 (1945). Apparently barred in trustee elections in Ohio. *See*, Ohio Rev. Code §1702.26.

140. State v. Doughty, 134 Ark. 435; 204 S.W. 968, 970 (1918).

141. Straughan v. Meyers, 268, Mo. 580; 187 S.W. 1159, 1162 (1916).

142. *In re* Crown Heights Hospital, Inc., 183 Misc. 563; 49 N.Y.S.2d 658 (1944). *And see*, Stratford v. Mallory, 70 N.J. L. 294, 58A. 347 (1904).

143. Opinions N.Y. Atty. Gen. (Dec. 9, 1946).

144. *Re* Excelsior Ins. Co., 38 Barb. (N.Y.) 297 (1863).

145. State *ex rel.* David v. Dudley, 23 Wash.2d 25; 158 P.2d 330 (1945).

146. *See* n. 139, above; and, Zachary v. Milan, 294 Mich. 622; 293 N.W. 770 (1940); Young v. Jebbett, 213 A.D. 774; 211 N.Y.S. 61 (1925).

147. Zachary case, n. 146, above.

148. David case, n. 145, above.

149. David case, n. 145, above.

150. Commissioner v. Vandegrift, 232 Penna. 53; 81 A. 153 (1911); *Re* Pioneer Paper Co., 36 How. Pr. (N.Y.) 105 (1864).

151. N.Y. Gen. Corp. L. §20 (omitted in N.Y. Bus. Corp. L. and N-P-C Law); Petition of Serenbetz, 46 N.Y.S.2d 475 (1943); *affd.*, 267 A.D. 836; 46 N.Y.S.2d 127 (1944); *see*, McGoldrick v. Rotwein, 127 N.Y.L.J. 508, col. 6 (Feb. 6, 1952), *unrep. dec.*

152. N.Y. Not-for-Profit Corp. L. §610. *Cf.* ABA Model N-P-C Act §7.27 (1986 Exposure Draft); Calif. Corp. Code §707(a); Annot., 44 A.L.R. 3rd 1443; Gunzberg v. Gunzberg, 425 N.Y.S.2d 151 (App. Div. 1980).

153. State v. Cronan, 23 Nev. 437; 49 P. 41 (1897); *In re* Robert Clark, Inc., 186 A.D. 216; 174 N.Y.S. 314 (1919).

154. Amber v. Smith, 237 A.D. 226; 262 N.Y.S. 208 (1932); N.Y. Not-for-Profit Corp. L. §611.

155. *See*, Wyatt v. Armstrong, 186 Misc. 216; 59 N.Y.S.2d 502 (1945).

156. State v. Cronan, 23 Nev. 437; 49 P.41 (1897); Clarke case, n. 146, above; Prince v. Albin, 23 Misc.2d 194, 200 N.Y.S.2d 843.

157. *See* n. 83, above; State *ex rel.* Martin v. Chute, 34 Minn. 135; 24 N.W. 353 (1885). Delay may make the remedy futile. Stire v. Calogero, 144 S.2d 891 (La. 1962).

158. *See*, Appon v. Belle Isle Corp., 46 A.2d 749 (Del. 1946).

159. *See*, *In re* Weinstein, 203 Misc. 975; 119 N.Y.S.2d 457 (1953).

160. *See*, *In re* Bruder's Estate, 302 N.Y. 52; 96 N.E.2d 84 (1950).

161. *Dole v. International Brotherhood of Elec. Workers, Local . . .*, 727 F. Supp. 789 (D.C., N.Y., 1990).

162. *In re* Cedar Grove Cemetery Co., 61 N.J.L. 422; 39 A. 1024 (1898).

163. N.Y. Gen. Corp. L. §25; *In re* Empire State Supreme Lodge, 118 A.D. 616; 103 N.Y.S. 465, 103 N.Y.S. 1124 (1907); Burke v. Wiswall, 193 Misc. 14, 85 N.Y.S.2d 187 (1948).

164. N.Y.C. P.L.R. §§7801 *et seq.*

165. *In re* Lake Placid Co., 274 A.D. 205; 8 N.Y.S.2d 36 (1948).

166. *In re* Baldwinsville Fed. Sav. and Loan Assn., 268 A.D. 414; 51 N.Y.S.2d 816 (1944).

167. *In re* Workmen's Benefit Fund, 36 N.Y.S.2d 662 (1942); *appl. dism.*, 265 A.D. 176; 38 N.Y.S.2d 429 (1942); leave to *appl. den.*, 265 A.D. 991; 39 N.Y.S.2d 990 (1942). *And see,* Stansberry v. McCarty, 149 N.E.2d 683 (Ind. 1958).

168. *See* §256, above.

169. *In re* Flushing Hospital and Dispensary, 288 N.Y. 125; 41 N.E.2d 917 (1942); *reh. den.*, 288 N.Y. 735; 43 N.E.2d 356 (1942); and 289 N.Y. 654; 44 N.E.2d 626 (1942).

170. *In re* Bogart, 215 A.D. 45; 213 N.Y.S. 137 (1925).

171. *In re* Supreme Council C.R. and B.A., 142 A.D. 307; 127 N.Y.S. 143 (1911).

172. George v. Holstein-Friesian Assn. of America 238 N.Y. 513, 144 N.E. 776 (1924).

173. *In re* Washington Avenue Baptist Church, 215 A.D. 529; 214 N.Y.S. 259 (1926).

174. *See,* for typical forms, West's McKinney's Forms, N.Y. N-P-C Law §618.

175. *In re* Silaski, 175 A.D. 199; 161 N.Y.S. 513 (1916).

176. *See,* Ohio Rev. Code §1701.50.

177. Legis. Doc., N.Y. (1953) No. 65 (J); N.Y. Not-for-Profit Corp. L. §610.

178. *See* n. 101, 102, 103.

179. *Ibid.*, N.Y. Gen. Corp. L. §§23, 24 (oath must be taken by members and filed, if the records are not at the meeting) (repealed). See N.Y. N-P-C Law §§604, 610.

180. *See* n. 103–104, above; *see, In re* Remington Typewriter Co., 234 N.Y. 296; 137 N.E. 335 (1922).

181. Gow v. Consolidated Coppermines Corp., 19 Del. Ch. 172; 165 A. 136 (1933).

182. *In re* Wheeler, 2 Abb. Pr. N.Y.N.S. 361 (1866) (candidate); *In re* Chenango Co., 19 Wend. (N.Y.) 635 (1837) (officer).

183. *In re* Zenitherm Co., 95 N.J.L. 297; 113 A. 327 (1921).

184. State v. Merchant, 37 Ohio St. 251 (1881).

185. Thompson v. McLaughlin, 138 A.D. 711; 123 N.Y.S. 762 (1910); and *see* Aranow & Einhorn, *State Court Review of Corporate Elections,* 56 Colum. L. Rev. 155, 165 (1956); Gunzburg v. Gunzburg, 425 N.Y.S.2d 151 (App. Div., 1980); Annot., 44 A.L.R. 3rd 1443; Henn & Alexander, *Corporations,* 508 (3rd ed., 1983).

186. Standard Power and L. Co. v. Invest. Associates, Inc., 51 A.2d 572 (Del. 1947), Young v. Jebbett, 213 A.D. 774; 211 N.Y.S. 61 (1925); N.Y. Not-for-Profit Corp. L. §610(b).

187. *See* n. 145, above; *and see,* Gow v. Consolidated Coppermines Corp., 19 Del. Ch. 172; 165 A. 136 (1933). Great discretion, in Ohio: Ohio Rev. Code §1701.50.

188. *In re* Giant Portland Cement Co., 21 A.2d 697 (Del. 1941).

189. N.Y. Genl. Corp. L. §20 (omitted in N.Y. Bus Corp. Law and N.Y. N-P-C Law); *and see* §258 of this book.

190. Umatilla Water Users Assn. v. Irvin, 56 Ore. 414; 108 P. 1016 (1910); Triesler v. Wilson, 89 Md. 169; 42A. 926 (1899).

191. People v. Albany and S.R.R., 55 Barb. (N.Y.) 334 (1869).

192. *See*, Haslam v. Carlson, 46 R.I. 53; 124 A. 734 (1924); *In re* Gulla, 13 Del. Ch. 23; 115 A. 317 (1921).

193. Kauffman v. Meyberg, 59 Calif. App.2d 730; 140 P.2d 210 (1943).

194. N.Y. Genl. Corp. L. §20 (Omitted in N.Y. Bus. Corp. Laws and N.Y. N-P-C Law); Ohio Rev. Code §1701.50(C).

195. Ohio Rev. Code §1701.50; and *see* Henn & Alexander, *Corporations* 508 (3rd ed., 1983); 3 Oleck, *Modern Corporation Law* §1490 (1978 Suppl.).

26

PROXIES

[See Section 153.]

§260. WHAT IS A PROXY?

The word *proxy* has several meanings:

(a) the written authorization for one person (the bearer) to vote at a meeting, in place of the member who signed the paper; (b) the writing itself; (c) the person who carries the paper and casts the vote; or (d) the vote so-authorized, itself.[1]

The specific meaning of the word, in a particular case, thus must be governed by the context in which it is used. The right to employ proxies, in a corporation vote, is statutory, and did not exist in the common law.[2]

Today the use of proxy voting is so routine in all kinds of corporations that the 1986 Revised Model Nonprofit Corporation Act of the American Bar Association[3] does not bother to define the term, but says that "Unless the articles or bylaws prohibit or limit proxy voting, a member may appoint a proxy to vote or otherwise act for the member by signing an appointment form either personally or by an attorney-in-fact."[4] The revision allows eleven months' duration for a proxy, unless a different period (up to three years) is provided in it.

In business corporations, the use of proxies as instruments of manipulation and control of the corporation is now the paramount technique of power-gathering or exercise. It is not yet quite that in nonprofit corporations, but has been tending in the same direction since 1972. In that year the case of *Medical Committee for Human Rights v. S.E.C.*[5] led to revision of S.E.C. Proxy Rule 12a-8 in 1974 to enable corporation members to express their views effectively, especially as to corporate social responsibility.[6]

Voting by proxy is a practical necessity in modern organizations in today's world of constant travel and movement.

In business corporations, there now is a large and detailed body of law on proxy voting.[7] The law on business corporation proxy voting is quite complex in some respects, but there is no shortage of law on the subject.[8]

The same is not true of nonprofit organizations. As to them the law is fragmentary and confused. Yet the power to vote by proxy may be just as important in a nonprofit organization as in a business organization.

Proxy voting is not the same thing as the *voting trust*, although it is analogous; the voting trust passes title to stock to the voting trustee. See the end of this chapter for discussion (Section 270) on Voting Trusts, which now are permitted by such statutes as those of New York's Not-for-Profit Corporation Act.[9]

A proxy is essentially a deputization[10] of a person to serve as agent for the member, to vote on his behalf.[11]

The old common law view was that a member could vote only in person. But this rule has given way to the necessities of modern society.[12]

Though a member is unable to attend a meeting in person, usually he may vote by the use of a proxy.[13] In almost every state, however, some cases state that, because the common law gave no such right, the right must be based either on statute, the charter, or the bylaws.[14] Such cases also require strict *construction* of a proxy, in case of dispute, for the same reason.[15]

The proxy (person) need not be a member of the organization unless the bylaws so require.[16]

In most states, by statute, members of nonprofit organizations may vote by proxy.[17] In some states, voting by proxy is permitted only if the articles or bylaws specifically so provide.[18]

In some special types of nonprofit organizations, such as condominiums or cooperatives or credit unions or religious corporations, statutes sometimes forbid voting by proxy.[19]

The proxy holder is under a fiduciary duty, as an agent, to obey the directions given by the grantor of the proxy.[20]

A *"Datagram"* Proxy is a corporation's election of directors (using a toll-free phone number), without signature or identifying mark, is not reliable evidence as to the named shareholder or member, and is not entitled to a presumption of validity.[21]

Form No. 127

LIMITED PROXY

The undersigned hereby appoints _____ as my proxy, with full powers of substitution, to vote for _____ as indicated on this proxy, at the Annual Meeting of Club Condominium Building-B, Inc., to be held on March 1, 199 ___ at 3:30 p.m., at the Clubhouse, and any adjournment thereof.

Dated: _____, 199____.

Unit _____

All owners of the unit, or the owner designated as voting representative on a certificate signed by all owners of the unit must sign below.

_____

_____

_____

Vote for Four (4) Only.

_____ Herb _____

_____ Robert _____

_____ Rod _____

_____ Steve _____

_____ Thomas _____

_____ William _____

SUBSTITUTION OF PROXY

The undersigned, appointed as proxy above, does hereby designate _____ to substitute for me in the proxy set forth above.

Date:_____.

_____
Proxy

PLEASE RETURN PROXY TO THE SECRETARY OF THE ASSOCIATION.

§261. MEMBER'S PROXIES

A *proxy* is the authority (agency) given by one having the right to do a certain thing (*e.g.*, to vote) to another to do it for him. The term also may refer to the instrument, paper, or document which evidences the granting of such authority.[22] It is a grant of agency power to vote.[23] [*See,* Section 254.]

The common law rule was that voting at corporate meetings basically must be done in person. Neither a stockholder nor a member of a nonprofit corporation may grant a valid voting proxy, at common law, unless the right to do so is stated in the articles of incorporation, a general constitutional or statutory enactment, or in a valid bylaw.[24] But the power to use proxies is sufficiently stated by a general statute, even though the bylaws are silent on the subject.[25]

> This common law rule in respect of voting by proxy had its origin in reasons peculiarly applicable to the earlier forms of corporations; namely, municipal and charitable corporations. Membership in these was coupled with no pecuniary interest. The voting privilege was in the nature of a personal trust, committed to the discretion of the member as an individual, and hence not susceptible of exercise through delegation.[26]

In NPOs the right to vote by proxy serves to protect the right of a member to vote even though he/she is ill or constrained by some reason so as to be unable to be physically present for the voting. But in condominiums or cooperatives particularly the power to collect proxies from absent unit owners (members) serves to enable directors to perpetuate their control (office holding). This is why modern statutes, such as Florida's, recently forbade proxy voting in elections in such NPOs as condos. But the common-law view of proxies as basically not desirable still continues as a basic attitude of some people.

Even statutory authorization to provide for proxy voting in corporate bylaws does not assume inherent power in the members to do so, under this view. It contemplates only corporate decision to use or not use the power, unless there is an established custom of proxy voting already in being in the corporation.[27]

If a community association's bylaws invest the board of directors with the power to provide proper proxy forms and to mail those forms with the notice of annual meeting, forms provided and mailed by two members of the association are invalid.[28]

§262. STATUTORY PROXY RULES

> [Jeanne Frick made the original survey of statutes for 1980's updating of this section. It has been updated by the authors for this 1994 (6th) edition.]

Today statutes, charters or bylaws generally provide for proxy voting in corporations.[29]

The best way to ascertain the state of the law as to proxy voting in non-profit organizations is to examine the basic provisions of the several states. References are to voting by members, except as otherwise noted.[30] [*See* current amendments.]

Alabama:	Proxy voting allowed unless articles or bylaws provide otherwise (eleven months' maximum duration unless otherwise provided in the proxy).[31]
Alaska:	Similar to Model Act §15 (like above statement).[32]
Arizona:	Bylaws must be adopted and may provide for proxy voting by members.[33] Eleven month duration allowed.
Arkansas:	Members may vote in person or by proxy, unless the articles or bylaws require votes be cast in person. Proxies are valid for eleven months unless the member provides for a longer term in the appointment form.[34]
California:	Bylaws may provide manner of voting by members and how proxy voting shall be allowed. (Elaborate rules.) Proxies valid for eleven months unless otherwise provided in the proxy. Proxies may be limited or withdrawn by the articles or bylaws.[35]
Colorado:	Proxy voting allowed unless articles of incorporation otherwise provide (11 months' duration).[36]
Connecticut:	Proxy voting allowed unless articles or bylaws provide otherwise (11 months' maximum duration unless limited to a particular future meeting).[37]
Delaware	Proxy voting allowed unless articles provide otherwise (three years maximum duration unless proxy provides a longer period).[38]
District of Columbia:	Members of delegates may vote by proxy if bylaws so provide.[39] No proxy voting by members in cooperative associations.[40] (11 months duration).
Florida:	Members may vote by proxy unless the articles of incorporation or bylaws provide otherwise.[41] Coops may provide for proxies in their bylaws[42], but not credit unions.[43] No proxies in elections in condos.
Georgia:	Proxies may be used by members of business corporations,[44] and nonprofit corporations have generally similar powers.[45] Like the Model Act. No proxies may be used by credit unions.[46]
Hawaii:	Proxies are lawful for corporations.[47] Like the Model Act.
Idaho:	Members may vote by proxy.[48] Bylaws may provide for proxy voting in cooperative marketing associations.[49] No member,

officer, representative or delegate of a fraternal benefit society may vote by proxy.[50]

Illinois: Members may vote by proxy unless articles or bylaws provide otherwise (11 months' maximum duration unless otherwise provided in the proxy).[51]

Indiana: Voting in person or by proxy as the bylaws shall provide (11 months' maximum duration unless the proxy provides a longer time).[52]

Iowa: All members may vote by proxy unless bylaws or articles otherwise provided.[53] Not valid after 11 months unless provided in the proxy; no proxy vote in cooperatives.[54]

Kansas: Members may vote by proxy (three years' maximum duration unless proxy states a longer period).[55]

Kentucky: Members may vote by proxy unless articles or bylaws provide alternatives (11 months' duration unless proxy provides longer period).[56]

Louisiana: Members may vote by proxy unless articles or bylaws prohibit it, and directors may vote by proxy if so provided (up to three years if proxy so states[57]). No proxy voting in credit unions.[58]

Maine: Proxy voting forbidden in fraternal associations[59] and consumers' cooperatives.[60] Otherwise they are permitted (with maximum duration of 11 months, or bylaws may provide for them.[61]

Maryland: Proxy voting by members may be provided for by articles or bylaws (use of proxies seems to be assumed).[62] Voting by proxy is prohibited in agricultural[63] and consumer[64] cooperatives, and in fraternal benefit societies.[65] Members of credit unions may not vote by proxy.[66]

Massachusetts: Bylaws must provide rules for elections and the carrying out of purposes.[67] No specific provision. No proxies allowed in cooperatives.[68] No proxies after one year subsequent to incorporation of a credit union[69] No proxies in fraternal societies.[70]

Michigan: Provision as to proxies is like the 1986 Model Act. Three years' maximum duration, unless otherwise stated therein.[71] *See*, n. 4. new provision.[72]

Minnesota: Proxy voting not permitted unless authorized in the articles or bylaws, (11 months duration unless a different period is provided in the appointment form; 3 years maximum duration),[73] but directors may not vote by proxy.[74]

Mississippi: Proxy voting allowed unless prohibited by bylaws. Eleven months duration unless different period provided in appointment form. Three years maximum duration.[75] No proxy voting by credit unions.[76]

Missouri: Voting by proxy may be provided for in the bylaws,[77] and is specifically provided for in elections of directors of cooperatives.[78] Like the Model Act.

Montana: May vote by proxy unless bylaws or articles otherwise prohibit.[79] Like the Model Act.

Nebraska: Proxy voting is permitted unless articles or bylaws provide otherwise (11 months' maximum duration unless the proxy provides otherwise).[80]

Nevada: Proxies allowed in writing or by electronic transmission. Proxies valid for 6 months unless otherwise provided in the proxy but not to exceed 7 years from creation.[81]

New Hampshire: Voting by proxy prohibited in consumers' cooperative associations.[82] Vague bylaws powers.[83]

New Jersey: Specific provision, since 1983. Eleven months' (or as provided) duration, or up to three years.[84]

New Mexico: Proxy allowed unless prohibited by bylaws (up to 11 months unless otherwise in proxy).[85]

New York: Proxy voting permitted, unless articles or bylaws provide otherwise.[86] Lack of a bylaw does not abridge the right.[87] Directors may not vote by proxy.[88]

North Carolina: Proxy voting allowed unless articles or bylaws provide otherwise (11 months' maximum duration unless the proxy provides otherwise).[89]

North Dakota: Proxy voting allowed unless articles or bylaws provide otherwise (11 months' maximum duration unless the proxy provides otherwise).[90] No proxy voting in credit unions and fraternal benefit societies.[91]

Ohio: No proxy voting by members (except organizations which are members) unless the articles or bylaws so provide.[92]

Oklahoma: Proxy voting allowed (three years maximum duration, unless the proxy provides for a longer period.[93]

Oregon: Like the Model Act rules.[94]

Pennsylvania: Proxy voting allowed if bylaws so provide (11 months' maximum duration unless a longer period, up to three years, is provided therein.)[95]

Rhode Island: Proxy voting may be provided for by articles or bylaws.[96] Like the Model Act.

South Carolina: Vague bylaw powers,[97] but proxy voting may be provided for by bylaws of cooperative market associations[98] and rural electric coops.[99] No proxies in cooperative credit unions.[100]

South Dakota: Proxy voting allowed,[101] in articles or bylaws.[102] Like the Model Act.

Tennessee: Proxy voting allowed.[103] Like the Model Act.

Texas: Proxy voting by members permitted unless articles or bylaws provide otherwise (11 months' maximum duration unless otherwise provided in the proxy).[104]

Utah: Members may vote by proxy unless articles or bylaws provide otherwise.[105] No time limit on proxy.

Vermont: Proxy voting allowed.[106] Like the Model Act.

Virginia: Members may vote by proxy unless articles or bylaws provide otherwise (11 months' maximum duration unless otherwise provided in the proxy).[107]

Virgin Islands: Vague bylaw powers; apparently may provide for proxy voting.[108]

Washington: Proxy permitted unless articles or bylaws provide otherwise.[109]

West Virginia: Proxy voting allowed.[110] Like the Model Act.

Wisconsin: Members may vote by proxy unless articles or bylaws provide otherwise (11 months' maximum duration unless otherwise provided in the proxy).[111] No proxy voting in credit unions.[112]

Wyoming: Voting by proxy allowed.[113] Like the Model Act.

The foregoing summaries of state statutes and rules should suffice to convey a fair idea of the present status of the law on voting by proxy. Many state statutes contain special additional rules applicable to certain specific types of organizations. The summaries here provided contain the major provisions on the subject.

§263. MODEL ACT PROXY RULES

One pattern is immediately apparent—that of the states whose statutes are based on the Model Nonprofit Corporations Act of the American Bar Association's Section of Corporation, Banking and Business Law.[114] The 1986 Revision Draft has substantially the same rules as in 1964, renumbered (7.24). These statutes are based on Section 15 of the old Model Act and Sections 7.21, 7.24 of the new. Close similarity to that section is found in the statutes of Alabama, Connecticut, Delaware, Illinois, Indiana, Kansas, Louisiana, Minnesota, Nebraska, North Carolina, North Dakota, Texas, and Wisconsin. But some of these states' provisions are not necessarily copied from the Model Act; they are only coincidentally similar. Mississippi and Tennessee adopted the 1986 A.B.A. Revised Model Nonprofit Corporation Act in 1987.

The Model Corporation Acts of this section of the American Bar Association (more particularly the Model Business Corporation Act) have been severely criticized. The gist of the criticism is that these models are weighted in favor of directors and officials (management) as against members (shareholders).[115]

Similar criticism is warranted as to such provisions of the Model Nonprofit Corporations Act as the placing of bylaw powers in the directors rather than the members,[116] or the provision of cumulative voting for members[117] and vitiation of that provision by the provision elsewhere of classes of directors[118] (making "bullet" voting futile).

But the Model Act's provisions as to voting by proxy should not be summarily categorized as "pro-management," even though proxies may be forbidden by the articles or bylaws (the original "management" may grant or withhold). After all, there must be an original managing group to organize the corporation, usually; and we must appeal to self-interest if we want to encourage entrepreneurs in nonprofit as in business organizations.

§264. DIRECTORS' PROXY VOTING

The real question is "Should there be proxy voting in nonprofit organizations?", regardless of the defects of any particular statute or suggested statute.

In a case involving proxy voting in a political party committee organization, the New Jersey Superior Court held that proxy voting should not be permitted, reiterating the old arguments against it.[119] The court said:

> To permit unit rule and proxy voting in the absence of legislative approval,
> is to permit an abdication from the position of trust ascribed to a committeeman. . .[120]

This refers to a *committeeman; i.e.,* to a delegate or representative. It does not refer to a member generally. Indeed, the court specifically stated that it was referring to "the question of the duties of those with representative status."[121]

This, it is submitted, is the core of the old objection to proxy voting—it is an objection to proxy voting by *representatives*, meaning *delegates, trustees,* or *directors*, not by *members* as such.

The state nonprofit corporation statutes almost uniformly omit any specific provision for directors' or trustees' powers to vote by proxy. Some statutes specifically bar voting by representatives or delegates in certain types of organizations, such as fraternal benefit societies or cooperative associations.[122] Other statutes specifically *permit* proxy voting in certain types of organizations.[123]

Yet, in practice, many nonprofit organizations blithely ignore the legal theories and *do* provide for proxy voting by delegates, trustees, or directors, in their articles or bylaws. It is difficult, sometimes, for a trustee to be physically present at a meeting, and yet he may be very anxious to vote for or against a specific proposal. Often the proposal is a narrow one, calling for a "yes" or "no" only, on a clear issue or choice. Most people see no real reason why such a *decision* cannot be voted by proxy.

On the other hand, case decisions, mostly old ones (and the old Minnesota statute[124]), have held that a trustee or director may not vote by proxy, because he may not delegate his control and management.[125] It is hard to see how a director delegates any discretion if he grants a proxy to vote "yes" or "no" on a specific question only.

Ohio's (and other) statutes governing decisions by members of the executive committee of a nonprofit board of trustees permit decisions to be made "by a writing or writings signed by all of its members" unless otherwise provided in the bylaws or ordered by the trustees.[126] This is analogous to voting by proxy.

What is said here of corporations is equally applicable to unincorporated associations. It is general practice to use corporation law and practice as analogous in unincorporated associations. Some court decisions expressly so state. In one case involving proxy voting by members of an executive committee of an unincorporated association, which was forbidden for corporation trustees, such voting was viewed as invalid even though customarily employed by that association.[127]

It is submitted that the modern statutes permitting directors to act by "a writing,"[128] the specific grant of authority for directors to vote by proxy and the actual practice of many organizations mentioned above, are sound, provided that they are confined to narrow specific vote issues. As the statutes pertaining to proxy voting by members clearly indicate,[129] it now is well established that members of nonprofit organizations can (and should) be able to vote by proxy. The old rule, which is suspicious of proxy voting has outlived its usefulness.

Florida eliminated the use of proxies in voting for members of a condo board, beginning Jan. 1, 1992. Use of proxies to perpetuate themselves in office has been a very questionable aspect of condo board operation. Now the board must give 60 days' notice of an election with a request for volunteers to run for election to the board, with a resumé from volunteers of their background data, to be sent by the board in a second mailing to unit owners, with ballot submission by a date stated. No quorum is to be required; the ballots cast shall determine the election.[130]

Oleck has advised inclusion of proxy voting power in bylaws of organizations for which he was (and is) counsel. No case of objection or abuse, or trouble of any kind, has resulted. The organizations concerned have found the provision to be convenient. Of course, the provision should be limited, not general, in nature.[131]

§265. FORM OF A PROXY

[*See also* Section 320.]

Many states require that proxies be executed in writing by the member or by his duly authorized agent.[132] But no particular form is required for nonprofit corporations.[133] Even the proxy of a corporate member need not be executed with all the formalities customary in a corporate document.[134] No witnessing nor even dating of the proxy is technically necessary in most states, although desirable for practical reasons.[135]

Even oral proxies are acceptable, when no statute or bylaw requires a writing.[136]

Use of telegrams or cablegrams and/or photocopies (or "faxes") of proxies now is permitted by state statutes; and this also applies to condos and coops and homeowners associations, while the statutory procedures often are made very specific.[137]

FORM NO. 128

Form of Proxy (general)

Know all men by these presents that I, the undersigned, a member of . . . .
Association, Inc., of . . . . (city), do hereby appoint . . . . ,
my true and lawful attorney-in-fact and proxy, to vote in my place and stead on
my behalf, as though I myself were present and voting, with power of substitution, at [state the time, place, and purpose of the meeting] or at any adjournment thereof, hereby revoking all previous proxies.

    [or] [State the extent or limits of discretion granted. Name the person
for whom the vote is to be cast if such express direction is intended.]
    . . . . Witness   . . . .

FORM NO. 129

Form of Proxy (Special)

Corporation   Date
    (Address)
    This is to certify that I, ____(name)____, a member in good standing in
_____ Corporation, do hereby designate _____(name)_____ of
____(address)____ to cast my vote at the _____(date)_____ meeting of the said
organization, in favor of [(or) opposed to] the proposal to (describe it) at that
meeting's balloting on that issue. The said _____(name)_____ is to act as my
proxy in voting on that issue only.

_____   _____
   Witness   Signature
                                                 (Name of member)

[See also the Index, as to other forms of proxies.]

FORM NO. 130

HOMEOWNER'S ASSOCIATION PROXY
HOMEOWNER'S ASSOCIATION, INC.
2701 _____ Drive
_____, (State)

ASSOCIATION MEETING PROXY

KNOWN ALL MEN BY THESE PRESENTS:

I, the undersigned, do hereby constitute and appoint _____

_____
(insert proxy name)

as my true and lawful attorney, substitute, and proxy for me and in my name, place, and stead, to vote at the meeting of Owners of the Homeowner's Association, Inc., to be held on Wednesday, September 6, 19___, at 6:30 p.m. in the _____ Room of the _____ Yacht & Country Club located at 6300 _____ Boulevard, _____, (State), and at any adjournment thereof, for the purpose of nominating and voting for one (1) director of said corporation; and I hereby revoke any Proxy or Proxies heretofore given by me to any person or persons whatsoever for the above purpose.

IN WITNESS WHEREOF, I hereunto set my hand and seal on this _____ day of _____, 19___.

_____
Signature(s) of Owner(s)

_____
Lot Number
or
UNIT NUMBER

FORM NO. 131

CONDO BOARD ELECTION PROXY

[See your state law limitations]

The undersigned hereby appoints _____ President or _____ as my proxy, with full powers of substitution, to vote for the nominees for director and the amendments to the By-laws as indicated on this proxy, at the Annual Meeting of _____, Inc. to be held on March 7, 199____ at 7:30 P.M., at the _____ Building, and any adjournment thereof.

Dated: _____, 199____.

Unit _____

The sole owner of the membership, or the owner designated as voting representative on a certificate signed by all owners of the membership must sign below.

_____

Vote for five (5) only.

_____	V	B	_____	B	L
_____	B	C	_____	B	N
_____	H	F	_____	C	W
_____	T	J	_____	B	Y
_____	_____				

(Write-in Candidate's Name)

Board members who are not here for the entire year may vote when away for extended periods if a speaker conference phone is used during the meeting so both the absent Board member and the Board members and unit owners present can hear the discussion. However, if three directors are present in person, which is a quorum, then the vote of absent directors is needed.

- -

1. Amendment to the By-Laws Article IV, Section 1 (a) (b) regarding number and qualifications, removal and vacancies.

❑   ❑

FOR   AGAINST

- -

2. Amendment to the By-Laws Article VII regarding the vote required to modify, amend or revoke the By-Laws.

❏   ❏

FOR   AGAINST

PLEASE RETURN TO THE FOLLOWING ADDRESS:

SECRETARY

_____, INC.
5940 _____ Street
_____, (State)

[*Note.* Proxy voting in elections of board members in Florida condominiums was almost entirely barred by statute beginning in 1992.]

§266. TYPICAL SPECIFIC STATUTORY PROVISIONS

New York's Not-for-Profit Corporation Act[138] has rather detailed provisions.

§609 Proxies

(a) Except as otherwise provided in the certificate of incorporation or the by-laws:

(1) Every member entitled to vote at a meeting of members or to express consent or dissent without a meeting may authorize another person or persons to act for him by proxy.

(2) Every proxy must be signed by the member or his attorney-in-fact. No proxy shall be valid after the expiration of eleven months from the date thereof unless otherwise provided in the proxy. Every proxy shall be revocable at the pleasure of the member executing it, except as otherwise provided in this section.

(3) The authority of the holder of a proxy to act shall not be revoked by the incompetence or death of the member who executed the proxy unless, before the authority is exercised, written notice of an adjudication of such incompetence or of such death is received by the corporate officer responsible for maintaining the list or record of members.

(4) Except when other provision shall have been made by written agreement between the parties, the record holder of capital certificates which he holds as pledgee or otherwise as security or which belong to another, shall issue to the pledgor or to such owner of such capital certificates, upon demand therefor and payment of necessary expenses thereof, a proxy to vote or take other action thereon.

(5) A member shall not sell his vote or issue a proxy to vote to any per-

son for any sum of money or anything of value, except as authorized in this
section and section 619 (Agreements as to voting).

(6) A proxy which is entitled "irrevocable proxy" and which states that
it is irrevocable is irrevocable when it is held by any of the following or a
nominee of any of the following:

(A) A pledgee.

(B) A person who has purchased or agreed to purchase the capital
certificates.

(C) A creditor or creditors of the corporation who extend or continue credit to the corporation in consideration of the proxy if the proxy states
that it was given in consideration of such extension or continuation of credit, the amount thereof, and the name of the person extending or continuing credit.

(D) A person who has contracted to perform services as an officer of
the corporation, if a proxy is required by the contract of employment, if the
proxy states that it was given in consideration of such contract of employment, the name of the employee and the period of employment contracted for.

(E) A person designated by or under an agreement under section
619.

(7) Notwithstanding a provision in a proxy, stating that it is irrevocable, the proxy becomes revocable after the pledge is redeemed, or the debt
of the corporation is paid, or the period of employment provided for in the
contract of employment has terminated, or the agreement under section
619 has terminated; and, in a case provided for in subparagraphs (6) (C)
or (D), becomes revocable three years after the date of the proxy or the
end of the period, if any, specified therein, whichever period is less, unless
the period of irrevocability is renewed from time to time by the execution
of a new irrevocable proxy as provided in this section. This paragraph does
not affect the duration of a proxy under subparagraph (2).

(8) A proxy may be revoked, notwithstanding a provision making it
irrevocable, by a purchaser of capital certificates without knowledge of the
existence of the provision unless the existence of the proxy and its irrevocability is noted conspicuously on the face or back of the capital certificate.

Federal statutes governing business corporation proxies are detailed and
comprehensive. They fall mostly within the supervision of the Securities and
Exchange Commission (S.E.C.).[140] These provisions are not *generally* applicable
to nonprofit corporations, but may apply in securities-type cases.

§267. IDENTIFICATION, AND CONFLICT, OF PROXIES

Any description of the proxy person that clearly identifies him is sufficient.
Thus, the designation, of "any member of the firm of $X \ldots \ldots Co$." is sufficient.[141]

If more than one proxy has been issued by a member, the one bearing or indicating the latest date or postmark governs.[142] If a communication with the member can be had, in time for the voting, he may clarify his intention.[143]

§268. SCOPE OF PROXY

The authority granted to (or in) a proxy may be general as though the member were present in person, or it may be expressly limited to certain acts or votes. But, within his apparent scope of authority, the acts of the proxy are binding on the member even if he exceeds the powers the member actually intended to give.[144] However, if the proxy acts in bad faith, the member may repudiate his acts, so long as nobody is adversely affected by such a repudiation.[145] But if he waits an unreasonable length of time before doing so, he may be estopped from repudiating the improper act of the proxy.[146]

§269. DURATION AND REVOCATION OF PROXIES

Some state statutes make a proxy valid for a limited period (*e.g.*, 11 months), unless it specifies a longer period of validity.[147] Other state statutes set a maximum duration, with no provision for increase even in the proxy itself.

The range of statutory duration provisions is illustrated by the following examples: Connecticut, Missouri, and Ohio (11 months, unless it provides a longer period),[149] Pennsylvania (three years maximum, if so stated therein);[150] Delaware (three years, unless it states a longer period);[151] California (three years maximum),[152] Florida (11 months).[153]

In general, a proxy always is revocable, except in the security-purpose arrangements permitted in some states for business corporations.[154] Also, in business corporations, a *proxy coupled with an interest* (*e.g.*, where the proxy-person has a pecuniary interest in the voting results) may be made irrevocable.[155] Excepting such circumstances, however, it is contrary to public policy for a proxy to be irrevocable.[156]

When any doubt exists about the irrevocability of a proxy, the member's desire to revoke must be honored. The proxy-person is left to his personal remedies against the member, if he is entitled to any.[157]

Some cases hold that, in the absence of a statute, even a proxy coupled with an interest is revocable.[158]

Death or incapacity (*e.g.*, insanity or the like) of the grantor revokes a proxy unless it is coupled with an interest or "given as security."[159] The granting of a second proxy, or notice to the corporation, revokes the first one.[160]

Statutes as to business corporations sometime provide that a proxy is not revoked by death unless actual notification of the death is given to the corporation before the proxy is exercised.[161] This rule may be applicable to nonprofit organizations in some cases. Of course, any of these rules are subject to statutory change.[162]

§270. VOTING AGREEMENTS (VOTING TRUSTS)

Members of a nonprofit corporation may provide for the manner in which they will vote, by signing an agreement for that purpose. Such agreements may be valid for a period of up to ten years. That is the law recommended by the 1986 Revision of the Model Nonprofit Corporation Act (Exposure Draft). The rule is limited in that "public-benefit" corporations may allow such agreements only for "a reasonable purpose not inconsistent with the corporation's public or charitable purposes." New York's statute [§619] provides for voting agreements.

If a corporation adopts such a rule (absent any statutory provision or court-established policy in the state) that should be stated in the articles or bylaws. This is because such agreement may separate voting power from beneficial interest of a member in the corporation.[163] It may amount to a *voting trust* if the votes are, in effect, transfer of membership (shares) to a voting trustee for a specific purpose or period of time. In a business corporation voting trust, the shareholders surrender their shares and receive voting trust certificates instead. These certificates can be bought and sold. Voting trusts are now widely employed by business corporations, as control devices, especially when granted to creditors, effective upon the insolvency of the corporation; as statutes now often permit.[164]

The voting trust is basically a business device, with complex corporate and tax law consequences,[165] although it may also serve to enable a minority group of members to have some degree of representation and effectiveness.[166] Forms of voting trusts may amount to complex securities—type contracts.[167]

Such voting agreements are seldom consistent with the democratic concept of nonprofit organization and operation in a membership corporation. They should be used only with caution, if at all, in nonprofit corporations. Ohio, for example, has held such agreements to be violations of members' rights to control corporation affairs.168 But, Florida's 1992 statute in effect allows such "grouping" of votes.[169] But Florida's 1992 statute in effect allows such "grouping" of votes.

POINTS TO REMEMBER

- Provide for proxy voting rights in the bylaws.
- Make detailed provisions as to members' proxies.
- Adopt a short duration period for proxies, (one to three months, maximum).
- Adopt a form of proxy for the organization.

- Do not give proxy powers to trustees, except as a calculated risk, and then only for specific (single issue or election) votes.

- Under such statutes as California's or New York's, that mix business and nonprofit activities, be especially careful of proxies that amount to security devices; among other things, they may involve S.E.C. regulation.

- Use voting agreements to secure representation for minority factions, but only with caution and no secrecy.

NOTES TO CHAPTER 26

1. *Oxford Universal Dictionary*, 1609 (1955 ed.); Henn & Alexander, *Corporations* §196 (3rd ed., 1983); 3 Oleck, *Modern Corporation Law*, c. 59 (1978 Supp.).

2. *Ibid.*; and *see*, 5 Fletcher, *Cyclopedia of the Law of Private Corporations* §§2050 *et seq.* (curr. ed.).

3. A.B.A. Model Nonprofit Corp. Act §7.24 (1986 Revision; Exposure Draft). Hereinafter cited as *Rev. M. NPCA*.

4. *Ibid.*, §7.24(a).

5. 432 F.2d 659 (D.C. Cir., 1970), vacated as moot, 404 U.S. 403 (1972). Discussed in 3 Oleck, *Modern Corporation Law*, new §1487A (1978 Supp.). *See*, L. Moody, *Securities Issues of Nonprofit Organizations*, in *Nonprofit Organization's Problems 1980*, p. 178 (Stetson Univ. 1980), as to S.E.C. supervision.

6. 17 C.F.R. §14-8 (1974). *But, c.f.*, Kixmiller v. S.E.C., 492 F.2d 641 (D.C. Cir. 1974). *And see, generally*, Mehren and McCarroll, *The Proxy Rules: A Case Study in the Administrative Process*, 29 Law and Contemp. Prob. 728 (1964).

7. Regulation 14a, Solicitation of Proxies, 17 C.F.R. 240.14a-8 (amended 1977). *See*, Axe, *Corporate Proxies*, 41 Mich. L. Rev. 38, 225 (1942); 5 Fletcher, *Cyclopedia of the Law of Private Corporations*, §§2050–2063 (curr. ed.); 3 Oleck, *Modern Corporation Law*, c. 59 (1978 Supp.); D.V. Austin, *Proxy Contests and Corporate Reform* (1965); B. Rogers, *Proxy Guide for Meetings of Stockholders* (1969); N.H. Kirshman, *Strategy of Corporate Proxy Contests*, 48 Los Ang. Bar Bull. 249 (1973).

8. *See, supra*, notes, and materials referred to in the cited works, *esp.* in Fletcher and Oleck.

9. As to this distinction *see*, Tompers v. Bank of America, 217 A.D. 691, 217 N.Y.S. 67 (1926), revg. 126 Misc. 753, 214 N.Y.S. 643; Simpson v. Nielson, 77 Cal. App. 297, 246 P. 342 (1926). N.Y. Not-for-Profit Corp. L. §619 (voting agreements).
   See, control of subservient nonprofit cemetery association by trustees of a cemetery lot business trust, through proxies; held to be against public policy as a violation of the members' right to control association affairs. Muth v. Maxton, 119 N.E.2d 162 (Ohio Com. Pl. 1954).

10. Cliffs Corp. v. United States, 103 F.2d 77, 80 (6th Cir. 1939).

11. *See*, Johnson v. Spartanburg Fair Assn., 41 S.E.2d 599 (S.C. 1947). Oral proxy is valid in some states. Pearson v. First Fed. S. and L. Assn. of T.S., 149 S.2d 891 (Fla. 1963). *But, c.f.*, proxy must be signed: Fla. St. §607.101.

12. *See*, Mackin v. Nicollet Hotel, Inc., 25 F.2d 783, 786 (8th Cir. 1928). *See*, Oleck, *Proxy Voting Power in Nonprofit Organizations*, 14 Clev.-Mar. L. Rev. 273 (1965).

13. *See*, 3 Oleck, *Modern Corporation Law*, c. 59 (1978 Supp.); Henn & Alexander, *Corporations*, §196 (3d ed. 1983).

14. *See*, Sagness v. Farmers Cooperative Creamery Co., 67 S.D. 379, 293 N.W. 365 (1940).

15. Wellington-Bull and Co. v. Morris, 132 Misc. 509, 230 N.Y.S. 122 (1928). But liberal construction was favored in Smith v. San Francisco and N.P.R. Co., 115 Calif. 584, 47 P. 582 (1897).

16. Gentry-Futch Co. v. Gentry, 90 Fla. 595, 106 S. 473 (1925); N.Y. Not-for-Profit Corp. L. §609(1).

17. N.Y. Not-for-Profit Corp. L. §609. *And see,* Anno. Calif. Corp. Code §9402; Conn. Gen. Stat. §33-471; Mo. Rev. Stat. §355.015(8); Fla. Stat. 617.0721; Del. Code Anno. tit. 8 §215(b). Not so at common law. Hart v. Sheridan, 168 Misc. 386, 5 N.Y.S.2d 820 (1938).

18. Ohio Rev. Code §1702.20; 15 Penna. Stat. §5759; Lo Curto v. River Edge Girl Scout Assoc., Inc., 59 N.J. Super. 408, 157 A.2d 862 (1960); Dixie Elec. Power Assn. v. Hosey, 208 S.2d 751 (Miss. 1968).

19. N.Y. Genl. Corp. L. §19. *But see,* State *ex rel.* Leavell v. Nelson, 387 P.2d 82 (Wash.), 99 A.L.R. 2d 231 (1963), allowing use of proxies in a cooperative apartment association. See Fl. St. §657.024; N.Y. N-P-C Law §609.

20. Blair v. F.H. Smith Co., 18 Del. Ch. 150, 156 A. 207 (1931); Matter of Ideal Mutual Ins. Co., 18 Misc.2d 127, 190 N.Y.S.2d 887 (1959); McClean v. Bradley, 299 F. 379 (6th Cir. 1924). *See* C.F., Safanda, *Proxy Voting by Commercial Bank Trust Departments,* 90 Banking L.J. 91 (1973).

21. *Parshalle v. Roy,* 567 A.2d 19 (Del. Ch. 1989).

22. Axe, *supra,* n. 7; Fletcher, *supra,* n. 2; text, *supra* at n. 1.

23. *See supra,* n. 1–5.

24. *See, supra,* n. 7, as to business corporations. As to nonprofit corporations *see,* Lo Curto v. River Edge Girl Scouts Assn., Inc., 59 N.J. Super. 408, 157 A.2d 862 (1960).

25. Vliet v. Smith, 153 N.Y.S.2d 1014 (1956), referring to N.Y. Gen. Corp. L. §19. Proxy voting historically has been a creature of statute: *In re* Schwartz and Gray, 77 N.J.L. 415, 72 A. 70 (S. Ct. 1909); Green v. Holzmueller, 1 Terry 16, 40 Del. 16, 5 A.2d 251, 253 (S. Ct. 1939).

26. Walker v. Johnson, 17 App. D.C. 144, 162 (1900).

27. Pohle v. Rhode Island Food Dealers Assn., 63 R.I. 91, 7 A.2d 267 (1939); and one instance of voting by *directors* is not sufficient to establish a corporate custom of proxy voting. *But see, In re* Tidewater Coal Exchange, 274 F. 1009 (D.C., N.Y. 1921) custom held not enough.

28. *Wymbs v. Conashaugh Lakes Community Ass'n, Inc.,* 616 A.2d 749 (Pa. Cmwlth., 1992).

29. *See* lists of case citations by states in 5 Fletcher, *Cyclopedia of the Law of Private Corporations,* 207 (curr. ed.); Oleck, *Modern Corporation Law,* cc. 47, 59 (1978 Supp.); RMN-P-C Act §7.24 (1986 Rev.).

30. Most of these citations of statutes below are from Oleck, *Proxies in Nonprofit Organization,* 14 Clev.-Mar. L. Rev. 273 (1965).

31. Code of Ala., tit. 10 §3A-31; like Model NPC Act §15; proposed §7.24 (1986).

32. Alaska St. §10.20.071 (approved 10-9-92); *see above,* n. 4.

33. Ariz. Rev. St. §10-033.

34. Ark. St. §4-28-212.

35. West's Ann. Cal. Corp. Code §5613.

36. C.R.S.A. §7-23-106.

37. C.G.S.A. §33-471.

38. 8 Del. C. §215.

39. DC Code 1981 §29-516.

40. DC Code 1981 §29-1114.

41. West's F.S.A. §617.0721.

42. West's F.S.A. §619.06.

43. Fla. Stat. 657.024.

44. Code, §14-2-722.

45. Code, §14-3-724.

46. Code, §7-1-661.

47. HRS §415B-43.

48. I.C. §30-3-58.

49. I.C. §22-2610.

50. I.C. §41-3203.

51. 805 ILCS 105/107.50.

52. IC 23-17-11-6.

53. I.C.A. §504A.15.

54. I.C.A. §498.18.

55. K.S.A. §17-6502.

56. KRS §273.201.

57. LSA-R.S. 12:232.

58. LSA-R.S. 6:647.

59. 24-A M.R.S.A. §4103.

60. 13 M.R.S.A. §1602.

61. 13 M.R.S.A. §604.

62. MD CORP & ASSNS §5-202.

63. MD CORP & ASSNS §5-521.

64. MD CORP & ASSNS §5-5A-02.

65. MD CORP & ASSNS §6-401.

66. MD FIN INST §6-211.

67. M.G.L.A. 180 §6A.

68. M.G.L.A. 157 §13.

69. M.G.L.A. 171 §11.

70. M.G.L.A. 176 §3.

71. M.C.L.A. 450.2421.

72. *Id.*

73. M.S.A. §317A.453

74. MBCA, section 302A.237.

75. Code 1972, §79-11-221.

76. Code 1972, §81-13-69.

77. V.A.M.S. 355.015 (8).

78. V.A.M.S. 357.090, 357.110.

79. MCA 35-2-539.

80. *See* Neb. Rev. St. §21-1914. Prohibited in cooperatives. Neb. Rev. St. §1335.

81. N.R.S. 82.321.

82. R.S.A. 301-A:1.

83. R.S.A. 295:5

84. N.J.S.A. 15A:5-18.

85. NMSA 1978, §53-8-15.

86. McKinney's N-PCL §602.

87. Flynn v. Kendall, 195 Misc. 221, 88 N.Y.S.2d 299 (1949); Azgi v. Ryan, 120 Misc. 2d 121, 465 N.Y.S.2d 414 (1983).

88. Craig Medicine Co. v. Merchants' Bank, 59 Hun. 561, 14 N.Y.S.2d 16 (1891).

89. G.S. §55A-32.

90. NDCC, 10-24-15.

91. NDCC, 6-06-10; NDCC, 26.1-15.1-04.

92. R.C. §§1702.20, 1702.21.

93. 18 OKL. St. Ann. §1060.

94. O.R.S. §65.231.

95. 15 Pa. C.S.A. §5759.

96. Gen. Laws 1956, §7-6-20.

97. Code 1976 §33-31-100.

98. Code 1976 §33-47-810.

99. Code 1976 §33-49-440.

100. Code 1976 §34-29-80.

101. SDCL 47-23-9.

102. SDCL 47-23-12.

103. T.C.A. §48-57-205.

104. Vernon's Ann. Texas Civ. St. Art. 1396-2.13.

105. V.C.A. 1953 §16-6-30.

106. 11 V.S.A. §2362

107. Code 1950, §13.1-847

108. 13 V.I.C. §495.

109. West's RCWA 24.03.085.

110. Code, §31-1-138.

111. W.S.A. 181.16.

112. W.S.A. 186.06.

113. W.S. 1977 §17-19-724.

114. (1964 revision) Committee on Corporate Laws of the A.B.A. (Joint Committee on Continuing Legal Education of the A.L.I. and A.B.A.). 133 South 36th St., Philadelphia 4, Pa.; and 1986 revision (Exposure Draft) (*See* n. 3,4).

115. Harris, *The Model Business Corporation Act; an Invitation to Irresponsibility*, 50 Northwestern Univ. L. Rev. 1 (1955).

116. Model Nonprofit Corp. Act. §12 (old).

117. *Ibid.*, §15.

118. *Ibid.*, §18.

119. Bontempo v. Carey, 64 N.J. Super. 51, 165 A.2d 222 (1960).

120. *Ibid.*, at 228.

121. *Ibid.*, at 229, citing Schwartze v. City of Camden, 77 N.J. Eq. 135, 75 A. 647 (Ch. 1910); O'Brien v. Fuller, 93 N.H. 221, 39 A.2d 220, 224 (S. Ct. 1944).

122. *See supra,* Colorado, Delaware, District of Columbia, *etc.*

123. *See, supra,* Florida, Idaho, Mississippi, *etc.*

124. Minn. St. Anno. §§317.22 (subd. 6), 317.20 (subd. 13).

125. Craig Medicine Co. v. Merchants Bank, 59 Hun. 561, 14 N.Y.S. 16 (1891) *re:* New Jersey law; Stevens v. Acadia Dairies, Inc., 15 Del. Ch. 248, 135 A. 846 (1927); Paxton v. Heron, 92 P. 15 (Colo. 1907); Lippman v. Kehoe Stenograph Co., 11 Del. Ch. 80, 95 A. 895 (1915); Perry v. Tuskaloosa etc. Co., 93 Ala. 364, 9 S. 217 (1891); *In re* Tidewater Coal Exchange, 274 F. 1009, 1011, at 1014 (D.C.S.D. N.Y. 1921) (unincorporated association; proxy viewed as invalid though customarily employed by executive committee); Greenberg v. Harrison, 143 Conn. 519, 124 A.2d 216 (1956).

126. Ohio Rev. Code §1702.33 (D). *See,* Note, *Extent to Which Corporate Directors May Act Without a Formal Board Meeting,* 11 Syracuse L. Rev. 68 (1959).

127. *In re* Tidewater Coal Exchange, *supra,* n. 125 *But see, supra,* n. 27.

128. *Supra,* at n. 125.

129. *Supra,* n. 31-113.

130. See, Fla. Condo Study Commission proposals CS/HB 1465 (Apr. 1991, eff. Jan. 1, 1992); 91 Community Up Date 4 (newsletter, May 1991, of Becker & Poliakoff of Fort Lauderdale, FL).

131. *See* the foregoing Sections.

132. N.Y. N-P Corp. L. §609. May be oral in some states.

133. White v. N.Y. *etc.* Society, 45 Hun. (N.Y.) 580 (1887).

134. Gow v. Consolidated Coppermines Corp., 19 Del. Ch. 172, 165 A. 136 (1933).

135. Commissioner of Banks v. Cosmopolitan Trust Co., 253 Mass. 205, 148 N.E. 609 (1925).

136. Hoene v. Pollak, 118 Ala. 617, 24 S. 349 (1898).

137. See, Fl. St. §§ 607.0722, 607.0724 (eff. July 1990); Fl. Admin. Code Rules 7D-23.002(1) and (2).

138. N.Y.N-P-C Law §609.

139. *Id.*

140. *See,* 3 Oleck, *Modern Corporation Law,* c. 59 (1978 Supp.).

141. *See,* Doris and Friedman, *Corporate Meetings, Minutes and Resolutions* (3d ed., New York, Prentice-Hall, Inc. 1951).

142. Elgin Natl. Industries, Inc. v. Chemetron Corp., 299 F. Supp. 367 (D.C. Del. 1969); Investment Associates, Inc. v. Standard P. and L. Corp., 48 A.2d 501 (Del. 1946); Standard L. and P. Corp. v. Invest. Assoc., Inc., 51 A.2d 572 (Del. 1947); latest proxy revokes the former.

143. Williams v. Sterling Oil of Okla., Inc., 267 A.2d 630 (Del. Ch. 1970). Pope v. Whitridge, 110 Md. 468; 73 A. 281 (1909).

144. *See,* Chounis v. Laing, 125 W. Va. 275;23 S.E.2d 628 (1942).

145. Blair v. F.H. Smith Co., 18 Del. Ch. 150; 156 A. 207 (1931).

146. Fidelity Bldg. and Loan Assn. v. Thompson, 25 S.W.2d 247 (Tex. Civ. App. 1930).

147. *E.g.,* New York (*see* §266 above). Gen. St. No. Car. §§55-68(b) followed in, Stein v. Capital Outdoor Advertising, Inc., 159 S.E.2d 351 (No. Car. 1968); Rev. St. Nebr. §§21-1914, 21-1915; La. St. Anno. §§12:232(C); 12:35(F).

148. Simpson v. Nielson, 77 Calif. App. 297; 246 P. 342 (1926).

149. Conn. Gen. Stat. §33-471; Mo. Rev. Stat. §355.120; Ohio Rev. Code §1702.20, 1702.21. *See,* Muth v. Maxton, 55 Ohio O. 263, 119 N.E.2d 162 (1954).

150. 15 Penna. Stat. §5759.

151. Del. Code Anno., tit. 8, §215.

152. Calif. Nonprofit Corp. L. §5613.

153. Fla. Stat. §617.0721.

154. *See* State *ex rel.* Everett Trust and Sav. Bk. v. Pacific W.P. Co., 22 Wash.2d 844; 157 P.2d 707 (1945); Henn and Alexander, *Corporations* §196 (3rd ed., 1983).

155. *See,* Ecclestone v. Indialantic, Inc., 319 Mich. 248; 29 N.W.2d 679 (1947); and, note, 16 LRA (n.s.) 1139.

156. Roberts v. Whitson, 188 S.W.2d 875 (Tex. Civ. App. 1945).

157. Sullivan v. Parkes, 69 A.D. 221; 74 N.Y.S. 787 (1902).

158. *See In re* Germicide Co., 65 Hun. (N.Y.) 606, 20 N.Y.S. 495 (1892).

159. In business corporations, pledge of stock, or the like. *See,* 3 Oleck, n.139; Henn and Alexander, *Corporations* §196 (3rd ed., 1983).

160. Schott v. Climax Molybdenum Co., 154 A.2d 221 (Del. Ch. 1959).

161. *E.g.,* Minn., N.Y., N.C., Ohio, Okla., Penna. *See* As to authenticating of proxies, 3 Oleck, *Modern Corporation Law,* §1491 (1978 Supp.).

162. N.Y. Not-for-Profit Corp. L. §609.

163. Warren v. Pym, 59 A.773 (N.Y. Eq., 1904); and *see,* Leavitt, *The Voting Trust,* c. 1 (1941).

164. Model Bus. Corp. Act §34; N.Y. Bus. Corp. L. §621; and *see* Hornstein, *Corporation Law & Practice* §221 (1959) for a form of Voting Trust Agreement; and Note, *Voting Trusts and Irrevocable Proxies,* 41 Temple L.Q. 480 (1968).

165. *See,* Henn and Alexander, *Corporations* §197, 198 (3rd ed., 1983); 3 Oleck, *Modern Corporation Law* §1472 (1978 Suppl.).

166. Oleck, n. 165, at §§1467-1472.

167. *See* forms in Oleck, n. 165, Forms 602-606.

168. Muth v. Maxton, 119 N.E.2d 162 (Ohio Com. Pl., 1954).

169. Fl. St. §617.0721 (3).

27

DIRECTORS AND TRUSTEES: SELECTION, STATUS, AND REMOVAL

[Caryl Kilinski and Scott Dwyer assisted in the research on this chapter and the next]

§271. STATUS OF A DIRECTOR OR TRUSTEE

Directors of nonprofit organizations (or *trustees,* as they often are titled in charitable, educational, and other eleemosynary organizations) usually are the mainsprings of their corporations, often far more than is the case in business organizations. In both kinds of organizations, a *director* or *trustee* is one of the persons elected or appointed to the board or group (however that group be titled) authorized to manage and direct the affairs of that company or corporation.[1] And a director or trustee is an *officer* of the organization.[2]

The body of persons elected by the shareholders (members) to manage the affairs of the corporation, by whatever name this body may be called, is the board of directors.[3]

In nonprofit organizations, these same terms often are used to designate the persons who are to manage and direct the organization affairs.[4]

A *director* of a corporation is a representative of the members. His status is akin to that of an elected legislator, but it also has many of the characteristics of an agent's position, and many of those of a trustee's position in a trust of property. But while a director's status resembles all of these, it is a distinct, special kind of status in itself.[5] In the last analysis, it is the status needed by a representative, as a practical matter, to carry on the affairs of the group which he represents.[6]

Even in business corporations, directors are often called *trustees.*

Use the title of "trustees". In nonprofit organizations, the term *trustees* conveys the idea of the functions of the officers of the board better than the word *directors* does. In most charitable organizations, the title of trustee is preferred.

Other terms also may be used, such as *councilor, governor, steward, guardian, warden, foreman,* or *master.*[7]

The 1986 Revision of the ABA Model Nonprofit Corporation Act proposed that directors no longer be viewed as trustee-type officers nor that founders' gifts be deemed assets in trust. L. A. Moody, *The Who, What and How of the RMNC Act,* p. 5, in Seminar Materials book of *Nonprofit Organizations,* Northern Kentucky Univ., Chase College of Law (Feb. 1988). Moody was the Chairperson of the ABA Subcommittee. This proposal is not acceptable to most people.

The general authority and status of trustees of a nonprofit corporation are similar to those of directors of other corporations, except that they are somewhat limited in their power to deal with the corporation's property.[8]

There is a split of views and authority as to whether a director of a charitable corporation, and perhaps even of a merely nonprofit (not charitable) corporation, should be held to the high standards of a trustee as in *trust law,* or of a director in ordinary business corporation law. The majority of writers' (usually teachers of *business* corporation or *tax* law) view sees the latter as the better rule.[9] The reason for this majority view has been stated as follows: "The trustee standard is excessively demanding for most directors of nonprofit organizations. Trustees are subject to the highest standards of care and fiduciary conduct. Directors of nonprofit organizations often have other full-time positions and perform their duties as an avocational community service. The 'prudent director' test is more realistic and more flexible than the trustee standards."[10] But in both business and nonprofit corporations, a corporate director has a duty to disclose misconduct of other directors in order to avoid personal liability for acquiescence.[11] [See the Section on Fiduciary Duty.]

In dealings with property, the express consent of the general membership (*e.g.,* two-thirds vote) often is required.[12]

A strong indication of the *trustee of property* nature of a director's position is apparent in that statutes often permit nonmembers of nonprofit corporations to be directors or officers.[13]

De facto directors or trustees. Persons who exercise the functions of directors under some seeming authority, despite their lack of true legal election or the like, are *de facto* directors.

This designation should not be confused with that of a *de facto corporation* (defectively incorporated).[14]

De facto directors may bind the corporation, although their tenure of office is open to direct attack[15] and sometimes to collateral attack.[16] But a person who wrongfully assumes the powers of a director may not use his de facto status as a defense for his acts.[17]

One who assumes to act as a director has the duties of a director.[18]

Trustee status in a nonprofit organization is not the same thing as the special status of a trustee of an express, private trust deed or indenture. Thus a church organization "trustee" or "steward" does not have personal responsibility and liability for a defective gate on church property, which fell and injured a child.[19] So, too, a bequest to the trustees of an institution is a bequest to the institution.[20]

§272. BOARD MANAGEMENT OF CORPORATE AFFAIRS

Status as a director means status as a member of the *board of directors*. This is important because the *board*—not the individual act of directors—must govern the corporation. [The importance of meetings in enabling directors to act is discussed in Chapter 29.]

Bylaws, the charter, or statutes may and do require that decision of certain special matters be made by the members. But in general, routine management of affairs lies in the hands of the board of directors.[21]

Even if directors wish to do so, they may not lawfully abdicate their authority or duties, in favor of anyone else.[22] The nature of the general management of a corporation is that the directors shall do the managing, in their own good discretion, except as the charter or bylaws provide otherwise, or as statutes require members' consents for special matters. To this the members agree by the very *contract of membership*. The relation of the members to the routine management of affairs is one primarily of request or suggestion.[23]

An agreement to place managing (directing) authority in one person, or even in one group of members, is illegal.[24] (An *executive committee* is a special case, and is treated below, in the chapter on committees.) An agreement for a director to be only nominal, while others actually run the corporation, is illegal.[25]

Directors must exercise reasonable care and high good faith in corporate affairs.[26] They may (and should) ask the advice and informative guidance of others.[27] But they must use their own judgment in coming to final decisions.[28] The members may not "sterilize" (make sterile or futile) the board of directors.[29]

Thus, in a nonprofit corporation, the power of control of day-to-day affairs rests in the board of directors. The members ordinarily cannot bind the corporation by contract.[30] On the other hand, the directors and officers are representatives, and their acts are subject to fair criticism by the members.[31]

Directors are presumed to use a reasonable degree of care and diligence, and are presumed to have a reasonably accurate knowledge of corporate affairs.[32]

All these rules suggest that it is unwise to attempt to vest too many specific control powers in the general membership. Aside from the clumsiness of a pure mass-meeting type of management, it is illegal if it makes puppets of the directors. However, attempts at such a system are common in nonprofit organizations. They seem very democratic and unobjectionable on casual inspection, but they often result in confusion and acrimonious disputes.

However, an opposite situation may exist when a nonprofit corporation is formed by a group of persons and *no* provision is made in the articles of incorporation for control by the members. In California, the incorporating directors and members were considered synonymous. Thus all control over the application of the nonprofit corporation's funds was vested exclusively in the Board of Directors, with probability that there then would be no input from outside sources.[33] Fortunately, California repealed §9603 in 1980.

§273. FIDUCIARY STATUS OF DIRECTORS

"It is well-established that a corporation officer occupies a position of trust in relation to his corporation. *Thomas v. Matthews* (1916), 94 Ohio St., 32, 43, 113 N.E. 669, 671. Such relationship imposes upon directors duties in the nature of a fiduciary obligation. *Id.*, see, also, *Radol v. Thomas* (C.A. 6, 1985), 772 F.2d 244, certiorari denied (1986), 477 U.S. 903, 106 S. Ct. 3272, 91 L.Ed. 2d 562. The principles which govern the fiduciary relationship between a corporation and its directors include a duty of good faith, a duty of loyalty, a duty to refrain from self-dealing, and a duty of disclosure. R.C. (Ohio) 1701.59(B) and 1701.60(A) (1); see also (citations)...."[34]

A director is a *fiduciary*.[35] A *fiduciary* holds a character status analogous to (but not quite as strict as) that of a trustee of an express trust of property.[36] It involves in essence a duty to act for the good of others rather than for one's own benefit.[37]

The chief fiduciary duty of a director is to exercise his powers for the benefit of the corporation.[38] He must exercise these powers for the benefit of all the members—not for only some of them[39]—with full honesty and reasonable efficiency.[40]

A director may, however, take advantage of an opportunity for personal benefit that arises because of his position, provided that no personal seizing of a corporate opportunity, or the like, is involved.[41] (See the next chapter.)

Breach of faith. Unfortunately, there are cases of breach of fiduciary duty by directors.[42] Some states hold directors personally liable only for "gross negligence."[43] Most states hold them personally liable for "ordinary negligence" in managing corporate affairs.[44]

Failure to properly supervise subordinates, or to use due care in choosing them, results in personal liability.[45] Good faith or good intentions do not purge improper conduct.[46]

"Proprietary" attitudes. Some trustees and officers of nonprofit organizations develop what can only be called a "proprietary" attitude, as though they were owners of the organization, not its servants. The improper and reprehensible nature of such an attitude, and of the decisions that flow from it, are obvious.

It is well for such persons to be reminded of the law applicable to high-handed use of managerial status. Statutes governing false statements, entries, or reports, of course, are stringent,[47] and misconduct results in personal liability.[48]

Public authorities and courts are particularly stern in cases of abuse of powers by trustees or officers of charitable (*e.g.*, religious, educational, etc.) organizations. For example, under the Ohio statutes, any interested persons may complain to the attorney-general. He will then begin court procedures in which the court may make any order suited to the situation.[49]

Any arrangement or contract of the organization in which a situation of conflicting loyalties is found will be subjected to strict scrutiny by the courts. Then the persons who seek to maintain the transaction must maintain the burden of proof of its propriety.[50]

The "National Religious Broadcasters" (Assn.) new Ethics and Financial Integrity Commission (EFICOM) (1989) *Standards of Ethics*, stated in its January 1990 meeting, require that the *Board* of Directors (Trustees) of Nonprofit Organizations have a *majority* who are *not members of the same family*. The president of the Evangelical Council for Financial Accountability (who was the administrator of EFICOM) said that family-controlled boards are not good practice, though legal. But ministries of under $100,000 annual donation income are *exempt* from the new Standard. Other big NPO watchdog groups require *independent boards*.[51]

§274. QUALIFICATIONS OF DIRECTORS

The definition of a board is, "an active and responsible governing body, holding regular meetings, whose members have no material conflict of interest and serve without compensation."[52]

The charter or bylaws of nonprofit corporations may establish the qualifications and classifications of directors.[53] *Classification* usually means division into not more than five *periods of office*, setting up a rotation of elections, of maintaining continuity of some experienced directors in office.

In most states, all directors must be over the age of 18 years, at least one must be a resident of the United States, and at least one must be a resident of the state of incorporation.[54]

Delaware and a few other states do not require state residence. Such absence of local attachment is unhealthy.[55] Such statutes represent a rather commercial bidding for corporate business (and income) by these states.

While it is not, strictly speaking, a "qualification," it should be remembered that the articles of incorporation usually must set forth the names and addresses of the original directors.[56]

If unqualified persons are elected as directors (*e.g.*, even in the charter) they are *de facto* directors.[57] But they may be removed from office.[58]

Directors in most states need not be members.[59]

Moral and personal-history qualifications may be—and often are—established for directors.[60]

Foreigners may be directors, provided usually that at least one director be a citizen.[61]

§275. NUMBER OF DIRECTORS

The size of the Board of Directors is extremely important in a nonprofit corporation. One author has suggested that the larger the size of the board, the greater the concentration of the board's powers in a few individuals. This reflects the tendency of some individuals to shirk their responsibilities and to lose interest in a nonprofit corporation's affairs.[62] On the other hand, it should be noted that, if the board of directors is too small, there will be inflexibility, little opportunity for injection of new ideas, and a serious risk of stagnation.

For nonprofit corporations most states require that there be at least three directors, while many require five.[63] Many states require that the charter set a maximum of from 15 to 21.[64] California permits a one-director "board,"[65] as does the 1986 Revision of the Model Nonprofit Corporation Act [proposed §8.01(c).] The A.B.A. proposals (also for one-person incorporations [proposed §2.01]) seem to be invitations to abuse of corporate status in nonprofit corporations as in business corporations.

For some special kinds of corporations—for example, cemetery corporations—special provisions concerning the number of directors may be made.[66]

Five incorporators usually are required, but only three directors. For the special corporations such as cemetery corporations, seven incorporators and three directors may be specified.[67]

Bylaws may make more specific numerical rules within the range permitted by the statutes.[68]

Many statutes also make special rules for changes in the number of directors.[69] Detailed procedures are specified in some statutes.[70]

§276. TRUSTEE-DIRECTORS IN CHARGE OF PROPERTY

A few states, by statute, permit the appointment of individual or corporate trustees to hold and care for the property of the corporation. New York, for example, approves if the charter or an amendment thereto so provides (excepting a YMCA). The charter must also provide rules for the trustees' selection and for the appointment of their successors. Specific powers and duties of the directors may then be vested in these *trustees*, concerning the specific property.[71]

These trustees thus closely resemble the trustees of an unincorporated association.[72]

A *group* (*e.g.*, such as a committee) that has autonomy (*e.g.*, over a welfare fund, or grievance committee for several branches of an organization) may be sued *as an entity*, in the group name.[73]

§277. (RESERVED)

§278. DIRECTORS' TERMS OF OFFICE

No precise limit to a director's term of office usually is found in nonprofit-corporation statues. This usually is left to the bylaws, but the New York statute now sets a limit of five years in some cases.[74]

A state statute limited the term of office of a director to one year, unless specifically otherwise stated in the corporation's articles of incorporation. A church endowment-fund (nonstock) corporation's articles of incorporation were claimed to be *not* controlled by this statute, because it was ex post facto (enacted after the articles were adopted), and a director claimed to have been elected (in effect) "for life." Virginia court *held* that the statute applies *retroactively*, because it is not an "interpretive" law, but goes to the basic regulation and limiting of "public" functions.[75]

A *rotating* system of elections now is widespread. It calls for election of at least one director every year. If a board consists of three members, three years is the term of office of any director. This method gives some assurance of continuity of experienced directors in office.[76]

An advantage of employing a system of staggering of the directors' terms of office is the assurance that the organization will not be subject to a quick turnover of board personnel. Also, persons both qualified and experienced will always be on the board.[77]

Another widely used system involves annual elections for the entire board.

Holdover directors. If elections of new directors are not held in due course, the old directors continue in office on a holdover status with their normal, full powers.[78] Holdover status continues until successors are duly elected.[79]

In such circumstances, the members should call a special election meeting (pursuant, where applicable, to statutory authority).[80]

Holdover directors are not forced to serve. They may outspokenly resign, or else resign by implication by refusing to continue to serve.[81]

It is reasonable to believe that holdover powers would not continue if the neglect to hold an election were deliberate, and intended as a device to continue to hold the office.

Under one state's approach, the statutes do not set an absolute limit to a director's term of office before he must seek re-election. Theoretically, a director could serve for life without having to seek re-election.[82] Under such law, the nonprofit corporation may become calcified. The opposite result may occur when the terms of the directors are made too short. The directors may never have enough time to thoroughly familiarize themselves with the corporation's affairs. Then the result may be that the staff in reality runs the corporation. The end result would be that the board of directors merely becomes a rubber stamp for the actions of the professional staff.[83]

§279. ELECTION OF DIRECTORS

See Chapter 24 on meetings and conventions of members and Chapter 25 on voting and elections.

If an irreconcilable deadlock among the members prevents the election of directors, a petition by one-half the members may be filed in the state court, for dissolution of the corporation. If a greater-than-majority number is required for the election, that number may file the petition. Or the number required by statute to file an ordinary dissolution of the corporation may do so.[84]

No express acceptance of election is necessary. Such acceptance is presumed, unless the person concerned indicates his intention not to accept.[85] In Pennsylvania, the naming of the directors in the articles of incorporation constitutes an affirmation that the directors have agreed to serve as such.[86]

Of course, the bylaws may require express acceptance. Acceptance also may be indicated by conduct. And once acceptance has expressly or impliedly been given, it may not be withdrawn; although, resignation of course is possible.[87]

§280. VACANT DIRECTORSHIPS

If a sufficient number of directors are left to make up a quorum, a vacancy on the board does not invalidate board actions.[88] Ordinarily, unless the bylaws, the charter, or statutes provide otherwise, vacancies should be filled by special elections by the members.[89] Bylaw rules covering vacancies are desirable.

A bylaw that authorized the directors who remain in office to choose a new director to fill a vacancy overrode another bylaw that required a 75 percent vote of directors in any business transaction.[90]

In an electric cooperative's bylaws its provisions as to removal of an officer or trustee, allowing any member to bring charges against him/her, is not per se the same thing as removal for cause. If the provisions are not clear they do not have effect "as a matter of law;" but court examination of evidence as to the intention of the bylaws must be made even where a declaratory judgment is sought.[91]

As to filling vacancies on the board, Ohio and New York's express enactments say:[92]

[*New York*] . . . If a vacancy remains unfilled for six months after it occurs, and by reason of the absence, illness, or other inability of one or more of the remaining directors a quorum of the board cannot be obtained, the remaining directors, or a majority of them, may appoint a director to fill such vacancy.

[*Ohio's* statute] (A) The office of a trustee becomes vacant if he dies or resigns, which resignation shall take effect immediately or at such other time as the trustee may specify.

(B) A trustee may be removed from office pursuant to any procedure therefor provided in the articles or in the regulations, and such removal shall create a vacancy in the board.

(C) Unless the articles or the regulations otherwise provide, the remaining trustees, though less than a majority of the whole authorized number of trustees, may, by the vote of a majority of their number, fill any vacancy in the board for the unexpired term. Within the meaning of this section, a vacancy exists in case the voting members increase the authorized number of trustees but fail at the meeting at which such increase is authorized, or an adjournment thereof, to elect the additional trustees provided for, or in case the voting members fail at any time to elect the whole authorized number of trustees.

In some states a director who is about to resign can vote on his successor.[93] This seems to be a very questionable view, conducive to abuse.

Statutes often give the power of election to the directors only when the members have had a reasonable period of time (*e.g.*, six months) themselves to fill the vacancy.

If the vacancy results from an increase in the number of directors, these statutes do not apply; the members must do the electing.[94] They hold a special election and need not wait for the annual election meeting.[95]

During dissolution period. While a corporation is being "wound up," in the process of dissolving it, vacancies in directorships may be filled by a majority vote of the remaining directors. If all the board positions are vacant, the former members may elect an entire board to carry through the winding-up process.[96]

When does a vacancy occur? In most cases, a vacancy on the board is the result of a resignation or a death. Permanent departure from the community may have the effect of a resignation.

Prolonged neglect or disability also may result in a vacancy. How long this must go on before having such an effect is best settled by a bylaw provision. A three-month absence has been held to be not long enough.[97]

Reduction in number of directors. A reduction in the number of directors, by an amendment of the charter, does not automatically create vacancies. The number in office drops as directors' terms of office expire. However, if the charter or bylaws provide that the directors may be removed without cause, immediate removals may be made.[98]

Vacancy by removal for cause. When a director is removed for cause, by legal proceedings, the same proceedings usually grant permission to fill the resulting vacancy, in accordance with the charter or bylaws if they cover this situation, and otherwise as the court may order.[99]

Notwithstanding that a shareholder's agreement requires maintenance in office of a particular director, such director may be removed for cause, since, implicit in any agreement to maintain a particular director in office, is the director's duty to fulfill faithfully the requirements of his office."[100]

§281. RESIGNATION OF DIRECTORS

A director (or officer) may resign at any time, ordinarily,[101] although existence of a contract of employment (and thus breach of that contract) may complicate the situation. In some cases, the resignation does not have to be accepted in order to be valid.[102] It also is possible to require acceptance by the board. This condition may be imposed by the charter or the bylaws or by contractual obligations.[103]

It can happen that a resignation is ineffective because it is not accepted, even though the affected director does not know this.[104] A mere provision that a director shall hold office for a specified period, or until his successor is elected, usually is not enough to produce such an effect.[105] Some states hold that service of legal process may legally be made on the resigning director or officer until the corporation acts on the resignation.[106]

Fraudulent resignations, intended to enable the director or officer to attack the corporation for its lack of such officers, of course are invalid. And the same is true of resignations that leave the organization uncared-for and unprotected,[107] or that are made for payment or gain.[108]

After he resigns, a director continues to be liable for acts he committed or concurred in before his resignation.[109] And he may not simply resume his office if he wishes to do so.[110]

The United Way was still grappling in 1993 with "trust and confidence issues" after director Aramony resigned amid allegations of misuse of funds. Only 73 percent of UW's members had paid their dues for 1993. Thus, there would be a $2.7 million shortfall of funds at the national association.[111]

If, after tendering his resignation, the director continues to act as such, and the resignation is not acted upon, he remains a director.[112] Similarly, if the resignation, in terms, is not to be effective until acted upon, he remains a director until it is acted upon.[113]

A resignation may be implied, as well as expressed.[114]

Withdrawal of resignation. A resignation may be withdrawn at any time before it is actually accepted.[115] The manner of revocation by contrary action (*e.g.*, attending meetings) is mentioned above.

If a resignation, by its terms, is intended to be effective at once, it thereafter may not be withdrawn.[116]

Form of resignation. No particular form or style is prescribed for resignations, unless by the charter or bylaws.[117] Oral resignation or resignation by conduct will suffice.[118] Nor, ordinarily, need it be announced to the public or to creditors.[119]

§282. SUSPENSION OR REMOVAL OF DIRECTORS

Most states now have statutory procedures for the removal or suspension of directors or officers. These procedures usually are based on charges of misconduct or abuse of trust, or on demands of accounting, or damages, or injunction for waste or improper transfer of assets.[120] They sometimes require court action[121] or action by the state's attorney-general.[122] Similar proceedings apply to improper[123] (usually fraudulent[124]) election to office.

Bylaw provisions often deal with this problem. They must be consistent with the statutes.[125]

These rules for directors must not be confused with rules governing expulsion of members in general. The latter are quite distinct. They are treated in a separate chapter, below.

Removal for cause always is possible, regardless of statutes. Every corporation has the inherent right to remove directors or officers for valid cause.[126]

Removal without cause also may be effected, if the charter, the bylaws, or a statute so provide.[127] Some states permit removal of purely administrative officers without cause.[128] Directors or officers who were elected on a *pro tem* basis may be so removed when no rule of removal only for cause is present.[129]

Examples of removal for cause. Unjustified attacks on the president, and refusal to cooperate with him, are cause for removal.[130]

Taking of corporate funds is cause for removal.[131]

Failure to disclose necessary information on business matters is cause for removal.[132]

Personal liability for *negligence* is touched on in Section 271. It would seem that negligence in performance of duties, if proved, would be good cause for removal from office.[133] But some cases have held that ordinary negligence, as distinguished from gross or willful negligence, is not sufficient cause.[134]

Disagreement or friction between directors or officers is not cause for removal except in extreme cases.[135]

Who may do the removing? In some states, such as Ohio or Florida, statutes permit removal of directors by the board of directors, with or without cause.[136] This does not affect the removed officer's rights under a contract, if he has one, but election, or bylaws as to terms of office, do not create contract rights.[137] Only members should remove officers elected by them.[138]

"A corporate shareholder's statutory right to remove any director, with or without cause, necessarily includes the right to remove the entire board of directors at one time."[139]

In some states, the rule is that directors may not remove other directors unless the bylaws or charter so provide. Removing must be done by those who selected. The members must act to remove a director,[140] the appointing authority acts in other cases.[141] Precise limitations may and should be put on bylaws that grant removal powers to the board of directors.[142]

Formalities of removal. The standard of formality customary in the organization must be maintained in removal proceedings. An accused director or officer must always be given a reasonable opportunity to defend himself.[143] But he may not vote on his own removal.[144] Removal is subject to court review.[145]

Notice of the charges, and reasonable opportunity to prepare and to speak and cross-examine in his own defense, always must be given.[146]

Improper removal. A director or officer who was improperly removed from office may obtain reinstatement by court order.[147]

The test or propriety of a removal is this: Did the removing authority act in good faith, and in accordance with the charter or bylaws, on due notice, giving due opportunity to be heard? If the answer is "yes," the courts seldom will interfere with the action of the organization.[148] Review of removal and expulsion procedures is more fully discussed in the next chapter below.

A valid bylaw, or clause in the articles, requiring a stated vote percentage for removal (by members or directors) bars removal (even for cause) by a lesser percentage.[149]

Court review of removal for cause is available.[150]

S.E.C. filing. If removal or replacement of a director may involve contractual or security agreements or interests, it may be necessary to comply with S.E.C. Proxy Statement notice rules; *e.g.*, in what amounts to a "takeover" or "tender offer" situation.[151]

POINTS TO REMEMBER

- Use the title *trustee* rather than *director*, in nonprofit organizations.
- But view a director as a kind of trustee of property.
- Let the board of trustees direct. Do not try to cut their powers too far.
- Do not rely on mass-meeting management.
- Clarify powers and duties in the bylaws.
- Provide qualification standards for directors or trustees.
- Keep the board at a practical numerical level.
- Do not make the board unwieldy with "window-dressing."
- Use a rotating system of terms of office.
- Provide clear election rules.
- Provide rules for filling vacancies.
- Provide rules for resignations.
- Provide rules for suspensions and removals—clear, procedural rules.
- Always provide for a hearing for an accused trustee or director.

- Beware of "securities" implications and SEC supervision in removal of "contractual" directors.

NOTES TO CHAPTER 27

1. Fl. St. §§617.0801–617.0834 (1992); 2 Oleck, *Modern Corporation Law*, cc. 39–41 (1978 Supp.) citing statutes and cases from all states, *and see*, 12A *Words and Phrases* 156 (with 1976 Supp.); Mease v. Warm Mineral Springs, Inc., 128 So.2d 174 (Fla. App. 1961) business corporation; State *ex rel.* Northeast Property Owners, Civic Assn. v. Kennedy, 117 Ohio App. 79, 181 N.E.2d 495 (1962) nonprofit corporation trustees. *And see*, Brandt v. Godwin, 3 N.Y.S. 807, 809 (1889); State v. Manning, 220 Iowa 525, 259 N.W. 213 (1935); Colonial Capital Co. v. General Motors Corp., 29 F.R.D. 514, 517 (D.C. Conn. 1961). Utilities Comm. v. General Tel. Co. of S.E., 189 S.E.2d 705 (N.C. 1972); Herald Co. v. Seawell, 472 F.2d 1081 (10th Cir. 1972).

2. State v. Whitmore, 126 Ohio St. 381, 185 N.E. 547, 551 (1933).

3. Restatement, *Conflict of Laws*, §164a. Arizona and Mississippi do not expressly require a board of directors. *See*, Kessler, *Statutory Requirement of a Board of Directors: A Corporate Anachronism*, 27 U. Chi. L. Rev. 696, 712, n. 76 (1960).

4. Balmford v. Grand Lodge A.O.U.W., 16 Misc. 4, 37 N.Y.S. 645, 646 (1896); *and see* (must have management and directory powers) Greek Catholic Congregation of B. of O. v. Plummer, 338 Pa. 373, 12 A.2d 435, 440, 127 *A.L.R.* 1008 (1940); *and see*, Ohio Rev. Code §1702.30.

5. Briggs v. Spaulding, 141 U.S. 132, 147, 11 S.Ct. 924, 35 L.Ed. 662 (1891); Stevens, *Corporations*, §143 (2d ed. 1949).

6. Henn & Alexander, *Corporations*, §203 (3d ed. 1983); Pepper v. Litton, 308 U.S. 295, 60 S.Ct. 238, 84 L. Ed. 281 (1939); Haluka v. Baker, 66 Ohio App. 308, 34 N.E.2d 68, 70 (1941).

7. N.Y. Gen. Corp. L. §3 (13); Ohio Rev. Code §1702.01 (K); *In re* Lake Placid Co., 274 A.D. 205, 81 N.Y.S. 2d 36 (1948); Balmford Case, above, n. 4; Plainview Plumbing & H. Co. v. Ethical Culture Society of L.I., Inc., 24 Misc.2d 1005, 205 N.Y.S.2d 419 (1960). N.Y. N-P-C Law §102.

8. Van Campen v. Olean General Hospital, 210 A.D. 204, 205 N.Y.S. 554 (1924), *affd.* without opinion, 239 N.Y. 615, 147 N.E. 219 (1925).

9. Stern v. Lucy Webb Hayes National Training School for Deaconesses and Missionaries, 381 F. Supp. 1003, 1013 (D.D.C. 1974).

10. Henn and Boyd, *Statutory Trends in the Law of Nonprofit Organizations: California Here We Come!*, 66 Cornell L. Rev. 1103 (1981).

11. Dotlich v. Dotlich, 475 N.E.2d 331 (Ind. App. 1985); and *see*, Note, *The Nonprofit Director's Fiduciary Duty: Toward a New Theory of the Nonprofit Sector*, 77 NW.U.L. Rev. 36 (1982).

12. *See* n. 8; N.Y. Not-for-Profit Corp. L. §509. But *contra*: Ohio Rev. Code §1702.36. Tex. Not-for Profit Corp. Act, Art. 1396, §5.08 permits the corporation to convey land if deed is signed by president and secretary, if supported by majority vote of the full board.

13. N.Y. N-P-C L. §701. *And see*, same rule for business corporations: People v. Lihme, 269 Ill. 351, 109 N.E. 1051, 1054 (1915).

14. *See*, Ridout v. State, 161 Tenn. 248, 30 S.W.2d 255, 257, 71 A.L.R. 830 (1930); Eaker v. Common School Dist. No. 73, 62 S.W.2d 778, 783 (Mo. App. 1933); Anno., 37 A.L.R.3d 277 (1971) as to de facto corporations.

15. Young v. Janas, 34 Del. Ch. 287, 103 A.2d 299 (1954); Stevens, *Corporations*, §160 (2d ed. 1949).

16. Matter of George Ringler & Co., 204 N.Y. 30, 97 N.E. 593 (1912).

17. Stevens, *Corporations*, 744 (2d ed. 1949). *See* as to duplicating of elections, East End Church of God v. Logan, 102 Ohio App. 552, 131 N.E.2d 439 (1956).

18. *Ibid.*, Henn & Alexander, *Corporations*, §§231–242 (3d ed. 1983).

19. Foppiano v. Baker, 3 Mo. App. 560 (1877, appendix digest).

20. New York Institution for Blind v. How's Executors, 10 N.Y. (6 Seld.) 84, 92 (1854).

21. 2 Oleck, *Modern Corporation Law*, c. 41 (1978 Supp. ed.); Church v. Young, 21 Ohio N.P. (n.s.) 569 (1919); Kaplan v. Block, 184 Va. 327, 31 S.E.2d 893 (1944); N.Y. Gen. Corp. L. §28; Gumpert v. Bon Ami Co., 251 F.2d 735 (2d Cir. 1958); D'Arcangelo v. D'Arcangelo, 137 N.J. Eq. 63, 43 A.2d 169 (1945); Lawnwood Medical Center vs. Cassimally, 471 S.2d 1346 (Fla. App. 1985); Gartell v. Knight, 546 F. Supp. 449 (D.C. Ala., 1982).

22. Wheeler v. Layman Foundation, 188 Ga., 267; 3 S.E.2d 645 (1939); Lawnwood, n.18.

23. Lord v. Equitable Life Assur. Society, 194.N.Y. 212, 228; 87 N.E. 443; 22 IRA (n.s.) 420 (1909); Anderson v. Grantsville North Willow Irrig. Co., 51 Utah 137; 169 P. 168 (1917).

24. *See*, Abbey v. Meyerson, 274 A.D. 389; 83 N.Y.S.2d 503; affd., 299 N.Y. 557; 85 N.E.2d 789 (1949).

25. Jackson v. Hooper, 76 N.J. Eq. 592; 75 A. 568 (1910); Zion v. Kurtz, 405 N.E.2d 681 (N.Y. 1980); Home Tel. Co. v. Darley, 355 F. Supp. 992 (D.C. Miss. 1973); Chris-Craft Ind., Inc. v. Piper Aircraft Corp. 480 F.2d 341 (2d Cir. 1973).

26. State *ex rel.* Blackwood v. Brast, 98 W. Va. 596; 127 S.E. 507 (1925); Ga. Code Ann. §14-3-830.

27. Miller v. Vanderlip, 285 N.Y. 116; 33 N.E.2d 51 (1941); Ohio Rev. Code Ann. §1702.30.

28. *See*, Marvin v. Solventol Chem. Pdts., Inc., 298 Mich. 296; 298 N.W. 782 (1941).

29. Manson v. Curtis, n. 14, N.Y. Gen. Corp. L. §27; N.Y. N-P-C Law §§602, 701, 707.

30. Clifford v. Fireman's Mut. Benev. Assn., 233 A.D. 260; 249 N.Y.S. 713 (1931), affd. 183 N.E. 175 (N.Y. 1932).

31. People *ex rel.* Ward v. Uptown Assn., 26 A.D. 297; 49 N.Y.S. 881 (1898).

32. Leterman v. Pink, 249 A.D. 164; 291 N.Y.S. 249 (1936), affd. 11 N.E. 781 (N.Y. 1937).

33. Calif. Corp. L. §9603.

34. *Wing Leasing, Inc. v. M. & B. Aviation*, 542 N.E.2d 671 (Ohio App. 1988, reported Oct. 1989).

35. Pepper v. Litton, 308 U.S. 295; 60 S.Ct. 238; 84 L. Ed. 281 (1939). *See*, W. Knepper, *Liability of Lawyer—Directors*, 40 Ohio St. L.J. 341–60 (1979); Note, *The Fiduciary Duties of Loyalty and Care . . . Directors and Trustees of Charitable Organizations*, 64 Va. L. Rev. 451 (1978); Marsh, *Governance for Non-Profit Organizations . . . (in) Cultural Institutions*, 85 Dick. L. Rev. 613 (1981); Brown, *The Not-For-Profit Corporation Director*, 28 Fedn. of Ins. Counsel Q. 69 (1977); Note, 77 NW. U. L. Rev. 36 (1982).

36. Svanoe v. Jurgens, 144 Ill. 507; 33 N.E. 955 (1893). *See* Vaughn v. Teledyne, 628 F.2d 1214 (9th Cir. 1980).

37. Haluka v. Baker, 66 Ohio App. 308; 34 N.E.2d 68, 70 (1941). *And see*, Trustees of Jesse P. Williams Hospital v. Nisbet, 191 Ga. 821; 14 S.E.2d 64, 76 (1941); *and note*, 59 Yale L.J. 151 (1949); Independent Optical v. Elmore, 289 S.2d 24 (Fla. App. 1974).

38. *See*, Citizens State Bank v. Adams, 140 Fla. 578; 193 S. 281 (1939); Pepper v. Litton, n. 22; Enyart v. Merrick, 148 Ore. 321; 34 P.2d 629 (1934); United States v. Byrum, 408 U.S. 125 (1972).

39. Atkins v. Hughes, 208 Calif. 508; 282 P. 787 (1929).

40. First Mortgage Bond Homestead Assn. v. Baker, 157 Md. 309; 145 A. 876 (1929); Junker v. Cory, 650 F.2d 1349 (5th Cir. 1981).

41. *See*, Solimine v. Hollander, 128 N.J. Eq. 228; 16 A.2d 203 (1940); Burg v. Horn, 380 F.2d 897 (D.C., N.Y. 1967).

42. *See* cases cited in, 2 Oleck, *Modern Corporation Law*, §961 (1978 Supp.). *See, for example,* Arkansas Valley Agric. Soc. v. Eichholtz, 45 Kan. 164, 25 P. 613 (1891).

43. Burkhart v. Smith, 161 Md. 398, 157 A. 299 (1931); Spiegel v. Beacon Participations, Inc., 297 Mass. 398, 8 N.E.2d 895 (1937).

44. Lippitt v. Ashley, 89 Conn. 451, 94 A. 995 (1915); Anderson v. Bundy, 161 Va. 1, 171 S.E. 501 (1933); Atherton v. Anderson, 99 F.2d 883 (6th Cir. 1938); Lewis v. S.&L.&E. Inc., 629 F.2d 764 (2nd Cir. 1980).

45. Briggs v. Spaulding, above n. 5; Rhoads, *Personal Liability of Directors for Corporate Management*, 65 U. Pa. L. Rev. 128 (1916); Note, 82 U. Pa. L. Rev. 364 (1934); Douglas, *Directors Who Do Not Direct*, 47 Harv. L. Rev. 1305 (1934); West v. Costen, 558 F. Supp. 564 (D.C. Va. 1983).

46. Manson v. Curtis, 223 N.Y. 313, 119 N.E. 559 (1918).

47. Ohio Rev. Code §§1702.54, 1702.56.

48. *Ibid.*, §1702.55. *See*, Oleck, *Proprietary Mentality and New Nonprofit Laws*, 20 Clev. St. L. Rev. 145 (1971). See n. 11.

49. *Ibid.*, §1713.31; Schelling v. Belcher, 582 F.2d 995 (5th Cir. 1978).

50. Geddes v. Anaconda Copper Min. Co., 254 U.S. 590, 41 S. Ct. 209, 65 L. Ed. 425 (1921).

51. *3 NonProfit Times* (12) 3 (March 1990).

52. 6 *NonProfit Times* (6) 1 (June 1992) (quoting the National Charities Information Bureau).

53. N.Y. Not-for-Profit Corp. L. §701; Ohio Rev. Code §1702.27. (C); Fla. Stat. §617.0802.

54. N.Y. Gen. Corp. L. §27. Need only one resident of the state; Ohio Rev. Code §1702.13. May be minors: Opinions Minn. Att'y-Gen. 102-E (June 25, 1951); Myott v. Greer, 204 Mass. 389, 90 N.E. 895 (1910); but Ga. Code Ann. §14-3-802 requires natural person over 18; Fla. St. §617.025 until 1982 permitted minors to be on Board of Directors as long as a majority of the Board's members competent to contract; Repealed by L. 1982, c.82–177 §21. *See* N.Y. N-P-C Law §602, 701, 707.

55. Ga. Code Ann. §14-3-802.

56. N.Y. Not-for-Profit Corp. L. §402; N.J. Rev. St., tit. 15; Fla. St. §617.0202.

57. Demarest v. Flack, 128 N.Y. 205; 25 N.E. 645 (1891), affd. 28 N.E. 645 (N.Y. 1891).

58. *In re* Ringler & Co., 204 N.Y. 30; 97 N.E. 593 (1912).

59. N.Y. Not-for-Profit Corp. L. §701.

60. *In re* Haecker, 212 A.D. 167; 207 N.Y.S. 561 (1925).

61. Opinions N.Y. Atty. Gen. (Jan. 17, 1912).

62. Taft, S., *Control of Foundations and Other Nonprofit Corporations*, 18 Clev. St. L. Rev. 478 (1969).

63. N.Y. Not-for-Profit Corp. L. §702; Ohio Rev. Code §1702.27 (A); Ohio Rev. Code §1702.05; Fla. St. §617.0803; Ga. Code Ann. §14-3-803; Ala. Code. tit. 10 §3A-35.

64. *Ibid.*, (minimum of three) (N.Y.).

65. Calif. Corp. Code §515(a) (1980).

66. *Ibid.*, §1401(u)(u).

67. N. 63–66.

68. N.Y. Not-for-Profit Corp. L. §702.

69. *Ibid.*, 801.

70. Ohio Rev. Code §1701.27 (B).

71. N.Y. Not-for-Profit Corp. L. §514.

72. *See* c. 5.

73. Marsh v. General Grievance Committee, 1 Ohio St.2d 165, 205 N.E.2d 571 (1965).

74. N.Y. N-P-C L. §703 (b); Ohio Rev. Code §1702.28.

75. *St. John's Protestant Episcopal Church Endowment Fund, Inc. v. Vestry of St. J.P.E. Church*, 377 S.E. 2d 375 (Va. 1989).

76. *See*, Ohio Rev. Code §1701.28.

77. Taft, S., *Control of Foundations and Nonprofit Corporations*, 18 Clev. St. L. Rev. 478 (1969).

78. N.Y. Not-for-Profit Law §703 (c).

79. *Ibid*; Eberts Cadillac Co. v. Miller, 159 N.W.2d 217 (Mich. App. 1968); Goldman v. Hickory House, Inc. 207 N.Y.S.2d 309, appeal dism. 10 A.2d 915 203 N.Y.S.2d 1002 (1960).

80. *Ibid.*, §22. *See* c.26. *And see, In Re*, Atwater, 85 N.Y.S.2d 738 (1948).

81. Almstead v. Dennis, 77 N.Y. 378 (1879).

82. 58 Cal. Op. Atty.-Genl. 442 (1975).

83. Sellin, H., ed., *Trustee and Director Duties and Obligations*, 9 Conf. of Char. Foundations 227, 279, N.Y.U. (1969). See n. 34.

84. N.Y. N-P-C Law §1102

85. Van Schaick v. Aron, 170 Misc. 520; 10 N.Y.S.2d 550 (1938).

86. 15 Pa. Cons. Stat. Ann. §7316 (b) (Purdon Supp. 1978); Cal. Corp. Code §7726; N.Y. Not-for-Profit Corp. L. §706.

87. Easterly v. Barber, 65 N.Y. 252 (1875).

88. Touchet, Inc., v. Touchet, 264 Mass. 499; 163 N.E. 184 (1928).

89. Sylvania & G.R. Co. v. Hoge, 129 Ga. 734; 59 S.E. 806 (1907).

90. Jacobson v. Moskowitz, 261 N.E.2d 613 (N.Y., 1970).

91. *Lee v. Joe Wheeler Elec. Membership Corp.*, 570 So. 2d 576 (Ala. 1990).

92. N.Y. Not-for-Profit Corp. L. §705. As to other states' statutes, *see*, People *ex rel.* Weber v. Cohn, 339 Ill. 121; 171 N.E. 159 (1930); Ohio Rev. Code §1702.29.

93. Mayo v. Interment Properties, 53 Calif. App. 2d 654; 128 P.2d 417 (1942).

94. Gold Bluff M. & L. Corp. v. Whitlock, 75 Conn. 699; 55 A. 175 (1903). *But see* Grassman v. Liberty Leasing Co., 295 A.2d 749 (Del. Ch. 1972).

95. Moon v. Moon Motor Car Co., 17 Del. Ch: 176; 151 A. 298 (1930).

96. N.Y. N-P-C Law §§1004, 1005, 1006, 1111.

97. Halpin v. Mutual Brewing Co., 20 A.D. 583; 47 N.Y.S. 412 (1897).

98. *In re* Manoca Temple Assn., 128 A.D. 796; 113 N.Y.S. 172 (1908).

99. *See*, Ohio Rev. Code §1702.29; N.Y. N-P-C Law §§623, 706, 714, 720.

100. Spingret v. Don & Bob Restaurants, 394 N.Y.S.2d 971 (App. Div., 1977).

101. 13 Am. Jur. 2d, "Corporations" §1113.

102. Dillon v. Berg. 326 F. Supp. 1214 (D.C. Del. 1971) Dillon v. Berg, 326 F. Supp. 1214 (D.C. Del. 1971), affd. 453 F.2d 876 (3rd Cir. 1971), relying on 8 Del. C. §§223, 223(a). *See*, C. Tuohey, *Corporate Director Resignation*, 33 Ark. L. Rev. 106–21 (1979).

103. Briggs v. Spaulding, 141 U.S. 132; 11 S.Ct. 924; 35 L. Ed. 662 (1891); Harris v. Cas. Recip. Exchange, 632 S.W.2d 714 (Tex. 1982); Shuckman v. Rubenstein, 164 F.2d 952 (6th Cir. 1947).

104. Petition of Serenbetz, 46 N.Y.S. 475; *affd.*, 267 A.D. 836; 46 N.Y.S.2d 127 (1944).

105. *In re* McNaughton's Will, 138 Wis. 179; 118 N.W. 997; 120 N.W. 288 (1909; *But see*, Security Investor Realty Co. v. Superior Court, 101 Calif. App. 450; 281 P. 709 (1929), that in such a case service of legal process on him is valid service on the corporation until it

accepts the resignation. And, similarly, until a successor is appointed, in, Timolate v. Held Co., 17 Misc. 556; 40 N.Y.S. 692 (1896); Zeltner v. Zeltner Brewing Co., 85 A.D. 387; 83 N.Y.S. 366 (1903).

106. *See* n. 105.

107. Gerdes v. Reynolds, 28 N.Y.S.2d 622 (1941).

108. *See* n. 93, above; Noel v. Drake, 28 Kans. 265 (1882).

109. Jacobus v. Diamond Soda W. Mfg. Co., 94 A.D. 366; 88 N.Y.S. 302 (1904).

110. Levi & Co., Inc. v. Feldman, 61 N.Y.S.2d 639 (1946).

111. Mehegan, S., (article) 7 *NonProfit Times* 6 (4) (June 1993).

112. Venner v. Denver Union Water Co., 40 Colo. 212; 90 P. 623 (1907).

113. Clark v. Oceano Beach Resort Co., 106 Calif. App. 574; 289 P. 946 (1930).

114. University of Maryland v. Williams, 9 Gill & J. (Md.) 365 (1838).

115. *In re* Fidelity Assur. Assn., 42 F. Supp. 973; revd. on other gds. 129 F.2d 442; *affd.*, 381 U.S. 608; 63 S. Ct. 807 (1943).

116. Levi case, n. 110.

117. Briggs case, n. 103.

118. *Ibid. See*, n. 102, Tuohey article.

119. Bruce v. Platt, 80 N.Y. 379 (1880).

120. N.Y. N-P-C Law §§623, 706, 714, 720.

121. *Ibid.* §§112, 623, 720. By directors alone: Ohio Rev. Code §1701.64(B)(2).

122. *Ibid.*, §§112, 623, 720.

123. N.Y. Exec. L. §63-b. *And see* c. 26.

124. In re Workmen's Benefit Fund, 36 N.Y.S.2d 662 (1942).

125. O'Neal v. Neider Co., 118 Ky. 62; 80 S.W. 451 (1904).

126. Walker v. Maas, 4 Misc. (N.J.) 230; 132 A. 322 (1926); Abberger v. Kulp, 156 Misc. 210; 281 N.Y.S. 373 (1935).

127. *See* n. 126; Bechtold v. Stillwagen, 119 Misc. 177; 195 N.Y.S. 66 (1922); Ohio Rev. Code §1701.64(B)(2); Ga. Code Ann. §14-3-808; Ala. Code, tit. 10-3A-35.

128. Brindley v. Walker, 221 Penna 287; 70 A. 794 (1908).

129. People *ex rel.* Manice v. Powell, 201 N.Y. 194; 94 N.E. 634 (1911); Ohio Rev. Code §1701.64(B)(2).

130. Guttman Silk Corp. v. Reilly, 189 A.D. 258; 178 N.Y.S. 457 (1919).

131. Green Bay Fish Co. v. Jorgensen, 165 Wis. 548; 163 N.W. 142 (1917). But a loan *to* the corporation is valid. Johndall v. Columbia Trotting Assn., 104 Ohio App. 118, 147 N.E.2d 101 (1956).

132. Oliphant v. Home Builders Co., 34 Calif. App. 720; 168 P. 700 (1917).

133. *See*, in §265, cases cited at n. 38–46.

134. Boardman Co. v. Petch, 186 Calif. 476, 199 P. 1047 (1921).

135. Mortimer v. McKeithan Lbr. Corp., 127 S.C. 266, 120 S.E. 723 (1923).

136. Ohio Rev. Code §1701.64(B)(2); Fla. St. §617.0808.

137. *Ibid.*

138. Fla. St. §607.154(2). *But see* §617.0842 Fla. Stat. (directors may remove officers with or without cause)

139. Scott County Tobacco Warehouses v. Harris, 201 S.2d 780 (Va., 1974).

140. Horn v. Kaupp, 147 N.W. 2d 607 (So. Dak. 1967); Whyte v. Faust, 281 Penna. 444, 127 A. 234 (1924); Anno. Calif. Corp. Code §303; Conn. Genl. Stat. Anno. §33–317.

141. Kiel v. Medart Mfg. Co., 46 S.W.2d 934 (Mo. App. 1932). See Fla. Stat. 617.0842(2).

142. *In re* Buckley, 183 Misc. 189, 50 N.Y.S.2d 54 (1944).

143. Kahn v. Colonial Fuel Corp., 198 N.Y.S. 596 (1923). A custom of informal action may be valid. Bylaw allowing removal without notice in invalid. Brevetti v. Tzougros, 42 Misc. (N.Y.) 2d 171, 247 N.Y.S.2d 295 (1964).

144. Hinkley v. Sagemiler, 191 Wis. 512, 210 N.W. 839 (1926).

145. N.Y. Genl. Corp. L. §25; Matter of Koch, 257 N.Y. 318, 178 N.E. 545 (1931); Matter of Teperman v. Atcos Baths, Inc., 4 Misc.2d 738, 158 N.Y.S. 2d 391 (1951). N.Y. N-P-C Law §618.

146. Piedmont Press Assn. v. Record Publ. Co., 156 S.C. 43; 152 S.E. 721 (1930).

147. *See,* State *ex rel.* Weingart v. Board of Officers of G.U.G.G., 144 Wis. 516, 129 N.W. 630 (1911); Welch v. Passaic Hospital, 59 N.J. L. 142; 36 A. 702 (1897); and local practice statutes.

148. *See,* State *ex rel.,* Blackwood v. Brast, 92 W.Va. 596, 127 S.E. 507 (1925).

149. Matter of Burkin, 136 N.E.2d 862 (N.Y., 1956); and see, Travers, *Removal of the Corporate Director,* 53 Iowa L. Rev. 389 (1967).

150. Grace v. Grace Institute, 226 N.E.2d 531 (N.Y., 1967); Brown v. North Ventura Road Devel., 30 Calif. Rptr. 568 (1963).

151. *E.g.,* U.S.C. §78n(f); and *see* Henn and Alexander, *Corporations* §§295 and 297 (3rd ed., 1983); S.E.C. Proxy Rules 14a-1 to 14a-12, etc.

28

DIRECTORS AND TRUSTEES: POWERS, DUTIES, AND LIABILITIES

§283. DIRECTORS' AND TRUSTEES' POWERS, IN GENERAL

In corporation law, the word *powers* means the bundle of legal rights or capacities of a corporation to act in a particular matter or in respect to a particular subject. Today the range of such powers is spelled out in detail in the corporation statutes of all the states.[1] These powers are exercised by the board of directors in most situations.

The *status* of a board member, in respect to *position* in the organization is discussed in the preceding chapter. His or her *powers* basically stem from that status, in a sense, but are more directly spelled out from the powers provisions of nonprofit corporation statutes. But directors of an applied research and service center of a university share a community of interest with other faculty, but if they also serve as bargaining agents in labor law type negotiations they may be deemed *management* officers under labor statutes if their duties are *managerial.*[2]

[Raymond L. Potts contributed the following two cases.]

A nonprofit director who failed to pay a plumbing contractor for work performed was found liable for breach of contract, even though a state statute shielded directors for breaches of duty that arose solely from their status. The court held that this statute did not immunize the defendant from liability because he was acting as an agent, not as a director, at the time he entered into the contract. Since he did not provide the contractor with full disclosure of the organization's legal status he was liable under the law of agency.[3]

Another court found that members of a condominium unit owners' association had standing to sue their director despite the lack of statutory author-

895

ity. The plaintiffs alleged that the director breached his fiduciary duty by appropriating an organizational opportunity for himself. The court circumvented the requirement for statutory standing by using a trial rule instead.[4]

Corporate (and thus, directors') powers should be distinguished from *purposes* of the corporation, though they are closely interwoven.[5]

Power theories. Under the minority view, the powers of directors or trustees of a corporation are deemed to be derived directly from the state, not delegated by the members. This is the so-called *concession,* or *fiat,* or *franchise* doctrine.[6] In most jurisdictions the prevailing view is that corporate powers are vested in the *artificial legal entity,* and thus in the general membership, by statute. This is variously called the *realist,* or *enterprise,* or *symbol* theory.[7] Under it, the members delegate powers to the directors.

Yet, even where the articles or bylaws limit the powers of directors, such provisions must not be inconsistent with laws.[8]

Another, not inconsistent, view is the *contract* theory, whereby the corporation, the members, and the state are deemed to contract for the grant and exercise of corporate authority.[9]

Nonprofit organizations can modify the fiduciary duties of their directors by placing further obligations on them in the articles of incorporation or bylaws. The courts have held that these governing documents constitute contracts between the organization and its members and are sufficient to bind the directors. As a result, many actions are brought as breaches of contract. Where the articles of incorporation, bylaws, or other governing documents spell out fiduciary duties of officers and directors, these actions often achieve the same result as fiduciary suits.

A condominium development corporation was held to have breached its fiduciary duty by failing to renew a fire insurance policy on a clubhouse. The obligation arose under the condominium association's bylaws, which required the maintenance of such coverage. Since the corporation failed to create a board of directors as required under the bylaws and maintained full control for itself, it was liable for the breach.[10]

Former members of a nonprofit corporation acquired standing to sue the organization and its directors under a breach of contract theory. The articles of incorporation required the directors to use corporation assets solely for the stated charitable purposes. The court found that this constituted a contract between the corporation and its members. This was sufficient to give the members standing to bring action against the defendants for the use of the assets for their own benefit. As a result, the directors could be held liable for violation of the fiduciary standards outlined in the articles of incorporation.[11]

Generally, the *entity* theory of corporate "personality" is not extended to unincorporated associations, which are viewed as *aggregate* groups similar to partnerships, as yet. Recent statutes and cases contrary to this view (see Sections 48 and 49) now are numerous enough to change the basic legal view of associations.

Basic rule. All these doctrines point to one major concept, of prime importance in nonprofit organizations. That is the basic rule that the legal entity (of the organization), rather than the board of directors, is the holder of legal power. The powers of the directors are not inherent in them, but inherently are in the organization as such.

Interpretation of statutes. In reading statutes that define the authority (powers) of trustees of nonprofit organizations, the above-stated principles must be kept in mind.

Thus, in a typical statute (Ohio's), trustees are defined as "the persons vested with the authority to conduct the affairs of the corporation. . . ."[12] And (in the same statute) it is stated that "Except where the law, the articles, or the regulations (bylaws) require that action be otherwise authorized or taken, all of the authority of a corporation shall be exercised by its trustees."[13]

These provisions were based on the Model Act of the American Law Institute, of which the "management-oriented" leaning has been remarked upon elsewhere herein.[14] That leaning continued in the 1986 proposals for revision of the American Bar Association-American Law Institute Model Act.

Ownership in the members; operation is by trustees. Underlying most nonprofit statutes and case law is the idea that directors or trustees are to *exercise the powers* (operate) the organization, but are *not to own* it. Their powers are managerial, *not proprietary*, in nature.[15]

For example, the trustees, not the members, are the proper persons to bring or defend suits in the corporation name.[16] A suit brought or defended by hundreds or thousands of members would be a mess.

But the power to act on behalf of an organization does not give to the agents ownership powers or rights within the organization.

The members, not the trustees, constitute the *body corporate* in most nonprofit, as well as business, corporations. Statutes, as well as case law, usually vest in the members the fundamental power to adopt or change rules (*e.g.*, articles and bylaws) for the government of most kinds of corporations.[17] They, rather than the trustees, have this fundamental power to adopt or change purposes and rules.[18] Most modern statutes allow amendment of the articles of incorporation without a provision allowing amendment in the articles or bylaws.[19]

A gross misconception is inherent in the old and new (1986) Model Nonprofit Corporations Act, where it grants the basic powers to directors unless the articles or bylaws provide otherwise. Those states that have blindly followed this "model" violate the essential idea of a nonprofit (tax exempt) organization. They thereby encourage use of nonprofit form for "proprietary" purposes.[20]

In the case of California, the statute of 1980 still allowed directors not only to effectively own the nonprofit corporation's assets but ultimately to benefit personally from its operation. First, in a nonprofit corporation formed without a provision for members, the directors were assumed to be the sole members.[21] Then as member/directors, they were permitted to establish a reasonable salary for themselves. Third, under the statute a nonprofit corporation may operate a business for profit as long as it is incidental to the corporation's main purpose.[22] Last, these member/directors may vote to dissolve the corporation and then as members be entitled in its distribution. Comment is super-fluous.

Trust nature of trustees' or directors' powers. Illumination of the real nature of a trustee's or a director's powers is found in statutes dealing with charitable, rather than "merely nonprofit," organizations.

For example, a trustee of a nonprofit *educational* corporation may not be given any compensation, and is not eligible to hold any office or agency to which a salary or emolument is attached, under the Ohio statute.[23]

The trustee of a charitable foundation holds legal title to the trust property and may not ratify any act that is in violation of the trust agreement. A trustee is a fiduciary to the trust and has only the power granted to him/her in the agreement. Any act in violation of the agreement is void.[24]

Special, limited provision is made for *fiscal trustees* who may hold and manage the endowment of a Y.W.C.A.[25]

In an incorporated *charitable trust (foundation)*, the trustees are the members of the corporation.[26]

In *credit unions*, the directors have special powers.[27] So, too, do the trustees of nonprofit medical care corporations.[28] For example, a labor dispute arbitrator, during collective bargaining for a paramedics union, ordered reinstatement of a paramedic discharged for poor performance by the medical director of the paramedic squad. The court held that the arbitrator exceeded his authority by dictating medical decisions legally delegated to the medical director. Directors are not mere powerless figureheads.[29] Where a corporation has only trustees, and no members, the trustees are deemed to be members when statutes speak of members.[30]

The implication of these illustrations is that a trustee or director of most nonprofit organizations has fiduciary management, not ownership, powers.

Board powers summarized. In general, the board of trustees or directors has the power and duty to carry on whatever transactions the corporation itself has the power and desire to carry on.[31] The power of the board is supreme in ordinary matters, so long as it is exercised lawfully and in lawful transactions.[32] Nor will the courts interfere unless illegal action, or action in bad faith, is shown.[33]

In a few states, such as New Jersey (by statute), the *charitable* corporation even may still have immunity against tort damages lawsuits for negligence.[34]

In extraordinary matters, however, the board may not govern, but the will of the general membership must rule—unless the charter or bylaws expressly permit the directors to do so. In such matters as a radical change of fundamental policy or purposes, or in dissolution or merger of the corporation, or matters of like importance, the power of decision rests in the members.[35]

Within the *purposes* and *powers* of the organization, the directors are free to change policies and short-range purposes. But unless the charter or bylaws expressly permit, they may not perform acts that amount to changes in fundamental purposes or methods of the organization.[36]

A rodeo cowboy brought action against the nonprofit Professional Rodeo Cowboys Association (PRCA) to get access to membership records, curtail a contract concerning the national finals rodeo competition, and dissolve the association. PRCA allowed the records to be copied. However, the court found that the PRCA articles of incorporation and *bylaws controlled* to give the board of directors, not the general membership, the power to contract, dissolve, or merge. Suit dismissed for lack of prosecution.[37]

§284. DIRECTORS' STANDARDS OF DILIGENCE AND CARE (PERSONAL LIABILITY)

[Mary Anne Rutherford contributed the cases concerning the business judgment rule in this section.]

The degree of diligence, skill, and care required of directors always is a relative matter. It depends on the organization's character, purpose, size, financial means, location, charter and bylaw provisions, and many other factors. In general, the directors must meet the standards applicable to agents who are almost trustees.[38]

Directors are usually held to the standard of diligence, skill, and care of an *ordinary man* in a like situation.[39] This is a vague enough standard to make it necessary to decide practically every case on its own peculiar facts. (See Section 271.)

If a director is to serve as such in a full-time capacity, he is held to the standard applicable to a man who is running his own business.[40] This high standard seldom applies in nonprofit corporations, where directors usually are part-time voluntary servants, deriving no pecuniary benefits from their work. But, on the other hand, the fact that they may be mere "window dressing" for the organization does not justify allowing them to act carelessly or with gross stupidity.[41]

A director is not ordinarily subject to the full liability of a trustee.[42] He is entitled to rely on the reports of officers and accountants, and on the advice of lawyers, within reasonable limits.[43] But he cannot escape personal liability *through nonmanagement*, by not attending meetings and by ignoring corporate affairs.[44]

William Aramony, the former president of the United Way of America (UWA) resigned following media accounts and allegations of mismanagement and a luxurious lifestyle. Sixty-seven local United Ways decided to withhold their dues to the main headquarters in response. In a 1992 poll by the *Non-Profit Times* and Barna Research, 65 percent of all Americans claim to have heard about the UWA situation involving Mr. Aramony. Of these, 59 percent said they were less likely to give to UWA due to the controversy.[45]

The former president of SADD (Students Against Drunk Driving) agreed to give up part of a lucrative pension and consulting contract he was awarded by his hand-picked board after the *Boston Herald* reported that the organization ran deficits of $557,824 in 1992 and $160,831 in 1991. An estimated quarter of

SADD's budget for 1993 would have been used to pay the former president's budget.[46]

If directors omit the reasonable precautions established by the bylaws, or by ordinary common sense, they may be grossly negligent, and may be held personally liable for resulting injuries or losses to the corporation.[47]

So long as a director exercises reasonable diligence and care, he is free from personal liability—when his poor judgment causes loss or injury to the corporation.[48] *Good faith* is the principal (but not the sole) test of the adequacy of a director's care and diligence.[49]

The *business judgment* rule is the *standard* for officers of a mutual-benefit nonprofit corporation formed to promote "single tax" law theory, which is more like a commercial than a charitable trust corporation in its purpose. Therefore, it is error for a trial court to use its equity powers to change its internal management rules or to enjoin a management decision to dissolve the corporation.[50] Similarly, condominium board members may use their "business judgment" to make material alterations, or without the usually required unit owners' vote, where they do not abuse their discretion or breach their trust duty with fraud or illegality or inequity; a decision to add exterior support pillars to balcony supports rather than disrupt residential conditions by rebuilding.[51] A director's (of condos and co-ops) decision (to stop a lessee's remodeling of his apartment), is valid if "reasonable" and in good faith, under a standard of review "analogous to the business judgment rule" applied to business corporation directors.[52]

Although the "business judgment rule" grants wide discretion to nonprofit officers and directors, they are still bound by the charter, bylaws, and other incorporating documents and subsequent amendments to them. These documents are viewed as the equivalent of contracts between and among the members and therefore binding on the business judgments of directors. Where a water company failed to obtain prior consent to rate hikes, the court denied protection under the "business judgment rule".[53]

Likewise, where a cooperative apartment housing complex through its directors has an existing lease with member/stock owners, the directors are not entitled to blanket application of the "business judgment rule" where the lease makes provisions for advance notice before the board can take action. The court stated that while the cooperative board clearly possesses the authority to make decisions regarding the complex, subject to the "business judgment rule," it nevertheless was required to comply with the notice provisions set forth in the lease prior to terminating it.[54]

Similarly, where the lease in a tenant cooperative provides for board approval on subleases for less than twelve months, the board is bound to follow the terms of the lease. Mr. and Mrs. Ludwig twice applied for permission to sublet their apartment according to lease requirements. Twice the board summarily denied the sublease applications. The court held that where the Board's actions clearly violate the express terms of the proprietary lease, the "business judgment rule" is inapplicable.[55]

Where the board of directors of a nonprofit legal services corporation make all the day-to-day decisions, there is no violation of the rules of professional conduct where the board of directors do not control or direct the professional judgment of the attorney. The "business judgment rule" applies to the daily operational decisions of the legal service corporation and are distinct and separate from the lawyer's decisions regarding the acceptance of clients and all case decisions, which are subject to the rules of professional conduct.[56]

The "business judgment rule" applies when there is a dispute between the homeowners, homeowners' association, and the developer over Planned Unit Development plans and assessments. Where the conduct of the directors is absent a showing of bad faith, dishonesty, or incompetence, the judgment of the directors will not be set aside by judicial action.[57]

In a Slip Copy of a yet unreleased-for-publication decision that addresses the growing problem of business going insolvent, the court has refused to allow the directors to hide behind the "business judgment rule." Here, the insurance commissioner has sued the former officers and directors for breaching their fiduciary duties. The nonmanagement directors tried to claim that they had no fiduciary duty because they were not involved in the daily operations and business decisions; and alternatively, that the "business judgment rule" protected them for liability should they be found to have a fiduciary duty. The court stated that directors had a duty of care based on the prudent man, prompted by self-interest, would exercise in the management of his/her own affairs standard. Under this standard, directors have a duty to attend regular board meetings and be informed of the material facts necessary to exercise their judgment.

If the director acts diligently and carefully in exercising his/her duties, then the "business judgment rule" protects him/her from liability. However, the shield of the "business judgment rule" is unavailable to directors who fail to exercise due care in the management of the corporation. The exercise of due care is a prerequisite to the applicability of the "business judgment rule" and consequently directors may still be held liable for damages caused by their lack of due care in carrying out their duties.[58]

Piercing the Corporate Veil. If a corporation is employed by a controlling director as his *alter ego*, which he governs and operates in detail, the "corporateness" may be ignored by the courts and he can be held personally liable for debts of the corporation.[59] The corporation may then be viewed as his mere *instrument* or agency.[60] The fact that an officer participates in a wrong cannot be excused by arguing that it was done in the course of his duties.[61] An officer has a *duty to disclose* misconduct of another (director), and is personally liable for acquiescence in the misdeed if he does not do so.[62]

Whistleblowing now tends to be viewed as proper duty, and not as "snitching".[63] The "morality" of criminals should not be the standard applied to directors of nonprofit organizations.

"Representative" Actions. If an officer of a corporation is clearly acting in a representative (not personal) capacity, as in signing a contract for a loan or guaranty, he is not personally liable on that obligation.[64]

Provisional Directors. Where, as in California, a deadlock among directors is broken by court appointment of a director to vote (one way or another) to break the deadlock, that "provisional director" is clothed with quasi-judicial immunity against civil law suits.[65]

Ordinarily, a director is not responsible for acts of other directors committed before he took office.[66]

Incompetence of a director is in itself no cause for him to be held personally liable for any losses caused by his inadequacy. The same is true of simple negligence, if it is not gross. The members have no one to blame but themselves if they elect incompetents or careless bunglers. Their only real relief is to choose more qualified people at the next election, unless the bylaws permit earlier replacement of an incompetent or negligent director.

Statutory standards. The relative freedom from all personal liability enjoyed by directors of nonprofit corporations is clarified by statutes in a number of states. The New York statute provides.[67]

> A director or officer shall not be liable under this Section if, in the circumstances, he discharged his duty to the corporation under Section 717 (Duty of Directors and Officers).

The Ohio statute exempts members, trustees, and officers from personal liability, similarly. Then it goes on, to hold personally liable, trustees who vote for or assent to: distribution of assets to members, contrary to law or the articles, improper distributions in dissolution, or improper loans; or trustees who fail to dissent promptly (and in writing) where impropriety occurs; or members who receive improper distribution; and then the statute permits contribution among trustees or members who may be found liable, sets a two-year statute of limitations (measured from the time of the violation), and gives credit rights against the corporation as well.[68]

In addition, as in most states, the Ohio statutes provide for fines to be imposed on persons who make or assist in making or filing false reports or certificates.[69]

Other statutes specifically exempt nonprofit corporations from certain statutory proceedings to enforce personal liability of directors, which proceedings are available for business corporations.[70]

Recent changes in statutory rules, tending to insulate directors and officers from personal liability for their own negligence in NPOs (in most states) are of three types: (1) "charter-option" (if so provided in articles) with exception for bad faith, disloyalty, intentional misconduct, knowing violation of law, and improper personal benefit; (2) "monetary cap" (limited damages); (3) "self-executing" (automatic if members take no action).

The SECs proxy rules limit these statutes by disclosure-statements requirements.[71]

Constitutional immunities as to testimony suspended. In many states, and in the federal courts, statutes now suspend the Constitutional privilege to refuse to testify on the ground of self-incrimination. These compulsory testimony statutes apply to directors. They deny the right to refuse to testify (granted by the Fifth Amendment), but grant immunity from prosecution for any criminal conduct revealed by such forced testimony.[72]

Joint liability. If directors are personally liable (in case of fraud or bad faith, they are jointly and severally liable), this means that a complaining party then may sue one of them, any of them, or all of them, as he chooses. Whichever one he sues is fully liable for the full amount of the loss suffered by the plaintiff.[73]

Criminal liability. Corporate crimes are discussed in Chapter 17.

A much-quoted case ruled that an officer or a director of a nonprofit corporation is not personally criminally liable for the violation of a penal statute by the corporation.[74] This should not be misunderstood. It means only that the criminal act of a nonprofit corporation ordinarily should not be imputed to an innocent director or officer. It does not mean that a director is immune against criminal liability for criminal conduct which he commits, aids, tolerates, or condones. For example, corporation officers who do not carry out their *charged* duty to ensure compliance with the terms of a settlement agreement may be held to be in *contempt of court* for the corporation's noncompliance.[75]

Breach of fiduciary duty, mismanagement of the corporation's investments, and *negligent selection, supervision and monitoring of an investment advisor and asset manager* are actionable claims against a director of a nonprofit corporation if the director conspires to deter other directors from investigating the services of an investment advisor and performs contrary to his *statutory duty to consider the corporation's long and short term needs*, financial requirements, expected total return on investments, price level trends and general economic conditions in selecting an asset manager.[76]

Breaches of fiduciary duty by directors of a corporation are breaches of *contract* to honestly and carefully direct the corporate activities, governed by the six year *statute of limitations*, not the two-year tort limitation.[77]

A complaint of "*waste*" of corporate assets by directors in giving corporate funding for a political support committee is not barred (not pre-empted) by the Federal Election Campaign Act.[78]

A *director's dissipation* of a restricted endowment fund of a hospital is a *breach of fiduciary duty*, not indemnified by alleged duty of the bank to be fiduciary to the directors. It is not such a "tort" as to be covered by the Illinois Contribution Act in an action by the Attorney-General against the director and the bank.[79]

Directors are liable for unlawful distribution of corporate assets in Louisiana if there is (1) unlawful distribution, payment or return, (2) of assets, (3) to members, (4) resulting from a vote by the director, (5) which was done without exercise of reasonable care and inquiry. A director who votes to authorize the unlawful distribution is individually liable for the full amount of the distribution. A director may get indemnity from the other directors-recipients if the director negligently consented or participated. Liability of a member who receives an unlawful distribution is limited to the amount of the distribution. Breach of fiduciary duty also exists where a corporation fails to receive the full value in return for sale of an asset.[80]

Under modern "Stakeholder Statutes" now enacted in most of the states in reaction against the late 1980's flood of "leveraged buyouts" and looting of corporations by "corporation raiders," the standard of "proper care" for directors is stated typically as follows:[81]

> (1) A director shall discharge his duties as a director ...
>> (c) in a manner he reasonably believes to be in the best interests of the corporation. ...
>> [relying on information, reports, opinions, etc. of persons, officers, employees, etc. that he "reasonably believes to be reliable"]

Fl. St. § 607.111(9) (1989) for *Business Corporations*:

"Board of directors; exercise of corporate powers—

(9) In discharging his duties, a director may consider such factors as ... long-term ... interests of the corporation and its shareholders, and the social, economic, legal and other effects of any action on the employees, suppliers, customers ... the communities and society ... and the economy. ..."

In effect, today, directors ought to take "long-term" view of what is appropriate, not a "short term" view.[82]

Most actions against directors are employment related, including actions for wrongful termination, harassment, or discrimination in the employment process. Less often, actions for claims alleging misuse of funds, antitrust violations, regulatory breaches, and civil rights abuses are filed, involving larger sums of money than employed related claims. Coverage for all of these actions should not be excluded in a D & O insurance policy.[83]

§285. RECORD OF PERSONAL CONDUCT

The one sure way for a director to protect himself against unfair personal liability is this. He must make sure that the written record indicates his good faith.

Whenever a matter arises in which any doubt of personal conduct may result, the director should insist that his views and acts be recorded. Thus, in a meeting, if a proposal is made which he believes to be of questionable propriety, he should state his dissent and objection. And he should make sure that his protest is recorded in the minutes, lest he be held personally liable.[84]

Whenever a director doubts the propriety of a contemplated corporate action, he should see that a written record of the objection is made, in verifiable form. This can be done by letter, memorandum, or other writing. Ordinarily such a paper would be objectionable as *self-serving evidence,* but it is both proper and desirable for self-defense purposes. Self-serving evidence is admissible when it is part of the whole transaction (*res gestae*), when it is not a mere fabrication, when it is acquiesced in by the other persons concerned, and when it is relevant.[85]

§286. DIRECTORS' DUTY TO REPORT (ANNUAL)

One of the paramount duties of directors of nonprofit corporations is to report to the members their activities and the state of the corporate finances and affairs. A director's freedom from liability for corporate debts may depend upon his filing of an annual report.[86]

Directors of most nonprofit organizations must report at least once a year, and more frequent reports are usually desirable. Statutes often require at least an annual report. The New York statute provides as follows:[87]

519. Annual Report of Directors

a. The board shall present at the annual meeting of members a report, verified by the president and treasurer or by a majority of the directors, or certified by an independent public or certified public accountant, or a firm of such accountants selected by the board, showing in appropriate detail the following:

1. The assets and liabilities, including the trust funds, of the corporation as of the end of a 12-month fiscal period terminating not more than six months prior to said meeting.

2. The principal changes in assets and liabilities, including trust funds, during the year immediately preceding the date of the report.

3. The revenue or receipts of the corporation, both unrestricted and restricted to particular purposes, for the year immediately preceding the date of the report.

4. The expenses or disbursements of the corporation, for both general and restricted purposes, during the year immediately preceding the date of the report.

5. The number of members of the corporation as of the date of the report, together with a statement of increase or decrease in such number during the year immediately preceding the date of the report, and a statement of the place where the names and places of residence of the current members may be found.

b. The annual report of directors shall be filed with the records of the corporation, and either a copy or an abstract thereof entered in the minutes of the proceeding of the annual meeting of members.

c. The board of a corporation having no members shall direct the president and treasurer to present at the annual meeting of the board a report in accordance with paragraph (a), but omitting the requirement of sub-paragraph (5). This report shall be filed with the minutes of the annual meeting of the board.

The annual report must be available for inspection by the members. A bylaw that bars access to it, or to lists of members, is invalid.[88]

The right of directors to inspect and make extracts of records of the corporation usually is absolute.[89] A director may inspect them even in order to organize a rival corporation, but in such circumstances he will not be permitted to copy the lists.[90]

The New York statute requires directors to file an adequate *report*, not necessarily an accountant's detailed statement.[91]

The making of false reports, or the failure to make reports lawfully required by a public officer, or the keeping of false financial records, is a crime.[92]

Audit Committees. Today many corporations have established *audit committees* to monitor such aspects of corporate operations as financial reporting and internal controls; these are in addition to outside auditors. The S.E.C. and American Institute of Certified Public Accountants have endorsed this idea; and the New York Stock Exchange requires such committees in its listed companies, and that the directors in such committees be independent.

FORM NO. 131
Annual Report
(Illinois)

Annual Report

General Not-for-Profit Corporation Act

For 19_____

_____
File No.

(*Filing Fee $_____*)

Secretary of State of Illinois

CORPORATE NAME

REGISTERED AGENT

REGISTERED OFFICE

CITY, STATE, ZIP CODE

DO NOT WRITE IN THIS SPACE

Filing fee . . . . $_____

Penalty . . . . $_____

Clerk _____

USE A TYPEWRITER IN COMPLETING THIS REPORT

1. The printed information above is the exact format maintained on file by the secretary of state. If any portion does not agree with your records you must acquire and file proper forms for correction.

2. The above corporation organized under the laws of the state of _____, pursuant to the provisions of "The General

Not-For-Profit Corporation Act" of the state of Illinois hereby makes the following report:

3. The names and respective addresses of its officers and directors are:

Name	Office	Address Number and Street	City	State
	President			
	Secretary			
	Treasurer			
	Director			
	Director			
	Director			
	Director			
	Director			
	Director			
	Director			
	Director			

NOTE: List all directors above: Illinois Corporations must have at least **three** directors.

4. The following is a brief statement of the character of the affairs which the corporation is actually conducting.

5. If a foreign corporation, the address of its principal office in the state of its incorporation is:

_____

Number and Street   City   State or County

IN WITNESS WHEREOF, the undersigned corporation has caused this report to be executed in its name by its_____

(President, Vice-President, Secretary, Assistant Secretary, Treasurer, Receiver, or Trustee)

This _____ Day of,_____A.D. 19_____

Place
(Corporate Seal)   Exact corporation name
Here   By _____
(Signature of President, Vice-President, Secretary,
Assistant Secretary, Treasurer, Receiver, or Trustee.)

State of _____

County of _____   S.S.

I, _____, notary public, do hereby certify that on the _____ day of _____, A.D. 19_____, _____ personally appeared before me, and being first sworn by me acknowledged that _____ he signed the foregoing document in the capacity therein set forth and declared that the statements therein contained are true.

IN WITNESS WHEREOF, I have hereunto set my hand and seal the day and year before written.

Place
(Notarial Seal)
Here

_____

Notary Public

Notice

Under the General Not-For-Profit Corporation Act this annual report must be properly executed with notarial seal affixed and filed in the office of the secretary of state prior to March 1st of each year. If filed on time, a filing fee of $_____ only is required by statute. If filed later, a statutory penalty of $_____ must be added.

§287. COMPENSATION OF DIRECTORS OR OFFICERS

[See: D.A. Weeks, 1993 *Salary Survey*, 8 *Nonprofit Times* (1) 19 (Jan. 1994).]

Basic in any nonprofit corporation is the rule that directors and officers make no pecuniary profit out of the corporation.[93] This does not mean they may not receive salary or compensation for services.

A typical statute provides:[94]

> The fixing of salaries of officers, if not done in or pursuant to the bylaws, shall require the affirmative vote of a majority of the entire board, unless a higher proportion is set by the certificate of incorporation or bylaws.

The statute clearly permits compensation to directors or officers only in accordance with rules deliberately adopted.[95] It is basic in the concept of a nonprofit corporation that the directors, officers and employees receive no more than reasonable compensation for their services.[96]

The prohibition against payment of compensation to trustees of educational charitable corporations, found in some states (*e.g.*, Ohio Rev. Code §1713.30), also often forbids such trustees to be officers or agents of the corporation.

Even when proper bylaw authority exists some states require that there be an express contract for the payment of compensation, even for extraordinary services.[97] No state permits compensation merely because the services were rendered with expectation of payment.[98] Payment for past services must rest both on proper authority and on an actual or implied agreement.[99]

If the board is empowered to grant salaries, only it—not the president—may do so.[100]

A corporation may not pay to its officers, as bonuses, amounts which have no relation to the value of services rendered.[101]

Obviously, agreements among directors or officers to award salaries to each other (based on what amounts to a division of profits) are against public policy and are void.[102]

The reasonableness of compensation voted by directors to a director may be scrutinized by the courts. If it is unreasonable, wasteful, excessive, or in any way improper, the court may order it returned to the corporation.[103]

The rights of officers are discussed in a separate Chapter below.

It should be quite clear that bylaws must be carefully drawn to govern the compensation of directors and officers. Approval of such bylaws by the membership is the best method. Approval by the directors alone is a constant source of suspicion and dispute.

Directors' fees. With the bylaw authorization required by statute, it is quite proper to grant fees to directors for attending meetings.[104] But the directors may not vote for themselves.[105] Fees vary from about $10 per meeting to as high as hundreds of dollars.

The 1986 American Law Institute—American Bar Association Revised Model Nonprofit Corporation Act (§8.12) recommends overruling of the common law doctrine that directors may not set their own compensation.

Florida's new NPC statute, effective July 1991, provides that "unless the articles of incorporation or the bylaws provide otherwise," the board of directors may fix the compensation of directors.[106]

Expense accounts. Payment of reasonable expense accounts for executives is valid if properly authorized.[107] The principle is that an employer may reimburse an employee for money he lays out on the employer's behalf. The outlay to be repaid must have been expressly or tacitly authorized by the employer.[108]

Trustees of charitable organizations. In organizations that are charitable, rather than merely nonprofit in nature, some statutes make special rules regarding compensation. These rules apply to organizations such as schools, hospitals, and other charitable bodies.

The Ohio statute governing educational corporations, for example, states that

> No trustee ... shall be eligible to any office or agency of the corporation to which a salary or emolument is attached, nor shall the trustees be allowed any salary, emoluments, or perquisites, except the right of free ingress to the grounds, rooms, and building of the corporation.[109]

Objective, disinterested trusteeship, not affected by personal advantage or profit, is what such a statute seeks to ensure. The purpose, to prevent "proprietary" handling of charitable funds is plain. (See Section 283.)

Evasions of this rule, by use of *executive committee*, or *administrative committee*, or other devices, are contrary to the intent of the statute. Such evasion, and their effects, are discussed below in the sections on committees.

Pension and insurance plans. In order to attract and hold capable officers and employees, many organizations now provide pension and insurance coverage for them. The lack of social security, hospitalization, insurance, or retirement coverage in many nonprofit organizations has caused great difficulty in getting and keeping capable administrators. [See Section 288.]

Tax and other aspects of pension plans and the like are too specialized to warrant discussion here. Special works should be consulted.[110] For example, use of contributing or noncontributing pension plans involve tax questions as well as internal policy and financial questions.

Fringe benefits. Both nonprofit and business organizations now find it important to offer numerous *fringe benefits* in order to attract and keep well-qualified personnel. These may include payment of moving expenses, reimbursement of loss on sale of a house, help in buying a new home, travel and entertainment allowances, use of organization automobiles and facilities, vacation allowances, reimbursement for surrender of pension benefits lost because of change of employment, severance benefits, and other fringe benefits. Special works should be consulted as to these matters.[111]

§288. LITIGATION EXPENSES OF DIRECTORS OR OFFICERS

[See Section 446.]

Modern statutes sometimes expressly provide for reimbursement of trustees, directors, or officers for expenses of litigation resulting from their official status.[112] Ohio's provision, for example, not only permits such indemnification, but also allows additional compensation in such cases if the articles, bylaws, or members so provide or agree.[113]

D and O Insurance. Directors' and officers' liability insurance coverage for their officers' possible liability is now a routine part of corporation coverage. These are termed "D and O policies." Booklets on the current practice in such coverage can be obtained free, on request, from such companies as INA Corporation (Insurance Company of North America), 1600 Arch Street, Philadelphia, Pa., 19101.

Directors and officers insurance may cover costs incurred in defending state court action for wrongful discharge against a director, even if the settlement agreement admits no wrongful conduct by the director. Wrongful allegations are enough for indemnification.[114]

Many state statutes today recognize the right of directors and officers to be reimbursed for expenses of litigation resulting from their official status. When a director or officer is sued by a member, he must defend himself, usually on the basis of the validity of his official acts.

In some states, a director is held to be entitled to be indemnified for the expenses of such a lawsuit whenever it served to preserve the corporation's property. But, in most states, statutory authority for such reimbursement is required.[115]

Statutes usually provide that authority for indemnification must be stated in the charter or bylaws or by a general resolution.[116] The expenses covered are litigation costs and attorney's fees. Specific assessment procedures are stated, usually requiring formal approval by a court.[117]

The basis for indemnity, of course, is successful defense by the director or officer who is attacked.[118] If the court finds him to be in the wrong, he certainly is not entitled to reimbursement. He need not actually win an affirmative decision, but he must vindicate himself.[119]

When a director defends himself against a *criminal* charge, these statutes do not allow reimbursement of expenses by the corporation.[120] These statutes apply only to civil suits; that is, to *any civil proceedings*, even those before a referee.[121] And they apply also in federal suits.[122]

The 1986 Draft of the Revised Model Nonprofit Corporations Act [§8.51(a)(3)] proposes that indemnification be allowed in criminal proceedings if the accused (indicted) director "had no reasonable cause to believe his or her conduct was unlawful." It is not likely that this proposal will be accepted by legislatures that know what human nature and conduct really are like.

The 1986 Draft of the Revised Model Nonprofit Corporation Act proposed an elaborate and lengthy statute designed to shield directors and officers from liability except in extraordinarily gross cases of misconduct. [Subchapter E therein.]

§289. PERSONAL INTERESTS IN CORPORATE CONTRACTS

[Raymond L. Potts contributed some of this section.]

California's revised Nonprofit Corporation Act in 1980 introduced the startling rule that as many as 49 percent of the board may be "interested" personally in their corporation's deals (contracts, *etc.*).[123] New York's statute permits self-dealing if the transaction is fair.[124] In Florida, a *statute permitting* a contract between two corporations with common or *"interested"* directors, when approved by the shareholders (members), places the *burden on the interested* (or, common) directors to prove their good faith and also the inherent fairness of the contract to the corporation.[125] The 1986 American Law Institute-American Bar Association Revision of the Model Nonprofit Corporation Act echoed the California rule and also included permission for their friends and relatives.[126] The New York rule may have some merit in some cases. The A.B.A. and California rule is hardly able to be justified in most cases.

A director or officer of a nonprofit corporation in most states may have no personal interest in a corporate contract, unless this is specifically authorized by the corporation. A typical statute states.[127]

[N.Y. N-P-C Law §715.]
Interested directors and officers

(a) No contract or other transaction between a corporation and one or more of its directors or officers, or between a corporation and any other corporation, firm, association, or other entity in which one or more of its directors or officers are directors or officers, or have a substantial financial interest, shall be either void or voidable for this reason alone or by reason alone that such a director or directors or officer or officers are present at the meeting of the board, or of a committee thereof, which authorizes such contract or transaction, or that his or their votes are counted for such purpose:

(1) If the material facts as to such director's or officer's interest in such contract or transaction and as to any such common directorship, officership, or financial interest are disclosed in good faith or known to the board or committee, and the board or committee authorizes such contract or transaction by a vote sufficient for such purpose without counting the vote or votes of such interested director or officer; or

(2) If the material facts as to such director's or officer's interest in such contract or transaction and as to any such common directorship, officership, or financial interest are disclosed in good faith or known to the members entitled to vote thereon, if any, and such contract or transaction is authorized by vote of such members.

(b) If such good faith disclosure of the material facts as to the director's or officer's interest in the contract or transaction and as to any such common directorship, officership, or financial interest, is made to the directors or members, or known to the board or committee or members authorizing such contract or transaction, as provided in paragraph (a), the contract or transaction may not be avoided by the corporation for the reasons set forth in paragraph (a). If there was not such disclosure or knowledge, or if the vote of such interested director or officer was necessary for the authorization of such contract or transaction at a meeting of the board or committee at which it was authorized, the corporation may avoid the contract or transaction unless the party or parties hereto shall establish affirmatively that the contract or transaction was fair and reasonable as to the corporation at the time it was authorized by the board, a committee, or the members.

(c) Common or interested directors may be counted in determining the presence of a quorum at a meeting of the board or of a committee which authorizes such contract or transaction.

(d) The certificate of incorporation may contain additional restrictions on contracts or transactions between a corporation and its directors, or officers, or other persons and may provide that contracts or transactions in violation of such restrictions shall be void or voidable.

(e) Unless otherwise provided in the certificate of incorporation or the bylaws, the board shall have authority to fix the compensation of directors for services in any capacity.

(f) The fixing of salaries of officers, if not done in the bylaws, shall require the affirmative vote of a majority of the entire board unless a higher proportion is set by the certificate of incorporation or bylaws.

This statute is similar to the New York Business Corporation Law provision (§713), and applies to officers as well as directors. It typifies the business-proprietary attitude of the New York statute. It is contrary to the idea of fiduciary, not-for-personal-profit *service*.

In the absence of such authorization, a director's contract with his corporation is invalid.[128]

It is obvious that a director is to act for his corporation's—not his own—benefit. A director is liable for breach of his fiduciary duty in most states if either he votes for or influences a corporate decision to transact business with another entity in which he is indirectly or directly beneficially interested.[129]

For example, a corporation director who obtained *personal* (*inurement*) assets or funds by violation of the fiduciary duty to protect its assets (duty of loyalty), may be subjected to "*constructive trust*" of those assets or proceeds in Illinois, and *thus restitution* of those assets may be enforced by courts; sale of property to the corporation by director with misstatements of size, zoning, and mortgage encumbrance.[130]

This does not mean that a director or officer may touch nothing connected with the corporation. If no contract relationship and no loss or disadvantage to the corporation is involved, he is as free to act as anyone else.[131]

For example, he may validly buy bonds of the corporation in the open market, if as an investment and not on the basis of "inside" information.[132] But transactions taking advantage of fiduciary status or knowledge, even with third persons, are invalid and will result in forced return of profits.[133]

The "business judgment rule" does not bar an inquiry into whether the directors of a charitable organization are disinterested when they are charged with misfeasance.[134]

For example, on August 29, 1972, the Cleveland *Plain Dealer* reported the filing of a civil action for $372,000 by the Ohio Attorney-General against a former university trustee, charging that the trustee had ignored a conflict of interest and violation of public trust in selling insurance coverage to the university staff. An attempt to indict the same trustee criminally had returned no indictment in 1971 because of the allegedly narrow scope of Ohio's conflict-of-interest statute.

If authorization for directors or officers to deal with the corporation is provided in the charter, bylaws, or a resolution, greater freedom of action is permitted. But any contract is voidable if unfairness, fraud, or even unreasonableness is shown.[135] Any challenge of the good faith of a director or officer should lead the courts to scrutinize the transaction sharply,[136] especially in a seizure of a "corporate opportunity."[137]

An injunction was held to be proper when nonprofit directors undersold corporate assets to a business they owned. It was held that the injunction against such future sales was proper even though the improper use was not occurring at the time of trial.[138]

Self-interested transactions by nonprofit directors are not sufficient alone to find a breach of fiduciary duty. Under the for-profit standard directors may engage in activities that benefit their own personal or business ends if they do not interfere with the purpose of the nonprofit corporation or endanger its assets.

A director of an incorporated foundation who ousted his fellow directors in order to install his wife and children on the board, used the organization's stock holdings in other corporations to elect himself to the directorships of those businesses, and sold foundation stock to a corporation which he chaired, did not violate his fiduciary duty. The court stated that the fundamental question was one of fairness to the organization.[139]

The governing documents of unincorporated associations have the same effect on the fiduciary duties of organizational officials as the articles of incorporation and bylaws do for nonprofit corporations.

A union constitution was held to be a contract between the international and local branches and the members. Violations of the constitution that amounted to a breach of fiduciary duty gave the members a cause of action in contract. Therefore, a union official who used his power for personal gain in violation of the constitution could be held liable.[140]

Voting by *"interested" directors.* A director who is personally interested in a corporate contract should not vote on it. It is invalid unless its approval is sufficient without counting his vote.[141] [See n. 116]

When a director can be shown to have dominated the board, the fact that a sufficient number of votes (even without his vote) approved the transaction does not validate it.[142]

Transactions between corporations having common directors. A transaction between two corporations that have a common director is subject to the same principles as transactions of a director through third persons. A challenge may bring close scrutiny by the courts. Good faith and fairness then must be proven by the directors.[143]

Where two or more corporations have common directors, this is called *interlocking directorate.*[144] When joint voting is found to occur, aiming at joint management, problems of *anti-trust* law may arise.[145] In banking associations, trust companies, and the like, the anti-monopoly rules of Section 8 of the Clayton Anti-Trust Act[146] may apply.

Voting control by charitable foundations. Use of foundations as personal holding companies has been a problem in recent years. This is discussed elsewhere in this book.[147]

§290. ADVISORY BOARDS OR COUNCILS

Many nonprofit corporations have found that use of an *advisory board* or *council* is helpful to the organization. Such a board or council is not the controlling, operating board of directors, but adds useful assistance, especially in educational, civic, social welfare, and other kinds of organizations that have public service purposes. They also serve as devices for honoring friends of the organization, with a "status" designation.

The creation, nature, and purposes, limitations, control, and other aspects of such boards or councils is best illustrated by a sample form of the *regulations* of such a body. This example was drafted by the author in 1985 for a nonprofit organization dedicated to assisting, educating, and placing in jobs, women recently widowed or divorced or otherwise cast adrift.

FORM NO. 132
Advisory Board of Council
Regulations (Bylaws)

ASC Regulations—Adopted by the Board of _____ **Corporation**
on Sept. _____ **, 19_____**
Advisory and Support Council (ASC)
of _____ **—Regulations of ASC**

Article I—Name

The name of this (ASC) Council shall be the Advisory and Support Council of _____, herein referred to as ASC, in distinction from but in cooperation with _____ Corporation.

Article II—Purposes

The purposes of ASC shall be to act in an advisory and supportive capacity to the _____ Board and its directors, when requested to do so by the Board; and to assist and encourage individual projects approved by that board.

Article III—Objectives

The specific objectives of ASC shall be, in the order of their primacy:

Section 1:   To serve as advisors to the Board, either individually or collectively.

Section 2:   To advocate and encourage projects of the Board in the community through personal contacts and help, insofar as individual ASC members wish to do so.

Section 3:   To actively solicit members for ASC, so as to maintain and expand support for _____.

Section 4: To plan and produce programs, projects, and other functions to raise funds for expenses not otherwise provided for in the regular budget and program.

Article IV—Membership

ASC membership shall be:

Section 1: Non-sectarian, non-partisan, and nonprofit, in accordance with the charter of _____ and the laws of the State of _____ and the USA.

Section 2: Open to corporations, civic, service, and professional organizations, as well as interested individuals who support the objectives of _____ and ASC.

Article V—Dues

Section 1: Annual individual membership shall be entirely voluntary; but dues shall be contributed by corporate members at the rate of $50 per year.

Section 2: Dues are payable by corporations upon joining, and thereafter on July 1 annually.

Section 3: A corporate member is in good standing when dues are paid.

Section 4: Any corporate member whose dues are not current by September 1 shall be removed from the ASC roster; however, such member may be reinstated on payment of delinquent dues.

Article VI—Fiscal Responsibility

Section 1: The ASC fiscal year shall commence on the second day of July and end on the next first day of July.

Section 2: An Auditing Committee shall be appointed by the Board from among the ASC members in May. The committee shall audit the treasurer's records within ten days after the close of the treasurer's term of office and shall report to ASC at its next meeting.

Article VIII—Officers

Section 1: The officers of ASC shall be a Chairperson, past-Chairperson, Chairperson-elect, Secretary, and Treasurer; which persons shall compose the Executive Committee of ASC.

Section 2: ASC officers shall serve for a term of one year and may be re-elected for one additional term. This does not preclude anyone from serving in that office at a later date.

Section 3: ASC officers shall be elected by ASC from its active members in good standing at the May meeting and be installed at the June meeting to serve for a term or until their successors are elected. Initially, however, the first slate of officers shall take office immediately following the election.

Section 4: Any ASC officer resigning or failing to adequately perform the duties of the office may be replaced by the Executive Committee for the completion of his or her term.

Article VIII—Nominations and Elections

Section 1: ASC officers shall be elected in May from among the individual members in good standing.

Section 2: ASC nominating committee shall be appointed by the Chairperson in April to present a slate of officers to the May meeting. Nominations may also be made from the floor.

Section 3: ASC officers shall be eligible to serve no more than two consecutive terms. Six months or more shall be considered a term of office in determining eligibility for re-election.

Section 4: The Chairperson of the official Board of Directors shall be an *ex-officio* member of the ASC Executive Committee and may attend any or all ASC general or committee meetings, to observe or advise.

Article IX—Duties of Officers

Section 1: The President of _____ shall be the principal officer of the organization; and see to active liaison between ASC and the Board of Directors, and shall:

a. Attend ASC and ASC Executive Committee meetings.

b. Serve as *ex-officio* member of all ASC committees except the nominating committee.

c. Sign all orders upon the treasurer for disbursements as directed by the organization board.

d. Be responsible for keeping the Board of Directors apprised of ASC activities, including the following:

    I. Statement of annual goals;

    II. Specific plans for programs, solicitations, and/or projects;

    III. Monthly membership reports;

    IV. Progress reports of ASC activities;

    V. Any requests for staff assistance;

    VI. Any requests for seed money needed to initiate any program or project;

    VII. Treasurer's report including transfer of funds to or from _____.

Section 2: The immediate past-Chairperson of ASC shall:

a. Serve as an advisor to the Chairperson;

b. Serve on the Executive Committee of ASC;

c. Chair the awards committee;

d. Chair the ASC nominating committee.

Section 3:   The Chairperson-elect shall:

a. Perform all duties of the Chairperson in the absence of that person;

b. Become Chairperson after the Chairperson's term has expired or should he or she be unable to complete the elected term;

c. Serve as an *ex-officio* member, without vote, of all ASC committees except the nominating committee;

d. Become chairperson of the Fund Raising Committee;

e. Serve in such other capacity as may be requested by the President.

Section 4:   The Vice-Chairperson shall:

a. Perform the duties of the Chairperson in the absence of the Chairperson and the Chairperson-elect;

b. Become Chairperson of the Membership Committee;

c. Serve in such capacities as may be requested by the President.

Section 5:   The ASC Secretary shall:

a. Take and record accurate minutes of the proceedings of all meetings of the ASC Council and its Executive Committee;

b. Conduct the correspondence of the Council;

c. Preserve in a permanent file all minutes, correspondence and other official records of ASC.

Section 6:   The ASC Treasurer shall:

a. Have charge of all monies of ASC and report thereon at all of its meetings;

b. Collect dues from ASC members and furnish proper receipts;

c. Keep a list of names, addresses, phone numbers, and occupations of ASC members.

d. Prepare any requests for payment of bills, and secure approval of ASC Chairperson and present them to _____ Treasurer for payment;

e. Keep an itemized record, in a permanent file, of ASC receipts and expenditures;

f. Forward promptly to _____ Treasurer all monies received for membership dues, project funds, fees, and contributions, properly identified;

g. Serve as an *ex-officio* member of the ASC Finance Committee;

h. Deliver to the successor within fifteen days of expiration of term of office, all books, records and papers, requesting receipt therefore.

Section 7:   Each ASC officer, except the Treasurer, shall deliver to the successor immediately after retiring from office all accounts, records, books, papers and other property belonging to the ASC or _____ organization.

Article X—Meetings

Section 1:   Regular ASC meetings shall be held on the fourth Friday of the month unless otherwise scheduled by the Chairperson.

Section 2:   ASC Executive Committee shall meet as necessary in special meetings to conduct business, fill vacancies, plan, or set goals.

Section 3:   The June meeting shall be designated the annual ASC meeting, at which time reports summarizing the year's activities shall be given and new officers installed. This meeting may be special function to which all members of ASC, _____, friends, and celebrities are invited.

Section 4:   Special ASC meetings also may be called by the President, by any five members or by the Board of Directors, provided that all ASC members are notified of time, place and purpose of such meeting.

Section 5:   A quorum shall consist of those ASC members attending a regular or properly called meeting.

Section 6:   Motions shall pass by a majority vote.

Article XI—Standing Committees

Section 1:   The ASC Standing Committees shall be Fund Raising, Membership, Public Relations, Foundations, and Education.

Section 2:   Committee chairpersons and members shall be appointed by the ASC Chairperson for a term of one year and may be reappointed for one additional year.

Section 3:   The ASC Fund Raising Committee shall be comprised of a chairperson and at least two members. It shall be the duty of the Fund Raising Committee to present to members specific programs, projects, and/or special events, which may be profitable to conduct; and to solicit participation of other committees and ASC members, set goals, establish guidelines, and execute plans of ASC.

Section 4:   The ASC Membership Committee shall consist of a chairperson and two or more members. It shall be the duty of the membership committee to promote, expand and orient membership.

Section 5:   The ASC Public Relations Committee shall be composed of the chairperson and two or more members. It shall be the duty of the Public Relations Committee to present programs and other activities through available news media, flyers, speakers bureau, and newsletter.

Section 6:   The ASC Foundation chairman shall assemble a team of professional people with expertise in soliciting bequests, grants
and other contributions, so as to establish a permanent trust
fund to insure the continuing service of _____
to the community.

Section 7:   The ASC Education Committee shall promote public awareness of, and support for, the organization and its programs.

Article XII—Parliamentary Procedure

The rules of parliamentary practice that shall govern all proceedings of the
ASC Council and its Executive Committee shall be Oleck & Green, "Parliamentary Law and Practice For Nonprofit Organizations" (American Law Institute—American Bar Association Joint Committee, 2d ed. 1991).

Article XIII—Amendments

Section 1:   All proposed amendments to these Regulations shall be presented to the President for Executive Committee consideration prior to presentation to the ASC organization.

Section 2:   Final adoption of these Regulations or any revisions or
amendments thereto shall be contingent upon the approval
of the Board of Directors.

Article XIV—Dissolution

Upon dissolution of the (ASC or _____) organization all assets
remaining after payment of any outstanding expenses, all records, files, or
other property belonging to ASC shall be delivered to _____ or to
the Board of Directors thereof, or their legal successors in nonprofit type work.

POINTS TO REMEMBER

- Routine affairs are for the board of trustees or directors to decide.
- Extraordinary affairs are for the members to decide.
- Fundamental changes in policy or purposes must be approved by the gen-
eral membership.
- An honest director who uses reasonable care and diligence has no per-
sonal liability for corporate debts or obligations.
- Directors guilty of fraud or bad faith are personally, jointly, and severally
liable.
- Insist on written records of objections or doubtful decisions or acts.
- Be sure to prepare and file at least an annual report on the organization's
finances and affairs.
- Provide in the bylaws for compensation of directors and officers. Provide
also for reimbursement of litigation expenses.

- Do not give compensation to trustees of charitable organizations, directly or indirectly.

- Include power in the bylaws for directors and officers to deal with the corporation. But include protective restrictions. Generally discourage such transactions.

- Do not allow use of the organization as a tax dodge or business holding device by anyone or any group.

- Do not allow trustees or officers to make the organization a proprietary device. Use trustees' and/or members' proper powers to prevent abuse.

- Remember that directors and trustees often must serve as financial experts. If they are not such experts, they must obtain expert guidance and assistance or face personal liability.

NOTES TO CHAPTER 28

1. Fla. St., §617.0302 is typical. It says that every nonprofit corporation, unless otherwise provided in its articles of incorporation, shall have the list of powers set forth in that section of the statute. This long has been the rule; *see,* Frelish v. Saugerties, 70 Hun. (N.Y.) 589, 24 N.Y.S. 182 (1893); Bradley v. State *ex. rel.* Hill, 111 Ga. 168, 36 S.E. 630 (1900); Penberthy Electromelt Co. v. Star City Glass Co., 135 S.E.2d 289 (W. Va. 1964); Williams v. United Most Worshipful . . . , 140 S.2d 206 (La. App. 1962).

2. Board of Regents of Regency Universities System v. Illinois Educational Labor Relations Board, 520 N. E. 2d 1150 (Ill. App. 1988).

3. **Benjamin Plumbing Inc. v. Barnes**, 470 N.W.2d 888 (Wis 1991).

4. **Kirtley v. McClelland**, 562 N.E.2d 27 (Ind. Ct. App. 1991).

5. *See,* Oleck, *Modern Corporation Law,* §603 (1978 Supp.); Brooks v. State Board of Funeral Dir. and Emb., 233 Md. 98, 195 A.2d 728 (1963); Frelish case, *supra; In re* Society for Social Responsibility in Science, Inc., 9 Bucks. (Pa.) 42 (1959).

6. *Ibid.; and see,* Henn and Alexander, *Corporations,* §78 (3d ed. 1983).

7. *Ibid.,* Stevens on *Corporations,* §1 (2d ed. 1949); 1 Hornstein, *Corporation Law and Practice,* §12 (1959); Coastal Pharmaceutical Co. v. Goldman, 213 Va. 831, 195 S.E.2d 848 (1973).

8. *Runcie v. Bankers Trust Co.,* 6 N.Y.S. 2d 623 (1938); N.Y. BCL §§55-2-06.

9. Dartmouth College v. Woodward, 17 U.S. (4 Wheat.) 518, 4 L Ed. 629 (1819).

10. *Munder v. Circle One Condominium, Inc.,* 596 So.2d 144 (Fla. 4th DCA 1992).

11. *Brenner v. Powers,* 584 N.E. 2d 569 (Ind. Ct. App. 1992).

12. Ohio Rev. Code §1702.01(L).

13. *Ibid.,* §1702.30.

14. Model Nonprofit Corp. Act §17.

15. A religious leader's personal estate may not take funds solicited for his religious organization. *In re* Estate of Muhammed, 520 N. E. 2d 795 (Ill. App. 1987).

16. Church v. Young, 21 Ohio N.P. (n.s.) 569, 29 Ohio Dec. 477 (1919).

17. Ohio Rev. Code §§1702.04(B), 1702.10. But control vests in trustees in a Y.M.C.A., Ohio Rev. Code §1715.24; Maxwell v. Northwest Ind., Inc., 339 N.Y.S.2d 347 (1972).

18. Veterans of World War I v. Levy, 70 Ohio L. Abs. 49, 118 N.E.2d 670 (1954).

19. Fla. Stat. §617.1001; Ga. Code Ann. §14-3-1001; Ala. Code §10-3A-80.

20. *See*, Oleck, *Proprietary Mentality and the New Nonprofit Corporation Laws*, 20 Clev. St. L. Rev. 145 (1971).

21. Cal Corp. Code, §9603 (1978). Also, §5233 (1980) allows self-dealing within "reasonable" limits.

22. Cal. Corp. Code. §9200(2)(1978); and §5233 (1980) permitting self-dealing.

23. Ohio Rev. Code §1713.30.

24. *Mark Twain Kansas City Bank v. Kroh Bros. Development Co.*, 829 P.2d 907 (Kan. 1992).

25. Ohio Rev. Code §§1715.29–1715.31.

26. *Ibid.*, §1719.01.

27. Id., §1733.13.

28. *Ibid.*, §1737.

29. *County of Hennepin v. Association of Paramedics*, 464 N.W. 2d 578 (Minn. App. 1990).

30. Ohio Rev. Code., §1702.14.

31. Templeman v. Grant, 75 Colo. 519; 227 P. 555 (1924); Berkeley County Court v. Martinsburg and P. Turnpike Co., 94 W. Va. 246; 115 S.E. 448 (1922).

32. Ayres v. Hadaway, 303 Mich. 589; 6 N.W.2d 905 (1942). But conditions attached to a gift must be followed: Ohio Society for Crippled Children v. McElroy 175 Ohio St. 49, 191 N.E.2d 543, 100 A.L.R.2d 1202 (1963).

33. Conrick v. Houston Civic Opera Assn., 99 S.W.2d 382 (Tex. Civ. App. 1936); Levin v. Sinai Hospital, 186 Md. App. 174; 46 A.2d 298 (1946) Central N.Y. Bridge Assn., Inc. v. American Contract Bridge League, Inc., 339 N.Y.S.2d 438 (N.Y. Supp. 1972) not-for-profit corporation's actions in excess of granted powers may be *ultra vires.*

34. Jacobs v. North Jersey Blood Center, 411 A.2d 210 (N.J. Super., 1979).

35. Commercial National Bank v. Weinhard, 192 U.S. 243; 24 S.Ct. 253, 48 L. Ed. 425 (1904); *and see*, Ballantine, *Corporations* 120 (rev. ed. 1946).

36. *See* n. 28, above; Zion v. Kurtz, 405 N.E. 2d 681 (N.Y. 1980).

37. *Powers v. Professional Rodeo Cowboys Ass'n*, 832 P.2d 1099 (Colo. App., 1992).

38. *See* Briggs v. Spaulding, 141 U.S. 132, 147, 11 S.Ct. 924; 35 L. Ed. 662 (1891); Citizens Building, Loan and Sav. Assn. v. Coriell, 34 N.J. Eq. 383, 392 (1881); Home Tel. Co. v. Darley, 355 F. Supp. 992 (D.C. Miss. 1973); D. Shoneyfeldt, *Personal Liability Maze of Corporate Directors and Officers*, 58 Nebr. L. Rev.692-717 (1979).

39. Syracuse Television, Inc. v. Channel 9, Syracuse, Inc. 273 N.Y.S.2d 16 (N.Y. Sup. Ct. 1966); Weidner v. Engelhart, 176 N.W.2d 509 (No. Dak. 1970); Anderson v. Akers, 7 F. Supp. 924 (D.C., Ky, 1934); modified, 86 F.2d 518 (6th Cir. 1936), revd. 302 U.S. 643 (1937) (directors of unsound mind, relieved of liability); N.Y. Not-for-Profit Corp. L. §717; Meyers v. Moody, 693 F.2d 1196 (D.C., Tex., 1982).

40. People v. Mancuso, 255 N.Y. 463, 469; 175 N.E. 177; 76 A.L.R. 514 (1931). *See*, Mulcahy, R., *Foundation Trustees—Selection, Duties, and Responsibilities*. 13 U.C.L.A. L. Rev. 1060, 1071 (1961); note, *The Charitable Corporation*, 64 Harv. L. Rev. 1168, 1174 (1951). *Contra:* Lynch v. John Redfield Foundation, 9 Cal. App.3d 293, 299, 88 Cal. Rptr. 86, 89 (1970); Holt v. College of Osteopathic Physicians and Surgeons, 61 Cal.2d 750, 394 P.2d 932 (1964). Gifts made to a charitable corporation were held in trust by the corporate directors for the charitable corporation's purposes. *Id.* at 935. *See*, Pasley, *Nonprofit Corporations—Accountability of Directors and Officers*, 21 Bus. Law 621 (1976).

41. Gibbons v. Anderson, 80 F. 345, 350 (W.D. Mich. 1897); Cushing, *The Liability of the Inactive Corporate Director*, 8 Columbia L. Rev. 18 (1908).

42. Stern v. Lucy Webb Hayes National Training School for Deaconesses and Missionaries, 381 F. Supp. 1003, 1013 (D.D.C. 1974). However, a contrary view states that the law should recognize that the charitable trust and the charitable corporation have much more in common with each other than each has with its private counterpart. The important differences among charities relate not to their form but to their function. In the area of fidu-

ciary duties, a law of charities is needed. Karst, *The Efficiency of the Charitable Dollar: An Unfulfilled State Responsibility*, 73 Harv. L. Rev. 433, 436 (1960). Thus, the director should be bound by the same duty as that of a trustee. An appropriate title would be "quasi-trustee." The reason for this is that the quasi-trustee never gets title to property as does a trustee, and the quasi-trustee would be held to a higher duty of care. *Id.* at 547.

43. Pool v. Pool, 22 S2d 131 (La. App. 1945); Litwin v. Allen, 25 N.Y.S.2d 667, 719 (1940); Ohio Rev. Stat. 1702.30; N.Y. Not-for-Profit Corp. §717(b).

44. Bowerman v. Hamner, 250 U.S. 504, 513; 39 S.Ct. 549; 63 L. Ed. 1113 (1919); Stern v. Lucy Webb, 381 F. Supp. 1003, 1014 (D.D.C. 1974).

45. *See* Keenan, (article) 6 *NonProfit Times* (5) 1 (May 1992); Keenan, (article) 6 *NonProfit Times* (9) 1 (Sept. 1992).

46. Mehegan, S., (article) 7 *NonProfit Times* (6) 4 (June 1993).

47. Charitable Corp. v. Sutton, 2 Atk. 400; 26 Engl. Reprint 642; Briggs case, n. 31, above. A minority of the board members may enjoin a threatened breach of trust by the majority; the power of the attorney-general is not exclusive. Holt v. College of Osteopathic Phys. and Surg., 61 Cal.2d 750, 394 P.2d 932, 40 Cal. Rptr. 244 (1964), noted, 16 Hastings L.J. 479 and 629 (1965).

48. *See* Abbot v. Waltham Watch Co., 260 Mass. 81; 156 N.E. 897 (1927); and Citronelle— Mobile Gathering, Inc. v. O'Leary, 499 F. Supp. 871 (Ala. 1980) director is liable for tort of another that he authorizes or approves.

49. Rous v. Carlisle, 14 N.Y.S.2d 498; *affd.*, 15 N.Y.S.2d 721 (1939); Goff v. Emde, 32 Ohio App. 216; 167 N.E. 699 (1928); Beard v. Achenbach Memorial Hospital Assn. 170 F.2d 859, 862, (10th Cir. 1948). Calif. Corp. Code §5230 (1980) adopts the "prudent man" (not trustee) standard of duty.

50. *Fairhope Single Tax Corp. v. Rezner*, 527 So. 2d 1232 (AL 1987) (reh. den. 1988); W. Fletcher, *Cyclopedia of Corporations* §2104, at 425 (1976).

51. *Russo v. Turin*, Civ. # CA-89-601 (Fla. Cir. Ct., 1990); Fla. St. § 607.0830 requires directors to consider social, legal, economic and other relevant factors.

52. *Levandusky v. One Fifth Avenue Aptmt. Corp.*, 553 N.E.2d 1317 (N.Y. 1990) unanimous opinion.

53. *Leon L. Clardy, et al., vs. Tri-Community Water System*, 591 So.2d 65, (Ala. 1991).

54. *Marco A. Longo, Jr., et al., vs. Town 'N Harbour Owners Corp.*, 180 A.D.2d 779, 580 N.Y.S.2d 427 (N.Y. App. Div. 1992).

55. *Eleanor Ludwig, et al., vs. 25 Plaza Tenants Corp.*, 184 A.D.2d 623, 584 N.Y.S.2d 907 (N.Y. App. Div. 1992).

56. *The Bank of Hartford, Inc., vs. Alda Bultron, et al.*, 1992 WL 436242 (Conn. Sup. Ct.)

57. *Maj. Gen. Guy H. Goddard, Ret., Robert M. Stone, et al., vs. Fairways Development General Partnership, et al.*, 426 S.E.2d 828, 832 (S.C. Ct. App. 1993).

58. This opinion has not been released for publication in the permanent law reports. Until released it is subject to revision or withdraw. *Zack Stamp, Director of Insurance for the State of Illinois, as Liquidator of Pine Tops Insurance Co., vs. Ralph E. Batastini, W. Carroll Bumpers, Milton D. Faber, et al.*, 1993 WL 56149 (Ill. App. 1Dist.).

59. Macaluso v. Jenkins, 420 N.E.2d 251 (Ill. App. 1981).

60. Commonwealth v. Colonial Motor Sales, Inc., 420 N.E.2d 20 (Mass. App., 1981) Liability for tampering with automobile's odometer in a sale. *Cf.*, Hauser Motor Co. v. Byrd, 377 S.2d 773 (Fla. App. 1980).

61. National Survival Game, Inc. v. Skirmish, 603 F. Supp. 339 (D.C., N.Y., 1985).

62. Dotlich v. Dotlich, 475 N.E.2d 331 (Ind. App., 1985).

63. *Ibid.*

64. Solar Supply, Inc. v. Arctic Air, Inc., 400 S.2d 924 (La. App., 1981).

65. Latt v. Superior Court (Kaufman) 212 Calif. Rptr. 380 (App., 1985). For other examples

of *fiduciary duty*, see: Hall-Hottel Co. v. Oxford Square Co-op., 446 N.E.2d 25 (Ind. App. 1983); Raven's Cove case, 171 Calif. Rptr. 334 (App., 1981); Matter of Koszuth, 43 B.R. 104 (1984).

66. Solimine v. Hollander, 128 N.J. Eq. 228; 16 A.2d 203 (1940).

67. N.Y. Not-for-Profit Corp. L. §719(e). Knowingly misleading conduct results in liability. First Natl. Bank v. Level Club, 241 A.D. 433; 272 N.Y.S. 273 (1934); Fl. St. §617.0825.

68. Ohio Rev. Code §1702.55; Ga. Code Ann. §§14-3-851 through 14-3-856.

69. *Ibid.*, §1702.99. As to false entries and statements, *see, Ibid.* §1702.54.

70. Walker Memorial Baptist Church v. Saunders, 173 Misc. 455; 17 N.Y.S.2d 842 (1940); *affd. without op.*, 259 A.D. 1010; 21 N.Y.S.2d 512 (1940); *revd on other gds.*, 285 N.Y. 462; 35 N.E.2d 42 (1941); *rehearing den.*, 286 N.Y. 607; 35 N.E.2d 944 (1941); Lewis v. S.L.& E., Inc., 629 F.2d 764 (2d Cir. 1980).

71. J.J. Hands, *Living with Limited Liability, Natl. L.J.* 21 (July 4, 1988).

72. Ohio Rev. Code §§2945.44, 3901.23.

73. Kugelman v. Hirschman, 22 Misc. 533; 49 N.Y.S. 1012 (1898); *and see* n. 68.

74. People v. Smith, 190 Misc. 871; 74 N.Y.S.2d 845 (1947).

75. *Connolly v. J.T. Ventures*, 851 F.2d 930 (7th Cir., IL, 1988).

76. *S.H., Helen R. Scheuer Family Foundation, Inc., By and Through Scheuer v. 61 Associates*, 582 N.Y.S. 2d 662 (A.D. 1 Dept. 1992).

77. *Bibo v. Jeffrey's Restaurant*, 770 P.2d 290 (AK 1989), overruling *Blake v. Gilbert*, 702 P.2d 631 (Alaska); AS 09.10.050, 09.10.070.

78. *Stern v. General Elec. Co.*, 924 F.2d 472 (2d Cir., N.Y., 1991).

79. *People v. Community Hospital of Evanston*, 545 N.E.2d 226 (Ill. App., 1989).

80. *Mary v. Lupin Foundation*, 609 So. 2d 184 (La., 1992).

81. *Fl. St.* § 617.0830 (eff. July 1, 1991) for *Nonprofit Corporations.*

82. *See also Fl. St.* § 606.0830(3) (1989), and similar statutes in Idaho, Indiana, Maine, Minnesota, New Mexico, New York, etc. And see papers in a *Stetson Univ. College of Law* (First Annual) *Corporate Governance Symposium*, titled *Corporate Malaise—Stakeholder Statutes: Cause or Cure?* (Feb. 2, 1991).

83. *D & O Yes or No? Directors and Officers Insurance for the Volunteer Board*, National Center for Community Risk Management & Insurance, 1828 L St., NW, Suite 505, Washington, D.C. 20036; telephone: 202-785-3891; Tremper, C., (article) 6 *NonProfit Times* (9) 23 (Sept. 1992).

84. Tillman v. Wheaton-Haven Recreational Assoc., 517 F.2d 1141 (4th Cir. 1975), 580 F.2d 1222 (4th Cir. 1978): The Board of Directors of a nonprofit corporation which operated a community swimming pool passed a rule prohibiting blacks from using the pool. Before passing the rule, the board consulted an attorney who confirmed the propriety of such a rule. The Court of Appeals held the directors who had voted for the rule personally liable for violating the federal statute prohibiting racial discrimination. However, the members who did not vote for the rule or who had not attended the meeting were not held liable. The court distinguished between the director who is alleged to have been negligent in the performance of his duties and the director who is alleged to have intentionally breached a federal statute. In the former case, the director may plead due diligence as a defense, while in the latter there is no excuse for ignorance of the law.

85. Richardson, *Evidence* §§415-149 (7th ed. 1948); Ohio Rev. Code §1702.55(C). Directors have both the power and the duty to inspect records. Hyman v. Jewish Chronic Disease Hospital, 15 N.Y.2d 317, 206 N.E.2d 338 (1965).

86. Mountain States Supply Inc. v. Mountain States Feed and Livestock Co., 425 P.2d 75 (Mont. 1967); Fisher Provision Co. v. Lo Patin, 237 N.W.2d 562 (Mich App. 1975).

87. N.Y. Not-for-Profit Corp. L. §519; Ohio Rev. Code §1702.16 requires an "annual meeting."

88. Davids v. Sillcox, 297 N.Y. 355, 79 N.E.2d 440 (1948).

89. Henshaw v. American Cement Corp., 252 A.2d 125 (Del. Ch. 1969) (based on 8 Del. C. §220); Pilat v. Broach Systems, Inc., 108 N.J. Super. 88, 260 A.2d 13 (1969); Leisner v. Kent Investors, Inc., 307 N.Y.S.2d 293 (Sup. Ct. 1970); Javits v. Investors League, 92 N.Y.S.2d (1949); *but see,* Ohio Rev. Code §1702.15 and *see,* Chavco Investment Co. v. Pybus, 613 S.W.2d 806 (Tex. 1981).

90. *Ibid.*

91. Hamilton v. Patrolmen's Benevolent Assn. 88 N.Y.S.2d 683 (1949); and, above N.Y. N-P-C-L. §519(a).

92. *See* c. 1; and n. 69.

93. N.Y. Penal L. §665; Fla. Stat. §617.0505; Ga. Code Ann. §14-3-112; Ala. Code, tit. 10 §3A-44.

94. N.Y. Not-for-Profit Corp. L. §715.

95. Hawaiian Intnatl. Finances, Inc. v. Pablo, 488 P.2d 1172 (Hawaii 1971); Knapp v. Rochester Dog Protective Assn., 235 A.D. 436; 257 N.Y.S. 356 (1932); Vervars v. Young, 539 F.2d 966 (3rd Cir. 1976); cf. Hight Equip. v. Shelton, 103 S.2d 615 (Fla. 1958) as to implied contract for salary.

96. Fla. Stat. §617.0505. Moore v. Anadalsie Hospital, Inc., 284 Ala. 259, 224 So.2d 617 (1969). The sole limitation on a doctor's salary at a nonprofit corporation is that his charges be reasonable. There is no prohibition against the physician personally benefiting. *Id.,* at 620.

97. Dixmoor Golf Club, Inc. v. Evans, 325 Ill. 612; 156 N.E. 785 (1927).

98. Alexander v. Equitable Life Assur. Soc., 233 N.Y. 300; 135 N.E. 509 (1922); *revg.,* 196 A.D. 963; 188 N.Y.S. 908 (1921).

99. Stafford's Estate v. Progressive Natl. Farm Loan Assn., 207 La. 1097; 22 S.2d 662 (1945).

100. Vredenburg v. Internatl. Trade Exhibition, Inc., 166 La. 390; 117 S. 437 (1928).

101. Rogers v. Hill, 289 U.S. 582 (1933).

102. Pence v. West Side Hospital, 265 Ill. App. 560 (1932).

103. Albers v. Villa Moret, 46 Calif. App.2d 54; 115 P.2d 238 (1941); Worley v. Dunkle, 62 A.2d 699 (N.J. Eq. 1948). Rogers v. Hill, 289 U.S. 582; 53 S.Ct. 731 (1933); *revg.,* 60 F.2d 109 (1932).

104. *See,* 19 C.J.S., *Corporations,* §805.

105. *In re* Aksel Arnessen, 127 N.Y.L.J. 1359, col. 5 (Apr. 4, 1952) (unrep. decis., Supr. Ct.); O'Malley v. Casey, 589 P.2d 1388 (Colo. App. 1979).

106. Fl. St. §617.0801, enacted in Fl. Session L. 1990 Regular Session Chap. 90–179 § 45 (eff. July 1, 1991).

107. *See* Cohn v. Columbia Pictures Corp., 128 N.Y.L.J. 725, col. 3 (Oct. 7, 1952) (unrep. decis., Supr. Ct.).

108. Gimbel Bros. v. Brook Shopping Centers, 499 N.Y.S.2d 435 (1986).

109. Ohio Rev. Code §1713.30.

110. *See,* 2 Oleck, *Modern Corporation Law,* §§1003–1023 (1978 Supp.).

111. *Ibid.*

112. Ohio Rev. Code §1702.12(E); Calif. Nonprofit Corp. L. §5239.

113. *Ibid.*

114. *Wayne County Neighborhood Legal Services v. National Union Fire Ins. Co.,* 971 F. 2d 1 (6th Cir. (Mich.), (1992).

115. Solimine v. Hollander, 129 N.J. Eq. 264; 19 A.2d 344 (1941) (no statute). But statute usually is required. Bailey v. Bush Terminal, 293 N.Y. 735; 56 N.E.2d 739 (1944).

116. N.Y. Bus. Corp. L. §§721–725; N.Y. N-P-C Law §§722, 723, 726.

117. *Ibid.,* §725; N.Y. N-P-C Law §725, 726.

118. Bysheim v. Miranda, 45 N.Y.S.2d 473 (1943).

119. Tichnor v. Andrews, 193 Misc. 1050; 85 N.Y.S.2d 760; *affd. without op.*, 275 A.D. 749; 90 N.Y.S.2d 920 (1949).

120. Petition of Schwartz, 94 F. Supp. 129 (D.C. N.Y. 1950).

121. Dornan v. Humphrey, 278 A.D. 1010; 106 N.Y.S.2d 142; *affd.*, 279 A.D. 1040; 112 N.Y.S.2d 585 (1952).

122. Cohen v. Beneficial Indust. L. Corp., 337 U.S. 541; 69 S. Ct. 1221 (1949).

123. Calif. Corp. Code §5227 (1980). *See also* the text, at n. 141.

124. N.Y. N-PCL §715. *E.g.*, a loan to the corporation: R.J. Eustrom Corp. v. Interceptor Corp., 555 F.2d 277 (10th Cir. 1977).

125. *Woodstock Enterprises, Inc. v. International Moorings and Marine, Inc.*, 524 So. 2d 1313 (LA App. 1988). Fla. St. § 617.0832 (eff. 1991).

126. Rev. M.NPC Act §8.13.

127. N.Y. N-PCL. §715; *cf.*, Calif. N-PCL. §5333 (1980).

128. Knapp v. Rochester Dog Protective Assn., 285 A.D. 436; 257 N.Y.S. 356 (1937).

129. Stern v. Lucy Webb, 381 F. Supp. 1003, 1014 (D.D.C. 1974); Gilbert v. McLeod Infirmary, 219 S.C. 174, 64 S.E.2d 524 (1951).

130. *Forkin v. Cole*, 548 N.E.2d 795 (Ill. App. 1989); and see Fl. St. § 617.0832 (eff. July 1, 1991).

131. Kratzer v. Day, 12 F.2d 724 (9th Cir. Wash. 1926). *See*, note, 35 Columbia. L. Rev. 289 (1935). Durfee v. Durfee and Canning, 323 Mass. 187; 80 N.E.2d 522 (1948); Marcus v. Otis, 168 F.2d 649 (2d Cir. 1948), 169 F.2d 148 (2d Cir. 1948).

132. Seymour v. Spring Forest Cemetery Assn., 144 N.Y. 333; 39 N.E. 365; 26 L.R.A. 859. *See* cases in 76 A.L.R. 439. *See also*, Wyman v. Bowman, 127 F.257; 273 (8th Cir. Iowa 1904).

133. *See* Kleinsasser v. McNamara, 129 Calif. App. 49; 18 P.2d 423 (1933) (sale of land, third-person deal); Johnson v. Kaiser, 104 Mont. 261; 65 P.2d 1179 (1937).

134. *S.H., Helen R. Scheuer Family Foundation, Inc., By and Through Scheuer v. 61 Associates*, 582 N.Y.S. 2d 662 (A.D. 1 Dept. 1992).

135. Todd v. Temple Hospital Assn., 273 P. 595 (Cal. App. 1928).

136. Knudsen v. Burdett, 67 S.D. 20; 287 N.W. 673 (1939); Gall v. Cowell, 118 W. Va. 263; 190 S.E. 130 (1937).

137. City of Miami v. Smith, 551 F.2d 1370 (D.C., Fla., 1977). Failure to recognize fiduciary duty is enough, even if no active dishonesty is shown. Robinson v. Watts Detective Agency, 685 F.2d 729 (D.C. Mass., 1982).

138. **Butterworth v. Anclote Manor Hospital, Inc.**, 566 So.2d 296 (Fla. 2d DCA 1990).

139. **Oberly v. Kirby**, 1990 WL 183884 (Del. Supr. 1990).

140. **Shea v. McCarthy**, 953 F.2d 29 (2d Cir. 1992).

141. *See* n. 125; Elggren v. Wooley, 64 Utah 183; 228 P. 906 (1924); Todd case, n. 102.

142. Dixmoor Golf Club v. Evans, 325 Ill. 612; 156 N.E. 785 (1927).

143. *See*, Lazenby v. Henderson, 241 Mass. 177; 135 N.E. 302 (1922); and note, 29 Columbia L. Rev. 338 (1929); Calif. Civ. Code (1941) §311; *and see*, Brainard v. De La Mantanya, 18 Calif.2d 502; 116 P.2d 66 (1941), 2 Oleck, *Modern Corporation Law*, 758–762 (1978 Supp.).

144. *See*, 2 Oleck, *Modern Corporation Law*, 758 (1978 Supp.) giving illustrative cases.

145. *Ibid.*, vol. 3, §1469.

146. 38 Stat. 732, 15 U.S.C. §19 (1963).

147. *See* the Index for discussions of this problem; *and see* 3 Oleck, *Modern Corporation Law*, §1471 (1978 Supp.); and Oleck, *Foundations used as Business Devices*, 9 Clev.-Mar. L. R. 339 (1960).

29

OFFICERS AND MANAGERS

[See also Chapter 42 on *Management, Generally.*]

§291. WHAT IS AN OFFICER?

[*Note:* Because *directors* and *trustees* are *officers*, much of what is said in Chapters 27 and 28 applies also to officers other than directors.]

The Model Nonprofit Corporation Act (§8.40; Revised Draft of 1986) says that "(a) Unless otherwise provided in the articles or bylaws, a corporation shall have a president, a secretary, a treasurer and such other officers as are appointed by the board"; and it adds [subs.(c)] that "the same individual may simultaneously hold more than one office in a corporation," unwise as that may be in most cases.

But *Internal Revenue Ruling* 57-246 (I.R.B. 1957-23, 15) says that ". . . an officer of a corporation is an employee . . . but a corporate director not serving as an officer of the company is not an employee." And Revenue Ruling 69-421, C.B. 1969-2, 59 says that (with one exception) "attorneys, CPA's and other professional individuals . . . (*e.g.,* serving the corporation) . . . are not employees."

It is obvious, as these examples show, that the word "officer" in corporation law has different meanings in different connections. The statutes are vague in their definitions, when they have any descriptions at all, merely referring to persons "elected or appointed" to positions of authority.[1]

Any person elected or appointed to an office or position of authority in an organization is an *officer.*

An *office,* in the sense of employment, is a position of trust and confidence, in which the holder is lawfully invested with some portion of the organization's powers.[2] The office holder is vested and charged by the appointing group with the power and duty to exercise certain functions.[3]

A corporation officer holds an office and performs duties prescribed by the charter, bylaws, or general laws. He is elected by the directors or members at a fixed rate of compensation. He occupies a fiduciary relation to the members. And he must devote to his duties such time and effort as are reasonably required.[4]

By contrast, an *employee* does not hold any *office*, usually is employed by the managing officer, who also determines his compensation, is subordinate to and controlled by the officers, bears little or no fiduciary relation to the members, and usually works a specified schedule of days or hours.[5]

A director or trustee is an officer.[6] An *officer* is subject to control by the members and directors, is not an owner of corporate assets, and carries out the policies formulated by the directors or members.[7] Exercise of judgment and discretion is one of the principal tests of officer status.[8] Unlike directors, officers are primarily agents of the corporation, subject to usual rules of agency law, including the fiduciary duties of agents.[9] All officers are agents of the corporation, but not all agents are officers.[10]

An *officer* is any person who holds a position of authority and trust in an organization—whether civil, political, social, military, or ecclesiastical.[11]

More specifically, an officer is a person lawfully invested with an office (a trust-status employment on behalf of the employing group).[12] He has been vested and charged by the appointing group with the power and duty to exercise certain functions.[13]

An officer enjoys greater importance, dignity, independence, tenure, and authority than other employees. These *differences of degree* chiefly differentiate between *officers* and *employees*.[14] An officer far more often than an employee must take an oath, give bond, and execute duties prescribed by general or internal law.[15]

The officer is usually elected rather than appointed or hired by contract, serves for a fixed period of time, and has a permanence of status absent in most ordinary employment.[16]

Ministerial officers are those whose offices give them no real discretion as to what is to be done, and place them under the mandate of superiors.[17]

An *officer de facto* has practical possession and operation of office under some color of valid selection and authority, but lacks *complete* legal right or validity.[18] For example, an officer elected in a vote that is being attacked as improper, or whose resignation is for some reason ineffective, is an officer *de facto*. He has the powers of the office until his election is legally invalidated by due procedures or his position is clearly shown to be not that of an officer.[19]

A *usurping officer* (more accurately, a *usurper*) has neither legal right nor even color of right to the office.[20]

An *officer de jure* is in all ways legally and properly selected, qualified, and entitled to the office.[21]

Statutory provisions. Most state statutes contain few and brief provisions about nonprofit corporation officers.

Ohio's, like most statutes, lists the customary titles of officers, and permits use of other titles as may be provided in the articles or bylaws or resolutions. Officers need not be trustees, and two or more offices may be held by the same person. Officers must be elected annually unless otherwise provided in the articles or bylaws. The appointing or electing authority determines officers' authority and duties. Officers may be removed, with or without cause, by the appointing authority, without prejudice to contract rights, and vacancies for any reason may be filled by the same authority.[22]

Minnesota's statute is similar, though shorter.[23]

§292. SELECTION OF OFFICERS

In nonprofit organizations, the officers must be chosen as the bylaws (and sometimes the charter) provide.[24]

Every corporation has the power to appoint the officers it needs and within statutory limits (see Section 287), to fix their compensation.[25] This holds during the winding up of a corporation that is being dissolved.[26]

Bylaws may make provisions not inconsistent with law or the charter regulating the number, times, and manner of choosing, qualifications, terms of office, official designations, powers, duties, and compensation of officers; they may also define a vacancy in office and the manner of filling it.[27]

When the bylaws do not cover the situation, *de facto* selection (or continuation in office) is effective.[28]

See also Chapters 27, 28.

§293. RESTRICTIONS ON OFFICERS (COMPENSATION, MISCONDUCT, AND INTERESTS IN CONTRACTS)

See Chapter 27. In many large nonprofit corporations there is a great disparity in salary between the president and the other officers. Today the president quite frequently does as well financially as his counterparts in private industry. This is particularly true if all the various kinds of benefits are included, such as club memberships and free housing. This occurs quite frequently in large hospitals and in universities.[29] However, with respect to the smaller foundations and other types of nonprofit corporations, the opposite is true. Due to small size, many organizations' boards apparently do not feel that they are capable of paying a proper salary. In 1971, it was estimated that 30 percent of the estimated $20 billion worth of work managed by nonprofit corporations was done by volunteers.[30] The percentage was about 40 percent in 1988. Thus, it appears that a major portion of all charitable money is controlled by individuals who contribute their time and resources for little or no pay.

NPO Salaries in six figures are strongly disfavored by most Americans; they would be less likely to contribute to NPOs having such salary levels. See, NPT/Barna Research survey of 1992. Chart, 6 *NonProfit Times* (10)1(Oct. 1992).

Loans to officers, directors, or employees, other than bonds or similar securities normally used in public trade, may not lawfully be given by their NP organization; but if such a loan is made the duty to repay applies, and its illegality is not a defense to avoid repayment.[31]

Nonprofit corporation statutes sometimes limit the *power* of removal as well as the legal right.[32] This limitation applies primarily to removal by action of public officers (attorneys-general).

The law sometimes results in the strange spectacle of an officer being kept in office against the express (and sometimes justified) wishes of the organization, even where there has been a violation of official duties.[33] But the rules are apparently intended to prevent removals by other than internal action, in private organizations not affecting any particular public interest. Thus, too, discharge of an employee could not be prevented by federal grant-making agency rules, because federal outsiders do not have power to invade the internal affairs and control of state-authorized domestic corporations.[34]

Some state statutes limit the term of office of officers to one year, unless the articles or bylaws provide otherwise.[35] (See Section 291, at n. 22, Ohio.)

In banking-type mutual corporations, when banking statutes apply, employment contracts cannot fasten liability on the corporation. Such statutes usually grant the right to dismiss officers and other employees "at pleasure," without liability for breach of contract.[36]

California's new statutes, since 1980, are very favorable to officers.[37] So, too, are the provisions proposed in the 1986 Revised Model Nonprofit Corporations Act.

On being above criticism. Managers occasionally attempt to place themselves in a status above criticism. Provisions to this effect are not valid.

Thus, when a union constitution contained a provision that suppressed the protests of members against the actions of officers, this provision was held to be illegal and unenforceable.[38]

Tenure. Rights to remain in office, under special rules such as colleges and universities have, are governed by special rules (*e.g.,* school law or college law). Until quite recently this law was thought to be fairly clear. *Tenure* was a special, limited privilege. Thus, a faculty member, dismissed by his college in 1964, could not specifically enforce his contract under *general* law.[39]

But then, in a series of cases, faculty members demanded, and received, full-scale hearings (and, in effect, trials) before their college administrators could dismiss them even for cause, or even when their hiring had been only on a "try-out" basis. The reasons for giving them such tenure-like rights were the *general* constitutional rights of due process, equal protection of the laws, and the like. If a teacher alleged violation of his civil rights, that almost certainly raised issues of fact that made a trial inevitable, and dismissal "on the pleadings and on the law" almost impossible. When the timidity of administrators was added to this, plus the ready availability of aid to any teacher from the American Association of University Professors (A.A.U.P.), it seemed that a mere hiring of a teacher practically amounted to grant of tenure (while tenure seemed to mean absolute job security). Of course such a state of affairs led to complaints that tenure had become a protection for incompetents (and worse), and that tenure should be abolished. But then the tide began to turn in 1971 and 1972, back to a more balanced interpretation of the meaning of tenure. The subject is a big one, and special works and cases on school law, college law, administrative law, constitutional law, et cetera, must be studied.[40] The same concepts sometimes have been applied in hospitals and other organizations, and even to administrators.[41]

[See also the next section.]

§294. STATUS AND TENURE OF OFFICERS

See the discussion at the end of Section 293.

See Chapter 27 for acceptance of office, removal, and other matters of tenure and status.

All corporations have an inherent power to remove officers for cause. Some statutes permit removal with or without cause.[42]

Contract status as an officer (*e.g.*, being *hired* for a set term) may bar removal or suspension without cause—even when bylaw permits such removal.[43] But the corporation still has the *power* to remove, in some states, though not the legal right.[44] If it does remove, it then becomes liable for breach of contract.[45]

§295. OFFICERS' POWERS, IN GENERAL

Bylaws, charters, and statutes govern officers' powers. Their provisions are far too variable to justify more than very general descriptions. But whatever the powers and limitations of officers, well-drawn bylaws specify them with *strict precision*.[46]

Since the board of directors is the governing and managing force in a corporation, no one officer has the power to act individually for the corporation.[47] Even the powers of the president are, in a sense, no more than those of a single director.[48] But there is the general tendency to view the president as the manager of the corporation. Some courts will presume corporation approval of a contract that is executed in due form by its president, despite absence of such approval in the records.[49]

Certainly if one officer is given general management powers, he has implied power to do anything reasonably necessary or proper in the corporation's affairs.[50] (See the preceding chapter.)

Agency law applies to officers, all of whom are agents of the corporation in varying degrees.[51] If an officer acts without authority, and the corporation did not hold him out to have such authority, the corporation is not liable.[52] The knowledge of an officer is imputed to his corporation, just as the knowledge of any agent about his principal's business is deemed to be shared by his principal.[53] If an officer acts without revealing that he is acting as an agent, (for an *undisclosed principal*) he is personally liable.[54]

Power to execute documents or instruments often is given to a certain officer. (The corporation as such cannot execute documents.) Those who deal with the officer must understand that this power is granted within certain limits as an *administrative* power. They are bound to look into the actual extent of his power, and not merely to take it at his word. Otherwise they may find that he has exceeded his authority and that the corporation is not bound.[55]

However, when the officer is the president, who has a general power of management, the corporation may be bound even when he exceeds his power to execute instruments.[56]

No officer can commit a corporation to something that its charter does not authorize, nor can the corporation ratify such an *ultra vires* act.[57] But limitations of powers that are in the bylaws do not bind third persons unless they know of them.[58]

§296. EXPRESS AND IMPLIED POWERS (ACTUAL AND APPARENT POWERS)

Although the powers of officers are limited by the charter and bylaws, these limitations are often overlooked when they are set up as bars to the just claim of third persons.[59] Third persons need only use reasonable caution, not suspicious caution, in ascertaining the extent of the authority of officers with whom they deal.[60] Yet they must not fail to use reasonable caution. The corporation, too, is entitled to be protected from liability for unauthorized acts of its officers.[61]

Express and implied powers. Officers' *express* powers are set forth in the bylaws or the charter. These express powers carry the *implied* power to do such other (unstated) acts as are reasonably necessary to effectuate the express powers and functions of the officer. Thus, an officer who is expressly empowered to lend out the funds of the corporation is thereby impliedly empowered to receive payment of those funds for the corporation.[62]

Implied powers always arise from express, intended powers.

Actual and apparent powers. Uncertainties about officers' powers arise mostly from the appearance of power and authority where in fact there is none.

If the corporation's conduct makes an officer appear to have power that in fact it did not grant him, the corporation is bound as to third persons who are misled by these appearances. But if the appearance is created only by the officer's own words or conduct, this does not bind the corporation.[63]

This, the rule of *indoor management,* may be summed up thus: Third persons are bound to look reasonably closely at the *external appearances* of a corporation; but are not bound to search through its indoor management.[64] Acts by corporate officers that the corporate conduct makes to seem validly authorized are presumed to be in fact so authorized.[65]

Alien Officers

The Republic of Transkei, one of the homelands created by South Africa, formed a nonprofit corporation in the United States for the purpose of disseminating trade and tourism information about Transkei. The president of the nonprofit corporation could not change his visitor emigration status to intra-company transferee status because the employee-president was not primarily engaged in managerial activities. Public relations and lobbying activities also disqualified the president.[66]

§297. OFFICER'S LIABILITIES

Specific rules as to officers' immunity from civil liability now are statutory in some states. See, for example, Florida Statute §§617.0831 (eff. 1992) and 617.0834 (eff. 1992). See, D.L. Shoneyfeldt, Personal Liability Maze of Corporate Directors and Officers, 58 Nebr. L. Rev. 692–717 (1979).

See the preceding chapter as to absence of liability as long as a trustee or a director is not guilty of fraud or bad faith. A 1987 Amendment to Chapter 607 of the Florida NPO corporations statute gave considerable immunity to *officers*, as well as *directors*, for many kinds of actions such as self-dealing in policy matters, in IRC § 501(c) corporations. This also is the rule proposed by the 1986 Revised Model NPC Act of the A.B.A.

Liability for making or filing false statements or reports, unauthorized loans, and other misconduct is treated in Chapter 28. Distinctions should be noted among tort (civil) and criminal liability, personal liability, organization liability for acts of officers and agents, and answerability to the organization or to third persons or state and federal authorities.

An officer is an agent. As such he ordinarily has no personal liability for the debts of his principal, the corporation. But a position of trust that gives him a fiduciary responsibility increases his susceptibility to liability as an agent.

The 1986 Model Nonprofit Corporation Act (revised) proposed to treat officers as ordinary "prudent" persons, not as fiduciaries. [in §§8.30, 8.41, 8.42.]. Florida Stat. §§617.0831, 617.1405 and 617.0834 (eff. 1992).

In general, an officer's personal liability, like that of any agent, arises out of *agency law* rules.[67] Thus, he is liable if he fails to reveal that he is acting for the corporation. He then is acting for an *undisclosed principal* and thereby binds himself.[68] Or, if he clearly exceeds his authority, he is personally liable.[69] Or, if he acts without any authorization, he binds himself, not the corporation.[70] (But see Sections 293, 295.)

Officers are subject to the modern *compulsory testimony* statutes described elsewhere, and other liabilities. (See the Index.)

Ratification of unauthorized acts. An act of an officer, done without authorization, may be ratified by the board of directors, if he could have been previously authorized.[71]

Acceptance of the benefits of an unauthorized act, with knowledge of the facts, is implied ratification.[72] In some states, presence of the *corporate seal* on a written instrument raises a rebuttable presumption of authorization.[73]

Judgment against a debtor who is the sole stockholder, director, president and treasurer of a (business) corporation may be satisfied out of the moneys of the corporation, under Illinois law.[74]

Directors who refuse to make certain repairs requested by a condo association unit owner, because they believed those repairs (in good faith) to be unwarranted, are protected from legal liability under the "business judgment" rule.[75]

Where an officer of a nonprofit corporation is estopped from performing his responsibilities, because of misconduct, and there is no other officer available, the district court may, after application of an interested party, protect and preserve, take charge of, administer, and oversee disposition of the property. The district court must act consistently with the corporation's articles of incorporation.[76]

Simple negligence alone is not enough to make an officer or director personally liable, under Louisiana statute.[77]

Officers and agents of a center ("home") for mentally retarded children are liable, under *nondelegable* duty of care, to protect and care for the children; similar to a common carrier's duty of care (exception to respondeat superior standard).[78]

A nonprofit corporation, which extended loans to promote development, brought a collection action against the Secretary of a corporation, which failed to make payments due on a note. The court held that a signing secretary is personally liable where the promissory note creates unambiguous personal liability of the signors, even though the payors had signed "as its President" and "as its Secretary." In Florida there is statutory presumption that the signor is personally liable.[79]

Criminal Liability of NPO Officers

[Earl F. Hack, III did the research for the rest of this section.]

Criminal prosecutions of NPOs are rare. Of about 200,000 serious federal prosecutions in 1984–7, only 1,569 were organizations, and of 1,221 of those convicted less than 1 percent were other-than-profit business organizations. About half of all corporation prosecutions also involve officers and employees.[80]

In the much publicized *Bakker* case, he was convicted of 24 counts of fraud in selling "partnerships" in his NPC.[81] In that religious corporation case an aide to the chairman of the board also was convicted of evading over a half million dollars in income taxes owed on misappropriated assets.[82]

Embezzlement (by fraudulent transfers) of a hospital NPC's assets by a sole director was not protected by the alleged consent of the hospital.[83]

The Contemporary Arts Center (NPC) in Cincinnati and its director were indicted in April 1990 for exhibiting photos alleged to be obscene (homo-erotic; nude males and minors), but were acquitted by a jury on Oct. 5, 1990.[84]

Operating *unlicensed day care centers* may be criminal for officers of NPC as well as profit corporations, under current statutes.[85]

§298. DELEGATION OF POWERS

[*See also*, Section 305.]

An officer, like any agent, may delegate only purely administrative powers, not his discretionary powers. He may not have someone else make the discretionary decisions called for by the office. But he may have other persons assist him in purely ministerial work, or to enable him to perform his fundamental function as an officer.[86]

Power granted to an officer in the sense of special trust and personal reliance on his wisdom, faithfulness, or discretion, may not be delegated at all.[87]

§299. POWERS AND DUTIES OF THE PRESIDENT

As for all officers, the charter and bylaws can, and should, specify the powers and duties of the president.

In the absence of such provisions, he may be a figurehead with no real powers to bind the corporation.[88] But some cases hold that if, by nature of the organization, he seems to have authority, the corporation will be bound by such acts of his that could be authorized or ratified by the directors.[89]

Of course, if the corporation expressly or impliedly ratifies, or adopts his unauthorized acts, it cannot later deny his authority to act.[90] And if he has express powers, he also has the implied powers necessary to effectuate them— such as the power to hire an attorney when he must protect corporate legal rights.[91] Thus, if he is authorized to make a bond issue, he may retain an attorney to draft the necessary contracts.[92]

If the corporation allows him to manage its affairs, it may not suddenly deny his authority to a person who relied on it.[93]

In many states, statutes expressly assign to the president (together with the secretary) the duty of filing certain reports, such as financial reports.[94] Other documents also must be signed by him, such as a certificate of consolidation with another organization[95] or a certificate of dissolution.[96]

(See, below, Forms of *Annual Reports* that should be signed and filed by the president, or by the secretary under the president's direction.)

If he is given general management powers, he may do all things reasonably necessary to accomplish his task.[97] But his management powers ordinarily are less than those of a president of a business corporation. His general management powers do not authorize him to borrow money or issue notes for the corporation.[98]

For examples of the powers and duties usually vested in the president, see the forms for articles of association in Chapter 6, for charters in Chapter 19, and for bylaws in Chapter 23. *See also,* for many forms respecting directors and officers, 6 *Am. Jur. Legal Forms* §§74:1011 *et seq.*

Note that the titles *president* and *chairman of the board* sometimes are interchangeable. Other titles may be used instead of *president: supreme guardian, chancellor,* or other terms.

The *president* of a corporation usually is the proper officer to sign corporation contracts.[99]

A private university chancellor's *promise* (as an agent) of tenure in four years to physician/associate professor was not binding where the plaintiff knew, or should have known, that grant of tenure is a prerogative of the *faculty,* especially where the appointment was described as "special"—dependent on grants, institution needs, etc.[100]

FORM NO. 133
Annual (Biennial) Report
(Maine)

**NONPROFIT CORPORATION
STATE OF MAINE
BIENNIAL REPORT as of December 31, 19 . . .
for**

————————————————————————————————

To the Secretary of State of the State of Maine:
Pursuant to 13-B MRSA §1301 to undersigned corporation executes and delivers for filing the following biennial report.

    1. The jurisdiction of its incorporation is .... (State)
    2. The address of the registered office of the corporation in Maine is
    ....
(See 13-B MRSA §304(1) and §1212(1))
    ....
(street, city, state and zip code)
    and the name of its registered agent at such address is ....

Foreign corporation should complete:
The address of its registered or principal office in its jurisdiction of incorporation is ....
....
(street, city, state and zip code)
    3. The activities in which the corporation is actually engaged in the State of Maine, briefly stated, are ....
    ....

4. Names of officers and their business or residence addresses (including street or rural route number, town or city, state and zip code) are:

Officers	Address
Pres.	....
	....
Treas.	....
	....
Sec....................................	....
	....
Clerk	....
	....

5. Date and location of last annual meeting to elect directors was held on ......, 19 .., in..

(Complete the following if applicable.)

6. The material changes that have occurred since December 31st with respect to the facts set forth hereinabove are as follows:

Dated: ....
                                                    (Exact name of corporation)
                                  By..
                                                    (signature)
                                  ....
                                  (type or print name and capacity of signer)
                                  (*See §1301(3) below as to who may sign)

....
NAME OF
CORPORATION

TITLE 13-B

§1301. Biennial report of domestic and foreign corporations; excuse

1. Biennial report. Each domestic corporation, unless excused as provided in subsection 5, and each foreign corporation authorized to carry on activities in this State shall deliver for filing, within the time prescribed by this Act, a biennial report to the Secretary of State setting forth:

A. The name of the corporation and the jurisdiction of its incorporation;

B. The address of the registered office of incorporation in this State and the name of its agent for service of process if a domestic corporation, or its registered agent if a foreign corporation, in this state at such address, including the street or rural route number, town or city, county and state; and in the case of a foreign corporation, the address of its registered or principal office in its jurisdiction of incorporation;

C. A brief statement of the character of the activities in which the corporation is actually engaged in this State;

D. The names and business or residence addresses of the officers of the corporation, including the street or rural route number, town, city and state; and

E. The date and place of the last annual meeting of the members to elect the directors of the corporation.

STATE OF INCORPORATION

2. Information contained in biennial report. The information contained in the biennial report shall be given as of the close of business on the last day of the 2nd calendar year of the biennium for which the report is filed, including, where applicable, the calendar year in which the corporation is organized. If, between such date and the date of execution of the report, any material change has occurred with respect to any fact required to be set forth in the report, such change shall also be stated.

*3. Execution. The biennial report shall be executed as provided by section 104, except that signing by any one of the president, a vice-president, the secretary, the treasurer or an assistant secretary, without a 2nd signature, shall be deemed valid under section 104, subsection 1, paragraph B, subparagraph (2).

4. Filing. The biennial report shall be delivered for filing between the first day of January and the first day of June of the year next succeeding the 2nd calendar year of the biennium for which the report is to be made. One copy of the report shall be delivered for filing to the Secretary of State, who shall file the report if he finds that it conforms to the requirements of this Act. The Secretary of State shall promulgate rules and regulations to provide that approximately 1/3 of the biennial reports shall be filed in each calendar year.

5. Certificate of fact. The Secretary of State, upon application by any corporation and satisfactory proof that it has ceased to carry on activities, shall file a certificate of the fact and shall give a duplicate certificate to the corporation. Thereupon, such corporation shall be excused from filing biennial

reports with the Secretary of State so long as the corporation in fact carries on no activities.

6. Vote to carry on activities. The members entitled to vote or, if none, the directors of a corporation which has been excused pursuant to subsection 5 may vote to resume carrying on activities at a meeting duly called and held for such a purpose. A certificate executed and filed, as provided in sections 104 and 106 setting forth that a members' or director' meeting was held, the date and location of the meeting and that a majority of the members or directors voted to resume carrying on activities, shall authorize such corporation to carry on activities; and after such certificate is filed, it shall be required to file biennial reports.

§1302. Failure to file biennial report; incorrect report; penalties

PLEASE NOTE: This report must be completed and returned on or before June 1st. For ease in returning, completed report may be folded and mailed in a window envelope to:

1. Failure to file biennial report. Any corporation which is required to deliver a biennial report for filing, as provided by section 1301, and which fails to deliver its properly completed biennial report to the Secretary of State, shall pay, after January 1, 1981, the sum of $00 for each failure to so file on time. Upon failure to file a biennial report and to pay the penalty, the Secretary of State shall, after January 1, 1981, revoke a foreign corporation's authority to carry on activities in this State and suspend a domestic corporation from carrying on activities. He shall use the procedures set forth in section 1210, relative to revoking the right of foreign corporations to carry on activities in this State, for suspending domestic corporations. A foreign corporation whose authority to carry on activities in this state has been revoked under this subsection and which wishes to carry on activities again in this state must be authorized as provided in section 1202. A domestic corporation which has been suspended under this subsection may be reinstated by filing the current biennial report and by paying the penalty for the current biennium and for each biennium that it has failed to file a biennial report.

2. Nonconformity. If the Secretary of State finds that any biennial report delivered for filing does not conform with the requirements of section 1301, he may return the report for correction.

3. Time limit specified. If the biennial report of a corporation is not received by the Secretary of State within the time specified in section 1301, the corporation shall be excused from the liability provided in this section and from any other penalty for failure to timely file the report if it establishes, to the satisfaction of the Secretary of State, that its failure to file was the result of excusable neglect and it furnishes the Secretary of State with a copy of such report within 30 days after it learns of the nondelivery of the original report.

Secretary of State
Corporation & UCC Division
State Office Building
Augusta, Maine 04333

FORM NO. 134
Report—Excuse Application
(Maine)

**NONPROFIT CORPORATION
STATE OF MAINE
APPLICATION FOR EXCUSE**

Filing Fee

For Use by the Secretary of State
File No. _____
Fee Paid_____
C. B._____
Date _____

TO: SECRETARY OF STATE
STATE OFFICE BUILDING
AUGUSTA, MAINE 04333

President
Treasurer
Clerk or Secretary

I,..
(Title)

of ....
a corporation duly organized under the laws of the State of Maine, certify that said corporation ceased to carry on activities on ......, 19 ... Application is made to be excused from further filing biennial reports with the Secretary of State, so long as the corporation in fact carries on no activities, in accordance with 13-B M.R.S.A., Section 1301.

....
Signed

STATE OF MAINE

....ss.   ...., 19........

    Then personally appeared the above-named.. and made oath to the truth of the statements contained in the above application by him subscribed.

Before me,..
Notary Public
Justice of the Peace

....

FOR SECRETARY OF STATE'S USE ONLY

EXCUSE IS GRANTED   ...., 19........

....
Deputy Secretary of State

§300. POWERS AND DUTIES OF THE VICE-PRESIDENT

The vice-president is next in rank below the president. He takes over the president's functions in the event of the absence, incapacity, or death of the president.[101] Whether or not he then has the power to bind the organization by his acts (*e.g.*, contracts) depends on whether or not the president has such powers. Bylaws should provide for this situation.

    The office of vice-president ordinarily has no other inherent powers. The vice-president may not bind the corporation unless the charter or bylaws or a resolution specifically so provide.[102]

    Some state statutes require (or permit) that the vice-president sign certificates of corporate consolidation or dissolution.[103]

    For examples of the powers and duties usually vested in the vice-president, see the forms of articles of association in Chapter 6, of charters in Chapter 19, and of bylaws in Chapter 23.

    Selection of several vice-presidents, each with separate functions (often merely honorary), now is commonplace.

    Sometimes the title *executive vice-president* is used to indicate general management powers and duties.

§301. POWERS AND DUTIES OF THE SECRETARY

Importance of a nonprofit organization's *secretary*, and details of his or her duties are (spelled out in detail) more substantial than most people understand.[104] The secretary is an administrative officer usually charged with the care and keeping of the corporate records, minutes, and seal.[105] He also usually takes minutes at meetings.

The office of secretary ordinarily has no other inherent powers. The secretary usually is presumed to have no discretionary executive power to bind the corporation, unless such authority is shown.[106] But if he is held out as having such power, the corporation may be estopped to deny that he actually did have it, when third persons reasonably rely on the appearances.[107] And if he is given actual authority, even orally, the authority is effective.[108]

Some state statutes require that the secretary (with the president) sign certificates of corporate consolidation or dissolution[109] and also certain financial reports.[110]

For examples of the powers and duties usually vested in the secretary, see the forms of articles of association in Chapter 6, of charters in Chapter 19, and of bylaws in Chapter 23.

Selection of an assistant secretary, or of recording and corresponding secretaries with separate functions, now is commonplace.

§302. POWERS AND DUTIES OF THE TREASURER

[*See also* Sections 304, 305.]

The treasurer ordinarily is the custodian and the disbursing and accounting agent for the corporate funds, able to disburse them only as directed by the directors or other constituted authority.[111]

The office of treasurer has no other inherent powers. The treasurer may not bind the corporation, unless the charter, bylaws, or a resolution so provide.[112] But if the corporation holds him out as having apparent authority, it may be bound by his acts, as far as third persons who reasonably rely on the appearance are concerned.[113] Despite his title he has no power to borrow, or to draw or issue funds, notes, checks, or other financial paper, unless he is authorized to do so.[114]

Treasurers have gained increased prestige as executives in recent years.[115]

A charitable (religious) corporation's treasurer had no power to sign an agreement for sale of its real property, where there was no signature by the president or vice-president as the statute required, and its broker and attorney authorization was ineffective to empower the treasurer. Massachusetts construes officers' powers narrowly.[116]

Pennsylvania has a Uniform Fiduciaries Act designed to relieve banks of the responsibility of seeing that authorized corporate fiduciaries use entrusted funds for proper purposes. However, where there is a rubber-stamp restrictive endorsement, stating that checks are to be deposited only to the credit of the depositor, the bank can be held responsible, under the U.C.C., for deposits made to an officer's personal account.[117]

For examples of the powers and duties usually vested in the treasurer, see the forms of articles of association in Chapter 6, of charter in Chapter 19, and of bylaws in Chapter 23.

Selection of assistant treasurers, or of comptroller, treasurer, cashier, and auditor, each with separate functions, now is commonplace.

§303. EXECUTIVE MANAGERS (EXECUTIVE SECRETARY)

As for all officers, the charter and bylaws can, and should, specify the powers and duties of the executive manager (or the executive secretary or executive vice-president), if there is such an office.

Professional nonprofit organization managers. Many nonprofit organizations employ an executive secretary (general manager). This officer, who often is a professional, usually is a full-time paid employee who runs the daily routine business of the organization. The 1993 survey of salaries of executives of NPOs dropped from a median of $51,000 in 1992 to $50,350. For complete surveys on the various kinds of NPOs address Abbott, Langer & Associates, Inc., 548 First St., Crete, IL. 60416 (708-672-4200). See, D.A. Weeks, 1993 Salary Survey, 8 *Nonprofit Times* (1) 19 (Jan. 1994).

The work of the *association executive* has become a profession in itself.[118] There is an American Trade Association Executive organization (A.T.A.E.), having its own high code of ethics,[119] with offices in Washington, D.C. Trade Association Management firms now are found in most major cities.[120]

Managers' functions. In the absence of specific provisions in the charter or bylaws, a general manager's powers are just about those of the corporation.[121] He may hire administrative employees,[122] obtain legal advice on corporate problems,[123] and enter into other routine contracts.[124] But it must at once be emphasized that these broad powers apply only in the absence of charter or bylaw provisions, and that they apply *only in routine business, not in extraordinary (major decision) matters.*[125]

For major matters, such as an amalgamation, sale of assets, and other drastic decisions, the general manager has no power to decide the organization's fate or choice of direction.[126] And the powers he exercises in even routine matters must be only those reasonably necessary. He ordinarily (in the absence of emergency) cannot make decisions such as whether to borrow or issue notes, without the board of directors' approval.[127]

Third persons are entitled to rely on a general manager's apparent authority to do reasonably necessary acts in routine matters.[128]

If an officer is given general manager's powers, his lesser powers as an officer do not limit his broader powers as a general manager.[129]

Qualifications of managers. Bylaws may and should specify qualifications for office as a manager, particularly for the *executive secretary* (general manager). Beyond this, the highest qualification in terms of a personnel expert's analysis are important.[130]

Special types of organizations. In such special kinds of nonprofit organizations as schools, asylums, hospitals, and the like, special types of managers are required.

Thus, in a college, the *dean* is a managing officer as well as head of the faculty. Special rules and customs apply, usually, for such situations.

For example, in law schools, the powers and limitations of deans are stated or implied in the rules of the Section of Legal Education of the American

Bar Association, the Constitution of the Association of American Law Schools, and in Ohio (for instance) the Constitution of the League of Ohio Law Schools.[131]

Similar collateral rule-making authorities exist as to hospitals,[132] religious organizations, and so forth. In addition, in many states special statutes are provided for educational, religious, social welfare, and other types of nonprofit organizations, and for their officers.

§304. FINANCIAL MANAGERS OF TRUST ASSETS

[See the Chapter on Management]

[*Note*: The balance of this chapter is a reprint (of extracts) with permission of the National Association of College and University Attorneys, of extracts from an article by John W. Wheeler, Esq. of New York City, titled "Fiduciary Responsibilities of Trustees in Financing of Private Institutions of Higher Education," 2 J. Coll. & U.L. 210. Section titles and numbers have been changed to fit this volume's numbering]

. . . When the so-called Paley Report[133] was written in 1957, it was not very prophetic to the extent that it said, "Everyone gladly grants to the trustee bodies the difficult task . . . of . . . managing funds." There have been changes. There was (and is) an increasing interest . . . in the investment policies . . . , sometimes on political rather than economic grounds, such as the attempt to require that universities refrain from purchasing stocks from companies which are located in South Africa or have military contracts with the Department of Defense . . .

In 1819, the United States Supreme Court held that under English law, a charitable trust was valid only by virtue of the English Statute of Charitable Uses and was, therefore, invalid in Virginia which had repealed that statute along with other English statutes after the American Revolution.[134] Although subsequent research revealed that the English courts had upheld charitable trusts prior to the enactment of the Statute of Charitable Users and that, therefore, the premise of the Supreme Court's decision was wrong, the courts of various jurisdictions (*e.g.*, New York, Virginia, Maryland) accepted both that premise and decision as correct. Accordingly, if the courts in such states were to uphold the validity of a charitable gift (which they were prone to do) they were forced to conclude that the donor had not intended to create a technical trust but to vest absolute title in the corporate recipient subject to the donor's restrictions as to the preservation of the principal and use of income. Thus, in New York, by judicial decision, the transfer to a charitable corporation for one or more of its corporate purposes does not create a strict trust even if words of express trust are used in the conveying instrument.[135]

The answer to any given question in this area can thus vary among 50 states, depending upon the particular state's laws as to the nature of a charitable transfer, whether it constitutes a true trust, or an outright gift, or something in between: a conditional gift.

In New York, the *St. Joseph's Hospital* rule has, since 1969, been codified by the Legislature in Section 513 of New York's Not-for-Profit Corporation Law[136] although that statute did not apply to all educational corporations until the New York Not-for-Profit Corporation Law was "bridged" to education corporations under the New York Education Law[137] including specially chartered institutions such as Columbia University, effective September 1, 1973.[138] In other states, the "Uniform Management of Institutional Funds Act," drafted by the National Conference of Commissioners on Uniform State Laws and by it approved and recommended for enactment in all of the states, has been enacted into law.

The points which follow assume that the answer is not provided by express statutory provision.

Legal Investments in General

With respect to investments, are the trustees strict trustees or are they something else, more resembling directors of business corporations? In the area of investments, in New York, at least, corporate law, rather than trust law, governs.

In 1951, the New York Attorney General expressed his official opinion that the powers of trustees of an educational corporation in respect to the administration and investment of funds do not differ from those of directors of a business corporation.[139] In that ruling he stated:

> Unless modified by statute, charter, or bylaw, the powers of the trustees of an educational, religious, or charitable corporation in respect to the administration and investment of the corporation's funds are fundamentally no different than that of a director of a business corporation in respect to the administration of the property held by the corporation.

In that opinion, the attorney general held that trustees of educational corporations were not limited to the statutory list of permissible trust investments which was then in force, but could invest in such securities as they deemed advisable so long as they exercised care and prudence "in the same degree that a man of common prudence ordinarily exercises in his own affairs." Ordinarily, it is not safe to rely on the opinion of an attorney general without judicial ratification; but, in the area of charitable corporation law, the attorney general's opinion is worth more than it might ordinarily be, because, in most states, he would be the person most likely to attack the transaction if, indeed, it involved a breach of trust.

In New York, the attorney general's opinion has been substantially ratified by statute. The investment power of the governors of New York charitable corporations is now controlled by §513 of the New York Not-for-Profit Corporation Law which provides as follows:

(b) Except as may be otherwise permitted under article eight of the estates, powers and trusts law or section 522 (Release of restrictions on use or investment), the governing board shall apply all assets thus received to the purposes specified in the gift instrument and to the payment of the reasonable and proper expenses of administration of such assets. The governing board shall cause accurate accounts to be kept of such assets separate and apart from the accounts of other assets of the corporation. Unless the terms of the particular gift instrument provide otherwise, the treasurer shall make an annual report to the members (if there be members) or to the governing board (if there be no members) concerning the assets held under this section and the use made of such assets and of the income thereof.

The legislative history of §513 indicates that the Legislature intended to have corporate laws apply to all matters of investment and administration of restricted funds. For example, the Revisers' Notes and Comments contain the following statement:

This Section [513] provides increased flexibility in the administration of funds received by not-for-profit corporations for specific purposes that fall within any of its corporate purposes. This Section codifies St. Joseph's Hospital v. Bennett, 281 N.Y. 115, 22 NE 2d 305, (1939) *but goes beyond that decision in providing the framework for the administration of such assets within the principles of the corporation law rather than the trust law. . . . As compared with the trust law, the section gives the directors greater freedom of investment*, including the pooling of two or more funds. (Underscoring added.). . .[141]

§305. INVESTMENT MANAGERS

Delegation of Authority to Make Investment Decisions

It would appear to be legally proper for the trustees to delegate to a third party investment manager decisions on investments of the university's funds under certain conditions.

Let us assume that an individual manager for the university's portfolio of investments could be appointed, who could be highly compensated, perhaps by sharing in the gains and losses from investments made under his direction. The investment manager would operate within general guidelines given him by the trustees with reference to (i) the objectives of investments, (ii) the type and size of commitments to any one situation, (iii) the appropriateness of investments for the university's portfolio, and (iv) in other general respects. Within these guidelines, the manager would be free to make final investment decisions and to commit the university's funds. The manager would make prompt and frequent reports to the trustees with respect to his investment decisions and with respect to the performance of the funds under his management.

The delegation would seem to be legally unobjectionable so long as the above procedures are followed and provided (i) the term of his contract is not unreasonably long and can be terminated promptly on agreed terms and (ii) his compensation is reasonable.

The Restatement of the Law of Trusts states:

> In the case of a *charitable corporation* duties of a somewhat similar character to those of the trustee of a *charitable trust* rest upon members of the controlling board, whether they are called directors or trustees. The extend of the duties is not always the same as the extent of the duties of individual trustees holding property for charitable purposes. It may be proper, for example, for the board to appoint a committee of its members to deal with the investment of the funds of the corporation, the board merely exercising a general supervision over the actions of the committee. (Underscoring and matter in brackets added.)[142]

It can be argued from the *Restatement's* position that the delegation by the trustees to an individual of power to deal with the investment of funds under the general supervision of the trustees would be legally permissible.

There are apparently no judicial decisions directly in point. However, a respected secondary source states that, under business corporation standards, it is clear that:

> The directors or trustees of a corporation ... can certainly delegate authority to act for and represent the corporation to subordinate officers and agents, even in matters involving the exercise of judgment and discretion, when they are expressly authorized to do so by appointment of committees and subordinate officers and agents.[143]

By statute, in New York, the governing board of a nonprofit corporation may delegate their authority to invest institutional funds, contract with independent advisors, and compensate the chosen advisors.[144] The board must exercise due care in choosing investment advisors, however.[145] Further, the board is relieved of all liability for investment and reinvestment of institutional funds after the delegation of investment power.[146]

How much may such an investment manager be lawfully paid? There is probably no objection, based on the tax laws, to the hiring of investment counsel on a highly compensated basis, so long as the compensation is reasonable in the light of that received by other investment managers. On this point, the assistant attorney general indicated informally that his office might object to compensation in excess of the compensation allowed as commissions to a trustee of a charitable trust charged with the duty of managing its funds. No principal commissions are permitted to be paid to such a trustee under New York law.[147] This restriction suggested by the assistant attorney general would, if followed, present considerable practical difficulties for an educational corporation in obtaining the services of a highly skilled individual, who would no doubt request a higher rate of compensation than that informally suggested by the assistant attorney general. Although the matter is not entirely free from doubt, and notwithstanding the informal opinion of the Assistant Attorney General, it would not seem to be unlawful for a university to pay such an investment manager that amount which he would be able to command from other investors with comparable portfolios.

An appropriate university trustees' bylaw covering this subject might read substantially as follows:

FORM NO. 135 Investment Manager Bylaw

"*Investment Manager.* The Trustees, on the recommendation of the Committee on Finance, may hire for a reasonable period, with right of prompt termination on agreed terms, an individual, firm, or corporation to buy, sell, and otherwise deal with the investment funds of the University subject to the general supervision of the Trustees, acting by the Committee on Finance or its subcommittee, the Committee on Investments, and in accordance with guidelines established by the Trustees or either of such Committees, with respect to (i) the objectives of investment, (ii) the type and size of commitments to any one situation, (iii) the appropriateness of investments for the University's portfolio, and (iv) in such other respects as the Trustees or either of the Committees may deem appropriate, from time to time, and to pay to such investment manager a reasonable rate of compensation. Such investment manager shall be required to make prompt and frequent reports to the Trustees or either of such Committees with respect to investment decisions and the performance of the funds under his management."

A university's retention of multiple investment managers might be preferable, for comparative performance would better enable the Trustees to judge the work of each manager. . . .

POINTS TO REMEMBER

- Routine affairs are for the board of trustees or directors to decide.
- Extraordinary affairs are for the members to decide.
- Fundamental changes in policy or purposes must be approved by the general membership.
- An honest director who uses reasonable care and diligence has no personal liability for corporate debts or obligations.
- Directors guilty of fraud or bad faith are personally, jointly, and severally liable.
- Insist on written records of objections or doubtful decisions or acts.
- Be sure to prepare and file at least an annual report on the organization's finances and affairs.
- Provide in the bylaws for compensation of directors and officers. Provide also for reimbursement of litigation expenses. (D and O Insurance)
- Do not give compensation to trustees of charitable organizations, directly or indirectly.

- Include power in the bylaws for directors and officers to deal with the corporation. But include protective restrictions. Generally discourage such transactions.

- Do not allow use of the organization as a tax dodge or business holding device by anyone or any group.

- Do not allow trustees or officers to make the organization a proprietary device. Use trustees' and/or members' proper powers to prevent abuse.

- Remember that directors and trustees often must serve as financial experts. If they are not such experts, they must obtain expert guidance and assistance or face personal liability.

- Consider the advisability of employing an inside (house counsel) investment manager.

NOTES TO CHAPTER 29

1. Oleck, *Modern Corporation Law*, c. 40 (1978 Supp.) lists the statutes of all states. *And see*, 29 *Words and Phrases* 288 *et seq.* (1988 Supp.) for many definitions and cases. California's business statute formerly referred to a chairman of the board and a chief financial adviser as officers: Calif. Corp. Code §112(a) (1977) (repealed). See N.Y. N-PCL §713.

2. Board of Chosen Freeholders of Hudson County v. Brenner, 25 N.J. Super. 557; 96A.2d 776, 780 (1953); Sparks v. Board of Library Trustees of Carter County, 197 Okla. 132; 169 P.2d 201, 204 (1946); Potter v. Patee, 493 S.W.2d 58 (Mo. App. 1973).

3. State v. Bratton, 148 Tenn. 174, 253 S.W. 705, 706 (1923).

4. Flight Equipment and Engineering Corp. v. Shelton, 103 S.2d 615, 623 (Fla. 1958).

5. *Ibid.*

6. Monroe v. Schofield, 135 F2d 725, 726 (10th Cir. 1943), Sinram v. Wa Ken Const. and Realty Corp., 196 Misc. 496, 94 N.Y.S.2d 491, 492 (1949). *But see*, Jackson v. County Trust Co., 176 Md. 505, 6A2d 380, 382 (1939) (director may not act alone, as an "officer").

7. Griswold v. United States, 36 F. Supp. 714, 717 (D.C. Mass. 1941).

8. *See*, Colonial Capital Co. v. General Motors Corp. 29 F.R.D. 514, 517 (D.C. Conn. 1961); Public Employees Rel. Comm. v. Dade County Police Ben. Assn., 467 S.2d 987 (Fla., 1985).

9. *See*, Kempin, *The Corporate Officer and the Law of Agency*, 44 Va. L. Rev. 1273 (1958). Agent may be criminally liable: People v. Gilmore, 273 Ill. 143, 112 N.E. 458 (1916) (steward's sale of liquor).

10. *See*, Wills v. Rowland and Co., 117 A.D. 122, 102 N.Y.S. 386 (1907).

11. Illinois Commerce Commission v. Cleveland, C., C. and S. L. Ry., 320 Ill. 214 150 N.E. 678, 682 (1926).

12. *See*, 2 Oleck, *Modern Corporation Law*, §§963–969 (1978 Supp.).

13. State v. Bratton, 148 Tenn. 174, 253 S.W. 705, 706 (1923); Margolis v. Allen Morg. and Loan Corp., 268 S.2d 714 (La. App. 1972).

14. Jefferson County v. Case, 244 Ala. 56; 12 S.2d 343, 346 (1943).

15. *See* n. 14, above; McClendon v. Board of Health, 141 Ark. 114; 216 S.W. 289, 290 (1919).

16. Hyde v. Board of Commissioners, 209 Ind. 245; 198 N.E. 333, 337 (1935).

17. Vose v. Deane, 7 Mass. 280 (1811).

18. Johnson v. State, 27 Ga. App. 679; 109 S.E. 526, 527 (1921). *And See*: South Seas Corp. v. Saklan, 525 F. Supp. 1033 (D.C. N. Mariana Isl., 1981).

19. *See* n. 18; *and see,* City of Terre Haute v. Burns, 69 Ind. App. 7; 116 N.E. 604 (1917); Wendt v. Berry, 154 Ky. 586; 157 S.W. 1115, 118; 45 L.R.A. (n.s.) 1101 (1913); Petition of Serenbetz, 46 N.Y.S.2d 475 (1943); affd., 267 A.D. 836; 46 N.Y.S.2d 127 (1944); Mahoney Mineral Co. v. Anglo-California Bank, 104 U.S. 192 (1881).

20. Smith v. City of Jefferson, 75 Ore. 179; 146 P. 809, 812 (1915).

21. People v. Brautigan, 310 Ill. 472; 142 N.E. 208, 211 (1923). *And see,* n. 18, as to *de facto* and *de jure.*

22. Ohio Rev. Code §1702.34; Ga. Code Ann., §14-3-843, (b); Ala. Code, tit. 10 §3A-35.

23. Minn. Stat. Anno. §317A.341.

24. N.Y. Not-for-Profit Corp. L. §713.

25. N.Y. Bus. Corp. L. §202; Ala. Code, 10-3A-44; Fla. Stat. §617.021(4); Ga. Code Ann. § 14-3-302; N.Y. N-PCL §§202, 515.

26. *Ibid.* §1006. N.Y. N-PCL §§515.

27. N.Y. Not-for-Profit Corp. L. § 713; Fla. Stat. §617.0840; Ga. Code Ann. §14-3-840. Model Business Corporation Act (American Bar Foundation) §42 allows the directors to provide for a committee of less than all directors which can act as the entire board for routine matters.

28. Petition of Serenbetz, 46 N.Y.S.2d 475 (1943); affd. 267 A.D. 836, 46 N.Y.S.2d 127 (1944).

29. Zurcher, A., *The Foundation Manager: A Profile,* 10 Conf. on Char. Foundations 63, 210, N.Y.U. (1969).

30. *Id.* at 65.

31. Fl. St. § 617.0833; Fl. Sess. L. 1990, Chap. 90–179 § 56 (eff. July 1, 1991).

32. N.Y. Genl. Corp. L. §130 (repealed). See N.Y. N-PCL §714.

33. *See,* Fiske v. Beatty, 206 A.D. 349; 201 N.Y.S. 441; *affd. without op.,* 238 N.Y. 598; 144 N.E. 907 (1924) (removal of church vestrymen and wardens refused); Walker Memorial Baptist Church v. Saunders, 173 Misc. 455; 17 N.Y.S.2d 842; *affd. without op.,* 259 A.D. 1010; 21 N.Y.S.2d 512; *revd. on other gds.,* 285 N.Y. 462; 35 N.E.2d 42; *rehear. den.,* 286 N.Y. 607; 35 N.E.2d 944 (1941).

34. Weiss v. Opportunities for Cortland County, 40 A.D.2d 45, 337 N.Y.S.2d 409 (3d Dept. 1972).

35. Term not to exceed three years. Ala. code, tit. 10, §3A-41.

36. *See* Copeland v. Melrose Natl. Bk., 254 N.Y. 632; 173 N.E. 898 (1930); under National Banking Act, 12 U.S.C.A. §24.

37. *E.g.,* Calif. Corp. Code §§5210, 5211(a)(7), 5227, 5230, etc. (1980).

38. Schrank v. Brown, 192 Misc. 80; 80 N.Y.S.2d 452 (1948).

39. Felch v. Findlay College, 119 Ohio App. 357, 200 N.E.2d 353 (1963); motion to certify dismissed 1964; *and see,* Byse, *Academic Freedom, Tenure, and the Law: A Comment on Worzella v. Board of Regents,* 73 Harv. L. Rev. 304 (1959); Byse and Joughin, *Tenure in American Higher Education* (Ithaca, Cornell Univ. Press. 1959); Blackwell, *College Law* (Wash., D.C., Amer. Council on Educ. 1961).

40. *See,* Kahn and Solomon, *Untenured Professors' Rights to Reappointment,* 20 Clev. St. L. Rev. (3) 522 (Sept. 1971); Flaherty, *Probationary Teachers and the "Expectancy of Continued Employment"* 20 Clev. St. L. Rev. (3) 533 (Sept. 1971); McFarland, *Suability of School Boards and School Board Members,* 21 Clev. St. L. Rev. (2) 181 (May 1972); Simcox v. Board of Education, 443 F.2d 40 (Cir. App., Ill., 1971); Orr v. Trinter, 444 F.2d 128 (6th Cir. Ohio 1971) revg. 318 F. Supp. 1041 (D.C. Ohio 1971); Fooden v. Board of Governors, 268 N.E.2d 15 (Ill. 1971); Jones v. Hopper, 410 F.2d 1323 (C.A. Colo. 1970), 90 S.Ct. 1111 (1970); Roth v. Board of Regents, 310 F. Supp. 972 (D.C. Wis. 1970), note, 16 Wayne St. L. Rev. 252 (1969); Monroe v. Trustees, 99 Cal. Rptr. 129, 491 P.2d 1105 (1971); Powell v. Board of Higher Education, 325 N.Y.S.2d 14 (Supr. Ct., N.Y. County, 1971). *See,* as to current cases, the current issues of the A.A.U.P. *Bulletin* (magazine).

41. *See,* Powell case, n. 40.
     In 1987 Prof. Michael Swygert, of Stetson University College of Law, led a movement for restoration of the view that tenure is a conditional privilege and not a legal right.

42. Inherent power; *see, In re* Koch, 257 N.Y. 318, 178 N.E. 545 (1931) (religious corporation); Removal with or without cause; Ohio Rev. Code §1702.34; Minn. Stat. Anno §317.21; *and see* N.Y. N-PCL §§ 623, 706, 714, 720, 112.

43. Cuppy v. Stollwerck Bros., 216 N.Y. 591, 111 N.E. 249 (1916).

44. *See* n. 22, 23 (*e.g.,* Minn., Ohio).

45. *Ibid.; and see,* N.Y. Bus. Corp. L. §§716, 715; N.Y. N-PCL §§623, 706, 714, 720.

46. Ohio Rev. Code §§1702.11 (A)(9); 1702.34; *and see,* State *ex rel.* Northeast Property Owners Civic Assn. v. Kennedy, 117 Ohio App. 79, 178 N.E.2d 608 (1962) (lawfully dismissed officers may be removed by *quo warranto* proceeding, if the constitution and bylaws have been followed).

47. Wait v. Nashua Armory Assn., 66 N.H. 581; 23 A. 77; 14 L.R.A. 356 (1891); *and see* n. 6 (Jackson case) as to directors.

48. Button v. Diversified Resources Corp., 634 F.2d 1313 (6th Cir., 1981); Knopf v. Alma Park, Inc., 107 N.J. Eq. 140; 152 A. 919; affg., 105 N.J. Eq. 299; 147 A. 590 (1929).

49. Note, *Ann. Cas.* 1917 A, 360; *and see* n. 56.

50. Sun Printing and Publishing Assn. v. Moore, 183 U.S. 642; 22 S.Ct. 240; 46 L.Ed. 366; (1902); Henn, Corporations §255 (2d ed., 1970); East Central Okla. Elec. Co-op, Inc. v. Oklahoma Gas and Elec. Co., 505 P.2d 1324 (Okla. 1973).

51. Silver Spring Development Corp. v. Gnertler, 262 A.2d 749 (Md. 1970); Wills v. Rowland and Co., 117 A.D. 122, 102 N.Y.S. 386 (1907); Gilbert v. Sharkey, 80 Ore, 323, 156 P. 789 (1916); *see* above, n. 9, 10; Herald Co. v. Seawell, 472 F.2d 1081 (10th Cir. 1972).

52. Security Bldg. and Loan Assn. v. Seibert, 41 P.2d 556 (Calif. App. 1935).

53. Axelrod v. Premier Photo Service, Inc. 173 S.E.2d 383 (W. Va. 1970); Tinley v. Ammerman, 150 Okla. 215, 299 P. 918 (1931).

54. Carlesimo v. Schwebel, 197 P.2d 167 (Calif. App. 1948); *and see* n. 68.

55. Catholic Foreign M. Society v. Oussani, 215 N.Y. 1 (1915).

56. *See* Rosenthal v. 34th St. Shop, 129 Misc. 822; 222 N.Y.S. 733 (1927); and, note, *Ann. Cas.* 1917A, 360. But *see* Burlington Industries v. Foil, 284 N.C. 740, 202 S.E.2d 591 (1974): (Where act undertaken by corporate president relates to matters outside the corporation's ordinary course of business, corporation not bound unless there was express authorization by the board of directors); and *see* Templeton v. Nocona Hills Owners, 555 S.W.2d 534 (1977): (State statute provided that board of directors and not president, is charged with corporate affairs duties; so president's authority must be found to be derived elsewhere).

57. State Exch. Bank v. Simms. 266 S.W. 1111 (Tex. Civ. App. 1924).

58. Arts, Inc. v. Bowles, 38 A.2d 660 (Mun. App., D.C. 1944).

59. Saint Clair v. Rutledge, 115 Wis. 583; 92 N.W. 234 (1902).

60. *Restatement, Agency* §§159, 165–167.

61. *See* American Business Credit Corp. v. First State Bank, 385 So.2d 1080 (Fla. 4th DCA, 1980): (Bank held to have duty to inquire into the authority of corporate president to borrow money or execute documents); and, Kentucky-Pennsylvania O.&G. Corp. v. Clark, 57 S.W.2d 65 (Ky., 1933).

62. Meyer v. Glenmoor Homes 246 Cal. App. 2d 242, 54 Cal. Rptr. 786, 55 Cal. Rptr. 502 (1966): (In order to have implied authority, an agent must be performing an act that is appropriate in the ordinary course of the corporation's business); and, New York Mortgage Co. v. Garfinkel, 179 N.E. 33 (N.Y., 1931).

63. Diversification Consultants, Inc. v. Candy-Gram, Inc., 264 N.E.2d 788 (Ill. App. 1970); Rathbun v. Snow, 123 N.Y. 343, 10 L.R.A. 255 (1890).

64. Louisville N.A. and C.R. Co. v. Louisville Trust Co., 174 U.S. 552, 573; 19 S.Ct. 817; 43 L.Ed. 1081 (1899); Real Estate Capital Corp. v. Thunder Corp., 287 N.E.2d 838 (Ohio Ops. 1972).

65. Demings v. Supreme Lodge Knights of Pythias, 131 N.Y. 522, 527; 30 N.E. 572 (1892).

66. *Republic of Transkei v. I.N.S.*, 923 F.2d 175 (D.C. Cir. 1991).

67. Gilbert v. Sharkey, 80 Ore. 323; 156 P. 789; *and see* above n. 9, 10 (1916).

68. Carlesimo v. Schwebel, 197 P.2d 167 (Calif. App.); *and see* n. 54 (1948).

69. *See* Vulcan Corp. v. Cabden Mach. Wks., 336 Ill. App. 394; 84 N.E.2d 173 (1949); Island Winds Condo v. Wettingfield, 440 S.2d 455 (Fla. App. 1983); Calif. Nonprofit Corp. Code, §5239(a)(1).

70. Security Bldg. and Loan Assn. v. Seibert, 41 P.2d 556 (Calif. App.); Whitford v. Laidler, 94 N.Y. 145 (1883).

71. *See,* Ballentine on Corporations, §60 (rev. ed. 1946); Scientific . . . v. Plessey, 510 F.2d 15 (2d Cir. 1974).

72. Rachelle Enterprises, Inc. v. U.S., 169 F. Supp. 266 (Ct. Cl. 1959); Roth v. Embotelladora Nacional, Inc., 2 N.Y.2d 864, 161 N.Y.S.2d 128, 141 N.E.2d 617 (1957); Snyder v. Freeman, 266 S.E.2d 593 (N.C., 1980); Gillespie v. DeWitt, 280 S.E.2d 736 (N.C. App., 1981).

73. Bryant v. Lakeside Galleries, Inc., 402 Ill. 466, 84 N.E.2d 412 (1949); Robertson v. Burstein, 105 N.J.L. 375, 146 A. 355, 65 A.L.R. 324 (1929).

74. *Boatmen's Natl. Bk of S. L. v. Smith*, 706 F. Supp. 30 (D.C., IL., 1989).

75. *Lillian Schoniger v. Yardarm Beach Homeowners Assn., Inc.*, 523 N.Y.S.2d 523 (2d Dept., App. Div., 1990). The test of the rule is absence of fraud, self-dealing, or unconscionability.

76. *Matter of Will of Coe*, 826 P.2d 576 (N.M. App. 1992).

77. *Louisiana World Exposition v. Federal Ins. Co.*, 864 F.2d 1147 (5th Civ., LA, 1989).

78. *Stropes by Taylor v. Heritage House Children's Center of Shelbyville, Inc.*, 547 N.E.2d 244 (Ind. 1989).

79. *Tampa Bay Economic Development Corp. v. Edman*, 598 So.2d 172 (Fla. 2d DCA 1992); West-'s F.S.A. § 673.403(2)(b) (1991).

80. *Parker, Criminal Sentencing Policy for Organizations*, 26 *Amer. Crim. L. Rev.* 513, 521 (n.21), 522 (n.23) (1989).

81. *United States v. Bakker*, D.C. No. Car.; Oct. 5, 1989; and see *In re Heritage Village Church and Missionary Fellowship, Inc.*, 2 Bkcy. R. 1000 (Bkcy. Ct., D. So. Car., 1988).

82. *Ibid.*, report in *N.Y. Times*, p. A12 (July 26, 1989).

83. *People v. Wood*, 451 N.W.2d 563 (Mich. App. 1990).

84. *N.Y. Times* report, p.1 (Apr. 8, 1990); and most newspapers of Oct. 6, 1990.

85. *See,* Ariz. Rev. S. §36-916; Okl. Stat., Tit. 6331-878.

86. *See,* Gerrish Dredging Co. v. Bethlehem S. Corp., 247 Mass. 162; 141 N.E. 867 (1923).

87. *See,* Dewey v. National Tank Maint. Corp., 233 Iowa 58; 8 N.W.2d 593 (1943).

88. Wait v. Nashua Armory Assn., 66 N.H. 581; 23 A. 77 (1891); Lyndon Mill Co. v. Lyndon Literary and Biblical Inst., 63 Vt. 581; 22 A. 575 (1891); Anderson Est., Inc., v. Puget Sound Sav. and L. Assn., 171 Wash. 378; 18 P.2d 5 (1933); Weinbert Clinic and Research Labs., Inc. v. Weinberg; 105 N.J. Eq. 690; 149 A. 362 (1930).

89. *See,* Kline v. Thompson, 206 Wis. 464; 240 N.W. 128 (1932); Berend v. Benwood-Linze Co., 192 S.W.2d 660 (Mo. App. 1946). *And see,* Annot., 53 A.L.R.2d 1421 (1957).

90. Colton Manor Co. v. Davis, 106 N.J. Eq. 76; 150 A. 10 (1930).

91. Argue v. Monte Regio Corp., 115 Calif. App. 575; 2 P.2d 54 (1931): but *see,* Robert Nanney Chevrolet v. Evans & Moses, 601 S.W.2d 441 (Mo., 1980).

92. *See* n. 91.

93. Hackney v. York, 18 S.W.2d 923 (Tex. Civ. App. 1929).

94. *See* 15 Pa. C.S.A. §5553.

95. Ohio Rev. Code §1702.41(B).

96. Ohio Rev. Code §1702.47(F).

97. Sun Printing and Publ. Assn. v. Moore, 183 U.S. 642; 22 S.Ct. 240, 46 L. Ed. 366 (1902).

98. People's Bank v. St. Anthony's Rom. Cath. Church, 109 N.Y. 512 (1888); and note, 12 A.L.R. 130n.

99. *Thompson Elec., Inc. v. Bank One, Akron*, 525 N.E.2d 761 (OH 1988).

100. *Gottlieb v. Tulane University of Louisiana*, 529 So.2d 128 (LA App. 1988).

101. Anderson v. Campbell, 176 Minn. 411; 223 N.W. 624 (1929).

102. *Ibid.*, Clements v. Coppin, 61 F.2d 552 (9th Cir. 1932); Nelson v. Central Metr. Bk., 185 Minn. 449, 241 N.W. 585 (1932).

103. Ohio Rev. Code §1702.47(F).

104. *The Association Secretary: A Working Profile,* 89 *Community Up-Date* (clients newsletter) 1 (Aug., 1989) by Becker, Poliakoff & S. law firm of Fort Lauderdale, Florida, available on request, presumably.

105. Meyer v. Glenmoor Homes, Inc., 54 Cal. Rptr. 786 (App. 1966); Helberg v. Zuck, 201 Iowa 860, 208 N.W. 209 (1926); *see,* Doris and Friedman, *Corporate Secretary's Manual and Guide* (rev. ed.; New York; Prentice-Hall, Inc. 1949); Choka, *Six Check Lists for Corporate Secretary,* 5 Prac. Law 85 (1959); and as to minutes, *see,* Field v. Oberwartmann, 16 Ill. App.2d 376, 148 N.E.2d 600 (1958).

106. Hopkins v. Paradise Hts. Fruit Growers Assn., 58 Mont. 404; 193 P. 389 (1920); Citizens Development Co. v. Kypawya Oil Co., 191 Ky. 183; 229 S.W. 88 (1921). *Contra:* People's Sav. Bk v. Hine, 131 Mich. 181; 91 N.W. 130 (1902) (as to business corporations).

107. Hopkins case, n. 106.

108. Leary v. Blanchard, 48 Me. 269 (1860).

109. Ohio Rev. Code §1702.47(F).

110. 15 Pa. C.S.A. §5553.

111. *See,* Green Bay Fish Co. v. Jorgensen, 165 Wis. 548; 163 N.W. 142 (1917); and n. 114. Also Doris (ed.), *Corporate Treasurer's Handbook* (New York: Prentice-Hall, Inc. 1950).

112. Coney Island Auto Race Co. v. Boynton, 87 A.D. 251; 84 N.Y.S. 347 (1903).

113. First Natl. Bk. v. Levine, 136 Misc. 355; 239 N.Y.S. 655 (1930).

114. *See* n. 111; *see* Grossman and Co., Inc. v. Merchants Refrig. Co., 255 A.D. 146; 5 N.Y.S.2d 494 (1938).

115. *See,* as to financial men as corporate leaders, 81 *Time* Mag. (10) 85 (Mar. 8, 1963).

116. *Bisceglia v. Bernadine Sisters . . . Order . . .*, 560 N.E.2d 567 (Mass. App. 1990).

117. *Lehigh Presbytery v. Merchants Bancorp, Inc.*, 600 A.2d 593 (Pa. Super, 1991).

118. *See* Duncan (ed.), *Trade Association Management,* c. 21 (rev. ed.; Chicago: Natl. Institute for Commercial and Trade Organization Executives, 1948).

119. *Ibid.*, (Duncan), p. 184.

120. Look under the heading "Association Management" in yellow page phone directories or in business directories.

121. Memorial Hosp. Assn. v. Pacific Grape Pdts. Co., 290 P.2d 481 (Calif. 1955); Sun Printing and Publ. Assn. v. Moore, 183 U.S. 642; 22 S.Ct. 240; 46 L.Ed. 366 (1902); *and see,* Freeman v. River Farms Co., 5 Calif.2d 431, 55 P.2d 199 (1936); Matson v. Alley, 141 Ill. 284, 31 N.E. 419 (1892); Stevens on Corporations, 769 (2d ed. 1949); Annot., 53 A.L.R.2d 1421 (1957).

122. *See*, Holeman, *Condominium Management* (Prentice-Hall, 1980); and, *Fund Raising Management* (Magazine) 224-7th St., Garden City, N.Y. 11530; and, Manross v. Uncle Sam Oil Co., 88 Kans. 237; 128 P. 385 (1912).

123. Hackney v. York, 18 S.W.2d 923 (Tex. Civ. App. 1929).

124. *See*, Warren v. Littleton O.C.B. Co., 204 N.C. 288; 168 S.E.2d 226 (1933).

125. Potts v. Wallace, 146 U.S. 689; 13 S.Ct. 196; 36 L. Ed. 1135 (1892).

126. *Ibid.*

127. *See*, People's Bank v. St. Anthony's Rom. Cath. Church, 109 N.Y. 512 (1888); as to notes, *see*, 12 A.L.R. 130 n. But he may have this power in "business-type" situations in some states. *See*, National Surety Co. v. Wingate, 153 Okla. 132; 5 P.2d 376 (1931).

128. Farmers Fund, Inc. v. Tooker, 207 A.D. 37; 201 N.Y.S. 592 (1923); *Restatement, Agency* §73.

129. *See*, Conde Nast Press, Inc. v. Cornhill Publ. Co., 255 Mass. 480; 152 N.E. 240 (1926).

130. *E.g.*, as to trade association executive, *see*, Duncan (ed.), *op. cit. supra.*, n. 118.

131. Address inquiries, as to these, to the American Bar Assn. in Chicago, the Assn. of American Law Schools in Washington, D.C., and for the League of Ohio Law Schools, to the Secretary of the Ohio Supreme Court in Columbus, Ohio.

132. *See*, Hospital Accreditation References [Amer. Hosp. Assn., Chicago, Ill., (curr. ed.)] *But, see* n. 39, that outside authorities' rules (*i.e.*, federal grant-making agencies) have no power to take over control of internal affairs and policies of state-chartered private corporations.

133. *The Role of the Trustees of Columbia University*, published privately by Columbia University, 1957.

134. The Trustees of the Philadelphia Baptist Association v. Hart's Baptist Association, 17 U.S. 1 (1819).

135. St. Joseph's Hospital v. Bennett, 281 N.Y. 115 (1939).

136. McKinney, *Consolidated Laws of New York*, Annotated, Book 37, *Not-for-Profit Corporation Law* ("N—PCL").

137. McKinney, *Consolidated Laws of New York*, Annotated, Book 16, *Education Law ("Ed. Law")*.

138. N—PCL, §103(a); *Ed. Law*, §§2(3), 214 and 126-a(1)(b).

139. 1951 Op. Atty. Genl. 159.

140. N—PCL, §513(b).

141. Legislative Document (1970) No. 11, pp. 110–111.

142. *Restatement (Second) Trusts*, §379, comment b.

143. 2 Fletcher, *Corporations*, §495, p. 510 (curr. ed.)

144. N.Y. Nonprofit Corp. L., §514(a).

145. N.Y. Nonprofit Corp. L., §§514(b), 717.

146. *Id.*

147. McKinney, *Consolidated Laws of New York*, Annotated, Book 58A, *New York Surrogate's Court Procedure* §2309(5). *See, generally*, IV *Scott on Trusts*, §390 (current ed. _____).

30

MEETINGS OF DIRECTORS

[*See* Chapter 24 as to Meetings of Members]

§306. DIRECTORS' MEETINGS, IN GENERAL

Meetings may be *regular*—at the time and place appointed by statute, charter, bylaws, or other positive provision, or *special*—for special or limited purposes specially stated to the parties concerned. *Black's Law Dictionary 886* (5th ed. 1979). But see, below, § 311.

A *meeting*, in the law of corporations or associations, is an assembly of persons for the purpose of discussing or acting upon a matter or matters of common interest.[1] As to parliamentary procedure see the Index and Chapter 51.

A conference of two members of a board, without notice to a third member, is not a "meeting" of the board.[2]

Where *no provision* is made for calling special meetings, *customary* methods of calling meetings (in a church) were not enough to override statute regulations; e.g., board special meeting to dismiss the pastor, with no notice to members, was *void*. Bethlehem Baptist Church v. Henderson, 522 S. 2d 1339 (La. App. 1988). Whatever the name given to such an assembly, it is a meeting if it satisfies the description stated above. Thus, a "communication" is the term used by the Masonic Order.[3] A "session" of the board of supervisors is a meeting,[4] so is a "sitting."[5]

The essential idea conveyed by the word "meeting" is the consultation and discussion conducted by an assembled deliberative body.[6] But today, actual "in person" meetings may not be necessary, since they can communicate by conference call on telephones, or on closed-circuit television. It is enough if ". . . all directors participating can simultaneously hear each other during the meeting."[7]

Original and adjourned sessions of a meeting are part of the same "meeting."[8]

A convention of delegates is a "meeting of corporation" just as is a gathering of members or trustees.[9]

Statutory requirements. Most state statutes make few or no mandatory rules about trustees' meetings. They rarely say that directors or trustees must meet in order to act. For example, Florida's statute says that directors "may" hold regular or special meetings in or out of the state.[10] Some states, such as Pennsylvania, have no provisions about directors' meetings in their nonprofit statutes.

A typical modern nonprofit statute, that of Ohio, says only that meetings may be called by certain officers, may be within or without the state, should be based on written notice, and do not need notice of adjournment other than that given at the original meeting. All these provisions are not applicable if the articles or bylaws provide otherwise.[11]

The only other provision in this typical statute deals with the usual requirement of a majority of the trustees to constitute a quorum; again, unless the articles or bylaws provide otherwise.[12]

Meeting ordinarily is required. When the board of directors has the power to act, it must act as a board. The management of a corporation is intrusted to the directors (trustees) as a group—not as so many individuals. Independent action by one director or by several directors is not action by the board, and ordinarily is not effective or binding on the corporation.[13]

Even if they wish to do so, the members may not lawfully turn the board's general powers over to an individual.[14]

Except in certain special situations, the directors or trustees cannot bind the organization by their acts unless they act as a *duly assembled* board.[15] However, use of communications equipment, such as conference calls, can constitute *assembly*.[16]

Action even by a majority of the board members will not suffice if the members act as individuals[17]—particularly when they act without the knowledge or consent of the remaining members of the board.[18] Nor, ordinarily, is a collection of separate consents from all of the directors legally equivalent to a board meeting and decision.[19] But the Michigan, Minnesota, Ohio, and Pennsylvania statutes expressly permit such consents if they are made in writing.[20] (See Section 308.)

Usually, a certain formality is required in calling and holding the meeting. A casual gathering of the board members, of which no record is kept, is not a legally effective meeting.[21]

In one instance, all the directors attended a general meeting of the members and voted there on a resolution before the meeting. This was held to be ineffective as an action of the board. The directors had voted as members; and the matter was not one on which the board ordinarily would have acted.[22] This holding seems to carry the theory of board management to an illogical extreme.

Irregular practices. It is no secret that many meetings of directors are held by telephone—one director calling the others and polling each on a particular matter. Later, when the decision has been reached, the record is made to give the impression that a meeting actually has been held.

Many times, too, one interested member of the board will collect the oral consents of others in a series of individual luncheons or other such meetings.

Although this manner of obtaining agreement usually results in no protest, it is not a sound practice. The rules are flouted only at the risk of later trouble.

It is wiser to hold meetings on due notice and with due formality, keeping due record.[23]

Actions taken without meetings are discussed in Section 308.

§307. WHERE MAY DIRECTORS MEET?

Unless the bylaws provide otherwise, boards of directors may meet either within or without the home state of the organization. Specific statutes may require meetings to be within the state in very special cases.[24] But, within or without the state, the meeting must be called in a reasonably convenient place—though not necessarily in the organization's home office or center.[25] It will not do ordinarily, for example, to call a meeting on the top of Mount Everest.

Some states' statutes provide that a meeting is valid, no matter where it is held, if the directors all consent; in California they may hold meetings as they see fit.[26] Most statutes generally permit meetings of directors[27] or of members[28] to be held anywhere.

The general rule, then, is that directors may meet at any place convenient or necessary, provided that proper notice and full consent of the board members are given.[29] If the meeting is held outside the state contrary to the wishes of some of the directors when unanimous consent to such a meeting is required, the meeting is invalid. For example, the execution of notes pursuant to authority granted at such a meeting has been held to be improper because the required consents of all the directors had not been obtained. The notes in question were held to be invalid.[30]

Obviously, those directors who without protest attend such a meeting will not later be heard to say the meeting was invalid.[31]

§308. ACTIONS TAKEN WITHOUT MEETINGS

The principal purpose of the rule (see Section 307) that directors must meet and act *as a board* is to protect creditors and other interested third parties. If no rights of creditors are affected and no violation of public policy is involved, the acts of directors may be binding and effective without proper meeting. Many nonprofit organizations go along happily without much regard for the formalities and without getting into any trouble.

When the members generally acquiesce in such a slipshod course of procedure, and when the acts of the directors are not otherwise beyond the scope of their powers, their acts are binding and effective, though no meetings were held.[32] By the same principle, when the directors or members acquiesce in a particular act, though they know that no proper meeting was held to authorize it, they are bound by it.[33] Their acquiescence amounts to ratification.

If the directors are also all the members, they cannot disown their action in one capacity by protesting it in another capacity.[34]

It is possible, too, for members expressly or by implication to waive such a defect as the failure to hold a meeting. Such a waiver binds the members who did the waiving.[35]

The general equitable principles of *waiver* and *estoppel* apply to nonprofit organizations and to their directors, officers, and members. (See Sections 312 and 313.)

Case decisions. The following examples illuminate the attitude of the courts toward actions unauthorized by proper meetings of directors:

1. A corporation, without holding a meeting, granted a mortgage of its property to secure the repayment of a loan to the corporation. The mortgage was held to be invalid.[36]

2. A corporation began a lawsuit with the authorization of its directors but without proper authorization by a meeting. The action was held to have been improperly commenced.[37]

3. A corporation decided to go into voluntary insolvency without proper authorization by a meeting. The decision was held to be improper.[38]

4. A corporation made a general sale of its assets without proper meeting and consents. The sale was held to be improper.[39]

5. Action without a proper meeting was held to be binding and effective when the directors of a corporation had authorized the ordering of some advertising.[40] A different decision, based on the artificial technicality, would have unjustly enriched the corporation at the expense of the advertising (radio) company. (Such use of one's own improper conduct as a defense against liability for one's own acts is forbidden by the equitable doctrine of estoppel.)

6. The making of an ordinary employment contract without a meeting could not later be disowned because of the technical deficiency.[41] The need for immediate decision justified assuming the members' assent.

7. Legal action to enforce a member's past-due debt to the corporation, without formal meeting-approval, was upheld.[42]

Statutes validating action without meeting. Modern statutes in some states (*e.g.*, Ohio Rev. Code Sec. 1702.25) expressly authorize the doing of acts, without a meeting, which could be done at a meeting of trustees or of members. These statutes require the making of a written record of the action, signature by the trustees or members who would have been entitled to notice of a meeting, and filing with the corporate records. See the provisions of Michigan, Minnesota, and Pennsylvania, above, in Section 306.

Most of the cases cited above involved business acts and obligations. Those who deal with nonprofit organizations should understand that the members usually will not be personally bound without their reasonably clear consent. Estoppel will not be invoked as strictly against them as against members of business organizations.

§309. SUNDAY OR HOLIDAY MEETINGS

Statutes in a number of states declare contractual arrangements made on a Sunday, or on certain holidays, invalid. Local statutes should be consulted on this point.

Certain acts accomplished at meetings are contractual without being so entitled. Care must be exercised where Sunday laws apply. It has been held that the adoption of a bylaw is *not* subject to a Sunday law's restrictions.[43]

Under certain statutes, a contract made at a Sunday meeting is absolutely void. It cannot be ratified by later action.[44] But if a statute provides that a meeting is itself not void, but only *voidable*, the act in question may be either voided or validated at a later (non-Sunday) meeting.[45]

§310. WHO CALLS DIRECTORS' MEETINGS

Clear provision as to who may or should call meetings is important. Bylaws usually contain some such provision. It is well that they be precise, not only in listing alternative officers but in specifying the conditions for descent of authority. Then, if someone violates these provisions, his lack of authority to call a meeting is clear.[46]

In one case, where the bylaws did not specify who had the authority to call a meeting, the president was held to have that authority.[47]

Ordinarily the chairman of the board is given the primary power to *call* a board meeting. Often the *sending of notices* is made the secretary's responsibility. The secretary of the organization usually is also chosen as the secretary of the board—but sometimes it is better to have different persons, lest the all-too-human desire for self-aggrandizement and "empire building" operate against the best interest of the organization as a whole.

Provisions for the calling of a meeting at the request of a certain number of directors are also desirable. Provisions for a call at the request of a certain number of members are less common. Without such provision, members ordinarily may not call meetings of the board of directors.[48]

If the officer who should call a meeting fails or neglects to do so, and if no express system of alternatives is found in the bylaws, the officer next in rank should do so. If need be, *any* other officer may do so.[49] If the charter or bylaws list several officers who may call a meeting, with no order of priority, any one of these officers may do so.[50]

If directors actually receive notice of a call, and minor defects in the call exist, this does not make the call ineffective, nor the meeting invalid.[51] If all the members of the board attend, such defects do not invalidate the meeting.[52]

Excepting possible instances of unanimity in which nobody is adversely affected, the members may not call a board meeting by action contrary to the bylaw provisions.[53]

§311. NOTICE OF DIRECTORS' MEETINGS, IN GENERAL

Unless a meeting of directors is a *stated meeting* (listed as a regular one in the charter or bylaws) or unless it is fixed by custom, notice must be given to all the directors.[54] The requirement that all receive notice ordinarily applies to any meeting of any committee, board, or deliberative body.[55] But if the charter, the bylaws, or a resolution of the directors set a time and place for a regular meeting, no notice need be given.[56]

Disregard of such rules of notice does not in itself justify third persons who dealt with the corporation in attacking the validity of that corporate action.[57] Nor, on the other hand, may they flatly insist that such action was valid if such a defect materially affected the rights of the members.[58] But 48-hours telephone notice now is valid in California.[59]

Lack of notice does not invalidate a meeting if all the directors attend and participate without objection.[60] Their presence amounts to a waiver of the defect.[61]

Notice need not be given if it would be unlawful. For example, statutes often forbid sending notice to an enemy-alien in a time of war.[62]

Failure to give notice may be excused, if no serious harm is done. In an emergency, for example, the officers on hand may act as the situation requires. Their acts will not automatically be invalidated by the failure to follow proper form.[63] Actually, there is a general rule that giving of due notice will be presumed, unless evidence to the contrary is introduced.[64]

Notice of special meetings must be given, subject to the general rules. But third parties are not prejudiced by the fact that a meeting is special rather than regular. Creditors, for example, are entitled to assume that a meeting is a regular one, whether or not notice was duly given in the calling of the meeting.[65]

The A.B.A. 1986 Revised Model Nonprofit Corporation Act [§ 8.22(b)] proposes that *special* meetings notices need not state the *purpose* of the meeting. A more permissive rule cannot be imagined. It almost invites managerial coups.

Adjournments. When a duly called meeting adjourns to another time, no notice of its reassembly is required—even to directors absent from the first session—unless bylaws specifically require another sending of notice.[66] Only if the adjournment resolution failed to specify the time or place for continuation must notice be sent.[67]

Directors who together do not constitute a quorum may not adjourn a meeting until another time to cure the lack of a quorum. No meeting at all is valid in such a case without statutory authority. No meeting was constituted to transact any business.[68] Even if a bylaw permits such action, its validity is doubtful if it adversely affects a member or a third person.

How to give notice. Bylaws usually specify the manner in which notice shall be given to directors. Mailing of written notice a few (*e.g.*, five or ten) days in advance is usually required. In the absence of such a rule, it is still wise to send written notice by mail. The mailing in ordinary course raises a prima facie presumption of delivery of the notice to the address of the recipient, and to him.[69]

A few less recent cases have held that actual delivery of personal notice must be proven if the giving of notice becomes an issue.[70] But few people expect (or get) such notice, except in small local clubs or in special cases.

§312. WAIVER OF NOTICE

Waiver of notice is touched upon in Section 308.

In many older cases, it was held that a director may waive the giving of notice before a meeting is held, but not afterward.[71] But cases and statutes now tend to hold that a waiver after the meeting also is valid, especially when the members approved the action taken at the meeting.[72]

In practice this problem seldom arises. Waivers made after the meeting usually are back-dated, and proof of the back-dating is very difficult. Moreover, the principles of estoppel, unjust enrichment, and protection of innocent parties are more effective than arguments about formal improprieties.

§313. CONTENTS OF THE NOTICE

Usually, no particular form is prescribed for notices, so long as they contain the necessary information. Even the purpose of the meeting need not be stated unless the bylaws require it. If there is no statement of the purpose, a notice implies that the meeting will deal with any matters that generally come before such a meeting of such a body[73]—unless the meeting is called for action in an emergency situation, where unusual powers and actions will be necessary.[74]

Oral notice is sufficient, if this is the custom of the organization, despite a technical requirement of written notice in the bylaws or in a statute,[75] but is not preferred practice where written notice is required.

Statement of time and place is essential,[76] unless the bylaws provide for time and place. No signature need be on the notice to validate it, even when the notice must be written.[77]

§314. FREQUENCY OF MEETINGS

Meetings of directors may be called as often as reasonably necessary. This is left largely to the discretion of the authorized officers. Often the bylaws rule on the frequency of the meetings. Abuses, or unreasonable frequency of calls, are improper.[78]

§315. QUORUMS AND VOTING AT DIRECTORS' MEETINGS

When no express rule is stated in the charter or in the bylaws, a majority of the members of the board constitute a *quorum*.[79] If fewer than that number assemble, those present cannot act as a board, and have no alternative but to disperse.[80] A quorum for any action ordinarily is a majority,[81] but the bylaws or articles may provide otherwise, within statutory limits (*e.g.*, two directors in California, now.)[82]

Action at the meeting, too, ordinarily goes by majority vote.[83] A majority of those *voting* controls, regardless of how many are present.[84]

Unless the record of a meeting shows otherwise, a quorum is presumed to have been present.[85]

The bylaws or charter may make special provisions for quorums—perhaps not requiring a majority. But less than one-third of the board usually does not constitute a legal quorum.[86]

Greater-than-majority-vote rules. Many current statutes permit bylaw requirements for quorums and voting to vary from one-third to four-fifths. A requirement of unanimity in voting usually is viewed as too drastic.[87] But a quorum requirement of five-sixths of the directors has been found valid.[88] A two-thirds vote requirement has been found valid.[89] But drastic rules may conflict with public policy concerning the due powers of the board of directors.[90]

Tricking a director into attending, in order to obtain a quorum, is improper. His attendance may not be counted.[91] However, a director who claims that he has been tricked into attending should not stay and participate in the meeting, or his presence may count in forming a quorum.[92]

For ratifications, the quorum requirements that govern original actions apply.[93]

Vacancies on the board do not invalidate its action if its quorum requirements are met.[94]

The vote or presence of an "interested" director (see below) may not be counted.[95] But California now allows "interested" ones to count, up to 49 percent, and the 1986 Revision of the Model Nonprofit Corporation Act echoes the same rule proposal; comment on such law is waste of effort.

If vacancies reduce the board to less than a quorum, the board must fill the vacancies before it can act upon other matters.[96]

What if some members leave a meeting? A quorum must be present not only to begin a meeting, but also to carry on board or group action.[97] If some directors leave the meeting, and less than a quorum remain, ordinarily there can be no legally effective board or group action.[98]

But if the withdrawal is unreasonable, or intended to hamstring action, the ones who remain may legally act, just as though a quorum were present.[99] If directors intentionally absent themselves from a board meeting in order to prevent a quorum, they may not set aside the election of a director by the other directors.[100]

California and New York *expressly provide* that when a *quorum* is *once present* at a meeting, it is *not broken* by subsequent *walkout* of directors or members, and remaining persons may adjourn ("continue") the meeting.[101]

Quorum is *not* broken by a *provoked*, noncapricious walkout.[102]

For various state statutes and case decisions on "walkouts" see:

Oleck & Green, *Parliamentary Law & Practice for Nonprofit Organizations*, 2nd ed., (American Law Institute—American Bar Association, 1991); and see *C.J.S., Parliamentary Law* §4 (1950) as to adjourned meetings. Also:

NY Bus. Corp. L. §608(c), (d):

(c) "When a quorum is once present to organize a meeting, it is not broken by the subsequent withdrawal of any shareholders."

(d) "The shareholders present may adjourn the meeting despite the absence of a quorum."

NY Not-for-Profit Corp. L. §708(d):

"Except as otherwise provided in this chapter, the vote of a majority of the directors present *at the time of the vote*, if a *quorum is present at such time*, shall be the act of the board."

Id. §707:

"Unless a greater proportion is required by this chapter or by the certificate of incorporation or a by-law adopted by the members, a majority of the entire board shall constitute a quorum for the transaction of business, except. . . ."

CA Corps. Code §9211(a)(8):

". . . A meeting at which a *quorum is initially present* may continue to transact business notwithstanding the withdrawal of (some) *directors*, if any action taken is approved by at least a majority of the required quorum for such a meeting, or such greater number as is required by this decision, the articles or bylaws."

The American Bar Association's Revised Model Nonprofit Corporation Act of 1987 (really only its "*Subcommittee* on Model NPC Law of the Business Law Section") expressly says in its *Official Comment to Section 8.24*: "Section 8.24(b) *authorizes quorum breaking* by requiring a quorum to be present when a vote is taken. . . . If a director is about to lose a vote, he or she can leave the meeting before the vote is taken thereby breaking the quorum . . . [but] *should consider* his or her duties of care and loyalty."

This is only one of the provisions and attitudes that have led most able lawyers and legislators to ignore the ABA "Model." It says: "If a quorum is present when a vote is taken, the affirmative vote of a majority of directors present is the act of the board unless this Act, the articles or bylaws require the vote of a greater number of directors." Florida adopted this provision in its new

Not-for-Profit Corporation Act §617.0824 effective 1991, to the surprise of this writer. Such deliberate obstructionism is hardly consistent with the trustee (at least, fiduciary) nature of elected officials.

Obviously, a well drawn set of bylaws should expressly forbid such destructive "quorum breaking."

What of those who attend only to protest? Those members who attend a meeting only to protest lack of due notice, or lack of power to act, should not be counted in establishing a quorum.[103]

"Interested" directors. A director who has a personal interest in the matter before a meeting (*e.g.*, ownership of property proposed for purchase by the organization) may not be counted in determining the presence of a quorum.[104] (See also the Index.) This is the rule in most states.

Note, however, that the New York and California statutes are very permissive in this respect.[105] Such provisions almost invite abuses.

Modern nonprofit corporation statutes often expressly forbid a director to have any direct or indirect personal interest in contracts of the corporation. But they usually permit such an interest if the charter or the bylaws authorize it, or if two-thirds of the directors vote for it.[106] A modern trend in some states is to validate such transactions if full and open disclosure is made.[107] Similar rules apply to business corporations.[108] In the absence of express permissive provisions in the charter or bylaws, a contract with an "interested" director usually is invalid in most states (not in California).[109]

It is certain that dealings between a director and the corporation are open to court scrutiny and may create suspicion and dissension. In a nonprofit organization, it usually is wise to permit no such dealings—excepting directors whose functions normally require them within predictable limits. For example, the incorporating attorney often is also a director of the corporation. It is unfair to subject him to suspicion just because he is especially useful to the organization. His personal interest in a contract (such as a pension plan or a wage plan) does not disqualify him for quorum and voting purposes.[110]

§316. HOW TO CONDUCT DIRECTORS' MEETINGS

Most directors' meetings proceed with a minimum of formality. In larger organizations more formality is customary, and advisable.

The president of the organization ordinarily is also chairman of the board, and presides at its meetings. But other provisions may be made in the bylaws.[111]

Oral "yes"-or-"no" voting is the general rule. It is valid unless the bylaws provide otherwise.[112] Clear failure to oppose the proposition during voting may amount to assent, if the purpose and conclusion of the vote are evident.[113]

One who opposes a proposal should state his opposition clearly and demand that it be noted in the record. Thereby he may prove his stand later, and he may avoid liability when impropriety is present. He also enables himself to fight the decision later.[114]

Minutes should be taken and kept, whether or not by specific requirement.[115]

Reduction of decisions to formal resolutions, though ordinarily not required, is often very advisable.[116]

Previous decisions may be changed or revoked if nobody's "vested" rights under those decisions will thereby be injured.[117]

Voting is treated in a separate chapter, below.

The agenda. It is always well to have an *agenda* (schedule of sequence, by subjects) for the meeting to follow. This preserves order and prevents disputes about the priority of subjects. Often a general agenda is set forth in the bylaws, subject to change either by agreement or in the discretion of the chairman.

In board meetings a typical order of business is:

1. Assembly.
2. Call to order.
3. Roll call (names should be noted in the minutes).
4. Announcement of a quorum (the fact should be noted in the minutes).
5. Reading of the minutes of the previous meeting.
6. Correction (if necessary) of the minutes.
7. Approval of the minutes (as corrected.)
8. Reports of officers.
9. Reports of committee chairmen.
10. Old business.
11. Elections (if any).
12. New business.
13. Appointment of committees or of officers to study or deal with the new matters.
14. Choice of time and place for the next meeting.
15. Adjournment.
16. Collation (optional).

Director's counsel. Note that a director may have the right to the presence and advice of his own counsel at the director's meetings;[118] however, the bylaw should be explicit as to the presence of counsel at meetings.

§317. FORMS FOR CALLING MEETINGS

[*See* the Index of Forms, and Chapter 24.]

Statutory provisions about meetings usually deal with the minimum requirements of certain notices or calls—not their form. Unless the bylaws specify details of form, no special form is prescribed by law for calling meetings of members or directors.

In a few states, *official* forms are provided for some purposes. Some forms in this volume indicate their official nature [as in Maine's, and those of Washington, D.C.], while some official forms are prescribed by Georgia, Kansas, Michigan, Nevada, Oregon, North Dakota, and Washington. [See, 5 Oleck, *Modern Corporation Law Forms* 625, 626A, 627, 642, 643, 946, 1156, and more (1978 supp. ed.).]

The following forms are suggestions. As in use of any forms, other than official ones, they should not be followed slavishly, but should be adapted to the particular organization and situation.

FORM NO. 136
Call of Members' Meeting by the President

Mr. . . . ., Secretary

l. . . . . Assn., Inc.

Please take notice the regular annual (or a special) meeting of the members of the . . . . Association is to be (and hereby is) called for (date, hour, place).

[Statement of the usual purposes of the meeting is added. But this is more important in the *Notice* than in this *Call.*]

This is to request and direct that you, as Secretary, send due notice of this meeting to all the members of this Association, in accordance with the provisions of the bylaws.

Dated: . . . . . ., 19 . .   . ., President

[*Note:* For calls of special meetings, a statement of purposes of the meeting is essential.]

FORM NO. 137
Call of Members' Meeting by Directors

Mr. . . . ., President

. . . . Assn., Inc.

We, the undersigned, being directors of the . . . . Association, pursuant to Article . . . . . . , Section . . . . . . , of the Bylaws of the said Association, do hereby request (and direct) that you call a special meeting of the general membership of this Association to be held (date, hour, place) for the purpose(s) of:

[State briefly the purpose or purposes.]

Dated: . . . . . ., 19 . .

. . . .

. . . .

. . . .

[*Note:* This call may be addressed to the president, to the secretary, or to another officer authorized to issue notices and arrange the meeting.]

FORM NO. 138
Request by a Member for the Calling of a Meeting

. . . . . . , 19. .

Mr.. . . . . , President
. . . . Assn., Inc.
. . . . (address)
Dear Mr.. . . . . :

On my own behalf, and also as spokesman for . . . . . . , ... , ... , and . . . . . . , all of us being members of the . . . . . . Association, and pursuant to the laws of the State of . . . . . . , and to the Charter and Bylaws of this Association, we do request [or *direct* (if the Bylaws grant this power to member-groups)] that you call a special meeting of the Association's full membership (date, hour, place) for the purpose(s) of:

[State briefly the purpose or purposes],

and for the transaction of such other business and affairs as may properly come before the said meeting.

. . . .
. . . .
. . . .

§318. FORMS FOR NOTICE OF MEETINGS

FORM NO. 139
Notice of Annual Meeting of Members

. . . . Association, Inc.
. . . . (address)

Dear Member (or name him):

Please take notice that the annual meeting of the general membership of the . . . . Association, Inc. will be held at (place, date, hour) for the regular election of Directors (Trustees), and for the transaction of such other matters as may come before the said meeting.

[State briefly any special matters to be discussed.]

If you are unable to attend in person, you may give your written proxy for the voting to a member who will be present, in accordance with Article . . . . . . , Section . . . . . . , of the Association Bylaws.

Cordially yours,

. . . .
Secretary

[*Note.* Forms of proxies appear below.]

FORM NO. 140
Notice of Adjourned Meeting

[*Note.* The sending of notice of an adjourned meeting is usually advisable, though it is not actually required unless the bylaws so specify.]

.... Association, Inc.
.... (address)
.... (date)

Dear Member (or name him):

The regular (special) meeting of the members (Directors) of the .... Association, called for ......, 19.., was adjourned until ......, 19.., to be reconvened at ......p.m. (a.m.) at (address). The adjournment was resolved upon because [state the reason].

The meeting will reconvene at (place, date, hour) for the purposes specified in the original notice of meeting dated ......, 19 ... These purposes were, and are:

[State the purposes.]

Cordially yours,

....

Secretary

FORM NO. 141
Notice of Special Meeting of Members

.... Association, Inc.
.... (address)
.... (date)

Dear Member (or name him):

Please take notice that a special meeting of the members of the .... Association, Inc. will be held (place, date, hour) for the following purpose(s):

1. To approve or disapprove a resolution for [state the purpose] recommended by (name or committee).

2. To consider and decide upon a proposal to [state the proposal].

3. To act upon any matters related or pertinent to the above-stated purpose(s).

(or)

To act upon any other matters that may be brought before the said meeting.

If you cannot attend, you are respectfully urged to give your written proxy for voting to a member who will be present at the meeting, in accordance with the provisions of Article . . . . . . , Section . . . . . . , of the Association Bylaws.

By Order of the President (Board of Directors).

Cordially yours,

....
Secretary

FORM NO. 142
Notice of Regular Meeting of Directors

. . . . Association, Inc.
. . . .(address)

To the Board of Directors (Trustees) of . . . . Association, Inc.

Please take notice that pursuant to Article . . . . . . , Section . . . . . . , of the Association Bylaws, a regular meeting of the members of the Board of Directors (Trustees) will be held (place, date, hour).

[It is good practice to briefly outline the business other than routine matters that will be considered.]

If you will not be able to attend, please so advise the undersigned at your earliest convenience.

Dated:. . . . . . , 19. .

....
Secretary

FORM NO. 143
Notice of Special Meeting of Directors

[This follows Form No. 133, except that it describes the meeting as *special* rather than regular, and it *must* state the purpose of the meeting—for example, as follows:]

Mr. . . . .   (date)
. . . . .Street
(city) (state) (zip code)
. . . .

TO: ALL TRUSTEES

Gentlemen:

Pursuant to the direction of (President) . . . . . . , please be advised that there will be a Special Meeting of the Trustees of the . . . . . . School, on Friday, April . . . . . . , 19. .4:00 p.m., at the School, in order to pass on the amended Articles of Incorporation and Bylaws (regulations) of the Corporation, in conformity with the affiliation agreement with . . . . College.

Your attendance at this meeting is requested.

Enclosed herewith are copies of the Amended Articles of Incorporation and Regulations of the Corporation, for study by you meanwhile.

With personal regards, I am

> Secretary
> H. . . . L. O . . . . . .
> (title)

HLO:wm
encl/

§319. FORM OF WAIVER OF NOTICE

FORM NO. 144
Waiver of Notice (General Form)

I (We), the undersigned, being a member (all the members) of the . . . . Association, Inc., of . . . . (home city), do hereby waive any and all notice of a (regular) (special) meeting of the (members) (Directors) of the said Association as required by the Bylaws and statutes, and pursuant to the laws of the State of . . . . . . , do hereby consent to the holding of a (regular) (special) meeting of (members) (Directors) on (date, hour, place) and any adjournments thereof, for the purpose of

[State the purpose of the meeting],

and do consent to the transaction of any business, in addition to that stated above, that may properly come before the said meeting.

Dated: . . . . . . , 19 . . , in the City of . . . . , State of . . . .

. . . .
. . . .
. . . .

[*Note*: If publication of notice is required by the local law or the Bylaws, the waiver should mention and waive this requirement too.]

§320. FORMS OF PROXIES FOR MEETINGS

[See, in Chapter 26, the discussion of proxies, and forms.]

FORM NO. 145
General Proxy for Annual Meeting

Know all men by these presents that I, ... , a member in good

standing of the . . . . Association, Inc., do hereby appoint and constitute . . . . [a member], of . . . . . . (city), State of . . . . . ., my true and
lawful proxy and attorney-in-fact, to act and vote in my place and stead, at the
annual meeting of the said Association to be held (place, date), or on any
other day when the said meeting thereafter may be held by adjournment or
otherwise, according to the laws of the State of . . . .

I do hereby grant to the said . . . . (name) full power and
authority to act on my behalf in the voting for the election of Directors at the
said meeting, and in any other matters which may come before the said meeting, as fully as I myself could do if then and there personally present, with full
power of substitution and revocation, and do hereby ratify and confirm all that
the said . . . . (name), my proxy, there and then may do in my place and stead.

In witness whereof I have hereunto set my hand and seal this . . . . . . day of
. . . . . . , 19 . . .

[*Note:* This also may be stated in the plural and signed by several members, who thus all will be represented by the same proxy-person.]

FORM NO. 146
Proxy Limiting Discretion in Voting

[The general form is the same as Form No. 136. The second paragraph
is replaced, however, by this:]

The said . . . . (name), my (our) proxy, is to vote in favor of
. . . . (name), and against the proposal to (state the proposal purpose), but in all other respects is to have full discretion in any and all voting
at the said meeting, as fully as I (we) myself (ourselves) would have if then and
there personally present.

[The proxy may also specify and limit the period during which it is to be
valid.]

[A corporation's proxy should refer to the resolution appointing the
proxy, and should bear the corporate seal as well as the signature of the corporation's designated officer, or even of two officers.]

FORM NO. 147
Revocation of Proxy

The undersigned hereby cancels and revokes his proxy dated . . . . . . , 19
. . , given to . . . . (name) to vote at the regular (special) meeting of
members to be held on . . . . . . , 19 . . , or adjournments thereof, or any other
meeting of the members of . . . . Association, Inc., called for the purpose of [state the purpose].

Witness my hand and seal this . . . . . . day of . . . . . . , 19 . . , at
. . . . (city), State of . . . .

. . . .(L.S.)

§321. FORMS FOR PROOF OF NOTICE

FORM NO. 148
Affidavit of Mailed Service of Notice

State of . . . .
County of . . . . SS:

. . . . , being duly sworn, deposes and says that (s)he is the Secretary of . . . . Association, Inc., of . . . . (city), State of . . . . , and that on the . . . . . . day of . . . . . . , 19 . . , (s)he caused a notice of a regular (special) meeting of the members (Directors) of the said Association, a copy of which is annexed hereto and made a part hereof, to be deposited in the United States Post Office at . . . . (place), each in a sealed postpaid envelope, duly addressed to each member (Director) of the said Association, in accordance with the Association's records of addresses to his last-known address.

....
Secretary

Subscribed and sworn to before
me this . . . . . . day of
. . . . . . , 19 . .

Notary Public

FORM NO. 149
Affidavit of Personal Service of Notice

[This follows the foregoing form, except that the service of notice is described thus:]
by personally delivering to, and leaving with each Director (or, with Mr. J. . . . . . .J. . . . . . .) a true copy thereof.

FORM NO. 150
Affidavit of Publication of Notice

State of . . . .
County of . . . . SS:

. . . . , being duly sworn, deposes and says that he is the Secretary of the . . . . Association, Inc., of . . . . (city), State of

. . . ., and that pursuant to the orders of the Board of Directors (or, President) of the said Association, he did on . . . . . ., 19 . ., cause a notice of the regular (special) meeting of the members (Directors) of the said Association, a copy of which is annexed hereto and made a part hereof, to be published in the (city) *Daily Blat*, a newspaper of general circulation, circulated in . . . . . . County wherein the home office of the said Association is located, on . . . . . . (date), ... (date), and . . . . . . (date), as required by the Bylaws of the Association (or, laws of the State of . . . .).

. . . .
Secretary

Subscribed and sworn to before
me this . . . . . . day of
. . . . . ., 19 . .
. . . .
Notary Public

[Note that a *Publisher's Affidavit of Publication of Notice* should be obtained from the newspaper and retained for record purposes.]

POINTS TO REMEMBER

- Hold meetings on formal written notice.
- Make the time and place reasonable. Hold meetings at the home office unless all directors agree on another location.
- Give adequate notice (ten days, ordinarily).
- State in the notice the purpose of the meeting.
- Do not rely on informal decisions reached over the telephone or at luncheons.
- Take minutes at every meeting. Record approvals and dissents.
- Remember that informal-decision transactions may be binding—impossible to repudiate.
- Do not meet on Sundays or holidays.
- Specify in the bylaws who may call meetings.
- Avoid adjourned carry-over meetings.
- Get waivers (before the meeting begins) when inadequate notice or none is sent.
- Establish a form of notice for the organization.
- Hold meetings neither too often nor too seldom.
- Beware of quorum rules. Make them clear. Follow them.
- Avoid "interested" director transactions.
- Use an agenda for the meeting; and do not depart from it without good reason.

- Do not copy legal "forms" *verbatim*; adapt them to your particular organization and purposes.

NOTES TO CHAPTER 30

1. 57 C.J.S., *Meeting* 1044 (Curr. Supp.); Sacramento Newspaper Guild v. Sacramento County Board of Supervisors, 69 Cal. Rptr. 480, 485, 487, 26 Cal. App. 2d 41 (1968); American Brass Co. v. Ansonia Brass Workers' Union Local 445, I.U.M., M. & S. W., 140 Conn. 457, 101 A.2d 291, 293 (1953); State *ex rel.* Wayne v. Sims, 141 Va. 302, 90 S.E.2d 288, 295 (1955); Abeles v. Adams Engr. Co., 165 A.2d 555 (N.J. 1960); Prunier v. Commissioner, 248 F.2d 818 (Tax Ct. 1957); Notes, 26 Fordham L. Rev. 339 (1957); 11 Syracuse L.R. 68 (1959); Henn, *Corporations* (casebook) 346–357, 285–301 (2d ed. 1986).

2. Gallagher v. Unemployment Compensation Board of Review, 148 Pa. Super. 228, 24 A.2d 627 (1942).

3. State v. Goodwyn, 83 W.Va. 255, 98 S.E. 577 (1919).

4. People *ex rel.* Ward v. Chicago and E.I. Ry. Co., 365 Ill. 202, 6 N E 2d 119, 121 (1936); Turpin v. Haggerty, 47 Weekly L. Bull. (Ohio) 809.

5. Town of Hodgenville v. Kentucky Utilities Co., 250 Ky. 195, 61 S.W.2d 1047 (1933).

6. Board of Education of Marshall County v. Baugh, 240 Ala. 391, 199 S. 822, 825 (1941). *See,* Hurley v. Ornsteen, 42 N.E.2d 273 (Mass. 1942); Note, 11 Syracuse L.R. 68 (1959).

7. Revised Model Nonprofit Corporations Act (1986 Exposure Draft) §8.20(c). *See eg,* Minn. Stat. Ann. §317A.231 (Supp. 1993); Comp. Stat. Mich. §450.2521.

8. Atterbury v. Consolidated Coppermines Corp., 26 Del. Ch. 1, 20 A.2d 743, 749 (1941). *But see,* Burkelo v. Washington County, 38 Minn. 441, 38 N.W. 108 (1888).

9. Di Silvestro v. Sons of Italy Grand Lodge, 130 Misc. 494, 223 N.Y.S. 791, 795 (1927).

10. Fla. Stat. §617.0820 (1991).

11. Ohio Rev. Code §1702.31. *See,* Frantz Mfg. v. EAC, 501 A.2d 401 (Del. 1985).

12. *Ibid.,* §1702.32.

13. Cammeyer v. United German Lutheran Churches, 2 Sandf. Ch. (N.Y. 1844) 186; Moffatt v. Niemitz, 102 N.J. Eq. 112; 139 A. 798 (1928); Knapp v. Rochester Dog Protective Assn., 235 A.D. 436; 257 N.Y.S. 356 (1932); Curtis v. Pipeline Corp., 370 S.W.2d 764 (Tex. Civ. App. 1963). *In re* Hawaii Times, 53 B.R.560 (1985).

14. Kaplan v. Block, 183 Va. 327; 31 S.E.2d 893 (1944).

15. City of Floydada v. Gilliam, 111 S.W.2d 761 (Tex. Civ. App. 1937); Bayer v. Beran, 49 N.Y.S.2d 2 (1944); Ohio Rev. Code §1702.31.

16. Calif. Corp. Code §5211 (a)(b) (1980); and n. 7.

17. Mosell Realty Corp. v. Schofield, 183 Va. 782; 33 S.E.2d 774 (1945).

18. Flick v. Jordan, 74 Ind. App. 314; 129 N.E. 42 (1920); Hurley v. Ornsteen, 311 Mass. 477; 42 N.E.2d 273 (1942).

19. Coleman v. Northwestern Mutual Life Ins. Co., 273 Mo. 620; 201 S.W. 544 (1917) (motion for rehearing denied).

20. Comp. Mich. §450.2525; Minn. Stat. Ann §317A.239, Ohio Rev. Code §1702.25; Penna. Stat. 15–5727; Ga. Code Ann. §14-3-704.

21. Lycette v. Green River Gorge Assn., 21 Wash. 2d 589; 153 P.2d 873 (1944).

22. Gashwiler v. Willis, 33 Calif. 11, 19; 91 *Am. Dec.* 607 (1867).

23. For the contrary view *see,* Stevens, *Hornbook on Corporations,* §145 (2d ed. 1949).

24. Saltmarsh v. Spaulding, 147 Mass 224; 17 N.E. 316 (1888); George v. Holstein-Friesian Assn., 238 N.Y. 513, 521; 144 N.E. 776 (1944); N.Y. Not-for-Profit Corp. L §710.

25. Hackler v. International Travelers Assn., 165 S.W. 44 (Tex. Civ App. 1914); Russian Rein-surance Co. v. Stoddard, 211 A.D. 132; 207 N.Y.S. 574 (1925).

26. Calif. Corp. Code §5211 (a) (b) (1980).

27. Ohio Rev. Code §1702.31 (B); Ga. Code Ann. §14-3-820.

28. N.Y. Not-for-Profit Corp. L. §603 (a); Ohio Rev. Code §1702.17 (B).

29. George v. Holstein-Friesian Assn., 238 N.Y. 513, 521; 144 N.E. 776 (1944). Schroder v. Scotten, Dillon Co. 299 A.2d 431 (Del. Ch. 1972).

30. Lorenze Co. v. Penn-Louisiana O & G. Co., 155 La. 749; 99 S. 586 (1924).

31. Wood v. Boney, 21 A. 574 (N.J. 1891); N.Y. Not-for-Profit Corp. L §711 (c).

32. Baker v. Smith, 41 R.I. 17; 102 A. 721; Bayer v. Beran, 49 N.Y.S.2d 2 (1944).

33. Hurley v. Ornsteen, 311 Mass. 477; 42 N.E.2d 273 (1942).

34. Remilling v. Schneider, 185 N.W.2d 493 (No. Dak. 1971); Temple Enterprises, Inc. v. Cowles, 164 Ore. 133, 100 P.2d 613 (1940); Simonson v. Helburn, 198 Misc. 430, 97 N.Y.S.2d 406 (1950); Winters v. Shelton, 357 P.2d 284 (Ore. 1960).

35. Morisette v. Howard, 62 Kan. 463, 63. P. 756 (1901).

36. Lycette v. Green River Gorge Assn., 41 Wash. 2d 859; 153 P.2d 873 (1944).

37. Douglas Development Corp. v. Carillo, 64 N.Y.S.2d 747 (1946).

38. Re Joseph Field & Co., Inc., 38 F. Supp. 506 (D.C. N.J. 1941). *But contra*, condemnation action without a meeting, sustained: Kountz v. Morris, 58 N.J.L. 303; 33 A. 252 (1895); *affd.*, 58 N.J.L. 695; 34 A. 1099 (1896).

39. Mosell Realty Corp. v. Schofield, 183 Va. 782, 33 S.E.2d 774, (1945).

40. Bayer v. Beran, 49 N.Y.S.2d 2 (1944).

41. Scott v. Superior Sunset Oil Co., 144 Calif. 140; 77 P. 817 (1904).

42. Elliot v. Sibley, 101 Ala. 344; 13 S. 500 (1893).

43. Cheney v. Canfield, 158 Calif. 342; 111 P. 92 (1910).

44. Smith v. Mills, 199 Miss. 367; 24 S. 2d 864 (1946).

45. Flynn v. Columbus Club, 21 R.I. 534; 45 A. 551 (1900).

46. Jackson v. Dillehay, 209 Ark. 707; 192 S.W.2d 354 (1946).

47. Johnston v. Livingston Nursing Home, Inc., 211 S.2d 151 (Ala. 1968).

48. Re Allied Fruit and Export Co., Inc., 243 A.D. 52; 276 N.Y.S. 153 (1934).

49. Whipple v. Christie, 122 Minn. 73; 141 N.W. 1107 (1913).

50. Jackson case, n. 46.

51. Morris v. Y. & B. Corp., 198 N.C. 705; 153 S.E. 327 (1930).

52. Ohio Rev. Code §1702.19; N.Y. Not-for-Profit Corp. L. §§708, 711; Ga. Stat. Anno. §14-3-823.

53. *Re* Allied Fruit, n. 48.

54. Forest City Box Co. v. Barney, 14 F.2d 590 (8th Cir. 1926); Ohio Rev. Code §1702.31; Knox v. C.I.R., 323 F.2d 84 (5th Cir. 1963); Cirricione v. Polizzi, 220 N.Y.S.2d 741 (1961).

55. Lycette v. Green River Gorge Assn., 21 Wash. 2d 859; 153 P.2d 873 (1944).

56. Holcombe v. Trenton White City Co., 80 N.J. Ch. 122; 82 A. 618 (1912); Ann. Calif. Corp. Code §5211(a); N.Y. Not-for-Profit Corp. L. §711.

57. Colcord. v. Granzow, 137 Okla. 194; 278 P. 654; 64 *A.L.R.* 699 (1928).

58. *See*, United States v. Interstate R.R., 14 F.2d 328 (D.C. Va. 1926).

59. Calif. Corp. Code §5211 (a) (2) (1980).

60. Osbourne v. Locke Steele Chain Co., 218 A.2d 526 (Conn. 1966); Zachary v. Milin, 294 Mich. 622, 293 N.W. 770 (1940); Ohio Rev. Code §1702.19.

61. N.Y. Not-for-Profit Corp. L. §§711, 708; Lippman v. Kehoe Stenograph Co., 11 Del. Ch. 80, 95 A. 895 (1915); *Union Hosp. Ass'n of Bronx ex rel. Shumofsky v. Carty,* 586 N.Y.S.2d 798 (N.Y.A.D. 1 Dept., 1992) (trustees authorized takeover of one hospital by another).

62. N.Y. N-PCL §108(b).

63. *In re* Argus Co., 138 N.Y. 557; 34 N.E. 388 (1893); Vaught v. Ohio County Fair Co., Ky. L. Rev. 1471; 49 S.W. 426 (1899).

64. Chase v. Tuttle, 55 Conn. 455; 12 A. 874 (1888); Balfour Guthrie Inv. Co. v. Woodworth, 124 Calif. 169; 56 P. 891 (1899); Santa Fe Hills Golf and C. Club v. Safehi Realty Co. 349 S.W.2d 27 (Mo. 1961).

65. Colcord v. Granzow, 137 Okla. 194; 278 P. 654 (1961).

66. Clark v. Oceano Beach Resort Co., 106 Calif. App. 574; 289 P. 946 (1930); N.Y. Not-for-Profit Corp. L. §711 (d).

67. Thompson v. Williams, 76 Calif. 153; 18 P. 153 (1888).

68. Noremac, Inc. v. Centre Hill Court, 178 S.E. 877 (Va. 1935); N.Y. Not-for-Profit Corp. L. §711 (d).

69. See, Harrison v. Welsh, 295 Penna. 501; 145 A. 507 (1929); 1 Williston, *Contracts,* §84 (3d ed. 1957); Ohio Rev. Code §1702.31; (requires notice in writing by personal delivery, mail or telegram).

70. Bank of Little Rock v. McCarthy, 55 Ark. 473; 18 S.W. 759 (1892).

71. Holcombe v. Trenton, 80 N.J. Eq. 122; 82 A. 618 (1912); *affd.,* 82 N.J. Eq. 364; 91 A. 1069 (1913); Lippman v. Kehoe Stenograph Co., 11 Del. Ch. 80; 95 A. 895 (1915).

72. N.Y. Not-for-Profit Corp. L. §711; (waiver by directors sufficient); Chambers v. Sterling Auto M. Co., 163 N.Y.S. 574 (1917); Clark Realty Co. v. Douglas, 46 Nev. 378, 212 P. 466 (1923).

73. *Ibid. In re* Argus Co., 138 N.Y. 557, 558, 34 N.E. 388 (1893); Homan v. Fir. Pdts. Co., 123 Wash. 260; 212 P. 240 (1923).

74. Mercantile Library Hall Co. v. Pittsburgh Library Assn., 173 Penn. 30; 33 A, 744 (1896).

75. O'Rourke v. Grand Opera House Co., 47 Mont. 459; 133 P. 965 (1913).

76. Hackler v. International Travelers Assn., 165 S.W. 44 (Tex. Civ. App. 1914); Ohio Rev. Code §1702.32; N.Y. Not-for-Profit Corp. L. §711 (a); (notice not required when time and place in bylaws).

77. Bell v. Standard Quicksilver Co., 146 Calif. 699; 81 P. 17 (1905).

78. United Growers Co. v. Eisner, 22 A.D. 1, 47 N.Y.S. 906 (1897).

79. Sargent v. Webster, 13 Metc. (Mass.) 497, 46 *Am. Dec.* 743 (1847); Ohio Rev. Code §1702.32; N.Y. Not-for-Profit Corp. L. §707; Matter of Rye Psych. Hosp., 488 N.E.2d 63 (N.Y. 1985).

80. *See* n. 79; Leavitt v. Oxford and Geneva S.M. Co., 3 Utah 265; 1 P. 356 (1883); Parucki v. Polish National Catholic Church, 114 Misc. 6; 186 N.Y.S. 702 (1920); *In re Hawaii Times,* 53 B.R. 560 (1985).

81. *In re* McGovern, 180 Misc. 508; 44 N.Y.S.2d 132, 137 (1943); N.Y. Not-for-Profit Corp. L. §707. But a majority of the trustees in office constitutes a *quorum* for filling a vacancy in the board. Ohio Rev. Code §1702.32.

82. Calif. Corp. Code §5211 (a) (7) (1980); Rev. Model NPCL §8.24 (1986 Draft).

83. Kaplan v. Block, 183 Va. 327; 31 S.E.2d 893 (1944); N.Y. Not-for-Profit Corp. L. §708(d); Minn. Stat. Ann. 317A.235.

84. Crowley v. Commodity Exchange, Inc., 141 F.2d 182 (2d Cir. 1944); Reed v. National Order of D. of I., 95 Misc. 695; 160 N.Y.S. 907 (1916); *affd.* 177 A.D. 949; 164 N.Y.S. 1110 (1917); 222 N.Y. 529; 118 N.E. 1075 (1917), but *cf.,* N.Y. Not-for-Profit Corp. L. §708; Ohio Rev. Code §1702.32.

85. Coombs v. Harford, 99, Me. 426; 59 A. 529 (1904).

86. Not less than one-third. Comp. L. Mich. §450.2523; N.Y. Not-for-Profit Corp. L. §707, greater number than majority may be required for voting: Ohio Rev. Code §1702.32; two directors: Calif. Corp. Code §5211 (a) (7) (1980).

87. See n. 86; Benintendi v. Kenton Hotel, Inc., 294 N.Y. 112, 60 N.E.2d 829 (1945). See for statutes of all states as to business corporation voting rules, and for "control agreements" as to voting, 3 Oleck, *Modern Corporation Law*, c. 57, 58 (1978 supp.); analogies may be drawn for nonprofit organizations.

88. Wohl v. Avon Elec. Supp., Inc., 55 N.Y.S.2d 252 (1945); Olincy v. Merle Norman Cosmetics, Inc., 19 Calif. Rptr. 387 (Calif. App. 1962).

89. *In re* Lake Placid Co., 274 A.D. 205; 81 N.Y.S.2d 36 (1948).

90. Opinions N.Y. Atty. Gen. (Dec. 14, 1948).

91. Zachary v. Milin, 294 Mich. 622; 293 N.W. 770 (1940).

92. Dillon v. Berg. 326 F. Supp. 1214 (D.C. Del. 1971).

93. Belle Isle Corp. v. MacBean, 49 A. 2d 5 (Del. 1946); noted, 45 *Mich. L. Rev.* 630 (1947).

94. Castle v. Lewis, 78 N.Y. 13 (1879); *In re* Hellborn-Hamburger, Inc., 128 N.Y.L.J. 249 col. 2 (Aug. 14, 1952); *but see* n. 80. After one resignation, three-fifths of a six-man board was not deemed valid. Continental TV Corp. v. Caster, 191 N.E.2d 607 (Ill. App. 1963); N.Y. N-PCL §705.

95. Crump v. Bronson, 168 Va. 527; 191 S.E. 663 (1937); Hein v. Gravelle Farmers Elevator Corp., 164 Wash. 309; 2 P.2d 741 (1931); Holcomb v. Forsythe, 210 Ala. 484; 113 S. 516 (1927). See n. 104, 105.

96. Belle Isle case, n. 93; Parucki v. Polish National Catholic Church, 114 Misc. 6, 186 N.Y.S. 702 (1920); Currie v. Matson, 33 F. Supp. 454 (D.C. La. 1940).

97. *In re* Gulla, 13 Del. Ch. 23, 115 A. 317 (1921), related case, 13 Del. Ch. 1, 114 A. 596 (1921).

98. N.Y. Not-for-Profit Corp. L. §708 (d).

99. Duffy v. Loft, Inc., 17 Del. Ch. 376; 152 A. 849 (1930); Commissioner v. Vandegrift, 232 Penna. St. 53; 81 A. 153 (1911).

100. *Matter of Gearing v. Kelly*, 11 N.Y.2d 201, 182 N.E.2d 391 (1962). *Cf., Tomlinson v. Loew's, Inc.*, 36 DE Ch. 516, 134 A.2d 518 (1957), rearg. den. 37 DE Ch. 8, 135 A.2d 136 (1957) where minority directors argued that they were protecting the shareholders' right to elect.

101. *New York Business Corporate Law §608(c), (d)*; CA Corp. Code §9211(a)(8); N.Y.N.P.C. Law §708(d). See below.

102. *Lehigh Presbytery v. Merchants Bancorp, Inc.*, 600 A.2d 593 (Pa. Super, 1991).

103. Gulla case, n. 97; Vandegrift case, n. 99.

104. *See* cases in n. 95; *but see*, N.Y. Not-for-Profit Corp. L §715(c); Calif. Corp. Code §5227 (1980) and Comp. L. Mich. § 450.1545a.

105. *Ibid.* N.Y. and Calif., and Mich.

106. N.Y. Not-for-Profit Corp. L. §715.

107. *Ibid.*, Comp. L. Mich. §450.1545(a).

108. Piccard v. Sperry Corp., 48 F. Supp. 465 (D.C.N.Y.); *affd.*, 152 F.2d 462 (2d Cir. 1946); *cert. den.*, 328 U.S. 845, 66 S. Ct. 1024 (1946).

109. Knapp v. Rochester Dog Protective Assn., 235 A.D. 436; 257 N.Y.S. 356 (1932); but *c.f.*, Calif. code §5227 (1980).

110. Piccard case, n. 108.

111. Benson v. Keller, 37 Ore. 120, 132, 60 P. 918 (1900).

112. Barkin Constr. Co. v. Goodman, 221 N.Y. 156; 116 N.E. 770 (1917).

113. Herring-Curtis Co. v. Curtiss, 120 Misc. 733; 200 N.Y.S. 7 (1923); Ohio Rev. Code §1702.55 (c); N.Y. Not-for-Profit Corp. L. §719 (b).

114. *See* n. 113.

115. Butts v. Gaylord State Bank, 156 Misc. 552; 282 N.Y.S. 1 (1935). But failure to take minutes does not affect corporate existence. Gale-Hasslacher Corp. v. Carmen Contracting Corp., 219 N.Y.S.2d 212 (1961).

116. *See* n. 115.

117. Ohio Rev. Code §1702.24; Staats v. Biograph Co., 236 F. 454 (2d Cir. 1916). As to conflicts of interest, and voidability of decisions, *see*, Annot. 33 A.L.R. 2d 1060, 1064 (1954).

118. Selama-Dindings Plantations, Ltd. v. Durham, 216 F. Supp. 104 (D.C., Ohio 1963); *contra*: Jacobson v. Moskowitz, 261 N.E.2d 613 (N.Y. 1970); *see also*, Burt v. Irvine Co., 36 Calif. Rptr. 270 (App., 1964) sustaining objection to director bringing a stenographer and attorney.

31

COMMITTEES

§322. IMPORTANCE OF COMMITTEES

Detailed statutory provisions as to corporation committees are now found in the statutes of almost every state. Florida's statute [§607.0825] is typical in being quite lengthy and precise in delineating the proper powers and limitations of various kinds of business corporation committees. Florida's nonprofit corporation statute [§617.0825] is even more detailed. So is the 1986 statute in the Revised Model Nonprofit Corporations Act [§8.25]. All three of these statutes place the power to appoint committees in the board of directors, unless the articles or bylaws provide otherwise, but expressly limit the authority of a committee as to certain actions.[1]

A *committee* is a person or a group of persons elected or appointed to consider, investigate, and sometimes to act upon, a matter or category of business activities that is referred to it.[2] Committees may be created by the bylaws, or by resolutions, of the directors or members, or by designation by the president. A *subcommittee* is a division of a committee, charged by the latter with consideration or determination of a part of the latter's functions.[3]

Usually a group, rather than one person, is appointed as a committee. If a single person is appointed, he is called a *committee of one.*

Committees do much of the most important work of nonprofit organizations. Far more than in business organizations, the work of nonprofit organizations is done by true cooperation among the members.

The nature of committees often is misunderstood. The fact that committee findings and decisions are usually accepted and followed tends to create a mistaken impression.

The committee fundamentally is an administrative, not an executive device. It is a technique for research or supervision. It is not essentially a repository of executive powers—though it often has such power. The committee ordinarily is an *assistance* to the executive officers. It is not itself the executive.

Nevertheless, actual management or decision of a matter may be entrusted to a committee. Not long ago,[4] a committee that had autonomy (*e.g.*, a welfare fund or grievance committee for several branches of the organization) was allowed to be sued *as an entity*, under its own name. Delegation of any authority of the trustees, to an *executive committee,* for example, is specifically permitted by statute in many states.[5] Usually statutes permit the bylaws to provide for committees and their authority.[6]

In most cases, a committee is a group of members or trustees, appointed by the chief executive officers *to study and make recommendations* about a particular matter.

§323. DELEGATION OF AUTHORITY TO A COMMITTEE OR AGENT

The power of the board of directors, and of officers, to delegate their administrative (ministerial) authority, is touched on in the foregoing chapters. But the procedural constraints that apply to the board itself, such as in an action without meetings, notice and waiver, *quorum, etcetera,* apply also to the committee appointed by the board.[7]

In general, there is an inherent power, in the board and in officers, to delegate to committees the performance of administrative (ministerial) acts.[8] This means the study of any matter, or even the management of routine matters.[9] Management of the organization's routine affairs may be entrusted to a committee, as well as to an officer or agent.[10]

Even the doing of such important executive acts as the making of contracts or leases may be delegated to a committee.[11]

Power to delegate authority is not clearly defined in most nonprofit corporation statutes, except as to the executive committee (see Section 325).

Although the power to delegate *administrative* duties is clear, the power to delegate *discretionary* (executive) duties or powers is not so simple. The board of directors may not freely give away the discretionary power inherent in it.[12]

But the power to delegate even discretionary authority is an inherent power of the directors and officers. How far it extends depends on the necessity for the delegation.[13]

Certain powers may not be delegated at all. Statutes, the charter, and the bylaws may (and do) confer certain powers expressly (or by implication) on specific officers or on the board.[14] The board of directors, for example, may not completely turn over to others the power to exercise the authority of the board.[15] The appointment of even an *executive committee* must not amount to an abandonment of the board powers to that committee.[16]

Continued responsibility of the delegating authority. When the board, or the officers, delegate authority to committees or agents, they continue to be responsible for the proper exercise of this authority.[17] They must maintain a general supervision over the exercise of the powers that they have delegated.[18] If they negligently permit the delegate to abuse the delegated powers, they may be liable for the consequences of that abuse.[19]

Division or delegation of duties or powers to committees or subgroups, by whatever name or title given to such group, is a kind of committee assignment. Thus, a nonprofit corporation, organized to establish a community college, sought to *force* a higher education *board* to establish a junior college *district* in their area, through a writ of mandamus. Full relief was granted when the trial court issued a writ ordering the board to consider the proposal. It is not proper for the trial court to push the manner or method of review to be used, in a writ of mandamus.[20]

§324. APPOINTMENT OF COMMITTEES

Fundamentally, the power to delegate authority springs from the board of directors. The board often vests this power (the power to appoint committees or agents) in the president. Often the charter or bylaws give express powers of this kind to the president or to other officers. But the power continues to reside in the board. Any such power not expressly placed elsewhere by the charter and bylaws, or by statutes, lies in the board.[21]

The power of the board to delegate authority is most dramatically expressed by the appointment of an *executive committee*. Statutes in many states now expressly recognize this power; but they often require that it be stated in the bylaws.[22] But with or without such statutes, the appointment of even such a powerful committee is valid.[23]

Use resolutions for appointments. Although valid oral appointments of committees and committee members often are made, it is better to keep written records of such appointments—at least in the minutes.

Carefully drafted resolutions are advisable. They prevent later disputes and recriminations. Most important, they clarify one crucial issue: the appointment may have *the effect of a contract*. If no clear record is available, the difficulties that may arise are easy to imagine.[24]

State the purpose and powers clearly. Once it is decided to appoint a committee, it is important to delineate its functions and powers. Often it is wise to state also the limitations on its powers. Overlapping authority of committees is a frequent source of friction.

In organizations having wide geographic distributions of members, it is practically essential that written instructions be distributed to committee members. In other cases, clear descriptions should be given in the minutes.

Let it function. The responsibility to see that a committee does not abuse its powers does not justify meddling or interfering with its work. Board members sometimes harass a committee by such interference.

One good way to prevent both abuse and interference is this: Make the president or chairman of the board a member *ex officio* of every committee. This has a salutary effect.

Warnings:

1. Do not form committees merely to distribute titles or flatter members. The glamour soon wears off and skepticism develops.

2. Do not form committees merely for publicity purposes. The members ultimately will resent such deception.

3. Do not form committees merely to muzzle obstreperous members. This only gives them added material and vehicles for blocking action.

4. Do not form committees merely to bury unpleasant issues. Such issues always seem to arise again. It is better to try to solve them at once.

§325. TYPES OF COMMITTEES

In most organizations, committees are of three general types:

1. *Standing committees* carry on continuing functions. Usually they attend to regular administration of internal affairs. They include the executive committee, finance committee, budget committee, membership committee, grievance committee, standardization committee (*e.g.*, in trade associations), sometimes an ethics committee (*e.g.*, in professional associations), and an audit committee in larger organizations.

2. *Administrative committees* closely resemble the standing committees but are concerned only with administrative matters. They are useful mostly in larger organizations. In practice they often amount to subcommittees to assist the standing committees. Often they are made necessary by the size or unwieldiness of a large board of directors. They may be appointed, for example, to deal with special phases of executive committee work, or to aid the finance, budget, membership, and other committees. A clubhouse or building committee is a typical administrative committee; or a compensation or investment committee.

3. *Special committees* are formed as problems arise. Often they are temporary and may be called *temporary* or *project* committees. The matters with which they are concerned may range from special aspects of administration to special services and research, and safety or public interest.

Special committees should be appointed only when necessary. (The question of need for committees sometimes brings the appointment of a *committee on committees*.) Typical special committees are a nominating committee and a committee to arrange a particular social affair.

For descriptions of various types of committees, and provisions for them, see Chapter 6 (Unincorporated Associations and Bylaws) and Chapter 23 (Bylaws).

Note that in the absence of statutory provision, delegation of authority (especially discretionary power) is strictly construed in most decisions,[25] often being viewed as improper abdication of duties of the board of directors.[26]

§326. COMMITTEES TO MONITOR CORPORATE ACTIVITIES

It has been suggested that the same principles utilized in business organizations for evaluating the performance of profit corporation managers and staff be used for nonprofit corporations.[27] Of course, the nonprofit corporation often cannot be divided into clear-cut segments or centers as is traditionally done in business corporation analysis. However, those who advocate emulation of business practices also advocate the employment of analytical techniques for determining each corporation segment's ability to deliver services at the lowest cost.[28] To monitor such a program, committees may be established, each one to review the performance of a particular aspect or segment to make sure that it is cost efficient with respect to the services it is delivering. If it is not efficient, then the committee should recommend a course of change, even to recommending that the jobs of the employees, or the service, be terminated. In the case of a "public interest" supervision committee, toleration of cost usually should be reasonably practical. Cost alone is not a sufficient measure for evaluating the service rendered by a part of, or an entire, nonprofit corporation. If the aforementioned approach should be widely adopted, there would be the prospect that many areas of charitable endeavor would be abandoned for the sake of cost efficiency.

§327. EXECUTIVE COMMITTEE

Use of *executive committees* by nonprofit as well as by business organizations now is widespread.[29] Delegation of managerial authority is also often made to officers,[30] or even at times to persons having no affiliation with the organization.[31]

In nonprofit organizations, delegation of such power may not be given to outsiders; indeed, statutes today often require that the members of the executive committee must be trustees.[32] The California statute that permits power concentration (by contract) in a person or persons even *outside* the corporation,[33] is a contradiction of the concept of altruistic or voluntaristic status.

The power of the board of directors or trustees to appoint an executive committee is an inherent power.[34] So, generally, is the power to delegate authority to officers and agents as well.[35]

The executive committee is a kind of sub-board of directors, and normally should act as a unified or collective group. Yet, lack of a formal meeting does not invalidate its actions, if the members later agree in writing to a decision reached without a meeting.[36]

In general, the executive committee is subject to the same rules that apply to the trustees or directors.[37]

For full treatment of the executive committee, see, *Role and Responsibilities of Executive Committees* (1969), published by International Publications Service. It is a product of Central Institute of Research and Training in Public Cooperation (ed.).

Complete abdication of the board by transfer of its power to the executive committee is improper.[38] Thus, surrender of board powers to a management company for 20 years was held to be against public policy.[39] Yet, a five-year grant of complete authority over editorial policy, to an editor of a newspaper, was held to be valid.[40]

It has been held that where it was the custom of the executive committee to meet informally, the corporation was estopped from questioning the lack of formality.[41]

Ordinarily, the charter or bylaws (usually the bylaws) may (and do) set forth the power to appoint an executive committee, and the rules regarding exercise of this power.[42] Some statutes (*e.g.*, New York) state that the articles or bylaws *may* provide for an executive committee.[43] Others, (*e.g.*, Ohio) state that directors may appoint an executive committee *unless* the articles provide otherwise.[44] Minnesota's new statute provides that committees may be formed by a resolution approved by a majority of the board.[45]

An executive committee usually is empowered to exercise all of the power of the board of directors at times when the board is not in session. It executes the policy of the board in routine affairs during intervals between board meetings. Almost invariably it consists of a number of the directors themselves, or of a combination of directors and officers. It must follow the general directions of the board.[46]

The executive committee may manage the routine affairs of the corporation, but it may not take extraordinary or drastic action, such as liquidating the organization, on its own discretion.[47] Also, it ordinarily may not run corporate affairs for an unduly long period without meetings or decisions by the board itself.[48] In fact, the authorization for the appointment of an executive committee (the bylaw, charter provision, or resolution) is invalid if it fails to set reasonable limits on the authority of the committee.[49]

This committee, like all committees, must act by a *quorum*, and by majority vote, unless other provisions are expressly made.[50] It may not delegate its powers—not even to one of its own members.[51]

Calling a meeting of the board of directors suspends the power of the executive committee to act until after the meeting of the board.[52]

If an executive committee deals with third persons, the usual rules of express, implied, and apparent authority of agents apply.[53] If, for example, the corporation impliedly ratifies the unauthorized act of the committee, by accepting its benefits, the corporation will be estopped from later denying the committee's authority to perform that act.[54]

The committee may validly act only within the limits of its real purpose— interim supervision. Thus, it may not change the officers or their salaries, amend bylaws, or expel or change committee members.[55] But if the power to fix salaries, or some other such routine discretionary power, is given to the committee by the board, it may validly exercise such a power.[56]

It should be clear that the functions and powers of an executive committee depend on the charter and bylaw provisions, on statutory limitations that require action by directors themselves in certain matters, and on the purpose for which the committee was established. Its powers largely are those implied in, or necessary to, the purpose for which it was formed, as declared in the bylaw or resolution for its formation.[57] Attempts of executive committees to usurp control, and to exclude some of the board members from this control, are uniformly condemned.[58]

Oblique and indirect attempts to usurp control also should be condemned. Appointment of relatives is a common abuse of power, and appointment of relatives of powerful officers to executive committees was carefully scrutinized by a New York court.[59]

"Control agreements" and executive committees. Attempts by a few members to fasten their personal control onto a nonprofit corporation often revolve about the executive committee.

In business corporations, perpetuation of control can be accompanied by stockholders' and pre-incorporators' agreements, voting trusts, and other devices.[60] But in nonprofit corporations, the executive committee often is deemed to be the best device. Control by *investors*, for their protection, is discussed elsewhere herein (*e.g.*, under the New York and California *nonprofit business* corporation statutes).

Attempts to control are, of course, contrary to the purpose of nonprofit organizations in society, and are difficult to accomplish if any organized resistance is offered.

When the incorporators draft the charter and bylaws to suit themselves, and elect themselves to the board of directors and to the executive committee, they can grasp control. But the next elections may oust them. And the members can at any time amend the bylaws or even the charter. Attempts to enforce discriminatory, or control-purpose rules cannot overcome a vigorous defense of members' rights.

The very presence of oligarchic rules in the charter or bylaws may defeat their own purpose. Few members may join or long remain in an organization after they discover such rules.

Control of dual power groups. A common device for gaining or holding control of charitable corporations (*i.e.*, schools or hospitals) is use of dual power control groups.

Thus, a school or hospital often needs no membership, under modern statutes, other than the board of trustees. The board, in such organizations, literally holds the corporation's property in trust for corporate purposes.

By forming a nonprofit corporation with a few members, plus a board of trustees, most of whom are not members, two power groups are created. They tend to neutralize each other, both often performing their duties perfunctorily.

The "managers" provide for granting of control power to themselves as officers, usually placing themselves in the members group. If they are trustees they often cannot get any salaries or compensation.[61]

Often the "managers" have themselves appointed as the *executive committee*, by the trustees, who are grateful for the honor of being appointed as trustees of a public service organization.

Where statutes require members of the executive committee to be trustees, as many do,[62] the title of *administrative committee*, or the like, is employed. Or, the bylaws simply grant wide powers to the officers (the "managers").

The trustees then are subordinated to the members, who have final amendment powers. Meanwhile, the members are kept content with jobs in administration, and salaries, or with other favors from the organization's managers. Trustees' and members' meetings are called as seldom as possible.

The officers or administrative committee often run such an organization well, in practice. But the evasion of the principle of control of operations by a disinterested board is unhealthy.

Probably, in such a device, the members could be deemed to be a class of trustees, and thus not entitled to compensation, as above noted, in case of challenge of the managerial group. Such challenges are surprisingly seldom offered.

This device is typical of the "proprietary mentality" in nonprofit organizations.[63] A determined board of trustees, of course, can upset such a plan by exercising its statutory powers. So, too, the members can upset it by amending the articles or bylaws.

Such seizure of power, of course, may lead to the destruction of the organization. Sometimes, individual lethargy or self-interest allows the aggressive managerial group to remain in power indefinitely.

In order to minimize the possibility of the executive committee usurping the board of directors' power and control, the following rules should be observed in setting up the committee:

1. Spell out the committee's powers when creating it.

2. Require that certain designated actions of the committee be approved by the board of directors before implementation.

3. Require keeping of minutes of the executive committee at each of its meetings, and have them reviewed promptly by the board of directors.

4. Control the executive committee's membership and actions by establishing maximum periods and rules of membership.[64]

5. Keep the committee's term of office short.

§328. COMMITTEE PERSONNEL

It is good policy to decide in advance the size, makeup, kind of personnel, functions, and other aspects of each important committee.

Size of committees. Experienced association and corporation experts affirm that most committees should be small and compact. Practical experience conflicts with the recurrent impulse to assign many members to each committee, in the hope that there will be strength in numbers. Appointing officers sometimes try to assign every member to some committee, in order to give every member something to do. This theory seldom works out successfully in practice.

It is a sad truism that few men are leaders and doers. Most people are not self-starters. They prefer to let somebody else do the work, while they sit back and offer occasional criticism. In committee work, the presence of many members often is a hindrance rather than a help.

One answer to the problem is the use of one major committee, plus a number of specialized subcommittees. This system seems to work fairly well, but it requires much organization work at the top, and multiplies time-wasting formalities.

For most purposes a committee of three, five, or at most seven members seems to be most effective.

Florida's new NPC statute, effective July 1, 1991, states that "Each committee of directors must have two or more members. . . ." Thus, a "one-man committee" would be improper in Florida.[65]

Personnel. Tact and consideration are essential in selecting the personnel for various committees. Knowledge of the characteristics and habits of the members is crucial. Some people work well in teams, while others simply cannot work in harness with others. The *prima donna* type will be happy only in the spotlight; other members may work hard and shun applause. But all members should be assumed to enjoy attention and applause, until they clearly indicate the contrary.

Special knowledge, experience, or contacts of any member should be carefully considered. Almost everyone likes to do what he understands, and dislikes trying to do something that is strange or difficult for him.

The amount of time that a member can and will devote to committee work should be periodically checked. A simple questionnaire is desirable for this purpose.

Chain of command. The bylaws or administrative regulations should set up a practical system for committee work, cooperation, supervision, and reports.

If there are grades or levels of authority or function, these should be made clear in advance. Otherwise conflicts and frictions are bound to develop. The plan should specify to whom reports are to be made, when, and by whom.

Interference with a committee's proper powers, functions, and independence should be prevented. This is one of the duties of the president or chairman of the board.

Committee chairmen. Everything that has been said about selecting committeemen applies especially to selecting the committee chairman. The chairman usually makes or breaks his committee.

Qualifications and leadership should be the primary criteria for selection of committee chairmen. Political favoritism should be avoided. Meritorious past performance counts, but the necessities of the position should guide the selection.

The authority of the chairman must be supported by the appointing authority, lest the committee run the chairman.

§329. COMMITTEE MEETINGS AND REPORTS

See Chapters 24 and 27 on meetings, generally, and forms for meetings, and Chapter 25 on voting.

Preparation is the simple secret of successful committee meetings. If a meeting is held after proper study of the problems involved, with a comprehensive agenda, and with necessary data and documents at hand, effective work and decision usually will follow.

Committee meetings usually are conducted with little formality.

Time and place. Committee meetings can often be held just before or just after a general meeting. Otherwise, a regular schedule of meetings is advisable. The time and place of every meeting should be suited to the committee members' convenience and preferences, subject to the requirements of the committee's work.

Choice of a good place for the meeting is important. Many organizations favor dinner meetings, at which the committee work follows a pleasant and fraternal repast. Use of the organization's quarters for meetings of committees should be encouraged.

Written advance notice should usually be given.

Expenses. Insofar as the organization can afford to foot the bills for committee work, it is good policy to do so. Most committeemen do not relish paying to do committee work. Whenever possible the organization should pay at least travel and other out-of-pocket expenses.

Reports. Brevity is the best quality in a report. Nothing is more tedious than a long-winded committee report.

The elements of a committee report are:

1. Reason for appointment of the committee.

2. Basic problems involved.

3. Summary of study or action.

4. Conclusions or recommendations.

Thanks and expressions of appreciation *always* should be extended to the committee members by the appointing authority. It is most impolite and unwise to take such work for granted. Lack of appreciation has a deadly dampening effect on the enthusiasm of committee members.

Publication to the general membership of a summary of the report often is both useful and impressive.

FORM NO. 151

Executive Committee Report (and Meeting Agenda)

[This form was written by the author, in his capacity as President of a state association of schools, and as a member *ex officio* of the Executive Committee of that association. It served as the Committee Report *and* as the Agenda for the organization's executive meeting to adopt, reject, or change the decisions of the committee.]

April . . . , 19. .   H............................ L.O........................

....School

                                        of .... College
                                        .... Street
                                        ....
LEAGUE OF . . . . SCHOOLS

Executive Committee
REPORT—AGENDA
for the
SPRING MEETING, 19 . .

(S. . . . . . .Hotel, A. . . . . . , May 16; 9:30 a.m.)

FROM: H . . . . . . L. O . . . . . . , President, for the Executive Com-
                   mittee (M . . . . . . C . . . . . . , Secy.-Treas.; C. . . . . . F
                   . . . . . . , R . . . . . . H . . . . . . , O . . . . . . S . . . . . .).
TO: Deans of all . . . . . schools, and for Members of Faculties
                   of all . . . . Schools.
FOREWORD: In past years, each outgoing League President customarily
                   has delivered a "President's Address" at the annual spring
                   meeting. This year, instead of such an address, the Presi-
                   dent submits this Report to all member schools, in
                   advance of the meeting and for use thereat.
                   This report also is intended to serve as the Agenda for the
                   Spring 19 . . General Meeting. It incorporates suggestions
                   made by the members of the Executive Committee, and is
                   the Report of the Executive Committee. Hopefully, it
                   should expedite the conduct of the business of the meet-
                   ing. Suggested motions are included.
WELCOMES: To visitors attending the meeting (*e.g.*, members of . . . . . .
                   Committee on . . . . . . Education, and others attending).
AGENDA   1. Acceptance or correction of minutes of the previous
ITEM   meeting. Minutes were distributed to all Deans some time
                      ago. Secretary moves that the minutes of the May 19 . .
                      meeting be approved.
AGENDA   2. Reports of officers: (a)   This Report-Agenda;
ITEM   (b)   Treasurer's Report.
                                                    M . . . . . . C . . . . . . (. . .)
                   Outline Committee Report.
AGENDA   3. M . . . . . . C . . . . . . (. . .)
ITEM   Report of League's Liaison Representative to the Special
AGENDA   4. Committee of the . . . .
ITEM   R . . . . . . B . . . . . . (. . .)
                      Report of the League's Representative (member ex offi-
                      cio)
AGENDA   5. on the . . . . . . Judicial Council.

ITEM   C . . . . . F . . . . . . (. . .)
                                            Report of League's Liaison Representative to . . . . . .

AGENDA   6. . . . . . . Ethics Committee.

ITEM   J . . . . . . S . . . . . . (. . . . . .)

AGENDA   Old business.

ITEM   7.

AGENDA   New business.

ITEM   8.

. . . . . . SEMINARS

AGENDA
ITEM
9.

The Executive Committee recommends that the Spring . . . . . . Seminar be moved to the Fall. Inclement weather in March is the motivating reason for this suggested change. It is the Committee's belief that the work session should be held on the Saturday of the Joint Meeting of the . . . . . . and the . . . . . . Examiners. While this change may dictate the necessity of having the Spring Meeting in . . . . . . , the Committee believes that the Fall is more desirable and that a day which brings the Deans to . . . . . . for other business is a suitable day for the Faculties to hold their work sessions.

Motion that the League . . . . . . Seminars be held in the Fall, in conjunction with the Joint Conference with the . . . . . . Examiners.

PLANNING OF PROFESSIONAL CONFERENCES, ETC.

The Executive Committee recommends generally to the new officers and Executive Committee that plans be made and executed, aimed at carrying forward the new emphasis of the League on professional and cooperative functions of the League.

In this connection, thanks are due to participants, for the fine March 19 . . . . Seminars, directed by J . . . . . . S . . . . . . (. . .), W . . . . . . G . . . . . . (. . . . .), and J . . . . . . S . . . . . . (. . . . .) and delivered by Messrs. H . . . . . . (. . . . .), S . . . . . . (. . . . .), B . . . . . . and G . . . . . . (. . . . .), K . . . . . . (. . . . .), S . . . . . . (. . . . . .), S . . . . . . (. . . . .), S . . . . . . (. . . . . .), M . . . . . . (. . . . . .), and S . . . . . . (. . . . .).

LEAGUE RELATIONS WITH THE . . . . . .

AGENDA
ITEM
10. As directed by the League's May 19 . . Meeting, a Committee on League Relations with the . . . . . . was appointed, consisting of S . . . . . . H . . . . . . (. . . .), Chairman, R . . . . . . K . . . . . . (. . .), and J . . . . . . M . . . . . . (. . . .). The committee was asked by the President to develop the facts

surrounding the institution of and the operation of the
. . . . . . Institute. The committee rendered a report to the
executive Committee in October. . . . Motion by . . . . . . ,
duly seconded, was adopted: Motion that the findings of
the Executive Committee be approved, and that the
League suggest that all . . . . . . schools interested in participation in the . . . . . . , communicate directly with the
latter.

. . . . . . EVIDENCE STANDARDS

AGENDA ITEM
11. In connection with a case concerning admission of
. . . . . . dropped by other . . . . . . schools, the Executive
Committee contemplated a possible revision of Article
VIII, Section 10, of the Constitution, to provide more precise Standards as to what constitutes proper investigation
by the admitting school in such cases. A member of the
Faculty of a . . . . . . school, appointed to study this matter,
as a committee of one, did not deliver a report.
In view of the change in League emphasis, away from
"watch dog" functions, the Executive Committee suggests
that study of such revision be made by the new Executive
Committee if the League so desires.
Motion that the Executive Committee be instructed to
study possible revision and greater detailing of Art. VIII,
Sec. 10, of the Constitution.

. . . . . . SCHOOL ENROLLMENT INCREASE

AGENDA ITEM
12. Increasing enrollment in . . . . . . schools is occurring now
and probably will continue. This imposes greater burdens
on . . . . . . schools, and requires greater support of . . . . . .
schools.
Motion that the new President be instructed to communicate to all . . . . . . School, University, or other chief administrative officers the view of the League that a decided
increase in support of their . . . . . . schools is vitally necessary.

AGENDA ITEM
13. Assessment for 19 . . Secretary moves that each member
school be assessed $. . . . dues for 19 . .

NOMINATING COMMITTEE

AGENDA ITEM
14. Nominations by Nominating Committee consisting of
M . . . . . . D . . . . . . (. . . .), Chairman, and J . . . . . . S
. . . . . . (. . . .), for President, Secretary-Treasurer, and one
member of the Executive Committee (three-year term).

AGENDA ITEM
15. Introduction of new President; turnover of the rostrum to
him.

[*NOTE*: Files of the outgoing President will be turned over at once to the new President.]

Remarks

The executive Committee congratulates the . . . . . . school and its parent college on the reaffiliation that has, among other things, changed the name of this member law school to ". . . . . School of . . . . College."

The Executive Committee congratulates . . . . . . University . . . . . . School on the breaking of ground for the construction of the new building that will be its new home when completed.

The Executive Committee strongly urges the new officers and Executive Committee to be bold and energetic in implementing the clearly expressed desire of member schools for more and better cooperation and activities aimed at making the League of . . . . . . Schools above all a fine Society of professional . . . . . . educators, as well as an association of . . . . . . education institutions.

The Executive Committee suggests to the new Officers and new Executive Committee that a carefully planned program of support and "propaganda" on behalf of . . . . . . schools (vis-a-vis university administrators and others) is a legitimate and desirable part of the functions of the League.

POINTS TO REMEMBER

- Committees are the basic apparatus for nonprofit organization work.
- Delegation of functions to committees is both legal and useful.
- Do not delegate discretionary powers to bind the organization, except with precise limitation.
- Delegate administrative work freely.
- Delegate decision-making power very cautiously.
- Continue to supervise the execution of delegated authority.
- Use written resolutions for committee appointments. State purposes, powers, and limitations.
- Do not use committees as a political device.
- Distinguish among the different types of committees.
- Use an executive committee if necessary. Do not use it if it is not necessary.
- Set up precise rules for this committee.
- Do not try to use it as a control device.
- Choose committee personnel with care.
- Set up a plan for committee work and cooperation.
- Keep committee reports brief.
- Thank committees for work done.

NOTES TO CHAPTER 31

1. Clarke Memorial College v. Monaghan Land Co., 257 A.2d 234 (Del. Ch. 1969); and *see*, McMullen, *Committees of the Board of Directors*, 29 Bus. Law 755 (1974); Henn and Alexander, *Corporations* §212 (3rd ed., 1983); 2 Oleck, *Modern Corporation Law* §958 (1978 supp.).

2. Oleck & Green, *Parliamentary Law and Practice for Nonprofit Organizations*, c. 12 (Amer. Law Inst.-Amer. Bar Assn. Joint Comm. 2d ed., 1991); Schulte v. Ideal Food Pdt. Co., 208 Iowa 767, 226 N.W. 174 (1929); *and see* Keesey, *Modern Parliamentary Procedure* 113 (1974); Robert, *Rules of Order Newly Revised* (1970); Sturgis, *Standard Parliamentary Procedure* 175 (2d ed. 1966).

3. Barenblatt v. United States, 100 U.S. App. D.C. 13, 240 F.2d 875, 878. (D.C. Cir. 1957).

4. Marsh v. General Grievance Committee, 1 Ohio St.2d 165, 205 N.E.2d 571 (1965). *See generally*, 92. A.L.R.2d 499.

5. Ohio Rev. Code §1702.33.

6. *Ibid.*, §1702.11(A)(8). *See also*, Grange, *Corporation Law for Officers and Directors*, c. 35 (1940); Prentice-Hall, *Directors' and Officers' Ency. Manual*, 103 (1955).

7. Rev. Model NPC Act §8.25(c) [1986 Draft.]; and *see*, Kolb, *Delegations of Authority to Committees, 9 U. of Baltimore L. Rev. 189 (1980).*

8. *See*, Schulte v. Ideal Food Pdts. Co., 208 Iowa 767; 226 N.W. 174 (1929); Calif. Corp. Code §5212 (1980).

9. *See*, n.8.*See*, Note, *The Executive Committee in Corporate Organization—Scope of Powers*, 42 Mich. L. Rev. 133 (1943).

10. *See*, n.8 and 9, Wallace v. International Trade Exhibition, Inc., 170 La. 55, 127 S. 362 (1930).

11. Holwick v. Walker, 6 Calif. App.2d 669; 45 P.2d 374 (1935).

12. *See* cc. 27, 28.

13. Social Security Board v. Warren, 142 F.2d 974 (8th Cir. 1944). But a grant of powers may be implied as well as expressed. Hahnemann Hospital v. Golo Slipper Co., 135 Penna. Super. 395, 5 A.2d 603 (1939).

14. *See*, Dewey v. Natl. Tank Maint. Corp., 233 Iowa 58; 8 N.W.2d 593 (1943).

15. Lane v. Bogert, 116 N.J. Eq. 454; 174 A. 217; Farmers' Gin Co. v. Kasch, 277 S.W. 746 (Tex. Civ. App. 1925).

16. Note, *The Executive Committee in Corporate Organization—Scope of Powers*, 42 Mich. L. Rev. 133 (1943).

17. Martin v. Hardy, 251 Mich. 413; 232 N.W. 197 (1930).

18. *Ibid.*

19. *See*, Hoit and Co. v. Detig, 320 Ill. App. 179; 50 N.E.2d 602 (1943).

20. *State ex rel. Lake of the Ozarks Community College Steering Comm., Inc. v. Coordinating Bd. for Higher Educ.*, 802 S.W.2d 533 (Mo. App. 1991).

21. *See*, the foregoing sections. Ga. Code Ann. §22-2602(a) (also requires two members of the board of directors to be on each committee); Ala. Code, tit. 10, §223 (board of directors remains responsible for the committee's acts).

22. N.Y. Not-for-Profit Corp. L. §712.

23. Harris v. Harris, 137 Misc. 73; 241 N.Y.S. 474 (1930).

24. *See*, 5 Oleck, *Modern Corporation Law*, c.99 (1978 Supp.) for many forms of resolutions for many purposes. The results of lack of a clear, recorded decision are illustrated by Houghtaling v. Upper Kittaning Brick Co., 92 Misc. 228, N.Y.S. 540 (1915).

25. *See*, Fletcher, *Private Corporations* §522.2 (curr. ed.).

26. *See* Kennerson v. Burbank Amusement Co., 260 P.2d 823 (Calif. App. 1953); Note, 6 Ark. L. Rev. 486 (1952); Kolb article, *See* n.7.

27. Cyert, *Management of Nonprofit Organizations*, 8 (1977).

28. *Ibid.*, 12–13.

29. *See*, 2 Oleck, *Modern Corporation Law*, §958 (1978 Supp.); Comment, *Corporate Management by an Executive Committee*, 25 Albany L. Rev. 93 (1961).

30. Hoyt v. Thompson's Exr., 19 N.Y. 207 (1859).

31. *See, In re* Lone Star Shipbuilding Co., 6 F.2d 192 (2d Cir. 1925) *contra*: Long Park, Inc. v. Trenton-New Brunswick Theatres Co., 297 N.Y. 174, 77 N.E.2d 633 (1948); Noted. 61 Harv. L. Rev. 1251 (1948).

32. Steigerwald v. A.M. Steigerwald Co., 9 Ill. App.2d 31, 132 N.E.2d 373 (1955); and use of directors from other corporations is improper; 1955 Op. Atty.-Genl. (N.Y.) Mar.; and executive committee members must be trustees: Ohio Rev. Code §1702.33.

33. Calif. Nonprofit Corp. Code, tit. 1,§§5210,5231(b).

34. Syracuse Television, Inc. v. Channel 9, Syracuse, Inc., 273 N.Y.S.2d 16 (Sup. Ct. 1966); McNeil v. Boston Chamber of Commerce, 154 Mass. 277, 28 N.E. 245 (1891); Harris v. Harris, 137 Misc. 73, 241 N.Y.S. 474 (1930); *and see*, Gordon, *Business Leadership in the Large Corporation*, 46 *et passim* (Brookings Institute, 1945).

35. Jones *v.* Williams, 139 Mo. 1, 39 S.W. 486, 490 (1897); San Antonio Joint Stock Land Bank v. Taylor, 129 Tex. 335, 105 S.W.2d 650, 654 (1937).

36. Ohio Rev. Code §1702.33(D); Caldwell v. Mutual Reserve Fund Life Assn., 53 A.D. 245 65 N.Y.S. 826 (1900).

37. Wingate v. Bercut, 146 F.2d 725 (9th Cir. 1944).

38. Lane v. Bogert, 116 N.J. Eq. 454, 174 A. 217 (1934).

39. Sherman and Ellis, Inc. v. Indiana Mut. Casualty Co., 41 P.2d 588 (7th Cir. 1930) *cert. den* 282 U.S. 893, 51 S.Ct. 107, 75 L.Ed. 787 (1930).

40. Jones v. Williams, 139 Mo. 1, 39 S.W. 486 (1897).

41. Superior Portland Cement v. Pacific Coast Cement Co., 205 P.2d 597 (Wash. 1949).

42. *See* N.Y. Not-for-Profit Corp. L. §712.

43. N.Y. Not-for-Profit Corp. L. §712. *See generally*, as to statutes and powers, 2 Oleck, *Modern Corporation Law*, c. 39 (1978 Supp.) listing provisions of all states.

44. Ohio Rev. Code §1702.33.

45. Minn. Stat. Anno. §317A.241.

46. Wallace v. International Trade Exhibition, Inc., 170 La. 55; 127 S. 362 (1930); Tempel v. Dodge, 89 Tex. 69; 32 S.W. 514; 33 S.W. 222 (1895); First Natl. Bk. v. Commercial Trav. Home Assn., 108 A.D. 78; 95 N.Y.S. 454; *affd.*, 185 N.Y. 575; 78 N.E. 1103 (1906). Note, *The Executive Committee in Corporate Organization—Scope of Powers*, 42 Mich. L. Rev. 33 (1943); Minn. Stat. Anno. §317A.241.

47. *See*, Fensterer v. Pressure Lighting Co., 85 Misc. 621; 149 N.Y.S. 49; Lawrence v. Atlantic P. and P. Corp., 298 P. 246 (5th Cir. 1924), *cert. denied*, 266 U.S. 606, 45 S.C.T. 92, 69 L. Ed. 464 (1924); Wash. Rev. Code §24.03.115.

48. *See*, Sherman and Ellis v. Indiana Mut. Cas. Co., 41 P.2d 688 (7th Cir. 1930); *see* n. 39, 40.

49. *See*, Ryder v. Bushwick R. Co., 134 N.Y. 83; 31 N.E. 251 (1892).

50. Marshall v. Industrial Federation of America, 84 N.Y.S. 85 (1903); Peurifoy v. Loyal, 154 S.C. 267; 151 D.E. 579 (1930); *but see* n.36.

51. Caldwell v. Mutual Reserve Fund L. Assn., 53 A.D. 215; 65 N.Y.S. 826 (1900).

52. *See*, Commercial Wood and C. Co. v. Northampton P.C. Co., 190 N.Y. 1; 82 N.E. 750 (1907).

53. *See* Chapter 28.

54. *See,* Respess v. Rex Spinning Co., 191 N.C. 809; 153 S.E. 391 (1926).

55. Tempel case, n.24; Hayes v. Canada, A. and P.S.S. Co., Ltd. 181 F. 289 (1st Cir. 1910).

56. Wallace case, n.46; Haldeman v. Haldeman, 176 Ky. 635; 197 S.W. 376, 382 (1917); and San Antonio Joint S.L. Bk. v. Taylor, 129 Tex. 335; 105 S.W.2d 650 (1937).

57. *See,* Wingate v. Bercut, 146 F.2d 725 (9th Cir. 1944).

58. Hayes case, n.55; Robinson v. Benbow, 298 F. 561, 570 (4th Cir. 1924).

59. Sovin v. Shahmoon Industries, Inc., 220 N.Y.S.2d 760 (1961).

60. *See,* 3 Oleck, *Modern Corporation Law,* c. 58 (1978 Supp.).

61. Ohio Rev. Code §1713.30.

62. *Ibid., See* §1702.33(A).

63. *See,* Oleck, *Proprietary Mentality and the New Nonprofit Corporation Laws,* 20 Clev. St. L. Rev. 145 (1971).

64. McMullen, *Committees of the Board of Directors,* 29 Bus. Law. 755 (1974); Kolb, *Delegation of Authority to Committees,* 9 U. of Baltimore L. Rev. 189 (1980).

65. Fl. St. § 617.0825(3); *Fl. Session L.* 1990, Chap. 90–179 § 51(3).

32

AGENTS, EMPLOYEES, AND VOLUNTEERS

[Steven D. Overly contributed research materials for this chapter.]

§330. AGENTS, EMPLOYEES, AND VOLUNTEERS, IN GENERAL

[See the Index for specific terms and definitions such as *Officers, Agents, Employees, etc.*]

California, New York, Texas, Florida, Pennsylvania, Illinois, Ohio, and Michigan account for half of all people employed by nonprofit organizations, according to a 1990 Census Bureau study. Some 7.8 million people are employed in nonprofit organizations, representing 6.7 percent of all U.S. employees. There are 3,120 persons employed in nonprofits per 100,000 population, compared to 46,513 for all persons employed per 100,000 population. The Northeast region of the United States has more than 4,000 nonprofit employees per 100,000 population. The Midwest ranked second, followed by the West, and then the South.[1]

Although their employees, agents, and volunteers are the most important assets of many nonprofit organizations, there is surprisingly little data available about their nature, numbers, and efficiency, and less about their individual participation and value.[2] On the other hand, attention to the nature and compensation of management personnel has been intense. For example, a current hornbook on corporation law devotes 31 heavily footnoted pages to "management compensation."[3] *Volunteers* are not employees,[4] and have been excluded from the Fair Labor Standards Act (FLSA) protections,[5] except in a private nonprofit organization operation of a school, hospital or commercial-type activity.[6] An individual is not an employee unless he or she is economically dependent on the organization.[7]

An *agent* is a person who acts for or in place of another by authority from the latter.[8] An *employee* is a person who works under direct supervision and control, for salary or wages, when both the purpose and means of his work are selected by the employer.[9] If an agent (employee) acts only for the benefit of the employer and not out of personal malice or negligence, he or she is not personally liable; *e.g.*, where a hospital corporation agent is not acting from personal reasons in cutting off a staff physician's operating room privileges.[10]

Agency is any relationship in which one person acts for or represents another, with the latter's consent.[11] The agent basically follows the purpose of his principal, but uses means of his own selection in so doing.[12] The *law of agency* governs this relationship; it is too large a subject to be discussed here.

Employee is synonymous with *servant*,[13] and distinct from *agent* or *officer*.[14] The term usually is implied to clerks, laborers, or workmen, but seldom to officers or agents.[15] But sometimes it is used to signify anyone who exercises a function on behalf of an employer, for compensation.[16]

Whether or not a particular employee has *agency* powers is a question of intention, as expressed in the bylaws or other regulations. *Apparent* authority may suffice to enable him to bind the organization by his acts (contracts). Even a humble employee may have a limited agency for some purposes; *e.g.*, a janitor—to buy floor wax; or a truck driver—to buy a tankful of gasoline.

All officers of a corporation are agents, but not all agents of the corporation are officers.[17]

The board of directors, and the officers, have the right to delegate to agents the performance of ministerial functions.[18] And they have the power to discharge such employees as well as hire them.[19] The effect of contracts of employment in such cases is sketched in Chapter 30.

The power of delegation is inherent, though it usually is limited by statutes and bylaws.[20]

Officers may be employees. Ordinarily, a trustee, director, or officer of a nonprofit organization also may be an employee. His functions as an officer then may be (and must be) distinct from those performed as an employee. As to exception of charitable corporation trustees, see Chapters 28 to 30.

Thus, a president of a corporation (*i.e.*, as an officer) may also perform routine work (*e.g.*, supervision of production), and be an employee in the latter capacity, for *workmen's compensation* purposes,[21] or *unemployment compensation* purposes.[22]

Note that local statutes and cases should be consulted regarding inclusion or exclusion of nonprofit organization employees from such compensation coverage. These subjects are too complex for discussion here. Some state statutes exclude employees of nonprofit or charitable organizations.

Alien Employees

All employers, profit or nonprofit, are legally obliged to verify the *immigration law status* of employees hired since November 1986, when the Immi-

gration Reform & Control Act took effect. They must use Immigration & Nat-
uralization Service Form I-9, showing data about the employee, and keep it
available for inspection, under penalty of fines for failure to do so. Knowing
hiring or retention of an illegal alien is a crime, with fines of up to $3000
and/or six months jail.[23]

Employee Contracts

If a restrictive covenant not to compete, in a contract for employment, is
clear on its face and no fraud, collusion, overreaching or unequal bargaining
power is present, the court will not substitute contractual terms. Liquidated
damages for breach of an employment contract are valid if they are not a
"penalty."[24]

A nonprofit corporation (hospital) may restrict, by contract, its employees from taking similar positions in the same county within one year following
termination of employment. Injunction to prohibit the employee from taking
such a position does not create a restriction of trade and is proper if the
employer has a proper protectable interest, and the time and place restrictions
of the injunction are reasonable.[25]

§331 VOLUNTEERS

In 1991 President Bush proposed a model state statute to protect NPO
volunteers (in nonwillful or wanton conduct) and approved development of a
privately funded center for their protection from personal liability and expensive insurance (which over half the states provide only to directors and officers). All NPOs now tax exempt under IRC § 501(c) would be covered. Nonprofits' Risk Mgmt. Insur. Inst.; Wash., D.C., is *source*.[26]

Statutory regulation, governing the provisions of volunteer services, is
increasingly prevalent. Currently, many statutes provide for the retention and
training of volunteers in such areas of public interest as care of the aged, education of children, and community health. Notably, some of these laws provide
that volunteers shall be indemnified or protected by the state for claims against
them arising out of the scope of their volunteer service.[27]

Twenty bills to shield volunteers from liability were introduced in state
legislatures in 1992. California, Colorado, and Delaware passed bills in 1992.
The District of Columbia passed a volunteer protection bill in January of
1993.[28]

Many states pass laws that protect volunteers from claims against them
that arose in the course of the volunteer activity as long as the volunteer can
show that there is no evidence of willful misconduct or gross negligence.

For example, Cal. Health & Saf. Code §429.64 (1993) regulates flu and
pneumonia vaccines and those local government or private, nonprofit agencies which administer such vaccines. §429.64 (f) of this code states that "No
private, nonprofit volunteer agency whose involvement with an immuniza-

tion program governed by this section is limited to the provision of a clinic site or promotional and logistical support pursuant to subdivision (c), or any employee or member thereof, shall be liable for any injury caused by an act or omission in the administration of the vaccine or other immunizing agent to a person 60 years of age or older or to members of high-risk groups identified by the U.S. Public Health Service, if the immunization is performed pursuant to this section in conformity with applicable federal, state, or local governmental standards and the act or omission does not constitute willful misconduct or gross negligence."

Cal. Food & Agr. Code §5239(a): There shall be no personal liability to a third party for monetary damages on the part of a volunteer director or volunteer executive officer of a nonprofit corporation subject to this part, caused by the director's or officer's negligent act or omission in the performance of that person's duties as a director or officer, if all of the following conditions are met:

(1) The act or omission was within the scope of the director's or executive officer's duties.

(2) The act or omission was performed in good faith.

(3) The act or omission was not reckless, wanton, intentional, or grossly negligent.

(4) Damages caused by the act or omission are covered pursuant to a liability insurance policy issued to the corporation, either in the form of a general liability policy or a director's and officer's liability policy. In the event that the damages are not covered by a liability insurance policy, the volunteer director or volunteer executive officer shall not be personally liable for the damages if the board of directors of the corporation and the person had made all reasonable efforts in good faith to obtain available liability insurance.

§5239 (b) defines "volunteer" as the rendering of services without compensation.

Legislators play an important role in the area of Volunteer Liability. For example, Representative John Edward Porter (R-IL) is reintroducing legislation that would encourage states to exempt individual volunteers from tort liability if they were acting in good faith and within the scope of duties to the organization. The volunteer would still be liable if his or her behavior constituted "willful and wanton misconduct." The measure is backed by 250 organizations. However, the legislation is opposed by the Association of Trial Lawyers of America.[29]

A District of Columbia law that took effect in March of 1993 provides full immunity from civil liability for volunteers with 501 (c) (3) organizations that have operating expenses under $100,000.00. Volunteers of organizations with budgets above that threshold are required to maintain a $200,000/$500,000 package of liability insurance. The legislation, the Nonprofit Corporation Act, is still subject to congressional review but resembles legislation already in effect in many other jurisdictions.[30]

The Kansas House Public Health Committee heard arguments March 8, 1993, that the state's Charitable Doctor law should be expanded to include protection from liability for clinics that charge fees as long as those fees are means-tested. Current law makes doctors who render free care "state employees" and brings them under the $500,000 liability cap of the State Tort Claims Act. The bill, S.B. 14, would bring indigent care clinics under the law and allow them to charge fees graduated according to means. Richard Morrissey, director of the state's Office of Local and Rural Health Systems, asked that the bill be expanded to include volunteers who participate in child immunization programs.[31]

A Florida legislative plan that would grant doctors immunity from malpractice claims, thereby allowing doctors to volunteer services at public health clinics, is near completion. Physician groups expect a flood of new volunteers once malpractice immunity is granted.[32]

A volunteer protection act passed the Florida legislature in 1993. The act will protect volunteers at large who perform any service for a nonprofit without "willful or wanton misconduct." Connecticut, Arizona, and North Carolina were considering similar legislation in 1993.[33]

Volunteer immunity statutes do not always provide complete protection. For example, action was brought against owners of individual condominium units to recover for injuries sustained when a person slipped and fell on stairways in the common area. The court held that the owners were not entitled to immunity from civil tort liability under the statute providing immunity in certain circumstances to the volunteer officer or director of the association managing a common interest residential development. The owners of the individual condominium units could be held liable for the injuries the plaintiff sustained in the common area, even if the owners thought they had delegated the duty of control and management to a separate legal entity.[34]

NPO Liability for Volunteer's Negligence

The determination of whether a party may be held vicariously liable for the torts of another depends on whether the tortfeasor is characterized as a servant. A servant has been defined as one employed to perform services in the affairs of another and who is subject to the other's control or right to control with respect to the physical conduct in the performance of the services. Occasionally, courts hold charitable organizations vicariously liable for the acts of their volunteers.

In *Wilson v. St. Louis Area Counsel, Boy Scouts of America*, 845 S.W.2d 568 (Mo. App. E.D. 1992), the parents of a Boy Scout who was killed during troop activity brought an action against the St. Louis Area Council (Council) and the Boy Scouts of America, Inc. The court held that Council was not vicariously liable for any negligence of the troop leaders. Council is an umbrella organization. It charters individual troops and tries to assure itself that the troop will have responsible adult leadership. Council does not choose or in any way directly supervise the scoutmaster, who is selected by the troop.

Another example of courts not holding Boy Scouts of America (BSA) vicariously liable occurred in *Anderson v. Boy Scouts of America, Inc.*, 589 N.E.2d 892 (Ill. App. 1 Dist. 1992). In this case, a fourteen-month-old child was injured when she was run over by a local Boy Scout leader, Daniel Searle, as he was backing out of a driveway after delivering craft materials that were to be used for a scouting project. The court found no evidence that the national or district organization had any direct supervisory powers over the local troop leader and found no evidence that they had exercised control over Mr. Searle on the date at issue. In light of the lack of such evidence, the court held that Mr. Searle was not the agent of BSA or the district council, thereby relieving BSA and the district council from any vicarious liability.

Some courts, however, have found nonprofit organizations to be vicariously liable for the acts of their volunteers. For example, workers for a nonprofit refugee center volunteered to remove a fire escape which a town house owner had donated to the center. A fire resulted from a torch used to remove the fire escape. The court held that the volunteer status of an employee does not shield the owner from vicarious liability where a dangerous activity is involved, even though there is no master-servant relationship formed between the owner and the volunteering employees.[35]

In the Whetstone case, the issue involved a religious organization's liability for the negligence of one of its deacons who volunteered his services and was not compensated for those services. At the time of the accident, members of the Faith and Truth Church's Board of Deacons shared the responsibility of assisting in the remodeling of the church. The board members were expected to use their own vehicles when running errands such as picking up building supplies. The defendant was involved in an automobile accident. The court analyzed whether a master-servant relationship existed and decided to reverse the trial court decision and hold Faith and Truth vicariously liable for the negligence of Mr. Dixon in causing the accident in question. Mr. Dixon was "more than a casual volunteer" and was classified as a "non-employee leader" of Faith and Truth. Both the church membership and the Board of Deacons had the right to exercise control over Mr. Dixon. The court stated:

> If the facts presented in this case do not support a finding of vicarious liability, then we find it difficult to imagine a situation wherein vicarious liability could be imposed on a charitable organization for the acts of its volunteer. The effect of this conclusion would be to reinstate the doctrine of charitable immunity, contrary to the Supreme Court's dictates.[36]

Masters and employers are answerable for the damages occasioned by their servants in the exercise of the functions in which they are appointed. A person who volunteers services without an agreement for or expectation of reward may be a servant of one accepting such services. A charitable organization's right to control the activities of a volunteer is the determining factor in deciding whether a volunteer is in fact a "servant" of that charity. To determine the right to control, the court considers:

(1) the degree of contact between the charity and the volunteer,

(2) the degree to which the charity orders the volunteer to perform specific actions, and

(3) the structural hierarchy of the charity.

In this case, Vanno was an adult leader in the St. Andrew Catholic Church's New Youth Organization (SANYO). He allegedly sexually molested a 14-year-old member of the church. Plaintiffs alleged the church should be held vicariously liable. The church defendants could be held liable for Vanno's actions if the Plaintiffs proved two things: (1) that Vanno was the church defendants' servant, and (2) that Vanno committed the tort in question in the course and scope of his duties as the church defendants' servant. The court concluded that Vanno was not a servant for the purposes of vicarious liability. Therefore, the court refused to hold the church vicariously liable for the acts of Vanno.[37]

Volunteers must be acting in their "duty as a volunteer" before the not-for-profit corporation can be held vicariously liable for the negligence of a volunteer. Concession-stand operators (volunteer firefighters) at a not-for-profit corporation's fundraiser sold beer to a person who appeared to be "somewhat drunk." This patron of the concession stand was involved in an automobile accident after leaving the fundraiser. The victims of the accident alleged that the city should be held vicariously liable for the negligence of the firefighters who had served alcohol that evening. However, the court determined that the participation of these volunteer firefighters in fundraising activities was not deemed to constitute "duty as volunteer firemen" within the meaning of the civil liability provision of the General Municipal Law. As a result, the court held that the city was not vicariously liable.[38]

The purpose for which gratuitous services are rendered may be a significant consideration in determining liability. An end of season pizza party initiated, supervised and funded solely by players' parents, absent any sanction by the football league, did not appear purposed at advancing the league's interest in providing a program for competitive youth football. Thus, the league was not liable for injuries sustained at the party.[39]

The right to control the mode and manner by which tasks are performed is the key component in determining the existence of a master-servant or loaned servant relationship. A music festival organizer did not retain the right to control the mode and manner by which local volunteers (Jaycees) performed traffic control duties on an adjacent campground, and is not liable for injuries caused by their neglect, when traffic control was the contractual duty of the campground owner who chose to use volunteers in place of professional traffic officers.[40]

Injuries caused by the negligence of a driver, who volunteered to transport a basketball recruit from the airport to a hotel, can be attributed to the community college involved under the doctrine or respondeat superior, because the college's coach had the right to control and did govern the driver's performance.[41]

In selecting employees or volunteers, the master "must exercise a degree of care commensurate with the nature and danger of the business . . . and the nature and grade of service for which the servant is intended." The selection of child-care personnel inherently necessitates a relatively high standard of care to be considered reasonable.[42]

Volunteers' Standing to Sue an NPO

A parishioner may maintain suit against an unincorporated association (church) for injuries suffered when he fell through a roof while voluntarily making repairs requested by the pastor.[43]

Two key factors comprise the gratuitous employee relationship: "[f]irst, control of one for whom the service is done . . . [and] second, whether the primary purpose underlying the act is to serve another." Neither a relationship of gratuitous employee nor that of independent contractor exists when, on his own initiative, a camper joins a group voluntarily undertaking to construct a footbridge on distant camp property and is injured in the process.[44]

Survivors brought action against a nonprofit sailing organization to recover for the deaths of two volunteer trainee sailors, who perished in a race. The court held that the plaintiffs could add general maritime survival claims, for the decedent's pain and suffering before death, to their Death on the High Seas claim (DOHSA).[45]

Court-Ordered Volunteers

Court-ordered volunteers, or people who are required to perform community service as part of their sentence or probation for crime, have contributed millions of hours to nonprofits in the last 20 years. Such volunteers are usually appreciated even though they may display poor attitudes or refuse to show up altogether. Community service is a sentencing tool in California, Florida, New Jersey, North Carolina, Michigan, Colorado, Oregon, and elsewhere. According to New Jersey statistics, 1.8 million hours of service was performed there by some 26,000 court-ordered volunteers in 1992. In California, 40 percent of the 50,000 volunteers it placed in 1992 were placed in nonprofits. According to Herbert Hoelter, director of the National Center for Institutions and Alternatives in Alexandria, Virginia, "the theory is, if the community is violated by the crime, then the community ought to get directly paid back." Times of service range from 30 to 60 hours for lower court cases to more than 100 for lesser federal crimes. There are problems with court-ordered volunteer systems. Volunteers who are not complying, not doing the job, should be sent back to the court. There is no hard evidence that the programs reduce recidivism or cut costs of incarceration. Also, the volunteers add another layer of bureaucracy to the probation system.[46]

Paid Volunteers

The $268 million (for 1990–1993 period) National & Community Service Act was signed into law in Nov. 1990 by President Bush, despite "reservations about the wisdom of employing 'paid volunteers' to the extent contemplated." Low-income youths were expected to be encouraged by this.[47]

Bartering of volunteer work in exchange for other volunteer efforts (e.g., for later collection, or exchange for a different kind) now is being systematized in the United States. Some people favor this idea, and some call this "payment" devoid of altruism.[48]

Volunteer Training

Volunteer training guides as well as publications for and about volunteers are available from Energize, Inc., 5450 Wissahickon Ave., Philadelphia, PA 19144, or call toll free 1-800-395-9800 for a catalog.

Volunteer Employees' Workers' Compensation

First Amendment is not violated by inclusion of a church in a Workers' Compensation program.[49]

A psychiatrist on the staff of a state psychiatric center volunteered to share staff assignment at nonprofit private hospitals. He subsequently sued the private hospitals seeking overtime pay and compensation for services rendered to patients previously treated at the state hospital. The court held that the psychiatrist had no claim for compensation other than his state hospital salary. Further, he had no reasonable expectation of overtime payment from the private hospitals where he had volunteered to work.[50]

A volunteer ambulance driver sued for workers' compensation benefits after he was injured in a volleyball game held to raise funds for the ambulance service. The court held that the ambulance service is exempt from liability from workers' compensation insurance requirements because it is an institution maintained and operated wholly as a public charity.[51]

The California Labor Code §§ 3352(b) and (i) excludes from workers' compensation coverage those persons performing services for a religious or charitable organization "in return for aid or sustenance only" and those individuals rendering voluntary service to a nonprofit organization without expectation of remuneration other than incidentals. An indigent laborer paid $5 per hour by a church out of its benevolent assistance fund, for various odd jobs he performed on church property, did not receive sums gauged to equate to his necessaries of life, nor did he donate his services with charitable intent. His employment relation carries with it the respective benefits and responsibilities of workers' compensation coverage.[52]

A volunteer assistant pitching coach neither worked under any express or implied employment contract, nor could he be considered an employee by appointment under the Workers' Compensation Act of Colorado, because the head baseball coach lacked authority to hire or appoint volunteers.[53]

Volunteer Blood Donors [AIDS Infection]

The right of access to the courts, as expressed in Article I § 10 of the Washington State Constitution, and the interest of an AIDS contaminated patient in obtaining redress from a person potentially liable for infecting him through the donation of AIDS tainted blood, operate in favor of compelling a blood center to disclose information identifying the donor.[54]

§332. STATUTORY AGENTS

Many nonprofit corporation statutes now require all corporations to designate a *statutory agent* to represent the organization. He becomes the person upon whom any legal process, notice, or demand may be served; and may be either a natural person or licensed "corporation service company" (corporation).[55]

The statutory agent must reside in the county where the corporation has its principal place of business. His designation is filed with the secretary of state. If he dies, resigns, or moves away, another person must be similarly designated.[56] Failure to obey such a statute may result in cancellation of the corporate charter.[57]

(See also the forms in chapters on incorporation.)

FORM NO. 152
Designation of Statutory Agent

Designation of Registered Office
and Registered Agent
Domestic Corporation

1. Name of corporation _____

2. Address, including city, street, number, and county, of registered office ___

_____

3. Name of registered agent _____

4. The address of the registered office of the corporation and the business address of the registered agent of the corporation, as designated, are identical.

5. The designation of registered office and agent as above set forth was authorized by a resolution duly adopted by the board of directors of the corporation.

IN TESTIMONY WHEREOF, this statement is signed by the _____ president and _____ secretary, this the _____ day of _____, A.D. 19 _____.

_____

_____ president.

_____

_____ secretary

State of _____

County of _____

This is to certify that on this _____ day of _____, 19__, before me, a notary public, personally appeared _____ and _____, each of whom, being by me first duly sworn, declared that he signed the foregoing document in the capacity indicated, that he was authorized to sign, and that the statements therein contained are true.

Witness my hand and official seal, this _____ day of _____, 19__.

_____   _____
                                          Notary Public

(Seal)

My commission expires: _____

FORM NO. 153
Change of Statutory Agent (and/or Office)
(Illinois)

[See for Florida's form: Fla. Certif. 114 (12/16/77).]

FORM NP-11   Do Not Write in This Space
ONE COPY ONLY TO BE FILED   Date _____
FILING FEE   Filing Fee $_____
                                    Clerk _____
Please read instructions on back before
attempting to execute.

CERTIFICATE OF CHANGE OF REGISTERED AGENT
AND REGISTERED OFFICE BY
A FOREIGN OR DOMESTIC CORPORATION
under the
GENERAL NOT-FOR-PROFIT CORPORATION ACT

TO Secretary of State, Springfield, Illinois:

The undersigned corporation, organized and existing under the laws of the State of _____ for the purpose of changing its registered agent and its registered office, or both, in Illinois, as provided by the "General Not-for-Profit Corporation Act." of Illinois, represents that:

1. The name of the corporation is _____

2. The address, including street and number, if any, of its present registered office (*before change*) is:_____

_____

3. Its registered office (*including street and number, if any change in the registered office is to be made*) is hereby changed to_____

_____ (_____) (_____)

(County)   (Zip Code)

4. The name of its present registered agent, (*before change*) is_____

5. The name of the new registered agent is _____

6. The address of its registered office and the address of the office of its registered agent, as changed, will be identical.

7. Such change was authorized by resolution duly adopted by the board of directors.

IN WITNESS WHEREOF, the undersigned corporation has caused this report to be executed in its name by its President and its _____ Secretary, this _____ day of _____, 19___.

(
Place
Corporate Seal
Here
)

By _____

_____
(*Exact Corporate Title*)

(*Its _____ President*)

_____
(*Its _____ Secretary*)

[*NOTE: This "change" must be signed by both officers, but may be verified by either.*]

STATE OF _____
COUNTY OF _____   ss

I, _____, a Notary Public, do hereby certify that on the _____ day of _____, A.D. 19___, personally appeared before me, _____, and being first duly sworn by me, acknowledges that _____ signed the foregoing document in the capacity therein set forth and declared that the statements therein contained are true.

IN WITNESS WHEREOF, I have hereunto set my hand and seal the day and year before written.

(
Place
Notorial Seal
Here
)

_____
Notary Public

FORM NO. 154
Change of Agent's Address
(Maine)

NONPROFIT CORPORATION

Filing Fee $ This Space for Use by
                                                     Secretary of State

For Use by the Secretary of State
File No. _____
Fee Paid_____
C. B. _____
Date _____

**STATE OF MAINE
NOTIFICATION BY REGISTERED
AGENT OF CHANGE IN
REGISTERED OFFICE**

Pursuant to 13-B MRSA §305 (3) or §1212 (2), the undersigned registered agent for one or more domestic or foreign corporations gives notice of the following change of business address which is the registered office in Maine for each corporation listed:

FIRST: Name of registered agent*_____

SECOND: Address of former registered office_____

               _____

                              (street, city, state, and zip code)

THIRD: Address of new registered office _____

               _____

                              (street, city, state, and zip code)

FOURTH: Notice of the above change in registered office has been sent to each of the following corporations by the undersigned as registered agent of each:

Name of Corporation	Jurisdiction of Incorporation if Other than Maine

*Registered agent of a corporation may be a person or corporation. If a person, it must be manually signed. If the registered agent is a corporation the name of the corporation should be typed, and the document must be signed (1) by the clerk or secretary *or* (2) by the president or a vice-president and by the secretary or an assistant secretary, or such other officer as the by-laws may designate as a 2nd certifying officer *or* (3) if there are no such officers, then by a majority of the directors or by such directors as may be designated by a majority of the directors then in office *or* (4) if there are no such directors, then by the members or such of them as may be designated by the members at a lawful meeting.

FORM NO. 155
Notice of Resignation of Agent

NONPROFIT CORPORATION

Filing Fee $ This Space for Use by
                                                         Secretary of State

For Use by the Secretary of State
File No. _____
Fee Paid_____
C. B._____
Date _____

STATE OF MAINE
NOTICE OF RESIGNATION
OF REGISTERED AGENT
OF

_____

Pursuant to 13-B MRSA §305 (2) or §1212 (3) you are hereby notified that the undersigned has resigned as the registered agent of _____, a corporation, whose address is _____.
Domestic corporation complete:

    *A copy of the notice of resignation has been mailed to _____,
                                       (insert name)
    at _____such person being
                 (mailing address)
    the _____of the corporation.
Foreign corporation complete:

      A copy of the notice of resignation has been mailed to the corpo-
    ration at its last registered or principal office in its jurisdiction of incor-
    poration, as filed with the Secretary of State, which is: _____

_____

Dated: _____

_____   _____
                                   (Signature of registered agent)

By _____

                                  (signature)

Legibly print or type name
and capacity of all signers   _____
13-B MRSA §104.   (type or print name and capacity)

By _____

                                  (signature)

_____

(type or print name and capacity)

---

*A copy of the resignation notice must be mailed to the corporation in care of an officer who is not the resigning registered agent, at the address of such officer as shown by the most recent annual report of the corporation. The name of the person to whom the copy is mailed and the corporate office held must be specified in the notice filed.

Appointment of registered agent terminates 30 days after filing notice of resignation by the Secretary of State.

§333. APPOINTMENT AND DISCHARGE OF AGENTS

The power of directors and officers to appoint and discharge agents is, in practice, usually vested by the bylaws in one executive officer. The president is usually given the power. Procedures should also be in the corporation regulations.

Once an agent is appointed, he becomes the agent of the corporation— not of the officer who appointed him nor of the one(s) who elected him.[58]

The revocability of the agency is treated in Chapter 29, especially in Section 293. The description of an agency as *irrevocable* does not make it so unless it is *coupled with an interest* in the subject of the agency.[59]

School and college law problems, in recent years, have confused the problem by injecting questions as to *tenure* rights of employees, officers, and administrators. In 1964, a dismissal of a college faculty member still could not be countered by demanding specific performance of his contract.[60] An employee did not have permanent job security because of constitutional arguments, at that time, although academic freedom was involved.[61] But by 1971, there were many cases holding that constitutional protection of civil rights gave what amounted to job security similar to *tenure* even for untenured faculty members.[62] This, in turn, was under attack as an improper use of civil rights concepts for the protection of incompetence or worse.[63] The subject is complex and specialized. Works on school law and constitutional law must be consulted.

In 1993 the problem was still unresolved. *See,* Swygert and Gozansky, *Desirability of Post-Tenure Performance Reviews of Law Professors,* 15 Stetson L. Rev. 355 (1986).

The rules of ratification, apparent authority, and so forth, which apply to agents' acts, are treated in Chapters 27, 28, and 29, on officers and directors.[64]

Modern cases and rules, and the effects of *tenure,* AAUP, and other influences are summarized in Section 293.

Recklessness in hiring or retaining a dangerous or incompetent employee makes the corporation liable for *punitive* damages for the torts of that employee. This is "complicity" (blameworthiness) of the employer.[65]

Defamation by or to persons in a hiring capacity is conditionally privileged if made upon proper occasion, from proper motive, in proper manner, and based upon reasonable cause.[66] However, a recent survey of executives nationwide indicates that 68 percent of executives think that it is harder to check the references of a prospective employees, citing the fact that companies are increasingly reluctant to release anything but basic employment information. Despite the trend, 55 percent of the executives stated that they would hire an employee if one of several references was negative.[67]

A church does not violate the Age Discrimination in Employment Act [29 U.S.C. § 626] by considering age when appointing pastors, when it had a stated policy to do so. A minister's lawsuit for violation of the act was properly dismissed, as a violation of the "free exercise" clause of the First Amendment.[68]

Agents' and Employees' Dismissal

Dismissal of an untenured teacher by a college is not intentional "interference with prospective economic advantage" unless the teacher can show (1) a reasonably certain existing prospective contract with another school, and (2) violation of procedural rules.[69]

Refusal of an at-will employee *to work with another* employee (an anesthesiologist) because of alleged drug-use-incompetence of the latter, unless supported by proof of the incompetence, is valid reason for dismissing the objector. Subjective opinion is not enough, but there must be proof of a reason that invokes public policy. Employee does not have ground for action for wrongful discharge.[70]

A client usually may discharge an *attorney* without liability for breach of contract, and this includes in-house counsel. The attorney (in-house) status bars his/her claim for wrongful discharge.[71]

A physician waives all rights to sue a nonprofit hospital for breach of contract, when his/her hospital privileges are terminated without malice, if he/she acknowledges in his/her application that the hospital has absolute immunity from civil liability for acts of the hospital taken for the purpose of achieving and maintaining an acceptable level of patient care.[72]

An unsigned draft contract may be used as an indication of the intent to contract, and to satisfy the statute of frauds, in a breach of contract action by a terminated employee, if the employer admits in memoranda, answer and a signed deposition to the terms of the draft contract.[73]

When a *doctor* sues a hospital for suspending his or her *staff privileges,* the court should consider whether the hospital complied with federal and state procedural safe guards. It is no longer necessary to determine whether the hospital is public, private or quasi-public.[74]

Wrongful discharge can be proved by evidence indicating that the employee was exercising a *job-related right or complying with a public duty when discharged.* When an employee was discharged after he disclosed information about dangerous conditions and potential physical abuse of the residents of a center for the mentally retarded, the evidence was sufficient for a jury to find wrongful discharge. Wrongful discharge of an employee is an intentional tort. By statute, directors are not shielded, in many states, from gross negligence or intentional torts.[75]

An employee may delay suit for wrongful termination, for ten months, and not be barred by laches if he/she is awaiting the outcome of the employer's appeal of his/her related unemployment compensation claim, even if the employer is prejudiced by the delay.[76]

A terminated at-will employee has no right to the benefits of termination procedures set forth in an employees' manual where there is no evidence that there was a contractual understanding of the right to such benefits at the time of employment.[77]

A terminated employee sued, seeking review of a private nonprofit hospital's grievance review committee that sustained his termination. The court held that certiorari (through CPLR article 78) was not available to review the termination. A private nonprofit employer may fire an at-will employee at any time absent an express contractual agreement to the contrary.[78]

Racially motivated discharge of an employee, by a nonprofit corporation, was not established by evidence indicating that a black employee's picture remained on exhibit after being defaced, her child was left unsupervised in a day-care center during a fire drill and she was not given complete information on grievance procedures.[79]

Constructive discharge of an employee occurs when an employer's illegal discriminatory acts foster a climate in the work place that would compel a reasonable person to resign. Age discrimination exists where an employee is evaluated negatively immediately after the employer merges with another company, the employee is treated as incapable and uneducable, the employee's supervisor asks her to quit (citing her age and image), and the employee's job is given to the person charged with training her. Reinstatement is the preferred remedy in Age Discrimination in Employment Act (ADEA) cases, however front pay is appropriate when reinstatement is not feasible.[80]

Personality conflicts are not enough to demonstrate a discriminatory *hostile work environment* that is actionable under Title VII of the Civil Rights Act of 1964. An employer is not legally liable for firing an employee who is not performing satisfactorily, even though the employee was discharged less than six months after he filed a civil rights action against his employer.[81]

A nonprofit hospital can not terminate by contract an employee who has AIDS and evict him from his ancillary housing tenancy "with or without cause" unless it is prepared to give a non-disability discrimination reason. Such action violates the Americans with Disabilities Act of 1990.[82]

An employer that employs under 13 full-time and part-time employees is not subject to suit for age and disability discrimination in Nebraska.[83]

A university, that is organized as a nonprofit religious organization, is exempt from the Fair Employment and Housing Act, even if it receives state funding. Thus, a terminated employee who was discharged for having intercourse outside of marriage could not use the Act to recover for discrimination on the basis of marital status, sex and pregnancy.[84]

A valid claim for retaliatory discharge requires that the employee has been discharged, in retaliation for the employee's actions, and that the discharge is against public policy. A medical school professor, demoted from his position as chairman of the department of radiology or as chief of services at an affiliated hospital, for alleging fraud by hospital employees, has no retaliatory discharge action if still tenured and receiving a salary increase. There is no action for retaliatory demotion in Illinois.[85]

A dental hygienist who insisted on "sharing her faith" in Christ with patients in the dentist's office, despite repeated warnings from the employer to desist because of patients' complaints, disqualified herself for unemployment compensation when she was discharged.[86]

A discharged employee who refused to submit to an examination and who refused to consider the employer's offer of reemployment is not entitled to future medical and health continuation benefits.[87]

State Action Requirement for Civil Rights Suits

In order for the illegal act of a private actor to confer liability on the state under § 1983, there must be an agreement between the private and state actors to violate the plaintiff's constitutional rights. In one case, a jail counselor was discharged by a private not-for-profit corporation which provided mental health services to a county jail. The court would not allow the joinder of the corporation and the county jail under § 1983 because there was no illegal state action or agreement to violate the plaintiff's constitutional rights.[88]

A *discharged director* of a nonprofit mental health institute brought a civil rights claim, under 42 U.S.C.A. § 1983, against state officials for civil malicious prosecution. The courts have recognized that a *criminal malicious prosecution* action exists under § 1983. However, the second circuit held that a cause of action for *civil malicious prosecution* is present under § 1983 only where the stock shows "conscious-shocking" behavior so egregious as to work a deprivation of a constitutional dimension.[89]

The government must exercise sufficient control over a nonprofit facility for the facility to be a "state actor." If insufficient control exists then a discharged employee cannot maintain a civil rights action under § 1983.[90]

Lay-Offs

When an employee association brought suit against an employer for falsely telling them that the company would not shut down and that their *jobs were secure*, the federal court took jurisdiction over all claims that required interpretation of a collective bargaining agreement, under § 301 of the Labor Management Relations Act.[91]

Under ERISA (Employee Retirement Income Security Act), an employer must not misrepresent to laid-off employees that voluntary termination of their employment benefits would not be available for their participation while the employer is privately considering the option of the employees' participation, thus inducing the employees to accept an alternate plan with lesser payout. The employer has a fiduciary duty to fairly disclose the progress of its serious considerations and plans.[92]

Under the COBRA amendments to ERISA, employers must provide laid-off employees with meaningful continuation *health care coverage*, identical to that provided for employees, for up to 18 months, or until the employee obtains an alternate source of health insurance.[93]

Unemployment Insurance for Employees

A nonprofit organization, which provided educational and training seminars to individuals and businesses, exercised *control* over its regional representative in that it determined his territory, approved all sales, and prohibited him from representing other similar organizations. Thus, the representative was an *employee*, and not an *independent contractor*, for purposes of unemployment compensation.[94]

Employee Manuals' Effects

Employees of nonprofit corporations can overcome the presumption of at-will employment by showing enforceable contract rights in an "employee handbook." However, a disclaimer in the handbook, stating that the policies are not part of an employment contract, operates to preserve the at-will presumption. Recently, the court looked to a *handbook disclaimer* to justify the at-will presumption even though a "*policy manual*," stating termination and discipline procedures, contained no such disclaimer.[95]

Employee Handbook's express provision that the handbook is not to be viewed as a contract, as was understood by a plaintiff-employee, made him an *at-will* employee who could be terminated at any time.[96]

An employer (college or hospital) is estopped from denying the binding effects of its (faculty affairs committee's) manual provisions regarding probational employee (faculty members') employment contracts, where the employer (college) caused the employee (faculty) to rely on the manual as part of its rules and regulations, even though it had refused to formally adopt the manual.[97]

Rules applicable to employees in a nonprofit organization, often incorporated in the contract of employment (e.g., by reference), such as American Association of University Professors (AAUP) tenure (termination) guidelines, in a private university's faculty handbook, are not so incorporated unless fairly clearly meant (by the university) to be so attached. Refusal (or neglect) by trustees to include them, after a specific request by a faculty member, means that they are not included.[98]

For an employees' manual document to create enforceable *contract relations* it must be more than a list of vacation times, holidays, leaves, and so on. It must have a detailed procedure as to dismissal, etc.; otherwise it does not overcome the *presumption* of "at will" employment.[99]

Employee handbook provisions are not contracts insofar as they are distributed to *management* personnel only to advise them as to policies regarding employees under their supervision, and were not reasonably relied upon as contractual as to them.[100]

§334. STATUS OF AN AGENT OR EMPLOYEE

(See section above)

An officer has certain rights that are inherent in his office (see Chapter 29) but a mere agent or employee has not.[101] The method of selection, duties, and tenure of an officer are defined in the corporation charter, the bylaws, and the statutes.[102] But an agent's or an employee's status depends on his contract of employment, unless the bylaws or charter make special provision for it.

Thus, an attorney who was employed to take oaths as to documents was held to be an officer.[103] And a college's *faculty members* were held to be officers under a tax statute applying to property occupied by the *college's officers.*[104] But a foreman is not an officer.[105] Nor are the members of a committee to liquidate the corporation necessarily officers because of this appointment.[106]

If the charter or bylaws do not create an office, there is no such office— or officer.[107]

A general manager may or may not be an officer, depending on the method of creation of the position, and on its scope of authority.[108] Certainly, the word *manager* is not equivalent to *officer.*[109] But in modern practice, this title usually connotes status equivalent to that of an officer.[110]

Interference by agents or employees. When an agent or employee or officer oversteps propriety, by interfering with contract or other rights of other persons or organizations, he is not personally liable if he induced the breach in good faith and for the benefit of the corporation.[111]

Denial of promotion because of political affiliation is a violation of First Amendment rights of employees of public organizations.[112]

A college's failure to give timely notice to a probationary teacher that it did not intend to renew that teacher's contract of employment did not constitute automatic re-appointment with tenure.[113]

School administrators do not have "tenure" in administrative positions, and may be removed by the board for any reason that does not violate statutory or constitutional rights (e.g., such as First Amendment right of free speech and religious beliefs).[114]

A university professor has no "property right" protected by the Fourteenth Amendment if denied *emeritus* status.[115]

An employee of a city-supported *private community action organization,* bringing suit against the city for allegedly improper dismissal, comes under the statutory (Art. 78) proceedings rules covering misconduct of persons not employed/controlled by the city, and not under city employment-contract rules. Thus the Art. 78 (short, four-month) limitation period bars his suit brought years after the dismissal by administrative hearings.[116]

"Apparent" (seeming) *agents* of an NPO, such as in a nonprofit hospital, may bind the (seeming) employer by their tortious conduct, if an injured plaintiff's acceptance of them as agents was reasonable.[117]

At-will status of an employee is not converted into contractual (permanent) employment by her compliance with the employer's requirement that she move to a residence within 30 minutes responsive-time distance from the workplace, within two months after starting work. Conversion of at-will status to permanent status (requiring good cause for termination) must be independent consideration that is "detriment" to the employer and corresponding "benefit" to the employee.[118]

Employees as Third Party Beneficiaries

Where a nonprofit corporation receives federal grants for projects, an employee of the corporation is not automatically a third party beneficiary of the corporation's contract with the granting agency. In order for an employee to be a third party beneficiary, the language of the contract must clearly evidence the intent to permit enforcement by the third party or it must appear that no one other than the third party can recover if the promisor breaches the contract.[119]

A school nurse in a school district is not entitled to credit there for time spent assigned to part-time work at a parochial school.[120]

§335. COMPULSORY TESTIMONY

Like officers and directors, agents of corporations now are subject in many states and in certain federal matters to compulsory testimony statutes.

These statutes, contrary to Constitutional guarantees, compel a witness to testify even when he may tend to incriminate or degrade himself by so doing. But they bar prosecution for the witness' crimes revealed by him in so testifying.[121]

§336. EMPLOYEE COMPENSATION

(See, above, Sections 329 *et seq.*)

American NPO salaries in 1991, according to a survey of several surveys, showed higher salaries on the east and west coasts and lowest ones in the southwest, north central and mountain states; but the south paid the most to fund raisers while fringe benefits such as vacation time were highest in the midwest. The highest-budget-organizations paid the highest executive-director salaries (e.g., $5 million budget meant average $81,737 salary for executive director; under $100,000 budget meant $27,083). Median salaries nationwide were $48,000 for chief executives but $71,000 for chief legal officers and $14,560 for clerks. Averages were $52,789 for executive directors, $36,827 for development directors, $27,574 for program managers, $16,937 for secretaries. Executive "perks" of various kinds most commonly included a car allowance and spouse travel expenses, while officers' membership fees in professional associations were paid by 75 percent of NPOs. Major health and welfare groups seemed to pay the highest median salaries.[122]

According to a survey conducted by management consultant Towers Perrin of New York, top management officials in nonprofit corporations received a 4.8 percent merit increase in salary in 1992. Incentive pay programs, tied to productivity gains are a growing trend. Nonprofit employees are working a longer week but are getting more benefits, such as retirement benefits. Such organizations, in 1992, employed 8 million people, 10 percent of the U.S. labor force. Nonprofit groups represent the fastest growing sector in the service economy. Salaries of nonprofit employees are in general 10 to 15 percent lower than comparable jobs in the private sector.[123]

Nonprofit chief executive salaries rose 5.3 percent in 1992 according to a survey by the Greater Washington Society of Association Executives (GWSAE). The average chief executive's salary was $116,487.00. Payroll represents 32.6 percent of association budgets.[124]

Compensation for executives of larger nonprofit corporations must be reported annually to the federal, state, and some local governments. Salaries should also be reported to one or more watchdog organizations.[125]

The Fair Labor Standards Act (FLSA) applies to wages and hours of workers in private industry.[126] Its limited application to workers in nonprofit organizations is noted in Section 321 as regards *volunteer* workers. Its provisions as to minimum wage, child labor, equal pay, *etc.* are too specialized to warrant detailed treatment here. It does not apply to executives, administrators, professionals, or outside salespersons.[127]

Minimum wage laws set by Congress, at about $4.25 per hour in 1993 (and subject to change as inflation may require) should be noted.[128] *Overtime* work (over 40 hours) is basically payable at one and a half rate.[129] Special rules apply to hospitals and patient care institutions.[130]

Social Security exemptions' options are provided for private nonprofit organizations operated exclusively for charitable, religious, educational, literary, scientific, or humane purposes, under the Federal Insurance Contributions Act (FICA).[131] Their employees may elect coverage by filing a certificate waiving tax exemption and listing all concurring employees.[132] In addition, an employer's certification must also be filed.[133] This is effective for eight years. Other waiver rules apply as well.[134]

Miscellaneous employee benefits lists may include workers' compensation, pension plans, accident and health insurance, sick leave, life insurance, unemployment insurance, severance pay, *etc.*[135] Fringe benefits such as cars, hospitalization, dental care coverage, and the like are much appreciated, especially as they are not usually reported as taxable income.[136] Pension plans probably are the biggest single concern of most employees nowadays.[137] Expense accounts are dearly beloved by the higher ranking executive employees.[138]

Congress recently (1993) proposed a $150,000 cap on compensation that can be used for calculating benefits and contributions to tax-qualified retirement plans. The cap is now $235,840. The American Society of Association executives says that the cap will disadvantage nonprofits in their competitive search for top employees.[139]

A nonprofit corporation's welfare and benefits program is subject to regulation under the federal Employee Retirement Income Security Act (ERISA) only if the members have sufficient "commonalty of interest" and are a "homogenous employee organization." An organization that offers membership to employees, employers, and independent contractors is subject to state insurance laws due to lack of commonality of the members' interests.[140]

Agreement on compensation in advance is important, lest retroactive compensation be viewed as improper distribution of the corporation's assets.[141]

Liability insurance coverage (*D. and O.* policies) covering directors and officers also apply to agents and employees in some cases. Such coverage is expressly authorized by statutes in some states.[142] The 1986 Draft Revision of the Model Nonprofit Corporations Act presented a very complete coverage for "director, officer, employee, or agent," past or present, of the corporation or of some group to which he or she was lent as an agent.[143]

Income Withholding Proceedings

In income withholding proceedings, a nonprofit employer must be given an evidentiary hearing to determine whether it was in fact the spouse's employer and to determine the amount to be withheld from a spouse's income, before payments can be ordered for maintenance and support after divorce.[144]

§337. PERSONNEL POLICIES (REGULATIONS)

Nonprofit organizations should have high moral standards in all phases of their activities. Within the boundaries of fair and reasonable use of funds, employees should be treated with particularly scrupulous fairness. The niggardly compensation paid by many public organizations is well known. The effects of such policy, in discouraging able people from seeking employment there, are equally apparent.

Certainly, directors' and trustees' caution in use of organization funds does not justify niggardliness to organization employees, from whom hard work is expected. It is good policy to reward faithful service on the organization's behalf. In the long run it almost always benefits the organization itself, by spurring employees to greater enthusiasm and efforts on its behalf.

Rules and regulations. Experienced organizations almost always have, and keep current, written rules and regulations for the guidance of agents and employees. These regulations serve to answer most of the questions that arise in routine operations. They are most helpful and valuable, not only for purposes of efficiency but also for morale purposes. They are internal law, very often.[145]

For example, educational organizations generally issue annual *catalogs* or *bulletins* for the guidance of applicants, students, and administrators.[146] *Faculty manuals*, often amounting to whole volumes, are issued to faculty members and administrative personnel.[147]

Membership in appropriate other organizations (*e.g.*, of faculty members in professional societies, of students in national student organizations, of trade association executives in their national organization) should be encouraged. Nonprofit organization employees often are professional people, and must maintain a high standard of knowledge and ability.

Contented, enthusiastic employees are the secret of success of nonprofit organizations. After all, they are not likely to get rich working for most social service or charitable organizations.

Their principal rewards are moral satisfaction, interest in their work, a degree of security if not wealth, and a happy organization in which to work. It is both the duty and to the interest of the nonprofit organizations to build and maintain fine personnel policies.

Continuing (or beginning) as an employee, after receiving a copy of the *organization's manual*, can amount to *incorporation of the manual's terms* into the employment contract; but is not an implied contract if the employer retained the right to modify unilaterally the manual's terms and no term of employment was stated in the manual.[148]

A teacher's right to personal liberty is not violated when allegedly false and defamatory charges against him were in his *personnel file*, but were removed from it without having been disclosed.[149]

Supervision of Employees

(See sections above)
[Jeffrey L. Winn did research for the balance of this subsection.]

The usual rules of *respondeat superior* apply to nonprofit as well as profit organizations. Thus, a labor union representative's failure to prevent conduct specifically threatened by a local's member on a picket line will not cause tort liability of the international union which had no control or domination over the local union or its picket line.[150]

Constructive notice of public records was held not to be enough to make a union liable in tort done by its members if there was no showing of instigation or ratification of the act by the union leadership.[151]

A nonprofit institute may be liable for a sexual assault on a minor in a hospital room when it allowed employees to "hang-out" in an empty nurses' station near that room; summary judgment for the institute was denied.[152]

A hospital was not liable for a psychologist's coercing a mental patient into sexual relations when such unprofessional conduct was unexpected and not done for the employer's purposes.[153]

A mental health organization may be liable for negligent supervision of its employee, a minister-therapist, who persuaded a female patient to engage in sex with him; e.g., negligent hiring or supervision.[154]

But if the conduct of the employee is "reasonably incidental" to the employee's activities, such as a physician's relation to a mental patient in a mental health center, location and timing of the improper sexual relations may be relevant. Thus sex after taking the patient off the premises, after a counseling session, or even a month after cancellation of therapy, may be close enough to bind the clinic.[155]

Sexual abuse of children in a day center was held to be so contrary to the employer's purposes as to be departure from employment.[156]

A plaintiff must show that an employee's bad conduct or incompetence was discovered, or discoverable by the employer's use of reasonable supervision, in order to hold the employer liable for the employee's misconduct or incompetence.[157]

Instructing an employee (a professor) to refrain from injecting his personal religious beliefs into his teaching work is not a violation of his/her rights of freedom of speech.[158]

§338. ORGANIZATION LIABILITY FOR EMPLOYEES AND AGENTS

[Gretchen L. Henry and Tammy N. Giroux contributed material for this section.]

A town sanitation worker brought a civil rights action against unincorporated political associations in connection with a coercive political contribution scheme. The court held that it was not necessary to prove the participation of every member in order to impose § 1983 liability. The association could be held liable for the actions of its members who were responsible for solicitation and who were working within the scope of their general apparent authority in carrying out the coercive scheme.[159]

An African-American union member filed an action against a union alleging racial discrimination under 42 U.S.C. § 1981 and Title VII, based on discrimination in the dissemination of work information and employment referrals, and retaliation. Based on the plaintiff's allegations, the court held that the union member had an actionable cause against the union.[160]

The Plaintiff, a waitress, was injured when she tripped over coats dropped on the floor by an association of football players who were having a pizza party with their families. The court held that the members were not agents of the association because the pizza party was merely an informal gathering. The party did nothing to further the purpose underlying the existence of the association. Therefore, the association was not liable.[161]

A charitable institution is immune from liability to its beneficiaries if due care has been exercised in the selection and retention of the servants and agents. Immunity of charitable institution does not extend to a person who is not a beneficiary. While a spectator at a parade conducted as part of the Urbanna Oyster Festival, the Plaintiff, Evelyn Straley, was negligently injured when she was struck in the eye by a piece of candy thrown into the crowd of spectators by an unidentified person dressed as a clown. The Defendant filed a plea of charitable immunity. The court held that the Defendant owed a duty of reasonable care to Ms. Straley since she was a mere invitee and not a beneficiary of the charitable institution. The charity could not be protected by charitable immunity in this situation.[162]

An interscholastic athletic association is not vicariously liable for the actions of a referee at a school wresting tournament if the conduct of the match is in the sole control of the referee, the work is highly specialized, the referee provides his own uniforms, and the referee is paid by the job, even though the association tests and ranks the referees, assigns them to matches and provides a check list of things to do before, during, and after the match. Such a referee is an independent contractor, not an agent. The association has no duty to supervise the matches or to require that the referees be employees.[163]

The doctrine of assumption of risk has been abandoned in Michigan except in cases involving employer/employee relationships and cases involving express contractual assumption of risk.[164]

Sexual Harassment

The Equal Employment Opportunity Commission regulations state that an employer is responsible for the acts of its agents and supervisory employees, with respect to sexual harassment, regardless of whether the specific acts complained of were authorized. The employer is responsible even if the acts complained of were forbidden by the employer, and regardless of whether the employer knew or should have known of the occurrence of the acts. These regulations apply to nonprofit as well as for profit corporations.[165]

Criminal Liability

The court, in the *Jund* case, held that an unincorporated political association is capable of committing criminal violations and found liability under the Racketeer Influenced and Corrupt Practices Act (RICO). Liability was imposed on the associations, in connection with a coercive solicitation scheme, because the fruits of the violations went to the coffers of the associations themselves, not to the members who actually solicited.[166]

In 1994 RICO was applied, by the Supreme Court, to violent picketing of abortion clinics by anti-abortion (pro-life) organization members.

Hospital Liability

A hospital's duties include reasonable care and maintenance of safe and adequate facilities and equipment, selecting and retaining only competent physicians, overseeing all persons who practice medicine within all hospital walls as to patient care, and formulating, adopting and enforcing adequate rules and policies to assure quality care for patients. In order for a hospital to be charged with negligence under the *corporate liability doctrine*, the hospital must have actual or constructive knowledge of the defect or procedures that created harm. Also, the hospital's negligence must have been a substantial factor in bringing about harm to the injured party.[167]

The theory of *ostensible or apparent authority* holds hospitals vicariously liable for the acts of *nonemployees* who are providing services to patients in the hospital. The plaintiff must demonstrate that: (1) he reasonably believed an agency relationship existed; (2) the belief was created by an act or omission on the part of the agent or institution; and (3) the plaintiff detrimentally relied on the relationship.[168]

A patient, who suffered brain damage while in the care of an emergency room doctor and hospital, brought a medical malpractice action against the hospital. The court held the evidence was sufficient to support a jury finding that the hospital represented by act, conduct or statement that the physician was its employee or agent, even though the doctor was actually employed by a professional association and not the hospital.[169]

Hospitals are no longer viewed as a facility in which various independent contractors perform services. The hospital itself is viewed as the ultimate care giver. It is the hospital that patients look to if they are unnecessarily injured. One method of finding a hospital liable is to characterize the physician as the *ostensible or apparent agent* of the hospital under the doctrine of respondeat superior. An alternative method is to sue the hospital for *negligent credentialing*.[170]

A clinic that has its name on medical records (not the physicians), and gets payment for the physicians' services, may be liable for their negligence.[171]

A contract for a physician to treat a state's (group's) prisoners makes the state (group!) vicariously liable for his negligence, even though he is an independent contractor. [True for NPOs!][172]

Insurance Coverage

When an unincorporated association has an insurance coverage policy for its members, agents, or volunteers, the association will have a duty to defend against any claims or suits arising under that coverage. The Toledo Shrine Club's insurance policy contained the following provision:

LIABILITY COVERAGE–WHO IS AN INSURED?

"Anyone volunteering service to you is an "insured" while using a covered "auto" you don't own, hire or borrow to transport your clients or other persons to activities necessary to your business. Anyone else who furnishes that "auto" is also an insured."

Michael Scavo, a member of the Toledo Shrine Club, was driving to Celina, Ohio, to participate in a Shrine Club parade when he was involved in an automobile accident. To defend against the Plaintiff's claim, Shrine Club's insurer argued that Mr. Scavo's vehicle was not used in an activity for the business of the Shrine Club on the day of the accident since Mr. Scavo and his passengers had stopped at the Mercer County Elks Club near Celina to play a round of golf before proceeding to the parade. The defense contended that the golf game was not a Shrine activity and was in actuality a voluntary activity by Scavo.

The court held the Shrine Club liable for this automobile collision under the "Volunteer" endorsement of its automobile liability insurance. The court viewed the accident as a risk created by the trip to the hotel to prepare for the Shrine parade. Therefore, the risk was within the scope of liability defined in the policy and its "Volunteer" endorsement.[173]

An insurance policy that includes a provision excluding voluntary labor prevents a volunteer from suing an organization for injury that allegedly occurred during the course and in the scope of the volunteer's activity for the organization. At an ethnic festival, a volunteer, Romano, was injured when he fell in a hole inside the tent. The insurance at issue had an exclusion that provided that "this insurance does not apply to 'bodily injury,' 'personal injury,' or medical payments to any person . . . volunteering services to you arising out of or in the course of work performed on your behalf." The court determined Romano was a volunteer who had been injured in the course of work at the festival, thereby excluding him from coverage under the insurance contract.[174]

FORM NO. 156
Personnel Policy Regulations

[This set of Personnel Policies is from a university faculty booklet issued for the guidance of university employees. It is adaptable for use by other types of organizations, by judicious editing and amplifications, with the rules peculiar to the specific *kind* of organization.]

As Approved by
The Board of Trustees
(date)

FACULTY PERSONNEL POLICIES

201   PROCEDURES OF APPOINTMENT AND PROMOTION IN RANK.
        Members of the Faculty are Appointed and promoted by the Board of
        Trustees on nomination by a college or school and recommendation
        by the President.

201.1   PROCEDURES FOR NOMINATION. Nominations for appointment or promotion shall be made by the responsible department or school with concurrence of the Dean or Director. Nominations of department chairmen shall be made by the Dean or Director with advice of the department or school concerned and with advice of an *ad hoc* committee of senior faculty members, which, at his discretion, he may appoint for the purpose. Persons nominated for joint appointments shall receive joint consideration.

201.2   EVIDENCE OF QUALIFICATION FOR NOMINATION. Nominations for appointment or promotion shall be accompanied by the academic and personal qualification of nominees as stipulated in Section 202, including relevant biographical data, evidence of academic degrees and honors, a statement of publications and other professional achievements, and no less than three confidential letters of recommendation from responsible academic sources. Letters of recommendation accompanying nominations for appointment or promotion to the rank of professor shall be solicited from scholars or practitioners of acknowledged regional or national authority in the nominees' fields of study.

201.3   TERMS OF APPOINTMENT. Appointments to the Faculty shall be for specified terms or with indefinite tenure, as stipulated in Section 204.

   (a) *Instructor.* An instructor shall be appointed for one academic year and may be reappointed annually for no more than three additional years. Reappointment to a fourth year as an instructor shall be accompanied by notice of termination, unless advancement in rank is simultaneously recommended.

   (b) *Assistant Professor.* An assistant professor shall be appointed for a period of one to three years, subject to termination for cause, and may be reappointed for additional one- to three-year periods. Except as stipulated in Section 204, however, the cumulative years of appointment in The . . . . . . University in the ranks of instructor and assistant professor shall not exceed seven without promotion to associate professor with tenure.

   (c) *Associate Professor and Professor.* A first appointment to the Faculty in the rank of associate professor or professor may be with tenure or for a term of no more than four years. At the conclusion of such a term, he shall receive tenure or his appointment shall be terminated.

201.4   NOTICE OF RENEWAL OR TERMINATION OF APPOINTMENT. Written notice of renewal or termination of a term appointment without tenure shall be given to members of the faculty no later than March 1 during the first year of academic service, and no later than December 15 of the second and third years, and after the third year of service notice of termination of an appointment shall be given at least 12 months in advance. (This change was approved by the Board of Trustees on March 14, 19 . . .)

201.5   NEPOTISM. No person shall be appointed or employed when, in the judgment of the University, his term of employment or advancement, or his standards of conduct, are subject to the authority of another appointee or employee related by blood or marriage.

202   STANDARDS FOR APPOINTMENT AND PROMOTION IN RANK. Appointment and promotion to the Faculty shall be on the basis of merit without regard to race, color, religion, sex, age, national, or ethnic origin. In addition to requirements of formal education, the relevant standards are teaching ability, creative achievement, professional service, and professional bearing.

202.1   STANDARDS OF PROFESSIONAL MERIT.

(a) *Teaching*: The highest standards are comprehensive knowledge of the field of study, thorough preparation, intense interest in students as well as sensitivity to student interests, open-mindedness, independence, and integrity, and above all, intellectual enthusiasm which is transmitted to students.

(b) *Creative Achievement*: The standard of scholarship requires a working commitment to inquiry research and to creative achievement. The University obligation for the generation of new knowledge and practices imposes a responsibility for creativity, whether in inquiry and investigation, writing, design and production, or in the performing and fine arts. In the best of scholars and the best of teachers, creative inquiry is joined with effective classroom teaching.

(c) *Professional Service*: A university faculty member is "a citizen, a member of a learned profession, and an officer of an educational institution."* After a period of personal growth in which he is encouraged to develop his abilities as a teacher and creative scholar, a faculty member may properly be expected to assume increased responsibility, in keeping with his professional interest, for the government of the University, the standards of his discipline, and the welfare of the civic community.

(d) *Professional Bearing*: Personal qualities which have a direct relation to the professional standing of a faculty member, his colleagues, or the University are, of course, relevant when considering his appointment or promotion.

202.2   APPOINTMENT AND PROMOTION BY RANK. Possession of an earned doctorate or its equivalent, if such is a recognized standard of attainment in any discipline or field of study, is normally required of all appointments above the rank of instructor.

---

*AAUP and AAU; 1940 Statement of Principles on Academic Freedom and Tenure.

(a) *Instructor.* An instructor is appointed primarily upon evidence from a fully accredited institution of graduate or professional study that he holds a master's degree or its equivalent, is well-advanced upon doctoral or comparable study, if such is required in his discipline, exhibits good promise as a teacher and original scholar, and possesses the qualities for professional development.

(b) *Assistant Professor.* Appointment or promotion to the rank of assistant professor is based upon demonstrated teaching ability, as attested by his colleagues, graduate advisers, and qualified students, and upon indications of creative scholarship and a willingness to assume responsibility in departmental, college, and University affairs.

(c) *Associate Professor.* Appointment or promotion to the rank of associate professor is based on sustained high-quality performance in teaching and the evidence of a growing capacity for scholarship, as well as upon evidence that the candidate can assume responsibility for participating in the government of the University and the activities of his professional associations. Inasmuch as appointment or promotion to this rank entails tenure (Section 204, below), the University and the appointee assume an obligation to one another and to the academic community which must be weighed carefully. It is, in many ways, the most important appointment to be conferred or accepted.

(d) *Professor.* Appointment or promotion to the rank of professor is based on sustained excellence in teaching and demonstrated performance in scholarship. A professor is the highest ranking officer of instruction, and as such participates effectively in the government of the University and in his professional associations. In addition to those qualities demanded for the rank of associate professor, the candidate for professor shall have a regional or national reputation as a scholar or practitioner in his field, as may be required for professional success in his field.

202.3 APPOINTMENT OF DEPARTMENT CHAIRMEN

(a) *Duties:* The Chairman (1) shall have general administrative responsibility for the Department's program and budget, subject to approval by the Dean of the College; (2) shall recommend to the Dean appointments, promotions, salary adjustments, dismissals, and the conferment of tenure with regard to the Department faculty; (3) shall encourage and promote Department morale, research and scholarship, and quality teaching; and (4) shall cultivate democratic management by sharing information on all matters of general department interest with all the members of the Department on regular contract (defined as constituting Instructor, Assistant Professors, Associate Professors, and Professors) at appropriate intervals, and by accepting majority opinion on actions, except insofar as he shall decide otherwise, in which case he should give his reasons and invite comments.

(b) *Method of Selection*: The Dean of the College shall meet with the College's elected Faculty Council members and the President of the University or his representatives. Together they shall determine the method of choosing the selection committee. The committee established to make recommendations on the selection may differ from case to case according to the particular situation at the time in the department concerned. Considerations involved in deciding on the selection committee may include the size of the department, the relative strengths of subspecialties within the department, the administrative policies and procedures of the previous chairman, the state of morale in the department, the degree of cooperation between the department and related departments, and perhaps numerous other factors. Normally, however, the selection committee will be composed of faculty elected by the department on regular contract, although faculty members from one or more related disciplines or professional fields may be added. The selection committee may choose to use the services of one or more consultants. The committee will solicit recommendations and interview prospective appointees. The committee will recommend to the Dean and the President or their representatives the names of individuals considered acceptable for appointment.

All the persons involved in the selection will work closely together in attempting to achieve agreement on the individual who will finally be offered the chairmanship through the customary procedure of the University.

(c) *Review and Continuance*: A Department Chairman will serve for four years at the pleasure of the Dean. He shall be eligible for appointment to successive four-year terms. In May of the third year, the Dean shall solicit the individual opinions of the Department faculty on regular contract, expressed by secret ballot, on the Chairman's reappointment. If the Chairman lacks the support of the majority, the Dean may, nonetheless, decide contrariwise, in which case he shall so inform the faculty and invite their comments. If the chairman is not to be reappointed, the above-mentioned method for the selection of a successor shall be undertaken.

A Department Chairman appointed to that position before the activation of the . . . . University shall have his term of office defined as having begun September 1, 19 . . , 19 . . , 19 . . , or 19 . . , at the discretion of the Dean of the College. Others serving at the time this policy is adopted shall have their initial term commence on September 1 following their appointment.

202.4 APPOINTMENT OF DEANS OF COLLEGES

(a) *Duties*: The Dean of a College (1) shall have general administrative responsibility for the program and budget of the College, subject to approval by the President of the University; (2) shall recom-

mend to the President appointments, promotions, salary adjust
ments, dismissals, and the conferment of tenure with regard to the
College faculty; (3) shall encourage and promote College morale,
research and scholarship, and quality teaching; and (4) shall cultivate democratic management by sharing information on all matters of general College interest with all the members of the College faculty and by consulting them on all significant notions as
required by the College Bylaws.

(b) *Method of Selection*: The Dean of Faculties shall meet with the college's elected Faculty Control members and the President of the
University or his representative. Together they shall determine the
method of choosing the selection committee. The committee
established to make recommendations on the selection may differ
from case to case according to the particular situation at the time
in the college concerned. Considerations involved in deciding on
the selection committee may include the size of the college, the
relative strength of departments within the college, the administrative policy and procedures of the previous dean, the state of
morale in the college, the degree of cooperation between the college and other colleges, and perhaps numerous other factors. Normally, however, the selection committee will be composed of faculty elected by the faculty of the college on regular contract,
although faculty members from one or more other colleges may
be added. The selection committee may choose to use the services
of one or more consultants. The committee will solicit recommendations and interview prospective appointees. The committee
will recommend to the Dean of Faculties and the President or his
representative the names of individuals considered acceptable for
appointment. These names shall have been approved by the majority of the Department Chairmen in the College. All the persons
involved in the selection will work closely together in attempting
to achieve agreement on the individual who will finally be offered
the appointment through the customary procedure of the University.

(c) *Review and Continuance*: The Dean of a College shall serve at the
pleasure of the President. In May of every third year, however, the
Dean of Faculties shall solicit the individual written opinions of the
College's tenured faculty on the Dean's performance in office.
Normally, the Dean shall enjoy the confidence of at least a major-
ity of his tenured faculty in order to continue in the position.

The Dean of a College appointed to that position before the
activation of The . . . . University shall have his term of
office defined as having begun September 1, 19 . . . Others serving
at the time this policy is adopted shall have their accession to
office deemed to have commenced on September 1 following their
appointment.

203   ACADEMIC FREEDOM. The .... University subscribes to
        the 1940 Statement of Principles on Academic Freedom and Tenure
            of the American Association of University Professors and the Asso-
            ciation of American Universities (as shown in Attachment A).

203.1   THE RIGHT TO DEMONSTRATE AND PROTEST ON UNIVERSITY
        PROPERTY. It is recognized that free speech is essential in a democ-
        ratic society. As individuals or as groups, the faculty are permitted to
        demonstrate and protest on University property in opposition to Uni-
        versity, City, State, National, or International Policy provided they do
        not violate any applicable local, state, or federal law, and no acts are
        performed which 1) cause damage to property (personal or Universi-
        ty); 2) cause physical injury to any individual; 3) prevent any student
        from attending class, entering or leaving any University facility, or
        attending any special program on University property; 4) prevent
        administrative officers, faculty, students, employees, or invited guests of
        the University from performing duties they are authorized to perform;
        5) block the normal business of the University, particularly classroom
        or laboratory instruction; and 6) block pedestrian or vehicle traffic.
        Disciplinary procedures which may be taken against any faculty mem-
        ber or members charged with actions contrary to these policies shall
        be as such as are provided in paragraph 204.5 below.

204   TENURE. Tenure is the prerogative of a qualified faculty member to
        appointment on a continuing basis, without arbitrary or discriminato-
        ry treatment, subject to abrogation only for certain imperatives and
        after due process. Tenure is the guaranty of academic freedom, and
        thus embraces the obligation of the faculty member to maintain the
        highest standards of his profession. It is awarded, therefore, in recog-
        nition of professional competence and not simply as a condition of
        employment.

204.1   CRITERIA FOR AWARDING TENURE. Tenure may be granted after
        a probationary period of term appointments. This period shall be lim-
        ited to a total of seven years, provided, however, that no more than
        three years of full-time service in other fully accredited institutions
        which grant a baccalaureate or higher degree need be credited.
        Appointment to the full-time rank of associate professor shall be
        accompanied by notifications as to the presence or absence of tenure
        unless a probationary period is stipulated for a first appointment in the
        University. No appointment to the rank of instructor or assistant pro-
        fessor shall be with tenure, excepting any assistant professor who may
        have received or been nominated for tenure on or before September
        15, 19 . . . Persons who may hold concurrent faculty appointments and
        administrative positions shall have tenure only in their faculty capaci-
        ties. Failure of a letter of appointment to mention tenure means that
        no tenure was granted.

204.2   PROCEDURES FOR AWARDING TENURE. No later than 12 months
        before the terminal date of his probationary period of term appoint-

ments, an assistant professor shall receive written notice that he will be promoted to associate professor with tenure or that his appointment is to be terminated. An associate professor or professor first appointed in the University at that rank without tenure shall receive written notice no later than 12 months before expiration of his appointment that he will receive tenure or that his appointment is to be terminated. Procedures for nomination and presentation of evidence of qualification for tenure are as provided in paragraphs 201.1 and 201.2 above, for appointments and promotions.

204.3   DISMISSAL OF PERSONNEL WITH TENURE. A faculty member may be subject to dismissal during his appointment for cause or for general reasons of University reorganization or financial exigency. In cases of dismissal because of reorganization or financial considerations, the faculty member shall receive notice no less than 12 months prior to his release. Grounds for dismissal for cause shall extend to incompetence, violation of professional standards, neglect of duty, personal dishonesty or misconduct, and conviction of felony.

204.4   PROCEDURES FOR DISMISSAL FOR CAUSE. No faculty member shall be dismissed for cause without due process. Proceedings for such dismissal shall be conducted by the President and other Academic Officers, the appropriate committee of the Faculty Council, and the respondent according to the 1958 Statement of Procedural Standards in Faculty Dismissal Proceedings of the American Association of University Professors and the Association of American Universities, as shown in Attachment B.

204.5   PROCEDURES FOR DISCIPLINARY ACTION RESULTING FROM DEMONSTRATIONS AND PROTESTS ON UNIVERSITY PROPERTY. No faculty member shall be disciplined for actions specified in paragraph 203.1 above without due process. Disciplinary proceedings shall be conducted by the President and/or other delegated academic officers before the Faculty Judiciary Committee of the Faculty Council following the determination of a basis for action upon a review of the charges by the Faculty Affairs Committee. A respondent or respondents shall have 1) the right to have a reasonable length of time prior to the hearing, a written statement concerning the alleged misconduct; 2) the right to remain silent or to cease answering questions at any time he believes he may be incriminating himself or that his personal or constitutional rights are being infringed upon; 3) the right to confront witnesses against him; 4) the right to counsel; 5) the right to present witnesses and a defense in his behalf; 6) the right to the attendance of witnesses from among employees and students of ...... University; 7) the right to a written transcript of the hearing if he so requests; 8) the right to reasonable privacy in which to conduct the hearing; and 9) the right to remain in his appointed position during proceedings involving him; provided no immediate harm to himself or others is threatened by his continuance, and to continue to receive his pay, unless legal considerations forbid.

205 RESIGNATION. A faculty member has an obligation to the University upon voluntary termination of his appointment. He shall give notice of his intent to resign no less than three months before termination of his service at the end of any academic quarter.

206 RETIREMENT. The services of all university faculty members shall terminate on June 30th following the date at which they reach the age of 70 years, or upon their 70th birthday, if that falls on June 30th, provided that in exceptional circumstances any faculty member may be reappointed at rank for terms of one to three years thereafter.

207 PAYMENT OF SALARY.

208 FACULTY BENEFITS.

209 FACULTY TRAVEL.

210 LEAVES OF ABSENCE. Short leaves of a day or two for professional purposes which entail no interruption of regular work require no more than oral notification to the department chairman. Sick leaves or leaves to attend scientific or professional meetings of no more than one week, during which time the department can assume the absent member's responsibilities, require oral permission of the department chairman or dean. For extended leaves which will interrupt department routine or burden the faculty member's colleagues, a formal request must be submitted. Formal request is required for the following extended leaves, both with and without pay.

210.1 LEAVES WITH PAY.

(a) *Military Leave.* As a general rule, faculty members who participate in military reserve programs should take their training during the summer months. Leave with pay will be granted, however, to members of the National Guard and other armed forces for annual two-week periods of service.

(b) *Judicial Leave.* Leave with pay is granted when a faculty member is called for jury duty or to testify as a principal or expert witness before any court or governmental hearing body.

(c) *Professional Leave.* Full-time leave with prorated pay is granted to members of the Faculty under the following conditions. The period of leave must be used for professional benefit to the faculty member, his discipline, or the University. Thus leave may be requested for purpose of research, writing, or other independent creative work; to assume a temporary professional position without compensation, such as the editorship of a scholarly journal; for completion or extension of higher education or training; or for the purposes which the President and other Academic Officers may find compelling.

A faculty member, at the rank of assistant professor or above, is eligible for professional leave after six consecutive years of full-time service in the University, at least two years of which have been at the rank of assistant professor or above. Second and subsequent professional leaves are awarded wholly on a showing of merit or need, except that a minimum of two academic years of full-time service in the University must elapse between the end of one such leave and the beginning of another.

Leave may be granted for one, two, or three consecutive academic quarters, with pay as follows: full pay for the first quarter, one-half pay for the second quarter, and one-quarter pay for the third quarter. Under no circumstances may the recipient of professional leave with pay accept employment for compensation, academic or other, during the period of his leave, although he is encouraged to seek supplemental grants or awards for independent research or training. Periods of professional leave are credited as service in the University for purposes of promotion, tenure, increments, and faculty benefits.

(d) *Sick Leave.* (See Section 208, Faculty Benefits.)

210.2   LEAVES WITHOUT PAY.

(a) *Military Service Leave.*

(b) *Special Leave.* Leave without pay may be granted for study, research, professional employment, election or appointment to public office, or other personal reasons. Periods of leave without pay may or may not be credited as professional service in consideration of promotion, tenure, and increments, depending on the circumstances of the leave. University benefits may continue during a period of special leave with approval of the President, provided, in any case, that the faculty member on leave makes proper arrangements for payment of premiums in all contributory benefit programs.

210.3   APPLICATION FOR EXTENDED LEAVES. All extended leaves of absence, with or without pay, are granted by the Board of Trustees upon recommendation of the President. Applications for professional leave with pay and special leave without pay must be submitted at a sufficiently advanced date that they will reach the Board of Trustees for its consideration at least one full academic quarter before the beginning of leave. Applications for other extended leaves shall be submitted at the earliest practicable date.

(a) *Professional Leave with Pay.* Except in the circumstance that an application may initially be recommended by the President, the applicant for professional leave with pay shall submit a written request to his department chairman stating in detail the purpose and program of the proposed leave, the places where the applicant is to be, the positions he is to hold, and whether and in what amount supplemental funds have been solicited or received. After departmental review, the application, together with applicant's up to-date curriculum vitae, shall be forwarded to the Dean or Director for review. It shall thereafter be sent to the President, who shall act with the advice of the appropriate committee of the Faculty on all questions of merit.

(b) *Other Extended Leaves*: Application procedures for other extended leaves shall be as above for professional leave with pay, except that the extent of information required may vary and the President may seek the advice of the appropriate committee of the faculty at his discretion.

211   GRANTS AND CONTRACTS FOR RESEARCH, TRAINING, AND OTHER PURPOSES. All proposals to outside agencies for financial support of University projects in excess of $500 for research, training, institutes, seminars, facilities, equipment, or other University activities or purchases shall be submitted to the Academic Vice-President, according to procedures that he shall establish. All such grants or contracts shall be negotiated by the Academic Vice-President, acting with advice of responsible faculty members and officers, and shall be accepted for the University by the Board of Trustees on recommendation of the President. No grant or contract shall be negotiated or accepted by the University which stipulates a level of compensation or employee benefits for any faculty member in excess of that stipulated in his annual appointment contract, or which commits any faculty member to a type or extent of employment to which he, his department, and the Dean or Director have not been parties. All monies received under the terms of any such grant or contract shall be received by the chief financial officer and disbursed by him according to University policies and procedures.

212   CONSULTING AND OTHER EXTRAMURAL EMPLOYMENT. Faculty members are frequently called upon to render professional counsel or service to public or private agencies for which compensation is direct and in excess of the terms of University contracts. Properly transacted, such services fulfill a responsibility of the University to the community at large and provide invaluable professional experiences to faculty members. It is understood, however, that such activities shall in no way limit the extent or quality of a faculty member's obligation to the University or his profession. In no event shall he accept a regular salary or annual retainer for his counsel or services without the written consent of the chairman of the department and the dean of the college, or use the name, symbol, or address of The . . . . . . University in any extramural employment agreement. University facilities, equipment, and materials may be used for such purposes only with the express consent of the University and according to explicit terms for reimbursement. Department chairmen shall at all times be kept informed of the extramural employment of faculty members, and shall submit a detailed report of such activities to the Dean in the spring quarter of each academic year. It is expected that consulting activities for compensation will be at a fee level equal or above the level gener-

ally charged by private practitioner in the community for the same service. Consulting activities should make a demonstrable contribution to the enrichment of the teaching and/or research competence of the faculty member. With advice from appropriate officers of the University, the President may order suspension of any extramural employment.

213   CANDIDACY FOR PUBLIC OFFICE. A faculty member may run for or accept elective or appointive office under the following conditions. He shall in all cases submit a full statement of his proposed campaign activities and of the responsibilities of the office which he may assume. When, in the judgment of the University, those activities and responsibilities will conflict with his professional obligations, he shall submit a written application for reduced levels of employment and compensation in the University, or for special leave of absence without pay, at such a date that it will come before the Board of Trustees for its consideration at least one full academic quarter before the assumption of the said activities or responsibilities. Submission of statements and applications shall be according to procedures set forth in paragraph 210.3, Application for Extended Leaves.

Attachment A

1940 Statement of Principles on Academic Freedom and Tenure of the American Association of University Professors and the Association of American Universities:

(a) The teacher is entitled to full freedom in research and in the publication of the results, subject to the adequate performance of his other academic duties; but research for pecuniary return should be based upon an understanding with the authorities of the institution.

(b) The teacher is entitled to freedom in the classroom in discussing his subject, but he should be careful not to introduce into his teaching controversial matter which has no relation to his subject. Limitations of academic freedom because of religious or other aims of the institution should be clearly stated in writing at the time of the appointment.

(c) The college or university teacher is a citizen, a member of a learned profession, and an officer of an educational institution. When he speaks or writes as a citizen, he should be free from institutional censorship or discipline, but his special position in the community imposes special obligations. As a man of learning and an educational officer, he should remember that the public may judge his profession and his institution by his utterances. Hence, he should at all times be accurate, should exercise appropriate restraint, should show respect for the opinions of others, and should make every effort to indicate that he is not an institutional spokesman.

Attachment B

19 .. STATEMENT ON PROCEDURAL STANDARDS IN FACULTY DISMISSAL PROCEEDINGS

FOREWORD

The following statement on Procedural Standards in Faculty Dismissal Proceedings has been prepared by a joint committee representing the Association of American Colleges and the American Association of University Professors. It is intended to supplement the 1940 Statement of Principles on Academic Freedom and Tenure by providing a formulation of the "academic due process" that should be observed in dismissal proceedings. However, the exact procedural standards here set forth "are not intended to establish a norm in the same manner as the 1940 Statement of Principles of Academic Freedom and Tenure, but are presented rather as a guide . . ." (The statement was approved by the American Association of American Colleges in January, 1958, and by the American Association of University Professors in April, 1958.)

INTRODUCTORY COMMENTS

Any approach toward settling the difficulties which have beset dismissal proceedings on many American campuses must look beyond procedure into setting and cause. A dismissal proceeding is a symptom of failure; no amount of use of removal process will help strengthen higher education as much as will the cultivation of conditions in which dismissals rarely if ever need occur.

Just as the board of control or other governing body is the legal and fiscal corporation of the college, the faculty are the academic entity. Historically, the academic corporation is the older. Faculties were formed in the Middle Ages, with managerial affairs either self-arranged or handled in course by the parent church. Modern college faculties, on the other hand, are part of a complex and extensive structure requiring legal incorporation, with stewards and managers specifically appointed to discharge certain functions.

Nonetheless, the faculty of a modern college constitute an entity as real as that of the faculties of medieval times, in terms of collective purpose and function. A necessary precondition of a strong faculty is that it have firsthand concern with its own membership. This is properly reflected both in appointments to and in separations from the faculty body.

A well-organized institution will reflect sympathetic understanding by trustees and teachers alike of their respective and complementary roles. These should be spelled out carefully in writing and made available to all. Trustees and faculty should understand and agree on their several functions in determining who shall join and who shall remain on the faculty. One of the prime duties of the administrator is to help preserve understanding of those functions. It seems clear on the American college scene, that a close positive relationship exists between the excellence of colleges, the strength of their faculties, and the extent of faculty responsibility in determining faculty membership. Such a condition is in no way inconsistent with full faculty awareness of institutional factors with which governing boards must be primarily concerned.

In the effective college, a dismissal proceeding involving a faculty member on tenure, or one occurring during the term of an appointment will be a rare exception, caused by individual weakness and not by an unhealthful setting. When it does come, however, the college should be prepared for it, so that both institutional integrity and individual human rights may be preserved during the process of resolving the trouble. The faculty must be willing to recommend the dismissal of a colleague when necessary. By the same token, presidents and governing boards must be willing to give full weight to a faculty judgment favorable to a colleague.

One persistent source of difficulty is the definition of adequate cause for the dismissal of a faculty member. Despite the 1940 Statement of Principles on Academic Freedom and Tenure and subsequent attempts to build upon it, considerable ambiguity and misunderstanding persist throughout higher education, especially in the respective conceptions of governing boards, administrative officers, and faculties concerning this matter. The present statement assumes that individual institutions will have formulated their own definitions of adequate cause for dismissal, bearing in mind the 1940 Statement and standards which have developed in the experience of academic institutions.

This statement deals with procedural standards. Those recommended are not intended to establish a norm in the same manner as the 1940 Statement of Principles on Academic Freedom and Tenure, but are presented rather as a guide to be used according to the nature and traditions of particular institutions in giving effect to both faculty tenure rights and the obligations of faculty members in the academic community.

PROCEDURAL RECOMMENDATIONS

1. Preliminary Proceedings Concerning the Fitness of a Faculty Member. When reason arises to question the fitness of a college or university faculty member who has tenure or whose term appointment has not expired, the appropriate administrative officers should ordinarily discuss the matter with him in personal confidence. The matter may be terminated by mutual consent at this point; but if an adjustment does not result, a standing or *ad hoc* committee elected by the faculty and charged with the function of rendering confidential advice in such situations should informally inquire into the situation, to effect an adjustment if possible, and if none is effected, to determine whether in its view formal proceedings to consider his dismissal should be instituted. If the committee recommends that such proceedings should be begun, or if the president of the institution, even after considering a recommendation of the committee favorable to the faculty member, expresses his conviction that a proceeding should be undertaken, action should

be commenced under the procedures which follow. Except where there is disagreement, a statement with reasonable particularity of the grounds proposed for the dismissal should then be jointly formulated by the president and the faculty committee; if there is disagreement, the president or his representative should formulate the statement.

2. Commencement of Formal Proceedings.

   The formal proceedings should be commenced by a communication addressed to the faculty member by the president of the institution, informing the faculty member of the statement formulated, and inform- ing him that, if he so requests, a hearing to determine whether he should be removed from his faculty position on the grounds stated will be conducted by a faculty committee at a specified time and place. In setting the date of the hearing, sufficient time should be allowed the faculty member to prepare his defense. The faculty member should be informed, in detail or by reference to published regulations, of the pro- cedural rights that will be accorded to him. The faculty member should state in reply whether he wishes a hearing, and, if so, should answer in writing, not less than one week before the date set for the hearing, the statements in the president's letter.

3. Suspension of the Faculty Member.

   Suspension of the faculty member during the proceedings involving him is justified only if immediate harm to himself or others is threatened by his continuance. Unless legal considerations forbid, any such suspension should be with pay.

4. Hearing Committee.

   The committee of faculty members to conduct the hearing and reach a decision should either be an elected standing committee not previously concerned with the case or a committee established as soon as possible after the president's letter to the faculty member has been sent. The choice of members of the hearing committee should be on the basis of their objectivity and competence and of the regard in which they are held in the academic community. The committee should elect its own chairman.

5. Committee Proceeding.

   The committee should proceed by considering the statement of grounds for dismissal already formulated, and the faculty member's response written before the time of the hearing. If the faculty member has not requested a hearing, the committee should consider the case on the basis of the obtainable information and decide whether he should be removed; otherwise the hearing should go forward. The committee, in consultation with the president and the faculty member, should exer- cise its judgment as to whether the hearing should be public or private. If any acts are in dispute, the testimony of witnesses and other evidence concerning the matter set forth in the president's letter to the faculty member should be received.

The president should have the option of attendance during the hearing. He may designate an appropriate representative to assist in developing the case, but the committee should determine the order of proof, should normally conduct the questioning of witnesses, and, if necessary, should secure the presentation of evidence important to the case.

The faculty member should have the option of assistance by counsel, whose function should be similar to those of the representative chosen by the president. The faculty member should have the additional procedural rights set forth in the 1940 Statement of Principles on Academic Freedom and Tenure, and should have the aid of committee, when needed in securing the attendance of witnesses. The faculty member or his counsel and the representative designated by the president should have the right, within reasonable limits, to question all witnesses who testify orally. The faculty member should have the opportunity to be confronted by all witnesses adverse to him. Where unusual and urgent reasons move the hearing committee to withhold this right, or where the witness cannot appear, the identity of the witness, as well as his statements, should nevertheless be disclosed to the faculty member. Subject to these safeguards, statements may when necessary be taken outside the hearing and reported to it. All of the evidence should be duly recorded. Unless special circumstances warrant, it should not be necessary to follow formal rules of court procedure.

6. Consideration by Hearing Committee.

   The committee should reach its decision in conference, on the basis of the hearing. Before doing so, it should provide an opportunity for the faculty member or his counsel and the representative designated by the president to argue orally before it. If written briefs would be helpful, the committee may request them. The committee may proceed to decision promptly, without having the record of the hearing transcribed, where it feels that a just decision can be reached by this means; or it may await the availability of a transcript of the hearing if its decision would be aided thereby. It should make explicit findings with respect to each of the grounds of removal presented, and a reasoned opinion may be desirable. Publicity concerning the committee's decision may properly be withheld until consideration has been given to the case by the governing body of the institution. The president and the faculty member should be notified of the decision in writing and should be given a copy of the record of the hearing. Any release to the public should be made through the president's office.

7. Consideration by Governing Body.

   The president should transmit to the governing body the full report of the hearing committee, stating its action. On the assumption that the governing board has accepted the principle of the faculty hearing committee, acceptance of the committee's decision would normally be expected. If the governing body chooses to review the case, its review should be based on the record of the previous hearing, accompanied by opportunity for argument, oral or written or both, by the principals at the hearing or their representatives. The decision of the hearing committee should either be sustained or the proceeding be returned to the committee with objections specified. In such a case the committee should reconsider taking account of the stated objections and receiving new evidence if necessary. It should frame its decision and communicate in the same manner as before. Only after study of the committee's reconsideration should the governing body make a final decision overruling the committee.

8. Publicity.

Except for such simple announcements as may be required, covering the time of the hearing and similar matters, public statements about the case by either the faculty member or the administrative officers should be avoided so far as possible until the proceedings have been completed. Announcement of the final decision should include a statement of the hearing committee's original action, if this has not previously been made known.

POINTS TO REMEMBER

- Distinguish between officers and other agents.
- Distinguish agents and other employees.
- Remember that directors and officers are agents.
- Set up rules in the bylaws as to agents and employees as well as officers.
- Appoint at least one personnel officer.
- Remember the compulsory testimony statutes.
- Establish fair personnel policies.
- Check local statutes as to unemployment, workmen's compensation, and other applicable statutes as to nonprofit organization employee coverage.
- Make, and keep current, organization rules and regulation for agents and employees. Then, *follow* the rules that have been published.
- Set up reasonable compensation terms, within the practical resources of the organization; but remember the biblical saying: "Thou shalt not muzzle the ox that treadeth out the corn." *Slander of an accrediting officer (inspector)* is actionable *tort. M. Nazeri. Missouri Valley* College, #75201 MO Supr. Ct., Aug. 17, 1993.

NOTES TO CHAPTER 32

1. 7 *NonProfit Times* (2) 4 (Feb. 1993).
2. *See,* Conard, *Corporations in Perspective,* 111, 365 (1976); Maslow, *A Theory of Human Moti-*

vation, 50 Psychological Rev. 370 (1943); McClelland & Burnham, *Power Is the Great Motivator*, 1976 Harv. Bus. Rev. 861.

3. Henn and Alexander, *Corporations*, 663–694 (3rd ed., 1983). See, Board of Regents v. Illinois Educ. L. R. Board, 520 N.E.2d 1150 (Ill. App., 1988): Classification of "managers" of course affects compensation; *e.g.*, some services are more like "community of interest" than "managerial." In re Estate of Muhammad, 520 N.E.2d 795 (Ill. App. 1987): Management compensation may not be paid out of funds solicited for "religious" use if it is a profit for a religious leader's personal estate. And see, below, n.111.

4. Rogers v. Schenkel, 162 F.2d 596 (2d Cir., 1947).

5. 29 U.S.C. §203; Turner v. Unification Church, 473 F. Supp. 367 (D.C., R.I. 1978); *Black's Law Dictionary* 1413 (5th ed., 1979).

6. 29 U.S.C. §203(s); Wage & Hour Div., *Field Operations Handbook* 10, c.16.

7. *See*, Brennan v. Partida, 492 F.2d 707 (5th Cir., 1974); Nunnelly v. Farmers Insur. Exchange, 564 P.2d 231 (Okl. 1977); Dunlop v. Dr. Pepper-Pepsi C. B. Co., 529 F.2d 298 (6th Cir., 1976).

8. English v. Dhane, 286 S.W.2d 666 (Tex. Div. App. 1956); Stephenson v. Golden, 279 Mich. 710, 276 N.W. 849 (1937); *and see* Black's *Law Dict.* 59 (5th ed., 1979); and 2A *Words and Phrases*, 515 *et seq.* (Supp.).

9. Cornell v. Ohio State Univ. Hospitals, 521 N.E.2d 857 (Ohio Ct. Cl., 1987); Young v. Demos, 70 Ga. App. 577, 28 S.E. 2d 891, 893 (1944); Aberdeen Aerie No. 24 of F.O.E. v. United States, 50 F.Supp. 734, 736–738 (D.C. Wash. 1943); Black's *Law Dict.* 471 (5th ed. 1979); and 14 *Words and Phrases* 524, *et seq.* (Supp.). *See* (president, employed as production supervisor, for a salary, held to be an "employee" for workmen's compensation coverage) Williams v. Williams Insulation Materials, Inc., 91 Ariz. 89, 370 P.2d 59, 63 (1962). *See* (Unemployment Compensation Act applicability) Smith v. Brooklyn Bar Assn., 266 A.D. 1038. 44 N.Y.S.2d 620, 621 (1943). *See* (Social Security Act applicability) Matcovith v. Anglem, 134 P.2d 834, 837 (9th Cir. 1943); Hayes v. Morse, 474 F.2d 1265 (8th Cir. 1973).

10. Salaymeh v. Interqual, Inc., 508 N.E.2d 1155 (Ill. App., 1987).

11. Doane Agr. Service, Inc. v. Coleman, 254 F.2d 40, 43 (6th Cir. 1958). Freeman v. Navarre, 47 Wash.2d 760, 289 P.2d 1015, 1019 (1955).

12. State v. Bond, 94 W. Va. 255, 118 S.E. 276, 279 (1923).

13. Gooden v. Mitchell, 2 Terry (Del.) 501, 21 A.2d 197, 200 (1941).

14. Essex County Country Club v. Chapman, 113 N.J.L. 182, 173 A. 591, 592 (1934).

15. Keefe v. City of Monroe, 9 La. App. 545, 120 S. 102 (1929).

16. Hopkins v. Cromwell, 89 A.D. 481, 85 N.Y.S. 839 (1903).

17. *See* Wills v. Rowland and Co., 117 A.D. 122, 102 N.Y.S. 386 (1907).

18. *See*, Schulte v. Ideal Food Pdts. Co., 208 Iowa 767, 226 N.W. 174 (1929).

19. Fells v. Katz, 256 N.Y. 67, 175 N.E. 516 (1931).

20. Social Security Board v. Warren, 142 F.2d 974 (8th Cir. 1944) 2 Oleck, *Modern Corporation Law* §958 (1978 Supp.).

21. *See*, n.9, Williams case. But note that statutes may bar workmen's compensation coverage for nonprofit organizations.

22. *See*, n.9, Smith case. But note that statutes may bar unemployment compensation coverage for nonprofit organizations.

23. Articles, 90 *Community Up-Date* (Newsletter) 4 (Mar. 1990) publ. by Becker, Poliakoff & Streitfeld law office, Fort Lauderdale, FL 33312-6525.

24. *Geisinger Clinic v. Di Cuccio*, 606 A.2d 509 (Pa. Super. 1992).

25. *Sarah Bush Lincoln Health Center v. Perket*, 605 N.E. 2d 613 (Ill. App. 4 Dist., 1992).

26. 4 *NonProfit Times* (10)1 (Jan. 1991).

27. *See e.g. N.Y. Pub. Health Law* § 3607 (maternal and child health volunteers); *N.Y. Pub. Off. Law* § 17 (volunteers defined by state and indemnified for tort claims against them arising from scope of services); *N.Y. Exec. Law* § 546 (senior home helper program); *N.Y. Educ. Law* § 4212 (background checks and training of volunteers working with disabled children); *N.Y. Pk. & Rec. Law* § 323 (conservation corps volunteers provided status of employees for work related tort claims). *See also Fla. Stat.* § 410.201 *et. seq.* (elderly volunteers rendering services to aged get credit towards own personal care); *Fla., Stat.* § 110.501 *et. seq.* authorizes state agencies to retain volunteers and reimburse their incidental expenses), *Fla. Stat.* § 125.9501 *et. seq.* authorizes county governments to retain volunteers and reimburse their incidental expenses); *Fla. Stat.* § 230.23 (recognizes use and benefit of school volunteers); *Fla. Stat.* § 385.103 (community health volunteers protected by state from personal liability).

28. Mehegan, Sean, (article) 7 *NonProfit Times* (3) 6 (March 1993).

29. *Porter Reintroduces Volunteer Protection Act*, LIABILITY WEEK, February 8, 1993, at No. 6, Vol. 8.

30. *D.C. To Get Volunteer Protection Law*, LIABILITY WEEK, January 25, 1993, at No. 4, Vol. 8.

31. *Kansas Bill Would Expand "Charitable Doctor" Law*, LIABILITY WEEK, March 15, 1993, at No. 11, Vol. 8.

32. *State Assumes Liability for Volunteer Doctors in Clinics*, MIAMI HERALD, January 11, 1993, at Section B, page 1.

33. 7 *NonProfit Times* (5) 1 (May 1993).

34. *Ruoff v. Harbor Creek Community Association*, 13 Cal. Rptr. 2d 755 (Cal. App. 4 Dist. 1992).

35. *Levy v. Currier*, 587 A.2d 205 (D.C. App. 1991).

36. *Whetstone v. Dixon*, No. 92 0123, 1993 La. App. LEXIS 1032 (La. Ct. App. 1st Cir. Mar. 5, 1993).

37. *Doe v. The Roman Catholic Church for the Archdiocese of New Orleans, et. al.*, No. 91-CA-0988, 1993 La. App. LEXIS 870 (La. Ct. App. 4th Cir. Feb. 26, 1993).

38. *Haskell v. Chautauqua County Fireman's Fraternity, Inc.*, 590 N.Y.S.2d 637 (A.D. 4 Dept. 1992).

39. *Cnota v. Palatine Area Football Ass'n.*, 592 N.E.2d 196 (Ill. App. 1 Dist. 1992).

40. *Beddia v. Goodin*, 957 F.2d 254 (6th Cir. (Ohio), 1992).

41. *Foster v. Board of Trustees of Butler County Community College*, 771 F. Supp. 1122 (D. Kan. 1991).

42. *Broderick v. King's Way Assembly of God Church*, 808 P.2d 1211 (Alaska 1991). *Cf. Infant C. v. Boy Scouts of America, Inc.*, 391 S.E. 2d 322 (Va. 1990) (exception to charitable immunity exists for a charity's failure to exercise due care in the selection and retention of employees).

43. *Crocker v. Barr*, 409 S.E. 2d 368 (S.C. 1991).

44. *Cottam v. First Baptist Church of Boulder*, 756 F. Supp. 1433 (D. Colo. 1991).

45. *McAleer v. Smith*, 791 F. Supp. 923 (D.R.I., 1992).

46. Stepneski, R, (article) 7 *NonProfit Times* (6) 1, 29–30 (June 1993).

47. Sterne article, 4 *NonProfit Times* (9)1 (Dec. 1990).

48. Keenan article, 5 *NonProfit Times* (9)3 (Dec. 1991).

49. *South Ridge Baptist Church v. Industrial Comm. of Ohio*, 911 F.2d 1203 (6th Cir., 1990).

50. *Nemani v. United Health Services, Inc.*, 565 N.Y.S.2d 884 (A.D. 3 Dept. 1991).

51. *Sloan v. Voluntary Ambulance Service*, 826 S.W. 2d 296 (Ark. App. 1992).

52. *Hoppmann v. Workers' Compensation Appeals Board*, 277 Cal. Rptr. 116 (Cal. App. 6 Dist 1991).

53. *Mesa County Valley School District No. 51 v. Goletz*, 821 P.2d 785 (Colo. 1991).

54. *Doe v. Puget Sound Blood Center*, 819 P.2d 370 (Wash. 1991). *Cf. Borzillieri v. American Nat. Red Cross*, 139 F.R.D. 284 (W.D.N.Y. 1991) (AIDS infected patient may only discover information from donor by written interrogatories concerning the blood center's procedures and may not seek information aimed at identity of donor or for suit against donor personally); *Snyder v. Makhjian*, 593 A.2d 318 (N.J. 1991) (AIDS infected patient may seek limited discovery of blood donors to examine potential negligence claims against blood center).

55. *See*, Ga. Code Ann., §14-3-501; *also* Ohio Rev. Code §1702.06(A). As to Corporation Service Companies, *see* 1 Oleck, *Modern Corporation Law*, c. 11 (1978 Supp.); Pasadena Medi Center Assn. v. Superior Ct., 108 Cal. Rptr. 828, 511 P.2d 1180 (1973); Rev. Model Nonprofit Corp. Act §5.01 (1986 draft).

56. *See*, for lengthy details of procedure, Ohio Rev. Code §1702.06.

57. *Ibid.*, §1702.06(M).

58. *See*, Ploen v. Aetna Cas. & Sur. Co., 525 N.Y.S.2d 522 (Supr. Ct. 1988); and, Kidd v. New Hampshire Traction Co., 74 N.H. 160, 66 A. 127 (1907). See, generally, D.L. Kurtz, *Board Liability* (1988).

59. Frink v. Roe, 70 Calif. 296, 11 P. 828 (1886); Eduardo Firnandez v. Compania v. Longino and Collins, 199 La. 343, G.S.2d 137, 142 (1942).

60. Felch v. Findlay College, 200 N.E.2d 353 (Ohio App. 1964).

61. *See*, Byse, *Academic Freedom, Tenure, and the Law; A Comment on Worzella v. Board of Regents*, 73 Harv. L. Rev. 304 (1959); Byse and Coughin, *Tenure in American Higher Education* (1959); Blackwell, *College Law*, c. 3 (1961).

62. *See, Symposium on School Law*, 20 Clev. St. L. Rev. (3) 522 (1971), for a series of articles citing many cases.

63. *Ibid.*

64. *See* also, Santarsiero v. Green Bay Transport, Inc., 249 Wis. 303; 24 N.W.2d 659 (1946).

65. *Southern American Insur. Co. v. Gabbert-Jones, Inc.*, 769 P.2d 1194 (KA App. 1989).

66. *Rutherford v. Presbyterian University Hosp.*, 612 A.2d 500 (Pa. Super., 1992).

67. 7 *NonProfit Times* (3) 31 (March 1993).

68. *Minker v. Baltimore Annual Conference of United Methodist Church*; D.C. Cir. Ct. App., (Jan. 19, 1990).

69. *Wereblood v. Columbia College of Chicago*, 536 N.E.2d 750 (IL App. 1989).

70. *Seery v. Yale-New Haven Hospital*, 554 A.2d 757 (CN App. 1989).

71. *Nordley v. Northern States Power Co.*, 465 N.W.2d 81 (Minn. App. 1991).

72. *Everett v. St. Ansgar Hosp.*, 974 F.2d 77 (8th Cir. (N.D.), 1992).

73. *Bowers v. Jones*, 978 F.2d 1004 (7th Cir. (Ind.), 1992).

74. *Allison v. Centre Community Hosp.*, 604 A.2d 294 (Pa. Cmwlth. 1992).

75. *Hirsovescu v. Shangri-La Corp.*, 831 P.2d 73 (Or. App. 1992).

76. *Long v. Tazewell/Pekin Consol. Communication Center*, 602 N.E. 2d 856 (Ill. App. 3 Dist., 1992).

77. *Rutherford v. Presbyterian University Hosp.*, 612 A.2d 500 (Pa. Super., 1992).

78. *Fiammetta v. St. Francis Hosp.*, 562 N.Y.S. 2d 777 (A.D. 2 Dept. 1990).

79. *Kizer v. Children's Learning Center*, 962 F.2d 608 (7th Cir. (Ill.), 1992).

80. *Acrey v. American Sheep Industry Ass'n*, 981 F.2d 1569 (10th Cir. (Colo.), 1992).

81. *Valdez v. Mercy Hosp.*, 961 F.2d 1401 (8th Cir. (Iowa), 1992).

82. *Downtown Hosp. (Booth House) v. Sarris*, 588 N.Y.S. 2d 748 (N.Y. City Civ. Ct., 1992).

83. *Steier v. Crosier Fathers of Hastings*, 492 N.W. 2d 870 (Neb., 1992).

84. *Arriaga v. Loma Linda University*, 13 Cal. Rptr. 2d 619 (Cal. App. 4 Dist., 1992).

85. *Hindo v. University of Health Sciences/Chicago Medical School, Winick, Falk*, 604 N.W. 2d 463 (Ill. App. 2 Dist., 1992).

86. *Vander Laan v. Mulder*, 443 N.W. 2d 491 (Mich. App. 1989).

87. *Beauford v. Father Flanagan's Boys' Home*, 486 N.W. 2d 854 (Neb., 1992).

88. *Cunningham v. Southlake Center for Mental Health, Inc.*, 924 F.2d 106 (7th Cir. 1991); 42 U.S.C.A. § 1983.

89. *Easton v. Sundram*, 947 F.2d 1011 (C.A. 2 (N.Y.), 1992).

90. *Wolotsky v. Huhn*, 960 F.2d 1331 (6th Cir. (Ohio), 1992).

91. *Milne Employees Ass'n v. Sun Carriers*, 960 F.2d 1401 (9th Cir. 1991).

92. *Drennan v. General Motors Corp.*, 977 F. 2d 246 (6th Cir. (Ohio), 1992).

93. *Coble v. Bonita House, Inc.*, 789 F. Supp. 320 (N.D. Cal. 1992).

94. *Claim of Froehlich*, 584 N.Y.S. 2d 953 (N.Y.A.D. 3 Dept., 1992).

95. *Bykonen v. United Hosp.*, 479 N.W. 2d 140 (N.D. 1992).

96. *Robinson v. Christopher Greater Area Rural Health Planning Corp.*, 566 N.E.2d 768 (Ill. App. 1991).

97. *Arneson v. Board of Trustees of McKendree College*, 569 N.E. 2d 252 (Ill. App. 1991); *Daymon v. Hardin County General Hospital*, 569 N.E.2d 316 (Ill. App. 1991); *Semerau v. Village of Schiller Park*, 569 N.E.2d 183 (Ill. App. 1991).

98. *Olivier v. Xavier University*, 553 S. 2d 1004 (La. App., 1989).

99. *Bjorn v. Associated Regional and University Pathologists, Inc.*, 567 N.E.2d 417 (Ill. App. 1991).

100. *Lawrence v. Edwin Shaw Hospital*, 566 N.E.2d 1256 (Ohio App. 1988, reported 1991).

101. Vardeman v. Penna. Mut. L. Ins. Co., 125 Ga. 117; 54 S.E. 56 (1906).

102. *See*, n.101, State v. Lewis, 141 S.C. 207; 139 S.E. 386 (1927).

103. *In re* St. Lawrence and A.R. Co., 133 N.Y. 270; 31 N.E. 218 (1892).

104. Williams College v. Assessors of Williamstown, 167 Mass. 505, 45 N.E. 394 (1897).

105. *See*, Simmons v. Defiance Box Co., 148 N.C. 544; 62 S.E. 435 (1908).

106. Wills case, n.17.

107. Kramer v. State, 16 Ala. App. 40; 75 S. 185 (1917) (cashier: not an officer because not in bylaws): Knoxville Water Co. v. E. Tenn. Natl. Bk., 123 Tenn. 364; 131 S.W. 447 (1910).

108. Vardeman case, n.101, (held to be an employee).

109. State *ex rel.* Matre v. Berg, 195 Wis. 73; 217 N.W. 736 (1928).

110. *See*, §293.

111. *See*, Oleck, *Modern Corporation Law* §1692 (1978 Supp.); and this applies to officers as well; Taylor v. Cowit, 244 N.Y.S.2d 845 (1963); and to directors: Marin v. Jacuzzi, 36 Cal. Rptr. 880 (App. 1964). See above, cases in n.3, 10.

112. *Rutan v. Republic Party of Illinois*, 848 F.2d 1396 (7th Cir., 1988).

113. *Cohen v. Board of Trustees of University of M. and D. of New Jersey*, 867 F.2d 1455 (3rd Cir., NJ 1989).

114. *Hooks v. Smith*, 781 S.W. 2d 522 (Ky. App. 1989).

115. *Samad v. Jenkins*, 845 F.2d 660 (6th Cir., OH 1988).

116. *Foster v. City of N.Y.*, 549 N.Y.S. 2d 707 (App. Div., 1st Dept., 1990).

117. Ring (article)—*Trial* (Mag.) 16–22 (May 1988); citing *Irving v. Doctor's Hospital of Lake Worth*, 415 So. 2d 55 (FL 4th D.C. App. 1982); and Jaar case, 474 So.2d 239.

118. *Lavery v. Southlake Center for Mental Health*, 566 N.E.2d 1055 (Ind. App., 1991).

119. *Oursler v. Women's Interart Center, Inc.*, 566 N.Y.S.2d 295 (A.D. 1 Dept. 1991).

120. *Cole v. Board of Educ. of Syosset Cent. School Dist.*, 562 N.Y.S.2d 209 (App. Div. 1990).

121. *E.g., see*, N.Y. CPL Art.50 §190.40 *but see* (does not apply to certification of pleadings) People v. Lorch, 171 Misc. 469, 13 N.Y.S.2d 155 (1939). *And see*, Ohio Rev. Code §§2945.44, 3901.23.

122. J. Fisch article, 5 *NonProfit Times* (7) Insert p. 2 (Oct. 1991).

123. Leenan, (article) 6 *NonProfit Times* 7 (3) (July, 1992).

124. 7 *NonProfit Times* (6) 1 (June 1993). For copies of the study and details including type of association, membership, geographic scope, budget, and number of employees, call Laura Krotky at 202-429-9370.

125. *Bryce, H., Financial Strategic Management for Nonprofit Organizations 2nd*, (Prentice Hall 1992). (201) 767-5937.

126. 29 U.S.C. §206, 207 *etc.; see*, Note, *Scope of Coverage of F.L.S.A.*, 30 Wash. & Lee L. Rev. 149 (1973); Note, *Assertion of Statutory Rights* . . . ,1981 Brigham Young L. Rev. 361.

127. 29 U.S.C. §213(a)(1).

128. *Ibid.* §206(a)(1).

129. *Id.* §207(a)(1); Shearer v. E. Brame Trucking, 245 N.W.2d 84 (Mich. App. 1976).

130. 29 C.F.R. §778.601(b,c).

131. 20 C.F.R. §404.1026(a); IRC §501(c)(3).

132. Forms SS 15, SS 15a.

133. 20 C.F.R. §404.1026(b)(1,2).

134. *Ibid.*, subd.(c).

135. *See*, Paine, *Flexible Compensation*, 1974 Financial Executive 56; Gordon & LeBeau, *Employee Benefits*, 1970 Harv. Bus. Rev. 93; Ellig, *Competitiveness of Employee Benefits Systems*, 1974 Compensation Rev. 8.

136. *See, e.g.*, IRC §§162(h), 105, 106.

137. *See, Ibid.* §§401 *et seq.*; Young, *Pension and Profit Sharing Plans* (1977).

138. Rothschild & Soberheim, *Expense Accounts*, 67 Yale L.J. 1363 (1958); and *see*, Morrisey v. Curran, 650 F.2d 1267 (2d Cir., 1981).

139. 7 *NonProfit Times* (4) 1 (April 1993).

140. *Derby Ass'n Trust, Inc. v. Department of Ins. and Finance*, 835 P.2d 149 (Or. App. 1992).

141. Dowdie v. Texas Amer. Oil. Co., 503 S.W.2d 647 (Tex. App. 1973); *and see*, n.135, 138, above; Lewis v. Ricklis, 440 N.Y.S.2d 658 (App., 1981).

142. Calif. Corp. Code §317(i); N.Y. Bus. Corp. L. §727; and *see*, Dankloff v. Bowling Proprietors Assn., 331 N.Y.S.2d 109 (1972); Bishop, *Law of Corp. Officers and Directors*, c.8 (1981).

143. Rev. Model Nonprofit Corp. Act §8.57 (1986 Draft).

144. *Rooney v. Rooney*, 478 N.W. 2d 545 (Minn. App. 1991).

145. Internal regulations are not laws in a general or jurisdictional sense, but are laws for particular and special situations and purposes only. 13 Ohio Jur.2d, Corporations §655.

146. Samples may be obtained free from most institutions, on request.

147. Many schools, for example, issue brochures on "Faculty Personnel Policies" and "Faculty Bylaws," etc.

148. *Jackson v. Action for Boston Community Development, Inc.*, 525 N.E.2d 411 (MA 1988).

149. *Brandt v. Board of Co-op. Educational Services*, 845 F.2d 416 (2d Cir., NY 1988).

150. *Laborers' Intnatl. Union of N.A. v. Rayburn Crane Service, Inc.*, 559 So. 2d 1219 (Fla. 2d DCA, 1990).

151. *International Jai-Alai Players Assn. v. Sports Palace, Inc.*, 564 So. 2d 281 (Fla. 5th DCA, 1990).

152. *Donson v. Baez*, 1991 WL 26995 (D.C. Del., Feb. 21, 1991).

153. *Ode v. Swift*, 570 So. 2d 1209 (Ala., 1990); and see *Moman v. Gregerson's Foods, Inc.*, 570 So. 2d 1215 (Ala., 1990).

154. *Doe v. Samaritan Counseling Center*, 791 P.2d 344 (Alaska 1990); *Richard H. v. Larry D.*, 243 Cal. Rptr. 807 (Cal. App. 1988); 2 Fla. Jr. 2d, Agency & Empl., § 91; 45 A.L.R. 4th 289; *Insinga v. La Bella*, 543 So. 2d 209 (Fla. 1989).

155. *Doe v. Samaritan Counseling Center*, above.

156. *Worcester Insur. Co. V. Fells Acres Day School, Inc.*, 558 N.E.2d 958 (Mass., 1990).

157. *Perkins v. Dean*, 570 So. 2d 1217 (Ala., 1990).

158. *Bishop v. Aronov*, 926 F.2d 1066 (11th Cir., Ala., 1991).

159. *Jund v. Town of Hempstead*, 941 F.2d 1271 (2nd Cir. (N.Y.), 1991).

160. *Malone v. Pipefitters' Ass'n Local Union 597*, 774 F.Supp. 490 (N.D. Ill. 1991).

161. *Cnota v. Palatine Area Football Ass'n*, 592 N.E. 2d 196 (Ill. App. 1 Dist. 1992).

162. *Straley v. Urbanna Chamber of Commerce*, 413 S.E.2d 47 (Va. 1992).

163. *Aetna Cas. & Sur. Co. v. Arizona Interscholastic Ass'n*, 841 P.2d 1384 (Ariz. App. Div. 2, 1992).

164. Finkler v. Toledo Ski Club, 577 N.E. 2d 1114 (Ohio App., 6 Dist. 1989).

165. Panken, Torsone and Starr, *Sexual Harassment in the Workplace: Employer Liability for the Sins of the Wicked*, C588 ALI-ABA 201 (1991), *see, North v. Madison Area Ass'n for Retarded Citizens-Developmental Centers Corp.*, 844 F.2d 401 (7th Cir. (Wis.), 1988); *Morgan v. Massachusetts General Hospital*, 901 F.2d 186 (1st Cir. (Mass.), 1990); *Miller v. Lidenwood Female College*, 616 F. Supp. 860 (E.D. Mo. 1985); *Giorgio v. Verdugo Hills Hospital*, 258 Cal. Rptr. 426 (Cal. App. 2 Dist. 1989).

166. *Jund v. Town of Hempstead*, 941 F.2d 1271 (2nd Cir. (N.Y.), 1991).

167. *Thompson v. Nason Hospital*, 591 A.2d 703 (Pa. 1991).

168. Koob, *Special Problems of the Hospital as Defendant, Corporate Liability; Nursing Malpractice*, C655 ALI-ABA 55 (1991).

169. *Baptist Memorial Hospital System v. Smith*, 822 S.W. 2d 67 (Tex. App.—San Antonio 1991).

170. Griffith, Parker, *With Malice Toward None: The Metamorphosis of Statutory and Common Law Protections for Physicians and Hospitals in Negligent Credentialing Litigation*, 22 Tex. Tech. L. Rev. 157 (1991).

171. *Medi-Stat, Inc. v. Kustierin*, 792 S.W.2d 869 (Ark. 1990).

172. *Medley v. No. Car. Dept. of Corrections*, 393 S.E.2d 288 (N.C. App. 1990); *West v. Atkins*, 108 S. Ct. 2250 (1988).

173. *Commercial Union Ins. Co. v. Scavo*, No. 1297, 1992 Ohio App. LEXIS 965 (Ohio Ct. App. Mar. 4, 1992).

174. *Romano v. Northland Insurance Co.*, No. 92-0237, 1993 Wisc. App. LEXIS 247 (Wisc. Ct. App. Mar. 9, 1993).

33

FREEDOM TO ASSOCIATE

[*See also* Chapter 34]

CONSTITUTIONAL/CIVIL RIGHTS

[Kirk Bauer and Thomas J. Walsh contributed to research for this chapter and Chapter 34.]

§339. RIGHT OF FREE CHOICE OF ASSOCIATES, IN GENERAL

"*Civil rights*" law changes in recent years expanded between 1960–80 and contracted after 1980.[1] Chief among the affected rights, in nonprofit corporations' law, is the First Amendment provision that "Congress shall make no law . . . abridging . . . the right of the people peaceably to assemble. . . ." Free speech, picketing, demonstrations, etc., of NPOs or members, are not unlimited. Thus, abortion-opponent views that are carried to the point of substantial amounts of harassment and name calling against patrons of abortion clinics may be enjoined by courts, or restricted by court order.[1a] And violent, anti-abortion picketing may be criminal under RICO law since early 1994, ruled the Supreme Court [*See also*, Section 339.]

State Action: A major difficulty in this area of law is the limitation that views the constitutional rule as being concerned, first and foremost (if not solely) with *state action*. A leading case, *Roberts v. United States Jaycees*,[2] for example, held that a state's *public accommodations* laws, that forbid racial or religious discrimination in places of public accommodation, may validly limit a private association's membership—exclusiveness rules. This is in addition to a similar view set forth in the Federal Civil Rights Act.[3] The *Roberts* case distinguished between organizations for "intimate association," which have personal relationships (and thus more choice of associates), and those for "expressive association" (with less free choice of associates). But, if a "*compelling*" *government interest* is involved, the courts may interfere more strongly with freedom of choice of associates.[4] Some state anti-discrimination statutes prohibit discrimination with regard to the advantages or privileges offered to the public, but allow discrimination in membership or ownership of a club that provides "public accommodations."[5] For example, a men's fishing and hunting club, with a clubhouse and grounds, limited (300) membership, and nonprofit, neverthe-less is a "place of *public accommodation,* resort or amusement" under state anti-discrimination law where there is *no real selectivity* of members. Statutes do not abridge the members' rights of association by requiring (in effect) admission of women.[6]

Thus a group (*e.g.,* Republicans) may validly exclude persons (Democrats) who hold different political views,[7] but government protection of *classes* of persons might interfere with a "Free Ireland" club's barring of Irish-Americans of the Protestant religion.

An AIDS service group may properly exclude and enjoin a protester from attending its workshops, without denying the protester freedom of speech, if no government official coerced, encouraged, or suggests actions taken by the group (i.e. state action). State action does not exist where the city and county merely fund and oversee the workshops of the AIDS group.[8]

Hospital Privileges in a private nonprofit hospital, and revocation by the hospital, are not "state action" violating due process constitutional rights, even though hospitals are "public bodies" under the state law and the county commissioners could appoint most of the hospital board (but had no other control). *Weston v. Carolina Medicorp, Inc.,* _____ S.E.2d _____ (N.C. App., Apr. 2, 1991).

Reasonableness of Restrictions: Membership restrictions, such as age restriction (no children under 12 years of age) in a condominium association of retirees (over 60), if it is not used as a device to exclude certain classes of people from desirable housing, is not unconstitutional.[9] The reasonableness of the restriction is the test.[10] For example, the promotion of safety and preservation of inter/scholastic competition are important government interests that allow a public school athletic league to enforce its rules denying a male junior high student the opportunity to play on a girls hockey team. The court gives such state action intermediate scrutiny under state equal protection guarantees.[11]

Firing of school employees because of their association with the school superintendent (i.e., by abolishment of their positions) if a decision to abolish was motivated in large part by this association, is basis for the award of damages under *U.S. Code §1983* as violation of their constitutional freedom of association.[12]

Racial, religious, sexual and other discrimination continue to be world-wide problems, as well as American problems.[13] Most Americans (except a few bigots) now view religious bigotry and discrimination as contemptible and irreligious. But racial (color) discrimination, aimed mostly at black people, has not yet been eradicated. Vicious organized anti-Semitic (including black) groups increased their venom in the early nineties.

Today, the right of a white member to bring a black guest into his social club is upheld.[14] Many cases have tested the extent to which private racial discrimination is permitted by the Civil Rights Act of 1964 in exempting from its coverage "a private club or other establishment open to the public." If tenuous reasons are given for excluding a black applicant, the organization may be held to be not really a *private* (hunting and fishing) *club.*[15]

New York City's *Local Law 63*, prohibiting discrimination in private clubs that provide benefits to persons other than their own members, was upheld as valid exercise of police powers in *N.Y. State Club Assn. Inc. v. City*, by the New York Court of Appeals on Feb. 17, 1987. [See text, below, at n. 30, 31.]

State courts can review membership rules of a private organization when membership is an economic necessity.[16] Religious organizations may establish their own rules for internal discipline and government.[17] In 1987 the Supreme Court ruled that Title VII of the 1964 Civil Rights Act does not bar the use of religious tests for employment by a (Mormon) Church, nor does the First Amendment. *Corp. of the Presiding Bishop v. Amos*, #86–179 (June 1987).

Tillman v. Wheaton—Haven Recreation Assn., Inc. is an illuminating case.[18] An able commentator said as follows of that case:[19]

In this case the plaintiffs were denied membership in a neighborhood swimming pool organized as a nonprofit corporation. The court significantly held that the exemption applied to the civil rights Act of 1866[20] as well as to that of 1964 and devoted most of its attention to an examination of whether the 'club' was in fact *private* on the basis that it was owned, operated, and controlled by its members and financed by their payment of substantial dues for the exclusive use of members and their guests, despite the fact it was exempt from state income taxation, constructed under special exceptions to local zoning ordinances, and lacked significant standards other than racial for admission to membership. In so holding it would appear that the court has departed from the standards which at least one author predicted would be applied to the exemption; i.e., genuine selectivity, absence of an integral part in the recreational activity of community, and lack of public support. All were lacking ingredients in the case and the court chose instead the standard of membership control.

The Supreme Court, reversing the lower court, held that a private nonprofit association may not deny membership where the civil rights statute (42 U.S.C. §1982) would be violated when the only criterion for selection was race.

An important case, in this connection, was *Moose Lodge No. 107 v. Irvis*, decided by the United States Supreme Court.[21] Of that case, it was said:[22]

The Supreme Court ruled that racially discriminatory guest policies of a membership club (conceded to be private) did not violate the equal protection clause of the fourteenth amendment in that state action was not involved. The fact that the lodge was licensed by the state liquor board did not sufficiently implicate the staff in the lodge's discriminatory practices. The court did hold, however, that the state liquor board's requirement that every club licensee adhere to its bylaws involved the state in sanctioning discriminatory practices and that any action by the state to enforce such a rule would be enforced.

As far as refusal to admit certain groups is concerned, private discrimination is not absolutely prohibited. For instance, voluntary associations may limit use of their facilities in the sale of personal property; thus discrimination on the basis of *sex*, in sale of liquor by private clubs and organizations, was not prohibited.[23] But this kind of discrimination is crumbling fast, as recent cases and rulings include *sexism* and *age-ism* as violations of constitutional rights.[24]

In a case where a nonprofit athletic club denied use of its facilities to everyone except its members and their guests, and the club was not connected to a larger establishment that was a public accommodation, civil rights were held not to have been violated by its refusing to admit blacks.[25] A club with community-oriented activities in 1977 was held to be free to restrict membership to *men only*, because no government supervision applied to an essentially private activity.[26] The tests for determining whether a club is private or not were discussed in *Cornelius v. Benevolent Protective Order of Elks*,[27] in 1974.

A private yacht club's lease of dock land (for $1/year) from a city was deemed sufficient "state action" to allow a court to enjoin discrimination.[28] But a tavern was held not to be legally a private club for the purpose of discrimination against women.[29]

In early 1987 the Supreme Court ruled that a California statute forbidding exclusion of women by Rotary Clubs is valid, because such clubs involve the right to business-people contacts;—the right to earn a living. California cases already had so held in case decisions[30], and so had New York[31] in cases involving golf clubs and the like. Only time will tell what will be the effects of the Reagan Administration's filling of the Supreme Court bench with "conservatives" and "strict constructionists."

Supreme Court rulings and government commands in the Bush administration, especially in 1991 barring abortion counselling by Family Planning NPOs that receive any federal funds, utterly confused the constitutional-rights-state-laws conflicts. The problems are so many and so fluid that they must be considered on the basis of 1994 daily newspaper (rather than law book) reports; political tactics and religious factions pressures dominated NPO rights and limitations in 1993.

§340. CONSTITUTIONAL FREEDOM OF ASSOCIATION

[Kirk Bauer contributed much of Sections 339 and 340.]

[See the preceding Section.]

Besides the previously-outlined First Amendment rules as to freedom of *assembly*, free choice of one's associates and freedom to join together into voluntary associations, are impliedly guaranteed by the Constitutional protection of freedom of speech and assembly, freedom of religion, and a generalized freedom of association.[32] A group of persons wishing to incorporate in order to advocate unpopular views (*e.g.*, homosexual freedom) may or may not be denied incorporation, depending on the public policy of the particular state.[33] Where the express purpose was to promote reform of laws which discriminated against homosexuals, it was held that such purpose is legal.[34] On the other hand, in another state the secretary of state's denial of approval of an application for incorporation for a proposed nonprofit corporation which had as its purpose promotion of homosexual freedom was held to be correct because the purpose was contrary to the public policy of Ohio.[35] However, a school student senate denial of funds to an association of *homosexual* students violates their First Amendment rights, according to a federal case originating in Arkansas.[36] But, church discrimination against gay members is privileged exercise of religious liberty.[37]

Freedom to belong to a voluntary association is not specifically guaranteed by the Constitution.[38] The Supreme Court has interpreted the Constitution to include the right of association as fundamental.[39] In the past the Supreme Court interpreted the First Amendment to mean "the right of the people peacefully to assemble *in order to* petition the government." The right of *petition* was deemed primary, with assembly as only the means to obtain the right.[40] A long list of cases today holds the right to associate as fundamental, and action by a state to curtail the right is subject to severe scrutiny by the courts.[41]

United States *Supreme Court* rulings, such as the 1991 limitation of women's freedom in abortion matters and of other civil rights freedoms, promise continuing narrowing of "freedom of association." This fluid situation in constitutional law must be expected to become more and more "conservative" as the Supreme Court attitudes and personnel become ever more affected by the Reagan-Bush appointments to the bench.

The question of freedom *not* to associate has been settled, as yet, only as to a few, limited matters. Thus state-compelled acceptance of Negroes into labor unions was upheld as a valid regulation of employment.[42] An employee was required to join a union in order to retain his job.[43] A lawyer was forced to join his state's bar association by court-ordained integration of the state bar.[44]

Most anti-discrimination statutes serve two general state interests: providing *equal access* to a particular opportunity and *affirming the equal dignity* and worth of excluded individuals. The Supreme Court's reasoning in "right to discriminate" cases suggests that it will not protect an association's membership choices unless the association is organized for specific expressive purposes. Absent this, the Court characterizes the burden imposed by a non-discrimination statute as an incidental abridgment of protected speech which is easily justified by the state's compelling interest in combating discrimination.[45] For example, an honor society rejection of a membership candidate because of his father's criticism may be violation of their free speech rights.[46] A regulation by a Transit Authority, requiring a permit for a NPO's *free-speech* activities on its (Authority's) property, violates the First Amendment.[47]

Vast growth of the power of nonprofit organizations, in recent years, and weakening of traditional methods of control by members, has caused widespread concern. A growing public awareness of the problem may lead to re-examination of the laws governing freedom of association.[48]

Court supervision of internal affairs of nonprofit organizations must not interfere with their constitutional freedom to make their own rules as to function.[49] Court unfamiliarity with their purposes and practices should cause caution in interfering.[50]

Various factors are considered by the courts in deciding whether to review the internal affairs of a nonprofit organization. These include: the nature of the injury; social interest in permitting such conduct; the burden on the association and on the court in intervening; the party's need for membership; and the alternatives available.[51]

The government can overcome freedom of association objections to subpoenas of bank records, which indicate the identities of members of a nonprofit organization, by showing compelling need. Recently, compelling need was shown in a case against a barter organization where there was a good faith investigation of possible violations of federal money laundering statutes.[52]

The right of a person to associate with others is fundamental. Although such rights may not be "abridged," they are not absolute.[53] They are subject to limitation if a particular restriction is needed in order to protect the state or prevent political, economic or other injuries.[54] The emphasis of the Supreme Court opinions on whether the governmental interest or a legitimate state interest is involved, or how substantial it is, or if that interest is "compelling," in the past usually depended on the writer of the opinion.[55] Today the Court seems to require a state that interferes with freedom of association to show a compelling governmental interest that needs protection.[56]

For example, dictation of manner of peoples' organization into an association in a political party, by *state Election Law* rules *controlling selection of delegates* and makeup of *county executive committees* or parties for state and county conventions, is unconstitutional violation of freedom of association.[57] But, a government agent's refusal to take action to notify prospective refugees (Soviet and eastern European aliens) that a certain NPO (Ukrainian-American Bar Assn.) was offering free service to such aliens, is not a violation of the first Amendment right to freedom of association.[58]

Individuals and society must be protected from harm *by groups*, as to reputation,[59] religious freedom,[60] free speech,[61] or the like, of persons; or as to public interest in such things as advocacy of legislation opposed by the group,[62] or availability of services of physicians in hospitals, unrestrained by a medical society's restrictions.[63] Exercise of monopoly power by groups requires the placing of community (social) interests above that of private groups.[64]

The old rule that states generally may not validly enact law or take action governing religion, except for "*compelling state interest*" protection, was modified by a 1990 Supreme Court decision regarding use of peyote in religious ceremonies, in Oregon, by Native American Church members. The court said that a state or local government is free to require *everyone* to comply with *a law that is generally valid.* Two church members were denied unemployment benefits for ingesting peyote in church ceremonies.[65] The Supreme Court re-introduced the "compelling state interest" rule in early 1994 in applying RICO law to anti-abortion picket violence. [See also § 36, above.]

In a charge of wrongdoing by a church, the courts must decide: (1) whether the organization is in fact a *"religious society"*; (2) whether its conduct was *"religious expression"*; and if both (1) and (2) are answered in the affirmative, then (3) if the alleged conduct is so harmful as to involve *"compelling state interest"* in discouraging such conduct even while allowing religious freedom.[66]

A religious academy's First Amendment freedom is not violated by a town *school committee's review* of the *credentials* of the academy's *teachers*, or visit to observe the quality of the teaching, or the gathering of written information about the school.[67]

The problems of validity of group action (*i.e.*, freedom of association) are so complex that no detailed treatment of them can be given here. Reference should be made to special studies of the subject. One remarkably thorough study, exhaustively annotated, is a lengthy note entitled: "Developments in the Law—Judicial Control of Actions of Private Associations," in the 1963 *Harvard Law Review*.[68] (See also Sections herein.)

Despite these complications, the basic nature of the constitutional freedom of the association remains constant.[69] A well-stated summary of the nature of the right is this.[70]

> To summarize the discussion of the right of association, then, one may say first that there is no specific statement of such a right in either the national Constitution or in any of the state constitutions. It is, however, a right cognate to those of free speech and free assembly. Associations have a place of particular importance in a democracy, whether they are associations of laborers, professional men, or electors and office seekers. They serve as a training ground for group participation, organization, and management of people and programs, and for democratic acceptance of the majority will. They can also serve as a potential influence for improvement of communication between the individual and the government.

§341. ASSERTION OF RIGHT TO ASSOCIATION

There is little doubt that a person is entitled to his right to freedom of association. The right of an association to assert *its* constitutional rights, on the other hand, is not as obvious. But under certain circumstances an association has standing to assert questions affecting its members and their freedom to associate.[71] Thus, private schools have standing to challenge a federal statute forbidding the schools' exclusion of blacks.[72] The NAACP, and other organizations, were held entitled to assert the constitutional rights of their members.[73]

An association may assert the legal right to free association for itself, at least in its constitutionally protected activities;[74] for instance, when it challenges a requirement of disclosure of its membership list.[75]

Individuals must sometimes exhaust their administrative remedies prior to litigation. For example, an equestrian has no right to bring private action under the Amateur Sports Act if she/he is not chosen for the American international competition team. He/she must exhaust administrative remedies under the Act.[76]

A student's relationship with a college or university is "contractual in nature," and the student's failure to pursue all reasonable avenues for preventing harm, as catalog and handbook provided, may bar his claim of mistreatment.[77] [See, "Members Manuals" etc.]

A club's membership list has First Amendment privacy protection against a Franchise Tax Board administrative subpoena (random audits) of its state income tax records, even though it was a **discriminatory** club and the inquiry was meant to enforce a regulation against discrimination.[78]

Privileges entitle the physician to use facilities, and often to admit patients, but are not "employment" nor a right to employment.[79]

§342. *DELECTUS PERSONAE* AND FREEDOM TO ASSOCIATE

Delectus personae means *the choice of the person.*[80] The term refers to the right of a partner to choose with whom he wishes to associate himself in a partnership. It refers to the exercise of personal choice and preference in the admission of new members into an existing partnership.[81]

Because an *unincorporated* association is, in its essence, a form of multi-partner partnership, the principle of *delectus personae* is relatively easy to apply to such associations. (See Chapter 6.)

For an *incorporated* association, a slightly disconcerting note is introduced by the law or corporations. The doctrine of *delectus personae* does not apply to *stock* corporations.[82] Stock ordinarily must be freely transferable. Any person who acquires the stock may then become a member (shareholder) in the corporation. In the absence of special agreements or provisions, no choice of new stockholders is available to the existing stockholders (other than the choice of a buyer or grantee by the one who gives up his shares).

But in nonprofit corporations, there is usually no need to preserve the free transferability of property (shares of stock). The limitation on *delectus personae* does not ordinarily apply to corporations that are simply incorporated nonprofit associations.

Criminal associations. Besides the principle of *delectus personae,* certain other limits on the right of association do exist. For example, association for criminal purposes (as in "Murder, Inc.") clearly is illegal. But this means association in illegal *activities,* in the sense of criminal conspiracy—not merely association with persons who have criminal records. In essence, association for illegal (or perhaps merely undesirable-in-public-view!) *purposes* is what is illegal.[83] The doubtful quality of this rule of law is obvious when the "illegality" is questionable.

Laws that forbid association with persons having known criminal records have been declared to be unconstitutional in a number of interesting cases.[84]

One may choose one's friends from among the highest or the lowest types of people so long as no illegal activity is carried on. An overt act is necessary to convert mere association into conspiracy;[85] but an actual agreement to commit such an act is itself sufficient criminal act at common law—even if the persons change their minds and do nothing further.[86] Statutes in many states now require an overt act, except in conspiracy to commit a felony on the person of another, or to commit burglary or arson.[87]

Right to incorporate. Incorporation statutes place implied restrictions on the right to associate in corporate form. The necessity for approvals by administrative agencies and for acceptance of the charter by the secretary of state, and other such requirements, are regulatory. It is obvious that some kinds of charters will be refused to known criminals. These matters are discussed in Chapter 13.

Property Rights in Expulsion of Members

See, in this text, § 347 below, *Elgin v. Montgomery Farm Bureau,* 549 S. 2d 486 (Ala. 1989).

Membership Restriction in NPOs

[Bruce Z. Walker contributed most of the rest of this section.]

There now is a recognized right of "exclusive association," by which private organizations *may* follow discriminatory practices.

Public Accommodations

States limit private clubs' restriction rules by invoking "public accommodation" laws. These laws guarantee, to individuals, freedom from discrimination in the use of facilities defined as "public accommodations," such as restaurants. Public accommodations are entities which make goods or services *available to the public.* As the entities become more public in nature, associational rights of the members decrease.[88]

The Supreme Court has held constitutional a state's law defining criteria which automatically made an organization a public accommodation, thus subjecting the club to antidiscrimination laws.[89]

Another method of limiting clubs' membership exclusion rules is through use of the *Civil Rights Act of 1964.* Thus, an entire swim club facility, including a snack bar, was held to be a place of public accommodation within the meaning of Title II of the Act.[90]

Freedom of association has been interpreted to include classifications of *"intimate"* and *"expressive"* associations. Marriages, family relationships, and *other* relationships which involve *strong emotional ties* have been protected, because they can be considered intimate. However, this type of constitutional protection is rare. While the right to associate and exclude associates for "expressive" purposes is recognized, it is not absolute. State infringement of that right is allowed upon a showing of a compelling state interest. Thus, an association's freedom of choice must be balanced against the state's interest in ending discrimination against its citizens.[91]

For example, the relationship among *Rotary Club* members has been held to be one *not* deserving of "intimate association" protection. Also, the *Jaycees* organization has been held to be outside the intimate-association protection. In determining classification of groups, courts have considered chapter and organization size, dropout rate, participation by strangers, *selectivity* as to members, and *criteria* for judging applicants.[92]

The club was held not exempt from Title II of the Act, because: (1) the club's membership procedures were not genuinely selective on a reasonable basis; (2) the origins of the club suggested that it was intended to serve as a community pool for area families; and (3) the club's facilities were regularly used by nonmembers. Other factors to be considered in determining whether a club is "public" within the meaning of the Act are: membership control over operations; history of the organization; advertising; profit/nonprofit distinction; and formalities observed by the club.[93]

Membership organizations, similar to the Boy Scouts of America, that do not operate from or supply access to a particular facility or location, do not qualify as places of *public accommodation*, which are protected under Title II of the Civil Rights Act. Accordingly, a boy, who was excluded from the Boy Scouts, because he was unwilling to profess belief in a supreme being, was denied a civil rights action against the Boy Scouts.[94]

Religious or Racial Discrimination

Courts have also applied the *Fair Housing Act*, which provides that it is unlawful to refuse to sell or rent because of an individual's religion or sex.[95]

In *United States v. Columbus Country Club* (above), a widow whose *husband* was a *member* of a country club was *not* allowed to become an annual member because of the club's restriction of annual membership to Roman Catholics.

The Fair Housing Act exempts from its prohibitions nonprofit institutions associated with religious organizations, which *may* limit sale or rental of dwellings to members of that religion. Also, a private club, which as incidental to its primary purpose provides lodging, may discriminate in the rental or occupancy of such lodging. The court held that Congress did not intend to prohibit religious-based discrimination in instances like these.[96]

But rejection of *black families* seeking membership in a *nonreligion*-based club constituted discrimination within the meaning of Title II of the Civil Rights Act of 1964. The court made this finding even though the defendant had not discriminated uniformly.[97]

A not-for-profit equal opportunity organization brought suit against the

New York Times, alleging that the *Times* violated the Fair Housing Act by indicating preference for race in its housing advertisements. The court held that the Fair Housing Act prohibits all advertising that indicates a racial preference.[98]

Gender Discrimination

In the *Columbus Country Club* case (above), the widow was not allowed to become an annual member because the club also had a restriction of membership to *males*. Memberships were to be passed on to sons or other male relatives as long as they were Roman Catholic.

The court stated that although the bylaws had since been modified to conform to the requirements of the Fair Housing Act, it remanded the case for determination of whether the "real world" actions of the club conformed to the statutory requirements of the Act and whether past violations had been remedied.[99]

When a *Rotary Club* Chapter admitted three women as regular members its charter was revoked by Rotary International. The Supreme Court held that no First Amendment violation would result by requiring all-male Rotary clubs to admit women to membership. Rotary clubs are large and encourage a steady stream of new members, and one stated club purpose was to promote *diversity* of interests in membership. And there is a compelling governmental interest in eliminating discrimination against women.[100]

Likewise, the Supreme Court upheld a Minnesota *Human Rights Act*, thus allowing women to join a historically male organization. The *Jaycees* allowed women to attend chapter meetings and to participate, but barred women from holding office, voting, and receiving certain awards. The court stated that this type of gender discrimination warranted abridgement of the Jaycees' associational freedoms. Admission of women as regular members would not seriously hamper constitutionally protected activities.[101]

Although some interest in a right to exclusiveness must be acknowledged, recent decisions have narrowed the range of allowable discrimination, because the American society can no longer tolerate unjustified suppression of people by "classes."[102]

Women and members of (ethnic, religious, etc.) groups may not be excluded from *private* country *clubs* (e.g., "men's"), and may sue under the state's civil rights law, in California. In a divorce settlement, a woman (in business) may claim (the husband's) club membership.[103]

New York City's *Human Rights Law*, which forbids discrimination by private clubs that have over 400 members, is not an unconstitutional violation of the First Amendment.

The Supreme Court has ruled that "private club" *exemption* from the ban on *discrimination* in clubs that offer "public accommodation" (*e.g.*, such as restaurant service) does not apply to groups with over 400 members that are not classified as *religious* or *benevolent*. It upheld (unanimously) a New York City law aimed at eradicating discrimination against *women* and racial minorities in large private clubs.[104]

[Greg Isaacson contributed the next four cases.]

When a female university undergraduate brought a claim of gender discrimination against eating clubs which serve only male university students at Princeton University, the New Jersey Supreme Court held that the clubs had a *"symbiotic relationship"* with Princeton. The private clubs supplied an essential service which was not provided by the public accommodation. Thus, the clubs *lost their private character* and become subject to laws against discrimination. Impermissible gender discrimination was found.[105]

A city, suing a private club for racial and sexual discrimination in its membership policies, is entitled to discover the names and addresses of membership applicants rejected during the past decade, provided that the club first notifies the applicants in order to give them the opportunity to seek protection from disclosure.[106]

A private club, with fixed limited membership, that is part of no formal national organization and uses a highly selective membership process, is a purely private social group entitled to First Amendment protection of its membership list under the freedom of intimate association.[107]

Equal access to commercial opportunities represents a much greater state interest than providing equal access to other types of advantages or intangible benefits. Claims based upon "nothing more than the plaintiff's desire to socialize in a particular private setting" try to establish a right to the very thing that the freedom of private association presupposes the plaintiff may not do absent others' consent.[108]

Membership Discrimination, Insurance

Screening of prospective members of a nonprofit organization, such as a condominium association, must be carefully drawn so as not to violate civil rights (e.g., such as race, religion, etc. freedoms). If an insured organization intentionally violates these rights, public policy forbids insurance indemnification of the insured for an expense caused by such discriminatory conduct; such as, a damages award or case settlement expense.[109]

§343. LABOR UNIONS

The points that follow are indicated simply to show the nature and the right of association in labor law. Full discussion of labor law is available in many other works.[110] [See also the discussions in Chapter 6.]

In early common law, association of workmen into groups for advancement of their interests as employees was viewed as criminal syndicalism.[111] This was much like criminal conspiracy.[112] In 1842, this view was reversed in the celebrated Massachusetts case of *Commonwealth v. Hunt.*[113] Thereafter, many cases affirmed the right of workmen to join together, in labor unions or otherwise, for the advancement of their common interests.

Today such associations are valid so long as they do not contemplate or use unlawful means or methods.[114] An attempt by a Colorado statute to regulate unions by requiring that they be incorporated was made in 1943. It was held to be unconstitutional, in 1944, as a restriction on the right to assembly and free speech.[115]

Unions have been held not to be illegal combinations in restraint of trade.[116] The accusation of overbearing power has been made with increasing frequency and bitterness since World War II. When labor unions can, through sheer force, establish higher wage scales and security for some unskilled laborers than for college professors, perhaps it is time for a rebalancing.

Despite the Colorado decision mentioned above, it is believed by many competent and fair-minded persons that compulsory incorporation of labor unions is a just and practical solution to many problems. The decision that such regulation is unconstitutional is viewed as artificial, illogical, and unrealistic. Under such reasoning, statutes that require incorporation of banks and insurance companies also would be unconstitutional. Now that labor unions are giant business organizations, public toleration of shadowy irresponsibility no longer is justifiable. (See Chapter 6.) Power should entail responsibility—at least in the sense of *noblesse oblige.*

The full-scale entry of the great unions into the political arena was approved by the Supreme Court in 1948, in the important case of *United States v. C.I.O.*[117] That case held unconstitutional a section[118] of the Taft-Hartley Act that prohibited contributions or expenditures by corporations or unions in relation to federal elections. This decision practically invited labor unions to dominate the nation by full use of their powerfully organized forces. To infer that the right of association is also the right to dominate society by organization of one group or class is a breathtaking inference, indeed.

As to limitations for the protection of the public, see Section 339.[119] As to mandatory admission of members, see the next chapter.

Recent tendencies to view nonprofit unincorporated associations (*i.e.,* labor unions) as equivalent to corporate entities have been touched on in Chapter 6. In particular, this tendency became marked in 1964.[120]

However, in the *United Steelworkers of America, AFL-CIO v. R.H. Bouligney, Inc.,*[121] the Court refused to treat a union as a corporation for federal diversity jurisdiction purposes, stating that it was a matter for legislative consideration.

§344. "HATE" ORGANIZATIONS

Such organizations as the "Ku Klux Klan," the "American Neo-Nazi Party," and the "Nation of Islam" organization fall into the category of groups whose avowed purposes may be lawful, at least technically, but some of whose members' activities and real purposes are openly racist and bigoted.

In some such organizations, "hate-mongering" is openly avowed. Some are openly and violently anti-Semitic, anti-Negro, anti-Catholic, or anti-something. Their destructive tendencies and effects have been the subject of deep public concern in recent years; Canada has adopted criminal statutes to control "hate propaganda."[122]

Canada's highest court ruled Dec. 13, 1990, that hate propaganda does not have the protection of freedom of speech. A Canadian federal statute to this effect was upheld by a 4 to 3 decision in a lawsuit challenging the statute brought by a school teacher who had been convicted of preaching hatred of Jews in his classroom. This applies to group propaganda as well as to individual hate mongering.[123]

Hate-crime legislation has been adopted (beginning in 1980) in all but three or four states; the latest (in 1990) to adopt such law was Vermont. This applies to hate-mongering by or against groups as well as individuals. There also now is in effect a federal *Hate Crimes Statistics Act* that requires the U.S. Department of Justice to compile data about bigotry-based crimes. As of 1990, only Arkansas, Nebraska, Utah, and Wyoming had not yet adopted such statutes. Bigotry-based crimes now usually entail heavier penalties than other similar crimes, especially for institutional vandalism and harassment. Statutes now often provide for civil causes of action for victims of such hate-based crimes as swastika graffiti and cross-burnings. The trend towards increased governmental action to punish hate crimes is expected to continue.[124]

State statutes, more than federal ones, provide the best checks on sick/evil hate conduct, under the Reagan-Bush Supreme Court justices tendencies today (1993).

Florida has a statute requiring distributors of hate leaflets to put their names and addresses on their scurrilous propaganda.[125] This is a limited but effective idea, because hatemongers usually seek the safety of anonymous and/or law-protected shields against the anger of their victims.

Most of the hate-mongers specialize in "group defamation," which is constitutionally protected freedom to libel and slander groups of people, as contrasted with laws protecting individuals from direct, personal defamation.[126] The right to criticize public officials, even untruly or unfairly, as long as such criticism is not willfully malicious, must be distinguished from hate-mongering directed against racial or religious or other groups.[127]

In the past three decades, a number of "super-patriot" organizations have attracted public attention. While not necessarily in the category of "hate organizations" *as organizations*, they have been used as havens of seeming respectability by some vicious hate-mongers.[128]

There is something very distasteful, not to say dangerous, about an organization in which the members in effect say to nonmembers, "I am a better American than you." One is minded of Samuel Johnson's saying that "patriotism is the last refuge of a scoundrel."

In 1987 the Supreme Court ruled that "racist discrimination" criminal law applies to *ethnic* discrimination or defamation (*e.g.*, against Jews and Arabs in the case) and is grounds for tort action for damages as well as criminal prosecution.[129]

Yet, patriotic organizations are fine things, in the vast majority of cases. It is the "hate organizations" that poison society.

The writers' personal opinions of hate organizations, and of those who organize and operate them, are unprintable. But this discussion will deal only with their technical status.

Such organizations rely for protection on the constitutional privileges that they are eager to deny to the objects of their respective hatreds. These are the usual privileges of free speech, free press, free assembly, and so on.

Where their activities become "clear and present danger," as in the case of use of masks and disguises by the "Ku Klux Klan," statutes in many states now forbid such activities.[130] The history of the Klan clearly indicates how hatred eventually converts sincere thought into vicious actions, and how hate organizations attract the lowest social strata of society and the sickest minds.

A more useful type of regulatory statute requires the registration of members of organizations consisting of 20 or more persons, when the taking of an oath by members is part of the organization's operations. Such organizations are required to register sworn copies of their constitutions, bylaws, rules, oaths, and lists of officers and members. New York's statute, adopted in 1923, has been upheld by the Supreme Court as a valid exercise of the police power.[131]

Such registration statutes are highly desirable. The kind of person who makes hatred his occupation or avocation is best kept under careful public observation. Although such people relish public attention to their blatherings, they are often not so enthusiastic about public knowledge of their personal backgrounds and activities.[132]

The final irony in these organizations often is their violent breast-beating about Communism. By identifying anti-Communism with themselves, they become the best assistants that Communism can have. They suggest to the bulk of reasonable people that there must be a public choice between them and the Communists. Then, after a good look, most people are tempted to prefer the Communists, as the lesser of two evils.

The liking of many of the hate-mongers for fascism and dictatorship (by them, of course) was made clear in the period just before, and since, World War II. It would appear that many professional "hate" organizations are in the category of open, anti-democracy societies. How long a free democracy can tolerate such organizations is a serious question.[133]

§345. SUBVERSIVE (SEDITIOUS) ORGANIZATIONS

"Hate" organizations are just as dangerous and subversive as Communist or Fascist organizations. But the term *subversive* usually is applied primarily to Communist or Fascist organizations, which aim at the overthrow of the government by force and violence. Properly speaking, to *subvert* means to overthrow or ruin; or to undermine morals, allegiance, or faith; or to corrupt.[134]

More accurately, the term *seditious* should be applied to Communist, Fascist, and other totalitarian organizations. *Sedition* is an insurrectionary attempt, by words but not by action, to disturb the peace of the state; it tends to, but does not strictly amount to, treason.[135] In English law, it includes words aimed at fostering ill will among different classes or groups of subjects (which includes hate-mongering).[136]

In the United States, *treason* consists only in levying war against the United States, adhering to their enemies, or giving them aid or comfort.[137]

Guilt by association. The Smith Act of 1940, dealing with sedition and subversion, makes it unlawful knowingly to be a member of, or to be affiliated with, any subversive or seditious "society, group, or assembly of persons."[138] This is a *guilt by association* statute.

Similar statutes (termed *criminal conspiracy* or *criminal syndicalism* laws) are found in many states today.[139] Other such laws are found in labor statutes, where union officers must sign an oath that they are not Communists;[140] in alien laws, for deportation of Communists on the basis of association with such organizations;[141] and in "political party" statutes,[142] and in other statutes dealing with Communism.

A 1982 decision of the Supreme Court held that the Communist Party is exempt from the Federal Elections Commission regulation that requires political parties to reveal the names of contributors in presidential elections, because the danger of public hostility and harassment of members of the Communist Party is great enough to outweigh the government interest in this case.[143]

Loyalty oaths often are required for public employment and for other purposes. They usually require an oath that the person has not been, and is not, a member of a subversive organization. Such statutes have been upheld so long as they are employment tests, rather than *ex post facto* "bills of attainder."[144] *Attainder* means loss of real and personal rights, as punishment, without trial, by legislative enactment.[145] Attainder, forbidden by the Constitution, was implied in some of these laws.

New York's Feinberg Law in 1949 provided a solution to this problem. It required that lists of subversive organizations be prepared by the board of education after hearings. Then applicants for public positions would have to swear that they had not been members of any of the organizations thus publicly proscribed. Membership was tantamount to self-disqualification for public employment, although hearings were provided for. This statute has been held to be constitutional.[146]

Statutes that create guilt-by-association on the basis of *innocent* membership in a subversive organization, especially in the *past* are *ex post facto* laws, or *bills of attainder*, and are unconstitutional.[147]

Yet, refusal of public office to members of subversive organizations can hardly be called suppression of freedom of speech or limitation of the right of association.

The federal government has copied the idea of the Feinberg law. The Attorney-General prepared and published lists of national organizations of subversive character beginning in 1954 and 1955. Here, reasonable warning and due process are preserved.

State nonprofit statutes. Most state statutes (*e.g.,* Ohio's) provide that nonprofit corporations may be formed "for any purpose or purposes *for which natural persons lawfully* may associate themselves."[148] (See Chapter 15.)

Some cases say that only the words of the articles of incorporation may be used to determine the validity of purpose, in granting or withholding a charter.[149] Other cases say that other (outside) facts also may be considered.[150] The writer believes that all facts should be considered by a properly constituted agency; lip service to decency does not prove decency of the speaker.

Private organizations as "public" subjects. A private organization that performs a public function has a "public character" and is subject to criticism, if that is not malicious, without legal recourse, just as is a public official or public matter. Thus a private nursing home organization that accepts private mental patients placed in it by the state, for care, becomes a "public figure" for libel and slander law purposes.[151]

POINTS TO REMEMBER

- Freedom of association is a basic right.
- Action by a group usually is more effective than individual action.
- *Delectus personae* applies to nonprofit organizations.
- Limitations on freedom of association do exist, in criminal matters, licensing, and incorporation laws.
- Some limitations exist in labor unions, too.
- "Hate" organizations are still permitted to operate but are slowly being brought under regulation.
- Subversive organizations are subject to many regulations, and the number of regulations is growing.
- "Guilt by association" in certain organizations now is created by statutes, and the number of statutes is growing.
- "Loyalty oaths" are a chief basis for "guilt by association," when the association is with subversive organizations.
- Purposes and actions that are unlawful or improper for individuals usually also are unlawful or improper for organizations.

NOTES TO CHAPTER 33

1. An extensive literature on this (mainly constitutional) law is available, and much case law. *See,* for example: G.D. Cox article, 12 Natl. L.J. (23)3 (Feb. 12, 1990); L.J. Barker, *Civil*

Liberties and the Constitution: Cases and Commentaries (Prentice-Hall, 1986); Note, 104 Harv. L. Rev. 1835 (1991); Univ. of Texas, *Our Freedoms: Rights and Responsibilities* (U. of Tex., 1985); J.W. Montgomery, *Human Rights and Human Dignity* (Zondervan Pub., 1986); R. Sherman article, 12 Natl. L.J. (37)3 (May 21, 1990).

1a. *Operation Rescue v. Women's Health Center, Inc.,* 18 FLW–S559 (Fla. 10/28/93); 16A Am. Jur. 2d Constitutional Law § 519 (1993 pocket supp., p. 109).

2. 104 S. Ct. 3244, 82 L. Ed. 2d 462 (1984).

3. 42 U.S.C. §§164 *et seq. See,* Dorsen, *The Model Anti-Discrimination Act,* 4 Harv. J. on Legis. 212 (1966) as to states' statutes.

4. 104 S. Ct. at 3252.

5. *Maine Human Rights Com'n v. Le Club Calumet,* 609 A.2d 285 (Me., 1992).

6. *Concord Rod & Gun Club, Inc. v. Massachusetts Commission Against Discrimination,* 524 N.E.2d 1364 (MA 1988); *Roberts v. U.S. Jaycees,* 104 S. Ct. 3244, 3249–50, 82 L.Ed. 2d 462 (1984); *New York State Club Association v. City of New York,* 108 S. Ct. 2225 (1988); *Directors of Rotary International v. Rotary Club of Duarte,* 107 S. Ct. 1940, 1945, 95 L.Ed. 2d 474 (1987).

7. Democratic Party v. Wisconsin, 450 U.S. 105 (1981).

8. *Weaver v. AIDS Service of Austin, Inc.,* 835 S.W. 2d 798 (Mo. App. E.D., 1992).

9. White Egret Condominium, Inc. v. Franklin, 379 S.2d 346 (Fla. 1980); U.S. Const. Amend. 14; Fla. Stat. §718.112(3); Pomerantz v. Woodlands Section 8 Association, 479 S.2d 794 (Fla. 4th D.C. App. 1985).

10. *See,* for example, Golden v. Biscayne Bay Yacht Club, 521 F.2d 344 (5th Cir. 1975); but compare Perkins v. New Orleans Athletic Club, 429 F. Supp. 661 (D.C. La. 1976); and Davis v. Attic Club, 371 N.E.2d 903 (Ill. App. 1977); and Kiwanis Club of Great Neck, Inc. v. Board of Trustees of Kiwanis Intnatl., 363 N.E.2d 1378 (N.Y. 1977). More generally, *see,* Henkin, *The Rights of Man Today* (1978); Sachs, *Sexism and the Law* (1978); Walker, *American Politics and the Constitution* (1978). Note, *Discrimination in Private Social Clubs.* 1970 Duke L.J. 1181; D. Fellman, *The Constitutional Right of Association* (Chicago; Univ. of Chicago Press, 1963); H. Kalven, *The Negro and the First Amendment* (Chicago; Univ. of Chicago Press, 1966); Rice, *Freedom of Association* (N.Y.; N.Y. Univ. Press. 1962).

11. *Kleczek v. Rhode Island Interscholastic League, Inc.,* 612 A.2d 734 (R.I., 1992).

12. *Franklin County School Board v. Page,* 540 So. 2d 891 (FL 1st DCA 1989).

13. *See, Human Rights and Third World Development* (Greenwood Press, 1985); M.A. Eissen, *Case Law on Article 5 of the Convention for Protection of Human Rights* (Council of Europe, 1986); Holland, *Clubs and the Race Relations Act of 1968,* 122 New L.J. 258 (1972); and n.1.

14. Bell v. Kenwood Golf and Country Club, Inc., 313 F. Supp. 753 (D.C., Md., 1970).

15. Durham v. Red Lake Fishing & Hunting Club, Inc., 666 F. Supp. 954 (D.C. Tex. 1987). *See* cases cited in, Note, *The Private Club Exemption to the Civil Rights Act of 1964; A Study in Judicial Confusion,* 44 N.Y.U.L. Rev. 1112 (1969); M. Galen, *Private Clubs: Round Two at the Supreme Court,* 9 Natl. L.J. (29)1(Mar. 30, 1987).

16. Treister v. American Academy of Orthopaedic Surgeons, 396 N.E. 2d 1225 (Ill. App. 1979).

17. Wheeler v. Roman Catholic Archdiocese of Boston, 389 N.E.2d 966 (Mass. 1979). Antioch Temple, Inc. v. Pareka, 422 N.E.2d 1337 (Mass., 1981) (Courts forbidden to try disputes about church property or administration on issues of religious doctrine); *see, Washington Brief,* 9 Natl. L.J. (29)5(Mar. 30, 1987).

18. 410 U.S. 431, 93 S.Ct. 1090, 35 L.Ed.2d 403 (1973). Annot., 49 A.L.R. Fed. 590 (1980) (Private Club coverage under 42 U.S.C. §1983); Annot., 50 A.L.R. Fed. 516 (1980) (Public college refusal of recognition to, or permit meetings of, student homosexual organizations on campus).

19. L. Moody, *Not-for-Profit Corporations—A Survey of Recent Cases,* 21 Clev. St. L. Rev. (3) 26, at 38 (1972).

20. Citing 42 U.S.C. §§1981, 1982.

21. 92 S.Ct. 1965, 407 U.S. 163, 32 L.Ed. 627 (1972). Flagg Bros. Inc. v. Brooks, 436 U.S. 149, 56 L.Ed.2nd 185, (1978) (State's acquiescence in private conduct does not make that conduct that of the state for purposes of the Fourteenth Amendment); Annot., 37 A.L.R. Fed. 601 (1978) (Conduct of private college as state action for purposes of Fourteenth Amendment).

22. *See* n. 19.

23. Davis v. Attic Club, 371 N.E.2d 903 (Ill. App. 1977).

24. *See*, n. 26 and 29 below. *And see* works on civil rights (constitutional) law.

25. Perkins v. New Orleans Athletic Club, 429 F. Supp. 661 (D. Ct. La. 1976).

26. Kiwanis Club of Great Neck Inc. v. Board of Trustees of Kiwanis Intl., 363 N.E.2d 1378 (N.Y. 1977).

27. 382 F. Supp. 1182 (D.C. Conn. 1974).

28. Golden v. Biscayne Bay Yacht Club, 521 F.2d 344 (5th Cir. 1975).

29. Seiderberg v. McSorley's Old Ale House, Inc., 317 F. Supp. 593 (D.C. N.Y. 1970).

30. Rotary Club of Duarte v. Board of Directors of Rotary Intnatl., 178 Cal. App. 3rd 1035, 1048-50, 224 Cal. Rptr. 213, 219–21 (1986); Bohemian Club v. Fair Employment or Housing Comm., 187 Cal. App. 3rd 1, 6; 231 Cal. Rptr. 769, 770 (1986.)

31. N.Y. State Club Assn., Inc. v. City; N.Y. Ct. App., Feb. 17, 1987, cert. gtd. and arguments heard by U.S. Supr. Ct. (#86-1836) in Feb. 1988. See, M. Galen *article* in 9 Natl. L. J. (29) 1 (Mar. 30, 1987); L. Greenhouse *article* in N.Y. Times (Feb. 24, 1988).

32. U.S. Const., First and Fourteenth Amendments. *See* Horn, *Groups and the Constitution* (1956); Fellman, *The Constitutional Right of Association* (1963); N.A.A.C.P. v. Button, 371 U.S. 415, 9 L. Ed.2d 405 (1963) 83 S. Ct. 328; N.A.A.C.P. v. Alabama *ex rel.* Patterson, 357 U.S. 449; 78 S. Ct. 1163; 2 L. Ed.2d 1488 (1958); State v. Turner, 183 Kan. 496, 328 P.2d 735 (1958); *Developments in the Law—Judicial Control of Actions of Private Associations*, 76 Harv. L. R. 983, 1055 (1963); Abernathy, *The Right of Association*, 6 So. Car. L.Q. 32 (1953); Rice, *Freedom of Association* (New York: N.Y.U. Press, 1962); Douglas, *The Right of Association*, 65 Columbia L.R. 1361 (1963); Note, 112 U. Pa. L.R. 647 (1964); Note, 23 Albany L.R. 153 (1964). Rice, *The Constitutional Right of Association*. 16 Hastings L.J. 491 (1965); Pasley, *Exclusion and Expulsion from Nonprofit Organizations—The Civil Rights Aspect*, 14 Clev.-Mar. L. Rev. 203 (1965).

33. Application of Thom, 33 N.Y.2d 609, 301 N.E.2d 542 (1973); *and see* above, chapter on corporate names; and NAACP v. Alabama, 84 S. Ct. 1302 (1964); Kusper v. Pontikas, 94 S. Ct. 303 (1973); Annot. 33 L.Ed.2d 865; 89 A.L.R.2d 964; Re Grand Jury, 633 F.2d 754 (9th Cir., Calif. 1980).

34. Gay Activists Alliance v. Lorenzo, 31 N.Y.2d 965, 293 N.E.2d 255, 341 N.Y.S.2d 108 (1973), rev'g 66 Misc.2d 456, 320 N.Y.2d 994 (Sup. Ct. 1971).

35. State *ex rel.* Grant v. Brown, 313 N.E.2d 847, 39 Ohio St.2d 112, (1974), *cert. den.* 95 S.Ct. 1110.

36. *Gay and Lesbian Students Association v. Johns*, 850 F.2d 361 (8th Cir. AR 1988).

37. *Dignity Twin Cities v. Neuman Center*, 472 N.W. 2d 355 (Minn. App. 1991).

38. *See* U.S. Const., First and Fourteenth Amendments.

39. NAACP v. Alabama, 357 U.S. 449, 2 L.Ed. 2d 1488 (1958); Healy v. James, 408 U.S. 169, 33 L.Ed. 2d 266, (1972); Democratic Party v. Wisconsin, 450 U.S. 107, 67 L.Ed. 2d 82 (1981).

40. U.S. v. Cruikshank, 92 U.S. 542, 23 L.Ed. 588 (1876).

41. *See* Curle v. Ward, 59 A.D. 2d 286, 399 N.Y.S. 2d 308, *mod.* 46 N.Y. 2d 1049, 416 N.Y.S. 2d 549, 389 N.E. 2d 1070 (1977) (To justify interference with associational freedom, state must show an interest that is "compelling" and of great importance to the state; and the state must prove such interest); Sawyer v. Sandstrom, 615 F. 2d 311 (5th Cir. 1980) (Statute upheld if it proscribes conduct which threatens public safety or causes breach of peace).

42. N.Y. Civ. Rights L. §43; Railway Mail Assn. v. Corsi, 326 U.S. 88, 65 S.Ct. 1483, 89 L. Ed. 2072 (1945); Railway Employees' Dept. v. Hanson, 351, U.S. 225; 76 S.Ct. 714, 100 L.Ed. 1112 (1956); Lathrop v. Donohue, 367 U.S. 820 81 S.Ct. 1826, 6 L. Ed.2d 1191 (1961). N.L.R.B. v. Mansion House Center Mgt. Corp., 473 F.2d 471 (8th Cir. 1973).

43. *See*, Wellington, *The Constitution, the Labor Union and "Governmental Action."* 70 Yale L.J. 345, 355 (1961).

44. Lathrop case, n.42. But states ordinarily could not compel admission, Medical Society of Mobile County v. Walker, 245 Ala. 135, 16 S.2d 321 (1944); Trautwein v. Harbourt, 40 N.J. Super, 247, 123 A.2d 30 (1956). Even if exclusion was based on malice. Terbeil v. Clifford, 32 Utah 222, 72 A. 921 (1909).

45. *State Power and Discrimination by Private Clubs: First Amendment Protection for Nonexpressive Associations*, 104 Harv. L. Rev. 1835 (1991).

46. *Danglev v. Yorktown Cent. Schools*, U.S. Dist. Ct., N.Y.; Aug. 14, 1991.

47. *Community for Creative Non-Violence v. Turner*, 893 F. 2d 1387 (D.C. Civ., 1990).

48. *See, Developments in the Law*, above, n.32 at 989 *a seq*, and Rice, *Freedom of Association*, above, n.25. Attorney General v. Bailey, 386 Mass. 367, 436 N.E. 2d 139, *cert. den.*, 859 U.S. 970, 74 L.Ed 2d 282, (1982) [State statute that required private schools to report names and addresses of children (to the Commissioner of Education) does not unduly burden right to associate].

49. NAACP cases, n.33; Ross v. Ebert, 275 Wis. 523, 82 N.W.2d 315. State action also is constrained. Gideon v. Wainright, 372 U.S. 335, 83 S.Ct. 792, 9 L. Ed.2d 799 (1963). *See* State Bd. of Ed. v. National Collegiate Athletic Assoc., 273 So.2d 912 (La. App. 1973) (court mentions violation of civil rights as cause for judicial interference with the internal affairs of a private association).

50. Whipple v. Fehsenfeld, 173 Kans. 427, 249 P.2d 538 (1952); *cert. den.* 346 U.S. 813 (1953); Chaffee, *The Internal Affairs of Associations Not for Profit*, 43 Harv. L. Rev. 993, 1027 (1930).

51. *See*. Chaffee, *Developments in the law—Judicial Control of Actions of Private Associations*, 76 Harv. L.R. 983 (1963).

52. *National Commodity and Barter Ass'n v. U.S.*, 951 F.2d 1172 (10th Cir. 1991).

53. United States Civil Serv. Com. v. National Assoc. of Letter Carriers, 413 U.S. 548, 37 L.Ed. 2d 796 (1973); Buckley v. Valeo, 424 U.S. 1, 46 L.Ed. 2d 659, (1976); Democratic Party v. Wisconsin, 450 U.S. 107, 67 L.Ed. 2d 82 (1981).

54. Sawyer v. Sandstrom, 615 F. 2d 311 (5th Cir. 1980); Beller v. Middendorf, 632 F.2d 788 (9th Cir. 1980) *reh. den.*, 647 F.2d 80, *cert. den.*, 454 U.S. 855, 70 L.Ed. 2d 150, (1981), *reh. den.*, 454 U.S. 1069, 70 L.Ed. 2d 605 (1981).

55. Uphaus v. Wyman, 360 U.S. 72, 3 L.Ed. 2d 1090, *reh. den.*, 361 U.S. 856, 4 L.Ed. 2d 95, *rev.* 364 U.S. 388, 5 L.Ed. 2d 148 (1960)(Balance public interest against right to associate); Jenness v. Fortson, 403 U.S. 431, 29 L.Ed. 2d 554 (1971) (A major state interest); Re Primus, 436 U.S. 412, 56 L.Ed. 2d 417 (1978) (A major state interest); Barenblatt v. United States, 360 U.S. 109, 3 L.Ed. 2d 1115, *reh. den.*, 361 U.S. 854, 4 L.Ed. 2d 93 (1959) (Compelling government interest); Williams v. Rhodes, 393 U.S. 23, 21 L.Ed. 2d 24, (1968) (Compelling government interest).

56. *See* note 55, Curle v. Wood, 399 N.Y.S. 2d 308, *mod.*, 46 N.Y. 2d 1049, 389 N.E. 2d 1070 (1979).

57. *Heitmanis v. Austin*; U.S. 6th Cir., Mich., Mar. 29, 1990.

58. *Ukrainian-American Bar Assn., Inc. v. Baker*, D.C. Cir. Ct. App. (Jan. 26, 1990).

59. Unexplained expulsion: Anthony v. Syracuse Univ.; 224 A.D. 478, 251 N.Y.S. 435 (1928).

60. Randolph v. First Baptist Church, 68 Ohio L. Abs., 100, 120 N.E.2d 486 (1954).

61. Madden v. Atkins, 4 N.Y.2d 283, 151 N.E.2d 73 (1958).

62. Mitchell v. International Assn. of Machinists, 196 Calif. App.2d 786, 16 Cal. Rpts. 813 (1961).

63. Falcone v. Middlesex County Medical Society, 34 N.J. 583, 170 A.2d 791 (1961).

64. *See* Falcone case, n.63; Chaffee, n.51.

65. *Employment Div. v. Smith*, U.S. Supr. Ct. (#88-1213) (6-3 decision) (Apr. 30, 1990).

66. *Snyder v. Evangelical Orthodox Church*, 264 *Calif. Rptr* 640 (App. Ct., 1989).

67. *New Life Baptist Church Academy v. Town of East Longmeadow*, U.S. 1st Circ. Ct. (Sept. 7, 1989).

68. 76 Harv L.R. 983-1160 (1963). Freedom of association is a basic right. De Jonga v. Oregon, 289 U.S. 353, 57 S.Ct. 255, 81 L.Ed. 278 (1937).

69. Wieman v. Updegraff, 344 U.S. 183, 195, 73 S.Ct. 215, 97 L.Ed. 216 (1952).

70. Abernathy, *The Right of Association*. 6 So. Car. L.Q. 32–77 (1953). *And see*, n.32 Hernandez v. Banco de Las Americas, 571 P.2d 1033 (Ariz. 1976).

71. *See*. 16 Am.Jur. 2d, *Constitutional Law* §535; and, Note, *Associational Standing and Due Process* 61 B.U.L.Rev. 174 (1981).

72. Runyon v. McCrary, 427 U.S. 160 *app.*, 569 F. 2d 124 (4th Cir. 1976), and *cert. den.*, 439 U.S. 927, 58 L.Ed. 2d 320 (1976).

73. Bates v. Little Rock, 361 U.S. 516. (1960); NAACP v. Button, 371 U.S. 415, 9 L.Ed. 2d 405 (1963).

74. N.A.A.C.P. v. Button, n.55, 371 U.S. 416; Carson v. Pierce, 719 F.2d 931 (Cir. App., Mo. 1983); Bronson v. Board of Education, 573 F.Supp. 767 (D.C. Ohio 1983).

75. *See*. N.A.A.C.P. v. Alabama, 357 U.S. 449, n.56; Gibson v. Florida Legislative Investig. Comm., 372 U.S. 539 (1963).

76. *Dolan v. U.S. Equestrian Team, Inc.*, 608 A.2d 434 (N.J. Super. A.D., 1992).

77. *Smith v. Ohio State University*, 557 N.E. 2d 857 (Ohio Ct. Clm. 1990).

78. *Pacific-Union Club v. Superior Court* (State Franchise Tax Board), 283 Cal. Rptr. 287 (App. 1991). See, as to EEOC and Title VII coverage, *E.E.O.C. v. University Club of Chicago*, 763 F. Supp. 985 (D.C. Ill, 1991).

79. *Saint Louis v. Baystate Medical Center, Inc.*, 568 N.E.2d 1181 (Mass. App. 1991).

80. Johnston v. Winn, 105 S.W.2d 398, 400 (Tex. Civ. App. 1937). *But see*, n.42,43.

81. People v. Herbert, 162 Misc. 817; 295 N.Y.S. 251, 253 (1937).

82. Adams v. St. Clair, 185 Miss. 416, 188 S. 559, 560 (1939).

83. Saint Louis v. Roche, 120 Mo. 541; 31 S.W. 915 (1895); Coker v. Fort Smith, 162 Ark. 357; 258 S.W. 388; *see*, Sayre, *Criminal Conspiracy*, 35 Harv. L. Rev. 393 (1922); Communist Party v. Subversive Activities Control Board, 367 U.S. 1, 81 S.Ct. 1357 6 L. Ed.2d 625 (1961). Thus, incorporation was denied to a group that meant to associate for the purpose of advocating a change in the law forbidding homosexual activities. Gay Activists Alliance v. Lomenzo, 66 Misc.2d 456, 320 N.Y.S.2d 994 (Sup. Ct. 1971). *See*, for criticism of this (forbidding an effort to *advocate* change of a law), L. Moody article cited above, n.19 at pp. 35–36 (where the purposes proposed by the Gay Activists Alliance, in its rejected charter, are set forth).

84. *See*, n.83, Lanzetta v. New Jersey, 366 U.S. 451, 59 S.Ct. 618, 83 L. Ed. 888 (1939); Sawyer v. Sandstrom, above, n.41 (Forbidding association with user of drugs violates First Amendment). U.S. v. Lowe, 654 F.2d 562 (9th Cir. 1981) (Probation rules limiting association right may be valid). Tyra v. State, 644 S.W.2d 865 (D.C., Tex. 1982) (Probation naming ten persons to be avoided is valid).

85. United States v. Kissel, 218 U.S. 601; 31 S.Ct. 124; 54 L. Ed. 1168 (1910); McCloskey v. Charleroi Mt. Club, 134 A.2d 873 (Pa. 1957).

86. Commonwealth v. Judd, 2 Mass. 329; 3 Am. Dec. 54 (1807). Yates v. U.S., 354 U.S. 298, 70 L.Ed2d 1356 (1956) [Government may punish under Smith Act (18 U.S.C. §2385) the advocacy of forcible action to overthrow the government, not mere abstract theory).

87. N.Y. Rev. Penal L. §105.20; People v. Daniels, 105 Calif. 262; 38 P. 720 (1894).

88. Comment, *Members' Liability for Dues, Fees, Fines, and Assessments in Nonprofit Associations and Corporations*, 19 *U. of San Fran. L.R.* 393, 415–17 (1985); Note, *Roberts v. United States Jaycees: Does the Right of Freedom of Association Imply an Absolute Right to Private Discrimination?*, Utah L.R. 373, 380 (1986).

89. *New York State Club Association, Inc. v. City of New York*, 108 S. Ct. 2225 (1988).

90. Note, *Roberts v. United States Jaycees: Does the Right of Freedom of Association Imply an Absolute Right to Private Discrimination?*, Utah L.R. 373, 376 (1986); Comment, *Member Liability for Dues, Fees, Fines, and Assessments in Nonprofit Associations and Corporation*, 19 *U. San Fran. L.R.* 393, 415 (1985).

91. *Roberts v. U.S. Jaycees*, 468 U.S. 609, 623 (1984); *Griswold v. Connecticut*, 381 U.S. 479, 483 (1964).

92. *Board of Directors of Rotary Intl. v. Rotary Club of Duarte*, 481 U.S. 537, 546–47 (1987).

93. *United States v. Landsowne Swim Club*, 713 F. Supp. 785 (E.D. Pa. 1989).

94. *Welsh v. Boy Scouts of America*, 787 F. Supp. 1511 (N.D. Ill. 1992).

95. *United States v. Columbus Country Club*, WL 149935 (E.D. Pa. 1989).

96. *U.S. v. Columbus Country Club*, WL 149935 (E.D. Pa. 1989).

97. *United States v. Landsowne Swim Club*, 713 F. Supp. 785 (E.D. Pa. 1989).

98. *Ragin v. New York Times Co.*, 923 F.2d 995 (2d Cir. 1991).

99. *United States v. Columbus Country Club*, WL 149935 1, 3, 6 (E.D. Pa. 1989).

100. *Board of Directors of Rotary Intl. v. Rotary Club of Duarte*, 481 U.S. 537, 543, 546–47, 549 (1987).

101. *U.S. v. Columbus Country Club*, WL 149935 (E.D. Pa. 1989).

102. See *E.E.O.C. v. University Club*, 763 F. Supp. 122 (D.C. Ill., 1991).

103. *Warfield v. Peninsula Gold & Country Club*, 214 Cal. App. 3rd 646; appeal rejected by Calif. Supr. Ct. (Jan. 25, 1990).

   Club's restaurant, bar, etc., for guests, has "businesslike characteristics, as in: *Board of Directors of Rotary Intnatl. v. Rotary Club*, 481 U.S. 537 (1987). See G.D. Cox article: 12 *Natl. L. J.* 23 3 (Feb. 12, 1990).

104. *New York State Club Association, Inc. v. City of New York*, 108 S. Ct. 2225 (1988).

105. *Frank v. Ivy Club*, 576 A.2d 241 (N.J. 1990), *cert. denied*, 111 S. Ct. 799 (U.S.N.J. 1991).

106. *Olympic Club v. Superior Court*, 282 Cal. Reptr. 1 (Ca. App. 1 Dist. 1991).

107. *Pacific-Union Club v. Superior Court*, 283 Cal. Rptr. 287 (Cal. App. 1 Dist. 1991).

108. *State Power and Discrimination by Private "Clubs": First Amendment Protection for Nonexpressive Associations*, 104 Harv. L. Rev. 1835 (1991).

109. *Ranger Insurance Co. v. Bal Harbour Club, Inc.*, 14 Fla. L. W. 416 (Fla., Aug. 31, 1989). See (short article), 89 *Community Up-Date* 3 (Nov. 1989; publ. by Becker, Poliakoff & Streitfeld law firm, Fort Lauderdale, Fla.).

110. See (all with curr. supp.): Newman, *Labor Law*, Forkosch, *Labor Law*, Teller, *Labor Law*.

111. *Ibid.*

112. Rex v. Journeymen Tailors of Cambridge, 8 Mod (Engl.) 10; Commonwealth v. Pullis (one of the "Cordwainers' Cases"), discussed in Abernathy, *The Right of Association*, 6 So. Car. L.Q. 82, 50 (1953); "Case of the Journeymen Cordwainers," Yates, *Selected Cases* (N.Y.) Ill.; People v. Fisher, 14 Wend. (N.Y.) 9; 28 Am. Dec. 501 (1835); Sayre, *Criminal Conspiracy*, 35 Harv. L. Rev. 393 (1922).

113. Commonwealth v. Hunt. 4 Metc. (Mass.) Ill. (1842). And *see*, Columbus Education Assn. v. Columbus City School Distr., 623 F.2d 1155 (6th Cir. 1980) (Union representative is allowed to be a passionate advocate); Carter v. Kurzejeski, 706 F.2d 835 (8th Cir. 1983) (Federal employees may join labor unions, under First Amendment).

114. *See* notes, 28 Am. Dec. 529; 95 A.L.R. 10; Clayton Act, 38 U.S. Stat. 730 lit. 15 U.S.C.A.; §

12, *etc.*; National Industrial Recovery Act of 1933; 44 U.S. Stat. 195; and subsequent labor statutes.

115. American Federation of Labor v. Reilly, 113 Colo. 90; 155 P.2d 145; 160 A.L.R. 873 (1944).

116. Bedford Cut Stone Co. v. Stone Cutters' Assn. of No. Amer., 274 U.S. 37; 47 S.Ct. 522, 71 L.Ed. 916, 54 A.L.R. 791 (1927).

117. United States v. C.I.O. 335 U.S. 105; 68 S.Ct. 1349, 92 L. Ed. 1849 (1948).

118. But union members cannot be forced to pay dues for financing political campaigns. International Assn. of Machinists v. Stroat, 367 U.S. 740 81 S.Ct. 1784, 6 L. Ed.2d 1141 (1961). *And see* (freedoms in unions), N.L.R.B. v. General Motors Corp., 373 U.S. 732; 83 S.Ct. 1453, 10 L. Ed.2d 670 (1963); Retail Clerks Int. Assn. v. Schermerhorn, 373 U.S. 746, 83 S.Ct. 1461, 10. L. Ed.2d 678 (1963).

119. At n. 35–68; *and see*, n. 118.

120. Miasga v. International Union of Operating Engineers, A.F.L. C.I.O., 196 N.E.2d 324 (Ohio App. 1964); Oleck *Nonprofit Associations as Legal Entities*, 13 Clev.-Mar. L. Rev. 350 (1964).

121. U.S. Steelworkers of America v. R.H. Boulingny, Inc. 382 U.S. 145, 86 S. Ct. 272, 15 L. Ed.2d 217 (1965).

122. *See*, Brown and Stern, *Group Defamation in the United States*, 13 Clev.-Mar. L. Rev. 7 (1964); part of a Symposium on Group Defamation, 13 Clev.-Mar. L. Rev. 1–117 (1964) containing articles by Supreme Court Assoc. Justice Tom Clark, Senator Thomas H. Kuchel (Calif.) and others. Canada has adopted statutes to control "hate propaganda," in its Criminal Code §267A; *see* M. Cohen, *The Hate Propaganda Amendments*, 9 Alberta L. Rev. 103 (1970).

123. News Report, *St. Petersburg Times*, p. 21A (Dec. 14, 1990).

124. R. Sherman article, 12 *Natl. L.J.* (37) 3 (May 21, 1990).

125. Fla. St., §836.11; and *see also*, Georgia State Advisory Committee to U.S. Commission on Civil Rights, *Perceptions of Hate Group Activity in Georgia* (Dec. 1982); Kaust, *The Freedom of Intimate Association*, 89 Yale L.J. 624 (1980).

126. *See*, n. 122

127. New York Times Co. v. Sullivan, 84 S.Ct. 710, 376 U.S. 254, 11 L. Ed.2d 686, 95 A.L.R.2d 1412 (1964).

128. Some "survivalist" organizations have been found to be "covers" for hate organizations and actually engaged in murder, robbery, and other crimes. They often seem to like military camouflage clothing.

129. St. Francis College v. Al-Khazraji, #85-2169 (1987); and Shaare Tefila Congregation v. Cobb, #85-2156 (1987).

130. For lists of statutes, and comments, *see*, Gellhorn (ed.) *The States and Subversion*, Append. A. (1952 and Supp.); and n. 10 above. *See also* citations above, n. 20; and note, 32 Geo. Wash. L. Rev. 139 (1963); 17 U. Miami L. Rev. 223 (1962); 15 Vand. L. Rev. 634 (1962).

131. New York *ex rel.* Bryant v. Zimmerman, 278 U.S. 63, 49 S.Ct. 61, 73 L.Ed. 184 (1928).

132. *See* the Florida statute, above, n. 125

133. *See*, n. 122

134. Webster's *3d New Internat'l. Dict.*, 2281 (1961).

135. Arizona Pub. Co. v. Harris, 20 Ariz. 446, 181 P. 373, 375 (1919).

136. State v. Shepherd, 177 Mo. 205; 76 S.W. 79 (1903).

137. U.S. Const. art. 3 §3 cl. 1; *see*, Young v. U.S. 62; 24 L. Ed. 992, 97 U.S. 39, 62 (1877).

138. *See*, §2(3) of the Act, in 54 U.S. Stat. 670.

139. *E.g.*, Alabama, California, New York, *etc. See*, Gellhorn (ed.), *The States and Subversion*, Append. A. (curr. supp.).

140. American Communications Assn. V. Douds, 339 U.S. 382, 70 S.Ct. 674, 94 L.Ed. 925 (1950).

141. United States *ex rel.* Kaloudis v. Shaughnessy, 180 F.2d 489 (2d Cir. 1950)

142. Communist Party v. Peek, 20 Calif.2d 536; 127 P.2d 889 (1942).

143. Federal Elections Comm. v. Hall-Tyner Election Campaign Committee, 678 F.2d 416 (2d Cir.) *cert. den.* 459 U.S. 1145, 74 L. Ed.2d 992 (1982).

144. Garner v. Board of Public Works, 341 U.S. 716, 71 S.Ct. 909, 95 L. Ed. 1317 (1951).

145. State v. Graves, 352 Mo. 1102; 182 S.W.2d 46, 54 (1944).

146. Adler v. Board of Education, 342 U.S. 485, 72 S.Ct. 380, 96 L. Ed. 517 (1952).

147. Wieman v. Updegraff, 344 U.S. 183, 73 S.Ct. 215, 97 L.Ed. 216 (1952).

148. Ohio Rev. Code §1702.03; Fla. St. §617.01.

149. Association for the Preservation of Freedom of Choice v. Shapiro, 214 N.Y.S.2d 383, 9 N.Y.2d 376, 174 N.E.2d 487 (1961).

150. *In re* Fraternidad Hispana-Americana, 39 Misc.2d 100, 240 N.Y.S.2d 110 (1963). *See also,* Henn and Alexander, *Corporations* §§181–184 (3d ed. 1983). Note that a corporation cannot be "defamed" for tort-damages purposes, unless it shows injury to its business relations, or loss of revenue, resulting from the defamation. *See,* Eason Publications v. Atlanta Gazette, Inc., 233 S.E.2d 232 (Ga. App. 1977).

151. Doctors Convalescent Center, Inc. v. East Shore Newspapers, Inc., 244 N.E.2d 373 (Ill. App. 1968). *See,* as to "qualified privilege" to defame: Ashe v. Hatfield, 300 N.E.2d 545 (Ill. App. 1973). *See* as to "public matter" vulnerability: Gertz v. Robert Welch, Inc., 94 S. Ct. 2997 (1974); Demsky v. Double, 126 A.2d 915 (Pa. 1956) a copy sent to League of Women Voters is privileged because such organization might aid in obtaining an investigation. And "fair comment" on schools, churches and charitable organizations is privileged: Prosser and Keeton, *Torts* 831 (5th ed., 1984) citing cases.

34

DISCIPLINARY AND ASSOCIATIONAL RIGHTS

[See constitutional law cases in Chapter 33.]

§346. WHAT ARE ASSOCIATIONAL RIGHTS?; INTERESTS?

[*See* Chapter 27 as to Directors' Associational and Removal Bases]
Removal of a *director* may be "without cause," by members of a nonprofit corporation, as to directors elected by the members; and by two-thirds vote of the
board as to those elected by the board, or by majority vote for missing a specified number of meetings, if the articles or bylaws so provided when his or her
term began. These rules are the policy proposed in the Revised Model Nonprofit Corporation Act of 1986.[1] *Termination* of a member's association with the
organization may be by a "fair and reasonable" procedure, with 15 days' notice,
a hearing, and other formalities, according to that same Model Act's provision.[2]

In well-organized and well-run nonprofit organizations, express bylaws
make provision for the inevitable problems of members' rights *vis-a-vis* the
organization and *vice-versa*. In some states the statutes state that bylaws *must* be
adopted (by the members), and *may* provide "the conditions upon which, and
the time when, membership of any member in the association shall cease; the
mode, manner, and effect of expulsion of a member . . . *et cetera*. . . ."[3] It would
be wiser to *require* that conditions for membership and expulsion be placed in
the bylaws, thus avoiding trouble in the future.

Constitutional law aspects of associational interests and rights have been
much discussed in recent years. (See the preceding chapter, esp. §340.)

Much of the problem, in this technical aspect, is the question of what is
and what is not such "state action" as to justify the invoking of the federal
authority on a basis of federal constitutional law.[4] The whole matter is in a state
of flux, and is likely to be unsettled for some years to come.

The interests of a member in his position and status in an organization
are called his *associational* rights. Conversely, the rights of the organization in
the same relation are similarly termed.[5]

Statutory provisions. Most state statutes contain few, and sketchy, provisions about associational rights *as such.* Provisions as to voting, qualifications, office holding, and the like, of course are part of associational rights. But little is said, usually, about such things as discipline or expulsion of members.

For example, the Ohio statute, one of the most modern and complete, contains only a few references to this important matter. The most pertinent provision is that

> Membership in a corporation may be terminated in the manner provided
> by law, the articles, or the regulations (bylaws), and upon the termination
> of membership for any cause, such fact and the date of termination shall
> be recorded in the membership book.[6]
>
> Unless the articles or the regulations (bylaws) otherwise provide, all the
> rights and privileges of a member in the corporation and its property shall
> cease on termination of his membership.[7]

The latter provision makes it clear that a member of a club, whose membership is terminated, has no rights as to club assets other than those specifically given to him (if any) by the articles or bylaws.[8] Obviously, this is only if the termination of his membership is lawful and proper.

Another provision of the Ohio statute *permits* the bylaws to include rules as to

> The qualifications, admission, voluntary withdrawal, censure, and suspen-
> sion of members, and the termination of membership . . .[9] (and) the spec-
> ification of their relative rights and privileges among themselves and in the
> property of the corporation.[10]

In the case of charitable organizations (educational, religious, or the like), even in dissolution of the organization, the members have no property rights as to its assets. The assets must be applied to similar purposes, under court direction.[11] Members do not have property rights in assets of other than charitable corporations (*i.e.*, in case of dissolution).[12]

Reading the various provisions together, the Ohio statute indicates that a member has no property rights in a nonprofit organization, unless it is charitable in nature. However, he waives these rights, by joining, except insofar as the articles or bylaws preserve them for him. In the absence of any provision in the articles or bylaws, he retains his property rights in a dissolution of the corporation, if it is not a charitable organization.

Nevertheless, common sense tells us that associational rights of a member include much more than property interests alone. The relation of a member to his fellow members and to the organization, and of them to him, include many other interests, duties, and rights.[13]

Such interests are established and measured largely by the charter and bylaws. One who joins an organization agrees, at least impliedly, that the charter and bylaws shall determine his rights and status in relation to the organization and his fellow members.

But it is clear that a member is entitled to fair and reasonable treatment by his fellow members. It cannot be denied that he has some kind of interest (if only a moral interest) in the organization. And this interest is entitled to protection.

Religious Organizations: First Amendment rules, applied to State actions pursuant to the Fourteenth Amendment, allow religious hierarchies to establish their own organizations' rules as to internal government and discipline.[14] Thus a teacher in a "Christian" school may be "not renewed" when her employment contract year ends, when she had become pregnant, if the school administrators honestly (not as a pretext) believe that their religion holds that children's mothers should stay at home.[15] And a state statute that exempts religiously affiliated child care centers from state licensing requirements does not violate the establishment clause of the constitution.[16]

Expulsion of members is the principal problem in this area of organizational activities and law.

Clearly, money damages often will not suffice to heal the harm caused by unjust expulsion of a member.[17] Courts are reluctant to interfere in disputes between private associations and their members.[18] Nevertheless, courts are obliged to afford legal protection of the rights of members.[19] For example, a country club that is a "private organization" rather than a "business establishment" under the meaning of California's Unruh Civil Rights Act may terminate the membership of a divorced wife who received her membership in a divorce settlement because of its policy of issuing family memberships to adult males only. However, the divorced wife must receive "fair procedure" as a component of due process associated with her expulsion from the enjoyment of the club facilities.[20]

Courts can, and do, review the propriety of an expulsion.[21] They will do so especially when economic interests of a member are involved,[22] or when constitutional rights of a member are affected.[23]

Protection of tenure rights. "Tenure" in an academic community commonly refers to *status* granted usually after a probationary period, which protects a teacher from dismissal except for serious misconduct or incompetence; the primary function of tenure is the preservation of academic freedom.[24] *De facto* tenure means a justifiable expectation of continued employment. However, a mere expectancy of tenure is not considered to be enough to create a property right in the employment.[25] Generally, tenured professors may be discharged only for cause, and only with some reasonable measure of due process.[26] A nontenured teacher has no constitutional right to a hearing prior to a decision not to rehire. Yet, if the decision not to rehire was made by reason of the teacher's exercise of the First Amendment rights, he or she may have a claim for re-employment.[27] Absence of an explicit contractual provision relating to tenure does not always foreclose the possibility that a teacher has a property interest in re-employment.[28] Tenure may be lost in an emergency retrenchment program,[29] and a state may deny tenure to a university teacher for any or no reason, except for a reason which violates his constitutional rights.[30]

In the late 1980's a strong criticism of the abuses of tenured status, by some university professors, aroused great interest but little action. Professors Michael I. Swygert (Stetson University) and Nathaniel E. Gozansky (Emory University) published an article: *The Desirability of Post-Tenure Performance Reviews of Law Professors*[31] that pointed out the dangerous conversion of the concept of tenure (protection from unjust administrative abuse of faculty members) into a lifetime guaranty of privilege and no further hard work, for the holders of tenured status.[32] This phenomenon had been observed before, in 1948, by Professor William Prosser, and by others.[33]

Court-ordered admission of members. In the past, it has consistently been held that a nonprofit organization could not be forced to accept an applicant as a member.[34] Even arbitrary rejection had been upheld.[35]

But where economic interests have been involved (*e.g.*, the need to belong to a union in order to earn a living), courts have compelled acceptance of applicants for membership.[36] Discriminatory rejections (race, creed, or color in a union) have been overridden,[37] in some cases, and upheld in others.[38] A baseball league cannot exclude coaches in wheelchairs from being on the field, under the Americans with Disabilities Act, without an individualized assessment on the nature, duration, and severity of risk posed by the coach.[39] Some leading cases in which economic interests were involved were rejections of applications of physicians for membership in a county medical society and on a hospital staff.[40] The court ordered that the applicants be accepted, as they could not practice in hospitals if not members.[41]

A rule of a high school athletic association, that excludes students over 19 from competing is analyzed with respect to rationality and broad overinclusiveness under the equal protection clause. Such rules are rationally related to the legitimate interests of promoting safety and competition and of eliminating the practice of keeping athletes out of competition in order to extend their eligibility.[42]

Eligibility rules, for participation in an athletic association at a state school, are reviewed for conformity with substantive due process and equal protection by applying the rational basis test. A rule may be found to be overbroad, even if it is rationally related to the state's legitimate interest of establishing priority of class room education over participation in athletic activities.[43]

A promise of future membership has been held to be unenforceable, absent fraud.[44]

Former members of a nonprofit corporation have standing to bring a declaratory action to determine their membership status and rights. If the former members have a statutory right to vote at the meetings where their memberships were revoked, then they have standing to maintain a breach of contract action if the statutes were violated. Former members do not have status to bring *quo warranto* action to determine their rights to hold office in the corporation if those rights are too remote. Membership status must be resolved before former members can bring a derivative action for the benefit of the corporation.[45]

Lifetime membership in a nonprofit organization is a vested right. Only resignation or dishonorable expulsion can terminate a tenure for life. However, if a majority vote of members can change the membership provisions in the articles of incorporation, then the membership rights cannot be considered to be lifetime rights.[46]

A minor and his father brought suit against a nonprofit corporation which operated a youth baseball league to challenge the league's failure to select the minor for the league all-star team. The court held that the plaintiffs lacked *standing* under the Nonprofit Corporation Law of 1988, in equity or at law, because they had no *special relation* to the corporation by virtue of being a member, officer or member of another body, even though they might have been injured by the corporation's action.[47]

An equestrian brought action against two nonprofit amateur athletic associations because they did not choose her to be a member of the American world competition team. The court held that she must exhaust her remedies under the Amateur Sports Act before any legal action is proper. The Act creates no private action and requires arbitration.[48]

Payment of Dues

A campus group cannot define its membership to be all those who pay a mandatory student activity fee, in part, to the group. The membership should be defined as those who seek membership. Otherwise, *automatic membership* transgresses the proscription against forced association.[49]

A member's relation to his/her NPO is basically contractual, in that he/she impliedly or expressly agrees to certain activities, and *impliedly excludes* certain other activities. If the association uses his/her *dues* to promote *contrary* views, it violates his/her rights. In 1990, the Supreme Court ruled that a California bar group that did that violated the First Amendment rights of 21 lawyers who did not want their dues spent to promote such causes as nuclear disarmament and handgun control. They were entitled to *withhold their dues* from the state bar association.[50]

A dues paying member of a homeowners' association in a private development is bound (by implied contract) to support the association by paying dues, etc.[51]

Student organizations challenged the validity of a mandatory student activity fee collected by the University of California to fund the actions of the nonprofit student body government organization. The court held that the university had constitutional authority to assess the fee as a condition of enrollment. Further, the fee was held not to deprive students of their right of association because membership was voluntary despite the mandatory fee. The fee did not deprive the students of freedom of speech because the organization's political activity, though controversial, was necessary and related to the university's educational purposes.[52]

§347. COURT REVIEW OF MEMBER'S RIGHTS

In general, courts will not *re-try* the case when called upon to review the proceedings of a nonprofit organization that suspended or expelled a member. The court review will usually be limited to consideration of whether or not the organization's rules were reasonable and/or were properly enforced, with "due process."[53] In other words, the court will ascertain whether the bylaws were the rules that governed the organization's proceedings, whether good faith was shown, and whether any general laws or constitutional rights were violated.[54]

What the court wants to see in the organization's proceedings is a fair hearing, the member's right to be heard, and enforcement of the organization's reasonable rules. If these were present, the court would not intervene, ordinarily.

Religious Views

[See preceding chapters]
The Evangelical Lutheran Church in America, launched in 1988 through merger of three previous Lutheran groups and now the fourth largest U.S. Protestant denomination (5.3 million members), has adopted a set of *disciplinary rules* (and procedures in violations) for its *ministry*. These rules are quite specific (e.g., as to what is or is not acceptable conduct) as to ministerial office, in such matters as marital conduct, family treatment, alcohol or drug use, debts, etc. This is, in effect, a new body of *private law* of a group of NPOs.[55]

A religious organization's members who were required to take their public (high) school *AIDS-education classes* may be free to take or avoid those classes depending on whether or not their *religion* so mandated; and this is a material question of fact, not a matter for summary judgment.[56]

A public school teacher's occasional *wearing of a headwrap*, as a symbol of her religion (African Hebrew Israelite of Ethiopia), is a constitutionally protected expression (cultural and religious) if sincere, though it might be insubordinate misconduct if not so protected by law.[57]

§348. PROPERTY RIGHTS AS THE BASES OF PROTECTION: GENERAL RULES

As a result of historical accidents in the development of the common law, the special courts of Equity were the principal ones to establish protection of social and *relational* interests.[58] The Equity courts were prompt to protect property rights, but slow to protect purely *moral* rights.[59]

The development of law concerning membership rights was further hindered because most of the cases arose out of membership in unincorporated associations. The originally vague status of such organizations is discussed in

Chapter 6. When doubtful *moral* rights, in a hazy *associated but not cohesive group* were presented to the courts, they tended to recoil from such foggy problems.

Nevertheless, some cases did get to be heard, and some basic rules were established for associational rights and interests. Certain general rules emerged.[60]

In the older cases, no legal protection of a member's interest was available unless he could show that this interest amounted to a *property right* that had some pecuniary value.[61] Nor has this view entirely disappeared. It recurs often in modern decisions.[62] It is based on the idea that courts cannot give any effective relief (*e.g.*, in expulsion of a member) because they cannot force people to be fair to each other.[63] But this difficulty has not caused all courts to admit defeat. Even years ago, some courts refused to permit administrative difficulties to prevent the doing of justice.[64]

What property rights suffice? Under the narrow old rules, not every interest in associational relations was (or is) sufficient property right to deserve legal protection.[65]

Interest in a social club, or even in a church, can be a right to share property owned by the club, such as funds, furniture, land, or a building.[66]

In a social club or a socio-mutual organization, an interest in death-benefit levies is protectable.[67] But a member of a yacht club has no right to a refund of his initiation fee ($2000) when expelled less than two years after joining, unless there is provision for refunds in the club rules; courts avoid interference in internal decisions in the absence of fraud or arbitrariness.[68]

Under the old rules, interests in associational relations were too vague, private, and "merely moral" in nature to win court acceptance and protection.[69] (See Section 321.)

Labor unions. Labor unions present a somewhat different situation. Social and purely relational interests here are distinctly secondary to pecuniary interests—viz., the right to work and to earn a living. Membership here has an obvious pecuniary value; and this long has been recognized as sufficient basis for Equity relief, even under the old view.[70] (See Section 345, next to last paragraph, and Chapter 6.)

In addition, statutory provisions protecting associational rights in unions now are relatively plentiful. The National Labor Relations Act, amended by the Labor Management Relations Act of 1947 and subsequently, covers this subject.[71] This now is amplified in the Labor-Management Reporting and Disclosure Act of 1959 (45 U.S.C. 151), and the Welfare and Pension Plans Disclosure Act of 1962 (29 U.S.C. 301–309) and their amendments.

Trade and professional organizations. There is little doubt that membership in a trade association often has pecuniary value. Membership in some trade associations is almost a prerequisite for the carrying on of business.[72]

The pecuniary value of membership in a professional society, such as a medical society or bar association, is not so clear. A duly licensed doctor or lawyer can practice in many localities without belonging to any society. But in other localities, lack of membership may be very damaging.[73]

In states such as Florida, that have an "integrated bar," membership is essential.[74]

This is why the newer decisions [see Section 345, last paragraph] forcing acceptance of a physician by a hospital or a medical society, seem to be sound.[75] So, too, are decisions requiring a lawyer to join an "integrated bar" in his state.[76]

§349. NATURAL RIGHTS AS THE BASES OF PROTECTION

Throughout the course of the decisions mentioned in the preceding sections, dissatisfaction with the *property basis* of protection of associational rights has been apparent. Many of the old decisions showed that the courts recognized the artificial historical causations of the rules that constrained them.

It was evident to many people, then as now, that the right to decent treatment by one's associates is a *natural right*—not one that needs to be justified on artificial *property* grounds. A number of decisions flatly rejected the old constraints and protected these rights even where no property basis could be shown.[77] Some authorities urged that declaratory judgments be used for this purpose, on the theory that they would at least clarify issues.[78]

The fault was in the administrative inadequacies of the courts, rather than in the problem itself. Such a default by the courts was almost inexcusable, in the light of the great legal maxim that "where there is a right, there is a remedy."[79]

The "new" rule of natural rights. In 1947 the rule of *natural rights* in association relations was solidly declared by the United States Court of Appeals, in the celebrated case of *Berrien v. Pollitzer.*[80] It settled, as the new rule, the rule advocated by rebellious earlier decisions.[81]

The "new rule" of protection of *natural rights* of members in nonprofit organizations clearly is sound.[82]

The federal Civil Rights Law of 1964 is, in effect, a codification of ideas of *natural rights* of all human beings. It is quite consistent with the foregoing discussion.

§350. FINES, SUSPENSION, AND EXPULSION OF MEMBERS: GENERAL RULES

The old rule as to fines, suspension, or expulsion of members is stated in the foregoing sections. The rule emerging from newer legal decisions is discussed in the section that follows this one.

Suspension and removal of directors and officers are discussed in the chapters on directors and officers.

The *implied control*[83] that membership creates strongly affects the suspension or expulsion of a member. By joining the organization, every member expressly or impliedly submits to the internal rules of the organization. He agrees to abide by the rules in the charter and bylaws and thus submits to any reasonable changes therein that are made in accordance with them and/or in accordance with the law.

Under the *contract theory*, an improper expulsion is breach of contract.[84] Even membership itself may have property (economic) value.[85]

The contract theory makes the articles and bylaws the terms of agreement.

All this creates at least a prima facie presumption that, if a member is suspended or expelled, this is in accordance with the rules to which he agreed. When he appeals to a court, the court ordinarily will look first at the *proceedings* whereby he was suspended or expelled. If these proceedings were conducted as the charter and bylaws provided, fairly, and as they reasonably should have been conducted, no inquiry into the basis for the action will be made.[86] If the proceedings were conducted unfairly, or not in accordance with the charter or bylaws, then the court can and will look at the facts, and grant relief.[87]

A member who appeals to the courts must show that he has employed and exhausted every remedy available to him under the internal rules of the organization, unless such steps clearly would be useless in the situation.[88] It has been indicated that if one member of a house committee acts improperly in suspending or fining another member, the first may be personally liable.[89]

Injunction from a threatened suspension or expulsion can be had, in a proper case.[90]

Statutory grounds. Special statutory rules apply in some cases. One such case is that of a labor union. Another is that in which racial or religious discrimination is involved.

For labor unions, civil rights statutes apply in a growing number of states. They prohibit racial or religious discriminations in admission of members.[91] This prohibition, of course, applies also to expulsion of members. *Right to work* statutes, in some states, also may apply (*e.g.*, in Florida).

Admission of members fundamentally remains a matter of *delectus personae*, except where the right to earn a living depends on the membership, as discussed in preceding sections.

Due process is not violated by a school's *disciplining* of a violent student by imposing two *penalties*, one by the principal (summary suspension) and one by the superintendent after due hearings (two, in fact).[92]

Suspension of students for publishing an unofficial school newspaper did not violate their First Amendment rights.[93]

Expulsion of a private social club member requires *notice and a hearing*, comporting with its bylaws.[94]

Membership may be governed by implied conditions, such as continued ownership of land in the place where a club is located.[95]

Expulsion of a student from school, based on charges by some students that she had distributed drugs, which charges were given with the accusers' names, is not invalidated by the school's not having given her the names of some additional accusers; she received adequate *due process*.[96]

When a nonprofit horse club *terminated the membership* of a participant on the grounds of unsportsmanlike conduct and continued disruptive behavior at meetings and shows, the former member sued. Slander and libel charges were unsuccessful because statements, made by the directors and officers, were made without malice. The former member failed to show the elements necessary for intentional infliction of emotional distress. There were no facts to indicate alleged tortious interference of business relationship.[97]

Under Florida law, the confidentiality of communications given in a *peer review* setting are governed by the law where the reviewing nonprofit corporation is incorporated. Thus, Illinois law governed to make privileged a disciplinary proceeding of a voluntary association of real estate appraisers, incorporated in Illinois, even though Florida was the forum state of the fraud action involved.[98]

Physicians and hospitals are *immune from liability* for their actions, under the Health Care Quality Improvement Act (HCQIA), where they are acting as a *professional review body* that imposes *monitoring or suspension* on a physician, if they reasonably believe that the action furthered quality health care, fact gathering, notice and hearing, and that the action taken was warranted.[99]

§351. DETAILS OF EXPULSION AND OTHER DISCIPLINARY ACTION

See the Index as to the forms setting forth *Procedural Rules* for this purpose. Preceding sections set forth the general rules on expulsions and suspensions of members. The illustrations below deal with the details of such disciplinary procedures. Of course, if an organization's bylaws or constitution provide specific procedures for revocation of membership, they must be followed.[100]

Often the rules of an organization differentiate between members "in good standing" and others. Thus payment of dues usually is a prerequisite. An unhappy member is not "in good standing" if he pays his dues into *escrow* instead of to the treasurer.[101]

If a bylaw authorizes only suspension or expulsion of members, this does not include authority to levy fines.[102]

If a bylaws authorizes only "disciplinary measures and punishments," this does not authorize expulsion.[103]

Expulsion *without notice and hearing* is invalid, even if the bylaws so provide. Opportunity for a hearing must be given.[104]

If the bylaws require a two-thirds vote of the members for an expulsion, the directors may not themselves expel a member.[105]

Where bylaws make no provision as to notice and a hearing, *notice* nevertheless *must be given*, and *reasonable opportunity to be heard must be given*. Notice by registered mail is preferable.[106] Notice in a newspaper is insufficient, when a vote by the members (and thus a meeting) is required.[107]

Power to expel members resides in the general membership, unless it clearly is delegated elsewhere by the charter or bylaws.[108]

If the bylaws require that re-admission be on a two-thirds vote by the members or executive committee, re-admission is not spelled out by a lesser action than this.[109]

If the charter is silent, a bylaw amendment that reduces the number of members is valid.[110]

A bylaw that imposes a fine on members of a milk association for failure to contribute a set quantity of milk is void.[111]

If bylaws of a trade association of discount companies require members to report suspicious transactions by clients, failure to do so may result in punishment as the bylaws direct. But such failure does not warrant outside legal action for damages, as between members.[112]

If a club has permitted certain conduct on the part of a member for an extended period of time, it may not suddenly decide that such behavior is grounds for suspension.[113]

An expulsion trial or hearing must be fairly conducted.[114]

Notice of hearing must allow enough time for preparation of a defense.[115]

Notice must state the charges.[116]

The accused member must have the right to cross-examine witnesses who testify against him.[117]

No constitutional privilege against double jeopardy applies; the accused person, though acquitted, may be tried again on the same charge later.[118] [What is "good cause" for censure or expulsion of a member is a matter for the organization's authorities (*e.g.*, board of directors where the bylaws so provided), not for the court substituting its discretion for that of the board, unless abuse of discretion is fairly clear.[119]] Nor does acquittal in criminal court prevent expulsion by the organization for the same offense.[120]

Performance of proper civil duties is not a ground for expulsion (*e.g.*, a doctor testifying against another in court proceedings).[121]

Incorrect procedure, not in conformity with the organization's rules, invalidates an expulsion.[122]

A member may not have court relief unless he has exhausted his remedies under the organization's rules.[123] But the internal rules must be reasonable.[124] Nor need he appeal within the organization where it obviously would be futile.[125] For example, when the nonprofit National Association of Securities Dealers (NASD) imposed *sanctions* on one of its members, the District Court refused to exercise jurisdiction, over a motion seeking to enjoin imposition of the sanctions because the member had not exhausted his administrative remedies.[126]

All aspects of expulsion proceedings must be proper. Thus, where a doctor had received a registered mail notice of disciplinary action according to the bylaws of a college of surgeons, but had not been informed of the charges, nor allowed to confront his accusers, the proceedings were not valid.[127]

A county fireman's appeal of his dismissal (for using drugs) through the state civil service procedure barred action under the labor union grievance (arbitration) procedure. He could use either procedure, but not both. Fl. St. § 447.401 (1989).[128]

§352. ANNUAL REPORTS OF NONPROFIT ORGANIZATIONS: FAILURE TO FILE

Failure of an organization to file required reports to state authorities may result in *disciplinary action against the organization itself.* Some states require biennial reports; most require annual reports, usually to the Department of State.

Florida, for example, even supplies forms for sworn annual filing each year. There is a filing fee. The form calls for names and addresses of officers and directors, corporate name and address, date of incorporation, the Federal Employer Identification Number, and name and address of registered agent.[129] Also, salaries of officers must be stated, amount of charitable contributions, and other financial information to help prevent abuse of nonprofit status.[130]

Penalties. Failure to file means that the corporation shall not be permitted to maintain or defend lawsuits in the state.[131] This can be cured by filing and by paying back fees due; a very mild punishment. But the corporation *can* be dissolved or barred from the state, though this seldom is done.[132]

[See also, in the Index, "Dissolution."]

Other Corporate Responsibilities. Increasing governmental supervision of nonprofit corporations has been the rule in recent years, even under the Reagan administration. Disciplinary proceedings by states and the federal authorities can be expected to escalate, despite politicians' protestations of intention to cut down the "intrusion" of government into private enterprise.[133]

Thus, a fraternal organization that gave only 2.8 percent of its gross income to charitable purposes, while getting most of its income from sales of food and liquor, was held to be not entitled to charitable property tax exemption, even though it had had exemption for ten years prior.[134] [See Chapter 3 on Mixtures of Profit and Nonprofit Purposes and Operations].

POINTS TO REMEMBER

- Constitutional (Civil Rights) law applies to nonprofit organizations, with a few exceptions.

- *Associational rights* of members now are protected as *natural rights.*

- Protection of *property rights* was the old rule. This rule continues in many courts. It protects only rights that have a monetary value.

- Trade-association, labor-union, and professional-association rights often are pecuniary interests and are fairly sure of protection in all states.

- Fines, suspension, and expulsion of members can be imposed. But the charter and/or bylaws should make provision for them. Otherwise they may be barred.

- Courts tend not to interfere if internal procedural rules have been followed fairly.

- Notice, and opportunity to be heard, *always* must be given.

- Statutory *civil rights* apply especially in cases of racial or religious discrimination, and in labor unions.

- Make bylaw provisions for disciplinary proceedings very precise. Follow them very strictly.

- Remember that courts now tend to favor protection of associational rights. The old, absolute rule of *delectus personae* is dwindling in importance.

NOTES TO CHAPTER 34

1. Rev. Model NPC Act §8.08 (1986 Exposure Draft).

2. *Ibid.* §6.21.

3. Fla. St. §619.06 (nonprofit cooperative associations).

4. *See,* Pasley, *Exclusion and Expulsion from Non-Profit Organization—The Civil Rights Aspect,* 14 Clev.-Mar. L. Rev. 203 (1965); Frieden, *Judicial Review of Expulsion Actions in Voluntary Associations,* 6 Washburn L.J. 160 (1966); Chafee, *The Internal Affairs of Associations Not-for-Profit,* 43 Harv. L. Rev. 993 (1930); Paglia v. Staten Island Little League, 66 Misc.2d 626, 322 N.Y.S.2d 37 (Sup. Ct. 1971). The Public Health and Welfare, 42 U.S.C. §2000 (1970); 42 U.S.C.A. 1981 (which applies to private action); Walacz v. Brewer, 315 F. Supp. 431 (D.C. Ala. 1970); Boudreaux v. Baton Rouge Marine Contracting Co., 437 F.2d 1011 (5th Cir. 1971); Annot., 20 A.L.R.2d 344, 374 (1951); Tillman v. Wheaton-Haven Recreation Assn., Inc., 451 F.2d 1211 (9th Cir. 1971) as to the exemption of private clubs from the Civil Rights Act of 1964 (42 U.S.C.A. §§1981–1982); Moose Lodge No. 107 v. Irvis, 92 S.Ct. 1965 (1972).

5. *See,* Stampolis v. Lewis. 180 Pa. Super. 285, 142 A.2d 348 (1958); *In re* Sautter's Estate, 142 Neb. 42, 5 N.W.2d 263, 268 (1942); Lowe v. Public Service Commission, 116 Utah 376, 210 P.2d 558, 561 (1949); *In re* Midwest Athletic Club, 161 F.2d 1005, 1008 (7th Cir. 1947), as to the nature and characteristics of association. *And see,* Note, *Judicial Protection of Membership in Private Associations,* 14 West Res. L. Rev. 346 (1963).

6. Ohio Rev. Code §1702.13(C). Compare Fla. St. §619.06.

7. *Ibid.,* §1702.13(D).

8. Chestnut Beach Association v. May, 4 Ohio App. 217, 184 N.E. 856 (1933). And see below, at n.68.

9. Ohio Rev. Code §1702.11(A)(2).

10. *Ibid.,* §1702.11(A)(4).

11. Ohio Rev. Code §1702.49(D)(2).

12. *Ibid.,* §1702.49(D)(3); Fla. St. §617.011.

13. *See, Developments in the Law—Judicial Control of Actions of Private Associations,* 76 Harv. L. Rev. 983 (1963). *And see* the preceding chapter.

14. Wheeler v. Roman Catholic Archdiocese of Boston, 389 N.E.2d 966 (Mass. S.J. 1979).

15. Ohio Civil Rts. Comm. v. Dayton Christian Schools, 766 F. 2d 932 (6th Cir. 1985), revd. 106 S. Ct. 2718 (1986).

16. Forest Hills Early Learning Ctr. v. Grace Baptist Church, 4th Cir., Va. (May 6, 1988).

17. Rowen v. Morris, 219 Ala. 639, 123 S. 222, 223 (1929); Lavalle v. Societe St. Jean Baptiste, 17 R.I. 680, 24 A. 467, 469 (1892).

18. Local 57. Brotherhood of Painters v. Boyd, 245 Ala. 227, 16 S.2d 705, 711 (1944); Hopson v. Swansy, 1 S.W.2d 413 (Tex. Civ. App. 1927).

State *ex rel.* Ohio School Athletic Assoc. v. Judges of Court of Common Pleas, 173 Ohio St. 239, 181 N.E. 2d 261 (1962); Robinson v. Illinois High School Assoc., 45 Ill. App. 277, 195 N.E. 2d 38, *cert. den.* 85 S.Ct. 647, *reh. den.* 85 S.Ct. 1022 (1965); Jackson v. American Yorkshire Club, 340 F.Supp. 628 (D.C., Iowa, 1971); Nelson v. Texas State Teachers Assoc., 629 S.W. 2d 151 (Tex. Civ. App. 1982); Lawrence v. Ridgewood Country Club, 635 S.W. 2d 665 (Tex. Civ. App. 1982) (Courts will seldom interfere with internal disciplinary processes of a private club unless the club violates its own rules); Annot., 74 A.L.R. 2d 783 (1960).

19. Chafee, *Internal Affairs of Associations Not for Profit*, 43 Harv. L. Rev. 993, 1020 (1936). *See* the preceding chapter; and *see*, James v. Camden City Council No. 10 of N.J. Civil Serv. Assoc., 188 N.J. Super. 251, 457 A.2d 63 (1982) (If rules of association violate public policy, court may intervene to protect rights of members).

20. *Warfield v. Peninsula Golf & Country Club*, 16 Cal. Rptr. 2d 243 (Cal. App. 1 Dist., 1993).

21. Even in cases involving complex questions of religious doctrine, Randolph v. First Baptist Church, 120 N.E.2d 485 (Ohio Com. Pl. 1954); Slaughter v. New St. John M.B. Church, 8 La App. 430.

22. Falcone v. Middlesex County Med. Soc., 34 N.J. 582, 170 A.2d 791 (1961).

23. *E.g.*, free speech: DeMille v. American Fed. of Radio Artists, 31 Calif. 139, 187 P.2d 769 (1947), *cert. den.* 333 U.S. 876. *See* the preceding chapter.

24. Drano v. Providence College, 383 A.2d 1033 (R.I. 1978).

25. N.Y. Institute of Tech. v. State Div. of Human Rights, 386 N.Y.S.2d 685, 40 N.Y.2d 316, 353 N.E.2d 598, (1976).

26. Johnson v. Univ. of Pittsburgh, 435 F.Supp. 1938 (D.C.Pa. 1977).

27. Cherry v. Burnett, 444 F.Supp. 324 (D.C.Md. 1977).

28. Perry v. Sindermann, 408 U.S. 593, 92 S.Ct. 2694, 33 L. Ed.2d 570 (1972).

29. Klein v. Board of Higher Education of City of N.Y., 434 F. Supp. 1113 (D.C. N.Y. 1977).

30. Megill v. Board of Regents of State of Florida, 541 F.2d 1073 (C. App. Fla. 1976).

31. 15 Stetson L. Rev. (2) 355 (1986).

32. 1 J. Legal Educ. 257, 259 (1948). *See also*, Olswange & Fantel, *Tenure and Periodic Performance Review*, 7. J. of College & Univ. Law 1, 25 (1981); and *cf.*, Amer. Assn. of Univ. Profs., *1940 Statement of Principles on Academic Freedom and Tenure*, 39 (1984); R.P. Chait & A.T. Ford, *Beyond Traditional Tenure*, 174–181 (1982).

33. *Ibid.*

34. Barazani v. Brighton and M.B. Chamber of Commerce, 20 Misc.2d 844, 194 N.Y.S.2d 426 (1959); Ross v. Ebert, 275 Wis. 523 82 N.W.2d 315; Sebastian v. Quarter Century Club, 327 Mass. 178, 97 N.E.2d 412 (1951). Hackenthal v. California Medical Assoc., 187 Cal.Rptr. 811 (1982) (Private organizations usually have discretion as to who may be or not be members; Matthews v. Bay Head Improvement Assoc. 95 N.J. 306, 471 A.2d 355, *cert. den.* 53 U.S.L.W. 3236 (U.S. Sup. Ct. 1984).

35. Trautwein v. Harbourt, 40 N.J. Super. 247, 123 A.2d 30, *cert. den.* 125 A.2d 233 (1956); Arnstein v. A.S.C.A.P. 29 F. Supp. 388 (D.C.N.Y. 1939).

36. Clark v. Curtis, 273 A.D. 797, 76 N.Y.S.2d 3, affd, 297 N.Y. 1014, 80 N.E.2d 536 (1948); Thorman v. Intntl. Alliance of T.S.E., 49 Calif.2d 29, 320 P.2d 494 (1958); Seligman v. Toledo Moving Picture Operators Unions, 38 Ohio App. 137, 98 N.E.2d (1947); *and see* note, 18 Rutgers L.R. 704 (1964). Treister v. American Academy of Orthopaedic Surgeons, 78 Ill.App. 3d 746, 396 N.E. 2d 1225, *app. den.*, 79 Ill.2d 630 (1980); Vanderbilt Museum v. American Assoc. of Museums, 449 N.Y.S. 2d 399 (1982).

37. Betts v. Easley, 161 Kans. 459, 169 P.2d 831 (1946).

38. Oliphant v. Brotherhood of Locomotive Firemen, 156 F. Supp. 89 (D.C., Ohio 1957), *cert. den.* 355 U.S. 898 (1957).

39. *Anderson v. Little League Baseball, Inc.* 794 F. Supp. 342 (D. Ariz., 1992).

40. Pinsker v. Pacific Coast Society of Orthodontists, 12 Cal.3d 541, 116 Cal. Rep. 245, 526 P.2d 253 (1974). Westlake Community Hospital v. Superior Court of Los Angeles County, 131 Cal.Rptr. 90, 551 P.2d 410 (1976) Hospital's bylaws rule that hospital staff member waives right of personal redress for any disciplinary action violates public policy.

41. Falcone v. Middlesex County Med. Soc. 62 N.J. Super. 184, 162. A.2d 324, 331 (1960); note, 75 Harv. L.R. 1183 (1962); Group Health Coop. v. Ring County Med. Soc., 39 Wash.2d 586, 237 P. 737, 755 (1951). And, a hospital was forced to accept an osteopath on its courtesy staff, in Greisman v. Newcomb Hosp., 40 N.J. 389, 192 A.2d 817 (1963). Noted, 18 Rutgers L.R. 704 (1964), *and see*, Virgin v. Amer. College of Surgeons, 42 Ill. App.2d 352, 192 N.E. 2d 414 (1963); noted, 60 N.W.L.R. 241 (1955); Treister v. American Academy of Orthopaedic Surgeons, 396 N.E.2d 1225 (Ill. App. 1979). *See*, n.4.

42. *Thomas v. Greencastle Community School Corp.*, 603 N.E. 2d 190 (Ind. App. 5 Dist., 1992).

43. *Indiana High School Athletic Ass'n, Inc. v. Schafer*, 598 N.E. 2d 540 (Ind. App. 5 Dist., 1992).

44. *Cora v. Spanish Naturopath Society, Inc.*, 562 N.Y.S. 2d 766 (A.D. 2 Dept. 1990).

45. *Brenner v. Powers*, 584 N.E. 2d 569 (Ind. App. 3 Dist. 1992).

46. *Id.*

47. *Keranko By and Through Keranko v. Washington Youth Baseball, Inc.*, 584 A. 2d 1082 (Pa. Cmwlth. 1990).

48. *Dolan v. U.S. Equestrian Team, Inc.*, 608 A.2d 434 (N.J. Super. A.D., 1992).

49. *Carroll v. Blinken*, 957 F.2d 991 (2nd Cir. (N.Y.), 1992).

50. U.S. Supr. Ct. (unanimous decision), June 4, 1990.

51. *Douglas Manor Assn., Inc. v. Popovich*, 562 N.Y.S.2d 170 (App. Div., 1990).

52. *Smith v. Regents of University of California*, 3 Cal. Rptr. 2d 384 (Cal. App. 1 Dist. 1992).

53. Terrell v. Palomino Horse Breeders, 414 N.E.2d 332 (Ind. App. 1980); Jackson v. American Yorkshire Club, 340 F.Supp. 628 (D.C., Iowa 1971); State ex.rel. Barfield v. Florida Yacht Club, 106 So.2d 207 (Fla. Dist. Ct. App. 1958), *cert. den.* 111 So.2d 40 (Fla. 1959); Smith v. Kern County Medical Assoc., 19 Cal. 2d 263, 120 P.2d 874 (1942).

54. Robinson v. Illinois High School Assoc., 195 N.E.2d 38, *supra* n.18. (Association may enforce its own rules with no court interference, absent fraud, or unreasonable conduct by the association); Rutledge v. Gulian, 93 N.J. 113, 459 A.2d 680 (1983) (Courts will invalidate an expulsion that was based on considerations that violate public policy); Scheirer v. International Show Car Assoc., 717 P.2d 464 (Cal. App. 1983).

55. Geo. W. Cornell (Associated Press), *Lutheran Church Spells Out Moral Rules for Clergy*, St. Petersburg Times (Religion section) 5E (Jan. 20, 1990).

56. *Ware v. Valley Stream High School Dist.*; N.Y. Ct. App.; (Dec. 19, 1989); with two dissents.

57. *Mississippi Employment Security Comm. v. McGlothin*, 556 So. 2d 324 (Miss. 1990) (with several dissenting opinions).

58. Oleck, *Historical Nature of Equity Jurisprudence*, 20 Fordham L. Rev. 23 (1951).

59. *See* Oleck, *Maxims of Equity Reappraised*, 6 Rutgers L. Rev. 528 (1952).

60. *See*, Chafee, *The Internal Affairs of Associations Not for Profit*, 43 Harv. L. Rev. 993 (1930). For more recent cases, *see*, note, 175 A.L.R. 438, 506–23. *And see*, the preceding chapter.

61. Rigby v. Connol, L.R. 14 Ch. Div. 482 (Engl. 1880).

62. Minton v. Leavell, 297 S.W. 615 (Tex. Civ. App. 1927); Gibson v. Singleton, 149 Ga. 502; 101 S.E. 178 (1930).

63. Baird v. Wells, 44 Ch. Div. 661; 59 L.J. Ch. 673; 33 L.T. 312; 39 W.R. 61; 6 T.L.R. 229 (Engl., 1890).

64. *See*, as to some of the older cases that rejected "property rights" as the sole basis of relief, comment, 37 Yale L.J. 368 (1927).

65. *See*, Pound, *Equitable Relief Against Defamation and Injuries to Personality*, 23 Harv. L. Rev. 640, 677 (1916).

66. Loubat v. Le Roy 15 Abb. N.C. 1, rev'd. 40 Hun (N.Y.) 546; 17 Abb. N.C. (N.Y.) 512; 1 N.Y. St. R. 178 (1886); Allee v. James, 68 Misc. 141; 123 N.Y.S. 581 (1910); Minton v. Leavell, 297 S.W. 615 (Tex. Civ. App. 1927); Smith v. Dicks, 197 N.C. 355; 148 S.E. 484 (1929). Church property interest: Randolph v. First Baptist Church, 120 N.E.2d 485 (Ohio Com. Pl. 1954).

67. Universal Lodge No. 14, F. and A. Masons v. Valentine, 134 Md. 505; 107A. 531 (1919); Holmes v. Brown, 146 Ga. 402; 91 S.E. 408 (1917); Von Arx v. San Francisco Gruetli Verein, 113 Calif. 377; 45 P. 685 (1896).

68. Solomon v. Edgewater Yacht Club, Inc., 519 N.E. 2d 429 (Ohio Mun. 1987). And see above, at n.8.

69. Walsh, *Equity*, §52 (1930); *McClintock, Equity*, §161 (2d ed. 1948); Chafee article, n.60 Smith, *Law of Associations*, 91 (1914). As to religious societies, *see*, Boyles v. Roberts, 222 Mo. 613, 642; 121 S.W. 805 (1909).

70. Heasley v. Operative Plasterers and C.F. Int. Assn., Local No. 31, 324 Penna. 257; 188 A. 206 (1936); Spayd v. Ringing Rock Lodge No. 665, Brotherhood of R.R.T. 270 Penna. 67; 113 A. 70; 14 A.L.R. 1443 (1921); Fales v. Musicians' Protective Union, Local 198, A.R. of M., 40 R.I. 34; 99 A. 823 (1917); Summers, *Legal Limitations of Union Disciplines*, 64 Harv. L. Rev. 1649 (1951); Annot. 21 A.L.R.2d 1397.

71. 29 U.S.C.A. §101, amending §§82(3,5), 9(3). And in England, under the Trade Union Acts of 1871 and 1878, *see*, Amalgamated Society v. Braithwaite, 2 A.C. 440 (H.L., Engl. 1922); note, *The Judicial Resolution of Factional Disputes in Labor Unions*, 30 Columbia L. Rev. 1625 (1930).

72. Strong v. Minneapolis Automobile Trade Assn., 151 Minn. 406; 186 N.W. 800 (1922). *See*, n.41 Treister case; Annot. 72 A.L.R. 3rd 422 (1976).

73. *See*, Weyrens v. Scotts Bluff Medical Society, 133 Nebr. 814; 277 N.W. 378 (1938) (expelled physician claimed loss of hospital connections would caused pecuniary loss; but medical society not compelled to reinstate him); Ewald v. Medical Society, 144 A.D. 128 N.Y.S. 886 (1911) (expulsion for outside conduct). *But see*, n.41, *contra*.

74. The American Judicature Society is dedicated to advancement of the idea of "the integrated bar." Under this view, one State bar association rules lawyers in the state, and membership in the bar association is required of all lawyers in that state. Many states now have an "integrated bar." *See*, Note, 47 J. Amer. Jur. Soc. (9) 203 (Feb. 1964).

75. Falcone case, n.41; *see* Anno., 89 A.L.R.2d 964 (1963); Pinsker v. Pacific Coast Society of Orthodontists, 81 Cal. Rptr. 623, 460 P.2d 495 (1969); *see*, note, *Judicial Review-Professional Association—Inquiry into Exclusion from Membership, 72 W. Va. L. Rev. 420 (1970)*; see generally, Ridesut, *Admission to Non-Statutory Associations Controlling Employment*, 30 Modern L. Rev. 389 (1967); Akers, *Professional Associations and the Legal Regulation of Practice*, 2 Law and Soc. Rev. 463 (1968).

76. Lathrop v. Donohue, 367 U.S. 820, 81 S.Ct. 1826, 6 L. Ed.2d 1191 (1961).

77. *See* cases in note, 175 A.L.R. 438, 509–23; comment, 37 Yale L.J. 368 (1927).

78. *E.g.*, McCormick, *Equity*, §161 (2d ed. 1948).

79. Oleck, *Maxims of Equity Reappraised*, 6 Rutgers L. Rev. 528 (1952).

80. Berrien v. Pollitzer, 83 U.S. App. D.C. 23; 165 F.2d 21 (1947); Noted, 33 Cornell L.Q. 579 (1943); 36 Geo L.J. 692 (1948); 34 Va. L. Rev. 352 (1948); 34 Yale L.J. 999 (1949).

81. In n.77, and in the foregoing sections; and *see*, Chaffee, *Internal Affairs of Associations Not for Profit*, 43 Harv. L. Rev. 993 (1930); Lawrence v. Ridgewood Country Club, 635 S.W.2d 665 (Tex. Civ. App., 1982).

82. Berrien v. Pollitzer, 83 U.S. App. D.C. 23; 165 F.2d 21 (1947); note, 33 Cornell L.Q. 579 (1948); 36 Geo. L.J. 692 (1948); 34 Va. L. Rev. 352 (1948); 34 Yale L.J. 999 (1949). *See also*, other illustrative cases; International Union of Steam and O. Engrs. v. Owens, 119 Ohio St. 94; 162 N.E. 386 (1928) (union member's suit to enjoin expulsion of local's members for failure to strike); Evans v. Royal Arcanum, 223 N.Y. 497; 120 N.E. 93; 1 A.L.R. 163, 169 (expulsion for refusal to pay increase in amount of assessment in benefit association); Williams v. District Executive Board, 1 Penna. Dist. and County Rep. 31; noted, 7

Cornell L.Q. 261 (1921) (union nominee for salaried office, action to enjoin distribution of ballots with his name omitted).

83. Slaughter v. New St. John M.B. Church, 8 La. App. 430; Riko Enterprises, Inc. v. Seattle Supersonics Corp., 357 F. Supp. 521 (D.C. N.Y. 1973). *But see*, (criticism), Laski, *The Personality of Associations*, 29 Harv. L. Rev. 404, 420 (1916).

84. Farrall v. District of Columbia A.A.U., 153 F.2d 647 (D.C. Cir. 1946). *But see*, Smith v. Kern County Med. Assn., 19 Calif.2d 263, 120 P.2d (1942). Scott v. East Alabama Educational Foundation, Inc., 417 S.2d 572 (Ala. 1982) (Constitution and bylaws constitute a contract among the association's members, binding while in effect).

85. Bernstein v. Alameda-Contra Costa Med. Assn., 130 Calif.2d 241, 293 P.2d 862 (1956); Berrien v. Pollitzer, 165 F.2d 21 (D.C. Cir. 1947); Reid v. Medical Society, 156 N.Y.S. 780, 783 (1915).

86. McConville v. Milk Wagon Drivers' Union, Local 226, 106 Calif. App. 596, 289 P. 352 (1930); Monroe v. Colored Screwmen's Benev. Assn., 135 La. 893, 66 S.360 (1914); Stevenson v. Holstein Friesian Assn., 30 F.2d 625 (2d Cir. 1929); N.Y. Not-for-Profit Corp. L. §601; Ohio Rev. Code §§1702.11 (A)(2,4); 1702.50; *See also* n. 20 above, *Warfield* case.

87. Lawson v. Hewel, 118 Cal. 613, 50 P. 763, 49 L.R.A. 400 (1897); Lo Bianco v. Cushing, 115 N.J. Eq. 358, 171 A. 778 (1934); Krause v. Sander, 66 Misc. 601, 122 N.Y.S. 54, *affd.* without op. 143 A.D. 941, 127 N.Y.S. 1128 (1911); Universal Lodge No. 14, F. and A. Masons v. Valentine, 134 Md. 505, 107A. 531 (1919); *and see*, Braemer, *Disciplinary Procedures for Trade and Professional Associations*, 23 Bus. Law. 959 (1968); *See also* n. 20 above, *Warfield* case.

88. Shay v. Lovely, 276 Mass. 159; 176 N.E. 791 (1931); Moody v. Farrington, 227 Ill. App. 40; Krause case, n.87, above; Sims v. University Interscholastic League, Ill. S.W.2d 814 (Tex. Civ. App. 1937); revd. on other gds., 133 Tex. 605; 131 S.W.2d 94 (1939); noted, 16 Tex. L. Rev. 410 (1938); Branham v. Benevolent and Protective Order of Elks, Lodge No. 942, 427 S.W.2d 572 (Ky., 1968).

89. Kokolas v. Johnson City Lodge No. 311, Loyal Order of Moose, 66 Misc.2d 39, 319 N.Y.S.2d 668 (Sup. Ct. 1971).

90. Chaffee article, n.60; Pinsker and Falcone cases, n.41.

91. N.Y. Civil Rights L. §43; Railway Mail Assn. v. Corsi, 293 N.Y. 315; 56 N.E.2d 721 (1944); *and see*, Simpson, *Fifty Years of American Equity*, 50 Harv. L. Rev. 171, 201 (1936).

92. *Reasoner by Reasoner v. Meyer*, 766 S.W.2d 161 (MO App. 1989).

93. *Bystrom v. Fridley High School*, 686 F.Supp. 1387 (D.C., MN, 1988).

94. *Boca West Club, Inc. v. Levine*, 578 So. 2d 14 (Fla. 4th DCA, 1991).

95. *Id.*

96. *Jones v. Board of Trustees of Pascaquola Mun. S. School Dist.*, 524 So. 2d 968 (MS 1988).

97. *Tibke v. McDougall*, 479 N.W. 2d 898 (S.D. 1992).

98. *Anas v. Blecker*, 141 F.R.D. 530 (M.D. Fla., 1992).

99. *Fobbs v. Holy Cross Health System Corp.*, 789 F. Supp. 1054 (E.D. Cal. 1992)

100. Kokolas v. Johnson City Lodge No. 311, Loyal Order of Moose, 66 Misc.2d 39, 219 N.Y.S.2d 668 (Sup. Ct. 1971). *See also* Leon v. Chrysler Motors Corp. 358 F. Supp. 877 (D.C. N.J. 1973) aff'd 474 F.2d 1340 (3rd Cir. 1973) (stringent withdrawal-of-membership procedure upheld); Kendler v. Rutledge, 396 N.E.2d 1309 (Ill. App. 1979). But (cf.) *see*, Quaker City Yacht Club v. Williams, 59 Pa. Com. W. Ct. 256, 429 A.2d 1204 (1981) invalidating suspension of a member where bylaws did not provide for reasonable notice.

101. American Hungarian Federation v. Nadas, 519 N.E.2d 677 (Ohio App. 1987).

102. Merchants' Ladies Garment Assn. v. Coat House of W.M. Schwartz, 152 Misc. 130; 273 N.Y.S. 317 (1934).

103. Pepe v. Missanellese Society, 141 Misc. 7; 252 N.Y.S. 70 (1930).

104. Briggs v. Technocracy, 85 N.Y.S.2d 735 (1948). Arizona Osteopathic Medical Assoc. v. Fridena, 10 Ariz.App. 232, 457 P.2d 945, *vacated*, 105 Ariz. 291, 463 P.2d 825, *cert. den.* 90 S.Ct. 2201 (1970) (If membership is necessary for his profession or trade, the member has a right to reasonable notice of hearing and reasonable opportunity to be heard); Curran v. Mount Diablo Council of the Boy Scouts of America, 195 Cal.Rptr. 325, *app. dism.*, 104 S.Ct. 3574 (1984).

105. Weinberg v. Carson, 196 Misc. 74; N.Y.S.2d 398 (1949).

106. *Ibid.*

107. *Ibid.*

108. *Ibid.*; but (cf.) *see* Everglades Protective Syndicate, Inc. v. McKinney, 391 S.2d 262 (Fla. App., 1980) that very little reason for expulsion may suffice for it, in a private club rules.

109. Felman v. Far Dressers' Union, 29 N.Y.S.2d 174 (1941).

110. Keeler v. N.Y. Hide Exchange, 231 A.D. 450; 257 N.Y.S. 432 (1931).

111. Monroe Dairy Assn. v. Webb, 40 A.D. 49; 57 N.Y.S. 572 (1899).

112. Weissman v. Birn, 56 N.Y.S.2dc 269; *affd.* without opinion, 270 A.D. 757; 59 N.Y.S.2d 917 (1946).

113. Spiegelman v. Engineers Country Club, Inc., 316 N.Y.S.2d 358 (Sup. Ct. 1970).

114. Blenko v. Schmeltz, 362 Pa. 365, 67 A.2d 99 (1949); *e.g.*, a relative of the complainant may not be a judge; Meads case, below, n.116.

115. Gallaher v. American Legion, 154 Misc. 281, 277 N.Y.S. 81 (1934); *affd.* by memo, 242 A.D. 604, 271 N.Y.S. 1109 (1934); Terrell v. Palomino Horse Breeders, 414 N.E.2d 332 (Ind. 1980).

116. People *ex rel.* Meads v. Alpha Lodge No. 1, 13 Misc. 677, 35 N.Y.S. 214 (1895); *affd.* by memo, 40 N.Y.S. 1147 (1896). Hackenthal v. California Medical Assoc., 187 Cal.Rptr. 811, *supra* n.34; Applebaum v. Board of Directors, 104 Cal.App. 3d 648, 163 Cal.Rptr. 831 (1980).

117. Pales v. Musicians' Protective Union, 40 R.I. 35, 99 A. 328 (1917). Brooks v. Engar, 259 A.D. 333, 19 N.Y.S.2d 114 (1940); *affd.* 284 N.Y. 767, 31 N.E.2d 514 (1940).

118. Rueb v. Render, 24 New Mex. 534, 174 P. 992 (1918).

119. Van Daele v. Vinci, 264 N.E.2d 41 (Ill. App. 1970) (grocery cooperative).

120. Miller v. Hennepin County Med. Soc., 124 Minn. 314, 144 N.W. 1091 (1914).

121. Bernstein v. Alameda—Contra Costa Med. Assn. 139 Calif. App.2d 241, 293 P.2d 352 (1956).

122. Joseph v. Passaic Hospital Assn., 26 N.J. 557, 141 A.2d 18 (1958). *See*, Kendler v. Rutledge, 396 N.E.2d 1309 (Ill. App. 1979).

123. Bernstein case, n.121; Branham v. Benevolent Protective Order of Elks, Lodge No. 942, 427 S.W.2d 572 (Ky., 1968); Peters v. Minnesota Dept. of Ladies of G.A.R., 239 Minn. 133, 58 N.W.2d 58 *affd.* 245 Minn. 563, 73 N.W. 2d 621 (1955); Taylor v. Favorito, 74 N.E.2d 768 (Ohio 1947).

124. Two-year wait for appeal hearing by members is not reasonable. Savior v. Harkins, 11 N.J. 435, 94 A.2d 825 (1953).

125. Thorman v. Intnatl Alliance of Theatrical S.E., 49 Calif. 2d 629, 320 P.2d 494, 498 (1958); Taylor case, n.123; Love v. Grand Temple Daughters, I.B.P.O.E. of W., 325 N.Y.S. 2d 368 (App. 1971).

126. *J.W. Gant & Associates, Inc. v. National Ass'n of Securities Dealers, Inc.*, 791 F. Supp. 1022 (D. Del., 1992).

127. Virgin v. American College of Surgeons, 192 N.E.2d 414 (Ill. App. 1963). *And see*, note, *Judicial Protection of Membership in Private Associations*, 14 Wes. Res. L.R. 346 (1963); Frieden, *Judicial Review of Expulsion Actions in Voluntary Associations*, 6 Washburn L.J. 160 (1966). *See*, Kendler v. Rutledge, 396 N.E.2d 1309 (Ill. App. 1979).

128. *Metropolitan Dade County v. Dade County Assn. of Firefighters, Local 1403,* 575 So. 2d 289 (Fla. 3rd DCA, 1991).

129. Fla. St. §§607.1622, 617.1622

130. *Id.*;

131. *Id.* §607.1622(8), 617.1622(8)

132. *Id.*

133. *See,* Henn and Alexander, *Corporations,* 27–35 (3rd ed., 1983).

134. Indiana State Bd. of Tax Commrs. v. Fraternal Order of Eagles, Lodge No. 255, 521 N.E. 2d 678 (Ind. 1988).

35

ACCOUNTING FOR NONPROFIT ORGANIZATIONS

[Section 352 was contributed in 1988 by Richard P. Lancaster (J.D.; C.P.A.); and most of the rest of this chapter was contributed by Robert L. McIntyre, Jr. (J.D.; C.P.A.); updating in 1993 was done by Stewart.]

§353. ACCOUNTING FOR NONPROFIT ORGANIZATIONS, IN GENERAL

[Accountant duties and liabilities to *third persons*, in financial review reports or certified audits, are found only where a relation similar to *privity of contract* is shown; the accountant's duty runs primarily to the party contracting for the accounting services.][1] [There is a cause of action against an accounting partnership where the accountants hired by a nonprofit organization allegedly have knowledge of illegal acts and conceal them, divert funds, and fail to withdraw in the face of a conflict of interest, even though courts do not generally regard the accountant-client relationship as a fiduciary relationship. There is no cause of action against the individual accountants absent allegations that the partnership is insolvent or can't pay its debts.][2]

The keeping of accounting records in business enterprises has been standard practice since time immemorial. This century has seen rapid sophistication in economic recordkeeping. Besides being vital for business decisions, the government has required it for compliance with income tax laws.

The nonprofit organization has grown sophisticated too. Good financial management and governmental requirements dictate the keeping of accurate accounting records.

Because the variety of nonprofit organizations is so diverse, the accounting problems are diverse. However, the same basic tenets seem to recur throughout.

The subject of accounting for nonprofit organizations was one the mass market literature seemed to have overlooked. Practically all accounting instruction for nonprofit organizations had been adapted from commercial accounting literature, until Malvern J. Gross, Jr., published the *Financial and Accounting Guide for Nonprofit Organizations* (1973). This book is viewed by many persons as the authority in the field.[3]

In fact, the American Institute of Certified Public Accountants has only recently adopted a statement of position. This was done in a formal statement of position entitled *Accounting Principles and Reporting Practices for Certain Nonprofit Organizations.*[4] This statement of position applies to almost all nonprofit organizations. There are two exceptions, however. The first group is those in which the AICPA has issued specific industry audit guides. They are: Hospitals (1972), Colleges and Universities (1973), Voluntary Health and Welfare Organizations (1974), and State and Local Governmental Units (1974).[5] The second group not covered is those entities that operate essentially as commercial business for the benefit of their members, such as pension plans, mutual insurance companies, mutual banks, trusts, and farm cooperatives.[6]

Note: For many nonprofit organizations, complex "accrual accounting" is burdensome and unnecessary. *See,* Smith, *Accounting for Librarians,* 77 at n. 20 (1983). Reporting based on cash receipts and disbursements may be adequate enough to permit an independent auditor to describe the result as in conformity with generally accepted accounting principles. *See,* AICPA, *Statement of Position* 78–10, at 10. [The *Financial Accounting Standards Board* current recommendations should be consulted.]

[Mention must be made of FASB Financial Accounting Series #017 (elements of financial statements) 12/85 and No. 006 (9/18/86) replacing Concepts Statement No. 3; of AICPA (above cited) Principles (*etc.*) for Certain Nonprofit Organizations; FASB Standards 56 for hospital-related organizations and Concepts #4 for nonbusiness organizations. FASB'S Exposure Draft (of Dec. 23, 1986) on Depreciation in nonprofit organizations would apply to church property.]

Types of organizations intended to be included are:

- Cemetery organizations
- Civic organizations
- Fraternal organizations
- Labor unions
- Libraries
- Other cultural institutions
- Performing arts organizations
- Political parties
- Private elementary and secondary schools
- Private and community foundations
- Professional associations

- Public broadcasting stations
- Religious organizations
- Research and scientific organizations
- Social and country clubs
- Trade associations
- Zoological and botanical societies[7]

The uses of financial statements of nonprofit organizations should influence the content and format, so they will be meaningful.

A wide variety of persons and groups are interested in the financial statements of nonprofit organizations. Among the principal groups are: (a) contributors to the organization, (b) beneficiaries of the organization, (c) the organization's trustees or directors, (d) employees of the organization, (e) governmental units, (f) the organization's creditors and potential creditors, and (g) constituent organizations.

A principal purpose of the financial statements of a nonprofit organization is to communicate the ways in which resources have been used in carrying out the organization's objectives. That requires reporting the nature and amount of available resources, the uses made of the resources, and the net change in fund balances during the period. In addition, while adequate measures of program accomplishment generally are not available in the context of present financial statements, the financial statements should identify the principal programs of the organization and their costs. A third aspect of nonprofit financial reporting is disclosure of the degree to which the organization's board has flexibility or is restricted by donors in determining how the resources have been or will be used. A fourth aspect is that the financial statements of a nonprofit organization should help the reader to evaluate the organization's ability to carry out its fiscal objectives.[8]

An important factor in developing the accounting practices of a nonprofit organization is to contrast the differences between commercial and nonprofit organizations.

The AICPA's statement of position on *Accounting Principles and Reporting Practices for Certain Nonprofit Organizations* requires that financial statements of nonprofit organizations be prepared using the accrual method of accounting if they are to be in conformity with generally accepted accounting principles. The requirement is only that the financial statement be presented on the accrual basis and not that the books be kept on that basis throughout the year.[9]

Transfers and Appropriations. The funds of a nonprofit organization are usually segregated into many different funds, some restricted and others not. Management can legally transfer funds between nonrestricted funds, and frequently does to balance the budgets. This transfer of money between funds is easy to confuse with an expense, if it is not clearly designated a transfer in the financial statements.

Appropriations are internal authorizations for future expenditures. Appropriations are used when specific sums within a fund are designated for a particular purpose. They do not represent an expenditure, but only management's intended use. Great care needs to be taken so appropriations are not confused with expenses.

A very important new requirement of the AICPA is the reporting requirement that financially interrelated organizations present combined financial statements. Specifically, combined financial statements are required when one nonprofit organization has control over another. Control means the ability, direct or indirect, to cause the direction of the management and policies whether through ownership, by contract or otherwise.

Combined financial statements are also required if any of the following circumstances exist:

a. Separate entities solicit funds in the name of, and with the expressed or implicit approval of, the reporting organization and substantially all of the funds solicited are intended by the contributor or are otherwise required to be transferred to the reporting organization or used at its discretion, or

b. A reporting organization transfers some of its resources to another separate entity whose resources are held for the benefit of the reporting organization, or

c. A reporting organization assigns functions to a controlled entity whose funding is primarily derived from sources other than public contributions.

Exceptions are provided for loosely affiliated local organizations who operate autonomously in determining their program activities, and under certain circumstances religious organizations are also exempted.[10]

One reason for adoption of the requirement for combined financial statement reporting is to curb abuses such as transferring funds in a good year to a control foundation thereby causing the excess of revenues over expenses to be minimal. In this way the organization could cite its low "excess" or even its "deficit" in soliciting contributions from its supporters. Accordingly, this fictional "need" for contributions is highlighted.

Thereafter, the amount transferred to the controlled foundation could be transferred back.

Hopefully, the requirement of combined financial statements in financially interrelated organizations will curb this abuse.[11]

In October 1978 the AICPA adopted the position that nonprofit organizations should capitalize purchased fixed assets at cost and donated fixed assets at their fair value on the date of the gift. They also adopted the position that nonprofit organizations which had not previously capitalized their fixed assets, should do so retroactively.

In conjunction with this capitalization of fixed assets the AICPA position is that to comply with generally accepted accounting principles exhaustible fixed assets should be depreciated over their estimated useful lives.

Exempted from the requirement of depreciation are those non-exhaustible assets such as landmarks, monuments, cathedrals, and historical treasures. Also exempt are houses of worship.[12]

Study of sample *Statements of Income, etc.* of various organizations is the best method for deciding precisely what form should be used for a specific organization.[13]

§354. WHAT IS ACCOUNTING?

Accounting is "the art of recording, classifying and summarizing in a significant manner and in terms of money, transactions and events which are of a financial character and interpreting the results thereof."[14] For a comprehensive text covering all aspects of accounting and its impact for nonprofit organizations see: *Financial and Accounting Guide for Nonprofit Organizations*[15] by Gross and Warshauer, partners in the public accounting firm of Price Waterhouse and Co. Nonprofit organization accounting is similar to that in business organizations in all but a few matters.[16] The main difference stems from the nonprofit's emphasis on accountability and program, as against the commercial's matching of revenue against expenses to measure profit.[17]

"There are six major areas where the accounting principles of nonprofits are likely to differ from those of a similar for-profit organization: 1. cash basis or accrual-basis accounting, 2. fund-accounting, 3. fixed assets 4. transfer appropriations 5. grants, pledges and non-cash contributions (of appreciated property for example) and 6. funds solicitation activities.[18]

§355. STANDARDS AND SOURCES

Uniform accounting standards are obviously desirable in order to allow understanding of reports about varied organizations and activities. Standards in the United States are set by the Financial Accounting Standards Board (F.A.S.B.). Also, the AICPA (see above, Section 352) *Statements of Position* and numerous guides such as "*Audits of Nonprofit Organizations*", "*Accounting Principles and Reporting Practices for Certain Nonprofit Organizations*", and various guides for specific types of organizations, such as "*Audit Guide for Voluntary Health and Welfare Organizations.*"[19]

Major *changes* in the way that NPOs present their *financial statements* were recommended by the Not-for-Profit Task Force of the American Institute of CPAs, researched also by the Financial Accounting Standards Board in 1989–90. For example, unconditional pledges of contributions were to be recorded as receivables under the new rules, which would improve the picture given in a statement. Address FASB at P.O. Box 5116, 401 Merritt 7, Norwalk, Ct. 06856-5116.[20]

New accounting rules favored by the Financial Accounting Standards Board (Norwalk, CT) in late 1992 shift the focus to the NPO rather than its funds. "Required statements include a statement of financial position (i.e., a balance sheet), a statement of activities, and a statement of cash flows."[21]

In fall of 1992, the Financial Accounting Standards Board started releasing exposure drafts of its new rules for accounting. The second draft, on accounting for contributions, drew only 75 responses suggesting change. The financial display first draft drew fewer than 100 letters. The FASB board was to vote on the final approval in June of 1993. Those interested in the final version of the rules should write to the FASB address listed above.

In addition, there are specific "industry-wide" association publications that often treat the special accounting problems of their member organizations. Also, the *"Uniform Fiduciary Accounting Guide"* of the American Bar Association and American Law Institute typifies attempts to provide uniform accounting manuals.[22]

National Directory of Volunteer Accounting Programs (2d edition) may be obtained for postage and handling fee of $6, from Accountants' for the Public Interest, 1012–14th Street, N.W. (Suite 906), Washington, D.C. 20005. It lists over 260 volunteer accounting programs available to NPOs and others.[23]

Microcomputers software based on such uniform statements of principles as the ALI-ABA manual also are available.

Internal Controls are vitally important systems for eliminating possible theft and misappropriation of assets. They are usually based on procedures to make detection probable. Among the most important examples of controls are: budgets, dual-signature requirements, check impression devices, lock boxes, fidelity insurance, background checks on employees, checking of references, and the like.

"Creative" Accounting that abuses NPO accounting standards, as by concealing exorbitant fund raising or administrative costs, were decried in 1992 by NASCO (Natl. Assn. of State Charity Officials').[24]

One example of *"creative accounting"* occurred when an Illinois charity hired a Texas fund raiser. The charity garnered more than $2.5 million in the first year, but spent only $100,000 on its beneficiary patients. The rest went to the Texas fundraiser, who made at least $600,000 in profit. The Illinois Attorney General sued the charity, asking for triple damages of $24 million. The Pennsylvania and Connecticut Attorneys General have also sued the Illinois charity for trying to offset its fundraising costs with contributions of $2.6 million in surplus vegetable and flower seeds, baby foods, cereal, and grass seed. These "gifts in kind" also helped the charity qualify for government payroll deduction campaigns. It seems that the goods were overvalued paper transfers that had nothing to do with what donors were told in fundraising letters. Further, the transfers were arranged by a procurement agency. The Illinois charity had no knowledge that it had donated $2.3 million in seeds to two Texas charities.[25]

In another "creative accounting" case, Viking Penguin donated 350,000 books to a charity in Oklahoma City. The Oklahoma charity donated the books in turn to another charity at a value of $1,056,160. Two of the five truckloads of books were donated to an Atlanta charity at a stated value of $422,464. Then one truckload was donated to a California nonprofit at a stated value of $322,000. Thus the books offset the fundraising costs of two or three different organizations. The value of the goods-in-kind didn't reflect the market value of the goods. The donation appeared on the books even though the Oklahoma charity acted as agent for the donor and passed the donation along.

These types of "creative accounting" practices should obviously be discouraged. Though these goods-in-kind transactions fall within the accounting guidelines, the press and the public see these "paper transactions" as deceiving.[26]

Charities facing problems in accounting with state regulators and oversight organizations have formed a Coalition for Nonprofit Accountability to lobby for changes in the accounting regulatory rules. For information on the Coalition contact Bob Frank of Robert Frank & Co., chairman, (202) 628-5224.

§356. TREASURER'S DUTIES

The primary responsibility for a corporation's accounting is the treasurer's. He or she should have the aid of a professional accountant, of course, unless the operation is quite small.

The treasurer must set up and maintain adequate accounting records, usually in respect to: financial records and statements, budget planning and supervision, safeguarding of financial assets, and compliance with the various governmental financial reporting requirements.[27] In larger organizations the treasurer also must supervise the personnel who handle these matters. A major aspect of a good treasurer's work is the continued analysis of ongoing reports, in order to spot financial problems before they become impossible to handle.[28]

[See also Directors' and Officers' Duties, Chapter 29.]

Securities:

The treasurer (and others) should be aware that some kinds of financial paper do not necessarily look like stocks or bonds, but are "securities" that bring S.E.C. supervision. For example, a country club's form solicitation of initiation fees was held to be such a "security" as to invoke S.E.C. Rule 10b5 sanctions.[29]

Internal Revenue Service (IRS) standards as to tax-exempt (or taxable) activities of course are ongoing supervision matters. See the chapters on Tax Exemption (and Index) as to these. Consult a tax attorney for such problems.

Accountant "Opinion Shopping", aimed at getting some accountant to uphold a doubtful procedure or activity, now may bring (rather than avoid) S.E.C. and other investigation and intervention.[30]

§357. STATE ACCOUNTING REQUIREMENTS

Today it is important that nonprofit organizations determine that their accounting system and reporting are adequate to assure compliance with the various states' registration and reporting requirements, including submission of its financial reports to certain agencies of the state. Registration usually requires reports on: *soliciting funds; holding property,* and *doing business* in the state.[31]

Increasingly, nonprofit organizations have become subject to statutory legal requirements for their accounting principles, including the use of accrual-basis reporting and reporting in accordance with generally accepted accounting principles.[32] In New York, for example, the Not-For-Profit Corporation Law[33] requires that

(a) The board shall present at the annual meeting of members a report, verified by the president and treasurer or by a majority of the directors, or certified by an independent public or certified public accountant or a firm of such accountants selected by the board, showing in appropriate detail the following:

   (1) The assets and liabilities, including the trust funds, of the corporation as of the end of a twelve month fiscal period terminating not more than six months prior to said meeting.

   (2) The principal changes in assets and liabilities, including trust funds, during said fiscal period.

   (3) The revenue or receipts of the corporation, both unrestricted and restricted to particular purposes during said fiscal period.

   (4) The expenses or disbursements of the corporation, for both general and restricted purposes, during said fiscal period.

   (5) The number of members of the corporation as of the date of the report, together with a statement of increase or decrease in such number during said fiscal period, and a statement of the place where the names and places of residence of the current members may be found.

(b) The annual report of directors shall be filed with the records of the corporation and either a copy or an abstract thereof entered in the minutes of the proceedings of the annual meeting of members.

(c) The board of a corporation having no members shall direct the president and treasurer to present at the annual meeting of the board a report in accordance with paragraph (a), but omitting the requirement of subparagraph (5). This report shall be filed with the minutes of the annual meeting of the board.

§358. BOOKKEEPING

Establishment of bookkeeping systems for the nonprofit organization should not be difficult since, once the appropriate accounting standards, procedures and reporting practices are identified, there are numerous alternative methods available. One alternative is certain to accommodate the organization's needs given its budget and its reporting constraints. For example, the volume and accounting complexity of the transactions may require that the bookkeeping records be updated anywhere from daily to annually. It must also be determined whether the treasurer can keep the books himself or if part or full-time professional help is needed. These factors will also determine whether the bookkeeping can be most economically maintained manually, through a mere checkbook record, by a manual one-write system, or whether automated assistance is needed, such as a data processing service bureau, or the organization's own computer and attendant personnel. In establishing the bookkeeping system, assistance from similar nonprofits and knowledgeable professionals can be invaluable, particularly in light of the recent technological explosion in the use of computers and new bookkeeping and financial reporting software programs becoming available almost daily.[34]

Computers and Nonprofit Accounting:

Recent advances in the speed and capabilities of small business computers and the programs for financial reporting and budgeting, when coupled with the drastic reductions in prices, should revolutionize the small nonprofits' accounting and reporting abilities. The speed and ease of operation of these new systems make daily controls and reports available economically even where the treasurer must do the work himself.

Robert L. McIntyre, Jr.[35] has had excellent experience in small nonprofits with *Accounting Partners* by Star Software, Inc. and *Easy Accounting* by DAC Software, Inc., both software programs compatible with many different computers. The administrative services personnel with Price Waterhouse & Co. and Alexander Grant & Company advised that some of the most popular systems for larger nonprofits are *Soloman III, Computec,* and *Open Systems.* For excellent reviews of these and other software programs see *P C World* magazine. *See also* the Bibliography in Chapter 2.

POINTS TO REMEMBER

- Accounting is a profession in itself; not an amateur's work.
- Bookkeeping, too, requires special knowledge and ability.
- Get qualified people to do this work, if you yourself are not so qualified.
- Follow the applicable standards, and avoid trouble.
- View the treasurer as an officer of great importance.
- Beware of changing requirements of State Reports rules.
- Use computers if your records are complex.

NOTES TO CHAPTER 35

1. William Iselin and Co., Inc. v. Landau, 71 N.Y.2d 420, 522 N.E.2d 21 (1988).

2. *Nate B. & Frances Spingold Foundation v. Wallin, Simon, Black and Co.,* 585 N.Y.S. 2d 416 (N.Y.A.D. 1 Dept, 1992).

3. M. Gross, Jr. and W. Warshauer, Jr., Now titled: *Financial Accounting Guide for Nonprofit Organizations* (1979).

4. *Accounting Principles and Reporting Practices for Certain Nonprofit Organizations*, Draft Copy as of October 10, 1978; approved as a final statement of position by the American Institute of Certified Public Accountants.

5. *Ibid.*, p. 2.

6. *Id.*, p. 3.

7. *Id.*, pp. 3, 4.

8. *Id.*, pp. 5, 6.

9. *Accounting Principles and Reporting Practices for Certain Nonprofit Organizations*, Draft Copy as of October 10, 1978, American Institute of Certified Public Accountants, pp. 6, 7.

10. *Ibid.*, pp. 18–20.

11. Speech by Lester I. Wolosoff, Member of the Subcommittee on Nonprofit Organizations, Accounting Standards Division, American Institute of Certified Public Accountants, given November 15, 1978 in Tampa, Florida.

12. *Accounting Principles and Reporting Practices for Certain Nonprofit Organizations*, Draft Copy as of October 10, 1978, pp. 45, 46.

13. *See also* such articles as: Tsaklanganos, *Sense and Nonsense in Financial Reporting by Nonprofit Organizations*, 27 Michigan State U. Business Topics (1) 25–33 (1979).

14. AICPA, *Accounting Research Terminology Bulletin*, No. 1, at 9–90 (1961).

15. Gross and Warshauer, above, n. 3. (Hereafter cited as *G. & W text.*)

16. G. & W. text, p. 10.

17. *Ibid.*, pp. 13–15.

18. *Id.*

19. G. Smith, *Accounting for Librarians*, 6–7 (1983).

20. 3 *Nonprofit Times* (7) 7 (Oct. 1989).

21. D. Harr article, 6 *NonProfit Times* (11) 4 (Nov. 1992).

22. Whitman, Brown & Kramer, *Uniform Fiduciary Accounting Guide* (ALI-ABA; Phila., Pa., 1984).

23. *Note*, 4 *NonProfit Times* (12)5 (Mar. 1991).

24. B. H. Bush article, 6 *NonProfit Times* (11) 1 (Nov. 1992).

25. Huntsinger, J., 7 *NonProfit Times* (2) 24, 26 (Feb. 1993).

26. *Id.*

27. G. & W. text, pp. 4–5.

28. *Ibid.*, p. 337. *See*, for example, Kellogg, *How to Find Negligence and Misrepresentation in Financial Statements* (1979).

29. Silver Hill Country Club v. Sabieski, 55 Calif. 2d 811, 361 P.2d 906 (1961).

30. *See*, M. Middleton, *SEC Targets "Opinion Shopping"*, 8 Natl. L. J. (2)1 (Sept. 23, 1985).

31. G. & W. text, p. 454.

32. *Ibid.*, p. 24.

33. N.Y. N-P-C L. §519

34. *See*, G. & W. text, p. 470.

35. Contributor and writer of Sections 356, 357 noted at beginning of this chapter.

36

RELIGIOUS ORGANIZATIONS

[See the *Index* as to specific topics]

[Many (perhaps half) of all church differences/conflicts can be avoided/resolved if ministers/officers are trained/skilled in the law/practices of Nonprofit Corporations. A church is a *corporate* as well as a religious organization, and needs able *business management* as well as faith.]

§359. RELIGIOUS ORGANIZATIONS IN GENERAL

Religious corporations include not only churches, but all corporations created for religious purposes. Unincorporated churches are congregations or societies that have religious purposes but are not incorporated.[1]

    The name of a religious corporation need not indicate its corporateness. This also is true in many states for charitable, benevolent, regents-supervised schools, and professional societies.[2]

    In secular aspects, these organizations are governed by state law.[3] Special provisions for each of the various denominations (as to incorporation and management) are found in some states.[4] Management is by fiduciary-type directors (with specially limited powers);[5] but in 1993 members sued the Christian Science Church Trustees for alleged continued waste of church funds.

    Religious corporations usually are nonprofit. A religious corporation is composed of a legal entity and a spiritual entity. The acts of one entity will not necessarily affect the other entity.[6] Thus, only members of a church in its corporate form, as opposed to the church in its spiritual form, may vote in the corporate elections.[7]

    Powers of a religious corporation are similar to those of other nonprofit corporations. Some states impose limitations upon the amount of property that a religious corporation may own at any time. Michigan allows religious[8] corporations to hold property that "may be needful for its proper purposes."[9]

    Some states have extensive statutory provisions for specific religious denominations.[10] If a particular denomination is not provided for in the statutes, a religious corporation may incorporate under the general religious corporation statute or under the general not-for-profit corporation statutes, depending upon that state's statutory scheme.[11]

Religious corporations, like other organizations, sometimes cease to operate. Such *de facto* dissolution causes it to be legally extinct. This is provided for in some states when the following circumstances exist:[12]

1. Failure to carry on religious worship, or failure to use its property for religious worship, for a period of two years;
2. A decrease in membership, either in numbers or financial strength, such that for a period of two years it has been impossible to maintain services or to protect its property from dilapidation.

Religious "societies" must be distinguished from religious corporations. The purpose of a religious society is to maintain religious exercises, support the ministry, and promote the growth and efficiency of the church with which the group is aligned.[13] Business aspects of a religious corporation, and the implementation of its secular affairs, are subject to the laws of the state and also to judicial scrutiny. Courts will not interfere with the religious or spiritual affairs of a religious corporation or its ecclesiastical decisions.[14] Judicial interference in ecclesiastical or doctrinal affairs may be invoked only insofar as is necessary in order to ascertain the civil or property (not doctrinal) rights of a party.[15] Other matters that warrant judicial interference include fraud, collusion, or arbitrary conduct on the part of church authorities.[16] Cults and religion-flavored rackets sometimes trouble society. Courts have acknowledged that a cult may be as much a religious organization as any other form of more traditional religion, and these cults are equally subject to state laws.[17]

Typical Church Organization

A typical "setup" of a religious corporation is that of a Presbyterian church in Florida. It states as follows (in outline):

> It is a religious corporation, incorporated under the laws of Florida. Its purpose is to conduct religious worship, instruction and other institutional activities connected therewith of a religious, educational, charitable and benevolent character. The church obtains its guidance from the beliefs, rules and orders of the Presbyterian Church, U.S.A.
>
> The officers of the corporation consist of the Elders and Deacons of the church. The elders are elected by the congregation and their function is to supervise the spiritual development of the local church. The membership consists of the congregation. Rights of the members include:
>
> 1. The right to receive the annual report and any recommendation concerning the holding and control of church property,
> 2. The right to approve the election process for nominating elders and deacons, and the right to elect the deacons and elders,
> 3. The right to approve the salaries of the pastor and associate pastor, and
> 4. The right to receive a copy of the operating budget of the church.
>
> The corporate structure is divided into the Session and the Diaconate. The Session consists of the Elders, which is the administrative body.

The Diaconate is subordinate to the Session and coordinates the ministry in overseeing the physical needs of the congregation, stewardship development, property development and management, financial matters and other matters that address the effectiveness of the church ministry. Where the Session focuses its activities on its members, the Diaconate controls the maintenance and use of the church property.

The church provides financial support for various projects, including mission posts in Bangladesh, Korea and Taiwan. The Diaconate also supervises other committees, including the building, grounds, congregational service, fellowship, stewardship development, and budget and finance committees.

Elections of officers are based upon the nominations of a nominating committee. The corporate charter provides that the committee shall be made up of two members designated by the Session, and the remaining committee members composed of active members selected by the congregation. The pastor is required to serve on the committee, but in an ex officio capacity. The committee is selected annually, and no member may serve more than three years consecutively.

§360. CONSTITUTIONAL BASES OF U.S. "CHURCH AND STATE" LAW

[*Note:* See the index as to specific matters. Many cases and problems as to religions, church, etc., are treated in other chapters herein.] The Constitution of the United States expressly provides that:

(1) "Congress shall make no law respecting an establishment of religion, or prohibiting the free exercise thereof, . . ." [Amend. I].

(2) ". . . (N)o religious test shall ever be required as a qualification to any office or public trust under the United States." [Article VI, cl. 3].

(3) ". . . No state shall make or enforce any law which shall abridge the privileges or immunities of citizens of the United States;. . . ." [Amend. XIV, §1].

For exhaustive outlines of sources, books, articles, etc. analyzing these provisions and topics, see H.J. Vogel (compiler), *Law and Religion; A Compilation of Syllabi For Courses Taught In American Law Schools* (Hamline Univ. School of Law, Nov. 1990) 286 pp., for the Amer. Assn. of Law Schools, Section on Law and Religion.[18]

Religious Constitutionality Test

"States may not make laws that inhibit the free exercise of religion. The freedom to hold religious beliefs and opinions is absolute. . . . The government may not evaluate the benefits of religious practice including the truth or falsity of statements about the benefits of religious practices under any circumstances. . . .

"States may not make laws respecting the establishment of religion. Courts interpret this clause broadly to prohibit laws that aid one religion, aid all religions, or prefer one religion over another. . . .

"In most cases a law must satisfy each part of a three-part test to withstand any Establishment Clause challenge: (1) the law must have a secular legislative purpose; (2) the principal or primary effect of the law must neither advance nor inhibit religion; and (3) the law must not foster 'an excessive government entanglement with religion.' "[19]

Church Secrets were privileged (e.g., names of priests accused of child sexual abuse); subpoenas quashed, because of "pastoral privilege"; by Circuit Judge Fitzgerald at request of Roman Catholic Archdiocese of Chicago. Cook County state's attorney office to file appeal.[20]

Civil Court jurisdiction over religious disputes is generally barred by the First Amendment's "free exercise" rule, although not over disputes about property or about criminal matters. But if the state has a "compelling interest" in the issue it may accept jurisdiction.[21] [See page 1112.]

For example, courts will, with reluctance, resolve temporal church issues but will not resolve spiritual issues including doctrine and basic beliefs of the church. Under Religious Corporations law, a Baptist church is governed solely by the members. The church bylaws and constitution govern issues relating to deacon's status and powers. However, if the bylaws allow deacons to have absolute veto power over the conduct of financial matters, the bylaws violate the purpose of Religious Corporation Law. The temporal financial matters of the church should be in the control of elected trustees, subject to approval of its membership. Members must be removed only according to the bylaws of the church.[22]

The state has no constitutional right to know a person's membership in, support for, belief in, or practice of religious activities. The state also has no right to probe into the internal operations of a church, without limitation or compelling purpose. Freedom of privacy of belief and association is implicit in the First Amendment. The state may, however, in Texas, investigate a church under the Texas Non-Profit Corporation Act and require the church to comply with a narrow summons to show its entitlement to tax-exempt status. Such an investigation is only an incidental burden on the free exercise of religion.[23]

When a minister brings action against his or her church, civil courts must generally enforce rulings made by the highest church authority which has heard a matter of religious doctrine. The court can only question such rulings in cases of fraud by the church. The court can only rule contrary to church authority when the court's decision is based upon principles which have no reference to religious doctrines or rulings.[24]

The Synod, that paid a property and liability insurance premium for a member church, is entitled to all the right, title and interest in the property and assets of an insolvent member church, including the fire insurance proceeds, where the constitutional documents of the member church provide that the Synod has such rights. The court cannot interfere in church governance to determine if there has been breach of fiduciary duty between the member church and the Synod, even though rights to church property may be affected incidentally.[25]

A Quaker organization refused to pay the military portion of their taxes. The court held that the free exercise of religion clause is violated by generally applicable social regulation only if it is specifically directed at religious practice, or attempts to regulate religious beliefs, communication of religious beliefs, or the raising of children in those beliefs. The regulation was enforceable even though the desire to withhold certain taxes was a fundamental tenet of the members.[26]

A New York statute, that allows religious organizations to discriminate on the basis of religion in their capacity as employer and landlord of a public accommodation, does not entitle a Jewish group to exert pressure on a resort facility to cancel a contract with "Jews for Jesus." Discrimination engaged in by third parties who use speech or other expressive conduct to coerce primary actors to violate anti discrimination statutes can be constitutionally outlawed.[27]

A state may order medical treatment for a dangerously ill child, despite the religious objections of its parents (Jehovah's Witnesses).[28] On the same day the same court held that a competent adult (with a minor child) was free to refuse life-saving medical treatment, despite the state's interest in its citizens.[29]

A city ordinance that bans the killing of animals during religious rites is unconstitutional according to the U.S. Supreme Court (1993).[30]

§361. RELIGIOUS ORGANIZATIONS' IMPORTANCE

There are about 350,000 tax exempt church organizations in the United States. (See statistics and other data hereinabove at §§ 1, 4, 10, 336, et passim.) Their influence and importance are too well known to require emphasis here.

Religious institutions are the *most favored* of all types of nonprofit organizations in the United States; including educational and charitable aspects of their work. Thus, Florida tax exemption of real and personal property used *predominantly for religious purposes* does not require annual application for renewal of exemption (as *other* types of exemption must apply annually), though a certified statement of continued use for religious purpose is required to be sent to the Department of Revenue.[31]

A "*church*" is *defined* by statutes in some states, for tax exemption purposes, in general terms as "any organization" of persons who indicate adherence to a religious assemblage bound together by such manifestations as a certain source of beliefs/rules and no substantial private investment of assets. Sale of books and tapes by such an organization, with profits obtained from the sales being used for group purposes, is entitled to statutory *sales tax exemption* of churches.[32]

For example, intangible *personal property tax exemption* was specifically granted by Florida statutes, which defined them as ". . . Churches and ecclesiastical or denominational organizations, or established physical places for worship in this state at which nonprofit religious services and activities are regularly conducted and carried on, and also . . . church cemeteries." This also included "parochial, church and nonprofit private schools" and "physical facilities . . . providing charitable services, a reasonable percentage of which shall be without cost to those unable to pay. . . ."[33]

§362. RELIGIOUS SECULAR MIXTURES

[See Chapter 3.]

Profit-Seeking Operations of churches often include bingo games, retirement home operations, leasing of its facilities, flea markets, bake sales; and nowadays various much more sophisticated income-seeking ventures, both alone and in collaboration with other organizations both profit and nonprofit in their nature. [See, herein, Chapter 3.]

Church and business and other profit and nonprofit *mixtures* are favored by some business executives as valuable public-relations and social-responsibility operations.[34]

These *mixtures* include such diverse projects as low rent housing, publishing, real estate, communications and computer sharing, financial underwriting, and manufacturing; which in turn employ sale-leasebacks, tax-exempt bond issues, syndications, joint ventures, and sharing of personnel and equipment. [See, herein, Chapter 3.].[35]

The Florida Statute provides a detailed set of *criteria* for determining profit or nonprofit status of an asset of an applicant for tax exemption; it is based mainly on the "*reasonableness*" of salaries, loans, trades, charges, and so on.[36]

Income from regular, but not merely occasional business activity such as rental of church property, is taxable "unrelated business income." but income from volunteer services, bingo weekly games, sales of contributed goods, or services only for members or employees or students, is not taxable.[37]

State and municipal governments can create constitutional problems when they mix religion with secular issues. For example, the use of religious symbols on a city's seal violates the Establishment Clause of the Constitution.[38]

Holding of a Roman Catholic mass at a municipal festival violated the First Amendment if the town is (at least) a sponsor.[39]

When a church and pastor sued to challenge the constitutionality of a school district's refusal to allow the church to show religious films in school facilities, the court held that school facilities are limited forums. As such, the facilities are not open to religious uses by policy or practice. The school district's refusal did not violate free speech.[40]

Since a school board had approved past Christmas programs at a school, a limited public forum or a designated public forum had been created. Thus, a Christian magician should have been allowed to use the auditorium, unless the school district expressly adopted a new policy that treated all programs with a religious theme equally.[41]

Courts *lawfully may* deal with application and enforcement of such matters as (for instance) real property legal aspects in matters in which religious organizations may be involved; though courts may not constitutionally delve into matters of ecclesiastical freedom.[42]

A National Labor Relations Act clause requiring inquiry into religious doctrine for employees in organizations historically opposed to labor organizations violates constitutional (First Amendment) law.[43]

§363. RELIGIOUS TAX EXEMPTION

[Some of the following cases were contributed by James F. Haggerty].

When the facts on which tax exemption status are clear, the exemption of property from taxation is a matter of law.[44]

[See "Tax Exemption", in the Index.]

When the question of taxability of a religious organization involves the constitutionality of an exemption statute, the circuit court must hear the case de novo prior to the Supreme Court's determination of the constitutionality of the statute. The circuit court must also determine whether the taxpayer is a religious entity.[45]

To determine whether a church or religious association is bona fide and entitled to property tax exemption, the court considers the sincerity of the organization's beliefs in the light of all evidence, and determines whether the beliefs are held in good faith. Tax exemption is not allowed where the forms of religious organization are erected for the sole purpose of cloaking a secular enterprise with the legal protections of religion.[46]

Under the First Amendment, any subsidy benefiting religious organizations must result from the natural inclusion of religion within the perimeter of a broad circle of nonsectarian groups also benefiting from the subsidy. A statute that granted exemption, from use tax, to religious publications violated the establishment clause because it did not have a secular objective, and its primary effect was to advance religion.[47]

A charitable institution does not lose its tax exempt status merely because persons who are unable to pay for its services are required to do so, as long as the institution makes no profit and all funds are used to further the institution's charitable goals.[48]

Supporters of pro-choice abortion-rights view do not have *"standing"* to bring suit challenging the tax-exemption of the (anti-abortion view) Catholic church.[49]

Contribution Tax

Contribution Tax. In late 1992 churches in Berkeley, California were ordered to pay taxes on *contributions* (60¢ per $1000 received) and also to *register* like other nonprofit organizations. City finance director Sonali Bose reported that only half of the 600 NPOs in that city had registered yet. The tax is based on the unanimous ruling of the U.S. Supreme Court in 1990 (*Jimmy Swaggart Ministries v. Calif. Board of Equalization*, 110 S. Ct. 688 (1990)) upholding the California sales tax on religious organizations as well as other NPOs. The trend seems to be to require churches to pay such taxes as other NPOs are required to do, said Joe Conn, a spokesman for Americans United for Separation of Church and State, based in Silver Spring, Maryland.[50] But in 1993 the I.R.S. held the church to be tax exempt.

Payments to Church of Scientology for instruction, in the nature of psychiatry, could not be deducted as contributions to a religious organization.[51] But in 1993 the I.R.S. held the church to be tax exempt.

IRS administration of charitable deductions for *quid pro quo* contributions to various religious organizations is actionable if that administration is inconsistent.[52]

Sales and Use Tax

A "use tax" on a church use of consumer goods (cleaning supplies, etc.) bought from out-of-state church-affiliated suppliers does not violate the church's free-exercise rights; no exemption.[53]

Church sales and use tax (even on bibles) is valid in some states; but not in others; no constitutional right to exemption.[54] Exemption of religious publications from sales tax did not violate equal protection law in Texas, but it did in North Carolina.[55]

Property Tax

In Florida and Illinois, a tax exemption will apply to nonreligious use of property by a tax-exempt church (as a parking lot) where the religious use is the *"predominant"* or "most significant" activity on land whereon multiple-type activities are conducted.[56] For example, *church housing* used by *non-member visiting missionary* persons was *held tax exempt* by *Illinois.*[57] There, temporary non-use of a church parsonage on retirement of pastor does not cause loss of property tax exemption of that parcel.[58] But, *church land (park)* next to its caretakers' residence, though used for meditation (religious), was held *not tax exempt* by *Illinois because also used for grazing* of horses.[59]

In New York, portions of a nonprofit religious corporation's property, used as residences for its faculty, staff, students and their families is "necessary and reasonably incidental" to the primary or major purpose of the facility, if the primary purpose of providing religious educational instruction would be seriously undermined if the corporation could not provide the housing. Such property is exempt from property tax.[60]

In Ohio, a building used exclusively as its regional headquarters by a church is not tax exempt if no public worship services are conducted there.[61] Also in Ohio, property used by a church as a noisebuffer zone is not "essential ... to facilitate public worship." Tax exemption for it was denied.[62]

A real property tax exemption statute, that limits the exemption to dedicated church property buildings related to church purposes and the land on which the buildings are located, does not include a transmission tower and tower house used to broadcast Christian programming produced elsewhere, in Arkansas.[63]

In Indiana, a religious corporation doing broadcasts of religion, using apartments only for program workers, has property tax exemption for the apartments.[64]

Florida, Nevada, and South Dakota may portion religious property on a pro rata basis according to its religious use. For example, a religious society, that operated two church camps, is entitled to only one exemption under a statute providing that agricultural land owned by a religious society and used exclusively for religious purposes is exempt from taxation. The church camp is entitled to only a pro rata property tax exemption because the property was not used "exclusively" for religious purposes, to the extent that it was rented, for non-religious activities, to persons and organizations not affiliated with the church, in South Dakota.[65]

A Roman Catholic *nursing home* was entitled to complete exemption from state *ad valorem* taxes, when operating as an IRS approved charitable corporation, though *one-third* of its residents were private *paying patients*, because none of its income was used as "for profit" operations. Florida's *pro rata rule* as to charitable versus profit purpose (and tax) proportions would not be applied.[66]

Church land in two parcels, five miles apart and each divided into 25 tracts (called "churches") and each 40 acres, gets tax exemption only for 146 acres used actually for religious purposes, in Nevada.[67]

Leased property is exempt in some states and not in others, *church school property leased from* a landowner was *held* to be *tax exempt* in *Florida*, Skycrest Baptist Church (Clearwater), 508 So.2d 1314 (FL 2d DCA (June 1987). But *Illinois refused* tax exemption for a *building leased* by a college for *dormitory* use.[68] In Illinois, vacant lots *leased* by a church for parking are not exempt from property tax under a tax exemption statute that applies only to parking areas *owned* by the church.[69]

To qualify as a "church" (e.g., for tax exemption) an organization must satisfy the court as to its

distinct legal existence

recognized creed

form of worship

distinct ecclesiastical government

formal code or doctrine and discipline

places of worship

religious history

membership distinct from other groups or denomination

ordained ministers

prescribed studies for ministry

regular congregations

religious schools for the young

schools for ministers

Not all these factors need to be met, but enough of them to qualify under the Tax Code. Spiritual Outreach Society did not, the court held.[70]

§364. RELIGIOUS ORGANIZATION OFFICERS AND AGENTS

[Julian A. Sanchez did research for some of this section.]

[See the Index]

Unemployment Compensation

New York, by statute, excludes persons who perform duties of a religious nature at a place of worship from unemployment insurance coverage. Thus, an English teacher, who had been employed at a nonprofit religious high school, was ineligible and was charged with more than $4000 in recoverable benefits.[71] Church secretaries, who are appointed by a pastor and board of deacons and have mainly secular duties (not of a religious nature), are not excluded from unemployment insurance coverage. The "elected appointed official exclusion" from unemployment insurance coverage applies only to persons with authority or responsibility within religious organizations.[72]

Employment Disputes

Employment disputes of a church organization and its employees (pastors and others) concerning their status are inherently religious matters, not subject to jurisdiction of civil courts under the first Amendment's separation of church and state.[73] For example, if a professor of a religious educational institution performs "ministerial functions" the court must abstain, under the First Amendment, from the exercise of jurisdiction over employment disputes concerning the professor, including a dispute about the institution's denial of tenure to the professor.[74] However, a denomination (church) *superintendent's oral promise* to obtain a more suitable position as pastor in another church, for the plaintiff, may be an enforceable contract, depending on usual contract-validity-test law: and the minister's lawsuit to enforce the (employment) contract may *not* be barred by invoking the Constitution's First Amendment. The claim: alleged age discrimination and breach of contract, in the suit by a Methodist minister.[75]

A priest's tort damages suit against the bishop and Church, for firing him, is an ecclesiastical matter, not within civil court jurisdiction.[76] But, a clergyman's property right in his office may be resolved by a civil court, if no religious doctrine is in issue, using property law principles, after examining church charters, state laws, and other pertinent documents.[77]

The constitutional bar against interference in religious matters did not apply to alleged *defamation of a minister* who had resigned and been dismissed, when the statements were outside his denomination; they were not internal religious matters.

But a religious corporation could bring a defamation action on the basis of alleged defamatory statements about a minister who was the principal spokesman for the organization.[78]

Title VII prohibition of discrimination does not bar dismissal of a teacher from a parochial school for conduct inconsistent with its religious doctrine; e.g., against divorcee marriage.[79] However, a religious order operating a university has no religious based privilege to discriminate against aged employees.[80]

A state *statute limiting the term* of office of a director to one year, unless otherwise provided in the organization's (a church endowment fund, nonstock corporation) articles of incorporation, is not a mere interpretive rule, but goes to the limiting and regulation of public functions, and therefore applies retroactively to the fund's existing articles. This prevented interpretation of terms of office as being "for life."[81]

Liability for Agents and Officers

TV ministries' scandals recently have endangered the honored status of religious organizations. The Internal Revenue Service in 1989 reported that it was *auditing* the finances of 23 television ministries and expected to challenge the tax exemption of some evangelists. Key issues in these cases were suspicion of hiding of income, engaging in political activities, and self enrichment of officers as well as failure to pay taxes on unrelated business income. Some ministries already had been forced to pay substantial federal income tax, interest and penalties.[82]

The National Religious Broadcasters (NRB) recently eliminated its Ethics and Financial Integrity Commission, which was set up in 1987 to accredit 501 (c) 3 members with incomes over $500,000. Since 1993, members making over $500,000 yearly must receive approval from the Evangelical Council for Financial Accountability, an *outside* organization, set up by the NRB to monitor fiscal improprieties. Those members making under $500,000 yearly must still report to the NRB's ethics committee. The NRB continues to oppose the reinstatement of the Fairness Doctrine, which requires that broadcasters air discussion of vital public issues and provide opposing viewpoints.[83]

Massachusetts federal bankruptcy court ordered a church to return $6.5 million donated by a former member, finding that the church officers had used *undue influence* to get the money.[84]

A Minnesota (Hennepin Co.) trial court held a Christian Science church liable for punitive damages for the "negligence" of a C.S. nurse and practitioner for "nontreatment" of a man in a diabetic coma, resulting in his death. [Lundman v. McKown, 91–8197 (Aug. 1993).]

Claims of "professional malpractice" by pastors are not favored by the courts, because training of ministers is not that of professionals in medicine or psychology, and also involves problems of separation of church and state.[85]

However, *clergyman malpractice lawsuits* (that also may involve their churches in some cases) are multiplying. For example, a nontherapist counselor's advice to a suicidally inclined person who killed himself was held not to hold the church and pastor liable, such liability being unreasonably demanding and against public policy.[86]

Proper supervision of the pastor is a question of fact.[87] Proved negligence of the church in hiring or retaining a pastor who sexually assaulted boys in the congregation would result in liability of the church conference.[88] Where a pastor forced a wife, in counseling her and her husband, to have sex with him, the pastor is liable in tort, but not the church because it had not been negligent in hiring or retaining the pastor.[89]

If the local church is independent of the national church it is probably not an "agency" to bind the national by its pastor's misconduct.[90] But, when a child abuse victim brought action against a church for sexual abuse by a pastor, the court held that an award of punitive damages, remitted to $187,000, is not against public policy and does not violate the free exercise or establishment clause of the U.S. Constitution. Church officials had knowingly placed the pastor where he could sexually abuse boys, had failed to supervise him, and had refused to deal with the allegations of sexual abuse until threatened with public disclosure.[91] However, in Louisiana, parents had no negligence cause of action against a church pastor who had counselled the church youth director, when the youth director molested their child, for failing to warn of the director's potential danger. This was not a "special relationship" to the plaintiffs, and thus involved no special duty to them.[92]

A Catholic priest's counsel to a parishioner-woman about her marital problems, plus her pregnancy by him led to a $100,000 damages verdict against him, for her husband, followed by divorce and her marriage to the priest.[93]

A Washington State jury awarded $130,000 damages to a woman seduced by her minister, despite their church doctrine of teaching the desirability of a "spiritual connection" with someone other than one's spouse; she was divorced and then banished from the church when she broke off the affair.[94]

The classic court case about clergy misconduct torts involved a minister who refused to let a reluctant parishioner-woman leave his yacht for a month after a sea voyage, while he tried to reconvert her. He was held liable for "false imprisonment" damages.[95]

A priest who damaged an abortion clinic and injured its employee was held personally liable, but not his religious order or bishop, as he exceeded his "course and scope of authority." His *order* was a "corporation sole" (one man—bishop—incorporation) under Alabama Code 1975 §10-4-4, and its priests are not agents *per se*.[96]

Negligence of a pastor in operating an automobile was not imputed to his diocese in a Kansas case.[97]

A minister's alleged affair with the wife while counseling a husband and wife, is an "intentional tort" and not "malpractice," as it is an abandonment of employment and does not bind the church as a "religious activity."[98]

A church was held liable for "tortious invasion of her rights" of an unmarried woman who had an affair with a man, by the church minister's public castigation of her *after she withdrew from the church*. She impliedly consented to *religious discipline* while she was a member, but not after she ceased to be a member.[99]

False imprisonment and intentional infliction of emotional distress, in a brainwashing claim, does not exist where a religious organization deprives a minor of her financial resources, restricts her diet, imposes a grueling work schedule on her, limits her physical possessions, and limits her access to means of communication absent any threat of force. However, the minor can recover for the wrongful death of her father due to the exacerbation of his heart disease while he searched for her. The minor's mother can recover for intentional infliction of emotional distress, and libel where the religious organization released an erroneous report that the child had been beaten at home.[100]

The right of inspection of corporate records does not apply to a non-profit church that is incorporated without stock. Church members, who are expelled after they filed suit to inspect the financial records of their church to investigate conversion of church property to non-church uses, lack standing to sue as they are no longer members. Thus, a plaintiff may lose standing during litigation. The court has no "ecclesiastical jurisdiction," and cannot review church disciplinary action or reinstate expelled church members, even if the discipline proceeding is contrary to church procedure. The court may, however, protect civil or property rights of church members.[101]

§365. CHURCH-STATE CONFLICTS

[See Section 359, above]

Officers and directors of churches and other religious corporations are given a high degree of *immunity from civil liability* in most aspects of management, especially in corporations recognized as tax exempt by the U.S. Internal Revenue Code, Sections 501(c)(3), 501(c)(4), 401(c)(5) and 501(c)(6); e.g., religious/charitable in their nature. Unless such officer's conduct is quite clearly unreasonable, self-enriching, reckless or in bad faith, it will not be open to attack in the courts.[102]

Religious reasons for violating laws are not valid in most cases. Separation of church and state does not mean that criminal conduct is immunized. Thus, government infiltration of some church "sanctuary movement" groups is constitutional. "The government's interest in controlling immigration outweighs (the clergy's) purported religious interest." Eight defendants (5 clergy) were convicted of illegally aiding Central American persons to enter the USA through Arizona. The prosecution used tape recordings of church meetings, obtained without warrants.[103] *Contra:* Infiltration by agents wearing "body bugs" was held to be violation of the First Amendment.[104] An airport authority may reasonably regulate the solicitation of contributions in an airport without violating free speech, in view of the inconvenience to passengers and the burden placed on officials by the solicitation activity. However, free speech is violated when the authority bans the distribution of literature.[105]

"Compelling State Interest"

"Compelling state interest" justifies state legislation/action even in religious matters, and is not a violation of the rule of separation of church and state (First Amendment). But in 1990 the Supreme Court ruled that a state is free to make laws applicable to *all* organizations, including religious ones.[106] The U.S. Supreme Court ruled in 1993 that a city may not ban animal sacrifice during religious rites.[107] The *Religious Freedom Restoration Act (RFRA)* was enacted Nov. 16, 1993 to restore the rule that a "compelling state interest" must exist to justify state action.

Ohio's Supreme Court held that it had a "compelling state interest" in forcing the taking of a blood sample from a rape suspect despite his claim of religious freedom (as a Jehovah's Witness) against such blood tests in his church doctrine.[108]

Compelling state interests justify state imposition of liability for fraud in recruiting members by brainwashing devices, despite First Amendment (free exercise) constitutional law. California Supreme Court (6 to 1) ordered trials of aggrieved members' claims.[109]

A 1984 federal law requiring public schools to allow student religious groups to use school facilities, if they allow other extracurricular groups to do so, was upheld as constitutional by the Supreme Court (8 to 1): a federally assisted Omaha secondary school.[110]

A court order to a divorced (noncustodial) parent to take their child to church, or give up custody to the father so that he could do so, violated the Virginia constitution's provision that nobody be compelled to frequent or support religious worship.[111]

Religious Discrimination

A religious organization is not "discriminated against" by a city ordinance barring display of a Chanukah Menorah in the airport public area. A *Religious Display* (a Menorah) in Grand Rapids, Mich. public Calder Plaza, does not violate First Amendment when that public forum is (1) traditionally open to all citizens equally and (2) a private group elected it. (9 to 6 decision).[113]

Abortion Right was upheld by the Supreme Court in 1992 as constitutional, despite religious activists' fierce opposition. Shift of the debate to state courts, as local issues, began to grow.[114]

Designation of a building as a landmark (which was entitled to special government protection) did not amount to violation of a church's First Amendment rights.[115]

A city ordinance regulating ritual sacrifices of animals is not valid, and does violate First Amendment rights of a church, accord to the U.S. Supreme Court (1993).[116]

A mortgage on church property, to secure a loan, may be adjudicated by a civil court, though the court may not adjudicate religious or spiritual disputes.[117]

Members of a *church* with *black* congregation could *sue under civil rights* statutes for discriminatory *repudiation of a contract* for sale of a school building to the church.[118]

Church refusal to renew a lease of property to a "gay" member because of its policy against homosexuality is a privileged exercise of religious freedom.[119]

A city's sale of land to a (Hasidic) religious organization does not violate neighborhood residents' First Amendment or equal protection rights.[120]

§366. RELIGIOUS SCHOOL ACTIVITIES

A religious academy's First Amendment freedom is not violated by a town's school committee review of the credentials of the academy teachers, or visit to observe the quality of teaching, or gathering of written information about the school.[121]

Federal funding of supplies for sectarian schools violates the Constitution. Federal courts in Kansas City (in 1989) and Louisville and New Orleans (in 1990) have so ruled. Almost all of the non-public schools in the New Orleans area are religious-affiliated and three-fourths of these are Roman Catholic. Also, a Canadian (Ontario) Court of Appeal ruled in 1990 that "state-authored religious indoctrination"—e.g., "teaching students Christian Doctrine as if it were the exclusive means of teaching morality—amounts to religious coercion in the classroom" for a child raised in the Baha'i faith.[122]

U.S. Department of Education executives have had an "off the top" policy of allocating remedial education funds, giving first priority to religious (private) schools, which reduces the funds available to public schools. Two federal district court decisions ordered the federal agency to stop this discriminatory local school district procedure.[123]

A church teaching that parents are ordered by God to educate their own children (*at home*), and not allow teaching by teachers who took courses based upon secular humanism, does not excuse violation of state "compulsory attendance" for all schools. Home "school" is not a "private school." The statute does not offend due process rules (14th Amend.). Requirement of "certificated" teachers does not violate first Amendment.[124]

Religious institutions may participate in publicly sponsored social welfare (teenage sex counseling) activities, and are not barred by the "establishment" clause of constitutional law.[125]

A city may close a city block and lease it to a church school, after much public debate and expert testimony, said a Louisiana court.[126]

In 1991 California's Supreme Court ruled (5 to 2) that prayers at a public high school graduation ceremony violate the constitution's separation of church and state. Such prayer "sends a powerful message that it (the school district) approves of the prayer's religious content," said the majority opinion.

Federal district courts have barred such prayer ceremonies in public schools in Iowa and Rhode Island, and upheld them in Pennsylvania and Virginia. The U.S. Supreme Court was expected to rule on an appeal from the 1990 Rhode Island decision in its 1991–2 term. And a Minnesota school board in 1991 approved silent (not spoken) prayers at high school graduations, after being threatened with loss of state financial aid.[127]

Lee v. Weisman, a Supreme Court decision of June 21, 1992, ruled (5 to 4) that officially sponsored *public* school graduation ceremonies that present *prayers* are unconstitutional coercion of the persons attending, violating the "establishment of religion" prohibition. This does not apply to private (Religious) schools.[128]

Distribution by students of religious literature in high schools was upheld in 1991 by a federal district judge in Philadelphia, as "free speech" if it does not interfere with public school activities. Similar federal court ruling in New York and Indiana and New Jersey in 1991 approved distribution of bibles in public schools.[129]

Such prayers and distributions in religious private schools have been held to be valid, even though some public (state) licensing and supervision of schools are involved. And barring a fund raiser with religious arguments from a school district is unconstitutional violation of free speech and equal protection.[130]

Reading of Bible for 5 minutes daily in a public school fifth grade in Fernando Beach, Florida, authorized by the Nassau County School Board, was discontinued when an ACLU lawsuit for a family objecting was settled by the Board paying attorney fees and $15,000 in damages to the objecting family.[131]

§367. CHURCH ZONING

[Ilene Marie Harrison did research for some of the cases in this supplement section.]

A zoning ordinance, that prohibits home-church worship in a single family home in a residential neighborhood, does not infringe on the constitutional right to freedom of religion.[132]

A group of orthodox Jews successfully obtained a conditional use permit, which grants rights beyond the scope of the local zoning restrictions and allows the operation of a synagogue in a residential neighborhood.[133]

The Alabama Supreme Court held that a church parking lot, that is separated from a church building in a residential neighborhood, cannot qualify for the same zoning exception as the church building.[134]

In the *LeBanc* case, the court entertained and reinforced arguments, advanced by an orthodox Jewish group, that to deny their right to create a residential synagogue was tantamount to a violation of their civil rights.[135]

A Florida church was denied an injunction to prevent the city from enforcing zoning ordinances which prevented operation of a homeless shelter on church property in a residential neighborhood. In denying the protective injunction, the court said that the church must demonstrate that the homeless shelter was not a public nuisance.[136]

The application of zoning restrictions, to religious organizations, may require the consideration of whether the area is zoned residential or commercial. One recent case held that zoning ordinances, that restrict churches from an industrial commercial zone, raise constitutional issues about the freedom of religion.[137]

The private religious practices of an individual can also be restricted by zoning. An Ohio court recently held that a homeowner's right to religious freedom is not violated by a zoning ordinance that prohibits the construction of crosses in the homeowner's front yard.[138]

A center for Pastoral Counseling is not "religious purpose" for zoning exemption purposes.[139]

Denial of a church application to expand its parking facilities, by requiring it to establish its right by clear and convincing evidence, is not a valid zoning exception to freedom of religion, when granting of a conditional use permit would be prima facie valid on the facts of the case.[140]

A city "Landmark Law" barring replacement of a 60 year old church building by a tower office building, though it limits the church income does not violate First Amendment, because "free exercise" can be carried on elsewhere.[141]

A city decision to sell to a synagogue, for religious school and faculty residence construction in an urban renewal plan, is not a violation of the Establishment clause of the Constitution.[142]

Religious Land Use (Licensing) Laws

[See Chapter 13.]

§368. CHURCH POLITICKING

[See Section 359 above.]

Political mixing of church and state by some U.S. denominations (e.g., of their politico-preachers) approached a point of danger to the nation and to the churches (but notably not by the Mormon church) in the 1988, 1990, and 1992 political election campaigns.[143]

Court decisions and law on boundaries of religious activity in political elections or office are vague. The main current issue is religious leaders' pressure as to pro or anti-abortion views/action of political officers or in elections. Excommunication (or threats of it) against Catholic politicians/officials, such as that in the adopting of a strong anti-abortion statute in Guam after threats by the local archbishop, brought prompt Attorney-General-Opinion declaration that the statute was an unconstitutional violation of women's rights of privacy. Thus, Florida Supreme Court Justice Leander Shaw was specifically (and futilely) targeted by anti-abortion groups for (money-raising) defeat in the

November 1990 retention-election-voting, because of his pro-choice decision, which attack threatened independence of the judiciary. Direct political action/force violates church-state separation law.[144]

Abuses of religious nonprofit organization status and public confidence, by (a few) what can only be called "religious racketeers," on TV and other mass-appeal media, obviously present most immediate general problems for leading non-profit religious organization officers. Left unchecked, such abuses are bound to have (already have had) destructive effects on many honorable organizations and the clergy in general. Not even the shocking call of an ayatollah for the murder of a free-speaking critic/novelist can equal the erosive effects of TV evangelists' sex and self-enrichment scandals. Treatment of such abuses by recourse to the (Federal) *Racketeering Influenced Corrupt Organizations Act* (RICO lawsuits), both criminal and civil, in federal and state courts, seems to be the most effective approach to a cure for these abuses. There have been scandalous eras in religious organizations' history before. Hopefully, the present wave of cynicism can and will be cured by prompt renewal of leadership for decency and morality and *responsibility*, (rather than for political and personal power), by leaders of religious organizations. The 1992 Republican convention was a shocking exhibition of political power playing by religious organization leaders.[145]

The U.S. Supreme Court's (5 to 4) decision, in May 1991, barring revelation to a pregnant woman (even if poor or ignorant, or even if a raped child) of the existence of abortion as a possible option, when she consults family planning *organizations that receive any federal fund support*, was a clearly religious-faction decision. Most people view that decision as a blatant violation of womens' rights and especially freedom of speech of physicians and other persons active in family planning organizations.[146]

A judge was held to have improperly injected his own sense of religion in sentencing TV evangelist Jim Bakker to 45 years in jail for fraud. In sentencing, the judge spoke of being "ridiculed as saps from money-grubbing preachers or priests." This violated "due process."[147]

§369. RELIGIOUS ORGANIZATIONS BIBLIOGRAPHY

[See the general Bibliography herein in Chapter 2, § 16.].
There are thousands of books, articles, court decisions, and other writings about religion and religious organizations. A few "starter" items are set forth here, making no pretensions to exhaustive listing, in this section.

For a big compilation of up-to-date citations on the subject, including the court case decisions, see the fine (286 page) compilation made in late 1990 for the Association of American Law Schools, Section on Law and Religion, Committee on Curriculum and Interdisciplinary Contracts, by Prof. Howard J. Vogel of Hamline University School of Law, 1536 Hewitt Ave., St. Paul, Minnesota, 55104; Tel. #(612) 641-2081. $10/copy, plus postage ($1.50).[148]

A few relatively recent books are:

- H. Berman, Law and Revolution (1983).
- L. Buzzard, Schools: They Haven't Got a Prayer (1982).
- T. Curry, The First Freedoms (1986).
- M. Eliad (ed.), Encyclopedia of Religion (1987).
- K. Greenawalt, Religious Convictions and Political Choice (1988).
- Miller & Flowers, Toward a Benevolent Neutrality (1987).
- R. Neuhaus, The Naked Public Square (2d ed., 1986).
- M. Perry, Morality, Politics, and Law (1988).
- A. Reichley, Religion in American Public Life (1985).
- D.B. Robertson (ed.), Voluntary Associations (1966).
- T. Shumate, The First Amendment (1985).
- Wilson & Drakeman, Church and State in American History (1987).
- Yearbook of American Churches (Natl., Council of Churches of Christ).

§370. NONPROFIT (CHURCH) ORGANIZATION

Religious organizations should inform potential members, and others, of their goals, policies and beliefs. Distribution of a simple statement of "what the church is" might be helpful to outline expectations and avoid any misunderstanding.

FORM NO. 157

NP Organization Statement of "What It Is"

[A Verbatim Copy of a Published Statement-Pamphlet of the _____ Church.]

_____ Church
(A Minnesota Organization)

What Is This Church?

The _____ Church Is a Liberal Protestant Religious Community . . .

To Be Liberal means that we believe in growth.

To Believe in Growth means that all truth is relevant to the person, group, place, time and circumstances.

In Other Words, to be Liberal means that there are no absolutes of truth, belief, faith or achievements. What is true, helpful and creative for one day and people may be false or meaningless and destructive for another people in another day.

We Are Proud of the beliefs, faith and achievements of our ancestors, but we do not stop there.

We Inherit many beliefs, but we go on to develop our own.

We Grow up in the faith we inherit, but we establish our own as soon as we are able to do so.

We Respect and accept the achievements of those who have gone before us but we feel under obligation to win our victories in our own way.

What We Hold for ourselves in our relationship with those who have gone before us we also hold for our children in their relations with us.

We Teach Our Children the truth as we see it. We bring them up in our faith. We expose them to our forms of devotion. We introduce them to our problems and we encourage their participation in our achievements.

But, Far More Important, for it lies beneath and beyond all this, we seek to inspire in our children the necessity and glory of going beyond what they inherit to find their own faith, to create their own forms and to solve their own problems, in their own way through their own religion.

When We Say That Our Church Is Protestant . . .

We Mean that we are democratic.

The Control and Management of our church rests entirely within the membership of the church.

There is no denominational control over us.

There are no obligations imposed on us from without.

There are no specially endowed persons designated to look after us.

There is no priesthood or clergy to assume our religious responsibilities.

Each Person is responsible. No one may expect another to look after one's own religious interest, meet one's own religious obligations or solve one's own problems.

On the Other Hand no person should ever attempt to impose his or her religious convictions, conclusions, or forms on any other person.

The Priesthood of All Believers, which is what we have been describing, means that each one is personally responsible. Each person must interpret the Scriptures, incorporate traditions, recognize problems, and seek solutions for one's self. In simple words, each person must determine his or her own religion.

In Practical Terms this means we would rather make our own mistakes and endure the confusion involved in living and growing in our own way than have the dubious and dangerous comfort and unity that is purported to come through authoritative direction and control.

When We Say That We Are a Religious Community . . .

We Mean that our primary and indeed sole purpose as a church is to provide the kind of provocative, encouraging and supportive environment in which **some** persons will be able to find a richer and more meaningful life. This same objective is sometimes described as growing in wisdom, in stature and in the goodness of God.

When We Seek to provide an environment which will be helpful to some, we have no intention of excluding anyone. Just as there is no one above or beyond us to whom we look for guidance and control so there is no one who cannot participate in our religious community if he or she chooses to do so.

Our Religious Community is founded on and sustains itself through our common concern for that which makes all good possible and makes possible the growth of all that is good and true and just and worthy.

Since There Is No Absolute Truth and no final perfection we do not expect all people, not even those in our own religious community, to believe the same, feel the same, seek the same economic, social or political goals, use the same methods, or agree always on what is true, good, just and worthy.

One Result of These Attitudes which would be expected and is indeed confirmed in reality, is that our church is characterized by a great deal of diversity in personality, belief, interest, taste, achievement and concern.

Because We Believe in the necessity of religion for the growth of the individual and the preservation and enhancement of society;

And Because We Believe in the validity of diversity and the capacity of the spirit to express itself in unlimited ways and to grow through the sharing of interest, insight and concern;

We Welcome to Our Religious Community anyone who believes that a person can grow in understanding appreciation and service of the good and who believes that such growth is necessary both for the individual and the race and who would like to unite with others of life mind and desire.

NOTES TO CHAPTER 36

1.   N.Y. Relig. Corp. L. §2.

2.   N.Y. Not-for Profit Corp. Law §301; Ohio Rev. Code §1715.12.

3.   *See New Magnolia Baptist Church Inc. v. Ellerker*, 353 So.2d 204 (Fla. App. 1977); *United*

Methodist Church, Baltimore, 1990 WL 21141 (D.C. App.); *See* the text and cases in §359, n. 18–30.

4. *E.g.,* N.Y. Relig. Corp. L. art. 4 (Presbyterian), art. 5 (Roman Catholic), art. 7 (Baptist), etc.

5. N.Y. Relig. Corp. L. §5. For detailed discussion of the old New York system with forms, see, Oleck, *New York Corporations,* c. 95 (New York: Robert Slater Corp., 1959 Supp.); and see, Ohio Rev. Code §1715.20.

6. Walker Memorial Baptist Church Inc. v. Saunders, 173 Misc. 455, 17 N.Y.S.2d 842 (1940). But a church was held liable for enforcing an "unreasonable" doctrine of no medical treatment. Lundman v. McKown, 91–8197 (D.C. Minn., Aug. 1993).

7. Fiske v. Beaty, 201 N.Y.S. 441, 445 (App. Div. 1923).

8. 112. Mich. Comp. Laws Ann. §458.27.

9. *Ibid.*; cf., available for *all* corporations: 1986 Rev. Model Nonprofit Corp. Act, §3.02(4).

10. N.Y. Relig. Corp. Law., Art. 3, *et seq.*

11. Fla. Stat. §617.2001; N.Y. Relig. Corp. Law §2a,b.

12. Fla. Stat. §617.2005.

13. First Presbyterian Church v. Dennis, 178 Iowa 1352, 161 N.W. 183 (1917).

14. St. John's Presbytery v. Central Presbyterian Church of St. Petersburg, 102 So. 2d 714 (Fla. 1958). The courts will decline jurisdiction; e.g., in a property-dedication dispute: Archdiocese of Miami v. Sama; 519 So. 2d 28 (Fla. 3rd Dist. Ct. App., 1987).

15. Cadman Memorial Congregational Society of Brooklyn v. Kenyon, 279 A.D. 1015, 111 N.Y.S.2d 808 (1952). Kelley v. Riverside Boulevard Independent Church of God, 44 Ill. App. 3d 673, 358 N.E.2d 696 (1976).

16. Epperson v. Myers, 58 So. 2d 150 (Fla. 1952).

17. Leuken v. Our Lady of the Roses, 97 Misc. 2d 1201, 410 N.Y.S.2d 793 (1978).

18. See also: J. Witte, Jr., *Tax Exemption of Church Property,* 64 So. Cal. L. Rev. 363–415 (1991); and Church/State Symposium, 22 Cumb. L. Rev. 471–680 (1991–92).

19. *Judge Elizabeth Kovachevich, in Church of Scientology Flag Services Orgn., Inc. v. City of Clearwater, FL.* FLW Fed. D 38 (Fed. D.C., Tampa; Feb. 4, 1991).

20. Note, 15 *Natl. L.J.* (13) 6 (Nov. 30 1992).

21. *State v. Motherwell,* 788 P.2d 1066 (Wash. 1990) *yes* in prevention of child abuse. *Higgins v. Maher,* 258 Calif. Rptr. 757 (App. 1989) *not* as to dismissal of a priest for disciplinary reasons; cf., *United Methodist Church, B.A.C. v. White,* 571 A.2d 790 (D. C. App. 1990). *Burgess v. Rock Creek Baptist Church,* 734 F. Supp. 30 (D.C., D.C., 1990) *yes* as to property disputes. *McConell v. Episcopal Diocese of Ga.,* 381 S.E.2d 126 (Ga. App. 1989) *not* as to a minister's employment agreement; *ibid., Willitts v. Roman Catholic Archbishop of Boston,* 581 N.E. 2d 475 (Mass. 1991); and see, *Olson v. Magnuson,* 457 N.W.2d 394 (Minn. App. 1990).

22. *Ward v. Jones,* 587 N.Y.S. 2d 94 (N.Y. Sup. 1992).

23. *Word of Faith World Outreach Center Church, Inc. v. Morales,* 787 F. Supp. 689 (W.D. Tex. 1992) (governor's attempt to produce records, seek forfeiture of charter, dissolve and appoint receiver).

24. *Lewis v. Lake Region Conference of Seventh Day Adventists,* 779 F. Supp. 72 (E.D. Mich. 1991).

25. *Upstate New York Synod of Evangelical Lutheran Church in America v. Christ Evangelical Lutheran Church of Buffalo,* 585 N.Y.S. 2d 919 (A.D. 4 Dept. 1992).

26. *United States v. Philadelphia Yearly Meeting of Religious Soc'y of Friends,* 753 F. Supp. 1300 (E.d. Pa. 1990; U.S.C.A. Const. Amend. 1; 26 U.S.C. (1982 Ed.) §6332(c)(1).

27. *Jews for Jesus, Inc. v. Jewish Community Relations Council of New York, Inc.,* 968 F. 2d 286 (2nd Cir. 1992).

28. *In the Matter of McCauley,* #S-5413 (Mass. supr. Jud. Ct., Jan. 15, 1991).

29. *Norwood Hospital v. Munoz,* #N5417 (Mass. Supr. Jud. Ct., Jan. 15, 1991).

30. *Church of Lukumi Babalu Aye, Inc. v. City of Hialeah,* 113 S. Ct. 2217 (U.S. Fla., Jun 11, 1993).

31. *Florida Statutes* §§196.011(3), (4); 196.196.

32. *The Way International v. Limbach,* 552 N.E. 2d 908 (Ohio 1990).

33. *Florida Statutes* §§199.072(b) 1.2.3 (repealed 1985), relating to intangible personal property taxes.

34. See. *Rose-Ackerman (ed.). Economies of Nonprofit Organizations* (1986).

35. *The Nonprofit as Entrepreneur:* Development Options . . . (Inst. for Professional and Executive Development, 1985); Firstenberg, *Managing for Profit in a Nonprofit World* (1986).

36. *Florida Statutes* §§196.195, 196.196., 196.197, 196.1975, etc.

37. IRS Publication 598, *Tax on Unrelated Business Income.* Or call your state-located IRS "Forms Only" toll-free number, such as Florida: 1-800-424-3676 in Jacksonville.

38. *Harris v. City of Zion,* 927 F.2d 1401 (7th Cir., Ill., 1991). Appeal to the U.S. Supreme Court was voted by the city council. A cross on the city seal was the cause of the case.

39. *Doe v. Village of Crestwood, Ill.,* 917 F.2d 1476 (7th Cir., Ill. 1990).

40. *Lamb's Chapel v. Center Moriches Union Free School Dist.,* 959 F.2d 381 (2nd Cir. (N.Y.), 1992).

41. *Travis v. Owego-Apalachin School Dist.,* 927 F.2d 688 (2nd Cir. (N.Y.), 1991).

42. *New Magnolia Baptist Church, Inc. v. Ellerker,* 353 So. 2d 204 (Fl. App. 1977).

43. *Wilson v. N.L.R.B.,* 6th Cir., Dec. 4, 1990.

44. *Our Savior Lutheran Church v. Dept. of Revenue,* 562 N.E.2d 1198 (1990).

45. *New Vrindaban Community, Inc. v. Rose,* 419 S.E. 2d 478 (W. Va., 1992).

46. *Waushara County v. Graf,* 480 N.W. 2d 16 (Wis. 1992).

47. *Thayer v. South Carolina Tax Com'n,* 413 S.E. 2d 810 (S.C. 1992).

48. *Resurrection Lutheran Church v. Department of Revenue,* 571 N.E. 2d 989 (Ill. App. 1 Dist. 1991).

49. In re U.S. Catholic Conference, 885 F. 2d 1020 (2d Cir., N.Y., 1989).

50. Note, *St. Petersburg (FL) Times,* Religion Section, p. 3E (Aug. 15, 1992).

51. *Neher v. C.I.R.,* 382 F.2d 848 (6th Cir., 1988), overruled by U.S. Supr. Ct. in 1989.

52. *Powell v. U.S.,* 945 F. 2d 374 (11th Cir., FL., 1991).

53. *Hope Evangelical Lutheran Church v. Iowa Dept. of Revenue,* 463 N.W.2d 76 (Iowa 1990).

54. *Jimmy Swaggart Ministries v. Calif. Board of Equalization,* 110 S. Ct. 688 (1990).

55. *Texas Monthly v. Bullock,* § 87–1245; Tex. (Aug. 1988); cf., *Finlator v. Powers,* U.S. 4th Cir., N.C. (May 10, 1990).

56. *Grady v. Hausman,* 509 So. 2d 1316 (Fla. DCA 1987). But, *cf.,* loss of exemption by a fraternal lodge as to a building used for social purposes by members, as purpose use must be "exclusively" of exempt kind. *Morton Temple Assn. v. Dept. of Revenue,* 511 N.E. 2d 892 (Ill. App. 1987); *Lutheran Child & Family Service v. Dept. of Revenue,* 513 N.E. 2d 587 (Ill. App. 1987).

57. *Evangelical Alliance v. Dept. of Revenue,* 517 N.E. 2d 1178 (IL App. 1987).

58. *Our Savior Lutheran Church v. Dept. of Revenue,* 562 N.E.2d 1198 (Ill. App. 1990).

59. *Illinois Conference of U.C.C. v. Illinois Department of Revenue,* 518 N.E.2d 755, (IL App. 1988).

60. *Hapletah v. Assessor of Town of Fallsburg,* 590 N.E. 2d 1182 (N.Y. 1992).

61. *Christian Church of Ohio v. Limbach,* 560 N.E.2d 199 (Ohio 1990).

62. *Full Gospel Apostolic Church v. Limbach,* 546 N.E. 2d 403 (Ohio 1989); but, *cf., Brith Emeth v. Limbach,* 514 N.E. 2d 874 (Ohio 1987); *Matter of Worley,* 377 S.E. 2d 270 (N.C. App. 1989);

63. *Agape Church, Inc. v. Pulaski County,* 821 S.W. 2d 21 (Ark. 1991).

64. *Le Sea Broadcasting Corp. v. State Board of Tax Commrs.*, 525 N.E.2d 637 (IN Tax Ct., 1988).

65. *Lutherans Outdoors in South Dakota, Inc. v. South Dakota State Bd. of Equalization*, 475 N.W. 2d 140 (S.D. 1991).

66. *Markham v. Broward County Nursing Home*, 540 So. 2d 940 (FL 4th DCA 1989).

67. *Simpson v. International Community of Christ*, 796 P.2d 217 (Nev. 1990).

68. *Wheaton College v. Department of Revenue*, 508 N.E.2d 1136 (IL App. 1987).

69. *Faith Christian Fellowship of Chicago, Illinois, Inc. v. Department of Revenue*, 589 N.E. 2d 796 (Ill. App. 1 Dist., 1992).

70. *Spiritual Outreach Society (S.O.S.) v. Commissioner* (U.S. 8th Cir. Ct. App.), Harmon & Ladd column, 5 *NonProfit Times* (3)29 (June 1991).

71. *Claim of Klein*, 585 N.E. 2d 809 (N.Y.S. 1991).

72. *Matter of Faith Bible Church*, 582 N.Y.S. 2d 841 (A.D. 3 Dept. 1992).

73. *United Methodist Church, Baltimore Annual Conference v. White*, 1990 WL 21141 (D.C. App.)

74. *Alicea v. New Brunswick Theological Seminary*, 608 A.2d 218 (N.J., 1992).

75. *Minker v. Baltimore Annual Conference of United Methodist Church.* #89-7009; D.C. Circ. Ct. App.: Jan. 19, 1990.

76. *Strata v. Patin*, §85–14546: LA Civ. Dist. Ct., Orleans Parish, 1988.

77. *Lily of the Valley Spiritual Church v. Sims*, 523 N.E.2d 999 (IL App. 1988).

78. *Gorman v. Swaggart*, 524 So. 2d 915 (LA App. 1988).

79. *Little v. Wuerl*, U.S. 3rd Dist., PA., 1991.

80. *Soriano v. Xavier University Corp.*, 687 F. Supp. 1188 (D.C., OH 1988).

81. *St. John's Protestant Episcopal Church Endowment fund, Inc. v. Vestry of St. J. P. E. Church*, 377 S.E.2d 375 (VA 1989).

82. J. Luther (article), Associated Press, in *St. Petersburg* (FL) *Times*, p. 3A (Mar. 14, 1989). And see, L. Martz and G. Carroll, *Ministry of Greed* (Newsweek book, Weidenfeld & Nicolson, 260 pp., 1988).

83. McIlquham, J., (article) 7 *Non Profit Times* (4) 2 (April 1993).

84. *In re, The Bible Speaks* (Church), §86—40392; U.S. Dist. Ct., MA, May 1988.

85. *White v. Blackburn*, 787 P.2d 1315 (Utah App., 1990); cf., *Olson v. Magnuson*, 457 N.W.2d 394 (Minn. App., 1990).

86. *Nally v. Grace Community Church of the Valley*, 763 P.2d 948 (CA 1988), cert. denied by U.S. Supreme Court (Apr. 1989): See. Rouse (note), *Clergy Malpractice*, 16 No. Ky. L. Rev. 383 (1989).

87. *Erickson v. Christenson*, 781 P.2d 383 (Ore. App., 1989).

88. *Mt. Zion State Bank & Methodist Church*, 556 N.E. 2d 1270 (Ill. App. 1990).

89. *Byrd v. Faber*, 565 N.E.2d 584 (Ohio 1991). See: Hanson, Clergy Malpractice: Suing Ministers . . . , 39 Drake L. Rev. (3) 597–616 (1989–90).

90. *Eckler v. General Council of Assemblies of God*, 784 S.W.2d 935 (Tex. App., 1990).

91. *Mrozka v. Archdiocese of St. Paul and Minneapolis*, 482 N.W. 2d 806 (Minn. App., 1992).

92. *Miller v. Everett*, 576 So. 2d 1162 (La. App. 1991).

93. *Strata v. Patin*, §85–14546: LA Civ. Dist. Ct., Orleans Parish, 1988.

94. *Edwards v. McDonald*, WA Pierce County Super. Ct., Tacoma: Oct. 1988.

95. *Whittaker v. Sandford*, 85 A. 399 (Maine Sup. Jud. Ct., 1912).

96. *Wood v. Benedictine Society of Alabama, Inc.*, 530 So. 2d 801 (AL 1988).

97. *Brillhart v. Scheier*, 758 P.2d 219 (KA 1988).

98. *Strock v. Pressnell*, 527 N.E.2d 1235 (OH 1988).

99. *Guinn v. Church of Christ of Collinsville*, §62–154: OK Ct.: Jan. 17, 1989.

100. *George v. International Society for Krishna Consciousness of California*, 4 Cal. Rptr 2d 473 (Cal. App. 4 Dist. 1992).

101. *Fowler v. Bailey*, 844 P.2d 141 (Okl., 1992).

102. Fl. Stat. §§ 617.0830 et seq. (eff. July 1, 1991).

103. *United States v. Aguilar*, §86–1208; U.S. 9th Cir. Ct. App., San Francisco (Mar. 30, 1989).

104. *Presbyterian Church v. U.S.*; 9th Cir., AZ (Mar. 15, 1989).

105. *International Society for Krishna Consciousness, Inc. v. Lee*, 112 S. Ct. 2701 (U.S.N.Y., 1992); *Lee v. International Society for Krishna Consciousness, Inc.*, 112 S. Ct. 2709 (U.S. N.Y., 1992).

106. *Employment Division v. Smith*, # 85-12, 13, U.S. Supr. Ct. (6–2) (Apr. 17, 1990); see S. Wermeel, Washington Docket, *Wall Street Journal*, p. 85 (Apr. 30, 1990); *cf., First Covenant Church of Seattle v. City of Seattle*, 787 P. 2d 1352 (Wash. 1990): and Supreme Court left intact a religiously motivated ban on dances at public schools in Purdy, Missouri high school (Apr. 16, 1990).

107. *Church of Lukum: Babalu Aye, Inc. v. City of Hialeah*, 113 S. Ct. 2217 (U.S. Fla., June 11, 1993).

108. *State v. Biddings*, 550 N.E. 2d 975 (Ohio app., 1988, reported May 1990); and see. *Snyder v. Evangelical Orthodox Church*, 264 Calif. Rptr. 640 (App. 1989); *Ware v. Valley Stream H.S. Dist.*, 50 N.E. 2d 420 (N.Y. 1989).

109. *Molko v. Holy Spirit Association for the Unification of World Christianity*, 762 P.2d 46 (CA 1988); *cf., Sapa Najin v. Gunter*, 857 F.2d 463 (8th Cir., NE 1988). U.S. Supreme Court dismissed the church's appeal from the Molko case decision on May 22, 1989.

110. *Westside Community Board of Educ. v. Mergens*; #88–1957; U.S. Supr. Ct.; report in 12 *Natl. L.J.* (41) 15 (June 18, 1990).

111. *Carriso v. Blevins*, 402 S.E.2d 235 (Va. App. 1991).

112. *Lubavitch Chabad House, Inc. v. City of Chicago*, 917 F.2d 341 (7th Cir., 1990).

113. Americans United for Separation of Church and State v. City of Grand Rapids, #90–2337; (U.S. 6th Cir., Nov. 16, 1992).

114. Planned Parenthood v. Casey, 112 S. Ct. 2791 (1992); R. Sherman, The War to Heat Up, 15 *Natl. L.J.* (13) 1 (Nov. 30, 1992).

115. *Rector, Wardens and Members of the Vestry of St. Bartholomew's Church v. City of N.Y.*, 728 F. supp. 958 (D.C., N.Y., 1990); see articles, *St. Petersburg Times*, p. 2E (Dec. 14, 1991).

116. *Church of Lukum: Babalu Aye, Inc. v. City of Hialeah*, 113 S. Ct. 2217 (U.S. Fla., 1993).

117. *African Methodist Episc. Zion church v. Zion Hill Methodist Church, Inc.*, 534 So. 2d 224 (AL 1988).

118. *New Christian Valley M.B. Church v. Board of Educ.*, (D.C., IL) 704 F. Supp. 868 (1989).

119. *Dignity Twin Cities v. Neuman Center*, 472 N.W. 2d 355 (Minn. App. 1991).

120. *Southside Fair Housing Committee v. City of N.Y.*, 928 F.2d 1336 (2d Cir., 1991).

121. *New Life Baptist Church Academy v. Town of East Longmeadow*, U.S. 1st Cir.; Sept. 7, 1989.

122. Religious News Service (two reports), in *St. Petersburg Times*, p. 16E (Religion section) (Apr. 7, 1990).

123. *Barnes v. Cavazos* (Louisville, Ky., D.C., Judge Charles M. Allen). and _____ v. _____ (Kansas City, MO., D.C., Judge Joseph E. Stevens, Jr., Feb., 1990), Religion Digest, *St. Petersburg Times*, p. 4E (Mar. 3, 1990).

124. *People v. De Jonge*, 449 N.W. 2d 899 (Mich. App. 1989) (publ. 1990); Mich. C.L.A. §§380.1561, 380.1599, 388.553.

125. *Bowen v. Kendrick*, 108 S. Ct. 2562 (1988).

126. *Coliseum Square Association v. City of New Orleans*, 528 So. 2d 205 (La. 4th Cir. App. 1988).

127. *Lee v. Weisman*, #90–1014; U.S. 1st Cir., Providence, R.I. (Mar. 1991); citing *Lemon v. Kurtz-*

man*, 403 U.S. 602 (1971). Bush administration lawyers seek to scrap the *Lemon* case tests. Religious News Service article, *St. Petersburg (FL) Times*, p. E3 (May 25, 1991), and p.2 (Aug. 3, 1991).

128. Editorial, *Voice of Reason*, No. 41, p. 2 (*Newsletter of Americans for Religious Liberty*, Spring 1992).

129. Paulsen case, N.Y., U.S. 2d Cir., Feb. 7, 1991. *Berger v. Rensselaer Central School Corp.*, #L. 90–19, Ind., May 1991.

      Religion Digest (p. 8E), *St. Petersburg (FL) Times*, (May 25, 1991).

130. *Traves v. Owego-Appalachian School dist.*, 927 F.2d 688 (2d Cir., N.Y., 1991).

131. Religion Digest, *St. Petersburg (FL) Times*, p. 8E (Feb. 9, 1991).

132. *Christian Gospel Church, Inc. v. City and County of San Francisco*, 896 F. 2d 1221 (9th Cir. (Cal.), 1990), *cert. denied*, 111 S. Ct. 559 (U.S. 1991).

133. *Lucas Valley Homeowners Ass'n, Inc. v. County of Marin (Chabad of North Bay, Inc.)*, 284 Cal. Rptr. 427 (Cal. App. 1 Dist. 1991).

134. *Ex parte Fairhope Bd. of Adjustment and Appeals*, 567 So. 2d 1353 (Ala. 1990).

135. *LeBlanc-Sternberg v. Fletcher*, 781 F. Supp. 261 (S.D.N.Y. 1991).

136. *First Assembly of God of Naples, Florida, Inc. v. Collier County*, 775 F. Supp. 383 (M.D. Fla. 1991).

137. *Cornerstone Bible Church v. City of Hastings*, 948 F.2d 464 (8th Cir. (Minn.), 1991).

138. *Elsaesser v. Hamilton Bd. of Zoning Appeals*, 573 N.E. 2d 733 (Ohio App. 1990).

139. *Needham Pastoral Counseling Center, Inc. v. Board of Appeals*, 557 N.E. 2d 43 (Mass. App. 1990).

140. *Our Saviour's Evangelical Lutheran Church v. City of Naperville*, 542 N.E. 2d 1158 (Ill. App. 1989).

141. *Rector, Wardens & Members of Vestry of St. Bartholomew's Church v. City of N.Y.*, 914 F.2d 343 (2d Cir., N.Y., 1990).

142. *Southside Fair Housing Committee v. City of N.Y.*, 750 F. Supp. 575 (D.C., N.Y., 1990).

143. Jeanne Pugh, *Church State Line Blurs for Myopic Denominations*, St. Petersburg (FL) Times, Religion Section (E)2 (July 9, 1988).

144. *St. Petersburg Times*, p. 4B; and Religion Section, p. 3E (Mar. 24, 1990).

145. See, J. Turley, *Laying Hands on Religious Racketeers: Applying civil RICO to Fraudulent Religious Solicitation*, 29 Wm. & Mary L. Rev. 441–500 (1988).

146. *Rust v. Sullivan*, S. Ct. _____. (May 23, 1991); see R. Marcus (article) *Washington Post* (May 24, 1991).

147. *U.S. v. Bakker*, #89–5687 (4th Cir. Feb. 11, 1991).

148. H.J. Vogel, *Law and Religion: A Compilation of Syllabi for Courses Taught in American Law Schools* (Nov. 1990).

37

CONDOMINIUMS AND COOPERATIVES

[Matthew R. Danahy contributed the 1988 first outline of this chapter. It was updated and expanded in 1993 by Oleck and Stewart.]

§371. CONDOMINIUMS AND COOPERATIVES, IN GENERAL

[Christopher D. Marone did research for some of this section.]

Condominiums and cooperatives have both been the subject of extensive statutory regulations in all states. In Florida, for instance, separate statutes regulate each,[1] and it appears that most states follow this arrangement.

While authorities and state statutes differ on the definition of the term "condominium," it has generally come to refer to a multi-unit residential, industrial or commercial building "each of whose residents or unit owners enjoys exclusive ownership of his individual apartment or unit, holding a fee simple title thereto, while retaining an undivided interest, as a tenant in common, in the common facilities and areas of the building and grounds which are used by all residents [or unit owners] of the condominium."[2] Thus, the concept of "condominium" consists of two principal elements: "(1) separate ownership of a part of a building (apartment), coupled with (2) common ownership with other apartment owners in the land or such parts of the building as are intended for common use."[3] As a result, the condominium has been characterized as a "welding of two distinct tenures, one in severalty and the other in common."[4]

On the other hand are the cooperatives. They are organizations for mutual help and service among and to their members ... (especially) food producers, marketers, and consumers. They may be for profit as well as not for profit. Individuals and organizations may be members. Their powers and liabilities are set forth in local statutes. [See Section 38.]

Community Associations: By 1985 it was estimated that there were 90,000 community associations of various types in the United States. Fifteen percent of the population was said to belong to some such association.[5]

Condo law trends, typified by Florida's amendments to its Chapter 718 statute (effective April 1, 1992), require 14 day written notice of owners' meetings, allow proxy voting except in board elections, arbitration before court suit by unit owners, stern election voting rules, open records for buyers, bidding on contracts of over $5000 or a year duration, and more. Florida has almost 16,000 condo associations, with nearly 900,000 units housing probably well over a million people.[6]

Condo-Governing Statutes

Florida's extensive revisions of its condo (chap. 718) statute, effective April 1, 1992, made changes in many provisions, and emphasizes an Ombudsman and advisory council for the state division governing condos.[7]

Florida's NPC statute states specifically that its provision authorizing *classes* of members, and *chapter* or affiliate subdivision organizations' *voting* by chapters or classes, do not apply to condominium associations.[8]

Also, liability immunities of officers, given by Fl. St. § 617.0831, does not apply to condo or coop directors appointed by the developers. *Ibid.* § 53 of Fl. Sess. L. 90-179.

Statutory condo right to sue the developer does not bar unit owner's right to sue for defect in his unit.[9]

In 1991 Florida amended its condo statute to abolish *proxy voting* for board offices among unit owners and permit the state to fine association officers and directors who knowingly violate state condo laws or rules. It also created a *state ombudsman* to report on condo matters and serve as a liaison between the state and unit owners.[10]

Detailed rules as to *bonding* of persons who hold or pay out association funds are provided in state statutes, usually applicable to sums over 10,000 and/or condos or coops of over 50 units.[11]

The *State Condominium Act* limits the *powers* of a Condo Association to those expressly stated in the Act, in Florida, since the decision of the Florida Supreme Court in 1985 in *Towerhouse v. Millman*, 475 So. 2d 674. In the same year that Court gave developers the right to develop schemes *solely* to frustrate *regulatory control* of "master associations," in *Dept. of Business Regulation v. Siegel*, 479 So. 2d 112. In 1987, that Court held that *municipal ordinance* rules against *age discrimination* in housing overrides restrictions in the Condominium documents, in *Metropolitan Dade County Fair Housing & Employment Appeals Board v. Sunrise Mobile Home Park*, 12 F.L.W. 346. The results of such decisions have been to drive out many marginal developers, with positive (not negative) effects on use of condominiums for housing.[12]

State statutes governing condominium developments do not preempt *municipal zoning* or other *ordinances* adopted by municipalities; e.g., mobile home park.[13]

In New York, the state "Condo & Coop. Abuse Relief Act" applies to other injured parties as well as those who signed self-dealing leases.[14] There, *forfeiture of a condo* allegedly used as a drugs-sale depot is a valid constitutional civil penalty.[15]

Homestead exemptions from *real property taxes* (e.g., up to $25,000 value in Florida) usually apply to condo and other unit ownership. Rates and procedures vary from state to state and from time to time, of course. Application usually must be made for such exemptions, and annual renewal filings. Florida's "homestead" tax exemption does not apply to a debtor's interest in a year-to-year lease of a condo unit; bankruptcy proceeding case.[16]

A *declaration of condominium*, like other legal instruments, may be "reformed" by a court of equity, in a case of mutual *mistake*, so as to express the true intention of the parties; and parole evidence is admissible for this purpose. But *statutes*, such as Florida's, extensively regulate condominiums today, stating precise rules for *amending* a condominium declaration [FL St. §718.110]. In a strongly criticized decision, however, the Florida Supreme Court allowed equity reformation-for-mistake in such a situation, despite the statute in the state.[17]

The court interprets covenants contained in condominium declarations by looking to the intent of the parties, especially the grantor. The court construes covenants without extrinsic evidence where plain terms of the covenant are sufficiently clear.[18]

Condominium form of land *ownership*, approved by statute, does not make simultaneous *nonownership interests* in that land per se illegal. A developer's *retention* of the right to control some driveway and parking in the condo parking areas, for purpose of allocation of some limited parking rights, clearly expressed in the declaration, is valid if for *reasonable* uses.[19]

Setting of a minimum price at which a unit owner may resell is a valid condo association declaration rule to protect property values and for screening of new residents for financial means and social suitability; it is not per se price fixing or unreasonable restriction.[20]

Restrictive covenants in a condo declaration of condominium are viewed with disfavor unless they relate to a general plan of which a purchaser has notice. Rejection of an application for a front screen door installation is not arbitrary per se.[21]

Condominium Conversion

A statute (District of Columbia) permitting conversion of an apartment building to a condominium by majority (51 percent) vote of eligible tenants is constitutionally valid. It does not violate the "due process of law" clause of the constitution.[22]

In conversion of an apartment house to a condo or coop, in New York, continued state-statutory tenancy for certain nonpurchasers violates the landlord's due process rights under a consent judgment (a contract), and takes his property without compensation, without reducing the housing shortage enough to *substantially* advance a state interest.[23] Also in New York, in eviction-type *cooperative conversion* of an apartment building, the adequacy of notice to tenants may be tested (as to materiality of an omission under state statutes) by *federal securities law* decisions interpreting analogous law.[24]

Condo unit buyer may have tort action for fraud against engineering firm that give false information as to condition of the apartment building when it was about to be converted to a condo, despite lack of contractual privity, in Florida.[25]

A *city ordinance* providing rights for tenants in *condominium conversion* evictions does not impliedly authorize a municipal rent-equity board to require that the "converter" offer a "conversion eviction package" where no eviction is intended. It is not a general empowering ordinance for the board, in Massachusetts.[26]

Condominium Contracts

Oral promise to build golf course, leading a buyer to buy a condo unit for resale, is not actionable *misrepresentation* where the buyer was an experienced realty investor and the *contract* had a statement that only the writings, not oral statements, were to be relied upon. A buyer's right to sue for misrepresentation by the condo developer must be based on reasonable reliance; e.g., childish reliance by a professional investor is not reasonable.[27]

Misrepresentations by a New York mortgage company's Florida investment advisor (with whom it had an agency relation), as to value of Florida condos mortgaged, is enough to give jurisdiction (long-arm statute) for fraud claims in New York courts.[28]

Whether a unit (townhouse) buyer was reasonable in relying on the condominium (vendor) *agent's statement* that recreational areas would be built, in a claim of fraudulent misrepresentation, is a jury question.[29]

Assurances of free use of recreational facilities were fraud where the unit owner had to be a paying member to use these facilities.[30]

Brochures featuring "Meticulous Construction" are fraud where condo walls were destroyed by water because of bad construction.[31]

A buyer's failure to check on zoning law as to occupancy by tenants (not owners) bars his claim as to oral representations as to leasing of townhouse condo units.[32]

Assurances of a panoramic view entitle the purchaser of a condo unit to enjoin blocking construction by the developer.[33]

Violation of later-enacted statutory amendment (bar) of rulees as to *escalation of rates*, in a condo recreation lease, will not be found by a court unless the agreement terms clearly show intent to make escalation available under statutory rules.[34]

A lessee using condo space for a restaurant has enough "interest" in the condo to have "standing" to seek injunction against its assignments of parking space, even though not a unit owner.[35]

Corporate condo project owner has cause of action against lenders who made a loan commitment, but then did not give loans on units in the condo.[36]

A tennis/pool recreation facility owner (transferee from original developer) may sue the association to collect unit owners' fees obligations, despite absence of specific provision (in package sales) for such a right to have the association perform such services. This does not violate the Condominium Act nor antitrust laws, being of common interest to all units.[37]

Mechanic's Lien laws apply to condo *improvement* or *repair* work as well as to others. *Double payment* may be required if a contractor does not pay his suppliers; for example, after being paid by the condo association. A contractor's Affidavit and Final *Release* of Lien should be obtained in order to avoid trouble. If the contract is over $2,500 the association may have to record a *Notice* of Commencement in the office of the Circuit Court Clerk; best done before work begins.[38]

A statute requiring a municipality to provide or pay for municipal services to condominiums, but not apartment complexes, does not violate equal protection. Such statutes have a reasonable basis to foster the goal of individual home ownership.[39]

§372. HISTORY OF CONDOMINIUMS

While scholars have long debated the origins of the condominium, there can be no doubt that the condominium concept is an ancient one. "There is at least one record of the sale of a part of a building, in ancient Babylon . . . nearly two centuries before the birth of Christ."[40] Yet the extent to which the condominium concept was used in Roman times is uncertain. Nevertheless, it appears that "the word condominium is derived from the Latin word meaning joint dominion or co-ownership."[41]

There is more agreement on the fact that "during the latter middle ages, when massive walls were built around many European communities for purposes of defense and building space consequently became scarce, the condominium concept flourished."[42] It is not surprising that the first known statutory recognition of condominiums occurred in Europe—in the Napoleonic Code of 1804.[43]

Long before the United States adopted the condominium form "the statutes of other countries, including Spain, Italy, Germany, Belgium and France, denoted rights and obligations of such ownership."[44] However, most of these laws "never used the term condominium, but used such names as horizontal property or similar attempts at descriptive terminology which are just as poor."[45]

"The condominium concept did not take root in this country until after Puerto Rico . . . had experimented with this form of ownership" beginning in 1951.[46] Since that time, starting with Hawaii and ending with Vermont, all 50 states, the District of Columbia and the Virgin Islands "have passed enabling statutes, many of which follow the model condominium statute drafted by the FHA."[47]

Growth of the Condominium

It has been only recently, especially in the last two decades, that the condominium has become a common form of property ownership. "According to a survey of the Urban Land Institute, there were only 500 condominium projects nationwide in 1962, representing approximately 50,000 condominium units. Census data indicate that the number of condominium units in the United States grew to 436,000 in 1970."[48] In 1989, new privately owned condominium units started numbered 118,000 in the United States.[49]

"Florida has experienced the most phenomenal condominium growth."[50] One factor is the rapidly increasing value of real property in Florida, particularly along the East and West coasts. "By 1972 approximately 85,000 units had been constructed in Florida at a total value in excess of $1.5 billion."[51] By 1992, there were 1,067 rental condominiums in Florida for public lodging, with some 41,639 rental units.[52]

"In 1975, the Department of Housing and Urban Development identified 12,500 different projects representing more than 1 million condominiums in the United States. By early 1982, condominium sales had risen to 12 percent of total sales by real estate agents in America."[53] By 1989, condominium sales rose to 13.5 percent of all sales, including multiple-family houses.[54]

§373. TYPES OF CONDOMINIUMS

Virtually any residential, industrial, commercial or recreational enterprise can use the condominium form. "Condominiums are not limited to apartments,—cluster homes, townhouses, commercial structures of offices and other uses, campsites, parking spaces, hotels and other projects have been committed to the condominium form of ownership."[55]

A list of some possibilities include:[56]

1. "Single high rise apartments . . . entirely residential . . .
2. A single . . . building, with a mixed . . . ownership of residentially and commercially utilized space.
3. Single high rise apartment ownership . . . residential . . . , with commercially utilized space . . . operated by commercial tenants under lease.
4. Single high rise apartment condominiums with . . . commercial areas reserved for the sponsor or other owner, with various easements and reciprocal obligations existing between the condominium and the other owner or owners.
5. Commercial condominium buildings. . . .

6. Varieties of recreational developments, such as ski resorts, golf courses, beach clubs, (*etc.*) . . .

7. Educational or government used facilities shared in usage and ownership by several independent localities."[57]

[For typical condominium litigation case problems in 1987–88 see below, footnote 180]

§374. TIMESHARING CONDOMINIUMS

"In the mid-1970s, a new form of condominium ownership, the timesharing condominium, was developed."[58] This form of ownership is most commonly found in resort or vacation areas. "In essence, the timesharing concept involves communal ownership, with term occupancy, for a specified time interval each year, usually one to four weeks, that is geared to the actual use of the unit at a fraction of the whole unit cost."[59]

There are three basic formats used to allocate the ownership rights of timesharing condominiums. "First, in the time span or tenancy in common format, buyers are deeded an undivided interest in a particular unit as tenants in common with other buyers of the unit. At the same time, the buyers agree to limit their use of the unit to a designated time period."[60] "Second, in the interval ownership format, purchasers are granted an estate for years for the agreed time period each year. This revolving estate for years lasts for the expected useful life of the property. At that point, all owners become tenants in common in the property. Third, under a vacation license, a developer retains ownership and agrees to allow buyers to use the premises for a stated number of years."[61]

Some states have now enacted legislation to specifically authorize and regulate the timesharing condominium, including Florida.[62]

§375. COMMERCIAL CONDOMINIUMS

As noted earlier, condominiums are not limited to residential apartments, but include commercial condominiums. However, there has been a more limited acceptance of the commercial condominium until recently.

"The advantages of owning a commercial condominium are: 1) rent increases are avoided; 2) an owner cannot be evicted to make room for more important tenants; 3) well located and constructed units tend to increase in value."[63] There are disadvantages as well, and they include: "1) the owner is locked into a particular location; 2) additional space is more difficult to obtain; 3) rent is totally tax deductible while commercial condominium owners are limited to tax deduction for mortgage interest, taxes, depreciation and maintenance expenses; and 4) funds otherwise available for inventory and business expansion are tied up by the condominium purchase."[64]

§376. ORGANIZING A CONDOMINIUM

Every state has enacted laws establishing and regulating the condominium. It has been held that "the requirements for qualifying as a condominium are specifically provided for in the law and must be" strictly complied with.[65] Further, many states' laws expressly state that all condominiums must conform to the particular state's condominium statute.[66]

The procedure most commonly used permits the establishment of a condominium by the use of three types of instruments: 1) the declaration or master deed; 2) the bylaws or declaration of restrictions; and 3) the deeds to the individual units. [The individual can sell (deed) his unit to another person,[67] subject to association rules.]

1. The Declaration

"The declaration is the primary instrument by which property is committed to a condominium plan of ownership."[68] The declaration of condominium "spells out the extent of the interest that each purchaser acquires and the rights and liabilities of the unit owners."[69] By recording the declaration "the last act in creation of the condominium is accomplished and the condominium comes into existence."[70]

The FHA Model Act suggests provisions to be included in the declaration, which most states follow. These suggestions include: "The declaration should describe the land, each unit and the common elements. It should conform to the formalities required of instruments conveying or encumbering real property and it should be recorded. It should provide for the establishment of an association of owners, a method of sharing common expenses, the percentage of votes assigned to each apartment, and procedure governing management of the building."[71]

2. ByLaws [See *Association Rules*, below]

Condo operation rules *enforcement,* such as licensing of managers and document retention for at least a year, may involve fines and other penalties. Enforcement by authorities (e.g., Florida Bureau of Condominiums) involves Bureau as well as statute rules. See, for example, the list of records required to be preserved, in Fla. Stat. §718.111(12) plus Rule 61B-23.002 of Fla. Division of Land Sales, Condos, & Mobile Homes (eff. Nov. 23, 1993).

The bylaws may include the following: "The election of a board of managers, their terms of office, powers and duties and election of officers of the board, a yearly accounting to the unit owners, notice to unit owners of board meetings, maintenance repair and replacement of the common elements, the adoption of rules and regulations for the use of units and common areas."[72]

It has been held that "as long as the bylaws are reasonable they are binding."[73] Thus, any limitations on the bylaws should be placed in the declaration. "The declaration is the basic charter of fundamental rights. It is the proper place where limitations on such rights should be placed."[74]

3. Deeds to Individual Units

"Ownership of a unit in a condominium is evidenced by individual [unit] deeds which should contain a direct reference to the declaration which has already been recorded, and an accurate description of the property and of the [unit] number as set out in the declaration."[75] The FHA Model Act provides that deeds of units shall include:

"1) Description of land as provided in the declaration or the exact address of the property together with the page and date of recording the declaration; 2) The apartment number and any other data necessary for identification of the apartment; 3) Statement of the use for which the apartment is intended and restrictions on its use; 4) The percentage of undivided interest appertaining to the apartment in the common area or facilities; and 5) Any further details deemed desirable."[76] [These deeds are transferable; *see* note 67.]

§377. OPERATIONAL ASPECTS OF CONDOS

Before a new condominium can be put into operation, a number of steps must be taken, including: "1) Election, in accordance with the bylaws, of a governing board by the unit owners; 2) election of officers; 3) appointment of committees; 4) transfer of control from the developer to the newly-elected board; 5) hiring a new building manager (if the owners desire); 6) review of the insurance purchased by the developer; 7) review by the board of completion of the building in accordance with plans and specifications; 8) adoption of rules [and restrictions]"[77] governing units, common areas and so forth.

Condominium Association Legal Actions

[See also Chap. 44]

A common type of class action involves members of a condominium association. This kind of procedure is well illustrated by the 1981 Florida Rule of Civil Procedure 1.221—Condominium Associations:

"Rule 1.221.

After control of a condominium association is obtained by unit owners other than the developer, the association may institute, maintain, settle or appeal actions or hearings in its name on behalf of all unit owners concerning matters of common interest, including, but not limited to, the common elements; the roof and structural components of a building or other improvements; mechanical, electrical and plumbing elements serving an improvement or a building; representations of the developer pertaining to any existing or proposed commonly used facilities; and protesting *ad valorem* taxes on commonly used facilities. If the association has the authority to maintain a class action under this section, the association may be joined in an action as a representative of that class with reference to litigation and disputes involving the matters for which the association could bring a class action under this section. Nothing herein limits any statutory or common-law right of any individual unit owner or class of unit owners to bring any action which may otherwise be available. An action under this rule shall not be subject to the requirements of Rule 1.220."[78]

The condo association has a duty to protect unit owners and guests from foreseeable crimes by third persons.[79]

A *recreation association,* though a *separate entity* owning land, for use of condo unit owners as a swimming pool, required condo unit owners' unanimous consent to assess unit owners for the cost; it is a "condominium association."[80]

Members of a *housing association* who made an initial contribution in starting an association are entitled to interest on their contributions, in a *bankruptcy.*[81]

Class action may be brought by the condo association for construction defects (water, undrained, under the foundation) where all unit owners are members and state civil procedure law is followed.[82]

A condominium association cannot receive attorney fees as a "prevailing party" under *Fla. Stat.* § 718.303(1) (1989) where the relief granted is considerably different from the relief sought.[83]

A condominium association's lien relates back to the time that declaration of condominium is recorded. Such a lien runs with the land and binds subsequent mortgage interests.[84]

Statute giving the condo association the right to sue the developer as to common areas does not bar individual unit owners' rights to sue (standing) for breach of contract as to construction of the building other than the common areas (as to which there is a derivative cause of action).[85]

Trustees of a condo association have power to carry on *litigation* about common areas and facilities, which includes the power to settle claims in (or before) litigation, and to enter into contracts on behalf of the unit owners group. *Trustees* of a condominium signed a *release* of a roofing company after leaks caused damage to the condo and to units. Held not effective to bar individual unit owners' claims for damages to individual units. Trustees govern "common areas."[86]

Class action by an owners association is often valid for objecting to tax valuation assessment by the state Department of Revenue or appraiser. Owners not willing to join must have some means to opt out.[87]

A single condominium unit owner, not the association, is a "person injured" for purposes of an award of damages from a Residential Contractors' Recovery Fund when an association of unit owners prevails against a contractor and developer no longer doing business.[88]

The doorman of a condominium is an employee of the association, not the individual unit owners. Thus, a doorman, who was injured as a result of a unit owners' negligence, may sue the unit owner and is not limited to the exclusive remedy provision of the Workers' Compensation Act.[89]

Association Rules [See *Bylaws*, above]

Civic-residential *association rules* requiring homeowners or builders to submit building construction plans to the association are valid, though an accompanying requirement of payment of a fee for such review is not. Thus, deed restrictions that barred prefabricated homes were valid, unless consent of the association be granted.[90]

No preliminary injunction may be had by a unit owner who challenges the validity of a regulation of his condominium, unless he can show clear justification (and irreparable injury) for such swift court decision.[91]

Master deed provisions are paramount in analyzing condo unit owners' rights. Thus, a 12-year-old girl residing in an "adult" condo community is not a valid "*companion*" under the basic rule exemptions; nor is an unmarried non-spouse person. But, a 12-year-old visiting her mother about twice a week is okay.[92]

California's statute permitting private mobile home parks to adopt *rules limiting* residence to persons of *minimum age* of 25 years old or older is constitutional and enforceable. (CA Civil Code §798.76).[93]

Condo rules documents, limiting display of the flag to certain designated occasions, involve "state action" enough to warrant invocation of the 14th Amendment in judicial enforcement of private agreements, because judicial enforcement of a declaration of condominium is state action.[94]

Declaration of condominium, which allows pets to be kept, is superior to *Rules and Regulations* (bylaws) that bars pets.[95] A condominium association may, by proper rules and regulations, adopt a county dog leash law and enforce that law on common grounds of the condominium.[96]

A condo owners' association may amend its declaration to prohibit leasing of units, and this is not *per se* invalid against existing ownership rights of unit owners if it is *reasonable* in light of the surrounding circumstances, even-handed, and made in good faith.[97]

Rules as to priorities and required consents for unit mortgages, especially in cases of defaults and foreclosures, are very complex as to legal status and various parties' rights. Also, rules as to homeowners associations and coops often are different from condo rules in some details. Careful study of the state's current laws should be made whenever a mortgage is involved, or assessment vs. mortgage rules.[98]

Condo association may reasonably *interpret* its own *rules*; e.g., viewing flower box planters as "structures" requiring association approval.[99]

A condominium association may get a permanent injunction that prohibits a condominium resident from communicating with the condominium's security guards and office staff, except in emergencies, without violating the resident's right to free speech, when the resident is boisterous, offensive, or obnoxious to the point of causing irreparable harm. A finding of civil or criminal contempt for violating the order requires that the underlying order is valid and that the resident had sufficient notice of restraints imposed on his/her behavior.[100]

A *condominium* unit owner's installation of an air conditioner through the wall, in violation of association rules, may be removed by summary judgment injunction obtained by the association *board of managers.*[101]

The fact that others besides unit owners or members benefit from a condo's activities (e.g., use of roadways, or adjoining land security benefits) does not make such benefits improper, unless violations of voting rights or the declaration, or the like, are involved.[102]

Operation of a day-care home is not permitted in a purely "residential" condominium; it is a business.[103]

Condominiums' Design Defects

A general *contractor* who settled claims against him for *defects* in the building in a condominium, if he did so in good faith is protected from all equitable indemnity claims from vicariously-liable persons, such as derivatively-liable tortfeasors.[104]

A condominium developer, who was sued by a condominium home-owners association for construction defects, is not entitled to an action for equitable indemnity from the unit owners. An affirmative defense that the unit owners misused the property would provide equivalent relief.[105]

A condominium board of directors may sue the developer for design defects that it discovers, if at all, only when it acts promptly upon "discovery" of the flaw, not if it delays. Under statutes of repose (such as Florida Statute § 718.203) implied warranties of fitness on roofs, wiring, plumbing, and so on are open to attack for only three years from the date of the grant of a certificate of occupancy, or one year after transfer to the condo association, whichever is later, but not more than five years later in any case. Prompt analysis by engineers should be made for the association when a serious design defect is discovered. (But a 15-year period is possible in some cases.)[106]

When a condominium association brought suit against the condominium *developer,* in his corporate and individual capacity, for fire damages to an uninsured clubhouse recreation center, the court held that the developer corporation breached its *fiduciary duty* by failing to renew a fire policy on the clubhouse. The developer corporation had the duty to maintain insurance under the association *bylaws.* However, the developer could not be held personally liable absent fraud, self-dealing, unjust enrichment, or betrayal of trust.[107]

An amendment to *Fla. Stat.* § 718.203 (1991) eliminates implied warranties of fitness in condominium design by architects and engineers. However, the amendment does not affect common law tort actions against architects and engineers.[108]

When a condominium association receives a settlement from a developer for repairs necessary after an apartment building was changed into a condominium, neither the settlement nor the Illinois contribution statute bars a third party claim against the architect who was involved.[109]

Building code violations do not per se make a condo architect liable to unit owners in a negligence suit if he designed units by first determining that (in his professional opinion) only one exit was required for each, and then getting a city building permit on which he relied as he was entitled to do.[110]

Condo association suit against the developer's architect, for costs of repair of defective design, cannot claim these costs under a negligent malpractice basis for the suit, nor a warranty basis [under Moorman Mfg. Co. v. National Tank Co., 435 N.E. 2d 443 (Ill. 1982)]; it may not have damages for purely economic loss in a tort action; only physical harm or personal injury damages are allowed under tort principles.[111]

Tender of Fees

A condo unit owner's tender of fees, marked by a *letter of protest* of their assessment, is not an improper tender and is not vitiated by the protest.[112]

Payment and terms of "*security deposits*" required by condos and coops are governed by detailed rules in the statutes of most states, and usually are similar to those rules applied to landlords and associations.[113]

Statutory authority for the condominium association's *board of directors to assess* units for common expenses benefiting less than all units does not justify a "move-in fee" when the condo documents provide expressly for pro rata allocation of expenses among unit owners except in cases of owner negligence. This was a clear limitation, not overridden by the statute.[114]

It is not against public policy for a declaration of condominium to charge a late fee for dues not timely paid.[115]

Common Elements

Unit owners may sue, over defects in common areas, but must represent the interests of other owners.

Garage space just behind a condo parking area is not a "limited common area" under the declaration of condominium. The unit owners may be enjoined from using that space even if the sale contract spoke of two parking spaces as part of the purchase of a unit.[116]

In a unit owner's claim of use of a restricted yard area of a condo, the area was deemed a common element, the repair of which was included in the association's responsibility for structural maintenance.[117]

A condominium association sued a utility when the utility enlarged its easement by placing its underground transformers above ground. The court held that the use of an easement cannot be enlarged to injure the servient estate, unless the right to enlarge is established by prescription or agreement with the servient landowner.[118]

Air space above condo units and condo land is "common element," and a taking by building an additional storey without general-owners'-consent is cause of action for damages.[119]

A "development" containing condominiums and single-family homes and undeveloped land and common-use (club) land and facilities, involves cross-contract rights, which give legal rights (and obligations) in common areas;

such as, limited rights in common areas that are not supported by one particular corporation (e.g., a single-family homeowners association paying for maintenance could demand an accounting from the condo association as to expenses paid by the homeowners association). Use of a roadway partially on the
subdivision part of the development, by condo unit owners, was upheld on the
basis of their legal status as "invitees" there.[120]

Condo Officers' and Trustees' Liability

[See c. 17 § 181]

Officers of a condominium association have a *fiduciary* duty to warn unit
owners of serious defects or dangers in the building [FL St. §718.111(1)(a)],
but this fiduciary relation does not extend to *prospective purchasers* of units
(although duty to them may exist in developers and builders).[121]

Condo association *president* had implied *authority* to grant an easement for
installing an underground sewage line to a temple on the association's land,
where members of the temple were all only condominium unit owners.[122]

Trustees who approved a balcony construction that interfered with the
light in plaintiff's (lower) condo unit, are not liable for damages when the
deed of trust provided for liability only for willful breach of trust, even though
their lack of notice to the lower owner was unduly casual.[123]

A *unit owner's bankruptcy trustee* may properly reject claims of the unit owner's condominium for common charges that were not "perfected" before bankruptcy petition was filed; this, under a trustee's "strong-arm" powers.[124]

Rent Escalation in Leases

Statutory restriction of rent escalation clauses in recreational leases of
condos usually attempts to end the tactic of tying rent rates in a lease to such
things as the constantly changing national Consumer Price Index. But leases
(or declarations) ante-dating the statutory amendment sometimes may become
totally voided by enforcement of the statutory limitation. The rule seems to be
full of uncertainties.[125]

Escalation clauses in recreation or land leases of condo property had been
made void under Fla. Stat. § 718.401(8)(a) of 1985, but changes under *preexisting* agreements were held to be effective unless the lessor agreed to be
bound by changes in the Condo Act, c. 718.[126]

Unconscionable rent escalation clauses are void if they violate new statutes.[127]

Condo/Coop. Meeting Notice

Number of days notice required for the annual meeting and/or budget
adoption of a condo or coop. now is fourteen (14) days under the amended
Florida Condo and Coop. Act, and the requirement of getting a certificate of
mailing from the Post Office as proof of notice of a meeting also no longer is
specified by the statute. Notice affidavit by an officer of the corporation is suf-

ficient, unless bylaws provide otherwise. Also, voting or service on the board by a delinquent unit owner are stated by this statute to be deemed inherent in the ownership, and the bylaws may not make such delinquency a bar to such voting or service.[128]

[See additional illustrative cases, below, in footnote[170].]

§378. HISTORY OF COOPERATIVES

A cooperative can be defined as "a democratic association of persons organized to furnish themselves an economic service under a plan that eliminates entrepreneur profit and that provides for substantial equality in control and ownership."[129] There are some distinctive features that distinguish cooperatives from other business structures. Generally, these include "democratic control and voting, the distribution of economic benefits on an equal basis or in proportion to the use made of the association facilities, limited return on capital and the fact of doing most of their business with their own members."[130]

It should be mentioned that a condominium is "a specialized type of cooperative . . . [in which] each member owns his [unit], subject to such mortgage as he might have, and in addition holds his proportionate ownership of halls, elevators and all other common parts of the realty. With respect to the group ownership, a condominium is not significantly different from any other cooperative. The organization to protect the common interests of the owners, whether it be an unincorporated association, a corporation or a trust, is for practical purposes, truly a cooperative."[131]

Cooperatives have commonly been used for the creation of housing, but cooperatives are and have been used for many other purposes. Cooperatives for housing purposes "are relatively new, having first become important with the housing shortage which followed the first World War."[132]

The first consumer cooperative is usually attributed to the "Equitable Pioneers Society, organized in 1844 . . . in . . . England."[133] But the emergence in the United States of a firm policy with regard to cooperatives "came in 1875, when the . . . Rochdale principles were adopted at the convention of the National Grange of the Patrons of Husbandry."[134] These principles are still used when stating the fundamentals of cooperatives, and emphasize the democratic character of such an enterprise. They are: "1) charging of local prevailing prices; 2) limited interest on capital investment; 3) refunds in proportion to purchases; 4) sale for cash and not for credit; 5) sex equality; 6) one vote for each member; 7) regular and frequent meetings."[135] Landlord-tenant law basically is inappropriate for cooperative apartment agreements.[136]

Types of Cooperatives; a Functional Classification.

There are a great number of purposes for which the cooperative form may be used. The different types of cooperatives include: "Consumer cooperatives (consumer stores, housing cooperatives, condominiums, electric, telephone and other utility cooperatives, and health cooperatives) marketing cooperatives, business purchasing cooperatives, workers productive cooperatives, financial cooperatives (such as credit unions and savings and loan associations); insurance cooperatives, labor unions, trade associations, self-help cooperatives"[137] and agricultural cooperatives.[138]

§379. ORGANIZING A COOPERATIVE

Legislation

"Practically all jurisdictions have adopted legislation permitting the formation of cooperative associations or the conversion of existing business organizations of other types to the cooperative pattern."[139] And while the principle of cooperatives has generally been favored in State and Federal legislation, "farmers' cooperatives appear to have received public support to a greater degree than cooperatives generally. Some differentiation in treatment designed to encourage agricultural or related activities has customarily been sustained."[140] Florida follows this arrangement by the use of three separate statutes relating to cooperatives: Fla. Stat., Ch. 719 gives the general requirements to form a cooperative; Fla. Stat. Ch. 618 gives the requirements for agricultural cooperative marketing associations; and Fla. Stat. Ch. 619 gives the requirements for forming nonprofit cooperative associations.

Statutes providing for the creation of cooperative associations have "been held not to be unconstitutional as special legislation, or as violative of the due process clause of the Fourteenth Amendment."[141] Such statutes have also "been held valid as against contentions that it controlled or burdened interstate commerce, regulated or restricted the freedom of the market in interstate commerce, or was in conflict with the established policy of the state.[142]

The language of a statute which authorizes the incorporation of a cooperative association "should be given a reasonably liberal construction as to the purposes for which such corporations may be formed and the courts have liberally construed the cooperative marketing acts in order to accomplish the object for which they were created."[143] Thus, horse racing and wagering, as supportive activities, have been held to be valid activities."[144]

Formation

There are several activities that precede the organization of a cooperative. These are conducted by a promoter or sponsor, whose job it is to "(1) arouse cooperative interest; (2) sign up cooperators; (3) obtain financial subscriptions; (4) complete requirements for actual operation."[145] "A promoter stands in a fiduciary relation to both the corporation as a separate legal entity and the stockholders—including those who it is anticipated will buy such stock as well as those presently within the class—and he is bound to exercise the utmost good faith in dealing with them."[146]

While the requirements for formation of cooperatives are contained under state law and must be followed, particularly with respect to condominiums, generally requirements for forming a cooperative include: "(1) Drafting the charter and basic documents; (2) Executing, filing and recording of the charter; (3) Meetings for completion of the organization and (4) Adoption of bylaws."[147]

§380. OPERATIONAL ASPECTS OF COOPS

Statutory Control

An electrical cooperative can *waive* a city's compliance with a statute, which prohibits the city from supplying power to customers outside its territorial limits, by an *unwritten policy* allowing the city to serve locations out of its territory near the city power lines.[148]

Even though an independent nonprofit electrical cooperative is not entitled to governmental immunity, the Johnson Act precludes federal court jurisdiction over a suit by a customer where utility rates are approved by the state.[149]

Indian governmental entities are immune from execution under the doctrine of tribal sovereign immunity. However, a Native Alaskan cooperative association waived any possible tribal immunity when it agreed to arbitration of a dispute in a suit to enforce an arbitration award. The normal presumption in favor of the immunity of native groups is inapplicable when the group claims exemption from debt.[150]

In Montana, the Territorial Integrity Act (1971) aids in the resolution of disputes, between electrical cooperatives and electrical utilities, over what company will provide services to new customers.[151]

Financing Cooperatives

The United States Rural Electrification Administration (REA) is an agency that makes and guarantees loans to electrification cooperatives set up to furnish electric power to rural areas. The REA takes security interests in the physical assets and the respective rights and interest of each party to the wholesale power contract. An Illinois court recently held that the REA may intervene in state court proceedings to protect its rights. The REA also may enjoin those proceedings where intervention is not allowed.[152]

Co-op Rentals

In a cooperative housing corporation, 80 percent or more of the gross income, for the taxable year in which the taxes and interest are paid, must be derived from tenant-stockholders. The tenant-stockholders are allowed deductions for the amounts paid to the co-op to the extent that such amounts represent the tenant-stockholder's proportionate share of real estate taxes and mortgage interest.[153]

Cooperatives—Sale of Shares

If a residential co-op member claims that the corporation sold his shares of stock at a price below their fair market value, he must show appraisals of the shares or other evidence as to the value of his apartment.[154]

"It is well settled that the imposition of a waiver of option fee upon outgoing shareholders who wish to sell their shares on the open market, rather than resell them to the cooperative association at book value, is a valid exercise of a cooperative board's power as granted by statute and the corporate by-laws, and as interpreted by case law."[155]

Coop Director's Standard of Care

Directors' decision (to stop lessee's remodeling in his coop apartment) is valid if "reasonable" and in good faith, under a standard of review "analogous to the *business judgment* rule;" applicable to condos and coops.[156]

When a dairyman sued his cooperative for breach of fiduciary duty and breach of a milk marketing contract, the court held that if the written agreement is unambiguous, no parol evidence of prior or contemporaneous agreements or understandings, tending to vary the written agreement, is admissible. There is no *breach of fiduciary duty* absent any evidence that the cooperative failed to seek the best available market price for the milk or due to the cooperative's failure to notify the dairyman sooner about the loss of a good market for milk.[157]

If a tenant has stipulated that his coop actually has fulfilled its duty to repair a roof leak, in a settlement of his suit to avoid a special assessment, he cannot then obtain a court hearing and introduction of evidence, if he presents no issue of material fact in his renewed application.[158]

Coop Tenant Eviction

Where a nonprofit landlord's certificate of incorporation imposed various governmental restrictions on a cooperative apartment project, the conduct of the cooperative was not private and was sufficiently entwined with the government to trigger due process protections for the tenants, including proper notice and reasons for eviction.[159]

Coop Tax Rules

Loss carryback for tax deductions claimed by Subchapter S agricultural cooperatives, that are social clubs or membershihp organizations, are prohibited where they are losses incurred in furnishing services, insurance, goods or other items of value to members. Such cooperatives have to pass investment tax credits onto their patrons.[160]

A telephone cooperative cannot obtain a refund of sales taxes, collected on the rates it charges its customers, to the extent that the charges are in excess of its costs.[161]

Coop. Customer Land Rights

An electric cooperative customer impliedly consents to entry on the customer's land, by the coop's agents, to check up on condition of the electric equipment there and its possible misuse; that is not actionable trespass.[162]

Coop. Conversion

In a proposed *conversion* of an apartment house into cooperative ownership, the Attorney General under Art. 23-A of the N.Y. General Business Law (Martin Act), in an application for acceptance of the plan, must *notify* the petitioners within 180 days of the filing if he cannot make a decision as to an excessive number of long-term vacancies. Violation of the "excessive etc." provision of N.Y. Gen. Bus. L. § 352-e, subd. 2, is not a "deficiency" in the plan contemplated by that section.[163]

§381. CONDOMINIUMS AND COOPERATIVES COMPARED

Cooperatives have certain characteristics that distinguish them from other business organizational forms. While no single characteristic is all-controlling, generally a cooperative has the following characteristics: "(1) Control and ownership of each member is substantially equal; (2) Members are limited to those who will avail themselves of the services furnished by the association; (3) Transfer of ownership is prohibited or limited; (4) Capital investment receives either no return or a limited return; (5) economic benefits pass to the members on a substantially equal basis or on the basis of their patronage of the association; (6) members are not personally liable for obligations of the association in absence of a direct undertaking or authorization by them; (7) death, bankruptcy or withdrawal of one or more members does not terminate the association: (8) services of the association are furnished primarily for the use of the members."[164]

In comparing condominiums with cooperatives, cooperative apartments best illustrate the similarities and differences between the two forms. In a cooperative of this type, each owner has "(1) an interest in the entity owning the building; and (2) a lease entitling him to occupy a particular [unit] within the building."[165]

"Although the condominium has been regarded as just one form of cooperative . . . a division between . . . cooperatives and condominiums . . . has crystalized."[166] In this sense, a cooperative has come to indicate "a corporate or business trust entity holding title to the premises and granting rights of occupancy to particular apartments by means of proprietory leases or similar arrangements."[167] On the other hand, the condominium "refers specifically to schemes of individual ownership of individual units usually organized pursuant to statutory authority."[168] While both cooperatives and condominiums have advantages and disadvantages, "[t]he consensus of modern writers is that the advantages of the condominium system far outweigh both its disadvantages and the advantages of the cooperative venture."[169]

A cooperative housing venture now often is treated as very similar to unit ownership in a condominium, the stock assignments being allocated in proportion to the individual unit value, and both basically being viewed by the legislatures like any other interest in real property.[170]

Some advantages of the condominium include the following.

Tax Advantages

"The deductions for interest on a mortgage and for property taxes from income for federal income tax purposes are available to the unit owner of a condominium."[171] While these deductions are also available to cooperators, "[t]here is a danger of tenant cooperators being unable to take this deduction if the amount of the cooperative's gross income in any year falls below 80 percent."[172] But note the 1986 Tax Code amendments.[173] Also in this area, a condominium owner may "deduct uninsured casualty losses unconnected with a trade of business, while a member in a cooperative can't."[174] Finally, the tax assessment in a condominium is an individual assessment on the unit and its share of the common elements. In the cooperative, there is one tax bill on the entire building. If some owners don't pay their share, the others must pay for them or face tax foreclosure proceedings.

Financing Advantages

"The condominium owner may mortgage his real estate interest as he sees fit. If he does, the mortgage only covers his unit and its share of the common elements."[175]

In a cooperative, "the mortgage covers the entire property. If any substantial number of tenants default, the foreclosure would wipe out all tenants. To avoid this, non-defaulting unit owners would have to carry the defaulting owners."[176]

Psychological Advantages

"The condominium owner holds title to the unit."[177] He owns his own unit, in fee simple, the same as an individual who buys a home. "The social status that is said to be the natural concomitant of home ownership (as opposed to leasing—as in a cooperative) attaches to the condominium unit."[178]

"By contrast, the property of the cooperative, including the shareholders apartment, is owned by the corporate entity."[179] "He has no direct ownership of real estate, but is only the owner of a member certificate or a corporate share or shares."[180]

§382. CREDIT UNIONS: COOPS [See "Credit Unions" in the Index]

Bankers complain that Credit Unions are really tax-free banks competing in business and should be taxed as a $20 billion-a-year business of taking-and-lending money. They are filing lawsuits and lobbying to restrict the CUs at least as to rent-free quarters in government buildings and freedom to enroll anyone in their specific *or related* "common bond" basis of membership. Florida, for example, in 1990 had 365 credit unions with 2.5 million members and $9.1 billion in assets. Nationally there were about 15,000 CUs with 62 million members and $215 billion in assets. They are (F)inancial Cooperatives enabling people to pool their funds and give financial services to their members, and they do pay taxes on "unrelated business activities."[181]

Rhode Island's governor closed 45 financial institutions, including 35 credit unions, in 1991 (a "bank holiday" for a week) because of insolvency caused by management making too many bad *commercial* loans. Embezzlement by its president of $15 million caused failure of the biggest CU and triggered the collapse. But the frightened depositors were assured by the governor that the state treasury (or taxpayers' money) would bail out their organizations. Most states (such as Florida) have federal depositors' insurance and do not engage in such commercial lending as ruined the R.I. institutions.[182]

Only governmental authorities, not borrowers, may question whether a loan properly used terms beyond those permitted by statute. There is no penalty provided by Congress under Federal Credit Union Act § 107 (12 U.S.C. § 1757).[183]

§383. SUMMARY OF CONDO UNIT OWNER RIGHTS AND RESPONSIBILITIES

[This was issued by the Florida Department of Business Regulation, Division of Florida Land Sales, Condominium & Mobile Homes; Tallahassee, FL (in 1985).]

For more information contact: The Education Section,
Bureau of Condominiums, Johns Building, Tallahassee,
Florida 32301-1927 (904) 488-0725 or toll free in
Florida 1-800-342-8081

Other Informational Brochures
on Condominiums by
Division of Florida Land Sales
Condominiums and Mobile Homes

Condominium Living in Florida
Guide to Purchasing a Condominium Unit
Insuring the Condominium: An Insurance Guide
for the Condominium Unit Owners
Condominium and Cooperative Conversions

You may obtain copies of these materials from your local library or from the Division of Florida Land Sales,

Condominiums and Mobile Homes from the Tallahassee office or:

Suite 903
1313 North Tampa Street
Tampa, Florida 33602
(813) 272-3845
or
Emerald Hills Plaza II
4651 Sheridan Street, Suite 480
Hollywood, Florida 33021
(305) 963-1440

The information contained herein is based on
existing law and is subject to change.

May, 1985

Introduction

The State of Florida, through its Condominium and Cooperative Acts, provides for a number of rights for owners of condominium and cooperative units. These rights are balanced with several major responsibilities tied to these forms of real property ownership. The purpose of this brochure is to summarize unit owners' rights and responsibilities under the Condominium Act (Chapter 718 of the Florida Statutes) and the Cooperative Act (Chapter 719 of the Florida Statutes). The rights are listed in the order that they appear in the statutes. The specific statute reference is listed after each right. You should refer to that section of the statute for the exact language of the designated provision. For a copy of these statutes or for more information pertaining to these rights and responsibilities, you may contact: The Education Section, Bureau of Condominiums, Johns Building, Tallahassee, Florida 32301-1927, (904) 488-0725. Toll free in Florida 1-800-342-8081.

Rights

Unit owners have the right to . . .

1. Exclusive ownership of the condominium unit, exclusive lease of the cooperative unit. Section 718.103(23) and Section 719.103(14)

2. Membership in the association. Section 718.104(4)(i) and Section 719.105(1)

3. Vote as described in the declaration of condominium or cooperative documents. [Not proxy-elections now.]

4. Veto any changes in the share of ownership or common expenses and material alterations in their unit unless the declaration as originally recorded provides for less than 100% approval for such changes. Section 718.110(4) and Section 719.106(3)

5. Full voting rights appurtenant to the unit. Section 718.106(2)(d), no provision in the Cooperative Act

6. Use of the common elements and association property without payment of a fee unless such use is the subject of a lease between the association and the unit owner. Section 718.111(4), no provision in the Cooperative Act

7. Inspect the condominium or cooperative records at reasonable times. Make or obtain copies of the records at the reasonable expense, if any, of the association member. Section 718.111(12) and Section 719.104(2) *(Copies not provided for in Chapter 719)

8. Inspect all association insurance policies at any reasonable time. Section 718.111(11)(a) and Section 719.104(3)

9. Inspect minutes of all meetings of unit owners and the board at any reasonable time. Section 718.111(12)(a) 6. and Section 719.106(1)(e)

10. Receive a financial report of the actual receipts and expenditures of the association annually. Section 718.111(13) and Section 719.104(5)

11. Vote by proxy. Section 718.112(2)(b) 1. and Section 719.106(1)(b)

12. Right to revoke a proxy. Section 718.112(2)(b)2. and Section 719.106(1)(b)

13. Receive 48-hour notice, posted conspicuously on the condominium or cooperative property, of board meetings. Section 718.112(2)(c) and Section 719.106(1)(c)

14. Be permitted admission to all board meetings at which a quorum of the board is conducting condominium or cooperative business. Section 718.112(2)(c), Section 719.106(1)(c) and Rule 7D-23.01(1), Florida Administrative Code

15. Be advised, in the posted notice described in item 13, when the board meeting is meeting for the purpose of considering assessments and the nature of any such assessments. Section 718.112(2)(c) and Section 719.106(1)(c)

16. Be nominated from the floor to be a candidate for board membership. Section 718.112(2)(d)1. and Section 719.106(1)(d)

17. Receive at least 14 days' written notice of the annual meeting. The notice must also be posted in a conspicuous place on condominium property. Section 718.112(2)(d)2. and Section 719.106(1)(d)

18. Receive not less than 14 days written notice of budget adoption meetings and a copy of the proposed budget (Section 718.112(2)(e), condominiums). Receive not less than 30 days written notice of budget adoption meetings and a copy of the proposed budget (Section 719.106(1)(f), cooperatives)

19. Object, along with a majority of the other unit owners, to any budget over 115 percent of the previous year's assessments. Section 718.112(2)(e) and Section 719.106(1)(f). In developer controlled associations, a majority of the unit owners must approve an assessment for any year greater than 115 percent of the prior year's assessment. Section 718.112(2)(e) and Section 719.106(1)(f)5

20. Pay assessments on a quarterly or more frequent basis. Section 718.112(2)(g) and Section 719.106(1)(g)

21. Join with a majority of the other unit owners to recall any board member. Section 718.112(2)(k) and Section 719.106(1)(k)

22. Arbitration of dispute involving recall of board members. Only one side needs to submit this type of dispute and the result will be binding on both parties. Section 718.112(2)(k), no provision in the Cooperative Act

23. Apply to the circuit court for the appointment of a receiver if the association fails to fill vacancies on the board sufficient to constitute a quorum. Section 718.1124 and Section 718.1064

24. Expect maintenance of the common elements by the association. Section 718.113(1) and Section 719.103(2)

25. Require the association to enforce a recorded claim of lien against their condominium parcels by filing a notice of contest of lien. Section 718.116(4)(a), and Section 719.108(4)

26. Receive written notice from the association 30 days before foreclosure action is filed. Section 718.116(5)(b), no provision in the Cooperative Act

27. Require the association to provide a certificate showing the amount of unpaid assessments against them with respect to their parcels. Section 718.116(7) and Section 719.108(6)

28. Receive notification of any special assessment which shall state the specific purpose of the special assessment. Upon completion of the project any excess funds will be considered common surplus. If the funds are not used for the purpose intended, the funds will be returned to the unit owners. Section 718.116(9), no provision in the Cooperative Act

29. Receive notice from the association of its exposure to liability in excess of insurance coverage protecting it against legal action within a reason-

able time so the unit owners have the opportunity to intervene and defend on their own behalf. Section 718.119(3), no provision in the Cooperative Act

30. Use the common elements, common areas and recreation facilities serving their condominium/cooperative according to the association's properly adopted rules and regulations. Sections 718.106, 718.123 and Section 719.105, 719.109

31. Obtain access to any available franchised or licensed cable television service without charge to receive such service except those charges normally paid for like services by residents of single family homes except for installation charges agreed to between the residents and providers of the service. Section 718.1232, no provision in the Cooperative Act

32. Arbitration of disputes based on voluntary submission of both sides to the arbitration proceedings. Section 718.1255, no provision in the Cooperative Act

33. Bring action for damages or for injunctive relief, or both, against the association, another unit owner, directors designated by the developer or any director who willfully and knowingly fails to comply with Chapters 718, 719, or the association and condominium/cooperative documents. The prevailing party is entitled to recover reasonable attorney's fees. Section 718.303(1) and Section 719.303(1)

Responsibilities

Under Florida law, unit owners have the responsibility to . . .

1. Pay their shares of the common expenses as defined in the statute and their documents. Sections 718.103(7), 718.115, 718.116, and Sections 719.103(6), 719.107, and 719.108

2. Use the common elements in a manner which will not hinder or encroach on the rights of the other unit owners. Section 718.106(3) and Section 719.105(2)

3. Provide access to their units to the association for the maintenance, repair, or replacement of any common elements or for making emergency repairs necessary to prevent damage to the common elements or to other unit or units. Section 718.111(5) and Section 719.104(1)

4. Not make any alterations to their units which would adversely affect the safety or soundness of the common elements or any portion of the condominium property which is to be maintained by the association. Section 718.113(3), no provision in the Cooperative Act

5. Comply with the provisions of Chapters 718 and 719, the declaration of condominium or documents creating the cooperative, the articles of incorporation and the bylaws. Section 718.303(1) and Section 719.303(1)

6. Comply with provisions of the declaration, association bylaws or rules as the condominium documents may provide for the levying of a fine for failure to comply. Section 718.303(3), no provision in the Corporate Act Section

718.119(2) of the Condominium Act states that a unit owner may be personally liable for the acts and omissions of the association in relation to the use of the common elements. Section 607.074 of the Corporate Act contains similar provisions applicable to cooperatives. Unit owners should therefore, take on the additional responsibilities of:

1. Attending and participating in all unit owner meetings.
2. Attending or reading the minutes of all board meetings.
3. Voting on all issues and elections.
4. Cooperating with other unit owners in day-to-day community life.
5. Bringing any concerns or problems to the attention of the board of directors.
6. Serving on the board of directors when needed.
7. Being familiar with the provisions of their condominium/cooperative documents.

Criminal-injury-liability of unit owners is proportionate to "control" by them.

L.M. Dial article, 41 *Pinellas County Review* (1)5 (Jan. 1, 1993).

§384. CONDOMINIUM FORMS

[See also, "Bylaws," etc.; "Leases," etc., Forms.]

FORM No. 158

Condominium
Bylaws
of
_____ Yacht Club Condominium,
Building B, Incorporated
[5940 _____ Plaza:
High-Rise Buildings and Grounds
(in the _____ Yacht and Country Club Area)
_____, Florida 33707]
[valid when appended to the recorded Declaration of Condominium]

Chapter 1

Identify

Section 1. These are the Bylaws of _____ YACHT CLUB CONDOMINIUM, BUILDING B, INC., called The Association by these Bylaws, a nonprofit corporation formed under Florida Statutes Chapter 718, which Association, located on the lands described in the Declaration of Condominium in the Prospectus of the Development (_____ Realty Development Division) dated March 3, 19___, came into the control of its unit owners other than the developer in 19___.

Section 2. The office of the Association shall be at 5940 _____ Plaza, _____, FL 33707, in _____ County.

Section 3. The Association shall use the Calendar Year as its fiscal year.

Section 4. The seal of the Association shall bear its name and the words "Condominium Nonprofit Corporation."

Chapter II

The Association

Section 1. The owners of the condominium units shall be the members of this Association.

Section 2. The owners of units may be individual persons or legal entities capable of ownership of real property under the laws of Florida.

Section 3. Upon acquiring title to a unit the owner of it shall become a member of the Association, and upon that owner conveying or transferring said ownership that membership shall automatically cease.

Section 4. Meetings of the members shall be held at the condo building.

Section 5. Annual meetings of the members of the Association shall be held on the first Thursday of March in each year, except that if that date falls on a legal holiday then the meeting shall be held on the first secular day thereafter. At the Annual Meeting the members may transact such business of the Association as may properly be brought up at such meetings under Florida law. The hour and place of that meeting shall be set by the board of directors.

Section 6. Special meetings of the members may be called by the President, or by the Secretary upon the written requests of five (5) members, and such requests shall state the purpose(s) of the proposed meeting.

Section 7. Notices of annual or special meetings shall be mailed by the Secretary to every member, stating the time and place and purpose(s), addressed to each member's address as listed on the membership rolls, at least fourteen days before the annual and five days before a special meeting date. Mailing, duly certified by a written statement of the Secretary, shall be deemed service of notice.

Section 8. Minutes of all meetings shall be kept by the Secretary and be available for inspection by members at reasonable business hours, and retained for seven years.

Section 9. A quorum for meetings shall consist of at least 51 percent of the total number of unit owners, except as provided otherwise by these bylaws for certain specific decisions. If a quorum cannot be obtained because of failure of members to attend, then those present may adjourn the meeting to a new date certain duly noticed to all members for not more than ten days thereafter, and at that later-noticed meeting a quorum shall consist of those members then present.

Section 10. Voting at meetings of members shall be by one vote per condo unit, and a majority vote rules, except as provided otherwise by these bylaws for certain specific decisions. If a unit is owned by more than one person the person entitled to cast that unit's vote shall be designated by a written certificate signed by all the co-owners of record on the Association rolls. If a corporation owns a unit, its certificate for the person casting its vote shall be signed by its president or secretary. Certificates of designation of the person to vote on behalf of a unit may be revoked by an owner of a share of that unit.

Section 11. Members may vote by written proxy, general or special in nature, filed with the secretary seven (7) days before the meeting hour; but a proxy may be revoked by the owner, particularly by attending the meeting in person. A proxy may be valid for no more than ninety days after its date and only for the particular meeting or its adjourned (continued) sessions.

Section 12. The Order of Business at a meeting of members shall be as follows:

   a. Roll call.
   b. Proof of notice of meeting or waiver thereof.
   c. Reading and correction of minutes of the preceding meeting.
   d. Reports of officers.
   e. Reports of committees.
   f. Election voting (if an election meeting).
   g. Old business.
   h. New business.
   i. Adjournment.

Section 13. Parliamentary procedure at members' meetings, insofar as not provided for herein or in the bylaws or the statutes of Florida, shall be according to *Oleck & Green, Parliamentary Law and Practice for Nonprofit Organizations* (ALI-ABA, 2d ed., 1991). General guidance on principles and concepts of good operation of nonprofit organizations shall be based on *Oleck & Green, Nonprofit Corporations, Organizations & Associations* (6th edition, 1994, Prentice Hall, Inc., Englewood Cliffs, NJ); with annual supplements.

Section 14. A unit owner in this condominium association may lease that owner's unit to a tenant who will occupy the unit subject to the bylaws and other rules of the association, subject also to the following provisions:

   a. The consent of the board of director's president, in writing, must be obtained before the lease is granted, and that consent shall not be denied for reasons of racial or religious or other such civil rights discrimination; but the leasing of units basically is not favored in this condominium. The board shall have the power to adopt rules regulating the method by which approval shall be granted.
   b. No more than a maximum of seven units in the condominium may be leased-out at any one time, and no further leasing shall be permitted when seven units have been leased, until one or more of those leases has

ended; the unit owners agreeing that this is a unit-owner residential association in its essence and that such essence-quality should be maintained.
The "loan" of a condominium unit shall be prohibited. Where a unit is
occupied by a person or persons other than the recorded owner or his
family members and such occupancy exceeds thirty (30) days in a calendar year, such occupancy shall be deemed to be a lease or rental of the
unit, and the provisions of Section 14(a) above, shall apply.

c. A lessor shall continue to be fully responsible to the association as a unit
owner, and the lessee shall be responsible as a unit occupant.

d. Leases may be made only once a year, and only for residential, not business, occupance, and shall be for a minimum of six months and a maximum of two years in duration, with renewal options subject to the limitations above stated (subd. b) as to total number of leases in effect at the
time of renewal.

e. Leasehold law as to condominiums stated in Florida Statute §718.401
shall apply to leases insofar as that statute is relevant, such as its provisions as to the lessor's obligations, reservation of possession or control of
the leased property, conspicuousness of disclosure of reservations, subordination to mortgages or liens, escalation clauses, etc.

Chapter III

Management

Section 1. The Board of Directors of the Association shall manage its regular affairs. The Board shall consist of seven (7) directors elected by the unit
owners. All directors shall be members of the Association or designees of the
developer as to units unsold by the developer. Directors shall be elected by
majority vote at the Annual Meetings of the Association, to be for terms respectively of one year each for two directors in 19___, of two years each for two
directors in 19___, and of three years each for three directors in 19___, and
similar numbers thereafter (2 one-year in 19___) (2 two-year in 19___) (3
three-year in 19___) so as to maintain experienced (rotating) board membership.

Section 2. Directors may be removed, with or without cause, by a written
vote of a majority at a meeting called by 10 percent of owners, and vacancies
on the board may be filled by special or general election by the owners. Termination of ownership of a director shall also be termination of that person's
membership on the board. Interim vacancies on the board, pending such special election, shall be filled by the remaining directors' votes.

Section 3. In managing the Association affairs, the board may do all things
reasonably lawful, necessary, and proper for such purposes, including enforcement of the Condominium Articles and Bylaws and functions stated in the
Florida laws, and also:

a. To prepare and propose an annual operating budget, for approval by the members invited as detailed below in Chapter V Section 1, to pay for the common expenses of the common areas for the coming year, plus a reasonable reserve for upkeep and repair and replacement of common elements and for contingencies.

b. To prepare and present a detailed report for the Annual Meeting of the owners.

c. To select or change legal counsel for the Association when necessary.

d. To select or change the fiscal depository of the Association.

e. To select or change maintenance and operation personnel, and set their salaries.

f. To assess and collect assessments, and funds for reserves.

g. To furnish by mail or personal delivery a complete financial report for each unit owner for the preceding fiscal year, showing management and services fees, security costs, taxes, utilities costs, insurance costs, recreation costs, grounds care costs, other administrative costs, reserves for various purposes, and other relevant data; such reports also going, upon written requests, to mortgagees, insurers, guarantors and other interested parties entitled thereto. Audited reports shall be employed if so requested by the Association membership by 60 percent vote.

Section 4. All books, records and documents of the Association such as the Declaration of Condominium, Bylaws, Minutes, financial reports, proxies, and the like, shall be available for inspection by unit owners of their guarantors or mortgagees or insurers, in the office of the Association at reasonable business hours.

Section 5. A management agent may be employed (or changed) by the Board to see to routine operation of the Association properly and functions, at a salary to be set by the Board, but always under the overriding authority and powers and duties of the Association Board of Directors and Officers.

Section 6. Directors shall receive no compensation for their services as directors, and if specifically retained to perform specific services as an officer shall be reasonably compensated for such employment only to the extent specifically authorized in advance by a two-thirds vote of the Board.

Section 7. Regular Board meetings shall be held, as determined by the Board, at least in January, July, September, and November, on at least four days notice by personal notice or by mail, phone or telegram for each meeting, on dates set by the President. (See Chapter II, Section 5 for the Annual Meeting.)

Section 8. Special meetings of the Board may be called by the President on four days notice personally or by mail or telephone or telegram, stating the time and place and purpose(s), or by the President or Secretary on similar notice on written request of two or more directors.

Section 9. All unit owners shall be invited to attend all Board meetings, by notice conspicuously posted at least three days in advance, except in an emergency. If assessments are to be considered, that fact, and the nature thereof, shall be specifically stated in the notices.

Section 10. Waiver of notice of a meeting of the Board may be made, in writing, by a director, and attendance without specific objection by the director shall be deemed waiver of notice.

Section 11. Minutes of board meetings shall be made and kept available for inspection by owners during reasonable business hours, and retained for seven years.

Section 12. A quorum of directors shall be a majority of the Board. If no quorum is present at the beginning of a meeting, it may be adjourned by the vote of a majority of those present to a date certain, at least three days later, at which time those present then shall constitute a quorum.

Section 13. The Board shall obtain Fidelity Bonding coverage for each director, at Association expense.

Section 14. The officers of the Association shall be elected at the Annual Meeting of Members by the unit owners, on nomination by a committee to be named by the President, or from the floor, to hold office for one year, at the pleasure of the Board of Directors, subject to removal by a majority vote of the Board with or without cause, and replaced when necessary, at the next meeting of the Board, for the balance of the year. The officers shall be elected by the board:

a. President; the chief executive officer, who presides at all meetings, with the powers usual for a president of a nonprofit condominium association in Florida law.

b. Vice President; to act in the place of the president, when the President is absent or unable to act, and to perform such other duties as the Board may specify for this officer. If the President and Vice President are unable to act, the board of directors shall appoint some other member of the board to do so on an interim basis.

c. Secretary; to keep minutes of meetings and books and records, and to send notices and reports as specified herein and by law.

d. Treasurer; to have charge of Association funds and securities, and to keep written accounts and records of financial receipts and disbursements, and be responsible for moneys and valuables and supervision of assets in depositaries of the Association. The Treasurer shall be bonded at Association expense.

Section 15. No lessee shall be elected to serve as an officer or member of the board of directors.

Chapter IV

Assessments

Section 1. Each unit owner shall share that percentage of the common expenses, and own that percentage of the common surplus, in direct proportion to the percentage of the common elements of the Association owned by said unit owner. Assessments for the common expenses shall be secured by a lien against the condo unit against which it is made, in favor of the Association, with priority status except as to the institutional first mortgage purchase lien on the unit. Assessments shall be made not less frequently than quarterly, in advance of need for the sums.

Section 2. Special assessments may be decided by the board with the approval of the majority of unit owners.

Chapter V

Annual Budget

Section 1. Pursuant to Chapter III Section 3a of these Bylaws, the Board of Directors shall send notices and copies of the proposed budget before a proposed meeting for adopting a budget for the next fiscal year, not less than thirty days before the Annual Meeting, inviting all unit owners to attend. The budget shall be adopted by majority vote of the unit owners, after amendments (if any) to the specific proposals are voted by the unit owners.

Section 2. The Annual Budget shall show in detail the amounts for all classifications of functions and expenses involved, at least as detailed as the list in Florida Statutes Section 718.504(20). It also shall show reserve accounts for probable capital and deferred maintenance expenses based on estimated life and replacement costs of reserve items such as roofs, painting, paving, and the like.

Section 3. Budgets exceeding 115 percent of the preceding year's budget assessments shall be adopted in accordance with Florida Statute Section 718.112(2)(f).

Chapter VI

Amendments

Section 1. Amendments of these Bylaws may be made only by two-thirds vote of members of the Association, on at least fourteen days notice of a meeting at which the proposed (stated) amendment's details will be presented; the notice stating the reason(s) for the proposal(s), as provided in Florida Statutes Section 718.112(2)(i).

Chapter VII

Mortgagees' Notices

Section 1. Institutional mortgagees of purchase money mortgages of units, shall, upon written request to the Association identifying the unit and name and address and lien-type of the mortgagee and mortgagor, be entitled to timely notice of

a. Any casualty or condemnation loss affecting a substantial part of the affected unit or condo;

b. Any delinquency in payment of assessments or charges by such unit owner that is unpaid for 60 days;

c. Any cancellation, material modification, or lapse of the fidelity bond or insurance policy maintained by the Association;

d. Any proposed action that would require the consent of a specified percentage of first mortgage holders, guarantors, or insurers.

Chapter VIII

Adoption (Amendment) of Bylaws

The forgoing amended Bylaws of _____ Yacht Club Condominium, Building B, Inc., a Florida nonprofit corporation, were adopted by the unit owners of the Association at a duly convened meeting held at the condominium on _____, 19___.

> Certified by
>
> _____
>
> (Name)
> Secretary

FORM NO. 159

Condominium Purchase
(Set of Documents)
Yacht Club Condominium,
Building B
Purchase Agreement

THIS AGREEMENT, made and entered into this _____ day of _____, A.D. 19___, by and between _____ CORPORATION, formerly known as _____ CORPORATION, a Delaware corporation authorized to do business in the State of Florida, hereinafter referred to as the "Seller," and whose mailing address is ——————— ————, and whose out of town address is ———————————, hereinafter referred to as the "Purchaser,"

WITNESSETH

WHEREAS, the Purchaser desires to purchase a living unit in _____ _____ YACHT CLUB CONDOMINIUM, BUILDING B, a condominium situated in _____ County, Florida, upon real estate described as follows:

That certain condominium parcel described as Unit Number ————————
together with its appurtenances as described in the Declaration of Condominium of
———————————— YACHT CLUB CONDOMINIUM, BUILDING B, and related
documents as recorded in OR. Book 5505, Pages 1080 through 1138, and the plat
thereof recorded in Condominium Plat Book 67, Pages 121 through 132, all in the
Public Records of ———————————— County, Florida.

WHEREAS, the Purchaser desires to acquire from the Seller, and the Seller desires to convey to the Purchaser, a condominium parcel as aforesaid described, to wit: the condominium unit described as Unit Number _____
in said Declaration of Condominium above described, together with appurtenances thereto, said Unit not having been previously occupied.

NOW, THEREFORE, in consideration of the mutual covenants herein contained, it is agreed between the parties hereto that Purchaser shall buy and Seller shall sell the above described property under the following terms and conditions:

ORAL REPRESENTATIONS CANNOT BE RELIED UPON AS CORRECTLY STATING THE REPRESENTATIONS OF THE DEVELOPER. FOR CORRECT REPRESENTATIONS REFERENCE SHOULD BE MADE TO THIS CONTRACT AND THE DOCUMENTS REQUIRED BY THE FLORIDA STATUTES SECTION 718.503 TO BE FURNISHED BY A DEVELOPER TO A PURCHASER OR LESSEE.

1. Purchase Price $ _____
   Authorized Extras $ _____
   _____ $ _____
   _____ $ _____
   _____ $ _____
   _____ $ _____
   Total Purchase Price $ _____

The above total purchase price shall be paid to the Seller as follows:
a. Cash deposit made herewith $ _____
b. Balance of required 10 percent
   deposit to be made on or
   before _____ $ _____
c. Balance upon the closing of this
   transaction by cashier's check,
   bank draft or certified check, as
   adjusted for prorations
                                      $ _____
        Total $ _____
d. In addition to the above, Purchaser will be required to pay to the Condominium Association at closing the sum of $100, to be used by the Association for a capital improvement and working capital reserve.

_____
_____
_____
_____
_____
_____
_____
_____

2. This transaction shall be closed on or before _____.
The closing shall take place at such place as may be designated by seller or by any mortgagee.

3. In the event there are unsold units at the date of closing and if the Seller should retain any of said units, it may rent them on a _____ _____ basis notwithstanding anything to the contrary which may be contained in the proposed Declaration of Condominium. Seller reserves the right to maintain model apartments in the condominium from which to conduct sales in the condominium project until all units in the project are sold.

4. a. Insurable fee simple title to the condominium parcel shall be conveyed by warranty deed, free and clear of all encumbrances, except for the provisions of the Declaration of Condominium and related documents and restrictions, reservations and easements of record.

b. At the time of closing of this transaction Seller will deliver to Purchaser, at Seller's expense, an owner's title insurance binder in the face amount of the purchase price of said condominium unit, which binder may be subject to standard title insurance exceptions and will be subject to the provisions of the Declaration of Condominium and related documents recorded in the Public Records of _____ County, Florida. Seller further agrees to place all proper revenue stamps on the deed, with the Purchaser to pay the cost of recording same. Taxes, insurance and any other portable items will be prorated as of the date of closing.

5. From the date of closing, the Purchaser will be liable for the payment of assessments, if any, allocable to the subject proposed condominium unit. Purchaser will also be liable for his pro rata share of the monthly maintenance fee which said pro rata share shall be collected at the time of closing. In the event Purchaser fails to close on the date and at the time provided herein, Purchaser will nevertheless be liable for payment of monthly maintenance fees and assessments, if any, from the date the closing otherwise should have been held pursuant to the terms of this Agreement.

6. At the time of closing herein, Purchaser (if more than one purchaser, designation shall be made by a written statement filed with the Secretary of the Association pursuant to the Declaration of Condominium naming who shall serve as proxy) shall automatically be a member in _____ YACHT CLUB CONDOMINIUM, BUILDING B, INC., a nonprofit Florida corporation, which corporation administers the affairs of the condominium. Such

membership shall entitle the holder thereof to one (1) vote in the management affairs of the nonprofit corporation, in accordance with the provisions of the Articles of Incorporation of said Association.

7. In the event that the Purchaser should fail to pay any sums due under this Purchase Agreement to the Seller within ten (10) days from the date that same becomes due, or should fail or refuse to execute any and all of the necessary documents and instruments required of him promptly and when requested by the Seller, or should in any other manner fail to conform strictly with the terms and conditions of this Purchase Agreement, then, at Seller's option, this Agreement shall immediately become null and void and shall no longer be binding upon any of the parties hereto. In such event any and all deposits or payments made under this Agreement shall be retained by the Seller as liquidated and agreed damages. It is understood by the parties hereto that this provision is placed in the Agreement for the specific reason that nonperformance by the Purchaser in accordance with this agreement will have an adverse financial effect upon the Seller by reason of said apartment having been withdrawn from the market; that the Purchaser acknowledges that this is a fair provision to protect the Seller in the event of default on the part of the Purchaser. In the event Seller defaults under this Purchase Agreement, the Purchaser's sole remedies shall be the return of any deposits paid, together with interest earned thereon, or the remedy of specific performance.

8. The Purchaser hereby agrees to conform with and abide by all of the terms, conditions and provisions of the Declaration of Condominium recorded in the Public Records of _____ County, Florida, relative to the property hereinabove described.

9. Purchaser understands and agrees that Seller is contracting with him/her personally and agrees that this Purchase Agreement or any of the rights hereunder may not be transferred or assigned by the Purchaser without first obtaining the written consent of the Seller.

10. The parties both agree that any changes in the proposed layout of the unit hereinabove described or any additional work done at the request of Purchaser by the Seller shall, prior to the commencement of such work or the alteration of said unit, be reduced to writing and executed by both the Purchaser and the Seller wherein the parties hereto agree to such changes, alterations, or additions, and the cost of same.

11. This Purchase Agreement is subject to Purchaser being approved for membership in the _____ YACHT CLUB CONDOMINIUM, BUILDING B, INC. Application shall be made at the time of signing of this Agreement, or a reasonable time thereafter, with said approval to be obtained in writing prior to closing, otherwise a refund shall be given and all further liability hereunder shall terminate.

12. It is agreed by and between the parties hereto that time is of the essence of this Agreement and that all covenants and agreements herein contained shall extend to and be obligatory upon the heirs, executors, administrators, and assigns of the respective parties.

13. This Agreement constitutes the entire Agreement between the parties and merges and extinguishes all prior negotiations, and no modifications hereto shall be valid unless and until it is in writing and signed by the parties hereto.

14. Pursuant to Section 718.503, Florida Statutes, the Purchaser acknowledges that he has received a copy of the floor plan of the unit and a copy of the prospectus or offering circular required by Section 718.503, Florida Statutes, simultaneously herewith with the exception of the following (if all received, so indicate):

THIS AGREEMENT IS VOIDABLE BY PURCHASER BY DELIVERING WRITTEN NOTICE OF THE PURCHASER'S INTENTION TO CANCEL WITHIN FIFTEEN (15) DAYS AFTER THE DATE OF EXECUTION OF THIS AGREEMENT BY THE PURCHASER, AND RECEIPT BY PURCHASER OF ALL OF THE ITEMS REQUIRED TO BE DELIVERED TO HIM BY THE DEVELOPER UNDER SECTION 718.503, FLORIDA STATUTES. THIS AGREEMENT IS ALSO VOIDABLE BY PURCHASER BY DELIVERING WRITTEN NOTICE OF THE PURCHASER'S INTENTION TO CANCEL WITHIN FIFTEEN (15) DAYS AFTER THE DATE OF RECEIPT FROM THE DEVELOPER OF ANY AMENDMENT WHICH MATERIALLY ALTERS OR MODIFIES THE OFFERING IN A MANNER THAT IS ADVERSE TO THE PURCHASER. ANY PURPORTED WAIVER OF THESE VOIDABLE RIGHTS SHALL BE OF NO EFFECT. PURCHASER MAY EXTEND THE TIME FOR CLOSING FOR A PERIOD OF NOT MORE THAN FIFTEEN (15) DAYS AFTER THE PURCHASER HAS RECEIVED ALL OF THE ITEMS REQUIRED. PURCHASER'S RIGHT TO VOID THIS AGREEMENT SHALL TERMINATE AT CLOSING.

---

15. All notices by one party to the other given pursuant to this Agreement shall be in writing and may be served upon either party by personal delivery or certified mail at the following addresses:

For Seller: _____ Corporation
                          6000 _____ Boulevard
                          _____, Florida 33707
For Purchaser: _____
                          _____
                          _____

16. Information regarding the type, thickness, R-value and location of insulation which is installed in each part of the condominium unit, or surrounding the same, is shown in the following table. All R-values described are based upon information received from the manufacturer of the insulation materials and do not constitute representations or warranties by the Seller.

Table of Insulation Data

Portion of Unit Insulated	Insulation Type	Thickness	R-Value
Exterior Walls	Sprayed Insulation	3/4"	5.26
	or		
	Blanket Insulation	1"	4.16
Roof	Lightweight Insulating Concrete	4.5" avg.	7.5+

17. Radon is a naturally occurring radioactive gas that, when it has accumulated in a building in sufficient quantities, may present health risks to persons who are exposed to it over time. Levels of radon that exceed federal and state guidelines have been found in buildings in Florida. Additional information regarding radon and radon testing may be obtained from your county public health unit.

IN WITNESS WHEREOF, the parties hereto have set their hands and seals the day and year first hereinabove written.

Witnesses:

_____ _____ (Seal) _____ (Date)

_____ _____ (Seal) _____ (Date)

As to Purchaser   PURCHASER

Witnesses: CORPORATION

_____ By _____ (Seal) _____

_____ (Date)

As to Seller   Project Manager _____

                                    _____ Development Division

                                    of _____ Group

                                                                SELLER

Contract Addendum for Building B

THIS ADDENDUM is made this _____ day of _____ _____, 1988, with respect to the Purchase Agreement entered into between _____ CORPORATION, as Seller, and _____, as Purchaser, dated _____, 19___, for the purchase of Unit

_____, _____ Yacht Club Condo-
minium, Building B., hereinafter "Purchase Agreement."

Included with the purchase of the condominium unit, Purchaser shall
receive the exclusive right to use carport parking space number _____,
hereinafter "Carport", as shown on the attached Exhibit "A" under the following terms and conditions:

a) Seller, its successors or assigns shall have the right to construct a parking
   garage "Parking Garage 2" where the Carport is located, with the parking
   garage to serve this condominium and _____ Yacht Club
   Condominium, Building C that may be developed on property adjacent
   to the east of Parking Garage 2.

b) Upon commencement of construction of the Parking Garage 2, Purchaser shall be deemed to have released and transferred any right, title, interest or claim that he has in the Carport to Seller.

c) In consideration for Purchaser releasing all interest in the Carport, Purchaser shall be assigned a parking space, "Parking Space" in the Parking
   Garage 2 as a limited common element appurtenant to the condominium unit. Purchaser shall select the Parking Space from the spaces allocated to _____ Building B in the Parking Garage 2 and
   shall be allowed to select based chronologically on the date the purchase
   of the condominium unit is closed with respect to the date that owners
   of other units in Building B selecting parking spaces close.

d) The provisions of this Addendum shall survive the closing of the purchase
   of the condominium unit.

IN WITNESS WHEREOF, the parties have executed this Addendum
the date and year first above written.

Witnesses:

_____   _____

_____   _____

As to Purchaser   "PURCHASER"

_____   CORPORATION

_____   By: _____

As to Seller   Project Manager

                                                       "SELLER"

```
┌─────────────────────────┐
│                         │
│     PLAT SKETCH         │
│                         │
└─────────────────────────┘
```

Real Property Sales Disclosure

In accordance with Rule 2-13-03 of the Florida Real Estate Statutes, the buyer is hereby notified of the following costs for which he may be charged in the transaction on

_____

_____

IN A CASH SALE WITH NO MORTGAGES INVOLVED

> —recording of the Deed

IF NEW MORTGAGE IS TO BE OBTAINED BY THE BUYER

> —the costs will include service fees to lending institution, discount point, document tax, recording of mortgage, required survey, title policy for lender, prorated and prepaid escrows for real estate taxes and insurance, recording of the Deed, intangible tax on mortgage, appraisal fee, credit report, mortgage company attorney's fee.

IF EXISTING MORTGAGE IS TO BE ASSUMED

> —assumption fee or transfer fee, recording of the Deed, reimbursement of seller's escrow account on assumption of existing mortgage.

IF PERSONAL ATTORNEY IS RETAINED BY THE BUYER

> —Attorney's fees

It is understood that _____ REALTOR, is agent for the Sellers and that any commission due from the sale of this property will be paid by the Sellers.

Purchaser acknowledges this instrument has been read and signed before any contract to purchase real estate has been signed.

_____   ACKNOWLEDGED BY:

Date

_____   _____

Salesman   Buyer

_____   _____

Broker   Buyer

Yacht Club Condominiums
Receipt for Condominium Documents

The undersigned acknowledges that the documents checked below have been received or, as to plans and specifications, made available for inspection.

YACHT   CLUB   CONDOMINIUM-BUILDING_____
_____ Plaza, _____, Florida 33707

Place a check in the column by each document received or, for the plans and
specifications, made available for inspection.
If an item does not apply, place "N/A" in the column.

Document	Received
Prospectus Text	X
Declaration of Condominium	X
Articles of Incorporation	X
Bylaws	X
Estimated Operating Budget	X
Form of Agreement for Sale or Lease	X
Rules and Regulations	N/A
Covenants and Restrictions	N/A
Ground Lease	N/A
Management and Maintenance Contracts for More than One Year	N/A
Renewable Management Contracts	N/A
Lease of Recreational and Other Facilities to be Used Exclusively by Unit Owners of Subject Condominium	N/A
Form of Unit Lease if a Leasehold	N/A
Declaration of Servitude	N/A
Sales Brochures	X
Phase Development	X
Description (See 718.503 (2) (k) and 504 (14))	N/A
Lease of Recreational and other facilities to be used by unit owners with other condominiums (See 718.503(2) (h))	N/A
Description of Management for Single condominiums (See 718.503 (2) (k))	N/A
Description of Management of Multiple condominiums (See 718.503 (2) (k))	X
Conversion Inspection Report	N/A
Conversion Termite Inspection Report	N/A
Plot Plan	X
Floor Plan	X
Survey of Land and Graphic Description of Improvements	X
Executed Escrow Agreement	X
Plans and Specifications (Made Available)	X

THE PURCHASE AGREEMENT IS VOIDABLE BY BUYER DELIV-
ERING WRITTEN NOTICE OF THE BUYER'S INTENTION TO

CANCEL WITHIN 15 DAYS AFTER THE DATE OF EXECUTION OF THE PURCHASE AGREEMENT BY THE BUYER, AND RECEIPT BY THE BUYER OF ALL OF THE DOCUMENTS REQUIRED TO BE DELIVERED TO HIM BY THE DEVELOPER. BUYER MAY EXTEND THE TIME FOR CLOSING FOR A PERIOD OF NOT MORE THAN 15 DAYS AFTER THE BUYER HAS RECEIVED ALL OF THE DOCUMENTS REQUIRED. BUYER'S RIGHT TO VOID THE PURCHASE AGREEMENT SHALL TERMINATE AT CLOSING.

Executed this _____ day of _____, 19_____.

_____
Purchaser or Lessee

_____
Purchaser or Lessee

Memorandum to Purchasers—_____ CONDOMINIUM
COLONY CONDOMINIUM
COLONY ESTATES

Subject: Membership Availability _____ Yacht & Country Club

Due to the limited number of condominium golf memberships available in the _____ Yacht & Country Club, it is necessary that we restrict the allocation of such memberships to those who apply and qualify for memberships within thirty (30) days after the date of their closing.

A waiting list has been established for those who elect to apply for golf membership after the expiration of the aforementioned thirty (30) day period. To be on this waiting list, one must apply and be accepted in the Club as an owner golf member. Initiation fee and dues will be as stipulated at time of approval of application.

Purchasers of homesites or condominiums that are still in the process of being developed or constructed, may join the Club upon payment of applicable initiation fees and have the option to place their membership in an inactive status with no payment of monthly dues until on or before the closing date of the purchase of their new condominium or homesite.

Acknowledged:

_____
_____
_____
(Date)

Condominium Association Membership Application

( )_____ Yacht Club Condominiums

( )_____ Yacht and Country Club Condominiums

Association:_____ Series _____ Bldg: _____ Apt: _____

Estimated Monthly Maintenance Fee for Above Apartment . . . $ —————

Name: _____

            (First)   (Middle)   (Last)

Local Address (if Visiting): —————————————Phone —————————

Home Address: _____

_____ Zip:_____

Home Phone: (___)_____ Age:_____ Lifetime Occupation_____

      (Area Code)

Position Attained _____ Retired _____

Family Consists of the Following Who Will Occupy the Apartment:

Name _____ Relationship _____ Age _____

Name _____ Relationship _____ Age _____

Name _____ Relationship _____ Age _____

Any special health problems? _____

Your Doctor in the St. Petersburg area: _____

In case of emergency, notify: _____

     Address _____ Zip_____

     Phone (___)_____ Relationship _____

       Area Code

     What months do you intend to occupy the apartment? _____

     Will you have an automobile here? _____ How many? _____

     Interests: Golf ( ) Tennis ( ) Boating ( ) Fishing ( )

           Swimming ( ) Cycling ( ) Other:_____

     Pets: No ( ) Yes ( ) If "Yes", please complete "Pet Information Form"

     Are you interested in a Membership in the _____ Yacht
and Country Club? Yes ( ) No ( ) Golf ( ) Social ( )

**THE INFORMATION CONTAINED IN THIS APPLICATION WILL
BE HELD IN STRICT CONFIDENCE.**

Date _____ Signature _____

Date _____ Signature _____

Accepted by: _____ Title _____ Date _____

Final Section
Congratulations!

We are delighted to welcome you to the communities of _____ Yacht & Country Club. In order for your closing and "moving in" to progress smoothly, there are a few simple items you should be aware of:

1. If you are getting a loan to purchase your new condominium, please contact your sales representative for names and lenders who can quote competitive rates, and process your loan quickly and efficiently. In any event, you should make loan application within 5 days of contract, because favorable interest rates and mortgage plans have created an overload in the industry, and loans are not being processed as speedily as is necessary.

2. Your color selections should be made at time of contract, so that carpet can be ordered in plenty of time for proper installation.

3. You should plan to have a preliminary inspection of your unit at contract, and a final inspection before closing. Our Field Engineer is _____ _____, and all items pertaining to construction and interior finishing of your unit should be referred to Mr. _____ at 813-_____-_____, and to schedule your inspections. If you are planning to have a "mail-away" closing, Mr. _____ will meet you on your next visit to this area.

4. Questions concerning Property Management should be referred to _____. Common elements, pool, entrances, parking spaces, keys, guarantees, security etc . . . are managed by Mr. _____. Your "move-in" date should be on a week-day, and must be scheduled through Mr. _____ _____. Please call 813-_____-_____ to have Mr. _____ assign your parking space, and give you keys and instructions regarding our security system. You should plan to meet with Mr. _____ immediately after your closing. If you are closing by mail, please notify Mr. _____ when you will be arriving.

5. You should contact Florida Power at 813-895-8711 and arrange for electricity, and General Telephone at 1-800-282-2525 for telephone service. If you plan to receive cable TV, contact _____ Cable at 813-579-8400 to activate service.

6. Your closing will be conducted by _____, who will also write your Title Insurance. Before your closing, one of their representatives will contact you to inform you of the precise dollar amount required at closing. All monies due at closing must be cash or certified or cashiers check made payable to: _____ Trust Account." Their telephone number is 813_____-_____.

Again, welcome to _____ Yacht & Country Club, and do please call us if we may help you in any way.

_____
Sales Director

Form No. 160

CONDO RULES/REGULATIONS

RULES AND REGULATIONS

for

_____ YACHT CLUB
CONDOMINIUM BUILDING B

[*See:* Lewis A. Schiller, *Limitations on the Enforceability of Condominium Rules,* 22 Stetson L. Rev. 1133-1168 (1993).]

Approved by Majority Vote of the Members of the
_____ **Yacht Club Condominium**
Building B Association, Inc.
5940 _____
_____**,Florida 33707**
May/June, 1993

Issued by the Board of Directors of the Association

Rules & Regulations for
_____ **Yacht Club Condominium Building B**

Introduction

The following rules are intended as a guide for compatible and enjoyable living with those with whom you share the building. For further clarification, please consult your Condominium Documents, Section 18 as amended, the Board of Directors or the Property Manager.

General

1. Owners are responsible for the actions of guests and tenants and are accountable for their compliance with all Building rules.

2. No storage is allowed in any common area, including the hallways outside

your entrance doorway. Unless specifically approved by the Board of Directors, no storage or unauthorized installations are permitted on the roof or in any storage area except those assigned to your unit.

3. Please be discreet—wear cover-ups when using the elevators and hallways on your way to and from the pool area. No one is to be barefooted at any time in the halls, elevators, lobbies, Captain's Quarters or any other common area.

4. Bicycles are not allowed inside the Condominium Building at any time. Adequate storage is provided in the garage areas.

5. TV's, radios, stereos, musical instruments, etc. must not disturb neighbors. Please keep the volume low.

Security and Fire Protection

1. Help keep our building safe and secure. See that the main entrance doors are closed and locked as you enter or leave the building. Do not offer to let any person into the building or hold the door open for them unless you are certain that they belong inside.

2. Use discretion in giving keys to others, including friends, service personnel, etc. so that building security is not compromised.

3. No solitations of any kind are allowed on the premises.

4. There is no admittance to the roof, elevator control room, pump room, fire control room, and all mechanical and electrical control rooms except by authorized personnel or in emergencies.

5. The Fire Marshall advises that hallways, stairways and stairwells must be kept clear at all times and that any missing or defective fire-fighting equipment must be reported immediately. Failure to observe these rules may result in suspension of our fire insurance.

6. Smoking in elevators and all common areas is illegal in Florida.

7. In the past, there have been occasional incidents of vandalism in the Building. If you see or hear anything suspicious, immediately notify Security (381-3104).

Moving

Owners or authorized lessees must notify the Board of Directors or the Maintenance Employee at least two days in advance of the scheduled arrival of a moving van or furniture deliveries. However, special authorization may be obtained for Saturday moving by giving at least two weeks notice and paying a fee to cover the cost of the Maintenance Employee being called in. This fee is established at $150 but may be revised from time to time by the Board of Directors.

Deliveries of furniture and similar items are permitted only between the hours of 7:30 a.m. and 4:30 p.m., Monday through Friday.

Owners will be responsible for any damage done by movers or delivery personnel.

Rentals

The minimum term that a unit may be rented is 6 months and only one time each 12 month period beginning with the effective date of the lease. Because our condominium is not a "time share" building, no unit may be bought, loaned or sold as a time sharing arrangement.

Balconies

1. Do not feed birds or ducks on or from balconies. Do not cook on or use barbecue grills on balconies at any time. Do not hang towels or laundry on balconies.
2. When cleaning your balcony, do not use excess water which will cascade down onto your neighbors' balconies below you. Under no circumstances should a hose be connected and used to clean balconies. Dirty water may discolor or stain furniture on balconies below you.

Interior Tile Floors. If you have interior ceramic tile floors, please remember that such floors transmit noise to units below. Please take care not to disturb your neighbors.

Captain's Quarters

1. The Captain's Quarters rooms are reserved for the exclusive use of owners or tenants and guests residing with them or accompanied by them. *They are not to be used by guests or by persons under 16 years of age unless accompanied by an adult owner or tenant.*
2. All persons using the rooms are responsible for keeping the premises clean and orderly at all times. The owner(s) or tenant(s) hosting the event are financially responsible for any damage that they or their guests cause to the rooms.
3. In order to entertain a group in the Captain's Quarters, a reservation must be made with the Maintenance Employee at least 24 hours in advance. A security deposit of $50 must be made at the time the reservation is made; the deposit will be returned if the facilities are left in a neat and clean condition.
4. The owner or tenant making the reservation will inspect the rooms with the Maintenance Employee before the party and again afterwards in order for the security deposit to be returned.
5. Private parties will be limited to a maximum of 36 persons unless approved otherwise in advance by the Board of Directors.
6. All parties will end on or before 11 p.m. Cleaning of the rooms should

begin immediately after and must be completed by 12 noon the following day.

7. Because of past damage to the table and equipment, the Association does not furnish cue sticks for the pool table.

Recycling

We have a recycling program underway in the Building. Please neatly stack newspapers to be recycled in the designated areas on each floor. Do not include magazines of any kind. Place other recyclable items in the bins as marked (to be installed when the City implements a total recycling program).

Trash and Garbage

1. All non-recyclable trash, including glass of any kind, must be placed in securely-tied plastic bags.

2. Do not put loose garbage of any kind, such as liquids, coffee grounds, cat litter, etc. down the trash chute.

Pets

1. Pets are not allowed unless a pet application has been approved in writing by the Board of Directors, and then only one pet, weighing less than 20 pounds, per unit. Pets must be hand-carried when in the hallways, elevators, lobbies or the garage. An exception is a seeing-eye dog for the sight impaired. Failure to observe the rules regarding pets may result in rescinding the pet authorization.

2. When outside in the Building B property areas, the pet must be hand leashed. Do not walk your pet where it might damage the shrubs and plantings.

3. A pet walking area has been designated along the road on the northeast side of the building. Pet waste must be removed from grounds immediately and disposed of properly by the pet owner.

Parking and Garages

1. Owners and guests must park in assigned spaces or in areas marked for parking. Unattended vehicles may not be left in the front entrance area or adjacent driveways.

2. Because assigned parking spaces are limited common areas, our maintenance employee will do general cleaning. However, grease and oil leakage and stains are the responsibility of the unit owner or lessee.

3. Parking spaces may not be used for storage.

4. The speed limit in the garage and driveways is 10 miles per hour.

5. Recreation vehicles are permitted to park in parking lots for a maximum of 72 hours. No commercial vehicles are permitted to park except when supplying services, and then only in parking lots.

6. Bicycles and tricycles are to be parked in designated areas only and never on walkways.

Car Washing

1. Car washing facilities are available in the South (new) garage for the use of Building B residents only. Hose, broom and squeegee are available in the locked storage area and must be returned to the storage area after use.

2. After washing a vehicle, the floor area should be rinsed down to remove dirt, debris and residual soap and then squeegeed to force all standing water down the drain.

Shopping Carts; Valet Luggage Racks

Shopping carts and valet luggage racks are located in the separate storage locations for your convenience. *Please return the carts and racks promptly to the storage rooms rather than leaving them on your floor*; others often are waiting to use them.

Pool and Spa

Rules governing the use of the pool, spa and recreation area have been established in conjunction with the County Health Department and are listed below. All owners, tenants and guests are expected to abide by these rules.

1. Pool hours: 7 a.m. to 11 p.m.
2. *Warning*: No lifeguard is on duty. Residents and guests swim at their own risk.
3. Shower before entering pool or Jacuzzi.
4. No animals in pool or on pool deck.
5. No food or drink in pool or on deck.
6. No children wearing diapers in pool or Jacuzzi at any time.
7. No children under age 12 permitted in the sauna or Jacuzzi unless accompanied by an adult.
8. No floats of any kind allowed in pool.
9. No ball playing, running or rough play in pool area.
10. Maximum pool load: 50 persons.
11. No diving permitted.

Observations, Suggestions and Complaints

If you have suggestions or a complaint, please contact the management company, Professional Bayway Management, Inc.—telephone 866–3115. However, if you have a complaint about another resident, it must be put in writing.

If your complaint is of a nature that requires immediate action, call Security.

Useful Phone Numbers

Emergency–911
Security (Gatehouse)- _____
Police- _____
Fire- _____
Professional Management Company- _____ Emergency:- _____

Issued by the Board of Directors and Approved by Association Members.
6/93

FORM NO. 161
Condo Form For Amending Documents
to Adopt New Statutory Provisions
of Florida 1991–2 Amendments

_____ **YACHT CLUB CONDOMINIUM BUILDING**
C/O _____ **MANAGEMENT**
5901_____ BOULEVARD, SUITE
ST. PETERSBURG, FL 33715

_____ 24, 1992

Dear Unit Owner(s):

Two laws became effective this year which made several changes in the Florida Condominium Act, Florida Statute 718. Those which are most important for the owners to be aware of are embodied in many of the enclosed proposed amendments to condominium documents. With the exception of the proposed change to Sec. _____ of the Bylaws, which is a reversion to earlier language, all of the changes to the Declaration and to the Bylaws are directed by additions to the law. The proposed revisions to our Articles of Incorporation are to facilitate operation of day to day activities and conform to our other documents.

Enclosed, along with the proposed amendments is a ballot. Please indicate your vote for each amendment in the space provided, place the completed ballot in the enclosed return envelope, indicate your unit number on the outside, the authorized voting member must initial where indicated and return by mail in the enclosed stamped envelope (Continental U.S. ONLY) to our management group, _____ Management Company so as to arrive no later than _____ 31, 1992, at which time the votes will be counted. The approved amendments will then be submitted to the Clerk of

Courts for recording, as required by law. After recording each unit owner will be furnished a copy of the amendments for guidance and inclusion in your condominium documents.

Your vote is very important for, as you know, sixty six 2/3 percent of our members must approve most changes before they can be effected.

_____

_____
    President

_____ YACHT CLUB CONDOMINIUM BUILDING AMENDMENTS TO DECLARATION OF CONDOMINIUM

XII
COMMON BENEFITS

It is proposed to add the following as additional language to existing language; no current language being affected. See Article _____, Section _____ for present text of existing language:

> Nor may the Association convey, mortgage or lease Association real property except under the conditions stated in this paragraph.

XXII
MAINTENANCE, ALTERATION AND IMPROVEMENT

Section 1.(b)(2) *Except for the installation of approved hurricane shutters*, not to paint or otherwise decorate or change the appearance of any portion of the exterior of the condominium building, including, but not limited to, balconies or terraces.

It is proposed to add the following as additional language to existing language; no current language being affected. See Article _____, Section _____ for present text existing language:

> However, any unit owner wishing to install hurricane shutters may do so if the design, method of operation, color and other pertinent factors comply with the specifications adopted by the Board of Directors. The unit owner shall be responsible for ensuring that the plans for the proposed installation are submitted to the Board for review. If it becomes necessary for the Association to expend funds to assure timely completion of the installation or to correct defects in workmanship, or to defend itself against any action arising from the installation or related thereto, such funds shall be secured by a lien against the condominium parcel on which the shutters were installed. The installation, maintenance and repair of such shutters shall

not be deemed to be a material alteration or substantial addition to the common elements.

AMENDMENTS TO BYLAWS

III
THE ASSOCIATION

It is proposed to add the following as additional language to existing language; no current language being affected. See Article _____ Section _____ for present text of existing language:

> Proxies cannot be used for the election of directors. Limited proxies may be used to establish a quorum; to waive or reduce reserves; to waive certain financial statement requirements; to amend the various condominium documents and for any other matter which requires a vote of the unit owners.

IV
ADMINISTRATION

It is proposed to add the following as additional language to existing language; no current language being affected. See Article _____, Section _____ for present text of existing language:

> In electing Directors the following procedures shall be adhered to: At least 60 days prior to the election the Association shall mail or deliver to each unit owner a first notice of the election.

> Any unit owner desiring to be a candidate for the Board of Directors shall advise the Association, in writing, at least 40 days before the election.

> Within the next five days and no later than 35 days before the election, the present Board of Directors must hold a meeting to accept additional nominations. Any unit owner may nominate themselves or, if written permission is granted by the person, any other unit owner.

> At least 40 days before the election, the Association must mail or deliver a second notice of the election along with the list of candidates. Candidates may submit, at least 35 days before the election, a summary of their qualifications, not to exceed one 8 1/2 by 11 page, which shall be enclosed with this notice.

> There is no quorum requirement for the election of directors, but at least 20% of the eligible voters must cast ballots. However, if no more candidates have filed notice of intent to run than there are positions to be filled on the Board, then no balloting or election is required. No proxies are allowed in electing Directors and only the ballots mentioned above, which may be returned to the Association by mail or presented in person at the election, will be counted.

It is proposed to add the following as additional language to existing language; no current language being affected. See Article _____, Section

_____ for present text of existing language;

> No officer, director or manager shall solicit, offer to accept or accept any-
> thing of value, for which such person has not paid a true and just consid-
> eration, from any person or business providing or proposing to provide
> goods or services to the Association.

Sec. 5. Organization Meeting. The first meeting of the newly elected Board
of Directors shall be held within ten (10) days after the annual members
meeting, at such time and place as shall be fixed by the Board. No notice
shall be necessary to the newly elected directors in order to legally constitute such meeting, providing all members of the Board shall be present.

Section 8. Notice of Meetings to Unit Owners. Meetings of the Board of
Directors shall be open to all unit owners as shall meetings of committees
appointed by the Board, or a member of the Board, to make recommendations to the Board regarding the Association budget or to take action on
behalf of the Board. Notices of meetings shall be posted conspicuously forty
eight (48) hours in advance for the attention of unit owners, except in an
emergency. Notice of any meeting where assessments against unit owners
are to be considered for any reason shall specifically contain a statement
that assessments will be considered and the nature of such assessments.

Sec. 18. Secretary. The Secretary shall keep the minutes of all meetings of
the Board of Directors, and the minutes of all meetings of the Association;
shall have charge of such books and papers as the Board of Directors may
direct; shall send notices and reports as specified herein and by law; and
shall, in general, perform all of the duties incident to the office of Secretary. If the Board so desires it may combine the offices of Secretary and
Treasurer.

VI
ANNUAL BUDGET

It is proposed to add the following as an additional paragraph to existing language; no current language being affected. See Article _____
for present text of existing language:

> Reserve and operating funds of the Association may be commingled for
> purposes of investment, but separate ledgers must be maintained for each
> account and they may not be commingled with other accounts not belong-
> ing to the Association.

AMENDMENTS TO ARTICLES OF INCORPORATION

III
POWER

Sec. 3.2f. To make and amend reasonable rules and regulations respecting use
of the property in the condominium, other than the restrictions contained in
the Declaration of Condominium; as allowed in the Florida Condominium Act.

IV
REGISTERED AGENT AND OFFICE

The registered agent for the Association <u>and the location of the office have been filed with the Florida Secretary of State.</u> The Board shall have the authority to change the registered agent and office from time to time.

X
AMENDMENTS

c.2.a. Such approvals must be by not less than seventy-five per cent of the entire membership of the Board of Directors and by not less than <u>sixty</u> six <u>and</u> two <u>thirds</u> per cent of the votes of the entire membership of the Association; or

> *Appendix:* 1. Ballot
> 2. Return Envelope]

Form No. 162
Modern (1993) Forms for *Condo* Annual Meeting
and *Election*, under the *new* Florida Statutes

_____ CONDOMINIUM BUILDING "B"

February 3, 1993

Dear Unit Owner(s):

The Annual Membership meeting of the _____ Yacht Club Condominium Building "B" will be held March 4, 1993 at 2:30 P.M., at the POOL-SIDE recreation room.

Documents pertinent to the official conduct of this meeting are enclosed:

1. Official Meeting Notice and Meeting Agenda. (A)
2. Ballot for the election to the Board of Directors. (B)
3. Information sheet on candidates. (C)
4. Proxy for Annual Meeting. (D)
5. Directions for Election Procedures. (E)
6. A BALLOT Envelope and TWO Return Envelopes.

ELECTION

This meeting will differ from previous meetings in one important aspect. There has been a change in Florida law and in the rules promulgated thereunder by the Division of Florida Land Sales, Condominiums and Mobile

Homes, which will make things somewhat more complicated. Under the new law and rules, the voting for the five Directors' positions must be done by *secret ballot*, which may be mailed in advance or cast at the annual meeting. Voting for members of the Board *can no longer be done by proxy*. The winners will be determined by the plurality of votes received.

Even though a quorum is not required to hold an election, *a minimum of 20% of the owners must cast a ballot in order for election to be legal.*

MARK YOUR BALLOT AND PLACE IT IN THE "BALLOT" ENVELOPE, SEAL IT AND PLACE THE BALLOT ENVELOPE INSIDE THE RETURN ENVELOPE. PLEASE SIGN YOUR NAME AND UNIT NUMBER ON THE OUTSIDE OF THE RETURN ENVELOPE WHERE INDICATED. FAILURE TO DO SO WILL NULLIFY YOUR VOTE.

PROXY VOTING CERTIFICATE

Although proxies cannot be used to elect Directors, they are important to meet the quorum requirement for our Annual Meeting. We need representation from 51% of the units in order to have the Annual Meeting and such a meeting is required by both Florida law and your Condominium Documents.

If a quorum is not obtained for the meeting, we will have to go to the inconvenience and expense of another attempt to hold the meeting. Please, use the plain self-addressed envelope for the Proxy, *NOT* the return envelope in which you placed your Ballot. We must use separate envelopes so as to first establish a quorum initially, then count the ballots.

Please do yourself and your Association a large favor, and return your papers to us NOW.

Sincerely,

_____
Property Manager

NOTICE

ANNUAL MEETING OF THE MEMBERSHIP
_____ YACHT CLUB CONDOMINIUM BUILDING "B"

a Florida Corporation Not For Profit

_____

YOU ARE HEREBY NOTIFIED THAT THE ANNUAL MEETING OF THE MEMBERSHIP OF _____ YACHT CLUB CONDOMINIUM BUILDING "B" INC., will be held on Thursday, March 4, 1993 at 2:30 P.M., in the "POOLSIDE Recreation Room, located at _____, Florida.

AGENDA

(1) Call to order
(2) Establish Quorum
(3) Approve minutes of last annual meeting (enclosed)
(4) The election of Five (5) unit owners to serve on the Board of Directors (no quorum required).
(5) Officers reports.
(6) Unit owner concerns

There will be a meeting of the Board of Directors immediately following the adjournment of the Annual Meeting of the Membership for the sole purpose of appointing officers.

BOARD OF DIRECTORS MEETING
AGENDA

(1) Call to order
(2) Establish quorum
(3) Appoint officers
(4) Set date for next meeting
(5) Adjourn

I HEREBY CERTIFY that this notice has been mailed by depositing same in a post office in a sealed envelope, by regular mail, to each of the members of Yacht Club Condominium Building "B" Inc., at the address as it appears on the books of the Association.

DATED at _____ , Florida, this 3rd day of February, 1993.

_____
Property Manager

YACHT CLUB CONDOMINIUM "B" BUILDING
BOARD CANDIDACY FOR 1993
INFORMATION SHEET

Candidate No. 1.

_____ – *UNIT #404*
_____
_____

Retired—Former Field Engineer with General Electric.
Normally leave area June thru September.

_____ *UNIT #802 INCUMBENT*
_____
_____

Graduate of the University of Illinois & Michigan with degrees in Chemistry & Chemical Engineering. Staff Engineer in Gulf Oil Research & Development.

First Chairman of the Board of Building "B" and served three (3) years.

_____ – *UNIT #201*   *INCUMBENT*
_____
_____

Member of Condominium "B" Board for the past three (3) years, served as President for the last two (2) years. Acted as Negotiating Committee which successfully negotiated an equitable settlement with the developer U.S.X. Corp., Realty Division.

Professional Experience:
Served in the Army Air Corps and Air Force from 1942 until 1948 as pilot instructor and combat pilot. Retired medically with the rank of Major.

Employed by Rex Nord, Inc. from 1952 until 1973, after graduating from Texas A & M University. Positions held were Product Engineer, District Sales Engineer and District Sales Manager of engineered equipment.

From 1973 to 1988 held several positions with U.S. X. Engineers and Consultants, Inc., such as Senior Project Engineer, Contract Manager, Manager of Mining, Beneficiation Engineering and Project Manager

_____ – *UNIT PH #B*   *INCUMBENT*
_____
_____

Biographical Summary _____

Professional
Senior Partner, The Johnson-Layton Company, St. Petersburg and Los Angeles, a management consulting and business advisory firm. Also President of The Layton Group, an International Marketing organization. Formerly held management and executive positions in Human Resources and Administration with three Fortune 250 companies over a span of 28 years.

Personal
Married 39 years to Caroline. Three children and seven grandchildren. Native Iowan. B.A., Coe College; M.A., University of Illinois.

Experience as Condominium Director
Member of Building "B" Board since 1991, serving as Secretary. Formerly President of two other condominium developments in Memphis, Tennessee, 1984–86 and 1988–90.

_____ – *UNIT #104*   *INCUMBENT*
_____
_____

Rate Analyst–Florida Power Corporation.
Computer Science Instructor–St. Petersburg Jr. College.
Graduate–University of Florida–Engineering.
_____ – *UNIT #1003*

_____

_____

1979–1989 Executive Vice President of E. Merck (Pharmaceuticals Chemicals).
1953–1979 Vice President of Color & Chemicals Div. Inmont Corporation.
Board of Directors–Tenants Company, London, England.
Board of Directors–Scientific App. & Mfrs. Assoc.
Board of Directors–Upper Montclair C.C.
Civic Activities:
Deputy Mayor–Village of Stewart Manor, N.Y.
Zoning Board–Borough of Allendale, N.J.
Coach–Football & Soccer

_____ – *UNIT $303*

_____

_____

Born May 3, 1920–Age 72
Married to my wife Helen for 45 years, and have a daughter–Valerie.
Served in the U.S. Army–Corps. of Engineers, for 4 years during World War II, which included 3 years in the European Theater of Operations, and 1 year in the Pacific Theater of Operations. I was awarded a Battle Field Officer's Commission.
Graduated from the University of Pittsburgh with a B.S. degree in Business Administration.
Retired after 44 years of service in various U.S. Steel Corp. subsidiaries. Some positions held during my career included Laborer, Crane Operator, Moulder or Cast Iron objects, Accounting Trainee, Financial Analyst, Director of Cost Planning, Manager of Auditing and Manager of Accounting.

ELECTION PROCEDURES

Effective January 1, 1992, the election procedures for the election of Directors has changed considerably. Please read and follow the procedures set forth below:

The ballot you have received will be a secret ballot and will not be opened until the Annual Membership meeting by a Ballot Counting Committee.

Read the enclosed information sheet on the candidates and then mark your ballot with "x's." Once you have voted place your ballot in the "BALLOT" envelope, seal it, and enclose it in the self-addressed envelope with the signature line. Do not sign or show any identification on the "BALLOT" envelope. On the *outer* envelope, fill in your unit number and signature of the authorized representative. (If husband and wife are not sure who is the authorized voter, have both sign.) Please print your name above the signature.

DO NOT VOTE FOR MORE THAN FIVE (5) CANDIDATES

_____YACHT CLUB CONDOMINIUM, BUILDING B, INC.

_____   _____, FLORIDA_____

Minutes of the Annual Meeting of the Membership
Thursday, March 5, 1992—Poolside Recreation Room

Board of Directors Members Present: _____ _____

Representing Professional Bayway Management Co. (PBM): _____

Others Present (in person or by signed proxy): 45 unit owners

The annual meeting was called to order at 6:35 P.M. by Board President _____ _____. Proof of notice of the meeting was verified and it was established that a quorum was present.

_____ called for volunteers to serve as tellers to tally the votes to elect a Board of Directors. _____ _____ were appointed. It was announced that the meeting would be interrupted at the point the vote tally was complete. It was also clarified that only personally cast votes were valid (no proxies for election of directors).

1. *Minutes.*—The minutes of the 1991 annual meeting were read by Secretary _____. A motion _____ and second _____ to accept the minutes as read was approved.

2. *Storage Cages.*—After completing a tally of the votes cast by written ballot, _____ announced that the proposal to permit owners who wished to have their storage cages enlarged to do so received 34 in favor and 11 opposed. Since the change required a 2/3 majority (49 votes), the proposal was not approved.

3. *Officers' Reports.*_____ reported that the change to a calendar fiscal year had gone smoothly. The Association posted a deficit of $1,161.71 for the old fiscal year (ending 8/31/91), but showed positive variances to budget of $1,409.20 for the three months ending 12/31/91 and $316.57 for the month ending 1/31/92. The reserve accounts are on budget; the total reserves currently stand at approximately $225,000.

4. *Results of Election*
_____ reported the following election results for Board of Directors members:

Candidate 1_____   29 votes
Candidate 2_____   57
Candidate 3_____   53
Candidate 4_____   59
Candidate 5_____   58
Candidate 6_____   51

It was announced that the new Board would meet immediately following the annual meeting in order to elect officers.

5. *Unfinished Business.*

   a. _____ announced that in order to avoid problems with boxes left outside storage cages, all boxes for disposal must be broken down flat.

   b. Residents continue to bring bicycles into the hallways and elevators, even though the rules booklet prohibits doing so. After discussion of various alternatives, it was decided that the only appropriate action that could be taken at this time was to send a letter to the residents involved asking them to keep their bicycles in the designated storage areas.

   c. _____ pointed out that although the rules booklet is helpful, especially for new residents, it was approved only by the Board of Directors when issued in 1991. Technically, such a document requires approval of 75% of the membership, which will be solicited when a revision is prepared later this year.

6. *New Business*

   a. ADT will be conducting an inspection of fire systems on March 19 and must have access to all units. Unoccupied units will be entered only by two or more authorized persons.

   b. Re-instituted water restrictions require that cars be washed only on Tuesdays and Saturdays. The Board has established the period from 9 a.m. to 5 p.m. for this purpose. The maintenance employee will remove the hose at all other times. Residents are reminded once again of the importance of using the squeegee to remove excess water and prevent a slip hazard. Further investigation of non-residents of Building B using the car washing area will be conducted.

7. *Termination of Former Maintenance Employee.* _____ read a report of an investigation into the facts surrounding the discharge of the former maintenance employee. Subsequently, a motion _____ and a second _____ to approve the action of the Management Company and the Board was approved unanimously.

8. *Unit Owners' Concerns and Comments*

   a. The decorative items for the elevator areas on each floor have been ordered and are expected to be in place in the next four weeks.

   b. _____ reported that 17 owners have signed up for the pest control service. The cost will be $10 per month, billed directly to owners by the supplier, _____ Pest Control Services.

Also, 23 owners have signed up for the individual air conditioning/furnace inspection and preventive maintenance service. The work will be done in April and October of each year at a cost of $29.29 per visit.

Additional owners interested in these services should contact _____ at _____.

_____ thanked _____ for his excellent work on these projects.

    c. Two owners were given special recognition for their volunteer services in connection with the pool _____ and grounds _____.

There being no further business, the meeting was adjourned at 7:33 p.m.

Respectfully submitted,

_____
Secretary

Form No.163
Minutes of a Special Meeting of the Board of Directors
YACHT CLUB CONDOMINIUM, BUILDING B, INC.

_____   _____, FLORIDA_____

January 29, 1993–Captain's Quarters

Board Members Present: _____

Representing _____ *Management Co. (PBM):* _____

Others Present:
_____ – Construction Consultant
_____ – FRMSC Co.
_____ – Shephard Painting
_____ – Shephard Painting

    The meeting was called to order at 8:40 a.m. by President _____. The purpose of the meeting was to review the problems with two types of water intrusion into the building: (1) during rainstorms primarily coming from a southwest direction, with the most severe occurring in master bedroom areas in Units 201 and 401 and in the south storage areas, and (2) leakage around sliding glass doors, which is more generic, occurring in a number of units and frequently causing ceiling stains in units below. A third issue, that of drilling out and re-setting weep holes on the balconies, would be dealt with separately.

_____ presented his analysis of problem #1, which indicates that cracks have developed in or near certain construction joints where the poured columns meet with the concrete block wall filler. The materials involved are dissimilar, and expansion and contraction is causing the stucco finish on the building to crack. allowing water intrusion during a driving rain.

_____ commented that in his opinion, part of the problem is due to the lack of control joints at the corners in question, which he termed a design issue. He added that he felt that even when control joints were installed in Building B, some were not executed properly. He pointed out that this situation had been described in his inspection report at the time of Building B's settlement with USX. _____ commented that it was Building B Board's understanding that USX was going to ensure that the leakage problem was solved, but apparently that did not happen. He added that he felt it was _____ responsibility to ensure that outcome. _____ said that when the work was completed in 1990 there were no leaks. _____ replied that the leaks in her unit have never stopped since she moved in (1987).

_____ expressed the opinion that the work done was still under warranty. _____ pointed out that his warranty is explicit in excluding problems caused by new cracks.

The Board and guests toured the areas in question on the second floor and then resumed the meeting.

As for solutions, _____ recommended that a brush grade caulking compound be applied, then the area re-coated with Elastomeric. _____ concurred. _____ agreed that his company would carry out that treatment on the three walls in question at no cost to Building B, but that if the leakage persists, the matter will need to be reviewed and a cost determined for any additional work needed.

_____ offered to "ride" the area for a closer look and also to inspect the work at both the caulking and Elastomeric stages and report the results to the Board.

With regard to the sliding doors, _____ said that in his view the problem was caused by lack of flashing and/or failure to seal the casings properly. He added that for a long-term, lasting solution, he had previously recommended that all doors be taken out of their frames and a flashing pan installed. The group discussed potential costs, and the number $750 to $1,000 per door was mentioned. _____ disagreed with that solution, suggesting instead that using a good sealant would be sufficient. He acknowledged that the life of such a treatment would probably be five years, at which time re-sealing would probably be needed. Cost of this approach was estimated in the $100–$150 range per door.

After further discussion, it was decided that the sealing solution would be attempted as an experiment, with a water test to be performed after the installation.

Messrs. _____ departed, and the Board continued the meeting to discuss the problem of the weep holes, some of which were not installed with enough pitch to carry off water. This issue has come to light in connection with the balcony repairs and tiling. _____ had estimated that about 250–275 weep holes may need treatment, and an estimate of $35–40 per hole has been obtained. The work must be done before tile is laid. (For the balconies already tiled, the installer apparently has found none that are a problem.)

After discussion, the Board unanimously approved a motion _____ second, _____ to engage _____ Coating to re-check the balconies, determine the number of holes that actually need to be re-drilled, report the estimated cost to the Board and begin the work so that the tiling can proceed. Cost of the project will be an Association expense.

There being no further business, the meeting was adjourned at 10:30 a.m.

Respectfully submitted,

_____

Secretary

NOTES TO CHAPTER 37

1. See Fla.Stat.c. 718 as to condominiums; Fla.Stat.cc. 618, 619, 719 as to cooperatives; Fla. Stat 617 as to corporations not for profit.

2. 15A Am.Jur.2d, *Condominiums and Cooperative Apts.* §1.

3. Vol. I, *Law of Condominium* §3 (1967).

4. W.K. Kerr, *Condominium—Statutory Implementation*, 38 St. John's L.Rev. 1 (1963).

5. *See*, Natl. L. J. p. 1 (Jan. 14, 1985); Hyatt, *Condominium and Homeowner Associations Practice: Community Association Law* (ALI-ABA, 1981).

6. L. Griffin, article *St. Petersburg Times*, City Times Section, p. 1 (Nov. 24, 1991).

7. See: Community Up-Date (newsletter), vol. 91 (June 1991) of Becker & Poliakoff of Fort Lauderdale, FL.

8. Fl. St. § 617.0601 subd. (c); Fl. Session L. 1990, Chap. 90–179 § 34(c).

9. Cigol v. Leader Development Corp., 557 N.E. 2d 1119 (Mass. S.J. 1990).

10. *St. Petersburg Times*, p. 4B (Apr. 27, 1991).

11. See, Fl. St. §§ 718.112(2)(j); 719.1061(k).

12. (Articles, series) in 88 *Community Up-Date* (newsletter) No's. 4, 5, 6 (Apr., May, June 1988) (Becker, Poliakoff & Streitfeld [law firm], Fort Lauderdale, FL 33312–6525).

13. *Orange West, Ltd. v. City of Winter Garden*, 528 So. 2d 84 (FL App. 1988).

14. *Coliseum Park Apartments Co. v. Coliseum Tenants Corp.*, 742 F. Supp. 128 (D.C., N.Y., 1990).

15. *U.S. v. Certain Real Property and Premises Known as 38 Whalers Cove Dr.*, 747 F. Supp. 173 (D.C., N.Y. 1990).

16. See, Fl. St. § 196.011; Fl. Admin. Code Rule 12D-7.001; 91 *Community Up-Date* 1 (Jan. 1991; Becker & P. law firm newsletter, Fort Lauderdale, FL 33312–6525); *In re Tenorio*, 107 B.R. 787 (Bkcy. Ct., D.C., Fla. 1990).

17. *Providence Square Assn., Inc., v. Biancardi*, 507 So. 2d 1366 (FL 1987); criticized in Note, 17 *Stetson L. Rev.* (2)447 (1988).

18. *American Holidays, Inc. v. Foxtail Owners*, 821 P. 2d 577 (Wyo. 1991).

19. *Commercial Wharf East Condo Assn. v. Waterfront Parking Corp.*, 552 N.E.2d 66 (Mass. S.J., 1990).

20. *Oper v. Riverwood Condo. Assn.*, 563 So. 2d 110 (Fla. 3rd DCA, 1990); Fl. St. §§ 542.15 et seq., 718.104(5).

21. *Sprunk v. Creekwood Condo. Unit Owners Assn.*, 573 N.E. 2d 197 (Ohio App. 1989, publ. 1991).

22. *Hornstein v. Barry*, 560 A.2d 530 (D.C. App., 1989).

23. *19th Street Associates v. State*, N.Y. App. Div., Apr. 23, 1991.

24. *State v. Rachmani Corp.*, 525 N.E.2d 704 (NY 1988).

25. *Bay Garden Manor Condo. Assn., Inc. v. James D. Marks Associates, Inc. & H.N.A., Inc.*, 16 *Fla. L. W.* 455 (Fl. App. 1991).

26. *Perry v. Boston Rent Equity Board*, 537 N.E.2d 580 (MA 1989).

27. *Kline v. Resort Investment Corp.*, 547 So. 2d 495 (Ala., 1989).

28. *Holmes v. First Meridian Planning Corp.*, 547 N.Y.S.2d 928 (App. Div., 1989).

29. *Leake v. Sunbelt Ltd. of Raleigh*, 377 S.E.2d 285 (NC App., 1989).

30. *Palm Aire Country Club Apts. Condo v. FPA Corp.*, 15 Fla. L. W. D. 806 (Apr. 6, 1990).

31. *HOW Insur. Co. v. Patriot Fin. Svc. of Tex.*, 1990 WL 29770 (Tex. App., Austin, 1990).

32. *Difillipo v. Hidden Ponds Associates*, 537 N.Y.S.2d 222 (App. Div. 1989).

33. *Baker v. Promenade Developers*, 15 Fla. L. W. 110 (Fla. App., 1990).

34. *Sky Lake Gardens Recreation, Inc. v. Sky Lake Gardens Nos. 1, 3 & 4, Inc.*, 574 So. 2d 1135 (Fla. 3d DCA, 1991).

35. *Jamlynn Investments Corp. v. San Marco Residences*, 544 So. 2d 1080 (Fla. 2d D.C.A., 1989).

36. *Walsh v. City Mortgage Services, Inc.*, 103 B.R. 502 (D.C., La., 1989).

37. *Kesl, Inc. v. Racquet Club of Deer Creek*, 574 So. 2d 251 (Fla. DCA, 1991); Fl. St. § 718.114; *Chatham Condo Assn. v. Century Village, Inc.*, 597 F.2d 1002 (5th Cir., 1979).

38. Fla. Stat., c. 713; discussed in 80 *Community Up-Date* 1 (May 1990) Newsletter of Becker, Poliakoff & Streitfeld law office, Fort Lauderdale, FL.

39. *New Jersey State League of Municipalities v. State*, 608 A.2d 965 (N.J. Super. A.D., 1992).

40. Vol. I, *Law of Condominium* §31 (1967).

41. *Real Estate Transactions*, Condominium Law and Practice, Vol. I, Part I, 1–3 (1985).

42. Vol. I, *Law of Condominium* §32 (1967).

43. 15A Am.Jur.2d, *Condominiums and Cooperative Apts.* §6.

44. Clurman, Jackson and Hebard, *Condominiums and Cooperatives*, 3 (2d ed. 1984).

45. *Id.*

46. 15A Am.Jur.2d, *Condominiums and Cooperative Apts.* §7.

47. *Florida Condominiums—Developer Abuses and Securities Law Implications Create A Need For A State Regulatory Agency*, 25 U.Fla.L.Rev. 350 (1973).

48. Clurman, Jackson and Hebard, *Condominiums and Cooperatives*, 2 (2d ed. 1984).

49. U.S. Bureau of the Census, *Statistical Abstract of the United States*: 1991 (111th edition.) Washington, D.C., 1991.

50. *Florida Condominiums—Developer Abuses and Securities Law Implications Create A Need For A State Regulatory Agency*, 25 U.Fla.L.Rev. 350, 351 (1973).

51. *Id.*

52. *1992 Florida Statistical Abstract*, University Press of Florida, Gainesville (26th edition) 1992.

53. Clurman, Jackson and Hebard, *Condominiums and Cooperatives*, 2 (2d ed. 1984).

54. U.S. Bureau of the Census, *Statistical Abstract of the United States*: 1991 (111th edition.) Washington, D.C., 1991.

55. R. Kratovil and R. Werner, *Real Estate Law*, 498 (8th ed. 1983).

56. Clurman, Jackson and Hebard, *Condominiums and Cooperatives*. 10, 11 (2d ed. 1984).

57. *Id.*

58. R. Kratovil and R. Werner, *Real Estate Law*, 524 (8th ed. 1983).

59. W. Milligan and A. Bowman, *Real Estate Law*, 208 (1984).

60. R. Kratovil and R. Werner, *Real Estate Law*, 524 (8th ed. 1983).

61. *Id.*, at 525.

62. Fla. Stat. §718.1045 *et. seq.* (1991).

63. R. Kratovil and R. Werner, *Real Estate Law*, 526 (8th ed. 1983).

64. *Id.* at 526.

65. Susskind v. 1136 Tenants Corp., 43 Misc.2d 588; 251 NYS 2d 321, 327 (1964).

66. Fla. Stat. §718.102 (1991).

67. *See*, for example: Blue Lakes Apartments v. Geo. Jowing, Inc., 464 S.2d 705 (Fla. App. 1985).

68. 15 A Am.Jur.2d, *Condominiums and Cooperative Apartments*, §14.

69. Pepe v. Whispering Sands Condominium Association, Inc., 351 So. 2d 755, 757 (1977).

70. State Savings and Loan Association v. Kavaian Development Company, 445 P.2d 109, 116 (Hawaii 1968).

71. FHA Model Act §11.

71a. 93 *Community Update* 1 (Dec. 1993) issued by Becker & Poliakoff (attys.) of Fort Lauderdale, Fl. 33312.

72. FHA Model Act §19.

73. Ryan v. Baptiste, 565 S.W. 2d 196,198 (Tex. 1978).

74. R. Kratovil and R. Werner, *Real Estate Law*, 505 (8th ed. 1983).

75. 15A Am.Jur.2d, *Condominiums and Cooperative Apartments*, §18.

76. FHA Model Act §12.

77. Hennessey, *Practical Problems of Residential Condominium Operation*, 2 Conn.L.Rev. 12 (1969).

78. Fla.R.Civ.P., Rule 1.221 (1993).

79. Moody v. Cawdrey & Associates, Inc., 721 P.2d 708 (Hawaii App., 1986); Frances T. v. Village Green Owners Assn.; #L.A.31873; Calif. Supr. Ct. (Sept. 4, 1986).

80. *Downey v. Jungle Den Villas Recreation Assn., Inc.*, 525 So. 2d 438 (FL 5th D.C. App. 1988).

81. *In re Mandalay Shores Co-Op Housing Assn., Inc.*, 87 B.R. 184 (Bkcy. Ct., FL, 1988).

82. *Villa Sierra Condo. Assn. v. Field Corp.*, 787 P.2d 661 (Colo. App., 1990).

83. *Village of Kings Creek Condominium Ass'n, Inc. v. Goldberg*, 596 So. 2d 1195 (Fla. 3d DCA 1992).

84. *American Holidays, Inc. v. Foxtail Owners*, 821 P.2d 577 (Wyo. 1991).

85. *Cigal v. Leader Development Corp.*, 557 N.E.2d 1119 (*Mass. S.J.*, 1990).

86. *Golub v. Milpo, Inc.*, 522 N.E.2d 954 (MA 1988).

87. *Brazilian Court Hotel Condo. Owners Assn. v. Walker*, 584 So. 2d 609 (Fla. 4th DCA, 1991).

88. *Shelby v. Arizona Registrar of Contractors*, 834 P.2d 818 (Ariz. 1992) (claim of negligence, breach of warranty, and misrepresentation).

89. *Holmes v. Roth*, 14 Cal. Rptr. 2d 315 (Cal. App. 2 Dist., 1992).

90. *Spring Hill Civic Assn. v. Richard*, _____ So. 2d _____ (FL 5th D.C. App., June 6, 1988).

91. *Caruso v. Board of Managers of Murray Hill Terrace Condo.*, 550 N.Y.S.2d 548 (N.Y. Co. Sup. Ct., 1990).

92. *Shadow Lake Village Condo Assn., Inc. v. Zampella*, 569 A.2d 288 (N.J. Super., App. D., 1990).

93. *Schmidt v. Court*, L.A. #32110; Calif. Supr. Ct. (Mar. 27, 1989).

94. *Gerber v. Longboat Harbor North Condo, Inc.*; (Fla. D.C.; Nov. 17, 1989).

95. *Parkway Gardens Condo Assn., Inc. v. Kinser*, 536 So.2d 1076 (FL 4th DCA, 1988).

96. *Korman v. Pond Apple Maintenance Ass'n, Inc.*, 607 So.2d 489 (Fla. App. 4 Dist., 1992).

97. *Worthinglen Condo. Unit Owners Assn. v. Brown*, 566 N.E.2d 1275 (Ohio App. 1989, reported 1991).

98. See, The Priority of Association, 91 *Community Up-Date*, p. 1 (Feb. 1991; Newsletter of Becker & Poliakoff, P.A.; Fort Lauderdale, FL 33312-6525).

99. *Yorkshire Village Community Assn. v. Sweasy*, 524 N.E.2d 237 (IL App. 1988).

100. *River Towers Ass'n v. McCarthy*, 482 N.W.2d 800 (Minn. App., 1992).

101. *Board of Managers v. Lent*, 538 NYS2d 824 (2d Dept., App. Div., 1989).

102. *Toepper v. Brookwood Country Club Road Assn., Inc.*, 561 N.E.2d 1281 (Ill. App. 1990); *Kirtley v. McClelland*, 562 N.E.2d 27 (Ind. App. 1990); Members may bring derivative action (have "standing to sue") against officers despite lack of express statutory authority.

103. *Orange West, Ltd. v. City of Winter Garden*, 528 So. 2d 84 (FL App. 1988).

104. *Far West Financial Corp. v. D & S., Co., Inc.*, 760 P.2d 399 (CA 1988).

105. *Lauriedale Associates, Ltd. v. Wilson*, 9 Cal. Rptr. 2d 774 (Cal. App. 1 Dist., 1992).

106. *Almand Construction Co., Inc. v. Evans*, 14 *Fla. Law Weekly* 331 (July 7, 1989), citing *Kelly v. School Board*, 435 So. 2d 804 (Fla. 1983). See (short article), 89 *Community Up-Date* 1 (Nov. 1989; publ. by Becker, Poliakoff & Streitfeld law firm, Fort Lauderdale, FL).

107. *Munder v. Circle One Condominium, Inc.*, 596 So. 2d 144 (Fla. 4th DCA 1992).

108. *See* C.S.S.B. 2334 by Dudley, Ch. 92-49 (1992).

109. *Granville Beach Condominium Ass'n v. Granville Beach Condominiums, Inc.*, 592 N.E. 2d 160 (Ill. App. 1 Dist. 1992).

110. *Edward J. Siebert v. Bayport Beach & Tennis Club Assn., Inc.*, 573 So. 2d 889 (Fla. DCA 1991); citing, *Humhosco v. Dept. of H. & R.S.*, 476 So. 2d 258 (Fla. DCA 1985).

111. *2314 Lincoln Park West Condo. v. Mann*, 555 N.E.2d 346 (Ill. 1990).

112. *Gascoyne v. Bay Towne Property Owners Assn., Inc.*, 575 So. 2d 671 (Fla. 2d DCA, 1991) citing cases from Ky., N.M., and Okla.

113. See, Fl. St. § 718.112(2)(i) (eff. Oct. 1, 1990).

114. *Westbridge Condominium Assn., Inc. v. Lawrence*, 554 A.2d 1163 (D.C. App. 1989).

115. *Carnes v. Meadowbrook Executive Bldg. Corp.*, 836 P.2d 1212 (Kan. App. 1992).

116. *334 Barry In Town Homes, Inc. v. Farago*, 563 N.E.2d 856 (Ill. App. 1990).

117. *Aglione v. Stonegate at Grasmere Condo 1*, 565 N.Y.S.2d 559 (App. Div., 1991).

118. *Villager Condominium Ass'n, Inc. v. Idaho Power Co.*, 829 P.2d 1335 (Idaho 1992).

119. *Grey v. Coastal States Holding Co.*, 578 A.2d 1080 (Conn. App. 1990).

120. *Englewood Golf, Inc. v. Englewood Golf Condominium Villas Assn., Inc.*, 547 So. 2d 1050 (Fla. 3d DCA, 1989).

121. *Maillard v. Dowdell*, 528 So.2d 512 (FL 3d D.C.Appl. 1988); *Kole v. Amfac, Inc.*, 750 P.2d 929 (Hawaii 1988) danger of golf balls flying into condo pool area from adjacent golf course (known as a danger by the officers).

122. *Rothfleisch v. Cantor*, 534 So. 2d 823 (FL 4th DCA, 1989). FL Stat. §§718.111(10, 11); 692.01.

123. *Newport Condominium Assn. v. Talman Home Fed. Sav. & L. Assn.*, 545 N.E.2d 136 (Ill. App., 1989).

124. *In re Mishkin*, 85 B.R. 18 (Bkcy. Ct., S.D., NY 1988).

125. See, Recent Developments . . . (article), in 91 Community Update 1 (Mar. 1991), newsletter of Becker & Poliakoff (Fort Lauderdale, FL 33312) about Fla. St. § 718.4015; *Sky Lake Gardens Recreation, Inc. v. Sky Lake Gardens No. 1, 394, Inc.*, 16 *Fla. L. W.* D317 (Fla. 3rd DCA 1991).

126. *Sky Lake Gardens Recreation, Inc. v. Sky Lake Gardens*, 567 So. 2d 1026 (Fla. 3rd DCA 1990); *Assn. of Golden Glades Condo Club v. Security Mgmt. Corp.*, 557 So. 2d 1350 (Fla. 1990) [and see 1991 decision, above] in n. 120.

127. *Beeman v. Island Breakers. A Condo, Inc.* 577 So.2d 1341 (Fla. 3rd DCA 1991); FL. St. § 718.122 (1987).

128. *90 Community Up-Date* 3 (Apr. 1990) (newsletter of Becker, Poliakoff, & Streitfeld law offices, Fort Lauderdale, Fla.).

129. I. Packel, *The Organization and Operation of Cooperatives*, 2 (4th ed. 1970).

130. 18 Am.Jur.2d, *Cooperative Associations*, §2 (1985).

131. I. Packel, *The Organization and Operation of Cooperatives*, 3–4, (4th ed. 1970).

132. *Real Estate Transactions*, Cooperative Housing Law and Practice, Vol. 2, 1-1 (1985).

133. I. Packel, *The Organization and Operation of Cooperatives*, 11 (4th ed. 1970).

134. *Id.*, 11.

135. *Id.*, 12.

136. Kohler v. Snow Village, Inc., 475 N.E.2d 1298 (Ohio App. 1984).

137. 11–23 (Packel).

138. *See*, for example: Christian County Farmers Supply Co. v. Supply Co. v. Rivard, 476 N.E.2d 452 (Ill. App. 1985); State v. Franklin Co. Coop Inc., 464 S.2d 120 (Also Civ. App. 1985).

139. 18 Am.Jur.2d, *Cooperative Associations*, §5.

140. *Id.*, §6.

141. *Id.*, §11.

142. *Id.*, §11.

143. *Id.*, §11.

144. Ocala Breeder Sales v. Div. of Pari-Mutuel Wagering, 464 S.2d 1272 (Fla. App. 1985).

145. I. Packel, *The Organization and Operation of Cooperatives*, 46 (4th ed. 1970).

146. 18 Am.Jur.2d, *Corporations*, §109.

147. I. Packel, *The Organization and Operation of Cooperatives*, 63–86 (4th ed. 1970).

148. *Illinois Valley Elec. Co-op., Inc. v. City of Princeton*, 594 N.E. 2d 347 (Ill. App. 3 Dist., 1992).

149. *Brooks v. Sulphur Springs Valley Elec. Co-op.*, 951 F.2d 1050 (9th Cir. 1991).

150. *Hydaburg Co-op Ass'n of Hydaburg v. Hydaburg Fisheries*, 826 P.2d 751 (Alaska 1992).

151. *Yellowstone Valley Electric Cooperative, Inc. v. Montana Power Company*, 822 P.2d 102 (Mont. 1991).

152. *United States v. Elec. Convenience Co-op. Co.*, 922 F.2d 429 (7th Cir. 1991); 28 U.S.C.A. § 1345.

153. 14 Nat'l L.J. (50)5 (August 17, 1992).

154. *Goldberg v. Linden Towers Cooperative #5, Inc.*, 538 N.Y.S.2d 263 (App. Div., 2d Dept., 1989).

155. *Badowski v. Roosevelt Terrace Cooperative, Inc.*, 538 N.Y.S.2d 563 (App.Div., 2d Dept., 1989).

156. *Levandusky v. One Fifth Avenue Aptmt. Corp.*, 553 N.E.2d 1317 (N.Y. 1990) unanimous opinion.

157. *Simon v. National Farmers Organization, Inc.*, 829 P.2d 884 (Kan 1992).

158. *Twelve Lions Renaissance Corp. v. 684 Owners Corp.* , 550 N.Y.S.2d 296 (App. Div., 1st Dept., 1990).

159. *512 East 11th Street HDFC v. Grimmet*, 581 N.Y.S. 2d 24 (N.Y.A.D. 1 Dept., 1992).

160. *Landmark, Inc. v. U.S.*, 25 Cl. Ct. 100 (1992).

161. *Pioneer Telephone Co-op. Inc. v. Oklahoma Tax Com'n*, 832 P.2d 848 (Okl., 1992).

162. *McCaig v. Talladega Pub. Co., Inc.*, 544 So. 2d 875 (Ala., 1989).

163. *Fraiman v. Abrams*, 549 N.Y.S.2d 915 (Sup. Ct., 1989).

164. I. Packel, *The Organization and Operation of Cooperatives*, 4–5 (4th ed. 1970).

165. 15A Am.Jur.2d, *Condominiums and Cooperative Apartments*, §4.

166. *Real Estate Transactions*, Condominium Law and Practice, Vol. 1, Part 1, 1–6 (1985).

167. *Id.*

168. *Id.*

169. 15A Am.Jur.2d, *Condominiums and Cooperative Apartments*, §5.

170. *Drew Associates of N.J. v. State of N.J., Dept. of Community Affairs*, 584 A.2d 807 (N.J. 1991).

171. *Real Estate Transactions*, Condominium Law and Practice, Vol. 1, Part 1, 1 (1985).

172. *Id.*

173. §644(c) (of 1986) permits co-ops to elect deduction of separate taxes and interest.

174. *Id.*

175. I. Packel, *The Organization and Operation of Cooperatives*, 14 (4th ed., 1970).

176. R. Kratovil and R. Werner, *Real Estate Law*, 528 (8th ed., 1983).

177. *Id.*

178. *Real Estate Transactions*, Condominium Law and Practice, Vol. 1, Part 1, 2 (1985).

179. A. Ferrer and C. Stecker, *Law of Condominium*, 6–7 (1967).

180. R. Kratovil and R. Werner, *Real Estate Law*, 528 (8th ed., 1983).
    [*Condominium Cases*: Some illuminating recent decisions are: Developer's fiduciary duty: Old Port Cove Prop. Owners Assn., Inc. v. Ecclestone, 500 S.2d 331 (Fla. 4th DCA, 1986).
    Bylaws and Mortgages: St. Paul Fed. Bank v. Wesby, 501 N.E.2d 707 (Ill. App. 1987).
    Statutes of limitations: Conquistador Condo. v. Conquistador Corp., 500 S.2d 346 (Fla. 4th DCA, 1987).
    Material Alterations: Islandia Condo. Assn., Inc. v. Vermut, 501 S.2d 741 (Fla. 4th DCA, 1987).
    Condo terminology ("unit"; "parcel"); Welleby Condo. Assn. One, Inc. v. W. Lyon Co., 522 S.2d 35 (Fla. 4th DCA, 1988).
    Board "business judgment" standard: Farrington v. Casa Solana Condo Assn., 517 S.2d 70 (Fla, 3rd DCA, 1987).
    Condo age limitations: Roth v. Normandy Shores Yacht and Country Club, Inc., 511 S.2d 658 (Fla. 4th DCA, 1987).
    Reformation of condo instrument in mistakes: Providence Square Assn., Inc., v. Biancardi, 507 S.2d 1366 (Fla. 1987); M. Campbell, *Reformation of Condo Declarations . . .* , 17 Stetson L. Rev. (2) 447 (1988).]

181. H. Huntley, Credit Union Face Challenges to Their Non-Profit Status, *St. Petersburg Times*, p. I (Dec. 23, 1990).

182. Associated Press Reports, *St. Petersburg Times*, p. 1A (Jan. 3, 1991); p. 10A (Jan. 4, 1991).

183. *Payne v. Mundaca Investment Corp.*, 562 N.E.2d (Ind. App. 1990).

38

TRADE ASSOCIATIONS

[Peter E. Lanning contributed much of this chapter in 1988 §§ 384–392.]

§385. TRADE ASSOCIATIONS, IN GENERAL

[See above Section 156, How to Organize a Trade Association.]
A trade association is a nonprofit organization of businesses, usually competitors, brought together out of the desires of members to improve their economic status. Trade associations take many forms. They may consist of businesses engaged in one level of a product industry, or they may consist of members representing various functional levels. In fact, a trade association can also consist of members who are themselves other trade associations.[1] Whatever the makeup of the association, its primary function is to promote the business interests of its members.

Just as trade associations come in many shapes and sizes, trade associations perform a variety of activities designed to improve economic conditions. Some, but certainly not all, of these activities would include promotional campaigns, market and product research, education, programs to gather and disseminate information about an industry or profession, meetings, conferences, trade shows, and promulgating standards of conduct and practices.[2] Associations may also conduct litigation[3] and have been held to be privileged to interfere with the business of a third party in order to protect public and membership interests.[4]

Origin of Trade Associations

It is suggested that the origin of modern trade, business, and professional associations can be traced to the merchant and craft guilds of the middle ages.[5] Medieval guilds performed many functions, such as caring for the sick and the families of imprisoned members, as well as defining the scope of work that guild members could undertake. However, the primary function of these guilds centered on promoting the production of high quality goods at fair prices.[6]

The earliest trade associations in the United States were organized in the middle of the nineteenth century. These early trade associations included The National Association of Wool Manufacturers (1864), The Manufacturing Chemists Association (1872), The American Iron Association (1855), The American Association of Nurserymen (1875), The Writing Paper Manufacturers Association (1861), The American Dental Trade Association (1882), and the American Institute of Laundering (1883).[7] Like trade associations, associations for the professions were organized during the same time period.[8]

§386. PUBLIC ATTITUDES TOWARDS TRADE ASSOCIATIONS

Divergent views are expressed by different people as to the social utility of trade associations. On one hand, associations consisting of competing businesses have led many to sound the alarm that business is engaged in a conspiracy against the public. Thus, the trade association has been called ". . . the principal instrument of restrictive practices. . . ."[9] Another writer has said that, "the real core of the trade association movement . . . has lain in its attack on free competition."[10] On the other hand, it is stated that the trade association, as "an association for political, commercial, or manufacturing purposes, or even for those of science and literature, is a powerful and enlightened member of the community."[11]

Although the attitudes toward these associations have varied, it cannot be doubted that they occupy a privileged niche among organizations. Because trade associations are generally formed for purposes other than the accumulation of organizational profits, they are accorded tax exempt status. Lest these organizations become a shelter for abuses, the Internal Revenue Service has taken the lead in attempts to regulate the privilege. The remainder of this chapter treats the basic tax law regarding the exempt status of trade associations, and also considers the limits which have been placed upon this privilege. It should be noted that *professional associations* and other similar (occupational) organizations raise many of the same issues and also are considered.

§387. GENERAL TAX LAW ASPECTS OF TRADE ASSOCIATIONS

The main provisions in the tax code concerning trade associations are Section 501(c)(6) which discuss tax exemption generally, and Sections 511–513 which cover "unrelated business income" of exempt organizations.

The tax exempt status of trade associations is governed by Section 501(c)(6), which exempts from income taxation ". . . business leagues, chambers of commerce, real estate boards, or professional football leagues . . . not organized for profit and no part of the net earnings of which inures to the benefit of any private shareholder or individual."[12] If a trade association is to enjoy the status of exemption from income taxation under 501(c)(6), it must generally be classified as a *business league* within the meaning of that term, as it is interpreted in relevant treasury regulations and court decisions. The term *business league* is defined by the Internal Revenue Service as follows:

> A business league is an association of persons having some common interest, the purpose of which is to promote such common interest and not to engage in a regular business of a kind ordinarily carried on for profit. It is an organization of the same general type as a chamber of commerce or board of trade. Thus, its activities should be directed to the improvement of business conditions of one or more lines of business as distinguished from the performance of particular services for individual persons. An organization whose purpose is to engage in a regular business of a kind ordinarily carried on for profit, even though the business is conducted on a cooperative basis or produces only sufficient income to be self-sustaining, is not a business league. . . . Organizations otherwise exempt are taxable upon their unrelated business income.[13]

The code section, and the regulation contained in the text above set forth specific criteria which an organization must satisfy in order to qualify as a tax-exempt business league. In general, an organization's purpose must be to improve the business conditions of one or more lines of business, it must refrain from performing services for specific individuals, and none of the benefits of its earnings may inure to the benefit of its members.[14] It should be noted that the regulation also prohibits the undertaking of activities normally engaged in for profit. However, it has been suggested that this test is more or less subsumed by the others, even though occasional reference is made to this factor in decisions.[15]

§388. LINE OF BUSINESS TEST

An association must promote the common interests of one or more lines of business.[16] Pursuant to the *line of business* test, an association qualifies for tax exemption if its purpose is to further the common business interests of all members within a particular industry,[17] or all components of an industry within a set geographic area.[18] An association will not qualify as a tax-exempt business league if it furthers the interests of only a specific portion of an industry or community. For example, the United States Supreme Court has held that an association composed of only holders of Midas Muffler franchises does not satisfy the line of business test, and does not qualify for the privilege of tax exemption. The court reasoned that this association benefited only Midas Muffler dealers and did very little to advance the economic or other goals of the muffler-dealer industry in general.[19] Other groups who have failed to satisfy the line of business requirement include groups composed of entities that sell a single brand of automobile,[20] have licenses to sell a single patented product,[21] or bottle one type of soft drink.[22]

§389. COMMON INTEREST TEST

The second requirement established by the tax regulations is that a trade association not engage in activities consisting of the rendering of services to individual members; trade association activities must be for the benefit of the industry it purports to represent at large.[23] For example, a nonprofit organization, formed by carriers engaged in transoceanic passenger service, was not entitled to tax exempt status when the organization's primary activity was operating a service to arrange for the booking of passengers on ships of association members.[24] It has also been determined that a trade association whose principal activity is the provision of worker's compensation insurance to its members is not entitled to exemption, because this activity is the provision of services to individuals.[25] A barber and beauty shop association which sold insurance to its members has been treated similarly.[26] Further examples of this principle are not necessary. Suffice it to say that a review of the rulings shows that it is well established.[27]

§390. INUREMENT OF EARNINGS TEST

Another condition upon the tax-exempt status of trade and other similar associations is that none of the organization's earnings inure to the benefit of its members.[28] In theory, it could be said that any earnings of the association, which in some way were put to the task of making the organization more effective and efficient, inure to the benefit of the members. In practice, however, the requirement has not been read so broadly. In fact, the *inurement* concept can be read only to exclude the direct or indirect distribution of money. For example, tax exemption was denied to an association that provided financial aid to members, even though this activity was a relatively minor portion of its activities.[29] A violation of the inurement concept is also found when an association undertakes the act of reimbursing the litigation and judgment costs of individual members in malpractice suits.[30] The cases forbidding reimbursement of litigation costs should not be read to prohibit involvement of a trade association in litigation which is for the general benefit of an industry.[31]

§391. INCIDENTAL ACTIVITIES TEST

Thus far, trade associations have been discussed as though they are single-function organizations. However, they often undertake a variety of activities which, if considered alone, might or might not qualify the organization for the privilege of tax exemption. In general, a multi-function association need not worry about losing its tax-exempt status if it engages in activities which taken alone might jeopardize its privilege. A trade association may engage in nonexempt activities so long as these activities are incidental.[32] The term *incidental* can mean incidental in the sense that the provision of a service is only a collateral benefit of a program to achieve a broader purpose.[33] For example, the fact that members of an association received a benefit from quality-control testing at the plants of members was incidental to the association's purpose in seeing to the production of higher quality plywood.[34] Incidental can also mean that a service is only a small part of the association's total activities. One case held that a leather and shoe association's provision of bulletins containing tax, freight, credit and other valuable information, apparently a service to individuals, was incidental to its educational and promotional programs aimed at improving the industry in general.[35] On the other end of the spectrum, an activity which amounts to no more than providing services is not incidental when it accounts for over fifty percent of the association's time.[36] One court has rejected the mathematical approach on the ground that bookkeeping practices could too easily be altered so as to subvert the approach.[37]

§392. UNRELATED BUSINESS INCOME TEST

A trade association's incidental activities may not jeopardize its overall exempt status, and yet a tax may be imposed on any income derived from these sources. *Unrelated business income* means ". . . gross income derived by an organization from any unrelated trade or business . . . regularly carried on by it . . ."[38] Unrelated trade or business is defined as any activity not ". . . substantially related to the basis for its exemption under section 501 . . ."[39] It has been suggested that the test for determining whether an activity is an unrelated trade or business is similar to the test for determining whether an activity, not incidental in nature, would jeopardize an organization's tax-exempt status.[40]

§393. ADVERTISING BY TRADE ASSOCIATIONS

Trade associations often conduct advertising and promotional campaigns in favor of the trade, industry, or profession they represent. Generally, the fact that a trade association advertises will not effect its tax exempt status, so long as individual members are not named or otherwise identified. Naming of specific association members or their products would, presumably, be tantamount to providing advertising services to particular individuals. Therefore, generic advertisements (*e.g.*, a campaign for Washington state apples) are permissible.[41]

Advertising, even if it might be viewed as providing a specific service to members, may not be fatal to overall tax-exempt status, because it might well be only incidental to a larger purpose served by the campaign. For example, a television advertisement run by a plywood association, which briefly flashed a trademark of wood sold by some of its members, was viewed as incidental to the main message which promoted the use of plywood in general.[42]

§394. INDUSTRIAL RESEARCH BY TRADE ASSOCIATIONS

Industrial research of many types is an increasingly important function of trade associations.[43] For tax purposes the benefits of these programs will be seen as benefiting an industry at large if the results are made available to all participants in the industry, including those who are not members of the association conducting the research. If the results are restricted only to association members the program may lead to a denial or revocation of tax exemption, or at least of unrelated business income.[44]

§395. LITIGATION BY TRADE ASSOCIATIONS

[See the chapter on Litigation.]

Trade associations are often involved in litigation.[45] In general, involvement in litigation will not jeopardize the association's tax exempt status as long as the desired result is one of common interest to the association's constituency.[46] Involvement in litigation goes too far when the association finances the individual disputes of its members. Thus, the payment of cost and judgment expenses in litigation involving the malpractice of individual members is providing a service, and may lead to revocation of tax exempt status.[47]

Trade Associations may use constitutional rights to prevail in litigation. After the state of Ohio established a formula for reimbursing Medicaid providers for service related expenses, an association of Medicaid providers sued for declaratory and injunctive relief. The court held that the association had a cause of action under 42 U.S.C.A. §1983 and that the association had been deprived of procedural *due process* concerning their legitimate property interest. The rates established had to be reasonable and adequate.[48]

Nonprofit trade associations can find out, through declaratory action, whether they have complied with legal regulations.[49]

An association of gasoline franchisees brought suit for breach of warranties when the franchisor required them to buy an unleaded gasoline that was unmerchantable because it damaged engines. The court held that claims could be maintained for consequential damages in the form of lost profits and lost secondary profits. Further, lost profit damages could be sought for breach of warranty.[50]

Standing to Sue

[Most of the following subsection was contributed by Marguerite A. DeYoung.]

"Standing" is a legal doctrine to ensure that the plaintiffs have sufficient interest in the issues brought before the court to adequately advocate their position. The law in regard to a trade association's ability to bring suit is well established, and specifically addressed by the Supreme Court in *Hunt v. Washington State Apple Advertising Comm'n*, 432 U.S. 333 (1977). Here the high court articulated a three-part test for associational standing which has been repeatedly cited, even in recent case law:

> "[A]n association has standing to bring a suit on behalf of its members when: (a) its members would otherwise have standing to sue in their own right; (b) the interests it seeks to protect are germane to the organization's purpose; and (c) neither the claim asserted nor the relief requested requires the participation of individual members in the lawsuit." Id. at 343, 97 S.Ct. at 2441.

This test takes into account both the constitutional dimensions of standing as well as the concern that the association properly represent its members in the particular suit. This law has been valid from 1977 to the present.

In *Kansas Health Care Ass'n v. Kansas DSRS*, 958 F.2d 1018 (10th Cir. 1992), the association represented Kansas nursing homes and instituted this challenge to Kansas Medicaid reimbursement plans and the implementation of regulations affecting the reimbursement schedule for nursing home providers who cared for Medicaid recipients. The Court of Appeals determined that the health care association had proper standing to bring a suit on behalf of its members on the basis of the three-part test for associational standing set forth in *Hunt*.

The court determined that under the *Hunt* test, an association has standing only if neither the claim asserted nor the relief requested requires the participation of individual members in the lawsuit. Also, even in the absence of a direct injury to the association itself, the association could have standing solely as the representative of its members.[51]

Similarly, an ambulance association that serviced Medicaid recipients had "standing" as an association, to sue on behalf of for-profit ambulance companies providing services to Medicaid recipients. The suit forced the commissioner of the city human resources administration to negotiate in good faith with the association regarding the fee reimbursement schedule. The court found that good faith negotiation was a required ministerial task of the commissioner.[52]

The Florida Restaurant Association was granted standing to seek declaratory and injunctive relief against Hillsborough County on the basis of the application of the three-prong test, which confers standing to an association to sue for the benefit of its members who are more directly affected by the governmental action than the association itself: (1) a substantial number of the association's members, although not necessarily a majority, are substantially affected by the challenged rule; (2) the subject matter of the rule is within the association's general scope of interest and activity; and (3) the relief requested is the type appropriate for a trade association to receive on behalf of its members.[53]

In *Fla. League of Cities v. DER*, 603 So.2d 1363 (Fla. 1st DCA 1992) the city, county, and association of cities challenged the proposed rule establishing minimum standards for waste management and disposal. The court applied the three-prong test espoused in *Florida Restaurant Ass'n,* set forth in Section 3, and determined that the association of cities did in fact have standing. In addition, the court cites to Section 120.54(4)(a), Florida Statutes (1989), which provides that: "[a]ny substantially affected person may seek an administrative determination of the invalidity of any proposed rule on the ground that the proposed rule is an invalid exercise of delegated legislative authority." Because one of the purposes of the Administrative Procedure Act was to expand the public's access to governmental agency activities, both trade and professional associations are accorded standing to represent the interests of their injured members. As such, a trade or professional association should be able to institute a rule challenge even though it is acting solely as the representative of its members. To do so the association must demonstrate the fulfillment of the *Hunt* prerequisites to standing.[54]

In fact, a nonprofit trade association of milk producers has standing to challenge provisions of the milk marketing orders issued by the Secretary of Agriculture, even though there are on-going rule making procedures to adopt new orders, because enjoining the enforcement of the old orders would redress the producers' on-going injuries.[55]

A declaratory judgment action challenging the fee and disclosure requirements adopted for a statewide waste management program was brought by a not-for-profit association of chemical recycling businesses in *Ohio Chem. Recyclers Ass'n v. Fisher,* 607 N.E.2d 852 (Ohio App. 10th 1992). After the businesses had individually attempted to resolve these matters, the companies formed the nonprofit trade association filing this action for declaratory and injunctive relief.

The court refused to deny standing to the association merely on the basis that it had not participated in the initial rule-making proceeding determining the administrative regulation of fee and disclosure requirements. Constitutional challenges to an administrative proceeding are a proper subject matter for a declaratory judgment action, and an administrative agency is without jurisdiction to determine the constitutional validity of a statute, thereby granting the association standing to seek relief.[56]

A trade association has standing to bring suit on behalf of its members if the members would otherwise have standing to sue in their own right, the interests it seeks to protect relate to its purpose, and neither the claim asserted nor the relief requested requires participation of individual members. To seek a writ of mandamus, the association must be beneficially interested in the outcome, a party with special interest or particular right above the interest held by the public at large. However, if the question is one of public right and the object of mandamus is to enforce public policy, a trade association has standing to seek a writ of mandamus under the public interest exception to the "beneficial interest" requirement.[57]

A trade association of general contractors brought an action against the

City of Jacksonville in *Northeastern Florida Chapter v. City of Jacksonville, Fla.*, 951 F.2d 1217 (11th Cir. 1992). The association challenged the city's contract set-aside program for minority business enterprises. Ultimately, the court determined that the association lacked standing to challenge such a program, unless its individual members had standing to litigate their claims.

A plaintiff, to properly invoke Article III standing, must:

> "(1) demonstrate injury of a direct, personal, economic or noneconomic, actual or threatened, real and not hypothetical nature; (2) show injury resulting from defendant's violation of a constitutional or statutory right; and (3) satisfy the court that plaintiff is within the zone of interests intended to be protected by the constitution or statute. Plaintiff must also show that the injury is likely to be redressed by a favorable decision."[58]

Cases arising from shipping, trade, etc. with foreign nations present an added dimension to general trade association standing to sue in within the United States. In the *Matter of Oil Spill By The Amoco Cadiz*, 954 F.2d 1279 (7th Cir. 1992), involving the oilspill off the coast of France by the American corporation of Amoco, French trade associations sought to bring suit in the United States to collect damages. The court dealt with the issue of whether a foreign trade association could bring suit in a U.S. court. Accordingly, the court articulated that, generally, the question in each case is who is the real party in interest. This often depends on the law of the place creating the claim. The court thus turned to the law of France to discover whether the trade associations are authorized to represent the interests of their members. As such, French law stated that a trade association may represent its members' collective interests in litigation, but may represent the members' individual interests only if the association's charter expressly gives it that right. The association had no such express right and was thus precluded from bringing suit.[59]

§396. LOBBYING BY TRADE ASSOCIATIONS

[See the next chapter.]

An association may pursue legislative matters without much fear of losing its tax exemption as a business league. In fact, an organization whose sole purpose is to advocate the desirability or undesirability of legislation of interest to an industry is held to be entitled to the privilege of tax exemption.[60]

Lobbying may have an effect on the deductability of dues paid by members to the association. Dues are deductible so long as the association confines its activities to such functions as appearances before legislative bodies, or individual legislators or committees. Dues may not be deductible if the association becomes involved in efforts to persuade the general electorate. This is impermissible "grass rooting," as it is called in the treasury regulations.[61]

Trade Association Challenge to Legislation

The state may change the method of making employer contributions to a teachers' retirement fund association without impairing the teachers' contractual rights, even though the fund is thereby allegedly made actuarially unsound.[62]

A association of Black teachers, all or whom were terminated after they failed the Texas teacher competency test, sued alleging disparate impact and disparate treatment under Title VII of the Civil Rights Act. However, the difference in pass rates between white and black teachers was not significant enough to prove disparate impact. Intent to discriminate, which indicates disparate treatment, could not be proved to the court.[63]

Statute requiring that all teachers be paid on a uniform basis does not justify their association efforts to "grandfather" salary entitlements for some employees, nor to "freeze" some who failed to finish additional course work. Teachers' association should demand reclassification of *all*[64]

An association of out-of-state ticket manufacturers sued to declare a Minnesota statute invalid because the statute required that all tickets sold in Minnesota be manufactured in Minnesota. The court held that the requirements of the law violated the commerce clause.[65]

A statute completely outlawing the taking of oysters from a bay by any mechanized dredge or rake unconstitutionally impairs perpetual oyster harvesting leases which allowed the use of any implements or appliances.[66]

A state statute, limiting to 115% of "reasonable charges" the amount that physicians could charge Medicare patients, is constitutional.[67]

A statute that restricts chiropractors and other health care providers from direct solicitation of patients who have been recently involved in automobile accidents violates the commercial free speech of the health care providers. The state may only prohibit commercial speech that is false, deceptive, misleading, or that proposes an illegal transaction. The state must choose a reasonable means of directly advancing a substantial governmental interest—though not the least restrictive means.[68]

The State Highway and Transportation Commission may place logo signs, which announce vendors of food, fuel, and lodging at highway exits, on highway right-of ways, despite the objections of a nonprofit corporation which represents vendors of outdoor advertising.[69]

The state can constitutionally ban the use of the names "accountant" and "accounting" by non licensed persons only where the use of those generic terms would potentially mislead the public. Unlicensed persons can use the terms if they further state that they are not licensed by the state or that the services they perform are not required to be licensed by the state.[70]

A plumbers' association sued to challenge the constitutionality of a New Jersey statute which permitted only licensed master plumbers to act as plumbing contractors. The statute was held to be too broad, in that it expanded the exclusive jurisdiction of plumbers beyond buildings and structures, depriving piping contractors and laborers of their prior employment opportunities.[71]

Where amendments to regulations have general application, are promulgated pursuant to the rule-making authority of an agency, and are complete with a finding of no adverse economic impact on small businesses, the agency need only provide a rational basis for the regulation amendments. Nonprofit trade unions that challenge the amendments are not entitled to a hearing before adoption of the amendments.[72]

§397. TRADE SHOWS

A nonprofit association may be organized primarily to conduct conventions and trade shows. Whether or not the association is exempt as a business league will depend on the *common interest* test. For example, an association which allows only members to participate in the show will be providing services to individuals and will not qualify for exemption. But the same association will be exempt if non-members are also allowed to participate.[73]

An organization which is otherwise exempt from income taxation may earn taxable unrelated business income from a trade show. A series of revenue rulings have defined the tests of when an association will be held to realize unrelated business income from money taken in from the rental of exhibit space. In order to avoid having rental space income taxed, the association must not advertise that selling and order taking will be permitted.[74] Furthermore, this practice may not be specifically permitted [75] or condoned.[76] Positive steps that an association may take in order to avoid the unrelated business income pitfall include efforts to prohibit sales and order taking, as well as encouraging exhibitors to use educational and communications displays.[77]

§398. ILLEGAL ACTIVITIES

Surprising as it sounds, a trade association may sometimes engage in illegal activities without jeopardizing its overall tax-exempt status, so long as the illegal activities are only incidental to the broader purposes or activities of the association.[78] This aspect of the tax law may be important to trade associations because they often are the defendants in antitrust litigation.[79] (See the chapter on Antitrust Laws.)

A teachers' union agreement with the Board of Education, expanding the *statutory* recall rights of teachers who were laid off is null and void.[80]

A nonprofit insurance federation, representing domestic and foreign insurance companies, can not use individual medical underwriting to exclude individuals from small-group health insurance. Such a policy is contrary to the Unfair Insurance Practices Act.[81]

§399. TRADE ASSOCIATION TRENDS

[Michael Willis contributed most of this section.]

Two main differences between §501(c)(3) "charitable" and §501(c)(6) "*trade association*" *tax exemption* tests are that the first may not lobby and second not get "charitable gifts."[82]

But significant profit-making activities of a trade association, as by *rebates* regularly bigger than expenditures, are not proper "services" and are taxable as unrelated business income.[83] Thus, profits from insurance policies offered to members are not tax exempt.[84]

"*Standing to sue*" of a trade association is granted only when the association is directly "affected" or "aggrieved."[85]

Setting of *industry standards* by an association does not per se make it liable for injuries related to those standards, while *supervision* of them *may* cause liability.[86]

Antitrust violations by association members may cause civil liability of the association if the standards that it set gave "apparent" authority to violate the antitrust law, or it acted unreasonably in its self-regulation.[87] Some few cases holding politically motivated *boycotts* to be exempt from antitrust law seem to be in a state of doubt, and limited to their particular facts.[88]

Membership Termination: Property Rights

The older "per se" rule as to *exclusion* of association members for improper reasons is being overruled by recent case decisions dealing with a more liberal "rule of reason."[89] A termination of a trade association member's membership is a nullity if shown to have been done in bad faith.[90]

Termination of membership of a NPO (Farm Bureau) member, for "the interest of the membership as a whole," as provided in the bylaws, is not violation of due process, and does not invade his claimed property right to continued membership benefits such as the right to continue his policy with an insurer who sold policies to members, nor is it interference with his (insurance) contract.[91]

§400. FORMS

A few sample Forms of a few aspects of trade (occupational) associations are set forth in this chapter. See the Index for many more.

FORM NO. 164
Preamble to Professional Association
Constitution

[Note: This form also asserts "labor union" status, which is not done in most professional associations.]

We the members of this Association do hereby declare that henceforth this organization shall be known as the (city/town) Police Officers' Association.

We the members of the (city/town) Police Officers' Association do declare and pledge the protection of our autonomy as a free body of American citizens, in our capacity as public employees.

The objective of the (city/town) Police Officers' Association shall be to advance the moral, social, and material standing of the members of the Association by honorable and lawful means. As a labor organization, the Association shall endeavor to achieve collective bargaining with binding arbitration.

The (city/town) Police Officers' Association shall be of corporate unity pursuant to the right and liberty of free association under natural and common law, the law of the Constitution of the United States of America and the State of _____, to promote and to protect the welfare of one another, and to provide financial and legal assistance, subject to the discretion of the Executive Board in accordance with the Constitution and Bylaws of this Association.

FORM NO. 165
Membership Eligibility Clauses
in Professional Association Constitution

Section 1. Any commissioned police officer or turnkey assigned to the Metropolitan Police Department may apply for membership in the Police Officers' Association.

Section 2. Admission to the association is voluntary. Written applications shall be made to the executive board. A file of said applications shall be maintained by the financial secretary.

Section 3. Upon their date of appointment, all commissioned police officers or turnkeys shall be eligible to apply for membership in the Association.

Section 3A. Applicants eligible for membership in the association may apply for membership during the initial period of one year following their date of appointment to the department without assessment of fees. Any applicant applying for membership after the initial period of one year has lapsed, must pay a compensation fee equal to the normally assessed dues for the period subsequent to the expiration of the initial one year following his appointment to the department to the time of application for membership in the Association, the said sum not to exceed $100.

Section 3B. All reinstated commissioned officers of this department who were not members of the association at the time of their termination and who have not been on the department for two or more years at the time of termination shall be governed in terms of eligibility by Article One, Section 3A.

Section 3C. All reinstated commissioned officers of this department who were members of this association in good standing upon their termination may reactivate their membership without cost by written application within 90 days of reinstatement. Should this period lapse, Article One, Section 3A shall determine eligibility.

Section 4. Extraordinary applications for membership shall be considered by the executive board. Approval of such applicants must be a two-thirds vote of those present at an executive board meeting with a *quorum.*

Section 5. Should any objections by any active member of this association to any applicant arise, such objections shall be submitted in writing to the executive board which shall consider the objections and the questioned application.

FORM NO. 166
Dues Rules of
Professional Association

Section 1. The active membership dues shall be one percent of a five-year patrolman's salary each pay period, payable through the payroll deduction plan.

Section 2. POA members who retired prior to July 1, 19___, when a blanket life insurance policy for all SLPOA members became effective, shall have the option, unless already forfeited, of maintaining a $1,000 life insurance policy with a special dues payment of $42.00 per annum, payable January 1st, of each year.

Section 3. Any assessments must be submitted to the active membership of the Association for approval.

Section 4. It shall be the duty of all members to pay the dues and fees of the association when due; support the association and its members; and abide by the rules, regulations and Bylaws of the Association. In the event a member of the association willfully violates any of the provisions of the constitution or Bylaws, or any lawfully adopted resolution of the executive board or general membership, he may be fined, suspended or expelled from membership in the association or removed from office in accordance with the provisions of Article 1, Section 7 and its subsections. Any fine or delinquent dues, fee or assessment not paid within 30 days shall constitute a debt to the association which may be collected by the association through judicial action to collect, the amount owed plus interest, court costs, and the Association's reasonable attorney fees. The executive board may adopt detailed trial procedures in specific cases, a copy of which shall be served on the charged member at a reasonable time before his hearing date.

Section 5. Suspended members shall not be required to pay dues during the period of his/her suspension.

FORM NO. 167
Membership Invitation/Application
of a Professional Association

Dear Fellow Educator:

The Association of Teachers, Inc. (A.T.) is dedicated to improving the life style of teachers throughout the country. Examples of services provided through A.T. are listed below. To receive information on any of the following items, please check (4) the appropriate box and return to Association of Teachers, Inc.

Thank You, _____, President

P.S. Staff personnel are also eligible for membership!

☐ State Retirement Information National Buying Discounts
☐ Tax Shelter Annuity Part Time Income Opportunities
☐ High Yield Tax Deferred Insurance Programs Grocery Coupons
☐ Education Video Tapes and Software Group Health/Disability
☐ Credit Cards: For prescreening give SS# _____

Name _____
         First   M.I.   Last

Address _____

_____
         City   State   Zip

Home Phone (____) _____ School Phone (____) _____
         Area   Area

School System _____ Subject/Grade _____
JOIN BY PHONE—For faster service call toll free 1-800- _____,
California residents call 1-800- _____.

POINTS TO REMEMBER

- Trade Associations must protect an entire trade or industry, rather than only some of those in that trade or industry.
- Remember that *public* interests, as well as those of people in the trade, must be protected.
- Expect Federal Tax Law to be the main test of propriety or impropriety of actions.
- Expect scrutiny under Antitrust Law too.

NOTES TO CHAPTER 38

1. G. Lamb and C. Shields, *Trade Association Law and Practice*, 3 (1971).

2. G. Webster, *The Law of Associations*, 1-12-1-13 (1971).

3. Mutation Mink Breeders Ass'n v. Low Nierenberg Corp., 23 F.R.D. 155 (S.D. N.Y. 1959) (trade association held to have standing to sue under the Lanham Act to restrain a business's misleading use of a name or mark.) See also, Florida Bar v. Furman, 376 So.2d 378 (Fla. 1979) (Bar Association action against legal secretary for engaging in the unauthorized practice of law.)

4. Middlesex Concrete P. & E. Corp. v. Carteret Industrial Ass'n, 37 N.J. 507, 181 A.2d 774 (1962).

5. G. Webster, *The Law of Associations*, 1-3, 1-8-1-10 (1971).

6. *Id.* at 1-3.

7. G. Lamb and C. Shields, *Trade Association Law and Practice*, 5 (1971).

8. G. Webster, *The Law of Associations*, 1-10-1-11 (1971).

9. G. Lamb and C. Shields, *Trade Association Law and Practice*, 4 (1971).

10. *Id.* at 4.

11. *Id.* at 4-5.

12. IRC. §501(c)(6) (1985).

13. Treas. Reg. §1.501(c)(6)-1 (1958).

14. *See*, IRC. §501(c)(6) (1985); Treas. Reg. §1.501(c)(6)-1 (1958).

15. G. Lamb and C. Shields, *Trade Association Law and Practice*, 245 (1971).

16. Treas. Reg. §1.501(c)(6).

17. Commissioner v. Chicago Graphics Arts Federation, Inc., 128 F.2d 424 (7th Cir. 1942); Crooks v. Kansas City Hay Dealer's Ass'n, 37 F.2d 83 (8th Cir. 1929).

18. American Plywood Ass'n v. United States, 267 F. Supp. 830 (W.D. Wash. 1967); National Leather & Shoe Finders Ass'n v. Commissioner, 97 T.C. 121 (1947).

19. National Muffler Dealer's Ass'n v. United States, 440 U.S. 482 (1979).

20. Rev. Rul. 67-77, 1967-1 C.B. 138.

21. Rev. Rul. 58-294, 1958-1 C.B. 244.

22. Rev. Rul. 68-182, 1968-1 C.B. 263 [IRS. announces its nonacquiescence in Pepsi-Cola Bottler's Ass'n v. United States, 369 F.2d 250 (7th Cir. 1966). The court in Pepsi-Cola held that an association of Pepsi-Cola bottlers was entitled to tax exemption as a business league even though the association consisted of members who bottled only Pepsi-Cola brand. The validity of the decision has been question by others. *See*, National Muffler Ass'n v. United States, 440 U.S. 482 (1979).]

23. Rev. Rul. 74-228, 1974-1 C.B. 136.

24. *Id.* at 136.

25. Rev. Rul. 74-81, 1974-1 C.B. 135.

26. Associated Master Barbers & Beauticians of America, Inc., 69 T.C. 53 (1977).

27. *See*, Rev. Rul. 73-411, 1973-2 C.B. 180; Rev. Rul. 65-14, 1965-1 C.B. 236; Rev. Rul. 70-591, 1970-2 C.B. 153; Rev. Rul. 80-287, 1980-2 C.B. 185 (Nonprofit lawyer referral service operated by local bar associations is exempt as a business league because the activity improved conditions in the legal profession as a whole. Under the guidelines of the association, lawyers who accepted a referral were required to remit the reduced fee paid by clients for the initial interview to the service. The IRS did not view this activity as a provision of services to individuals).

28. IRC. §501(c)(6) (1985).

29. Rev. Rul. 67-251, 1967-2 C.B. 196.

30. *National Chiropractic Ass'n, Inc. v. Birmingham*, 96 F. Supp. 874 (N.D. Iowa 1951).

31. *See infra*, §394.

32. *American Plywood Ass'n v. United States*, 267 F. Supp. 830 (W.D. Wash. 1967).

33. *Id.* at 830.

34. *Id.* at 830.

35. *National Leather & Shoe Finders Ass'n*, 9 T.C. 121 127 (1947).

36. *Indiana Retail Hardware Ass'n v. United States*, 336 F.2d 988 (Ct. Cl. 1966).

37. *Southern Hardwood Traffic Ass'n v. United States*, 68-1 U.S.T.C. ¶9295 (W.D. Tenn. 1968).

38. IRC. §512(a) (1993).

39. IRC. §513(a) (1993).

40. G. Lamb and C. Shields, *Trade Association Law and Practice*, 250 (1971).

41. *Washington State Apples, Inc.*, 46 B.T.A. 64 (1942).

42. *American Plywood Ass'n v. United States*, 267 F. Supp. 830 (W.D. Wash. 1967).

43. G. Lamb and C. Shields, *Trade Association Law and Practice*, 245 (1971).

44. Rev. Rul. 70-187, 1970-1 C.B. 131.

45. *See supra*, text and accompanying notes at §384.

46. Rev. Rul. 67-175, 1967-1 C.B. 139 (Association of growers and processors of agricultural products in a given region hired attorneys to bring an action to secure an injunction to stop a factory from polluting the air in this area. This ruling stated that the association's activity would not jeopardize its tax exempt status under section 501(c)(6) because this activity was in the furtherance of common interests.).

47. *See supra* at §390.

48. *Ohio Academy of Nursing Homes, Inc. v. Barry*, 564 N.E. 2d 686 (Ohio 1990).

49. *See e.g., Ingredient Communication Council, Inc. v. Lundgren*, 4 Cal. Rptr. 2d 216 (Cal. App. 3 Dist. 1992) (warnings found insufficient under Safe Drinking Water and Toxic Enforcement Act concerning carcinogenic and toxic substances).

50. *AM/PM Franchise Ass'n v. Atlantic Richfield Co.*, 584 A. 2d 915 (Pa. 1990).

51. *Kansas Health Care Ass'n v. Kansas DSRS*, 958 F.2d 1018 (10th Cir. 1992).

52. *Ambulance Ass'n of Greater New York, Inc. v. Grinker*, 564 N.Y.S. 2d 279 (A.D. 1 Dept. 1990).

53. *Hillsborough County v. Florida Restaurant Ass'n*, 603 So.2d 587 (Fla. 2d DCA 1992).

54. *Fla. League of Cities v. DER*, 603 So.2d 1363 (Fla. 1st DCA 1992).

55. *Minnesota Milk Producers Ass'n v. Madigan*, 956 F.2d 816 (8th Cir. (Minn.), 1992).

56. *Ohio Chem. Recyclers Ass'n v. Fisher*, 607 N.E.2d 852 (Ohio App. 10th 1992).

57. *Driving School Ass'n of California v. San Mateo Union High School Dist.*, 14 Cal. Rptr. 908 (Cal. App. 1 Dist., 1992).

58. *Northeastern Fla. Chapter v. City of Jacksonville, Fla.* 951 F.2d 1217 (11th Cir. 1992).

59. *Matter of Oil Spill By The Amoco Cadiz*, 954 F.2d 1279 (7th Cir. 1992).

60. Rev. Rul. 61-177, 1961-2 C.B. 117.

61. Treas. Reg. §1.162-20 (1969).

62. *Minneapolis Teachers Retirement Fund Ass'n v. State*, 490 N.W. 2d 124 (Minn. App., 1992).

63. *Frazier v. Garrison I.S.D.*, 980 F. 2d 1514 (5th Cir. (Tex.), 1992).

64. *California Teachers Assn. v. Governing Board*, 276 Cal. Rptr. 222 (App., 1990).

65. *National Ass'n of Fund Raising Ticket Manufacturing v. Humphrey,* 753 F. Supp. 1465 (D. Minn. 1990).

66. *State v. Leavins,* 599 So. 2d 1326 (Fla. App. 1 Dist., 1992).

67. *New York State Soc. of Orthopaedic Surgeons, Inc. v. Gould,* 796 F. Supp. 67 (E.D.N.Y., 1992).

68. *Gregory v. Louisiana Bd. of Chiropractic Examiners,* 608 So. 2d 987 (La., 1992).

69. *Missouri Outdoor Advertising Ass'n, Inc. v. Missouri State Highways and Transp. Com'n,* 826 S.W. 2d 342 (Mo. banc. 1992).

70. *Moore v. California State Bd. of Accountancy,* 9 Cal. Rptr. 2d 358 (Cal. 1992).

71. *Mechanical Contractors Ass'n of New Jersey, Inc. v. State,* 605 A.2d 743 (N.J. Super. A.D. 1992).

72. *Gasda Ltd. v. Adduci,* 582 N.Y.S. 2d 525 (A.D. 3 Dept. 1992).

73. American Woodworking Machinery and Equipment Show, Inc. v. United States, 249 F. Supp. 392 (M.D. N.C. 1966).

74. Rev. Rul. 75-517, 1975-2 C.B. 221.

75. Rev. Rul. 75-519, 1975-2 C.B. 226.

76. Rev. Rul. 75-518, 1975-2 C.B. 225.

77. Rev. Rul. 75-516, 1975-2 C.B. 220.

78. United States v. Omaha Livestock Traders Exchange, 366 F.2d 749 (8th Cir. 1966).

79. I.S. Bass, T. Belcher, W. Dallas, S. Egan, J. Latwin, R.B. Rich, *Trade Associations and the Antitrust Laws,* 46 Brooklyn L. Rev. 179 (1980).

80. *Board of Educ. of Depew Free School Dist. v. Depew Teachers Orgn., Inc.,* 562 N.Y.S.2d 275 (App. Div., 1990).

81. *Insurance Federation of Pennsylvania, Inc. v. Foster,* 587 A.2d 865 (PA. 1990).

82. Houck, *With Charity for All,* 1984 *Yale L. J.* 1415, at 1432.

83. *Carolinas Farm & Power Equip. Dealers Assn. v. U.S.,* 699 F.2d 167 (4th Cir., 1983).

84. *Professional Insur. Agents of Mich. v. Comr.,* 726 F.2d 1097 (6th Cir. 1984).

85. See, *American Booksellers Association v. Randall,* 481 A.2d 919 (PA Super. 1984).

86. *Meyers v. Donnatucci,* 531 A.2d 398 (NJ Super., 1987); *Steel Joist Institute, Inc. v. J. H. Mann, Inc.,* 171 So. 2d 625 (FL DCA, 1977).

87. *American Society of Mechanical Engineers, Inc. v. Hydrolevel Corp.,* 456 U.S. 556 (1982); and see, *Arizona v. Maricopa County Medical Society,* 457 U.S. 332 (1982); Greenblatt (article), 38 *U. Miami L. Rev.* 741, 759 (1984); Ledman (article), 47 *Ohio State L. J.* 729, 738 (1986).

88. Mahoney, *A Market Power Test for Noncommercial Boycotts,* 93 *Yale L. J.* 523 (1984).

89. *Phil Tolkan Datsun, Inc. v. Greater M. Datsun D. Advertising Association, Inc.,* 672 F.2d 1280 (7th Cir. 1982); *Rothery Storage v. Atlas Van Lines,* 792 F.2d 210 (D.C. Cir. 1986).

90. *Automotive Elec. Service Corp. v. Assn. of Automotive Aftermarket Distributors,* 747 F. Supp. 1483 (D.C., N.Y., 1990).

91. *Elgin v. Montgomery County Farm Bureau,* 549 So. 2d 486 (Ala. 1989).

39

LOBBYING AND POLITICAL ACTION

[Section 402 and parts beyond in this Chapter were contributed by Phyllis Chew.]

§401. LOBBYING, IN GENERAL

Outline of *lobbying* and *grassrooting* law is set forth herein in Chapter 17 at Section 190. The Internal Revenue Code provisions, and case decisions, limiting a tax-exempt organization's *propaganda* or "attempting to influence legislation," are there summarized. The distinction between an *action* organization (*e.g.*, a taxable one) and nonpartisan research and analysis (*e.g.*, valid activities) is the most important item. For example, a city bar association that *rates candidates* for judicial positions (elective or appointive) is participating in *political campaigns* on behalf of candidates for public office, and does *not* qualify for tax-exempt status as a charitable and educational organization under I.R.C. §501(c)(3).[1]

Members' Objection to Lobbying

Members of a state bar association (California) may withhold their dues if the association uses the money to campaign for political or social causes to which they object; e.g., campaigning for causes such as nuclear weapons freeze and handgun control. A state bar association (integrated bar) resembles a labor union more than a government agency, and thus may not use members' dues to support political or ideological views (such as gun control) not approved by its members; it is supposed to use them for regulating and improving legal services. Misuse of dues violates the First Amendment.[2]

PACs

Political Action Committees, often referred to as PACs, are a source of widespread concern today; many people fearing that they corrupt democracy by buying the votes of state and federal legislators and officers (*e.g.*, by campaign fund "contributions"). Thus, in 1984 Florida legislators got $4.1 million of the $7.1 million raised by special interest groups.[3] Lobbyists in that state were said to "wield more power than politicians."[4] Churches then were reported to be exercising great "corporate clout" as stockholders in major American business corporations, with the National Council of Churches' 19 Protestant denominational orders and 210 Roman Catholic orders and dioceses owning about $10 billion worth of stock in United States companies.[5] They affected matters from nuclear arms agreements to industrial-social policies. Lists of big money contributions to political office-holders were published, as illustrations of "The best legislatures that money can buy."[6]

But a counter-current of tendencies to limit the propaganda is a constant restraining factor. For example, in 1986 several state courts (in California and New Hampshire) and federal circuit courts forebade even state bar associations from using mandatory dues of members for any propaganda other than matters germane to their administration-of-justice functions.[7] And, in a New York case, a coalition of special-interest groups was held to "lack standing" as taxpayers to challenge the constitutionality under State Finance Law of a Prison Construction Act.[8]

§402. FEDERAL LOBBYING LAW

[This Section is based on a report issued in March 1985 by the National Federation of State Humanities Councils, 12 South 6th Street, Minneapolis, Minn. 55402; titled Lobbying By NonProfit Organizations: A Summary of the Regulations.]

Nonprofit organizations are the ones most affected by laws that *limit lobbying*, because they can lose their vital tax-exempt status if they violate the law. Campaign *contributions* are not the same thing, and are subject to other rules.

Foreign lobbyists are a separate, and often secretive, problem. See, for example: S. Goldberg, *Japan's Lobbyists Keep Trade Door Open in U.S.*, Tampa *Tribune* (Bus. Section) Part 2. (Nov. 3, 1985).

On May 29, 1984 the federal Office of Management and Budget (OMB) created new rules to govern lobbying by nonprofit groups that receive federal grants or contracts took effect. These new rules allow lobbying only with use of *non*-federal funds. They are based on the general regulations that bar such use of federal funds as trips to Washington to exercise legislative persuasion with congresspeople.[9]

Three main federal laws govern nonprofit's lobbying:

1. 18 U.S. Code §1913 (barring use of federal funds by federal employees for lobbying). This, in effect, bars similar action by nonprofit groups, as it involves criminal punishment for the guilty official or employee.

2. Internal Revenue Code [especially §501(c)(3)], as revised by Tax Reform Act of 1976 (barring "substantial"—over 5% of organization revenues—use for lobbying by nonprofit groups) but allowing "election" to spend up to 20 percent of its first $500,000 expenditures, etc.—Maximum $1 million/year); up to 25 percent on "grass-roots" lobbying.[10]; But as far as the IRS law is concerned, lobbying is only such activity as involves spending of money. What effects the 1984 and 1986 Tax Reform laws will have is not likely to be apparent for many years.

3. *OMB Circular A-122* (establishing cost principles for nonprofit groups). This divides lobbying into (a) *direct* communications with legislatures or their members or employees, and (b) *grass-roots* communications to persuade the general public to press legislators. Exceptions allowed are (a) testimony responding to *written request* by legislators, (b) nonpartisan *research* or analysis, (c) communications not *primarily* trying to influence, (d) routine *discussion*-type communications with organization members, and (e) defensive activities to *preserve* organization tax-exempt status.

But the new OMB rules now cover "legislative liaison" (*e.g.*, attending or recording legislative work sessions), for which federal funds may not be used. And, most important, nonprofit groups must report not only expenditures of federal funds in lobbying, but also of private funds for lobbying, if they seek federal grants. This last worries some groups, which view it as an infringement on freedom of speech and other rights.[11] Since 1978, the IRS also has been issuing *revenue rulings* on *grass-rooting* expenses, and other aspects of lobbying's effect on tax exemption. A heavy tax excise penalty and loss of exemption for continued violations are the chief IRS sanctions; not to mention possible criminal proceedings. *See,* as to 1976 tax-reform changes (Conable-Muskie Act), J. Nix (article), 81 W. Va. L. Rev. 407 (1979). For "election" under the tax law, use Treasury (IRS) Form 5768.

Lobbying is a useful and honorable instrument for democratic persuasion of legislators, as long as it is not abused. Few people would urge that it be outlawed. The same is not true for "campaign contributions," which now are so massive as to cause people to talk often about "The best congress (or, legislature) that money can buy." Persuasive argument or evidence-providing is one thing; cash "gifts" another kind of "persuasion" entirely.

§403. STATE LOBBYING LAW

State regulation of lobbyists is partly based on the federal rules. Florida's law is fairly typical of what little regulation is required by the states. Its statute is relatively detailed and specific:

§11.045 Lobbyists: registration and reporting; exemptions; penalties.

§11.05 Oath by lobbyist; penalty for false swearing.

§11.06 Member of committee may administer oath.

§11.061 State employee lobbyists; registration; recording attendance; penalty; exemptions.

§11.062 Use of state funds for lobbying prohibited; penalty. ch 106 Campaign Financing.

Election Law also applies to the use of lobbyists and lobbying (see Sections which follow). In the enforcement of state regulation the election laws often provide the most complete coverage of the subject of "political" action.

Lobbyists: Definition

A *lobbyist* is any person other than a member of a legislature or one of its duly authorized aides who seeks to encourage the passage, defeat or modification of any legislation in the Senate or the House of Representatives or any committee thereof.[12]

Lobbyists, in general seem to have been quite unregulated in the past. The law with respect to lobbyists and their related activities today still is very limited. The *Florida Statute* sets out *registration requirements* for persons who engage in political lobbying.[13] It requires a lobbyist to submit a semi-annual statement of expenditures and sources of funds.[14] It provides that lobbyists, if in doubt concerning the law governing them, shall submit written queries, for an advisory opinion, to a special committee of the legislature; and they may appear and discuss it in person.[15] A list of all registered lobbyists, and of all advisory opinions, is maintained by the joint legislative office of the state.

Penalties for violations of the lobbyist laws are provided.[16] The penalties are based on reporting alleged violations to the President of the Senate or the Speaker of the House. Sanctions for violations may include reprimand, censure, probation, or prohibition from lobbying for that legislative term.

There are special statues regarding state employees and related lobbying activities. The statute prohibits the use of state funds for lobbying purposes.[17] State employees engaging in lobbyists activities must register as lobbyists, and failure to do so may result in deductions in their salaries of amounts equal to time spent on lobbying. State funds used in lobbyist activities may also be deducted from state employees' salaries.

The Florida Constitution[18] contains the "sunshine amendment." This amendment provides that former legislators and statewide elected officers are prohibited from lobbying their former governmental bodies or agencies for a period of two years following their vacation of office. The Florida Supreme Court invalidated a proposed change in this provision,[19] because "clearly the primary purpose for which the sunshine amendment was adopted was to impose stricter standards on public officials in order to avoid conflicts of interests."[20]

The amendment embodies four important state concerns:

1. The public's right to know an official's interest.
2. The deterrence of corruption and conflicting interest.
3. The creation of public confidence in state officials.
4. Assistance in detecting and prosecuting officials who have violated the law.

Part of the sunshine amendment was specifically designed to prevent those having control over the affairs of public agencies from influencing, or potentially influencing, decisions when they appear as compensated advocates.[21]

The few rules set out above comprise the bulk of Florida law relating to lobbyists and their activities. The law is silent concerning the methods and tactics that lobbyists may employ. Penalties are, however, provided for lobbyists who use false statements.

It appears that lobbyists are free to employ whatever means they choose in order to achieve the results they, or their principals, desire. A lobbyist, in essence, may be the hired gun of a principal whose purpose may remain undisclosed. The potential for corruption in this system is evident.

Many lobbyists are employed by businesses. They represent special interests and not the public at large. Some counterbalance is provided by the lobbying work of public-interest nonprofit organizations.

§404. POLITICAL COMMITTEES AND COMMITTEES OF CONTINUOUS EXISTENCE

"Political Committees" are divided into two classes by some state statutes:[22] a "political committee," and a "committee of continuous existence." An organization must choose which type of committee it wishes to employ.

A *political committee* is one which may support or oppose political candidates, issues or parties. It may make independent expenditures. A *committee of continuous existence* may contribute to the expenses of candidates or political committees. It may not make independent expenditures not support nor oppose specific issues, unless it is registered as a political committee.

Contributions to Committees

The amount which may be contributed to a committee of continuous existence is unlimited as long as 25 percent of its income is derived from dues and assessments of members. There is a $500 limit on the amount which may be contributed by any person to a political committee supporting one or more candidates. There are no limits as to the amount which may be contributed to committees organized solely to support or oppose a particular issue (issues committee).

The United States Court of Appeals, Fifth Circuit, in a 1980 case,[28] reviewed a decision by a lower court wherein a Florida law,[29] limiting the amount that any person may contribute to a committee organized to urge the passage of a constitutional amendment, was held to be unconstitutional. The circuit court affirmed the decision, stating that the law abridged important First Amendment rights and did not tend to prevent corruption or promote disclosure of large contributors. For the same reasons, the restrictions on contributions to committees for candidates are maintained. Contributions to issue committees, however, are unlimited.

The Florida statutes set out the amounts that may be contributed by any person, political committee, or committee of continuous existence to any candidate.[30] The limit is $500 for a candidate for countrywide office or in an election on less then a countrywide basis, a candidate for legislative multi-county office, or a candidate for county court judge or circuit judge. There is a $500 limit as to a candidate for retention as judge of a District Court of Appeal, and $500 limitation for a candidate for statewide office or retention as Justice for the Supreme Court.

§405. POLITICAL ACTIVITIES

[See "Freedom of Association"—Chap. 33]
State legislation to limit unfair political activity of profit and nonprofit organizations (e.g., use of corporation funds—of investors), being a "compelling state interest" to prevent use of such funds to swing voting or elections, may validly limit both business and nonprofit corporations (excluding media corporations).[23]

The United States Office of Personnel Management (OPM) new regulations now permit "*advocacy*" *charities* to participate in the Combined Federal Campaign; e.g., if they provide human health and welfare services, assistance, or programs. NPOs must apply to OPM and demonstrate their qualifications, while charities with annual budgets under $50,000 may submit instead their IRS Form 990 reports instead of an independent audit.[24]

A nonprofit promoter whose name was on bills posted in violation of an antipostering law won his suit challenging the law because the law was unconstitutionally vague. The phrase "violation . . . [that] continues on a regular and ongoing basis" was completely undefined in the statute and implied liability on any person whose name appeared on a handbill.[25]

Nonprofit corporations providing hospital-related services brought an Article 78 proceeding to challenge an administrative decision not to reimburse Medicaid extended to alternative level care patients. The administrative decision was found to be arbitrary and capricious because the statute contained no exception regarding types of care to which it applied. Thus, there is a strong presumption that no exception was intended.[26]

A ban on NPO "pro life" campaign contributions violates constitutional free-speech rights (with three test-features for exemption for NPOs from Fed. Elec. Campaign Act).[27]

§406. POLITICAL COMMITTEES: COMPOSITION AND DUTIES

A political committee is defined as "a combination of two or more individuals, or a person other than an individual, the primary or incidental purpose of which is to support or oppose any candidate, issue, or political party, and which accepts contributions or makes expenditures during a calendar year in an aggregate amount in excess of $500, or the sponsor of a proposed constitutional amendment by initiative intending to seek the signatures of registered electors." Such committees are required to register.[31]

A *statement of organization* must be filed, containing basic information about the committee, the names of the officers, and its anticipated political activities. This statement must be filed within 10 days after organization or within 10 days after information has been received causing the organization to think that it will fall into the category of a committee. If formed within 10 days of an election, it must file immediately. Any change in information must be filed within 10 days. Statements are filed with the division of elections.

If organized to address issues involved in only one county, then the organization must file with the supervisor of elections of that county. If support involves a municipality, then filing is with an officer of that municipality.

Each political committee must appoint a campaign treasurer and designate a campaign depository.[32] These data must be filed with the statement of organization. The treasurer has the responsibility for keeping detailed accounts of contributions and expenditures and deposits and withdrawals. Regular reports on contributions and expenditures must be filed. The committee may appoint up to three deputy treasurers who may be authorized to carry out the duties of the treasurer. A treasurer or deputy may resign. A successor must be appointed immediately.

Campaign depositories must be designated by each committee for the purpose of depositing all contributions and disbursing all expenditures. Campaign depositories may be any bank, savings and loan, or credit union authorized to do business in the state. Secondary depositories may be designated in individual counties. These depositories may only forward contributions to the primary depository. Contributions to secondary depositories must be forwarded before the end of the first business day following the deposit.[33]

§407. CAMPAIGN FINANCES

Campaign accounts must be kept separate from all other accounts, and each must be identified as a campaign account of a named committee.[34] The checks of the account must contain at least:[35]

1. Name of committee

2. Account number and name of bank and

3. Space for:

    a. Amount of expenditure

    b. Signature of treasurer or deputy

    c. Purpose of expenditure, and

    d. Name of payee

The committee may have a savings account for funds that are not currently needed. A certificate of deposit may also be purchased in the committee's name.[36]

The committee may maintain a petty cash fund. The amount of the fund and purposes for which it may be used are limited. Petty cash cannot be used to buy time, space, or services from any media.[37]

Credit cards may be obtained by the committee for travel-related expenditures. The card must reflect that it is a campaign account and be in the name of the committee. A copy of the credit-card agreement between the committee and the bank and a list of all persons authorized to use the card must be filed with the secretary of state. These cards expire no later than midnight of the last day of the month of the general election.[38]

Contributions received by the committee must be deposited in the primary campaign account. These deposits must be accompanied by a deposit slip which states the name of the contributor and the amount contributed.[39]

A committee may not accept cash contributions or contributions by cashier's check in excess of $100.00. If contributions are received less than five days prior to the election, they must be returned to the contributor.[40]

In-kind contributions may be received if, at the time of making such contribution, the contributor places a fair market value on the contribution.[41]

§408. COMMITTEE REPORTS

Political committees must file regular reports of contributions and expenditures. The Florida statute, like many others, sets out the time requirements for filing. Each report must contain the following information.[42]

1. The full name, address and occupation of each contributor, together with the amount and date of the contribution;

2. The name and address of each political committee with which the reporting committee made a transfer of funds, together with the amount and date of transfer;

3. Each loan for campaign purposes to or from the committee, together with name, address, occupation, and principal place of lenders and endorsers, as well as date and amount of loan;

4. A statement of each contribution, rebate, refund, or receipt not listed in a, b, c, or d.

5. The total sum of all loans, in-kind contributions and other receipts

6. The full name and address of each person to whom expenditures have been made; the amount, date, and purpose of each expenditure; the name and address of, and office sought by, each candidate on behalf of whom the expenditure was made. Petty cash expenditures need not be reported

7. The full name and address of each person receiving an expenditure for services or salary not otherwise reported, together with the amount, date, and purpose

8. Total amount withdrawn and spent for petty cash purposes

9. Total sum of expenditures

10. Amount and nature of any savings accounts or certificates of deposits and institutions that hold these accounts

11. A list of all credit card purchases and amount. A copy of each statement must be included in the next report; and

12. Contributions which are returned must also be reported.

If a political committee disbands, it must notify the filing officer and file a final report.

Political Activity Reports

While PAC's (Political Action Committees) of both profit and nonprofit organizations are causing much concern today (*e.g.*, leading to danger of having "The best legislatures that money can buy"), these committees also *do* have *constitutional rights*, such as the one to petition the Congress or legislature for redress of grievances. Thus, a *statute* requiring activity *reports* from such committees [*e.g.*, Fla. St. §106.07(8)(b) (of 1987) as to Division of Elections, Florida Elections Commission, and a fine of $50/day for delay or late filing of the required report] is not applicable when the committee has no activity to report.

"The condition triggering the penalty machinery is the obligation timely to file a report. In the event, however, that no funds have been received or expended, section 106.07(7) specifically provides that 'the filing of the required report for that period is waived.' Thus, if a *report* is not due, it cannot be deemed late. . . .

"The state's concern with keeping track of individuals and committees engaged in raising and expending political money, *see Falzone v State*, 500 So. 2d 1337 (Fla. 1987), simply does not rise to a compelling state interest when persons or entities are only potential mangers of funds and are not engaged in political activity. . . ."[43]

Lobbying Regulation

The essence of *illegality* in lobbying by NPOs is the expenditure of money to influence legislation, because lobbying by NPOs is basically a proper function of such organizations that are tax-exempt under IRC §501(c)(3). I.R.S. 1990 Regulations on P.L. 94-455 § 1307 (1976) sets percentage limitations based on exempt-purpose expenditures.[44]

Committees of Continuous Existence

A "committee of continuous existence" is defined in this state's statute, as any group, organization, or association, or other such entity, which is certified pursuant to its provisions.[45]

Two criteria which must be met in order to qualify as a committee of continuous existence:[46]

1. It must be organized and operated in accordance with a written charter or set of bylaws which contains procedures for the election of officers and directors and which clearly defines membership.

2. At least 25 percent of the income is derived from dues and assessments payable on a regular basis by its membership.

Any group seeking to become a committee of continuous existence must file an application with the state's department of state, division of elections. The division reviews the application and determines if the group meets the criteria, and then notifies the organization.

Regular reports of contributions and expenditures are required to be filed with the division of elections, with duplicates filed with the supervisor of elections in the county in which the committee maintains its books. Requirements for what and when to file are set out, and are similar to those for political committees. All reports must be filed on forms provided by the division of elections.

In addition to regular reports, committees of continuous existence must also file annual reports in January of each year.

The division of elections must revoke the committee's certification if it ceases to meet the criteria for a committee of continuous existence.

§409. A COMPARISON OF FEDERAL REGULATIONS AND STATE RULES

The Federal scheme for political committees is substantially the same as Florida's. There are some differences in time requirements as to contribution limitations, *etc.*, in the *Code of Federal Regulation.*[47]

The most significant distinction between the Florida and federal system is found in the Federal Election Campaign Act of 1971.[48] This Act prohibits corporations and labor organizations from using their general treasury funds to make contributions or expenditures in connection with federal elections. Corporations and labor organizations may, however, use their funds to set up political committees. These committees are called Separate Segregated Funds (SSF) because the funds of the committee must be kept separate from the funds of the corporation or labor organization.

An SSF must register as a political committee. If the fund is solely for the purpose of financing state and local politics, it is not considered a political committee under the Act.

An SSF must disclose the name of its *connected organization*. A "connected organization" is the corporation or labor organization which directly or indirectly established the SSF. The connected organization financially supports the SSF and may exercise control over it. The connected organization may exercise control through the adoption of bylaws and the appointment of SSF officials. Connected organizations may also determine which candidates receive contributions for the SSF.

The Florida statute forbids buying of speaker time at a political meeting,[49] and limits the amounts spent or retained,[50] permits endorsements by groups that file them,[51] limits poll and survey campaigns,[52] and provides various penalties for violations of the law.

How sternly such rules are enforced in any state at any time may well be a function of the local political situation.

§410. "POLITICAL" FINANCES

Current data on PAC and other political campaign finance reports may be obtained from the state and federal offices listed by the Federal Election Commission by writing to: The Federal Election Commission Washington, D.C. 20463.

Lobbyists often chase funds for schools and colleges, but critics say that this *politicizes* academic projects. Congress is not composed of the kind of experts who should be the ones to evaluate scientific and other academic projects; peer review is a much better basis for grants of taxpayers' money.[53]

Omnibus Reconciliation Act became law on Aug. 11 1993, eliminating the *tax deduction* for lobbying expenses, But chambers of commerce and associations' local and county level lobbying was exempted, and reporting and penalty requirements were lessened. Chambers spending less than $2000/yr. were exempted.[54]

§411. FORMS FOR LOBBYING AND PACS

FORM NO. 168
Statement of Organization of Political Committee (Florida)

STATEMENT OF ORGANIZATION OF POLITICAL COMMITTEE
Supporting or Opposing any Candidate, Issue, or Political Party
and which Accepts Contributions or Makes Expenditures During a
Calendar Year in An Aggregate Amount in Excess of $100.
(Section 106.03, Florida Statutes)

1. Full Name of Committee	Date

Mailing Address (If Post Office Box or Drawer, Add Street Address)

City	County	Telephon e

2.   Affiliated or Connected Organizations (Includes Other Committees of Continuous Existence and Political Committees)

Name of Affiliated or Connected Organization	Mailing Address	Relationship

3.   Area, Scope and Jurisdiction of the Committee

4.   Identify by Name, Address and Position, the Custodian of Books and Accounts

Full Name	Mailing Address	Committee Title or Position

5.   List by Name, Address and Position, other Principal Officers. Including Officers and Members of the Finance Committee, if Any:

Full Name	Mailing Address	Committee Title or Position

FORM NO. 168 (continued)

Statement of Organization of Political Committee—Page 2

6. List by Name, Address, Office Sought, and Party Affiliation each Candidate or Other Individual that this Committee is Supporting.

Full Name	Mailing Address	Office Sought	Party

7. List Any Issues this Committee is Supporting:

List Any Issues this Committee is Opposing:

8. If this Committee is Supporting the Entire Ticket of a Party, Give Name of Party:

9. In the Event of Dissolution, What Disposition Will be Made of Residual Funds?

10. List all Banks, Safety Deposit Boxes, or other Depositories used for Committee Funds:

Name of Bank or Depository and Account Number	Mailing Address

11. List all Reports Required to be Filed by this Committee with Federal Officials and the Names, Addresses, and Positions of Such Officials, if any:

Report Title	Dates Required To Be Filed	Name and Position of Official	Mailing Address

State of _____   _____ County

    I, _____, being duly sworn, depose (affirm) and say that the information in this Statement of Organization is complete, true, and correct.

       (seal)   _____
                          (Signature of Chairman of Political Committee)

Subscribed and sworn to (affirmed) before me this _____ day of _____,
A.D., 19____.

                                _____
                                Notary Public

My Commission Expires _____ 19____

FORM NO. 169
Appointment of Campaign Treasurer and Campaign Depository (Florida)

APPOINTMENT OF CAMPAIGN TREASURER AND DESIGNATION OF CAMPAIGN DEPOSITORY FOR POLITICAL COMMITTEE ((S. 106.021(1), Florida Statutes)	CHECK APPROPRIATE BOX ☐ ORIGINAL APPOINTMENT ☐ DEPUTY TREASURER ☐ REAPPOINTMENT OF TREASURER ☐ SECONDARY DEPOSITORY

1. Committee Name	2. Mailing Address		
3. City	4. County	5. State	6. Zip Code

The following person has been appointed to serve as Campaign Treasurer ☐, Deputy Treasurer ☐, for the above named Committee.

7. Name (typed)	8. Street Address	9. Telephone
10. City	11. County	12. State	13. Zip Code

The following bank has been designated as the Primary Depository ☐, Secondary Depository ☐.

14. Bank Name	Street Address		
16. City	17. County	18. State	19. Zip Code

I will notify you of any additions or changes to these appointments.

20. Typed Name of Chairman	21. Signature of Chairman

Sworn and Subscribed before me this _____ day of _____,

19____ at _____, _____ County, Florida.

My commission expires _____ 19____

(seal)

_____
Notary Public

Campaign Treasurer's Acceptance of Appointment

I, _____, do hereby accept the appointment as Campaign Treasurer ☐,
(Please Print or Type)

Deputy Treasurer ☐ for the _____ Committee. As a duly regis-

tered voter in _____ County, Florida, I am qualified to accept this appointment.

_____
Date

_____
Signature of Campaign Treasurer

FORM NO. 170
Committees of Continuous Existence Application/Report (Florida)

COMMITTEES OF CONTINUOUS EXISTENCE

(Section 106.04(4), Florida Statutes)

☐ APPLICATION FOR CERTIFICATION   ☐ CHANGE OF INFORMATION

☐ ANNUAL REPORT FOR THE PERIOD OF _____ THROUGH _____

1. Full Name of Committee	Date
Mailing Address (If Post Office Box or Drawer, Please Add Street Address)	Telephone

City	County	Zip Code

2.   Affiliated or Connected Organizations (Includes Other Committees of Continuous Existence and Political Committees)

Name of Affiliated or Connected Organization	Mailing Address	Relationship

3.   Area, Scope and Jurisdiction of the Committee

4.   Identify by Name, Address and Position, the Custodian of Books and Accounts

Full Name	Mailing Address	Committee Title or Position

5.   List by Name, Address and Position, other Principal Officers. Including Officers and Members of the Finance Committee, if Any:

Full Name	Mailing Address	Committee Title or Position

FORM NO. 170 (continued)

Committees of Continuous Existence—Page 2

6. List by Name, Address, Office Sought, and Party Affiliation each Candidate or Other Individual that this Committee is Supporting.

Full Name	Mailing Address	Office Sought	Party

7. List Any Issues this Committee is Supporting:

List Any Issues this Committee is Opposing:

8. If this Committee is Supporting the Entire Ticket of a Party, Give Name of Party:

9. Is This a Continuing Committee?   ☐ Yes   ☐ No

10. In the Event of Dissolution, What Disposition Will be Made of Residual Funds?

11. List all Banks, Safety Deposit Boxes, or other Depositories used for Committee Funds:

Name of Bank or Depository and Account Number	Mailing Address

12. List all Reports Required to be Filed by this Committee with Federal Officials and the Names, Addresses, and Positions of Such Officials, if any:

Report Title	Dates Required To Be Filed	Name and Position of Official	Mailing Address

State of _____   _____ County

I, _____, being duly sworn, depose (affirm) and say that the information in this Application (or Annual Report) is complete, true, and correct. I further certify that a member-ship list will be made available for inspection, if deemed necessary by the Division of Elections.

(seal)   _____
                         (Signature of Chairman of Continuous Existence Committee)

Subscribed and sworn to (affirmed) before me this _____ day of _____,
A.D., 19____.

My Commission Expires _____ 19____   _____
                                            Notary Public

POINTS TO REMEMBER

- Lobbying that is open, honest, and with concern for the public interest, is lawful and valuable.

- Special-interest lobbying must be reasonable, and not contrary to public interest, to be lawful.

- PACs that "buy" influence are enemies of the people.

- Federal lobbying law is largely governed by tax law (*e.g.*, tax-exemption law).

- OMB Circular A-122 should be studied.

- State lobbying law is relatively mild.

- State regulation usually consists of registration and reporting rules.

NOTES TO CHAPTER 38

1. *Association of the Bar of City of New York v. C.I.R.*, 2d Cir. (US) Ct. App., Sept. 27, 1988.

2. *Keller v. State Bar of California*, 110 S. Ct. 2228 (1990); *Abood v. Detroit Board of Educ.*, 97 S. Ct. 1782 (same rule as to labor union dues.)

3. St. Petersburg *Times*, p. 1D (Mar. 31, 1985). Obviously this subject involves "compelling state interests," and thus state regulation is constitutional. See, Falzone v. State, 500 S.2d 1337 (Fla. 1987); Fla. St. § 106.03; U.S. Const., Amend 1.

4. *Ibid.*, p. 1B (Mar. 31, 1985).

5. *Ibid.*, Religion Section, p. 13 (Mar. 30, 1985).

6. *Id.*, Hollman and Travis, *Curbs are Sought on the Power of PACs*, (Special Section—For a Better Florida) pp. 31–36 (Apr. 1985).

7. Gibson v. Florida Bar, U.S. 11th Cir. Ct. App. (Oct. 1986).

8. N.Y. State Coalition for Criminal Justice v. Coughlin, 474 N.E.2d 607 (N.Y., 1984).

9. *See*, Federal Publ. #2–84, *Lobbying By Nonprofit Organizations*.

10. *See*, Section 190.

11. *See* the National Federal Report (pamphlet) cited at the beginning of this Section; and also: National Assembly of State Arts Agencies, *Arts Organizations Lobbying and the Law* (rev. ed., 1982). Wash., D.C. Independent Sector, *Layman's Guide to Lobbying Without Losing Your Tax-Exempt Status* (curr. ed.) Wash., D.C.
    Ornstein and Elder, *Interest Groups, Lobbying and Policymaking* (1978); Congress. Q. Press; Wash., D.C.)
    Living with A-122: A Handbook for Nonprofit Organizations (OMB Watch; Wash., D.C. 1984).

12. *See* Fla. Stat. §§11.061(1), 11.05(1).

13. *Ibid.*, §11.045; Falzone v. State, 500 S.2d 1337 (Fla. 1987).

14. *Id.* §11.045(3).

15. *Id.* §11.045(4).

16. *Id.* §11.045(6).

17. *Id.* §11.061.

18. Fla. Const., Art. II §8.

19. Askew v. Firestone, 421 S.2d 151 (Fla., 1982).

20. Plante v. Smothers, 372 S.2d 933 (Fla., 1979).

21. Fla. Const., Art. II §8(6).

22. *E.g.*, Fla. Stat., c. 106; and *see*, Fla. Dept. of State, *Handbook for Committees* (1985).

23. *Austin v. Michigan Chamber of Commerce*, 58 U.S.L.W. 4371 (U.S. Supr. Ct., 1990).

24. Harmon and Weiss, *Tax Monthly for Exempt Organizations*, p. 2 (July 1988) (Washington, DC).

25. *Sulzer v. Environmental Control Bd. of City of New York*, 566 N.Y.S.2d 595 (A.D. 1 Dept. 1991).

26. *Hospital Ass'n of New York State v. Axelrod*, 565 N.Y.S.2d 884 (A.D. 3 Dept 1991).

27. *Federal Election Comm. v. Mass. Citizens for Life, Inc.*, 107 S. Ct. 616 (1986); *Austin v. Mich. Chamber of Commerce*, 110 S. Ct. 1391 (1990); *Faucher v. Fed. Elec. Comm.*, 743 F. Supp. 64 (D.C., Me. 1990); 55 FR 40397 (No. 192).

28. Let's Help Florida v. McCrory, (11th Cir. 1980), affd. 454 U.S. 1130 (1981), cert. den. 454 U.S. 1142 (1981).

29. Fla. Stat. §108.08.

30. *Id.* §106.08.

31. *Id.* §106.03; and *see* Askew v. Firestone, 421 S.2d 151 (Fla. 1982).

32. *Id.* §106.21

33. *Id.* §106.05.

34. *Id.*; and *see*, Plante v. Smothers, 372 S.2d 933 (Fla., 1979).

35. *Fla. Stat.* §106.11

36. *Id.* §106.141.

37. *Id.* §106.12.

38. *Id.* §106.125.

39. *Id.* §106.05.

40. *Id.* §106.09.

41. *Id.* §106.055.

42. *Id.* §106.07.

43. *PAC for Equality v. Dept. of State*, 542 So. 2d 459 (FL 2d D.C. App., 1989).

44. See, Smucker (of Independent Sector) article in *Grantsmanship Center* Winter 1991 Whole NP Catalog, p. 11.

45. *Fla. Stat.* §106.04.

46. *Id.*

47. C.F.R., tit. 11.

48. 2 U.S.C. §§431–455 (1985).

49. Fla. Stat. § 106.15.

50. *Id.* § 106.141.

51. *Id.* § 106.144.

52. *Id.* § 106.17.

53. D. Dahl, article, *St. Petersburg (Fl.) Times,* p. 1 (Jan. 10, 1994).

54. For IRS information phone (202) 463-5580. *See also,* S. Carruthers, note, 376 *AFTL Journal* 25 (Jan. 1994).

40

AFFILIATIONS

[*See also* the chapter on Mergers and Consolidations, and Chapter 3 on Mixtures.]

§412. AFFILIATION OF ORGANIZATIONS, IN GENERAL

Affiliation is defined as "Act or condition of being affiliated, allied, or associated with another person, body or organization. Imports less than membership in an organization, but more than sympathy, and a working alliance to bring to fruition the . . . program of an . . . organization, as distinguished from mere cooperation. . . ."[1]

The term often also is applied to parent-subsidiary corporations, where one effectively controls the other. In a business corporation this may involve the Investment Company Act,[2] for companies that directly or indirectly own five percent or more of the voting stock of a subsidiary (*e.g.*, such as a "Holding Company").[3]

Affiliated organizations may be parent-and-subsidiary, or brother-and-sister organizations, or other, more complex contractual relatives.[4]

In modern nonprofit organizations work, the affiliation of two or more corporations, or even of many in a *consortium*, in order to accomplish mutually agreeable objectives, now is very commonplace. Such contractual arrangements have many advantages and a few disadvantages.

Court approval of an agreement affiliation, by a "show cause" order, after advertised notice and hearing, is a wise step in the procedure of contracting for an affiliation.

Attorney general approval is similarly helpful. *See,* for example, Section 413, Form 172, last line.

Any two or more nonprofit corporations incorporated for kindred purposes under or by general or special laws may agree to consolidate or affiliate. But if the agreement is contrary to any law governing any one of the constituent organizations, a single dissenting member can have it set aside as *ultra vires* (beyond the powers).[5] Yet, consolidations of groups having different rules (even of different religious groups) is perfectly proper.[6]

Some states now permit the merger of a corporation for profit with one organized not for profit as long as the latter is the remaining entity.[7] But the actual I.R.S. and other-state attitudes toward such operations will not be clear for years yet to come.

Combinations may be effected on the charter level, while local-level (*e.g.*, bylaw) rules remain distinct. This often happens in affiliations of educational, or of labor or fraternal organizations. Thus, affiliation of a local union with an *international* (area of entire-trade) group may leave the bylaws of the local in effect, though they differ from those of the parent body, and even limit its powers over the local.[8] Consolidation or affiliation is a *contractual* arrangement.

The form of consolidation or affiliation agreement may be almost anything desired, subject to the laws of contracts and general corporation laws.[9]

Thus, an affiliation is proper between two colleges, wherein one will grant the degrees for both, and in which a common name is used while neither is liable for the debts or obligations of the other.[10]

For example, a college of law or medical school may affiliate with a university, change its name to that of the university, consolidate the two faculties, and yet remain largely autonomous as to its own internal finance and administration under its own board of overseers or trustees.[11]

§413. AUTONOMY OF AFFILIATES

The first problem in contemplating an affiliation of organizations is usually the concern of the board and members of each organization that such affiliation may cause loss of autonomy and independence, or liability for the actions of another organization.

Given legitimate purposes, the tests of continued separateness of identities will be: (1) Were the records or assets or personnel intermingled or kept separate? (2) Were the formalities of separate procedures, meetings, and government, intermingled or kept separate? (3) Were the financial resources of each adequate, or did inadequate funding and/or draining of assets lead to predictable trouble for the subsidiary? (4) Were the respective organizations held out to be independent or interdependent? (5) Was the overall purpose of each organization an independent one or a mere side aspect of that of another organization?[12] For example, were they independent entities or mere instrumentalities?

The ultimate test is whether or not the organizations were (are) in *allied* or in *subsidiary* relationships. If they are allied, but continue to act procedurally as separate entities, they are affiliates and not mere instrumentalities of others.[13]

If they are affiliated, their relationship is governed by the contract (charter) to which they agreed.[11]

A corporation may be deemed to be "in business" if it *controls* a *subsidiary* corporation (e.g., owns all its stock), in that it is acting through a corporate *agency*; subsidiary's actions become ground for *venue* in the county where the subsidiary was domiciled, just as with any other agency.[15]

A condo developer's subsidiary relationship to a lessor does not *per se* bind the lessor to obligations assumed only by the developer.[16]

§414. AFFILIATES' RELATIONSHIPS ILLUSTRATED

[See the preceding section]

[Nelon Kirkland contributed this Section]

Rights in property held by affiliates have been governed through their contract provisions. For instance, where there existed an agreement between an affiliate fraternal lodge and its fraternal order, that any property acquired by the affiliate would revert to the order, that was held to be a valid provision and not against public policy.[17] Even contractual clauses requiring the local affiliate to get the consent of the parent organization before selling any of the affiliate's property have been held to be valid, and not considered unreasonable restraints.[18]

It seems that a true affiliation can be more beneficial than a consolidation or merger, when the entities wishing to associate with one another also want to retain some independence. Such an arrangement can be contractually defined to the mutual benefit of all parties.

One good example of such relationships is to be found in the health care field. Small hospitals (nonprofit and profit) are finding that they cannot compete with larger hospital chains.[19] Also, the lone hospital corporation now finds that large hospital chains have concentrated on "acute care hospitals . . . and . . . operate psychiatric and other special facilities, health maintenance and preferred-provider organizations, freestanding emergency centers, health insurance, home health care and other ancillary services."[20]

It is important to recognize the future legal ramifications of such affiliations. The relationship among the affiliates will be governed by their contract. However, as for liability among and within the organizations to *third* parties, many questions remain unanswered. Such questions have been considered in the health care field, where, in a typical case, a hospital was alleged to be "unlawfully engaging in the practice of medicine through its radiology contract." The complaint was dismissed. The court said: "the crux of the matter . . . is whether the relationship between the radiologist and the patients of the hospital has been so destroyed as to allow the hospital to become the medical practitioner."[21]

But, all in all, affiliation can be a viable alternative to merger or consolidation where all the organizations involved wish to retain their separate identities while sharing in the benefits of group participation. By utilizing *joint ventures* the organizations do not merge or consolidate.

A recent trend in the area of nonprofit "consolidations" involves many nonprofit hospitals. These organizations do not actually merge or consolidate, but rather they form joint ventures. The joint ventures are in the form of shared-service agreements. For example, hospitals can join with commercial laboratories for the purpose of creating separate laboratory facilities that provide "pre-admission diagnostic testing and reference laboratory services for other hospitals and physicians on the medical staffs of other hospitals."[22] By engaging in such a joint venture, the hospital can share the investment expenses with the commercial laboratories for facilities and equipment. "At the same time the hospital will assure itself a flow of non-patient revenues ... and reduce the costs of in-patient services provided by the hospital itself."[23]

NCNA

In 1989 a new *National Council of Nonprofit Associations*, representing 28 associations with 10,000 nonprofit organizations, was begun. The organization was incorporated in Washington, D.C., with offices on both coasts. It is a counterpart to the *Independent Sector*, which represents over 650 big nonprofit organizations. For more data on locals and affiliations, address *The Union Institute's Center for Public Policy* (Washington, D.C.) and the *Center for Non-Profit Corporations* (Trenton, N.J.).[24]

QUANTUM

Associations of associations have made available some *association services* organizations to assist them in *foreign* countries, such as "*Quantum*" in Europe, based in Geneva, Switzerland. Cooperation without loss of identity is offered. Address: 18, Rue des Moraines, CH-1227 Carouge/Geneva.

International Associations of Associations

Grants and contributions to the American Council for Voluntary International Action (InterAction), an association of 136 international organizations, totaled $2.1 billion as of 1991. InterAction plans to unify private independent organizations to participate in foreign government aid programs. Currently, aid to foreign governments is 80% government supplied. InterAction wants to see at least half of all aid to foreign governments handled by private or unilateral agencies. Such Non-Government Organizations (NGOs) will attempt to manage and control funds more efficiently.[25]

Fund Raising Affiliations

Associations (affiliations) of fund raising organizations may cut costs and increase income of many (or even all) the participants. A successful example is NCDC (National Catholic Development Conference, Inc.), which uses meetings, conferences, and tested materials, including four-day seminar conventions annually, etc. For information address: 86 Front St., Hempstead, N.Y. 11550; Tel. # (516) 481-6000; Fax: (516) 489-9287. For example, request a copy of the NCDC "Precepts of Stewardship" pamphlet.

A *coalition of associations* of persons licensed to work in clinical psychotherapy services has "standing" to intervene in administrative proceedings to challenge the validity of rules proposed by a state Board of Social Therapy, as its members would be subject to those rules.[26]

Associations of Associations

In Illinois about 17,000 NPOs now have a new professional association ("Illinois Association of Nonprofit Organizations") to offer information and training and other assistance to 501(c)(3) organizations.[27]

An "*association of associations*" is illustrated by the "*California Association of Nonprofits, Inc.*" [P.O. Box 1478, Santa Cruz, CA 95061-1478]. In its promotional circular in 1989, it said of itself:

"Who Is CAN?"

"CAN is its nonprofit agency members. The CAN Board of Directors is chosen by the membership in bi-annual elections. The board is made up of California nonprofit agency and coalition executive directors and other professionals expert in the area of proposal writing, lobbying, fiscal management, nonprofit law and personnel benefits. All board members and technical advisors have extensive experience with nonprofits and a proven commitment to strengthening the nonprofit field.

"The CAN Staff includes acknowledged leaders in nonprofit administration, fiscal management and innovative project development."

"Board of Directors"

[Names and Organizations]

Then the circular continued:

"What Is CAN?"

"The California Association of Nonprofits, Inc. is a private, nonprofit, tax-exempt membership organization. Our purpose is to help nonprofit agencies in California work together to strengthen our sector.

"CAN member groups are large and small, traditional and alternative, state-wide and local. Members include nonprofits providing programs for children, the elderly, minorities, women and the disadvantaged, as well as cultural, educational, health, and environmental services.

"Working together, California nonprofits have the collective strength to obtain the same benefits and savings available to large businesses, government, and other trade associations. Mutual interest advocacy results in increased respect, appreciation, and effectiveness for the nonprofit sector.

"What CAN Does"

"We are your 'extra staff.' We negotiate advantageous rates for a variety of products and services and also lobby, network, and provide technical assistance for California nonprofit agencies. As one executive director expressed it, 'We need an association to provide support services to save money; information services to help agencies cope; and advocacy to strengthen the nonprofit voice.' CAN regularly surveys members to determine what additional services they would like to see developed.

"Through regional workshops, 'hotline' consultation services, and its monthly newsletter, the **CAN Alert**, CAN makes valuable management information available to members. In addition, CAN's research and development projects are continually finding new ways to support the nonprofit sector."

The CAN circular then set forth the *services* it offered:

FORM NO. 171
Membership Application
of
Association of Associations
[Of the California Association of Nonprofits, Inc. (see above)]

S E R V I C E S

- **CAN Provides a Growing Number of Services to Nonprofit Member Agencies**

- **Employee Benefits**

Comprehensive insurance coverages tailored for nonprofits and made available at special rates, including health, life, dental, and vision. Workers compensation and long-term disability coverages are being developed. These and other programs are offered through our subsidiary, Nonprofit Administrators Corporation (NAC).

- **Liability Insurance**

CAN's Sponsored Liability and Property Insurance Program provides a broad range of liability coverages, including property and casualty, directors' and officers' liability, and volunteer coverage. The Sponsored Liability program is the first step toward formation of a liability risk pool.

- **Subscription to the CAN Alert**

This newsletter (published ten times a year) keeps members in touch with relevant issues and events; strategies for reducing costs; fundraising; networking with other nonprofits; training opportunities; developments in volunteer and personnel management; new products and services; and more. Back issues are available.

• Unemployment Tax Trust

CAN members have access to two "pooled trust" programs (in both Northern and Southern California) which cut unemployment tax costs in half during the first year in participation.

• Tax-Deferred Annuity—403(b)—Program

This program allows nonprofit agency employees to save with before-tax dollars.

• Seminars and Workshops

Free or low-cost workshops and seminars for nonprofit managers are offered regularly throughout the state. The emphasis is on acquiring new resources and managing current ones more effectively.

• Group Purchasing

Significant discounts on office supplies and equipment and special rates on numerous other products and services. An equipment leasing plan is also being developed.

• Managers' Hotline

A starting point for problem-solving and resource location. Provides free assistance with administrative, fiscal, and personnel problems using the expertise of CAN staff and a panel of technical advisors.

• CAN's Personnel Policies and Procedures Manual

A comprehensive guide for nonprofits in all aspects of personnel management. Also available on diskette.

• Section 125 Premium Only Plan (POP)

Everything a nonprofit agency needs to install a pre-tax insurance premium contribution plan for its employees, resulting in substantial savings for both the agency and its employees.

• Credit Union

Member agencies and employees have access to the Provident Central Credit Union. Services include free interest-checking, low-interest Visa card, 15 offices statewide, more than 30,000 ATMs nationwide, and a wide range of financial services.

• Lobbying

CAN's Sacramento lobbyist keeps us regularly informed on issues affecting our members. CAN sponsors legislation aimed at furthering the nonprofit sector, and opposes unfavorable legislation.

• HandsNet

CAN is responsible for the resource development HandsNet, a statewide pilot computer network funded by Apple Computer and Hands Across America, which focuses on the needs of agencies serving the hungry and homeless.

CALIFORNIA ASSOCIATION OF NONPROFITS INC.

MEMBERSHIP APPLICATION

(Annual Dues $35)

1. Agency Name: _____

2. Address: _____

   City: _____ Zip Code: _____ County: _____

3. Telephone: _____

4. Contact Person: _____

5. Title: ☐ Executive Director / CEO   ☐ Program Manager / Coordinator

   ☐ Associate / Asst. Director   ☐ Business Manager

   ☐ Other:

6. Name of Executive Director / CEO (If different from above): _____

7. Year Agency Incorporated: _____

8. Number of Paid Employees: _____

9. Number of Volunteers: _____ (estimate if exact number unknown)

10. Annual Budget: ☐ Less than $100,000   ☐ $1,000,000 - $2,999,999

    ☐ $100,000 - $199,000   ☐ $3,000,000 - $4,999,999

    ☐ $200,000 - $499,999   ☐ $5,000,000 or Greater

    ☐ $500,000 - $999,999

11. 501(c) (3) Status: ☐ Yes ☐ No   Other status: _____

12. How did you hear about CAN (check all applicable)?

    ☐ Current CAN Member   ☐ CAN seminar / workshop

    ☐ *CAN ALERT* newsletter   ☐ Other meeting

    ☐ Mail Solicitation   ☐ Other: (specify) _____

13. Number of different clients served annually: ☐ 1 - 99   ☐ 1000 - 4999

    ┌─── For CAN Official Use Only ───┐   ☐ 100 - 499   ☐ 5000 - 9999
    │ Member # _____ Mail Code: 70   │   ☐ 500 - 999   ☐ 10,000 or more
    │ Date Received _____ Check # ___ │
    │ _____ A - Major _____ B - Beneficiary │
    └──────────────────────────────────┘

                                                              OVER ➡

P.O. Box 1478 • SANTA CRUZ, CA 95061-1478 • (408) 458-1955 • (800) 345-4226

AGENCY CLASSIFICATION

In order to know our member agencies and organizations better, CAN has begun using a classification system for non-profits recently developed by the National Center for Charitable Statistics, a program of the Independent Sector.

■ Major Group Code

Circle <u>one</u> category that <u>best</u> describes your agency's primary purpose.* Please circle only one. For more detailed information on the categories listed below please see attached.

A. Arts, Culture, Humanities

B. Education Instruction and Related - Formal & Non-Formal

C. Environmental Quality, Protection & Beautification

D. Animal Related

E. Health - General & Rehabilitation

F. Health - Mental Health, Crisis Intervention

G. Health - Mental Retardation/Develpmentally Disabled

H. Consumer Protection, Legal Aid

I. Crime & Delinquency Prevention - Public Protection

J. Employment/Jobs

K. Food, Nutrition, Agriculture

L. Housing/Shelter

M. Public Safety, Emergency Preparedness & Relief

N. Recreation, Leisure, Sports, Athletics

O. Youth Development

P. Human Service, Other Including Multipurpose (also, Social Services Individual & Family)

Q. International/Foreign

R. Civil Rghts, Social Action, Advocacy

S. Community Improvement, Community Capacity Building

T. Grant Making/Foundations

U. Research, Planning, Science, Technology, Technical Assistance

V. Voluntarism, Philanthropy & Charity

W. Religion Related/Spiritual Development

■ Beneficiary Code

Circle up to 5 categories that best describe the people that benefit from your agency's services. For more detailed information on the categories listed below please see attached.

A. All/General Public/Beneficiary Group Not Identified

AGE

B. Infants/Babies

C. Children & Youth

D. Aging/Elderly/Senior Citizens/Retired

SEX

E. Boys

F. Boys/Men

G. Girls

H. Girls/Women

I. Men

J. Women

RACE

K. Asian/Pacific Islander

L. Blacks

M. Hispanics

N. Native AmericanAmerican Indian

O. Minorities - Other Specified Racial/Cultural Groups NEC:

P. Minorities - General, Group not Specified

OTHER BENEFICIARIES

Q. Disabled - General/Unspecified

R. Disabled, Mentally/Emotionally

S. Disabled, Physically

T. Immigrants/Newcomers/Refugees/Stateless

U. Members/Affiliates (Organizations)

V. Members (Individuals)

W. Military/Veterans

X. Offenders/Ex-Offenders

Y. Poor/Economically Disadvantaged

Z. Other Named Group NEC

A—MAJOR GROUP CODE DESCRIPTIONS

Note: Intended to classify each entity according to its primary purpose, major field/area of service or operation, or type of institution.

A ARTS, CULTURE, HUMANITIES: Includes all entities whose activities focus primarily on the broad areas of the arts, culture, and/or the humanities. It is suggested that the various arts schools (*e.g.*, School of Music, School of Ballet) be classified in this group rather than in the Major Group B for Education/Instruction and Related-Formal & Nonformal.

B EDUCATION/INSTRUCTION AND RELATED-FORMAL & NON-FORMAL: Includes all entities whose activities focus primarily on the provision of formal/academic (degrees, diploma, certificate) educational opportunities. Also, use this code to classify entities which provide opportunities for supplementing and continuing education outside the framework of formal institutions such as schools, colleges, universities; and further, to classify associations, councils, professional groups which support, promote, or otherwise aid education or are affiliated with educational institutions.

C ENVIRONMENTAL QUALITY, PROTECTION & BEAUTIFICATION: Includes all entities whose activities focus primarily on the preservation and protection of the planetary human environment and thereby the enhancement of environmental quality. Also includes entities whose activities focus primarily on environmental beautification and environmental health and safety.

D ANIMAL RELATED: Includes all entities whose activities focus primarily on animals or animal related concerns of one or more types.

E HEALTH—GENERAL & REHABILITATION: Includes all entities whose activities focus primarily on the promotion of wellness of individuals, the treatment of disease or other health problems, and the rehabilitation of the disabled. Health entities having a more general or broad health purpose (i.e., inclusive of mental health and developmental disabilities, indistinguishable from physical health) are classified here. Entities specializing in Mental Health and Developmental Disabilities are assigned codes F and G. Also included in this group are health entities engaged in the prevention or treatment of specific diseases and research for the arresting or cure of those diseases.

F HEALTH—MENTAL HEALTH, CRISIS INTERVENTION: Includes all entities whose activities focus primarily on the promotion of mental health and treatment of mental illness. All types of crisis intervention groups such as "hot lines" and "suicide prevention" are also included here.

G HEALTH—MENTAL RETARDATION/DEVELOPMENTALLY DISABLED: Includes all entities whose activities focus primarily on helping individuals who, as a result of inadequately developed intelligence, are severely impaired in their ability to learn and adapt to the demands of society.

H CONSUMER PROTECTION, LEGAL AID: Includes all entities whose activities focus primarily on consumerism types of concerns; i.e., safety of consumer goods, protection of consumer rights and educating the public about the same. Legal Aid includes all forms of legal assistance to individuals and groups, including litigation (class action).

I CRIME & DELINQUENCY PREVENTION—PUBLIC PROTECTION: Includes all entities whose activities focus primarily on the prevention of crime and juvenile delinquency and protection of the public from antisocial elements.

J EMPLOYMENT/JOBS: Includes all entities whose activities focus primarily on various types of assistance in helping people find jobs, training them to obtain jobs and making appropriate referrals for employment.

K FOOD, NUTRITION, AGRICULTURE: Includes all entities whose activities focus primarily on the production/collection and distribution of food, and related activities in the area of nutrition. Also classified here are various agricultural entities.

L HOUSING/SHELTER: Includes all entities whose activities focus primarily on the provision of various forms of assistance related to the housing needs of individuals, families, and communities. Housing, involving some form of care or social service support (*e.g.*, Group Homes), is classified under Major Group P for Human Service, Other Including Multipurpose.

M PUBLIC SAFETY, EMERGENCY PREPAREDNESS & RELIEF: Includes all entities whose activities focus primarily on preventing disasters to the extent possible and providing relief and assistance to the victims of disasters of every type. Disasters may be human-caused or natural (*e.g.*, earthquakes).

N RECREATION, LEISURE, SPORTS, ATHLETICS: Includes all entities whose activities focus primarily on meeting the recreation needs of individuals and communities. Entities engaged in sports, athletics and leisure time activities are classified here. Those engaged in working with serving youth groups are not classified here but in a separate Major Group O, for Youth Development.

O YOUTH DEVELOPMENT: Includes all entities whose activities focus primarily on working with children and youth groups in a variety of ways for character building and personality and leadership development purposes. While many of these entities use recreational programs as a method, their purpose is youth development and for that reason they are classified in this separate group and not in the Major Group, Recreation, etc.

P HUMAN SERVICE, OTHER INCLUDING MULTIPURPOSE (ALSO, SOCIAL SERVICES INDIVIDUAL & FAMILY): Includes all entities whose activities focus primarily on some particular personal social service, as well as those that provide a variety of different social or human services. Some of these entities also provide services classified under other Major Groups such as employment, health, education but do not have a focus in these areas and are therefore classified here. Thus, multipurpose entities such as the American Red Cross are classified here. Also, human service organizations which operate under the auspices of particular religious groups (Catholic, Jewish, etc.) are also classified here and not under the Major Group W, for Religion Related/Spiritual Development.

Q INTERNATIONAL/FOREIGN: Includes all entities whose activities focus primarily on various aspects of international life or which involve or concern foreign nations and peoples. Services of these entities may be performed in the U.S. (*e.g.*, foreign policy analysis) or abroad (*e.g.*, provision of overseas relief assistance).

R CIVIL RIGHTS, SOCIAL ACTION, ADVOCACY: Includes all entities whose activities focus primarily on broad issues of fundamental rights and/or some form of social action to cause social change. These entities, generally, attempt to influence public policy decision-making to assert and sustain basic rights.

S COMMUNITY IMPROVEMENT, COMMUNITY CAPACITY BUILDING: Includes all entities whose activities focus primarily on strengthening, unifying, and building community spirit and increasing the capacity of various community organizations to improve the quality of life for all. Methods used to achieve these goals include fund raising, problem solving, human needs assessment, partnership/coalition building, etc.

T GRANT MAKING/FOUNDATIONS: Includes all entities whose activities focus primarily on grant making (*i.e.*, funding programs or agencies).

U RESEARCH, PLANNING, SCIENCE, TECHNOLOGY, TECHNICAL ASSISTANCE: Includes all entities whose activities focus primarily on conducting general research, planning, and evaluation. Public policy research institutions (*e.g.*, The Brookings Institution, The American Enterprise Institute) should be classified in this group. Entities conducting specialized research, planning, etc., in particular fields such as health, education, or food should not be classified here but under the appropriate Major Group. Entities whose primary purpose is to help other organizations do a better job at whatever they are doing (technical assistance) are also classified here.

V VOLUNTARISM, PHILANTHROPY AND CHARITY: Includes all entities whose activities focus primarily on the promotion and advocacy of voluntary action and initiative or volunteer work.

W RELIGION RELATED/SPIRITUAL DEVELOPMENT: Includes all entities whose activities focus primarily on the religious indoctrination or spiritual development of their members and other individuals. Human service (social service) entities functioning under religious auspices (e.g., Lutheran Social Service) are classified under Major Group P, Human Service, Other Including Multipurpose. Church, synagogue, temple, mission, etc., are also classified here.

B—BENEFICIARY CODE DESCRIPTIONS

Note: Beneficiary refers to a primary beneficiary group. Entities may serve or benefit others in addition to the primary beneficiary group.

A ALL/GENERAL PUBLIC/BENEFICIARY GROUP NOT IDENTIFIED: For entities not specifying or focusing on assistance to a particular client, recipient or beneficiary group. Services are available to all or may benefit all.

Age

B INFANTS/BABIES: For entities whose primary beneficiaries are infants or babies generally under age five.

C CHILDREN & YOUTH: For entities whose primary beneficiaries are children and youth generally between the ages of 5 and 19. May also benefit others such as parents and families.

D AGING/ELDERLY/SENIOR CITIZENS/RETIRED: For entities whose primary beneficiaries/clients are those who are characterized by any of these terms. No specific age demarkation is stated because the age criteria may vary according to different entities. However, most of these entities specializing in helping this beneficiary/client group usually include this description in their names (*e.g.*, Area Agency on Aging, Senior Center) or imply it in their program focus.

Sex

E BOYS: For entities whose primary beneficiaries are boys, generally between the ages of 5 and 19.

F BOYS/MEN: For entities whose primary beneficiaries are males regardless of age.

G GIRLS: For entities whose primary beneficiaries are girls, generally between the ages of 5 and 19.

H GIRLS/WOMEN: For entities whose primary beneficiaries are females regardless of age.

I MEN: For entities whose primary beneficiaries are males age 19 and above.

J WOMEN: For entities whose primary beneficiaries are females age 19 and above.

Race

K ASIAN/PACIFIC ISLANDER: For entities whose primary beneficiaries are individuals who indicate their race as Japanese, Chinese, Filipino, Korean, Asian Indian, Vietnamese, Hawaiian, Guamanian, or Samoan and by other nationality groups belonging to that geographical area.

L BLACKS: For entities whose primary beneficiaries are persons who indicate their race as Black or Negro.

M HISPANICS: For entities whose primary beneficiaries are persons of Spanish origin or descent, including Mexican, Puerto Ricans, Cubans, Spaniards, and those whose origins are from Spanish speaking countries of Central and South America.

N NATIVE AMERICAN/AMERICAN INDIAN: For entities whose primary beneficiaries are persons who classify themselves as American Indian, Eskimo, Aleut or by the name of one of the Indian tribes.

O MINORITIES—OTHER SPECIFIED RACIAL/CULTURAL GROUPS NEC: For entities whose primary beneficiaries are members of some racial/cultural/ethnic group not included under codes K through N above.

P MINORITIES—GENERAL, GROUP NOT SPECIFIED: For entities whose primary beneficiaries are minorities (individuals) and minority groups in general, *i.e.*, without reference to any particular minority group.

Other Beneficiaries

Q DISABLED—GENERAL/UNSPECIFIED: For entities whose primary beneficiaries are persons with some form of disability (physical, mental), however, the particular disability is not specified.

R DISABLED, MENTALLY/EMOTIONALLY: For entities whose primary beneficiaries are persons who experience some form of mental/emotional disability.

S DISABLED, PHYSICALLY: For entities whose primary beneficiaries are physically disabled persons.

T IMMIGRANTS/NEWCOMERS/REFUGEES/STATELESS: For entities whose primary beneficiaries are immigrants (also known as newcomers), refugees and those without any nationality (stateless).

U MEMBERS/AFFILIATES (ORGANIZATIONS): For entities whose primary beneficiaries are other exempt organizations including those with which they maintain special relationships (chapter, member, affiliate). Most of the national organizations (*e.g.,* Family Service America) will use this beneficiary code. The exact nature of national/local relationships may vary but may include election to national board, payments of dues by formula or sharing in fund-raising results.

V MEMBERS (INDIVIDUALS): For entities whose primary beneficiaries are those who hold "membership," usually by paying dues, fees, etc., for specified periods. In most cases, members of these entities receive certain direct benefits (*e.g.,* members of particular religious groups).

W MILITARY/VETERANS: For entities whose primary beneficiaries are members of the armed forces of the U.S. and veterans of these forces.

X OFFENDERS/EX-OFFENDERS: For entities whose primary beneficiaries are those who are convicted of some form of criminal behavior and are either serving a sentence or have recently completed serving the terms of legal punishment.

Y POOR/ECONOMICALLY DISADVANTAGED: For entities whose primary beneficiaries are persons (or families) who are identified as poor/economically disadvantaged. No income level is specified as a poverty index because it may vary from entity to entity.

Z OTHER NAMED GROUP NEC: This code will be used to identify any other beneficiary group which may be mentioned by the entity being coded but is not identified in this taxonomy (*e.g.,* various school or college student groups).

§415. AFFILIATION CONTRACTS

Use of *foundations* as "controlled" affiliates of other corporations is often desired by executives of schools, churches, and other nonprofit organizations, as well as by business corporations. Abuses of tax-exempt status, in "holding company" foundations, especially by family or "close" corporations, was checked by the 1970 Tax Reform Act. *See,* Chapter 7.

When the tax and corporation laws are not abused, the use of foundations as affiliates of other corporation is sound policy when done for proper purposes, such as for the exercise of social responsibility by other (including business) corporations. This is so even when the setting up of a charitable foundation is partly motivated by the founder's desire for advantageous "public relations."

Courts are often asked to interpret affiliation Contracts. For example, where an association of hospitals contracted with a health maintenance organization for certain services to groups of subscribers, and terms were unambiguous, the hospitals may not claim breach of contract when the HMO provided "nontraditional" services to others on different terms. The plain language governs.[28]

§416. FORM OF AFFILIATION CONTRACT

FORM NO. 172
Affiliation Contract
(Foundation and University)

[*Note*: This is based on an agreement between a university and its affiliated foundation.]

**Agreement
of
Affiliation**

THIS AGREEMENT is entered into by and between the _____ UNIVERSITY, an institution of higher education and an agency of the State of, _____, hereinafter referred to as "University," and the _____ UNIVERSITY FOUNDATION, a corporation organized under the provisions of the _____ Nonprofit Corporations Act, hereinafter referred to as "Foundation."

WITNESSETH:

WHEREAS, the University, pursuant to RCW 28B.30.150 § (23), may accept such gifts, grants, conveyances, devices, and bequests, whether real or personal property, in trust or otherwise, for the use or benefit of the University, its colleges, schools, or departments;

WHEREAS, the University has from its express power to receive such gifts, grants, conveyances, devises, and bequests of real and personal property from whatever source, the implied power to solicit same;

WHEREAS, pursuant to RCW 28B.30.150, § (18), the University has the authority to enter into such contracts as the Board of Regents deem essential to University purposes; and

WHEREAS, Foundation was formed for the exclusive purpose of raising, receiving, managing and distributing funds for the benefit of University, Article III. of its Articles of Incorporation stating in part:

This Corporation is organized and shall operate exclusively to receive, hold, invest, and administer funds and property and to make expenditures to or for the benefit of the _____ University . . . thereby promoting, supporting, developing, and extending the educational services and undertakings of the university; and, in furtherance thereof, to support and conduct any and all scientific, literary, charitable and educational activities permitted both to an organization exempt under Section 501 (c) (3) of the Internal Revenue Code, or acts amendatory thereof or supplementary thereto, and by Chapter 24.03 of the revised code of _____, as now or hereafter amended.

To that end, it shall be within the purpose of the Foundation to conduct such activities and to operate in such a manner as shall be designed or intended to facilitate or enhance the educational, cultural, living, and operational conditions at the University; to provide support for, maintaining, enlarging, and extending the curricula, services, faculty, staff, and the real or personal properties of the University; and, to provide financial or other assistance to the students, faculty, and staff of the University in their efforts to acquire new knowledge and to extend the educational endeavors of the University.

WHEREAS, the University has determined the Foundation is the most appropriate organization and means to enhance, coordinate, and exchange the beneficial receipt of such gifts, grants, conveyances, devises, and bequests, and shall be the official fund-raising organization for the University.*

THEREFORE, the parties agree as follows:

I. Definitions

A. Whereinafter the terms of Board of Regents, Board, or Regents are used, these shall specifically refer to the University Board of Regents.

B. Whereinafter the terms Board of Trustees or Trustees are used, these shall specifically refer to the Foundation Board of Trustees.

C. Whereinafter the term development council is used, this shall specifically refer to the University committee which reports to the president of the University composed of the executive vice president, the vice president— academic and provost, the vice president—business and finance, the dean of the graduate school, and the director of development, or comparable or successor members of the University administration as the Board of Regents or president may determine.

II. Responsibilities of the Foundation

A. Fund Raising

Foundation, its trustees, officers, and members agree to provide solicitation, consultation, and other related services in efforts to maximize gifts, grants, conveyances, devises, and bequests of real or personal property from various sources, to the University or to the Foundation for the benefit of the University. To that end, the Foundation shall plan, direct, coordinate and conduct activities for raising funds from private sources, including:

1. An annual giving program.
2. Capital campaigns.
3. Deferred giving programs.
4. Special project campaigns.

B. *Coordination with University*

It is understood that the activities of the Foundation are to be conducted for the benefit of the University and must be consistent with University's plans, programs and policies. It is therefore agreed that the Foundation shall:

1. Not solicit or accept gifts, grants, conveyances, devises, bequests, or otherwise from any source for a use specified by the donor which is unlawful or inconsistent with the University's goals and objectives.

2. Coordinate its annual giving program with University's alumni relations office.

3. Coordinate all capital and special project campaigns with University.

4. Refer all proposals for funding which the Foundation receives directly from colleges, departments, faculty, staff or other units of the University to the development council for assessment, prioritization and recommendation.

5. Provide professional and volunteer consultations to the University administration, faculty, staff, and various University constituencies on development and fund-raising projects.

6. Conduct its public relations and publication program in support of the development and fund-raising activities in coordination with the office of university relations.

7. Maintain a master calendar of solicitation activities including mailings, events, and programs and coordinate these events with the University.

8. Maintain a donor relations file for all development contacts to minimize overlap and multiple solicitations.

9. Process, accept, and acknowledge all gifts and grants from private sources. The Board of Regents reserves the right to accept or reject any gifts offered by the Foundation or the conditions thereof of any such gifts and grants.

C. *Management and Use of Funds*

1. Gifts and grants designated for special use ("designated funds").

    a. Any gift, grant, conveyance, devise and bequest received by Foundation, the principal of which is designated by the donor or testator for a lawful specific University purpose shall, immediately following receipt, be delivered to the University for the designated purpose.

    b. Any gift, grant, conveyance, devise and bequest received by Foundation, the income from which is designated by the donor or testator for a specific University purpose, shall be retained by the Foundation, invested and managed as provided in subparagraph C.3., except where funds are received by the Foundation which relate to an endowment asset held by the University, such funds shall immediately following receipt be delivered to the University.

2. Undesignated gifts and grants ("undesignated funds").

   a. Any gift, grant, conveyance, devise and bequest received by the Foundation, the principal or income of which has not been designated for a special use by the donor or testator shall be invested, managed, used and distributed as provided in subparagraphs C.3. and C.4.

3. Investment of gifts.

   a. The Foundation shall invest and manage all funds and property it receives, other than designated funds described in subparagraph C.1.(a) and (b) above.

   b. The Foundation shall maintain a separate accounting of undesignated funds received and gains, profits, and losses resulting from the investment thereof. Further, the Foundation shall maintain such accounting for each designated fund it manages.

   c. Notwithstanding any contrary provisions in this agreement, provided that this is not inconsistent with the specific fund involved, the Foundation may commingle assets it receives, invest and manage the same in a common investment fund or funds, subject to any restrictions imposed by the donor or testator and subject to the separate accounting requirements of subparagraph 3.(b) immediately above.

4. Transfer of funds. The Foundation shall transfer funds to the University as follows:

   a. The net income from designated endowment funds managed by the Foundation in monthly, quarterly or semi-annual installments for use by the University for the specific purpose stated by the grantor or testator.

   b. All undesignated funds quarterly, semi-annually or annually, for such use or uses as the Foundation designates, less amounts expended for the Foundation expenses in accordance with provision II(5) herein.

      1. The Foundation shall not make any award or grant, the proposed use of which is inconsistent with University policies.

      2. All proposals for awards and grants from the Foundation shall be submitted to the University for review, prioritization and recommendation to the Foundation. The University shall forward all such proposals to the Foundation with its recommendation and prioritization.

      3. All awards and grants shall be made by transfer of funds from the Foundation to the University for the use designated by the Foundation and accepted by the University.

5. Payment of expenses. It is understood and agreed that the Foundation will expend undesignated funds and/or the income or gains therefrom for its operating expenses, including the payment of reasonable compensation for services actually rendered in the operation of the Foundation. The University and the Foundation shall agree on an annual bud-

get which identifies expected revenue sources and proposed expenditures from undesignated funds for the Foundation operating expenses.

D. *Reports and Accounting*

The Foundation shall:

1. Provide the University with a copy of its annual financial statement, audited by a certified public accounting firm selected by the Foundation.
2. Provide the University with an annual report outlining the investment policies and performance of the Foundation and the activities of the Foundation.
3. Permit designated representatives of the University, or the state auditor's office to examine its records during reasonable business hours.
4. Acknowledge in writing all gifts it receives. As appropriate, the University shall also acknowledge gifts received.

E. *The Foundation May Contract with the University*

The Foundation may elect to engage the office of the University development by contract, from time to time, to secure performance of some of the duties of the Foundation identified herein.

III. Responsibilities of the University

A. The University shall utilize the services of the director of the University development and other employees to provide staff services for the University for the performance of the University activities and responsibilities undertaken herein by the University. The Foundation may employ its own personnel for the performance of activities and responsibilities undertaken herein by the Foundation.

B. In consideration of the performance by the Foundation of activities and duties identified in provision II. herein, the University agrees:

1. To make available to the Foundation office space at no cost to the Foundation. In addition, the University will provide access to the University services, including consumable office supplies, postage, use of audiovisual equipment and services, computer services, duplicating, printing and publication services, and other services and supplies available to a University department in accordance with normal University procedures.
2. To provide full accounting services for the Foundation at no cost, but the University shall have no liability or responsibility for the accuracy of information supplied by the Foundation.
3. To provide services through the office of University development, pursuant to specified contractual arrangements, from time to time.

C. The University shall cooperate with the Foundation in the development of its fund-raising programs and campaigns, including providing information, data, plans, speakers, facilities for meetings on the University campus and such other materials and services as may reasonably be necessary for the successful conduct of fund-raising programs and campaigns.

D. The University will review the terms of any proferred gift to the Foundation to determine whether such terms are consistent with the policies, programs, goals and objectives of the University and whether acceptance may impose financial hardship upon the University. The University shall complete such review within a reasonable time and respond to the Foundation in writing. If any terms are deemed unacceptable, they shall be identified and the basis therefor stated.

E. The University shall, not less than annually, provide the Foundation with its projects, policies, programs, goals and objectives for the Foundation's consideration in developing fund-raising programs and campaigns for the University's benefit, which are not inconsistent with such projects, policies, programs, goals and objectives.

IV. Operational Considerations

A. The Foundation and the University agree that at all times, and for all purposes of this agreement, that the Foundation is a separate legal entity, in the performance of this agreement and other activities to be undertaken by the Foundation, and shall act in an independent, separately legal capacity and not as an employee, agent, or representative of the University. The Foundation and the University shall be responsible for their own acts and responsible to each other for any negligent acts which cause damage to other.

B. The Foundation shall have the right to receive or purchase patents and copyrights, inventions, discoveries, and processes; to apply for and aid in the processing of applications for patents and copyrights donated to it as recipient; hold, manage, use, and develop the same; sell, license, or otherwise dispose of the same; and collect royalties thereon; provided, that it is mutually agreed that patents and copyrights developed by faculty and other employees of the University will continue to be received, held, and managed by the University research foundation, development corporation or research corporation of _____, at the sole discretion of the University patent and copyright committee in accordance with the stated policies and regulations of the University.

C. The Foundation acknowledges that endowment assets currently held by the University and previously donated to the University as recipient, will continue to be managed and invested, and the income thereof to be disbursed and dedicated, and to be otherwise the responsibility of the University, unless transfers of such assets are specifically and individually authorized by the board of regents.

V. Assignment

This agreement is not assignable by the Foundation either in whole or in part without prior written approval of the Board of Regents, nor by the University without the prior written approval of the board of trustees of the Foundation.

VI. Amendments and Notices

A. It is mutually understood and agreed any alteration or variation of the terms of the Foundation's articles of incorporation or the bylaws of the Foundation which affect the ability of the Foundation to carry out its responsibilities under this agreement shall be submitted for approval of the Board of Regents of the University. No amendment to this agreement shall be valid unless made in writing and signed by both parties. No oral understandings or agreements not incorporated herein and no alterations or variations of the terms hereof unless made in writing between both parties shall be binding on either of the parties.

B. All official notices required under this agreement shall be given as follows:

Notice to the University: Vice President—Business and Finance
(address)
Notice to the Foundation: President
(address)

VII. Termination

This agreement may be terminated by either party effective upon written notice to the other party at least 60 days in advance thereof. If for any reason this agreement is terminated or the Foundation is dissolved or liquidated all assets of the Foundation shall either revert or be transferred to the University on or before the date of termination.

VIII. Enforcement

This agreement shall be construed and enforced in accordance with, and the validity and performance hereof shall be governed by, the laws of the state of _____, 19___.

*Pending any amendments to this Agreement, responsibility for fund-raising activities of the athletic departments and the Club Foundation shall remain with the department subject to such coordination with the _____ foundation as the president of the University may decide from time to time or as may be mutually agreed by the Department and the _____ Foundation.

IN WITNESS WHEREOF, this agreement has been executed by and on behalf of the parties hereto on this _____ day of _____

BOARD OF REGENTS   BOARD OF TRUSTEES

_____ University   _____University Foundation

_____   _____
President   Chair

_____   _____
Secretary   Secretary

Approved as to form:

By: _____
Assistant Attorney General

NOTES TO CHAPTER 39

1. *Black's Law Dictionary*, 54 (5th ed., 1979). Affiliation agreement between a national foundation and a local chapter does not per se give the local chapter authority to bind the national in the local lease of a building. Bank of Waukegan v. Epilepsy Foundation of America, 516 N.E.2d 1337 (Ill. App. 1987).

2. 15 U.S.C. §80a-2.

3. *See* 3 Oleck, *Modern Corporation Law* §1469 (1978 Supp.).

4. Henn and Alexander, *Corporations*, 355 (3rd Ed., 1983).

5. Davis v. Congregation Beth Tephilas Israel, 40 A.D. 424; 57 N.Y.S. 1015 (1899).

6. *In re* Young Women's Assn., 169 A.D. 734, 155 N.Y.S. 838 (1916); Eitel v. John N. Norton Memorial Infirmary, 441 S.W.2d 438 (Ky. 1969).

7. Fla. Corp. Not-for-Profit Act §617.1805.

8. Kunze v. Weber, 197 A.D. 319; 188 N.Y.S. 644 (1919).

9. For a form, *see* the record on appeal in, *In re* Walker 276 N.Y. 567; 12 N.E.2d 579 (1937).

10. Opinions of Ohio Atty-Genl. (1933) 759 (p. 644).

11. The author arranged such an affiliation in Ohio in 1963 for a law school; and Wake Forest University has a somewhat parallel arrangement of this type with Bowman-Gray Medical School.

12. *See* cases cited in Henn and Alexander, *Corporations* §148 (3rd ed., 1983); and esp., Middendorf v. Fuqua Industries, Inc., 623 F.2d 13 (6th Cir. 1980); Camelot Carpets v. Metro Distrib., 607 S.W.2d 746 Mo. App. 1980).

13. Herman v. United Auto, Aircraft & Agricultural Implement Workers, 264 Wis. 562, 59 N.W.2d 475, 478 (1953). See above, n.1, Bank case.

14. Knights of the Ku Klux Klan v. Francis, 79 Calif. App. 383, 249 P. 539, 540 (1926).

15. *Ex Parte Charter Retreat Hosp., Inc.*, 538 So. 2d 787 (AL 1989).

16. *Sky Lake Gardens Recreation, Inc. v. Sky Lake Gardens No's 1, 3, & 4, Inc.*, 567 So. 2d 1026 (Fla. 3rd DCA 1990).

17. Grand Lodge of Iowa v. Osceola Lodge, No. 18, 178 N.W.2d 362, 368 (Iowa, 1970).

18. Grand Lodge of N.H. v. Union Lodge, No. 32, 111 N.H. 241, 279 A.2d 590, 593 (1972).

19. Dooley and Johnson, *Trends in the Industry*, 58 Fla. Bar J. 139 (1984), citing cases on health care organizations' affiliates; M. Marks, *Help for Hospitals*, St. Petersburg (Fl.) Times, Business Section, 14 (June 13, 1988).

20. *Ibid.*

21. *Ibid.*

22. *See*, Trickel, *Focus on Consolidation by Not For Profit Hospitals*, 58 Fla. Bar J. 142 (1984).

23. *Ibid.*

24. Article, 3 *NonProfit Times* (7) 1 (Oct. 1989).

25. Cohen, S.F., (article) 6 *NonProfit Times* (9) 1 (Sept. 1992).

26. *Coalition of Mental Health Professions v. D.P.R.*, 546 So. 2d 27 (Fla. 1st D.C.A., 1989).

27. 3 *NonProfit Times* (12) 4 (March 1990).

28. *Aultman Hospital Assn. v. Community Mut. Ins. Co.*, 544 N.E.2d 920 (Ohio 1989).

41

ANTITRUST RULES AND NONPROFIT OPERATIONS

[This is a contributed chapter, by Frank J. Nawalanic, Patent Counsel, Midland-Ross Corporation, Cleveland, Ohio. He updated it for the 1980 edition, and the authors added a few citations] [Meg A. Christiansen, Rajjina Grace Singh, and Peggy (Margaret) Hoyt contributed material for the 6th edition.]

§417. APPLICATION OF ANTITRUST LAWS

Nonprofit organizations are generally held to the same requirements as for-profit entities with regard to violations of the antitrust laws. However, the year 1994 could see the federal government take advantage of its antitrust exemption with the institution of a countrywide managed health care program with enforcement aid from the IRS and the elimination of the antitrust exemption for baseball enjoyed since 1922. As nonprofit organizations continue to grow and expand, they undoubtedly will attract continued antitrust litigation, attention, and legislation. [In 1988 the U.S. Department of Justice said that it properly enforces the Clayton Act (15 U.S.C. §18); but the National Association of Attorneys General said that the DOJ does so poor a job that the NAAG will challenge mergers that they believe to be anticompetitive. G.J. Werden, *Market Delineation Under the NAAG Horizontal Merger Guidelines: Reality or Illusions?* 35 Clev. St. L. Rev. (4) 403 (1986–7; issued in 1988).]

At first glance, it would appear repugnant to equate or associate non-profit organizations with the antitrust laws. This reaction stems from a clash between the basic definition of a nonprofit organization—one that is not intended to and does not produce monetary gain except as reasonable salaries paid employees for actual services rendered[2]—with the basic purpose of the antitrust laws: to insure competitive business.[3] On its face, a nonprofit organization would hardly be guilty of conspiring to restrain trade because its purpose is not so oriented.

[It is the *anti-competitive* aspect of an action that calls anti-trust laws into effect. Thus, a wholesale cooperative does not automatically violate the *Sherman Anti-Trust Act* when it expels a retail member without providing any procedure for challenging the expulsion, "unless the cooperative possesses market power or exclusive access to an element essential to effective competition."[4]]

Yet nonprofit organizations have recently demonstrated a rapid growth into big business.[5] Along with such growth, abuses of the nonprofit status also have occurred.[6] Simply put, some men are using altruistic form to further their financial gain.

Nonprofit status has traditionally been delegated and regulated by state law. It is becoming increasingly clear that state law is expanding the types of organizations allowed nonprofit status, thus inviting more abuses of the status to exist.[7]

It is with this understanding that the applicability of the antitrust laws to nonprofit corporations will be considered.

Rural Telephone Service Company, Inc., a nonprofit, cooperative telephone company, was granted monopolist status by the State of Kansas to provide telephone service to subscribers in northwest Kansas. Rural Telephone publishes and distributes an annual telephone directory containing white-page listings and yellow-page advertising. Feist Publications is a private Kansas corporation that distributes a competing telephone directory. Rural Telephone declined Feist Publications' 1978 offer to purchase its white-page listings. Feist nevertheless copied the white-page listings and incorporated them into its own directory. Rural Telephone sued Feist Publications for violation of its copyright and Feist Publications counterclaimed with a Sherman Act violation, which forms the basis for this case.

On appeal the court held that: (1) rural telephone's refusal to deal was insufficient to constitute actual or threatened harm to competition within the meaning of the Sherman Act, and (2) even if Rural Telephone had anticompetitive intent when it refused to license its white-pages listings to publisher, anticompetitive intent alone was insufficient to establish violation of §2 of the Sherman Act.[8]

On September 25, 1990, Gregory F. Daniel, M.D., filed suit against the American Board of Emergency Medicine (The Board), a not-for-profit corporation, for refusing to permit him to take its certifying examination for Diplomate in emergency medicine. In an amended complaint filed in 1991, Dr. Daniel asserted antitrust violation of sections 1 and 2 of the Sherman Act.

The court adopted the reasoning in *Summit Health, Ltd., et al v. Pinhas,* 111 S.Ct. 1842 (1991), finding that the exclusion of the skilled medical services of even one physician from a large metropolitan health care market is potentially actionable and that Dr. Daniel's §1 Sherman Act claim may have merit. The court further found unquestionably that the Board certifies emergency medicine physicians throughout the United States and, in doing so, is engaged in and affects interstate commerce. Dr. Daniel has therefore established a sufficient nexus between the alleged trade restraint and interstate commerce and has thereby shown an adequate jurisdictional basis for his Sherman Act claims to proceed. Dr. Daniel has also demonstrated that where the Board is the only national organization that certifies emergency medicine physicians that they allegedly possess monopoly power in the market for Board-certified emergency medicine physicians, and this prima facie showing of monopoly may be used to infer that there is a dangerous probability that defendants' alleged attempt to monopolize the market will succeed.[9]

A Realtor filed suit after a local association of state brokers denied him access to its multiple listing service on the basis that he did not belong to the association. The court held that the association violated anti trust laws when it denied access to the listing service to nonmembers. The American Society of Association Executives (ASAE) has filed an amicus brief in an attempt to overturn the decision at the Supreme Court level. The Solicitor General has also been invited to file a brief indicating the position of the United States.[10]

The owner of a condominium recreation club may bring suit against the condo association, rather than against each unit owner, and this does not violate anti-trust law, where collection of fees by the association impliedly was the intention in the original declaration provisions as to *package* sales or leases of units.[11]

The circuit court of appeals is the proper place for a nonprofit hospital to seek to enjoin the Federal Trade Commission (FTC) from proceeding against the hospital on an antitrust claim.[12]

In 1993, the Federal Trade Commission blocked attempts by the Seventh-Day Adventists to swap their nonprofit hospital for a for-profit hospital owned by a consortium in Florida. The FTC blocked the trade because of the "anti competitive" nature of the circumstances that would have resulted. Punta Gorda, Florida, would have lost its only nonprofit hospital. Further, the consortium would have owned all of the city's major acute-care facilities.[13]

Development and Purpose of the Antitrust Laws

Any discussion of the antitrust laws is premised on the belief that it is socially acceptable for an individual to compete in trade and commerce for profit.[14] However, engagement in trade is principally due to selfishness and not selflessness.[15] It naturally follows that the selfish desire to engage in trade for profit would injure the public if left unchecked. History shows that such basic considerations as these led the ancient empires of Sumeria, Babylonia, Athens, and Rome to initiate checks on competition to prevent destruction of competitors.[16]

In England and America, regulation of trade practices began to develop under a common law doctrine. One author has divided the trade practices regulated under common law into four areas: (1) unfair trade practices: (2) unfair competition; (3) unreasonable restraint of trade; and (4) combinations or agreements to monopolize.[17]

However, the common law proved to be incapable of handling the competitive restraints of the 19th Century; namely, the trusts, pools, and holding companies resulting and continuing from the large-scale business ventures formed to feed and supply the armed forces during the Civil War.[18] First, the common law did not develop as a uniform body; and second, contracts in restraint of trade at common law were unenforceable; they did not give rise to a civil cause of action and were not criminally unlawful.[19]

Also, state legislation proved only partially successful because the interstate activities of the "trusts" were largely beyond the reach of intrastate activity.[20] Further, some state legislation even facilitated the growth of holding companies.[21] It was in this background that the Sherman Act came into existence.

Contrary to the views of at least one well-known authority,[22] there is both legislative[23] and judicial[24] support for the proposition that the Sherman Act codified the common law, although in doing so it was given a far broader reach than the common law prohibitions against trade restraint.[25]

An Approach to the Nonprofit Organization—Antitrust Analysis

At common law, the purpose of the defendant organization was a factor to be weighed in determining the legality of the trade restraint asserted.[26] Hence, the approach taken here with respect to nonprofit organizations will be to determine if the nature of such organizations will result in any form of an antitrust immunity or exemption and if so, to ascertain to what extent the immunity or exemption exists.

§418. ANTITRUST EXEMPTIONS APPLICABLE TO NONPROFIT ORGANIZATIONS

According to this analysis, it is more logical to first set forth the nature and extent of exemptions granted to certain characteristically nonprofit activities before applying antitrust "elements" by rote. Noticeably absent from considerations are trade associations which have been deleted for obvious reasons, and publicly regulated utility companies, insurance companies, etc. which have been deleted because of the complex state and federal laws governing such companies.

§419. STATUTORY EXEMPTIONS

1.) *Agricultural Cooperatives.* Statutory antitrust exemptions for agricultural cooperatives are found in
   a.) Section 6 of the Clayton Act declaring that nonprofit agricultural

organizations are not to be considered "illegal combinations or conspiracies in restraint of trade",[27]

b.) Section 1 of the Capper-Volstead Act (sometimes referred to as the "Magna Carta" of cooperatives) authorizing persons engaged in the production of agricultural products to act together in associations with or without capital stock and to collectively process, prepare for market, handle, and market such products;[28]

c.) Section 2 of the Capper-Volstead Act authorizing the Secretary of Agriculture to prohibit any agricultural association from monopolizing or restraining trade.[29]

The policy underlying these exemptions is to permit the individual farmer to compete effectively in the concentrated markets in which he buys and sells[30] by organizing into cooperative associations which may be nonprofit or profit in nature.[31] At the turn of the century, the small farmer may well have been deserving of such special status, but since the statutory exemption was passed, cooperatives have considerably grown in size and number.[32]

Whatever the justification for such policy, Supreme Court decisions have interpreted the cooperative statutory exemption. The first decision was rendered in *United States v. Borden Co.*,[33] which set forth the "Other Person's Rule," holding that the exemption to agricultural cooperatives did not extend to combinations or conspiracies in restraint of trade between an agricultural cooperative and others who would not qualify as such. The second decision rendered in *Maryland and Virginia Milk Producers' Association v. United States*[34] held that cooperatives could not engage in predatory trade practices. The third Supreme Court decision, *Sunkist Growers, Inc. v. Winckler and Smith Citrus Products Co.*[35] held that intra-enterprise conspiracy as applied to three separate cooperatives having substantially the same members were exempt from an antitrust violation despite allegations of conspiracy. The fourth decision, *Case-Swayne Co., Inc. v. Sunkist Growers Inc.*,[36] held the exemption inapplicable because the co-op included, as its members, nonproducing processors, a class of persons not entitled to the exemption. In its last decision, *Nat. Broiler Markt'g Ass'n. v. United States*,[37] the court held that a cooperative of vertically-integrated poultry processors could not qualify for the exemption because six of its members did not own breeder flocks, hatcheries, or grow-out facilities and thus were not "farmers." Under the *Case-Swayne* decision, the poultry processors were not entitled to an exemption.

Hence, it appears settled that the antitrust exemption given the agricultural cooperatives does not extend to predatory trade practices,[38] that the power vested in the Secretary of Agriculture was not exclusive or primary jurisdiction,[39] and that the exemption will be strictly construed to cover only "farmers" who, in the traditional sense, either own land or till the soil. On the other hand, several cases have held that because of the exemption, natural cooperative association growth may proceed without limitation even to the point of a total monopoly.[40]

The question of the applicability of the exemption for vertically integrated processors who are also farmers has not yet been decided. In view of the Supreme Court's policy to strictly construe any antitrust exemption, it is submitted that the court will analyze the activities of such an association to determine if the association will offer any significant "competitive advantage" to the processing business of its members and if such an advantage is found, the exemption will be denied.

The farmers' agricultural marketing cooperatives' exemption is not unlimited, and is tested largely by whether or not the cooperative is protecting its own, or its members' valid interests.[41]

2.) *Labor Unions.* In 1908, the Supreme Court in the *Danbury Hatters* case[42] held that a boycott by labor organizations and their members to compel unionization of the boycotted manufacturer violated the Sherman Act. To counteract this decision, the Clayton Act, when passed in 1914, contained two sections exempting labor from certain antitrust prohibitions. The first section provided that labor was not a "commodity or article of commerce" and the organization of labor shall not be a violation of antitrust laws.[43] The second antitrust exemption basically prevented any restraining order or injunction from issuing to prevent a labor dispute.[44] In 1932, the Norris-LaGuardia Act broadened labor's exemption by expanding the definition of a labor dispute[45] and forbidding injunctions from issuing in a wide variety of labor union activities.[46]

In *United States v. Hutcheson,*[47] the Supreme Court declared that the Sherman, Clayton and Norris-LaGuardia Acts would have to be construed together to actively determine the status of labor's exemption in the antitrust area. So long as the unions active in their self interest did not combine with nonlabor groups,[48] the statutory exemption applied. Agreements between unions and nonlabor parties, if exempt from the antitrust laws, are therefore exempt on the basis of a nonstatutory exemption. Several Supreme Court decisions have carved out such a nonstatutory exemption giving assent to joint activities between labor and nonunion parties where considerations of a national labor policy outweigh those of a national antitrust policy.[49] The cases indicate that the courts will take a case-by-case, balancing approach, to determine if restraints imposed by the labor-nonlabor agreements are restraints by labor acting in its own interests (thus entitling labor to a nonstatutory exemption) or if the restraints are imposed as a result of labor joining an employer conspiracy (thus denying labor the nonstatutory exemption).

A Supreme Court case[50] indicates that the nonstatutory labor exemption may be construed more narrowly than in the past. In that case, the court held that a valid union objective (organization) could violate the antitrust laws if the means or methods (secondary picketing resulting in agreements imposing direct restraints on business which would not have resulted from elimination of competition in the ordinary labor organization's activities) chosen to achieve the goal violate the antitrust laws.

Labor union exemption from the law is not unlimited, and is tested largely by whether or not the union is protecting its own, or its members', valid interests.[51]

3.) *Nonprofit Institutions.* In 1938, Congress specifically exempted certain nonprofit institutions from the price discrimination provisions of the Robinson-Patman Act.[52] The legislation was prompted in good part by a letter from the president of the Hospital Bureau of Standards and Supplies, calling attention to hospital supply bills increasing 20 percent[53] as a result of the passage of the Robinson-Patman Act, eliminating price discrimination. Both the Senate[54] and the House[55] reasoned that a price discrimination exemption should apply to eleemosynary institutions.

Prior to a 1976 Supreme Court decision, three cases considered the nonprofit exemption. In the *General Shale Products* case,[56] the statute was construed as not repealing price discrimination exemptions but adding to existing exemptions because such exemptions were provided for after the passage of the Robinson-Patman Act. Hence, the court held that the exemptions are specifically limited to those set forth in the nonprofit statute and the statute would not be construed otherwise. In *Students Book Co. v. Washington Law Book Co.*[57] the court held that the nonprofit statute was not applicable in a price discrimination suit to sales at a university campus bookstore because, "the books sold were not for the use of the universities, but for resale at profit."[58] Finally, in *Logan Lanes, Inc. v. Brunswick Corp.*[59] the court came to grips with the statute. In that case, summary judgment was granted dismissing a suit brought by a private bowling alley against a manufacturer of bowling equipment for discriminately selling similar equipment at a lower price to a state university for use in the university's student union. The reduced price sales allegedly resulted in the private bowling concern having to charge higher prices for bowling than that charged by the university. The court held that the Nonprofit Institutions Act prohibited maintenance of an antitrust action in this instance, stating that (i) the word "supplies" in the statute included not only stock materials and provisions needed to carry on daily operations, but also "embraces anything required to meet the institution's needs, whether it is consumed or otherwise disposed of or, whether it constitutes or becomes part of, a material object utilized to enable the institution to carry on its activities,"[60] and (ii) even if the public were shown to have substantially used the university's bowling lanes, the exemption would still be applicable because the purchases of the bowling facilities were made by a nonprofit institution for its own use.

In *Abbot Laboratories v. Portland Retail Druggists Association, Inc.,*[61] an association of commercial pharmacies in the Portland area maintained that price discounts granted nonprofit hospitals by pharmaceutical firms enabled the hospitals to sell their products at lower prices than retail pharmacies. The hospital pharmacies operated as profit centers and net profits were used to support other hospital functions. The ninth circuit[62] rejected an argument for a broad exemption because the hospital pharmacies performed a proper hospital function and held the exemption applicable only to the drugs consumed (i.e., used) by the hospital patients. The exemption did not apply to drug resales by the hospital to the private consumer. The Supreme Court noted that the exemption was limited and did not apply to all pharmaceutical products purchased by the hospitals. The exemption applied only to supplies purchased by the hospitals for the hospitals' own use "in the sense that such use is a part of and promotes the hospital's intended institutional operation in the care of persons who are its patients."[63] The court then categorized all possible prescription sales by a hospital's pharmacy and concluded that sales in connection with in-patient treatment, emergency room patients, out-patient use on hospital premises, take-home prescription for in-patients and emergency room patients, and dispensing of drugs to hospital employees, physicians, staff members, students, and their dependents, qualified for the antitrust exemption. The exemption did not apply to prescription renewals by former patients, walk-in customers (except in an "emergency"), and nondependents of hospital employees, physicians, staff members, and students.

In summary, an antitrust exemption will exist, on a case-by-case basis, for goods purchased by a nonprofit institution if the institution, itself, uses the goods purchased in a manner compatibly linked with its nonprofit purpose.

A hospital could not be sued for antitrust violation if it did not have enough market power to affect the market in denying staff privileges to two doctors, [Flegal v. Christian Hospital, 92-3773, U.S. 6th Cir. Ct. App., Sept. 14, 1993.]

Phillip M. Bloom, M.D., a former employee of Hennepin Faculty Associates, sued Hennepin County Board of Commissioners, Hennepin County Medical Center (HCMC), a not-for-profit corporation, Hennepin Faculty Associates (HFA), a not-for-profit corporation, and various others alleging antitrust and contractual violations in connection with his discharge. Specifically, Dr. Bloom alleged that HFA and others have entered into a market allocation conspiracy to monopolize the End Stage Renal Disease (ESRD) market in the Twin Cities in violation of state and federal antitrust laws.

The court granted the defendants' Hennepin County Board of Commissioners, Hennepin County Medical Center, and Hennepin Faculty Associates motion for summary judgment holding that they were immune from antitrust claims under the Local Government Antitrust Act and the state action doctrine where Minnesota Statute specifically authorizes the activities undertaken by the defendants and where plaintiff has produced no evidence of a market allocation scheme.[64]

A corporation's "value" had to be $1 million in order for Clayton Act §8 to bar a director sitting on the boards of two competing corporations, until 1990, when Congress raised the minimum "value" to $10 million and also added three more *de minimis* rules exempting certain other violations.[65]

§420. JUDICIAL EXEMPTIONS

1.) *State and Federal Government Action.* It should be obvious that the federal government cannot be held to violate the antitrust laws.[66] But the Supremacy Clause of the Constitution[67] did not make such conclusion obvious for state governmental action until *Parker v. Brown*[68] was decided in 1943. The Supreme Court held in the *Parker* case that state government activities directed by its legislature and imposed by the state as a sovereign would not be prohibited by reason of the antitrust laws.

Several Supreme Court cases have defined the exemption to exist in a limited context. In *Goldfarb v. Virginia State Bar*[69] the exemption was not applicable to a minimum fee schedule for lawyers because the anticompetitive effects of the fee schedule were not directed by the state acting as a sovereign. The Supreme Court determined that, even though the fee schedule was regulated by the state bar, an administrative agency of the Virginia Supreme Court, no Virginia statute referred to lawyers' fees and the Virginia Supreme Court had not specifically required the use of such schedules. On the other hand, the exemption was applied in *Bates v. State Bar of Arizona*[70] to approve, with respect to the antitrust issue, a ban on attorney advertising directly imposed by the Arizona Supreme Court. The anticompetitive restraint (advertising ban) was part of a comprehensive regulatory system clearly articulated and firmly expressed as state policy and actively supervised by the Arizona State Supreme Court as its policymaker. In *Cantor v. Detroit Edison,*[71] the exemption was denied on the basis that a state subdivision approval of an anticompetitive light-bulb distribution program engaged by publicly regulated utility could not be deemed as acting as an agent of the state since the state's policy was neutral on the question where the utility should or should not have a light-bulb distribution program. *Cantor* indicates that a state regulatory board cannot be used as a "straw man" for other interests. Finally, in *City of Lafayette, La. v. La. Power and Light Co.,*[72] the Supreme Court held that municipalities organized under state law are not automatically entitled to the *Parker* exemption on the basis that cities are not themselves sovereign. The court did note that a city's actions would not need specific, detailed legislative authorization to invoke a *Parker* defense and a showing that the state legislature contemplates a type of activity challenged as anticompetitive would suffice. *City of Lafayette* indicates that antitrust immunity for state entity actions may only apply to activities for which the entity was authorized to engage in by the state.

Construing the Supreme Court cases noted above, it appears that if nongovernmental entities and persons engage in anticompetitive activities under the "umbrella" of "state regulations," three criteria must be met for an antitrust exemption under *Parker.*

1. The anticompetitive activity has to be commanded by the state acting as a sovereign.
2. The anticompetitive activity must be supervised by the state.
3. The anticompetitive activity is tied to or is necessary to effect the accomplishment of a legislative goal.[73]

2.) *Group Solicitation of Favorable Governmental Action.*

If an organization is *compelled,* by the *state,* to act in a specific way, that amounts to a state act rather than an independent act chosen by the organization.[74]

But *counties and cities* do not have the immunity-resulting privilege equal to the state's, because they are not "sovereign." They do have such equality only when the state authorized them to have such effect.[75]

As to state-imposed restraints, an organization may invoke the *state-action immunity* "only if the state compels it to perform the disputed action."[76]

A Puerto Rico *government instrumentality* (corporation), for ocean freight transportation, is not subject to antitrust law under the Local Government Antitrust Act.[77]

Related to the above section on governmental immunity is the effect given to conspiring businessmen procuring legislative or executive action favorable to business activity under the assertion of political activity rights.[78] The question was decided by the Supreme Court in *Eastern Railroad Presidents Conference v. Noerr Motor Freight, Inc.*,[79] holding that joint efforts by businessmen organized in a trade association to procure favorable anticompetitive legislation was not a Sherman Act violation. Rationale for the *Eastern Railroad* holding was that the Sherman Act did not invade the area of legitimate political activity[80] and to do so would encroach on the right of group petition, a freedom appended to the Bill of Rights.[81] The court noted that an exception existed for "publicity campaigns" influencing (as opposed to seeking) governmental action which is a "mere *sham* to cover what is actually nothing more than an attempt to interfere directly with the business relationships of a competitor."[82] The *Noerr* doctrine was reiterated and broadened in *United Mine Workers v. Pennington*,[83] the court holding that a union's actions in concert with large coal companies to influence a public official to set minimum wages for government purchases of coal was not an antitrust violation.

The *Noerr* doctrine was significantly narrowed in *California Motor Transport Co. v. Trucking Unlimited*[84] where defendants were alleged to have conspired to monopolize the transportation of goods by instituting state and federal proceedings resisting and defeating applications for highway carrier permits. The court held that First Amendment considerations guaranteed group rights to use state and federal agencies and courts respecting their interests vis-a-vis their competitors, but such right "does not necessarily give them immunity from the antitrust laws."[85] The court concluded that, if the filing of many baseless claims interfered with the rights of the aggrieved party to have free and unlimited access to agencies and courts, the activity would amount to a sham, not protected by the *Noerr* doctrine. In *Otter Tail Power Co. v. United States*,[86] the court noted the filing of repetitive lawsuits based on insubstantial claims evidenced a purpose to suppress competition and constitutes a sham. The practical effect of *Trucking Limited* and *Otter Tail* under the liberal Civil Procedure discovery rules may eliminate the *Noerr* doctrine. A recent ninth circuit case[87] has interpreted *Trucking Unlimited* to apply only in those instances where specific activities, required to be alleged in the pleadings, could bar the aggrieved party's access to a governmental body.

Lower court decisions, prior to *Trucking Unlimited*, have held *Noerr* not applicable to instances where false information was submitted to government officials,[88] to efforts influencing the sale of products to public officials acting under competitive bidding statutes,[89] to efforts to utilize government powers conferred upon a private agency for illegal ends,[90] and to attempts to use illegal means to influence governmental officials.[91] Because the rationale for the *Noerr* doctrine is the same for legislative, executive, or judicial actions, the vitality of the *Noerr* doctrine must await case law interpretation in light of *Trucking Unlimited.*

The Noerr-Pennington Doctrine protects associations and businesses from antitrust liability when they make concerted efforts to restrain or monopolize trade in order to petition the government. For example, antitrust immunity exists, under the Noerr-Pennington doctrine, for anti-abortion organizations and their members who threaten and intimidate abortion clinic personnel and patients, because their actions are valid efforts to influence government action against abortion.[92]

The American Medical Association (AMA) claimed that their campaign against chiropractors was insulated from antitrust liability due to the Noerr-Pennington doctrine. The court held that the acts and policies of the AMA aimed to achieve a boycott against chiropractors, not genuine legislative action.[93]

Lawyers, who agreed to stop representing indigent criminal defendants, until the District of Columbia increased their compensation, were price-fixing under the Sherman Act. Because there was no political activity involved, the Noerr-Pennington doctrine could not shield them from antitrust liability.[94]

3.) *The Professions.*

a.) *Professional Sports.* In 1992, the Supreme Court in *Federal Baseball Club v. National League,*[95] held that baseball was exempt from the antitrust laws. The exemption was affirmed in *Toolson v. New York Yankees, Inc.,*[96] in 1953, and in *Flood v. Kuhn*[97] in 1972. While granting an exemption to baseball, the Supreme Court denied such exemptions to boxing[98] and football,[99] and in *Flood* expressly affirmed lower court decisions, refusing to recognize the exemptions for professional basketball,[100] hockey,[101] bowling,[102] and golf.[103]

[The 1986 case of *United States Football League v. National Football League [634 F. Supp. 1155]* dealt with 1961 legislation exempting transfer of a league's television rights to one (not three) networks.]

Of interest only is the rationale underlying the baseball exemption which is simply grounded on *stare decisis.* In the *Toolson, Radovich,* and *Flood* cases, the court referred to congressional legislation as the means to subject baseball to the federal antitrust laws.[104]

In March 1993, Florida Democrat Bob Graham and Republican Connie Mack along with Ohio Democrat Howard Metzenbaum introduced legislation designed to eliminate major league baseball's 71-year exemption from federal antitrust laws. "Justice Oliver Wendell Holmes' 1922 landmark opinion that baseball 'cannot be considered interstate commerce' appears not only wrong but ludicrous when viewed in the context of 1993."

Today, baseball consists of 28 valuable coast-to-coast franchises. Its operations exert a major impact on taxes, local communities' economies, and cable television rates. In 1992, baseball's ownership cartel blocked a $115 million dollar offer for the San Francisco Giants from St. Petersburg, Florida, owner Bob Lurie. This marks the third time in 10 years that St. Petersburg has been jilted by a franchisee using the threat of moving to Florida as a lever to pry more concessions out of its host city.[105]

b.) *The Learned Professions.* In an early common-law decision, *The Nympth,* rendered by Justice Story, "trade" excluded professions and the liberal arts,[106] and Supreme Court cases have cited this language with approval.[107] Thus, at least in dicta, the learned professions were immune from antitrust violations.[108] In 1940, the appellate court for the District of Columbia in the first *American Medical Association* case[109] held that the field of medicine was trade and can be subjected to a "restraint of trade." In the second *A.M.A.* case,[110] the Supreme Court reserved its decision on the definition of trade to include medicine,[111] saying that if the purpose and effect of the alleged conspiracy was a restraint of business, it would be sufficient for an antitrust violation. The rationale which afforded the professions any special consideration was vague. The Supreme Court noted that ethical considerations of the relationships between patient and physician are quite different from usual considerations involving ordinary commercial matters,[112] and that such forms of business competition may be demoralizing to the ethical standards of a profession which would directly affect the community.[113] Further, the Supreme Court has indicated that external activities of a professional group as opposed to internal activities receive different antitrust considerations.[114]

The "learned profession" exemption was squarely presented to the Supreme Court in *Goldfarb v. Virginia State Bar.*[115] In *Goldfarb* a minimum fee schedule for lawyers was held to be a *per se* violation of the antitrust laws. The court noted that it had never ruled on the "learned profession" exemption and then held that the "nature of an occupation, standing alone, does not provide sanctuary from the Sherman Act . . . nor is the public service aspect of professional practice controlling in determining whether §1 includes professions."[116] While denying an antitrust exemption to the learned profession, a footnote[117] in the *Goldfarb* decision indicated that it would not be realistic to view the practice of professions as interchangeable with business activities, and certain practices adopted by the professions relating to their public service aspects which otherwise would constitute an antitrust violation may not be a Sherman Act violation.

Any rational thought that *Goldfarb* could be interpreted as granting the learned professions "special treatment" under the antitrust laws' rule-of-reason approach was blunted in *National Society of Professional Engineers v. U.S.*[118] In the *Engineers* case, an ethical canon prohibited competitive bidding. This prohibition, while not a *per se* violation of the antitrust laws, nevertheless violated the Sherman Act unless it could be justified under "rule of reason". The Society argued that the bidding restraint was justified because competitive bidding would result in inferior work with consequent risks to public safety and health. While the court rejected this argument on its merits, it went farther and applied the traditional rule-of-reason test set forth in the *Chicago Board of Trade*[119] case. Thus, any ethical restraint imposed by the professions having an overall anticompetitive effect will be barred by the Sherman Act, and it is difficult to determine, at this time, what ethical business or commercial restraints can be imposed on professionals despite language to the contrary[120] by the court.

Following *Goldfarb*, several courts have considered professional association rules allegedly constituting "tie-ins" affecting trade. The ninth circuit[121] would not dismiss an antitrust complaint based on a dental society rule conditioning its membership on membership in other dental societies even though membership was not a prerequisite to the practice of dentistry. The court noted that the rule was not so obviously designed to improve dental services to the public as to justify dismissal. On the other hand, the third circuit,[122] while reversing summary judgment granted to a professional association who issued certification only to its members, noted that it may be possible for the association to develop a factual case under *Goldfarb* for not applying liability concepts in the context of for-profit businesses. In another tie-in case[123] alleging that certification by a board was required for employment, summary judgment was refused on the factual issue of whether the tie-in was commercial (*per se* liability) or noncommercial (subject to rule-of-reason).

A direct competitive restraint in the form of a bylaw of the NCAA restricting the number of coaches which certain member colleges may employ was upheld by the fifth circuit to be reasonable and not a violation of the antitrust laws.[124] The court disavowed any antitrust exemption for the NCAA because it was a nonprofit organization with educational objectives, and likened the bylaw to a market division scheme, normally a *per se* antitrust violation. However, the court noted the footnoted expression in *Goldfarb* and applied the *Chicago Board of Trade* rule-of-reason test to the bylaw, concluding that its purpose was to actually preserve foster competition by maintaining parity among the schools. The holding was further qualified by noting that, if subsequent developments indicated that the bylaw did not achieve its purpose, it would then be held to be unreasonable. Obviously, if the bylaw in question is, in fact, a *per se* restraint, the *Goldfarb* case requires it to be stricken.

It is submitted that the *Goldfarb* and *Engineers* cases clearly hold that a judicially created antitrust exemption, as set forth in *Parker* and *Noerr* or as created for labor, will not exist for the learned professions. On the other hand, the Supreme Court has indicated that certain, non *per se*, trade restraints imposed by professional associations having a bona fide public service purpose may be tolerated. Massachusetts School of Law (Andover, Mass.) began antitrust lawsuit against American Bar Assn., (Nov. 23, 1993; U.S. Dist. Ct., Phila; PA) charging that ABA uses its accrediting powers to inflate the cost of legal education, with a small group of deans and professors acting as a dictatorial cartel. MSL was refused accreditation by the ABA. *Mass. School of Law v. ABA*, 93-CV-6206, E.D. PA. See Myers, Law Schools, 16 *Natl. L.J.* (14)4 (Dec. 6, 1993).

A bar association and its committee members are not subject to anti-trust liability in a lawsuit alleging unauthorized practice of law. *Lender's Service, Inc. v. Dayton Bar Assn.*, 758 F. Supp. 429 (D.C., Ohio, 1991).

§421. ANTITRUST VIOLATION "ELEMENTS" APPLIED TO NONPROFIT ORGANIZATIONS

Because the antitrust laws are complex bodies of various statutory laws, it is perhaps a misnomer to refer to "elements" of an antitrust violation. Insofar as a Sherman §1 violation is concerned, the activity complained of must be (1) in interstate commerce; (2) a restraint of trade (*per se* or *rule of reason*); and, (3) a contract, combination, or conspiracy.[125] A similar breakdown exists for Sherman §2 violations dealing with monopoly.[126]

A. Interstate Commerce

Two tests are applied in determining if a particular activity is within interstate commerce. The first test defines interstate commerce to embrace any activity, including local activity, within the flow of interstate commerce.[127] The second test defines interstate commerce to cover activity, including local activity, which has a substantial *effect* on the flow of interstate commerce.[128] A Supreme Court decision has indicated that "substantial" need not be very significant.[129] The two theories are supposedly reconcilable by noting that they are additive in nature.

The U.S. Supreme Court held that the interstate requirement of antitrust litigation is satisfied by simple allegations that a health care institution's conspiracy against a doctor affected interstate commerce, even without demonstrating an actual effect on interstate commerce.[130]

A suit was brought alleging that a group of Ivy League colleges known as the Ivy Overlap Group unlawfully conspired to restrain trade in violation of §1 of the Sherman Act, 15 U.S.C. §1 (1990), by collectively determining the amount of financial assistance awarded to students. All of the colleges except for Massachusetts Institute of Technology, a nonprofit institution of higher education, settled out of court.

The court held that: (1) college was engaged in "commerce" for purposes of Sherman Act coverage; (2) rule of reason analysis was appropriate, rather than determination that agreement was per se violative of the Sherman Act; and (3) agreement was an illegal horizontal price-fixing arrangement, even though the college claimed it was necessary to conserve student assistance resources and provide access to colleges on part of deserving needy students from various backgrounds.

After the trial was completed, Congress passed the Higher Education Amendments of 1992. Pub.L. No. 102–325, 106 Stat. 448 (1992). Section 1544 of the Amendments makes lawful, for a two year period, certain Ivy Overlap Group activity, which is the subject of this civil action. In general, institutions of higher education may: (1) voluntarily agree with any other institution of higher education to award financial aid not awarded under the Higher Education Act of 1965 to students attending those institutions only on the basis of demonstrated financial need for such aid; and (2) discuss and voluntarily adopt defined principles of professional judgment for determining student financial need for aid not awarded under the Higher Education Act of 1965. Institutions of higher education shall not discuss or agree with one another on the prospective financial aid award to a specific common applicant for financial aid. No inference of unlawful contract, combination, or conspiracy shall be drawn from the fact that institutions of higher education engage in conduct authorized by this section.[131]

B. Restraint of Trade

It is commonly agreed that nonprofit organizations are engaged in trade or commerce within the meaning of the Sherman Act.[132] Hence, nonprofit institutions can engage in restraints of trade.[133]

Again, for simplicity, restraints of trade may be classified into two categories, those that constitute *per se* violations (inherently unlawful) and those that amount to violations by application of the rule of reason. Theoretically, the *per se* doctrine evolved from application of the rule of reason to numerous, similar fact situations involving the same restraints of trade amounting to antitrust violations.[134] What activities are currently deemed *per se* violations are beyond the scope of this book. In any event, *Goldfarb*, by analogy, dictates that when clear *per se* violations are found, the noneconomic or public service purposes of true nonprofit corporations will not serve as a defense.

The rule-of-reason application may be likened to a gradient. At the top of the gradient are activities falling short of *per se* violations, and at the bottom are activities clearly not amounting to restraints of trade. Somewhere on this scale, the nonprofit purpose will result in some "reasonable" restraint of trade. To the extent the nonprofit purpose is concerned with public service similar to public service aspects of the learned professions, the *Goldfarb* rationale will apply. To the extent the nonprofit purpose exceeds that of the learned profession (i.e., charitable) and is linked to the activity supposedly constituting a trade restraint, a more "significant" trade restraint should be permitted notwithstanding the *Chicago Board of Trade* test set forth in the *Engineers* case. Prior to the *Goldfarb* and *Engineers* decisions, the courts were following a case-by-case approach to nonprofit restraints of trade, either harmonizing the restraint to the nonprofit purpose or disavowing the restraint from the nonprofit purpose, and thereby holding the restraint a violation.[135] After the *Goldfarb* and *Engineers* decisions, case law development will have to be awaited to determine what weight, if any, the courts will assign the nonprofit purpose to the trade restraints incurred.

Area hospitals were sued for *discriminatory pricing* in giving *discounts* to a large health insurance provider, in restraint of trade. But the Illinois Supreme

Court held that this was not actionable under the Antitrust Acts, because this price discrimination was not *predatory* nor *refusal* to deal, nor *conspiratorial.*[136]

In 1990, the Justice Department began investigating price fixing of financial aid packages and tuition by colleges. Since then the Department has filed an antitrust suit against Ivy League schools. A motion to dismiss a suit, involving price fixing of tuition and financial aid, was denied by a federal district court.[137]

The profit motive may involve nonprofit organizations in improper activities. A *joint venture* between a durable medical equipment provider (for profit) and a nonprofit hospital unreasonably *restricted competition* by channeling their patient's choice of medical equipment through undue influence on home health care nurses. The nurses were coerced to preferentially recommend the preferred vendor and to exclude a competing vendor's access to hospital patients. The court held that both the nonprofit and profit corporations had specific intent to monopolize the market and had tortiously interfered with business relations, giving rise to actionable antitrust injury.[138]

A hospital and medical equipment vendor and others violate antitrust laws by directing to themselves their patients' purchases of equipment.

"Restraint of Trade" or "Price fixing" by groups of schools (e.g., "Ivy" types) in giving financial aid to students may be violations of the Sherman Act.[139]

When the Professional Golf Association banned golf clubs with U-shaped grooves, the professional golf players challenged the rule as an antitrust violation. The district court properly granted a preliminary injunction prohibiting enforcement of the rule.[140]

Sale of pipe couplings by an *association* of pipe manufacturers was not unlawful *restraint of trade.*[141]

To prove a violation of Section 2 of the Sherman Act, the plaintiff must show that the defendants engaged in anti-competitive behavior to foreclose competition *without any legitimate business purpose.*[142]

A complaint of *"restraint* of trade" (Sherman Act) that did not show market analysis to support its allegation of the required *"injury"* to competitors, was properly dismissed as insufficient.[143]

C. Contract, Combination, etc.

Again, the scope of nonprofit organizations and the antitrust laws must necessarily limit the analysis to a general treatment of the "step" which has resulted in a restraint of trade.

It should seem clear that nonprofit status will not immunize nonprofit organizations from associations with profit business concerns leading to violations of the antitrust laws. This necessarily follows from the analysis of the agricultural cooperative and labor union immunities which do not cover such situations.

Another area of speculation lies in a monopolization charge against a nonprofit corporation. Because nonprofit organizations generally do not expand by merger or acquisition, such charge, if made, would be based on a "natural" monopoly. This area is not completely settled with respect to profit-going concerns,[144] it is currently unresolved with respect to the statutory exemption relating to agricultural cooperatives,[145] and it is suggested that nonprofit status would be placed somewhere in the middle with substantial weight being given to the use of such monopoly power.[146]

An organizer of a tennis contest has no action under the Sherman Act unless he can show *monopoly* by a sponsor of many tennis tournaments.[147]

§422. TRENDS IN ANTITRUST APPLICATION TO NONPROFIT ORGANIZATIONS

Since this chapter was originally published, the Supreme Court has ruled on a number of antitrust exemptions (cited herein) and has consistently limited the application of statutory and judicially created exemptions. At the same time, the Federal Trade Commission and the U.S. Department of Justice have and continue to attack activities of professional associations and nonprofit corporations which the government believes are restraints of trade.[148] It is not surprising that the Supreme Court would hold that the public service aspect of a nonprofit association does not justify any direct (*Goldfarb*) or indirect (*Engineers*) attempt on the part of the association to fix the price at which its members would do business. In doing so, the Supreme Court also denied any antitrust exemption to any nonprofit organization and applied traditional business tests to determine the legality of any restraints effected by nonprofit associations. Almost as an afterthought and possibly because of the wide-scale implications of its rulings, the Supreme Court did note that special considerations of the nonprofit or public service aspects of an organization may justify certain restraints if effected by business organized for profit.

It appears that two types of activities engaged in by nonprofit organizations will come under the scrutiny of the antitrust laws. The first activity will be the actual business activity of the organization, itself. For example, if United Way and another charitable fund raising association had a difference of opinion concerning fund disbursements and United Way disassociated its name from the other fund raising association, United Way may be subjected to an antitrust action based on a boycott principle.[149] The second type of activity will be rulings and practices instituted by a nonprofit organization which affects either activities of business entities or the conduct of its members. Clearly, ethical codes will come under attack, especially if they can be interpreted as effecting price restraints. More significant though is an attack on the accreditation given by the American Medical Association to medical schools[150] or the required approval by the National Conference of Catholic Bishops for Roman Catholic religious publications.[151] The NCAA bylaw noted above[152] is yet another example. If the NCAA could not enforce the regulation under attack, its actual existence would be threatened.

It is submitted that any nonprofit activity allegedly resulting in a restraint of trade could be successfully defended if (i) the activity was compatibly linked to a truly nonprofit or humanitarian purpose and (ii) the activity resulted from uniformly applied and nondiscriminatory considerations in the manner of a "due process" requirement. Thus, the United Way could defend its fund disbursements if it followed an objective, uniformly applied code. The same test would apply to acts of accreditation, admittance, ethical codes, etc. provided that the act or regulation was also compatibly linked to a valid purpose.

Alarm has been expressed that the nonprofit form is being abused by profit-centered individuals.[153] Some abuses will now be controlled by the application of antitrust laws to nonprofit organizations. Unfortunately, the antitrust laws will apply to all nonprofit organizations.

[*See:* Parzych, K.M., *Primer to Antitrust Law and Regulatory Policy* (1987), *see also* Amer. Bar Assn. *Treble Damages Remedy* (1986); Werden *article*, 35 Clev. St. L. Rev. (4) 403 (1986–7).]

Anti-Trust Mergers

[Michael B. Vigodsky did research for this subsection.]

The Clayton Act of 1914, like the Sherman Act, is meant to outlaw business mergers that reduce competition. In 1989 the Act was applied to mergers of nonprofit hospitals, but only if actual reduction of competition occurred, not if the merger actually caused other competitors to increase competition.[154]

Restraint of trade (e.g., constraining practice of a profession or occupation by others) also can be a violation of the Sherman Act by a nonprofit organization.[155]

Merger of nonprofit hospitals was held valid in one federal district court and not valid in another in 1989. Reduction of competition, and necessity to preserve valuable services, collided; the Sherman Act and the Clayton Act both require analysis of the product and the geographic markets involved.

There is no clear rule as to which view will prevail.[156]

NOTES TO CHAPTER 41

1. The subject matter of this chapter first was drafted as an article by Mr. Nawalanic published in 21 Cleve. St. L. Rev. (1) 97, and subsequently revised and amplified by him for the 1980 edition. *See,* Parzych, *Prim er to Antitrust Law and Regulatory Policy* (1987); *Treble Damages Remedy* (A.B.A. 1986); *Corporate Concentration: National and International Regulation* (U. of Michigan 1981).

   For other basic materials *see:* Note, *Antitrust and Nonprofit Entities,* 94 Harv. L. Rev. 802 (1981); Hansmann, *Role of Nonprofit Enterprise,* 89 Yale L. J. 835 (1980). And, that antitrust law applies to nonprofits: United States v. Topco Assoc., 405 U.S. 596, 610 (1982); Sasso, *Antitrust Law Affects All But A Few NPO's,* Pinnelas County Rev. (Fl.), (Jan. 6, 1984).

2. H. Oleck, *Nonprofit Uses and Abuses,* 19 Cleve. St. L. Rev. 207, 211 (1970).

3. "The heart of our national economic policy long has been faith in the value of competition. In the Sherman and Clayton Acts, as well as in the Robinson-Patman Act, Congress

was dealing with competition, which it sought to prevent." FTC v. Sinclair Refining Co., 261 U.S. 463, 475–76 (1923). *See also*, United States v. South-Eastern Underwriters Ass'n., 322 U.S. 533, 559 (1944); Washington State School Directors Ass'n v. Department of Labor and Indus., 510 P.2d 818 (Wash. 1973). (*See also*: Bodner, *Antitrust Restrictions on Trade Association Membership and Participation: Recent Developments*, 24 N.Y.L.S. L. Rev. 907–920 (1979).)

4. Northwest Wholesale Stationers v. Pacific Stationery, #83-1368; U.S. Supreme Ct. (June 1985).

5. *See, Power Pools—Private Foundations*, 13 U.C.L.A. L. Rev. 938 (1966). Note that the 1969 Tax Reform Act somewhat curtailed such organizations by imposing a 4 percent tax on net investment income of private foundations (now 2 percent).

6. *Supra* note 2 at 209. *See, e.g.,* Collins v. Main Line Bd. of Realtors, 304 A.2d 493 (Pa. 1973) (nonprofit corporation found to be engaging in a restraint of trade).

7. H. Oleck, *Proprietary Mentality and the New Nonprofit Corporation Laws*, 20 Cleve. St. L. Rev. 145 (1971).

8. *Rural Telephone Service Company, Inc. v. Feist Publications, Inc.*, 957 F.2d 765 (10th Cir. 1992).

9. *Daniel v. American Board of Emergency Medicine, et al.*, 802 F.Supp. 912 (W.D.N.Y. 1992).

10. 6 *NonProfit Times* (5) 41 (May 1992); *See DeKalb Board of Realtors, Inc. and Metropolitan Multi-List, Inc. v. Fletcher L. Thompson and Empire Real Estate Board, Inc.*, 934 F.2d 1566 (11th Cir. 1991); 112 S. Ct. 1259 (U.S. 1992).

11. *Kesl, Inc. v. Racquet Club of Deer Creek*, 574 So. 2d 251 (Fla. DCA. 1991); *Chatham Condo Assn. v. Century Village, Inc.*, 597 F.2d 1002 (5th Cir., 1979).

12. *Ukiah Adventist Hosp. v. F.T.C.*, 981 F. 2d 543 (D.C. Cir., 1992) (administrative complaint by the FTC about possible section 7, Clayton Act, violation).

13. Mehegan, Sean, (article) 7 *NonProfit Times* (4) 4 (March 1993).

14. J. Van Cise, *Understanding the Anti-Trust Laws* 1 (1970 ed.).

15. W. and A. Durant, *The Lesson of History* 54 (1968); J. Van Cise, *supra* note 14 at 3; by legislative acts such as the Homestead Act and constitutional rewards in the form of limited monopolies to inventors and authors of original works, our government implicitly accepts such premise as true.

16. J. Van Cise, *supra* note 14 at 3.

17. V. Kalinowski, 16 *Bus. Org. Anti-Trust and Trade Regulation* 1–39, §1.03.

18. J. Van Cise, *supra* note 14 at 14, 15. *See also* E. Kinter, *An Anti-Trust Primer* 1–15 (1964).

19. V. Kalinowski, *supra* note 17 at 1–35.

20. J. Van Cise, *supra* note 14 at 15.

21. E. Kinter, *supra* note 18 at 10.

22. Dewey, *The Common-Law Background of Anti-Trust Policy* 41 Va. L. Rev. 759 (1955).

23. *See* 21 Cong. Rec. 1765 (1890).

24. Standard Oil Co. v. United States, 221, U.S. 1 (1911); Apex Hosiery Co. v. Leader, 310 U.S. 469 (1940).

25. Loewe v. Lawlor, 208 U.S. 274 (1908); Northern Sec. Co. v. United States, 193 U.S. 197 (1904); cases cited note 24 *supra*.

26. *See* Coons, *Non-Commercial Purpose—Sherman Act*, 56 Nw. U.L. Rev. 705 (1962); *Judicial Control of Actions of Private Associations*, 76 Harv. L. Rev. 983, 1044 (1963).

27. 15 U.S.C. §17 (1963).

28. 7 U.S.C. §291 (1964).

29. 7 U.S.C. §291, 292 (1964).

30. *Anti-Trust Developments*, 1955–1968, 208 (1968).

31. *See* c.37, and Index, herein.

32. E. MacIntyre, *Cooperatives*, 26 A.B.A. Anti-Trust L.J. §§125, 126 (1964); *c.f.* J. Noakes, *Exemption for Cooperatives* 19 A.B.A. Anti-Trust L.J. §§407, 410 (1961).

33. 308 U.S. 188 (1939). *See also*, Bergjans Farm Dairy Co. v. Sanitary Milk Producers, 241 F. Supp. 476 (E.D. Mo. 1965).

34. 362 U.S. 458 (1962). In the *Maryland* case a dairy cooperative attempted to purchase a dairy distributor. The dairy cooperative controlled 80 to 85 percent of the milk produced in the area. Held, that allegations of Sherman §2 violation of illegal monopoly, that allegations of Sherman §1 violation of illegal conspiracy, and that allegations of Clayton §7 violation of illegally acquiring dairy's business, all stated valid causes of action.

35. 370 U.S. 19 (1962).

36. Case-Swayne Co., Inc. v. Sunkist Growers, Inc. 389 U.S. 384 (1967).

37. Nat. Broiler Markt'g Ass'n v. United States, ——————————— U.S. ———————————
——, 56 L. Ed.2d 728 (1978).

38. Tillamook Cheese and Dairy Ass'n. v. Tillamook County Creamery Ass'n., 358 F.2d 115 (9th Cir. 1966); April v. National Cranberry Ass'n., 168 F. Supp. 919 (D. Mass. 1958); United States v. King, 250 F. 908 (D. Mass. 1916); *supra* note 33.

39. United States v. Dairy Co-op Ass'n., 49 F.Supp. 475 (D. Ore. 1943); Cape Cod Food Products v. National Cranberry Ass'n., 119 F.Supp. 900 (D. Mass. 1954); Bergjans Farm Dairy Co. v. Sanitary Milk Producers, 241 F.Supp. 476 (E.D. Mo. 1965); Tillamook Cheese and Dairy Ass'n. v. Tillamook Co. Cream Ass'n., 358 F.2d 115 (9th Cir. 1966).

40. Cape Cod Food Products v. National Cranberry Ass'n., 119 F.Supp. 900 (D. Mass. 1954); United States v. Maryland and Virginia Milk Producers Ass'n., 167 F.Supp. 45 (D.C. Cir. 1958), *modified* 362 U.S. 458 (1962).

41. See, 7 U.S.C. §291; 15 U.S.C. §17; and see n.51.

42. Loewe v. Lawler, 208 U.S. 274 (1908).

43. U.S.C. §17 (1963). *See* Philadelphia World Hockey Club, Inc. v. Philadelphia Hockey Club, Inc., 351 F.Supp. 462 (D.C. Pa. 1972) (labor organization must qualify to receive exemption).

44. 29 U.S.C. §52 (1965).

45. 29 U.S.C. §113 (c) (1965).

46. 29 U.S.C. §104 (1965).

47. 312 U.S. 219 (1941). *See also*, Allen-Bradley Co. v. Local Union No. 3, International Brotherhood of Electrical Workers, 325 U.S. 797 (1944).
    "We have two declared congressional policies which it is our responsibility to try to reconcile. The one seeks to preserve a competitive business economy; the other to preserve the right of labor to organize to better its conditions through the agency of collective bargaining. We must determine here how far Congress intended activities under one of these policies to neutralize the results envisioned by the other." 325 U.S. at 806.

48. United States v. Hutcheson, 312 U.S. 219, at 223 (1941).

49. United States v. Hutcheson, *Id*; Allen-Bradley Co. v. Local Union No. 3, International Brotherhood of Electrical Workers, *supra* note 47; Pennington v. United Mine Workers of America, 381 U.S. 657 (1965); Jewel Tea Co. v. Associated Food Retailers, 381 U.S. 761 (1965); Local Union 189, Amalgamated Meat Cutters, and Butchers Workmen of North America v. Jewel Tea Co., 381 U.S. 676 (1965).

50. Connel Construction Co., Inc. v. Plumbers and Steamfitters Local 100, 421 U.S. 616 (1975).

51. See, *Associated General Contractors, Inc. v. Calif. State Council of Carpenters*, 459 U.S. 519 (1983); and see n.41.

52. "Nothing in §§13–13b and 21a of this title, shall apply to purchases of their supplies for their own use by schools, colleges, universities, public libraries, churches, hospitals, and charitable institutions not operated for profit." 15 U.S.C. §13c (1963).

53. "The 2,700 voluntary nonprofit hospitals of the country spend over 150 million dollars a

year on foodstuffs and supplies for the care of the needy sick, who would otherwise be a burden on federal, state, and municipal institutions.

"Because of the charitable nature of their work many suppliers have hitherto allowed these institutions special prices on their purchases. This the Robinson-Patman Act now prohibits and as a consequence, hospital supply bills are increasing about 20 percent." S. Rep. No. 1769, 75th Cong., 3d Sess. 1 (1938).

54.   "The purpose of the Robinson-Patman Act, to prohibit price discrimination between purchasers in interstate commerce where competition would thereby be lessened, does not seem to apply as to eleemosynary institutions as they are not operated for profit. The act does forbid such favors as might now be granted by sellers to such institutions." S. Rep. No. 1769, 75th Cong., 3d Sess. 1 (1938).

55.   "The committee does not feel that the wholesome purpose of the Robinson-Patman Act will be interfered with by the enactment of this bill to make certain that favors in price which are occasionally extended to eleemosynary institutions, because of the character of the institution, do not fall under the ban of the act." H.R. Rep. No. 2161, 75th Cong., 3d Sess. 1 (1938).

56.   General Shale Products Corp. v. Struck Const. Co., 37 F.Supp. 598, 603 (W.D. Ky. 1941), *aff'd. 132 F.2d 425 (6th Cir. 1942), cert. denied* 318 U.S. 780 (1943).

57.   232 F.2d 49 (D.C. Cir. 1955), *cert. denied* 350 U.S. 988 (1956).

58.   *Id.* at 45 n.6.

59.   378 F.2d 212 (9th Cir. 1967), *cert. denied* 389 U.S. 898 (1967).

60.   *Id.* at 216.

61.   Abbot Laboratories v. Portland Retail Druggists Association, Inc., 425 U.S. 1 (1976).

62.   Abbot Laboratories v. Portland Retail Druggists Association, Inc., 501 F.2d 486 (9th Cir. 1974).

63.   Abbot Laboratories v. Portland Retail Druggists Association, Inc., *supra* note 61 at 14.

64.   *Bloom v. Hennepin County, et al.,* 783 F.Supp 418 (D. Mn. 1992).

65.   Antitrust Amendments Act of 1990; P.L. 101–588 (1990).

66.   U.S. v. Rock Royal Cooperative, Inc., 307 U.S. 533, 560 (1939).

67.   U.S. Const., art. VI, §2.

68.   Parker v. Brown, 317 U.S. 341 (1943).

69.   Goldfarb v. Virginia State Bar, 421 U.S. 733 (1975).

70.   Bates v. State Bar of Arizona, 433 U.S. 350 (1977).

71.   Cantor v. Detroit Edison Co., 428 U.S. 579 (1976).

72.   City of Lafayette, La. v. La. Power and Light Co., ——————— U.S. ————— —————, 55 L. Ed.2d 364 (1978).

73.   *See also Retail Liquor Dealers Assn. v. Midcal Aluminum, Inc.,* 445 U.S. 97 (1980).

74.   *United States v. Title Insurance Rating Bureau,* 700 F.2d 1247, at 1252 (9th Cir., 1983).

75.   American Bar Association Antitrust Section, *Antitrust Law Developments* 609 (2d ed., 1984). See, *Community Communications Co. v. City of Boulder,* 455 U.S. 40, at 54 (1982).

76.   *United States v. Southern Motor Carriers Rate Conference,* 702 F.2d 1247, at 1252 (9th Cir., 1983).

77.   *Capital Freight Services, Inc. v. Trailer Marine Transport Corp.,* 704 F. Supp. 1190 (D.C., NY, 1989).

78.   In United States v. Association of American Railroads, 4 F.R.D. 510, 527 (D. Neb. 1945), this issue was considered with the court holding that group solicitation activities, lawful in themselves under the first amendment of the Constitution, may become unlawful if done in concert within a board scheme of conspiracy.

79.   Eastern Railroad Presidents Conference v. Noerr Motor Freight, Inc., 365 U.S. 127 (1961).

80.   "To hold that the government retains the power to act in this representative capacity and

yet hold, at the same time, that the people cannot freely inform the government of their wishes would impute to the Sherman Act a purpose to regulate, not business activity, but political activity, a purpose which would have no basis whatever in the legislative history of the Act." *Id.* at 137.

81. "The right of the people to inform their representatives in government of their desires with respect to the passage or enforcement of laws cannot properly be made to depend upon their intent in doing so." *Id.* at 139. *See also* dissent in United States v. Robel, 389 U.S. 258 283 n.1 (1967), saying that the right of association is an extension of protection afforded by the First Amendment and whether the right to associate is an independent First Amendment right is yet to be decided.

82. *Id.* at 144.

83. United Mine Workers of America v. Pennington, 381 U.S. 657 (1965). "Joint efforts to influence public officials do not violate the anti-trust laws even though intended to eliminate competition. Such conduct is not illegal, either standing alone or as part of a broader scheme itself violative of the Sherman Act," at 670.

84. California Motor Transport Co. v. Trucking Unlimited, 405 U.S. 508 (1972).

85. *Id.* at 513.

86. Otter Tail Power Co. v. United States, 410 U.S. 366 (1973).

87. Franchise Realty Interstate Corp. v. San Francisco Local Joint Executive Board of Culinary Workers, 542 F.2d 1076 (9th Cir. 1976) *cert. denied*, 430 U.S. 940 (1977).

88. Woods Exploration and Prod. Co. v. Aluminum Co. of America, 497 Anti-Trust and Trade Regulation Reporter, A-1, D-1 (9th Cir. 1971).

89. George R. Whitten Jr., Inc. v. Paddock Pool Builders, Inc., 424 F.2d 25 (1st Cir. 1970), *cert. denied*, 400 U.S. 850 (1970).

90. Union Carbide and Carbon Corp. v. Nisley, 300 F.2d 561 at 593 (10th Cir. 1961) *petition for cert. dismissed*, 371 U.S. 801 (1962).

91. Sacramento Coca-Cola Bottling Co., Inc. v. Chauffeurs, Teamsters, and Helpers Local No. 150, 505 Anti-Trust and Trade Regulation Reporter A-1 (9th Cir. 1971).

92. *National Organization for Women, Inc. v. Scheidler*, 765 F. Supp. 937 (N.D. Ill. 1991).

93. *Wilk v. American Medical Ass'n*, 895 F.2d 352 (7th Cir. (Ill.)) *cert. denied*, 111 S. Ct. 513 (U.S. 1990).

94. *FTC v. Superior Court Trial Lawyers Ass'n*, 493 U.S. 411 (U.S. Dist. Col. 1990).

95. Federal Baseball Club of Baltimore, Inc. v. National League of Professional Baseball Clubs, 259 U.S. 200 (1922).

96. Toolson v. New York Yankees, Inc., 346 U.S. 356 (1953).

97. Flood v. Kuhn, 407 U.S. 238 (1972). *See also* Salerno v. American League of Professional Baseball Clubs, 1970 Trade Cas. §72,996 (S.D.N.Y. 1969), *aff'd* 1970 Trade Cas. §73,276 (2d Cir. 1970), *cert. denied*, 400 U.S. 1001 (1971).

98. United States v. International Boxing Club, 348 U.S. 236 (1955).

99. Radovich v. National Football League, 352 U.S. 445 (1957).

100. Washington Pro. Basketball Corp. v. National Basketball Ass'n., 147 F.Supp. 154 (S.D.N.Y. 1956).

101. Peto v. Madison Square Garden Corp., 1958 Trade Cas. §69,106 (S.D.N.Y. 1958).

102. Washington State Bowling Proprietors Ass'n. v. Pacific Lanes, Inc., 356 F.2d 371 (9th Cir. 1966), *cert. denied*, 384 U.S. 963 (1966).

103. Deesen v. Professional Golfers' Ass'n. of America, 358 F.2d 165 (9th Cir. 1966), *cert. denied*, 385 U.S. 846 (1966).

104. "We think that if there are evils in this field [baseball] which now warrant application to it of the anti-trust laws, it should be by legislation."
    Toolson v. New York Yankees, 346 U.S. 356 (1953).
    "But Federal Baseball held the business of baseball outside the scope of the Act. No

other business claiming the coverage of those cases has such an adjudication. We therefore conclude that the orderly way to eliminate error or discrimination, if any there be, is by legislation and not by court decision."

Radovich v. National Football League, 352 U.S. 445 (1957).

"And what the Court said in Federal Baseball in 1922 and what it said in Toolson in 1953, we say again here in 1972: the remedy, if any is indicated, is for congressional, and not judicial, action."

Flood v. Kuhn, 407 U.S. 238 (1972).

105. United Press International, March 17, 1993.

106. ". . . the word 'trade' is often and, indeed, generally used in a broad sense, as equivalent to occupation, employment, or business, whether manual or mercantile, wherever any occupation, employment, or business is carried on for the purpose of profit, or gain, or a livelihood, not in the liberal arts or in the learned professions, it is constantly called a trade."

The Nympth, 18 F. Cas. (No. 10,388) 506,507 (C.C. Me. 1834).

107. Atlantic Cleaners and Dyers v. United States, 286 U.S. 427, 435–36 (1931); United States v. National Ass'n. Real Estate Boards, 339 U.S. 485, 490–91 (1949).

108. "Of course medical practitioners . . . follow a profession and not a trade, are not engaged in the business of making or vending remedies but in prescribing them."

Federal Trade Commission v. Raladam Co., 283 U.S. 643, 653 (1930).

109. United States v. American Medical Ass'n., 110 F.2d 703 (D.C. Cir. 1940), *cert. denied*, 310 U.S. 644 (1940).

110. American Medical Ass'n. v. United States, 130 F.2d 233 (D.C. Cir. 1942), *aff'd* 317 U.S. 519 (1943).

111. "Much argument has been addressed to the question of whether a physician's practice of his profession constitutes trade under §3 of the Sherman Act. In the light of what we shall say with respect to the charge laid in the indictment, we need not consider or decide this question." *Id.* at 528.

Note that "trade" under a §3 Sherman violation may be different than that for other Sherman Act violations.

See Annot. 76 L.Ed. 1209.

112. United States v. Oregon State Medical Ass'n., 343 U.S. 326 at 336 (1952).

113. Semler v. Oregon State Bd. of D. Examiners, 294 U.S. 608 at 612 (1934).

114. United States v. Oregon State Medical Ass'n., 343 U.S. 326 at 336 (1952).

115. *Supra*, note 69.

116. *Id.* at 787.

117. *Id.* at 787, footnote 17.

118. National Society of Professional Engineers v. United States, ——————— U.S. — ———————, 55 L.Ed2d 637 (1978).

119. "The true test of legality is whether the restraint imposed is such as merely regulates and perhaps thereby promotes competition or whether it is such as may suppress or even destroy competition."

Chicago Board of Trade v. United States, 246 U.S. 231 at 238 (1917).

120. *Supra* note 118 at 653 (L.Ed.2d), footnote 22. The court appears to analogize the public service aspect of the learned professions to a marketing scheme restraint instituted for product safety which would be upheld under the rule of reason provided there is "no anticompetitive effect."

121. Boddicker v. Arizona State Dental Ass'n., 549 F.2d 626 (9th Cir. 1977).

122. Bogus v. American Speech and Hearing Ass'n., 582 F.2d 277 (8th Cir. 1978).

123. Veizaga v. The National Board for Respiratory Therapy, No. 75 C 3430 (N.D. Ill. 1977) reported in [1978] 801 *Antitrust and Trade Regulation Reporter* (BNA), A-19.

124. Hennessey v. National Collegiate Athletic Ass'n., 564 F.2d 1136 (1976). *See also*, Board of Regents of the Univ. of Oklahoma v. National Collegiate Athletic Ass'n., 561 P.2d 499 (Okla. 1977) where the same NCAA rule was held to be a reasonable restraint of trade. The Oklahoma Supreme Court rejected the *per se* finding of the trial court and applied a rule-of-reason test to determine that the bylaw in question was reasonable.

125. J. Van Cise, *supra* note 14 at 29–34; and n.4.

126. *Id.* at 34.

127. Radiant Burners, Inc. v. Peoples Gas Light and Coke Co., 364 U.S. 656 (1961); United States v. Central States Theatre Corp., 187 F.Supp. 114 (D. Neb. 1960). (Both *per se* violations.)

128. Hotel Phillips, Inc. v. Journeymen Barbers, Hairdressers, Cosmetologists, and Proprietors Intern. Union of America, 195 F.Supp. 664 (W.D. Mo. 1961) *aff'd* 301 F.2d 443 (8th Cir. 1962); Elizabeth Hospital, Inc. v. Richardson, 269 F.2d 167 (8th Cir. 1959); Lieberthal v. North Country Lanes, Inc., 221 F.Supp. 685 (S.D.N.Y. 1963). (All-not *per se* violations.)

129. Hospital Bldg. Co. v. Rex Hospital Trustees, 425 U.S. 738 (1976) holding that hospital's purchases of out-of-state supplies, management fees paid to out-of-state corporations, and financing from out-of-state lenders have a substantial effect on commerce even if market price not affected or business of out-of-state persons affected by local restraint doesn't fail. *See also* Goldfarb v. Virginia State Bar, *supra* note 69.

130. *Summit Health, Ltd. v. Pinhas*, 111 S. Ct. 1842 (U.S. Cal., 1991).

131. *United States of America v. Brown University in Providence, State of Rhode Island, et al.*, 805 F.Supp. 288 (E.D. Pa. 1992). See below, n.139.

132. *Supra* at 34.

133. *See* [1977] 813 *Antitrust and Trade Regulation Reporter*, AA-1, [1977] 812 *Antitrust and Trade Regulation Reporter*, A-23; and [1977] 811 *Antitrust and Trade Regulation Reporter*, A-8, where FTC reform bill (S. 1288) attacked for provision including nonprofit groups under FTC authority and similar house measure (H.R. 3816) passed by House Commerce Committee with nonprofit provision deleted.

134. Rule of reason re-endorsed in The White Motor Co. v. United States, 372 U.S. 253 (1963); United States v. E. I. DuPont de Nemours and Co., 351 U.S. 377 (1955) (but not as to *per se* violations); United States v. Parke, Davis and Co., 362 U.S. 29 (1960); Klor's v. Broadway-Hale Stores, 359 U.S. 207 (1959); *see supra*, n.4.

135. *See* Application of American Society for Testing and Materials, 231 F.Supp. 686 (E. D. Pa. 1968) holding that nonprofit charitable organization did not violate antitrust laws but that such organization could conceivably violate antitrust laws under different fact situations; Travelers Ins. Co. v. Blue Cross of Western Penn., 298 F.Supp. 1109 (W. D. Pa. 1969) holding that state's nonprofit laws are silent on trade and therefore alleged activities would have to be investigated; Marjorie Webster Jr. Col v. Middle States Ass'n. of C. and S.S., *cert. denied*, 400 U.S. 965 (1970) holding noncommercial purpose justified incidental trade restraint; Deesen v. Professional Golfer's Ass'n. of Amer., 358 F.2d 165 (9th Cir. 1966), *cert. denied*, 385 U.S. 846 (1966) holding that membership denial in professional sports association was reasonable; STP Corp. v. United States Auto Club, Inc., 286 F.Supp. 146 (S. D. Ind. 1968), no arbitrary abuse of power found by nonprofit rulesmaking body; Nankin Hospital v. Michigan Hospital Services, 361 F.Supp. 1199 (E.D. Mich. 1972) and Roafire Alarm Co. v. Royal Indemnity Co., 202 F.Supp. 166 (E. D. Tenn. 1962) *aff'd* 313 F.2d 635 (6th Cir. 1963), regulations of nonprofit organizations have been tested for reasonableness.

136. *Laughlin v. Evanston Hospital*, 550 N.E.2d 986 (Ill., 1990).

137. *Kingsepp v. Wesleyan University*, 763 F. Supp. 22 (S.D.N.Y 1991). *See also* Miller, *Are Colleges Fixing Prices*, 250 The Nation Company Inc. No 11 (March 19, 1990).

138. *Key Enterprises of Delaware, Inc. v. Venice Hospital*, 919 F.2d 1550 (11th Cir. Fla., 1990).

139. E.B. Smith, Comment, 24 *U. of San Fran. L. Rev.* 653 (1990); see above at n.131.

140. *Gilder v. PGA Tour, Inc.*, 936 F.2d 417 (9th Cir. (Ariz.), 1991).

141. *Clamp-All Corp. v. Cast Iron Soil Pipe Institute* (1st Cir., MA, 1988).

142. *Eureka Urethane, Inc. v. PBA, Inc.*, 746 F.Supp. 915 (E.D. Mo., 1990).

143. *Les Shockley Racing, Inc. v. National Hot Rod Assn.*; U.S. 9th Cir. (C.D. Calif.) #88-5748, 9–6; *12 Natl. L. J.* (34) 29 (Apr. 30, 1990). *See also Re-Alco Industries, Inc. v. National Center for Health Education, Inc., et al.*, 812 F.Supp. 387 (S.D.N.Y. 1993).

144. *Antitrust Developments, supra* note 30 at 35–36.

145. Authorities cited note 39 *supra.*

146. *See* weight given to such use of power in American Football League v. National Football League, 323 F.2d 124 (4th Cir. 1963); Deesen v. Professional Golfer's Ass'n. of America, 358 F.2d 165 (9th Cir. 1966), *cert. denied*, 385 U.S. 846 (1966). *See supra*, n.3, 4.

147. *Volvo North America Corp. v. Men's International Professional Tennis Council*, 687 F. Supp. 800 (D.C., NY, 1988).

148. *See* [1978] 853 *Antitrust and Trade Regulation Reporter*, A-4. But see, above, the beginning of Section 387; 35 Clev. St. L. Rev. (4) 403 (1986–7).

149. Associated In-Group Donors v. United Way, Inc., No. C233112 (Calif. Super. Ct., Los Angeles, 3/28/78) *noted in* [1978] 860 *Antitrust and Trade Regulation Reporter*, D-4.

150. *See* FTC comment on AMA accreditation in [1977] 815 *Antitrust and Trade Regulation Reporter*, A-2.

151. Costello Publishing Co. v. Rotelle, No. 76-1930 (D.D.C. 10/19/76), *noted in*, [1976] 789 *Antitrust and Trade Regulation Reporter*, A-25.

152. *Supra*, note 124.

153. *Supra*, notes 5, 6, 7. In 1978 the Justice Dept. refused an antitrust exemption that hospitals sought to curb costs. *N.Y. Times*, p. A 16 (June 14, 1978).

154. *United States v. Carillon Health System*, 707 F. Supp. 840 (D.C. Va., 1989); *United States v. Rockford Memorial Corp. . . .* , #89-1900 (D.C., Ill.; Nov. 27, 1989).

155. *Schachar v. American Academy of Ophthalmology, Inc.*, 870 F.2d 397 (7th Cir., 1989); and see *Community Hospital of Andalusia, Inc. v. Tomberlin*, 712 F. Supp. 170 (D.C. Ala., 1989).

156. Leonard & Rosch, *Courts Split on Clayton Act Use . . .* , 12 *Natl. L. J.* (12) 18 (Nov. 27, 1989); citing *U.S. v. Carillon Health System & C.H. of R.V.*, 107 F. Supp. 840 (W.D., Vir., 1989); *U.S. v. Rockford Memorial Corp. & S.A. Corp.* (D.C., Ill., 1989).

42

MANAGEMENT TECHNIQUES IN NONPROFIT ORGANIZATIONS

[*See also*, Chapter 29 (Officers and Managers), especially Section 304 (Financial Managers) and Section 305 (Investment Managers).]

§423. "MANAGEMENT," IN GENERAL

Business Management is a major field of study in itself, with an extensive literature and many schools and colleges of business management.[1] *Management* is supervision, control, and guidance of a group of people and things in an organization or enterprise; and a *manager* is the person chosen or appointed to supervise, direct and administer the affairs of the organization or group.[2] *Discretionary authority* and power to direct some (or all) of the activities of the organization is implied in the title of "manager" or in whatever term is used to indicate such power; often today the term *executive director* or *executive vice president* or *executive secretary* is employed for designation of the *chief* manager. Sometimes the term *managing agent* is used to designate "the person invested by a corporation with general powers involving the exercise of judgment and discretion."[3]

Texts used in college courses on business management often devote their opening chapters to the history, philosophy, and general *theory* of management.[4] They usually are vague as to the *legal* status and *specific duties, powers* and *liabilities* of specific categories or levels of managers and management functions. A legal treatise on business corporations[5] contains many chapters and sections devoted to detailed exposition of these specifics.

Today the tendency is to view the fiduciary nature of management to be owed primarily to the corporation, and only little to the members (shareholders) as such, even in closely-held corporations. Harris v. Mardan Business Systems, Inc., 421 N.W.2d 350 (Minn. App. 1988).

"The Management" is a term signifying the dominant or guiding group of managers of an organization. It refers to the board of directors (or, trustees) *together with* the *chief officers* of the organization. It does not include lesser officers or managers, nor ordinary employees, nor necessarily the main office employees, except those who are vested with important authority.

Officers are persons holding positions of trust and/or authority. The term means such office-holders as the *president, vice president, treasurer, secretary,* and the like, in corporations. "In determining whether one is an *officer* or *employee,* important tests are the tenure by which a position is held, whether its duration is defined by the statute or ordinance (or bylaw) creating it, or whether it is temporary or transient, or for a time fixed only by agreement; whether it is created by an appointment or election, or merely by a contract of employment by which the rights of the parties are regulated; whether the compensation is by a salary or fees fixed by law, or by a sum agreed upon by the contract of hiring."[6]

[Decision enforcement by managers (e.g., by nonprofit organizations' tribunals) with respect to internal affairs, will usually be deemed conclusive in the absence of fraud, mistake, collusion, or arbitrariness. Solomon v. Edgewater Yacht Club, Inc., 519 N.E.2d 429 (Ohio Mun. 1987).]

Charitable Funds Management is service work done by specialists who help NPOs to manage their supervision, investment and disbursement of charitable fund assets. Thus, a major company in that field, Wachovia C.F.M. of Atlanta, offers (in its 1991 brochure) services that include "investment management, custodial or master custody services, tax reporting and consulting, fund accounting and foundation administration," and other services. An *Organization providing administrative services to charities qualifies as (tax) exempt,* under a 1992 Tax Court decision; *The Council for Bibliographic and Information Technologies v. Commissioner.* This overrules the I.R.S. policy of viewing such organizations as *not* charitable, even if their primary purpose is to aid the charities, when that aid/service is not their exclusive function.[7]

Volunteers, "Evangelizing" of "young volunteers" is the main purpose of *Energize, Inc.* (5450 Wissahickon Ave., Philadelphia, PA 19144), publisher of such works as *Children As Volunteers* (2d ed. 1991), and conductor of workshops on the subject.

Begun in 1989, the first AMTEC (Association and Membership Organization Technology Exposition and Conference) was held Nov. 1–2, 1989, at (and by) INFORUM Center in Atlanta, Georgia (250 Williams St.). At that conference and show center, displays and demonstrations and discussions of the most advanced technological resources for NPOs were (and annually will be) offered to those attending. Inquire at Phone 404-220-2700 or FAX 404-220-2720.

For management information sources, see the *Bibliography* herein. Also, such "associations of associations" as: Independent Sector, 1828 "L" Street N.W., Washington, D.C. 20036; Foundation Center, 79 Fifth Ave., N.Y.C. 10003; National Center for Nonprofit Boards, 2000 "L" St. N.W., Washington, D.C. 20036; the schools for NPOs (see Index); National Executive Service Corps, 257 Park Ave. So., N.Y.C. 10010; etc.

§424. QUALIFICATIONS OF MANAGERS

Statutes, governmental agency regulations, and corporation bylaws often state specific rules as to qualifications that may, or must, be satisfied for certain specified officer positions.

Statutes of most states require that most *directors* be over the age of 18 years.[8] Some statutes (*e.g.*, Florida and New York) may say that the charter or bylaws of nonprofit corporations—in New York, may and in Florida, must—establish the qualifications and classifications of officers and/or directors.[9] *Classifications* mean division of a board into directors elected at different times (*e.g.*, three to five divisions), in order to *rotate* the board membership in part, so as to maintain continuity of some experienced directors on the board at all times. Some states (*e.g.*, Minnesota) permit *minors* to be directors.[10]

Special qualifications for office, set forth in the charter or bylaws, may be any reasonable ones. For example, it may be required, in a professional association that all *members* must be licensed to practice that profession, but that all *officers* must have at least three years of experience in active practice of that profession; or other moral or personal-history qualifications may be required.

Managers' qualifications requirements are often *implied* by the nature of the organization. Thus, a manager of a scientific research organization obviously ought to have adequate training in, or familiarity with, the particular branch of science dealt with. Ordinarily, too, a denominational religious organization would want its executives to be members of that denomination. Yet, experience has shown that in a church-related college, for example, teachers who adhere to other denominations or other religions often are the best people available in their subject specialties, and generally get along very amicably with colleagues of other faiths. The use of religious tests for employment, or sex, national origin, or other such criteria, may be illegal breaches of the civil rights of applicants, and should be required only where fully justified by the inherent nature of the employment.[11]

Job qualifications should obviously be analyzed, stated in an *employee's manual*, and required of employees, including the chief management employees. For example, people employed in accounting work should be knowledgeable about bookkeeping; truck drivers should be knowledgeable about heavy motor vehicles; and so on. The same is true as to managers; they should be knowledgeable about organization work, personnel, finance, and other aspects of their jobs. Ideally there should be *job descriptions* written by (or under the guidance of) the board of directors, including an outline of the executive director's functions and qualifications. Cronyism and nepotism are even more destructive in nonprofit organizations than they are in business corporations; the voluntarism of NPOs fades rapidly if members become convinced that favoritism rather than qualifications is the key to status or position in the organization.

§425. TRAINING OF NPO MANAGERS

People who wish to obtain positions as *managers* in nonprofit organizations can prepare (educate) themselves for this kind of work, in the "Lincoln tradition" of self-education. Or they can attend schools that offer the necessary courses. In both methods, certain basic subjects (or, courses) are important; and these are indicated in the following suggested curriculum of study:

1. *Introduction to Nonprofit Organizations*: A survey course to introduce beginning students to the numbers, kinds, functions and practices of modern nonprofit organizations.
    [Text: Oleck & Stewart, *Nonprofit Corporations, Organizations & Associations*, cc. 1–6 (6th ed., Prentice-Hall, 1994)]

2. *Nonprofit Organizations' Law*: Legal rights and obligations of members, officers, agents, and third parties. A survey course, using select, illuminating sections from NPO works and from a college level, general business law course syllabus.
    [Text: Oleck & Stewart, *Nonprofit Corporations, Organizations, & Associations*; or, Hopkins, *Law of Tax-Exempt Organizations* (3rd ed., John Wiley & Sons, 1979)]

3. *Principles of Management of NPOs*. An analysis of the management functions of planning, organizing, directing, and controlling an NPO; emphasizing differences from management of a business (profit-oriented) organization.
    [Text: *See* works cited in footnote 1]

4. *Introductory Accounting for NPOs*: Financial Accounting, with emphasis on the concepts and standards for NPO corporate accounting.
    [Text: *NPO Standards of the American Accountants Society* (1979–80); and extracts from a college level business accounting syllabus; and/or (text) such as *Bookkeeping for Nonprofit Organizations* (1980), Public Management Inst., Detroit).]

5. (a) *Finances of NPOs*: Sources and management of NPO moneys, properties, investments, fund-raising, and the like.
    [Text: Gross, *Financial and Accounting Guide for Nonprofit Organizations* (3rd ed., Ronald Press, 1978); and materials from *Association of Association Executives* publications (Washington, D.C.).]

    (b) *Fund-Raising Careers*: Similar to (5a), but emphasizing the latter kind of materials, and various finance materials from organizations such as bank *trust departments* or *public relations* training courses.

6. *Comparative NPOs:* An outline of the characteristics and differences of the chief types of NPOs, such as charities, religious organizations, trade associations, country clubs, schools, labor unions, fraternal orders, chambers of commerce, civic associations, foundations, *etc.*
   [Text: Various works on each of the specific types of organizations mentioned above, plus others; and bylaws and other literature obtained from various, specific types of organizations.]

7. *Parliamentary Procedure (Meetings and Conventions) of NPOs:* How to plan, organize, and supervise meetings and conventions of NPO's and their boards, committees, elections, and so forth.
   [Text: Oleck & Green, *Parliamentary Law & Practice for Nonprofit Organizations* (Amer. Law Inst.-Amer. Bar Assn. Comm., 2d ed., 1991); or Robert's *Rules of Order* (current ed.)

8. *Sociology of NPOs:* Extracts from books on sociology.

9. *Political and Civic NPOs:* Extracts from books on political science.

10. *Charitable NPOs:* Extracts from books on charity organizations and programs.

11. *Religious NPOs:* Extracts from books on church organizations and activities.

12. *Etcetera:*

Apprenticeship, and Training Programs

On-the-job-training, by the officers of organizations, has long been the chief method of obtaining skilled management personnel for nonprofit organizations. Often, in the past, persons trained and/or experienced in other fields of endeavor have shifted to NPO work. Thus, someone already knowledgeable about accounting work or real property management can adapt quickly to the special nature of such work in a NPO setting, if given some guidance. Too often, in the past, persons with no particularly appropriate background have been thrown into a NPO position, to sink or swim.

Today the availability of training courses on various aspects of NPO management work is increasing rapidly. Since 1979, for example, the Association of American Law Schools has encouraged programs on NPO law and education; with over thirty law schools that have offered programs or courses in the field: *e.g.,* at Arizona State University, Cleveland State University, Cornell University, Duke University, Stetson University, Syracuse University, Wake Forest University, University of California (Los Angeles), University of Pennsylvania, University of South Carolina, University of Texas, Yale University, *etc.* College (undergraduate) courses have long been offered at Antioch College, Long Island University, Stetson University, Wake Forest University, and other schools, under rubrics of sociology, business law, economics, political science, *etc.*

Special seminars on NPOs (especially on tax-exempt organizations) are often offered by such associations as the "Independent Sector" organization

(Washington, D.C.), the American Law Institute—American Bar Association Joint Committee on CLE (ALI-ABA), various schools, and by various bar associations, trade associations, and learned societies. These are usually advertised in law and business periodicals.

By 1991 there were many training programs for NPO management, not only by seminar/conference organizers and even law schools (e.g., Stetson University's annual conference and law school semester-long courses), but also in *degree* programs. The latter programs were being offered (according to the *Non-Profit Times*): *Northeast/Mid Atlantic*: Brandeis U., Central Michigan U., CUNY Baruch College (proposed), Clark U. (proposed), Eastern College, Geo. Washington U., New School (N.Y.C.), Seton Hall U., SUNY Stony Brook, Tufts U., U. of Pittsburgh; *Midwest*: Case Western Res. U., Hamline U., Roosevelt U., U. of Missouri K.C.; *South*: Georgia State U. (proposed), U. of Virginia (D.C. area) (proposed); *West*: Golden Gate U., Regis College, U. of Judaism in Los Angeles, U. of San Francisco. Also, *certificates* in NPO management were being offered by: American U., Calif. State Long Beach, CWRU, Columbia U., Geo. Washington U., Metropolitan State Denver, New School (N.Y.C.), N.Y.U., Regis College, R.P.I., Roosevelt U., Rutgers U., San Francisco State, Sangamon State, Sonoma State, Springfield College, Tufts U., U. of Denver, V.P.I. *Short* (few days) *workshops* were offered by Antioch New England, N.Y.U., Springfield College, and Tufts U.[12]

Since 1971 there have been a number of training "Support Centers" for NPOs (in many cities nationwide) conducting "Management Workshops" and other programs. Address: The Support Center of Washington, D.C.; 2001 "O" St., N.W.; Washington, D.C. 20036; tel. # (202) 833-0300.

The Nonprofits' Risk Management & Insurance Institute, in Washington, D.C., advises nonprofit organizations nationwide on legal liability, risk management, insurance purchasing, and employee benefits.[13]

Management Training "Masters Degree"

A typical modern graduate-degree-in-NPO-management *program* is that of the New School for Social Research in New York City, which in 1991 in its catalog of its Graduate School of Management and Urban Policy said:

Curriculum

The curriculum of the Nonprofit Management program has been developed to provide students with the knowledge and skills needed for effective management and leadership in the nonprofit sector. To that end, the curriculum consists of three components through which students fulfill the degree requirement of forty-two credits—a required schoolwide core of twelve credits, a required program core of fifteen credits, and fifteen credits of elective courses.

[Descriptions of all courses.]

The **schoolwide core** of four required courses equips students with basic analytic skills and an understanding of major theories of management and organizational behavior.

MM 240   Economic Analysis
MM 250   Policy Analysis
MM 260   Quantitative Methods
MM 270   Management and Organizational Behavior

Five required **program core** courses build on the knowledge and skill base developed in the school wide core, providing students with an understanding of key nonprofit management functions and issues while sharpening their analytic and decision making capabilities.

MF 301   Fund Raising and Development
MF 311   Theory and Practice of Nonprofit Management
MF 332   Financial Management in Nonprofit Organizations
MM 101   Laboratory in Issue Analysis (full-time students)
or
MM 417   Managerial Decision Making (part-time students)
MF 335   Advanced Seminar in Nonprofit Management

The third group of courses in the master's program consists of the five **elective courses** that students may organize, in consultation with an academic advisor, to suit their individual academic and professional interests and goals. This flexibility is possible given the broad array of courses offered by the Nonprofit Management program, by other programs in the Graduate School, and by other divisions of the university. Elective courses offered in Nonprofit Management include:

MF 303   Personal Solicitation of Charitable Gifts
MF 305   Market Research and Strategic Planning for Fund Raising
MF 306   The Role of Foundations
MF 308   The Governance of Nonprofit Organizations
MF 310   The Law of Nonprofit Organizations
MF 312   Corporate Philanthropy
MF 313   The Voluntary Tradition
MF 314   Ethics, Professionalism, and Leadership in Nonprofit Organizations
MF 315   Marketing in Nonprofit Organizations
MF 322   Direct Mail Fund Raising
MF 323   Grantsmanship: Government, Corporations, and Foundations
MF 326   The Development of Planned Giving Programs
MF 330   Nonprofit Organizations and the Shaping of Public Policy
MF 336   Social Movements and Social Policy
MF 337   The Nonprofit Manager and Public Benefit Strategies
MF 340   Strategic Planning in Nonprofit and Public Organizations
MF 345   International Nonprofit Management

MF 350　　　Critical Issues in Nonprofit Management
MF 400　　　Independent Study

§426. HOW TO GET GOOD MANAGERS

There are many books on management that include much discussion of what *is* a good manager, what to *look for* in a good one, and *how to get* good ones.[14] Many books are devoted *entirely* to this last subject. And there are numerous articles written on the subject, in various periodicals.[15] This is important because at least one out of every ten people employed in the United States may properly be classified as a "manager" or "executive" with some degree of authority.

　　The following list of items sets forth, in outline, necessary documents, and procedures to be followed in selecting and obtaining good executives:

A. *Preliminary Data*:

　1. Job description,

　2. Chief qualifications desired,

　3. Criteria that are paramount (especially, salary),

　4. Organization's major objectives,

　5. Organization's major needs,

　6. Current personnel—market situation.

B. *Recruiting Method(s)*:

　1. Internal promotion (gets a "known quantity" and is good for general morale),

　2. External search (form letters inviting applications, *etc.*) (This gets "new blood," avoids jealousies, gives wider choice).

　3. Training program(s),

　4. Media (press releases, *etc.*)

　5. Employment agencies, (headhunters),

　6. Advertising (*Wall Street Journal*, and/or local, *etc.*).

C. *Interview Bases*:

　1. Resumes (or, *Vita*), in advance,

　2. References (before, or after, interview),

　3. Tests (examinations),

　4. Visits and personal interviews,

　5. Checking of references and qualifications allegations,

　6. Affirmative action aspects.

D. *Selection Board Action*: In NPOs a vote (or at least a sampling of opinions of the board or committee) is usually required and/or desirable.

Association management companies can be retained for managing nonprofit organizations. Most big cities have several such companies.

Consultant services (companies and individual experts), linking NPOs and contract trainers, speakers, etc., now are available, especially for fund raising and development of volunteer programs. For example, *Independent Sector* of Washington, D.C., or Patton Consulting Services of Hamilton, Mass. 01982.

The *great dangers* in recruiting are similar in business organizations and NPOs; *e.g.*, tendencies towards nepotism, favoritism, cronyism, and failure to thoroughly check out (even a private detective agency should be used, in many cases) allegations of candidates, prior employment record, references, and some personal history aspects not referred to in applications, such as apparent standard of living, *etc.* Even such personal matters as the general state of the marriage of the candidate may be highly significant. All these matters require reasonable investigation, but must not be carried to the point of invasion of civil rights to privacy.

Head hunting (pirating): is the most popular (and often the most successful) of recruitment methods, in many respects. It is the straightforward *raiding* of other organizations, in order to obtain the services of experienced and proven managers. This usually requires the ability to offer better pay or other inducements. Head hunting is used with most evident success in the field of higher education; where it is generally believed that this is the best assurance of getting high quality deans, presidents, and department heads, as well as top professors. But the practice of hiring away top-quality managers is not confined to any one type of business or nonprofit organization. It has drawbacks as well as advantages. For example, it may cost more than it is worth, or it may unduly inflate the ego of the person who is so courted, while it embitters inside managers who are passed over for promotion. But, all in all, it is the method of choice in most large NPOs for recruiting top management prospects.

Management Contracts

A 20-year *management contract* of a hospital with a *management company* can be terminated only if the management company commits a *material* breach of contract; its mere unilateral raising of rates is not material enough if the hospital can override it.[16]

A corporation may not evade liability on a contract with a former member (shareholder) by dissolving the corporation and transferring its assets to a newly organized corporation. But the claimant is entitled to the assets (as source of payment) only insofar as the old corporation did not get a fair price for its assets.[17]

A condominium owners' association obtained a default judgment against its managers for mismanagement of funds. The default could not be set aside, even though the managers were Canadian citizens, unfamiliar with state laws, acting *pro se*, and had filed a timely answer without the required $160 appearance fee.[18]

Exclusive-management-agent contract *termination* by a coop. association can be the basis of a damages action by the agent if published reasons given by the association officers are malicious in fact, and may be the basis of an action for specific performance of its (contract's) termination-formalities requirements.[19]

Form No. 173

NPO MANAGEMENT CONTRACT

Management Agreement

THIS MANGEMENT AGREEMENT (the "Agreement") is made and entered into this_____18th day of July, 199___, by and between CONDOMINIUM, BUILDING "B", ASSOCIATION, INC., a Florida corporation not for profit (the "Association"), and MANAGEMENT COMPANY, a Florida corporation, (PBM).

W I T N E S S E T H :

WHEREAS, the Association is a non-profit corporation organized for the administration and operation of CONDOMINIUM, BUILDING "B", ASSOCIATION, INC. (the "Condominium"); and

WHEREAS, the Association desires to employ a managing agent for said Condominium Association; and

WHEREAS, the chief operating officer of PBM has extensive experience in the operation and administration of condominiums and the duties and responsibilities of the Association.

NOW THEREFORE, in consideration of the premises, and of the mutual covenants and other considerations hereinafter set forth, the parties hereto agree as follows:

1. *Definitions.* The term used in this Management Agreement shall have the meaning as set forth in the Declaration of Condominium and Chapter 718 of the Florida Statutes (the "Condominium Act"), unless the context otherwise requires.

2. *Employment.* The Association hereby employs PBM and PBM hereby accepts said employment on the terms and conditions provided for in this Management Agreement.

3. *Exclusiveness.* The management provided for herein shall be exclusively performed by PBM under the direct control and supervision of the Association.

4. *Term.* The term of this Agreement shall extend from September 1, 199___ until August 31, 199___ and thereafter shall continue in full force and affect from year to year with an increase in compensation of 6% over each the previous years unless terminated:

(a) By notice in writing given by either party to the other not less than one (1) month prior to the expiration of the term of this agreement and any renewal thereof, or

(b) In accordance with the provisions of Paragraph 13.

5. *Powers and Duties of PBM.*

(a) PBM will designate a Property Manager for the Association. The Property Manager shall be at the cost of PBM and be directly responsible to the Association's Board of Directors for administration of Managerial services. In the event PBM wishes to substitute a Property Manager, the Association agrees to accept the appointment for a probationary period of sixty (60) days. Upon completion of the probationary period, the Board shall advise PBM as to whether or not the Association wishes to have another manager assigned to the Condominium Association and PBM shall comply with the request within a period not to exceed sixty (60) days.

(b) PBM shall have fiduciary responsibility to the Association through its Board of Directors, and shall have the powers of the Association under the direction of the Association's Board of Directors in performance of the duties provided for in this Agreement in accordance with the Association's approved yearly budget. PBM shall further have the powers of the Association to monitor and enforce the rules and regulations of the Association and such other rules and regulations as the Board of Directors shall, from time to time, properly adopt.

6. *Services, Duties and Obligations of PBM.* PBM shall provide the following services which shall include, but not be limited to:

(a) Hire, supervise, pay and discharge in PBM's name with Association approval all non-administrative personnel necessary to properly operate and maintain the Condominium consistent with the approved budget. All such personnel shall be supervised by PBM and all compensation for the services of such personnel shall be considered an expense of the Association. PBM shall, in its sole discretion, cause to be discharged all persons unnecessary or undesirable by either PBM or the Association.

(b) Cause the Common Elements, including the Limited Common Elements and any recreation facilities, to be maintained, repaired and replaced, as set forth in the Declaration, including interior and exterior cleaning and repairs and alterations to plumbing, electrical work, carpentry, painting, decorating and such other incidental alterations or changes therein as may be proper. Ordinary repairs, replacements or alterations involving an expenditure of more than $500.00 for any one item and that is not budgeted for shall be made only with the prior written approval of the Association. EMERGENCY REPAIRS immediately necessary for the preservation or safety of the Condominium Property or for the safety of Unit Owners, tenants or other persons, or required to avoid suspension of any necessary service in or about the Condominium Property, may be made by PBM without the prior approval of the Association;

(c) Cause all acts and things to be done in or about the Condominium as is necessary to comply with any and all orders or requirements affecting the premises, placed thereon by an governmental authority having jurisdiction thereof, subject to the limitation with respect to the amount of expenditure involved which requires Association approval, as set forth in Subparagraph (b) above, and subject also to specific instructions from the Association not to comply with such orders or requirements because the Association intends to contest same;

(d) Solicit, analyze recommend and negotiate contracts for execution by the Association for the services of contractors for garbage and trash removal, vermin extermination and other services; the purchase of all tools, equipment and supplies which shall be necessary to properly maintain and operate the Condominium; and make all such contracts and purchases in either the Association or PBM's name after receipt of the Association's approval to do so;

(e) Shall cause to be effected and maintained to the extent obtainable with insurance carriers selected by the Association, in such amounts as required under the Declaration and as the Association shall designate in writing, recommend modifications or additional coverages, prepare claims when required and follow-up payment, and act as the Association representative in negotiating settlement pursuant to Association instructions and to submit to the Association such insurance, including, but not limited to fire, liability, workmen's compensation and other such insurance required by the Declaration and as the Association may deem necessary or advisable;

(f) Make a careful inspection and review of all bills received for services, work and supplies ordered in connection with maintaining and operating the Condominium, pay all such bills, including but not limited to water charges, sewer charges and assessments assessed with respect to the Common Elements, if any, as and when the same shall become due and payable by making the required disbursements for the Association, to take advantage of all discounts on behalf of the Association. PBM is hereby granted authority to make any disbursements or expenditures provided in the approved budget at PBM's own discretion.

(g) Bill Unit Owners for Common Expenses and use its best efforts to collect same. In this regard, the Association hereby authorizes PBM to make demand for all regular and special assessments and charges which may be due the Association, and to assist the Association by way of making, recording, satisfying and foreclosing the Association's lien therefore, or by way of other legal process or otherwise, as may be required for the collection of such assessments.

All such collection procedures shall be approved by the Association and all legal action shall be initiated by the Association through the Association's attorney, at the expense of the Association;

(h) Shall reply to and, where reasonable, attending to the complaints of the Unit Owners or their tenants;

(i) Shall prepare and file the necessary forms for unemployment insurance, Social Security taxes, withholding taxes and all other forms, reports and returns required by any federal, state or municipal authority;

(j) Deposit all funds collected from the Unit Owners or otherwise accruing to the Association in a special bank account or accounts of the Association and selected by the Association, (in which PBM may be an authorized signatory) in a bank or savings and loan association in Pinellas County, Florida, with suitable designation indicating their source, separate from other funds of PBM. In the event interest is earned on any account, such interest shall accrue to the benefit of the Association;

(k) Maintain in accordance with generally accepted accounting standards the books of account, check books, copies of minutes and other records of the Association at PBM's office;

(l) In conjunction with the accountant for the Association, if any, prepare an annual financial report of the operations of the Association for the year then ended. A copy of each annual report shall be sent by PBM to each Unit Owner;

(m) Prepare and submit at least 60 days prior to the fiscal year end to the Association a recommended operating budget setting forth the anticipated income and expenses of the Condominium for the ensuing year; notify the Unit Owners of annual and all other Assessments for Common Expenses determined by the Board as more particularly set forth in the Bylaw.

(n) Cause a representative of its organization to attend meetings of the Unit Owners and of the Board. Meetings of the Board of Directors shall be held Monday through Thursday between the hours of 9 A.M. and 10 P.M. Should the manager and or secretary be required to attend meetings outside of the aforementioned time a charge of FIFTY DOLLARS ($50.00) per hour and THIRTY FIVE DOLLARS ($35.00) per hour respectively will be payable to PBM.

(o) Prepare and send out all notices of Board meetings and members' meetings and such other letters and reports as the Board may request;

(p) Maintain records sufficient to describe its services hereunder and such financial books and records, in accordance with prevailing accounting standards sufficient to identify the source of all funds collected by it as Manager and the disbursement there of. Such records shall be kept at the office of PBM and shall be available for inspection by the Unit Owners at reasonable times. These records shall be kept in accordance with Section 718.111(11) of the Condominium Act. The Manager shall perform a continual internal audit of its financial records relative to its services as Manager for the purpose of verifying same, but no independent or external audit shall be required of PBM. The Association shall have the right to an annual external independent audit provided the cost there of and the employment of such auditor be by the Association directly and not through PBM, such independent audit shall be at the office of PBM;

(q) PBM shall provide the Board by the 20th of each month with a set of statements showing by month and year to date:

(i) dollar amount of each disbursement;

(ii) the names of the members of the Association who are delinquent in payment of their required contribution to common expenses and the amount of each delinquency:

(iii) dollar amount of common expenses collected;

(iv) dollar amount of each disbursement as compared with budgeted expenses by budget categories;

(v) the names and amount of all other delinquent accounts;

(vi) Association income;

(vii) particulars of accounts, deposits, securities and any other instruments respecting investment income;

(viii) all accounting and financial reporting which is required under the terms of this agreement to be provided by PBM shall be in accordance with generally accepted accounting principles and practices.

(r) Recommend to the Association retainment or employment of attorneys, accountants and such other experts and professionals whose services PBM may reasonably require to effectively perform its duties hereunder; and

(s) PBM Shall maintain, manage and supervise the recreational facilities and Common elements operated by the Association for the use of its members; enforce rules and regulations as may be established by the Association, from time to time, concerning the use thereof; and generally to do all things necessary and appropriate for the beneficial use of such facilities, subject to the direction of the Association.

(t) PBM shall coordinate and administer Association approvals for sale, rent, or lease of units as provided in Association Bylaws and Board Actions, and use all reasonable efforts to collect fees and fines.

(u) PBM shall designate, subject to the Board of Directors approval, certain bonded employees who will be authorized to disburse funds of the Association. All payment by check shall require two signatures.

(v) PBM shall monitor all contractual work for proper compliance and performance, receive and analyze bills for same, recommending payment for those deemed proper.

(w) PBM shall maintain a complete inventory of Association property, including supplies, tools and equipment, verify its presence and condition annually, with files indicating such details.

The specific services, obligations and responsibilities to provide maintenance and/or management to the Unit Owners, the amount of money to be paid, the time schedule as to how often the services will be performed, and the minimum number of personnel to be employed to provide maintenance of management services is as set forth on Exhibit A attached hereto and made a part hereof.

7. *Reimbursed Expenses*. The Association authorizes PBM to perform any act or do anything necessary or desirable in order to carry out its duties hereunder, and everything done by PBM hereunder shall be done as agent of the Association and all obligations or expenses incurred thereunder, PBM shall not be obliged to make any advance to or for the account of the Association, nor to pay any amount except out of funds held or provided as aforesaid, nor shall PBM be obliged to incur any liability or obligation unless the Association shall furnish PBM with the necessary funds for the discharge thereof. If PBM shall voluntarily advance, for the Association's account, any amount for the payment of any proper obligation or necessary expense connected with the maintenance or Operation of the Condominium or otherwise, PBM may, reimburse itself out of the first collections from the Unit Owners. PBM shall confer fully with the Association in the performance of its duties hereunder.

8. *Indemnification*. PBM shall not be liable to the Association for any loss or damage not caused by PBM's own negligence or willful misconduct. The Association will indemnify and save harmless PBM from any liability for damages, costs and expenses for injury to any person or property in, about and in connection with the Condominium, from any cuse whatsoever, unless such injury shall be caused by PBM or PBM's employees own negligence or willful misconduct.

9. *Compensation*. As compensation for its services hereunder, the Association shall pay to MANAGEMENT the sum of Seven Hundred Eighty-seven Dollars and Fifty Cents ($787.50) per month for the first TWELVE (12) MONTHS; Eight Hundred Eleven Dollars and Thirteen Cents ($811.13) for the SECOND TWELVE (12) MONTHS; and Eight Hundred Thirty-five Dollars and Forty-Six Cents ($835.46) for the THIRD TWELVE (12) MONTHS. Such compensation shall be payable monthly in advance during the term of this Agreement.

10. *Office Facilities*. PBM will provide its own office facilities, office maintenance and office staff thereof at its own expense.

11. *Normal Work Week/Holidays*. The normal work week shall be Monday through Friday, 40 hours per week. At least one Property Manager shall be directly available (on call) for emergencies, including nights, weekends and holidays. Holidays observed by office staff are 8 days per year, and are as posted by PBM at the start of each calendar year.

12. *Liaison Officer*. The Board shall designate a single individual who shall be authorized to deal with P.B.M. on any matter relating to the management of the Association. P.B.M. is directed not to accept directions or instructions with regard to the management of the Association from anyone else. In the absence of any other designation by the Board, the President of the Association shall have this authority.

13. *Termination.* (A) This Agreement may be terminated with cause by either party at any time during its initial term or any extension thereof by written notice of at least two (2) months duration, provided that with respect to the Association giving notice to P.B.M. the Board shall take the steps set out in the order below.

(B) The Board shall submit to P.B.M. in writing stated reasons why it considers that P.B.M. is not fulfilling its contractual obligations whereupon P.B.M. shall within a reasonable time, not to exceed Thirty (30) days take steps to rectify and/or remove the cause for such stated dissatisfaction.

(C) In the event that P.B.M. fails to take reasonable steps to rectify an/or remove the stated cause for dissatisfaction, and the Board continues to be dissatisfied with P.B.M., the Board shall call a meeting of the Board for the purpose of considering the termination of this agreement. In the event the Board votes to terminate the agreement they may do so upon providing 30 days written notice to P.B.M.

(D) Upon termination of this Agreement:

(a) PBM shall as soon as possible thereafter render a final account to the Corporation;

(b) PBM shall surrender to the Association all contracts, records, files and other documents or information which may be pertinent to the continuing operation of the Property. The Association shall provide access to PBM at all reasonable times and upon reasonable notice to all such contracts, records, files and other documents or information subsequent to termination of this Agreement; and

(c) The Association shall assume the obligation of any and all contracts which PBM has properly made for the purpose of arranging services to be provided pursuant to this Agreement.

14. *Notices.* Unless otherwise stated herein, all notices which the parties hereto may desire or be required to give hereunder shall be deemed to have been properly given and shall be effective when, and if, sent by United States regular mail, postage prepaid, addressed to the Association, c/o President, Florida, 33707 and to PBM at Boulevard, Suite 203, Florida 33715, or to such other address as either of the parties may designate in writing.

15. *Benefit.* This Management Agreement and every provision hereof shall bind, apply to and run in favor of the Association and PBM and respective successors in interest, and may not be changed, waived or terminated orally. Neither of the parties may assign this Management Agreement without the written consent of the other.

16. *Severability.* If any Paragraph, Subparagraph, sentence, clause, phrase or word of this Management Agreement shall be or is, for any reason, held or declared to be inoperative or void, such holding will not affect the remaining

portions of this Management Agreement and it shall be construed to have been the intent of the parties hereto to have agreed without such inoperative or invalid part therein and the remainder of this Agreement, after the exclusion of such parts, shall be deemed and held to be as valid as if such excluded parts had never been included therein.

IN WITNESS WHEREOF, the parties hereto have executed this Agreement this 18th day of July, 199——————.

Signed, sealed and delivered
the presence of: ———————————— CONDOMINIUM,
                                    BUILDING "B", ASSOCIATION,
                                    INC., a Florida corporation not for
                                    profit

———————————————————— By: ————————————————————
                                                        Its President
———————————————————— By: ————————————————————
                                                        Director

As to the Association   (CORPORATE SEAL)

                                    ——————————MANAGEMENT
                                    COMPANY,a Florida corporation

———————————————————— By: ————————————————————
                                                        Its Vice-President

————————————————
As to PBM   (CORPORATE SEAL)

EXHIBIT A
TO MANAGEMENT AGREEMENT

The number of units constructed in CONDOMINIUM "B", ASSOCIATION, INC., A CONDOMINIUM, are SEVENTY-FOUR (74). As set forth in Paragraph 9 of the Management Agreement, PBM shall be entitled to collect as compensation TEN DOLLARS AND SIXTY FOUR CENTS ($10.64) per unit, per month, the first twelve (12) months, TEN DOLLARS AND NINETY-SIX CENTS ($10.96), the second twelve (12) months, and ELEVEN DOLLARS AND TWENTY-NINE CENTS ($11.29), the third twelve (12) months.

1. *"On-Site Supervisory Services."* Subparagraphs (b) and (r) of Paragraph 6 of the Management Agreement shall be designated as "On-Site Supervisory Ser-

vices" and shall be allocated twenty percent (20%) of the compensation. These services to be performed shall be provided on a five (5) day per week basis. At no time shall there be less than two (2) persons employed by manager for the purpose, among others, of providing the services specified therein. There shall be no resident manager living at the condominium complex.

2. *"Administrative Services."* Subparagraphs (a), (c), (d), (e), (g), (h), (k), (l), (m), (n), (o), (q), (r), (s), (t), (u), (v) and (w) of Paragraph 6 of the Management Agreement shall be designated as "Administrative Services" and shall be allocated forty percent (40%) of the compensation. The services to be performed shall be provided on an as-needed basis. At no time shall there be less than one (1) person employed by PBM for the purpose, among others, of provided the services specified therein.

3. *"Accounting Services."* Subparagraphs (f), (g), (i), (j), (k), (l), (m), (p) and (q) of the Management Agreement shall be designated as "Accounting Services" and shall be allocated forty percent (40%) of the compensation). Certain of the services as designated in the above paragraphs contain areas of responsibility which will be performed on either a weekly, monthly, quarterly or annual basis, or more frequently as needed in accordance with generally accepted accounting principles, or as may be required by any federal, state or municipal authority.

§427. THE ELEMENTS OF "MANAGEMENT PROCESS"

[Leo D. Gomez contributed materials for Sections 426–429.]

Financial and nonfinancial resources available to nonprofit organizations are often barely adequate, and demand skill and care in their management. Thus, two considerations—(1) the significance of the problems addressed by nonprofit organizations, and (2) the frequent lack of sufficient resources needed to address them—place a heavy burden of responsibility on those who manage nonprofit organizations, to do so intelligently and efficiently.[20]

One of the responses of the nonprofit sector to these concerns has been to become more "management conscious."[21] Simply stated, the management process is described as (1) planning, (2) organizing, and (3) controlling.[22]

Planning is the process of determining what an organization is, what its objectives or goals are, and what alternatives exist for reaching the goals. This procedure exists on a variety of levels within each organization.

Organizing, the second major step, requires *division* of the work of the organization. Like planning, organizing is process-oriented, and requires allocation and reallocation of authority and responsibility to carry out the plans. Interpersonal relationships play an important role in organizing, since this is how a manager combines available resources—the largest parts of which are *people*—to achieve the organization's goals.[23]

Controlling the third segment in the management process, is the link to planning. Controlling seeks to answer the questions: "Did we achieve what we initially set out to do?", and, "Were our objectives met?" It tries to ensure efficient use of resources. Controlling may include such activities as constructing work plans and reviewing progress. The results of these procedures are fed back to the planning segment, in the management process. Thus, the last step in management is to *evaluate* how well the organization has done in achieving its objectives, and then to repeat the process. These elements of management process are widely recognized in the business world.[24]

§428. "SYSTEMS APPROACH" TO MANAGING

Business management principles are not mutually exclusive; in practice, organizations combine, exclude, and tailor them to their specific needs.[25]

Of the business management techniques practiced by nonprofit organizations, perhaps the most important is the *systems approach* to managing.[26] The systems approach provides the foundation for some of the most modern business management principles being applied in nonprofit organizations.

The systems approach to management is based upon *general systems theory*, which asserts that if the operation of an entity is to be understood, it (the entity) must be viewed as a *system*. A system is defined as "a number of independent parts functioning as a whole for some purpose.[27]

The systems approach to management is always evolving, thus it is difficult to define "systems management" in a precise and technical manner. However, the following definition is probably as accurate as is possible:

> *Systems Management*—Management (the process of working with and through other persons to define and achieve the objectives of a formal organization) that is characterized by the following practices:
> (1) Views the organization both as a system within its own system and as a subsystem of a larger environmental system; (2) takes a holistic approach, using techniques of analysis that emphasize the interrelationships among the component parts of the organization; (3) uses flexible, changing organizational structures, served by computerized information plans, to keep structure adjusted to changing tasks; (4) designs information flow and uses qualitative techniques to strengthen decision-making; and (5) views the organization as a social structure and as a series of human/ machine relationships.[28]

The systems approach is very useful to nonprofit organizations, since it takes all of the relationships and inter-dependencies present in the system into account, and provides a valuable tool for the manager in a nonprofit setting.[29]

§429. MANAGEMENT INFORMATION SYSTEM (MIS)

In some nonprofit organizations, managers employ a Management Information System (MIS) as the guiding principle for their programs. An MIS, simply defined, is a network established to provide organization managers with information that will assist them in the decision-making process.[30] A more complete definition has been furnished by the MIS Committee of the Financial Executives Institute:

> An MIS is a system designed to provide selected decision-oriented information needed by management to plan, control, and evaluate the activities of the corporation. It is designed within a framework that emphasizes profit planning, performance planning, and control at all levels. It contemplates the ultimate integration of required business information subsystems, both financial and non-financial, within the company.[31]

MIS personnel generally perform six sequential and distinct steps to operate the MIS properly. The initial step requires a determination as to what information is needed within the organization, when it will be needed, and in what form it will be needed.[32]

The second step is pinpointing and gathering data that will provide needed information. If the data collected does not relate properly to informational needs, it will be impossible to generate the needed information.[23]

Summarizing, and analyzing the data are respectively the third and fourth steps to be completed by MIS personnel. In these stages computers are very helpful.[34]

The final two steps consist of transmitting the information obtained through data analysis to appropriate managers, and having managers actually use the information. The performance of the final two steps results in managerial decision-making.[35]

The procedure for establishing an MIS can be broken down into four stages: (1) planning for the MIS, (2) designing the MIS, (3) implementing the MIS and (4) improving the MIS.

[The setting up of an MIS requires equipment and procedures too technical for inclusion here. See works on that subject.[36]]

[*Guide forms and tables*, often prepared by others, are useful management equipment; *e.g., Reference (Table) Guide 1988*, is a Tax and Reporting Compliance list of forms and directions for nonprofit organizations, published in *Nonprofit Times* (Apr. 1988 issue).]

§430. MANAGEMENT BY OBJECTIVES (MBO)

A popular modern business management technique is *management by objectives* (MBO). A concise, yet comprehensive definition of the MBO system of management contains several provisions:[37]

> MBO is a systems approach to managing an organization, *any* organization. It is not a technique, or just another program, or a narrow area of the process of managing. Above all, it goes far beyond mere budgeting even though it does encompass budgets in one form or another.

First, those accountable for directing the organization determine where they want to take the organization or what they want it to achieve during a particular period, establishing the overall objectives and priorities.

Second, all the key managerial, professional and administrative personnel are required, permitted, and encouraged to contribute their maximum efforts to achieving the overall objectives.

Third, the planned achievement (results) of all key personnel is blended and balanced to promote and realize the greater total results for the organization as a whole.

Fourth, a control mechanism is established to monitor progress compared to objectives and feed the results back to those accountable at all levels.[38]

The MBO system is initiated by establishing overall objectives for the whole organization for the target period. In a church, for example, one of the overall objectives might be to attain a specific increase in the number of church members. After the top management of the organization has established these broad objectives, they add up the sum total of the results that must be accomplished by all the managers of that organization. In other words, at the end of the target period, the total of the results accomplished by all the managers must add up to, at least, the overall objectives that were set earlier.[39]

The management by objectives principle can be adapted to any organization, provided that the organization has a clearly-defined purpose. Only the type and substance of the objectives will differ. In a school system, the objective might be to provide educational benefits at various cost levels. The overall objective for a charitable institution might be to provide a certain level of money assistance.

Once the major objectives have been approved, the next step is to transform them into the required action each manager must take. The objective-setting process is complete when each of the managers, at all levels, has been given objectives that, when added together, will equal the overall objectives of the particular enterprise.

The methods by objectives approach to management developed in an environment of profit oriented business organizations. As a result, both writers and practicing managers in nonprofit organizations have raised important questions concerning MBO systems and its value in the absence of the profit motive. See Borst and Montana, for example [n. 21, at p. 143].

Undoubtedly, there are significant differences between profit-making and nonprofit enterprises. However, they both use elements of the same management process. Although not all business management techniques will work in the nonprofit sector, it is important to recognize that some business management principles are being applied effectively in various organizations in the nonprofit sector. If nonprofit groups wish to function efficiently and productively in a rapidly changing society, they must demonstrate a willingness to consider the possible benefits of applying business management principles to their organizations.

§431. IRS STANDARDS FOR MANAGEMENT

Supervision for nonprofit organizations' financial management is touched on at various points in this work. (See the Index.) State supervision by attorneys-general, theoretically the main body of such superintendence, in fact usually is scanty or nonexistent. In practice the federal authorities have most influence and effect.

IRS "Prohibited Transactions." The Internal Revenue Code Section 503 (b) treatment of tax exemption of private charitable foundations, as set forth in the tax reform amendments of 1970, is a key provision for determining the propriety of organization transactions. It enumerates certain prohibited transactions.[40] Most states have placed the "prohibited transactions" list in their nonprofit corporation laws, so that the IRS view now is the general rule as to what is, and what is not, proper conduct of officers and directors in their respects. (See Chapters 28–32).

§432. SECURITIES OF NONPROFIT ORGANIZATIONS

Many nonprofit organizations violate the securities laws because they believe those laws to be not applicable to them; both state and federal laws. This may lead to severe personal (also, criminal) liabilities of officers and trustees as well as the corporation itself. Little has been written about securities law as to non-profits; much about business corporations.[41]

What is "a security"? Securities law apply to bonds and debentures, some membership certificates, condominium purchase and operation instruments, many voting proxies, contracts of retirement homes, et cetera. The tests of what is a security are chiefly these: 1) Investment of money or assets, 2) A common enterprise, 3) Expectation of income on the investment (benefits) (profits) from the efforts of others [United Housing Foundation v. Forman, 421 U.S. 837, 848, 851 (1975).]

For example, transferable membership in a tennis club [Riviera Operating Co., CCH Fed. Securities L. Rep. Par. 81,569 (Mar. 8, 1978)]. Or, membership in a scholarship trust fund to pay college fees [Scholarship Counselors, Inc. v. Waddle, 507 S.W.2d 138 (Ky. App. 1974) (on death, resignation or moving away)]. But redeemable membership certificates of a country club, worth half the membership fee and not interest bearing, are *not* securities. [Dunwoody Country Club of Atlanta, Inc. v. Fortson, 253 S.E.2d 700 (Ga. 1979).]

S.E.C. Proxy Solicitation rules as to details of disclosure required may bring in unexpected S.E.C. supervision rules [3 Oleck, *Modern Corporation Law* §§732 (unregistered securities), 1481, 1468, 1487 et passim (1978 supp.)].

Securities Exemptions: Various exemptions are extended by the federal and state (Blue Sky) laws. An important one is Securities Act of 1933 §3(a)(4), which, with exceptions, excludes securities (not for private purposes) of "religious, education, benevolent, fraternal, charitable, or reformatory purposes and not for pecuniary profit." The Uniform Securities Act [U.L.A. §402(a)(g)] in all but a very few additional states excludes social and athletic organizations. "Private," and "small," and "intra-state" offerings also are excluded from (or held to lesser) *registration* requirements. [See Moody article n.41, at p. 192.]

Forms. Almost any carefully drawn form for a securities issue is extremely detailed and lengthy; too long for inclusion in this treatise. See examples in 2 Oleck, *Modern Corporation Law*, especially §695.1 *et seq.* (pp. 32–191) (1978 supp.).

§433. S.E.C. "SECURITIES" TRANSACTIONS

The Securities and Exchange Commission has been steadily expanding the applicability of its supervision over "securities" and "deceptive" or "self-serving" practices of corporation officers and directors. Almost any kind of interest in a venture or in property, if represented by some writing or graphic form, and that produces the income or "benefits" resulting from efforts of other persons or organizations, might be deemed to be a "security."

The 10b-5 Rule governing fraudulent transactions[42] now may be applied to "securities" of *nonprofit* as well as of profit corporations.[43] The Supreme Court has adopted criteria for example, for deciding if a share in a coop comes under the Securities Act, in *United Housing Foundation v. Forman.*[44]

An interest in a nonprofit condominium or mutual-type organization, for instance, might readily be brought under this S.E.C. supervision. Then manipulative, deceptive, or fraudulent devices or practices by nonprofit organization officers or directors may result in S.E.C. punitive action as well as in personal liability in damages to aggrieved "security holders" since the U.S. Supreme Court's 1971 decision in *Superintendent of Insurance of State of N.Y. v. Bankers Life and Casualty Co.*[40] But in 1976 that court limited personal liability for damages only to cases of *knowing* (*scienter*) and not merely negligent violations, in *Ernst & Ernst v. Hochfelder.*[46] Also, both individuals and the corporation itself may sue the erring officer, under the rule of *Blue Chip Stamps v. Manor Drug Stores.*[47] And any misrepresentation will suffice if it was likely to induce a reasonable complaining plaintiff to act upon the officer's representation, according to *TSC Industries, Inc. v. Northway, Inc.*[48] Even the usual fraudtort element of *reliance* as a prerequisite to a tort action for damages was viewed as unnecessary in a *nondisclosure* (failure to disclose facts) situation, in *Fridrich v. Bradford.*[49]

The California nonprofit statute,[50] effective 1980, as amended in 1992, and the American Bar Association 1986 Revised Model Nonprofit Corporation Act, based on it, set out lengthy rules that in essence, hardly do much to control self-dealing and immunity for directors, especially in noncharitable corporations. But the California concept is not yet the general view, and ought not to be, in the opinion of many people.

Probably the usual business type applications of the federal securities laws will be applied to nonprofit organizations too. The main ones are Section 16 for "insider trading," Section 9(a) for antimanipulation rules, Rule 10b-5 for antifraud, Section 16(b) for "short-swing profits," and Rule 10b-5 for corporate mismanagement.

The Securities Acts Amendments of 1975 charged with S.E.C. with various duties for the better control of securities dealings and marketing.[51]

Also, the Foreign Corrupt Practices Act of 1977[52] amending the Securities Exchange Act of 1934, and governing bribery and other abuses with foreign officials, and the Domestic and Foreign Investment Improved Disclosure Act of 1977[53] amending Title II of the securities statute, both can be applied to utilization of nonprofit as well as of business organization securities. Any direct or indirect beneficial interest in an equity security, certainly of 5 percent or more of its class, may involve organization officers' liabilities.[54]

The "investment contract" tests of *S.E.C. v. W.J. Howey Co.*[55] were applied in 1977 to a nonprofit organizations' (union) member's interest in a pension plan.[56] This decision is probably going to prevail.[57] This tendency is evident in a nonprofit organization's solicitation of country club membership initiation fees being treated as securities,[58] for example. It, therefore, is plain that S.E.C. Rule 10b-5 (fraud, treated as tort and crime) and other S.E.C. rules may be applied in nonprofit as well as in profit organizations, and thus to their directors and officers.[59]

[Robert Roselli did research work for the rest of this section.]

State, as well as federal, law applies to such NPO activities as *"securities" transactions*, and may even lead to revocation of charter.[60]

Such action as *divestment of investments* in South Africa because of that country's racial policies may involve S.E.C. and state law, and might even be deemed a violation of trust law.[61]

In *securities transactions*, such laws as the "new" California NPO statute are more permissive than traditional trust law, though not quite as permissive as that state's business law.[62] Also, ordinary strict *filing and registration requirements* sometimes are not applied to issues of "stock" by nonprofit organizations, in California.[63]

California enacted a permissive *standard of care* for unpaid directors of NPOs of public benefit corporations such as March of Dimes or the like.[64] But those standards were repealed in 1990.

If the transaction (*e.g.*, a lease) is deemed not *a security* (in a co-op housing project), because housing and not profit is the primary purpose, securities laws will not apply.[65]

New York also specifically allows an NPO to place *investment authority* in its officers or committees, but says that the members of the board of directors will be liable if they are negligent in selecting such officers.[66]

In Georgia, purchasers of lots in a housing development and nonequity members of an adjacent nonprofit country club alleged that the sale of *equity memberships* in the club and the sale of the undeveloped lots were sales of unregistered *securities*. The court held that the interests were not securities because the persons bought the lots to use them rather than derive profits from the entrepreneurial efforts of the developers.[67]

§434. "D. AND O. INSURANCE" FOR OFFICERS AND DIRECTORS

[*See* Section 446.]

The possibility of heavy damage suits against officers and directors becomes especially serious when an "S.E.C.-type" situation occurs. That is because the issuance of "securities" brings into being a class of numerous possible investors, who then become a potentially numerous class of lawsuit claimants.

In business corporations today protection by purchase of "Directors and Officers Insurance" (D. and O. Insurance), at corporation expense, is a normal precaution. Without it many competent executives would refuse to accept office and its consequent exposure to suits.

Today nonprofit organization officers and directors also should obtain such protection, especially when some kind of "securities issue" is contemplated.

Since about 1970 the offering of D. and O. Insurance has become a new branch of the insurance industry. Various companies now offer insurance protection for corporate officers and directors.

For an informative booklet on current trends in this area, one may write to INA, 1600 Arch Street, Philadelphia, Pa. 19101.

Special coverage for NPO agents, volunteers, officers and organizations now is offered by some companies. For example coverage protects against financial costs in legal defense and settlement of claims of discrimination, wrongful dismissal, inefficient administration or supervision, waste of assets, misleading reports or misrepresentation, and defamation. Also, discount purchasing programs are offered.[68]

A nonprofit medical care provider can be reimbursed for *directors' and officers' liability insurance* premiums by Medicare, because liability insurance does not constitute "remuneration" to the directors. The cost of liability insurance is "related to patient care".[69]

§435. FORMS OF STAFF POLICIES (MANUALS)

It is good management sense to supply to all members of the staff a clearly-worded "Staff Manual," stating the rules of the organization's management and/or office procedures. Employment contracts often are subject to *employee manual* provisions.[20]

Some typical provisions are the following ones

FORM NO. 174

Staff Policies
[Based on the rules of a statewide foundation.]

1. *Employment and Reporting Relationships*:
   Executive Director: The executive director is hired by and reports to the board of directors.
   Other Administrative Staff: Other members of the administrative staff are hired by and report to the executive director.
   Employment Contracts: All personnel employed full time will be provided with contracts. The conditions of employment shall be as established in the individual employment contracts.
   Termination of Employment: No fault termination of employment, consistent with individual contracts, is authorized during the first six months of employment. After the first six months, termination of employment is unsatisfactory performance of the conditions of employment (contract and/or job description).

2. *Compensation*:
   Compensation Range. The range of compensation for each staff position is established by the board upon recommendation of the executive director. Once established, the range is adjusted annually to reflect changes in the cost of living. Such adjustment is automatic unless suspended by the Board for budgetary reasons or for policy reasons (*e.g.*, compliance with federal wage guidelines).
   Compensation Level: Employees may be hired at any point within the compensation range, based upon qualifications and experience. Once hired, employees receive an annual step increase for added experience and proficiency equal to 1/20th of the compensation range for the position, until the maximum level has been reached. Such increases are automatic unless suspended by the Board for budgetary or for policy reasons.
   Payroll: Time and Attendance. Paychecks are issued at the office every other Friday, starting with the second Friday of the fiscal period, and cover the preceding two weeks of work. Employees shall fill out time and attendance records showing overtime, compensatory time, sick leave and annual leave prior to receiving compensation. Payroll withholding and other deductions shall be as authorized by the board and as required by federal and state law.

3. *Reimbursement*:
   Employees will be reimbursed for expenses incurred in carrying out their responsibilities. Reimbursement shall be for actual cost, or as governed

by specific policies of the board (e.g., travel reimbursement policies). Receipts are normally required.

4. *Work Schedule*:
   The office observes the work calendar of administrative offices within the system. Office hours are from 9 to 5, with 40 minutes for lunch or other work breaks, totaling _____ hours per week. Flexible office hours for individual staff members are authorized when approved by the executive director. Compensatory time off for overtime worked is authorized on an "equal time" basis. Sick leave is one day per month, to a maximum accumulation of _____ days. Annual leave is _____ work days for secretarial help. Annual leave for other staff personnel is established in employment contracts.

5. *Allowance in Lieu of Benefits*:
   A special allowance in lieu of a group benefit program is provided all full-time employees. This allowance, which is intended to cover the costs of health insurance, life insurance, accident insurance, and a retirement program, etc., is computed by multiplying base pay by_____ percent. Employees may choose to receive this benefit allowance as an addition to taxable income (part of their pay check), or to have it deposited by _____ in tax-sheltered programs.

6. *Procedure for Evaluation*:
   There shall be an annual evaluation of the performance of the executive director based upon the job description for that position and any specific directives issued by the board during the year. This evaluation shall be conducted by the executive committee at a special session at the regular quarterly board meeting. Other staff members will be evaluated annually by the executive director based upon their contracts, job descriptions and special instructions during the period.

7. *Grievance Procedures*:
   Any employee having an employment grievance shall present such grievance to the executive director. If the executive director's resolution of the grievance proves unsatisfactory, the employee may appeal to the personnel subcommittee of the Board. If the resolution of the grievance proves unsatisfactory after it has been evaluated and a decision rendered by the personnel subcommittee, the employee may appeal to the _____ board for final determination.

8. *Equal Opportunity*:
   _____ is an equal opportunity employer, in accordance with federal and state laws.

9. *Travel Reimbursement*:
   Background: Mileage (for trips of more than _____ miles round trip) or actual cost of commercial coach travel (receipt required) is paid for official trips. The mileage rate is the rate set by the federal government (as of _____ this rate is _____ mile).

Per diem costs are reimbursed as follows: actual cost of hotel rooms up to $_____ per day for persons in travel status. Food allowance of $_____ for each 24 hours in travel status (portions are pro-rated on an hourly basis). Of this $_____ allowance, $_____ is held in a reserve account (discretionary fund) to cover the cost of receptions, business lunches, and if sufficient funds are available (if the account balance is over $_____), of coffee and rolls provided at meals. In cases in which _____ provides meals for board members or staff (except for occasional business lunches with clients), the cost of such meals is deducted from the per diem allowance in addition to the $_____ withheld. Actual individual cost is deducted where this is known; otherwise, the total cost is pro-rated to the total number of persons participating in the meal (spouses are charged for spouses). This second amount deducted is held in a reserve account (meals provided fund) to cover payment of meal bills. Receipts are required for hotel rooms, and should cover only the cost of lodging.

Travel Status: Board members and staff making trips of more than three hours in total are considered to be in a travel status for the duration of the trip. Board members and staff attending board meetings in their immediate locality are considered to be in a travel status for the duration of the meeting (although they would be expected to stay overnight at home rather than at the hotel unless this would be, in their judgment, a serious inconvenience).

Insufficient Funds: In an occasional case in which per diem paid at a meeting is not sufficient to cover deductions for discretionary fund and food provided, the amount short will be carried in a board member receivable account and charged against per diem earned at a subsequent meeting.

There will be no reimbursement for car rental expenses for board members. Taxi, bus and personal car expenses, as always, are allowed. Exceptions on approval in writing by chair. (Note: The committee does not wish to disallow hotel room expenses for board members who reside in the city in which a board meeting is being held. However, board members are asked to use good sense and remember our budget limitations.)

FORM NO. 175
Members' Participation Survey
SURVEY

for the guidance of the officers of the _____ Fellowship.

Please do not sign your name. Husbands and wives are requested to fill out separate questionnaires. Answer as many or as few items as you desire.

WHO ARE WE?

I am a member ☐   a friend ☐
Before coming here I had a previous association with a
Church ☐   Fellowship ☐
I was a member of another religious organization ☐
I never had a previous religious association ☐
How do you consider yourself? (check as many as you choose)
Agnostic ☐   Atheist ☐   Christian ☐   Humanist ☐   Jew ☐
Theist ☐   Other _____

WHAT BROUGHT ME HERE?

I was one of the original organizers ☐ I read the ad in the (newspaper/magazine) ☐   Other publicity ☐   A friend told me ☐

WHAT DO I WANT?

I am satisfied with the present format of a half hour discussion, followed by a one hour program ☐   I would prefer more structure ☐   more formality ☐   religious readings ☐   philosophical readings ☐   music programs on other religions ☐   would you be willing to tell us of your personal life and philosophy ☐   would you like to hear this from others in the group ☐   how many minor children do you have who would like a class in religious education ☐

I would like to see this Fellowship grow   ☐ would not   ☐ indifferent ☐   should we ambition to acquire our own meeting place ☐

WHAT WILL I PAY FOR THESE THINGS?

I am willing to give ____ hours per week, _____ weeks per year.
I am willing to give $_____ per year. Our current budget averages about $_____ per person).

NOTES TO CHAPTER 41

1. *See,* for example: Anthes, E., Cronin, J., and Jackson, M., *The Nonprofit Board Book* (Independent Comm. Consult., W. Memphis, Ark., 1983). And for an exhaustive bibliography, address: The Institute for Nonprofit Organization Management, at *The Independent Sector,* 1828 L Street, N.W., Washington, D.C. 20036, Tel. (202) 223-8100.

Anthony, R.N. and Herzlinger, R., *Management Control in Non-Profit Organizations*, (Richard D. Irwin, Inc., Norwood, Ill., 1975).

Borst, D. and Montana, P.J., (eds.), *Managing Nonprofit Organizations* (AMACOM, N.Y., 1977).

Buchele, R.B., *The Management of Business and Public Organizations*, (McGraw-Hill, N.Y., 1977).

Callaghan et al, *Governance Course Syllabus: A Master's Level Curriculum on Managing Nonprofit Organizations* (Independent Sector, Washington, D.C. 1985).

Certo, S.C., *Principles of Modern Management*, (Wm. C. Brown Co., Publ., Dubuque, Iowa, 1980).

Conrad, W. and Glenn, W., *The Effective Voluntary Board of Directors* (Chicago, Swallow Press, 1976).

Hill, M. *Management Rights* (Bureau of Natl. Affairs; Wash., D.C., 1986).

McConkey, D.D., *MBO for Nonprofit Organizations*, (AMACOM, N.Y., 1975).

O'Connell, B., *Effective Leadership in Voluntary Organizations* (Chicago, Follett Publ. Co., 1976).

Zaltman, G. (ed.), *Management Principles for Non-Profit Agencies and Organizations*, (AMACOM, N.Y., 1979).

2. *Black's Law Dictionary*, 865 (5th ed., 1979) citing court decisions from Arkansas, Oklahoma, Washington, D.C. and *Ballentine's Law Dictionary*, 769, 770 (3rd ed., 1969) cites decisions from Illinois, Kansas, Pennsylvania, and the U.S. Supreme Court, and also Am. Jur., A.L.R., and A.L.R. 2d. *See also*, K.M. Brown, *Applied Empirical Research and NPO Management: Survey and Recommendations* (U. of San Francisco, Institute for NPO Management) 38 pp. (1986).

3. *Ballentine's (supra)*, p. 770, citing similar authorities and a Nebraska court decision. *See also*, *Webster's New World Dictionary*, 889, 890 (College ed. 1962); and *Oxford Universal Dictionary*, 1197 (1955).

4. *E.g.*, Flippo & Munsinger, *Management*, c.1 (3rd ed., 1975), citing (at pp. 24, 25) various learned articles on these subjects. *Cf.*, Kahn, *Organizing: A Guide for Grassroots Leaders* (1982). And *see*, n.1.

5. *E.g.*, Oleck, *Modern Corporation Law* (6 volumes) (1978 supp. ed.).

6. *Black's Law Dictionary*, 977 (5th ed., 1979); and *see* herein the chapter on Officers and Managers.

7. Harmon, Ladd & Acosta column, 6 *NonProfit Times* (11) 46 (Nov. 1992).

8. N.Y. Bus. Corp. L. §701; Fla. Stat. 617.0802; N.Y. N-PCL §§701.

9. N.Y. Not-For-Profit Corp. L. §701; Fla. Stat. 617.0202.

10. Minn. Atty. Gen. Opinions, 102-E (June 25, 1951).

11. *See* Chapter 32 §332.

12. 4 *NonProfit Times* (10)22 (Jan. 1991), and p. 18 (Mar. 1991).

13. *See* 6 *NonProfit Times* (7) 16 (July 1992).

14. *See*, for example: Usis, *The Executive Job Market* (1965); Sands, *How to Select Executive Personnel* (1963); Mascon, *Management: Individual and Organizational Effectiveness* (1981).

15. *See* journals in the particular field, such as *Chronicle of Higher Education* for colleges, *National Law Journal* for law, *etc.*

16. *UHS-Qualicare, Inc. v. Gulf Coast Community Hosp., Inc.*, 525 So. 2d 746 (MS 1987).

17. *Morris v. Macione*, 546 So. 2d 969 (Miss., 1989).

18. *Board of Directors of the Edelweiss Owners' Ass'n v. McIntosh*, 822 P.2d 1080 (Mont. 1991).

19. *American Ideal Mgt., Inc. v. Dale Village Inc.*, 567 So. 2d 497 (Fla. 4th D.C.A., 1990).

20. G. Zaltman (ed.), *Management Principles for Nonprofit Agencies and Organizations* (AMACOM, New York, 1979) p. 1.

21. D. Borst and P.J. Montana (eds.), *Managing Nonprofit Organizations*, (AMACOM, New York, 1977), p. 2.

22. *Ibid.*

23. *Id.*, p. 3.

24. *Id.*

25. R.B. Buchele, *The Management of Business and Public Organizations*, (McGraw Hill, 1977), p. 23.

26. R.W. Anthony and R. Herzlinger, *Management Control in Nonprofit Organizations*, (Richard D. Irwin, Inc., Norwood, Ill., 1975), p. 13.

27. S.C. Certo, *Principles of Modern Management*, (Wm. C. Brown Co., Publishers, Dubuque, Iowa, 1980), p. 37.

28. R.B. Buchele, *The Management of Business and Public Organizations*, n.25, at p. 41.

29. Borst and Montana, *Managing Nonprofit Organizations*, n.21, at p. 58.

30. Certo, *Principles of Modern Management*, n. 27, at p. 484.

31. R.W. Holmes, "Twelve Areas to Investigate for Better MIS," *Financial Executive*, (July, 1970), p. 24.

32. Certo, *Principles of Modern Management*, p. 484.

33. *Ibid.*, p. 485.

34. *Ibid.*

35. *Ibid.*

36. Such as: D.F. Stollen and R.L. Van Horn, *Design of an MIS* (Rand Corp., Santa Monica, Calif., 1958).

37. Borst and Montana, *Managing Nonprofit Organizations* (AMACOM, N.Y., 1977), p. 47.

38. *Ibid.*

39. D.D. McConkey, *MBO for Nonprofit Organizations* (AMACOM, N.Y., 1975), p. 17.

40. U.S.C. §§4941–4945; Treas. Regs. §1.501(a)-1.

41. *See*, for example, Volume 2 (and big supplement), Oleck, *Modern Corporation Law*, Chaps. 34–36 (1978 suppl.). A valuable study is: Moody, *Securities Issues of Non-Profit Organizations*, in, Stetson Seminar (Book of Materials) on *Nonprofit Organizations Problems 1980*, pp. 178–201 (1980).]

42. Securities Exchange Act of 1934 §10(b); and S.E.C. Rule 10b-5. *And see* definitions and exemptions in I.R.S. Reg. §230.144 (1978) and Moody article, n.41.

43. Silver Hills Country Club v. Sobieski, 55 Cal.2d 811, 361 P.2d 906 (1961). *See* n.41.

44. 421 U.S. 837 (1975).

45. 404 U.S. 6, 13 n.9, 92 S.Ct. 165, 30 L.Ed.2d 128 (1971).

46. 425 U.S. 185, 96 S.Ct. 1375, 47 L.Ed.2d 668 (1976).

47. 421 U.S. 723, 95 S.Ct. 1917, 44 L. Ed. 539 (1975).

48. 426 U.S. 438, 96 S.Ct. 2126, 48 L.Ed. 757 (1976).

49. 542 F.2d 307 (6th Cir. 1976), *cert. den.* 429 U.S. 1053 (1977).

50. Cal. Nonprofit Corp. L. §§5047, 5047.5, 5233–5237 (1992).

51. 15 U.S.C. §78K-1; Publ. L. 94-29 §7 (1975).

52. 15 U.S.C. §78a *et. seq.*; Sec. Exch. Act of 1934 tit. 1; Publ. L. 95-213 (1977).

53. *Ibid.*, *tit.* II.

54. 2 Oleck, *Modern Corporation Law* c.34 §736, p. 208 (1978 Supp.) *addendum* 1–3.

55. 328 U.S. 293 (1946); followed in United Housing Foundation, Inc. v. Forman, 421 U.S. 837 (1975).

56. Daniel v. Brotherhood of Teamsters, 561 F.2d 1223 (7th Cir. 1977). *But see, contra,* Robinson v. United Mine Workers of America, 435 F. Supp. 245 (D.C. D.C. 1977).

57. *Ibid.*, Robinson case.

58. Silver Hills Country Club v. Sobieski, 55 Cal.2d 811, 361 P.2d 906 (1961).

59. 3 Oleck, *Modern Corporation Law* §1697 (1978 Supp.) pp. 277–322.

60. *Matter of Jesus Loves You*, 40 B.R. (1984).

61. Troyer, S. & B., *Divestment of So. Afr. Investments: The Legal Implications for Foundations, Other Charitable Institutions, and Pension Funds*, 74 Geo. L. J. 127 (1985).

62. *Cal. Corp. Code* §§5233–5237 (1988). *Cf.*, NJ Stat. Ann. §15A-6-11 (1988).

63. *Cal. Corp. Code* §25100 (1988).

64. *Cal. Corp. Code* §5231.5 (1988) (repealed in 1990, c. 107 (A.B. 2292), §3.

65. *United Housing Foundation, Inc. v. Foreman*, 429 U.S. 1009 (1975).

66. N.Y. *Not-For-Profit Corp. L.* §514(a) and (b) (1988).

67. *Rice v. Branigar Organization, Inc.*, 922 F.2d 788 (11th Cir. 1991).

68. For reference data, for example, address: Partnership Umbrella, Inc., 102 S. Alfred St., Alexandria, VA 22314.

69. *Mercy-Douglass Center, Inc. v. Department of Public Welfare*, 601 A.2d 913 (Pa. Cmwlth. 1992)

70. See, Goldhor v. Hampshire College, 521 N.E.2d 1381 (Mass. App. 1988). But *cf.*, Lurton v. Muldon Motor Co., 523 S.2d 706 (Fla. App. 1988).

43

FUND RAISING

[Susan L. Filson and Deborah L. Hunter-Conley contributed material for this chapter.]

§436. FUND RAISING: INFORMATION SOURCES

[*See* the *General Bibliography*, herein, Section 16.]
[Some sources of guidance about fund raising, in no particular order of weight or classification, are the following (in addition to works cited by Filson in the following sections)]:

(Book) *Activists Guide to Religious Funders* (Center for Third World Organizing, 3861 Martin Luther King, Jr. Way; Oakland, CA 94609; 415-654-9601; $25; 1989). Guidelines, techniques, and people in raising money from religious organizations.

Ammon-Wexler, Jill and Catherine Carmel. *How to Create a Winning Proposal* (Santa Cruz, Calif.; Mercury Communications Corporation, 1978).

Coleman, William E. *Grants in the Humanities* (N.Y., Neal-Schuman Publ., Inc., 1980).

Decker, Virginia A. and Larry E. Decker. *The Funding Process: Grantsmanship and Proposal Development* (Charlottesville, Va., Community Collaborators, 1978).

Flanagan, Joan. *The Successful Volunteer Organization* (Chicago; Contemporary Books, Inc., 1981).

Gaby, Patricia and Gaby, Daniel. *Non-Profit Organization Handbook* (N.J.; Prentice-Hall, Inc., 1980).

Grant Writer's Handbook 1978–79 (San Francisco, Public Management Inst. 1978).

Hall, Mary. *Developing Skills in Proposal Writing* (2nd ed.; Portland, Or.; Continuing Education Publications, 1977).

Public Service Materials Center. *Corporate Fund Raising Directory Curr. Edition*.

Rados, Daniel. *Marketing for Nonprofit Organizations* (Mass., Auburn House Publ. Co., 1981).

White, Virginia P. *Grants: How to Find Out About Them and What to Do Next* (N.Y., Plenum Press, 1976).

Whole Nonprofit Catalog, a compendium of resources for nonprofit organizations, The Grantsmanship Center, P.O. Box 220, Los Angeles, CA 90017, quarterly, lists many titles.

Williams, M. Jane (ed.) *FRI Foundations Handbook* (3rd ed., Plymouth Meeting, Penn., Fund Raising Institute, 1975).

Wolf, Thomas. *The Nonprofit Organization* (N.J.; Prentice Hall, 1984).

Collections of "papers" presented at NPO Conferences often amount to "books." See, for example the materials presented at the 1991 National Catholic Development Conference and Exposition (5 days) in Washington, D.C. Address the National Catholic Development Conference, 86 Front St., Hempstead, N.Y. 11550.

Fund Raising Data Centers

There are a number of organizations that furnish information useful in relation to fund raising. For example:

National Information Bureau, Inc.
419 Park Avenue South
New York, N.Y. 10016
(212) 532-8595

and:

Independent Sector (a consortium)
National Center for Charitable Statistics
701 North Fairfax Street
Alexandria, Va. 22314

and:

National Charities Information Bureau
1841 Broadway
New York, N.Y. 10023

Fund Raising Schools

[See Chap. 1, §1, and Chap. 42 §424]

The *Fund Raising School* of the new Center on Philanthropy at Indiana University is a leading organization among the many that offer courses/seminars on fund raising. It offers three-, four- and five-day and two-week (basic and intensive) courses in various cities (all year) all across the U.S.A. For details write to P.O. Box 269, San Rafael, CA 94915, or call toll free number 1-800-962-6692, or the Indiana Center number: (317) 274-7063.

In 1992 its tuition fees for various courses ranged from $195 to $595.

Disclosure Rule

The 1987 tax law amendments now require NPOs that do not have §
501(c)(3) status to disclose conspicuously if their solicitations are not tax-
deductible. Also all NPOs must have available to the public, at their main
offices, a copy of their tax returns for the previous three years. 2 *Nonprofit Times*
(2) editorial (May 1988).

§437. NATURE OF FUND RAISING, IN GENERAL

"To give away money is an easy matter, and in any man's power. But to
decide to whom and to give it, and how much and when, and for what purpose and how, is neither in every man's power—nor an easy matter. Hence,
it is that such excellence is rare, praiseworthy and noble."[1]

We know that there are hundreds of thousands of nonprofit organizations in the United States today, and that almost every American belongs to or
works with dozens of them in his or her lifetime.[2] A nonprofit organization is
"one that is not used for the personal financial enrichment of any of its members or managers, and no portion of the money or property which is permitted to inure to the benefit of any private individual, *except as a proper grant*
according to its state-approved purpose, *or* as salaries paid for employee-type
services rendered to the organization."[3]

Fund raising may be done by profit-seeking as well as nonprofit organizations. For a nonprofit organization, *fund raising* can be defined as the art and
practice of directing and motivating individuals to bestow contributions on the
organization for the support of a specified program.[4] Fund raising is often the
most important activity of the nonprofit organization. The organization purpose
is often to provide a service to some community.[5] But without private or government funding many of these organizations would be unable to provide minimal programs and services. The kind of support needed to keep a nonprofit
organization alive can often only be generated through extensive fund raising.

Fund Raising Standards

The world of philanthropy is based on trust—people give to charities
trusting that the money will be used for good. Highly ethical standards are
expected to be habitually practiced by voluntary and charitable groups.
A 15-page statement on ethics was approved by *Independent Sector*, a nonprofit
coalition that works to increase giving and volunteerism by citizens. Two of the
values adopted are openness and honesty in reporting and accountability to
the public.[6]

A 1990 survey by Nonprofit Times/Opinion Research Corporation found that Americans continued to make donations to charity, at a higher rate-of-persons donating (76 percent) than in the 1989 survey (which was 69 percent). Less than 40 percent viewed fundraisers (persons) as trustworthy. But lawyers, stockbrokers, politicians, and auto salesmen were viewed as even less trustworthy (respectively voted—"trustworthy"—were 30 percent, 20 percent, 14 percent, 7 percent, and 5 percent). Physicians were voted trustworthy by 71 percent and TV anchorpersons by 54 percent.[7]

In 1994 the public opinion of almost all kinds of human activity was even more distrustful, while fund raising solicitations had become so numerous as to be viewed as a nuisance by many people.

National Charities Information Bureau, Inc. in 1988 issued its (1988) "*Standards in Philanthropy*", which were expected by NCIB to be universally useful for nonprofits generally, although to be used rather more flexibly by organizations under three years old or with annual budgets of less than $100,000. One change from the 1987 Standards was that there now should be no specific percentage listed for fund raising, as there had been one in the past. Another change was increased use of the words "usually" and "normally."[8]

The American Association of Fund Raising Counsel (AAFRC) prohibits members from *accepting custody of funds* intended for client institutions and proscribes *percentage compensation* in the recent revision of its Standards of Membership and Professional Conduct.[9] Similarly, the National Society of Fund Raising Executives in 1992 passed a revised set of ethics and standards for its members. The new standards explicitly call for banning percentage and commission compensation for professional fund raisers.[10]

In late 1988, the *Internal Revenue Service* issued quite *specific guidelines* that must be followed by "merely nonprofit" (not charitable) organizations in *disclosing* the *non-deductible* nature of contributions to them, by such groups as clubs, unions, business or professional associations, and political committees. These govern only organizations getting over $100,000/yr. gross, as to direct solicitation material. Specific disclaimer wordings are provided by the IRS. $1000/day penalties are provided for up to $10,000; more for deliberate violations.[11]

An international fund-raising organization, the *World Fund Raising Council*, began in fledgling form in 1989, to establish international standards of certification, provide forums, and promote sound fund-raising personnel and practices. *Address* Gale Clarke of National Society of Fund Raising Executives for data.[12]

Fund Raising Contracts

When a nonprofit charitable corporation raises money to benefit a public arts festival within a city, the funds generated do not become city funds. The city does not have control over the funds, but does have an obligation to maintain control over the subject matter of a contract with the nonprofit entity and to require accountability for the funds. The nonprofit corporation with which a city contracts, or to which it contributes funds does not become an agency of the city.[13]

Fund Raising Overhead

In all likelihood, donors rarely decide to make contributions to charities with the information on how much is spent on the purpose versus how much is spent on fund raising and administrative costs. Individual donors responsible for over 85 percent of the $100 billion given to charity annually have no meaningful opportunity to learn about fund raising costs. In the past, legislatures have controlled fund raising costs by imposing fund raising expenditure limits on charities. Between 1960 and 1980, 28 states and many municipalities imposed fund raising limits on charities. Most placed ceilings on fund raising costs. The limits ranged from 25 percent to 50 percent of annual revenues. If a charity exceeds the limit, it can no longer participate in fund raising. The regulators acted upon the belief that a charity was illegitimate if it spent too much revenue on fund raising.

Perceptions of legitimacy and the provision of social good are central to the direct public support of a charity through contributions and to the maintenance of indirect governmental support through the tax law. Donors have a right to information that allows them to make informed decisions. Mandatory disclosure rules attempt to improve the operation of the marketplace for solicitation of funds by providing all potential contributors with basic financial information about the charity.[14]

Donors are becoming more interested in how their money is being used. They are becoming consumer oriented, perceiving that they want the most for their money. The proportion of contributions that goes to pay fund raising costs has become important to people.

According to a survey conducted by *The NonProfit Times* and Barna Research, only 8 percent of 1009 adults questioned would contribute to an organization if more than 50 percent of the money donated went to fund raising costs.[15]

Americans are generous, but they can also be naive about where their charitable contributions go. "A lot of people aren't well educated about fundraising and are under the impression that all charities are run by volunteers," said Margret Bower, Associate Director of the Council of Better Business Bureaus' Philanthropic Advising Service. "A lot of times people are shocked when they find out that people are paid [to fundraise]."

People are being paid and some are paid very well. The Ohio Attorney General's Office estimates that professional fundraisers collected nearly $27 million in Ohio in the 14 months ending December 31, 1991. An estimated 31 percent of that was used for charitable purposes.[16]

Most corporations are flooded with funding requests from charitable organizations. But in deciding which of these appeals to honor, companies use a wide variety of procedures. The firm of Cummins, Krasik and Hohl Co. generally follows one underlying principle when it comes to deciding which charities to donate to. It will not give money to causes that use professional fundraisers. "We only make donations in which all of the proceeds go to charity," Ralph Krasik explains. "That doesn't happen when professional fundraisers are involved, because the fundraisers are paid some preset percentage of the money they raise."[17]

Blatant abuses in the area of fundraising overhead have outraged the public. Some of the more recent cases are outlined below.

The IRS is attempting to retroactively strip the tax exempt privileges of the United Cancer Council (UCC), a now defunct nonprofit organization. In filing the suit, the IRS is attempting to establish a "commensurate means" test for direct mail expenses. At the center of the conflict is a contract that the UCC made with a direct mail firm. The contract allegedly allowed the mail firm to reap a 98 percent expense ratio while retaining co-ownership of the donor list at the expense of the charity. The U.S. Postal Service has already stripped UCC of its nonprofit mailing privileges because it considers the co-ownership of the donor list to be a commercial co-venture, in violation of postal rules for nonprofit mailing privileges.[18]

According to the Council of Better Business Bureaus' charity rating guide, The National Cancer Research Institute, a project of the Walker Cancer Research Institute, spent less than 2 percent of the $6.6 million it garnered in contributions on cancer research in 1991. Its direct mail literature claims that 6.4 percent of its money goes to program services, and 44.7 percent goes to public education. Walker's public education is no more than basic information about cancer printed on the back of solicitation letters. Walker is one of several charities whose professional fund-raiser, Watson and Hughey, now in business as Direct Response Consulting Services, was charged with fraudulent fundraising activities in 10 states. The case was settled in 1991 for $2.1 million.

In contrast, the National Charities Information Bureau says the American Cancer Society spends about 80 cents of every dollar on research and other charitable purposes.[19]

Heaven's Children solicited funds by telephone to grant the dying wishes of terminally ill children. An exposé was published charging that only 13 percent of the $220,000 raised went to these children. The charity claimed that solicitation was also advocacy for the cause because it made the public aware of terminally ill children. Equating the use of an organization's name to raise funds for public education and advocacy is deceptive.[20]

In 1986 the Massachusetts Attorney General sued the postal workers' union and their solicitor, Telco. Approximately $450,000 was collected for terminally ill children. Only $10,000 was given to charity and $70,000 went toward sending union members to a national conference in San Francisco. The rest of the contributions went to Telco.[21]

Supporters of politicians do not have a "license to commit fraud" in fund raising, by soliciting donations and "loans."[22]

A Connecticut study of local charities using hired telephone solicitors showed that the charities received on average only 25 percent of the money collected and in one instance as little as 4.92 percent was retained by the charity.[23]

National Charities Information Bureau in 1990, for example, accused MADD (Mothers Against Drunk Driving) of "creative accounting" in declaring that 29 cents of every dollar raised went to "Programs" when in fact 72 cents of every dollar went to fund raising, and that "MADD's major activity . . . is conducting a direct-mail and telemarketing campaign." MADD denied becoming "A Money Machine."[24]

In a consumer action column, the author warns readers of charities with similar names. For example, the Make a Wish Foundation of Tampa Bay collected $54,882 during part of 1991 and spent $68 percent on the wishes. The Children's Wish Come True Foundation's professional solicitors raised $93,279 during the first six months of 1992 and used less than 2 percent for charitable purposes. (The Foundation went out of business in June due to poor contributions.) Most of the money raised went to solicitors. The Suncoast Children's Dream Fund spent a total of $105,100 in 1992. Of that, 65 percent was spent on fulfilling dreams. Individual donors should investigate each organization before giving money.[25]

Protection of an organization's name and reputation is important. For example, the Swiss-registered World Wide Fund for Nature is a nonprofit group that holds the copyright to the organization's two greatest assets: the familiar panda logo and the letters WWF. These symbols are zealously guarded and are protected with the threat of legal action for copyright infringement. The symbols are so important because they are recognized worldwide as representing nature conservation and this gives the national organization its main fundraising asset. WWF International's priority has been to maintain common standards and goals to keep the contributions coming in from the national organizations that are responsible for most of the fundraising.[26]

The use of an organization's funds should be carefully considered. With its high ceilings, skylights, and picture windows, the new building of the United States Audubon Society does not seem like the likely headquarters of a nonprofit organization. The 101-year-old building in downtown Manhattan, complete with gargoyles and Romanesque arched windows, was recently renovated at a cost of roughly $14 million. The Society paid $10 million for the building.[27]

Contributions and Compensation

Once you might have thought that the money you gave to a highly respected charity would be well spent. Not any more. In February, the United Way admitted that it paid its president William Aramony an annual salary and benefits totaling $463,000 plus lavish perks such as Concorde flights costing $40,700 and chauffeured limousines costing $92,265. There was also a reported $2 million loan to a for-profit merchandising company run by Aramony's son Robert. Complaints from donors forced Aramony to resign. Just how unusual is this compensation?

The 10 highest paid charity executives average an annual salary of

$277,050 with leaders in national groups averaging $150,000. Some charity chiefs can expect annual bonuses of 15–40 percent of their base salary for meeting prescribed goals. Are charities squandering donations on overpaid executives?[28]

At least 99 of 122 major nonprofit organizations pay their leaders $100,000 or more. The president of Mount Sinai Medical Center in New York City earned $799,492 in salary and $26,249 in benefits. The National Charities Information Bureau, a New York-based watchdog group, has seen in the last year a heightened interest in nonprofits' executive pay. "A guy who works at a plant or something, when he's asked to make a donation and then sees what some of these guys make, he's bound to get upset," spokesman Daniel Langan said.[29]

Professional solicitor compensation may not be limited (e.g., to 25 percent), by statute, in charity-related solicitations.[30]

§438. MECHANICS OF FUND RAISING

The Development Philosophy

In order to determine the kind of approach needed in a nonprofit organization's fund-raising campaign, there needs to be an understanding of the motivation behind philanthropy. *Philanthropy* can be defined as the "voluntary sharing by an individual of his or her worldly goods, in whatever degree, with those of his or her fellow creatures who are less fortunately circumstanced than he or she."[31] A development, or fund raising, philosophy is realized by asking some fundamental questions, such as:

1. Why do people/corporations/foundations give?
2. Why do people volunteer?[32]

The answers to these questions can help the nonprofit organization's fund raisers to target a campaign or strategy which will induce donations and volunteerism.

Americans are among the most generous people in the world. Statistics show that, in recent years, individuals donated annually nearly $110 billion to the nation's 300,000 organized charities. About $3.3 billion come from foundations, $6.0 billion are received from corporations and other businesses to make up the staggering (1992 sum of) $124.3 billion total.[33]

Also noteworthy is where the money goes. Religious organizations usually get about 46 percent of the chunk, coming out to approximately $56.7 billion. The next closest recipients are usually the health, education, and hospital categories, each with about $10 billion. From there, in descending order, are social welfare, "other" charities, arts and humanities, civic, and public recipients.[34]

People give for various reasons. Results from a survey sponsored by the Save the Children Federation showed that 60 percent of Americans who give do so out of a sense of moral obligation.[35] Another 35 percent give for their own personal satisfaction in helping others, and about two percent said they gave to assuage guilt.[36]

Why do people volunteer? According to the United States Census Bureau, a majority of volunteers, 60 percent, do so out of a desire to help people, and a substantial number, 38 percent, do so out of a sense of duty.[37] Aside from this, the fact is that many people volunteer to fulfill their own needs. Many motives beyond generosity prompt giving of time and money, and it is important for the fund raiser to know this.[38] In the words of a philosopher, "Does not the Christian depend for his salvation on the beggar? No beggars, no Christian charity."[39] In other words, volunteerism, like the law, can be a two-edged sword. On one side, an indispensable resource to keep the nonprofit organization going, and on the other, a method of fulfilling the giver's inherent need to feel important and worthwhile. It is to these inward motivations that the nonprofit organization's fundraisers must appeal as well. This theory must be a meritorious one, for an estimated thirty-eight million people over the age of thirteen annually volunteer their time and efforts for nonprofit organizations, bringing the total volunteer time in hours to over six billion hours of work each year.[40]

The Fund-Raising Hierarchy

The fund-raising hierarchy includes the various people who are the actual fund raisers of the nonprofit organization. Each is important in his or her own way. It helps to understand the role that each plays in the overall fund-raising scheme. These people include the chief executive officer, chief development officer, board of trustees, and professional consultants.

As Richard D. Cheshire, president of the University of Tampa, has put it, the basic responsibilities of the *chief executive officer* of a nonprofit organization are to "plan, promote, and preside."[41] He or she is the chief decision-maker, and the chief planner as to time, space, people, and money.[42] In this capacity, the *president* of the organization is critical to any fund-raising program. He or she is the most visible person of the organization, and thus must be a model of the image that the prospective donors want to see.

The *chief development officer* is the one who is in charge of drafting the plan which sets forth the specific objectives of the nonprofit organization and the ways and means of achieving them.[43] This officer must be actively involved in all aspects of the organization in order to be able to identify its ideals and needs.

The chief development officer often is in charge of the *development office* of the organization. The development office has two main functions: public relations and fundraising.[44] The essential task of this office is to help the chief executive to secure the needed resources in order to enable the nonprofit organization to achieve its monetary goals, through, among other means, researching the giving potential of prospective donors, organizing and implementing and fund-raising strategy, and managing the force of volunteers.[45]

The board of trustees of an organization is its governing body. They have responsibility for the establishment, growth, and viability of the fund-raising campaign.[46] Most trustees are prominent citizens of a particular area, and many have strong ties of allegiance to the organization's board on which they serve. The trustees *should* all be donors, but they *must* all be fund raisers.[47]

Consultants are professional outside counsel, who can bring expert know-how and skilled personnel, along with knowledge of proven techniques, with them to the hiring organization.[48] The professional fund raiser is an outsider, however, and is not an emotionally involved component of the fund-raising hierarchy. He or she also works for a fee; thus, less of the money raised actually goes to the organization needing it.[49]

Certification of fundraisers (by the NSFRE, AHP, CFRE, or ACFRE) has little influence in a hiring decision. It may be far more valuable for a fundraiser to have rigorous training, ample reasoning, and sound experience.[50]

The Annual Fund Campaign

The annual fund campaign is basically a comprehensive plan designed to fit the financial needs of the nonprofit organization. The philosophy behind the annual fund campaign is that "an all-inclusive, coordinated strategy can better concentrate efforts and produce results than can a series of special campaigns."[51]

There are *four major tiers of giving* which must be understood before implementing the annual fund campaign.[52] It is helpful to picture the levels as a pyramid. At the base of the pyramid are the annual gifts. These consist of a large number of donors, usually making relatively small gifts. These gifts are generally used for the organization's current year-to-year needs.[53]

[Dues, or even "training" fees, may be a basic resource, of course. Church "auditing" fees of the Church of Scientology once were held to be tax-deductible. Foley v. C.I.R., 844 F. 2d 94 (2d Cir. 1988).] See Chapter 36.

At the second level are the gift clubs or memorial gifts. These include a smaller number of donors who belong to a continuing "club."[54] These donors give larger amounts of money than the annual givers, and they do it yearly. They give mostly unrestricted funds that are used wherever they are most needed.[55] Memorial gifts, also in this tier, are one-time gifts, usually given in memory of a deceased person or in honor of one who is still living.[56] Donors of memorial gifts are generally not interested in gift-club memberships.

The third tier of giving is the capital gift. This category consists of an even smaller number of donors with sufficient assets to make large gifts, often a large sum of money earmarked for a particular project or for capital needs.[57]

The top level of the pyramid is the deferred or estate gift. This is a gift given by one of a small, select group of people, intended for future use, generally in the form of trusts or lump-sum bequests.[58] Within these four levels of giving, there are many specific kinds of gifts.

Before any successful fund-raising program can begin, the organization seeking money must establish its purpose and goals.[59] The goals should be periodically reviewed and revised, to keep them current and salable.[60] Donors don't give gifts simply to give money away. They like to know how their donations are being used.

   The next step in the development plan of the nonprofit organization is to research and identify potential donors. Keeping good records on those affiliated with a particular organization, such as alumni, parishioners, and patrons, is a good way to start.[61] Identify the prospects through researching their past giving history. A good rule-of-thumb is to follow the "80-20 rule," which is that eighty percent of the money raised will come from twenty percent of the donors.[62] That is to say, don't waste time cultivating prospects without a high giving potential. Instead, it is more advantageous to concentrate on fewer, more promising sources.

   The old fundraising axiom that says that 80 to 90 percent of an organization's support comes from 10 to 20 percent of the donors is still true today. Organizations continually research their donor base hoping to expand their donor lists. Some library materials that may be useful are:[63]

Marquis Whos's Who: An annual publication that lists an individual's birthplace, parents, family, occupation, clubs, organizations, and religious affiliation.

Standard and Poor's Register: Lists top companies, what they make, and their executives.

Martindale-Hubbell Law Directory, the *American Medical Association Directory*, and the *Medical Specialist Directory*: Volumes are organized by state, city, and alphabetically by name.

10K Compaq Disclosure: A computer database that provides information on the prospective donor and that individual's company.

Annual Reports: If the prospect's company is large enough, the library may hold a copy of this document. Or, contact the company directly.

Business Dateline Ondisc, Periodical Ondisc, and *Infotrac*: Computer databases that provide newspaper and magazine articles on any given subject.

Dun & Bradstreet Business Locator: Provides brief sketches of companies.

   The fundraisers of colleges and universities had to cope with less in 1992 by realigning staff, targeting prospects more closely, and focusing on the ultimate beneficiaries of their efforts—the students. Educational institutions are increasingly focusing on alumni, parents, and unaffiliated prospects to increase donations. For example, the University of South Carolina's targeting of unaffiliated donors led to the donation of an island, to be used for environmental research. New technologies, for example, 10-minute videotape primers on endowments, have been successful. Computer research, telemarketing equipment, and statistical analysis have increased response to direct mailing efforts. Nationwide teleconferencing, with people able to call in a pledge on their credit cards, is expected to be the new means of garnering contributions.[64]

   Once all the prospects have been identified, a *case statement* should be prepared for them. The case statement is merely the nonprofit organization's sales pitch.[65] It is made in order to show the value and needs of the organization, clearly and persuasively, to prospective donors.[66] The volunteer force is then given their assignments and the actual fund raising begins.

There are a myriad of techniques used to induce prospective donors to give. Some of these include matching gifts, challenge gifts, and the afore-mentioned gift clubs. Matching gifts have historically been almost the exclusive domain of educational institutions.[67] Now, however, hospitals, the media, and the arts are also using this method of fund raising in their campaigns. A *matching gift* program is one in which a corporation, or other business, makes an offer to match the contributions of its employees, dollar-for-dollar, up to a set figure.[68] The Counsel for the Advancement and Support of Education (CASE) issues publications which contain the specifics for all matching-gift corporations.[69]

A *challenge gift* is a single, large pledge made by an individual, foundation, or corporation, for an organization, that will come to the organization when, and if, certain conditions or "challenges" are met.[70] Often the board of trustees of an organization will make an initial challenge. This campaign technique is an interesting way to create motivation in the donor arena.[71]

As mentioned earlier, gift clubs are a continuing plan of giving. They are basically membership programs, called gift clubs because contributors often receive some form of tangible recognition for their gifts, anything from calendars, to tickets to events.[72] The only qualification for membership in a gift club is that an individual give a standard sum of money to the organization on a regular basis, usually annually.[73]

Other examples of annual fund campaign techniques include reunion giving, corporate underwriting, federated fund raising, and person-to-person solicitation.[74]

Fund Raising Trends in 1993

Del Martin, vice president of Alexander O'Neill Hass & Martin, Inc., a national fundraising consulting firm based in Atlanta has identified the top ten fundraising trends for the future based on her firm's experience with the non-profit sector. 1. Giving will increase at the greatest rate in history from 1998 to 2002. 2. Strong volunteers will become the most precious (and rare) commodity a nonprofit can have. 3. Capital campaign goals will cease to be "comprehensive" and revert to being for "new money" or will become ongoing campaigns. 4. Public/private partnerships will be part of all large campaigns/projects. 5. Giving to a profitable nonprofit hospital will not exist by 2000. 6. Direct mail will be used primarily as a prospecting tool, (not fundraising). 7. Tax-advantageous charitable deductions will continue to deteriorate. 8. Unrestricted corporate giving will all but disappear. 9. There will be increasing (and enormous) pressure for fundraising to be completely staff driven. 10. "High touch" will replace "high tech" in the successful development office.[75]

§439. BASIC TOOLS OF FUND RAISING

The tools of fund raising include the skills and techniques used in implementing fundraising activities. They are the means by which the nonprofit organization's primary development goal is reached, that goal being monetary. There are many different approaches used, some creative, some novel, and some tried and true old standbys. The most popular of these "tools" are the telephone campaign, direct mailout, and special events campaign.

Telephone campaigns are an effective means of fund raising, because they add a somewhat personal touch to an organization's efforts.[76] They are utilized in any situation where there are too many donors to reach personally. A team of volunteers can reach thousands of potential donors in a short period of time, with virtually no overhead to the nonprofit organization.[77] A 1993 *Non-Profit Times/* Barna Research study revealed that while women say they dislike telemarketing and direct mail appeals more than men do, they actually give more to those appeals.[78]

Consumers who call 800 or 900 numbers are often identified by Caller ID signals for the purpose of future marketing and solicitation contact. The Direct Marketing Association (DMA) supports legislative or regulatory efforts that require suppliers of Automatic Number Identification to offer consumers the option of blocking the Caller ID signal on a per-call basis. The DMA Guidelines for Marketing by Telephone also require that telephone marketers who receive or collect consumer data as a result of a telephone marketing contact, and who intend to rent, sell or exchange those data for direct marketing purposes, should notify the consumer of that fact.[79]

Direct mail is probably the most widely-used form of fund raising in the United States today, and accounts for over one half of the monies raised for United States' charities each year.[80] Estimates show that over seven billion pieces of direct-mail solicitation are sent out each year by nonprofit organizations.[81] Out of these torrents of letters only a very few will ever be answered.[82] Using the mails is expensive, but an increasingly popular way to raise money for everything from political causes to educational institutions and charities.[83] Although it seems like a waste of time and money, judging by these statistics, various nonprofit organizations have proved that the direct-mail method of fund-raising works, by actually raising over $10 billion per year.[84]

Letters sent in response to direct mail fundraisers often seem like letters written to a friend. Many correspondents are elderly and their unsteady handwriting conveys a level of trust; one that is more and more at odds with the spread of skepticism facing fundraisers.[85]

Some legislators want to end the "free lunch" for a consumer group that uses state mailings for membership and fundraising drives. Since 1988, the Citizen's Utility Board—a nonprofit utility watchdog group—has been able to solicit funds by including its literature in such bulk state mailings as drivers license renewal notices, auto registration forms, and tax refund checks. The

Board pays no postage for this dissemination of information. The legislators have introduced legislation that would require the Board to share this privilege with other nonprofit groups in the state on a rotating basis. Of the 1,676 other nonprofit groups in Illinois, groups such as the United Way and the Red Cross will also benefit.

According to the U.S. Postal Service, not-for-profit groups pay $.11 per envelope for bulk mailings while standard patrons pay $.29. If the Board has to pay this increased cost out of its budget, it will make it harder to wage expensive legal battles against the utility companies. The Board's budget depends entirely on contributions from individual consumers. The Board has an annual budget of $1.5 million raised from $10 donations from 150,000 contributors. Most of the budget is spent on legal fees. The majority of members join the organization in response to the information sent out in the state mailings. If the Board loses this benefit, it would have to pay $16,500 for each fundraising effort. This would probably put the Board out of business.

The legislators say they simply want to give other groups the same benefit. The intent of the legislation is to give access to the mails to other groups. The bill won committee approval in 1993 and awaited further action.[86]

See Ch. 1 §7. for a discussion of the postal privilege accorded to nonprofit organizations.

Special-event fund raising is an excellent way, not only to raise money, but also to increase participation in the organization, identify new members, and develop good public relations, at the same time.[87] Donors love special events; the more glamorous, the better. A special event can be defined as a "dramatized effort to promote an idea, a cause, or a program" with the purpose being "to improve relationships with an organization's public, develop understanding, and strengthen support through increased effort and contributions."[88] Special events are risky, though. There are a vast number of factors which can affect their success, such as weather conditions, other competing events, and timing.

A most useful, detailed survey, published by *Independent Sector*, in 1988, titled *Giving and Volunteering in the United States*, gives demographics, attitudes and motivations of present-day American philanthropy. For instance: almost half of all U.S. contributions to charity today come from households with incomes below $30,000/yr.[89]

Computerizing an organization's fundraising (or grant making) operations involves a lot more data entry work than fast typing. The data is the most important part. How to do it is spelled out in detail in this very useful, short article:

> M.T. Segall, Building a Computer Database: How to Do It Right the First Time, 4 *NonProfit Times* (11)23 (Feb.1991). The *N-P Times* carries many advertisements for NPO computer equipment.

The Grantsmanship Center is one of the largest fundraising training organizations. To get information about its training programs, call the Registrar at: (213) 482-9860 or (800) 421-9512.

§440. SPECIAL TYPES OF FUND RAISING

There are some specialized forms of fund raising which go beyond the basic annual fund campaign. Many nonprofit organizations never get into these areas with their fund-raising endeavors, but a great many find them very attractive. Some of these special types are deferred giving programs, capital campaigns, foundation support, and government grants.

Deferred Giving Programs

The *deferred giving* program has been defined as the "systematic and aggressive encouragement of gifts to an institution . . . by means of life income plans, bequests, insurance contracts, annuities, and other methods."[90] This concept had its inception in 1969 with the advent of the 1969 Tax Reform Act, which added to the provisions allowing "deferred gifts" to be made to nonprofit organizations.[91] The term *deferred giving* is actually something of a misnomer, because these are current gifts, with immediate tax benefits for the donor, and an irrevocable contribution for the organization, even though the bulk of the gift is to be received at a later date.[92] There are several different kinds of deferred-giving plans used today. In addition to the standard bequest of money to a nonprofit organization through one's will, other, more creative types of deferred bequests are also employed.

Donors may make gifts during their lifetimes, giving instructions as to the disposition of the property at death. This is generally called a *living trust*.[93] There are four basic requirements needed to create a valid living trust: a designated beneficiary, a *res*, a designated trustee, and actual delivery of the *res* to the trustee with the intent to pass title.[94] Living trusts can save time by escaping the delays of probate, as well as saving money by avoiding probate costs and estate taxes.

A *charitable gift annuity plan* is one in which a donor irrevocably transfers money or property to an organization, where such an organization promises, in exchange, to pay the donor a fixed amount, annually, for life.[95] These annuities are part gift and part purchase. The amount of the gift annuity's annual payment depends upon the donor's age at the time the gift was made; and the full amount becomes available to the organization only upon the death of the donor.[96]

A *charitable remainder trust* is a life-income plan whereby a donor irrevocably transfers assets to a trust, which pays to him or her income annually for life based on a fixed percentage.[97] The donor is also entitled to take a tax deduction on the property contributed when the gift is made, while assuring him or her an increased cash flow for life.[98]

In a *pooled-income fund trust*, a donor irrevocably transfers money or property to a pooled-income fund maintained by the recipient organization, and that organization signs a contract to pay the donor an annual income for life.[99] A pooled-income fund is a trust maintained by the nonprofit organization receiving these irrevocable gifts, where such gifts are comingled with the gifts of other like donors.[100] The income from the fund is paid, in *pro rata* shares, to all of the donors. At the death of the last donor, the remainder of the *res* is turned over the to the organization.[101] The same basic advantages as those previously mentioned are present in this type of program as well.

Capital Campaigns

Another special type of fundraising is the capital campaign. A *capital campaign* is a concentrated effort, by an organization, to raise a specified amount of money over an extended period of time, for a specified project.[102] This kind of program differs from the annual fund campaign, in that funds solicited through the annual fund campaign are unrestricted in nature, and those obtained through a capital campaign are designated for a specific purpose.[103] A capital campaign can be, and is, often carried on in conjunction with a non-profit organization's annual fund drive.

Foundations

[See Chapter 7.]

A *foundation* is a "nongovernmental, nonprofit organization, with funds and program managed by its own trustees or directors, which was established to maintain or aid social, educational, charitable, religious or other activities serving the common welfare, primarily by making grants to other nonprofit organizations."[104] The area of foundation giving is a vast, complicated one, going far beyond the scope of this chapter. A basic overview, however, is warranted in light of the massive amounts of money given to persons and organizations through private foundations.

Private foundations usually account for about $2.6 billion in support to nonprofit organizations each year.[105] In the United States today, there are over 25,000 foundations with a total of over 35 billion in assets.[106] Each year, over one million proposals for foundation grants are submitted, but less than seventy thousand are actually funded.[107]

To apply for a foundation grant, it is necessary to find a foundation that funds similar projects.[108] There are several different categories of foundations, including, but not limited to, family foundations, corporate foundations, and community foundations.[109] An organization must determine which to solicit. There is a publication called the *Foundation Grants Index*, which is put out by the Foundation Center, that serves this purpose.[110] The organization should also obtain more detailed information on pertinent foundations through publications such as the *Foundation Directory*[111] or the *Source Book Profile Directory*, also put out by the Foundation Center.[112]

A detailed, formal proposal must then be submitted to the foundation, if required.[113] If not, in smaller foundations, a proposal letter will suffice.[114] Once the proposal has been submitted, the foundation will begin to process it and make a decision. Various factors enter into a foundation's decision to award a grant. These include policy and changes, availability of funds, perceived merits of the proposal, competing proposals, and prior commitments of the foundation.[115] The whole decision-making process usually takes approximately four to six months.[116]

Government Funding

Government funding is a popular method of fund raising. The two major mechanisms for conveying funds to support nonprofit organization's projects are grants and contracts.[117] Government programs use both, while private foundations rarely use contracts.[118] In 1958, Congress passed the *Grant Act of 1958*, which authorized all federal agencies, having the power to enter into contracts, to give grants instead.[119]

To apply for government funding, the same preliminary research as for foundations is necessary.[120] The *Catalog of Federal Domestic Assistance* is a useful guide in this endeavor,[121] as is the *Federal Register, Federal Assistance Programs Retrieval System, Commerce and Business Daily* and others.[122] Once the initial research is completed, the same kind of formal proposal is to be submitted to the appropriate governmental agency.[123]

Government contracts are almost always used when the government is procuring services from a profit-making organization.[124] They can also be used to procure services from nonprofit organizations.[125] Grants are usually used to support research, training, and service programs based on unsolicited proposals.[126] The Federal Grants and Cooperative Agreement Act of 1978 provides a guide to be used for the determination of what kind of funding is to be given in specific situations.[127]

There are a multitude of types of grants available to the nonprofit organization. These include: broad block grants, specific categorical grants, project grants, service grants, developmental grants, research grants, training grants, and staffing grants, *et al.*[128]

Recipients of government grants are subject to the regulations of the *Code of Federal Regulations*, the individual granting agency, and also the conditions attached to the particular grant, while organizations contracting with the government are bound by the *Federal Procurement Regulations* and the *Armed Service Procurement Regulations.*[129]

While inflation and federal spending cutbacks have diminished the volume of government grants given, they are still a very viable mode of fund raising.

Individuals and nonprofit organizations that receive benefits from the federal government have a private right of action for monetary and non-monetary damages, against the federal government, under the Rehabilitation Act, if the government discriminates against them in awarding benefits because of their handicap. However, if the organization seeks to change policy (regulatory) rather than to receive money (proprietary) then the organization must exhaust its remedies under the Administrative Procedure Act.[130]

Funds in a Medicare provider's funded depreciation account are funds "available," if not contractually committed to ongoing projects, and must be considered in evaluating financial need for borrowing and the reimbursability of Medicare provider's interest expenses.[131]

The Student Loan Default Prevention Initiative Act and its regulations are not invalid on the ground of retroactivity, even though they make past student default rates grounds for termination from the Guaranteed Student Loan (GSL) program. Member schools have no "vested right" to participate in the GSL program.[132] However, the Secretary of Education cannot arbitrarily and capriciously rule a college ineligible to participate in the guaranteed student loan program. The Secretary must articulate a rational basis for determinations, contemporaneous with its decisions, and present the decisions in reviewable format.[133]

In California, a non-profit modern dance corporation was denied National Endowment for the Arts (NEA) grants because the applicants refused to certify that the funds awarded would not be used to promote or produce obscene material. The court held that the NEA requirement was unconstitutionally vague because it left the determination of obscenity in the hands of the NEA. Further the requirement violated the First Amendment because it created a chilling effect on speech.[134]

Funds borrowed from the Department of Housing and Urban Development (HUD), to be used for the elderly, cannot be used to build a center that is used partially for a church school as a "related facility," unless the borrower complies with HUD regulatory prerequisites. The United States can seek to recover such funds.[135] The government can recover Public Health Service Act grant money, used to construct a hospital, if the hospital is subsequently transferred to an ineligible for-profit entity.[136]

§441. GOVERNMENT REGULATIONS ON SOLICITATIONS (SELECTED STATES)

[See Chapter 8.]

The Model Act Concerning the Solicitation of Funds for Charitable Purposes was developed six years ago by the National Association of State Charity Officials and a "private sector" (nonprofit) advisory group. Many of the fundraising bills now being introduced in many states contain features of the Model Act. Some of the act's more noteworthy features are: (1) The Model Act would register only counsel with custody of contributions, not paid solicitors. However, both counsel and paid solicitors must file a bond. (2) Required advertising disclosures and contract requirements of cause marketing agreements between corporations and nonprofits. (3) A uniform registration code, adopted nationwide, with a uniform registration form.[137]

Proposed House Bill 733 is the first attempted federal regulation of direct mail fundraising. Under the bill, the Postal Service would have to determine compliance. Disclosures required of charitable organizations in mail solicitation include: (1) its legal name and address; (2) whether it is tax exempt and whether contributions are tax deductible; (3) the intended use of the contribution, whether the program exists or is just planned, and the purpose of the solicitation; (4) provision by the charity of financial information to anyone requesting it. The bill also requires conspicuous and legible language and applies to radio and television commercials.[138]

For more nationwide consumer information, The *Consumer Information Catalog*, listing 200 consumer guides, is available free by writing for a Consumer Information Catalog, Pueblo, Colorado, 81009 or by calling (719) 948-4000. The catalog is revised quarterly.

Florida

On October 1, 1984, the Florida Solicitation of Charitable Contributions Act became effective, repealing the former Florida Solicitation of Charitable Funds Act.[139] This act comprises chapter 496 of the Florida statutes.[140] It provides for control over the solicitation and fund-raising practices of Florida's charitable organizations.

Requirements for registration of these organizations are set out in §496.405 of the statutes; each charitable organization is required to register with the Division of Consumer Services of the Department of Agriculture and Consumer Services before being allowed to solicit funds.[141] Included in the registration application is a laundry list of information to be filled in. In this list are the organization's name and purpose, address, names and addresses of trustees and directors, custodian of financial records, names of those in charge of the solicitation within the organization, purpose for the funds, anticipated fund-raising costs, and a financial statement covering the complete disclosure of all fiscal activities of the organization during the preceding year.[142]

Exemptions from this registration include charitable organizations not receiving contributions in excess of $25,000 during its fiscal year, those which only solicit within their own membership, and those which solicit in the name of some specified person where all of the money is given directly to the beneficiary.[143]

All nonexempt charitable organizations, professional solicitors and their sponsors (such as police and fire groups) in Florida must register with the Florida Department of Agriculture and Consumer Services. Professional solicitors must also post a $50,000 bond with the department. Upon request, all nonexempt organizations must provide a financial report or budget within 14 days. Consumers can call (800) 435-7352 to find out if an organization is registered.[144]

The Division of Consumer Services of the Department of Agriculture and Consumer Services is empowered to enforce all provisions of the act as well as impose appropriate penalties for violations.[145]

Florida Licensing. Under the new (1992) law, *registration is required* of persons or organizations who will solicit funds; failure to register first is a third-degree felony. Consultant fund raisers must pay a filing fee of $200, and professional solicitors must file a $50,000 bond.[146]

In 1989, Florida stopped keeping track of charitable solicitations, on the theory that requiring *registration and reports* of charities and professional solicitors was ineffective. In 1991, the state's attorney-general reported that a task force study of the effects of the radical Florida policy found it to be a failure.

Supreme Court decisions had stopped the states from governing what percentage of their "take" the solicitors may keep for themselves. People simply do not usually *ask* the solicitors for detailed revelations of their practices. In Florida, by early 1991 it was a fact that "As long as they don't (didn't!?) tell any outright lies or otherwise misrepresent themselves, fundraisers can (could?!) pretty much do whatever they want."[147]

In 1991, Florida reinstituted registration requirements for nonprofit organizations, fund raisers and fundraising counsel (consultants) which it had abolished two years earlier. The new law also requires solicitors to state where additional information can be had from the Division of Consumer Services (and the phone number). The rule became effective Jan. 1, 1992.[148]

[*Addendum (1986)*: (Oleck)

County Permits for solicitations of contributions are required in Florida; *e.g.*, in Pinellas County (St. Petersburg—Clearwater) a five member Charitable Solicitations Board (volunteers) is appointed by the County Commission. It rarely meets and very rarely penalizes anyone, although it can invoke fines and jail sentences. A 17-page County Ordinance is largely ignored. The county charitable-solicitations officer is an officer of the department of social services and is hopelessly overburdened with other duties. [D. Olinger, *Charity Control Ineffective in County*, St. Petersburg *Independent*, p. 1 (Sept. 20, 1986).]

The Florida department of state, division of licensing has proposed much stricter rules for fund raising organizations and solicitors. [St. Petersburg *Times*, p. 3B (Sept. 4, 1986) (K. Ovack article)]. In many states (*e.g.*, North Carolina Federal Court) a requirement of *licensing of professional solicitors* has been held to be unconstitutional under the First Amendment [National Federation of the Blind of N.C., Inc. v. Riley, 635 F. Supp. 256 (D.C., No. Car., 1986). *See* the next Section.] [In 1988 Florida added a statutory requirement that people who raise $5000 or more, *for someone else*, register and report to the Department or State, and excess amounts must be used for other needy people in similar circumstances. There are fines and civil penalties for violations of this rule.]

A *citizens' association's* legal "standing" to challenge actions (or inactions) of a county authority is almost zero unless some extraordinary "special injury" can be shown by the person or organization affected. [Upper Keys Citizens Assn., Inc. v. Monroe County, 467 S.2d 1018 (Fla. 3rd D.C. App., 1985).]

Maryland

A Maryland law, passed in the last day of the 1992 session, restricts the amount of money collected during in-home or door-to-door solicitations to

$200. The statute also requires that solicitors present the donors with a pledge form that must include the solicitor's name, organization name and address, date and amount of solicitation, donor's name, and a statement telling the donors that they have 20 days to cancel pledges. Another form to rescind pledges must also be distributed. Solicitors can receive pledges of over $200 only if actual payment is not made at the initial solicitation.[149]

Massachusetts

Massachusetts, in 1993, limited the fundraising activities by the state's police and their associations by using the state's conflict-of-interest laws. Police associations are notorious for their high-pressure tactics and deceptive practices. The Massachusetts State Ethics Commission says that the officers and their agents may not imply that official action will depend on a donation, send stickers or decals for cars, engage in fundraising while on duty, use official resources for fundraising (telephones, copy and fax machines, and stationary), or show badges or wear uniforms while fundraising.[150]

Michigan

Michigan also incorporates many of these same restrictions in one of the nation's most rigorous laws directed at all public safety solicitations. Michigan's public safety solicitation regulations go into effect December 18, 1993, and create separate registration and enforcement procedures for the attorney general's Charitable Trust Section to administer. A violation of the regulations may result in civil penalties up to $5,000. In Michigan, professional solicitors, working for public-safety entities, must post a $25,000 bond, which is increased yearly, based on the amount of contributions raised. Michigan also provides a toll-free number for consumer complaints against public safety solicitation organizations.[151]

New York

New York's laws on the solicitation and collection of funds for charitable purposes are contained in Article 7-A of the New York Consolidated Laws.[152] This article provides for the *registration* of charitable organizations in order to solicit funds, as does the Florida law.[153] The same pertinent information is required for such registration in New York, but its *exemption* provisions are significantly more detailed.[154]

In New York, all religious organizations, fraternal, patriotic, social, alumni organizations, and historical societies are exempt when contributions are confined to their membership, as opposed to the general public.[155] Any charitable organization receiving funds from a united fund or community chest will be exempt, but only if it complies with the other exemption requirements.[156] In some instances, veteran's associations and volunteer firemen's auxiliaries are also exempt.[157]

Professional fund raisers are required to register with the secretary of state and post a surety bond, as in Florida, but the exact amount of such bond is not specified.[158]

In New York, the attorney general, instead of the department of state, has the power to enforce violations of the article as enumerated.[159]

Ohio

In the Ohio Revised Code, there is also a provision mandating the *registration* of nonprofit organizations before soliciting of funds is allowed.[160] The same basic information is required here as in New York and Florida.[161] An *annual financial report* is also required of registrants, and such must be filed with the application in the attorney general's office.[162]

These sections of the code are generally not applied to religious organizations, nor to most educational institutions, where contributions are confined to the membership.[163] All organizations where solicitation is only within its membership are exempt from registering.[164]

In Ohio, *professional fund raisers* are required to register as an organization would. These applications must be in writing and under oath, submitted with a twenty-five thousand dollar surety bond, to a surety authorized to do business in the state.[165]

This code contains a penalties provision,[166] with authority in the attorney general to enforce the provision.[167]

Texas

Texas is considering a bill to register solicitors, requiring the filing of solicitation notices, financial reports of campaigns, and a $25,000 bond. But, the bill was not expected to be heard in the 1993 session.[168]

Utah

Utah's new fundraising statute requires in-person and telephone solicitors to display or read information cards to prospective donors. The information to be read includes the amount of funds "to remain available for application to the charitable purpose." Utah's law probably violates the U.S. Supreme Court's decision in *Riley* where the court determined that such a requirement is mandated speech that would have a chilling effect on solicitation. The law further requires that funds be deposited in a Utah Bank, a possible violation of the commerce clause. Further, registration of fundraisers may be revoked without due process by the Division of Consumer Protection. Financial reporting by 501 (c)(3) organizations is not required. A statement that financial disclosure statements are available from the state would not be required in initial solicitations. Such a law may be found unconstitutional.[169]

Utah, in a 1993 bill amending its fundraising law, would require charities to file quarterly financial reports within 30 days of each quarter during the first year a charity is registered with the state.[170]

Virginia

Virginia has passed a law authorizing cities and towns to force nonprofit bingo operators to devote a certain percentage of their receipts to charitable activities. The law was passed in response to a Richmond report indicating that local charities devoted just 2 percent of the $4 million gross take in 1992 to humanitarian programs. The law took effect July 1, 1993. Richmond has determined that charities using bingo operations for fundraising will have to set aside 6 percent of their proceeds for human-service programs starting October 1, 1993.[171]

Other States

In response to abuse of fundraising ethics rules, the states have continued to propose a dizzying collection laws to curb deceptive practices.

Bills have been introduced in Idaho and Delaware to regulate fundraising. Alaska may also reintroduce a 1992 bill in its 1993 term.

Delaware's bill would require registration by nonprofits' fundraising counsel and professional solicitors, fees, bonding, and other requirements. Contracts signed by nonprofits with solicitors would have a 10-day cancellation clause.

Idaho's bill, which would establish a Charitable Solicitation Act, contains no registration provisions. The bill simply states that "it is unlawful . . . to utilize any unfair, false, deceptive, misleading or unconscionable act or practice" in the course of solicitation.

Registration fees for charities in Connecticut could be raised to $250 (up from the current, 1992, $20) under proposed legislation. A proposed bill in Connecticut would also require that solicitors file contracts with nonprofits with the state, to be advertised in a local newspaper where the fundraising campaign is being conducted. Solicitor fees would increase to $1,000 from $120.

Rhode Island, currently, in its registration requirements, demands a list of names and salaries of all persons employed by nonprofits earning more than $12,500. Pending 1993 legislation would increase that figure to $30,000.[172]

The Attorney-General is the authority exclusively clothed with authority to enforce the Illinois Solicitation Act and prosecute violations of it.[173]

California's new law requiring commercial fundraisers for charities to register, effective January 1, 1990, applies to persons or organizations that receive the donations and/or control the solicitations.[174]

Fund Raisers' Registration Costs increased to $20,000 bonds for solicitors in Massachusetts and $50,000 in Florida for 1992, and registration fees were $800 in New York and $1000 in Tennessee.[175]

A recent survey of charity officials, by the American Association of Fund-Raising Counsel (AAFRC), outlines the concerns of charity officials as well as

a comparison of the legislation and registration forms in states that require registration of professional fund raising counsel, professional solicitors, and commercial co-venturers. The survey is available from AAFRC for $25 per copy. Check
or money order to: AAFRC, 25 West 43rd St., Suite 820, New York, NY 10036[176]

§442. FIRST-AMENDMENT IMPLICATIONS IN FUND RAISING

Significant issues of constitutional law have arisen with respect to fund raising
and solicitation by nonprofit organizations. Most of these have roots in the
First Amendment of the Constitution. Twenty-three states have passed laws limiting a fund raiser's expenses and fees to approximately 25 percent of all gross
receipts.[177] There have been many situations where such laws, and others like
them, have been challenged as unconstitutional.

The United States Supreme Court decided this issue in *Secretary of State of
Maryland v. Joseph H. Munson Co.*[178] In this case, the Court held a Maryland
statute, prohibiting charitable organizations making solicitations from paying
expenses of more than 25 percent of the total funds raised, unconstitutional.[179]
The Court determined that such a provision constituted a direct restriction on
protected First Amendment activity, in that it "included within its sweep impermissible applications."[180] Because of this, the statute was held "fundamentally
defective."[181]

In the prior case of *Village of Schaumburg v. Citizens for a Better Environment,
et al.*,[182] the Supreme Court ruled that an Illinois town violated the First Amendment rights of a nonprofit organization by refusing to grant a solicitation permit because of a town ordinance limiting such permits to organizations using
at least 75 percent of their gross receipts for *charitable* (not collection expenses) purposes.[183] The Court held that the ordinance was unconstitutionally overbroad and violated the First and Fourteenth Amendments, in that it did not
serve a sufficiently strong subordinating interest that the village was entitled to
protect, that being the prevention of fraud and protection of residential privacy.[184]

Another interesting case dealing with First Amendment issues is *Larson v.
Valente*.[185] In that case, the Supreme Court held unconstitutional a Minnesota
statute which imposed certain registration requirements only on religious organizations that solicited less than 50 percent of their funds from members, on
the grounds that such statute violated the Establishment Clause of the First
Amendment.[186] The Court said that the "clearest command of the Establishment Clause is that one religious denomination cannot be officially preferred
over another."[187] A rule granting such a preference is suspect, and is constitutional only if justified by a compelling governmental interest.[188]

One case in which the Supreme Court ruled in favor of the State is
Heffron v. International Society for Krishna Consciousness, Inc., et al.[189] In this case,
a Minnesota state fair rule requiring that the sale and distribution of any material be from a duly licensed location on the fairgrounds, was upheld on

grounds that it did not violate the Free Exercise Clause of the First Amendment, as applied to members of the Hare Krishna religious sect.[190] The Court held that the state's interest in maintaining public order was sufficient to satisfy the "significant governmental interest" requirement.[191] The Court noted that, while the propagation of the Krishnas' views are within the purview of the First Amendment, these rights are not absolute and are subject to time, place, and manner restrictions.[192]

[Reginald Stambaugh, Rana Holz, and Patricia Cullen contributed cases for the rest of this section.]

(See Chapter 8)

State attempts to control fund raising abuses have been held (by the Supreme Court) to be violations of First Amendment and other liberties when they are broadly worded. The aspects most likely to be deemed valid are provisions requiring registration, financial disclosure reports, and modest fees to finance administration of regulation.[193]

Defining solicitation of funds to include the sale of property, including books, pamphlets, subscriptions, etc., sold under the express or implied representation that the proceeds of the sale will be used for charitable purposes, is constitutional.[194]

In Clearwater Florida, the Church of Scientology attacked the constitutionality of a local ordinance which required charitable organizations to file registration statements or make available private disclosure statements to their members. The court upheld the ordinance since the law had a secular legislative purpose, did not foster excessive government entanglement with religion, and its primary effect neither advanced nor inhibited religion.[195]

An ordinance that banned solicitations between 5 p.m. and 9 p.m. Monday through Friday, and all of Saturday and Sunday (year round), was held to be an unreasonable and unnecessary burden both on potential soliciting activities and upon residents who wished to hear the solicitor's message.[196]

Since a beggar is a solicitor, with a financial motive for speaking, begging could be viewed as commercial speech. Consequently, begging may be entitled to the free speech protections afforded to commercial speech.[197]

An ordinance, that requires an organization either to file the written contract between it and a professional fund raiser or a statement summarizing the compensation to be received by the professional fund raiser, does not violate First Amendment rights. An organization may also constitutionally be required to describe their purpose and the intended use for collected funds, or to disclose any conflict of interest which might affect the charity, or to disclose, upon request, the estimated percentage of money collected that will actually go to charity.[198]

When a state statute completely bans police personnel from soliciting for the benefit of law enforcement, and the state subsequently enacts an exception to the statute permitting police personnel to solicit funds for construction of a memorial to slain police officers, the state has discriminatorily favored one charity over another, violating equal protection.[199]

When a charitable organization challenged the constitutionality of an ordinance that prohibited roadway solicitations, the court held that the ordinance was narrowly tailored to a governmental interest in public safety. There was a real danger to the public which justified the prohibition of street solicitation.[200]

The people, through the attorney general, may enjoin professional telephone solicitors along with the heads of the nonprofit law enforcement support organizations, from fund raising by telephone without violating the First Amendment, if the solicitation misinforms and defrauds the public.[201]

The federal court must abstain from enjoining a state court preliminary injunction, prohibiting an association of police officers from soliciting contributions from Port Authority tenants, if a federal injunction would infringe on the legitimate authority of state court to resolve disputes which come before them and would be interfering with the state's important interest in enforcing its courts' judgments and orders, the "*Younger* abstention doctrine."[202]

In a recent action concerning the constitutionality of a New York law imposing a registration charge of $80 on professional solicitors, the U.S. District Court for New York held the law did not violate the First Amendment or the Equal Protection clause. The plaintiffs challenged the law stating that the fee was an unconstitutional tax and prior restraint on expression, and that by requiring the fee from professional solicitors while exempting officers, volunteers, and employees of charities, the law violated the Fourteenth Amendment. The Court held that charitable solicitations are protected speech under the First Amendment, but that general registration fees are permissible if there is a reasonable connection between the fee and the administrative and enforcement costs of registration. The Court also found that the exemption of some solicitors did not violate the Fourteenth Amendment, since the law appeared to be prudent and was devised to protect the public from unsupervised fundraising activities.[203]

The Cancer Fund of America challenged the Solicitation of Funds for Charitable Purposes Act of Pennsylvania on the grounds that it regulates free speech but is not content-neutral because it exempts certain organizations including fire fighters, veterans organizations, and religious groups. The Act requires disclosure in solicitations of the percentage of total contributions to activities associated with the fundraising. The Court held that even if a regulation has an operational discriminatory effect on certain speakers, the regulation will be upheld if the government's purpose is not related to the content of the speech.

The Fund was also held to have violated the sections of the Act prohibiting utilization of unfair or deceptive acts or practices or engaging in any fraudulent conduct that creates a likelihood of confusion or misunderstanding or using a name, symbol, or statement so closely related or similar to that used by another charitable organization that it would tend to confuse or mislead a solicited person.

The Fund disclaims affiliation with several other charitable cancer organizations in one part of its solicitation materials and disclaims association with the American Cancer Society in a later segment of the materials. The Court held that the similar name and deceptive disclaimer create a likelihood of confusion.[204]

Solicitation of funds for charitable purposes constitutes a "speech" interest within the protection of the First Amendment. Yet cities continue to promulgate ordinances limiting various types of fund raising efforts.

For example, a religious organization in Houston challenged a *street-ordinance* prohibiting solicitation of funds for charitable purposes from occupants of vehicles. As access to the streets has long been an essential element of free speech, the ban had to be closely scrutinized. Despite valid traffic control and safety concerns, the city failed to meet its burden of proof as it failed to enforce the provision evenhandedly against such commercial solicitors as newspaper or frozen dessert vendors. Consequently, the court refused to enforce the ordinance.[205]

The U.S. District Court struck down a New York City statute prohibiting loitering in public places as well as panhandling, begging, and soliciting in the public transportation (e.g., subway) facilities. The court could not draw a meaningful distinction between soliciting for charity and begging. Therefore, the court designated the public transit system as public fora, analogizing them to the city's airport terminals.[206]

Fund Raising Solicitors

Many nonprofit organizations are using commercial fund raising techniques and professional solicitors to further their efforts. By doing this, these organizations do not lose their First Amendment rights. A body of protections has been developing, in recent years, which affords nonprofit and commercial solicitors many of those rights traditionally reserved for charitable entities. The gravamen for barring of a state action in these cases is the *arbitrary enforcement* of such provisions by governmental entities.

As to a provision which requires disclosure of the name and address of the organization which would benefit from the contribution, the courts have held this requirement to be not unduly burdensome on the charity; and it achieves the narrow aim that potential donors should be able to verify the authenticity of a solicitation.[207]

In *Telco*, the court defended not only the professional fund raiser's right to guard the interests of charitable entities, but also his individual right to substantial First Amendment protections. Even in regard to purely commercial speech, the state must meet standards very similar to those regarding charitable solicitations before it can regulate a targeted commercial activity. A four-part standard is set forth in *Central Hudson Gas & Electric Corp. v. Public Service Comm'n*, 447 U.S. 557, 100 S. Ct. 2343, 65 L. Ed. 2d 341 (1980). The speech must concern a lawful activity and not be misleading. The government interest asserted must be substantial. Then, if both of these inquiries yield positive results, the court must examine whether the regulation directly advances the interest asserted and whether or not it is more extensive than necessary to serve the interest.[208]

Statutes forbidding telephone solicitations of charitable contributions, by professional solicitors, and limiting their compensation, are unconstitutional invasions of free speech.[209]

Parts of the Indiana statute governing fund raising and solicitation were declared unconstitutional under the First Amendment, for requiring disclosure (to solicitees) of the percentage (or fee arrangement) of the professional solicitor's company.[210]

A state (NC) statute regulating rates of fees to professional fund raising solicitors is not validly narrow enough to avoid conflict with "free speech" if it uses vague terms such as "reasonable" and "excessive" as to the amounts or percentages of their fees.[211]

A new study on the National Change of Address Service by a congressional subcommittee warns that the Postal Service is undermining privacy by disclosing the names and addresses of customers against their wishes. In response, Rep. Don Wise (D-W.V.), chair of the House Subcommittee on Government Information, Justice and Agriculture, introduced legislation in 1993 to prevent the Postal Service from providing address corrections.[212]

Florida's Supreme Court in 1990 struck down, as unconstitutional, a state statute of 1989 that banned political fund raising during the state's 60-day annual legislative session. The plaintiff (Jack Dodd, Republican candidate for Agriculture Commissioner) had challenged the law as giving incumbents an advantage over challengers for office. The state's argument was that its purpose was to cut down corrupt "sale" of office. Lower courts had ruled that it was a vague and too-broad infringement on freedom of speech. The Supreme Court ruling was one sentence (6 to 0).[213]

An airport authority may reasonably regulate the solicitation of contributions in an airport without violating free speech, in view of the inconvenience to passengers and the burden placed on officials by the solicitation activity. However, free speech is violated when the authority bans the distribution of literature.[214]

Requesting an injunction against solicitation practices, that are found by a court to be misleading and deceptive, is a sufficiently tailored remedy to satisfy the First Amendment prohibition against prior restraints on freedom of speech.[215]

First Amendment free speech protection has not been violated when a state established fund raising drive, managed by a Principal Fund Raising Organization, excludes a charitable organization from membership on a campaign committee.[216]

Required Contributions

New York's "Son of Sam" law requires that an accused or convicted criminal's income, from published works about his crime, be deposited into a nonprofit escrow account for the benefit of the victims of crime. The law was found to be inconsistent with the First Amendment guarantee of free speech.[217]

A terminated United Parcel Service employee sued claiming that she was terminated for refusing to comply with her employer's directive that she donate time and money to the United Way Fund (the Fund). Maryland, by statute prohibits coercion or intimidation in soliciting contributions. However, the court held that the Fund is not a social or economic association or organization, but is a charitable institution not included in the provisions of the statute.[218]

The Illinois Voluntary Payroll Deduction Act allows Illinois state employee to direct a specific portion of their pay to qualified community charities. The Act was found to be constitutional when several tax-exempt nonprofit corporations, that did not qualify to receive funds, challenged the Act.[219]

§443. CREATIVE FUND RAISING

[See the preceding sections.]

There have been many nonprofit organizations in this country with creative approaches to fundraising. The most innovative group of organizations seems to be that which includes the arts, museums and theaters.

The Children's Museum of Denver, in Denver, Colorado, publishes various booklets for children for sale to different corporations, at a profit for the museum.[220] The museum develops the idea and format for each booklet, and then matches it with a corporation that can use it as a premium for its customers.[221] An activity guide about responsible pet care, titled "Kids and Pets," is one such example. This booklet was sold to Nine-Lives Dry Cat Food.[222] This venture generates over $200,000 for the Children's Museum per year.[223]

Denver's Holiday Festival of Trees, sponsored by the city's Artreach program, is a four-day festival which helps support the nonprofit organization's efforts to bring the arts to Denver's elderly, handicapped, institution inmates, and other disadvantaged citizens.[224] In 1982, this event yielded $90,000.[225] For the festival, individuals, corporations, or any other entity can decorate a Christmas tree and donate it for sale. All of the trees are collected and shown at a lavish cocktail party, to which admission is charged, and a silent auction is held to sell the trees.[226] The proceeds are used to fund Artreach.[227]

In 1976, the Greater Minneapolis Chamber of Commerce created the Five Percent Club, whereby Minnesota businesses were invited to donate five percent of their taxable incomes to the community's social, arts, and cultural programs.[228] The purpose of this program was, and is, to encourage more businesses to increase their level of giving.[229] Recognition within the community and business world is the main incentive, but luncheons and banquets are also given to honor members of the club.[230]

Palm Beach County, Florida, has an interesting way of raising money for the arts. In 1982, the county passed a local-option, tourism-development tax.[231] This took the form of a two percent hotel-motel tax that provides funds to promote tourism in the county.[232] The money collected from the tax is split, with 30 percent of the total going to Palm Beach County's arts programs.[233] This tax program is expected to provide over one million dollars per year in support to the arts.[234] This type of tax is popular because the tax is paid by visitors to the area, as opposed to residents, who reap the benefits.[235] The Palm Beach County Council of the Arts is the nonprofit organization in charge of distributing the funds.[236]

NOTES TO CHAPTER 43

1. Wm. K. Grasty & K.G. Sheinkopf, *Successful Fundraising*, introduction, citing Aristotle (1982).

2. See *supra*, Chapter 1 of this treatise.

3. *Id.* at §2.

4. David F. Long, *How to Organize and Raise Funds for Small Nonprofit Organizations* 3–4 (1979).

5. Grasty & Sheinkopf, *supra* n.1, at 19.

6. Proprietary to the United Press International, Dec. 27, 1991.

7. 3 *NonProfit Times* (12) 1 (March 1990).

8. *ESLM Quarterly*, 3 (Independent Sector, Summer 1988).

9. 6 *NonProfit Times* (3)22 (March 1992).

10. *NonProfit Times*, March, 1993.

11. See, Harmon, Curran & Townsley, *Tax Monthly for Exempt Organizations*, p. 1 (Dec. 1988); a Washington, DC law firm. See *IRS Publ.* 1391 (1988).
    See, Prentice Hall *Non-Profit Tax Letter*, bi-weekly ($9.95/mo., plus shipping).

12. Article, 3 *NonProfit Times* (2)3 (May 1989).

13. *Baltimore Arts Festival, Inc. v. Mayor and City Council of Baltimore*, 607 A.2d 1 (Md. 1992).

14. 64 So.Cal. Law Rev. 605 (March, 1991).

15. Keenan, (article) 6 *NonProfit Times* 6 (1) (June 1992).

16. *Chicago Tribune*, Dec. 7, 1992.

17. *Business First-Columbus*, Dec. 14, 1992.

18. Mcilquham, J., (article) 6 *NonProfit Times* (9) 1 (Sept. 1992).

19. *St. Petersburg Times*, p. B1, June 1, 1993.

20. 1 *Chronicle of Philanthropy*, April 18, 1989 at 25; 64 So.Cal. Law Rev. 605 (March, 1991).

21. *Boston Globe* (August 14 and 15, 1986); 64 So.Cal. Law Rev. 605 (March, 1991).

22. *(State) v. Caucus Distributors, Inc.* (a nonprofit corporation for Lyndon H. La Rouche, Jr.); affg. a cease and desist order; Alaska Supr. Ct. (June 15, 1990) 12 *Natl. L. J.* (43) 6 (July 2, 1990).

23. 1 *Chronicle of Philanthropy*, May 2, 1989 at 25 64 So.Cal. Law Rev. 605 (March, 1991).

24. J. Harper (article), p. 1, *St. Petersburg (FL) Times* (Oct. 18, 1990).

25. *Tampa Tribune*, March 19, 1993.

26. *Newspaper Publishing PLC, The Independent*, January 1, 1993.

27. *Financial Times*, January 20, 1993.

28. *Money* Magazine, May, 1992.

29. *Tampa Tribune*, April 5, 1993.

30. Shannon v. Telco Communications, Inc., 824 F. 2d 150 (1st Cir., Mass., 1987); Also, State ex rel. Olson v. W.R.G. Enterprises, 314 N.W. 2d 842 (N.D. 1982). See Section 413.

31. Dennis, L.B.: *The Limits of Giving: New Realities in Lean Times, Vital Speeches of the Day* (March 1, 1983) at 298.

32. Development Steering Committee of Major Orchestras, American Symphony Orchestra League Professional Development Seminar on Fund Raising, (1983).

33. Associated Press Report (N.Y. City) May 27, 1993.

34. McIlquham, article, 7 *NonProfit Times*, (6) 1, 27 (June 1993).

35. Carl Bakal, *Charity U.S.A.*, 39 (1979).

36. *Id.*

37. *Id.* at 77.

38. George Kirstein, *Better Giving: The New Needs of American Philanthropy*, 2 (1975).

39. Kirstein, *supra* at 3 [citing Jacques Barzun, *The House of Intellect* 180 (1959).]

40. Fred Schnaue, *Giving U.S.A.*, 42 (1980).

41. Grasty & Sheinkopf, *supra* n.1, at 4.

42. *Id.*

43. *Id.* at 5.

44. *Id.* at 7.

45. *Id.*

46. Long, *supra* n.4, at 170.

47. Grasty & Sheinkopf, *supra* n.1, at 12.

48. *Id.* at 16.

49. Tivnan, E.: *Bittersweet Charity: The High Cost of Fundraising*, (New York, August 15, 1983) at n.8 at 27.

50. McIlquham, J., 7 *NonProfit Times* (6) 3 (June 1993).

51. Grasty & Sheinkopf, *supra* n.1, at 20.

52. *Id.* at 21.

53. *Id.*

54. *Id.* at 22.

55. *Id.* at 76.

56. *Id.* at 22.

57. *Id.*

58. *Id.*

59. T.E. Broce, *Fund Raising*, 17 (1979).

60. *Id.* at 18.

61. Grasty & Sheinkopf, *supra* n.1, at 26.

62. *Id.* at 27.

63. 7 *NonProfit Times* (5) 38 (May 1993).

64. Fisher, B., 7 *NonProfit Times* (6) 1, 27 (June 1993).

65. Grasty & Sheinkopf, *supra* n.1, at 38.

66. Broce, *supra* n.59, at 21.

67. Grasty & Sheinkopf, *supra* n.1, at 44.

68. *Id.*

69. *Id.*

70. Broce, *supra* n.59, at 49.

71. *Id.* at 50.

72. Grasty & Sheinkopf, *supra* n.1, at 76.

73. *Id.*

74. *Id.* at 47–52.

75. 7 *Nonprofit Times* (2) 28 (Feb. 1993).

76. Grasty & Sheinkopf, *supra* n.1, at 99.

77. *Id.* at 100.

78. 7 *NonProfit Times* (4) 29 (April 1993).

79. 7 *NonProfit Times* (2) 28 (February 1993).

80. Bakal, *supra* n.35, at 339.

81. Dudar, Helen, Neither Snow, Nor Rain, Nor Gloom of Night Can Stop Sanky Perlowin, *Ms. Magazine* (April, 1980) at 54.

82. ————————————, Dear Friend, Send Money, *Changing Times* (August. 1982) at 56.

83. *Id.*

84. Grasty & Sheinkopf, *supra* n.1, at 127.

85. Mill Hollow Corp. *DM News,* March 9, 1992.

86. *Gannett News Service,* March 8, 1993.

87. T.W. Tenbrunsel, *The Fund Raising Resource Manual,* 165 (1982).

88. Grasty & Sheinkopf, *supra* n.1, at 159.

89. Address, I.S., Suite 1200, 1828 L. Street N.W., Washington, D.C. 20036.

90. Broce, *supra* n.59, at 137.

91. Grasty & Sheinkopf, *supra* n.1, at 217.

92. *Id.*

93. *Id.* at 230.

94. *Id.* at 231.

95. Broce, *supra* n.59, at 139.

96. Grasty & Sheinkopf, *supra* n.1, at 233.

97. Broce, *supra* n.59, at 138.

98. Grasty & Sheinkopf, *supra* n.1, at 234.

99. Broce, *supra* n.59, at 138.

100. Grasty & Sheinkopf, *supra* n.1, at 238.

101. *Id.* at 239.

102. Broce, *supra* n.59, at 46.

103. Grasty & Sheinkopf, *supra* n.1, at 241.

104. The Foundation Center, *The Foundation Directory* (M. Lewis, 8th ed., 1981).

105. Dennis, *supra* n.31, at 298.

106. Grasty & Sheinkopf, *supra* n.1, at 263.

107. Schnaue, *supra* n.40, at 15.

108. Tenbrunsel, *supra* n.87, at 124.

109. *Id.* at 125.

110. The Foundation Center, *Foundation Grants Index* (1983).

111. The Foundation Center, *Foundation Directory* (8th ed. 1981).

112. The Foundation Center, *Foundation Center Source Book Profiles* (8th ed. 1981).

113. Tenbrunsel, *supra* n.87, at 124.

114. *Id.*

115. Broce, *supra* n.59, at 118.

116. Grasty & Sheinkopf, *supra* n.1, at 272.

117. Robert Lefferts, *The Basic Handbook of Grants Management,* 50 (1983).

118. *Id.*

119. *Id.* at 51.

120. Tenbrunsel, *supra* n.87, at 88.

121. Superintendent of Documents, *Catalog of Federal Domestic Assistance* (Government Printing Office, curr. ed.).

122. Tenbrunsel, *supra* n.87, at 91.

123. *Id.* at 88.

124. Lefferts, *supra* n.117, at 52.

125. *Id.*

126. *Id.*

127. *Id.* at 52–53.

128. Virginia White, *Grants: How to Find Out About Them and What To Do Next,* (1975).

129. Lefferts, *supra* n.117, at 51.

130. *JL. v. Social Sec. Admin.,* 971 F. 2d 260 (9th Cir. (Cal.), 1992.).

131. *Sentara-Hampton General Hosp. v. Sullivan,* 980 F. 2d 749 (D.C. Cir., 1992).

132. *Association of Accredited Cosmetology Schools v. Alexander,* 979 F. 2d 859 (D.C. Cir., 1992).

133. *Atlanta College of Medical and Dental Careers, Inc. v. Alexander,* 792 F. Supp. 114 (D.D.C. 1992).

134. *Bella Lewitzky Dance Foundation v. Frohnmayher,* 754 F. Supp. 774 (C.D. Cal. 1991).

135. *United States v. Flake,* 783 F. Supp. 762 (E.D.N.Y. 1992).

136. *United States v. St. James Parish, Louisiana,* 792 F. Supp. 1419 (E.D. La. 1992).

137. 7 *NonProfit Times* (5) (May 1993).

138. Bush, B.H., 7 *NonProfit Times* (6) 8 (June 1993); *See also,* 7 *NonProfit Times* (4) 12 (April 1993).

139. 1984 Fla. Laws 84–310.

140. Fla. Stat. Chap. 496.

141. Fla. Stat. §496.03.

142. §496.03.

143. Fla. Stat. §496.406.

144. *St. Petersburg Times* (June 1, 1993).

145. Fla. Stat. §496.22.

146. K. Colton (article), 6 *NonProfit Times* (10)4 (Oct. 1992).

147. J. Harper, Deregulation of solicitors called a mistake, *St. Petersburg Times* (FL.), 1B (Feb. 4, 1991).

148. 5 *NonProfit Times* (2)1 (May 1991).

149. 7 *NonProfit Times* (3) 14 (March 1993).

150. 7 *NonProfit Times* (5), (3) (March, May, 1993).

151. *Id.*

152. N.Y. Executive Law §171-a-177.

153. N.Y. Executive Law §172.

154. §172-a.

155. §172-a(2)(b).

156. §172-a(2)(e).

157. §172-a(2)(f).

158. §173(1).

159. §175.

160. Ohio Rev. Code Ann. §1716.02.

161. §1716.02.

162. §1716.04.

163. §1716.03(A), (C)

164. §1716.03(D)

165. §1716.05.

166. §1716.99.

167. §1716.16

168. Bush, B.H., 7 *NonProfit Times* (6) 8 (June 1993).

169. Bush, B.H., 7 *NonProfit Times* (6) 8 (June 1993).

170. *Id.*

171. 7 *NonProfit Times* (5) 6 (May 1992).

172. 7 *NonProfit Times* (4) 8 (April 1993)

173. *City of Evanston v. Evanston Fire Fighters Assn.*, 545 N.E.2d 252 (Ill. App., 1989).

174. 3 *Non-Profit Times* (12) 5 (March 1990).

175. B.H. Bush, Regulation Watch, 5 *NonProfit Times* (8)6 (Nov. 1991).

176. 6 *NonProfit Times* (7) 4 (July 1992).

177. Tivnan, *supra* n.49, at 28.

178. 52 U.S.L.W. 4875 (1984); and *see* National Federation case in the preceding Section.

179. *Id.* at 4876.

180. *Id.*

181. *Id.*

182. 444 U.S. 620 (1980).

183. *Id.*; National Federation of the Blind v. Riley, 635 F. Supp. 256 (D.C., No. Car., 1986).

184. *Id.* at 635–638.

185. 456 U.S. 228 (1982).

186. *Id.* at 244–255.

187. *Id.* at 245–246.

188. *Id.*

189. 452 U.S. 640 (1981).

190. *Id.* at 642.

191. *Id.*

192. *Id.*

193. See, Harris, Holley & McC. article in 24 *U. of San Fran. L. Rev.* 571–652 (1990).

194. *Church of Scientology Flag Services Org., Inc. v. City of Clearwater,* 756 F. Supp. 1498 (M.D. Fla. 1991).

195. *Church of Scientology Flag Services Org., Inc. v. City of Clearwater,* 756 F. Supp. 1498 (M.D. Fla. 1991). The Clearwater ordinance modeled a Houston ordinance. *See, International Society for Krishna Consciousness v. City of Houston Tex.,* 689 F.2d 541 (5th Cir. Tex. 1982).

196. *People v. Nassau/Suffolk Neighborhood Network, Inc.,* 574 N.Y.S. 2d 243 (N.Y. Vill. Ct., 1991).

197. *Loper v. New York City Police Department,* 766 F. Supp. 1280 (S.D.N.Y. 1991).

198. *Famine Relief Fund v. State of W. Va.,* 905 F.2d 747 (4th Cir. (W. Va.), 1990).

199. *Auburn Police Union v. Tierney,* 756 F. Supp. 610 (D. Me. 1991).

200. *Association of Community Organizations for Reform Now v. St. Louis County,* 930 F.2d 591 (8th Cir. (Mo.), 1991).

201. *People by Abrams v. New York State Federation of Police Inc.,* 590 N.Y.S. 2d 573 (N.Y.A.D. 3 Dept., 1992).

202. *Port Authority Police Benev. Ass'n, Inc. v. Port Authority of New York and New Jersey Police Dept.,* 973 F. 2d 169 (3rd Cir. (N.J.), 1992).

203. *National Awareness Foundation v. Abrams,* 1993 U.S. Dist. Lexis 1435.

204. *Commonwealth of Penn. v. Cancer Fund of America, Inc.,* 620 A. 2d 647, (1993).

205. *City of Angeles Mission Church v. City of Houston,* 716 F. Supp. 982 (S.D. Tex. 1989).

206. *Young v. New York City Transit Authority,* 729 F. Supp. 341 (S.D. N.Y. 1990).

207. *Telco Communications, Inc. v. Barry,* 731 F. Supp. 670 (D.C. N.J. 1990).

208. *Project 80's, Inc. v. City of Pocatello,* 876 F.2d 711 (9th Cir. 1988) (commercial solicitors case).

209. *WRG Enterprises, Inc. v. Crowell,* 758 S.W.2d 214 (TN 1988).

210. *Indiana Voluntary Fireman's Association, Inc. v. Pearson,* U.S. Dist. Ct., IN, Nov. 29, 1988.

211. *Riley v. National Federation of the Blind of NC, Inc.,* 108 S. Ct. 2667 (1988); and see, *L. Blumenthal* (article) on U.S. Supr. Ct. (June 1988 decision) in 2 *NonProfit Times* (5)1 (Aug. 1988).

212. 7 *NonProfit Times* (2) 1 (Feb. 1993).

213. Associated Press report, *St. Petersburg Times,* p. 4B (Apr. 19, 1990).

214. *International Society for Krishna Consciousness, Inc. v. Lee,* 112 S. Ct. 2701 (U.S.N.Y., 1992); *Lee v. International Society for Krishna Consciousness, Inc.,* 112 S. Ct. 2709 (U.S.N.Y., 1992).

215. *Commonwealth by Preate v. Events Intern., Inc.,* 585 A.2d 1146 (Pa. Cmwlth. 1991).

216. *Fund for Community Progress, Inc. v. Kane,* 943 F.2d 137 (1st Cir. (R.I.), 1991).

217. *Simon and Schuster, Inc. v. Members of The New York Crime Victims Bd.,* 112 S. Ct. 501 (1991).

218. *Ball v. United Parcel Service, Inc.,* 602 A.2d 1176 (Md. 1992).

219. *Pilsen Neighbors Community Council v. Netsch,* 960 F.2d 676 (7th Cir. (Ill.), 1992).

220. Clurman, I., The Art of Solvency, *Horizon* (June, 1982) at 45.

221. *Id.* at 46.

222. *Id.*

223. *Id.* at 45.

224. Blomster, W., Diamonds and Firs, *Horizon* (June, 1983) at 49.

225. *Id.*

226. *Id.* at 50.

227. *Id.*

228. Golightly, B., The Five-Percent Solution, *Horizon* (Nov./Dec., 1983) at 37.

229. *Id.* at 38.

230. *Id.*

231. Forsthoffer, J.P., Taxes for Arts Sale, *Horizon* (Oct., 1984) at 41.

232. *Id.*

233. *Id.*

234. *Id.*

235. *Id.* at 42.

236. *Id.* at 41.

44

LAWSUITS AND LITIGATION

§444. CORPORATIONS AS PARTIES IN LAWSUITS

Litigation involving a *legal fiction*, such as a *corporate person* (entity) and the mirror image of individual persons who are its members (or, shareholders), is sure to become confused when it involves *constitutional* (human) rights. Above all, *procedural* law is bound to be complicated when one party is many persons at the same time. Although designation of a corporation as a party in a lawsuit now is simple under modern practice statutes,[1] the legal rights of members of the corporation, especially in civil rights matters, are now quite complex. For example, Fourteenth Amendment "due process" clause rules may make service of legal process a constitutional law question when a "foreign corporation" (out-of-state) resident business agent is served.[2] And it required a 1985 Congressional addition to the Equal Access to Justice Act[3] to allow nonprofit and public interest organizations (as well as small business firms) to receive attorneys' fees in civil suits in which they prevailed against unjustified governmental (administrative agency) oppression.[4]

Corporation litigation *procedure* is quite complex, in other words.[5] Often, today, interaction of state law with federal law is involved; *e.g.*, with the federal rules of civil procedure, which override state law that contradicts the federal rules, in many cases,[6] especially those that involve "securities"[7] or "diversity of citizenship."[8]

"The growing body of federal corporation law is tending to become stricter as most state corporate statutory standards become increasingly permissive."[9]

A corporation may invoke the attorney-client privilege of secrecy.[10] But a corporation (or unincorporated association, in many cases) may not appear "in person" in a legal proceeding, but must appear by a licensed attorney, except in a few minor kinds of cases, in almost all states.[11]

Even a *de facto* corporation can be sued, and usually can sue.[12] In federal courts, corporate capacity to sue or be sued is decided by the law of the state of incorporation.[13]

Failure to file reports, or failure of a foreign corporation to qualify (register) in the jurisdiction, may result in suspension of the capacity to sue or defend.[14]

The complaint against a corporate defendant, or by a corporate plaintiff, must state the corporate nature of the party, and in what state it was incorporated. A statement may be given "on information and belief" if the precise facts (dates, state) are not certainly known.[15] A statement that the party is a "foreign corporation" is sufficient, if true.[16]

Corporate stock in nonprofit organizations, operating social and recreational clubs, is subject to execution, levy, and sheriff's sale.[17]

Process ordinarily must be served on a corporation by personal delivery of a copy to an officer or managing agent within the state.[18] In most states the secretary-of-state may be the agent for this purpose.[19] Special rules apply to automobile accident lawsuits[20]—especially concerning foreign and "public" corporations—and in certain other matters.[21] Ordinary rules apply to *substituted service* by mail to, and other special procedures.

Litigation, process service, and procedure are especially complex for corporations. No detailed discussion of such legal practice and procedure is warranted here. Most of the rules of practice that apply to nonprofit corporations are those that apply to all corporations.

Local practice and procedure codes and texts, and works on corporations, should be consulted insofar as corporate parties to litigation are concerned.[22]

The organization, and not an individual member, ordinarily must be the party to enforce corporate rights.[23] But *see*, "Derivative Actions."

An NPO may sue in the corporation name in case involving a tradename.[24] See, S. Bachmann, *Nonprofit Litigation* (J. Wiley and Sons, N.Y.C., 1992), 425 pp., $95.

Attorney Fees and Attorneys

A nonprofit *corporation* for prevention of cruelty to children may appear *in propia persona* (itself) as its representative, and need not appear by attorney, when starting and carrying on a child-protection legal proceeding.[25]

A pastor cannot represent a church, on an appeal from an order enforcing fines for failure to file financial disclosures required by the Campaign Reform Act because, even if the church was a de facto corporation, the pastor was not a corporate officer. Also, the pastor was not an attorney and thus could not represent an unincorporated association.[26]

A corporation is *not* entitled to claim rights to utilize the courts "*in forma pauperis.*"[27]

A contract term, entitling a homeowners' association to "costs of collection" in litigation against a defaulting homeowner, includes attorney fees.[28]

The trial court has broad discretion to award attorney fees to legal service organizations that provide pro bono representation to indigent clients in matrimonial matters.[29]

Under the "equitable fund doctrine" an attorney may receive fees on considerations of *quantum meruit* and prevention of unjust enrichment if by instituting and pursuing successful litigation, he confers a benefit on a group or class of persons who hold a common fund. That doctrine may apply to actions taken to benefit taxpayers, such as a recent case where an attorney prevailed in a suit against nonprofits that were improperly exempted from payment of city water and sewer charges. However, the equitable fund doctrine does not apply to litigation necessary to get the fee. Such litigation does not provide any benefit to the city or the taxpayers.[30]

When a nonprofit news organization prevailed in its suit to access district court decisions, it was not entitled to attorneys fees under the Freedom of Information Act because the public benefit, afforded by the suit, was minimal, the publisher had personal motive to bring suit, and the government's position had a reasonable basis in the law.[31]

A group of personal care providers and residents of group homes, who successfully challenged a zoning exclusion of group homes from residential and agricultural districts, are not entitled to attorneys fees under the federal Civil Rights Attorney's Fees Awards Act or federal Fair Housing Act. A zoning appeal is not a "lawsuit" entitled to attorney's fees where it is part of an administrative agency process in common pleas court.[32]

Prevailing Civil Rights plaintiffs are entitled to reasonable attorney fees. The determination of reasonableness is made by reference to standards established in dealings between paying clients and the private bar.[33]

A city attorney may defend, without conflict, both a police officer and the city in a civil rights action against the city if the city agrees to indemnify the officer or takes positions consistent with the officer. However, police disciplinary proceedings should be referred to outside counsel.[34]

A nonprofit association, representing a self-insured municipality, can be required to pay for a city employee's independent counsel if the insured could be prejudiced by the insurer's representation. For example, the insurer might not vigorously defend a punitive damages claim against the insured if the insurer has excluded punitive damages through contract.[35]

If a derivative suit is based primarily on the corporate, rather than an individual, right, attorney fees are within the discretion of the court.[36]

Award of attorney fees may depend on the discretion of the trial judge, applies to corporate actions rather than individual members' suits, and requires compliance with procedural rules.[37]

Homeowners may be required to pay attorney fees in their association's enforcing an injunction about satellite dishes, where they had notice and opportunity to be heard before fees were awarded.[38]

SLAPP (Strategic Lawsuit Against Public Participation) suits, frivolous suits brought against public interest groups, can be discouraged by statutes that award sanctions and attorney's fees to the public interest groups that can prove that the SLAPP suits were frivolous.[39]

Petition for review of a corporate medicaid provider corporation may be *verified* by the corporation's attorney, and need not be verified only by an officer of the corporation.[40]

A nonprofit corporation, representing property owners, had sanctions, including the costs of preparing a motion for sanctions, as well as attorney fees, imposed against it for directing factually frivolous claims, and bad faith motions to strike or dismiss, in its action against a water district and its directors arising out of the district's imposition and continuation of a water hookup moratorium.[41]

The court must set forth specifically its reasons for the amount of attorney fees awarded.[42]

A nonprofit North Dakota Insurance Guaranty Association is liable to an attorney retained by an insolvent insurer for post insolvency attorney fees and expenses.[43]

In Florida, former directors who sue a nonprofit corporation seeking review of corporate records are entitled to attorney fees from the corporation.[44]

A charitable nonprofit child care organization, as beneficiary, sued to modify an accounting proceeding order fixed compensation for legal services to an estate. The court held that services that ordinarily could have been performed by the executor could not be considered in setting the amount of compensation for legal services to the estate.[45]

Nonprofit petitioners may waive the attorney-client privilege by putting privileged matters at issue in their affirmative defenses.[46]

[The rest of this subsection was contributed by Chris Likens.]

Attorney fees in NPO litigation follow the general guidelines set by courts and legislatures in general litigation matters. "Generally parties to litigation are responsible for their own Counsel fees and costs unless otherwise provided by statutory authority, agreement of parties, or some other recognized exception," *Wrenfield Homeowners Assoc., Inc. v. De Young*, 600 A.2d 960 (Pa.Super. 1991). Most of the case law in this area surrounds statutes and courts interpretations of the statutes.

It is first important to determine who is the attorney entitled to collect the fee. The Colorado Court of Appeals held that the prohibition against unlicensed legal representation does not impermissibly impinge upon the constitutional right to free exercise of religion when applied to prevent a pastor from representing his church. *People v. LaPorte Church of Christ* 830 P.2d 1150, 1152 (Colo. App. 1992) (Pastor could not represent his church on appeal from an order enforcing a fine for failure to file financial disclosures after church contributed to a political cause in violation of Campaign Reform Act).

In the past, counsel for NPO's have had the option of hourly or contingent fee agreements. When the litigation seeks injunctive or declaratory relief, hourly fee contracts are necessary, however when the NPO seeks damages contingent fees proved a convenient way to conduct the suit. The Supreme Court has substantially changed the legal landscape in this area in *City of Burlington v. Dague* 60 USLW 4717 (1992) (Fee shifting statutes in the Solid Waste Disposal Act do not permit fee enhancement of the fee award beyond the lodestar amount to reflect the fact that a parties attorneys were retained on a contingent-fee basis). Thus, attorneys will no longer be compensated for assuming the risk of contingent fee agreements, but instead will only be paid (if they are a prevailing party) on a lodestar concept.

By far, most of the cases deal with attorney fee awards under statutes. Most of the statutes provide for an award of fees if the plaintiff is the prevailing party.

> ... the Supreme Court has established certain contours regarding the threshold question of what constitutes a prevailing party.
>
> 1) Plaintiff must prevail on something concrete ...
>
> 2) Plaintiff must prevail on the final merits on the case ... interim issues will not suffice
>
> 3) Plaintiff may prevail through means other that a final judgment ... A happy settlement may make the plaintiff into a prevailing party[47]

A good example of fees pursuant to statute is *Athens County Property Owners Assoc., Inc. v. City of Athens*, 1992 WL 353859 (Ct. App. Ohio 1992), *stay granted* 607 NE 2d 654 (Ohio 1993), *jurisdiction overruled* 66 Ohio St. 3d 1459 (Ohio 1993). (Association brought action against city for failure to provide property records on computer diskette when city offered hard copy of records. Trial court's denial of fees to Association as prevailing party was abuse of discretion).

However, when pursuing an award of fees the NPO must be careful to comply with all of the requirements of the statute. When all of the provisions are not met, the courts will not award fees. *Biose Cent. Trades & Labor Council, Inc. v. Board of Ada County Commissioners* 831 P.2d 535 (Idaho 1992) (Labor council failed to send written demand 10 days prior to commencement of action, or bring action for damages, both being a precondition for an award of fees under the state statute). *Downey Community Hosp. v. Wilson et al* 977 F.2d 470 (9th Cir. 1992) (Award of attorneys fees under ERISA health benefits plan in action against hospital could not include costs of litigation in state court which was not brought under ERISA).

The NPO must also consider that the statutory provisions for an award of fees can be a double-edged sword. Courts may interpret statutes that are ambiguous to allow a successful defendant to collect fees and costs. *Cowiche Canyon Conservancy v. Bosley* 828 P.2d 549 (Wash. 1992) (award of fees to defendant as prevailing party under state statute). While "the statute is not a model of clarity ... if the legislature had intended an award of fees only to the prevailing Plaintiff, the reference to 'prevailing party' need not be in the statute at all." *Id.* at 560. *See also East Lizard Butte Water Corp. v. Howell* 837 P.2d 805 (Idaho 1992) (award of fees and costs based upon frivolous defense reversed upon finding that defense created a material issue of fact enabling reversal of summary judgment for plaintiff).

Courts have also demonstrated a great ability to interpret statutory language in fee cases. *Idaho Branch, Inc. of the Associated General. Contractors of America, Inc. v. Nampa Highway Dist. No. 1, et al* 846 P.2d 239 (Idaho App. 1993)(statutory language awarding fees "in any commercial transaction" held to include commercial transactions between the parties only, thus association's actions against highway districts for violation of state constitutional provisions in purchase of equipment was outside scope of statute). *See also Kleine-Albrandt v. Lamb* 597 N.E..2d 1310 (Ind. App. 5 Dist. 1992)(Nonprofit legal association entitled to award of fees as prevailing party even though the client did not incur any legal expense).

Courts may also look to the equities of the case in its determination. *The New York Times v. PHH Mental Health Services* 18 FLW S167 (Fla. 1993)(NPO acting on behalf of state agency who wrongfully denied access to records held not responsible to pay fees where court found statute was ambiguous and NPO acted in good faith).

NPO attorneys may also note who they can collect fees from in the event their client goes insolvent. *Zuger v. North Dakota Ins. Guar. Ass'n.* 494 N.W. 2d 135 (N.D. 1992)(Attorney retained by medical malpractice insurer to defend hospitals had no claim against hospitals after the insurer became insolvent). Generally, persons who have not contracted for legal services have no obligation to pay for those services, even though they receive benefit from them. *Id.* at 139.

Courts also place limits on the award of fees. Generally, the award is within the discretion of the judge, and the time will be analyzed as what is reasonable. *Wrenfield Homeowners Assoc. v. DeYoung* 600 A.2d 960 (Pa. Super. 1991). The judge will normally award fees only for the successful part of the litigation. *Mississippi State Chp. Operation Push v. Mabus* 788 F. Supp. 1406 (N.D. Miss. 1992)(NPO entitled to fees for initial litigation which resulted in determination of violations of Voting Rights Act, but no fee award for unsuccessful appeal of remedial legislation). *See also Soler v. G&U, Inc.* 801 F. Supp. 1056 (S.D.N.Y. 1992) (success under Federal Labor Standards Act by NPO representing migrant workers was limited as they failed to prevail on issue of housing, therefore award of fees based on that part of litigation was reduced on appeal).

The calculation of attorneys hours. is also restricted by the courts in certain instances. *Protect the Peninsula's Future v. Clallam County* 833 P.2d 406 (Wash. App. Div.2 1992) *rev. den.* 121 Wash. 2d 1011 (Wash. 1993)(Fees awarded to NPO limited to those incurred before settlement was reached with the county). Also, in *Soler v. G&U, Inc. supra,* the court reduced the award of fees where the attorneys had improperly commingled several activities under one time entry. Even where the court would normally award a fee if the activities were listed separately, by combining on time records activities such as "phone call" and "research", the court held that it could not carry out its function of evaluation of reasonableness. The court threw out over 73 hours of billable time.

While the judge has discretion in awarding fees, it is not unlimited discretion. *Korman v. Pond Apple Maintenance Ass'n, Inc.* 607 So.2d 489 (Fla. 4th

DCA 1992)(Trial court erred in not setting forth specifically how it arrived at award of fees to condominium association as prevailing party). *But see River Towers Ass'n. v. McCarthy* 482 N.W.2d 800 (Minn. App. 1992)(trial court could award fees to condominium association as prevailing party without requiring a detailed accounting, although appellate court noted that it generally advises against such practice).

Courts may also award fees pursuant to agreement between the parties. Many contracts provide for an award of fees to the prevailing party of litigation resulting from the contractual relationship. *Marshall v. Munro* 845 P.2d 424 (Alaska 1993) (fee award to prevailing party reversed where appellate court reversed portion of suit which made party a "prevailing party").

As with statutory interpretation, courts will interpret terms of the contract between the parties in its discretion. *Wrenfield Homeowners Assoc. v. DeYoung* 600 A.2d 960 (Pa. Super. 1991)(contract term entitling association to "costs of collection" included attorneys fees). The court, citing *Marrcinak v. Southeastern Green School Dist.* 544 A.2d 1025 (Pa. Super. 1988) noted "in construing a contract 'each and every part of it must be taken into consideration and given effect, if possible, and the intention of the parties must be ascertained from the entire instrument.' " *Id.* at 963.

Much of the current NPO attorney fees litigation arises in the west, perhaps due to the intense environmental battles which are currently being waged. It seems likely that other areas of the country will see more of this type of litigation as environmental groups continue to grow, and the federal government continues to assess its environmental policies and legislation. The award of attorney fees to a successful plaintiff is extremely important to most NPO's, most of which are not financial Goliaths. The trend seems to be a greater number of instances where fees can be awarded, limited by a restriction on the *amount* of fees awarded (*City of Burlington v. Dague, supra*) and in any event involving a closer scrutiny of the billing methods and what is considered *reasonable* under a lodestar concept. Just how costly this will prove to NPO's and their ability to successfully challenge existing and new legislation has yet to be determined.

Bars to Legal Action

A NPO association of electric-power plant organizations is not entitled to *intervene* in a "Clean Water Act" lawsuit brought by a private citizen.[48]

If a nonprofit organization's complaint in intervention is stricken because of the organization's failure to obtain counsel essential to prosecution, the suit is barred by res-judicata.[49]

The Attorney General is barred by res judicata from bringing suit to recover charitable assets donated by a religious organization, and allegedly used to form a corporation, where the religious organization had brought a similar proceeding that failed.[50]

A "statute of limitations" is one that limits the time in which a plaintiff may start action after the cause "accrues"; and a "statute of repose" is one that might bar an action before the cause "accrues" (e.g., a malpractice statute of 5 years, might expire before the plaintiff *discovers* that he was injured by a hospital or physician, and thus might bar access to the courts).[51]

A ten year statute of limitations barred recovery of damages for asbestos floors installed in 1976 and 1977 in a nonprofit North Carolina hospital.[52]

Negligence claims, made against nonprofit medical centers that provide "patient care," may be barred by a four year statute of limitations in Illinois.[53]

Laches bars an association of subdivision residents from claiming that they are entitled to an equitable easement over land where they knew, for nine years, that the developer had retained the disputed land and maps had been changed to preclude the inclusion of the land in the common area.[54]

An arbitration agreement should be interpreted so as to effectuate its purpose to minimize adversarial disputes. Thus, a proceeding by an Education Association against a Board of Education as to proper distribution of an "Excellence in Teaching" fund should be decided by the arbitrator rather than treated by the courts when the board tried to enjoin the association's request for arbitration under its collective bargaining agreement.[55]

A bill of review, to reinstate a case, is not warranted where the case is dismissed for failure to prosecute when the failure to act is due to some mistake on the part of office personnel, if the opposing party has done no wrong.[56]

"Voluntary cessation" of an action does not render a case moot unless the defendants can show lack of reasonable expectation of recurrence. However, the Forest Service's cancellation of a timber sale, challenged by environmental societies, is not "voluntary cessation" if prompted by the environmental groups' successful administrative appeal.[57]

Defamation of a group such as a corporation is actionable, as a *tort*, by the injured organization, but is actionable (as a tort) by individual members only if they are few enough (e.g., less than 60) to be individually identified and personally injured. *General attack* on a group such as "all lawyers" or "all doctors" or "all Catholics" usually is not actionable tort, although *criminal law* sanctions may be applied against the hate-monger in many jurisdictions.[58] Slander of an accrediting agency inspector is a tort. *Nazeri v. Missouri Valley College*, #75201, MO Supr. Ct., Aug. 17, 1993.

A nonprofit coalition is not entitled to declaratory or injunctive relief against a State Water Resources Control Board absent allegations that the Board's action caused or threatened to cause, injury to any particular person or entity.[59]

A condominium association's claim asking the court to decide whether the condo had adequately demonstrated negligence or misconduct of the contractor, so that it could terminate a contract alleged to be unfair, is a mere request for an advisory opinion, not a valid "cause of action."[60]

Damages

Nonprofit organizations were originally exempted from punitive damages in an 1846 case in England, *Feoffees of Heriot's Hospital v. Ross*, 8 Eng. Rep. 1508.

The *Heriot's* case established a general rule that nonprofits were *immune* from tort liability. Though England repudiated the rule later, American courts picked up the original decision and carried it forth to establish charitable immunity. In past decisions, immunity was denied if the nonprofit had insurance. But, an entity that was not insured could not be sued. And, if punitive damages were awarded as a result of outrageous conduct, insurance coverage was usually denied.

Currently, there is no common-law rule in America exempting religious or nonprofit organizations from punitive damage awards. Certainly, nonprofits *must not* be exempt from rules of reasonable societal behavior.[61]

Punitive damages may be awarded when there is fraud, actual malice, deliberate violence or oppression, when there is willful conduct, gross negligence or outrage, because of evil motive or reckless indifference to the rights of others. Such damages are not favored in the law.[62]

In Alabama, if an award of punitive damages is proper, a portion of that punitive damage award may not be allocated to a nonprofit organization or to an entity other than the plaintiff.[63]

Punitive damage are not available against a governmental entity in a breach of contract action. Loss of corporate value to the nonprofit that sued the government entity was not proved because the government could not have foreseen, at the time the contract was signed, that breach would cause the destruction of the nonprofit corporation.[64]

A $5 million punitive damages award against a religious corporation for infliction of mental anguish on a former member was excessive when that sum was one and a half times its total assets. This was not that outrageous. Reduced to $2 million.[65]

A university president may be held liable to an improperly dismissed professor for punitive damages (and so too the university itself).[66]

Torts of a charitable organization may be held to be actionable only to a stated ("cap") maximum award of damages, by statute; this is not unconstitutional in some states, but is in many states.[67]

There cannot be a $100,000 limit on damage claims against a charitable hospital while at the same time there is a $200,000 limit on all other charitable organizations, without violating equal protection.[68]

Security-for-costs rule in shareholder cases does not apply to NPO corporation.[69]

Jurisdiction

The charter of the American Red Cross authorizes it "to sue and be sued in courts of law and equity, State or Federal, within the jurisdiction of the United States." This charter clause grants original federal jurisdiction over a claim against the Red Cross brought by a patient who acquired the AIDS virus from blood supplied by the Red Cross.[70]

The "case or controversy" requirement of Article III of the Constitution requires that an association suffer some actual injury or face threatened injury, fairly traceable to the action challenged and likely to be redressed by favorable decision, before the federal court can exercise jurisdiction. A bar association has standing to challenge a state statute prescribing the number of judges on the superior court if it alleges that it is, in its own right, a civil litigant in the courts and has suffered inordinate delays in litigation due to the unconstitutionality of the statute and the shortage of judges available.[71]

The state Supreme Court lacks jurisdiction over a petition challenging the sale of public land where the decision to sell is not a final decree from a formal adjudicative proceeding.[72]

The Federal Communications Commission has jurisdiction over disputes between inter-exchange carriers and the nonprofit corporations, that were formed to perform services for local telephone companies, following the breakup of AT&T.[73]

A New York corporation that acts as agent for a foreign corporation is covered by the New York long-arm statute as to jurisdiction; so is a church for sexual abuse by its agent.[74]

New York has no personal jurisdiction over a New Hampshire Insurance Guarantee Association, standing in the shoes of an insolvent New Hampshire Insurer involved in litigation in New York.[75]

A Canadian corporation attending a trade show in Illinois annually, to take orders for fishing lodges reservations, is not "doing business" there for court jurisdiction purposes.[76]

Citizens suits against strip mines, brought under the Surface Control and Reclamation Act, must be brought in the district in which the complained of mine is located. The requirement cannot be waived by consent or actions of the parties.[77]

Parties

A damages lawsuit against a condo unit owner does not require that the homeowners association also be named as a party defendant, even when the unit owner is the president of the association who wrongfully had a car owned by a visitor to the condo towed away.[78]

A school (college) is not entitled to sue a student loan program corporation (that had federal guaranty support) for violation of that corporation's contract with a college student.[79]

Due Process

An incorporated homeowner's association whose common streets and areas are subjected to a foreclosure action is not entitled to the same statutory notice provisions as apply to private individuals under Oklahoma Mechanics and Materialmen's lien laws.[80]

A formal hearing must be held before the HRS can withhold Medicaid reimbursements from a nonprofit hospital to collect unpaid revenue assessments.[81]

The Department of Health and Human Services may not terminate or reduce financial assistance, to a nonprofit Head Start Program, without notice and a hearing.[82]

An order, by the Director of Water Resources, that denied the right of an association of farmers to start a water diversio project to replenish ground water, affects the association's substantial rights in a special proceeding. Thus, the order is final and appealable when entered, even though the Director retained jurisdiction over the matter.[83]

A nonprofit public interest group, that intervened in a products liability suit against a manufacturer of breast implants, is not entitled to an order requiring the filing of, and access to, all discovery materials, where a confidentiality agreement and protective order, entered into by the parties, exists, and where relevance and admissibility has not been demonstrated.[84]

The county's notice of a public hearing, on a proposal to purchase and lease a horse racing track, must only substantially comply with the notice statute. The county need not inform the taxpayers of the true nature of a lease-purchase agreement.[85]

Venue

Where a corporate venue statute indicates that a corporation's residence or location shall be deemed to be where its registered office is maintained, venue is proper in the county of the registered office for both profit and non-profit corporations.[86]

Administrative Review

A circuit court must vacate or modify agency decisions if the substantial rights of the party seeking review are prejudiced by findings, inferences, conclusions, or decisions of the order or if the order violates statutory or constitutional provisions, exceeds agency authority or jurisdiction, or represent abuse or clearly unwarranted exercise of discretion. The agency order also must not be made upon unlawful procedures, be affected by other error of law, or be clearly wrong in view of the evidence on the whole record.[87]

Judicial review under California's Environmental Quality Act (CEQA) is limited to whether the agency has abused its discretion by not proceeding as required by law or by making a determination not supported by substantial evidence.[88]

A nonprofit claimant need not exhaust its administrative remedies if it can show that an administrative remedy would be patently inadequate, exhaustion of remedies would be futile, or that grave irreparable harm would result from requiring exhaustion of administrative remedies.[89]

A State Board of Examiners may vote to delay the issuance of bonds to fund cultural projects if its decision is discretionary and reasonable. Such a decision does not warrant a writ of mandamus to force the issuance of the bonds.[90]

When a city council recites in its minutes that there is a consensus that a conditional use permit, that has not been put to use within one year from approval date, is still valid, that recitation is not a reviewable interpretation of a local ordinance. Thus, the Land Use Board of Appeals must remand such a local land use decision back to the local government for interpretation.[91]

An association may not demand that a public official perform his duty through mandamus unless it first makes an express and distinct request that the official perform the duty.[92]

An administrative hearing by the Illinois Racing Board, that denied a horsemen's association the racing dates it wanted, violated the association's due process rights when the track involved was given evidence after the hearing was half over, allowed only an hour lunch break to examine evidence, and not allowed to address competitors' contentions, or to cross-examine other participants.[93]

FORM NO. 176

Attorney-Retainer Agreement
[Based on a retainer of a law firm to represent a Police Officers' Association]

AGREEMENT effective July 1, 19 _____ , between the _____ Police Officers' Association, a Not For Profit _____ Corporation, which is also an organization of commissioned employees of the _____ Metropolitan Police Department, hereinafter called the Client, and _____, hereinafter called the Attorneys.

1. The Client hereby retains and employs the Attorneys, and the Attorneys hereby accept the retainer and employment upon the terms and conditions hereinafter set forth.

2. The term of this Agreement shall begin on July 1, 19 _____, and shall terminate on June 30, 19 _____.

3. For all services rendered by the Attorneys under this Agreement relating to the organizational and business matters of the _____ Police Officers' Association and intradepartmental police matters of the members of the Association, the Client shall pay the Attorneys for the following retainer fees:

For Services Performed between July 1, 19 _____ and June 30, 19 _____– $3,000.00 per month.

For Services Performed between July 1, 19 _____ and June 30, 19 _____– $3,250.00 per month.

For Services Performed between July 1, 19 _____ and June 30, 19 _____– $3,500 per month.

Matters included within the monthly retainer shall include appearances by members of the Client before the Board of Police Commissioners, the Retirement Board and State and Federal Grand Juries, and shall also include services in connection with citizen appeal hearings. Moreover, Attorneys agree to attend monthly Executive Board meetings, occurring on the 3rd Saturday of the month for the purpose of updating and answering questions of the Executive Board regarding pending and prospective cases and Client agrees to place Attorneys on the top of its agenda for this purpose.

The above paragraph pertaining to retainer matter shall be subject to the following proviso:

> Within 60 days after any change in present circumstances which has the effect of providing the _____ Metropolitan Police Officers with collective bargaining and binding arbitration, the Attorneys and representatives of the Client shall renegotiate the terms of this retainer agreement. Said renegotiation shall take into consideration any anticipated change in the duties, responsibilities and expenditure of time occasioned by reason of said change in circumstances.

Additionally, the Association shall furnish to the Attorneys the number of active dues paying members on the date of the execution of the Agreement and thereafter shall report the number of active dues paying members every six months. If the number of dues paying members at any six month reporting date differs from the number on the effective date of this Agreement, the retainer shall be adjusted upward 5 percent for each additional 75 members and shall be reduced 5 percent for each decrease of 75 members. These adjustments shall be computed against the retainer fee then in effect and the new retainer fee shall be in effect for six months until the next report of membership to the Attorneys, when the retainer shall again be set using the most recent report of active dues paying members to compute an adjustment to the retainer for the next six months.

4. The Attorneys shall be authorized to perform all services on behalf of the Client or its members upon the direction of the President or Chairman of the Legal Committee of Client Association. For all services rendered by the Attorneys under this Agreement relating to all matters other than those specified in Paragraph 3, above, the Client shall pay the Attorneys on the basis of the amount of time spent on such matters, at the following hourly rate:

For Services Performed by partners between July 1, 19 ____ and June 30, 19 ____–$80 per hour.

For Services Performed by partners between July 1, 19 ____ and June 30, 19 ____–$85 per hour.

For Services Performed by partners between July 1, 19 ____ and June 30, 19 ____–$90 per hour.

For Services Performed between July 1, 19 ____ and June 30, 19 ____ by associates of the Attorneys–$75 per hour except that if during the period July 1, 19 ____ and June 30, 19 ____ the Attorneys increase their associates' customary hourly rate generally for all other clients of the Attorneys, that same increase will apply to the Client _____ Police Officers' Association to the extent that the associates' rate does not exceed the partners' rate for the year in which the associates' rate is increased.

Additionally, the Attorneys will prepare and furnish to members of the Client Association and their spouses, Wills of a non-complex nature for a charge of $25 per Will. An additional charge will be made for Wills of a complex nature, and arrangements will be made with the individual member requesting the Will regarding such additional charges prior to the preparation of such Wills.

5. Furthermore, when the Attorneys, by mutual agreement, are engaged by members of the Client or their immediate families on personal legal matters, the Attorneys shall provide services at a rate not to exceed 75 percent of their regular billing rates in effect at the time said services are rendered on matters normally billed at hourly rates and on personal injury matters, undertaken on a contingent fee basis, shall provide services at a rate not to exceed 25 percent of the gross recovery on matters settled without litigation and 30 percent of the gross recovery after a lawsuit has been filed. However, nothing contained in this paragraph (Number 5) shall be construed to require members of the Client to utilize the services of the Attorneys on personal matters nor to require the Attorneys to undertake said matters.

6. Attorneys shall provide Client with a monthly statement setting forth the nature of the matter with the services rendered, the date or dates thereof, and the charges for the time devoted to such matters, and payment shall be made within 30 days after the receipt of said statement.

7. The Attorneys are authorized to incur reasonable expenses attendant upon the handling of Client's matters, including but not limited to the ordering of copies of reports and other documents, photocopying of papers, court costs, photographs, preparation of transcripts, printing of briefs and long distance telephone calls. The Client will reimburse the Attorneys for all expenses upon the presentation by the Attorneys, from time to time, of an itemized account of such expenditures.

8. The rights and obligations of the Client under the Agreement shall inure to the benefit of and shall be binding upon the successors and assigns of the Client and any Association or organization which may result from a reorganization or redesignation of the Client's current status as a Not For Profit Corporation, or the creation of or affiliation with a labor organization.

9. This instrument contains the entire Agreement of the parties. It may not be changed orally, but only by an Agreement in writing signed by the party against whom enforcement of any waiver, change, modification, extension or discharge is sought.

IN WITNESS WHEREOF, the parties have executed this Agreement on the _____ day of _____, 19 ____.

ATTEST: _____ POLICE OFFICERS'
                                                         ASSOCIATION, a Corporation

(Seal)

_____   By _____
Secretary   President

                                                         _____(Attorneys)

                                         By _____

§445. UNINCORPORATED ASSOCIATIONS AS PARTIES IN LAWSUITS

The vague legal status of unincorporated associations causes great difficulties. Some of these difficulties are discussed in Chapter 5. The lack of legal "entity" or "personality" is the root of most of the trouble. (See the next section and Chapter 5.)

When litigation of any kind is the problem, the rules governing unincorporated associations are complicated. A good article by Nolen L. Brunson of the South Carolina Bar, in the *South Carolina Law Quarterly*, required 30 pages of terse summary to *sketch* the principal problems.[94] And this article, which considered both profit and nonprofit associations, made no pretense of covering all the ramifications!

The literature on the subject is not extensive and is in the last analysis rather inconclusive.[95] Special kinds of associations (such as mutual benefit associations, boards of trade, or trust groups) themselves are so specialized as to be subject in most states to special statutes.[96] A trust, of course, may as a general rule sue or be sued in the trustee's name. Brunson, in his discussion, simply dismisses trusts as too specialized to warrant discussion. He concentrates on labor unions, fraternal orders, and churches. He also eliminates federal matters: the Federal Rules of Civil Procedure[97] make state law determinative if the suit is in the federal court only for jurisdictional reasons. Under the Federal Rules, associations may sue or be sued in the association name for the purpose of enforcing, for or against it, a substantive right existing under the Constitution or the laws of the United States.[98]

States have adopted many and varied statutes on procedure in litigation involving unincorporated associations. Limitations of space prevent their full discussion here. Reference should be made to such scholarly and detailed studies as that of Brunson, mentioned above.[99]

Joinder of parties. Because an unincorporated association is a group of individuals—not a legal entity—at common law, the use of *class actions* (*i.e.*, one person acting for all of the members of the class or group) is the fundamental procedural device. Suit in the name of the association, or against it by name, is impossible at common.[100] It is generally held, however, that failure to raise the question of the capacity of the association to sue or be sued in its own name is a waiver of the objection, and such an objection cannot be raised for the first time on appeal.[101] It has also been held that an unincorporated association which has held itself out as capable of contracting in the association name is estopped when sued on its contract, or for negligence in performing the contract, to assert that it is not capable of being sued in such name.[102]

Statutes now expressly authorize such class actions in many states[103] and in the federal courts.[104]

In some states statutes also permit "class action" suit in the common name by or against any groups of persons associated and carrying on transactions in that common name.[105] Some states have similar statutes that permit such actions *by*, as well as against, such associations, in the common name, if they carry on activities.[106] In England and most states, an unincorporated association may sue or be sued in the common name just as if it were a corporation.[107] Today the law favors this view.

A *statute* allowing unincorporated associations to sue or be sued in their own names is *prospective*; no presumption of retroactivity is spelled out merely by statements of the sponsors of the legislation; in a *substantive* statute such as this.[108]

If common interests are present, an unincorporated association (hunters using a camp regularly, and socializing) may be liable as an entity, for negligence of its servants in giving whiskey to one who injured the victim.[109]

A nursing home's association (*un*incorporated *or* incorporated) has standing to sue on behalf of its members who otherwise could sue on their own, about an association's interests, where individual participation is not required; but not on behalf of parties that are not members nor equivalent-to-membership parties.[110]

A *member* of an unincorporated association, injured by tort of another member (church member placing a ladder) may not sue the association for damages, in Indiana; old rule continued.[111] But members may sue their unincorporated association in other states.[112]

"An association may have standing (to sue) solely as the representative of its members."[113]

In most states statutory remedies are viewed as additions to the method of common law class suit.[114] But in a few states the statutory remedies are said to be exclusive.[115] The justification for this latter view is hard to see.

Under some of these statutes, the association must have carried on some activities ("done business") in the state before the common-name-action-right can arise. In other states no such preliminary activity need have occurred.[116] This latter rule is found, usually, where the statute authorizes the designation of a single representative (officer) to sue or be sued in the name of the association.[117] One type of statute implies that *all the members* are being sued, while the other implies that suit is against the *entity.*

Venue. Insofar as *venue* is concerned, the type of statute would seem to decide whether suit should be brought in the association's home county (where the representative is) or in any county (where a member is). But the law is very vague on this point.[118]

Of course, suit usually may be brought in the county where the cause of action arose.

Service of process. Under the common law rules, legal process must be served on each member if he is to be bound.[119] But where suit by or against a representative is authorized, service on the representation binds all the members.[120] Sometimes the statutes permit service to be made on others besides the named representative.[121] In other cases, service on any member may suffice, if it is such service and on such a person as to reasonably assure adequate notice to the association's members.[122]

Enforcement of judgment. Enforcement of claims in debtor-creditor relations is far too complicated to permit more than the merest outline here. For these matters, reference should be made to specialized works.[123]

It is generally held that only those members personally served with process are personally bound in action against an unincorporated association, when the action is "at law" for a money debt.[124] It has been held that in a class action liability attaches only to common assets.[125]

In equity proceedings, where a specific order, decree, or injunction is granted in a representative (class) action, all the members are bound.[126]

In some states (but not all) the personal service on representatives makes them personally liable.[127] And the jointly owned association property is bound by a judgment against the association.[128]

In many states, even where statutes permit action against the association in its common name, the personal liability of the members on a money judgment is not barred.[129] If the association assets are insufficient to satisfy the judgment, a new action usually must be brought against individual members, on the basis of the first judgment.[130] And statutes then usually permit such personal action only if the member being sued had authorized or ratified the act that formed the basis of the original claim.[131] If this collection action is successful, the member may be able to obtain contribution from other members by joining them in the suit as parties defendant, or by separate suit. His right to contribution will then be governed by the law of torts, or of contracts, or of other law applicable to the original transaction. As to this, see the discussions of liabilities of officers, members, agents, and others elsewhere herein. As to rights to contribution or indemnity, see the standard works on torts, contracts, negotiable instruments, or whatever other law applies to the case.

Suggested statute Nolen L. Brunson, whose article is mentioned previously,[132] has suggested a draft uniform statute to cover these matters. His proposed statute would read as follows:

Suit: An action may be commenced against an unincorporated association in any county in which the association does business, or has an agent, or maintains an office.

Process: Service of process upon an unincorporated association doing business in this state may be had upon any agent of the association.

Judgment: Execution of a judgment against an unincorporated association may be levied against its property, or the joint property of its members.

Upon the return of execution levied upon the joint property unsatisfied, individual property of the members may be levied upon as follows:

1. If the member is a nonresident, by a new action commenced against him by regular process and service of summons, or seizure of his property by attachment.

2. If the member is a resident, by a notice served upon him personally after judgment, apprizing him that at a stated time and place, a motion will be made to enter judgment against him personally.

At the new and subsequent proceeding, whether it is the new action under (1) or (2), the prior judgment against the association shall be *res judicata* as to matters actually litigated therein.

To this proposed statute, there is suggested only one change, insofar as nonprofit associations are concerned. In the first clause (on *suit*), the words *does business* might better be *carries on activities.*

Finally, the writer of this book urges (with no real expectation of acceptance) a more sweeping proposal. This is simply to require that all nonprofit organizations be incorporated—excepting perhaps a few, special, very small, local ones.[133] Thereby, most of the vast study already applied to corporations could be turned to the benefit of nonprofit organizations. This move would, with one blow, cut through most of the artificial knots into which unincorporated associations have been tied. (See the next section.)

§446. NONPROFIT UNINCORPORATED ASSOCIATIONS AS LEGAL ENTITIES

[See Chapter 5.]

[This section is a shortened, updated version of the note by Oleck, entitled, "Nonprofit Associations as Legal Entities," 13 Cleve.-Mar. L. Rev. 350.]

Unincorporated associations long have been a problem to the law. They are analogous to partnerships, and yet not partnerships; analogous to corporations, and yet not corporations; analogous to joint tenancies, and yet not joint tenancies; analogous to mutual agency, and yet not mutual agency.[134] The most baffling of all are the nonprofit unincorporated associations.

Piecemeal attempts to make legal order and sense of these organizations have not solved the basic question. Thus statutes requiring the filing of certificates of doing business under an assumed name treat a symptom, not the problem itself.[135]

Modern studies of the subject express the same bafflement as did earlier studies, plus growing impatience with the slovenly law that permits such uncertainty to continue so long. For example, the application of constitutional rights to associations has involved the question of whether or not they are "persons" (*i.e.*, "legal entities") for purposes of the privilege against self-incrimination.[136] Certainly the drafters of the Constitution could not foresee the modern proliferation of associations, both incorporated and unincorporated.

Straightforward legislative attempts to force associations to settle into some specific form (*e.g.*, corporate entity) have been futile. Thus a Colorado statute requiring labor unions to incorporate was held to be unconstitutional as an unlawful invasion of "freedom of speech" and of "freedom of assembly."[137] This contrasts strangely with the common requirement that a national bank, for example, must be a "body corporate," as must other banks, insurance "companies," or public utilities.[138]

A helpful appellate decision in Ohio was the case of *Miazga v. International Union of Operating Engineers, A.F.L.-C.I.O., Local 18.*[139]

In the *Miazga* case, the plaintiff and other members sued the union (a nonprofit unincorporated association) for damages for defamation. The defense was the usual demurrer, based on the usual argument that a member of an unincorporated association is a co-principal in a joint enterprise, and thus in effect sues himself if he sues the association. The defense cited a long line of cases so holding.

Judge Skeel pointed out that, since 1955, Ohio's statutes have provided that an unincorporated association may contract or sue to be sued "as an entity" under its own name.[140] Such provisions are now found in many states.[141]

Ohio's statute seemingly permits execution only against the assets of the association but has been interpreted otherwise,[142] while some statutes expressly permit execution also against assets of members in some situations.[143]

Judge Skeel then referred to the common law origin of the theory of non-liability in the law of partnership.[144] He said that, while this may be reasonable for small unincorporated associations, it is "completely outmoded" for a labor union consisting of thousands of members.[145]

He then ruled that "such as association . . . should be like any other corporate entity, held legally responsible as an association in a proper case for injuries inflicted by its wrongful acts not only to members of the public but to its members as well." He pointed out that the use of the legal fiction of legal entity of an organization has been, and still is, determined by the courts rather than by legislative action, and that there is no statutory provision to this effect even as to corporations in Ohio or in most states.[146] Judicial control of the actions of private associations fills what otherwise would be a vacuum in the law.[147]

The Ohio Supreme Court affirmed the *Miazga* decision and held that under Chapter 1745 a member of an unincorporated association has the right to sue his union as an entity.[148] This doctrine was expanded in *Tanner v. Loyal Order of Moose*.[149] In *Tanner* the Ohio Supreme Court gave the broadest possible interpretation to the language of Chapter 1745, by deciding that any unincorporated association may sue or be sued by members or nonmembers as a legal entity.[150]

Prior efforts to solve the problem have employed various devices to fasten liability on unincorporated associations, such as the concept of conspiracy.[151] Some courts have held a union to be not liable for injury done by a member,[152] while others have held it to be liable.[153] Under federal labor law, unions are considered to be legal entities; under bankruptcy law a nonprofit association may go into voluntary bankruptcy as an entity.[154]

Many states have applied to nonprofit associations the *co-principal doctrine,* which treats them as partnerships, imputing negligence from one member to another, including the injured member himself.[155] There is some logical basis for this only in the case of a small organization, not in the case of a large one.[156] A large group (Temple of the Mystic Shrine) was held to be liable for an injury to a member.[157] In labor union cases the doctrine has been invoked frequently.[158]

As to unions, the tendency has been to hold them liable for intentional acts.[159] So, too, if a union owes a duty of representation to a member,[160] but not if a matter of business judgment is involved.[161]

The *Tanner* case, and its conclusion that all unincorporated nonprofit associations shall be treated as legal entities, is wise and sound. This view will require clarification of the status of officers, trustees, and members, *vis-a-vis* each other and *vis-a-vis* third persons. The constitutional problem of privilege of an association against self-incrimination is a good example of the problems involved even as to incorporated associations.[162] It is now to be settled whether or not corporate norms or some other standards shall be applied to internal and external relations or unincorporated nonprofit associations.

A member of an unincorporated church was allowed to sue his own "partnership" for tortious actions (negligence) of an association agent in *Joseph v. Calvary Baptist Church*, 500 N.E.2d 250 (Ind. App. 1986); but this is the minority view. *See* 7 C.J.S. Associations §51 and cases cited therein; and *Edwards v. Natl. Speleological Soc., Inc.*, 502 S.2d 337 (Ala. 1987); *Leppert v. Lakebreeze Homeowners Assn., Inc.*, 500 S.2d 250 (Fla. 1st DCA, 1986); *American Legal Foundation v. F.C.C.*, 808 F.2d 84 (C.A., D.C., 1987).

§447. DERIVATIVE ACTIONS AND CLASS ACTIONS

[See, Section 490.]

In corporations, when a dissident (minority) member of the corporation is not able to obtain justice within the corporation's rules and procedures, he may be able to invoke court intervention in order to obtain justice. His (or her) right to have the court support his claim by acting as one who *derives* his rights from the failure of the usual corporation authorities that act properly, is called a *derivative action*. Only the members of a nonprofit corporation have standing to bring a derivative action.[163] There is a large body of law about this subject in business corporation (shareholder) cases,[164] and New York specifically allows such suit by five percent of the members in nonprofit corporations.[165]

A *derivative suit* is an action based on injury to the corporation (and thus to the member)—to enforce a corporate right—wherein the corporation itself is joined as a necessary party defendant, and recovery of a judgment is in favor of (and for) the corporation.[166] Demand for action by the directors usually is a condition precedent, before members may act to bring suit.

A *personal action* is one brought by the member for direct injury to his *individual* rights, such as a denial of his right to inspect books and records.[167]

A *class action* (or, *representative* action) is one in which one or more members of a class (*e.g.*, such as a number of shareholders or members who are denied the same personal right) sue for themselves or for all to whom the right was denied.[168]

In order to bring a derivative action the member (shareholder) must show his current (at time of wrong) interest in the corporation, a demand for action by the directors unless such demand obviously would have been futile,[169] his "equity" position in the matter, his representative quality in bringing suit, and (in some states) his ability to post security for the expenses of the defendant(s) if his claim is unwarranted.[170]

The many problems involved in derivative and/or class actions are mainly encountered in business corporation (shareholder) matters; and they are mainly matters of practice and procedure, largely governed by practice acts rather more than corporation (especially nonprofit corporation) law.[171]

In order to bring a derivative action for the benefit of a nonprofit corporation, the plaintiff must first have membership status.[172]

Plaintiffs have standing to bring a derivative action to challenge the propriety of actions taken by a board of directors of a nonprofit corporation, as equitable shareholders, even if they are not shareholders of record and have not received the shares they claim they are entitled to by operation of law, under the probate code.[173]

Representational Standing

According to the U.S. Supreme Court, an organization must meet a three pronged test in order to have representational standing to sue on behalf of its members. It must establish that "(a) its members would otherwise have standing to sue in their own right; (b) the interests it seeks to protect are germane to the organization's purpose; and (c) neither the claim asserted nor the relief requested requires the participation of individual members in the lawsuit."[174]

In order to maintain a taxpayer's action to set aside a contract between a nonprofit corporation and a county board of supervisors, a taxpayer must establish taxpayer status and allege an official act which causes waste or injury, imperils public interest, or is calculated to work public injury, or to produce some public mischief.[175]

A nonprofit refugee center and Antonio Diaz as representative of a *class* sued to enjoin enforcement of a municipal ordinance prohibiting solicitation of employment from a vehicle or by a pedestrian on a public street. The court held that the ordinance did not violate the First Amendment right of free expression and was not overbroad.[176]

Citizens groups, such as those active in enforcing environmental (clean air) regulations, must show how they are affected by *state administrative agency rulings* in specific cases in which they wish to *intervene.*[177]

An organization of insurance agents may validly request the state Commissioner of Insurance to have an administrative hearing as to (unlawful) selling of insurance by banks.[178]

A party may join (or start) legal action if he/she/it can show *sufficient stake* (standing) in an otherwise justiciable issue; *e.g.,* "personal" actual or threatened harm. This is a jurisdictional issue. Thus, "pro-choice" parties may *not* sue the Catholic church as to its tax exemption for its political action in elections of only anti-abortion candidates for public office, because only the I.R.S. may object to tax-exemption violations (or the Attorney General).[179]

[Mia M. Snyder did research for the rest of this subsection.]

An individual or association seeking to join with a party in a lawsuit, because they are "interested" in the result of that suit, must show "standing" (under Article 3 of the Constitution); e.g., that he/she/it will be seriously affected by the outcome of the suit. The nature of the claimant's interest (the party), rather than the issue itself, is the critical concern.[180]

Thus the "Coalition of Mental Health Professions" had "standing" to intervene in administrative proceedings of a state agency in a proposal of new rules to govern clinical social workers and counselors.[181]

But a Society of Ophthalmology and the state Medical Association were not sufficiently "substantially affected" to challenge elimination of a rule authorizing optometrists to administer certain topical eye drugs; had no "standing" as to that.[182]

National Federation of Federal Employees did not have standing to challenge the Army's decision to use private contractors, instead of employees of the Fort Sill Directorate of Logistics, to perform certain supply functions; the Federation was only "marginally" affected.[183]

In a suit by a private citizens' group under the Clean Water Act, the group organization must give 60 day prior notice before bringing the legal action.[184]

The League of Latin American Citizens brought action under the Voting Rights Act to challenge certain Texas counties' at-large method of electing trial judges. When the League lost the suit, an intervening state trial judge was denied attorney's fees because the League's action was not frivolous, unreasonable or without foundation. Attorney's fees are only awarded to those who participated in order to establish and rectify a violation of civil rights.[185]

An oceanfront property owners association challenged a Department of Environmental Protection amendment that reduced the Departments territorial scope of regulation on the water front and extended the waterfront permit requirements to inland properties. The court held the amended rule invalid because it exceeded the Waterfront Development Act's underlying purpose of regulating commerce along the waterfront.[186]

A local florists trade association did have standing to challenge an adverse ruling (allowing Mexican producers of cut flowers to "dump" their goods in the United States) by the International Trade Commission.[187]

Jai-Alai players' association does not have enough "standing" (direct injury to it or its members) to contest an application of fronton owners to the Florida Pari-Mutuel Commission for changes in playing dates. Such speculative remote injury to players is not the kind that such a Commission is designed to protect.[188]

A nonstock hospital corporation, along with other institutional healthcare providers, brought action claiming that their exclusion from a health insurer's preferred provider organization was unreasonable, discriminated against providers and violated Virginia's statute. The court held that a selection procedure based on price negotiations did not unreasonably discriminate among providers.[189]

§448. INDEMNIFICATION OF OFFICERS AND DIRECTORS

[See Chapter 28, Section 288; and also Section 433.]

Litigation expenses of officers and directors are summarized above, in Section 288. Today the right to such indemnification, and its conditions, are largely treated in statutes in most states, especially as regards business corporations. In recent years, a big increase in lawsuits against officers and directors of nonprofit corporations has made the subject an important one to them as well.[190]

The Model Nonprofit Corporation Act (1986 Draft) adopts the view that directors of a nonprofit corporation are akin to business corporation directors more than to trustees.[191] This Model Act[192] includes civil and criminal proceedings, and includes counsel fees as well as other expenses of directors and directors acting as agents or employees of others on behalf of his corporation.[193] *Good faith* is the main test of protection by this statute.[194] Advances as well as reimbursements of expenses are covered.[195] Both mandatory and court-ordered indemnification are covered.[196] Board vote is required on indemnification, or approval by special counsel of the board.[197] Officers and employees and agents are included.[198] Bylaws must be consistent with this Model[199] (*sic*). And insurance coverage may be bought by the corporation.[200]

But sometimes such indemnification is against public policy, as in a case of negligent approval of false statements in a securities issue circular,[201] or false statements in an insurance application.[202]

See also, as to "D and O Insurance," Section.

§449. CONSTITUTIONAL PROBLEMS IN NPO LITIGATION

[See, section 442, and the Index.]

Collisions between state corporation and practice law, and constitutional rights, have been numerous in nonprofit organizations litigation in recent years.

Because that has been especially true of religious organizations' cases, the following examples are set forth, to suggest how the courts handles these problems.

Since the leading case of *Watson v. Jones*[203] in 1872 the courts have followed the "absolute principle of judicial deference to internal ecclesiastical decisions."[204] In most cases this deference was (and is) the rule "whenever the questions of discipline, or faith, or ecclesiastical rule, custom, or law have been decided by the highest of these church judicatories to which the matter has been carried."[205]

One alternative rule applies in disputes about *property*. In the *Hull* case[206] that rule said (and says) that civil courts may employ "neutral principles of law" in resolving property disputes, if that will avert underlying doctrinal disputes.[207]

In tax exemption cases, individuals who challenge the tax-exempt status of a church have *standing* to do so *as voters*, when they object to infringement of their individual rights to participate on equal terms in *political* matters,[208] such as about what law governs abortion rights.

A church has the right to discriminate against people in its employ who refuse to follow its religious policy, as in discharging an employee because of his or her sexual (homosexual) preferences.[209]

The *Hull* case rule as to property disputes was held not to apply when the dispute was basically governed by internal ecclesiastical rule; or, at least was ruled to be not applicable, and the *Watson* rule was followed, by Florida in 1985.[210] That was because an ecclesiastical court had ruled specifically about the property in question.[211]

Religious freedom is not unconstitutionally impaired by the government, requiring minimum wage law, (labor law) compliance by an evangelical group that runs numerous commercial businesses.[212] Use of a city's zoning authority to forbid a church to operate a shelter for homeless people on its premises violates the First Amendment.[213] A college may be held liable in damages for an injury sustained by a student in an assault in the college parking lot;[214] which probably would also be true of a church parking lot especially in a non-charitable function, such as a bazaar sale.[215]

The tendency to avoid interference with church organization activities is neatly illustrated by the exemption of a *bingo* (money-raising) activity, from strict application of a two-days-a-week-limitation statute. The leasing of the premises to a second religious organization, for bingo games on other days of the week, was held to be no violation of the statute.[216]

Illustrative Cases:

The Hyde Amendment's restriction on the use of federal funds to pay for abortions in certain instances does not prohibit the state from funding abortions, even though federal matching funds are being received by the state, if accounting measures are used to ensure that state funds entirely are used to pay for abortion services.[217]

A nonprofit family planning clinic can obtain an injunction to prohibit protesters' antiabortion activities on their commercial private property. Such protesters have no First Amendment or state constitutional right to access private property. The injunction can constitutionally limit sign size and can reach anyone served with it.[218]

Courts do not generally interfere with the internal affairs of a private organization unless a personal liberty or property right is threatened.[219]

The fact that a witness in a trial had been "disfellowshipped" by her church (Jehovah's Witnesses) may not be used to impeach her testimony. "Evidence of *religious belief or lack* thereof" may not be used to "enhance or impair a witness' credibility" (citations).[220]

A suspended fraternity and its members, at a private school, are not entitled to the due process guarantees accorded to students at state schools unless the state involved itself in the private university activities. Absent state involvement the court may not challenge the university's actions if the university substantially complied with its published guidelines or rules regarding procedures and disciplinary proceedings.[221]

Advertisements for luxury apartments depicting only white models violate the Civil Rights Act.[222]

A party to a lawsuit involving constitutionality of a statute (state or federal) must serve notice and a copy of his/her/its brief on the Attorney-General and file proof of service with the Clerk of the Supreme Court.[223]

Constitutional issues often arise in trade association litigation. An association has no vested right to statutory procedure when a procedural statute is amended between nisi prius and an appellate decision. The reviewing court has to apply the latest version of the law.[224]

Property owners challenged an agency's authority to broaden the definition of "family" in administrative regulations to include two adult lifetime partners. The court held that the regulations were in the scope of the state division of housing and community renewal agency's rule-making authority. Further, the new "family" definition was not too vague and was consistent with legislative intention and policies. The court found no unconstitutional taking without compensation.[225]

In South Carolina, property owners sued to enjoin a nonprofit organization from starting a group residence in a residential subdivision. The South Carolina Supreme Court held that a group home would not infringe upon the subdivision's restrictive covenant that prohibited use of the property for other than private residential purposes. The mentally handicapped adults were guaranteed rights under the Fair Housing Amendments Act. Any other result would be contrary to state and federal public policy and law prohibiting housing discrimination against the handicapped.[226]

A charitable organization is not entitled to legal fees in opposing a municipality's regulatory ordinance.[227]

A statute, giving the park commission the right to regulate the use and operation of motor vehicles, or to ban them entirely, does not entitle the commission to select a particular class, motorcycles, for prohibition.[228]

A church had a statutory right to *participate* in hearings conducted by the Department of Liquor Control on a proposed transfer of a license to a nearby retail store. However, churches do *not* have the right to *appeal* departmental decisions or to compel the department to take particular action.[229]

In Lynchburg, Virginia, the city industrial development authority brought action seeking to find out if it could issue bonds that would enable a church-related, nonprofit, private university to purchase and construct facilities in the city. The Virginia Supreme Court held that the bond issue would violate the Establishment of Religion Clause of the Virginia and Federal Constitutions. The University had a policy of equipping young people for an evangelistic ministry. A substantial portion of the school's function was directed toward its religious mission.[230]

A public school district that allowed an openly religious fund-raiser thus created a limited public forum, and then may not deny an application to use a school auditorium for a religious-theme fund raiser; that denial would violate the 14th Amendment equal protection clause and First Amendment free speech clause.[231]

[Rana Holz contributed the analysis of the following case.]

The Supreme Court in 1990 took a controversial step backwards by upholding a Michigan statute requiring corporations to make *all* independent political expenditures through a *separate fund* solicited expressly for political purposes. The aim of the statute was to reduce the chance that corporations will use funds from their sizable corporate treasuries to unfairly influence the outcome of elections and other political actions. Although the majority agreed that expressive rights were implicated in this case, they believed the statute was sufficiently tailored to serve a valid constitutional state interest.

The dissenters were bitterly opposed to the provision. Justice Scalia [citing this treatise—by Oleck—among others] took the unusual step of reading his dissent from the bench, saying that the provision is "incompatible with the absolutely central truth of the First Amendment: that government cannot be trusted to assure, through censorship, the 'fairness' of the political debate." By prohibiting a corporation from spending its own funds on this form of political speech, it has the same effect as prohibiting any other *person* from speaking. Scalia believes that while commercial corporations may not have a public persona as sympathetic as that of public broadcasters (who were expressly immune from the provision), they nonetheless are entitled to the same protections. The majority did note three characteristics which would exempt an organization from this rule [as established in *FEC v. Massachusetts Citizens for Life, Inc.*, 479 U.S. 238 (1986)]: (1) the organization must have been formed for the express purpose of promoting political ideas and cannot engage in business activities; (2) there must not be shareholders or other personnel so affiliated with the entity as to have a claim on its assets or earnings; and (3) the organization must be independent from the influence of business corporations.[232]

Standing

Three requirements for "Standing" to sue of a NPO, to challenge administrative action, are (1) "standing" of one or more of its members, (2) whether the interests asserted are included in the NPO purposes, and (3) the claim or relief sought do not require individual member participation.[233]

A nonprofit environmental group filed suit to permanently enjoin a Clean Water Act permittee from violating monitoring and reporting requirements of its permit. The court held that the environmental association had standing because the group's *members had standing to sue in their own right.*[234]

Standing, under the Administrative Procedure Act, is given to persons whose *substantial interest will be affected* by agency decisions. An environmental organization, that wanted to challenge the proposed use of a botanical site purchased under the Conservation and Recreation Lands statute (CARL), had standing because its members are presently using the property in a manner consistent with the purposes and intent of the CARL program.[235]

When a nonprofit organization and other private plaintiffs sued a landowner for removing trestles on a railroad right-of-way, in violation of a Shoreline Management Act, the court denied standing to the members because they failed to comply with the requirements of the *rule relating to class actions,* owned no property adjacent to or even in the vicinity of the area, and *could not show that they were damaged.*[236]

The *alleged harmful effects,* on members of an organization that sued to review an environmental impact statement and to set aside a master plan to resettle the Love Canal area, were enough to afford the organization standing in an Article 78 proceeding.[237]

Where an agency creates judicial review of an administrative decision that is broader than the review provided for in the statute creating the agency, the statute controls. Thus, a State Air Pollution Control Board can't extend standing to "other persons aggrieved" where the statute creating the Board grants standing to challenge only to an aggrieved "owner" of the pollution source.[238]

A contractors association has "*standing*" to bring suit to enjoin a school board from requiring that public construction contracts contain a "prevailing wage" provision that will affect bids on projects of the board.[239]

Property owners near a poultry processing plant do not have "standing" for their Citizens for Clean Air Group to challenge an air pollution permit for expansion of the plant (Rockingham Poultry, Inc.).[240]

An NPO standing to sue for declaratory or injunctive relief on behalf of its members if this serves the corporate purposes and individual participation is not necessarily required; but not in appeals of administrative law applicable only to individuals.[241]

Nonprofit organizations have standing to contest an initiative, brought by the Governor, if the nonprofit has been involved in promoting the interests of those most likely to be affected by the initiative, or in lobbying and advocacy efforts regarding the subject of the initiative.[242]

A physician in a private hospital, whose hospital privileges or employment were terminated, must exhaust all the hospital rules procedures (remedies) before seeking court (judicial) review; unless such attempt would have been futile.[243]

A nonprofit corporation has standing to bring action against real estate agents based on alleged racial steering by the agents where the nonprofit diverted its time and money from counseling to investigate the alleged discrimination. Compensatory damages for the nonprofit are warranted in such a case.[244]

State legislative leaders and environmental associations have standing to challenge a governor's executive order abolishing an existing Department of Natural Resources (DNR) and establishing a new department if they have substantial interest in the dispute and would be detrimentally affected by the litigation in a manner different than the citizenry at large.[245]

A nonprofit corporation has standing to challenge the construction of a city dam where a majority of the members own land around the river, and use the river, and the purpose of the corporation is to preserve cold-water resources.[246]

The president of an association of fur trappers has standing to bring a declaratory action against a city to challenge an anti-trapping ordinance if he/she has an interest in preserving his/her business opportunity and economic well-being.[247]

Taxpayers in a homeowners' association have standing to seek to enjoin ultra vires acts of governing authorities. However, the county does not act ultra vires when it hires a private firm to mass reappraise property in the county if there is legislative authority to hire the private firm, even though the county may have committed procedural irregularities in entering the contract. The homeowners' association has no standing to sue the private firm hired by the county for return of county funds.[248]

Citizens' associations have standing to challenge federal agency decisions if there is a threatened injury which can be fairly traced to the conduct of the defendant and which can be redressed by judicial decision.[249]

A contractor's association does not have standing to challenge a city's affirmative action program absent any injury caused by coercion of the members to alter subcontracting procedures.[250]

An association of contractors does not have standing to challenge a county's minority business enterprise program unless they have an injury that can be traced to the program and which is redressable by the court. To cause injury, the program must have required them to compete on an uneven economic playing field or must have barred them from competing on some contracts.[251]

[Ben W. Subin contributed the analysis of the following case.]

The recent case of *Lujan v. Defenders of Wildlife* involved a nonprofit environmental organization called the Defenders of Wildlife (Defenders), which sought judicial review of the Department of Interior's interpretation of the Endangered Species Act (Act) of 1973.[252] The Act mandated that federal agencies' actions must not threaten species or their habitats. [253] In 1986, the Secretary of the Interior ruled that the Act was not applicable to U. S. projects overseas.[254] The nonprofit environmental group, Defenders of Wildlife, filed suit in opposition to the Secretary's narrow interpretation of the Act. Defenders argued that it had the right to sue because of its members' vocational interest in the habitat, which would become adversely affected by the Secretary's narrow interpretation.[255] In the alternative, Defenders reasoned that it had the right to sue because the Endangered Species Act has a "citizen's suit" provision allowing "any person to sue any agency" whose actions are violative of the statute.[256]

The court ruled that the environmental group opposed to the Department's narrow interpretation of the act did not have standing to sue under federal law.[257] Continuing to narrow the doctrine, Scalia wrote that the plaintiff could not prove an adequate injury-in-fact to have standing. The court reached this conclusion based on an analysis of the plaintiff's affidavits. The court ruled that since the plaintiff's members had not made specific plans to return to the region specified to the lawsuit it did not satisfy the injury-in-fact requirement.[258] The injury must be "actual or imminent" to be an injury-in-fact. Scalia held that an environmental plaintiff is injured by government action only if it has "used the area effected by the challenged activity".[259] Scalia explicitly rejected the plaintiff's theory that individuals with an "aesthetic or vocational" interest in a species or ecosystem could be injured unless such individuals were specifically working within the geographic boundaries of a species or ecosystem.[260]

§450. LITIGATION FORMS

[Sample pleading and practice forms set forth here were provided by Peter J. Thayer of East Chicago, Ind. They are extracts from an actual case brought *against the Trustees* of an Ohio nonprofit organization in a *dispute about proposed transfer of assets from the private organization to state control.*]

[These samples are meant only to suggest the "flavor" of such litigation. Obviously it would take a volume in itself to illustrate the many various kinds of litigation procedures that might be used.]

[The assets consist of a property and a memorial to perpetuate the memory of a distinguished person. A meeting had approved transfer of the assets to the state.]

FORM NO. 177

Motion for Temporary Injunction

IN THE COURT OF COMMON PLEAS OF_____ COUNTY,

_____ Avenue	:
Plaintiff	:
—vs—	CASE NO._____
THE EXECUTIVE COMMITTEE OF THE_____ MEMORIAL ASSOCIATION, et al	: :
_____ Avenue	:
Defendants	: :

MOTION FOR TEMPORARY RESTRAINING ORDER AND FOR PRELIMINARY INJUNCTION

Pursuant to Civil Rule 65(A) and upon notice to be given to defendants or their attorneys, plaintiff moves the court to issue a temporary restraining order:

1. Enjoining and restraining any conveyance, transfer, and/or donation of the tract of land known as the _____ Area, said tract being 5.693

acres situated in the Southwest Quarter of Section _____, Township _____ South, Range _____ East, in the City of _____, _____ County, State _____, the property of the _____ Memorial Association, to the City of _____, _____.

2. Enjoining and restraining any conveyance, transfer, and/or donation to the Governor, State of _____ and/or the _____ Historical Society as to the _____ Memorial, _____ Home and Museum, said real estate which is situated in the State of _____, the County of _____, the township of _____, _____ and the City of _____, or any money, securities, and credits held by the _____ Memorial Association, or any tangible personal property of the Memorial Association, including but not limited to printed materials, exhibits, furnishings, and items held for sale.

3. Enjoining and restraining named President _____ from serving as President of the _____ Memorial Association.

AFFIDAVIT

_____, being first duly sworn, states that he is the plaintiff and a Trustee of the _____ Memorial Association, and that he gives the affidavit upon information and belief.

Affiant states that the following allegations are true as he verily believes:

1. The tract of land known as the _____ Area will be transferred to the City of _____ as provided by Ordinance No. _____ which, unless the defendants are restrained from conveying said tract of land to the City of _____, will:

A. Result in the transfer, conveyance, and/or donation of the assets of the _____ Memorial Association in contravention of the Bylaws, Code of Regulations, Articles of Incorporation, and State statutes governing nonprofit corporations.

B. Result in the breach of fiduciary duties of the officers of a nonprofit corporation.

2. The tracts of land known as the _____ Memorial, _____ Home and Museum as well as accompanying assets, grounds, and personal property will be transferred to the _____ Historical Society as provided by House Bill _____ which, unless the defendants are: restrained from conveying said property and assets to the State of _____, will:

A. Result in the transfer, conveyance, and/or donation of the assets of the _____ Memorial Association in contravention of the Bylaws, Code of Regulations, Articles of Incorporation, and State statutes governing nonprofit corporations.

B. Result in the abuse of corporate powers and ultra vires acts.

C. Result in the usurpation of powers.

SWORN TO and subscribed before me, a Notary Public, in and for the County of _____ State of _____, this _____ day of June 19____.

_____

NOTARY PUBLIC

FORM NO. 178

Complaint Against Trustees

IN THE COURT OF COMMON PLEAS OF _____
COUNTY, _____

                                                   :

_____ Avenue

_____

   Plaintiff   :

   —vs—   CASE NO._____

THE EXECUTIVE COMMITTEE OF   :
THE_____ MEMORIAL   :
ASSOCIATION,
_____ Avenue   :

_____ Avenue   :

                                            COMPLAINT

                                                   :

_____ , MD
Vice President,
Memorial Association   :

_____

Secretary,
Memorial Association

_____

Treasurer,
Memorial Association

Defendants

CLAIM I

1. Plaintiff is a Trustee and a member of the _____ Memorial Association, _____, _____.

2. The Plaintiff institutes this action in application to the Court for an order of injunction to restrain the defendants from conveying, transferring, and/or donating said real and personal property referred to below to the Governor, State of _____, _____ Historical Society, or City of _____, in contravention of the Articles of Incorporation, Bylaws, and Code of Regulations of the _____ Memorial Association, and Chapter 1702, Sections 1702.33 and 1702.39(A), _____ Revised Code.

3. The defendant, Executive Committee of the Memorial Association, is a body duly appointed pursuant to Article IV of the Bylaws of the _____ Memorial Association and Chapter 1702, Section 1702.33, _____ Revised Code, to manage and conduct the ordinary course of business.

4. Defendants, Mr. _____, Vice President, Mr. _____, Vice President, Mr. _____, Vice President, Mr. _____, Secretary and Mr. _____, Treasurer, are the duly elected officers of the _____ Memorial Association as provided by Article III and Article IV of the Code of Regulations of the _____ Memorial Association, and the officers in this complaint in relation to the validity, approval, and conveyance of said real and personal property referred to below.

5. _____ is the named President of the Association and the named officer in this complaint in relation to the validity, approval, and conveyance of said real and personal property referred to below, but is named in contravention of Article IV of the Code of Regulations of the _____ Memorial Association.

6. The _____ Memorial Association is a nonprofit corporation organized and operated by authority of Chapter 1702, Revised Code and its Articles of Incorporation for the purpose of erecting and maintaining in perpetuity the _____ Memorial and all necessary real estate on which to place said memorial and for roads, ways, places, and parks leading thereto and for the beautification of the place surrounding said mausoleum, and to acquire and hold the _____ Home and to hold all property, both real and personal, and money and choses in action of every description coming into possession of this association, in trust for the uses and purposes hereinbefore set forth for carrying out the objects of the association and to provide for and hold in trust an endowment fund for the purpose of guarding, maintaining, and perpetuating said places mentioned in Articles of Incorporation. Said Articles of Incorporation were adopted October 1, _____, and filed with the Secretary of State on October 8, _____.

7. Plaintiff believes that on or about November 2, _____, the Trustee and members of the _____ Memorial Association did approve a resolution authorizing and directing the Board of Trustees to negotiate with the _____ Historical Society for the transfer of all assets of the _____ Memorial Association to the State of _____ and authorizing the officers of the _____ Memorial Association to take all appropriate actions and to execute any and all documents necessary to complete said transfer to the State of _____. Plaintiff cast a dissenting vote as to this said resolution.

8. It is believed, and therefore alleged, that said resolution authorizing and directing the actions of the Board of Trustees and Officers of the _____ Memorial Association referred to in paragraph seven (7) above is in contravention of the Articles of Incorporation of the _____ Memorial Association as referred to in paragraph six (6) above. Such resolution is therefore null and void.

9. By virtue of Chapter 1702, Section 1702.39(A), Revised Code, the _____ Memorial Association and Board of Trustees, in approving such resolution, was required to comply with the provisions of Chapter 1702, Section 1702.39(A) by holding a meeting for such purposes after first giving proper notice to each member of the Association accompanied by a copy or summary of the terms of the transaction. The defendant, former President of the _____ Memorial Association and member of the Executive Committee, _____, and the defendant former Secretary of the _____ Memorial Association and member of the Executive Committee, _____, and the _____ Memorial Association did not comply with the requirements of such statutes in failing to call a meeting for the announced purpose of approving the above-named resolution and in failing to give prior notice to each Association member accompanied by a copy or summary of the terms of the transaction. Such resolution as referred to in paragraph seven (7) above is therefore null and void.

For the foregoing reasons, passage of this aforesaid resolution and the conveyance of said properties to the State of _____ constitute an abuse of corporate powers, are ultra vires acts, and are in contravention of the Bylaws, Articles of Incorporation, and Code of Regulations of the _____ Memorial Association and contravene Chapter 1702, Section 1702.39, _____ Revised Code.

Plaintiff is entitled to an injunction enjoining such abuse of corporate and ultra vires acts and the execution and performance of the resolution.

CLAIM II

1. Pursuant to the resolution approved on or about November 2, _____, by the members of the _____ Memorial Association authorizing and directing the Board of Trustees to neogiate with the _____ Historical Society for the transfer of all assets of the _____ Memorial Association to the State of _____ and authorizing the officers of the _____ Memorial Association to take

all appropriate actions and to execute any and all documents necessary to complete said transfer to the State of _____, a bill (HB _____ and SB _____) was drafted and submitted to each house of the _____ General Assembly authorizing the State of _____ to accept the assets of the _____ Memorial Association. This said bill is in conflict with the resolution aforementioned in that a major asset of the _____ Memorial Association known as the _____ Area was deleted from the bill.

2. It is believed and therefore alleged that the conflict in the wording of the bill and the resolution is a result of the fact that the Executive Committee and Officers of the _____ Memorial Association negotiated with the _____ Historical Society and derived an agreement with said Society which contained less property and assets of the _____ Memorial Association than had been offered to the State through said resolution. Such negotiations by the Executive Committee and Officers of the _____ Memorial Association violates the provisions of the resolution passed by the Trustees and members of the _____ Memorial Association on or about November 2, _____, referred to in Claim I, paragraph Seven (7), and is a usurpation of the powers of the Trustees and contravenes Article IV of the Bylaws of said Association, and contravenes the Code of Regulations as well as Chapter 1702, Section 1702.39(A) of the _____ Revised Code.

3. The bill and resolution in question involving the usurpation of power by the Executive Committee and Officers of the _____ Memorial Association are null and void, and it is alleged that the defendants, unless restrained by the court, will continue the usurpation of power by conveying said property and assets to the State of _____.

Plaintiff is entitled to an injunction enjoining the defendants from usurping the powers of the Trustees and from transferring any property and assets of the _____ Memorial Association to the State of _____.

CLAIM III

1. _____ is the named President of the _____ Memorial Association, but is named in contravention of Article IV of the Code of Regulations of the _____ Memorial Association because he is not a Trustee of said Association as set forth in such Article.

2. _____ is the Mayor of the City of _____ and in this capacity signed an ordinance No. passed by the Council of the City of _____ on February 27 19 ___. This ordinance approved the acceptance of a tract of land known as the _____ Area consisting of 5.693 acres to be donated to the city of _____ to be used as Green space. This ordinance was brought about by the fact that on or about February 27, 19___, _____, as named President of the _____ Memorial Association, with the approval of the Executive Committee, did offer the donation of said land known as the _____ Area, which land is the

property of the _____
Memorial Association to the City of _____.

3. Said action mentioned in paragraph two (2) is in contravention of _____ Revised Code Chapter 1702, Section 1702.39, and this action was not presented to the Trustees and members in a properly called meeting for said purpose, with due notice as required by said Section, and is in contravention of Article IV of the Bylaws of the Association because said action did not have the vote and approval of the members of the _____ Memorial Association.

4. The naming of _____ as President of the _____ Memorial Association as well as the actions of _____ as President of said Association and the actions of the Executive Committee as mentioned previously in paragraphs 1, 2, and 3 of Claim III are null and void, and it is alledged that these defendants will continue the violations of Article 4 of the Code of Regulations, Article IV of the Bylaws of the Association and Chapter 1702, Section 1702.39 of the _____ Revised Code unless restrained by the court. Plaintiff is entitled to an injunction enjoining these said defendants from contravening the Bylaws and Code of Regulations of the _____ Memorial Association and from contravening Chapter 1702, Section 1702.39 of the _____ Revised Code.

5. Plaintiff is entitled to an injunction enjoining the said defendants from conveying, transferring, and/or donating said _____ Area to the City of _____.

CLAIM IV

1. Plaintiff adopts by reference the statements contained in paragraph 2 of Claim III.

2. This said action was a breach of the fiduciary responsibility of the President and Executive Committee of the _____ Memorial Association in that it divested the Association of valuable interests and lands of the Association without proper ratification by the full membership of the Association.

3. Plaintiff is entitled to an injunction enjoining the said defendants from further breaching their fiduciary duties by conveying, transferring, and/or donating said Area to the City of _____.

WHEREFORE, plaintiff applies to this Court:

A. For a permanent injunction restraining the defendant's Executive Committee of the _____ Memorial Association, named President _____

former President _____,

former Secretary _____,

Vice-President _____,

Vice-President _____,

Vice-President _____,

Secretary _____,
Treasurer _____,
all being, except for _____, members of the Executive Committee of
the _____ Memorial Association, from conveying, transferring,
and/or donating assets of the _____ Memorial Association to the
State of _____, namely the _____ Memorial, the
_____ Home and Museum, in contravention of the Articles of Incorporation, Code of Regulations, and Bylaws of the said Association, and State
statutes governing them, abuse of corporate powers, ultra tires acts, usurpation
of powers of the Trustees and members of the _____ Memorial
Association.

B. For a permanent injunction restraining the defendants named above
from transferring, conveying, and/or donating assets of the _____
Memorial Association, namely the _____ Area, to the City of
_____ in contravention of the Articles of Incorporation, Code of
Regulations, and Bylaws of the said Association, and State statutes governing
them, abuse of corporate powers, ultra vires acts, usurpation of powers of the
Trustees, and members of the _____ Memorial Association.

_____
                PROSE
_____ Avenue

_____, being first duly sworn, states that he has
read the foregoing Complaint and it is true as he verily believes.

_____

STATE OF _____, COUNTY OF _____,
SS: _____
_____ SWORN TO and subscribed before me, a
Notary Public, for the County of _____,
State of _____ this 19th day of June, 19____.

_____
          NOTARY PUBLIC

FORM NO. 179

Trustees' Motion for Summary Judgment
(Supporting Memorandum)

IN THE COURT OF COMMON PLEAS
OF _____ COUNTY, _____

```
*******************************************************
```

_____,   *
                                         *
                                         *   Case No. _____
                                         *
Plaintiff,   *
—vs—   *   MOTION FOR SUMMARY
                                         *   JUDGMENT
The Executive Committee of the   *
                                         *
_____   *
Memorial Association,   *
et al.,   *
Defendants   *

```
*******************************************************
```

Defendants move the Court to enter pursuant to Rule 56 of the _____ Rules of Civil Procedure a Summary Judgment in Defendants' favor dismissing the action of Plaintiff on the ground that no genuine issue as to any material fact exists and that Defendants are entitled to a judgment as a matter of law.

This Motion is based upon:

1. The Complaint, and Answer to Defendants.
2. The Affidavit attached hereto.
3. The Exhibits attached to said Affidavit.

_____, Attorney for Defendants
_____ Street, P.O. Box _____

MEMORANDUM IN SUPPORT OF MOTION
FOR SUMMARY JUDGMENT

The attached Affidavit clearly shows that the Secretary of the Association, _____, would be qualified to testify with regard to the matters in the Affidavit, and that as Secretary he is in possession of the minutes of the Association, as well as the minutes of the Trustees, and the minutes of the Executive Committee.

The minutes of the Special Meeting of the Trustees at 11:00 a.m. on November 2, 19___, reflects the action of the Trustees in authorizing the Executive Committee to enter into certain negotiations, and further that if those negotiations were fruitful the Officers would be authorized to execute any necessary documents.

The minutes of the Association meeting at 12:00 noon on November 2nd, 19___, approved the action of the Trustees in authorizing the negotiations and in authorizing the execution of instruments.

These actions of the Trustees and the Association were pursuant to the minutes of the Executive Committee of October 25th, 19___, the meeting of October 25th, 19___ having merely been action by the Executive Committee asking for authority to proceed.

The minutes of the Executive Committee of March 2nd 19___ reflect specifically that the Executive Committee understands that there must be a General Meeting of the Association before any official action could be taken as shown by the following statement in the said minutes:

> "As a result of further discussion, it was determined by the Executive Committee that under no circumstances could the transfer of the _____ property be made to the City of _____ until such time as it was certain that the proposed House Bill would be approved by the Legislature and signed by the Governor.
>
> The Executive Committee also agreed that when and if the _____ Historical Society is authorized to assume responsibility that the transfer of the deed could not be made until a general meeting of the _____ Memorial Association was held and the action approved and ratified by a majority of members."

It is therefore very apparent that it is premature to be bringing an action to restrain any transfers.

The facts of the matter are that the Bill before the General Assembly of _____ has only been adopted by the House of Representatives of said Assembly and has not been acted upon by the State Senate in said Assembly, and of course, has not been submitted to the Governor for signature. If a Bill is finally adopted and signed by the Governor and becomes law, then and only then would the terms be known in order that the issue could be submitted to the members of the Association for them to ascertain whether they are willing to make the transfer on the conditions that may exist in the legislation.

In so far as the issue of _____ being validly the President of the Association, again the Secretary is in possession of the Articles of Incorporation, the Code of Regulations, and the Bylaws of the Association, and could testify as to their content. These Bylaws, Code of Regulations, and Articles of Incorporation are attached to the Affidavit.

[Note: These are
omitted, herein.]

The Court will note that there is no requirement in any of these instruments dealing with the necessity that the President of the Association be a

Trustee. Article IV permits the Trustees to select the Secretary from outside the Board of Trustees, but it does not restrict who may or may not be the President of the Association.

The Court's attention is respectfully called to _____ Revised Code 1702.34 which provides among other things:

"Unless the Articles or Regulations otherwise provide, none of the officers need to be Trustees."

It is therefore apparent that there is no requirement that the President be a Trustee, and that _____ is serving legally as President.

Since the statute clearly settles the question of the validity of _____ serving as President and the minutes clearly reflect that the action is premature at best, there remains no issue, and the case should be dismissed.

_____
Attorney for Defendants

FORM NO. 180
Trustees' Motion for Summary Judgment
(Supporting Affidavit)

IN THE COURT OF COMMON PLEAS
OF _____ COUNTY, _____

****

_____,	*
	*
	* Case No. _____
Plaintiff,	*
—vs—	* AFFIDAVIT IN SUPPORT
The Executive Committee of the	* OF MOTION FOR
_____	* SUMMARY JUDGMENT
Memorial Association,	*
et al.,	*
Defendants	*

****

State of _____

              ss.

_____ County:

_____,, being first duly sworn according to law, deposes and says:

    1. I am Secretary of the _____ Memorial Association, the above-named Defendant, and I was the Secretary during all the times mentioned

herein. I have personal knowledge of the matters hereinafter referred to, and make this Affidavit in support of Defendants' motion for summary judgment.

2. As Secretary a true copy of the Articles of Incorporation of the _____ Memorial Association, and a true copy of the Code of Regulations of the _____ Memorial Association, and a true copy of the Bylaws of the _____ Memorial Association are within my jurisdiction and possession.

3. That Exhibit "A" attached hereto is a true copy of the Articles of Incorporation of the _____ Memorial Association. That attached hereto as Exhibit "B" is a true copy of the Code of Regulations of the _____ Memorial Association. Attached hereto as Exhibit "C" is a true copy of the Bylaws of the _____ Memorial Association.

4. That as Secretary of the _____ Memorial Association I have control of and am in possession of the minutes of Regular and Special meetings of the Executive Committee of the _____ Memorial Association, minutes of the Trustees of the _____ Memorial Association, and the minutes of the _____ Memorial Association.

5. That Exhibit "D" attached hereto is a true copy of the minutes of the Special Meeting of the Executive Committee of the _____ Memorial Association of Tuesday, October 25, 19___ at 1:00 o'clock p.m. That Exhibit "E" attached hereto is a true copy of the minutes of the Trustees' Meeting, being a Special Meeting of the Trustees of the _____ Memorial Association held at 11:00 a.m. on Wednesday, November 2nd, 19___. That Exhibit "F" attached hereto is a true copy of the minutes of the Fifty-Fifth Annual Meeting of the _____ Memorial Association held at 12:00 o'clock noon on the second day of November, 19___. That Exhibit "G" attached hereto is a true copy of the minutes of the 55th Annual Meeting of the Trustees of the _____ Memorial Association held on the second day of November, 19___. That Exhibit "H" attached hereto is a true copy of the minutes of the Executive Committee at a Special Meeting of the Executive Committee of the _____ Memorial Association held at 2:00 p.m. on March 2nd, 19___.

Sworn to before me and subscribed in my presence this _____ day of July, A.D., 19___.

_____
NOTARY PUBLIC

FORM NO. 181

Motion to Dismiss

IN THE COURT OF COMMON PLEAS
OF _____ COUNTY, _____

_____,	*
Plaintiff,	*
	* Case No. _____
—vs—	*
The Executive Committee of the	* MOTION TO DISMISS
_____	*
Memorial Association,	*
et al.,	*
Defendants	*
	*

    Plaintiff moves the Court to dismiss the Defendants' motion for Summary Judgment on the grounds that there are genuine issues as to material facts and the Defendants are not entitled to judgment as a matter of law.

    In support of this motion the Plaintiff refers to the pleadings herein, the Defendants' motion for summary judgment and his supporting papers, and the memorandum, affidavit, and exhibits of the plaintiff hereto attached.

_____

Attorney for Plaintiff

PROOF OF SERVICE

    The plaintiff served the foregoing on the attorney for the defendants, _____ Street, _____, _____ by personal service on August 3, 19_____.

_____

Attorney for Plaintiff

MEMORANDUM IN SUPPORT OF MOTION TO DISMISS

    The attached Affidavit clearly shows that the Plaintiff would be qualified to testify with regard to the matters in the Affidavit, and that as a Trustee he is in possession of the Articles of Incorporation of the _____ Memorial Association as well as the Code of Regulations, Bylaws, minutes of membership meetings, minutes of the Board of Trustees, and minutes of the Executive Committee.

The minutes of the Special Meeting of the Trustees at 11:00 a.m. on November 2, 19___, as contained in Exhibit "E" of the Defendants' Affidavit in Support of Motion for Summary Judgment, contrary to the Defendants' contentions, do not reflect any action by the Trustees authorizing the Executive Committee to enter into any negotiations, nor do the aforementioned minutes authorize the Officers of said Association to execute any documents as a result of any negotiation by the Executive Committee. Said minutes only refer to negotiations conducted by the Board of Trustees. Such negotiations have never taken place.

[The balance of the memorandum, and supporting Affidavit and other papers, and copies of minutes, are omitted here.]

FORM NO. 182

Court Finding and Summary Judgment

IN_____PLEAS,_____COUNTY,_____

_____

Plaintiff,   :

                                               Case No._____

—vs—   :

THE EXECUTIVE COMMITTEE   :   FINDING ON MOTION

of THE_____   :   FOR SUMMARY JUDGMENT

MEMORIAL ASSOCIATION, et al.,   :

                                               :

Defendants   :

                                               :

On consideration of the Motion for Summary Judgment and the Motion to dismiss the Motion for Summary Judgment and the arguments, the Court finds that the latter Motion is not well-taken and overrules the same. However, the Court will consider the Affidavit and Exhibits of the plaintiffs which accompany the Motion to dismiss as evidence contra to the Motion for Summary judgment.

The Court finds that on the evidence and admissions of both sides, the copies of the Articles of Incorporation, the Code of Regulations and the Bylaws marked as Exhibits of the defendants on the Motion for Summary Judgment do not contain certain Amendments thereto or are incomplete in minor details as shown by plaintiff's Exhibits, but that said differences are shown in plaintiff's Exhibits and the differences are not pertinent and have no bearing on this case.

The Court further finds that the pertinent statute, Sec. 1702.34, states "Unless the Articles or the regulations otherwise provide, none of the officers need be a trustee" and that neither the article nor the regulations in this case restrict the right to office to a trustee. The meaning of the statute and the

Code of regulations is clear and neither requires the use of inferences to discover their meaning. Tradition is not binding in this case and if there was such a tradition the Trustees chose to depart from it when they voted unanimously to elect _____ to the office of President. (Defendants' Exhibit "G".)

Although the prayer of the Complaint is silent as to this matter, the Court finds from the evidence that _____ is the validly elected President of the _____ Memorial Association.

The Court further finds that Defendants' Exhibit "E" which is a copy of the Minutes of the Trustees' Meeting of November 2, 19___, shows that it was resolved by the Board of Trustees:

"That the officers . . . be authorized and directed to take all *appropriate actions* . . . to complete said transfer."

(Underline added)

This resolution was passed with 15 yes votes, 1 abstention, and 1 no vote.

The Court finds that at the Fifty-Fifth Annual Meeting on November 2, 19___, of the Memorial Association (Minutes—Defendants' Exhibit "F"), the membership evidenced an intention to *negotiate* with the Historical Society and the State of _____ to *effect a proposal* for the transfer of ownership by a vote of 36 yes votes, 0 no votes, and 2 abstentions.

The same Minutes reflect that the membership resolved that the Board be directed to *negotiate* and that the officers be authorized to take *all appropriate actions.*

On March 2, 19___ the Executive Committee met in special session and discussed the action of the membership in directing the Trustees to *negotiate* and the officers to take all *appropriate action.* (Defendants' Exhibit "H".) At this March 2, 19___ meeting, the Executive Committee of which the officers are members, agreed consistent with their duty to take *appropriate action* that the _____ property could not be transferred until such time as it was certain that the proposed House Bill would be approved by the Legislature and signed by the Governor. The Executive Committee also determined and recognized that their duty to take *appropriate action* was, when and if a definite proposal was received in regard to all areas of the transfer, to submit that proposal to the members of the Association for ratification and approval by a majority of the members.

No definite proposal has been received.

The Executive Committee and the Officers have not acted in contravention of the Articles, Code of Regulations, Bylaws, or pertinent sections of the Revised Code, and their recognition of the duty to submit the proposal to the membership when and if received indicates an intention to continue to act within their authority.

The above findings of the Court are based on evidence submitted by both parties and there is no genuine issue as to any material fact.

Reasonable minds could come to but one conclusion and that conclusion is adverse to the party against whom the Motion is made.

Negotiations and appropriate action have been authorized, but until final action by the legislature is had there is no proposal to submit to the general membership. Until there is a proposal there can be no certain injury to which the extraordinary remedy of injunction can be directed.

The request for injunction is premature and the Motion for Summary Judgment will be sustained.

Entry may be drawn accordingly.

_____
JUDGE

Copy:

POINTS TO REMEMBER

- Distinguish between civil suit rules for incorporated and for unincorporated associations.
- Look first to local practice statutes.
- Follow general corporation law where incorporated associations are concerned.
- In federal cases, the Federal Rules permit suit by or against the association as an entity.
- Use state law first; federal law is harder to invoke, ordinarily.
- Consult labor law, for labor unions; trust law, for trusts; insurance law, for mutual associations; condominium law for resident associations; etc.
- Use *class actions* whenever possible.
- Try to serve process on all important members.
- Pick the county for suit with care. Best sue where the cause for action arose.
- Refer to debtor-creditor law texts and statutes for enforcement of judgments.
- Try to avoid enforcement of claims against individual members.
- Beware of constitutional law re-interpretations by the courts.
- Do not try to be your own lawyer.

NOTES TO CHAPTER 44

1. *See,* Henn, *Corporations* (casebook), c. 19 (2d ed., 1986); 1 Oleck, *Modern Corporation Law,* c.2 (1978 Supp.); Bachmann, *Nonprofit Litigation* (1992).

2. Eagle-Picher Industries, Inc. v. Proverb, 464 S.2d 658 (Fla. 4th DCA, 1985); Sierra Holding v. Inn Keepers Supply Co., 464 S.2d 652 (Fla. 4th DCA, 1985).

3. Congr. H.R. 2378 (1985).

4. 8 Civil Liberties Alert (4)2 (ACLU; Oct. 1985).

5. *See,* for example, Henn and Alexander, *Corporations* (casebook), 1019–1146 (3rd ed., 1983) on corporate litigation alone.

6. 28 U.S.C.; Hanna v. Plumer, 85 S. Ct. 1136 (1965).

7. *See*, Annot., 30 A.L.R. 3rd 1088.

8. For diversity jurisdiction a corporation is a citizen of the place of its incorporation and also of its principal place of business. 28 U.S.C. §§1331 *et seq*; Jergon v. Blue Dot Inv., 659 F.2d 31 (5th Cir., 1981).

9. Henn, *Corporations* (casebook) 979 (2d ed., 1986).

10. *See*, Weissenberger, . . . *Attorney-Client Privilege*, 65 Iowa L. Rev. 899 (1980); Upjohn Co. v. U.S., 101 S. Ct. 677 (1981).

11. K.M.A., Inc. v. General Motors Accep. Corp., 652 F.2d 398 (5th Cir., 1981); Remole Soil Service, Inc. v. Benson, 215 N.E.2d 678 (Ill. App. 1966); Union Sav. Assn. v. Home Owners Aid, Inc., 23 Ohio St.2d 60, 262 N.E.2d 558 (1970); N.Y.C.P.L. and R. §321(a); Oliver v. Mid-Town Promoters, Inc., 156 N.Y.S.2d 833, 2 N.Y.2d 63, 138 N.E.2d 217 (1956); Ashley-Cooper Sales Service, Inc. v. Brentwood Mfg. Co., 168 F. Supp. 742 (D.C., Md. 1958).

12. First Baptist Church v. Branham, 90 Calif. 22, 27 P. 60 (1891); Beckstrom Co. v. Armstrong, 220 Ill. App. 598 (1921). But, held that it cannot sue; Rogers v. Toccoa Power Co., 161 Ga. 524, 131 S.E. 517, 44 A.L.R. 534 (1926); Note, *Defective Formation and Suits in Corporate Name*, 84 U. Pa. L. Rev. 514 (1936).

13. Fed. Rules Civ. Prac., Rule 17(b). *See* G. R. Sponaugle and Sons, Inc. v. McKnight Const. Co., 304 A.2d 339 (Del. Super. 1973). See n.8.

14. *See*, chapter on foreign corporations. *See* Mather Const. Co. v. United States, 475 F.2d 1152 (Ct. Cl. 1973).

15. N.Y.C.P.L. and R. §§3015(b), 3023.

16. Grassi v. La Sociedad Bancaria D.C., 213 A.D. 629, 210 N.Y.S. 705 (1925).

17. Icardi v. National Equipment Rental, 378 S.2d 113 (Fla. D.C.A. 1980); Fla. Stat. §§56.061, 678–317.

18. N.Y.C.P.L. and R. §311(1). *See* Keske v. Square D Co., 58 Wis.2d 307, 206 N.W.2d 189 (1973). Fla. Genl. Corp. Act. §607.0504.

19. *Ibid.*; Olson v. Jordan, 181 Misc. 942, 43 N.Y.S.2d 348 (1943). In Ohio, as in many states, a "statutory agent" must be designated; and if he cannot be found, the Secretary of State may be served. Ohio Rev. Code §1702.06.

20. N.Y. Veh. and Traf. L. §§253, 254.

21. Foreign corporations: N.Y. Bus. Corp. L. §306. Note that a "public corporation" is a governmental one. *See*, Keyes, *Some Controversial Aspects of the Public Corporation* (English), 70 Pol. Sci. Q. (Mar. 1955); N.Y. N-PCL §§306, 307.

22. *For example*, Oleck, *New York Corporations*, c. 79 (New York: Matthew Bender Co. 1959 Supp.) contains details of the New York practice, subject to New York's new practice and corporation laws, and forms for litigation involving corporations. *See also*, as to damages, Oleck, *Damages to Persons and Property*, §371 (New York: Central Book Co. 1961 revision); Henn and Alexander, n.5.

23. Carroll v. Beaumont, 18 S.W.2d 813 (Tex. Civ. App. 1927), enforcement of a charitable corporation's trust agreement. *But see, contra*, that club members cannot bring a class action to impose a constructive trust on fees received from 50,000 members; each one must sue separately: Onofrio v. Playboy Club of N.Y., Inc., 15 N.Y.2d 740, 205 N.E.2d 308 (1965), revg. 20 A.D.2d 3, 244 N.Y.S.2d 485 (1963).

24. MAS Nussing, Inc. v. Burke, 523 S. 2d 909 (La. App. 1988).

25. *Matter of Sharon B. (Westchester County Society for Prevention of Cruelty to Children)*, 530 N.E.2d 832 (NY 1988).

26. *People ex rel. Meyer v. LaPorte Church of Christ*, 830 P. 2d 1150 (Colo. App. 1992).

27. *FDM Manufacturing Co., Inc. v. Scottsdale Insurance Co.*, 855 F.2d 213 (5th Cir., LA, 1988).

28. *Wrenfield Homeowners Ass'n, Inc. v. DeYoung*, 600 A.2d 960 (Pa. Super. 1991).

29. *In re Marriage of Ward*, 4 Cal. Rptr. 2d 365 (Cal. App. 4 Dist. 1992).

30. *Baksinski v. Northwestern University*, 595 N.E. 2d 1106 (Ill. App. 1 Dist., 1992).

31. *Tax Analysts v. U.S. Dept. of Justice,* 965 F.2d 1239 (2nd Cir. (Conn.), 1992).

32. **Human Development of Erie, Inc. v. Zoning Hearing Bd. of Millcreek TP.,** 600 A.2d 658 (Pa. Cmwlth. 1991).

33. *Davis v. City and County of San Francisco,* 976 F. 2d 1536 (9th Cir. (Cal.), 1992) (fire department employment discrimination).

34. *Minneapolis Police Officers Federation v. City of Minneapolis,* 488 N.W. 2d 817 (Minn. App., 1992).

35. *Illinois Mun. League Risk Management Ass'n v. Siebert,* 585 N.E. 2d 1130 (Ill. App. 4 Dist. 1992).

36. *Lane v. Head,* 566 So. 2d 508 (Fla. 1990); Fl. St. § 607.147(5).

37. See, *Walker v. Tri-County Elec. Membership Corp.,* 1990 WL 120721 (Tenn. App.); *Stueve v. Northern Lights, Inc.,* 797 P.2d 130 (Idaho 1990); *Lane v. Head,* 555 So. 2d 508 (Fla. DCA 1990).

38. *Baker v. Heatherwood Homeowners Assn.,* 587 So 2d 938 (Ala. 1991).

39. *Entertainment Partners Group, Inc. v. Davis,* 590 N.Y.S. 2d 979 (N.Y. Sup., 1992) (frivolous suit brought against community leaders who opposed business' application for special zoning permit to operate restaurant and nightclub).

40. *Indiana Dept. of Public Welfare v. Chair Lance Service, Inc.* 523 N.E. 2d 1373 (IN 1988).

41. *Lockary v. Kayfetz,* 974 F. 2d 1166 (9th Cir. (Cal.), 1992).

42. *Korman v. Pond Apple Maintenance Ass'n, Inc.,* 607 So. 2d 489 (Fla. App. 4 Dist., 1992).

43. *Zuger v. North Dakota Ins. Guar. Ass'n,* 494 N.W. 2d 135 (N.D., 1992).

44. *Myakka Valley Ranches Imp. Ass'n Inc. v. Bieschke,* 610 So. 2d 3 (Fla. App. 2 Dist., 1992).

45. *Matter of Jones,* 562 N.Y.S. 2d 568 (A.D. 2 Dept. 1990).

46. *First Southern Baptist Church of Mandarin, Florida, Inc. v. First Nat. Bank of Amarillo,* 610 So. 2d 452 (Fla. App. 1 Dist., 1992).

47. Bachmann, Steve, *Nonprofit Litigation. A Practical Guide with Forms and Checklists.* John Wiley & Sons, Inc., 1992.

48. *Manasota-88, Inc. v. Tidwell,* 896 F.2d 1318 (11th Cir., Fla., 1990).

49. *Te-Ta-Ma Truth Foundation of Uri, Inc. v. Vaughan,* 835 P.2d 938 (Or. App., 1992).

50. *People ex rel. Burris v. Progressive Land Developers, Inc.,* 602 N.E. 2d 820 (Ill., 1992).

51. *McCollum v. Sisters of Charity of Nazareth Health Corp.,* 799 S.W.2d 15 (Ky. 1990).

52. *Forsyth Memorial Hosp., Inc. v. Armstrong World Industries, Inc.,* 418 S.E. 2d 529 (N.C. App. 1992).

53. *Solich v. George and Anna Portes Cancer Prevention Center of Chicago, Inc.,* 606 N.E. 2d 572 (Ill. App. 1 Dist., 1992).

54. *Murray v. Countryman Creek Ranch,* 838 P.2d 431 (Mont. 1992).

55. *Board of Education of Watertown City School Dist. v. Watertown Educ. Assn.,* 549 N.Y.S.2d 652 (Ct. App., 1989).

56. *Mathews v. Harris Methodist, Fort Worth,* 834 S.W. 2d 582 (Tex. App.-Fort Worth, 1992) (claim for negligent removal of a decedent's corneas).

57. *Oregon Natural Resources Council, Inc. v. Grossarth,* 979 F. 2d 1377 (9th Cir. (Or.), 1992) (case moot).

58. *Kutner & Reynolds, Advanced Torts; Cases and Materials,* 513–516 (1989); Annot., 52 A.L.R. 4th 618 (1987); Note, *Group Defamation,* 64 *Tex. L. Rev.* 591 (1985).

59. *State Water Resources Control Bd. v. Office of Administrative Law (Bay Planning Coalition),* 16 Call. Rptr. 2d 25 (Cal. App. 1 Dist., 1993).

60. *Breakers of Fort Walton Beach Condos., Inc. v. Atlantic Beach Mgmt., Inc.,* 552 So. 2d 274 (Fla. DCA, 1989).

61. 15 *National Law Journal,* (27) 17 (March 8, 1993).

62. *Homewood Fishing Club v. Archer Daniels Midland Co.,* 605 N.E. 2d 1140 (Ill. App. 4 Dist., 1992) (suit by club over pollution of lake owned by the club).

63. *Smith v. States General Life Ins. Co.*, 592 So. 2d 1021 (Ala. 1992). *See contra Fuller v. Preferred Risk Life Ins. Co.*, 577 So. 2d 878 (Ala. 1991) (stating that the court may order a defendant who receives a punitive damage award to pay part of the award to either a state general fund or fund that serves a public purpose or advances the cause of justice).

64. *Torrance County Mental Health Program, Inc. v. New Mexico Health and Environmental Dept.*, 830 P.2d 145 (N.M. 1992).

65. *Wollersheim v. Church of Scientology of Calif.*, 260 *Calif. Rptr.* 331 (App., 1989).

66. *Gibson v. Kentucky State University*, 799 S.W.2d 38 (Ky., 1990).

67. *English v. New England Medical Center*, 541 N.E.2d 329 (Mass. S.J., 1989). cap o.k.; not o.k. in *Branigan v. Usitalo*, 587 A.2d 1232 (N.H. 1991); and Florida (3rd D.C.A. 1991).

68. *Hanvey v. Oconee Memorial Hosp.*, 416 S.E. 2d 623 (S.C. 1992).

69. *Leppert v. Lake Breeze Homeowners Assn., Inc.*, 500 S.2d 250 (Fla. App. 1986).

70. *American National Red Cross v. S.G.*, 112 S. Ct. 2465 U.S.N.H., 1992).

71. *Los Angeles County Bar Ass'n v. Eu*, 979 F. 2d 697 (9th Cir. (Cal.), 1992) (statute found constitutional).

72. *Southern Utah Wilderness Alliance v. Board of State Lands and Forestry of State*, 830 P.2d 233 (Utah, 1992).

73. *Allnet Communication Service, Inc. v. National Exchange Carrier Ass'n, Inc.*, 965 F.2d 1118 (D.C. Cir., 1992).

74. *New York Marine Managers, Inc. v. M.V. Topor*, 715 F. Supp. 783 (D.C., N.Y., 1989); *Olson v. Magnuson*, 457 N.W. 2d 394 (Minn. App. 1990).

75. *Pitco Frialator v. Guaranty Fund Management Services*, 590 N.Y.S. 2d 989 (N.Y. Sup., 1992).

76. *St. Mary of the Plains College v. Higher Education Loan Program of Kansas, Inc.*, 724 F. Supp. 803 (D.C., Kan. 1989).

77. *Save Our Cumberland Mountains, Inc. v. Lujan*, 963 F. 2d 1541 (D.C. Cir., 1992).

78. *Griffith v. Faltz*, 785 P.2d 119 (Ariz. App., 1990).

79. *St. Mary of the Plains College v. Higher Education Loan Program of Kansas, Inc.*, 724 F. Supp. 803 (D.C., Kan. 1989).

80. *Pavestone v. Interlock Pavers, Inc.*, 771 P.2d 236 (OK App. 1989).

81. *Campbellton-Graceville Hosp. v. Department of Health and Rehabilitative Services*, 610 So. 2d 82 (Fla. App. 1 Dist., 1992).

82. *Salt Lake Community Action Program, Inc. v. Sullivan*, 785 F. Supp 1013 (D.D.C. 1992).

83. *In re Applications A 14137, A 14138A, A 14138B, and A14139*, 480 N.W. 709 (Neb. 1992).

84. *Mirak v. McGhan Medical Corp.*, 142 F.R.D. 34 (D. Mass., 1992).

85. *Stanfield v. Polk County*, 492 N.W. 2d 648 (Iowa, 1992).

86. *State ex rel. Vaughn v. Koehr*, 835 S.W. 2d 543 (Mo. App. E.D., 1992).

87. *Bel-O-Mar Interstate Planning Com'n v. West Virginia Com'n on Aging*, 423 S.E. 2d 867 (W. Va., 1992) (commission has discretion to reduce number of area aging agencies).

88. *Local and Regional Monitor v. City of Los Angeles (City Centre Development)*, 16 Cal. Rptr. 358 (Cal. App. 2 Dist., 1992) (nonprofit corporation could not mandate second environmental impact report).

89. *Dioxin/Organochlorine Center v. Washington State Dept. of Ecology*, 837 P.2d 1007 (Wash., 1992).

90. *Brewery Arts Center v. State Bd. of Examiners*, 843 P.2d 369 (Nev., 1992).

91. *Weeks v. City of Tillamook*, 844 P.2d 914, (Or. App., 1992).

92. *Florida Pharmacy Ass'n, Inc. v. Strong*, 604 So. 2d 529 (Fla. App. 1 Dist., 1992).

93. *Balmoral Racing Club, Inc. v. Illinois Racing Bd.*, 603 N.W. 2d 489 (Ill., 1992).

94. Brunson, *Some Problems Presented by Unincorporated Associations in Civil Procedure*, 7 S.C. Law Q. 396–426 (1955).

95. *See*, Comment, *Unincorporated Assns: Diversity Jurisdiction and the A.L.I. Proposal*, 1965 Duke L.J. 329; Note, *Hazards of Enforcing Claims Against Unincorporated Associations in Florida*, 17 U. Fla. L.R. 211 (1964); Lloyd, *Actions Instituted by or Against Unincorporated Bodies*, 12 Mod. L. Rev. 408 (1949); Sturgis, *Unincorporated Associations as Parties to Actions*, 33 Yale L.J. 383 (1924); Note, 9 Can. B. Rev. 223 (1931); Wrightington, *Unincorporated Associations and Business Trusts* 425 (2d ed., 1923); Dodd, *Dogma and Practice of Associations and Business Trusts*, 425 (2d., 1923); Dodd, *Dogma and Practice of Associations*, 42 Harv. L. Rev. 977 (1929); Note, 29 N.C. Law Rev. 335 (1951); Magill, *The Suability of Labor Unions*, 1 N.C. Law Rev. 81 (1922); Note, 7 Minn. L. Rev. 42 (1922); 1 N.C. Law Rev. 81 (1922); Note, 7 Minn. L. Rev. 42 (1922); Holdoegel, *Jurisdiction Over Partnerships*, 11 Iowa L. Rev. 193 (1926); Warren, *Corporate Advantages Without Incorporation* 544 (1929); Crane, *Liability of Unincorporated Associations for Tortious Injury to a Member*, 16 Vand. L. Rev. 319 (1963).

96. *See*, as to mutual associations and insurance: Ann., 88 A.L.R. 164; as to boards of trade: Ann., 141 A.L.R., 789; as to trust groups: Ann., 71 A.L.R. 898.

97. Fed. Rules Civ. Proc., Rule 17(b).

98. *Ibid.* AFL-CIO v. Ogilvie, 465 F.2d 221 (C.A. Ill. 1972). Especially labor unions: United Mine Workers v. Coronado Coal Co., 259 U.S. 344 (1922). Judgment enforceable only against the organization's assets, 29 U.S.C.A. §185.

99. *See* n.94; and §446. *See* Silliman v. Dupont, 302 A.2d 327 (Del. Super. 1972) (10 Del. C. §3904 permits associations to be sued in the name presented to the public).

100. United Packing House Workers v. Boynton, 240 Iowa 212, 35 N.W.2d 881 (1949); State *ex rel.* W. Va. State Lodge, Fraternal Order of Police v. City of Charleston, 133 W. Va. 403; 56 S.E.2d 763; Ann., 149 A.L.R. 510 (1949); and, in equity too: Milam v. Settle, 127 W. Va. 271; 32 S.E.2d 269 (1944); State *ex rel.* Glass Bottle Blowers Assn. of U.S. and Canada v. Silver, 155 S.E.2d 564 (W. Va. 1967). O'Bryant v. Veterans of Foreign Wars, 376 N.E.2d 521 (2dD.C.A. Ind. 1978).

101. United case, n.100; Coughlin v. Iowa High School Athletic Assn., 150 N.W.2d 660 (Iowa 1967); 149 A.L.R. 516.

102. Askew v. Joachim Memorial Home, 234 N.W.2d 226 (N.D. 1975).

103. N.Y.C.P.L. and R. §901. *And see* Brunson article, n.94, for many other statutes.

104. Fed. Rules Civ. Proc., Rule 23(a); Ohio Rev. Code §§1745.01–1745.04.

105. The purpose of a class action, as a tool of judicial administration is to enable representative party or parties to litigate, in a single lawsuit, legal questions common to a class of persons. *See*, Dubose v. Harris, 434 F. Supp. 227 (D.C. Conn. 1977). *And see*: Ohio Rev. Code Sec. 1745.01. Even against a *committee* that has autonomy (*e.g.*, welfare fund, or grievance committee for several branches) may be sued as an entity. Marsh v. General Grievance Committee, 1 Ohio St.2d 165, 205 N.E.2d 571 (1965).

106. Mich. Compiled Laws § 600.2051.

107. *See* the next Section, below. Even without a statute. Knight and Searle v. Dove [1964] 2 All. E.R. 307; noted in 80 Law Q. Rev. 326 (1964); Rivard v. Chicago Firefighters Union, 494 N.E.2d 756 (Ill. App. 1986).

108. *Rivard v. Chicago Firefighters Union, Local No. 2*, 522 N.E.2d 1195 (IL 1988); S.H.A., c. 110 Par. 2.209.1.

109. *Ermert v. Hartford Insur. Co.*, 559 So. 2d 467 (La., 1990). [See § 417.]

110. *Ohio Academy of Nursing Homes, Inc. v. Barry*, 523 N.E.2d 523 (OH App. 1987), *cert. den.*, June 1987; published July 1988.

111. *Calvary Baptist Church v. Joseph*, 522 N.E.2d 371 (IN Supr. Ct., 1988).

112. *See Cox v. Thee Evergreen Church A/K/A Evergreen Church*, 1992 WL 148116 (July 1, 1992).

113. *Blue Cross v. Protective Life Insurance Co.*, 527 So. 2d 125 (AL Civ. App. 1987; reported Aug. 1988); citing *Warth v. Weldin*, 422 U.S. 490, 511, 95 S. Ct. 2197, 2211, 45 L. Ed. 2d 343 (1975); cf. *Society of the Plastics Industry, Inc. v. County of Suffolk*, 573 N.E. 2d 1034 (N.Y. 1991).

114. Lyons v. American Legion Post No. 650, 175 N.E.2d 733 (Ohio 1961); McNulty v. Higginbotham, 252 Ala. 218, 40 S.2d 414 (1949).

115. *See*, Elliot v. Greer Presbyterian Church, 181 S.C. 84, 186 S.E. 651 (1936).

116. N.Y. Genl. Assns. L. §13, 14.

117. *Ibid.*

118. *See,* Brunson article, n.94, at pp. 415, 416.

119. Johnson v. Albritton, 101 Fla. 1285; 134 S. 563 (1931). Failure to serve all members of an unincorporated association may constitute the fatal defect of lack of an indispensable party. *Developments in the Law, Multiparty Litigation in Federal Courts,* 71 Harv. L. Rev. 874 (1958).

120. Slaughter v. Amer. Baptist Publ. Society, 150 S.W. 224 (1912).

121. McGinn v. Morrin, 158 Misc. 666; 286 N.Y.S. 410; *affd.,* 247 A.D. 770; 286 N.Y.S. 411 (1936).

122. Brotherhood of R.R. Trainmen v. Agnew, 170 Miss. 604; 155 S. 205 (1934).

123. Oleck, *Debtor-Creditor Law* (New York: Central Book Co. 1959 Supp.).

124. Montgomery Ward v. Langer, 168 F.2d 182, 189 (1948); Pennover v. Neff, 95 U.S. 714 (1877); Fall v. Eastin, 215 U.S. 1 (1909).

125. Thomas v. Dean, 432 S.W.2d 771 (Ark. 1968).

126. Masonic Widows and Orphans v. Hieatt Bros., 197 Ky. 301; 247 S.W. 34 (1923); Jacobs v. Murphy, 245 Ala. 260; 16 S.2d 859 (1944); Griefll v. Dullea, 66 Calif. App.2d 986; 153 P.2d 581.

127. *Restatement, Judgments,* §86, Comment i.

128. N.Y. Genl. Assns. L. §15; Ohio Rev. Code §1745.02.

129. Conn. Genl. Stat. Ann. §52–76; Lawler v. Murphy, 58 Conn. 294, 20 A. 457 (1889); and Ohio, *see,* n. 97. *See* the next section.

130. Montgomery Ward case, n. 124.

131. N.Y. Genl. Assn. L. §16; N.J. Stat. Ann. §2 A:64–5; *and see,* Flagg v. Nichols, 307 N.Y. 96, 120 N.E.2d 513 (1954).

132. In the text, at n. 94.

133. *See generally,* Marshall v. International Longshoremen's and Warehousemen's Union, 57 Cal.2d 781, 371, 371 P.2d 987. 23 Cal. Rptr. 403 (1962).

134. Cousin v. Taylor, 115 Ore. 472, 239 P. 96, 41 A.L.R. 750 (1925); People v. Herbert, 162 Misc. 817, 295 N.Y.S. 251 (1937); Blair v. Southern Clay Mfg. Co., 173 Tenn. 571, 121 S.W.2d 570 (1938); Stone v. Guth, 232 Mo. 217, 102 S.W.2d 738 (1937); Security-First Natl. Bank v. Cooper, 62 Cal. App.2d 653, 145 P.2d 722 (1943); *and see,* Wrightington, *Unincorporated Assns. and Business Trusts* (1923); 3 C.J.S., *Agency,* §259; Crane, *Law of Partnership* 537 (1952).

135. Bacon v. Gardner, 38 Wash.2d 299, 299 P.2d 523 (1951); Notes, 39 Yale L.J. 874 (1930); 18 Calif. L. Rev. 707 (1930); Anno. L.R.A. 1915D, 982. L.R.A. 1916D, 335; 45 A.L.R. 198 (1926); 59 A.L.R. 55 (1929).

136. Confusion as to "entity" or "group of individuals" concepts was criticized in, Note, *Constitutional Rights of Associations to Assert the Privilege Against Self-Incrimination,* 112 U. Pa. L. Rev. 394 (1964), citing Hale v. Henkel, 201 U.S. 43 (1906) that associations are not "persons," and Supreme Court difficulties in cases involving unincorporated associations. Under the decision in, United States v. White, 322 U.S. 694, 700 (1944), associations again were denied the privilege available to "persons." Hale v. Henkel's artificial separation of associations from their agents still confuses decisions in self-incrimination cases, but seems consistent with the trend towards "entity."

137. American Federation of Labor v. Reilly, 113 Colo. 90, 155 P.2d 145, 160 A.L.R. 873 (1944).

138. *See,* 1 Oleck, *Modern Corporation Law* §26 (1978 Supp.), citing typical statutes, and cases.

139. 196 N.E.2d 324 (Ohio Ct. of Appeals, 8th Dist., #26670, Opinion Feb. 14, 1964); Skeel writing the opinion; Silbert and Corrigan concurring.

140. Ohio Rev. Code, §1745.01.

141. *See,* N.J. Stat. Anno., tit. 2A, c. 64; N.Y.C.P.L. and R., §1025; Okla. Stat. Anno., tit. 12, §182.

142. Ohio Rev. Code §1745.02 speaks only of execution against association assets, but a case held that the statutory right to sue the "entity" is one in addition to the right to hold the members of an unincorporated association (American Legion Post) personally liable: Lyons v. American Legion Post No. 650 Realty Co., 17S N.E.2d 733 (Ohio 1961).

143. As to the federal view, that an association is an entity for suit (venue, jurisdiction) purposes, but that tort liability applies only to members generally, *see*, Sperry Products v. Assn. of Amer. R.R., 132 F.2d 408 (2d Cir. 1942), *cert. den.* 63 S.Ct. 1031; Nehemiah v. Athletics Congress of U.S., 765 F.2d 42 (1985).

144. *See*, DeVillars v. Hessler, 363 Pa. 498, 70 A.2d 333 (1950), 14 A.L.R.2d 470; Anno., 14 A.L.R.2d 473 (1950).

145. *See*, Crane, *Liability of Unincorporated Association of Tortious Injury to a Member*, 16 Vand. L. Rev. 319 (1963), citing Marshall v. International Longshoremen's and W. Union, 57 Cal.2d 781, 22 Cal. Rptr. 211, 371 P.2d 987 (1962), *and see* Inglis v. Operating Engrs. Local Union No. 12, 18 Cal. Rptr. 187; *affd.* 23 Cal. Rptr. 403, 373 P.2d 467 (1962).

146. Citing, 1 Oleck, *Modern Corporation Law*, c. 1, 2 (1978 Supp.).

147. *See*, Note, *Development in the Law: Judicial Control of Actions of Private Associations*, 76 Harv. L. Rev. 983 (1963).

148. 205 N.E.2d 884 (Ohio 1965).

149. 44 Ohio St.2d 49, 337 N.E.2d 625 (Ohio 1975).

150. *See generally*, Burlington, *Unincorporated Associations; Tanner v. Loyal Order of Moose*, 9 Akron L. Rev., 602–608 (1976).

151. Wallick v. International Union of Elec., R. and M.W., 90 Ohio L. Abs. 584 (1962). Compare, Meriwhether v. Atkin, 137 Mo. App. 32, 119 S.W. 36 (1909), which held an association not to be bound through its members who acted might be; American Art Works v. Republican State Committee, 177 Okla. 420, 60 P.2d 786 (1936) political committee members not liable; Magness v. Chicora Chapter, 193 So. Car. 205, 8 S.E.2d 344 (1940) members held liable; Mitterhausen v. South Wisconsin Conference Assn., 245 Wis. 353, 14 N.W.2d 19 (1944) trustee-members held liable: Note, *Liability of Members and Officers of Non-Profit Associations for Contracts and Torts*, 42 Calif. L. Rev. 812 (1954).

152. Benoit v. Amalgamated Local 229 U.E.R.M.W., 188 A.2d 499 (Conn. 1963).

153. United Brotherhood of Carpenters and J. of Amer. v. Humphreys, 127 S.E.2d 98 (Va. 1962).

154. *See*, c.5. Associations can be taxed as corporations: *see*, Sarner, article, 20 N.Y.U. Inst. Fed. Tax. 609 (1962). *And see*, n. 136, 141, 146.

155. Anno., 14 A.L.R.2d 473 (1950); DeVillars v. Hessler, 363 Pa. 498, 70 A.2d 333 (1950).

156. Crane, article, n. 145. But in a small group (*e.g.*, a three- or five-man partnership) the individual members deny association (partnership) status too, when that is inconvenient; as in refusal of workmen's compensation coverage to an injured employee or a partnership of farmers, in, Campos v. Tomoi, 122 N.W.2d 473 (Neb. 1963).

157. Thomas v. Dunne, 131 Colo. 20, 279 P.2d 427 (1955).

158. Crane, article, n. 145; Marchitto v. Central R. Co. of N.J., 9 N.J. 456, 88 A.2d 851 (1952).

159. International Assn. of Machinists v. Gonzales, 78 S.Ct. 923, 356 U.S. 617, 2 L.Ed.2d 1018 (1958); Morton v. Local 20, Teamsters, Chauffeurs, and Helpers Union, 200 F. Supp. 653 (N.D. Ohio 1961) awarded punitive damages.

160. Fray v. Amalgamated Meat Cutters, *etc.*, 9 Wis.2d 631, 101 N.W.2d 782 (1960). But no duty was required in Marshall v. International Longshoremen's and W. Union, Local 6, 57 Cal.2d 781, 22 Cal. Rptr. 211, 371 P.2d 987 (1962).

161. Finnegan v. Penna. R. Co., 76 N.J. Super. 71, 183 A.2d 779 (1962); *but see* (no special duty involved) Marshall case, *supra*. n. 95.

162. *See* comments at n.149.

163. *Basich v. Board of Pensions of Evangelical Lutheran Church in America*, 493 N.W. 2d 293 (Minn. App., 1992) (congregation and ministers not "members" of the denomination or board of pensions).

164. *See*, Hornstein, *Shareholder's Derivative Suit in the U.S.*, 1967 J. Bus. L. 282 (1967); 3 Oleck, *Modern Corporation Law*, c. 63 (1978 supp.); Henn and Alexander, *Corporations* §§358–381 (3rd ed., 1983).

165. N.Y. NPCL §623; Henn and Boyd, *Statutory Trends* . . . , 66 Cornell L.R. 1103, 1123 (1981).

166. Price v. Gurney, 324 U.S. 100 (1945); Koster v. Lumbermen's Mutual Cas. Co., 330 U.S. 578, 522 (1947).

167. Durr v. Paragon Trading Corp., 270 N.Y. 464, 1 N.E.2d 967 (1936); *Black's Law Dictionary* 27 (5th ed., 1979).

168. Huester v. Gilmour, 13 F. Supp. 630 (D.C. Pa., 1936); James v. Ahmanson & Co., 460 P.2d 464 (Calif. 1964).

169. Aronson v. Lewis, 473 A.2d 805 (Del., 1984).

170. *See*, n.164, Hornstein at p. 286, and Oleck, c. 63; Henn and Alexander, *Corporations* §§358–381 (3rd ed., 1983).

171. *E.g.*, such as Uniform Class Actions (12 U.L.A. Supp.) Act; Fed. Rules Civ. Proc., Rules 23, 23.1; but *c.f.*, N.Y. Bus. Corp. L. §§720,627 (security for expenses), *etc.*

172. *Brenner v. Powers*, 584 N.E. 2d 569 (Ind. App. 3 Dist. 1992).

173. *Norton v. National Research Foundation*, 141 F.R.D. 510 (D. Kan., 1992).

174. *Associated General Contractors of California, Inc. v. Coalition for Economic Equity*, 950 F.2d 1401 (9th Cir. 1991); *see also Kansas Health Care Ass'n, Inc. v. Kansas Dept. of Social and Rehabilitative Services*, 958 F.2d 1018 (10th Cir. (Kan.), 1992); *Save Ourselves, Inc. v. U.S. Army Corps of Engineers*, 958 F.2d 659 (5th Cir. (La.), 1992); *Retired Chicago Police Ass'n v. City of Chicago*, 141 F.R.D. 477 (N.D. Ill., 1992);

175. *Schulz v. Warren County Bd. of Sup'rs*, 581 N.Y.S. 2d 885 (N.Y.A.D. 3 Dept., 1992).

176. *Central American Refugee Center-Carecen (N.Y.) v. City of Glen Cove*, 753 F. Supp. 437 (E.D.N.Y. 1990).

177. *Matter of BASF Corp., Chemical Division*, 528 So. 2d 162 (LA App. 1988); *Costain Florida, Inc. v. Metropolitan Dade County*, 528 So. 2d 35 (FL App. 1988).

178. *First Union Natl. Bk. of Ga. v. Independent Insur. Agents of Ga., Ins.*, 398 S.E.2d 254 (Ga. App. 1990).

179. *In re U.S. Catholic Conference*, 885 F.2d 1020 (2d Cir., N.Y., 1989), affd, without op. by U.S. Supr. Ct. (Apr. 30, 1989), reported in *Baltimore Sun*, and *St. Petersburg Times* (May 1, 1990).

180. *National Federation of Federal Employees & Cheney*, 883 F.2d 1038 (D.C. Cir., 1989); citing *Flast v. Cohen*, 88 S. Ct. 1942 (1968).

181. *Coalition of Mental Health Professions v. Dept. of Professional Regulation*, 546 So. 2d 27 (Fla. D.C. App., 1989).

182. *State of Florida, Board of Optometry v. Florida Society of Ophthalmology*, 538 So. 2d 878 (Fla. D.C.A., 1988), rev. denied 542 So. 2d 1333 (Fla. 1989).

183. *National Federation of Federal Employees v. Cheney*, 883 F.2d 1038, 1042 (D.C. Cir. 1989).

184. *National Environmental Foundation v. ABC Rail Corp.*, 926 F.2d 1096 (11th Cir., Ala., 1991).

185. *League of United Latin Amer. Citizens v. Clements*, 923 F.2d 365 (5th Cir. 1991).

186. *Long Beach Township Oceanfront Property Owners Ass'n v. New Jersey Dep't of Envtl. Protection*, 584 A. 2d 820 (N.J. Super. A.D. 1990).

187. *Florex, et al. v. U.S. and Floral Trade Council of Davis*, 705 F. Supp. 582 (Ct. of Intnatl. Trade, 1989).

188. *International Jai-Alai Players Assn. v. Florida Pari-Mutuel Commission*, 561 So. 2d 1224 (Fla. 3rd DCA, 1990).

189. *HCA Health Services of Virginia, Inc. v. Metropolitan Life Ins. Co.*, 752 F. Supp. 202 (E.D. Va. 1990).

190. Model Nonprofit Corp. Act (1986 Revision Draft), Subchap. E (1); Comment of ABA committee.

191. Stern v. Lucy Webb Hayes Natl. Training School, 38 F. Supp. 1003 (D.C., D.C., 1974).

192. (Rev.) Model NPC Act (1986 draft) §§8.50–8.58.

193. *Ibid.* §8.50.

194. *Id.* §8.51.

195. *Id.* §8.53.

196. *Id.* §8.52, 8.54.

197. *Id.* §8.55.

198. *Id.* §8.56.

199. *Id.* §8.58.

200. *Id.* §8.57. But if §§8.51, 8.52, 8.53, or 8.54 are employed, that must be reported in writing to the members. *Id.* §16.21.

201. **Globus v. Law Research Service, Inc.**, 418 F.2d 1272 (2d Cir., 1969), cert. den. 397 U.S. 913 (1970).

202. **Shapiro v. American Home Assur. Co.**, 584 F. Supp. 1245 (D.C., Mass., 1984).

203. 80 U.S. (13 Wall.) 679, 20 L.Ed. 666 (1872).

204. **York v. First Presbyterian Church**, 474 N.E.2d 716 (Ill. App., 1984).

205. *Watson v. Jones*, 80 U.S. 679, 727, 20 L.Ed. 666, 676 (1872). *See*, for example, *First Baptist Church v. Owens*, 474 S. 2d 638 (Ala., 1985).

206. *Presbyterian Church v. Mary Elizabeth Blue Hull Mem. Presb. Church*, 393 U.S. 440, 21 L.Ed. 658 (1969).

207. *Jones v. Wolf*, 443 U.S. 595, 61 L.Ed. 2d 775 (1979).

208. **Abortion Rights Mobilization, Inc. v. Regan**, 544 F. Supp. 471 (D.C., N.Y., 1982).

209. **Madsen v. Erwin**, 481 N.E.2d 1160 (Mass. S.J., 1985).

210. **Townsend v. Teagle**, 467 S. 2d 772 (Fla. 1st D.C. App., 1985).

211. **Serbian Eastern Orthodox Diocese v. Milivojevich**, 426 U.S. 696, 49 L.Ed. 2d 151 (1976).

212. **Alamo Foundation v. Secretary of Labor**, #83–1935; U.S. Supr. Ct. (Apr., 1986), affg. 8th Cir. Ct. App.; Natl. L.J. (May 6, 1985); St. Petersburg, *Times* (Apr. 24, 1985).

213. **St. John's Evangelical Lutheran Church v. City of Hoboken**, 479 A.2d 935 (N.J. Super., 1985).

214. *Peterson v. San Francisco Community College Dist.*, 205 Cal. Rptr. 842, 685 P.2d 1193 (1985).

215. *See*, Oleck, *Tort Law Practice Manual*, c. 17 (1982), citing: **Williams v. First United Church of Christ**, 40 Ohio App. 2d 187, 318 N.E.2d 562 (1974).

216. **State v. South County Jewish Federation**, 491 S.2d 1183 (Fla. 4th D.C. App., 1986); Fla. Stat. §849.093 (11).

217. *Boley v. Miller*, 418 S.E. 2d 352 (W. Va., 1992).

218. *Family Planning Alternatives, Inc. v. Pruner*, 15 Cal. Rptr. 2d 316 (Cal. App. 6 Dist., 1993).

219. *Brenner v. Powers*, 584 N.E. 2d 569 (Ind. App. 3 Dist. 1992).

220. *Parker v. Jones Community Hospital*, 549 So. 2d 443 (Miss., 1989). The old common law requirement that a witness have belief in God has long been abandoned.

221. *Mu Chapter of Delta Kappa Epsilon, by Swett v. Colgate University*, 578 N.Y.S. 2d 713 (A.D. 3 Dept. 1992).

222. *Ragin v. Harry Macklowe Real Estate Co., Inc.*, 801 F. Supp. 1213 (S.D.N.Y., 1992).

223. *Holdredge Co-op Assn. v. Wilson*, 463 N.W.2d 312 (Nebr. 1990); Nebr. S. Ct. Rules of Practice, Rule 9, subd. E.

224. *Texas County Irrigation & Water Ass'n & Water Comm'n v. Oklahoma Water Resources Bd.*, 803 P. 2d 1119 (Okl. 1990); 75 O.S. Supp. 1989, § 306; 82 O.S. Supp. 1989, § 1020.6.

225. *Rent Stabilization Ass'n v. Higgins*, 562 N.Y.S. 2d 962 (A.D. 1 Dept. 1990).

226. *Rhodes v. Palmetto Pathway Homes, Inc.*, 400 S.E. 2d 484 (S.C. 1991).

227. *Church of Scientology Flag Services Orgn. v. City of Clearwater*, 773 F. Supp. 321 (D.C. Fl. 1991).

228. *American Motorcyclist Ass'n v. Park Com'n of City of Brockton*, 592 N.E. 2d 1314 (Mass. 1992).

229. *First Church of the Nazarene of Cincinnati v. Ohio Dep't of Liquor Control*, 565 N.E. 2d 872 (Ohio App. 1989).

230. *Habel v. Industrial Development Authority of the City of Lynchburg*, 400 S.E. 2d 516 (Va. 1991); Const. Art. 1, § 16; U.S.C.A. Const. Amend. 1.

231. *Travis v. Owego-Apalachin School Distr.* (U.S. 2d Cir., N.Y., Feb. 18, 1991).

232. *Austin v. Michigan Chamber of Commerce*, 58 U.S.L.W. 37 (March 27, 1990).

233. *Society of the Plastics Industry, Inc. v. County of Suffolk*, 573 N.E. 2d 1034 (N.Y. 1991); *Ohio State Pharmaceutical Assn. v. Wickham*, 573 N.E. 2d 148 (Ohio App. 1989, publ. 1991).

234. *Arkansas Wildlife Federation v. Bekaert Corp.*, 791 F. Supp. 769 (D. Mass., 1992).

235. *Friends of the Everglades, Inc. v. Board of Trustees of Internal Imp. Trust Fund*, 595 So. 2d 186 (Fla. 1st DCA 1992).

236. *Cowiche Canyon Conservancy v. Bosley*, 828 P.2d 549 (Wash. 1992).

237. *Ecumenical Task Force of Niagara Frontier, Inc. v. Love Canal Area Revitalization Agency*, 583 N.Y.S. 2d 859 (N.Y.A.D. 4 Dept, 1992).

238. *Citizens for Clean Air v. Com., ex rel. State Air Pollution Control Bd.*, 412 S.E. 2d 715 (Va. App. 1991).

239. *Louisiana Associated General Contractors, Inc. v. Calcasieu Parish School Bd.*, 586 So. 2d 1354 (La. 1991).

240. Virginia Court of Appeals (Dec. 11, 1991).

241. *Northern Woods Civic Assn. v. City*, 508 N.E. 2d 676 (Ohio App. 1986). (Zoning case). *Contra: American Legal Foundation v. F.C.C.* 808 F. 2d 84 (D.C. Cir., 1987).

242. *League of Women Voters v. Eu (Wilson)*, 9 Cal. Rptr. 2d 416 (Cal. App. 3 Dist., 1992).

243. *Nemazee v. Mt. Sinai Medical Center*, 564 N.E.2d 477 (Ohio 1990).

244. *City of Chicago v. Matchmaker Real Estate Sales Center, Inc.*, 982 F. 2d 1086 (7th Cir. (Ill.), 1992).

245. *House Speaker v. Governor*, 491 N.W. 2d 832 (Mich. App., 1992).

246. *Trout Unlimited Muskegon White River Chapter v. City of White Cloud*, 489 N.W. 2d 188 (Mich. App., 1992).

247. *Miller v. City of Manchester*, 834 S.W. 2d 904 (Mo. App. E.D., 1992).

248. *City of Atlanta v. North by Northwest Civic Ass'n, Inc.*, 422 S.E. 2d 651 (Ga, 1992).

249. *Waterford Citizens' Ass'n v. Reilly*, 970 F. 2d 1287 (4th Cir. (Va.), 1992) (citizen suit to force the EPA to review procedures required under the National Historic Preservation Act).

250. *Hunt Paving Co., Inc. v. City of Indianapolis*, 800 F. Supp. 740 (S.D. Ind., 1992).

251. *Cone Corp. v. Hillsborough County*, 983 F. 2d 197 (11th Cir. (Fla.), 1993).

252. *Lujan v. Defenders of Wildlife*, 112 S.Ct. 2130 (1992).

253. 112 S.Ct. at 2135.

254. *Id.*

255. 112 S.Ct. at 2138.

256. 112 S.Ct. at 2142.

257. *Lujan*, 112 S.Ct. at 2130.

258. *Id.*

259. *Id.*

260. *Id.*

45

AMENDMENTS, EXTENSIONS, AND MERGERS

[See also, Chapter 40, *Affiliations.*]

[Bruce Kremers and Nelon Kirkland aided in the updating research for this chapter.]

§451. AMENDMENTS AND CORRECTIONS OF CHARTERS

An *amendment* of an organization's governing document or documents may be either a *revision* or a *correction* of that writing, meant to correct errors or better to state its intended meaning or purpose. Rather precise statutory requirements concerning amendments of, and changes in, corporation chapters apply in almost every state. These statutes specify what must be *stated* in a certificate of correction or amendment, *who* must *sign, subscribe,* or *acknowledge* it, and so forth.[1]

A typical statute states examples of what may be amended (*e.g.*, name, purposes, etc.), voting requirements (usually majority vote), who may vote (usually the members), filing procedures, and filing fees.[2] No procedures other than those stated in the statute are proper, ordinarily.[3]

Amendments to conform the articles of incorporation to the actual practices of the organization are common.[4]

Statements of continued existence. Many state statutes now require all non-profit corporations to file with the secretary-of-state periodic statements of their continued existence and operation.[5] Often these must be filed every five years, or three years.

Corporations that are required to report to other state authorities (*.e.g.*, charitable organizations) may be exempt from this requirement.[6]

Failure to file usually may be cured by later filing and payment of a penalty fee.[7] (See §351: *Annual Reports.*)

These reports are the basis of listing by the secretary-of-state, with the Tax Commissioner, of dormant or delinquent organizations.[8] While not actually amendments, such reports serve to keep current some record of organizations' actual practices.

Continued failure to file such statements results in cancellation of the articles of incorporation.[9]

FORM NO. 183
Statement of Continued Existence
[Official Form: Ohio]

Prescribed by Ted W. Brown Secretary of State C-119	Corporation Number_____ Approved _____ Date_____ Fee_____ **FOR OFFICIAL USE ONLY**

STATEMENT OF CONTINUED EXISTENCE

_____ (Name of Corporation) _____, a corporation not for profit organized under the provisions of Chapter 1702 of the Revised Code (or previous laws, or under special provisions of the Revised Code, or created prior to September 1, 1851 and having elected to be governed by subsequent laws and whose articles or other documents are filed with the Secretary of State), and not specifically exempted by this section, makes the following verified statement to the Secretary of State:

1. Corporation name _____.
2. Location of principal office_____
   (City, Village or Township & County)
3. Date of incorporation_____
4. The corporation is still actively engaged in exercising its corporate privileges.
5. a. Name of statutory agent _____
   b. Address of agent_____
   _____

IN WITNESS WHEREOF, said _____ has caused this

statement to be executed by an officer (trustee, three members in good standing) duly authorized in the premises, this _____ day of _____, 19____.

_____

(Name of Corporation)

By _____

(Title)

FILING FEE: $_____

Corrections. Corrections of errors in the charter usually require the filing of formal amendatory certificates with the secretary of the state of original incorporation.[10] But such corrections may not impair rights already acquired by anyone under the original wording of the charter.[11] And the form, language, and contents of such amendatory certificates are usually specified in the state's corporation statutes.[12]

Amendments. Amendments (changes) in charters may be made in the same way as corrections. Usually they do not require two-thirds approval by the directors or members, unless the charter or bylaws themselves so specify. This is because they do not import the *nunc pro tunc* (*now for then:* retroactive) effect that is present in a correction. In most cases, the statutes permit the filing of amendatory certificates on the basis of a simple majority vote obtained at a duly called meeting.[13]

The charter of statutory rules for amendments must be followed closely. In some cases the charter, bylaws, constitution, or other internal rules can (and do) provide for a higher percentage of approval than simple majority.[14] They also can (and do) provide for *repeal* of existing rules.[15]

Even unanimous adoption by the board of directors of an amendment to the original articles of incorporation is not effective if it does not comply with the state's statute about amendments in the absence of express provisions for them in the charter or by-laws; e.g., a statute requiring two-thirds vote of voting members at a meeting in such a case.[16]

"Unless otherwise provided in the articles of incorporation, members may amend the articles of incorporation, without action by the directors, at a meeting for which notice of the changes to be made is given," in Florida.[17]

A corporation is prohibited from amending its bylaws so as to impair a member's vested contractual rights.[18] And this principle probably can be extended to protect reasonable apprehension of irreparable harm to property or other rights.[19] On the other hand, corporate stock held by a nonprofit corporation is subject to execution levy and sheriff's sale under the procedures set forth in the Uniform Commercial Code.[20]

No powers not obtainable in an original incorporation may be obtained by use of amendments.[21] Nor may obligations and office-rights be eliminated by this device. Thus, reduction of the number of directors does not eliminate the extra directors until their terms expire or they resign.[22]

Adoption of an amendment, by vote, is not effective until the amendatory certificate is duly filed, and even then there may be a delay stated.[23]

See the next section below for the *tests* of validity of amendments to bylaws.

Approvals. All the administrative *approvals* required for filing an original charter (see Chapter 13) must be obtained for the amendatory certificate.[24] However, this requirement probably does not hold true for changes in merely internal regulations.[25]

Chapters and branches. Changes and amendments in the charters of branch organizations usually require the approval of the parent organizations.

Unincorporated associations. No filing of charters, nor therefore of amendments, may be required for unincorporated associations. But they are not free to do as they please. They must be constrained by the rules of parent bodies, as well as by their own internal rules. They may also be constrained by possible loss of tax-exempt status and by the general requirement of administrative approvals for public-welfare organizations.

The vague legal status of unincorporated associations here again produces legal problems without clear answers.

Forms. Statutory forms of amendment certificates are too highly specialized in each state to warrant provision of a *general* form here; however, it should be noted that merely filling in the blanks of a standard form may leave wide gaps in the actual outlook of a corporation not-for-profit, notwithstanding the form's legal sufficiency. In fact, a few states (*e.g.,* Florida) do not have many official forms for filling out and filing of any documents. Local texts and statutes must be consulted.[26]

Importance of statutory *form* cannot be overemphasized. To neglect statutory rules is to invite rejection of the amendatory certificate. Even a simple change in name must be in the precise statutory form.[27]

State changes in the law. All charters are granted subject to the reserved right of the state to change the law or to amend or repeal charters. If such an amendment or change occurs, by due process, there is no valid basis for complaint so long as contract rights are not destroyed.[28] Even in business corporations, such vested rights as a pre-emptive right to buy stock may be cut off by such amendment followed by corporate action.[29] And the state's motives are immaterial.[30] (See §452.)

Restated charter. When a series of amendments have been made, over a period of time, a corporation may (and should) file a "restated" articles of incorporation, in order to integrate all the changes into one final amended form. (See an example in the Form 193 which follows in this section.) Some jurisdictions permit such restatements to occur without a vote of the members. However, where this is so, coincident amendment may occur only if the requirements with respect to amendments are complied with, and the provisions being amended are identified. Such restated charter can then be executed, acknowledged, and filed in accordance with the provisions relating to the filing of amendments to articles of incorporation.[31]

Conversion into NPC. If a specific statute (for conversion of a profit school into a nonprofit school) is intended by the legislature to be followed, rather than the general NPC statute, then *all* the provisions of the special statute apply; *e.g.*, barring use of government bonds to support the school.[32]

§452. FORMS OF AMENDMENTS

FORM NO. 184
Resolution Adding a New Article

RESOLVED: That the provision of the articles of incorporation of this corporation are hereby amended by the addition of a New Article _____ to read as follows:

(here set out the new article.)

[An existing article being amended must be correctly identified by the numerical or other designation given it in the articles of incorporation; for example, if the article is designated as "Four" in the articles of incorporation, then it should be so identified in the resolution and not be identified as "4," or "IV," or "Fourth." If a new article is being added, it should be given the next succeeding numerical designation of the same kind (Arabic, Roman, cardinal, or ordinal) used to identify the other article provisions.]

FORM NO. 185
Resolution of Amendment

RESOLVED: That the provision of the articles of incorporation of this corporation which now reads:

(here quote the entire provision being amended)

is amended to read as follows:

(here set out the provision as amended).

[If an existing provision being amended is not given any separate numerical or other designation in the articles of incorporation, then it is necessary to quote the present wording of the provision for purposes of identification. The provision being amended must be a complete provision and should not consist merely of a phrase or clause.]

FORM NO. 186
Minutes of Amendment Vote (Meeting)

**CERTIFICATE OF AMENDMENT
IN MINUTES OF
GENERAL MEETING.**

At the general meeting held at _____
on October 5, 19_____, two-thirds of the Members and the Board of Directors present, a motion was made by R. F., seconded by S. B., President, that the following amendment be added to and made part of the Charter-by-Law of the Corporation:

> Upon the *dissolution* of the Corporation, the Board of Trustees shall, after paying or making provision for the payment of all the liabilities of the Corporation, dispose of all of the assets of the Corporation in such manner, or to such Organization or Organizations organized and operated exclusively for charitable, educational, Religious or scientific purposes as shall at the time qualify as an exempt organization or organizations under Section 501(c)(3) of the Internal Revenue Code 1954.

The proposed amendment was voted on by all present and approved.

After discussion by the Members as to the Corporations status, S. B., our President, volunteered to go to the New York State Division of Corporations, and proceed to have the Corporation status brought up to date.

A motion to adjourn was made by A. F., seconded by S. B. Motion carried.

Meeting adjourned at 9.15 p.m.

W. F.
Secretary General

Approved, S. B.
President.

State of New York,   ss:
County of New York

On this August 4, 19_____, before me personally appeared S. B. and W. F., to me known and known to me to be the individuals described in, and who executed the foregoing certificate, and they thereupon duly acknowledged to me that they executed the same.

[Notary Public]

FORM NO. 187
Certificate of Amendment of Articles

CERTIFICATE OF AMENDMENT OF THE CERTIFICATE OF INCORPORATION
OF

_____

(Pursuant to Article 2, Section 3 of the Religious Corporations Law of the State of New York)

It is hereby certified that:

FIRST: That the name of the corporation is:

SECOND: The certificate of incorporation of the corporation was filed and recorded in the County Clerk's Office of New York County on January 16, 19___.

THIRD: The Corporation was formed under the Religious Corporation Law.

FOURTH: The amendment of the certificate of incorporation affected by this certificate of amendment is to additionally add to a previous certificate of amendment authorized and voted by a Board of Directors on October 5, 19____, notarized on March 16, 19____ and certified by the County Clerk and Clerk of the Supreme Court of New York County on April 14, 19____, on what happens with the assets of the Corporation upon the dissolution.

FIFTH: To accomplish the foregoing amendment Article SECOND of the Certificate of incorporation of the corporation is hereby amended to read as follows:

> Notwithstanding any other provisions of these articles, the corporation is organized exclusively for one or more of the following purposes: religious, charitable, scientific, testing for public safety, literary or educational purposes, or to foster national or international amateur sports competition (but only if no part of its activities involve the provision of athletic facilities or equipment), or for the prevention of cruelty to children or animals, as specified in section 501(c)(3) of the Internal Revenue Code of 1954, and shall not carry on any activities not permitted to be carried on by a corporation exempt from Federal income tax under section 501(c)(3) of the Internal Revenue Code of 1954.

SIXTH: No approval or consent of any body or officer is required to be endorsed upon or annexed to this certificate of amendment of the certificate of incorporation prior to its delivery to the County Clerk of New York County for filing and recording.

IN WITNESS WHEREOF, we have subscribed this document on this August 4, 19_____ and do hereby affirm, under the penalties of perjury, that the statements contained therein have been examined by us and are true and correct.

_____

S. B., Legal President

_____

W. B., Secretary General

State of New York,
County of New York   ss:

On this August 4, 19_____ before me personally appeared S. B. and W. F., to me known and known to me to be the individuals described in, and who executed the foregoing certificate, and they thereupon duly acknowledged to me that they executed the same.

[Notary Public]

FORM NO. 188
Secretary of State Certificate of
Filing of Articles of Amendment

_____
FILE NUMBER   DOMESTIC

State of Washington | Department of State

I, **BRUCE K. CHAPMAN**, Secretary of State of the State of Washington and custodian of its seal, hereby certify that

ARTICLES OF AMENDMENT TO
ARTICLES OF INCORPORATION
UNIVERSITY FOUNDATION

of _____

a domestic corporation of ____(Amending Article II)_____ Washington,

_____

_____

_____

was filed for record in this office on this date, and I further certify that such Article remain on file in this office.

> In witness whereof I have signed and have affixed the seal of the State of Washington to this certificate at Olympia, the State Capital,

_____

_____

[Articles of Amendment are attached hereto.]

BRUCE K. CHAPMAN
SECRETARY OF STATE

FORM NO. 189
Articles of Amendment
(Illinois)

To be Filed
In Duplicate
Filing Fee $_____

(DO NOT WRITE
IN THIS SPACE)

Date _____
Filing Fee $ _____
Clerk _____

FORM NP-35
Articles of Amendment
to the
Articles of Incorporation
under the
General Not-For-Profit Corporation Act

To _____, Secretary of State, Springfield, Illinois:

The undersigned corporation, for the purpose of amending its Articles of Incorporation and pursuant to provisions of Section 35 of the "General Not-for-Profit Corporation Act" of the State of Illinois, hereby executes the following Articles of Amendment:

1. The name of the corporation is: _____

2. There are _____ members,
   (Insert "no" or "some")

having voting rights with respect to amendments:

(*Strike paragraphs (a), (b), or (c) not applicable*)

3. (a) At a meeting of the members, at which a quorum was present, held on _____, 19_____ same receiving at least two-thirds (2/3) of the votes entitled to be cast by the members of the corporation present or represented by proxy at such meeting.

   (b) By a consent in writing signed by all members of the corporation entitled to vote with respect thereto,

   (c) At a meeting of directors (members having no voting rights with respect to amendments) held on _____, 19 _____, same receiving the votes of a majority of the directors then in office, the following amendment or amendments were adopted in the manner prescribed by the "General Not-for-Profit Corporation Act" of the State of Illinois:

IN WITNESS WHEREOF, the undersigned corporation has caused these Articles of Amendment to be executed in its name by its _____ President, and its _____ Secretary, this _____ day of _____, 19_____.

(Exact Corporate Title)

By _____

Its _____ President

Its _____ President

Place
(CORPORATE SEAL)
Here

STATE OF _____
COUNTY OF _____ } ss.

I, _____, a Notary Public, do hereby certify that on the _____ day of _____, 19_____, _____

(Acknowledgment by either officer is sufficient)

personally appeared before me and, being first duly sworn by me, acknowledged that _____ he signed the foregoing document in the capacity therein set forth and declared that the statements therein contained are true.

IN WITNESS WHEREOF, I have hereunto set my hand and seal the day and year before written.

Place
(NOTARIAL SEAL)
Here

Notary Public

FORM NO. 190
Articles of Amendment
(North Carolina)

ARTICLES OF AMENDMENT
TO THE CHARTER OF

_____

(Name of Corporation)

The undersigned nonprofit corporation, for the purpose of amending its articles of incorporation, and in accordance with the provision of Section 55 A-36 of the North Carolina Nonprofit Corporation Act, hereby sets forth:

I

Name of the corporation _____

II

At a regularly convened meeting of the directors/members (strike word inapplicable) of the corporation held on the _____ day of _____, A.D. 19_____, the following amendment to the articles of incorporation was adopted:

III
(Strike inapplicable paragraph)

There are no members of the corporation having voting rights. The above amendment received the affirmative vote of a majority of the directors in office.

or

The corporation has members with voting rights. A quorum was present at the meeting held on the above date; and the said amendment received at least two-thirds of the votes entitled to be cast by members present or represented by proxy at such meetings.

IN TESTIMONY WHEREOF, the corporation has caused this document to be executed in its name by its President and Secretary this _____ day of _____, A.D. 19_____.

_____

By: _____
                        President

_____
                        Secretary

STATE OF _____
COUNTY OF _____

This is to certify that on this the _____ day of _____ _____, A.D. 19_____, personally appeared before me _____ _____ and _____, each of whom, being by me first duly sworn, deposes and says that he signed the foregoing "Articles of Amendment" in the capacity indicated, and that the statements therein contained are true and correct.

_____
Notary Public

My Commission expires: _____

FORM NO. 191
Certificate of Amendment
(Ohio)

[This form illustrates the corporation certification of the amendments filed. It does not attempt to state the actual amendment involved, which will vary in each case.]

**CERTIFICATE OF AMENDMENT
OF ARTICLES OF INCORPORATION
OF
. . . . . . SCHOOL
OF . . . . . . COLLEGE**

. . . . , President, and . . . . . . , Secretary, of . . . . . . School of . . . . . . College, an . . . . . . corporation not for profit, with its principal office located at . . . . . . , ... , do hereby certify that at a meeting of the Members of the said corporation duly called and held on the . . . . . . day of April, 19 . . , and at a meeting of the Trustees of the said corporation duly called and held on the . . . . . . day of April, 19 . . , at both of which meetings respectively quorums of Members and Trustees were present, the following resolution was duly adopted to amend the articles of incorporation of the said corporation:

**AMENDMENT OF THE ARTICLES OF INCORPORATION
OF
. . . . SCHOOL
OF . . . . COLLEGE
A Nonprofit Corporation**

RESOLVED, that the Articles of Incorporation of . . . . . . School of . . . . . . College be, and hereby are, amended in their entirety to be and to read as follows:
[Then, set out the newly adopted provisions.]

IN WITNESS WHEREOF, ..., President, and . . . . . ., Secretary, of . . . . . .
School of . . . . . . College, a nonprofit corporation, acting for and on
behalf of said corporation, have hereunto set their hands and affixed the
corporate seal this . . . . . . day of April, 19 . . .

                                                        (Signed)

   [Seal]

                              _____

                                          . . . .
                                                        (Signed)

                              _____

                                          . . . .

                              FORM NO. 192
                           Certificate of Amendment
                                (California)

                        CERTIFICATE OF AMENDMENT
                                    OF
                        ARTICLES OF INCORPORATION

JOHN DOE and RICHARD ROE certify:
   1. That they are the president and secretary, respectively, of _____
   _____
                         (insert correct name of corporation)
   a California corporation.
   2. That at a meeting of the board of directors of said corporation, duly held
      at _____, California, on _____, the
               (city or town)   (date)
      following resolution was adopted:
            "RESOLVED: That Article _____
      (insert correct designation)
      of the _____ articles of incorporation of this corporation be
      amended to read as follows:
                     (here set out the article as amended)."

   3. That a meeting of the members of said corporation, duly held at
      _____, California, on _____, a resolution was
            (city or town)   (date)
      adopted, and the wording of the amended article as set forth in the mem-
      bers' resolution is the same as that set forth in the directors' resolution
      in Paragraph 2 of this certificate.

   4. That the number of members who voted affirmatively for the adoption of
      said resolution is _____, and that the number of mem-
      bers constituting a quorum is _____.

_____
JOHN DOE, President

_____
RICHARD ROE, Secretary

Each of the undersigned declares under penalty of perjury that the matters set forth in the foregoing certificate are true and correct. Executed at _____, California, on _____.
(city or town)   (date)

_____
JOHN DOE, President

_____
RICHARD ROE, Secretary

SEC/STATE FORM LL-37 (REV. 1-75)

FORM NO. 193
Restated Charter

RESTATED CHARTER OF
.... CLUB, INC.

WHEREAS, the Corporation has been in existence as a nonprofit corporation under the laws of the State of North Carolina since September 25, 19_____, and,

WHEREAS, the Charter of the Corporation has been amended several times and upon the resolution of its corporate members and directors dated October 19, 19_____, it is deemed in the best interest of the Corporation that its Charter and the several amendments thereto be integrated into one *restated* Charter; moreover, this restated Charter merely restates the original Articles of Incorporation as supplemented and amended and that there are no further changes, amendments, or discrepancies between the original Articles of Incorporation as amended and the provisions of this restated Charter;

NOW, THEREFORE, pursuant to authority of the Board of Directors and the corporate members, the Corporation does hereby restate its Charter as follows:

A. The name of the Corporation shall be .... CLUB, INC.

B. The duration of the corporation shall be perpetual.

C. The purposes for which the Corporation is formed are as follows:

1. To promote and maintain an organization of persons who are interested in motor vehicles and travel of all kinds and further to encourage, develop, and promote safe and convenient travel services and facilities within the states of North Carolina and South Carolina;

2. To promote the construction, maintenance, and use of safe, economical, and adequate systems of transportation for its members and to promote, advocate, and encourage the construction, betterment, and maintenance of proper and necessary highways in the states of North Carolina and South Carolina and to promote and maintain guidance and information for the traveling public;

3. To furnish advice, information, and assistance of all kinds to users and operators of vehicles and crafts of all kinds operated on land, water, or in the air and to maintain offices in North Carolina and South Carolina or elsewhere for the purpose of rendering the services for which the corporation is formed;

4. To initiate, sponsor, and in any manner cooperate in the securing of reasonable legislation for the advancement, promotion, and protection of the interest of motor vehicular traffic, air traffic, or any other form of travel and to protect the owners and users of said conveyances against unjust or unreasonable legislation;

5. To generally function and carry on the operations of a travel agency and to encourage both domestic and international travel by members of the corporation and the general public and to promote and advertise the beauties and points of historical interest in the states of North Carolina and South Carolina;

6. To promote and encourage the development of a spirit of cooperation and courtesy among the users of all modes of transportation and travel and to generally maintain the rights and privileges of all persons interested in travel, and to this end encourage proper safety and law enforcement in connection with the use of streets, highways, and other modes of travel;

7. To affiliate with any other similar local or national organization under such terms and conditions as may be deemed advisable by the Board of Directors;

8. To exercise any power to carry out any of the purposes for which this corporation has been organized; to buy, sell, lease, or mortgage real or personal property; to borrow and lend money with or without security; to collect fees and dues from its members as well as donations and other payments and fees and generally to perform and carry out contracts of every kind for any lawful purpose.

D. The corporation shall have at least two classes of membership which shall be designated general members and associate members. The corporation may have such other classes of membership as may be provided for in the Bylaws of the corporation. Both classes of membership should be entitled to such benefits from the corporation as may be decided from time to time by the Board of Directors; however, only general members shall have voting rights.

The qualifications and fees charged for membership in the corporation shall be as provided for in the Bylaws of the corporation or at the direction of the Board of Directors. No member, either general, associate, or otherwise, shall have any rights to the property of the corporation and shall, upon termination of membership, be entitled only to the refund of the pro-rata membership fee which was paid.

Upon dissolution or liquidation, the property and assets of the corporation shall be distributed and applied first to all liabilities and obligations of the corporation, including any assets held by the corporation upon special conditions or limited uses. Any remaining assets shall then be distributed to such charitable organizations as shall be designated in the plan of dissolution which shall be adopted by the Directors of the corporation.

E. The Board of Directors of the corporation shall be elected by the general members at the corporation's annual meeting or at any special meeting called specifically for that purpose. The method of election or Directors shall be as set forth in the Bylaws.

F. The address of the registered office of the corporation shall be . . . . Street, ... , ... County, North Carolina and the name of the registered agent of the corporation at said address is . . . .

G. The number of persons constituting the Board of Directors of the corporation shall be set by the Bylaws. The existing Board of Directors of the corporation shall continue to serve until their successors have been elected by the general members.

IN TESTIMONY WHEREOF, ... Club, Inc. has caused these articles of Restatement of its Charter to be signed in its name by its President, and its corporate seal to be hereto affixed and attested by its Secretary, this 24th day of October, 19 . . . , all in pursuance of authority duly given by resolution of its corporate members.

.... CLUB, INC.

By...
                                                 President

ATTEST:

....
                    Secretary

STATE OF NORTH CAROLINA
COUNTY OF . . . .

This is to certify that on this the 24th day of October, 19 . . , personally appeared before me and . . . . , each of whom, being by me first duly sworn, deposes and says that they signed the foregoing Restated Charter of

.... Club, Inc., in the capacity indicated below their names, and that the statements therein contained are true and correct.

....
Notary Public

My commission expires: ....

§453. AMENDMENTS OF BYLAWS

Methods for adoption of bylaws are discussed in Chapter 22.[33]

Bylaws, like charters, are subject to the reserved power of the state to amend the law (see the second to last paragraph in Section 450). For example, if a statute is enacted that has the effect of nullifying an existing bylaw, this is a perfectly proper exercise of the state's reserved powers.[34]

Bylaws also are equivalent to contracts among the members of the organization; that is, they establish by agreement certain relations and duties among the members. But there are agreements that contain provisions (express or implied) for their own amendment, pursuant to agreed or legally established procedures. They should not conflict with the articles of incorporation, which (incidentally) may place the power to amend them in the board of directors.[35] Equitable concerns and relationships among the members, officers, and directors may limit the amendment of the bylaws.[36] State statutes now sometimes place bylaw-amendment power in the board unless expressly reserved by the members in the articles of incorporation.[37]

The power to amend its bylaws from time to time is inherent in a corporation.[38] But such amendment may not validly affect a particular member or group of members if it violates rights vested under a special contract arrangement with the organization.[39] In such case, the *power* of the organization to amend its bylaws operates effectively, but its *right* to do so is barred so far as the affected members are concerned. The bylaw amendment is effective, but a breach of contract has been committed by adoption of the amendment. And in a case where great injustice or hardship may result, an injunction against enforcement of the amendment undoubtedly is possible.[40]

Tests of an amendment's validity. An amendment of bylaws is valid if it is:

1. Not violative of vested contract rights[41] (but note that an amendment is invalid only for the member whose rights are violated).
2. Consistent with the charter[42] (because the charter is the supreme internal law of the organization).
3. Consistent with the general law[43] (because private law may not validly negate or alter public law).
4. Reasonable[44] (unreasonable, capricious, and arbitrary internal rules that offend reason and good sense are disfavored by the law).
5. Practical[45] (able to be complied with; not impossible to obey).

It has been held that although a member of a cooperative may contract to be bound by the organization's internal regulations, passed both before and *after* entering into such contract, *future* bylaws may *not* validly impair existing contracts between the association and its members. That is, each bylaw is a contract between the organization and its members and cannot be so abrogated, in the sense that a "special" contract cannot be abrogated.[46]

Who has power to amend bylaws? Bylaws themselves should contain detailed rules as to how they may be amended or repealed. Well-drawn bylaws do contain such provisions. (See the forms of bylaws in Chapter 6 for unincorporated associations, and in Chapter 23, for corporations.) Various methods for amendment may be provided.[47]

Fundamentally, the power to amend or repeal bylaws rests in the members, not in the directors.[48] When the bylaws do not state how they may be amended, the directors have no power to amend them.[49]

Statutes in some states have given to the directors the power to adopt or amend bylaws, as long as the articles so provide or no contrary provision appears in the articles of incorporation or the bylaws. But such provision continues to be subordinate to the *members'* right to do so.[50]

The power of the members is such that they even may adopt bylaws that are unwise, if they wish. For example, a bylaw that required no notice to members for the adoption of amendments clearly was unwise. But it was held to be not so unreasonable and unfair as to be illegal, especially when no member objected to its adoption.[51]

The members do have the power, however, to vest in the board of directors the power to adopt amendments. This they may do either by resolution or by approval of a bylaw provision to this effect.[52] The charter, or statutes applicable to certain actions, may grant this power to the board of directors.[53]

The Model Nonprofit Corporation Act[54] vests the primary power to adopt amendments in the board of directors. This rather "proprietary minded" provision is inconsistent with the concept of a nonprofit organization, and fortunately has been ignored in most states.

Even when the members do grant directors the power to amend bylaws, the amendatory powers of the members continue to be paramount. Nor may the directors then amend the bylaws that grant amendatory powers to them, unless the clear intent of these enabling rules is that they may do so. Even when the charter grants amendatory powers to the directors by express statutory authority, the power of the members to override and to amend director-adopted rules is supreme.[55]

Experience has shown that the granting of amendatory powers to the directors is safe and practical when these powers apply only to routine or procedural affairs. Too-great powers are a great temptation: they sometimes suggest to the directors means to perpetuate power. The destructive potentialities of overcentralization must be balanced against the danger of destructive inertia and slowness when such powers are too widely scattered.

How bylaws are amended. See the forms in Chapters 6 and 23, which exemplify amendment procedures. The bylaws more often than the charter contain these rules. Some statutes set forth amendment procedures. The prescribed procedures must be followed if the amendment is to be valid.[56] See Chapter 22 about adoption of bylaws. Rules for meetings and notice are the same as those for other actions by the members.[57]

De facto *amendment.* If the members consistently ignore a bylaw, or act contrary to its provisions, its repeal or amendment may be a practical fact (*de facto*) without any formal amendment procedure.[58] Such conduct by the directors is equally effective when they have the power to amend the bylaws.[59] Whether or not such conduct amounts to a permanent amendment *de facto* or applies only to the particular transaction depends on the facts—particularly on the length of time involved and the number of conflicting acts.[60]

However, simply because the method of adoption or amendment is termed *waiver* or *de facto*, does not mean that the substance need not be scrutinized. A waiver period of seven years was held not to validate bylaws that produced an unfair advantage for a group of members, or some other unlawful result.[61]

The person who claims that a *de facto* amendment has been effected by custom or usage has the burden of proving it.[62]

Waiver of a bylaw rule in a particular instance, by express or implied consent of the organization or members, does not amount to permanent amendment.[63]

§454. EXTENSION AND REVIVAL OF EXISTENCE

A few states still require that the certificate of incorporation state the number of years a corporation is to endure. In most states duration may be perpetual, or is deemed to be perpetual if no term is stated.[64]

In practice most attorneys who prepare certificates of incorporation state that the duration of the corporation shall be perpetual. Terms are stated in years only in special cases.

Statutes now provide for any desired extension of the existence of the corporation when a term of years has been stated. Amendatory certificates must be filed; and their contents and form of execution are prescribed by statutes.[65] The statute must be consulted in each state.[66]

Extension certificates must almost always be filed before the stated term of years has expired.[67] Filing after that time is permitted in very few states.[68] In Florida this must be done within three years.[69]

After the term of existence has expired, corporate existence may be *revived* (not extended) in most cases by filing certificates of revival in accordance with other statutory provisions.[70] Here, too, precise statutory rules and forms are provided in the various states, and these must be followed closely.[71]

For either extension or revival the consent of the members must be obtained.[72] And in both cases, obligations of the old corporation continue in the extended or revived corporation.[73]

Approvals of administrative authorities often are required just as in the filing of original charters.[74]

See, Section 450, *statements of continued existence.*

§455. CONSOLIDATIONS AND MERGERS

[See Chapter 40, *Affiliations.*]

The amalgamation of two or more nonprofit corporations into one is a *consolidation* or a *merger.*[75]

Thus, one corporation may absorb another (merger),[76] or both may go out of existence while a new corporation appears—under a new name or under one of the old names (consolidation).[77] The term *affiliation* refers to the consolidation of one organization with, and often as a branch of, another organization; or a special association of the two organizations for some joint purpose. (Affiliation is treated in detail, in Chapter 40.)

Purchase and transfer of assets of one corporation by (and to) a second corporation is not a consolidation or merger.[78] Nor is mere ownership of all the shares of one corporation by another,[79] not the leasing of all assets of one by another corporation.[80] A bequest to one of two merging organizations has been held to go to the surviving corporation.[81]

Some states permit a business corporation to change its status to that of nonprofit corporation simply by filing a petition in circuit court. The nonprofit corporation is the surviving organization, and is deemed to have succeeded to all rights, liabilities, and assets of its business corporation predecessor.[82]

However, many of those same states have failed to provide for the reverse situation. That is, there is no provision allowing a nonprofit corporation to switch its form to that of a business corporation simply by amending its charter and filing a petition. Thus, where such a situation arises, dissolution and reorganization appear to be the only solution.[83]

Procedure. Most statutes provide for arrangement of the merger agreement by the trustees of both corporations. Then the members of each vote approval. Filing of a certificate of consolidation in the form required by the statutes is made by officers of the dominant (or either) corporation.[84] [See the forms in Section 451 as to amendments, and Section 455 as to mergers.]

Certificate of consolidation. Statutes in practically all states now provide for the filing of a certificate of consolidation to effectuate a merger agreement. In some states special forms are required for domestic nonprofit corporations,[85] while other forms are required for consolidations with foreign nonprofit corporations.[86] Rules for execution of these forms are equally specific. But in some states the forms and procedures set forth in the general corporation statutes are all that have been provided.

Two-thirds approval by the members of each constituent corporation and approval by administrative authorities (as in an incorporation) often are required.[87] Administrative or court approval authorities often also have statutory power to modify the consolidation certificate or agreement.[88]

Succession to rights. After a merger or consolidation the surviving corporation succeeds to all the rights, powers, liabilities, and obligations of the merged original corporations.[89]

Creditors' rights. In consolidations of nonprofit corporations, the old corporations cease to exist except insofar as in necessary in order to preserve bequests, or for specific other reasons, or as the approving authority directs. The new corporation assumes all the obligations and liabilities of the constituent corporations.[90] Consolidation without state approval is unlawful.[91]

If creditors of either corporation have specific liens on specific property, these liens continue. They even may attach to after-acquired property—for example, under open-end mortgages.[92]

If fraudulent transfers are involved, creditors may have them set aside.[93] And if a consolidation results in a new corporation that is insolvent, presumably the entire consolidation is invalid as to creditors.[94] Then, if fraud is shown, personal liability on the part of the guilty persons may result.[95]

Liability for affiliates or subsidiaries. Statutory rules as to liabilities of the surviving corporation in a merger are clear.[96] In affiliations the rules are not clear.[97]

Affiliation, with provision for nonliability for each affiliate for the debts of the other, is possible.[98] But it is questionable whether such a provision is binding as to creditors without notice of the provision.

Each claim of liability of an affiliate for the acts or debts of another affiliate must be viewed in the light of its particular facts. In a proper case the courts will "pierce the corporate veil" and hold one affiliate liable for the debts or obligations of another.[99]

The same is true as to corporate members of associations.[100]

"Charities" may merge only with charities, in some states.[101]

Anti-Trust law. See above, the chapter on Anti-Trust law for NPO's says that it properly enforces the Clayton Act, etc. The National Association of Attorneys-General in 1988 said that the DOS does so poor a job that the NAAG will challenge mergers that seem to be anticompetitive. G.J. Werden, *Market Definition* . . . 35 Clev. St. L. Rev. (4) 403 (1986–7) [Issued in 1988].

State officials may invoke federal antitrust law to break up corporate mergers, and so may any opponent who can show anti-competition effects; and this applies to (divestiture) even of completed mergers. This was a California merger of Lucky and Alpha Beta supermarket chains. But in private litigant cases the claimant "must prove threatened loss or damage to his own interests."[102]

Statutes authorizing mergers of corporations do not unconstitutionally destroy minority-of-members' (shareholders') rights, and are *not breaches of fiduciary duties* of directors *per se.*[103]

Where a corporation's *entire assets* are sold or transferred to another corporation, the latter is not liable for the debts of the former unless the latter is a continuation of the former, or the transaction is really a merger or consolidation, or the purpose is fraudulent evasion of liability, or the latter is a reincarnation of the seller, or there is continuity of the enterprise in effect.[104]

Nonprofit corporations faced with threatened "*corporate takeover*" by "*corporation raiders*" have more than the ordinary ability to defend themselves. This is because they usually are quite clearly affected with a *public interest; i.e.*, are public service in nature; and it is against public policy to allow speculators to enrich themselves in a way that injures the public interest. The 1990 case of *Poynter-Jamison Ventures Ltd. Partnership v. Times Publishing Co.*, involving the nonprofit *Poynter Institute* which serves as a holding company controlling the *St. Petersburg Times, Congressional Quarterly*, etc., is an example. The Poynter Institute is an NPO dedicated to improving journalism, and operates on 85.7 of the *dividends* distributed by *Times*, while the attacking (Bass interests) Partnership gets only 5.7% of them though owning 40% of the voting stock. Bass sought a change in his return rate, by forcing use of an available cheap *redemption right* as to the voting stock, which would make the dividend rates better proportioned to the voting stock percentages. The Institute could point to new statutes requiring directors to consider "public," "community," "social," and other effects of their decisions and held out for protection of those (over new shareholders') rights.[105]

This case was settled in late 1990. The Institute remained independent. Bass was bought out. But Bass' allegation of breach of fiduciary duty (to shareholders) by the directors collides with the "business judgment" rule that governs most decisions of the board members, with which courts should hesitate to interfere.[106]

If a nonprofit corporation merges with an electrical distribution cooperative, thereby changing the delegation of price fixing duties, any electrical distribution cooperative which was a member of the merged cooperative, must continue its duty to purchase electricity from the merged corporation if its contract recognizes that the merged cooperative could take in new members.[107]

§456. FORMS FOR MERGERS AND CONSOLIDATIONS

FORM NO. 194
Articles of Merger-Consolidation
(Illinois)

File in Duplicate
Filing Fee $_____   **FORM NP-40**   _____

                                                   Date Paid........................
                                                   Filing Fee $ ....
                                                   Clerk................................

                                                   _____

ARTICLES OF MERGER-CONSOLIDATION
(STRIKE IN APPLICABLE WORD)
UNDER THE
GENERAL NOT-FOR-PROFIT CORPORATION ACT

To _____ _____, Secretary of State, Springfield, Illinois.

The undersigned corporations, pursuant to Section 40 of the "General Not-for-Profit Corporation Act" of the State of Illinois, hereby execute the following articles of merger/consolidation:

1. The names of the corporations proposing to merge/consolidate are as follows:

_____

_____

_____

_____

_____

2. The name of the surviving/new corporation shall be_____.

3. The plan of merger/consolidation is as follows:

(Strike any paragraph (a), (b), or (c) not applicable)

4. Some or all of the members of each corporation named in paragraphs (a) and (b) hereof have voting rights and the plan of merger/consolidation was adopted

(a) at a meeting of the members of

_____ held on _____, 19_____.

_____ held on _____, 19_____.

_____ held on _____, 19_____.

A quorum of the members entitled to vote thereon of such corporation respectively was present at each such meeting; and such plan of merger/consolidation received at least two-thirds of the votes entitled to be cast by members present or represented by proxy at each such meeting; or (b) by a consent in writing signed by all members entitled to vote with respect thereto of

_____, _____,

_____, _____,

(c) None of the members of any corporation named in this paragraph (c) has voting rights, and the plan of merger/Consolidation was adopted at a meeting of the board of directors of

_____ held on _____, 19_____.

_____ held on _____, 19_____.

_____ held on _____, 19_____.

such plan receiving the vote of a majority of the directors then in office of each such corporation.

IN WITNESS WHEREOF each of the undersigned corporations has caused these articles of merger/consolidation to be executed in its name by its

_____ president and by its _____ secretary on
this _____ day of _____, 19_____.

                                        _____
                                                   (Exact Corporate Title)
                Place   By_____
         (CORPORATE SEAL)   Its _____ President
                Here

                                        _____

                                                   Its _____ President

                                        _____
                                                   (Exact Corporate Title)
                Place   By_____
         (CORPORATE SEAL)   Its _____ President
                Here

                                        _____

                                                   Its _____ President

STATE OF _____ ⎫
COUNTY OF _____ ⎬ ss.
                                  ⎭

     I, _____, a Notary Public, do hereby certify that on the
_____, day of _____, A.D. 19_____, personally appeared
before me _____, who declares that he is the _____
of _____, one of the corporations executing the foregoing
document, and being first duly sworn, acknowledged that he signed the foregoing articles in the capacity therein set forth and declared that the statements
therein contained are true.
     IN WITNESS WHEREOF, I have hereunto set my hand and seal the day
and year before written.

                Place   _____
         (NOTARIAL SEAL)   Notary Public
                Here

STATE OF _____ ⎫
COUNTY OF _____ ⎬ ss.
                                  ⎭

     I, _____, a Notary Public, do hereby certify that on the
_____ day of _____, A.D. 19____, personally
appeared before me _____, who declares that he is the
_____ of _____, one of the corporations
executing the foregoing document, and first being duly sworn, acknowledged

that he signed the foregoing articles in the capacity therein set forth and declared that the statements therein contained are true.

IN WITNESS WHEREOF, I have hereunto set my hand and seal the day and year before written.

Place

(NOTARIAL SEAL)

Here

_____

Notary Public

FORM NO. 195

Articles Of Merger (Domestic)

(Washington, D.C.)

ARTICLES OF MERGER

OF DOMESTIC CORPORATIONS

INTO

_____

To: The Recorder of Deeds, D.C.

Washington, D.C.

Pursuant to the provisions of the District of Columbia Nonprofit Corporation Act, the undersigned corporations adopt the following Articles of Merger for the purpose of merging them into one of such corporations:

FIRST: The following Plan of Merger was approved by each of the undersigned corporations:

(Insert Plan of Merger)

SECOND: As to each of the undersigned corporations, the Plan of Merger was adopted in the following manner:

(Note 1)

Date:_____

(CORPORATE SEAL)

_____

Corporate name

Attest:

By_____

Its President or Vice President

_____

Its Secretary or Assistant Secretary

(CORPORATE SEAL)

_____

Corporate name

Attest: By _____
Its President or Vice-President

_____
Its Secretary or Assistant Secretary

Note 1. As to each of the corporations parties to the merger, insert whichever of the following statements is applicable:

    a. "The Plan of Merger was adopted by _____ at a meeting of its members held on _____, at which a quorum was present, the Plan of Merger received at least two-thirds of the votes which members present or represented by proxy at such meeting were entitled to cast."

    b. "The Plan of Merger was adopted by _____ by a consent in writing signed by all members entitled to vote in respect thereof."

    c. "The Plan of Merger was adopted by _____ at a meeting of the Board of Directors held on _____, and received the vote of a majority of the Directors in office, there being no members having voting rights in respect thereof."

MAIL TO:	**FEES DUE**	
OFFICE OF THE RECORDER OF DEEDS, D.C.	Filing Fee	$_____
CORPORATION DIVISION	Indexing Fee	_____
SIXTH AND D STREETS, N.W.		_____
WASHINGTON, D.C. 20001	Total	$_____

MAKE CHECK PAYABLE TO
RECORDER OF DEEDS, D.C.

FORM NO. 196
Articles of Merger (Foreign and Domestic)
(Washington, D.C.)

**ARTICLES OF MERGER
OF DOMESTIC AND FOREIGN CORPORATIONS
INTO**

_____

To: The Recorder of Deeds, D.C.
    Washington, D.C.

    Pursuant to the provisions of the District of Columbia Nonprofit Corporation Act, the undersigned domestic and foreign corporations adopt the following Articles of Merger for the purpose of merging them into one of such corporations:

FIRST: The names of the undersigned corporations and the States, including the District of Columbia, under the laws of which they are respectively organized, are:

NAME OF CORPORATIONS   **STATE**

....

....

....

SECOND: The laws of the State under which such foreign corporation is organized permit such merger.

THIRD: The name of the surviving corporation is _____ and it is to be governed by the laws of the District of Columbia, or State of _____.

FOURTH: The following Plan of Merger was approved by each of the undersigned corporations:

(Insert Plan of Merger)

FIFTH: As to each of the undersigned corporations, the Plan of Merger was adopted in the following manner:

(Notes 1 and 2)

SIXTH: If the surviving corporation is to be governed by the laws of any state or country other than the District of Columbia, it agrees that it may be served with process in the District of Columbia in any proceeding for the enforcement of any obligation of any domestic corporation which is a party of such merger; and that a copy of such process may be mailed to the following address: _____. It irrevocably appoints the Recorder of Deeds for the District of Columbia as its agent to accept the service of process in any such proceeding.

Date:_____

(CORPORATE SEAL)

Attest:

_____
Corporate name

By _____
Its President or Vice President

_____
Its Secretary or Assistant Secretary

(CORPORATE SEAL)

Attest:

_____
Corporate name

By _____
Its President or Vice-President

_____
Its Secretary or Assistant Secretary

Note 1. As to each of the domestic corporations parties to the _____ merger, insert whichever of the following statements is applicable:

    a. "The Plan of Merger was adopted by ———————————— at a meeting of its members held on ———————————— at which a quorum was present, and the Plan of Merger received at least two-thirds of the votes which members present or represented by proxy at such meeting were entitled to cast."

    b. "The Plan of Merger was adopted by ———————————— by a consent in writing signed by all members entitled to vote in respect thereof."

    c. "The Plan of Merger was adopted by ———————————— at a meeting of the Board of Directors held on ————————————, and received the vote of a majority of the Directors in office, there being no members having voting rights in respect thereof."

2. As to each of the foreign corporations parties to the merger insert the following statement:

    a. The Plan of Merger was approved by the undersigned foreign corporation in the manner prescribed by the laws of the state under which it is organized.

MAIL TO:	**FEES DUE**	
OFFICE OF THE RECORDER OF DEEDS, D.C.	Filing Fee	$_____
	Indexing Fee	_____
CORPORATION DIVISION		_____
SIXTH AND D STREETS, N.W.	Total	$_____
WASHINGTON, D.C. 20001		

MAKE CHECK PAYABLE TO
RECORDER OF DEEDS, D.C.

FORM NO. 197
Articles of Consolidation (Domestic)
Maine

Filing Fee (See Sec. 1401)

This Space for Use by
Secretary of State

For Use by the Secretary of State
File No. _____
Fee Paid_____
C. B._____
Date _____

NONPROFIT CORPORATION
STATE OF MAINE
ARTICLES OF CONSOLIDATION
OF

_____

A MAINE CORPORATION
AND

_____

A MAINE CORPORATION
INTO

_____

Pursuant to 13-B MRSA §904, the undersigned corporations, execute and deliver for filing the following Articles of Consolidation:

FIRST: The name of the new corporation is _____.

SECOND: The plan of consolidation is set forth in Exhibit _____ _____ attached hereto and made a part hereof.

THIRD: As to each participating corporation, the plan of consolidation was adopted in the following manner: ("X" one box only for each corporation.)

Name of corporation _____.

☐   a.   By the members at a meeting on _____, 19_____, at which a quorum was present and such plan received at least a majority of the votes which members were entitled to cast.

☐   b.   If the Articles of Incorporation require more than a majority vote, by members at a meeting on _____, 19_____, and such plan received at least the percentage of votes of the members required by the Articles of Incorporation.

☐   c.   By the written consent of all members entitled to vote with respect thereto, dated _____, 19_____, without resolution of the board of directors.

☐   d.   There being no members, or no members entitled to vote thereon, the plan was adopted by a majority vote of the board of directors in office at a meeting held on _____, 19_____.

Name of corporation ─────────────────.

☐   a.   By the members at a meeting on _____, 19_____, at which a quorum was present and such plan received at least a majority of the votes which members were entitled to cast.

☐   b.   If the Articles of Incorporation require more than a majority vote, by the members at a meeting on _____, 19_____, and such plan received at least the percentage of votes of the members required by the Articles of Incorporation.

☐   c.   By the written consent of all members entitled to vote with respect thereto, dated _____, 19_____, without resolution of the board of directors.

☐ d.   There being no members entitled to vote thereon, the plan was adopted by a majority vote of the board of directors in office at a meeting held on _____, 19_____.

FOURTH: The address of the registered office of _____

is _____.

                                (street, city, state and zip code)

The address of the registered office of _____

is _____

                                (street, city, state and zip code)

FIFTH: Effective date of the consolidation (if other than the date of filing of the Articles) is _____, 19_____.

(Not to exceed 60 days after filing date of articles.)

Dated: _____

I certify that I have custody of the minutes showing the above action by the members of

_____
           (name of corporation)

_____
(signature of clerk, secretary, or asst. secretary)

Legibly print or type name
and capacity of all signers
13-B MRSA §104.

I certify that I have custody of the minutes showing the above action by the members of

_____
           (name of corporation)

_____
(signature of clerk, secretary, or asst. secretary)

_____
           (name of corporation)

By_____
            (signature)

_____
    (type or print name and capacity)

By_____
            (signature)

_____
   (type or print name and capacity)*

_____
           (name of corporation)

By_____
            (signature)

_____
   (type or print name and capacity)

By_____
            (signature)

_____
   (type or print name and capacity)

    'The name of the corporation should be typed, and the document must be signed (1) by the clerk or secretary *or* (2) by the president or a vice-president and by the secretary or an assistant secretary, or such other officer as the bylaws may designate as a second certifying officer *or* (3) if there are no such officers, then by a majority of the directors or by such directors as may be designated by a majority of directors then in office *or* (4) if there are no such directors, then by the members or such of them as may be designated by the members at a lawful meeting.

FORM NO. MNCPA-10E

Form #198
CONSOLIDATION OF TWO NPOs
(RESOLUTION)

A RESOLUTION
APPROVING THE PROPOSED PLAN
OF CONSOLIDATION OF
THE _____ _____ FELLOWSHIP, INC.
AND THE
_____ FELLOWSHIP OF _____ INC.
AND DIRECTING THAT SAID PLAN
BE SUBMITTED TO A VOTE
OF THE MEMBERSHIP

Be it resolved by the Board of Trustees of The _____ _____ Fellowship, Inc., at a special meeting of the Fellowship and the said Board of Trustees duly noticed and convened that the proposed Plan of Consolidation of The _____ Fellowship, Inc. and the _____ Fellowship of _____ Inc., having been adopted by majority vote of the membership as required by the Bylaws, is approved and;

    Be it further resolved by said Board of Trustees that the said Plan of Consolidation be submitted to a vote of the members of The _____ ____ _____ Fellowship, Inc., at a special meeting of said membership which is called for 7:00 P.M. on Saturday, January, _____, 199___, at the _____ _____ Club, 4720 _____ Causeway.

    Be it further resolved by the Board of Trustees, that a summary of the Plan of Consolidation shall be given to each member as provided by law, by mail postmarked at least seven (7) days prior to such meeting.

    I certify that this resolution was adopted this eighth day of January, 199___.

_____
_____ _____, President

The _____ _____
_____ Fellowship, Inc.

Attest:

_____
Secretary

Form # 199
CONSOLIDATION—SUMMARY
FOR MEMBERS' APPROVALS
[SCHEMATIC OUTLINE]

Summary of the Plan of Consolidation

PROCEDURE

Pursuant to Section _____ of the _____ Not-For-Profit Corporation Act, the _____ _____ Fellowship Inc., and the _____ Fellowship of _____ _____ Inc., propose to consolidate into a new Not-For-Profit Corporation. The Boards of Trustees of both existing corporations have adopted resolutions approving the proposed plan and directing that it be submitted to a vote of the members having voting rights at 7:00 P.M. on Saturday, _____ 26, 199___, at the _____ _____ Club, 4720 _____ Causeway. This summary is provided to the members of both corporations pursuant to Section _____ _____ _____ Statutes. The plan of consolidation shall be adopted upon receiving at least two thirds of the votes of members present. Upon adoption, the articles of consolidation shall be executed by each corporation and filed with the Secretary of State. Upon filing, the Secretary of State will issue a certificate of consolidation, whereupon the consolidation will become effective and the separate existence of the existing non-profit corporations (_____ _____ and _____) will cease and the new corporation shall succeed to all assets and liabilities and property of the prior existing corporations. See Section _____, _____ Statutes, for a more detailed explanation.

Substance of Plan

NAME

The name of the new corporation shall be either _____ _____ _____ Fellowship, Inc. or such other name as may be selected by the membership of both corporations at the meeting for approval of the consolidation.

NOT-FOR-PROFIT
TAX EXEMPT STATUS

The corporation shall be prohibited from engaging in activities which would endanger its tax exempt status.

POWERS

The corporation shall have all powers, rights, privileges, and immunities and benefits granted to similar corporations under the laws of the State of _____
_____.

MEMBERSHIP

The corporation is open to membership without regard to race, color, sex, affectual or sexual orientation, age, national origin or handicap, and without requiring adherence to any particular _____ or _____
_____ belief or creed.

ADMISSION TO MEMBERSHIP

Admission to membership shall be provided by the Bylaws.

TERM OF EXISTENCE

Perpetual existence

INITIAL MEMBERS

The initial members are all members of _____ and _____
_____. Members may resign or persons may obtain membership, prior to adoption of Bylaws, by written notice to the president or registered agent and a statement of sympathy with the purposes and objectives of this corporation.

INCORPORATORS

_____ _____ and _____ _____

BOARD OF TRUSTEES

Comprised of at least five members, staggered terms by group (after the initial Board), President, Vice President, Secretary and Treasurer elected by Board members. President and Vice President must be members of the Board. President and Secretary (and Vice President in the absence of the President) are authorized to execute legal documents on behalf of the corporation. Regular meetings of the Board (unless Bylaws provide otherwise) on first _____ _____ of each month.

INITIAL BOARD OF TRUSTEES
AND INITIAL OFFICERS

The initial Board is comprised of the current officers of _____ ___ and Board members of _____. This Board will elect from its members a President and Vice President and will elect a Secretary and Treasurer. These officers and Board members will serve until a new Board is elected as provided in the Bylaws. The Initial Board of Trustees is comprised of:

J_____ H_____   330_____d St. North,
                                        _____, _____33710
S_____ S_____-H_____   2391 _____ St. _____
                                        _____, _____33710
D_____ H_____   2391 _____ St. _____
                                        _____, _____33710
J_____ O_____   6251 _____ Avenue. _____
                                        _____, _____33707
R_____ T_____   7150 _____ _____ #23-E
                                        _____ Beach, _____
                                        33706
G_____ M_____   1722 _____ Rd.
                                        _____, _____34624
J_____ F_____   7636 _____ St. _____
                                        _____, _____34647

OTHER OFFICERS: STAFF

May be provided by Bylaws

MEETINGS

Annual business meeting as provided by Bylaws. Other meetings as provided in Bylaws, or, prior to adoption of Bylaws, as determined by Board of Trustees. Twenty days notice of such meetings by mail to members. Initial business meetings within 120 days to adopt Bylaws, establishing a date to elect successors to initial Board of Trustees. Thirty days notice of such meeting. Thirty percent constitutes a quorum. Bylaws may provide for a different quorum.

BYLAWS

Minimum of two-thirds vote of members present and voting required for adoption.

AMENDMENTS TO ARTICLES OF CONSOLIDATION

Minimum of two-thirds vote of members present and voting required.

RESIDENT AGENT FOR
SERVICE OF PROCESS

M_____ D _____ is initial Resident Agent. Room 210, _____ _____ Street, _____, _____, _____ 33701

FORM NO. 200
Articles of Consolidation (Foreign and Domestic)
(Maine)

Filing Fee (See Sec. 1401)

This Space for Use by
Secretary of State

For Use by the Secretary of State
File No. _____
Fee Paid_____
C. B._____
Date _____

NONPROFIT CORPORATION
STATE OF MAINE
(CONSOLIDATION OF DOMESTIC
AND FOREIGN CORPORATIONS)
ARTICLES OF CONSOLIDATION
OF

_____

AND

_____

INTO

_____

Pursuant to 13-B MRSA §906, the undersigned domestic and foreign corporations execute and deliver for filing the following Articles of Consolidation for the purpose of consolidating them into a new corporation:

FIRST: The names of the undersigned corporations and the states under the laws of which they are respectively organized:

Name of Corporation   State

SECOND: The laws of the state of _____ under which the foreign corporation is organized permit such consolidation and said corporation has complied with the applicable provisions of such laws.

THIRD: The name of the new corporation is _____ which corporation is to be governed by the laws of the state of _____. If such corporation is to be governed by the laws of a state other than Maine, the corporation agrees that it may be served with process in the state of Maine in any proceeding for the enforcement of any obligation of any domestic corporation which is a party to such consolidation. The corporation irrevocably appoints the Secretary of State of Maine as its agent to accept service of process in any such proceedings and the address to which the Secretary of State shall mail a copy of any process in such proceeding is _____.

FOURTH: The plan of consolidation is set forth in Exhibit _____ _____ attached hereto and made a part hereof.

FIFTH: As to each domestic corporation, the plan of consolidation was adopted in the following manner: ("X" one box only.) Name of corporation _____.

☐   a.   By the members at a meeting on _____, 19_____ at which a quorum was present and such plan received at least a majority of the votes which members were entitled to cast.

☐   b.   If the Articles of Incorporation require more than a majority vote, by the members at a meeting on _____ 19_____, and such plan received at least the percentage of votes of the members required by the Articles of Incorporation.

☐   c.   By the written consent of all members entitled to vote with respect thereto, dated _____, 19_____, without resolution of the board of directors.

☐   d.   There being no members, or no members entitled to vote thereon, the plan was adopted by a majority vote of the board of directors in office at a meeting held on _____ _____, 19_____.

SIXTH: The address of the registered office of _____ , the participating domestic corporation is: _____

_____
(street, city, state and zip code)

The address of the registered office of _____

, the participating foreign corporation is* _____

_____
(street, city, state and zip code)

SEVENTH: Effective date of the consolidation (if other than date of filing of the Articles) is _____, 19_____.

(Not to exceed 60 days after filing date of articles.)

Dated: _____

I certify that I have custody of the
minutes showing the above action
by the members of

_____
(name of corporation)

By_____
(signature)

_____
(name of corporation)

_____
(type or print name and capacity)

_____
(signature of clerk, secretary, or asst. secretary)

By_____
(signature)

Legibly print or type name
and capacity of all signers
13-B MRSA §104.

_____
(type or print name and capacity)*

_____
(name of corporation)

I certify that I have custody of the
minutes showing the above action
by the members of

By_____
(signature)

_____
(name of corporation)

_____
(type or print name and capacity)

_____
(signature of clerk, secretary, or asst. secretary)

By_____
(signature)

_____
(type or print name and capacity)

_____

*Give address of registered office in Maine. If the corporation does not have a registered office in Maine the address given should be the principal or registered office in the state of incorporation.

**The name of the corporation should be typed, and the document must be signed (1) by the clerk or secretary *or* (2) by the president or a vice-president and by the secretary or an assistant secretary, or such other officer as the bylaws may designate as a second certifying officer *or* (3) if there are no such officers, then by a majority of the directors or by such directors as may be designated by a majority of directors then in office *or* (4) if there are no such directors, then by the members or such of them as may be designated by the members at a lawful meeting.

FORM NO. MNCPCA-10E

§457. INTERSTATE MERGERS AND CONSOLIDATIONS

Corporations of different states may, where permitted by statute, merge or consolidate with each other.[108] A typical statute setting forth both the right to consolidate or merge, and the necessary procedure, is found in the Ohio Revised Code.[109]

The foreign corporation must have the power under its state law to merge with other states' corporations.[110] Some statutes that authorize consolidation or merger of corporations refer only to those corporations located within that state.[111] This is considered insufficient authority for consolidation or merger with foreign corporations.[112]

Where a foreign corporation has merged with a domestic one, but failed to file a certificate of merger, it has been held, that consent under a merger agreement, to assume all liabilities of the domestic corporation will cause the foreign corporation to consent, by implication, to the jurisdiction of the domestic corporation's state.[113] Thus, the foreign corporation will be estopped to deny jurisdiction over it in the domestic corporation's state, because of a mere technicality, such as failing to file a certificate of merger.[114]

Anti-Trust Law may apply to mergers and consolidations, especially interstate combinations. See, Chapter 40, and Section 454 above.

POINTS TO REMEMBER

- See local statutes for procedures and forms for corrections or amendments of charters or bylaws.
- Include rules for changes when you draft a charter or bylaws. Preferably, put these rules in bylaws.
- Beware of contract rights when making amendments.
- Remember to file statements of continued existence.
- Do not try to get, by amendment, powers that may not be obtained originally.
- Remember that the state reserves the power to change laws and charters.
- Use the tests for validity of amendments (Sections 450, 452)
- Do not give away the members' basic powers to control important amendments.
- Beware of amendments by custom or usage.

- Beware of waivers of rules; keep waivers to a minimum.
- File necessary extension certificates in time.
- Draft consolidation or merger agreements with care and in detail.
- File certificates for all consolidations or mergers.
- Remember creditors' rights.
- Treat *affiliations* as basically contract matters, but beware of state and anti-trust law limitations. (See Chapter 39.)

NOTES TO CHAPTER 45

1. For digests of the statutes of all states *see*, 3 Oleck, *Modern Corporation Law*, c. 52 (1978 Supp.). For definition of amendments of various special kinds, *see*, Ballentine's *Law Dictionary* 67, 68 (3rd ed. 1969). As to statute *effects* see Hamilton, *Corporations*, c. 19 (2nd ed., 1986); Soderquist & S., *Corporations Cases*, c. 15 (3rd ed. 1991)

2. *E.g.*, Fla. Stat. §§617.1001–617.1009; Ohio Rev. Code §1702.38.

3. Opinions, Ohio Atty-Gen. (1931), 3429.

4. *See*, East End Church of God v. Logan, 102 Ohio App. 552, 75 Ohio L. Abs. 29, 131 N.E.2d 439 (1956).

5. *E.g.*, Ohio Rev. Code §1702.59.

6. *Ibid.*

7. *Id.*

8. *Id.*

9. *Id.*

10. N.Y. Bus. Corp. L §105. But not in Fla. Stat. cc.617 or 607. N.Y. N-CPL §105.

11. Fla. Stat. 617.0124 (3); N.Y. N-PCL §105.

12. N.Y. Not-for-Profit Corp. L. §803; Fla. Stat. §617.0124.

13. N.Y. Not-for-Profit Corp. L. §802. Ohio Rev. Code §1702.38; Fla. Stat. §§617.0124, 617.1001–617.1006.

14. *See*, as to following the rules: Charter Oak Council v. Town of New Hartford, 121 Conn. 466; 185 A. 575 (1936).

15. N.Y. Not-for-Profit Corp. L. §602.

16. *Ponder v. Guiteau*, 528 So. 2d 184 (LA App. 1988).

17. Fla. Stat. §617.1002(2) (eff. July 1, 1991); Fl. 1990 Sess. L., Chap. 90–179 §§65 (eff. July 1, 1991).

18. Surf Club v. Long, 325 So.2d 66 (Fla. App. 1976); First Florida Bank v. Financial Transaction Systems, Inc., 522 S. 2d 891 (Fla. App. 1988).

19. Cash v. Surf Club, 436 S.2d 970 (Fla. 3rd D.C. App., 1983).

20. Icardi v. National Equipment Rental, Inc., 378 S.2d 113 (Fla. 5th D.C. App., 1980).

21. N.Y. Not-for-Profit Corp. L. §801; Opinions N.Y. Att'y Gen. (1935) 229, 373; St. Lawrence University v. Trustees of Theological School of St. Lawrence University, 269 N.Y.S.2d 285 (1966); but *cf.*, 282 N.Y.S.2d 746 (1967).

22. Opinions, N.Y. Att'y Genl. (1911), 460, *In re* Manoca Temple Assn., 128 A.D. 796; 113 N.Y.S. 172 (1908); *See also Fla. Stat.* 617.1009; N.Y. Not-for-Profit Corp. L. §804.

23. Cabana v. Holstein-Friesian Assn., 112 Misc. 262; 183 N.Y.S. 658; modified as to other mat-

ters, 196 A.D. 842; 188 N.Y.S. 277; *affd without op.*, 233 N.Y. 644; 135 N.E. 953 (1922); *In re* Eaton, 276 A.D. 7; 92 N.Y.S.2d 867 (1949).

24. N.Y. Not-for-Profit Corp. L. §804; Italian Hospitalization Society v. State Dept. of Social Welfare. 178 Misc. 183; 34 N.Y.S.2d 385 (1942); Ohio Rev. Code §1702.38. *Fla. Stat* §§617.01201, 617.1006.

25. Fla. Stat. §617.10. (Repealed by s. 38, ch. 92–173.]

26. *E.g.*: For New York, *see*, Oleck, *New York Corporations* §525 (New York: Robert Slater Co., 1959); and for all states, 5 Oleck, *Modern Corporation Law* (1978 Supp.); and for Florida, *see*, Nadler, *Fla. Corp. Law*, Forms 18–23 (Curr. Ed.).

27. N.Y. Bus. Corp. L. §§303, 615, 801(b)(1); Sykes v. People, 132 Ill. 32; 23 N.E. 391 (1890). *See* n. 14, above. See N.Y. N-PCL §§303, 801, 802, 803, 804.

28. Greenwood v. Freight Co., 105 U.S. 13, 19; 26 L.Ed. 961 (1881); N.Y. Genl. Corp. L. §5. *Due process* means: not unreasonable or destructive of contract rights. Ware Lodge No. 435 v. Harper, 236 Ala. 334; 182 S. 59 (1938); Berea College v. Commonwealth of Kentucky, 211 U.S. 45 (1908); *In re* Opinion of the Justices, 300 Mass. 607; 14 N.E.2d 468 (1938).

29. Milwaukee Sanitarium v. Swift, 238 Wis. 628; 300 N.W. 760, 138 A.L.R. 521 (1941); Ohio Rev. Code §1701.15; Federal United Corp. v. Havender, 24 Del. Ch. 318; 11 A.2d 331 (1940); Note, 53 Wis. L. Rev. 482 (1953).

30. Ramapo Water Co. v. City of N.Y., 236 U.S. 579; 35 S.Ct. 442; 59 L.Ed. 731 (1915). But *cf.*, State Highway Commission v. Wieczorek, 248 N.W.2d 369 (S.D., 1976).

31. Fla. Stat. §617.1007.

32. *State v. Palm Beach County*, 575 So. 2d 652 (Fla. 1991).

33. *See also*, concerning their purpose: Van Atten v. Modern Brotherhood of America, 131 Iowa 232; 108 N.W. 313 (1906); Griffith v. Klamath Water Assn., 68 Ore. 402, 137 P. 226 (1913); State v. Ostrander, 318 P.2d 284 (Ore., 1957), Fla. Stat. 617.0206.

34. Saint John of Vizzini Assn. v. Cavallo, 134 Misc. 152; 234 N.Y.S. 683 (1929).

35. State *ex rel.* Schwab v. Price, 121 Ohio 114; 167 N.E. 366 (1929); Hornaday v. Goodman, 167 Ga. 555; 146 S.E. 173 (1928); Cabana v. Holstein-Friesian Assn., n.21; Associated Press v. Emmett 45 F. Supp. 907 (S.D. Calif. 1942); State v. Ostrander, 318 P.2d 284 (Ore., 1957); Florida Bar v. Town, 174 S.2d 395 (Fla., 1965).

36. *See*, Coleman v. Coleman, 191 S.2d 460 (Fla. 1st D.C. App., 1966).

37. *See*, R.M. Leisner article, 50 Fla. Bar J. 33 (1976); and Fla. St. §617.0206.

38. Steen v. Modern Woodmen of America, 296 Ill. 104; 129 N.E. 546 (1920); Interstate Bldg. and L. Assn. v. Wooten, 113 Ga. 247; 38 S.E. 738 (1901); Lambert v. Fishermen's Dock Co-op, Inc., 61 N.S. 596, 297 A.2d 566 (1972).

39. Farrier v. Ritzville, 116 Wash. 522; 199 P. 984 (1921).

40. *See*, Hueftle v. Farmers Elevator Assn., 145 Nebr. 424; 16 N.W.2d 855 (1944); Born v. Beasley, 145 Tenn. 64; 235 S.W. 62 (1921).

41. *See* n.38, above; and *see*, Brotherhood's Relief and Comp. Fund v. Cagnina, 155 S.2d 820 (Fla. 2d D.C. App., 1963).

42. Tempel v. Dodge, 89 Tex. 69; 33 S.W. 222, 514 (1895); Brooks v. State, 26 Del. 1; 79 A. 790 (1911).

43. Farrier case, n.39; Davids v. Sillcox 297 N.Y. 355; 79 N.E.2d 440; *rehear. den.*, 298 N.Y. 618; 81 N.E.2d 353 (1948); and *see*, Abbey Properties Co. v. Presidential Ins. Co., 119 S.2d 74 (Fla. 2d D.C. App., 1960).

44. Matthews v. Associated Press, 136 N.Y. 333; 32 N.E. 981 (1893); Saltman v. Nesson, 201 Mass. 534; 88 N.E. 3 (1909); Superior Bedding Co. v. Serta Associates, Inc., 353 F. Supp. 1143 (D.C. Ill. 1973); *but see* n.48 below.

45. *See* n.44.

46. *See*, 61 A.L.R. 3rd 976 (Coop. Assns.).

47. N.Y. Not-for-Profit Corp. L. §602; Fla. Stat. §§617.013(3) (now discretionary); 617.0206.

48. State *ex rel.* Carpenter v. Kreutzer, 100 Ohio 246; 126 N.E. 54 (1919).

49. Croughan v. N.Y. Mutual Benev. Society, 179 A.D. 211; 166 N.Y.S. 161 (1917).

50. Calif. Nonprofit Corp. L. §5250 (eff. 1980); *See* Fla. Stat. 617.0206.

51. *In re* Flushing Hospital and Dispensary, 288 N.Y. 125; 41 N.E.2d 917 (1942). *See* n.33. In Flushing, a meeting was required; there had been no objections for seven years.

52. Hingston v. Montgomery, 97 S.W. 202 (Mo. App., 1906).

53. *See* Fla. Stat. §617.0202.

54. §34 therein; and §10.21 in the 1986 Revision draft.

55. Rogers v. Hill, 289 U.S. 582; 53 S.Ct. 731; 77 L.Ed 1385 (1933); 88 A.L.R. 744; no cert. gtd., 289 U.S. 716; 53 S.Ct. 593; 77 L.Ed. 1469; revg., 62 F.2d 1079 (2d Cir., N.Y.); revg., 60 F.2d 109 (2d Cir., N.Y.); Templeton v. Grant, 75 Colo. 519; 227 P. 555 (1924).

56. Noble v. California, etc., Assn., 98 Calif. App. 230; 276 P. 636 (1929). For a good discussion of bylaw adoption (in a business corporation case) *see*, Benintendi v. Kenton Hotel, Inc., 181 Misc. 897; 45 N.Y.S.2d 705; *affd.*, 50 N.Y.S.2d 843; modified, 294 N.Y. 112; 60 N.E.2d 829 (1945); *and, note*, 45 Columbia L. Rev. 960 (1945).

57. *See* c.24 (meetings), 25 (voting), *etc.*

58. *In re* Ivey and Ellington, 42 A.2d 508 (Del. 1945); Pomeroy v. Westaway, 70 N.Y.S.2d 449 (1947); Elliott v. Lindquist, 94 Pittsb. L.J. 295 (Allegh. Co. Ct. Com. Pl., Penna.).

59. Hill v. American Co-op. Assn., 195 La. 590; 197 S.241 (1940).

60. *See*, note, 3 La. L. Rev. 235 (1940).

61. *In re* Flushing Hospital, 388 N.Y. 125, 41 N.E.2d 917 (1942).

62. Belle Isle Corp. v. MacBean, 49 A.2d 5 (Del. 1946).

63. Grand Valley Irrig. Co. v. Fruita Improv. Co., 37 Colo. 483; 86 P. 324 (1906) (waiver by members of publication of notice of assessment). *And see*, State *ex rel.* Lieghley v. Potter, 42 Ohio App. 489; 182 N.E. 242 (1932) (waiver of executor's failure to record change in ownership of shares for voting in business corporation).

64. *See* c.19.

65. *See e.g.* N.Y. Not-for-Profit Corp. L. §§802–804; *Fla. Stat.* 617.1001–617.1006. These are constitutional. Keetch v. Cordner, 90 Utah 423; 62 P.2d 273 (1936). For forms of all states *see*, 5 Oleck, *Modern Corporation Law* (1978 Supp.).

66. *See* n.65.

67. *See, Nonprofit Corporations in Florida*, §9.5 (Fl. Bar, 1981).

68. *Ibid.*

69. Loeffler v. Federal Supply Co., 187 Okla. 373; 102 P.2d 862 (1940).

70. *See*, Note, *Statutory Revival of Corporate Existence*, 28 Calif. L. Rev. 195 (1940).

71. *See* n.62. For forms of all states *see*, 5 Oleck, *Modern Corporation Law* (1978 supp.); N.Y. N-PCL §§801, 802, 803.

72. Lyon-Gray L. Co. v. Gibraltar L. Ins. Co., 247 S.W. 652 (Tex. Civ. App. 1922). Court order to revive is improper. *In re* Wessel, Nickel and Gross, 176 Misc. 824; 28 N.Y.S.2d 76 (1941).

73. First Presbyterian Church v. National State Bank, 57 N.J.L. 27; 29 A. 320 (1894); Fla. Stat. §617.1106.

74. *Fla. Stat.* §§617.1006, 617.01201.

75. Ohio Rev. Code §1702.41 (trustees of each corporation arrange the agreement); *ibid.* §1702.42 (members of each vote approval; may involve a "greater than majority" vote if the articles or bylaws so provide); *ibid.* §1702.43 (filing of certificate of merger); *ibid.* §1702.44 (consolidation of rights and liabilities); *ibid.* §1702.45 (merger with foreign cor-

poration permitted); *ibid.* §1702.46 (consolidation of rights and liabilities in merger with foreign corporation).

76. Merger: Fla. Stat. §§617.1101–617.1107.

77. Consolidation: Ohio Rev. Code §1702.41.

78. 19 Am. Jur. 2d, Corporations §1493.

79. St. Peterburg Sheraton Corp. v. Stuart, 242 S.2d 185 (Fla. 2d D.C. App., 1970).

80. 19 Am. Jur. 2d, Corporations §1494.

81. First National Bank v. General Assembly Mission, 610 S.W.2d 927 (Ky. App., 1981).

82. Fla. Stat. §§617.1805–617.19.

83. Op. Atty. Gen. (Fl.) 072–399 (Nov. 9, 1972).

84. *See* the Ohio provisions, n.75; Fla. Stat. §§617.1101–617.1106.

85. N.Y. Not-for-Profit Corp. L. §904; Fla. Not-for-Profit Act. §617.1105.

86. *Ibid.* §906 and §617.1107, respectively.

87. *Ibid.* At common law, unanimous consent is required. Garrett v. Reid Cushion L. and C., 34 Ariz. 245; 270 P. 1044. *See* the rule as to "greater than majority" approval (optional) in the Ohio statute, n.75; Fla. Stat. §617.1103 (at least a majority required).

88. Garrett v. Reid-Cushion L. and C. Co., 34 Ariz. 245, 270 P. 1044 (1928); N.Y. Not-for-Profit Corp. L. §907.

89. Knightstown Lake Property Owners Assn. v. Big Blue River Conservancy Distr., 383 N.E.2d 361 (Ind. App. 1978). *See*, West Publ. Co., key number 589; Fla. Stat. §617.1106.

90. Even for punitive damages: Celotex Corp. v. Pickett, 490 S.2d 35 (Fla. 1986); this is the majority rule. *See also*, Klein v. Fisher Foods, Inc., 6 Ohio Misc. 84, 216 N.E.2d 647 (1965); N.Y. Not-for-Profit Corp. L. §906; *and see* Globe Indemnity Co. v. McDowell, 159 S.W.2d 822 (Mo. App., 1942); *and note*, 14 Tulane L. Rev. 273 (1940); Huff v. Warden and Keeper of Prison, 118 Misc. 681; 194 N.Y.S. 862 (1922); *In re* Record Club of America, Ins., 28 B.R. 996 (D.C. Pa., 1983); Engel v. Teleprompter, 703 F.2d 127 (C.A., Tex., 1983).

91. Jones v. Rhea, 130 Va. 345; 107 S.E. 814 (1921); Agoodash Achim, Inc. v. Temple Beth El, 147 Misc. 405; 263 N.Y.S. 81 (1933); Fla. Stat. §617.056; Knightstown Lake Property Owners Assn. v. Big Blue River Conservancy Distr., 383 N.E.2d 361 (Ind. App., 1978); Ruddy v. Norco Local 4–750, 359 S.2d 957 (La., 1978).

92. *In re* New York, S. and W.R. Co., 109 F.2d 988 (3d Cir. 1940); *cert. den.,* 310 U.S. 633; 60 S.Ct. 1075; Note, 26 Va. L. Rev. 104 (1939).

93. Anno., 149 A.L.R. 799; Oleck, *Debtor-Creditor Law* c. 5 (New York: Central Book Co., 1959 Supp.; Wm. Hein Co., 1986 reprint).

94. Ann., 15 A.L.R. 1148.

95. *See*, Brown v. Ramsdell, 227 A.D. 224; 237 N.Y.S. 573 (1929); Umstead v. Durham Hosiery Mills, Inc., 578 F. Supp. 342 (D.C., N.C., 1984).

96. *See, above,* n.75, 87–92.

97. *But see above,* c.40.

98. *Ibid.*

99. *See* 4 Oleck, *Modern Corporation Law,* c.71 (1978 Supp.); and as to liability of corporate members of an association, *see, Ibid.* §1795; *and see,* Note, *Liability of a Corporation for Acts of a Subsidiary or Affiliate,* 71 Harv. L. Rev. 1122 (1958).

100. *Ibid.*

101. Ohio Rev. Code §1702.41(A). And both should be corporations: Trinity Pentecostal Church v. Terry, 660 S.W.2d 449 (Mo. App., 1983).

102. U.S. Supr. Ct. (9 to 0 decision), Apr. 30, 1990; *Assoc. Press* report (May 1, 1990).

103. *Rosenstein v. CMC Real Estate Corp.*, 522 N.E.2d 221 (IL App. 1988).

104. *Elizabeth Gamble Deaconess Home Association v. Turner Construction Co.*, 526 N.E.2d 1368 (OH Com. Pl., 1987, publ. 1988).

105. Fla. Stat. §§607.111(9); 606.111; 606.0830(3); and similar statutes in N.Y., Ind., Minn., etc.; *Poynter-Jamison Ventures Ltd. Partnership v. Times Publishing Co.*, (M.D. Fla. 1990) #90–144–Div.–T–17(a). See 1993 *St. Petersburg Times* reports.

106. *International Insur. Co. v. Johns*, 874 F.2d 1447 (11th Cir., 1989).

107. *Rural Electric Convenience Cooperative Company v. Soyland Power*, 606 N.E. 1269 (Ill. App. 4 Dist., 1992).

108. 36 Am. Jur. 2d 391.

109. Ohio Rev. Code §1702.45.

110. *Id.* §1702.45(A).

111. St. Louis, I. M. & S. RR. v. Berry, 113 U.S. 465 (1885).

112. *Ibid.*

113. Armour Handicrafts, Inc. v. Miami Decorating and Design Center, Inc., 471 N.Y.S. 2d 607, 609 (1984).

114. *Ibid.*

46

FOREIGN ORGANIZATIONS AND ACTIVITIES

[Robert W. Darnell and Mary Klimis assisted in the updating research for this chapter.]

§458. WHAT IS A FOREIGN CORPORATION OR ASSOCIATION?

International Corporations are treated in the next chapter.

A *"foreign* corporation" means a nonprofit corporation formed under the laws of another state.[1] "Foreign" means *nonresident* when applied to corporations or associations. The term usually refers to American corporations incorporated in a state other than the one in which its activities are being scrutinized. The term "alien" corporation sometimes is used to describe a corporation organized under the laws of a foreign nation.[2] "Domestic" corporation means one incorporated locally; while "domesticated corporation" means a foreign corporation that has duly registered and been licensed to do business in the state.[3]

Fairly detailed provisions as to foreign nonprofit corporations are now found in the statutes of most states.[4] Of chief importance are the rules regarding "penalties for failure to qualify" (be licensed) to do business within the state; that is, to do more than purely "interstate" business.[5] But a "federal" corporation doing business in a particular state may be considered to be exempt from such penalties, and viewed the same as a domestic corporation.[6]

Foreign-ness is important in tax law and in determining jurisdiction in federal courts.[7] But our chief concern here is to determine what state or federal *control* applies to out-of-state activities of nonprofit organizations.

A foreign corporation that is merely *registered* (licensed to carry on activities) in a state does not thereby acquire *citizenship* in that state for federal jurisdictional purposes.[8]

Reincorporation in a second state creates a second corporation having the same name and paternity. The second corporation is a *citizen* of the second state.[9] But if the second incorporation is arranged by the first *corporation*, rather than by its *members*, the courts may not recognize a new citizenship in the second state.[10] For federal jurisdictional purposes, the citizenship in either state ordinarily may be used.[11]

Facts in each case must decide whether it is better to reincorporate or merely to register in each state in which activities are carried on. Usually it is advisable to incorporate local branches and to affiliate them under the master charter and bylaws of the parent organization.

§459. LICENSING AND REGISTRATION IN OTHER STATES

Most incorporation statutes expressly or impliedly authorize corporations to carry on activities outside the state.[12] But corporations (and associations), not being natural persons, are not protected by the privileges-and-immunities clause of the Constitution. In effect, this means that states lawfully may discriminate (within reason) against foreign organizations,[13] if the discrimination bears a rational relation to a legitimate state purpose.[14] Thus a tax exemption for homes for the aged owned by Florida corporations only was held to be unreasonable.[15] The burden of requiring a certificate of qualification is not *per se* unconstitutional.[16]

The states, out of comity, may (and do) permit organizations of other states to carry on activities within their borders.[17] And they may (and do) attach conditions.[18]

However, once the foreign corporation has fulfilled the conditions laid down by the state, thereafter the state must extend equal protection of its laws to this corporation.[19]

An *offshore* corporation, such as a lending company officed in the Cayman Islands, cannot be forced to register like a sister-state's corporation for a mortgage foreclosure here, but may be required to provide information about its operation, short of registration.[20]

Special factors, such as the nature of cooperatives, may warrant special treatment.[21]

Insofar as the foreign activities constitute *interstate business*, the states may *not* regulate them, although they may subject the corporation or association to the service of legal process.[22] Usually statutes permit service of process on any agent or clerk in any office or agency maintained within the state, in actions connected with that office or agency.[23] And in other cases, service may be made by leaving process with any person in charge of the local office, in any lawsuit arising out of any activities in the state.[24]

Both incorporated and unincorporated associations are subject to regulation and licensing requirements in other states as well as in their home states.[25]

A state's taxation of foreign activities carried on within its borders by foreign organizations, in purely interstate commerce, is not lawful.[26] But taxation based on the value of local property or local activities is lawful.[27]

A business need not have presence in the state for the state to force an out-of-state company to collect use taxes that in-state customers owe on purchases. However, the out-of-state company must have a "substantial nexus" with the taxing state, as required by the commerce clause.[28]

A corporation that is granted a *certificate of authority* to do business in the state does not thereby acquire powers that it did not possess in its home state.[29]

State regulation and taxation of even purely interstate activities is permitted by special acts of Congress for such matters as workers' compensation and unemployment insurance.[30]

Foreign business corporations may not qualify as nonprofit corporations even though actually operated as nonprofit organizations by their stockholders.[31]

As federal jurisdiction is not necessarily based on diversity of citizenship, a national association may enjoin use of its name or symbol even by a local organization without qualifying as a foreign corporation.[32]

Typical registration statute. The statutes of all states require substantially the same registration procedure for foreign corporations. For example, the Florida, New York, and Ohio statutes lay down these rules.[33]

1. No activities (other than purely interstate affairs) may be carried on in the state by a foreign corporation unless first a *certificate of authority* is filed with the secretary-of-state.

2. In order to obtain such a certificate, the corporation must present to the secretary-of-state a *statement* of its name and state of incorporation (signed by its president, vice-president, secretary, treasurer, managing director, or attorney-in-fact) and the address of its office within the state; the activities it proposes to carry on (which must also be valid under its charter); and a *designation* of the secretary-of-state as its agent for the service of legal process against it *in* the state. Annexed to this must be a certificate by the officer in its home state who has custody of its original certificate of incorporation, or of the special statute that created it, that it is an existing corporation in its home state.[34]

3. Licensing is permitted only of such activities as a domestic corporation could carry on.[35]

4. The name of the foreign corporation must be distinctive. If it is similar to that of a local organization, a certificate granting the latter's consent must be annexed.[36]

When the *statement* and *designation* are filed, and the fees are paid the secretary of state issues to the corporation a *certificate of authority.*[37] [See forms, in the next section herein.]

License fees. Filing fees for foreign corporations vary from state to state, and are changed periodically. They usually are in the $50 to $100 range.[38]

Approvals required. If the proposed activities would require administrative approvals if carried on by domestic organizations (see Chapter 13), similar approval certificates must be obtained and annexed to the statement and designation, or endorsed on it.[39]

Thus, where court approval of the articles of a domestic nonprofit corporation is required, the foreign corporation applying must obtain such approval.[40]

Surrender of authority. Whenever it wishes to discontinue activities in the state, the foreign corporation may file with the department of state a certificate to this effect, revoking the designation of the secretary-of-state as its agent. The form of this certificate is prescribed by local statutes.[41]

Such surrender may not lawfully be used as a device to cut off existing claims, contract rights, or pending actions.[42]

In some states a formal certificate of surrender of authority to do business is required, showing payment of all fees, taxes, workmen's compensation, and the like.[43]

It should be remembered that the holding of property in the state, by a foreign corporation, may be viewed as the doing of business. Thus holding real estate for investment purposes has been so viewed.[44]

Dissolution of the foreign corporation, in its home state, may be certified to the local secretary-of-state as the basis for surrender of license to do business.[45] But mere retirement from activity, of a foreign corporation, does not exempt it from the duty to pay fees and make reports.[46]

The common practice of simply discontinuing activities in the foreign state, without bothering to file a certificate of surrender of authority, is quite unwise. Besides causing annoyance, it results in a continuation of state regulatory rights that some day may cause embarrassment to the organization.

Franchise taxes and license fees. Such taxes as apply to domestic organizations also apply to foreign organizations doing business in the state. That is of chief importance in cases of related business income of nonprofit organizations.

For example, franchise taxes based on real property owned within the state are levied on most foreign corporations.[47] But often no tax is levied on deposits of money or securities in a state.[48]

As to exemptions of charitable organizations from taxation, see Chapters 9 to 12.

§460. MODEL NONPROFIT CORPORATION ACT PROPOSALS

The law governing foreign corporations developed chiefly out of court-case decisions over the past century, modified by piecemeal legislative action. A unified proposal, for a statute that integrates the many case and statute rules into one coherent whole, is the American Bar Association Committee proposal in the 1986 "Exposure Draft" of the Revised Model Nonprofit Corporation Act, Chapter 15. Whether this proposal is sound, or too permissive, will be argued for years.

The proposed statute provides (Subchapter A) for requirement of a certificate of authority. But it immediately lists a minimum of eleven corporate acts that *shall not* be deemed to "constitute transacting business," and thus shall not warrant state regulation; *e.g.*, such as conducting "activities concerning internal corporate affairs," maintaining offices, selling or soliciting, owning assets, etcetera, in the state.[49] These seem to have been copied in the Florida Nonprofit Corporations Act §617.1501. Many of these activities have been held to constitute "doing business" by many court decisions.[50] Failure to register, where registration should be made, would be punished only by a requirement to do so before the corporation may use the courts of the host state.[51] The official comment says that the policy should be "not to impose draconian penalties."[52]

These few examples should suffice to show how permissive the A.B.A. proposal is. The probability of its adoption by many states is quite high. For an analysis see, Oleck, *Mixtures of Profit and Nonprofit Corporate Purposes and Operations*, in Nonprofit Organizations Seminar (coursebook), Northern Kentucky Univ. Chase College of Law (Feb. 1988),—No. Ky. L. Rev.—(late 1988); and L. Moody paper supporting the proposed revisions, in the same coursebook.

Mississippi and Tennessee promptly adopted the proposed revised statute in 1987; a few states thereafter, with many variations.

§461. EFFECT OF FAILURE TO REGISTER IN OTHER STATES

Most states impose injunctions and penalties for the carrying on of local activities by foreign corporations (or their assigns) without registration and licensing. This holds particularly for the solicitation of contributions and the making of contracts. (See Chapters 8, 13, and 17.)

Often a penalty (fine or imprisonment), or injunction, may be imposed on the local agent who acts without complying with the licensing statutes.[53]

Statutory corporate penalties for transacting business without license, or when license has expired or has been cancelled, may be from $250 to $10,000, plus any fees that should have been paid, plus interest.[54] The statute of limitations period in such cases often is about five years.[55]

Nevertheless, if violation of this licensing requirement is not wilful, the secretary-of-state often has authority to remit the forfeit, or part of it; or the court in which the penalty action is brought may do so.[56] Sometimes, if statutes so provide, the officers and members of the foreign corporation may be held liable as partners.[57]

In most states the chief penalty for not registering is that the foreign corporation or its assigns may not enforce its local contracts in the courts of the state.[58] In courts in some states such contracts are absolutely void.[59] But this does not mean that suits in federal courts also are barred.[60] Filing *after* the making of a contract may not validate that contract in some state courts.[61] Lack of filing does not invalidate the contract or conveyance in others.[62]

Many modern statutes permit the defaulting corporation to cure its failure to register, usually by registering and paying back taxes and fees plus a penalty fee.[63] In such states, the contracts of a foreign corporation are not void. The corporation may later file for license, pay a penalty per year (*e.g.*, $500), plus stated other fees, and then sue in the local courts to enforce its contracts; and in no state may failure to register with all due formality as a foreign corporation be punished by injunction against all activity in the state.[64]

Unjust enrichment of local residents at the expense of unlicensed foreign corporations is not tolerated. For example, actions in the local courts are permitted for recovering back money paid under a void contract.[65] Actions based on *noncontractual* obligations such as torts *may* be carried on even without licensing.[66] And contracts made outside the state may be enforced even without licensing.[67] This last suggests that contracts to contribute, for example, always should be accepted (made) in the home state of a charitable corporation.

In some states certain *moneyed* organizations (*e.g.*, banking or insurance) are exempted from the licensing requirements.[68] A foreign credit union, for example, is not required to register in order to enforce its local contracts.[69]

Although the maintenance of action on a contract is barred for nonregistration, this does not bar the bringing of a counterclaim when action is begun against the foreign corporation.[70]

Injunction by the state's attorney-general is authorized when unlicensed activities are carried on.[71]

Court Venue

A foreign corporation transacting business in another state may be barred from that state's statutory grant of choice of venue of the courts for lawsuits there.[72] It may then be required to defend a *transitory* action against it in any county of the state chosen by its adversary party in a lawsuit there.[73]

§462. WHAT IS "DOING BUSINESS"?

In general, the duty to file in foreign states depends on how much activity is carried on in those states. [But see Section 459.]

Isolated, occasional transactions are interstate commerce, which the states may not regulate. But if the organization is *operating in the foreign state*, it is subject to regulation by that state.

The problem boils down to a question of whether or not the foreign organization is *doing business* in the state.

Thousands of conflicting cases and dozens of articles deal with what is and what is not *doing business*. No detailed excursion into this controversial problem is warranted in a work of this kind. Reference should be made to local cases, digests, and articles.[74]

In recent years, the tests of jurisdiction of courts over foreign corporations have included some new concepts and terminology. Besides the old term, *doing business*, such concepts as *presence, contacts, nexus of activity, center of gravity*, and other words and phrases have been employed.[75]

In 1958 Congress passed Public Law 85-554, providing that a corporation is to be deemed a citizen of the state where it has its principal place of business, as well as of the state where it was incorporated, and thus cannot avoid trial in Federal Court in the state where it does its main business.[76]

Modern "*Long Arm*" statutes, now found almost everywhere in the United States, also take jurisdiction over even small "contact" or "activity" of a foreign corporation in the state concerned.[77]

An example of "minimum contacts" of nonprofit corporations, that suffice to constitute "doing business," is this: The American Association of Museums was held to be subject to personal jurisdiction under New York's *long-arm* statute for purporting to have accreditation and evaluation power over museums in New York state, although its office was in Washington, D.C.[78]

Even the amount of business expected to be carried on in the state may affect the statutory requirement to register,[79] although occasional isolated sales will not have such effect.[80] Many states treat the question on an *ad hoc*, case-by-case basis.[81] The foreign corporation is presumed to be doing business in the state where it was incorporated, or has its principal place of business.[82] In the case of a nonprofit corporation, its performance of any of the functions for which it was organized, in the host state, gives long-arm jurisdiction to that state.[83]

Activities of a foreign corporation agent, soliciting business in Illinois, even in a car owned by the foreign corporation, are not enough to constitute "doing business" in Illinois for jurisdiction purposes over the foreign corporation.[84]

The mother of a child who was injured while attending a nonprofit camp in Vermont brought an action for personal injury in New York where the child lived. The court found that the Vermont incorporated camp was not doing business in New York because it had no offices, no real-estate, no bank accounts and no employees in New York. Further, Vermont was the proper place for venue because the injury occurred there and the facility alleged to have been negligently maintained was there. Also, the Vermont court was closer to the residences of the potential witnesses.[85]

§463. LAWSUITS BY OR AGAINST FOREIGN ORGANIZATIONS

See Chapter 44.[86]

Statute of Limitations

State statutes that toll the Statutes of Limitations for lawsuits against foreign corporations that have not registered may be sternly interpreted against those corporations, particularly as to long-arm jurisdiction for corporations that do not have anyone in the state upon whom process can be served. This does not usually violate the 14th Amendment equal protection of the laws clause.[87]

§464. FORMS FOR FOREIGN CORPORATIONS

FORM NO. 201
Application for Registration
of Foreign Corporation
(Illinois)

(Illinois FORM NP-71)

To Be filed in Duplicate

Date Paid.........................
Filing Fee $ ....
Clerk................................

Application for Certificate of Authority of
(Original or Amended)
Foreign Corporation
under the
General Not-for-Profit Corporation Act

To Secretary of State, Springfield, Illinois:

_____, a corporation organized and existing under and by virtue of the laws of the _____ of _____ desiring admission into the state of Illinois, for the purpose of conducting its affairs in said state, hereby makes application for a _____ certificate of authority and submits the following statement pursuant to the "General Not-for-Profit Corporation Act," of Illinois:

    1. —The above corporation was duly incorporated under the laws of the _____ of _____ on the _____

day of _____, A.D. 19_____ for a term of _____
years.

      2. —The address of the principal office in the state or country under the
laws of which it is organized is: _____

      3. —The address of the proposed registered office of the state of Illinois
will be located at _____ street in the city of _____
_____ (_____),
          (ZIP CODE)
County of _____, and the name of its proposed registered
agent in this state at such address is: _____

      4. —The corporation is admitted or qualified to conduct its affairs in the
following states and countries other than Illinois:

      5. —The names of its officers and directors and their addresses are as fol-
lows:

NAME	Street and No.	City and State
President		
Secretary		
Treasurer		
Director		
Director		
Director		
Director		
Director		

      6. —The purpose or purposes for which it was organized which it pro-
poses to pursue in conducting its affairs in this state are:

      IN WITNESS WHEREOF, the undersigned corporation has caused this
application to be executed in its name by its
President and its _____ Secretary, this _____
day of _____, A.D. 19_____

                                                _____
                                              (EXACT CORPORATE TITLE)
             PLACE
         (Corporate Seal)
             HERE
                        By_____
                               Its _____ President

                                _____
                               Its _____ President

STATE OF _____
COUNTY OF _____ } ss.

I, _____, a Notary Public, do hereby certify that on the
_____ day of _____, A.D. 19_____, personally appeared
before me _____, and being first duly sworn by me, acknowledged
that he signed the foregoing document in the capacity therein set forth and
declared that the statements therein contained are true.

IN WITNESS WHEREOF, I have hereunto set my hand and seal the day
and year before written.

PLACE
(Notarial Seal)
HERE

_____
Notary Public

Filing Cover
Illinois Form NP-71
Box _____ File _____

**Application for
Certificate of Authority of
Foreign Corporation under
the General Not-for-Profit
Corporation Act of**

**(file in Duplicate)
New Application**
Filing Fee $_____

Amended Application
Filing Fee $_____

FORM NO. 202
Application for Amended Registration
of Foreign Corporation
(Washington, D.C.)

APPLICATION FOR
AMENDED CERTIFICATE OF AUTHORITY
OF

_____

To: The Recorder of Deeds, D.C.
    Washington, D.C.

      Pursuant to the provisions of the District of Columbia Nonprofit Corporation Act, the undersigned corporation applies for an Amended Certificate of Authority to conduct its affairs in the District of Columbia, and for that purpose submits the following statement:

      FIRST: A Certificate of Authority was issued to the corporation by your office on _____, 19 _____, authorizing it to conduct its affairs in the District of Columbia.

      SECOND: The corporate name of the corporation has been changed to

_____

_____ (Note 1)

      THIRD: It desires to pursue in the conduct of its affairs in the District of Columbia other or additional purposes than those set forth in its prior Application for a Certificate of Authority, as follows:

_____

_____ (Note 2)

Date:_____

(CORPORATE SEAL)

                                         _____

Attest: Corporate name

                                By_____

                                   Its President or Vice President

_____
      Its Secretary or Assistant Secretary

Notes: 1. If the corporate name has not been changed, insert "No change."
         2. If no other additional purposes are proposed, insert "None."

MAIL TO:	FEES DUE	
OFFICE OF THE RECORDER OF DEEDS, D.C.	Filing Fee	$_____
CORPORATION DIVISION	Indexing Fee	_____
SIXTH AND D STREETS, N.W.		_____
WASHINGTON, D.C. 20001	Total	$_____

MAKE CHECK PAYABLE TO
RECORDER OF DEEDS, D.C.

FORM NO. 203
Nonprofit Foreign Corporation Statement
for License Application
[Official Form: Ohio]

Prescribed by   APPROVED

_____   By _____

SECRETARY-OF-STATE   Date _____

                                                       Fee $ _____

**FOREIGN CORPORATION
NOT-FOR-PROFIT
STATEMENT FOR LICENSE CERTIFICATE**

_____, a foreign corporation organized not for profit, desiring to exercise its corporate privilege in the State of Ohio, pursuant to the provisions of Chapter 1703 of the Foreign Corporation Act of Ohio, does hereby certify as follows:

FIRST: That its corporate name is _____

_____

SECOND: That it is a corporation incorporated under the laws of the State of _____

THIRD: That the location of its principal office outside of the State of Ohio is _____

FOURTH: That the corporate privileges it proposes to exercise in the State of Ohio are as follows: _____

_____

FIFTH: That the location of its principal office in the State of Ohio is

_____

SIXTH: That it hereby constitutes and appoints _____, a resident of the county in which the principal office of the corporation in the State of Ohio is located, as its agent upon whom process against the corporation may be served within the State of Ohio. The complete residence address of said person is _____.

SEVENTH: That it hereby irrevocably consents that such process may be served on the person above named and his successors so long as the authority of such agent and his successors shall continue and that service of process may be made upon the Secretary-of-State of Ohio in the event that person or persons so designated cannot be found, or in the other events provided for by the Foreign Corporation Act of Ohio.

EIGHTH: That attached hereto is a Certificate of Good Standing, or of Subsistence, certified by the Secretary-of-State, or other proper official, of the state of incorporation, setting forth:

1. The exact corporate title;

2. The date of incorporation; and

3. That the corporation is in good standing or is a subsisting corporation.
IN WITNESS WHEREOF, said _____ has hereunto affixed its corporate seal and has caused this application to be executed by its officers thereunto duly authorized, this _____ day of _____ _____ 19_____.

_____

By_____

STATE OF   }
COUNTY OF   } ss.

_____, being first duly sworn, deposes and says that he is the _____ of _____, the corporation described in the foregoing application, and that the statements contained in said application are true as he verily believes.

_____

Sworn to before me and subscribed in my presence, this _____ _____ day of _____ 19_____.

_____
NOTARY PUBLIC
My Commission Expires _____

FILING FEE $00.00

FORM NO. 204
Statement and Designation by Foreign Corporation
(New York)

Statement and designation of _____ *Association, Inc., a foreign corporation, pursuant to §210 of the New York General Corporation Law.*

1. The state of its incorporation is the State of _____

2. Its office within the State of New York is to be located at number _____ West _____ Street, _____ (city), New York.

3. The business it proposes to carry on in the State of New York is [state briefly the proposed activities]; and these activities are valid under the certificate of incorporation of the said corporation.

4. It hereby designates the Secretary of the State of New York as its agent upon whom all process in any legal actions or proceedings against it may be served within the State of New York.

5. [Optional] Annexed hereto is a copy of its certificate of incorporation, duly certified by _____, the public officer having custody of

the original certificate. [Note below the requirement of additional approval certificates in some cases.]

6. It hereby agrees to use with its name in the State of New York the suffix *Incorporated*, so that its name will appear as _____ Association, Inc.

7. Annexed hereto is a certificate of the officer in its state of incorporation who is authorized so, to certify that it is an existing corporation in that state.

In witness whereof the said corporation has caused this instrument to be executed in its name by its president, this _____ day of ____ _____ 19_____.

_____ Assn., Inc.

By _____ President

[Annexed Certificate(s)]
[Attach License Fee]

FORM NO. 205
Statement of Change of Registered
Agent and/or Office
(Washington State)

STATE OF WASHINGTON
OFFICE OF SECRETARY OF STATE
CORPORATIONS AND TRADEMARKS DIVISION
OLYMPIA, WASHINGTON 98501

STATEMENT OF CHANGE OF REGISTERED OFFICE,
REGISTERED AGENT, OR BOTH

NONPROFIT CORPORATIONS

> **FILING FEE $_____**

Pursuant to the provisions of Title 24.03.055 or 24.03.345 of the Washington Nonprofit Corporation Act, the undersigned corporation, organized under the laws of the state or county of _____, submits the following statement for the purpose of changing its registered office, registered agent, or both, in the state of Washington.

1. Name of corporation: _____

_____

2. Address of former registered office:_____

_____

3. Address to which the registered office is to be changed (include street

and number or rural route and box number, city and zip code): _____

_____

4. P.O. box address, if any, which may be used for mailing purposes only:

_____

_____

5. Name of former registered agent: _____

6. Name of present registered agent: _____

7. The address of the registered office of the corporation in Washington and the business address of the registered agent of the corporation, as changed, will be identical.

8. This change was authorized by resolution duly adopted by the board of directors of the corporation.

IN TESTIMONY WHEREOF, this statement is signed by the President or Vice-President on _____, 19_____.

_____
(Signature)   (Title)

Subscribed and sworn to before me on _____, 19_____.

_____

Notary public in and for the

(Notarial Seal)   state of_____

residing at_____

FORM NO. 206
Surrender of Registration
(Illinois)
Form NP-82

To Be Filed in Triplicate   Date Paid
Filing Fee $_____   Filing Fee $_____
                                       Clerk

APPLICATION FOR CERTIFICATE OF WITHDRAWAL
UNDER THE
GENERAL NOT-FOR-PROFIT CORPORATION ACT

To Secretary of State, Springfield, Illinois:

The undersigned corporation for the purpose of withdrawing from the state of Illinois, and pursuant to the provisions of Section 82 of the "General Not-for-Profit Corporation Act" of the State of Illinois, hereby represents:

1.—The name of the corporation is _____ and the state

or country under the laws of which it is organized is _____.

_____

    2.—That it (a) surrenders its authority to conduct affairs in Illinois, (b) hereby revokes the authority of its registered agent in Illinois to accept service of process, and (c) hereby consents that service of process in any action or proceeding based upon any cause of action arising in Illinois during the time the corporation was authorized to conduct its affairs in Illinois may hereafter be made on such corporation by service thereof on the Secretary of the State of Illinois.

    3.—The address to which the Secretary of State of the State of Illinois may mail a copy of any process against the corporation that may be served on him is_____

    IN WITNESS WHEREOF, the undersigned corporation has caused this application to be executed in its name by its _____ President and by its _____ Secretary this _____ day of _____ , A.D. 19_____.

PLACE
(Corporate Seal)
HERE

_____
(Exact Corporate Title)

By_____

    Its _____ President

_____

    Its _____ Secretary

STATE OF

COUNTY OF } ss.

    I, _____, a Notary Public, do hereby certify that on the _____ day of _____, 19_____,

_____

    personally appeared before me and being first duly sworn by me, acknowledge he signed the foregoing document in the capacity therein set forth and declared that the statements therein contained are true.

    IN WITNESS WHEREOF, I have hereunto set my hand and seal the day and year before written.

PLACE
(Notarial Seal)
HERE

_____
Notary Public

POINTS TO REMEMBER

- Do not confuse citizenship rights of individuals with those of corporations or associations.

- It usually is best to incorporate branches separately in each state, and to affiliate them under the master charter and bylaws of the parent organization.

- The licensing rules of the various states differ.

- Do not register if only occasional transactions are conducted in the foreign state. That is *interstate commerce.*

- If in doubt—register.

- File reports in all states where property is owned.

- Accept all contracts in the home office.

- Follow local statutes when registering in other states.

- Get necessary administrative approvals there.

- Study the statutory requirements of any state in which a contract is to be made or performed.

- Get a state license approval before soliciting funds in any state.

- Expect the state to claim jurisdiction over your organization, whenever you carry on any activity.

- Be familiar with the "Long Arm" statutes.

- File notice of withdrawal if you cease to operate in another state.

NOTES TO CHAPTER 46

1. Ohio Rev. Code §1702.01(B); 20 C.J.S. *Corporations* §1783. The Wisconsin State Investment Board was held to be a "foreign corporation" insofar as it operated in Ohio. Opinions Ohio Atty. Genl. (1953), 2719; Walker, *Foreign Corporation Law: A Current Account,* 47 N.C.L. Rev. 733 (1985); *In re* Grand Lodge, 110 Pa. 613, 1 A.582 (1885); *In re* Ewles' Estate, 105 Utah 507, 143 P.2d 903, 905 (1943); Restatement, Conflict of Laws §153.

2. *See,* State *ex rel.* Cartwright v. Hillcrest Investments Ltd., 630 P.2d 1253 (Okl. 1981).

3. Okl. Stat., tit. 18 §1.2 (4) (former Bus. Corp. Act).

4. *See,* Walker article, n.1; and, Fessler, *Codification and the Nonprofit Corporation: the philosophical choices, pragmatic problems and drafting difficulties encountered in the formulation of a new Alaska Code,* 33 Mercer L. Rev. 543 (1982); Henn and Boyd, *Statutory Trends in the Law of Nonprofit Organizations: California, Here We Come,* 66 Cornell L. Rev. 1103 (1981); Darlow, *Michigan Nonprofit Corporations,* 62 Mich. B.J. 530 (1983); Hubbard, *Missouri Nonprofit Corporations,* 39 J. Mo. B. 209 (1983); *The New Jersey Nonprofit Corporation Act,* 112 N.J.L.J. (1983); Compton and Perelson, *1983 Amendments to the New Mexico Business Corporation Act and Related Statutes,* 14 N.M.L. Rev. 371 (1984); Leiser, *The Foreign Non-Profit Corporation and the Mystique of Jurisdiction,* 1976 Detr. Coll. L. Rev. 257.

5. Eg. Calif. Corp. Code, §2259; Alaska Stat. § 10.06.713; *Fla. Stat.* 617.1502 Ohio Rev. Code §1703.28, and *see* statutes of all states, in Oleck, *Modern Corporation Law,* c. 37, and as to

fees c. 10 (1978 Supp.); and as to "doing business" *see*, Ibid. §829 (1978 Supp.), and Henn, *Corporations* (casebook) 87–117 (2d ed., 1986); Rev. Model Nonprofit Corp. Act, c. 15 (1986 revision).

6. Commonwealth v. First Pennsylvania Overseas Finance Corp., 229 A.2d 896 (Pa. 1967).

7. As to franchise tax, *see*, Smith v. Lewis, 211 Calif. 294; 295 P. 37 (1930). As to federal jurisdiction, *see* Saltzman v. Birrell, 78 F. Supp. 778 (S.D.N.Y. 1948), Doctor v. Harrington, 196 U.S. 579; 25 S.Ct. 355, 49 L.Ed. 606 (1905).

8. Baltimore and O.R. Co. v. Harris, 12 Wall. (U.S.) 65; 20 L.Ed. 354 (1870).

9. Clark v. Barnard, 108 U.S. 436; 2 S.Ct. 878; 27 L.Ed. 780 (1883).

10. Carolina and N.W.R. Co. v. Town of Clover, 34 F.2d 480 (W.D., So. Car. 1929).

11. Clark case, n.9; Note, 72 A.L.R. 105; 20 C.J.S., *Corporations* §1795; Beale, *Corporations of Two States*, 4 Columbia L. Rev. 391 (1904).

12. *E.g.*, meetings may be held outside the state: Ohio Rev. Code §1702.17(B); carry on activities outside the state: 5 Ann. L. Mass., c. 158 §10, "carry on its operations . . . in any state . . . or country." Fla. Stat. §617.0302(8).

13. Paul v. Virginia, 8 Wall. (U.S.) 168; 19 L.Ed. 357 (1868); Quong Wing v. Kirkendall, 223 U.S. 59, 62; 32 S.Ct. 192; 56 L.Ed. 350 (1912).

14. Western and Southern Life Ins. Co., v. State Board, 100 S.Ct. 2017 (1981). *Cf.*, Missouri Pacific RR. v. Kirkpatrick, 652 S.W. 2d 128 (Mo. 1983).

15. Miller v. Board of Pens. of United Presbyterian, 431 S.2d 350 (Fla. 5th D.C. App., 1983).

16. Neogard Corp. v. Malott & P.-G., 106 Calif. 3rd 213, 164 Calif. Rptr. 813 (1980); Bianco v. Concepts 100, Inc., 436 A.2d 206 (Pa. Sup. 1981).

17. Bank of Augusta v. Earle, 13 Pet. (U.S.) 519, 588; 10 L.Ed. 274 (1839).

18. Blake v. McClung, 172 U.S. 239, 256; 19 S.Ct. 165; 43 L.Ed. 432 (1898); Green Val. School, Inc. v. Nyquist, 72 Misc.2d 889, 340 N.Y.S.2d 234 (1972).

19. WHYY, Inc. v. Borough of Glassboro, 393 U.S. 117, 89 S.Ct. 286, 21 L.Ed.2d 242 (1968); State *ex rel.* Cartwright v. Hillcrest, 630 P.2d 1253, (Okla. 1981); Anno. 48 L.Ed. 2d 1296.

20. Batavia, Ltd. v. U.S. Dept. of Treasury, 393 S.2d 1207 (Fla., 1980).

21. Watergate South, Inc. v. Duty, 464 A.2d 141 (D.C. App., 1983).

22. *Restatement, Conflict of Laws*, §§174, 175; International Harvester Co. v. Commonwealth of Kentucky, 234 U.S. 579; 34 S.Ct. 944; 58 L.Ed. 1479 (1914); Note, 25 Columbia L. Rev. 204 (1925).

23. N.Y.C.P.L. and R. §§302, 311, 313. *See, e.g.*, Johnson v. Four States Enterprises, Inc. 355 F. Supp. 1312 (1972).

24. *Ibid.*

25. *Ibid; and see* State Board decision, above, n.1; N.Y. Genl. Assns. L. §§18, 19; Wis. Stat. §226.01; *e.g.*, a cooperative: Vilter Mfg. Co. v. Diarymen's League Coop. Assn., 84 N.Y.S.2d 445, *affd. without op.*, 275 A.D. 706, 769 88 N.Y.S.2d 248, 903 (1949).

26. Airway Elec. Appliance Corp. v. Day, 266 U.S. 71; 45 S.Ct. 12; 69 L.Ed. 169 (1924).

27. Baltic Mining Co. v. Commonwealth (Mass.), 231 U.S. 68; 34 S.Ct. 15; 58 L.Ed. 127 (1913).

28. *Quill Corp. v. North Dakota*, 112 S. Ct. 1904 (U.S.N.D., 1992).

29. Matter of Amer. Society for Prevention of Cruelty to Children, 446 N.Y.S.2d 108 (App. Div. 1982).

30. International Shoe Co. v. State of Washington, 326 U.S. 310; 66 S.Ct. 154; 90 L.Ed. 95; A.L.R. 1057 (1945); based on 26 U.S.C.A. §1606(a).

31. Opinions, Ohio Atty.-Genl. (1932), 4556.

32. Lyon v. Quality Courts United, 249 F.2d 790 (6th Cir. 1957).

33. Ohio Rev. Code §1703.27; Fla. Stat. §617.1503; N.Y.N-PCL §§1301, 1304.

34. *Ibid.*

35. Opinions, N.Y. Atty.-Genl. (1921), 307.

36. Ohio Rev. Code §1703.06. Unless the statute clearly so intends, a foreign corporation may not be required to change its name. Guyette v. C. & K. Development Co., 451 A.2d 1318 (N.H. 1982).

37. Ohio Rev. Code §1703.04; N.Y.N.-PCL §1305.

38. $75 in Ohio, Ohio Rev. Code §1703.04 (C); $225 in New York, N.Y. Exec. L. §96.9(a); $35 in Florida, Fla. Not-for-Profit Corp. Act §617.1503 [*See* amounts in current statutes.]

39. N.Y. N-PCL §1301.

40. Association for Preservation of Freedom of Choice, Inc. v. Simon, 22 Misc.2d 1016, 201 N.Y.S.2d 135, *app. dism.* 8 N.Y.2d 909, 204 N.Y.S.2d 150, 168 N.E.2d 826 (1960).

41. *Fla. Stat.* 617.1520; N.Y. N-PCL §1311.

42. *Ibid.*

43. Ohio Rev. Code §1703.17.

44. Opinions, Ohio Atty.-Genl. (1953), 2719.

45. Ohio Rev. Code §1703.17(D).

46. *Ibid.* §1703.17(F).

47. N.Y. Tax L. §209. As to authority to hold realty *see*, N.Y. N-PCL §1307.

48. *Ibid.*

49. Rev. Model NPC Act §1501 (1986 Draft).

50. *See* the Section on "doing business," below.

51. Rev. Model NPC Act §15.02(a)(1986 Draft).

52. *Ibid.*, Official Comment to §15.02.

53. *See*, Calif. Corp. Code, §2259; Ohio Rev. Code, c. 1716; 15 Penn. Stat. §6141; Fla. Stat. §617.1502; *and see*, Bogert, *Solicitation of Gifts for Charity*, 5 Hastings L.J. 96 (1954). As to injunction, As to officer or agent acts, *see*, Ohio Rev. Code §§1703.30, 1703.99. *See*, 2 Oleck, *Modern Corporation Law* §830 (1978 Supp.) for rules of all states; N.Y.N-PCL §1303.

54. Ohio Rev. Code §§1703.28, 1703.99.

55. *Ibid.*

56. *Ibid.*

57. Towle v. Beistle, 97 Ind. App. 241; 186 N.E. 344 (1933); Taylor v. Branham, 35 Fla. 297; 17 S. 552; 39 L.R.A. 362 (1895). Not without statutory basis. Pape v. Finch, 102 Fla. 425; 136 S. 496 (1931); Note, 41 Yale L.J. 309 (1931); Ladd, *Liability of Individuals, etc.*, 15 Iowa L. Rev. 285 (1930).

58. Fla. Stat. §617.1502; *Restatement, Conflict of Laws* §179; Chattanooga Natl. B. and L. Assn. v. Denson, 189 U.S. 408; 23 S.Ct. 630; 47 L.Ed. 870 (1903); C and C Products, Inc. v. Premier Indus. Corp., 275 So.2d 124 (Ala. 1972); Note, 25 Columbia L. Rev. 806 (1925); N.Y. N-PCL §1313.

59. Northern Bank and Trust Co. v. United Underwriters Sales Corp. of America, 474 S.W.2d 899 (Ark. 1971); *and see* Note, 25 Columbia L. Rev. 806 (1925).

60. David Lupton's Sons Co. v. Automobile Club of Amer., 225 U.S. 489; 32 S.Ct. 711; 56 L.Ed. 1177 (1912).

61. N.Y. N-PCL §1313.

62. Fla. Stat. §617.1502.

63. *See,* list of all states, in, 2 Oleck, *Modern Corporation Law,* c. 37 (1978 Supp.). *And see, for example,* Mass. Genl. L. Ann. c. 181 §9.

64. As to contracts (cure of default in registration) *see,* Ohio Rev. Code §1703.29; Conrad v. Rarey, 125 Ohio St. 326, 181 N.E. 444 (1932); Manhattan Terrazzo Brass Strip Co., Inc. v. Benzing and Sons, 72 Ohio App. 116, 50 N.E.2d 570 (1943). As to barring organization from the state (not permissible), *see* NAACP v. Alabama, 377 U.S. 288, 84 S.Ct. 1302, 12 L.Ed.2d 325 (1964), revg. 274 Ala. 544, 150 S.2d 677. Fla. Stat. §617.1502(4) ($500 to $1000 for each year of transacting business without authority).

65. Lasswell L. and L. Co. v. Lee Wilson and Co., 236 F. 322 (8th Cir. 1916); Gulf Chemical and Metallurgical Corp. v. Sylvan Chemical Corp., 122 N.J. Super. 499, 300 A.2d 878 (1973).

66. Northwest Ready Roofing Co. v. Antes, 117 Nebr. 121; 219 N.W. 848 (1928); National Match Co. v. Empire S. and I. Co., 227 Mo. App. 1115; 58 S.W.2d 797 (1933).

67. *Restatement, Conflict of Laws* §178; Brace v. Gauger Korsmo Constr. Co., 36 F.2d 661 (8th Cir. 1929).

68. N.Y. N-PCL §§1301, 1304.

69. Walsh v. Mazzariello, 189 Misc. 433; 71 N.Y.S.2d 806 (1947).

70. Rolle v. Rolle, 201 A.D. 698; 194 N.Y.S. 661 (1922); Capin v. S. & H. Packing, 636 P.2d 1223 (Ariz., 1981).

71. N.Y. N-PCL §1303.

72. Such as Fla. Stat. §47.051.

73. United Engines, Inc. v. Citmoco Services, Inc., 418 S.2d 409 (Fla., 1982).

74. *See,* Isaacs, *An Analysis of Doing Business,* 25 Columbia L. Rev. 1018 (1925); 2 Oleck, *Modern Corporation Law,* c. 37 (1978 Supp.); Henn and Alexander, *Corporations,* §136 (3d ed., 1983); 17 Fletcher, *Cyc. of Corporations,* §8464 (perm. ed.); Stevens, *Corporations,* §206 (2d ed., 1949); International Shoe Co. v. State of Washington, 326 U.S. 310, 66 S.Ct. 154, 90 L.Ed. 95, 161 A.L.R. 1057 (1945); Vt. Stat. Ann., tit. 12 §855 (1959); Ill. Rev. St. c. 110 §17 (1968); McGee v. International Life Insur. Co., 355 U.S. 220, 78 S.Ct. 199, 2 L.Ed.2d 223 (1957); *Restatement Conflict of Laws,* §§42, 75, 77, 84, 86 (tent. draft No. 3, 1956); *Developments in the Law, State-Court Jurisdiction,* 73 Harv. L. Rev. 909, 919–935 (1960); Dym v. Gordon, 41 Misc. (N.Y.)2d 657; 25 N.Y.S.2d 656 (1963, Supr. Ct., Nassau County), *and see* the (free) bimonthly pamphlet, *The Corporation Journal* (New York: Corporation Trust Co.) giving late cases and developments.

75. *Ibid.* Leiser, *The Foreign Non-Profit Corporation and the Mystique of Jurisdiction,* 1976 Det. Coll L. Rev. 257.

     See, Grayson, *Federal Courts: Jurisdiction over foreign corporations,* 22 Harv. Int'l L.J. 688 (1981); Darrell, *Minimum Contacts,* 30 Drake L. Rev. 171 (1980); Friedman, *Constitutional Law—Jurisdiction: To be subject to forum state's personal jurisdiction, foreign corporation must reasonably expect to defend suit,* 51 Miss. L. J. 121 (1980).

76. 28 U.S.C. §1332; *see,* 2 Oleck, *Modern Corporation Law,* c. 37, §829 (1978 supp.).

77. *See,* for example, Clark, *Nationwide Service of Process for Citizens of the Forum in Personal Injury Cases Against Business,* 1969 U. of Illinois L. For. 488. *See also, e.g.,* Ohio Rev. Code Ann. §2307.38.2; Mont. Rev. Code Ann. Title 25 ch. 20, M.R.Civ.P., Rule 4B.

78. Estate of Vanderbilt, 441 N.Y.S. 2d 153 (Super. Ct., 1981).

79. Fla. Stat. §607.1501

80. *Ibid.* §607.1501.

81. Mis Cal 204, Ltd. v. Upchurch, 465 S.2d 326 (Miss., 1985).

82. Oliver Promotions, Ltd. v. Tams-Witmark Music Library, Inc., 535 F. Supp. 1224 (D.C., N.Y., 1982).

83. Galatz v. Eighth Judicial Distr. Ct., 683 P.2d 26 (Nev., 1984).

84. *Longo vs. AAA-Michigan*, 569 N.E.2d 927 (Ill. App. 1990).

85. *Marks v. Farm and Wilderness Foundation*, 753 F. Supp. 523 (S.D.N.Y. 1991); N.Y. McKinney's
     CPLR 301, 302(a); 28 U.S.C.A. §1404.

86. *See also*, n.74; and Ohio Rev. Code §§1703.19, 1703.191, 1703.23, 1703.29; N.Y. N-PCL
     §§1314, 1315.

87. *See*, G.D. Searle & Co. v. Cohn, 102 S.Ct. 1137 (1982).

47

INTERNATIONAL NONPROFIT ORGANIZATIONS

[See also the preceding chapter: *Foreign Organizations and Activities*]

§465. ORIGIN OF MODERN INTERNATIONAL ASSOCIATIONS˙

˙Charles D. Svoboda contributed research for this section. He cited the following selected Bibliography, in a pre-published note in, *Pinellas County (FL.) Review*, (Feb. 10, 1984) p.6:

Bennett, A. LeRoy, *International Organizations, Principles and Issues*, Englewood Cliffs, NJ: Prentice-Hall, 1977.

Feld, Werner J. & Jorlan, Robert S., *International Organizations, A Comparative Approach*, New York, NY: Praeger Press, 1983.

Friedlander, Walter A., *International Social Welfare*, Englewood Cliffs, NJ: Prentice-Hall, 1975.

Handbook of the Nations and International Organizations, New York, NY: Time, Inc., Editors of Life Magazine, 1966.

International Encyclopedia of the Social Sciences, New York, NY: The Free Press, 1968.

Kirgis, Frederic L. Jr., *International Organizations in Their Legal Setting*, St. Paul, MN: West Publishing, 1977.

Marts, Arnold C., *Man's Concern for His Fellow Man*, Geneva, NY: Humphrey Press, 1961.

Oleck, Howard L., *Nonprofit Corporations, Organizations and Associations*, [6th ed., Englewood Cliffs, NJ: Prentice-Hall, 1994.] [He cited the 5th ed.]

Patterns of Cooperation, Washington, DC: Department of State, Date Unknown.

Reuter, Paul, *International Institutions*, New York, NY: Rinehard & Co., 1958.

White, Lyman C., *International Non-Governmental Organizations*, New Brunswick, NJ: Rutgers University Press, 1951.

Ancient religious organizations were probably the first nonprofit international associations. Today the modern religious associations continue to be the most important nonprofit international associations; *e.g.*, Judaism is the oldest continuous one, and Roman Catholicism the largest one.

An international association usually organizes in one country and then becomes "international" by having other such organizations in other countries join with it, or does so through treaties among various nations. Some of these organizations are "government"; that is, formed and/or financed by a national government, in whole or in part.

The 1978 Yearbook of International Organizations broke nongovernmentals down into 20 divisions. Examples of these divisions included: Religion, Social Sciences, Politics, Law, Social Welfare, Health, and Education. The top five categories, by number of organizations in existence, were: Health & Medicine—306; Commerce & Industry—273; Science—190; Technology—147; and Education and Youth—134.

In 1859 a young Swiss banker named Jean Henri Dunant, shocked by seeing thousands of dead and wounded, unattended soldiers on the battlefield near Solferino, Italy, wrote a book titled *Un Souvenir de Solferino*. Published in Geneva, it inspired the Swiss government to invite representatives of 17 countries to a "Geneva Convention," to form an organization for care of war casualties and prisoners, and to promulgate a constitution for what became the *International Red Cross* in 1864.

The International Red Cross is a prime example of non-religious-based, nonprofit, international organizations. It has been a model for other nonprofit associations, both national and international. Accompanying such organizations in their formation and operation, are various treatises on international law, of which a prime example is the 1625 book on international law written by the jurist Hugo Grotius. The Hanseatic League and other international business organizations, past and present, are sources of experience, too.

In 1984 the American Council for Voluntary International Action came into being, to concentrate on private voluntary organization work in the Third World. For generations, such organizations have worked to help the poor and dispossessed, but especially since World War II, when such organizations became very active—such as CARE, Church World Service, Catholic Relief Services, and the Jewish immigrant aid society HIAS. American Council of Voluntary Agencies in Foreign Service (ACVAFS) formed a voluntary umbrella agency. And in 1981 a grouping coalesced, called PAID—Private Agencies in International Development. Then, in late 1984 the two groups merged, to become *Interaction*—120 organizations joined in voluntary international service for Third World aid alone.[1] There are other, more specialized organizations too, such as AMNESTY INTERNATIONAL.

§466. WHAT IS AN "INTERNATIONAL NONPROFIT ORGANIZATION"?

[Beverly J. Ness, Richard E. Kramer and Gigi Garber Skipper contributed material for this section.]

Some kinds of nonprofit organizations carry on international activities regularly. Charitable, professional, and educational associations; sports organizations; scientific, cultural, religious, missionary, and other groups; churches, international trade, social, and fraternal societies are all common examples.

Protection of a client's assets in a foreign country often takes the form of organizing a legal entity (corporation) under foreign laws—creating an international corporate entity.[2] The foreign corporation is an artificial legal person, for most purposes separate from the individual members.[3] It generally is entitled to protection by, and is under the jurisdiction of, the country where it is incorporated.[4]

In general, the "corporate veil" will be pierced when the state views the alien "owners" as unfriendly to it.[5] This often turns on the matter of who "controls" the corporation.[6]

In the '70s and '80s the *transnational* American corporation was seen by some people as a new phenomenon, changing the world. It was viewed with a mixture of awe and alarm. For example, it was described thus:

> Possessed of size, allied with the United States government and its universities, foreign economies and cultures are penetrated, dominated, and conquered by the American-based enterprise that masters research, understands application, and most important is able to organize and energize men to action.[7]

The size and scope of American corporations' involvements in foreign countries had grown big enough, and worrisome enough, to inspire issuance in 1977, by the Antitrust Division of the U.S. Department of Justice, of an *Antitrust Guide for International Operations.*[8]

The **Encyclopedia of Associations** today includes two volumes devoted to International Organizations. Part 2 is an index volume that is indexed in the following manner:

1. Geographic index by country
2. Executive index—alphabetic index of executives by name, which gives the address and a cross reference to the description listing
3. Name and key word index

Part 1 gives descriptive listings for each international organization, which includes the address, phone number, year founded, number of members, budget, languages, brief description of activities and purpose, publications, and conventions.

Some examples of international nonprofit organizations are:

InterAction—Washington, D.C., umbrella organization of 143 private groups engaged in international humanitarian service; established in 1984; 2.1 billion contributions.

PLAN International—$165 million multinational child sponsorship organization.

Worldwide Fund for Nature (WWF)—A conservation group founded in 1961 in Switzerland, WWF has 1.5 million members and a $25 million budget. It is an umbrella group for 23 national groups and maintains a library. Formerly the World Wildlife Fund.

Save the Children Fund—Oldest nonsectarian international aid organization. Established in Sweden and the United Kingdom after World War I.

OXFAM—A nonmembership group founded in England in 1942, it provides food and shelter in depressed areas of the world.

Doctors Without Borders (Medicins Sans Frontiers)—The world's largest independent emergency medical aid organization provides medical assistance to crisis-stricken areas. Founded in 1971, it has 3500 members and a $20 million budget.

International Committee of the Red Cross (ICRC)—Founded in 1863 in Switzerland and known for its neutrality while rendering aid during times of crisis.

Greenpeace International—Founded in the Netherlands in 1971, the goal of its 2 million members is to curb irresponsible uses of the environment and wildlife.

Conservation International—A Washington, D.C.,-based group of corporations and individuals in 15 countries interested in environmental protection and conservation. Founded in 1987.

Amnesty International—Human rights group of 700,000 members founded in England in 1961 working toward the release of all prisoners of conscience.

International Federation for Human Rights—Founded in 1922 in France, it is a nonpolitical and nonaligned international human rights organization.

Definitions[9]

Use of the term "foreign" corporation is not a clear enough definition, because, in the United States, that means merely incorporated in another state. (See the preceding chapter). The terms IGO (international governmental organization) and INGO (international nongovernmental organization) are sometimes used. The U.N. Economic and Social Council (ECOSOC) defines INGO as: "Any international organization which is not established by intergovernmental agreements shall be considered as a nongovernmental organization

..., including organizations which accept members designated by governmental authorities, provided that such membership does not interfere with the free expression of the views of the organization."[10]

Yearbook of International Organizations

The editors of this Yearbook use *seven criteria* for classifying a nongovernmental organization as one that should be included in that annual (also requiring that the organization be oriented to three or more countries).[11]

1. *Aims*: Must be genuinely international.
2. *Members*: Must be individual or collective participation with full voting rights, from at least three countries. Membership open to any qualified individual or entity in the organization's area of operations. No one national group may control the organization.
3. *Structure*: Constitution must give members the right to periodically elect a governing body and officers.
4. *Officers*: If officers are all of the same nationality, to facilitate management, that does not necessarily disqualify the organization; but then there should be rotation (at designated intervals) of headquarters and officers among the various member countries.
5. *Finance*: Substantial contributions must come from at least three countries.
6. *Relations with other organizations*: Entities formally connected with another organization are not necessarily excluded, but evidence must show that they elect their own officers and each leads an independent life.[12]
7. *Activities*: Evidence of current activity must be available; otherwise they will be treated as "dissolved" or "dormant."

Transnational Corporation: This is defined as one involved in movement of tangible or intangible items across national boundaries, in which at least one actor is not an agent of a government or of an intergovernmental organization.

Multinational Corporation: This is an enterprise that operates in many parts of the world, without having a specific home base, and also one that has an office in one country and branches in several others.[13] A listing of (nonprofit) Multinational Enterprises (MNE) is available in the *Encyclopedia of Associations*[14] annual.

§467. REGULATION OF INTERNATIONAL ORGANIZATIONS

[Beverly J. Ness and Louise B. Fields contributed material for this section.]

[*Note* that the term *MNE* (Multinational Enterprise) is used in this section, to include international groups of *various* kinds; nonprofit, for profit, intergovernmental, *etc.*]

There has been a proliferation of writing concerning the regulation of MNEs during the past few years.[15] Generally, these writings center on *Codes of Conduct*, which are supranational quasi-legislation. The formulation of a code of conduct that is internationally accepted is a difficult task that requires political sensitivity. Internationally accepted codes of conduct, however, are extremely important (politically and socially) to the attorney involved with the nonprofit corporation abroad.[16] The present goal of most of the codes is to improve the economic position of less developed countries (LDCs).[17]

The need for a supranational code of conduct was evidenced in the Middle East war of 1973 when OPEC's (cartel) price increase caused world inflation along with overproduction of commodities. The resulting effect of the Middle East war on the economics of the Third World was to make the LDCs more dependent on U.S. and other aid and MNEs.[18] The LDCs often view the MNEs as the major obstacle to their economic development.[19]

The tendency of the LDCs is to nationalize business in order to control and regulate MNEs. The LDCs are in a position to demand U.N. consideration in the development of the codes because they outnumber the developed countries, even though they maintain lesser economic positions. As a result of the input of the LDCs, the overriding theme of these codes is to control the power and activities of the MNEs which are based largely in the U.S., western Europe, or Japan.

There are presently over a dozen international codes of conduct in various stages of development. The most important and comprehensive of these works, although the most difficult to formulate, are from the United Nations. Other types of codes emanate from private or trade sources or from regional efforts. The increasing international economic dysfunction emphasizes the need for new ways to manage world economy equitably and efficiently.[20] Proliferation of writings in this area has been so rapid that by the time information is published it is out of date. Usually, the best up-to-date bibliography of codes of conduct may be found in looseleaf services.[21]

The following are some of the types or sources of codes of conduct:

United Nations Codes of Conduct:

A. Code of Conduct for Liner Conferences.[22] "This is the first piece of international economic legislation to be completed."[23]

B. Code on Restrictive Business Practices.[24] First to be embodied in a General Assembly resolution.

C. Regulation of Multinational Enterprises.[25]

D. Regulation of Technology Transfer.

E. Agreements Regarding Corrupt Practices.

F. Codes of International Organizations, such as Labor Policies (Unions), and Infant Formula (product) sales.

G. Codes of Regional Organizations, such as OECD (Economic Co-operation and Development) Guidelines.

H. Private Codes, such as that of the International Chamber of Commerce code on business self-regulation.

Some collisions between a nation's political and social policies and the policies of transnational corporations are almost inevitable. International treaties thus far have been the chief method for dealing with these problems, but have not been very satisfactory in practice. Efforts to develop an unofficial but morally binding system of Codes of Conduct for multinational corporations have shown promise,[26] but now are laboring in the morass of U.N. politics.

The European Company (C.E.C.)

In 1970 a statute was proposed by the "Commission of the European Communities" (C.E.C.) for formation of corporations that would be western "European"—not French, German, or any other single nationality. Such corporations would be called *Societas Europaea*, or "SE," and would be transnational in basic structure.[27] While such corporations would be mainly large multinational *business* corporations, the possibility of their use for nonprofit purposes also might be available.

Difficulties of membership of Britain in the C.E.C., and other problems, delayed the enactment of the proposed statute. Also, even after enactment, the statutes of the member nations would have to be amended accordingly.

But there are many important *nongovernmental* international organizations, and there long have been many. They have served (and serve) for worthy purposes in all phases of human society and life.[28] Many are private corporations, not connected with a nation's, or group of nation's, political or diplomatic life. They are citizens (nationals) of their countries of origin, as private corporations usually are.[29]

Judging a Charity

Following the resignation of the president of United Way, the Council of Better Business Bureaus has added CEO salaries to its "Annual Charity Index," a guide that profiles over 200 U.S. charities. If one is interested in the same information regarding international relief groups, contact InterAction, which in 1992 adopted tough new standards for member charities. To be phased in over the next year, InterAction will provide a list of its standards, a list of its members, or a list of members active in a particular part of the world, like Somalia. Send a stamped, self-addressed envelope to 1717 Massachusetts Avenue, N.W., Suite 801, Washington, D.C. 20036.[30]

The IRS has released Revenue Procedure 92–94, which helps private foundations to determine whether a foreign organization is recognized by the IRS as a charity qualifying for tax-free distributions. In the past, in order to avoid taxable expenditures, foundations had to make decisions about donations based on "reasonable judgment" or "a good faith determination" by their counsel. Now, foreign grantees providing appropriate affidavits will relieve foundations from the expense of obtaining opinions of counsel. The affidavits should contain a description of activities, corporate documents, an analysis of whether the organization is publicly supported under the tax code, and statements that the organization meets the basic requirements of U.S. charitable status.[31]

§468. REGISTRATION OF FOREIGN CORPORATIONS

Chapter 46 discusses the requirements of the various states of the United States as to "qualification" or "registration" of *foreign corporations* in each state. That discussion is basically applicable to corporations from other countries as well as from other states.

In some places, such as Canada, the statutes require registration almost exactly in the same way as do states of the United States; subject to similar penalties, but also such penalties as prohibition of mortgage loans, *etc.* Much alike are the laws of the Provinces of Alberta,[32] British Columbia,[33] Manitoba,[34] New Brunswick,[35] Nova Scotia,[36] Ontario,[37] Quebec,[38] and Saskatchewan.[39] They closely resemble the statutes of the United States.

In practically all places, jurisdiction and applicability of the statutes turns on what each state or country deems to be "doing business"[40] by the foreign corporation in that state or country.[41]

The classic case on "doing business" in the United States still is *International Shoe Company v. State of Washington.*[42]

§469. PRACTICAL APPROACH TO INTERNATIONAL NONPROFIT ORGANIZATION

As is evident in the thumbnail sketch of international organizations law, in the foregoing sections, there is plenty of *international law*, and much law about international *government-related* organizations. But there is very little available about *private nonprofit, nongovernmental organizations.*

Neither is the law as to "foreign corporations" of much help. (See Chapter 46 on foreign corporations.) That term usually refers to conflicts of law as between states of the United States—*i.e.*, a foreign corporation is one incorporated under the law of another state but operating in the host state.

As to corporations from other *countries*, they are more accurately described as foreign in the sense of being composed of *alien* (noncitizen) members.

Yet, for lack of more ample material, we must consider Chapter 46 discussions of *qualification and registration* of foreign corporations that are *doing business* in another state. Similar qualification and registration requirements are sure to be found in most nations. In some countries only their own citizens may form corporations. And the "company law" (corporation law) of many countries (even of England, France, or Germany) is quite different from American law in many respects.

WITS—*Worldwide Information and Trade Systems*; computerized data on foreign markets and companies, at Department of Commerce.

FCS—*Foreign Commercial Service*, a Department of Commerce service abroad.

U.S. Customs Catalogs—on various countries' practices and rules.

Nongovernmental sources of information include the following:

Banks with international departments.

Law Firms with international practice.

Accounting Firms with international practice.

Publications such as "Exporters' Encyclopedia," etc.

Chambers of Commerce in each country and area.

Law School Professors who teach corporation law or allied subjects in each country.

U.S. Business and Nonprofit Organizations already there.

§470. ORGANIZING AN INTERNATIONAL NONPROFIT CORPORATION

For illustrative purposes the actual advice given to organizers of a proposed "International Tictactoe Corporation" is set forth here. The sport of tictactoe (not the actual sport of the group described) is popular in the United States, other North and South American countries, Australia, many countries in Europe, and a few countries in Asia and Africa. There already was, in being, an American (National) Tictactoe Corporation.

Procedure—Outline of Advice to the Organizers

1. Hold a meeting of the organizers to decide
   a. Who will be the incorporators?
      They must be respected citizens, knowledgeable about Tictactoe, and willing and able to serve. Seven or nine names should be used; two from the state or province where incorporation will be done, and the others from various countries.
   b. Where to incorporate. [See No. 9.]
      It can be any convenient state where one or two of the incorporators reside.
   c. Appoint a committee to research political, social and economic climate of relevant-country as indicated in Sections 436–438. Also retain a foreign-country lawyer, for counsel, at once.

    d. Make inquiry (ask advice) of authorities in the foreign jurisdiction; such as the minister of foreign business there. It is amazing how much help can be obtained by just asking for advice.

2. Draft, but do not file, a Constitution and/or Bylaws that describe the purpose and operations of the corporation.

3. Retain a lawyer in the selected state, to file the Articles of Incorporation. Also, designate the lawyer (or the proposed Executive Secretary) to be the corporation's Registered Agent in the state of incorporation.

4. Agree on "Purpose Clause" for incorporation, stating that:

    a. It should set forth the international nature and purposes intended— e.g., to hold Annual World Championship Contests in Tictactoe, and to popularize and improve the game; and that

    b. The Articles and Bylaws of the International Tictactoe Corporation shall be binding on National corporations that are formed under (or in association with) the International.

5. State in the Articles the agreement (clearance) to use the sport's name (Tictactoe) with no conflict with the existing National (and/or State) corporation in the state of incorporation (and in other places if there are several such organizations).

6. State in the Articles the usual disclaimers as to forbidden transactions, self-dealing, etc.

7. File the Articles, and become a corporation.

8. Put the Bylaws (and/or Constitution) into final, formal order and adopt them at the organization meeting, and elect officers.

9. Make sure that the laws of the state of incorporation do not conflict with the purposes and procedures of the Tictactoe International [see item 1 (b) herewith].

10. Make detailed rules (and forms) for National or State Tictactoe Corporations that are to be affiliated with the International.

11. Set up (and revise when necessary or desirable) the rates and system of financial and other support of National and State affiliates.

12. Above all check the laws and customs of each country in which the International and its affiliates are to operate.

       Make sure that the International (and local affiliates insofar as can be done) obey the national or state laws and rules of every country or state in which the corporation "does business."

Sources of Guidance

Government sources of legal information useful in dealing with the problems of international organizations and operations include the following:[43]

    ITA—U.S. Commerce Department, *International Trade Administration*. A clearing house of information.

OBR—*Overseas Business Reports*; country-by-country; largely on taxes and investment rules. This includes country desk information service, in response to queries.

[*See:*

Seki, *Antitrust Guide for International Operations*, 32 Business Lawyer 1633–1656 (1977).

Note, *Codes of Conduct for Multinational Corporations*, 33 Business Lawyer 1799–1820 (1978).

Nixon, *Controlling the Transnationals? Political Economy and the U.N. Code of Conduct*, 11 Intnatl. J. of Sociology of Law, 83–103 (1983).

U.N. Commission on Transnational Corporations, *Report of the Secretariat on draft Code on Transnational Corporations*, 23 Intnatl. Legal Materials 602-640 (1984).

Thomas, *Host State Treatment of Transnational Corporations*, 7 Fordham Intnatl. L.J. 467–500 (1984).]

[*See also:* Surbeck (article) 33 Amer. U.L. Rev. 125 (1983).

Comment, 78 Amer. J. Intnatl. L. 859 (1984).

Forsythe (comment), 31 Amer. U.L. Rev. 833 (1982).

Wortley (article), 54 British Yearbook of Intnatl. L. 143 (1984).]

Geolex (Shorewood, Wis. 53211-2106)

Provides English Translations of foreign laws.

For information call (Toll free)
1-800-446-0906.

International Bar Association

Address inquiries to:
Lorna Macleod,
International Bar Association,
2 Harewood Place, Hanover Square,
London W1R 9HB England
Tel: +44 (0)71 629 1206
Fax: +44 (0)71 409 0456

FORM NO. 207
International Nonprofit Corporation
Articles of Incorporation
(Draft for Ratification)

Application for Incorporation

Corporation Name: International _____ Association, Inc. Organized as a nonprofit, worldwide sports corporation in _____, Florida, on March 10, 19___.

The general nature of the object of the Association is to stimulate the formation of National _____ Associations throughout the world; to give information on the game of _____; to promote construction developments in playing equipment and the improvement of the rules of play; to create interest by promoting world championship games between nations. Further, it is the intention of this Association to undertake to promote international _____ tournaments between nations throughout the world where the National _____ Association of that particular nation is a member of our International _____ Association, Inc.

The membership of the International _____ Association, Inc. and the manner of admission shall be as follows:

Any one National _____ Association of any nation having qualified under the Constitution and Bylaws of the International _____ Association, Inc. may be duly proposed for membership and voted on by the Board of Directors of the International Association, Inc.

The term of existence for this corporation shall be perpetual.

Names and Residences of Subscribers:

_____, Apt. 7 Bldg. 4, _____ Road, _____

_____, Florida, U.S.A.

_____, Nippon I.L.C., _____ Bldg., 4-Chome,

_____, Chuo-Ku, Tokyo, Japan.

_____, _____, Avenue North, _____,

_____, Florida, U.S.A.

_____, 25-B _____ Street, ——————,

_____ Canada.

The main office of the corporation shall be at Apt. 7 Bldg. 4, _____ Florida, U.S.A. with _____ as the registered agent.

[Add the disclaimer clauses as to forbidden transactions, self-dealing, etc.]

The officers of the Association shall be a President, a First Vice-President, a Second Vice-President, a Treasurer, and a Secretary.

Nominations for officers of the Association shall be made from the floor, or by the reading of mailed-in nominations at the annual meeting. Mailed-in votes must be in plain envelopes and be in the hands of the President at least ten (10) days before the annual meeting date. The election of the Association's officers shall take place at the time of and at the place of the annual meeting of the Association. Currently serving officers may be nominated to succeed themselves with the exception of the President, who may not hold office as President for more than four (4) years. If there be more than one nominee for an office, then, and only then shall the voting be by secret ballot; otherwise, the secretary shall be directed to cast a single vote for the single nominee for each office. Each nominee must receive a majority of the total votes cast to be elected. In the event there are more than two (2) candidates for any office, a run-off vote shall be had between the two (2) candidates receiving the greatest number of votes on the first ballot. Each official elected shall hold office for two years or until his successor in office has been elected. This shall apply to officers and directors of the Association.

Officers who are to serve until the first election or appointment under the articles of incorporation are:

_____, President
_____ First Vice-President
_____, Second Vice-President
_____, Treasurer
_____, Secretary

The first Board of Directors shall consist of the following:

_____, Apt. 7 Bldg. 4, _____ Road, _____
_____, Florida, U.S.A.
_____, Nippon I.L.C., _____ Bldg., 4-Chome
_____, Chuo-Ku, Tokyo, Japan.
_____, _____, Avenue North, _____
_____, Florida, U.S.A.
_____, 25-B _____ Street, _____,
_____, Canada.

The Constitution, Bylaws, or Playing Rules of the Association may be made, altered, or rescinded by sending copies of suggested changes to all Board members at least forty (40) days prior to the annual meeting, at which time they will be placed on the agenda for discussion and voted upon—a two-thirds majority of votes cast being necessary to make any changes *or* sending suggested changes to all members of the Board and asking the President to call a mail vote within forty (40) days—a two-thirds majority necessary to make any changes.

All members of the Board shall have the privilege of voting, either by mailed-in ballot or by voting at the annual meeting.

We, the undersigned, subscribe to the foresaid Articles of Incorporation of the International _____ Association, Inc. and hereby affix our signatures in approval.

_____
President and Registered Agent

_____
First Vice-President

_____
Second Vice-President

_____
Treasurer

_____
Secretary

I hereby accept the responsibility as Registered Agent for the International _____ Association, Inc.

_____
Registered Agent

Dated this _____ day of _____, 19___.

FORM NO. 208
Request for Guidance (Letter of Inquiry)
[Based on correspondence of a "Universal-Religion"
organization with its office in the U.S.A.]

Letterhead

The Ministry or Secretary of   (Date)
Educational Matters, and Tourism
Republic of _____
    (Address)

To the attention of His Excellency the Minister.

Your Excellency,

We wish to submit our Memorandum to the consideration of the Government of the Republic of _____, with the request of due attention and also timely suggestions. [Memo describing this organization is enclosed.]

Needless to say we are interested only in the positive and effective realization of the humane and Divine fundamentals, essentials and ideals of all the respectable Religions, Faiths, Mystic Orders and Spiritual Philosophies or Traditions, with neither ill-will, hatred, prejudice, disrespect or defiance toward anyone. We strive for due respect of all the devotional forms of beliefs and cults, and we defend this vital right under all circumstances because we hold that the expressions of Human Conscience are as sacred as life itself. We remain, as a matter of fact, completely above all doctrinal differences and without fancy pauses, or vain rhetorics and self-aggrandizement. We earnestly seek that WRONG BE RIGHTED, STOLEN GOODS RESTORED, OFFENSIVE CRITICISM SUPPRESSED, PETTY COMPETITION ELIMINATED and the true WORLD PEACE HUMAN BROTHERLINESS ENHANCED and SPIRITUAL COMMUNION BE ESTABLISHED through the sincere and practical cooperation of all the willing religious, mystic, philosophical and Spiritual organizations throughout the world, unitedly, by means of true Spiritual Communion.

In no way does (a) *politics*, (b) *worldly gains, gossip, gigantism, glamour and glory*, (c) *any specific religious hegemony or Church supremacy*, (d) *any sort of worldly happening*, or (e) *even onesided religious propaganda and proselytism ever come with in our scope of interest or biased sectarian action* . . .

With the hope of an early reply, we heartily wish the people of the Republic of ————————————— the greatest prosperity and happiness, and we beg to remain, Your Excellency,

Most Faithfully,

(Signature)_____
Officer

§471. FUTURE OF INTERNATIONAL NONPROFIT CORPORATIONS

[Beverly J. Ness contributed material for some of this section.]

The U.N. Center on Transnational Corporations held a special session of the committee and a ministerial meeting in 1986, and hoped to finalize its code in 1987. But the developing nations oppose because they deem the code unfair to them. For up to the minute data, call U.N. Secretariat for the Commission on Transnationals, Economic and Social Council: (212) 754-1234.

There is little doubt that the number and influence of international nonprofit corporations is growing and will continue to grow.[44] Especially in the "developing nations" there is statutory effort to cut down dependency on foreign business corporations, but much less of such effort in respect to foreign nonprofit corporations.[45] The cultural, as well as the economic, impact of transnational organizations is great enough to change substantially the cultural and economic aspects of the developing countries, and even of developed countries.[46]

A growing tendency of transnational corporations is to join with other similar organizations, in joint ventures and special affiliations and contract arrangements, that increase their individual potential.[47]

Establishment of U.N. *Guidelines* as to transnational enterprise, already done, has shown little effect or probability of effect.[48] A more likely form of cooperative action to regulate international enterprise is the 1977 U.S. Department of Justice (Antitrust Division) "Antitrust Guide for International Operations."[49] Already there have been a number of cooperative treaties and agreements, along these lines, between the United States and several other countries.[50] More such agreements are almost certain to be reached, with substantial effect on international corporation enterprise.[51]

Growth of the International Nonprofit Sector

The American Association of Fund Raising Counsel reports that the international nonprofit sector is growing rapidly. In 1991, the total amount given to international affairs was over 2 percent of all giving, at $2.59 billion. The fastest growing organizations are those addressing global concerns such as environmental, animals welfare and conservation organizations. InterAction, the American Council for Voluntary International Action has increased its membership by over one third since 1984. As the number of Non-Governmental Organizations (NGOs) grows worldwide, the private sector will have more opportunity to work to solve world problems. Cross cultural adaptation will be important in communication with countries such as Japan. In the Soviet Union, Goodwill Industries has found that the concept of philanthropy needs revival. There is a growing demand from international affiliates to use only local staff in order to foster the ideas of empowerment and partnership internationally.[52]

Growth of the international nonprofit sector has prompted the Encyclopedia of Associations to extend its geographic scope by providing contact information and descriptions for nearly 800 newly identified multinational and binational organizations and national groups based outside the United States. Over 45 percent of the associations listed are located in Asian and Pacific countries. More than 10 percent of the listings represent newly formed European nonprofits. For information on the Encyclopedia of Associations, contact Gale Research Inc., 835 Penobscot Bldg., Detroit, Michigan 48226-4094. Phone: (313)961-2242. Toll Free: (800)347-4253. Facsimile: (313)961-6815.

News of developments among organizations in many nations, and law changes, is available from INTWORLSA *Bulletin* (a publication of the International Third World Legal Studies Association), Internatl. Center for Law in Development, 777 United Nations Plaza, New York, NY 10017, USA. It includes news from other international organizations as well; relevant even if not nonprofit.

International Giving

The greatest percentage increase in giving in 1991 was in the area of international affairs, with an 11.2 percent increase over 1990 and a total revenue figure of $2.59 billion. The increase in international giving is being attributed to the Gulf War and to changes in the Soviet Union. Awareness of the global nature of the economy and international problems should continue to drive the trend toward international giving.[53]

Fundraising for Somalia

From January through early December 1992, $11 million was raised for Somalia by American groups—only a tenth of the $110 million raised in a six-month period from 1984–85 to fight the Ethiopian famine. The American Council of Voluntary International Action (InterAction), a Washington, D.C. based group of 143 private groups engaged in international humanitarian service, is actively involved. The International Committee of the Red Cross (ICRC) has committed a third of its global budget—$196 million—to the Somalian relief effort. Save the Children, CARE, UNICEF, International Rescue Committee, and World Vision International are a few of the organizations contributing to this effort.[54]

Grants and contributions to the American Council for Voluntary International Action (InterAction), an association of 136 international organizations, totaled $2.1 billion as of 1991. InterAction plans to unify private independent organizations to participate in foreign government aid programs. Currently, aid to foreign governments is 80% government supplied. InterAction wants to see at least half of all aid to foreign governments handled by private or unilateral agencies. Such Non-Government Organizations (NGOs) will attempt to manage and control funds more efficiently.[55]

International Currency Exchanges for Fund Raising

For some big, international charities buying *bad debts* owed to U.S. companies by Third World countries is a profitable way to obtain funds. Paying the U.S. companies in dollars, the NPO then gets payment from the Third World country in local currency. The local currency is worth more to them if not traded at international exchange rates. Instead, in a "debt for development" transaction, based on U.S. banks' willingness to take discounted (less than the face value of) foreigners' debts, instead of mere promises of payment, and the Third World country's (for a fee) desire to keep their currency from going overseas only to be called in for some of that country's scarce U.S. or other hard currencies, a *cut-rate swap* is made. The difference in values goes to the charity. The same process is used with "blocked funds" of foreign countries. But these deals involve risk of loss of both money and a charity's reputation.[56]

Ukraine International Associations

Early in 1990, an English-language weekly newspaper of the "Association for Cultural Relations with Ukrainians Abroad" announced the holding of the "Founding Congress" there, in Kiev, of an organization calling itself "The Union of the Working People of Ukraine for Socialist Restructuring." It was said to have been formed by "a tractor-parts-production association and a potato-growing research institute in Kiev as well as several state and collective farms . . . to take issue with the political tension . . . " Its declared purpose was "to counteract the activities of those who aim all their efforts at meetings and confrontations with the Party and the authorities . . . " In other words it was a *nonprofit political-action organization*, similar in purpose to some NPOs in the USA and elsewhere. In another part of the *NFU* newspaper, same issue, was an article about meetings of USSR religious leaders urging "Reconciliation on the basis of all-forgiveness . . . (to) take the place of disturbances and confrontation" wracking the Soviet empire. The parallels with American socio-political NPC organizations are striking; but *governmental inspiration* seems to be a probable factor in some such associations.[57]

Note: In 1991 the Ukraine became an independent nation, as did Russia.

Philanthropy in the Former Soviet Union

Goodwill Industries reports that the concept of philanthropy needs revival in the former Soviet Union, even though Soviet philanthropy had deep roots in the church. Goodwill is working with the Association for Charity and Culture in the former Soviet Union to instill the twin concept of giving and private enterprise by importing used clothing to a thrift shop and using the funds obtained by selling the clothes to buy property for an orphanage.[58]

Alternate Summit to Teach Russians to Fish for Themselves: While Russian President Boris Yeltsin and American President Bill Clinton met in a Summit Conference in Vancouver on April 2, 1993, another Summit hosted by the Canadian charitable foundation Philanthropy Without Frontiers was taking place. Entitled "Building an Enabling Environment for a Civil Society," the goals of the symposium included the importance of the independent voluntary sector in Russia to address the humanitarian needs experienced in transition and the importance of providing expertise and sharing experiences as well as monetary contributions.[59]

European International Associations

The first European conference on multinational corporation giving was held in Washington, D.C., in June of 1993. The conference, planned by the Washington, D. C.-based Council on Foundations, hosted giving managers of U.S. and European multinational corporations doing business in Europe. Sessions explored social, political, and economic issues affecting corporate interests and multinational giving.[60]

Working in Europe: For Americans who wish to work for charities in Europe, an understanding of the charity's particular mission and the church-related moral culture is required to find work in management of European charities.[61]

The European Foundation Center (EFC) was inaugurated on the day the Berlin Wall was dismantled. The opening up of Central and Eastern Europe and the radical shifts that followed have highlighted a need to foster socio-political and economic cooperation, which the EFC feels can't be done by governments alone. EFC's goal is to reinforce European awareness of the key role foundations and corporate and institutional grant-givers play in the new Europe. EFC's Orpheus Programme provides an information service on the activities of foundations and corporate funders in Europe. So far, EFC has been helpful in setting up an international alliance of the independent sector. EFC is now the primary contact between the European Community and the foundations of Europe.[62]

European NPOs now seek (and get) support in the USA, and USA organizations do the same in Europe.[63]

Japanese Charitable Institutions

"Japan at the American Grassroots" (a five city, all-day conference) in 1991 dealt with Japanese companies' civic leadership activities and programs in the U.S.A., with NPOs. For records of this, address: Corporate Philanthropy Report, 2727 Fairview Ave. East, Suite D, Seattle, WA 98102-3199.

Japan has been trying (in 1990–2) to establish wider contacts in the USA through NPO's organized in the USA.

Japanese contributions to nonprofit organizations have remained the same in 1991 as in 1990, at about $300 million. Japanese corporate foundations operating in the U.S. rose in number from three to twenty-five between 1984 and 1991. In general, it serves the interests of Japanese companies to develop programs for community giving and volunteering. Benefits result from the good will generated with state and local government officials. Favorable tax status may benefit Japanese subsidiaries filing returns in the United States. More than $100 million was donated to American colleges and universities by the Japanese in the 1990s. Such donations may benefit the Japanese "corporate recruitment strategy" and their interest in educating the next generation of American employees and consumers.[64]

On March 10, 1993, Kyodo News Service reported that the Bank of Tokyo (BOT) will donate $250,000 to UNICEF, a "principal collateralized interest reduction bond." The bond was originally issued by the Philippine government with a face value of $250,000, due in 2017. The debt is scheduled to be reimbursed to UNICEF by the Philippine government at 70 percent of face value with the money to be used for projects promoting education for children. The donation is the first of its kind from a Japanese bank.

Pacific Rim NPOs

A Pacific Nonprofit Leadership Program was being planned in 1993 for Seattle University. The program will address leadership issues involved in the needs of charitable movements in Western Canada, Japan, Taiwan, Korea, China, and many other Pacific Rim countries as will as Washington's own 28,000 nonprofits.[65]

Mexico-Central America NPOs

A joint declaration was signed in 1993 between the Washington, D.C.-based Council on Foundations and the Mexican Center for Philanthropy. The accord encourages cross-border giving and fosters a stronger nonprofit sector in Mexico. The Mexican center has published a list of philanthropic organizations in Mexico and has established a training center in Mexico City.[66]

The U.S. and Mexico recently (1993) signed a tax treaty that could give the IRS the authority to certify Mexican exempt organizations and permit U.S. taxpayers to take deductions on contributions to qualifying Mexican organizations. After ratification, Mexican taxpayers will receive comparable tax advantages for gifts to U.S. charities.[67]

Human Rights Organizations

A human rights nongovernmental organization (NGO) is a private association, which devotes significant resources to the promotion and protection of human rights, which is independent of both governmental and political groups that seek direct political power, and which does not itself seek such power. As a collection of independent national, regional, and international NGOs, human rights NGOs seek to hold governments accountable to internationally defined standards of human rights. The most common strategy employed by these NGOs is public exposure and pressure.[68]

Fact finding by a credible organization such as Amnesty International, the International Commission of Jurists, the Watch Committees, or the International Federation of Human Rights followed by release of a report to the media, can be effective. Other tools of exposure are the urgent action network (UA), human rights awards, and accompaniment of threatened human rights leaders. Often quiet diplomacy behind the scenes is used.[69]

Another technique is the use of nongovernmental human rights tribunals.[70]

NPO Abortion Policy Funding: In 1984, President Reagan announced the Mexico City Policy under which the United States government would cease to provide financial assistance to foreign NGOs that perform or actively promote abortion as a method of family planning. The Agency for International Development ("AID") had authority to distribute funds subject to this policy. In 1985, several NGOs brought suit in the U.S. District Court for the District of Columbia challenging the constitutionality of the AID policy on the basis that it unconstitutionally interfered with their ability to exercise their rights of freedom of association and freedom of speech.

In *DKT Memorial Fund Ltd. v. Agency for Int'l Dev.*, 887 F.2d 275 (D.C. Cir. 1989), the appellate court held that the AID policy did not violate DKT's constitutional rights, noting that DKT's right to associate had not been impaired by the AID policy, since no foreign NGO had actually avoided associating with DKT because of the policy.

In *Planned Parenthood Fed'n of America v. Agency for Int'l Dev.*, 915 F.2d 59 (2d Cir. 1990), the U.S. Court of Appeals for the Second Circuit held that the impairment of Planned Parenthood Federation of America's constitutional rights to speech, association, and privacy the United States' policy on population planning was permitted, because the policy furthered the legitimate governmental objective of not funding abortions and was implemented in the least restrictive manner. Liberalization is progressing in 1994.

Indigent Asylum Seekers: In 1993 the U.S.A. policy on abortion rights swung the other way. The Minnesota Lawyers International Human Rights Committee (MLIHRC), a nonprofit human rights organization established in 1983, provides legal services to victims of political, religious, and social persecution. The Pro Bono Asylum Project (the Project) as model program is described in: Frey and Udagama, *Assisting Indigent Political Asylum Seekers In the United States: A Model For Volunteer Legal Assistance*, 13 Hamline L. Rev. 661 (1990).

Environmental Protection

In 1991, the Protocol on Environmental Protection to the Antarctic Treaty (Madrid Protocol) was approved. Negotiated over a three-year period, the Protocol, together with annexes, is the most comprehensive multilateral document ever adopted on the international protection of the environment. The negotiations leading to the Protocol were marked by unprecedented NGO participation. Two environmental protection NGOs played a direct role in negotiations, and a number of others, such as Greenpeace, were represented on national delegations. Their success is shown by the final text, which reflects their concerns and objectives.

Debt-for-Nature and Development Swaps: In a debt-for-nature swap, a country's debt is cancelled in exchange for the debtor country's commitment to use a given amount of local currency funds to protect national resources, establish environmental programs, or train people in natural resource conservation or management. Debt-for-nature swaps have two purposes: to reduce foreign debt and to protect endangered habitats. The economic purpose is short term, while the environmental purpose is long term.

In a debt-for-nature swap, non-governmental organization (NGO) seeks out threatened environmental resources in countries with outstanding national debt and proposes a swap transaction to the government and central bank of the debtor country. After approval, the NGO purchases the debt of the debtor country at a substantial discount. The NGO presents the debt to the central bank of the debtor country for redemption in local currency. The debt is officially retired and the NGO uses the local currency proceeds to fund environmental projects in the debtor country.

NGO's that have completed debt-for-nature swaps are Conservation International, World Wildlife Fund, and the Nature Conservancy. Countries that have already set up debt-for-nature swaps are Bolivia, Brazil, Costa Rica, Dominican Republic, Ecuador, Madagascar, Mexico, and the Philippines. Tropical rain forests are a common target for preservation.

Similar to the debt-for-nature swap, a nonprofit organization such as UNICEF would purchase the debt of a debtor country from a creditor commercial bank. Then UNICEF would sell the paper back to the debtor government and receive local currency, which would allow UNICEF to expand its aid programs.

On March 4, 1993, Reuters Limited reported that Bolivia reached agreement with all of its commercial bank creditors to clear its remaining $180 million debt through several methods, including bonds for social and environmental projects. In 1988 Bolivia's commercial bank debt was $678 million. By mid-1992, it had been cut by 70.6 percent with an innovative string of deals of $0.11 to the dollar, including debt-for-nature, debt repackaging, and debt forgiveness.

On March 1, 1993, Inter Press Service reported that the Philippine government is going ahead with a plan to set aside the Subic forest as a national park under a $25 million debt-for-nature swap sponsored by the Worldwide Fund for Nature (WWF) and the U.S. Aid for International Development (USAID).

In *Business Mexico,* January 1993, reportedly the Inter-American Development Bank plans to forgive $100 million of debt in return for the Mexican government's commitment to plant trees around Mexico City. The World Bank, the United Nations Development Program and the United Nations Educational Program have established a Global Environment Facility with $1.4 billion in funds to finance conservation programs in developing countries over the next three years.

On October 8, 1992, States News Service reported that Congress has finalized a plan to help Mexico and eight other nations make vital environmental improvements by allowing them to pay off debts to the United States under more favorable conditions if they devote their savings to conservation measures. The other countries are Brazil, Panama, Peru, Chile, El Salvador, Honduras, the Dominican Republic, and Jamaica.

Communist/Dictatorship Countries

There are some exchanges among persons or groups from communist and/or dictatorships countries, with groups or people from democratic/capitalist states, usually in INGO (intergovernmental) association settings. Seminars for medical associations' exchanges of technical studies are among the most common ones.

But truly private nonprofit organizations are viewed with suspicion by most Soviets or juntas, let alone supreme rulers or Ayatolahs. It is probable that this state of affairs will continue, with variations depending on the political and/or revolutionary winds of a particular time and place.

The best illustration of this is an incident from a group trip in the mid-eighties, by co-author Oleck, to China and to the U.S.S.R. In China, there was a polite welcome for technical and business people by the officials, with some friendly-seeming exchanges of ideas and data.

In Russia, at an evening meeting with a group of lawyers and law professors, the author proposed the forming of a private nonprofit international association for the study of voluntaristic group development of the law of such groups. The communist party bureaucrat (Aparatchik) in charge signalled "silence" to the Russians present, by the unsubtle gesture of cutting his fingertips swiftly across his throat. Then he said: "There is no need for such a group in the Soviet Union, because everything is nonprofit in the U.S.S.R."

POINTS TO REMEMBER

- International law is an uncertain thing, today.

- Organize at home, and open branches or affiliates abroad, if that wil suffice.

- Retain foreign counsel, at once.

- Study the laws and practices of the countries in which the organization will operate; and then obey them.

- Expect a cool reception in many foreign countries, and a hostile one in many.

- Do not compromise your own principles merely for the sake of approval by foreign bureaucrats.

NOTES TO CHAPTER 47

1. 2 World Development Forum (21) 3 (Nov. 30, 1984) (San Francisco, Cal. 94101; P.O. Box 789).

2. Oleck, *Modern Corporation Law* §12 (1978 Supp.), quoting H. Gallagher, *The Private Corporate Entity on the International Plane*, 34 Neb. L. Rev. 47–58 (1954–5). *See* also, Conard, *Corporations in Perspective*, 4–6, 75–93 (1976).

3. *Ibid.*, Ballantine, *Corporations* §118 (1946).

4. Sinclair Pipe Line Co. v. State Comm. of Rev. and Tax, 184 Kan. 713, 339 P.2d 341 (1959). *See*, Johnson (ed.), *Attack on Corporate America*, c. 6 (multinational corporations) (1978).

5. Domke, *The Control of Corporations*, 3 Intnatl. L.Q. 52 (1950); Kronstein, *The Nationality of International Enterprises*, 52 Col. L. Rev. 983 (1952).

6. Galbraith, *The Concept of Countervailing Power* (1952); Domke, above, n.5.

7. D. Baum, *The Global Corporation: An American Challenge to the Nation-State?*, 1970–71 Corporate Practice Commentator 435–470; Robertson, *International Firms Dilute Nationalism*, Toronto *Globe and Mail*, B2 (Sept. 28, 1968); L. Solomon, *Multinational Corporations and the Emerging World Order*, 8 Case Wes. Res. U. J. of Intnatl. L. 329 (1976).

8. CCH Trade Reg. Rep. No. 266, Part II (Feb. 1, 1977); noted in H. Seki, *The Justice Department's New Antitrust Guide for International Operations*, 32 Bus. Law. 1633 (July 1977); 1978 *Corporate Counsel's Annual* 1429.

9. *See*, H. Merillat (ed.), *Legal Advisers and International Organizations* 13 (1966).

10. Feld & Jordan, *International Organizations: A Comparative Approach* 438 (1983).

11. R. Covalescu (ed.), *Yearbook of International Organizations 1985–86*, 1592 (22nd ed. 1985). *See also*: A. Bennett, *International Organizations* (3rd ed. 1984); F. Kirgis, *International Organizations in Their Legal Setting* (1977); D. Bowett, *Law of International Institutions* (3rd ed., 1975); G. Maris, *International Law* (1984); C. Jenks, *Proper Law of International Organizations* (1962); M. Akehurst, *Modern Introduction to International Law* (3rd ed., 1977); Falk, Kratovil & Mendlovitz, *International Law: A Contemporary Perspective* (1985).

12. Covalescu, n.11, at 1593.

13. *Ibid.*

14. Published by Gale Publ. Co.; Detroit (*see* current issue).

15. Reynolds, *Clouds of Codes: The New International Economic Order Through Codes of Conduct: A Survey*, 75 Law. Lib. J. 315–354 at 316 (1982 updated on Jan. 1983).

16. *Importance of Role of Guidelines for International Application*, 57 Austl. L. J. 249 (1983).

17. *See 4 Encyc. of Associations* (1984–85), p. 318.

18. *Id.* the term "multinational" is preferred in the West; "transnational" is favored by the U.N.

19. *See supra* note l. LCDs seem to overlook the problems of overpopulation, misallocation of resources, and the lack of industrial and technological expertise, not to mention ineffective bureaucracy and outdated economic systems (and costly bigotry).

20. *See, Towards the New International Economic Order: Analytical Report on Developments . . . since the Sixth Special Session of the General Assembly*, U.N. Sales No.E. 82 II.A. 7 (1982).

21. *See*, T. Nawaz, *The New International Economic Order: A Bibliography* (1980) (Westport, Conn,; Greenwood) and *The New International Economic Order: A Selective Bibliography*, U.N. Doc. ST/LIB/SER.B/30 (1980): *See also* E. Browndorf & S. Riemer, *Bibliography of Multinational Corporations and Foreign Direct Investment* (1981–date) (Dobbs Ferry: Oceana). This is a two volume looseleaf which is part of K. Simmonds, *Multinational Corporation Law* (1978–date).

22. *See supra*, note 17.

23. *See, International Shipping Legislation*: Report of the Working Group on International Shipping Legislation on Its Third Session . . . from 5 to 18 January 1972, U.N. Doc. TD/D/C.4/93 (1972) & TD/B/C.4/93/Corrs. 1–2 (1972): *See also* Shah, *The 'U.N. Liner Code of Conduct': Some Key Issues*, 16 Eur. Transp. L. 491 (1981); Kuyper, *The European Communities and the Code of Conduct for Liner Conferences*, 12 Neth. Y.B. Int'l L. 73 (1977).

24. *See supra*, n. 17, at 329. *See*, N. Horn, ed., *Legal Problems of Codes of Conduct for Multinational Enterprise* (1981).

25. *See supra* note 17 at 329, *citing* G.A. Res. 35/63, U.N. GAOR Supp. (No. 48) at 123, U.N. Doc. A/35/48 (1980) (*Declaring the Set of Multilaterally Agreed Equitable Principles and Rules for the Control of Restrictive Business Practices*, U.N. Doc. TD/RBP/CONF/10 (1980), reprinted in 19 Int'l Legal Mat. 813 (1980).

26. S. Chance, *Codes of Conduct for Multinational Corporations*, 33 Bus. Law. 1799 (1978).

27. *See*, L. White, *International Non-Governmental Organization* (1951); and n.11.

28. *See*, Brownlie, *Principles of Public International Law*, c.19 (2d ed. 1973); Greig, *International Law* 397 (2d ed. 1976).

29. *See*, C. Schmitthoff, *European Company Law Texts* 173 (1974); Vagts and Welde, *The Societas Europaea: A Future Option for U.S. Corporations?*, 29 Bus. Law. 823 (1974); A. Conrad, *Corporations in Perspectiv* §350 (1976); Golbert & Nun, *Latin American Laws and Institutions* (1982); Schwartz, *International Business Ventures*, 6. N.C. J. Intntl. L. & Comm. Reg. 181 (1981); U.S. Dept. of Commerce, *Overseas Business Reports* (curr. issues).

30. 113 U.S. News & World Report 83 (21), Nov. 30, 1992.

31. 7 *NonProfit Times* (2) 46 (Feb. 1993).

32. Alberta Rev. Stat., c. 53 §§147–162.

33. Brit. Col. Rev. Stat., c. 67 §§186–205.

34. Manitoba Rev. Stat., c. 43 §321.

35. New Brunswick Rev. Stat., c. 33 §125A, Companies Act (amend).

36. Nova Scotia Rev. Stat., c. 74 §39 (amend.).

37. Ontario Rev. Stat., c. 71 §§345–356.

38. Quebec Rev. Stat. §2(10) *et seq.*

39. Saskatchewan Rev. Stat., c. 124 §§190–212.

40. *See*, 2 Oleck, *Modern Corporation Law*, §829 (1978 Supp.). *See*, for example: Allenberg Cotton Co. v. Pittman, 419 U.S. 20, 95 S.Ct. 260, 42 L.Ed.2d 195 (1974); Ministers Life and Cas. Union v. Haase, 30 Wis.2d 339, 141 N.W.2d 287 (1966), appl. dism. 385 U.S. 205, 87

S.Ct. 407, 17 L.Ed.2d 301 (1966), *reh. den.* 385 U.S. 1033, 87 S.Ct. 739, 17 L.Ed.2d 681 (1967); Prudential Fed. Sav. and Loan Ass'n. v. Wm. Pereira and Associates, 16 Utah2d 365, 401 P.2d 439 (1965).

41. Corporation Trust Co. (C.T. Corporation System), 277 Park Ave., New York, N.Y. 10017, provides to attorneys, on request, an annual booklet of cases on "What Constitutes Doing Business."

42. 326 U.S. 310, 66 S.Ct. 154, 90 L.Ed. 95, 161 A.L.R. 1057 (1945). *And see,* Note, *Conflict of Laws,* 26 Geo. Wash. L. Rev. 735 (1958), commenting on it and on the case of McGee v. International Life Ins. Co., 355 U.S. 220, 78 S.Ct. 199, 2 L.Ed.2d 223 (1958).

43. These are mostly intended for business operations, but are applicable to nonprofit organizations in many points.

44. *See,* L. Solomon, *Multinational Corporations and the Emerging World Order,* 8 Case Wes. Res. U.J. of Intnatl. Law 329 (1976); 1977 Corporate Counsel's Annual 10 65–166.

45. *Ibid.;* and, Fayerweather, *The Internationalization of Business,* 403 Annals 1, 4–5 (1972); Horowitz, *Capitalism, Communism, and Multinationalism,* in, *The New Sovereigns* 133–137 (1975); Barnett and Muller, *Global Reach: The Power of the Multinational Corporations* 137 (1974).

46. *Ibid.;* and, Said and Simmons, *The Politics of Transition,* in, *The New Sovereigns* 27 (1975); Turner, *Multinational Companies and the Third World,* c.8 (1973); United Nations, *The Impact of Multinational Corporations* 45 (1974).

47. Friedman and Beguin, *Joint International Business Ventures in Developing Countries* (1971); Stopford and Wells, *Managing the Multinational Enterprise* 152 (1972). *And see,* Rubin, *Corporations and Society: The Remedy of Federal and International Incorporation,* 23 Amer. L. Rev. 263 (1973).

48. *See,* Chance, *Codes of Conduct for Multinational Corporations,* 33 Bus. Law. 1799 (1978).

49. CCH Trade Reg. Rep. No. 266, Part II (Feb. 1, 1977); BNA Antitrust and Trade Reg. Rep. No. 799 at E-1 (Feb. 1, 1977).

50. Seki, *The Justice Department's New Antitrust Guide for Internatl. Operations—A summary and Evaluation,* 32 Bus. Law. 1633 (1977), citing examples; 1978 *Corporate Counsel's Annual* 1431.

51. *See,* generally, *Legal Problems for Multinational Corporations* (Symposium issue), 10 Law Am. 265–423 (1978); *c.f.,* Baker, *Critique of the Antitrust Guide: A Rejoinder,* 11 Cornell Intntl. L.J. 215–61 (1978); *and see,* Wang, *Code of Conduct and Taxation of Transnational Corporations,* 8 Ga. J. Int. and Comp. L. 809–22 (1978); Wriston, *People, Politics and Productivity: The World Corporation in the 1980's,* 49 N.Y.S.B. J. 190–3(1977); Chance, *Codes of Conduct for Multinational Corporations,* 33 Bus. Law. 1799–1820 (1978); Siqueiros, 8 Calif. West. Intntl. L.J. 1–21 (1978). *See also* the citations, especially n.10–16.

52. Cohen, S.F., (article) 6 *NonProfit Times* (9) 1 (Sept. 1992).

53. Keenan, L. (article), 6 *NonProfit Times* (7) 1 (July, 1992); *Giving USA 1992,* The American Association of Fund Raising Counsel Trust for Philanthropy.

54. Stepneski, R., (article) 7 *NonProfit Times* (1), 1 (Jan. 1993).

55. Cohen, S.F., (article) 6 *NonProfit Times* (9) 1 (Sept. 1992).

56. D. Johnston (article), 2 *NonProfit Times* (6)1 (Sept. 1988).

57. 10 *News from Ukraine* (10) 1, 3 (Mar. 1990). For (free) copies of *NFU* address Ukraine Society, 6 Zolotl Varota S1. 252601, Kiev, Ukr. SSR.

58. Cohen, S.F., (article) 6 *NonProfit Times* (9) 1 (Sept. 1992).

59. Boyd, D., (article) **Vancouver Sun**, B1 (April 2, 1993).

60. 7 *NonProfit Times* (3) 1 (March 1993).

61. Cohen, S.F., (articles) 7 *NonProfit Times* (2), 1 (Feb. 1993).

62. 7 *NonProfit Times* (1) 5 (January 1993).

63. See, S.C. Freeman (article), 6 *NonProfit Times* (10)1 (Oct. 1992).

64. Grunberg, Greg, *Land of the Rising Funds*, (article), *The Grantsmanship Center Whole Nonprofit Catalog*, Summer 1992. *See also Japanese Corporate Connection: A Guide for Fundraisers*, ($90); *Directory of Japanese Giving*, ($190); *Inside Japanese Support* ($195), The Taft Group, 1-800-877-8238.

65. 7 *NonProfit Times* (4) 1 (April 1993).

66. 7 *NonProfit Times* (1) 1 (January 1993).

67. 7 *NonProfit Times* (5) 41 (May 1993).

68. Wiseberg, *Protecting Human Rights Activists and NGOs: What More Can Be Done?*, 13 Human Rights Quarterly 525 (Nov. 1991); Blaser, *How To Advance Human Rights Without Really Trying: An Analysis of Nongovernmental Tribunals*, 14 Human Rights Quarterly 339 (Aug. 1992); Whelan, *The Challenge of Lobbying for Civil Rights in Northern Ireland: the Committee on the Administration of Justice*, 14 Human Rights Quarterly 149 (May, 1992).

69. *Id.*

70. *Id.*

48

INSOLVENCY, BANKRUPTCY, AND REORGANIZATION

[Colleen Braden contributed a portion of this chapter.]

§472. WHAT IS INSOLVENCY LAW?

State insolvency law in the United States has been largely a matter of statutory provisions that are disjointed and fragmentary. This at least in part is the result of the pre-emption of bankruptcy law by the federal government, based on the Constitution's reservation to Congress of all bankruptcy law authority.[1] The Constitution gives to Congress the power "to establish uniform laws on the Subject of Bankruptcy throughout the United States."[2]

Taking the Florida statutes as fairly typical, one finds a section about the preferential position of the state as to a debtor's assets;[3] a section about false statements concerning building and loan associations;[4] some sections about decedents' estates in the Probate Code;[5] and some other disjointed provisions—none particularly applicable to nonprofit organizations. There are other provisions about debtors and creditors, plus a clear-cut statutory system (requirement) specifically related to nonprofit organizations in *distribution* of assets. [Fl. St. §617.1406].

Specific provisions for problems of insolvency of nonprofit organizations have been rare in most states. The statutes of Ohio, for example, define the meaning of the word *insolvency* as applied to nonprofit corporations, and then say no more about it.[6] But since 1992 Indiana has expressly required NPO articles to provide for insolvency plans. [See n.19.]

Ohio's statute says simply that "insolvent" means that the corporation is "unable to pay its obligations as they become due in the usual course of its affairs."[7]

The comment of the legislative committee in the adoption of the definition was this: "As the word 'insolvent' is used a few times in the chapter, it should be defined. The equity definition has been adopted." The old American Bar Association Model Nonprofit Corporation Act used the same definition, but the 1986 Revision Proposal omitted this term from its list of definitions.[8]

Insolvency law for nonprofit organizations, therefore, must be found elsewhere than in the nonprofit organizations statutes.

There are, for legal purposes, two kinds of *insolvency*, equity insolvency and bankruptcy insolvency.

Equity insolvency. In the general sense, *insolvency* means inability to pay debts as they fall due; inability to pay bills in the regular and ordinary course of business.[9] For most purposes this is insolvency, even though the financial embarrassment may be merely temporary.

Such insolvency is termed *equity insolvency*, in order to distinguish it from bankruptcy insolvency.[10] It is sufficient, for most purposes, under the laws of almost all the states, to justify the use of debtor-creditor insolvency statutes and remedies. For example, receivership proceedings may be begun, [11] and even corporate reorganization proceedings under the Federal Bankruptcy Act may be commenced.[12]

Bankruptcy insolvency. For bankruptcy purposes, and for a few other purposes, the work *insolvency* has a special meaning, by virtue of its definition in the old, now replaced Bankruptcy Act and in the new Act: It occurs when the aggregate of the debtor's property, exclusive of any property which he (or it) may have conveyed, transferred, concealed, removed, or permitted to be concealed or removed, with intent to defraud, hinder, or delay his (or its) creditors, shall not at fair valuation be sufficient in amount to pay his (or its) debts.[13]

The same definition was adopted for some purposes in other statutes, such as the New York statute governing the making of a *general assignment* of assets for the benefit of creditors.[14] This definition refers to an accountant's version of insolvency—*book insolvency*—an excess of liabilities over assets. It means real, rather than merely temporary, financial collapse.[15]

The kind of insolvency determines the kinds of remedies and procedures open to creditors or to the debtor.

All modern insolvency law aims at the same general solution. This is the gathering (*marshalling*) of the assets of the debtor, their liquidation, and their *pro rata* distribution among the creditors. It proceeds on the equitable premise that "equality is equity."[16]

The subject of debtor-creditor relations and law is enormously complex. For short analyses of the various aspects *see* Oleck, *Debtor-Creditor Law* (1986 reprint, Wm. Hein Co., Buffalo, N.Y.). The ordinary procedures, such as judgment enforcement, attachment, garnishment, execution sales, preferences, and fraudulent conveyances cannot be adequately discussed here. Reference must be made to special texts: multi-volume sets, such as Collier's.

The Shifting Duties of Officers and Directors

Bankruptcy causes fundamental changes in the nature of corporate relationships; interests of shareholders become subordinated to the interests of creditors. As a practical matter, directors and officers of an insolvent corporate debtor can protect themselves by obtaining prior court approval of any transaction outside the ordinary course of the debtor's business.[17]

Grounds for Appointment of a Receiver

General receivership statutes recognize insolvency as a proper circumstance in which appointment of a receiver is authorized. Nevertheless, insolvency alone is generally not a sufficient ground to warrant the appointment of a receiver, even in the case of a corporation.[18]

Member/Beneficiary Interests in Insolvency of NPO5

[This subsection was contributed by Kevin Bearley.]

The *cy pres* doctrine may be applicable in dissolution proceedings after insolvency to determine the distribution of assets. The *cy pres* doctrine is applicable when a condition imposed by a donor has proven impracticable. The doctrine allows the court to determine a means of using the property that will most approximately carry out the donor's intent. A modified *cy pres* doctrine, called the doctrine of *approximation*, permits the court to direct the application of property to some charitable purpose that falls within the general purpose of the donor when it has become impossible or illegal to carry out the particular purpose and when the donor has manifested a more general intention to devote the property to charitable purposes. The result of a too strict adherence to the words of the donor often would cause the defeat rather than the accomplishment of the donor's charitable purpose.

Under Texas law, where the particular charitable purpose for which a trust was created becomes impossible of achievement or illegal or impractical, the trust does not fail if the settlor has shown a general intention that his property shall be used for charitable purposes. In *Salisbury v. Ameritrust Texas*, 1993 WL 65468 (Bankr. N.D.Tex.), Bishop College became insolvent and filed for bankruptcy. The College, by way of a will, was the sole named beneficiary of a trust. The will did not provide for the trust's termination and distribution of assets upon Bishop College's failure. Instead the will provided for annual payments to the College from the trust in perpetuity. Furthermore, the will contained no language earmarking the income provided by the trust. Therefore, the College had been using the trust's resources to provide scholarships to minority students.

The court in *Salisbury* first of all determined that the trust was not property of Bishop College's estate as classified under §541 of the Federal Bankruptcy Code (1992). Therefore, the trust could not be liquidated by the trustee and distributed to the creditors. However, because the purpose of the trust had been frustrated, the court exercised its *cy pres* power and authorized that the property be applied to some other particular charitable purpose falling within the general intention of the settlor. In selecting the other particular charitable purpose, the court chose a public charity that was as near as possible to the one designated by the settlor.

Courts in other states have also taken the initiative in determining the proper distribution of assets when no formal plan of dissolution has been adopted by an insolvent not-for-profit organization. In *The Council for Bibliographic and Information Technologies v. Commissioner of Internal Revenue*, 1992 WL 145276 (Tax Court), the debtor was a nonprofit Ohio corporation whose members consisted of public and academic libraries. The Council's Articles of Incorporation provided that upon liquidation, all assets were to be distributed for one or more tax exempt purposes or would be distributed to the Federal government or a State or local government for a public purpose. The court held that this plan for asset distribution upon dissolution of the organization was overly broad and did not address the way in which specific assets were to be distributed. Therefore, the court decided that it would determine the best purpose for any remaining assets following the Council's dissolution.

Courts have also looked to an organization's Articles of Incorporation when determining whether to extend tax exempt status to the organization. In *American Baptist Homes of the Midwest v. State*, 1992 WL 15482 (Minn. Tax), the court was faced with a decision as to whether or not American Baptist was in fact a nonprofit organization. To help in its decision, the court looked to the organization's Articles of Incorporation. The articles specifically stated that all of American Baptist's assets shall be used exclusively for religious and charitable purposes and if American Baptist is liquidated or dissolved, then all of the assets shall be distributed only to nonprofit organizations affiliated with the American Baptist Churches, U.S.A., whose purposes are charitable, educational, and religious. Furthermore, the articles specifically prohibited any member, trustee, director, or officer of American Baptist from sharing in the distribution of any assets upon dissolution. The court held that because the assets could not be distributed to private individuals upon the dissolution of American Baptist, but instead had to be used in a manner consistent with the formulation of the organization as described in its Articles of Incorporation, that American Baptist was in fact a nonprofit organization and was afforded tax exempt status.

Insolvency—Distribution of Assets

Many states have statutes that govern the distribution of assets upon dissolution of specific not-for-profit organizations. *Fla. Stat.* §657.063 (1992) provides for the asset distribution of involuntarily liquidated credit unions. Under this statute, the National Credit Union Administration will appoint a liquidator who shall proceed with the liquidation of the assets by sale or transfer and conversion of the assets into cash or liquid investments in order to pay the creditors and in preparation for the distribution of assets to members on account of shares and deposits. The liquidator may enter into agreements for the sale or transfer of loans and other assets with the assumption of outstanding share and deposit accounts, which assumption constitutes full and complete distribution to members on account of shares and deposits.

Fla. Stat. §657.064 (1992) determines the procedure for the distribution of assets when a credit union voluntarily liquidates. This statute provides that when all assets from which there is a reasonable expectancy of realization have been fully paid, the remaining liquidation proceeds shall be paid and distributed to the members, ratably according to the balances in the share accounts as of the close of the last business day preceding the date of the resolution of the board of directors recommending the dissolution of the credit union.

The issue that often arises concerning the asset distribution of a credit union is whether an individual or entity should be classified as a creditor or a member of the credit union. In *Sisters of the Presentation of the Blessed Virgin Mary of Aberdeen v. National Credit Union Administration Board,* 961 F. 2d 733 (1992), the petitioner claimed that it was a creditor of Franklin Credit Union and was, therefore, entitled to preference over the members in the distribution of assets upon Franklin's dissolution. The court found that by applying for and accepting the insurance available for member accounts, the petitioner impliedly agreed that its account was a member account and that it was to be treated as a member of Franklin for purposes of classification and treatment of its account. Therefore, the court held that the petitioner was a member to the extent of its uninsured shares for purposes of asset distribution under the priority schedule.

The concern over the asset distribution of nonprofit organizations has prompted many states to enact legislation addressing this issue. Most states already have statutes that require organizations to set up a plan for asset distribution upon liquidation in its Articles of Incorporation. However, too few nonprofits adhere to this requirement or update their articles as assets that are added to and transferred out of the organization. There is a sense that the concern over the liquidation and distribution of assets is too remote for consideration when a not-for-profit is in its infancy. However, when the nonprofit is faced with insolvency, the process of liquidating and distributing the assets ends up in the court system because of this poor planning process. In order to alleviate the courts of this burden, many states have passed legislation that mandates how the assets of a liquidating nonprofit organization will be distributed.

Fla. Stat. § 617.1406 (1992) requires that a plan providing for the distribution of assets be adopted by a nonprofit corporation in the following manner:

> **617.1406 Plan of distribution of assets.**—A plan providing for the distribution of assets, not inconsistent with this act or the articles of incorporation, must be adopted by a corporation in the following manner:
>
> (1) If the corporation has members entitled to vote on a plan of distribution of assets, the board of directors must adopt a resolution recommending a plan of distribution and directing its submission to a vote at a meeting of members entitled to vote thereon, which may be either an annual or a special meeting. Written notice setting forth the proposed plan of distribution or a summary thereof must be given to each member entitled to vote at such meeting in accordance with the articles of incorporation or the bylaws. Such plan of distribution shall be adopted upon receiving at least a majority of the votes which the members present at such meeting or represented by proxy are entitled to cast.

(2) If the corporation has no members or if its members are not entitled to vote on a plan of distribution, such plan may be adopted at a meeting of the board of directors by a majority vote of the directors then in office.

(3) A plan of distribution of assets must provide that:

(a) All liabilities and obligations of the corporation be paid and discharged, or adequate provisions be made therefor;

(b) Assets held by the corporation upon condition requiring return, transfer, or conveyance, which condition occurs by reason of the dissolution, be returned, transferred, or conveyed in accordance with such requirements;

(c) Assets received and held by the corporation subject to limitations permitting their use only for charitable, religious, eleemosynary, benevolent, educational, or similar purposes, but not held upon a condition requiring return, transfer, or conveyance by reason of the dissolution, be transferred or conveyed to one or more domestic or foreign corporations, trusts, societies, or organizations engaged in activities substantially similar to those of the dissolving corporation, as provided in the plan of distribution of assets;

(d) Other assets, if any, be distributed in accordance with the provisions of the articles of incorporation or the bylaws to the extent that the articles of incorporation or the bylaws determine the distributive rights of members, or any class or classes of members, or provide for distribution to others; and

(e) Any remaining assets be distributed to such persons, trusts, societies, organizations, or domestic or foreign corporations, whether for profit or not for profit, as specified in the plan of distribution of assets.

(4) A copy of the plan of distribution of assets, authenticated by an officer of the corporation and containing the officer's certificate of compliance with the requirements of subsection (1) or subsection (2) must be filed with the Department of State.

History.—s. 81, ch. 90–179.

In 1991, Indiana enacted legislation requiring all nonprofit organizations to provide in the Articles of Incorporation how the assets will be distributed upon dissolution of the nonprofit. Although the nonprofit must provide how the assets will be distributed, this requirement does not necessarily mean the nonprofit must specify the exact individuals or organizations. For example, the nonprofit may provide for flexibility in the distribution by authorizing the board of directors to distribute the assets consistent with the Internal Revenue Code. The ability to distribute the assets upon dissolution to nonprofit members depends upon the nonprofit's category. First, if the nonprofit is a mutual benefit corporation, the Articles of Incorporation may provide that the members will receive the assets upon dissolution of the nonprofit. This option is a significant benefit for mutual benefit members. If the nonprofit is a public benefit or religious corporation then the members cannot receive the assets upon dissolution of the corporation. Public benefit or religious corporations are restricted to distributing assets to an organization organized for public or charitable purpose, a religious corporation, the United States, a state, or a 501(c)(3) entity.[19]

A Utah statute created the Industrial Loan Guarantee Corporation (ILGC), a private nonprofit corporation intended to guarantee thrift deposits until those deposits were federally insured. Upon insolvency of the ILGC and its dependent thrifts, those aggrieved could not use the state as an alter ego to obtain a greater recovery than allowed by the statutes creating the ILGC.[20]

An association of nonprofit shippers' contracted with a common carrier to haul freight and received payment from a member of the association. Subsequently, the association became insolvent before the carrier was paid. The member was found to be individually liable to the common carrier due to an implied agency relationship.[21]

§473. COMPOSITION; CREDITORS' AGREEMENT

A *composition,* or *creditors' agreement,* is a compromise between an insolvent debtor and all (or substantially all) of his creditors. In it, the creditors agree to accept less than full-payment, in order to get quicker payment and to avoid legal proceedings.[22]

Such a composition may be agreed upon without any legal proceedings, or even while a bankruptcy proceedings is going on. In these circumstances, it often is called *common law composition* (in the first case) or *composition in bankruptcy.* Its chief advantage is that it enables the debtor to continue to operate, and to try to make good.[23]

The primary distinction between a composition agreement under state common law and a court-confirmed plan for the payment of debts under the federal bankruptcy law is that the former is a voluntary agreement based on contract law and the latter is a statutory proceeding in which creditors are required to participate.[24]

§474. GENERAL ASSIGNMENT FOR BENEFIT OF CREDITORS

An *assignment for the benefit of creditors* is the voluntary transfer of some or all of the debtor's property in trust to a third person for the purpose of liquidation and distribution of proceeds among the debtor's creditors in payment of their claims. A *general assignment* for the benefit of creditors refers only to a transfer of *all* of the debtor's property, except that which is exempt by law. Most states provide for this procedure by statute.[25]

Short but precise statutes as to procedures in a "general assignment for the benefit of creditors" are found in most states. The Florida statute as to this, for example, requires only five pages in its code, including forms.[26]

A *general assignment for the benefit of creditors* is an assignment of the assets of the insolvent to a trustee (*assignee*), to pay all debts of the insolvent so far as the value of the assets will allow when liquidated.[27] It is largely governed by statutory rules of notice and other procedures.[28]

Most states permit the assignee to gather out-of-state assets, as well as assets within the states.[29] Some states, such as California, Iowa, and Kentucky, permit local creditors to seize local assets, in defiance of the claims of out-of-state creditors.[30]

Unlike bankruptcy, if the assignment is done informally, as an extra-judicial, common law proceeding, the preceding can be handled without public knowledge or public record. On the other hand, it has been generally recognized that this (common law) mechanism, as opposed to bankruptcy, is totally inadequate to assure an equitable treatment of all creditors simply because the assignee is practically a free agent and the procedure does not involve any judicial control or supervision of the assignment.[31]

The assignee under a general assignment for the benefit of creditors is included within the definition of a "custodian" under the Bankruptcy Code. Thus, once a bankruptcy case is commenced, the assignee is subject to the "custodian" provisions of the Code.[32]

Sale or disposition of assets. A general sale of assets, or other disposition of them, is not the same thing as a general assignment for the benefit of creditors.

Under the nonprofit statutes of some states, special provision is made for sale or disposition of assets.[33] Trustee authorization and consent of the members of the organization are required.[34] Such sales usually require compliance with other statutes, such as *bulk sales laws*,[35] which call for formal notice to creditors.

Such sales are final unless promptly challenged, for cause, by dissenting members, usually within 90 days.[36] Similar sales, with court approval or by court order, also are covered by statutes.[37]

While a general assignment is a type of liquidation procedure, this is not necessarily true of a sale or disposition of assets even when it amounts to a bulk sale.

§475. RECEIVERSHIP

A *receiver* is a disinterested person or corporation appointed by a court, on application by a debtor or by a creditor, to receive and hold the assets of the debtor for ultimate distribution among all the creditors.[38] The court decides how the distribution is to be made, and the receiver then makes it.[39] The receiver is the court's agent and officer for this purpose.[40]

The procedure for the appointment of a receiver now is largely statutory.[41] In ordinary proceedings in state courts the receiver is called an *equity receiver*. In bankruptcy proceedings, the *bankruptcy receiver* is a mere temporary custodian of the assets who is soon replaced by the *trustee in bankruptcy*.[42] Besides the principal receiver, *ancillary receivers* may be appointed in other states, to collect assets there, and to dispose of them as the principal receiver directs.[43]

The chief distinguishing feature between an equity and a statutory receivership is the amount of discretion which may be exercised by the court. In equity, virtually all decisions affecting the receivership are discretionary with the court. When a statutory receivership is involved, however, the supervising court has little or no discretion, particularly as to the issue of appointment.[44]

A receiver may be appointed at any time, when in the discretion of an equity court such a seizure of assets is necessary. For example, such an appointment may be made even without notice to the organization, when mis-application of assets by officers occurs, even while the organization is solvent.[45] But the allegations (and then proof) of fraud or improper conduct must be clear and convincing.[46]

Receivers also are appointed, under statutory rules, as custodians of assets in corporation dissolution of annulment proceedings;[47] in foreclosures against cor-porations;[48] when corporate officers are found to be misbehaving in corporate matters;[49] when corporate assets need to be protected and no officers are present in the state;[50] in liquidations of foreign corporations;[51] and in certain other cases. But the power of equity courts to appoint receivers when they are needed does not depend on any statutory authorization.[52] A statute that attempted to oust equi-ty courts from this power would be unconstitutional in many states.[53]

On the other hand, there is no authority for appointing a receiver and dissolving a corporation when it is solvent, and such dissolution will not be for the best interest of the members.[54] Appointment of a receiver is a last resort to be used when no other remedy is available.[55]

Appointment of a receiver is an extraordinary remedy which must be exercised with caution as it is in derogation of the fundamental right of the legal owner to possession of his property.[56]

Like the assignee for the benefit of creditors, a receiver is also included within the definition of a "custodian" under the Bankruptcy Code.[57]

A statutory grant of qualified immunity to agents of a state (Maryland) Deposit Insurance Fund Corporation, acting as *Receiver* for a savings and loan corporation, extends to tort actions as well as to other kinds of claims.[58]

Distribution by receivers follows the so-called *rule of absolute priority*: (1) bondholders, (2) general creditors, (3) members.[59] This rule ordinarily requires payment in full to one category of creditors before payment is made to the next class.

Turnover of the debtor's property to the bankruptcy trustee is the general rule and excuse from compliance is the exception. Therefore, the party opposing turnover must demonstrate affirmatively how creditors will be better served if the receiver is retained. While the bankruptcy court has the power to leave a pre-petition receiver in place, it may not appoint one.[60]

A nonprofit corporation that issued bonds for financing churches was forced into state court receivership due to the promoters' misdeeds. The corporation brought action seeking a determination of the priority of the debtor's liens as opposed to liens of the bond holders. The court held that the trustee had the authority to issue first deeds of trust to the debtors, so that modification agreements, under which debtors' liens become equal to those of the bond holders, were valid and enforceable.[61]

The Federal Savings and Loan Insurance Corporation (FSLIC) does not have sole and exclusive jurisdiction to deal with (adjudicate) insolvent *savings and loan associations'* debts and creditors. If its procedures are inadequate, a claimant may have disputed state law claims resolved by state courts.[62]

§476. BANKRUPTCY, IN GENERAL

The "old" Bankruptcy Act of 1898 was repealed in 1978, and replaced by a revised statute. But a century of experience (and decisions) with the old statute is not to be wasted. A wealth of cases and rulings under the old Act is applicable to most of the provisions of the new act. This statute is lengthy and complicated.[63]

Both incorporated and unincorporated organizations are subject to the "corporation" provisions of the Act. Nonprofit unincorporated associations are given special treatment.[64] The Act applies, with limitations stated below, to associations, which are treated as though they were corporations, under the Bankruptcy Act.[65]

The commission of an "act of bankruptcy" such as the old statute required in involuntary bankruptcy,[66] is no longer required. But bankruptcy still may be "voluntary" or "involuntary" (brought by creditors).[67]

Exemption of nonprofit organizations. Nonprofit corporations are *not subject to involuntary bankruptcy.*[68] They *cannot* be forced into bankruptcy by creditors.[69] Creditors are obliged to follow state law proceedings against insolvent nonprofit organizations.

Neither are nonprofit unincorporated associations subject to involuntary bankruptcy.[70] The test of exemption from involuntary bankruptcy is the nonprofit character of the organization.[71]

Thus, a social club was held to be nonprofit, for this purpose.[72] So, too, a cooperative marketing association was deemed to be nonprofit,[73] but not a gambling club.[74] In bankruptcy the test of nonprofit status is not necessarily the purpose for which an organization was established, but rather the manner in which it operates.[75]

Nonprofit corporations and associations *are eligible for voluntary bankruptcy.*[76] A voluntary written petition is filed asking to be adjudicated a bankrupt.[77] It may be filed even after state insolvency proceedings are under way.[78] Bankruptcy Courts and Federal District Courts may be used.

Authority to file a bankruptcy petition must be found in the instruments of the corporation and applicable state law. Most often this authority rests with those individuals who have management control of the corporation. In most states, such management control is deposited with the board of directors.[79]

The filing of a petition in bankruptcy is a matter of law which requires representation by a licensed attorney. Thus, when a non-attorney officer or director files a petition in bankruptcy on behalf of the corporation, such an act constitutes the unauthorized practice of law and requires dismissal of the petition. Moreover, the subsequent entry of an appearance by an attorney on behalf of the corporation will not cure the initial impermissible filing.[80]

Removal of a board of directors that authorizes an attorney to file a petition will not invalidate the board's authorization so as to warrant dismissal.[81]

It is grounds for dismissal if a director acts beyond his scope of authority in approving the filing of a bankruptcy petition.[82]

It is not well settled whether corporate officer and directors have the authority to approve the filing of a petition in bankruptcy while state receivership proceedings are pending.[83]

A *referee in bankruptcy* may be designated by the court to supervise the proceedings.[84] The chief administrative functionary—a *trustee in bankruptcy*—normally is elected by the creditors to administer the assets of the bankrupt.[85] Appointment of the trustee's attorney is subject to the discretion of the court.[86] The procedures for filing of claims, and for distribution, were and are complicated.[87]

Filing of the petition in bankruptcy amounts to an immediate (anticipatory) breach of existing contracts, and the affected parties may file their claims without completing performance of the affected contracts.[88]

The old statute set up a (now changed—See Section 476) detailed *order of priority* for payments of claims.[89] Lienholders were paid first out of the property, subject to their respective liens.[90] Then administrative costs were paid,[91] then wages up to $600 for each claimant,[92] and so on.[93] Now a new order of priorities is described in Section 492.

Corporations *were* required to file an application for *discharge* within six months. This they seldom did, as they rarely continued to operate after a bankruptcy.[94] For others, adjudication as a bankrupt was deemed to be application for discharge.[95] But discharge could be waived, in writing.[96] Fraudulently obtained discharges could be revoked, on application of an interested party, within one year.[97] Discharge could be denied for improper conduct, such as fraud, or improper preservation of records, or tampering with records.[98]

Discharge currently means the release of a debtor from all his debts except those which are excepted by the Code. Under the current Bankruptcy Code, discharge is available only to individuals.[99]

Corporations and partnerships receive an indirect discharge in a reorganization case under Chapter 11 when their plan is confirmed. However, under section 1141(d)(3), a corporate or partnership debtor that proposes a plan which *liquidates* and *discontinues* its business does not receive a discharge when its plan is confirmed.[100]

Excepted corporations. Insurance, banking, building and loan, and municipal corporations could not use Bankruptcy Act relief. They generally had to follow state law, under the supervision of state authorities.[101]

Terminology has been changed in the present statute; *e.g.*, a "bankrupt" is now termed a "debtor," and "adjudication" as a bankrupt now is termed the "order for relief." Much of the old pejorative implication of bankruptcy now is no longer suggested.

Old *Chapter XI Arrangements* were voluntary extensions of time for a debtor to pay, under court supervision.[102] They were *pro rata*,[103] could not include secured debts,[104] were simple systems of reorganization,[105] and were rarely used by nonprofit organizations.

Old *Chapter X Corporate Reorganizations* were available to nonprofit corporations,[106] involved state law,[107] and had to be voluntary.[108] They were complex[109] and required special treatises as guides.[110]

A bankruptcy trustee's "strong-arm" powers permit him to reject a condominium's common-areas charges made before filing of the bankruptcy, as claims that were not properly "perfected."[111]

A bankruptcy trustee who keeps substantial sums of trust estate money in a noninterest bearing checking account is guilty of breach of his duty.[112]

Illegal activities by a labor union's members may be enjoined by the affected employer (debtor-airline), under the *Norris LaGuardia Act*, in a bankruptcy proceeding.[113]

§477. PRESENT (NEW) BANKRUPTCY LAW

The "new" Bankruptcy Act is Title 11 of the United States Code.[114] The new Title 11 is divided into a new system of Chapters: Chap. 1—General Provisions; Chap. 2—Case Administration Rules; Chap. 3—Creditors and Debtors and Assets; Chap. 4—Liquidation; Chap. 5—Municipal Corporation Insolvency; Chap. 11—Reorganization; Chap. 13—Individual Debtor Extensions; and, Chap. 15—U.S. Trustees. In effect Chapter 11 replaces the old statute's Chapters VIII, X, XI, and XII.

In 1984 the Bankruptcy Act Amendments plus a Federal Judgeship Act[115] divided the jurisdiction of bankruptcy courts into *bankruptcy courts* with exclusive jurisdiction over *reorganization* cases, and the *federal district courts* with jurisdiction over *civil proceedings* arising in or from bankruptcy cases, but able to refer such cases to the bankruptcy courts.

Definitions of important categories of debtors or of their members have been made specific.[116] Thus a 20 percent control makes the holder of it an "affiliate." Notice and hearing rules are sharpened.[117]

Acts of bankruptcy no longer are criteria for involuntary bankruptcy or reorganization. Instead, three claimants may start such proceedings if they hold $5,000 aggregate (over secured amounts) in claims; if there are 12 or more claimants; one $5,000 claimant may do so if there are less than 12 in all.[118]

Bankruptcy judges no longer may attend first meetings of creditors.[119]

The *order of priorities* of payment of claims now is slightly changed from its old sequence. Now it must be: first, administrative expenses; second, claims arising after involuntary proceedings were begun; third, unsecured wages, fourth, employee pension system contributions claims; fifth, unsecured claims of $900 per person for amounts deposited for goods or services never delivered; and sixth, tax claims.[120] Presumably, then, the fixed principle of priorities in *distribution* of assets thereafter largely continues as in the old cases, with some changes (See, §492.)

"Insider" and other "preferences" in payments may be set aside.[121]

Liquidation proceedings may be converted to Chapter 11 or 13 proceedings at the debtor's request.[122]

Elaborate reorganization rules are set up under new Chapter 11.[123] S.E.C. participation is provided for.[124]

The priorities of *distribution* in bankruptcy, under U.S. Code §726, are different from the former system. [See, §492.]

There are many other new provisions and variations on the old rulings and decisions. But as far as nonprofit organizations are concerned the bulk of law about their insolvency or reorganization seems to continue to be the bits and pieces touched on herein in the preceding sections of this chapter.[125] Thus, involuntary bankruptcy still seems not applicable to nonprofit organizations.[126] And most parts of the Act still seem to be much the same as before 1979.

Reorganization

New Chapter 11 of the Bankruptcy Act is of concern to most corporations as the vehicle for planning and executing a re-arrangement of debts and claims in such a way as to allow the corporation to continue to exist and operate, while preserving as much as possible of the creditors' (reduced) interests in its assets. The role of the S.E.C. is much reduced. Court supervision, and *confirmation* of the *plan*, is based on eleven statutory criteria.[127] The S.E.C. serves as an advisory agency.[128] Unless that is a principal purpose of the plan, the fact that it will modify or avoid taxes is not fatal;[129] but if it is such an avoidance the secretary of the treasury or appropriate state officer may object.[130]

When the incorporators of a health care center voted to reorganize and to become a subsidiary of another health center, they did so in return for contractual commitments by the parent health center. In a subsequent contractual dispute, the court held that the parent center need not provide legally enforceable benefits exactly as anticipated by the subsidiary, as long as the potential for long term benefit for the subsidiary remains and the purposes of the contract have not changed.[131]

Conversion or Dismissal of Voluntary Bankruptcy

A Chapter 11 debtor must show that it can regain lost assets essential to its operation before the passage of time has materially prejudiced its claim to a share in its market or its other business prospects. It must also show that it will have startup capital and that it can propose a confirmable plan after recovery of its assets to withstand a motion to convert or dismiss. A debtor Minnesota nonprofit corporation could not withstand a motion to dismiss by the U.S. Trustee where it had no significant assets other than a parcel of real-estate in foreclosure and had no discernible business activity.[132]

Debts to Nonprofit Educational Institutions

Individual debtors are not discharged from any debt for an educational loan under section 523(a)(8) of the Bankruptcy Code, including extensions of credit when the following factors are present: (1) the student was aware of the credit extension and acknowledges the money owed; (2) the amount owed was liquidated; and (3) the extended credit was defined as "a sum of money due to a person."[133]

A student loan made by a nonprofit institution is not generally dischargeable, unless the debt will impose an undue hardship on the debtor and the debtor's dependents.[134] "Undue hardship" means "something more" than a tight budget or present inability to pay, for the purpose of discharging student loans that are nondischargeable under § 523 (a)(8) of the Bankruptcy Code. Undue hardship is determined after the conclusion of the debtor's Chapter 13 plan and depends on the totality of the circumstances involved.[135]

The role of a nonprofit organization, in disseminating information to prospective law student borrowers about loans from for profit lenders, is not sufficient to trigger the statutory exception to discharge of student loans in bankruptcy.[136]

A credit union is *not* a nonprofit institution for purposes of the nondischarge of student loans under section 523(a)(8) of the Bankruptcy Code.[137]

Bank loans, guaranteed by nonprofit educational institutions, and the extension of credit for educational expenses are educational loans and are nondischargeable in bankruptcy. However, nonprofit educational institutions cannot withhold the debtor's transcript without violating automatic bankruptcy stays.[138]

Foreclosures

In order for an automatic bankruptcy stay to toll a statute of limitation on a foreclosure action, the property must be "property of the estate." Where a nonprofit institution was forced to sell its property by sheriff's deed, before filing bankruptcy, the statute was not tolled. Thus, a foreclosure suit by the mortgagee was time barred.[139]

Dissolved Corporations

A dissolved Florida corporation is eligible for Chapter 11 relief, but only to accomplish ordinary liquidation of assets, unless its corporate status is reinstated. An administratively dissolved corporation may file a petition under Chapter 7 of the Code unless the law of the state of incorporation expressly forbids such filing.[140]

Bankrupt Contributors (Tithing)

Many courts have ruled that money set aside for religious tithing is disposable income, and thus, the debtor must forego this expenditure in order to receive confirmation of his Chapter 13 Plan.[141] Where discontinuation of tithing would curtail a debtor's right to fully participate in his religion, it has been held that such tithing constitutes a reasonable necessary expense.[142] A bankruptcy court does not violate the First Amendment by concluding that a proposed level of tithing in a particular case is *excessive*, and thus not reasonable necessary.[143]

Religious constitutional privilege applies: Bankrupt debtors' assets were held to be exempt from their creditors' claims, to the extent of the amounts due to their church under its *tithing* rules. *In re* Green, HK87–00354; Bankruptcy Ct. (Chapter 13 case), Grand Rapids, Mich. (June 1987).

Bankruptcy and Retirement Annuities Held by Non-profit Corporations

A debtor professor participated in a retirement plan through a nonprofit legal reserve life insurance company which provided a fixed retirement annuity to fund the retirement plan. In adversary proceedings the court held that the debtor professor's interest in the supplemental retirement annuities, which could be surrendered for cash value at any time before the annuity payments began, could not be exempted, due to public policy, from estate property even though the annuity contracts contained antialienation and assignment provisions enforceable under both federal tax law and state law.[144]

National Credit Union Administration

New (1991) procedures were stated in regulations as to federal CU's revocations of charters, involuntary liquidations and creditor claims.[145]

POINTS TO REMEMBER

- Distinguish between *equity insolvency* and *bankruptcy insolvency*.
- See local law about basic creditors' rights and judgment enforcement.
- Use common law *composition* (agreement), if possible, when in financial difficulties.
- Use *general assignments* as a simple form of liquidation.
- Use *receivership* for emergency, protective, and time-gaining liquidations.
- Use *bankruptcy* only as a last resort.
- See the statutes about priorities and distribution.
- Ordinarily, use state law and procedures.
- Know about the new Bankruptcy Act rules, but call in corporation reorganization or liquidation experts.
- Use voluntary proceedings rather than await probable involuntary proceedings.

NOTES TO CHAPTER 48

1. For a history *see*, Oleck, *Debtor-Creditor Law* §§1,39 (1959 Supp.; 1986 reprinted., Wm. Hein Co., Buffalo, N.Y.) and Noel, *History of the Bankruptcy Law* 36 (1919); Friedman, *A History of American Law* 238–245 (1973); Collier, *Bankruptcy* (curr. ed.).

2. U.S. Const., Art. I, Sec. 8, cl. 4. *See*, Symposium, 58 *No. Car. L. Rev.* 667 (1980).

3. Fla. Stat. §215.07.

4. *Ibid.* §836.06.

5. *Id.* §§731 *et seq.*

6. Ohio Rev. Code §1702.01(M).

7. *Ibid.*

8. Committee Comment 1955, Banks-Baldwin Ohio Corp. L. Anno. (1970 ed.), Anno. to §1702.01. *And see,* Model Nonprofit Corp. Act. §2(h); *cf.,* 1986 Revision Draft.

9. Northern State Const. Co. v. Robbins, 457 P.2d 187 (Wash. 1969); Ackman v. Walter E. Heller and Co., 307 F.Supp. 958 (S.D., N.Y. 1968) based on N.Y. Stock Corp. L. §15; Smith v. Witherow, 102 F.2d 638, 640 (3d Cir.); People v. Biscailuz, 95 Calif. App.2d 635; 213 P.2d 753, 756 (1950); U.C.C. §1–201(23).

10. Oleck, *Debtor-Creditor Law* 13, 14 (1986 reprinted., Wm. Hein Co., Buffalo, N.Y.); Finn v. Meighan, 325 U.S. 300; 65 S.Ct. 1147, 1149; 89 L.Ed. 1624 (1945).

11. Royal Academy of Beauty Culture v. Wallace, 226 Ind. 383; 78 N.E.2d 32 (1948).

12. Old Bankruptcy Act §§170(3), 179, 216(8). [1977, old statute.]

13. *Ibid.* §1(19)(old Act); 11 U.S.C. §101(26)(new Act).

14. N.Y. Debt. and Cred. L. §13; N.Y.L. 1950 c. 758, §3.

15. Bowery v. Vines, 178 Tenn. 98; 156 S.W.2d 395 (1941).

16. *See,* Oleck, *Debtor-Creditor Law* c. 1, note 5; Oleck, *Maxims of Equity Reappraised,* 6 Rutgers L. Rev. 528, 543–546 (1952).

17. Michael L. Cook, "Duty of Care Owed by Officers and Directors to Creditors of an Insolvent Corporation," *ALI-ABA Course of Study, Chapter 11 Business Reorganizations* at 405, 406 (citing *Commodity Futures Trading Com'n v. Weintraub,* 471 U.S. 343, 354–55 (U.S. Ill. (1985)). *See also, Matter of Engineering Products Co., Inc.,* 121 B.R. 246, 249 (Bankr. E.D. Wis. 1990).

18. 8 Theodore Eisenberg, *Debtor-Creditor Law* ¶ 33.03 at 33-26 (1992); *Andreae v. Andreae,* 1992 WL 43924 at 8, Fed. Sec. L. Rep. p. 96,571 (Del. Ch. 1992); *Bay Point Yacht Harbor, Inc. by Gerbig v. Jersey Cent. Power & Light, Co.,* 598 A.2d 916 (N.J. Super. A.D. 1991); *Adinolfi v. Adinolfi,* 562 N.Y.S. 2d 528 (N.Y. App. Div. 1990); *Twinjay Chambers Partnership v. Suarez,* 556 So. 2d 781 (Fla. 2d DCA 1990).

19. *Boyle, K., NonProfit Corporation Act of 1991: Introduction to Significant Changes.* Indiana Bar Association, April 1992.

20. *Prows v. State,* 822 P.2d 746 (Utah 1991).

21. *Central States Trucking Co. v. J.R. Simplot Co.,* 965 F.2d 431 (7th Cir. (N.Y.), 1992).

22. Russell v. Douget, 171 S. 501 (La. App. 1936); Anderman v. Meier, 91 Minn. 413, 98 N.W. 327 (1904); note, 108 A.L.R. 650; *and see* Fla. Stat. §607.07401 (court approval of stockholders derivative action).

23. *See,* Billig, *A Realistic Approach to the Study of Insolvency Law* 16 Cornell L.Q. 542 (1931); *see* n.11, above; Glenn, *Liquidation* §91 (1935); Hanna and MacLachlan, *Cases on Creditors' Rights* 256 *et passim* (5th ed 1957).

24. 8 Theodore Eisenberg, *Debtor-Creditor Law* ¶ 34.02 at 34-21 (1992).

25. 5 Theodore Eisenberg; *Debtor-Creditor Law* ¶ 24.02 (1992); *See also, Martin v. U.S. Trust Co. of N.Y.,* 690 S.W. 300 (Tex. Ct. App. 1985). *See eq. Fla. Stat.* §§ 727.101 *et seq.,* (1991); *N.J. Stat. Ann.* § 2A:19-6 (West 1991).

26. Fla. Stat. c. 727.

27. *In re* Bradley, 27 F.Supp. 475, 477 (E.D. Ky. 1939); Jensen v. Friedman, 79 Calif. App.2d 494; 179 P.2d 855, 858 (1947); Fagan v. LaGloria Oil and Gas Co., 494 S.W.2d 624 (Tex. Civ. App. 1973).

28. *E.g.,* Fla. Stat. §§727.101–727.116; Ohio Rev. Code, c. 1313; N.Y. Debt. and Cred. L. §3;

Tex. Codes Ann., *Business and Commerce*, ch. 23; *and see*, Reich, *Assignments for Benefit of Creditors*, 57 Com. L.J. 57 (Jan. 24, 1952); and Oleck, *Debtor-Creditor Law* §30 note 10, above.

29. *See*, Clark v. Williard, 294 U.S. 211; 55 S.Ct. 356; 79 L.Ed. 865; 98 A.L.R. 347 (1935); noted, 23 Geo. L. Rev. 545 (1935).

30. Lackmann v. Supreme Council, 142 Calif. 22; 75 P. 583 (1904); *see*, Moore and Countryman, *Cases on Debtors' and Creditors' Rights* 417 n (1951).

31. 5 Theodore Eisenberg *Debtor-Creditor Law* ¶ 24.02 at 24-10 (1992); Alexander L. Paskay, *Creditor's Rights* at 295 (1991).

32. 11 U.S.C. § 101(11) (B) (1991). *See eg.* 11 U.S.C. §§ 543(a), 543(b), 543(d)(1) (1991); *In re Constable Plaza Associates, L.P.*, 125 B.R. 98 (Bankr. S.D.N.Y. 1991); *In re Lee*, 126 B.R. 978 (Bankr. S.D. Ohio 1991).

33. *E.g.*, Ohio Rev. Code §1702.39.

34. *Ibid.*

35. Ohio Rev. Code, c. 1313.

36. Ohio Rev. Code §1702.39(C).

37. *Ibid.* §1702.40.

38. Westgate v. Westgate, 294 Mich. 88; 292 N.W. 569, 571 (1940); Akers v. Corbett, 138 Fla. 730; 190 S. 28 (1939). *See*, Oleck, *Debtor-Creditor Law* c. 7 (1986 reprinted., Wm. Hein Co., Buffalo, N.Y.). Revised Model Nonprofit Corp. Act §14.32 (1986 Draft).

39. Lone Star Bldg. and L. Assn. v. State, 153 S.W.2d 219 (Tex. Civ. App. 1941); Williams v. Messick, 177 Md. 605; 11 A.2d 472; 129 A.L.R. 1035 (1940).

40. Hanno v. Superior Court, 30 Calif. App.2d 639; 87 P.2d 50 (1939); note, *State or Federal Control Over Receiverships*, 48 Harv. L. Rev. 1400 (1935); Lazarus v. Home Bldg. and L. Assn., 132 N.J. Eq. 36; 26 A.2d 563 (1942).

41. *See*, Fla. Stat. § 617.1432 (Receivership or Custodianship); *and see* Ohio Rev. Code §2333.22; N.Y.C.P.I. and R. §§6401–6405; Hayes, Green and Co. v. Moore, 5 Ohio N.P. 220, 5 Ohio D. 520 (1899); Carmody-Forkosch, *New York Practice*, c. 42 (8th ed. 1963); Am. Jur. 2d, *Executions*, §§675–729, 676–725, 682 (Fraud and Deceit), 683 et passim (1978 Supp.); Clark, *Procedure Necessary to Secure Appointment of Ancillary Receiver in Equity*, 24 Va. L. Rev. 20 (1937); and as to forms, *see*, 4 Clark, *Receivers*, Forms 15–27 (3rd ed. 1959); *and see*, Hanna and MacLachlan, *Cases on Creditors' Rights*, 960 et seq. (5th ed. 1957).

42. (Old) Bankruptcy Act §§1(31), 2a(3).

43. Restatement, *Conflict of Laws* 2d c.14, topic 2 "Receiverships" 438.

44. 8 Theodore Eisenberg *Debtor-Creditor Law* § 33.02 at 33-10 and 33-11 (1992); *See also*, Hawkins v. Twin Montana, Inc., 810 S.W. 2d 441 (Tex. App. - Fort Worth, 1991); *Puma Enterprises Corp. v. Vitale*, 566 So. 2d 1343 (Fla. 3d DCA 1990).

45. Southern Maryland Agric. Assn. v. Magruder, 81 A.2d 592 (Md. 1951); Carmody, n.41, above.

46. Rabinowitz v. Steinberg, 112 N.Y.S.2d 758 (1952).

47. Ohio Rev. Code §1701.90; Fla. Stat. § 617.1432; N.Y. N-PCL §§1111, 1202, 112.

48. N.Y. N-PCL §§1111, 1202.

49. *Ibid.* §§623, 706, 714, 720, 1111, 1202.

50. *Ibid.* 1111, 1202.

51. N.Y.C.P.L. and R. §6401; Betz v. N.J. Refrigerating Co., 231 A.D. 553, 248 N.Y.S. 35 (1931).

52. Popper v. Supreme Council, 61 A.D. 405, 407, 70 N.Y.S. 637 (1901).

53. N.Y. Const. art. 6, §1.

54. *In re* Sentinel Pub. Co., 113 Ohio St. 608, 149 N.E. 882 (1925); Martin Oil Co. v. Clokey, 277 So.2d 343 (Ala. 1973).

55. Lafayette Realty Corp. v. Moller, 215 N.E.2d 859 (Ind. 1966).

56. *Twinjay Chambers Partnership v. Suarez,* 556 So. 2d 781 (Fla. 2d DCA 1990).

57. 11 U.S.C. § 101(11)(A) & (C) (1991).

58. *Laws v. Thompson,* 554 A.2d 1264 (MD App. 1989); MD Code §§10–101 *et. seq.,* 10–101 note.

59. Established in: Northern Pac. Ry. v. Boyd, 228 U.S. 482; 33 S.Ct. 554; 57 L.Ed. 931 (1913); Case v. Los Angeles L. Co., 308 U.S. 106; 60 S.Ct. 1 (1939); *see,* Oleck, *Debtor-Creditor Law* 170 *et seq.* note 10.

60. *In re California Gardens Apartments, Ltd.,* 130 B.R. 509 (Bankr. S.D. Ohio 1991); *In re Northgate Terrace Apartments, Ltd.,* 117 B.R. 328 (Bankr. S.D. Ohio 1990); 11 U.S.C. § 105(b) (1991).

61. *In re Church and Institutional Facilities Dev. Corp.,* 122 B.R. 958 (Bkrtcy. N.D. Tex. 1991).

62. *ABC Plumbing & Heating Co., Inc. v. Vernon Savings & Loan Association,* 257 Cal. Rptr. 139 (App., 1989).

63. *See,* Collier, *Bankruptcy* (12th Vol., 14th Ed., 1978, with Cum. Supp.); Nadler, *Debtor Relief* (1962 Supp. Ed); Oleck, *supra* n.10.

64. (Old) Bankruptcy Act §1(8) (as to business organizations); as to nonprofit associations, *see,* Matter of William McKinley Lodge, 4 F.Supp. 280 (S.D.N.Y. 1933). *Now see,* 11 U.S.C. §101(8).

65. *In re* Missco Homestead Assn. Inc., 86 F.Supp. 511 (E.D. Ark. 1949), *affd.* 185 F.2d 280 (8th Cir. 1950); *In re* Midwest Athletic Club, 161 F.2d 1005 (7th Cir. 1947); *In re* Poland Union, 77 F.2d 855 (2d Cir. 1935); *In re* Philadelphia Consistory, 40 F.Supp. 645 (E.D. Pa. 1941); *In re* Michigan Sanitarium and Benev. Assn., 20 F.Supp. 979 (E.D. Mich. 1937). 11 U.S.C. §101(8).

66. (Old) Bankruptcy Act §3(a, b). *Now see* 11 U.S.C. §§301, 303.

67. *Ibid.* §1(6). *Now see* 11 U.S.C. §§ 301. 303.

68. *Ibid.* §303(a); Matter of Supreme Lodge of the Masons Annuity, 286 F. 180 (N.D. Ga. 1923); 2 Amer. B.R. (n.s.) 429.

69. *See,* 1, Collier, *Bankruptcy* 634 (14th Ed., 1966, with Cum Supp.).

70. *Ibid.;* and cases, n.65.

71. *Ibid.*

72. Matter of Elmsford Country Club, 50 F.2d 238 (S.D.N.Y. 1931).

73. Matter of Wisconsin Co-op. Milk Pool, 119 F.2d 999 (7th Cir. 1941).

74. Matter of Deauville, Inc., 52 F.2d 963 (D. Nev. 1931).

75. *In re* Missco Homestead Assn., above, n. 53.

76. Bankruptcy Act §§4 a, b; 303(a); *and see,* for an interesting discussion, Reese, *Cy Pres. Powers of the Federal Bankruptcy Courts—New Hope for Financially Distressed Charities,* 5 Ford. Urb. L.J. 435 (1977).

77. *Ibid.;* Collier, *op. cit. supra,* n. 63 ¶3.601.

78. *In re* Harriman, 35 F.Supp. 50 (S.D.N.Y. 1939).

79. *In re Protho Exp., Inc.,* 130 B.R. 517 (Bankr. M.D. Tenn. 1991); *Matter of Quarter Moon Livestock Co., Inc.,* 116 B.R. 775 (Bankr. D. Idaho 1990).

80. *In re Elshiddi Enterprises, Inc.,* 126 B.R. 785 (Bankr. E.D. Mo. 1991); *In re Global Const. & Supply, Inc.,* 126 B.R. 573 (Bankr. E.D. Mo. 1991); *In re Bellerive Springs Bldg. Corp.,* 127 B.R. 219 (Bankr. E.D. Mo. 1991); *In re Video Systems Design & Sales, Inc.,* 129 B.R. 196 (Bankr. W.D. Mo. 1991).

81. *In re Wynco Distributors, Inc.,* 126 B.R. 131 (Bankr. D. Mass. 1991).

82. *In re M & M Commercial Services, Inc.,* 115 B.R. 212 (Bankr. E.D. Mo. 1990).

83. *See In re Kreisers, Inc.,* 112 B.R. 996 (Bankr. D.S.D. 1990) (officers and directors permitted to pass a resolution to file bankruptcy despite a state court order in a receivership proceeding not to do so.); *United States v. Vanguard Investment Co., Inc.,* 907 F.2d 439 (4th Cir.

(N.C.), 1990) (president had no authority to file voluntary bankruptcy after court had appointed a temporary receiver and issued a temporary restraining order ending authority of officers and directors).

84. (Old) Bankruptcy Act §22.

85. *Ibid.* §44a; New Act is 11 U.S.C. §702.

86. (Old) Bankruptcy Act, Gen. Order 44; Matter of Christ's Church of the Golden Rule, 165 F.2d 1007 (9th Cir. 1948).

87. *See* n.63.

88. Central Trust Co. of Ill. v. Chicago Auditorium Assn., 240 U.S. 581 (1916). *See,* Melville, *Disclaimer of Contracts in Bankruptcy,* 15 Modern L. Rev. 28 (1952).

89. (Old) Bankruptcy Act §64a.

90. *In re* Stratton, 53 F.Supp. 131 (S.D. Calif. 1943), *affd.* as American Surety Co. of N.Y. v. Sampsell, 148 F.2d 986, *affd.* 327 U.S. 269, 66 S.Ct. 571, 90 L.Ed. 663 (1946), Ginsberg v. Lindel, 107 F.2d 721 (8th Cir. 1939).

91. (Old) Bankruptcy Act §64a(1).

92. *Ibid.* §64a(2); *and see* Collier, n. 63 at ¶64.201.

93. *See* n.63.

94. (Old) Bankruptcy Act §14a.

95. *Ibid.*

96. *Ibid.*

97. *Ibid.* §15.

98. *Ibid.* §14c.

99. Alexander L. Paskay, *Creditor's Rights* at 153 (1991); 11 U.S.C. § 727(a) (1991); *Matter of Liberty Trust Co.,* 130 B.R. 467 (W.D. Tex. 1991).

100. Alexander L. Paskay, *Creditor's Rights* at 156 (1991). *See also In re Wood Family Interests, Ltd.,* 135 B.R. 407 (Bankr. D. Colo. 1989); *Teamsters' Pension Trust Fund of Philadelphia and Vicinity v. Malone Realty Co.,* 82 B.R. 346 (E.D. Pa. 1988).

101. (Old) Bankruptcy Act c. XI §§306(3), 321, 322.

102. *Ibid.* §306(1).

103. *See,* Collier *on Bankruptcy,* n. 63

104. *Ibid.*

105. (Old) Bankruptcy Act §§106(3), 4b; Sims v. Fidelity Assur. Assn., 129 F.2d 442 (4th Cir. 1942), *affd. on other gds.,* 318 U.S. 608; 63 S.Ct. 807, 87 L.Ed. 498 (1943); Matter of Pacific States S. and L. Assn., 27 F.Supp. 1009 (S.D. Cal. 1939).

106. Missco case, above, n. 65; Grand Lodge, Knights of Pythias v. O'Connor, 95 F.2d 477 (5th Cir 1938); Collier, Oleck, and Nadler works cited n.63.

107. Price v. Gurney, 324 U.S. 100; 65 S.Ct. 513, 89 L.Ed. 562 (1945).

108. (Old) Bankruptcy Act §§126, 4b.

109. *See,* 7 Collier, *Bankruptcy* (14th Ed. 1977, with Cum. Supp.) for forms; Blum *The Law and Language of Corporate Reorganization,* 17 U. Chicago L. Rev. 565 (1950).

110. *See,* Collier, Nadler, Oleck works cited at n.63.

111. *In re Mishkin,* 85 B.R. 18 (Bkcy. Ct., S.D., NY 1988).

112. *In re Consupak, Inc.,* 87 B.R. 529 (Bkcy. Ct., IL 1988).

113. *In re Ionosphere Clubs, Inc.,* 108 B.R. 901 (N.Y. Bkcy. D.C., 1990).

114. Cite as 11 U.S.C. §1 *et seq.*

115. Publ. L. 98–353 §101 *et seq.* (1984).

116. 11 U.S.C., c. 1.

117. *Id.* §102(1).

118. *Id.* §303.

119. *Id.* §341.

120. *Id.* §507.

121. *Id.* §547.

122. *Id.* §706.

123. *Id.* §1102 *et seq.*

124. *Id.* §1109.

125. For details *see* Collier on *Bankruptcy* (current supp.).

126. 11 U.S.C. §303(a).

127. *Id.* §1129.

128. *Id.* §1109.

129. *Id.* §346(j)(1).

130. *Id.* §1129(d).

131. *Bok. v. Northeast Health,* 599 A.2d 815 (Me. 1991).

132. *In re Minnesota Alpha Foundation,* 122 B.R. 89 (Bkrtcy. D. Minn. 1990).

133. 11 U.S.C. § 523(a)(8) (1991); *In re Merchant,* 958 F.2d 738 (6th Cir. (Mich.), 1992).

134. *In re Berthiaume,* 138 B.R. 516 (Bkrtcy. W.D. Ky. 1992).

135. *In re Claxton,* 140 B.R. 64 (S.D.N.Y., 1992).

136. *In re Pilcher,* 139 B.R. 948 (Bkrtcy. P. Ariz, 1992).

137. *In re Sinclair-Ganos,* 133 B.R. 382 (Bankr. W.D. Mich. 1991).

138. *In re Merchant,* 958 F.2d 738 (6th Cir. (Mich.), 1992).

139. *Illinois Service Federal Sav. and Loan Ass'n of Chicago v. Academy of St. James College Preparatory,* 592 N.E. 2d 126 (Ill. App. 1 Dist. 1992).

140. *In re Aurora Investments, Inc.,* 134 B.R. 982 (Bankr. M.D. Fla. 1991); *Matter of Tri-Angle Distributors, Inc.,* 102 B.R. 151 (Bankr. M.D. Ind. 1989).

141. *See generally,* Bruce E. Kosub & Susan K. Thompson, "The Religious Debtor's Conviction to Tithe as the Price of a Chapter 13 Discharge," 66 *Tex. L. Rev.* 873 (1988). *See eg. In re Tamez,* 110 B.R. 9 (Bankr. S.D. Ca. 1990); *In re Reynolds,* 83 B.R. 684 (Bankr. W.D. Mo. 1988).

142. *In re Bien,* 95 B.R. 281 (Bankr. D. Conn. 1989).

143. *In re McDaniel,* 126 B.R. 782 (Bankr. D. Minn. 1990).

144. *Richardson v. TIAA/CREF,* 123 B.R. 540 (E.D.N.C. 1991).

145. 56 FR 56921 (No. 216) (1991).

49

DISSOLUTION AND ANNULMENT

[See, as to winding-up of a dissolved organization, and transfer of its assets Chapter 50.]

[Michael S. Hayworth assisted in updating this chapter.]

§478. METHODS OF DISSOLUTION

Many small nonprofit organizations end their existence informally, by simply ceasing to function. They do not hold meetings, give no notice to anybody, and just drift apart. This ordinarily causes no trouble if nobody is harmed by it, no creditors are left unpaid, and nobody objects—at least as to noncharitable organizations. It is unwise, nevertheless. Somebody may unexpectedly object later. In that case the former members may be surprised to find themselves accused of improper conduct. It is better to be sure, and to dissolve the organization with proper formality. In the case of a charitable trust organization, proper procedure is highly important.

Few aspects of the law of nonprofit organizations are more thoroughly covered by statutes than the dissolution of such organizations. The Model Nonprofit Corporation Act (1986 Revision) of the American Bar Association provides lengthy and detailed rules, divided into four parts of Chapter 14:

Subchapter A—Voluntary Dissolution

Subchapter B—Administrative Dissolution (More usually termed Involuntary Dissolution)

Subchapter C—Judicial Dissolution (e.g., Under court supervision)

Subchapter D—Miscellaneous (e.g., deposit of unique or unclaimed assets with the state treasurer, for ultimate delivery to unlocated creditors or members)

For example, the Ohio and Florida statutes provide detailed rules as to procedure for voluntary dissolution,[1] public notice,[2] winding up of affairs,[3] court jurisdiction over the winding up of affairs when petitioned to intervene,[4] use of a receiver by the court in such case,[5] involuntary, judicially supervised dissolution proceedings,[6] and appointment of a receiver or provisional trustee.[7] Statutes in other states often are similarly lengthy and detailed.

Nonprofit corporations can be dissolved by:

1. Repeal of the enabling statute under which they were incorporated.

2. Death or withdrawal of substantially all the members without replacement by new members.

3. Surrender of the charter by voted action of the members (with or without court supervision) in accordance with statutory procedures.

4. Expiration of the stated period of duration of the corporate existence, without extension or revival.

5. Annulment of the charter by the state authorities for improper corporate conduct.

6. Court order, on the application of creditors or members, in accordance with statutory procedures.

Unincorporated associations can be dissolved by methods 2 and 6, above, and also by:

a. Voluntary voted action of the members.

b. Expiration of the period of duration of the association's existence—if one is stated in the articles of association.

c. Action by the state authorities, for improper association conduct.

The state that granted the charter is the only one that can dissolve a corporation. Neither another state nor Congress can do so.[8] But without dissolving the corporation a state *can* wind up its activities in that state. This holds for both foreign and domestic corporations.[9]

Mere inactivity of the organization does not ordinarily bring its dissolution.[10] But administrative statutes in many states do provide for periodic "cleanouts" of charters dormant or abandoned (even for one year) by the state's corporation department or attorney-general, especially in cases of prolonged (two or three years) nonpayment of franchise taxes, or failure to file required reports.[11]

In some states the secretary of state is required by statutes to certify for dissolution any corporation that fails to file a report within 90 days after the date provided by law.[12] However, such statutes usually add a method of curing such default by later filing, payment of a fee, and obtaining a *certificate of reinstatement.*[13]

As has been mentioned (see Chapter 48), a sale of assets of an organization may amount to abandonment of activity. Nevertheless, even a sale of all assets is not necessarily, in itself, a dissolution of the organization.[14]

Nor does the appointment of a receiver necessarily have this effect,[15] because a receiver may rehabilitate an organization as well as liquidate it.[16] Not even a general assignment for the benefit of creditors necessarily results in dissolution, because it need not always provide for cessation of activities.[17]

Injunctive relief, as in alleged unfair trade practices, may be brought only by the attorney general, although consumers and competitors have private right of action. Monroe Medical Clinic, Inc. v. Hospital Corp. of Amer., 522 S. 2d 1362 (La. App. 1988).

§479. VOLUNTARY DISSOLUTION (WITHOUT COURT SUPERVISION)

Voluntary dissolution of a nonprofit corporation or association may be decided by the members, in accordance with charter and bylaw rules. In the case of a corporation, state approval is required.[18]

Statutes in practically every state now specify how corporations may voluntarily dissolve, and what percentage of the members must consent. At common law unanimous consent of all the members was necessary,[19] but this rule is out. Thus, in California, Ohio, Delaware and Minnesota a majority vote by the members is enough; and a majority vote by the directors suffices when the corporation has not begun activities or has been adjudicated a bankrupt, or when its stated duration has expired.[20]

A two-thirds vote of the members—not a simple majority—is required in some states[21]; for example[22], in New York,[23] South Dakota,[24] and Colorado.[25]

In reorganization proceedings under new Federal Bankruptcy Act Chapter 11 (see Chapter 47), voluntary dissolution also may be effected, in accordance with the rules of that federal statute.[26]

The decision to dissolve or not to dissolve must be in good faith. Fraudulent or oppressive decisions, even by a large plurality of the members, may be set aside by the courts.[27] On the other hand, improper hamstring action, by a minority, also may be oppressive. In such cases the appointment of a receiver to effect dissolution may be granted by a court of equity, where the facts warrant drastic action.[28] (See Section 480 on involuntary dissolution.)

The charter or bylaws may potentially affect the right to dissolve. Some bylaws or charters prohibit dissolution so long as (for example) 15 members vote to continue.

Procedure. In most cases members agree upon a voluntary dissolution by adopting a resolution at a duly called meeting. In a few states the proper number may sign the certificate of dissolution without a meeting. Often the original resolution is first adopted by the directors and then submitted to the members for the approval required by the local statute. In many states a *surrender of franchise* may be filed before any corporate activities have been begun.

Articles of dissolution must be filed in almost every state. These must be prepared, executed, acknowledged, and filed as the statute specifies. The forms and filing procedures vary from state to state, and local statutory rules must be strictly followed.[29]

Statutes also lay down express rules for the sending and publication of notice to creditors, for clearance (and obtaining and filing of certificates of clearance) with state tax departments and for other allied matters.

Typical dissolution statutes. The New York statute, which is fairly typical, requires the following formalities.[30]

1. Dissolution by voluntary vote, without court supervision, is accomplished by filing with the secretary of state a certificate entitled *Certificate of Dissolution of (name of corporation).*

2. Consent for the filing must be (1) by unanimous vote of all the members entitled to vote; or (2) by two-thirds vote, in person or by proxy at a proper meeting, of members entitled to vote; or (3) for corporations having over 500 members, by a two-thirds vote.

3. Approval of the dissolution must be endorsed on or affixed to the certificate by a justice of the state's supreme court, or by other appropriate approving administrative board or commission or body.[31]

4. Even after the filing, the corporation continues to exist for the purpose of meeting its obligations and for winding up its affairs.[32] And dissolution may not be used as a device to impair any trust agreements or property rights thereunder.[33]

The statute is not mandatory. Other procedures also are available.[34]

The Ohio statute, on the other hand, allows the trustees to dissolve the corporation by resolution when (1) the corporation has become bankrupt or made a general assignment for the benefit of creditors, (2) with court consent when a receiver has been appointed, (3) when a sale of substantially all assets has been made, or (4) when the duration of the corporation has expired.[35]

Dissolution by resolution of the members, in Ohio, needs only a majority vote, unless the articles or bylaws provide a higher voting requirement. Of course, the voting must be done at a meeting called on due notice to all members whether or not entitled to vote thereon.[36]

Public notice of dissolution also must be given, in Ohio, by publication in a newspaper of general circulation, in the county where the corporation's principal office is located. Also, notice by mail, or personally, must be given to all creditors of, or claimants against, the dissolved corporation.[37]

FORM NO. 209
Statement of Intent to Dissolve (Maine)

Filing Fee $————   This Space for Use by
                                                    Secretary of State

For Use by the
Secretary of State
File No................
Fee Paid..............
C. B. ....
Date...................

Nonprofit Corporation

State of Maine
Statement of Intent to Dissolve
of

By Vote of the Members or Directors

Pursuant to 13-B MRSA §1101, the undersigned corporation executes and delivers for filing the following statement of intent to dissolve the corporation.

FIRST: The names and respective addresses of its officers and directors are:

Title	*Name*	*Address*
President	_____	_____
Treasurer	_____	_____
Secretary	_____	_____
Clerk	_____	_____
Directors:	_____	_____
	_____	_____
	_____	_____
	_____	_____

SECOND: Exhibit A attached hereto is a copy of the resolution adopted
             by (check one):
☐ The members of the corporation entitled to vote.
☐ The directors of the corporation, there being no members or no members entitled to vote.

THIRD: Number of Members/
                                                           Directors
                                                     Entitled to Vote
Number of Members/
        Directors
  Entitled to Vote   Voting *for* and *Against*

_____   _____

Dated: _____   _____
                                          (name of corporation)

                                         By_____
                                                   (signature)

                                         _____
                                         (type or print name and capacity)

Legibly print or type name   >   By_____
and capacity of all signers   (signature)
13-B MRSA §104

                                         _____
                                         (type or print name and capacity)

I certify that I have custody of the
minutes showing the above action by the
members.

_____
(signature of the clerk, secretary,
  or asst. secretary)

_____

    Notice of the filing of this statement shall be mailed to each known cred-
itor of the corporation pursuant to §1101(2) and to the State Tax Assessor.

    *The name of the corporation should be typed, and the document must
be signed (1) by the clerk or secretary *or* (2) by the president or a vice-president and by the secretary or an assistant secretary, or such other officer as the
bylaws may designate as a 2nd certifying officer *or* (3) if there are no such officers, then by a majority of the directors or by such directors as may be designated by a majority of the directors then in office *or* (4) if there are no such
directors, then by the members or such of them as may be designated by the
members at a lawful meeting.

FORM NO. 210
Articles of Dissolution
(Illinois)

FORM NP-48

To Be Filed	**Date Paid**
in Triplicate	**Filing Fee $_____**
Filing Fee $_____	
	Clerk

**Articles of Dissolution Pursuant to Section 48
of the "General Not-for-Profit Corporation Act"**

To Alan J. Dixon, Secretary of State, Springfield, Illinois:

The undersigned corporation, for the purpose of dissolving, and pursuant to the provisions of the "General Not-for-Profit Corporation Act" of the State of Illinois relating to the dissolution of said corporation, hereby executes the following articles of dissolution:

1. Name of corporation is _____
2. There are _____ members, having voting rights with
   (insert "no" or "none")

respect to resolutions to dissolve the corporation, and the following resolution was adopted in the manner prescribed by the "General Not-for-Profit Corporation Act" of the state of Illinois

(Strike paragraphs (a), (b), or (c) not applicable)

(a) at a meeting of members, at which a quorum was present, held on _____ 19___ same receiving at least two-thirds (2/3) of the votes entitled to be cast by the members of the corporation present or represented by proxy at such meeting:

(b) by a consent in writing signed by all members of the corporation entitled to vote with respect thereto:

(c) at a meeting of directors (members having no voting rights with respect to dissolutions) held on _____, 19___, same receiving the votes of a majority of the directors then in office:

(Set out resolution to dissolve here)

★ 3. All debts, obligations, and liabilities of the corporation have been paid and discharged, or adequate provision has been made therefor.

★ 4. All the remaining property and assets of the corporation have been transferred, conveyed, or distributed in accordance with the provisions of the "General Not-for-Profit Corporation Act" of this state.

★ 5. There are no actions pending against the corporation in any court, or adequate provision has been made for the satisfaction of any judgment, order, or decree which may be entered against it in any pending action.

IN WITNESS WHEREOF, the undersigned corporation has caused these articles to be executed in its name by its _____ President and its _____ Secretary this _____ day of _____, A.D. 19___.

_____
(Exact Corporate Name)

Place
(CORPORATE SEAL)
Here

By _____
       Its _____ President

By _____
       Its _____ Secretary

STATE OF _____ } ss.
County of _____

I, _____, a Notary Public, do hereby certify that on the _____ day of _____, A.D. 19— _____, _____ personally appeared before me and being first duly sworn by me acknowledged that _____ signed the foreging document in the capacity therein set forth and declared that the statements therein contained are true.

IN WITNESS WHEREOF, I have hereunto set my hand and seal the day and year before written.

_____
Notary Public

Place
(NOTARIAL SEAL)
Here

(Illinois—"Back")
FORM NP-48

Box—_____.   File—_____.

Articles of Dissolution
Pursuant to Section 48 of the "General Not-
for-Profit Corporation Act"
OF

_____

*Note: Nothing should be inserted in Paragraphs 3, 4, and 5 of the Articles of Dissolution as these are statements of fact required under the Statute. Set out resolution to dissolve in space preceding paragraph 3. Suggested resolution: Resolved that the corporation be dissolved.

To be Filed in Triplicate
Filing Fee $0.00

FORM NO. 211 Certificate of Dissolution (Ohio)

[This form is based on the Certificate of Voluntary Dissolution of an incorporated foundation.]

_____ FUND
CERTIFICATE OF VOLUNTARY DISSOLUTION

H _____ T.C _____, President, and M. J. R. _____, Secretary of L _____ C.H _____ Fund, an Ohio Nonprofit Corporation, Articles of Incorporation of which were filed in the Office of the Secretary of State on the 14th day of August 19___ as "H _____ Fund" and amended Articles of which changing the name to "L _____ C. H _____ Fund" were filed in the Office of the Secretary-of-State on February 10, 19____, do hereby certify that at a meeting of the Voting Members of said Corporation duly called and held for such purpose on Tuesday, October 2, 19____ at which meeting all of said Members were present, the following Resolution of Dissolution, which had been given unanimous approval by the _____ Trustees of L _____ C. H _____ Fund at their meeting held immediately prior to said meeting of the Voting Members, was adopted by unanimous vote:

Whereas, on December 21, 19___ the Trustees of L _____ C. H _____ Fund by the Announcement hereinafter set forth, declared their intention to effect the complete liquidation of this Fund and formally dissolve the corporation before October 5, 19___:

ANNOUNCEMENT
BY
_____ FUND

"The Trustees of L _____ C. H _____
Fund—H _____ T. C _____ ; J _____
C. V _____, and L _____ B. W _____
announce that this is their intention to effect the complete liquidation of said
Fund and formally dissolve the corporation before October 5, 19___.

L _____ C. H _____ Fund, a corporation not-
for-profit under the Laws of Ohio, was created at the direction of L
_____ C. H _____ on August 12, 19___ to carry out
his long-considered charitable desire. It was organized under the name of H
_____ Fund and continued under that name until changed by
amendment on February 10, 19___ , to clear certain confusion which had
arisen as to its purposes and indicate more clearly that L _____
C. H _____ was the donor of all contributions to the Fund.
L _____ C. H _____ was President of the
Fund from its incorporation on August 12, 19___ until his death at _____
Village, Ohio, on October 5, 19___.

It was Mr. H _____'s hope that it might be possible to
effect a complete distribution of the assets of the Fund and terminate its corporate existence within five years from the date of his death. This would mean
on or before October 5, 19___. The _____ Trustees were
given complete discretion in this as well as in all other matters. Perhaps the
most important of these was not only to determine the beneficiaries, but to use
principal as well as income in the payments of grants. In spite of many problems, they formed the belief more than a year ago that by continuing to work
diligently Mr. H _____'s hope as to complete liquidation of the
Fund within the five-year period could be realized.

The many large grants from principal which have been publicly reported
were made pursuant to such a policy of liquidation.

Nearly 100 applications are now pending. These involve far greater sums
than the Trustees could consider granting in the light of commitments already
made and of allocations planned. Because no further requests can be considered, the Trustees ask that no more applications for grants be made.

L _____ C. H _____ FUND

By _____
President and Trustee

_____
Vice-President, Treasurer,
and Trustee

J ———— C ————

_____
                    Trustee

December 21, 19___

Now, therefore, be it resolved, that in order to carry out the intention expressed in the foregoing Announcement the following resolution be and it hereby is adopted:

Resolved, that L _____ C. H _____ Fund, a corporate not-for-profit under the laws of Ohio, elects to be dissolved voluntarily in the manner provided in Section 1702.47 of the Nonprofit Corporation Law of Ohio, and that the President and Secretary be and they hereby are authorized to file a Certificate of Voluntary Dissolution with the Secretary of the State of Ohio.

In the proposed dissolution and winding up, the Trustees and Officers intend to proceed as promptly as may prove to be advisable and to complete their duties within the limiting date which they have voluntarily set for themselves as not later than Janurary 15, 19___, unless events now unforeseeable shall require the Trustees to alter their plans in order that they may more effectively carry out their duties in compliance with Section 1702.49 of the Nonprofit Corporation Law of Ohio. The Trustees and Officers believe that all the assets of L _____ C. H _____ Fund will be applied not later than January 15, 19___ toward the carrying out of the charitable purposes stated in its Articles of Incorporation.

We further certify that:

First: The name of the Corporation is L _____ C. H _____ Fund;

Second: The place where its principal office in Ohio is located is _____ Building, _____ 14, Ohio;

Third: The names, titles, and complete Post Office addresses of its Trustees and Officers are:

Name and Title	Street	City and State
H_____ T. C _____ President and Trustee		_____, Ohio
L _____ B. W _____ Vice-President, Treasurer and Trustee		_____, Ohio
J _____ C. V _____ Trustee		_____, Ohio
M. J. R _____ Secretary		_____, Ohio

Fourth: The name and address of the Statutory Agent is M. J. R _____, _____ Building, _____ Ohio;

Fifth: We the undersigned have been authorized to execute and file this Certificate by the resolution adopted as hereinabove set forth declaring that the Corporation elects to wind up its affairs and dissolve.

In Witness Whereof, said H _____ T. C_____ President, and M. J. R_____, Secretary, of L _____ C. H_____ Fund, acting for and on behalf of said Corporation have hereunto subscribed their names and caused the seal of said Corporation to be hereunto affixed this second day of October, 19__

L _____ C. H _____ FUND

H____ T. C ____

By _____

President

Attest: M. J. R _____

_____

Secretary

[Seal]

[*Note:* Attached, must be evidence of payment of taxes up to date.]

FORM NO. 212
Revocation of Dissolution (Washington, D.C.)

STATEMENT OF REVOCATION
OF
VOLUNTARY DISSOLUTION PROCEEDINGS
OF

_____

To: The Recorder of Deeds, D.C.

Washington, D.C.

Pursuant to the provisions of the District of Columbia Nonprofit Corporation Act, the undersigned corporation submits the following statement of revocation of voluntary dissolution proceedings:

FIRST: The name of the corporation is _____

SECOND: A resolution recommending that the voluntary dissolution proceedings be revoked was adopted in the following manner:

(Note 1)

Date_____

_____
Corporate name

(CORPORATE SEAL)
Attest:

By_____
Its President or Vice-President

_____
Its Secretary or Assistant Secretary

Note 1.   Insert whichever of the following statements is applicable:
   (a) "The resolution recommending that the voluntary dissolu-
       tion proceedings be revoked was adopted at a meeting of
       members held on _____ at which a quo-
       rum was present, and the resolution received at least two-
       thirds of the votes which members present or represent-
       ed by proxy at such meeting were entitled to cast."
   (b) "The resolution recommending that the voluntary dissolu-
       tion proceedings be revoked was adopted at a meeting of
       the Board of Directors held on _____,
       and received the vote of a majority of the Directors in
       office, there being no members having voting rights in
       respect thereof."

MAIL TO:	**FEES DUE**	
OFFICE OF RECORDER OF DEEDS, D.C.	Filing Fee	$
CORPORATION DIVISION	Indexing Fee	
SIXTH AND D STREETS, N.W.		_____
WASHINGTON, D.C. 20001	Total	$

MAKE CHECK PAYABLE TO
RECORDER OF DEEDS, D.C.

§480. VOLUNTARY DISSOLUTION (WITH COURT SUPERVISION)

In a number of states voluntary dissolution of a corporation may be carried on
with court supervision on the petition of a creditor, of a member, of the attorney-general, or of an interested person; or if the members generally so desire.[38]
In some states voluntary dissolution *should* be carried on under court supervision.[39] Such a requirement protects creditors and other interested parties, who
then may resist the dissolution, or have it nullified, if they can show a good
cause.[40]

Deadlock. One of the principal purposes of statutes for court-supervised dissolutions is to deal with the problem of deadlock in the corporation. The General Statutes of North Carolina (Art. 8, Section 55A-53 of its Nonprofit Corporation Act) contain typical provisions. If the directors are divided into two equal fractions, or the members are evenly divided so that they cannot elect a board (consisting of an even number), a petition for voluntary dissolution may be filed with the state court.[41] Appointment of a *Provisional Director,* in order to resolve a deadlock, is available in some states, while *arbitration* is used in some states.[42]

In some states this form of proceeding is expressly denied to religious, educational, or municipal corporations.[43] These types of nonprofit corporations are subject to state administrative board regulation.

In states where statutory procedures exists, the statute must be followed closely, and the deadlock must be certain.[44]

Notice of the proceeding to dissolve must be given to the state's attorney-general.[45] The petition may be filed by the members or by the directors.[46] Even *de facto* directors may be counted in such a petition.[47]

The *test* of whether or not the court should approve such a petition is, in the discretion of the court, whether or not it is in fact (ultimately) *beneficial* to the interests of the members.[48]

Where the charter or bylaws require a greater-than-majority vote for elections, and the directors are so divided that they cannot reach a decision for action, or the members similarly cannot elect directors, a formula is specified by some recent statutes: in such cases, the petition may be filed by the number of members able to vote under the charter or bylaws, and the voting percentage for elections specified in the charter or bylaws, plus one.[49]

The form of such petition is not specified. It usually must be detailed in order to explain why such dissolution is necessary.[50] Schedules showing the names and residences of all the members, all debts and assets, an inventory of property, and a list of all books and records, usually must accompany the petition.[51]

Formal hearings must be held, and a quick decision must be reached.[52]

Court supervision, generally. In any dissolution, when any interested party petitions for court supervision, the court may, in its discretion, issue orders regarding publication of notice, filing of claims, and other such matters.[53]

§481. INVOLUNTARY DISSOLUTION

[See also §481.]

The involuntary dissolution of a nonprofit corporation or association may result from certain kinds of *improper* conduct, or simply from lack of *proper* conduct. This section deals with dissolution. The next section deals with annulment (forfeiture) of charters.

Expiration of charter. If a charter states a period of duration of corporate existence, and this period expires without action to extend or revive it (see Chapter 45), the corporation thereupon dies (dissolves) automatically.[54] No court adjudication is necessary in such a case.[55] Ordinarily, corporate existence may be continued, if necessary, only for (and just long enough for) winding up its affairs.[56]

Nonuser of charter (inactivity). Failure to use the corporate powers (*inactivity*), if prolonged, may result in dissolution of the corporation, upon proceedings by the state's attorney general or suit by the members.[57] Statutes now often set a two-year period of inactivity as the basis for action by the attorney-general to cancel a charter.[58]

Until the corporation is officially dissolved it is open to creditors' claims and suits, unless they are enjoined by the dissolution proceedings.[59] But it sometimes is said that prolonged inactivity is equivalent to a surrender of the charter, and that this occurs automatically, without any action to dissolve the corporation.[60]

Defective incorporation. If an attempted (or alleged) incorporation was defective to the extent that *de jure* status was not achieved, and this has not been remedied, the state's attorney-general or secretary of state may bring *quo warranto* proceedings to dissolve the corporation. (See Chapters 13 and 19.) This holds especially if a charter was filed by fraudulent conduct or for fraudulent purposes.[61] In a few states private persons may bring *quo warranto* actions.[62] [See Note 93].

Insolvency. If the corporation is insolvent, or lacks assets for securing rights of those who deal with it, and if it is necessary for the protection of creditors, judicial dissolution can be had.[63] (See Chapter 48.)

Failure of purpose. If the objects of the corporation have wholly failed, or are entirely abandoned, or if their accomplishment is impracticable, judicial dissolution can be had.[64]

Dissolution by equity court decree. In the past it was argued by some courts that they had no inherent equity power to dissolve a corporation, and that this power could only be statutory in origin.[65]

Today, it is well-settled that equity courts can order the dissolution of a corporation (by appointment of a receiver)[66] when this is necessary in order to protect creditors or members. And no statutory authority is required for this purpose.[67]

This power is exercised cautiously. For example, if a less drastic order than one to dissolve will suffice, it will be used. Thus, if removal of the persons responsible for the trouble will do, that will be ordered, and dissolution by the receiver will not be ordered by the court.[68]

The common bases for exercise of the equity power of the courts in these cases are: (1) fraud on the members,[69] (2) mismanagement by directors or officers.[70] (3) dissension that disables the corporation.[71] This is now largely governed by the statutes.[72]

Statutory affirmation of this general power of the equity courts now is found in many jurisdictions (*e.g.*, Arizona, California, District of Columbia, Illinois, Louisiana, Massachusetts, Minnesota, North Carolina, Pennsylvania, Rhode Island, Washington, and West Virginia.)[73]

Continued denial of the inherent power of the equity courts in this respect, except in extraordinary cases of hardship and in "public-interest" organizations, continues in New York.[74] In that state, however, a large number of express statutes exist, making the restriction of equity power largely academic. Thus, there are statutes for YMCA's and YWCA's,[75] for insurance-type organizations,[76] banking-type organizations,[77] and educational corporations.[78]

These statutes (in all the states where they exist) usually specify grounds and procedures.[79] Some are narrow and some are quite broad in scope.[80] The specifications of grounds are sometimes rather odd. Thus, in New York statutes, the proceeding is brought by the state's attorney-general, on application by an interested party, in cases of (1) insolvency of the corporation for one year, (2) failure to pay notes or other evidences of debt for one year, (3) inactivity for one year, or (4) securities frauds.[81] But the New York statute does not apply to religious, municipal, public-benefit, and regents-supervised school corporations, except to aid the administrative agencies that govern (and may dissolve) these types of organizations.[82] And personal liability may be found in cases of fraud.[83] The New York and Ohio statutes also lay down detailed procedures that must be followed.[84] In Florida, the person instigating a complaint to the Department of Legal Affairs must pay court costs and expenses, Fla. Stat. §617.2003.

Compulsory testimony. In some states, the statutes for involuntary dissolutions contain provisions for compulsory testimony by members, agents, and officers. Protection of the Constitutional privilege against self-incrimination is continued, however, by guarantees against prosecution for the witness' criminal conduct thus revealed.[85] Special procedures as to notice to the attorney-general and court granting of immunity often are part of these provisions.[86]

Bankruptcy court reorganizations. If a corporation is ordered to be dissolved in the process of reorganization in a bankruptcy court (see Chapter 40), a new corporation may be formed to take its place, pursuant to the same order and proceedings. A certificate of dissolution, or the filing of the new certificate of incorporation (with explanatory details) suffices in this situation to dissolve the old corporation.[87] But regents-supervised educational corporations must follow special rules laid down by such authorities.[88]

Illustrative Cases

Liquidation of a savings and loan association requires filing of notice by the state department in charge of such organizations, allows change of venue (county), and is a civil action subject to judicial review.[89]

An association dissolved by proclamation of a Secretary of State is entitled to the remedies provided in the city or state's Administrative Code for persons who have interests in foreclosed property at the time of its acquisition by the city involved, which includes the remedy of release provided in the code.[90]

Oppressive conduct by the members of a nonprofit corporation does not justify involuntary dissolution of a viable nonprofit corporation, unless the conduct substantially defeats the reasonable expectations held by the minority shareholders in committing their capital to a particular enterprise. Imposition of a $20 surcharge, on members who could not host one meeting of a hunting club per year, is not sufficiently oppressive action.[91]

When a nonprofit corporate officer engages in improper conduct and breach of fiduciary trust, he is estopped from acting as liquidating trustee or from asserting a claim to the property of a corporation at the time of involuntary dissolution.[92]

Board members of a nonprofit corporation, who had not resigned and who were not given notice of meetings in disputes among directors over records removals and meetings without notice, had *standing* to bring *involuntary dissolution* proceedings.[93]

§482. ANNULMENT (FORFEITURE) OF CHARTER

[See also §480.]

A corporation's charter may be annulled by state action, because of the corporation's abuse or neglect of its powers, privileges, or duties.

Any serious offense against corporation laws or other laws, or abuse or usurpation of powers or privileges, may result in state action to annul the corporation's charter.[94] Such a forfeiture of charter may be effected only by formal court proceedings, and after a judgment, on action brought by the state.[95] Usually it turns on the meaning and interpretation of a statute. Because only the legislature has the power to revoke or annul charters, its language in authorizing the state's solicitor or attorney-general to execute this power is determinative.[96]

Some statutes specifically require the attorney-general to bring *quo warranto* proceedings "on the relation of any person."[97] Even without such a statute, however, any complaint from any person is almost certain to start inquiry by the attorney-general's office. [See Note 62].

Misuse of powers is a prime ground for annulment of charter.[98] Fraud in incorporating or in written reports (or, failure to file such reports) are other grounds.[99] So is failure to pay taxes.[100] If the abuse is not too serious, some states merely oust the corporation from its improperly seized powers, without annulment of the charter.[101]

A very few states' statutes are automatic in their operation. Violation by a corporation is, *ipso facto*, forfeiture of the charter in these states, without any further proceedings.[102] In most states, legal action by the state is necessary.[103]

And the courts are not quick to order forfeitures of charters, as they generally dislike forfeitures of any kind.[104]

Only the state authority can bring such action, even when it is instigated
by a private citizen.[105]

Criminal conduct by a corporation is discussed in Chapter 17. Of course,
such conduct usually results in forfeiture of charter.

Activities that are considered to be injurious to the public are common
sources of state action. Such is the case, for example, when a corporation practices professions such as law, medical, or dentistry, which only licensed individuals lawfully may do.[106]

Quo warranto proceedings. State proceedings brought by the attorney-general to oust a corporation from improper activities, or to forfeit its charter, are
usually called *quo warranto* (by what authority) proceedings.[107]

Express statutory provisions for such procedures are found in all jurisdictions.[108] In most cases, the attorney-general brings such proceedings, in equity courts, for a decree or order to dissolve (annul) the corporation.[109]

Tax delinquency. In some states failure to pay taxes results in suspension
of the charter. Then, when payment is made (if made within statutory time limits, *e.g.*, three months), a certificate to this effect may be filed (with penalty,
e.g., $50) and the charter is revived.[110]

In some states such a failure does not result in immediate forfeiture of
the charter, but bars legal suits in the state's courts by the corporation.[111] In
other states the corporation does not lose its capacity to sue.[112] Often a whole
table of tax and filing penalties and procedures for late payment, or for revival
after forfeiture for nonpayment, is set up by the statute.[113]

State tax commissions usually turn over to the attorney-general, periodically, lists of delinquent corporations. Then the corporation is notified to pay
up, or to incur forfeiture proceedings or other penalties.[114] This applies to both
foreign and domestic corporations. Revocation of the certificate of authority of
a foreign corporation is equivalent to forfeiture of the charter in that state.[115]

Even dissolved corporations must pay taxes while they are being wound
up.[116]

The suspended status of a corporation, before it is reviewed by subsequent payment of taxes and penalties, may not be used as the basis for barring
legitimate rights that accrue during or after the period of suspension.[117]

Annual reports to state. See, notes 99, 105. See, in Chapter 34, Section 351.
Also, as to annulment and dissolution (*e.g.*, for failure to file annual report)
effects on property interests, see Chapter 50.

FORM NO. 213
Petition for Reinstatement
(Washington, D.C.)

PETITION FOR REINSTATEMENT OF
ARTICLES OF INCORPORATION
OF

_____

To: The Recorder of Deeds, D.C.
    Washington, D.C.

Pursuant to the provisions of the District of Columbia Nonprofit Corporation
Act, the undersigned corporation hereby petitions and applies for a Certificate
of Reinstatement of a proclaimed domestic corporation:

FIRST: The name of the corporation at the time of publication of the
proclamation was _____ (Note 1)

SECOND: The new name by which the corporation will hereafter be
known is _____ (Note 2)

THIRD: The Certificate of Incorporation was revoked on September
_____, 19___, for failure and/or refusal to file any
annual report for two consecutive years, next proceeding June 30, 19___.

FOURTH: The address, including street and number, of its registered
office in the District of Columbia is _____ and the name of its
registered agent at such address is _____.

FIFTH: This petition is accompanied by all delinquent reports together
with requisite filing fees, and penalties required by the District of Columbia
Nonprofit Corporation Act.

Date._____
(CORPORATE SEAL)

_____
                                                      Corporate name

Attest: By _____
                                      Its President or Vice-President

_____

Its Secretary or Assistant Secretary

Notes 1. The period for reservation of the corporate name has not
          expired, or if such period has expired, that the name is avail-
          able for corporate use pursuant to the provisions of the Act.

       2. The period of reservation of the corporate name has expired
          and it is not available for corporate use pursuant to the provi-

sions of the Act, then, the proclaimed corporation shall set forth in the petition the new name by which it will hereafter be known.

MAIL TO:	**FEES DUE**	
OFFICE OF RECORDER OF DEEDS, D.C.	Filing Fee	$
CORPORATION DIVISION	Indexing Fee	
SIXTH AND D STREETS, N.W.		——
WASHINGTON, D.C. 20001	Total	$

MAKE CHECK PAYABLE TO
RECORDER OF DEEDS, D.C.

Organizations supervised by state agencies. In many states some of the *quo warranto* powers of the attorney-general specifically do not apply to certain types of nonprofit organization. State administrative agencies have their own rules for control and regulation of domestic, religious, public benefit, municipal, and regents-supervised educational corporations.[118] But the courts sometimes tend to override such exceptions when perversion or willful disregard of corporate propriety occurs.[119] And it should be noted that the statutory exceptions apply only to *certain* specified quo warranto suits by the attorney-general, not to all of them.

Statute of limitations. Often the statutes set a period of limitation on the bringing of *quo warranto* proceedings. A five-year statute of limitations is often provided.[120]

Prescriptive rights. In some states, if a corporation has been permitted to exercise powers not properly within its authority for a long time (*e.g.*, 20 years), the statute of limitations is viewed as having run. Put otherwise, the corporation then has a legal right to continue what otherwise might be deemed beyond its authority, and quo warranto proceedings may not be brought.[121]

Waiver of forfeiture. A state may waive grounds for a forfeiture by continuing to treat the corporation as one in good standing (*e.g.*, by accepting the required reports) while it has notice of the neglect or improper act. *Estoppel* rules apply, but the rules of *laches* (undue delay) do *not* apply to a state.[122]

Procedure. No attempt to set forth the annulment procedure of any state is appropriate here. These procedures vary greatly from state to state, and often are quite complex. Local statutes and texts must be consulted.[123]

Ordinarily, a verified petition must be filed, a receiver may be appointed by the court, injunctions may be issued, pending litigation may be stayed by court order, claimants notified to present claims, and other dissolution procedures may be employed.[124]

Hearing of all parties is had, often before a special master or commissioner appointed by the court. Then an order is issued, and a certified copy effecting dissolution is filed with the secretary of state.[125]

§483. TYPICAL STATE STATUTE SYSTEM (FOR DISSOLUTION OR ANNULMENT OF CHARTER)

[Sarah A. Schenk prepared this outline of the statutory provisions of Florida (a fairly typical enactment)]

Dissolution of NPOs in Florida

Domestic Corporations:

617.1401 Voluntary dissolution of corporation prior to conducting its affairs.

617.1402 Dissolution of corporation.
617.1403 Articles of dissolution.
617.1404 Revocation of dissolution.
617.1405 Effect of dissolution.
617.1406 Plan of distribution of assets.
617.1420 Grounds for administrative dissolution.
617.1421 Procedure for and effect of administrative dissolution.
617.1422 Reinstatement following administrative dissolution.
617.1423 Appeal from denial of reinstatement.
617.1430 Grounds for judicial dissolution.
617.1431 Procedure for judicial dissolution.
617.1432 Receivership or custodianship.
617.1433 Decree of dissolution.
617.2003 Proceedings to revoke articles of incorporation or charter or prevent its use.

Foreign Corporations:

617.1520 Withdrawal of foreign corporation.
617.1530 Grounds for revocation of authority to conduct affairs.
617.1531 Procedure for and effect of revocation.
617.1532 Appeal from revocation.
617.1533 Reinstatement following revocation.

Dissolution of Churches:

617.2004 Extinct churches and religious societies; property.
617.2005 Extinct churches and religious societies; dissolution.

POINTS TO REMEMBER

- Dissolution may be voluntary or involuntary.
- Voluntary dissolution may be with or without court supervision.

- Involuntary dissolution may be begun by members, creditors, or interested third persons.

- Annulment (forfeiture) of charter in most states can be effected only by state action by the attorney-general.

- Do not simply abandon the organization. Take legal steps to dissolve it. File a certificate.

- Follow local statutes closely. The procedure *is statutory*, and quite precise.

- Be sure to pay taxes and get clearance certificates from all supervisory agencies.

- Oppressive decisions to dissolve can be set aside.

- In case of deadlock consider the wisdom of dissolving and of starting a new organization.

- Beware of expiration of the charter.

- Avoid improper conduct, lest forfeiture of charter, and imposition of personal liability, result.

- Winding-up procedures must be remembered; the filing of a certificate of dissolution is not necessarily the end (see the next chapter).

- Plan the distribution of assets before you dissolve the corporation; especially the *cy pres* system if it is a charitable organization.

NOTES TO CHAPTER 49

1. Ohio Rev. Code §1702.47; Fla. Stat. §§617.1401, 617.1402.

2. *Ibid.* Ohio §1702.48; Fla. §617.1402(1).

3. *Ibid.* Ohio §1702.49; Fla. §617.1405.

4. *Ibid.* Ohio §1702.50.

5. *Ibid.* Ohio §1702.51; Fla. §617.1432.

6. *Ibid.* Ohio §1702.52; Fla. §§617.1430–617.1443

7. *Ibid.* Ohio §1702.53; Fla. §§617.05(2), 617.1432

8. *Restatement, Conflict of Laws* §157; *and see*, State v. Atlantic City and S.R. Co., 77 N.J.L. 465; 72 A. 111 (1909).

9. *Restatement, Conflict of Laws* §162.

10. *See*, Coleman v. Woodland Hills Co., 72 Ga. App. 92; 33 S.E.2d 20 (1945); Inasmuch Gospel Mission v. Mercantile Trust Co., 40 A.2d 506, 509 (Md. 1945).

11. N.Y. Gen. Corp. L. §71; N.Y. Tax L. §203-a; Ohio Rev. Code §5727.54; Fla. Stat. §§617.1420–617.1423. *See also*, Henn and Alexander, *Corporations*, 990, 1151 (3rd ed., 1983), esp. §349 as to rights of dissenting shareholders in dissolution of business corporations, and §383 as to preferential rights of shareholders when shares are of different "classes."

12. Ohio Rev. Code §5727.54.

13. *Ibid.* §5727.56; Fla. Stat. 617.1422.

14. Schneider v. Schneider, 347 Mo. 102; 146 S.W.2d 584 (1940).

15. State v. Dyer, 200 S.W.2d 813 (Tex. 1947); *and see* Chapter 48.

16. *See*, Oleck, *Debtor-Creditor Law* c. 7 (1986 reprint, Wm. Hein Co., Buffalo, N.Y.).

17. McKey v. Swenson, 232 Mich. 505; 205 N.W. 583 (1925).

18. *In re* North American Coal and Mining Co., 99 Minn. 475, 109 N.W. 1116 (1906); *and see*, Leventhal v. Atlantic Finance Corp., 316 Mass. 194; 55 N.E.2d 20 (1944); Fla. Stat. §617.1403.

19. Barton v. Enterprise Bldg. and L. Assn., 114 Ind. 226; 16 N.E. 486 (1888).

20. Cal. Corp. Code §§9924, 6610; Del. Code, Tit. 8 §275; Minn. St. §302A.721; Ohio Rev. Code §1702.47(D); Fryer and Haglund, *New California Corporation Law*, 7 Pepperdine L. Rev. 1 (1979); Henn and Boyd, *Statutory Trends in Law of NPAs*, 66 Cornell L. Rev. 1103, 1125 (1981).

21. Del. Code (*see* n. 20).

22. Minn. S.A. (*see* n. 20).

23. N.Y. Not-for-Profit Corp. L. §1002(a).

24. Farmers Union Coop. Br. v. Palisade Farmers Union Local No. 714, 69 S.D. 126; 7 N.W.2d 293 (1942).

25. Colo. Rev. Stat. Tit. 7 §26–102.

26. *See*, Cary, *Liquidation of Corporations in Bankruptcy Reorganization*, 60 Harv. L. Rev. 173 (1946); Oleck, *op cit.* n. 16 *supra* cc. 8–15.

27. Hayman v. Brown, 176 Misc. 176; 26 N.Y.S.2d 898 (1941); *In re* Paine, 200 Mich. 58; 166 N.W. 1036 (1918); White v. Kincaid, 149 N.C. 415; 63 S.E. 109; L.R.A. (n.s.) 1177 (1908).

28. *See* n. 16; Flemming v. Heffner and Flemming, 263 Mich. 561; 248 N.W. 900 (1933); People *ex rel.* Seeman v. Greer College, 302 Ill. 538; 135 N.E. 80 (1922); Ann., 43 A.L.R. 242; 61 A.L.R. 1212; 91 A.L.R. 648, 665; Meiselman v. Meiselman, 295 S.E.2d 249 (N.C. App. 1982).

29. Automatic Canteen Co. of America v. Wharton, 358 F.2d 587 (2d Cir. 1966); Trippett v. Commissioner, 118 F.2d 764 (5th Cir. 1941); City of Newark v. Joseph Hollander, 136 N.J. Eq. 539; 42 A.2d 872 (1945).

30. N.Y. Not-for-Profit Corp. L. §1002, 1003.

31. See Chapter 13.

32. N.Y. Not-for-Profit Corp. L. §1005, *In re* Mohr's Estate, 175 Misc. 706; 24 N.Y.S.2d 977 (1946); Fla. Stat. 617.1405.

33. N.Y. Not-for-Profit Corp. L. §1005; Fla. Stat. 617.1405.

34. Saint John of Vizzini v. Cavallo, 134 Misc. 152; 234 N.Y.S. 683 (1929).

35. Ohio Rev. Code §1702.47(C).

36. *Ibid.* §1702.47(D).

37. *Id.* §1702.48.

38. Ohio Rev. Code §1702.52; *In re* Buse and Caldwell, 328 Penna. 211, 195 A.9(1937); N.Y. Not-for-Profit Corp. L. §1001–1010, 1012; Fla. Stat. §617.1402.

39. Florida: *see*, Fla. Stat. Anno. §617.05 Maine: *see*, Elston v. Elston and Co., 131 Me. 149; 159 A.731 (1932). Massachusetts: *see*, 180 Anno. L. Mass. §11A. Missouri: *see*, State *ex rel.* New First Natl. Bk. v. White, 223 Mo. App. 36; 7 S.W.2d 474 (1928). New Jersey: *see*, *In re* Reade, 99 N.J. Eq. 282; 132 A. 477 (1926). Washington: *see*, Moore v. Los Lugos G.M., 172 Wash. 570; 21 P. 2d 253 (1933).

40. *See* Moore case, Elston case, in n. 37.

41. Ohio Rev. Code §1702.52(A) (4); 15 Penna. St. §8001; N.J. Stat. Anno. §14 A:12-7; *see* Anno. 13 A.L.R. 2d 1251; N.Y. NPCL §§1001, 1002, 1102.

42. N.J. Stat. §14A: 12-7; Del. Genl. Corp. L. §353; Hetherington and Dooley, *Illiquidity and Exploitation*, 63 Va. L. Rev. 1, 20 (1977); Oleck, *Modern Corporation Law*, §§1984 *et seq.* (1978 Supp.).

43. N.Y. Gen. Corp. L. §100. *See* digests of statutes of all states in 4 Oleck, *Modern Corporation Law*, c. 79 (1978 Supp.).

44. *In re* Lakeland Development Corp., 152 N.W.2d 758 (Minn. 1967); *In re* Acker, 124 N.Y.S.2d 298 (1953).

45. *In re* Society of Justice, 233 N.Y. 691; 193 N.Y.S. 954 (1922).

46. *In re* McLoughlin, 176 A.D. 653; 163 N.Y.S. 547 (1917).

47. *In re* Manoca Temple Assn., 128 A.D. 796; 113 N.Y.S. 172 (1908).

48. *See,* Cachules v. Finklestein, 279 A.D. 173; 109 N.Y.S.2d 272 (1951); *In re* Acker, 124 N.Y.S.2d 298 (1953); Ohio Rev. Code §1702.52(A) (4) (1978); N.Y. N-PCL §§1001, 1002, 1102.

49. N.Y. Gen. Corp. L. §103; amended by N.Y. Laws 1951, c. 717. For many forms for dissolution, from many states, *see,* 5 Oleck, *Modern Corporation Law* (Vol. of Forms) (1978 Supp.).

50. Ohio Rev. Code §1702.52(B).

51. N.Y. N-PCL §1103.

52. *Ibid.* §§1104, 1111, 1113, 1106, 1107.

53. N.Y. Not-for-Profit Corp. L. §1001–1010, 1012; *In re* Mohr's Estate, 175 Misc. 706; 24 N.Y.S.2d 977 (1941); *In re* Italian Benevolent Institute, 127 N.Y.S.2d 396 (1953); Ohio Rev. Code §1702.52.

54. Eagle Pass Realty Co. v. Esparza, 474 S.W.2d 624 (Tex. 1971); Clark v. Brown, 108 S.W. 421 (Tex. Civ. App. 1908) rev. on other gds., 108 S.W. 421 (1909); Bonfils v. Hayes, 70 Colo. 336; 201 P. 677 (1925).

55. *In re* Friedman, 177 A.D. 755; 164 N.Y.S. 892 (1917); Ohio Rev. Code §1702.47 (C) (4).

56. Kash v. Lewis, 224 Ky., 679; 6 S.W.2d 1098 (1928); ann., 47 A.L.R. 1288, 1326, 1594. Sometimes statutes set a three-year period for winding up.

57. 180 Anno. L. Mass. §11B; N.Y. Gen. Corp. L. §30; *see,* State v. Dilbeck, 297 S.W. 1049 (Tex. Civ. App. 1927); State *ex inf.* Gentry v. Ramona Kennel Club, 8 S.W.2d 1 (Mo. 1928).

58. *See* n. 55; People v. Stilwell, 157 A.D. 839; 142 N.Y.S 881 (1913); affg., 78 Misc. 96; 138 N.Y.S. 693; Nicolai v. Maryland Agric. and Mech. Assn., 96 Md. 323; 53 A. 965 (1903).

59. Kincaid v. Dwinelle, 59 N.Y. 548 (1875).

60. Combes v. Milwaukee and M. R. Co., 89 Wis. 297; 62 N.W. 89; 27 L.R.A. 369 (1895); and People v. Stilwell, n. 58.

61. Floyd v. State *ex rel.* Baker, 177 Ala. 169; 59 S. 280 (1912); N.Y. N-PCL §1101.

62. Rouse v. Wiley, 440 S.2d 1023 (Ala. 1983).

63. Ohio Rev. Code §1702.52(A) (2) (b).

64. *Ibid.* §1702.52(A) (2) (c).

65. Attorney-General *ex rel.* Pattee v. Stevens, 1 N.J. Eq. 369; 22 Am. Dec. 526 (1831); People *ex rel.* Seeman v. Greer College, 302 Ill. 538; 135 N.E. 80 (1922).

66. *See* Chapter 48.

67. Flemming v. Heffner and Flemming, 263 Mich. 561; 248 N.W. 900 (1933); Greer College case, n. 63; ann. 43 A.L.R. 242; 61 A.L.R. 1212; 91 A.L.R. 648, 665.

68. Brennan v. Rollman, 151 Va. 715; 145 S.E. 160 (1928). *And see,* Schneider v. Schneider, 347 Mo. 102; 146 S.W.2d 584 (1940); Schuster v. Largman, 308 Penna, 520; 162 A. 305 (1932).

69. Bailey v. Proctor, 160 F.2d 78 (1st Cir. 1947); Drob v. National Memorial Park, Inc., 41 A.2d 589, 597 (Del. 1945); Goodwin v. Van Cotzhauser, 171 Wis. 351; 177 N.W. 618 (1920); Whitman v. Fuqua, 549 F. Supp. 315 (D.C. Penna., 1982).

70. *See* n. 65, above; Loney v. Consolidated Water Co., 122 Calif. App. 350; 9 P.2d 888 (1932); *and see,* Hornstein, *A Remedy for Corporate Abuse,* 40 Columbia L. Rev. 220 (1940).

71. Flemming case, n. 67; Cowin v. Salmon, 248 Ala. 580; 28 S.2d 633 (1946).

72. Application of Landau, 183 Misc. 876; 51 N.Y.S.2d 651 (1944); Meiselman Case, n, 28.

73. *See,* comment, 41 Mich. L. Rev. 714, 721 (1943).

74. People v. Volunteer Rescue Army, Inc., 262 A.D. 237; 28 N.Y.S.2d 994 (1941) (religious corporation: equity dissolution granted because of perversion of its purpose).

75. N.Y. Not-for-Profit Corp. L. §1404.

76. N.Y. Insur. L. §§510–546.

77. N.Y. Bank L. §§600–634.

78. N.Y. Educ. L. §§220, 221, 223.

79. *See,* Religious Press Assn. v. Sunday School Times Co., 151 Penna. Super. 69; 29 A.2d 344 (1942); Hornstein article, n. 68, above; Ohio Rev. Code §1702.52.

80. Short, but broadly conceived provision: Conn. Gen. Stat. §33–489; moderately detailed, broad provision: Ohio Rev. Code §1702.52, lengthy, broad equity powers provision: W. Va. Code §31-1-81.

81. N.Y. Gen. Corp. L. §71 (Omitted in N.Y. N-PCL).

82. *Ibid.* §§72, 81.

83. *Ibid.* §§73–76, 130; Ohio Rev. Code §1702.52; See N.Y. N-PCL §§1113, 1111, 1202.

84. For various dissolution procedures, in all states, *see,* 5 Oleck, *Modern Corporation Law,* c. 78, 79 (1978 Supp.). *See* N.Y. N-PCL §§1109, 1113, 706, 714, 1110, 1202.

85. People v. Lorch, 171 Misc. 469, 13 N.Y.S.2d 155 (1939).

86. N.Y. Gen. Corp. L. arts. 6–8; N.Y. Penal. L. §2447.

87. N.Y. Gen. Corp. L. §9-b(3); *and see* Ohio Rev. Code §1701.86 (D); N.Y. N-PCL §302.

88. *See* the analogous sale of assets situations in Ohio Rev. Code §1713.24.

89. *Matter of Liquidation of United Sav. & L. Assn. of Gary,* 543 N.E.2d 211 (Ind. App. 1989).

90. *172 East 122 St. Tenant's Association v. Schwarz* (NY Ct. App., Apr. 6, 1989).

91. *Gee v. Blue Stone Heights Hunting Club, Inc.,* 604 A.2d 1141 (Pa. Cmwlth. 1992).

92. *Matter of Will of Coe,* 826 P.2d 576 (N.M. App. 1992).

93. *In re Krewe of Crescent City, Inc.,* 532 So. 2d 897 (LA App. 1988).

94. Anno. Mo. Stat. §352.240; Ohio Rev. Code §§1702.52, 2733.02–2733.39. *See,* Sheard, *Forfeiture of Nonprofit Corporations' Charters,* 14 Clev.-Mar. L. Rev. 253 (1965).

95. Nicolai v. Maryland Agric. and Mech. Assn., 96 Md. 323, 53 A. 965 (1903); People v. Stilwell, 157 A.D. 839, 142 N.Y.S. 881 (1913), affg. 78 Misc. 96, 138 N.Y.S. 693; Amer. Home Benefit Assn. v. United Amer. Benefit Assn., 63 Idaho 754, 125 P.2d 1010 (1942); State v. Dyer, 200 S.W.2d 813 (Tex. 1947).

96. *See* n. 94.

97. Anno. Mo. Stat. Sec. 352.240.

98. State v. Retail Credit Men's Assn., 163 Tenn. 450; 43 S.W.2d 918 (1931); Commonwealth v. Neptune Club, 321 Penna. 574; 184 A. 542 (1936). *See,* Sheard, above, n. 87.

99. Fla. Stat. §§617.1430, 617.2003, 617.1530. N.Y. N-PCL §1101. Bergeron v. Belisle, 256 Mich. 225; 239 N.W. 277 (1931); Bunn v. City of Laredo, 213 S.W. 320 (Tex. Civ. App. 1919); Holman v. State, 105 Ind. 569; 5 N.E. 702 (1886).

100. Nebraska Central Bldg. and L. Assn. v. Yellowstone, Inc., 141 Nebr. 679; 4 N.W.2d 762 (1942); Frederic G. Krapf and Son, Inc. v. Gorson, 243 A.2d 713 (Del. 1968).

101. State *ex rel.* Colburn v. Oberlin Bldg. and L. Assn., 35 Ohio St. 258 (1879).

102. *See,* Fidelity Met. Corp. v. Risley, 175 P.2d 592 (Calif. App. 1946); A.R. Young Constr. Co. v. Dunne, 123 Kans. 176; 254 P.323 (1927). Usually such a statute is conditional: revival will follow payment of a penalty. *See,* Wax v. Riverview Cemetery Co., 2 Ter. (Del.) 424; 24 A.2d 431 (1942).

103. *See* n. 91, Amer. Home Benefit Assn. v. United Amer. Benefit Assn., 63 Idaho 754; 125 P.2d 1010 (1942); State v. Dyer, 200 S.W.2d 813 (Tex. 1947).

104. *See*, State *ex rel.* Smith v. Hutchinson Gas Co., 125 Kans. 337; 264 P. 44 (1928). *See*, n. 95.

105. Fla. Stat. §§617.1430, 617.2003, 617.1530. *See*, note, 32 Iowa L. Rev. 558 (1947); and, People v. Dashaway Ass'n., 84 Calif. 114; 24 P. 277 (1890). *See*, Monroe Medical Clinic, Inc., v. Hospital Corp. of Amer., 522 S. 2d 1362 (La. App. 1988).

106. *See* c. 2; People v. Pacific Health Corp., 12 Calif.2d 156; 82 P.2d 429; 119 A.L.R. 1284 (1928); *In re* Cooperative Law Co., 198 N.Y. 479; 92 N.E. 15; 32 L.R.A. (n.s.) 55 (1910); People v. California Protective Corp., 76 Calif. App. 354; 244 P. 1089 (1926); State v. Lumbermen's Clinic, 186 Wash. 384; 58 P.2d 812 (1936); People v. United Medical Service, Inc., 362 Ill. 442; 200 N.E. 157 (1936); 103 A.L.R. 1229, 1240n; Carter v. Berberian, 434 A.2d 255 (R.I. 1981).

107. 44 *Am. Jr.* 2d Quo Warranto §§41–44; 74 C.J.S., Quo Warranto §12.

108. *See* Ohio Rev. Code §§1702.52, 2733.02–2733.39; Del. Super. Ct. Civ. Rule 81; Del Code Anno., tit. 8 §§136, 323. Must have court approval: People v. B.C. Associates, 22 Misc. 2d 43, 194 N.Y.S.2d 353 (1959). *See* N.Y. N-PCL §§112, 1101.

109. *See* n. 105, *and see*, Southerland *ex rel.* Snider v. Decimo Club, Inc., 16 Del. Ch. 183, 142 A. 786 (1928).

110. N.Y. Tax L. §203-a(7); Bengel v. Kenney, 126 Calif. App. 735; 14 P.2d 1031 (1932).

111. *See*, Stephens County v. J.N. McCammon, 122 Tex. 148; 54 S.W.2d 880 (1932). *And see*, Nebraska Central Bldg. and L. Assn. v. Yellowstone, Inc., 141 Nebr. 679; 4 N.W.2d 762 (1942); Bank of America Nat. Trust and Sav. Ass'n. v. Morse, 508 P.2d 194 (Or. 1973).

112. M. and S. Const. and Engineering Co. v. Clearfield State Bank, 467 P.2d 410 (Utah 1970).

113. N.Y. Tax L. §§203-a (1–10).

114. *Ibid.* §§203(1), 217.

115. See above, n. 110.

116. *Ibid.* §§191, 209(3).

117. Poritzky v. Wachtel, 176 Misc. 633; 27 N.Y.S.2d 316 (1941). *See*, Moore v. Occupational S. & H.R. Comm., 591 F.2d 991 (4th Cit., 1979); Kerney v. Cobb, 658 S.W.2d 128 (Tenn. App., 1983); Barker-Chadsey v. W.C. Fuller, 448 N.E.2d 1983 (Mass. App., 1983); Creditors Protective Assn. v. Baksay, 573 P.2d 766 (Or. App., 1978).

118. N.Y. Gen. Corp. L. §130 (omitted in N.Y. N-PCL); Walker Memorial Baptist Church v. Saunders, 173 Misc. 455; 17 N.Y.S.2d 842; *affd, without op.*, A.D. 1010; 21 N.Y.S.2d 512; *revd. on other gds.*, 285 N.Y. 462; 35 N.E.2d 42; *rehear. den.*, 286 N.Y. 607; 35 N.E.2d 944 (1941).

119. People v. Volunteer Rescue Army, Inc., 262 A.D. 237; 28 N.Y.S.2d 994 (1941).

120. Ohio Rev. Code §2733.35; *and see* Anno., 174 A.L.R. 1217; People v. Society of St. Joseph P.D.C., 177 Misc. 419, 30 N.Y.S.2d 551 (1941).

121. Ohio Rev. Code §2733.35; *and see* Thomas v. England, 71 Calif. 456, 12 P. 491 (1886) as to the nature of "prescription."

122. *See*, State *ex inf.* Hadley v. Delmar Jockey Club, 200 Mo. 34, 92 S.W. 185, 98 S.W. 539 (1906); People *ex rel.* Shedd, 241 Ill. 155, 89 N.E. 332 (1909); State v. Bailey, 19 Ind. 452 (1862).

123. *See* the Florida charter forfeiture grounds in Fla. Stat. §§617.2003, 617.1530, 812.035.

124. Ohio Rev. Code §1702.52(B, C).

125. *Ibid.* §1702.52 (D, E).

50

EFFECTS OF DISSOLUTION, AND TRANSFER OF PROPERTY

[See Chapter 49 as to causes and procedures of dissolution]

[Michael S. Hayworth assisted in the updating of this chapter.]

§484. "WINDING UP" A DISSOLVED ORGANIZATION

Dissolution and liquidation of a corporation, with court supervision that helps to assure propriety, must be begun with regular court proceedings, not summary process or speed, which are proper only after the initial question of dissolution has been determined through ordinary process.[1]

Filing of a certificate of dissolution is a formal declaration of the decision to dissolve a corporation, or of compliance with a legal order to do so. Corporate assets and liability do not magically vanish then.

In fact, the filing of a certificate of dissolution often is only the formal beginning of actual dissolution of the organization. Much may remain to be done for the purpose of *winding up* its affairs and liquidating and distributing its assets—or arranging for continued use of assets if they are held in trust for a specific (usually, charitable) purpose.

This is why a corporation continues to exist, under statutory provisions, in order to make practicable the winding-up process.[2] This is true in both voluntary and involuntary dissolutions, except that in the latter case the management of assets usually is in the hands of a court-designated custodian rather than of the trustees.[3]

Indeed, in many states the first thing that the trustees must do, after filing of the certificate of dissolution, is to give public notice. In a voluntary dissolution the trustees are charged with this duty.[4] In an involuntary dissolution, which is under court supervision, the court proceedings are matters of public record; in addition, the receiver or other liquidation manager must give notice to all interested persons.[5]

Public notice usually includes advertising of notice once a week, on two successive weeks, in a newspaper of general circulation in the county in which the principal office of the corporation is or was to be located. It also must include written notice by mail to all known creditors of, and to all known claimants against, the dissolved corporations.[6]

Duration of winding-up procedures. In some cases, where few or no assets and claimants exist, the winding-up process is of short duration. Sometimes the filing of the certificate of dissolution actually is the end of the corporation in fact as well as legally.

In other cases the process is quite lengthy and detailed. It may involve real difficulties, for example, in the case of a foundation or other charitable organization which is committed to a program that must be supervised through to completion.

A valuable technique to solve such problems was developed by the late Harold T. Clark, the attorney-president of the famous Hanna Foundation of Cleveland. His final fund plan, in essence, employed a small (three-man) liquidating board of trustees (unincorporated), to supervise completion of grants and programs to which all remaining assets were committed. A bank-depository-trustee was charged with the detailed payment of disbursements and keeping of financial records. Filing of the liquidation plan with the secretary of state, in addition to (and after) the filing of the certificate of dissolution, assured proper public notice and supervision.[7]

Forms developed and used by Harold T. Clark for the "Leonard Hanna, Jr. Final Fund" are set forth below, in this chapter.

Statutes in some states set up a maximum period of three years for the completion of winding-up procedures.[8] In some state statutes, completion is required within "a reasonable time," or "as speedily as is practicable."[9]

In one case the process still was going on 11 years later. The courts said that this was too long, in rejecting an obligation in favor of the corporation.[10]

Typical statutory rules. Using Ohio's statute (and New York's) as typical, the legal process of winding up usually involves the following general rules:[11]

The corporation continues to exist, but only for winding-up purposes. Pending claims and legal proceedings may be carried through to judgment; or stayed by court order in judicial dissolution cases.

Process may be served on the liquidation manager or trustees; or on the statutory agent if the proper person cannot be served.

Liquidating trustees may carry on business, enter or complete contracts as necessary, fill vacancies, buy or sell or mortgage assets as necessary, pay obligations, incur new ones as necessary, and generally do everything reasonably necessary to effectively liquidate the organization.

In *charitable* organizations, assets must be held in trust for the charitable purpose; and if the purpose cannot be achieved in whole or in part, the assets must be applied as directed by the court in an action brought for that purpose by the trustees or the corporation, with the attorney-general being joined as a party in the action (*i.e.*, to a similar charitable purpose). (See the section on *cy pres*, Section 486.)

In noncharitable nonprofit organizations, assets may be distributed as articles or bylaws provide; and if there are no provisions, then according to a plan adopted by a vote of the members; and if the members fail to adopt a plan, then according to a plan adopted by the trustees.

During the winding-up period, though the trustees carry on the liquidation, the members may make decisions by vote as they ordinarily may do, for winding-up purposes. But they may not violate the rule that assets of charitable organizations must go towards charitable purposes.

Officers appointed by the trustees may act for the corporation.

And at any time, court supervision of the winding-up process may be invoked.[12]

In addition, court jurisdiction over voluntary dissolution steps and questions is described in detail.[13] In involuntary dissolution, which is under court supervision, of course the court's powers are even wider.[14]

Similarity to business procedures. The winding up of a nonprofit organization is largely a matter of businesslike liquidation, though the nonprofit basis of course has great importance. When doubts arise, analogy to solutions employed by business corporations is very helpful.[15]

For example, business continues, with the aim of closing out affairs.[16] Legal counsel may be retained to collect claims and for other purposes.[17] If such counsel is retained, and if the corporation's assets warrant it, the attorney should file a special lien for fees, thus protecting his right to payment as against other creditors.[18] A liquidator may be appointed if the trustees cannot agree.[19]

Gifts may continue to be received.[20] The organization's name may continue and its protection may be continued, even as against members.[21]

Corporate assets become trust funds as to creditors[22] and members,[23] in all corporations, profit or nonprofit. In a charitable organization, of course, they are trust funds for all purposes.[24] (See, in this chapter, Section 488 minority members' rights in property transfers.)

Arbitration of disputes may be employed, if not barred by prior agreement or by the articles or bylaws.[25]

Such arbitration is possible for the same reason that a corporation in the winding up process may sue or be sued.[26] Court enforcement of an arbitration agreement requires that there be shown a valid agreement and a dispute about an arbitrable issue.[27]

§485. EFFECTS OF DISSOLUTION

Common law rules. Upon the filing of a certificate of dissolution, or at the expiration of its term, a corporation ceases to be a legal entity, under common law rules. It therefore cannot sue or be sued as an entity.[28] But even under the common law, dissolution does not wipe out liabilities previously accrued against the corporation or its members.[29] Nevertheless, the corporation no longer can hold title to property,[30] nor transfer title,[31] nor enter into contracts.[32] It is as though the "artificial person" had died.

Modern rules. It is obvious that the common law view, which is very logical if a corporation is viewed as a "person" (who has *died*), is hopelessly impractical. As a result it has been changed by statute in most jurisdictions.

Modern statutes empower the directors or trustees of a dissolved corporation to continue in office for the purpose of winding up affairs. In most states they may do so in the corporate name, but in a few they may do so in their own names. They may thus sue or be sued, or hold and convey property for the corporation.[33]

The problem of how long the winding-up powers may continue has been mentioned in the preceding section. Three years, or a "reasonable time," are common periods set by the statutes.[34]

Absent a statute providing otherwise, dissolution of a nonprofit corporation is the same as corporate death and terminates its existence.[35]

Many of the statutes make the directors *trustees* of the assets for the winding-up process.[36] As such they are held to a very high standard of conduct[37] and are subject to personal liability for improper or negligent conduct.[38]

In a few states (Illinois, Minnesota, Pennsylvania, and Washington), the winding-up process must or may precede the dissolution—avoiding some of the theoretical difficulties presented by the situation.[39]

In most states the directors simply continue in office—unless a court designates other persons, as in a receivership. Election of officers and appointment of necessary agents continues, but by the directors. They may even elect new directors, by majority vote. If none are left, the remaining members may elect directors.[40]

Acceptance of gifts and bequests may continue during the winding-up period.[41]

The obligation to pay taxes and debts continues.[42]

Executory contracts are not wiped out by dissolution.[43] But insolvency law may give a receiver or other liquidator an option to affirm or reject contracts.[44]

In a few cases contracts of employment sometimes were held to be abrogated by the "legal death" of the employer.[45] But this depends largely on the implied intention of the parties in the contract. Some cases find that dissolution is a breach of contract, and that it gives the employee a claim for damages.[46]

Except as the contract or insolvency statutes may provide,[47] dissolution does not terminate a lease of property, in the United States.[48] If the lease occupancy is not continued by the corporate lessee, the lessor has a claim for damages for breach of lease.[49] Modern emergency rent laws make special rules for certain areas, and should be consulted.

Though the corporation ordinarily cannot be forced point for point to perform contracts, in this period, it can be held liable for damages for breach of contract.[50]

§486. DISPOSITION OF PROPERTY (CY PRES DOCTRINE)

The law on disposition of property held by nonprofit organizations is rather vague. It is not well-settled whether property donated as a gift should revert to the donor (or his heirs) on dissolution of the donee organization, *escheat* (be forfeited) to the state, or go to the members.

In some states the old common law rule is followed, that such property goes to the state on the dissolution of a nonprofit organization, even one such as a mutual insurance corporation.[51] This, of course, is a great temptation to see to it that no property is left at the time of dissolution. But in most states such property is distributed among the members.[52]

This refers to organizations of a merely nonprofit, not charitable, nature. Charitable corporation property, of course, is trust property that must be used solely for charitable purposes. (See Section 483, outlining the Ohio statutory rules on this point, which are typical.)

Cy pres doctrine. The problem is that many nonprofit organizations commonly receive donations and gifts of property. And in many cases the donor had no intention of making a gift to the members individually. The intention of a donor should govern, *as nearly as is possible*, when literal effect cannot be given to it (*e.g.*, after the dissolution of the donee). The legal rule to this effect is termed the *cy pres doctrine*.

This view of the "trust" nature of assets of a nonprofit corporation may be summarized thus:[53] [*Restatement (2d) of Trusts* § 399].

"If property is given in trust to be applied to a particular charitable purpose, and it is or becomes impossible or impracticable or illegal to carry out the particular purpose, and if the settlor manifested a more general intention to devote the property to charitable purposes, the trust will not fail, but the court will direct the application of the property to some charitable purpose which falls within the general charitable intention on the settlor."

If the grant to a nonprofit organization is limited to a particular object, or to a specific institution only, and there is no general charitable intent, then if that object becomes impossible, or that institution dies, the doctrine of *cy pres* may not apply, and the asset may revert to the grantor or his estate.[54]

In some states (*e.g.*, New York) the common law doctrine of cy pres was replaced by statutes setting down rules for court supervision of such distributions of property.[55] (*See also,* Section 492.)

A good summary of the modern standards for application of the *cy pres* doctrine to nonprofit corporations is this one, from a 1986 New York Court of Appeals decision.[56]

> "Under the quasi cy pres standard of the Not-For-Profit Corporation Law, a Supreme Court Justice in determining whether to approve the plan of distribution proposed by the corporation's board, and if not to what other charitable organizations distribution should be made, should consider (1) the source of the funds to be distributed, whether received through public subscription or under the trust provision of a will or other instrument; (2) the purposes and powers of the corporation as enumerated in its certificate

of incorporation; (3) the activities in fact carried out and services actually provided by the corporation; (4) the relationship of the activities and purposes of the proposed distributee(s) to those of the dissolving corporation, and (5) the bases for the distribution recommended by the board."

Taxpayers' interests. A taxpayer has standing to sue to contest a charitable corporation's gift of its assets to another charitable corporation; but the transfer as such is valid under the *cy pres* doctrine.[57] Some courts recognize this kind of *standing to sue*,[58], but others do not accept such individual suit by a mere member of the public.[59] Thus, if a corporation that administers a trust for orphanages should dissolve, the fund should go to another organization having the same purpose, as nearly as possible. It is a rule of trust law. The gift for such a purpose is viewed as a trust in most states.[60]

The ascertaining of the intention of a donor, and the consequent treatment of the property, are fundamentally questions of trust law. If the intention is clear, the problem is simple. If the intention is uncertain, rules of interpretation under charitable trust law apply. This is only incidentally a matter of corporation or association law. Special texts on trusts must be consulted.[61] (See also, Chapter 7, other sections in this chapter, and Chapter 49).

Statutory court supervision of disposition of assets, on dissolution of nonprofit corporations, is the solution in some states. Thus, in New York, any member or creditor, or the attorney-general, may petition for court supervision and direction as to disposition of assets under the cy pres doctrine. Procedures as to notice to interested parties, hearing, and other matters are provided for.[62]

Modern statutory rule. Distinction between charitable and merely nonprofit organizations is the basis of the modern statutory rule as to distribution of assets. (See the Ohio provision description in Section 483[63] and at n. 55).

Where the organization is charitable (*i.e.*, religious, educational, or the like), the members are deemed to have no claim to the property.[64] The property must go to another, similar charity, as described in the Ohio statute. In some states there is escheat to the state, in the case of property bought by the organization; and sometimes return to the donor in the case of donated property.[65]

In merely nonprofit organizations, too, there may be assets acquired partly by dues payment and partly by gifts.

When gifts cannot be identified as to who donated them, or for what specific purpose, another difficulty arises. If the funds are mixed with those of the members, the tendency is to distribute the gift among them.[66] If no creditors or members are found, it goes to the state.[67]

In some decisions concerning corporations the cy pres doctrine is not followed. In this view, when *any* corporation dissolves, the excess assets are distributed among the members, regardless of the sources of those assets.[68]

When the organization is not for public charity or trust purposes, the problem is simple. In a private club, for example, where no trust property (gift for a public-benefit purpose) is concerned, simple distribution of excess assets among the members is the rule.[69]

Disaffiliation of branch or subsidiary. A disaffiliation of a chapter, branch, or subsidiary of an organization is not necessarily a dissolution, though it may be.

For example, the disaffiliation of a labor union local from the international involves problems as to disposition of funds. This has been a difficult problem for the courts. Various theories and doctrines have been applied in various cases. Unincorporated associations are particularly difficult to handle in disaffiliations.

This subject is too specialized to warrant discussion here, as there are six distinct groups of case law doctrine on the problem. Special studies should be consulted.[70]

Provision should be made in the articles and bylaws of both the parent and subsidiary organizations for this possibility. Even so, such provisions probably are not binding if they are improper or unfair.[71]

Minority-Group-of-Members' Interest in Property Transferred: See Section 489 *et seq.*

Illustrative Cases on Property Transfer

[Richard F. Askins did the research for the rest of this section.]

A member of a nonprofit organization may have property rights based on: (1) contract, (2) bylaws, (3) state statutes, or (4) constitutional law. Constitutional questions are the most complex of these bases. Thus, membership does not, per se, give property interests in such a membership benefit as insurance policy coverage, on alleged "due process" basis, when membership is terminated by lawful expulsion. And a bylaw basis for expulsion eliminates the argument that tortuous interference with the insurance coverage occurred.[72]

An association in which membership is not voluntary, such as a state bar association, may advance social and political views with which its members disagree (in some cases), by lobbying and filing "amicus" briefs in lawsuits, without thereby being necessarily charged with violating their individual interests in dues and other assets. So held the California high court in 1989; but review by the U.S. Supreme Court held that a member may get back his dues payment if it is used in a way not impliedly approved by the member. The constitutional rights of the member are protected. A bar association view as to gun laws is not part of the bar and law practice improvements to which members impliedly agreed to contribute their dues.[73] However, a state university may constitutionally allocate a portion of mandatory student activity fees to a group, with whose speech some students disagree, if the allocation is spent on campus.[74]

A homeowner's association has "standing" to protect rights of its members in a lawsuit about a deal to obtain a recreation-site city-approval, although it would affect the members' rights in loss of use of the common area; individually they are not necessary parties.[75]

Under Virginia statutory law, a nonstock corporation is without authority to dispose of all of its property or assets without the adoption of a resolution by the board or a vote by the membership at a membership meeting.[76]

A NPO owning an athletic field as its only asset may sell it and distribute the proceeds, where it received the land with no limitations on its use or disposition and specifically so provided in its articles of incorporation; and the city mayor's "dedicating" it to the use of the city's children is a nullity when there was no evidence that he was authorized to speak for the corporation.[77]

A college professor's interest in *"tenure"* is not "property."[78]

A member's interest in the loss of value caused to his horse by cancellation of its association (AQHA) registration certification does not entitle him to claim deprivation of his property right (due to decrease in value of an unregistered horse) where the cancellation was in accordance with bylaws.[79]

A nonprofit performing rights organization sued the owner of a chain of retail stores, for copyright license fees, after the stores played the organization's radio broadcasts during regular business hours. The court held that the home-type exemption, in the Copyright Act applied to allow such use of public performances.[80]

The Bayh-Dole Act grants nonprofit research institutions private title to all inventions developed through federal funding. Such federal contractors are not required to share royalties with the inventor.[81]

§487. DISTRIBUTION OF ASSETS

[*See also* Section 492.]

Distribution of assets of charitable organizations is treated in the preceding sections. True distribution occurs only in merely nonprofit (not charitable) organizations, ordinarily.

After the problem of disposition of trust-purpose property is settled, free assets of the organization belong to the members generally, as in a business corporation or association.[82]

First, however, assets usually are liquidated, and the debts and obligations of the organization must be paid.[83] The assets often are said to be a *trust fund* for the creditors.[84] If they are given to the members, while creditors are unpaid, the creditors may recover them (if the actual assets are traceable) and may sue the directors personally.[85] The liability of the directors then is primary, and that of the members is secondary.[86] The member who receives such funds often is said to hold them in trust for the creditors.[87] The trust fund doctrine applies to assets of a dissolved corporation held by any third party, including officers or directors, as long as the assets are traceable and have not been acquired by a bonafide purchaser.[88] Liability cannot be wiped out by merely effecting some kind of corporate transformation.[89]

In a few states the order of distribution priorities is established by statute. In insolvency cases, insolvency statutes usually set up such priorities.[90]

Unclaimed property in the possession of the organization, and unclaimed debts, may go to the state at once, and sometimes must be reported and paid after the expiration of a waiting period set by statute.[91]

Pro rata distribution of free assets among the members is the general rule, unless the charter, bylaws, or special agreements provide otherwise.[92] Such distribution ordinarily is only to members in good standing. Provisions regarding distribution upon dissolution should be made in the charter or bylaws.

Often even where nontrust property is concerned, the members vote to give the assets to another organization rather than take them themselves.

The real property of an involuntarily dissolved nonprofit corporation does not revert to the grantors or to a liquidating trustee where a framework for the distribution of assets is provided in the articles of incorporation. The articles in question required the conveyance to an institution of similar objectives.

After dissolution, a nonprofit corporation has no power to dispose of its property, except as specifically authorized by law or judicial order.[93]

In the District of Columbia, church trustees brought an action alleging that statutory distribution of church assets upon dissolution was improper. The statute required church property to revert to the persons, heirs and assigns of the contributors of the property. The court applied the neutral property disposition rule to avoid entanglement in religion. The statute was held to be presumptively valid. Further, the court found that the statute neither violated the free exercise clause nor placed a substantial burden on the observation of central religious beliefs.[94]

FORM NO. 214
Certificate of Actions Taken for Winding Up

Forms for Winding Up

[Based on Final Forms in Winding Up of an Ohio Foundation.]

L . . . . . . C. H . . . . . .FUND
An Ohio Nonprofit Corporation in Voluntary Dissolution
Secretary of State, State of Ohio—No. . . . .
Office of the Attorney-General—State of Ohio Charitable Trust
Registration No. . . . , 19 . . .

Certificate of Actions Taken to Complete "Winding Up Affairs of the Corporation," Together with the Final Accounting Thereof.

H . . . . . . T. C . . . . . . , President, and M. J. R. . . . . . . , Secretary of L . . . . . . C. H . . . . . . Fund, an Ohio Nonprofit Corporation, Articles of incorporation of which were filed in the Office of the Secretary of State on the 14th day of August, 19 . . as "H . . . . . . Fund" and amended Articles of which changing the name to "L . . . . . . C. H . . . . . . Fund" were filed in the office of the Secretary of State on February 10, 19 . . . , hereby certify that the following is a true and correct report of actions taken to complete the voluntary dissolution of L . . . . . . C. H . . . . . . Fund. It is likewise the Final Accounting of the

Winding Up of Affairs of L . . . . . . C. H . . . . . . Fund in compliance with Sections 1702.47, 1702.48, and 1702.49 of The Nonprofit Corporation Law of Ohio.

I.

In accord with Section 1702.47 of The Nonprofit Corporation Law of Ohio, a Resolution of Dissolution was duly adopted October 2, 19 . . by all of the Corporate Members of L . . . . . . C. H . . . . . . Fund, with the unanimous approval of the three Trustees of the Corporation.

II.

The Certificate of Voluntary Dissolution was duly filed in the Office of T . . . . . . W. B . . . . . . , Secretary of State of the State of Ohio, at Columbus, Ohio, on October 4, 19 . . , and recorded on Roll B-. . . . , at Frame . . . . . . of the Records of Incorporation and Miscellaneous Filing.

III.

Following the filing of the Certificate of Voluntary Dissolution, all requirements of Section 1702.48 of The Nonprofit Corporation Law of Ohio were complied with forthwith.

IV.

The steps which the three Trustees and Corporate Members of L. . . . . . C. H . . . . . . Fund found necessary to take to make possible the liquidation of the Fund before January 15, 19. . , together with the reasons therefor, were fully set forth in a statement which the Directors of L. . . . . C. H . . . . . . Final Fund caused to be printed on March 15, 19. . , when the two leading newspapers of Cleveland were not being published because of a strike which lasted one hundred sixteen (116) days from November 30, 19. . . to April 8, 19. . . Said statement was given wide circulation and saved L. . . . . C. H . . . . . . Final Fund burdensome correspondence with applicants for grants throughout the United States.

There is attached hereto, marked Exhibit "A," and made a part hereof a copy of said printed statement of March 15, 19. . , which had the following explanatory heading:

"L. . . . . . C. H . . . . . . FINAL FUND"

Directors and Officers

. . . . . . Building,
. . . . . . 14, Ohio

H. . . . . . T. C . . . . . .
Chairman
J. . . . . . B. W . . . . . .   March 15, 19. . .

Vice Chairman
C. . . . . E. S . . . . . .

"An unincorporated Fund created by unanimous vote of H. . . . . .T. C. . . . . , L. . . . .B. W. . . . . , and J. . . . .C. V. . . . . , they being all the Trustees and Corporate Members of L. . . . . .C. H. . . . .Fund, an Ohio Corporation, not-for-profit, in voluntary dissolution, to give assurance that all requirements of Section 1702.49 of the Nonprofit Corporation Law of Ohio are fully met."

V.

There is also attached hereto, marked Exhibit "B," and made a part hereof, a photostatic copy of the Trust Agreement mentioned in the statement of March 15, 19. . . This Agreement was made as of January 14, 19. . . between L. . . . .C. H. . . . . Fund, an Ohio corporation not-for-profit, and THE . . . . BANK OF . . . . . . , a national banking association of . . . . . . , Ohio, and assented to by H. . . . . .T. C. . . . . . , C. . . . . .E. S. . . . . . , and J. . . . .B. W. . . . . . , in order to create a charitable trust to be known as L. . . . . .C. H. . . . .FINAL FUND. This charitable trust was registered on or about March 15, 19. . . in the office of the Attorney-General, State of Ohio, under Registration No. . . . 19. . .

VI.

There is also attached hereto, marked Exhibit "C," and made a part hereof, a signed copy of Report of A . . . . . . A. . . . . & Co., ... East . . . . . . Street, ... 14, Ohio, designated as follows:

"L . . . . . C. H . . . . . Fund"
Financial Statements for the
Period September 1, 19. . . to
January 18, 19. . (Date of Liquidation)
Together with Auditors' Report

A . . . . . . A . . . . . . & Co. have been the authorized Auditors of L . . . . . . C. H . . . . . Fund, beginning as of March 15, 19. . . and continuing through the final audit hereinabove mentioned. Said Report contains the following statement:
"*Liquidation of the Fund*:
    "On October 4, 19. . , the Trustees filed with the Secretary-of-State of the State of Ohio a Certificate of Voluntary Dissolution of L . . . . . . C. H . . . . . . Fund, thereby carrying out the hope and wishes of Mr. H. . . . . . that the Fund might be dissolved within five years of the date of his death. The Trustees substantially completed the liquidation on January 14, 19 . . , by transferring the then remaining net assets of the Fund, subject to certain grants made but not

disbursed, to the newly created L . . . . . . C. H . . . . . Final Fund (an unincorporated charitable trust). The liquidation was completed on January 18, 19. . ."

VII.

L . . . . . . C. H . . . . . Fund, an Ohio Charitable Corporation in Voluntary Dissolution under Section 1702.47, et seq. of The Corporation Law of Ohio, having made this its Final Accounting of Complete Dissolution, is notifying the Secretary-of-State of the State of Ohio by separate letter that it is withdrawing the name of M. J. R. . . . . . . as Statutory Agent.

IN WITNESS WHEREOF, said H . . . . . . T. C . . . . . President, and M. J. R. . . . . . . Secretary of L . . . . . . C. H . . . . . FUND, acting for and on behalf of said Corporation, have hereunto subscribed their names and caused the seal of said Corporation to be hereunto affixed this sixth day of September, 19. . .

L . . . . . . C. H . . . . . FUND

By _____H . . . . . . T. C . . . . . ._____
                    President

[SEAL]

Attest   M.J.R. . . . . . ._____
                    Secretary

STATE OF OHIO   } SS:
COUNTY OF. . . . . .

BEFORE ME, a Notary Public in and for said County, personally appeared H . . . . . . T. C . . . . . ., President and M. J. R. . . . . ., Secretary of L . . . . . . C. H . . . . . FUND, an Ohio nonprofit corporation in voluntary dissolution, which corporation executed the foregoing instrument, who acknowledged that the seal affixed to said instrument is the corporate seal of said corporation; that they did sign and seal said instrument as such President and Secretary in behalf of said Corporation and by authority of its Board of Trustees and of all its Corporate Members; and that said instrument is their free act and deed individually and as such President and Secretary, and the free and corporate act and deed of said L . . . . . . C. H . . . . . . Fund.

IN TESTIMONY WHEREOF, I have hereunto subscribed my name and affixed my official seal at C . . . . . ., Ohio, this sixth day of September, 19. . .
. . . . . .

_____
Notary Public

STATE OF OHIO   } SS: E.D.W. . . . ., Attorney-at-Law
COUNTY OF. . . . . .   Notary Public for the State of Ohio.

BEFORE ME, a Notary Public in and for said County, pe appeared H . . . . . . T. C . . . . . ., and M. J. R. . . . . ., President and Secretary respectively of L . . . . . . C. H . . . . . FUND, an Ohio nonprofit who separately acknowledged that they signed the foregoing instrument and that the same is their free act and deed as President and Secretary respectively of said L . . . . . . C. H . . . . . . Fund and for the uses and purposes therein set forth.

IN TESTIMONY WHEREOF, I have hereunto subscribed my name and affixed my official seal at . . . . . . , Ohio, this sixth day of September, 19. . .

[Seal]   E. D. W . . . .
_____
E. D. W . . . . . . , Attorney-at-Law
Notary Public for the State of Ohio

[*Exhibit "A"* (attached) is any published statement(s) regarding the dissolution and its reasons and procedures.]
[*Exhibit "B"* (attached). See the next form.]
[*Exhibit "C"* (attached). See the form after the next one, below.]

FORM NO. 215
Liquidation Trust Agreement

EXHIBIT "B"

L. . . . . . C. H . . . . . . FINAL FUND

TRUST AGREEMENT

This Trust Agreement is made and entered into at . . . . . . , Ohio, as of this fourteenth day of January, 19. . , by and between L . . . . . . C. H . . . . . . FUND, an Ohio Corporation not for profit, (hereinafter sometimes referred to as the Fund), and THE . . . . . . BANK OF . . . . . . , a national banking association of . . . . . . , Ohio, (hereinafter referred to as Trustee), and assented to by H . . . . . . T. C . . . . . . , C . . . . . . E. S. . . . . . . , and J . . . . . . B. W . . . . . . (hereinafter referred to as Directors), in order to create a charitable trust to be known as L . . . . . . C. H . . . . . . Final Fund (hereinafter sometimes referred to as Final Fund).

1. Since the death on October 5, 19. . , of L . . . . . . C. H . . . . . . , the creator of the L . . . . . . C. H . . . . . . Fund, the officers and trustees of the Fund have worked diligently to carry out the wishes of Mr. H. . . . . . . with respect to the charitable uses and purposes to which the assets of the Fund were to be devoted and to meet his hope that there might be a final termination of the Fund within a period of approximately five years from the date of his death.

2. In carrying out the wishes and purposes of Mr. H . . . . . . during the period which has elapsed since his death, the officers and trustees of the Fund have effected the distribution of over . . . . . . Dollars for charitable purposes, principally in the areas of health, education, and the arts.

3. The Fund has informed the Directors of certain grants in the total

amount of . . . . . . Dollars which the fund has made but has not distributed. These grants shall, as soon as practicable, be distributed by the Trustee upon the terms and conditions set forth by the Directors, consistent with the terms of the minutes of the Fund of September 5, 19. . , a copy of which has been furnished the Trustee.

4. The Fund has caused to be assigned, transferred, conveyed, delivered, and set over unto the Trustee the property described in Schedule A hereto attached and made a part hereof, to be held, managed, and distributed by the Trustee upon the trusts and for the uses and purposes hereinafter set forth.

5. The trust created by this Agreement is organized and shall be operated exclusively for charitable, scientific, or educational purposes, or for the prevention of cruelty to children or animals, and the entire income and principal of the trust property held hereunder shall be held and distributed solely for such purposes. No part of its net earnings shall inure to the benefit of any individual, no substantial part of its activities shall be carrying on propaganda or otherwise attempting to influence legislation, and it shall not participate in or intervene in (including the publishing or distributing of statements) any political campaign on behalf of any candidate for public office. If by reason of change in Section 501(c) of the United States Internal Revenue Code, or otherwise, the carrying out of any of said purposes would cause the Final Fund to be subject to federal income tax, no further distributions shall be made for such non-exempt purpose or purposes. Subject to this limitation, the authority of the Directors with respect to distributions shall be unlimited.

6. H . . . . . T. C . . . . . . , C . . . . . E. S . . . . . . , and J . . . . . . B. W . . . . . . are hereby designated as Directors of L . . . . . . C. H . . . . . . Final Fund. The Directors shall have the sole authority to designate, subject to the terms of this Agreement, the beneficiaries, the amounts, and the methods of payment of the grants to be made hereunder. They may also affix to such grants such conditions as they deem necessary or advisable. The Directors may from time to time designate their successors and the time for such successors to commence their duties. Any such designation may be revoked at any time prior to the time therein provided for the designated director to assume his duties. All provisions hereof shall be applicable alike to originally named Directors and to successor Directors. All decisions of the Directors shall be concurred in by at least two Directors. All directions, designations, and revocations of the Directors shall be in writing, shall be signed by at least two of the Directors, and shall be effective upon delivery to the Trustee.

7. The Directors shall from time to time direct the Trustee to distribute the entire net income of the trust and so much, or all, of the principal as the Directors from time to time shall deem advisable for the charitable purposes set forth in paragraph 5 above. The Trustee shall make the distributions so directed, in trust, or otherwise, upon the terms and conditions specified by the Directors.

8. It is hoped that the entire trust property will be distributed within a period of two years from the date hereof, but if the Directors find a longer

period to be necessary or advisable, then such distribution shall be made within a further period not to exceed three additional years. Any funds not distributed or committed at the termination of this trust shall be paid over and distributed to the trust held by the Trustee for the benefit of The . . . . . . Foundation as provided in the Resolution of the Board of Directors of The . . . . . . Bank of . . . . . . adopted August 9, 19. . .

9. The L . . . . . . C. H . . . . . . Fund has endeavored to pay, and believes that it has paid all of its obligations which are concurrently ascertainable and payable, but there are certain relatively minor expenses in connection with its dissolution which must be paid at a later date and it is recognized that there may possibly be other expenses. Consequently, the Trustee is authorized and directed to pay any and all valid obligations of L . . . . . . C. H . . . . . . Fund presented to it and reasonably believed by it to be proper and valid obligations of the L . . . . . . C. H . . . . . . Fund. In connection with the payment of any such obligations, the Trustee may consult with the Directors.

10. With respect to any trust property held hereunder, and until final distribution thereof, the Trustee shall have, together with all other powers given it by law, the following powers:

1. To manage, control, sell, exchange, lease for any term irrespective of the duration of the trust, convey, transfer, invest, and reinvest the trust property or any part thereof, upon such terms and in such manner as it, in its discretion, shall deem for the best interests of the trust estate without limitation by any statutory provision or restriction as to the investment of trust funds by trustees or fiduciaries generally now or hereafter enacted or prescribed; to improve, manage, protect, and subdivide any real property from time to time held hereunder, to dedicate parks, streets, highways, and alleys, and to vacate any subdivision or part thereof; to resubdivide said real property as often as desired; to contract to sell; to sell on any terms; to partition; to exchange said real property or any part thereof, for other real or personal property; to grant easements or charges of any kind; to release, convey, or assign any right, title, or interest in or about said real property; to handle, mortgage, control, dispose of, and deal with said real property and any and every part thereof and all rights and privileges pertaining thereto in any way in which it would be lawful for any person owning the same to handle, control, or dispose of or deal with the same, whether similar to or different from the ways above specified, and purchasers from the Trustee shall not be required to see to the application of the purchase money, and persons dealing with the Trustee shall not be required to see that the terms hereof are complied with.

2. To exercise, buy, or sell subscription and conversion rights; to participate in or dissent from reorganizations, recapitalizations, consolidations, mergers, exchanges, or other capital readjustments, and liquidations and creditors and security holders' arrangements; to exercise voting rights and to issue proxies, discretionary or otherwise, upon or in connection with any

stock or other securities in the trust estate as it shall determine to be proper.

3. To adjust, compromise, compound, release, and discharge all debts and claims owing to or by the trust estate; to employ suitable agents or attorneys, at the expense of the trust, if it deems it necessary or advisable in the administration of the trust, but the Trustees shall not be liable for any neglect, omission, or wrongdoing of any such agents or attorneys, provided reasonable care shall have been exercised in their selection.

4. To register or hold title to stocks, bonds, or other securities or property in its own name or in the name of its nominee without disclosing the trust or to hold the same in bearer form; but the Trustee shall be liable for any wrongful act of its nominee with respect to any property held in the name of such nominee.

5. To make any division or distribution directed hereunder in cash or in kind, at its discretion, and to select and allocate to any division or distribution particular trust property, but property divided or distributed in kind shall, except as otherwise specifically provided herein, be taken at its fair market value, or, if the same has no readily ascertainable market value, then at such value as the Trustee shall determine.

6. To determine, in case of uncertainty, whether money or property coming into its hands hereunder shall be treated as principal or income; and to apportion expenses, taxes, gains, or losses to principal or income as it shall deem just.

7. The Trustee shall keep accurate records showing all receipts, disbursements, and other transactions involving the trust estate. All such records shall be the property of the Trustee, but they, together with the trust property and all evidences thereof, shall be available for inspection and for the purpose of making copies, during the Trustee's usual business hours, to the Directors. The Trustee shall regularly furnish the Directors full information regarding all receipts, disbursements, and assets of the trust.

8. With respect to any real estate held hereunder, the Trustee shall have all of the power and authority herein before given it, but anything herein to the contrary notwithstanding, with respect to the property known as . . . . . . Farm, shall take only such action, either in regard to the maintenance and operation of such farm or the disposition thereof, as shall be directed by the Directors, unless or until such right of direction is waived in writing by them.

11. For its services hereunder, the Trustee shall receive reasonable compensation in accordance with its regular schedule of compensation in effect at the time such services are rendered. For their services, the Directors shall receive compensation in such reasonable amounts as they from time to time shall determine. All compensation may be paid by the Trustee from income quarterly as earned.

[*Note.* Check local statutes as to the voting of compensation by directors to themselves.]

In witness whereof, L . . . . . . C. H . . . . . Fund has caused its corporate name to be hereunto subscribed and its corporate seal hereunto affixed by H . . . . . . T. C . . . . . ., its President, and M. J. R . . . . . ., its Secretary, thereunto duly authorized The . . . . . . Bank of . . . . . . has caused its corporate name to be hereunto affixed by C . . . . . . S. B . . . . . ., Vice-President and Trust Officer and R . . . . . . E. S . . . . . ., Vice-President and Trust Officer, thereunto duly authorized, at . . . . . ., Ohio, this 25th day of January, 19 . .

Signed, sealed, and acknowledged
in the presence of—
L . . . . . . C. H . . . . . . FUND

	By H . . . . . . T. C . . . . . .
	President
C . . . . . . A. D	
	And M. J. R . . . . . .
	Secretary
M . . . . . . K	
Assented to by	THE N . . . . . . BANK OF . . . . . .
H . . . . . . T. C	By G. P. F . . . . . .
C . . . . . . E. S . . . . . . [Seal]	Vice-President and Trust Officer
J . . . . . . B. W	And B. E. S . . . . . .
	Vice-President and Trust Officer

STATE OF OHIO   } SS:
COUNTY OF. . . . . .

STATE OF OHIO   } SS:
COUNTY OF. . . . . .

Before me, a Notary Public, in and for said County, personally appeared H . . . . . . T. C . . . . . ., President, and M. J. R . . . . . ., Secretary of L . . . . . . C. H . . . . . . Fund, the corporation which executed the foregoing instrument, who acknowledged that the seal affixed to said instrument is the corporate seal of said corporation; that they did sign and seal said instrument as such President and Secretary in behalf of said Corporation and by authority of its Board of Trustees; and that said instrument is their free act and deed individually and as such President and Secretary and the free and corporate act and deed of said L . . . . . . C. H . . . . . . Fund.

In testimony whereof, I have hereunto subscribed my name and affixed my official seal at . . . . . ., Ohio, this 25th day of January 19. . .

[Seal]

M . . . . . . K . . . . . .

EXHIBIT "A"
TO AGREEMENT OF TRUST
BY AND BETWEEN
L . . . . C. H . . . . FUND
AND
THE N . . . . . . BANK OF . . . . . . , TRUSTEE
TO BE KNOWN AS L . . . . . . C. H . . . . . . FINAL FUND

The following described property is hereby assigned, transferred, conveyed, and delivered to The N . . . . . . Bank of C . . . . . . , pursuant to the
Agreement of Trust by and between said Bank and L . . . . . . C. H . . . . . .
Fund, dated January 14, 19 . . to which Agreement this Exhibit is attached
and made a part thereof:

Par Value	Bonds
$1,200,000	U.S. Treasury Bills dated April 15, 19 . . due April 15, 19 . .
1,940,000	U.S. Treasury Bills dated September 6, 19 . . due March 7, 19 . . .
3,220,000	U.S. Treasury Bills dated August 16, 19 . . due February 14, 19 . . .
300,000	U.S. Treasury Notes 4 7/8% dated November 15, 19 . . due November 15, 19 . . , with February 15, 19 . . and subsequent coupon attached.
4,000	U.S. Treasury Notes 2 5/8% dated April 15, 19. . due February 15, 19. . , with February 15, 19. . coupons attached.

Principal Cash in the sum of $4,138.35

Income Cash in the sum of $50,749.85

Real Estate

Property situated in the Village of . . . . . . , County of . . . . . . , State of
Ohio, of record in the name of The . . . . . . Bank of . . . . . . , Trustee, known
as . . . . . . Farm. This property was deeded to The . . . . . . Bank of . . . . . . ,
Trustee, on January 27, 19 . . by L . . . . . . C. H . . . . . . Fund recorded in . . . . . .
County records February 9, 19. . as Document # . . . . . . Title to this property
is now subject to an easement granted to the State of Ohio Highway Department in April of 19 . . for highway purposes, and also subject to an easement
granted to the . . . . . . Gas Company in July of 19. . to lay pipe lines along
. . . . . . Road and . . . . . . Road upon special conditions set forth in said option.

Farm Equipment

All farm equipment and personal property at . . . . . . Farm consisting of three trucks, two tractors with equipment, power lawn mowers, tools, and all other items and equipment located on said premises used in connection with the operation of the farm.

Cash

Funds on deposits in L . . . . . . C. H . . . . . . Fund . . . . . . Farm Operating Account amounting to $3,873.14.

Accounts Receivable

Any and all income and/or principal which might at any time become payable or distributable to L . . . . . . C. H . . . . . . Fund from any source whatsoever, including, but without limiting the generality of the foregoing.

a. The following trusts with The . . . . . . Bank of . . . . . . Trustee, known as L
. . . . . . , Development Trusts: University Hospitals of . . . . . . C. H . . . . . .
-House Division # . . . . . . created by Exhibit B dated May 2, 19. . attached
to Development Trust Agreement dated March 10, 19 . . . . Hospital
for Crippled and Convalescent Children Division # . . . . . . created by
Exhibit C dated May 2, 19 . . attached to Development Trust Agreement
dated March 10, 19. . .

b. Income from L . . . . . . C. H . . . . . . Fund known as The . . . . . . Plaza
Beautification Fund # . . . . . . created under agreement dated January 11,
19 . . , as set forth in Exhibit B attached to said Trust Agreement.

In witness whereof, L . . . . . . C. H . . . . . . Fund has caused its corporate name to be hereunto subscribed and its corporate seal hereunto affixed by H . . . . . . T. C . . . . . . , its President, and M. J. R . . . . . , its Secretary, thereunto duly authorized at . . . . . . , Ohio, this 25th day of January, 19 . . .

Signed, sealed, and acknowledged
in the presence of—   L . . . . . . C. H . . . . . . FUND

C . . . . . . A. D . . . . . .   [Seal]

                                                       By H . . . . . . T. C . . . . . .
                                                                          President

M . . . . . . K . . . . . .   And M. J. R . . . . . .
Secretary   Secretary

STATE OF OHIO   } SS:
COUNTY OF. . . . . .

Before me, a Notary Public, in and for said County, personally appeared H . . . . . . T. C . . . . . . , President, and M. J. R . . . . . , Secretary of L . . . . . C. H . . . . . . Fund, the corporation which executed the foregoing instrument, who acknowledge that the seal affixed to said instrument is the corporate seal of said corporation; that they did sign and seal said instrument as such President and Secretary in behalf of said Corporation and by authority of its Board of Trustees; and that said instrument is their free act and deed individually and as such President and Secretary and the free and corporate act and deed of said L . . . . . . C. H . . . . . . Fund.

In testimony whereof, I have hereunto subscribed my name and affixed my official seal at . . . . . . , Ohio, this 25th day of January, 19 . . .

[Seal] M . . . . . . K . . . . . .
Notary Public

M . . . . . . K . . . . . . Notary Public
My commission expires Mar. 27, 19 . .

As evidencing the correctness of the foregoing Exhibit, the undersigned have hereunto subscribed their names, the date, and year first above written.

THE . . . . . . BANK OF . . . . . .
By G . . . . . . F . . . . . .
Vice President

And R . . . . . E. F . . . . . .
Trust Officer
Vice President

FORM NO. 216
Financial Statement in Winding Up (Liquidation)

Exhibit "C"

L . . . . . . C. H ——————— Fund
Financial Statements for the
Period September 1, 19 . . to
January 18, 19 . .(Date of Liquidation)
Together with Auditors' Report

A . . . . . . & Co.
. . . . . . East . . . . . . Street,
. . . . . . 14, Ohio
A . . . . . . A . . . . . . & Co.
. . . . . . East . . . . . . Street
. . . . . . 14, Ohio
February 21, 19 . .

To the Board of Trustees,
     L . . . . . . C. H . . . . . . Fund:

We have examined the statements of changes in fund balances and income and disbursements of L . . . . . . C. H . . . . . . FUND (an Ohio Corporation not for profit) for the period from September 1, 19 . . , to January 18, 19 . . (date of liquidation). The scope of our examination, which is described in the following paragraphs, included all of the procedures which we considered necessary.

The records of the Fund were maintained generally on the cash receipts and disbursements basis.

Liquidation of the Fund:

On October 4, 19 . . , the Trustees filed with the Secretary-of-State of the State of Ohio a Certificate of Voluntary Dissolution of L . . . . . . C. H . . . . . . Fund, thereby carrying out the hope and wishes of Mr. H . . . . . . that the Fund might be dissolved within five years of the date of his death. The Trustees substantially completed the liquidation on January 14, 19 . . , by transferring the then remaining net assets of the Fund, subject to certain grants made but not disbursed, to the newly created L . . . . . . C. H . . . . . . Final Fund (an unincorporated charitable trust). The liquidation was completed on January 18, 19 . . .

We verified the transfer in liquidation of the net assets of the Fund at January 14, 19 . . , to the L . . . . . . C. H . . . . . . Final Fund. The following assets were transferred:

	Carrying Value
Description	
Principal Funds—	
U.S. Government obligations ($6,664,000 face amount) at cost	$6,616,852
. . . . . . Farm real estate and equipment at value assigned by Trustees	415,270
Cash	4,138
Total principal funds	$7,036,260
Income Funds—	
Cash	$ 50,750
. . . . . . Farm operating cash (excluded from the records of L . . . . . . C. H . . . . . . Fund)	$ 3,873
Total transfer to L . . . . . . C. H . . . . . . Final Fund	$7,090,883

The following contributions, authorized by the Trustees but not disbursed at January 14, 19 . . , were assumed by the L . . . . . . C. H . . . . . . Final Fund:

. . . . . . Bureau of the Welfare Federation	$ 100,000
City of . . . . . . Greenhouse	300,000

. . . . . . Aquarium	300,000
The . . . . . . Museum of Natural History	500,000
The . . . . . . Garden of Greater	250,000
The Garden Center of Greater	
500,000	
. . . . . . Recreation Foundation, Inc.	41,500
. . . . . . Recreation Foundation, Inc.	
Matching fund	15,000
. . . . . . Historical Society Matching Fund	300,000
	$2,306,500

Securities Transactions:

All securities transactions during the period were traced to brokers' confirmations, bank advices, or other supporting data. Gains and losses on sales of securities were computed.

All purchases of investment securities during the period were stated at cost.

Cash:

Principal and income cash receipts and disbursements for the period, as reflected in the records of the Fund, were accounted for and were traced to supporting data.

Income from Investments:

Dividend income for the period was accounted for by reference to published data. Income from U.S. Treasury bills redeemed was verified by reference to receipt of proceeds.

Principal Distributions:

Cash distributions for the period were compared to endorsed cancelled bank vouchers; the distribution of securities to the . . . . . . Plaza Beautification Fund was compared to the signed trust agreement. All distributions during the period were traced to the minute book for authorization by the Trustees.

Administrative Expenses:

Major disbursements for administrative expenses were traced to supporting invoices or vouchers, and all such disbursements were traced to cancelled bank vouchers on which payee's endorsements were noted. Major expenses were authorized by action of the Trustees.

. . . . . . Farm Operations:

Disbursements for . . . . . . Farm were reviewed for the period and compared to cancelled bank vouchers on which payee's endorsements were noted.

Trustee Minutes:

We have read the minutes of the meetings held by the Board of Trustees from September 1, 19 . . , to January 18, 19 . . (date of liquidation). We noted that all contributions, security purchases and sales, and other significant transactions reflected in the records of the Fund during the period September 1, 19 . . , to January 18, 19 . . (date of liquidation), had been authorized or approved by action of the Board of Trustees.

In our opinion, the accompanying statements of the L . . . . . . C. H . . . . . .

Fund, present fairly, on a cash receipts and disbursements basis, the changes in fund balances, income and disbursements, charitable distributions, and distribution in liquidation to L . . . . . . C. H . . . . . . Final Fund for the period September 1, 19 . . , to January 18, 19 . . (date of liquidation).

Very truly yours,

A . . . . . A . . . . . & Co.

by . . . .
_____
(title)

EXHIBIT I

L . . . . . . C. H . . . . . . Fund
Statement of Changes in Principal Funds Balance
for the Period September 1, 19 . . to
January 18, 19 . . (Date of Liquidation)

Principal Balance September 1, 19 . .		$5,195,192
Excess of Proceeds over Carrying Value of		
Securities Sold		4,095,265
		$9,290,457
Distributions:		
In cash—		
The . . . . . . Society for the Blind	$ 75,000	
The . . . . . . Foundation	100,000	
. . . . . Recreation Foundation, Inc.	8,725	
. . . . . . Academy-H		
Educational Fund	100,000	
. . . . . . University	25,000	
In securities—		
The . . . . . . Plaza Beautification		
Fund, U.S. Government obligations,		
maturity value $1,950,000,		
carrying value	1,945,472	2,254,197
		$7,036,260
Transfer in Liquidation to L . . . . . . C.		
H . . . . . . Final Fund:		
Cash	4,138	
U.S. Government obligations		
($6,664,000 face amount) at cost	6,616,852	
. . . . . . Farm real estate and equipment,		
at value assigned by Trustees	415,270	$7,036,260
Principal Balance January 18, 19 . .		$ —

EXHIBIT II

L . . . . . . C. H . . . . . FUND
INCOME FUNDS
STATEMENT OF INCOME AND DISBURSEMENTS
AND CHANGES IN ACCUMULATED INCOME BALANCE
FOR THE PERIOD SEPTEMBER 1, 19 . . TO
JANUARY 18, 19 . . (DATE OF LIQUIDATION)

Income from Investments:

Dividends	$ 40,030
Interest on U.S. Government obligations	18,391
Income derived from charitable trusts	
created by L . . . . . . C. H	
Fund	10,741
Total income from investments	69,162

Disbursements:

Administrative expenses—	
Trustees' fees and salaries	$ 86,395
Officers' salaries	17,000
Legal and professional fees	50,560
Bank agency fees	20,000
Office salary and other	1,670
Total administrative expenses	$175,625
Transferred to . . . . . . Farm for operating purposes	18,367
Total disbursements	193,992
Excess of disbursements over income	$124,830
Balance Income Funds September 1, 19 . .	175,580
$ 50,750	
Transfer in Liquidation to L . . . . . . C. H	
Final Fund	50,750
Balance Income Funds January 18, 19 . .	$ —

FORM NO. 217
Notice of Withdrawal of Statutory Agent

L . . . . . .—C. H . . . . .Fund

. . . . . .—, Ohio

September 6, 19 . .

Honorable T . . . . . .—W. B. . . . . . .
Secretary of State of Ohio
Columbus, Ohio
Dear Mr. B. . . . . . .:

Notice is hereby given to you that, pursuant to the Certificate of Voluntary Dissolution filed on October 4, 19. . , Roll . . . . , Frame . . . . . .—, the liquidation of L . . . . . .—C. H . . . . . . Fund having been completed on January 18, 19. . , the name of M. J. R . . . . . . is hereby withdrawn as Statutory Agent.

Very truly yours

H . . . . . . T. C . . . . . .

President

Attest—   [SEAL]

M. J. R . . . . . .

Secretary

FORM NO. 218

Secretary of State's Certificate of Complete Liquidation

UNITED STATES OF AMERICA
STATE OF OHIO
OFFICE OF THE SECRETARY-OF-STATE   }

I, T . . . . . .—W. B . . . . . .

Secretary-of-State of the State of Ohio, do hereby certify that the foregoing is an exemplified copy, carefully compared by me with the original record now in my official custody as Secretary-of-State, and found to be true and correct, of the

CERTIFICATE OF COMPLETE LIQUIDATION

OF

L . . . . . . C. H . . . . . . FUND

filed in this office on the 13th day of September, A. D. 19. . , and recorded on Roll . . . . . .—, Frame . . . . . .—of the Records of Incorporations.

WITNESS my hand and official seal at Columbus, Ohio, this 14th day of October, A. D. 19 . .

[STATE SEAL]   T . . . . . .—W. B . . . . . .—

T . . . . . .—W. B . . . . . .—

SECRETARY-OF-STATE

---

§488. MINORITY MEMBERS' RIGHTS IN ORGANIZATION-PROPERTY TRANSFERS

[Sections 487–491 below in this chapter, are from an article by B. Richard Sutter, titled "Death of Charitable Trust Corporation Law," in 20 Cleve. St. L. Rev. (2)233 written for a seminar (on Nonprofit Law) at Cleveland State University. The paper has been shortened and updated.]

Since the subject of nonprofit corporations covers such a broad area, this (discussion) is limited to "Type B corporations"[95] (*i.e.*, the "charitable" type) as described in the New York Not-for-Profit Corporations Law. These classifications of the statutory concept (Types A,B,C,D) look to the *general* purpose of the organization, rather than to a very *specific* purpose,[96] or to whether or not stock is issued.[97] The New York law further provides for the possibility of any corporation having multiple and overlapping purposes,[98] thus providing a very rational and simple (though debatable as to policy) test to apply for classification purposes.[99]

It is generally felt that the *administrative* machinery for enforcement of nonprofit gifts is inadequate. . .[100]

The purpose of this paper is to sketch the development of *minority rights* in one narrow area—that of nonprofit property transfer, and especially in religious or charitable organizations. Representative state statutes, as well as case law, are used in order to demonstrate the confusing lack of uniformity in this area.

§489. THEORETICAL BASES OF MINORITY MEMBERS' RIGHTS IN ASSETS

At common law, gifts to a religious society were given with the implied trust that they be used *only* for the specific purpose for which the society was founded.[101] However, the United States Supreme Court in *Watson v. Jones*[102] said that so long as no trust was imposed when the property was acquired for a religious organization, none would be *implied* for the purpose of expelling those whose ideas of religious truth had changed. Further, as to the rule of trusts, Professor Bogert[103] indicated that implied trusts to further the dogma of the church do not necessarily represent the desires of the donor, especially where dogmas and creeds have lost their importance in this century.

The Ohio courts have uniformly held that in congregational disputes (even where property transfers are involved), majority actions will not be enjoined by minorities.[104] In the case of *Mack v. Huston*,[105] the defendants (a group of members of a Unitarian church in Cleveland), through a majority vote, had given their church property to a black separatist group on a lease-back arrangement. The plaintiffs, representing minority interests, sought an injunction on several grounds, all of which were rejected by the court. In looking at the church regulations, the court said that this was *not* a disposal of all assets, which would have required a two-thirds vote of the members. Further, since the regulations did not cover a partial disposition (75 percent of all assets were involved in the transfer), the court would look to the portion of the Ohio code[106] providing for a *majority* vote in the disposition of all, or substantially all, of a nonprofit corporation's assets. After supervising a second vote, the court held that a majority of the members *present* and constituting a quorum could dispose of substantially all of the corporation's assets in the manner they had attempted. The court added:

> This Court would be disappointed and disillusioned if at a later date it developed that the actions of the membership of the Society. . .were only the first step in a two-step procedure to change the location or terminate the operation.[107]

Subsequently, it was revealed in a newspaper that the operations of the church were indeed terminating, and that the members were looking for a new locale.[108]

In light of past decisions in this area, the *Mack*[109] court probably would have come up with the same result had they used an implied trust theory. Perhaps the failure to use this theory indicates the reluctance of the courts to use legal fictions, and a tendency to rely more heavily on statutory requirements. The trend in Ohio seems to be away from the implied trust, except where lack of good faith can be shown.[110] Texas is another jurisdiction that will not interfere in church property transfers until all ecclesiastical appeals have been exhausted.[111] Apparently they also follow the doctrine of *Watson v. Jones*,[112] and will not allow an implied trust to defeat the property transfers of a majority.[113] New York's statute[114] seems to have. . .obliterated trust law as far as nonprofit corporations of the type being discussed. This concept is treated below.

Other jurisdictions, however, favor an implied trust theory. This is so perhaps because of their reluctance to get involved in ecclesiastical matters, or perhaps because of the equitable nature of the remedy, or even because of their desire to refrain from causing resentment among devoted members.[115] In Minnesota, it has been held that property acquired by a church is impressed with a trust in favor of the church doctrine.[116] Arkansas,[117] Indiana,[118] and Virginia[119] are among other jurisdictions that still recognize an implied trust to a limited extent.

In light of the Supreme Court's holding in the *Presbyterian Church* case,[120] it appeared that the state courts have a precedent for denying the implied trust doctrine when looking at majority transfers. With this theory not available, minority interests may have to rest on statutory provisions, trust or deed provisions, or corporate bylaw provisions.[121]

Subsequent to *Presbyterian Church*, the Supreme Court decided the case of *Jones v. Wolf*,[122] in which the court, addressing this issue of church property transfers, held that a State is constitutionally entitled to adopt a "neutral principles of law" analysis to determine if such transfers are valid. This theory may take into consideration the deeds, state statutes governing the holding of church property, the local church's charter and the general church's constitution.[123] The court appears to be directing courts to use an "objective" basis in determining the validity of a transfer, and once again stresses that courts are to avoid any inquiry into religious doctrines.[124]

The doctrine of implied trusts,. . .a legal fiction,[125] has been used in the past to limit majority rule. . . .

With the absence of a very specific creed or doctrine, how can a member of a nonreligious, nonprofit corporation[126] claim that an implied trust should be found to prevent the transfer of corporate assets? While not using the words "implied trust," the court in *Lefkowitz v. Cornell University*[127] was able to prevent the transfer of property by the majority interest on a similar theory; *i.e.*, specific purpose. Cornell University, as the recipient of a fully staffed aerodynamics research laboratory, wished to sell the lab and put the money to use for general education purposes. The court said that the fact that Cornell had treated this as a *specific purpose* gift estopped them from selling it for *general purposes*. Also, the court said that Cornell must show how the sale of the property would promote the best interest of carrying out the charitable purposes of the trust. Despite the "changing times" (there was no longer a need for a propeller test lab) and the nature of the gift ("advancement of science and education"[128]), the court was able to come up with a means of preventing a property transfer, only to reverse itself and restore the condition of legal confusion a year later.[129]

While New York was rejecting and then accepting the use of "changing times" and upholding and then rejecting minority interests in the *Cornell*[130] case, Connecticut was putting a great deal of reliance on it in the case of *Dagget v. Children's Center.*[131] That case involved the religious affiliations of the board of directors of an orphanage. The original grantor had specified that the board of directors be comprised solely of Protestants. The court overlooked that specific provision by stating that "(t)he change in the religious make-up of the Center's board of managers has not affected the operation of the center."[132] Further, after looking at the desire not to discriminate and the fact that the original gift was valued at only 1/2 percent of the operating revenue of the foundation, the court was able to conclude that the purpose of the gift was *general* enough to allow the majority interest to prevail.

It would seem from these cases that if a member can show a very *specific* purpose in the operation of the nonprofit corporation, he probably can enforce the proposed disposition to that purpose. However, because a nonprofit corporation is tested by its *actual* rather than its *stated* purposes,[133] most corporations involve themselves in purposes broad enough to encompass the problem presented in the *Cornell*[134] situation. The possibility of a minority member prevailing in an action to prevent a majority transfer is greatly diminished if the purposes of the corporation are broad in scope.

§490. CHANGE IN TRUST LAW IN NEW YORK

Section 513 of the New York Not-for-Profit Corporation Act. . .statute makes Type B corporations *full owners* (not merely trustees) of all corporate assets. . .The statute makes the transfer of assets fully discretionary with the board of directors. . . .

This section was purportedly passed to give these types of corporations flexibility in the administration of their funds within the principles of corporation law, rather than trust law. . .[135]

Nowhere[136] else were corporate directors given the power that New York gives them. . .(at the time) [But *see* the 1986 A.B.A. Model Nonprofit Corporation Act Revision proposals.]

§491. WHO MAY ENFORCE MINORITY MEMBERS' RIGHTS IN PROPERTY?

There is little doubt that an outside trustee may hold a trust to its *specific* purpose within the framework of the nonprofit corporation. . .[137]

It has been held that the attorney-general, through *quo warranto* proceedings,[138] can enforce minority rights where there has been a misuse of the charitable gift.[139] However, this is a common law power of enforcement, and it is generally considered a very passive method.[140] Several states (*e.g.*, California,[141] Illinois,[142] New York,[143] Ohio,[144] have set up procedures for investigation and enforcement by the attorney-general. Texas,[145] on the other hand, only provides that the attorney-general's office is the proper party in an enforcement action, but provides for no method of initial investigation.[146]

Some states are silent as to the role of enforcement by the attorney-general,[147] or deny him the right of enforcement altogether.[148] Professor Bogert[149] states that because the attorney-general is a political officer with duties in (and pressures from) the state government, he has little time for enforcing charitable gifts. Thus, it appears that the attorney-general's office is not the best place to initiate litigation where minority interests are at stake.[150]

Because a director of a nonprofit corporation is a fiduciary,[151] a member (majority or minority) can bring an action where there has been a breach of faith in the property transfer. Since some statutes assume the good faith of the director in a property transfer,[152] it would seem that breach of faith becomes a difficult matter for the minority member to prove. . .

It would seem that presently, the best the minority members can hope for, where there are nonprofit statutes, is to attack the statutory requirements as was done in the *Mack*[153] case. In the case of *Davis v. Congregation Beth Tephila Israel*,[154] one member of a nonprofit corporation was allowed to maintain an action to prevent a property transfer. The case involved a consolidation agreement by two religious corporations with no attempt to comply with the statutory requirements of merger.[155] The court said that since this was an *ultra vires* act, a single dissenting member of either congregation could maintain an action to set aside the agreement. The case decisions in this area have added to the confusion of who may maintain an action. For instance, one Ohio Court[156] said that members, *not* the trustees of the nonprofit corporation, were vested with the powers to adopt, and presumably enforce, the fundamental principles of the society. Another Ohio court[157] has said that trustees, having the powers vested in them, are the proper parties to bring an action. The author suggests that the best view is that the trustee actually is vested with power to act for the benefit of all members.[158] With this in mind, it would seem that all a member would have to do is show that the director (trustee) did not act for the benefit of all the members of the corporation in transferring the corporate assets. Yet case law and statutes indicate that, whether or not it *should* be, this is not always the test used.[159]

Ohio provides that directors may mortgage any and all property of a non-profit corporation without the vote of a single member.[160] Ohio, by statute, also provides for court supervision of corporate property sales at any time.[161] This procedure, however, is not mandatory for all nonprofit corporations, according to the court in *Fenn College v. Nance*.[162] In that case, Fenn sought a declaratory judgment on whether it could cease functioning as an educational institution and transfer its assets to a newly created state university without court supervision. In answering the question affirmatively, the court said that since Fenn's Articles of Incorporation gave it broad plenary powers

". . .(i)t is abundantly clear that Fenn has full and complete legal authority. . .to enter into the (a)greement and. . .(i)t need not even have resorted to the Court to have such action sanctioned."[163]

New York[164] provides that leave of court (under Gen. Corp. L. §50 and Relig. Corp. L §12) is necessary in order to transfer property of a religious society.[165] However, New York too has case law to effect that court approval is not necessary. In the *Sun Assets*[166] case, the defendant church was alleged to have failed to convey the church property pursuant to a contract to sell. The church claimed that since it had not sought the court's supervision, the contract entered into was void. The court rejected this argument by stating that the court can always give approval *after* the contract is entered into. Since this case involved two purchasers of the same property, the holding of the case seems to be contra to the purpose of the statute,[167] which is to give the court supervisory powers over the sales of property of religious corporations. The problem presented in *Sun Assets*[168] probably never would have arisen if the court had supervised the sale *before* the contracts were entered into.

Texas[169] provides that one-tenth of the voting members is a quorum sufficient to transfer property. Also, the recordation of a deed of conveyance is prima facie evidence that a resolution of conveyance was duly adopted by the members. . .[170]

§492. MEMBERS' DERIVATIVE ACTIONS TO ENFORCE PROPERTY RIGHTS

[See, Section 446.]

Several writers have suggested corporate remedies in the area of nonprofit corporation litigation.[171] While not citing these authorities, the court in *Atwell v.*

Bide-a Wee Home Association[172] seems to bear out these advocates. In that case, the plaintiffs brought a derivative action on behalf of the defendant nonprofit corporation. Defendant was alleged to have destroyed animals entrusted to its care. The court agreed with the defendant's contention that plaintiffs were not voting members. However, the court went on, the mere fact that one of the plaintiffs had contributed to the corporation gives her standing to bring a derivative action. The significance of this case is that it was decided *before* the New York Not-for-Profit Corporation law was passed (which allows members' derivative actions).[173] However forward-looking this decision may appear on its face, it is tempered by the earlier decision of *In re Dissolution of Cleveland Savings Society*[174] which dismissed the derivative action of the members because they represented personal interests, as opposed to corporate interests. Therefore, derivative actions will only be supported by the courts (if they are supported at all) where the minority members can show that corporate interests are at stake. . .

. . .With the provisions of the New York statutes, these cases, and the writers who advocate such a position, a strong argument can be made for allowing derivative actions—as well as other corporate remedies.[175]

There have been varying suggestions for degrees of control, from intracorporate board control[176] to infrastructural[177] ("private initiative") enforcement. . . .

Admittedly, it is difficult to balance control and enforcement with initiative and philanthropy and still come up with a viable policing mechanism that will not stifle nonprofit growth. To this end, the only hope seems to be to either adopt a uniform nonprofit statute with enforcement sections that will work,[178] or set up a separate policing agency not unlike what the SEC does for profit-oriented corporations. . . .[179]

Dissenters' Appraisal Rights, such as are available in business corporation law, are statutory rights to be "bought out," if shareholders are a minority who object to some extraordinary matters, such as a sale of substantially all assets of the organization.[180] The same concept might be employed as a settlement device in nonprofit corporations.

§493. FIXED ORDER OF PRIORITIES

In a liquidation, the order or priorities in distribution of assets is treated herein in Chapters 48, 49. A good guide is the order of priorities set forth in the Bankruptcy Act (11 U.S.C. §726) for bankruptcy liquidations:

1. Secured creditors (whose collateral has been liquidated by the estate).
2. Post-petition lenders (who made loans after filing of the bankruptcy).
3. Creditors whose court-ordered protection is inadequate.
4. Administrative expenses (fees of trustees in bankruptcy, and attorneys).

5. Involuntary-gap creditors (whose claims arose after filing of the petition, but before court order as to payments).

6. Employee claims (wages of $2000 or less, earned within 90 days prior; and contributions to employee benefit plans).

7. [Grain farmers and fishermen (in the Bankruptcy Act list).]

8. Consumer claims (deposits, layaways, etc., up to $900 per person).

9. Tax-lien claims and unsecured tax claims.

10. Duly filed unsecured claims of creditors.

11. Subordinated claims (by agreement or court-ordered).

12. Late unsecured claims (filed with no acceptable excuse for delay).

13. Fines and penalties.

14. Post-petition interest on claims.

15. Any assets remaining then go to the corporation members, if this is a merely nonprofit group; to another organization (cy pres doctrine) if it is "charitable". [See §475.]

FORM NO. 219
Notice of Dissolution (Court-Supervised)

[Court name, circuit county, *etc.*]
NOTICE TO CREDITORS
In the dissolution of _____ Corporation, of
_____, (State):
    All creditors and persons holding claims or demands on the said corpo-
ration, are hereby notified of the filing of a petition for dissolution of said cor-
poration, and are directed to present their claims or demands to [Clerk of the
Court] at his office at [Address] on or before [Date].
        [Dated]   Clerk's Title and Signature
            [Seal of the Court.]   Attorney for Petitioner[Name, Address]

FORM NO. 220
Order Directing Publication of Notice
of Dissolution (Court-Supervised)

File No. _____.   [Court name, circuit county, *etc.*]
Case Title {   ORDER

In the matter of _____ Corporation
Petition for Dissolution

    It is ordered by this court that Notice of the said Petition be published
for _____ days in the _____ (Newspaper Name),

a newspaper for general circulation in _____ County,_____ (State), between the dates of _____,,
19___, and _____, 19___.

     Done and Ordered in Chambers _____, State, this
_____ day of _____, 19___

Dated   Signature

[Seal of the Court]   _____

                             _____ Judge of _____ Court

POINTS TO REMEMBER

- Filing of a certificate of dissolution does not end corporate affairs (except where winding up precedes dissolution).
- Winding up of activities must be completed.
- Debts must be paid, so far as there are assets available.
- Statutes now provide a winding-up period (usually three years).
- Directors continue to serve and manage affairs.
- They may continue to employ agents and officers.
- Executory contracts and leases are not wiped out; liability for breach continues.
- Trust-type property is subject to special rules.
- In some states, all property is free from personal claims of the members.
- *Cy pres doctrine* rules apply (trust law). These rules vary from state to state.
- Free assets go first to pay creditors; then, to members.
- Make provisions for dissolution and distribution in the charter (briefly), and in the bylaws (fully).
- When in doubt as to members' rights to share in distribution of assets, give the assets to another nonprofit organization with similar purposes.
- Remember that majority members have a fiduciary duty to be fair as to minority members' rights in organization property; and the same is even truer as to the duties of trustees.

NOTES TO CHAPTER 50

1. Olano v. Marigny Royal, 464 S.2d 774 (La. App., 1985); Note, *Dissolution of Public Charity Corporations: Preventing Improper Distribution of Assets*, 59 Tex. L. Rev. 1429 (1981).

2. *See* detailed discussions in 4 Oleck, *Modern Corporation Law* cc. 76–81 (1978 Supp.). For good typical state statutory provisions *see*: Ohio Rev. Code §1702.49(A); N.Y. N-PCL §§1004, 1005, 1006, 1111.

3. *See* the preceding chapter.

4. Ohio Rev. Code §1702.48.

5. *See* Oleck, *Debtor-Creditor Law*, c.7 (1959 Supp. Ed.); *and see*, Ohio Rev. Code §1702.52(C,D).

6. Ohio Rev. Code §1702.48.

7. Personal communications and discussions with Mr. Clark, in Cleveland.

8. *E.g.* Del. Code Ann. tit. 8, §278.

9. Ohio Rev. Code §1702.49; N.Y. N-PCL §§1004, 1005, 1006, 1111. *And see* Holiday v. Cornett, 224 Ky. 356, 6 S.W.2d 497 (1928) (no time stated in the Kentucky statute in question); five years in the old Alabama statute. *See* the next section.

10. Delpad v. Rapport, 119 N.Y.S.2d 675 (1953).

11. Ohio Rev. Code §1709.49; *and see* N.Y. N-PCL §§1004, 1005, 1006, 1111 *See*, Alford, *Disposition of Assets Upon Failure of a Charitable Trust or Corporation*, 9 Utah L. Rev. 217 (1964).

12. *Ibid. See, e.g.*, Lockwood v. OFB Corp., 305 A.2d 636 (Del. Ch. 1973).

13. Ohio Rev. Code §1702.50.

14. *See* the preceding chapter.

15. *See*, 4 Oleck, *Modern Corporation Law*, (1978 Supp.).

16. Garibaldi v. Yonkers, 198 Misc. 1100, 102 N.Y.S.2d 200, *affd. mem.* 278 A.D. 571, 102 N.Y.S.2d 426 (1951); N.Y. N-PCL §§1004, 1005, 1006, 1111.

17. Application of Peters, 271 A.D. 518, 67 N.Y.S.2d 305, modified 296 N.Y. 974, 73 N.E.2d 560 (1947); Laurendi v. Cascade Devel. Co., 5 Misc.2d 688, 165 N.Y.S.2d 832, affd. 4 A.D.2d 852, 167 N.Y.S.2d 240 (1957) (dissolution for tax delinquency).

18. Aetna Casualty and Surety Co. v. Atom Foreign Auto Parts, Inc., 455 N.Y.S.2d 531 (Sup. Ct., 1982).

19. Gutwirth and Errante Homes, Inc. v. Jacobowitz, 81 N.Y.S.2d 607 (1948).

20. *In re* Mohr's Estate, 175 Misc. 706, 24 N.Y.S.2d 977 (1941).

21. Glen-Dale, Inc. v. Abt, 133 N.Y.S.2d 353 (1954); Country Tweeds, Inc. v. Clyde Fashions, Ltd., 286 A.D. 49, 145 N.Y.S.2d 267 (1955).

22. Horan v. John F. Trommer, Inc. 129 N.Y.S.2d 539, affd. 283 A.D. 774, 128 N.Y.S.2d 595 (1954).

23. *In re* Estate of Sheresky, 157 N.Y.S.2d 829 (1956).

24. As to discussion distribution, *see*, Ohio Rev. Code §1702.49 (D)(2,3).

25. *See*, 1 Oleck, *Modern Corporation Law*, §201 (1978 Supp.). But see Matter of Ehrlich, 5 A.D.2d 272, 171 N.Y.S.2d 502 (1958), reversed in 1959, sub. nom. Milton L. Ehrlich, Inc., n. 26.

26. Milton L. Ehrlich, Inc. v. Unit Frame & Floor Corp., 184 N.Y.S.2d 334 (1959).

27. Marben Realty Co. v. Sweeney, 448 N.Y.S.2d 196 (App. Div., 1982).

28. Chicago Riding Club v. Avery, 305 Ill. App. 419; 27 N.E.2d 636 (1940); Fitts v. National Life Assn., 130 Ala. 413; 30 S. 374 (1901) (3 years); ann., 47 A.L.R. 1288. And action under way at the time abates. Sturges v. Vanderbilt, 73 N.Y. 384. *See also*, Marcus, *Suability of Dissolved Corporations*, 48 Harv. L. Rev. 675 (1945).

29. Dick v. Petersen, 90 Colo. 83; 6 P.2d 923 (1931).

30. Klorfine v. Cole, 121 Ore. 76; 252 P. 708 (1927).

31. Bradley v. Reppell, 133 Mo. 545; 32 S.W. 645 (1895).

32. *In re* Solomon, 16 N.Y.S.2d 472 (1939).

33. *See*, Anno. Calif. Corp. Code §9860; Conn. Gen. Stat. §33-489; Del. Code Anno., tit. 8, §278; Fla. Stat. Anno. §617.1405; N.Y. Gen. Corp. L. §29; Ohio Rev. Code §1702.49.

34. *See*, at n. 8,9; *and see*, Watts v. Vanderbilt, 45 F.2d 968 (2d Cir. 1930); Marshall v. Wittig, 205 Wis. 510, 238 N.W. 390 (1931).

35. *Matter of Will of Coe*, 826 P.2d 576 (N.M. App. 1992).

36. Bunn v. City of Laredo, 213 S.W. 320 (Tex. Civ. App. 1919).

37. *Ibid.; see*, Marine Trust Co. v. Tralles, 147 Misc. 426; 263 N.Y.S. 750 (1933).

38. *See* n. 33, above; State *ex rel.* Stoddard v. District, 108 Mont. 51; 88 P.2d 34 (1939); Young v. Blandin, 215 Minn. Ill; 9 N.W.2d 313 (1943).

39. Ill. Anno. Stat., 805/105/112.20; Minn. Stat. Anno. §302A.031; 15 Pa: Stat. Anno. §2105; Rev. Code Wash. §24.03.240.

40. Garibaldi v. Yonkers, 198 Misc. 1100; 102 N.Y.S.2d 200; *affd., without op.*, 278 A.D. 571; 102 N.Y.S.2d 426 (1951). Peters v. State, 271 A.D. 518; 67 N.Y.S.2d 305; *modified on other gds.*, 296 N.Y. 974, 73 N.E.2d 560 (1947) (retainer of a lawyer); N.Y. N-PCL §§ 1004, 1005, 1006, 1111.

41. *In re* Mohr, 175 Misc. 706; 24 N.Y.S.2d 977 (1941).

42. Updike v. U.S., 8 F.2d 913 (8th Cir. 1925); 6 Williston, *Contracts* §1960 (3d ed. 1978).

43. Kalkhoff v. Nelson, 60 Minn. 284; 62 N.W. 332 (1895); ann., 47 A.L.R. 1368.

44. *See* Oleck, *Debtor-Creditor Law*, c. 7 *et passim* (1986 reprint, Wm. Hein Co., Buffalo, N.Y.).

45. *See*, People v. Globe Mutual L. Ins. Co., 64 How. Pr. (N.Y.) 240; 91 N.Y. 174 (1883).

46. Central Trust Co. of Ill. v. Chicago Auditorium Assn., 240 U.S. 581; 36 S.Ct. 412; 60 L.Ed. 811 (1916); L.R.A. 1917B, 580; 6 Williston, *Contracts* §1960 (3d ed. 1978). But voluntary participation in the distribution may amount to abandonment of employment contract. *See*, Leak v. Halaby Galleries, Inc., 49 S.W.2d 858. (Tex. Civ. Ann. 1932); DuSeSoi v. United Refining, 540 F. Supp. 1260 (D.C.Pa. 1982).

47. *See* n. 44.

48. Perry v. Shaw, 152 Fla. 765; 13 S.2d 811 (1943); 147 A.L.R. 352; ann., 147 A.L.R. 360; Cummington Realty Asso. v. Whitten, 239 Mass. 313; 132 N.E. 53; 17 A.L.R. 527, 532 (1921).

49. *See* n. 48; ann., 111 A.L.R. 556, 560; 147 A.L.R. 366. Such dissolution may make the members (shareholders) the lessee, instead of the dissolved corporation. *See*, Everett Credit Union v. Allied Ambulance Service, Inc., 424 N.E.2d 1142 (Mass. App. 1981); City of Springfield v. Schaffer, 423 N.E.2d 797 (Mass. App. 1981).

50. Kalkhoff case, n. 43; Schlieder v. Dielman, 44 La. A. 462; 10 S. 934 (1892); and as to specific performance, *see*, Oleck, Specific Performance of Builders' Contracts, 21 Fordham L. Rev. 156 (1952).

51. Titcomb v. Kennebunk Mutual F. Ins. Co., 79 Me. 315; 9 A. 732 (1887); *and see*, Clarke v. Armstrong, 151 Ga. 105; 106 S.E. 289 (1921).

52. Neptune Fire Engine and Hose Co. v. Board of Educ., 166 Ky. 1; 178 S.W. 1138 (1915); Huber v. Martin, 127 Wis. 412; 105 N.W. 1031; 3 L.R.A. (n.s.) 653 (1906).

53. *See*, Boston Seaman's Friend Society v. Atty.-Gen., 398 N.E.2d 721 (Mass. 1980); Wesley United Methodist Church v. Harvard College, 366 Mass. 247, 251, 316 N.E.2d 620 (1974); and see, note 61.

54. Board of Selectmen of Provincetown v. Attorney General, 447 N.E.2d 677 (Mass App. 1983); Matter of Gerber, 652 P.2d 937 (Utah, 1982).

55. N.Y. Pers. Prop. L. §12; Real Prop. L. §113; now EPTL 8-1.1(c)(j). See, Bogert, *Trusts and Trustees* §431 at 490 (curr. ed.); 4 Scott, *Trusts* §399, at 3084 (3rd ed., curr. supp.).

56. Matter of Multiple Sclerosis Service Organization of New York, Inc., 68 N.Y.2d 32, 496 N.E.2d 861, 862 (1986).

57. Gordon v. Baltimore, 267A.2d 98 (Md. App. 1970).

58. *Ibid.*

59. Carroll Park Manor Community Assn. v. Board of County Commissioners, 437 A.2d 689 (Md. Ct. Spec. App. 1982).

60. Crane v. Morristown Foundation, 120 N.J. Eq. 583; 187 A. 632, 635 (1936); People v. Braucher, 258 Ill. 604; 101 N.E. 944, 946 (1913); Tincher v. Arnold, 147 F. 665 (7th Cir. 1906).

61. Alford, *Disposition of Assets Upon Failure of a Charitable Trust or Corporation*, 9 Utah L. Rev. 217(1964). *See*, Bogert, *Law of Trusts* (14 Vols.; St. Paul, Minn.: West Publ. Co., 2d ed. 1964 with 1978 Supp.). Bogert, *Proposed Legislation Regarding State Supervision of Charities*, 52 Mich. L. Rev. 633 (1954); or Bogert, *Trusts 529–531 (5th ed. 1973). See discussions in Note, Charitable Trusts: Termination by Judicial Decree*, 28 Wash. L. Rev. 76 (1953).

   Note, *Cy Pres Doctrine and Anonymous Donors*, 6 Stanford L. Rev. 729 (1954).

   Fisch, *American Acceptance of Charitable Trusts*, 28 Notre Dame Law. 219 (1953).

   Granirer, *Charitable Gifts—Reversion. . .* , 22 Queens Bar Bull, 94 (1959).

   Gray, *Charitable Trusts*, 16 Modern L. Rev. 95 (1953).

   McClean, *Charitable Trusts. . .and Cy Pres*, 1 U.B.C.L. Rev. 727 (1963).

   Restatement (2d) Trusts, §399, Comments i, q (1959).

   Scott, *Law of Trusts* (6 Vols.; Boston: Little Brown; 3d Ed. 1967 with Curr. Supp.), esp. Vol. 4. §§399.2, 399.3.

   Scott, *Trusts for Charitable and Benevolent Purposes*, 58 Harv. L. Rev. 548 (1945).

   Sheridan, *The Cy Pres Doctrine*, 32 Can. B. Rev. 599 (1954).

62. N.Y. Not-for-Profit Corp. L. §1008; *In re* Italian Benevolent Institute, 127 N.Y.S.2d 396 (1953); *In re* Mohr's Estate, 175 Misc. 706; 24 N.Y.S.2d 977 (1941).

63. Ohio Rev. Code §1702.49.

64. Danville Cemetery v. Mott, 136 Ill. 289; 28 N.E. 54 (1891); People v. Trustees of College of California, 38 Calif. 166 (1869); Late Corporation of Church of Jesus Christ of Latter Day Saints v. U.S., 136 U.S. 1; 10 S.Ct. 792; 34 L.Ed. 478 (1889); 14 C.J.S., Charities §§67, 77.

65. Clarke v. Armstrong, 151 Ga. 105; 106 S.E. 289 (1921); Coe v. Washington Mills Relief Society, 149 Mass. 543; 21 N.E. 966 (1889); ann., 47 A.L.R. 1336. Alford, *Disposition of Assets Upon Failure of a Charitable Trust or Corporation*, 9 Utah L. Rev. 217 (1964).

66. *See* cases in n. 52, above; Franklin County v. Blake, 283 Ill. 292; 119 N.E. 288 (1918); McAlhany v. Murray, 89 S.C. 440; 71 S.E. 1025; 35 L.R.A. (n.s.) 895 (1911).

67. *See* n. 66.

68. Huber case, n. 52, above; McAlhany case, n. 66, above; First Christian Church v. Jefferson Standard L. Ins. Co., 183 Ga. 167; 187 S.E. 729 (1936); Mobile Temperance Hall Assn. v. Holmes, 189 Ala. 271; 65 S. 1020 (1914).

69. *See* n. 52, 11.

70. *See*, Svete, *Disposition of Local's Funds Upon Disaffiliation*, 12 Clev.-Mar. L. Rev. 539 (1963).

71. Svete article, above, n. 70.

72. *Elgin v. Montgomery County Farm Bureau*, 549 S. 2d 486 (Ala. 1989).

73. *Keller v. California*, 767 P. 2d 1020 (Calif., 1989), reversed by U.S. Supr. Ct. (1990).

74. *Carroll v. Blinken*, 957 F.2d 991 (2nd Cir. (N.Y.), 1992).

75. *River Birch Assn. v. City of Raleigh*, 388 S.E. 2d 538 (N.C., 1990). Cf., *International Primate Protec. League v. Admin.*, 895 F. 2d 1056 (5th Cir. 1990).

76. *Princess Anne Hills Civic League, Inc. v. Susan Constant Real Estate Trust*, 413 S.E.2d 599 (Va. 1992).

77. *Fort Payne v. Fort Payne Athletic Assn*, 567 So. 2d 1260 (Ala. 1990).

78. *Staheli v. University of Mississippi*, 854 F.2d 799 (5th Cir., MS, 1988). See Oleck, *Debtor-Creditor Law*, c. 13 (Reprint Edition, William S. Hein Co.; Buffalo, NY, 1986).

79. *Burge v. American Quarter Horse Assn.*, 782 S.W. 2d 353 (Tex. App., 1990).

80. *Broadcast Music, Inc. v. Claire's Boutiques, Inc.*, 949 F.2d 1482 (7th Cir. 1991). *See also Diagnostic Unit Inmate Council v. Motion Picture Ass'n of America, Inc.*, 953 F.2d 376 (8th Cir. 1992) (inmates contend that prison situations fall into exception to copyright law).

81. *Platzer v. Sloan-Kettering Institute for Cancer Research*, 787 F. Supp. 360 (S.D.N.Y. 1992).

82. *See* n. 69; Di Prete v. Vallone, 48 A.2d 250 (R.I. 1946); Jones v. Peck, 63 Calif. App. 397; 218 P. 1030 (1923). *See*, Alford, *Disposition of Assets Upon Failure of a Charitable Trust or Corporation*, 9 Utah L.R. 217 (1964).

83. Wilson v. Lucas, 185 Ark. 183; 47 S.W.2d 8 (1932); *In re* Pacific Coast B. & L. Assn., 15 Calif.2d 134; 99 P.2d 251 (1940); Franklin v. Watson, 69 N.Y.S.2d 444 (1946).

84. *See*, 4 Oleck, *Modern Corporation Law*, c. 78, 79 (1978 Supp.).

85. Pierce v. U.S. 255 U.S. 398, 41 S.Ct. 365, 65 L.Ed. 197 (1921); Rochelle v. Oates, 241 Ala. 372, 2 S.2d 749 (1941); Dick v. Petersen, 90 Colo. 83, 6 P.2d 923 (1931).

86. N.J. Stat. Anno. §14A:6–12; *and see*, Note, *Disposition of Assets of Charitable Corporation Upon Dissolution*, 1 U.C.L.A. L. Rev. 117 (1953).

87. *See* n. 85, 86, Koch v. U.S., 138 F.2d 850 (10th Cir. 1943).

88. Hunter v. Fort Worth Capital Corp., 620 S.W.2d 547 (Tex. 1981); Norton, *Relationship of Shareholders to Corporate Creditors Upon Dissolution,. . ."Trust Fund" Doctrine*, 30 Bus. Law 1061, 1074 (1975).

89. United States v. Ashland Oil Co., 537 F. Supp.—(D.C., Tenn. 1982); Stone v. First Wyoming Bank, 625 F.2d 332 (10th Cir., 1980).

90. *See*, Waldner v. Equitable Loan Society, 60 F. Supp. 372 (D.C. 1945); Oleck, *Debtor-Creditor Law*, §36 (1959 Supp. Ed.).

91. Calif. Code Civ. Proc. §§1300 *et seq.*

92. Ohio Rev. Code Sec. 1702.49 (D)(3): plan to be made by members, or by trustees if members fail to act, in absence of express provisions in articles or bylaws. *See* Williams v. Renshaw, 220 A.D. 39, 220 N.Y.S. 532 (1927).

   Depositors in a savings society own the beneficial interest in its surplus. *In re* Dissolution of Springfield Savings Society, 12 Ohio App.2d 120, 231 N.E.2d 314 (1966); 12 Ohio Misc. 51 (1965); 12 Ohio Misc. (1967).

   A society for savings has authority to transfer its assets for other property, as well as for money. *In re* Dissolution of Cleveland Savings Society, 91 Ohio Abs. 289 (1961).

   As to derivative rights and procedures, *see*, *In re* Dissolution, 90 Ohio Abs. 3, 183 N.E.2d 234 (1962).

93. *Matter of Will of Coe*, 826 P.2d 576 (N.M. App. 1992).

94. *Prince v. Firman*, 584 A. 2d 8 (D.C. App. 1990); D.C. Code 1981, §29-911; U.S.C.A. Const. Amend. 1.

95. N.Y. Not-for-Profit Corp. Act, §201(b). Type B defined as having nonbusiness purposes that are charitable, religious, educational, scientific, literary, cultural, or prevention of cruelty to children or animals. Some of the specific purposes for which Type B corporations may include the following:

   Afro-American Experience (Cultural, Educational)

   Alcoholics Benevolent Society (Charitable, Educational)

   Arboretum Association (Educational, Scientific)

   Arts Council (Cultural, Literary)

   Autistic Children (Charitable, Educational)

Aviation Institute (Scientific)

Biocharacterization of Populations (Scientific)

Fine Arts Society (Cultural)

General Charitable Organizations

Health Consumers' Alliance (Educational)

Heart Research Fund (Charitable, Educational)

Housing Improvement Association (Charitable, Educational)

Law Services Committee (Charitable)

Leadership Training (Educational)

Training Orchestra (Educational)

Youth Involvement Program (Cultural, Educational)

Youth Center (Cultural, Educational)

For forms concerning these and many other types of nonprofit corporations consult West-'s McKinney's (N.Y.) Not-for-Profit Corp. L. forms under §201. Other types of nonprofit corporations fall under different categories; *e.g.*, Type A includes nonbusiness, nonpecuniary corporations formed for athletic or patriotic purposes; Type C for the lawful business purpose of achieving a lawful public or quasi-public objective.

96. Ohio Rev. Code, tit. 17 generally. Over 26 general chapter headings on types of corporations are described in the statute.

97. Mich. Comp. L. Anno., §450.2201, 450.2303.

98. N.Y. Not-for-Profit Corp. Act. §201(c).

99. For a critical analysis of the New York statute, *see* Oleck, *Proprietary Mentality and the New Nonprofit Corporation Laws*, 20 Cleve. St. L. Rev. 145 (1971).

100. Alford, *The Disposition of Assets Upon Failure of a Charitable Trust or Corporation: Policy Relationship to Enforcement of Charities*, 9 Utah L. Rev. 217 (1964–65).

101. Ferraria v. Vasconellos, 31 Ill. 25 (1863); Hale v. Everret, 16 Am. Rep. 82, 53 N.H. 9 (1868).

102. 80 U.S. (13 Wall.) 679 (1871) dictum.

103. Bogert, *Trusts and Trustees*, §398 (2d Ed., 1964 with curr. Supp.).

104. Heckman v. Mees, 16 Ohio Rep. 584 (1849). Majority breakaway upheld on the grounds that implied trust is for the benefit of the majority. Wiswell v. First Congregational Church, 14 Ohio St. 31 (1862). Court would not find implied trust for creedless Unitarian church. Keyser v. Stansifer, 6 Ohio Rep. 364 (1834). Majority held the property in fee simple, thereby solving the court's dilemma of implied trusts. Katz v. Goldman, 33 Ohio App. 150 (1929). No implied trust to support orthodox Judaism. Majority was allowed to specify the use of the property.

105. 256 N.E.2d 271 (Comm. Pleas. Ohio 1970).

106. *Supra*, n. 96, §1702.39.

107. *Supra*, n. 96, at 281.

108. Cleveland *Plain Dealer*, Feb. 20, 1971, at 2-B, col. 1.

109. *Supra*, n. 105.

110. Ohio Rev. Code, §1702.54. *See also* Gochenour v. Cleveland Terminal Bldg. Co., 118 F.2d 89 (C.C.A. Ohio 1941). Fiduciaries charged with handling affairs honestly and in good faith.

111. Groce, *Authority of Officers to Convey for Church*, 22 Bay. L. Rev. 222 (1970).

112. *Supra*, n. 102.

113. *Supra*, n. 111.

114. *Supra*, n. 98, §513.

115. Chafee. *The Internal Affairs of Associations Not for Profit*, 43 Harv. L. Rev. 992, 1026 (1930).

116. Veltman v. DeBoer, 118 N.W.2d 808 (Minn. 1962). Due notice of meeting and right of all members to be heard apparently would suffice for majority transfer.

117. Holiman v. Dovers, 366 S.W.2d 197 (Ark. 1963).

118. Stansberry v. McCarty, 149 N.E.2d 683 (Ind. 1958). Majority rule final unless property rights of members, all of whom have interest in property, are violated.

119. Barber v. Caldwell, 152 S.E.2d 23 (Va. 1967). Majority cannot divert property to support conflicting doctrines.

120. Presbyterian Church in the United States v. Mary Elizabeth Blue Hall Memorial Presbyterian Church, 393 U.S. 440 (1969). In reversing the Georgia Supreme Court's finding of an implied trust in favor of the loyal members, the United States Supreme Court said that in order to decide if the implied trust has been breached, a civil court must necessarily involve itself in the relative importance of religious doctrines—plainly forbidden by the First Amendment of the Constitution.

121. Kauper, *Church Autonomy and the First Amendment: the Presbyterian Church Case*, Sup. Ct. Rev. 347 (1969).

122. Jones v. Wolf, 443 U.S. 595 (1979).

123. *Id.* at 602–606.

124. *Id* at 603.

125. Elliot, *Majority Control of the Property of Independent Churches*, 12 Kan. L. Rev. 436 (1963–64).

126. *Supra*, n. 96.

127. 62 Misc.2d 95, 308 N.Y.S.2d 85 (Sup. Ct. 1970).

128. *Supra*, n. 115, 62 Misc.2d 95 at 96, 308 N.Y.S.2d 85 at 87 (1970).

129. Lefkowitz v. Cornell, 316 N.Y.S.2d 264 (App. Div. 1970), affd. 322 N.Y.S.2d 717 (N.Y. 1971).

130. *Supra*, n. 127, 128.

131. 28 Conn. Sup. 468, 266 A.2d 72 (1970).

132. *Supra*, n. 131, 28 Conn. Sup. 468, 266 A.2d 72 at 75 (1970).

133. *See above*, cc. 1–2.

134. *Supra*, n. 127.

135. *Supra*, n. 98, §513. Legislative Studies and Reports.

136. For a discussion of corporate property sales on a state-by-state basis, *See* 4 Oleck, *Modern Corporation Law*, §1710–§1762 (1978 Supp.).

137. St. Joseph's Hospital v. Bennett, 281 N.Y. 115, 22 N.E.2d 305 (1939). Use of income for anything other than perpetual fund would be violation of testator's intent.

138. State ex rel. Attorney General v. Norcross, 132 Wis. 534, 112 N.W. 40 (1907). *Quo warranto* is a redress of a public wrong, or the enforcement of a public right. *See*, for example, Fla. Stat. §§A5S3, A5S5 542.03.

139. Commonwealth v. Seventh Day Baptists, 317 Pa. 358. 176 A. 17 (1935); Lefkowitz v. Lebensfeld, 417 N.Y.S.2d 715 (App. Div. 1979).

140. Bogert and Oaks, *Cases on the Law of Trusts*, 699 (Foundation Press, 4th ed., 1967).

141. Ann. Cal. Gov. Codes, §12580 *et seq.*

142. Ill. Rev. Stats., c. 14 §51 *et seq.*

143. N.Y. Est., Powers and Trusts L., §8–1.4.

144. Ohio Rev. Code, §109.23 et seq.

145. Tex. Civ. Stat., §4412(a).

146. Bogert, *Proposed Legislation Regarding State Supervision of Charities*, 52 Mich. L. Rev. 633 at 647 (1952). A bill, which would have given the attorney general broad powers of enforcement, was defeated by the Texas legislature. Apparently strong pressure was put on by church groups and wealthy trustors to defeat the bill.

147. *E.g.*, Colo. Rev. Stat. Tit. 7 §50–101 to 114.

148. Tenn. Code Anno., tit. 23, §2809. Although this section says that the attorney-general and the governor (together) may direct that an action be brought, the courts have interpreted this to mean that the attorney-general alone has no authority under the statute to bring an action to recover misappropriated charitable funds. State ex rel. Tennessee Children's Home Society v. Hollinsworth, 193 Tenn. 491, 246 S.W.2d 345 (1952).

149. *Supra*, n. 146.

150. Souhegan National Bank v. Kenison, 92 N.H. 117, 26 A.2d 26 (1942). Admission that the attorney-general is forced, by an overload in work, to move sporadically.

151. *See*, herein, Chaps. 28, 29.

152. Texas Not-for-Profit Corp. Act. §1396-5.08 provides that recordation of deed is prima facie evidence of proper procedure by director in transfer of property.

153. *Supra*, n. 105.

154. 40 App. Div. 424, 57 N.Y.S. 1015 (1899). *See also* Agoodash Achim of Ithaca v. Temple Beth-El, 147 Misc. 405, 263 N.Y.S. 81 (Sup. Ct. 1933).

155. N.Y. Rel. Corp. L., §12.

156. Veterans of W.W.I. v. Levy, 70 Ohio Abs. 49, 118 N.E.2d 670 (1954).

157. First United Presbyterian Church of New Concord v. Young, 21 Ohio Nisi Prius (N.S.) 569, 29 Ohio Dec. 477 (1919). Minority members must go through trustees to enjoin property transfer.

158. *See*, herein, Chaps. 28, 29.

159. Tex. Rev. Civ. Stat., art. 5523a provides that any person who has a right of action against a trustee in a conveyance of property must do so within ten years. While one court has ruled that this is a statute of limitations to bar an action by a member: Dall v. Lindsey, 237 S.W.2d 1006 (Tex. Civ. App. 1951); another court has said that since the trustee did not have authority to sell, the ten-year period did not affect an action brought against him: Burrow v. McMahon, 384 S.W.2d 124 (Tex. Sup. Ct., 1964).

160. *Supra*, n. 96, §1702.36.

161. *Supra*, n. 96, §1702.40 and §1715.39.

162. 33 Ohio Op.2d 292, 4 Ohio Misc. 183, 210 N.E.2d 418 (1965).

163. *Id.*, 33 Ohio Op.2d 292 at 296, 4 Ohio Misc. 183 at 189, 210 N.E.2d 418 at 422 (1965).

164. *Supra*, n. 1.

165. Wilson v. Ebenezer Baptist Church, Inc., 187 N.Y.S.2d 861 (1963); Church of God of Prospect Plaza v. Fourth Church of Christ, Scientist, 442 N.Y.S.2d 986 (1981).

166. Sun Assets Corp. v. English Evangelic Lutheran Church of the Ascension of Borough Park, 185 N.Y.S.2d 695 (1963). *See also* Application of Margolin, 183 N.Y.S.2d 36 (1963).

167. *See, supra*, n. 166.

168. *Supra*, n. 166.

169. Tex. Nonprofit Corp. Act. art. 1396-2.12. See also Ill. Gen. Not-for-Profit Corp. Act, §163 al5.

170. Tex. Nonprofit Corp. Act, art. 1396-5.08.

171. Oleck, *Nonprofit Types, Uses, and Abuses* 1970, 19 Clev. St. L. Rev. 207 (1970). *See also* Lesher. *The Nonprofit Corporation—A Neglected Stepchild Comes of Age*, 22, Bus. Law. 951 (1967).

172. 59 Misc.2d 321, 299 N.Y.S.2d 40 (Sup. Ct. 1969).

173. *See*, N.Y. Not-for-Profit Corp. L.

174. 90 Ohio Law Abs. 3, 183 N.E.2d 234 (1962).

175. *See*, herein, Section 445; and 3 Oleck, *Modern Corporation Law*, c. 63 (1978 Supp.).

176. Taft, *Control of Foundations and Other Nonprofit Corporations*, 18 Clev. St. L. Rev. 478 (1969).

177. Alford, *supra*, n. 100.

178. *E.g., see*, herein, proposed Uniform Act of Nonprofit Organizations, a licensing commission, state supreme court supervision, and intervention by "any interested person," in prior editions of this treatise.

179. *Ibid.*

180. See, Buxbaum, *The Dissenters' Appraisal Remedy*, 23 U.C.L.A. L. Rev. 1229 (1976); Henn and Alexander, *Corporations* §349 (3rd ed., 1983). And *see*, Burkins (article), *St. Petersburg Times* p. 1 *et seq.* (Business Section) (Nov. 10, 1986).

51

PARLIAMENTARY LAW

RULES OF ORDER

See §507

[*Note*: Oleck & Green, *Parliamentary Law & Practice for Nonprofit Organizations* (2d ed., 1991; American Law Inst.-Amer. Bar Assn. Join Comm.) is available from American Law Institute, 4025 Chestnut St., Philadelphia, PA 19104. The First Edition, referred to in the main text of the Fifth Edition of this treatise is revised and updated in the Second Edition. A paperback "handbook" of 160 pages.

The handbook is described by the ALI-ABA Executive Director, as one that "addresses itself to nonprofit organizations in the context of relevant statutory materials and case law, in format that permits ready access to specific questions, lay or legal." It is suggested that the handbook be used in conjunction with this treatise.]

* * * *

[John Waldeck of Canton, Ohio, a distinguished member of the American Institute of Parliamentarians, National Association of Parliamentarians, contributed this chapter in its original form. *Note*: This chapter is in *two parts*. Part II begins at §500; and the footnote numbers there begin with n. 1 again. The first part was specially written for this treatise; and the second part also, but the second part was prepublished in 21 Clev. St. L. Rev. (1) 85. Both have been shortened and updated.]

"Parliamentary law gets its name and basic principles from the Parliament of Great Britain. It was brought to the colonies with the common law and other political institutions of England. Jefferson, as presiding officer of the Senate, looked to the procedure of Parliament as his guide and prepared his manual from English precedents. The state legislatures and local governmental bodies copied from Congress. But the procedure of the state legislatures, local legislative bodies and voluntary associations now differs greatly from the procedure of Parliament and Congress."[1]

Among the sources which govern parliamentary law, listed in order of priority, are: 1) constitutional rules, 2) fundamental legal principles, 3) statutory rules of charter provisions, 4) adopted rules, 5) adopted parliamentary authority, 6) parliamentary law, 7) customs and usages, and 8) judicial decisions.[2]

I. Origin and Development of Parliamentary Procedure (Waldeck)

[See also, Chapters 24 and 27.]

§494. WHAT IS PARLIAMENTARY PROCEDURE?

[*See*, Waldeck, *Parliamentary Procedure for Nonprofit Organizations* (Doctoral Thesis, unpublished, in Cleveland State University Law Library).]

Parliamentary procedure has been called a blind spot in the law.[3]

It has not always been so. For the first 100 years of our country's history, parliamentary law was the exclusive subject of study and writing by lawyers, such as Thomas Jefferson,[4] Luther S. Cushing,[5] Rufus Waples,[6] and Thomas B. Reed,[7] until 1876. . . .

(Until just recently) the leading works and articles on parliamentary procedure for the last 100 years have been written by laymen with backgrounds as varied as an army general,[8] a W.A.C. colonel,[9] a professor of public speaking,[10] a psychiatrist,[11] a veterinarian.[12] sociologist,[13] a semanticist,[14] an almanacist,[15] a priest,[16] a sister,[17] and a lawyer's wife.[18]

The laymen writers have produced more than 200 publications on parliamentary procedure,[19] with more than 55 currently in print.[20] One of them, *Robert's Rules of Order*, is the oldest nonfiction best seller of all time,[21] at over 2 million copies,[22] second only to the Bible.

Organization activity in the field of parliamentary procedure has been carried on by associations not of lawyers but of laymen, such as the American Institute of Parliamentarians,[23] the National Association of Parliamentarians,[24] and Toastmasters International,[25] with a combined membership of perhaps 200,000. The membership of the American Bar Association in 1985 was over 300,000.[26]

. . . Parliamentary *procedure*. It is defined in *Webster's Dictionary* as "of, according to, or based upon parliamentary law,"[27] Parliamentary *law* has been defined as:[28]

> The rules and usages of parliament or of deliberative bodies by which their procedure is regulated. A rule of parliamentary law is a rule created and adopted by the legislative or deliberative body it is intended to govern.

The ambivalent nature of parliamentary law is shown in its definition as applying both to public legislatures and private deliberative bodies.

Parliamentary procedure has developed for over 1,000 years from the time of the first English parliament in 959, called together by King Edgar.[29] The word "parliament" is derived from the French "parler," meaning "to speak" or to "parley" between parties. . . .[30]

§495. LAWYER-WRITERS ON PARLIAMENTARY LAW

. . . Thomas Jefferson wrote the first American manual of parliamentary law, *Jefferson's Manual*. . . .[31] In a letter . . . he wrote on February 20, 1800 he said.[32]

> So little has the parliamentary branch of the law been attended to, that I not only find no person here, but not even a book to aid me. . . . . .

He also said:[33]

> The voice of the majority decides; for the lex majoris partis is the law of all councils, and elections . . . where not otherwise expressly provided.

It is ironic that Jefferson's *Manual* has not been adopted as part of the rules of the Senate[34] but is the parliamentary authority of the House, where debate is closed by majority vote.[35] A . . . nationwide poll revealed that 63 percent of public opinion favored a curb on filibusters, a parliamentary tactic possible under the Senate rule that allows one-third plus one vote to delay closing debate and making a decision.[36]

Under Senate Rule 22, debate was closed by a two-thirds vote until March 7, 1975, when one-third plus one vote could keep debate open to filibuster. Effective May 8, 1975, Rule 22 was changed to close debate by a three-fifths vote by sixty senators, or vote of forty-one to keep debate open. To prevent filibusters, debate after cloture is limited to one hour for each senator for a limit of one hundred hours.[37]

Jefferson's *Manual* served as a bridge from the British practice to the American rules, and as a basis for both legislative and nonlegislative rules of procedure in the United States today, except for the laymen-writers who follow Robert's *Rules of Order* written by an army general in 1876 . . .

The first writer in America to prepare a manual of parliamentary procedure for the use of nonlegislative assemblies was Luther S. Cushing, an outstanding lawyer, who write his popular *Manual of Parliamentary Practice* in 1844 . . .[38]

He prepared an outstanding work on legislative rules of procedure, entitled *Lex Parliamentaria Americana*, published in 1856.[39] It was from this work that Cushing prepared his *Manual* for nonlegislative groups, based on what he considered to be common parliamentary law. Cushing cited no legal decisions. . . .

Rufus Waples, LL.D., . . . wrote *A Handbook of Parliamentary Practice* published in 1883 . . .[40]

Waples did not cite case law to support his system of parliamentary procedure, saying that judicial decisions did not cover the field, were not sufficiently uniform, and merely covered the issue in litigation.[41] But Waples pointed out that there was no rule in parliamentary law, however seemingly unimportant, on which important litigation might not turn.[42]

The next writer . . . for the use of nonlegislative organizations was Thomas B. Reed (1839–1902), who served as Speaker of the House of Representatives and had been educated as a lawyer . . . *Reed's Rules: A Manual of General Parliamentary Law*, published in 1894,[43] . . . said that the purpose of the book was to present the rules of general parliamentary law in such a way as to be understood by those who presided over meetings, and by those who wished to participate in the proceedings of deliberative bodies. . . .

The first work on parliamentary law for nonlegislative organizations to cite case law was the 1914 edition of *Cushing's Manual* as edited by Albert S. Bolles. . . .[44]

§496. LAYMEN-WRITERS ON PARLIAMENTARY PROCEDURE

. . . Henry Martyn Robert (1837–1923), . . . published his . . . *Rules of Order* in 1876 . . . Robert was a graduate of West Point in 1857, . . . and rose to the rank of general, . . . serving in the Washington Territory and the defenses of Washington, D.C. during the Civil War.[45] Robert did not follow the law of majority rule, but created his own special rules of two-thirds vote requirements. Robert declared that the fundamental principles of parliamentary law required a two-thirds vote in certain situations,[46] of which he listed 17.[47] The rules of the House of Representatives require a two-thirds vote in only four instances. . . .[48]

Robert based his theories on special rules adopted by Congress, and on what he thought was required for harmony in ordinary societies[49]. . . . The courts have applied the rule of "lex majoris partis" as authority for action by the majority, instead of following a rule requiring a two-thirds vote.[50]

Robert invented a rule that members not voting are to be counted as voting in the affirmative.[51] The courts have held otherwise.[52] Likewise, Robert said that a plurality vote never elects anyone to office.[53] The courts have held the common law rule to be that a plurality elects.[54] Robert also devised his own rules on debate, limiting speeches to 10 minutes each, and that a member could speak only twice during debate.[55]

Robert created a special rule on actions to reconsider, saying that a motion to reconsider had to be moved by a member who voted with the prevailing side.[56] Thus, those not on the prevailing side were without remedy to reconsider an action. The action of a majority in disregard of this rule has been upheld by the courts.[57]

Among other special rules on reconsidering action, Robert invented a motion to reconsider and to be entered on the minutes of the next meetings . . .[58]

Robert's Rules of Order, in various editions had sold over 2 million copies as of 1979.[59] Ten editions had been published by 1985.

Robert's Rules . . . is the basis used by the majority of laymen-writers who produced the over 200 titles shown in a bibliography of the subject prepared by the American Institute of Parliamentarians.[60] The *Subject Guide to Books in Print*, 1985 showed that about 55 publications on parliamentary procedure then were in print . . .[61]

§497. DEFECTS IN NONLAWYER-WRITTEN PARLIAMENTARY PROCEDURE

The ... state of parliamentary procedure was criticized by a past president of the American Bar Association[62] ... David F. Maxwell ... "one of the few great lawyer-parliamentarians,"[63] said that ... it was high time that the law profession became active in the field of parliamentary law on the conduct of meetings of voluntary organizations.

Paul Mason ... has pointed out ... that the courts will apply the rules of parliamentary law as laid down by judicial decisions and not according to General Robert[64] ... Many of the rules in parliamentary manuals, by Robert or other laymen, are not parliamentary law, and ... there is no assurance that an organization can follow them and have its actions upheld by a court of law.[65]

Adoption of highly technical and complex rules of procedure as bylaws, as found in Robert's *Rules*, has been criticized by others too.[66]

Ernest S. Wooster criticized Robert's *Rules of Order* as outdated in operation, and as to the archaic terminology and the need for reform.[67] The manual of procedure for meetings of the Parent-Teachers Association, with 12 million members, has been criticized by a ... professor of education.[68]

§498. CURRENT INFLUENCES ON PARLIAMENTARY LAW

Effort towards reform by modernizing terms and return to case law, has been made by Alice F. Sturgis of California (not a lawyer), in the second edition of her book *Standard Code of Parliamentary Procedure*, published in 1966[69] ... Howard L. Oleck ... (at her request) read part of her manuscript revision, and made a few suggestions.[70]

Joseph F. O'Brien, a professor of public speaking at Pennsylvania State College, has written a textbook entitled *Parliamentary Law for the Layman*, published in 1952 ...[71]

Marguerite Grumme is the author of *Basic Principles of Parliamentary Law and Protocol*,[72] for nonlegislative organizations ...

Henry A. Davidson, M.D., a psychiatrist, is the author of *Handbook for Parliamentary Practice*, published in 1955 ...[73]

[*See also*, L. Deschler, *Handbook of Parliamentary Procedure* (1976) and R. Kessey, *Modern Parliamentary Procedure* (1974); G. Hills, *Managing Corporate Meetings* (1977); L. Place, *Parliamentary Procedure Simplified* (1976); F. Stevenson, Pocket *Primer of Parliamentary Procedure* (5th ed. 1974); H. Oleck *et al.*, *Parliamentary Law for Nonprofit Organizations* (1979); Oleck & Green, *Parliamentary Law & Practice for Nonprofit Organizations* (2d ed., 1991) (see description, above, at the beginning of this chapter).]

Among the national organizations ... is the American Institute of Parliamentarians ... consisting primarily of teachers of high school and college level, as well as of instructors in adult education.[74] Its program includes the teaching and examination of members for certification as professional parliamentarians. Another national organization is the National Association of Parliamentarians, which has a quarterly publication devoted to parliamentary questions.[75] The answers or opinions . . . based on . . . *Robert's Rules of Order* . . . have . . . been published in book form.[76] It also has a program of instruction and registration for professional parliamentarians.

An international organization, active in instruction in parliamentary procedure, is Toastmasters International, with 7,270 clubs in 50 countries and over 170,000 members.[77] A membership publication, *The Toastmaster*, appears monthly, containing educational articles on parliamentary procedure.

The 20th Edition of *Encyclopedia of Associations* (Gale Research Co., Detroit, 1994, Vol. I, 9991) lists also the International Training in Communication Clubs (formerly the International Toastmistress Clubs) with 27,000 members, . . . and a bimonthly publication titled *ITC Communicator*.

The duty of a member to learn the rules of parliamentary procedure, and to speak up and participate in meetings, has been the subject of a pamphlet entitled "How Parliamentary Law Protects You," printed in 1,250,000 copies by a national religious organization.[78]

§499. COURTS' VIEWS OF PARLIAMENTARY PROCEDURE

The courts, . . . have recognized and applied common parliamentary law in the following situations: where an organization had not adopted rules of parliamentary procedure,[79] in the absence of an adopted rule,[80] gaps in the rules of procedure,[81] where the bylaws did not provide adequate parliamentary rules,[82] and to test the action taken at a meeting.[83] Common parliamentary law has been defined as the ordinary custom and usage of parliamentary procedure; and the courts have accepted as authorities on the point involved such writers as Jefferson,[84] Cushing,[85] Reed,[86] Trow,[87] and Robert.[88] However, it has been held that *Robert's Rules of Order* is not binding, and need not be followed by any and all corporations in conducting a stockholder's meeting.[89]

Judicial decisions have been made as to the nature and effect of motions and rules of parliamentary procedure, such as a motion to amend,[90] a substitute motion,[91] a second to a motion,[92] to postpone indefinitely,[93] to table,[94] to close debate,[95] call for a division,[96] a point of order,[97] appeal the decision of the chair,[98] point of information,[99] adjourn,[100] recess,[101] to fix the time of the next meeting,[102] reconsider,[103] reconsider and enter on the minutes,[104] and to rescind . . .[105]

The courts have held that . . . articles or constitution, regulations, and rules of an association constitute a contract between a member and the association,[106] and among the members.[107] The majority have the power to adopt a set of rules that becomes a contract binding on all the members.[108] Becoming a member is an agreement to be governed by the constitution, bylaws, and rules of procedure of an organization.[109] If a parliamentary manual is adopted by reference as a part of the bylaws, the rules therein become the law applicable and are enforceable as a contract right by a member.[110]

§500. STATUTORY PARLIAMENTARY LAW

The development of modern codes has replaced much of parliamentary procedure with law. The 1964 Model Nonprofit Corporation Act,[111] as adopted in part by Ohio,[112] and some other states[113] and the District of Columbia, had sections that apply to actions formerly covered by the rules of parliamentary procedure, such as rescinding,[114] call for meetings, place of meetings, notice of meeting, time of meeting, adjourning, waiver of notice, voting,[115] quorums,[116] time of notice,[117] rights of members,[118] officers' duties,[119] and nominations and elections.[120] The Illinois nonprofit statute apparently was the model for the 1964 Model Nonprofit Corporations Act. Codes of other states, of course, have similar effects. The 1986 Model Nonprofit Corporation Act, apparently based on the 1980 California statute, contains similar sections, more permissive for management than before.

Another modern code to apply law to the conduct of meetings of nonprofit corporations and associations is the Not-for-Profit Corporation Law of New York,[121] with sections applying to membership, voting, meetings, notice of meetings,[122] quorums,[123] and other elements of meetings. (The California Nonprofit Corporation statute of 1980 and the 1986 A.B.A. proposed revision also has such provisions.)

Federal statutory law has been created to control the parliamentary procedure of labor unions, in the "Bill of Rights" of the Landrum-Griffin Act of 1959.[124] The act provides equal rights for union members to nominate candidates, to vote in elections or referendums, to attend meetings, to participate in deliberations, and for voting on the business of meetings, subject to reasonable rules pertaining to the conduct of meetings.[125]

However, the rise of modern code law has stopped short of providing detailed rules for the conduct of meetings. It is in this legal vacuum that the parliamentary manuals of laymen are still used.

Deliberative bodies have the right and power to make rules of procedure, given to them by general laws, statutes, and constitutional provisions, or by inherent power.[126] The Model Nonprofit Corporation Act sets forth authority for the corporate bylaws or regulations to include rules for the conduct of meetings. These were employed in the parts adopted by Ohio, for example . . .[127]

Ohio, like Florida and other states, has a "sunshine law" that requires that most meetings of governmental bodies be open to the public and press, with notice given and minutes kept.[128] Executive closed sessions, for some purposes, are permitted by such statutes.[129]

II. Parliamentary Procedure Becomes Law (Waldeck)

[See also Sections 497 and 498, and Chapters 24 and 27.]

§501. COMMON LAW THEORY OF PARLIAMENTARY PROCEDURE

Parliamentary procedure is common law, developed under the doctrine of *stare decisis* in the courts, precedents in the legislatures, and by common usage and custom in nonlegislative assemblies.[1]

The common parliamentary law of England in use at the time of the American Revolution and the Declaration of Independence became the parliamentary law of the United States of America . . .[2]

The court test is the law, customs, and usages of similar bodies in like cases, or in analogy to them.[3]

When rules or orders have been established by a legislature, they become the law of that body for such purposes, and are binding upon legislators as the law to govern them in such proceedings; and this is called parliamentary law. Legislators may not arbitrarily depart from such law and conduct meetings by other rules not known or adopted by such body.[4]

The United States Supreme Court has looked to the general rule of parliamentary bodies and applied it as the general law of such bodies in reviewing legislation passed by Congress.[5]

Deliberative assemblies . . . must be governed by rules of procedure to which each member must conform. In the absence of special rules of procedure adopted by such an assembly, or of superior law, its procedure is governed by the general parliamentary law.[6] All proceedings in meetings should be had in accordance with and subject to the incidents of the ordinary procedure of parliamentary assemblies . . .[7]

A proper regard for established rules of procedure will cause little trouble and avoid cases in court.[8]

The courts will follow the fundamental rules of parliamentary practice governing assemblies to protect the rights of the minority against the will of the majority.[9]

. . . In the absence of any provision in the laws of an association, . . . common parliamentary principles in use by all deliberative assemblies may be resorted to in considering the regularity of the proceedings.[10]

Common parliamentary law has been found and enforced by the courts in reconsideration,[11] time of doing business,[12] mode of voting,[13] action by less than a quorum,[14] unanimous consent,[15] adjourning,[16] questions of order and appeal,[17] absence of rules,[18] meaning of a parliamentary bylaw,[19] refusal of elections by member to office,[20] conduct of meeting,[21] less than quorum adjourning,[22] and election of officers.[23]

In a private corporation case, the court followed the common-law rule as to majority vote of a *quorum* of six member board vote of three to two, with one abstaining, as sufficient to adopt a resolution, and applying to both private corporations and public bodies.[24]

§502. CONTRACT THEORY OF PARLIAMENTARY PROCEDURE

[Mark J. Horne assisted research updating of this section.]

Parliamentary procedure is a contract in nonlegislative assemblies. Parliamentary procedure can be made a part of the bylaws and thus become a contract between the member and the association. A bylaw is a contract between the corporation and its members,[25] among the shareholders,[26] and even a void bylaw may become a valid contract.[27]

Where a parliamentary manual has been adopted, it becomes the law applicable, and a plaintiff has the right by contract to its proper application. An action in expulsion contrary to its terms is unauthorized, and the proper remedy is an order of reinstatement in a mandamus action.[28]

The majority of an association has the power to make a contract of rules binding upon all the members, directors, officers, and agents. The consent of all parties, as in the case of ordinary contracts, is not necessary to pass effective bylaws.[29]

The constitution, bylaws, rules, and regulations constitute a contract between the members and the association. When the association departs from that contract, it is not reasonable to require that a member conform to those rules to secure relief from such unauthorized acts.[30]

Power and authority to change the bylaws is conferred on an association by the acceptance of a contract reserving the right to do so.[31]

The rules and regulations of an Ohio corporation have all the force of a contract between the corporation and its members and between the members themselves, and a regulation on a *quorum* is valid and binding.[32]

The charter and bylaws of a business corporation constitute a binding contract between the shareholders. The contract cannot be altered except according to the terms of the contract.[33]

The bylaws are a part of the contract of membership and a member is bound by them.[34] Where the bylaws give authority to 10 members to continue an organization, the action by a majority in dissolution is invalid as a breach of the contractual obligation in the bylaws, and is invalid.[35]

Under statutory power to make bylaws, the membership application, constitution, and bylaws of membership corporations are the contract by which a member is bound.[36]

The contract between members created by the bylaws is of limited scope. A breach of the bylaws is not actionable in law for damages as a tort or breach of contract, but the remedy is punishment of the offending member according to the bylaws.[37]

The relationship of members to each other and to an organization is contractual, and the articles of association or bylaws constitute the terms of the contract.[38] Becoming a member of an organization is an agreement to be governed by the constitution and bylaws of that organization. Suspension as a communist supporter according to the terms of the constitution and bylaws was held proper.[39]

The rights of union members and their duties are defined in the contract made by the constitution, bylaws, and rules not inconsistent with the Landrum-Griffin Act of 1959.[40]

A member of a membership corporation makes valid bylaws a part of his membership and is bound thereby, and must pay dues when they are increased by the body, where he did not withdraw or resign.[41]

§503. LEGISLATIVE PARLIAMENTARY PROCEDURE

One of the reasons given for the argument that parliamentary procedure is not law is that the courts will not enforce the rules of parliamentary procedure where state legislatures are concerned. Joseph F. O'Brien, author of *Parliamentary Law for the Layman*,[42] cites six cases to support his claim, from Robert Luce's book *Legislative Process*.[43] They both admit that *People v. Devlin*,[44] which is discussed herewith, is contrary to their theory . . .

One of the six cases, *Illinois v. Hatch*,[45] is strongly in favor of enforcing parliamentary law by applying parliamentary usage as laid down by all writers on parliamentary law to interpret Constitutional requirements, and to apply it where the constitution, statutes, or rules are silent. In the case of *State v. Brown*,[46] the court merely said that rules may be suspended by action of the body, the same position taken in parliamentary law. The right to suspend, amend, or rescind rules was also upheld in *Railway v. Gill*.[47] The common parliamentary-law rule that the majority rules was likewise upheld in *Schweizer v. Terr. of Oklahoma*,[48] which overruled the theory of Robert and O'Brien that it takes a two-thirds vote to suspend rules. In the case of *Manigault v. Ward*,[49] the Court recognized there was a diversity of opinion among the states as to the status of parliamentary law and judicial review. The federal court applied the South Carolina rule, and said it would look behind the state seal on a bill and examine the parliamentary procedure as set forth in the journals.

In the case of *People v. Devlin*,[50] the court allowed evidence to be introduced to impeach legislative journals and to show the real parliamentary situation.

A comprehensive review of common parliamentary law was made by the court in *Brake v. Callison*, which held that the established parliamentary law of England in force at the time of the American Revolution applied, and had not been changed by statute.[51] The courts have followed universal legislative procedure,[52] usual parliamentary procedure,[53] and parliamentary law methods,[54] in testing legislative actions.

. . . An organization (that) adopts . . . rules of a legislative nature in its manual, tends to confuse . . . officers as well as members with these complicated and obsolete rules. Robert's *Rules of Order* . . . (is helpful) for suggestions as to relevant parliamentary usage of deliberative assemblies . . .[55]

A mayor, lawfully presiding-over a public body meeting, has implied authority to maintain order. He has discretionary power, as presiding officer, to insist upon orderly recognition of speakers (as per Jefferson's Manual, in this case), and to make quick judgments as to the method to use in maintaining order.[56]

Members of the Chicago City Council were entitled to a roll-call vote on a voice vote to adjourn by an oral request without formal motion, after the mayor declared a meeting adjourned and left, under its own rules of order and by parliamentary law cases. Evidence was presented from the clerk's journal, two transcripts by hired court reporters, and network news video tapes.[57]

The distinction made by courts between legislative parliamentary law and parliamentary procedure for private organizations is illustrated by a case concerning a New York Senate rule. This rule allows a senator or to be "present" and vote on a "fast roll call" when in fact he is in the hospital, by reporting to the clerk, with a presumption that he votes in the affirmative. The court refused to review the legislative process, which might violate the principle of separation of powers.[58]

§504. RULE-MAKING POWER OF GROUPS

Deliberative groups have the right and power to adopt rules of parliamentary procedure for the conduct of meetings. The rule-making power is given by the general parliamentary law, constitutional provisions, *ex-necessitate rei*,[59] and now by code in the Model Nonprofit Corporation Act,[60] other state acts,[61] and by federal code.

The power and authority to enact rules that will apply to parliamentary situations, where the code law and charter do not provide otherwise, was recognized early by the courts, in holding that directors may proceed by resolution to appoint inspectors of elections as prescribed in duly adopted bylaws.[62]

In pre-code cases, the power to adopt rules of procedure lay in the stockholder-member, and not in the directors, unless authorized by law, articles, or by action of the stockholders.[63] The board of directors usually has no authority to amend such rules, for the basic power to make bylaws and regulations for the government of a corporation basically lies in the members . . ."[64]

This power to adopt rules is not lost to the stockholders by delegation of authority to the directors to make and alter bylaws.[65] The bylaws ultimately come into existence by action of the *members* of the corporation.[66] [*Proposal of model bylaws* is not binding until adopted by a state or organization. Settler v. Hopedale Foundation, 400 N.E.2d 577, 580 (1980).]

A deliberative body such as a town meeting may not pass procedural rules which will tightly bind the body in subsequent meetings.[67] The rules and regulations made by a church or by long and established custom and usage will be enforced by the court, if not in conflict with civil law.[68]

In the absence of evidence to the contrary, it will be presumed that a meeting was held in accordance with the statutes, charter, and bylaws.[69] It will not be presumed that a voluntary association is governed by the commonly accepted parliamentary rules.[70]

The Landrum-Griffin Act requires labor organizations to adopt a constitution and bylaws providing procedures for the following: qualifications for or restrictions on membership,[71] the calling of regular and special meetings,[72] the selection of officers and stewards, and of any representatives to other bodies composed of labor organizations' representatives, the manner in which each officer is elected or appointed or otherwise selected,[73] the disciplining or removal of officers or agents for breaches of their trust,[74] the imposition of fines or suspensions and expulsion of members; these provisions including the grounds of such action and any provisions made for notice, hearing, judgment on the evidence, and appeal procedures.[75]

Under this Act, a court tested a meeting procedure of a union, according to parliamentary law, and held the main purpose of a call for division of the house was to test the chair's obviously incorrect announcement about a vote.[76]

A meeting of a county political party was not legally organized (and actions were null and void) until it adopted rules. One way to adopt rules is to pass a resolution that the rules of a specific (named) work on parliamentary law should govern the meeting. In this case, a question of order was held to take precedence over a pending question, requiring no second, and not amendable nor debatable, citing Robert's *Rules of Order*.[77]

§505. PARLIAMENTARY LAW IN ARTICLES OF INCORPORATION OR ASSOCIATION

Some parliamentary law applies to the articles of incorporation by provisions of the code law directly or by provisions giving the power to the directors or members, in the various states.

In the (old) Model Nonprofit Corporation Act, as adopted by many states and the District of Columbia, the articles of incorporation *may* contain any provision, not inconsistent with law, for the regulation of the internal affairs of the corporation . . .

Where a provision in the articles is inconsistent with the bylaws, the articles are controlling.[78]

The regulations in the Model Act govern (*unless* otherwise provided in the articles, or in most cases by the bylaws) the conduct of meetings, as follows: stating that power lies in the board of directors to alter, amend, or repeal bylaws; who may call special meetings of members; the proper content and time of notices of meetings of members; the right to vote; the right to vote by proxy; the rule of simple-majority vote; that a majority of the directors is a quorum and may act by majority vote of a quorum; and that the directors shall have the sole voting power when there are no members or when members have no right to vote.

The Model Act makes no flat rule but *allows* the articles to determine the following: if greater than majority vote is required, rules for executive or other committees, for cumulative vote, for classes of voters, or for government when there are no members. The articles or bylaws are to set forth members' rights, officers' qualifications and manner of election or appointment, and use of classes of membership.

In Ohio the articles may set forth any qualifications for and classification of membership. The board of trustees may adopt amended articles that are in force at that time, or the voting members at a meeting called for such purpose may adopt such amended articles by the same vote as required to adopt an amendment. The trustees may adopt bylaws for their own government, not inconsistent with the articles or regulations.[79]

§506. PARLIAMENTARY LAW IN BYLAWS

Some elements of parliamentary law are found in the bylaws. At common law,[80] and under parliamentary procedure, the power to adopt, amend, or repeal bylaws was in the members. Now, by the Model Act, the power is vested in the directors, *unless* the articles or bylaws provide otherwise.[81] (The old rule was, and is, more appropriate.)

For membership control, the power over the bylaws should be reserved to the members. The bylaws may contain any provision for the regulation and management of the corporate affairs not inconsistent with law or the articles. This makes the articles superior to the bylaws. There are no provisions for the procedure of amending bylaws in the Model Act, so such a procedure should be written in by the lawyers.

In the Model Act, the bylaws *must* provide for the notice of directors' meetings, election, or appointment or term of officers. The initial bylaws are adopted by the board of directors.

The rules in the Model Act will apply, *unless* the bylaws provide otherwise, in the following parliamentary situations: place of meeting, quorum for members' meetings, quorum for directors' meetings, and vote by proxy. For individual membership control, proxy voting must be barred by the bylaws or articles.

The Model Act makes no rule in other parliamentary matters but leaves them to be determined in the bylaws; *e.g.*, such as: time of the annual meeting, voting by mail, kind of notice for directors' meetings, and officers in the organization other than president and secretary.

In Ohio, the trustees may adopt bylaws for their own government not inconsistent with the articles or regulations.[82]

The Model Act gives the directors the authority to adopt *emergency* bylaws that may be practical and necessary during an emergency resulting from an attack on the United States or any nuclear or atomic disaster.[83] This provision has been adopted by Virginia.[84]

In New York, the . . . Not-for-Profit Corporation Law, effective September 1, 1970 . . . follows the Model Business Corporation Act, giving more control to the directors and less to the members.[85]

The Landrum-Griffin Act requires that labor unions adopt bylaws and a constitution and file a copy thereof with the secretary-of-labor.[86]

Bylaws become the law,[87] or the private statutes,[88] of the corporation, when enacted by the members for the regulation of its affairs. A corporation may make any bylaws for the call and conduct of meetings and elections that are not contrary to statute, articles, general law, or public policy.[89]

Where there is an inconsistency between two bylaws, the one most recently adopted modifies the first.[90] Where the certificate of incorporation and bylaws conflict in respect to election of directors, the certificate will control.[91]

Members are bound by the constitution and bylaws, and are conclusively presumed to know them.[92] Even a fugitive from justice is entitled to protection of corporate bylaws.[93]

A Michigan appeal court held that a vote on a proposed amendment to bylaws of a credit union, conducted over a period of five days in two different locations, was valid in conforming to "general parliamentary procedure," cited in *Corpus Juris Secundum* definition of "meeting," although it did not follow the definition in Robert's *Rules of Order.*[94]

§507. PROBABLE FUTURE OF PARLIAMENTARY LAW

The exact nature of parliamentary law, like the nature of all law, is yet to be fully discovered . . .

The nature of parliamentary law as to *majority rule* by stockholders in a meeting has been held to be *substantive* law rather than merely procedural, in a conflict of laws case. The Venezuelan law, requiring that derivative actions be authorized by vote at a stockholders' meeting, is substantive rather than procedural; and, under the New York conflicts of laws rules, it governed in a stockholders' derivative action in the New York federal court.[95]

Parliamentary procedure is enforceable both where *property* rights are concerned, and also where it involves *personal* rights. The concept of parliamentary law as a *natural right* is commented on by the court in *Berrien v. Pollitzer*[96] and by Howard L. Oleck in this book . . .[97]

The majority voting rule (majority vote prevails) is final unless it violates a contractual right, property right, or a liberty protected by the Constitution or general laws, and only if a basic right is violated does a court have jurisdiction to review tyrannical action by the majority over the minority.[98]

The better view is one giving priority to personal rights or natural rights. The courts must see to it that a membership corporation does not become a vehicle for personal-profit use or abuse.[99]

Certain rules in the conflict of laws among the states have developed concerning parliamentary law. Under the "Massachusetts Rule," a stockholder's derivative action is barred unless it is approved by an independent majority of stockholders.[100]

The aspects of parliamentary law in use in international organizations that have been recognized are termed "international parliamentary law."[101]

... Sometimes the rules of procedure are just as imprtant in their application as is constitutional law ... Such rules of procedure are law because they have the same importance and nature as other law derived from constitutions ...[102]

Jefferson said, in the introduction to his *Manual*, on the importance of adhering to rules:[103]

> It is much more material that there should be a rule to go by, than what that rule is; that there may be a uniformity of proceeding in business, not subject to the caprice of the Speaker, or capriciousness of the members. It is very material that order, decency, and regularity be preserved in a dignified public body.

But the development of this law goes on daily. For example, the doctrine of *lex majoris partis* is alive and well, as an Iowa case shows ...[104]

The *lawyer-writers* now are appearing in the *Index of Legal Periodicals* with articles on parliamentary problems of shareholders' meetings[105] on parliamentary procedure as a tool for the successful lawyer,[106] on simplification of rules of order,[107] and with a survey of nonlegislative procedure ...[108]

[The direction of parliamentary procedure as *law* is epitomized in the handbook on the subject: Oleck & Green, *Parliamentary Law and Practice for Nonprofit Organizations* (Amer. Law Inst.—Amer. Bar Assn. Joint Comm., 2d. ed. 1991).][109]

The American Bar Association—American Law Institute handbook brings lawyers back into the field of parliamentary law and procedure. This manual (Oleck and Green, above) should take its place with Jefferson's *Manual* and Robert's *Rules of Order*. It is the first major work in which the parliamentary law of the courts and the statutes and the parliamentary practice of writers on parliamentary procedure [*Rules of Order*] have been researched and combined in a joint-effort of the American Bar Association and the American Law Institute, by a group of students and lawyers, to make a unified system of the rules of parliamentarians and lawyers.

§508. PARLIAMENTARY LAW "RULES OF ORDER" OUTLINE

Rules of Order

Parliamentary Rules Summarized

Based on *Oleck & Green, Parliamentary Law and Practice for Nonprofit Organizations* (2d ed., 1991; Amer. Law Inst.—Amer. Bar Assn. Committee on CLE) 180 pp.; available from American Law Inst., 4025 Chestnut St., Philadelphia, PA 19104. [See that book as to details.]

I. *Priority (Privileged) Motions*

In their order of priorities:

1. Motion to *Adjourn* (or set time for adjourning)
Mover may not interrupt other speaker; a "second" is required; no debate; may be amended for clarity; majority vote carries.

2. Motion to *Recess*
Mover may not interrupt other speaker; a "second" is required; no debate; may be amended; majority vote carries.

3. (Motion on) Point of *Privilege*-Requested
Mover may interrupt other speaker; no "second" required; no debate; no amendment; either no vote required (or majority vote carries).

II. *Subsidiary Motions*

4. Motion to *Table (Postpone)* Temporarily
Mover may not interrupt other speaker; a "second" is required; no debate; no amendment; majority vote carries.

5. Motion to *Close Debate*
Mover may not interrupt other speaker; a "second" is required; no debate; no amendment; majority vote carries.

6. Motion to *Limit Debate* (or *Prolong* it)
Mover may not interrupt other speaker; a "second" is required; limited debate; limited amendment; two-thirds vote carries.

7. Motion to *Postpone* to a *Specified Time*
Mover may not interrupt other speaker; a "second" is required; limited debate; limited amendment; majority vote carries.

8. Motion to *Refer* the matter *to a Committee*
Mover may not interrupt other speaker; a "second" is required; limited debate; limited amendment; majority vote carries.

9. Motion to *Amend*
Mover may not interrupt other speaker; a "second" is required; debatable (except in undebatable-type motion); limited amendment; majority vote carries.

10. Motion to *Table Permanently* (or Indefinitely)

> Mover may not interrupt other speaker; a "second" is required; debatable; no amendment; majority vote carries.

III.   *Main Motions (on Substantive Matters)*

> Mover may not interrrupt other speaker; a "second" is required; debatable; may be amended; majority vote carries.

IV.   *Incidental Motions* (no Priority-Rank)

(a) *Point of Order*

> Mover may interrupt; no "second" required; no debate or amendment or vote (except if chairperson submits the question to the meeting).

(b) *Request* for *(Point of) Information*

> Mover may interrupt other speaker; no "second" required; no debate; no amendment; no vote.

(c) *Objection to Consideration* of a Matter

> Mover may interrupt other speaker; no "second" required; no debate; no amendment; two-thirds vote (in "negative") required.

(d) *Motion to Withdraw* the *Motion*

> Mover may interrupt other speaker; no "second" required; no debate; no amendment; majority vote carries.

(e) *Motion to Divide the Pending Motion*

> Mover may not interrupt other speaker; authorities divided as to "second" or debate or amendment; "no vote" or "majority vote" if chairperson so rules.

(f) *Appeal from a Ruling*

> Mover may interrupt other speaker; a "second" is required; debatable; no amendment; majority vote carries.

(g) *Motion* to *Reconsider* a Matter

> Authorities are divided as to right to interrupt other speaker or to debate; a "second" is required; no amendment; majority vote carries.

(h) *Motion to Rescind*

> Mover may not interrupt other speaker; a "second" is required; debatable; divided authority as to amendment or vote required.

       (i) Motion to *"Take from the Table" (Resume Consideration)*
           of a *Tabled Matter*
              Mover may not interrupt other speaker; a "second"
              is required; no debate; no amendment; majority vote
              carries.

     Stating the Proposal: Usually stated as "Mr. (Ms.) Chairperson, I *move that*
.... (state it), because ... (state *why,* if appropriate)."
     Motion to Amend: This is a complex matter; *e.g.,* as to amending a proposed amendment, *etc.* (*See* the handbook.)
[*Note:* These outline-summaries are *not* complete statements of rules. Each item listed above is covered by an entire *Section* in the *Oleck & Green, Parliamentary Law and Practice for Nonprofit Organizations* (2d ed., 1991; ALI-ABA).]
     NOTE: The above outlines of *Motions* at Meetings are only rough *rules of thumb,* subject to various special exceptions and limitations. Adoption of a specific, detailed set of Parliamentary Law rules is vitally important, in order to avoid disputes as much as is possible, and to promote cooperation.

POINTS TO REMEMBER

- Rules of procedure for meetings should be provided in the bylaws.
- Make parliamentary procedure rules as detailed as possible; but do not try to write a book on it in the bylaws.
- Adopt some authority on parliamentary procedure as a guide for situations not covered by law of bylaws (*e.g.,* Oleck handbook, or etc.).
- Remember that laymen's books are not legally binding on organizations, unless so agreed among the members, and are disfavored by courts.
- Use law-based books, preferably, for parliamentary rules.
- Have the rules drafted by an attorney.
- Lack of parliamentary procedure rules can convert a minor difference of opinion into a major crisis.
- Clearly stated rules of procedure (*e.g.,* at a meeting) promote cooperation.
- Make sure that the minutes correctly state what was agreed.

NOTES TO CHAPTER 51

1. Beitelspacher v. Risch, 671 P.2d 1068, 1077 (Idaho, 1983), quoting Mason's *Manual of Legislative Procedure.* (*see* n, 61, 62) (Calif. State Printing Office, 1962); *cf.,* 59 Am. Jur. 2d, Parliamentary Law.

2. Mark J. Horne, term paper in a seminar conducted by the author (Oleck) in late 1985; based on Beitelspacher case, n, 1; Traino v. McCoy, 455 A.2d 602, 607 (N.J. Super. 1982).

3. Maxwell, *Books for Lawyers,* 41 A.B.A.J. 950 (Oct. 1955).

4. Jefferson, *Manual of Parliamentary Practice for the Use of the Senate of the United States* (New York: Clark and Maynard, 1874). (First edition 1801).

5. Cushing, *Manual of Parliamentary Practice* (rev. by Frances P. Sullivan) (Baltimore: I. and M. Ottenheimer, 1950). (First edition 1844.)

6. Waples, *Handbook of Parliamentary Practice* (Chicago: Callaghan and Co., 1883).

7. Reed, *Reed's Parliamentary Rules: A Manual of General Parliamentary Law* (Chicago: Rand McNally and Co., 1898). (First edition 1894.)

8. Robert, *Robert's Rules of Order*, newly revised (Chicago: Scott, Foresman and Co., 1970). (First edition 1876.)

9. Hobby, *Mr. Chairman* (Oklahoma City: Economy Co., 1936).

10. O'Brien, *Parliamentary Law for the Layman* (New York: Harper and Bros., 1952).

11. Davidson, *Handbook of Parliamentary Procedure* (New York: Ronald Press, 1955).

12. Gilbert, *Parliamentary Procedure in City Councils*, 4 Parliamentary J. (1) 19 (Chicago: American Institute of Parliamentarians) (Jan. 1963).

13. Lehman, *Parliamentary Procedure* (New York: Doubleday and Co., 1962).

14. Hayakawa, On Conducting Meetings with Ease and Authority, *San Francisco Chronicle* (magazine section) This World, May 13, 1951, p. 21.

15. Golenpaul, Parliamentary Procedure, *Information Please Almanac*, 1964 (New York: Simon and Schuster) 477 (1964).

16. Keller, *How Parliamentary Law Protects You, Christopher Notes No. 103* (New York: The Christophers, 18 E. 48th St., 1960).

17. Anger, Sister Mary A., *Introductory Course in Parliamentary Procedure*,5 Parliamentary J. (1)3 (Chicago: American Institute of Parliamentarians, Jan. 1964).

18. Sturgis, *Sturgis' Standard Code of Parliamentary Procedure* (New York: McGraw-Hill Book Co., 2d ed. 1966).

19. English, Ed., *Parliamentary Bibliography*, 226 titles (Chicago: American Institute of Parliamentarians, 1961).

20. *Subject Guide to Books in Print*, 1984–1985 (New York: Bowker Co., 1985).

21. Hackett, *60 Years of Best Sellers 1895–1955*, p. 76 (New York: Bowker Co., 1956).

22. Robert, *op cit. supra*, n. 8, at title page (1964).

23. American Institute of Parliamentarians, Inc., Fort Wayne, Ind.

24. National Association of Parliamentarians, Inc., Kansas City, Missouri

25. Toastmasters International, Inc., Santa Anna, California.

26. Report of the Standing Committee on Membership, Annual Report of the American Bar Assn, A.B.A. Journal (Jan. 1986).

27. *Webster's Dictionary, Unabridged*, p. 1643 (Springfield, Mass.: Merriam Co., 1961).

28. Landes v. State *ex rel.* Pros. Atty., 160 Ind. 479, 67 N.E. 189 (1903).

29. Dietz, *Political and Social History of England*, 18 (New York: Macmillan Co., 1937).

30. *Webster's Dictionary, op. cit. supra*, n. 27.

31. Jefferson, *op cit. supra*, n. 4.

32. Mayo, *Jefferson Himself*, 203 (Boston: Houghton Mifflin Co., 1942).

33. Jefferson, *op cit. supra*, n. 4, at 91.

34. Senate Procedure, 85th Congress, 2nd Session, State Document No. 93, 264 (1958).

35. Rules and Manual, United States House of Representatives, 85th Congress, 2nd Session, House Document No. 485,499 (1959).

36. Harris, Harris Survey, *Cleveland Plain Dealer*, April 17, 1964, p. 22.

37. Congressional Quarterly Almanac 1975, p. 35. Rule XXII, Standing Rules of the Senate (U.S.), S. Res. 274 and S. Res. 389, 96 Cong., Nov. 14, 1979 and March 25, 1980, respectively.

38. Cushing, *op cit. supra*, n. 5.

39. Cushing, *Lex Parliamentaria Americana* (Boston: Little, Brown and Co., 1856).

40. Waples, *op cit. supra*, n. 6.

41. *Id.*, at 258.

42. *Id.*, at 255.

43. Reed, *op cit. supra*, n. 7.

44. Cushing, *Cushing's Manual of Parliamentary Practice* (rev. by Albert S. Bolles) (Philadelphia: John C. Winston Co., 1914).

45. Smedley, *The Great Peacemaker* (Los Angeles: Borden Co., 1955).

46. Robert, *op cit. supra*, n. 8, at 109.

47. *Id.*, at 205.

48. House Rules, *op cit. supra*, n. 35, at 247.

49. Robert, *op cit. supra*, n. 8, at 183.

50. Crawford v. Gilchrist, 64 Fla. 41, 59 S. 963 (1912).

51. Robert, *op cit. supra*, n. 8, at 193.

52. Caffey v. Veale, Mayor, 193 Okla. 444, 145 P.2d 961 (1944).

53. Robert, *op cit. supra*, n. 8, at 191.

54. Lawrence v. Ingersoll, 88 Tenn. 52, 12 S.W. 422 (1889).

55. Robert, *op cit. supra*, n. 8, at 178.

56. *Id.*, at 156.

57. People *ex rel.* John C. Locke v. Common Council of City of Rochester, 5 Lans. S.C. Rep. (N.Y.) 11 (1871).

58. Robert, *op cit. supra*, n. 8, at 165.

59. Hackett, *op cit. supra*, n. 21.; and inquiries in 1979.

60. English, *op cit. supra*, n. 19.

61. *Subject Guide to Books in Print*, 1985, 4238 (N.Y.-Bowker Co. 1985).

62. Maxwell, *op cit. supra*, n. 3.

63. Carmack, Evolution in Parliamentary Procedure, The Speech Teacher, (1) 35 (Jan. 1962).

64. Mason, The Nature of Rules, State Government, National Legislative Conference, Spring 1963, p. 101.

65. Mason, The Legal Side of Parliamentary Procedure, *Today's Speech*, November 1956, p. 9.

66. Givens, *The Landrum-Griffin Act and Rules of Procedures for Union Meetings*, 12 Labor Law J. 477 (June 1961).

67. Wooster, There's a Revolution Going On, *The Toastmaster*, 12 (Toastmasters International, Santa Anna, California: Oct. 1961).

68. Kvaraceus, William C., The P.T.A. Is a Waste of Time, *Sat. Evening Post*, May 2, 1964, p. 6.

69. Sturgis, *op cit. supra*, n. 18.

70. Mrs. Sturgis is in Piedmont, California.

71. O'Brien, *op cit. supra*, n. 10.

72. Grumme, *Basic Principles of Parliamentary Law and Protocol* (St. Louis: Revell Co., 1963).

73. Davidson, *op cit. supra*, n. 11.

74. *Supra*, n. 23.

75. *Official Opinions*, Parliamentary Journal, National Association of Parliamentarians, Kansas City, Missouri.

76. National Association of Parliamentarians, Parliamentary Questions and Answers (Kansas City: Graphic Laboratory, 1962).

77. *Supra*, n. 25.

78. Keller, *op cit. supra*, n. 16.

79. Ostrom v. Greene, 161 N.Y. 353, 55 N.E. 919 (1900).

80. Young v. Jebbett, 211 N.Y.S. 61 (Ct. of App. 1925).

81. Mixed Local of Hotel and Restaurant Employees Union Local No. 548 and others v. Hotel and Restaurant Employees International Alliance and Bartenders International League of America and others, 212 Minn. 587, 4 N.W.2d 771 (1942).

82. *In re* Election of Directors of Bushwick Savings and Loan Ass'n, 70 N.Y.S.2d 478, 189 Misc. 316 (1947).

83. Marvin v. Manash, 153 P.2d 251 (Ore. Sup. Ct. 1944).

84. Miller v. Ohio, 3 Ohio St. 475 (1854); Kimball v. Marshall, 44 N.H. 465 (1863); Hicks v. Long Branch Commission, 69 N.J.L. 300; Wood v. Town of Milton, 197 Mass. 531, 84 N.E. 332 (1908).

85. Brake v. Callison, 122 F. 722 (S.D., Fla. 1903); Hill v. Goodwin, 56 N.H. 441 (1876); Richardson v. Union Congregational Society of Francestown, 58 N.H. 187 (1877); State *ex rel.* Southey v. Lasher, 71 Conn. 540, 42 A. 636, 44 L.R.A. 197 (1899); Kimball v. Marshall, *supra*, n. 84; State *ex rel.* Attorney General v. Anderson, 45 Ohio St. 196, 12 N.E. 656 (1887); Wood v. Town of Milton, *supra*, n. 84; Hicks v. Long Branch Commission, *supra*, n. 84; Rushville Gas Company v. City of Rushville, 121 Ind. 206, 23 N.E. 72 (1889); State *ex rel.* Laughlin v. Porter, 113 Ind. 79; O'Neill v. Tyler, 3 N.D. 47, 53 N.W. 434 (1892).

86. Wood v. Town of Milton, *supra*, n. 84.

87. Strain v. Mims, 123 Conn. 275, 193 A. 754 (Ct. App. 1937); Trow, *The Parliamentarian* (New York: Gregg Publishing Co., 1933).

88. Shelby v. Burns, 153 Miss. 392, 121 S. 113 (1929); Marvin v. Manash, *supra*, n. 80.

89. Abbey Properties Co., Inc. v. Presidential Insurance Company, 119 S.2d 74 (Fla. C.A. 1960).

90. Hood v. City of Wheeling, 85 W. Va. 578, 102 S.E. 259 (1920); State *ex rel.* Davis v. Cox, 105 Neb. 75, 178 N.W. 913 (1924).

91. Casler v. Tanzer, 134 Misc. 48, 234 N.Y.S. 571 (1929).

92. Commonwealth of Pennsylvania *ex rel.* Fox, v. Chace, 403 Pa. 117, 168 A.2d 569 (1961); Shoults v. Alderson, 55 Cal. App. 527, 205 P. 809 (1921).

93. Zeiler v. Central Railway Company, 84 Md. 304, 35 A. 932 (1896); Wood v. Town of Milton, *supra*, n. 84.

94. Wright v. Wiles, 173 Tenn. 384, 117 S.W.2d 736, 119 A.L.R. 456 (1938); Goodwin v. State Board of Administration, 210 Ala. 453, 102 S. 718 (1925).

95. Wall v. London and Northern Assets Corp., Eng. Law Rep. Chancery Div. 469 (1898 W. 1178) (1898).

96. Pevey v. Aylward, 205 Mass. 102, 91 N.E. 315 (1920); Kimball v. Lamprey, 19 N.H. 215 (1848).

97. State *ex rel.* Southey v. Lasher, *supra*, n. 85.

98. People *ex rel.* Locke v. Common Council of City of Rochester, 5 Lans. S.C. Rep. (N.Y.) 11 (1871); American Aberdeen-Angus Breeder's Association v. S.C. Fullerton, 325 Ill. 323, 156 N.E. 314 (1927); Duffy v. Loft, Inc. 17 Del. Ch. 140, 151, 223 (1930).

99. Field v. Oberwortmann 16 Ill. App.2d 376, 148 N.E.2d 600 (1958).

100. Vogel v. Parker, Clerk of the Borough of Fair Lawn, 118 N.J.L. 521 (. . .); Strain v. Mims, *supra*, n. 87.

101. Shelby v. Burns, *supra*, n. 88; Ex Parte U. Mirande, on Habeas Corpus, 73 Cal. 265 (. . .).

102. *In re* Election of Directors of Bushwick Savings and Loan Ass'n., *supra*, n. 79; Noremac, Inc. v. Centre Hill Court, Inc. 178 S.E. 877 (Va. 1935); Clark v. Oceano Beach Resort Co., 106 Cal. App. 579, 289 P. 946 (1930).

103. Sagness v. Farmers Co-Operative Creamery Co., of Baltic and Dell Rapids, 67 S.D. 379, 293 N.W. 365 (1940); Mansfield v. O'Brien, 273 Mass. 515, 171 N.E. 487 (1930).

104. First Buckingham Community, Inc. v. Malcolm, 177 Va. 710, 15 S.E.2d 54 (Ct. App. 1941).

105. United States v. Interstate R. Co., 14 F.2d 328 (W.D., Va. 1926).

106. Rueb v. Rehder, 24 N.M. 534, 174 P. 992 (1918).

107. St. Regis Candies, Inc. v. Hovas., 8 S.W.2d 574 (Tex. Civ. App. 1928).

108. Cheney v. Canfield, 158 Cal. 342, 111 P.92 (1910).

109. Rosen v. District Council No. 9 of New York City of The Brotherhood of Painters, Decorators and Paperhangers of America *et al.*, 198 F.Supp. 46 (S.D., N.Y. 1961).

110. People *ex rel.* Thomas Godwin v. The American Institute of City of New York, 44 How. Prac. 486 (N.Y. 1873).

111. Committee on Corporate Laws, American Bar Association, Model Business Corporation Act; Published by the Joint Committee on Continuing Legal Education of the American Law Institute and the American Bar Association, Philadelphia; (Revised 1964), Handbook D, Model Nonprofit Corporation Act. *See* the 1986 Revision Proposals cited at various points; Chapters 24 and 27.

112. Ohio Rev. Code, c. 1702 (Nonprofit Corporation Law).

113. Ill. Anno. Stat., c. 32, Sec. 163a, *et seq.* (1943) (preceding the Model Act); Wis. Stat., c. 181 (1953); Mo. Rev. Stat., c. 355 (1955); No. Car. Gen. Stat., c. 55 A (1955); Ala. Code Recomp., tit. 10, c. 3A (1955); Va. Code, tit. 13.1, c. 8 (1956); No. Dak. Century Code, c. 10–24 (1959); Neb. Rev. Stat., c. 21, Art. 19 (1959); Tex. Civ. Stat., tit. 32, ch. 9, art. 1396 (1962); Ore. Rev. Stat., c. 61 (1959); District of Columbia Code, tit. 29, c. 53 (1962); Utah Code Anno. tit. 16, c. 6 (1963).

114. Ohio Rev. Code §1702.24.

115. *Id.*, §§1702.17–1702.20.

116. *Id.*, §1702.22.

117. *Id.*, §1702.02.

118. *Id.*, §1702.13.

119. *Id.*, §1702.34.

120. *Id.*, §1702.26.

121. N.Y. Not-for-Profit Corp. L., Book 37. *McKinney's Consol. Laws of New York*; St. Paul, West, c 1970.

122. *Id.*, §§601, 603–605, 609, 611, 612.

123. *Id.*, §608.

124. 73 Stat. 522 (1959); 29 U.S.C. §411.

125. *Id.*, §101 (a)(1).

126. Witherspoon v. State *ex rel.* West, 138 Miss. 310, 103 S. 134 (1925).

127. Ohio Rev. Code. §1702.11.

128. *Ibid.* §121.22.

129. Dayton Newspapers v. Dayton, 28 Ohio App. 95, 274 N.E.2d 766 (1971).

* * *

1. L. Cushing, *Manual of Parliamentary Practice*, 5 (1950).

2. Brake v. Callison, 122 F. 722 (S.D. Fla. 1903), *cert. denied* 194 U.S. 638 (1904).

3. Kerr v. Trego, 47 Pa. 292 (1864); Mixed Local v. Hotel and R. Employees, 212 Minn. 587, 4 N.W.2d 771 (1942); Koth v. Congregation C.U.B., 430 N.Y.S.2d 786 (1980).

4. People v. Devlin, 33 N.Y. 269, 88 Am. Dec. 377 (1865).

5. United States v. Ballin, 144 U.S. 1 (1892).

6. Witherspoon v. State, 138 Miss. 310, 103 So. 134, 137 (1925).

7. Mansfield v. O'Brien, 271 Mass. 515, 171 N.E. 487, 489 (1930).

8. Strain v. Mims, 123 Conn. 275, 193 A. 754, 758 (1937).

9. Terre Haute Gas Corp. v. Johnson, 221 Ind. 499, 45 N.E.2d 484, 489 (1942); cf., Boisdore v. Bridgman 439 S.2d 1266 (La. App. 1983).

10. Marvin v. Manash, 175 Ore. 311, 153 P.2d 251, 254 (1944).

11. People v. Davis, 284 Ill. 439, 120 N.E. 326, 328 (1819); Chanhassen Est. v. City, 342 N.W.2d 335 (Minn. 1984).

12. Kimball v. Marshall, 44 N.H. 465 (1863).

13. Richardson v. Union Congregational Society of Francestown, 58 N.H. 187 (1877); Governing Board v. Panill, 659 S.W.2d 670 (Tex. Civ. App. 1983).

14. Board of Supervisors Oconto County v. Hall, 47 Wis. 208, 2 N.W. 291 (1879).

15. Brown v. Winterport, 79 Me. 305, 9 A. 844, 845 (1879).

16. O'Neil v. Tyler, 3 N.D. 47, 53 N.W. 434, 437 (1892); Green v. Amer. Cast Iron, 446 S.2d 16 (Ala. 1984).

17. State v. Lashar, 71 Conn. 540, 42 A. 636 (1899).

18. Ostrom v. Greene, 161 N.Y. 353, 55 N.E. 919, 922 (1900).

19. Commonwealth v. Vandergrift, 232 Pa. 53, 81 A. 153, 154 (1911).

20. State *ex rel.* Hatfield v. Farrar, 89 W. Va. 232, 109 S.E. 240 (1921).

21. Young v. Jebbett, 213 App. Div. 774, 211 N.Y.S. 61 (App. Div. 1925); State v. Bibb, 470 N.E.2d 257 (Ohio App. 1984).

22. Shelby v. Burns, 153 Miss. 392, 121 So. 113 (1929); Rock v. Thompson, 426 N.E.2d 891 (Ill. 1981).

23. *In re* Election of Directors of Bushwick Sav. and Loan Ass'n, 189 Misc. 316, 70 N.Y.S.2d 478 (Sup. Ct. 1947).

24. Equity Investors, Inc. v. Ammest Group, Inc., 563 P.2d 531 (Kan. App., 1977).

25. Farmers Cooperative Co. v. Birmingham, 86 F.Sup. 201, 223 (N.D. Iowa 1949).

26. Hornsby v. Lohmeyer, 364 Pa. 271, 72 A.2d 294, 299 (1950).

27. Palmer v. Chamberlin, 191 F.2d 532, 536 (5th Cir. 1951).

28. People *ex rel.* Godwin v. American Institute of New York, 44 How. Pr. 468, 63 Am. Dec. 776n (1873).

29. Cheney v. Canfield, 158 Cal. 342, 111 P. 92 (1910).

30. Rueb v. Rehder, 24 N.M. 534, 174 P. 992 (1918).

31. Steen v. Modern Woodmen of America, 296 Ill. 104, 129 N.E. 546 (1920).

32. State *ex rel.* Schwab v. Price, 121 Ohio St. 114, 167 N.E. 366 (1929).

33. St. Regis Candies, Inc. v. Hovas, 8 S.W.2d 574 (Tex. Civ. App. 1928).

34. Cubana v. Holstein-Friesian Ass'n of America, 196 App. Div. 842, 188 N.Y.S. 277 (App. Div. 1921).

35. St. John of Vizzini v. Cavallo, 134 Misc. 152, 234 N.Y.S. 683 (Sup. Ct. 1929).

36. Associated Press v. Emmett, 45 F.Supp. 907, 918 (S.D. Cal. 1942).

37. Weissman v. Birn, 270 App. Div. 757, 56 N.Y.S.2d 269, *aff'd mem.*, 59 N.Y.S.2d 917 (App. Div. 1945).

38. Anderson v. Amidon, 114 Minn. 202, 130 N. 1002 (1911).

39. Rosen v. Dist. Council No. 9 of New York City of the Board of Painters Decorators and Paperhangers of America, 198 F.Supp. 46 (S.D.N.Y. 1961).

40. Cleveland Orchestra Committee v. Cleveland Federation of Musicians, Local No. 4, 303 F.2d 229, 230 (6th Cir. 1962).

41. Associated General Contractors of America, New York State Chapter, Inc. v. Lapardo Bros. Excavating Contractors, Inc., 43 Misc.2d 825, 252 N.Y.S.2d 486, 488 (Sup. Ct. 1964).

42. J. O'Brien, *Parliamentary Law for the Layman* (1952).

43. R. Luce, *Legislative Procedure* (1922).

44. People v. Devlin, 33 N.Y. 269, 88 Am. Dec. 377 (1865).

45. People *ex rel.* Harless v. Hatch, 33 Ill. 9 (1863).

46. State v. Brown, 33 S.C. 151, 11 S.E. 641, 643 (1890).

47. St. Louis and S.F. Ry. Co. v. Gill, 54 Ark. 101, 15 S.W. 18, 19 *aff'd* 156 U.S. 649 (1891).

48. Schweizer v. Territory, 5 Okl. 297, 47 P. 1094 (1897).

49. Manigault v. S.M. Ward and Co., 123 F. 707, 716 (D.S.C. 1903); *cf.*, Kentucky High School A.A. v. Jackson, 569 S.W.2d 185 (Ky. 1978).

50. People v. Devlin, 33 N.Y. 269, 88 Am. Dec. 377 (1865).

51. Brake v. Callison, 122 F. 722 (S.D. Fla. 1903), *cert. denied*, 194 U.S. 638 (1904).

52. State *ex rel* Coleman v. Lewis, 181 S.C. 10, 186 S.E. 625 (1936).

53. Hood v. City of Wheeling, 85 W. Va. 578, 102 S.E. 259 (1920).

54. State *ex rel.* Coleman v. Lewis, 181 S.C. 10, 186 S.E. 625 (1936).

55. Posner v. Bronx County Medical Society, 19 App. Div.2d 89, 241 N.Y.S.2d 540, 544 (App. Div. 1963).

56. Arrington, Mayor of Seat Pleasant v. Moore, 258 A.2d 909 (Md. App. 1976). Television news tapes and six photos were available as proof of the disorder, in this case.

57. Roti v. Washington, Mayor of Chicago, 450 N.E.2d 456 (Ill. App., 1983).

58. Heinbach v. State of N.Y., 454 N.Y.S.2d 993 (App. Div., 1982).

59. Witherspoon v. State, 138 Miss. 310, 103 S. 134, 137 (1925).

60. Model Nonprofit Corp. Act §5 (L) (1964) (To make and alter bylaws for the administration and regulation of the affairs of the corporation.)

61. Ohio Rev. Code Ann. §1702.11 (Page 1964) (The regulations . . . may provide . . . the manner of conducting . . . meetings of members . . . or their elected representatives or delegates.)

62. *In re* Election of Directors of the Mohawk and Hudson R.R. Co., 19 Wend. 135, 13 N.Y. Common Law Rep. 556 (Sup. Ct. 1838).

63. North Milwaukee Town-Site Co. No. 2 v. Bishop, 103 Wis. 492, 79 N.W. 785 (1899).

64. State v. Kreutzer, 100 Ohio St. 246, 126 N.E. 54, 55 (1919).

65. Rogers v. Hill, 289 U.S. 582 (1933).

66. Hopewell Baptist Church of Hartford v. Craig, 143 Conn. 593, 124 A.2d 220, 222 (1956).

67. Town of Exeter v. Kanick, 104 N.H. 157, 181 A.2d 638, 640 (1962).

68. Schumann v. Dally, 29 S.W.2d 422, 426 (Tex. Civ. App. 1930).

69. Abbey Properties Co. v. Presidential Ins. Co., 119 So.2d 74 (Dist. Ct. Fla. 1960).

70. Gipson v. Morris, 31 Tex. Civ. App. 645, 73 S.W. 85 (Tex. Civ. App. 1903).

71. Landrum-Griffin Act. §201(a), 29 U.S.C. §431 (1964).

72. *Id.* at (f).

73. *Id.* at (g).

74. *Id.* at (h).

75. *Id.* at (i).

76. Pignotti v. Sheet Metal Workers Union, 477 F.2d 825 (8th Cir., 1973).

77. Ryan v. Grimm, 254 N.Y.S.2d 462 (App. Div. 1964).

78. Model Nonprofit Corp. Act §29 (1964); Ala. Code tit. 10-3A-61; D.C. Code §29–53; Fla. Stat. §617.021; Ill. Ann. Stat. ch. 32, §163a28; Iowa Code Ann. §504A.29; Mo. Rev. Stat. §355.045; Neb. Rev. Stat. §21-1928; N.C. Gen. Stat. §55A-7; N.D. Cent. Code §10-24-29; Ohio Rev. Code Ann. §1702.30; Ore. Rev. Stat. §61.095; Tex. Rev. Civ. Stat. art. 1396-3.02; Utah Code Ann. §16-6-46; Va. Code Ann. §13.819; Wash. Rev. Code Ann. §24.03.025; Wis. Stat. Ann. §181.31.

79. Ohio Rev. Code Ann. §1702.30 (1964).

80. Lawson v. Hewel, 118 Cal. 613, 50 P. 763 (1897).

81. Model Nonprofit Corp. Act §34 (1964).

82. Ohio Rev. Code Ann. §1702.30 (1964).

83. Model Nonprofit Corp. Act. §12A (1964).

84. Va. Code Ann. §13.1-824. (1964).

85. N.Y. Not-for-Profit Corp. Law, Book 37 (1970).

86. Landrum-Griffin Act §201(a), 29 U.S.C. §431 (1964).

87. Weisblum v. LiFalco Mfg. Co., 193 Misc. 473, 84 N.Y.S.2d 162, 166 (Sup. Ct. 1947).

88. Elliot v. Lindquist, 356 Pa. 385, 52 A.2d 180, 182 (1947).

89. Brooker v. First Fed. Sav. and Loan Ass'n, 215 Ga. 277, 110 S.E.2d 360, 362, *cert. denied* 361 U.S. 916 (1959).

90. New England Trust Co. v. Penobscot Chem. Fibre Co., 142 Me. 286, 50 A.2d 188, 191 (1946).

91. *In re* Election of Directors of Radiant Knitting Mills, Inc., 20 Misc.2d 915, 194 N.Y.S.2d 232, 234 (Sup. Ct. 1959).

92. Schroeder v. Meridian Imp. Club, 36 Wash.2d 925, 221 P.2d 544 (1950).

93. Bickston v. Federal Firearms Corp. of Cal., 38 Cal. Rptr. 793, 796 (Cal. App. 1964).

94. Casazza v. Dept. of Commerce, 350 N.W.2d 855 (Mich. App., 1984).

95. Hausman v. Buckley, 299 F.2d 696 (2d Cir. 1962).

96. Berrien v. Pollitzer, 165 F.2d 21 (D.C. Cir. 1947).

97. *See* Chapters 1 and 2.

98. Stansberry v. McCarty, 238 Ind. 338, 249 N.E.2d 683, 686 (1958).

99. Hungarian Freedom Fighters Federation, Inc. v. Samson, 30 Misc.2d 354, 219 N.Y.S.2d 348, 355 (Sup. Ct. 1961).

100. Hausman v. Buckley, 299 F.2d 696, 705 (2d Cir. 1962).

101. Jessup, *International Parliamentary Law*, 51 Am. J. Int'l. L. 396 (April, 1957).

102. Gooch, *The Legal Nature of Legislative Rules of Procedure*, 12 Virginia L. Rev. 529 (May, 1926).

103. T. Jefferson, *A Manual of Parliamentary Practice for the Use of the Senate of the United States* 14, (1874).

104. Adams v. Fort Henry School Dist., 182 N.W.2d 132 (Iowa 1970).

105. Dewolfe, *Problems at Shareholders Meetings*, 52 Chi, B. Rec. 188 (1971).

106. Karcher, *Essential Tool for the Successful Lawyer*, 43 Fla. B.J. 440 (1969).

107.   Bradley, *Toward Simplified Rules of Order*, 11 N.H.B.J. 195 (1969).

108.   Gannen, *Overview of American Non-Legislative Procedure*, 61 Law Lib. J. 296 (1968).

109.   American Law Institute—Amer. Bar Assn. Joint Comm.; office: 4025 Chestnut St., Philadelphia, Pa. 19104.

CLOSING WORDS

"There's only one right way to wrap up a meeting . . . (s)it back down and identify what we had just agreed to do . . . First, you recap the salient points . . . Next you ask for what you want . . . Third, state the benefits of what you are proposing . . . (O)ften people give you exactly what you asked for. . . . "
H. Maskay, article, 43 *Successful Meetings* (1) 24 (Jan. 1994, Part 1).

INDEX

G